Financial Accounting Standards Board
401 Merritt 7, P.O. Box 5116, Norwalk, Connecticut 06856-5116

ORIGINAL PRONOUNCEMENTS

As Amended
2007/2008 Edition

ACCOUNTING STANDARDS
as of June 1, 2007

VOLUME II
FASB STATEMENTS OF STANDARDS 121–159

Published by the
Financial Accounting Standards Board

NOTICE TO USERS OF THE *ORIGINAL PRONOUNCEMENTS, AS AMENDED*

This year's edition of the Financial Accounting Standard Board's (FASB) *Original Pronouncements, As Amended* has been revised and updated to include the following new pronouncements:

FAS157: Fair Value Measurements

Statement 157, which was issued in September 2006, defines fair value, establishes a framework for measuring fair value in generally accepted accounting principles, and expands disclosures about fair value measurements. Statement 157 applies under other accounting pronouncements that require or permit fair value measurements. Accordingly, Statement 157 does not require any new fair value measurements.

FAS158: Employers' Accounting for Defined Benefit Pension and Other Postretirement Plans

Statement 158, which was issued in September 2006, requires employers to fully recognize the obligations associated with single-employer defined benefit pension, retiree healthcare, and other postretirement plans in their financial statements. The standard makes it easier for investors, employees, retirees, and others to understand and assess an employer's financial position and its ability to fulfill the obligations under its benefit plans.

Statement 158 requires an employer to:

1. Recognize in its statement of financial position an asset for a plan's overfunded status or a liability for a plan's underfunded status
2. Measure a plan's assets and its obligations that determine its funded status as of the end of the employer's fiscal year (with limited exceptions)
3. Recognize changes in the funded status of a defined benefit postretirement plan in the year in which the changes occur. Those changes will be reported in comprehensive income (i.e., net periodic benefit cost or other comprehensive income) of a business entity and in changes in unrestricted net assets of a not-for-profit organization.

Statement 158 applies to public or private business entities and nongovernmental not-for-profit organizations that sponsor one or more single-employer defined benefit plans.

FAS159: The Fair Value Option for Financial Assets and Financial Liabilities

Statement 159, which was issued in February 2007, provides companies with an option to report selected assets and liabilities (principally financial assets and financial liabilities) at fair value. The objective of Statement 159 is to reduce both complexity in accounting for financial instruments and the volatility in earnings caused by measuring related assets and liabilities differently. Statement 159 also establishes presentation and disclosure requirements designed to facilitate comparisons between companies that choose different measurement attributes for similar types of assets and liabilities.

Statement 159 requires companies to provide additional information that will help investors and other users of financial statements to more easily understand the effect of the company's choice to use fair value on its earnings. It also requires entities to display the fair value of those assets and liabilities for which the company has chosen to use fair value on the face of the balance sheet. Statement 159 does not eliminate disclosure requirements included in other accounting standards, including requirements for disclosures about fair value measurements included in FASB Statements No. 157, *Fair Value Measurements,* and No. 107, *Disclosures about Fair Value of Financial Instruments.*

FIN48: Accounting for Uncertainty in Income Taxes

Interpretation 48, which was issued in June 2006, increases the relevancy and comparability of financial reporting by clarifying the way companies account for uncertainty in income taxes. Interpretation 48 prescribes a consistent recognition threshold and measurement attribute, as well as clear criteria for subsequently recognizing, derecognizing, and measuring such tax positions for financial statement purposes. The Interpretation also requires expanded disclosure with respect to the uncertainty in income taxes.

FASB Staff Positions

Various new FASB Staff Positions (FSPs) listed below have been included in Volume III of *Original Pronouncements, As Amended.* The FSPs contain application guidance which has been exposed for comment and approved by the Board.

- FSP FAS 13-2, "Accounting for a Change or Projected Change in the Timing of Cash Flows Relating to Income Taxes Generated by a Leveraged Lease Transaction"
- FSP FAS 123(R)-5, "Amendment of FASB Staff Position FAS 123(R)-1"
- FSP FAS 123(R)-6, "Technical Corrections of FASB Statement No. 123(R)"
- FSP FAS 126-1, "Applicability of Certain Disclosure and Interim Reporting Requirements for Obligors for Conduit Debt Securities"
- FSP FAS 158-1, "Conforming Amendments to the Illustrations in FASB Statements No. 87, No. 88, and No. 106 and to the Related Staff Implementation Guides"
- FSP FIN 39-1, "Amendment of FASB Interpretation No. 39"
- FSP FIN 46(R)-7, "Application of FASB Interpretation No. 46(R) to Investment Companies"
- FSP FIN 48-1, "Definition of *Settlement* in FASB Interpretation No. 48"
- FSP EITF 00-19-2, "Accounting for Registration Payment Arrangements"
- FSP AUG AIR-1, "Accounting for Planned Major Maintenance Activities."

AN INTRODUCTION TO THE *ORIGINAL PRONOUNCEMENTS, AS AMENDED*

Volumes I and II contain the Statements of Financial Accounting Standards issued by the Financial Accounting Standards Board (FASB) from its inception in 1973 to June 1, 2007. Volume III contains the following materials issued by the American Institute of Certified Public Accountants or its committees and the Accounting Principles Board through June 1973 and by the FASB to June 1, 2007:

- Accounting Research Bulletins
- Accounting Principles Board Opinions
- Interpretations of Accounting Research Bulletins and Accounting Principles Board Opinions
- FASB Interpretations
- FASB Technical Bulletins
- FASB Staff Positions
- FASB Statements of Accounting Concepts

In this edition, all pronouncements amended by subsequent pronouncements reflect those amendments. Unless a complete paragraph or footnote has been deleted or added, additions and deletions as a result of amendments are not identified. The numerical sequence of the paragraphs or footnotes has not been changed as the result of any amendments; consequently, where complete paragraphs or footnotes have been deleted as a result of an amendment, that deletion is noted as follows:

[This paragraph (footnote) has been deleted. See Status page.]

Additionally, where new paragraphs have been added as the result of an amendment, they are numbered with the number of the preceding paragraph and a capital letter, such as 59A, and where new footnotes have been added they are numbered with the number of the preceding footnote and a lowercase letter, such as 3a.

The Introduction, Background Information, and Basis for Conclusions sections have not been changed to reflect amendments made to the pronouncements. Those sections remain as issued.

In rare instances, brackets have been used to show material that has been effectively amended by a subsequent pronouncement or for editorial changes that have been made to make the sentence read more smoothly.

Pronouncements that have been superseded but are still applicable for some entities due either to delayed effective dates of the superseding pronouncement or to scope exceptions have been updated for any amendments and are shaded to indicate that they have been superseded. Pronouncements that have been completely superseded and may no longer be applied are omitted from this edition; however, a Status page is retained for those omitted pronouncements.

A Status page at the beginning of each pronouncement identifies (a) the source of the changes to the pronouncement, (b) other pronouncements affected by that pronouncement, and (c) the principal effective date. The Status page can be used to identify which pronouncement (and paragraph within it) created an amendment. The pronouncement creating the amendment must be reviewed to see the amendment as it was originally issued and, if applicable, subsequently amended. For users who need to determine the provisions of a pronouncement at a particular point in time, the original pronouncements as they were originally issued, which are marked with shading and sidebars to indicate deletions and additions, can be found in the electronic Financial Accounting Research System (FARS) or the loose-leaf edition of *Original Pronouncements.*

The Status page also identifies, where applicable, other interpretive pronouncements and releases (including Special Report implementation guidance and FASB Staff Positions) that further clarify that pronouncement. Where applicable, the Status pages also identify related Accounting Standards Executive Committee (AcSEC) pronouncements, which include both Statements of Position (SOPs) and Practice Bulletins (PBs). In addition, the Status pages of applicable pronouncements reflect either the impact of a given pronouncement on an Emerging Issues Task Force (EITF) Issue (for example, resolves, nullifies, or affects that Issue) or the relationship of an EITF Issue to a given pronouncement (for example, interpretive of or related to). An interpretive Issue is one in which the Task Force reached a consensus that interprets certain guidance in an existing original pronouncement. A related Issue is one in which the topic of the Issue is related to the topic of the original pronouncement but either there was no consensus reached or the consensus is not interpretive.

The appendixes and Topical Index (included in Volume III) refer to the pronouncements contained in all three volumes. Appendix A presents a current list of AICPA Practice Bulletins, audit and accounting Guides, and Statements of Position. Appendix B presents a schedule of all amended and superseded standards. Appendix C lists the effective dates of all pronouncements included in the *Original Pronouncements, As Amended.* That appendix also presents the complete effective date and transition paragraphs of more recent pronouncements whose effective dates and transition provisions are such that they might initially be applied in annual financial statements issued on or after June 1, 2007. Appendix D lists all EITF Issues discussed to date and their current status.

Volume II
ORIGINAL PRONOUNCEMENTS
As Amended
FASB Statements of Standards 121–159
as of June 1, 2007

TABLE OF CONTENTS

Table of Contents

Table of Contents

Statements of

Financial Accounting Standards

No. 121 through No. 159

Statement of Financial Accounting Standards No. 121
Accounting for the Impairment of Long-Lived Assets and for Long-Lived Assets to Be Disposed Of

STATUS

Issued: March 1995

Effective Date: For fiscal years beginning after December 15, 1995

Affects: Replaces APB 16, paragraph 88(d)
      Amends APB 17, paragraph 31
      Amends APB 18, paragraph 19(h)
      Amends AIN-APB 30, Interpretation No. 1
      Amends FAS 15, paragraphs 28 and 33
      Amends FAS 19 by adding paragraph after paragraph 62
      Amends FAS 34, paragraph 19
      Amends FAS 51, paragraph 14
      Amends FAS 60, paragraph 48
      Amends FAS 61, paragraph 6
      Replaces FAS 66, footnote 5
      Amends FAS 67, paragraphs 3, 24, and 28
      Deletes FAS 67, paragraph 16
      Replaces FAS 67, paragraph 25
      Amends FAS 71, paragraphs 9 and 10 and by adding paragraph after paragraph 10
      Amends FAS 101, paragraph 6

Affected by: Paragraph 3 amended by FAS 142, paragraph D10(a)
      Paragraph 3(b) replaced by FAS 139, paragraph 7(a)
      Paragraphs 4, 6, and 27 amended by FAS 142, paragraphs D10(b), D10(c), and D5(b), respectively
      Paragraph 12 deleted by FAS 142, paragraph D10(d)
      Paragraph 147 amended by FAS 139, paragraph 7(b), and FAS 142, paragraph D10(e)
      Superseded by FAS 144, paragraph C1

Issues Discussed by FASB Emerging Issues Task Force (EITF)

Affects: Resolves EITF Issue No. 84-28
      Partially resolves EITF Issue No. 85-36
      Affects EITF Issues No. 90-16, 93-4, and 93-11

Statement of Financial Accounting Standards No. 122
Accounting for Mortgage Servicing Rights

an amendment of FASB Statement No. 65

STATUS

Issued: May 1995

Effective Date: Prospectively for fiscal years beginning after December 15, 1995

Affects: Amends FAS 65, paragraphs 1, 10, 15, 19, and 30
　　　　Amends FAS 65 by adding paragraphs after paragraph 30
　　　　Replaces FAS 65, paragraphs 16 through 18 and footnote 6
　　　　Replaces FTB 87-3, paragraph 9

Affected by: Superseded by FAS 125, paragraph 232, and FAS 140, paragraph 351(c)

Issues Discussed by FASB Emerging Issues Task Force (EITF)

　Affects: Nullifies EITF Issues No. 86-39 and 92-10
　　　　Partially nullifies EITF Issue No. 86-38

Statement of Financial Accounting Standards No. 123
Accounting for Stock-Based Compensation

STATUS

Issued: October 1995

Effective Date: For fiscal years beginning after December 15, 1995

Affects: Amends ARB 43, Chapter 13B, paragraph 2
Deletes ARB 43, Chapter 13B, paragraph 15
Amends APB 25, paragraph 4
Replaces APB 25, paragraph 19
Deletes APB 25, footnote 5
Replaces APB 29, footnote 4
Amends AIN-APB 25, Interpretation No. 1
Amends FAS 5, paragraph 7
Amends FAS 21, footnote 3
Amends FAS 43, paragraph 2
Amends FAS 105, paragraph 14(c)
Amends FAS 107, paragraph 8(a)
Amends FAS 109, paragraph 36(e)
Amends FAS 112, paragraphs 5(d) and 9
Amends FIN 28, paragraph 2
Amends FIN 31, footnote 1
Amends FIN 38, paragraph 2
Supersedes FTB 82-2

Affected by: Paragraphs 8 and 36 amended by FAS 141, paragraph E16
Paragraph 9 amended by FAS 144, paragraph C15
Paragraph 44 amended by FAS 148, paragraph 2(d)
Paragraph 45 replaced by FAS 148, paragraph 2(e)
Paragraph 49 replaced by FAS 128, paragraph 167(a)
Paragraph 49 amended by FAS 135, paragraph 4(u)
Paragraphs 50 and 357 amended by FAS 128, paragraphs 167(b) and 167(c), respectively
Paragraph 52 replaced by FAS 148, paragraph 2(a)
Paragraphs 52A and 52B added by FAS 148, paragraphs 2(b) and 2(c), respectively
Paragraph 53 amended by FAS 148, paragraph 2(f)
Paragraph 358 amended by FAS 128, paragraph 167(d), and FAS 135, paragraph 4(u)
Paragraph 359 and footnote 26 replaced by FAS 128, paragraph 167(e)
Paragraph 359 amended by FAS 135, paragraph 4(u)
Paragraph 360 replaced by FAS 128, paragraph 167(f)
Paragraph 361 deleted by FAS 128, paragraph 167(g)
Superseded by FAS 123(R), paragraph D6

Other Interpretive Pronouncement: FTB 97-1

AICPA Accounting Standards Executive Committee (AcSEC)

Related Pronouncements: SOP 76-3
SOP 93-6
SOP 94-6

Issues Discussed by FASB Emerging Issues Task Force (EITF)

  Affects: EITF Issue No. 84-8

  Interpreted by: Paragraph 8 interpreted by EITF Issues No. 96-18 and 97-2
                   Paragraphs 9 and 10 interpreted by EITF Issue No. 96-18
                   Paragraph 11 interpreted by EITF Issue No. 97-2

  Related Issues: EITF Issues No. 97-12, 00-8, 00-12, 00-15, 00-16, 00-18, and 01-1 and Topics No. D-83
                   and D-90

SUMMARY

This Statement establishes financial accounting and reporting standards for stock-based employee compensation plans. Those plans include all arrangements by which employees receive shares of stock or other equity instruments of the employer or the employer incurs liabilities to employees in amounts based on the price of the employer's stock. Examples are stock purchase plans, stock options, restricted stock, and stock appreciation rights.

This Statement also applies to transactions in which an entity issues its equity instruments to acquire goods or services from nonemployees. Those transactions must be accounted for based on the fair value of the consideration received or the fair value of the equity instruments issued, whichever is more reliably measurable.

Accounting for Awards of Stock-Based Compensation to Employees

This Statement defines a *fair value based method* of accounting for an employee stock option or similar equity instrument and encourages all entities to adopt that method of accounting for all of their employee stock compensation plans. However, it also allows an entity to continue to measure compensation cost for those plans using the *intrinsic value based method* of accounting prescribed by APB Opinion No. 25, *Accounting for Stock Issued to Employees.* The fair value based method is preferable to the Opinion 25 method for purposes of justifying a change in accounting principle under APB Opinion No. 20, *Accounting Changes.* Entities electing to remain with the accounting in Opinion 25 must make pro forma disclosures of net income and, if presented, earnings per share, as if the fair value based method of accounting defined in this Statement had been applied.

Under the fair value based method, compensation cost is measured at the grant date based on the value of the award and is recognized over the service period, which is usually the vesting period. Under the intrinsic value based method, compensation cost is the excess, if any, of the quoted market price of the stock at grant date or other measurement date over the amount an employee must pay to acquire the stock. Most fixed stock option plans—the most common type of stock compensation plan—have no intrinsic value at grant date, and under Opinion 25 no compensation cost is recognized for them. Compensation cost is recognized for other types of stock-based compensation plans under Opinion 25, including plans with variable, usually performance-based, features.

Stock Compensation Awards Required to Be Settled by Issuing Equity Instruments

Stock Options

For stock options, fair value is determined using an option-pricing model that takes into account the stock price at the grant date, the exercise price, the expected life of the option, the volatility of the underlying stock and the expected dividends on it, and the risk-free interest rate over the expected life of the option. Nonpublic entities are permitted to exclude the volatility factor in estimating the value of their stock options, which results in measurement at *minimum value.* The fair value of an option estimated at the grant date is not subsequently adjusted for changes in the price of the underlying stock or its volatility, the life of the option, dividends on the stock, or the risk-free interest rate.

Nonvested Stock

The fair value of a share of nonvested stock (usually referred to as restricted stock) awarded to an employee is measured at the market price of a share of a nonrestricted stock on the grant date unless a restriction will be imposed after the employee has a vested right to it, in which case fair value is estimated taking that restriction into account.

Employee Stock Purchase Plans

An employee stock purchase plan that allows employees to purchase stock at a discount from market price is not compensatory if it satisfies three conditions: (a) the discount is relatively small (5 percent or less satisfies this condition automatically, though in some cases a greater discount also might be justified as noncompensatory), (b) substantially all full-time employees may participate on an equitable basis, and (c) the plan incorporates no option features such as allowing the employee to purchase the stock at a fixed discount from the lesser of the market price at grant date or date of purchase.

Stock Compensation Awards Required to Be Settled by Paying Cash

Some stock-based compensation plans require an employer to pay an employee, either on demand or at a specified date, a cash amount determined by the increase in the employer's stock price from a specified level. The entity must measure compensation cost for that award in the amount of the changes in the stock price in the periods in which the changes occur.

Disclosures

This Statement requires that an employer's financial statements include certain disclosures about stock-based employee compensation arrangements regardless of the method used to account for them.

The pro forma amounts required to be disclosed by an employer that continues to apply the accounting provisions of Opinion 25 will reflect the difference between compensation cost, if any, included in net income and the related cost measured by the fair value based method defined in this Statement, including tax effects, if any, that would have been recognized in the income statement if the fair value based method had been used. The required pro forma amounts will not reflect any other adjustments to reported net income or, if presented, earnings per share.

Effective Date and Transition

The accounting requirements of this Statement are effective for transactions entered into in fiscal years that begin after December 15, 1995, though they may be adopted on issuance.

The disclosure requirements of this Statement are effective for financial statements for fiscal years beginning after December 15, 1995, or for an earlier fiscal year for which this Statement is initially adopted for recognizing compensation cost. Pro forma disclosures required for entities that elect to continue to measure compensation cost using Opinion 25 must include the effects of all awards granted in fiscal years that begin after December 15, 1994. Pro forma disclosures for awards granted in the first fiscal year beginning after December 15, 1994, need not be included in financial statements for that fiscal year but should be presented subsequently whenever financial statements for that fiscal year are presented for comparative purposes with financial statements for a later fiscal year.

Statement of Financial Accounting Standards No. 123

Accounting for Stock-Based Compensation

CONTENTS

INTRODUCTION

1. This Statement establishes a **fair value**[1] based method of accounting for **stock-based compensation plans.** It encourages entities to adopt that method in place of the provisions of APB Opinion No. 25, *Accounting for Stock Issued to Employees,* for all arrangements under which employees receive shares of stock or other equity instruments of the employer or the employer incurs liabilities to employees in amounts based on the price of its stock.

2. This Statement also establishes fair value as the measurement basis for transactions in which an entity acquires goods or services from nonemployees in exchange for equity instruments. This Statement uses the term *compensation* in its broadest sense to refer to the consideration paid for goods or services, regardless of whether the supplier is an employee or not. For example, employee compensation includes both cash salaries or wages and other consideration that may be thought of more as means of attracting, retaining, and motivating employees than as direct payment for services rendered.

3. Opinion 25, issued in 1972, requires compensation cost[2] for stock-based employee compensation plans to be recognized based on the difference, if any, between the quoted market price of the stock and the

---

[1]Terms defined in Appendix E, the glossary, are set in **boldface type** the first time they appear.

[2]This Statement refers to recognizing *compensation cost* rather than *compensation expense* because part of the amount recognized in a period may be capitalized as part of the cost to acquire an asset, such as inventory.

amount an employee must pay to acquire the stock. Opinion 25 specifies different dates for the pertinent quoted market price of the stock used in measuring compensation cost, depending on whether the terms of an award[3] are fixed or variable, as those terms are defined in Opinion 25.

4. Since 1972, **stock options** and other forms of stock-based employee compensation plans have become increasingly common. Also, option-pricing models have become widely used for measuring the value of stock options and similar equity instruments other than those issued to employees as compensation. Opinion 25 has been criticized for producing anomalous results and for providing little general guidance to use in deciding how to account for new forms of stock-based employee compensation plans. Several FASB Interpretations and Technical Bulletins have dealt with specific kinds of plans, and the Emerging Issues Task Force has considered numerous related issues.

5. Because of the perceived deficiencies in Opinion 25, early in the 1980s the AICPA's Accounting Standards Executive Committee, the staff of the Securities and Exchange Commission, most of the larger accounting firms, industry representatives, and others asked the Board to reconsider the accounting specified in Opinion 25. This Statement, which is the result of that reconsideration, establishes an accounting method based on the fair value of equity instruments awarded to employees as compensation that mitigates many of the deficiencies in Opinion 25. The Board encourages entities to adopt the new method. However, this Statement permits an entity in determining its net income to continue to apply the accounting provisions of Opinion 25 to its stock-based employee compensation arrangements. An entity that continues to apply Opinion 25 must comply with the disclosure requirements of this Statement, which supersede the disclosure requirements of paragraph 19 of Opinion 25. This Statement also supersedes or amends other accounting pronouncements listed in Appendix D. Appendix A explains the reasons the Board decided not to require recognition of compensation cost for stock-based employee compensation arrangements measured in accordance with the fair value based method described in this Statement.

STANDARDS OF FINANCIAL ACCOUNTING AND REPORTING

Scope and Alternative Accounting Methods

6. This Statement applies to all transactions in which an entity acquires goods or services by issuing equity instruments[4] or by incurring liabilities to the supplier in amounts based on the price of the entity's common stock or other equity instruments. Therefore, it applies to all transactions in which an entity grants shares of its common stock, stock options, or other equity instruments to its employees, except for equity instruments held by an employee stock ownership plan.[5]

7. The accounting for all stock-based compensation arrangements with employees or others shall reflect the inherent rights and obligations, regardless of how those arrangements are described. For example, the rights and obligations embodied in a transfer of stock to an employee for consideration of a nonrecourse note are substantially the same as if the transaction were structured as the grant of a stock option, and the transaction shall be accounted for as such. The terms of the arrangement may affect the fair value of the stock options or other equity instruments and shall be appropriately reflected in determining that value. For example, whether an employee who is granted an implicit option structured as the exchange of shares of stock for a nonrecourse note is required to pay nonrefundable interest on the note affects the fair value of the implicit option.

[3]This Statement uses the term *award* as the collective noun for multiple instruments with the same terms granted at the same time either to a single employee or to a group of employees. An award may specify multiple vesting dates, referred to as graded vesting, and different parts of an award may have different expected lives.

[4]An entity may conditionally transfer an equity instrument to another party under an arrangement that permits that party to choose at a later date or for a specified time whether to deliver the consideration for it or to forfeit the right to the conditionally transferred instrument with no further obligation. In that situation, the equity instrument is not *issued* until the issuing entity has received the consideration, such as cash, an enforceable right to receive cash, other financial instruments, goods, or services, agreed to by the parties to the transaction. For that reason, this Statement does not use the term *issued* for the grant of stock options or other equity instruments subject to service or performance conditions (or both) for vesting.

[5]AICPA Statement of Position No. 93-6, *Employers' Accounting for Employee Stock Ownership Plans*, specifies the accounting by employers for employee stock ownership plans.

Accounting for Transactions with Other Than Employees

8. Except for transactions with employees that are within the scope of Opinion 25, all transactions in which goods or services are the consideration received for the issuance of equity instruments shall be accounted for based on the fair value of the consideration received or the fair value of the equity instruments issued, whichever is more reliably measurable. The fair value of goods or services received from suppliers other than employees frequently is reliably measurable and therefore indicates the fair value of the equity instruments issued. The fair value of the equity instruments issued shall be used to measure the transaction if that value is more reliably measurable than the fair value of the consideration received.[6] A common example of the latter situation is the use of the fair value of tradable equity instruments issued in a business combination to measure the transaction because the value of the equity instruments issued is more reliably measurable than the value of the business acquired.

9. This Statement uses the term *fair value* for assets and financial instruments, including both liability and equity instruments, to refer to the amount at which the asset could be bought or sold in a current transaction between willing parties, that is, other than in a forced or liquidation sale. Quoted market prices in active markets are the best evidence of fair value and shall be used as the basis for the measurement, if available. If quoted market prices are not available, the estimate of fair value shall be based on the best information available in the circumstances. The estimate of fair value shall consider prices for similar assets and the results of valuation techniques to the extent available in the circumstances. Examples of valuation techniques include the present value of estimated expected future cash flows using a discount rate commensurate with the risks involved, option-pricing models, matrix pricing, option-adjusted spread models, and fundamental analysis.

10. If the fair value of the goods or services received is not reliably measurable, paragraph 8 of this Statement requires that the measure of the cost of goods or services acquired in a transaction with other than an employee be based on the fair value of the equity instruments issued. However, this Statement does not prescribe the **measurement date,** that is, the date of the stock price on which the fair value of the equity instrument is based, for a transaction with a non-employee (paragraphs 70-73).

Accounting for Transactions with Employees

11. This Statement provides a choice of accounting methods for transactions with employees that are within the scope of Opinion 25. Paragraphs 16-44 of this Statement describe a method of accounting based on the fair value, rather than the **intrinsic value,** of an employee stock option or a similar equity instrument. The Board encourages entities to adopt the fair value based method of accounting, which is preferable to the Opinion 25 method for purposes of justifying a change in accounting principle under APB Opinion No. 20, *Accounting Changes.*[7] However, an entity may continue to apply Opinion 25 in accounting for its stock-based employee compensation arrangements. An entity that does so shall disclose pro forma net income and, if presented, earnings per share, determined as if the fair value based method had been applied in measuring compensation cost (paragraph 45).

12. The fair value based method described in paragraphs 16-44 of this Statement applies for (a) measuring stock-based employee compensation cost by an entity that adopts that method for accounting purposes and (b) determining the pro forma disclosures required of an entity that measures stock-based employee compensation cost in accordance with the intrinsic value based method in Opinion 25. Neither those paragraphs (16-44) nor subsequent paragraphs (45-54) of this Statement affect application of the *accounting* provisions of Opinion 25 by an entity that continues to apply it in determining reported net income.

---

[6]The consideration received for issuing equity instruments, like the consideration involved in a repurchase of treasury shares, may include intangible rights. FASB Technical Bulletin No. 85-6, *Accounting for a Purchase of Treasury Shares at a Price Significantly in Excess of the Current Market Price of the Shares and the Income Statement Classification of Costs Incurred in Defending against a Takeover Attempt*, provides pertinent guidance.

[7]Opinion 20, paragraph 8, provides that initial adoption of an accounting principle for a transaction that the entity has not previously had to account for is not a change in accounting principle.

13. For convenience, in describing the fair value based method, paragraphs 16-44 of this Statement refer only to *recognition* or *accounting* requirements. However, those provisions apply equally in determining the pro forma amounts that must be disclosed if an entity continues to apply Opinion 25.

14. An entity shall apply the same accounting method—either the fair value based method described in this Statement or the intrinsic value based method in Opinion 25—in accounting for all of its stock-based employee compensation arrangements. Once an entity adopts the fair value based method for those arrangements, that election shall not be reversed.[8]

15. Equity instruments granted or otherwise transferred directly to an employee by a **principal stockholder** are stock-based employee compensation to be accounted for by the entity under either Opinion 25 or this Statement, whichever method the entity is applying, unless the transfer clearly is for a purpose other than compensation.[9] The substance of a transaction in which a principal stockholder directly transfers equity instruments to an employee as compensation is that the principal stockholder makes a capital contribution to the entity and the entity awards equity instruments to its employee. An example of a situation in which a direct transfer of equity instruments to an employee from a principal stockholder is not compensation cost is a transfer to settle an obligation of the principal stockholder unrelated to employment by the reporting entity.

Valuation of Equity Instruments Issued for Employee Services

Measurement Basis

16. Frequently, part or all of the consideration received for equity instruments issued to employees is past or future employee services. Equity instruments issued to employees and the cost of the services received as consideration shall be measured and recognized based on the fair value of the equity instruments issued. The portion of the fair value of an equity instrument attributed to employee services is net of the amount, if any, that employees pay for the

instrument when it is granted. Paragraphs 17-25 of this Statement provide guidance on how to measure the fair value of stock-based employee compensation. Paragraphs 26-33 provide guidance on how to attribute compensation cost to the periods in which employees render the related services. Appendix B, which is an integral part of this Statement, provides additional guidance on both measurement and attribution of employee compensation cost.

Measurement Objective and Date

17. The objective of the measurement process is to estimate the fair value, based on the stock price at the **grant date,** of stock options or other equity instruments to which employees become entitled when they have rendered the requisite service and satisfied any other conditions necessary to earn the right to benefit from the instruments (for example, to exercise stock options or to sell shares of stock). Restrictions that continue in effect after employees have earned the rights to benefit from their instruments, such as the inability to transfer **vested** employee stock options to third parties, affect the value of the instruments actually issued and therefore are reflected in estimating their fair value. However, restrictions that stem directly from the forfeitability of instruments to which employees have not yet earned the right, such as the inability either to exercise a nonvested option or to sell **nonvested stock,** do not affect the value of the instruments issued at the vesting date, and their effect therefore is not included in that value. Instead, no value is attributed to instruments that employees forfeit because they fail to satisfy specified service- or performance-related conditions.

Measurement Methods

Awards that call for settlement by issuing equity instruments

18. The fair value of a share of nonvested stock awarded to an employee shall be measured at the market price (or estimated market price, if the stock is not publicly traded) of a share of the same stock as if it were vested and issued on the grant date. Nonvested stock granted to employees usually is referred to as **restricted stock,** but this Statement reserves that term for shares whose sale is contractually or

---

[8]APB Opinion No. 22, *Disclosure of Accounting Policies,* requires an entity to include a description of all significant accounting policies as an integral part of the financial statements. The method used to account for stock-based employee compensation arrangements is an accounting policy to be included in that description.

[9]That accounting has been required since 1973 in accordance with AICPA Accounting Interpretation 1, "Stock Plans Established by a Principal Stockholder," of Opinion 25.

governmentally restricted after the shares are vested and fully outstanding. The fair value of a share of restricted stock awarded to an employee, that is, a share that will be restricted after the employee has a vested right to it, shall be measured at its fair value, which is the same amount as a share of similarly restricted stock issued to nonemployees.

19. The fair value of a stock option (or its equivalent) granted by a **public entity** shall be estimated using an option-pricing model (for example, the Black-Scholes or a binomial model) that takes into account as of the grant date the exercise price and expected life of the option, the current price of the underlying stock and its expected **volatility,** expected dividends on the stock (except as provided in paragraphs 32 and 33), and the risk-free interest rate for the expected term of the option. For options that a U.S. entity grants on its own stock, the risk-free interest rate used shall be the rate currently available on zero-coupon U.S. government issues with a remaining term equal to the expected life of the options. Guidance on selecting other assumptions is provided in Appendix B. The fair value of an option estimated at the grant date shall not be subsequently adjusted for changes in the price of the underlying stock or its volatility, the life of the option, dividends on the stock, or the risk-free interest rate.

20. A **nonpublic entity** shall estimate the value of its options based on the factors described in the preceding paragraph, except that a nonpublic entity need not consider the expected volatility of its stock over the expected life of the option. The result of excluding volatility in estimating an option's value is an amount commonly termed **minimum value.**

21. It should be possible to reasonably estimate the fair value of most stock options and other equity instruments at the date they are granted. Appendix B illustrates techniques for estimating the fair values of several options with complicated features. However, in unusual circumstances, the terms of a stock option or other equity instrument may make it virtually impossible to reasonably estimate the instrument's fair value at the date it is granted. For example, it may be extremely difficult, if not impossible, to reasonably estimate the fair value of a stock option whose exercise price decreases (or increases) by a specified amount with specified changes in the price of the underlying stock. Similarly, it may not be possible to reasonably estimate the value of a convertible instrument if the conversion ratio depends on the outcome of future events.

22. If it is not possible to reasonably estimate the fair value of an option or other equity instrument at the grant date, the final measure of compensation cost shall be the fair value based on the stock price and other pertinent factors at the first date at which it is possible to reasonably estimate that value. Generally, that is likely to be the date at which the number of shares to which an employee is entitled and the exercise price are determinable. Estimates of compensation cost for periods during which it is not possible to determine fair value shall be based on the current intrinsic value of the award, determined in accordance with the terms that would apply if the option or similar instrument had been currently exercised.

Employee stock purchase plans

23. If an employee stock purchase plan satisfies all of the following criteria, the plan is not compensatory. Therefore, the discount from market price merely reduces the proceeds from issuing the related shares of stock.

a. The plan incorporates no option features other than the following, which may be incorporated:
   (1) Employees are permitted a short period of time—not exceeding 31 days—after the purchase price has been fixed to enroll in the plan.
   (2) The purchase price is based solely on the stock's market price at date of purchase, and employees are permitted to cancel participation before the purchase date and obtain a refund of amounts previously paid (such as those paid by payroll withholdings).
b. The discount from the market price does not exceed the greater of (1) a per-share discount that would be reasonable in a recurring offer of stock to stockholders or others or (2) the per-share amount of stock issuance costs avoided by not having to raise a significant amount of capital by a public offering. A discount of 5 percent or less from the market price shall be considered to comply with this criterion without further justification.
c. Substantially all full-time employees that meet limited employment qualifications may participate on an equitable basis.

24. A plan provision that establishes the purchase price as an amount based on the lesser of the stock's market price at date of grant or its market price at date of purchase is, for example, an option feature that causes the plan to be compensatory. Similarly, a plan in which the purchase price is based on the

stock's market price at date of grant and that permits a participating employee to cancel participation before the purchase date and obtain a refund of amounts previously paid is a compensatory plan.

Awards that call for settlement in cash

25. Some awards of stock-based compensation result in the entity's incurring a liability because employees can compel the entity to settle the award by transferring its cash or other assets to employees rather than by issuing equity instruments. For example, an entity may incur a liability to pay an employee either on demand or at a specified date an amount to be determined by the increase in the entity's stock price from a specified level. The amount of the liability for such an award shall be measured each period based on the current stock price. The effects of changes in the stock price during the **service period** are recognized as compensation cost over the service period in accordance with the method illustrated in FASB Interpretation No. 28, *Accounting for Stock Appreciation Rights and Other Variable Stock Option or Award Plans.* Changes in the amount of the liability due to stock price changes after the service period are compensation cost of the period in which the changes occur.

Recognition of Compensation Cost

26. The total amount of compensation cost recognized for an award of stock-based employee compensation shall be based on the number of instruments that eventually vest. No compensation cost is recognized for awards that employees forfeit either because they fail to satisfy a service requirement for vesting, such as for a **fixed award,** or because the entity does not achieve a **performance condition,** unless the condition is a target stock price or specified amount of intrinsic value on which vesting or exercisability is conditioned. For awards with the latter condition, compensation cost shall be recognized for awards to employees who remain in service for the requisite period regardless of whether the target stock price or amount of intrinsic value is reached.[10] Previously recognized compensation cost shall not be reversed if a vested employee stock option expires unexercised.

27. For purposes of this Statement, a stock-based employee compensation award becomes vested when an employee's right to receive or retain shares of stock or cash under the award is not contingent on the performance of additional services. Typically, an employee stock option that is vested also is immediately exercisable. However, if performance conditions affect either the exercise price or the exercisability date, the service period used for attribution purposes shall be consistent with the assumptions used in estimating the fair value of the award. Paragraphs 309 and 310 in Appendix B illustrate how to account for an option whose exercise price depends on a performance condition.

28. An entity may choose at the grant date to base accruals of compensation cost on the best available estimate of the number of options or other equity instruments that are expected to vest and to revise that estimate, if necessary, if subsequent information indicates that actual forfeitures are likely to differ from initial estimates. Alternatively, an entity may begin accruing compensation cost as if all instruments granted that are subject only to a service requirement are expected to vest. The effect of actual forfeitures would then be recognized as they occur. Initial accruals of compensation cost for an award with a performance condition that will determine the number of options or shares to which all employees receiving the award will be entitled shall be based on the best estimate of the outcome of the performance condition, although forfeitures by individual employees may either be estimated at the grant date or recognized only as they occur.[11]

29. Compensation cost estimated at the grant date for the number of instruments that are expected to vest based on performance-related conditions, as well as those in which vesting is contingent only on future service for which the entity chooses to estimate forfeitures at the grant date pursuant to paragraph 28, shall be adjusted for subsequent changes in the expected or actual outcome of service- and performance-related conditions until the vesting date. The effect of a change in the estimated number of shares or options expected to vest is a change in an estimate, and the cumulative effect of the change on current and prior periods shall be recognized in the period of the change.

---

[10]The existence of a target stock price that must be achieved to make an option exercisable generally affects the value of the option. Option-pricing models have been adapted to value many of those *path-dependent* options.

[11]For convenience, the remainder of this document refers to options or shares *expected to vest* because referring specifically to both acceptable methods of accounting for forfeitures by individual employees each time the point is mentioned would be too unwieldy.

30. The compensation cost for an award of equity instruments to employees shall be recognized over the period(s) in which the related employee services are rendered by a charge to compensation cost and a corresponding credit to equity (paid-in capital) if the award is for future service. If the service period is not defined as an earlier or shorter period, the service period shall be presumed to be the period from the grant date to the date that the award is vested and its exercisability does not depend on continued employee service (paragraph 27). If an award is for past services, the related compensation cost shall be recognized in the period in which it is granted.

31. Compensation cost for an award with a graded vesting schedule shall be recognized in accordance with the method described in Interpretation 28 if the fair value of the award is determined based on different expected lives for the options that vest each year, as it would be if the award is viewed as several separate awards, each with a different vesting date. If the expected life or lives of the award is determined in another manner, the related compensation cost may be recognized on a straight-line basis. However, the amount of compensation cost recognized at any date must at least equal the value of the vested portion of the award at that date. Appendix B illustrates application of both attribution methods to an award accounted for by the fair value based method.

32. Dividends or dividend equivalents paid to employees on the portion of an award of stock or other equity instruments that vests shall be charged to retained earnings. Nonforfeitable dividends or dividend equivalents paid on shares of stock that do not vest shall be recognized as additional compensation cost. The choice of whether to estimate forfeitures at the grant date or to recognize the effect of forfeitures as they occur described in paragraph 28 also applies to recognition of nonforfeitable dividends paid on shares that do not vest.

33. If employees receive only the dividends declared on the class of stock granted to them after the stock becomes vested, the value of the award at the grant date shall be reduced by the present value of dividends expected to be paid on the stock during the vesting period, discounted at the appropriate risk-free interest rate. The fair value of an award of stock options on which dividend equivalents are paid to employees or are applied to reduce the exercise price pursuant to antidilution provisions shall be estimated based on a dividend payment of zero.

Additional Awards and Modifications of Outstanding Awards

34. The fair value of each award of equity instruments, including an award of **reload options,** shall be measured separately based on its terms and the current stock price and related factors at the date it is granted.

35. A modification of the terms of an award that makes it more valuable shall be treated as an exchange of the original award for a new award. In substance, the entity repurchases the original instrument by issuing a new instrument of greater value, incurring additional compensation cost for that incremental value. The incremental value shall be measured by the difference between (a) the fair value of the modified option determined in accordance with the provisions of this Statement and (b) the value of the old option immediately before its terms are modified, determined based on the shorter of (1) its remaining expected life or (2) the expected life of the modified option. Appendix B provides further guidance on and illustrates the accounting for modifications of both vested and nonvested options.

36. Exchanges of options or changes to their terms in conjunction with business combinations, spinoffs, or other equity restructurings are modifications for purposes of this Statement. However, a change to the terms of an award in accordance with antidilution provisions that are designed, for example, to equalize an option's value before and after a stock split or a stock dividend is not a modification of an award for purposes of this Statement.

Settlements of Awards

37. An entity occasionally may repurchase equity instruments issued to employees after the employees have vested rights to them. The amount of cash or other assets paid (or liabilities incurred) to repurchase an equity instrument shall be charged to equity, provided that the amount paid does not exceed the value of the instruments repurchased. For example, an entity that repurchases for $10 a share of stock on the date it becomes vested does not incur additional compensation cost if the market price of the stock is $10 at that date. However, if the market price of the stock is only $8 at that date, the entity incurs an additional $2 ($10 – $8) of cost. An entity that settles a nonvested award for cash has, in effect, vested the award, and the amount of compensation cost measured at the grant date but not yet recognized shall be recognized at the date of repurchase.

38. For employee stock options, the incremental amount, if any, to be recognized as additional compensation cost upon cash settlement shall be determined based on a comparison of the amount paid with the value of the option repurchased, determined based on the remainder of its original expected life at that date. As indicated in paragraph 37, if stock options are repurchased before they become vested, the amount of unrecognized compensation cost shall be recognized at the date of the repurchase.

39. The accounting shall reflect the terms of a stock-based compensation plan as those terms are mutually understood by the employer and the employees who receive awards under the plan. Generally, the written plan provides the best evidence of its terms. However, an entity's past practice may indicate that the **substantive terms** of a plan differ from its written terms. For example, an entity that grants a **tandem award** consisting of either a stock option or a cash stock appreciation right (SAR) is obligated to pay cash on demand if the choice is the employee's, and the entity thus incurs a liability to the employee. In contrast, if the choice is the entity's, it can avoid transferring its assets by choosing to settle in stock, and the award qualifies as an equity instrument. However, if an entity that nominally has the choice of settling awards by issuing stock generally settles in cash, or if the entity generally settles in cash whenever an employee asks for cash settlement, the entity probably is settling a substantive liability rather than repurchasing an equity instrument. The substantive terms shall be the basis for the accounting.

40. To restrict control to a limited group, for example, the members of a particular family, a nonpublic entity may obligate itself to repurchase its equity instruments for their fair value at the date of repurchase. In practice, such an obligation is not deemed to convert the stock to a liability. This Statement is not intended to change that view of the effect of a fair value repurchase agreement for a nonpublic entity. Thus, a nonpublic entity may grant or otherwise issue to employees equity instruments subject to such a repurchase agreement. The repurchase agreement does not convert those equity instruments to liabilities, provided that the repurchase price is the fair value of the stock at the date of repurchase.

Accounting for Tax Consequences of Equity Instruments Awarded to Employees

41. Income tax regulations specify allowable tax deductions for stock-based employee compensation arrangements in determining an entity's income tax li-

ability. Compensation cost recognized under this Statement is measured based on the fair value of an award to an employee. Under existing U.S. tax law, allowable tax deductions are generally measured at a specified date as the excess of the market price of the related stock over the amount the employee is required to pay for the stock (that is, at intrinsic value). The **time value** component of the fair value of an option is not tax deductible. Therefore, tax deductions generally will arise in different amounts and in different periods from compensation cost recognized in financial statements.

42. The cumulative amount of compensation cost recognized for a stock-based award that ordinarily results in a future tax deduction under existing tax law shall be considered to be a deductible temporary difference in applying FASB Statement No. 109, *Accounting for Income Taxes*. The deferred tax benefit (or expense) that results from increases (or decreases) in that temporary difference, for example, as additional service is rendered and the related cost is recognized, shall be recognized in the income statement. Recognition of compensation cost for an award that ordinarily does not result in tax deductions under existing tax law shall not be considered to result in a deductible temporary difference in applying Statement 109. A future event, such as an employee's disqualifying disposition of stock under existing U.S. tax law, can give rise to a tax deduction for an award that ordinarily does not result in a tax deduction. The tax effects of such an event shall be recognized only when it occurs.

43. Statement 109 requires a deferred tax asset to be evaluated for future realization and to be reduced by a valuation allowance if, based on the weight of the available evidence, it is more likely than not that some portion or all of the deferred tax asset will not be realized. Differences between (a) the deductible temporary difference computed pursuant to paragraph 42 and (b) the tax deduction inherent in the current fair value of the entity's stock shall not be considered in measuring either the gross deferred tax asset or the need for a valuation allowance for a deferred tax asset recognized under this Statement.

44. If a deduction reported on a tax return for a stock-based award exceeds the cumulative compensation cost for that award recognized for financial reporting, the tax benefit for that excess deduction shall be recognized as additional paid-in capital. If the deduction reported on a tax return is less than the cumulative compensation cost recognized for financial reporting, the write-off of a related deferred tax asset in

excess of the benefits of the tax deduction, net of the related valuation allowance, if any, shall be recognized in the income statement except to the extent that there is remaining additional paid-in capital from excess tax deductions from previous stock-based employee compensation awards accounted for in accordance with the fair value based method in this Statement. In that situation, the amount of the write-off shall be charged against that additional paid-in capital. If an entity that continued to apply Opinion 25 subsequently adopts the fair value based method in this Statement, only the additional paid-in capital recognized from excess tax deductions for awards accounted for under the fair value based method pursuant to the transition provisions of paragraph 52 is available to absorb any such write-offs.

Disclosures

45. Regardless of the method used to account for stock-based employee compensation arrangements, the financial statements of an entity shall include the disclosures specified in paragraphs 46–48. All entities shall disclose the following information in the "Summary of Significant Accounting Policies" or its equivalent:[11a]

a. The method used—either the intrinsic value method or the fair value based method—to account for stock-based employee compensation in each period presented
b. For an entity that adopts the fair value recognition provisions of this Statement, for all financial statements in which the period of adoption is presented, a description of the method of reporting the change in accounting principle
c. If awards of stock-based employee compensation were outstanding and accounted for under the intrinsic value method of Opinion 25 for any period for which an income statement is presented, a tabular presentation of the following information for all periods presented:
   (1) Net income and basic and diluted earnings per share as reported
   (2) The stock-based employee compensation cost, net of related tax effects, included in the determination of net income as reported
   (3) The stock-based employee compensation cost, net of related tax effects, that would

have been included in the determination of net income if the fair value based method had been applied to all awards[11b]
   (4) Pro forma net income as if the fair value based method had been applied to all awards
   (5) Pro forma basic and diluted earnings per share as if the fair value based method had been applied to all awards.

The required pro forma amounts shall reflect the difference in stock-based employee compensation cost, if any, included in net income and the total cost measured by the fair value based method, as well as additional tax effects, if any, that would have been recognized in the income statement if the fair value based method had been applied to all awards. The required pro forma per share amounts shall reflect the change in the denominator of the diluted earnings per share calculation as if the assumed proceeds under the treasury stock method, including measured but unrecognized compensation cost and the excess tax benefits credited to additional paid-in capital, were determined under the fair value based method. Examples of the required tabular presentation are included in Appendix B of FASB Statement No. 148, *Accounting for Stock-Based Compensation—Transition and Disclosure.*

46. An entity with one or more stock-based compensation plans shall provide a description of the plan(s), including the general terms of awards under the plan(s), such as vesting requirements, the maximum term of options granted, and the number of shares authorized for grants of options or other equity instruments. An entity that uses equity instruments to acquire goods or services other than employee services shall provide disclosures similar to those required by this paragraph and paragraphs 47 and 48 to the extent that those disclosures are important in understanding the effects of those transactions on the financial statements.

47. The following information shall be disclosed for each year for which an income statement is provided:

a. The number and weighted-average exercise prices of options for each of the following groups of options: (1) those outstanding at the beginning of the year, (2) those outstanding at the end of the

[11a]APB Opinion No. 22, *Disclosure of Accounting Policies,* paragraph 15, introduces the term *Summary of Significant Accounting Policies* and expresses a preference for disclosure of accounting policies preceeding the notes to financial statements or as the initial note.

[11b]For purposes of applying the guidance in this Statement, *all awards* refers to awards granted, modified, or settled in fiscal periods beginning after December 15, 1994—that is, awards for which the grant date fair value was required to be measured under this Statement.

year, (3) those exercisable at the end of the year, and those (4) granted, (5) exercised, (6) forfeited, or (7) expired during the year.

b. The weighted-average grant-date fair value of options granted during the year. If the exercise prices of some options differ from the market price of the stock on the grant date, weighted-average exercise prices and weighted-average fair values of options shall be disclosed separately for options whose exercise price (1) equals, (2) exceeds, or (3) is less than the market price of the stock on the grant date.

c. The number and weighted-average grant-date fair value of equity instruments other than options, for example, shares of nonvested stock, granted during the year.

d. A description of the method and significant assumptions used during the year to estimate the fair values of options, including the following weighted-average information: (1) risk-free interest rate, (2) expected life, (3) expected volatility, and (4) expected dividends.

e. Total compensation cost recognized in income for stock-based employee compensation awards.

f. The terms of significant modifications of outstanding awards.

An entity that grants options under multiple stock-based employee compensation plans shall provide the foregoing information separately for different types of awards to the extent that the differences in the characteristics of the awards make separate disclosure important to an understanding of the entity's use of stock-based compensation. For example, separate disclosure of weighted-average exercise prices at the end of the year for options with a fixed exercise price and those with an indexed exercise price is likely to be important, as would segregating the number of options not yet exercisable into those that will become exercisable based solely on employees' rendering additional service and those for which an additional condition must be met for the options to become exercisable.

48. For options outstanding at the date of the latest statement of financial position presented, the range of exercise prices (as well as the weighted-average exercise price) and the weighted-average remaining contractual life shall be disclosed. If the range of exercise prices is wide (for example, the highest exercise price exceeds approximately 150 percent of the lowest exercise price), the exercise prices shall be segregated into ranges that are meaningful for assessing the number and timing of additional shares that may be issued and the cash that may be received as a result of

option exercises. The following information shall be disclosed for each range:

a. The number, weighted-average exercise price, and weighted-average remaining contractual life of options outstanding

b. The number and weighted-average exercise price of options currently exercisable.

Earnings per Share Implications

49. FASB Statement No. 128, *Earnings per Share,* requires that employee stock options, nonvested stock, and similar equity instruments granted to employees be treated as potential common shares in computing diluted earnings per share. Diluted earnings per share shall be based on the actual number of options or shares granted and not yet forfeited, unless doing so would be antidilutive. If vesting is contingent upon factors other than continued service, such as the level of future earnings, the shares or options shall be treated as contingently issuable shares in accordance with paragraphs 30–35 of Statement 128. If stock options or other equity instruments are granted or forfeited during a period, the shares issuable shall be weighted to reflect the portion of the period during which the equity instruments were outstanding.

50. In applying the treasury stock method of Statement 128, the assumed proceeds shall be the sum of (a) the amount, if any, the employee must pay, (b) the amount of compensation cost attributed to future services and not yet recognized, and (c) the amount of tax benefits, if any, that would be credited to additional paid-in capital. Statement 128 provides detailed examples of the treatment of stock compensation plans accounted for under Opinion 25 in earnings per share computations. Although the related cost and tax amounts will differ if the fair value based accounting method in this Statement is applied, the principles in Statement 128 remain applicable.

Effective Date and Transition

51. The requirement in paragraph 8 of this Statement shall be effective for transactions entered into after December 15, 1995.

52. If an entity elects to adopt the recognition provisions of this Statement for stock-based employee compensation in a fiscal year beginning before December 16, 2003, that change in accounting principle shall be reported using any one of the following methods:

a. *Prospective method.* Apply the recognition provisions to all employee awards granted, modified, or settled after the beginning of the fiscal year in which the recognition provisions are first applied.

b. *Modified prospective method.* Recognize stock-based employee compensation cost from the beginning of the fiscal year in which the recognition provisions are first applied as if the fair value based accounting method in this Statement had been used to account for all employee awards granted, modified, or settled in fiscal years beginning after December 15, 1994.

c. *Retroactive restatement method.* Restate all periods presented to reflect stock-based employee compensation cost under the fair value based accounting method in this Statement for all employee awards granted, modified, or settled in fiscal years beginning after December 15, 1994. Restatement of periods prior to those presented is permitted but not required. The restated net income and earnings per share of prior periods shall be determined in a manner consistent with the requirements of paragraphs 12, 13, and 45 of this Statement.

Accounting for modifications and settlements of awards initially accounted for in accordance with Opinion 25 is discussed and illustrated in Appendix B. Awards are considered to be accounted for under Opinion 25 only if they were issued in fiscal periods beginning before December 15, 1994 (that is, the grant date fair value of the awards was never required to be measured under this Statement).

52A. If an entity elects to adopt the recognition provisions of this Statement for stock-based employee compensation in fiscal years beginning after December 15, 2003, that change in accounting must be reported using either the method described in paragraph 52(b) or the method described in paragraph 52(c).

52B. An entity that elects the transition method described in paragraph 52(b) or 52(c) may need to report an adjustment to additional paid-in capital as of the beginning of the first period for which stock-based employee compensation cost is accounted for in accordance with the fair value based method. For awards that are unvested or, in the case of certain variable awards, unexercised as of the beginning of that period, that adjustment shall be determined as follows:

a. The carrying amounts of unearned or deferred compensation (contra-equity accounts), stock-based compensation liabilities, and the related deferred tax balances recognized under Opinion 25, if any, shall be reversed.

b. The stock-based compensation liabilities and related deferred tax balances determined under this Statement shall be recognized.

c. The difference between the amounts reversed in (a) and the amounts recognized in (b) shall be reported as an adjustment to additional paid-in capital as of the beginning of the period. No cumulative effect of a change in accounting principle shall be presented.

Examples of determining and recording that adjustment are included in Appendix B of Statement 148. For those entities that elect retroactive restatement, any effect on additional paid-in capital or retained earnings arising from the restatement of periods subsequent to the period of initial application of the fair value based method but prior to the earliest period for which an income statement is presented should be reported as an adjustment to those accounts as of the beginning of the earliest period for which an income statement is presented. The transition adjustment as well as the effect of restatement of intervening periods, if any, should be disclosed in the year of adoption.

53. The disclosure requirements of this Statement shall be effective for financial statements for fiscal years beginning after December 15, 1995, or for the fiscal year for which this Statement is initially adopted for recognizing compensation cost, whichever comes first. Pro forma disclosures required by paragraph 45 of this Statement shall include the effects of all awards granted in fiscal years that begin after December 15, 1994. Pro forma disclosures for awards granted in the first fiscal year beginning after December 15, 1994 need not be included in financial statements for that fiscal year but shall be presented subsequently whenever financial statements for that fiscal year are presented for comparative purposes with financial statements for a later fiscal year.

54. During the initial phase-in period, the effects of applying this Statement for either recognizing compensation cost or providing pro forma disclosures are not likely to be representative of the effects on reported net income for future years, for example, because options vest over several years and additional awards generally are made each year. If that situation exists, the entity shall include a statement to that effect. The entity also may wish to provide supplemental disclosure of the effect of applying the fair value based accounting method to all awards made in fiscal years beginning before the date of initial adoption that were not vested at that date.

> **The provisions of this Statement need
> not be applied to immaterial items.**

This Statement was adopted by the affirmative votes of five members of the Financial Accounting Standards Board. Messrs. Foster and Leisenring dissented.

Messrs. Foster and Leisenring dissent from the issuance of this Statement because they believe that the compensation associated with employee stock options should be recognized as a cost in the financial statements and disagree with the decision to permit that cost to be reflected only in pro forma disclosures. They agree with the Board's conclusion that employee stock options represent compensation and that the amount of associated cost can be determined with sufficient reliability for recognition in financial statements. Messrs. Foster and Leisenring believe that, having reached those conclusions, the Board should accept the conclusion of paragraph 9 of FASB Concepts Statement No. 5, *Recognition and Measurement in Financial Statements of Business Enterprises,* that disclosure is not a substitute for recognition in financial statements for items that meet recognition criteria.

Messrs. Foster and Leisenring believe that a high level of controversy and a perceived threat to accounting standard setting in the private sector as discussed in paragraphs 57-62 are inappropriate reasons for not requiring recognition in financial statements of an item that meets the recognition criteria of Concepts Statement 5.

Messrs. Foster and Leisenring further believe that the effect of this Statement on improving disclosure of compensation cost for those entities that choose not to adopt the fair value based method is substantially diminished because the Statement does not require disclosure of the pro forma effect on net income and earnings per share in summarized interim financial data required by APB Opinion No. 28, *Interim Financial Reporting.* They believe that comparable data presented on a quarterly basis is important to financial analysis.

While Messrs. Foster and Leisenring concur with the conclusion that fair value of employee stock options is the appropriate measure of compensation cost, they do not agree that the grant date method of accounting as described in paragraphs 16-44 results in the best measure of that cost. As discussed in paragraphs 155-160, the Board's decision to look to certain events that occur after the grant date in measuring compensation cost, by, for example, adjusting for forfeitures after that date, is inconsistent with its decision to base compensation cost on a grant date stock price. Messrs. Foster and Leisenring believe that a more understandable, representationally faithful, and consistent measure of the compensation granted in an employee stock option would be achieved by measuring the fair value of all vested options at the vesting date. As explained in paragraphs 96 and 167, employee stock options are not issued until the vesting date. At that date, the employer and employee have fulfilled their obligations under the agreement that offers the stock options and consequently the options are issued and can then be measured.

Despite their belief that vesting date measurement would result in a superior measure of compensation cost, Messrs. Foster and Leisenring would have accepted the modified grant date method and assented to issuance of this Statement if the cost determined under that method was required to be recognized rather than only disclosed. Notwithstanding the shortcomings of the modified grant date method of measuring compensation expense, it is significantly better than the continued failure to recognize compensation cost in financial statements—the result of applying Opinion 25.

Members of the Financial Accounting Standards Board:

Dennis R. Beresford,	Anthony T. Cope	Robert H. Northcutt
Chairman	John M. Foster	Robert J. Sweiringa
Joseph V. Anania	James J. Leisenring	

Appendix A

BASIS FOR CONCLUSIONS

CONTENTS

Appendix A

BASIS FOR CONCLUSIONS

Introduction

55. This appendix summarizes considerations that Board members deemed significant in reaching the conclusions in this Statement. It includes reasons for accepting certain approaches and rejecting others. Individual Board members gave greater weight to some factors than to others.

56. Accounting for stock-based employee compensation plans is a pervasive subject that affects most public entities and many nonpublic entities. Opinion 25 continues to be criticized for producing anomalous results and for lacking an underlying conceptual rationale that helps in resolving implementation questions or in deciding how to account for stock-based compensation plans with new features. A frequently cited anomaly is that the requirements of Opinion 25 typically result in the recognition of compensation cost for performance options but no cost is recognized for fixed options that may be more valuable at the grant date than performance options. Critics of Opinion 25 also note that long-term fixed options granted to employees are valuable financial instruments, even though they carry restrictions that usually are not present in other stock options. Financial statements prepared in accordance with the requirements of Opinion 25 do not recognize that value. The resulting financial statements are less credible than they could be, and the financial statements of entities that use fixed employee options ex-

tensively are not comparable to those of entities that do not make significant use of fixed options. Because of the various criticisms of Opinion 25, in March 1984, the Board added a project to its agenda to reconsider accounting by employers for stock-based compensation plans.

Why the Board Decided Not to Require Fair Value Accounting

57. In June 1993, the Board issued an Exposure Draft on accounting for stock-based compensation that would have replaced Opinion 25 with an accounting method based on recognizing the fair value of equity instruments issued to employees, regardless of whether the instrument was a share of stock, a fixed or performance option, or some other instrument, with measurement based on the stock price at the date the instrument was granted. Requiring all entities to follow the fair value based method in the Exposure Draft would have (a) resulted in accounting for stock-based employee compensation that was both internally consistent and also consistent with accounting for all other forms of compensation, (b) "leveled the playing field" between fixed and variable awards, and (c) made the accounting for equity instruments issued to employees more consistent with the accounting for all other free-standing equity instruments[12] and the related consideration received.

58. That Exposure Draft was extraordinarily controversial. The Board's due process is intended to ensure that the views of all interested parties are heard and fully considered. The Board not only expects but actively encourages debate of the issues and proposals in an Exposure Draft, and the final Statement

---

[12]A *free-standing* equity instrument is one that is not embedded in a compound instrument with other, nonequity, components. For example, convertible debt is a compound instrument with both liability and equity components. The call option on common stock that is part of convertible debt is not a free-standing equity instrument, and it is not currently accounted for separately from the liability component.

generally benefits from information the Board receives during that debate. Both the Board and its constituents usually learn from the debate, with the result that the Board's views and the views of many of its constituents generally move closer together during the debate.

59. Unlike other highly controversial topics, the controversy on accounting for stock-based compensation escalated throughout the exposure process. The main point of contention was whether compensation cost should be recognized for stock options with fixed terms that are at-the-money[13] at the date they are granted. Constituents gave different reasons for opposing cost recognition, with many expressing concerns about whether the fair value of employee stock options at the grant date can be estimated with sufficient reliability. Most respondents urged the Board to expand disclosures about stock-based employee compensation arrangements rather than to change the basic accounting method in Opinion 25. The specific comments of respondents to the Exposure Draft and later comments made as the Board redeliberated the issues are discussed later in this appendix.

60. The debate on accounting for stock-based compensation unfortunately became so divisive that it threatened the Board's future working relationship with some of its constituents. Eventually, the nature of the debate threatened the future of accounting standards setting in the private sector.

61. The Board continues to believe that financial statements would be more relevant and representationally faithful if the estimated fair value of employee stock options was included in determining an entity's net income, just as all other forms of compensation are included. To do so would be consistent with accounting for the cost of all other goods and services received as consideration for equity instruments. The Board also believes that financial reporting would be improved if all equity instruments granted to employees, including instruments with variable features such as options with performance criteria for vesting, were accounted for on a consistent basis. However, in December 1994, the Board decided that the extent of improvement in financial reporting that was envisioned when this project was added to its technical agenda and when the Exposure Draft was issued was not attainable because the de-

liberate, logical consideration of issues that usually leads to improvement in financial reporting was no longer present. Therefore, the Board decided to specify as preferable and to encourage but not to require recognition of compensation cost for all stock-based employee compensation, with required disclosure of the pro forma effects of such recognition by entities that continue to apply Opinion 25.

62. The Board believes that disclosure of the pro forma effects of recognizing compensation cost according to the fair value based method will provide relevant new information that will be of value to the capital markets and thus will achieve some but not all of the original objectives of the project. However, the Board also continues to believe that disclosure is not an adequate substitute for recognition of assets, liabilities, equity, revenues, and expenses in financial statements, as discussed more fully later in this appendix. The Board chose a disclosure-based solution for stock-based employee compensation to bring closure to the divisive debate on this issue—not because it believes that solution is the best way to improve financial accounting and reporting.

Alternative Accounting Methods

63. When the Board decided not to require recognition of compensation cost determined by the fair value based method, it also decided that it was important to avoid explicitly or implicitly endorsing arguments against the Exposure Draft that the Board did not find credible. For example, endorsing the argument that an at-the-money option has no value or that financial statements should exclude the values of financial instruments that are difficult to measure would misrepresent the Board's views and likely would impede efforts to improve financial reporting in other areas—especially for other financial instruments, some of which are more complex and may be more difficult to value than employee stock options. The Board's reasons for rejecting those arguments are discussed in paragraphs 76-117 of this appendix.

64. The Board also decided that improved disclosure alone—regardless of the nature of the disclosure—is not sufficient. The Board thus encourages entities to adopt the fair value based accounting method described in this Statement. That method permits an entity to avoid in its financial statements the effects of

---

[13]For convenience, this appendix uses the terms *at-the-money, out-of-the-money,* and *in-the-money* commonly used by option traders to denote an option with an exercise price that *equals, exceeds,* or *is less than,* respectively, the current price of the underlying stock.

Opinion 25 that encourage fixed plans and discourage plans with variable, performance-based features. Providing an alternative accounting method does not achieve as level a playing field for fixed and performance-based plans as the Board and some of its constituents would like. However, it establishes a mechanism that can result in a more level playing field over time if many entities eventually choose the fair value based accounting method. It also provides a means by which improved accounting for stock-based employee compensation can evolve through the voluntary actions of entities and their advisors without the Board's having to undertake another reconsideration of this topic.

65. Some respondents asked the Board to permit a plan-by-plan choice between the intrinsic value based method in Opinion 25 and the fair value based method established by this Statement. Those respondents argued that permitting a choice on a plan-by-plan basis would result in a more level playing field than this Statement does because entities could avoid the volatility in compensation cost for performance-based awards that often results from Opinion 25's requirements while continuing to report zero expense for most fixed awards.

66. The Board decided not to permit a plan-by-plan choice of accounting method. The overriding objective of this project was to improve the accounting for stock-based employee compensation by superseding Opinion 25's inconsistent requirements for fixed and variable awards with accounting standards that would result in more relevant and representationally faithful financial statements. That overriding objective could not be achieved without developing an internally consistent accounting method for all stock-based employee compensation awards, which in turn would result in a more level playing field for fixed and performance-based awards. Providing a plan-by-plan choice would permit an entity to choose whichever method it expected to produce the lower reported cost for each award. Permitting that choice was not among the objectives of this project.

67. The Board notes that permitting a plan-by-plan choice of accounting method would still be biased in favor of fixed awards and therefore would not level the playing field because entities would continue to be required to report compensation cost for performance-based awards while reporting no cost for fixed, at-the-money stock options. Permitting a plan-by-plan choice of method also would eliminate any possibility that evolution alone, perhaps

including the development of improved methods of valuing employee stock options, would eventually result in better accounting for stock-based employee compensation.

68. Permitting a plan-by-plan choice also would result in more complicated financial statements. Entities would need to explain which method was used for which plans and why, as well as provide disclosures to help users of the financial statements understand the effects of the accounting choices and to put all entities' reporting on a comparable basis.

Pro Forma Disclosure of the Effects of Applying Fair Value Based Accounting

69. Because this Statement permits an entity to choose either of two different methods of accounting for its stock-based employee compensation arrangements, pro forma disclosures of net income and earnings per share computed as if the fair value based method had been applied are required in the financial statements of an entity that chooses to continue to apply Opinion 25. Those disclosures will give investors, creditors, and other users of the financial statements more comparable information, regardless of the accounting method chosen. The pro forma disclosures also will make available better information than Opinion 25 provides about the costs of stock-based employee compensation.

Accounting for Equity Instruments Issued for Consideration Other Than Employee Services

70. The Exposure Draft was the result of a comprehensive reconsideration of accounting issues related to the measurement and recognition of stock-based compensation paid to employees for their services. The Board's deliberations that led to the Exposure Draft also considered current accounting principles for other issuances of equity instruments. The Exposure Draft covered accounting for all issuances of equity instruments for consideration other than cash, which may consist of goods, services, or noncash financial instruments. Issuances of equity instruments for cash rarely raise significant accounting issues.

71. That the cost of employee services measured by the fair value of equity instruments issued in exchange for them should be recognized in determining the employer's net income is not a new notion. Indeed, recognition of consideration received and the cost incurred as that consideration is used in an entity's operations is fundamental to the accounting for

equity instruments. Therefore, the Board decided that the choice of continuing to apply Opinion 25 should be limited to issuances of equity instruments for employee services that fall within the scope of Opinion 25. All other issuances of equity instruments should be recognized based on the fair value of the consideration received or the fair value of the equity instrument issued, whichever is more reliably measurable.

72. The appropriate date at which to measure an issuance of equity instruments for consideration other than employee services usually is a relatively minor issue. Generally, an issuer of equity instruments receives the consideration for them—whether it is cash, another financial instrument, or an enforceable right to receive financial instruments, goods, or services in the future—almost immediately after the parties agree to the transaction. If a longer time elapses between agreement and receipt of consideration, neither the issuer nor the other party may have a unilateral obligation under the contract during that period. That is, the distinction between grant date and vesting date may not be clearly present in many situations other than stock-based employee compensation. For some transactions, such as business combinations, in which the measurement date can be a significant issue, other accounting pronouncements specify the date of the stock price on which the measurement should be based. Therefore, this Statement does not specify the measurement date for determining the fair value of equity instruments issued to other than employees.

73. An initial draft of portions of this Statement was distributed for comment to task force members and other constituents. That draft would have excluded stock options issued to independent contractors from the transactions to which an entity may apply Opinion 25 in determining net income. Some respondents objected to that exclusion because, in practice, the scope of Opinion 25 has been extended to include many option recipients treated as independent contractors for tax purposes. Some Board members believe that application of Opinion 25 to service providers that are not employees is inappropriate. However, the Board decided that resolving the issue of whether Opinion 25 has been applied correctly is outside the scope of this Statement. The Board expects to consider at a future date the need for a pronouncement about the scope of Opinion 25.

Why Stock-Based Employee Compensation Is a Cost That Should Be Recognized in Financial Statements

74. Paragraphs 75-117 of this appendix discuss the reasons for the Board's principal conclusions on recognition and measurement issues, which support the Board's belief that recognition of stock-based employee compensation cost determined according to the fair value based method is preferable to continued application of Opinion 25 with only pro forma disclosures of the effect of recognizing stock-based employee compensation cost. That discussion begins with the basic issue of why employee stock options give rise to recognizable compensation cost.

75. The Board's conclusion that recognizing the costs of all stock-based employee compensation, including fixed, at-the-money stock options, is the preferable accounting method stems from the following premises:

a. Employee stock options have value.
b. Valuable financial instruments given to employees give rise to compensation cost that is properly included in measuring an entity's net income.
c. The value of employee stock options can be estimated within acceptable limits for recognition in financial statements.

Employee Stock Options Have Value

76. An option or warrant to buy an entity's stock for a fixed price during an extended future time period is a valuable right, even if the ways in which the holder can exercise the right are limited. Investors pay cash to buy stock options and warrants that generally have fewer restrictions than employee stock options, and unrestricted options and warrants are traded daily in financial markets. The additional restrictions inherent in employee stock options, such as the inability to transfer the option to a third party for cash, cause the value of an employee stock option to be less than the value of an otherwise identical tradable option at any time before the expiration date, but the restrictions do not render employee stock options valueless.

77. Employees rarely pay cash to acquire their employee stock options. Instead, employees provide services to their employer in exchange for cash, stock options, and other employee benefits. Even if employees are required to pay a nominal amount of cash for their options, it usually is far less than the fair value of the options received. The majority of the consideration an employer receives for employee

stock options is employee services. Nonrecognition of compensation cost implies either that employee stock options are free to employees or that the options have no value—neither of which is true.

78. Some respondents argued that an employee stock option has value only if the employee ultimately realizes a gain from it. The Board does not agree. Many traded options ultimately expire worthless; that does not mean that the options had no value either when they were written or at any other time before they expired. An employee stock option has value when it is granted regardless of whether, ultimately, (a) the employee exercises the option and purchases stock worth more than the employee pays for it or (b) the option expires worthless at the end of the option period. The grant date value of a stock option is the value *at that date* of the right to purchase an entity's stock at a fixed price for an extended time period. Investors pay cash to acquire that right—employees provide services to acquire it.

Valuable Financial Instruments Given to Employees Give Rise to Compensation Cost That Is Properly Included in Measuring an Entity's Net Income

79. Employees provide services for which employers pay compensation. The components of an employee's total compensation package are, to some extent, flexible. The compensation package, for example, might include more cash and less health insurance, or the package might include stock options and less cash. Some employers even offer employees a choice between predetermined amounts of cash and stock options.

80. Large employers have included stock options in the compensation packages of upper echelon management for many years, and some employers recently have adopted broad-based plans that cover most of their full-time employees. A stated objective of issuing stock options is to align employee interests with those of shareholders and thereby motivate employees to work to maximize shareholder value. In addition, many start-up and other cash-poor entities provide stock options to make up for cash wages and other benefits that are less than those available elsewhere. Many respondents from younger, rapidly growing entities said that their success was attributable in large part to their extensive use of stock options; without stock options, they could not have attracted and retained the employees they needed.

81. Some respondents said that stock options are not direct compensation for services rendered and thus are not comparable to cash salaries and wages. Rather, stock options usually have other objectives, such as to attract valuable employees and to encourage them to stay with the employer by requiring a period of service before their options vest and become exercisable. Stock options, like other forms of incentive compensation, also are intended to motivate employees to perform better than they might have without the incentive. Stock-based compensation awards often are intended to compensate employees for incremental efforts beyond the basic performance required to earn their salaries or wages. Respondents that made those points generally said that the value of stock options is not a compensation cost that should be recognized in the entity's financial statements.

82. The Board acknowledges that employee stock options, as well as other forms of stock-based compensation, usually are not direct substitutes for a stated amount of cash salaries. That does not, however, imply that the value of options issued to employees is not a recognizable cost. Group medical and life insurance, disability insurance, employer-paid memberships in health clubs, and the like also are not direct compensation like cash salaries because the amount of benefit that an individual employee may receive does not necessarily vary directly with either the amount or the quality of the services rendered. However, virtually everyone agrees that the costs of those benefits are properly deducted in determining the entity's net income. Like employee stock options, benefits such as medical insurance and pensions are compensation in the broad sense of costs incurred to attract, retain, and motivate employees. It has long been an established practice that, even if employee benefits are paid—directly or indirectly—with shares of the employer's stock, the value of the stock issued to the employee or the service provider is a cost to be reported in the employer's income statement.

83. Some opponents of recognizing compensation cost for stock options acknowledge that stock options are recognizable compensation, but they say that a requirement to recognize that compensation would have adverse economic consequences because many entities would reduce or eliminate their stock option programs. However, some of the same respondents also said that Opinion 25's bias in favor of fixed awards at the expense of awards with performance conditions, options with indexed exercise prices, and the like should be eliminated because that bias has undesirable economic consequences. It deters employers from using more performance-based awards,

which those respondents consider preferable to fixed options in many situations.

84. The Board's operating precepts require it to consider issues in an even-handed manner, without intentionally attempting to encourage or to discourage specific economic actions. That does not imply that improved financial reporting should not have economic consequences; a change in accounting standards that makes available more relevant and representationally faithful financial information often will have economic consequences. For example, the availability of the new information resulting from application of this Statement may lead an entity to reassess the costs and benefits of its existing stock option plans. If a reassessment reveals that the expected benefits of a stock option plan do not justify its costs, a rational response would be to revise or eliminate the plan. However, an entity presumably would not restrict or eliminate a stock option program whose motivational effect on employees is expected to make a net contribution to reported results of operations. To do so would not be rational because continuing the plan would be expected to increase revenues (or to decrease other expenses) more than enough to offset the reported compensation cost. In addition, many small, emerging entities told the Board that stock options often substitute for higher cash wages or other benefits, such as pensions. Significantly reducing those option programs would not make economic sense if employees would demand equal or greater cash wages or other benefits to replace the lost stock options.

85. Some people told the Board that a requirement to recognize compensation cost might bring additional discipline to the use of employee stock options. Unless and until the stock price rises sufficiently to result in a dilutive effect on earnings per share, the current accounting for most fixed stock options treats them as though they were a "free good." Stock options have value—employee stock options are granted as consideration for services and thus are not free.

86. Some respondents said that recognizing the compensation cost stemming from stock options would, by itself, raise the cost of capital of all entities that use options extensively. An individual entity's cost of capital would rise only if its lenders or buyers and sellers of its stock had previously been misled by the accounting under Opinion 25 to believe that

fixed, at-the-money employee stock options have no value and thus impose no cost on the entity. If that were the situation for an individual entity or a group of entities, any increase in cost of capital would result from new, relevant information. Making available at an acceptable cost information that is helpful in making investment, credit, and similar decisions is the overriding objective of financial reporting.

87. Some respondents that agreed with the Board's conclusion that accounting standards, by themselves, are highly unlikely to have negative economic consequences noted that the market abhors uncertainty. Reducing uncertainty can reduce the cost of capital. Therefore, recognizing in financial statements the cost of all stock-based compensation measured in a reasonable and internally consistent manner might lower rather than raise an entity's cost of capital. Financial statement users no longer would have to decide how to consider the cost of stock options in their analysis of an entity, knowing that whatever method they chose would be based on inadequate information. With amounts recognized and measured on a reasonable and consistent basis that takes into account detailed information generally available only to the entity, users might still choose to modify or use the available information in different ways, but they would have a reasonable starting point for their analysis.

Expenses and capital transactions

88. Some respondents pointed out that the definition of expenses in FASB Concepts Statement No. 6, *Elements of Financial Statements,* says that expenses result from outflows or using up of assets or incurring of liabilities (or both). They asserted that because the issuance of stock options does not result in the incurrence of a liability, no expense should be recognized. The Board agrees that employee stock options are not a liability—like stock purchase warrants, employee stock options are equity instruments of the issuer. However, equity instruments, including employee stock options, are valuable financial instruments and thus are issued for valuable consideration, which often is cash or other financial instruments but for employee stock options is employee services. Using in the entity's operations the benefits embodied in the asset received results in an expense, regardless of whether the consideration is cash or

other financial instruments, goods, or services.[14] Moreover, even if shares of stock or other equity instruments are donated to a charity, the fair value of the instruments issued is recognized together with other charitable contributions in determining the issuer's net income. The Board recently reaffirmed that general principle in FASB Statement No. 116, *Accounting for Contributions Received and Contributions Made.*

89. Others noted that the issuance of an employee stock option is a capital transaction. They contended that capital transactions do not give rise to expenses. As discussed in paragraph 88, however, issuances of equity instruments result in the receipt of cash, other financial instruments, goods, or services, which give rise to expenses as they are used in an entity's operations. Accounting for the consideration received for issuing equity instruments has long been fundamental to the accounting for all free-standing equity instruments except one—fixed stock options subject to the requirements of Opinion 25.

90. Some respondents also asserted that the issuance of an employee stock option is a transaction directly between the recipient and the preexisting stockholders in which the stockholders agree to share future equity appreciation with employees. The Board disagrees. Employees provide services to the entity—not directly to the individual stockholders—as consideration for their options. Carried to its logical conclusion, that view would imply that the issuance of virtually any equity instrument, at least those issued for goods or services rather than cash or other financial instruments, should not affect the issuer's financial statements. For example, no asset or related cost would be reported if shares of stock were issued to acquire legal or consulting services, tangible assets, or an entire business in a business combination. Moreover, in practice today, even if a stockholder directly pays part of an employee's cash compensation (or other corporate expenses), the transaction and the related costs are reflected in the entity's financial statements, together with the stockholder's contribution to paid-in capital. To omit such costs would give a misleading picture of the entity's financial performance.

91. The Board sees no conceptual basis that justifies different accounting for the issuance of employee stock options than for all other transactions involving either equity instruments or employee services. As explained in paragraphs 57-62, the Board's decision not to require recognition of compensation expense based on the fair value of options issued to employees was not based on conceptual considerations.

Prepaid compensation

92. The Exposure Draft proposed that an asset, prepaid compensation, be recognized at the date stock-based employee compensation awards are granted; the prepaid compensation would represent the value already conveyed to employees for services to be received in the future. Later, compensation cost would have been incurred as the benefits embodied in that asset were used up; that is, as the employees rendered service during the vesting period.

93. Many respondents objected to the recognition of prepaid compensation at the grant date. They said that, unlike most other amounts paid to suppliers before services are received, the proposed prepaid compensation for nonvested stock-based employee compensation did not meet the definition of an asset in paragraph 25 of Concepts Statement 6, which defines assets as "probable future economic benefits obtained or controlled by a particular entity as a result of past transactions or events" (footnote reference omitted). Prepaid fees for legal services, consulting services, insurance services, and the like represent probable future economic benefits that are controlled by the entity because the other party to the transaction has entered into a contract to provide services to earn the fees. The service provider is not entitled to walk away from its obligation to render the services that are the subject of the contract by merely foregoing collection of the fee for services not rendered. Although courts rarely enforce specific performance under a service contract, a construction contractor, for example, cannot decide unilaterally not to finish a building after digging the foundation without being subject to legal action for monetary damages by the other party to the contract. Contracts sometimes specify the damages to be paid if the contract is broken. In other circumstances, such as prepaid rent or insurance, the purchaser of the service may be able to successfully sue for specific performance—the right to occupy an office or to be reimbursed for fire damage, for example.

---

[14]Concepts Statement 6, paragraph 81, footnote 43, notes that, in concept, most expenses decrease assets. However, if receipt of an asset, such as services, and its use occur virtually simultaneously, the asset often is not recorded.

94. Those respondents said that employee stock options do not represent probable future benefits that are controlled by the employer at the date the options are granted because employees are not obligated to render the services required to earn their options. The contract is unilateral—not bilateral—because the entity has only conditionally transferred forfeitable equity instruments and is obligated to issue the instruments *if and when* the employee has rendered the specified service or satisfied other conditions. However, the employee is not obligated to perform the services and may leave the employer's service without being subject to damages beyond the loss of the compensation that would have been paid had the services been rendered.

95. The Board agreed that an entity does not obtain an asset for future service to be rendered at the date employee stock options are granted. Therefore, this Statement does not require recognition of prepaid compensation at the grant date. Rather, the cost of the related services is accrued and charged to compensation cost only in the period or periods in which the related services are received. At the grant date, awards of stock-based employee compensation are fully executory contracts. Once employees begin to render the services necessary to earn the compensation, execution of the contracts has begun, and recognition of the services already received is appropriate. The Board's conclusions on how to attribute compensation cost to the periods in which the entity receives the related employee services are discussed further in paragraphs 196-203.

96. An equity instrument may be conditionally transferred to another party under an agreement that allows that party to choose at a later date whether to deliver the agreed consideration for it, which may be goods or services rather than cash or financial instruments, or to forfeit the right to the instrument conditionally transferred, with no further obligation. In that situation, the equity instrument is not *issued* for accounting purposes until the issuing entity has received consideration for it and the condition is thus satisfied. The grant of an employee stock option subject to vesting conditions is an example of such a conditional transfer. For that reason, this Statement does not use the term *issued* to refer to the grant of a stock option or other equity instrument that is subject to service or performance conditions for vesting. The Board's conclusion that the entity receives no asset at the date employee stock options are granted is consistent with that use of the term *issued*. That conclusion about the issuance date of employee stock options, in turn, has implications for the appropriate date at which to measure the value of the equity instruments issued. This Statement requires a measurement method that combines attributes of both grant date and vesting date measurement. The Board's conclusions on measurement date and method are discussed in paragraphs 149-154.

The usefulness and integrity of the income statement

97. An entity's income statement reports the revenues from and the costs of its operations. Under Opinion 25, part of a cost, compensation to employees, is not reported in the income statements of most entities that issue fixed stock options. Some entities use fixed stock options more extensively than other entities do, and reported operating expenses thus are understated to differing degrees. Comparisons between entities of profit margins, rates of return, income from operations, and the like are impaired to the extent that entities continue to account for their stock-based employee compensation according to the provisions of Opinion 25.

98. To illustrate the lack of comparability under Opinion 25, assume that Companies A, B, and C each report $6 million of total compensation cost. Company A does not grant fixed stock options to its employees, but Companies B and C do. The value of fixed stock options as a percentage of the total compensation package for employees of Companies B and C are 20 percent and 40 percent, respectively. Total compensation cost for Company A is $6 million, as reported in its financial statements. Although Companies B and C report the same amount of compensation cost as Company A, actual compensation is $7.5 million for Company B and $10 million for Company C. The three companies are not competing for capital on a level playing field because their financial statements are not comparable.

99. Some opponents of recognizing compensation cost for stock options are concerned about the adverse effect they contend it would have on their income statements. The effect of recognizing compensation cost for employee stock options should be neither more nor less adverse than the effect of recognizing a comparable amount of depreciation (or any other) cost. Recognition of depreciation always reduces a company's profit or increases its loss. Entities would look more profitable on paper if they discontinued depreciating their assets, but no one recommends not recognizing depreciation to eliminate its adverse effect on the income statement. The

Board believes that the rationale that a potentially adverse effect on income statements argues against recognition is no more compelling for compensation than it is for any other cost.

The cost of employee stock options is not "recognized" in earnings per share

100. Primary earnings per share represents the entity's earnings (the numerator) divided by the number of common and common equivalent shares outstanding (the denominator). Some respondents that opposed recognizing compensation cost for employee stock options said that to do so would "double count" the effect of issuing stock options. The dilutive effect of any in-the-money stock options is included in the denominator of earnings per share, and a reduction in net income (the numerator) would, in their view, create an inappropriate dual effect.

101. The Board disagrees. A transaction that results in an expense and also increases, actually or potentially, the number of shares outstanding properly affects both the numerator and denominator of the earnings per share calculation. If an entity issues stock, stock options, or stock purchase warrants for cash and uses the cash received to pay expenses, earnings are reduced and more common equivalent shares are outstanding. Even in applying the requirements of Opinion 25, granting nonvested (so-called restricted) stock decreases the numerator (earnings) and increases the denominator (shares outstanding). In both of those examples, the effect on income appropriately reflects the use of the consideration received (either cash or employee services) for issuing equity instruments.

Disclosure is not a substitute for recognition

102. FASB Concepts Statement No. 5, *Recognition and Measurement in Financial Statements of Business Enterprises,* says:

> Since recognition means depiction of an item in both words and numbers, with the amount included in the totals of the financial statements, disclosure by other means is *not* recognition. Disclosure of information about the items in financial statements and their measures that may be provided by notes or parenthetically on the face of financial statements, by supplementary information, or by other means of financial reporting is not a substitute for recognition in financial statements for items that meet recognition criteria. [paragraph 9]

103. Many respondents contended that improved disclosures about employee stock options in the notes to financial statements would be as useful as recognition of compensation cost in the income statement. A specific disclosure proposal submitted by a group of providers and users of financial statements and endorsed by the largest accounting firms was illustrated in Appendix E of the Exposure Draft. Most respondents, including some that had previously endorsed that proposal, agreed that the proposed disclosures were too extensive and included some items that more properly belong in a proxy statement. The Board received several other proposals for disclosures in lieu of recognition during the exposure period and during its redeliberations of the conclusions in the Exposure Draft. Some of those proposals included a measure of the value of options granted during the year, but most focused largely on greatly expanding the detailed data disclosed about stock-based employee compensation plans.

104. As discussed in paragraphs 57-62, the Board's decision to encourage but not to require recognition of compensation cost for the fair value of stock-based employee compensation was not based on acceptance of the view that disclosure is an adequate substitute for recognition in the financial statements. If disclosure and recognition were equal alternatives, the arguments for only disclosing either detailed information about stock-based employee compensation awards or the amount of unrecognized cost would apply equally to other costs such as depreciation, warranties, pensions, and other postretirement benefits.

105. The Board believes that the pro forma disclosures required by this Statement will mitigate to some extent the disadvantages of permitting disclosure in lieu of recognition. To disclose only additional details about options granted, vested, forfeited, exercised, expired, and the like would permit only the most sophisticated users of financial statements to estimate the income statement impact of recognizing all compensation costs. Many individual investors and other users of financial statements could not, and even the more sophisticated users would have available less information than the entity itself has on which to base estimates of value and related compensation cost related to employee stock options. The Board's continuing belief that disclosure is not an adequate substitute for recognition of items that qualify for recognition in financial statements is the reason for this Statement's establishment of the fair value based accounting method as preferable for purposes

of justifying an accounting change and for encouraging entities to adopt it.

106. The Board did not specifically address during its formal deliberations whether pro forma disclosures of the effects on net income and earnings per share of applying the fair value based method should be included in summarized interim financial data required by APB Opinion No. 28, *Interim Financial Reporting.* That question arose late in the process of drafting this Statement when some Board members noted that comparable information about earnings and earnings per share presented on a quarterly basis would be important to financial analysis. Other Board members agreed but thought that it was too late in this extraordinarily controversial project to add a requirement for pro forma disclosures in summarized interim financial data. Therefore, this Statement does not require those disclosures. If a need for pro forma disclosures on a quarterly basis becomes apparent, the Board will consider at a later date whether to require those disclosures.

The Value of Employee Stock Options Can Be Estimated within Acceptable Limits for Recognition in Financial Statements

107. The value of employee services rendered is almost always impossible to measure directly. For that reason, accounting for the cost of employee services is based on the value of compensation paid, which is presumed to be an adequate measure of the value of the services received. Compensation cost resulting from employee stock options is measured based on the value of stock options granted rather than on the value of the services rendered by the employee, which is consistent with the accounting for other forms of employee compensation.

108. Trading of options in the financial markets has increased significantly in the last 20 years. During that time, mathematical models to estimate the fair value of options have been developed to meet the needs of investors. Some employers and compensation consultants have used variations of those models in considering how much of a compensation package should consist of employee stock options and in determining the total value of a compensation package that includes stock options. Many that have been using option-pricing models for those purposes said that the existing models are not sufficiently accurate for accounting purposes, although they are adequate for comparing the value of compensation packages across entities and for estimating the value of options

in designing compensation packages. Those respondents generally said that a more precise measure is needed for measuring compensation cost in the income statement than for comparing the value of total compensation, including options, paid by various entities or in determining how many options to grant an employee.

109. The Board disagrees with the distinction made by those respondents. One important use of financial statements is to compare the relative attractiveness of investment and lending opportunities available in different entities. Therefore, increasing the comparability of financial statements is a worthy goal, even if all entities use a measurement method that is less precise than the Board or its constituents might prefer.

110. The derivative markets have developed rapidly with the introduction of new kinds of options and option-like instruments, many of which are long term and nontraded—or even nontransferable. For example, interest rate caps and floors, both of which are forms of options, are now common. Often, option components are embedded in other instruments, and both the seller and the purchaser of the instrument need to evaluate the value added by each component of a compound instrument. Mathematical models that extend or adapt traditional option-pricing models to take into account new features of options and other derivative securities also continue to be developed. Sometimes decisions have been made based on inadequate analysis or incomplete models, resulting in large and highly publicized losses for one party to a contract. Those instances usually lead to additional analysis of the instruments in question and further refinement of the models. However, market participants—whether they consider themselves to be traders, investors, or hedgers—continue to commit billions of dollars to positions in options and other derivatives, based at least in part on analysis using mathematical pricing models that are not perfect.

111. The Exposure Draft noted that uncertainties inherent in estimates of the fair value of employee stock options are generally no more significant than the uncertainties inherent in measurements of, for example, loan loss reserves, valuation allowances for deferred tax assets, and pension and other postretirement benefit obligations. All estimates, because they are estimates, are imprecise. Few accrual-based accounting measurements can claim absolute reliability, but most parties agree that financial statement recognition of estimated amounts that are approximately right is preferable to the alternative—

recognizing nothing—which is what Opinion 25 accounting recognizes for most employee stock options. Zero is not within the range of reasonable estimates of the value of employee stock options at the date they are granted, the date they vest, or at other dates before they expire, with the possible exception of deep-out-of-the-money options that are near expiration. Even those latter options generally have a nominal value until very shortly before expiration.

112. Many respondents said that the Exposure Draft inappropriately compared the imprecision in estimating the value of employee stock options with similar imprecisions inherent in estimating, for example, the amount of an entity's obligation to provide postretirement health care benefits. They said that because postretirement health care benefits eventually result in cash payments by the entity, the total obligation and related cost are "trued up" over the entity's life. In contrast, the value of employee stock options estimated at the grant date is not trued up to reflect the actual gain, if any, that an employee realizes from an award of employee stock options. Those respondents asserted that the lack of true-up makes it necessary for the estimated value of employee stock options that forms the basis for recognizing the related compensation cost to be more precise than an estimate of the value of the same entity's obligation for postretirement health care benefits.

113. The Board questions that perceived distinction between the relative importance of the precision of estimates of the value of employee stock options and the precision of other estimates inherent in financial statements. Although the total amount of any expense that is ultimately paid in cash will necessarily equal the total of the amounts attributed to each of a series of years, the appropriate amount to attribute to any individual year is never trued up. Nor can the precision of the reported total obligation be determined at any date while it is being incurred. For example, the total cost of a postretirement health care plan will be trued up only if the plan is terminated. Investors, creditors, and other users of financial statements must make decisions based on a series of individual years' financial statements that covers less than the entire life of the entity. For costs such as postretirement health care benefits, the true-up period for an individual employee (or group of similar employees) may be decades, and even then the total amount cannot be separated from amounts attributed to other employees. Concern about the reliability of estimates of the value of employee stock options and the related cost seem equally applicable to annual estimates of, for example, obligations for postretirement benefits and the related cost.

114. The respondents that emphasized the importance of truing up the total cost of a stock-based employee compensation award generally were adamantly opposed to exercise date accounting—the only accounting method for employee stock options that would true up interim cost estimates to equal the total gain, if any, an employee realizes. The Board rejected exercise date accounting for conceptual reasons, as discussed in paragraph 149. However, deferring final measurement of a transaction until enough of the related uncertainties have been resolved to make reasonably reliable measurement possible is the usual accounting response to measurement difficulties for virtually all other transactions except an award to an employee of fixed stock options.

115. The standard Black-Scholes and binomial option-pricing models were designed to estimate the value of transferable stock options. The value of transferable stock options is more than the value of employee stock options at the date they are granted primarily for two reasons. First, transferable stock options can be sold, while employee stock options are not transferable and can only be exercised. Second, an employee can neither sell nor exercise nonvested options. Nonvested employee options cannot be exercised because the employee has not yet fully paid for them and is not obligated to do so. Options other than employee options rarely include a lengthy period during which the holder may choose to walk away from the right to the options.

116. The measurement method in this Statement reduces the estimated value of employee stock options below that produced by an option-pricing model for nonforfeitable, transferable options. Under the method in this Statement, the recognized value of an employee stock option that does not vest—and thus is never issued to the employee—is zero. In addition, the estimated value of an employee stock option is based on its expected life rather than its maximum term, which may be considerably longer. Paragraphs 155-173 explain why the Board believes those adjustments are appropriate and sufficient to deal with the forfeitability and nontransferability of employee stock options.

117. The Board continues to believe that use of option-pricing models, as modified in this Statement, will produce estimates of the fair value of stock options that are sufficiently reliable to justify recognition in financial statements. Imprecision in those estimates does not justify failure to recognize

compensation cost stemming from employee stock options. That belief underlies the Board's encouragement to entities to adopt the fair value based method of recognizing stock-based employee compensation cost in their financial statements.

The Major Measurement Issues

118. Having concluded that stock-based compensation awards, including fixed employee stock options, give rise to compensation cost that should be measured and recognized, the Board considered more detailed measurement and recognition issues.

Measurement Date for Compensation Cost

119. The measurement date for equity instruments awarded to employees is the date at which the stock price that determines the measurement of the transaction is fixed. The Board decided to retain the provisions of the Exposure Draft that the measurement date for equity instruments awarded to employees (and subsequently issued to them if vesting conditions are satisfied) and the related compensation cost is to be measured based on the stock price at the grant date. The Board also decided that the measurement method for public entities should be fair value. The reasons for those conclusions are discussed in paragraphs 120-153.

Alternative measurement dates

120. Possible measurement dates[15] include the date an award of employee stock options or similar instruments is granted *(grant date)*, the date on which an employee has completed the service period necessary for the award to vest *(vesting date)*, the dates on which an employee renders the related services *(service date)*, the date on which all service-related conditions expire *(service expiration date)*, and the date an award is exercised or expires *(exercise date)*.

Grant date

121. Advocates of grant date measurement note that the employer and employee come to a mutual understanding of the terms of a stock-based compensation award at the grant date and that the employee begins to render the service necessary to earn the award at that date. They therefore consider use of the grant

date stock price appropriate in measuring the transaction. In deciding whether to grant shares of stock, for example, and how many shares to award an individual employee, both parties to the agreement presumably have in mind the current stock price—not the possible stock price at a future date. If compensation cost were measured based on the stock price at a later date, such as the date at which the award vests, the amount of compensation cost that could result from an award would not be known when an entity decides how many shares to grant.

122. Advocates of grant date measurement also consider it to be consistent with generally accepted concepts and practices applied to other equity instruments. They note that changes in the price of an issuer's stock after the parties agree to the terms of a transaction in which equity instruments are issued generally do not affect the amount at which the transaction is recognized. Grant date measurement is based on the view that equity instruments are issued to employees—not just conditionally transferred to them—at the grant date because the entity becomes unilaterally obligated at that date. To be fully consistent with that premise, application of grant date measurement would reflect at the grant date the effect of all restrictions inherent in vesting requirements in estimating the value of the instrument considered to be effectively issued at the grant date. For example, the value of an option with a performance vesting condition would be reduced to reflect both the likelihood that the performance condition will not be satisfied and the likelihood that an employee will not continue in service until the end of the vesting period. Because the option is considered to have been issued to the employee at the grant date, initial estimates would not be subsequently adjusted to reflect differences between estimates and experience.

123. To illustrate, if an employee stock option is considered to be issued at the grant date, the effects of its forfeitability, nonexercisability, and any other restrictions that are in effect during the vesting period but that are removed after the equity instrument vests would be estimated at the grant date and not subsequently adjusted. Changes in the value of an entity's equity instruments, whatever the source, are not reflected in its income statement. For example, if an entity grants 10,000 options, of which 8,000 are expected to vest, the final measurement of com-

---

[15]The various measurement dates discussed refer to the dates of the stock price on which fair value and the related cost are based—not the date at which accounting based on estimates begins. For example, most advocates of vesting date measurement would begin accruing compensation cost as soon as employees begin to render the service necessary to earn their awards.

pensation cost in accordance with a strict application of grant date measurement would be based on the value of 8,000 options estimated at the grant date, regardless of whether all 10,000 options or only 4,000 options eventually vested.

Vesting date

124. Proponents of measuring the value of equity instruments awarded to employees and the related compensation cost based on the stock price at the date the award vests note that employees have not earned the right to retain their shares or options until that date. They suggest that a more descriptive term for the *grant date* would be *offer date* because the entity makes an offer at that date and becomes unilaterally obligated to issue equity instruments to employees if the employees render the necessary service or satisfy other conditions for vesting. Employees effectively accept the offer by fulfilling the requisite conditions (generally rendering services) for vesting. Proponents contend that the transaction between the employer and employee should not be finally measured until both parties have fulfilled their obligations under the agreement because the employee has only a conditional right to the equity instruments and the instruments thus are not actually issued until that date.

125. Advocates of vesting date measurement consider that method to be consistent with accounting for the issuance of similar equity instruments to third parties for either cash or an enforceable right to receive cash or other assets in the future. At the date a stock purchase warrant, for example, is issued and measured, the investor need not satisfy obligations to provide further assets or services to the issuer to become eligible to retain and exercise the warrant. For the same reason, vesting date advocates do not think that measurement of the transaction should be held open after the vesting date. Once an employee stock option becomes vested, they contend that the employee is in much the same position as a third-party holder of a stock purchase warrant.

Service date

126. Service date measurement can be described as a variation of vesting date measurement because, in both methods, measurement of the transaction between an employer and its employees is held open until employees have rendered the services necessary to earn their awards. Advocates of service date measurement, however, point out that the earning of

a stock-based compensation award—like the earning of other forms of compensation—is a continuous process. They say that the related compensation cost should be measured based on the stock prices during the period the service is rendered—not solely on the stock price at either the beginning or the end of that period.

127. Advocates of service date measurement prefer it to vesting date measurement because the latter adjusts the value (and related cost) of the service received in, for example, year 1 of a two-year vesting period based on stock price changes that occur in year 2. Moreover, the increment (or decrement) in value attributable to year 1's service is recognized in year 2. In their view, to retroactively adjust the value of consideration (in this situation, employee services) already received for future issuance of an equity instrument is to treat awards of equity instruments to employees as if they were liabilities until the employees have vested rights to them. Because an entity that grants stock options is obligated only to issue its own stock, not to transfer its assets, those that favor service date accounting contend that measuring nonvested awards as if they were liabilities is inappropriate.

128. Under service date measurement, a proportionate number of the shares in a grant of shares of stock subject to vesting requirements, for example, would in concept be measured based on the stock price each day that an employee renders service. In practice, the results of daily accrual probably would be reasonably approximated by basing the amount of compensation cost recognized each accounting period on the average stock price for that period.

Service expiration date

129. The service expiration date, sometimes referred to as the *portability date,* is the date at which all service-related conditions that may change the terms under which employees may exercise their stock options expire. Awards of employee stock options generally specify a limited period of time, often 90 days but sometimes a shorter or even no period, after termination of service during which employees with vested options may exercise them. The options are canceled if they are not exercised by the end of that period. If the exercise period is 90 days after termination, the service expiration or portability date is 90 days before the maximum term of the options expires. If the options are exercised before then, the exercise date would be the measurement date. (For an

award of stock subject to vesting requirements, the service expiration date is the date at which service-related restrictions on the sale of the stock lapse, which usually would be the same as the vesting date.)

130. Advocates of service expiration date measurement argue that a limitation on exercise of an option after termination of service, say to 90 days, effectively reduces the term of a vested option to 90 days. On the day that an employee's rights to that option vest, the employee holds an option whose effective term is 90 days, regardless of its stated term. Each additional day of service until the service expiration date extends the life of the option by one day. Advocates also generally note that equity of an entity arises from transactions between the entity and its owners in their role as owners, not as suppliers, employees, creditors, or some other role. Advocates of service expiration date measurement do not consider an employee stock option to be an outstanding equity instrument as long as the employee must render additional service to extend the term of the option. Until then, the ongoing transaction is one between an entity and its employees in their role as employees in which the entity incurs a liability to pay for employee services. Thus, they say that it is appropriate to treat the option as a liability until all service-related restrictions expire (or the option is exercised, whichever comes first).

131. Supporters of service expiration date measurement also note that it would be easier to apply than earlier measurement dates. If the period after which service-related conditions expire is short, such as 90 days, most of the option's value at that time is likely to be made up of its intrinsic value, which is readily measurable. If the option has no intrinsic value at that time, its total value also is likely to be low, and concerns about how well traditional option-pricing models measure that value would be mitigated by the short life of the option.

Exercise date

132. Some that favor exercise date measurement of stock-based employee compensation awards do so because they consider call options written by an entity on its stock to be liabilities rather than equity instruments. They acknowledge that those options, including both employee stock options and stock purchase warrants, do not qualify as liabilities under the definition in paragraph 35 of Concepts Statement 6 because they do not obligate the entity to transfer its assets to the holder and thus lack an essen-

tial characteristic of a liability. Those that hold this view generally favor revising the conceptual distinction between liabilities and equity instruments so that an obligation to issue stock at a fixed price would qualify as a liability.

133. Advocates of exercise date measurement note that an obligation to issue stock at a price that may be less than its market price at the date of the transaction has the potential to transfer value from the preexisting stockholders to holders of the call options. In their view, that potential makes the obligation a liability of the entity, even though the entity is not obligated to transfer its own assets to the holders of the options. Other advocates of exercise date measurement contend that the gain, if any, that an employee realizes upon exercise of a stock option appropriately measures the total compensation paid. They are less concerned about the conceptual distinction between liabilities and equity because they see little, if any, practical difference between an employee stock option and a cash bonus indexed to the price of the entity's stock.

134. Exercise date advocates also note that measurement at that date is simple and straightforward. Concerns about how to apply option-pricing models initially developed for traded options to forfeitable, nontransferable employee options, how to estimate expected long-term volatility, and the like do not apply if final measurement is based on the gain, if any, that an employee realizes by exercising an option. The usual response to major problems in measuring the effects of a transaction is to defer final measurement until the difficulties are resolved. Exercise date measurement might be appropriate for that reason, regardless of more conceptual considerations.

Measurement Method for Compensation Cost

135. This Statement specifies fair value as the basic method for measuring awards of equity instruments, including stock options, to employees as compensation. Not only the appropriate measurement method but also the meaning of *fair value*—especially at the grant date—were contentious issues during the exposure period. Moreover, respondents' views on the measurement method often were closely linked to their views on the measurement date question. The possible measurement methods, together with differences, if any, in how they might be applied at various possible measurement dates are discussed in paragraphs 136-148. The reasons for the Board's conclusions on measurement date and method are then explained.

Intrinsic value

136. The intrinsic value of an option at any point during its term is the difference between its exercise price and the current price of the underlying stock. Intrinsic value thus excludes the value of the right to purchase the underlying stock at a fixed price for a specified future period—its time value. Respondents that favored measuring employee stock options at their intrinsic value generally said that intrinsic value is easily measured and understood. Some also noted that employees cannot convert the time value of their options to cash.

137. Intrinsic value measurement might be combined with any of the measurement dates discussed in paragraphs 120-134. However, the vast majority of the advocates of intrinsic value would accept only intrinsic value measurement at the grant date. They generally said that Opinion 25 has "worked well" and that the Board should not change its requirements but merely supplement them with additional disclosures. However, some respondents went further and said that grant date-intrinsic value accounting—Opinion 25's method for fixed plans—should be applied to variable plans as well. Adopting that suggestion would result in recognition of no compensation cost for all options that are at-the-money when granted, implying that at-the-money options have no value. The inaccuracy of that implication already has been discussed (paragraphs 76-78).

138. Respondents that favored extending grant date-intrinsic value measurement to variable plans said that the result would be a level playing field for fixed and variable plans. The Board believes that adopting a grant date-intrinsic value method for all options would level the playing field at the cost of making financial statements even less relevant and representationally faithful than they are when Opinion 25 is the basis of measuring stock-based employee compensation cost. That is not an acceptable outcome of a project that was undertaken with the overriding objective of improving financial reporting. An *exercise date*-intrinsic value method also would level the playing field, and some Board members think that it would enhance the relevance and representational faithfulness of financial statements.

Minimum value

139. The so-called minimum value method derives its name from the theory underlying its calculation. The idea is that a person who wishes to purchase a call option on a given stock would be willing to pay *at least* (perhaps more important, the option writer would demand *at least*) an amount that represents the benefit (sacrifice) of the right to defer payment of the exercise price until the end of the option's term. For a dividend-paying stock, that amount is reduced by the present value of the expected dividends because the holder of an option does not receive the dividends paid on the underlying stock.

140. Minimum value thus can be determined by a present value calculation. It is (a) the current price of the stock reduced by the present value of the expected dividends on the stock, if any, during the option's term minus (b) the present value of the exercise price. Present values are based on the risk-free rate of return. For a 10-year option with an exercise price of $50 on a stock with a current price of $50 and expected dividends of $.25 paid at the end of each quarter—an expected annual dividend yield of 2 percent—minimum value is computed as shown below. The risk-free interest rate available for 10-year investments is 7 percent.

Current stock price	$50.00
Minus:	
Present value of exercise price[16]	24.83
Present value of expected dividends	7.21
Minimum value	$17.96

Investing $24.83 at a 7 percent risk-free interest rate for 10 years would give the investor $50, which is the amount needed to exercise the option. However, an investor who held the stock rather than the option would receive dividends during the term of the option with a present value of $7.21. The net benefit from deferring payment of the exercise price thus is $17.96.

141. Minimum value also can be computed using an option-pricing model and an expected volatility of effectively zero. (Standard option-pricing models do not work if the volatility input is zero because the models use volatility as a divisor, and zero cannot be

---

[16]Present value calculations reflect daily compounding.

a divisor. Using an expected volatility of, say, 0.001 avoids that problem.) In the above example, using an option-pricing model with an expected volatility of effectively zero, a risk-free rate of 7 percent, an expected dividend yield of 2 percent, and an option term of 10 years results in a minimum value of $16.11. That is lower than the amount calculated using simple present value techniques ($16.11 versus $17.96) because the calculations inherent in option-pricing models assume that both the stock price and dividends will grow at the same rate (if the dividend assumption is stated as a constant yield). The assumed growth rate is the difference between the risk-free interest rate and the dividend rate, which is 5 percent (7 percent – 2 percent) in this example.

142. For a stock that pays no dividends, minimum value is the same regardless of which method is used, and the lower the expected dividend yield, the less difference between the results of the two methods. This Statement permits only nonpublic entities to measure their options at minimum value (paragraphs 174-178 explain the Board's conclusions on nonpublic entities), and many of the nonpublic entities that use employee stock options extensively pay either no or relatively low dividends. Moreover, the expected life of employee stock options with a contractual term of 10 years often is substantially shorter, which also reduces the amount of potential difference. In addition, models are available that compute value based on a fixed dividend amount, rather than a constant dividend yield. Therefore, the Board acceded to the request of some respondents to permit either method of computing minimum value.

Fair value

143. Because it ignores the effect of expected volatility, the minimum value method differs from methods designed to estimate the fair value of an option, such as the Black-Scholes and binomial option-pricing models and extensions or modifications of those original models. Expected volatility provides much of the value of options—especially relatively short-term options. Even for longer term options such as most employee stock options, the level of expected volatility accounts for a significant part of the difference in the values of options on different stocks. Option holders benefit from the volatility of stocks because they have the right to capture increases in the price of (and related return on) the underlying stock during the term of the option without having to bear the full risk of loss from stock price decreases. The maximum amount that the holder of a call option can

lose is the premium paid to the option writer—which represents the right to benefit from price increases without the corresponding risk of loss from price decreases during the option term. In contrast, the holder of a share of the underlying stock can lose the full value of the share.

144. The fair value of the option whose minimum value was computed in paragraphs 140 and 141 thus is more than either $17.96 or $16.11. The fair value of that option depends on the expected volatility of the underlying stock. If the expected long-term volatility of the stock in the example is 35 percent, the fair value of the option is approximately $23.08. Volatility and its effect on option value are defined and explained more fully in Appendixes E and F.

What is the fair value of an employee stock option?

145. The Exposure Draft applied to employee stock options the same definition of fair value that is used elsewhere in the authoritative literature. That definition and the related guidance, which are quoted in paragraph 9, focus first on the price at which a willing buyer and a willing seller would be willing to exchange an item in other than a forced or liquidation sale and require the use of quoted market prices for the same or similar items if they are available. However, the definition mentions several valuation techniques, including option-pricing models, that are acceptable for estimating fair value if quoted market or other exchange prices for the item or a similar item are not available.

146. Some respondents apparently focused solely on the part of the definition that refers to the price a willing buyer would pay for an item. They said that the objective of determining the fair value of an employee stock option should be to determine the amount of cash compensation employees would be willing to trade for their stock options. Those respondents mentioned several reasons, such as the relatively large amount of most employees' personal financial wealth that is tied to the fortunes of their employer or employees' need for cash to pay current expenses, that might make most employees unwilling to pay as much as a third party might pay for a given stock option.

147. The Board rejected that view of the meaning of the *fair value* of an employee stock option. The fair values of other financial instruments do not take into account either the source of the funds with which a

buyer might pay for the instrument or other circumstances affecting individual buyers. A logical extension of that view could result in a different "fair value" for identical options in a single grant for each employee who receives an award, even if the expected life is the same for each option.

148. Moreover, the definition of fair value places equal emphasis on the amount a willing (and presumably rational) seller would demand for the item. The estimated fair value of employee stock options, like the estimated fair value of other financial instruments for which market prices are not available, may not reflect all of the factors that an individual willing buyer or willing seller would consider in establishing an exchange price. That does not make it inappropriate to estimate the fair value of the item using a valuation technique that takes into account the theoretical effect on buyers and sellers as a group of the various features of the instrument. In addition, market prices are usually set at the margin. An option writer would seek the highest bidder with the capacity to buy the option. That bidder would be the pertinent "willing buyer."

Conclusions on Measurement Date and Method

149. After considering both the written responses to the Discussion Memorandum, *Distinguishing between Liability and Equity Instruments and Accounting for Instruments with Characteristics of Both,* and comments made at the public hearing on that document (refer to Appendix C), the Board decided early in 1992 not to pursue possible changes to the conceptual definitions of liabilities and equity. Instead, the Board decided to seek resolution of issues on accounting for stock-based compensation within the context of the conceptual definitions set forth in Concepts Statement 6 under which a call option written by an entity on its stock is an equity instrument rather than a liability. The Board decided not to pursue exercise date measurement on conceptual grounds because it is more consistent with viewing call options written as liabilities.

150. Each of the other possible measurement dates had advocates among the Board members in deliberations preceding issuance of the Exposure Draft. Even at that time, most Board members thought that a reasonable conceptual case could be made for either the vesting date or the service date. On balance, however, the Board agreed that a variation of grant date measurement was appropriate, and that was what the Exposure Draft proposed. In reaching that

conclusion, Board members generally found persuasive the argument that measurement at the grant date bases the compensation cost stemming from a stock-based compensation award on the stock price at the date the parties agree to its terms. As discussed in paragraphs 92-96, the Board also concluded in the Exposure Draft that an asset—prepaid compensation—should be recognized at the grant date because the Board was persuaded at that time that a forfeitable equity instrument conditionally transferred to an employee could be considered "issued," which is an important part of the rationale for grant date accounting. However, Board members subsequently agreed with the majority of respondents that said that an entity that grants stock-based compensation does not receive an enforceable right to employee services at the grant date. That conclusion raises an additional question about the appropriateness of grant date accounting versus some version of vesting date accounting.

151. An overwhelming majority of respondents favored grant date measurement. They generally emphasized the importance of basing the measure of the related cost on the stock price at the date the parties agree to the terms of an award. Most of those respondents, however, did not support the fair value based measurement method in the Exposure Draft. Most that opposed the Exposure Draft on that basis said that traditional option-pricing models, even modified to take into account the effect of forfeitability and nontransferability, did not fully reflect all of the factors that would affect the fair value of an employee stock option at the grant date. For example, an employee or a third party to whom an option is issued that is neither exercisable nor transferable for the first part of its life presumably would want to pay less for the option because of those restrictions. Similarly, many respondents pointed out that liquidity adds value and that the fair value of shares of "restricted" or "letter" stock is less than the value of unrestricted stock of the same entity.

152. Most respondents that took that view favored continued measurement of employee stock options at intrinsic value on the grounds that fair value could not be measured with reasonable reliability at the grant date. Others, however, suggested reducing the estimated fair value of both stock options and nonvested stock at the grant date to reflect additional restrictions during the vesting period. For example, some suggested a reduction in value by an arbitrary percentage, say, 10 percent for each year of the vesting period. The Board considered both that and other

possible, but more complicated, ways of taking restrictions during the vesting period into account.

153. The Board reaffirmed its conclusion in the Exposure Draft that public entities should account for their stock options and other equity instruments at fair value. A fair value basis is consistent with the measurement principles applied to other issuances of equity instruments and to other forms of compensation paid to employees. Equity instruments other than employee stock options and the consideration received for them are recognized at their fair values on the dates the instruments are issued. For example, the initial recognition of debt issued with detachable stock purchase warrants is based on the relative fair values of the debt and the warrants at the date of issuance—not on a calculated minimum value of the warrants. Similarly, a share of stock or a warrant issued to settle an obligation to pay for services other than employee services would be measured at fair value. Other forms of compensation paid to employees, including cash, other assets, pension benefits, and the like are initially measured at the fair value of the asset given up or the liability incurred. The Board does not believe that concerns about measurement are a sufficient reason to measure compensation paid in stock options on a different basis.

154. Paragraphs 165-173 discuss the modifications to standard option-pricing models to take into account the nontransferability of vested employee stock options. The Board's intent in this Statement is for the guidance in both the standards section and the guidance and illustrations in Appendix B to be sufficiently broad that employers may adopt future refinements in models that improve their application to employee stock options without requiring the Board to amend this Statement.

Restrictions that apply only during the vesting period

155. This Statement requires recognition of no compensation cost for awards that do not vest, as proposed in the Exposure Draft. Even so, some respondents said that an additional reduction in value is needed for awards of employee stock options that do vest to reflect their nonexercisability before they vested. Those respondents did not consider the use of expected life sufficient to reflect both the nontransferability and nonexercisability of nonvested options.

156. Board members generally agreed that investors who might purchase equity instruments with restrictions similar to those in a nonvested award of employee stock compensation (including nonvested shares of stock, which in effect are options for which the entire exercise price is employee services) would take those restrictions into account in determining how much they would be willing to pay for the instruments. However, employees do not pay the full value of their options at the grant date, although they may pay a nominal amount for each option granted. If they fully paid for their options at the grant date, the options would not be subsequently forfeitable, and the restrictions stemming from forfeitability would not exist. An investor who pays cash or other enforceable consideration for an option subject to restrictions similar to those in a nonvested employee stock option could not be required subsequently to forfeit entirely any benefit inherent in the instrument if the investor did not fulfill additional requirements.

157. Restrictions that apply to awards of stock-based employee compensation only during the period before they become vested stem entirely from the forfeitability of nonvested awards, which in turn stems from employees' not yet having satisfied the conditions necessary to earn their awards and having no enforceable obligation to do so. That conclusion is consistent with not recognizing prepaid compensation at the grant date. Some Board members believe that conclusion calls for measuring both the value of the equity instrument and the related compensation cost based on the stock price at the vesting date—the date the instrument is issued. Other Board members agree that vesting date measurement may be conceptually appropriate; nevertheless, they consider it important to base the measure of compensation cost stemming from awards of employee stock options on the stock price at the date the entity decides how many options to award to an employee—the grant date.

158. Respondents' overwhelming opposition to vesting date measurement and the potential resulting volatility in reported net income during the vesting period would make it less likely that entities would voluntarily adopt the fair value based method if it were based on the stock price at the vesting date. The choice of accounting methods in this Statement provides an opportunity for entities to improve their accounting for employee stock options. Therefore, on balance, the Board decided to retain the Exposure Draft's provision that compensation cost should be measured based on the stock price at the grant date. However, the Board does not consider it necessary also to reflect in the measurement of fair value restrictions that no longer apply after employee stock

options become vested and nonforfeitable. To do so would be inconsistent with the employee stock options' being issued at the vesting date (paragraph 96). The measurement method in the Exposure Draft combined features of both grant date and vesting date measurement because it adjusted for the effect of the difference, if any, between estimated and actual forfeitures due to failure to render the requisite service or to satisfy performance conditions. The measurement method in this Statement also is a hybrid of grant date and vesting date accounting for the same reason.

159. Some respondents that favored reducing the value of nonvested employee stock options for restrictions that stem from their forfeitability were opposed to similar reductions in the value of shares of nonvested stock. They noted similar situations in which the value of shares of an entity's stock that are involved in other employee compensation or benefit arrangements is not reduced below the market price of an unrestricted share at the date compensation is measured even though individual employees may not be able to realize the value of the stock for many years. Examples are stock transferred to employee stock ownership plans, an entity's contributions of its own stock to either defined benefit or defined contribution pension plans, and deferred compensation arrangements designed to permit employees to defer payment of income taxes.

160. As mentioned earlier, the Board views shares of nonvested stock as employee stock options in which the exercise price consists entirely of employee services. Therefore, the Board believes that any reduction in the value of stock-based compensation to reflect restrictions during the vesting period would have to apply to both nonvested options and nonvested shares of stock. The Board is concerned that applying such a reduction to the stock-based employee compensation covered by this Statement would raise questions about the appropriateness of making similar value reductions in other situations in which shares of an entity's stock are used to provide employee benefits.

Option-pricing models and fair value

161. A quoted market price, if one is available, is the best measure of the fair value of an asset, liability, or equity instrument. In its deliberations leading to this Statement, the Board was not able to identify currently available quoted market prices or negotiated prices for employee stock options that would qualify

as a price at which a willing buyer and a willing seller would exchange cash for an option. Some employers have offered employees a choice between a specified amount of cash or a specified number of options on the employer's stock. However, the Board understands that the terms of those arrangements generally do not result from negotiation between the employer and employee(s). The Board also was told that employers often offer a relatively low alternative cash amount to induce employees to choose options.

162. Market prices for employee stock options may become available in the future, perhaps through arrangements that permit employees to purchase their options by trading a specified amount of cash compensation for them on clearly unbiased terms. If so, the foregone cash compensation—not an estimated fair value of the options—would be recognized as compensation cost, and no adjustments for expected option forfeitures and nontransferability would be needed.

163. It also is conceivable, although unlikely, that options between parties other than employers and employees that are subject to essentially the same restrictions as employee stock options might be developed and traded. For example, a third-party option might in concept be made forfeitable under certain conditions, and the option contract might specify that the options can only be exercised—not transferred to another party. The provisions of this Statement are not intended to preclude use of quoted market prices to determine the fair values of employee stock options if such prices become available. However, various implementation questions would need to be considered, such as how to treat options that are forfeited. Because neither quoted nor negotiated market prices existed when the Board developed this Statement, it has not considered those issues. This Statement specifies the basic method and assumptions to be used in estimating the fair values of employee stock options in the absence of a quoted market price. Specifically, this Statement requires the use of an option-pricing model, and it also specifies how to reduce the amount resulting from use of a traditional option-pricing model to reflect the unique restrictions inherent in employee stock options.

164. The Board recognizes that many entities and their auditors are not familiar with option-pricing models and the inherent mathematics. However, software to apply the models is widely available and easy to use for one who is familiar with electronic spreadsheets and similar tools. Selecting the appropriate assumptions to use as inputs to the models is not easy,

but entities and their advisors must select similar assumptions about the future in many other areas of accounting. Understanding the details of the inherent mathematical formulas is not necessary, just as it is not necessary for an entity to understand the precise computations an actuary might use to estimate the amount of a liability for pension benefits.

Adapting option-pricing models for employee stock options

165. Paragraphs 166-173 explain the reasons for the specified adjustments to the results of standard option-pricing models to reflect differences between the terms of employee stock options and the traded options for which option-pricing models were initially developed.

Forfeitures before vesting

166. This Statement uses the term *forfeiture* to refer only to an employee's failure to earn a vested right to a stock-based employee compensation award because the specified vesting requirements are not satisfied. In other words, a vested award is no longer subject to forfeiture as this Statement uses that term, although the term of a vested award may be truncated by termination of service. Some respondents said that previously recognized compensation cost should be reversed to income if an option expires unexercised because its exercise price exceeds the market price of the stock. Some of those respondents interpreted the notion of forfeiture to include all situations in which employees do not realize gains on their options—for whatever reason. This Statement does not permit reversal of compensation cost in that situation because to do so would be inconsistent with the nature of an employee stock option (an equity instrument of the employer) and with both grant date and vesting date accounting. As with other equity instruments, the cost recognized for an employee stock option stems from use of the consideration received—not from subsequent changes in the value of the equity instrument. Moreover, to be internally consistent, recognizing income when an option expires out-of-the-money would call for recognizing additional compensation cost when the stock price increases as well—the result would be exercise date accounting.

167. This Statement requires that the compensation cost for an award of employee stock options reflect the number of options that actually vest. That is the same as the provision of the Exposure Draft, although the rationale is somewhat different. The Exposure Draft explained that provision as a means of adjusting the grant date value of an award of forfeitable stock-based employee compensation to reflect the risk of forfeiture. The measurement method in this Statement is intended to be consistent with an entity's having no enforceable right to future employee services or other consideration for forfeitable awards. An award of stock-based employee compensation does not result in the issuance of equity instruments until the award is vested. Recognizing compensation cost only for the number of instruments actually issued (vested) is consistent with that view of the nature of a nonvested award.

168. The Exposure Draft proposed that an entity be required to estimate expected forfeitures at the grant date, with subsequent adjustments if actual forfeitures differed from estimates. Some respondents said that permitting accrual of compensation cost for all awards not yet forfeited, with reversals of previously accrued compensation cost for subsequently forfeited awards, would reduce the implementation cost of this Statement. The Board decided to permit that method of accounting for forfeitures for cost-benefit reasons. However, accrual of compensation cost during the service period based on expected forfeitures, with subsequent adjustments as necessary, remains an acceptable method. Respondents asked how changes in estimates of forfeitures (and performance outcomes) during the vesting period should be attributed. The Board concluded that the effects of retroactively applying a change in estimate during the vesting period should be recognized at the date of the change.

Inability to transfer vested employee stock options to third parties

169. The value of a transferable option is based on its maximum term because it rarely is economically advantageous to exercise, rather than sell, a transferable option before the end of its contractual term. Employee stock options differ from most other options in that employees cannot sell their options—they can only exercise them.[17] To reflect the effect of

---

[17]Some employees may be permitted to place their nontransferable options in a trust for the benefit of family members or otherwise to transfer vested options to family members. However, the options remain nontransferable in the hands of the trust or family member. The transfer thus does not affect the value of the option—both the option holder and the option writer (the employer) know it may be economically advantageous for the holder to exercise the options before maturity because exercise remains the only available means to terminate exposure to future price changes.

employees' inability to sell their vested options, this Statement requires that the value of an employee stock option be based on its expected life rather than its maximum term.

170. For example, a 10-year option with an exercise price of $50 on a stock with a market price of $50 might be valued at $25.89, assuming that the stock's volatility is 30 percent, it pays a dividend of 1 percent, and the risk-free interest rate is 7.5 percent. After 5 years, when the stock price has risen to $75, an option holder might wish to realize the gain on the option, thereby terminating exposure to future price changes. The fair value of a 5-year option with an intrinsic value of $25 ($75 - $50) on the same stock is $39.86, assuming that the stock's volatility is now 35 percent, the dividend yield remains at 1 percent, and the current risk-free rate for 5-year maturities is 7 percent. If the option is transferable, the holder could sell it for $39.86 rather than exercise it and receive only the intrinsic value of $25. An employee who does not wish to remain exposed to future price changes in the underlying stock after 5 years can only exercise the option and sell the stock obtained upon exercise—realizing only the gain of $25 in intrinsic value. The employee is unable to realize the option's remaining time value of $14.86 ($39.86 – $25) because of its nontransferability. In other words, an employee who exercises an option with a contractual term of 10 years after only 5 years receives the benefit of only a 5-year option. Because the economic effect of holding a nontransferable rather than a transferable option is to make early exercise significantly more likely, the Board's conclusion stated in the Exposure Draft was that estimating the fair value of an employee stock option based on its expected life, later adjusted to actual life, rather than its maximum term is a logical and practical means of reducing the option's value to reflect its nontransferability.

171. Many respondents objected to the Exposure Draft's proposed subsequent adjustment of expected life to actual life. They generally pointed to the resulting counterintuitive effect that higher expense would be recognized for an option that runs for its full contractual term because its exercise price always exceeds the stock price than for an option that is exercised relatively early in its contractual term because the stock price increased rapidly.

172. As discussed in Appendix C, the Board held a roundtable discussion in April 1994. Participants were invited to submit papers and discuss with other participants, the Board, and its staff potential changes to the measurement method proposed in the Exposure Draft. The papers presented by academic researchers generally agreed that use of expected life is the appropriate way to adjust for the nontransferability of employee stock options. They also agreed with other respondents that the expected life estimated at the grant date should not be subsequently adjusted if actual life differs from expected life because that would produce a counterintuitive result. The participants in the roundtable also discussed several features that affect the expected life of an employee stock option, such as the relationship between expected life and expected volatility and the effect of the nonlinear relationship between option value and option life. Several factors considered helpful in estimating expected life are incorporated in the guidance on selecting assumptions in Appendix B.

173. The Board reaffirmed its conclusion in the Exposure Draft that the appropriate way to reflect the effect on an option's fair value of an employee's inability to sell vested options is to use the option's expected life rather than its contractual term in estimating fair value using an option-pricing model. However, the Board also agreed with respondents and researchers that the Exposure Draft's requirement to adjust compensation cost to reflect the effect of a difference between expected life and actual life should be eliminated. The Board believes that eliminating that requirement will reduce the costs of complying with this Statement. Not adjusting option value to reflect differences between initial estimates and later estimates or outcomes—at least not after the vesting date—also is generally consistent with the Board's conclusion that equity instruments awarded to employees are issued at the vesting date. The value recognized for equity instruments issued in other situations is not changed by subsequent events. An argument could be made that changes in expected life should be reflected until the vesting date, but to do so without also reflecting changes in the price of the underlying stock during the vesting period would have the same counterintuitive results as the Exposure Draft's requirement to reflect differences between expected life and actual life.

Nonpublic Entities

Measurement

174. An emerging entity whose stock is not yet publicly traded may offer stock options to its employees. In concept, those options also should be measured at fair value at the grant date. However, the Board recognizes that estimating expected volatility for the stock of a newly formed entity that is rarely traded, even privately, is not feasible. The Board therefore decided to permit a nonpublic entity to omit expected volatility in determining a value for its options. The result is that a nonpublic entity may use the *minimum value* method discussed and illustrated in paragraphs 139-142. Options granted after an entity qualifies as a public entity must be measured using the procedures specified for public entities. Paragraphs 273-287 in Appendix B provide guidance on how to determine the assumptions required by option-pricing models, including expected volatility for a publicly traded stock that has little, if any, trading history.

175. The Exposure Draft included a provision that permitted a nonpublic entity to use the minimum value method except when its stock was traded with sufficient frequency to reasonably estimate expected volatility. Several respondents to the Exposure Draft thought that "traded with sufficient frequency" would be difficult to judge and that few nonpublic entities would likely incorporate volatility into their measurements on that basis. The Board decided to permit any nonpublic entity to exclude volatility from its measurement of option value. However, a nonpublic entity may incorporate volatility if it desires to do so.

176. Some respondents to the Exposure Draft suggested that there is no reason for different measurement methods for public and nonpublic entities. They believe all entities should use the same method and that requiring public entities to report higher compensation cost based on fair value creates a bias against them. Some respondents endorsed using minimum value for all entities. Others said that the need for special guidance for nonpublic entities was additional evidence that the Exposure Draft's proposals were flawed and that the Board should abandon its approach.

177. A solution suggested by other respondents was to require all entities to use the same expected volatility, such as the historical volatility of a market index. They believe that would ease application of the Statement, mitigate the differences in an entity's transition from nonpublic to public, and improve comparability by reducing the subjectivity of the estimate of volatility.

178. The Board believes that mandating the same estimate of expected volatility for use by all entities would impair, rather than improve, comparability because the volatilities of different entities differ. The use of minimum value by nonpublic entities is a practical solution to the difficulties of estimating expected volatility for a nonpublic entity. For a public entity, estimating the fair value of its options is practicable because an estimate of expected volatility can be made.

Definition of a public entity

179. The Exposure Draft defined a public entity consistent with definitions used in FASB Statements, except that an entity with only publicly traded debt, not equity securities, would be classified as a nonpublic entity. The Exposure Draft definition also drew from the definition in AICPA Statement on Auditing Standards No. 26, *Association with Financial Statements,* which makes it clear that a subsidiary of a public entity also is a public entity. Some respondents objected to considering a subsidiary of a public entity that, by itself, would not meet that definition to be a public entity for purposes of this Statement. They believe that whether an entity is owned by a public entity is not relevant to the measure of a nonpublic subsidiary's options. They also said that awards related to the subsidiary's stock may be better employee incentives than awards related to the parent company's stock.

180. The Board recognizes that the accounting consequences of classifying a subsidiary as a public entity may limit the types of award that it chooses to grant. For example, an entity might choose not to grant an option on the stock of a wholly owned subsidiary combined with a repurchase agreement for the stock issued upon exercise because that award would be treated as a liability in consolidated financial statements. If classification as nonpublic were extended to subsidiaries, the effect of the provisions of paragraph 40 that permit nonpublic entities with mandatory fair value stock repurchase agreements to treat awards as equity instruments even though the entity is effectively obligated to transfer its assets to the holder would be to permit a consolidated public entity to treat effective liabilities to employees of those subsidiaries as if they were equity instruments. The

Board believes that would be an inappropriate result. The Board notes that an award of the parent's equity instruments could include a subsidiary performance criterion, at least partially achieving the goal of relating incentive compensation of subsidiary employees to subsidiary performance.

181. Some respondents to the Exposure Draft suggested that a newly public entity should continue to be classified as nonpublic for some period. Others suggested that a public entity whose stock is thinly traded should be classified as nonpublic. In contrast, some respondents suggested that a nonpublic entity that expected to go public within a certain period should be classified as a public entity. The Board decided that the most straightforward approach would be to determine public or nonpublic status based on an entity's characteristics at the date an award is granted.

Other Measurement Issues

Reload Options and Options with a Reload Feature

182. Reload options are granted upon exercise of previously granted options whose original terms provide for the use of shares of stock that the employee has held for a specified period of time, referred to as *mature shares,* rather than cash to satisfy the exercise price. At the time of exercise using mature shares, the employee is automatically granted a reload option for the same number of shares used to exercise the original option. The exercise price of the reload option is the market price of the stock at the date the reload option is granted; its term is equal to the remainder of the term of the original options.

183. Because a reload feature is part of the options initially awarded, the Board believes that the value added to those options by the reload feature ideally should be considered in estimating the fair value of the initial award at its grant date. However, the Board understands that no reasonable method currently exists to estimate the value added by a reload feature.

184. Some respondents to the Exposure Draft suggested that an option with a reload feature can be valued at the grant date as a "forward start option" commencing at the date or dates that the option is "reloaded." The forward start option's value would be added to the value of the option granted with a reload feature to determine the total value of the award. However, the forward start option formula calls for a number of subjective inputs, such as the number of

expected reloads, the expected timing of each reload, and the expected total rate of return on the stock. Also, because an employee can take advantage of the reload feature only with shares already held, the employer would need to estimate (a) the number of employees who are expected to pay the exercise price with those shares rather than with cash and (b) their holdings of mature shares.

185. Others suggested that a reload feature be treated as if it merely extended the life of an option to its maximum term because the term of a reload option granted upon exercise of an option with mature shares cannot extend beyond the expiration date of the original option. Under that view, the fair value of an option with a reload feature would be estimated based on its maximum term, regardless of the expected life of the original option. However, that method understates the value of the reload feature because the value of an option on a dividend-paying stock is reduced by the present value of the dividends expected to be paid during the term of the option. The holder of an option subject to a reload feature, however, receives the dividends paid on stock obtained by exercising the option early and also is granted a reload option. Further, the holder of a reload option can effectively realize a gain by selling the stock acquired on exercise without forfeiting the opportunity to benefit from future increases in the price of the underlying stock, which also makes the reload option worth more than an otherwise identical option without a reload feature even if its value is based on its contractual life.

186. The Board continues to believe that, ideally, the value of an option with a reload feature should be estimated at the grant date, taking into account all of its features. However, at this time, it is not feasible to do so. Accordingly, the Board concluded that the best way to account for an option with a reload feature is to treat both the initial grant and each subsequent grant of a reload option separately.

Modifications of Awards

187. An employer and employee may agree to modify the terms of an award of stock options or similar instruments. The Board concluded that the effects of a modification of terms are indistinguishable from the effects of an exchange of the existing equity instrument for a new instrument. For example, the same transaction might be described either as a decrease in the exercise price of an outstanding option or as the repurchase (and subsequent cancellation) of

the existing option in exchange for a new option with a lower exercise price. The economics of the transaction are the same regardless of how it is described. In effect, the employee surrenders, and the employer repurchases, the existing instrument in exchange for another instrument.

188. The repurchase of an equity instrument generally is accounted for based on the fair values of the instrument repurchased and the consideration paid for it. For example, if an entity repurchases shares of common stock at an amount significantly in excess of the current market price of the shares, the excess is presumed to be attributable to stated or unstated rights the issuer receives in addition to the shares surrendered, such as an agreement that the stockholder will not purchase additional shares. The Board concluded that a modification of the terms of a stock-based compensation award should be accounted for based on a comparison of the fair value of the modified option at the date it is granted and the value at that date of the old option that is repurchased (immediately before its terms are modified) determined based on the shorter of (a) its remaining initially estimated expected life or (b) the expected life of the modified option. If the fair value of the modified option exceeds the value of the old option repurchased, the entity recognizes additional compensation cost for the difference.

189. The method in the Exposure Draft for determining the additional compensation cost arising from a modification of an award was revised based on comments received and because of changes in the proposed measurement method for measuring compensation cost. As discussed in paragraph 173, under the measurement method in this Statement, the expected life estimated at the grant date is not subsequently adjusted to the actual life in determining the value of options granted. The "true-up" approach in the Exposure Draft significantly influenced the proposed method for modifications, which based the fair value of the original option on its remaining contractual life at the date of modification. However, under this Statement's requirements, no changes are made to the value of an instrument determined at the grant date. Therefore, the Board believes that determining the value of the original option at the date of modification using the shorter of the expected life of the modified option or the remaining portion of the expected life of the original option is consistent with not truing up the initial measure of compensation cost for a change in option life. It also precludes the possibility of a counterintuitive result, namely, a reduction of

compensation cost, which some respondents said could result from certain minor modifications. Using the shorter of the expected life of the modified option or the remaining portion of the expected term of the original option precludes net credits to compensation cost arising from modifications of an award.

190. An employee generally will accept a modification only if its effect is to increase the value of the instrument the employee holds. For example, the maximum term of an award of stock options may be extended or the exercise price may be lowered. Some respondents asked that the Statement address the accounting for cancellations of existing awards or for modifications of existing awards that reduce the value of the instrument held by the employee. The Board discussed those situations and believes that the circumstances under which an employer could unilaterally cancel or reduce the value of an award to an employee without substituting another form of compensation would be rare. The Board decided that it was not practical to consider the appropriate accounting for such an unusual—perhaps nonexistent— transaction except in the context of a specific set of facts.

191. Exchanges of equity instruments or changes to their terms in conjunction with a business combination accounted for as a pooling of interests are not considered modifications for purposes of this Statement. The Board recognizes that entities have essentially no discretion in revising the terms of outstanding equity awards if the business combination is to qualify as a pooling of interests. However, there are no similar criteria for other equity transactions, such as a business combination accounted for as a purchase. Therefore, an exchange or modification of an equity instrument as a result of a purchase business combination, spinoff, or other equity restructuring is considered a modification for purposes of this Statement. The terms of an equity instrument also may be modified pursuant to a stock dividend or a stock split without changing the value of the instruments that the employee holds. For example, an adjustment to an option's exercise price designed to equalize the holder's value before and after a stock split or a stock dividend is not a modification for purposes of this Statement.

192. Some respondents suggested that the criteria in EITF Issue No. 90-9, "Changes to Fixed Employee Stock Option Plans as a Result of Equity Restructuring," should be used to determine whether additional compensation should be recognized for equity restructurings under the fair value based method in this

Statement. EITF Issue 90-9 is written in the context of Opinion 25's intrinsic value measurement method. The Board believes that the requirements in this Statement for accounting for modifications of awards, including those resulting from equity restructurings, are more appropriate for the fair value based method because those requirements are based on comparing fair values before and after a modification. As with all other Opinion 25-related authoritative literature, the consensus on EITF Issue 90-9 continues to apply for an entity that recognizes compensation cost based on Opinion 25.

193. Some respondents requested additional guidance on the accounting for cash settlements or modifications of nonvested awards. Paragraphs 35-40 of this Statement provide that guidance, and Appendix B illustrates the accounting for cash settlements and modifications.

194. Appendix B also illustrates accounting for cash settlements and modifications of options granted before or after initial application of this Statement. Generally, whether the entity has chosen to recognize compensation cost under the fair value based method or to disclose the pro forma effects of that method does not affect the illustrations.

195. An entity that has disclosed the pro forma effects of adopting this Statement for several years may choose to adopt the cost recognition method in this Statement. In that situation, subsequent modifications of awards for which pro forma disclosures were made should be accounted for as if cost had been recognized under the fair value based method as shown in the illustrations for modifications of awards granted after adoption of this Statement (Illustrations 5(a)-5(d)). Doing so will make the financial statements for periods after adoption more consistent for comparative purposes with the pro forma disclosures made for any prior years presented.

Recognizing Compensation Cost over the Service Period

Attribution Period

196. This Statement continues the provisions of Opinion 25 and Interpretation 28 that stock-based compensation cost is to be recognized over the period or periods during which the employee performs the related services. If the service period is not defined as an earlier or shorter period, the service period is presumed to be the vesting period. If the award is for past service, compensation cost is recognized when the award is granted.

197. The Board considered whether the attribution period for employee stock options should extend beyond the vesting date, perhaps to the service expiration date (paragraphs 129-131), even though the measurement date is the grant date. Advocates of that method, which might be considered consistent with amortization of postretirement health care benefits over the period to *full eligibility date,* contend that employees have not earned the full benefit to which they are entitled until termination of service no longer shortens the life of the option. They would use the longer attribution period to allocate the time value of an option.

198. Most respondents that addressed this issue agreed with the Exposure Draft that the attribution period should not extend beyond the vesting date. However, some respondents suggested attribution over the option's expected life, which would be consistent with the method described in paragraph 197. They believe that the option serves as an incentive during its entire life and that attribution over the longer period "better matches" revenues and costs.

199. Although amortization of the time value of an option beyond the vesting date has some conceptual appeal, the Board concluded that no compelling reason exists to extend the attribution period beyond the period now used for stock options that give rise to compensation cost. The Board notes that the decision on when to exercise a vested option is the employee's. The right to exercise an option has been earned by the date the option becomes vested.

200. As discussed in paragraph 96, options are issued to employees at the vesting date. Some advocates of vesting date accounting say that a logical extension of that view would call for recognition of the full amount of the compensation cost at the vesting date, once the equity instrument has been fully earned and issued to the employee. However, the cost of services received in exchange for other employee benefits with a vesting period, such as pensions and other postemployment benefits, generally is recognized in the periods in which the services are received even if the benefits are not yet vested. Although those employee benefit plans generally result in the incurrence of liabilities rather than the issuance of equity instruments, the Board decided that the form of eventual settlement should not change the general principle that the costs of employee services are recognized over the periods in which employees are required to render service to earn the right to the benefit.

Awards with Graded Vesting

201. Interpretation 28 requires that compensation cost for a variable award with a graded vesting schedule, such as an award that vests 25 percent per year over 4 years, be accrued as if the grant were a series of awards rather than a single award. Each award in the series is accounted for as if it had its own separate service period and vesting date. That method attributes a higher percentage of the reported cost to the earlier years than to the later years of the service period because the early years of service are part of the vesting period for later awards in the series. For example, cost attributed to the first year of service includes not only the amount that vests in that year but also one-half of the award that vests in the second year, one-third of the award that vests in the third year, and so on.

202. The Exposure Draft acknowledged that the Interpretation 28 method of recognizing compensation cost is more complicated than others and may be considered illogical if an award with graded vesting is viewed as a single award rather than a series of linked awards. Therefore, it proposed that an award with graded vesting would be attributed ratably to individual years of service. Some respondents recommended that the cost of awards that vest in a graded pattern should be attributed using the method in Interpretation 28.

203. As noted in paragraph 31, an entity may estimate the fair value of an award of stock options with graded vesting using different estimated lives for each group of options depending on the length of the vesting period for that group. If the entity uses that method, the Board concluded that it would be logically consistent to require the attribution pattern specified by Interpretation 28. If the entity does not use different estimated lives but rather uses either an average life for the entire award or different lives based on considerations other than the vesting period for each group, it may use either the Interpretation 28 approach or an approach that ratably allocates compensation cost over the service period. However, to be consistent with the attribution pattern required for other employee benefit plans, the cumulative compensation cost recognized at any date must at least equal the value of the portion of the award that is vested. For example, if an award vests over 3 years, with 50 percent vested after the first year, and 25 percent in each of the next 2 years, cost accrued by the end of the first year must at least equal the amount attributable to 50 percent of the award.

Dividends

204. This Statement requires that dividends paid on shares of nonvested stock that are not expected to, and do not, vest be recognized as additional compensation cost during the vesting period. If an employee terminates service and forfeits nonvested stock but is not required to return dividends paid on the stock during the vesting period, the Board concluded that recognizing those dividends as additional compensation is appropriate.

205. The fair value of a share of stock in concept equals the present value of the expected future cash flows to the stockholder, which includes dividends. Therefore, additional compensation does not arise from dividends on nonvested shares that eventually vest. Because the measure of compensation cost for those shares is their fair value at the grant date, recognizing dividends as additional compensation would effectively double count the dividends.

206. The recipient of an award of nonvested stock may not receive dividends paid on the stock during the vesting period. In that situation, the Board concluded that the value of the award at the grant date should be the fair value of a dividend-paying share of the stock reduced for the present value of the dividends that will not be received during the vesting period.

207. Some employee stock options are *dividend protected,* which means that the exercise price is adjusted downward during the term of the option to take account of dividends paid on the underlying stock that the option holder does not receive. The effect of that adjustment of the exercise price is to remove the effect of dividends as a factor that reduces the value of a stock option on a dividend-paying stock. The usual method of applying an option-pricing model to estimate the value of a dividend-protected option is to assume a dividend payment of zero on the underlying stock, and this Statement requires use of that method.

Settlements of Stock-Based Compensation Awards

208. This Statement deals primarily with equity instruments, such as stock options, issued to employees as compensation. Ordinarily, an entity settles stock options upon exercise by issuing stock rather than by paying cash. However, an entity sometimes may choose to repurchase an employee stock option for a cash payment equal to the intrinsic value of the option when it is exercised.

209. Under some stock-based compensation plans, an entity incurs a liability to its employees, the amount of which is based on the price of the entity's stock. An example of the latter is a cash SAR under which an employee receives upon "exercise" a cash payment equal to the increase in the price of the employer's common stock from a specified level. For example, if the price of the stock increases from $25 to $35 per share, employees receive a $10 cash payment for each SAR held.

210. In addition, some tandem plans offer employees a choice of receiving either cash or shares of stock in settlement of their stock-based compensation awards. For example, an employee may be given an award consisting of a cash SAR and a stock SAR with the same terms. A stock SAR is the same as a cash SAR except that it calls for settlement in shares of stock with an equivalent value. Exercise of one cancels the other. The employee can demand settlement either in cash or in shares of stock.

211. Opinion 25 provides that the amount of cash paid to settle an earlier award of stock or stock options is the final measure of the related compensation cost. An entity's repurchase of stock shortly after the employee acquired that stock upon exercise of an option is considered *cash paid to settle an earlier award,* and compensation cost is adjusted accordingly. Under Opinion 25, a stock SAR is a variable award because the number of shares to which an employee is entitled cannot be determined at the grant date. Compensation cost for a stock SAR thus is finally measured when the SAR is exercised, which produces the same compensation as for a cash SAR. However, a stock SAR and a stock option with similar terms, both of which qualify as equity instruments under the definitions in Concepts Statement 6, result in different amounts of compensation cost under Opinion 25. For example, no compensation cost is recognized for an award of 100 stock options at $25 per share if the market price of the stock is $25 at the grant date even if the stock price is $35 when the options are exercised. However, if an identical transaction involved an award of stock SARs rather than stock options, compensation cost of $1,000 [100 shares × ($35 − $25)] is recognized.

212. One reason for the Board's undertaking a comprehensive review of Opinion 25 was a concern that the differing results produced for stock-based compensation awards that call for settlement by issuing stock and those that call for settlement in cash were, at best, difficult to understand and explain. While it may be appropriate for cash plans and stock plans to result in different total charges to income, no common thread to distinguish between cash and stock plans is apparent in Opinion 25. For example, some awards that result in the entity's issuing equity instruments, such as stock SARs, are treated as if the entity had incurred a liability. Similar awards, such as stock options, are treated as equity instruments unless they are eventually settled in cash, at which time the accounting is adjusted to produce the same results as if the entity had incurred a liability rather than issued an equity instrument at the grant date.

213. Some constituents contend that the amount of compensation cost recognized for stock-based compensation awards should not differ solely because one award calls for settlement in stock and another calls for settlement in an equivalent amount of cash. Others are not concerned with differing results for stock plans and cash plans, but they note that the provisions of Opinion 25 sometimes produce results that are inconsistent with those for similar transactions in equity instruments issued to outside parties. For example, the repurchase of stock from an investor who recently acquired it by exercising a stock purchase warrant would not be accounted for as if it were the settlement of a liability.

214. As discussed in Appendix C, late in 1988 the Board set aside work on stock compensation issues to await progress on its broader project on distinguishing between liability and equity instruments. The main reason for that decision was concern about whether applying the current distinction between liabilities and equity instruments and the different effects on income stemming from repurchase of an equity instrument versus settlement of a liability produced appropriate results for stock-based compensation plans. Because the Board subsequently decided not to pursue substantive changes to the conceptual definitions of liabilities and equity, it considered accounting for stock-based compensation awards in the context of the definitions in Concepts Statement 6.

215. Concepts Statement 6 distinguishes between liabilities and equity on the basis of whether an instrument obligates the issuer to transfer its assets (or to use its assets in providing services) to the holder. A liability embodies such an obligation, while an equity instrument does not. A call option that an entity writes on its own stock, such as an employee stock option, is an equity instrument because its settlement requires only the issuance of stock, which is not the

issuer's asset. The entity's obligation under a cash SAR, on the other hand, is a liability because its settlement requires the transfer of assets to the holder.

216. Whether an instrument qualifies as a liability or an equity instrument of its issuer depends on the nature of the obligation embodied in it—not on the means by which it is actually settled. In other words, the characteristics of a liability are present from the date it is incurred. Settlement of a liability by issuing equity instruments, such as shares of stock, whose value is the same as the amount of the liability does not change the nature of the obligation settled—the transaction is the settlement of a liability. Similarly, the repurchase of an equity instrument for cash does not convert the equity instrument to a liability—the transaction still is the repurchase of an equity instrument.

217. The Board decided that the principles outlined in paragraph 216 apply to obligations incurred to employees under stock-based compensation awards as well as to similar obligations incurred to other parties. Those principles provide the basis for dealing with both awards that call for settlement in stock and awards that call for settlement in cash (or other assets of the entity). The former are equity instruments when issued, and their subsequent repurchase for cash equal to their value does not call for an adjustment to previously recognized compensation cost. The latter are liabilities, and their settlement calls for an adjustment to previously recognized compensation cost if the settlement amount differs from the carrying amount of the liability.

218. The Board also concluded that the conceptual distinctions between liabilities and equity instruments provide a reasonable way of accounting for tandem plans that offer a choice of settlement in stock or in cash. An entity that grants a tandem award consisting of either a stock option or a cash SAR, for example, is obligated to pay cash upon demand if the choice of settlement is the employee's. The contract gives the entity no discretion to avoid transferring its assets to the employee if the employee elects settlement in cash. The entity thus has incurred a liability. If the choice is the entity's, however, it can avoid transferring assets simply by electing to issue stock, and the award results in the issuance of an equity instrument. However, this Statement requires accounting for the substantive terms of a plan. If an entity nominally has the choice of settling awards under a tandem plan by issuing stock but regularly does so by paying cash, or if the entity settles awards in cash

whenever employees ask for cash settlement, the instrument awarded likely is a substantive liability of the entity.

Stock Repurchase Agreements of Closely Held Entities

219. Many respondents to the Discussion Memorandum on distinguishing between liabilities and equity noted that closely held entities commonly specify that shares of stock granted or otherwise issued to employees cannot be transferred to a third party but can only be sold to the issuer. Often, the holder is required to sell, and the issuer is required to repurchase, the stock at a price that reasonably approximates fair value at the date of repurchase. In a family-owned entity, a repurchase agreement may apply to all of the stock outstanding, or it may apply only to shares held by employees and others that are not members of the founding family.

220. In concept, stock that its issuer must repurchase for fair value at the date of repurchase is a liability rather than an equity instrument because the issuer is obligated to transfer its assets to the holder. To treat all of those instruments as liabilities, however, would be troublesome because an entity with repurchase agreements for all of its common stock would report no equity. In practice, the existence of a mandatory fair value repurchase agreement, by itself, is not considered to convert to a liability an instrument that otherwise would qualify as equity. Future work on the Board's liability-equity project will consider the effect of a mandatory fair value repurchase agreement. The Board therefore concluded that this Statement should not change current practice concerning the effect of a mandatory fair value repurchase agreement applicable to the stock of a nonpublic entity.

221. Some respondents to the Exposure Draft asked that mandatory repurchases under all formula-based plans be considered repurchases at fair value that are accounted for as the repurchase of an equity instrument. Others requested that additional criteria be provided to establish whether the formula in a plan produces a repurchase price equivalent to fair value. The Board believes that the terms of formula value repurchase plans are too diverse to specify the circumstances, if any, in which a formula-based value might be fair value. Whether the terms of a particular plan produce a repurchase price that is a reasonable estimate of fair value and whether the plan is subject to additional compensation cost needs to be assessed on a case-by-case basis (paragraphs 37-40).

Accounting for Tax Effects of Stock Compensation Awards

222. The provisions of the Exposure Draft on accounting for the tax effects of awards of stock-based employee compensation were based on recognizing an asset, prepaid compensation, for the fair value of an award at the grant date. For awards of stock options, the financial reporting basis of that asset generally would exceed its tax basis at the grant date because the time value component of an option's value is not tax deductible. Therefore, a temporary difference would arise for which a deferred tax liability would be recognized under Statement 109. Because the Board decided that prepaid compensation should not be recognized at the grant date, the proposed tax accounting no longer could be applied.

223. Statement 109 retained Opinion 25's provisions on accounting for the income tax effects of stock-based employee compensation. The Board considered whether it should fundamentally change those requirements and decided not to, for the reasons explained in paragraphs 225-231.

224. The Board believes that recognition of deferred tax benefits related to stock-based awards for financial reporting should be based on provisions in the tax law that govern the deductibility of stock-based compensation. Some stock-based compensation plans result in tax deductions. Examples under existing U.S. tax law are so-called nonstatutory stock options (which are options that do not qualify for preferential tax treatment as incentive stock options) and nonvested stock. However, under existing U.S. tax law, an entity does not receive tax deductions for so-called incentive stock options (provided that employees comply with the requisite holding periods).

225. The Board believes that the recognition of compensation cost in an entity's income statement for an award that ordinarily results in tax deductions creates a deductible temporary difference for which deferred taxes are recognized under Statement 109. Paragraph 15 of Statement 109 describes temporary differences that are not associated with a particular asset or liability for financial reporting but that result from an event that has been recognized in the financial statements and, based on the provisions in the tax law, will result in deductible amounts in future years. Normally, tax deductions ultimately recognized for a stock option accounted for under this Statement will differ in amount from the compensation cost recognized for financial reporting. Compensation cost recognized for financial reporting under this Statement is measured as the fair value of the award at the grant date, which includes a time value component that is never tax deductible. Changes in the market value of the stock after the grant date do not affect the measurement of compensation cost recognized. Tax deductions are generally based on the intrinsic value of the award measured as the excess of the market price of the stock over the price, if any, the employee pays for the stock at a specified date. Changes in the market price of the stock between the date an award is granted and the exercise date directly affect the amount of the entity's tax deduction.

226. The Board decided that the amount of the temporary difference should be determined based on the compensation cost recognized for financial reporting rather than by reference to the expected future tax deduction (which would be estimated by the current intrinsic value of the award). The Board believes that approach is preferable because it is less complex to apply, will produce less volatility in reported net income, and will be consistent with the recognition of the tax effects of stock-based awards for those employers that continue to apply Opinion 25 for their stock-based employee compensation plans.

227. The temporary difference related to a stock-based award is measured by the cumulative compensation cost recognized rather than the expected future tax deduction based on the present intrinsic value of the award. Therefore, a deferred tax asset recognized for that temporary difference should be reduced by a valuation allowance only if, based on the weight of the available evidence, the entity expects future taxable income will be insufficient to recover the deferred tax asset in the periods the tax deduction for the stock-based award will be recognized or in an applicable carry-back or carry-forward period.

228. The amount of stock-based compensation that is deducted on the tax return may exceed the compensation cost recognized for financial reporting. This Statement requires that the tax benefits of deductions in excess of compensation cost be recognized as additional paid-in capital when they are initially recognized. The Board agrees with the conclusion of the Accounting Principles Board in Opinion 25 that the additional tax benefits are attributable to an equity transaction.

229. Alternatively, the deductible amount on the tax return may be less than the cumulative compensation cost recognized for a particular stock-based award.

The Board concluded that the write-off of the related deferred tax asset in that situation should be recognized in the income statement except to the extent that there is paid-in capital arising from excess tax deductions from previous awards under stock-based employee compensation arrangements accounted for using the fair value based method described in this Statement. The Board believes that it would be inappropriate for an entity to use credits to paid-in capital from awards accounted for under Opinion 25 to offset the write-off of a deferred tax asset related to compensation cost measured using the fair value based method in this Statement because those credits generally result from awards for which no compensation cost has been recognized. To use those credits would overstate an entity's cumulative net income.

230. This Statement does not permit retroactive application to determine the fair value of stock-based awards granted before this Statement's effective date. The Board believes that it would not be practical to determine the appropriate amount of excess tax deductions that would have been credited to paid-in capital had the fair value based method been applied to awards granted before the effective date of this Statement. After the effective date of this Statement, entities that continue to apply Opinion 25 are required to determine not only the pro forma net income effects of the fair value based method but also the pro forma equity effects in determining the tax benefits for excess tax deductions that would have been recognized in paid-in capital had the fair value based method in this Statement been applied to recognize compensation cost. Paid-in capital for tax benefits resulting from awards granted before the effective date of this Statement are still available for applying paragraph 17 of Opinion 25 because this Statement does not change the accounting for tax effects under Opinion 25. Entities also are precluded from offsetting the write-off of a deferred tax asset against the tax benefits of excess deductions or tax credits reported as paid-in capital from stock-based arrangements that are outside the scope of this Statement, such as employee stock ownership plans.

231. An entity sometimes may realize tax benefits for an award that ordinarily does not result in a tax deduction because an employee receiving the stock does not comply with a holding period required by the tax law for favorable tax treatment for the recipient. The Board decided that the resulting tax benefit from such a disqualifying disposition should be recognized in the period that the event occurs. The benefit of any deduction recognized in the income statement is limited to the tax benefit for the cumulative compensation cost previously recognized for financial reporting. Any excess benefit should be recognized as an increase to paid-in capital.

Employee Stock Purchase Plans and Other Broad-Based Plans

232. The Exposure Draft applied to broad-based employee stock option plans and broad-based plans that permit employees to purchase stock at a discount from market value *(employee stock purchase plans)* the same recognition and measurement provisions as those proposed for all other stock-based plans. Many respondents said that broad-based plans should be exempted from the proposed requirement to recognize compensation cost for the fair value of the benefit given to employees. They noted that Opinion 25, paragraph 7, considers broad-based plans that meet certain specified criteria to be *noncompensatory,* with no compensation cost recognized even if the purchase price is less than the price of the underlying stock at the measurement date. Respondents also pointed out that Opinion 25 cites an employee stock purchase plan that qualifies under Section 423 of the Internal Revenue Code as an example of a noncompensatory plan.

233. The Internal Revenue Code provides that employees will not be immediately taxed on the difference between the market price of the stock purchased and a discounted purchase price if several requirements in Section 423 are met. The requirements are generally the same as those in paragraph 7 of Opinion 25, with the following additions:

a. The option price may not be less than the lesser of (1) 85 percent of the market price when the option is granted or (2) 85 percent of the price at exercise.
b. The term of the option cannot exceed 5 years from the grant date if the purchase price is 85 percent or more of the market price at the exercise date. If the purchase price can turn out to be less than 85 percent of the stock price at exercise, the term of the option cannot exceed 27 months from the grant date. For example, 27 months is the maximum term of a *look-back option* in which the purchase price equals the lower of 85 percent of the stock price at the grant date or at the exercise date.

234. In the past few years, some employers have granted fixed, 10-year stock options to substantially all employees. Those awards differ from Section 423

employee stock purchase plans because the exercise price usually equals the stock price at the date of grant and the term is longer. Although those options generally do not qualify as *noncompensatory* under Opinion 25, no compensation cost is typically recognized for them because of the intrinsic value method specified in Opinion 25. In this Statement, the phrase *broad-based* plans includes long-term fixed stock options issued to substantially all of an entity's employees as well as Section 423 plans.

235. In supporting the noncompensatory treatment of broad-based plans, respondents said that the primary purpose of those plans is not to compensate employees for services rendered. Rather, broad-based plans are aimed at encouraging employees to become stakeholders, thereby leading to greater employee loyalty and an interest in increasing shareholder value, and at raising capital over time without incurring the stock issuance costs related to a public offering. Many respondents asserted that the purchase discount offered to employees was comparable to the stock issuance costs avoided by issuing the stock to employees rather than to the public. The purchase discount is viewed as an inducement for employees to participate in the plans or as a cost of raising capital. Some respondents suggested that the noncompensatory provisions of Opinion 25 should be not only retained but also broadened to encompass options with a 10-year term.

236. The Board found merit in the argument that a small percentage discount in a broad-based plan offered to employees is an inducement that is analogous to a discount routinely offered to stockholders and others or to avoided stock issuance cost. The Board decided that the purchase discount in a broad-based plan is noncompensatory if the discount from the market price does not exceed the greater of the following two thresholds:

a. The per-share discount that would be reasonable in a recurring offer of stock to stockholders or others. For example, some entities offer a purchase discount to shareholders participating in a dividend reinvestment program. The Board related this threshold to a recurring discount because it did not want a percentage discount justified by an isolated rights offering that might involve an above-normal discount.

b. The per-share amount of stock issuance costs avoided by not having to raise a significant amount of capital by a public offering. Some respondents suggested that this threshold should be based on the per-share avoided stock issuance

costs for a public offering of only the number of shares expected to be issued to the employees. The Board rejected that suggestion. Per-share amounts would tend to be higher for a small public offering because many of the costs are more fixed than variable. The Board agreed to include this threshold in the standard because of the long-term impact of broad-based plans, which some respondents indicated provide a significant source of capital *over time.* The Board does not want this threshold used to justify a higher percentage discount as noncompensatory simply based on a short-term focus.

237. Some constituents expressed concern about the effort and related costs to justify the purchase discount granted to employees. The Board discussed whether a specified discount should be established for cost-benefit reasons as a safe harbor for a noncompensatory discount. It decided to specify that a purchase discount of 5 percent or less automatically complies with the Statement's limitations on the amount of purchase discount allowed for noncompensatory broad-based plans. The Board chose 5 percent because, based on available data, it believes that amount is closer to the average cost of most public offerings than is the 15 percent discount effectively used as a safe harbor under Opinion 25. A discount in excess of 5 percent is permitted if an entity can justify it under the criteria in paragraph 23.

238. Having decided that a reasonable percentage discount (such as 5 percent) can be included in a noncompensatory broad-based plan, the Board considered how compensation cost should be determined for a broad-based plan that includes a higher percentage discount than could be considered noncompensatory. Should the cost computation include the entire discount or only the portion that exceeds the amount that would, by itself, qualify as noncompensatory? The Board decided that if an employee stock purchase plan includes an excessively high discount that cannot be justified under the criteria in paragraph 23(b), the plan is compensatory and the entire discount should be used in determining compensation cost. The Board rejected the notion that an employee stock purchase plan could be accounted for as partially compensatory and partially noncompensatory.

239. The Board considered respondents' requests that broad-based plans with look-back options be considered noncompensatory and noted that a look-back option can have substantial value because it enables the employee to purchase the stock for an

amount that could be significantly less than the market price at date of purchase. A look-back option is not an essential element of a broad-based plan aimed at promoting broad employee stock ownership; a purchase discount also provides inducement for participation. The Board concluded that broad-based plans that contain look-back options cannot be treated as noncompensatory. The consequences of other option features are discussed in paragraphs 240 and 241.

240. Under some employee stock purchase plans, the purchase price is fixed at the grant date (for example, as a percentage of the market price at the grant date) and an enrollment period is provided for employees to decide whether to participate. Technically, the availability of an enrollment period after the purchase price has been fixed constitutes an option feature that has time value. However, for practical reasons, the Board decided that an enrollment period not in excess of 31 days is not a disqualifying option feature that would otherwise preclude a plan from being treated as noncompensatory.

241. To facilitate employee participation and eliminate the need for lump-sum payments, employee stock purchase plans typically stipulate that participating employees pay for stock purchases by payroll withholding during a period preceding the date of purchase. Under some plans, employees are permitted to cancel their participation in the plan before the purchase date and obtain a refund of amounts previously withheld. If a plan permits a participating employee to cancel participation in the plan after the purchase price has been fixed, that cancellation ability is an option feature. The Board decided that a plan in which the purchase price is fixed at the grant date and participating employees may cancel their participation before the purchase date and obtain a refund of previous withholdings is indistinguishable from a fixed-price option and therefore should be treated as compensatory. In contrast, a plan in which the purchase price is based *solely* on the *purchase-date* market price embodies no valuable option feature. Even if the plan enables participating employees to cancel their participation before the purchase date and obtain a refund of previous withholdings, that plan might qualify as noncompensatory.

242. The Board considered attempting to simplify determining the fair value of an employee stock purchase plan that incorporates a look-back option by establishing a specified percentage of the stock price at the grant date, such as 20 percent, that could be

considered fair value. The Board rejected that idea largely because determining an appropriate percentage that would produce a reasonable substitute for fair value for a wide variety of plans did not seem feasible. Moreover, the Board understands that, given the choice of using a specified amount or determining an amount based on its own circumstances, many entities do not select the specified amount without first determining the alternative amount.

Disclosures

243. Paragraphs 244-261 discuss the basis for the Board's conclusions on the required disclosures of this Statement other than the pro forma disclosures required by paragraph 45. The basis for the Board's conclusions on those pro forma disclosures is discussed in paragraph 69.

244. Some respondents suggested that the Board provide percentage guidelines to specify when both the pro forma disclosures of the effects of applying the fair value based method and the disclosures in paragraphs 46-48 could be omitted on the grounds of immateriality. The Board decided not to do so because it believes an entity can best determine the materiality of the disclosures in its individual circumstances. In addition, different percentage criteria likely would be needed for different disclosures, for example, the materiality of some items might be best evaluated in terms of the effect on reported net income, while the materiality of other items might be better evaluated in the context of number of shares outstanding. Specifying those guidelines for individual disclosures could unduly complicate this Statement. The Board notes, however, that the general guidance provided at the end of each Statement on application of its provisions to immaterial items applies to both accounting and disclosure requirements.

Disclosures Similar to Those Required by Opinion 25

245. The Board concluded that the disclosures specified in paragraphs 46-48 should be required for all entities regardless of the method used to account for stock-based employee compensation. The disclosures required by Opinion 25 thus are superseded by this Statement, regardless of the method an entity uses to account for stock-based employee compensation cost.

246. The Exposure Draft proposed continuing the disclosures required by Opinion 25, including the

number of shares under option, the option price, the number of shares for which options are exercisable, the number of shares exercised, and the exercise prices. In applying Opinion 25, many entities have disclosed only the range of exercise prices of options, which is not very helpful in understanding the potential increase in outstanding shares by option exercises, especially if the range is wide. The Exposure Draft proposed disclosing the weighted-average exercise prices of options outstanding, granted, and exercised.

247. Many respondents expressed support for the proposed disclosures. Others said that additional information about options outstanding at the date of the financial statements would be useful. They generally requested more information helpful in evaluating "potential future dilution," "option overhang," or potential capital contributions from outstanding options. They suggested the need for more information about options whose exercise prices are greater than, equal to, or less than the current stock price. Those respondents said that weighted-average information, although important, is not sufficient for those assessments because, by itself, it provides no information helpful in evaluating the likelihood that options will be exercised in the future. Disclosure of the number of options outstanding at each exercise price, or at least by ranges of exercise prices, was suggested.

248. The Board concurred and decided to require disclosure of the range of exercise prices (as well as the weighted-average exercise price) and the weighted-average remaining contractual life for the options outstanding as of the date of the latest statement of financial position presented. If the overall range of exercise prices is wide (for example, the highest exercise price exceeds approximately 150 percent of the lowest exercise price), the Board decided to require further segregation of those prices into narrower ranges that are meaningful for assessing the likelihood and consequences of future exercises. The Board also decided that the number and weighted-average exercise price of options that are currently exercisable at that date should be disclosed for each range.

249. The Board decided not to specify strict criteria for when further segregation should be required. The 150 percent example in paragraph 48 is meant to be a guideline. An entity should exercise its judgment in providing the most meaningful disclosures.

Disclosures of Method and Significant Assumptions Used to Determine Fair Value

250. The Exposure Draft proposed requiring disclosure of the method and significant assumptions used to estimate the fair value of options. About half of the respondents that commented on the proposed disclosures supported that requirement; others considered those disclosures unnecessary if compensation cost is recognized. Many respondents opposed disclosure of expected dividends, and a fewer number also opposed disclosure of the expected volatility. They said they feared that those disclosures raised the potential for future litigation if the disclosures were misconstrued as a commitment to declare future dividends or a forecast of future stock prices. Others suggested that disclosure of assumptions should not be required because entities might have to reveal confidential information about possible future changes in dividend rates and the like.

251. As explained in paragraphs 273-287 of Appendix B, the assumptions about expected volatility and dividends needed to comply with this Statement generally should be based on historical experience, adjusted for *publicly available information* that may indicate ways in which the future is reasonably expected to differ from the past. In addition, required disclosures of potentially sensitive assumptions in other areas, such as expected rates of salary increases used in measuring pension cost for a period, apparently have not led to litigation or other problems. Moreover, after the Exposure Draft was issued, the SEC began requiring registrants to disclose the underlying assumptions, including expected volatility and dividends, if they choose to comply with the recently expanded proxy disclosures about the value of options granted to executives by disclosing the "present value" of the options at the grant date.

252. The Exposure Draft did not propose requiring disclosure of expected lives of stock options, principally because that assumption was required to be subsequently adjusted to actual life in measuring compensation cost. Some respondents said that disclosure of expected lives would be useful, especially should the Board decide not to require "true up" of expected life to actual life—which is the conclusion that the Board reached (paragraph 173).

253. The Board therefore concluded that disclosure of the method and significant assumptions used in estimating the fair values of stock options should be required. The assumptions used in an option-

pricing model can significantly affect the estimated value of stock options, and therefore disclosure of the assumptions used will assist in understanding the information provided by entities in their financial statements.

Other Required Disclosures

254. The Exposure Draft proposed requiring entities with both fixed and indexed or performance-based plans to provide separate disclosures for the different types of plans. Some respondents to the Exposure Draft requested additional guidance on the situations in which separate disclosures would be necessary and what information should be provided separately for fixed plans and other plans. The Board decided that separate disclosures should be provided to the extent that differences in the characteristics of the awards make those disclosures important to an understanding of the entity's use of stock-based compensation. This Statement gives examples of such circumstances rather than specifying detailed requirements. The Board recognizes that entities differ in the extent to which they use various forms of stock-based employee compensation. An entity should exercise its judgment in providing detailed information that is useful in its own situation.

255. The Exposure Draft proposed, and this Statement retains, required disclosure of the weighted-average fair values of options granted during the year, along with the weighted-average exercise prices. That disclosure will allow a reader to compute the ratio of option value to stock value at grant date, which is commonly used for comparisons between entities and in assessing the perceived reasonableness of option valuations. Reference to a ratio helps in comparing, for example, the estimated value of an option on a $20 stock with one on a $90 stock. However, that ratio generally is used only for options whose exercise prices equal the stock price at the grant date.

256. For example, if both the $20 stock and the $90 stock paid dividends of approximately 1.5 percent and other factors such as expected lives of the options, historical stock price volatility, and future prospects were similar, one might question estimated fair values of options on the 2 stocks with similar terms if the ratio of fair value to stock price is 20 percent for the $20 stock and 40 percent for the $90 stock. Those ratios might be comparable, however, if the exercise price of the first option is $20 (equal to the stock price at grant date) but the exercise price of the sec-

ond option is $75 ($15 less than the stock price at grant date). To combine in the same ratio options with exercise prices that equal, exceed, and are less than the stock price at the grant date would produce a meaningless amount. Accordingly, this Statement requires separate disclosure of weighted-average fair values and exercise prices of options granted at exercise prices that equal the stock price at the grant date and those whose exercise prices differ from the grant date stock price.

257. During the Board's redeliberations of the proposals in the Exposure Draft, questions arose about whether the disclosures required by this Statement were generally consistent with current disclosures for other potentially dilutive financial instruments. APB Opinion No. 15, *Earnings per Share,* says:

> The use of complex securities complicates earnings per share computations and makes additional disclosures necessary. The Board has concluded that financial statements should include a description, in summary form, sufficient to explain the pertinent rights and privileges of the various securities outstanding. Examples of information which should be disclosed are dividend and liquidation preferences, participation rights, call prices and dates, conversion or exercise prices or rates and pertinent dates, sinking fund requirements, unusual voting rights, etc. [paragraph 19]

That paragraph could be interpreted to apply to employee stock options, although entities generally have not done so because Opinion 25 specifically deals with stock-based awards to employees. The Board believes that the disclosures required by this Statement are generally consistent with disclosures long required for other potentially dilutive securities.

258. During its deliberations leading to the Exposure Draft, the Board received several proposals for disclosures in lieu of cost recognition for stock-based compensation, the most comprehensive of which was submitted by a group of preparers and users of financial statements and was endorsed by the six largest accounting firms. That proposal was included in the Exposure Draft as Appendix E.

259. As discussed earlier, many respondents to the Exposure Draft supported additional disclosures as a substitute for measurement and recognition of compensation cost. The notice to recipients asked

whether any of the additional disclosure items in Appendix E should be added to the required disclosures, assuming that recognition of compensation cost was required. Few respondents suggested additional disclosure items, and some said that none of the additional disclosure items in Appendix E's example were warranted. The Board therefore did not expand the required disclosures to include items from Appendix E of the Exposure Draft.

260. During its deliberations, especially after the Board had initially decided to require disclosure of pro forma information rather than recognition of compensation cost determined by the fair value based method, some constituents asserted that disclosure of a single point estimate of the fair value of employee stock options was not appropriate. They said that the assumptions used in option-pricing models are too subjective or that available option-pricing models are inappropriate for estimating the fair value of employee stock options with their inherent differences from tradable options. They suggested that the Board require only disclosure of a range of possible values for employee stock options.

261. As discussed earlier in this appendix and in Appendix B, the Board believes that option-pricing models, adjusted as this Statement specifies for the differences between the typical employee stock option and a tradable option for which the models were initially developed, will produce estimated values for employee stock options that will be within acceptable limits for recognition in financial statements. The Board also believes that it has required disclosure of the basic information needed to understand the effects of stock-based compensation plans. An entity may, of course, disclose additional information it considers pertinent to readers of its financial statements. For example, an entity may disclose supplemental information, such as a range of values calculated on the basis of different assumptions, provided that the supplemental information is reasonable and does not discredit the information required by this Statement (paragraph 364).

Benefits and Costs

262. The mission of the FASB is to "establish and improve standards of financial accounting and reporting for the guidance and education of the public, including issuers, auditors, and users of financial information" (FASB *Rules of Procedure*, page 1). In fulfilling that mission the Board strives to determine that the expected benefits of the information resulting from a new standard will exceed the perceived costs. The objective and implicit benefit of issuing an accounting standard are the increased credibility and representational faithfulness of financial reporting as a result of the new or revised accounting. However, the value of that incremental improvement to financial reporting and most of the costs to achieve it are subjective and cannot be quantified. Likewise, the costs of *not* issuing an accounting standard are impossible to quantify.

263. The Board's consideration of each individual issue in a particular project includes the subjective weighing of the incremental improvement in financial reporting against the incremental cost of implementing the identified alternatives. At the end of that process, the Board considers the accounting provisions in the aggregate and must conclude that issuance of the standard is a sufficient improvement in financial reporting to justify the related costs.

264. The Board concluded that the expected benefits resulting from this Statement will exceed the related costs. Although required recognition using the fair value based method of determining compensation cost for stock-based employee compensation would have provided greater benefits, the representational faithfulness and credibility of the information provided by the financial statements and notes, taken as a whole, will be improved even if the results of that method are only reflected in disclosure of pro forma information. Entities that choose to adopt the fair value based method will be better able to establish plans that they believe provide the best incentives with less need to "design around" accounting standards. Opinion 25's distinction between fixed and variable awards effectively encourages fixed stock options and discourages performance awards. Encouraging one form of award at the expense of another not only imposes the cost of treating accounting requirements as a significant factor in plan design but also may encourage selection of plans that an entity might not otherwise choose.

265. The Board has attempted to mitigate the incremental costs of complying with this Statement wherever possible without detracting from its objectives. For example:

a. A nonpublic entity is permitted to use the so-called minimum value method to value its options.
b. Entities may choose to estimate the number of options or other equity instruments that are ex-

pected to vest and to revise that estimate, if necessary, if subsequent information indicates that actual forfeitures are likely to differ from initial estimates. Alternatively, an entity may begin
recognizing compensation cost as if all instruments granted are expected to vest, with recognition of actual forfeitures as they occur.

c. The grant-date estimate of expected option life is
not adjusted to actual outstanding life, as was
proposed in the Exposure Draft. The Board believes that elimination of that requirement will reduce the costs of complying with this Statement.

d. If there is a range of reasonable assumptions
about the factors that are used in option-pricing
models, entities are to use the low end of the
range. That should somewhat simplify the decisions involved in determining appropriate
assumptions.

Effective Dates and Transition

266. The Exposure Draft proposed two effective
dates: one for its disclosure provisions, including pro
forma disclosures of its effects on net income and
earnings per share, and a later date for adopting its
recognition provisions in the financial statements.
Because this Statement does not require an entity to
adopt the fair value based method of accounting for
stock-based employee compensation (although the
Board encourages entities to do so), the question of
effective date pertains almost entirely to the required
pro forma disclosures. An entity may adopt the fair
value based method of accounting for its stock-based
employee compensation cost as soon as the Statement is issued or at any date thereafter. The only restriction is that the new method must be applied *as of*
the beginning of the fiscal year in which it is adopted.

267. The Board decided that a lengthy transition period for the required pro forma disclosures is not necessary. The fair value based method to be used in
those disclosures has been debated and widely publicized for several years. The measurement method in
this Statement is similar to the one in the Exposure
Draft, and the areas of change, such as not adjusting
for the effect of a difference between initially estimated expected and actual lives of options, should
ease implementation. Therefore, the Board decided
that the required pro forma disclosures should begin
with awards granted in fiscal years beginning after
December 15, 1994 (that is, awards granted in 1995
fiscal years). However, the Board recognizes that the
issuance of this Statement relatively late in 1995

might make it difficult for some entities with fiscal
years ending in December to gather the information
necessary to disclose pro forma information in their
1995 financial statements. The Board thus decided that
required presentation of pro forma information
should begin with financial statements for 1996,
which also should include the pro forma disclosures
for 1995 if comparative financial information is
presented.

268. This Statement deals separately with issuances
of equity instruments to acquire employee services in
transactions that are included in the scope of Opinion 25 and other issuances of equity instruments to
acquire goods or services. For the latter transactions,
this Statement essentially codifies current best practice, which is to measure the transaction at the fair
value of the consideration received or the fair value
of the equity instrument issued, whichever is more
reliably measurable. The Board decided that the effective date of that provision should be transactions
entered into after December 15, 1995, because the
provisions are not expected to result in a significant
change in practice.

269. The Exposure Draft proposed prospective application of the new method of accounting for stock-
based employee compensation plans, that is, the new
method would be applied only to awards granted after a specified date. This Statement retains prospective application. Some respondents were concerned
about the inherent "ramp-up" effect on compensation
cost as additional awards are granted and the first
awards to which the new method applies move
through their vesting periods. Those respondents
generally suggested either requiring or permitting
retroactive application to all awards that are not
vested at the effective date.

270. The Board recognizes the potential for misleading implications caused by the ramp-up effect of prospective application of a new accounting or pro
forma disclosure requirement for a recurring transaction. However, the Board continues to question the
feasibility of retroactive application of the fair value
based method of accounting, which could involve
several years depending on the length of the vesting
period. (Some constituents even objected to having
to apply the fair value based method to awards
granted in 1995, but before this Statement was issued.) For example, field test participants reported
that estimating what assumptions they might have
used for expected option lives, volatility, or dividends

for grants made several years in the past was problematical. The Board decided that requiring retroactive application would be excessively burdensome. Permitting either retroactive or prospective application would detract from the comparability of the information reported by different entities. Instead, the Board decided that entities should be required to alert readers of the financial statements if amounts of compensation cost determined using the fair value based method that are reflected in the pro forma disclosures or recognized are not indicative of future amounts when the new method will apply to all outstanding, nonvested awards.

Appendix B

ILLUSTRATIVE GUIDANCE FOR APPLYING THE STANDARDS

CONTENTS

Appendix B

ILLUSTRATIVE GUIDANCE FOR APPLYING THE STANDARDS

Introduction

271. This appendix, which is an integral part of the requirements of this Statement, discusses further the fair value based method of accounting for stock-based employee compensation and illustrates its application to specific awards. The examples and related assumptions in this appendix are illustrative only; they may not represent actual situations.

272. The guidance in paragraphs 273-287 on selecting assumptions for use in an option-pricing model applies equally to (a) an entity that applies the fair value based method in accounting for its stock-based employee compensation cost and (b) an entity that accounts for its stock-based employee compensation in accordance with Opinion 25 and discloses the pro forma information required by paragraph 45. Except where noted, the illustrations in paragraphs 288-356 assume that the reporting entity had adopted the fair value based method of accounting for compensation cost before the transactions illustrated. However, had the entity continued to account for its stock-based employee compensation cost in accordance with Opinion 25, it would follow the same procedures in preparing the pro forma disclosures required by this Statement.

Selecting Assumptions for Use in an Option-Pricing Model

273. This Statement requires a public entity to estimate the fair value of an employee stock option using a pricing model that takes into account the exercise price and expected life of the option, the current price of the underlying stock, its expected volatility, the expected dividends on the stock, and the current risk-free interest rate for the expected life of the option. As indicated in paragraph 19, a U.S. entity issuing an option on its own stock must use as the risk-free interest rate the implied yield currently available on zero-coupon U.S. government issues with a remaining term equal to the expected life of the option that is being valued. Guidance on selecting the other assumptions listed in paragraph 19 is provided in the following paragraphs.[18]

274. In estimating the expected volatility of and dividends on the underlying stock, the objective is to approximate the expectations that likely would be reflected in a current market or negotiated exchange price for the option. Similarly, the objective in estimating the expected lives of employee stock options is to approximate the expectations that an outside party with access to detailed information about employees' exercise behavior likely would develop based on information available at the grant date.

275. The Board recognizes that in most circumstances there is likely to be a range of reasonable expectations about future volatility, dividends, and option life. If one amount within the range is a better estimate than any other amount, that amount should be used. If no amount within the range is a better estimate than any other amount, it is appropriate to use an estimate at the *low* end of the range for expected volatility and expected option life, and an estimate at the *high* end of the range for expected dividends. (Computed option value varies directly with expected volatility and life, but it varies inversely with expected dividends.) That approach is similar to the one used in FASB Interpretation No. 14, *Reasonable Estimation of the Amount of a Loss,* which requires accrual of the minimum amount in a range of reasonable estimates of the amount of a loss if no amount within the range is a better estimate than any other amount.

276. Expectations about the future generally are based on past experience, modified to reflect ways in which currently available information indicates that the future is reasonably expected to differ from the past. In some circumstances, identifiable factors may indicate that unadjusted historical experience is a relatively poor predictor of future experience. For example, if an entity with two distinctly different lines of business disposes of the one that was significantly less volatile and generated more cash than the other,

---

[18]The guidance on assumptions in this Statement, especially the expected lives of employee stock options, benefited from several working papers discussed at an informal roundtable discussion on measuring the value of employee stock options the Board held on April 18, 1994. Some of those papers have subsequently been published.

historical volatility, dividends, and perhaps lives of stock options from the predisposition period are not likely to be the best information on which to base reasonable expectations for the future.

277. In other circumstances, historical information may not be available. For example, an entity whose common stock has only recently become publicly traded will have little, if any, historical data on the volatility of its own stock. In that situation, expected volatility may be based on the average volatilities of similar entities for an appropriate period following their going public. Similarly, an entity whose common stock has been publicly traded for only a few years and has generally become less volatile as more trading experience has been gained might appropriately place more weight on the more recent experience. It also might consider the stock price volatilities of similar entities.

278. Not all of the general guidance on selecting assumptions provided in paragraphs 273-277 is repeated in the following discussion of factors to be considered in selecting specific assumptions. However, the general guidance is intended to apply to each individual assumption. The Board does *not* intend for an entity to base option values on historical average option lives, stock volatility, or dividends (whether stated as a yield or a dollar amount) without considering the extent to which historical experience reasonably predicts future experience.

Expected Lives of Employee Stock Options

279. The value of an award of employee stock options may be based either on an appropriately weighted average expected life for the entire award or on appropriately weighted lives for subgroups of the award based on more detailed data about employees' exercise behavior. Paragraphs 281 and 282 each discuss a different way to incorporate a range of expected lives in estimating option value rather than effectively assuming that all employees hold their options for the weighted-average life.

280. Factors to consider in estimating the expected life of an award of stock options include:

a. The vesting period of the grant. The expected life must at least include the vesting period. In addition, if all other factors are equal, the length of time employees hold options after they first become exercisable may vary inversely with the length of the vesting period. For example, employees may be more likely to exer-

cise options shortly after the options vest if the vesting period is four years than if the vesting period is only two years.
b. The average length of time similar grants have remained outstanding in the past.
c. Expected volatility of the underlying stock. On average, employees may tend to exercise options on highly volatile stocks earlier than on stocks with low volatility.

281. Segregating options into groups for employees with relatively homogeneous exercise behavior may also be important. Option value is not a linear function of option term; value increases at a decreasing rate as the term lengthens. For example, a two-year option is worth less than twice as much as a one-year option if all other assumptions are equal. That means that calculating estimated option value based on a single weighted-average life that includes widely differing individual lives will overstate the value of the entire award. Segregating options granted into several groups, each of which has a relatively narrow range of lives included in its weighted-average life, reduces that overstatement. For example, the experience of an entity that grants options broadly to all levels of employees might indicate that top-level executives tend to hold their options longer than middle-management employees hold theirs and that hourly employees tend to exercise their options earlier than any other group. In addition, employees who are encouraged or required to hold a minimum amount of their employer's equity instruments, including options, might on average exercise options later than employees not subject to that provision. In those situations, segregating options by groups of recipients with relatively homogeneous exercise behavior and determining the related option values based on appropriate weighted-average expected lives for each group will result in an improved estimate of the fair value of the total award.

282. Rather than estimating expected life directly, an entity may wish to estimate it indirectly, using an option-pricing model that has been modified to compute an option value using an assumed stock price at which the options would be expected to be exercised. For example, an entity's experience might show a large increase in option exercises when the stock price first reaches 200 percent of the exercise price. If so, that entity might compute an option value using a pricing model that implicitly determines a weighted-average life based on exercise at an assumed price of 200 percent of the exercise price. The model would assume exercise of the option at each point on the inherent probability distribution of possible stock

prices at which the expected price at exercise is first reached. On branches of the binomial tree on which the stock price does not reach 200 percent of the exercise price but is in-the-money at the end of the contractual term, the model would assume exercise at that date. The expected life is then computed as the weighted-average life of the resulting binomial tree. That method recognizes that employees' exercise behavior is related to the path of the stock price.

283. Segregating options into groups based on the exercise behavior of the recipients also may be important if the technique in paragraph 282 is used. For example, an employer's experience might indicate that hourly employees tend to exercise for a smaller percentage gain than do more highly compensated employees.

Expected Volatility

284. Volatility is a measure of the amount by which a price has fluctuated or is expected to fluctuate during a period. The measure of volatility used in the Black-Scholes option-pricing model is the annualized standard deviation of the continuously compounded rates of return on the stock over a period of time. Generally, at least 20 to 30 price observations made at regular intervals are needed to compute a statistically valid standard deviation. For long-term options, historical volatility generally should be calculated based on more—probably many more—than 30 observations. The concept of volatility is defined more fully in the glossary. One method of calculating historical average annualized volatility based on weekly price observations is illustrated in Appendix F. As discussed further in the following paragraph, an entity may need to adjust historical average annualized volatility to estimate a reasonable expected volatility over the expected life of an option.

285. Factors to consider in estimating expected volatility include:

a. The historical volatility of the stock over the most recent period that is generally commensurate with the expected option life.
b. The length of time an entity's stock has been publicly traded. If that period is shorter than the expected life of the option, historical volatility should be computed for the longest period for which trading activity is available. A newly public entity also should consider the historical volatility of similar entities following a comparable period in their lives. For example, an entity that has been publicly traded for only one year that

grants options with an average expected life of five years might consider the pattern and level of historical volatility of more mature entities in the same industry for the first six years the stocks of those entities were publicly traded.
c. The mean-reversion tendency of volatilities. For example, an entity with insufficient trading history on which to base an estimate of historical volatility might take into account mean-reversion tendencies (sometimes called *shrinkage*). A newly public entity with a trading history of only 1 year might have a historical volatility of 60 percent, while the mean volatility of an appropriate peer group is only 35 percent. Until a longer series of historical data is available, the entity might use an expected volatility of approximately 47.5 percent [(.60 + .35) ÷ 2]. A more mature entity also should consider mean-reversion tendencies and other reasons for which expected future volatility may differ from past volatility. For example, if an entity's stock was extraordinarily volatile for some identifiable period of time because of a failed takeover bid or a major restructuring, that period might be disregarded in computing historical average annual volatility.
d. Appropriate and regular intervals for price observations. In general, weekly price observations should be sufficient for computing long-term historical volatility. The price observations should be consistent from period to period. For example, an entity might use the closing price for each week or the highest price for the week, but it should not use the closing price for some weeks and the highest price for other weeks.

Expected Dividends

286. Standard option-pricing models generally call for expected dividend yield. However, the models may be modified to use an expected dividend amount rather than a yield. An entity may use either its expected yield or its expected payments. If the latter, the entity's historical pattern of increases in dividends should be considered. For example, if an entity's policy generally has been to increase dividends by approximately 3 percent per year, its estimated option value should not assume a fixed dividend amount throughout the expected life unless there is evidence that supports that assumption.

287. Generally, the assumption about expected dividends should be based on publicly available information. An entity that does not pay dividends and has no plans to do so would assume an expected dividend

yield of zero. However, an emerging entity with no history of paying dividends might expect to begin paying dividends during the expected lives of its employee stock options. Those entities may use an average of their past dividend yield (zero) and the mean dividend yield of an appropriately comparable peer group. For example, it would not be appropriate for a young, rapidly growing entity to base its expected dividend yield on the average dividend yield of the entities in the Standard & Poor's 500 Index.

Illustrative Computations

Illustration 1—Fixed Stock Option

288. Company S, a public entity, grants options with a maximum term of 10 years to its employees. The exercise price of each option equals the market price of its stock on the grant date. All options vest at the end of three years (cliff vesting). The options do not qualify for tax purposes as incentive stock options. The corporate tax rate is 34 percent.

289. The following table shows assumptions and information about options granted on January 1, 2000.

Options granted	900,000
Employees granted options	3,000
Expected forfeitures per year	3%
Stock price	$50
Exercise price	$50
Expected life of options	6 years
Risk-free interest rate	7.5%
Expected volatility	30%
Expected dividend yield	2.5%

290. Using as inputs the last 6 items from the table above, the Black-Scholes option-pricing model modified for dividends determines a fair value of $17.15 for each option. Using the same assumptions, a binomial model produces a value of $17.26. A difference between a Black-Scholes model and a binomial model grant-date valuation of an option generally arises from the binomial model's fully reflecting the benefit in limited circumstances of being able to exercise an option on a dividend-paying stock before its expiration date when it is economic to do so. (If Company S paid no dividends, both the Black-Scholes and the binomial models would determine a fair value of $22.80, holding other assumptions constant.) Although some available software modifies the Black-Scholes model to attempt to take that ben-

efit into account, the result may not be exactly the same as a binomial model. The following illustrations use a fair value of $17.15, but $17.26 is equally acceptable.

291. Total compensation cost recognized over the vesting period will be the fair value of all options that actually vest, determined based on the stock price at the grant date. This Statement allows an entity either to estimate at the grant date the number of options expected to vest or to recognize compensation cost each period based on the number of options not yet forfeited. An adjustment to eliminate compensation cost previously recognized for options that were subsequently forfeited is recognized when the forfeitures occur. This example assumes that Company S estimates at the grant date the number of options that will vest and subsequently adjusts compensation cost for changes in the assumed rate of forfeitures and differences between expectations and actual experience. None of the compensation cost is capitalized as part of the cost to produce inventory or other assets.

292. The estimate of the expected number of forfeitures considers historical employee turnover rates and expectations about the future. Company S has experienced historical turnover rates of approximately 3 percent per year for employees at the grantees' level having nonvested options, and it expects that rate to continue. Therefore, Company S estimates the total value of the award at the grant date based on an expected forfeiture rate of 3 percent per year. Actual forfeitures are 5 percent in 2000, but no adjustments to cost are recognized in 2000 because Company S still expects actual forfeitures to average 3 percent per year over the 3-year vesting period. During 2001, however, management decides that the rate of forfeitures is likely to continue to increase through 2002, and the assumed forfeiture rate for the entire award is changed to 6 percent per year. Adjustments to cumulative cost to reflect the higher forfeiture rate are made at the end of 2001. At the end of 2002 when the award becomes vested, actual forfeitures have averaged 6 percent per year, and no further adjustment is necessary.

Cliff vesting

293. The first set of calculations illustrates the accounting for the award of options on January 1, 2000, assuming that the entire award vests at the end of three years, that is, the award provides for cliff vesting rather than graded vesting. (Paragraphs 298-305

illustrate the accounting for an award assuming graded vesting in which a specified portion of the award vests at the end of each year.) The number of options expected to vest is estimated at the grant date to be 821,406 (900,000 × .97 × .97 × .97). Thus, as shown in Table 1, the estimated value of the award at January 1, 2000 is $14,087,113 (821,406 × $17.15), and the compensation cost to be recognized during each year of the 3-year vesting period is $4,695,704 ($14,087,113 ÷ 3). The journal entries to recognize compensation cost follow.

For 2000:

Compensation cost	4,695,704	
Additional paid-in capital— stock options		4,695,704

To recognize compensation cost.

Deferred tax asset	1,596,539	
Deferred tax expense		1,596,539

To recognize the deferred tax asset for the temporary difference related to compensation cost ($4,695,704 × .34 = $1,596,539).

The net after-tax effect on income of recognizing compensation cost for 2000 is $3,099,165 ($4,695,704 – $1,596,539).

294. In the absence of a change in estimate or experience different from that initially assumed, the same journal entries would be made to recognize compensation cost and related tax effects for 2001 and 2002, resulting in a net after-tax cost for each year of $3,099,165. However, at the end of 2001, management changes its estimated employee forfeiture rate from 3 percent to 6 percent per year. The revised number of options expected to vest is 747,526 (900,000 × .94 × .94 × .94). Accordingly, the revised total compensation cost to be recognized by the end of 2002 is $12,820,071 (747,526 × $17.15). The cumulative adjustment to reflect the effect of adjusting the forfeiture rate is the difference between two-thirds of the revised cost of the award and the cost already recognized for 2000 and 2001. The related journal entries and the computations follow.

At December 31, 2001 to adjust for new forfeiture rate:

Revised total compensation cost	$12,820,071
Revised cumulative cost as of 12/31/01 ($12,820,071 × ⅔)	$ 8,546,714
Cost already recognized in 2000 and 2001 ($4,695,704 × 2)	9,391,408
Adjustment to cost at 12/31/01	$ (844,694)

The related journal entries are:

Additional paid-in capital— stock options	844,694	
Compensation cost		844,694

To adjust compensation cost and equity already recognized to reflect a higher estimated forfeiture rate.

Deferred tax expense	287,196	
Deferred tax asset		287,196

To adjust the deferred tax accounts to reflect the tax effect of increasing the estimated forfeiture rate ($844,694 × .34 = $287,196).

For 2002:

Compensation cost	4,273,357	
Additional paid-in capital— stock options		4,273,357

To recognize compensation cost ($12,820,071 ÷ 3 = $4,273,357).

Deferred tax asset	1,452,941	
Deferred tax expense		1,452,941

To recognize the deferred tax asset for additional compensation cost ($4,273,357 × .34 = $1,452,941).

At December 31, 2002, the entity would examine its actual forfeitures and make any necessary adjustments to reflect compensation cost for the number of shares that actually vested.

Table 1—Fixed Stock Option—Cliff Vesting

Year	Total Value of Award	Pretax Cost for Year	Cumulative Pretax Cost
2000	$14,087,113 (821,406 × $17.15)	$4,695,704 ($14,087,113 ÷ 3)	$4,695,704
2001	$12,820,071 (747,526 × $17.15)	$3,851,010 [($12,820,071 × ⅔) − $4,695,704]	$8,546,714
2002	$12,820,071 (747,526 × $17.15)	$4,273,357 ($12,820,071 ÷ 3)	$12,820,071

295. For simplicity, the illustration assumes that all of the options are exercised on the same day and that Company S has already recognized its income tax expense for the year without regard to the effects of the exercise of the employee stock options. In other words, current tax expense and current taxes payable were recognized based on income and deductions before consideration of additional deductions from exercise of the employee stock options. The amount credited to common stock (or other appropriate equity account) for the exercise of the options is the sum of (a) the cash proceeds received and (b) the amounts credited to additional paid-in capital for services received earlier that were charged to compensation cost. At exercise, the stock price is assumed to be $70.

At exercise:

Cash (747,526 × $50)	37,376,300	
Additional paid-in capital—stock options	12,820,071	
Common stock		50,196,371

To recognize the issuance of stock upon exercise of options.

296. The difference between the market price of the stock and the exercise price on the date of exercise is deductible for tax purposes because the options do not qualify as incentive stock options. The benefit of tax return deductions in excess of compensation cost recognized results in a credit to additional paid-in capital. Tax return deductions that are less than compensation cost recognized result in a debit to additional paid-in capital to the extent that the benefit of

tax deductions from stock-based compensation awards in excess of compensation cost recognized based on the fair value method have been previously credited to capital. To the extent that insufficient credits are available in additional paid-in capital, a charge is made to income tax expense in the period of exercise (paragraph 44). With the stock price at $70 at exercise, the deductible amount is $14,950,520 [747,526 × ($70 − $50)]. The entity has sufficient taxable income, and the tax benefit realized is $5,083,177 ($14,950,520 × .34).

At exercise:

Deferred tax expense	4,358,824	
Deferred tax asset		4,358,824

To write off deferred tax asset related to deductible stock options at exercise ($12,820,071 × .34 = $4,358,824).[19]

Current taxes payable	5,083,177	
Current tax expense		4,358,824
Additional paid-in capital—stock options		724,353

To adjust current tax expense and current taxes payable to recognize the current tax benefit from deductible compensation cost upon exercise of options. The credit to additional paid-in capital is the tax benefit of the excess of the deductible amount over the compensation cost recognized: [($14,950,520 − $12,820,071) × .34 = $724,353].

297. If instead the options had expired unexercised, the additional paid-in capital—stock options account

---

[19]Individual entries to the deferred tax asset account do not add to $4,358,824 due to rounding differences.

would have been closed to other paid-in capital. Previously recognized compensation cost would not be reversed. Similar to the adjustment for the actual tax deduction realized described in paragraph 296, whether part or all of the deferred tax asset of $4,358,824 is charged to additional paid-in capital or to income tax expense is determined by applying paragraph 44.

Graded vesting

298. Paragraph 31 of this Statement provides for use of either the attribution method described in Interpretation 28 or a straight-line method for awards with graded vesting depending on the approach used to estimate the value of the option award. Both methods are illustrated and use the same assumptions that follow. Company S awards 900,000 options on January 1, 2000, that vest according to a graded schedule of 25 percent for the first year of service, 25 percent for the second year, and the remaining 50 percent for the third year. Each employee is granted 300 options.

299. Table 2 shows the calculation of the number of employees and the related number of options expected to vest. Using the expected 3 percent annual forfeiture rate, 90 employees are expected to terminate during 2000 without having vested in any portion of the award, leaving 2,910 employees to vest in 25 percent of the award. During 2001, 87 employees are expected to terminate, leaving 2,823 to vest in the second 25 percent of the award. During 2002, 85 employees are expected to terminate, leaving 2,738 employees to vest in the last 50 percent of the award. That results in a total of 840,675 options expected to vest from the award of 900,000 options with graded vesting. As provided in paragraph 28, Company S could have chosen to recognize cost based on the number of options granted and recognized forfeitures as they occur; that method is not illustrated.

Table 2—Fixed Stock Option—Graded Vesting—Expected Amounts

Year	Number of Employees	Number of Vested Options
	Total at date of grant 3,000	
2000	$3,000 - 90\ (3,000 \times .03) =\ 2,910$	$2,910 \times 75\ (300 \times 25\%) =\ 218,250$
2001	$2,910 - 87\ (2,910 \times .03) =\ 2,823$	$2,823 \times 75\ (300 \times 25\%) =\ 211,725$
2002	$2,823 - 85\ (2,823 \times .03) =\ 2,738$	$2,738 \times 150\ (300 \times 50\%) =\ \underline{410,700}$
		Total vested options $\underline{840,675}$

Circumstances in which Interpretation 28 attribution is required

300. If the value of the options that vest over the three-year period is estimated by separating the total award into three groups according to the year in which they vest because the expected life for each group differs significantly, the fair value of the award and its attribution would be determined as follows. (Paragraphs 281 and 283 discuss segregation of options into groups that vest.) The estimated weighted-average expected life of the options that vest in 2000 is assumed to be 2.5 years, resulting in a value of $11.33 per option.[20] The estimated weighted-average expected life of the options that vest in 2001 is assumed to be 4 years, resulting in a value of $14.32 per option. The estimated weighted-average expected life of the options that vest in 2002 is assumed to be 5.5 years, resulting in a value of $16.54 per option. Table 3 shows the estimated compensation cost for the options expected to vest.

---

[20]To simplify the illustration, the fair value of each of the 3 groups of options is based on the same assumptions about expected volatility, expected dividend yield, and the risk-free interest rate used to determine the value of $17.15 for the cliff-vesting options (paragraph 290). In practice, each of those assumptions would be related to the expected life of the group of options being valued, which means that at least the risk-free interest rate and perhaps all three assumptions would differ for each group.

Table 3—Fixed Stock Option—Graded Vesting—Expected Cost

Year	Vested Options	Expected Life	Value per Option	Compensation Cost
2000	218,250	2.5 years	$11.33	$ 2,472,773
2001	211,725	4.0 years	14.32	3,031,902
2002	410,700	5.5 years	16.54	6,792,978
	840,675			$12,297,653

301. Compensation cost is recognized over the periods of service during which each group of options is earned. Thus, the $2,472,773 cost attributable to the 218,250 options that vest in 2000 is allocated to the year 2000. The $3,031,902 cost attributable to the 211,725 options that vest at the end of 2001 is allocated over their 2-year vesting period (2000 and 2001). The $6,792,978 cost attributable to the 410,700 options that vest at the end of 2002 is allocated over their 3-year vesting period (2000, 2001, and 2002).

302. Table 4 shows how the $12,297,653 expected amount of compensation cost determined at the grant date is attributed to the years 2000, 2001, and 2002.

Table 4—Fixed Stock Option—Graded Vesting— Computation of Expected Cost

	Pretax Cost to Be Recognized		
	2000	2001	2002
Options vesting in 2000	$2,472,773		
Options vesting in 2001	1,515,951	$ 1,515,951	
Options vesting in 2002	2,264,326	2,264,326	$ 2,264,326
Cost for the year	$6,253,050	$ 3,780,277	$ 2,264,326
Cumulative cost	$6,253,050	$10,033,327	$12,297,653

Circumstances in which straight-line attribution is permitted

303. Company S assumes a single weighted-average expected life of five years for the entire award of graded vesting options because the expected lives of each group of options that vest are not expected to be significantly different. Other assumptions except for expected life are the same as in the previous illustration. Company S elects to recognize compensation cost on a straight-line basis.

304. Using an estimated weighted-average expected life of 5 years results in a value of $15.87 per option. The same number of options are expected to vest as shown in the previous illustration, 840,675, based on estimated forfeitures. Total compensation cost to be attributed in a straight-line pattern over the 3-year vesting period is $13,341,512 (840,675 × $15.87). Compensation cost recognized at any date must be at least equal to the amount attributable to options that are vested at that date. For example, if this same op-

tion award vested 50 percent in the first year of the 3-year vesting period, at least $6,670,756 ($13,341,512 × 50%) would be recognized in the first year.

305. The estimated value of the award is adjusted to reflect differences between expected and actual forfeitures as illustrated for the cliff-vesting options, regardless of which method described in paragraph 31 is used to estimate value and attribute cost for the graded vesting options. For example, if the actual forfeiture rate is 5 percent rather than 3 percent in 2000, the compensation cost for the options that vest in 2000 (attributed under the Interpretation 28 method) is adjusted to $2,421,788 (2,850 × 75 × $11.33), reflecting the reduction in the number of employees [2,850 = 3,000 − (3,000 × .05)] whose first 75 options became vested at December 31, 2000. Compensation cost for the options expected to vest in 2001 and 2002 also is recomputed to reflect the actual forfeitures in 2000. Similar adjustments are made to reflect

differences, if any, between expected and actual forfeitures in those years. Total compensation cost at the end of 2002 reflects the number of vested options at that date.

Illustration 2—Performance-Based Stock Option

Illustration 2(a)—Option award under which the number of options to be earned varies

306. Illustration 2(a) shows the computation of compensation cost if Company S grants a performance-based stock option award instead of a fixed stock option award. Under the plan, employees vest in differing numbers of options depending on the increase in market share of one of Company S's products over a three-year period. On January 1, 2000, Company S grants to each of 1,000 employees an award of up to 300 10-year options on shares of its common stock. If by December 31, 2002, market share increases by at least 5 percentage points, each employee vests in at least 100 options at that date. If market share increases by at least 10 percentage points, another 100 options vest, for a total of 200. If market share increases by more than 20 percentage points, each employee vests in 300 options. Company S's stock price on January 1, 2000, is $50, and other assumptions are the same as in Illustration 1. The fair value at the grant date of an option expected to vest is $17.15. The estimated fair value of the entire performance-based award depends on the number of options that are expected to be earned during the vesting period. Accruals of cost are based on the best estimate of market share growth over the three-year vesting period, and adjusted for subsequent changes in the expected or actual market share growth. Paragraph 28 requires accruals of cost to be based on the best estimate of the outcome of the performance condition. Therefore, Company S is not permitted to estimate a percentage likelihood of achieving a performance condition and base accruals on an amount that is not a possible outcome.

307. Table 5 shows the compensation cost recognized in 2000, 2001, and 2002 if Company S estimates at the grant date that it is probable that market share will increase between 10 and 20 percentage points. That estimate remains reasonable until the end of 2002, when Company S's market share has increased over the 3-year period by more than 20 percentage points. Thus, each employee vests in options on 300 shares.

308. As in Illustration 1, Company S experiences actual forfeiture rates of 5 percent in 2000, and in 2001 changes its estimate of forfeitures for the entire award from 3 percent to 6 percent per year. In 2001, cumulative compensation cost is adjusted to reflect the higher forfeiture rate. By the end of 2002, a 6 percent forfeiture rate has been experienced, and no further adjustments for forfeitures are necessary. Through 2000, Company S estimates that 913 employees ($1,000 \times .97 \times .97 \times .97$) will remain in service until the vesting date. At the end of 2001, the number of employees estimated to vest is adjusted for the higher forfeiture rate, and the number of employees expected to vest in the award is 831 ($1,000 \times .94 \times .94 \times .94$). The value of the award is estimated initially based on the number of options expected to vest, which in turn is based on the expected level of performance, and the fair value of each option. Compensation cost is initially recognized ratably over the three-year vesting period, with one-third of the value of the award recognized each year, adjusted as needed for changes in the estimated and actual forfeiture rates and for differences between estimated and actual market share growth.

Table 5—Performance-Based Stock Option—Number of Options Varies

Year	Total Value of Award	Pretax Cost for Year	Cumulative Pretax Cost
2000	$3,131,590 ($17.15 × 200 × 913)	$1,043,863 ($3,131,590 ÷ 3)	$1,043,863
2001	$2,850,330 ($17.15 × 200 × 831)	$856,357 [($2,850,330 × ⅔) – $1,043,863]	$1,900,220
2002	$4,275,495 ($17.15 × 300 × 831)	$2,375,275 ($4,275,495 – $1,900,220)	$4,275,495

Illustration 2(b)—Option award under which the exercise price varies

309. Illustration 2(b) shows the computation of compensation cost if Company S grants a performance-based stock option award under which the exercise price, rather than the number of shares, varies depending on the level of performance achieved. On January 1, 2000, Company S grants to its chief executive officer (CEO) 10-year options on 10,000 shares of its common stock, which are immediately exercisable. The stock price at the grant date is $50, and the initial exercise price also is $50. However, that price decreases to $30 if the market share of Company S's products increases by at least 10 percentage points by December 31, 2001, and provided that the CEO continues to be employed by Company S.

310. Company S estimates at the grant date the expected level of market share growth, the exercise price of the options, and the expected life of the options. Other assumptions, including the risk-free interest rate and the service period over which the cost is attributed, need to be consistent with those estimates. Company S estimates at the grant date that its market share growth will be at least 10 percentage points over the 2-year performance period, which means that the expected exercise price of the options is $30, resulting in an estimated option value of $22.64.[21] Compensation cost of $226,400 (10,000 × $22.64) would be accrued over the expected 2-year service period. Paragraph 19 of this Statement requires the value of both fixed and performance awards to be estimated as of the date of grant. Paragraph 26, however, calls for recognition of cost for the number of instruments that actually vest. For this performance award, Company S also selects the expected assumptions at the grant date if the performance goal is not met. If market share growth is not at least 10 percentage points over the 2-year period, Company S estimates that the CEO will exercise the options with a $50 exercise price in 5 years. All other assumptions would need to be consistent, resulting in an estimated option value of $15.87.[22] (For convenience, the illustration assumes that all options are expected to be exercised on the same date.) Total compensation cost to be recognized if the performance goal is not met would be $158,700 (10,000 ×

$15.87). During the two-year service period, adjustments to expected amounts for changes in estimates or actual experience are made and cost recognized by the end of that period reflects whether the performance goal was met.

Illustration 3—Stock Option with Indexed Exercise Price

311. Company S instead might have granted stock options whose exercise price varies with an index of the stock prices of a group of entities in the same industry. Assume that on January 1, 2000, Company S grants 100 options on its stock with a base exercise price of $50 to each of 1,000 employees. The options have a maximum term of 10 years. The exercise price of the options increases or decreases on December 31 of each year by the same percentage that the index has increased or decreased during the year. For example, if the peer group index increases by 10 percent in 2000, the exercise price of the options during 2001 increases to $55 ($50 × 1.10). The assumptions about the risk-free interest rate and expected life, dividends, volatility, and forfeiture rates are the same as in Illustration 1. On January 1, 2000, the peer group index is assumed to be 400. The dividend yield on the index is assumed to be 1.25 percent.

312. Each indexed option may be analyzed as an option to exchange 0.1250 (50 ÷ 400) "shares" of the peer group index for a share of Company S stock, that is, to exchange one noncash asset for another noncash asset. An option to purchase stock for cash also can be thought of as an option to exchange one asset (cash in the amount of the exercise price) for another (the share of stock). The gain on a cash option equals the difference between the price of the stock upon exercise and the amount—the "price"—of the cash exchanged for the stock. The gain on an option to exchange 0.1250 "shares" of the peer group index for a share of Company S stock also equals the difference between the prices of the 2 assets exchanged.

313. To illustrate the equivalence of an indexed option and the option above, assume that an employee exercises the indexed option when Company S's stock price has increased 100 percent to $100 and the peer group index has increased 75 percent, from 400

---

[21]Option value is determined using a $50 stock price, $30 exercise price, 3-year expected life, 6.5 percent risk-free interest rate, 2.5 percent dividend yield, and .30 volatility.

[22]Option value is determined using a $50 stock price, $50 exercise price, 5-year expected life, 7.5 percent risk-free interest rate, 2.5 percent dividend yield, and .30 volatility.

to 700. The exercise price of the indexed option thus is $87.50 ($50 × 1.75). The employee's realized gain is $12.50.

Price of Company S stock	$100.00
Less: Exercise price of option	87.50
Gain on indexed option	$ 12.50

That is the same as the gain on an option to exchange 0.1250 "shares" of the index for one share of Company S stock:

Price of Company S stock	$100.00
Less: Price of a "share" of the peer group index (.1250 × $700)	87.50
Gain on exchange	$ 12.50

314. The Black-Scholes or binomial option-pricing models can be extended to value an option to exchange one asset for another. The principal extension is that the volatility of an option to exchange two noncash assets is based on the relationship between the volatilities of the prices of the assets to be exchanged—their **cross-volatility.** In a cash option, the amount of cash to be paid involves no risk, that is, it is not volatile, so that only the volatility of the stock needs to be considered in estimating the option's value. In contrast, the value of an option to exchange two noncash assets depends on possible movements in the prices of both assets—in this example, a "share" of the peer group index and a share of Company S stock. Historical cross-volatility can be computed directly by measuring the stock price in "shares" of the peer group index. For example, the stock price was 0.1250 "shares" at the grant date and 0.1429 (100 ÷ 700) "shares" at the exercise date. Those share amounts then are used to compute cross-volatility. Cross-volatility also can be computed indirectly based on the respective volatilities of Company S stock and the peer group index and the correlation between them. The cross-volatility between Company S stock and the peer group index is assumed to be 26.5 percent.

315. In a cash option, the assumed risk-free interest rate (discount rate) represents the return on the cash that will not be paid until exercise. In this example, an equivalent "share" of the index, rather than cash,

is what will not be "paid" until exercise. The dividend yield on the peer group index of 1.25 percent therefore is used in place of the risk-free interest rate as an input to the Black-Scholes model.

316. The exercise price for the indexed option is the value of an equivalent "share" of the peer group index, which is $50 (0.1250 × 400). The fair value of each option granted is $9.78 based on the following inputs:

Stock price	$50
Exercise price	$50
Dividend yield	2.50%
Discount rate	1.25%
Volatility	26.5%
Expected life	6 years

The value of the entire award would be based on the number of options expected to vest. That cost would be recognized over the service period as shown in Illustration 1.

Illustration 4—Option with Exercise Price That Increases by a Fixed Amount or a Fixed Percentage

317. Some entities grant options with exercise prices that increase by a fixed amount or a constant percentage periodically rather than by the percentage change in an index. For example, the exercise price of the options in Illustration 1 might increase by a fixed amount of $2.50 per year. Binomial option-pricing models can be adapted to accommodate exercise prices that change over time.

318. Options with exercise prices that increase by a constant percentage also can be valued using an option-pricing model that accommodates changes in exercise prices. Alternatively, those options can be valued by deducting from the discount rate the annual percentage increase in the exercise price. That method works because a decrease in the risk-free interest rate and an increase in the exercise price have a similar effect—both reduce the option value. For example, the exercise price of the options in Illustration 1 might increase at the rate of 5 percent annually. For that example, Company S's options would be valued based on a risk-free interest rate of 2.5 percent (7.5% – 5%). Holding all other assumptions constant

from Illustration 1, the value of each option granted by Company S would be $12.34.

Illustration 5—Modifications and Cash Settlements

Illustration 5(a)—Modification of vested options granted after adoption of this Statement

319. The following examples of accounting for modifications of the terms of an award are based on Illustration 1, in which Company S granted its employees 900,000 options with an exercise price of $50 on January 1, 2000. At January 1, 2004, after the options have vested, the market price of Company S stock has declined to $40 per share, and Company S decides to reduce the exercise price of the outstanding options to $40. In effect, Company S issues new options with an exercise price of $40 and a contractual term equal to the remaining contractual term of the original January 1, 2000, options, which is 6 years, in exchange for the original vested options. Company S incurs additional compensation cost for the excess of the fair value of the modified options issued over the value of the original options at the date of the exchange measured as shown in paragraph 320. The modified options are immediately vested, and the additional compensation cost is recognized in the period the modification occurs.

320. The fair value on January 1, 2004, of the modified award, based on a 3-year expected life, $40 current stock price, $40 exercise price, 7 percent risk-free interest rate, 35 percent volatility, and a 2.5 percent dividend yield, is $10.82. To determine the amount of additional compensation cost arising from the modification, the value of the original vested options assumed to be repurchased is computed based on the shorter of (a) the remaining expected life of the original options or (b) the expected life of the modified options. In this example, the remaining expected life of the original options is two years, which is shorter than the expected life of the modified options (three years). The resulting computed value at January 1, 2004, of the original options based on a $40 current stock price, a $50 exercise price, a risk-free interest rate of 7 percent, expected volatility of 35 percent, and a 2.5 percent dividend yield is $5.54 per option. Thus, the additional compensation cost stemming from the modification is $5.28 per option, determined as follows:

Fair value of modified option at January 1, 2004	$10.82
Less: Value of original option at January 1, 2004	5.54
Additional compensation cost to be recognized	$ 5.28

Compensation cost already recognized during the vesting period of the original award is $12,820,071 for 747,526 vested options (refer to Illustration 1). For simplicity, it is assumed that no options were exercised before the modification. Previously recognized cost is not adjusted. Additional compensation cost of $3,946,937 (747,526 vested options × $5.28) is recognized on January 1, 2004, because the modified options are fully vested.

Illustration 5(b)—Cash settlement of vested options granted after adoption of this Statement

321. Rather than modify the option terms, Company S offers to settle the original January 1, 2000 options for cash at January 1, 2004. The value of each option is estimated in the same way as illustrated in the preceding example, resulting in a value of $5.54. Company S recognizes the settlement as the repurchase of an outstanding equity instrument, and no additional compensation cost is recognized at the date of settlement unless the cash payment exceeds $5.54. Previously recognized compensation cost for the fair value of the original options is not adjusted.

Illustration 5(c)—Modification of nonvested options granted after adoption of this Statement

322. This example assumes that Company S granted its employees 900,000 options with an exercise price of $50, as in Illustration 1. At January 1, 2001, 1 year into the 3-year vesting period, the market price of Company S stock has declined to $40 per share, and Company S decides to reduce the exercise price of the options to $40. The 3-year cliff-vesting requirement is not changed. In effect, Company S grants new options with an exercise price of $40 and a contractual term equal to the 9-year remaining contractual term of the options granted on January 1, 2000, in exchange for the original nonvested options. The expected life of the repriced options is five years. Company S incurs additional compensation cost for the excess of the fair value of the modified options issued over the value of the original options at the date of the exchange determined in the manner set forth in

paragraph 320. Company S adds that incremental amount to the remaining unrecognized compensation cost for the original options at the date of modification and recognizes the total amount over the remaining two years of the three-year vesting period.

323. The fair value at January 1, 2001, of the modified options, based on a 5-year expected life, $40 current stock price, $40 exercise price, 7 percent risk-free interest rate, 35 percent volatility, and a 2.5 percent dividend yield, is $13.60 per option. The computed value of the original options at the date of modification used to measure additional compensation cost is based on an expected life of five years because the remaining expected life of the original options and the expected life of the modified options both are five years. The resulting value of the original options, based on a current stock price of $40 and an exercise price of $50, with other assumptions the same as those used to determine the fair value of the modified options, is $10.77. Thus, the additional compensation cost stemming from the modification is $2.83, determined as follows:

Fair value of modified option at January 1, 2001	$13.60
Less: Value of original option at January 1, 2001	10.77
Incremental value of modified January 1, 2001, option	$ 2.83

324. On January 1, 2001, the remaining balance of unrecognized compensation cost for the original options is $11.43 per option.[23] The total compensation cost for each modified option that is expected to vest is $14.26, determined as follows:

Incremental value of modified option	$ 2.83
Unrecognized compensation cost for original option	11.43
Total compensation cost to be recognized	$14.26

That amount is recognized during 2001 and 2002, which are the two remaining years of the service period.

Illustration 5(d)—Cash settlement of nonvested options granted after adoption of this Statement

325. Rather than modify the option terms, Company S offers to settle the original January 1, 2000 grant of options for cash at January 1, 2001. Because the stockprice decreased from $50 at the grant date to $40 at the date of settlement, the estimated fair value of each option is the same as in Illustration 5(c), $10.77. If Company S pays $10.77 per option, it would recognize that cash settlement as the repurchase of an outstanding equity instrument and total compensation cost would not be remeasured. However, the cash payment for the options effectively vests them. Therefore, the remaining unrecognized compensation cost of $11.43 per option also would be recognized at the date of settlement.

Illustration 5(e)—Modification of vested options granted before adoption of this Statement

326. This example assumes that a modification similar to Illustration 5(a) above occurred on January 1, 1998, and that the original award was granted before Company S adopted this Statement.[24] Thus, Company S recognized no compensation cost for the original options accounted for in accordance with Opinion 25 because the exercise price equaled the stock price at the measurement (grant) date. To better illustrate the accounting distinction, all other assumptions are the same as in Illustration 5(a). Therefore, the fair value of the modified option is assumed to be $10.82, as determined in paragraph 320.

327. Because no compensation cost was recognized for the original options, the modified options are treated as a new grant. Compensation cost of $10.82 is recognized for each outstanding option at the date of the modification. However, if immediately before their terms were modified, the original options had been in-the-money and thus had intrinsic value at the date of modification, that intrinsic value would be excluded from the amount of compensation cost recognized. For example, if a modification of terms occurred in conjunction with a spinoff, the original options might have intrinsic value of, say, $2 each, just before their terms are modified. In that situation, if the fair value of a modified option is $16.50, only

---

[23]Using a value of $17.15 for the original option as in Illustration 1 results in recognition of $5.72 ($17.15 ÷ 3) per year. The unrecognized balance at January 1, 2001 is $11.43 ($17.15 − $5.72) per option.

[24]For purposes of the pro forma disclosures required by paragraph 45 of this Statement, the method in Illustrations 5(e) through 5(g) applies only to modifications and cash settlements of awards granted before the beginning of the fiscal year for which that paragraph is initially applied. A modification or cash settlement of an award for which compensation cost has been included in pro forma disclosures since it was granted would be treated in the pro forma disclosures in the same manner as in Illustrations 5(a) through 5(d).

$14.50 ($16.50 – $2) of compensation cost would be recognized at the date of the modification. The intrinsic value is excluded from compensation cost because the employees could have exercised their options immediately before the modification and received the intrinsic value without affecting the amount of compensation cost recognized. Only the time value of the modified options is additional compensation cost.

Illustration 5(f)—Modification of nonvested options granted before adoption of this Statement

328. This example of a modification of an option assumes that an award originally accounted for according to Opinion 25 is not yet vested when it is modified. Company S grants an option with an exercise price of $47 when the stock price is $50 and the option cliff-vests after 3 years. Opinion 25 requires compensation cost of $3 ($50 – $47) to be recognized over the vesting period at the rate of $1 per year. After two years of that three-year cliff-vesting period, Company S adopts the accounting method for cost recognition encouraged by this Statement. It also decides to reduce the exercise price of the options to $40, which is the current price of the stock. For convenience, the value of the modified option on the date of the modification is again assumed to be $10.82 (paragraph 320), which consists entirely of time value.

329. Company S had recognized compensation cost of $2 under Opinion 25 at the date of modification for each option that had not been forfeited. After the modification, the remaining amount of compensation cost to be recognized during the final year of the 3-year service period is $9.17 for each option that vests, determined as follows:

Fair value of modified option	$10.82
Less: Value of original option, based on 1-year remaining life[25]	2.65
Incremental value of modified option	8.17
Plus: Remaining unrecognized cost for original option	1.00
Compensation cost to be recognized	$ 9.17

The value of the original option deducted from the fair value of the modified option to determine the amount of compensation cost to recognize is based on a one-year life because that is the remaining term

of the vesting period. To maintain consistency with (a) the requirements of this Statement for accounting for plan modifications and (b) the principal difference between this Statement and Opinion 25—accounting for the time value of an option—the vesting period is used as the expected life of the original option. The life of an option beyond the vesting period is not pertinent to the accounting under Opinion 25.

Illustration 5(g)—Cash settlement of vested options granted before adoption of this statement

330. This example assumes that a cash settlement of the options described in Illustration 5(a) above occurred on January 1, 1998, and that the original options were granted before Company S adopted the accounting method for cost recognition encouraged by this Statement. Thus, Company S recognized no compensation cost for the original award accounted for in accordance with Opinion 25 because the exercise price equaled the stock price at the measurement (grant) date. All other assumptions are the same as in Illustration 5(a). Therefore, the amount of the cash payment and the fair value of the out-of-the-money option at the date of cash settlement are $10.82, as determined in paragraph 320.

331. Because no cost was recognized for the original award, the cash settlement of the out-of-the-money options for $10.82 each is treated as a new grant. Compensation cost of $10.82 is recognized for each outstanding option at the date of settlement. However, if the original options had been in-the-money and thus had intrinsic value immediately before the settlement, that intrinsic value would be excluded from the amount of compensation cost recognized for the reasons cited in Illustration 5(e), paragraph 327.

Illustration 6—Options Granted by a Nonpublic Entity

332. Company P, a nonpublic entity, grants 100 stock options on its stock to each of its 100 employees. The options cliff-vest after three years. The fair value of the stock and the exercise price of the options is $5, the expected life of the options is 8 years, and the risk-free interest rate is 7.5 percent. Company P calculates a *minimum value* for each option. The so-called minimum value does not take into account the expected volatility of the underlying stock.

---

[25]Other assumptions are $40 stock price, $47 exercise price, expected volatility of 30 percent, risk-free interest rate of 5 percent, and dividend yield of 2.5 percent.

Fair value of stock	$5.00
Present value of exercise price (compounded daily)	2.74
Minimum value of each option	$2.26

333. An option-pricing model can also be used to compute the minimum value of Company P's options if the volatility assumption is set to near zero (say, 0.001), resulting in the same $2.26. If Company P expected to pay dividends, the minimum value of the options would be further reduced to reflect the present value of the expected dividends that the option holder will not receive. Assuming a 1 percent dividend yield over the 8-year expected life of the options, an option-pricing model results in a minimum value of $1.87.

334. Alternatively, the present value of the expected dividends would be computed as $.30, using 32 quarterly (8-year expected life) payments of $.0125 [($5.00 × .01) ÷ 4], and a quarterly interest rate of 1.875 percent (7.5 percent annual rate). That amount would be deducted from the minimum value of an option on a stock that pays no dividends computed in paragraph 332, resulting in a minimum value of $1.96 ($2.26 − $.30). The $0.39 present value of the dividends computed using the option-pricing model ($2.26 − $1.87) differs from the $0.30 present value computed by directly discounting dividend payments because the option-pricing model assumes that dividends will grow with increases in the stock price (if the dividend assumption is stated as a constant yield). The assumed growth rate is the difference between the risk-free interest rate and the dividend rate. In this example, that difference is 6.5 percent (7.5% − 1%). Either method of computing minimum value is acceptable in applying this Statement.

Illustration 7—Tandem Plan—Stock Options or Cash SARs

335. A plan in which employees are granted awards with two separate components, in which exercise of one component cancels the other, is referred to as a tandem plan. In contrast, a **combination plan** is an award with two separate components, both of which can be exercised.

336. The following illustrates the accounting for a tandem plan in which employees have a choice of either stock options or cash SARs. Company S grants to its employees an award of 900,000 stock options

or 900,000 cash SARs on January 1, 2000. The award vests on December 31, 2002, and has a contractual life of 10 years. If an employee exercises the SARs, the related stock options are canceled. Conversely, if an employee exercises the options, the related SARs are canceled.

337. The tandem award results in Company S's incurring a liability because the employees can demand settlement in cash, and Company S therefore is obligated to pay cash upon demand. If Company S could choose whether to settle the award in cash or by issuing stock, the award would be an equity instrument because Company S would have the discretion to avoid transferring its assets to employees (unless Company S's past practice is to settle most awards in cash, indicating that Company S has incurred a substantive liability as indicated in paragraph 39). In this illustration, however, Company S incurs a liability to pay cash, which it will recognize over the service period. The amount of the liability will be adjusted each year to reflect the current stock price. If employees choose to exercise the options rather than the SARs, the liability is settled by issuing stock.

338. In concept, the fair value of the expected liability at the grant date is $14,087,113 as computed in Illustration 1 because the value of the SARs and the value of the stock options are equal. However, this Statement does not require accounting for the time value of the cash SARs at the grant date because the compensation cost stemming from the award must be finally measured as the intrinsic value of the SARs at the exercise (or expiration) date. Accordingly, at the end of 2000, when the stock price is $55, the amount of the liability is $4,107,030 (821,406 cash SARs expected to vest × $5 increase in stock price). One-third of that amount, $1,369,010, is recognized as compensation cost for 2000. At the end of each year during the vesting period, the expected liability is remeasured based on the current stock price. As provided in paragraph 28, Company S has the choice of estimating forfeitures at the grant date or accruing cost for the total grant and adjusting for forfeitures as they occur. After the vesting period, the expected liability is remeasured for all outstanding vested awards.

Illustration 8—Tandem Plan—Phantom Shares or Stock Options

339. The illustration that follows is for a tandem plan in which the components have different values after the grant date, depending on the movement in

the price of the entity's stock. The employee's choice of which component to exercise will depend on the relative values of the components when the award is exercised.

340. Company S grants to its CEO an immediately vested award consisting of two measurable parts:

a. 1,000 phantom stock units (units) whose value is always equal to the value of 1,000 shares of Company S's common stock.
b. Options on 3,000 shares of Company S stock with an exercise price of $50 per share.

At the grant date, Company S's stock price is $50 per share. The CEO may choose whether to exercise the options or to cash in the units at any time during the next five years. Exercise of all of the options cancels all of the units, and cashing in all of the units cancels all of the options. The cash value of the units will be paid to the CEO at the end of five years if the option component of the tandem award is not exercised before then.

341. With a 3-to-1 ratio of options to units, exercise of 3 options will produce a higher gain than receipt of cash equal to the value of 1 share of stock if the stock price appreciates from the grant date by more than 50 percent. Below that point, one unit is more valuable than the gain on three options. To illustrate that relationship, the results if the stock price increases 50 percent to $75 are:

	Units		Exercise of Options	
Market value	$75,000	($75 × 1,000)	$225,000	($75 × 3,000)
Purchase price	0		150,000	($50 × 3,000)
Net cash value	$75,000		$ 75,000	

342. If the price of Company S's common stock increases from $50 to $75, each part of the tandem grant will produce the same net cash inflow (ignoring transaction costs) to the CEO. If the price increases only to $74, the value of 1 share of stock exceeds the gain on exercising 3 options, which would be $72 [3 × ($74 − $50)]. But if the price increases to $76, the gain on exercising 3 options, $78 [3 × ($76 − $50)], exceeds the value of 1 share of stock.

343. At the grant date, the CEO could take $50,000 cash for the units and forfeit the options. Therefore, the total value of the award at the grant date must exceed $50,000 because at stock prices above $75, the CEO receives a higher amount than would the holder of 1 share of stock. To exercise the 3,000 options, the CEO must forfeit the equivalent of 1,000 shares of stock, in addition to paying the total exercise price of $150,000 (3,000 × $50). In effect, the CEO receives only 2,000 shares of Company S stock upon exercise. That is the same as if the option component of the tandem award consisted of options to purchase 2,000 shares of stock for $75 per share.

344. The cash payment obligated by the units qualifies the award as a liability of Company S. The maximum amount of the cash liability, which is indexed to the price of Company S's common stock, is $75,000 because at stock prices above $75, the CEO will exercise the options.

345. In measuring compensation cost, the award may be thought of as a *combination*—not tandem—grant of (a) 1,000 units with a value at grant of $50,000 and (b) 2,000 options with a strike price of $75 per share. Compensation cost is measured as the combined value of the two parts.

346. The expected volatility of Company S stock is assumed to be 30 percent, the risk-free interest rate is 7 percent, Company S stock pays no dividend, and the expected life of the options is 5 years. Using those assumptions, the fair value of an option with an exercise price of $75 is $12.13 when the price of Company S's stock price is $50. Therefore, the total value of the award at the grant date is:

Units (1,000 × $50)	$50,000
Options (2,000 × $12.13)	24,260
Value of award	$74,260

347. Compensation cost recognized at the date of grant (the award is immediately vested) therefore would be $74,260. That amount is more than either of the components by itself, but less than the total cost that would be computed if both components (1,000 units and 3,000 options with an exercise price of $50) were exercisable. Because granting the units creates a liability, changes in the liability that result from increases or decreases in the price of Com-

pany S's stock price would be recognized each period until exercise, except that the amount of the liability would not exceed $75,000.

Illustration 9—"Look-Back" Options

348. Some entities offer options to employees under Section 423 of the Internal Revenue Code, which provides that employees will not be immediately taxed on the difference between the market price of the stock and a discounted purchase price if several requirements are met. One requirement is that the option price may not be less than the smaller of (a) 85 percent of the market price when the option is granted or (b) 85 percent of the price at exercise. An option that provides the employee the choice of (a) or (b) may not have a term in excess of 27 months. Options that provide for the more favorable of two (or more) exercise prices are referred to as "look-back" options. A look-back option with a 15 percent discount from the market price at either grant or exercise is worth more than a fixed option to purchase stock at 85 percent of the current market price because the holder of the look-back option cannot lose. If the price rises, the holder benefits to the same extent as if the exercise price were fixed at the grant date. If the stock price falls, the holder still receives the benefit of purchasing the stock at a 15 percent discount from its price at the date of exercise.

349. For example, on January 1, 2000, when its stock price is $50, Company S offers its employees the opportunity to sign up for a payroll deduction to purchase its stock at either 85 percent of the stock's current price or 85 percent of the price at the end of the year when the options expire, whichever is lower. The exercise price of the options is the lesser of (a) $42.50 ($50 × .85) or (b) 85 percent of the stock price at the end of the year when the option is exercised. For simplicity, the first set of calculations assumes that Company S pays no dividends, its expected volatility is .30, and the risk-free interest rate available for the next 12 months is 6.8 percent.

350. The value of that look-back option can be estimated at the grant date by breaking it into its components and valuing the option as a combination position. In this situation, the components are:

- 0.15 of a share of nonvested stock
- 0.85 of a 1-year call option held with an exercise price of $50.

Supporting analysis for the two components is discussed below.

351. Beginning with the first component, an option with an exercise price that equals 85 percent of the value of the stock at the exercise date will always be worth 15 percent (100% − 85%) of the stock price upon exercise. For a stock that pays no dividends, that option is the equivalent of 15 percent of a share of the stock. The holder of the look-back option will receive *at least* the equivalent of 0.15 of a share of stock upon exercise, regardless of the stock price at that date. For example, if the stock price falls to $40, the exercise price of the option will be $34 ($40 × .85), and the holder will benefit by $6 ($40 − $34), which is the same as receiving 0.15 of a share of stock for each option.

352. If the stock price upon exercise is more than $50, the holder of the look-back option receives a benefit that is worth more than 15 percent of a share of stock. At prices of $50 or more, the holder receives a benefit for the difference between the stock price upon exercise and $42.50—the exercise price of the option (.85 × $50). If the stock price is $60, the holder benefits by $17.50 ($60 − $42.50). However, the holder cannot receive *both* the $17.50 value of an option with an exercise price of $42.50 *and* 0.15 of a share of stock. In effect, the holder gives up 0.15 of a share of stock worth $7.50 ($50 × .15) if the stock price is above $50 at exercise. The result is the same as if the exercise price of the option were $50 ($42.50 + $7.50), and the holder of the look-back option held 85 percent of a 1-year call option with an exercise price of $50 in addition to 0.15 of a share of stock that will be received if the stock price is $50 or less upon exercise.

353. A standard option-pricing model can be used to value the 1-year call option on 0.85 of a share of stock represented by the second component. Therefore, the compensation cost for the look-back option at the grant date is:

• 0.15 of a share of nonvested stock ($50 × 0.15)	$ 7.50
• Call on 0.85 of a share of stock, exercise price of $50 ($7.56 × .85)	6.43
Total grant date value	$13.93

354. For a look-back option on a dividend-paying stock, both the value of the nonvested stock component and the value of the option component would be adjusted to reflect the effect of the dividends that the employee does not receive during the life of the option. The present value of the dividends expected to

be paid on the stock during the life of the option, which is one year in the example, would be deducted from the value of a share that receives dividends. One way to accomplish that is to base the value calculation on shares of stock rather than dollars by assuming that the dividends are reinvested in the stock.

355. For example, if Company S pays a quarterly dividend of 0.625 percent (2.5% ÷ 4) of the current stock price, 1 share of stock would grow to 1.0252 (the future value of 1 using a return of 0.625 percent for 4 periods) shares at the end of the year if all dividends are reinvested. Therefore, the present value of 1 share of stock to be received in 1 year is only 0.9754 of a share today (again applying conventional compound interest formulas compounded quarterly) if the holder does not receive the dividends paid during the year.

356. The value of the option component is easier to compute; the appropriate dividend assumption is used in the option-pricing model in determining the value of an option on a whole share of stock. Thus, the compensation cost for the look-back option if Company S pays quarterly dividends at the annual rate of 2.5 percent is:

- 0.15 of a share of nonvested stock
  ($50 × 0.15 × 0.9754) $ 7.32
- Call on 0.85 of a share of stock,
  $50 exercise price, 2.5% dividend
  yield ($6.78 × 0.85)   5.76

Total grant date value $13.08

The first component, which is worth $7.32 at the grant date, is the minimum amount the holder benefits regardless of the price of the stock at the exercise date. The second component, worth $5.76 at the grant date, represents the additional benefit to the holder if the stock price is above $50 at the exercise date.

Illustration of the Earnings per Share Computation

357. An illustration of the computation of earnings per share follows. Under Statement 128, stock options, stock appreciation rights, and other awards to be settled in stock are potential common shares for purposes of computing earnings per share. In applying the treasury stock method, all dilutive potential common shares, regardless of whether they are exercisable, are treated as if they had been exercised. The treasury stock method assumes that the proceeds upon exercise are used to repurchase the entity's stock, reducing the number of shares to be added to outstanding common stock in computing earnings per share. The proceeds assumed to be received upon exercise include the exercise price that the employee pays, the amount of compensation cost measured and attributed to future services but not yet recognized, and the amount of any tax benefits upon assumed exercise that would be credited to additional paid-in capital. The assumed proceeds exclude any future tax benefits related to compensation cost to be recognized in income.

358. Under paragraph 28 of this Statement, an entity has the choice of estimating forfeitures in advance or recognizing forfeitures as they occur. However, the weighted-average number of options outstanding, rather than the number of options expected to vest, would be used in computing diluted EPS. In addition, the average net unrecognized compensation cost would include the options not expected to vest. For this illustration, a total of 4,600,000 options are assumed to be outstanding from current year's and prior years' grants. The weighted-average exercise price of outstanding options is assumed to be $40. The average stock price during 2000 is assumed to be $52. To simplify the illustration, it is assumed that (a) all outstanding options are the type that upon exercise give rise to deductible compensation cost for income tax purposes, and (b) no tax benefit upon exercise would be credited to additional paid-in capital; that is, the tax deduction based on current intrinsic value is less than the amount of cost recognized for financial statement purposes.

359. Computation of assumed proceeds for diluted earnings per share:

- Amount employees would pay if the weighted-average number of options outstanding were exercised using the weighted-average exercise price (4,600,000 × $40) $184,000,000
- Average unrecognized compensation balance during year[26]   17,700,000

Assumed proceeds $201,700,000

360. Assumed repurchase of shares:

- Repurchase shares at average market price during the year ($201,700,000 ÷ $52)   3,878,846
- Incremental shares to be added (4,600,000 − 3,878,846)   721,154

The number of shares to be added to outstanding shares for purposes of the diluted earnings per share calculation is 721,154.

361. [This paragraph has been deleted. See Status page.]

Illustrative Disclosures

362. An illustration of disclosures of an entity's compensation plans follows. The illustration assumes that compensation cost has been recognized in accordance with the provisions of this Statement for several years. The amount of compensation cost recognized each year includes both costs from that year's grants and from prior years' grants. The number of options outstanding, exercised, forfeited, and expired each year includes options granted in prior years. The additional disclosures that would be required if the entity had elected to continue to recognize compensation cost in accordance with Opinion 25 are presented in paragraph 363.

* * *

Stock Compensation Plans

At December 31, 2006, the Company has four stock-based compensation plans, which are described below. The Company accounts for the fair value of its grants under those plans in accordance with FASB Statement 123. The compensation cost that has been charged against income for those plans was $23.3 million, $28.7 million, and $29.4 million for 2004, 2005, and 2006, respectively.

Fixed Stock Option Plans

The Company has two fixed option plans. Under the 1999 Employee Stock Option Plan, the Company may grant options to its employees for up to 8 million shares of common stock. Under the 2004 Managers' Incentive Stock Option Plan, the Company may grant options to its management personnel for up to 5 million shares of common stock. Under both plans, the exercise price of each option equals the market price of the Company's stock on the date of grant and an option's maximum term is 10 years. Options are granted on January 1 and vest at the end of the third year under the 1999 Plan and at the end of the second year under the 2004 Plan.

The fair value of each option grant is estimated on the date of grant using the Black-Scholes option-pricing model with the following weighted-average assumptions used for grants in 2004, 2005, and 2006, respectively: dividend yield of 1.5 percent for all years; expected volatility of 24, 26, and 29 percent, risk-free interest rates of 6.5, 7.5, and 7 percent for the 1999 Plan options and 6.4, 7.4, and 6.8 percent for the 2004 Plan options; and expected lives of 6, 5, and 5 years for the 1999 Plan options and 5, 4, and 4 years for the 2004 Plan options.

---

[26]Average unrecognized compensation balance is determined by averaging the beginning-of-the-year balance of cost measured and unrecognized and the end-of-the-year balance of cost measured and unrecognized. The assumed amount is $17,700,000 based on ongoing cost recognition for stock options granted in the current year and prior years.

A summary of the status of the Company's two fixed stock option plans as of December 31, 2004, 2005, and 2006, and changes during the years ending on those dates is presented below:

	2004		2005		2006	
Fixed Options	Shares (000)	Weighted-Average Exercise Price	Shares (000)	Weighted-Average Exercise Price	Shares (000)	Weighted-Average Exercise Price
Outstanding at beginning of year	4,500	$34	4,600	$38	4,660	$42
Granted	900	50	1,000	55	950	60
Exercised	(700)	27	(850)	34	(800)	36
Forfeited	(100)	46	(90)	51	(80)	59
Outstanding at end of year	4,600	38	4,660	42	4,730	47
Options exercisable at year-end	2,924		2,873		3,159	
Weighted-average fair value of options granted during the year	$15.90		$17.46		$19.57	

The following table summarizes information about fixed stock options outstanding at December 31, 2006:

	Options Outstanding			Options Exercisable	
Range of Exercise Prices	Number Outstanding at 12/31/06	Weighted-Average Remaining Contractual Life	Weighted-Average Exercise Price	Number Exercisable at 12/31/06	Weighted-Average Exercise Price
$25 to 33	1,107,000	3.6 years	$29	1,107,000	$29
39 to 41	467,000	5.0	40	467,000	40
46 to 50	1,326,000	6.6	48	1,326,000	48
55 to 60	1,830,000	8.5	57	259,000	55
$25 to 60	4,730,000	6.5	47	3,159,000	41

Performance-Based Stock Option Plan

Under its Goals 2010 Stock Option Plan adopted in 2002, each January 1 the Company grants selected executives and other key employees stock option awards whose vesting is contingent upon increases in the Company's market share for its principal product. If at the end of 3 years market share has increased by at least 5 percentage points from the date of grant, one-third of the options under the award vest to active employees. However, if at that date market share has increased by at least 10 percentage points, two-thirds of the options under the award vest, and if market share has increased by 20 percentage points or more, all of the options under the award vest. The number of shares subject to options under this plan cannot exceed 5 million. The exercise price of each option, which has a 10-year life, is equal to the market price of the Company's stock on the date of grant.

The fair value of each option grant was estimated on the date of grant using the Black-Scholes option-pricing model with the following assumptions for 2004, 2005, and 2006, respectively: risk-free interest rates of 6.5, 7.6, and 7.4 percent; dividend yield of 1.5 percent for all years; expected lives of 6, 6, and 7 years; and volatility of 24, 26, and 29 percent.

A summary of the status of the Company's performance-based stock option plan as of December 31, 2004, 2005, and 2006, and changes during the years ending on those dates is presented below:

Performance Options	2004		2005		2006	
	Shares (000)	Weighted-Average Exercise Price	Shares (000)	Weighted-Average Exercise Price	Shares (000)	Weighted-Average Exercise Price
Outstanding at beginning of year	830	$46	1,635	$48	2,533	$51
Granted	850	50	980	55	995	60
Exercised	0		0		(100)	46
Forfeited	(45)	48	(82)	50	(604)	51
Outstanding at end of year	1,635	48	2,533	51	2,824	55
Options exercisable at year-end	0		780	46	936	47
Weighted-average fair value of options granted during the year	$16.25		$19.97		$24.32	

As of December 31, 2006, the 2.8 million performance options outstanding under the Plan have exercise prices between $46 and $60 and a weighted-average remaining contractual life of 7.7 years. The Company expects that approximately one-third of the nonvested awards at December 31, 2006, will eventually vest based on projected market share.

Employee Stock Purchase Plan

Under the 1987 Employee Stock Purchase Plan, the Company is authorized to issue up to 10 million shares of common stock to its full-time employees, nearly all of whom are eligible to participate. Under the terms of the Plan, employees can choose each year to have up to 6 percent of their annual base earnings withheld to purchase the Company's common stock. The purchase price of the stock is 85 percent of the lower of its beginning-of-year or end-of-year market price. Approximately 75 to 80 percent of eligible employees have participated in the Plan in the last 3 years. Under the Plan, the Company sold 456,000 shares, 481,000 shares, and 503,000 shares to employees in 2004, 2005, and 2006, respectively. Compensation cost is recognized for the fair value of the employees' purchase rights, which was estimated using the Black-Scholes model with the following assumptions for 2004, 2005, and 2006, respectively: dividend yield of 1.5 percent for all years; an expected life of 1 year for all years; expected volatility of 22, 24, and 26 percent; and risk-free interest rates of 5.9, 6.9, and 6.7 percent. The weighted-average fair value of those purchase rights granted in 2004, 2005, and 2006 was $11.95, $13.73, and $15.30, respectively.

* * *

363. If compensation cost has been determined by applying Opinion 25 as permitted by this Statement (paragraph 5), the total compensation cost disclosed in the first paragraph of the illustrative disclosures would need to be revised to reflect the cost recognized under Opinion 25. The following paragraph would replace that paragraph; all other disclosures about the plans and related assumptions would be required.

* * *

At December 31, 2006, the Company has four stock-based compensation plans, which are described below. The Company applies APB Opinion 25 and related Interpretations in accounting for its plans. Accordingly, no compensation cost has been recognized for its fixed stock option plans and its stock purchase plan. The compensation cost that has been charged against income for its performance-based plan was $6.7 million, $9.4 million, and $0.7 million for 2004, 2005, and 2006, respectively. Had compensation cost for the Company's four stock-based compensation plans been determined based on the fair value at the grant dates for awards under those plans consistent with the method of FASB Statement 123, the Company's net income and earnings per share would have been reduced to the pro forma amounts indicated below:

		2004	2005	2006
Net income	As reported	$347,790	$407,300	$479,300
	Pro forma	$336,828	$394,553	$460,398
Primary earnings per share	As reported	$1.97	$2.29	$2.66
	Pro forma	$1.91	$2.22	$2.56
Fully diluted earnings per share	As reported	$1.49	$1.73	$2.02
	Pro forma	$1.44	$1.68	$1.94

* * *

Supplemental Disclosures

364. In addition to the information required by this Statement, an entity may disclose supplemental information that it believes would be useful to investors and creditors, such as a range of values calculated on the basis of different assumptions, provided that the supplemental information is reasonable and does not discredit the information required by this Statement. The alternative assumptions should be described to enable users of the financial statements to understand the basis for the supplemental information. For example, if in the previous example the Company estimated in 2004 that its expected stock price volatility over the next 6 years was within a range of 24 to 32 percent in which no amount was a

better estimate than any other amount, its use of a 24 percent volatility assumption is consistent with paragraph 275, which indicates that using an estimate at the low end of the range for expected volatility is appropriate in that circumstance. The Company could, however, choose to disclose supplementally the weighted-average fair value of stock options granted during the year (and related effect on the pro forma disclosures) based on the midpoint or the high end of the range of expected volatility. However, presenting supplemental disclosures based on, for example, an expected volatility assumption of 18 percent would not be appropriate because the Company had already concluded in making its calculations that an 18 percent assumption is below the range of reasonable assumptions. Presenting supplemental disclosures of the value of stock options based on an approach contrary to the methodology specified in this Statement, such as reflecting an additional discount related to the nontransferability of nonvested stock options, is similarly inappropriate. However, the Company's supplemental disclosures could include the intrinsic value of stock options exercised during the year.

Appendix C

BACKGROUND INFORMATION

365. In 1984, the Board added to its agenda a project to reconsider APB Opinion No. 25, *Accounting for Stock Issued to Employees.* On May 31, 1984, an FASB Invitation to Comment, *Accounting for Compensation Plans Involving Certain Rights Granted to Employees,* was issued based on the November 4, 1982, AICPA Issues Paper, *Accounting for Employee Capital Accumulation Plans.* The Board received 144 letters of comment.

366. From 1985 through 1988, the Board considered accounting for stock-based compensation and conducted research on various aspects of those plans, including how existing option-pricing models might be adapted to measure the fair value of employee stock options.

367. The issues were complex and highly controversial. Still, each time the issue was raised, Board members voted unanimously that employee stock options result in compensation cost that should be recognized in the employer's financial statements.

368. As with all FASB projects, the Board's discussions of stock compensation were open to public observation, and its tentative conclusions on individual

issues were reported in its weekly *Action Alert.* During the Board's deliberations from 1985 to 1988, more than 200 letters were received that commented on, and usually objected to, tentative conclusions reported in *Action Alert.* That was unusual because most of the Board's constituents await publication of an Exposure Draft before they submit comments.

369. Some Board members and others were troubled by the differing results of stock-based compensation plans that called for settlement in cash and those that called for settlement in stock. But exercise date accounting for all plans is the only way to achieve consistent results between cash and stock plans, and that accounting was not considered to be consistent with the definitions of liabilities and equity in FASB Concepts Statement No. 6, *Elements of Financial Statements.* It also would be inconsistent with current accounting for stock purchase warrants, which are similar to employee stock options except that warrants are issued to outsiders rather than to employees.

370. A part of the financial instruments project on the Board's agenda considers whether changes to the concepts of liabilities and equity are needed. Late in 1988, the Board decided to set aside specific work on stock compensation while it considered broader questions of how to distinguish between liabilities and equity and the implications of that distinction.

371. In August 1990, a Discussion Memorandum, *Distinguishing between Liability and Equity Instruments and Accounting for Instruments with Characteristics of Both,* was issued. The Discussion Memorandum framed and discussed numerous issues, some of which bear directly on deciding how to account for employee stock options. The Board received 104 comment letters and in March 1991 held a public hearing on the issues, at which 14 commentators appeared.

372. More than 90 percent of the respondents to the Discussion Memorandum said that an entity's obligation to issue its own stock is an equity instrument because the entity does not have an obligation to transfer its assets (an entity's own stock is not its asset), which is an essential characteristic of a liability. In February 1992, the Board decided not to pursue possible changes to the conceptual distinction between liabilities and equity and to resume work on the stock compensation project within the present conceptual framework.

373. In March 1992, the Board met with several compensation consultants and accountants to discuss

current practice in valuing employee stock options and accounting for stock compensation. The compensation consultants generally agreed that current accounting provisions heavily affect the design of stock compensation plans. They said that there were far fewer variable (or performance) plans than fixed plans because of the required accounting for variable plans. The compensation consultants also said that the Black-Scholes and other option-pricing models were used to value various types of employee stock options for purposes other than accounting. Grant date measures were relied on to provide comparisons to other compensation arrangements.

374. A task force of accountants, compensation consultants, industry representatives, and academics was formed to assist in the project. Accounting for stock compensation was addressed at 19 public Board meetings and at 2 public task force meetings in 1992 and 1993. The Board's tentative conclusions on individual issues were reported in *Action Alert*. During 1992 and the first part of 1993, more than 450 comment letters were received, mostly objecting to the tentative conclusions. Many of the letters proposed disclosure in lieu of cost recognition for stock compensation. Several of the commentators submitted alternatives to the Board; the most comprehensive disclosure proposal was included as an appendix to the Exposure Draft.

375. In June 1993, the Board issued an FASB Exposure Draft, *Accounting for Stock-based Compensation*, that would have required recognizing compensation cost for all awards of stock-based compensation that eventually vest, based on their fair value at the grant date. The Board and KPMG Peat Marwick conducted a field test of the provisions of the Exposure Draft. In addition, other organizations provided information about their own test applications of the Exposure Draft.

376. As discussed in Appendix A, the Exposure Draft was extraordinarily controversial. The Board received 1,786 comment letters, including approximately 1,000 form letters, on the Exposure Draft. The vast majority of respondents objected to the recognition of compensation cost for fixed employee stock options—sometimes for reasons that had little to do with accounting. In March 1994, the Board held six days of public hearings in Connecticut and California. Representatives from 73 organizations presented testimony at those hearings. Several legislative proposals were introduced in Congress, both opposing and supporting proposals in the Exposure

Draft. A Sense of the Senate resolution was passed that the FASB "should not at this time change the current generally accepted accounting treatment of stock options and stock purchase plans." However, a second resolution was passed that "Congress should not impair the objectivity or integrity of the FASB's decision-making process by legislating accounting rules."

377. In April 1994, the Board held a public roundtable discussion with academic researchers and other participants on proposals the participants had submitted to improve the measure of the value of stock options. Also during 1994, the Board discussed accounting for stock-based compensation at 13 public Board meetings and at 1 public task force meeting.

378. In December 1994, the Board discussed the alternatives for proceeding with the project on accounting for stock-based compensation in light of the comment letters, public hearing testimony, and various meetings held to discuss the project. The Board decided to encourage, rather than require, recognition of compensation cost based on a fair value method and to pursue expanded disclosures. Employers would be permitted to continue to apply the provisions of Opinion 25. Employers that continued to apply Opinion 25 would be required to disclose the pro forma effects on net income and earnings per share if the new accounting method had been applied.

379. The Board discussed the details of the disclosure-based approach at six Board meetings in 1995. In 1995, 131 comment letters were received on the disclosure-based approach. In May 1995, an initial draft of the standards section and some of the other parts of this Statement were distributed to task force members and other interested parties that requested the draft; 34 comment letters were received. Appendix A discusses the basis for the Board's conclusions, including reasons for changes made to the provisions of the 1993 Exposure Draft.

Appendix D

AMENDMENTS TO EXISTING PRONOUNCEMENTS

380. FASB Technical Bulletin No. 82-2, *Accounting for the Conversion of Stock Options into Incentive Stock Options as a Result of the Economic Recovery Tax Act of 1981*, is superseded.

381. This Statement amends ARB No. 43, Chapter 13B, "Compensation Involved in Stock Option and Stock Purchase Plans," as follows:

a. The following sentences are added to the end of paragraph 2:

> FASB Statement No. 123, *Accounting for Stock-Based Compensation,* specifies a fair value based method of accounting for stock-based compensation plans and encourages entities to adopt that method for all arrangements under which employees receive shares of stock or other equity instruments of the employer or the employer incurs liabilities to employees in amounts based on the price of the employer's stock. However, Statement 123 permits an employer in determining its net income to continue to apply the accounting provisions of this section and Opinion 25 to all its stock-based employee compensation arrangements. Entities that continue to apply this section and Opinion 25 shall comply with the disclosure requirements of Statement 123.

b. Paragraph 15 is deleted.

382. APB Opinion No. 25, *Accounting for Stock Issued to Employees,* is amended as follows:

a. The following sentences are added to the end of paragraph 4:

> FASB Statement No. 123, *Accounting for Stock-Based Compensation,* specifies a fair value based method of accounting for stock-based compensation plans and encourages entities to adopt that method in place of the provisions of this Opinion for all arrangements under which employees receive shares of stock or other equity instruments of the employer or the employer incurs liabilities to employees in amounts based on the price of the employer's stock. Statement 123 permits an entity in determining its net income to continue to apply the accounting provisions of Opinion 25. If an entity makes that election, it shall apply Opinion 25 to all its stock-based employee compensation arrangements. If an entity elects to apply Statement 123, that election shall not be reversed. Entities that continue to apply Opinion 25 shall comply with the disclosure requirements of Statement 123.

b. Paragraph 19 is replaced by the following:

> *Disclosure.* Paragraphs 45-48 of FASB Statement No. 123, *Accounting for Stock-Based Compensation,* specify the disclosures related to stock-based employee compensation arrangements that shall be made in the financial statements.

c. Footnote 5 is deleted.

383. Footnote 4 of APB Opinion No. 29, *Accounting for Nonmonetary Transactions,* is replaced by the following:

> FASB Statement No. 123, *Accounting for Stock-Based Compensation,* applies to all transactions in which an entity acquires goods or services by issuing equity instruments or by incurring liabilities to the supplier in amounts based on the price of the entity's common stock or other equity instruments.

384. The following is added as a footnote to the end of the penultimate paragraph of AICPA Accounting Interpretation 1, "Stock Plans Established by a Principal Stockholder," of Opinion 25:

> *FASB Statement No. 123, *Accounting for Stock-Based Compensation,* specifies a fair value based method of accounting for stock-based compensation plans and encourages entities to adopt that method in place of the provisions of Opinion 25 for all arrangements under which employees receive shares of stock or other equity instruments of the employer or the employer incurs liabilities to employees in amounts based on the price of the employer's stock. Paragraph 15 of Statement 123 adopts the substance of this Interpretation regardless of the method chosen to account for stock-based compensation.

385. In the fourth sentence of paragraph 7 of FASB Statement No. 5, *Accounting for Contingencies,* the phrase *APB Opinion No. 25, Accounting for Stock Issued to Employees,* is replaced by *FASB Statement No. 123, Accounting for Stock-Based Compensation.*

386. In footnote 3 to paragraph 12 of FASB Statement No. 21, *Suspension of the Reporting of Earnings per Share and Segment Information by Nonpublic Enterprises,* the phrase *paragraph 15 of Chapter 13B, "Compensation Involved in Stock Option and Stock Purchase Plans," of ARB No. 43* is replaced by *paragraphs 45-48 of FASB Statement No. 123, Accounting for Stock-Based Compensation.*

387. In paragraph 2 of FASB Statement No. 43, *Accounting for Compensated Absences,* as amended by FASB Statement No. 112, *Employers' Accounting for Postemployment Benefits,* the phrase *APB Opinion No. 25, Accounting for Stock Issued to Employees,* is replaced by *FASB Statement No. 123, Accounting for Stock-Based Compensation.*

388. In paragraph 14(c) of FASB Statement No. 105, *Disclosure of Information about Financial Instruments with Off-Balance-Sheet Risk and Financial Instruments with Concentrations of Credit Risk,* the phrase *as well as APB Opinions No. 25, Accounting for Stock Issued to Employees, and No. 12* is replaced by *and No. 123, Accounting for Stock-Based Compensation, and APB Opinion No. 12.*

389. Paragraph 8(a) of FASB Statement No. 107, *Disclosures about Fair Value of Financial Instruments,* as amended by Statement 112, is amended as follows:

a. The phrase *No. 123, Accounting for Stock-Based Compensation,* is added before *and No. 43.*

b. The phrase *APB Opinions No. 25, Accounting for Stock Issued to Employees, and No. 12* is replaced by *APB Opinion No. 12.*

390. In paragraph 36(e) of FASB Statement No. 109, *Accounting for Income Taxes,* the phrase *paragraphs 41-44 of FASB Statement No. 123, Accounting for Stock-Based Compensation, and* is added after *refer to.*

391. In paragraph 5(d) of Statement 112, the phrase *APB Opinion No. 25, Accounting for Stock Issued to Employees,* is replaced by *FASB Statement No. 123, Accounting for Stock-Based Compensation.*

392. The following is added as a footnote to the end of the second sentence of paragraph 2 of FASB Interpretation No. 28, *Accounting for Stock Appreciation Rights and Other Variable Stock Option or Award Plans:*

*FASB Statement No. 123, Accounting for Stock-Based Compensation, specifies a fair value based method of accounting for stock-based compensation plans (including those that involve variable plan awards) and encourages entities to adopt that method in place of the provisions of Opinion 25 for all arrangements under which employees receive shares of stock or other equity instruments of the employer or the employer incurs liabilities to employees in amounts based on the price of the employer's stock. Statement 123 permits an entity in determining its net income to continue to apply the accounting provisions of Opinion 25. If an entity makes that election, it shall apply Opinion 25 (including this Interpretation) to all its stock-based employee compensation arrangements.

393. The following is added to the end of footnote 1 to paragraph 3 of FASB Interpretation No. 31, *Treatment of Stock Compensation Plans in EPS Computations:*

FASB Statement No. 123, *Accounting for Stock-Based Compensation,* specifies a fair value based method of accounting for stock-based compensation plans (including those that involve variable plan awards) and encourages entities to adopt that method in place of the provisions of Opinion 25.

394. The following is added as a footnote at the end of paragraph 2 of FASB Interpretation No. 38, *Determining the Measurement Date for Stock Option, Purchase, and Award Plans Involving Junior Stock:*

*FASB Statement No. 123, Accounting for Stock-Based Compensation, specifies a fair value based method of accounting for stock-based compensation plans (including those that involve variable plan awards) and encourages entities to adopt that method in place of the provisions of Opinion 25.

Appendix E

GLOSSARY

395. This appendix contains definitions of certain terms or phrases used in this Statement.

Combination plan
An award with two (or more) separate components, all of which can be exercised. Each part of the award is actually a separate grant, and compensation cost is measured and recognized for each grant.

Cross-volatility
A measure of the relationship between the volatilities of the prices of two assets taking into account the correlation between price movements in the assets.

Fair value
The amount at which an asset could be bought or sold in a current transaction between willing parties, that is, other than in a forced or liquidation

sale. Quoted market prices in active markets are the best evidence of fair value and are to be used as the basis for measurement, if available. If quoted market prices are not available, the estimate of fair value is based on the best information available in the circumstances. The estimate of fair value considers prices for similar assets and the results of valuation techniques to the extent available in the circumstances. Examples of valuation techniques include the present value of estimated expected future cash flows using a discount rate commensurate with the risks involved, option-pricing models, matrix pricing, option-adjusted spread models, and fundamental analysis.

Fixed award

An award of stock-based employee compensation for which vesting is based solely on an employee's continuing to render service to the employer for a specified period of time, that is, an award that does not specify a performance condition for vesting. This Statement uses the term *fixed award* in a somewhat different sense than Opinion 25 uses the same or similar terms because Opinion 25 distinguishes between fixed awards and variable awards, while this Statement only distinguishes between fixed awards and performance awards. For example, Opinion 25 does not consider stock appreciation rights (SARs), regardless of whether they call for settlement in stock or in cash, to be fixed awards because the number of shares to which an employee is entitled is not known until the exercise date. This Statement considers an SAR that calls for settlement in stock to be substantially the same as a fixed stock option. A cash SAR is an indexed liability pursuant to this Statement, and the measurement date is the settlement (exercise) date because that is consistent with accounting for similar liabilities—not because a cash SAR is a variable award.

Grant date

The date at which an employer and an employee have a mutual understanding of the terms of a stock-based compensation award. The employer becomes contingently obligated on the grant date to issue equity instruments or transfer assets to employees who fulfill vesting requirements. Awards made under a plan that is subject to shareholder approval are not deemed to be granted until that approval is obtained unless approval is essentially a formality, for example, management and the members of the board of directors control enough votes to approve the plan. The grant date of an award for current service may be the end of a fiscal period instead of a subsequent date when an award is made to an individual employee if (a) the award is provided for by the terms of an established formal plan, (b) the plan designates the factors that determine the total dollar amount of awards to employees for that period (for example, a percentage of net income), and (c) the award is attributable to the employee's service during that period.

Intrinsic value

The amount by which the market price of the underlying stock exceeds the exercise price of an option. For example, an option with an exercise price of $20 on a stock whose current market price is $25 has an intrinsic value of $5.

Issuance of an equity instrument

An equity instrument is issued when the issuing entity receives the agreed-upon consideration, which may be cash, an enforceable right to receive cash or another financial instrument, goods, or services. An entity may conditionally transfer an equity instrument to another party under an arrangement that permits that party to choose at a later date or for a specified time whether to deliver the consideration or to forfeit the right to the conditionally transferred instrument with no further obligation. In that situation, the equity instrument is not *issued* until the issuing entity has received the consideration. For that reason, this Statement does not use the term *issued* for the grant of stock options or other equity instruments subject to service or performance conditions (or both) for vesting.

Measurement date

The date at which the stock price that enters into measurement of the fair value of an award of employee stock-based compensation is fixed.

Minimum value

An amount attributed to an option that is calculated without considering the expected volatility of the underlying stock. Minimum value may be computed using a standard option-pricing model and a volatility of effectively zero. It also may be computed as (a) the current price of the stock reduced to exclude the present value of any expected dividends during the option's life minus (b) the present value of the exercise price. Different methods of reducing the current price of the stock for the present value of the expected dividends, if any, may result in different computed minimum values.

Nonpublic entity

Any entity other than one (a) whose equity securities trade in a public market either on a stock exchange (domestic or foreign) or in the over-the-counter market, including securities quoted only locally or regionally, (b) that makes a filing with a regulatory agency in preparation for the sale of any class of equity securities in a public market, or (c) that is controlled by an entity covered by (a) or (b).

Nonvested stock

Shares of stock that cannot currently be sold because the employee to whom the shares were granted has not yet satisfied the vesting requirements necessary to earn the right to the shares. The restriction on sale of nonvested stock is due to the forfeitability of the shares. A share of nonvested stock also can be described as a nonvested employee stock option with a cash exercise price of zero—employee services are the only consideration the employer has received for the stock when the option is "exercised," and the employer issues vested, unrestricted shares to the employee.

Performance condition or performance award

An award of stock-based employee compensation for which vesting depends on both (a) an employee's rendering service to the employer for a specified period of time and (b) the achievement of a specified performance target, for example, attaining a specified growth rate in return on assets or a specified percentage increase in market share for a specified product. A performance condition might pertain either to the performance of the enterprise as a whole or to some part of the enterprise, such as a division.

Principal stockholder

One who either owns 10 percent or more of an entity's common stock or has the ability, directly or indirectly, to control or significantly influence the entity.

Public entity

Any entity (a) whose equity securities trade in a public market either on a stock exchange (domestic or foreign) or in the over-the-counter market, including securities quoted only locally or regionally, (b) that makes a filing with a regulatory agency in preparation for the sale of any class of equity securities in a public market, or (c) that is controlled by an entity covered by (a) or (b).

Reload option and option granted with a reload feature

An option with a reload feature is one that provides for automatic grants of additional options whenever an employee exercises previously granted options using shares of stock, rather than cash, to satisfy the exercise price. At the time of exercise using shares, the employee is automatically granted a new option, called a *reload option* for the same number of shares used to exercise the previous option. The number of reload options granted is the number of shares tendered, and the exercise price of the reload option is the market price of the stock on the date the reload option is granted. All terms of the reload option, such as expiration date and vesting status, are the same as the terms of the previous option.

Restricted stock

Shares of stock for which sale is contractually or governmentally restricted for a given period of time. Most stock grants to employees are better termed *nonvested stock* because the limitation on sale stems solely from the forfeitability of the shares before employees have satisfied the necessary service or performance requirements to earn the rights to the shares. Restricted stock issued for consideration other than employee services, on the other hand, is fully paid for immediately, that is, there is no period analogous to a vesting period during which the issuer is unilaterally obligated to issue the stock when the purchaser pays for it, but the purchaser is not obligated to buy the stock. This Statement uses the term *restricted stock* to refer only to fully vested and outstanding stock whose sale is contractually or governmentally restricted. (Refer to the definition of *nonvested stock.*)

Service period

The period or periods during which the employee performs the service in exchange for stock options or similar awards. If the service period is not defined as an earlier or shorter period, the service period is presumed to be the vesting period. However, if performance conditions affect either the exercise price or the exercisability date, this Statement requires that the service period over which compensation cost is attributed be consistent with the related assumption used in estimating the fair value of the award. Doing so will require estimates at the grant date, which will be subsequently adjusted as necessary to reflect experience that differs from initial expectations.

Stock option

A contract that gives the holder the right, but not the obligation, either to purchase or to sell a certain number of shares of stock at a predetermined price for a specified period of time.

Stock-based compensation plan

A compensation arrangement under which one or more employees receive shares of stock, stock options, or other equity instruments, or the employer incurs a liability(ies) to the employee(s) in amounts based on the price of the employer's stock.

Substantive terms

The terms of a stock-based compensation plan as those terms are mutually understood by the employer and the employee who receives a stock-based award under the plan. Although the written terms of a stock-based compensation plan usually provide the best evidence of the plan's terms, an entity's past practice may indicate that some aspects of the substantive terms differ from the written terms.

Tandem plan

An award with two (or more) components in which exercise of one part cancels the other(s).

Time value

The portion of the fair value of an option that exceeds its intrinsic value. For example, an option with an exercise price of $20 on a stock whose current market price is $25 has intrinsic value of $5. If the fair value of that option is $7, the time value of the option is $2 ($7 – $5).

Vest or Vested

To earn the rights to. An employee's award of stock-based compensation becomes vested at the date that the employee's right to receive or retain shares of stock or cash under the award is no longer contingent on remaining in the service of the employer or the achievement of a performance condition (other than the achievement of a target stock price or specified amount of intrinsic value). Typically, an employee stock option that is vested also is immediately exercisable.

Volatility

A measure of the amount by which a price has fluctuated (historical volatility) or is expected to fluctuate (expected volatility) during a period. The volatility of a stock is the standard deviation of the continuously compounded rates of return on the stock over a specified period. That is the same as the standard deviation of the differences in the natural logarithms of the stock prices plus dividends, if any, over the period. The higher the volatility, the more the returns on the stock can be expected to vary—up or down. Volatility is typically expressed in annualized terms that are comparable regardless of the time period used in the calculation, for example, daily, weekly, or monthly price observations.

The *rate of return* (which may be positive or negative) on a stock for a period measures how much a stockholder has benefited from dividends and appreciation (or depreciation) of the share price. Return on a stated rate increases as compounding becomes more frequent, approaching e^{rate} as a limit as the frequency of compounding approaches continuous. For example, the continuously compounded return on a stated rate of 9 percent is $e^{(.09)}$. (The base of the natural logarithm system is e, which is a constant, transcendental number, the first 5 digits of which are 2.7183.) Stock price changes are log-normally distributed, but continuously compounded rates of return on stocks are normally distributed.

The expected annualized volatility of a stock is the range within which the continuously compounded annual rate of return is expected to fall roughly two-thirds of the time. For example, to say that a stock with an expected continuously compounded rate of return of 12 percent has a volatility of 30 percent means that the probability that the rate of return on the stock for 1 year will fall between -18 percent (12% – 30%) and 42 percent (12% + 30%) is approximately two-thirds. If the stock price is $100 at the beginning of the year and it does not pay dividends, the year-end price would be expected to fall between $83.53 ($100 × e$^{(-.18)}$) and $152.20 ($100 × e$^{(.42)}$) approximately two-thirds of the time.

For the convenience of those who are not familiar with the concept of volatility, Appendix F provides more information on volatility and shows one way in which an electronic spreadsheet may be used to calculate historical volatility based on weekly price observations.

Appendix F

CALCULATING HISTORICAL VOLATILITY

Introduction

396. As discussed in paragraphs 273-278 of Appendix B, estimating expected long-term future volatility generally begins with calculating historical volatility for a similar long-term period and then considering the effects of ways in which the future is reasonably expected to differ from the past. For some mature entities, unadjusted long-term historical volatility may be the best available predictor of future long-term volatility. However, this appendix should be read in the context of paragraphs 284 and 285 of Appendix B, which mention factors that should be considered in determining whether historical volatility is a reasonable indicator of expected future volatility.

397. The concept of volatility and the reason that it is an important factor in estimating the fair value of an option is well explained in various texts on option-pricing models and the use of derivative financial instruments. However, those texts are generally directed more at mathematicians than at accountants, and one without an extensive background in statistics and mathematics may find them difficult to understand. During the exposure process and the field test, the staff received numerous requests for help in understanding the notion of volatility, especially for an illustration of how to compute historical volatility. This appendix responds to that request.

398. The goal of this appendix is not to explain the development of traditional option-pricing models and why they are valid. Sources for that information are available. Several currently available articles and texts that explain option-pricing models and the place of volatility in option value are listed at the end of this appendix. This appendix is intended to help someone familiar with the use of electronic spread-

sheets to compute historical volatility in three common situations. The illustrations do not provide a rigorous explanation of the mathematical concepts underlying the computations. In addition, the illustrations do not illustrate the only possible way of calculating historical volatility; for example, observations at daily or monthly, rather than weekly, intervals might have been used.

399. This appendix also is not intended to deemphasize the importance of adjusting historical volatility, however computed, to reflect ways in which future volatility is reasonably expected to differ from historical volatility for entity-specific reasons.

Volatility Is a Standard Deviation

400. The needed assumption about expected volatility for use in the traditional Black-Scholes and binomial option-pricing models is the *annualized* standard deviation of the differences in the natural logarithms of the possible future stock prices. Natural logarithms are needed to compute the continuous rate of return reflected in the change from one stock price to another, plus dividends, if any. A standard deviation is a statistical method used to convert a series of natural logarithms of stock price changes into a single, usable statistic—volatility. Like rates of return, volatility can be measured over any time period. For convenience and consistency, volatility is generally expressed on an annual basis even if the measurement period is longer or shorter than one year.

Computing Historical Volatility for a Stock That Pays No Dividends

401. The first step in computing historical volatility is to gather the necessary stock prices. The expected lives of employee stock options generally are several years long, so weekly (perhaps even monthly) stock price observations generally should be sufficient. (Volatility estimates for shorter-term options, such as 30-, 60-, or 90-day options commonly traded on exchanges, generally rely on daily, or even more frequent, stock price observations). The consistency of the time intervals between observations is critical—determining the frequency of the observations is not as critical, although the frequency of observations likely will affect the computed volatility. The time intervals between price observations should be as uniform as possible; for example, the weekly stock closing price could be used for all observations. It would not be appropriate to use the weekly closing price for

some observations and, for example, the average weekly price for other observations in the same calculation.

402. The Board is not aware of any research that demonstrates conclusively how long the historical period used to estimate expected long-term future volatility should be. However, informal tests and preliminary research tends to confirm the intuitive expectation that long-term historical volatility generally predicts long-term future volatility better than short-term historical volatility predicts long-term future volatility. Paragraph 285 of this Statement says that estimates of expected future long-term volatility should be based on historical volatility for a period that approximates the expected life of the option being valued. For example, if the expected life of an employee stock option is three years, historical volatility might be based on weekly closing stock prices for the most recent three years. In that situation, approximately 157 weekly stock price observations would be needed (52 observations per year for 3 years plus the initial observation).

403. For convenience, the illustrative calculations are based on only 20 price observations, which is generally considered to be the minimum number of sample observations necessary to compute a statistically valid estimate of standard deviation. Therefore, the table shows the calculation of the annualized historical volatility based on 19 weeks of stock price activity. More than 20 price observations would be necessary for long-term employee stock options; more observations also would improve the statistical validity of the estimate of expected volatility.

404. In the following table, column B contains the 20 stock price observations for the 19-week period. Each cell in column C contains the ratio of the stock price at the end of that week to the stock price at the end of the preceding week. That is designated by the symbol P_n/P_{n-1}. For example, in week 4, the number in column C is computed as the week 4 stock closing price ($48.50) divided by the week 3 stock closing price ($51.00), or 0.95098. Column D is the natural logarithm (the mathematical expression Ln) of the amount computed in column C. The weekly volatility estimate is the standard deviation of the amounts shown in column D. Most, if not all, electronic spreadsheets include a standard deviation function that will automatically compute the standard deviation of a series of amounts.

Table 1

A	B	C	D
Date	Stock Price	P_n/P_{n-1}	$Ln(P_n/P_{n-1})$
Week 0	$50.00		
Week 1	51.50	1.030000	0.029559
Week 2	52.00	1.009709	0.009662
Week 3	51.00	0.980769	-0.019418
Week 4	48.50	0.950980	-0.050262
Week 5	46.50	0.958763	-0.042111
Week 6	45.75	0.983871	-0.016261
Week 7	50.50	1.103825	0.098782
Week 8	53.50	1.059406	0.057708
Week 9	51.75	0.967290	-0.033257
Week 10	53.25	1.028986	0.028573
Week 11	54.50	1.023474	0.023203
Week 12	56.00	1.027523	0.027151
Week 13	53.50	0.955357	-0.045670
Week 14	52.00	0.971963	-0.028438
Week 15	55.00	1.057692	0.056089
Week 16	56.25	1.022727	0.022473
Week 17	58.00	1.031111	0.030637
Week 18	55.50	0.956897	-0.044060
Week 19	56.00	1.009009	0.008969
Weekly Volatility			**0.041516**
Annualized Volatility	$0.041516\sqrt{52}$		**0.299**

405. Weekly volatility must be converted to an annualized measure of volatility before it can be used in most option-pricing models. To convert from periodic to annualized volatility, the periodic volatility is multiplied by the square root of the number of periods in a year. In this example, weekly observations are used. There are 52 weeks in a year, so weekly volatility is multiplied by the square root of 52 to convert it to annualized volatility. If monthly stock price observations were used, the monthly volatility would be multiplied by the square root of 12 to convert to annualized volatility. Likewise, daily volatility would be multiplied by the square root of the number of trading days in the year to compute annualized volatility (about 260). The annualization calculation is independent of the number of observations used to compute the periodic historical volatility. For example, whether 20 or 157 weeks of data are used to compute weekly volatility, that weekly volatility must be multiplied by the square root of 52 to convert it to annual volatility.

Computing Historical Volatility for a Dividend-Paying Stock

406. Computing volatility for a dividend-paying stock is very similar to computing volatility for a stock that does not pay dividends. The only difference is an adjustment for dividends paid. Because volatility is defined as the standard deviation of the total return on a stock, dividend payments, which are part of the total return, affect the computation. The price change resulting solely from the effect of dividend payment on the stock price must be removed from the price observations used to calculate volatility.

407. As discussed in paragraph 401, stock price observations used in the calculations should be separated by uniform time periods. When gathering data, it is important to observe the payment of dividends. If an ex-dividend date occurs between two price observations, the per-share dollar amount of the dividends should be noted. For example, if the ex-dividend date for a dividend of one dollar occurs between the third and fourth weekly price observations, that payment should be noted when gathering stock price observations. In computing historical volatility, dividends must be added to the stock price after the ex-dividend date before the ratio in column C (the price after the

dividend to the price before the dividend) is computed. Note that the market reflects the effect of a dividend payment on the stock price on the ex-dividend date, not the date of the cash distribution, because the ex-dividend date is the last date that a seller, rather than a purchaser, of stock is entitled to the dividend.

408. The following table illustrates the computation of historical volatility based on weekly stock closing prices for a company that pays a dividend of $1 between both the week 3 and week 4 price observations and the week 15 and week 16 price observations.

Table 2

A	B	C	D
Date	Stock Price	P_n/P_{n-1}	$Ln(P_n/P_{n-1})$
Week 0	$50.00		
Week 1	51.50	1.030000	0.029559
Week 2	52.00	1.009709	0.009662
Week 3	51.00	0.980769	-0.019418
Week 4	48.50		
Dividend Adjusted	49.50	0.970588	-0.029853
Week 5	46.50	0.958763	-0.042111
Week 6	45.75	0.983871	-0.016261
Week 7	50.50	1.103825	0.098782
Week 8	53.50	1.059406	0.057708
Week 9	51.75	0.967290	-0.033257
Week 10	53.25	1.028986	0.028573
Week 11	54.50	1.023474	0.023203
Week 12	56.00	1.027523	0.027151
Week 13	53.50	0.955357	-0.045670
Week 14	52.00	0.971963	-0.028438
Week 15	55.00	1.057692	0.056089
Week 16	56.25		
Dividend Adjusted	57.25	1.040909	0.040094
Week 17	58.00	1.031111	0.030637
Week 18	55.50	0.956897	-0.044060
Week 19	56.00	1.009009	0.008969
Weekly Volatility			**0.040799**
Annualized Volatility	$.040799\sqrt{52}$		**0.294**

409. The only difference between Table 2 and Table 1 is the necessary adjustment in Table 2 for the dividend payments made between the week 3 and week 4 observations and between the week 15 and week 16 observations. In each case, the ratio of the current period stock price to the prior period stock price must

be adjusted for the dividend payment. For example, the pre-dividend week 3 observation is used in the ratio of the week 3 stock price to the week 2 stock price. Then, the post-dividend week 4 stock price must be adjusted by the amount of the dividend payment before the ratio of the week 4 stock price to the week 3 stock price is computed in column C (both stock prices in the ratio must be eitherpre-dividend or post-dividend). That adjustment is necessary to isolate the price change effect in the change from week 3 to week 4 that is independent from the stock price decrease caused by the dividend payment.

Computing Historical Volatility for a Stock That Has Split

410. If a stock split occurs during the historical period over which volatility is to be calculated, an adjustment much like the one for a dividend payment is required for that split. For computing the ratio of the stock prices around the period of the split, the prices must be shown in consistent form, that is, either pre-split or post-split. For example, in Table 2, if a stock split had occurred between the week 16 and week 17 stock price observations, the price observed in week 17 would be $29 instead of the $58 shown in the table. For computing column B, the ratio of the week 16 stock price to the week 15 stock price would be unchanged, but the ratio of the week 17 to the week 16 price would need adjustment. The split-adjusted week 17 stock price of $29 should be divided by the split-adjusted week 16 stock price, which is $28.125. After the adjustment is made for the stock split, the calculation of historical volatility is the same as in Table 2. If the only difference from

the Table 2 stock price changes is the stock split, the historical volatility would be the same as the volatility computed in Table 2 because the stock split would not alter the relative size of the random stock price changes that volatility measures.

Sources for Further Information about Option-Pricing Models and Volatility

411. The following sources provide further information on option-pricing models and the relationship of volatility to option value:

*   Black, Fischer, and Myron Scholes. "The Pricing of Options and Corporate Liabilities." *The Journal of Political Economy 81,* 3 (May-June 1973): 637-654.
*   Cox, John C., and Mark Rubinstein. *Option Markets.* Englewood Cliffs, N.J.: Prentice-Hall, Inc., 1985.
*   Figlewski, Stephen, William L. Silber, and Marti G. Subrahmanyam, eds. *Financial Options: From Theory to Practice.* New York: New York University, Business One Irwin, 1990.
*   Hull, John C. *Options, Futures, and Other Derivative Securities.* Englewood Cliffs, N.J.: Prentice-Hall, Inc., 1993.
*   Smithson, Charles W., Clifford W. Smith, Jr., and D. Sykes Wilford. *Managing Financial Risk.* New York: Richard D. Irwin, Inc., 1995.

Those sources include the classic works in which the Black-Scholes and binomial option-pricing models were first developed and other sources that may be useful.

Statement of Financial Accounting Standards No. 123 (revised 2004)
Share-Based Payment

STATUS

Issued: December 2004

Effective Date: For public entities that do not file as small business issuers—as of the beginning of the first interim or annual reporting period that begins after June 15, 2005; for public entities that file as small business issuers—as of the beginning of the first interim or annual reporting period that begins after December 15, 2005; for nonpublic entities—as of the beginning of the first annual reporting period that begins after December 15, 2005

Affects: Deletes ARB 43, Chapter 13B
Supersedes APB 25
Deletes APB 28, paragraph 30(j) and footnote 8
Amends APB 29, footnote 4
Supersedes AIN-APB 25, Interpretation No. 1
Amends FAS 5, paragraph 7
Amends FAS 43, paragraph 2(d)
Amends FAS 95, paragraphs 19, 23, and 27
Amends FAS 107, paragraph 8(a)
Amends FAS 109, paragraph 36(e)
Amends FAS 112, paragraph 5(d)
Supersedes FAS 123
Amends FAS 128, paragraphs 20 through 23 and 151 and footnotes 12 and 13
Replaces FAS 128, paragraphs 157 through 159
Amends FAS 133, paragraph 11(b)
Supersedes FAS 148
Amends FAS 150, paragraphs 17 and D1
Supersedes FIN 28
Supersedes FIN 38
Supersedes FIN 44
Amends FIN 46(R), footnotes 18 and 23
Supersedes FTB 82-2
Amends FTB 97-1, the Reference, paragraphs 1 through 3, 5 through 10, 12 through 15, 17, 18, 20, 21, and 24 and footnotes 2, 7, and 13

Affected by: Paragraphs 32 and A229 amended by FSP FAS 123(R)-4, paragraph A1
Paragraphs 38 and A23 amended by FAS 154, paragraph C13
Paragraphs A102, A170, A240(d)(1), and E1 amended by FSP FAS 123(R)-6, paragraphs 8, 10, 4, and 12, respectively
Paragraph E1 effectively amended by FAS 159, paragraph C2

Other Interpretive Releases: FASB Staff Positions FAS 123(R)-1 through FAS 123(R)-6

AICPA Accounting Standards Executive Committee (AcSEC)

Related Pronouncements: SOP 76-3
SOP 93-6

Issues Discussed by FASB Emerging Issues Task Force (EITF)

Affects: Nullifies EITF Issues No. 84-13, 84-18, 84-34, 85-45, 87-23, 88-6, 90-7, 95-16, 97-5, 97-12, 00-15, and 00-23 and Topics No. D-18, D-91, and D-93
Resolves EITF Issue No. 84-8

Interpreted by: No EITF Issues

Related Issues: EITF Issues No. 96-18, 97-2, 97-14, 00-8, 00-12, 00-16, 00-18, 00-19, 01-1, 01-6, 02-8, and 06-11 and Topics No. D-83, D-90, and D-98

SUMMARY

This Statement is a revision of FASB Statement No. 123, *Accounting for Stock-Based Compensation.* This Statement supersedes APB Opinion No. 25, *Accounting for Stock Issued to Employees,* and its related implementation guidance.

Scope of This Statement

This Statement establishes standards for the accounting for transactions in which an entity exchanges its equity instruments for goods or services. It also addresses transactions in which an entity incurs liabilities in exchange for goods or services that are based on the fair value of the entity's equity instruments or that may be settled by the issuance of those equity instruments. This Statement focuses primarily on accounting for transactions in which an entity obtains employee services in share-based payment transactions. This Statement does not change the accounting guidance for share-based payment transactions with parties other than employees provided in Statement 123 as originally issued and EITF Issue No. 96-18, "Accounting for Equity Instruments That Are Issued to Other Than Employees for Acquiring, or in Conjunction with Selling, Goods or Services." This Statement does not address the accounting for employee share ownership plans, which are subject to AICPA Statement of Position 93-6, *Employers' Accounting for Employee Stock Ownership Plans.*

Reasons for Issuing This Statement

The principal reasons for issuing this Statement are:

a. **Addressing concerns of users and others.** Users of financial statements, including institutional and individual investors, as well as many other parties expressed to the FASB their concerns that using Opinion 25's intrinsic value method results in financial statements that do not faithfully represent the economic transactions affecting the issuer, namely, the receipt and consumption of employee services in exchange for equity instruments. Financial statements that do not faithfully represent those economic transactions can distort the issuer's reported financial condition and results of operations, which can lead to the inappropriate allocation of resources in the capital markets. Part of the FASB's mission is to improve standards of financial accounting for the benefit of users of financial information. This Statement addresses users' and other parties' concerns by requiring an entity to recognize the cost of employee services received in share-based payment transactions, thereby reflecting the economic consequences of those transactions in the financial statements.
b. **Improving the comparability of reported financial information by eliminating alternative accounting methods.** Over the last few years, approximately 750 public companies have voluntarily adopted or announced their intention to adopt Statement 123's fair-value-based method of accounting for share-based payment transactions with employees. Other companies continue to use Opinion 25's intrinsic value method. The Board believes that similar economic transactions should be accounted for similarly (that is, share-based compensation transactions with employees should be accounted for using one method). Consistent with the conclusion in the original Statement 123, the Board believes that those transactions should be accounted for using a fair-value-based method. By requiring the fair-value-based method for all public entities, this Statement eliminates an alternative accounting method; consequently, similar economic transactions will be accounted for similarly.
c. **Simplifying U.S. GAAP.** The Board believes that U.S. generally accepted accounting principles (GAAP) should be simplified whenever possible. Requiring that all entities follow the same accounting standard and eliminating Opinion 25's intrinsic value method and its related detailed and form-driven implementation guidance simplifies the authoritative literature.

d. **Converging with international accounting standards.** This Statement will result in greater international comparability in the accounting for share-based payment transactions. In February 2004, the International Accounting Standards Board (IASB), whose standards are followed by entities in many countries, issued International Financial Reporting Standard (IFRS) 2, *Share-based Payment.* IFRS 2 requires that all entities recognize an expense for all employee services received in share-based payment transactions, using a fair-value-based method that is similar in most respects to the fair-value-based method established in Statement 123 and the improvements made to it by this Statement. Converging to a common set of high-quality financial accounting standards for share-based payment transactions with employees improves the comparability of financial information around the world and makes the accounting requirements for entities that report financial statements under both U.S. GAAP and international accounting standards less burdensome.

Key Provisions of This Statement

This Statement requires a public entity to measure the cost of employee services received in exchange for an award of equity instruments based on the grant-date fair value of the award (with limited exceptions). That cost will be recognized over the period during which an employee is required to provide service in exchange for the award—the requisite service period (usually the vesting period). No compensation cost is recognized for equity instruments for which employees do not render the requisite service. Employee share purchase plans will not result in recognition of compensation cost if certain conditions are met; those conditions are much the same as the related conditions in Statement 123.

A nonpublic entity, likewise, will measure the cost of employee services received in exchange for an award of equity instruments based on the grant-date fair value of those instruments, except in certain circumstances. Specifically, if it is not possible to reasonably estimate the fair value of equity share options and similar instruments because it is not practicable to estimate the expected volatility of the entity's share price, a nonpublic entity is required to measure its awards of equity share options and similar instruments based on a value calculated using the historical volatility of an appropriate industry sector index instead of the expected volatility of its share price.

A public entity will initially measure the cost of employee services received in exchange for an award of liability instruments based on its current fair value; the fair value of that award will be remeasured subsequently at each reporting date through the settlement date. Changes in fair value during the requisite service period will be recognized as compensation cost over that period. A nonpublic entity may elect to measure its liability awards at their intrinsic value through the date of settlement.

The grant-date fair value of employee share options and similar instruments will be estimated using option-pricing models adjusted for the unique characteristics of those instruments (unless observable market prices for the same or similar instruments are available). If an equity award is modified after the grant date, incremental compensation cost will be recognized in an amount equal to the excess of the fair value of the modified award over the fair value of the original award immediately before the modification.

Excess tax benefits, as defined by this Statement, will be recognized as an addition to paid-in capital. Cash retained as a result of those excess tax benefits will be presented in the statement of cash flows as financing cash inflows. The write-off of deferred tax assets relating to unrealized tax benefits associated with recognized compensation cost will be recognized as income tax expense unless there are excess tax benefits from previous awards remaining in paid-in capital to which it can be offset.

The notes to financial statements of both public and nonpublic entities will disclose information to assist users of financial information to understand the nature of share-based payment transactions and the effects of those transactions on the financial statements.

How This Statement Changes Practice and Improves Financial Reporting

This Statement eliminates the alternative to use Opinion 25's intrinsic value method of accounting that was provided in Statement 123 as originally issued. Under Opinion 25, issuing stock options to employees generally resulted in recognition of no compensation cost. This Statement requires entities to recognize the cost of employee services received in exchange for awards of equity instruments based on the grant-date fair value of those awards (with limited exceptions). Recognition of that compensation cost helps users of financial statements to better understand the economic transactions affecting an entity and to make better resource allocation decisions. Such information specifically will help users of financial statements understand the effect that share-based compensation transactions have on an entity's financial condition and results of operations. This Statement also will improve comparability by eliminating one of two different methods of accounting for share-based compensation transactions and thereby also will simplify existing U.S. GAAP. Eliminating different methods of accounting for the same transactions leads to improved comparability of financial statements because similar economic transactions will be accounted for similarly.

The fair-value-based method in this Statement is similar to the fair-value-based method in Statement 123 in most respects. However, the following are the key differences between the two:

a. Public entities are required to measure liabilities incurred to employees in share-based payment transactions at fair value. Nonpublic entities may elect to measure their liabilities to employees incurred in share-based payment transactions at their intrinsic value. Under Statement 123, all share-based payment liabilities were measured at their intrinsic value.

b. Nonpublic entities are required to account for awards of equity instruments using the fair-value-based method unless it is not possible to reasonably estimate the grant-date fair value of awards of equity share options and similar instruments because it is not practicable to estimate the expected volatility of the entity's share price. In that situation, the entity will account for those instruments based on a value calculated by substituting the historical volatility of an appropriate industry sector index for the expected volatility of its share price. Statement 123 permitted a nonpublic entity to measure its equity awards using either the fair-value-based method or the minimum value method.

c. Entities are required to estimate the number of instruments for which the requisite service is expected to be rendered. Statement 123 permitted entities to account for forfeitures as they occur.

d. Incremental compensation cost for a modification of the terms or conditions of an award is measured by comparing the fair value of the modified award with the fair value of the award immediately before the modification. Statement 123 required that the effects of a modification be measured as the difference between the fair value of the modified award at the date it is granted and the award's value immediately before the modification determined based on the shorter of (1) its remaining initially estimated expected life or (2) the expected life of the modified award.

e. This Statement also clarifies and expands Statement 123's guidance in several areas, including measuring fair value, classifying an award as equity or as a liability, and attributing compensation cost to reporting periods.

In addition, this Statement amends FASB Statement No. 95, *Statement of Cash Flows,* to require that excess tax benefits be reported as a financing cash inflow rather than as a reduction of taxes paid.

How the Conclusions of This Statement Relate to the FASB's Conceptual Framework

FASB Concepts Statement No. 1, *Objectives of Financial Reporting by Business Enterprises,* states that financial reporting should provide information that is useful in making business and economic decisions. Recognizing compensation cost incurred as a result of receiving employee services in exchange for valuable equity instruments issued by the employer will help achieve that objective by providing more relevant and reliable information about the costs incurred by the employer to obtain employee services in the marketplace.

FASB Concepts Statement No. 2, *Qualitative Characteristics of Accounting Information,* explains that comparability of financial information is important because information about an entity gains greatly in usefulness if it can be compared with similar information about other entities. Establishing the fair-value-based method of accounting as the required method will increase comparability because similar economic transactions will be accounted for similarly, which will improve the usefulness of financial information. Requiring the fair-value-based method also enhances the neutrality of the resulting financial reporting by eliminating the accounting bias toward using certain types of employee share options for compensation.

Completeness is identified in Concepts Statement 2 as an essential element of representational faithfulness and relevance. To faithfully represent the total cost of employee services to the entity, the cost of services received in exchange for awards of share-based compensation should be recognized in that entity's financial statements.

FASB Concepts Statement No. 6, *Elements of Financial Statements,* defines *assets* as probable future economic benefits obtained or controlled by a particular entity as a result of past transactions or events. Employee services received in exchange for awards of share-based compensation qualify as assets, though only momentarily—as the entity receives and uses them—although their use may create or add value to other assets of the entity. This Statement will improve the accounting for an entity's assets resulting from receipt of employee services in exchange for an equity award by requiring that the cost of such assets either be charged to expense when consumed or capitalized as part of another asset of the entity (as permitted by U.S. GAAP).

Costs and Benefits

The mission of the FASB is to establish and improve standards of financial accounting and reporting for the guidance and education of the public, including preparers, auditors, and users of financial information. In fulfilling that mission, the Board endeavors to determine that a proposed standard will fill a significant need and that the costs imposed to meet that standard, as compared with other alternatives, are justified in relation to the overall benefits of the resulting information. The Board's consideration of each issue in a project includes the subjective weighing of the incremental improvement in financial reporting against the incremental cost of implementing the identified alternatives. At the end of that process, the Board considers the accounting provisions in the aggregate and assesses the perceived benefits and the related perceived costs on a qualitative basis.

Several procedures were conducted before the issuance of this Statement to aid the Board in its assessment of the expected costs associated with implementing the required use of the fair-value-based accounting method. Those procedures included a review of the comment letters received on the Exposure Draft, a field visit program, a survey of commercial software providers, and discussions with members of the Option Valuation Group that the Board established to provide information and advice on how to improve the guidance in Statement 123 on measuring the fair value of share options and similar instruments issued to employees in compensation arrangements. That group included valuation experts from the compensation consulting, risk management, investment banking, and academic communities. The Board also discussed the issues in the project with other valuation experts, compensation consultants, and numerous other constituents. After considering the results of those cost-benefit procedures, the Board concluded that this Statement will sufficiently improve financial reporting to justify the costs it will impose.

The Effective Dates and Transition Requirements of This Statement

This Statement is effective:

a. For public entities that do not file as small business issuers—as of the beginning of the first interim or annual reporting period that begins after June 15, 2005
b. For public entities that file as small business issuers—as of the beginning of the first interim or annual reporting period that begins after December 15, 2005
c. For nonpublic entities—as of the beginning of the first annual reporting period that begins after December 15, 2005.

This Statement applies to all awards granted after the required effective date and to awards modified, repurchased, or cancelled after that date. The cumulative effect of initially applying this Statement, if any, is recognized as of the required effective date.

As of the required effective date, all public entities and those nonpublic entities that used the fair-value-based method for either recognition or disclosure under Statement 123 will apply this Statement using a modified version of prospective application. Under that transition method, compensation cost is recognized on or after the required effective date for the portion of outstanding awards for which the requisite service has not yet been rendered, based on the grant-date fair value of those awards calculated under Statement 123 for either recognition or pro forma disclosures. For periods before the required effective date, those entities may elect to apply a modified version of retrospective application under which financial statements for prior periods are adjusted on a basis consistent with the pro forma disclosures required for those periods by Statement 123. Nonpublic entities that used the minimum value method in Statement 123 for either recognition or pro forma disclosures are required to apply the prospective transition method as of the required effective date.

Early adoption of this Statement for interim or annual periods for which financial statements or interim reports have not been issued is encouraged.

Statement of Financial Accounting Standards No. 123 (revised 2004)

Share-Based Payment

CONTENTS

INTRODUCTION

1. This Statement requires that the cost resulting from all **share-based payment transactions**[1] be recognized in the financial statements. This Statement establishes **fair value** as the measurement objective in accounting for **share-based payment arrangements** and requires all entities to apply a fair-value-based measurement method in accounting for share-based payment transactions with **employees** except for equity instruments held by **employee share ownership plans.** However, this Statement provides certain exceptions to that measurement method if it is not possible to reasonably estimate the fair value of an award at the **grant date. A nonpublic entity** also may choose to measure its liabilities under share-based payment arrangements at **intrinsic value.** This Statement also establishes fair value as the measurement objective for transactions in which an entity acquires goods or services from nonemployees in share-based payment transactions. This Statement uses the terms *compensation* and *payment*

---

[1]Terms defined in Appendix E, the glossary, are set in **boldface type** the first time they appear.

in their broadest senses to refer to the consideration paid for goods or services, regardless of whether the supplier is an employee.

2. This Statement amends FASB Statement No. 95, *Statement of Cash Flows,* to require that **excess tax benefits** be reported as a financing cash inflow rather than as a reduction of taxes paid.

3. This Statement replaces FASB Statement No. 123, *Accounting for Stock-Based Compensation,* and supersedes APB Opinion No. 25, *Accounting for Stock Issued to Employees.* This Statement also supersedes or amends other pronouncements indicated in Appendix D. Appendix A is an integral part of this Statement and provides implementation guidance on measurement and recognition of compensation cost resulting from share-based payment arrangements with employees. Appendix B provides the basis for the Board's conclusions, and Appendix C provides background information. Appendix E defines certain terms as they are used in this Statement, and Appendix F indicates the effect of this Statement on the status of related authoritative literature, including American Institute of Certified Public Accountants (AICPA) literature, Emerging Issues Task Force (EITF) issues, and Statement 133 implementation issues.

STANDARDS OF FINANCIAL ACCOUNTING AND REPORTING

Scope

4. This Statement applies to all share-based payment transactions in which an entity acquires goods or services by **issuing** (or offering to issue) its shares, **share options,** or other equity instruments (except for equity instruments held by an employee share ownership plan)[2] or by incurring liabilities to an employee or other supplier (a) in amounts based, at least in part,[3] on the price of the entity's shares or other equity instruments or (b) that require or may require **settlement** by issuing the entity's equity shares or other equity instruments.

Recognition Principle for Share-Based Payment Transactions

5. An entity shall recognize the goods acquired or services received in a share-based payment transaction when it obtains the goods or as services are received.[4] The entity shall recognize either a corresponding increase in equity or a liability, depending on whether the instruments granted satisfy the equity or liability classification criteria (paragraphs 28–35). As the goods or services are disposed of or consumed, the entity shall recognize the related cost. For example, when inventory is sold, the cost is recognized in the income statement as cost of goods sold, and as services are consumed, the cost usually is recognized in determining net income of that period, for example, as expenses incurred for employee services. In some circumstances, the cost of services (or goods) may be initially capitalized as part of the cost to acquire or construct another asset, such as inventory, and later recognized in the income statement when that asset is disposed of or consumed.[5]

6. The accounting for all share-based payment transactions shall reflect the rights conveyed to the holder of the instruments and the obligations imposed on the issuer of the instruments, regardless of how those transactions are structured. For example, the rights and obligations embodied in a transfer of equity shares to an employee for a note that provides no recourse to other assets of the employee (that is, other than the shares) are substantially the same as those embodied in a grant of equity share options. Thus, that transaction shall be accounted for as a substantive grant of equity share options. The **terms** of a share-based payment award and any related arrangement affect its value and, except for certain explicitly excluded features, such as a **reload feature,** shall be reflected in determining the fair value of the equity or liability instruments granted. For example, the fair value of a substantive option structured as the exchange of equity shares for a nonrecourse note will differ depending on whether the employee is required

[2]AICPA Statement of Position 93-6, *Employers' Accounting for Employee Stock Ownership Plans,* specifies the accounting by employers for employee share ownership plans.

[3]The phrase *at least in part* is used because an award of share-based compensation may be indexed to both the price of an entity's shares and something else that is neither the price of the entity's shares nor a market, performance, or service condition.

[4]An entity may need to recognize an asset before it actually receives goods or services if it first exchanges share-based payment for an enforceable right to receive those goods or services. Nevertheless, the goods or services themselves are not recognized before they are received.

[5]This Statement refers to recognizing *compensation cost* rather than *compensation expense* because any compensation cost that is capitalized as part of the cost to acquire or construct an asset would not be recognized as compensation expense in the income statement.

to pay nonrefundable interest on the note. Assessment of both the rights and obligations in a share-based payment award and any related arrangement and how those rights and obligations affect the fair value of an award requires the exercise of judgment in considering the relevant facts and circumstances.

Measurement Principle for Share-Based Payment Transactions

7. If the fair value of goods or services received in a share-based payment transaction with nonemployees is more reliably measurable than the fair value of the equity instruments issued, the fair value of the goods or services received shall be used to measure the transaction.[6] In contrast, if the fair value of the equity instruments issued in a share-based payment transaction with nonemployees is more reliably measurable than the fair value of the consideration received, the transaction shall be measured based on the fair value of the equity instruments issued. A share-based payment transaction with employees shall be measured based on the fair value (or in certain situations specified in this Statement, a **calculated value** or intrinsic value) of the equity instruments issued.

Measurement Date for Share-Based Payment Transactions with Nonemployees

8. This Statement does not specify the **measurement date** for share-based payment transactions with nonemployees for which the measure of the cost of goods acquired or services received is based on the fair value of the equity instruments issued. EITF Issue No. 96-18, "Accounting for Equity Instruments That Are Issued to Other Than Employees for Acquiring, or in Conjunction with Selling, Goods or Services," establishes criteria for determining the measurement date for equity instruments issued in share-based payment transactions with nonemployees.

Accounting for Share-Based Payment Transactions with Employees

9. The objective of accounting for transactions under share-based payment arrangements with employees

is to recognize in the financial statements the employee services received in exchange for equity instruments issued or liabilities incurred and the related cost to the entity as those services are consumed.

10. An entity shall account for the compensation cost from share-based payment transactions with employees in accordance with the fair-value-based method set forth in paragraphs 11–63 of this Statement. That is, the cost of services received from employees in exchange for awards[7] of share-based compensation generally shall be measured based on the grant-date fair value of the equity instruments issued or on the fair value of the liabilities incurred. The fair value of liabilities incurred in share-based transactions with employees shall be remeasured at the end of each reporting period through settlement. Paragraphs 23–25 and 38 set forth exceptions to the fair-value-based measurement of awards of share-based employee compensation.

Certain Transactions with Related Parties and Other Economic Interest Holders

11. Share-based payments awarded to an employee of the reporting entity by a **related party** or other holder of an **economic interest** in the entity as compensation for services provided to the entity are share-based payment transactions to be accounted for under this Statement unless the transfer is clearly for a purpose other than compensation for services to the reporting entity. The substance of such a transaction is that the economic interest holder makes a capital contribution to the reporting entity, and that entity makes a share-based payment to its employee in exchange for services rendered. An example of a situation in which such a transfer is not compensation is a transfer to settle an obligation of the economic interest holder to the employee that is unrelated to employment by the entity.

Employee Share Purchase Plans

12. An employee share purchase plan that satisfies all of the following criteria does not give rise to recognizable compensation cost (that is, the plan is noncompensatory):

---

[6] The consideration received for issuing equity instruments, like the consideration involved in a repurchase of treasury shares, may include stated or unstated rights. FASB Technical Bulletin No. 85-6, *Accounting for a Purchase of Treasury Shares at a Price Significantly in Excess of the Current Market Price of the Shares and the Income Statement Classification of Costs Incurred in Defending against a Takeover Attempt*, provides pertinent guidance.

[7] This Statement uses the term *award* as the collective noun for multiple instruments with the same terms and conditions granted at the same time either to a single employee or to a group of employees. An award may specify multiple vesting dates, referred to as graded vesting, and different parts of an award may have different expected terms. Provisions of this Statement that refer to *an award* also apply to a portion of an award.

a. The plan satisfies at least one of the following conditions:
 (1) The terms of the plan are no more favorable than those available to all holders of the same class of shares.[8]
 (2) Any purchase discount from the market price does not exceed the per-share amount of share issuance costs that would have been incurred to raise a significant amount of capital by a public offering. A purchase discount of 5 percent or less from the market price shall be considered to comply with this condition without further justification. A purchase discount greater than 5 percent that cannot be justified under this condition results in compensation cost for the entire amount of the discount.[9]
b. Substantially all employees that meet limited employment qualifications may participate on an equitable basis.
c. The plan incorporates no option features, other than the following:
 (1) Employees are permitted a short period of time—not exceeding 31 days—after the purchase price has been fixed to enroll in the plan.
 (2) The purchase price is based solely on the market price of the shares at the date of purchase, and employees are permitted to cancel participation before the purchase date and obtain a refund of amounts previously paid (such as those paid by payroll withholdings).

13. A plan provision that establishes the purchase price as an amount based on the lesser of the equity share's market price at date of grant or its market price at date of purchase is an example of an option feature that causes the plan to be compensatory. Similarly, a plan in which the purchase price is based on the share's market price at date of grant and that permits a participating employee to cancel participation before the purchase date and obtain a refund of amounts previously paid contains an option feature that causes the plan to be compensatory. Illustrations 19 (paragraphs A211–A219) and 20 (paragraphs A220 and A221) provide guidance on determining whether an employee share purchase plan satisfies the criteria necessary to be considered noncompensatory.

14. The **requisite service period** for any compensation cost resulting from an employee share purchase plan is the period over which the employee participates in the plan and pays for the shares.

Measurement Principle for Share-Based Payment Transactions with Employees

15. The cost of services received by an entity as consideration for equity instruments issued or liabilities incurred in share-based compensation transactions with employees shall be measured based on the fair value of the equity instruments issued or the liabilities settled. The portion of the fair value of an instrument attributed to employee service is net of any amount that an employee pays (or becomes obligated to pay) for that instrument when it is granted. For example, if an employee pays $5 at the grant date for an option with a grant-date fair value of $50, the amount attributed to employee service is $45.

Measurement of Awards Classified as Equity

Measurement objective and measurement date for equity awards

16. The measurement objective for equity instruments awarded to employees is to estimate the fair value at the grant date of the equity instruments that the entity is obligated to issue when employees have rendered the requisite service and satisfied any other conditions necessary to earn the right to benefit from the instruments (for example, to exercise share options). That estimate is based on the share price and other pertinent factors, such as expected **volatility,** at the grant date.

17. To satisfy the measurement objective in paragraph 16, the **restrictions** and conditions inherent in equity instruments awarded to employees are treated differently depending on whether they continue in effect after the requisite service period. A restriction that continues in effect after an entity has issued instruments to employees, such as the inability to transfer **vested** equity share options to third parties or the

[8]A transaction subject to an employee share purchase plan that involves a class of equity shares designed exclusively for and held only by current or former employees or their beneficiaries may be compensatory depending on the terms of the arrangement.
[9]An entity that justifies a purchase discount in excess of 5 percent shall reassess at least annually, and no later than the first share purchase offer during the fiscal year, whether it can continue to justify that discount pursuant to paragraph 12(a)(2) of this Statement.

inability to sell vested shares for a period of time, is considered in estimating the fair value of the instruments at the grant date. For equity share options and similar instruments, the effect of nontransferability (and nonhedgeability, which has a similar effect) is taken into account by reflecting the effects of employees' expected exercise and post-vesting employment termination behavior in estimating fair value (referred to as an option's *expected term*).

18. In contrast, a restriction that stems from the forfeitability of instruments to which employees have not yet earned the right, such as the inability either to exercise a nonvested equity share option or to sell **nonvested shares,** is not reflected in estimating the fair value of the related instruments at the grant date. Instead, those restrictions are taken into account by recognizing compensation cost only for awards for which employees render the requisite service.

19. Awards of share-based employee compensation ordinarily specify a **performance condition** or a **service condition** (or both) that must be satisfied for an employee to earn the right to benefit from the award. No compensation cost is recognized for instruments that employees forfeit because a service condition or a performance condition is not satisfied (that is, instruments for which the requisite service is not rendered). Some awards contain a **market condition.** The effect of a market condition is reflected in the grant-date fair value of an award.[10] Compensation cost thus is recognized for an award with a market condition provided that the requisite service is rendered, regardless of when, if ever, the market condition is satisfied. Illustrations 4 (paragraphs A86–A104), 5 (paragraphs A105–A110), and 10 (paragraphs A127–A133) provide examples of how compensation cost is recognized for awards with service and performance conditions.

20. The fair-value-based method described in paragraphs 16–19 uses fair value measurement techniques, and the grant-date share price and other perti-

nent factors are used in applying those techniques. However, the effects on the grant-date fair value of service and performance conditions that apply only during the requisite service period are reflected based on the outcomes of those conditions. The remainder of this Statement refers to the required measure as fair value.

Nonvested and restricted equity shares

21. A nonvested equity share or nonvested equity **share unit** awarded to an employee shall be measured at its fair value as if it were vested and issued on the grant date. A **restricted share**[11] awarded to an employee, that is, a share that will be restricted after the employee has a vested right to it, shall be measured at its fair value, which is the same amount for which a similarly restricted share would be issued to third parties. Illustration 11(a) (paragraphs A134–A136) provides an example of accounting for an award of nonvested shares.

Equity share options

22. The fair value of an equity share option or similar instrument shall be measured based on the observable market price of an option with the same or similar terms and conditions, if one is available (paragraph A7).[12] Otherwise, the fair value of an equity share option or similar instrument shall be estimated using a valuation technique such as an option-pricing model. For this purpose, a *similar instrument* is one whose fair value differs from its intrinsic value, that is, an instrument that has **time value.** For example, a share appreciation right (SAR) that requires net settlement in equity shares has time value; an equity share does not. Paragraphs A2–A42 provide additional guidance on estimating the fair value of equity instruments, including the factors to be taken into account in estimating the fair value of equity share options or similar instruments as described in paragraph A18.

---

[10]Valuation techniques have been developed to value path-dependent options as well as other options with complex terms. Awards with market conditions, as defined in this Statement, are path-dependent options.

[11]Nonvested shares granted to employees usually are referred to as *restricted shares,* but this Statement reserves that term for fully vested and outstanding shares whose sale is contractually or governmentally prohibited for a specified period of time.

[12]As of the issuance of this Statement, such market prices for equity share options and similar instruments granted to employees are generally not available; however, they may become so in the future.

Equity instruments for which it is not possible to reasonably estimate fair value at the grant date

Equity instruments granted by a nonpublic entity for which it is not possible to reasonably estimate fair value at the grant date because it is not practicable to estimate the expected volatility of the entity's share price

23. A nonpublic entity may not be able to reasonably estimate the fair value of its equity share options and similar instruments because it is not practicable for it to estimate the expected volatility of its share price. In that situation, the entity shall account for its equity share options and similar instruments based on a value calculated using the historical volatility of an appropriate industry sector index instead of the expected volatility of the entity's share price (the calculated value).[13] Paragraphs A43–A48 and Illustration 11(b) (paragraphs A137–A142) provide additional guidance on applying the calculated value method to equity share options and similar instruments granted by a nonpublic entity.

Equity instruments with terms that make it not possible to reasonably estimate fair value at the grant date

24. It should be possible to reasonably estimate the fair value of most equity share options and other equity instruments at the date they are granted. Appendix A illustrates techniques for estimating the fair values of several instruments with complicated features. However, in rare circumstances, it may not be possible to reasonably estimate the fair value of an equity share option or other equity instrument at the grant date because of the complexity of its terms.

25. An equity instrument for which it is not possible to reasonably estimate fair value at the grant date shall be accounted for based on its intrinsic value, remeasured at each reporting date through the date of exercise or other settlement. The final measure of compensation cost shall be the intrinsic value of the instrument at the date it is settled. Compensation cost for each period until settlement shall be based on the change (or a portion of the change, depending on the percentage of the requisite service that has been rendered at the reporting date) in the intrinsic value of the instrument in each reporting period. The entity

shall continue to use the intrinsic value method for those instruments even if it subsequently concludes that it is possible to reasonably estimate their fair value.

Reload options and contingent features

26. The fair value of each award of equity instruments, including an award of options with a reload feature (reload options), shall be measured separately based on its terms and the share price and other pertinent factors at the grant date. The effect of a reload feature in the terms of an award shall not be included in estimating the grant-date fair value of the award. Rather, a subsequent grant of reload options pursuant to that provision shall be accounted for as a separate award when the reload options are granted.

27. A contingent feature of an award that might cause an employee to return to the entity either equity instruments earned or realized gains from the sale of equity instruments earned for consideration that is less than fair value on the date of transfer (including no consideration), such as a clawback feature (paragraph A5, footnote 44), shall not be reflected in estimating the grant-date fair value of an equity instrument. Instead, the effect of such a contingent feature shall be accounted for if and when the contingent event occurs.

Awards Classified as Liabilities

Criteria for classifying awards as liabilities

28. Paragraphs 29–35 of this Statement provide guidance for determining whether certain financial instruments awarded in share-based payment transactions are liabilities. In determining whether an instrument not specifically discussed in paragraphs 29–35 should be classified as a liability or as equity, an entity shall apply generally accepted accounting principles (GAAP) applicable to financial instruments issued in transactions not involving share-based payment.

Applying the classification criteria in Statement 150

29. FASB Statement No. 150, *Accounting for Certain Financial Instruments with Characteristics of both Liabilities and Equity,* excludes from its scope instruments that are accounted for under this Statement. Nevertheless, unless paragraphs 30–35 of this

---

[13]Throughout the remainder of this Statement, provisions that apply to accounting for share options and similar instruments at fair value also apply to calculated value.

Statement require otherwise, an entity shall apply the classification criteria in paragraphs 8–14 of Statement 150, as they are effective at the reporting date, in determining whether to classify as a liability a **freestanding financial instrument** given to an employee in a share-based payment transaction. Paragraphs A230–A232 of this Statement provide criteria for determining when instruments subject to this Statement subsequently become subject to Statement 150 or to other applicable GAAP.

30. In determining the classification of an instrument, an entity shall take into account the deferrals contained in FSP FAS 150-3, "Effective Date, Disclosures, and Transition for Mandatorily Redeemable Financial Instruments of Certain Nonpublic Entities and Certain Mandatorily Redeemable Noncontrolling Interests under FASB Statement No. 150, *Accounting for Certain Financial Instruments with Characteristics of both Liabilities and Equity*." In addition, a call option[14] written on an instrument that is not classified as a liability because of the deferrals in FSP FAS 150-3 (for example, a call option on a mandatorily redeemable share for which liability classification is deferred under FSP FAS 150-3) also shall be classified as equity while the deferral is in effect unless liability classification is required under the provisions of paragraph 32 of this Statement.

Classification of certain awards with repurchase features

31. Statement 150 does not apply to outstanding shares embodying a conditional obligation to transfer assets, for example, shares that give the employee the right to require the employer to repurchase them for cash equal to their fair value (puttable shares). A put-table (or callable) share[15] awarded to an employee as compensation shall be classified as a liability if either of the following conditions is met: (a) the repurchase feature permits the employee to avoid bearing the risks and rewards normally associated with equity share ownership for a reasonable period of time from the date the requisite service is rendered and the share is issued,[16,17] or (b) it is probable that the employer would prevent the employee from bearing those risks and rewards for a reasonable period of time from the date the share is issued. For this purpose, a period of six months or more is a *reasonable period of time*. A puttable (or callable) share that does not meet either of those conditions shall be classified as equity.[18]

32. Options or similar instruments on shares shall be classified as liabilities if (a) the underlying shares are classified as liabilities or (b) the entity can be required under any circumstances[18a] to settle the option or similar instrument by transferring cash or other assets.[18b] For example, an entity may grant an option to an employee that, upon exercise, would be settled by issuing a mandatorily redeemable share that is not subject to the deferral in FSP FAS 150-3. Because the mandatorily redeemable share would be classified as a liability under Statement 150, the option also would be classified as a liability.

Awards with conditions other than market, performance, or service conditions

33. An award may be indexed to a factor in addition to the entity's share price. If that additional factor is not a market, performance, or service condition, the award shall be classified as a liability for purposes of this Statement, and the additional factor shall be re-

---

[14]Refer to the definition of *share option* in Appendix E.

[15]A put right may be granted to the employee in a transaction that is related to a share-based compensation arrangement. If exercise of such a put right would require the entity to repurchase shares issued under the share-based compensation arrangement, the shares shall be accounted for as puttable shares.

[16]A repurchase feature that can be exercised only upon the occurrence of a contingent event that is outside the employee's control (such as an initial public offering) would not meet condition (a) until it becomes probable that the event will occur within the reasonable period of time.

[17]An employee begins to bear the risks and rewards normally associated with equity share ownership when all the requisite service has been rendered.

[18]SEC registrants are required to consider the guidance in ASR No. 268, *Presentation in Financial Statements of "Redeemable Preferred Stocks."* Under that guidance, shares subject to mandatory redemption requirements or whose redemption is outside the control of the issuer are classified outside permanent equity.

[18a]A cash settlement feature that can be exercised only upon the occurrence of a contingent event that is outside the employee's control (such as an initial public offering) would not meet condition (b) until it becomes probable that event will occur.

[18b]SEC registrants are required to consider the guidance in ASR 268. Under that guidance, options and similar instruments subject to mandatory redemption requirements or whose redemption is outside the control of the issuer are classified outside permanent equity.

flected in estimating the fair value of the award.[19] Paragraph A53 provides examples of such awards.

Evaluating the terms of a share-based payment award in determining whether it qualifies as a liability

34. The accounting for an award of share-based payment shall reflect the substantive terms of the award and any related arrangement. Generally, the written terms provide the best evidence of the substantive terms of an award. However, an entity's past practice may indicate that the substantive terms of an award differ from its written terms. For example, an entity that grants a **tandem award** under which an employee receives either a stock option or a cash-settled SAR is obligated to pay cash on demand if the choice is the employee's, and the entity thus incurs a liability to the employee. In contrast, if the choice is the entity's, it can avoid transferring its assets by choosing to settle in stock, and the award qualifies as an equity instrument. However, if an entity that nominally has the choice of settling awards by issuing stock predominately settles in cash, or if the entity usually settles in cash whenever an employee asks for cash settlement, the entity is settling a substantive liability rather than repurchasing an equity instrument. In determining whether an entity that has the choice of settling an award by issuing equity shares has a substantive liability, the entity also shall consider whether (a) it has the ability to deliver the shares[20] and (b) it is required to pay cash if a contingent event occurs (paragraph 32).

Broker-assisted cashless exercises and minimum statutory withholding requirements

35. A provision that permits employees to effect a **broker-assisted cashless exercise** of part or all of an award of share options through a broker does not re-

sult in liability classification for instruments that otherwise would be classified as equity if both of the following criteria are satisfied:[21]

a. The cashless exercise requires a valid exercise of the share options.
b. The employee is the legal owner of the shares subject to the option (even though the employee has not paid the exercise price before the sale of the shares subject to the option).

Similarly, a provision for either direct or indirect (through a net-settlement feature) repurchase of shares issued upon exercise of options (or the vesting of nonvested shares), with any payment due employees withheld to meet the employer's minimum statutory withholding requirements[22] resulting from the exercise, does not, by itself, result in liability classification of instruments that otherwise would be classified as equity. However, if an amount in excess of the minimum statutory requirement is withheld, or may be withheld at the employee's discretion, the entire award shall be classified and accounted for as a liability.

Measurement objective and measurement date for liabilities

36. At the grant date, the measurement objective for liabilities incurred under share-based compensation arrangements is the same as the measurement objective for equity instruments awarded to employees as described in paragraph 16. However, the measurement date for liability instruments is the date of settlement. Accordingly, liabilities incurred under share-based payment arrangements are remeasured at the end of each reporting period until settlement.

Measurement of liability awards of public entities

37. A **public entity** shall measure a liability award under a share-based payment arrangement based on

---

[19]For this purpose, an award of equity share options granted to an employee of an entity's foreign operation that provides for a fixed exercise price denominated either in the foreign operation's functional currency or in the currency in which the employee's pay is denominated shall not be considered to contain a condition that is not a market, performance, or service condition. Therefore, such an award is not required to be classified as a liability if it otherwise qualifies as equity. For example, equity share options with an exercise price denominated in Euros granted to employees of a U.S. entity's foreign operation whose functional currency is the Euro are not required to be classified as liabilities if those options otherwise qualify as equity. In addition, such options are not required to be classified as liabilities even if the functional currency of the foreign operation is the U.S. dollar, provided that the employees to whom the options are granted are paid in Euros.

[20]Federal securities law generally requires that transactions involving offerings of shares under employee share option arrangements be registered, unless there is an available exemption. For purposes of this Statement, such requirements do not, by themselves, imply that an entity does not have the ability to deliver shares and thus do not require an award that otherwise qualifies as equity to be classified as a liability.

[21]A broker that is a related party of the entity must sell the shares in the open market within a normal settlement period, which generally is three days, for the award to qualify as equity.

[22]Minimum statutory withholding requirements are to be based on the applicable minimum statutory withholding rates required by the relevant tax authority (or authorities, for example, federal, state, and local), including the employee's share of payroll taxes that are applicable to such supplemental taxable income.

the award's fair value remeasured at each reporting date until the date of settlement. Compensation cost for each period until settlement shall be based on the change (or a portion of the change, depending on the percentage of the requisite service that has been rendered at the reporting date) in the fair value of the instrument for each reporting period. Illustration 10 (paragraphs A127–A133) provides an example of accounting for an instrument classified as a liability using the fair-value-based method.

Measurement of liability awards of nonpublic entities

38. A nonpublic entity shall make a policy decision of whether to measure all of its liabilities incurred under share-based payment arrangements at fair value or to measure all such liabilities at intrinsic value.[23] Regardless of the method selected, a nonpublic entity shall remeasure its liabilities under share-based payment arrangements at each reporting date until the date of settlement. The fair-value-based method is preferable for purposes of justifying a change in accounting principle under FASB Statement No. 154, *Accounting Changes and Error Corrections*. Illustration 10 (paragraphs A127–A133) provides an example of accounting for an instrument classified as a liability using the fair-value-based method. Illustration 11(c) (paragraphs A143–A148) provides an example of accounting for an instrument classified as a liability using the intrinsic value method.

Recognition of Compensation Cost for an Award Accounted for as an Equity Instrument

Recognition of compensation cost over the requisite service period

39. The compensation cost for an award of share-based employee compensation classified as equity shall be recognized over the requisite service period, with a corresponding credit to equity (generally, paid-in capital). The requisite service period is the period during which an employee is required to provide service in exchange for an award, which often is the

vesting period. The requisite service period is estimated based on an analysis of the terms of the share-based payment award.

40. The requisite service period may be explicit or it may be implicit, being inferred from an analysis of other terms in the award, including other explicit service or performance conditions. The requisite service period for an award that contains a market condition can be derived from certain valuation techniques that may be used to estimate grant-date fair value (paragraph A60). An award may have one or more **explicit, implicit,** or **derived service periods;** however, an award may have only one requisite service period for accounting purposes unless it is accounted for as in-substance multiple awards.[24] Paragraphs A59–A74 provide guidance on estimating the requisite service period and provide examples of how that period should be estimated if an award's terms include more than one explicit, implicit, or derived service period.

41. The **service inception date** is the beginning of the requisite service period. If the service inception date precedes the grant date (paragraph A79), accrual of compensation cost for periods before the grant date shall be based on the fair value of the award at the reporting date. In the period in which the grant date occurs, cumulative compensation cost shall be adjusted to reflect the cumulative effect of measuring compensation cost based on fair value at the grant date rather than the fair value previously used at the service inception date (or any subsequent reporting date). Illustration 3 (paragraphs A79–A85) provides guidance on the concept of *service inception date* and how it is to be applied.

42. An entity shall make a policy decision about whether to recognize compensation cost for an award with only service conditions that has a graded vesting schedule (a) on a straight-line basis over the requisite service period for each separately vesting portion of the award as if the award was, in-substance, multiple awards or (b) on a straight-line basis over the requisite service period for the entire award (that is, over the requisite service period of the last separately vesting portion of the award). However, the amount of compensation cost recognized at any date must at

---

[23]Consistent with the guidance in paragraph 23, footnote 13, a nonpublic entity that is not able to reasonably estimate the fair value of its equity share options and similar instruments because it is not practicable for it to estimate the expected volatility of its share price shall make a policy choice of whether to measure its liabilities under share-based payment arrangements at calculated value or at intrinsic value.

[24]An award with a graded vesting schedule that is accounted for as in-substance multiple awards is an example of an award that has more than one requisite service period (paragraph 42).

least equal the portion of the grant-date value of the award that is vested at that date. Illustration 4(b) (paragraphs A97–A104) provides an example of the accounting for an award with a graded vesting schedule.

Amount of compensation cost to be recognized over the requisite service period

43. The total amount of compensation cost recognized at the end of the requisite service period for an award of share-based compensation shall be based on the number of instruments for which the requisite service has been rendered (that is, for which the requisite service period has been completed). An entity shall base initial accruals of compensation cost on the estimated number of instruments for which the requisite service is expected to be rendered. That estimate shall be revised if subsequent information indicates that the actual number of instruments is likely to differ from previous estimates. The cumulative effect on current and prior periods of a change in the estimated number of instruments for which the requisite service is expected to be or has been rendered shall be recognized in compensation cost in the period of the change.

44. Accruals of compensation cost for an award with a performance condition shall be based on the probable[25] outcome of that performance condition—compensation cost shall be accrued if it is probable that the performance condition will be achieved and shall not be accrued if it is not probable that the performance condition will be achieved. If an award has multiple performance conditions (for example, if the number of options or shares an employee earns varies depending on which, if any, of two or more performance conditions is satisfied), compensation cost shall be accrued if it is probable that a performance condition will be satisfied. In making that assessment, it may be necessary to take into account the interrelationship of those performance conditions. Illustration 5 (paragraphs A105–A110) provides an example of how to account for awards with multiple performance conditions.

45. Previously recognized compensation cost shall not be reversed if an employee share option (or share unit) for which the requisite service has been rendered expires unexercised (or unconverted).

Estimating the requisite service period

46. An entity shall make its initial best estimate of the requisite service period at the grant date (or at the service inception date if that date precedes the grant date) and shall base accruals of compensation cost on that period. An entity shall adjust that initial best estimate in light of changes in facts and circumstances. The initial best estimate and any subsequent adjustment to that estimate of the requisite service period for an award with a combination of market, performance, or service conditions shall be based on an analysis of (a) all vesting and exercisability conditions, (b) all explicit, implicit, and derived service periods, and (c) the probability that performance or service conditions will be satisfied. For such an award, whether and how the initial best estimate of the requisite service period is adjusted depends on both the nature of those conditions and the manner in which they are combined, for example, whether an award vests or becomes exercisable when either a market or a performance condition is satisfied or whether both conditions must be satisfied. Paragraphs A59–A66 provide guidance on adjusting the initial estimate of the requisite service period.

Effect of market, performance, and service conditions on recognition and measurement of compensation cost

Market, performance, and service conditions that affect vesting or exercisability

47. If an award requires satisfaction of one or more market, performance, or service conditions (or any combination thereof), compensation cost is recognized if the requisite service is rendered, and no compensation cost is recognized if the requisite service is not rendered. Paragraphs A49–A51 provide guidance on applying this provision to awards with market, performance, or service conditions (or any combination thereof).

48. Performance or service conditions that affect vesting are not reflected in estimating the fair value of an award at the grant date because those conditions are restrictions that stem from the forfeitability of instruments to which employees have not yet earned the right. However, the effect of a market condition is reflected in estimating the fair value of an award at the grant date (paragraph 19). For purposes

---

[25]*Probable* is used in the same sense as in FASB Statement No. 5, *Accounting for Contingencies:* "the future event or events are likely to occur" (paragraph 3).

of this Statement, a market condition is not considered to be a vesting condition, and an award is not deemed to be forfeited solely because a market condition is not satisfied. Accordingly, an entity shall reverse previously recognized compensation cost for an award with a market condition only if the requisite service is not rendered.

Market, performance, and service conditions that affect factors other than vesting or exercisability

49. Market, performance, and service conditions (or any combination thereof) may affect an award's exercise price, contractual term, quantity, conversion ratio, or other factors that are considered in measuring an award's grant-date fair value. A grant-date fair value shall be estimated for each possible outcome of such a performance or service condition, and the final measure of compensation cost shall be based on the amount estimated at the grant date for the condition or outcome that is actually satisfied. Paragraphs A52–A54 provide additional guidance on the effects of market, performance, and service conditions that affect factors other than vesting or exercisability. Illustrations 5 (paragraphs A105–A110), 6 (paragraphs A111–A113), and 8 (paragraphs A121–A124) provide examples of accounting for awards with such conditions.

Recognition of Changes in the Fair Value or Intrinsic Value of Awards Classified as Liabilities

50. Changes in the fair value (or intrinsic value for a nonpublic entity that elects that method) of a liability incurred under a share-based payment arrangement that occur during the requisite service period shall be recognized as compensation cost over that period. The percentage of the fair value (or intrinsic value) that is accrued as compensation cost at the end of each period shall equal the percentage of the requisite service that has been rendered at that date. Changes in the fair value (or intrinsic value) of a liability that occur after the end of the requisite service period are compensation cost of the period in which the changes occur. Any difference between the amount for which a liability award is settled and its fair value at the settlement date as estimated in accordance with the provisions of this Statement is an adjustment of compensation cost in the period of settlement. Illustration 10 (paragraphs A127–A133) provides an example of accounting for a liability award from the grant date through its settlement.

Modifications of Awards of Equity Instruments

51. A **modification** of the terms or conditions of an equity award shall be treated as an exchange of the original award for a new award.[26] In substance, the entity repurchases the original instrument by issuing a new instrument of equal or greater value, incurring additional compensation cost for any incremental value. The effects of a modification shall be measured as follows:

a. Incremental compensation cost shall be measured as the excess, if any, of the fair value of the modified award determined in accordance with the provisions of this Statement over the fair value of the original award immediately before its terms are modified, measured based on the share price and other pertinent factors at that date.[27] The effect of the modification on the number of instruments expected to vest also shall be reflected in determining incremental compensation cost. The estimate at the modification date of the portion of the award expected to vest shall be subsequently adjusted, if necessary, in accordance with paragraphs 43–45 and other guidance in Illustration 13 (paragraphs A160–A170).

b. Total recognized compensation cost for an equity award shall at least equal the fair value of the award at the grant date unless at the date of the modification the performance or service conditions of the original award are not expected to be satisfied. Thus, the total compensation cost measured at the date of a modification shall be (1) the portion of the grant-date fair value of the original award for which the requisite service is expected to be rendered (or has already been rendered) at that date plus (2) the incremental cost resulting from the modification. Compensation cost shall be subsequently adjusted, if necessary, in accordance with paragraphs 43–45 and other guidance in Illustration 13 (paragraphs A160–A170).

c. A change in compensation cost for an equity award measured at intrinsic value in accordance

---

[26]A modification of a liability award also is accounted for as the exchange of the original award for a new award. However, because liability awards are remeasured at their fair value (or intrinsic value for a nonpublic entity that elects that method) at each reporting date, no special guidance is necessary in accounting for a modification of a liability award that remains a liability after the modification.

[27]As indicated in paragraph 23, footnote 13, references to *fair value* throughout paragraphs 24–85 of this Statement should be read also to encompass *calculated value.*

with paragraph 25 shall be measured by comparing the intrinsic value of the modified award, if any, with the intrinsic value of the original award, if any, immediately before the modification.

Illustrations 12–14 (paragraphs A149–A189) provide additional guidance on, and illustrate the accounting for, modifications of both vested and non-vested awards, including a modification that changes the classification of the related financial instruments from equity to liability or vice versa, and modifications of vesting conditions. Illustration 22 (paragraphs A225–A232) provides additional guidance on accounting for modifications of certain freestanding financial instruments that initially were subject to this Statement but subsequently became subject to other applicable GAAP.

Inducements

52. A **short-term inducement** shall be accounted for as a modification of the terms of only the awards of employees who accept the inducement. Other inducements are modifications of the terms of all awards subject to them and shall be accounted for as such.

Equity restructurings

53. Exchanges of share options or other equity instruments or changes to their terms in conjunction with an **equity restructuring** or a business combination are modifications for purposes of this Statement.

54. Except for a modification to add an antidilution provision that is not made in contemplation of an equity restructuring, accounting for a modification in conjunction with an equity restructuring requires a comparison of the fair value of the modified award with the fair value of the original award immediately before the modification in accordance with paragraph 51. If those amounts are the same, for instance, because the modification is designed to equalize the fair value of an award before and after an equity restructuring, no incremental compensation cost is recognized. Illustration 12(e) (paragraphs A156–A159) provides further guidance on applying the provisions of this paragraph.

Repurchases or cancellations of awards of equity instruments

55. The amount of cash or other assets transferred (or liabilities incurred) to repurchase an equity award shall be charged to equity, to the extent that the amount paid does not exceed the fair value of the equity instruments repurchased at the repurchase date. Any excess of the repurchase price over the fair value of the instruments repurchased shall be recognized as additional compensation cost. An entity that repurchases an award for which the requisite service has not been rendered has, in effect, modified the requisite service period to the period for which service already has been rendered, and thus the amount of compensation cost measured at the grant date but not yet recognized shall be recognized at the repurchase date.

Cancellation and replacement of awards of equity instruments

56. Cancellation of an award accompanied by the concurrent grant of (or offer to grant)[28] a **replacement award** or other valuable consideration shall be accounted for as a modification of the terms of the cancelled award. Therefore, incremental compensation cost shall be measured as the excess of the fair value of the replacement award or other valuable consideration over the fair value of the cancelled award at the cancellation date in accordance with paragraph 51. Thus, the total compensation cost measured at the date of a cancellation and replacement shall be the portion of the grant-date fair value of the original award for which the requisite service is expected to be rendered (or has already been rendered) at that date plus the incremental cost resulting from the cancellation and replacement.

57. A cancellation of an award that is not accompanied by the concurrent grant of (or offer to grant) a replacement award or other valuable consideration shall be accounted for as a repurchase for no consideration. Accordingly, any previously unrecognized compensation cost shall be recognized at the cancellation date.

Accounting for Tax Effects of Share-Based Compensation Awards

58. Income tax regulations specify allowable tax deductions for instruments issued under share-based

---

[28]The phrase *offer to grant* is intended to cover situations in which the service inception date precedes the grant date.

payment arrangements in determining an entity's income tax liability. For example, under U.S. tax law at the issuance date of this Statement, allowable tax deductions are generally measured as the intrinsic value of an instrument on a specified date. The time value component, if any, of the fair value of an instrument generally is not tax deductible. Therefore, tax deductions generally will arise in different amounts and in different periods from compensation cost recognized in financial statements.

59. The cumulative amount of compensation cost recognized for instruments classified as equity that ordinarily would result in a future tax deduction under existing tax law shall be considered to be a deductible temporary difference in applying FASB Statement No. 109, *Accounting for Income Taxes.* The deductible temporary difference shall be based on the compensation cost recognized for financial reporting purposes. The deferred tax benefit (or expense) that results from increases (or decreases) in that temporary difference, for example, an increase that results as additional service is rendered and the related cost is recognized or a decrease that results from forfeiture of an award, shall be recognized in the income statement.[29] Recognition of compensation cost for instruments that ordinarily do not result in tax deductions under existing tax law shall not be considered to result in a deductible temporary difference in applying Statement 109. A future event, such as an employee's disqualifying disposition of shares under U.S. tax law at the issuance date of this Statement, can give rise to a tax deduction for instruments that ordinarily do not result in a tax deduction. The tax effects of such an event shall be recognized only when it occurs.

60. The cumulative amount of compensation cost recognized for instruments classified as liabilities that ordinarily would result in a future tax deduction under existing tax law also shall be considered to be a deductible temporary difference. The deductible temporary difference shall be based on the compensation cost recognized for financial reporting purposes.

61. Statement 109 requires a deferred tax asset to be evaluated for future realization and to be reduced by a valuation allowance if, based on the weight of the available evidence, it is more likely than not that some portion or all of the deferred tax asset will not be realized.[30] Differences between (a) the deductible temporary difference computed pursuant to paragraph 59 of this Statement and (b) the tax deduction that would result based on the current fair value of the entity's shares shall not be considered in measuring the gross deferred tax asset or determining the need for a valuation allowance for a deferred tax asset recognized under this Statement.

62. If a deduction reported on a tax return for an award of equity instruments exceeds the cumulative compensation cost for those instruments recognized for financial reporting, any resulting realized tax benefit that exceeds the previously recognized deferred tax asset for those instruments (the excess tax benefit) shall be recognized as additional paid-in capital.[31] However, an excess of a realized tax benefit for an award over the deferred tax asset for that award shall be recognized in the income statement to the extent that the excess stems from a reason other than changes in the fair value of an entity's shares between the measurement date for accounting purposes and a later measurement date for tax purposes.

63. The amount deductible on the employer's tax return may be less than the cumulative compensation cost recognized for financial reporting purposes. The write-off of a deferred tax asset related to that deficiency, net of the related valuation allowance, if any, shall first be offset to the extent of any remaining additional paid-in capital from excess tax benefits from previous awards accounted for in accordance with this Statement or Statement 123. The remaining balance, if any, of the write-off of a deferred tax asset related to a tax deficiency shall be recognized in the income statement. An entity that continued to use Opinion 25's intrinsic value method as permitted by Statement 123 shall calculate the amount available for offset as the net amount of excess tax benefits that would have qualified as such had it instead adopted Statement 123 for recognition purposes pursuant to Statement 123's original effective date and transition method. In determining that amount, no distinction

---

[29]Compensation cost that is capitalized as part of the cost of an asset, such as inventory, shall be considered to be part of the tax basis of that asset for financial reporting purposes.

[30]Paragraph 21 of Statement 109 states, "Future realization of the tax benefit of an existing deductible temporary difference or carryforward ultimately depends on the existence of sufficient taxable income of the appropriate character (for example, ordinary income or capital gain) within the carryback, carryforward period available under the tax law." That paragraph goes on to describe the four sources of taxable income that may be available under the tax law to realize a tax benefit for deductible temporary differences and carryforwards.

[31]If only a portion of an award is exercised, determination of the excess tax benefits shall be based on the portion of the award that is exercised.

shall be made between excess tax benefits attributable to different types of equity awards, such as restricted shares or share options. An entity shall exclude from that amount both excess tax benefits from share-based payment arrangements that are outside the scope of this Statement, such as employee share ownership plans, and excess tax benefits that have not been realized pursuant to Statement 109, as noted in paragraph A94, footnote 82, of this Statement. Illustrations 4(a) (paragraphs A94–A96), 10 (paragraphs A132 and A133), 11(a) (paragraphs A135 and A136), and 14(a) (paragraphs A178–A180) of this Statement provide examples of accounting for the income tax effects of various awards.

Disclosures

64. An entity with one or more share-based payment arrangements shall disclose information that enables users of the financial statements to understand:

a. The nature and terms of such arrangements that existed during the period and the potential effects of those arrangements on shareholders
b. The effect of compensation cost arising from share-based payment arrangements on the income statement
c. The method of estimating the fair value of the goods or services received, or the fair value of the equity instruments granted (or offered to grant), during the period
d. The cash flow effects resulting from share-based payment arrangements.

Paragraphs A240 and A241 indicate the minimum information needed to achieve those objectives and illustrate how the disclosure requirements might be satisfied. In some circumstances, an entity may need to disclose information beyond that listed in paragraph A240 to achieve the disclosure objectives.

65. An entity that acquires goods or services other than employee services in share-based payment transactions shall provide disclosures similar to those required by paragraph 64 to the extent that those disclosures are important to an understanding of the effects of those transactions on the financial statements. In addition, an entity that has multiple share-based payment arrangements with employees shall disclose information separately for different types of awards under those arrangements to the extent that differences in the characteristics of the awards make separate disclosure important to an understanding of the entity's use of share-based compensation (paragraph A240).

Earnings per Share Implications

66. FASB Statement No. 128, *Earnings per Share,* requires that employee equity share options, nonvested shares, and similar equity instruments granted to employees be treated as potential common shares in computing diluted earnings per share. Diluted earnings per share shall be based on the actual number of options or shares granted and not yet forfeited, unless doing so would be antidilutive. If vesting in or the ability to exercise (or retain) an award is contingent on a performance or market condition, such as the level of future earnings, the shares or share options shall be treated as contingently issuable shares in accordance with paragraphs 30–35 of Statement 128. If equity share options or other equity instruments are outstanding for only part of a period, the shares issuable shall be weighted to reflect the portion of the period during which the equity instruments are outstanding.

67. Paragraphs 21–23 of Statement 128 provide guidance on applying the treasury stock method for equity instruments granted in share-based payment transactions in determining diluted earnings per share.

Amendments to Statement 95

68. Statement 95 is amended by adding the underlined wording as follows:

a. Paragraph 19, as amended by FASB Statements No. 117, *Financial Statements of Not-for-Profit Organizations,* and No. 149, *Amendment of Statement 133 on Derivative Instruments and Hedging Activities:*

Cash inflows from financing activities are:

a. Proceeds from issuing equity instruments
b. Proceeds from issuing bonds, mortgages, notes, and from other short- or long-term borrowing
c. Receipts from contributions and investment income that by donor stipulation are restricted for the purposes of acquiring, constructing, or improving property, plant, equipment, or other long-lived assets or establishing or increasing a permanent endowment or term endowment
d. Proceeds received[7a] from derivative instruments that include financing elements[7b] at inception

e. Cash retained as a result of the tax deductibility of increases in the value of equity instruments issued under share-based payment arrangements that are not included in the cost of goods or services that is recognizable for financial reporting purposes. For this purpose, excess tax benefits shall be determined on an individual award (or a portion thereof) basis.

b. Paragraph 23, as amended by FASB Statements No. 102, *Statement of Cash Flows— Exemption of Certain Enterprises and Classification of Cash Flows from Certain Securities Acquired for Resale,* and No. 145, *Rescission of FASB Statements No. 4, 44, and 64, Amendment of FASB Statement No. 13, and Technical Corrections:*

Cash outflows for operating activities are:

a. Cash payments to acquire materials for manufacture or goods[8d] for resale, including principal payments on accounts and both short- and long-term notes payable to suppliers for those materials or goods.

b. Cash payments to other suppliers and employees for other goods or services.

c. Cash payments to governments for taxes, duties, fines, and other fees or penalties and the cash that would have been paid for income taxes if increases in the value of equity instruments issued under share-based payment arrangements that are not included in the cost of goods or services recognizable for financial reporting purposes also had not been deductible in determining taxable income. (This is the same amount reported as a financing cash inflow pursuant to paragraph 19(e) of this Statement.)

d. Cash payments to lenders and other creditors for interest.

e. All other cash payments that do not stem from transactions defined as investing or financing activities, such as payments to settle lawsuits, cash contributions to charities, and cash refunds to customers.

c. Paragraph 27, as amended by Statement 117:

In reporting cash flows from operating activities, enterprises are encouraged to report major classes of gross cash receipts and gross cash payments and their arithmetic sum—the net cash flow from operating activities (the direct method). Enterprises that do so should, at a minimum, separately report the following classes of operating cash receipts and payments:[11]

a. Cash collected from customers, including lessees, licensees, and the like

b. Interest and dividends received[11a]

c. Other operating cash receipts, if any

d. Cash paid to employees and other suppliers of goods or services, including suppliers of insurance, advertising, and the like

e. Interest paid

f. Income taxes paid and, separately, the cash that would have been paid for income taxes if increases in the value of equity instruments issued under share-based payment arrangements that are not recognizable as a cost of goods or services for accounting purposes also had not been deductible in determining taxable income (paragraph 19(e))

g. Other operating cash payments, if any.

Enterprises are encouraged to provide further breakdowns of operating cash receipts and payments that they consider meaningful and feasible. For example, a retailer or manufacturer might decide to further divide cash paid to employees and suppliers (category (d) above) into payments for costs of inventory and payments for selling, general, and administrative expenses.

Effective Dates and Transition

69. This Statement is effective:

a. For public entities that do not file as **small business issuers**—as of the beginning of the first interim or annual reporting period that begins after June 15, 2005

b. For public entities that file as small business issuers—as of the beginning of the first interim or annual reporting period that begins after December 15, 2005

c. For nonpublic entities—as of the beginning of the first annual reporting period that begins after December 15, 2005.

The effective date for a nonpublic entity that becomes a public entity after June 15, 2005, and does not file as a small business issuer is the first interim or annual reporting period beginning after the entity becomes a public entity. If the newly public entity files as a small business issuer, the effective date is the first interim or annual reporting period beginning after December 15, 2005, for which the entity is a public entity.

70. This Statement applies to all awards granted after the required effective date. This Statement shall not be applied to awards granted in periods before the required effective date except to the extent that prior periods' awards are modified, repurchased, or cancelled after the required effective date and as required by paragraph 74. The cumulative effect of initially applying this Statement, if any, shall be recognized as of the required effective date (paragraphs 79–82).

71. As of the required effective date, all public entities and those nonpublic entities that used the fair-value-based method for either recognition or disclosure under Statement 123 shall apply the modified prospective application transition method (paragraphs 74 and 75). For periods before the required effective date, those entities may elect to apply the modified retrospective application transition method (paragraphs 76–78).

72. Nonpublic entities that used the minimum value method in Statement 123 for either recognition or pro forma disclosures are required to apply the prospective transition method (paragraph 83) as of the required effective date.

73. Early adoption of this Statement for interim or annual periods for which financial statements or interim reports have not been issued is encouraged.[32]

Modified Prospective Application

74. As of the required effective date, all public entities and those nonpublic entities that used the fair-value-based method for either recognition or disclosure under Statement 123, including such nonpublic entities that become public entities after June 15, 2005, shall adopt this Statement using a modified version of prospective application *(modified prospective application)*. Under modified prospective appli-

cation, this Statement applies to new awards and to awards modified, repurchased, or cancelled after the required effective date. Additionally, compensation cost for the portion of awards for which the requisite service has not been rendered that are outstanding as of the required effective date shall be recognized as the requisite service is rendered on or after the required effective date. The compensation cost for that portion of awards shall be based on the grant-date fair value of those awards as calculated for either recognition or pro forma disclosures under Statement 123. Changes to the grant-date fair value of equity awards granted before the required effective date of this Statement are precluded.[33] The compensation cost for those earlier awards shall be attributed to periods beginning on or after the required effective date of this Statement using the attribution method that was used under Statement 123, except that the method of recognizing forfeitures only as they occur shall not be continued (paragraph 80). Any unearned or deferred compensation (contra-equity accounts) related to those earlier awards shall be eliminated against the appropriate equity accounts.

75. An entity that does not choose modified retrospective application (paragraphs 76–78 of this Statement) shall apply the amendments to Statement 95 in paragraph 68 of this Statement only for the interim or annual periods for which this Statement is adopted.

Modified Retrospective Application

76. All public entities and those nonpublic entities that used the fair-value-based method for either recognition or disclosure under Statement 123, including such nonpublic entities that become public entities after June 15, 2005, may apply a modified version of retrospective application *(modified retrospective application)* to periods before the required effective date. Modified retrospective application may be applied either (a) to all prior years for which Statement 123 was effective[34] or (b) only to prior interim periods in the year of initial adoption if the required effective date of this Statement does not coincide with the beginning of the entity's fiscal year. An

---

[32]If an entity early adopts this Statement pursuant to paragraph 73, then the *required effective date* would be the first date in the initial period of adoption.

[33]The prohibition in paragraphs 74 and 76 of changes to the grant-date fair value of equity awards granted before the required effective date of this Statement does not apply if the entity needs to correct an error.

[34]A nonpublic entity shall apply this method to all prior years for which Statement 123's fair-value-based method was adopted for recognition or pro forma disclosures if that date is later than when Statement 123 was first effective.

entity that chooses to apply the modified retrospective method to all prior years for which Statement 123 was effective shall adjust financial statements for prior periods to give effect to the fair-value-based method of accounting for awards granted, modified, or settled in cash in fiscal years beginning after December 15, 1994, on a basis consistent with the pro forma disclosures required for those periods by Statement 123, as amended by FASB Statement No. 148, *Accounting for Stock-Based Compensation—Transition and Disclosure,*[35] and by paragraph 30 of APB Opinion No. 28, *Interim Financial Reporting.* Accordingly, compensation cost and the related tax effects will be recognized in those financial statements as though they had been accounted for under Statement 123.[36] Changes to amounts as originally measured on a pro forma basis are precluded.

77. If an entity applies the modified retrospective application method to all prior years for which Statement 123 was effective and does not present all of those years in comparative financial statements, the beginning balances of paid-in capital, deferred taxes, and retained earnings for the earliest year presented shall be adjusted to reflect the results of modified retrospective application to those prior years not presented. The effects of any such adjustments shall be disclosed in the year of adoption. If an entity applies the modified retrospective application method only to prior interim periods in the year of initial adoption, there would be no adjustment to the beginning balances of paid-in capital, deferred taxes, or retained earnings for the year of initial adoption.

78. The amendments to Statement 95 in paragraph 68 of this Statement shall be applied to the same periods for which the modified retrospective application method is applied.

Transition as of the Required Effective Date for both Modified Prospective and Modified Retrospective Transition Methods

79. Transition as of the required effective date for instruments that are liabilities under the provisions of this Statement shall be as follows:

a. For an instrument that had been classified as eq-

uity but is classified as a liability under this Statement, recognize a liability at its fair value (or portion thereof, if the requisite service has not been rendered). If (1) the fair value (or portion therof) of the liability is greater or less than (2) previously recognized compensation cost for the instrument, the liability shall be recognized first, by reducing equity (generally, paid-in capital) to the extent of such previously recognized cost and second, by recognizing the difference (that is, the difference between items (1) and (2)) in the income statement, net of any related tax effect, as the cumulative effect of a change in accounting principle.

b. For an outstanding instrument that previously was classified as a liability and measured at intrinsic value, recognize the effect of initially measuring the liability at its fair value, net of any related tax effect, as the cumulative effect of a change in accounting principle.[37]

80. As of the required effective date, an entity that had a policy of recognizing the effect of forfeitures only as they occurred shall estimate the number of outstanding instruments for which the requisite service is not expected to be rendered. Balance sheet amounts related to any compensation cost (excluding nonrefundable dividend payments), net of related tax effects, for those instruments previously recognized in income because of that policy for periods before the effective date of this Statement shall be eliminated and recognized in income as the cumulative effect of a change in accounting principle as of the required effective date.

81. Except as required by paragraph 80, no transition adjustment as of the required effective date shall be made for any deferred tax assets associated with outstanding equity instruments that continue to be accounted for as equity instruments under this Statement. For purposes of calculating the available excess tax benefits if deferred tax assets need to be written off in subsequent periods, an entity shall include as available for offset only the net excess tax benefits that would have qualified as such had the entity adopted Statement 123 for recognition purposes for all awards granted, modified, or settled in cash for fiscal years beginning after December 15, 1994. In

---

[35]For convenience, the remaining discussion in this Statement refers only to *Statement 123*. Those references should be understood as referring to Statement 123, as amended by Statement 148.

[36]This provision applies to all awards regardless of whether they were accounted for as fixed or variable under Opinion 25.

[37]If share-based compensation cost has been previously capitalized as part of another asset, an entity should consider whether the carrying amount of that asset should be adjusted to reflect amounts calculated pursuant to paragraphs 79(a) and 79(b).

determining that amount, an entity shall exclude excess tax benefits that have not been realized pursuant to Statement 109 (paragraph A94, footnote 82, of this Statement). An entity that previously has recognized deferred tax assets for excess tax benefits prior to their realization shall discontinue that practice prospectively and shall follow the guidance in this Statement and in Statement 109.

82. Outstanding equity instruments that are measured at intrinsic value under Statement 123 at the required effective date because it was not possible to reasonably estimate their grant-date fair value shall continue to be measured at intrinsic value until they are settled.

Nonpublic Entities That Used the Minimum Value Method in Statement 123

83. Nonpublic entities, including those that become public entities after June 15, 2005, that used the minimum value method of measuring equity share options and similar instruments for either recognition or pro forma disclosure purposes under Statement 123 shall apply this Statement prospectively to new awards and to awards modified, repurchased, or cancelled after the required effective date. Those entities shall continue to account for any portion of awards outstanding at the date of initial application using the accounting principles originally applied to those awards (either the minimum value method under Statement 123 or the provisions of Opinion 25 and its related interpretive guidance).

Required Disclosures in the Period This Statement Is Adopted

84. In the period that this Statement is adopted, an entity shall disclose the effect of the change from applying the original provisions of Statement 123[38] on income from continuing operations, income before income taxes, net income, cash flow from operations, cash flow from financing activities, and basic and diluted earnings per share. In addition, if awards under

share-based payment arrangements with employees are accounted for under the intrinsic value method of Opinion 25 for any reporting period for which an income statement is presented, all public entities shall continue to provide the tabular presentation of the following information that was required by paragraph 45 of Statement 123 for all those periods:

a. Net income and basic and diluted earnings per share as reported
b. The share-based employee compensation cost, net of related tax effects, included in net income as reported
c. The share-based employee compensation cost, net of related tax effects, that would have been included in net income if the fair-value-based method had been applied to all awards[39]
d. Pro forma net income as if the fair-value-based method had been applied to all awards
e. Pro forma basic and diluted earnings per share as if the fair-value-based method had been applied to all awards.

The required pro forma amounts shall reflect the difference in share-based employee compensation cost, if any, included in net income and the total cost measured by the fair-value-based method, as well as additional tax effects, if any, that would have been recognized in the income statement if the fair-value-based method had been applied to all awards. The required pro forma per-share amounts shall reflect the change in the denominator of the diluted earnings per share calculation as if the assumed proceeds under the treasury stock method, including measured but unrecognized compensation cost and any excess tax benefits credited to additional paid-in capital, were determined under the fair-value-based method.

85. A nonpublic entity that used the minimum value method for pro forma disclosure purposes under the original provisions of Statement 123 shall not continue to provide those pro forma disclosures for outstanding awards accounted for under the intrinsic value method of Opinion 25.

The provisions of this Statement need not be applied to immaterial items.

---

[38]The effect of the change for the period in which this Statement is adopted will differ depending on whether a public entity had previously adopted the fair-value-based method (or a nonpublic entity had adopted the minimum value method) of Statement 123 or had continued to use the intrinsic value method in Opinion 25.

[39]For paragraphs 84(c)–84(e), *all awards* refers to awards granted, modified, or settled in cash in fiscal periods beginning after December 15, 1994.

This Statement was adopted by the unanimous vote of the seven members of the Financial Accounting Standards Board:

Appendix A

IMPLEMENTATION GUIDANCE

CONTENTS

Appendix A

IMPLEMENTATION GUIDANCE

INTRODUCTION

A1. This appendix is an integral part of this Statement and provides implementation guidance that illustrates the fair-value-based method of accounting for share-based compensation arrangements with employees. Application of this Statement's provisions to actual situations will require the exercise of judgment; this appendix is intended to aid in making those judgments. Throughout this appendix, the phrase *fair value* is used to describe the measure resulting from the application of this Statement's fair-value-based method.[40]

FAIR VALUE MEASUREMENT OBJECTIVE AND ITS APPLICATION

A2. The measurement objective for equity instruments awarded to employees is to estimate the grant-date fair value of the equity instruments that the entity is obligated to issue when employees have rendered the requisite service and satisfied any other conditions necessary to earn the right to benefit from the instruments. That estimate is based on the share

---

[40]The implementation guidance in this Appendix also applies to nonpublic entities that use the calculated value method pursuant to paragraph 23.

price and other pertinent factors (including those enumerated in paragraph A18, if applicable) at the grant date and is not remeasured in subsequent periods under the fair-value-based method.

A3. A restriction[41] that continues in effect after the entity has issued instruments to employees, such as the inability to transfer vested equity share options to third parties or the inability to sell vested shares for a period of time, is considered in estimating the fair value of the instruments at the grant date.[42] For share options and similar instruments, the effect of non-transferability (and nonhedgeability, which has a similar effect) is taken into account by reflecting the effects of employees' expected exercise and post-vesting employment termination behavior in estimating fair value (referred to as an option's *expected term*).

A4. In contrast, a restriction that stems from the forfeitability of instruments to which employees have not yet earned the right, such as the inability either to exercise a nonvested equity share option or to sell nonvested shares is not reflected in the fair value of the instruments at the grant date.[43] Instead, those restrictions are taken into account by recognizing compensation cost only for awards for which employees render the requisite service.

A5. Reload features, and contingent features that require an employee to transfer equity shares earned, or realized gains from the sale of equity instruments earned, to the issuing entity for consideration that is less than fair value on the date of transfer (including no consideration), such as a clawback feature,[44] shall not be reflected in the grant-date fair value of an equity award. Those features are accounted for if and when a reload grant or contingent event occurs.

A6. The fair value measurement objective for liabilities incurred in a share-based payment transaction with employees is the same as for equity instruments awarded to employees. However, awards classified as liabilities are subsequently remeasured to their fair values (or a portion thereof until the requisite service has been rendered) at the end of each reporting period until the liability is settled.

Fair Value of Instruments Granted in a Share-Based Payment Transaction

A7. Fair value is defined in FASB Concepts Statement No. 7, *Using Cash Flow Information and Present Value in Accounting Measurements*, as follows:

> The amount at which that asset (or liability) could be bought (or incurred) or sold (or settled) in a current transaction between willing parties, that is, other than in a forced or liquidation sale. (Concepts Statement 7, Glossary of Terms)

That definition refers explicitly only to assets and liabilities, but the concept of *value in a current exchange* embodied in it applies equally to the equity instruments subject to this Statement. Observable market prices of identical or similar[45] equity or liability instruments in active markets are the best evidence of fair value and, if available, should be used as the basis for the measurement of equity and liability instruments awarded in a share-based payment transaction with employees. For example, awards to employees of a public entity of shares of its common stock, subject only to a service or performance condition for vesting (nonvested shares), should be measured based on the market price of otherwise identical (that is, identical except for the vesting condition) common stock at the grant date.

A8. If observable market prices of identical or similar equity or liability instruments of the entity are not available,[46] the fair value of equity and liability instruments awarded to employees shall be estimated

---

[41]Terms are defined in Appendix E, the glossary.

[42]For instance, if shares are traded in an active market, post-vesting restrictions may have little, if any, effect on the amount at which the shares being valued would be exchanged.

[43]Performance and service conditions are vesting conditions for purposes of this Statement. Market conditions are not vesting conditions for purposes of this Statement but market conditions may affect exercisability of an award. Market conditions are included in the estimate of the grant-date fair value of awards. Refer to paragraphs A52–A54.

[44]A clawback feature can take various forms but often functions as a noncompete mechanism: for example, an employee that terminates the employment relationship and begins to work for a competitor is required to transfer to the issuing entity (former employer) equity shares granted and earned in a share-based payment transaction.

[45]Determining whether an equity or liability instrument is similar is a matter of judgment, based on an analysis of the terms of the instrument and other relevant facts and circumstances.

[46]As of the issuance of this Statement, such market prices for equity share options and similar instruments granted to employees are generally not available; however, they may become so in the future.

by using a valuation technique that (a) is applied in a manner consistent with the fair value measurement objective and the other requirements of this Statement, (b) is based on established principles of financial economic theory[47] and generally applied in that field (paragraph A13), and (c) reflects all substantive characteristics of the instrument (except for those explicitly excluded by this Statement, such as vesting conditions and reload features). That is, the fair values of equity and liability instruments granted in a share-based payment transaction shall be estimated by applying a valuation technique that would be used in determining an amount at which instruments with the same characteristics (except for those explicitly excluded by this Statement) would be exchanged.

A9. An estimate of the amount at which instruments similar to employee share options and other instruments granted to employees would be exchanged would factor in expectations of the probability that the requisite service would be rendered and the instruments would vest (that is, that the performance or service conditions would be satisfied). However, as noted in paragraph A2, the measurement objective in this Statement is to estimate the fair value at the grant date of the equity instruments that the entity is obligated to issue when employees have rendered the requisite service and satisfied any other conditions necessary to earn the right to benefit from the instruments. Therefore, the estimated fair value of the instruments at grant date does not take into account the effect on fair value of vesting conditions and other restrictions that apply only during the requisite service period. Under the fair-value-based method required by this Statement, the effect of vesting conditions and other restrictions that apply only during the requisite service period is reflected by recognizing compensation cost only for instruments for which the requisite service is rendered.

Valuation Techniques

A10. In applying a valuation technique, the assumptions used should be consistent with the fair value measurement objective. That is, assumptions should reflect information that is (or would be) available to form the basis for an amount at which the instruments being valued would be exchanged. In estimating fair value, the assumptions used should not repre-

sent the biases of a particular party. Some of those assumptions will be based on or determined from external data. Other assumptions, such as the employees' expected exercise behavior, may be derived from the entity's own historical experience with share-based payment arrangements.

A11. The fair value of any equity or liability instrument depends on its substantive characteristics. Paragraph A18 lists the minimum set of substantive characteristics of instruments with option (or option-like) features that shall be considered in estimating those instruments' fair value. However, a share-based payment award could contain other characteristics, such as a market condition, that should be included in a fair value estimate. Judgment is required to identify an award's substantive characteristics and, as described in paragraphs A12–A17, to select a valuation technique that incorporates those characteristics.

A12. Valuation techniques used for employee share options and similar instruments estimate the fair value of those instruments at a single point in time (for example, at the grant date). The assumptions used in a fair value measurement are based on expectations at the time the measurement is made, and those expectations reflect the information that is available at the time of measurement. The fair value of those instruments will change over time as factors used in estimating their fair value subsequently change, for instance, as share prices fluctuate, risk-free interest rates change, or dividend streams are modified. Changes in the fair value of those instruments are a normal economic process to which any valuable resource is subject and do not indicate that the expectations on which previous fair value measurements were based were incorrect. The fair value of those instruments at a single point in time is not a forecast of what the estimated fair value of those instruments may be in the future.

Valuation Techniques for Share Options and Similar Instruments

A13. A **lattice model** (for example, a binomial model) and a **closed-form model** (for example, the Black-Scholes-Merton formula) are among the valuation techniques that meet the criteria required by this Statement for estimating the fair values of employee

[47]Established principles of financial economic theory represent fundamental propositions that form the basis of modern corporate finance (for example, the time value of money and risk-neutral valuation).

share options and similar instruments.[48] Those valuation techniques or models, sometimes referred to as *option-pricing models,* are based on established principles of financial economic theory. Those techniques are used by valuation professionals, dealers of derivative instruments, and others to estimate the fair values of options and similar instruments related to equity securities, currencies, interest rates, and commodities. Those techniques are used to establish trade prices for derivative instruments and to establish values in adjudications. As discussed in paragraphs A18–A42, both lattice models and closed-form models can be adjusted to account for the substantive characteristics of share options and similar instruments granted to employees.

A14. This Statement does not specify a preference for a particular valuation technique or model in estimating the fair values of employee share options and similar instruments. Rather, this Statement requires the use of a valuation technique or model that meets the measurement objective in paragraph 16 and the requirements in paragraph A8. The selection of an appropriate valuation technique or model will depend on the substantive characteristics of the instrument being valued.[49] For instance, the appropriate valuation technique or model selected to estimate the fair value of an instrument with a market condition must take into account the effect of that market condition. The designs of some techniques and models better reflect the substantive characteristics of a particular employee share option or similar instrument. Paragraphs A15–A17 discuss certain factors that an entity should consider in selecting a valuation technique or model for its employee share options or similar instruments.

A15. The Black-Scholes-Merton formula assumes that option exercises occur at the end of an option's contractual term, and that expected volatility, expected dividends, and risk-free interest rates are constant over the option's term. If used to estimate the fair value of instruments in the scope of this Statement, the Black-Scholes-Merton formula must be adjusted to take account of certain characteristics of employee share options and similar instruments that are not consistent with the model's assumptions (for

example, the ability to exercise before the end of the option's contractual term). Because of the nature of the formula, those adjustments take the form of weighted-average assumptions about those characteristics. In contrast, a lattice model can be designed to accommodate dynamic assumptions of expected volatility and dividends over the option's contractual term, and estimates of expected option exercise patterns during the option's contractual term, including the effect of **blackout periods.** Therefore, the design of a lattice model more fully reflects the substantive characteristics of a particular employee share option or similar instrument. Nevertheless, both a lattice model and the Black-Scholes-Merton formula, as well as other valuation techniques that meet the requirements in paragraph A8, can provide a fair value estimate that is consistent with the measurement objective and fair-value-based method of this Statement.

A16. Regardless of the valuation technique or model selected, an entity shall develop reasonable and supportable[50] estimates for each assumption used in the model, including the employee share option or similar instrument's expected term, taking into account both the contractual term of the option and the effects of employees' expected exercise and post-vesting employment termination behavior.

A17. An entity should change the valuation technique it uses to estimate fair value if it concludes that a different technique is likely to result in a better estimate of fair value (paragraph A23). For example, an entity that uses a closed-form model might conclude, when information becomes available, that a lattice model or another valuation technique would provide a fair value estimate that better achieves the fair value measurement objective and, therefore, change the valuation technique it uses.

SELECTING ASSUMPTIONS FOR USE IN AN OPTION-PRICING MODEL

A18. If an observable market price is not available for a share option or similar instrument with the same

---

[48]A Monte Carlo simulation technique is another type of valuation technique that satisfies the requirements in paragraph A8. Other valuation techniques not mentioned in this Statement also may satisfy the requirements in paragraph A8.

[49]Because an entity may grant different types of instruments, each with its own unique set of substantive characteristics, an entity may use a different valuation technique for each different type of instrument.

[50]The term *supportable* is used in its general sense: "capable of being maintained, confirmed, or made good; defensible" (*The Compact Oxford English Dictionary,* 2nd edition, 1998). An application is supportable if it is based on reasonable arguments that consider the substantive characteristics of the instruments being valued and other relevant facts and circumstances.

or similar terms and conditions, an entity shall estimate the fair value of that instrument using a valuation technique or model that meets the requirements in paragraph A8 and takes into account, at a minimum:

a. The exercise price of the option.
b. The expected term of the option, taking into account both the contractual term of the option and the effects of employees' expected exercise and post-vesting employment termination behavior. In a closed-form model, the expected term is an assumption used in (or input to) the model, while in a lattice model, the expected term is an output of the model (refer to paragraphs A26–A30, which provide further explanation of the expected term in the context of a lattice model).
c. The current price of the underlying share.
d. The expected volatility of the price of the underlying share for the expected term of the option.
e. The expected dividends on the underlying share for the expected term of the option (except as provided in paragraphs A36 and A37).
f. The risk-free interest rate(s) for the expected term of the option.[51,52]

A19. Paragraphs A20–A24 provide general guidance on estimating assumptions used in a valuation technique or model. Expanded guidance for specific assumptions, such as expected term, expected volatility, and expected dividends, is provided in paragraphs A25–A42.

A20. There is likely to be a range of reasonable estimates for expected volatility, dividends, and term of the option. If no amount within the range is more or less likely than any other amount, an average of the amounts in the range (the *expected value*) should be used. In a lattice model, the assumptions used are to be determined for a particular node (or multiple nodes during a particular time period) of the lattice and not over multiple periods, unless such application is supportable.

A21. Historical experience is generally the starting point for developing expectations about the future. Expectations based on historical experience should be modified to reflect ways in which currently available information indicates that the future is reasonably expected to differ from the past. The appropriate weight to place on historical experience is a matter of judgment, based on relevant facts and circumstances. For example, an entity with two distinctly different lines of business of approximately equal size may dispose of the one that was significantly less volatile and generated more cash than the other. In that situation, the entity might place relatively little weight on volatility, dividends, and perhaps employees' exercise and post-vesting employment termination behavior from the predisposition (or disposition) period in developing reasonable expectations about the future. In contrast, an entity that has not undergone such a restructuring might place heavier weight on historical experience. That entity might conclude, based on its analysis of information available at the time of measurement, that its historical experience provides a reasonable estimate of expected volatility, dividends, and employees' exercise and post-vesting employment termination behavior.[53]

A22. In certain circumstances, historical information may not be available. For example, an entity whose common stock has only recently become publicly traded may have little, if any, historical information on the volatility of its own shares. That entity might base expectations about future volatility on the average volatilities of similar entities for an appropriate period following their going public. A nonpublic entity will need to exercise judgment in selecting a method to estimate expected volatility and might do so by basing its expected volatility on the average volatilities of otherwise similar public entities. For purposes of identifying otherwise similar entities, an entity would likely consider characteristics such as industry, stage of life cycle, size, and financial leverage. Because of the effects of diversification that are

---

[51]The term *expected* in items (b), (d), (e), and (f) relates to expectations at the measurement date about the future evolution of the factor that is used as an assumption in a valuation model. The term is not necessarily used in the same sense as in the term *expected future cash flows* that appears elsewhere in FASB pronouncements.

[52]Items (d), (e), and (f) include the phrase *for the expected term of the option*. That phrase applies to both closed-form models and lattice models (as well as all other valuation techniques); however, if an entity uses a lattice model (or other similar valuation technique, for instance, a Monte Carlo simulation technique) that has been modified to take into account an option's contractual term and employees' expected exercise and post-vesting employment termination behavior, then items (d), (e), and (f) apply to the contractual term of the option.

[53]This paragraph is not intended to suggest either that historical volatility is the only indicator of expected volatility or that an entity must identify a specific event in order to place less weight on historical experience. Expected volatility is an expectation of volatility over the expected term of an employee share option or similar instrument; that expectation should consider all relevant factors in paragraph A32, including possible mean reversion. Paragraphs A31–A34 provide further guidance on estimating expected volatility.

present in an industry sector index, the volatility of an index should not be substituted for the average of volatilities of otherwise similar entities in a fair value measurement.

Consistent Use of Valuation Techniques and Methods for Selecting Assumptions

A23. Assumptions used to estimate the fair value of equity and liability instruments granted to employees should be determined in a consistent manner from period to period. For example, an entity might use the closing share price or the share price at another specified time as the "current" share price on the grant date in estimating fair value, but whichever method is selected, it should be used consistently. The valuation technique an entity selects to estimate fair value for a particular type of instrument also should be used consistently and should not be changed unless a different valuation technique is expected to produce a better estimate of fair value. A change in either the valuation technique or the method of determining appropriate assumptions used in a valuation technique is a change in accounting estimate for purposes of applying FASB Statement No. 154, *Accounting Changes and Error Corrections,* and should be applied prospectively to new awards.

A24. Not all of the general guidance provided in paragraphs A2–A23 is repeated in the following discussion of factors to be considered in selecting specific assumptions. However, the general guidance is intended to apply to each individual assumption.

Risk-Free Interest Rate(s) for the Expected Term of the Option

A25. Option-pricing models call for the risk-free interest rate as an assumption to take into account, among other things, the time value of money. A U.S. entity issuing an option on its own shares must use as the risk-free interest rates the implied yields currently available from the U.S. Treasury zero-coupon yield curve over the contractual term of the option if the entity is using a lattice model incorporating the option's contractual term. If the entity is using a closed-form model, the risk-free interest rate is the implied yield currently available on U.S. Treasury zero-coupon issues with a remaining term equal to the expected term used as the assumption in the model. For entities based in jurisdictions outside the United States, the risk-free interest rate is the implied yield currently available on zero-coupon government issues denominated in the currency of the market in

which the share (or underlying share), which is the basis for the instrument awarded, primarily trades. It may be necessary to use an appropriate substitute if no such government issues exist or if circumstances indicate that the implied yield on zero-coupon government issues is not representative of a risk-free interest rate.

Expected Term of Employee Share Options and Similar Instruments

A26. The fair value of a traded (or transferable) share option is based on its contractual term because rarely is it economically advantageous to exercise, rather than sell, a transferable share option before the end of its contractual term. Employee share options generally differ from transferable share options in that employees cannot sell (or hedge) their share options—they can only exercise them; because of this, employees generally exercise their options before the end of the options' contractual term. Thus, the inability to sell or hedge an employee share option effectively reduces the option's value because exercise prior to the option's expiration terminates its remaining life and thus its remaining time value. In addition, some employee share options contain prohibitions on exercise during blackout periods. To reflect the effect of those restrictions (which may lead to exercise prior to the end of the option's contractual term) on employee options relative to transferable options, this Statement requires that the fair value of an employee share option or similar instrument be based on its expected term, rather than its contractual term (paragraphs A3 and A18).

A27. The expected term of an employee share option or similar instrument is the period of time for which the instrument is expected to be outstanding (that is, the period of time from the service inception date to the date of expected exercise or other expected settlement). The expected term is an assumption in a closed-form model. However, if an entity uses a lattice model that has been modified to take into account an option's contractual term and employees' expected exercise and post-vesting employment termination behavior, the expected term is estimated based on the resulting output of the lattice. For example, an entity's experience might indicate that option holders tend to exercise their options when the share price reaches 200 percent of the exercise price. If so, that entity might use a lattice model that assumes exercise of the option at each node along each share price path in a lattice at which the early exercise expectation is met, provided that the option is vested and exercisable at that point. Moreover, such a model would assume exercise at the end of the contractual term on price paths along which the exercise expectation is not met but the options are in-the-money[54] at the end of the contractual term. That method recognizes that employees' exercise behavior is correlated with the price of the underlying share. Employees' expected post-vesting employment termination behavior also would be factored in. Expected term, which is a required disclosure (paragraph A240), then could be estimated based on the output of the resulting lattice.[55]

A28. Other factors that may affect expectations about employees' exercise and post-vesting employment termination behavior include the following:

a. The vesting period of the award. An option's expected term must at least include the vesting period.[56]
b. Employees' historical exercise and post-vesting employment termination behavior for similar grants.
c. Expected volatility of the price of the underlying share.[57]
d. Blackout periods and other coexisting arrangements such as agreements that allow for exercise to automatically occur during blackout periods if certain conditions are satisfied.
e. Employees' ages, lengths of service, and home jurisdictions (that is, domestic or foreign).

A29. If sufficient information about employees' expected exercise and post-vesting employment termination behavior is available, a method like the one described in paragraph A27 might be used because that method reflects more information about the instrument being valued (paragraph A15). However, expected term might be estimated in some other manner, taking into account whatever relevant and supportable information is available, including industry averages and other pertinent evidence such as published academic research.

A30. Option value increases at a decreasing rate as the term lengthens (for most, if not all, options). For example, a two-year option is worth less than twice as much as a one-year option, other things equal. Accordingly, estimating the fair value of an option based on a single expected term that effectively averages the differing exercise and post-vesting employment termination behaviors of identifiable groups of employees will potentially misstate the value of the entire award. Aggregating individual awards into relatively homogenous groups with respect to exercise and post-vesting employment termination behaviors and estimating the fair value of the options granted to each group separately reduces such potential misstatement. An entity shall aggregate individual awards into relatively homogenous groups with respect to exercise and post-vesting employment termination behaviors regardless of the valuation technique or model used to estimate the fair value. For example, the historical experience of an employer that grants options broadly to all levels of employees might indicate that hourly employees tend to exercise for a smaller percentage gain than do salaried employees.

Expected Volatility

A31. Volatility is a measure of the amount by which a financial variable, such as share price, has fluctuated (historical volatility) or is expected to fluctuate (expected volatility) during a period. Volatility is defined more fully in Appendix E. Option-pricing models require expected volatility as an assumption because an option's value is dependent on potential share returns over the option's term. The higher the volatility, the more the returns on the shares can be expected to vary—up or down. Because an option's value is unaffected by expected negative returns on the shares, other things equal, an option on a share with higher volatility is worth more than an option on a share with lower volatility. This Statement does not specify a method of estimating expected volatility; rather, paragraph A32 provides a list of factors that should be considered in estimating expected volatility. An entity's estimate of expected volatility should be reasonable and supportable.

---

[54]The terms *at-the-money, in-the-money,* and *out-of-the-money* are used to describe share options whose exercise price is equal to, less than, or greater than the market price of the underlying share, respectively.

[55]An example of an acceptable method for purposes of financial statement disclosures of estimating the expected term based on the results of a lattice model is to use the lattice model's estimated fair value of a share option as an input to a closed-form model, and then to solve the closed-form model for the expected term. Other methods also are available to estimate expected term.

[56]Under some share option arrangements, an option holder may exercise an option prior to vesting (usually to obtain a specific tax treatment); however, such arrangements generally require that any shares received upon exercise be returned to the entity (with or without a return of the exercise price to the holder) if the vesting conditions are not satisfied. Such an exercise is not substantive for accounting purposes.

[57]An entity also might consider whether the evolution of the share price affects an employee's exercise behavior (for example, an employee may be more likely to exercise a share option shortly after it becomes in-the-money if the option had been out-of-the-money for a long period of time).

A32. Factors to consider in estimating expected volatility include:

a. Volatility of the share price, including changes in that volatility and possible mean reversion[58] of that volatility, over the most recent period that is generally commensurate with (1) the contractual term of the option if a lattice model is being used to estimate fair value or (2) the expected term of the option if a closed-form model is being used.[59] For example, in computing historical volatility, an entity might disregard an identifiable period of time in which its share price was extraordinarily volatile because of a failed takeover bid if a similar event is not expected to recur during the expected or contractual term. If an entity's share price was extremely volatile for an identifiable period of time, for instance, due to a general market decline, that entity might place less weight on its volatility during that period of time because of possible mean reversion.

b. The implied volatility of the share price determined from the market prices of traded options or other traded financial instruments such as outstanding convertible debt, if any.

c. For public companies, the length of time an entity's shares have been publicly traded. If that period is shorter than the expected or contractual term of the option, the term structure of volatility for the longest period for which trading activity is available should be more relevant. A newly public entity also might consider the expected volatility of similar entities.[60] A nonpublic entity might base its expected volatility on the expected volatilities of entities that are similar except for having publicly traded securities.

d. Appropriate and regular intervals for price observations. If an entity considers historical volatility in estimating expected volatility, it should use intervals that are appropriate based on the facts and circumstances and that provide the basis for a reasonable fair value estimate. For example, a publicly traded entity would likely use daily price observations, while a nonpublic entity with shares that occasionally change hands at negotiated prices might use monthly price observations.

e. Corporate and capital structure. An entity's corporate structure may affect expected volatility (paragraph A21). An entity's capital structure also may affect expected volatility; for example, highly leveraged entities tend to have higher volatilities.

A33. A closed-form model, such as the Black-Scholes-Merton formula, cannot incorporate a range of expected volatilities over the option's expected term (paragraph A15). Lattice models can incorporate a term structure of expected volatility; that is, a range of expected volatilities can be incorporated into the lattice over an option's contractual term. Determining how to incorporate a range of expected volatilities into a lattice model to provide a reasonable fair value estimate is a matter of judgment and should be based on a careful consideration of the factors listed in paragraph A32 as well as other relevant factors that are consistent with the fair value measurement objective of this Statement.

A34. An entity should establish a process for estimating expected volatility and apply that process consistently from period to period (paragraph A23). That process (a) should comprehend an identification of information available to the entity and applicable factors such as those described in paragraph A32 and (b) should include a procedure for evaluating and weighting that information. The process developed by an entity will be determined by the information available to it and its assessment of how that information would be used to estimate fair value. For example, consistent with paragraph A21, an entity's starting point in estimating expected volatility might be its historical volatility. That entity also would consider the extent to which currently available information indicates that future volatility will differ from the historical volatility. An example of such information is implied volatility (from traded options or other instruments).

Expected Dividends

A35. Option-pricing models generally call for expected dividend yield as an assumption. However, the models may be modified to use an expected dividend amount rather than a yield. An entity may use either its expected yield or its expected payments. Additionally, an entity's historical pattern of dividend increases (or decreases) should be considered. For

---

[58]Mean reversion refers to the tendency of a financial variable, such as volatility, to revert to some long-run average level. Statistical models have been developed that take into account the mean-reverting tendency of volatility.

[59]An entity might evaluate changes in volatility and mean reversion over that period by dividing the contractual or expected term into regular intervals and evaluating evolution of volatility through those intervals.

[60]In evaluating similarity, an entity would likely consider factors such as industry, stage of life cycle, size, and financial leverage.

example, if an entity has historically increased dividends by approximately 3 percent per year, its estimated share option value should not be based on a fixed dividend amount throughout the share option's expected term. As with other assumptions in an option-pricing model, an entity should use the expected dividends that would likely be reflected in an amount at which the option would be exchanged (paragraph A10).

Dividend-Protected Awards

A36. Expected dividends are taken into account in using an option-pricing model to estimate the fair value of a share option because dividends paid on the underlying shares reduce the fair value of those shares and option holders generally are not entitled to receive those dividends. However, an award of share options may be structured to protect option holders from that effect by providing them with some form of dividend rights. Such *dividend protection* may take a variety of forms and shall be appropriately reflected in estimating the fair value of a share option. For example, if a dividend paid on the underlying shares is applied to reduce the exercise price of the option, the effect of the dividend protection is appropriately reflected by using an expected dividend assumption of zero.

A37. In certain situations, employees may receive the dividends paid on the underlying equity shares while the option is outstanding. Dividends or dividend equivalents paid to employees on the portion of an award of equity shares or other equity instruments that vests shall be charged to retained earnings. If employees are not required to return the dividends or dividend equivalents received if they forfeit their awards, dividends or dividend equivalents paid on instruments that do not vest shall be recognized as additional compensation cost.[61]

Other Considerations

Dilution

A38. Traded options ordinarily are written by parties other than the entity that issues the underlying shares, and when exercised result in an exchange of already outstanding shares between those parties. In contrast, exercise of employee share options results in the issuance of new shares by the entity that wrote the option

(the employer), which increases the number of shares outstanding. That dilution might reduce the fair value of the underlying shares, which in turn might reduce the benefit realized from option exercise.

A39. If the market for an entity's shares is reasonably efficient, the effect of potential dilution from the exercise of employee share options will be reflected in the market price of the underlying shares, and no adjustment for potential dilution usually is needed in estimating the fair value of the employee share options. For a public entity, an exception might be a large grant of options that the market is not expecting, and also does not believe will result in commensurate benefit to the entity. For a nonpublic entity, on the other hand, potential dilution may not be fully reflected in the share price if sufficient information about the frequency and size of the entity's grants of equity share options is not available for third parties who may exchange the entity's shares to anticipate the dilutive effect.

A40. An entity should consider whether the potential dilutive effect of an award of share options needs to be reflected in estimating the fair value of its options at the grant date. For public entities, the Board expects that situations in which such a separate adjustment is needed will be rare.

Credit Risk

A41. An entity may need to consider the effect of its credit risk on the estimated fair value of liability awards that contain cash settlement features because potential cash payoffs from the awards are not independent of the entity's risk of default. Any credit-risk adjustment to the estimated fair value of awards with cash payoffs that increase with increases in the price of the underlying share is expected to be de minimis because increases in an entity's share price generally are positively associated with its ability to liquidate its liabilities. However, a credit-risk adjustment to the estimated fair value of awards with cash payoffs that increase with decreases in the price of the entity's shares may be necessary because decreases in an entity's share price generally are negatively associated with an entity's ability to liquidate its liabilities.

Certain Contingent Features

A42. Contingent features that might cause an employee to return to the entity either equity shares

---

[61]The estimate of compensation cost for dividends or dividend equivalents paid on instruments that are not expected to vest shall be consistent with an entity's estimates of forfeitures (paragraphs 43–45).

earned or realized gains from the sale of equity instruments earned as a result of share-based payment arrangements, such as a clawback feature (refer to paragraph A5, footnote 44), shall not be reflected in estimating the grant-date fair value of an equity instrument. Instead, the effect of such a contingent feature shall be accounted for if and when the contingent event occurs. For instance, a share-based payment arrangement may stipulate the return of vested equity shares to the issuing entity for no consideration if the employee terminates the employment relationship to work for a competitor. The effect of that provision on the grant-date fair value of the equity shares shall not be considered. If the issuing entity subsequently receives those shares (or their equivalent value in cash or other assets) as a result of that provision, a credit shall be recognized in the income statement upon the receipt of the shares. That credit is limited to the lesser of the recognized compensation cost associated with the share-based payment arrangement that contains the contingent feature and the fair value of the consideration received.[62] Illustration 15 (paragraphs A190 and A191) provides an example of the accounting for an award that contains a clawback feature.

CALCULATED VALUE METHOD FOR CERTAIN NONPUBLIC ENTITIES

A43. Nonpublic entities may have sufficient information available on which to base a reasonable and supportable estimate of the expected volatility of their share prices. For example, a nonpublic entity that has an internal market for its shares, has private transactions in its shares, or issues new equity or convertible debt instruments may be able to consider the historical volatility, or implied volatility, of its share price in estimating expected volatility. Alternatively, a nonpublic entity that can identify similar public entities[63] for which share or option price information is available may be able to consider the historical, expected, or implied volatility of those entities' share prices in estimating expected volatility.

A44. This Statement requires all entities to use the fair-value-based method to account for share-based payment arrangements that are classified as equity instruments. However, if it is not practicable for a nonpublic entity to estimate the expected volatility of its share price, paragraph 23 of this Statement requires it to use the calculated value method.[64]

A45. For purposes of this Statement, it is not practicable for a nonpublic entity to estimate the expected volatility of its share price if it is unable to obtain sufficient historical information about past volatility, or other information such as that noted in paragraph A43, on which to base a reasonable and supportable estimate of expected volatility at the grant date of the award without undue cost and effort. In that situation, this Statement requires a nonpublic entity to estimate a value for its equity share options and similar instruments by substituting the historical volatility of an appropriate industry sector index for the expected volatility of its share price as an assumption in its valuation model. All other inputs to a nonpublic entity's valuation model should be determined in accordance with the guidance in paragraphs A2–A42.

A46. There are many different indices available to consider in selecting an appropriate industry sector index.[65] An appropriate industry sector index is one that is representative of the industry sector in which the nonpublic entity operates and that also reflects, if possible, the size of the entity. If a nonpublic entity operates in a variety of different industry sectors, then it might select a number of different industry sector indices and weight them according to the nature of its operations; alternatively, it might select an index for the industry sector that is most representative of its operations. If a nonpublic entity operates in an industry sector in which no public entities operate, then it should select an index for the industry sector that is most closely related to the nature of its operations. However, in no circumstances shall a nonpublic entity use a broad-based market index like the S&P 500, Russell 3000®, or Dow Jones

---

[62]The event is recognized in the income statement because the resulting transaction takes place with an employee (or former employee) as a result of the current (or prior) employment relationship rather than as a result of the employee's role as an equity owner.

[63]A nonpublic entity may have identified similar public entities that it uses to estimate the fair value of its shares or to benchmark various aspects of its performance (paragraph A22).

[64]It may not be possible for a nonpublic entity to reasonably estimate the fair value of its equity share options and similar instruments at the date they are granted because the complexity of the award's terms prevents it from doing so. In that case, paragraphs 24 and 25 of this Statement require that the nonpublic entity account for its equity instruments at their intrinsic value, remeasured at each reporting date through the date of exercise or other settlement.

[65]For example, Dow Jones Indexes maintain a global series of stock market indices with industry sector splits available for many countries, including the United States. The historical values of those indices are easily obtainable from its website.

Wilshire 5000 because those indices are sufficiently diversified as to be not representative of the industry sector, or sectors, in which the nonpublic entity operates.

A47. A nonpublic entity shall use the selected index consistently in applying the calculated value method (a) for all of its equity share options or similar instruments and (b) in each accounting period, unless the nature of the entity's operations changes such that another industry sector index is more appropriate.

A48. The calculation of the historical volatility of an appropriate industry sector index should be made using the daily historical closing values[66] of the index selected for the period of time prior to the grant date (or service inception date) of the equity share option or similar instrument that is equal in length to the expected term of the equity share option or similar instrument. If historical closing values of the index selected are not available for the entire expected term, then a nonpublic entity shall use the closing values for the longest period of time available. The method used shall be consistently applied (paragraph A23). Illustration 11(b) (paragraphs A137–A142) provides an example of accounting for an equity share option award granted by a nonpublic entity that uses the calculated value method.

ILLUSTRATIVE COMPUTATIONS AND OTHER GUIDANCE

Market, Performance, and Service Conditions

Market, Performance, and Service Conditions That Affect Vesting and Exercisability

A49. An employee's share-based payment award becomes vested at the date that the employee's right to receive or retain equity shares, other equity instruments, or assets under the award is no longer contingent on satisfaction of either a performance condition or a service condition. This Statement distinguishes among market conditions, performance conditions, and service conditions that affect the vesting or exercisability of an award[67] (paragraph 19). Other conditions affecting vesting, exercisability, exercise price,

and other pertinent factors in measuring fair value that do not meet the definitions of a market condition, performance condition, or service condition are discussed in paragraph A53.

A50. Analysis of the market, performance, or service conditions (or any combination thereof) that are explicit or implicit in the terms of an award is required to determine the requisite service period over which compensation cost is recognized and whether recognized compensation cost may be reversed if an award fails to vest or become exercisable (paragraphs 47 and 48). If exercisability or the ability to retain the award, for example, an award of equity shares may contain a market condition that affects the employee's ability to retain those shares is based solely on one or more market conditions, compensation cost for that award is recognized if the employee renders the requisite service, even if the market condition is not satisfied.[68] If exercisability (or the ability to retain the award) is based solely on one or more market conditions, compensation cost for that award is reversed if the employee does not render the requisite service, unless the market condition is satisfied prior to the end of the requisite service period, in which case any unrecognized compensation cost would be recognized at the time the market condition is satisfied. If vesting is based solely on one or more performance or service conditions, any previously recognized compensation cost is reversed if the award does not vest (that is, the requisite service is not rendered). Illustrations 4 and 5 (paragraphs A86–A110) are examples of awards in which vesting is based solely on performance or service conditions.

A51. Vesting or exercisability may be conditional on satisfying two or more types of conditions (for example, vesting and exercisability occur upon satisfying both a market *and* a performance or service condition). Vesting also may be conditional on satisfying one of two or more types of conditions (for example, vesting and exercisability occur upon satisfying either a market condition *or* a performance or service condition). Regardless of the nature and number of conditions that must be satisfied, the existence of a market condition requires recognition of compensation cost if the requisite service is rendered, even if

---

[66]If daily values are not readily available, then an entity shall use the most frequent observations available of the historical closing values of the selected index.

[67]Exercisability is used for market conditions in the same context as vesting is used for performance and service conditions.

[68]An award containing one or more market conditions may have an explicit, implicit, or derived service period (refer to Appendix E). Paragraphs A59–A74 provide guidance on explicit, implicit, and derived service periods.

the market condition is never satisfied. Even if only one of two or more conditions must be satisfied and a market condition is present in the terms of the award, then compensation cost is recognized if the requisite service is rendered, regardless of whether the market, performance, or service condition is satisfied (paragraphs A72–A74 provide an example of such an award).

Market, Performance, and Service Conditions That Affect Factors Other Than Vesting and Exercisability

A52. Market, performance, and service conditions may affect an award's exercise price, contractual term, quantity, conversion ratio, or other pertinent factors that are relevant in measuring an award's fair value. For instance, an award's quantity may double, or an award's contractual term may be extended, if a company-wide revenue target is achieved. Market conditions that affect an award's fair value (including exercisability) are included in the estimate of grant-date fair value (paragraph 49). Performance or service conditions that only affect vesting are excluded from the estimate of grant-date fair value, but all other performance or service conditions that affect an award's fair value are included in the estimate of grant-date fair value (paragraph 49). Illustra-

tions 5(b) (paragraphs A109 and A110), 6 (paragraphs A111–A113), and 8 (paragraphs A121–A124) provide further guidance on how performance conditions are considered in the estimate of grant-date fair value.

A53. An award may be indexed to a factor in addition to the entity's share price. If that factor is not a market, performance, or service condition, that award shall be classified as a liability for purposes of this Statement (paragraph 33). An example would be an award of options whose exercise price is indexed to the market price of a commodity, such as gold. Another example would be a share award that will vest based on the appreciation in the price of a commodity such as gold; that award is indexed to both the value of that commodity and the issuing entity's shares. If an award is so indexed, the relevant factors should be included in the fair value estimate of the award. Such an award would be classified as a liability even if the entity granting the share-based payment instrument is a producer of the commodity whose price changes are part or all of the conditions that affect an award's vesting conditions or fair value.

A54. The following flowchart provides guidance on determining how to account for an award based on the existence of market, performance, or service conditions (or any combination thereof).

Accounting for Awards with Market, Performance, or Service Conditions

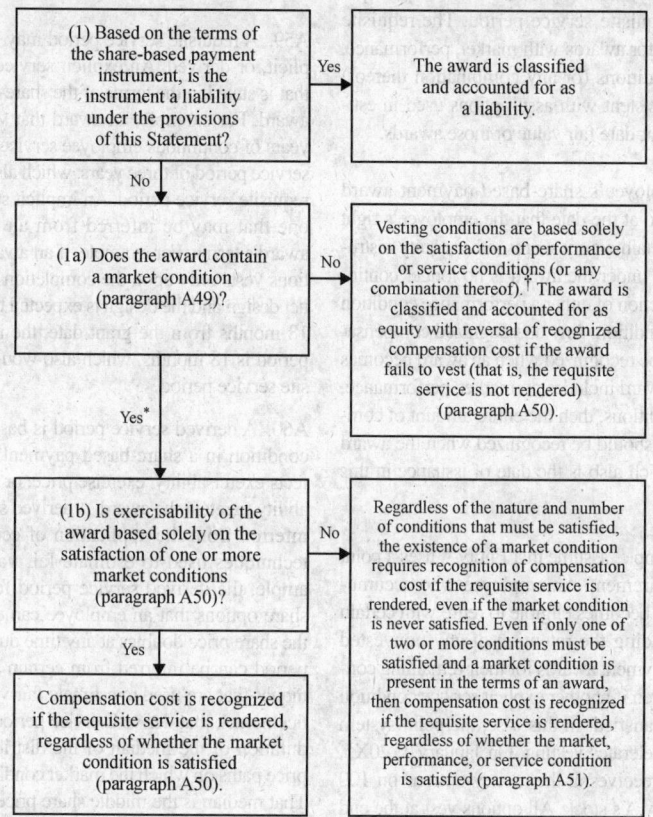

*The award should be classified and accounted for as equity. Market conditions are included in the grant-date fair value estimate of the award.

†Performance and service conditions that affect vesting are not included in estimating the grant-date fair value of the award. Performance and service conditions that affect the exercise price, contractual term, conversion ratio, or other pertinent factors affecting the fair value of an award are included in estimating the grant-date fair value of the award.

Estimating the Requisite Service Period of Awards with Market, Performance, and Service Conditions

A55. Paragraph 39 of this Statement requires that compensation cost be recognized over the requisite service period. The requisite service period for an award that has only a service condition is presumed to be the vesting period, unless there is clear evidence to the contrary. The requisite service period should be estimated based on an analysis of the terms of the award and other relevant facts and circumstances, including co-existing employment agreements and an entity's past practices; that estimate should ignore nonsubstantive vesting conditions. For example, the grant of a deep out-of-the-money share option award without an explicit service condition will have a derived service period.[69] If a market, performance, or

---

[69]Likewise, if an award with an explicit service condition that was at-the-money when granted is subsequently modified to accelerate vesting at a time when the award is deep out-of-the-money, that modification is not substantive because the explicit service condition is replaced by a derived service condition.

service condition requires future service for vesting (or exercisability), an entity cannot define a prior period as the requisite service period. The requisite service period for awards with market, performance, or service conditions (or any combination thereof) should be consistent with assumptions used in estimating the grant-date fair value of those awards.

A56. An employee's share-based payment award becomes vested at the date that the employee's right to receive or retain equity shares, other equity instruments, or cash under the award is no longer contingent on satisfaction of either a performance condition or a service condition. Any unrecognized compensation cost shall be recognized when an award becomes vested. If an award includes no market, performance, or service conditions, then the entire amount of compensation cost should be recognized when the award is granted (which also is the date of issuance in this case).

A57. For example, assume that Entity A uses a point system for retirement. An employee who accumulates 60 points becomes eligible to retire with certain benefits, including the retention of any nonvested share-based payment awards for their remaining contractual life, even if another explicit service condition has not been satisfied. In this case, the point system effectively accelerates vesting. On January 1, 20X5, an employee receives at-the-money options on 100 shares of Entity A's stock. All options vest at the end of 3 years of service and have a 10-year contractual term. At the grant date, the employee has 60 points and, therefore, is eligible to retire at any time.

A58. Because the employee is eligible to retire at the grant date, the award's explicit service condition is nonsubstantive. Consequently, Entity A has granted an award that does not contain a performance or service condition for vesting, that is, the award is effectively vested, and thus, the award's entire fair value should be recognized as compensation cost on the grant date. All of the terms of a share-based payment award and other relevant facts and circumstances must be analyzed when determining the requisite service period.

Explicit, Implicit, and Derived Requisite Service Periods

A59. A requisite service period may be explicit, implicit, or derived. An explicit service period is one that is stated in the terms of the share-based payment award. For example, an award that vests after three years of continuous employee service has an explicit service period of three years, which also would be the requisite service period. An implicit service period is one that may be inferred from an analysis of an award's terms. For example, if an award of share options vests only upon the completion of a new product design and the design is expected to be completed 18 months from the grant date, the implicit service period is 18 months, which also would be the requisite service period.

A60. A derived service period is based on a market condition in a share-based payment award that affects exercisability, exercise price, or the employee's ability to retain the award. A derived service period is inferred from the application of certain valuation techniques used to estimate fair value.[70] For example, the derived service period for an award of share options that an employee can exercise only if the share price doubles at any time during a five-year period can be inferred from certain valuation techniques that are used to estimate fair value.[71] In a lattice model, that derived service period represents the duration of the median of the distribution of share price paths on which the market condition is satisfied. That median is the middle share price path (the midpoint of the distribution of paths) on which the market condition is satisfied. The duration is the period of time from the service inception date to the expected date of market condition satisfaction (as inferred from the valuation technique). For example, if the derived service period is three years, the requisite service period is three years and all compensation cost would be recognized over that period, unless the market condition is satisfied at an earlier date, in which case any unrecognized compensation cost would be recognized immediately upon its satisfaction. If the requisite service is not rendered, all previously recognized compensation cost would be reversed. If the requisite service is rendered, the recognized compensation is not reversed even if the market condition is never satisfied.

---

[70]An entity that uses a closed-form model to estimate the grant-date fair value of an award with a market condition may need to use another valuation technique to estimate the derived service period.

[71]This example, and others noted in Appendix A, implicitly assume that the rights conveyed by the instrument to the holder are dependent on the holder's being an employee of the entity. That is, if the employment relationship is terminated, the award lapses or is forfeited shortly thereafter.

A61. An award with a combination of market, performance, or service conditions may contain multiple explicit, implicit, or derived service periods. For such an award, the estimate of the requisite service period shall be based on an analysis of (a) all vesting and exercisability conditions, (b) all explicit, implicit, and derived service periods, and (c) the probability that performance or service conditions will be satisfied. Thus, if vesting (or exercisability) of an award is based on satisfying both a market condition *and* a performance or service condition and it is probable that the performance or service condition will be satisfied, the initial estimate of the requisite service period generally is the longest of the explicit, implicit, or derived service periods. If vesting (or exercisability) of an award is based on satisfying either a market condition *or* a performance or service condition and it is probable that the performance or service condition will be satisfied, the initial estimate of the requisite service period generally is the shortest of the explicit, implicit, or derived service periods.

A62. For example, a share option might specify that vesting occurs after three years of continuous employee service *or* when the employee completes a specified project. The employer estimates that it is probable[72] that the project will be completed within 18 months. The employer also believes it is probable that the service condition will be satisfied. Thus, that award contains an explicit service period of 3 years related to the service condition and an implicit service period of 18 months related to the performance condition. Because it is considered probable that both the performance condition and the service condition will be achieved, the requisite service period over which compensation cost is recognized is 18 months, which is the shorter of the explicit and implicit service periods.

A63. As illustrated in paragraph A62, if an award vests upon the earlier of the satisfaction of a service condition (for example, four years of service) *or* the satisfaction of one or more performance conditions, it will be necessary to estimate when, if at all, the performance conditions are probable of achievement. For example, if initially the four-year service condition is probable of achievement and no performance condition is probable of achievement, the requisite service period is four years. If one year into the four-year requisite service period a performance condition becomes probable of achievement by the end of the second year, the requisite service period would be revised to two years for attribution of compensation cost (at that point in time, there would be only one year of the two-year requisite service period remaining).

A64. If an award vests upon the satisfaction of both a service condition *and* the satisfaction of one or more performance conditions, the entity also must initially determine which outcomes are probable of achievement. For example, an award contains a four-year service condition and two performance conditions, all of which need to be satisfied. If initially the four-year service condition is probable of achievement and no performance condition is probable of achievement, then no compensation cost would be recognized unless the two performance conditions and the service condition subsequently become probable of achievement. If both performance conditions become probable of achievement one year after the grant date and the entity estimates that both performance conditions will be achieved by the end of the second year, the requisite service period would be four years as that is the longest period of both the explicit service period and the implicit service periods. Because the requisite service is now expected to be rendered, compensation cost will be recognized in the period of the change in estimate (paragraph 43) as the cumulative effect on current and prior periods of the change in the estimated number of awards for which the requisite service is expected to be rendered. Therefore, compensation cost for the first year will be recognized immediately at the time of the change in estimate for the awards for which the requisite service is expected to be rendered. The remaining unrecognized compensation cost for those awards would be recognized prospectively over the remaining requisite service period.

A65. As indicated in paragraph A63, the initial estimate of the requisite service period based on an explicit or implicit service period shall be adjusted for changes in the expected and actual outcomes of the related service or performance conditions that affect vesting of the award. Such adjustments will occur as the entity revises its estimates of whether or when different conditions or combinations of conditions are probable of being satisfied. Compensation cost ultimately recognized is equal to the grant-date fair value of the award based on the actual outcome of

---

[72]*Probable* is used in the same sense as in FASB Statement No. 5, *Accounting for Contingencies:* "the future event or events are likely to occur" (paragraph 3).

the performance or service conditions (paragraph 49). If an award contains a market condition *and* a performance or a service condition and the initial estimate of the requisite service period is based on the market condition's derived service period, then the requisite service period shall not be revised unless (a) the market condition is satisfied before the end of the derived service period or (b) satisfying the market condition is no longer the basis for determining the requisite service period.

A66. How a change to the initial estimate of the requisite service period is accounted for depends on whether that change would affect the grant-date fair value of the award (including the quantity of instruments) that is to be recognized as compensation. For example, if the quantity of instruments for which the requisite service is expected to be rendered changes because a vesting condition becomes probable of satisfaction or if the grant-date fair value of an instrument changes because another performance or service condition becomes probable of satisfaction (for example, a performance or service condition that affects exercise price becomes probable of satisfaction), the cumulative effect on current and prior periods of those changes in estimates shall be recognized in the period of the change. In contrast, if compensation cost is already being attributed over an initially estimated requisite service period and that initially estimated period changes solely because another market, performance, or service condition becomes the basis for the requisite service period, any unrecognized compensation cost at that date of change shall be recognized prospectively over the revised requisite service period, if any (that is, no cumulative-effect adjustment is recognized). To summarize, changes in actual or estimated outcomes that affect either the grant-date fair value of the instrument awarded or the quantity of instruments for which the requisite service is expected to be rendered (or both) are accounted for using a cumulative effect adjustment, and changes in estimated requisite service periods for awards for which compensation cost is already being attributed are accounted for prospectively only over the revised requisite service period, if any.

Share-based payment award with a performance condition and multiple service periods

A67. On January 1, 20X5, Entity T enters into an arrangement with its chief executive officer (CEO) relating to 40,000 share options on its stock with an exercise price of $30 per option. The arrangement is structured such that 10,000 share options will vest or be forfeited in each of the next 4 years (20X5 through 20X8) depending on whether annual performance targets relating to Entity T's revenues and net income are achieved. All of the annual performance targets are set at the inception of the arrangement. Because a mutual understanding of the key terms and conditions is reached on January 1, 20X5, each tranche would have a grant date and, therefore, a measurement date, of January 1, 20X5. However, each tranche of 10,000 share options should be accounted for as a separate award with its own service inception date, grant-date fair value, and 1-year requisite service period, because the arrangement specifies for each tranche an independent performance condition for a stated period of service. The CEO's ability to retain (vest in) the award pertaining to 20X5 is not dependent on service beyond 20X5, and the failure to satisfy the performance condition in any one particular year has no effect on the outcome of any preceding or subsequent period. This arrangement is similar to an arrangement that would have provided a $10,000 cash bonus for each year for satisfaction of the same performance conditions. The four separate service inception dates (one for each tranche) are at the beginning of each year.

A68. If the arrangement had instead provided that the annual performance targets would be established during January of each year, the grant date (and, therefore, the measurement date) for each tranche would be that date in January of each year (20X5 through 20X8) because a mutual understanding of the key terms and conditions would not be reached until then. In that case, each tranche of 10,000 share options has its own service inception date, grant-date fair value, and 1-year requisite service period. The fair value measurement of compensation cost for each tranche would be affected because not all of the key terms and conditions of each award are known until the compensation committee sets the performance targets and, therefore, the grant dates are those dates.

A69. If the arrangement in paragraph A67 instead stated that the vesting for awards in periods from 20X6 through 20X8 was dependent on satisfaction of the performance targets related to the preceding award, the requisite service provided in exchange for each preceding award would not be independent of the requisite service provided in exchange for each successive award. In contrast to the arrangement described in paragraph A67, failure to achieve the annual performance targets in 20X5 would result in forfeiture of all awards. The requisite service provided in exchange for each successive award is dependent on the requisite service provided for each preceding award. In that circumstance, all awards have the same service inception date and the same grant date (January 1, 20X5); however, each award has its own explicit service period (for example, the 20X5 grant has a one-year service period, the 20X6 grant has a two-year service period, and so on) over which compensation cost would be recognized.[73]

Share-based payment award with a service condition and multiple service periods

A70. The CEO of Entity T enters into a five-year employment contract on January 1, 20X5. The contract stipulates that the CEO will be given 10,000 fully vested share options at the end of each year (50,000 share options in total). The exercise price of each tranche will be equal to the market price at the date of issuance (December 31 of each year in the five-year contractual term). In this fact pattern, there are five separate grant dates. The grant date for each tranche is December 31 of each year because that is the date when there is a mutual understanding of the key terms and conditions of the agreement—that is, the exercise price is known and the CEO begins to benefit from, or be adversely affected by, subsequent changes in the price of the employer's equity shares (refer to paragraphs A77 and A78 for additional guidance on determining the grant date). Because the awards' terms do not include a substantive future requisite service condition that exists at the grant date (the options are fully vested when they are issued), and the exercise price (and, therefore, the grant date) is determined at the end of each period, the service inception date precedes the grant date. The requisite service provided in exchange for the first award (pertaining to 20X5) is independent of the requisite service provided in exchange for each consecutive award. The terms of the share-based compensation arrangement provide evidence that each tranche compensates the CEO for one year of service, and each tranche should be accounted for as a separate award with its own service inception date, grant date, and

one-year service period; therefore, the provisions of paragraph 42 would not be applicable to this award because of its structure.

A71. If the arrangement described in paragraph A70 provided instead that the exercise price for all 50,000 share options would be the January 1, 20X5, market price, then the grant date (and, therefore, the measurement date) for each tranche would be January 1, 20X5, because that is the date at which there is a mutual understanding of the key terms and conditions. All tranches would have the same service inception date and the same grant date (January 1, 20X5). Because of the nature of this award, Entity T would make a policy decision pursuant to paragraph 42 of this Statement as to whether it considers the award as, in-substance, multiple awards each with its own requisite service period (that is, the 20X5 grant has a one-year service period, the 20X6 grant has a two-year service period, and so on) or whether the entity considers the award as a single award with a single requisite service period based on the last separately vesting portion of the award (that is, a requisite service period of five years). Once chosen, this Statement requires that accounting policy be applied consistently to all similar awards.

Share-based payment award with market and service conditions and multiple service periods

A72. On January 1, 20X5, Entity T grants an executive 200,000 share options on its stock with an exercise price of $30 per option. The award specifies that vesting (or exercisability) will occur upon the earlier of (a) the share price reaching and maintaining at least $70 per share for 30 consecutive trading days *or* (b) the completion of 8 years of service. That award contains an explicit service period of eight years related to the service condition and a derived service period related to the market condition.

A73. An entity shall make its best estimate of the derived service period related to the market condition (refer to paragraph A60 and Appendix E).[74] For this example, the derived service period is assumed to be six years. As described in paragraph A61, if an award's vesting (or exercisability) is conditional upon the achievement of *either* a market condition *or* performance or service conditions, the requisite service period is generally the shortest of the explicit, implicit, and derived service periods. In this example, the requisite service period over which compensation

---

[73]Because this award contains a performance condition, it is not subject to the attribution guidance in paragraph 42 of this Statement.

[74]The derived service period may be estimated using any reasonable methodology, including Monte Carlo simulation techniques.

cost should be attributed is six years (shorter of eight and six years).[75] Continuing with the example in paragraph A72, if the market condition is actually satisfied in February 20X9 (based on market prices for the prior 30 consecutive trading days) Entity T would immediately recognize any unrecognized compensation cost, because no further service is required to earn the award. If the market condition is not satisfied as of that date, but the executive renders the six years of requisite service, compensation cost shall not be reversed under any circumstances.

A74. The initial estimate of the requisite service period for an award requiring satisfaction of both market *and* performance or service conditions is generally the longest of the explicit, implicit, and derived service periods (paragraph A61). For example, if the award described in paragraph A72 required *both* the completion of 8 years of service *and* the share price reaching and maintaining at least $70 per share for 30 consecutive trading days, compensation cost would be recognized over the 8-year explicit service period. If the employee were to terminate service prior to the eight-year requisite service period, compensation cost would be reversed even if the market condition had been satisfied by that time.

Illustration 1—Definition of Employee

A75. This Statement defines employee as an individual over whom the grantor of a share-based compensation award exercises or has the right to exercise sufficient control to establish an employer-employee relationship based on common law as illustrated in case law and currently under U.S. Internal Revenue Service Revenue Ruling 87-41 (refer to Appendix E for a complete definition of the term *employee*). An example of whether that condition exists follows. Entity A issues options to members of its Advisory Board, which is separate and distinct from Entity A's board of directors. Members of the Advisory Board are knowledgeable about Entity A's industry and advise Entity A on matters such as policy development, strategic planning, and product development. The Advisory Board members are appointed for two-year terms and meet four times a year for one day, receiving a fixed number of options for services rendered at each meeting. Based on an evaluation of the relationship between Entity A and the Advisory Board members, Entity A concludes that the Advisory Board

members do not meet the common law definition of employee. Accordingly, the awards to the Advisory Board members are accounted for as awards to non-employees under the provisions of this Statement.

A76. The definition of employee in Appendix E states that nonemployee directors acting in their role as members of an entity's board of directors shall be treated as employees if those directors were elected by the entity's shareholders or appointed to a board position that will be filled by shareholder election when the existing term expires. However, that requirement applies only to awards granted to them for their services as directors. Awards granted to those individuals for other services should be accounted for as awards to nonemployees in accordance with paragraphs 5–8 of this Statement. Additionally, consolidated groups may have multiple boards of directors; this guidance applies only to (a) the nonemployee directors acting in their role as members of a parent entity's board of directors and (b) nonemployee members of a consolidated subsidiary's board of directors to the extent that those members are elected by shareholders that are not controlled directly or indirectly by the parent or another member of the consolidated group.

Illustration 2—Determining the Grant Date

A77. The definition of *grant date* requires that an employer and employee have a mutual understanding of the key terms and conditions of the share-based compensation arrangement (Appendix E). Those terms may be established through a formal, written agreement; an informal, oral arrangement; or established by an entity's past practice. A mutual understanding of the key terms and conditions means that there is sufficient basis for both the employer and the employee to understand the nature of the relationship established by the award, including both the compensatory relationship and the equity relationship subsequent to the date of grant. The grant date for an award will be the date that an employee begins to benefit from, or be adversely affected by, subsequent changes in the price of the employer's equity shares. In order to assess that financial exposure, the employer and employee must agree to the terms; that is, there must be a mutual understanding. Awards made under an arrangement that is subject to shareholder approval are not deemed to be granted until

---

[75]An entity may grant a fully vested deep out-of-the-money share option that would lapse shortly after termination of service, which is the equivalent of an award with both a market condition and a service condition. The explicit service period associated with the explicit service condition is zero; however, because the option is deep out-of-the-money at the grant date, there would be a derived service period.

that approval is obtained unless approval is essentially a formality (or perfunctory). Additionally, to have a grant date for an award to an employee, the recipient of that award must meet the definition of *employee* in Appendix E.

A78. The determination of the grant date shall be based on the relevant facts and circumstances. For instance, a look-back share option may be granted with an exercise price equal to the lower of the current share price or the share price one year hence. The ultimate exercise price is not known at the date of grant, but it cannot be greater than the current share price. In this case, the relationship between the exercise price and the current share price provides a sufficient basis to understand both the compensatory and equity relationship established by the award; the recipient begins to benefit from subsequent changes in the price of the employer's equity shares. However, if the award's terms call for the exercise price to be set equal to the share price one year hence, the recipient does not begin to benefit from, or be adversely affected by, changes in the price of the employer's equity shares until then.[76] Therefore, grant date would not occur until one year hence.

Illustration 3—Service Inception Date and Grant Date

A79. This Statement distinguishes between service inception date and grant date (refer to Appendix E of this Statement for definitions of *service inception date* and *grant date*). The service inception date is the date at which the requisite service period begins. The service inception date usually is the grant date, but the service inception date precedes the grant date if (a) an award is authorized,[77] (b) service begins before a mutual understanding of the key terms and conditions of a share-based payment award is reached, *and* (c) either of the following conditions applies: (1) the award's terms do not include a substantive future requisite service condition that exists at the grant date (refer to paragraph A83 for an example illustrating that condition) or (2) the award contains a market or performance condition that if not satisfied during the service period preceding the grant date and following the inception of the arrangement results in forfeiture of the award

(refer to paragraph A84 for an example illustrating that condition). In certain circumstances the service inception date may begin after the grant date (refer to paragraph A67 for an example illustrating that circumstance).

A80. For example, Entity T offers a position to an individual on April 1, 20X5, that has been approved by the CEO and board of directors. In addition to salary and other benefits, Entity T offers to grant 10,000 shares of Entity T stock that vest upon the completion of 5 years of service (the market price of Entity T's stock is $25 on April 1, 20X5). The share award will begin vesting on the date the offer is accepted. The individual accepts the offer on April 2, 20X5, but is unable to begin providing services to Entity T until June 2, 20X5 (that is, substantive employment begins on June 2, 20X5). The individual also does not receive a salary or participate in other employee benefits until June 2, 20X5. On June 2, 20X5, the market price of Entity T stock is $40. In this example, the service inception date is June 2, 20X5, the first date that the individual begins providing substantive employee services to Entity T. The grant date is the same date because that is when the individual would meet the definition of an employee. The grant-date fair value of the share award is $400,000 (10,000 × $40).

A81. If necessary board approval of the award described in paragraph A80 was obtained on August 5, 20X5, two months after substantive employment begins (June 2, 20X5), both the service inception date *and* the grant date would be August 5, 20X5, as that is the date when all necessary authorizations were obtained. If the market price of Entity T's stock was $38 per share on August 5, 20X5, the grant-date fair value of the share award would be $380,000 (10,000 × $38). Additionally, Entity T would not recognize compensation cost for the shares for the period between June 2, 20X5, and August 4, 20X5, neither during that period nor cumulatively on August 5, 20X5, when both the service inception date and the grant date occur. This is consistent with the definition of requisite service period, which states that if an award requires future service for vesting,[78] the entity cannot define a prior period as the requisite service period.

---

[76]Awards of share options whose exercise price is determined solely by reference to a future share price generally would not provide a sufficient basis to understand the nature of the compensatory and equity relationships established by the award until the exercise price is known.

[77]Compensation cost would not be recognized prior to receiving all necessary approvals unless approval is essentially a formality (or perfunctory).

[78]Future service in this context represents the service to be rendered beginning as of the service inception date.

A82. If the service inception date precedes the grant date, recognition of compensation cost for periods before the grant date shall be based on the fair value of the award at the reporting dates that occur prior to the grant date. In the period in which the grant date occurs, cumulative compensation cost shall be adjusted to reflect the cumulative effect of measuring compensation cost based on the fair value at the grant date rather than the fair value previously used at the service inception date (or any subsequent reporting dates) (paragraph 41).

A83. If an award's terms do not include a substantive future requisite service condition that exists at the grant date, the service inception date can precede the grant date. For example, on January 1, 20X5, an employee is informed that an award of 100 fully vested options will be made on January 1, 20X6, with an exercise price equal to the share price on January 1, 20X6. All approvals for that award have been obtained as of January 1, 20X5. That individual is still an employee on January 1, 20X6, and receives the 100 fully vested options on that date. There is no substantive future service period associated with the options after January 1, 20X6. Therefore, the requisite service period is from the January 1, 20X5 service inception date through the January 1, 20X6 grant date, as that is the period during which the employee is required to perform service in exchange for the award. The relationship between the exercise price and the current share price that provides a sufficient basis to understand the equity relationship established by the award is known on January 1, 20X6. Compensation cost would be recognized during 20X5 in accordance with paragraph A82.

A84. If an award contains either a market or a performance condition, which if not satisfied during the service period preceding the grant date and following the date the award is given results in a forfeiture of the award, then the service inception date may precede the grant date. For example, an authorized award is given on January 1, 20X5, with a two-year cliff vesting service requirement commencing on that date. The exercise price will be set on January 1, 20X6. The award will be forfeited if Entity T does not sell 1,000 units of product X in 20X5. In this example, the employee earns the right to retain the award if the performance condition is met and the employee renders service in 20X5 and 20X6. The requisite service period is two years beginning on January 1, 20X5. The service inception date (January 1, 20X5) precedes the grant date (January 1, 20X6). Compensation cost would be recognized during 20X5 in accordance with paragraph A82.

A85. In contrast, consider an award that is given on January 1, 20X5, with only a three-year cliff vesting explicit service condition, which commences on that date. The exercise price will be set on January 1, 20X6. In this example, the service inception date cannot precede the grant date because there is a substantive future requisite service condition that exists at the grant date (two years of service). Therefore, there would be no attribution of compensation cost for the period between January 1, 20X5, and December 31, 20X5, neither during that period nor cumulatively on January 1, 20X6, when both the service inception date and the grant date occur. This is consistent with the definition of requisite service period, which states that if an award requires future service for vesting, the entity cannot define a prior period as the requisite service period. The requisite service period would be two years, commencing on January 1, 20X6.

Illustration 4—Accounting for Share Options with Service Conditions

Illustration 4(a)—Share Options with Cliff Vesting

A86. Entity T, a public entity, grants at-the-money employee share options with a contractual term of 10 years. All share options vest at the end of three years (cliff vesting), which is an explicit service (and requisite service) period of three years. The share options do not qualify as incentive stock options for U.S. tax purposes. The enacted tax rate is 35 percent.

A87. The following table shows assumptions and information about the share options granted on January 1, 20X5.

Share options granted	900,000
Employees granted options	3,000
Expected forfeitures per year	3.0%
Share price at the grant date	$30
Exercise price	$30
Contractual term (CT) of options	10 years
Risk-free interest rate over CT	1.5 to 4.3%
Expected volatility over CT	40 to 60%
Expected dividend yield over CT	1.0%
Suboptimal exercise factor[79]	2

A88. This example assumes that each employee receives an equal grant of 300 options. Using as inputs the last 7 items from the table above, Entity T's lattice-based valuation model produces a fair value of $14.69 per option. A lattice model uses a suboptimal exercise factor to calculate the expected term (that is, the expected term is an output) rather than the expected term being a separate input. If an entity uses a Black-Scholes-Merton option-pricing formula, the expected term would be used as an input instead of a suboptimal exercise factor.

A89. Total compensation cost recognized over the requisite service period (which is the vesting period in this example) should be the grant-date fair value of all share options that actually vest (that is, all options for which the requisite service is rendered). Paragraph 43 of this Statement requires an entity to estimate at the grant date the number of share options for which the requisite service is expected to be rendered (which, in this illustration, is the number of share options for which vesting is deemed probable [80]). If that estimate changes, it shall be accounted for as a change in estimate and its cumulative effect (from applying the change retrospectively) recognized in the period of change. Entity T estimates at the grant date the number of share options

expected to vest and subsequently adjusts compensation cost for changes in the estimated rate of forfeitures and differences between expectations and actual experience. This illustration assumes that none of the compensation cost is capitalized as part of the cost of an asset.

A90. The estimate of the number of forfeitures considers historical employee turnover rates and expectations about the future. Entity T has experienced historical turnover rates of approximately 3 percent per year for employees at the grantees' level, and it expects that rate to continue over the requisite service period of the awards. Therefore, at the grant date Entity T estimates the total compensation cost to be recognized over the requisite service period based on an expected forfeiture rate of 3 percent per year. Actual forfeitures are 5 percent in 20X5, but no adjustments to cumulative compensation cost are recognized in 20X5 because Entity T still expects actual forfeitures to average 3 percent per year over the 3-year vesting period. At December 31, 20X6, management decides that the forfeiture rate will likely increase through 20X7 and changes its estimated forfeiture rate for the entire award to 6 percent per year. Adjustments to cumulative compensation cost to reflect the higher forfeiture rate are made at the end of 20X6. At the end of 20X7 when the award becomes vested, actual forfeitures have averaged 6 percent per year, and no further adjustment is necessary.

A91. The first set of calculations illustrates the accounting for the award of share options on January 1, 20X5, assuming that the share options granted vest at the end of three years. (Paragraphs A97–A104 illustrate the accounting for an award assuming graded vesting in which a specified portion of the share options granted vest at the end of each year.) The number of share options expected to vest is estimated at the grant date to be 821,406

---

[79]A suboptimal exercise factor of two means that exercise is generally expected to occur when the share price reaches two times the share option's exercise price. Option-pricing theory generally holds that the optimal (or profit-maximizing) time to exercise an option is at the end of the option's term; therefore, if an option is exercised prior to the end of its term, that exercise is referred to as *suboptimal*. Suboptimal exercise also is referred to as *early exercise*. Suboptimal or early exercise affects the expected term of an option. Early exercise can be incorporated into option-pricing models through various means. In this illustration, Entity T has sufficient information to reasonably estimate early exercise and has incorporated it as a function of Entity T's future stock price changes (or the option's intrinsic value). In this case, the factor of 2 indicates that early exercise would be expected to occur, on average, if the stock price reaches $60 per share ($30 × 2). Rather than use its weighted average suboptimal exercise factor, Entity T also may use multiple factors based on a distribution of early exercise data in relation to its stock price.
[80]Refer to paragraph A62, footnote 72.

$(900,000 \times .97^3)$. Thus, as shown in Table 1, the compensation cost to be recognized over the requisite service period at January 1, 20X5, is $12,066,454 (821,406 × $14.69), and the compensation cost to be recognized during each year of the 3-year vesting period is $4,022,151 ($12,066,454 ÷ 3). The journal entries to recognize compensation cost and related deferred tax benefit at the enacted tax rate of 35 percent are as follows for 20X5:[81]

Compensation cost	$4,022,151	
Additional paid-in		
capital		$4,022,151

To recognize compensation cost.

Deferred tax asset	$1,407,753	
Deferred tax benefit		$1,407,753

To recognize the deferred tax asset for the temporary difference related to compensation cost ($4,022,151 × .35 = $1,407,753).

The net after-tax effect on income of recognizing compensation cost for 20X5 is $2,614,398 ($4,022,151 − $1,407,753).

A92. Absent a change in estimated forfeitures, the same journal entries would be made to recognize compensation cost and related tax effects for 20X6 and 20X7, resulting in a net after-tax cost for each year of $2,614,398. However, at the end of 20X6, management changes its estimated employee forfeiture rate from 3 percent to 6 percent per year. The revised number of share options expected to vest is 747,526 $(900,000 \times .94^3)$. Accordingly, the revised cumulative compensation cost to be recognized by the end of 20X7 is $10,981,157 (747,526 × $14.69). The cumulative adjustment to reflect the effect of adjusting the forfeiture rate is the difference between two-thirds of the revised cost of the award and the cost already recognized for 20X5 and 20X6. The related journal entries and the computations follow.

At December 31, 20X6, to adjust for new forfeiture rate:

Revised total compensation cost	$10,981,157
Revised cumulative cost as of December 31, 20X6 ($10,981,157 × ⅔)	$ 7,320,771
Cost already recognized in 20X5 and 20X6 ($4,022,151 × 2)	8,044,302
Adjustment to cost at December 31, 20X6	$ (723,531)

The related journal entries are:

Additional paid-in capital	$723,531	
Compensation cost		$723,531

To adjust previously recognized compensation cost and equity to reflect a higher estimated forfeiture rate.

Deferred tax expense	$253,236	
Deferred tax asset		$253,236

To adjust the deferred tax accounts to reflect the tax effect of increasing the estimated forfeiture rate ($723,531 × .35 = $253,236).

For 20X7:

Compensation cost	$3,660,386	
Additional paid-in capital		$3,660,386

To recognize compensation cost ($10,981,157 ÷ 3 = $3,660,386).

Deferred tax asset	$1,281,135	
Deferred tax benefit		$1,281,135

To recognize the deferred tax asset for additional compensation cost ($3,660,386 × .35 = $1,281,135).

---

[81]In this example, Entity T has concluded that it will have sufficient future taxable income to realize the deferred tax benefits from its share-based payment transactions.

At December 31, 20X7, the entity would examine its actual forfeitures and make any necessary adjustments to reflect cumulative compensation cost for the number of shares that actually vested.

Table 1—Share Option—Cliff Vesting

Year	Total Value of Award	Pretax Cost for Year	Cumulative Pretax Cost
20X5	$12,066,454 (821,406 × $14.69)	$4,022,151 ($12,066,454 ÷ 3)	$4,022,151
20X6	$10,981,157 (747,526 × $14.69)	$3,298,620 [($10,981,157 × ⅔) − $4,022,151]	$7,320,771
20X7	$10,981,157 (747,526 × $14.69)	$3,660,386 ($10,981,157 ÷ 3)	$10,981,157

A93. All 747,526 vested share options are exercised on the last day of 20Y2. Entity T has already recognized its income tax expense for the year without regard to the effects of the exercise of the employee share options. In other words, current tax expense and current taxes payable were recognized based on income and deductions before consideration of additional deductions from exercise of the employee share options. Upon exercise, the amount credited to common stock (or other appropriate equity accounts) is the sum of the cash proceeds received and the amounts previously credited to additional paid-in capital in the periods the services were received (20X5 through 20X7). In this example, Entity T has no-par common stock and at exercise, the share price is assumed to be $60.

At exercise:

Cash (747,526 × $30) $22,425,780
Additional paid-in capital $10,981,157
    Common stock $33,406,937
To recognize the issuance of common stock upon exercise of share options and to reclass previously recorded paid-in capital.

Income taxes

A94. In this example, the difference between the market price of the shares and the exercise price on the date of exercise is deductible for tax purposes pursuant to U.S. tax law in effect at the date of this Statement's issuance (the share options do not qualify as incentive stock options). Realized benefits of tax return deductions in excess of compensation cost recognized are accounted for as a credit to additional paid-in capital.[82] With the share price of $60 at exercise, the deductible amount is $22,425,780 [747,526 × ($60 − $30)]. Entity T has sufficient taxable income to fully realize that deduction, and the tax benefit realized is $7,849,023 ($22,425,780 × .35).

At exercise:

Deferred tax expense $3,843,405
    Deferred tax asset $3,843,405
To write off the deferred tax asset related to deductible share options at exercise ($10,981,157 × .35 = $3,843,405).

Current taxes payable $7,849,023
    Current tax expense $3,843,405
    Additional paid-in
    capital $4,005,618
To adjust current tax expense and current taxes payable to recognize the current tax benefit from deductible compensation cost upon exercise of share options.

The credit to additional paid-in capital is the tax benefit of the excess of the deductible amount over the recognized compensation cost [($22,425,780 − $10,981,157) × .35 = $4,005,618].

A95. If instead the share options expired unexercised, previously recognized compensation cost would not be reversed. There would be no deduction on the tax return and, therefore, the entire deferred tax asset of $3,843,405 would be charged to income

---

[82]A share option exercise may result in a tax deduction prior to the actual realization of the related tax benefit because the entity, for example, has a net operating loss carryforward. In that situation, a tax benefit and a credit to additional paid-in capital for the excess deduction would not be recognized until that deduction reduces taxes payable.

tax expense[83] or additional paid-in capital, to the extent of any remaining additional paid-in capital from excess tax benefits from previous awards accounted for in accordance with this Statement or Statement 123 (paragraph 63).[84]

Cash flows from income taxes

A96. FASB Statement No. 95, *Statement of Cash Flows,* as amended by this Statement, requires that the realized tax benefit related to the excess of the deductible amount over the compensation cost recognized be classified in the statement of cash flows as a cash inflow from financing activities and a cash outflow from operating activities. Under either the direct or indirect method of reporting cash flows, Entity T would disclose the following activity in its statement of cash flows for the year ended December 31, 20Y2:

Cash outflow from operating activities:

Excess tax benefits from share-based payment arrangements	$(4,005,618)

Cash inflow from financing activities:

Excess tax benefits from share-based payment arrangements	$4,005,618

Illustration 4(b)—Share Options with Graded Vesting

A97. Paragraph 42 of this Statement provides for the following two methods to recognize compensation cost for awards with graded vesting: (a) on a straight-line basis over the requisite service period for each separately vesting portion of the award as if the award was, in-substance, multiple awards (graded vesting attribution method) or (b) on a straight-line basis over the requisite service period for the entire award (that is, over the requisite service period of the last separately vesting portion of the award), subject to the limitation noted in paragraph 42.[85] The accounting is illustrated below for both methods and uses the same assumptions as those noted in paragraphs A86–A88 except for the vesting provisions.

A98. Entity T awards 900,000 share options on January 1, 20X5, that vest according to a graded schedule of 25 percent for the first year of service, 25 percent for the second year, and the remaining 50 percent for the third year. Each employee is granted 300 share options. Table 2 shows the calculation as of January 1, 20X5, of the number of employees and the related number of share options expected to vest. Using the expected 3 percent annual forfeiture rate, 90 employees are expected to terminate during 20X5 without having vested in any portion of the award, leaving 2,910 employees to vest in 25 percent of the award (75 options). During 20X6, 87 employees are expected to terminate, leaving 2,823 to vest in the second 25 percent of the award. During 20X7, 85 employees are expected to terminate, leaving 2,738 employees to vest in the last 50 percent of the award. That results in a total of 840,675 share options expected to vest from the award of 900,000 share options with graded vesting.

Table 2—Share Option—Graded Vesting—Estimated Amounts

Year	Number of Employees	Number of Vested Share Options
	Total at date of grant 3,000	
20X5	3,000 – 90 (3,000 × .03) = 2,910	2,910 × 75 (300 × 25%) = 218,250
20X6	2,910 – 87 (2,910 × .03) = 2,823	2,823 × 75 (300 × 25%) = 211,725
20X7	2,823 – 85 (2,823 × .03) = 2,738	2,738 × 150 (300 × 50%) = 410,700
		Total vested options 840,675

---

[83]If employees terminated with out-of-the-money vested share options, the deferred tax asset related to those share options would be written-off when those options expire.

[84]A write-off of a deferred tax asset related to a deficiency of deductible compensation cost in relation to recognized compensation cost for financial reporting purposes shall not be reflected in the statement of cash flows because the unit of account for cash-flow purposes is an individual award (or portion thereof) as opposed to a portfolio of awards.

[85]The choice of attribution method for awards with graded vesting schedules is a policy decision that is not dependent on an enterprise's choice of valuation technique. In addition, the choice of attribution method applies to awards with only service conditions.

Graded vesting attribution method

A99. The value of the share options that vest over the three-year period is estimated by separating the total award into three groups (or tranches) according to the year in which they vest (because the expected life for each tranche differs). Table 3 shows the estimated compensation cost for the share options expected to vest. The estimates of expected volatility, expected dividends, and risk-free interest rates are incorporated into the lattice, and the graded vesting

conditions affect only the earliest date at which suboptimal exercise can occur. Thus, the fair value of each of the 3 groups of options is based on the same lattice inputs for expected volatility, expected dividend yield, and risk-free interest rates used to determine the value of $14.69 for the cliff-vesting share options (paragraphs A87 and A88). The different vesting terms affect the ability of the suboptimal exercise to occur sooner (and affect other factors as well, such as volatility), and therefore there is a different expected term for each tranche.

Table 3—Share Option—Graded Vesting—Estimated Cost

Year	Vested Options	Value per Option	Compensation Cost
20X5	218,250	$13.44	$ 2,933,280
20X6	211,725	14.17	3,000,143
20X7	410,700	14.69	6,033,183
	840,675		$11,966,606

A100. Compensation cost is recognized over the periods of requisite service during which each tranche of share options is earned. Thus, the $2,933,280 cost attributable to the 218,250 share options that vest in 20X5 is recognized in 20X5. The $3,000,143 cost attributable to the 211,725 share options that vest at the end of 20X6 is recognized over the 2-year vesting period (20X5 and 20X6). The $6,033,183 cost attribut-

able to the 410,700 share options that vest at the end of 20X7 is recognized over the 3-year vesting period (20X5, 20X6, and 20X7).

A101. Table 4 shows how the $11,966,606 expected amount of compensation cost determined at the grant date is attributed to the years 20X5, 20X6, and 20X7.

Table 4—Share Option—Graded Vesting—Computation of Estimated Cost

	Pretax Cost to Be Recognized		
	20X5	**20X6**	**20X7**
Share options vesting in 20X5	$2,933,280		
Share options vesting in 20X6	1,500,071	$1,500,072	
Share options vesting in 20X7	2,011,061	2,011,061	$ 2,011,061
Cost for the year	$6,444,412	$3,511,133	$ 2,011,061
Cumulative cost	$6,444,412	$9,955,545	$11,966,606

Straight-line attribution method

A102. Entity T could use the same computation of estimated cost, as in Table 3 above, but could elect to recognize compensation cost on a straight-line basis for all graded vesting awards. In that case, total com-

pensation cost to be attributed on a straight-line basis over each year in the 3-year vesting period is approximately $3,988,868 ($11,966,606 ÷ 3).[86] However, this Statement requires that compensation cost recognized at any date must be at least equal to the amount attributable to options that are vested at that

---

[86]Entity T also could use a single weighted-average expected life to value the entire award and arrive at a different amount of total compensation cost. Total compensation cost could then be attributed on a straight-line basis over the three-year vesting period.

date. For example, if 50 percent of this same option award vested in the first year of the 3-year vesting period, 436,500 options [2,910 × 150 (300 × 50%)] would be vested at the end of 20X5. Compensation cost amounting to $5,866,560 (436,500 × $13.44) attributable to the vested awards would be recognized in the first year.

A103. Compensation cost is adjusted for awards with graded vesting to reflect differences between estimated and actual forfeitures as illustrated for the cliff-vesting options, regardless of which method is used to estimate value and attribute cost.

A104. Accounting for the tax effects of awards with graded vesting follows the same pattern illustrated in paragraphs A94 and A95. However, unless Entity T identifies and tracks the specific tranche from which share options are exercised, it would not know the recognized compensation cost that corresponds to exercised share options for purposes of calculating the tax effects resulting from that exercise. If an entity does not know the specific tranche from which share options are exercised, it should assume that options are exercised on a first-vested, first-exercised basis (which works in the same manner as the first-in, first-out basis for inventory costing).

Illustration 5—Share Option with Multiple Performance Conditions

Illustration 5(a)—Share Option Award under Which the Number of Options to Be Earned Varies

A105. Illustration 5(a) shows the computation of compensation cost if Entity T grants an award of share options with multiple performance conditions. Under the award, employees vest in differing numbers of options depending on the amount by which the market share of one of Entity T's products increases over a three-year period (the share options cannot vest before the end of the three-year period). The three-year explicit service period represents the requisite service period. On January 1, 20X5, Entity T grants to each of 1,000 employees an award of up to 300 10-year-term share options on its common stock. If market share increases by at least 5 percentage points by December 31, 20X7, each employee

vests in at least 100 share options at that date. If market share increases by at least 10 percentage points, another 100 share options vest, for a total of 200. If market share increases by more than 20 percentage points, each employee vests in all 300 share options. Entity T's share price on January 1, 20X5, is $30 and other assumptions are the same as in Illustration 4(a) (paragraph A87). The grant-date fair value per share option is $14.69.[87] The compensation cost of the award depends on the estimated number of options that will vest. Entity T must determine whether it is probable[88] that any performance condition will be achieved, that is, whether the growth in market share over the 3-year period will be at least 5 percent. Accruals of compensation cost are initially based on the probable outcome of the performance conditions—in this case, different levels of market share growth over the three-year vesting period—and adjusted for subsequent changes in the estimated or actual outcome. If Entity T determines that no performance condition is probable of achievement (that is, market share growth is expected to be less than 5 percentage points), then no compensation cost is recognized; however, Entity T is required to reassess at each reporting date whether achievement of any performance condition is probable and would begin recognizing compensation cost if and when achievement of a performance condition becomes probable.

A106. Paragraph 44 of this Statement requires accruals of cost to be based on the probable outcome of performance conditions. Accordingly, this Statement prohibits Entity T from basing accruals of compensation cost on an amount that is not a possible outcome (and thus cannot be the probable outcome). For instance, if Entity T estimates that there is a 90 percent, 30 percent, and 10 percent likelihood that market share growth will be at least 5 percentage points, at least 10 percentage points, and greater than 20 percentage points, respectively, it would not try to determine a weighted average of the possible outcomes because that number of shares is not a possible outcome under the arrangement.

A107. Table 5 shows the compensation cost that would be recognized in 20X5, 20X6, and 20X7 if Entity T estimates at the grant date that it is probable that market share will increase at least 5 but less than

---

[87]While the vesting conditions in this illustration and Illustration 4 are different, the equity instruments being valued have the same estimate of grant-date fair value. That is a consequence of the modified grant-date method, which accounts for the effects of vesting requirements or other restrictions that apply during the vesting period by recognizing compensation cost only for the instruments that actually vest. (This discussion does not refer to awards with market conditions that affect exercisability or the ability to retain the award as described in paragraphs A49–A51.)

[88]*Probable* is used in the same sense as in Statement 5: "the future event or events are likely to occur" (paragraph 3).

10 percentage points (that is, each employee would receive 100 share options). That estimate remains unchanged until the end of 20X7, when Entity T's market share has increased over the 3-year period by more than 10 percentage points. Thus, each employee vests in 200 share options.

A108. As in Illustration 4(a) (refer to paragraph A90), Entity T experiences actual forfeiture rates of 5 percent in 20X5, and in 20X6 changes its estimate of forfeitures for the entire award from 3 percent to 6 percent per year. In 20X6, cumulative compensation cost is adjusted to reflect the higher forfeiture rate. By the end of 20X7, a 6 percent forfeiture rate has been experienced, and no further adjustments for forfeitures are necessary. Through 20X5, Entity T estimates that 913 employees $(1,000 \times .97^3)$

will remain in service until the vesting date. At the end of 20X6, the number of employees estimated to remain in service is adjusted for the higher forfeiture rate, and the number of employees estimated to remain in service is 831 $(1,000 \times .94^3)$. The compensation cost of the award is initially estimated based on the number of options expected to vest, which in turn is based on the expected level of performance and the fair value of each option.[89] The amount of compensation cost recognized (or attributed) when achievement of a performance condition is probable depends on the relative satisfaction of the performance condition based on performance to date. Entity T determines that recognizing compensation cost ratably over the three-year vesting period is appropriate with one-third of the value of the award recognized each year.

Table 5—Share Option with Performance Condition— Number of Share Options Varies

Year	Total Value of Award	Pretax Cost for Year	Cumulative Pretax Cost
20X5	$1,341,197 ($14.69 × 100 × 913)	$447,066 ($1,341,197 ÷ 3)	$447,066
20X6	$1,220,739 ($14.69 × 100 × 831)	$366,760 [($1,220,739 × ⅔) – $447,066]	$813,826
20X7	$2,441,478 ($14.69 × 200 × 831)	$1,627,652 ($2,441,478 – $813,826)	$2,441,478

Illustration 5(b)—Share Option Award under Which the Exercise Price Varies

A109. Illustration 5(b) shows the computation of compensation cost if Entity T grants a share option award with a performance condition under which the exercise price, rather than the number of shares, varies depending on the level of performance achieved. On January 1, 20X5, Entity T grants to its CEO 10-year share options on 10,000 shares of its common stock, which are immediately vested and exercisable (an explicit service period of zero). The share price at the grant date is $30, and the initial exercise price also is $30. However, that price decreases to $15 if the market share for Entity T's products increases by at least 10 percentage points by December 31, 20X6, and provided that the CEO continues to be employed by Entity T and has not previously exercised the options (an explicit service period of 2 years, which also is the requisite service period).

A110. Entity T estimates at the grant date the expected level of market share growth, the exercise price of the options, and the expected term of the options. Other assumptions, including the risk-free interest rate and the service period over which the cost is attributed, are consistent with those estimates. Entity T estimates at the grant date that its market share growth will be at least 10 percentage points over the 2-year performance period, which means that the expected exercise price of the share options is $15, resulting in a fair value of $19.99 per option.[90] Total compensation cost to be recognized if the performance condition is satisfied would be $199,900 (10,000 × $19.99). Paragraph 49 of this Statement requires that the fair value of both awards with service conditions and awards with performance conditions be estimated as of the date of grant. Paragraph 43 of this Statement also requires recognition of cost for the number of instruments for which the requisite service is provided. For this performance

---

[89]That amount would be adjusted as needed for changes in the estimated and actual forfeiture rates and for differences between estimated and actual market share growth.

[90]Option value is determined using the same assumptions noted in paragraph A87 except the exercise price is $15 and the award is not exercisable at $15 per option for 2 years.

award, Entity T also selects the expected assumptions at the grant date if the performance goal is not met. If market share growth is not at least 10 percentage points over the 2-year period, Entity T estimates a fair value of $13.08 per option.[91] Total compensation cost to be recognized if the performance goal is not met would be $130,800 (10,000 × $13.08). Because Entity T estimates that the performance condition would be satisfied, it would recognize compensation cost of $130,800 on the date of grant related to the fair value of the fully vested award and recognize compensation cost of $69,100 ($199,900 – $130,800) over the 2-year requisite service period related to the condition.[92] During the two-year requisite service period, adjustments to reflect any change in estimate about satisfaction of the performance condition should be made, and, thus, aggregate cost recognized by the end of that period reflects whether the performance goal was met.

Illustration 6—Other Performance Conditions

A111. While performance conditions usually affect vesting conditions, they may affect exercise price, contractual term, quantity, or other factors that affect an award's fair value prior to, at the time of, or subsequent to vesting. This Statement requires that all performance conditions be accounted for similarly. A potential grant-date fair value is estimated for each of the possible outcomes that are reasonably determinable at the grant date and associated with the performance condition(s) of the award (as demonstrated in Illustration 5(b), paragraphs A109 and A110). Compensation cost ultimately recognized is equal to the grant-date fair value of the award that coincides with the actual outcome of the performance condition(s).

A112. To illustrate the notion described in paragraph A111 and attribution of compensation cost when performance conditions have different service periods, assume Entity C grants 10,000 at-the-money share options on its common stock to an employee. The options have a 10-year contractual term. The share options vest upon successful completion of phase-two clinical trials to satisfy regulatory testing

requirements related to a developmental drug therapy. Phase-two clinical trials are scheduled to be completed (and regulatory approval of that phase obtained) in approximately 18 months; hence, the implicit service period is approximately 18 months. Further, the share options will become fully transferable upon regulatory approval of the drug therapy (which is scheduled to occur in approximately four years). The implicit service period for that performance condition is approximately 30 months (beginning once phase-two clinical trials are successfully completed). Based on the nature of the performance conditions, the award has multiple requisite service periods (one pertaining to each performance condition) that affect the pattern in which compensation cost is attributed.[93] The determination of whether compensation cost should be recognized depends on Entity C's assessment of whether the performance conditions are probable of achievement. Entity C expects that all performance conditions will be achieved. That assessment is based on the relevant facts and circumstances, including Entity C's historical success rate of bringing developmental drug therapies to market.

A113. At the grant date, Entity C estimates that the potential fair value of each share option under the 2 possible outcomes is $10 (Outcome 1, in which the share options vest and do not become transferable) and $16 (Outcome 2, in which the share options vest and do become transferable).[94] If Outcome 1 is considered probable of occurring, Entity C would recognize $100,000 (10,000 × $10) of compensation cost ratably over the 18-month requisite service period related to the successful completion of phase-two clinical trials. If Outcome 2 is considered probable of occurring, then Entity C would recognize an additional $60,000 [10,000 × ($16 – $10)] of compensation cost ratably over the 30-month requisite service period (which begins after phase-two clinical trials are successfully completed) related to regulatory approval of the drug therapy. Because Entity C believes that Outcome 2 is probable, it recognizes compensation cost in the pattern described. However, if circumstances change and it is determined at the end of year

---

[91]Option value is determined using the same assumptions noted in paragraph A87 except the award is immediately vested.

[92]Because of the nature of the performance condition, the award has multiple requisite service periods that affect the manner in which compensation cost is attributed. Paragraphs A55–A74 provide guidance on estimating the requisite service period.

[93]Paragraphs A55–A74 provide guidance on estimating the requisite service period of an award.

[94]The difference in estimated fair values of each outcome is due to the change in estimate of the expected term of the share option. Outcome 1 uses an expected term in estimating fair value that is less than the expected term used for Outcome 2, which is equal to the award's 10-year contractual term. If a share option is transferable, its expected term is equal to its contractual term (paragraph A26).

three that the regulatory approval of the developmental drug therapy is likely to be obtained in six years rather than four, the requisite service period for Outcome 2 is revised, and the remaining unrecognized compensation cost would be recognized prospectively through year six. On the other hand, if it becomes probable that Outcome 2 will not occur, compensation cost recognized for Outcome 2, if any, would be reversed.

Illustration 7—Share Option with a Market Condition (Indexed Exercise Price)

A114. Entity T grants share options whose exercise price varies with an index of the share prices of a group of entities in the same industry, that is, a market condition as defined in this Statement (refer to Appendix E). Assume that on January 1, 20X5, Entity T grants 100 share options on its common stock with an initial exercise price of $30 to each of 1,000 employees. The share options have a maximum term of 10 years. The exercise price of the share options increases or decreases on December 31 of each year by the same percentage that the index has increased or decreased during the year. For example, if the peer group index increases by 10 percent in 20X5, the exercise price of the share options during 20X6 increases to $33 ($30 × 1.10). On January 1, 20X5, the peer group index is assumed to be 400. The dividend yield on the index is assumed to be 1.25 percent.

A115. Each indexed share option may be analyzed as a share option to exchange 0.0750 (30 ÷ 400) "shares" of the peer group index for a share of Entity T stock—that is, to exchange one noncash asset for another noncash asset. A share option to purchase stock for cash also can be thought of as a share option to exchange one asset (cash in the amount of the exercise price) for another (the share of stock). The intrinsic value of a cash share option equals the difference between the price of the stock upon exercise and the amount—the price—of the cash exchanged for the stock. The intrinsic value of a share option to exchange 0.0750 "shares" of the peer group index for a share of Entity T stock also equals the difference between the prices of the two assets exchanged.

A116. To illustrate the equivalence of an indexed share option and the share option above, assume that an employee exercises the indexed share option when Entity T's share price has increased 100 percent to $60 and the peer group index has increased 75 percent, from 400 to 700. The exercise price of the indexed share option thus is $52.50 ($30 × 1.75).

Price of Entity T share	$60.00
Less: Exercise price of share option	52.50
Intrinsic value of indexed share option	$ 7.50

That is the same as the intrinsic value of a share option to exchange 0.0750 shares of the index for 1 share of Entity T stock:

Price of Entity T share	$60.00
Less: Price of a share of the peer group index (.0750 × $700)	52.50
Intrinsic value at exchange	$ 7.50

A117. Option-pricing models can be extended to value a share option to exchange one asset for another. The principal extension is that the volatility of a share option to exchange two noncash assets is based on the relationship between the volatilities of the prices of the assets to be exchanged—their **cross-volatility.** In a share option with an exercise price payable in cash, the amount of cash to be paid has zero volatility, so only the volatility of the stock needs to be considered in estimating that option's fair value. In contrast, the fair value of a share option to exchange two noncash assets depends on possible movements in the prices of both assets—in this example, fair value depends on the cross-volatility of a share of the peer group index and a share of Entity T stock. Historical cross-volatility can be computed directly based on measures of Entity T's share price in shares of the peer group index. For example, Entity T's share price was 0.0750 shares at the grant date and 0.0857 (60 ÷ 700) shares at the exercise date.

Those share amounts then are used to compute cross-volatility. Cross-volatility also can be computed indirectly based on the respective volatilities of Entity T stock and the peer group index and the correlation between them. The expected cross-volatility between Entity T stock and the peer group index is assumed to be 30 percent.

A118. In a share option with an exercise price payable in cash, the assumed risk-free interest rate (discount rate) represents the return on the cash that will not be paid until exercise. In this example, an equivalent share of the index, rather than cash, is what will not be "paid" until exercise. Therefore, the dividend yield on the peer group index of 1.25 percent is used in place of the risk-free interest rate as an input to the option-pricing model.

A119. The initial exercise price for the indexed share option is the value of an equivalent share of the peer group index, which is $30 (0.0750 × $400). The fair value of each share option granted is $7.55 based on the following inputs:

Share price	$30
Exercise price	$30
Dividend yield	1.00%
Discount rate	1.25%
Volatility	30%
Contractual term	10 years
Suboptimal exercise factor[95]	1.10

A120. The indexed share options have a three-year explicit service period. The market condition affects the grant-date fair value of the award and its exercisability; however, vesting is based solely on the explicit service period of three years. The at-the-money nature of the award makes the derived service period irrelevant in determining the requisite service period in this example; therefore, the requisite service period of the award is three years based on the explicit service period. The accrual of compensation cost would be based on the number of options for which the requisite service is expected to be rendered (which is not

addressed in this illustration). That cost would be recognized over the requisite service period as shown in Illustration 4(a) (paragraphs A86–A96).

Illustration 8—Share Unit with Performance and Market Conditions

A121. Entity T grants 100,000 share units (SUs) to each of 10 vice presidents (VPs) (1 million SUs in total) on January 1, 20X5. Each SU has a contractual term of three years and a vesting condition based on performance. The performance condition is different for each VP and is based on specified goals to be achieved over three years (an explicit three-year service period). If the specified goals are not achieved at the end of three years, the SUs will not vest. Each SU is convertible into shares of Entity T at contractual maturity as follows: (a) if Entity T's share price has appreciated by a percentage that exceeds the percentage appreciation of the S&P 500 index by at least 10 percent (that is, the relative percentage increase is at least 10 percent), each SU converts into 3 shares of Entity T stock, (b) if the relative percentage increase is less than 10 percent but greater than zero percent, each SU converts into 2 shares of Entity T stock, (c) if the relative percentage increase is less than or equal to zero percent, each SU converts into 1 share of Entity T stock, and (d) if Entity T's share price has depreciated, each SU converts into zero shares of Entity T stock.[96] Appreciation or depreciation for Entity T's share price and the S&P 500 index is measured from the grant date.

A122. The SUs' conversion feature is based on a variable target stock price (that is, the target stock price varies based on the S&P 500 index); hence, it is a market condition. That market condition affects the fair value of the SUs that vest. Each VP's SUs vest only if the individual's performance condition is achieved; consequently, this award is accounted for as an award with a performance condition (paragraphs A49–A51). This example assumes that all SUs become fully vested; however, if the SUs do not vest because the performance conditions are not achieved, Entity T would reverse any previously recognized compensation cost associated with the nonvested SUs.

---

[95] Refer to paragraph A87, footnote 79.

[96] This market condition affects the ability to retain the award because the conversion ratio could be zero; however, vesting is based solely on the explicit service period of three years, which is equal to the contractual maturity of the award. That set of circumstances makes the derived service period irrelevant in determining the requisite service period; therefore, the requisite service period of the award is three years based on the explicit service period.

A123. The grant-date fair value of each SU is assumed for purposes of this example to be $36.[97] For simplicity, this example assumes that no forfeitures will occur during the vesting period. The grant-date fair value of the award is $36 million (1 million × $36); management of Entity T expects that all SUs will vest because the performance conditions are probable of achievement. Entity T recognizes compensation cost of $12 million ($36 million ÷ 3) in each year of the 3-year service period; the following journal entries are recognized by Entity T in 20X5, 20X6, and 20X7:

Compensation cost	$12,000,000	
Additional paid-in capital		$12,000,000

To recognize compensation cost.

Deferred tax asset	$4,200,000	
Deferred tax benefit		$4,200,000

To recognize the deferred tax asset for the temporary difference related to compensation cost ($12,000,000 × .35 = $4,200,000).

A124. Upon contractual maturity of the SUs, four outcomes are possible; however, because all possible outcomes of the market condition were incorporated into the SUs' grant-date fair value, no other entry related to compensation cost is necessary to account for the actual outcome of the market condition. However, if the SUs' conversion ratio was based on achieving a performance condition rather than on satisfying a market condition, compensation cost would be adjusted according to the actual outcome of the performance condition (refer to Illustration 6, paragraphs A111–A113).

Illustration 9—Share Option with Exercise Price That Increases by a Fixed Amount or a Fixed Percentage

A125. Some entities grant share options with exercise prices that increase by a fixed amount or a constant percentage periodically. For example, the exercise price of the share options in Illustration 4(a) (paragraphs A86–A96) might increase by a fixed amount of $2.50 per year. Lattice models and other valuation techniques can be adapted to accommodate exercise prices that change over time by a fixed amount.[98]

A126. Share options with exercise prices that increase by a constant percentage also can be valued using an option-pricing model that accommodates changes in exercise prices. Alternatively, those share options can be valued by deducting from the discount rate the annual percentage increase in the exercise price. That method works because a decrease in the risk-free interest rate and an increase in the exercise price have a similar effect—both reduce the share option value. For example, the exercise price of the share options in Illustration 4 might increase at the rate of 1 percent annually. For that example, Entity T's share options would be valued based on a risk-free interest rate less 1 percent. Holding all other assumptions constant from Illustration 4(a) (refer to paragraph A87), the value of each share option granted by Entity T would be $14.34.

Illustration 10—Share-Based Liability (Cash-Settled SARs)

A127. Entity T, a public company, grants share appreciation rights (SARs) with the same terms and conditions as those described in Illustration 4(a) (paragraphs A86–A88). Each SAR entitles the holder to receive an amount in cash equal to the increase in value of 1 share of Entity T stock over $30. Entity T determines the grant-date fair value of each SAR in the same manner as a share option and uses the same assumptions and option-pricing model used to estimate the fair value of the share options in Illustration 4(a); consequently, the grant-date fair value of each SAR is $14.69 (paragraphs A87–A88). The awards cliff-vest at the end of three years of service (an explicit and requisite service period of three years). The number of SARs for which the requisite service is expected to be rendered is estimated at the grant date to be 821,406 ($900,000 \times .97^3$). Thus, the fair value of the award at January 1, 20X5, is $12,066,454 (821,406 × $14.69). For simplicity, this example assumes that estimated forfeitures equal actual forfeitures.

A128. Paragraph 37 of this Statement requires that share-based compensation liabilities be recognized at

---

[97]Certain option-pricing models, including Monte Carlo simulation techniques, have been adapted to value path-dependent options and other complex instruments. In this case, the entity concludes that a Monte Carlo simulation technique provides a reasonable estimate of fair value. Each simulation represents a potential outcome, which determines whether an SU would convert into three, two, one, or zero shares of stock.

[98]Such an arrangement has a market condition and may have a derived service period.

fair value or a portion thereof (depending on the percentage of requisite service that has been rendered at the reporting date) and be remeasured at each reporting date through the date of settlement;[99] consequently, compensation cost recognized during each year of the three-year vesting period (as well as during each year thereafter through the date of settlement) will vary based on changes in the award's fair value. At December 31, 20X5, the assumed fair value is $10 per SAR; hence, the fair value of the award is $8,214,060 (821,406 × $10). The share-based compensation liability at December 31, 20X5, is $2,738,020 ($8,214,060 ÷ 3) to account for the portion of the award related to the service rendered in 20X5 (1 year of the 3-year requisite service period). For convenience, this example assumes that journal entries to account for the award are performed at year-end. The journal entries for 20X5 are as follows:

Compensation cost $2,738,020
   Share-based
     compensation liability $2,738,020

To recognize compensation cost.

Deferred tax asset $958,307
   Deferred tax benefit $958,307

To recognize the deferred tax asset for the temporary difference related to compensation cost ($2,738,020 × .35 = $958,307).

A129. At December 31, 20X6, the fair value is assumed to be $25 per SAR; hence, the award's fair value is $20,535,150 (821,406 × $25), and the corresponding liability at that date is $13,690,100 ($20,535,150 × ⅔) because service has been provided for 2 years of the 3-year requisite service pe-

riod. Compensation cost recognized for the award in 20X6 is $10,952,080 ($13,690,100 − $2,738,020). Entity T recognizes the following journal entries for 20X6:

Compensation cost $10,952,080
   Share-based
     compensation
     liability $10,952,080

To recognize a share-based compensation liability of $13,690,100 and associated compensation cost.

Deferred tax asset $3,833,228
   Deferred tax benefit $3,833,228

To recognize the deferred tax asset for additional compensation cost ($10,952,080 × .35 = $3,833,228).

A130. At December 31, 20X7, the fair value is assumed to be $20 per SAR; hence, the award's fair value is $16,428,120 (821,406 × $20), and the corresponding liability at that date is $16,428,120 ($16,428,120 × 1) because the award is fully vested. Compensation cost recognized for the liability award in 20X7 is $2,738,020 ($16,428,120 − $13,690,100). Entity T recognizes the following journal entries for 20X7:

Compensation cost $2,738,020
   Share-based
     compensation liability $2,738,020

To recognize a share-based compensation liability of $16,428,120 and associated compensation cost.

Deferred tax asset $958,307
   Deferred tax benefit $958,307

To recognize the deferred tax asset for additional compensation cost ($2,738,020 × .35 = $958,307).

Table 6—Share-Based Liability Award

Year	Total Value of Award at Year-End	Pretax Cost for Year	Cumulative Pretax Cost
20X5	$8,214,060 (821,406 × $10)	$2,738,020 ($8,214,060 ÷ 3)	$2,738,020
20X6	$20,535,150 (821,406 × $25)	$10,952,080 [($20,535,150 × ⅔) − $2,738,020]	$13,690,100
20X7	$16,428,120 (821,406 × $20)	$2,738,020 ($16,428,120 − $13,690,100)	$16,428,120

---

[99]Paragraph 38 permits a nonpublic entity to measure share-based payment liabilities at either fair value (or, in some cases, calculated value) or intrinsic value. If a nonpublic entity elects to measure those liabilities at fair value, the accounting demonstrated in this illustration would be applicable.

A131. For simplicity, this illustration assumes that all of the SARs are exercised on the same day, that the liability award's fair value is $20 per SAR, and that Entity T has already recognized its income tax expense for the year without regard to the effects of the exercise of the employee SARs. In other words, current tax expense and current taxes payable were recognized based on taxable income and deductions before consideration of additional deductions from exercise of the SARs. The amount credited to cash for the exercise of the SARs is equal to the share-based compensation liability of $16,428,120.

At exercise:

Share-based
  compensation liability $16,428,120
    Cash (821,406 × $20) $16,428,120
To recognize the cash payment to employees from SAR exercise.

Income Taxes

A132. The cash paid to the employees on the date of exercise is deductible for tax purposes. Entity T has sufficient taxable income, and the tax benefit realized is $5,749,842 ($16,428,120 × .35).

At exercise:

Deferred tax expense $5,749,842
  Deferred tax asset $5,749,842
To write off the deferred tax asset related to the SARs.

Current taxes payable $5,749,842
  Current tax expense $5,749,842
To adjust current tax expense and current taxes payable to recognize the current tax benefit from deductible compensation cost.

A133. If the SARs had expired worthless, the share-based compensation liability account and deferred tax asset account would have been adjusted to zero through the income statement as the award's fair value decreased.

Illustration 11—Share-Based Equity and Liability Awards Granted by a Nonpublic Entity

Illustration 11(a)—Share Award Granted by a Nonpublic Entity

A134. On January 1, 20X6, Entity W, a nonpublic entity,[100] grants 100 shares of stock to each of its 100 employees. The shares cliff vest at the end of three years. Entity W estimates that the grant-date fair value of 1 share of stock is $7. The grant-date fair value of the share award is $70,000 (100 × 100 × $7). The fair value of shares, which is equal to its intrinsic value, is not subsequently remeasured. For simplicity, the example assumes that no forfeitures occur during the vesting period. Because the requisite service period is three years, Entity W recognizes $23,333 ($70,000 ÷ 3) of compensation cost for each annual period as follows:

Compensation cost $23,333
  Additional paid-in capital $23,333
To recognize compensation cost.

Deferred tax asset $8,167
  Deferred tax benefit $8,167
To recognize the deferred tax asset for the temporary difference related to compensation cost ($23,333 × .35 = $8,167).

Income taxes

A135. After three years, all shares are vested. For simplicity, this illustration assumes that no employees made an IRS Code §83(b) election[101] and Entity W has already recognized its income tax expense for the year in which the shares become vested without regard to the effects of the share award.

A136. The fair value per share on the vesting date, assumed to be $20, is deductible for tax purposes. Paragraph 62 of this Statement requires that excess tax benefits be recognized as a credit to additional paid-in capital. Tax return deductions that are less than compensation cost recognized result in a charge to income tax expense in the period of vesting unless

---

[100]The accounting demonstrated in this illustration also would be applicable to a public entity that grants share awards to its employees. The same measurement method and basis is used for both nonvested share awards and restricted share awards (which are a subset of nonvested share awards).

[101]IRS Code §83(b) permits an employee to elect either the grant date or the vesting date for measuring the fair market value of an award of shares.

there are any remaining excess tax benefits from previous awards accounted for in accordance with this Statement or Statement 123, in which case, the amount of any tax deficiency is first offset against additional paid-in capital. With the share price at $20 on the vesting date, the deductible amount is $200,000 (10,000 × $20). The entity has sufficient taxable income, and the tax benefit realized is $70,000 ($200,000 × .35).

At vesting:

Deferred tax expense	$24,500	
Deferred tax asset		$24,500

To write off deferred tax asset related to deductible share award at vesting ($70,000 × .35 = $24,500).

Current taxes payable	$70,000	
Current tax expense		$24,500
Additional paid-in capital		$45,500

To adjust current tax expense and current taxes payable to recognize the current tax benefit from deductible compensation cost upon vesting of share award. The credit to additional paid-in capital is the excess tax benefit: ($200,000 – $70,000) × .35 = $45,500.

Illustration 11(b)—Share Option Award Granted by a Nonpublic Entity That Uses the Calculated Value Method

A137. On January 1, 20X6, Entity W, a small nonpublic entity that develops, manufactures, and distributes medical equipment, grants 100 share options to each of its 100 employees. The share price at the grant date is $7.[102] The options are granted at-the-money, cliff vest at the end of 3 years, and have a 10-year contractual term. Entity W estimates the expected term of the share options granted as 5 years and the risk-free rate as 3.75 percent. For simplicity, the example assumes that no forfeitures occur during the vesting period and that no dividends are expected to be paid in the future, and the example does not reflect the accounting for income tax consequences of the awards.

A138. Entity W does not maintain an internal market for its shares, which are rarely traded privately. It has not issued any new equity or convertible debt instruments for several years and has been unable to

identify any similar entities that are public. Entity W has determined that it is not practicable for it to estimate the expected volatility of its share price and, therefore, it is not possible for it to reasonably estimate the grant-date fair value of the share options. Accordingly, Entity W is required to apply the provisions of paragraph 23 of this Statement in accounting for the share options under the calculated value method.

A139. Entity W operates exclusively in the medical equipment industry. It visits the Dow Jones Indexes website and, using the Industry Classification Benchmark, reviews the various industry sector components of the Dow Jones U.S. Total Market Index. It identifies the medical equipment subsector, within the health care equipment and services sector, as the most appropriate industry sector in relation to its operations. It reviews the current components of the medical equipment index and notes that, based on the most recent assessment of its share price and its issued share capital, in terms of size it would rank among companies in the index with a small market capitalization (or *small-cap* companies). Entity W selects the small-cap version of the medical equipment index as an appropriate industry sector index because it considers that index to be representative of its size and the industry sector in which it operates. Entity W obtains the historical daily closing total return values of the selected index for the five years immediately prior to January 1, 20X6, from the Dow Jones Indexes website. It calculates the annualized historical volatility of those values to be 24 percent, based on 252 trading days per year.

A140. Entity W uses the inputs that it has determined above in a Black-Scholes-Merton option-pricing formula, which produces a value of $2.05 per share option. This results in total compensation cost of $20,500 (10,000 × $2.05) to be accounted for over the requisite service period of 3 years.

A141. For each of the 3 years ending December 31, 20X6, 20X7, and 20X8, Entity W will recognize compensation cost of $6,833 ($20,500 ÷ 3). The journal entry for each year is as follows:

Compensation cost	$6,833	
Additional paid-in capital		$6,833

To recognize compensation cost.

---

[102]The AICPA Practice Aid, *Valuation of Privately-Held-Company Equity Securities Issued as Compensation,* describes best practices for the valuation of privately-held-company equity securities issued as compensation.

Table 7—Share Option Award Granted by a Nonpublic Entity That Uses the Calculated Value Method

Year	Total Calculated Value of Award	Pretax Cost for Year	Cumulative Pretax Cost
20X6	$20,500 (10,000 × $2.05)	$6,833 ($20,500 ÷ 3)	$6,833
20X7	$20,500 (10,000 × $2.05)	$6,834 ($20,500 × ⅔ – $6,833)	$13,667
20X8	$20,500 (10,000 × $2.05)	$6,833 ($20,500 – $13,667)	$20,500

A142. Assuming that all 10,000 share options are exercised on the same day in 20Y2, the accounting for the option exercise will follow the same pattern as in Illustration 4 (paragraph A93) and will result in the following journal entry.

At exercise:

Cash (10,000 × $7)	$70,000	
Additional paid-in capital	$20,500	
Common stock		$90,500

To recognize the issuance of shares upon exercise of options and to reclassify previously recognized paid-in capital.

Illustration 11(c)—Share-Based Liability Award Granted by a Nonpublic Entity That Elects the Intrinsic Value Method

A143. On January 1, 20X6, Entity W, a nonpublic entity that has chosen the accounting policy of using the intrinsic value method of accounting for share-based payments that are classified as liabilities in accordance with paragraph 38 of this Statement, grants 100 cash-settled SARs with a 5-year life to each of its 100 employees. Each SAR entitles the holder to receive an amount in cash equal to the increase in value of 1 share of Entity W stock over $7. The awards cliff-vest at the end of three years of service (an explicit and requisite service period of three years). For simplicity, the example assumes that no forfeitures occur during the vesting period and does not reflect the accounting for income tax consequences of the awards.

A144. Because of Entity W's accounting policy decision to use intrinsic value, all of its share-based payments that are classified as liabilities are recognized at intrinsic value (or a portion thereof, depending on the percentage of requisite service that has been rendered) at each reporting date through the date of settlement; consequently, the compensation cost recognized in each year of the three-year requisite service period will vary based on changes in the liability award's intrinsic value. At December 31, 20X6, Entity W stock is valued at $10 per share; hence, the intrinsic value is $3 per SAR ($10 – $7), and the intrinsic value of the award is $30,000 (10,000 × $3). The compensation cost to be recognized for 20X6, is $10,000 ($30,000 ÷ 3), which corresponds to the service provided in 20X6 (1 year of the 3-year service period). For convenience, this example assumes that journal entries to account for the award are performed at year-end. The journal entry for 20X6 is as follows:

Compensation cost	$10,000	
Share-based compensation liability		$10,000

To recognize compensation cost.

A145. At December 31, 20X7, Entity W stock is valued at $8 per share; hence, the intrinsic value is $1 per SAR ($8 – $7), and the intrinsic value of the award is $10,000 (10,000 × $1). The decrease in the intrinsic value of the award is $20,000 ($10,000 – $30,000). Because services for 2 years of the 3-year service period have been rendered, Entity W must recognize cumulative compensation cost for two-thirds of the intrinsic value of the award, or $6,667 ($10,000 × ⅔); however, Entity W recognized compensation cost of $10,000 in 20X5. Thus, Entity W must recognize an entry in 20X7 to reduce cumulative compensation cost to $6,667:

Share-based compensation liability	$3,333	
Compensation cost		$3,333

To adjust cumulative compensation cost ($6,667 – $10,000).

A146. At December 31, 20X8, Entity W stock is valued at $15 per share; hence, the intrinsic value is $8 per SAR ($15 – $7), and the intrinsic value of the award is $80,000 (10,000 × $8). The cumulative compensation cost recognized at December 31, 20X8, is $80,000 because the award is fully vested. The journal entry for 20X8 is as follows:

Compensation cost	$73,333	
Share-based compensation liability		$73,333

To recognize compensation cost ($80,000 – $6,667).

Table 8—Share-Based Liability Award at Intrinsic Value

Year	Total Value of Award at Year-End	Pretax Cost for Year	Cumulative Pretax Cost
20X6	$30,000 (10,000 × $3)	$10,000 ($30,000 ÷ 3)	$10,000
20X7	$10,000 (10,000 × $1)	$(3,333) [($10,000 × ⅔) – $10,000]	$6,667
20X8	$80,000 (10,000 × $8)	$73,333 ($80,000 – $6,667)	$80,000

A147. For simplicity, the illustration assumes that all of the SARs are settled on the day that they vest, December 31, 20X8, when the share price is $15 and the intrinsic value is $8 per share. The cash paid to settle the SARs is equal to the share-based compensation liability of $80,000.

At exercise:

Share-based compensation liability	$80,000	
Cash (10,000 × $8)		$80,000

To recognize the cash payment to employees for settlement of SARs.

A148. If the SARs had not been settled, Entity W would continue to remeasure those remaining awards at intrinsic value at each reporting date through the date they are exercised or otherwise settled.

Illustration 12—Modifications and Settlements

Illustration 12(a)—Modification of Vested Share Options

A149. The following examples of accounting for modifications of the terms of an award are based on Illustration 4(a) (paragraphs A86–A88), in which En-

tity T granted its employees 900,000 share options with an exercise price of $30 on January 1, 20X5. At January 1, 20X9, after the share options have vested, the market price of Entity T stock has declined to $20 per share, and Entity T decides to reduce the exercise price of the outstanding share options to $20. In effect, Entity T issues new share options with an exercise price of $20 and a contractual term equal to the remaining contractual term of the original January 1, 20X5, share options, which is 6 years, in exchange for the original vested share options. Entity T incurs additional compensation cost for the excess of the fair value of the modified share options issued over the fair value of the original share options at the date of the exchange, measured as shown in paragraph A150.[103] The modified share options are immediately vested, and the additional compensation cost is recognized in the period the modification occurs.

A150. The January 1, 20X9, fair value of the modified award is $7.14. To determine the amount of additional compensation cost arising from the modification, the fair value of the original vested share options assumed to be repurchased is computed immediately prior to the modification. The resulting fair value at January 1, 20X9, of the original share options is $3.67 per share option, based on their remaining contractual term of 6 years, suboptimal exercise

---

[103] A nonpublic entity using the calculated value would compare the calculated value of the original award immediately before the modification with the calculated value of the modified award unless an entity has ceased to use the calculated value, in which case it would follow the guidance in paragraphs 51(a) and 51(b) of this Statement (calculating the effect of the modification based on the fair value).

factor of 2, $20 current share price, $30 exercise price, risk-free interest rates of 1.5 percent to 3.4 percent, expected volatility of 35 percent to 50 percent and a 1.0 percent expected dividend yield. The additional compensation cost stemming from the modification is $3.47 per share option, determined as follows:

Fair value of modified share option at January 1, 20X9	$7.14
Less: Fair value of original share option at January 1, 20X9	3.67
Additional compensation cost to be recognized	$3.47

Compensation cost already recognized during the vesting period of the original award is $10,981,157 for 747,526 vested share options (refer to Illustration 4, paragraph A92). For simplicity, it is assumed that no share options were exercised before the modification. Previously recognized compensation cost is not adjusted. Additional compensation cost of $2,593,915 (747,526 vested share options × $3.47) is recognized on January 1, 20X9, because the modified share options are fully vested; any income tax effects from the additional compensation cost are recognized accordingly.

Illustration 12(b)—Share Settlement of Vested Share Options

A151. Rather than modify the option terms, Entity T offers to settle the original January 1, 20X5, share options for fully vested equity shares at January 1, 20X9. The fair value of each share option is estimated the same way as shown in Illustration 12(a) (refer to paragraphs A149 and A150), resulting in a fair value of $3.67 per share option. Entity T recognizes the settlement as the repurchase of an outstanding equity instrument, and no additional compensation cost is recognized at the date of settlement unless the payment in fully vested equity shares exceeds $3.67 per share option. Previously recognized compensation cost for the fair value of the original share options is not adjusted.

Illustration 12(c)—Modification of Nonvested Share Options

A152. This example assumes that Entity T granted its employees 900,000 share options with an exercise price of $30. At January 1, 20X6, 1 year into the 3-year vesting period, the market price of Entity T stock has declined to $20 per share, and Entity T decides to reduce the exercise price of the share options to $20. The 3-year cliff-vesting requirement is not changed. In effect, in exchange for the original nonvested share options, Entity T grants new share options with an exercise price of $20 and a contractual term equal to the 9-year remaining contractual term of the original share options granted on January 1, 20X5. Entity T incurs additional compensation cost for the excess of the fair value of the modified share options issued over the fair value of the original share options at the date of the exchange determined in the manner described in paragraph A150. Entity T adds that additional compensation cost to the remaining unrecognized compensation cost for the original share options at the date of modification and recognizes the total amount ratably over the remaining two years of the three-year vesting period.[104]

A153. The January 1, 20X6 fair value of the modified award is $8.59 per share option, based on its contractual term of 9 years, suboptimal exercise factor of 2, $20 current share price, $20 exercise price, risk-free interest rates of 1.5 percent to 4.0 percent, expected volatilities of 35 percent to 55 percent, and a 1.0 percent expected dividend yield. The fair value of the original award immediately prior to the modification is $5.36 per share option, based on its remaining contractual term of 9 years, suboptimal exercise factor of 2, $20 current share price, $30 exercise price, risk-free interest rates of 1.5 percent to 4.0 percent, expected volatilities of 35 percent to 55 percent, and a 1.0 percent expected dividend yield. Thus, the additional compensation cost stemming from the modification is $3.23 per share option, determined as follows:

Fair value of modified share option at January 1, 20X6	$8.59
Less: Fair value of original share option at January 1, 20X6	5.36
Incremental value of modified share option at January 1, 20X6	$3.23

A154. On January 1, 20X6, the remaining balance of unrecognized compensation cost for the original

---

[104]Because the original vesting provision is not changed, the modification has an explicit service period of two years, which represents the requisite service period as well. Thus, incremental compensation cost resulting from the modification would be recognized ratably over the remaining two years rather than in some other pattern.

share options is $9.79 per share option.[105] The total compensation cost for each modified share option that is expected to vest is $13.02, determined as follows:

Incremental value of modified share option	$ 3.23
Unrecognized compensation cost for original share option	9.79
Total compensation cost to be recognized	$13.02

That amount is recognized during 20X6 and 20X7, the two remaining years of the requisite service period.

Illustration 12(d)—Cash Settlement of Nonvested Share Options

A155. Rather than modify the share option terms, Entity T offers on January 1, 20X6, to settle the original January 1, 20X5, grant of share options for cash. Because the share price decreased from $30 at the grant date to $20 at the date of settlement, the fair value of each share option is $5.36, the same as in Illustration 12(c) (refer to paragraphs A152–A154). If Entity T pays $5.36 per share option, it would recognize that cash settlement as the repurchase of an outstanding equity instrument and no incremental compensation cost would be recognized. However, the cash settlement of the share options effectively vests them. Therefore, the remaining unrecognized compensation cost of $9.79 per share option would be recognized at the date of settlement.

Illustration 12(e)—Equity Restructurings

A156. In accordance with paragraph 54 of this Statement, accounting for a modification in conjunction with an equity restructuring requires a comparison of the fair value of the modified award with the fair value of the original award immediately before the modification, except as follows: If an award is modified to add an antidilution provision (that is, a provision designed to equalize an award's value before and after an equity restructuring) and that modification is not made in contemplation of an equity restructuring, a comparison of the fair value of the modified award and the fair value of the original award immediately before the modification is not required. Paragraphs A157–A159 provide additional guidance on accounting for modifications of awards in the context of equity restructurings.

Original award contains antidilution provisions

A157. For example, assume an award contains antidilution provisions. On May 1 there is an announcement of a future equity restructuring. On October 12 the equity restructuring occurs and the terms of the award are modified in accordance with the antidilution provisions. In this example, the modification occurs on October 12 when the terms of the award are changed. The fair value of the award is compared pre- and post-modification on October 12. The calculation of fair value is necessary to determine if there is any incremental value transferred as a result of the modification, and if so, that incremental value would be recognized as additional compensation cost. If there is no incremental fair value, no additional compensation cost would be recognized.

Original award does not contain antidilution provisions

A158. In this example, the original award does not contain antidilution provisions. On May 1 there is an announcement of a future equity restructuring. On July 26 the terms of an award are modified to add antidilution provisions in contemplation of an equity restructuring. On September 30 the equity restructuring occurs. In this example, there are two modifications to account for. The first modification occurs on July 26, when the terms of the award are changed to add antidilution provisions. Because the modification to add antidilution provisions on July 26 is done in contemplation of an equity restructuring, there must be a comparison of the fair value of the award pre- and post-modification on July 26. The pre-modification fair value is based on the award without antidilution provisions taking into account the effect of the contemplated restructuring on its value. The post-modification fair value is based on an award with antidilution provisions, taking into account the effect of the contemplated restructuring on its value. Any incremental value transferred would be recognized as additional compensation cost. Once the equity restructuring occurs, there is a second modification event on September 30 when the terms of the award are changed in accordance with the antidilution provisions. A second comparison of pre- and post-modification fair values is then required to determine whether any incremental value is transferred as a result of the modification. Changes to the terms

---

[105]Using a value of $14.69 for the original option as noted in Illustration 4 (refer to paragraph A88) results in recognition of $4.90 ($14.69 ÷ 3) per year. The unrecognized balance at January 1, 20X6, is $9.79 ($14.69 − $4.90) per option.

of an award in accordance with its antidilution provisions generally would not result in additional compensation cost if the antidilution provisions were properly structured. The incremental value transferred, if any, would be recognized as additional compensation cost.

A159. Assume the same facts as in paragraph A158 except the terms of the awards are modified on the date of the equity restructuring, September 30. In contrast to paragraph A158 in which there are two separate modifications, there is one modification that occurs on September 30 and the fair value is compared pre- and post-modification to determine whether any incremental value is transferred as a result of the modification. Any incremental value transferred would be recognized as additional compensation cost.

Illustration 13—Modifications of Awards with Performance and Service Vesting Conditions

A160. Paragraphs A49–A51 note that awards may vest based on service conditions, performance conditions, or a combination of the two.[106] A modification of vesting conditions is accounted for based on the principles in paragraph 51 of this Statement: total recognized compensation cost for an equity award that is modified shall at least equal the fair value of the award at the grant date unless, at the date of the modification, the performance or service conditions of the original award are not expected to be satisfied. If awards are expected to vest under the original vesting conditions at the date of the modification, an entity should recognize compensation cost if either (a) the awards ultimately vest under the modified vesting conditions or (b) the awards ultimately would have vested under the original vesting conditions. In contrast, if at the date of modification awards are not expected to vest under the original vesting conditions, an entity should recognize compensation cost only if the awards vest under the modified vesting conditions. Said differently, if the entity believes that the original performance or service vesting condition is not probable of achievement at the date of the modification, the cumulative compensation cost related to the modified award, assuming vesting occurs under the modified performance or service vesting

condition, is the modified award's fair value at the date of the modification. The following examples (paragraphs A161–A170) illustrate the application of those requirements.

A161. Illustrations 13(a)–13(d) are all based on the same scenario: Entity T grants 1,000 share options to each of 10 employees in the sales department. The share options have the same terms and conditions as those described in Illustration 4 (paragraphs A86–A87), except that the share options specify that vesting is conditional upon selling 150,000 units of product A (the original sales target) over the 3-year explicit service period. The grant-date fair value of each option is $14.69 (refer to Illustration 4(a), paragraph A88). For simplicity, this example assumes that no forfeitures will occur from employee termination; forfeitures will only occur if the sales target is not achieved. Illustration 13(e) is not based on the same scenario as Illustrations 13(a)–13(d) but, rather, provides an additional illustration of a Type III modification.

Illustration 13(a)—Type I (Probable-to-Probable) Modification

A162. Based on historical sales patterns and expectations related to the future, management of Entity T believes at the grant date that it is probable that the sales target will be achieved. At January 1, 20X7, 102,000 units of product A have been sold. During December 20X6, one of Entity T's competitors declared bankruptcy after a fire destroyed a factory and warehouse containing the competitor's inventory. To push the sales people to take advantage of that situation, the award is modified on January 1, 20X7, to raise the sales target to 154,000 units of product A (the modified sales target).[107] Additionally, as of January 1, 20X7, the options are out-of-the-money because of a general stock market decline.[108] No other terms or conditions of the original award are modified, and management of Entity T continues to believe that it is probable that the modified sales target will be achieved. Immediately prior to the modification, total compensation cost expected to be recognized over the 3-year vesting period is $146,900 or $14.69 multiplied by the number of share options expected to vest (10,000). Because no other terms or

---

[106]Modifications of market conditions that affect exercisability or the ability to retain the award are not addressed by this illustration.

[107]Notwithstanding the nature of the modification's probability of occurrence, the objective of this illustration is to demonstrate the accounting for a Type I modification.

[108]The examples in Illustration 13 assume that the options are out-of-the-money when modified; however, that fact is not determinative in the illustrations (that is, options could be in- or out-of-the-money).

conditions of the award were modified, the modification does not affect the per-share-option fair value (assumed to be $8 in this example at the date of the modification). Moreover, because the modification does not affect the number of share options expected to vest, no incremental compensation cost is associated with the modification.

A163. This paragraph illustrates the cumulative compensation cost Entity T should recognize for the modified award based on three potential outcomes: Outcome 1—achievement of the modified sales target, Outcome 2—achievement of the original sales target, and Outcome 3—failure to achieve either sales target. In Outcome 1, all 10,000 share options vest because the salespeople sold at least 154,000 units of product A. In that outcome, Entity T will recognize cumulative compensation cost of $146,900. In Outcome 2, no share options vest because the salespeople sold more than 150,000 units of product A but less than 154,000 units (the modified sales target is not achieved). In that outcome, Entity T will recognize cumulative compensation cost of $146,900 because the share options would have vested under the original terms and conditions of the award. In Outcome 3, no share options vest because the modified sales target is not achieved; additionally, no share options would have vested under the original terms and conditions of the award. In that case, Entity T will recognize cumulative compensation cost of $0.

Illustration 13(b)—Type II (Probable-to-Improbable) Modification

A164. It is generally believed that Type II modifications will be rare; therefore, this illustration has been provided for the sake of completeness. Based on historical sales patterns and expectations related to the future, management of Entity T believes that at the grant date, it is probable that the sales target (150,000 units of product A) will be achieved. At January 1, 20X7, 102,000 units of product A have been sold and the options are out-of-the-money because of a general stock market decline. Entity T's management implements a cash bonus program based on achieving an annual sales target for 20X7.[109] Concurrently, the sales target for the option awards is revised to 170,000 units of product A. No other terms or conditions of the original award are modified. Manage-

ment believes that the modified sales target is not probable of achievement; however, they continue to believe that the original sales target is probable of achievement. Immediately prior to the modification, total compensation cost expected to be recognized over the 3-year vesting period is $146,900 or $14.69 multiplied by the number of share options expected to vest (10,000). Because no other terms or conditions of the award were modified, the modification does not affect the per-share-option fair value (assumed in this example to be $8 at the modification date). Moreover, because the modification does not affect the number of share options expected to vest under the original vesting provisions, Entity T will determine incremental compensation cost in the following manner:

Fair value of modified share option	$ 8
Share options expected to vest under original sales target[110]	10,000
Fair value of modified award	$80,000
Fair value of original share option	$ 8
Share options expected to vest under original sales target	10,000
Fair value of original award	$80,000
Incremental compensation cost of modification	$ 0

A165. This paragraph illustrates the cumulative compensation cost Entity T should recognize for the modified award based on three potential outcomes: Outcome 1—achievement of the modified sales target, Outcome 2—achievement of the original sales target, and Outcome 3—failure to achieve either sales target. In Outcome 1, all 10,000 share options vest because the salespeople sold at least 170,000 units of product A. In that outcome, Entity T will recognize cumulative compensation cost of $146,900. In Outcome 2, no share options vest because the salespeople sold more than 150,000 units of product A but less than 170,000 units (the modified sales target is not achieved). In that outcome, Entity T will recognize cumulative compensation cost of $146,900 because the share options would have vested under the original terms and conditions of the award. In Outcome 3, no share options vest because the modified sales target is not achieved; additionally, no share

---

[109]The options are neither cancelled nor settled as a result of the cash bonus program. The cash bonus program would be accounted for using the same accounting as for other cash bonus arrangements.

[110]In determining the fair value of the modified award for this type of modification, an entity should use the greater of the options expected to vest under the modified vesting condition or the options that previously had been expected to vest under the original vesting condition.

options would have vested under the original terms and conditions of the award. In that case, Entity T will recognize cumulative compensation cost of $0.

Illustration 13(c)—Type III (Improbable-to-Probable) Modification

A166. Based on historical sales patterns and expectations related to the future, management of Entity T believes at the grant date that none of the options will vest because it is not probable that the sales target will be achieved. At January 1, 20X7, 80,000 units of product A have been sold. To further motivate the salespeople, the sales target (150,000 units of product A) is lowered to 120,000 units of product A (the modified sales target). No other terms or conditions of the original award are modified. Management believes that the modified sales target is probable of achievement. Immediately prior to the modification, total compensation cost expected to be recognized over the 3-year vesting period is $0 or $14.69 multiplied by the number of share options expected to vest (zero). Because no other terms or conditions of the award were modified, the modification does not affect the per-share-option fair value (assumed in this example to be $8 at the modification date). Since the modification affects the number of share options expected to vest under the original vesting provisions, Entity T will determine incremental compensation cost in the following manner:

Fair value of modified share option	$ 8
Share options expected to vest under modified sales target	10,000
Fair value of modified award	$80,000
Fair value of original share option	$ 8
Share options expected to vest under original sales target	0
Fair value of original award	$ 0
Incremental compensation cost of modification	$80,000

A167. This paragraph illustrates the cumulative compensation cost Entity T should recognize for the modified award based on three potential outcomes: Outcome 1—achievement of the modified sales target, Outcome 2—achievement of the original sales target and the modified sales target, and Outcome 3—failure to achieve either sales target. In Outcome 1, all 10,000 share options vest because the salespeople sold at least 120,000 units of product A. In that outcome, Entity T will recognize cumulative compensation cost of $80,000. In Outcome 2, Entity T will recognize cumulative compensation cost of

$80,000 because in a Type III modification the original vesting condition is generally not relevant (that is, the modified award generally vests at a lower threshold of service or performance). In Outcome 3, no share options vest because the modified sales target is not achieved; in that case, Entity T will recognize cumulative compensation cost of $0.

Illustration 13(d)—Type IV (Improbable-to-Improbable) Modification

A168. Based on historical sales patterns and expectations related to the future, management of Entity T believes that at the grant date it is not probable that the sales target will be achieved. At January 1, 20X7, 80,000 units of product A have been sold. To further motivate the salespeople, the sales target is lowered to 130,000 units of product A (the modified sales target). No other terms or conditions of the original award are modified. Entity T lost a major customer for product A in December 20X6; hence, management continues to believe that the modified sales target is not probable of achievement. Immediately prior to the modification, total compensation cost expected to be recognized over the 3-year vesting period is $0 or $14.69 multiplied by the number of share options expected to vest (zero). Because no other terms or conditions of the award were modified, the modification does not affect the per-share-option fair value (assumed in this example to be $8 at the modification date). Furthermore, the modification does not affect the number of share options expected to vest; hence, there is no incremental compensation cost associated with the modification.

A169. This paragraph illustrates the cumulative compensation cost Entity T should recognize for the modified award based on three potential outcomes: Outcome 1—achievement of the modified sales target, Outcome 2—achievement of the original sales target and the modified sales target, and Outcome 3—failure to achieve either sales target. In Outcome 1, all 10,000 share options vest because the salespeople sold at least 130,000 units of product A. In that outcome, Entity T will recognize cumulative compensation cost of $80,000 (10,000 × $8). In Outcome 2, Entity T will recognize cumulative compensation cost of $80,000 because in a Type IV modification the original vesting condition is generally not relevant (that is, the *modified* award generally vests at a lower threshold of service or performance). In Outcome 3, no share options vest because the modified sales target is not achieved; in that case, Entity T will recognize cumulative compensation cost of $0.

Illustration 13(e)—An Additional Illustration of a Type III (Improbable-to-Probable) Modification

A170. On January 1, 20X7, Entity Z issues 1,000 at-the-money options with a 4-year explicit service condition to each of 50 employees that work in Plant J. On December 12, 20X7, Entity Z decides to close Plant J and notifies the 50 Plant J employees that their employment relationship will be terminated effective June 30, 20X8. On June 30, 20X8, Entity Z accelerates vesting of all options. The grant date fair value of each option is $20 on January 1, 20X7, and $10 on June 30, 20X8, the modification date. At the date Entity Z decides to close Plant J and terminate the employees, the service condition of the original award is not expected to be satisfied because the employees cannot render the requisite service; therefore, any compensation cost recognized as of December 12, 20X7, for the original award would be reversed. At the date of the modification, the fair value of the original award, which is $0 ($10 × 0 options expected to vest under the original terms of the award), is subtracted from the fair value of the modified award $500,000 ($10 × 50,000 options expected to vest under the modified award). The total recognized compensation cost of $500,000 will be less than the fair value of the award at the grant date ($1 million) because at the date of the modification, the original vesting conditions were not expected to be satisfied.

Illustration 14—Modifications That Change an Award's Classification

A171. A modification may affect the classification of an award (for example, change the award from an equity instrument to a liability instrument). If an entity modifies an award in that manner, this Statement requires that the entity account for that modification in accordance with paragraph 51 of this Statement.

Illustration 14(a)—Equity-to-Liability Modification (Share-Settled Share Options to Cash-Settled Share Options)

A172. Entity T grants the same share options described in Illustration 4(a) (paragraphs A86–A90). The number of options for which the requisite service is expected to be rendered is estimated at the grant date to be 821,406 (900,000 × .97³). For simplicity, this example assumes that estimated forfeitures equal actual forfeitures. Thus, as shown in Table 9 (paragraph A177), the fair value of the award at

January 1, 20X5, is $12,066,454 (821,406 × $14.69), and the compensation cost to be recognized during each year of the 3-year vesting period is $4,022,151 ($12,066,454 ÷ 3). The journal entries for 20X5 are the same as those in paragraph A91.

A173. On January 1, 20X6, Entity T modifies the share options granted to allow the employee the choice of share settlement or net-cash settlement; the options no longer qualify as equity because the holder can require Entity T to settle the options by delivering cash. Because the modification affects no other terms or conditions of the options, the fair value (assumed to be $7 per share option) of the modified award equals the fair value of the original award immediately before its terms are modified on the date of modification; the modification also does not change the number of share options for which the requisite service is expected to be rendered. On the modification date, Entity T recognizes a liability equal to the portion of the award attributed to past service multiplied by the modified award's fair value. To the extent that the liability equals or is less than the amount recognized in equity for the original award, the offsetting debit is a charge to equity. To the extent that the liability exceeds the amount recognized in equity for the original award, the excess is recognized as compensation cost. In this example, at the modification date, one-third of the award is attributed to past service (one year of service rendered ÷ three-year requisite service period). The modified award's fair value is $5,749,842 (821,406 × $7), and the liability to be recognized at the modification date is $1,916,614 ($5,749,842 ÷ 3). The related journal entry follows.

Additional paid-in capital	$1,916,614	
Share-based compensation liability		$1,916,614

To recognize the share-based compensation liability.

A174. No entry should be made to the deferred tax accounts at the modification date. The amount of remaining additional paid-in capital attributable to compensation cost recognized in 20X5 is $2,105,537 ($4,022,151 – $1,916,614).

A175. Paragraph 51(b) of this Statement specifies that total recognized compensation cost for an equity award shall at least equal the fair value of the award at the grant date unless at the date of the modification the service or performance conditions of the original award are not expected to be satisfied. In accordance with that principle, Entity T will ultimately recognize cumulative compensation cost equal to the greater of (a) the grant-date fair value of the original equity award and (b) the fair value of the modified liability award when it is settled. To the extent that the recognized fair value of the modified liability award is less than the recognized compensation cost associated with the grant-date fair value of the original equity award, changes in that liability award's fair value through its settlement do not affect the amount of compensation cost recognized. To the extent that the fair value of the modified liability award exceeds the recognized compensation cost associated with the grant-date fair value of the original equity award, changes in the liability award's fair value are recognized as compensation cost.

A176. At December 31, 20X6, the fair value of the modified award is assumed to be $25 per share option; hence, the modified award's fair value is $20,535,150 (821,406 × $25), and the corresponding liability at that date is $13,690,100 ($20,535,150 × ⅔) because two-thirds of the requisite service period has been rendered. The increase in the fair value of the liability award is $11,773,486 ($13,690,100 − $1,916,614). Prior to any adjustments for 20X6, the amount of remaining additional paid-in capital attributable to compensation cost recognized in 20X5 is $2,105,537 ($4,022,151 − $1,916,614). The cumulative compensation cost at December 31, 20X6, associated with the grant-date fair value of the original equity award is $8,044,302 ($4,022,151 × 2). Entity T records the following journal entries for 20X6:

Compensation cost	$9,667,949	
Additional paid-in capital	$2,105,537	
Share-based compensation liability		$11,773,486

To increase the share-based compensation liability to $13,690,100 and recognize compensation cost of $9,667,949 ($13,690,100 − $4,022,151).

Deferred tax asset	$3,383,782	
Deferred tax benefit		$3,383,782

To recognize the deferred tax asset for additional compensation cost ($9,667,949 × .35 = $3,383,782).

A177. At December 31, 20X7, the fair value is assumed to be $10 per share option; hence, the modified award's fair value is $8,214,060 (821,406 × $10), and the corresponding liability for the fully vested award at that date is $8,214,060. The decrease in the fair value of the liability award is $5,476,040 ($8,214,060 − $13,690,100). The cumulative compensation cost as of December 31, 20X7, associated with the grant-date fair value of the original equity award is $12,066,454 (paragraph A172). Entity T records the following journal entries for 20X7:

Share-based compensation liability	$5,476,040	
Compensation cost		$1,623,646
Additional paid-in capital		$3,852,394

To recognize a share-based compensation liability of $8,214,060, a reduction of compensation cost of $1,623,646 ($13,690,100 − $12,066,454), and additional paid-in capital of $3,852,394 ($12,066,454 − $8,214,060).

Deferred tax expense	$568,276	
Deferred tax asset		$568,276

To reduce the deferred tax asset for the reduction in compensation cost ($1,623,646 × .35 = $568,276).

Table 9—Modified Liability Award—Cliff Vesting

Year	Total Value of Award	Pretax Cost for Year	Cumulative Pretax Cost
20X5	$12,066,454 (821,406 × $14.69)	$4,022,151 ($12,066,454 ÷ 3)	$4,022,151
20X6	$20,535,150 (821,406 × $25.00)	$9,667,949 [($20,535,150 × ⅔) − $4,022,151]	$13,690,100
20X7	$12,066,454 (821,406 × $14.69)	$(1,623,646) ($12,066,454 − $13,690,100)	$12,066,454

Income taxes

A178. For simplicity, this illustration assumes that all share option holders elected to be paid in cash on the same day, that the liability award's fair value is $10 per option, and that Entity T has already recognized its income tax expense for the year without regard to the effects of the settlement of the award. In other words, current tax expense and current taxes payable were recognized based on income and deductions before consideration of additional deductions from settlement of the award.

A179. The $8,214,060 in cash paid to the employees on the date of settlement is deductible for tax purposes. In the period of settlement, tax return deductions that are less than compensation cost recognized result in a charge to income tax expense except to the extent that there is any remaining additional paid-in capital from excess tax benefits from previous share-based payment awards available to offset that deficiency. The entity has sufficient taxable income, and the tax benefit realized is $2,874,921 ($8,214,060 × .35). As tax return deductions are less than compensation cost recognized, the entity must write off the deferred tax assets recognized in excess of the tax benefit ultimately realized from the exercise of employee stock options. Entity T has sufficient paid-in capital available from excess tax benefits from previous share-based payment awards to offset the entire tax deficiency. Therefore, the result is a debit to additional paid-in capital. The journal entries to reflect settlement of the share options are as follows:

Share-based		
compensation liability	$8,214,060	
Cash ($10 × 821,406)		$8,214,060

To recognize the cash paid to settle share options.

Deferred tax expense	$4,223,259	
Deferred tax asset		$4,223,259

To write off deferred tax asset related to compensation cost ($12,066,454 × .35 = $4,223,259).

Current taxes payable	$2,874,921	
Additional paid-in capital	$1,348,338	
Current tax expense		$4,223,259

To adjust current tax expense and current taxes payable for the tax benefit from deductible compensation cost upon settlement of share options.

A180. If instead of requesting cash, employees had held their share options and those options had expired worthless, the share-based compensation liability account would have been eliminated over time with a corresponding increase to additional paid-in capital. Previously recognized compensation cost would not be reversed. Similar to the adjustment for the actual tax deduction realized described in paragraph A179, all of the deferred tax asset of $4,223,259 would be charged to income tax expense except to the extent that there was any remaining paid-in capital available from excess tax benefits from previous share-based payment awards available to offset that deficiency when the share options expired.

Illustration 14(b)—Equity-to-Equity Modification (Share Options to Shares)

A181. Equity-to-equity modifications also are addressed in Illustrations 12 and 13. The following example is based on Illustration 4(a) (paragraphs A86–A96), in which Entity T granted its employees 900,000 options with an exercise price of $30 on January 1, 20X5. At January 1, 20X9, after 747,526 share options have vested, the market price of Entity T stock has declined to $8 per share, and Entity T offers to exchange 4 options with an assumed per-share-option fair value of $2 at the date of exchange for 1 share of nonvested stock, with a market price of $8 per share. The nonvested stock will cliff vest after two years of service. All option holders elect to participate, and at the date of exchange, Entity T grants 186,881 (747,526 ÷ 4) nonvested shares of stock. Because the fair value of the nonvested stock is equal to the fair value of the options, there is no incremental compensation cost. Entity T will not make any additional accounting entries for the shares regardless of whether they vest, other than possibly reclassifying amounts in equity; however, Entity T will need to account for the ultimate income tax effects related to the share-based compensation arrangement.

Illustration 14(c)—Liability-to-Equity Modification (Cash-Settled to Share-Settled SARs)

A182. This illustration is based on the facts given in Illustration 10 (paragraphs A127–A133): Entity T grants cash-settled SARs to its employees. The fair value of the award at January 1, 20X5, is $12,066,454 (821,406 × $14.69) (paragraph A127).

A183. At December 31, 20X5, the assumed fair value is $10 per SAR; hence, the fair value of the award at that date is $8,214,060 (821,406 × $10). The share-based compensation liability at December 31, 20X5, is $2,738,020 ($8,214,060 ÷ 3), which reflects the portion of the award related to the requisite service provided in 20X5 (1 year of the 3-year requisite service period). For convenience, this example assumes that journal entries to account for the award are performed at year-end. The journal entries for 20X5 are as follows:

Compensation cost	$2,738,020
Share-based compensation liability	$2,738,020

To recognize compensation cost.

Deferred tax asset	$958,307
Deferred tax benefit	$958,307

To recognize the deferred tax asset for the temporary difference related to compensation cost ($2,738,020 × .35 = $958,307).

A184. On January 1, 20X6, Entity T modifies the SARs by replacing the cash-settlement feature with a net-share settlement feature, which converts the award from a liability award to an equity award because Entity T no longer has an obligation to transfer cash to settle the arrangement. Entity T would compare the fair value of the instrument immediately before the modification to the fair value of the modified award and recognize any incremental compensation cost. Because the modification affects no other terms or conditions, the fair value, assumed to be $10 per SAR, is unchanged by the modification and, therefore, no incremental compensation cost is recognized. The modified award's total fair value is $8,214,060. The modified award would be accounted for as an equity award from the date of modification with a fair value of $10 per share. Therefore, at the modification date, the entity would reclassify the liability of $2,738,020 recognized at December 31, 20X5, as additional paid-in capital. The related journal entry is as follows:

Share-based compensation liability	$2,738,020
Additional paid-in capital	$2,738,020

To reclassify the award as equity.

Entity T will account for the modified awards as equity going forward following the pattern given in Illustration 4(a) (refer to paragraphs A86–A96), recognizing $2,738,020 of compensation cost in each of 20X6 and 20X7, for a cumulative total of $8,214,060.

Illustration 14(d)—Liability-to-Liability Modification (Cash-Settled SARs to Cash-Settled SARs)

A185. This illustration is based on the facts given in Illustration 10 (paragraphs A127–A133): Entity T grants SARs to its employees. The fair value of the award at January 1, 20X5, is $12,066,454 (821,406 × $14.69).

A186. At December 31, 20X5, the fair value of each SAR is assumed to be $5; hence, the fair value of the award is $4,107,030 (821,406 × $5). The share-based compensation liability at December 31, 20X5, is $1,369,010 ($4,107,030 ÷ 3), which reflects the portion of the award related to the requisite service provided in 20X5 (1 year of the 3-year requisite service period). For convenience, this example assumes that journal entries to account for the award are performed at year-end. The journal entries to recognize compensation cost for 20X5 are as follows:

Compensation cost	$1,369,010
Share-based compensation liability	$1,369,010

To recognize compensation cost.

Deferred tax asset	$479,154
Deferred tax benefit	$479,154

To recognize the deferred tax asset for the temporary difference related to compensation cost ($1,369,010 × .35 = $479,154).

A187. On January 1, 20X6, Entity T reprices the SARs, giving each holder the right to receive an amount in cash equal to the increase in value of 1 share of Entity T stock over $10. The modification affects no other terms or conditions of the SARs and does not change the number of SARs expected to vest. The fair value of each SAR based on its modified terms is $12. The incremental compensation cost is calculated per the method in Illustration 12:

Fair value of modified SAR award (821,406 × $12)	$9,856,872
Less: Fair value of original SAR (821,406 × $5)	4,107,030
Incremental value of modified SAR	5,749,842
Divide by three to reflect earned portion of the award	÷ 3
Compensation cost to be recognized	$1,916,614

A188. Entity T also could determine the incremental value of the modified SAR award by multiplying the fair value of the modified SAR award by the portion of the award that is earned and subtracting the cumulative recognized compensation cost [($9,856,872 ÷ 3) – $1,369,010 = $1,916,614]. As a result, Entity T will record the following journal entries at the date of the modification:

Compensation cost	$1,916,614	
Share-based compensation liability		$1,916,614

To recognize incremental compensation cost.

Deferred tax asset	$670,815	
Deferred tax benefit		$670,815

To recognize the deferred tax asset for the temporary difference related to additional compensation cost ($1,916,614 × .35 = $670,815).

Entity T will continue to remeasure the liability award at each reporting date until the award's settlement.

Illustration 14(e)—Equity-to-Liability Modification (Share Options to Fixed Cash Payment)

A189. Entity T grants the same share options described in Illustration 4(a) (paragraphs A86–A96) and records similar journal entries for 20X5 (paragraph A91). By January 1, 20X6, Entity T's share price has fallen, and the fair value per share option is assumed to be $2 at that date. Entity T provides its employees with an election to convert each share option into an award of a fixed amount of cash equal to the fair value of each share option on the election date ($2) accrued over the remaining requisite service period, payable upon vesting. The election does

not affect vesting; that is, employees must satisfy the original service condition to vest in the award for a fixed amount of cash. This transaction is considered a modification because Entity T continues to have an obligation to its employees that is conditional upon the receipt of future employee services. There is no incremental compensation cost because the fair value of the modified award is the same as that of the original award. At the date of the modification, a liability of $547,604 [(821,406 × $2) × (1 year of requisite service rendered ÷ 3-year requisite service period)], which is equal to the portion of the award attributed to past service multiplied by the modified award's fair value, is recognized by reclassifying that amount from additional paid-in capital. The total liability of $1,642,812 (821,406 × $2) should be fully accrued by the end of the requisite service period. Because the possible tax deduction of the modified award is capped at $1,642,812, Entity T also must adjust its deferred tax asset at the date of the modification to the amount that corresponds to the recognized liability of $547,604. That amount is $191,661 ($547,604 × .35), and the write-off of the deferred tax asset is $1,216,092 ($1,407,753 – $191,661). That write-off would be recognized in the income statement except to the extent that there is any remaining additional paid-in capital from excess tax benefits from previous share-based payment awards available to offset that deficiency. Compensation cost of $4,022,151 and a corresponding increase in additional paid-in capital would be recognized in each of 20X6 and 20X7 for a cumulative total of $12,066,454 (refer to Illustration 14(a)); however, that compensation cost has no associated income tax effect (additional deferred tax assets are recognized based only on subsequent increases in the amount of the liability).

Illustration 15—Share Award with a Clawback Feature

A190. On January 1, 20X5, Entity T grants its CEO an award of 100,000 shares of stock that vest upon the completion of 5 years of service. The market price of Entity T's stock is $30 per share on that date. The grant-date fair value of the award is $3,000,000 (100,000 × $30). The shares become freely transferable upon vesting; however, the award provisions specify that, in the event of the employee's termination and subsequent employment by a direct competitor (as defined by the award) within three years after vesting, the shares or their cash equivalent on the date of employment by the direct competitor must be returned to Entity T for no consideration (a clawback feature). The CEO completes five years of service and vests in the award. Approximately two years after vesting in the share award, the CEO terminates employment and is hired as an employee of a direct competitor. Paragraph A5 states that contingent features requiring an employee to transfer equity shares earned or realized gains from the sale of equity instruments earned as a result of share-based payment arrangements to the issuing entity for consideration that is less than fair value on the date of transfer (including no consideration) are not considered in estimating the fair value of an equity instrument on the date it is granted. Those features are accounted for if and when the contingent event occurs by recognizing the consideration received in the corresponding balance sheet account and a credit in the income statement equal to the lesser of the recognized compensation cost of the share-based payment arrangement that contains the contingent feature ($3,000,000) and the fair value of the consideration received.[111] The former CEO returns 100,000 shares of Entity T's common stock with a total market value of $4,500,000 as a result of the award's provisions. The following journal entry accounts for that event:

Treasury stock	$4,500,000
Additional paid-in capital	$1,500,000
Other income	$3,000,000

To recognize the receipt of consideration as a result of the clawback feature.

A191. If instead of delivering shares to Entity T, the former CEO had paid cash equal to the total market value of 100,000 shares of Entity T's common stock, the following journal entry would have been recorded:

Cash	$4,500,000
Additional paid-in capital	$1,500,000
Other income	$3,000,000

To recognize the receipt of consideration as a result of the clawback feature.

Illustration 16—Certain Noncompete Agreements and Requisite Service

A192. Paragraph 6 of this Statement requires that the accounting for all share-based payment transactions with employees or others reflect the rights conveyed to the holder of the instruments and the obligations imposed on the issuer of the instruments, regardless of how those transactions are structured. Some share-based compensation arrangements with employees may contain noncompete provisions. Those noncompete provisions may be in-substance service conditions because of their nature. Determining whether a noncompete provision or another type of provision represents an in-substance service condition is a matter of judgment based on relevant facts and circumstances. The following example in paragraphs A193–A197 illustrates a situation in which a noncompete provision represents an in-substance service condition.

A193. Entity K is a professional services firm in which retention of qualified employees is important in sustaining its operations. Entity K's industry expertise and relationship networks are inextricably linked to its employees; if its employees terminate their employment relationship and work for a competitor, the company's operations may be adversely impacted.

A194. As part of its compensation structure, Entity K grants 100,000 restricted share units (RSUs) to an employee on January 1, 20X6. The fair value of the RSUs represents approximately four times the expected future annual total compensation of the employee. The RSUs are fully vested as of the date of grant, and retention of the RSUs is not contingent on future service to Entity K. However, the units are transferred to the employee based on a 4-year delayed-transfer schedule (25,000 RSUs to be transferred beginning on December 31, 20X6, and on December 31 in each of the 3 succeeding years) if and only if specified noncompete conditions are satisfied. The RSUs are convertible into unrestricted shares any time after transfer.

---

[111]This guidance does not apply to cancellations of awards of equity instruments as discussed in paragraphs 55–57 of this Statement.

A195. The noncompete provisions require that no work in any capacity may be performed for a competitor (which would include any new competitor formed by the employee). Those noncompete provisions lapse with respect to the RSUs as they are transferred. If the noncompete provisions are not satisfied, the employee loses all rights to any RSUs not yet transferred. Additionally, the noncompete provisions stipulate that Entity K may seek other available legal remedies, including damages from the employee. Entity K has determined that the noncompete is legally enforceable and has legally enforced similar arrangements in the past.

A196. The nature of the noncompete provision (being the corollary condition of active employment), the provision's legal enforceability, the employer's intent to enforce and past practice of enforcement, the delayed-transfer schedule mirroring the lapse of noncompete provisions, the magnitude of the award's fair value in relation to the employee's expected future annual total compensation, and the severity of the provision limiting the employee's ability to work in the industry in any capacity are facts that provide a preponderance of evidence suggesting that the arrangement is designed to compensate the employee for future service in spite of the employee's ability to terminate the employment relationship during the service period and retain the award (assuming satisfaction of the noncompete provision). Consequently, Entity K would recognize compensation cost related to the RSUs over the four-year substantive service period.

A197. Illustration 15 (paragraphs A190 and A191) provides an example of another noncompete agreement. Illustration 15 and this illustration are similar in that both noncompete agreements are not contingent upon employment termination (that is, both agreements may activate and lapse during a period of active employment subsequent to the vesting date). A key difference between the two illustrations is that the award recipient in Illustration 15 must provide five years of service to vest in the award (as opposed to vesting immediately). Another key difference is that the award recipient in Illustration 15 receives the shares upon vesting and may sell them immediately without restriction as opposed to the RSUs, which

are transferred according to the delayed-transfer schedule. In Illustration 15, the noncompete provision is not deemed to be an in-substance service condition.[112]

Illustration 17—Tandem Award—Share Options or Cash-Settled SARs

A198. A tandem award is an award with two (or more) components in which exercise of one part cancels the other(s). In contrast, a **combination award** is an award with two separate components, both of which can be exercised.

A199. The following illustrates the accounting for a tandem award in which employees have a choice of either share options or cash-settled SARs. Entity T grants to its employees an award of 900,000 share options or 900,000 cash-settled SARs on January 1, 20X5. The award vests on December 31, 20X7, and has a contractual life of 10 years. If an employee exercises the SARs, the related share options are cancelled. Conversely, if an employee exercises the share options, the related SARs are cancelled.

A200. The tandem award results in Entity T's incurring a liability because the employees can demand settlement in cash. If Entity T could choose whether to settle the award in cash or by issuing stock, the award would be an equity instrument unless Entity T's predominant past practice is to settle most awards in cash or to settle awards in cash whenever requested to do so by the employee, indicating that Entity T has incurred a substantive liability as indicated in paragraph 34 of this Statement. In this illustration, however, Entity T incurs a liability to pay cash, which it will recognize over the requisite service period. The amount of the liability will be adjusted each year to reflect changes in its fair value. If employees choose to exercise the share options rather than the SARs, the liability is settled by issuing stock.

A201. The fair value of the SARs at the grant date is $12,066,454, as computed in Illustration 10 (paragraphs A127–A133), because the value of the SARs and the value of the share options are equal. Accordingly, at the end of 20X5, when the assumed fair value per SAR is $10, the amount of the liability is

---

[112]In making a determination about whether a noncompete provision may represent an in-substance service condition, the provision's legal enforceability, the entity's intent to enforce the provision and its past practice of enforcement, the employee's rights to the instruments such as the right to sell them, the severity of the provision, the fair value of the award, and the existence or absence of an explicit employee service condition are all factors that should be considered. Because noncompete provisions can be structured differently, one or more of those factors (such as the entity's intent to enforce the provision) may be more important than others in making that determination. For example, if Entity K did not intend to enforce the provision, then the noncompete provision would not represent an in-substance service condition.

$8,214,060 (821,406 cash-settled SARs expected to vest × $10). One-third of that amount, $2,738,020, is recognized as compensation cost for 20X5. At the end of each year during the vesting period, the liability is remeasured to its fair value for all SARs expected to vest. After the vesting period, the liability for all outstanding vested awards is remeasured through the date of settlement.

Illustration 18—Tandem Award—Phantom Shares or Share Options

A202. This illustration is for a tandem award in which the components have different values after the grant date, depending on movements in the price of the entity's stock. The employee's choice of which component to exercise will depend on the relative values of the components when the award is exercised.

A203. Entity T grants to its CEO an immediately vested award consisting of two parts:

a. One thousand phantom share units (units) whose value is always equal to the value of 1,000 shares of Entity T's common stock

b. Share options on 3,000 shares of Entity T stock with an exercise price of $30 per share.

At the grant date, Entity T's share price is $30 per share. The CEO may choose whether to exercise the share options or to cash in the units at any time during the next five years. Exercise of all of the share options cancels all of the units, and cashing in all of the units cancels all of the share options. The cash value of the units will be paid to the CEO at the end of five years if the share option component of the tandem award is not exercised before then.

A204. With a 3-to-1 ratio of share options to units, exercise of 3 share options will produce a higher gain than receipt of cash equal to the value of 1 share of stock if the share price appreciates from the grant date by more than 50 percent. Below that point, one unit is more valuable than the gain on three share options. To illustrate that relationship, the results if the share price increases 50 percent to $45 are:

	Units		Exercise of Options
Market value	$45,000 ($45 × 1,000)		$135,000 ($45 × 3,000)
Purchase price	0		90,000 ($30 × 3,000)
Net cash value	$45,000		$ 45,000

A205. If the price of Entity T's common stock increases to $45 per share from its price of $30 at the grant date, each part of the tandem grant will produce the same net cash payment (ignoring transaction costs) to the CEO. If the price increases to $44, the value of 1 share of stock exceeds the gain on exercising 3 share options, which would be $42 [3 × ($44 – $30)]. But if the price increases to $46, the gain on exercising 3 share options, $48 [3 × ($46 – $30)], exceeds the value of 1 share of stock.

A206. At the grant date, the CEO could take $30,000 cash for the units and forfeit the share options. Therefore, the total value of the award at the grant date must exceed $30,000 because at share prices above $45, the CEO receives a higher amount than would the holder of 1 share of stock. To exercise the 3,000 options, the CEO must forfeit the equivalent of 1,000 shares of stock, in addition to paying the total exercise price of $90,000 (3,000 × $30). In effect, the CEO receives only 2,000 shares of Entity T

stock upon exercise. That is the same as if the share option component of the tandem award consisted of share options to purchase 2,000 shares of stock for $45 per share.

A207. The cash payment obligation associated with the units qualifies the award as a liability of Entity T. The maximum amount of that liability, which is indexed to the price of Entity T's common stock, is $45,000 because at share prices above $45, the CEO will exercise the share options.

A208. In measuring compensation cost, the award may be thought of as a *combination*—not tandem—grant of (a) 1,000 units with a value at grant of $30,000 and (b) 2,000 options with a strike price of $45 per share. Compensation cost is measured based on the combined value of the two parts.

A209. The fair value per share option with an exercise price of $45 is assumed to be $10. Therefore, the total value of the award at the grant date is:

Units (1,000 × $30)	$30,000
Share options (2,000 × $10)	20,000
Value of award	$50,000

A210. Therefore, compensation cost recognized at the date of grant (the award is immediately vested) would be $30,000 with a corresponding credit to a share-based compensation liability of $30,000. However, because the share option component is the substantive equivalent of 2,000 deep out-of-the-money options, it contains a derived service period (assumed to be 2 years). Hence, compensation cost for the share option component of $20,000 would be recognized over the requisite service period.[113] That total amount of both components (or $50,000) is more than either of the components by itself, but less than the total amount if both components (1,000 units and 3,000 share options with an exercise price of $30) were exercisable. Because granting the units creates a liability, changes in the liability that result from increases or decreases in the price of Entity T's share price would be recognized each period until exercise, except that the amount of the liability would not exceed $45,000.

Illustration 19—Look-Back Share Options

A211. Some entities offer share options to employees under Section 423 of the U.S. Internal Revenue Code, which provides that employees will not be immediately taxed on the difference between the market price of the stock and a discounted purchase price if several requirements are met. One requirement is that the exercise price may not be less than the smaller of (a) 85 percent of the stock's market price when the share option is granted and (b) 85 percent of the price at exercise. A share option that provides the employee the choice of (a) or (b) may not have a term in excess of 27 months. Share options that provide for the more favorable of two (or more) exercise prices are referred to as look-back share options. A look-back share option with a 15 percent discount from the market price at either grant or exercise is worth more than a fixed share option to purchase stock at 85 percent of the current market price because the holder of the look-back share option is assured a benefit. If the price rises, the holder benefits to the same extent as if

the exercise price was fixed at the grant date. If the share price falls, the holder still receives the benefit of purchasing the stock at a 15 percent discount from its price at the date of exercise. An employee share purchase plan offering share options with a look-back feature would be compensatory because the look-back feature is an option feature (paragraph 12).

A212. For example, on January 1, 20X5, when its share price is $30, Entity T offers its employees the opportunity to sign up for a payroll deduction to purchase its stock at either 85 percent of the share's current price or 85 percent of the price at the end of the year when the share options expire, whichever is lower. The exercise price of the share options is the lesser of (a) $25.50 ($30 × .85) and (b) 85 percent of the share price at the end of the year when the share options expire.

A213. The look-back share option can be valued as a combination position.[114] In this situation, the components are as follows:

a. 0.15 of a share of nonvested stock
b. 0.85 of a 1-year share option held with an exercise price of $30.

Supporting analysis for the two components is discussed below.

A214. Beginning with the first component, a share option with an exercise price that equals 85 percent of the value of the stock at the exercise date will always be worth 15 percent (100% – 85%) of the share price upon exercise. For a stock that pays no dividends, that share option is the equivalent of 15 percent of a share of the stock. The holder of the look-back share option will receive *at least* the equivalent of 0.15 of a share of stock upon exercise, regardless of the share price at that date. For example, if the share price falls to $20, the exercise price of the share option will be $17 ($20 × .85), and the holder will benefit by $3 ($20 – $17), which is the same as receiving 0.15 of a share of stock for each share option.

A215. If the share price upon exercise is more than $30, the holder of the look-back share option receives a benefit that is worth more than 15 percent of a share of stock. At prices of $30 or more, the holder receives

---

[113]The share option component would not be remeasured because it is not a liability.

[114]This illustration presents one of several existing valuation techniques for estimating the fair value of a look-back option. In accordance with this Statement, an entity should use a valuation technique that reflects the substantive characteristics of the instrument being granted in the estimate of fair value.

a benefit for the difference between the share price upon exercise and $25.50—the exercise price of the share option (.85 × $30). If the share price is $40, the holder benefits by $14.50 ($40 − $25.50). However, the holder cannot receive *both* the $14.50 value of a share option with an exercise price of $25.50 *and* 0.15 of a share of stock. In effect, the holder gives up 0.15 of a share of stock worth $4.50 ($30 × .15) if the share price is above $30 at exercise. The result is the same as if the exercise price of the share option was $30 ($25.50 + $4.50) and the holder of the look-back share option held 85 percent of a 1-year share option with an exercise price of $30 in addition to 0.15 of a share of stock that will be received if the share price is $30 or less upon exercise.

A216. An option-pricing model can be used to value the 1-year share option on 0.85 of a share of stock represented by the second component. Thus, assuming that the fair value of a share option on one share of Entity T stock on the grant date is $4, the compensation cost for the look-back option at the grant date is as follows:

0.15 of a share of nonvested stock ($30 × 0.15)	$4.50
Share option on 0.85 of a share of stock, exercise price of $30 ($4 × .85)	3.40
Total grant date value	$7.90

A217. For a look-back option on a dividend-paying share, both the value of the nonvested stock component and the value of the share option component would be adjusted to reflect the effect of the dividends that the employee does not receive during the life of the share option. The present value of the dividends expected to be paid on the stock during the life of the share option (one year in the example) would be deducted from the value of a share that receives dividends. One way to accomplish that is to base the value calculation on shares of stock rather than dollars by assuming that the dividends are reinvested in the stock.

A218. For example, if Entity T pays a quarterly dividend of 0.625 percent (2.5% ÷ 4) of the current share price, 1 share of stock would grow to 1.0252 (the future value of 1 using a return of 0.625 percent for 4 periods) shares at the end of the year if all dividends are reinvested. Therefore, the present value of 1 share of stock to be received in 1 year is only 0.9754 of a

share today (again applying conventional compound interest formulas compounded quarterly) if the holder does not receive the dividends paid during the year.

A219. The value of the share option component is easier to compute; the appropriate dividend assumption is used in an option-pricing model in estimating the value of a share option on a whole share of stock. Thus, assuming the fair value of the share option is $3.60, the compensation cost for the look-back share option if Entity T pays quarterly dividends at the annual rate of 2.5 percent is as follows:

0.15 of a share of nonvested stock ($30 × 0.15 × 0.9754)	$4.39
Share option on 0.85 of a share of stock, $30 exercise price, 2.5% dividend yield ($3.60 × 0.85)	3.06
Total grant date value	$7.45

The first component, which is worth $4.39 at the grant date, is the minimum amount of benefits to the holder regardless of the price of the stock at the exercise date. The second component, worth $3.06 at the grant date, represents the additional benefit to the holder if the share price is above $30 at the exercise date.

Illustration 20—Employee Share Purchase Plans

A220. Paragraph 12 of this Statement stipulates the criteria that an employee share purchase plan must satisfy to be considered noncompensatory. One of those criteria specifies that substantially all employees that meet limited employment qualifications may participate on an equitable basis. Examples of limited employment qualifications might include customary employment of greater than 20 hours per week or completion of at least 6 months of service.

A221. Another criterion is that the terms are no more favorable than those available to all holders of the same class of shares. For example, Entity T offers all full-time employees and all nonemployee shareholders the right to purchase $10,000 of its common stock at a 5 percent discount from its market price at the date of purchase, which occurs in 1 month. The arrangement is not compensatory because its terms are no more favorable than those available to all holders of the same class of shares. In contrast, assume Entity C has a dividend reinvestment program that permits shareholders of its common stock the ability to reinvest dividends by purchasing shares of its common stock at a 10 percent discount from its market price on the date that dividends are distributed and Entity C offers all full-time employees the right to purchase annually up to $10,000 of its common stock at a 10 percent discount from its market price on the date of purchase. Entity C's common stock is widely held; hence, many shareholders will not receive dividends totaling at least $10,000 during the annual period. Assuming that the 10 percent discount cannot be justified as the per-share amount of share issuance costs that would have been incurred to raise a significant amount of capital by a public offering, the arrangement is compensatory because the number of shares available to shareholders at a discount is based on the quantity of shares held and the amounts of dividends declared. Whereas, the number of shares available to employees at a discount is not dependent on shares held or declared dividends; therefore, the terms of the employee share purchase plan are more favorable than the terms available to all holders of the same class of shares. Consequently, the entire 10 percent discount to employees is compensatory. If, on the other hand, the 10 percent discount can be justified as the per-share amount of share issuance costs that would have been incurred to raise a significant amount of capital by a public offering, then the entire 10 percent discount to employees is not compensatory.[115]

Illustration 21—Book Value Share Purchase Plans (Nonpublic Entities Only)

A222. Entity W, a nonpublic entity that is not an SEC registrant,[116] has two classes of stock: Class A is voting and held only by the members of the founding family, and Class B is nonvoting and held only by employees. The purchase price of Class B shares is a formula price based on book value. Class B shares require that the employee, six months after retirement or separation from the company, sell the shares back to the company for cash at a price determined by using the same formula used to establish the purchase price. Class B shares would be accounted for as liabilities pursuant to Statement 150 except during the indefinite deferral period established by FSP FAS 150-3, "Effective Date, Disclosures, and Transition for Mandatorily Redeemable Financial Instru-

ments of Certain Nonpublic Entities and Certain Mandatorily Redeemable Noncontrolling Interests under FASB Statement No. 150, *Accounting for Certain Financial Instruments with Characteristics of both Liabilities and Equity.*" Nevertheless, Class B shares may be classified as liabilities if they are granted as part of a share-based payment transaction and those shares contain certain repurchase features meeting criteria in paragraph 31 of this Statement; this example assumes that Class B shares do not meet those criteria.

A223. Determining whether a transaction involving Class B shares is compensatory will depend on the terms of the arrangement. For instance, if an employee acquires 100 shares of Class B stock in exchange for cash equal to the formula price of those shares, the transaction is not compensatory because the employee has acquired those shares on the same terms available to all other Class B shareholders and at the current formula price based on the current book value. Subsequent changes in the formula price of those shares held by the employee are not deemed compensation for services.

A224. However, if an employee acquires 100 shares of Class B stock in exchange for cash equal to 50 percent of the formula price of those shares, the transaction is compensatory because the employee is not paying the current formula price. Therefore, the value of the 50 percent discount should be attributed over the requisite service period. However, subsequent changes in the formula price of those shares held by the employee are not compensatory.

Illustration 22—Liability Classification and the Interaction of This Statement with Statement 150

Applying the Classification Criteria in Statement 150

A225. Statement 150 excludes from its scope instruments that are accounted for under this Statement. Nevertheless, unless paragraphs 30–35 of this Statement require otherwise, an entity shall apply the classification criteria in paragraphs 8–14 of Statement 150, as they are effective at the reporting date,

---

[115]If an entity justifies a purchase discount in excess of 5 percent, it would be required to reassess that discount at least annually and no later than the first share purchase offer during the fiscal year. If upon reassessment that discount is not deemed justifiable, subsequent grants using that discount would be compensatory.

[116]Because book value shares of public entities generally are not indexed to their stock prices, such shares would be classified as liabilities pursuant to this Statement.

in determining whether to classify as a liability a freestanding financial instrument given to an employee in a share-based payment transaction.

A226. In determining the classification of an instrument, an entity shall take into account the deferrals contained in FSP FAS 150-3. In addition, a call option[117] written on an instrument that is not classified as a liability because of the deferrals in FSP FAS 150-3 (for example, a call option on a mandatorily redeemable share for which liability classification is deferred under FSP FAS 150-3) also shall be classified as equity while the deferral is in effect unless liability classification is required under the provisions of paragraph 32 of this Statement.

Classification of Certain Awards with Repurchase Features

A227. Statement 150 does not apply to outstanding shares embodying a conditional obligation to transfer assets, for example, shares that give the employee the right to require the employer to repurchase them for cash equal to their fair value (puttable shares). A puttable (or callable) share[118] awarded to an employee as compensation shall be classified as a liability if either of the following conditions is met: (a) the repurchase feature permits the employee to avoid bearing the risks and rewards normally associated with equity share ownership for a reasonable period of time from the date the share is issued,[119,120] or (b) it is probable that the employer would prevent the employee from bearing those risks and rewards for a reasonable period of time from the date the share is issued. For this purpose, a period of six months or more is a *reasonable period of time*. A puttable (or callable) share that does not meet either of those conditions shall be classified as equity.[121]

A228. For example, an entity may grant shares under a share-based compensation arrangement that the employee can put (sell) to the employer (the entity) shortly after the vesting date for cash equal to the fair value of the shares on the date of repurchase. That award of puttable shares would be classified as a liability because the repurchase feature permits the employee to avoid bearing the risks and rewards normally associated with equity share ownership for a reasonable period of time from the date the share is issued (condition (a) in paragraph A227). Alternatively, an entity might grant its own shares under a share-based compensation arrangement that may be put to the employer only after the employee has held them for a reasonable period of time after vesting but at a fixed redemption amount. Those puttable shares also would be classified as liabilities under the requirements of this Statement because the repurchase price is based on a fixed amount rather than variations in the fair value of the employer's shares. The employee cannot bear the risks and rewards normally associated with equity share ownership for a reasonable period of time because of that redemption feature. However, if a share with a repurchase feature gives the employee the right to sell shares back to the entity for a fixed amount over the fair value of the shares at the date of repurchase, paragraph 55 of this Statement requires that the fixed amount over the fair value be recognized as additional compensation cost over the requisite service period (with a corresponding liability being accrued).

A229. Options or similar instruments on shares (for example, options on puttable or mandatorily redeemable shares) shall be classified as liabilities if (a) the underlying shares are classified as liabilities or (b) the

---

[117]Refer to the definition of *share option* in Appendix E.

[118]A put right may be granted to the employee in a transaction that is related to a share-based compensation arrangement. If exercise of such a put right would require the entity to repurchase shares issued under the share-based compensation arrangement, the shares shall be accounted for as puttable shares. That treatment is consistent with the definition of a freestanding financial instrument in Appendix E. It also is consistent with the notion of accounting for the substantive terms of a share-based compensation transaction, which reflects the rights conveyed to the holder and the obligations imposed on the issuer, regardless of how the transaction is structured (paragraph 6).

[119]A repurchase feature that can be exercised only upon the occurrence of a contingent event that is outside the employee's control (such as an initial public offering) would not meet condition (a) until it becomes probable that the event will occur within the reasonable period of time.

[120]An employee begins to bear the risks and rewards normally associated with equity share ownership when all the requisite service has been rendered.

[121]SEC registrants are required to consider the guidance in ASR No. 268, *Presentation in Financial Statements of "Redeemable Preferred Stocks."* Under that guidance, shares subject to mandatory redemption requirements or whose redemption is outside the control of the issuer are classified outside permanent equity.

entity can be required under any circumstances[121a] to settle the option or similar instruments by transferring cash or other assets.[121b] For example, an entity may grant an option to an employee that, upon exercise, would be settled by issuing a mandatorily redeemable share that is not subject to the deferral in FSP FAS 150-3. Because the mandatorily redeemable share would be classified as a liability under Statement 150, the option also would be classified as a liability.

Subsequent Accounting for Certain Freestanding Financial Instruments

A230. Once the classification of an instrument is determined, the recognition and measurement provisions of this Statement shall be applied until the instrument ceases to be subject to the requirements discussed in paragraph A231 of this Statement. Statement 150 or other applicable GAAP, such as FASB Statement No. 133, *Accounting for Derivative Instruments and Hedging Activities,* applies to a freestanding financial instrument that was issued under a share-based payment arrangement but that is no longer subject to this Statement.[122]

A231. A freestanding financial instrument ceases to be subject to this Statement and becomes subject to the recognition and measurement requirements of Statement 150 or other applicable GAAP when the rights conveyed by the instrument to the holder are no longer dependent on the holder being an employee of the entity (that is, no longer dependent on providing service). That principle should be applied to specific types of instruments subject to Statement 150 or other applicable GAAP as illustrated by the following examples:

a. A mandatorily redeemable share becomes subject to Statement 150 or other applicable GAAP when an employee (a) has rendered the requisite service in exchange for the instrument and (b) could terminate the employment relationship and receive that share.

b. A share option or similar instrument that is not transferable and whose contractual term is shortened upon employment termination continues to be subject to this Statement until the rights conveyed by the instrument to the holder are no longer dependent on the holder being an employee of the entity (generally, when the instrument is exercised).[123,124]

A232. An entity may modify (including cancel and replace) or settle a fully vested, freestanding financial instrument after it becomes subject to Statement 150 or other applicable GAAP. Such a modification or settlement shall be accounted for under the provisions of this Statement unless it applies equally to all financial instruments of the same class regardless of whether the holder is (or was) an employee (or an employee's beneficiary).[125] Following the modification, the instrument continues to be accounted for under Statement 150 or other applicable GAAP.

Illustration 23—Effective Dates and Transition Methods

Illustration 23(a)—Effective Dates and Transition Methods

A233. Tables 10–13 summarize guidance on the various transition methods permitted by this Statement and their relationship to its required effective dates.

[121a]A cash settlement feature that can be exercised only upon the occurrence of a contingent event that is outside the employee's control (such as an initial public offering) would not meet condition (b) until it becomes probable that event will occur.

[121b]SEC registrants are required to consider the guidance in ASR 268. Under that guidance, options and similar instruments subject to mandatory redemption requirements or whose redemption is outside the control of the issuer are classified outside permanent equity.

[122]This guidance is not intended to suggest that all freestanding financial instruments should be accounted for as liabilities pursuant to Statement 150, but rather that freestanding financial instruments issued in share-based payment transactions may become subject to Statement 150 or other applicable GAAP depending on their substantive characteristics and when certain criteria in paragraph A231 are met.

[123]A share option or similar instrument may become subject to Statement 150 or other applicable GAAP prior to its settlement. For instance, if a vested share option becomes exercisable for one year after employment termination, the rights conveyed by the instrument to the holder would no longer be dependent on the holder being an employee of the entity upon the employee's termination.

[124]Vested share options are typically exercisable for a short period of time (generally, 60 to 90 days) subsequent to the termination of the employment relationship. Notwithstanding the requirements of paragraph A231, such a provision, in and of itself, shall not cause the award to become subject to other applicable GAAP for that short period of time.

[125]A modification or settlement of a class of financial instrument that is designed exclusively for and held only by current or former employees (or their beneficiaries) may stem from the employment relationship depending on the terms of the modification or settlement. Thus, such a modification or settlement may be subject to the requirements of this Statement.

Table 10—Effective Dates and Transition Methods

Entity Classification[126,127]	First Applicable Reporting Period	Required Effective Date[128] (Periods Beginning After)	Transition Method at Required Effective Date	Optional Transition Method for Periods Prior to the Required Effective Date	
				MRA—All Periods[129]	MRA—Q1[130]
Public	Interim or Annual	6/15/05	MPA	MRA	MRA
SBI	Interim or Annual	12/15/05	MPA	MRA	MRA
NP-FV	Annual	12/15/05	MPA	MRA	N/A
ONP	Annual	12/15/05	Prospective	N/A	N/A

[126]Entities are classified by the following designations: Public (a public entity as defined in Appendix E that does not file as a small business issuer, which also is defined in Appendix E), SBI (a public entity as defined in Appendix E that files as a small business issuer), NP-FV (a nonpublic entity as defined in Appendix E that has adopted Statement 123's fair-value-based method for recognition or pro forma disclosures prior to the effective date of this Statement), and ONP (a nonpublic entity other than NP-FV).

[127]This table also applies to *foreign private issuers* (as defined in SEC Regulation C §230.405) that are Public (as designated in the preceding footnote). Foreign private issuers should initially apply this Statement no later than the interim (quarterly or other) or annual period beginning after the specified effective date for which U.S. GAAP financial information is required or reported voluntarily.

[128]Early adoption is encouraged, provided that the financial statements or interim reports for the periods before the required effective date have not been issued.

[129]The phrase *MRA–all periods* refers to an entity that adopts this Statement using the modified retrospective application method for all periods pursuant to Statement 123's original effective date (paragraph 76).

[130]The phrase *MRA–Q1* refers to an entity that adopts this Statement using a modified retrospective application method only for the annual period of this Statement's adoption (paragraph 76).

Tables 11–13 consider the impact of using the transition methods described in Table 10 on Entity D, which has a December 31 year-end for financial reporting purposes and has regularly granted share-based payment awards with 4-year cliff vesting service conditions in each of the past 10 years. Entity D is a public entity that does not file as a small business issuer and that has accounted for all share-based payment awards using Opinion 25.

Table 11—Example of Public Entity—December 31 Year-End: MPA

Reporting Period	Description of Effect of Using MPA Transition Method as of the Required Effective Date
1st Quarter 2005	Entity D recognizes compensation cost pursuant to Opinion 25 and includes disclosures pursuant to Statement 148.
2nd Quarter 2005	Entity D recognizes compensation cost pursuant to Opinion 25 and includes disclosures pursuant to Statement 148.
3rd Quarter 2005	Entity D applies this Statement to new awards granted and to modifications, repurchases, or cancellations on or after July 1, 2005. Compensation cost for the portion of awards for which the requisite service has not been rendered that are outstanding at July 1, 2005, shall be recognized using the measurement and attribution used for Statement 123's required pro forma disclosures as those services are received on or after July 1, 2005. If applicable, Entity D would recognize any cumulative effect adjustment as of July 1, 2005.
4th Quarter 2005	Same as 3rd quarter, except there would be no cumulative effect adjustment.
2005 Annual	For the year ended December 31, 2005, the financial statements reflect compensation cost pursuant to Opinion 25 for the first six months of the year and pursuant to this Statement for the second six months of the year.[131] The annual required pro forma disclosure reflects the recognition of compensation cost for the entire annual period. 2003 and 2004 would retain Opinion 25 and provide Statement 123's required pro forma disclosures.

---

[131]If an entity adopts this Statement using the modified prospective application method, an entity may not have information for an entire annual period. This Statement does not provide explicit guidance on how an entity should modify its annual disclosures in that event. An entity shall use judgment in applying this Statement's disclosure objectives and disclose that information deemed necessary for financial statement users to understand share-based payment transactions in the annual period of adoption and the impact of adopting this Statement.

Table 12—Example of Public Entity—December 31 Year-End:
MRA—All Periods

Reporting Period	Description of Effect of Using MRA—All Periods Transition Method as of the Required Effective Date
1st Quarter 2005	Entity D recognizes compensation cost pursuant to Opinion 25 and includes disclosures pursuant to Statement 148.
2nd Quarter 2005	Entity D recognizes compensation cost pursuant to Opinion 25 and includes disclosures pursuant to Statement 148.
3rd Quarter 2005	Same as 3rd quarter in Table 11, and Entity D would adjust financial statements for all periods prior to July 1, 2005, to give effect to the fair-value-based method of accounting for awards granted, modified, or settled in cash in fiscal years beginning after December 15, 1994, on a basis consistent with the pro forma disclosures required for those periods by Statement 123. For the nine months ended September 30, 2005, the financial statements reflect compensation cost as calculated under Statement 123 in the first six months of the year and under this Statement for the 3rd quarter of the year. Beginning balances should be adjusted for the earliest year presented to reflect MRA to those prior years not presented.
4th Quarter 2005	Same as 3rd quarter, except there would be no cumulative effect adjustment or adjustment of beginning balances.
2005 Annual	For the year ended December 31, 2005, the financial statements reflect compensation cost pursuant to Statement 123 for the first six months of the year and pursuant to this Statement for the second six months of the year. Fiscal years 2003 and 2004 would be adjusted to reflect compensation cost to give effect to the fair-value-based method of accounting for awards granted, modified, or settled in cash in fiscal years beginning after December 15, 1994, on a basis consistent with the pro forma disclosures required for those periods by Statement 123.
2006	Entity D's 2005 quarterly financial information presented for comparative purposes would reflect the adjustments made for the application of the MRA method to those periods.

Table 13—Example of Public Entity—December 31 Year-End: MRA—Q1

Reporting Period	Description of Effect of Using MRA—Q1 Transition Method as of the Required Effective Date
1st Quarter 2005	Entity D recognizes compensation cost pursuant to Opinion 25 and includes disclosures pursuant to Statement 148.
2nd Quarter 2005	Entity D recognizes compensation cost pursuant to Opinion 25 and includes disclosures pursuant to Statement 148.
3rd Quarter 2005	Same as 3rd quarter in Table 11, and Entity D would recognize compensation cost for the first two quarters of 2005 using its Statement 123 pro forma disclosure amounts. For the nine months ended September 30, 2005, the financial statements reflect compensation cost pursuant to Statement 123 for the first six months of the year and pursuant to this Statement for the 3rd quarter of the year.
4th Quarter 2005	Same as 3rd quarter, except there would be no cumulative effect adjustment.
2005 Annual	For the year ended December 31, 2005, the financial statements reflect compensation cost pursuant to Statement 123 for the first six months of the year and pursuant to this Statement for the second six months of the year. Fiscal years 2003 and 2004 would retain Opinion 25 and provide Statement 123's required pro forma disclosures.
2006	Entity D's 2005 quarterly financial information presented for comparative purposes would reflect the adjustments made for the application of the MRA method to those periods.

Illustration 23(b)—Transition Using the Modified Prospective Method

A234. Entity Z, a public company, granted SARs to certain employees on July 1, 2003, based on 100,000 shares and accounts for them under Opinion 25's intrinsic value method. The base price of $10 per share was equal to the fair value of the stock on July 1, 2003. The SARs provide the employees with the right to receive, at the date the rights are exercised, shares having a then-current value equal to the market appreciation since the grant date. The employees do not have the ability to receive a cash payment.[132] All of the rights vest at the end of three years and must be exercised one day after vesting. Entity Z's fiscal year ends on June 30 for financial reporting purposes. Entity Z adopts this Statement on July 1, 2005, using modified prospective application.

A235. The underlying stock price, compensation cost recognized, and related deferred tax benefit recognized under the intrinsic value method of Opinion 25 are as follows:

	2004	2005
Stock price at June 30	$12	$14
Compensation cost recognized	$66,667[133]	$200,000[134]
Deferred tax benefit at a 50 percent enacted tax rate	$33,333	$100,000

As of June 30, 2005, Entity Z has recognized a deferred tax asset of $133,333 ($33,333 + $100,000) and has increased additional paid-in capital by $266,667 ($66,667 + $200,000).

---

[132]Net-share-settled SARs are generally accounted for as equity instruments (unless such shares are liabilities themselves).

[133]$($12 − $10) \times 100,000 \times 1/3 = $66,667$

[134]$($14 − $10) \times 100,000 \times 2/3 − $66,667 = $200,000$

A236. The fair value on the grant date was $2.10 per SAR, or $210,000 ($2.10 × 100,000). Had Entity Z applied the fair-value-based method of accounting from the grant date, it would have recognized the following amounts related to the July 1, 2003, award:

	2004	2005
Compensation cost	$70,000[135]	$70,000
Deferred tax benefit at a 50 percent enacted tax rate	$35,000	$35,000

Under the fair-value-based method, Entity Z would have recognized a deferred tax asset at June 30, 2005, of $70,000 ($35,000 + $35,000) and an increase in additional paid-in capital of $140,000 ($70,000 + $70,000).

A237. As of July 1, 2005, when Entity Z adopts the fair-value-based method using the MPA, Entity Z estimates the number of equity instruments for which the requisite service is not expected to be rendered and recognizes, net of any related tax effect, an amount equal to the compensation cost that would not have been recognized in periods prior to the effective date for those instruments that are not expected to vest as a cumulative effect of a change in accounting principle to the extent that compensation cost had been recognized for those awards. To the extent that any contra-equity balances for unearned compensation cost had been recorded that are related to Entity Z's stock-based compensation arrangements, those balances would be charged against additional paid-in capital. There are no other transition adjustments necessary at July 1, 2005, as a result of adopting this Statement.

A238. During the 2006 fiscal year, Entity Z will recognize additional compensation cost of $70,000, and will have a deferred tax asset at June 30, 2006, of $168,333, consisting of $133,333 related to compensation cost recognized under Opinion 25 and $35,000 related to compensation cost recognized under this Statement. The awards will be fully vested on June 30, 2006.

A239. On July 1, 2006, Entity Z's stock price is $20 per share and all of the 100,000 SARs are exercised. Based on the exercise-date intrinsic value of $10 per share, Entity Z recognizes an aggregate tax deduction

of $1 million (100,000 SARs × ($20 − $10) appreciation), which is equal to the fair value of the shares issued to the employees. On a cumulative basis, Entity Z has recognized a deferred tax asset of $168,333. Total compensation cost recognized for the awards is $336,667, consisting of $266,667 recognized under Opinion 25 and $70,000 recognized under this Statement. On July 1, 2006, the following entries are made upon exercise:

| Deferred tax expense | $168,333 | |
| Deferred tax asset | | $168,333 |

To write off the deferred tax asset related to the SARs.

Current taxes payable	$500,000	
Current tax expense		$168,333
Additional paid-in capital		$331,667

To adjust current tax expense and current taxes payable to recognize the current tax benefit from deductible compensation cost upon exercise of SARs. The credit to additional paid-in capital is the excess tax benefit that results from the excess of the deductible amount over the compensation cost recognized [($1,000,000 − $336,667) × .50 = $331,667].

MINIMUM DISCLOSURE REQUIREMENTS AND ILLUSTRATIVE DISCLOSURES

A240. The minimum information needed to achieve the disclosure objectives in paragraph 64 of this Statement is set forth below. To achieve those objectives, an entity should disclose the following information:[136]

a. A description of the share-based payment arrangement(s), including the general terms of awards under the arrangement(s), such as the requisite service period(s) and any other substantive conditions (including those related to vesting), the maximum contractual term of equity (or liability) share options or similar instruments, and the number of shares authorized for awards of equity share options or other equity instruments. An entity shall disclose the method it uses for measuring compensation cost from share-based payment arrangements with employees.

b. For the most recent year for which an income statement is provided:

---

[135]$210,000 × ⅓ = $70,000

[136]In some circumstances, an entity may need to disclose information beyond that listed in this paragraph to achieve the disclosure objectives.

(1) The number and weighted-average exercise prices (or conversion ratios) for each of the following groups of share options (or share units): (a) those outstanding at the beginning of the year, (b) those outstanding at the end of the year, (c) those exercisable or convertible at the end of the year, and those (d) granted, (e) exercised or converted, (f) forfeited, or (g) expired during the year.

(2) The number and weighted-average grant-date fair value (or calculated value for a nonpublic entity that uses that method or intrinsic value for awards measured pursuant to paragraphs 24 and 25 of this Statement) of equity instruments not specified in paragraph A240(b)(1) (for example, shares of nonvested stock), for each of the following groups of equity instruments: (a) those nonvested at the beginning of the year, (b) those nonvested at the end of the year, and those (c) granted, (d) vested, or (e) forfeited during the year.

c. For each year for which an income statement is provided:

(1) The weighted-average grant-date fair value (or calculated value for a nonpublic entity that uses that method or intrinsic value for awards measured at that value pursuant to paragraphs 24 and 25 of this Statement) of equity options or other equity instruments granted during the year.

(2) The total intrinsic value of options exercised (or share units converted), share-based liabilities paid, and the total fair value of shares vested during the year.

d. For fully vested share options (or share units) and share options expected to vest at the date of the latest statement of financial position:

(1) The number, weighted-average exercise price (or conversion ratio), aggregate intrinsic value (except for nonpublic entities), and weighted-average remaining contractual term of options (or share units) outstanding.

(2) The number, weighted-average exercise price (or conversion ratio), aggregate intrinsic value (except for nonpublic entities), and weighted-average remaining contractual term of options (or share units) currently exercisable (or convertible).

e. For each year for which an income statement is presented:[137]

(1) A description of the method used during the year to estimate the fair value (or calculated value) of awards under share-based payment arrangements.

(2) A description of the significant assumptions used during the year to estimate the fair value (or calculated value) of share-based compensation awards, including (if applicable):

(a) Expected term of share options and similar instruments, including a discussion of the method used to incorporate the contractual term of the instruments and employees' expected exercise and post-vesting employment termination behavior into the fair value (or calculated value) of the instrument.

(b) Expected volatility of the entity's shares and the method used to estimate it. An entity that uses a method that employs different volatilities during the contractual term shall disclose the range of expected volatilities used and the weighted-average expected volatility. A nonpublic entity that uses the calculated value method should disclose the reasons why it is not practicable for it to estimate the expected volatility of its share price, the appropriate industry sector index that it has selected, the reasons for selecting that particular index, and how it has calculated historical volatility using that index.

(c) Expected dividends. An entity that uses a method that employs different dividend rates during the contractual term shall disclose the range of expected dividends used and the weighted-average expected dividends.

(d) Risk-free rate(s). An entity that uses a method that employs different risk-free rates shall disclose the range of risk-free rates used.

(e) Discount for post-vesting restrictions and the method for estimating it.

f. An entity that grants equity or liability instruments under multiple share-based payment arrangements with employees shall provide the information

---

[137]An entity that uses the intrinsic value method pursuant to paragraphs 24 and 25 of this Statement is not required to disclose the following information for awards accounted for under that method.

specified in paragraphs A240(a)–(e) separately for different types of awards to the extent that the differences in the characteristics of the awards make separate disclosure important to an understanding of the entity's use of share-based compensation. For example, separate disclosure of weighted-average exercise prices (or conversion ratios) at the end of the year for options (or share units) with a fixed exercise price (or conversion ratio) and those with an indexed exercise price (or conversion ratio) could be important. It also could be important to segregate the number of options (or share units) not yet exercisable into those that will become exercisable (or convertible) based solely on fulfilling a service condition and those for which a performance condition must be met for the options (share units) to become exercisable (convertible). It could be equally important to provide separate disclosures for awards that are classified as equity and those classified as liabilities.

g. For each year for which an income statement is presented:
   (1) Total compensation cost for share-based payment arrangements (a) recognized in income as well as the total recognized tax benefit related thereto and (b) the total compensation cost capitalized as part of the cost of an asset.
   (2) A description of significant modifications, including the terms of the modifications, the number of employees affected, and the total incremental compensation cost resulting from the modifications.

h. As of the latest balance sheet date presented, the total compensation cost related to nonvested awards not yet recognized and the weighted-average period over which it is expected to be recognized.

i. If not separately disclosed elsewhere, the amount of cash received from exercise of share options and similar instruments granted under share-based payment arrangements and the tax benefit realized from stock options exercised during the annual period.

j. If not separately disclosed elsewhere, the amount of cash used to settle equity instruments granted under share-based payment arrangements.

k. A description of the entity's policy, if any, for issuing shares upon share option exercise (or share unit conversion), including the source of those shares (that is, new shares or treasury shares). If as a result of its policy, an entity expects to repurchase shares in the following annual period, the entity shall disclose an estimate of the amount (or a range, if more appropriate) of shares to be repurchased during that period.

A241. An illustration of disclosures of a public entity's share-based compensation arrangements follows. The illustration assumes that compensation cost has been recognized in accordance with this Statement for several years. The amount of compensation cost recognized each year includes both costs from that year's grants and costs from prior years' grants. The number of options outstanding, exercised, forfeited, or expired each year includes options granted in prior years.

* * *

On December 31, 20Y1, the Entity has two share-based compensation plans, which are described below. The compensation cost that has been charged against income for those plans was \$29.4 million, \$28.7 million, and \$23.3 million for 20Y1, 20Y0, and 20X9, respectively. The total income tax benefit recognized in the income statement for share-based compensation arrangements was \$10.3 million, \$10.1 million, and \$8.2 million for 20Y1, 20Y0, and 20X9, respectively. Compensation cost capitalized as part of inventory and fixed assets for 20Y1, 20Y0, and 20X9 was \$0.5 million, \$0.2 million, and \$0.4 million, respectively.

Share Option Plan

The Entity's 20X4 Employee Share Option Plan (the Plan), which is shareholder-approved, permits the grant of share options and shares to its employees for up to 8 million shares of common stock. The Entity believes that such awards better align the interests of its employees with those of its shareholders. Option awards are generally granted with an exercise price equal to the market price of the Entity's stock at the date of grant; those option awards generally vest based on 5 years of continuous service and have 10-year contractual terms. Share awards generally vest over five years. Certain option and share awards provide for accelerated vesting if there is a change in control (as defined in the Plan).

The fair value of each option award is estimated on the date of grant using a lattice-based option valuation model that uses the assumptions noted in the following table. Because lattice-based option valuation models incorporate ranges of assumptions for inputs, those ranges are disclosed. Expected volatilities are based on implied volatilities from traded options on the Entity's stock, historical volatility of the Entity's stock, and other factors. The Entity uses historical data to estimate option exercise and employee termination within the valuation model; separate groups of employees that have similar historical exercise behavior are considered separately for valuation purposes. The expected term of options granted is derived from the output of the option valuation model and represents the period of time that options granted are expected to be outstanding; the range given below results from certain groups of employees exhibiting different behavior. The risk-free rate for periods within the contractual life of the option is based on the U.S. Treasury yield curve in effect at the time of grant.

	20Y1	20Y0	20X9
Expected volatility	25%–40%	24%–38%	20%–30%
Weighted-average volatility	33%	30%	27%
Expected dividends	1.5%	1.5%	1.5%
Expected term (in years)	5.3–7.8	5.5–8.0	5.6–8.2
Risk-free rate	6.3%–11.2%	6.0%–10.0%	5.5%–9.0%

A summary of option activity under the Plan as of December 31, 20Y1, and changes during the year then ended is presented below:

Options	Shares (000)	Weighted-Average Exercise Price	Weighted-Average Remaining Contractual Term	Aggregate Intrinsic Value ($000)
Outstanding at January 1, 20Y1	4,660	$42		
Granted	950	60		
Exercised	(800)	36		
Forfeited or expired	(80)	59		
Outstanding at December 31, 20Y1	4,730	$47	6.5	$85,140
Exercisable at December 31, 20Y1	3,159	$41	4.0	$75,816

The weighted-average grant-date fair value of options granted during the years 20Y1, 20Y0, and 20X9 was $19.57, $17.46, and $15.90, respectively. The total intrinsic value of options exercised during the years ended December 31, 20Y1, 20Y0, and 20X9, was $25.2 million, $20.9 million, and $18.1 million, respectively.

A summary of the status of the Entity's nonvested shares as of December 31, 20Y1, and changes during the year ended December 31, 20Y1, is presented below:

Nonvested Shares	Shares (000)	Weighted-Average Grant-Date Fair Value
Nonvested at January 1, 20Y1	980	$40.00
Granted	150	63.50
Vested	(100)	35.75
Forfeited	(40)	55.25
Nonvested at December 31, 20Y1	990	$43.35

As of December 31, 20Y1, there was $25.9 million of total unrecognized compensation cost related to nonvested share-based compensation arrangements granted under the Plan. That cost is expected to be recognized over a weighted-average period of 4.9 years. The total fair value of shares vested during the years ended December 31, 20Y1, 20Y0, and 20X9, was $22.8 million, $21 million, and $20.7 million, respectively.

During 20Y1, the Entity extended the contractual life of 200,000 fully vested share options held by 10 employees. As a result of that modification, the Entity recognized additional compensation expense of $1.0 million for the year ended December 31, 20Y1.

Performance Share Option Plan

Under its 20X7 Performance Share Option Plan (the Performance Plan), which is shareholder-approved, each January 1 the Entity grants selected executives and other key employees share option awards whose vesting is contingent upon meeting various departmental and company-wide performance goals, including decreasing time to market for new products, revenue growth in excess of an index of competitors' revenue growth, and sales targets for Segment X. Share options under the Performance Plan are generally granted at-the-money, contingently vest over a period of 1 to 5 years, depending on the nature of the performance goal, and have contractual lives of 7 to 10 years. The number of shares subject to options available for issuance under this plan cannot exceed five million.

The fair value of each option grant under the Performance Plan was estimated on the date of grant using the same option valuation model used for options granted under the Plan and assumes that performance goals will be achieved. If such goals are not met, no compensation cost is recognized and any recognized compensation cost is reversed. The inputs for expected volatility, expected dividends, and risk-free rate used in estimating those options' fair value are the same as those noted in the table related to options issued under the Share Option Plan. The expected term for options granted under the Performance Plan in 20Y1, 20Y0, and 20X9 is 3.3 to 5.4 years, 2.4 to 6.5 years, and 2.5 to 5.3 years, respectively.

A summary of the activity under the Performance Plan as of December 31, 20Y1, and changes during the year then ended is presented below:

Performance Options	Shares (000)	Weighted-Average Exercise Price	Weighted-Average Remaining Contractual Term	Aggregate Intrinsic Value ($000)
Outstanding at January 1, 20Y1	2,533	$44		
Granted	995	60		
Exercised	(100)	36		
Forfeited	(604)	59		
Outstanding at December 31, 20Y1	2,824	$47	7.1	$50,832
Exercisable at December 31, 20Y1	936	$40	5.3	$23,400

The weighted-average grant-date fair value of options granted during the years 20Y1, 20Y0, and 20X9 was $17.32, $16.05, and $14.25, respectively. The total intrinsic value of options exercised during the years ended December 31, 20Y1, 20Y0, and 20X9, was $5 million, $8 million, and $3 million, respectively. As of December 31, 20Y1, there was $16.9 million of total unrecognized compensation cost related to nonvested share-based compensation arrangements granted under the Performance Plan; that cost is expected to be recognized over a period of 4.0 years.

Cash received from option exercise under all share-based payment arrangements for the years ended December 31, 20Y1, 20Y0, and 20X9, was $32.4 million, $28.9 million, and $18.9 million, respectively. The actual tax benefit realized for the tax deductions from option exercise of the share-based payment arrangements totaled $11.3 million, $10.1 million, and $6.6 million, respectively, for the years ended December 31, 20Y1, 20Y0, and 20X9.

The Entity has a policy of repurchasing shares on the open market to satisfy share option exercises and expects to repurchase approximately one million shares during 20Y2, based on estimates of option exercises for that period.

Supplemental Disclosures

A242. In addition to the information required by this Statement, an entity may disclose supplemental information that it believes would be useful to investors and creditors, such as a range of values calculated on the basis of different assumptions, provided that the supplemental information is reasonable and does not lessen the prominence and credibility of the information required by this Statement. The alternative assumptions should be described to enable users of the financial statements to understand the basis for the supplemental information.

Appendix B

BASIS FOR CONCLUSIONS

CONTENTS

Appendix B

BASIS FOR CONCLUSIONS

INTRODUCTION

B1. This appendix summarizes considerations that Board members deemed significant in reaching the conclusions in this Statement. It includes reasons for accepting certain views and rejecting others. Individual Board members gave greater weight to some factors than to others.

WHY THE BOARD UNDERTOOK A PROJECT TO RECONSIDER STATEMENT 123

Statement 123's Provisions on Cost Recognition for Share-Based Payment Arrangements

B2. Statement 123 was issued in 1995. Its requirements for share-based employee compensation transactions were effective for financial statements for fiscal years beginning after December 15, 1995. As originally issued, Statement 123 established the fair-value-based method of accounting as preferable for share-based compensation awarded to employees and encouraged, but did not require, entities to adopt it. The Board's decision at that time was based on practical rather than conceptual considerations. Paragraphs 60 and 61 of Statement 123 stated:

> The debate on accounting for stock-based compensation unfortunately became so divisive that it threatened the Board's future working relationship with some of its constituents. Eventually, the nature of the debate threatened the future of accounting standards setting in the private sector.
>
> The Board continues to believe that financial statements would be more relevant and representationally faithful if the estimated fair value of employee stock options was included in determining an entity's net income, just as all other forms of compensation are included. To do so would be consistent with accounting for the cost of all other goods and services received as consideration for equity instruments. The Board also believes that financial reporting would be improved if all equity instruments granted to employees, in-

cluding instruments with variable features such as options with performance criteria for vesting, were accounted for on a consistent basis. However, in December 1994, the Board decided that the extent of improvement in financial reporting that was envisioned when this project was added to its technical agenda and when the Exposure Draft was issued was not attainable because the deliberate, logical consideration of issues that usually leads to improvement in financial reporting was no longer present. Therefore, the Board decided to specify as preferable and to encourage but not to require recognition of compensation cost for all stock-based employee compensation, with required disclosure of the pro forma effects of such recognition by entities that continue to apply Opinion 25.

B3. Statement 123 allowed entities to continue accounting for share-based compensation arrangements with employees according to the intrinsic value method in APB Opinion No. 25, *Accounting for Stock Issued to Employees,* under which no compensation cost was recognized for employee share options that met specified criteria. Public entities that continued to use the intrinsic value method were required to disclose pro forma measures of net income and earnings per share as if they had used the fair-value-based method. Nonpublic entities that continued to use the intrinsic value method were required to make pro forma disclosures as if they had used the minimum value method or the fair-value-based method for recognition.

Pertinent Events during the First Eight Years Statement 123 Was Applicable

B4. Before 2002, virtually all entities chose to continue to apply the provisions of Opinion 25 rather than to adopt the fair-value-based method to account for share-based compensation arrangements with employees. The serious financial reporting failures that came to light beginning in 2001 led to a keen interest in accounting and financial reporting issues on the part of investors, regulators, members of the U.S. Congress, and the media. Many of the Board's constituents who use financial information said that the failure to recognize compensation cost for most employee share options had obscured important aspects of reported performance and impaired the transparency of financial statements.

B5. The increased focus on high-quality, transparent financial reporting stemming from the financial reporting failures in the early years of the 21st century created a growing demand for entities to recognize compensation cost for employee share options and similar instruments—a demand to which entities began to respond. As of March 2003, when the Board added this project to its agenda, 179 public companies had adopted or announced their intention to adopt the fair-value-based accounting method in Statement 123. By May 2003, that number had grown to 276 public companies, of which 93 were companies included in the Standard & Poor's (S&P) 500 Index; those companies represented 36 percent of the index based on market capitalization.[138] By February 2004, the number had increased to 483 public companies, 113 of which represented 41 percent of the S&P 500 index based on market capitalization, and by July 2004, the number had increased to 753 public companies.

B6. The increased focus on financial reporting issues, including accounting for share-based compensation arrangements with employees, was accompanied by numerous requests from investors, regulators, and other users of financial statements for the Board to reconsider the cost recognition provisions of Statement 123. Although an increasing number of entities were voluntarily adopting the fair-value-based accounting method in Statement 123, it did not appear likely that voluntary adoption would extend to all entities, at least not in the foreseeable future. Voluntary adoption of Statement 123's fair-value-based accounting method by increasing numbers of entities provided improved information about the effects of share-based payment arrangements with employees on those entities and their shareholders. However, that voluntary adoption also resulted in less comparability across entities because of the alternative accounting methods Statement 123 permitted.

B7. The existence of alternative accounting methods for share-based compensation arrangements with employees, coupled with the failure of Opinion 25 to provide much general guidance on applying its intrinsic value method, had resulted in voluminous accounting guidance that constituents said was disjointed, rule-based, and form-driven.[139] Both the Board and the Emerging Issues Task Force (EITF) had responded to requests for guidance on a large number of implementation issues. For example, FASB Interpretation No. 44, *Accounting for Certain Transactions involving Stock Compensation,* addressed 20 implementation questions, many of which had 1 or more subquestions. The EITF addressed an additional 51 implementation issues in EITF Issue No. 00-23, "Issues Related to the Accounting for Stock Compensation under APB Opinion No. 25 and FASB Interpretation No. 44." Constituents asked the Board to simplify the existing accounting guidance on accounting for share-based payment arrangements, and some of those constituents noted that eliminating the alternative to continue using Opinion 25's accounting method would be the best way to achieve that simplification.

B8. In November 2002, the International Accounting Standards Board (IASB) issued an Exposure Draft, *Share-based Payment,* (ED2) that proposed a single, fair-value-based method to be used to account for all share-based compensation arrangements. Although the method that the IASB proposed in ED2 shared some important features of the fair-value-based method in Statement 123, it also differed in certain significant respects. Many of the differences involved secondary implementation issues rather than primary issues of fundamental principles.

B9. In November 2002, shortly after the IASB issued ED2, the FASB issued an Invitation to Comment, *Accounting for Stock-Based Compensation: A Comparison of FASB Statement No. 123,* Accounting for Stock-Based Compensation, *and Its Related Interpretations, and IASB Proposed IFRS,* Share-based Payment. The Invitation to Comment explained both the primary and secondary differences between the requirements of Statement 123 and the method proposed by the IASB. Most users of financial statements who responded to the Invitation to Comment urged the Board to undertake a project to require that entities account for share-based payment arrangements with employees using a fair-value-based

---

[138]Refer to Pat McConnell, Janet Pegg, Chris Senyek, and Dane Mott, "Companies That Currently Expense or Intend to Expense Stock Options Using the Fair Value Method," Bear Stearns (May 23, 2003), Bear Stearns update (February 12, 2004), and Bear Stearns update (July 20, 2004).

[139]That guidance was identified by the United States Securities and Exchange Commission (SEC) as an example of rules-based accounting standards. (SEC, *Study Pursuant to Section 108(d) of the Sarbanes-Oxley Act of 2002 on the Adoption by the United States Financial Reporting System of a Principles-Based Accounting System,* March 25, 2003 [www.sec.gov/news/studies/principlesbasedstand.htm]).

method. The majority of the preparers who responded did not support such a requirement. However, some of those preparers asked for additional guidance on applying the fair-value-based method in Statement 123.

B10. For the reasons discussed in paragraphs B4–B9, the Board concluded that the time had come to reconsider the provisions of Statement 123. Given that conclusion, the Board agreed with respondents to the Invitation to Comment that undertaking that reconsideration concurrently with the IASB's consideration of responses to ED2[140] would maximize the opportunity for convergence of U.S. and international accounting standards. Doing so would be consistent with the Board's commitment to work toward convergence to a set of high-quality accounting standards that can be used for both domestic and cross-border financial reporting.

Summary of Reasons for Undertaking a Project to Reconsider Statement 123

B11. After considering the factors discussed in paragraphs B4–B10, in March 2003, the Board added to its agenda a project to reconsider the existing guidance on accounting for share-based payment arrangements. This Statement is a result of that project. By requiring recognition of compensation cost for share-based payment arrangements with employees, this Statement responds to:

a. Requests from investors and others to improve the transparency, relevance, and comparability of information about the effects of share-based payment arrangements with employees on entities and their shareholders
b. The need to simplify the existing accounting guidance on share-based payment arrangements with employees by eliminating alternative accounting methods
c. The Board's commitment to work toward convergence to a set of high-quality accounting standards that can be used for both domestic and cross-border financial reporting.

SCOPE OF THIS STATEMENT

B12. As did Statement 123, this Statement includes in its scope all share-based payment transactions,

whether with employees or with counterparties who are not employees (nonemployees). The FASB project from which this Statement results encompasses reconsideration of all aspects of accounting for share-based payment arrangements. However, the Board decided to exclude from the scope of this Statement reconsideration of the measurement date for share-based payment transactions with nonemployees, which also was excluded from the scope of Statement 123. This Statement also excludes from its scope accounting for employee share ownership plans currently accounted for under AICPA Statement of Position 93-6, *Employers' Accounting for Employee Stock Ownership Plans.* In other words, this Statement reflects the Board's reconsideration of only those issues that were addressed in Statement 123.

B13. Most of the debate surrounding accounting for share-based payment has focused on arrangements with employees, and the Board concluded that mandating recognition of compensation cost measured at fair value for those arrangements was the most urgent aspect of this project. Moreover, cost is already recognized for share-based payment arrangements with nonemployees under Statement 123 and EITF Issue No. 96-18, "Accounting for Equity Instruments That Are Issued to Other Than Employees for Acquiring, or in Conjunction with Selling, Goods or Services," using a fair-value-based measure, albeit with a measurement date that may differ from the one this Statement prescribes for equity instruments issued to employees. Including guidance on share-based payment arrangements with nonemployees and guidance on accounting for shares held by employee share ownership plans would have delayed the issuance of this Statement.

B14. The Board may reconsider the issues addressed in Issue 96-18 in a later phase of this project. Although this Statement addresses issues with a focus on share-based payment transactions with employees, certain of its provisions are unrelated to the issues addressed in Issue 96-18. The Board understands that many entities have been analogizing to Statement 123's guidance in determining how to account for share-based payment transactions with nonemployees. However, because the Board did not specifically consider such items in the context of nonemployee transactions, it decided that, except for

---

[140]The IASB issued International Financial Reporting Standard (IFRS) 2, *Share-based Payment,* in February 2004. Refer to paragraphs B258–B269 of this appendix for a discussion of differences between this Statement and IFRS 2.

the amendment to Statement 95, no additional guidance should be provided in this Statement on accounting for share-based payment transactions with nonemployees.

RECOGNITION OF COMPENSATION COST FROM SHARE-BASED PAYMENT ARRANGEMENTS WITH EMPLOYEES

B15. The Board reaffirmed the conclusion reflected in Statement 123 that an entity should recognize compensation cost as a result of receiving employee services in exchange for valuable financial instruments, including equity share options. The reasons for that conclusion are discussed in paragraphs B16–B32. The Board also concluded that such compensation cost should be measured using a fair-value-based method similar to the one set forth in Statement 123. The reasons for the Board's conclusions on measurement of compensation cost are discussed in paragraphs B33–B60.

Employee Services Received in Exchange for Equity Instruments Qualify as Assets

B16. Some respondents to the Exposure Draft said that an entity does not receive an asset, and thus does not incur compensation cost, when it receives employee services in exchange for equity instruments. The Board disagrees; employers receive employee services in exchange for all forms of compensation paid. Those services, like services received from nonemployees, qualify as assets, if only momentarily because receipt of a service and its use occur simultaneously.

B17. FASB Concepts Statement No. 6, *Elements of Financial Statements,* paragraph 26, describes the three essential characteristics of an asset:

> . . . (a) it embodies a probable future benefit that involves a capacity, singly or in combination with other assets, to contribute directly or indirectly to future net cash inflows, (b) a particular entity can obtain the benefit

and control others' access to it, and (c) the transaction or other event giving rise to the entity's right to or control of the benefit has already occurred.

Employee services clearly have the capacity, in combination with other assets such as equipment, plant, or intangibles, to contribute to the employer's future net cash inflows by producing a product, which may itself be a service that is sold to customers. The employer can obtain the benefit and control others' access to it; an employee cannot provide the same services to more than a single employer simultaneously. By the time employee services (and the related cost or expense) are recognized, the employer has obtained the benefit.

B18. To summarize, employee services qualify as assets because they exhibit the three essential characteristics of an asset described in Concepts Statement 6. If employee (and other) services did not provide economic benefits, an entity would not be willing to pay any form of consideration, including cash salaries, for them. The nature of the consideration exchanged for employee services is not significant in determining whether those services qualify as assets. The consumption of the services received in exchange for the issuance of equity instruments (or the payment of assets) is the event that gives rise to compensation cost.[141]

Employee Services Exchanged for Equity Instruments Give Rise to Compensation Cost As Those Services Are Used

B19. Because an entity cannot store services, they qualify as separate or independent assets only momentarily. An entity's use of an asset results in an expense, regardless of whether the asset is cash or another financial instrument, goods, or services. (Generally accepted accounting principles in the United States require the cost of services to be capitalized as part of the cost of another asset in certain circumstances. In that situation, expense is recognized when that other asset, for example, inventory, is consumed or disposed of.) Concepts Statement 6, paragraph 81, footnote 43, notes that, in concept,

---

[141]Concepts Statement 6, paragraph 79, footnote 40, explains that point as follows: "Entities acquire assets (economic benefits), not expenses or losses, to carry out their production operations, and most expenses are at least momentarily assets. Since many goods and services acquired are used either simultaneously with acquisition or soon thereafter, it is common practice to record them as expenses at acquisition. However, to record an expense as resulting from incurring a liability is a useful shortcut that combines two conceptually separate events: (a) an exchange transaction in which an asset was acquired and (b) an internal event (production) in which an asset was used up."

most expenses decrease assets rather than increase liabilities. However, if receipt of an asset, such as services, and its use occur virtually simultaneously, the asset often is not recognized because it would be derecognized immediately.[142]

B20. Some who do not consider required cost recognition to be appropriate contend that the issuance of an employee share option is a transaction directly between the recipient and the preexisting shareholders. The Board disagrees. Employees provide services to the entity—not directly to individual shareholders—as consideration for their options. Carried to its logical conclusion, that view would imply that the issuance of virtually any equity instrument for goods or services, rather than for cash or other financial instruments, should not affect the issuer's financial statements. For example, no asset or related cost would be reported if shares of stock were issued to acquire legal or consulting services, tangible assets, or an entire business in a business combination. To omit such assets and the related costs would give a misleading picture of the entity's financial position and financial performance.

B21. To summarize, accounting for assets received (and the related expenses when the assets are consumed) has long been fundamental to the accounting for all freestanding equity instruments except one—fixed equity share options that had no intrinsic value at the grant date and were accounted for under the requirements of Opinion 25. This Statement remedies that exception.

Disclosure versus Recognition

B22. Having reaffirmed the conclusion that compensation cost from awards of equity instruments to employees, measured using the fair-value-based method, qualifies for recognition in the financial statements, the Board considered whether to eliminate the alternative to disclose, on a pro forma basis, the effects of that accounting in lieu of applying it for recognition purposes. Some respondents to the Exposure Draft and the Invitation to Comment said that the pro forma disclosures required by Statement 123 provided adequate financial information about share-based payment arrangements with employees. Similar comments were made in various public venues

during the Board's work leading to the issuance of this Statement. Some of those commentators asserted that whether information is disclosed in the notes or recognized in the financial statement is not important—either way, sophisticated users of financial information have access to the information they need.

Pro Forma Disclosure Is Not an Acceptable Substitute for Recognition

B23. The Board reaffirmed the conclusion in Statement 123 that pro forma disclosures are not an adequate substitute for recognition in the financial statements of compensation cost resulting from share-based payment arrangements with employees. Although the main reasons for that conclusion are essentially the same as in Statement 123, new information made available since the issuance of Statement 123 provided additional support for the Board's reasoning.

B24. Paragraph 9 of FASB Concepts Statement No. 5, *Recognition and Measurement in Financial Statements of Business Enterprises,* discusses recognition and disclosure:

> Since recognition means depiction of an item in both words and numbers, with the amount included in the totals of the financial statements, disclosure by other means is *not* recognition. Disclosure of information about the items in financial statements and their measures that may be provided by notes or parenthetically on the face of financial statements, by supplementary information, or by other means of financial reporting is not a substitute for recognition in financial statements for items that meet recognition criteria.

B25. Most of the users of financial statements who responded to either the Exposure Draft or the Invitation to Comment, as well as those who responded to the IASB's ED2 or the Exposure Draft that led to the issuance of FASB Statement No. 148, *Accounting for Stock-Based Compensation—Transition and Disclosure,* strongly supported recognition of the cost of employee services received in exchange for equity

---

[142]That footnote refers only to liabilities, but the same is true for equity. That is, issuing equity increases assets rather than resulting in an expense. The entity obtains assets in exchange for issuing equity instruments. For ease of discussion, this appendix also generally omits references to the interim step of recognizing an asset and uses shorthand phrases such as *the compensation cost resulting from awards of share-based compensation.*

instruments. Although the pro forma disclosures required by Statement 123 helped to mitigate the problems of nonrecognition of compensation cost, many financial statement users said that the failure of most entities to recognize that cost impaired the transparency, relevance, and comparability, as well as the credibility, of financial statements. In agreeing with those respondents, the Board noted that if disclosure and recognition were equal alternatives, the arguments for only disclosing the amount of compensation cost from share-based compensation arrangements with employees would apply equally to other costs incurred during a period, such as warranties, pensions, and other postretirement benefits. Disclosing but not recognizing those costs in the period in which they are incurred would cause reported net income to misrepresent the results of current operations.

B26. In addition to responses to the Exposure Draft, the Invitation to Comment, ED2, and the Exposure Draft that led to the issuance of Statement 148, the Board's conclusion that many users of financial statements support recognition of the cost of employee services received in exchange for share options and similar equity instruments was confirmed in a number of ways, including:

a. Numerous requests from users for the Board to add a project to its agenda to reconsider accounting for share-based payment arrangements with employees.
b. Responses to a survey of analysts and fund managers in 2001 by the Association for Investment Management and Research[143] (now the CFA Institute) in which 83 percent of respondents favored recognition of compensation cost for share-based payment arrangements with employees.
c. Responses to a recent survey[144] of 30 institutional investors in technology companies in which more than 90 percent supported recognition of compensation cost for employee share options. Approximately 70 percent of those analysts and portfolio managers also said that an analysis of an entity's share options is significant to their valuation of the entity and has the potential to influence their investment decisions.
d. Public comments made by various users of financial statements during the course of the Board's project on share-based payment.

e. Numerous nonbinding shareholder resolutions in which both institutional and individual investors urged entities to adopt Statement 123's fair-value-based method for recognition purposes.

Recognizing Compensation Cost for Employee Equity Share Options Does Not Inappropriately Double Count Their Effect

B27. Some respondents to the Invitation to Comment said that recognizing the cost of employee services received in exchange for employee share options would inappropriately "double count" the effect of granting share options. They noted that the dilutive effect of in-the-money share options is included in the denominator of diluted earnings per share. To reduce net income (the numerator of that ratio) by recognizing compensation expense based on fair value would, in their view, create an inappropriate dual effect on diluted earnings per share; this argument often is stated as "earnings per share would be hit twice."

B28. Earnings per share is a metric—no expense (cost), revenue, or other element of financial statements is "recognized" by including its effect only in earnings per share. A transaction that results in an expense and that also increases the number of common shares outstanding properly affects both the numerator and the denominator of earnings per share. An equity share option affects only potential dilutive common shares outstanding and thus affects only diluted earnings per share. If an entity issues equity shares, equity share options, or share purchase warrants for cash and uses the cash received to pay employee salaries, earnings are reduced and more actual or potential common shares are outstanding. Moreover, if an entity issues common shares in exchange for a depreciable asset, both the resulting depreciation expense and the increase in common shares outstanding reduce basic earnings per share. Recognition of the compensation cost resulting from awards of employee share options is no different from the accounting for other transactions in which use of the consideration received for issuing equity instruments reduces reported earnings, and the related equity instruments increase either actual or potential common shares outstanding.

---

[143] Association for Investment Management and Research (AIMR), "Survey on Accounting for Stock Options" (September 2001); electronic survey sent to more than 18,000 AIMR members worldwide to assess their response to a proposed agenda topic of the IASB.
[144] Merrill Lynch, "Tech Stock Options: The Invisible Cash Flow Drain" (February 3, 2004).

Potential Economic Consequences of Recognition of Compensation Cost

B29. Some respondents said that required recognition of compensation cost based on the fair value of employee share options may have undesirable economic consequences. They suggested that required recognition of compensation cost is likely to cause some entities to reduce, eliminate, or otherwise revise those arrangements. Some also contended that recognition of compensation cost for employee share options will raise the cost of capital for entities that make extensive use of those options.

B30. The Board's operating precepts require it to consider issues in an evenhanded manner, without attempting to encourage or to discourage specific actions. That does not imply that improved financial reporting should have no economic consequences. To the contrary, a change in accounting standards that results in financial statements that are more relevant and representationally faithful, and thus more useful for decision making, presumably would have economic consequences. For example, required recognition of compensation cost based on the provisions of this Statement would result in more comparable accounting for all forms of employee compensation. As a result, any decision to reassess and perhaps modify existing share-based payment arrangements would be based on financial information that better represents the economic effects of various forms of compensation.

B31. The Board understands that the vast majority of share options awarded to employees are fixed, at-the-money options for which entities that continued to use the accounting requirements of Opinion 25 recognized no compensation expense. The accounting under Opinion 25 treated most fixed share options as though they were a "free good," which implies that the services received in exchange for those options were obtained without incurring a cost. But employee services received in exchange for share options are not free. Share options are valuable equity instruments for which valuable consideration is received—consideration that should be recognized regardless of whether it is in the form of cash, goods, or services from employees or other suppliers. Accounting for fixed, at-the-money employee share options as though they impose no cost on the entity that

issues them may encourage their substitution for other forms of compensation, such as share options or other instruments with performance or market conditions, that may be preferable in a particular situation. Requiring recognition of compensation cost using the fair-value-based method increases the neutrality of financial reporting and removes what many consider to be an accounting incentive for an entity to choose a form of employee compensation—fixed, at-the-money share options—that may not be the most advantageous in its circumstances.

Conclusion on Recognition of Compensation Cost

B32. In summary, the Board reaffirmed the conclusions reflected in Statement 123 that:

a. Employee services exchanged for equity share options and other equity instruments give rise to a cost that is properly recognized in the issuing entity's financial statements.
b. Disclosure is not an adequate substitute for recognition.
c. Inclusion of employee share options and similar instruments in diluted earnings per share does not constitute recognition of compensation cost.

In light of those conclusions, which were considered in combination with recent events discussed in paragraphs B4–B10, the Board decided that to improve financial reporting it was necessary to require entities to recognize the compensation cost resulting from the consumption of employee services received in exchange for equity instruments.

HOW SHOULD COMPENSATION COST FROM SHARE-BASED COMPENSATION ARRANGEMENTS WITH EMPLOYEES BE MEASURED?

B33. Determining the appropriate measure of compensation cost from share-based compensation arrangements with employees requires resolving two fundamental issues:

a. The date at which the share price (and other pertinent factors) that enter into measurement of the fair value of an award of share-based payment is fixed—the measurement date issue[145]

b. The attribute used to measure the equity instruments awarded, and thus to measure the resulting compensation cost—the measurement attribute issue.

Once those two questions have been resolved, various issues arise about how to apply the measurement basis selected.

Why Grant Date Is the Appropriate Measurement Date

B34. The Board reaffirmed the conclusion reflected in Statement 123 that equity share options and other equity instruments awarded to employees (and subsequently issued to them if vesting conditions are satisfied) and the related compensation cost should be measured based on the share price and other pertinent factors at the date the award is granted. Paragraphs B35–B50 discuss the reasons for that conclusion, including the alternative measurement dates considered.

Alternatives to Grant Date as the Measurement Date

Vesting date

B35. Proponents of measuring the value of equity instruments awarded to employees and the related compensation cost based on the share price at the date the award vests noted that employees have not earned the right to retain their shares or options until that date. They suggested that a more descriptive term for *grant date* would be *offer date* because the entity makes an offer at that date and becomes obligated to issue equity instruments to employees if the employees render the requisite service or satisfy other conditions for vesting. Employees effectively accept the offer by fulfilling the requisite vesting conditions. Until both parties have fulfilled their obligations under the agreement, the employee has only a conditional right to the equity instruments to be issued. Accordingly, the transaction between the employer and employee should not be fixed until that date—that is, not until the vesting date.

B36. Advocates of vesting date measurement considered it to be consistent with accounting for the issuance of similar equity instruments to third parties for cash or other assets. At the date a share purchase warrant, for example, is issued and measured, the investor receives either the warrant itself or an enforceable right to receive and exercise the warrant without providing additional assets, including services, to the issuer. That is, the rights of the holder of a warrant at the date its fair value is measured and recognized are essentially the same as the rights of an employee at the date an equity share option or similar instrument becomes vested.

Service date

B37. Unlike most of the other alternatives described, service date measurement does not base the recognition of compensation cost stemming from share-based compensation arrangements on the share price on a single date. Rather, the share prices on the dates at which employees provide the service necessary to earn their awards are used. Under service date measurement, a proportionate number of the shares subject to a service condition for vesting, for example, would in concept be measured based on the share price each day that an employee renders service. In practice, the results of daily accrual generally could be reasonably approximated by basing the amount of compensation expense recognized each accounting period on the weighted-average share price for that period.

B38. Advocates of service date measurement pointed out that the earning of a share-based compensation award—like the earning of other forms of compensation—is a continuous process. They said that the related compensation cost should be measured based on the share prices during the period the service is rendered—not solely on the share price at either the beginning or the end of that period. In their view, service date measurement is most consistent with the current employee service model based on recognizing and measuring the cost of employee services as the service is rendered.

B39. Vesting date measurement effectively adjusts the value (and related cost) of the service received in, for example, year 1 of a two-year vesting period based on share price changes that occur in year 2. Moreover, the increment (or decrement) in value attributable to year 1's service is recognized in

---

[145]Possible alternative measurement dates do not refer to the date at which accounting for compensation cost begins. For example, most advocates of vesting date measurement would begin accruing compensation cost as soon as employees begin to render the service necessary to earn their awards. Rather, the measurement date issue concerns the date at which the share price and other pertinent factors that enter into the final measure of compensation cost are fixed.

year 2. Advocates of service date measurement contended that to retroactively adjust the value of consideration (in this situation, employee services) already received for future issuance of an equity instrument is to treat awards of equity instruments to employees as if they were liabilities until the employees have vested rights to them. Because an entity that grants share options is obligated only to issue its own shares, not to transfer its assets, advocates of service date measurement contended that measuring nonvested awards as if they were liabilities is inappropriate.

Service expiration date

B40. The service expiration date is the date at which all service-related conditions that may change the terms under which employees may exercise their stock options expire. Awards of employee stock options generally specify a limited period of time, often 60 or 90 days, after termination of service during which employees with vested options may exercise them. The options are cancelled if they are not exercised by the end of that period. If the exercise period is 90 days after termination, the service expiration date is 90 days before the maximum term of the options expires. If the options are exercised before then, the exercise date would be the measurement date. For an award of shares subject to vesting requirements, the service expiration date is the date at which service-related restrictions on the sale of the shares lapse, which usually would be the vesting date.

Component approaches to determining the measurement date

B41. The Board considered a version of service date and service expiration date measurement in its deliberations that led to the issuance of Statement 123, and respondents to the Exposure Draft of this Statement proposed several other versions of service expiration date measurement. Common to all those versions is the view that a limitation on the period of time an employee may exercise a vested option after termination of service, say to 90 days, effectively reduces the term of the option to 90 days (or whatever the length of the post-termination exercise period).[146] In effect, each day that an employee continues to render service after vesting results in a 1-day extension of the term of the 90-day option. Thus,

continued service after vesting is necessary to allow an employee to benefit from the time value of an option with an expected term that is longer than the vesting period. However, because an employee can immediately exercise a vested option and thus benefit from any intrinsic value as soon as the option vests, all versions of service expiration date measurement would call for separating the fair value of an option into its intrinsic value and time value components and recognizing each component differently.

B42. Advocates of those methods also contend that they would be easier to apply than earlier measurement dates. If the period after which service-related conditions expire is short, such as 90 days, concerns about how well traditional option-pricing models measure an option's fair value may be less significant than for a long-term option. Some suggest that use of the market price of a traded option (if the issuing entity has traded options) could be appropriate.

Exercise date

B43. Under exercise date measurement, the final measure of compensation cost is based on the share price at the date an employee exercises an option (or the date the option lapses or is otherwise settled). Some that favor exercise date measurement do so because they consider call options written by an entity on its shares to be liabilities rather than equity instruments. They acknowledge that neither employee share options nor share purchase warrants or other call options issued to third parties qualify as liabilities under the definition in Concepts Statement 6 because they do not obligate the entity to transfer its assets to the holder. Those instruments also do not qualify as liabilities under the criteria in FASB Statement No. 150, *Accounting for Certain Financial Instruments with Characteristics of both Liabilities and Equity*, for determining whether an equity-settled obligation embodied in a freestanding financial instrument should be classified as a liability. Those that hold this view generally favor revising the conceptual distinction between liabilities and equity instruments so that an obligation to issue a fixed number of shares at a fixed price would qualify as a liability.

B44. Other advocates of exercise date measurement contend that the intrinsic value, if any, that an employee realizes upon exercise of a share option appropriately measures the amount of compensation

---

[146]In concept, the post-termination exercise window specified by the terms of an award would be used in applying the service expiration date method. However, to simplify application, proponents of such methods generally suggest using an arbitrary period, usually 90 days, as a proxy for the post-termination exercise window, and this Statement discusses the methods in those terms.

paid. They see little, if any, practical difference between an employee share option and a cash bonus indexed to the price of the entity's shares.

B45. From a more pragmatic perspective, advocates note that exercise date measurement is simple and straightforward. The value of a share option upon exercise equals the difference between the exercise price and the market price of the underlying share at that date—its intrinsic value upon exercise. In effect, fair value and intrinsic value are equal at the exercise date. Recognition of compensation cost as an employee provides service before vesting (and recognition of gain or loss as the share price changes after vesting) might be based on the fair value of the option estimated using an option-pricing model. However, the aggregate measure of compensation cost will be the same under exercise date measurement regardless of the measurement method. Concerns about how to apply option-pricing models initially developed for traded options to forfeitable, nontransferable employee options are much less significant if final measurement is based on the intrinsic value, if any, that an employee realizes by exercising an option. The usual accounting response to major problems in measuring the effects of a transaction is to defer final measurement until the measurement difficulties are resolved. Exercise date measurement might be appropriate for that reason regardless of more conceptual considerations.

Conclusion on Measurement Date

B46. As noted in paragraph B34, the Board decided to retain grant date as the measurement date for share-based payment arrangements with employees. By definition, the grant date is the date at which an employer and an employee agree to the terms of a share-based compensation award. The Board concluded that the exchange of equity instruments for employee services should be measured at the date the parties agree to the exchange. In deciding whether and on what terms to exchange equity instruments for employee services, both parties to the agreement presumably base their decisions on the current fair value of the instrument to be exchanged—not its possible value at a future date. If compensation cost were measured based on the value of the equity instrument at a later date, such as the date at which the award vests, the resulting amount of compensation to be paid or received would not be known when the parties agree to the exchange. In that situation, recognized compensation cost would include both the

value of the consideration exchanged for services and the return to the holder of the instrument from subsequent changes in its value.

B47. The Board agreed with the conclusion in Statement 123 that equity instruments subject to service- or performance-based conditions are not issued until the entity has received the consideration for those instruments. However, because the entity becomes contingently obligated at the grant date to issue the instruments granted if employees satisfy the necessary conditions, the employees receive an equity interest in the entity at the grant date. The consideration an employee pays and the employer receives for that equity interest is future employee service. The Board concluded that the value of that service should be measured and recognized based on the share price at the date the parties reach a mutual understanding of the terms of the exchange and the employee begins to benefit from, or be adversely affected by, subsequent changes in the price of the employer's equity shares. In addition, a measurement date later than the grant date would result in recognition in the income statement of the effects of changes in the value of an equity interest, which the Board believes is inappropriate.

B48. An overwhelming majority of respondents to both the Invitation to Comment and the Exposure Draft who addressed the issue supported retaining the grant date as the measurement date. In addition to citing reasons similar to those in paragraphs B46 and B47 above, some respondents also pointed out that the compensation cost for employee equity share options and similar instruments that public entities have been either recognizing or disclosing for almost a decade has been based on grant date measurement. Retaining grant date measurement also achieves convergence with international accounting standards on this issue.

Definition of Grant Date

B49. The definition of grant date in this Statement is essentially the same as in Statement 123, which in turn was essentially the same as the notion of grant date used in practice under Opinion 25. Common to all those definitions is the notion of the grant date as the date an agreement or mutual understanding is reached. That is, the grant date is the date at which an employer and employee reach a mutual understanding of (agree to) the key terms and conditions of a share-based payment award. In reconsidering the definition of grant date, however, the Board noted that entities will need to apply that definition to a wide variety of share-based payment awards and that it sometimes may be difficult to determine when a mutual understanding of the key terms and conditionshas been reached. The Board therefore decided to clarify the concepts underlying the definition of grant date by adding the following sentence to the definition in Appendix E:

> The grant date for an award of equity instruments is the date that an employee begins to benefit from, or be adversely affected by, subsequent changes in the price of the employer's equity shares.

Some respondents to the Exposure Draft objected to the addition of that sentence. They said that a grant date has been reached when the parties to a share-based payment award have a mutual understanding of how its key terms, for example, the exercise price, will be established, even though the exact terms may not yet be known because they depend solely on a future market price. To illustrate, an award of equity share options may specify that the exercise price will be the market price of the underlying shares on a specified future date.

B50. The Board decided to retain the requirement that the grant date for an award of equity instruments is the date an employee begins to benefit from, or be adversely affected by, changes in the price of the employer's equity shares. Until that date, an employee is not subject to the risks and rewards associated with ownership of an equity instrument.

Why Fair Value Is the Relevant Measurement Attribute

B51. The Board reaffirmed the conclusion in Statement 123 that the fair value of equity instruments, including equity share options granted to employees, is the appropriate basis for measuring the related compensation cost. In reaffirming that conclusion, the Board considered the same alternatives to fair value that were discussed in Statement 123.

Alternatives to Fair Value as the Measurement Attribute

Intrinsic value

B52. The intrinsic value of an option is the difference between its exercise price and the current price of the underlying share. Intrinsic value thus excludes the value of the right to purchase the underlying share at a fixed price for a specified future period—its time value. Respondents that favored measuring employee share options at their intrinsic value generally said that intrinsic value is easily measured and understood. Some also noted that employees cannot convert the time value of their options to cash.

B53. Intrinsic value measurement might be combined with any of the measurement dates discussed in paragraphs B35–B50. However, the vast majority of the advocates of intrinsic value would only accept intrinsic value measurement at the grant date. They generally asserted that the recognition requirements of Opinion 25, coupled with the pro forma disclosure requirements of Statement 123, had provided users of financial statements with adequate information.

Minimum value

B54. The minimum value method derives its name from the theory underlying its calculation. The idea is that an investor who wishes to purchase a call option on a given share would be willing to pay *at least* (perhaps more important, the option writer would demand *at least*) an amount that represents the benefit (sacrifice) of the right to defer payment of the exercise price until the end of the option's term. For a dividend-paying share, that amount is reduced by the present value of the expected dividends during the time the option is outstanding because the holder of an option does not receive the dividends paid on the underlying share.

B55. Thus, the minimum value method reflects one part of the time value of an option—the value of the right to defer payment of the exercise price until the end of the option's term. But minimum value ignores what for many options is likely to be a greater part of time value—the right to benefit from increases in the price of the underlying share without being exposed to losses beyond the premium paid (sometimes termed *volatility value*). Advocates of minimum value generally contended that it would be too difficult to measure the volatility value component of time value (and thus of fair value) and that the resulting estimates of fair value would be too subjective for recognition in the financial statements. They noted that basing the measure of share options and similar instruments on a volatility of zero would produce a more objective measure than use of what they consider to be a subjective and difficult-to-audit expected volatility, which is needed to estimate fair value.

Conclusion on Measurement Attribute

B56. In reaffirming the conclusion in Statement 123 that equity instruments, including share options and similar instruments, awarded to employees as compensation should be measured at fair value, the Board noted that share options and other instruments that have time value are routinely traded in the marketplace at prices that are based on fair value—not on intrinsic value or minimum value. Consistent with that fact, other equity instruments and the consideration the issuing entity receives in exchange for them are recognized based on their fair values at the date the instruments are issued. For example, the initial recognition of debt issued with detachable share purchase warrants is based on the relative fair values of the debt and the warrants at the date of issuance—not on either the intrinsic value or the minimum value of the warrants. Similarly, an equity share or an equity share option issued in exchange for an asset other than employee services, such as a piece of equipment or legal services, and the related cost would be measured at either the fair value of the asset received or the fair value of the equity instrument issued, whichever is more reliably measurable. The Board sees no reason to measure compensation paid in equity share options or other equity instruments on a different basis. The Board concluded that it would not be feasible to measure directly the fair value of employee services received in exchange for employee share options or other equity instruments. Employee services generally are measured and accounted for based on the amount of consideration paid for them, regardless of the nature of the consideration. Thus, this Statement requires that the compensation cost for employee services received in exchange for equity instruments be based on the fair value of the instruments issued.

B57. Various valuation techniques are available for estimating the fair value of employee share options. Virtually any option-pricing model that is consistent with the fair value measurement objective and is applied in accordance with the guidance for its application discussed in paragraphs A2–A17 will result in an estimate of fair value that will be a more representationally faithful basis for recognition of compensation cost than either the intrinsic value or the minimum value of the options at the grant date. The grant-date intrinsic value method in Opinion 25 omits most of the factors that make an option valuable. Thus, it understates the value at the grant date of even those options for which Opinion 25's method does result in recognition of compensation cost. That is, the grant-date intrinsic value of an option fails to reflect the value of the holder's ability to benefit from increases in the price of the underlying share without being exposed to losses beyond the amount of the premium paid for the option. Minimum value reflects some, but not all, of the key factors that give a share option value. Moreover, Opinion 25's intrinsic value method often results in a higher (and more volatile) measure of compensation cost for a variable award, such as one with a market condition, than for an award that is similar except for the market condition, even though the presence of the condition reduces the value of the award.

B58. Even though measures of the grant-date intrinsic value of share options made by different entities presumably were comparable, the resulting financial statements were not necessarily comparable. For example, assume that in 2005 Entity A grants 500,000 share options with a total fair value of $1.5 million and an intrinsic value of zero. In the same year, Entity B, which is in the same industry, grants only 50,000 options with a fair value of $200,000 and an intrinsic value of zero. If the compensation cost for employee share options is recognized based on their intrinsic value at grant date, compensation cost reported by Entity A is understated by $1.5 million, while Entity B's is understated by only $200,000.

Is the Fair Value of Employee Share Options Measurable with Sufficient Reliability for Recognition in Financial Statements?

B59. Many respondents to the Exposure Draft and others who did not consider required recognition of compensation cost for employee services received in exchange for equity share options and similar instruments to be appropriate cited reliability concerns. Critics generally asserted that available valuation techniques, especially the Black-Scholes-Merton option-pricing formula and similar closed-form models, do not adequately take account of unique features of employee share options. They also pointed out that closed-form models may not be the best way to estimate the fair values of long-term options, even those without the unique features of employee share options, because those models are limited to single weighted-average assumptions for expected volatility and expected dividends. Some recommended deferring required recognition of compensation cost from employee share options until a better valuation technique for those instruments is developed. They contended that recognizing compensation cost based on fair value estimated using currently available valuation techniques would add an unacceptable level of measurement error to financial statements and impair their reliability and comparability.

B60. The Board did not find those assertions persuasive. During the course of its work on share-based payment, the Board and its staff devoted thousands of hours to understanding the available valuation models and how they can be applied to estimate the fair value of employee share options and similar instruments. That work encompassed discussions with many valuation experts, including those who developed some of the most widely used and familiar models. Based on that work, the Board concluded that entities can develop estimates of the fair value of equity instruments, including equity share options, awarded to employees that are sufficiently reliable for recognition in financial statements. The Board therefore concluded that use of the fair-value-based method required by this Statement will improve not only the relevance and reliability, but also the credibility, of financial statements. Without estimates, accrual accounting would not be possible. For example, financial statement amounts for loan loss reserves, valuation allowances for deferred tax assets, and pensions and other postretirement benefit obligations are based on estimates. For those and many other items in accounting that necessitate the use of estimates, companies are required to use appropriate measurement techniques, relevant data, and management judgment in the preparation of financial statements.[147] Few accrual-based accounting measurements can claim absolute reliability, but most parties agree that financial statement recognition of estimated amounts is preferable to the alternative—cash basis accounting.

Guidance on Estimating Fair Value

B61. Having concluded that fair value is the appropriate measurement attribute for measuring the value of the services received in exchange for equity instruments issued to employees and the related compensation cost, the Board considered what guidance to provide on estimating fair value.

General Guidance on Estimating Fair Value

B62. This Statement significantly enhances and clarifies Statement 123's guidance on estimating the fair value of equity share options and other equity instruments granted to employees. The FASB's Option Valuation Group (paragraph C20), as well as other valuation experts, provided valuable assistance in developing the revised guidance. This Statement requires that the fair value of an employee share option be based on an observable market price of an option with the same or similar terms and conditions if one is available. Although such market prices are not currently available, that requirement, together with the guidance in paragraphs A2–A42 of this Statement, clearly establishes the objective of the estimation process when fair value is estimated using a valuation technique. Moreover, market prices for equity share options with conditions similar to those in certain employee options may become available in the future.

Estimating the Fair Value of Employee Share Options Using a Valuation Technique Such as an Option-Pricing Model

B63. This Statement, as did Statement 123, provides more guidance on how to estimate fair value than other recently issued accounting standards generally provide. For example, FASB Statement No. 133, *Accounting for Derivative Instruments and Hedging Activities,* which requires derivative instruments, including options, to be measured at fair value, defines fair value but does not provide further guidance on how to apply valuation techniques if a market price is not available.[148] The Board noted that observable market prices rarely, if ever, will be available—either when the instrument is granted or subsequently—for some instruments, such as employee share options, to

---

[147]U.S. generally accepted accounting principles and generally accepted auditing standards currently address many circumstances in which entities use estimates. For example, APB Opinion No. 20, *Accounting Changes,* requires disclosure about changes in estimates. AICPA Statement of Position 94-6, *Disclosure of Certain Significant Risks and Uncertainties,* requires general disclosure in the notes to financial statements that the preparation of financial statements requires the use of estimates. AICPA Auditing Standards AU Section 380, "Communication with Audit Committees," addresses communicating certain estimates to the audit committee. In addition, the SEC has provided cautionary advice about public companies' disclosure of critical accounting policies used in financial statements (Cautionary Advice Regarding Disclosure about Critical Accounting Policies, Releases No. 33-8040, 34-45149; FR-60 [December 12, 2001]). Those required disclosures identify methods, estimates, and judgments that companies use in applying those accounting policies that have a significant impact on the results reported.

[148]In June 2004, the Board issued for comment an Exposure Draft, *Fair Value Measurements.* Except for the factors explicitly excluded from this Statement's fair-value-based measure (for example, refer to the items noted in paragraphs 18–20, 26, and 27 of this Statement), the guidance on estimating fair value in Appendix A of this Statement is consistent with, but more expansive than, the guidance that the Exposure Draft would establish.

which this Statement applies. In contrast, observable market prices often will be available for many of the instruments to which Statement 133 applies. In addition, Statement 133 generally is applied in a highly developed and sophisticated market environment, while this Statement will be applied broadly by entities with widely varying degrees of experience in estimating fair values. Numerous respondents to the Invitation to Comment asked the Board to revise, elaborate on, or clarify the guidance in Statement 123 on estimating the fair value of employee share options. The Board therefore concluded that providing guidance on estimating the fair value of employee share options continues to be appropriate. Respondents to the Exposure Draft generally agreed with the level of guidance provided for estimating the fair value of instruments granted to employees as compensation, although some respondents disagreed with certain aspects of that guidance or asked for additional guidance on estimating fair value.

Nature of the option-pricing model used

B64. As discussed in paragraphs A10–A17, closed-form models are one acceptable technique for estimating the fair value of employee share options. However, a lattice model (or other valuation technique, such as a Monte Carlo simulation technique, that is not based on a closed-form equation) can accommodate the term structures of risk-free interest rates and expected volatility, as well as expected changes in dividends over an option's contractual term. A lattice model also can accommodate estimates of employees' option exercise patterns and post-vesting employment termination during the option's contractual term, and thereby can more fully reflect the effect of those factors than can an estimate developed using a closed-form model and a single weighted-average expected life of the options.

B65. For the reasons discussed in paragraph B64, the Exposure Draft would have established a lattice model as preferable for purposes of justifying a change in accounting principle. Once an entity had adopted that valuation technique, it would have been prohibited from changing to a less preferable technique. Many of the respondents to the Exposure Draft who addressed the issue objected to establishing a lattice model as preferable and said that the guidance in the Exposure Draft would have been interpreted as effectively requiring most public entities to use a lattice model once the necessary data were available. Some of those respondents noted that other valuation techniques, such as a Monte Carlo simula-

tion technique, also generally would provide estimates of fair value that are superior to those resulting from use of a closed-form model, such as the Black-Scholes-Merton formula. Some respondents said that establishing a lattice model as preferable might inhibit future development of better models for estimating the fair value of employee share options.

B66. In light of the comments on the Exposure Draft, the Board decided not to establish a lattice model as preferable. The Board concluded that the objective of fair value measurements in paragraph A7, together with the discussion in paragraphs A8–A17, of how that objective might be achieved, is sufficient to help entities select a valuation technique that best fits their circumstances. Thus, the guidance in Appendix A of this Statement has been revised to remove the preferability of a lattice model and to clarify that neither a lattice model nor any other specific model is required.

B67. Valuation techniques for financial instruments, including employee share options, continue to evolve. Required recognition of compensation cost based on the fair value of employee share options may lead to the development of improved commercially available valuation techniques for those instruments.

B68. This Statement improves the guidance in Statement 123 on how to use an option-pricing model in estimating the fair value of an equity share option or similar instrument, including how to select the necessary assumptions. The FASB's Option Valuation Group, as well as other valuation experts, provided extensive help in developing those improvements. Paragraphs B63–B101 explain the Board's basis for its conclusions on applying an option-pricing-model or other valuation technique in estimating the fair value of employee share options.

Conditions and Restrictions That Apply Only during the Requisite Service Period

B69. This Statement retains the modified grant date method established in Statement 123, under which no compensation cost is recognized for awards for which the requisite service is not rendered. Respondents to both the Invitation to Comment and the Exposure Draft generally supported retaining that method.

B70. Investors who purchased equity instruments with restrictions similar to those in a nonvested award of employee share-based compensation (including both nonvested share options and nonvested shares) would take those restrictions into account in considering how much they would be willing to pay for the instruments. That is, a market price, if one existed, would reflect all restrictions inherent in the instrument, including restrictions that stem entirely from the forfeitability of the instruments if vesting conditions are not satisfied. Thus, a *pure* (as opposed to *modified*) grant date measure of fair value also would reflect all restrictions inherent in an award of share-based employee compensation, including vesting conditions and other restrictions that expire upon vesting. The recognized amount of compensation cost would not be subsequently adjusted to reflect the outcome of those conditions and other restrictions. The Board concluded, however, that in the absence of an observable market price for nonvested equity instruments similar to those awarded to employees, the effects of vesting conditions on fair value at the grant date are not measurable with sufficient reliability to serve as the final measure of compensation cost. Therefore, the Board decided to retain the modified grant date method required by Statement 123 under which the outcomes of all vesting conditions and other factors that apply only during the requisite service period are reflected in the ultimate measure of compensation cost.

B71. In addition, the Board noted that nonvested share-based employee compensation does not give rise to an asset at the grant date because the employer cannot require employees to render the requisite service or satisfy any other conditions necessary to earn their nonvested awards. Thus, at the grant date (or the service inception date), the employer does not yet control probable future economic benefits—in this case, employee services. That is in contrast to prepaid fees for legal services, consulting services, insurance services, and the like, which represent probable future economic benefits that are controlled by the entity because the other party to the transaction has entered into a contract to provide services to earn the fees. Unlike an employee with a nonvested award, the service provider is not entitled to walk away from its obligation to render the services that are the subject of the contract by merely foregoing collection of the fee for services not rendered.

B72. For the reason discussed in paragraph B71, this Statement does not require recognition of prepaid compensation (or any other asset) at the grant date. An investor who is not an employee transfers cash or other assets, such as an enforceable obligation to pay cash, for an equity instrument at the date it is issued. Thus, "pure" grant date accounting might be viewed

as appropriate only if the employer obtained an asset at the grant date, such as prepaid compensation, representing an enforceable right to receive employee services in the future. It also might be argued that the inappropriateness of recognizing prepaid compensation (that is, the fact that nonvested instruments have not yet been issued) supports vesting date accounting. However, the Board concluded for the reasons discussed in paragraphs B46–B48 that measurement based on the share price and other pertinent factors at the grant date is appropriate.

Inability to Transfer Employee Share Options to Third Parties and Other Restrictions That Continue after Vesting

B73. Equity instruments awarded to employees may carry restrictions that continue in effect after vesting. Under the modified grant-date method required by this Statement, the measurement objective is to estimate the fair value of the equity instruments to which employees become entitled when they have rendered the requisite service and satisfied any other conditions necessary to earn the right to benefit from the instruments. Consistent with that objective, the effect of restrictions that continue after an employee has a vested right to an instrument are reflected in estimating the fair value of the instrument at the grant date.

B74. Certain post-vesting restrictions, such as a contractual prohibition on selling shares for a specified period of time after vesting, are essentially the same as restrictions that may be present in equity instruments exchanged in the marketplace. For those restrictions, either a market price of a similar traded instrument or, if one is not available, the same valuation techniques used to estimate the fair value of a traded instrument are to be used to estimate the fair value of a similar instrument awarded to employees as compensation. However, the most common restriction embodied in equity instruments awarded to employees, the inability to transfer a vested share option to a third party, rarely, if ever, is present in traded share options.

B75. The value of a transferable option is based on its contractual term because it rarely is economically advantageous to exercise, rather than sell, a transferable option before the end of its contractual term. Employee share options differ from most other options in that employees cannot sell their options to third parties—they can only exercise them. The effect of that restriction is to increase the likelihood that an employee share option will be exercised before the end of its contractual term because exercise is the only available means to terminate the holder's exposure to future changes in the price of the underlying share. (Also refer to the discussion in paragraphs B80–B82 related to employees' inability to hedge their options.) Thus, this Statement requires that the value of a nontransferable employee share option be based on its expected term rather than its contractual term.

B76. Members of the Option Valuation Group, as well as many respondents to the Exposure Draft, agreed that the appropriate method of reflecting employees' inability to transfer their options to third parties is to base the estimate of fair value on the expected term of the options. However, some commentators suggested valuing a nontransferable option based on its contractual term and then reducing that amount by a percentage that is considered to reflect the discount that market participants would apply in determining an exchange price for a nontransferable option. A discount of as much as 50 percent was suggested. Commentators who favored that method said that it would provide a better estimate of the fair value of a nontransferable option and also would eliminate the need to estimate employees' expected exercise and post-vesting employment termination behavior. They asserted that many entities did not have the necessary information on which to base such estimates and that the estimates thus would be overly subjective as well as costly to develop.

B77. The Board carefully evaluated an alternative method of estimating the fair value of employee share options proposed by a group of constituents that would have used a percentage discount to reflect the effect of nontransferability. The Board and its staff discussed that proposed alternative method with members of the Option Valuation Group and other valuation experts, in addition to reviewing the results of pertinent academic research. Those discussions and review supported the Board's conclusion that the effect of the nontransferability of an employee share option is to make it likely that the option will be exercised before the end of its contractual term. Thus, estimating the option's fair value based on its expected term directly reflects the behavioral effect of nontransferability. The Board understands that use of the expected term may in some situations result in an estimated fair value that is as much as 50 percent lower than the fair value of an otherwise identical transferable option. Based on its discussions with valuation experts, together with its review of the relevant academic literature, the Board believes that marketplace participants would likely base their estimate of the appropriate percent discount for a nontransferable option on the difference between fair value estimated using the option's expected term and the value estimated using contractual term. In other words, incorporating employees' expected early exercise and post-vesting employment termination behavior in estimating the fair value of nontransferable options is the same process that would need to be applied to determine an appropriate percentage discount. The Board concluded that requiring entities to apply the process needed to determine an appropriate percentage discount would produce a more representationally faithful result than would an approach that presumes what the outcome of the process (the resulting percentage discount) would be.

B78. The Board also concluded that applying a similar percentage discount to determine the fair value of options with a variety of terms and conditions would be unlikely to faithfully represent the effects of nontransferability on each of those options. The result would be false comparability in which unlike things are made to look the same.

B79. Statement 123 required the same method of reflecting the effect on fair value of employees' inability to transfer their vested options to third parties that this Statement requires. However, in describing the expected term of an option, Statement 123 used the term *expected life*, and the related guidance focused primarily on estimating the weighted-average period of time employee share options were expected to remain outstanding. This Statement refers to the *expected term* of an option, which is based on the option's contractual term and employees' expected early exercise and post-vesting employment termination behavior. The valuation guidance and illustrations in Appendix A of this Statement discuss how expectations about those behaviors can be related to the intrinsic value of the option, among other factors. In using a lattice model, an option's expected term may be inferred based on the output of the model, but expected term is not a direct input to that model. Paragraph 282 of Statement 123 explained that method and indicated that entities might wish to use it.

Employees' inability to hedge call option positions

B80. Federal securities law precludes certain executives from selling shares of the issuer's stock that they do not own, and the Board understands that many public entities have established share trading policies that effectively extend that prohibition to other employees.

B81. Some respondents who did not consider requiring the fair-value-based method of accounting for employee share options to be appropriate noted that the theory underlying both closed-form and lattice option-pricing models involves replicating an option position with an offsetting position in the underlying security. Those opponents said that the inability of most employees to sell shares of their employer's stock that they do not own (to "short" the stock) calls for an additional (downward) adjustment to the fair value of a nontransferable option estimated using an option-pricing model. One method of determining that adjustment suggested by certain respondents to the Exposure Draft would discount the output of an option-pricing model by a rate that includes the employer's equity risk premium to reflect the presumably higher return required by an investor in an option that cannot be hedged.

B82. In addition to reviewing the relevant academic research, the Board discussed with experts in option valuation, including members of the Option Valuation Group, the effect of employees' inability to hedge their options positions on the fair value of employee options and its relationship to the inability to transfer vested options. Those experts agreed that nonhedgeability and nontransferability have the same effect on option value because both factors increase the likelihood that an employee share option will be exercised before the end of its contractual term. Thus, using the expected term rather than the contractual term of the option in estimating its fair value reflects the effects of both factors.

Effect of Potential Dilution on the Fair Value of Employee Share Options

B83. Some respondents to the Exposure Draft said that the effect of the potential dilution of the value of the underlying shares resulting from option exercise should be taken into account in estimating the fair value of all employee equity share options. Paragraph A38 explains why the exercise of an employee share option has the potential to dilute (decrease) the value of the underlying shares and thus decrease the employee's gain from exercising the option. Paragraph A39 then notes that the effect of potential dilution usually is already reflected in the market price of a public entity's shares and that applying a separate

discount for dilution rarely will be appropriate. For example, assume that the total market value of Entity D's 1 million common shares outstanding is $10 million on the date that it grants employee share options on 10,000 shares. If marketplace participants have anticipated that grant based on Entity D's past practice or other available information, the market price of $10 per share already reflects the market's assessment of the dilutive effect of that grant. Assuming that the market does not expect an offsetting increase in Entity D's share price as a result of the grant (and the only expected effect thus is dilution), the share price without the anticipated grant of 10,000 share options might be higher. Thus, the $10 share price used in estimating the fair value of the options already reflects the effect of potential dilution, and to include a separate discount for dilution would double count its effect.

B84. The Board's understanding of the effect of potential dilution on the fair value of an employee share option was based on and confirmed by discussion with members of the Option Valuation Group and other valuation experts. Thus, paragraph A40 of this Statement provides that an entity should consider whether the potential dilutive effect of an award of share options needs to be separately reflected in estimating the options' fair value at the grant date but notes that rarely will a public entity need to do so. In addition, the applicability of a separate adjustment for dilution in estimating the fair value of a nonpublic entity's share options may depend on how the fair value of its shares is determined.

Other Assumptions Needed to Estimate the Fair Value of Employee Share Options

B85. Paragraphs A31–A37 provide guidance on two additional assumptions needed to estimate the fair value of an employee share option using an option-pricing model—expected volatility of, and expected dividends on, the underlying shares. Paragraphs B86–B93 discuss that guidance, including comments by respondents to the Exposure Draft.

Expected volatility

B86. This Statement does not specify a method of estimating expected volatility; rather, paragraph A32 provides a list of factors to be considered in estimating expected volatility. In addition, paragraph A21 indicates that an entity might decide that historical volatility is a reasonable indicator of expected volatility but that the entity should consider ways in which future volatility is likely to differ from historical volatility. As with other aspects of estimating fair value, the objective is to determine the assumption about expected volatility that marketplace participants would be likely to use in determining an exchange price for an option.

B87. A majority of respondents to the Exposure Draft who discussed specific measurement issues supported a flexible approach to estimating expected volatility based on an indication of factors to be considered rather than a more inflexible approach that would specify a single method of determining expected volatility. Many respondents noted that such a flexible approach is consistent with a principles-based approach to standard setting. However, some respondents suggested that the Board either require or permit entities to use some form of standardized volatility assumption. For example, certain respondents suggested providing that historical volatility could be considered a "safe harbor" in all situations. Other respondents suggested use of the historical volatility of an index—either unadjusted or adjusted by the beta[149] of an entity's share price. Those suggestions were based on the view that even publicly traded entities cannot be expected to apply guidance such as that provided in paragraph A32 to develop reasonable estimates of the expected volatility of their share price. The Board rejected that view—the Board believes that public entities will be able to exercise appropriate judgment in estimating expected volatility, just as they do in other areas of accounting that require relatively high levels of management judgment. Establishing a single method for all entities to use in determining expected volatility would inevitably impair the representational faithfulness of the resulting information. For example, although use of unadjusted historical volatility may be appropriate for some entities (or even for most entities in some time periods), a marketplace participant would not use historical volatility without considering the extent to which the future is likely to differ from the past.

B88. The Board also is unaware of situations in which marketplace participants would base an estimate of the fair value of a share option either on the volatility of an index or on an index volatility adjusted by an entity's beta. Beta is not a measure of the volatility of an individual entity's shares; rather, an entity's beta is determined by comparing its volatility with the volatility of an index that represents the overall market. That measure does not reflect the unique risk inherent in an individual entity's share price because share price movements are not perfectly correlated with movements in the index. Accordingly, the suggested procedure of adjusting the volatility of an index by an entity's beta would not result in an appropriate surrogate for expected volatility.

B89. The Board also notes that public entities in the United States have for the past decade been required to estimate the expected volatility of their share price for either recognition or pro forma disclosures under Statement 123, and over 3,600 public entities in Canada are subject to similar requirements. Respondents to the Exposure Draft suggested additional factors that might be helpful in estimating expected volatility, such as the implied volatility of outstanding convertible debt, if any. The Board agreed with those suggestions. The Board concluded that entities should be able to use the improved guidance in Appendix A and build on their experience in developing estimates of expected volatility to appropriately comply with the requirements of this Statement.

Expected dividends and dividend protection

B90. Paragraphs A35–A37 provide guidance on estimating expected dividends on the underlying shares for use in an option-pricing model. As with other aspects of estimating fair value, the objective is to determine the assumption about expected dividends that would likely be used by marketplace participants in determining an exchange price for the option.

B91. Some employee share options are dividend protected. Dividend protection may take a variety of forms. For example, the exercise price of the option may be adjusted downward during the term of the option to take account of dividends paid on the underlying shares that the option holder does not receive. Alternatively, the option holder may receive the dividends or dividend equivalent payments in cash. The Exposure Draft would have carried forward Statement 123's requirement that either form of dividend protection be reflected by using an expected dividend assumption of zero in using an option-pricing model to estimate fair value. One respondent pointed out that different forms of dividend protection may have different effects on the fair value of the

---

[149]Beta is a measure of the volatility of a share relative to the overall volatility of the market. A beta of one is assigned to the volatility of the overall market. Thus, a beta of less than one indicates lower risk than the market; a beta of more than one indicates higher risk than the market.

related option. For instance, whether the option holder receives a cash payment during the option term or the exercise price is reduced affects a dividend-protected option's fair value. The Board agreed. The Board also noted that it is not feasible to anticipate all means by which an option holder may be provided full or partial dividend protection. Accordingly, this Statement requires that dividend protection be appropriately reflected in estimating the fair value of a dividend-protected option rather than specifying a single method of doing so.

B92. This Statement carries forward Statement 123's requirements on the treatment of nonrefundable dividends paid on shares of nonvested stock that the entity estimates will not, and that do not, vest. Those dividends are recognized as additional compensation cost during the vesting period. If an employee terminates service and forfeits nonvested stock but is not required to return dividends paid on the stock during the vesting period, the Board concluded that recognizing those dividends as compensation is appropriate.

B93. The fair value of a share of stock in concept equals the present value of the expected future cash flows to the stockholder, which includes dividends. Therefore, additional compensation does not arise from dividends on nonvested shares that eventually vest. Because the measure of compensation cost for those shares is their fair value at the grant date, recognizing dividends on nonvested shares as additional compensation would effectively double count those dividends. For the same reason, if employees do not receive dividends declared on the class of shares granted to them until the shares vest, the grant-date fair value of the award is measured by reducing the share price at that date by the present value of the dividends expected to be paid on the shares during the requisite service period, discounted at the appropriate risk-free interest rate.

Measurement of Equity Share Options Granted by a Nonpublic Entity

B94. Statement 123 permitted a nonpublic company to omit expected volatility (or to use an expected volatility of effectively zero) in estimating the value of its equity share options granted to employees. The result was a measure termed *minimum value*. The Board said in Statement 123 that, in concept, options granted by a nonpublic entity should be measured at fair value—the use of minimum value was only a practical response to the difficulties of estimating the expected volatility for a nonpublic entity.

B95. The Exposure Draft would have eliminated the minimum value method and required a nonpublic entity to make a policy choice of whether to measure its share options at their fair value at the grant date or at their intrinsic value through the date the options were exercised, lapsed, or otherwise settled. Many respondents to the Exposure Draft objected to that proposed requirement. Some said that it was not appropriate for a nonpublic entity to have a choice of accounting methods unless the same choice also was available to public entities. That is, those respondents objected to providing separate accounting methods for nonpublic and public entities because they think that the same transactions should be accounted for similarly by all entities regardless of their status as public or nonpublic. Other respondents said that both methods of accounting for options granted by a nonpublic entity would be unduly burdensome. In particular, respondents objected to the intrinsic value method because it would require estimates of the fair value of the entity's shares at each reporting date—estimates that for some nonpublic entities would not be required for any other purpose and that could be costly to obtain.

B96. The Board agrees with respondents who said that two entities should not use different methods to measure and account for their equity share options solely because one is public and the other is not, that is, that the basic measurement method should not be the subject of a policy choice. Therefore, the Board concluded that the fair-value-based measurement requirement should be the same for public entities and nonpublic entities. However, the Board recognizes that a nonpublic entity may have difficulty estimating the expected volatility of its share price because of the lack of frequent observations of the fair value of its shares. Accordingly, if it is not possible for a nonpublic entity to reasonably estimate the fair value of its equity share options and similar instruments because it is not practicable for the entity to estimate the expected volatility of its share price, this Statement requires that the entity measure its equity share options and similar instruments at a value calculated by substituting the historical volatility of an appropriate industry sector index for expected volatility in applying an option-pricing model. Illustration 11(b) in Appendix A provides guidance on the circumstances in which a nonpublic entity should use the historical volatility of an industry sector index and how to select an appropriate index.

B97. Although the Board concluded that the fundamental measurement requirements for equity share options should be the same for both public and nonpublic entities, the Board was persuaded by comments received on the Exposure Draft and the Invitation to Comment, as well as the additional cost-benefit procedures undertaken for nonpublic entities after the comment period on the Exposure Draft (paragraph B278), that a limited practicability exception is appropriate. The Board believes the requirements for nonpublic entities in this Statement will minimize the measurement differences between public and nonpublic entities without imposing an undue burden on nonpublic entities.

B98. The Board understands that relatively few small nonpublic entities offer share options to their employees, and those that do often are emerging entities that intend to make a future initial public offering. Many of those nonpublic entities that plan an initial public offering likely will be able to reasonably estimate the fair value of their equity share options and similar instruments using the guidance on selecting an appropriate expected volatility assumption provided in Appendix A. For those nonpublic entities for which it is not practicable to estimate expected volatility, the alternative measure in this Statement will impose minimal incremental cost over the minimum value method required by Statement 123, which required all of the same assumptions except for expected volatility. Determining the historical volatility of an appropriate industry sector index required for use in the calculated value alternative is a mechanical process that should not be difficult or costly to implement once the appropriate index is identified. In addition, because the calculated value does not omit expected volatility entirely, it should be a better surrogate for fair value than either the minimum value method in Statement 123 or the intrinsic value alternative proposed in the Exposure Draft.

B99. In deciding to require fair value as the measurement method for equity share options of nonpublic entities with a limited practicability exception, the Board acknowledged that estimating the expected volatility of a nonpublic entity's shares may be difficult and that the resulting estimated fair value may be more subjective than the estimated fair value of a public entity's options. However, the Board agrees with members of the Option Valuation Group that many nonpublic entities could consider internal and industry factors likely to affect volatility, and the average volatility of comparable entities, to develop an estimate of expected volatility. Using an expected volatility estimate determined in that manner often would result in a reasonable estimate of fair value.

B100. Some constituents questioned why the Board did not attempt to develop an alternative means for a nonpublic entity to reflect other factors, such as expected term, used in estimating the fair value of employee share options. The Board focused on expected volatility because it concluded that volatility is the only area in which a nonpublic entity is likely to encounter difficulties that are directly and uniquely related to its nonpublic status. In addition, to comply with the minimum value requirements of Statement 123, nonpublic entities were required to estimate other factors needed to estimate fair value or calculated value, such as the expected term of equity share options. Accordingly, the Board concluded that it would not be appropriate to provide a practicability exception for those assumptions.

B101. Some respondents suggested that any alternative measurement approach permitted for nonpublic entities also should apply to newly public entities. For much the same reasons cited in paragraph B99 for the Board's conclusion that many nonpublic entities should be able to reasonably estimate fair value, the Board decided not to extend the calculated value method to newly public entities. Once an entity "goes public," it should be able to identify comparable public entities and use the average volatility of those entities together with other internal and external data to develop a reasonable estimate of its expected volatility. Moreover, extending the practicability exception to newly public entities would require a definition of *newly public entity* because it is necessary to identify some point at which an entity no longer qualifies to use calculated value rather than fair value. The Board concluded that a logical and workable point is when an entity becomes a public entity—a term for which a longstanding definition in share-based payment accounting guidance is available (refer to Appendix E).

What If It Is Not Possible to Reasonably Estimate the Fair Value of an Equity Instrument at the Grant Date?

B102. Statement 123 provided that if it is not possible to reasonably estimate the fair value of an equity share option or similar equity instrument at the grant date, the final measure of compensation cost would be fair value estimated based on the share price and other factors at the first date at which reasonable estimation is possible. Paragraph 25 of this Statement instead requires that such an instrument continue to be measured at its intrinsic value at each reporting date until it is exercised or otherwise settled.

B103. In light of the variety of options and option-like instruments currently trading in external markets and the advances in methods of estimating their fair values, the Board expects that few instruments presently awarded to employees by public entities will fall into the category of instruments for which it is not possible to reasonably estimate fair value (or calculated value, for a nonpublic entity that qualifies to use that measure) at the grant date. For those that may, the Board is not aware of instances in which estimating fair value (or calculated value) at a date between grant and settlement will be significantly easier than estimating fair value at the grant date. In addition, the Board is concerned that continuing to permit the final measure of compensation cost to be based on the estimated fair value at the earliest date at which an entity decides such estimation is feasible might have unintended consequences. Requiring an entity to make a decision about whether it is possible to reasonably estimate fair value at the grant date and to follow the corresponding accounting treatment until settlement is more straightforward than Statement 123's original requirement. Therefore, the Board decided to require remeasurement of intrinsic value at each reporting date until settlement, even if the entity later concludes that it would be possible to reasonably estimate fair value (or calculated value) before the settlement date.

Reload Options

B104. Reload options are granted upon exercise of previously granted options whose original terms provide for the use of shares that the employee has held for a specified period of time, referred to as *mature shares,* rather than cash to satisfy the exercise price. At the time of exercise using mature shares, the employee is automatically granted a reload option for the same number of shares used to exercise the original option. The exercise price of the reload option often is the market price of the stock at the date the reload option is granted, and its term often is equal to the remainder of the term of the original options.

B105. Some respondents to the Exposure Draft, as well as some respondents to the Exposure Draft that preceded Statement 123, suggested that an option with a reload feature can be valued at the grant date as a "forward start option" commencing at the date or dates that the option is "reloaded." The forward start

option's value would be added to the value of the option granted with a reload feature to determine the total value of the award. However, the forward start option formula calls for a number of subjective assumptions, such as the number of expected reloads and the expected timing of each reload. In addition, because an employee can take advantage of the reload feature only with shares already held, the employer would need to estimate (a) the number of employees who are expected to pay the exercise price with those shares rather than with cash and (b) those employees' holdings of mature shares.

B106. Because a reload feature is part of the options initially awarded, the Board believes that the value added to those options by the reload feature ideally should be considered in estimating the fair value of the initial award at its grant date. However, the Board concluded that it is not feasible to do so at this time. Accordingly, the Board concluded that the best way to account for an option with a reload feature is to treat both the initial grant and each subsequent grant of a reload option as separate awards.

TRANSFERS OF SHARE-BASED PAYMENT TO EMPLOYEES BY ECONOMIC INTEREST HOLDERS

B107. Statement 123 required that an entity recognize compensation cost for equity instruments granted or otherwise transferred to an employee by a *principal shareholder* of the entity unless the transfer clearly was for a purpose other than compensation.[150] The Board concluded at that time that the substance of such a transaction is that the principal shareholder makes a capital contribution to the entity, which the entity uses to grant share-based compensation to the employee who receives the equity instruments. Paragraph 395 of Statement 123 defined a principal shareholder as:

> One who either owns 10 percent or more of an entity's common stock or has the ability, directly or indirectly, to control or significantly influence the entity.

B108. ED2 contained a similar provision, except that a direct transfer of equity instruments from any shareholder, not only a principal shareholder, to an

---

[150]An example of a situation in which a direct transfer of equity instruments to an employee from a principal shareholder (or other related party or economic interest holder) is not compensation cost is a transfer to settle an obligation of the principal shareholder unrelated to employment by the reporting entity.

employee as payment for services received by the reporting entity was to be recognized as share-based compensation. Most respondents to the Invitation to Comment and to ED2 who addressed this issue supported ED2's proposed requirement (which is in IFRS 2).

B109. The Board agreed that the scope of Statement 123's requirements for such transfers should be expanded to encompass transfers from any shareholder. However, the Board saw no reason to limit the provision to transfers by shareholders. Holders of other forms of economic interests in an entity, such as holders of convertible debt or other creditors, might see the likelihood of sufficient indirect benefit to themselves to justify compensating one or more of the employees of a reporting entity by transferring to those employees share-based payment of that entity.

B110. The Board intends the provision in paragraph 11 of this Statement to be applied by analyzing transactions in which a related party or a holder of an economic interest in the reporting entity transfers (or offers to transfer) share-based payment of the entity to an employee of the entity to determine whether the entity benefits from the transfer. If so, the transfer should be accounted for as share-based compensation to the employee and a capital contribution received from the transferring party. In broadening that requirement, the Board noted its belief that such a transfer is most likely to be made by a major shareholder or another holder of a significant economic interest in an entity.

Should This Statement's Requirements for Related Party and Other Economic Interest Holders Also Apply to Compensation Arrangements That Are outside the Scope of This Statement?

B111. The Board discussed whether the accounting for share-based payment awarded to an employee of the reporting entity by related parties or other holders of an economic interest in the entity also should apply to other forms of compensation arrangements that are outside of the scope of this Statement. The Board believes that, in concept, all forms of compensation paid to an entity's employees by related parties or other holders of economic interests in that entity should result in recognition of compensation cost if the entity effectively receives employee services as a result of such arrangements. However, the Board noted that broadening the scope of this Statement beyond transfers of the entity's share-based payment might require reconsidering other aspects of existing U.S. GAAP applicable to accounting for transactions with related parties. Thus, the Board decided not to expand the scope of this Statement beyond transfers of the entity's share-based payment.

EMPLOYEE SHARE PURCHASE PLANS

B112. Opinion 25 provided that an employee share purchase plan was noncompensatory if it satisfied four criteria: (a) substantially all full-time employees meeting limited employment qualifications might participate, (b) stock was offered to eligible employees equally or based on a uniform percentage of salary or wages, (c) the time permitted for exercise of an option or purchase right was limited to a reasonable period, and (d) the discount from the market price of the stock was no greater than would be reasonable in an offer of stock to shareholders or others. Opinion 25 gave as an example of a noncompensatory plan an employee share purchase plan that qualifies under Section 423 of the U.S. Internal Revenue Code, which may provide a discount of up to 15 percent from the market price of the shares.

B113. Statement 123 included more restrictive criteria than did Opinion 25 for an employee share purchase plan to be considered noncompensatory. Statement 123 provided an exemption only for plans that permitted all eligible employees meeting limited employment qualifications to participate and that (a) included no (or very limited) option features and (b) provided a discount that did not exceed the greater of (1) a discount that would be reasonable in an offering to shareholders or others or (2) the per-share amount of stock issuance costs avoided by not having to raise a significant amount of capital by a public offering. Statement 123 provided a "safe harbor" of 5 percent for applying the second criterion. A discount in excess of 5 percent was permitted only if an entity could justify it.

B114. The Exposure Draft would have established more stringent criteria than those in Statement 123 for an employee share purchase plan to be considered noncompensatory. Under the Exposure Draft, an employee share purchase plan could be considered noncompensatory only if (a) its terms were no more favorable than those available to all holders of the same class of shares and (b) substantially all eligible employees that met limited employment qualifications could participate on an equitable basis.

B115. Many of the respondents to the Exposure Draft who addressed employee share purchase plans said that the proposed criteria for determining whether a plan was noncompensatory were too restrictive. Many of those respondents noted that some entities raise significant amounts of capital through their employee share purchase plans at lower transaction costs than if the shares were issued by other means. Some respondents also said that looking only to whether the terms of a plan are no more favorable than those available to all holders of the same class of shares effectively looked at the issue from the employees' rather than the employer's perspective. They said that basing the criteria for a noncompensatory plan at least in part on the relative amount of proceeds the employer receives from issuance of shares would be more consistent with the employer perspective reflected in other requirements of the standard. The Board agreed and decided to supplement the criteria in the Exposure Draft with the Statement 123 criteria for determining whether an employee share purchase plan is compensatory, which include a focus on whether a per-share discount provided under an employee share purchase plan results in proceeds to the employer that are no less than the proceeds it would have received in a public offering of shares to raise a significant amount of capital.

B116. Many respondents to the Exposure Draft objected to elimination of Statement 123's 5 percent safe harbor for determining whether a plan is noncompensatory, and some even proposed restoring the effective 15 percent safe harbor in Opinion 25. The Board generally does not favor such bright lines or safe harbors, which are not consistent with a principles-based approach to accounting standards and may reduce the representational faithfulness of the financial statements. However, in this situation in which a bright-line criterion already exists, the Board agreed with respondents that maintaining that criterion could reduce implementation costs without necessarily sacrificing a significant degree of representational faithfulness. The Board therefore decided to continue the 5 percent test in Statement 123.

AWARDS CLASSIFIED AS LIABILITIES

Distinguishing between Awards of Liability Instruments and Awards of Equity Instruments

B117. Concepts Statement 6 distinguishes between liabilities and equity on the basis of whether an instrument obligates the issuer to transfer its assets (or

to use its assets in providing services) to the holder. A liability embodies such an obligation, while an equity instrument does not.[151] A call option that an entity writes on its own stock, such as an employee share option, is an equity instrument because its settlement requires only the issuance of stock, which is not the issuer's asset. An entity's obligation under a cash-settled SAR, on the other hand, is a liability because its settlement requires the transfer of assets to the holder.

B118. The Board concluded that the distinction between liabilities and equity instruments in Concepts Statement 6 provides a reasonable way of accounting for tandem awards that offer a choice of settlement in stock or in cash. An entity that grants tandem awards consisting of either a stock option or a cash-settled SAR, for example, is obligated to pay cash upon demand if the choice of settlement is the employee's. The contract gives the entity no discretion to avoid transferring its assets to the employee if the employee elects settlement in cash. The entity thus has incurred a liability. If the choice is the entity's, however, it can avoid transferring assets simply by electing to issue stock, and the award results in the issuance of an equity instrument. However, this Statement requires accounting for the substantive terms of a share-based payment arrangement, as discussed in paragraphs B119–B122, which in some circumstances may override the nominal settlement terms.

Applying Substantive Terms of an Arrangement in Determining Whether a Financial Instrument Qualifies as a Liability or as Equity

B119. Statement 123 (paragraph 39) noted that the substantive terms of a share-based payment arrangement might differ from its written terms and required that the substantive terms be the basis for the accounting. The example provided of substantive terms that might differ from the written terms involved a tandem award in which the choice of whether to settle in cash or equity instruments nominally is the entity's, but the entity generally settles in cash (or settles in cash whenever an employee asks for cash settlement). In that situation, Statement 123 indicated that the entity may have incurred a substantive liability.

B120. This Statement continues that requirement to consider the substantive terms of an arrangement in

---

[151]Under Statement 150, certain freestanding financial instruments that embody an obligation to issue equity instruments rather than to pay cash also are classified as liabilities. The interaction of this Statement with Statement 150 is discussed in paragraphs B130 and B131.

determining whether the arrangement gives rise to a liability or to an equity instrument. However, in certain recent projects, the Board has established criteria for liability recognition that may be more restrictive than the "substantive terms" requirement of Statement 123. For example, FASB Statement No. 143, *Accounting for Asset Retirement Obligations,* requires recognition of *legal obligations* associated with the retirement of a long-lived asset. Paragraph 2 of Statement 143 defines a legal obligation as one ". . . that a party is required to settle as a result of an existing or enacted law, statute, ordinance, or written or oral contract or by legal construction of a contract under the doctrine of promissory estoppel." *Black's Law Dictionary,* eighth edition, defines *promissory estoppel* as "the principle that a promise made without consideration may nonetheless be enforced to prevent injustice if the promisor should have reasonably expected the promisee to rely on the promise and if the promisee did actually rely on the promise to his or her detriment." It is not clear whether the counterparty (an employee, in this situation) to a contract that provides for settlement in either cash or shares at the election of the other party to the contract could use the doctrine of promissory estoppel to enforce cash settlement based on an entity's past practices.

B121. The Board and the EITF have encountered in other projects similar issues of whether a liability exists; some of those issues involve the current model for accounting for employee services, while others do not. For example, EITF Issue No. 00-19, "Accounting for Derivative Financial Instruments Indexed to, and Potentially Settled in, a Company's Own Stock," does not incorporate the same notion of a substantive liability that is included in this Statement. Thus, an instrument for which the entity incurs a substantive liability under this Statement might have been classified as equity had it instead been issued to a third party and thus been subject to Issue 00-19 (and vice versa).[152]

B122. The Board has on its agenda a project on distinguishing between liabilities and equity and accounting for instruments with characteristics of both liabilities and equity. In the course of that project, the Board expects to consider both the conceptual dis-

tinction between liabilities and equity and the appropriate criteria for liability recognition. That is, the Board's current project on liabilities and equity may result in changes to both the definition in Concepts Statement 6 and the criteria for liability recognition in various standards. The Board therefore decided not to consider changes to Statement 123's requirements for recognition of a substantive liability at this time. If progress on the Board's project on liabilities and equity suggests that this Statement's substantive liability provision (or any other aspects of this Statement's liability classification criteria) may be inappropriate, the Board will reconsider it at that time.

Certain Provisions That Do Not by Themselves Result in Liability Classification

B123. Paragraph 35 of this Statement states that a provision for employees to effect a broker-assisted cashless exercise of their options does not result in liability classification for instruments that otherwise would be classified as equity, provided that the exercise is valid and that the employee is the legal owner of the shares subject to the option. A broker that is a related party of the issuer must sell the shares on the open market within a normal settlement period, usually three days, for the provision not to be deemed to result in a liability. This Statement's provisions for broker-assisted cashless exercises are consistent with a related provision of Issue 00-23 concerning the accounting consequences under Opinion 25 of broker-assisted cashless exercises. Because a provision for broker-assisted cashless exercises does not obligate the employer to settle an option in cash or otherwise to transfer cash to the option holder, the Board concluded that such a provision does not result in the options subject to the provision qualifying as liabilities.

B124. Most respondents to the Exposure Draft who addressed the issue agreed with its provisions on broker-assisted cashless exercises, but a few asked that the final Statement explicitly indicate that a cashless exercise of only part of an award also qualifies. The Board agreed that that interpretation is consistent with the intent of the provisions for broker-assisted cashless exercises, and the wording of paragraph 35 has been revised accordingly.

---

[152]For instance, Issue 00-19 specifies that events or actions necessary to deliver registered shares are not controlled by a company and, therefore, except under limited circumstances, such provisions would require a company to assume that the contract would be net-cash settled (and therefore would be classified as either an asset or a liability). Federal securities law generally requires that transactions involving offerings of shares under employee share options be registered, unless there is an available exemption. Thus, employee share options might be classified as substantive liabilities if they were subject to Issue 00-19; however, for purposes of this Statement, the Board does not believe that employee share options should be classified as liabilities based solely on that notion.

B125. Paragraph 35 of this Statement also indicates that a provision for direct or indirect (by means of a net-settlement feature) repurchase of shares issued upon exercise of options (or vesting of shares) to meet the employer's minimum statutory withholding requirements does not, by itself, result in liability classification of instruments that otherwise would be classified as equity. Interpretation 44 also provided that exception for accounting under Opinion 25. In concept, the Board considers a provision for repurchase of shares at, or shortly thereafter, the exercise of options, for whatever reason, to result in the employer's incurrence of a liability. However, the Board decided for pragmatic reasons to continue the exception for direct or indirect repurchases to meet the employer's minimum statutory withholding requirements.

B126. Certain respondents to the Exposure Draft asked that the exception for minimum statutory withholding requirements be extended to encompass amounts in excess of the minimum statutory withholding requirements. As noted in paragraph B125, the Board included the exception for minimum statutory requirements for pragmatic rather than conceptual reasons. The Board therefore declined to extend the exception beyond the minimum statutory requirements to which the related exception in Opinion 25 and Interpretation 44 applied.

Conditions Other Than Market, Performance, or Service Conditions

B127. Paragraph 33 of this Statement requires that an award be classified and accounted for as a liability if it is indexed to a factor in addition to the entity's share price and that additional factor is not a market, performance, or service condition. For example, an award of share options with an exercise price that is indexed to changes in the price of a commodity is required to be classified as a liability. The Board concluded that the terms of such an award do not establish an ownership relationship because the extent to which (or whether) the employee benefits from the award depends on something other than changes in the entity's share price. That conclusion is consistent with the Board's conclusion in Statement 150 that a share-settled obligation is a liability if it does not expose the holder of the instrument to certain risks and rewards, including the risk of changes in the price of the issuing entity's equity shares, that are similar to those to which an owner is exposed.[153]

Classification of certain instruments indexed to an entity's own stock

B128. This Statement's definition of a performance condition provides that a performance measure may be defined by reference to the same performance measure of another entity or group of entities. For example, attaining a growth rate in earnings per share that exceeds the average growth rate in earnings per share of other entities in the same industry is a performance condition for purposes of this Statement. In addition, this Statement indicates that a market condition may relate to the achievement of (a) a specified price of the issuer's shares or a specified amount of intrinsic value indexed solely to the issuer's shares or (b) a specified price of the issuer's shares in terms of a similar (or index of similar) equity security (securities). In contrast, paragraph 5 of EITF Issue No. 01-06, "The Meaning of 'Indexed to a Company's Own Stock,'" states:

> . . . instruments within the scope of this Issue are considered *indexed to a company's own stock* within the meaning of Issue 00-19 and paragraph 11(a) of Statement 133 for the issuer provided that (1) the contingency provisions are not based on (a) an observable market, other than the market for the issuer's stock (if applicable), or (b) an observable index, other than those calculated or measured solely by reference to the issuer's own operations (for example, sales revenue of the issuer, EBITDA [earnings before interest, taxes, depreciation, and amortization] of the issuer, net income of the issuer, or total equity of the issuer), and (2) once the contingent events have occurred, the instrument's settlement amount is based solely on the issuer's stock.

Thus, certain instruments, such as an employee share option with an exercise price indexed to the S&P 500, will be classified differently depending on whether they are issued to employees or to third parties because this Statement effectively establishes a

---

[153]The scope of Statement 150 excludes dual-indexed obligations such as the one described, in which the amount, if any, that the holder of an instrument is entitled to receive upon settlement depends on both changes in the value of the entity's equity shares and changes not predominantly based on something else, in this case, changes in the commodity price. However, the Board concluded that the general principle could be applied in this situation, namely, that for a share-settled obligation to be classified as equity, the terms of an obligation must establish an ownership relationship.

definition of market condition that is specific to compensation arrangements. The Board decided to let that potential inconsistency stand for the present, pending progress on its liability and equity project.

Equity instruments with exercise prices denominated in a foreign currency

B129. The Exposure Draft would (implicitly) have required that all equity instruments with exercise prices denominated in a currency other than the currency of the market in which the underlying equity instrument primarily trades be accounted for as liabilities. Certain respondents to the Exposure Draft requested that this Statement include an exception for certain equity instruments with exercise prices denominated in a currency other than the reporting currency, similar to the exception provided in Issue 00-23. The Board agreed that a narrow exception to the requirements of paragraph 33 of this Statement would be appropriate. Accordingly, this Statement (paragraph 33, footnote 19) provides that an award of equity share options granted to an employee of an entity's foreign operation that provides for a fixed exercise price denominated either in the foreign operation's functional currency or in the currency in which the employee's pay is denominated shall not be considered to contain a condition that is not a market, performance, or service condition. Therefore, such an award is not required to be classified as a liability if it otherwise qualifies as equity. For example, equity share options with an exercise price denominated in Euros granted to employees of a U.S. entity's foreign operation whose functional currency is the Euro are not required to be classified as liabilities if those options otherwise qualify as equity. In addition, such options are not required to be classified as liabilities even if the functional currency of the foreign operation is the U.S. dollar, provided that the employees to whom the options are granted are paid in Euros. In this example, however, options with an exercise price denominated in, for instance, the British pound would be required to be classified as liabilities.

Interaction with Statement 150 in Classifying Awards as Liabilities or as Equity

B130. When Statement 123 was issued in 1995, financial instruments were classified as liabilities in accordance with the conceptual definition of liabilities in Concepts Statement 6, which focused on whether the obligations embodied in them called for settlement by transferring cash or other assets (liabilities) or by issuing equity instruments (equity). Statement 123's basis for conclusions indicated that the Board had on its agenda a project on distinguishing between liabilities and equity and accounting for financial instruments with characteristics of both that might change the distinction between liabilities and equity in Concepts Statement 6. As the first step in that reconsideration, in 2003 the Board issued Statement 150. Statement 150 establishes classification criteria for freestanding financial instruments under which some instruments that do not require the issuer to transfer its cash or other assets (either unconditionally or at the election of the holder) are classified as liabilities rather than as equity. Statement 150 also requires all freestanding instruments that call for settlement by transferring assets, including those issued in the form of mandatorily redeemable shares, to be classified as liabilities.[154] Obligations under share-based payment arrangements accounted for under this Statement are excluded from the scope of Statement 150 until they are no longer subject to this Statement. For example, mandatorily redeemable shares issued upon exercise of an employee share option are subject to Statement 150. Because of the potential overlap of this Statement and Statement 150, the Board considered how best to provide for the interaction between them.

B131. The Board considered amending Statement 150 to eliminate its scope exception for financial instruments accounted for under this Statement and decided not to make that amendment because some of the recognition and measurement requirements of Statement 150 differ from those in this Statement. Nevertheless, the Board believes that,

---

[154]Accounting for mandatorily redeemable shares varied before issuance of Statement 150, but those financial instruments usually were not treated as liabilities for accounting purposes. SEC regulations required public entities to display mandatorily redeemable instruments between total liabilities and equity on the balance sheet, but dividends on those instruments generally were not included with interest expense in determining net income.

in general, the classification of a freestanding financial instrument should be the same regardless of whether the instrument is issued in a share-based payment transaction or in a financing transaction. Therefore, the Board concluded that this Statement should require that an entity apply the criteria in paragraphs 8–14 of Statement 150 as they are effective at the reporting date in classifying freestanding financial instruments granted to employees under share-based payment arrangements. Paragraphs A225–A232 discuss the interaction of this Statement and Statement 150 in subsequent accounting for instruments that qualify as liabilities under those criteria.

Classification of Certain Instruments Issued by Nonpublic Entities

B132. In November 2003, the Board indefinitely deferred (through FSP FAS 150-3, "Effective Date, Disclosures, and Transition for Mandatorily Redeemable Financial Instruments of Certain Nonpublic Entities and Certain Mandatorily Redeemable Noncontrolling Interests under FASB Statement No. 150, *Accounting for Certain Financial Instruments with Characteristics of both Liabilities and Equity*") the effective date of the provisions of Statement 150 pertaining to the classification, measurement, and disclosure provisions for certain mandatorily redeemable financial instruments issued by entities that are not SEC registrants. The indefinite deferral applies to all mandatorily redeemable instruments that are not mandatorily redeemable on fixed dates for amounts that either are fixed or are determined by reference to an interest rate, currency, or other external index. Accordingly, an instrument granted to an employee by an entity that is not an SEC registrant that is redeemable upon the employee's retirement or death at the fair value of the instrument at the date of redemption is not subject to Statement 150 unless and until the Board rescinds that indefinite deferral. Classification of certain such instruments was dealt with in paragraph 40 of Statement 123. Those instruments would continue to be classified as equity as long as the indefinite deferral remains in effect in accordance with FSP FAS 150-3. In addition, for internal consistency, the Board concluded that call options written on instruments that continue to be classified as equity due to that indefinite deferral also should be classified as equity while the deferral is in effect.

Classification of Certain Awards with Repurchase Features

B133. Statement 150 does not apply to outstanding shares embodying a conditional obligation to transfer assets, for example, shares that give the employee the right to require the employer to repurchase them for cash equal to their fair value (puttable shares) awarded under share-based payment arrangements. The Exposure Draft did not provide guidance on puttable (or callable) shares issued in share-based payment arrangements. In addition, the Exposure Draft did not contain explicit provisions for freestanding put (or call) options on mandatorily redeemable shares that are subject to the deferral in FSP FAS 150-3. Under Statement 150, such freestanding options would be classified as liabilities although the underlying shares would continue to be classified as equity while the deferral is in effect. Some respondents to the Exposure Draft asked the Board to provide interim guidance on those two issues for entities to apply until the Board completes its project on liabilities and equity.

B134. The Board agreed that interim guidance on the two issues described in paragraph B133 would be appropriate, and paragraph 31 of this Statement accomplishes that. The interim guidance is based largely on practice under Interpretation 44 and Issue 00-23 because the Board believes that interim guidance, in general, should disrupt practice as little as possible. For that reason, the interim guidance in paragraph 31 about what constitutes *a reasonable period of time* continues the bright-line criterion of six months or more. The Board's reluctance to provide bright-lines has already been discussed (paragraph B116), and this Statement does not provide bright-line criteria in areas in which they do not already exist. However, the Board decided that in this situation in which a bright-line criterion already exists in practice, explicitly providing that entities should continue to use that criterion is preferable to effectively creating confusion on an issue that the Board is considering in another project.

B135. The Board continues to actively consider the distinction between liabilities and equity as part of its liability and equity project, which may eventually change the definitions in Concepts Statement 6. If so, further progress on that project may lead to changes in this Statement's distinction between awards of liability instruments and awards of equity instruments.

Measurement of Awards Classified as Liabilities

Public Entities

B136. This Statement requires public entities to base the measurement of their liabilities under share-based payment arrangements on fair value from incurrence until settlement. In contrast, Statement 123 required that awards of options and equivalent instruments, such as share appreciation rights that require the entity to settle in cash (cash-settled SARs),[155] that qualify as liabilities be measured based on their intrinsic value. Some respondents to the Exposure Draft asked that this Statement continue those provisions of Statement 123.

B137. Statement 123's requirement for intrinsic value measurement of cash-settled SARs and other liabilities continued the requirements of Opinion 25 for those instruments. At that time, the Board noted that whatever the attribute chosen for measuring those instruments initially and in subsequent periods, the final measure of compensation cost would be the amount of cash paid to settle the liability. For a cash-settled SAR, the cash paid would equal the intrinsic value of the instrument at the date it is settled. The main focus of Statement 123 was accounting for employee share options that were equity instruments—not accounting for cash-settled awards about which there had been little controversy. In addition, before Statement 123 was issued and entities began applying it (for either recognition or pro forma disclosures), many entities with share-based payment arrangements had little familiarity with option-pricing models. For those reasons, the Board decided in developing Statement 123 not to require measurement of cash-settled SARs at fair value.

B138. The Board believes that public entities should account for financial instruments issued to employees under share-based compensation arrangements based on their fair value regardless of whether the instruments are classified as liabilities or as equity. As discussed in paragraphs B56–B58, the Board concluded that fair value is the appropriate measurement attribute for equity instruments, such as share options or share appreciation rights that call for physical settlement by issuing shares (share-settled SARs). For the same reasons, fair value also is the appropriate measurement attribute for similar instruments, such as cash-settled SARs, that are liabilities.

B139. Public entities have been using option-pricing models to estimate the fair value of their equity share options since Statement 123 was issued in 1995. In addition, Statement 133 requires derivative instruments that are similar to cash-settled SARs and other liabilities incurred under share-based payment arrangements to be measured at fair value, which was not the case in 1995. The number and variety of both derivative instruments subject to Statement 133 and similar financial instruments granted to employees as share-based compensation have increased greatly. Finally, as indicated by the classification criteria established by Statement 150, the distinction between liabilities and equity continues to evolve, and the Board may make additional changes to that distinction. After taking all those considerations into account, the Board concluded that requiring public entities to account for liabilities incurred to employees under share-based payment arrangements at intrinsic value is no longer necessary or appropriate. Therefore, this Statement requires that public entities measure liabilities incurred under share-based compensation arrangements at fair value.

Nonpublic Entities

B140. The Exposure Draft would have required a nonpublic entity to make a policy decision of whether to account for its liabilities based on fair value or intrinsic value, which was essentially the same choice proposed in the Exposure Draft for equity instruments of a nonpublic entity. The Board decided for the reasons discussed in paragraphs B94–B101 to eliminate the choice of measurement method for equity instruments granted to employees of a nonpublic entity as compensation. However, for pragmatic reasons, the Board retained the choice of measurement method for liability awards of nonpublic entities. Thus, a nonpublic entity must make a policy decision of whether to measure all of its liability awards at fair value (or calculated value if the nonpublic entity qualifies to use that method for its equity instruments) or at intrinsic value until the date of settlement.

B141. In deciding to permit a nonpublic entity to account for its liability awards based on their intrinsic value, the Board noted that the amount of cash (or other assets) required to settle a liability will be the aggregate measure of compensation cost, regardless

---

[155]For convenience, the appropriate measurement attribute for liabilities incurred under share-based payment arrangements with employees is discussed in terms of cash-settled SARs, but the discussion applies equally to other liabilities, such as put options.

of the attribute used to measure those instruments initially and in subsequent periods. Thus, permitting a nonpublic entity to measure its liability awards, including cash-settled SARs and similar instruments, at intrinsic value reduces the cost that a nonpublic entity will have to incur to apply this Statement without misrepresenting the aggregate measure of compensation cost.

B142. The Board considered whether to extend the same choice between fair value and intrinsic value for liabilities to public entities and decided not to do so. The choice between fair value (or calculated value) and intrinsic value permitted a nonpublic entity is provided for the sole purpose of lowering the implementation cost of this Statement for nonpublic entities and is an exception from what the Board considers to be the preferable method. Most nonpublic entities have a limited number of users of their financial statements, and the cost-benefit tradeoff thus may be viewed somewhat differently than for a public entity. A public entity is likely to have both a larger number of investors and creditors who rely on its financial statements and more sophistication in using and estimating the value of derivatives such as options and option-like instruments than the average nonpublic entity does. Moreover, a public entity is required to account for its awards of equity instruments under share-based payment arrangements at fair value and should have no more difficulty estimating the fair value of its liabilities than it does in estimating the fair value of its equity instruments.

B143. The Board considered whether to require all nonpublic entities to measure their liability awards at intrinsic value. However, the Board understands that some nonpublic entities that plan an initial public offering wish to begin preparing their financial statements in accordance with the generally accepted accounting principles applicable to a public entity in reporting periods before the public offering. Moreover, because fair value is the conceptually preferable measurement attribute, the Board concluded that nonpublic entities should be permitted to use it. Accordingly, this Statement provides that a nonpublic entity may choose to account for all of its liability awards based on their fair value.

ATTRIBUTION OF COMPENSATION COST TO ACCOUNTING PERIODS

Attribution Period

B144. Statement 123 retained the provisions of Opinion 25 and Interpretation 28 that share-based compensation cost is to be recognized over the period or periods during which the employee performs the related services—the *requisite service period*.[156] Recognizing share-based compensation over the requisite service period is consistent with the manner in which other forms of compensation are recognized. This Statement continues that general requirement, but it explicitly defines the *requisite service period* and introduces the notion of the *service inception date*. This Statement also defines and provides guidance on *explicit, implicit,* and *derived* service periods.

B145. The Board considered whether the attribution period for employee share options should extend beyond the vesting date, perhaps to the service expiration date (paragraph B40), even though the measurement date is the grant date. Advocates of that method, which might be considered consistent with amortization of postretirement health care benefits over the period to *full eligibility date,* contended that employees have not earned the full benefit to which they are entitled until termination of service no longer shortens the life of the option. They would use the longer attribution period to allocate the time value of an option.

B146. Most respondents who addressed this issue agreed with the Exposure Draft that the attribution period should not extend beyond the vesting date. However, some respondents suggested attribution over the option's expected life, which would be consistent with the method described in paragraph B145. They said that the option serves as an incentive during its entire life and that attribution over the longer period would better match recognized compensation cost with the related benefits to the entity, for example, increased revenues.

B147. Although amortization of the time value of an option beyond the vesting date has some conceptual appeal, the Board concluded that no compelling reason exists to extend the attribution period beyond the

---

[156]An award may have multiple requisite service periods. For convenience, however, the discussion of attribution of compensation cost in this appendix refers only to a single *requisite service period*.

period now used for share options that give rise to compensation cost. The Board notes that the decision on when to exercise a vested option is the employee's. The right to exercise an option has been earned by the date the option becomes vested.

B148. As noted in paragraph B47, equity instruments are issued to employees when the entity has received the consideration for those instruments (usually, the vesting date). It might be argued that the full amount of the compensation cost resulting from an award of equity instruments should be recognized at the vesting date, once the equity instrument has been fully earned and issued to the employee. However, the cost of services received in exchange for other employee benefits with a vesting period, such as pensions and other postemployment benefits, generally is recognized in the periods in which the services are received even if the benefits are not yet vested. Although those employee benefit plans generally result in the incurrence of liabilities rather than the issuance of equity instruments, the Board decided that the form of eventual settlement should not change the general principle that the costs of employee services are recognized over the periods in which employees are required to render service to earn the right to the benefit.

Service Inception Date

B149. This Statement defines the service inception date as the date at which the requisite service period begins. The service inception date usually is the grant date. The service inception date precedes the grant date, however, if service that will count toward vesting begins before a mutual understanding of the key terms and conditions of a share-based payment award is reached *and* either of two conditions applies. Those conditions are (a) the award's terms do not include a substantive future requisite service condition that becomes effective at the grant date *or* (b) the award contains a market or performance condition that if not satisfied during the service period preceding the grant date and following the inception of the arrangement results in forfeiture of the award. Paragraphs A79–A85 further explain and illustrate application of the notion of a service inception date that precedes the grant date.

B150. The Board concluded that adding the notion of a service inception date that precedes the grant date would result in attribution of compensation cost in a manner that is more consistent with application of the current procedures for accounting for the consideration paid for employee services. The objective of that model is to attribute the cost of employee services to the periods in which employees render service in exchange for the consideration paid for those services. It is clear that in some situations, employee service that will count toward, and is necessary for, vesting will begin before the conditions for a grant date are present. In those situations, the Board concluded that the requisite service properly includes the period between the service inception date and the grant date.

B151. This Statement requires that compensation cost for each period between the service inception date and the grant date for an equity award be measured based on the share price and other pertinent factors in effect at each reporting date until the grant date occurs, at which time the estimate of the award's fair value, and thus the related compensation cost, is fixed. Because the grant date is, by definition, the date at which a mutual understanding of the key terms and conditions of an award is reached and because employees do not receive an equity interest before the grant date, it would be inappropriate to measure compensation cost based solely on the share price and other factors before that date. Accordingly, a cumulative adjustment is recognized in each period between the service inception date and the grant date for the portion of changes in fair value, if any, since the preceding reporting date. Because the measurement date for an equity award is the grant date, interim measures of compensation cost made in reporting periods before the grant date must be subsequently adjusted until the grant date occurs. The Board concluded that retrospective restatement for those differences was not necessary or appropriate, since compensation cost for each period was measured based on the share price and other pertinent factors that existed at the end of each period. Accordingly, the Board concluded that recognizing any needed cumulative adjustment in the period in which it arises would be the best available alternative.

Implicit and Derived Service Periods

B152. This Statement introduces the notions of implicit and derived service periods because an award of share-based employee compensation may not explicitly state a requisite service period or any stated service period may not, in substance, be the period over which employees must render service to benefit from an award.

B153. For instance, an award of share options might not state a service period but rather might provide that the award vests upon the completion of a new product design. That award has an implicit service period of 18 months if the design is expected to be completed in 18 months from the date of grant. Another award might state that it is fully vested at the grant date, but the award is deep out-of-the-money at that date. If, as is usually the case,[157] employees have only a limited period of time after termination of service to exercise a vested option, employees awarded such fully vested, deep out-of-the-money share options must provide service for some period of time in exchange for their awards. In other words, the employees' right to benefit from such an award substantively is contingent on satisfaction of a service condition although none is stated in the award. Thus, at the grant date, the award does not satisfy this Statement's definition of a vested award. Accordingly, the requisite service period must be derived from a valuation technique.

B154. Derived service periods are pertinent only for awards with market conditions. This Statement does not state a preference for a particular model, including a lattice model, for use in estimating the fair value of an equity share option, and it may be possible to estimate the fair value of certain options with market conditions using a closed-form model. However, the Board understands that it may be necessary to use another valuation technique to determine a derived service period.

Guidance on derived service periods

B155. The Exposure Draft would have required that a derived service period be determined based on the duration of the most frequent path (that is, the mode) of a path-dependent option-pricing model on which the market condition is satisfied. Certain respondents suggested use of either the weighted-average (the mean) or the median (the middle share price path—the midpoint of the distribution of paths—on which the market condition is satisfied).

B156. In reconsidering the guidance to be provided on determining a derived service period, the Board concluded that the median duration of the paths on which the condition is satisfied would provide a better measure of the period over which employees must render service to earn their options (the requisite service period). Because the median is less affected by extreme values than either the mode or the mean, the Board concluded that the median provides a more representationally faithful estimate of the requisite service period.[158]

Accounting for Changes in the Requisite Service Period

B157. This Statement (paragraph 46) provides guidance on when an entity should change its initial estimate of the requisite service period. For example, an award's terms might specify vesting at the date regulatory approval to market a new product is obtained. If the entity estimates at the grant date that regulatory approval will be obtained in two years, the initial estimate of the requisite service period is two years. If it becomes apparent after one year that it is probable that obtaining regulatory approval will instead take three years, the initial estimate of the requisite service period is changed to three years, of which two remain. The effect of that change will be reflected only prospectively, through a longer attribution period than initially estimated. The Board concluded that such a change in estimate is similar to a change in the estimated useful life of, for example, a piece of equipment that is reflected prospectively rather than by means of a cumulative adjustment in the year of the change.

Accounting for a Change in the Probable Outcome of an Award with Multiple Performance Conditions

B158. An award may contain multiple performance conditions, the outcome of each of which affects, for instance, the exercise price of share options granted or another factor that affects the fair value of the award. For example, an award of equity share options may specify that an employee will be entitled to 1,000 options with (a) an exercise price of $50 if the market share for a particular product has increased by 10 percent at the end of 2 years or (b) an exercise price of $40 if market share has increased by 20 percent at the end of 2 years. This Statement (paragraph 49) requires that the fair value of the award be estimated at the grant date under each potential outcome. The final measure of compensation cost will be based on the amount estimated at the

---

[157]Refer to paragraph A60, footnote 71, for a discussion of the assumption underlying many of the illustrations in this Statement. That is, if the employment relationship is terminated, the award lapses or is forfeited shortly thereafter.

[158]In a normal distribution, the mean, median, and mode are the same. However, if the distribution is skewed, those values may differ significantly.

grant date for the condition or outcome that is actually achieved. If it is deemed probable that the market share will increase by at least 10 percent but not more than 20 percent, accrual of compensation cost will be based on the fair value of the award according to the projected outcome of a 10 percent increase.[159] If the entity changes its estimate of the probable outcome at the end of the first year to a market share increase of 20 percent, a cumulative adjustment must be recognized to reflect the difference between the amount of compensation cost that has been accrued at that date and the amount that would have been accrued if a 20 percent increase in market share had been the original estimate of the probable outcome. Unlike the award in paragraph B157, this award has a different grant-date fair value that is to be recognized as compensation cost as a result of the change in estimate. The Board concluded that a cumulative adjustment is appropriate because it believes that the total amount of compensation cost recognized at the end of each period should be based on the information that is available at that date. That is the same rationale discussed in paragraphs B167 and B168 for the required cumulative adjustment if the estimated number of forfeitures changes during the requisite service period.

Certain Questions about the Effect of Subsequent Share Price Changes on Recognition of Compensation Cost

Why Is Compensation Cost Recognized for Vested Employee Share Options That Expire Worthless?

B159. Some respondents to the Exposure Draft or the Invitation to Comment and others questioned why compensation cost should be recognized for an award of share options that vests but that is not exercised and subsequently expires worthless. The premise of grant-date (and modified grant-date) accounting is that on the grant date (a) the employer and the employee come to a mutual understanding of the terms of a share-based payment arrangement, (b) the employer becomes contingently obligated to issue equity instruments to the employee in exchange for services to be rendered over the requisite service period, and (c) the employee begins to benefit from, or be adversely affected by, subsequent changes in

the price of the employer's shares. Equity instruments and the consideration the issuing entity receives in exchange for them are recognized based on their fair values at the date the instruments are issued. For equity instruments awarded to employees, this Statement requires that the estimate of fair value be based on the share price (and other pertinent factors) at the grant date.[160] That fair value estimate is not subsequently adjusted for either increases or decreases in the share price because the employee—not the employer—bears the risk of (and benefits from) share price changes after the grant date.

B160. Once an employee has rendered the requisite service and earned the right to a share option (or other equity instrument), the employer has already benefited from the services received. No change in compensation cost is recognized after vesting (unless the award is subsequently modified) because the exchange transaction is complete at that date—the employee has already rendered the requisite service and the employer has already issued equity instruments. To reverse compensation cost for an award that subsequently expires worthless would disregard the fact that the employer has received services in exchange for the instruments issued to the employee. The accounting for employee share options required by this Statement is substantively the same as the accounting for a share purchase warrant issued to a third party in exchange for cash or other assets. If the warrant expires worthless, the issuing entity retains the premium received (whether cash or services) and paid-in capital has increased by the amount of the premium, even though no shares ultimately were issued.

Why Is Compensation Cost Recognized for Share Options That Become Deep Out-of-the-Money before the Requisite Service Has Been Rendered?

B161. During the Board's redeliberation of the Exposure Draft, a question was raised about the recognition of compensation cost for certain employee share options and similar instruments that become deep out-of-the-money before an employee has earned the right to them, that is, before the employee has rendered all of the requisite service. The question is whether the exchange transaction entered into at

---

[159]Paragraph 44 requires that if an award has multiple performance conditions (for instance, each of which affects the number of options that will vest), compensation cost shall be accrued if it is probable that a performance condition will be satisfied.

[160]Refer to paragraph A2 for discussion of the fair value measurement objective under the modified grant-date method required by this Statement. This Statement provides an exception to grant-date fair value measurement for equity instruments for which it is not possible to reasonably estimate fair value. That exception is based on pragmatic rather than conceptual considerations.

the grant date may sometimes be effectively cancelled or nullified because the options granted have become so deep out-of-the-money that the employee has only a remote possibility of eventually being able to realize a profit by exercising them.

B162. To illustrate this view, consider an award of share options for which the market price of the underlying shares has decreased so significantly by the time 2 years of a 4-year requisite service period have passed that the share price would exceed the exercise price before the options expire on only, say, 30 of 1,000 possible paths in a lattice model used to estimate the fair value of the options. In that situation, some constituents contend that the options no longer are an effective part of the employee's compensation, and the options thus should be treated as if they were cancelled, with no further expense recognized. Those who hold this view consider it to be consistent with the requirement to estimate a derived service period for an option that is deep out-ofthe-money and fully vested at the grant date. (Refer to the definition of *derived service period* in Appendix E.)

B163. The Board disagreed with the view described in paragraphs B161 and B162. The employer and an employee are deemed to enter into an agreement at the grant date under which the employer becomes contingently obligated to issue options (or other equity instruments) when the employee has rendered the requisite service to earn the right to benefit from the instruments. Under the modified grant date method, the value of the services to be exchanged for equity instruments, and the related compensation cost, is measured based on the share price and other pertinent factors at the grant date. The employee rather than the employer bears the risk of (and benefits from) share price changes that occur after the grant date. Regardless of the extent of decreases (or increases) in the share price during the requisite service period, the employee is rendering service during that period to earn the *right* to benefit from the options, unless an action is taken to modify or cancel the contract. An employee who vests in an option that at the vesting date has only a small chance of being in-the-money before the end of its contractual term nevertheless has earned the *right* to benefit from that chance. In addition, the view described in paragraphs B161 and B162, like the view discussed in paragraphs B159 and B160, looks at the transaction from the employee's, rather than the employer's, perspective. The employer receives employee services throughout the requisite service period; under grant-date accounting, those services are measured based

on the share price at the grant date. Moreover, even if significant share price decreases during the requisite service period were deemed to effectively cancel an option, the accounting under this Statement would result in recognition of the remaining unrecognized compensation cost at the date of the cancellation.

B164. In contrast, the requirement to determine a derived service period for a deep out-of-the money, nontransferable option that by its stated terms is fully vested at the grant date merely recognizes that the employee must render service after the grant date to benefit from the option (refer to paragraph B153 and footnote 157 for discussion of the assumption about the limited period of time provided for exercise of a vested option after termination of service). In other words, the option is subject to a requisite service period even though it is nominally vested at the grant date. That requirement affects only the period over which compensation cost is recognized. The derived service period is determined at the grant date, and the amount of compensation cost to be recognized for an option that vests is not subsequently changed unless the option is modified to increase compensation cost.

Accounting during the Requisite Service Period for Awards Not Expected to Vest

B165. This Statement requires an entity to base accruals of compensation cost during the requisite service period on the estimated number of instruments for which the requisite service is expected to be rendered. That estimate is subsequently revised if it becomes evident that the actual number of instruments for which the requisite service is expected to be rendered is likely to differ from initial estimates. Statement 123 permitted entities either to use that method or to begin accruing compensation cost as if all instruments subject only to a service requirement were expected to vest and to recognize actual forfeitures as they occur.

B166. In deciding to eliminate the alternative that permitted recognition of the effects of forfeitures as they occur, the Board considered other areas of accounting in which similar estimates are made at initial recognition and subsequently adjusted if necessary, for example, recognition of coupon redemptions and promotional allowances in the retail industry. The Board sees no reason why estimating the number of instruments for which the requisite service is expected to be rendered will be more difficult than making similar estimates in those situations. Entities that have share-based payment arrangements with employees have had to keep track of the number of instruments granted and subsequently forfeited for purposes of either the recognition or the pro forma disclosure requirements of Statement 123. Until sufficient entity-specific information is available, start-up entities may base forfeiture estimates on the experience of other entities in the same industry.

Recognizing the Effect of a Change in the Number of Instruments for Which the Requisite Service Is Expected to Be Rendered

B167. This Statement (paragraph 43) requires an entity to revise its initial estimate of the number of instruments for which the requisite service is expected to be rendered if subsequent information indicates that the actual number of instruments for which the requisite service will be rendered is likely to differ from initial estimates. A cumulative adjustment to compensation cost for the effect on current and prior periods of a change in the estimated number of instruments for which the requisite service will be rendered is required to be recognized in the period of the change.

B168. The Board concluded that a cumulative effect adjustment for a change in the number of instruments for which the requisite service is expected to be rendered is appropriate because it believes that the total amount of compensation cost that has been recognized at the end of each period should be based on the information that is available at that date. Under Opinion 20, the effect of a change in an estimate is not recognized by retrospective restatement because the result of doing so would be to reflect in prior periods' financial statements the effects of information that was not available in those periods. The Board concluded that it would be equally inappropriate to recognize the effect of a change in the estimated number of instruments for which the requisite service will be rendered only prospectively because the result would be to not reflect in financial statements of the current and future periods the full effect of the information available in those periods. Accordingly, the Board concluded that recognizing a cumulative adjustment in the current period was the best available alternative.

Awards with Graded Vesting

B169. Statement 123 provided for two methods of accruing the compensation cost related to awards with graded vesting provisions, although the methods were not described as alternatives for the same set of

facts and circumstances. If the fair value of an award was determined based on different expected lives for the options that vest each year, compensation cost was required to be recognized separately over the life of each separately vesting portion. That was the method required for accounting under Opinion 25 by FASB Interpretation No. 28, *Accounting for Stock Appreciation Rights and Other Variable Stock Option or Award Plans.* That method considers an award with a graded vesting schedule to be in substance separate awards, each with a different vesting date. If the expected life of an award was determined in another manner, Statement 123 permitted the related compensation cost to be recognized on a straight-line basis over the total requisite service period for the entire award (that is, over the requisite service period of the last separately vesting portion of the award), provided that the amount of compensation cost recognized at any date at least equaled the fair value of the vested portion of the award at that date.

B170. The Exposure Draft would have required entities to use the first method described in paragraph B169. In other words, the Exposure Draft would have required an award with graded vesting to be accounted for as separate awards with different requisite service periods. In proposing to require that method, the Board noted that the length of the vesting period of an award is one important factor that influences the expected term of an option because employees cannot exercise nonvested options. In addition, as discussed in paragraph A30, estimates of employees' early exercise and post-vesting employment termination behavior, and thus the related estimates of fair value, are improved if employees are aggregated into groups with relatively homogenous behavior. The length of the vesting period is a significant determinant of that behavior.

B171. Many respondents to the Exposure Draft objected to its proposed method of recognizing compensation cost for awards with graded vesting schedules. Those respondents generally said that both they and employees consider an award with graded vesting to be a single award—not multiple awards. Some also said that the "front-loaded" recognition of compensation cost that results from considering an award with graded vesting to be multiple awards implies that the related employee services become less valuable as time passes, which is not the case. Many of those respondents also said that accounting for an award with graded vesting as effectively separate awards as proposed in the Exposure Draft would be unduly burdensome, especially for entities that grant awards that vest daily or monthly. They said that separately tracking each tranche of such an award for purposes of truing-up the associated tax benefit would be complicated and would require a redesign of their information systems. Certain respondents noted that a lattice model can be designed to take into account a graded vesting schedule. They said that the resulting estimated fair value for the entire award likely would not differ significantly from the weighted average of separately estimated values for each tranche.

B172. In reconsidering the proposed accounting for awards with graded vesting, the Board acknowledged that accounting for them as in substance multiple awards, each with its own requisite service period, is more complicated than accounting for them as a single award. The Board generally agreed with respondents that requiring the multiple-award method for all awards with graded vesting would be an unnecessary refinement. Accordingly, the Board decided to continue to provide a choice of attribution provisions for awards with graded-vesting schedules based only on service conditions. However, the Board eliminated the requirement in Statement 123 that compensation cost for an award with graded vesting be attributed to separate requisite service periods for each tranche if the fair values of each tranche are separately estimated based on the expected term of each tranche. One respondent noted that a lattice model with separate expected terms for each tranche could be used to estimate the fair value of an award with graded vesting, with a weighted-average expected term for the entire award estimated based on the results of the valuation. The Board agreed that an entity that uses such a method should not be precluded from using the straight-line method to attribute the compensation cost for the entire award, and this Statement thus does not link the choice of attribution method to the valuation method used.

Market Conditions, Performance Conditions, and Service Conditions

B173. In discussing the treatment of various conditions that can affect the vesting, exercisability, or exercise price of an award, paragraph 26 of Statement 123 provided that:

No compensation cost is recognized for awards that employees forfeit either because they fail to satisfy a service requirement for vesting, such as for a **fixed award,** or because the entity does not achieve a **performance condition,** unless the condition is a target stock price or specified amount of intrinsic value on which vesting or exercisability is conditioned. For awards with the latter condition, compensation cost shall be recognized for awards to employees who remain in service for the requisite period regardless of whether the target stock price or amount of intrinsic value is reached. [Footnote reference omitted.]

A fixed award was defined as one for which vesting is based solely on an employee's continuing to render service to the employer for a specified period of time. A performance award was defined as one for which vesting depends on both (a) an employee's rendering service for a specified period of time and (b) the entity's achievement of a specified performance target, such as attaining a specified growth rate for return on assets or a specified increase in market share for a specified product.

B174. The Board concluded that Statement 123's definitions might not clearly classify some conditions that affect vesting, exercisability, exercise price, or other pertinent factors used in determining the fair value of an award included in instruments awarded under share-based payment arrangements. Thus, this Statement revises the definitions of those conditions to more clearly distinguish between them, although the accounting effects of the revised conditions are not significantly different from the effects of those conditions in Statement 123. The most significant clarification is to separately define *market condition,* which Statement 123 included as one type of performance condition. This Statement defines market condition as a condition affecting the exercise price, exercisability, or other pertinent factors used in determining the fair value of an award that relates to the achievement of (a) a specified price of the issuer's shares or a specified amount of intrinsic value indexed solely to the issuer's shares or (b) a specified price of the issuer's shares in terms of a similar (or index of similar) equity security (securities).

B175. This Statement continues Statement 123's different accounting for market conditions and performance conditions.[161] That is, no compensation cost is recognized for awards that do not vest because a performance condition is not achieved, even though employees remain in service for the requisite service period. However, compensation cost is recognized for awards to employees who remain in service for the requisite service period regardless of whether (or when) a market condition is satisfied. Some respondents to the Exposure Draft objected to that provision, suggesting that performance and market conditions should be treated the same. Those respondents generally favored recognizing no cost for either if the condition is not satisfied.

B176. The Board decided to maintain the distinction between performance and market conditions, in part due to concerns about the measurability at the grant date of the expected outcomes associated with performance conditions. That is, the Board concluded that it would not be feasible to eliminate the distinction by reflecting the effects of both performance conditions and market conditions in an award's grant-date fair value and recognizing compensation for both if the requisite service is rendered. Although it would be possible, in theory, to estimate the grant-date fair value of an award with a performance condition, to do so would involve developing a probability distribution reflecting the likelihood that the entity will, for example, achieve a specified percentage increase in return on assets in a specified period of time. An entity might have little, if any, data on which to base such a probability distribution, and it would be unlikely to be able to obtain adequate pertinent information about similar awards made by similar entities. Also, the IASB proposed in ED2 a requirement to take into account the effects of performance conditions in estimating an award's fair value at the grant date. Respondents to ED2, as well as to the FASB's Invitation to Comment, generally objected to that proposal on the grounds that it would not be feasible to develop sufficiently reliable estimates of the probability of achieving performance conditions. The Board also was concerned about the potential inconsistency if the effects of performance conditions were taken into account in measuring fair value at the grant date unless the effects of service conditions were treated similarly.

B177. The Board also considered eliminating the different accounting for performance and market conditions by requiring recognition of no compensation cost if either type of condition is not satisfied, regardless of whether the requisite service has been rendered. However, based on discussions with members of the Options Valuation Group, the Board understands that the fair value of a share option with a market condition can be estimated at the grant date using valuation techniques developed for similar options that trade in external markets. The Board concluded that it would be inappropriate and illogical not to take advantage of relatively well-developed valuation techniques for those traded options in accounting for awards with market conditions. Therefore, this Statement continues to require recognition of compensation cost for awards with market conditions based on the fair value at the grant date, provided that the requisite service is rendered.

B178. The Board also notes that performance and market conditions are conceptually distinct. Including a performance condition in an award of share-based compensation requires an employee to contribute to achieving an increase in a specified measure of the entity's performance regardless of the extent to which that increase is reflected in the entity's share price. For example, a performance condition may require an increase of 15 percent in market share over a 2-year period. But the entity's share price may not increase accordingly, and may even decrease, even though that condition is achieved.

B179. Market conditions, on the other hand, pertain to the interaction between an entity's individual performance as reflected in its share price and changes in the environment in which it operates. For example, an award of share options with a market condition might have an exercise price that changes in accordance with (that is, is indexed to) changes in the relationship between the entity's share price and an index of the share prices of other entities in the same industry. Changes in measures of the entity's individual performance, such as achieving or not achieving a 15 percent increase in market share, will affect that award only to the extent that the increase is reflected in changes in the entity's share price relative to those of its competitors.

B180. Eliminating the distinction between performance conditions and market conditions would result

---

[161]References throughout the remainder of this appendix to conditions affecting the vesting, exercisability, exercise price, or other pertinent factors used in determining the fair value of an award use the terminology and related definitions as they appear in this Statement rather than as they appeared in Statement 123.

in only one class of performance-related conditions. That is, a *performance condition* would be defined to include both a performance condition and a market condition as defined in this Statement. In view of both the conceptual differences and the differences in measurability of those conditions, the Board concluded that providing different accounting for them continues to be appropriate.

MODIFICATIONS OF THE TERMS OR CONDITIONS OF EQUITY AWARDS

The Nature of a Modification of Terms or Conditions

B181. Statement 123 required that an entity recognize additional compensation cost if it modified the terms of an award to increase the award's value. Statement 123's basis for conclusions (paragraph 187) explained that a modification of terms is indistinguishable from an exchange of the existing equity instrument for a new instrument. That discussion continued in paragraph 188:

> The repurchase of an equity instrument generally is accounted for based on the fair values of the instrument repurchased and the consideration paid for it. For example, if an entity repurchases shares of common stock at an amount significantly in excess of the current market price of the shares, the excess is presumed to be attributable to stated or unstated rights the issuer receives in addition to the shares surrendered, such as an agreement that the stockholder will not purchase additional shares.

B182. In reconsidering the accounting for a modification of the terms of an award of employee share-based compensation, the Board reaffirmed the conclusion that such transactions generally are transfers of value from the entity to its employees that give rise to additional compensation cost. A modification of the terms of an equity instrument granted to employees as compensation is inherently a transaction between the entity and its employees in their role as employees—not in their role as holders of equity instruments. For instance, a common type of modification is the lowering of the exercise price of an option—a repricing—after a significant decrease in the price of the underlying share. Entities sometimes explain repricings as necessary to restore the incentive value of the options following a share price de-

crease. Entities provide that benefit to employees (and perhaps certain nonemployee service providers) if the original terms of an option are no longer deemed to provide adequate compensation.

Measuring the Effects of a Modification

B183. Statement 123 required that the effects of a modification be measured as the difference between the fair value of the modified award at the date it is granted and the award's value immediately before the modification determined based on the shorter of (a) its remaining initially estimated expected life or (b) the expected life of the modified award. That method precluded the counterintuitive result that certain modifications favorable to employees could result in reduced compensation cost. However, that advantage was gained by requiring a difficult-to-explain measurement procedure for the original award—a procedure whose result could not be described as consistent with the fair-value-based method.

B184. This Statement revises Statement 123 to require that the effects of a modification be measured by comparing the fair values (or calculated values for a nonpublic entity that qualifies to use that method) of the modified and original awards at the date of the modification, which is more consistent with the fair-value-based method of accounting for share-based payment arrangements. However, as noted in Statement 123's basis for conclusions, an employee generally will accept a modification only if its effect is to increase the value of the instrument the employee holds. For that reason, the Exposure Draft indicated that total recognized compensation cost for an award *rarely will be less* than the fair value of the award at the grant date unless at the date of the modification the performance or service conditions of the original award are not expected to be satisfied. Some respondents asked the Board to provide guidance on the circumstances, if any, in which a modification, by itself, would appropriately result in recognized compensation cost for the modified award that is less than the grant-date fair value of the original award. The Board decided that it was not feasible to provide criteria for identifying such an unusual—perhaps nonexistent—transaction. However, the Board agreed that the provision should be clarified. Therefore, this Statement indicates that total recognized compensation cost for an equity award shall at least equal the fair value of the award at the grant date unless at the date of the modification the performance or service conditions of the original award are not expected to be satisfied.

Additional Guidance on Accounting for a Modification

B185. This Statement provides more guidance than did Statement 123 on accounting for a modification of the terms or conditions of an award. Appendix A explains and illustrates that guidance. The reasons for the Board's conclusions on the more significant aspects of the additional guidance are discussed in paragraphs B186–B200.

Modifications of Service and Performance Vesting Conditions

B186. This Statement provides guidance on accounting for a modification of the vesting conditions of an award—Statement 123 did not provide explicit guidance on such modifications. The effect of a change in vesting conditions is measured in the same way as other modifications—by comparing the fair values of the award immediately before and after the modification. However, the amount of compensation cost recognized must at least equal the fair value of the original award at the grant date unless at the date of the modification it is not probable that the original vesting conditions will be satisfied. The combination of that requirement with the application of the modified grant-date method to performance conditions calls for additional discussion.

B187. Under the modified grant-date method, the effects of service and performance conditions are not reflected in the estimated fair value of the award at the grant date. Rather, grant-date fair value is estimated as if each condition was satisfied, and the effect of those conditions is reflected by recognizing compensation cost only for the awards that actually vest. Accrual of compensation cost during the requisite service period is based on the entity's expectation of the awards that will vest. Although the probability that a performance condition will be achieved can vary between zero and one, ultimately a performance condition either is or is not achieved, which means that compensation cost for an award with a performance condition is or is not accrued during the requi-

site service period.[162] If an award has multiple performance conditions (for example, if the number of options or shares an employee earns varies depending on which, if any, of two or more performance conditions is satisfied), compensation cost should be accrued if it is probable that a performance condition will be satisified. In making that assessment, it may be necessary to take into account the interrelationship of those performance conditions.

B188. In reconsidering the provisions of Statement 123, the Board divided modifications of performance- and service-vesting conditions into four categories:

a. **Type I: Probable-to-Probable.** A service or performance condition is changed in a way that does not affect the estimate of whether the award will vest. An example is a change from an original performance condition, which required a 20 percent increase in market share of Product A, to a modified requirement for a 22 percent increase in market share (or vice versa), when both conditions are expected to be satisfied.

b. **Type II: Probable-to-Improbable.** A service or performance condition is changed in a way that affects the estimate of whether the award will vest by substituting a condition that is not expected to be satisfied for one that was expected to be satisfied. An example is a change from an original performance condition that required a 20 percent increase in market share of Product A and was expected to be achieved to a requirement for a 25 percent increase in market share that is not expected to be achieved.

c. **Type III: Improbable-to-Probable.** A service or performance condition is changed in a way that affects the estimate of whether the award will vest by substituting a condition that is expected to be achieved for one that was not expected to be achieved. An example is a change from a performance condition that required a 20 percent increase in market share of Product A and was not expected to be achieved to a requirement for a 15 percent increase in market share that is expected to be achieved.

d. **Type IV: Improbable-to-Improbable.** A service or performance condition is changed in a way that does not affect the estimate of whether the award will vest by substituting one condition that is not expected to be achieved for another that also is not

---

[162]For simplicity, expected employee terminations before a performance condition is achieved are disregarded in the discussion. That is, even if a performance condition is achieved, some employees likely will have terminated service before the end of the requisite service period.

expected to be achieved. An example is a change from a performance condition that required a 25 percent increase in market share of Product A and was not expected to be achieved to a requirement for a 20 percent increase in market share that also is not expected to be achieved.

B189. Application of the required modification accounting to Types I and IV is relatively straightforward. No additional compensation cost would be recognized at the date of either a Type I or a Type IV modification because the modification changes neither the expectation of whether the vesting condition will be satisfied nor the fair value of the award (unless other terms also are changed). Employees are unlikely to accept Type II modifications (unless perhaps accompanied by changes in other terms or another form of consideration).[163]

Type III Modifications

B190. A Type III modification of a service or performance condition can result in recognition of compensation cost that is less than the estimated fair value of the award at the grant date if expectations about the probability of vesting are accurate. The following example illustrates that situation:

> On February 1, 20X5, an entity grants its vice president for marketing 5,000 at-the-money options with a provision that the awards will vest only if the market share of Product A increases 20 percent by January 31, 20X6. On September 1, 20X5, market share has increased only 12 percent, and the 20 percent goal is not expected to be achieved. On that date, the entity modifies the performance condition to require only a 15 percent increase in market share, which is expected to be achieved. The fair value of each option is $50 at the grant date and $30 on the date of the modification.

B191. The Board concluded that a Type III modification should be accounted for in the same way as other modifications. Thus, on the date of the modification, the fair value of the original award, which is $0 ($30 × zero options expected to vest under the original target) in the example, is subtracted from fair value of the modified award, or $150,000 ($30 × 5,000 options expected to vest under the modified target). If the modified target in the example

is ultimately satisfied, the total recognized compensation cost ($150,000) will be less than the fair value of the award at the grant date ($250,000) because at the date of the modification, the original vesting conditions were not expected to be satisfied. The Board considers that accounting for a Type III modification to be consistent with both the modified grant-date method and the requirements for accounting for a modification of the terms or conditions of an award. The Board also notes that its conclusions on Type III modifications would result in recognizing compensation cost that exceeds the fair value of the award at the grant date if the fair value of the award at the modification exceeds that amount. However, that situation may be less common than the one illustrated because failure to satisfy an original performance condition may be correlated with decreases in the price of the underlying share.

B192. Some respondents to the Exposure Draft favored adopting the requirements of IFRS 2 for Type III modifications. Under IFRS 2, the modification in the preceding example would be accounted for as a change only in the number of options expected to vest (from zero to 5,000), and the full grant-date fair value of the award ($250,000) would be recognized over the remainder of the service period. That result is the same as if the modified performance condition had been in effect at the grant date. If the fair value of the award at the modification date exceeds its fair value at the grant date, however, IFRS 2 would require recognition of the higher amount as compensation cost.

B193. The respondents who favored IFRS 2's accounting for Type III modifications generally were concerned about the necessary judgment about the probability of meeting the original performance condition required at the date of the modification to apply the method proposed in the Exposure Draft. In deciding to retain that method, the Board noted that judging whether it is probable that a performance condition will be satisfied is fundamental to applying the modified grant-date method. The Board also notes that the principles of accounting for a modification of an equity award in paragraph 51 of this Statement require that the amount of compensation cost recognized after a modification of the terms or conditions of an award at least equal the fair value of the award at the grant date, *unless at the date of the modification the performance or service conditions*

---

[163]Illustration 13 (paragraphs A160–A170) provides examples of Type I, II, III, and IV modifications and describes how the accounting for those modifications is consistent with the principles established in paragraph 51 of this Statement.

of the original award are not expected to be satisfied. The emphasized phrase is significant for Type III modifications of equity instruments. In a modification that makes it probable that a vesting condition will be achieved, the original vesting conditions ordinarily will not be expected to be achieved, and the grant-date fair value of the award thus is not a floor on the amount of compensation cost recognized.

A Modification That Changes the Classification of an Award from Equity to Liability

B194. The Board's conclusions on a modification of the terms of an award that changes its classification from an equity instrument to a liability are consistent with its conclusions on accounting for other modifications of awards of equity instruments. In particular, the minimum amount of compensation cost to be recognized is the fair value of the instrument at the date it was granted, unless at the modification date the original vesting conditions are not expected to be satisfied. To illustrate, if an entity modifies a vested award of share options to add a feature under which the employee may elect cash settlement of the intrinsic value of the options at the exercise date, a financial instrument that formerly was classified as equity instead will be classified as a liability because the entity is obligated to pay cash if the employee elects cash settlement. If the fair value of the award is $500,000 at the grant date and $400,000 at the modification date, no decrement to compensation cost is recognized at the modification date because the previously recognized grant-date fair value of the award is the minimum compensation cost. Rather, the fair value of the liability at the modification date is reclassified from paid-in capital to the liability resulting from the modification. If the liability subsequently is settled for $400,000 (or any amount less than $500,000), no increase in net income is recognized because compensation cost must at least equal the grant-date fair value of the original equity award. That grant date-fair value "floor" still applies because the award was an equity award at the date it was granted. The Board considered whether changes in the fair value of the liability subsequent to the modification date when the fair value of the liability is less than the grant-date fair value of the equity award should be recognized in other comprehensive income

rather than in paid-in capital. The Board decided that that issue would be better addressed in a broader project on other comprehensive income.[164] In reaching that decision, the Board noted that FASB Statement No. 130, *Reporting Comprehensive Income,* describes several potential items of other comprehensive income that could be addressed as part of a broader project in the future.

A Modification That Changes the Classification of an Award from Liability to Equity

B195. The Exposure Draft proposed that the principle that total compensation cost for a modified award must at least equal the grant-date fair value of the original award also would apply to a modification that changes the classification of an award from liability to equity. For example, if a vested award of cash-settled SARs was modified to replace required cash settlement with net share settlement, an instrument that qualified as a liability before the modification is effectively converted to an equity instrument. If the value of the liability was $500,000 at the grant date and is $400,000 immediately before the modification, the Exposure Draft would have required recognition of additional compensation cost of $100,000 at the date of the modification. That accounting produced the same result as if the award had been an equity instrument from the grant date.

B196. Some respondents to the Exposure Draft objected to that requirement on the grounds that the fair value of an award at the grant date is not relevant to liability awards, which are accounted for based on their fair value at each reporting date until exercise or other settlement. Those respondents said that a modification such as the one in paragraph B195 effectively settles the liability existing at the modification date in exchange for issuing an equity instrument with the same fair value, which is the way such modifications are accounted for under IFRS 2. The Board agreed with that view of the effect of a liability-to-equity modification and revised the Exposure Draft's requirements accordingly as illustrated in paragraphs A182–A184. Thus, in the preceding example, the award is accounted for as equity beginning at the date of the modification, with an effective grant-date fair value of $400,000.

---

[164]The Board noted that essentially the same issue arises for clawback provisions if the fair value of the consideration received exceeds the recognized compensation cost for the share-based payment arrangement that contained the contingent feature.

Share-Based Payment   FAS123(R)

Cancellations and Replacements

B197. The Board concluded that certain cancellations of awards accompanied by the grant of a replacement award are indistinguishable from modifications of the terms or conditions of the original award. For example, an entity might effectively reprice an award of share options with an exercise price of $50 by taking either of the following actions:

a. Modifying the terms of the award to lower the exercise price to $40
b. Cancelling the original award and concurrently granting a new award of share options with an exercise price of $40, a shorter contractual term, and subject to the same conditions as the original award.

In either case, the effect is the same—employees who previously had share options with an exercise price of $50 now have share options with an exercise price of $40.

B198. The Board considered what guidance to provide on distinguishing between a cancellation and grant of a replacement award that is substantively a modification and a cancellation of an award that should be accounted for as a settlement, with any replacement award accounted for separately. The Board concluded that a modification of an award, regardless of whether that modification is in the form of a cancellation of an existing award and grant of a replacement award, would be explained as such to the employees affected by the transaction. Thus, a cancellation and grant of (or offer to grant) a replacement award must occur concurrently if the transaction is to be accounted for as a modification. Otherwise, cancellation of an award is accounted for as a settlement in accordance with paragraphs 55 and 57 of this Statement.

Effect of Modifications on Determining Whether a Grant Date Has Occurred

B199. One criterion for determining whether a *grant date* has occurred under the definition in this Statement is that the employer and an employee must have reached a mutual understanding of the key terms and conditions of a share-based payment ar-

rangement. The effect of a modification is to change one or more of those terms or conditions, such as the exercise price of a share option.

B200. The Board considered whether multiple modifications of the same award might in some circumstances indicate that an employer and employees who benefit from the change(s) to their awards no longer have a mutual understanding of the award's key terms and conditions. The accounting result of a determination that such a mutual understanding does not exist would be to account for that award, and possibly similar awards, based on their estimated fair value at each reporting date until settlement. The Board considered several possible means of identifying awards to be accounted for as if a grant date has not yet occurred and concluded that each possible method could result in significant implementation problems. The Board also noted that most modifications of awards will result in recognition of incremental compensation cost. Accordingly, the Board decided not to establish special accounting requirements for multiple modifications of the same award.

Subsequent Accounting for Certain Freestanding Financial Instruments

B201. This Statement requires that the provisions of Statement 150, paragraphs 8–14, be applied in determining whether awards of freestanding financial instruments to employees as compensation qualify as liabilities. Paragraphs B202–B206 discuss subsequent accounting for certain financial instruments classified as liabilities in accordance with Statement 150.

B202. The Board considered when a financial instrument granted to an employee in a share-based payment transaction should cease to be accounted for under this Statement and should become subject to the requirements of other applicable GAAP, including Statements 133 and 150, as well as Issue 00-19.[165] This Statement deals with all aspects of measuring and recognizing financial instruments issued in exchange for employee services and the related compensation cost. In contrast, the financial instruments dealt with by other applicable generally accepted accounting principles, such as Statements 133 and 150, generally are issued in exchange

---

[165]The wording of the related paragraphs of the Exposure Draft dealt only with when an instrument ceases to be subject to this Statement and becomes subject to Statement 150. Respondents to the Exposure Draft pointed out that certain freestanding financial instruments may become subject to pronouncements other than Statement 150 when they cease to be subject to this Statement. The wording of this Statement has been revised in response to those comments.

FAS123(R)–133

for cash or other financial instruments, that is, in financing transactions. Therefore, those instruments generally give rise to interest cost or other cost of goods or services received rather than compensation cost. Accordingly, the Board concluded that this Statement should govern the accounting for a freestanding financial instrument granted to an employee until the rights conveyed to the holder of the instrument are no longer dependent on the holder's being an employee of the entity (that is, the rights are no longer dependent on continuing to provide service).

B203. An employee ordinarily is able to terminate service with vested shares (as opposed to share options or similar instruments) and still retain all rights inherent in the shares. Therefore, instruments such as mandatorily redeemable shares or other nonvested shares generally will become subject to Statement 150 upon vesting.

B204. A share option or similar instrument that is not transferable and whose contractual term is shortened upon employment termination continues to be subject to this Statement until the rights conveyed by the instrument to the holder are no longer dependent on the holder's being an employee of the entity (generally, when the instrument is exercised). However, vested share options are typically exercisable for a short period of time (generally, 60 to 90 days) subsequent to the termination of the employment relationship. The Board does not intend such a provision, in and of itself, to cause the award to become subject to other applicable GAAP for that short period of time.

B205. An entity may modify the terms of a fully vested, freestanding financial instrument after it becomes subject to Statement 150 or other applicable GAAP. The Board considers a modification of the terms of a financial instrument, such as a repricing of share options, held by current or former employees to be a transaction between the entity and those parties in their roles as employees rather than in their roles as holders of equity instruments. Any incremental value provided by the modification thus is additional compensation. Therefore, under this Statement, a modification that does not apply equally to all financial instruments of the same class regardless of whether the holder is or was an employee (or an employee's beneficiary) is a share-based payment transaction to be accounted for under the requirements of this Statement. Subsequently, the modified instrument will continue to be accounted for under Statement 150 or other applicable GAAP.

B206. Some classes of financial instruments are held only by current (or perhaps former) employees or their beneficiaries. The common shares of an entity that is wholly owned by its employee fall into that category. The Board concluded that modifications or settlements of such financial instruments may stem from the employment relationship depending on the terms of the modification or settlement. Thus, such a modification or settlement may be subject to the requirements of this Statement.

ACCOUNTING FOR INCOME TAX EFFECTS OF AWARDS OF SHARE-BASED COMPENSATION

Awards of Equity Instruments

B207. Consistent with the original provisions of Statement 123, the Board concluded that compensation cost recognized in the financial statements should be accounted for as a temporary difference under FASB Statement No. 109, *Accounting for Income Taxes.* Any deferred tax asset that is recognized for that temporary difference is not remeasured during the period that an award is outstanding for changes in the amount that would be deductible for tax purposes at subsequent balance sheet dates due to changes in the entity's share price but that are not recognized in measuring compensation cost.

B208. Under U.S. tax law at the date this Statement is issued, the tax deduction for an award of share-based compensation is based on the intrinsic value of the related instruments determined at a date after the grant date—generally the exercise date for share options (or equivalent instruments) and the vesting date for shares. The ultimate tax benefit for an equity award thus may be higher or lower than the temporary difference recognized for accounting purposes.

B209. The Board concluded that tax deductions in excess of recognized compensation costs that result from increases in intrinsic value after the grant date (that is, excess tax deductions) are due to changes in the price of an equity instrument. Therefore, the related tax effect (or excess tax benefit) should be an adjustment of paid-in capital. The result of that accounting is that the tax effects of an award of share-based employee compensation that qualifies as equity affect both the income statement and paid-in capital because the total tax deduction pertains to two separate transactions or events:

a. A transaction in which employees render services as consideration for an award of equity shares, equity share options, or other equity instruments. Use of those services in the entity's operations results in compensation cost, which is an income statement item.

b. An equity transaction, such as the exercise of share options or the vesting of shares. Changes in the share price after the grant date affect the amount of that equity transaction.

B210. If the tax benefit for an instrument is less than the amount of the related deferred tax asset, referred to as a *tax deficiency* in this discussion, this Statement requires, as did Statement 123, that the write-off of the deferred tax asset be recognized in the income statement except to the extent of any remaining paid-in capital arising from excess tax benefits from previous awards accounted for using the fair-value-based method. The Exposure Draft would have revised that provision to require that the full amount of a tax deficiency be recognized in the income statement. That proposal was based on viewing the tax effects of share-based compensation awards on an individual instrument basis; Statement 123's provisions, on the other hand, were consistent with accounting for the tax effects of awards on a group or portfolio basis.

B211. Some respondents to the Exposure Draft agreed with the method that it proposed. They generally said that the portfolio approach of netting tax deficiencies on some instruments against excess tax benefits on other instruments was not appropriate because one potential effect was to recognize in income a tax benefit on instruments awarded to an individual employee greater than the tax benefit received for those instruments.

B212. However, the majority of respondents to the Exposure Draft who addressed the issue disagreed with the proposed individual instrument requirement. They proposed a variety of other methods, including recognizing both excess tax benefits and tax deficiencies in the income statement or recognizing both in equity. Some respondents supported the original Statement 123 method. Most respondents said that the method they favored was more consistent with the income tax accounting principles in Statement 109. Many respondents who disagreed with the method in the Exposure Draft argued that the required tracking of tax effects of individual awards was unnecessarily complex. Some also said that the Exposure Draft method was inconsistent with other aspects of the fair-value-based accounting method, for example, reflecting the effects of employees' expected forfeiture and post-vesting employment termination behavior, that are based on a portfolio rather than an individual instrument approach.

B213. The Board rejected recognizing both excess tax benefits and tax deficiencies in the income statement because that view is consistent with viewing the entire tax deduction as the result of a single transaction in which employees render service in exchange for compensation in the form of equity instruments. As noted in paragraph B209, the Board concluded that the tax deduction results from both a compensatory transaction and a separate transaction in which the employer issues equity instruments to employees (or the award is otherwise settled, such as by expiration of a share option).

B214. The Board also rejected a method that would recognize both excess tax benefits and tax deficiencies in paid-in capital. The net result of recognizing the full amount of a tax deficiency in equity would be to recognize unrealized tax benefits for compensation cost as if they had been realized, which would overstate the entity's cumulative net income.

B215. Some respondents proposed a method of accounting for the tax consequences of awards of share-based compensation based on creation of a notional prepaid compensation asset on the grant date that exists as a notional reduction in equity. Under that method, a deferred tax liability would be recognized on the date an at-the-money share option is granted because that notional prepaid compensation asset is deemed to have no tax basis as it has no intrinsic value. As compensation cost was recognized over the requisite service period, the deferred tax liability would be eliminated by credits to income tax expense. Tax benefits, if any, realized upon exercise of the option then would affect only current taxes payable and paid-in capital. The net effect of that method would be that neither excess tax benefits nor tax deficiencies are recognized in the income statement. The Board rejected that method because it would result in recognition of a liability at the grant date that does not satisfy the definition of a liability. In addition, as discussed in paragraph B72, the Board concluded that an entity does not have a prepaid compensation asset at the grant date. It would be inconsistent with that conclusion to account for the tax consequences of an award of equity share options or similar instruments as if a prepaid compensation asset—notional or otherwise—was created at the grant date.

B216. The Board concluded that none of the methods discussed were clearly superior to the others in terms of consistency with the income tax accounting principles in Statement 109. The Board also noted that public entities already have been applying Statement 123's portfolio approach to recognizing excess tax benefits. That method not only is familiar, but also is somewhat easier to implement than the method in the Exposure Draft. Accordingly, this Statement continues the original Statement 123 method in which tax deficiencies are recognized in the income statement except to the extent of any remaining paid-in capital arising from excess tax benefits from previous awards subject to Statement 123.

B217. The Board was asked to specify which excess tax benefits are available as offsets to tax deficiencies. Because this Statement continues the fair-value-based method in Statement 123, the Board concluded that the "pool" of excess tax benefits available for offset should include those from all awards that were subject to Statement 123. That includes excess tax benefits recognized if the fair-based-method was adopted for recognition purposes, as well as those that would have been recognized had an entity that provided pro forma disclosures instead adopted Statement 123's fair-value-based method for recognition. However, excess tax benefits that have not been realized pursuant to Statement 109, as noted in paragraph A94, footnote 82, of this Statement, are not available for offset. The Board was informed by some constituents that a practice has developed whereby some entities recognized deferred tax assets for excess tax benefits before they were realized. The Board understands that such practice may be prevalent and therefore decided to provide transition guidance that requires an entity to discontinue that policy prospectively and follow the guidance in this Statement and Statement 109.

Awards of Liability Instruments

B218. This Statement provides guidance on accounting for the income tax effects of awards of liability instruments to employees in share-based payment transactions. Statement 123 did not address that issue because its required measurement date (settlement date) and measurement attribute (intrinsic value) for those liabilities were the same as the measurement date and attribute generally used for tax purposes. However, this Statement revises Statement 123 to require that awards of liability instruments by public entities be measured at fair value rather than intrinsic value. (Nonpublic entities may elect to use intrinsic value.) That requirement resulted in the need to address whether the excess of fair value over intrinsic value should be accounted for as a temporary difference under Statement 109. The Board concluded that it should.

Book and Tax Measurement Basis for Share Options

B219. The Board concluded that the deferred tax benefit for an award of share options recognized at the time the related compensation cost is recognized should be measured based on the fair value (or calculated value for certain nonpublic entities) of the options, including time value, because that method is consistent with the measurement of the related compensation cost. The Board does not consider a portion of the total difference between book and tax accounting for an award of share options to result from a difference in measurement basis (fair value and intrinsic value, respectively). At the date share options are exercised (or lapse unexercised at the end of their contractual term) and the actual tax deduction (if any) is determined, fair value (or calculated value) and intrinsic value are the same. At that date, either the employee has sacrificed the remaining time value upon early exercise or the time value has expired because the option has reached the end of its contractual term. Accordingly, the Board concluded that the difference between book and tax accounting under existing U.S. tax law results solely from different measurement dates and not from different measurement bases.

B220. Some respondents to the Exposure Draft favored the approach in IFRS 2 in which the deferred tax benefit is measured based on the intrinsic value of the award at the date the tax benefit is recognized. That approach is consistent with viewing the difference between book and tax accounting under existing U.S. tax law as resulting from different measurement attributes (fair value versus intrinsic value) as well as different measurement dates. The Board acknowledges that the IASB's conclusion is more consistent with the general approach to accounting for deferred taxes under both Statement 109 and IAS 12, *Income Taxes*. However, the Board decided to retain the existing departure from that basic tax-accounting model for the reasons noted above.

Accounting for the Deferred Tax Asset between Grant Date and Exercise Date

B221. Once a deferred tax asset pertaining to an award of share-based employee compensation is established as the related compensation cost is recognized, Statement 123 required that the effect of subsequent changes in the share price not be reflected in accounting for the deferred tax asset before that compensation is recognized for tax purposes. Rather, the deferred tax asset would be subsequently reduced by a valuation allowance only if, based on the weight of the available evidence, it is more likely than not that future taxable income[166] will be insufficient to recover the deferred tax asset in the periods the tax deduction for the award will be recognized (or in a carryback or carryforward period).

B222. Some commentators preferred the IFRS 2 approach to accounting for the deferred tax asset. IFRS 2 requires that the deferred tax asset be remeasured based on the share price at each reporting date before the deduction is recognized for tax purposes (or not recognized because an option is not exercised). The IASB concluded that reflecting changes in the share price before the deduction is recognized for tax purposes would be more consistent with other aspects of accounting for income taxes under its applicable accounting standard. As noted in paragraph B220 of this Statement, the FASB believes that treatment also could be viewed as conceptually consistent with Statement 109, but it decided for practical reasons to retain Statement 123's requirements. The Board also concluded that those requirements are consistent with its conclusion discussed in paragraphs B161–B164 of this Statement, in which a significant decrease in the share price after the grant date but before vesting does not result in ceasing to recognize compensation cost measured at the grant date.

AMENDMENTS TO STATEMENT 95

B223. FASB Statement No. 95, *Statement of Cash Flows*, requires an entity to provide a statement of cash flows that reports cash receipts and payments during the reporting period, classified according to whether they result from operating, investing, or financing activities. As originally issued, Statement 95 required all income tax payments (or refunds) to be classified as operating cash flows. In paragraph 92 of Statement 95, the Board explains that ". . . allocation of income taxes paid to operating, investing, and financing activities would be so complex and arbitrary that the benefits, if any, would not justify the costs involved." The Board continues to consider that conclusion generally accurate. However, it decided for the reasons discussed in paragraphs B224–B228 of this Statement to make an exception for the effects of excess tax benefits. Those excess tax benefits reduce the taxes otherwise payable when increases in the intrinsic value of equity instruments issued to employees are deductible for tax purposes but are not recognizable for accounting purposes.

B224. As discussed in paragraph B209, this Statement considers the tax effects of equity instruments awarded to employees to result from two transactions or events. Under that view, tax deductions that result from increases in intrinsic value after the grant date in excess of the grant-date fair value of the instruments awarded are considered to be due to an equity transaction, and the resulting excess tax benefits thus are recognized as an adjustment of paid-in capital. Thus, the tax effects of an award of share-based employee compensation affect both an income statement item and an equity item because the total tax deduction pertains to two separate transactions or events.

B225. For some entities, the tax savings realized upon employees' exercise of share options have significantly reduced the amount of income taxes otherwise payable. As a result, questions arose concerning the reporting of the net amount of taxes paid as an operating cash flow, especially since for income statement purposes the reduction in taxes otherwise payable is effectively accounted for as a part of the equity transaction when employees exercise their options (or shares vest). Some argued that the amount of the tax reduction should be classified in the statement of cash flows as resulting from a financing activity. In July 2000, the EITF considered that issue and concluded that entities should classify the amount of taxes paid as an operating cash payment

---

[166]Paragraph 21 of Statement 109 states, "Future realization of the tax benefit of an existing deductible temporary difference or carryforward ultimately depends on the existence of sufficient taxable income of the appropriate character (for example, ordinary income or capital gain) within the carryback, carryforward period available under the tax law." That paragraph goes on to describe the four sources of taxable income that may be available under the tax law to realize a tax benefit for deductible temporary differences and carryforwards.

because that is what Statement 95 required.[167] At that time, however, the Board agreed to reconsider the issue if it subsequently undertook a project on accounting for share-based payment.

B226. Advocates of retaining the original provisions of Statement 95 on classification of taxes paid, including many of the respondents to the Exposure Draft who addressed this issue, noted that the primary objective of a statement of cash flows is to provide relevant information about the cash receipts and cash payments of an enterprise during a period (Statement 95, paragraph 4). They pointed out that a reduction in taxes otherwise payable is not a cash receipt, nor is the related amount of taxes that would have been payable in the absence of a particular tax deduction a cash payment. Proponents of reporting the deemed tax saving as a result of excess tax benefits with cash flows from financing activities noted that net operating cash flows often are used as an indicator of the liquidity or "nearness to cash" of net income. For that reason, they advocated restricting operating cash flows, to the extent feasible, to the cash flow effects of transactions and events that enter into the determination of net income. The tax benefit in question, they pointed out, while not a cash receipt, is a "cash flow effect" of a financing activity that does not enter into the determination of net income.

B227. The Board acknowledges that both views on this issue have merit, but, on balance, it concluded that Statement 95 should be amended to report the tax reduction from excess tax benefits in the financing section of the statement of cash flows. The Board concluded that this item differs from other components of taxes paid that might be allocated among categories in the statement of cash flows because this item involves both compensation cost included in the income statement and an adjustment of paid-in capital as a result of an issuance of shares—a financing transaction. The Board also decided that the amendment of Statement 95 should apply to share-based payment transactions with nonemployees so that similar economic transactions are accounted for similarly. The amendment to Statement 95's treatment of taxes paid to report deemed tax savings from excess tax benefits as resulting from a financing activity also removes a potential point of nonconvergence with IFRS 2.

B228. The Board considered whether the cash flow statement should report an increase in operating cash flows and a decrease in financing cash flows in a reporting period in which there is a charge to paid-in capital as a result of the write-off of a deferred tax asset related to an award that did not result in deductible compensation cost. The Board decided not to require that presentation because it believes that the operating and financing sections of the cash flow statement should reflect only the effects of awards that generated tax savings from excess tax benefits.

DISCLOSURES

Objectives-Based Approach

B229. Because Statement 123 permitted entities to continue to use Opinion 25's requirements if they chose, many equity instruments granted to employees resulted in no compensation cost being recognized in the financial statements. As a consequence, Statement 123's disclosure requirements were developed in the context of recognition provisions that would not necessarily result in financial statements that adequately accounted for the economic effects of share-based payment arrangements with employees. Thus, one purpose of those disclosure requirements was to mitigate the inadequate accounting for share-based employee compensation arrangements under Opinion 25. The pro forma disclosures were the most obvious example of disclosures intended for that purpose, and this Statement eliminates those disclosures prospectively. The Board also reevaluated Statement 123's other disclosure requirements in light of this Statement's requirement to recognize the compensation cost from share-based payment arrangements in accordance with the fair-value-based method.

B230. The Board believes that a principal purpose of disclosures is to explain and elaborate on information recognized in the financial statements. The Board also notes that IFRS 2 establishes specific disclosure objectives for share-based payment arrangements and indicates minimum disclosures that would be needed to achieve each objective. Some respondents to the Invitation to Comment commented favorably on that approach, and the Board agrees that an objectives-based approach to disclosure requirements has merits. This Statement thus establishes

---

[167]Refer to EITF Issue No. 00-15, "Classification in the Statement of Cash Flows of the Income Tax Benefit Received by a Company upon Exercise of a Nonqualified Employee Stock Option."

four specific disclosure objectives (paragraph 64). Paragraph A240 indicates the minimum disclosures needed to achieve each objective, and paragraph A241 illustrates how the minimum requirements might be satisfied.

B231. Respondents to the Exposure Draft generally supported the objectives-based approach to disclosures, as well as the specific objectives proposed in the Exposure Draft. Some, however, asked the Board to establish a significance threshold below which some or all of the disclosures need not be provided. The Board notes that each of its Statements is accompanied by an indication that its provisions "need not be applied to immaterial items." The Board considers that general materiality provision to be preferable to establishing bright-line thresholds for a variety of items.

Information about the Nature and Terms of Share-Based Payment Arrangements

B232. The Board concluded that an important disclosure objective is to provide information that enables users of financial statements to understand the nature and terms of share-based payment arrangements with employees that existed during the reporting period and the potential effects of those arrangements on shareholders (paragraph 64(a)). Information needed to understand the potential effects of share-based payment arrangements on shareholders includes, but is not necessarily limited to, information about the potential transfer of value from preexisting shareholders to option holders upon exercise of in-the-money options. That objective was implicit in many of the disclosure requirements of Statement 123.

B233. The minimum disclosures this Statement specifies as necessary to achieve the objective discussed in paragraph 64 were required by Statement 123, and many of them also were required by Opinion 25. Thus, entities have for many years been disclosing items such as the nature and terms of share-based payment arrangements and a reconciliation of instruments outstanding at the beginning and end of the year. Those disclosures generally have been considered useful and have not been controversial.

B234. Statement 123 required entities to disclose the items specified in paragraph A240(b) of this Statement for each year for which an income statement was provided. Thus, an entity that presented comparative financial statements had to disclose, for example, the number and weighted-average exercise price of options granted, exercised, forfeited, or expired during a given year not only in the notes to that year's financial statements but also in the notes for succeeding years in which that year's financial statements are presented for comparative purposes. Although the Board continues to consider those disclosures important, it concluded that they are necessary only for the current year. The Board is not aware of a significant use or need for comparative disclosures of, for example, a reconciliation of the number of share options outstanding at the beginning of the year with those outstanding at the end of the year. Moreover, users who wish to see reconciliations for earlier years can consult the notes to the financial statements for those years. However, the Board concluded that the items specified in paragraph A240(c), such as the weighted-average grant-date fair values (or calculated values) of equity options and other equity instruments granted during the year, should be required for all periods presented to facilitate an understanding of trends.

B235. Statement 123 required disclosure of both (a) the weighted-average exercise price of options outstanding at the beginning of the year, those outstanding at the end of the year, and those granted, exercised, forfeited, or expired during the year and (b) the range of exercise prices of options outstanding at the date of the latest statement of financial position presented. The Board concluded that ranges of exercise prices are not an essential disclosure. The Board understands that ranges of exercise prices, by themselves, are not adequate to enable users to understand the potential increase in outstanding shares as a result of option exercises. Accordingly, the Board decided to retain only the required disclosure of weighted-average exercise prices. However, the Board emphasizes that paragraph A240(b) of this Statement specifies only minimum disclosures needed to achieve the objective of enabling users to understand the nature and general terms of share-based payment arrangements with employees that existed during the reporting period and the potential effects of those arrangements on shareholders. An entity that considers ranges of exercise prices also to be important in achieving that objective can provide that disclosure.

B236. This Statement requires disclosure of the total intrinsic value of options exercised (or share units converted) and share-based liabilities paid during the year (paragraph A240(c)). Some respondents questioned the need for intrinsic value disclosures in light of this Statement's focus on fair value. Under the modified grant date method, the amount of compensation cost recognized for awards of equity instruments ordinarily will differ from the value of the equity eventually issued (for example, upon vesting of nonvested shares or exercise of share options). The Board concluded that those intrinsic-value-based disclosures are important to provide information about the effect of outstanding share-based payment instruments on shareholders.

Information about the Effect of Compensation Cost on the Income Statement

B237. The Board concluded that information should be provided to enable users of the financial statements to understand the income statement effect of compensation cost arising from share-based payment arrangements with employees. Paragraph A240(g) specifies minimum disclosures needed to achieve that objective. Many of those disclosures, such as the total compensation cost recognized in income, also were required by Statement 123. However, the Board decided that certain other disclosures not specified by Statement 123 also are important in achieving the stated objective.

B238. To understand the effects of share-based payment arrangements on the income statement, users need to know not only the compensation cost recognized in income but also the related tax effects recognized in income. Users of financial statements, including many of those who responded to the Invitation to Comment, also asked for information to help understand the potential effects on future income statements of compensation cost resulting from outstanding awards. The Board considered that request to be both reasonable and consistent with the disclosure objectives. Accordingly, this Statement requires disclosure of total compensation cost related to nonvested awards that has not yet been recognized and the period over which it is expected to be recognized, as well as the total compensation cost capitalized as part of the cost of an asset (and thus recognizable in future years' income statements). Because that information should be readily available, the Board believes that the cost of disclosing it is not likely to exceed the related benefits.

B239. Some respondents said that certain of the minimum disclosures, such as the total amount of compensation cost, also should be required on a quarterly basis. The Board notes that paragraph 30 of APB Opinion No. 28, *Interim Financial Reporting,* specifies information to be included in quarterly financial reports, including information about changes in accounting principles or estimates and significant changes in financial position. The Board concluded that this Statement should not specify information about share-based compensation arrangements to be provided quarterly. Rather, entities should look to the general requirements of Opinion 28. The Board also notes that entities for which share-based compensation cost is significant may wish to provide additional information, including the total amount of that cost, on a quarterly basis to help users better understand their quarterly financial reports.

How the Fair Value of Goods or Services, Including Employee Services, Received as Consideration for Equity Instruments Issued Was Determined

B240. Another important objective of disclosures about share-based payment arrangements is to enable users of financial statements to understand how the fair value (or calculated value)[168] of the goods or services received, or the equity instruments issued, during the period was determined. This Statement requires that a public entity measure employee services received as consideration for equity instruments granted and liabilities incurred in share-based payment transactions with employees based on the fair value of the instruments issued. However, if the fair value of goods or services received in a share-based payment transaction with nonemployees is more reliably measurable than the fair value of the equity instruments issued, the fair value of the goods or services received should be used to measure the transaction. To understand the effects of share-based payment arrangements on the financial statements, users need to understand how the related fair value amounts were determined.

B241. The minimum disclosures specified in paragraph A240(f) of this Statement as necessary to enable users to understand how fair values were determined also were required by Statement 123.

---

[168] A nonpublic entity for which it is not possible to reasonably estimate the fair value of its share options and similar instruments because it is not practicable to estimate the expected volatility of its share price is required to account for its equity share options and similar instruments based on a calculated value (paragraph 23). Disclosures applicable to those instruments also apply if a calculated value rather than fair value is used. For convenience, that point generally is not noted in the remainder of the discussion of disclosure requirements.

However, because this Statement gives greater emphasis to lattice models than Statement 123 did, the required disclosures of the significant assumptions used to estimate the fair value of share-based compensation awards are revised to specifically encompass assumptions used in lattice models that employ a range of assumptions. For example, an entity that uses a valuation method in which different expected volatilities are used during the contractual term of an option is required to disclose the range of volatilities used.

B242. Some respondents to the Exposure Draft requested that the Board require disclosure of a sensitivity analysis of the effects of different assumptions about expected volatility and expected term. Paragraph A242 of this Statement indicates that an entity may wish to disclose additional information, such as a range of values calculated using different assumptions, if it believes that information would be useful to investors and creditors. However, the Board concluded that it is not necessary to require disclosure of such ranges or sensitivity analyses in all circumstances.

Information about Cash Flow Effects of Share-Based Payment Arrangements

B243. The Board concluded that an objective of the disclosures required by this Statement should be to provide information that enables users to understand the cash flow effects of share-based payment arrangements. The Board considers that objective to be consistent with the focus of users of financial statements on cash flows and with the overall financial reporting objective of providing information useful in assessing future cash flows.

B244. Although Statement 123 did not require the disclosures specified in paragraphs A240(i)–A240(k) of this Statement, entities likely disclosed certain of those items in the statement of cash flows if they were significant. Separate disclosure in the statement of cash flows of (a) the amount of cash received from exercise of share options and similar instruments and the related income tax benefits that were recognized in equity and (b) the amount of cash used to settle equity instruments granted under share-based payment arrangements will satisfy the related disclosure requirements of this Statement.

B245. The Board considered also requiring disclosure of the cash used to repurchase shares in conjunc-

tion with share-based payment arrangements. However, an entity may repurchase its shares for various reasons, and the Board concluded that distinguishing between shares repurchased for share-based payment arrangements and shares repurchased for other reasons would not always be feasible. Accordingly, the Board decided instead to require a description of the entity's policy for repurchasing shares in conjunction with share-based payment arrangements if such a policy exists, and the number of shares, if any, expected to be repurchased for that purpose in the following annual reporting period.

EFFECTIVE DATES AND TRANSITION

Effective Dates

Public Entities That Are Not Small Business Issuers

B246. The Exposure Draft's proposed effective date was for new awards and awards modified or settled in fiscal years beginning after December 15, 2004. Many respondents said that more time would be needed to adopt this Statement, often citing the ongoing implementation with the Sarbanes-Oxley Act[169] as a constraint on available resources. Moreover, the effective date proposed in the Exposure Draft was predicated on a targeted issuance date for this Statement of no later than November 15, 2004. In light of those comments and the fact that this Statement is being issued later than projected, the Board concluded that the effective date of this Statement should be deferred beyond the date proposed in the Exposure Draft.

B247. The Board also understands that users of financial statements expressly desire that the improvements to accounting for share-based compensation made by this Statement be reflected in financial statements as soon as possible. Moreover, the Board does not consider it necessary to defer the effective date as long as a year after this Statement is issued, as some respondents requested. Public entities have for many years been either recognizing, or disclosing the pro forma effects of recognizing, compensation cost based on the fair value of awards to employees. Even though the fair-value-based method in this Statement differs in certain respects from the one in Statement 123, those differences are not sufficient to warrant an extended transition period for larger public

---

[169]Public Law 107-204—July 30, 2002, Section 180(b)(1)(A)(v).

entities. Accordingly, after weighing the expressed desires of users of financial statements against what it is reasonable to expect of the entities that prepare those financial statements, the Board concluded that, for public entities that do not file as small business issuers, this Statement should be effective for new awards and those modified, repurchased, or cancelled in interim or annual reporting periods beginning after June 15, 2005.

Small Business Issuers

B248. Certain respondents asked the Board to permit *small business issuers* to apply this Statement's measurement provisions for nonpublic entities. Entities that file as small business issuers are, by definition, public entities, and the Board concluded that those entities should apply the measurement requirements for public entities. Those entities should be able to apply the guidance in Appendix A to develop reasonable estimates of the fair value of their share options and similar instruments. However, the Board recognizes that small business issuers, like nonpublic entities, may have fewer resources than do larger public entities to devote to implementing new accounting standards and thus may need additional time to do so. The Board therefore concluded that entities that file as small business issuers should be permitted to defer adoption of this Statement until their first interim or annual reporting period beginning after December 15, 2005.

Nonpublic Entities

B249. As with small business issuers, the Board concluded that nonpublic entities should be permitted additional time to adopt this Statement. Therefore, the effective date for nonpublic entities is fiscal years beginning after December 15, 2005. Statement 123 permitted nonpublic entities to use the minimum value method to estimate the value of their employee share options and similar instruments, and most nonpublic entities thus have not previously been using a fair-value-based method for recognition or pro forma disclosure purposes. Because it omits expected volatility, an estimate based on minimum value is not comparable to one based on fair value. In addition, a nonpublic entity for which it is not practicable to estimate the expected volatility of its share price will need time to identify or develop an appropriate industry sector index to use in determining the calculated value required by this Statement. Accordingly, the Board concluded that nonpublic entities should be required to apply this

Statement to new awards and to those modified, or settled (by means other than exercise or lapse) in fiscal years beginning after December 15, 2005.

Transition for Public Entities, Including Small Business Issuers

B250. The Board considered several alternatives for how public entities should accomplish the transition to this Statement, including full retrospective application with restatement of prior periods' financial statements, prospective application, and variations of each. The Board evaluated those alternatives in the context of the proposed requirements in its Exposure Draft of a proposed Statement, *Accounting Changes and Error Corrections,* which would replace Opinion 20 and FASB Statement No. 3, *Reporting Accounting Changes in Interim Financial Statements.* That Exposure Draft was issued for comment on December 15, 2003, as part of the Board's international convergence project. Under the provisions of that proposed Statement, a change in accounting principle would be applied retrospectively unless it is impracticable to determine either the cumulative effect or the period-specific effects of the change. Retrospective application would be deemed impracticable if it would require significant estimates as of a prior period, and it would not be possible to objectively determine whether information used to develop those estimates would have been available at the time the affected transactions or events would have been recognized in the financial statements or whether that information arose subsequently.

B251. If full retrospective application with restatement were practicable, the Board believes it would be the best transition method for this Statement because retrospective application would provide the maximum amount of comparability between periods and thus enhance the usefulness of comparative financial statements. However, the Board concluded that full retrospective application of the change in accounting principle to adopt this Statement would be impracticable because it could require an entity to make estimates as of a prior period. Although the guidance in this Statement on estimating the fair value of an award at the grant date is similar to the guidance that public entities have been following for either recognition or pro forma disclosure purposes under Statement 123, this Statement clarifies and elaborates on Statement 123's guidance. As a result, an entity might conclude that some aspects of its estimation method used in prior years should be changed, which could call for estimates of, for example, employees' expected early exercise and post-vesting employment termination behavior as of earlier periods. Other requirements of this Statement, for example, the method of measuring the effects of a modification of an award, also differ from the related requirements of Statement 123 and could require estimates as of an earlier period. The Board thus rejected full retrospective application.

Modified Prospective Application

B252. For public entities and nonpublic entities that used the fair-value-based method for recognition or pro forma disclosures under Statement 123, the Board also rejected full prospective application, that is, application only to new awards and to those modified or settled in fiscal periods beginning after the required effective date. Public entities have been for many years either recognizing or disclosing the pro forma effects of recognizing compensation cost from share-based payment arrangements with employees using a fair-value-based method that is similar to the method in this Statement. Accordingly, the Board concluded that all public entities and nonpublic entities that used the fair-value-based method for recognition or pro forma disclosures also should apply this Statement to the nonvested portion of awards granted before the required effective date and outstanding at the date of adoption. However, the grant-date fair value of those nonvested awards should not be adjusted for differences between the requirements of this Statement and those of Statement 123. That is, compensation cost for the nonvested portion of awards outstanding at the date of adoption should be recognized based on the previously estimated grant-date fair value and, except for the method of incorporating expected forfeitures before vesting, the same attribution method used for recognition or pro forma disclosures under Statement 123. Because previously estimated grant-date fair values will not be adjusted, modified prospective transition is practicable and will not impose significant costs. However, to enhance comparability, the Board concluded that entities that used the method permitted by Statement 123 of reflecting the effect of actual forfeitures of nonvested awards only as they occur should not continue to do so during the transition period. Thus, paragraph 80 of this Statement requires that an entity using that method adjust expected forfeitures as of the date of adoption.

Modified Retrospective Application

B253. The Exposure Draft would have precluded any form of retrospective application. Many respondents who addressed transition issues urged the Board to permit, if not require, a modified version of retrospective application in which the amounts used for prior periods presented would be the same as reported in the pro forma disclosures for those years. In reconsidering the transition alternatives in light of the comments received during the exposure period, the Board concluded that modified retrospective application should be permitted. As discussed in paragraph B252 of this Statement, using amounts previously reported in pro forma disclosures for prior years does not necessitate re-estimating fair values for those years and thus is neither impracticable nor costly to implement. However, regardless of whether this Statement is applied retrospectively as described, the pro forma amounts for prior years are available in the financial statements for those years. Thus, the Board concluded that modified retrospective application should not be required. Accordingly, this Statement permits all public entities and nonpublic entities that previously used the fair-value-based method in Statement 123 for either recognition or pro forma disclosures to choose between modified prospective or modified retrospective application.

Modified Retrospective Application Only to Beginning of Year of Adoption

B254. As noted in paragraph B247, the Board's balancing of the needs of users and preparers of financial statements resulted in an effective date of interim or annual periods beginning after June 15, 2005, for public entities that are not small business issuers. Thus, the effective date will fall in the middle of many public entities' fiscal years. The Board recognizes that some such entities may be concerned about the possible effects of a mid-year effective date on intra- and inter-year comparisons. Accordingly, the Board decided to permit an entity to choose to retrospectively apply this Statement (using the modified retrospective method) only to prior interim periods of the year of adoption.

Transition for Nonpublic Entities

B255. As noted in paragraph B249, one reason for providing a deferred effective date for nonpublic entities is that Statement 123 permitted those entities to use minimum value rather than fair value for recognition or pro forma disclosures. This Statement requires nonpublic entities that used the minimum value method under Statement 123 to adopt this Statement prospectively. Those entities have neither the grant-date fair value amounts for nonvested awards outstanding at the date of adoption of this Statement necessary for modified prospective transition nor the pro forma fair value disclosures for prior years necessary for modified retrospective application.

Transition Provisions for Awards for Which the Classification Changes from Equity to Liabilities

B256. Application of this Statement, combined with application of the classification provisions of Statement 150, may change the classification of a freestanding financial instrument granted to an employee from an equity instrument to a liability. The Board concluded that that change in classification should be made by recognizing a liability at its fair value (or portion thereof if the requisite service has not been rendered). If the fair value (or portion thereof) of the liability is greater than or less than previously recognized compensation cost for the instrument, the liability should be recognized, first, by reducing equity to the extent of such previously recognized cost, and second, by recognizing the difference in the income statement, net of any related tax effect, as the cumulative effect of a change in accounting principle. The Board does not consider it appropriate to continue to classify as equity an instrument that qualifies as a liability under this Statement. However, the Board also does not consider full retrospective application of changes in classification to be practicable because that transition method would require estimates of the fair value of the reclassified instruments for earlier periods. The Board thus concluded that reclassification of such instruments according to the transition guidance in this Statement is the best available alternative.

Effective Date and Transition Provisions for Nonpublic Entities That Become Public Entities after June 15, 2005

B257. Some constituents asked the Board to clarify the effective date and transition requirements for nonpublic entities that become public entities after June 15, 2005. That clarification is provided in paragraphs 69, 74, 76, and 83. In essence, those paragraphs indicate that a newly public entity should apply whatever provisions are applicable to its new status as of the beginning of the first interim or annual period after it becomes a public entity, taking into account whether it used the fair-value-based method or the minimum value method for recognition or pro forma disclosures under Statement 123. For example, paragraph 69 provides that the effective date for a nonpublic entity that becomes a public entity after June 15, 2005, and does not file as a small business issuer is the first interim or annual reporting period beginning after the entity becomes a public entity. If the newly public entity files as a small business issuer, the effective date is the first interim or annual reporting period beginning after December 15, 2005, for which the entity is a public entity.

CONVERGENCE OF U.S. AND INTERNATIONAL ACCOUNTING STANDARDS ON ACCOUNTING FOR SHARE-BASED PAYMENT TRANSACTIONS

B258. One potential benefit of this project is the opportunity for increased convergence of U.S. and international accounting standards on accounting for share-based payment transactions. At the time the Board added the project to its agenda early in 2003, the comment period on the IASB's ED2 was nearing its end, and the IASB was preparing to redeliberate its conclusions based on the comments received. Although the FASB's and the IASB's projects were at different stages (the FASB was working toward an Exposure Draft at the same time the IASB was working toward a final standard), both Boards considered it appropriate to cooperate to the extent feasible in considering the issues. Although the two Boards conducted their projects separately, the objective was to work together in understanding the issues and alternatives, with the objective of reaching compatible conclusions and thus furthering convergence of U.S. and international accounting standards on share-based payment. To a large extent, that objective was achieved. Accounting for share-based payment arrangements under this Statement and related accounting under IFRS 2 have the potential to differ in only a few areas. Those differences may be further reduced as the FASB progresses with the next phase of its project on accounting for share-based payment arrangements (refer to paragraphs B12–B14) as well as other convergence projects. In addition, the two Boards will consider whether to undertake additional work to further converge their respective accounting standards on share-based payment when the FASB has completed its project on accounting for share-based payment arrangements and its current project on distinguishing between liabilities and equity.

B259. The more significant differences between this Statement and IFRS 2 are:

a. Accounting for share-based payment arrangements with other than employees
b. Determining whether an employee share purchase plan gives rise to compensation cost
c. Measurement of share options granted by a nonpublic entity
d. Accounting for certain types of modifications of awards
e. Classification of certain instruments as liabilities or equity
f. Certain aspects of accounting for the income tax effects of an award of equity instruments.

Difference between Scope of This Statement and Scope of IFRS 2

B260. The Board's decision not to reconsider the existing guidance for share-based payment arrangements with nonemployees in developing this Statement may result, at least temporarily, in different accounting for those arrangements under U.S. GAAP and IFRS 2. The scope of IFRS 2 includes accounting for all share-based payment arrangements, regardless of whether the counterparty is an employee. All of those arrangements generally will be accounted for using the modified grant-date method that this Statement requires for share-based payment transactions with employees. In contrast, Issue 96-18 requires that grants of share options and other equity instruments to nonemployees be measured at the earlier of (a) the date at which a commitment for performance by the counterparty to earn the equity instruments is reached or (b) the date at which the counterparty's performance is complete. For many awards, the measurement date under Issue 96-18 will differ from the measurement date prescribed by IFRS 2, with a resulting difference in the amount of cost recognized for those awards.

Employee Share Purchase Plans

B261. For the reasons discussed in paragraphs B112–B116, this Statement retains the original Statement 123 criteria for determining whether an employee share purchase plan is compensatory or not. IFRS 2 contains more stringent criteria that are essentially the same as those proposed in the FASB's

Exposure Draft. The result of that difference is that some employee share purchase plans for which IFRS 2 requires recognition of compensation cost will not be considered to give rise to compensation cost under this Statement. An example is a plan that provides a 5 percent discount to employees that is not extended to other holders of the same class of shares. However, this Statement also includes an alternative criterion, which is essentially the same as the one in IFRS 2. Thus, if it so chooses, an entity generally would be able to satisfy both the requirements of this Statement and those of IFRS 2 in determining whether an employee share purchase plan is considered to be compensatory.

Equity Share Options Granted by a Nonpublic Entity

B262. IFRS 2 applies the same measurement requirements to employee share options regardless of whether the issuer is a public or a nonpublic entity. IFRS 2 contains the same accounting treatment as this Statement for financial instruments granted under share-based payment arrangements if the entity concludes that fair value cannot be reasonably estimated at the grant date. The IASB noted that share options granted by a nonpublic (or newly public) entity may fall into that category.

B263. This Statement requires that a nonpublic entity account for its options and similar equity instruments based on their fair value unless it is not practicable to estimate the expected volatility of the entity's share price. In that situation, the entity is required to measure its equity share options and similar instruments at a value calculated by substituting the historical volatility of an appropriate industry sector index for the expected volatility of its share price in applying an option-pricing-model.

Type III Modifications

B264. As indicated in paragraphs B192 and B193, the requirements of this Statement on accounting for Type III modifications differ from the related requirements of IFRS 2, which treat such modifications as affecting only the number of instruments that are likely to vest.

Distinguishing between Liabilities and Equity

B265. Currently, U.S. and international accounting guidance differ on various aspects of distinguishing between liabilities and equity and accounting for financial instruments with characteristics of both, and the FASB has an active project to reconsider portions of that guidance. In the meantime, related aspects of accounting for certain financial instruments issued to employees as compensation may differ under this Statement and under IFRS 2. For example, IFRS 2 does not distinguish between liabilities and equity using all the criteria established in Statement 150.

B266. This Statement does not attempt to analyze all potential differences between this Statement and IFRS 2 that stem from different U.S. and international accounting standards on liabilities and equity because at least some of those differences may be resolved when the FASB completes its project on that topic. As noted in paragraph B258, the FASB and the IASB will consider undertaking a joint project at that time to resolve any remaining differences between their standards on share-based payment.

Income Tax Effects of Equity Instruments Awarded to Employees

B267. The FASB's conclusion that the total tax deduction for an award of equity instruments arises from two transactions or events (paragraph B209) is consistent with the requirements of IFRS 2. However, the FASB and the IASB reached different conclusions on certain aspects of accounting for the income tax effects of equity instruments awarded to employees.

B268. In tax jurisdictions such as the United States, where the time value of share options generally is not deductible for tax purposes, IFRS 2 requires that no deferred tax asset be recognized for the compensation cost related to the time value component of the fair value of an award. A deferred tax asset is recognized only if and when the share options have intrinsic value that could be deductible for tax purposes. Therefore, an entity that grants an at-the-money share option to an employee in exchange for services would not recognize tax effects until that award was in-the-money. In contrast, this Statement requires recognition of a deferred tax asset based on the grant-date fair value of the award. The effects of subsequent decreases in the share price (or lack of an increase) are not reflected in accounting for the deferred tax asset until the related compensation cost is recognized for tax purposes. The effects of subsequent increases that generate excess tax benefits are recognized when they affect taxes payable.

B269. This Statement requires a portfolio approach in determining excess tax benefits of equity awards in paid-in capital available to offset write-offs of de-

ferred tax assets, whereas IFRS 2 requires an individual instrument approach. Thus, some write-offs of deferred tax assets that will be recognized in paid-in capital under this Statement will be recognized in determining net income under IFRS 2.

COST-BENEFIT CONSIDERATIONS

B270. The mission of the FASB is to establish and improve standards of financial accounting and reporting for the guidance and education of the public, including preparers, auditors, and users of financial information. In fulfilling that mission, the Board endeavors to determine that a proposed standard will fill a significant need and that the costs imposed to meet that standard, as compared with other alternatives, are justified in relation to the overall benefits of the resulting information. Although the costs to implement a new standard may not be borne evenly, investors and creditors—both present and potential—and other users of financial information benefit from improvements in financial reporting, thereby facilitating the functioning of markets for capital and credit and the efficient allocation of resources in the economy. However, the value of that incremental improvement to financial reporting and most of the costs to achieve it are subjective and cannot be quantified.

B271. The Board's consideration of each issue in a project includes the subjective weighing of the incremental improvement in financial reporting against the incremental cost of implementing the identified alternatives. At the end of that process, the Board considers the accounting provisions in the aggregate and assesses the related perceived costs on a qualitative basis.

B272. Several procedures were conducted before the issuance of the Exposure Draft to aid the Board in assessing the expected costs associated with implementing the required use of the fair-value-based accounting method. Those procedures included a field visit program, a survey of commercial software providers, and discussions with Option Valuation Group members and other valuation experts. In addition, the Board discussed this Statement's provisions with the Financial Accounting Standards Advisory Council, the User Advisory Council, the Small Business Advisory Committee, as well as with numerous constituents at four public roundtable meetings and at various other meetings.

B273. The Board uses the term *field test* to describe a formal application of a proposed Statement by a group of entities to their individual situations. The participating entities are provided with a description of the proposed approach (if an Exposure Draft has not yet been issued) and are asked to apply that approach either to current transactions or retroactively to one or more prior years. A field test may involve having the participating entities prepare financial statements in accordance with a proposed approach to accounting for a particular type of transaction. Field tests involve a significant commitment of resources by the participating entities—a commitment that the Board asks for only if it concludes that it cannot obtain the information it needs through field visits or other means. The Board conducted field tests in its deliberations that led to Statement 123 (paragraph C11 of this Statement).

B274. The Board uses the term *field visit,* on the other hand, to describe meetings with companies or firms to discuss a possible change in the accounting for a transaction, such as a share-based payment transaction. A field visit involves Board and staff members' meeting with individual entities at their offices or by means of a conference call to engage in an in-depth discussion of a proposed Statement. Entities participating in a field visit program are provided with a draft of the proposed requirements, together with a list of discussion questions. The questions focus on helping the Board and staff to better understand the costs and benefits of changing to the proposed approach, the operationality of the proposed approach, and any difficulties an entity might face in applying it.

B275. The Board concluded for its current project that field visits were an appropriate means of gathering information about the perceived costs of the proposed changes to Statement 123. The Board believes that field tests are more important for a proposed standard that would require an entirely new method of accounting, such as the original Statement 123, and, as mentioned in paragraph B273, field tests were conducted before issuance of Statement 123. That is not the situation with this Statement, which improves the fair-value-based method in Statement 123 rather than requiring an entirely new accounting method. Further, thousands of public entities have had many years of experience in estimating the fair values of their awards of share-based employee compensation—estimates that Statement 123 required for either recognition or pro forma disclosure purposes.

B276. The field visit program included discussions with 18 enterprises selected to achieve broad coverage of constituent enterprises based on market capi-talization, software used to value employee share options, filing status (public or nonpublic), industry membership, total number of employees, total awards outstanding, and types of awards outstanding. Field visit participants included preparers of financial statements, employee benefit consultants, and auditors. Before each field visit, participants received a package of materials, including a description of the proposed changes to Statement 123, a discussion of the type of information that could be incorporated into a lattice model, and questions for participants to consider.

B277. The Board also solicited information by means of a questionnaire survey of commercial software providers about the functionality of existing tracking and valuation software for employee share options and similar instruments. That survey asked about the functionality of existing software used to track grants of share-based compensation and to estimate the fair value of the related instruments. The survey also asked about the estimated costs and timing of availability of software with the ability to estimate fair value using a lattice model that incorporated information about employees' expected early exercise and post-vesting employment termination behavior.

B278. After comments were received on the Exposure Draft, the Board undertook additional cost-benefit procedures for nonpublic entities. Interviews were conducted with 13 constituents, selected to provide broad coverage of concerns related to nonpublic entities. The interviews covered detailed questions included in a questionnaire provided to interviewees before the date of the interviews. Questions covered included the types of share-based compensation used by nonpublic entities, how frequently awards are granted, how the current price of a nonpublic entity's share price is determined in complying with Opinion 25 and Statement 123, and the ways in which nonpublic entities might obtain information needed to apply the fair-value-based method, including likely costs that would be incurred to do so. In addition, cost-benefit issues were discussed at a meeting of the Small Business Advisory Committee held in May 2004.

B279. Based on the findings of the cost-benefit procedures, the Board concluded that this Statement will sufficiently improve financial reporting to justify the costs it will impose. Most of the expected benefits of required recognition of the cost of share-based compensation arrangements with employees using the fair-value-based method have been discussed already. In addition, existing guidance on accounting for share-based employee compensation is simplified because this Statement eliminates Opinion 25 and the guidance necessary to implement it (except for certain awards granted by nonpublic entities before the effective date of this Statement).

B280. Several of the Board's decisions are intended to mitigate the incremental costs of complying with this Statement. For example, an alternative measurement method based on substituting the historical volatility of an appropriate industry sector index for expected volatility (calculated value) also is provided for equity options and similar instruments granted by a nonpublic entity if it is not practicable to estimate the expected volatility of its share price. As a result, such nonpublic entities will incur minimal incremental costs in addition to those necessary to comply with the minimum value method in Statement 123. In addition, a nonpublic entity is not required to estimate the fair value (or calculated value) of its liability awards; instead, such an entity may elect to account for its liabilities based on their intrinsic value. Transition costs for public entities have been minimized by requiring that compensation cost for the nonvested portion of awards granted before the issuance of this Statement be based on the grant-date fair values previously estimated for recognition or pro forma disclosure purposes under Statement 123.

Appendix C

BACKGROUND INFORMATION

C1. APB Opinion No. 25, *Accounting for Stock Issued to Employees,* was issued in 1972. Opinion 25 required that compensation cost for an award of equity share options be measured at its intrinsic value, which is the amount by which the fair value of the underlying equity share exceeds the exercise price. Opinion 25 also established criteria for determining the date at which an award's intrinsic value should be measured; those criteria distinguished between awards whose terms are known (or fixed) at the date of grant and awards whose terms are not known (or variable) at the date of grant. Measuring the intrinsic values of fixed awards at the grant date generally resulted in little or no compensation cost being recognized for valuable equity instruments given to employees in exchange for their services. Additionally,

distinguishing between fixed and variable awards was difficult in practice, which resulted in a large amount of specialized and complex accounting guidance.

C2. In 1984, the Board added to its agenda a project to reconsider Opinion 25. On May 31, 1984, an FASB Invitation to Comment, *Accounting for Compensation Plans Involving Certain Rights Granted to Employees,* was issued based on the November 4, 1982, AICPA Issues Paper, *Accounting for Employee Capital Accumulation Plans.* The Board received 144 letters of comment.

C3. The issues raised in that Invitation to Comment were complex and highly controversial. Still, each time the issue was raised, Board members voted unanimously that employee share options result in compensation cost that should be recognized in the employer's financial statements.

C4. As with all FASB projects, the Board's discussions of stock compensation were open to public observations, and its tentative conclusions on individual issues were reported in its weekly *Action Alert.* During the Board's deliberations from 1985 to 1988, more than 200 letters were received that commented on, and usually objected to, tentative conclusions reported in *Action Alert.*

C5. Some Board members and others were troubled by the differing results of stock-based compensation plans that called for settlement in cash and those that called for settlement in stock. But exercise date accounting for all plans is the only way to achieve consistent results between cash and stock plans, and that accounting was not considered to be consistent with the definitions of liabilities and equity in FASB Concepts Statement No. 6, *Elements of Financial Statements.* It also would be inconsistent with current accounting for stock purchase warrants, which are similar to employee share options except that warrants are issued to outsiders rather than to employees.

C6. Part of the financial instruments project on the Board's agenda considers whether changes to the concepts of liabilities and equity are needed. Late in 1988, the Board decided to set aside specific work on stock compensation while it considered broader questions of how to distinguish between liabilities and equity and the implications of that distinction.

C7. In August 1990, an FASB Discussion Memorandum, *Distinguishing between Liability and Equity Instruments and Accounting for Instruments with*

Characteristics of Both, was issued. The Discussion Memorandum framed and discussed numerous issues, some of which directly related to how to account for employee share options. The Board received 104 comment letters and in March 1991 held a public hearing on those issues, at which 14 commentators appeared.

C8. More than 90 percent of the respondents to the Discussion Memorandum said that an entity's obligation to issue its own stock is an equity instrument because the entity does not have an obligation to transfer assets (an equity's own stock is not an asset), which is an essential characteristic of a liability. In February 1992, the Board decided not to pursue possible changes to the conceptual distinction between liabilities and equity and to resume work on the stock compensation project within the present conceptual framework.

C9. In March 1992, the Board met with several compensation consultants and accountants to discuss current practice in valuing employee share options and accounting for stock compensation. The compensation consultants generally agreed that current accounting provisions heavily affected the design of stock compensation plans. They said that there were far fewer variable (or performance) plans than fixed plans because of the required accounting for variable plans. The compensation consultants also said that the Black-Scholes-Merton formula and other option-pricing models were used to value various types of employee share options for purposes other than accounting. Grant date measures were relied on to provide comparisons to other compensation arrangements.

C10. A task force of accountants, compensation consultants, industry representatives, and academics was formed to assist in the project. Accounting for stock compensation was addressed at 19 public Board meetings and at 2 public task force meetings in 1992 and 1993. The Board's tentative conclusions on individual issues were reported in *Action Alert.* During 1992 and the first part of 1993, more than 450 comment letters were received, mostly objecting to the tentative conclusions. Many of the letters proposed disclosure in lieu of cost recognition for stock compensation. Several of the commentators submitted alternatives to the Board; the most comprehensive disclosure proposal was included as an appendix to the FASB Exposure Draft, *Accounting for Stock-Based Compensation,* issued in June 1993.

C11. The 1993 Exposure Draft would have required recognizing compensation cost for all awards of stock-based compensation that eventually vest, based on their fair value at the grant date. The Board and KPMG Peat Marwick conducted a field test of the provisions of the 1993 Exposure Draft. In addition, other organizations provided information about their own test applications of the 1993 Exposure Draft.

C12. The 1993 Exposure Draft was extraordinarily controversial; the Board received 1,789 comment letters. The vast majority of respondents objected to the recognition of compensation cost for fixed employee share options—sometimes for reasons that had little to do with accounting. In March 1994, the Board held six days of public hearings in California and Connecticut. Representatives from 73 organizations presented testimony at those hearings. Several legislative proposals were introduced in Congress, both opposing and supporting proposals in the 1993 Exposure Draft. A Sense of the Senate resolution was passed that the FASB "should not at this time change the current generally accepted accounting treatment of stock options and stock purchase plans." However, a second resolution was passed that "Congress should not impair the objectivity or integrity of the FASB's decision making process by legislating accounting rules."

C13. In April 1994, the Board held a public roundtable discussion with academic researchers and other participants on proposals the participants had submitted to improve the measure of the value of share options. Also during 1994, the Board discussed accounting for stock-based compensation at 13 public Board meetings and at 1 public task force meeting.

C14. In December 1994, the Board discussed the alternatives for proceeding with the project on accounting for stock-based compensation in light of the comment letters, public hearing testimony, and various meetings held to discuss the project. The Board decided to encourage, rather than require, recognition of compensation cost based on a fair-value-based method and to pursue expanded disclosures. Employers would be permitted to continue to apply the provisions of Opinion 25. Employers that continued to apply Opinion 25 would be required to disclose the pro forma effects on net income and earnings per share as if the new fair-value-based accounting method had been applied.

C15. The Board discussed the details of the disclosure-based approach at six public Board meetings in 1995. In 1995, 131 comment letters were received on the disclosure-based approach. In May

1995, an initial draft of the standards sections and some other parts of Statement 123 were distributed to task force members and other interested parties that requested the draft; 34 comments letters were received.

C16. Statement 123 was issued in October 1995 and was effective for share-based compensation transactions entered into in fiscal years that began after December 15, 1995. As originally issued, Statement 123 established a fair-value-based method of accounting for share-based compensation awarded to employees. The fair-value-based method of accounting requires that compensation cost for awards of share options be measured at their fair value on the date of grant. As opposed to the accounting under Opinion 25, the application of the fair-value-based method to fixed awards results in compensation cost being recognized when services are received in exchange for equity instruments of the employer. Statement 123 established as preferable the fair-value-based method and encouraged, but did not require, entities to adopt it. The Board's decision at that time to permit entities to continue accounting for share-based compensation transactions using Opinion 25 was based on practical rather than conceptual considerations.

C17. In the years following the issuance of Statement 123, users of financial statements, including institutional and individual investors, as well as many other parties expressed to the FASB their concerns that using Opinion 25's intrinsic value method results in financial statements that do not faithfully represent the economic transactions affecting the issuer, namely, the receipt and consumption of employee services in exchange for equity instruments.

C18. Beginning in 2002, a number of public companies began to adopt Statement 123's fair-value-based method of accounting. In connection with those decisions, a number of companies, as well as financial statement users, expressed concerns to the Board about the lack of comparability and consistency of reported results between periods caused by the ramp-up effect inherent in Statement 123's requirement to adopt the fair-value-based method prospectively. Such concerns led the Board to undertake a limited-scope project to reconsider the transition and disclosure provisions of Statement 123; that project resulted in the issuance of FASB Statement No. 148, *Accounting for Stock-Based Compensation—Transition and Disclosure,* in December 2002.

C19. In November 2002, shortly after the IASB issued a proposed IFRS, *Share-based Payment,* the

FASB issued an Invitation to Comment, *Accounting for Stock-Based Compensation: A Comparison of FASB Statement No. 123,* Accounting for Stock-Based Compensation, *and Its Related Interpretations, and IASB Proposed IFRS,* Share-based Payment. The Invitation to Comment explained both similarities of and differences between the requirements of Statement 123 and the method proposed by the IASB. The Board received 302 letters of comment in response to the Invitation to Comment, many of which commented only on the issue of whether the FASB should require recognition at fair value of compensation cost for employee share options. Most users of financial statements who responded to the Invitation to Comment urged the Board to undertake a project to require that entities account for share-based payment arrangements with employees using a fair-value-based method. The majority of the preparers who responded did not support such a requirement. However, some of those preparers asked for additional guidance on applying the fair-value-based method in Statement 123.

C20. In response to concerns about impaired usefulness, and a lack of transparency, of financial reporting resulting from the continued use of Opinion 25, and consistent with its commitment to the convergence of international accounting standards, the Board added a project to its agenda in March 2003 to reconsider Statement 123. Shortly after adding this project to its agenda, the Board established an Option Valuation Group to provide information and advice on how to improve the guidance in Statement 123 on measuring the fair value of share options and similar instruments issued to employees in compensation arrangements. That group included valuation experts from the compensation consulting, risk management, investment banking, and academic communities. The Board and staff met formally with that group and consulted frequently with its members.

C21. The Board deliberated issues in Statement 123, including the information received in the letters of comment on the Invitation to Comment, at 39 public meetings from March 2003 through March 2004. One of those meetings, held in October 2003, was a joint meeting of the FASB and the IASB. Additionally, the Board received 134 unsolicited letters of comment from various constituents during the deliberative process leading to the Exposure Draft that led to this Statement. Those respondents commented on various aspects of share-based payment and this project.

C22. During the fourth quarter of 2003, the Board conducted field visits related to the Exposure Draft that led to this Statement with various enterprises selected to achieve a broad coverage of constituent enterprises. Field visit participants included preparers of financial statements, employee benefit consultants, and auditors. Other cost-benefit procedures were performed and are described in paragraphs B270–B280.

C23. On March 31, 2004, the Board issued an FASB Exposure Draft, *Share-Based Payment,* with a comment period ending in June 2004. The Board received 14,239 comment letters in response to the 2004 Exposure Draft. In June 2004, the Board held four public roundtable meetings in California and Connecticut. Representatives from 73 organizations participated in those meetings.

C24. During the 108th Congress, several legislative proposals were introduced relating to the accounting for employee share options. On July 20, 2004, the United States House of Representatives passed H.R. 3574, the "Stock Option Accounting Reform Act." The Act's provisions prescribed detailed accounting guidance to be followed only for the chief executive officer and four other most highly compensated employees. On September 7, 2004, H.R. 3574 was referred to the Committee on Banking, Housing, and Urban Affairs of the United States Senate. The United States Senate did not take any action on H.R. 3574 or a similar companion bill, S. 1890, the "Stock Option Accounting Reform Act," before the adjournment of the 108th Congress.

C25. In May 2004, the FASB Small Business Advisory Committee met in Connecticut to discuss, among other things, matters related to the accounting for share-based compensation. During that meeting, committee members indicated that only a small percentage of small businesses issue share options, but they noted that behavior changes if the business plans to have an initial public offering. In August 2004, the Board undertook additional cost-benefit procedures to obtain additional information related to the concerns of small businesses. Interviews were conducted with various constituents, selected to provide a broad coverage of concerns related to small businesses. Board members also met in both private and public sessions with representatives of small businesses, including the National Venture Capital Association and the AICPA's Technical Issues Committee.

C26. The Board redeliberated the issues in the 2004 Exposure Draft at 21 public meetings from August 2004 through December 2004. Appendix B discusses the basis for the Board's conclusions.

Appendix D

AMENDMENTS TO EXISTING PRONOUNCEMENTS

Amendments Made by Statement 123 Carried Forward in This Statement with Minor Changes

D1. FASB Technical Bulletin No. 82-2, *Accounting for the Conversion of Stock Options into Incentive Stock Options as a Result of the Economic Recovery Tax Act of 1981,* is superseded.

D2. FASB Statement No. 5, *Accounting for Contingencies,* is amended as follows: [Added text is underscored and deleted text is struck out.]

a. Paragraph 7:

> This Statement supersedes both *ARB No. 50* and Chapter 6, "Contingency Reserves," of *ARB No. 43.* The conditions for accrual of loss contingencies in paragraph 8 of this Statement do not amend any other present requirement in an Accounting Research Bulletin or Opinion of the Accounting Principles Board to accrue a particular type of loss or expense. Thus, for example, deferred compensation contracts and stock issued to employees are excluded from the scope of this Statement. Those matters are covered, respectively, in *APB Opinion No. 12,* "Omnibus Opinion—1967," paragraphs 6–8, and ~~APB Opinion No. 25, "Accounting for Stock Issued to Employees"~~FASB Statement No. 123 (revised 2004), *Share-Based Payment.* Accounting for other employment-related costs is also excluded from the scope of this Statement except for postemployment benefits that become subject to this Statement through application of FASB Statement No. 112, *Employers' Accounting for Postemployment Benefits.*

D3. FASB Statement No. 43, *Accounting for Compensated Absences,* is amended as follows:

a. Paragraph 2(d), as amended by FASB Statement No 112, *Employers' Accounting for Postemployment Benefits:*

> Stock compensation plans that are addressed by ~~APB Opinion No. 25, "Accounting for Stock Issued to Employees"~~FASB Statement No. 123 (revised 2004), *Share-Based Payment.*

D4. FASB Statement No. 107, *Disclosures about Fair Value of Financial Instruments,* is amended as follows:

a. Paragraph 8(a), as amended by Statement 112:

> Employers' and plans' obligations for pension benefits, other postretirement benefits including health care and life insurance benefits, postemployment benefits, employee stock option and stock purchase plans, and other forms of deferred compensation arrangements, as defined in FASB Statements No. 35, *Accounting and Reporting by Defined Benefit Pension Plans,* No. 87, *Employers' Accounting for Pensions,* No. 106, *Employers' Accounting for Postretirement Benefits Other Than Pensions,* No. 112, *Employers' Accounting for Postemployment Benefits,* No. 123 (revised 2004), *Share-Based Payment,* and No. 43, *Accounting for Compensation Absences,* and ~~APB Opinions No. 25, *Accounting for Stock Issued to Employees,* and No. 12~~APB Opinion No. 12, *Omnibus Opinion—1967.*

D5. FASB Statement No. 112, *Employers' Accounting for Postemployment Benefits,* is amended as follows:

a. Paragraph 5(d):

> Stock compensation plans that are addressed by ~~APB Opinion No. 25, *Accounting for Stock Issued to Employees*~~FASB Statement No. 123 (revised 2004), *Share-Based Payment.*

Amendments to Existing Pronouncements

D6. This Statement replaces FASB Statement No. 123, *Accounting for Stock-Based Compensation.*

D7. This Statement supersedes APB Opinion No. 25, *Accounting for Stock Issued to Employees,* and the following related interpretations of Opinion 25:

a. AICPA Accounting Interpretation 1 of APB Opinion No. 25

b. FASB Interpretation No. 28, *Accounting for Stock Appreciation Rights and Other Variable Stock Option or Award Plans*

c. FASB Interpretation No. 38, *Determining the Measurement Date for Stock Option, Purchase, and Award Plans Involving Junior Stock*

d. FASB Interpretation No. 44, *Accounting for Certain Transactions involving Stock Compensation.*

D8. This Statement supersedes FASB Statement No. 148, *Accounting for Stock-Based Compensation—Transition and Disclosure.*

D9. All references to FASB Statement No. 123, *Accounting for Stock-Based Compensation,* are replaced by *FASB Statement No. 123 (revised 2004), Share-Based Payment.* All references to Statement 123 are replaced by *Statement 123(R).*

D10. This Statement supersedes ARB No. 43, Chapter 13B, "Compensation Involved in Stock Option and Stock Purchase Plans."

D11. APB Opinion No. 28, *Interim Financial Reporting,* is amended as follows:

a. Paragraph 30(j) and its related footnote 8, added by Statement 148:

> ~~The following information about stock-based employee compensation costs, disclosed prominently and in tabular form for all periods presented pursuant to the provisions of FASB Statement No. 148, *Accounting for Stock-Based Compensation-Transition and Disclosure,* if awards of stock-based employee compensation were outstanding and accounted for under the intrinsic value method of Opinion 25 for any period for which an income statement is presented:~~
>
> ~~(1) Net income and basic and diluted earnings per share as reported~~
> ~~(2) The stock-based employee compensation cost, net of related tax effects, included in the determination of net income as reported~~
> ~~(3) The stock-based employee compensation cost, net of related tax effects, that would have been included in the determination of net income if the fair value based method had been applied to all awards[8]~~

(4) Pro forma net income as if the fair value based method had been applied to all awards

(5) Pro forma basic and diluted earnings per share as if the fair value based method had been applied to all awards.

[8]For purposes of applying the guidance in this subparagraph, *all awards* refers to awards granted, modified, or settled in fiscal periods beginning after December 15, 1994—that is, awards for which the grant date fair value was required to be measured under FASB Statement No. 123, *Accounting for Stock-Based Compensation.*

D12. APB Opinion No. 29, *Accounting for Nonmonetary Transactions,* is amended as follows:

a. Footnote 4, as amended by Statement 123:

FASB Statement No. 123 (revised 2004), *Accounting for Stock-Based Compensation Share-Based Payment,* applies to all transactions in which an entity acquires goods or services by issuing its shares or other equity instruments (except for equity instruments held by an employee stock ownership plan) or by incurring liabilities to the supplier (a) in amounts based, at least in part, on the price of the entity's common stockshares or other equity instruments: or (b) that require or may require settlement by issuance of the entity's shares or other equity instruments.

D13. FASB Statement No. 109, *Accounting for Income Taxes,* is amended as follows:

a. Paragraph 36(e), as amended by Statement 123:

Expenses for employee stockshare options recognized differently for financial reporting and tax purposes (refer to paragraphs 41–44 58–63 of FASB Statement No. 123 (revised 2004), *Accounting for Stock-Based CompensationShare-Based Payment and paragraph 17 of APB Opinion No. 25, Accounting for Stock Issued to Employees*).

D14. FASB Statement No. 128, *Earnings per Share,* is amended as follows:

a. Paragraph 20, the heading preceding it, and its related footnote 12:

Stock-based compensation arrangements **Share-based payment arrangements**

Fixed awards and nonvested stockAwards of

share options and nonvested shares (as defined in FASB Statement No. 123 (revised 2004), *Accounting for Stock-Based Compensation Share-Based Payment*) to be issued to an employee[12] under a stockshare-based compensation arrangement are considered options for purposes of computing diluted EPS. Such stockshare-based awards shall be considered to be outstanding as of the grant date for purposes of computing diluted EPS even though their exercise may be contingent upon vesting. Those stockshare-based awards are included in the diluted EPS computation even if the employee may not receive (or be able to sell) the stock until some future date. Accordingly, all shares to be issued shall be included in computing diluted EPS if the effect is dilutive. The dilutive effect of stockshare-based compensation arrangements shall be computed using the treasury stock method. If the equity share options or other equity instruments are outstanding for only part of a stock based awards were granted during the period, the shares issuable shall must be weighted to reflect the portion of the period during which equity instruments awards were outstanding.

[12]The provisions in paragraphs 20–23 also apply to stockshare-based awards issued to other than employees in exchange for goods and services.

b. Paragraph 21 and its related footnote 13:

In applying the treasury stock method described in paragraph 17, the assumed proceeds shall be the sum of (a) the amount, if any, the employee must pay upon exercise, (b) the amount of compensation cost attributed to future services and not yet recognized,[13] and (c) the amount of excess tax benefits (both deferred and current), if any, that would be credited to additional paid-in capital assuming exercise of the options. Assumed proceeds shall not include compensation ascribed to past services. The excess tax benefit is the amount resulting from a tax deduction for compensation in excess of compensation expense recognized for financial reporting purposes. That deduction arises from an increase in the market price of the stock under option between the measurement date and the date at which the compensation deduction for income tax purposes is determinable. The amount of the tax benefit shall be determined by a "with-and-without" computation. Paragraph 63 of Statement 123(R) states that the amount deductible on an employer's tax return may be less than the cumulative compensation cost recognized for financial reporting purposes. If the deferred tax asset related to that resulting difference would be deducted from additional paid-in capital (or its equivalent) pursuant to that paragraph assuming exercise of the options, that amount shall be treated as a reduction of assumed proceeds.~~Paragraph 17 of APB Opinion No. 25, *Accounting for Stock Issued to Employees,* states that in some instances the tax deduction for compensation may be less than the compensation expense recognized for financial reporting purposes. If the resulting difference in income tax will be deducted from capital in accordance with that paragraph, such taxes to be deducted from capital shall be treated as a reduction of assumed proceeds.~~

---

[13]This provision applies only to those ~~stock~~share-based awards for which compensation cost will be recognized in the financial statements in accordance with ~~APB Opinion No. 25, *Accounting for Stock Issued to Employees,* or~~ Statement 123(R).

c. Paragraph 23:

Awards with a market condition, a ~~P~~performance condition, or any combination thereof ~~awards~~ (as defined in Statement 123(R)) shall be included in diluted EPS pursuant to the contingent share provisions in paragraphs 30–35 of this Statement.~~As discussed in paragraph 26 of Statement 123, targeted stock price options are not considered to be a performance award. However, because options with a target stock price have a market price contingency, the contingent share provisions of this Statement shall be applied in determining whether those options are included in the computation of diluted EPS.~~

d. Illustration 8—"Application of the Treasury Stock Method for Stock Appreciation Rights and Other Variable Stock Option Award Plans," paragraphs 157–159, is deleted because the accounting illustrated is based on Opinion 25 and its related interpretations, which are superseded by this Statement, and replaced with the following illustration:

Illustration 8—Application of the Treasury Stock Method to a Share-Based Payment Arrangement

157. Under this Statement options to be settled in stock are potential common shares for purposes of earnings per share computations. In applying the treasury stock method, all dilutive potential common shares, regardless of whether they are exercisable, are treated as if they had been exercised. The treasury stock method assumes that the proceeds upon exercise are used to repurchase the entity's stock, reducing the number of shares to be added to outstanding common stock in computing earnings per share. The proceeds assumed to be received upon exercise include the exercise price that the employee pays, the amount of compensation cost measured and attributed to future services but not yet recognized, and the amount of any tax benefits upon assumed exercise that would be credited to additional paid-in-capital. If the deferred tax asset related to that resulting difference would be deducted from additional paid-in capital (or its equivalent) assuming exercise of the options, that amount shall be treated as a reduction of assumed proceeds.

158. Under paragraph 43 of Statement 123(R), the effect of forfeitures is taken into account by recognizing compensation cost only for those instruments for which the requisite service has been rendered, and no compensation cost is recognized for instruments that employees forfeit because a service condition or a performance condition is not satisfied. The following example illustrates the application of the treasury stock method when share options are forfeited.

159. Entity L adopted a share option plan on January 1, 20X7, and granted 900,000 at-the-money share options with an exercise price of $30.[a] All share options vest at the end of three years (cliff vesting). At the grant date, Entity L assumes an annual forfeiture rate of 3 percent and therefore expects to receive the requisite service for 821,406 [900,000 × (.97³)] share options. On January 1, 20X7, the fair value of each share option granted is $14.69. Employees forfeited 15,000 stock options ratably during 20X7. The average stock

price during 20X7 is $44. Net income for the period is $97,385,602 (inclusive of $2,614,398 of share-based compensation, net of income taxes of $1,407,753). Entity L's tax rate is 35 percent. For the year ended December 31, 20X7, there are 25,000,000 weighted-average common shares outstanding. Entity L has sufficient previously recognized excess tax benefits in additional paid-in capi- tal from prior share-based payment arrangements to offset any write-off of deferred tax assets associated with its grant of share options on January 1, 20X7. All share options are the type that upon exercise give rise to deductible compensation cost for income tax purposes.

Computation of Basic EPS for the Year Ended December 31, 20X7:

Net income[b]	$ 97,385,602
Weighted-average common shares outstanding	25,000,000
Basic earnings per share	$ 3.90

Computation of assumed proceeds for diluted earnings per share:

Amount employees would pay if the weighted-average number of options outstanding were exercised using the average exercise price (892,500[c] × $30)	$ 26,775,000
Average unrecognized compensation cost in 20X7 (see computation)	10,944,050
Tax benefit deficiency that would be offset in paid-in capital (see computation)	(215,539)
Assumed proceeds	$ 37,503,511

Computation of average unrecognized compensation cost in 20X7:

Beginning of period

Unrecognized compensation cost (900,000 × $14.69)	$ 13,221,000

End of the period

Beginning of period	$ 13,221,000	
Annual compensation cost recognized during 20X7, based on estimated forfeitures	(4,022,151)[b]	
Annual compensation cost not recognized during the period related to outstanding options at December 31, 20X7, for which the requisite service is not expected to be rendered	(311,399)[d]	
Total compensation cost of actual forfeited options	(220,350)[e]	
Total unrecognized compensation cost, end of the period, based on actual forfeitures		8,667,100
Subtotal		21,888,100
Average total unrecognized compensation, based on actual forfeitures		$ 10,944,050

Computation of tax benefit:

Total compensation cost of average outstanding options	$ 13,110,825[f]
Intrinsic value of average outstanding options for the year ended December 31, 20X7 [892,500 × ($44 – $30)]	(12,495,000)
Excess of total compensation cost over estimated tax deduction	615,825
Tax benefit deficiency ($615,825 × .35)	$ 215,539

Assumed repurchase of shares:

Repurchase shares at average market price during the year ($37,503,511 ÷ $44)	852,353
Incremental shares (892,500 – 852,353)	40,147

Computation of Diluted EPS for the Year Ended December 31, 20X7:

Net income	$ 97,385,602
Weighted-average common shares outstanding	25,000,000
Incremental shares	40,147
Total shares outstanding	25,040,147
Diluted earnings per share	$ 3.89

---

[a]This guidance also applies if the service inception date precedes the grant date.

[b]Pre-tax annual share-based compensation cost is $4,022,151 [(821,406 × $14.69) ÷ 3]. After-tax share-based compensation cost included in net income is $2,614,398 ($4,022,151 – $1,407,753). ($4,022,151 × .35) = $1,407,753.

[c]Share options granted at the beginning of the year plus share options outstanding at the end of the year divided by two equals the weighted-average number of share options outstanding in 20X7: [(900,000 + 885,000) ÷ 2] = 892,500. This example assumes that forfeitures occurred ratably throughout 20X7.

[d]885,000 (options outstanding at December 31, 20X7) – 821,406 (options for which the requisite service is expected to be rendered) = 63,594. 63,594 options × $14.69 (grant-date fair value per option) = $934,196 (total fair value). $934,196 ÷ 3 = $311,399 (annual share-based compensation cost).

[e]15,000 (forfeited options) × $14.69 (grant-date fair value per option) = $220,350 (total fair value).

[f](892,500 × $14.69) = $13,110,825.

D15. FASB Statement No. 133, *Accounting for Derivative Instruments and Hedging Activities,* is amended as follows:

a. Paragraph 11(b):

Contracts issued by the entity that are subject to FASB Statement No. 123 (revised 2004), *Share-Based Payment*in connection with stock-based compensation arrangements addressed in FASB Statement No. 123, *Accounting for Stock-Based Compensation.* If any such contract ceases to be subject to Statement 123(R) in accordance with paragraph A231 of that Statement, the terms of that contract shall then be analyzed to determine whether the contract is subject to this Statement.

D16. FASB Statement No. 150, *Accounting for Certain Financial Instruments with Characteristics of both Liabilities and Equity,* is amended as follows:

a. Paragraph 17:

This Statement does not apply to obligations under stockshare-based compensation arrangements if those obligations are accounted for under APB Opinion No. 25, *Accounting for Stock Issued to Employees,* FASB Statement No. 123 (revised 2004), *Accounting for Stock-Based Compensation*Share-Based Payment, AICPA Statement of Position (SOP) 93-6, *Employers' Accounting for Employee Stock Ownership Plans,* or related guidance. However, this Statement does apply to a freestanding financial instrument that was issued under a ~~stock~~share-based compensation arrangement but is no longer subject to ~~Opinion 25,~~ Statement 123(R), SOP 93-6, or related guidance. For example, this Statement applies to mandatorily redeemable shares issued upon an employee's exercise of an employee ~~stock~~ share option.

b. Paragraph D1:

Nonpublic entity

Any entity other than one (a) whose equity securities trade in a public market either on a stock exchange (domestic or foreign) or in the over-the-counter market, including securities quoted only locally or regionally, (b) that makes a filing with a regulatory agency in preparation for the sale of any class of equity securities in a public market, or (c) that is controlled by an entity covered by (a) or (b). [Statement 123(R), paragraph ~~395~~E1]

D17. FASB Interpretation No. 46 (revised December 2003), *Consolidation of Variable Interest Entities,* is amended as follows:

a. Footnote 18:

The term *public entity* is defined in paragraph ~~395~~E1 of FASB Statement No. 123 (revised 2004), *~~Accounting for Stock-Based Compensation~~Share-Based Payment.*

b. Footnote 23:

The term *nonpublic entity* is defined in paragraph ~~395~~E1 of Statement 123(R).

D18. FASB Technical Bulletin No. 97-1, *Accounting under Statement 123 for Certain Employee Stock Purchase Plans with a Look-Back Option,* is amended as follows:

a. The Reference:

FASB Statement No. 123 (revised 2004), *~~Accounting for Stock-Based Compensation~~ Share-Based Payment,* paragraphs 12–14 and~~23 and 24, 232–242~~A211–A219~~348–356.~~

b. Paragraph 1:

The accounting guidance in this Technical Bulletin addresses the accounting under Statement 123(R) for certain employee stock purchase plans (ESPPs) with a look-back option. An example of a *look-back option* is a provision in an ESPP that establishes the purchase price as an amount based on the lesser of the stock's market price at the grant date or its market price at the exercise (or purchase) date. This Technical Bulletin does not address ~~the accounting for those plans under APB Opinion No. 25, *Accounting for Stock Issued to Employees*. It also does not address~~ the effect of those plans on earnings per share calculations.[1]

c. Paragraph 2:

Paragraph 12~~23~~ of Statement 123(R) establishes the criteria under which an ESPP should be evaluated to determine whether it qualifies for noncompensatory treatment. If a plan does not meet *all* of those criteria, the fair value method of accounting must be used. ~~Paragraph 24 notes that a plan provision such as a look-back option is one feature that causes an ESPP to be considered compensatory. Paragraph 239 explains in part the Board's rationale:~~

~~The Board considered respondents' requests that broad-based plans with look-back options be considered noncompensatory and noted that a look-back option can have substantial value because it enables the employee to purchase the stock for an amount that could be significantly less than the market price at date of purchase. A look-back option is not an essential element of a broad-based plan aimed at promoting broad employee stock ownership; a purchase discount also provides inducement for participation. The Board concluded that broad-based plans that contain look-back options cannot be treated as noncompensatory.~~

d. All references to *Illustration 9* or *Illustration 9 of Appendix B* of Statement 123 in paragraphs 3, 5, 6, 9, 10, 12–15, and 21 and footnote 7 are replaced by *Illustration 19* of Statement 123(R).

e. Footnote 2:

> The examples in Illustration 9-19 of Statement 123(R) and this Technical Bulletin illustrate the use of the Black-Scholes-Merton option-pricing modelformula (a closed-form model). It also may be acceptable to use other valuationa binomial option pricing models (for example, a lattice model) to value an award under an ESPP with a look-back option.

f. Paragraph 7:

> Although many ESPPs with a look-back option initially limit the maximum number of shares of stock that the employee is permitted to purchase under the plan (Type A plans), other ESPPs (Type B plans) do not fix the number of shares that the employee is permitted to purchase if the exercise date stock price is lower than the grant date stock price. In effect, an ESPP that does not fix the number of shares that may be purchased has guaranteed that the employee can always receive the value associated with *at least* 15 percent of the stock price at the grant date (the employee can receive much more than 15 percent of the grant date value of the stock if the stock appreciates during the look-back period). That provision provides the employee with the equivalent of a put option on 15 percent of the shares with an exercise price equal to the stock price at the grant date. In contrast, an employee who participates in a Type A plan is only guaranteed 15 percent of *the lower of* the stock price as of the grant date or the exercise date, which is the equivalent of a call option on 85 percent of the shares (as described more fully in paragraph 352A215 of Statement 123(R)). A participant in a Type B plan receives the equivalent of both a put option and a call option.

g. Paragraph 8:

> The following example illustrates that fundamental difference.[2a] [*Note:* the remainder of this paragraph is unchanged.]

[2a] The assumptions used for the numerical calculations in this Technical Bulletin are not intended to be the same as those in Illustration 19 of Statement 123(R). Rather, they are independent and designed to illustrate how the component measurement approach in Illustration 19 would be modified to reflect various features of employee stock purchase plans.

h. Paragraph 17:

> Likewise, although not a change to the terms of the ESPP, an election by an employee to increase withholding amounts (or percentages) for future services (Type F through Type H plans) is a modification of the terms of the award to that employee, which, in substance, is similar to an exchange of the original award for a new award with different terms. Accordingly, the fair value of an award under an ESPP with variable withholdings should be determined at the grant date (using the Type A, Type B, or Type C measurement approach, as applicable) based on the estimated amounts (or percentages) that a participating employee initially elects to withhold under the terms of the plan. Subsequent to the grant date (except as noted in paragraph 23), any increases in withholding amounts (or percentages) for future services should be accounted for as a plan modification in accordance with the guidance in paragraph 3551 of Statement 123(R).

i. Paragraph 18:

> Paragraph 3551 of Statement 123(R) explains the approach that should be used to account for a modification of the terms of an award as follows:

>> A **modification** of the terms or conditions of an equity award that makes it more valuable shall be treated as an exchange of the original award for a new award.[26] In substance, the entity repurchases the original instrument by issuing a new instrument of equal or greater value, incurring additional compensation cost for that any incremental value. The incremental value shall be measured by the difference between (a) the fair value of the modified option determined in accordance with the provisions of this Statement and (b) the value of the old option immediately before its terms are modified, determined based on the shorter of (1) its

~~remaining expected life or (2) the ex-~~
~~pected life of the modified option.~~
The effects of a modification shall be
measured as follows:

a. Incremental compensation cost
shall be measured as the excess,
if any, of the fair value of the
modified award determined in
accordance with the provisions of
this Statement over the fair value
of the original award immediately before its terms are modified, measured based on the share
price and other pertinent factors
at that date.[27] The effect of the
modification on the number of instruments expected to vest also
shall be reflected in determining
incremental compensation cost.
The estimate at the modification
date of the portion of the award
expected to vest shall be subsequently adjusted, if necessary, in
accordance with para-
graphs 43–45 and other guidance
in Illustration 13 (para-
graphs A160–A170).
b. Total recognized compensation
cost for an equity award shall at
least equal the fair value of the
award at the grant date unless at
the date of the modification the
performance or service conditions of the original award are not
expected to be satisfied. Thus, the
total compensation cost measured at the date of a modification
shall be (1) the portion of the
grant-date fair value of the original award for which the requisite
service is expected to be rendered
(or has already been rendered) at
that date plus (2) the incremental
cost resulting from the modification. Compensation cost shall be
subsequently adjusted, if necessary, in accordance with
paragraphs 43–45 and other
guidance in Illustration 13 (paragraphs A160–A170).
c. A change in compensation cost
for an equity award measured at
intrinsic value in accordance with

paragraph 25 shall be measured
by comparing the intrinsic value
of the modified award, if any,
with the intrinsic value of the
original award, if any, immediately before the modification.

Illustrations 12–14 (paragraphs A149–A189) provide additional guidance on, and illustrate the
accounting for, modifications of both
vested and nonvested awards, including a modification that changes the
classification of the related financial
instruments from equity to liability or
vice versa, and modifications of vesting conditions. Illustration 22 (paragraphs A225–A232) provides additional guidance on accounting for
modifications of certain freestanding
financial instruments that initially
were subject to this Statement but
subsequently became subject to other
applicable GAAP.

---

[26]A modification of a liability award also is accounted for as the exchange of the original award
for a new award. However, because liability
awards are remeasured at their fair value (or intrinsic value for a nonpublic entity that elects that
method) at each reporting date, no special guidance is necessary in accounting for a modification
of a liability award that remains a liability after
the modification.
[27]As indicated in paragraph 23, footnote 13, references to *fair value* throughout paragraphs 24–85 of this Statement should be read
also to encompass *calculated value*.

j. Paragraph 20:

Any decreases in the withholding amounts
(or percentages) should be disregarded for
purposes of recognizing compensation cost
unless the employee services that were valued at the grant date will no longer be provided to the employer due to a termination.
However, no compensation cost should be
recognized for awards that an employee forfeits because of failure to satisfy a service requirement for vesting. The accounting for decreases in withholdings is consistent with the
requirement in paragraph ~~26~~43 of Statement 123(R) that the total amount of compensation cost that must be recognized for an
award is based on the number of instruments

~~that vest rather than the number of instruments that are either granted or exercised~~for which the requisite service has been rendered (that is, for which the requisite service period has been completed).

k. Paragraph 24 and its related footnote 13:

> In some circumstances, applying the measurement approaches described in this Technical Bulletin at the grant date may not be practicable for certain types of ESPPs. ~~For example, an entity may not have access at a reasonable cost to the modeling capabilities needed to determine the fair value of plans with features in addition to or different from those described in this Technical Bulletin.~~ If it is *not practicable* to reasonably estimate fair value at the grant date, the guidance in paragraph ~~22~~25 of Statement 123(R) would apply.[13] Paragraph 25 of Statement 123(R) states:

>> An equity instrument for which~~If~~ it is not possible to reasonably estimate the ~~fair value ~~of an option or other equity instrument at the grant date~~at the grant date shall be accounted for based on its intrinsic value, remeasured at each reporting date through the date of exercise or other settlement. T~~the final measure of compensation cost shall be the ~~fair~~intrinsic value of the instrument at the date it is settled ~~based on the stock price and other pertinent factors at the first date at which it is possible to reasonably estimate that value.~~ Compensation cost for each period until settlement shall be based on the change (or a portion of the change, depending on the percentage of the requisite service that has been rendered at the reporting date) in the intrinsic value of the instrument in each reporting period. The entity shall continue to use the intrinsic value method for those instruments even if it subsequently concludes that it is possible to reasonably estimate their fair value. ~~Generally, that is likely to be the date at which the number of shares to which an employee is entitled and the exercise price are determinable. Estimates of~~

~~compensation cost for periods during which it is not possible to determine fair value shall be based on the current intrinsic value of the award, determined in accordance with the terms that would apply if the option or similar instrument had been currently exercised.~~

---

[13]Paragraphs ~~22~~24 and 25 of Statement 123(R) addresses circumstances in which the complexity of the terms of an~~characteristics of the~~ instrument prevent grant date measurement using available ~~option-pricing models~~rather than circumstances in which an entity considers the amount of recordkeeping involved to be excessive.

Appendix E

GLOSSARY

E1. This appendix contains definitions of certain terms or phrases used in this Statement.

Blackout period
> A period of time during which exercise of an equity share option is contractually or legally prohibited.

Broker-assisted cashless exercise
> The simultaneous exercise by an employee of a share option and sale of the shares through a broker (commonly referred to as a *broker-assisted exercise*).

> Generally, under this method of exercise:

> a. The employee authorizes the exercise of an option and the immediate sale of the option shares in the open market.
> b. On the same day, the entity notifies the broker of the sale order.
> c. The broker executes the sale and notifies the entity of the sales price.
> d. The entity determines the minimum statutory tax-withholding requirements.
> e. By the settlement day (generally three days later), the entity delivers the stock certificates to the broker.
> f. On the settlement day, the broker makes payment to the entity for the exercise price and the minimum statutory withholding taxes and remits the balance of the net sales proceeds to the employee.

Calculated value

A measure of the value of a share option or similar instrument determined by substituting the historical volatility of an appropriate industry sector index for the expected volatility of a nonpublic entity's share price in an option-pricing model.

Closed-form model

A valuation model that uses an equation to produce an estimated fair value. The Black-Scholes-Merton formula is a closed-form model. In the context of option valuation, both closed-form models and lattice models are based on risk-neutral valuation and a contingent claims framework. The payoff of a contingent claim, and thus its value, depends on the value(s) of one or more other assets. The contingent claims framework is a valuation methodology that explicitly recognizes that dependency and values the contingent claim as a function of the value of the underlying asset(s). One application of that methodology is risk-neutral valuation in which the contingent claim can be replicated by a combination of the underlying asset and a risk-free bond. If that replication is possible, the value of the contingent claim can be determined without estimating the expected returns on the underlying asset. The Black-Scholes-Merton formula is a special case of that replication.

Combination award

An award with two or more separate components, each of which can be separately exercised. Each component of the award is actually a separate award, and compensation cost is measured and recognized for each component.

Cross-volatility

A measure of the relationship between the volatilities of the prices of two assets taking into account the correlation between movements in the prices of the assets. (Refer to the definition of **volatility.**)

Derived service period

A service period for an award with a market condition that is inferred from the application of certain valuation techniques used to estimate fair value. For example, the derived service period for an award of share options that the employee can exercise only if the share price increases by 25 percent at any time during a 5-year period can be inferred from certain valuation techniques. In a lattice model, that derived service period represents the duration of the median of the distribution of share price paths on which the market condition is satisfied. That median is the middle share price path (the midpoint of the distribution of paths) on which the market condition is satisfied. The duration is the period of time from the service inception date to the expected date of satisfaction (as inferred from the valuation technique). If the derived service period is three years, the estimated requisite service period is three years and all compensation cost would be recognized over that period, unless the market condition was satisfied at an earlier date.[170] Further, an award of fully vested, deep out-of-the-money share options has a derived service period that must be determined from the valuation techniques used to estimate fair value. (Refer to the definitions of **explicit service period, implicit service period,** and **requisite service period.**)

Economic interest in an entity

Any type or form of pecuniary interest or arrangement that an entity could issue or be a party to, including equity securities; financial instruments with characteristics of equity, liabilities, or both; long-term debt and other debt-financing arrangements; leases; and contractual arrangements such as management contracts, service contracts, or intellectual property licenses.

Employee

An individual over whom the grantor of a share-based compensation award exercises or has the right to exercise sufficient control to establish an employer-employee relationship based on common law as illustrated in case law and currently under U.S. Internal Revenue Service Revenue Ruling 87-41.[171] Accordingly, a grantee meets the definition of an employee if the grantor consistently represents that individual to be an employee under common law. The definition of an employee for payroll tax purposes under the U.S. Internal Revenue Code includes common law employees. Accordingly, a grantor that classifies

---

[170]Compensation cost would not be recognized beyond three years even if after the grant date the entity determines that it is not probable that the market condition will be satisfied within that period.

[171]A reporting entity based in a foreign jurisdiction would determine whether an employee-employer relationship exists based on the pertinent laws of that jurisdiction.

a grantee potentially subject to U.S. payroll taxes as an employee for purposes of applying this Statement also must represent that individual as an employee for payroll tax purposes (unless the grantee is a leased employee as described below). A grantee does not meet the definition of an employee for purposes of this Statement solely because the grantor represents that individual as an employee for some, but not all, purposes. For example, a requirement or decision to classify a grantee as an employee for U.S. payroll tax purposes does not, by itself, indicate that the grantee is an employee for purposes of this Statement because the grantee also must be an employee of the grantor under common law.

A leased individual is deemed to be an employee of the lessee for purposes of this Statement if all of the following requirements are met:

a. The leased individual qualifies as a common law employee of the lessee, and the lessor is contractually required to remit payroll taxes on the compensation paid to the leased individual for the services provided to the lessee.
b. The lessor and lessee agree in writing to all of the following conditions related to the leased individual:
1. The lessee has the exclusive right to grant stock compensation to the individual for the employee service to the lessee.
2. The lessee has a right to hire, fire, and control the activities of the individual. (The lessor also may have that right.)
3. The lessee has the exclusive right to determine the economic value of the services performed by the individual (including wages and the number of units and value of stock compensation granted).
4. The individual has the ability to participate in the lessee's employee benefit plans, if any, on the same basis as other comparable employees of the lessee.
5. The lessee agrees to and remits to the lessor funds sufficient to cover the complete compensation, including all payroll taxes, of the individual on or before a contractually agreed upon date or dates.

A nonemployee director does not satisfy this definition of employee. Nevertheless, for purposes of this Statement, nonemployee directors acting in their role as members of a board of directors are treated as employees if those directors were (a) elected by the employer's shareholders or (b) appointed to a board position that will be filled by shareholder election when the existing term expires. However, that requirement applies only to awards granted to nonemployee directors for their services as directors. Awards granted to those individuals for other services shall be accounted for as awards to nonemployees for purposes of this Statement.

Employee share ownership plan
An employee benefit plan that is described by the Employment Retirement Income Act of 1974 and the Internal Revenue Code of 1986 as a stock bonus plan, or combination stock bonus and money purchase pension plan, designed to invest primarily in employer stock.

Equity restructuring
A nonreciprocal transaction between an entity and its shareholders that causes the per-share fair value of the shares underlying an option or similar award to change, such as a stock dividend, stock split, spinoff, rights offering, or recapitalization through a large, nonrecurring cash dividend.

Excess tax benefit
The realized tax benefit related to the amount (caused by changes in the fair value of the entity's shares after the **measurement date** for financial reporting) of deductible compensation cost reported on an employer's tax return for equity instruments in excess of the compensation cost for those instruments recognized for financial reporting purposes.

Explicit service period
A service period that is explicitly stated in the terms of a share-based payment award. For example, an award stating that it vests after three years of continuous employee service from a given date (usually the grant date) has an explicit service period of three years. (Refer to **derived service period, implicit service period,** and **requisite service period.**)

Fair value
The amount at which an asset (or liability) could be bought (or incurred) or sold (or settled) in a current transaction between willing parties, that is, other than in a forced or liquidation sale.

Freestanding financial instrument

A financial instrument that is entered into separately and apart from any of the entity's other financial instruments or equity transactions or that is entered into in conjunction with some other transaction and is legally detachable and separately exercisable.

Grant date

The date at which an employer and an employee reach a mutual understanding of the key terms and conditions of a share-based payment award. The employer becomes contingently obligated on the grant date to issue equity instruments or transfer assets to an employee who renders the requisite service. Awards made under an arrangement that is subject to shareholder approval are not deemed to be granted until that approval is obtained unless approval is essentially a formality (or perfunctory), for example, if management and the members of the board of directors control enough votes to approve the arrangement. Similarly, individual awards that are subject to approval by the board of directors, management, or both are not deemed to be granted until all such approvals are obtained. The grant date for an award of equity instruments is the date that an employee begins to benefit from, or be adversely affected by, subsequent changes in the price of the employer's equity shares. (Refer to the definition of **service inception date.**)

Implicit service period

A service period that is not explicitly stated in the terms of a share-based payment award but that may be inferred from an analysis of those terms and other facts and circumstances. For instance, if an award of share options vests upon the completion of a new product design and it is probable that the design will be completed in 18 months, the implicit service period is 18 months. (Refer to **derived service period, explicit service period,** and **requisite service period.**)

Intrinsic value

The amount by which the fair value of the underlying stock exceeds the exercise price of an option. For example, an option with an exercise price of $20 on a stock whose current market price is $25 has an intrinsic value of $5. (A non-vested share may be described as an option on that share with an exercise price of zero. Thus, the fair value of a share is the same as the intrinsic value of such an option on that share.)

Issued, issuance, or **issuing** of an equity instrument

An equity instrument is issued when the issuing entity receives the agreed-upon consideration, which may be cash, an enforceable right to receive cash or another financial instrument, goods, or services. An entity may conditionally transfer an equity instrument to another party under an arrangement that permits that party to choose at a later date or for a specified time whether to deliver the consideration or to forfeit the right to the conditionally transferred instrument with no further obligation. In that situation, the equity instrument is not *issued* until the issuing entity has received the consideration. For that reason, this Statement does not use the term *issued* for the grant of stock options or other equity instruments subject to vesting conditions.

Lattice model

A model that produces an estimated fair value based on the assumed changes in prices of a financial instrument over successive periods of time. The binomial model is an example of a lattice model. In each time period, the model assumes that at least two price movements are possible. The lattice represents the evolution of the value of either a financial instrument or a market variable for the purpose of valuing a financial instrument. In this context, a lattice model is based on risk-neutral valuation and a contingent claims framework. (Refer to **closed-form model** for an explanation of the terms *risk-neutral valuation* and *contingent claims framework*.)

Market condition

A condition affecting the exercise price, exercisability, or other pertinent factors used in determining the fair value of an award under a share-based payment arrangement that relates to the achievement of (a) a specified price of the issuer's shares or a specified amount of intrinsic value indexed solely to the issuer's shares or (b) a specified price of the issuer's shares in terms of a similar[172] (or index of similar) equity security (securities).

---

[172]The term *similar* as used in this definition refers to an equity security of another entity that has the same type of residual rights. For example, common stock of one entity generally would be similar to the common stock of another entity for this purpose.

Measurement date

The date at which the equity share price and other pertinent factors, such as expected volatility, that enter into measurement of the total recognized amount of compensation cost for an award of share-based payment are fixed.

Modification

A change in any of the terms or conditions of a share-based payment award.

Nonpublic entity

Any entity other than one (a) whose equity securities trade in a public market either on a stock exchange (domestic or foreign) or in the over-the-counter market, including securities quoted only locally or regionally, (b) that makes a filing with a regulatory agency in preparation for the sale of any class of equity securities in a public market, or (c) that is controlled by an entity covered by (a) or (b). An entity that has only debt securities trading in a public market (or that has made a filing with a regulatory agency in preparation to trade only debt securities) is a nonpublic entity for purposes of this Statement.

Nonvested shares

Shares that an entity has not yet issued because the agreed-upon consideration, such as employee services, has not yet been received. Nonvested shares cannot be sold. The restriction on sale of nonvested shares is due to the forfeitability of the shares if specified events occur (or do not occur).

Performance condition

A condition affecting the vesting, exercisability, exercise price, or other pertinent factors used in determining the fair value of an award that relates to both (a) an employee's rendering service for a specified (either explicitly or implicitly) period of time and (b) achieving a specified performance target that is defined solely by reference to the employer's own operations (or activities). Attaining a specified growth rate in return on assets, obtaining regulatory approval to market a specified product, selling shares in an initial public offering or other financing event, and a change in control are examples of performance conditions for purposes of this Statement. A performance target also may be defined by reference to the same performance measure of another entity or group of entities. For example, attaining a growth rate in earnings per share that exceeds the average growth rate in earnings per share of other entities in the same industry is a performance condition for purposes of this Statement. A performance target might pertain either to the performance of the enterprise as a whole or to some part of the enterprise, such as a division or an individual employee.

Public entity

An entity (a) with equity securities that trade in a public market, which may be either a stock exchange (domestic or foreign) or an over-the-counter market, including securities quoted only locally or regionally, (b) that makes a filing with a regulatory agency in preparation for the sale of any class of equity securities in a public market, or (c) that is controlled by an entity covered by (a) or (b). That is, a subsidiary of a public entity is itself a public entity. An entity that has only debt securities trading in a public market (or that has made a filing with a regulatory agency in preparation to trade only debt securities) is not a public entity for purposes of this Statement.

Related party

An affiliate of the reporting entity; another entity for which the reporting entity's investments in their equity securities would, absent the election of the fair value option under FASB Statement No. 159, *The Fair Value Option for Financial Assets and Financial Liabilities,* be required to be accounted for by the equity method; trusts for the benefit of employees, such as pension and profit-sharing trusts that are managed by or under the trusteeship of management; principal owners and management of the entity; members of the immediate families of principal owners of the entity and its management; and other parties with which the entity may deal if one party controls or can significantly influence the management or operating policies of the other to an extent that one of the transacting parties might be prevented from fully pursuing its own separate interests. Another party also is a related party if it can significantly influence the management or operating policies of the transacting parties or if it has an ownership interest in one of the transacting parties and can significantly influence the other to an extent that one or more of the transacting parties might be prevented from fully pursuing its own separate interests. This definition is the same as the definition of *related parties* in paragraph 24 of FASB Statement No. 57, *Related Party Disclosures.*

Reload feature and **reload option**

A reload feature provides for automatic grants of additional options whenever an employee exercises previously granted options using the entity's shares, rather than cash, to satisfy the exercise price. At the time of exercise using shares, the employee is automatically granted a new option, called a *reload option*, for the shares used to exercise the previous option.

Replacement award

An award of share-based compensation that is granted (or offered to grant) concurrently with the cancellation of another award.

Requisite service period (and **requisite service**)

The period or periods during which an employee is required to provide service in exchange for an award under a share-based payment arrangement. The service that an employee is required to render during that period is referred to as the *requisite service*. The requisite service period for an award that has only a service condition is presumed to be the vesting period, unless there is clear evidence to the contrary. If an award requires future service for vesting, the entity cannot define a prior period as the requisite service period. Requisite service periods may be explicit, implicit, or derived, depending on the terms of the share-based payment award.

Restricted share

A share for which sale is contractually or governmentally prohibited for a specified period of time. Most grants of shares to employees are better termed *nonvested shares* because the limitation on sale stems solely from the forfeitability of the shares before employees have satisfied the necessary service or performance condition(s) to earn the rights to the shares. Restricted shares issued for consideration other than employee services, on the other hand, are fully paid for immediately. For those shares, there is no period analogous to a requisite service period during which the issuer is unilaterally obligated to issue shares when the purchaser pays for those shares, but the purchaser is not obligated to buy the shares. This Statement uses the term *restricted shares* to refer only to fully vested and outstanding shares whose sale is contractually or governmentally prohibited for

a specified period of time.[173] (Refer to the definition of **nonvested shares.**)

Restriction

A contractual or governmental provision that prohibits sale (or substantive sale by using derivatives or other means to effectively terminate the risk of future changes in the share price) of an equity instrument for a specified period of time.

Service condition

A condition affecting the vesting, exercisability, exercise price, or other pertinent factors used in determining the fair value of an award that depends solely on an employee rendering service to the employer for the requisite service period. A condition that results in the acceleration of vesting in the event of an employee's death, disability, or termination without cause is a service condition.

Service inception date

The date at which the requisite service period begins. The service inception date usually is the grant date, but the service inception date may differ from the grant date (refer to Illustration 3, paragraphs A79–A85).

Settle, settled, or **settlement** of an award

An action or event that irrevocably extinguishes the issuing entity's obligation under a share-based payment award. Transactions and events that constitute settlements include (a) exercise of a share option or lapse of an option at the end of its contractual term, (b) vesting of shares, (c) forfeiture of shares or share options due to failure to satisfy a vesting condition, and (d) an entity's repurchase of instruments in exchange for assets or for fully vested and transferable equity instruments. The vesting of a share option is not a settlement as that term is used in this Statement because the entity remains obligated to issue shares upon exercise of the option.

Share option

A contract that gives the holder the right, but not the obligation, either to purchase (to call) or to sell (to put) a certain number of shares at a predetermined price for a specified period of time. Most share options granted to employees under

---

[173]Vested equity instruments that are transferable to an employee's immediate family members or to a trust that benefits only those family members are restricted if the transferred instruments retain the same prohibition on sale to third parties.

share-based compensation arrangements are call options, but some may be put options.

Share unit

A contract under which the holder has the right to convert each unit into a specified number of shares of the issuing entity.

Share-based payment (or compensation) arrangement

An arrangement under which (a) one or more suppliers of goods or services (including employees) receive awards of equity shares, equity share options, or other equity instruments or (b) the entity incurs liabilities to suppliers (1) in amounts based, at least in part,[174] on the price of the entity's shares or other equity instruments or (2) that require or may require settlement by issuance of the entity's shares. For purposes of this Statement, the term *shares* includes various forms of ownership interest that may not take the legal form of securities (for example, partnership interests), as well as other interests, including those that are liabilities in substance but not in form. *Equity shares* refers only to shares that are accounted for as equity.

Share-based payment (or compensation) transaction

A transaction under a share-based payment arrangement, including a transaction in which an entity acquires goods or services because related parties or other holders of economic interests in that entity awards a share-based payment to an employee or other supplier of goods or services for the entity's benefit.

Short-term inducement

An offer by the entity that would result in modification of an award to which an award holder may subscribe for a limited period of time.

Small business issuer

A public entity that is an SEC registrant that files as a small business issuer under the Securities Act of 1933 or the Securities Exchange Act of 1934. At the date this Statement was issued, a *small business issuer* was defined as an entity that meets all of the following criteria:

a. It has revenues of less than $25 million.
b. It is a U.S. or Canadian issuer.
c. It is not an investment company.
d. If the entity is a majority-owned subsidiary, the parent company also is a small business issuer.

However, regardless of whether it satisfies those criteria, an entity is not a small business issuer if the aggregate market value of its outstanding securities held by nonaffiliates is $25 million or more.

The definition of a small business issuer is a matter of U.S. federal securities law and is subject to change. The effective date provisions of this Statement for a small business issuer apply only to an entity that files as a small business issuer under the related definition at that date.

Tandem award

An award with two (or more) components in which exercise of one part cancels the other(s).

Terms of a share-based payment award

The contractual provisions that determine the nature and scope of a share-based payment award. For example, the exercise price of share options is one of the terms of an award of share options. As indicated in paragraph 34 of this Statement, the written terms of a share-based payment award and its related arrangement, if any, usually provide the best evidence of its terms. However, an entity's past practice or other factors may indicate that some aspects of the substantive terms differ from the written terms. The substantive terms of a share-based payment award as those terms are mutually understood by the entity and a party (either an employee or a nonemployee) who receives the award provide the basis for determining the rights conveyed to a party and the obligations imposed on the issuer, regardless of how the award and related arrangement, if any, are structured. Also refer to paragraph 6 of this Statement.

Time value of an option

The portion of the fair value of an option that exceeds its intrinsic value. For example, a call option with an exercise price of $20 on a stock

---

[174]The phrase *at least in part* is used because an award may be indexed to both the price of the entity's shares and something other than either the price of the entity's shares or a market, performance, or service condition.

whose current market price is $25 has intrinsic value of $5. If the fair value of that option is $7, the time value of the option is $2 ($7 – $5).

Vest, Vesting, or Vested

To earn the rights to. A share-based payment award becomes vested at the date that the employee's right to receive or retain shares, other instruments, or cash under the award is no longer contingent on satisfaction of either a service condition or a performance condition. Market conditions are not vesting conditions for purposes of this Statement.

For convenience and because the terms are commonly used in practice, this Statement refers to *vested* or *nonvested* options, shares, awards, and the like, as well as *vesting date*. The stated vesting provisions of an award often establish the requisite service period, and an award that has reached the end of the requisite service period is vested. However, as indicated in the definition of *requisite service period,* the stated vesting period may differ from the requisite service period in certain circumstances. Thus, the more precise (but cumbersome) terms would be *options, shares,* or *awards for which the requisite service has been rendered* and *end of the requisite service period.*

Volatility

A measure of the amount by which a financial variable such as a share price has fluctuated (historical volatility) or is expected to fluctuate (expected volatility) during a period. Volatility also may be defined as a probability-weighted measure of the dispersion of returns about the mean. The volatility of a share price is the standard deviation of the continuously compounded rates of return on the share over a specified period. That is the same as the standard deviation of the differences in the natural logarithms of the stock prices plus dividends, if any, over the period. The higher the volatility, the more the returns on the shares can be expected to vary—up or down. Volatility is typically expressed in annualized terms.

Appendix F

STATUS OF RELATED AUTHORITATIVE LITERATURE

F1. The following table reflects the current authoritative literature as of December 16, 2004, relating to share-based payment transactions that remain in effect upon issuance of this Statement.

AICPA Literature	Title
SOP 76-3	Accounting Practices for Certain Employee Stock Ownership Plans
SOP 93-6	Employers' Accounting for Employee Stock Ownership Plans

EITF Issue No.	Title
96-18	Accounting for Equity Instruments That Are Issued to Other Than Employees for Acquiring, or in Conjunction with Selling, Goods or Services
97-2	Application of FASB Statement No. 94 and APB Opinion No. 16 to Physician Practice Management Entities and Certain Other Entities with Contractual Management Arrangements
97-14	Accounting for Deferred Compensation Arrangements Where Amounts Earned Are Held in a Rabbi Trust and Invested
00-8	Accounting by a Grantee for an Equity Instrument to Be Received in Conjunction with Providing Goods or Services
00-12	Accounting by an Investor for Stock-Based Compensation Granted to Employees of an Equity Method Investee
00-16	Recognition and Measurement of Employer Payroll Taxes on Employee Stock-Based Compensation
00-18	Accounting Recognition for Certain Transactions involving Equity Instruments Granted to Other Than Employees
00-19	Accounting for Derivative Financial Instruments Indexed to, and Potentially Settled in, a Company's Own Stock
01-1	Accounting for a Convertible Instrument Granted or Issued to a Nonemployee for Goods or Services or a Combination of Goods or Services and Cash

EITF Issue No.	Title
01-6	The Meaning of "Indexed to a Company's Own Stock"
02-8	Accounting for Options Granted to Employees in Unrestricted, Publicly Traded Shares of an Unrelated Entity
D-83	Accounting for Payroll Taxes Associated with Stock Option Exercises
D-90	Grantor Balance Sheet Presentation of Unvested, Forfeitable Equity Instruments Granted to a Nonemployee

F2. Issuance of this Statement eliminates the need for the following EITF Issues (the status section in *EITF Abstracts* will be updated accordingly).

EITF Issue No.	Title	Effect of Statement on Consensus
84-8	Variable Stock Purchase Warrants Given by Suppliers to Customers	Resolved
84-13	Purchase of Stock Options and Stock Appreciation Rights in a Leveraged Buyout	Nullified— Unnecessary[175]
84-18	Stock Option Pyramiding	Nullified— Unnecessary
84-34	Permanent Discount Restricted Stock Purchase Plans	Nullified— Unnecessary
85-45	Business Combinations: Settlement of Stock Options and Awards	Nullified— Unnecessary
87-23	Book Value Stock Purchase Plans	Nullified— Unnecessary
88-6	Book Value Stock Plans in an Initial Public Offering	Nullified— Unnecessary
90-7	Accounting for a Reload Stock Option	Nullified— Unnecessary

---

[175]The consensus is considered no longer necessary because this Statement changed or eliminated the need for the guidance or because the guidance is considered an unnecessary level of detail.

EITF Issue No.	Title	Effect of Statement on Consensus
95-16	Accounting for Stock Compensation Arrangements with Employer Loan Features under APB Opinion No. 25	Nullified—Unnecessary
97-5	Accounting for the Delayed Receipt of Options Shares upon Exercise under APB Opinion No. 25	Nullified—Unnecessary
97-12	Accounting for Increased Share Authorizations in an IRS Section 423 Employee Stock Purchase Plan under APB Opinion No. 25	Nullified—Unnecessary
00-15	Classification in the Statement of Cash Flows of the Income Tax Benefit Received by a Company upon Exercise of a Nonqualified Employee Stock Option	Nullified—Unnecessary
00-23	Issues Related to the Accounting for Stock Compensation under APB Opinion No. 25 and FASB Interpretation No. 44	Nullified—Unnecessary
D-18	Accounting for Compensation Expense If Stock Appreciation Rights Are Cancelled	Nullified—Unnecessary
D-91	Application of APB Opinion No. 25 and FASB Interpretation No. 44 to an Indirect Repricing of a Stock Option	Nullified—Unnecessary
D-93	Accounting for the Rescission of the Exercise of Employee Stock Options	Nullified—Unnecessary

Impact of This Statement on Statement 133 Implementation Issues

F3. This Statement modifies the responses in the following Statement 133 Implementation Issues.

Statement 133 Implementation No.	Title
C3	Exception Related to Stock-Based Compensation Arrangements
E19	Methods of Assessing Hedge Effectiveness When Options Are Designated as the Hedging Instrument
G1	Hedging an SAR Obligation

Statement of Financial Accounting Standards No. 124
Accounting for Certain Investments Held by
Not-for-Profit Organizations

STATUS

Issued: November 1995

Effective Date: For fiscal years beginning after December 15, 1995

Affects: Amends FAS 60, paragraph 45
Replaces FAS 60, paragraph 46
Amends FAS 65, paragraph 4
Amends FAS 91, paragraph 3
Amends FAS 115, paragraph 4
Amends FAS 117, paragraph 168

Affected by: Paragraphs 3, 5, and 112 and footnote 6 amended by FAS 133, paragraph 535
Paragraph 3(a) amended by FAS 157, paragraph E17(a)
Paragraph 6 amended by FAS 133, paragraph 535, and FAS 159, paragraph C6
Paragraph 7 amended by FSP FAS 115-1/124-1, paragraph B3
Paragraph 112 amended by FAS 157, paragraph E17(b)
Footnote 3 replaced by FAS 157, paragraph E17(a)

Other Interpretive Release: FASB Staff Position FAS 115-1/124-1

AICPA Accounting Standards Executive Committee (AcSEC)

Related Pronouncements: SOP 01-6
PB 5
PB 6

Issues discussed by FASB Emerging Issues Task Force (EITF)

Affects: No EITF Issues

Interpreted by: Paragraph 11 interpreted by EITF Topic No. D-49

Related Issues: No EITF Issues

SUMMARY

This Statement establishes standards for accounting for certain investments held by not-for-profit organizations. It requires that investments in equity securities with readily determinable fair values and all investments in debt securities be reported at fair value with gains and losses included in a statement of activities. This Statement requires certain disclosures about investments held by not-for-profit organizations and the return on those investments.

This Statement also establishes standards for reporting losses on investments held because of a donor's stipulation to invest a gift in perpetuity or for a specified term.

This Statement is effective for annual financial statements issued for fiscal years beginning after December 15, 1995. Earlier application is encouraged. This Statement is applied either by restating the financial statements of all prior years presented or by recognizing the cumulative effect of the change in the year of the change. The expiration of restrictions on previously unrecognized net gains may be recognized prospectively.

Statement of Financial Accounting Standards No. 124

Accounting for Certain Investments Held by Not-for-Profit Organizations

CONTENTS

INTRODUCTION

1. This Statement establishes standards of financial accounting and reporting for certain investments in **securities**[1] and establishes disclosure requirements for most investments held by not-for-profit organizations.

2. Guidance for accounting for and reporting of investments held by not-for-profit organizations is currently provided primarily by the AICPA Guides listed in paragraph 22. This Statement is part of a broader FASB agenda project that considers several inconsistencies in that guidance. In addition, this Statement considers many of the same concerns that were examined for business enterprises in FASB Statement No. 115, *Accounting for Certain Investments in Debt and Equity Securities.* Because this Statement establishes standards for certain investments, provisions in the AICPA Guides that are inconsistent with this Statement are no longer acceptable *specialized*[2] accounting and reporting principles and practices.

STANDARDS OF FINANCIAL ACCOUNTING AND REPORTING

Scope

3. The measurement standards of paragraph 7 apply to investments in **equity securities** that have readily determinable fair values, except those described in paragraph 5, and to all investments in **debt securities** except as noted in paragraph 5. For purposes of this Statement, the fair value of an equity security is readily determinable if one of the following three criteria is met:

a. Sales prices or bid-and-asked quotations for the security are currently available on a securities exchange registered with the Securities and Exchange Commission (SEC) or in the over-the-counter market, provided that those prices or quotations for the over-the-counter market are publicly reported by the National Association of Securities Dealers Automated Quotations systems

---

[1]Words that appear in the glossary are set in **boldface type** the first time they appear.

[2]The term *specialized* is used to refer to the current accounting and reporting principles and practices in the existing AICPA Guides and Statements of Position that are neither superseded by nor contained in Accounting Research Bulletins, APB Opinions, FASB Statements, or FASB Interpretations.

or by Pink Sheets LLC. Restricted stock[3] meets that definition if the restriction terminates within one year.

b. For an equity security traded only in a foreign market, that foreign market is of a breadth and scope comparable to one of the U.S. markets referred to above.

c. For an investment in a mutual fund, the fair value per share (unit) is determined and published and is the basis for current transactions.

4. The reporting standards of paragraphs 8–16 apply to all investments held by not-for-profit organizations, except those described in paragraph 5.

5. This Statement does not apply to investments in equity securities that are accounted for under the equity method or to investments in consolidated subsidiaries. This Statement also does not apply to investments in derivative instruments that are subject to the requirements of FASB Statement No. 133, *Accounting for Derivative Instruments and Hedging Activities.* If an investment would otherwise be in the scope of this Statement and it has within it an embedded derivative that is subject to Statement 133, the host instrument (as described in Statement 133) remains within the scope of this Statement.

6. Generally accepted accounting principles other than those discussed in this Statement also apply to investments held by not-for-profit organizations. For example, not-for-profit organizations must disclose information required by FASB Statement No. 107, *Disclosures about Fair Value of Financial Instruments,* Statement 133, and FASB Statement No. 159, *The Fair Value Option for Financial Assets and Financial Liabilities.*

Accounting for Investments in Debt Securities and Certain Equity Securities

7. Investments in equity securities with readily determinable fair values and all investments in debt securities shall be measured at fair value in the statement of financial position.[3a]

Reporting Investment Gains, Losses, and Income

8. Pursuant to paragraph 22 of FASB Statement No. 117, *Financial Statements of Not-for-Profit Organizations,* gains and losses on investments shall be reported in the statement of activities as increases or decreases in unrestricted net assets unless their use is temporarily or permanently restricted by explicit donor stipulations or by law.

9. Pursuant to paragraph 20 of Statement 117, dividend, interest, and other investment income shall be reported in the period earned as increases in unrestricted net assets unless the use of the assets received is limited by donor-imposed restrictions. Donor-restricted investment income is reported as an increase in temporarily restricted net assets or permanently restricted net assets, depending on the type of restriction. This Statement does not specify methods to be used for measuring the amount of dividend and interest income.

10. Gains and investment income that are limited to specific uses by donor-imposed restrictions may be reported as increases in unrestricted net assets if the restrictions are met in the same reporting period as the gains and income are recognized, provided that the organization has a similar policy for reporting contributions received, reports consistently from period to period, and discloses its accounting policy.

Donor-Restricted Endowment Funds

11. A donor's stipulation that requires a gift to be invested in perpetuity or for a specified term creates a **donor-restricted endowment fund.** Unless gains and losses are temporarily or permanently restricted by a donor's explicit stipulation or by a law that extends a donor's restriction to them, gains and losses on investments of a donor-restricted endowment fund are changes in unrestricted net assets. For example, if a donor states that a specific investment security must be held in perpetuity, the gains and

---

[3]The fair value of restricted stock shall be measured based on the quoted price of an otherwise identical unrestricted security of the same issuer, adjusted for the effect of the restriction, in accordance with the provisions of FASB Statement No. 157, *Fair Value Measurements.*

[3a]Some investors, primarily health care organizations, indicated that because Statement 115 requires business entities to report changes in fair value of available-for-sale securities in a separate category of equity and to report held-to-maturity securities at amortized cost, users would be unable to make meaningful comparisons when not-for-profit organizations and business entities are engaged in the same industry. This Statement allows an organization with those comparability concerns to report in a manner similar to business entities by identifying securities as available-for-sale or held-to-maturity and excluding the unrealized gains and losses on those securities from an operating measure within the statement of activities. Investors that report a "performance indicator" as defined in the AICPA Accounting and Audit Guide, *Health Care Organizations,* shall refer to FSP FAS115-1 and FAS124-1, "The Meaning of Other-Than-Temporary Impairment and Its Application to Certain Investments," when determining impairment and evaluating whether the impairment is other than temporary.

losses on that security are subject to that same permanent restriction unless the donor specifies otherwise. However, if a donor allows the organization to choose suitable investments, the gains are not permanently restricted unless the donor or the law requires that an amount be retained permanently. Instead, those gains are unrestricted if the investment income is unrestricted or are temporarily restricted if the investment income is temporarily restricted by the donor.

12. In the absence of donor stipulations or law to the contrary, losses on the investments of a donor-restricted endowment fund shall reduce temporarily restricted net assets to the extent that donor-imposed temporary restrictions on net appreciation of the fund have not been met before the loss occurs. Any remaining loss shall reduce unrestricted net assets.

13. If losses reduce the assets of a donor-restricted endowment fund below the level required by the donor stipulations or law,[4] gains that restore the fair value of the assets of the endowment fund to the required level shall be classified as increases in unrestricted net assets.

Disclosures

14. For each period for which a statement of activities is presented, a not-for-profit organization shall disclose:

a. The composition of investment return including, at a minimum, investment income, net realized gains or losses on investments reported at other than fair value, and net gains or losses on investments reported at fair value
b. A reconciliation of investment return to amounts reported in the statement of activities if investment return is separated into operating and nonoperating amounts, together with a description of the policy used to determine the amount that is included in the measure of operations and a discussion of circumstances leading to a change, if any, in that policy.

15. For each period for which a statement of financial position is presented, a not-for-profit organization shall disclose:

a. The aggregate carrying amount of investments by major types, for example, equity securities, U.S. Treasury securities, corporate debt securities, mortgage-backed securities, oil and gas properties, and real estate
b. The basis for determining the carrying amount for investments other than equity securities with readily determinable fair values and all debt securities
c. The method(s) and significant assumptions used to estimate the fair values of investments other than financial instruments[5] if those other investments are reported at fair value
d. The aggregate amount of the deficiencies for all donor-restricted endowment funds for which the fair value of the assets at the reporting date is less than the level required by donor stipulations or law.

16. For the most recent period for which a statement of financial position is presented, a not-for-profit organization shall disclose the nature of and carrying amount for each individual investment or group of investments that represents a significant concentration of market risk.[6]

Effective Date and Transition

17. This Statement shall be effective for fiscal years beginning after December 15, 1995, and interim periods within those fiscal years. Earlier application is encouraged.

18. Unless this Statement is applied retroactively under the provisions of paragraph 19, the effect of initially applying this Statement shall be reported as the effect of a change in accounting principle in a manner similar to the cumulative effect of a change in accounting principle (APB Opinion No. 20, *Accounting Changes,* paragraph 19). The amount of the cumulative effect shall be based on a retroactive

---

[4]Donors that create endowment funds can require that their gifts be invested in perpetuity or for a specified term. Some donors may require that a portion of income, gains, or both be added to the gift and invested subject to similar restrictions. It is generally understood that at least the amount of the original gift(s) and any required accumulations is not expendable, although the value of the investments purchased may occasionally fall below that amount. Future appreciation of the investments generally restores the value to the required level. In states that have enacted its provisions, the Uniform Management of Institutional Funds Act describes "historic dollar value" as the amount that is not expendable.

[5]Paragraph 10 of Statement 107 requires organizations to disclose the method(s) and significant assumptions used to estimate the fair value of *financial instruments*.

[6]Paragraph 15A of Statement 107, as amended by Statement 133, requires organizations to disclose all significant concentrations of *credit risk* arising from financial instruments, whether from an individual counterparty or groups of counterparties.

computation, except that the expiration of restrictions on previously unrecognized gains and losses may be recognized prospectively.[7] A not-for-profit organization shall report the cumulative effect of a change in accounting on each class of net assets in the statement of activities between the captions "extraordinary items," if any, and "change in unrestricted net assets," "change in temporarily restricted net assets," and "change in permanently restricted net assets."

19. This Statement may be applied retroactively by restating the beginning net assets for the earliest year presented or, if no prior years are presented, for the year this Statement is first applied. The expiration of restrictions on previously unrecognized gains and losses may be recognized prospectively. In the period that this Statement is first applied, a not-for-profit organization shall disclose the nature of any restatement and its effect on the change in net assets and on each class of net assets for each period presented.

> **The provisions of this Statement need
> not be applied to immaterial items.**

This Statement was adopted by the affirmative votes of five members of the Financial Accounting Standards Board. Messrs. Beresford and Northcutt dissented.

Mr. Beresford disagrees with the standard in paragraph 7 that requires all investments in debt securities to be measured at fair value. Mr. Beresford believes this Statement should require a two-category approach. Under that approach, debt securities that an organization has the positive intent and ability to hold to maturity would be reported at amortized cost. Other debt securities and equity securities with readily determinable fair values would be reported at fair value. If a debt security is held to maturity, interim changes in that security's market value do not affect either the amount or timing of net cash flows to the entity. Consequently, Mr. Beresford agrees with the Board's conclusion in paragraph 58 of Statement 115 that "amortized cost is most likely to be relevant for those debt securities that will be held to maturity," and he believes that different accounting treatment is warranted for those debt securities. He believes that not-for-profit organizations should have the same ability as business enterprises to measure those securities at amortized cost.

Mr. Beresford also believes that more restrictive display requirements are necessary when amounts computed under a spending-rate or other budgetary method are included within an organization's measure of operations. He believes that users of financial statements might be misled if the amount reported within an operating measure is greater than the actual return for the period. He would limit the amount reported within the operating measure to actual gains and losses for the period—those amounts are based on the nature of the underlying transactions rather than on spending-rate or budgetary designations.

Mr. Northcutt disagrees with the standards in paragraphs 11–13, which prescribe the accounting for losses on the investments of donor-restricted endowment funds. Mr. Northcutt believes this Statement should require the method described in paragraphs 78 and 79, in which losses on investments of permanently restricted endowment funds reduce the net asset classes in which unappropriated net appreciation of the fund is reported and any additional losses reduce permanently restricted net assets. In Mr. Northcutt's view, the method required by paragraphs 11–13 has three main problems.

First, Mr. Northcutt believes that the method required by this Statement fails to acknowledge that not-for-profit organizations identify the assets of each endowment fund and the investment income earned by those assets because they have fiduciary responsibilities and must be able to demonstrate that they are complying with the donors' stipulations and applicable laws. Because the assets of an endowment fund

---

[7]Paragraph 17 of FASB Statement No. 116, *Accounting for Contributions Received and Contributions Made,* establishes standards for recognizing the expiration of donor-imposed restrictions. Those standards also apply to the expiration of donor-imposed restrictions on investment income, gains, and losses. A similar provision permitting prospective recognition of the expirations of restrictions is included in paragraphs 29 and 30 of Statement 116.

are known, classification of the net assets related to those assets is straightforward. First, the portion of the net assets that may never be spent because of donor or legal restrictions should be classified as permanently restricted net assets. Next, net appreciation for which restrictions on expenditure have not yet been met should be classified as temporarily restricted net assets. Finally, the remaining portion of net appreciation should be classified as unrestricted net assets. If a loss reduces the value of the assets of an endowment fund, the classification of the net assets related to the remaining assets follows the same procedure. If a loss reduces the assets of an endowment fund below the amount that must be maintained in perpetuity (historic dollar value), those assets are entirely unexpendable and all the net assets of that endowment fund should be classified as permanently restricted.

Mr. Northcutt acknowledges that the method he prefers must either define the assets of the fund or tolerate the effects of differing definitions. A definition requires a method for identifying when assets are removed from the fund for spending and thus are no longer present to absorb losses. Mr. Northcutt accepts the method provided in the Uniform Management of Institutional Funds Act for removing net appreciation—appropriation. He would define the assets of an endowment fund using appropriation because he believes the effects of management's discretion on classification of net assets are limited. An appropriation for expenditure does not change the class of net assets in which the appropriated amount is reported. An appropriation does not change when restrictions on net appreciation expire. When a loss occurs, only one classification of net assets is possible because an appropriation either was made or was not made prior to the loss. An appropriation can be made only when the fund has available net appreciation, and amounts appropriated may not be returned to the fund. The appropriation determines only the amount of net appreciation of a donor-restricted endowment fund that is available to absorb a future loss.

Mr. Northcutt recognizes that attributing significance to the act of appropriation for purposes of classifying losses on endowment funds may be viewed as inconsistent with the Board's decisions in Statements 116 and 117. He would be willing to amend Statement 117 to allow an exception only for this case.

Second, Mr. Northcutt believes that the method of accounting for losses described in this Statement can result in the classification of permanently restricted net assets and unrestricted net assets in a manner that is inconsistent with the definitions of those classes of net assets. That method can result in an overstatement of permanently restricted net assets, which could lead users to believe that there are more assets generating income for support of the organization than there actually are. That method also can result in an understatement of the net resources that an organization as a whole has available to meet current operating needs.

Third, Mr. Northcutt believes that the method described in paragraphs 11–13 of this Statement misclassifies the gains that restore the fair value of the assets of the endowment fund to the level required by donor stipulations or law. That method would report future gains as increases in unrestricted net assets, even though the amount of net resources that are expendable for current operating needs is unchanged. In effect, gains that must be retained in perpetuity because of a donor-imposed restriction will be reported as increases in unrestricted net assets, which makes sense only because it corrects the erroneous reporting of the year of the loss.

Appendix A

BACKGROUND INFORMATION

20. In March 1986, the Board added a project to its agenda to resolve certain inconsistent accounting practices of not-for-profit organizations. The Board identified five areas of inconsistency that persist, in part, because the specialized accounting principles and practices in the AICPA Guides for not-for-profit organizations contain inconsistent requirements. Accounting for investments, one of the five areas, was initially included in the financial instruments project, which was added to the Board's agenda in May 1986.

21. FASB Statement No. 115, *Accounting for Certain Investments in Debt and Equity Securities,* issued in May 1993, specifically excluded not-for-profit organizations from its scope. The Board decided to consider the issues about investments held by not-for-profit organizations after it resolved its agenda projects on accounting for contributions and financial statement display by those organizations. FASB Statements No. 116, *Accounting for Contributions Received and Contributions Made,* and No. 117, *Financial Statements of Not-for-Profit Organizations,* were issued in June 1993. In February 1994, the Board began deliberations to establish standards for reporting investments held by not-for-profit organizations.

22. Current guidance for accounting for and reporting of investments held by not-for-profit organizations is provided by the following four AICPA Guides:

a. *Audits of Colleges and Universities*
b. *Audits of Voluntary Health and Welfare Organizations*
c. *Audits of Providers of Health Care Services*
d. *Audits of Certain Nonprofit Organizations.*

The requirements in those Guides are similar in some respects. In other respects they differ from each other and from generally accepted accounting principles applicable to other entities. The inconsistencies lead to differences in accounting practices and, hence, to comparability and understandability problems. Further, three of the Guides permit accounting alternatives that lead to further inconsistencies within the subsector they cover.

23. In addition to the inconsistencies in the Guides, the Board identified other problems that this project should attempt to resolve:

a. *Greater relevance of fair value information.* Some believe that fair value information about investments is a more relevant measure of the ability of the organization's assets to support operations than cost-based information.
b. *LOCOM is not evenhanded.* The lower-of-cost-or-market method, which is required by one Guide and permitted by another, is not evenhanded because it recognizes the net diminution in value but not the net appreciation in the value of investments.
c. *Managing change in net assets.* Cost-based measures create situations in which decisions to sell certain securities may be based on the sale's effect on the change in net assets. Organizations may choose to sell appreciated securities to recognize the unrealized gains while choosing to retain other securities with unrealized losses. Similarly, organizations may choose to sell securities with unrealized losses while choosing to retain appreciated securities to reduce the change in net assets.
d. *Accounting based on intent.* Accounting standards based on the intent of management make the accounting treatment depend on the plans of management rather than the economic characteristics of an asset. Intent-based accounting impairs comparability.

24. The Board discussed the resolution of those problems at a number of public Board meetings. In March 1995, the Board issued the Exposure Draft, *Accounting for Certain Investments Held by Not-for-Profit Organizations.* The Board and staff analyzed the 86 comment letters received and obtained additional information from a field test of the proposed requirements for classification of losses on investments of endowment funds and from a meeting with rating agency analysts, officers of grant-making foundations, and others who use the financial statements of not-for-profit organizations. The concerns raised by respondents, field test participants, and users of financial statements were considered by the Board at additional public Board meetings. Throughout the project, the Board and staff consulted with the members of the FASB Task Force on Accounting Issues for Not-for-Profit Organizations, including discussing the Board's tentative decisions at a June 1994 public meeting. The Board decided that it could reach an informed decision without holding a public hearing.

Appendix B

BASIS FOR CONCLUSIONS

CONTENTS

Appendix B

BASIS FOR CONCLUSIONS

Introduction

25. This appendix summarizes considerations that Board members deemed significant in reaching the conclusions in this Statement. It includes reasons for accepting certain views and rejecting others. Individual Board members gave greater weight to some factors than to others.

Benefits and Costs

26. The mission of the Board is to establish and improve standards of financial accounting and reporting for the guidance and education of the public, including issuers, auditors, and users of financial information. In fulfilling that mission, the Board strives to determine that a proposed standard will fill a significant need and that the costs imposed to meet that standard, as compared with other alternatives, are justified in relation to the overall benefits of the resulting information. Present and potential donors, creditors, members, and others all benefit from improvements in financial reporting; however, the costs to implement a new standard may not be borne evenly by all parties. Further, the costs of not issuing a standard are impossible to quantify. Because there is no common gauge by which to judge objectively the costs to implement a standard against the need to improve information in financial statements, the Board's assessment of the costs and benefits of issuing an accounting standard is unavoidably subjective.

27. The benefits of reporting debt and certain equity securities at fair value are discussed in paragraphs 33–40. In addition to those benefits, fair value measurement resolves for those investments each of the problems discussed in paragraph 23 of Appendix A. This Statement enhances comparability by eliminating the inconsistencies in the current guidance for reporting carrying amounts of equity securities with readily determinable fair values and all debt securities. For those securities, this Statement also removes the bias implicit in LOCOM accounting, precludes opportunities for managing change in net assets through selective sale of securities, and eliminates the subjectivity of accounting based on management's intent.

28. The Board concluded that the overall benefits of the information provided by applying this Statement justify the costs that this Statement may impose. Because the AICPA Guides and FASB Statement No. 107, *Disclosures about Fair Value of Financial Instruments,* require that not-for-profit organizations disclose fair value information for investments reported at cost, organizations generally have the information systems that are needed to meet the requirements of this Statement. Although there will be transitional costs as not-for-profit organizations apply the requirements, the Board believes that the ongoing costs of applying this Statement should not be significantly greater than for existing requirements. The Board also believes that some of the costs this Statement imposes have been reduced in various ways: by limiting the scope of the measurement standards to equity securities whose fair values are readily determinable and to debt securities, by providing broad guidance and allowing some latitude in how information is reported in financial statements, and by eliminating requirements to disclose cost-based information for investments reported at fair value.

Scope

29. This Statement provides measurement standards for most investments held by not-for-profit organizations. Some not-for-profit organizations have more complex investment portfolios that include investments that are outside the scope of this Statement. A broader scope would have included investments such as interests in trusts, joint-venture agreements, oil and gas properties, real estate, and investments in closely held companies and partnerships. Those investments could have raised significant valuation issues that might not have been resolved in time to coordinate the implementation of this Statement with the implementation of Statements 116 and 117.

30. Most respondents to the Exposure Draft agreed with the Board's decision to limit the scope of this Statement. A few of those respondents said that the Board should consider carefully any requests to expand the scope to include investments that are not readily marketable. They were troubled by the subjectivity that may be necessary in estimating fair values. The Board understands that reliability is an important factor in financial reporting and, therefore, limited the scope for equity securities to those that have readily determinable fair values. The scope of

this Statement includes all debt instruments that are securities because the Board believes that sufficiently reliable estimates of fair value can be made for those instruments.

31. A few other respondents indicated that the scope should be expanded to include either all investments or all financial instruments. Provisions of the AICPA Guides remain in effect for measuring investments that are not within the scope of this Statement, including impairment of investments reported using cost-based measures. Where permitted by the relevant AICPA Guide, the Board does not discourage not-for-profit organizations from using fair value to measure investments that are outside the scope of this Statement; the Board limited the scope for practical reasons.

32. The Board decided to use the definitions of *security, equity security, debt security,* and *readily determinable fair value* that were developed in Statement 115 to ensure that this Statement and Statement 115 apply to the same investments. In the future, the Board expects to consider the accounting for other financial instruments held by business enterprises and not-for-profit organizations within the financial instruments project that is currently on its technical agenda.

Accounting for Certain Investments in Debt and Equity Securities

Relevance of Fair Values of Investments in Securities

33. The Board concluded that measuring investments in debt and equity securities at fair value in the financial statements provides information that is relevant and useful to present and potential donors, creditors, and others in making rational decisions about the allocation of resources to not-for-profit organizations—the first objective of financial reporting discussed in FASB Concepts Statement No. 4, *Objectives of Financial Reporting by Nonbusiness Organizations.*

34. Measuring those investments at fair value also serves to achieve the second objective of financial reporting—providing information that is useful in assessing the ability of the organization to provide services. Fair value more accurately measures the resources available to provide mission-related services because it portrays the market's estimate of the net future cash flows of those securities, discounted to reflect both time value and risk. "The assessment of

cash flow potential is important because it relates directly to the organization's ability to provide the goods and services for which it exists" (Concepts Statement 4, paragraph 45).

35. Fair value information assists users in assessing management's stewardship and performance—thus helping to meet the third objective of financial reporting discussed in Concepts Statement 4. Management must continually decide whether to hold an investment or to sell the investment and redirect resources to other investments or other uses. Fair value reports information useful in evaluating the performance of management in dynamic market conditions.

36. Many respondents to the Exposure Draft agreed with the Board about the relevance of fair value information. Creditors, rating agencies, regulators, and others that use the financial statements of not-for-profit organizations said fair value measures provide information that is useful to them in comparing and evaluating organizations and their managements. Because the goal of investing is to maximize returns commensurate with the risks undertaken, the only way to evaluate performance is to compare returns, adjusted for risk, to that of other entities or to common market indicators. Those financial statement users said that comparisons are reasonable only when securities and their returns are measured using fair value measures.

37. The ability to make meaningful comparisons between organizations is enhanced when securities are measured at fair value. Cost-based measures of the same security can vary significantly from organization to organization; fair value measures vary little, if at all. The value of securities, and all financial instruments, comes from the ability to convert them to their promised cash flows and to use the resulting cash to purchase the services, goods, and long-lived assets that the organization needs to conduct its activities. The cash flows associated with the securities do not depend on which organization owns them; thus, the measures of securities should not vary from organization to organization.

38. Some respondents were concerned primarily about reporting unrealized changes in fair value in their financial statements. Some that supported fair value measures said that changes in the fair values of securities should not be reported in the statement of activities until realized. They argued that the volatility that results from reporting unrealized gains and losses in change in net assets is unrepresentative of the results of operations of the organization and presents a false picture of the organization's stewardship abilities. Other respondents that favored cost-based measures said that not-for-profit organizations invest for long-term returns that support program activities and that temporary fluctuations in market values are irrelevant to managing the organization or its investment portfolio. They argued that fair value measures ignore those considerations. In their view, fair value measures focus on the effects of transactions and events that do not involve the organization and report opportunity gains and losses that should not be recognized until realized.

39. The Board concluded that to delay recognition of gains and losses until they are realized omits relevant information from the financial statements of not-for-profit organizations. To ignore fluctuations that actually occur fails to represent faithfully the risks inherent in investing activities, and to fail to report increases and decreases in value in periods when market conditions change impairs the credibility of financial statements. Recognizing only realized gains and losses in financial statements does not eliminate volatility in the change in net assets; instead, it provides opportunities to use selective sales of securities to manage that volatility. This Statement attempts to reduce opportunities to manage the reported change in net assets by selective sales of securities.

40. The requirement to report investments in equity securities with readily determinable fair values and all debt securities at fair value builds on current and evolving practices and requirements. Three of the four AICPA Guides permit organizations to report investments at fair value, and all four Guides require disclosure of fair value if investments are reported using a cost-based measure. FASB Statement No. 35, *Accounting and Reporting by Defined Benefit Pension Plans,* requires that all plan investments be reported at fair value because that reporting provides the most relevant information about the resources of a plan and its present and future ability to pay benefits when due. Statements 107, 115, and 119 also require that entities report fair value information about their financial instruments because that information is relevant to users of financial statements.

Consideration of Whether to Amend Statement 115

41. The Board considered amending Statement 115 to include not-for-profit organizations within its scope. In addition to not-for-profit organizations, Statement 115 excludes from its scope enterprises

whose specialized accounting practices include accounting for substantially all investments in debt and equity securities at market or fair value, with changes in value recognized in earnings (income) or in change in net assets. Those enterprises (principally brokers and dealers in securities, defined benefit pension plans, and investment companies) are excluded because the Board believes that their current accounting practices provide more relevant information for users of their financial statements. The specialized accounting practices of most not-for-profit organizations permit reporting investments at fair value with changes in fair value recognized in change in net assets, and a significant number of not-for-profit organizations presently do so. Accordingly, the Board considered whether an approach similar to those specialized accounting practices or the approach used in Statement 115 would result in more relevant information for the users of the financial statements of not-for-profit organizations.

42. Statement 115 identifies three categories of investments into which an enterprise classifies its investments. The accounting and reporting differ by category. Investments in debt securities that the enterprise has the positive intent and ability to hold to maturity are classified as *held-to-maturity securities* and are reported at amortized cost. Debt and equity securities that are bought and held principally for the purpose of selling them in the near term are classified as *trading securities* and reported at fair value, with unrealized holding gains and losses included in earnings.[8] Debt and equity securities not classified as either held-to-maturity securities or trading securities are classified as *available-for-sale securities* and reported at fair value, with unrealized holding gains and losses excluded from earnings and reported in a separate component of shareholders' equity.

43. The approach in Statement 115 resulted from a need to accommodate situations that are largely nonexistent in not-for-profit organizations. Some enterprises affected by Statement 115 (principally banks, thrifts, credit unions, and insurance companies) manage their interest rate risk by coordinating the maturity and repricing characteristics of their investments and their liabilities. Reporting unrealized holding gains and losses on only the investments, and not the related liabilities, could cause volatility in earnings that is not representative of how financial institutions

are affected by economic events. The Board concluded that accommodations similar to those in Statement 115 were unnecessary for not-for-profit organizations because (a) the purposes for which not-for-profit organizations hold investments generally do not relate investments to liabilities and (b) the change in net assets is not a performance measure comparable to earnings of a business enterprise.

44. Respondents to the Exposure Draft and task force members helped the Board identify the purposes for which not-for-profit organizations hold investments. Three of the primary purposes identified were endowment, funded depreciation, and short-term investment of operating cash surpluses. Organizations usually do not relate investment assets to liabilities when investing for those purposes. However, organizations may relate investment assets to specific liabilities when investing for other purposes. For many of those other purposes, the related liability is measured and periodically remeasured at the present value of estimated future cash flows using a discount rate commensurate with the risks involved. For example, the obligation to the beneficiary of an annuity agreement is measured at the present value of the payments to be made, the obligation to employees covered by a funded postretirement benefit plan is measured at the actuarial present value of the expected benefits attributed to periods of employee service, and the obligation to provide future service in continuing care retirement communities is measured at the present value of future net cash flows. This Statement's requirement to measure investment securities at fair value will eliminate situations where the adjustment of the liability is included in the change in net assets, but the change in the value of related investments is not.

45. In other identified relationships, such as many debt service funds, this Statement requires that the investments be measured at fair value, although the related liability is reported at historical proceeds. However, most respondents that supported a Statement 115 approach or its held-to-maturity category indicated that they did not coordinate maturities of the investments with the related liabilities. The Board concluded that the possibility for volatility that is not representative of how not-for-profit organizations are

---

[8]In addition to securities that are acquired with the purpose of selling them in the near term, Statement 115 also permits an enterprise to classify securities that it plans to hold for a longer period as *trading securities*. However, the decision to classify a security as trading should occur at acquisition; transfers into or out of the trading category should be rare.

affected by economic events is limited, both in the number of not-for-profit organizations potentially affected and in the amounts of investments and liabilities involved.

46. The Board also noted that the distinctions between the three categories of investments of Statement 115 are less relevant for not-for-profit organizations because the change in net assets is not a performance measure equivalent to earnings of a business enterprise. "[Not-for-profit] organizations generally have no single indicator of performance comparable to a business enterprise's profit" (Concepts Statement 4, paragraph 9). Although the magnitude of profits is generally indicative of how successfully a business enterprise performed, the same relationship is not true of a not-for-profit organization. The magnitude of change in net assets does not indicate how successfully a not-for-profit organization performed in providing goods and services. Further, because donor-imposed restrictions affect the types and levels of service a not-for-profit organization can provide, the change in each class of net assets may be more significant than the change in net assets for the organization as a whole (FASB Concepts Statement No. 6, *Elements of Financial Statements,* paragraph 106).

47. Because change in net assets is not a performance measure, the distinction between trading securities and available-for-sale securities is less relevant for not-for-profit organizations in reporting changes in fair value than that distinction is for business enterprises. Business enterprises distinguish between components of comprehensive income,[9] reporting certain changes in equity (net assets) in an income statement and other changes in net assets in a separate component of equity. The trading and available-for-sale categories are used to make those differentiations. In contrast, the statement of activities of a not-for-profit organization is like a statement of comprehensive income; it reports all changes in net assets. Reporting in a manner similar to Statement 115 introduces unnecessary complications by introducing separate components of equity within the three classes of net assets.

48. The Board concluded that fair value is more relevant to donors and other users of a not-for-profit organization's financial statements than the approach used in Statement 115. The Board decided that use of the three categories of investments prescribed in Statement 115 would add complexity without returning sufficient benefits for measurement or reporting purposes of not-for-profit organizations.

49. Some respondents, primarily health care organizations and their auditors, said that because Statement 115 requires business enterprises to report changes in fair value of available-for-sale securities in a separate category of equity and to report held-to-maturity securities at amortized cost, users would be unable to make meaningful comparisons when not-for-profit organizations and business enterprises are engaged in the same industry. This Statement allows an organization with those comparability concerns to report in a manner similar to business enterprises by identifying securities as available-for-sale or held-to-maturity and excluding the unrealized gains and losses on those securities from an operating measure within the statement of activities.

Debt Securities Held to Maturity

50. In addition to the three-category approach used in Statement 115, the Board considered a two-category approach. Under that approach, debt securities that the organization has the positive intent and ability to hold to maturity would be reported at amortized cost. Other debt securities and equity securities with readily determinable fair values would be reported at fair value. Two of the AICPA Guides permit the use of amortized cost for debt securities if a not-for-profit organization has the intent and ability to hold those securities to maturity. The Board considered whether that practice should continue and decided that amortized cost should not be permitted.

51. Respondents to the Exposure Draft that favored a two-category approach said that fair value information is less relevant for debt securities that are being held to maturity. They said that amortized cost provides relevant information because it focuses on the decision to acquire the asset, the earning effects of that decision that will be realized over time, and the ultimate recoverable value of the asset. If a debt security is held to maturity, the face value of the security will be realized, unless the issuer defaults, and all interim unrealized gains and losses will be reversed. In their view, increases and decreases in the fair value of

---

[9]Comprehensive income includes all changes in equity during a period except those resulting from investments by owners and distributions to owners (Concepts Statement 6, paragraph 70).

the debt security are not true gains and losses in investment value because the organization's cash flows are "locked in" at purchase.

52. Other respondents said that fair value information is as relevant for debt securities that are being held to maturity as it is for other investments. Increases or decreases in fair value reflect the success or failure of the strategy of purchasing and holding a longer-term rather than a shorter-term debt security in an environment of changing interest rates. For example, if an organization invests in a fixed-rate debt security and interest rates rise, the organization generally will receive less cash than if it had invested in a variable-rate security. That success (or failure) in maximizing the return on the organization's resources is relevant and should be reflected in the financial statements in the period the event (that is, the change in interest rates) occurs. In addition, fair value also reflects the risk that the cash flows will not be received as expected.

53. Some respondents that favored fair value measures mentioned that effective management of financial activities often requires a flexible investment strategy that is inconsistent with a held-to-maturity notion. They said that although many investment policies are based on long-term strategies, market fluctuations impact decisions to buy or sell specific instruments in order to achieve the organization's overall objectives. The Board believes that if an organization would sell a debt security to achieve its investment objectives, the organization does not have the positive intent to hold the security to maturity.

54. Other respondents that favored a two-category approach said they use a buy-and-hold strategy or "ladder" the maturities of their debt securities so that the organization can hold debt securities to maturity. Many of those respondents were concerned about volatility in the change in net assets, which would result if debt securities could not be reported at amortized cost when market interest rates changed. However, respondents that expressed that concern indicated that debt securities being held to maturity represent only a small portion of their portfolios. The Board noted that unless a portfolio was composed completely of debt securities being held to maturity, a two-category approach would not resolve concerns about volatility in change in net assets.

55. Respondents also said that not-for-profit organizations should have the same ability as business enterprises to report debt securities classified as held-to-maturity securities at amortized cost. Measuring an investment at (a) amortized cost if the organization has the positive intent and ability to hold it to maturity or (b) fair value if the organization does not have that intent bases the measurement on the intent of management rather than on the economic characteristics of the asset. Measurement based on the intent of management is one of the problems that this Statement attempts to resolve.

56. Statement 115 did not resolve the problem of accounting by intent. As discussed in paragraphs 43–48 of this Statement, the approach in Statement 115 resulted from a need to accommodate situations that are largely nonexistent in not-for-profit organizations. Thus, the Board concluded that allowing a not-for-profit organization to account for investments based on management's intent is unwarranted and that investments in equity securities with readily determinable fair values and all debt securities should be reported at fair value.

Determining Fair Values

57. The Board decided to use the term *fair value* in this Statement to avoid confusion between the terms *fair value* and *market value;* some constituents associate the term *market value* only with items that are traded on active secondary markets (such as exchange and dealer markets). However, the Board does not make that distinction and intends the term to be applicable whether the market for an item is active or inactive, primary or secondary.

58. The fair value of an asset is the amount at which the asset could be bought or sold in a current transaction between willing parties, that is, other than in a forced or liquidation sale. Quoted market prices in active markets are the best evidence of fair value and should be used as the basis for measurement, if available. Quoted market prices are easy to obtain and are reliable and verifiable. They are used and relied upon regularly and are well understood by donors, creditors, and other users of financial information.

59. Although quoted market prices are not available for all debt securities, the Board believes that a reasonable estimate of fair value can be made or obtained for the remaining debt securities required to be reported at fair value by this Statement. For debt securities that do not trade regularly or that trade only in principal-to-principal markets, the estimate of fair value should be based on the best information available in the circumstances. The estimate of fair value

should consider market prices for similar debt securities and the results of valuation techniques to the extent available in the circumstances. Examples of valuation techniques include the present value of estimated expected future cash flows using a discount rate commensurate with the risks involved, option-pricing models, matrix pricing, option-adjusted spread models, and fundamental analysis. The Board realizes that estimating fair value may require judgment but notes that a considerable degree of judgment also is needed when complying with other long-standing accounting and reporting requirements.

Financial Statement Presentation

Reporting Investment Gains, Losses, and Income

60. This Statement provides requirements for reporting changes in the fair value of investments in securities. The total change in fair value consists of both the change in the unpaid interest income on a debt security (or the unpaid accrued dividends on an equity security until the ex-dividend date) and the change in fair value that results from holding a security—the gain or loss, which can be either realized or unrealized. Gains and losses are recognized as changes in net assets in the periods in which they occur, and investment income is recognized as revenue in the period earned. Delaying recognition of restricted gains, losses, and income until the restrictions are met is inappropriate. The requirements of this Statement clarify, but do not change, the requirements of Statement 117.

61. Statement 117 establishes broad standards directed at critical display issues and allows organizations latitude to present information in a form that management believes is most meaningful to financial statement users. The Board decided that display guidance in this Statement also should focus on critical information that is essential in meeting the financial reporting objectives for all not-for-profit organizations.

62. The Board concluded that the most critical information—investment gains, losses, and investment income—should be recognized and reported in the statement of activities. Other critical information about the types of investments, their risks, and their returns should be disclosed, but organizations can decide whether that information is disclosed on the face of the statements or in the notes to financial statements.

63. The Board considered whether more restrictive display requirements were necessary for realized gains and losses, unrealized gains and losses, investment return, or the amounts computed under a spending-rate or other budgetary method for reporting endowment returns. By not prescribing specific standards in this Statement, the Board recognizes that differing financial statement display practices are probable. Statement 117 is not yet in effect for most organizations, and they are just beginning to explore reporting that complies with its requirements and responds to its flexibility. The Board believes that it is premature to conclude that reporting differences will be undesirable and that at this time it is best to allow latitude so that financial reporting practices may continue to evolve.

64. Most respondents supported the reporting flexibility that this Statement permits. However, several respondents said that users of financial statements might be misled if organizations use a spending-rate or total return policy[10] that reports in an operating measure an amount that exceeds the total investment return for the year. The Board noted that those respondents were not similarly concerned about reporting less than the total investment return in an operating measure, nor were they concerned about reporting net realized gains in an operating measure and net unrealized losses outside that measure, although the reporting in that latter case also may result in including an amount in an operating measure that exceeds the total investment return for the year. A few respondents said that distinctions between realized and unrealized amounts are acceptable because those distinctions are based on the underlying nature of the transaction, but spending-rate and total return amounts are computed using formulas. In general, the Board agrees that amounts reported in an organization's financial statements should be based on the nature of the underlying transactions

---

[10]In managing their endowment funds, some organizations use a spending-rate or total return policy. Those policies consider total investment return—investment income (interest, dividends, rents, and so forth) plus net realized and unrealized gains (or minus net losses). Typically, spending-rate or total return policies emphasize (a) the use of prudence and a rational and systematic formula to determine the portion of cumulative investment return that can be used to support operations of the current period and (b) the protection of endowment gifts from a loss of purchasing power as a consideration in determining the formula to be used.

rather than on budgetary designations—to report otherwise suggests the reported operating measure is being managed. In this case only, the Board agreed that amounts based on budgetary designations may be displayed because the necessary constraints are provided by the disclosures required by paragraph 14 of this Statement and paragraph 23 of Statement 117 (including its requirement that an operating measure, if reported, must appear in a financial statement that, at a minimum, reports the change in unrestricted net assets for the period).

Reporting Losses on Endowment Funds

65. Statement 117 requires that gains and losses be classified based on the existence or absence of donor-imposed restrictions or law that limits their use. Paragraph 129 of that Statement explains the application of that requirement to the net appreciation of endowment funds:

> . . . the Board concluded that if the law of the relevant jurisdiction, as interpreted by an organization's governing board, places permanent restrictions on some part of the net appreciation, that amount should be reported as permanently restricted net assets in the organization's financial statements. In the absence of such a law or a donor's explicit or clear implicit permanent restriction, net appreciation should be reported as unrestricted if the endowment's income is unrestricted or temporarily restricted if the endowment's income is temporarily restricted by the donor.

Some respondents to the Exposure Draft of Statement 117 raised questions about reporting losses on investments of endowments. The Board deferred consideration of those issues to this Statement.

66. The Board limited its consideration to losses on investments of endowment funds that are created by donor stipulations requiring that the gifts be invested in perpetuity or for a specified term. The classification of losses on investments of an endowment fund

created by a board designation of unrestricted funds is straightforward; the losses are classified as reductions in unrestricted net assets because all sources of that endowment fund—original amount, gains and losses, and interest and dividends—are free of donor restrictions.

67. The classification of losses on investments of an endowment fund created by a donor also is straightforward if the donor explicitly states in the gift agreement what is to occur in the event of a loss; the losses are classified in accordance with the donor stipulations. Similarly, a donor's explicit requirement that an organization hold a specific donated asset in perpetuity implies that the enhancements and diminishments of that asset (gains and losses) are subject to the same permanent restriction. In the absence of donor stipulations or law to the contrary, the Board concluded that losses on investments of a donor-restricted endowment fund should reduce temporarily restricted net assets to the extent that donor-imposed temporary restrictions on net appreciation of the fund have not been met before the loss occurs and that any remaining loss should reduce unrestricted net assets.

Fundamental conclusions about the classification of losses

68. In determining the method to be used to classify losses in the absence of explicit donor stipulations or law, the Board considered the Uniform Management of Institutional Funds Act (Uniform Act), which has been adopted in varying forms in at least 38 states and the District of Columbia. It says:

> The governing board may appropriate for expenditure for the uses and purposes for which an endowment fund[11] is established so much of the net appreciation, realized and unrealized, in the fair value of the assets of an endowment fund over the historic dollar value[12] of the fund as is prudent. . . .
>
> Unrealized gains and losses must be combined with realized gains and losses to insure

---

[11]The Uniform Act uses the term *endowment fund* to describe a fund with characteristics of a donor-restricted endowment fund, as defined in this Statement. Section 1(3) of the Uniform Act defines an endowment fund as:

> . . . an institutional fund, or any part thereof, not wholly expendable by the institution on a current basis under the terms of the applicable gift instrument.

[12]The Uniform Act defines *historic dollar value* in Section 1(5) as:

> . . . the aggregate fair value in dollars of (i) an endowment fund at the time it became an endowment fund, (ii) each subsequent donation to the fund at the time it is made, and (iii) each accumulation made pursuant to a direction in the applicable gift instrument at the time the accumulation is added to the fund.

that the historic dollar value is not impaired. [Section 2 and the comment to that section, footnotes added.]

Although the Uniform Act indicates that losses should be netted against gains and that realized and unrealized amounts should be considered equally in applying its provisions, the Act is silent about an organization's responsibility to restore a decrease in the value of the assets of an endowment fund. The Board concluded that a method for classifying losses of a donor-restricted endowment fund should not define an organization's fiduciary responsibilities to maintain the assets of the fund; each organization should determine its responsibilities in accordance with donor-imposed restrictions and law.

69. The Board also considered different interpretations of "the assets of an endowment fund," in part because the Uniform Act does not define that phrase. Different interpretations result in different determinations of which investment losses are losses of a donor-restricted endowment fund and how much of prior periods' appreciation can be netted with losses of the fund in the current period. Respondents' interpretations of the phrase differed. For example, some organizations that participated in the field test of the Exposure Draft interpreted the phrase to mean that assets purchased with a gift and assets purchased with its net appreciation are part of the endowment fund until a portion of the assets is removed by an appropriation for expenditure. Other participants said that in addition to those assets, assets purchased with investment income are part of the fund. Another participant said that assets purchased with net appreciation are not part of the fund at all. Without case law to help interpret the Uniform Act, the Board has no basis to adopt one interpretation and reject all others. The Board concluded that a method for classifying losses should accommodate different interpretations of "the assets of an endowment fund" but minimize the effects of differing interpretations on the classification of net assets.

70. The Board considered whether the ability to "appropriate for expenditure" granted by the Uniform Act should influence the classification of losses. Attributing significance to an act of appropriation would allow management's intent to influence the classification of net assets and is inconsistent with the Board's conclusions in Statements 116 and 117. Statement 116 requires that a restriction on temporarily restricted net appreciation expire when an expense is incurred for the restricted purpose, regardless of whether an amount is appropriated. In Statement 117, the Board concluded that decisions about when to appropriate resources should not influence their classification—net gains are reported in unrestricted or temporarily restricted net assets unless permanently restricted by the donor or law. The Board concluded that appropriation of a portion of net appreciation should not change the classification of a loss on an endowment fund.

71. The Board believes that inconsistent classification of net assets would result if it did not specify a method for classifying losses on investments of donor-restricted endowment funds. Donors generally are silent about losses on the investments of the funds they establish, and the Uniform Act is unclear about an organization's responsibilities when a loss occurs. Without explicit donor stipulations or law to determine the classification of losses on investments of endowment funds, organizations could arrive at different answers in similar circumstances.

72. The Board considered the three methods for classifying losses on investments of donor-restricted endowment funds that are discussed in paragraphs 73–82, as well as variations of those methods. All of the methods considered had some drawbacks. The Board believes that the method in this Statement for classifying losses is simple to apply and will result in greater comparability and consistency in classification of net assets so that users of financial statements may make better-informed decisions.

Method used in this Statement for classifying losses

73. The Board concluded that, in the absence of donor stipulations or law to the contrary, losses on the investments of a donor-restricted endowment fund reduce temporarily restricted or unrestricted net assets. The Board concluded that if a donor requires an endowment fund to be invested in perpetuity, permanently restricted net assets should equal the historic dollar value of the fund. The Uniform Act says, "Accounting entries recording realization of gains or losses to the fund have no effect upon historic dollar value. No increase or decrease in historic dollar value of the fund results from the sale of an asset held by the fund and the reinvestment of the proceeds in another asset" (comment to Section 1(5)). Unless historic dollar value changes, such as when a donor directs that gains be accumulated in the fund, neither gains nor losses affect permanently restricted net assets.

74. Whether a loss reduces temporarily restricted net assets, unrestricted net assets, or both depends on

where the net appreciation of the fund is classified at the time the loss occurs. First, to the extent that donor-imposed temporary restrictions on net appreciation have not been met prior to the loss, the loss reduces temporarily restricted net assets. The remaining loss reduces unrestricted net assets, which can be viewed as reducing any net appreciation classified in that net asset class and then reducing unrestricted net assets for any excess loss (that is, the amount by which the fair value of the assets of the fund is less than the historic dollar value). In other words, when losses exceed the net appreciation classified in temporarily restricted and unrestricted net assets, the excess loss reduces unrestricted net assets.

75. The Board concluded that the method used in this Statement is most consistent with the fundamental conclusions described in paragraphs 68–72. Under that method, different interpretations of "the assets of an endowment fund," especially differences in how and when net appreciation is removed from the fund, have a lesser effect on the classification of net assets. A loss that reduces the fair value of the assets of the endowment fund to historic dollar value and a loss that reduces the fair value below historic dollar value reduce the same net asset class, unrestricted net assets, unless restrictions on net appreciation have not been met prior to the loss. The effects of appropriation are minimized because the amounts appropriated for expenditure also are classified in unrestricted net assets (or will be reclassified to that net asset class shortly because the donor-imposed restrictions will be met when the amounts are spent).

76. A drawback of that method is that excess losses decrease unrestricted net assets even if the organization is not required by a donor-imposed restriction or law to use its unrestricted resources to restore immediately the value of the endowment fund to the level required by donor stipulations or law. Some respondents said that that drawback could be mitigated by requiring organizations to disclose the amount of the deficiency when the fair value of the assets of a donor-restricted endowment fund is less than the level required by the donor's restriction or law. The Board agreed and added that requirement. However, the field test results indicated that, except in the early years of an endowment fund, incidences of excess losses will be few because organizations generally accumulate net appreciation through policies that preserve and grow their endowment funds.

77. Because unrestricted net assets are reduced for the excess loss when the fair value of the assets of the endowment fund falls below the fund's historic dollar value, this Statement requires that unrestricted net assets be restored from future gains for that reduction. Some respondents said that that classification was confusing and that they would expect those gains to be classified as increases in permanently restricted net assets because they cannot be appropriated for expenditure. However, because the prior loss did not reduce permanently restricted net assets, the classification suggested by respondents would increase the amount of permanently restricted net assets beyond the level required by donor restrictions or law. Thus, gains that restore the fair value of the assets of the endowment fund to the fund's required level (historic dollar value) should be classified as increases to the same class of net assets that was previously reduced for the excess loss—unrestricted net assets. After the fair value of the assets of the endowment fund equals the required level, gains are again available for expenditure, and those gains that are restricted by the donor are classified as increases in temporarily restricted net assets.

Other methods considered

78. The Board also considered a method in which losses would reduce temporarily restricted and unrestricted net assets to the extent that unappropriated net appreciation is classified in those net asset classes, but the excess loss would reduce permanently restricted net assets if the donor required the fund to be invested in perpetuity or would reduce temporarily restricted net assets if the donor required the fund to be invested for a specified term. Most respondents that commented on the endowment loss provisions preferred that method.

79. That method would result in the same classification of net assets as this Statement except when the fair value of the assets of the endowment fund is less than historic dollar value. However, it cannot accommodate differing interpretations of "the assets of an endowment fund." Unless all organizations interpret the phrase in the same way, the calculation of the excess loss could differ, resulting in different classifications of net assets in similar circumstances. In addition, how and when an organization removes net appreciation from the fund also can affect classification of net assets. If an organization determines that appropriated amounts are unavailable to absorb losses on the investments of an endowment fund, an action of the governing board to appropriate an amount forces a larger reduction in permanently restricted net assets than would have occurred if that

amount had not been appropriated. The Board concluded that it is unacceptable to have differing classifications of net assets result from an action of the governing board. The Board rejected that method after evaluating it in light of the fundamental conclusions in paragraphs 68–72.

80. The Board also considered a second method that would allocate income, gains, and losses between the classes of net assets based on the proportionate interests of those classes in the investment pool—or the investments of each fund if investments were not pooled. Each time the fair value of the units related to permanently restricted net assets increased beyond historic dollar value, units with a value equal to the net appreciation would be transferred to temporarily restricted net assets (or unrestricted net assets if the donor did not restrict the use of income from the endowment). Each time a restriction expired, units with a value equal to the expired amount would be transferred from temporarily restricted net assets to unrestricted net assets. Income and gains on the units related to permanently restricted net assets would be classified as increases in temporarily restricted net assets if restricted by the donor to a specific use; otherwise, they would increase unrestricted net assets in accordance with paragraphs 8 and 9 of this Statement. Losses on those units would decrease permanently restricted net assets. Income, gains, and losses on the units related to unrestricted and temporarily restricted net assets would increase or decrease those net asset classes.

81. That second method results in similar classifications of net assets regardless of the interpretation of "the assets of an endowment fund" or whether amounts were appropriated. Further, it is the only method considered by the Board that does not reduce unrestricted net assets for a loss on investments of permanently restricted net assets. The method in this Statement and the other methods considered by the Board result in restriction of previously unrestricted gains when a loss occurs.

82. However, because that method allocates gains, losses, and income based on the proportionate interests of each net asset class, it can be inconsistent with some organizations' interpretations of their fiduciary responsibilities to maintain the assets of the endowment fund and to use the income earned by those assets in accordance with the donors' stipulations. That method's classification of losses is most consistent with an interpretation that an organization's fiduciary responsibilities do not extend to net appreciation of

previous periods; that is, net appreciation is not included in "the assets of an endowment fund." The Board rejected the second method after evaluating it in light of the fundamental conclusions in paragraphs 68–72.

Disclosures

83. Using an approach of broad standards for basic information similar to that used in Statement 117, the Board determined the information that is required to be disclosed without prescribing whether it should be disclosed on the face of the statements or in the notes. That approach allows an organization's management to report the information in a manner that is most useful to users of its financial statements. The disclosure requirements are not intended to limit the amount of detail or the manner of providing information; additional classifications and subclassifications may be useful.

84. The Board developed the disclosure requirements after consulting with its task force and with users of financial statements of not-for-profit organizations. It also considered existing disclosure requirements for investments reported at fair value, especially those found in Statements 35 and 115. The Board believes that the required disclosures provide information that is useful in assessing management's stewardship and the organization's liquidity and exposure to risk.

85. Some respondents questioned the need for the information about the composition of investment return or the reconciliation required if investment return is separated into operating and nonoperating amounts. Disclosures required for investment return reinforce the requirements of Statement 117 to (a) report information about revenues, gains, and losses by aggregating items into relatively homogeneous groups and (b) disclose information about the nature of a reported measure of operations if the definition of operations is not apparent from the face of the statement of activities. Users of financial information indicated that the disclosures required by paragraph 14 were especially useful in their work. The Board retained those requirements.

86. A few respondents suggested that additional guidance should be provided for the disclosure about "significant concentration of market risk or risk of physical loss" that was proposed in the Exposure Draft. Others suggested that the Board should quantify *significant*. The Board believes that management's judgment about concentrations and significance is in itself useful information. Therefore, the

Board chose not to define further those terms. The Board concluded that an entity should review its portfolio of investments to determine if any significant concentrations of market risk result from the nature of the investments or from a lack of diversity of industry, currency, or geographic location. The Board decided to delete the requirement to disclose information about the risk of physical loss.

87. The Board concluded that disclosure of realized gains and losses is necessary when investments that are reported at measures other than fair value are sold. Without that disclosure, information about total investment return may be misleading to donors, creditors, and other users of financial statements because the realized gains or losses reported will represent the activity of more than a single period; that is, the organization's change in net assets will include unrealized gains and losses accumulated in previous periods but not recognized until the year of sale.

88. However, the Board is not convinced that information about realized gains and losses or about the historical cost of investments is relevant and useful for investments reported at fair value when the changes in their fair values are reported in a statement of activities. Most respondents agreed. Both realized and unrealized net gains on endowment funds may be prudently spent in accordance with the Uniform Act. Thus, distinguishing between them does not enhance a user's assessment of an organization's ability to provide mission-related services and to pay debtors. Both realized and unrealized gains and losses are included in a statement of activities, and opportunities for managing change in net assets through selective sale of securities are greatly reduced by the requirements of this Statement. A user, therefore, does not need information about realized and unrealized gains and losses and about the historical cost of investments to determine if selective sales are occurring. Further, a user does not need the information to determine the potential tax consequences of management's decisions to sell or hold investments; realization of gains and losses has no tax consequences for most not-for-profit organizations.

89. The Board recognizes that information about realized and unrealized gains and losses and about historical costs of investments may be useful in some circumstances. For example, if a state adopted a modified form of the Uniform Act that allows a not-for-profit organization to spend only realized gains or if an organization pays taxes on realized gains and

losses, information that distinguishes between realized and unrealized amounts may be useful. Thus, this Statement does not preclude disclosing that information.

90. The Exposure Draft would have required that organizations disclose information about their investment objectives and about the contractual maturities of debt securities. Many respondents, including users of financial statements, asked the Board not to require those disclosures. Some said that information about investment objectives should not be required of not-for-profit organizations because Statement 115 does not require business enterprises to make that disclosure. Others said that organizations may have different objectives for different investment portfolios and that, as an organization's policies become more complex, investment objectives become more difficult to summarize. Still others said that the resulting disclosures might be "boilerplate" or would be meaningless without an accompanying disclosure of investment performance. A number of respondents said that information about contractual maturities was unnecessary when debt securities are reported at fair value. The Board decided that the information need not be disclosed.

Effective Date and Transition Method

91. The Board concluded that this Statement should be effective for fiscal years beginning after December 15, 1995. That effective date corresponds to the later effective date of Statements 116 and 117, which are effective for fiscal years beginning after December 15, 1995, for organizations with less than $5 million in total assets and $1 million in revenues. It was not possible to require the implementation of this Statement for the earlier effective date of Statements 116 and 117 (fiscal years beginning after December 15, 1994).

92. A few respondents said that smaller organizations might have difficulty implementing this Statement by its effective date. Because the AICPA Guides and Statement 107 require disclosure of the fair value of investments, organizations already have the necessary information systems in place. In addition, many not-for-profit organizations already report investments at fair value. Thus, the Board concluded that there is adequate time to develop the information required by this Statement. The Statement should not be difficult to implement, except perhaps for the release of restrictions on investment appreciation.

93. The Board decided to allow prospective treatment for the release of restrictions on previously unrecognized gains and losses. Determining the expiration of restrictions may be difficult or impossible if an organization no longer has the necessary records or if past procedures did not require those records. The Board permits similar treatment for expiration of restrictions on contributions in Statement 116.

94. Early application of this Statement is encouraged whenever practicable. Some respondents said that applying this Statement early may result in some loss of comparability of reporting between organizations during the transition period; however, the Board concluded that the benefits of early application outweigh its disadvantages. In addition, allowing early implementation will allow organizations that must implement Statements 116 and 117 on the earlier effective date to implement this Statement in the same fiscal year.

Appendix C

ILLUSTRATIVE EXAMPLES

Example of Classification of an Endowment Fund Loss

95. This example illustrates the classification prescribed by this Statement of a loss on investments of a donor-restricted endowment fund. Paragraph 12 of

this Statement requires that in the absence of donor stipulations or law to the contrary, losses on the investments of a donor-restricted endowment fund reduce temporarily restricted net assets to the extent that donor-imposed temporary restrictions on net appreciation of the fund have not been met before the loss occurs. Any remaining loss reduces unrestricted net assets. Paragraph 13 requires that if losses reduce the assets of a donor-restricted endowment fund below the level required by donor stipulations or law, gains that restore the fair value of the assets of the endowment fund to the required level are classified as increases in unrestricted net assets.

Year 1

96. At the beginning of year 1, NFP Organization received a gift of $1,000,000. The donor specified that the gift be used to create an endowment fund that will be invested in perpetuity with income to be used for the support of Program A. The investments purchased with the gift earned $30,000 of investment income. NFP Organization spent that income plus an additional $20,000 of unrestricted resources on Program A during the year. At the end of the year, the fair value of the investments was $1,047,000.

Transactions for year 1 are classified as increases or decreases in permanently restricted net assets, temporarily restricted net assets, or unrestricted net assets as follows:

| | Net Assets | | | |
Transactions	Unrestricted	Temporarily Restricted	Permanently Restricted	Total
Activity of Program A				
Board-designated resources[a]	$ 20,000			$ 20,000
Investment income		$ 30,000		30,000
Expenses	(50,000)			(50,000)
Release restriction[b]	30,000	(30,000)		
Subtotal	0	0		0
Investments				
Gift			$1,000,000	1,000,000
Gains[c]		47,000		47,000
Release restriction[b]	20,000	(20,000)		
Subtotal	20,000	27,000	1,000,000	1,047,000
End of year	$ 20,000	$ 27,000	$1,000,000	$1,047,000

a. The governing board designates $20,000 of unrestricted resources of the organization to be spent in support of Program A.
b. When $50,000 is spent in support of Program A, restrictions are released on the $30,000 of income and $20,000 of temporarily restricted gains according to the provisions of Statement 116. The restrictions on the gains expire even though the governing board chose to use unrestricted resources rather than sell some investments and use the proceeds for Program A.
c. The $47,000 gain is restricted to the same purpose as the income in accordance with the Uniform Act.

Year 2

97. On January 1, in accordance with its spending policy, the governing board of NFP Organization sold some investments for $25,000 and spent the proceeds on Program A. The remaining investments earned $30,000 of investment income, which NFP Organization also spent on Program A. At the end of the year, the fair value of the investments was $1,097,000.

Transactions for year 2 are classified as follows:

| Transactions | Net Assets | | | |
	Unrestricted	Temporarily Restricted	Permanently Restricted	Total
Activity of Program A				
Spending policy[d]		$ 25,000		$ 25,000
Investment income		30,000		30,000
Expenses	$(55,000)			(55,000)
Release restriction	55,000	(55,000)		0
Subtotal	0	0		0
Investments				
Spending policy[d]		(25,000)		(25,000)
Gains		75,000		75,000
Beginning of year	20,000	27,000	$1,000,000	1,047,000
End of year	$ 20,000	$ 77,000	$1,000,000	$1,097,000

d. When the governing board sells investments and uses the proceeds for the donor's specified purpose, the historic dollar value of the endowment fund does not change. Neither the decision by the governing board to appropriate net appreciation nor the sale of the investments changes the class of net assets in which the appropriated amount is reported. The $25,000 is classified as temporarily restricted net assets until the restriction is met by spending on Program A.

Year 3

98. On January 1, in accordance with its spending policy, the governing board of NFP Organization sold some investments for $28,000 and spent the proceeds on Program A. The remaining investments earned $30,000 of investment income, which NFP Organization also spent on Program A. At the end of the year, the fair value of the investments was $975,000.

Transactions for year 3 are classified as follows:

| Transactions | Net Assets | | | |
	Unrestricted	Temporarily Restricted	Permanently Restricted	Total
Activity of Program A				
Spending policy		$ 28,000		$ 28,000
Investment income		30,000		30,000
Expenses	$(58,000)			(58,000)
Release restriction	58,000	(58,000)		0
Subtotal	0	0		0
Investments				
Spending policy		(28,000)		(28,000)
Losses[e]	(45,000)	(49,000)		(94,000)
Beginning of year	20,000	77,000	$1,000,000	1,097,000
End of year[f]	$(25,000)	$ 0	$1,000,000	$ 975,000

e. According to the provisions of paragraph 12, the decline in the fair value of the assets of the endowment fund reduces temporarily restricted net assets by $49,000. The remaining loss reduces unrestricted net assets.

f. According to the provisions of paragraph 15(d), NFP Organization would disclose the $25,000 deficiency between the fair value of the investments of the endowment fund at the end of the year and the level required by donor stipulations or law. If NFP Organization had other donor-restricted endowment funds in deficit positions, it would disclose the aggregate amount of the deficiencies.

Year 4

99. On January 1, the governing board of NFP Organization could not apply its spending policy because the fair value of the investments was less than the historic dollar value of the fund; thus, no appreciation was available for expenditure. The investments earned income of $27,000, which NFP Organization spent on Program A. At the end of the year, the fair value of the investments was $1,005,000.

Transactions for year 4 are classified as follows:

| | Net Assets | | | |
	Unrestricted	Temporarily Restricted	Permanently Restricted	Total
Transactions				
Activity of Program A				
Investment income		$ 27,000		$ 27,000
Expenses	$(27,000)			(27,000)
Release restriction	27,000	(27,000)		0
Subtotal	0	0		0
Investments				
Gains[g]	25,000	5,000		30,000
Beginning of year	(25,000)	0	$1,000,000	975,000
End of year	$ 0	$ 5,000	$1,000,000	$1,005,000

g. According to the provisions of paragraph 13 of this Statement, because losses have reduced the assets of a donor-restricted endowment fund below the level required by donor stipulations or law ($1,000,000), the gains ($25,000) that restore the fair value of the assets of the endowment fund to the required level are classified as increases in unrestricted net assets. The remaining gains ($5,000) are available to be spent on Program A.

Example of an Organization That Separates Investment Return into Operating and Nonoperating Amounts

100. This example illustrates the disclosures required by paragraph 14 and a statement of activities that reports a portion of investment return within a measure of operations. Paragraph 14(a) requires an organization to disclose the composition of investment return including, at a minimum, investment income, net realized gains or losses on investments reported at other than fair value, and net gains or losses on investments reported at fair value. Paragraph 14(b) requires a reconciliation of investment return to amounts reported in the statement of activities if investment return is separated into operating and nonoperating amounts, together with a description of the policy used to determine the amount that is included in the measure of operations and a discussion of circumstances leading to a change, if any, in that policy. The reconciliation need not be provided if an organization includes all investment return in its measure of operations or excludes it from that measure entirely.

101. Statement 117 neither encourages nor discourages organizations from classifying items of revenues, expenses, and other changes in net assets as operating and nonoperating, but it requires that if an organization reports an intermediate measure of operations, it must do so within a financial statement that, at a minimum, reports the change in unrestricted net assets for the period. Statement 117 also specifies that if an organization's use of the term *operations* is not apparent from the details provided on the face of the statement of activities, a note to financial statements should describe the nature of the reported measure of operations or the items excluded from operations.

102. This example is illustrative only; it does not indicate a preferred method of reporting investment

return or defining operations. Organizations may separate investment return into operating and nonoperating amounts in ways that they believe will provide meaningful information to users of their financial statements. Distinctions may be based on:

a. The nature of the underlying transactions, such as classifying realized amounts as operating and unrealized amounts as nonoperating

b. Budgetary designations, such as classifying amounts computed under a spending-rate or total return policy as operating and the remainder of investment return as nonoperating

c. The reporting requirements for categories of investments used in Statement 115, such as classifying investment income, realized gains and losses, unrealized gains and losses on trading securities, and other-than-temporary impairment losses on securities (that is, all items included in net income of a business enterprise) as operating and classifying the remainder of investment return as nonoperating

d. Other characteristics that provide information that is relevant and understandable to donors, creditors, and other users of financial statements.

103. A statement of activities of Not-for-Profit Organization is illustrated below. Not-for-Profit Organization invests cash in excess of daily requirements in short-term investments; during the year, those investments earned $1,275. Most long-term investments of Not-for-Profit Organization's endowments are held in an investment pool, which earned income of $11,270 and had net gains of $15,450. Certain endowments are separately invested because of donors' requirements. The investments of those endowments earned income of $1,000 and increased in value by $1,500. One donor required that the net gains be added to the original endowment gift; that endowment's investment in the pool increased in value by $180.

Not-for-Profit Organization
Statement of Activities
Year Ended June 30, 19X1

	Unrestricted	Temporarily Restricted	Permanently Restricted	Total
Operating revenues, gains, and other support:				
Contributions	$ x,xxx	$ x,xxx		$xx,xxx
Fees	x,xxx			x,xxx
Investment return designated for current operations	11,025	4,500		15,525
Other	xxx			xxx
Net assets released from restrictions	xx,xxx	(xx,xxx)		
Total operating revenues, gains, and other support	xx,xxx	(x,xxx)		xx,xxx
Operating expenses and losses:				
Program A	xx,xxx			xx,xxx
Program B	x,xxx			x,xxx
Program C	x,xxx			x,xxx
Management and general	x,xxx			x,xxx
Fund raising	x,xxx			x,xxx
Total operating expenses	xx,xxx			xx,xxx
Change in net assets from operations	x,xxx	(x,xxx)		x,xxx
Other changes:				
Investment return in excess of amounts designated for current operations	10,992	3,798	$180	14,970
[Other items considered to be nonoperating]	x,xxx	x,xxx	xxx	x,xxx
	xxx	xxx	xxx	xxx
Change in net assets	$xx,xxx	$ x,xxx	$xxx	$xx,xxx

104. Not-for-Profit Organization would add the following illustrative text to its note to the financial statements that describes the measure of operations:

The board of trustees designates only a portion of the Organization's cumulative investment return for support of current operations; the remainder is retained to support operations of future years and to offset potential market declines. The amount computed under the endowment spending policy of the investment pool and all investment income earned by investing cash in excess of daily requirements are used to support current operations.

105. The following illustrative text and schedule would be added to a note to the financial statements

about investments to provide the information about the composition of return and the reconciliation of investment return required by paragraph 14:

State law allows the board to appropriate so much of the net appreciation as is prudent considering the Organization's long- and short-term needs, present and anticipated financial requirements, expected total return on its investments, price level trends, and general economic conditions. Under the Organization's endowment spending policy, 5 percent of the average of the fair value at the end of the previous 3 years is appropriated to support current operations. The following schedule summarizes the investment return and its classification in the statement of activities:

	Unrestricted	Temporarily Restricted	Permanently Restricted	Total
Dividends, interest, and rents (net of expenses of $565)	$ 8,400	$ 3,870		$ 12,270
Net realized and unrealized gains	12,342	4,428	$180	16,950
Return on long-term investments	20,742	8,298	180	29,220
Interest on short-term investments	1,275			1,275
Total return on investments	22,017	8,298	180	30,495
Investment return designated for current operations	(11,025)	(4,500)		(15,525)
Investment return in excess of amounts designated for current operations	$ 10,992	$ 3,798	$180	$ 14,970

106. Often, as in the example above, the amount of investment return designated for current operations is less than the total return on investments for the year. An organization may be able to designate an amount for the support of operations even if the total investment return for the year is less than the amount computed under a spending-rate policy; for example, when the organization designates part of its cumulative investment return from prior years to support its current operations. In that case, the operating and nonoperating amounts should be labeled to faithfully represent their natures. For example, the amount excluded from operations, which is negative, might be labeled "Investment return reduced by the portion of cumulative net appreciation designated for current operations."

Appendix D

AMENDMENTS TO EXISTING PRONOUNCEMENTS

107. FASB Statement No. 60, *Accounting and Reporting by Insurance Enterprises,* as amended by FASB Statement No. 115, *Accounting for Certain Investments in Debt and Equity Securities,* is amended as follows:

a. The following sentence is added at the end of paragraph 45:

A not-for-profit organization that conducts insurance activities should account for those investments in accordance with FASB Statement

No. 124, *Accounting for Certain Investments Held by Not-for-Profit Organizations.*

b. Paragraph 46 is replaced by the following:

Investments in equity securities that are not addressed by Statement 115 or Statement 124 because they do not have "readily determinable fair values" as defined by those Statements shall be reported at fair value. A business enterprise shall recognize changes in fair value as unrealized gains and losses reported, net of applicable income taxes, in a separate component of equity. A not-for-profit organization shall recognize the change in fair value in its statement of activities.

108. The following sentence is added at the end of paragraph 4 of FASB Statement No. 65, *Accounting for Certain Mortgage Banking Activities,* as amended by Statement 115:

Mortgage-backed securities held by not-for-profit organizations shall be reported at fair value in accordance with the provisions of FASB Statement No. 124, *Accounting for Certain Investments Held by Not-for-Profit Organizations.*

109. In paragraph 3 of FASB Statement No. 91, *Accounting for Nonrefundable Fees and Costs Associated with Originating or Acquiring Loans and Initial Direct Costs of Leases,* as amended by Statement 115, *of a business enterprise or change in net assets of a not-for-profit organization* is added at the end of the last sentence.

110. The last sentence of paragraph 4 of Statement 115 is replaced by the following:

> This Statement applies to cooperatives and mutual enterprises, including credit unions and mutual insurance companies, but does not apply to not-for-profit organizations. FASB Statement No. 124, *Accounting for Certain Investments Held by Not-for-Profit Organizations,* establishes standards for not-for-profit organizations.

111. In paragraph 168 of FASB Statement No. 117, *Financial Statements of Not-for-Profit Organizations,* the definition of *endowment fund* is replaced by the following:

> An established fund of cash, securities, or other assets to provide income for the maintenance of a not-for-profit organization. The use of the assets of the fund may be permanently restricted, temporarily restricted, or unrestricted. Endowment funds generally are established by donor-restricted gifts and bequests to provide a permanent endowment, which is to provide a permanent source of income, or a term endowment, which is to provide income for a specified period. The portion of a permanent endowment that must be maintained permanently—not used up, expended, or otherwise exhausted—is classified as permanently restricted net assets. The portion of a term endowment that must be maintained for a specified term is classified as temporarily restricted net assets. An organization's governing board may earmark a portion of its unrestricted net assets as a board-designated endowment (sometimes called funds functioning as endowment or quasi-endowment funds) to be invested to provide income for a long but unspecified period. A board-designated endowment, which results from an internal designation, is not donor restricted and is classified as unrestricted net assets.

Appendix E

GLOSSARY

112. This appendix contains definitions of terms or phrases as used in this Statement.

Debt security

Any security representing a creditor relationship with an enterprise. It also includes (a) preferred stock that by its terms either must be redeemed by the issuing enterprise or is redeemable at the option of the investor and (b) a collateralized mortgage obligation (CMO) (or other instrument) that is issued in equity form but is required to be accounted for as a nonequity instrument regardless of how that instrument is classified (that is, whether equity or debt) in the issuer's statement of financial position. However, it excludes option contracts, financial futures contracts, forward contracts, lease contracts, and swap contracts.

- Thus, the term *debt security* includes, among other items, U.S. Treasury securities, U.S. government agency securities, municipal securities, corporate bonds, convertible debt, commercial paper, all securitized debt instruments, such as CMOs and real estate mortgage investment conduits (REMICs), and interest-only and principal-only strips.
- Trade accounts receivable arising from sales on credit and loans receivable arising from consumer, commercial, and real estate lending activities of financial institutions and not-for-profit organizations are examples of receivables that do not meet the definition of *security;* thus, those receivables are not debt securities (unless they have been securitized, in which case they would meet the definition).

Donor-restricted endowment fund

An endowment fund that is created by a donor stipulation requiring investment of the gift in perpetuity or for a specified term. Also refer to **Endowment fund.**

Endowment fund

An established fund of cash, securities, or other assets to provide income for the maintenance of a not-for-profit organization. The use of the assets of the fund may be permanently restricted, temporarily restricted, or unrestricted. Endowment funds generally are established by donor-restricted gifts and bequests to provide a permanent endowment, which is to provide a permanent source of income, or a term endowment, which is to provide income for a specified period. The portion of a permanent endowment that must be maintained permanently—not used up, expended, or otherwise exhausted—is classified as permanently restricted net assets. The portion of a term endowment that must be maintained for a specified term is classified as temporarily restricted net assets. An organization's governing board may earmark a portion of its unrestricted net assets as a board-designated endowment (sometimes called funds functioning as endowment or quasi-endowment funds) to be invested to provide income for a long but unspecified period. A board-designated endowment, which results from an internal designation, is not donor restricted and is classified as unrestricted net assets.

Equity security

Any security representing an ownership interest in an enterprise (for example, common, preferred, or other capital stock) or the right to acquire (for example, warrants, rights, and call options) or dispose of (for example, put options) an ownership interest in an enterprise at fixed or determinable prices. However, the term does not include convertible debt or preferred stock that by its terms either must be redeemed by the issuing enterprise or is redeemable at the option of the investor.

Security

A share, participation, or other interest in property or in an enterprise of the issuer or an obligation of the issuer that (a) either is represented by an instrument issued in bearer or registered form or, if not represented by an instrument, is registered in books maintained to record transfers by or on behalf of the issuer, (b) is of a type commonly dealt in on securities exchanges or markets or, when represented by an instrument, is commonly recognized in any area in which it is issued or dealt in as a medium for investment, and (c) either is one of a class or series or by its terms is divisible into a class or series of shares, participations, interests, or obligations.

Statement of Financial Accounting Standards No. 125
Accounting for Transfers and Servicing of Financial Assets and Extinguishments of Liabilities

STATUS

Issued: June 1996

Effective Date: For transfers and servicing of financial assets and extinguishments
of liabilities occurring after December 31, 1996

Affects: Replaces APB 26, paragraph 3(a)
 Amends FAS 13, paragraph 20
 Amends FAS 22, footnote 1
 Amends FAS 65, paragraphs 1, 6, 9(a), 10, 15, and 34
 Deletes FAS 65, paragraphs 8, 11, 16 through 19, 30 and the paragraphs added by FAS 122,
  and footnotes 4 and 6
 Supersedes FAS 76
 Supersedes FAS 77
 Replaces FAS 105, paragraph 14(e)
 Replaces FAS 107, paragraph 8(b)
 Amends FAS 107, paragraph 28
 Amends FAS 115, paragraph 7
 Supersedes FAS 122
 Supersedes FTB 84-4
 Supersedes FTB 85-2
 Replaces FTB 86-2, paragraph 12
 Deletes FTB 87-3, paragraphs 1 through 7
 Replaces FTB 87-3, paragraph 9

Affected by: Paragraphs 4, 14, 31, and 243 amended by FAS 133, paragraph 536
 Paragraph 19 replaced by FAS 127, paragraph 5
 Superseded by FAS 140, paragraph 350

Other Interpretive Release: FASB Special Report, *A Guide to Implementation of Statement 125 on Accounting
 for Transfers and Servicing of Financial Assets and Extinguishments of Liabili-
 ties: Questions and Answers* (third edition) (Nullified by FAS 140)

Issues Discussed by FASB Emerging Issues Task Force (EITF)

Affects: Nullifies EITF Issues No. 85-40, 86-24, 86-39, 89-2, 92-10, and 94-9 and Topics No. D-13 and D-48
 Partially nullifies EITF Issues No. 84-5, 85-25, 86-18, 86-38, 87-30, 88-11, 88-17, 88-22, 89-4, 90-2, 92-2,
 and 96-10
 Resolves EITF Issues No. 84-21, 84-26, 85-26, 85-30, 85-34, 87-18, 87-25, and 94-4
 Partially resolves EITF Issues No. 84-20 and 87-20 and Topic No. D-14

Statement of Financial Accounting Standards No. 126
Exemption from Certain Required Disclosures about Financial Instruments for Certain Nonpublic Entities

an amendment of FASB Statement No. 107

STATUS

Issued: December 1996

Effective Date: For fiscal years ending after December 15, 1996

Affects: Amends FAS 107, paragraph 7

Affected by: Paragraph 2(c) replaced by FAS 133, paragraph 537
Paragraph 2(c) amended by FAS 149, paragraph 38
Paragraph 3 amended by FSP FAS 126-1, paragraph A5

Other Interpretive Release: FASB Staff Position FAS 126-1

SUMMARY

This Statement amends FASB Statement No. 107, *Disclosures about Fair Value of Financial Instruments*, to make the disclosures about fair value of financial instruments prescribed in Statement 107 optional for entities that meet all of the following criteria:

a. The entity is a nonpublic entity.
b. The entity's total assets are less than $100 million on the date of the financial statements.
c. The entity has not held or issued any derivative financial instruments, as defined in FASB Statement No. 119, *Disclosure about Derivative Financial Instruments and Fair Value of Financial Instruments*, other than loan commitments, during the reporting period.

This Statement shall be effective for fiscal years ending after December 15, 1996. Earlier application is permitted in financial statements that have not been issued previously.

Statement of Financial Accounting Standards No. 126

Exemption from Certain Required Disclosures about Financial Instruments for Certain Nonpublic Entities

an amendment of FASB Statement No. 107

CONTENTS

INTRODUCTION

1. The FASB received requests that it exempt certain entities from the requirements of FASB Statement No. 107, *Disclosures about Fair Value of Financial Instruments.* The Board concluded that the disclosures required by Statement 107 should be optional for certain nonpublic entities. The basis for the Board's conclusions is presented in the appendix to this Statement.

STANDARDS OF FINANCIAL ACCOUNTING AND REPORTING

2. Disclosures about the fair value of financial instruments prescribed in Statement 107 shall be optional for an entity that meets all of the following criteria:

a. The entity is a nonpublic entity.
b. The entity's total assets are less than $100 million on the date of the financial statements.
c. The entity has no instrument that, in whole or in part, is accounted for as a derivative instrument under FASB

Statement No. 133, *Accounting for Derivative Instruments and Hedging Activities,* other than commitments related to the origination of mortgage loans to be held for sale during the reporting period.

The criteria shall be applied to the most recent year presented in comparative financial statements to determine applicability of this Statement. If disclosures are not required in the current period, the disclosures for previous years may be omitted if financial statements for those years are presented for comparative purposes. If disclosures are required in the current period, disclosures about the fair value of financial instruments prescribed in Statement 107 that have not been reported previously need not be included in financial statements that are presented for comparative purposes.

3. For purposes of this Statement, a nonpublic entity is any entity other than one (a) whose debt or equity securities trade in a public market either on a stock exchange (domestic or foreign) or in the over-the-counter market, including securities quoted only locally or regionally, (b) that is a conduit bond

obligor for conduit debt securities[a] that are traded in a public market (a domestic or foreign stock exchange or an over-the-counter market, including local or regional markets), (c) that makes a filing with a regulatory agency in preparation for the sale of any class of debt or equity securities in a public market, or (d) that is controlled by an entity covered by (a), (b), or (c).

4. This Statement does not change the requirements of FASB Statements No. 115, *Accounting for Certain Investments in Debt and Equity Securities,* and No. 124, *Accounting for Certain Investments Held by Not-for-Profit Organizations* (including disclosures about financial instruments other than equity and debt securities that are measured at fair value in the statement of financial position), or any requirements, other than those specified in paragraph 2, for recogni-

tion, measurement, classification, or disclosure of financial instruments in financial statements.

Amendment to Statement 107

5. The following is added at the end of the second sentence of paragraph 7 of Statement 107:

> but is optional for those entities covered by FASB Statement No. 126, *Exemption from Certain Required Disclosures about Financial Instruments for Certain Nonpublic Entities.*

Effective Date

6. This Statement shall be effective for fiscal years ending after December 15, 1996. Earlier application is permitted in financial statements that have not been issued previously.

The provisions of this Statement need not be applied to immaterial items.

This Statement was adopted by the unanimous vote of the seven members of the Financial Accounting Standards Board:

Dennis R. Beresford,
Chairman
Joseph V. Anania

Anthony T. Cope
John M. Foster
James J. Leisenring

Robert H. Northcutt
Robert J. Swieringa

---

[a]*Conduit debt securities* refers to certain limited-obligation revenue bonds, certificates of participation, or similar debt instruments issued by a state or local governmental entity for the express purpose of providing financing for a specific third party (the conduit bond obligor) that is not a part of the state or local government's financial reporting entity. Although conduit debt securities bear the name of the governmental entity that issues them, the governmental entity often has no obligation for such debt beyond the resources provided by a lease or loan agreement with the third party on whose behalf the securities are issued. Further, the conduit bond obligor is responsible for any future financial reporting requirements.

Appendix

BACKGROUND INFORMATION AND BASIS FOR CONCLUSIONS

CONTENTS

Appendix

BACKGROUND INFORMATION AND BASIS FOR CONCLUSIONS

Introduction

7. This appendix summarizes considerations that were deemed significant by Board members in reaching the conclusions in this Statement. It discusses reasons for accepting certain views and rejecting others. Individual Board members gave greater weight to some factors than to others.

8. The Board issued an Exposure Draft, *Elimination of Certain Disclosures about Financial Instruments by Small Nonpublic Entities,* on September 20, 1996. The Exposure Draft proposed making the disclosures prescribed by Statement 107 optional for nonpublic entities with total assets of less than $10 million that do not hold or issue derivative instruments during the reporting period. The Board received 76 comment letters. The Board considered those comments and revised the Exposure Draft by clarifying this Statement's applicability and modifying the criteria for determining if the disclosures required by Statement 107 are optional. The Board concluded that it could reach an informed decision on the basis of existing information without a public hearing.

Benefits and Costs

9. The mission of the Board is to establish and improve standards of financial accounting and reporting for the guidance and education of the public, including issuers, auditors, and users of financial information. In fulfilling that mission, the Board strives to determine that a proposed standard will fill a significant need and that the costs imposed to meet that standard, as compared with other alternatives, are justified in relation to the overall benefits of the resulting information. Present and potential investors, creditors, and others benefit from improvements in financial reporting; however, the costs to implement a new standard may not be borne evenly by all parties. Further, the costs of not issuing a standard are impossible to quantify. Because there is no common gauge by which to judge objectively the costs to implement a standard against the need to improve information in financial statements, the Board's assessment of the costs and benefits of issuing an accounting standard is unavoidably subjective.

10. The Board has a commitment to consider potential disclosure differences between small and large companies on a case-by-case basis.[1] The Board recognizes that there is an incremental cost of applying Statement 107. The Board has long acknowledged that the cost of any accounting requirement falls disproportionately on small entities because of their

---

[1] "Board Responds to Concerns about 'Standards Overload,' " FASB *Status Report,* No. 150, November 22, 1983.

limited accounting resources and need to rely on outside professionals.[2]

11. In paragraph 79 of Statement 107, the Board observed:

> The Board considered whether certain entities should be excluded from the scope of this Statement. In particular, the Board considered the usefulness of the disclosures about fair value required by this Statement for small, nonpublic, or predominantly nonfinancial entities; a number of respondents to the 1990 Exposure Draft suggested exclusions on one or more of those bases. After considering the costs and benefits of those disclosures, the Board concluded that the disclosures are important and should be required for all entities, including small and nonpublic entities. The Board believes that the notion of "practicability" discussed in paragraph 15 ensures that excessive costs do not have to be incurred to comply with the disclosure requirements. In addition, the Board's decision to allow smaller entities additional time to apply the provisions of this Statement recognizes the fact that the costs of compliance can be reduced for those entities because the overall benefits of the information might be less than for larger entities.

12. Public accountants who serve smaller nonpublic entities informed the Board that the practicability provisions of Statement 107 have been useful in reducing the costs of complying with the Statement. However, they also reported that there is a cost of documenting compliance with the Statement, including the reasons why an entity concludes that estimating fair value is impracticable.

13. This Statement will result in some loss of information provided by the financial statements of certain nonpublic entities. However, the Board views that loss as temporary. The Board currently plans to address a number of issues involving the recognition and measurement of financial instruments. As those issues are resolved, the disclosures required by Statement 107 will change. The Board will have the opportunity to consider whether the entities to which this Statement applies should make the revised disclosures.

Fair Value Information in the Financial Statements of Smaller Nonpublic Entities

14. The Board has concluded in its Exposure Draft, *Accounting for Derivative and Similar Financial Instruments and for Hedging Activities,* that fair value is the most relevant measure for financial instruments. Nothing in this Statement changes that view. However, the Board concluded that the disclosures required by Statement 107 likely have limited utility to users of the financial statements of certain nonpublic entities. In reaching that conclusion, the Board considered (a) the types of financial instruments held by smaller nonpublic entities, (b) the extent to which those entities' financial statements already provide information about the fair value of financial instruments, and (c) the extent to which those entities make use of Statement 107's practicability provisions.

Types of Financial Instruments

15. Smaller nonpublic entities are less likely than larger entities to engage in complex financial transactions. Apart from cash and trade receivables, their financial assets tend to be traded securities, investments in other closely held entities, and balances with related parties. Their financial liabilities tend to be trade payables, variable-rate loans, and fixed-rate loans. In contrast, entities that engage in complex financial transactions or that have substantial risk associated with changes in the fair values of financial instruments are likely to use derivative financial instruments. This Statement does not apply to entities that held or issued derivative financial instruments, other than loan commitments, during the reporting period.

Information Already Provided in Financial Statements

16. The financial statements of entities covered by this Statement generally provide significant information about fair value of financial instruments, even without the requirements of Statement 107. Trade receivables and payables and variable-rate instruments are already carried at amounts that approximate fair value. Investments in securities addressed by Statements 115 and 124 are carried at fair value (as trading or available-for-sale) or, if carried at cost, the fair values are disclosed. Existing disclosures about fixed-rate long-term debt include information about interest rates and repayment terms. That information

---

[2] "FASB Analyzes Small Business Concerns about Accounting Standards," FASB *Status Report,* No. 181, November 3, 1986.

should allow users to estimate whether the fair value of the long-term debt is significantly different from the carrying amount.

Use of the Practicability Exception

17. The Board has been informed that smaller entities make frequent use of Statement 107's practicability exception when considering whether to disclose the fair value of many financial instruments, especially investments in other closely held entities and balances with related parties.

18. After considering the issues discussed in paragraphs 14-17, the Board concluded that, pending resolution of the underlying recognition and measurement issues, certain entities should have the option of not making disclosures mandated by Statement 107.

Factors Considered in Determining Scope

19. In considering which entities might be removed from the scope of Statement 107, the Board considered questions of size, financial activity, and ownership.

20. Previous FASB Statements that provided differential disclosure requirements have done so based on whether the entity is nonpublic. That criterion alone would have removed many large, nonpublic entities with complicated financial activities from the scope of Statement 107. The Board does not believe that it is appropriate to exempt those entities from the scope of Statement 107.

21. The Board decided that a size criterion was necessary to supplement the nonpublic criterion used in earlier pronouncements. The Exposure Draft proposed $10 million of total assets. The majority of the respondents to the Exposure Draft said that that amount was too low. The Board considered the nature of financial instruments in smaller nonpublic firms that do not use derivative financial instruments and decided that a higher threshold was acceptable. The Board settled on $100 million of total assets as an amount. In reaching its decision, the Board noted that exempting certain entities from current fair value disclosures is a practical matter and that the criteria used in paragraph 2 of this Statement are not meant to carry over into or influence future considerations about the usefulness of disclosures about financial instruments or other matters.

22. Some respondents said that total-asset size was not the best indicator of the relevance of disclosures about financial instruments. Some firms would not qualify for exemption as a result of having significant inventory or other physical assets. The Board considered changing the criterion to total financial instruments or to the amount of financial instruments not included within the scope of Statement 115 or Statement 124. While a criterion based on financial instruments may be more pertinent to the decision to exempt certain entities from the disclosure requirements in Statement 107, the Board decided that such a criterion would unnecessarily complicate the standard. The objective of this Statement is to reduce complexity for certain entities, and requiring them to make decisions as to what is and what is not a financial instrument would not contribute to that objective. A total-asset criterion is easier to apply and could accomplish much of the same effect.

23. A larger total-asset criterion also exempts more financial institutions and other entities with higher concentrations of financial instruments. Some Board members were concerned that disclosures about fair values of financial instruments are particularly relevant for those entities. However, the Board decided to exempt entities with less than $100 million of total assets that meet the other criteria in this Statement. In reaching that decision, the Board considered (a) available evidence about the composition of assets at smaller financial institutions and (b) regulatory requirements for reporting fair values to the Federal Deposit Insurance Corporation.

24. The Board had concluded in the Exposure Draft that an entity that uses derivative financial instruments subject to the requirements of Statement 119 should remain within the scope of Statement 107. Statements 119 and 107 interact with one another, and their requirements are not easily separated. More important, an entity that uses derivative financial instruments is not, by virtue of its utilization of complex financial instruments, the type of entity to which this Statement is intended to apply. Several respondents to the Exposure Draft indicated that the definition of derivative financial instruments in Statement 119 includes loan commitments and, as such, many entities would be precluded from applying this Statement. The Board agreed that loan commitments should not preclude entities from applying the provisions of this Statement.

25. Some respondents noted that the Exposure Draft was not clear on whether disclosures are required when previous periods are presented for comparative

purposes. The Board determined that it would not be cost beneficial to provide information for periods presented for comparative purposes unless those disclosures were presented in prior periods and the disclosures prescribed by Statement 107 are required in the current period. The following table presents the requirements for disclosures when prior periods are presented in comparative financial statements.

If Disclosures for the Current Period Are:	And Disclosures for Prior Periods Were:	Then Disclosures for Prior Periods Presented in Comparative Statements Are:
Optional	Optional	Optional
Optional	Required	Optional
Required	Optional	Optional
Required	Required	Required

Statement of Financial Accounting Standards No. 127
Deferral of the Effective Date of Certain Provisions
of FASB Statement No. 125

an amendment of FASB Statement No. 125

STATUS

Issued: December 1996

Effective Date: December 31, 1996

Affects: Replaces FAS 125, paragraph 19

Affected by: Superseded by FAS 140, paragraph 350

Statement of Financial Accounting Standards No. 127
Deferral of the Effective Date of Certain Provisions of FASB Statement No. 125

an amendment of FASB Statement No. 125

STATUS

Issued: December 1996

Effective Date: December 31, 1996

Affects: Replaces FAS 125 paragraph 19

Affected by: Superseded by FAS 140, Paragraph 350

Statement of Financial Accounting Standards No. 128
Earnings per Share

STATUS

Issued: February 1997

Effective Date: For financial statements for both interim and annual periods ending after December 15, 1997

Affects: Supersedes APB 15
      Amends APB 18, paragraph 18
      Replaces APB 18, footnote 8
      Amends APB 20, paragraphs 20, 21, 42 through 44, and 46 through 48
      Replaces APB 28, paragraph 30(b)
      Amends APB 30, paragraph 9
      Replaces APB 30, paragraph 12
      Deletes APB 30, footnote 3
      Supersedes AIN-APB 15, Interpretations No. 1 through 102
      Supersedes AIN-APB 20, Interpretations No. 1 and 2
      Amends FAS 21, paragraphs 12 and 14
      Deletes FAS 21, footnote 3
      Supersedes FAS 85
      Replaces FAS 123, paragraphs 49, 359, and 360 and footnote 26
      Amends FAS 123, paragraphs 50, 357, and 358
      Deletes FAS 123, paragraph 361
      Replaces FIN 28, paragraph 6
      Supersedes FIN 31
      Replaces FIN 38, paragraph 7
      Amends FTB 79-8, paragraph 2

Affected by: Paragraphs 15, 37, 148, and 149 amended by FAS 154, paragraph C19(c)
      Paragraphs 20 through 23 amended by FAS 123(R), paragraphs D14(a), D14(b), D9, and
        D14(c), respectively
      Paragraph 24 amended by FAS 150, paragraph C1
      Paragraph 28 amended by FAS 135, paragraph 4(v)
      Paragraph 59 amended by FAS 141, paragraph E17
      Paragraph 151 amended by FAS 123(R), paragraph D9
      Paragraphs 157 through 159 replaced by FAS 123(R), paragraph D14(d)
      Paragraph 171 amended by FAS 145, paragraph 9(i)
      Footnotes 12 and 13 amended by FAS 123(R), paragraphs D14(a) and D14(b)

AICPA Accounting Standards Executive Committee (AcSEC)

  Related Pronouncements: SOP 76-3
                    SOP 90-7
                    SOP 93-6

Issues Discussed by FASB Emerging Issues Task Force (EITF)

Affects: Partially nullifies EITF Issues No. 85-18 and 90-4
            Partially resolves EITF Issue No. 96-13

Interpreted by: Paragraph 8 interpreted by EITF Topic No. D-82
                   Paragraph 9 interpreted by EITF Topics No. D-42, D-53, and D-82
                   Paragraph 26 interpreted by EITF Topic No. D-53
                   Paragraph 29 interpreted by EITF Topic No. D-72
                   Paragraph 46 and footnote 18 interpreted by EITF Topic No. D-62
                   Paragraphs 60 and 61 interpreted by EITF Issues No. 03-6 and 04-12

Related Issues: EITF Issues No. 84-22, 90-19, 92-3, 99-7, 00-19, 04-8, and 05-1 and Topics No. D-15 and
                   D-98

SUMMARY

This Statement establishes standards for computing and presenting earnings per share (EPS) and applies to entities with publicly held common stock or potential common stock. This Statement simplifies the standards for computing earnings per share previously found in APB Opinion No. 15, *Earnings per Share,* and makes them comparable to international EPS standards. It replaces the presentation of primary EPS with a presentation of basic EPS. It also requires dual presentation of basic and diluted EPS on the face of the income statement for all entities with complex capital structures and requires a reconciliation of the numerator and denominator of the basic EPS computation to the numerator and denominator of the diluted EPS computation.

Basic EPS excludes dilution and is computed by dividing income available to common stockholders by the weighted-average number of common shares outstanding for the period. Diluted EPS reflects the potential dilution that could occur if securities or other contracts to issue common stock were exercised or converted into common stock or resulted in the issuance of common stock that then shared in the earnings of the entity. Diluted EPS is computed similarly to fully diluted EPS pursuant to Opinion 15.

This Statement supersedes Opinion 15 and AICPA Accounting Interpretations 1-102 of Opinion 15. It also supersedes or amends other accounting pronouncements listed in Appendix D. The provisions in this Statement are substantially the same as those in International Accounting Standard 33, *Earnings per Share,* recently issued by the International Accounting Standards Committee.

This Statement is effective for financial statements issued for periods ending after December 15, 1997, including interim periods; earlier application is not permitted. This Statement requires restatement of all prior-period EPS data presented.

Statement of Financial Accounting Standards No. 128

Earnings per Share

CONTENTS

INTRODUCTION

1. This Statement specifies the computation, presentation, and disclosure requirements for **earnings per share**[1] (EPS) for entities with publicly held **common stock** or **potential common stock.** This Statement's objective is to simplify the computation of earnings per share and to make the U.S. standard for computing earnings per share more compatible with the EPS standards of other countries and with that of the International Accounting Standards Committee (IASC).

2. In 1969, the AICPA issued APB Opinion No. 15, *Earnings per Share,* and by 1971 had published 102 Accounting Interpretations of Opinion 15. Given the widespread use of EPS data, the objective of Opinion 15 was to provide a standard so that earnings per share would be computed on a consistent basis and presented in the most meaningful manner. That objective also underlies this Statement.

3. Opinion 15 permitted a single presentation of "earnings per common share" for entities with simple capital structures. That presentation was similar to **basic EPS,** which is a common presentation outside the United States. However, Opinion 15 required that entities with complex capital structures present both "primary" and "fully diluted" EPS on the face of the

---

[1]Terms defined in Appendix E, the glossary, are set in **boldface type** the first time they appear.

income statement. The primary EPS computation included "common stock equivalents" in the denominator (the number of common shares outstanding). Only two other countries require presentation of primary EPS; all other countries that have EPS requirements require presentation of only basic EPS or both basic and fully diluted EPS.

4. In October 1993, the IASC issued a draft Statement of Principles, *Earnings per Share,* for public comment. Because earnings per share is one of the most widely used financial statistics, the IASC's goal was to initiate a common approach to the determination and presentation of earnings per share that would permit global comparisons. Even though EPS data may have limitations because of the different national methods for determining "earnings," the IASC and the FASB believe that a consistently determined denominator will be a significant improvement in international financial reporting.

5. The Board pursued its EPS project concurrently with the IASC to help achieve international harmonization of the accounting standards for computing earnings per share. The focus of the project was on the denominator of the EPS computation, not on issues about the determination of earnings. The IASC issued IAS 33, *Earnings per Share,* concurrently with the issuance of this Statement; the provisions in that Standard are substantially the same as those in this Statement.

STANDARDS OF FINANCIAL ACCOUNTING AND REPORTING

Scope

6. This Statement requires presentation of earnings per share by all entities that have issued common stock or potential common stock (that is, **securities** such as **options, warrants, convertible securities,** or **contingent stock agreements**) if those securities trade in a public market either on a stock exchange (domestic or foreign) or in the over-the-counter market, including securities quoted only locally or regionally. This Statement also requires presentation of

earnings per share by an entity that has made a filing or is in the process of filing with a regulatory agency in preparation for the sale of those securities in a public market. This Statement does not require presentation of earnings per share for investment companies[2] or in statements of wholly owned subsidiaries. Any entity that is not required by this Statement to present earnings per share in its financial statements that chooses to present earnings per share in its financial statements shall do so in accordance with the provisions of this Statement.

7. This Statement supersedes Opinion 15, AICPA Accounting Interpretations 1-102 of Opinion 15, AICPA Accounting Interpretations 1, "Changing EPS Denominator for Retroactive Adjustment to Prior Period," and 2, "EPS for 'Catch-up' Adjustment," of APB Opinion No. 20, *Accounting Changes,* FASB Statement No. 85, *Yield Test for Determining whether a Convertible Security Is a Common Stock Equivalent,* and FASB Interpretation No. 31, *Treatment of Stock Compensation Plans in EPS Computations.* It also amends other accounting pronouncements listed in Appendix D.

Basic Earnings per Share

8. The objective of basic EPS is to measure the performance of an entity over the reporting period. Basic EPS shall be computed by dividing **income available to common stockholders** (the numerator) by the **weighted-average number of common shares outstanding** (the denominator) during the period. Shares issued during the period and shares reacquired during the period shall be weighted for the portion of the period that they were outstanding.

9. Income available to common stockholders shall be computed by deducting both the dividends declared in the period on **preferred stock** (whether or not paid) and the dividends accumulated for the period on cumulative preferred stock (whether or not earned)[3] from income from continuing operations (if that amount appears in the income statement)[4] and also from net income. If there is a loss from continuing operations or a net loss, the amount of the loss shall be increased by those preferred dividends.

---

[2]That is, investment companies that comply with the requirements of the AICPA Audit and Accounting Guide, *Audits of Investment Companies,* to present selected per-share data.

[3]Preferred dividends that are cumulative only if earned shall be deducted only to the extent that they are earned.

[4]An entity that does not report a discontinued operation but reports an extraordinary item or the cumulative effect of an accounting change in the period shall use that line item (for example, *income before extraordinary items* or *income before accounting change*) whenever the line item *income from continuing operations* is referred to in this Statement.

10. Shares issuable for little or no cash consideration upon the satisfaction of certain conditions (**contingently issuable shares**) shall be considered outstanding common shares and included in the computation of basic EPS as of the date that all necessary conditions have been satisfied (in essence, when issuance of the shares is no longer contingent). Outstanding common shares that are contingently returnable (that is, subject to recall) shall be treated in the same manner as contingently issuable shares.[5]

Diluted Earnings per Share

11. The objective of **diluted EPS** is consistent with that of basic EPS—to measure the performance of an entity over the reporting period—while giving effect to all **dilutive** potential common shares that were outstanding during the period. The computation of diluted EPS is similar to the computation of basic EPS except that the denominator is increased to include the number of additional common shares that would have been outstanding if the dilutive potential common shares had been issued. In addition, in computing the dilutive effect of convertible securities, the numerator is adjusted to add back (a) any convertible preferred dividends and (b) the after-tax amount of interest recognized in the period associated with any convertible debt. The numerator also is adjusted for any other changes in income or loss that would result from the assumed conversion of those potential common shares, such as profit-sharing expenses. Similar adjustments also may be necessary for certain contracts that provide the issuer or holder with a choice between settlement methods.

12. Diluted EPS shall be based on the most advantageous **conversion rate** or **exercise price** from the standpoint of the security holder. Previously reported diluted EPS data shall not be retroactively adjusted for subsequent conversions or subsequent changes in the market price of the common stock.

No Antidilution

13. The computation of diluted EPS shall not assume conversion, exercise, or **contingent issuance** of securities that would have an **antidilutive** effect on earnings per share. Shares issued on actual conversion, exercise, or satisfaction of certain conditions for which the underlying potential common shares were antidilutive shall be included in the computation as outstanding common shares from the date of conversion, exercise, or satisfaction of those conditions, respectively. In determining whether potential common shares are dilutive or antidilutive, each issue or series of issues of potential common shares shall be considered separately rather than in the aggregate.

14. Convertible securities may be dilutive on their own but antidilutive when included with other potential common shares in computing diluted EPS. To reflect maximum potential dilution, each issue or series of issues of potential common shares shall be considered in sequence from the most dilutive to the least dilutive. That is, dilutive potential common shares with the lowest "earnings per incremental share" shall be included in diluted EPS before those with a higher earnings per incremental share.[6] Illustration 4 in Appendix C provides an example of that provision.

15. An entity that reports a discontinued operation or an extraordinary item in a period shall use income from continuing operations[7] (adjusted for preferred dividends as described in paragraph 9) as the "control number" in determining whether those potential common shares are dilutive or antidilutive. That is, the same number of potential common shares used in computing the diluted per-share amount for income from continuing operations shall be used in computing all other reported diluted per-share amounts even

---

[5]Thus, contingently issuable shares include shares that (a) will be issued in the future upon the satisfaction of specified conditions, (b) have been placed in escrow and all or part must be returned if specified conditions are not met, or (c) have been issued but the holder must return all or part if specified conditions are not met.

[6]Options and warrants generally will be included first because use of the treasury stock method does not impact the numerator of the computation.

[6a][This footnote has been deleted because the effective date of FASB Statement No. 154, *Accounting Changes and Error Corrections,* has passed.]

[7]Refer to footnote 4.

if those amounts will be antidilutive to their respective basic per-share amounts.[8]

16. Including potential common shares in the denominator of a diluted per-share computation for continuing operations always will result in an antidilutive per-share amount when an entity has a *loss* from continuing operations or a *loss* from continuing operations available to common stockholders (that is, after any preferred dividend deductions). Although including those potential common shares in the other diluted per-share computations may be dilutive to their comparable basic per-share amounts, no potential common shares shall be included in the computation of any diluted per-share amount when a loss from continuing operations exists, even if the entity reports net income.

Options and Warrants and Their Equivalents

17. The dilutive effect of outstanding **call options** and warrants (and their equivalents) issued by the reporting entity shall be reflected in diluted EPS by application of the **treasury stock method** unless the provisions of paragraphs 24 and 50-53 require that another method be applied. Equivalents of options and warrants include nonvested stock granted to employees, stock purchase contracts, and partially paid stock subscriptions.[9] Under the treasury stock method:

a. Exercise of options and warrants shall be assumed at the beginning of the period (or at time of issuance, if later) and common shares shall be assumed to be issued.

b. The proceeds from exercise shall be assumed to be used to purchase common stock at the average market price during the period.[10]

c. The incremental shares (the difference between the number of shares assumed issued and the number of shares assumed purchased) shall be included in the denominator of the diluted EPS computation.[11]

18. Options and warrants will have a dilutive effect under the treasury stock method only when the average market price of the common stock during the period exceeds the exercise price of the options or warrants (they are "in the money"). Previously reported EPS data shall not be retroactively adjusted as a result of changes in market prices of common stock.

19. Dilutive options or warrants that are issued during a period or that expire or are canceled during a period shall be included in the denominator of diluted EPS for the period that they were outstanding. Likewise, dilutive options or warrants exercised during the period shall be included in the denominator for the period prior to actual exercise. The common shares issued upon exercise of options or warrants shall be included in the denominator for the period after the exercise date. Consequently, incremental shares assumed issued shall be weighted for the period the options or warrants were outstanding, and common shares actually issued shall be weighted for the period the shares were outstanding.

Share-based payment arrangements

20. Awards of share options and nonvested shares (as defined in FASB Statement No. 123 (revised

---

[8]For example, assume that Corporation X has income from continuing operations of $2,400, a loss from discontinued operations of $(3,600), a net loss of $(1,200), and 1,000 common shares and 200 potential common shares outstanding. Corporation X's basic per-share amounts would be $2.40 for continuing operations, $(3.60) for the discontinued operation, and $(1.20) for the net loss. Corporation X would include the 200 potential common shares in the denominator of its diluted per-share computation for continuing operations because the resulting $2.00 per share is dilutive. (For illustrative purposes, assume no numerator impact of those 200 potential common shares.) Because income from continuing operations is the control number, Corporation X also must include those 200 potential common shares in the denominator for the other per-share amounts, even though the resulting per-share amounts [$(3.00) per share for the loss from discontinued operation and $(1.00) per share for the net loss] are antidilutive to their comparable basic per-share amounts; that is, the loss per-share amounts are less.

[9]Refer to paragraph 64.

[10]Refer to paragraphs 21, 47, and 48.

[11]Consider Corporation Y that has 10,000 warrants outstanding exercisable at $54 per share; the average market price of the common stock during the reporting period is $60. Exercise of the warrants and issuance of 10,000 shares of common stock would be assumed. The $540,000 that would be realized from exercise of the warrants ($54 × 10,000) would be an amount sufficient to acquire 9,000 shares ($540,000/$60). Thus, 1,000 incremental shares (10,000 − 9,000) would be added to the outstanding common shares in computing diluted EPS for the period.

A shortcut formula for that computation follows (note that this formula may not be appropriate for stock-based compensation awards [refer to paragraph 21]):

Incremental shares = [(market price − exercise price)/market price] × shares assumed issued under option; thus, [($60 − $54)/$60] × 10,000 = 1,000 incremental shares.

2004), *Share-Based Payment*) to be issued to an employee[12] under a share-based compensation arrangement are considered options for purposes of computing diluted EPS. Such share-based awards shall be considered to be outstanding as of the grant date for purposes of computing diluted EPS even though their exercise may be contingent upon vesting. Those share-based awards are included in the diluted EPS computation even if the employee may not receive (or be able to sell) the stock until some future date. Accordingly, all shares to be issued shall be included in computing diluted EPS if the effect is dilutive. The dilutive effect of share-based compensation arrangements shall be computed using the treasury stock method. If the equity share options or other equity instruments are outstanding for only part of a period, the shares issuable shall be weighted to reflect the portion of the period during which the equity instruments were outstanding.

21. In applying the treasury stock method described in paragraph 17, the assumed proceeds shall be the sum of (a) the amount, if any, the employee must pay upon exercise, (b) the amount of compensation cost attributed to future services and not yet recognized,[13] and (c) the amount of excess tax benefits, if any, that would be credited to additional paid-in capital assuming exercise of the options. Assumed proceeds shall not include compensation ascribed to past services. The excess tax benefit is the amount resulting from a tax deduction for compensation in excess of compensation expense recognized for financial reporting purposes. That deduction arises from an increase in the market price of the stock under option between the measurement date and the date at which the compensation deduction for income tax purposes is determinable. The amount of the tax benefit shall be determined by a "with-and-without" computation. Paragraph 63 of Statement 123(R) states that the amount deductible on an employer's tax return may be less than the cumulative compensation cost recognized for financial reporting purposes. If the deferred tax asset related to that resulting difference would be deducted from additional paid-in capital (or its equivalent) pursuant to that paragraph assuming exercise of the options, that amount shall be treated as a reduction of assumed proceeds.

22. If stock-based compensation arrangements are payable in common stock or in cash at the election of either the entity or the employee, the determination of whether such stock-based awards are potential common shares shall be made based on the provisions in paragraph 29. If an entity has a tandem [award] (as defined in Statement 123(R)) that allows the entity or the employee to make an election involving two or more types of equity instruments, diluted EPS for the period shall be computed based on the terms used in the computation of compensation expense for that period.

23. Awards with a market condition, a performance condition, or any combination thereof (as defined in Statement 123(R)) shall be included in diluted EPS pursuant to the contingent share provisions in paragraphs 30–35 of this Statement.

Written put options

24. Contracts that require that the reporting entity repurchase its own stock, such as written **put options** and forward purchase contracts other than forward purchase contracts accounted for under paragraphs 21 and 22 of FASB Statement No. 150, *Accounting for Certain Financial Instruments with Characteristics of both Liabilities and Equity,* shall be reflected in the computation of diluted EPS if the effect is dilutive. If those contracts are "in the money" during the reporting period (the exercise price is above the average market price for that period), the potential dilutive effect on EPS shall be computed using the **reverse treasury stock method.** Under that method:

a. Issuance of sufficient common shares shall be assumed at the beginning of the period (at the average market price during the period) to raise enough proceeds to satisfy the contract.
b. The proceeds from issuance shall be assumed to be used to satisfy the contract (that is, to buy back shares).
c. The incremental shares (the difference between the number of shares assumed issued and the number of shares received from satisfying the

---

[12]The provisions in paragraphs 20–23 also apply to share-based awards issued to other than employees in exchange for goods and services.

[13]This provision applies only to those share-based awards for which compensation cost will be recognized in the financial statements in accordance with Statement 123(R).

contract) shall be included in the denominator of the diluted EPS computation.[14]

Purchased options

25. Contracts such as purchased put options and **purchased call options** (options held by the entity on its own stock) shall not be included in the computation of diluted EPS because including them would be antidilutive. That is, the put option would be exercised only when the exercise price is higher than the market price and the call option would be exercised only when the exercise price is lower than the market price; in both instances, the effect would be antidilutive under both the treasury stock method and the reverse treasury stock method, respectively.

Convertible Securities

26. The dilutive effect of convertible securities shall be reflected in diluted EPS by application of the **if-converted method.** Under that method:

a. If an entity has convertible preferred stock outstanding, the preferred dividends applicable to convertible preferred stock shall be added back to the numerator.[15]

b. If an entity has convertible debt outstanding, (1) interest charges applicable to the convertible debt shall be added back to the numerator, (2) to the extent nondiscretionary adjustments based on income[16] made during the period would have been computed differently had the interest on convertible debt never been recognized, the numerator shall be appropriately adjusted, and (3) the numerator shall be adjusted for the income tax effect of (1) and (2).

c. The convertible preferred stock or convertible debt shall be assumed to have been converted at the beginning of the period (or at time of issuance, if later), and the resulting common shares shall be included in the denominator.

27. In applying the if-converted method, conversion shall not be assumed for purposes of computing di-

luted EPS if the effect would be antidilutive. Convertible preferred stock is antidilutive whenever the amount of the dividend declared in or accumulated for the current period per common share obtainable on conversion exceeds basic EPS. Similarly, convertible debt is antidilutive whenever its interest (net of tax and nondiscretionary adjustments) per common share obtainable on conversion exceeds basic EPS.

28. Dilutive securities that are issued during a period and dilutive convertible securities for which conversion options lapse, for which preferred stock is redeemed, or for which related debt is extinguished during a period shall be included in the denominator of diluted EPS for the period that they were outstanding. Likewise, dilutive convertible securities converted during a period shall be included in the denominator for the period prior to actual conversion. The common shares issued upon actual conversion shall be included in the denominator for the period after the date of conversion. Consequently, shares assumed issued shall be weighted for the period the convertible securities were outstanding, and common shares actually issued shall be weighted for the period the shares were outstanding.

Contracts That May Be Settled in Stock or Cash

29. If an entity issues a contract that may be settled in common stock or in cash at the election of either the entity or the holder, the determination of whether that contract shall be reflected in the computation of diluted EPS shall be made based on the facts available each period.[17] It shall be presumed that the contract will be settled in common stock and the resulting potential common shares included in diluted EPS (in accordance with the relevant provisions of this Statement) if the effect is more dilutive. A contract that is reported as an asset or liability for accounting purposes may require an adjustment to the numerator for any changes in income or loss that would result if the contract had been reported as an equity instrument for accounting purposes during the period. That

---

[14]For example, Corporation Z sells 100 put options with an exercise price of $25; the average market price for the period is $20. In computing diluted EPS at the end of the period, Corporation Z assumes it issues 125 shares at $20 per share to satisfy its put obligation of $2,500. The difference between the 125 shares issued and the 100 shares received from satisfying the put option (25 incremental shares) would be added to the denominator of diluted EPS.

[15]The amount of preferred dividends added back will be the amount of preferred dividends for convertible preferred stock deducted from income from continuing operations (and from net income) in computing income available to common stockholders pursuant to paragraph 9.

[16]Nondiscretionary adjustments include any expenses or charges that are determined based on the income (loss) for the period, such as profit-sharing and royalty agreements.

[17]An example of such a contract is a written put option that gives the holder a choice of settling in common stock or in cash. Stock-based compensation arrangements that are payable in common stock or in cash at the election of either the entity or the employee shall be accounted for pursuant to this paragraph.

adjustment is similar to the adjustments required for convertible debt in paragraph 26(b). The presumption that the contract will be settled in common stock may be overcome if past experience or a stated policy provides a reasonable basis to believe that the contract will be paid partially or wholly in cash.

Contingently Issuable Shares

30. Shares whose issuance is contingent upon the satisfaction of certain conditions shall be considered outstanding and included in the computation of diluted EPS as follows:

a. If all necessary conditions have been satisfied by the end of the period (the events have occurred), those shares shall be included as of the beginning of the period in which the conditions were satisfied (or as of the date of the contingent stock agreement, if later).

b. If all necessary conditions have not been satisfied by the end of the period, the number of contingently issuable shares included in diluted EPS shall be based on the number of shares, if any, that would be issuable if the end of the reporting period were the end of the contingency period (for example, the number of shares that would be issuable based on current period earnings or period-end market price) and if the result would be dilutive. Those contingently issuable shares shall be included in the denominator of diluted EPS as of the beginning of the period (or as of the date of the contingent stock agreement, if later).[18]

Paragraphs 31-34 provide general guidelines that shall be applied in determining the EPS impact of different types of contingencies that may be included in contingent stock agreements.

31. If attainment or maintenance of a specified amount of earnings is the condition and if that amount has been attained, the additional shares shall be considered to be outstanding for the purpose of computing diluted EPS if the effect is dilutive. The diluted EPS computation shall include those shares that would be issued under the conditions of the contract based on the assumption that the current amount of earnings will remain unchanged until the end of the agreement, but only if the effect would be dilutive. Because the amount of earnings may change in a future period, basic EPS shall not include such contingently issuable shares because all necessary conditions have not been satisfied. Illustration 3 in Appendix C provides an example of that provision.

32. The number of shares contingently issuable may depend on the market price of the stock at a future date. In that case, computations of diluted EPS shall reflect the number of shares that would be issued based on the current market price at the end of the period being reported on if the effect is dilutive. If the condition is based on an average of market prices over some period of time, the average for that period shall be used. Because the market price may change in a future period, basic EPS shall not include such contingently issuable shares because all necessary conditions have not been satisfied.

33. In some cases, the number of shares contingently issuable may depend on both future earnings and future prices of the shares. In that case, the determination of the number of shares included in diluted EPS shall be based on both conditions, that is, earnings to date and current market price—as they exist at the end of each reporting period. If *both* conditions are not met at the end of the reporting period, no contingently issuable shares shall be included in diluted EPS.

34. If the contingency is based on a condition other than earnings or market price (for example, opening a certain number of retail stores), the contingent shares shall be included in the computation of diluted EPS based on the assumption that the current status of the condition will remain unchanged until the end of the contingency period. Illustration 3 in Appendix C provides an example of that provision.

35. Contingently issuable potential common shares (other than those covered by a contingent stock agreement, such as contingently issuable convertible securities) shall be included in diluted EPS as follows:

a. An entity shall determine whether the potential common shares may be assumed to be issuable based on the conditions specified for their issuance pursuant to the contingent share provisions in paragraphs 30-34.

b. If those potential common shares should be reflected in diluted EPS, an entity shall determine their impact on the computation of diluted EPS by

---

[18]For year-to-date computations, contingent shares shall be included on a weighted-average basis. That is, contingent shares shall be weighted for the interim periods in which they were included in the computation of diluted EPS.

following the provisions for options and warrants in paragraphs 17-25, the provisions for convertible securities in paragraphs 26-28, and the provisions for contracts that may be settled in stock or cash in paragraph 29, as appropriate.[19]

However, exercise or conversion shall not be assumed for purposes of computing diluted EPS unless exercise or conversion of similar outstanding potential common shares that are not contingently issuable is assumed.

Presentation on Face of Income Statement

36. Entities with simple capital structures, that is, those with only common stock outstanding, shall present basic per-share amounts for income from continuing operations[20] and for net income on the face of the income statement. All other entities shall present basic and diluted per-share amounts for income from continuing operations and for net income on the face of the income statement with equal prominence.

37. An entity that reports a discontinued operation or an extraordinary item in a period shall present basic and diluted per-share amounts for those line items either on the face of the income statement or in the notes to the financial statements. Per-share amounts not required to be presented by this Statement that an entity chooses to disclose shall be computed in accordance with this Statement and disclosed only in the notes to the financial statements; it shall be noted whether the per-share amounts are pretax or net of tax.[21]

Periods Presented

38. Earnings per share data shall be presented for all periods for which an income statement or summary of earnings is presented. If diluted EPS data are reported for at least one period, they shall be reported for all periods presented, even if they are the same

amounts as basic EPS. If basic and diluted EPS are the same amount, dual presentation can be accomplished in one line on the income statement.

Terminology

39. The terms *basic EPS* and *diluted EPS* are used in this Statement to identify EPS data to be presented and are not required to be captions used in the income statement. There are no explicit requirements for the terms to be used in the presentation of basic and diluted EPS; terms such as *earnings per common share* and *earnings per common share—assuming dilution,* respectively, are appropriate.

Disclosure Requirements

40. For each period for which an income statement is presented, an entity shall disclose the following:

a. A reconciliation of the numerators and the denominators of the basic and diluted per-share computations for income from continuing operations.[22] The reconciliation shall include the individual income and share amount effects of all securities that affect earnings per share.[23] Illustration 2 in Appendix C provides an example of that disclosure.
b. The effect that has been given to preferred dividends in arriving at income available to common stockholders in computing basic EPS.
c. Securities (including those issuable pursuant to contingent stock agreements) that could potentially dilute basic EPS in the future that were not included in the computation of diluted EPS because to do so would have been antidilutive for the period(s) presented.

41. For the latest period for which an income statement is presented, an entity shall provide a description of any transaction that occurs after the end of the most recent period but before issuance of the financial statements that would have changed materially the number of common shares or potential common shares outstanding at the end of the period if the

---

[19]Neither interest nor dividends shall be imputed for the additional contingently issuable convertible securities because any imputed amount would be reversed by the if-converted adjustments for assumed conversions.

[20]Refer to footnote 4.

[20a][This footnote has been deleted because the effective date of Statement 154 has passed.]

[21]Paragraph 33 of FASB Statement No. 95, *Statement of Cash Flows,* prohibits reporting an amount of cash flow per share.

[22]Refer to footnote 4.

[23]An entity is encouraged to refer to pertinent information about securities included in the EPS computations that is provided elsewhere in the financial statements as prescribed by FASB Statement No. 129, *Disclosure of Information about Capital Structure,* and other accounting pronouncements.

transaction had occurred before the end of the period. Examples of those transactions include the issuance or acquisition of common shares; the issuance of warrants, options, or convertible securities; the resolution of a contingency pursuant to a contingent stock agreement; and the conversion or exercise of potential common shares outstanding at the end of the period into common shares.

Computational Guidance

42. The determination of EPS data as required by this Statement considers the complexities of the capital structures of some entities. The calculations also shall give effect to matters such as stock dividends or splits and business combinations. Guidelines for dealing with some common computational matters

and some complex capital structures are set forth in Appendix A. That appendix is an integral part of the requirements of this Statement.

Effective Date and Transition

43. This Statement shall be effective for financial statements for both interim and annual periods ending after December 15, 1997. Earlier application is not permitted. However, an entity is permitted to disclose pro forma EPS amounts computed using this Statement in the notes to the financial statements in periods prior to required adoption. After the effective date, all prior-period EPS data presented shall be restated (including interim financial statements, summaries of earnings, and selected financial data) to conform with the provisions of this Statement.

> The provisions of this Statement need not be applied to immaterial items.

This Statement was adopted by the unanimous vote of the seven members of the Financial Accounting Standards Board:

Dennis R. Beresford,	Anthony T. Cope	James J. Leisenring
Chairman	John M. Foster	Gerhard G. Mueller
Joseph V. Anania	Gaylen N. Larson	

Appendix A

COMPUTATIONAL GUIDANCE

CONTENTS

Appendix A

COMPUTATIONAL GUIDANCE

Introduction

44. This appendix, which is an integral part of the requirements of this Statement, provides general guidance to be used in the computation of earnings per share.

Computing a Weighted Average

45. The weighted-average number of shares discussed in this Statement is an arithmetical mean average of shares outstanding and assumed to be outstanding for EPS computations. The most precise average would be the sum of the shares determined on a daily basis divided by the number of days in the period. Less-precise averaging methods may be used, however, as long as they produce reasonable results. Methods that introduce artificial weighting, such as the "Rule of 78" method, are not acceptable for computing a weighted-average number of shares for EPS computations.

Applying the Treasury Stock Method

Year-to-Date Computations

46. The number of incremental shares included in quarterly diluted EPS shall be computed using the average market prices during the three months included in the reporting period. For year-to-date diluted EPS, the number of incremental shares to be included in the denominator shall be determined by computing a year-to-date weighted average of the number of incremental shares included in each quarterly diluted EPS computation. Illustration 1 (Full Year 20X1, footnote a) in Appendix C provides an example of that provision.

Average Market Price

47. In applying the treasury stock method, the average market price of common stock shall represent a meaningful average. Theoretically, every market transaction for an entity's common stock could be included in determining the average market price. As a practical matter, however, a simple average of weekly or monthly prices usually will be adequate.

48. Generally, closing market prices are adequate for use in computing the average market price. When

prices fluctuate widely, however, an average of the high and low prices for the period that the price represents usually would produce a more representative price. The method used to compute the average market price shall be used consistently unless it is no longer representative because of changed conditions. For example, an entity that uses closing market prices to compute the average market price for several years of relatively stable market prices might need to change to an average of high and low prices if prices start fluctuating greatly and the closing market prices no longer produce a representative average market price.

Options and Warrants and Their Equivalents

49. Options or warrants to purchase convertible securities shall be assumed to be exercised to purchase the convertible security whenever the average prices of both the convertible security and the common stock obtainable upon conversion are above the exercise price of the options or warrants. However, exercise shall not be assumed unless conversion of similar outstanding convertible securities, if any, also is assumed. The treasury stock method shall be applied to determine the incremental number of convertible securities that are assumed to be issued and immediately converted into common stock. Interest or dividends shall not be imputed for the incremental convertible securities because any imputed amount would be reversed by the if-converted adjustments for assumed conversions.

50. Paragraphs 51-53 provide guidance on how certain options, warrants, and convertible securities should be included in the computation of diluted EPS. Conversion or exercise of the potential common shares discussed in those paragraphs shall not be reflected in diluted EPS unless the effect is dilutive. Those potential common shares will have a dilutive effect if (a) the average market price of the related common stock for the period exceeds the exercise price or (b) the security to be tendered is selling at a price below that at which it may be tendered under the option or warrant agreement and the resulting discount is sufficient to establish an effective exercise price below the market price of the common stock obtainable upon exercise. When several conversion alternatives exist, the computation shall give effect to the alternative that is most advantageous to the holder of the convertible security. Similar treatment shall be given to preferred stock that has similar provisions or

to other securities that have conversion options that permit the investor to pay cash for a more favorable conversion rate.

51. Options or warrants may permit or require the tendering of debt or other securities of the issuer (or its parent or its subsidiary) in payment of all or a portion of the exercise price. In computing diluted EPS, those options or warrants shall be assumed to be exercised and the debt or other securities shall be assumed to be tendered. If tendering cash would be more advantageous to the option holder or warrant holder and the contract permits tendering cash, the treasury stock method shall be applied. Interest (net of tax) on any debt assumed to be tendered shall be added back as an adjustment to the numerator. The numerator also shall be adjusted for any nondiscretionary adjustments based on income (net of tax). The treasury stock method shall be applied for proceeds assumed to be received in cash.

52. The underlying terms of certain options or warrants may require that the proceeds received from the exercise of those securities be applied to retire debt or other securities of the issuer (or its parent or its subsidiary). In computing diluted EPS, those options or warrants shall be assumed to be exercised and the proceeds applied to purchase the debt at its average market price rather than to purchase common stock under the treasury stock method. The treasury stock method shall be applied, however, for excess proceeds received from the assumed exercise. Interest, net of tax, on any debt assumed to be purchased shall be added back as an adjustment to the numerator. The numerator also shall be adjusted for any nondiscretionary adjustments based on income (net of tax).

53. Convertible securities that permit or require the payment of cash by the holder of the security at conversion are considered the equivalent of warrants. In computing diluted EPS, the proceeds assumed to be received shall be assumed to be applied to purchase common stock under the treasury stock method and the convertible security shall be assumed to be converted under the if-converted method.

Restatement of EPS Data

Stock Dividends or Stock Splits

54. If the number of common shares outstanding increases as a result of a stock dividend or stock split[24] or decreases as a result of a reverse stock split, the computations of basic and diluted EPS shall be adjusted retroactively for all periods presented to reflect that change in capital structure. If changes in common stock resulting from stock dividends, stock splits, or reverse stock splits occur after the close of the period but before issuance of the financial statements, the per-share computations for those and any prior-period financial statements presented shall be based on the new number of shares. If per-share computations reflect such changes in the number of shares, that fact shall be disclosed.

Rights Issues

55. A **rights issue** whose exercise price at issuance is less than the fair value of the stock contains a bonus element that is somewhat similar to a stock dividend. If a rights issue contains a bonus element and the rights issue is offered to all existing stockholders, basic and diluted EPS shall be adjusted retroactively for the bonus element for all periods presented. If the ability to exercise the rights issue is contingent on some event other than the passage of time, the provisions of this paragraph shall not be applicable until that contingency is resolved.

56. The number of common shares used in computing basic and diluted EPS for all periods prior to the rights issue shall be the number of common shares outstanding immediately prior to the issue multiplied by the following factor: (fair value per share immediately prior to the exercise of the rights)/(theoretical ex-rights fair value per share). Theoretical ex-rights fair value per share shall be computed by adding the aggregate fair value of the shares immediately prior to the exercise of the rights to the proceeds expected from the exercise of the rights and dividing by the number of shares outstanding after the exercise of the rights. Illustration 5 in Appendix C provides an example of that provision. If the rights themselves are to be publicly traded separately from the shares prior to the exercise date, fair value for the purposes of this computation shall be established at the close of the last day on which the shares are traded together with the rights.

Prior-Period Adjustments

57. Certain APB Opinions and FASB Statements require that a restatement of the results of operations of a prior period be included in the income statement or summary of earnings. In those instances, EPS data

---

[24]Refer to ARB No. 43, Chapter 7B, "Capital Accounts—Stock Dividends and Stock Split-Ups."

given for the prior period or periods shall be restated. The effect of the restatement, expressed in per-share terms, shall be disclosed in the period of restatement.

58. Restated EPS data shall be computed as if the restated income or loss had been reported originally in the prior period or periods. Thus, it is possible that common stock assumed to be issued upon exercise, conversion, or issuance of potential common shares in accordance with the provisions of this Statement may not be included in the computation of restated EPS amounts. That is, retroactive restatement of income from continuing operations could cause potential common shares originally determined to be dilutive to become antidilutive pursuant to the control number provision in paragraph 15. The reverse also is true. Retroactive restatement also may cause the numerator of the EPS computation to change by an amount that differs from the amount of the retroactive adjustment.

Business Combinations and Reorganizations

59. When common shares are issued to acquire a business in a business combination, the computations of earnings per share shall recognize the existence of the new shares only from the acquisition date. In reorganizations, EPS computations shall be based on analysis of the particular transaction and the provisions of this Statement.

Participating Securities and Two-Class Common Stock

60. The capital structures of some entities include:

a. Securities that may participate in dividends with common stocks according to a predetermined formula (for example, two for one) with, at times, an upper limit on the extent of participation (for example, up to, but not beyond, a specified amount per share)
b. A class of common stock with different dividend rates from those of another class of common stock but without prior or senior rights.

61. The if-converted method shall be used for those securities that are convertible into common stock if the effect is dilutive. For those securities that are not convertible into a class of common stock, the "two-class" method of computing earnings per share shall be used. The two-class method is an earnings allocation formula that determines earnings per share for each class of common stock and participating security according to dividends declared (or accumulated) and participation rights in undistributed earnings. Under that method:

a. Income from continuing operations (or net income) shall be reduced by the amount of dividends declared in the current period for each class of stock and by the contractual amount of dividends (or interest on participating income bonds) that must be paid for the current period (for example, unpaid cumulative dividends).[25]
b. The remaining earnings shall be allocated to common stock and participating securities to the extent that each security may share in earnings as if all of the earnings for the period had been distributed. The total earnings allocated to each security shall be determined by adding together the amount allocated for dividends and the amount allocated for a participation feature.
c. The total earnings allocated to each security shall be divided by the number of outstanding shares of the security to which the earnings are allocated to determine the earnings per share for the security.
d. Basic and diluted EPS data shall be presented for each class of common stock.

For the diluted EPS computation, outstanding common shares shall include all potential common shares assumed issued. Illustration 6 in Appendix C provides an example of that provision.

Securities of Subsidiaries

62. The effect on consolidated EPS of options, warrants, and convertible securities issued by a subsidiary depends on whether the securities issued by the subsidiary enable their holders to obtain common stock of the subsidiary company or common stock of the parent company. The following general guidelines shall be used for computing consolidated diluted EPS by entities with subsidiaries that have issued common stock or potential common shares to parties other than the parent company:[26]

a. Securities issued by a subsidiary that enable their holders to obtain the subsidiary's common

---

[25]Dividends declared in the current period do not include dividends declared in respect of prior-year unpaid cumulative dividends. Preferred dividends that are cumulative only if earned are deducted only to the extent that they are earned.

[26]Refer to paragraphs 140 and 141.

stock shall be included in computing the subsidiary's EPS data. Those per-share earnings of the subsidiary shall then be included in the consolidated EPS computations based on the consolidated group's holding of the subsidiary's securities. Illustration 7 in Appendix C provides an example of that provision.

b. Securities of a subsidiary that are convertible into its parent company's common stock shall be considered among the potential common shares of the parent company for the purpose of computing consolidated diluted EPS. Likewise, a subsidiary's options or warrants to purchase common stock of the parent company shall be considered among the potential common shares of the parent company in computing consolidated diluted EPS. Illustration 7 in Appendix C provides an example of that provision.

As noted in paragraph 18 of APB Opinion No. 18, *The Equity Method of Accounting for Investments in Common Stock,* as amended by this Statement, the above provisions are applicable to investments in common stock of corporate joint ventures and investee companies accounted for under the equity method.

63. The if-converted method shall be used in determining the EPS impact of securities issued by a parent company that are convertible into common stock of a subsidiary company or an investee company accounted for under the equity method. That is, the securities shall be assumed to be converted and the numerator (income available to common stockholders) adjusted as necessary in accordance with the provisions in paragraph 26(a) and (b). In addition to those adjustments, the numerator shall be adjusted appropriately for any change in the income recorded by the parent (such as dividend income or equity method income) due to the increase in the number of common shares of the subsidiary or equity method investee outstanding as a result of the assumed conversion. The denominator of the diluted EPS computation would not be affected because the number of shares of parent company common stock outstanding would not change upon assumed conversion.

Partially Paid Shares and Partially Paid Stock Subscriptions

64. If an entity has common shares issued in a partially paid form[27] and those shares are entitled to dividends in proportion to the amount paid, the common-share equivalent of those partially paid shares shall be included in the computation of basic EPS to the extent that they were entitled to participate in dividends. Partially paid stock subscriptions that do not share in dividends until fully paid are considered the equivalent of warrants and shall be included in diluted EPS by use of the treasury stock method. That is, the unpaid balance shall be assumed to be proceeds used to purchase stock under the treasury stock method. The number of shares included in diluted EPS shall be the difference between the number of shares subscribed and the number of shares assumed to be purchased.

[27]Issuing common shares that are not fully paid is permitted in some countries.

Appendix B

BACKGROUND INFORMATION AND BASIS FOR CONCLUSIONS

CONTENTS

Appendix B

BACKGROUND INFORMATION AND BASIS FOR CONCLUSIONS

Introduction

65. This appendix summarizes considerations that were deemed significant by Board members in reaching the conclusions in this Statement. It includes rea-sons for accepting certain views and rejecting others. Individual Board members gave greater weight to some factors than to others.

Background Information

66. In 1991, the Board issued a plan for international activities (which was updated in 1995) that describes the FASB's role in international activities and pro-poses steps to increase the range and intensity of its

international activities.[28] An objective of the plan is to make financial statements more useful for investors and creditors by increasing the international comparability of accounting standards concurrent with improving the quality of accounting standards. One element of the plan is for the FASB to work toward greater international comparability of accounting standards by identifying projects that potentially could achieve broad international agreement in a relatively short time and by initiating cooperative international standards-setting projects.

67. An FASB Prospectus, *Earnings per Share,* was distributed for public comment in June 1993. The objective of the Prospectus was to inform the Board's constituents of a potential EPS project and to obtain information from them about the scope and importance of that project. The Prospectus explained that Opinion 15, as amended and interpreted, often had been criticized for having complex and arbitrary provisions and that, over the years, the FASB had received requests to reconsider EPS issues. In addition, it mentioned that the IASC had an EPS project on its agenda that provided an opportunity for the FASB to work with that international group toward achieving greater international comparability of EPS data.

68. The Prospectus explained that an EPS project would lend itself to a relatively narrow selection of issues and would not involve profound or divisive theoretical issues; thus, the Board concluded that an EPS project was a potential candidate for a successful cooperative international project. A majority of respondents to the Prospectus favored the Board's adding the project to its agenda in light of the agenda criteria. Most respondents indicated that the potential for international comparability should be an important consideration in the Board's agenda decision.

69. In March 1994, the Board added a project on earnings per share to its technical agenda to be pursued concurrently with the similar project of the IASC. The objective of the project was twofold: (a) to improve and simplify U.S. generally accepted accounting principles and (b) to issue a standard that would be compatible with international standards.

70. The IASC added an EPS project to its agenda in 1989 and issued a draft Statement of Principles, *Earnings per Share,* for public comment in October 1993. In June 1994, the IASC approved a Statement of Principles to be used as the basis for an IASC Exposure Draft. In November 1995, the IASC approved an Exposure Draft of a proposed International Accounting Standard, *Earnings per Share,* which was issued in January 1996.

71. In January 1996, the FASB issued an Exposure Draft, *Earnings per Share and Disclosure of Information about Capital Structure.* Part I of the Exposure Draft proposed computation, presentation, and disclosure requirements for earnings per share by entities with publicly held common stock or potential common stock, and Part II proposed disclosures about an entity's capital structure applicable to all entities. Part I was substantially the same as the IASC Exposure Draft. The Board received 104 comment letters in response to the FASB Exposure Draft. Most letters were supportive of the proposal. The IASC received 75 comment letters in response to its Exposure Draft. The concerns raised by respondents to both Exposure Drafts and the concerns expressed by the IASC were considered by the Board at public meetings in 1996. No formal field test was conducted on the FASB Exposure Draft; however, six respondents to the Exposure Draft noted that they had applied the provisions in Part I to their company's capital structure and generally had found that the requirements were not difficult to apply and resulted in minor changes, if any, from their current EPS computations.

72. The Board decided to issue the two parts of the Exposure Draft as separate Statements because of the differences in scope. That is, the Board did not want nonpublic entities that were excluded from the scope of Part I of the Exposure Draft to have to concern themselves with numerous provisions that were not applicable to them. FASB Statement No. 129, *Disclosure of Information about Capital Structure,* was issued concurrently with this Statement. The provisions of Statement 129 are essentially unchanged from those proposed in Part II of the Exposure Draft.

73. The FASB and the IASC exchanged information on the progress of their respective EPS projects during the deliberation and redeliberation processes, and the FASB considered the tentative decisions reached by the IASC on all issues. In addition, members of the IASC Steering Committee on Earnings per Share and the IASC staff participated in FASB meetings to

---

[28]FASB *Highlights,* "FASB's Plan for International Activities," January 1995.

discuss the differences between the tentative conclusions of the two standards-setting bodies. Similarly, members of the FASB and its staff participated in IASC meetings to discuss those differences. Both the FASB and the IASC agreed to modifications of their initial positions on issues that were not considered critical. In addition, some of the conclusions reached by the FASB were influenced by how those conclusions would simplify the computation of earnings per share. The FASB decided it could reach an informed decision on the project without holding a public hearing. In January 1997, the IASC approved IAS 33, *Earnings per Share,* which was issued about the same time as this Statement.

Benefits and Costs

74. One of the precepts of the Board's mission is to promulgate standards only when the expected benefits of the resulting information exceed the perceived costs of providing that information. The Board strives to determine that a proposed standard will fill a significant need and that the costs entailed in satisfying that need, as compared with other alternatives, are justified in relation to the overall benefits of the resulting information.

75. The Board concluded that EPS information provided to users in financial statements could be improved by simplifying the existing computational guidance, revising the disclosure requirements, and increasing the comparability of EPS data on an international basis. Some of the changes made to the EPS guidance in an effort to simplify the computation include (a) not considering common stock equivalents in the computation of basic EPS, (b) eliminating the modified treasury stock method and the 3 percent materiality provision, and (c) revising the contingent share provisions (including eliminating the requirement to restate prior EPS data in certain situations) and the supplemental EPS data requirements.

76. The Board expects that the costs to implement this Statement will include initial costs for education and the redesign of procedures used to compute EPS data but that any ongoing costs should be minimal. The Board believes that the benefits of simplifying the EPS computation and harmonizing with national and international standards-setting bodies will outweigh the costs of implementing this Statement.

Conclusions on Basic Issues

Scope

77. This Statement, which provides computation, presentation, and disclosure requirements for earnings per share, requires presentation of earnings per share by entities with publicly held common stock or potential common stock and by entities that are in the process of selling that stock to the public. Nonpublic entities are excluded from the scope because, generally, those entities have simple capital structures and few common stockholders; thus, EPS data may not be meaningful for users of their financial statements. In addition, nonpublic entities were excluded from the scope of Opinion 15 (as amended by FASB Statement No. 21, *Suspension of the Reporting of Earnings per Share and Segment Information by Nonpublic Enterprises*), and the Board was not aware of any new information that would suggest that those entities should be required to report EPS data. For similar reasons, the Board decided not to include in the scope of this Statement entities whose publicly traded securities include only debt. However, any entity that chooses to present EPS data should do so in accordance with this Statement.

78. Few respondents commented on the proposed scope of the Statement. Those that did suggested that the scope exemption in the Exposure Draft for investment companies registered under the Investment Company Act of 1940 be expanded to include investment companies, such as offshore mutual funds, that are not registered under the 1940 Act but that provide the same selected per-share data (in accordance with the AICPA Audit and Accounting Guide, *Audits of Investment Companies*). The Board agreed to make that change.

Objective of the Earnings per Share Computations

79. In discussing various issues about the computation of diluted EPS, the Board found it helpful to identify the objective of both basic and diluted EPS in order to reach consistent conclusions on those issues. The Board concluded that the objective of basic EPS is to measure the performance of an entity over the reporting period and that the objective of diluted EPS should be consistent with the basic EPS objective while giving effect to all dilutive potential common shares that were outstanding during the period.

80. Other objectives of diluted EPS that the Board considered and rejected were that it should be a predictor of dilution—a forward-looking number as opposed to one based on historic numbers—or that it should maximize dilution. In concluding that diluted EPS should be an extension of basic EPS—a historic, "for the period" number—the Board looked to FASB Concepts Statement No. 1, *Objectives of Financial Reporting by Business Enterprises,* which discusses the historical nature of accounting information, and FASB Concepts Statement No. 2, *Qualitative Characteristics of Accounting Information,* which discusses the "predictive value" of financial information. Concepts Statement 1 explains that users of financial statements may make predictions using financial information—information that is historical. Paragraph 53 of Concepts Statement 2 states in part:

> Users can be expected to favor those sources of information and analytical methods that have the greatest predictive value in achieving their specific objectives. Predictive value here means value as an *input* [emphasis in original] into a predictive process, *not value directly as a prediction.* [Emphasis added.]

81. The IASC initially concluded that the objective of diluted EPS should be to indicate the potential variability or risk attached to basic EPS as a consequence of the issue of potential common shares or to act as a warning signal of the potential dilution of basic EPS. Following that objective, diluted EPS would be computed using end-of-period shares and stock prices. The Board considers that objective to be relevant and useful but believes that it is preferable for diluted EPS to be computed in a manner consistent with the computation of basic EPS. After much discussion, the IASC agreed to require that diluted EPS be computed following the FASB objective because (a) diluted EPS computed following a performance objective can be presented in a time series and compared with diluted EPS of other periods and (b) a "warning signal" objective can be adequately conveyed through supplementary note disclosure.

82. To accommodate the concerns of the IASC, both the FASB and the IASC Exposure Drafts included disclosure requirements related to the IASC's warning signal objective. More than half of the respondents to the FASB Exposure Draft who commented on those disclosure requirements stated that they did not believe that the warning signal objective was relevant or useful, and some found the related disclosures confusing. Respondents to the IASC Exposure Draft made similar comments; they also encouraged the IASC to choose one objective. The FASB and the IASC decided to eliminate those disclosure requirements in response to the comments received.

Basic Earnings per Share

83. One of the main objectives of the Board's project on earnings per share was to issue a standard that would be compatible with those of the IASC and national standards-setting bodies. The biggest difference between Opinion 15 and other EPS standards is that Opinion 15 required presentation of primary EPS, which includes the dilutive effect of common stock equivalents. Currently, only two other countries require that primary EPS be presented. Thus, the first issue that the Board had to address was whether to eliminate the requirement to present primary EPS and replace it with a computation that does not consider the effects of common stock equivalents.

84. In making its decision to replace primary EPS with basic EPS, the Board considered the requirements of Opinion 15 to compute primary EPS, the criticisms about primary EPS, the arguments in favor of basic EPS, and the comments it had received from constituents prior to adding the project to its agenda.

Primary earnings per share

85. The rules used to compute primary EPS (Opinion 15 and its amendments and interpretations) had been criticized as being extremely complex and containing a number of arbitrary provisions. Those criticisms largely focused on the determination of convertible securities as common stock equivalents, specifically, the use of the Aa corporate bond rate for the common stock equivalency test, the two-thirds yield test for common stock equivalency, and the classification of a security as a common stock equivalent at issuance without regard to later events.

86. The complexity of Opinion 15 may have contributed to errors or to inconsistency in its application. Several empirical studies indicated that EPS rules often are misunderstood by preparers and auditors and are not always applied correctly. The primary EPS statistic itself had been widely criticized as not being useful. Considerable evidence showed that many users of financial statements think that primary EPS is based on an undiluted weighted-average number of common shares outstanding; that is, they think that primary EPS is computed without giving effect to common stock equivalents.

87. Because primary EPS assumes exercise and conversion of dilutive common stock equivalents, it includes a certain amount of dilution. Some said that the endpoints on the scale of dilution—from zero dilution to maximum dilution—would convey better information to financial statement users. Those critics said that the rules of Opinion 15 conceal part of the total potential dilution by presenting two numbers that include dilution rather than an undiluted and a diluted number.

88. Opinion 15 had drawn its strongest criticism from users (primarily financial analysts) and academics. Analysts' interest stemmed from the use of EPS in the computation of the price-earnings ratio, perhaps the most frequently cited statistic in the business of equity investment. In addition, analysts' earnings projections almost always are presented on a per-share basis. The Board did not receive many requests from other parties to comprehensively reconsider Opinion 15; therefore, it appeared that preparers and auditors had assimilated and accepted the rules. Most respondents to the EPS Prospectus agreed that basic EPS would be a simpler and more useful statistic than primary EPS. Most respondents to the Exposure Draft agreed that disclosing the full range of possible dilution using basic EPS and diluted EPS would reveal more useful information than the partial range of dilution disclosed with primary EPS and fully diluted EPS under Opinion 15. However, some respondents noted that that they did not find basic EPS to be a useful statistic and thought that users would focus only on diluted EPS.

89. The Board decided to replace primary EPS with basic EPS for the following reasons:

a. Presenting undiluted and diluted EPS data would give users the most factually supportable *range* of EPS possibilities. The spread between basic and diluted EPS would provide information about an entity's capital structure by disclosing a reasonable estimate of how much potential dilution exists.
b. Use of a common international EPS statistic has become even more important as a result of database-oriented financial analysis and the internationalization of business and capital markets.
c. The notion of common stock equivalents as used in primary EPS is viewed by many as not operating effectively in practice, and "repairing" it does not appear to be a feasible option.

d. The primary EPS computation is complex, and there is some evidence that the current guidance is not well understood and may not be consistently applied.
e. If basic EPS were to replace primary EPS, the criticisms about the arbitrary methods by which common stock equivalents are determined would no longer be an issue. If entities were required to disclose the details of their convertible securities, the subjective determination of the likelihood of conversion would be left to individual users of financial statements.

Computation of basic earnings per share

Weighted-average number of shares

90. In computing basic (and diluted) EPS, the Board agreed that use of a weighted-average number of shares is necessary so that the effect of increases or decreases in outstanding shares on EPS data will be related to the portion of the period during which the related consideration affected operations.

Contingently issuable shares

91. Contractual agreements (usually associated with purchase business combinations) sometimes provide for the issuance of additional common shares contingent upon certain conditions being met. The Board concluded that (a) consistent with the objective that basic EPS should represent a measure of the performance of an entity over a specific reporting period, contingently issuable shares should be included in basic EPS only when there is no circumstance under which those shares would not be issued and (b) basic EPS should not be restated for changed circumstances.

92. A few respondents to the Exposure Draft suggested that contingently issuable shares should never be included in the computation of basic EPS because basic EPS is supposed to be an EPS ratio with no dilution. They said that the denominator should include only actual shares outstanding. The Board considered that view but decided to retain the provision that "vested" contingently issuable shares should be considered in the computation of basic EPS because consideration for those shares has been received. The Board also agreed to retain the provision that contingently returnable shares should be treated in the same manner as contingently issuable shares. The IASC agreed to include a similar provision in IAS 33 in response to the comments received on its Exposure Draft (which did not include such a provision).

Diluted Earnings per Share

93. Securities (such as options, warrants, convertible debt, and convertible preferred stock) that do not have a current right to participate fully in earnings but that may do so in the future by virtue of their option or conversion rights are referred to in this Statement as potential common shares or potentially dilutive shares. That "potential dilution" is relevant to users because it may reduce the per-share amount of current earnings to be distributed by way of dividends in the future and may increase the number of shares over which the total market value of an entity is divided.

94. Whether option or conversion rights of potential common shares actually will be exercised is usually not determinable at an entity's reporting date. However, with the use of assumptions, it is possible to arrive at a reasonable estimate of what earnings per share would have been had common stock been issued for those securities. The Board concluded that the treasury stock method and the if-converted method prescribed in Opinion 15 should continue to be used in computing diluted EPS.

No antidilution

95. In computing diluted EPS, only potential common shares that are dilutive—those that reduce earnings per share or increase loss per share—are included. Exercise of options and warrants or conversion of convertible securities is not assumed if the result would be antidilutive, such as when a loss from continuing operations is reported. The sequence in which potential common shares are considered may affect the amount of dilution that they produce. The sequence of the computation was not specifically addressed in Opinion 15, but the IASC proposed that in order to maximize the dilution of earnings per share, each issue or series of potential common shares should be considered in sequence from the most dilutive to the least dilutive. The Board agreed with the IASC that that is a reasonable approach and included a similar provision in this Statement. Most respondents to the Exposure Draft agreed that sequencing potential common shares from the most dilutive to the least dilutive is a workable approach.

96. The Board also concluded that the "control number" for determining whether including potential common shares in the diluted EPS computation would be antidilutive should be *income from continuing operations* (or a similar line item above net in-

come if it appears on the income statement). As a result, if there is a loss from continuing operations, diluted EPS would be computed in the same manner as basic EPS is computed, even if an entity has net income after adjusting for a discontinued operation, an extraordinary item, or the cumulative effect of an accounting change. Similarly, if an entity has income from continuing operations but its preferred dividend adjustment made in computing *income available to common stockholders* in accordance with paragraph 9 results in a "loss from continuing operations available to common stockholders," diluted EPS would be computed in the same manner as basic EPS.

97. If *net income* were the control number as it was under Opinion 15, diluted EPS often would be the same number as basic EPS. The Board decided to change the control number to income from continuing operations because in the United States net losses are often the result of discontinued operations, extraordinary items, or accounting changes reported by the cumulative-effect method. The Board agreed that if an entity had income from continuing operations but had an accounting change that resulted in a net loss, its diluted net loss per share *should* include potential common shares (even though their effect would be antidilutive) and should not be the same as its basic net loss per share that does not include potential common shares. With income from continuing operations as the control number, the diluted net loss per share in that case would reflect the effect of potential common shares.

98. In addition, EPS data are more comparable over time if income from continuing operations is used as the control number. That is, for an entity that reports a net loss in the period solely because of the cumulative effect of an accounting change upon adopting a new accounting standard, that period's diluted net loss per share would reflect no dilution if net income were the control number and, thus, diluted net loss per share for the period would not be comparable with past or future diluted net income per-share amounts (which would reflect some dilution). The same would be true for an entity that makes a voluntary accounting change, reports discontinued operations, or reports extraordinary items that result in a net loss.

99. Respondents to the Exposure Draft agreed with the change in the control number from *net income* under Opinion 15 to *income from continuing operations* in this Statement. The IASC did not include a

control number provision in its Exposure Draft. In response to the comments received on the FASB Exposure Draft and the few comments on the issue received in response to the IASC Exposure Draft, the IASC agreed to include a provision in IAS 33 that requires *net profit from continuing ordinary activities* to be used as the control number in establishing whether potential common shares are dilutive or antidilutive.

Options and warrants and their equivalents

100. The issuance of common stock upon exercise of options and warrants produces cash inflows for the issuing entity but does not affect income. In computing earnings per share, an assumed issuance of stock increases the denominator but does not affect the numerator. The resulting reduction in earnings per share could be considered excessive if there were no adjustment for the use of the cash proceeds. The treasury stock method was meant to adjust for that situation by assuming that the cash proceeds from issuing common stock are used to acquire treasury shares. Thus, only the *net* assumed issuance of shares (common shares issued upon exercise less treasury shares acquired) is reflected in the denominator of the diluted EPS computation. Other methods that the Board considered in determining how to reflect the potential dilution of options and warrants in the computation of diluted EPS are discussed in paragraphs 101-104.

Imputed earnings method

101. Some countries use an imputed earnings method to compute diluted EPS. That method assumes that the proceeds from exercise of options and warrants are used to repay debt or are invested, for example, in government securities, rather than used to purchase treasury shares. Following the imputed earnings method, either the amount of interest that would have been saved (if the debt were repaid) or the income that would have been earned (on the investment) is added to the numerator of the computation, and the denominator is adjusted for the number of shares assumed to have been issued upon exercise of the options or warrants. The disadvantages of that method are that it requires an arbitrary assumption about the appropriate rate of earnings, it overstates dilution because it treats antidilutive potential common shares as if they were dilutive, and it gives the

same effect to all options and warrants regardless of the current market price.

Treasury stock method with a discounted exercise price

102. Another method that the Board considered was to discount the expected proceeds from exercise of options or warrants with long exercise periods to reflect the time value of money prior to applying the treasury stock method. The argument for that method is that because contracts with long exercise periods are not likely to be exercised for a considerable period of time, the exercise price should be discounted to its fair value at the balance sheet date, reflecting "time value" as one component of the value of an option or warrant. The main disadvantage of that method is that the determination of (a) the time periods over which to discount the options or warrants and (b) the applicable discount rate is subjective.

Maximum dilution method

103. The maximum dilution method assumes that all options and warrants are exercised and that the common shares issued upon exercise are added to the denominator with no change in the numerator. The principal disadvantage of that method is that an assumption that all potential common shares will convert without a change in earnings is both counterintuitive and unrealistic. It also would give the same effect to all options and warrants regardless of the current market price.

Graham-Dodd method

104. In computing diluted EPS, the Graham-Dodd method[29] takes into consideration all options and warrants, including those whose exercise price exceeds the market price of common stock. That method assumes that options and warrants are equivalent to additional outstanding common shares with the same aggregate market value as that of the options or warrants issued. The computation divides the total market value of all options and warrants by the current market price of the common stock to determine the number of additional common shares that would be equivalent to the value of outstanding options and warrants. Those additional common shares would be included in the denominator of the diluted EPS computation. In addition to showing the

---

[29]The method is described in Graham, Dodd, and Cottle, *Security Analysis: Principles and Technique,* 4th ed. (New York: McGraw-Hill, 1962).

dilutive effect of "out of the money" options and warrants, the Graham-Dodd method reflects more dilution as the value of options and warrants increases relative to the value of common stock. That method requires the use of option-pricing models at each reporting period to value options and warrants that are not traded.[30]

Treasury stock method

105. The Board decided to retain the treasury stock method from Opinion 15 because of its use in present practice, its relative simplicity and lack of subjectivity, and its adoption by the IASC (although the method is described differently in IAS 33). The method also reflects more dilution as the value of options and warrants increases relative to the value of common stock. That is, as the average market price of the stock increases, the assumed proceeds from exercise will buy fewer shares, thus, increasing the EPS denominator. The Board was concerned that the treasury stock method understates potential dilution because it gives no dilutive effect to options and warrants whose exercise prices exceed current common stock prices and, therefore, are antidilutive under the treasury stock method but may be dilutive sometime in the future. However, the Board was unable to identify another method that would address that concern that did not have its own set of disadvantages. To offset that concern, the Board decided to require disclosure in the notes to the financial statements of potential common shares not included in the computation of dilutive EPS because their impact would be antidilutive based on current market prices.

106. Another common criticism of the treasury stock method that the Board considered is that it assumes a hypothetical purchase of treasury stock. The Board recognizes that the funds obtained by issuers from the exercise of options and warrants are used in many ways with a wide variety of results that cannot be anticipated. Application of the treasury stock method in EPS computations represents a practical approach to reflecting the dilutive effect that would result from the issuance of common stock under option and warrant agreements at an effective price below the current market price.

107. The Board made one change to the treasury stock method prescribed in Opinion 15. This Statement requires that the average stock price for the period always be used in determining the number of treasury shares assumed purchased with the proceeds from the exercise of options or warrants rather than the higher of the average or ending stock price as prescribed by Opinion 15. The Board believes that use of the average stock price is consistent with the objective of diluted EPS to measure earnings per share for the period based on period information and that use of end-of-period data or estimates of the future is inconsistent with that objective. If purchases of treasury shares actually were to occur, the shares would be purchased at various prices, not at the price at the end of the period. In addition, use of an average stock price eliminates the concern that end-of-period fluctuations in stock prices could have an undue effect on diluted EPS if an end-of-period stock price were required to be used. Respondents to the Exposure Draft generally agreed with the requirement to use the average stock price.

108. Opinion 15 required that the "modified treasury stock" method be used if the number of shares of common stock obtainable upon exercise of outstanding options and warrants in the aggregate is more than 20 percent of the number of common shares outstanding at the end of the period. The Board found that the modified treasury stock method prescribed in Opinion 15 was not widely used in practice because few entities ever met the 20 percent test. For that reason, and in an effort to simplify the EPS computation and to be consistent with the IASC Standard, the Board decided not to include that method in this Statement. Respondents to the Exposure Draft generally agreed with the elimination of the modified treasury stock method.

Stock-based compensation arrangements

109. Fixed employee stock options (fixed awards) and nonvested stock (including restricted stock) are included in the computation of diluted EPS based on the provisions for options and warrants in paragraphs 17-25. Even though their issuance may be contingent upon vesting, they are not considered to be "contingently issuable shares" as that term is used in this Statement because to consider them contingently issuable shares would be a change from present practice and the provisions of IAS 33. However, because issuance of performance-based stock options (and performance-based nonvested stock) is contingent upon satisfying conditions in addition to

---

[30]Statement 123 generally requires that valuation only at the grant date.

the mere passage of time, those options and non-vested stock are considered to be contingently issu-able shares in the computation of diluted EPS. The Board decided that a distinction should be made only between time-related contingencies and contingen-cies requiring specific achievement.

110. The guidance in paragraph 21 for determining the assumed proceeds when applying the treasury stock method to an entity that has stock-based com-pensation arrangements is based on similar guidance in Statement 123, which was based on the provisions in paragraph 3 of FASB Interpretation No. 31, *Treatment of Stock Compensation Plans in EPS Computations.* The Board agreed that it would be appropriate to carry forward the remainder of the relevant guidance in paragraphs 4-6 of Interpreta-tion 31 into this Statement. That guidance has been incorporated into paragraphs 20, 22, and 29 of this Statement. Examples 1 and 2 from Appendix B of Interpretation 31 are included in Illustration 8 in Appendix C.

Written put options and purchased options

111. A number of respondents to the Exposure Draft requested that the Board address how written put op-tions, purchased put options, and purchased call op-tions should be included in the computation of di-luted EPS. Emerging Issues Task Force (EITF) Issue No. 87-31, "Sale of Put Options on Issuer's Stock," addresses put options sold by a company for cash that enable the holder to sell shares of the company's stock at a fixed price to the company. The EITF reached a consensus that the reverse treasury stock method should be used in computing the impact of those options on earnings per share. Under that method, the incremental number of shares to be added to the denominator is computed as the excess of shares that will be issued for cash at the then current market price to obtain cash to satisfy the put obligation over the shares received from satisfy-ing the puts. The Board agreed to include that ap-proach in this Statement for "in the money" contracts that require that the reporting entity repurchase its own stock.

112. The Board concluded that neither purchased put options nor purchased call options should be re-flected in diluted EPS because their effect would be antidilutive. A few respondents stated that entities should be permitted to aggregate the calls held by an entity on its own stock (purchased calls) with the op-tions or warrants it is attempting to hedge. Those re-

spondents suggested that the Board modify the trea-sury stock method to require that proceeds assumed to be received from the exercise of options be used to pay the strike price on the call option that the entity holds on its own stock (rather than assume that the proceeds received will be used to purchase treasury shares as required by the treasury stock method). The Board confirmed its position that securities that would have an antidilutive effect should not be in-cluded in the diluted EPS computation and that secu-rities should be considered separately rather than in the aggregate in determining whether their effect on diluted EPS would be dilutive or antidilutive.

Convertible securities

113. Other securities that could result in the issuance of common shares, in addition to options and war-rants, are debt and preferred stock that are convertible into common stock. The impact of those potential common shares on diluted EPS is determined by use of the if-converted method. That method recognizes that the holders of convertible preferred stock cannot share in distributions of earnings available to com-mon stockholders unless they relinquish their right to senior distributions. Conversion is assumed, and in-come available to common stockholders is deter-mined before distributions are made to holders of those securities. Likewise, the if-converted method recognizes that convertible debt can participate in earnings through interest or dividends, either as a se-nior security or as common stock, but not both.

114. The Board chose to retain the if-converted method prescribed in Opinion 15 in this Statement. There have been few criticisms of that method, and it is the method used by the IASC. One common criti-cism of the if-converted method is that conversion may be assumed when a convertible security appears likely to remain a senior security.

Contracts that may be settled in stock or cash

115. As discussed in paragraph 110, the guidance in Interpretation 31 has been brought forward into this Statement. Paragraph 6 of that Interpretation estab-lished a rebuttable presumption that when stock ap-preciation rights and other variable plan awards may be settled in stock or cash (at the election of either the holder or the reporting entity), the entity should pre-sume settlement in common stock and the dilutive potential common shares should be included in the EPS computation unless the presumption is over-come. The Board agreed that that guidance was

equally appropriate for other contracts that could be settled in stock or cash and thus included that guidance in paragraph 29 of this Statement. The Board believes that that approach is consistent with the objective of diluted EPS to reflect potential dilution that existed during the period. In circumstances in which the contract is reported as an asset or liability for accounting purposes (as opposed to an equity instrument) but the contract is presumed to be settled in common stock for EPS purposes, the Board believes it is appropriate to adjust income available to common stockholders for any changes in the fair value of the contract that had been recognized in income. Although all such contracts that provide the issuer or holder with a choice between settlement methods may not meet the definition of an option, warrant, convertible security, or contingently issuable share, they do meet the definition of potential common stock in paragraph 171 of this Statement.

Contingently issuable shares

116. In discussing the issue of the impact of contingently issuable shares on diluted EPS, the Board chose not to retain the requirements in Opinion 15 to (a) increase the numerator of the computation for possible future earnings levels and (b) restate prior EPS data for differences in actual and assumed earnings levels. The Board concluded that making assumptions about future earnings and restating for events that occur after the end of a period would be inconsistent with a "historic" objective. Thus, the Board decided to include contingently issuable shares in the computation of diluted EPS based only on current earnings (which are assumed to remain unchanged until the end of the contingency period) and to prohibit restatement.

117. The Board also was not in favor of permitting restatement of EPS data due to changes in market prices. The Board noted that restatement was prohibited for the impact of changes in market prices on the number of shares included in the denominator as a result of applying the treasury stock method. The Board decided to include shares contingent on market price in diluted EPS based on the end-of-period market price and to prohibit restatement.

118. Contingent stock agreements sometimes provide for shares to be issued in the future pending the satisfaction of conditions unrelated to earnings or market value (for example, opening a certain number of retail locations). Similar to its other conclusions, the Board decided (a) to include contingent shares in the computation of diluted EPS based on the assumption that the current status of the condition will remain unchanged until the end of the contingency period and (b) to prohibit restatement. Thus, if only half of the requisite retail locations have been opened, then no contingent shares would be included in the diluted EPS computation.

119. The Board considered including contingent shares on a pro rata basis based on the current status of the condition (such as half of the contingent shares for the example in paragraph 118). However, the Board was concerned that a pro rata approach would not be implemented easily and that it might make little sense in many instances, such as when it is readily apparent that the condition will not be met.

120. Some Board members were concerned about the inconsistency in when compensation cost for performance awards is included in the numerator of the diluted EPS computation (pursuant to Statement 123) and when the related contingent shares are included in the denominator of the same computation (pursuant to this Statement). The initial accruals of compensation cost for performance awards are based on the best estimate of the outcome of the performance condition. That is, compensation cost is estimated at the grant date for the options that are expected to vest based on performance-related conditions and that are accrued over the vesting period. However, pursuant to this Statement, diluted EPS would reflect only those shares (stock options) that would be issued if the end of the reporting period were the end of the contingency period. In most cases, performance awards will not be reflected in diluted EPS until the performance condition has been satisfied. The Board observed that (a) the focus of this Statement is the denominator of the EPS computation, not the determination of earnings, and (b) that treatment is consistent with current practice when compensation is associated with a contingent award.

121. Most respondents to the Exposure Draft agreed with the changes proposed for contingent stock agreements. A few respondents requested that the Board clarify as of what date contingently issuable shares should be included in the computations of basic and diluted EPS. The Board concluded that contingent shares should be deemed to be issued when all of the necessary conditions have been met and that those shares should be included in basic EPS on a weighted-average basis. In most cases, the shares would be included only as of the last day of the period because whether the condition has been satisfied

may not be certain until the end of the period. The Board concluded that contingent shares should be included in the denominator of the diluted EPS computation in a manner similar to other potential common shares; that is, as if the shares were issued at the beginning of the period (or as of the date of the contingent stock agreement, if later). However, for year-to-date computations, the Board agreed that contingent shares should be included on a weighted-average basis. That approach is similar to the method used for including incremental shares in year-to-date computations when applying the treasury stock method.

Presentation on Face of Income Statement

122. The Board agreed that EPS data should be presented prominently in the financial statements because of the significance attached by investors and others to EPS data and because of the importance of evaluating the data in conjunction with the financial statements. Thus, the Board concluded that both basic and diluted per-share amounts should be presented on the face of the income statement for income from continuing operations and net income. The Board agreed that, at a minimum, those per-share amounts should be presented on the face of the income statement to help users determine the impact of items reported "below-the-line."

123. The Board decided to give entities the option of presenting basic and diluted per-share amounts for discontinued operations, extraordinary items, and the cumulative effect of an accounting change either on the face of the income statement or in the notes to financial statements to address the concern that some constituents had with excessive information on the income statement. The extent of the data presented and the captions used will vary with the complexity of an entity's capital structure and the presence of transactions outside continuing operations.

124. The IASC Exposure Draft required presentation of only basic and diluted net income per share on the face of the income statement and encouraged presentation of other per-share amounts. Most respondents to the FASB Exposure Draft agreed with the requirements related to presentation of per-share amounts on the face of the income statement and in the notes to the financial statements and stated that the IASC should adopt the FASB's presentation approach. The IASC decided not to change its presentation requirements in its EPS standard but acknowledged that it will have to address presentation of per-share amounts other than net income per share as part of other related projects on its agenda.

125. The June 1996 FASB Exposure Draft, *Reporting Comprehensive Income,* would require presentation of a per-share amount for comprehensive income on the face of the statement of financial performance in which comprehensive income is reported. Per-share amounts are not required by that Exposure Draft for subtotals resulting from classifications within other comprehensive income. If that Exposure Draft is finalized as proposed, the Board will have to determine how comprehensive income per share should be computed to be in accordance with the provisions of this Statement.

126. The Board's decision to require a dual EPS presentation (basic and diluted EPS) for entities with complex capital structures regardless of the variance between basic and diluted EPS is a change from Opinion 15. Opinion 15 provided that fully diluted EPS did not have to be presented if the dilution caused by including all potential common shares in the computation was less than 3 percent of "simple" EPS, which includes no dilution. Similarly, primary EPS could be presented as simple EPS if the dilution caused by including common stock equivalents in the computation was less than 3 percent of simple EPS.

127. The Board decided to eliminate what is referred to as the "materiality threshold" for presentation of diluted EPS because (a) the requirement was used inconsistently, (b) in many cases, an entity had to compute fully diluted EPS to determine whether it met the 3 percent test, and (c) in any period that an entity's earnings per share fell out of the 3 percent range, Opinion 15 required fully diluted EPS to be shown for all periods presented. The Board concluded that requiring a dual presentation at all times by all entities with complex capital structures places all of the facts in the hands of users of financial statements at minimal or no cost to preparers and gives users an understanding of the extent and trend of potential dilution. The Board also noted that many entities currently present fully diluted EPS even when it does not differ by 3 percent from simple or primary EPS because when fully diluted EPS is compared over time, small differences may be relevant in assessing relative changes between periods.

128. Most respondents to the Exposure Draft agreed with the Board's conclusion that presenting both basic and diluted EPS on the face of the income statement would result in minimal or no additional cost to the preparer. However, many of those respondents requested that the Board retain a materiality threshold

similar to that in Opinion 15. They stated that presentation of diluted EPS when it is not materially different from basic EPS is an immaterial disclosure that could cause confusion (that is, multiple EPS amounts on the face of the income statement might be confusing to users). Some respondents also stated that the marginal costs of dual presentation would exceed the marginal benefits to the user community.

129. Because of those comments and the view of some respondents that diluted EPS is the more useful statistic, the Board initially decided that if only one per-share amount were to be required to be presented on the face of the income statement it should be diluted EPS, not basic EPS. The Board reasoned that a single presentation would eliminate any confusion that unsophisticated users might have with multiple EPS amounts and any confusion over which EPS number databases should include. In addition, presenting only diluted EPS on the face of the income statement would display the most meaningful information in the primary financial statements and would be another step toward simplification of the EPS guidance. The Board acknowledged the usefulness of providing a range of potential dilution and, therefore, agreed to retain the requirement that basic EPS should be presented in the notes to the financial statements as part of the required reconciliation of basic and diluted EPS.

130. Because of the international harmonization goal of the project, the FASB presented its initial decisions on income statement presentation to the IASC Steering Committee on Earnings per Share and the IASC Board in September 1996 as preliminary conclusions. The FASB indicated that it would reconsider those decisions based on the IASC's level of support for making similar changes to its proposed standard. The IASC decided to retain its requirement for equal prominence of basic and diluted EPS on the face of the income statement because it believes that there is valuable information content in the difference between the two numbers. The users in the United States with whom the FASB discussed its preliminary conclusions shared that view.

131. In the interest of international harmonization, the Board ultimately decided to retain the dual presentation requirement proposed in the Exposure Draft. The Board acknowledged that if it were to stay with its "diluted EPS only" preliminary conclusion, the resulting FASB and IASC EPS standards would have been substantially the same because EPS would be *computed* in the same manner even though

it would not be *presented* in the same manner. However, the Board believes it is most important to achieve harmonization in all aspects with the IASC, especially because the difference is only one of display, not one of a conceptual nature.

132. Consequently, both the FASB and the IASC agreed that dual presentation of basic and diluted EPS should be required in all instances, regardless of the difference between the two numbers. As noted in paragraph 89(a), the Board believes that, when compared with diluted EPS, basic EPS is useful as a benchmark for determining the amount of potential dilution. If basic and diluted EPS are the same amount, dual presentation can be accomplished in one line on the income statement. In response to the concerns of some respondents to the Exposure Draft that removal of the 3 percent materiality threshold will result in more variations in the concept of materiality than currently exists, the Board noted that the materiality box that states "The provisions of this Statement need not be applied to immaterial items" does not apply to the difference between two numbers.

Conclusions on Other Issues

Stock Dividends or Stock Splits

133. This Statement requires an entity that has a stock dividend, stock split, or reverse stock split after the close of the period but before issuance of the financial statements to compute basic and diluted EPS in those financial statements based on the new number of shares because those per-share amounts would have to be restated in the subsequent period. The IASC Exposure Draft proposed computing earnings per share in those situations based on the shares actually existing at the date of the financial statements. It also proposed disclosing a description of the subsequent event and pro forma EPS amounts in the financial statements of the period prior to the actual event.

134. Most respondents to the FASB Exposure Draft preferred the FASB restatement requirement over the IASC disclosure approach. Those respondents noted that reflecting the subsequent event in the current period would provide more useful, relevant, and meaningful information and would obviate the need for later restatement. In response to the comments it received on that issue and in the interest of harmonization, the IASC agreed to change from a disclosure approach to a requirement to restate, similar to that in this Statement.

Rights Issues

135. The IASC Exposure Draft proposed using the "theoretical ex-rights method" for adjusting EPS data for a bonus element contained in a rights issue offered to all existing stockholders. The FASB Exposure Draft proposed that the treasury stock method be used for making that adjustment. The Board initially decided not to use the IASC's proposed method because of the complexity of that method and the familiarity in the United States with the treasury stock method and because the treasury stock method achieves quite similar results. As noted by a few respondents to the Exposure Drafts, rights offerings are much more common outside the United States and use of the ex-rights method is established in international practice. In the interest of harmonization, the Board decided to accept the IASC's position on that issue and require use of the ex-rights method when adjusting both basic and diluted EPS for the bonus element in a rights issue.

Supplemental Earnings per Share Data

136. Opinion 15 required disclosure of supplemental EPS data. The purpose of those disclosures was to show what primary EPS would have been if the conversions or sales of securities had occurred at the beginning of the period being reported on rather than during the period. The Board concluded that requiring disclosure of similar information in this Statement was not consistent with the objective of basic and diluted EPS and, thus, decided not to include that requirement in this Statement. However, the Board agreed that it would be useful for financial statements to include a description of transactions that occur after the balance sheet date but before issuance of the financial statements that would have resulted in a material change in the number of common or potential common shares outstanding at the end of the period. Including that information will provide those that want to compute "pro forma" EPS information with the necessary data. Some respondents to the Exposure Draft suggested that information about post-balance-sheet transactions that occurred in periods other than the most recent period would not be useful. The Board decided to require disclosure of that information only for the current reporting period rather than, as proposed in the Exposure Draft, for all periods for which an income statement is presented.

Disclosure Requirements

137. The Board decided to require a reconciliation of the numerators and denominators of the basic and diluted EPS computations in this Statement because the reconciliation is simple and straightforward and will help users better understand the dilutive effect of certain securities included in the EPS computations. SEC Regulation S-K requires presentation of a statement that reasonably details the computation of earnings per share unless the computation can be clearly determined from the material contained in the annual report. The reconciliation required by this Statement should satisfy the SEC requirement and should not result in additional costs to preparers. The Board agreed that disclosing the nature and impact of each dilutive potential common share (or series of shares) included in the diluted EPS computation, as well as separately identifying those antidilutive potential common shares that could dilute earnings per share in the future, allows users to exercise their own judgment as to the "likely" EPS number.

138. Some respondents to the Exposure Draft did not support the reconciliation requirement and stated that (a) the costs to prepare it would exceed the benefit to users, (b) it would be complex and confusing, and (c) it is already required by the SEC. A number of respondents observed that the SEC has proposed eliminating its similar reconciliation requirement in Regulation S-K. The SEC has decided to postpone acting on that proposal in light of comments it has received regarding the usefulness of the reconciliation to investors and financial analysts and the similar proposed requirement in the FASB Exposure Draft. The comments received by the SEC reinforced the Board's position that the reconciliation contains information that is very useful to users of financial statements. However, in response to some of the comments it received, the Board agreed that insignificant reconciling items need not be itemized as part of the reconciliation and could be combined (aggregated).

139. The Exposure Draft would have required disclosure of information that would assist users of financial statements in assessing how basic EPS may be affected in the future due to the potential common shares still outstanding at the balance sheet date as well as the common stock price at that date. Those requirements were referred to as the "warning signal" disclosures because they were meant to address the IASC's warning signal objective for diluted EPS. However, as noted in paragraph 82, many respondents who commented on the warning signal disclosure requirement in the Exposure Draft stated that they did not believe that the warning signal objective was relevant or useful, and some found the related

disclosures confusing. Those respondents generally stated that the costs of the related disclosures would exceed the benefits and that those disclosures would be too complex. A number of respondents to the IASC Exposure Draft made similar comments, and some suggested that the disclosure requirement be made optional. Respondents also noted that some of the information is already required to be disclosed in the financial statements pursuant to other IASC standards. After reconsideration, both the FASB and the IASC agreed to eliminate the warning signal disclosure requirements from their respective standards.

Securities of Subsidiaries

140. This Statement is based on the current practice of deducting income attributable to the noncontrolling interest (minority interest) to arrive at consolidated net income in the consolidated financial statements. The October 1995 FASB Exposure Draft, *Consolidated Financial Statements: Policy and Procedures,* would change that practice to require that net income attributable to the noncontrolling interest be deducted from consolidated net income to arrive at an amount called *net income attributable to the controlling interest.* In addition, that Exposure Draft states that the computation of earnings per share in consolidated financial statements that include subsidiaries that are not wholly owned should be based on and designated as the amount of net income attributable to the controlling interest. Although consolidated net income would include the results of all consolidated operations, the EPS computation would continue to be based only on net income attributable to the controlling interest.

141. The consolidations Exposure Draft would not require disclosure of "income from continuing operations attributable to the controlling interest" if a noncontrolling interest exists. If that Exposure Draft is finalized as proposed, the Board will have to determine what the control number should be for entities that are required to present earnings per share for net income attributable to the controlling interest. Those and other related issues will be addressed before the Board finalizes its redeliberations on the proposed Statement on consolidated financial statements.

Effective Date and Transition

142. The Board decided that this Statement should be effective for financial statements issued for periods ending after December 15, 1997, including interim periods. The Board believes that that effective date provides adequate time for entities to make any needed modifications to their systems and procedures to conform with the provisions of this Statement. For comparability, the Board decided to require restatement of all prior-period EPS data presented (including interim and summary financial information) in the period of adoption.

143. Earnings per share is a widely quoted statistic; therefore, to enhance comparability among entities, the Board decided to prohibit early adoption of this Statement. Thus, entities are prohibited from presenting EPS data computed in accordance with this Statement on the face of the income statement prior to the required adoption date. However, the Board decided to permit entities to disclose pro forma EPS data in the notes to the financial statements prior to that date.

144. Most respondents to the Exposure Draft agreed with the proposed effective date; however, some respondents suggested that this Statement be effective as of the beginning of the year (for calendar-year entities) rather than as of the end of the year. Most respondents agreed with the Board that the benefits of restatement would exceed the related costs and that both the requirement to restate and the prohibition on early adoption would enhance the consistency and comparability of financial reporting. Due to the prohibition on early adoption, the Board decided to retain the effective date proposed in the Exposure Draft so that calendar-year entities will not have to wait until 1998 to adopt this Statement. That is, calendar-year entities will have to implement the Statement in the fourth quarter of 1997 (and restate back to January 1, 1997). An entity with a June 30, 1997 year-end will have to implement the Statement in its second quarter, the quarter ending December 31, 1997 (and restate its first-quarter results).

145. Some respondents indicated that restatement of all EPS data presented would be impracticable in some situations, especially for entities that present tables of 10-year selected data or that have had a number of changes in capital structure due to mergers or acquisitions. The Board acknowledged that it might be difficult to restate EPS data for 10 years, especially if there have been changes in capital structures. However, the Board decided to retain the requirement for restatement because it believes that the benefits far outweigh the costs. In conjunction with that decision, the Board noted that this Statement does not require presentation of EPS data for 10 years. It requires only that if EPS data are presented, those data must be computed in accordance with the

provisions of this Statement. Thus, entities that choose to present EPS data in summaries of earnings or selected financial data must restate that EPS data.

Other Literature on Earnings per Share

146. A number of respondents to the Exposure Draft suggested that the Board address changes to or continuation of other authoritative guidance on earnings per share, including that of the SEC and the EITF. Because one of the objectives of the EPS project was to simplify the EPS literature, the Board agreed to include in this Statement a table listing all non-FASB authoritative EPS literature and this Statement's impact, if any, on that literature. That table is presented in Appendix F as a reference tool. The Board did not deliberate any of the issues discussed in the other literature, except where specifically noted.

Appendix C

ILLUSTRATIONS

CONTENTS

Appendix C

ILLUSTRATIONS

Introduction

147. This appendix illustrates this Statement's application to entities with complex capital structures. Certain assumptions have been made to simplify the computations and focus on the issue at hand in each illustration.

Illustration 1—Computation of Basic and Diluted Earnings per Share and Income Statement Presentation

148. This example illustrates the quarterly and annual computations of basic and diluted EPS in the year 20X1 for Corporation A, which has a complex capital structure. The control number used in this illustration (and in Illustration 2) is income before extraordinary item because Corporation A has no discontinued operations. Paragraph 149 illustrates the

presentation of basic and diluted EPS on the face of the income statement. The facts assumed are as follows:

Average market price of common stock. The average market prices of common stock for the calendar-year 20X1 were as follows:

First quarter	$59
Second quarter	$70
Third quarter	$72
Fourth quarter	$72

The average market price of common stock from July 1 to September 1, 20X1 was $71.

Common stock. The number of shares of common stock outstanding at the beginning of 20X1 was 3,300,000. On March 1, 20X1, 100,000 shares of common stock were issued for cash.

Convertible debentures. In the last quarter of 20X0, 4 percent convertible debentures with a principal amount of $10,000,000 due in 20 years were sold for cash at $1,000 (par). Interest is payable semiannually on November 1 and May 1. Each $1,000 debenture is convertible into 20 shares of common stock. No de-

bentures were converted in 20X0. The entire issue was converted on April 1, 20X1, because the issue was called by the Corporation.

Convertible preferred stock. In the second quarter of 20X0, 600,000 shares of convertible preferred stock were issued for assets in a purchase transaction. The quarterly dividend on each share of that convertible preferred stock is $0.05, payable at the end of the quarter. Each share is convertible into one share of common stock. Holders of 500,000 shares of that convertible preferred stock converted their preferred stock into common stock on June 1, 20X1.

Warrants. Warrants to buy 500,000 shares of common stock at $60 per share for a period of 5 years were issued on January 1, 20X1. All outstanding warrants were exercised on September 1, 20X1.

Options. Options to buy 1,000,000 shares of common stock at $85 per share for a period of 10 years were issued on July 1, 20X1. No options were exercised during 20X1 because the exercise price of the options exceeded the market price of the common stock.

Tax rate. The tax rate was 40 percent for 20X1.

Year 20X1	Income (Loss) before Extraordinary Item[a]	Net Income (Loss)
First quarter	$3,000,000	$ 3,000,000
Second quarter	4,500,000	4,500,000
Third quarter	500,000	(1,500,000)[b]
Fourth quarter	(500,000)	(500,000)
Full year	$7,500,000	$ 5,500,000

[a]This is the control number (before adjusting for preferred dividends). Refer to paragraph 15.

[b]Corporation A had a $2 million extraordinary loss (net of tax) in the third quarter.

[c][This footnote has been deleted because the effective date of Statement 154 has passed.]

First Quarter 20X1

Basic EPS Computation

Net income		$3,000,000
Less: Preferred stock dividends		(30,000)[a]
Income available to common stockholders		$2,970,000

Dates Outstanding	Shares Outstanding	Fraction of Period	Weighted-Average Shares
January 1–February 28	3,300,000	2/3	2,200,000
Issuance of common stock on March 1	100,000		
March 1–March 31	3,400,000	1/3	1,133,333
Weighted-average shares			3,333,333

Basic EPS $0.89

The equation for computing basic EPS is:

$$\frac{\text{Income available to common stockholders}}{\text{Weighted-average shares}}$$

---

[a]600,000 shares × $0.05

First Quarter 20X1

Diluted EPS Computation

Income available to common stockholders		$2,970,000
Plus: Income impact of assumed conversions		
Preferred stock dividends	$ 30,000[a]	
Interest on 4% convertible debentures	60,000[b]	
Effect of assumed conversions		90,000
Income available to common stockholders + assumed conversions		$3,060,000
Weighted-average shares		3,333,333
Plus: Incremental shares from assumed conversions		
Warrants	0[c]	
Convertible preferred stock	600,000	
4% convertible debentures	200,000	
Dilutive potential common shares		800,000
Adjusted weighted-average shares		4,133,333

Diluted EPS $0.74

The equation for computing diluted EPS is:

$$\frac{\text{Income available to common stockholders} + \text{Effect of assumed conversions}}{\text{Weighted-average shares} + \text{Dilutive potential common shares}}$$

---

[a]600,000 shares × $0.05

[b]($10,000,000 × 4%) ÷ 4; less taxes at 40%

[c] The warrants were not assumed exercised because they were antidilutive in the period ($60 exercise price > $59 average price).

Second Quarter 20X1

Basic EPS Computation

Net income	$4,500,000
Less: Preferred stock dividends	(5,000)[a]
Income available to common stockholders	$4,495,000

Dates Outstanding	Shares Outstanding	Fraction of Period	Weighted-Average Shares
April 1	3,400,000		
Conversion of 4% debentures on April 1	200,000		
April 1–May 31	3,600,000	2/3	2,400,000
Conversion of preferred stock on June 1	500,000		
June 1–June 30	4,100,000	1/3	1,366,667
Weighted-average shares			3,766,667

Basic EPS $1.19

The equation for computing basic EPS is:

$$\frac{\text{Income available to common stockholders}}{\text{Weighted-average shares}}$$

---

[a] 100,000 shares × $0.05

Second Quarter 20X1

Diluted EPS Computation

Income available to common stockholders		$4,495,000
Plus: Income impact of assumed conversions		
Preferred stock dividends	$ 5,000[a]	
Effect of assumed conversions		5,000
Income available to common stockholders + assumed conversions		$4,500,000
Weighted-average shares		3,766,667
Plus: Incremental shares from assumed conversions		
Warrants	71,429[b]	
Convertible preferred stock	433,333[c]	
Dilutive potential common shares		504,762
Adjusted weighted-average shares		4,271,429

Diluted EPS $1.05

The equation for computing diluted EPS is:

$$\frac{\text{Income available to common stockholders} + \text{Effect of assumed conversions}}{\text{Weighted-average shares} + \text{Dilutive potential common shares}}$$

---

[a]100,000 shares × $0.05

[b]$60 × 500,000 = $30,000,000; $30,000,000 ÷ $70 = 428,571; 500,000 − 428,571 = 71,429 shares **OR**
[($70 − $60) ÷ $70] × 500,000 shares = 71,429 shares

[c](600,000 shares × 2/3) + (100,000 shares × 1/3)

Third Quarter 20X1

Basic EPS Computation

Income before extraordinary item	$ 500,000
Less: Preferred stock dividends	(5,000)
Income available to common stockholders	495,000
Extraordinary item	(2,000,000)
Net loss available to common stockholders	$(1,505,000)

Dates Outstanding	Shares Outstanding	Fraction of Period	Weighted-Average Shares
July 1–August 31	4,100,000	2/3	2,733,333
Exercise of warrants on September 1	500,000		
September 1–September 30	4,600,000	1/3	1,533,333
Weighted-average shares			4,266,666

Basic EPS

Income before extraordinary item	**$ 0.12**
Extraordinary item	**$(0.47)**
Net loss	**$(0.35)**

The equation for computing basic EPS is:

$$\frac{\text{Income available to common stockholders}}{\text{Weighted-average shares}}$$

Third Quarter 20X1

Diluted EPS Computation

Income available to common stockholders		$ 495,000
Plus: Income impact of assumed conversions		
Preferred stock dividends	$ 5,000	
Effect of assumed conversions		5,000
Income available to common stockholders + assumed conversions		500,000
Extraordinary item		(2,000,000)
Net loss available to common stockholders + assumed conversions		$(1,500,000)
Weighted-average shares		4,266,666
Plus: Incremental shares from assumed conversions		
Warrants	51,643[a]	
Convertible preferred stock	100,000	
Dilutive potential common shares		151,643
Adjusted weighted-average shares		4,418,309

Diluted EPS

Income before extraordinary item	**$ 0.11**
Extraordinary item	**$(0.45)**
Net loss	**$(0.34)**

The equation for computing diluted EPS is:

$$\frac{\text{Income available to common stockholders} + \text{Effect of assumed conversions}}{\text{Weighted-average shares} + \text{Dilutive potential common shares}}$$

Note: The incremental shares from assumed conversions are included in computing the diluted per-share amounts for the extraordinary item and net loss even though they are antidilutive. This is because the control number (income before extraordinary item, adjusted for preferred dividends) was income, not a loss. (Refer to paragraphs 15 and 16.)

---

[a][($71 − $60) ÷ $71] × 500,000 = 77,465 shares; 77,465 × 2/3 = 51,643 shares

Fourth Quarter 20X1

Basic and Diluted EPS Computation

Net loss	$(500,000)
Plus: Preferred stock dividends	(5,000)
Net loss available to common stockholders	$(505,000)

Dates Outstanding	Shares Outstanding	Fraction of Period	Weighted-Average Shares
October 1–December 31	4,600,000	3/3	4,600,000
Weighted-average shares			4,600,000

Basic and Diluted EPS

Net loss	$(0.11)

The equation for computing basic (and diluted) EPS is:

$$\frac{\text{Income available to common stockholders}}{\text{Weighted-average shares}}$$

Note: The incremental shares from assumed conversions are not included in computing the diluted per-share amounts for net loss because the control number (net loss, adjusted for preferred dividends) was a loss, not income. (Refer to paragraphs 15 and 16.)

(This page intentionally left blank.)

Full Year 20X1

Basic EPS Computation

Income before extraordinary item	$ 7,500,000
Less: Preferred stock dividends	(45,000)
Income available to common stockholders	7,455,000
Extraordinary item	(2,000,000)
Net income available to common stockholders	$ 5,455,000

Dates Outstanding	Shares Outstanding	Fraction of Period	Weighted- Average Shares
January 1–February 28	3,300,000	2/12	550,000
Issuance of common stock on March 1	100,000		
March 1–March 31	3,400,000	1/12	283,333
Conversion of 4% debenture on April 1	200,000		
April 1–May 31	3,600,000	2/12	600,000
Conversion of preferred stock on June 1	500,000		
June 1–August 31	4,100,000	3/12	1,025,000
Exercise of warrants on September 1	500,000		
September 1–December 31	4,600,000	4/12	1,533,333
Weighted-average shares			3,991,666

Basic EPS

Income before extraordinary item	**$ 1.87**
Extraordinary item	**$(0.50)**
Net income	**$ 1.37**

The equation for computing basic EPS is:

$$\frac{\text{Income available to common stockholders}}{\text{Weighted-average shares}}$$

Full Year 20X1

Diluted EPS Computation

Income available to common stockholders		$ 7,455,000
Plus: Income impact of assumed conversions		
Preferred stock dividends	$ 45,000	
Interest on 4% convertible debentures	60,000	
Effect of assumed conversions		105,000
Income available to common stockholders + assumed conversions		7,560,000
Extraordinary item		(2,000,000)
Net income available to common stockholders + assumed conversions		$ 5,560,000
Weighted-average shares		3,991,666
Plus: Incremental shares from assumed conversions		
Warrants	30,768[a]	
Convertible preferred stock	308,333[b]	
4% convertible debentures	50,000[c]	
Dilutive potential common shares		389,101
Adjusted weighted-average shares		4,380,767

Diluted EPS

Income before extraordinary item	**$ 1.73**
Extraordinary item	**$(0.46)**
Net income	**$ 1.27**

The equation for computing diluted EPS is:

$$\frac{\text{Income available to common stockholders} + \text{Effect of assumed conversions}}{\text{Weighted-average shares} + \text{Dilutive potential common shares}}$$

[a](71,429 shares × 3/12) + (51,643 shares × 3/12)
[b](600,000 shares × 5/12) + (100,000 shares × 7/12)
[c]200,000 shares × 3/12

149. The following illustrates how Corporation A might present its EPS data on its income statement. Note that the per-share amount for the extraordinary item is not required to be shown on the face of the income statement.

	For the Year Ended 20X1
Earnings per common share	
Income before extraordinary item	$ 1.87
Extraordinary item	(0.50)
Net income	$ 1.37
Earnings per common share—assuming dilution	
Income before extraordinary item	$ 1.73
Extraordinary item	(0.46)
Net income	$ 1.27

---

*[This footnote has been deleted because the effective date of Statement 154 has passed.]

150. The following table includes the quarterly qnd annual EPS data for Corporation A. The purpose of this table is to illustrate that the sum of the four quarters' EPS data will not necessarily equal the annual EPS data. This Statement does not require disclosure of this information.

	First Quarter	Second Quarter	Third Quarter	Fourth Quarter	Full Year
Basic EPS					
Income (loss) before extraordinary item	$ 0.89	$ 1.19	$ 0.12	$ (0.11)	$ 1.87
Extraordinary item	—	—	(0.47)	—	(0.50)
Net income (loss)	$ 0.89	$ 1.19	$(0.35)	$ (0.11)	$ 1.37
Diluted EPS					
Income (loss) before extraordinary item	$ 0.74	$ 1.05	$ 0.11	$ (0.11)	$ 1.73
Extraordinary item	—	—	(0.45)	—	(0.46)
Net income (loss)	$ 0.74	$ 1.05	$(0.34)	$ (0.11)	$ 1.27

Illustration 2—Earnings per Share Disclosures

151. The following is an illustration of the reconciliation of the numerators and denominators of the basic and diluted EPS computations for "income before extraordinary item and accounting change" and other related disclosures required by paragraph 40 for Corporation A in Illustration 1. **Note:** Statement 123(R) has specific disclosure requirements related to [share]-based compensation arrangements.

	For the Year Ended 20X1		
	Income (Numerator)	Shares (Denominator)	Per-Share Amount
Income before extraordinary item and accounting change	$7,500,000		
Less: Preferred stock dividends	(45,000)		
Basic EPS			
Income available to common stockholders	7,455,000	3,991,666	$1.87
Effect of Dilutive Securities			
Warrants		30,768	
Convertible preferred stock	45,000	308,333	
4% convertible debentures	60,000	50,000	
Diluted EPS			
Income available to common stockholders + assumed conversions	$7,560,000	4,380,767	$1.73

Options to purchase 1,000,000 shares of common stock at $85 per share were outstanding during the second half of 20X1 but were not included in the computation of diluted EPS because the options' exercise price was greater than the average market price of the common shares. The options, which expire on June 30, 20Y1, were still outstanding at the end of year 20X1.

Illustration 3—Contingently Issuable Shares

152. The following example illustrates the contingent share provisions described in paragraphs 10 and 30-35. The facts assumed are as follows:

- Corporation B had 100,000 shares of common stock outstanding during the entire year ended December 31, 20X1. It had no options, warrants, or convertible securities outstanding during the period.
- Terms of a contingent stock agreement related to a recent business combination provided the following to certain shareholders of the Corporation:
  - 1,000 additional common shares for each new retail site opened during 20X1
  - 5 additional common shares for each $100 of consolidated, after-tax net income in excess of $500,000 for the year ended December 31, 20X1.
- The Corporation opened two new retail sites during the year:
  - One on May 1, 20X1
  - One on September 1, 20X1.
- Corporation B's consolidated, year-to-date after-tax net income was:
  - $400,000 as of March 31, 20X1
  - $600,000 as of June 30, 20X1
  - $450,000 as of September 30, 20X1
  - $700,000 as of December 31, 20X1.

Note: In computing diluted EPS for an interim period, contingent shares are included as of the beginning of the period. For year-to-date computations, footnote 18 of this Statement requires that contingent shares be included on a weighted-average basis.

	First Quarter	Second Quarter	Third Quarter	Fourth Quarter	Full Year
Basic EPS Computation					
Numerator	$400,000	$200,000	$(150,000)	$250,000	$700,000
Denominator:					
Common shares outstanding	100,000	100,000	100,000	100,000	100,000
Retail site contingency	0	667[a]	1,333[b]	2,000	1,000[c]
Earnings contingency[d]	0	0	0	0	0
Total shares	100,000	100,667	101,333	102,000	101,000
Basic EPS	$ 4.00	$ 1.99	$ (1.48)	$ 2.45	$ 6.93

	First Quarter	Second Quarter	Third Quarter	Fourth Quarter	Full Year
Diluted EPS Computation					
Numerator	$400,000	$200,000	$(150,000)	$250,000	$700,000
Denominator:					
Common shares outstanding	100,000	100,000	100,000	100,000	100,000
Retail site contingency	0	1,000	2,000	2,000	1,250[e]
Earnings contingency	0[f]	5,000[g]	0[h]	10,000[i]	3,750[j]
Total shares	100,000	106,000	102,000	112,000	105,000
Diluted EPS	$ 4.00	$ 1.89	$ (1.47)[k]	$ 2.23	$ 6.67

[a] 1,000 shares × 2/3

[b] 1,000 shares + (1,000 shares × 1/3)

[c] (1,000 shares × 8/12) + (1,000 shares × 4/12)

[d] The earnings contingency has no effect on basic EPS because it is not certain that the condition is satisfied until the end of the contingency period (paragraphs 10 and 31). The effect is negligible for the fourth-quarter and full-year computations because it is not certain that the condition is met until the last day of the period.

[e] (0 + 1,000 + 2,000 + 2,000) ÷ 4

[f] Corporation B did not have $500,000 year-to-date, after-tax net income at March 31, 20X1. Projecting future earnings levels and including the related contingent shares are not permitted by this Statement.

[g] [($600,000 − $500,000) ÷ $100] × 5 shares

[h] Year-to-date, after-tax net income was less than $500,000.

[i] [($700,000 − $500,000) ÷ $100] × 5 shares

[j] (0 + 5,000 + 0 + 10,000) ÷ 4

[k] Loss during the third quarter is due to a change in accounting principle; therefore, antidilution rules (paragraph 15) do not apply.

Illustration 4—Antidilution Sequencing

153. The following example illustrates the antidilution sequencing provisions described in paragraph 14 for Corporation C for the year ended December 31, 20X0. The facts assumed are as follows:

- Corporation C had income available to common stockholders of $10,000,000 for the year 20X0.
- 2,000,000 shares of common stock were outstanding for the entire year 20X0.
- The average market price of the common stock was $75.

- Corporation C had the following potential common shares outstanding during the year:
  - Options (not compensation related) to buy 100,000 shares of common stock at $60 per share.
  - 800,000 shares of convertible preferred stock entitled to a cumulative dividend of $8 per share. Each preferred share is convertible into 2 shares of common stock.
  - 5 percent convertible debentures with a principal amount of $100,000,000 (issued at par). Each $1,000 debenture is convertible into 20 shares of common stock.
- The tax rate was 40 percent for 20X0.

Determination of Earnings per Incremental Share

	Increase in Income	Increase in Number of Common Shares	Earnings per Incremental Share
Options	0	20,000[a]	—
Convertible preferred stock	$6,400,000[b]	1,600,000[c]	$4.00
5% convertible debentures	3,000,000[d]	2,000,000[e]	1.50

Computation of Diluted Earnings per Share

	Income Available	Common Shares	Per Share	
As reported	$10,000,000	2,000,000	$5.00	
Options	0	20,000		
	10,000,000	2,020,000	4.95	Dilutive
5% convertible debentures	3,000,000	2,000,000		
	13,000,000	4,020,000	3.23	Dilutive
Convertible preferred stock	6,400,000	1,600,000		
	$19,400,000	5,620,000	3.45	Antidilutive

Note: Because diluted EPS *increases* from $3.23 to $3.45 when convertible preferred shares are included in the computation, those convertible preferred shares are antidilutive and are ignored in the computation of diluted EPS. Therefore, diluted EPS is reported as $3.23.

---

[a] [($75 – $60) ÷ $75] × 100,000
[b] 800,000 shares × $8
[c] 800,000 shares × 2
[d] ($100,000,000 × 5%) less taxes at 40%
[e] 100,000 debentures × 20

Illustration 5—Rights Issues

154. The following example illustrates the provisions for stock rights issues that contain a bonus element as described in paragraphs 55 and 56. The facts assumed are as follows:

- Net income was $1,100 for the year ended December 31, 20X0.
- 500 common shares were outstanding for the entire year ended December 31, 20X0.
- A rights issue was offered to all existing shareholders in January 20X1. The last date to exercise the rights was March 1, 20X1. The offer provided 1 common share for each 5 outstanding common shares (100 new shares).

- The exercise price for the rights issue was $5 per share acquired.
- The fair value of 1 common share was $11 at March 1, 20X1.
- Basic EPS for the year 20X0 (prior to the rights issuance) was $2.20.

As a result of the bonus element in the January 20X1 rights issue, basic and diluted EPS for 20X0 will have to be adjusted retroactively. The number of common shares used in computing basic and diluted EPS is the number of shares outstanding immediately prior to the rights issue (500) multiplied by an *adjustment factor*. Prior to computing the adjustment factor, the *theoretical ex-rights fair value per share* must be computed. Those computations follow:

Theoretical ex-rights fair value per share[a] $\quad$ $10 $\quad$ = $\quad$ $\dfrac{(500 \times \$11) + (100 \times \$5)}{(500 + 100)}$

Adjustment factor[b] $\qquad$ 1.1 $\quad$ = $\quad$ $11 ÷ $10

Denominator for restating basic EPS $\qquad$ 550 $\quad$ = $\quad$ 500 × 1.1

Restated basic EPS for 20X0 $\qquad$ $2.00 $\quad$ = $\quad$ $1,100 ÷ 550

Diluted EPS would be adjusted retroactively by adding 50 shares to the denominator that was used in computing diluted EPS prior to the restatement.

---

[a]The equation for computing the theoretical ex-rights fair value per share is:

$$\dfrac{\text{Aggregate fair value of shares prior to exercise of rights } + \text{ Proceeds from exercise of rights}}{\text{Total shares outstanding after exercise of rights}}$$

[b]The equation for computing the adjustment factor is:

$$\dfrac{\text{Fair value per share immediately prior to exercise of rights}}{\text{Theoretical ex-rights fair value per share}}$$

Illustration 6—Two-Class Method

155. The two-class method of computing basic EPS for an entity that has more than one class of nonconvertible securities is illustrated in the following example. This method is described in paragraph 61; as noted in that paragraph, diluted EPS would be computed in a similar manner. The facts assumed for the year 20X0 are as follows:

- Net income was $65,000.
- 10,000 shares of $50 par value common stock were outstanding.
- 5,000 shares of $100 par value nonconvertible preferred stock were outstanding.

- The preferred stock was entitled to a noncumulative annual dividend of $5 per share before any dividend is paid on common stock.
- After common stock has been paid a dividend of $2 per share, the preferred stock then participates in any additional dividends on a 40:60 *per-share* ratio with common stock. (That is, after preferred and common stock have been paid dividends of $5 and $2 per share, respectively, preferred stock participates in any additional dividends at a rate of two-thirds of the additional amount paid to common stock on a per-share basis.)

- Preferred stockholders have been paid $27,000 ($5.40 per share).
- Common stockholders have been paid $26,000 ($2.60 per share).

Basic EPS for 20X0 would be computed as follows:

Net income		$65,000
Less dividends paid:		
Preferred	$27,000	
Common	26,000	53,000
Undistributed 20X0 earnings		$12,000

Allocation of undistributed earnings:

To preferred:
$$0.4(5,000) \div [0.4(5,000) + 0.6(10,000)] \times \$12,000 = \$3,000$$
$$\$3,000 \div 5,000 \text{ shares} = \$0.60 \text{ per share}$$

To common:
$$0.6(10,000) \div [0.4(5,000) + 0.6(10,000)] \times \$12,000 = \$9,000$$
$$\$9,000 \div 10,000 \text{ shares} = \$0.90 \text{ per share}$$

Basic per-share amounts:

	Preferred Stock	Common Stock
Distributed earnings	$5.40	$2.60
Undistributed earnings	0.60	0.90
Totals	$6.00	$3.50

Illustration 7—Securities of a Subsidiary: Computation of Basic and Diluted Earnings per Share

156. The following example illustrates the EPS computations for a subsidiary's securities that enable their holders to obtain the subsidiary's common stock based on the provisions in paragraph 62. This example is based on current practice. Based on the provisions in the consolidations Exposure Draft, the presentation of earnings per share would differ from that illustrated in this example for an entity that includes subsidiaries that are not wholly owned. The facts assumed are as follows:

Parent corporation:

- Net income was $10,000 (excluding any earnings of or dividends paid by the subsidiary).
- 10,000 shares of common stock were outstanding; the parent corporation had not issued any other securities.

- The parent corporation owned 900 common shares of a domestic subsidiary corporation.
- The parent corporation owned 40 warrants issued by the subsidiary.
- The parent corporation owned 100 shares of convertible preferred stock issued by the subsidiary.

Subsidiary corporation:

- Net income was $3,600.
- 1,000 shares of common stock were outstanding.
- Warrants exercisable to purchase 200 shares of its common stock at $10 per share (assume $20 average market price for common stock) were outstanding.
- 200 shares of convertible preferred stock were outstanding. Each share is convertible into two shares of common stock.
- The convertible preferred stock paid a dividend of $1.50 per share.
- No intercompany eliminations or adjustments were necessary except for dividends.
- Income taxes have been ignored for simplicity.

Subsidiary's Earnings per Share

Basic EPS	$3.30	Computed:	$(\$3,600^a - \$300^b) \div 1,000^c$

Diluted EPS	$2.40	Computed:	$\$3,600^d \div (1,000 + 100^e + 400^f)$

Consolidated Earnings per Share

Basic EPS	$1.31	Computed:	$(\$10,000^g + \$3,120^h) \div 10,000^i$

Diluted EPS	$1.27	Computed:	$(\$10,000 + \$2,160^j + \$48^k + \$480^l) \div 10,000$

---

[a]Subsidiary's net income

[b]Dividends paid by subsidiary on convertible preferred stock

[c]Shares of subsidiary's common stock outstanding

[d]Subsidiary's income available to common stockholders ($3,300) increased by $300 preferred dividends from applying the if-converted method for convertible preferred stock

[e]Incremental shares from warrants from applying the treasury stock method, computed: $[(\$20 - \$10) \div \$20] \times 200$

[f]Shares of subsidiary's common stock assumed outstanding from conversion of convertible preferred stock, computed: 200 convertible preferred shares × conversion factor of 2

[g]Parent's net income

[h]Portion of subsidiary's income to be included in consolidated basic EPS, computed: $(900 \times \$3.30) + (100 \times \$1.50)$

[i]Shares of parent's common stock outstanding

[j]Parent's proportionate interest in subsidiary's earnings attributable to common stock, computed: $(900 \div 1,000) \times (1,000 \text{ shares} \times \$2.40 \text{ per share})$

[k]Parent's proportionate interest in subsidiary's earnings attributable to warrants, computed: $(40 \div 200) \times (100 \text{ incremental shares} \times \$2.40 \text{ per share})$

[l]Parent's proportionate interest in subsidiary's earnings attributable to convertible preferred stock, computed: $(100 \div 200) \times (400 \text{ shares from conversion} \times \$2.40 \text{ per share})$

Illustration 8—Application of the Treasury Stock Method to a Share-Based Payment Arrangement

157. Under this Statement, options to be settled in stock are potential common shares for purposes of earnings per share computations. In applying the treasury stock method, all dilutive potential common shares, regardless of whether they are exercisable, are treated as if they had been exercised. The treasury stock method assumes that the proceeds upon exercise are used to repurchase the entity's stock, reducing the number of shares to be added to outstanding common stock in computing earnings per share. The proceeds assumed to be received upon exercise include the exercise price that the employee pays, the amount of compensation cost measured and attributed to future services but not yet recognized, and the amount of any tax benefits upon assumed exercise that would be credited to additional paid-in capital. If the deferred tax asset related to that resulting difference would be deducted from additional paid-in capital (or its equivalent) assuming exercise of the op-

tions, that amount shall be treated as a reduction of assumed proceeds.

158. Under paragraph 43 of Statement 123(R), the effect of forfeitures is taken into account by recognizing compensation cost only for those instruments for which the requisite service has been rendered, and no compensation cost is recognized for instruments that employees forfeit because a service condition or a performance condition is not satisfied. The following example illustrates the application of the treasury stock method when share options are forfeited.

159. Entity L adopted a share option plan on January 1, 20X7, and granted 900,000 at-the-money share options with an exercise price of $30.[a] All share options vest at the end of three years (cliff vesting). At the grant date, Entity L assumes an annual forfeiture rate of 3 percent and therefore expects to receive the requisite service for 821,406 $[900,000 \times (.97^3)]$ share options. On January 1, 20X7, the fair value of each share option granted is $14.69. Employees forfeited 15,000 stock options ratably during 20X7. The

---

[a]This guidance also applies if the service inception date precedes the grant date.

average stock price during 20X7 is $44. Net income for the period is $97,385,602 (inclusive of $2,614,398 of share-based compensation, net of income taxes of $1,407,753). Entity L's tax rate is 35 percent. For the year ended December 31, 20X7, there are 25,000,000 weighted-average common shares outstanding. Entity L has sufficient previously recognized excess tax benefits in additional paid-in capital from prior share-based payment arrangements to offset any write-off of deferred tax assets associated with its grant of share options on January 1, 20X7. All share options are the type that upon exercise give rise to deductible compensation cost for income tax purposes.

Computation of Basic EPS for the Year Ended December 31, 20X7:

Net income[b]	$ 97,385,602
Weighted-average common shares outstanding	25,000,000
Basic earnings per share	$3.90

Computation of assumed proceeds for diluted earnings per share:

Amount employees would pay if the weighted-average number of options outstanding were exercised using the average exercise price (892,500[c] × $30)	$26,775,000
Average unrecognized compensation cost in 20X7 (see computation)	10,944,050
Tax benefit deficiency that would be offset in paid-in capital (see computation)	(215,539)
Assumed proceeds	$37,503,511

Computation of average unrecognized compensation cost in 20X7:

Beginning of period

Unrecognized compensation cost (900,000 × $14.69)	$13,221,000

End of the period

Beginning of period	$13,221,000	
Annual compensation cost recognized during 20X7, based on estimated forfeitures	(4,022,151)[b]	
Annual compensation cost not recognized during the period related to outstanding options at December 31, 20X7, for which the requisite service is not expected to be rendered	(311,399)[d]	
Total compensation cost of actual forfeited options	(220,350)[e]	
Total unrecognized compensation cost, end of the period, based on actual forfeitures		8,667,100
Subtotal		21,888,100
Average total unrecognized compensation, based on actual forfeitures		$10,944,050

[b]Pre-tax annual share-based compensation cost is $4,022,151 [(821,406 × $14.69) ÷ 3]. After-tax share-based compensation cost included in net income is $2,614,398 ($4,022,151 − $1,407,753). ($4,022,151 × .35) = $1,407,753.

[c]Share options granted at the beginning of the year plus share options outstanding at the end of the year divided by two equals the weighted-average number of share options outstanding in 20X7: [(900,000 + 885,000) ÷ 2] = 892,500. This example assumes that forfeitures occurred ratably throughout 20X7.

[d]885,000 (options outstanding at December 31, 20X7) − 821,406 (options for which the requisite service is expected to be rendered) = 63,594. 63,594 options × $14.69 (grant-date fair value per option) = $934,196 (total fair value). $934,196 ÷ 3 = $311,399 (annual share-based compensation cost).

[e]15,000 (forfeited options) × $14.69 (grant-date fair value per option) = $220,350 (total fair value).

Computation of tax benefit:

Total compensation cost of average outstanding options	$ 13,110,825[f]
Intrinsic value of average outstanding options for the year ended December 31, 20X7 [892,500 × ($44 – $30)]	(12,495,000)
Excess of total compensation cost over estimated tax deduction	615,825
Tax benefit deficiency ($615,825 × .35)	$ 215,539

Assumed repurchase of shares:

Repurchase shares at average market price during the year ($37,503,511 ÷ $44)	852,353
Incremental shares (892,500 – 852,353)	40,147

Computation of Diluted EPS for the Year Ended December 31, 20X7:

Net income	$ 97,385,602
Weighted-average common shares outstanding	25,000,000
Incremental shares	40,147
Total shares outstanding	25,040,147
Diluted earnings per share	$ 3.89

---

[f](892,500 × $14.69) = $13,110,825.

Appendix D

AMENDMENTS TO EXISTING PRONOUNCEMENTS

160. This Statement supersedes the following pronouncements:

a. APB Opinion No. 15, *Earnings per Share*
b. AICPA Accounting Interpretations 1-102 of Opinion 15
c. AICPA Accounting Interpretations 1, "Changing EPS Denominator for Retroactive Adjustment to Prior Period," and 2, "EPS for 'Catch-up' Adjustment," of APB Opinion No. 20, *Accounting Changes*
d. FASB Statement No. 85, *Yield Test for Determining whether a Convertible Security Is a Common Stock Equivalent*
e. FASB Interpretation No. 31, *Treatment of Stock Compensation Plans in EPS Computations.*

161. This Statement also amends other pronouncements issued by either the Accounting Principles Board or the Financial Accounting Standards Board that refer to Opinion 15. All such references appearing in paragraphs that establish standards or the scope of a pronouncement are hereby amended to refer instead to FASB Statement No. 128, *Earnings per Share.*

162. The last sentence of paragraph 18 and footnote 8 of APB Opinion No. 18, *The Equity Method of Accounting for Investments in Common Stock,* are replaced by the following:

> An investor's *share of the earnings or losses* of an investee should be based on the shares of *common* stock held by an investor.[8]

---

[8]Paragraph 62 of FASB Statement No. 128, *Earnings per Share,* discusses the treatment of common shares or potential common shares for purposes of computing consolidated EPS. The provisions of that paragraph also apply to investments in common stock of corporate joint ventures and investee companies accounted for under the equity method.

163. Opinion 20 is amended as follows:

a. The last sentence of paragraph 20 is replaced by the following:

> Presentation of per-share amounts for the cumulative effect of an accounting change shall be made either on the face of the income statement or in the related notes.

b. The parenthetical phrase in the second sentence of paragraph 21 is replaced by the following:

> (basic and diluted, as appropriate under FASB Statement No. 128, *Earnings per Share*)

c. In paragraphs 42 and 46, *(which are not common stock equivalents)* is deleted.

d. In the comparative statements in paragraphs 43, 44, and 47, in Note A in paragraph 47, and in the five-year summary in paragraph 48, *full* in *assuming full dilution* is deleted.

164. Paragraph 30(b) of APB Opinion No. 28, *Interim Financial Reporting,* is replaced by the following:

Basic and diluted earnings per share data for each period presented, determined in accordance with the provisions of FASB Statement No. 128, *Earnings per Share.*

165. APB Opinion No. 30, *Reporting the Results of Operations—Reporting the Effects of Disposal of a Segment of a Business, and Extraordinary, Unusual and Infrequently Occurring Events and Transactions,* is amended as follows:

a. Paragraph 9 is amended as follows:

   (1) In the first sentence, *APB Opinion No. 15,* is replaced by *FASB Statement No. 128, Earnings per Share.*

   (2) Footnote 3 is deleted.

b. Paragraph 12 is replaced by the following:

Earnings per share data for extraordinary items shall be presented either on the face of the income statement or in the related notes, as prescribed by Statement 128.

166. FASB Statement No. 21, *Suspension of the Reporting of Earnings per Share and Segment Information by Nonpublic Enterprises,* is amended as follows:

a. Paragraph 12 is amended as follows:

   (1) In the first sentence, *APB Opinion No. 15[3] and* is deleted.

   (2) In the second sentence, *Opinion No. 15 and* is deleted.

   (3) Footnote 3 is deleted.

b. In paragraph 14, *earnings per share and* and *APB Opinion No. 15 and* are deleted.

167. FASB Statement No. 123, *Accounting for Stock-Based Compensation,* is amended as follows:

a. Paragraph 49 is replaced by the following:

FASB Statement No. 128, *Earnings per Share,* requires that employee stock options, nonvested stock, and similar equity instruments granted to employees be treated as potential common shares in computing diluted earnings per share. Diluted earnings per share shall be based on the actual number of options or shares granted and not yet forfeited, unless doing so would be antidilutive. If vesting is contingent upon factors other than continued service, such as the level of future earnings, the shares or options shall be treated as contingently issuable shares in accordance with paragraphs 30-35 of Statement 128. If stock options or other equity instruments are granted during a period, the shares issuable shall be weighted to reflect the portion of the period during which the equity instruments were outstanding.

b. Paragraph 50 is amended as follows:

   (1) In the first sentence, *Opinion 15* is replaced by *Statement 128.*

   (2) In the second sentence, *FASB Interpretation No. 31, Treatment of Stock Compensation Plans in EPS Computations,* is replaced by *Statement 128.*

   (3) In the third sentence, *Interpretation 31* is replaced by *Statement 128.*

c. Paragraph 357 is amended as follows:

   (1) In the second sentence, *Under Opinion 15 and FASB Interpretation No. 31, Treatment of Stock Compensation Plans in EPS Computations* is replaced by *Under FASB Statement No. 128, Earnings per Share* and *common stock equivalents* is replaced by *potential common shares.*

   (2) In the third sentence, *common stock equivalents* is replaced by *potential common shares.*

d. Paragraph 358 is amended as follows:

   (1) The first three sentences are deleted.

   (2) In the fourth sentence, *, of which 4,500,000 are expected to vest* is deleted.

   (3) The seventh sentence is deleted.

e. Paragraph 359 and footnote 26 are replaced by the following:

Computation of assumed proceeds for diluted earnings per share:

- Amount employees would pay if all options outstanding were exercised using the weighted-average exercise price (4,600,000 × $40) $184,000,000
- Average unrecognized compensation balance during year[26] 17,700,000

Assumed proceeds $201,700,000

---

[26]Average unrecognized compensation balance is determined by averaging the beginning-of-the-year balance of cost measured and unrecognized and the end-of-the-year balance of cost measured and unrecognized. The assumed amount is $17,700,000 based on ongoing cost recognition for stock options granted in the current year and prior years.

f. Paragraph 360 is replaced by the following:

Assumed repurchase of shares:

- Repurchase shares at average market price during the year ($201,700,000 ÷ $52) 3,878,846
- Incremental shares to be added (4,600,000 – 3,878,846) 721,154

The number of shares to be added to outstanding shares for purposes of the diluted earnings per share calculation is 721,154.

g. Paragraph 361 is deleted.

168. Paragraph 6 of FASB Interpretation No. 28, *Accounting for Stock Appreciation Rights and Other Variable Stock Option or Award Plans,* is replaced by the following:

Stock appreciation rights and other variable plan awards are included in the computation of diluted earnings per share pursuant to the provisions of paragraphs 20-23 of FASB Statement No. 128, *Earnings per Share.*

169. Paragraph 7 of FASB Interpretation No. 38, *Determining the Measurement Date for Stock Option, Purchase, and Award Plans Involving Junior Stock,* is replaced by the following:

Paragraphs 20-23 of FASB Statement No. 128, *Earnings per Share,* provide guidance on when and how junior stock plans should be reflected in the diluted earnings per share computation.

170. In the first sentence of paragraph 2 of FASB Technical Bulletin No. 79-8, *Applicability of FASB Statements 21 and 33 to Certain Brokers and Dealers in Securities, and APB Opinion No. 15, Earnings per Share,* is deleted.

Appendix E

GLOSSARY

171. This appendix contains definitions of certain terms or phrases used in this Statement.

Antidilution (antidilutive)
An increase in earnings per share amounts or a decrease in loss per share amounts.

Basic earnings per share (basic EPS)
The amount of earnings for the period available to each share of common stock outstanding during the reporting period.

Call option
A contract that allows the holder to buy a specified quantity of stock from the writer of the contract at a fixed price for a given period. Refer to **option** and **purchased call option**.

Common stock (common shares)
A stock that is subordinate to all other stock of the issuer.

Contingent issuance
A possible issuance of shares of common stock that is dependent on the satisfaction of certain conditions.

Contingent stock agreement
An agreement to issue common stock (usually in connection with a business combination) that is dependent on the satisfaction of certain conditions. Refer to **contingently issuable shares**.

Contingently issuable shares (contingently issuable stock)
Shares issuable for little or no cash consideration upon the satisfaction of certain conditions pursuant to a contingent stock agreement. Refer to **contingent stock agreement**.

Conversion rate (conversion ratio)

The ratio of the number of common shares issuable upon conversion to a unit of a convertible security. For example, $100 face value of debt convertible into 5 shares of common stock would have a conversion ratio of 5 to 1.

Convertible security

A security that is convertible into another security based on a conversion rate; for example, convertible preferred stock that is convertible into common stock on a two-for-one basis (two shares of common for each share of preferred).

Diluted earnings per share (diluted EPS)

The amount of earnings for the period available to each share of common stock outstanding during the reporting period and to each share that would have been outstanding assuming the issuance of common shares for all dilutive potential common shares outstanding during the reporting period.

Dilution (dilutive)

A reduction in earnings per share resulting from the assumption that convertible securities were converted, that options or warrants were exercised, or that other shares were issued upon the satisfaction of certain conditions.

Earnings per share (EPS)

The amount of earnings attributable to each share of common stock. For convenience, the term is used in this Statement to refer to either earnings or loss per share.

Exercise price

The amount that must be paid for a share of common stock upon exercise of an option or warrant.

If-converted method

A method of computing EPS data that assumes conversion of convertible securities at the beginning of the reporting period (or at time of issuance, if later).

Income available to common stockholders

Income (or loss) from continuing operations or net income (or net loss) adjusted for preferred stock dividends.

Option

Unless otherwise stated in this Statement, a call option that gives the holder the right to purchase shares of common stock from the reporting entity in accordance with an agreement upon payment of a specified amount. As used in this Statement, options include, but are not limited to, options granted to employees and stock purchase agreements entered into with employees. Options are considered "securities" in this Statement. Refer to **call option.**

Potential common stock

A security or other contract that may entitle its holder to obtain common stock during the reporting period or after the end of the reporting period.

Preferred stock

A security that has rights that are preferential to common stock.

Purchased call option

A contract that allows the reporting entity to buy a specified quantity of its own stock from the writer of the contract at a fixed price for a given period. Refer to **call option**.

Put option

A contract that allows the holder to sell a specified quantity of stock to the writer of the contract at a fixed price during a given period.

Reverse treasury stock method

A method of recognizing the dilutive effect on earnings per share of satisfying a put obligation. It assumes that the proceeds used to buy back common stock (pursuant to the terms of a put option) will be raised from issuing shares at the average market price during the period. Refer to **put option.**

Rights issue

An offer to existing shareholders to purchase additional shares of common stock in accordance with an agreement for a specified amount (which is generally substantially less than the fair value of the shares) for a given period.

Security

The evidence of debt or ownership or a related right. For purposes of this Statement, it includes options and warrants as well as debt and stock.

Treasury stock method

A method of recognizing the use of proceeds that could be obtained upon exercise of options and warrants in computing diluted EPS. It assumes that any proceeds would be used to purchase common stock at the average market price during the period.

Warrant

A security that gives the holder the right to purchase shares of common stock in accordance with the terms of the instrument, usually upon payment of a specified amount.

Weighted-average number of common shares outstanding

The number of shares determined by relating (a) the portion of time within a reporting period that common shares have been outstanding to

(b) the total time in that period. In computing diluted EPS, equivalent common shares are considered for all dilutive potential common shares.

Appendix F

OTHER LITERATURE ON EARNINGS PER SHARE

172. The following table addresses changes to or continuation of other authoritative guidance on earnings per share, including that of the SEC and the EITF. For each item, this table either discusses the impact of this Statement, if any, or indicates reasons that specific items are beyond the scope of this Statement. This table is presented in this Statement for use as a reference tool. The Board did not deliberate any of the issues contained in the literature listed in this table, except where specifically noted.

Note: Current SEC, EITF, and AICPA guidance has been quoted, paraphrased, or restated to facilitate the reader's understanding of the effect of this Statement.

Status Legend:

Affirmed = Consensus is carried forward (with or without modifications).

N/A = Issue is either outside the scope of or unaffected by Statement 128.

Nullified = Consensus is overturned (either entirely or partially, as noted).

Pending = The SEC staff has indicated that it will consider amending or rescinding the guidance prior to the effective date of Statement 128.

Resolved = Guidance is provided by Statement 128 on issues previously unresolved by EITF.

Bold numbers in brackets refer to related paragraphs in Statement 128.

Status after Statement 128	Current Guidance	Effect of Statement 128
N/A	**Staff Accounting Bulletin (SAB) 64 Topic 3C: Redeemable Preferred Stock** SAB 64 states that if the initial fair value of redeemable preferred stock is less than the mandatory redemption amount, the carrying amount of the stock should be increased to the mandatory redemption amount through periodic accretions charged against retained earnings. Those periodic accretions are treated in the same manner as a dividend on nonredeemable preferred stock for EPS computations. That is, dividends on the preferred stock and accretions of their carrying amounts cause income or loss available to common stockholders (the EPS numerator) to be less than reported income.	The Board expects to address the accounting for preferred stock in its project on distinguishing between liability and equity instruments. Statement 128 does not address numerator issues relating to the EPS computation. Statement 128 permits an adjustment only for preferred dividends in computing income available to common stockholders. The SEC guidance for redeemable preferred stock continues to apply. [9]

Status after Statement 128	Current Guidance	Effect of Statement 128
	Topic 6B: Accounting Series Release (ASR) No. 280—*General Revision of Regulation S-X*	
N/A	ASR 280 states that income or loss available to common stockholders should be reported on the face of the income statement when it is materially different in quantitative terms from reported net income or loss or when it is indicative of significant trends or other qualitative considerations.	The disclosure requirement is due, in part, to the provisions in Topic 3C; similar provisions are not included in Statement 128. Statement 128 does not require income available to common stockholders to be presented on the face of the income statement. The SEC disclosure guidance continues to apply.
	SAB 68 **Topic 5Q: Increasing Rate Preferred Stock**	
N/A	SAB 68 states that the discount resulting from the issuance of increasing rate preferred stock should be amortized over the period preceding commencement of the perpetual dividend through a charge to retained earnings and a corresponding increase in the carrying amount of the preferred stock. Those periodic increases are treated in the same manner as a dividend on nonredeemable preferred stock for EPS computations. That is, dividends on the preferred stock and accretions of their carrying amounts cause income or loss available to common stockholders (the EPS numerator) to be less than reported income.	The Board expects to address the accounting for preferred stock in its project on distinguishing between liability and equity instruments. Statement 128 does not address numerator issues relating to the EPS computation. Statement 128 permits an adjustment only for preferred dividends in computing income available to common stockholders. The SEC guidance for increasing rate preferred stock continues to apply. [9]

SAB 83

Topic 4D: Earnings per Share Computations in an Initial Public Offering

Pending

The guidance in SAB 83 is applicable to registration statements filed in connection with an initial public offering (IPO) of common stock. SAB 83 states that potentially dilutive instruments with exercise prices below the IPO price that are issued within a one-year period prior to the initial filing of the IPO registration statement should be treated as outstanding for all reported periods (current and prior), in the same manner as shares issued in a stock split are treated. However, in determining the dilutive effect of the issuances, a treasury stock approach may be used.

This method should be applied in the computation of EPS for all prior periods, including loss years in which the impact of the incremental shares is antidilutive.

Statement 128 would permit those potentially dilutive common shares to be included only in the computation of *diluted* EPS and only from the date of issuance. In essence, SAB 83 permits an entity involved in an IPO to treat those potentially dilutive common shares as outstanding common shares in the computation of both basic and diluted EPS for all reported periods. [17]

Statement 128 does not permit incremental shares to be included in the computation of diluted EPS when an entity has a loss from continuing operations (as the effect is antidilutive). [13, 15, 16]

The SEC guidance continues to apply to SEC registrants involved in an IPO that have issued such potentially dilutive common shares.

Status after Statement 128	Current Guidance	Effect of Statement 128
	EITF Topic No. D-15—Earnings-per-Share Presentation for Securities Not Specifically Covered by APB Opinion No. 15	
N/A	Topic D-15 (an SEC Observer announcement) states that when situations not expressly covered in Opinion 15 occur, they should be dealt with according to their substance. It also provides the two following general principles that must be considered in analyzing new securities in order to reflect the most appropriate EPS presentation.	Although not expressly stated, this broad concept is implicit in Statement 128.
Pending	1. Securities that enable the holder to participate with common shareholders in dividends over a significant period of time should be reflected in EPS using the two-class method if that method is more dilutive than other methods.	Statement 128 requires use of the two-class method for participating securities that are not convertible into common stock (the if-converted method should be used for all convertible securities). **[60, 61]**
Pending	2. Contingent issuances should be reflected in fully diluted EPS if those contingent issuances have at least a reasonable possibility of occurring.	The contingent-share provisions in Statement 128 are fairly specific and do not permit an entity to consider the probability of a contingent issuance occurring. **[30]**

EITF Topic No. D-42—The Effect on the Calculation of Earnings per Share for the Redemption or Induced Conversion of Preferred Stock

N/A

Topic D-42 (an SEC Observer announcement) states that if a registrant redeems its preferred stock, the excess of the fair value of the consideration transferred to the holders of the preferred stock over the carrying amount of the preferred stock should be subtracted from net income to arrive at net income available to common stockholders in the computation of EPS. Similarly, if convertible preferred stock is converted to other securities issued by the registrant pursuant to an inducement offer, the excess of the fair value of all securities and other consideration transferred to the holders of the convertible preferred stock over the fair value of securities issuable pursuant to the original conversion terms should be subtracted from net income to arrive at net income available to common stockholders.

The Board expects to address the accounting for preferred stock in its project on distinguishing between liability and equity instruments. Statement 128 does not address numerator issues relating to the EPS computation. Statement 128 permits an adjustment only for preferred dividends in computing income available to common stockholders. The SEC guidance for redemption or induced conversion of preferred stock continues to apply. [9]

Status after Statement 128	Current Guidance	Effect of Statement 128
N/A	**ETTF Topic No. D-53—Computation of Earnings per Share for a Period That Includes a Redemption or an Induced Conversion of a Portion of a Class of Preferred Stock** Topic D-53 (an SEC Observer announcement) is related to Topic D-42. Topic D-53 states that if a registrant effects a redemption or induced conversion of only a *portion* of the outstanding securities of a class of preferred stock, any excess consideration should be attributed to those shares that are redeemed or converted. For purposes of determining whether the "if converted" method is dilutive for the period, the shares redeemed or converted should be considered separately from those shares that are not redeemed or converted.	The Board expects to address the accounting for preferred stock in its project on distinguishing between liability and equity instruments. Statement 128 does not address numerator issues relating to the EPS computation. The SEC guidance for redemption or induced conversion of preferred stock continues to apply. The "if converted" provisions in Statement 128 do not address how to determine whether a convertible security is antidilutive when there has been a partial conversion. [26-28]
Nullified	**ETTF Issue No. 85-18—Earnings-per-Share Effect of Equity Commitment Notes** Issue 85-18 states that shares contingently issuable under equity commitment notes and equity contracts should *not* be included in EPS computations. Those shares are considered contingently issuable because the company has an option of paying in cash or stock.	Statement 128 contradicts the consensus reached. Statement 128 states that contracts that may be settled in stock or cash should be presumed to be settled in stock and reflected in the computation of diluted EPS unless past experience or a stated policy provides a reasonable basis to believe otherwise. [29]
Affirmed	Issue 85-18 states that equity contracts that specifically require the issuance of common stock to repay debt should be included in the EPS computations as potentially dilutive securities.	Statement 128 supports the consensus reached; equity contracts that require payment in stock should be considered potentially dilutive securities (convertible debt). [26-28]

	EITF Issue No. 87-31—Sale of Put Options on Issuer's Stock	In computing diluted EPS, Statement 128 requires use of the reverse treasury stock method to account for the dilutive effect of written put options and similar contracts that are "in the money" during the reporting period. [24]
Affirmed	Issue 87-31 prescribes use of the reverse treasury stock method to account for the dilutive effect of written put options that are "in the money" during the period.	
	Note: The EITF combined the consensuses in this Issue with the consensuses in Issue No. 96-13, "Accounting for Derivative Financial Instruments Indexed to, and Potentially Settled in, a Company's Own Stock."	
	EITF Issue No. 88-9—Put Warrants	
N/A	The EITF superseded its consensus on this Issue for companies with publicly traded stock in Issue 96-13.	N/A

Status after Statement 128	Current Guidance	Effect of Statement 128
Nullified	**EITF Issue No. 90-4—Earnings-per-Share Treatment of Tax Benefits for Dividends on Stock Held by an Employee Stock Ownership Plan (ESOP)** Issue 1: Dividends on preferred stock held by an ESOP should be deducted from net income, net of any applicable income tax benefit, when computing primary EPS. Issue 2: The second issue was addressed by the EITF in Issue No. 92-3, "Earnings-per-Share Treatment of Tax Benefits for Dividends on Unallocated Stock Held by an Employee Stock Ownership Plan (Consideration of the Implications of FASB Statement No. 109 on Issue 2 of EITF Issue No. 90-4)."	Statement 128 has no provisions related to primary EPS and, thus, nullifies the consensus of Issue 90-4. However, it seems appropriate to make a similar deduction for dividends on preferred stock held by an ESOP when computing both basic and diluted EPS if that preferred stock is considered outstanding (that is, if the ESOP shares are allocated).
	EITF Issue No. 90-19—Convertible Bonds with Issuer Option to Settle for Cash upon Conversion Issue 90-19 provides EPS guidance for companies that issue debt instruments that are convertible into a fixed number of common shares. Upon conversion, the issuer either is required or has the option to satisfy all or part of the obligation in cash as follows:	

Instrument A: If the issuer must satisfy the obligation entirely in cash, the instrument does not have an impact on primary or fully diluted EPS other than that the conversion spread must be recognized as a charge to income.

Affirmed*

Statement 128 implicitly supports the consensus reached; this type of security does not meet the definition of potential common stock. [171]

Instrument B: If the issuer may satisfy the entire obligation in either stock or cash equivalent to the conversion value, the instrument is treated as convertible debt for purposes of computing primary and fully diluted EPS.

Affirmed*

Statement 128 implicitly supports the consensus reached. Contracts that may be settled in stock or cash should be presumed to be settled in stock and reflected in the computation of diluted EPS unless past experience or a stated policy provides a reasonable basis to believe otherwise. [29]

Instrument C: If the issuer must satisfy the accreted value of the obligation in cash and may satisfy the conversion spread in either cash or stock, the instrument does not have an impact on primary EPS but impacts fully diluted EPS as convertible debt.

Affirmed*

Statement 128 implicitly supports the consensus reached for diluted EPS. [29]

Status after Statement 128	Current Guidance	Effect of Statement 128
	EITF Issue No. 92-3—Earnings-per-Share Treatment of Tax Benefits for Dividends on Inoculated Stock Held by an Employee Stock Ownership Plan (Consideration of the Implications of FASB Statement No. 109 on Issue 2 of EITF Issue No. 90-4)	Statement 128 provides no guidance on common stock held by an ESOP. The guidance in AICPA Statement of Position (SOP) 93-6, *Employers' Accounting for Employee Stock Ownership Plans*, continues to apply as does the consensus in EITF Issue 92-3. AICPA Statement of Position 76-3, *Accounting Practices for Certain Employee Stock Ownership Plans*, continues to apply for "grandfathered" shares.
N/A	Issue 92-3 states that tax benefits related to dividends paid on unallocated common stock held by an ESOP, which are charged to retained earnings, should not be an adjustment to net income for purposes of computing EPS.	
	SOP 93-6 was issued in November 1993. Under SOP 93-6, dividends paid on unallocated ESOP shares are not treated as dividends for financial reporting purposes and, therefore, do not affect the if-converted EPS computations.	

EITF Issue No. 94-7—Accounting for Financial Instruments Indexed to, and Potentially Settled in, a Company's Own Stock

Resolved

Issue 94-7 addresses the classification of certain contracts (forward sales, forward purchases, purchased put options, and purchased call options) that are settled in a variety of ways (physical, net share, or net cash) as equity instruments or assets-liabilities and specifies the treatment of changes in the fair value of those instruments. The Issue does not address EPS treatment.

Note: The EITF combined the consensuses in this Issue with the consensuses in Issue 96-13.

Statement 128 states that contracts that may be settled in stock or cash should be presumed to be settled in stock and reflected in the computation of diluted EPS unless past experience or a stated policy provides a reasonable basis to believe otherwise. [29]

In computing diluted EPS, Statement 128 requires use of the reverse treasury stock method to account for the dilutive effect of written put options and similar contracts that are "in the money" during the reporting period. Statement 128 states that purchased options should not be reflected in the computation of diluted EPS because to do so would be antidilutive. [24, 25]

EITF Issue No. 96-1—Sale of Put Options on Issuer's Stock That Require or Permit Cash Settlement

Resolved

Issue 96-1 provides guidance similar to Issue 94-7 and relates only to written put options settled in a variety of ways. The Issue does not address EPS treatment.

Note: The EITF combined the consensuses in this Issue with the consensuses in Issue 96-13.

Refer to discussion on Issue 94-7.

Status after Statement 128	Current Guidance	Effect of Statement 128
Resolved	**EITF Issue No. 96-13—Accounting for Derivative Financial Instruments Indexed to, and Potentially Settled in, a Company's Own Stock** Issue 96-13 codifies the consensuses provided in Issues 87-31, 94-7, and 96-1 into a framework that can be applied to a variety of similar financial instruments settled in a variety of different ways. With the exception of the consensus on use of the reverse treasury stock method in Issue 87-31, Issue 96-13 does not address EPS treatment.	Refer to discussion on Issue 94-7.

Statement of Financial Accounting Standards No. 129
Disclosure of Information about Capital Structure

STATUS

Issued: February 1997

Effective Date: For financial statements for periods ending after December 15, 1997

Affects: Deletes APB 10, paragraphs 10 and 11
Deletes FAS 47, paragraph 10(c)

Affected by: No other pronouncements

Other Interpretive Release: FASB Staff Position FAS 129-1

AICPA Accounting Standards Executive Committee (AcSEC)

Related Pronouncement: PB 14

Issues Discussed by FASB Emerging Issues Task Force (EITF)

Affects: No EITF Issues

Interpreted by: Paragraph 4 interpreted by EITF Issues No. 00-19 and 03-6
Paragraph 8 interpreted by EITF Issue No. 00-19

Related Issues: EITF Issues No. 86-32, 98-5, 00-27, and 05-2 and Topic No. D-98

SUMMARY

This Statement establishes standards for disclosing information about an entity's capital structure. It applies to all entities. This Statement continues the previous requirements to disclose certain information about an entity's capital structure found in APB Opinions No. 10, *Omnibus Opinion—1966,* and No. 15, *Earnings per Share,* and FASB Statement No. 47, *Disclosure of Long-Term Obligations,* for entities that were subject to the requirements of those standards. This Statement eliminates the exemption of nonpublic entities from certain disclosure requirements of Opinion 15 as provided by FASB Statement No. 21, *Suspension of the Reporting of Earnings per Share and Segment Information by Nonpublic Enterprises.* It supersedes specific disclosure requirements of Opinions 10 and 15 and Statement 47 and consolidates them in this Statement for ease of retrieval and for greater visibility to nonpublic entities.

This Statement is effective for financial statements for periods ending after December 15, 1997. It contains no change in disclosure requirements for entities that were previously subject to the requirements of Opinions 10 and 15 and Statement 47.

Statement of Financial Accounting Standards No. 129

Disclosure of Information about Capital Structure

CONTENTS

INTRODUCTION

1. In conjunction with its project to supersede the provisions for computing earnings per share (EPS) found in APB Opinion No. 15, *Earnings per Share,* the Board reviewed the disclosure requirements specified in that Opinion. The Board noted that although some of the disclosures were not necessarily related to the computation of earnings per share, they provided useful information. Because nonpublic entities were excluded from the scope of Opinion 15 and that Opinion's disclosure requirements regarding capital structure are not required elsewhere, the Board decided to include those disclosure requirements in this Statement and make them applicable to all entities. In addition, the Board decided to incorporate related disclosure requirements from other Opinions or Statements into this Statement for ease of use. The specific disclosures required by this Statement were previously required by APB Opinion No. 10, *Omnibus Opinion—1966,* Opinion 15, and FASB Statement No. 47, *Disclosure of Long-Term Obligations,* for entities that were subject to the requirements of those standards.

2. The following terms and definitions are used in this Statement:

a. *Securities*—the evidence of debt or ownership or a related right. For purposes of this Statement, the term *securities* includes options and warrants as well as debt and stock.

b. *Participation rights*—contractual rights of security holders to receive dividends or returns from the security issuer's profits, cash flows, or returns on investments.

c. *Preferred stock*—a security that has preferential rights compared to common stock.

STANDARDS OF FINANCIAL ACCOUNTING AND REPORTING

Scope

3. This Statement applies to all entities, public and nonpublic, that have issued securities addressed by this Statement.

Information about Securities

4. An entity shall explain, in summary form within its financial statements, the pertinent rights and privileges of the various securities outstanding. Examples of information that shall be disclosed are dividend and liquidation preferences, participation rights, call prices and dates, conversion or exercise prices or rates and pertinent dates, sinking-fund requirements, unusual voting rights, and significant terms of contracts to issue additional shares.[1]

---

[1] Disclosure of this information about securities previously was required by Opinion 15, paragraph 19.

5. An entity shall disclose within its financial statements the number of shares issued upon conversion, exercise, or satisfaction of required conditions during at least the most recent annual fiscal period and any subsequent interim period presented.[2]

Liquidation Preference of Preferred Stock

6. An entity that issues preferred stock (or other senior stock) that has a preference in involuntary liquidation considerably in excess of the par or stated value of the shares shall disclose the liquidation preference of the stock (the relationship between the preference in liquidation and the par or stated value of the shares).[3] That disclosure shall be made in the equity section of the statement of financial position in the aggregate, either parenthetically or "in short," rather than on a per-share basis or through disclosure in the notes.

7. In addition, an entity shall disclose within its financial statements (either on the face of the statement of financial position or in the notes thereto):

a. The aggregate or per-share amounts at which preferred stock may be called or is subject to redemption through sinking-fund operations or otherwise; and

b. The aggregate and per-share amounts of arrearages in cumulative preferred dividends.[4]

Redeemable Stock

8. An entity that issues redeemable stock shall disclose the amount of redemption requirements, separately by issue or combined, for all issues of capital stock that are redeemable at fixed or determinable prices on fixed or determinable dates in each of the five years following the date of the latest statement of financial position presented.[5]

Amendments to Existing Pronouncements

9. Paragraphs 10 and 11 of Opinion 10 are deleted as well as the heading preceding paragraph 10.

10. Paragraph 10(c) of Statement 47 is deleted.

Effective Date and Transition

11. This Statement shall be effective for financial statements for periods ending after December 15, 1997. It contains no change in disclosure requirements for entities that were previously subject to the requirements of Opinions 10 and 15 and Statement 47.

> **The provisions of this Statement need not be applied to immaterial items.**

This Statement was adopted by the unanimous vote of the seven members of the Financial Accounting Standards Board:

Dennis R. Beresford, *Chairman*	Anthony T. Cope	James J. Leisenring
	John M. Foster	Gerhard G. Mueller
Joseph V. Anania	Gaylen N. Larson	

---

[2]Disclosure of this information about changes in securities previously was required by Opinion 15, paragraph 20. Footnote 5 to Opinion 15 referred to paragraph 10 of APB Opinion No. 12, *Omnibus Opinion—1967*. That paragraph requires, among other things, disclosure of the changes in the number of shares of equity securities during at least the most recent annual fiscal period and any subsequent interim period presented to make the financial statements sufficiently informative. The disclosure required by paragraph 5 of this Statement meets that requirement.

[3]Disclosure of this information about liquidation preferences previously was required by Opinion 10, paragraph 10.

[4]Disclosure of this information about preferred stock previously was required by Opinion 10, paragraph 11.

[5]Disclosure of this information about redemption requirements previously was required by Statement 47, paragraph 10(c).

Appendix

BACKGROUND INFORMATION AND BASIS FOR CONCLUSIONS

CONTENTS

Appendix

BACKGROUND INFORMATION AND BASIS FOR CONCLUSIONS

Introduction

12. This appendix summarizes considerations that were deemed significant by Board members in reaching the conclusions in this Statement. It includes reasons for accepting certain views and rejecting others. Individual Board members gave greater weight to some factors than to others.

Background Information

13. In March 1994, the Board added a project on earnings per share to its technical agenda to be pursued concurrently with a similar project of the International Accounting Standards Committee (IASC). The objective of the Board's project was twofold: (a) to improve and simplify U.S. generally accepted accounting principles and (b) to issue a standard that would be compatible with international standards.

14. In January 1996, the Board issued an FASB Exposure Draft, *Earnings per Share and Disclosure of Information about Capital Structure.* Part I of the proposed Statement included provisions related to the computation and presentation of earnings per share and was not applicable to nonpublic entities. Part II of the proposed Statement included disclosure requirements for information about capital structure and was applicable to all entities. The Board re-

ceived 104 comment letters on the Exposure Draft, most of which commented only on the earnings per share provisions in Part I. The few letters that addressed Part II generally supported the Board's intent to centralize capital structure disclosure requirements.

15. The Board decided to issue Part II as a separate Statement because of its applicability to non-public entities. The Board was concerned that if it included those disclosure requirements in the final Statement on computing earnings per share, nonpublic entities might not be aware of the existence of those disclosure requirements and their wider applicability.

Conclusions on Basic Issues

Scope

16. This Statement is applicable to all entities that have issued securities addressed by this Statement. The Board believes that all of the required disclosures will be useful to users of financial statements of entities that have issued any type of security covered by this Statement, whether or not those securities are publicly held. The scope of this Statement is unchanged from that of the standards that previously contained its disclosure requirements (Opinions 10 and 15 and Statement 47), except for the elimination of the exemption of nonpublic entities from the provisions of Opinion 15. That exemption was provided by FASB Statement No. 21, *Suspension of the Reporting of Earnings per Share and Segment Information by Nonpublic Enterprises,* which was amended by FASB Statement No. 128, *Earnings per Share.*

Disclosure Requirements

17. Opinion 15 required disclosure of descriptive information about securities that is not necessarily related to the computation of earnings per share. The Board considered limiting that disclosure to information about only those securities that affect or could affect the computation of basic and diluted EPS. However, the Board decided not to limit the disclosure requirement because it contains useful information about the capital structure of an entity that is not required elsewhere.

18. This Statement also requires disclosure of information about (a) the liquidation preference of preferred stock and (b) redeemable stock that previously had been required to be disclosed by Opinion 10 and Statement 47, respectively. Those disclosure requirements were incorporated into this Statement because the Board believes that it is useful to include all disclosure requirements related to an entity's capital structure in the same standard.

Effective Date

19. The Board decided that this Statement should be effective for financial statements for periods ending after December 15, 1997. That effective date corresponds to the effective date of Statement 128. This Statement contains no change in disclosure requirements for entities that were previously subject to the requirements of Opinions 10 and 15 and Statement 47.

Statement of Financial Accounting Standards No. 130
Reporting Comprehensive Income

STATUS

Issued: June 1997

Effective Date: For fiscal years beginning after December 15, 1997

Affects: Amends APB 28, paragraphs 2 and 30(a)
Amends FAS 52, paragraph 13
Amends FAS 80, paragraph 5
Amends FAS 87, paragraphs 37 and 38
Amends FAS 109, paragraphs 35 and 36
Amends FAS 115, paragraphs 13, 15(c), 15(d), and 16

Affected by: Paragraphs 17, 19, and 20 amended by FAS 158, paragraphs F4(a) through F4(c), respectively
Paragraph 21 deleted by FAS 158, paragraph F4(d)
Paragraph 27 amended by FAS 135, paragraph 4(w)
Paragraph 130 amended by FAS 158, paragraph F4(e)
Paragraph 131 amended by FAS 154, paragraph C19(d), and FAS 158, paragraph F4(f)
Paragraph 132 amended by FSP FAS 158-1, paragraph 13

AICPA Accounting Standards Executive Committee (AcSEC)

Related Pronouncement: SOP 02-2

SUMMARY

This Statement establishes standards for reporting and display of comprehensive income and its components (revenues, expenses, gains, and losses) in a full set of general-purpose financial statements. This Statement requires that all items that are required to be recognized under accounting standards as components of comprehensive income be reported in a financial statement that is displayed with the same prominence as other financial statements. This Statement does not require a specific format for that financial statement but requires that an enterprise display an amount representing total comprehensive income for the period in that financial statement.

This Statement requires that an enterprise (a) classify items of other comprehensive income by their nature in a financial statement and (b) display the accumulated balance of other comprehensive income separately from retained earnings and additional paid-in capital in the equity section of a statement of financial position.

This Statement is effective for fiscal years beginning after December 15, 1997. Reclassification of financial statements for earlier periods provided for comparative purposes is required.

Statement of Financial Accounting Standards No. 130

Reporting Comprehensive Income

CONTENTS

INTRODUCTION

1. This Statement establishes standards for reporting and display of comprehensive income and its components in a full set of general-purpose financial statements. It does not address issues of recognition[1] or measurement for comprehensive income and its components.

2. Historically, issues about income reporting were characterized broadly in terms of a contrast between the so-called current operating performance (or dirty surplus) and the all-inclusive (or clean surplus) income concepts. Under the current operating performance income concept, extraordinary and nonrecurring gains and losses are excluded from income. Under the all-inclusive income concept, all revenues, expenses, gains, and losses recognized during the period are included in income, regardless of whether they are considered to be results of operations of the period. The Accounting Principles Board largely adopted the all-inclusive income concept when it issued APB Opinion No. 9, *Reporting the Results of Operations,* and later reaffirmed the concept when it issued APB Opinions No. 20, *Accounting Changes,* and No. 30, *Reporting the Results of Operations— Reporting the Effects of Disposal of a Segment of a Business, and Extraordinary, Unusual and Infrequently Occurring Events and Transactions.*

---

[1]"Recognition is the process of formally recording or incorporating an item in the financial statements of an entity. Thus, an asset, liability, revenue, expense, gain, or loss may be recognized (recorded) or unrecognized (unrecorded). *Realization* and *recognition* are not used as synonyms, as they sometimes are in accounting and financial literature" (Concepts Statement No. 6, *Elements of Financial Statements,* paragraph 143; footnote reference omitted).

3. Although the Board generally followed the all-inclusive income concept, occasionally it made specific exceptions to that concept by requiring that certain changes in assets and liabilities not be reported in a statement that reports results of operations for the period in which they are recognized but instead be included in balances within a separate component of equity in a statement of financial position. Statements that contain those exceptions are FASB Statements No. 12, *Accounting for Certain Marketable Securities,*[2] No. 52, *Foreign Currency Translation,* No. 80, *Accounting for Futures Contracts,* No. 87, *Employers' Accounting for Pensions,* and No. 115, *Accounting for Certain Investments in Debt and Equity Securities.*

4. Some users of financial statement information expressed concerns about the increasing number of comprehensive income items that bypass the income statement. Currently, an enterprise is required to report the accumulated balances of those items in equity. However, because of the considerable diversity as to how those balances and changes in them are presented in financial statements, some of those users urged the Board to implement the concept of comprehensive income that was introduced in FASB Concepts Statement No. 3, *Elements of Financial Statements of Business Enterprises* (which was superseded by FASB Concepts Statement No. 6, *Elements of Financial Statements*), and further described in FASB Concepts Statement No. 5, *Recognition and Measurement in Financial Statements of Business Enterprises.*

5. As a first step in implementing the concept of comprehensive income, this Statement requires that all items that meet the definition of components of comprehensive income be reported in a financial statement for the period in which they are recognized. In doing so, this Statement amends Statements 52, 80, 87, and 115 to require that changes in the balances of items that under those Statements are reported directly in a separate component of equity in a statement of financial position be reported in a financial statement that is displayed as prominently as other financial statements. Items required by accounting standards to be reported as direct adjustments to paid-in capital, retained earnings, or other nonincome equity accounts are not to be included as

components of comprehensive income. (Refer to paragraphs 108-119.)

STANDARDS OF FINANCIAL ACCOUNTING AND REPORTING

Scope

6. This Statement applies to all enterprises that provide a full set of financial statements that report financial position, results of operations, and cash flows.[3] This Statement does not apply to an enterprise that has no items of other comprehensive income in any period presented or to a not-for-profit organization that is required to follow the provisions of FASB Statement No. 117, *Financial Statements of Not-for-Profit Organizations.*

7. This Statement discusses how to report and display comprehensive income and its components. However, it does not specify when to recognize or how to measure the items that make up comprehensive income. Existing and future accounting standards will provide guidance on items that are to be included in comprehensive income and its components.

Definition of Comprehensive Income

8. Comprehensive income is defined in Concepts Statement 6 as "the change in equity [net assets] of a business enterprise during a period from transactions and other events and circumstances from nonowner sources. It includes all changes in equity during a period except those resulting from investments by owners and distributions to owners" (paragraph 70).

9. In Concepts Statement 5, the Board stated that "a full set of financial statements for a period should show: Financial position at the end of the period, earnings (net income) for the period, comprehensive income (total nonowner changes in equity) for the period, cash flows during the period, and investments by and distributions to owners during the period" (paragraph 13, footnote references omitted). Prior to issuance of this Statement, the Board had neither required that an enterprise report comprehensive income, nor had it recommended a format for displaying comprehensive income.

---

[2]Statement 12 was superseded by Statement 115.

[3]Investment companies, defined benefit pension plans, and other employee benefit plans that are exempt from the requirement to provide a statement of cash flows by FASB Statement No. 102, *Statement of Cash Flows—Exemption of Certain Enterprises and Classification of Cash Flows from Certain Securities Acquired for Resale,* are not exempt from the requirements of this Statement if they otherwise apply.

Use of the Term Comprehensive Income

10. This Statement uses the term *comprehensive income* to describe the total of all components of comprehensive income, including net income.[4] This Statement uses the term *other comprehensive income* to refer to revenues, expenses, gains, and losses that under generally accepted accounting principles are included in comprehensive income but excluded from net income. This Statement does not require that an enterprise use the terms *comprehensive income* or *other comprehensive income* in its financial statements, even though those terms are used throughout this Statement.[5]

Purpose of Reporting Comprehensive Income

11. The purpose of reporting comprehensive income is to report a measure of all changes in equity of an enterprise that result from recognized transactions and other economic events of the period other than transactions with owners in their capacity as owners. Prior to the issuance of this Statement, some of those changes in equity were displayed in a statement that reports the results of operations, while others were included directly in balances within a separate component of equity in a statement of financial position.

12. If used with related disclosures and other information in the financial statements, the information provided by reporting comprehensive income should assist investors, creditors, and others in assessing an enterprise's activities and the timing and magnitude of an enterprise's future cash flows.

13. Although total comprehensive income is a useful measure, information about the components that make up comprehensive income also is needed. A single focus on total comprehensive income is likely to result in a limited understanding of an enterprise's activities. Information about the components of comprehensive income often may be more important than the total amount of comprehensive income.

Reporting and Display of Comprehensive Income

14. All components of comprehensive income shall be reported in the financial statements in the period in which they are recognized. A total amount for comprehensive income shall be displayed in the financial statement where the components of other comprehensive income are reported.

Classifications within Comprehensive Income

15. This Statement divides comprehensive income into net income and other comprehensive income. An enterprise shall continue to display an amount for net income. An enterprise that has no items of other comprehensive income in any period presented is not required to report comprehensive income.

Classifications within net income

16. Items included in net income are displayed in various classifications. Those classifications can include income from continuing operations, discontinued operations, extraordinary items, and cumulative effects of changes in accounting principle. This Statement does not change those classifications or other requirements for reporting results of operations.

Classifications within other comprehensive income

17. Items included in other comprehensive income shall be classified based on their nature. For example, under existing accounting standards, other comprehensive income shall be classified separately into foreign currency items, gains or losses associated with pension or other postretirement benefits, prior service costs or credits associated with pension or other postretirement benefits, transition assets or obligations associated with pension or other postretirement benefits, and unrealized gains and losses on certain investments in debt and equity securities. Additional classifications or additional items within current classifications may result from future accounting standards.

Reclassification adjustments

18. Adjustments shall be made to avoid double counting in comprehensive income items that are displayed as part of net income for a period that also had been displayed as part of other comprehensive income in that period or earlier periods. For example,

---

[4]This Statement uses the term *net income* to describe a measure of financial performance resulting from the aggregation of revenues, expenses, gains, and losses that are not items of other comprehensive income as identified in this Statement. A variety of other terms such as *net earnings* or *earnings* may be used to describe that measure.

[5]Paragraph 40 of Concepts Statement 5 states that "just as a variety of terms are used for net income in present practice, the Board anticipates that total nonowner changes in equity, comprehensive loss, and other equivalent terms will be used in future financial statements as names for comprehensive income."

gains on investment securities that were realized and included in net income of the current period that also had been included in other comprehensive income as unrealized holding gains in the period in which they arose must be deducted through other comprehensive income of the period in which they are included in net income to avoid including them in comprehensive income twice. Those adjustments are referred to in this Statement as *reclassification adjustments.*

19. An enterprise shall determine reclassification adjustments for each classification of other comprehensive income. The requirement for a reclassification adjustment for Statement 52 foreign currency translation adjustments is limited to translation gains and losses realized upon sale or upon complete or substantially complete liquidation of an investment in a foreign entity.

20. An enterprise may display reclassification adjustments on the face of the financial statement in which comprehensive income is reported, or it may disclose reclassification adjustments in the notes to the financial statements. Therefore, for all classifications of other comprehensive income, an enterprise may use either (a) a gross display on the face of the financial statement or (b) a net display on the face of the financial statement and disclose the gross change in the notes to the financial statements.[6] Gross and net displays are illustrated in Appendix B. An example of the calculation of reclassification adjustments for Statement 115 available-for-sale securities is included in Appendix C.

21. [This paragraph has been deleted. See Status page.]

Alternative Formats for Reporting Comprehensive Income

22. An enterprise shall display comprehensive income and its components in a financial statement that is displayed with the same prominence as other financial statements that constitute a full set of financial statements. This Statement does not require a specific format for that financial statement but requires that an enterprise display net income as a component of comprehensive income in that financial statement. Appendix B provides illustrations of the components of other comprehensive income and to-

tal comprehensive income being reported below the total for net income in a statement that reports results of operations, in a separate statement of comprehensive income that begins with net income, and in a statement of changes in equity.

23. Although this Statement does not require a specific format for displaying comprehensive income and its components, the Board encourages an enterprise to display the components of other comprehensive income and total comprehensive income below the total for net income in a statement that reports results of operations or in a separate statement of comprehensive income that begins with net income.

24. An enterprise may display components of other comprehensive income either (a) net of related tax effects or (b) before related tax effects with one amount shown for the aggregate income tax expense or benefit related to the total of other comprehensive income items.

25. An enterprise shall disclose the amount of income tax expense or benefit allocated to each component of other comprehensive income, including reclassification adjustments, either on the face of the statement in which those components are displayed or in the notes to the financial statements. Alternative formats for disclosing the tax effects related to the components of other comprehensive income are illustrated in Appendix B.

Reporting Other Comprehensive Income in the Equity Section of a Statement of Financial Position

26. The total of other comprehensive income for a period shall be transferred to a component of equity that is displayed separately from retained earnings and additional paid-in capital in a statement of financial position at the end of an accounting period. A descriptive title such as *accumulated other comprehensive income* shall be used for that component of equity. An enterprise shall disclose accumulated balances for each classification in that separate component of equity on the face of a statement of financial position, in a statement of changes in equity, or in notes to the financial statements. The classifications shall correspond to classifications used elsewhere in the same set of financial statements for components of other comprehensive income.

---

[6]If displayed gross, reclassification adjustments are reported separately from other changes in the respective balance; thus, the total change is reported as two amounts. If displayed net, reclassification adjustments are combined with other changes in the balance; thus, the total change is reported as a single amount.

Interim-Period Reporting

27. APB Opinion No. 28, *Interim Financial Reporting,* clarifies the application of accounting principles and reporting practices to interim financial information, including interim financial statements and summarized interim financial data of publicly traded companies issued for external reporting purposes. An enterprise shall report a total for comprehensive income in condensed financial statements of interim periods.

Amendments to Existing Pronouncements

28. APB Opinion No. 28, *Interim Financial Reporting,* is amended as follows:

a. In the first sentence of paragraph 2, as amended by FASB Statement No. 95, *Statement of Cash Flows,* the term *comprehensive income,* is inserted before *and cash flows.*

b. In paragraph 30(a), the phrase *and net income* is replaced by *net income, and comprehensive income.*

29. In the last sentence of paragraph 13 of FASB Statement No. 52, *Foreign Currency Translation,* the phrase *separately and accumulated in a separate component of equity* is replaced by *in other comprehensive income.*

30. FASB Statement No. 80, *Accounting for Futures Contracts,* is amended as follows:

a. In the third sentence of paragraph 5, *a separate component of stockholders' (or policyholders') equity* is replaced by *other comprehensive income.*

b. In the last sentence of paragraph 5, as amended by FASB Statement No. 115, *Accounting for Certain Investments in Debt and Equity Securities,* the phrase *shall be included as part of other comprehensive income and* is inserted after *those assets.*

31. FASB Statement No. 87, *Employers' Accounting for Pensions,* is amended as follows:

a. In the last sentence of paragraph 37, as amended by FASB Statement No. 109, *Accounting for In-come Taxes,* the phrase *as a separate component (that is, a reduction) of equity* is replaced by *in other comprehensive income.*

b. Paragraph 38 is amended as follows:

(1) In the first sentence, *the balance accumulated in a* is inserted before *separate.*

(2) The following sentence is added to the end of paragraph 38:

> Eliminations of or adjustments to that balance shall be reported in other comprehensive income.

32. FASB Statement No. 109, *Accounting for Income Taxes,* is amended as follows:

a. In the first sentence of paragraph 35, *other comprehensive income,* is inserted after *extraordinary items.*

b. In the first sentence of paragraph 36, *to other comprehensive income or* is inserted after *credited directly.*

33. FASB Statement No. 115, *Accounting for Certain Investments in Debt and Equity Securities,* is amended as follows:

a. Paragraph 13 is amended as follows:

(1) In the second sentence, *as a net amount in a separate component of shareholders' equity until realized* is replaced by *in other comprehensive income.*

(2) In the last sentence, *a separate component of shareholders' equity* is replaced by *other comprehensive income.*

b. In paragraph 15(c), *recognized in a separate component of shareholders' equity* is replaced by *reported in other comprehensive income.*

c. In the first sentence of paragraph 15(d), *such as accumulated other comprehensive income,* is inserted after *shareholders' equity.*

d. In the last sentence of paragraph 16, both references to *the separate component of equity* are replaced by *other comprehensive income.*

Effective Date and Transition

34. The provisions of this Statement shall be effective for fiscal years beginning after December 15, 1997. Earlier application is permitted. If comparative financial statements are provided for earlier periods, those financial statements shall be reclassified to reflect application of the provisions of this Statement. The provisions of this Statement that require display of reclassification adjustments (paragraphs 18-21) are not required, but are encouraged, in comparative financial statements provided for earlier periods. Initial application of this Statement shall be as of the beginning of an enterprise's fiscal year; that is, if the Statement is adopted prior to the effective date and during an interim period other than the first interim period, all prior interim periods of that fiscal year shall be reclassified.

> **The provisions of this Statement need not be applied to immaterial items.**

This Statement was adopted by the affirmative votes of five members of the Financial Accounting Standards Board. Messrs. Cope and Foster dissented.

Messrs. Cope and Foster dissent from this Statement because it permits an enterprise to display the items of other comprehensive income identified in this Statement with less prominence and to characterize them differently from other items of comprehensive income that are currently included in net income. The Board's conceptual framework does not define earnings or net income, nor does it provide criteria for distinguishing the characteristics of items that should be included in comprehensive income but not in net income. The qualitative characteristics of the items currently classified as items of other comprehensive income have not been conceptually distinguished from those items included in net income. Messrs. Cope and Foster believe that items of other comprehensive income can be as significant to measurement of an enterprise's economic and financial performance as those items of comprehensive income that are currently included in measuring net income, and that the comparability and the neutrality of reported information are adversely affected if some items of comprehensive income are omitted from reports on economic and financial performance. Therefore, they have concluded that this Statement should have required that items of other comprehensive income be reported in a statement of financial performance, preferably in a single statement in which net income is reported as a component of comprehensive income.

Messrs. Cope and Foster believe that a primary objective in undertaking a project on reporting comprehensive income was to significantly enhance the visibility of items of other comprehensive income. They do not believe that this Statement will achieve that objective. Messrs. Cope and Foster think that it is likely that most enterprises will meet the requirements of this Statement by providing the required information in a statement of changes in equity, and that displaying items of other comprehensive income solely in that statement as opposed to reporting them in a statement of financial performance will do little to enhance their visibility and will diminish their perceived importance. Thus, it is their view that this Statement will inappropriately relegate certain items of comprehensive income to a lesser standing, having less visibility than other items of comprehensive income that are included in net income, and will do so for the foreseeable future.

Another objective of the project on reporting comprehensive income was to encourage users of financial statements to focus on the components that constitute comprehensive income rather than limiting their analyses solely to the amounts reported as net income and earnings per share. The current, apparent market fixation on earnings per share is evidence that some users exclude other measures of performance from their analyses. Messrs. Cope and Foster believe that permitting items of other comprehensive income to be reported solely in a statement of changes in equity does not achieve the foregoing objective and may, in fact, divert the attention of some users of financial statements from those items of comprehensive income, thereby diminishing their understanding of the economic and financial performance of the reporting enterprise. For users of financial statements to fully understand and appropriately analyze the economic and financial performance of an enterrise, all items of other comprehensive income must be reported in a statement of financial performance, as was proposed in the Exposure Draft of this Statement.

Messrs. Cope and Foster believe that the Board inappropriately failed to respond to the clear and unequivocal call from users of financial statements for the transparent presentation of all items of comprehensive income, whose request is acknowledged in paragraphs 40 and 41 of this Statement. While many respondents to the Exposure Draft asserted that users would be confused by the presentation of comprehensive income, the users that testified at the public hearing on this project categorically denied that that would be the case.

Messrs. Cope and Foster also note that, as evidenced by the basis for conclusions in the Exposure Draft, the Board held views similar to theirs when it issued that document. The stated objective in the Exposure Draft was "to issue a Statement that requires that an enterprise report all components of comprehensive income in one or two statements of financial performance for the period in which those items are recognized." Messrs. Cope and Foster believe that the basis for conclusions supporting this Statement provides little, if any, rationale as to why, having determined at the time it issued the Exposure Draft that comprehensive income is clearly a measure of financial performance, the Board subsequently concluded it should not require presentation of comprehensive income in a statement of financial performance

(paragraphs 58-67). In fact, paragraph 67 of this Statement acknowledges the conceptual superiority of displaying comprehensive income in a statement of performance.

Finally, based on the Board's tentative conclusions, at this time it seems that a future standard on accounting for hedging and derivative instruments likely will provide that certain gains and losses on transactions in derivative instruments not be included in the determination of net income when they occur, but be reported as items of other comprehensive income. Much concern recently has been expressed about derivative instruments and their effects on the financial position and performance of various enterprises. The Board's project on accounting for derivative instruments and hedging activities was undertaken to enhance the visibility and understanding of those transactions and their effects on financial position and performance. Messrs. Cope and Foster believe that if certain of those effects are reported as items of other comprehensive income, application of this Statement in conjunction with that reporting is likely to do little to achieve that objective. In their view, that is inappropriate, particularly when the potential for significant impact that derivative instruments have on an enterprise's performance is an important concern.

Members of the Financial Accounting Standards Board:

Appendix A

BACKGROUND INFORMATION AND BASIS FOR CONCLUSIONS

CONTENTS

Appendix A

BACKGROUND INFORMATION AND BASIS FOR CONCLUSIONS

Introduction

35. This appendix summarizes considerations that were deemed significant by Board members in reaching the conclusions in this Statement. It includes reasons for accepting certain approaches and rejecting others. Individual Board members gave greater weight to some factors than to others.

Background Information

36. The term *comprehensive income* was first introduced in Concepts Statement 3, which was issued in December 1980. However, the term comprehensive income was used to communicate the same notion as *earnings* in FASB Concepts Statement No. 1, *Objectives of Financial Reporting by Business Enterprises,* which was issued in November 1978.[7] The Board decided to use comprehensive income rather than earnings in Concepts Statement 3 because it wanted to reserve earnings for possible use to designate a different concept that was narrower than comprehensive income.

37. In Concepts Statement 5, the Board concluded that comprehensive income and its components should be reported as part of a full set of financial statements for a period. The Board also described earnings as part of comprehensive income in that Concepts Statement, indicating that earnings was narrower than comprehensive income, and provided illustrations of possible differences between earnings and comprehensive income. Earnings was described as being similar to net income in current practice, except for cumulative effects of changes in accounting principles, which are included in present net income but are excluded from earnings.

38. In December 1985, Concepts Statement 6 superseded Concepts Statement 3, expanding the scope to encompass not-for-profit organizations. Concepts Statement 6 does not alter the definition of comprehensive income provided in Concepts Statement 3.

39. Prior to the issuance of this Statement, the Board had not required that comprehensive income and its components be reported as part of a full set of financial statements. However, several accounting standards required that certain items that qualify as components of comprehensive income bypass a statement of income and be reported in a balance within a separate component of equity in a statement of financial position. Those items are:

a. Foreign currency translation adjustments (Statement 52, paragraph 13)
b. Gains and losses on foreign currency transactions that are designated as, and are effective as, economic hedges of a net investment in a foreign entity, commencing as of the designation date (Statement 52, paragraph 20(a))
c. Gains and losses on intercompany foreign currency transactions that are of a long-term-investment nature (that is, settlement is not planned or anticipated in the foreseeable future), when the entities to the transaction are consolidated, combined, or accounted for by the equity method in the reporting enterprise's financial statements (Statement 52, paragraph 20(b))
d. A change in the market value of a futures contract that qualifies as a hedge of an asset reported at fair value pursuant to Statement 115 (Statement 80, paragraph 5)
e. A net loss recognized pursuant to Statement 87 as an additional pension liability not yet recognized as net periodic pension cost (Statement 87, paragraph 37)
f. Unrealized holding gains and losses on available-for-sale securities (Statement 115, paragraph 13)
g. Unrealized holding gains and losses that result from a debt security being transferred into the available-for-sale category from the held-to-maturity category (Statement 115, paragraph 15(c))
h. Subsequent decreases (if not an other-than-temporary impairment) or increases in the fair value of available-for-sale securities previously written down as impaired (Statement 115, paragraph 16).

40. Users of financial statements expressed concerns about the practice of reporting some comprehensive

---

[7]Comprehensive income also is the concept that was referred to as earnings in other conceptual framework documents: *Tentative Conclusions on Objectives of Financial Statements of Business Enterprises* (December 1976), FASB Discussion Memorandum, *Conceptual Framework for Financial Accounting and Reporting: Elements of Financial Statements and Their Measurement* (December 1976), FASB Exposure Draft, *Objectives of Financial Reporting and Elements of Financial Statements of Business Enterprises* (December 1977), and FASB Discussion Memorandum, *Reporting Earnings* (July 1979).

income items directly within a balance shown as a separate component of equity. Among those expressing concerns was the Association for Investment Management and Research (AIMR). In its 1993 report, *Financial Reporting in the 1990s and Beyond,* the AIMR urged the Board to implement the concept of comprehensive income for several reasons. Two of those reasons were to discontinue the practice of taking certain items of comprehensive income directly to equity and to provide a vehicle for addressing future accounting issues, such as the display of unrealized gains and losses associated with financial instruments. In that report, the AIMR noted that it has long supported the all-inclusive income concept.

41. The Accounting Policy Committee of the Robert Morris Associates also indicated support for what it referred to as an all-inclusive income statement at a 1995 meeting with the Board by stating that "net income should include the effect of *all* of the current period's economic transactions and other activity of the entity."

42. There is also international precedent for moving toward an all-inclusive income concept. In 1992, the United Kingdom Accounting Standards Board (ASB) issued Financial Reporting Standard (FRS) 3, *Reporting Financial Performance.* That standard introduced a "statement of total recognized gains and losses" as a supplement to the "profit and loss account," which is equivalent to the U.S. income statement. The amount for "recognized gains and losses relating to the year" in the statement of total recognized gains and losses is analogous to comprehensive income.

43. Largely in response to the precedent set by the ASB, other international standard setters have focused attention on reporting financial performance. As part of its efforts to promote international harmonization, the Board discussed reporting comprehensive income with the ASB as well as with standard setters from the International Accounting Standards Committee (IASC), the Canadian Institute of Chartered Accountants, the Australian Accounting Research Foundation, and the New Zealand Society of Accountants.

44. In July 1996, the IASC issued an Exposure Draft, *Presentation of Financial Statements,* which included a proposed requirement for a new primary financial statement referred to as a "statement of nonowner movements in equity." The purpose of that statement would be to highlight more prominently gains and losses, such as those arising from revaluations and deferred exchange differences, that are not reported in the income statement under existing IASC standards.[8] The IASC's proposed requirement is similar in concept to this Statement's requirement for reporting comprehensive income and the ASB's requirement for a statement of total recognized gains and losses.

45. In addition to users' concerns about reporting comprehensive income items in equity and the desire for international harmonization, the project on reporting comprehensive income became more urgent because of the increasing use of separate components in equity for certain comprehensive income items. In that regard, a recent motivating factor for adding the comprehensive income project to the Board's technical agenda was the Board's financial instruments project, which is expected to result in additional comprehensive income items.

Financial Instruments Project

46. Many financial instruments are "off-balance-sheet." In the derivatives and hedging portion of the financial instruments project, the Board has proposed that all derivative instruments should be recognized and measured at fair value. Moreover, Board members believe that most, if not all, financial instruments ultimately should be recognized and measured at fair value because fair values generally are more decision useful (that is, more relevant), more understandable, and more practical to use than cost or cost-based measures.

47. The use of fair values to measure financial instruments necessarily raises questions about how the resulting gains and losses should be reported. Certain constituents expressed concern that using fair values will (a) cause more gains and losses to be recognized than currently are recognized and (b) increase the volatility of reported net income.

48. While measuring financial instruments at fair value results in recognizing gains and losses on those

---

[8]In redeliberations of the IASC Exposure Draft, the proposed requirement for a separate statement of nonowner movements in equity has been modified. As of April 1997, the IASC tentatively decided to require that an enterprise present, as a separate component of its financial statements, a statement showing (a) the net profit or loss for the period, (b) each item of income and expenses and gains and losses which, as required by other standards, are recognized directly in equity, and the total of those items, (c) the total of both item (a) and item (b) above, and (d) the cumulative effect of changes in accounting policy and the correction of fundamental errors.

instruments, it does not necessarily follow that those gains and losses must be reported in the income statement as part of net income. The Board believes that it is appropriate and consistent with the definition of comprehensive income provided in the Concepts Statements to include some gains and losses in net income and to exclude others from net income and report them as part of comprehensive income outside net income. Furthermore, reporting separately gains and losses in a financial statement would make those gains and losses more transparent than if they were only included within the equity section of a statement of financial position.

49. In response to the concerns discussed in paragraphs 40-48, the Board added a project on reporting comprehensive income to its agenda in September 1995. The Board's objective was to issue a Statement that requires that an enterprise report all components of comprehensive income in a financial statement that is displayed with the same prominence as other financial statements that constitute a full set.

50. An FASB Exposure Draft, *Reporting Comprehensive Income,* was issued in June 1996. The Board received 281 comment letters on the Exposure Draft, and 22 individuals and organizations presented their views at a public hearing held in November 1996.[9] In addition, the Board discussed the Exposure Draft in meetings with constituents, the Financial Instruments Task Force, and the Financial Accounting Standards Advisory Council. The comments from those groups, comment letters, and public hearing testimony were considered by the Board during its redeliberations of the issues addressed by the Exposure Draft at public meetings held in 1997. This Statement is a result of those Board meetings and redeliberations.

Benefits and Costs

51. In accomplishing its mission, the Board follows certain precepts, including the precept to promulgate standards only when the expected benefits of the information exceed the perceived costs. The Board endeavors to determine that a standard will fill a significant need and that the costs imposed to meet that standard, as compared to other alternatives, are justified in relation to the overall benefits of the resulting information.

52. Based on the recommendations by users of financial statements, the increasing use of separate accounts in equity for certain comprehensive income items, and issues arising in the financial instruments project, the Board concluded that a standard on reporting comprehensive income was needed. This Statement should help facilitate a better understanding of an enterprise's financial activities by users of financial statements because it will result in enhanced comparability within and between enterprises by providing more consistency as to how the balances of components of other comprehensive income and changes in them are presented in financial statements. Moreover, this Statement provides a method for reporting comprehensive income that should prove helpful in addressing and resolving issues that potentially include items of comprehensive income now and in the future. Because enterprises already accumulate information about components of what this Statement identifies as other comprehensive income and report that information in a statement of financial position or in notes accompanying it, the Board determined that there would be little incremental cost associated with the requirements of this Statement beyond the cost of understanding its requirements and deciding how to apply them.

Conclusions on Basic Issues

Scope

53. The Board decided to limit the project's scope to issues of reporting and display of comprehensive income so that it could complete the project in a timely manner. The Board concluded that timely completion was important because of the project's relationship to the project on accounting for derivatives and hedging activities.

54. Although the scope of the project was limited to issues of reporting and display, the Board recognizes that other more conceptual issues are involved in reporting comprehensive income. Such issues include questions about when components of comprehensive income should be recognized in financial statements and how those components should be measured. In addition, there are conceptual questions about the characteristics of items that generally accepted accounting principles require to be included in net income versus the characteristics of items that this Statement identifies as items that are to be included in comprehensive income outside net income. Furthermore, there are several items that generally accepted

---

[9]The public hearings on the comprehensive income Exposure Draft and the June 1996 FASB Exposure Draft, *Accounting for Derivative and Similar Financial Instruments and for Hedging Activities,* were held jointly.

accounting principles require to be recognized as direct adjustments to paid-in capital or other equity accounts that this Statement does not identify as being part of comprehensive income. (Refer to paragraphs 108-119.) The Board expects to consider those types of issues in one or more broader-scope projects related to reporting comprehensive income.

55. The Board considered whether not-for-profit organizations should be permitted to follow the provisions of this Statement and decided that those organizations should continue to follow the requirements of Statement 117. Because Statement 117 requires that those organizations report the change in net assets for a period in a statement of activities, those organizations already are displaying the equivalent of comprehensive income.

Issues Considered

56. The issues considered in this project were organized under the following general questions: (a) whether comprehensive income should be reported, (b) whether cumulative accounting adjustments should be included in comprehensive income, (c) how components of comprehensive income should be classified for display, (d) whether comprehensive income and its components should be displayed in one or two statements of financial performance, and (e) whether components of other comprehensive income should be displayed before or after their related tax effects.

Reporting of comprehensive income

57. The Board considered the following issues about reporting comprehensive income: (a) whether all items that are or will be recognized under current and future accounting standards as items of comprehensive income should be reported in a statement of financial performance, (b) whether a total amount for comprehensive income should be displayed, (c) how the total amount of comprehensive income should be labeled or described, and (d) whether a per-share amount for comprehensive income should be displayed.

Reporting all items of comprehensive income in a statement of financial performance

58. The Exposure Draft proposed that changes in the accumulated balances of income items currently required to be reported directly in a separate component of equity in a statement of financial position (unrealized gains and losses on available-for-sale-securities, minimum pension liability adjustments, and translation gains and losses) should instead be reported in a statement of financial performance. In deliberations leading to the Exposure Draft, the Board noted that those items would be included in a statement of financial performance under the all-inclusive income concept.

59. Some respondents to the Exposure Draft stated that information about the components of other comprehensive income already was available elsewhere in the financial statements and that it was unnecessary for the Board to require that information to be reported separately and aggregated into a measure of comprehensive income. Other respondents agreed that the components of other comprehensive income should be displayed in a more transparent manner. However, a majority of those respondents indicated that until the Board addresses the conceptual issues discussed in paragraph 54, it was premature for the Board to require that the components be reported in a statement of financial performance.

60. Most respondents to the Exposure Draft asserted that the requirement to report comprehensive income and its components in a statement of financial performance would result in confusion. Much of that confusion would stem from reporting two financial performance measures (net income and comprehensive income) and users' inability to determine which measure was the appropriate one for investment decisions, credit decisions, or capital resource allocation. Many of those respondents argued that the items identified as other comprehensive income were not performance related and that it would be not only confusing but also misleading to require that those items be included in a performance statement. Finally, some respondents indicated that comprehensive income would be volatile from period to period and that that volatility would be related to market forces beyond the control of management. In their view, therefore, it would be inappropriate to highlight that volatility in a statement of financial performance. Other respondents said that comprehensive income was more a measure of entity performance than it was of management performance and that it was therefore incorrect to argue that it should not be characterized as a performance measure because of management's inability to control the market forces that could result in that measure being volatile from period to period.

61. Many respondents suggested that the Board could achieve the desired transparency for the components of other comprehensive income by requiring that they be displayed in an expanded statement of changes in equity or in a note to the financial statements. Respondents said that either of those types of display would be more acceptable than display in a performance statement because the components of other comprehensive income would not be characterized as being performance related.

62. In response to constituents' concerns about the requirement in the Exposure Draft to report comprehensive income and its components in a statement of financial performance, the Board considered three additional approaches in its redeliberations. The first approach would require disclosure of comprehensive income and its components in a note to the financial statements. The second approach would require the display of comprehensive income and its components in a statement of changes in equity. The third approach would require the reporting of comprehensive income and its components in a financial statement that is displayed with the same prominence as other financial statements, thereby permitting an enterprise to report the components of comprehensive income in one or two statements of financial performance as proposed by the Exposure Draft or in a statement of changes in equity if that statement was presented as a financial statement.

63. The Board decided against permitting an enterprise to disclose comprehensive income and its components in a note to the financial statements. The Board acknowledged that it could justify note disclosure because it would provide important information in the interim while the conceptual issues surrounding comprehensive income reporting were studied in more depth. However, the Board decided that such disclosure would be inconsistent with the Concepts Statements, which both define comprehensive income and call for the reporting of it as part of a full set of financial statements. The Board also agreed that only disclosure of comprehensive income and its components was inconsistent with one of the objectives of the project, which was to take a first step toward the implementation of the concept of comprehensive income by requiring that its components be displayed in a financial statement.

64. The Board also decided against requiring that an enterprise display comprehensive income and its components in a statement of changes in equity. APB Opinion No. 12, *Omnibus Opinion—1967,* requires that an enterprise report changes in stockholders' equity accounts other than retained earnings whenever both financial position and results of operations are presented. However, paragraph 10 of Opinion 12 states that "disclosure of such changes may take the form of separate statements or may be made in the basic financial statements or notes thereto." The Board agreed that it was important for information about other comprehensive income and total comprehensive income to be displayed in a financial statement presented as prominently as other financial statements that constitute a full set of financial statements. Because Opinion 12 permits an enterprise to report changes in equity in a note to the financial statements, the Board agreed that if it required an enterprise to display comprehensive income and its components in a statement of changes in equity that it would first have to implement a requirement for all enterprises to provide such a statement. The Board also acknowledged that the Securities and Exchange Commission requires that public enterprises provide information about changes in equity but, similar to Opinion 12, those requirements permit an enterprise to display that information in a note to the financial statements.[10] The Board noted that some enterprises might not have items of other comprehensive income and decided that it would be burdensome to require that those enterprises provide a statement of changes in equity when the impetus for that requirement did not apply to them. The Board also noted that some enterprises might have only one item of other comprehensive income and that those enterprises might prefer to report that item below net income in a single statement instead of creating a separate statement of changes in equity to report that amount.

65. The Board decided that it could achieve the desired transparency for the components of other comprehensive income and at the same time be responsive to the concerns of its constituents by permitting a choice of displaying comprehensive income and its components (a) in one or two statements of financial performance (as proposed by the Exposure Draft) or (b) in a statement of changes in equity. The Board

---

[10]SEC Regulation S-X, Section 210.3-04, "Changes in Other Stockholders' Equity," states that "an analysis of the changes in each caption of other stockholders' equity presented in the balance sheets shall be given in a note or separate statement. This analysis shall be presented in the form of a reconciliation of the beginning balance to the ending balance for each period for which an income statement is required to be filed with all significant reconciling items described by appropriate captions."

decided that if an enterprise opted to display comprehensive income in a statement of changes in equity, that statement must be presented as part of a full set of financial statements and not in the notes to the financial statements.

66. The Board also decided that until it addresses the conceptual issues surrounding the reporting of comprehensive income, it should not require presentation of comprehensive income as a measure of financial performance. Consequently, the Board agreed to eliminate references to comprehensive income as a performance measure in the standards section of the final Statement. Therefore, this Statement requires that all items that are recognized under accounting standards as components of comprehensive income be reported in a financial statement that is displayed with the same prominence as other financial statements that constitute a full set of financial statements that report financial position, results of operations, and cash flows.

67. The Board decided to encourage an enterprise to report comprehensive income and the components of other comprehensive income in an income statement below the total for net income or in a separate statement of comprehensive income that begins with net income as originally proposed by the Exposure Draft. The Board believes that displaying comprehensive income in an income-statement-type format is more consistent with the Concepts Statements and therefore is conceptually superior to displaying it in a statement of changes in equity. That type of display also is consistent with the all-inclusive income concept. Furthermore, display of comprehensive income in an income-statement-type format provides the most transparency for its components. Also, it may be more practical for an enterprise that has several items of other comprehensive income to display them outside a statement of changes in equity. Finally, display in an income-statement-type format is consistent with the Board's desire to implement a broader-scope project on comprehensive income that ultimately could move toward reporting comprehensive income and its components in a statement of financial performance.

Displaying a total for comprehensive income

68. The Board decided to retain the requirement in the Exposure Draft to display a total amount for comprehensive income in the financial statement in which its components are displayed regardless of whether an enterprise chooses to display those components in an income-statement-type format or in a statement of changes in equity. The Board agreed that that total will demonstrate articulation between an enterprise's financial position at the end of the period and all aspects of its financial activities for the period, thereby enhancing the understandability of the statements. Also, that total will provide enhanced comparability between enterprises by providing a benchmark for users.

Describing the total for comprehensive income

69. The term *comprehensive income* is used consistently in this Statement to describe the total of all components of comprehensive income, including net income. However, the Board decided not to require that an enterprise use that term in financial statements because it traditionally has not specified how particular amounts should be labeled and often has simply required that a "descriptive label" be used. In practice, a variety of terms, such as net income, net earnings, or earnings, are used to describe the total appearing at the bottom of a statement that reports the results of operations.

70. Many respondents to the Exposure Draft indicated that the term comprehensive income should not be used. They said that the term is misleading because the amount is neither "comprehensive" nor "income." Although the Exposure Draft did not require use of the term comprehensive income, its consistent usage throughout the document (and in its title) gave respondents the impression that it was required.

71. The Board discussed whether using the term comprehensive income would be misleading. The Board agreed that comprehensive income is "income" because changes in equity (changes in assets and liabilities) are identified by the Concepts Statements as revenues, expenses, gains, and losses. The Board acknowledged that comprehensive income will never be completely "comprehensive" because there always will be some assets and liabilities that cannot be measured with sufficient reliability. Therefore, those assets and liabilities as well as the changes in them will not be recognized in the financial statements. For example, the internally generated intangible asset often referred to as intellectual capital is not presently measured and recognized in financial statements. The Board agreed that comprehensive income is "comprehensive" to the extent that it includes all recognized changes in equity during a period from transactions and other events and

circumstances from nonowner sources. The Board acknowledged that there are certain changes in equity that have characteristics of comprehensive income but that are not presently included in it. (Refer to paragraphs 108-119.) Those items may be addressed in a broader-scope project on comprehensive income.

72. In considering other terminology that could be used to describe the aggregate total referred to by this Statement as comprehensive income, the Board acknowledged that in paragraph 13 of Concepts Statement 5, the terms *comprehensive income* and *total nonowner changes in equity* are used as synonyms: "A full set of financial statements for a period should show . . . comprehensive income (total nonowner changes in equity) for the period" (footnote reference omitted). In paragraph 40 of that Concepts Statement the Board noted that:

> Just as a variety of terms are used for net income in present practice, the Board anticipates that total nonowner changes in equity, comprehensive loss, and other equivalent terms will be used in future financial statements as names for comprehensive income.

Nonetheless, the term comprehensive income is used consistently throughout the remainder of Concepts Statement 5 and throughout Concepts Statement 6.

73. In its redeliberations, the Board discussed whether it should continue using the term comprehensive income in this Statement. The Board believes that as a result of the Exposure Drafts on comprehensive income and derivatives and hedging, the term comprehensive income has become more familiar and better understood. Although some constituents argued that the items described as other comprehensive income are not "true" gains and losses, they are defined as gains and losses by the Concepts Statements. Therefore, the Board decided that it is appropriate to continue using the term comprehensive income rather than total nonowner changes in equity in this Statement.

74. The Board also reasoned that once it addresses the conceptual issues in a broader-scope project on comprehensive income, it can consider requiring comprehensive income to be reported in a statement of financial performance. If comprehensive income was ultimately to be reported in a statement of financial performance, the term comprehensive income is more descriptive of a performance measure than are other terms such as total nonowner changes in equity. Therefore, the Board decided that it would be instructional to continue using the term comprehensive income throughout this Statement. However, it decided to clarify that the term comprehensive income is not required and that other terms may be used to describe that amount. The Board decided to make that clarification by including a footnote reference to paragraph 40 of Concepts Statement 5 in this Statement.

Displaying per-share amounts for comprehensive income

75. The Exposure Draft proposed that a public enterprise should display a per-share amount for comprehensive income. The Board thought that it was important that comprehensive income receive appropriate attention and was concerned that it could be perceived as being inferior to measures such as net income if a per-share amount were not required. Moreover, the Board decided that a requirement to display a per-share amount would impose little or no incremental cost on an enterprise.

76. Most respondents were opposed to the requirement for a per-share amount for comprehensive income. They argued that a per-share amount would give comprehensive income more prominence than net income and would result in confusion, especially if analysts quote earnings per share for some enterprises and comprehensive income per share for others. Many respondents suggested that until the Board addresses the conceptual issues involved in reporting comprehensive income (such as when components of comprehensive income should be recognized in financial statements, how those components should be measured, and the criteria for inclusion of those items in net income or in other comprehensive income), it was premature to require a per-share amount for it.

77. The Board decided to eliminate the requirement for a per-share amount for comprehensive income in this Statement. The Board agreed with those respondents that said the conceptual issues involved in reporting comprehensive income should be addressed before requiring a per-share amount. Furthermore, the Board thought that a requirement for a per-share amount was inconsistent with its decisions to (a) permit an enterprise to display comprehensive income and its components in a statement of changes in equity and (b) not require an enterprise to report comprehensive income as a performance measure.

Including cumulative accounting adjustments in comprehensive income

78. In addressing what items should be included in comprehensive income, the Board considered whether the effects of certain accounting adjustments related to earlier periods, such as the principal example in current practice—cumulative effects of changes in accounting principles—should be reported as part of comprehensive income. Revenues, expenses, gains, and losses of the current period—including those that bypass the income statement and go directly to equity—are all clearly part of comprehensive income and were not at issue.

79. The Board considered the definition of comprehensive income in Concepts Statement 5, which states that "comprehensive income is a broad measure of the effects of transactions and other events on an entity, comprising *all recognized changes in equity* (net assets) of the entity during a period . . . except those resulting from investments by owners and distributions to owners" (paragraph 39; footnote reference omitted; emphasis added). Concepts Statement 5 further indicates that comprehensive income includes cumulative accounting adjustments. The Board continues to support that definition and, therefore, decided to include cumulative accounting adjustments as part of comprehensive income.

80. The Board considered two alternatives for displaying cumulative accounting adjustments in financial statements: (a) include cumulative accounting adjustments in comprehensive income by displaying them as part of other comprehensive income and (b) include cumulative accounting adjustments in comprehensive income by continuing to display them as part of net income.

81. The first alternative, display cumulative accounting adjustments as part of other comprehensive income, would have allowed the Board to begin to implement the concept of earnings as described in Concepts Statement 5, because cumulative accounting adjustments would no longer be included in net income. Concepts Statement 5 describes *earnings* as "a measure of performance for a period and to the extent feasible excludes items that are extraneous to that period—items that belong primarily to other periods" (paragraph 34, footnote reference omitted). Earnings, so defined, excludes cumulative effects of changes in accounting principle. Nonetheless, earnings have been included in net income since

Opinion 20. As a result, earnings is similar to, but not necessarily the same as, net income in current practice.

82. The Board committed at the outset to limit the project's scope to display of comprehensive income. The Board's decision to continue to display cumulative accounting adjustments as part of net income resulted more from adherence to that scope commitment than to the merits of the arguments for either alternative.

Display of components of comprehensive income

83. The Board considered two issues related to the display of components of comprehensive income: (a) whether comprehensive income should be divided into two broad display classifications, net income and other comprehensive income, and (b) how other comprehensive income should be classified for display in a financial statement.

Dividing comprehensive income into net income and other comprehensive income

84. The Board decided that comprehensive income should be divided into two broad display classifications, net income and other comprehensive income. The Board reasoned that the division would generally preserve a familiar touchstone for users of financial statements.

85. For similar reasons, the Board also decided not to change the remaining display classifications of net income (that is, continuing operations, discontinued operations, extraordinary items, and cumulative-effect adjustments).

Display classifications for other comprehensive income

86. The Board looked to both the Concepts Statements and current practice in considering how the components of other comprehensive income might be classified for purposes of display. The Concepts Statements provide general guidance about classification, with homogeneity of items being identified as a key factor and the need to combine items that have essentially similar characteristics (and the need to segregate those that do not have similar characteristics) being emphasized.

87. In identifying current practice, the Board considered the results of an FASB staff study of a sample of

financial statements that revealed that most enterprises classify balances of items of other comprehensive income in the equity sections of their statements of financial position according to the accounting standards to which those items relate. Because those accounting standards result in items of comprehensive income that are quite different from one another (for example, the items arising under Statement 52 on foreign currency are quite different from those arising under Statement 87 on pensions), the staff's findings were that existing practice is consistent with the guidance in the Concepts Statements.

88. Based on those considerations, the Board decided that the classification of items of other comprehensive income should be based on the nature of the items. The Board also concluded that the current practice of classifying items according to existing standards generally is appropriate at the present time. However, future standards may result either in additional classifications of other comprehensive income or in additional items within current classifications of other comprehensive income.

89. The Board also considered the need to display reclassification adjustments. Those adjustments are necessary to avoid double counting certain items in comprehensive income. For example, gains realized during the current period and included in net income for that period may have been included in other comprehensive income as unrealized holding gains in the period in which they arose. If they were, they would have been included in comprehensive income in the period in which they were displayed in other comprehensive income and must be offset in the period in which they are displayed in net income.

90. The current-period change in the balance of particular items of other comprehensive income could be displayed gross or net. If reported gross, reclassification adjustments are reported separately from other changes in the balance; thus, the total change is displayed as two amounts. If reported net, reclassification adjustments are combined with other changes in the balance; thus, the total change is displayed as a single amount. Both approaches are illustrated in Appendix B, Format A.

91. The Board decided that an enterprise should use a gross display for classifications of other comprehensive income where it is practicable to ascertain the amount of reclassification adjustments for particular items within that classification. The Board concluded that it should be practicable for an enterprise to calculate reclassification adjustments for securities and other financial instruments and for foreign currency translation items but that it is not practicable for an enterprise to calculate reclassification adjustments for minimum pension liability adjustments. Therefore, an enterprise is required to use a gross display for classifications of other comprehensive income resulting from gains and losses on securities and other financial instruments and for foreign currency items and to use a net display for the classification of other comprehensive income resulting from minimum pension liability adjustments.

92. The Board decided that under a gross display, an enterprise could display reclassification adjustments either as a single section within other comprehensive income or as part of the classification of other comprehensive income to which those adjustments relate (such as foreign currency items or gains and losses on available-for-sale securities). However, if all reclassification adjustments are displayed in a single section within other comprehensive income, they should be descriptively labeled so that they can be traced to their respective classification within other comprehensive income. For example, the reclassification adjustments should be labeled as relating to available-for-sale securities or foreign currency items.

93. The notice for recipients of the Exposure Draft asked if it would be practicable to determine reclassification amounts for (a) gains and losses on available-for-sale securities, (b) foreign currency items, and (c) minimum pension liability adjustments. A majority of the respondents that commented on reclassification adjustments generally agreed that it would be practicable to determine reclassification adjustments for available-for-sale securities and foreign currency items but that it would not be practicable to determine a reclassification adjustment for minimum pension liability adjustments.

94. In response to other comments from constituents about reclassification adjustments, the Board decided to (a) include an example illustrating the calculation of reclassification adjustments for available-for-sale securities, (b) clarify that the requirement for a reclassification amount for foreign currency translation adjustments is limited to translation gains and losses realized upon sale or complete or substantially complete liquidation of an investment in a foreign entity, (c) encourage, but not require, reclassification adjustments for earlier period financial statements presented for comparison to the first period in which

this Statement is adopted, and (d) permit an enterprise to display reclassification adjustments on the face of the financial statement where comprehensive income is reported or in a note to the financial statements. Therefore, for all classifications of other comprehensive income other than minimum pension liability adjustments, an enterprise may either (1) use a gross display on the face of the financial statement or (2) use a net display on the face of the financial statement and disclose the gross changes in the notes to the financial statements.

95. The Board also decided that an enterprise should display the accumulated balance of other comprehensive income in the equity section of the statement of financial position separately from retained earnings and additional paid-in capital and use a descriptive title such as *accumulated other comprehensive income* for that separate component of equity. So that users of financial statements are able to trace the component of other comprehensive income displayed in a financial statement to its corresponding balance, the Board decided that an enterprise should disclose accumulated balances for each classification in that separate component of equity on the face of a statement of financial position, in a statement of changes in equity, or in notes to the financial statements. Each display classification should correspond to display classifications used elsewhere in the same set of financial statements for components of other comprehensive income.

Display of comprehensive income in one or two statements of financial performance

96. The Exposure Draft proposed that an enterprise should be required to display the components of comprehensive income in either one or two statements of financial performance. In addressing whether comprehensive income should be displayed in one or two statements of financial performance, the Board noted that accounting standards in the United Kingdom require that the equivalent to comprehensive income be displayed in two statements. The Board concluded that a two-statement approach might be preferred by many constituents. However, some enterprises with few items of other comprehensive income might prefer to display comprehensive income by means of a single statement and they should not be prohibited from doing so.

97. Respondents to the Exposure Draft provided mixed views about whether the Board should permit

a choice of displaying comprehensive income in one statement or two statements of financial performance. Of the respondents that agreed with the Board's decision to permit a choice of one or two statements, some stated that the preparer should be allowed to decide which format best depicts the enterprise's other comprehensive income items. Most of the respondents that disagreed with the Board's decision to permit a choice of one or two statements indicated that the Board should mandate the two-statement approach because that type of display could alleviate confusion by clearly distinguishing between net income and comprehensive income. Based on comments from constituents, the Board found no compelling reason to eliminate either the one-statement approach or the two-statement approach for those enterprises that choose to display comprehensive income in an income-statement-type format.

98. The Board also decided that an enterprise should use a "reconciled" format for reporting comprehensive income whereby the components of other comprehensive income are the reconciling amounts between net income and comprehensive income. That format makes the relationship between net income and comprehensive income more apparent and might better facilitate the transition to reporting comprehensive income.

99. Under a reconciled format, an enterprise that chooses to display comprehensive income in an income-statement-type format by using two statements should begin the second statement with net income, the bottom line of the first statement. An enterprise that chooses to display comprehensive income in an income-statement-type format by using one statement should include net income as a subtotal within that statement. An enterprise that chooses to display comprehensive income in a statement of changes in equity should display net income in that statement in such a way that it can be added to the components of other comprehensive income to arrive at total comprehensive income. Appendix B includes illustrations of a one-statement and two-statement approach as well as two illustrations of a statement-of-changes-in-equity approach.

Display of related tax effects

100. The Board had two competing objectives in considering whether the components of other comprehensive income should be displayed before or after their related tax effects. The first objective was to

facilitate the traceability of reclassification adjustments from other comprehensive income to net income. Because the corresponding net income components generally are displayed before tax, to achieve that objective, reclassification adjustments must be displayed before tax and, consequently, other comprehensive income items also must be displayed before tax in a financial statement.

101. The second objective was to show clearly how other comprehensive income items change the accumulated balance in equity. Because accumulated other comprehensive income is displayed in the equity section of a statement of financial position net of tax, to achieve that objective, it is necessary to display the changes that are incorporated into that balance net of tax.

102. Some Board members were more concerned about the traceability of reclassification adjustments from other comprehensive income to net income than they were about the transfer of other comprehensive income items to their accumulated balance in equity. Therefore, they favored a display whereby an enterprise would show all components of other comprehensive income on a before-tax basis and display the tax effects of those items on one line, similar to the way in which the tax effects for income from continuing operations are displayed.

103. Other Board members thought that a net-of-tax display would be acceptable as long as adequate disclosure of the related tax effects was provided so that before-tax amounts could be ascertained. Furthermore, because of its decision to permit an enterprise to display comprehensive income and its components in a statement of changes in equity, the Board thought that a net-of-tax display of the components of other comprehensive income would be more practical in that statement because other items in that statement are displayed net of related tax effects.

104. The Board concluded that regardless of whether a before-tax or net-of-tax display was used, adequate disclosure of the amount of income tax expense or benefit allocated separately to individual components of other comprehensive income should be provided. Furthermore, the Board concluded that the tax disclosure provisions should be an integral part of the comprehensive income standard.

105. The Board decided that an enterprise should be permitted a choice of whether to display components

of other comprehensive income on a before-tax basis or on a net-of-tax basis. Both display formats provide adequate information as long as disclosures of the related tax effects are provided.

Conclusions on Other Issues

Including Prior-Period Adjustments in Comprehensive Income

106. The Board considered whether items accounted for as prior-period adjustments should be included in comprehensive income of the current period. Opinion 9, as amended by FASB Statement No. 16, *Prior Period Adjustments,* requires that prior-period adjustments be reflected as retroactive restatements of the amounts of net income (and the components thereof) and retained earnings balances (as well as other affected balances) for all financial statements presented for comparative purposes. In single-period financial statements, prior-period adjustments are reflected as adjustments of the opening balance of retained earnings. The Board decided that because of the requirement for retroactive restatement of earlier period financial statements, items accounted for as prior-period adjustments are effectively included in comprehensive income of earlier periods and, therefore, should not be displayed in comprehensive income of the current period.

Statement of Cash Flows Reporting

107. The Board considered whether the operating section of an indirect-method statement of cash flows or the reconciliation provided with the operating section of a direct-method statement of cash flows should begin with comprehensive income instead of net income as is required by FASB Statement No. 95, *Statement of Cash Flows.* When items of other comprehensive income are noncash items, they would become additional reconciling items in arriving at cash flows from operating activities and would add additional items to the statement of cash flows without adding information content. Thus, the Board decided not to amend Statement 95.

Other Items Reported in Equity

108. Certain items are presently recorded in equity that some respondents to the Exposure Draft thought should be considered as items of other comprehensive income. Those items are discussed below.

Deferred compensation expense and unearned ESOP shares

109. The Board considered whether unearned or deferred compensation expense, which is shown as a separate reduction of shareholders' equity pursuant to APB Opinion No. 25, *Accounting for Stock Issued to Employees,* should be included as an item of other comprehensive income. Paragraph 14 of Opinion 25 requires recognition of unearned compensation as a separate reduction of shareholders' equity if stock is issued in a plan before some or all of the services are performed by the employee. According to Opinion 25, in the subsequent periods in which the employee performs services to the employer, the employer is required to reduce the unearned compensation amount in shareholders' equity and recognize compensation expense for a corresponding amount. Therefore, those transactions have both equity and expense characteristics.

110. The Board also considered whether a reduction of shareholders' equity related to employee stock ownership plans (ESOPs) should be included as an item of other comprehensive income. AICPA Statements of Position 76-3, *Accounting Practices for Certain Employee Stock Ownership Plans,* and 93-6, *Employers' Accounting for Employee Stock Ownership Plans,* provide guidance on accounting for three types of ESOPs: leveraged, nonleveraged, and pension reversion.[11] The accounting for a leveraged ESOP results in a direct reduction to shareholders' equity in the form of a debit to unearned ESOP shares both when an employer issues shares or sells treasury shares to an ESOP and when a leveraged ESOP buys outstanding shares of the employer's stock on the open market. As ESOP shares are committed to be released (SOP 93-6) or are released (SOP 76-3), unearned ESOP shares are credited and, depending on the purpose for which the shares are released, (a) compensation cost, (b) dividends payable, or (c) compensation liabilities are debited. Transactions in which unearned ESOP shares are credited and compensation cost is debited have both equity and expense characteristics.

111. The Board agreed that it could be argued that the direct reductions to shareholders' equity under Opinion 25 and SOP 93-6 that will eventually be

recognized as compensation expense are items of other comprehensive income. However, because those transactions involve the company's own stock, an argument also could be made that those are transactions with owners and hence are not other comprehensive income. In other words, those types of transactions have both equity (transaction with owners) characteristics and expense (comprehensive income) characteristics.

112. The Board concluded that it was beyond the scope of the project to determine whether deferred compensation expense and reductions to equity related to ESOPs were items of other comprehensive income. Therefore, until it makes a definitive decision about those items in a broader-scope project on comprehensive income, those transactions are to be considered as equity transactions and are not to be included as other comprehensive income.

Taxes not payable in cash

113. A reorganized enterprise may suffer net operating losses prior to reorganization that provide it with significant tax advantages going forward. SOP 90-7, *Financial Reporting by Entities in Reorganization Under the Bankruptcy Code,* requires that a reorganized enterprise record a "full tax rate" on its pretax income although its actual cash taxes paid are minimal because of those net operating loss carryforwards. "Taxes not payable in cash" are reported in the income statement as an expense with a corresponding increase to paid-in capital in shareholders' equity.[12]

114. One respondent to the Exposure Draft contended that the amount credited to paid-in capital for taxes not payable in cash represented a "significant economic or cash flow benefit" and "is a change in equity from nonowner sources." Therefore, that respondent suggested that that amount should be included as an item of other comprehensive income.

115. The Board agreed that the credit to paid-in capital resulting from taxes not payable in cash is not a transaction with an owner. However, the Board decided that that credit derives from the accounting required upon reorganization that results in adjustments to equity accounts based on reorganization

[11]SOP 93-6 superseded SOP 76-3 and is required for ESOP shares acquired after December 31, 1992. Employers are permitted, but not required, to apply the provisions of SOP 93-6 to shares purchased by ESOPs on or before December 31, 1992, that have not been committed to be released as of the beginning of the year of adoption.

[12]Under SOP 90-7, "benefits realized from preconfirmation net operating loss carryforwards should first reduce reorganization values in excess of amounts allocable to identifiable assets and other intangibles until exhausted and thereafter be reported as a direct addition to paid-in capital."

value. Therefore, although taxes not payable in cash is not a transaction with an owner, it does not qualify as comprehensive income because the credit to paid-in capital stems from transactions and accounting that took place upon reorganization. In effect, the credit to paid-in capital for taxes not payable in cash adjusts transactions that were recorded in equity in an earlier period and does not result from the current-period debit to income tax expense. Therefore, the Board decided that taxes not payable in cash should not be included as an item of other comprehensive income. In a broader-scope project, the Board may consider whether the initial accounting upon reorganization that results in adjustments to equity accounts based on reorganization value should result in the recognition of comprehensive income. If so, that would ultimately affect the reporting of taxes not payable in cash as part of comprehensive income.

Gains and losses resulting from contracts that are indexed to a company's shares and ultimately settled in cash

116. One respondent to the Exposure Draft indicated that the Board should consider whether a gain or loss arising from a contract that is indexed to a company's shares and ultimately settled in cash should be considered as an item of other comprehensive income. EITF Issue No. 94-7, "Accounting for Financial Instruments Indexed to, and Potentially Settled in, a Company's Own Stock,"[13] addresses four types of freestanding contracts that a company may enter into that are indexed to, and sometimes settled in, its own shares: (a) a forward sale contract, (b) a forward purchase contract, (c) a purchased put option, and (d) a purchased call option. Those contracts may be settled by physical settlement, net share settlement, or net cash settlement.

117. Issue 94-7 indicates that contracts that give the company a choice of net cash settlement or settlement in its own shares are equity instruments and should be measured initially at fair value. If such contracts are ultimately settled in cash, the amount of cash paid or received should be an adjustment to contributed capital. The Board considered whether the amount of cash paid or received (which represents a loss or gain on the contract) should be included as an item of other comprehensive income.

118. In Issue 94-7, the Emerging Issues Task Force reached a consensus that contracts that give the company a choice of net cash settlement or settlement in its own shares are equity instruments. Comprehensive income excludes all changes in equity resulting from investments by owners. Therefore, the Board decided that until it addresses that issue in a broader-scope project, a net cash settlement resulting from a change in value of such a contract should be treated as a change in value of an equity instrument and should not be considered as an item of comprehensive income.

Other paid-in capital transactions not addressed

119. The Board recognizes that there may be other transactions that are reported as direct adjustments to paid-in capital or other equity accounts that have characteristics similar to items that the Board has identified as other comprehensive income. Instead of addressing those transactions on a piecemeal basis, the Board decided that transactions required by generally accepted accounting principles to be recognized in paid-in capital or other similar nonincome equity accounts are not to be displayed as other comprehensive income. However, the Board may collectively address those types of transactions in a broader-scope project on comprehensive income.

Display of Other Comprehensive Income under the Equity Method of Accounting

120. Under APB Opinion No. 18, *The Equity Method of Accounting for Investments in Common Stock,* an investor records its proportionate share of the investee's net income (net loss) as investment income along with a corresponding increase (decrease) to the investment account. Several respondents to the Exposure Draft asked the Board to address the question of how an investor should record its proportionate share of the investee's other comprehensive income.

121. Paragraph 19(e) of Opinion 18 states that a transaction of an investee of a capital nature that affects the investor's share of stockholders' equity of the investee should be accounted for as if the investee were a consolidated subsidiary. Therefore, an investor records its proportionate share of the investee's equity adjustments for other comprehensive income

---

[13]Issue 94-7 was combined with and codified in EITF Issue No. 96-13, "Accounting for Sales of Options or Warrants on Issuer's Stock with Various Forms of Settlement."

(unrealized gains and losses on available-for-sale securities, minimum pension liability adjustments, and foreign currency items) as increases or decreases to the investment account with corresponding adjustments in equity. Under this Statement, an enterprise may elect to display other comprehensive income in an income-statement-type format (below net income or in a separate statement beginning with net income) or in a statement-of-changes-in-equity format.

122. The Board decided that the format in which an investee displays other comprehensive income should not impact how an investor displays its proportionate share of those amounts. Therefore, regardless of how an investee chooses to display other comprehensive income, an investor should be permitted to combine its proportionate share of those amounts with its own other comprehensive income items and display the aggregate of those amounts in an income-statement-type format or in a statement of changes in equity.

Other Comprehensive Income of Subsidiaries

123. The October 1995 FASB Exposure Draft of a proposed Statement, *Consolidated Financial Statements: Policy and Procedures,* would require that a portion of the net income or loss of a subsidiary that is not wholly owned be attributed to the noncontrolling interest (minority interest) on the basis of its proportionate interest in the subsidiary's net income or loss. The net income attributable to the noncontrolling interest would be deducted from consolidated net income to arrive at an amount called *net income attributable to the controlling interest.* If that Statement is finalized as proposed, the Board will have to determine whether other comprehensive income will be attributed to the noncontrolling and controlling interests on the same basis as items of net income and how the amounts attributed to those interests will be displayed.

Interim-Period Reporting

124. The Exposure Draft proposed that a publicly traded enterprise should be required to report an amount for total comprehensive income in condensed financial statements of interim periods issued to shareholders. In its redeliberations, the Board acknowledged that requiring information about total comprehensive income without requiring information about its components might result in a limited understanding of an enterprise's activities and considered whether it also should require a publicly

traded enterprise to report the components of other comprehensive income at interim periods.

125. The Board was concerned that adding a requirement for interim-period financial information about the components of other comprehensive income might create a disincentive for voluntary reporting of interim financial information, particularly for those enterprises that disagree with the annual reporting of comprehensive income. The Board decided that if there is a significant difference between total comprehensive income and net income in interim periods, an enterprise would be inclined to explain that difference by disclosing the components. Furthermore, the Board decided that it should not alter the Exposure Draft's interim-period reporting requirements by mandating additional information. Therefore, the Board decided to retain the requirement for a publicly traded enterprise to report total comprehensive income in condensed financial statements of interim periods issued to shareholders.

Effective Date and Transition

126. The Board proposed in the Exposure Draft that this Statement should be effective for fiscal years beginning after December 15, 1996, for all enterprises. That effective date was established under the presumption that a Statement would be issued in the first quarter of 1997. Because the Statement was not issued until late in the second quarter of 1997, the Board decided to postpone the effective date until fiscal years beginning after December 15, 1997. In deciding on that effective date, the Board agreed that the costs and start-up time associated with implementing this Statement should be minimal and that, with the exception of reclassification adjustments, an enterprise will only be displaying information currently available in a different format.

127. The Board also decided to permit an enterprise, for fiscal years beginning prior to December 16, 1997, initially to apply the provisions of this Statement for a fiscal year for which annual financial statements have not previously been issued. If the Statement is adopted prior to the effective date and during an interim period other than the first interim period, all prior interim periods of that fiscal year must be reclassified.

128. The Board decided that an enterprise should be required to apply the provisions of this Statement to comparative financial statements provided for earlier periods to make them comparable to the financial

statements for the current period. An enterprise should not encounter difficulties in reclassifying earlier periods' financial statements because the information required to be displayed by this Statement previously was displayed in the statement of changes in equity, the equity section of the statement of financial position, or in notes to the financial statements. The Board decided not to require, but to encourage, an enterprise to display reclassification adjustments for earlier period financial statements presented for comparison to the first period in which this Statement is adopted.

Appendix B

ILLUSTRATIVE EXAMPLES

129. This appendix provides illustrations of reporting formats for comprehensive income, required disclosures, and a corresponding statement of financial position. The illustrations are intended as examples only; they illustrate some recommended formats. Other formats or levels of detail may be appropriate for certain circumstances. An enterprise is encouraged to provide information in ways that are most understandable to investors, creditors, and other external users of financial statements. For simplicity, the illustrations provide information only for a single

period; however, the Board realizes that most enterprises are required to provide comparative financial statements.

130. Brackets are used to highlight certain basic totals that must be displayed in financial statements to comply with the provisions of this Statement. This Statement requires not only displaying those certain basic totals but also reporting components of those aggregates. For example, it requires reporting information about unrealized gains and losses on available-for-sale securities, foreign currency items, gains or losses associated with pension or other postretirement benefits, prior service costs or credits associated with pension or other postretirement benefits, and transition assets or obligations associated with pension or other postretirement benefits.

131. The illustrations use the term *comprehensive income* to label the total of all components of comprehensive income, including net income. The illustrations use the term *other comprehensive income* to label revenues, expenses, gains, and losses that are included in comprehensive income but excluded from net income. This Statement does not require that an enterprise use those terms in its financial statements. Other equivalent terms, such as *total nonowner changes in equity,* can be used as labels for what this Statement refers to as comprehensive income.

Format A: One-Statement Approach

Enterprise
Statement of Income and Comprehensive Income
Year Ended December 31, 20X9

Revenues		$140,000
Expenses		(25,000)
Other gains and losses		8,000
Gain on sale of securities		2,000
Income from operations before tax		125,000
Income tax expense		(31,250)
Income before extraordinary item		93,750
Extraordinary item, net of tax		(30,500)
[Net income		63,250]
Other comprehensive income, net of tax:		
Foreign currency translation adjustments[a]		8,000
Unrealized gains on securities:[b]		
Unrealized holding gains arising during period	$13,000	
Less: reclassification adjustment for gains included in net income	(1,500)	11,500
Defined benefit pension plans:[c]		
Prior service cost arising during period	(1,600)	
Net loss arising during period	(1,000)	
Less: amortization of prior service cost included in net periodic pension cost	100	(2,500)
Other comprehensive income		17,000
[Comprehensive income		$ 80,250]

Alternatively, components of other comprehensive income could be displayed before tax with one amount shown for the aggregate income tax expense or benefit:

Other comprehensive income, before tax:		
Foreign currency translation adjustments[a]		$10,666
Unrealized gains on securities:[b]		
Unrealized holding gains arising during period	$17,333	
Less: reclassification adjustment for gains included in net income	(2,000)	15,333
Defined benefit pension plans:[c]		
Prior service cost arising during period	(2,133)	
Net loss arising during period	(1,333)	
Less: amortization of prior service cost included in net periodic pension cost	133	(3,333)
Other comprehensive income, before tax		22,666
[Income tax expense related to items of other comprehensive income		(5,666)]
Other comprehensive income, net of tax		$17,000

---

*[This footnote has been deleted. See Status page.]

[a]It is assumed that there was no sale or liquidation of an investment in a foreign entity. Therefore, there is no reclassification adjustment for this period.

[b]This illustrates the gross display. Alternatively, a net display can be used, with disclosure of the gross amounts (current-period gain and reclassification adjustment) in the notes to the financial statements.

[c]This illustrates the gross display. Alternatively, a net display can be used, with disclosure of the gross amounts (prior service cost and net loss for the defined benefit pension plans less amortization of prior service cost) in the notes to financial statements.

Format B: Two-Statement Approach

**Enterprise
Statement of Income
Year Ended December 31, 20X9**

Revenues	$140,000
Expenses	(25,000)
Other gains and losses	8,000
Gain on sale of securities	2,000
Income from operations before tax	125,000
Income tax expense	(31,250)
Income before extraordinary item	93,750
Extraordinary item, net of tax	(30,500)
[Net income	$ 63,250]

**Enterprise
Statement of Comprehensive Income
Year Ended December 31, 20X9**

[Net income		$63,250]
Other comprehensive income, net of tax:		
Foreign currency translation adjustments[a]		8,000
Unrealized gains on securities:[b]		
Unrealized holding gains arising during period	$13,000	
Less: reclassification adjustment for gains included in net income	(1,500)	11,500
Defined benefit pension plans:[c]		
Prior service cost arising during period	(1,600)	
Net loss arising during period	(1,000)	
Less: amortization of prior service cost included in net periodic pension cost	100	(2,500)
Other comprehensive income		17,000
[Comprehensive income		$80,250]

Alternatively, components of other comprehensive income could be displayed before tax with one amount shown for the aggregate income tax expense or benefit as illustrated in Format A.

---

*[This footnote has been deleted. See Status page.]

[a]It is assumed that there was no sale or liquidation of an investment in a foreign entity. Therefore, there is no reclassification adjustment for this period.

[b]This illustrates the gross display. Alternatively, a net display can be used, with disclosure of the gross amounts (current-period gain and reclassification adjustment) in the notes to the financial statements.

[c]This illustrates the gross display. Alternatively, a net display can be used, with disclosure of the gross amounts (prior service cost and net loss for defined benefit pension plans less amortization of prior service cost) in the notes to financial statements.

Format C: Statement-of-Changes-in-Equity Approach (Alternative 1)

Enterprise
Statement of Changes in Equity
Year Ended December 31, 20X9

	Total	Comprehensive Income[a]	Retained Earnings	Accumulated Other Comprehensive Income	Common Stock	Paid-in Capital
Beginning balance	$561,500		$ 88,500	$23,000	$150,000	$300,000
Comprehensive income						
Net income	63,250	$63,250	63,250			
Other comprehensive income, net of tax						
Unrealized gains on securities, net of reclassification adjustment (see disclosure)	11,500	11,500				
Foreign currency translation adjustments	8,000	8,000				
Defined benefit pension plans:						
Net prior service cost (see disclosure)	(1,500)	(1,500)				
Net loss	(1,000)	(1,000)				
Other comprehensive income		17,000		17,000		
Comprehensive income		$80,250				
Common stock issued	150,000				50,000	100,000
Dividends declared on common stock	(10,000)		(10,000)			
Ending balance	$781,750		$141,750	$40,000	$200,000	$400,000

Disclosure of reclassification amount:[b]

Unrealized holding gains arising during period		$13,000
Less: reclassification adjustment for gains included in net income		(1,500)
Net unrealized gains on securities		$11,500
Prior service cost from plan amendment during period		$(1,600)
Less: amortization of prior service cost included in net periodic pension cost		100
Net prior service cost arising during period		(1,500)
Net loss arising during period		(1,000)
Defined benefit pension plans, net		$ (2,500)

---

[a] Alternatively, an enterprise can omit the separate column labeled "Comprehensive Income" by displaying an aggregate amount for comprehensive income ($80,250) in the "Total" column.

[b] It is assumed that there was no sale or liquidation of an investment in a foreign entity. Therefore, there is no reclassification adjustment for this period.

Format D: Statement-of-Changes-in-Equity Approach (Alternative 2)

Enterprise
Statement of Changes in Equity
Year Ended December 31, 20X9

Retained earnings		
Balance at January 1	$ 88,500	
Net income	63,250	[$ 63,250]
Dividends declared on common stock	(10,000)	
Balance at December 31	141,750	
Accumulated other comprehensive income[a]		
Balance at January 1	23,000	
Unrealized gains on securities, net of reclassification adjustment (see disclosure)		11,500
Foreign currency translation adjustments		8,000
Defined benefit pension plans:		
Net prior service cost (see disclosure)		(1,500)
Net loss		(1,000)
Other comprehensive income	17,000	17,000
Comprehensive income		[$ 80,250]
Balance at December 31	40,000	
Common stock		
Balance at January 1	150,000	
Shares issued	50,000	
Balance at December 31	200,000	
Paid-in capital		
Balance at January 1	300,000	
Common stock issued	100,000	
Balance at December 31	400,000	
Total equity	$781,750	

Disclosure of reclassification amount:[b]

Unrealized holding gains arising during period	$ 13,000
Less: reclassification adjustment for gains included in net income	(1,500)
Net unrealized gains on securities	$ 11,500
Prior service cost from plan amendment during period	$ (1,600)
Less: amortization of prior service cost included in net periodic pension cost	100
Net prior service cost arising during period	(1,500)
Net loss arising during period	(1,000)
Defined benefit pension plans, net	$ (2,500)

[a]All items of other comprehensive income are displayed net of tax.

[b]It is assumed that there was no sale or liquidation of an investment in a foreign entity. Therefore, there is no reclassification adjustment for this period.

All Formats: Required Disclosure of Related Tax Effects Allocated to Each Component of Other Comprehensive Income

Enterprise
Notes to Financial Statements
Year Ended December 31, 20X9

	Before-Tax Amount	Tax (Expense) or Benefit	Net-of-Tax Amount
Foreign currency translation adjustments	$10,666	$(2,666)	$ 8,000
Unrealized gains on securities:			
Unrealized holding gains arising during period	17,333	(4,333)	13,000
Less: reclassification adjustment for gains realized in net income	(2,000)	500	(1,500)
Net unrealized gains	15,333	(3,833)	11,500
Defined benefit pension plans:			
Prior service cost from plan amendment during period	(2,133)	533	(1,600)
Less: amortization of prior service cost included in net periodic pension cost	133	(33)	100
Net prior service cost arising during period	(2,000)	500	(1,500)
Net loss arising during period	(1,333)	333	(1,000)
Defined benefit pension plans, net	(3,333)	833	(2,500)
Other comprehensive income	$22,666	$(5,666)	$17,000

Alternatively, the tax amounts for each component can be displayed parenthetically on the face of the financial statement in which comprehensive income is reported.

All Formats: Disclosure of Accumulated Other Comprehensive Income Balances

Enterprise
Notes to Financial Statements
Year Ended December 31, 20X9

	Foreign Currency Items	Unrealized Gains on Securities	Defined Benefit Pension Plans	Accumulated Other Comprehensive Income
Beginning balance	$ (500)	$25,500	$(2,000)	$23,000
Current-period change	8,000	11,500	(2,500)	17,000
Ending balance	$7,500	$37,000	$(4,500)	$40,000

Alternatively, the balances of each classification within accumulated other comprehensive income can be displayed in a statement of changes in equity or in a statement of financial position.

All Formats: Accompanying Statement of Financial Position

Enterprise
Statement of Financial Position
December 31, 20X9

Assets:

Cash	$ 150,000
Accounts receivable	175,000
Available-for-sale securities	112,000
Plant and equipment	985,000
Total assets	$1,422,000

Liabilities:

Accounts payable	$ 112,500
Accrued liabilities	78,583
Liability for pension benefits	130,667
Notes payable	318,500
Total liabilities	$ 640,250

Equity:

Common stock	$ 200,000
Paid-in capital	400,000
Retained earnings	141,750
[Accumulated other comprehensive income	40,000]
Total equity	781,750
Total liabilities and equity	$1,422,000

Appendix C

ILLUSTRATIVE EXAMPLES OF THE DETERMINATION OF RECLASSIFICATION ADJUSTMENTS

132. This Statement requires that an enterprise determine reclassification adjustments for each classification of other comprehensive income. An enterprise may display reclassification adjustments on the face of the financial statement in which comprehensive income is reported, or it may disclose reclassification adjustments in the notes to the financial statements.

133. This appendix provides illustrations of the calculation of reclassification adjustments for Statement 115 available-for-sale securities. Illustration 1 is of available-for-sale equity securities, and Illustration 2 is of available-for-sale debt securities. The illustrations are intended as examples only; they do not represent actual situations.

134. Illustrations 1 and 2 involve a nonpublic enterprise that follows the practice of recognizing all unrealized gains and losses on available-for-sale securities in other comprehensive income before recognizing them as realized gains and losses in net income. Therefore, the before-tax amount of the reclassification adjustment recognized in other comprehensive income is equal to, but opposite in sign from, the amount of the realized gain or loss recognized in net income.

Illustration 1: Statement 115 Available-for-Sale Equity Securities

135. The available-for-sale equity securities in this illustration appreciate in fair value. On December 31, 1997, Enterprise purchased 1,000 shares of equity securities at $10 per share, which it classified

as available for sale. The fair value of the securities at December 31, 1998 and December 31, 1999 was $12 and $15, respectively. There were no dividends declared on the securities that were sold on December 31, 1999. A tax rate of 30 percent is assumed.

Calculation of Holding Gains

	Before Tax	Income Tax	Net of Tax
Holding gains recognized in other comprehensive income:			
Year ended December 31, 1998	$2,000	$ 600	$1,400
Year ended December 31, 1999	3,000	900	2,100
Total gain	$5,000	$1,500	$3,500

Amounts Reported in Net Income and Other Comprehensive Income for the Years Ended December 31, 1998 and December 31, 1999

	1998	1999
Net income:		
Gain on sale of securities		$ 5,000
Income tax expense		(1,500)
Net gain realized in net income		3,500
Other comprehensive income:		
Holding gain arising during period, net of tax	$1,400	2,100
Reclassification adjustment, net of tax	0	(3,500)
Net gain (loss) recognized in other comprehensive income	1,400	(1,400)
Total impact on comprehensive income	$1,400	$ 2,100

Illustration 2: Statement 115 Available-for-Sale Debt Securities

136. The available-for-sale interest-bearing debt securities (bonds) in this illustration were purchased at a premium to yield 6.5 percent. Interest income is included in net income based on the historical yield, and the bonds decline in fair value during the first two years in which they are held.

137. On December 31, 1995, registration of Micki Inc.'s 8-year, 8 percent debentures, interest payable annually, became effective and the entire issue of $10,000,000 was sold at par. At the end of each of the next four years, the closing prices and the related market interest rates to maturity were as follows:

December 31	Price ($000)	Yield (%)
1996	$102.6	7.5
1997	107.3	6.5
1998	96.1	9.0
1999	92.2	10.5

138. On December 31, 1997, Enterprise purchased $1,000,000 of Micki Inc.'s bonds on the open market at 107.3 and classified them as available for sale. Enterprise continued to hold the bonds until December 31, 1999, at which time they were sold at 92.2. Enterprise prepared the following schedules in relation to the bonds:

Cost-Based Carrying Amount, Interest Income, and Premium Amortization

	(a) Beginning Carrying Value	(b) Cash Interest Received [8% × par]	(c) Interest Income [(a) × 6.5%]	(d) Premium Amortization [(b) − (c)]	(e) Ending Carrying Value [(a) − (d)]
Year					
1997					$1,073,000
1998	$1,073,000	$80,000	$69,745	$10,255	1,062,745
1999	1,062,745	80,000	69,078	10,922	1,051,823

Calculation of Before-Tax Holding Loss

Year Ended 12/31	(a) Ending Carrying Value	(b) Ending Fair Value	(c) Change in Fair Value	(d) Premium Amortization	(e) Holding Loss [(c) + (d)]
1997	$1,073,000	$1,073,000	$ 0		
1998	1,062,745	961,000	(112,000)	$10,255	$(101,745)
1999	1,051,823	922,000	(39,000)	10,922	(28,078)

Net-of-Tax Holding Losses
(Assume a Tax Rate of 30 Percent)

	Before Tax	Income Tax	Net of Tax
Holding losses recognized in other comprehensive income:			
Year ended December 31, 1998	$(101,745)	$30,523	$(71,222)
Year ended December 31, 1999	(28,078)	8,423	(19,655)
Total loss	$(129,823)	$38,946	$(90,877)

Amounts Reported in Net Income and Other Comprehensive Income
for the Years Ended December 31, 1998 and December 31, 1999

	1998	1999
Net income:		
Interest income	$ 69,745	$ 69,078
Loss on sale of bonds		(129,823)
Income tax (expense) benefit	(20,923)	18,223
Amounts realized in net income	48,822	(42,522)
Other comprehensive income (OCI):		
Holding loss arising during period, net of tax	(71,222)	(19,655)
Reclassification adjustment, net of tax		90,877
Net (loss) gain recognized in other comprehensive income	(71,222)	71,222
Total impact on comprehensive income	$(22,400)	$ 28,700

139. The following before-tax entries would be made to record the purchase, accrue interest (using the effective interest method based on cost), recognize the change in fair value, and record the sale:

December 31, 1997:

Investment in bonds	$1,073,000	
Cash		$1,073,000

To record purchase of bond

December 31, 1998:

Cash	80,000	
Investment in bonds		10,255
Interest income (to earnings)		69,745

To record interest income on the bond, amortize the premium, and record cash received

Unrealized holding loss (to OCI)	101,745	
Investment in bonds		101,745

To adjust carrying amount of bond to fair value

Accumulated OCI	101,745	
Unrealized holding loss		101,745
Interest income	69,745	
Retained earnings		69,745

To close nominal accounts to real accounts at year-end

December 31, 1999:

Cash	80,000	
Investment in bonds		10,922
Interest income (to earnings)		69,078

To record interest income on the bond, amortize the premium, and record cash received

Unrealized holding loss (to OCI)	28,078	
Investment in bonds		28,078

To adjust carrying amount of bond to fair value

Accumulated OCI	28,078	
Unrealized holding loss		28,078

To close nominal account to real account at year-end

Cash	922,000	
Loss on sale of securities (to earnings)	129,823	
Investment in bonds		922,000
Reclassification adjustment (to OCI)		129,823

To record sale of bond

Reclassification adjustment	129,823	
Accumulated OCI		129,823
Retained earnings	60,745	
Interest income	69,078	
Loss on sale of securities		129,823

To close nominal accounts to real accounts at year-end

Statement of Financial Accounting Standards No. 131
Disclosures about Segments of an Enterprise and Related Information

STATUS

Issued: June 1997

Effective Date: For fiscal years beginning after December 15, 1997

Affects: Amends ARB 43, Chapter 12, paragraph 5
Replaces ARB 43, Chapter 12, paragraph 6
Deletes ARB 51, paragraph 19
Amends APB 28, paragraph 30
Supersedes FAS 14
Supersedes FAS 18
Replaces FAS 19, paragraph 59C(c) and footnote 5a
Amends FAS 19, footnote 5d
Supersedes FAS 21
Supersedes FAS 24
Supersedes FAS 30
Amends FAS 51, footnote 3
Replaces FAS 69, paragraph 8(c) and footnote 4
Amends FAS 69, footnote 7
Amends FTB 79-4, paragraphs 1 and 3
Replaces FTB 79-4, paragraph 2
Amends FTB 79-5, paragraphs 1 and 2
Supersedes FTB 79-8

Affected by: Paragraph 9 amended by FSP FAS 126-1, paragraph A6
Paragraphs 18, 25, 27, 28, and 123 amended by FAS 135, paragraph 4(x)
Paragraphs 31 and 32 amended by FAS 154, paragraph C19(e)
Paragraph 33 amended by FAS 135, paragraph 4(x), and FAS 154, paragraph C19(e)

Other Interpretive Release: FASB *Highlights,* "Segment Information: Guidance on Applying Statement 131," December 1998 (in *Current Text* Section S30)

Issues Discussed by FASB Emerging Issues Task Force (EITF)

Affects: No EITF Issues

Interpreted by: Paragraph 17 interpreted by EITF Issue No. 04-10
Paragraphs 18, 27, and 28 interpreted by EITF Topic No. D-70

Related Issues: No EITF Issues

SUMMARY

This Statement establishes standards for the way that public business enterprises report information about operating segments in annual financial statements and requires that those enterprises report selected information about operating segments in interim financial reports issued to shareholders. It also establishes standards for related disclosures about products and services, geographic areas, and major customers. This Statement supersedes FASB Statement No. 14, *Financial Reporting for Segments of a Business Enterprise,* but retains the requirement to report information about major customers. It amends FASB Statement No. 94, *Consolidation of All Majority-Owned Subsidiaries,* to remove the special disclosure requirements for previously unconsolidated subsidiaries. This Statement does not apply to nonpublic business enterprises or to not-for-profit organizations.

This Statement requires that a public business enterprise report financial and descriptive information about its reportable operating segments. Operating segments are components of an enterprise about which separate financial information is available that is evaluated regularly by the chief operating decision maker in deciding how to allocate resources and in assessing performance. Generally, financial information is required to be reported on the basis that it is used internally for evaluating segment performance and deciding how to allocate resources to segments.

This Statement requires that a public business enterprise report a measure of segment profit or loss, certain specific revenue and expense items, and segment assets. It requires reconciliations of total segment revenues, total segment profit or loss, total segment assets, and other amounts disclosed for segments to corresponding amounts in the enterprise's general-purpose financial statements. It requires that all public business enterprises report information about the revenues derived from the enterprise's products or services (or groups of similar products and services), about the countries in which the enterprise earns revenues and holds assets, and about major customers regardless of whether that information is used in making operating decisions. However, this Statement does not require an enterprise to report information that is not prepared for internal use if reporting it would be impracticable.

This Statement also requires that a public business enterprise report descriptive information about the way that the operating segments were determined, the products and services provided by the operating segments, differences between the measurements used in reporting segment information and those used in the enterprise's general-purpose financial statements, and changes in the measurement of segment amounts from period to period.

This Statement is effective for financial statements for periods beginning after December 15, 1997. In the initial year of application, comparative information for earlier years is to be restated. This Statement need not be applied to interim financial statements in the initial year of its application, but comparative information for interim periods in the initial year of application is to be reported in financial statements for interim periods in the second year of application.

Statement of Financial Accounting Standards No. 131

Disclosures about Segments of an Enterprise and Related Information

CONTENTS

INTRODUCTION

1. This Statement requires that public business enterprises[1] report certain information about operating segments in complete sets of financial statements of the enterprise and in condensed financial statements of interim periods issued to shareholders. It also requires that public business enterprises report certain information about their products and services, the geographic areas in which they operate, and their major customers. The Board and the Accounting Standards Board (AcSB) of the Canadian Institute of Chartered Accountants (CICA) cooperated in developing revised standards for reporting information about segments, and the two boards reached the same conclusions.

2. This Statement supersedes FASB Statements No. 14, *Financial Reporting for Segments of a Business Enterprise,* No. 18, *Financial Reporting for Segments of a Business Enterprise—Interim Financial Statements,* No. 24, *Reporting Segment Information in Financial Statements That Are Presented in Another Enterprise's Financial Report,* and No. 30, *Disclosure of Information about Major Customers.* It amends FASB Statement No. 94, *Consolidation of*

---

[1]For convenience, the term *enterprise* is used throughout this Statement to mean public business enterprise unless otherwise stated.

All Majority-Owned Subsidiaries, to eliminate the requirement to disclose additional information about subsidiaries that were not consolidated prior to the effective date of Statement 94. It also amends APB Opinion No. 28, *Interim Financial Reporting,* to require disclosure of selected information about operating segments in interim financial reports to shareholders. Appendix C includes a list of amendments to existing pronouncements.

Objective and Basic Principles

3. The objective of requiring disclosures about segments of an enterprise and related information is to provide information about the different types of business activities in which an enterprise engages and the different economic environments in which it operates to help users of financial statements:

a. Better understand the enterprise's performance
b. Better assess its prospects for future net cash flows
c. Make more informed judgments about the enterprise as a whole.

That objective is consistent with the objectives of general-purpose financial reporting.

4. An enterprise might meet that objective by providing complete sets of financial statements that are disaggregated in several different ways, for example, by products and services, by geography, by legal entity, or by type of customer. However, it is not feasible to provide all of that information in every set of financial statements. This Statement requires that general-purpose financial statements include selected information reported on a single basis of segmentation. The method the Board chose for determining what information to report is referred to as the management approach. The management approach is based on the way that management organizes the segments within the enterprise for making operating decisions and assessing performance. Consequently, the segments are evident from the structure of the enterprise's internal organization, and financial statement preparers should be able to provide the required information in a cost-effective and timely manner.

5. The management approach facilitates consistent descriptions of an enterprise in its annual report and

various other published information. It focuses on financial information that an enterprise's decision makers use to make decisions about the enterprise's operating matters. The components that management establishes for that purpose are called *operating segments.*

6. This Statement requires that an enterprise report a measure of segment profit or loss and certain items included in determining segment profit or loss, segment assets, and certain related items. It does not require that an enterprise report segment cash flow. However, paragraphs 27 and 28 require that an enterprise report certain items that may provide an indication of the cash-generating ability or cash requirements of an enterprise's operating segments.

7. To provide some comparability between enterprises, this Statement requires that an enterprise report certain information about the revenues that it derives from each of its products and services (or groups of similar products and services) and about the countries in which it earns revenues and holds assets, regardless of how the enterprise is organized. As a consequence, some enterprises are likely to be required to provide limited information that may not be used for making operating decisions and assessing performance.

8. Nothing in this Statement is intended to discourage an enterprise from reporting additional information specific to that enterprise or to a particular line of business that may contribute to an understanding of the enterprise.

STANDARDS OF FINANCIAL ACCOUNTING AND REPORTING

Scope

9. This Statement applies to public business enterprises. Public business enterprises are those business enterprises that have issued debt or equity securities or are conduit bond obligors for conduit debt securities[1a] that are traded in a public market (a domestic or foreign stock exchange or an over-the-counter market, including local or regional markets),

---

[1a]*Conduit debt securities* refers to certain limited-obligation revenue bonds, certificates of participation, or similar debt instruments issued by a state or local governmental entity for the express purpose of providing financing for a specific third party (the conduit bond obligor) that is not a part of the state or local government's financial reporting entity. Although conduit debt securities bear the name of the governmental entity that issues them, the governmental entity often has no obligation for such debt beyond the resources provided by a lease or loan agreement with the third party on whose behalf the securities are issued. Further, the conduit bond obligor is responsible for any future financial reporting requirements.

that are required to file financial statements with the Securities and Exchange Commission, or that provide financial statements for the purpose of issuing any class of securities in a public market. This Statement does not apply to parent enterprises, subsidiaries, joint ventures, or investees accounted for by the equity method if those enterprises' "separate company" statements also are consolidated or combined in a complete set of financial statements and both the separate company statements and the consolidated or combined statements are included in the same financial report. However, this Statement does apply to those enterprises if they are public enterprises and their financial statements are issued separately. This Statement also does not apply to not-for-profit organizations (regardless of whether the entity meets the definition of a public entity as defined above) or to nonpublic enterprises. Entities other than public business enterprises are encouraged to provide the disclosures described in this Statement.

Operating Segments

Definition

10. An *operating segment* is a component of an enterprise:

a. That engages in business activities from which it may earn revenues and incur expenses (including revenues and expenses relating to transactions with other components of the same enterprise),
b. Whose operating results are regularly reviewed by the enterprise's chief operating decision maker to make decisions about resources to be allocated to the segment and assess its performance, and
c. For which discrete financial information is available.

An operating segment may engage in business activities for which it has yet to earn revenues, for example, start-up operations may be operating segments before earning revenues.

11. Not every part of an enterprise is necessarily an operating segment or part of an operating segment. For example, a corporate headquarters or certain functional departments may not earn revenues or may earn revenues that are only incidental to the activities of the enterprise and would not be operating segments. For purposes of this Statement, an enterprise's pension and other postretirement benefit plans are not considered operating segments.

12. The term *chief operating decision maker* identifies a function, not necessarily a manager with a specific title. That function is to allocate resources to and assess the performance of the segments of an enterprise. Often the chief operating decision maker of an enterprise is its chief executive officer or chief operating officer, but it may be a group consisting of, for example, the enterprise's president, executive vice presidents, and others.

13. For many enterprises, the three characteristics of operating segments described in paragraph 10 clearly identify a single set of operating segments. However, an enterprise may produce reports in which its business activities are presented in a variety of different ways. If the chief operating decision maker uses more than one set of segment information, other factors may identify a single set of components as constituting an enterprise's operating segments, including the nature of the business activities of each component, the existence of managers responsible for them, and information presented to the board of directors.

14. Generally, an operating segment has a *segment manager* who is directly accountable to and maintains regular contact with the chief operating decision maker to discuss operating activities, financial results, forecasts, or plans for the segment. The term segment manager identifies a function, not necessarily a manager with a specific title. The chief operating decision maker also may be the segment manager for certain operating segments. A single manager may be the segment manager for more than one operating segment. If the characteristics in paragraph 10 apply to more than one set of components of an organization but there is only one set for which segment managers are held responsible, that set of components constitutes the operating segments.

15. The characteristics in paragraph 10 may apply to two or more overlapping sets of components for which managers are held responsible. That structure is sometimes referred to as a matrix form of organization. For example, in some enterprises, certain managers are responsible for different product and service lines worldwide, while other managers are responsible for specific geographic areas. The chief operating decision maker regularly reviews the operating results of both sets of components, and financial information is available for both. In that situation, the components based on products and services would constitute the operating segments.

Reportable Segments

16. An enterprise shall report separately information about each operating segment that (a) has been identified in accordance with paragraphs 10-15 or that results from aggregating two or more of those segments in accordance with paragraph 17 and (b) exceeds the quantitative thresholds in paragraph 18. Paragraphs 19-24 specify other situations in which separate information about an operating segment shall be reported. Appendix B includes a diagram that illustrates how to apply the main provisions in this Statement for identifying reportable operating segments.

Aggregation criteria

17. Operating segments often exhibit similar long-term financial performance if they have similar economic characteristics. For example, similar long-term average gross margins for two operating segments would be expected if their economic characteristics were similar. Two or more operating segments may be aggregated into a single operating segment if aggregation is consistent with the objective and basic principles of this Statement, if the segments have similar economic characteristics, and if the segments are similar in each of the following areas:

a. The nature of the products and services
b. The nature of the production processes
c. The type or class of customer for their products and services
d. The methods used to distribute their products or provide their services
e. If applicable, the nature of the regulatory environment, for example, banking, insurance, or public utilities.

Quantitative thresholds

18. An enterprise shall report separately information about an operating segment that meets any of the following quantitative thresholds:

a. Its reported revenue, including both sales to external customers and intersegment sales or transfers, is 10 percent or more of the combined revenue, internal and external, of all operating segments.
b. The absolute amount of its reported profit or loss is 10 percent or more of the greater, in absolute amount, of (1) the combined reported profit of all operating segments that did not report a loss or

(2) the combined reported loss of all operating segments that did report a loss.
c. Its assets are 10 percent or more of the combined assets of all operating segments.

Operating segments that do not meet any of the quantitative thresholds may be considered reportable, and separately disclosed, if management believes that information about the segment would be useful to readers of the financial statements.

19. An enterprise may combine information about operating segments that do not meet the quantitative thresholds with information about other operating segments that do not meet the quantitative thresholds to produce a reportable segment only if the operating segments share a majority of the aggregation criteria listed in paragraph 17.

20. If total of external revenue reported by operating segments constitutes less than 75 percent of total consolidated revenue, additional operating segments shall be identified as reportable segments (even if they do not meet the criteria in paragraph 18) until at least 75 percent of total consolidated revenue is included in reportable segments.

21. Information about other business activities and operating segments that are not reportable shall be combined and disclosed in an "all other" category separate from other reconciling items in the reconciliations required by paragraph 32. The sources of the revenue included in the "all other" category shall be described.

22. If management judges an operating segment identified as a reportable segment in the immediately preceding period to be of continuing significance, information about that segment shall continue to be reported separately in the current period even if it no longer meets the criteria for reportability in paragraph 18.

23. If an operating segment is identified as a reportable segment in the current period due to the quantitative thresholds, prior-period segment data presented for comparative purposes shall be restated to reflect the newly reportable segment as a separate segment even if that segment did not satisfy the criteria for reportability in paragraph 18 in the prior period unless it is impracticable to do so. For purposes of this Statement, information is impracticable to present if the necessary information is not available and the cost to develop it would be excessive.

24. There may be a practical limit to the number of reportable segments that an enterprise separately discloses beyond which segment information may become overly detailed. Although no precise limit has been determined, as the number of segments that are reportable in accordance with paragraphs 18-23 increases above 10, the enterprise should consider whether a practical limit has been reached.

Disclosures

25. An enterprise shall disclose the following for each period for which an income statement is presented:

a. General information as described in paragraph 26
b. Information about reported segment profit or loss, including certain revenues and expenses included in reported segment profit or loss, segment assets, and the basis of measurement, as described in paragraphs 27-31
c. Reconciliations of the totals of segment revenues, reported profit or loss, assets, and other significant items to corresponding enterprise amounts as described in paragraph 32
d. Interim period information as described in paragraph 33.

However, reconciliations of balance sheet amounts for reportable segments to consolidated balance sheet amounts are required only for each year for which a balance sheet is presented. Previously reported information for prior periods shall be restated as described in paragraphs 34 and 35.

General information

26. An enterprise shall disclose the following general information:

a. Factors used to identify the enterprise's reportable segments, including the basis of organization (for example, whether management has chosen to organize the enterprise around differences in products and services, geographic areas, regulatory environments, or a combination of factors and whether operating segments have been aggregated)
b. Types of products and services from which each reportable segment derives its revenues.

Information about profit or loss and assets

27. An enterprise shall report a measure of profit or loss and total assets for each reportable segment. An enterprise also shall disclose the following about each reportable segment if the specified amounts (a) are included in the measure of segment profit or loss reviewed by the chief operating decision maker or (b) are otherwise regularly provided to the chief operating decision maker, even if not included in that measure of segment profit or loss:

a. Revenues from external customers
b. Revenues from transactions with other operating segments of the same enterprise
c. Interest revenue
d. Interest expense
e. Depreciation, depletion, and amortization expense
f. Unusual items as described in paragraph 26 of APB Opinion No. 30, *Reporting the Results of Operations—Reporting the Effects of Disposal of a Segment of a Business, and Extraordinary, Unusual and Infrequently Occurring Events and Transactions*
g. Equity in the net income of investees accounted for by the equity method
h. Income tax expense or benefit
i. Extraordinary items
j. Significant noncash items other than depreciation, depletion, and amortization expense.

An enterprise shall report interest revenue separately from interest expense for each reportable segment unless a majority of the segment's revenues are from interest and the chief operating decision maker relies primarily on net interest revenue to assess the performance of the segment and make decisions about resources to be allocated to the segment. In that situation, an enterprise may report that segment's interest revenue net of its interest expense and disclose that it has done so.

28. An enterprise shall disclose the following about each reportable segment if the specified amounts (a) are included in the determination of segment assets reviewed by the chief operating decision maker or (b) are otherwise regularly provided to the chief operating decision maker, even if not included in the determination of segment assets:

a. The amount of investment in equity method investees
b. Total expenditures for additions to long-lived assets other than financial instruments, long-term customer relationships of a financial institution, mortgage and other servicing rights, deferred policy acquisition costs, and deferred tax assets.

Measurement

29. The amount of each segment item reported shall be the measure reported to the chief operating decision maker for purposes of making decisions about allocating resources to the segment and assessing its performance. Adjustments and eliminations made in preparing an enterprise's general-purpose financial statements and allocations of revenues, expenses, and gains or losses shall be included in determining reported segment profit or loss only if they are included in the measure of the segment's profit or loss that is used by the chief operating decision maker. Similarly, only those assets that are included in the measure of the segment's assets that is used by the chief operating decision maker shall be reported for that segment. If amounts are allocated to reported segment profit or loss or assets, those amounts shall be allocated on a reasonable basis.

30. If the chief operating decision maker uses only one measure of a segment's profit or loss and only one measure of a segment's assets in assessing segment performance and deciding how to allocate resources, segment profit or loss and assets shall be reported at those measures. If the chief operating decision maker uses more than one measure of a segment's profit or loss and more than one measure of a segment's assets, the reported measures shall be those that management believes are determined in accordance with the measurement principles most consistent with those used in measuring the corresponding amounts in the enterprise's consolidated financial statements.

31. An enterprise shall provide an explanation of the measurements of segment profit or loss and segment assets for each reportable segment. At a minimum, an enterprise shall disclose the following:

a. The basis of accounting for any transactions between reportable segments.
b. The nature of any differences between the measurements of the reportable segments' profits or losses and the enterprise's consolidated income before income taxes, extraordinary items, and discontinued operations (if not apparent from the reconciliations described in paragraph 32). Those differences could include accounting policies and policies for allocation of centrally incurred costs that are necessary for an understanding of the reported segment information.

c. The nature of any differences between the measurements of the reportable segments' assets and the enterprise's consolidated assets (if not apparent from the reconciliations described in paragraph 32). Those differences could include accounting policies and policies for allocation of jointly used assets that are necessary for an understanding of the reported segment information.
d. The nature of any changes from prior periods in the measurement methods used to determine reported segment profit or loss and the effect, if any, of those changes on the measure of segment profit or loss.
e. The nature and effect of any asymmetrical allocations to segments. For example, an enterprise might allocate depreciation expense to a segment without allocating the related depreciable assets to that segment.

Reconciliations

32. An enterprise shall provide reconciliations of all of the following:

a. The total of the reportable segments' revenues to the enterprise's consolidated revenues.
b. The total of the reportable segments' measures of profit or loss to the enterprise's consolidated income before income taxes, extraordinary items, and discontinued operations. However, if an enterprise allocates items such as income taxes and extraordinary items to segments, the enterprise may choose to reconcile the total of the segments' measures of profit or loss to consolidated income after those items.
c. The total of the reportable segments' assets to the enterprise's consolidated assets.
d. The total of the reportable segments' amounts for every other significant item of information disclosed to the corresponding consolidated amount. For example, an enterprise may choose to disclose liabilities for its reportable segments, in which case the enterprise would reconcile the total of reportable segments' liabilities for each segment to the enterprise's consolidated liabilities if the segment liabilities are significant.

All significant reconciling items shall be separately identified and described. For example, the amount of each significant adjustment to reconcile accounting methods used in determining segment profit or loss

---

1a–1b[These footnotes have been deleted because the effective date of FASB Statement No. 154, *Accounting Changes and Error Corrections,* has passed.]

to the enterprise's consolidated amounts shall be separately identified and described.

Interim period information

33. An enterprise shall disclose the following about each reportable segment in condensed financial statements of interim periods:

a. Revenues from external customers
b. Intersegment revenues
c. A measure of segment profit or loss
d. Total assets for which there has been a material change from the amount disclosed in the last annual report
e. A description of differences from the last annual report in the basis of segmentation or in the basis of measurement of segment profit or loss
f. A reconciliation of the total of the reportable segments' measures of profit or loss to the enterprise's consolidated income before income taxes, extraordinary items, and discontinued operations. However, if an enterprise allocates items such as income taxes and extraordinary items to segments, the enterprise may choose to reconcile the total of the segments' measures of profit or loss to consolidated income after those items. Significant reconciling items shall be separately identified and described in that reconciliation.

Restatement of previously reported information

34. If an enterprise changes the structure of its internal organization in a manner that causes the composition of its reportable segments to change, the corresponding information for earlier periods, including interim periods, shall be restated unless it is impracticable to do so. Accordingly, an enterprise shall restate those individual items of disclosure that it can practicably restate but need not restate those individual items, if any, that it cannot practicably restate. Following a change in the composition of its reportable segments, an enterprise shall disclose whether it has restated the corresponding items of segment information for earlier periods.

35. If an enterprise has changed the structure of its internal organization in a manner that causes the composition of its reportable segments to change and if segment information for earlier periods, including interim periods, is not restated to reflect the change, the enterprise shall disclose in the year in which the change occurs segment information for the current period under both the old basis and the new basis of segmentation unless it is impracticable to do so.

Enterprise-Wide Disclosures

36. Paragraphs 37-39 apply to all enterprises subject to this Statement including those enterprises that have a single reportable segment. Some enterprises' business activities are not organized on the basis of differences in related products and services or differences in geographic areas of operations. That is, an enterprise's segments may report revenues from a broad range of essentially different products and services, or more than one of its reportable segments may provide essentially the same products and services. Similarly, an enterprise's segments may hold assets in different geographic areas and report revenues from customers in different geographic areas, or more than one of its segments may operate in the same geographic area. Information required by paragraphs 37-39 need be provided only if it is not provided as part of the reportable operating segment information required by this Statement.

Information about Products and Services

37. An enterprise shall report the revenues from external customers for each product and service or each group of similar products and services unless it is impracticable to do so. The amounts of revenues reported shall be based on the financial information used to produce the enterprise's general-purpose financial statements. If providing the information is impracticable, that fact shall be disclosed.

Information about Geographic Areas

38. An enterprise shall report the following geographic information unless it is impracticable to do so:

a. Revenues from external customers (1) attributed to the enterprise's country of domicile and (2) attributed to all foreign countries in total from which the enterprise derives revenues. If revenues from external customers attributed to an individual foreign country are material, those revenues shall be disclosed separately. An enterprise shall disclose the basis for attributing revenues from external customers to individual countries.

[1c][This footnote has been deleted because the effective date of Statement 154 has passed.]

b. Long-lived assets other than financial instruments, long-term customer relationships of a financial institution, mortgage and other servicing rights, deferred policy acquisition costs, and deferred tax assets (1) located in the enterprise's country of domicile and (2) located in all foreign countries in total in which the enterprise holds assets. If assets in an individual foreign country are material, those assets shall be disclosed separately.

The amounts reported shall be based on the financial information that is used to produce the general-purpose financial statements. If providing the geographic information is impracticable, that fact shall be disclosed. An enterprise may wish to provide, in addition to the information required by this paragraph, subtotals of geographic information about groups of countries.

Information about Major Customers

39. An enterprise shall provide information about the extent of its reliance on its major customers. If revenues from transactions with a single external customer amount to 10 percent or more of an enterprise's revenues, the enterprise shall disclose that fact, the total amount of revenues from each such customer, and the identity of the segment or segments reporting the revenues. The enterprise need not disclose the identity of a major customer or the amount of revenues that each segment reports from that customer. For purposes of this Statement, a group of entities known to a reporting enterprise to be under common control shall be considered as a single customer, and the federal government, a state government, a local government (for example, a county or municipality), or a foreign government each shall be considered as a single customer.

Effective Date and Transition

40. This Statement shall be effective for fiscal years beginning after December 15, 1997. Earlier application is encouraged. Segment information for earlier years that is reported with corresponding information for the initial year of application shall be restated to conform to the requirements of this Statement unless it is impracticable to do so. This Statement need not be applied to interim financial statements in the initial year of its application, but comparative information for interim periods in the initial year of application shall be reported in financial statements for interim periods in the second year of application.

The provisions of this Statement need not be applied to immaterial items.

This Statement was adopted by the affirmative votes of six members of the Financial Accounting Standards Board. Mr. Leisenring dissented.

Mr. Leisenring dissents from the issuance of this Statement because it does not define segment profit or loss and does not require that whatever measure of profit or loss is reported be consistent with the attribution of assets to reportable segments.

By not defining segment profit or loss, this Statement allows any measure of performance to be displayed as segment profit or loss as long as that measure is reviewed by the chief operating decision maker. Items of revenue and expense directly attributable to a given segment need not be included in the reported operating results of that segment, and no allocation of items not directly attributable to a given segment is required. As a consequence, an item that results directly from one segment's activities can be excluded from that segment's profit or loss. Mr. Leisenring believes that, minimally, this Statement should require that amounts directly incurred by or directly attributable to a segment be included in that segment's profit or loss and that assets identified with a particular segment be consistent with the measurement of that segment's profit or loss.

Mr. Leisenring supports trying to assist users as described in paragraph 3 of this Statement but believes it is very unlikely that that will be accomplished, even with the required disclosures and reconciliation to the entity's annual financial statements, because of the failure to define profit or loss and to impose any attribution or allocation requirements for the measure of profit or loss.

Mr. Leisenring supports the management approach for defining reportable segments and supports requiring disclosure of selected segment information in condensed financial statements of interim periods issued to shareholders. Mr. Leisenring believes, however, that the definitions of revenues, operating profit or loss, and identifiable assets in paragraph 10 of Statement 14 should be retained in this Statement and applied to segments identified by the management approach. Without retaining those definitions or some other agreed-to

definition of segment profit or loss, Mr. Leisenring believes that the objective of presenting segment information would more likely be met by retaining the requirements of Statement 14 and amending that Statement to define segments and require disclosure of interim segment information consistent with the provisions of this Statement.

Members of the Financial Accounting Standards Board:

Dennis R. Beresford,	Anthony T. Cope	James J. Leisenring
Chairman	John M. Foster	Gerhard G. Mueller
Joseph V. Anania	Gaylen N. Larson	

Appendix A

BACKGROUND INFORMATION AND BASIS FOR CONCLUSIONS

CONTENTS

Appendix A

BACKGROUND INFORMATION AND BASIS FOR CONCLUSIONS

Introduction

41. This appendix summarizes considerations that were deemed significant by Board members in reaching the conclusions in this Statement. It includes reasons for accepting certain approaches and rejecting others. Individual Board members gave greater weight to some factors than to others.

Background Information

42. FASB Statement No. 14, *Financial Reporting for Segments of a Business Enterprise,* was issued in 1976. That Statement required that business enterprises report segment information on two bases: by industry and by geographic area. It also required disclosure of information about export sales and major customers.

43. The Board concluded at the time it issued Statement 14 that information about components of an enterprise, the products and services that it offers, its foreign operations, and its major customers is useful for understanding and making decisions about the enterprise as a whole. Financial statement users observe that the evaluation of the prospects for future cash flows is the central element of investment and lending decisions. The evaluation of prospects requires assessment of the uncertainty that surrounds both the timing and the amount of the expected cash flows to the enterprise, which in turn affect potential cash flows to the investor or creditor. Users also observe that uncertainty results in part from factors related to the products and services an enterprise offers and the geographic areas in which it operates.

44. In its 1993 position paper, *Financial Reporting in the 1990s and Beyond,* the Association for Investment Management and Research (AIMR) said:

> [Segment data] is vital, essential, fundamental, indispensable, and integral to the investment analysis process. Analysts need to know and understand how the various components of a multifaceted enterprise behave economically. One weak member of the group is analogous to a section of blight on a piece of fruit; it has the potential to spread rot

over the entirety. Even in the absence of weakness, different segments will generate dissimilar streams of cash flows to which are attached disparate risks and which bring about unique values. Thus, without disaggregation, there is no sensible way to predict the overall amounts, timing, or risks of a complete enterprise's future cash flows. There is little dispute over the analytic usefulness of disaggregated financial data. [pages 59 and 60]

45. Over the years, financial analysts consistently requested that financial statement data be disaggregated to a much greater degree than it is in current practice. Many analysts said that they found Statement 14 helpful but inadequate. In its 1993 position paper, the AIMR emphasized that:

> There is no disagreement among AIMR members that segment information is totally vital to their work. There also is general agreement among them that the current segment reporting standard, Financial Accounting Standard No. 14, is inadequate. Recent work by a subcommittee of the [Financial Accounting Policy Committee] has confirmed that a substantial majority of analysts seek and, when it is available, use quarterly segment data. [page 5]

46. The Canadian Institute of Chartered Accountants (CICA) published a Research Study, *Financial Reporting for Segments,* in August 1992. An FASB Research Report, *Reporting Disaggregated Information,* was published in February 1993. In March 1993, the FASB and the Accounting Standards Board (AcSB) of the CICA agreed to pursue their projects jointly.

47. In May 1993, the FASB and the AcSB jointly issued an Invitation to Comment, *Reporting Disaggregated Information by Business Enterprises.* That Invitation to Comment identified certain issues related to disclosure of information about segments, solicited comments on those issues, and asked readers to identify additional issues. The boards received 129 comment letters from U.S. and Canadian respondents.

48. In late 1993, the FASB and the AcSB formed the Disaggregated Disclosures Advisory Group to advise and otherwise support the two boards in their efforts to improve disaggregated disclosures. The members

of the group included financial statement issuers, auditors, financial analysts, and academics from both the United States and Canada. In January 1994, the FASB and the AcSB began discussing changes to Statement 14 and *CICA Handbook* Section 1700, "Segmented Information." The two boards met with and otherwise actively solicited the views of analysts and preparers of financial statements about possible improvements to the current segment reporting requirements. FASB and AcSB members and staff also discussed disaggregated disclosures at meetings of several groups of analysts, including the AIMR's Financial Accounting Policy Committee.

49. In 1991, the AICPA formed the Special Committee on Financial Reporting (the Special Committee) to make recommendations to improve the relevance and usefulness of business reporting. The Special Committee, which comprised financial statement auditors and preparers, established focus groups of credit analysts and equity analysts to assist in formulating its recommendations. The Special Committee issued its report, *Improving Business Reporting— A Customer Focus,* in 1994. That report listed improvements in disclosures of business segment information as its first recommendation and included the following commentary:

> . . . for users analyzing a company involved in diverse businesses, financial information about business segments often is as important as information about the company as a whole. Users suggest that standard setters assign the highest priority to improving segment reporting because of its importance to their work and the perceived problems with current reporting of segment information. [page 68]

50. The report of the Special Committee listed the following as among the most important improvements needed:

a. Disclosure of segment information in interim financial reports
b. Greater number of segments for some enterprises
c. More information about segments
d. Segmentation that corresponds to internal management reports
e. Consistency of segment information with other parts of an annual report.

Similar recommendations had been made in each of the last 20 years in evaluations of corporate reporting conducted by the AIMR.

51. The two boards reached tentative conclusions about an approach to segment reporting that was substantially different from the approach in Statement 14 and Section 1700. Key characteristics of the new approach were that (a) information would be provided about segments of the enterprise that corresponded to the structure of the enterprise's internal organization, that is, about the divisions, departments, subsidiaries, or other internal units that the chief operating decision maker uses to make operating decisions and to assess an enterprise's performance, (b) specific amounts would be allocated to segments only if they were allocated in reports used by the chief operating decision maker for evaluation of segment performance, and (c) accounting policies used to produce the disaggregated information would be the same as those used in the reports used by the chief operating decision maker in allocating resources and assessing segment performance.

52. In February 1995, the staffs of the FASB and the CICA distributed a paper, "Tentative Conclusions on Financial Reporting for Segments" (Tentative Conclusions), to selected securities analysts, the FASB Task Force on Consolidations and Related Matters, the Disaggregated Disclosures Advisory Group, the FASB's Emerging Issues Task Force, the Financial Accounting Standards Advisory Council, the AcSB's list of Associates,[2] and members of representative organizations that regularly work with the boards. The paper also was announced in FASB and CICA publications and was sent to anyone who requested a copy. Board and staff members discussed the Tentative Conclusions with various analyst and preparer groups. Approximately 80 comment letters were received from U.S. and Canadian respondents.

53. In January 1996, the FASB and the AcSB issued virtually identical Exposure Drafts, *Reporting Disaggregated Information about a Business Enterprise.* The FASB received 221 comment letters and the AcSB received 73 comment letters in response to the Exposure Drafts. A field test of the proposals was conducted in March 1996. A public meeting was held in Toronto in October 1996 to discuss results and concerns with field test participants. Other interested

---

[2]Associates are individuals and organizations with a particular interest in financial reporting issues that have volunteered to provide an outside reaction to AcSB positions at an early stage in the AcSB's deliberations.

parties attended a public meeting in Norwalk in October 1996 to discuss their concerns about the proposals in the Exposure Drafts. The FASB decided that it could reach an informed decision on the project without holding a public hearing.

54. The FASB and the AcSB exchanged information during the course of redeliberating the proposals in their respective Exposure Drafts. AcSB members and CICA staff attended FASB meetings, and FASB members and staff attended AcSB meetings in late 1996 and in 1997 to discuss the issues raised by respondents. Both boards reached agreement on all of the substantive issues to achieve virtually identical standards for segment reporting in the United States and Canada. Members of the Segment Disclosures Advisory Group (formerly the Disaggregated Disclosures Advisory Group) discussed a draft of the standards section in March 1997.

55. The International Accounting Standards Committee (IASC) issued an Exposure Draft of a proposed International Accounting Standard that would replace International Accounting Standard IAS 14, *Reporting Financial Information by Segment,* in December 1995. Although many of its provisions are similar to those of the FASB and AcSB Exposure Drafts, the IASC's proposal is based on different objectives and is different from those Exposure Drafts. A member of the IASC Segments Steering Committee participated in FASB meetings during the redeliberations of the Exposure Draft, and members of the FASB participated in meetings of the IASC Segments Steering Committee. Many of the respondents to the Exposure Drafts encouraged the FASB and the AcSB to work closely with the IASC to achieve similar standards for segment reporting. The IASC expects to issue a standard on segment reporting later in 1997. Although there likely will be differences between the IASC's requirements for segment reporting and those of this Statement, the boards expect that it will be possible to prepare one set of segment information that complies with both the IASC requirements and those of this Statement.

56. This Statement addresses the following key issues:

a. What is the appropriate basis for defining segments?
b. What accounting principles and allocations should be used?
c. What specific items of information should be reported?

d. Should segment information be reported in condensed financial statements for interim periods?

Defining Operating Segments of an Enterprise

57. The Board concluded that the *industry approach* to segment disclosures in Statement 14 was not providing the information required by financial statement users and that disclosure of disaggregated information should be based on operating segments. This Statement defines an operating segment as a component of an enterprise (a) that engages in business activities from which it may earn revenues and incur expenses, (b) whose operating results are regularly reviewed by the enterprise's chief operating decision maker to make decisions about resources to be allocated to the segment and to assess its performance, and (c) for which discrete financial information is available.

58. The AIMR's 1993 position paper and the report of the AICPA Special Committee criticized Statement 14's industry segment approach to reporting segment information. The AIMR's position paper included the following:

> FAS 14 requires disclosure of line-of-business information classified by "industry segment." Its definition of segment is necessarily imprecise, recognizing that there are numerous practical problems in applying that definition to different business entities operating under disparate circumstances. That weakness in FAS 14 has been exploited by many enterprises to suit their own financial reporting purposes. As a result, we have seen one of the ten largest firms in the country report all of its operations as being in a single, very broadly defined industry segment. [page 60]

The report of the Special Committee said that "[financial statement users] believe that many companies define industry segments too broadly for business reporting and thus report on too few industry segments" (page 69).

59. The report of the AICPA Special Committee also said that "... the primary means to improving industry segment reporting should be to align business reporting with internal reporting" (page 69), and the AIMR's 1993 position paper recommended that:

> ... priority should be given to the production and dissemination of financial

data that reflects and reports sensibly the operations of specific enterprises. If we could obtain reports showing the details of how an individual business firm is organized and managed, we would assume more responsibility for making meaningful comparisons of those data to the unlike data of other firms that conduct their business differently. [pages 60 and 61]

Almost all of the users and many other constituents who responded to the Exposure Draft or who met with Board and staff members agreed that defining segments based on the structure of an enterprise's internal organization would result in improved information. They said that not only would enterprises be likely to report more detailed information but knowledge of the structure of an enterprise's internal organization is valuable in itself because it highlights the risks and opportunities that management believes are important.

60. Segments based on the structure of an enterprise's internal organization have at least three other significant advantages. First, an ability to see an enterprise "through the eyes of management" enhances a user's ability to predict actions or reactions of management that can significantly affect the enterprise's prospects for future cash flows. Second, because information about those segments is generated for management's use, the incremental cost of providing information for external reporting should be relatively low. Third, practice has demonstrated that the term *industry* is subjective. Segments based on an existing internal structure should be less subjective.

61. The AIMR and other users have commented that segment information is more useful if it is consistent with explanatory information provided elsewhere in the annual report. They note that the business review section and the chairman's letter in an annual report frequently discuss the enterprise's operations on a basis different from that of the segment information in the notes to the financial statements and the management's discussion and analysis section, which is required by SEC rules to correspond to the segment information provided to comply with Statement 14. That appears to occur if the enterprise is not managed in a way that corresponds to the way it defines segments under the requirements of Statement 14. Segmentation based on the structure of an enterprise's internal organization should facilitate consistent discussion of segment financial results throughout an enterprise's annual report.

62. Some respondents to the Exposure Draft opposed the Board's approach for several reasons. Segments based on the structure of an enterprise's internal organization may not be comparable between enterprises that engage in similar activities and may not be comparable from year to year for an individual enterprise. In addition, an enterprise may not be organized based on products and services or geographic areas, and thus the enterprise's segments may not be susceptible to analysis using macroeconomic models. Finally, some asserted that because enterprises are organized strategically, the information that would be reported may be competitively harmful to the reporting enterprise.

63. The Board acknowledges that comparability of accounting information is important. The summary of principal conclusions in FASB Concepts Statement No. 2, *Qualitative Characteristics of Accounting Information,* says: "Comparability between enterprises and consistency in the application of methods over time increases the informational value of comparisons of relative economic opportunities or performance. The significance of information, especially quantitative information, depends to a great extent on the user's ability to relate it to some benchmark." However, Concepts Statement 2 also notes a danger:

> Improving comparability may destroy or weaken relevance or reliability if, to secure comparability between two measures, one of them has to be obtained by a method yielding less relevant or less reliable information. Historically, extreme examples of this have been provided in some European countries in which the use of standardized charts of accounts has been made mandatory in the interest of interfirm comparability but at the expense of relevance and often reliability as well. That kind of uniformity may even adversely affect comparability of information if it conceals real differences between enterprises. [paragraph 116]

64. The Board was concerned that segments defined using the approach in Statement 14 may appear to be more comparable between enterprises than they actually are. Statement 14 included the following:

> Information prepared in conformity with [Statement 14] may be of limited usefulness for comparing an industry segment of one enterprise with a similar industry segment of

another enterprise (i.e., for interenterprise comparison). Interenterprise comparison of industry segments would require a fairly detailed prescription of the basis or bases of disaggregation to be followed by all enterprises, as well as specification of the basis of accounting for intersegment transfers and methods of allocating costs common to two or more segments. [paragraph 76]

65. Statement 14 explained why the Board chose not to develop a detailed prescription of the bases of disaggregation:

> ... differences among enterprises in the nature of their operations and in the extent to which components of the enterprise share common facilities, equipment, materials and supplies, or labor force make unworkable the prescription of highly detailed rules and procedures that must be followed by all enterprises. Moreover, ... differences in the accounting systems of business enterprises are a practical constraint on the degree of specificity with which standards of financial accounting and reporting for disaggregated information can be established. [paragraph 74]

Those same considerations persuaded the Board not to adopt more specific requirements in this Statement. Both relevance and comparability will not be achievable in all cases, and relevance should be the overriding concern.

66. The AICPA Special Committee, some respondents to the Exposure Draft, and other constituents recommended that the Board require that an enterprise use an alternative method of segmentation for external reporting if its internal organization is not based on differences in products and services or geography. Some specifically recommended adoption of the proposal in the IASC Exposure Draft that was commonly referred to as a "safety net." The IASC Exposure Draft approach to identifying primary and secondary operating segments calls for review of management's organization of segments, but both primary and secondary segments are required to be defined either on the basis of related products and services or on the basis of geography. That is, regardless of management's organization, segments must be grouped either by related products and services or by geographic areas, and one set must be presented as primary segments and the other as secondary segments.

67. The Board recognizes that an enterprise may not be divided into components with similar products and services or geographic areas for internal purposes and that some users of financial statements have expressed a desire for information organized on those bases. However, instead of an alternative method of segmentation, which would call for multiple sets of segment information in many circumstances, the Board chose to require disclosure of additional information about products and services and about geographic areas of operations for the enterprise as a whole if the basic segment disclosures do not provide it.

68. One reason for not prescribing segmentation along bases of only related products and services or geography is that it is difficult to define clearly the circumstances in which an alternative method that differs from the management approach would be applied consistently. An enterprise with a relatively narrow product line may not consider two products to be similar, while an enterprise with a broad product line may consider those same two products to be similar. For example, a highly diversified enterprise may consider all consumer products to be similar if it has other businesses such as financial services and road construction. However, an enterprise that sells only consumer products might consider razor blades to be different from toasters.

69. A second reason for rejecting that approach is that an alternative method of segmentation would increase the cost to some enterprises to prepare the information. A management approach to defining segments allows enterprises to present the information that they use internally and facilitates consistent descriptions of the components of an enterprise from one part of the annual report to another. An enterprise could be organized by its products and services, geography, a mixture of both products and services and geography, or other bases, such as customer type, and the segment information required by this Statement would be consistent with that method of organization. Furthermore, the enterprise-wide disclosures about products and services will provide information about the total revenues from related products and services, and the enterprise-wide disclosures about geography will provide information about the revenues and assets of an enterprise both inside and outside its home country. If material, individual foreign country information also is required.

70. The Board recognizes that some enterprises organize their segments on more than one basis. Other

enterprises may produce reports in which their activities are presented in a variety of ways. In those situations, reportable segments are to be determined based on a review of other factors to identify the enterprise's operating segments, including the nature of the activities of each component, the existence of managers responsible for them, and the information provided to the board of directors. In many enterprises, only one set of data is provided to the board of directors. That set of data generally is indicative of how management views the enterprise's activities.

Reportable Segments

71. The Board included a notion of reportable segments, a subset of operating segments, in this Statement by defining aggregation criteria and quantitative thresholds for determining which operating segments should be reported separately in the financial statements.

72. A so-called pure management approach to segment reporting might require that an enterprise report all of the information that is reviewed by the chief operating decision maker to make decisions about resource allocations and to assess the performance of the enterprise. However, that level of detail may not be useful to readers of external financial statements, and it also may be cumbersome for an enterprise to present. Therefore, this Statement uses a modified management approach that includes both aggregation criteria and quantitative thresholds for determining reportable operating segments. However, an enterprise need not aggregate similar segments, and it may present segments that fall below the quantitative thresholds.

Aggregation of Similar Operating Segments

73. The Board believes that separate reporting of segment information will not add significantly to an investor's understanding of an enterprise if its operating segments have characteristics so similar that they can be expected to have essentially the same future prospects. The Board concluded that although information about each segment may be available, in those circumstances the benefit would be insufficient to justify its disclosure. For example, a retail chain may have 10 stores that individually meet the definition of an operating segment, but each store may be essentially the same as the others.

74. Most respondents commented on the aggregation criteria in the Exposure Draft. Many said that the

criteria were unreasonably strict, to the extent that nearly identical segments might not qualify for aggregation. Some respondents linked their concerns about competitive harm and too many segments directly to the aggregation criteria, indicating that a relaxation of the criteria would significantly reduce those concerns. To better convey its intent, the Board revised the wording of the aggregation criteria and the introduction to them. However, the Board rejected recommendations that the criteria be indicators rather than tests and that the guidance require only the expectation of similar long-term performance of segments to justify aggregation because those changes might result in a level of aggregation that would cause a loss of potentially valuable information. For the same reason, the Board also rejected suggestions that segments need be similar in only a majority of the characteristics in paragraph 17 to justify aggregation. The Board recognizes that determining when two segments are sufficiently similar to justify aggregating them is difficult and subjective. However, the Board notes that one of the reasons that the information provided under Statement 14 did not satisfy financial statement users' needs is that segments with different characteristics in important areas were at times aggregated.

Quantitative Thresholds

75. In developing the Exposure Draft, the Board had concluded that quantitative criteria might interfere with the determination of operating segments and, if anything, might unnecessarily reduce the number of segments disclosed. Respondents to the Exposure Draft and others urged the Board to include quantitative criteria for determining which segments to report because they said that some enterprises would be required to report too many segments unless specific quantitative guidelines allowed them to omit small segments. Some respondents said that the Exposure Draft would have required disclosure of as many as 25 operating segments, which was not a result anticipated by the Board in its deliberations preceding the Exposure Draft. Others said that enterprises would report information that was too highly aggregated unless quantitative guidelines prevented it. The Board decided that the addition of quantitative thresholds would be a practical way to address respondents' concerns about competitive harm and proliferation of segments without fundamentally changing the management approach to segment definition.

76. Similar to the requirements in Statement 14, the Board decided to require that any operating segment that constitutes 10 percent or more of reported revenues, assets, or profit or loss be reported separately and that reportable segments account for at least 75 percent of an enterprise's external revenues. The Board decided to retain that guidance for the quantitative thresholds because it can be objectively applied and because preparers and users of financial statements already understand it.

77. Inclusion of quantitative thresholds similar to those in Statement 14 necessitates guidance on how to report operating segments that do not meet the thresholds. The Board concluded that enterprises should be permitted to aggregate information about operating segments that do not meet the thresholds with information about other operating segments that do not meet the thresholds if a majority of the aggregation criteria in paragraph 17 are met. That is a more liberal aggregation provision than that for individually material operating segments, but it prohibits aggregation of segments that are dissimilar.

78. Paragraph 125 of Concepts Statement 2 states that ". . . magnitude by itself, without regard to the nature of the item and the circumstances in which the judgment has to be made, will not generally be a sufficient basis for a materiality judgment." That guidance applies to segment information. An understanding of the material segments of an enterprise is important for understanding the enterprise as a whole, and individual items of segment information are important for understanding the segments. Thus, an item of segment information that, if omitted, would change a user's decision about that segment so significantly that it would change the user's decision about the enterprise as a whole is material even though an item of a similar magnitude might not be considered material if it were omitted from the consolidated financial statements. Therefore, enterprises are encouraged to report information about segments that do not meet the quantitative thresholds if management believes that it is material. Those who are familiar with the particular circumstances of each enterprise must decide what constitutes *material*.

Vertically Integrated Enterprises

79. The Board concluded that the definition of an operating segment should include components of an enterprise that sell primarily or exclusively to other operating segments of the enterprise if the enterprise is managed that way. Information about the components engaged in each stage of production is particularly important for understanding vertically integrated enterprises in certain businesses, for example, oil and gas enterprises. Different activities within the enterprise may have significantly different prospects for future cash flows, and users of financial statements have asserted that they need to know results of each operation.

80. Some respondents to the Exposure Draft opposed the requirement to report vertically integrated segments separately. They said that the segment results may not be comparable between enterprises and that transfer prices are not sufficiently reliable for external reporting purposes. The Board considered an approach that would have required separate reporting of vertically integrated segments only if transfer prices were based on quoted market prices and if there was no basis for combining the selling segment and the buying segment. However, that would have been a significant departure from the management approach to defining segments. The Board also was concerned that the criteria would be unworkable. Therefore, the Board decided to retain the Exposure Draft's provisions for vertically integrated segments.

Accounting Principles and Allocations

81. The Board decided that the information to be reported about each segment should be measured on the same basis as the information used by the chief operating decision maker for purposes of allocating resources to segments and assessing segments' performance. That is a management approach to measuring segment information as proposed in the Exposure Draft. The Board does not think that a separate measure of segment profit or loss or assets should have to be developed solely for the purpose of disclosing segment information. For example, an enterprise that accounts for inventory using a specialized valuation method for internal purposes should not be required to restate inventory amounts for each segment, and an enterprise that accounts for pension expense only on a consolidated basis should not be required to allocate pension expense to each operating segment.

82. The report of the AICPA Special Committee said that the Board "should allow companies to report a statistic on the same basis it is reported for internal purposes, if the statistic is reported internally. The usefulness of information prepared only for [external] reporting is questionable. Users want to understand management's perspective on the company and

the implications of key statistics." It also said that "key statistics to be reported [should] be limited to statistics a company has available . . ." (page 72).

83. Respondents to the Exposure Draft had mixed reactions to its measurement guidance. Very few suggested that the Board require allocations solely for external reporting purposes. Most agreed that allocations are inherently arbitrary and may not be meaningful if they are not used for management purposes. No respondents suggested that intersegment transfers should be reported on any basis other than that used internally. However, some respondents recommended that information about each segment be provided based on the accounting principles used in the enterprise's general-purpose financial statements. Some observed that unadjusted information from internal sources would not necessarily comply with generally accepted accounting principles and, for that reason, might be difficult for users to understand. Other respondents argued that comparability between enterprises would be improved if the segment information were provided on the basis of generally accepted accounting principles. Finally, a few questioned the verifiability of the information.

84. The Board decided not to require that segment information be provided in accordance with the same generally accepted accounting principles used to prepare the consolidated financial statements for several reasons. Preparing segment information in accordance with the generally accepted accounting principles used at the consolidated level would be difficult because some generally accepted accounting principles are not intended to apply at a segment level. Examples include allocation of the cost of an acquisition to individual assets and liabilities of a subsidiary using the purchase method of accounting, accounting for the cost of enterprise-wide employee benefit plans, accounting for income taxes in an enterprise that files a consolidated income tax return, and accounting for inventory on a last-in, first-out basis if the pools include items in more than one segment. In addition, there are no generally accepted accounting principles for allocating joint costs, jointly used assets, or jointly incurred liabilities to segments or for pricing intersegment transfers. As a consequence, it generally is not feasible to present segment profitability in accordance with generally accepted accounting principles.

85. The Board recognizes that segment information is subject to certain limitations and that some of that information may not be susceptible to the same de-

gree of verifiability as some other financial information. However, verifiability is not the only important qualitative characteristic of accounting information. Verifiability is a component of reliability, which is one of two characteristics that contribute to the usefulness of accounting information. The other is relevance, which is equally important. Concepts Statement 2 states:

> Although financial information must be both relevant and reliable to be useful, information may possess both characteristics to varying degrees. It may be possible to trade relevance for reliability or vice versa, though not to the point of dispensing with one of them altogether. . . . trade-offs between characteristics may be necessary or beneficial.
>
> In a particular situation, the importance attached to relevance in relation to the importance of other decision specific qualities of accounting information (for example, reliability) will be different for different information users, and their willingness to trade one quality for another will also differ. [paragraphs 42 and 45]

86. It is apparent that users are willing to trade a degree of reliability in segment information for more relevant information. The AIMR's 1993 position paper states:

> Analysts need financial statements structured so as to be consistent with how the business is organized and managed. That means that two different companies in the same industry may have to report segment data differently because they are structured differently themselves. [page 20]

But, as previously noted, the position paper says that, under those circumstances, analysts "would assume more responsibility for making meaningful comparisons of those data to the unlike data of other firms that conduct their business differently" (page 61).

87. The Board believes that the information required by this Statement meets the objective of reliability of which both representational faithfulness and verifiability are components. An auditor can determine whether the information reported in the notes to the financial statements came from the required source by reviewing management reports or minutes from meetings of the board of directors. The information is not required to be provided on a specified basis, but

the enterprise is required to explain the basis on which it is provided and to reconcile the segment information to consolidated enterprise totals. Adequate explanation and an appropriate reconciliation will enable a user to understand the information and its limitations in the context of the enterprise's financial statements. The auditor can test both the explanation of segment amounts and the reconciliations to consolidated totals. Furthermore, because management uses that information in its decision-making processes, that information is likely to be highly reliable. The information provided to comply with Statement 14 was more difficult to verify in many situations and was less reliable. Because it was prepared solely for external reporting purposes, it required allocations that may have been arbitrary, and it was based on accounting principles that may have been difficult to apply at the segment level.

88. Paragraph 29 requires amounts allocated to a segment to be allocated on a reasonable basis. However, the Board believes that the potential increased reliability that might have been achieved by requiring allocation of consolidated amounts is illusory because expenses incurred at the consolidated level could be allocated to segments in a variety of ways that could be considered "reasonable." For example, an enterprise could use either the number of employees in each segment or the segment's total salary expense in relation to the consolidated amounts as a basis for allocating pension expense to segments. Those two approaches to allocation could result in significantly different measures of segment profit or loss. However, both the number of employees and the total salary expense might be reasonable bases on which to allocate total pension expense. In contrast, it would not seem reasonable for an enterprise to allocate pension expense to a segment that had no employees eligible for the pension plan. Because of the potential for misleading information that may result from such allocations, the Board decided that it is appropriate for this Statement to require that amounts allocated to a segment be allocated on a reasonable basis.

89. The Board also considered explicitly requiring that revenues and expenses directly incurred by or directly attributable to an operating segment be reported by that segment. However, it decided that, in some cases, whether an item of revenue or expense is attributable to an operating segment is a matter of judgment. Further, such an explicit requirement would be an additional modification of the management approach to measurement. While the Board decided not to include an explicit requirement, it believes that many items of revenue or expense clearly relate to a particular segment and that it would be unlikely that the information used by management would omit those items.

90. To assist users of financial statements in understanding segment disclosures, this Statement requires that enterprises provide sufficient explanation of the basis on which the information was prepared. That disclosure must include any differences in the basis of measurement between the consolidated amounts and the segment amounts. It also must indicate whether allocations of items were made symmetrically. An enterprise may allocate an expense to a segment without allocating the related asset; however, disclosure of that fact is required. Enterprises also are required to reconcile to the consolidated totals in the enterprise's financial statements the totals of reportable segment assets, segment revenues, segment profit or loss, and any other significant segment information that is disclosed.

91. In addition, the advantages of reporting unadjusted management information are significant. That practice is consistent with defining segments based on the structure of the enterprise's internal organization. It imposes little incremental cost on the enterprise and requires little incremental time to prepare. Thus, the enterprise can more easily report segment information in condensed financial statements for interim periods and can report more information about each segment in annual financial statements. Information used by management also highlights for a user of financial statements the risks and opportunities that management considers important.

Information to Be Disclosed about Segments

92. The items of information about each reportable operating segment that must be disclosed as described in paragraphs 25-31 represent a balance between the needs of users of financial statements who may want a complete set of financial statements for each segment and the costs to preparers who may prefer not to disclose any segment information. Statement 14 required disclosure of internal and external revenues; profit or loss; depreciation, depletion, and amortization expense; and unusual items as defined in APB Opinion No. 30, *Reporting the Results of Operations—Reporting the Effects of Disposal of a Segment of a Business, and Extraordinary, Unusual and Infrequently Occurring Events and Transactions,* for each segment. Statement 14

also required disclosure of total assets, equity in the net income of investees accounted for by the equity method, the amount of investment in equity method investees, and total expenditures for additions to long-lived assets. Some respondents to the Exposure Draft objected to disclosing any information that was not required by Statement 14, while others recommended disclosure of additional items that are not required by this Statement. This Statement calls for the following additional disclosures only if the items are included in the measure of segment profit or loss that is reviewed by the chief operating decision maker: significant noncash items, interest revenue, interest expense, and income tax expense.

93. Some respondents to the Exposure Draft expressed concern that the proposals would increase the sheer volume of information compared to what was required to be reported under Statement 14. The Board considers that concern to be overstated for several reasons. Although this Statement requires disclosure of more information about an individual operating segment than Statement 14 required for an industry segment, this Statement requires disclosure of information about only one type of segment—reportable operating segments—while Statement 14 required information about two types of segments—industry segments and geographic segments. Moreover, Statement 14 required that many enterprises create information solely for external reporting, while almost all of the segment information that this Statement requires is already available in management reports. The Board recognizes, however, that some enterprises may find it necessary to create the enterprise-wide information about products and services, geographic areas, and major customers required by paragraphs 36-39.

94. The Board decided to require disclosure of significant noncash items included in the measure of segment profit or loss and information about total expenditures for additions to long-lived segment assets (other than financial instruments, long-term customer relationships of a financial institution, mortgage and other servicing rights, deferred policy acquisition costs, and deferred tax assets) if that information is reported internally because it improves financial statement users' abilities to estimate cash-generating potential and cash requirements of operating segments. As an alternative, the Board considered requiring disclosure of operating cash flow for each operating segment. However, many respondents said that disclosing operating cash flow in accordance with FASB Statement No. 95, *Statement of Cash Flows,* would require that they gather and process information solely for external reporting purposes. They said that management often evaluates cash generated or required by segments in ways other than by calculating operating cash flow in accordance with Statement 95. For that reason, the Board decided not to require disclosure of cash flow by segment.

95. Disclosure of interest revenue and interest expense included in reported segment profit or loss is intended to provide information about the financing activities of a segment. The Exposure Draft proposed that an enterprise disclose gross interest revenue and gross interest expense for all segments in which reported profit or loss includes those items. Some respondents said that financial services segments generally are managed based on net interest revenue, or the "spread," and that management looks only to that data in its decision-making process. Therefore those segments should be required to disclose only the net amount and not both gross interest revenue and expense. Those respondents noted that requiring disclosure of both gross amounts would be analogous to requiring nonfinancial services segments to disclose both sales and cost of sales. The Board decided that segments that derive a majority of revenue from interest should be permitted to disclose net interest revenue instead of gross interest revenue and gross interest expense if management finds that amount to be more relevant in managing the segment. Information about interest is most important if a single segment comprises a mix of financial and nonfinancial operations. If a segment is primarily a financial operation, interest revenue probably constitutes most of segment revenues and interest expense will constitute most of the difference between reported segment revenues and reported segment profit or loss. If the segment has no financial operations or only immaterial financial operations, no information about interest is required.

96. The Board decided not to require the disclosure of segment liabilities. The Exposure Draft proposed that an enterprise disclose segment liabilities because the Board believed that liabilities are an important disclosure for understanding the financing activities of a segment. The Board also noted that the requirement in FASB Statement No. 94, *Consolidation of All Majority-Owned Subsidiaries,* to disclose assets, liabilities, and profit or loss about previously unconsolidated subsidiaries was continued from APB Opinion No. 18, *The Equity Method of Accounting for Investments in Common Stock,* pending completion of the project on disaggregated disclosures.

However, in commenting on the disclosures that should be required by this Statement, many respondents said that liabilities are incurred centrally and that enterprises often do not allocate those amounts to segments. The Board concluded that the value of information about segment liabilities in assessing the performance of the segments of an enterprise was limited.

97. The Board decided not to require disclosure of research and development expense included in the measure of segment profit or loss. The Exposure Draft would have required that disclosure to provide financial statement users with information about the operating segments in which an enterprise is focusing its product development efforts. Disclosure of research and development expense was requested by a number of financial statement users and was specifically requested in both the report of the AICPA's Special Committee and the AIMR's 1993 position paper. However, respondents said that disclosing research and development expense by segment may result in competitive harm by providing competitors with early insight into the strategic plans of an enterprise. Other respondents observed that research and development is only one of a number of items that indicate where an enterprise is focusing its efforts and that it is much more significant in some enterprises than in others. For example, costs of employee training and advertising were cited as items that often are more important to some enterprises than research and development, calling into question the relevance of disclosing only research and development expense. Additionally, many respondents said that research and development expense often is incurred centrally and not allocated to segments. The Board therefore decided not to require the disclosure of research and development expense by segment.

Interim Period Information

98. This Statement requires disclosure of limited segment information in condensed financial statements that are included in quarterly reports to shareholders, as was proposed in the Exposure Draft. Statement 14 did not apply to those condensed financial statements because of the expense and the time required for producing segment information under Statement 14. A few respondents to the Exposure Draft said that reporting segment information in interim financial statements would be unnecessarily burdensome. However, users contended that, to be timely, segment information is needed more often than annually and that the difficulties of preparing it

on an interim basis could be overcome by an approach like the one in this Statement. Managers of many enterprises agree and have voluntarily provided segment information for interim periods.

99. The Board decided that the condensed financial statements in interim reports issued to shareholders should include disclosure of segment revenues from external customers, intersegment revenues, a measure of segment profit or loss, material changes in segment assets, differences in the basis of segmentation or the way segment profit or loss was measured in the previous annual period, and a reconciliation to the enterprise's total profit or loss. That decision is a compromise between the needs of users who want the same segment information for interim periods as that required in annual financial statements and the costs to preparers who must report the information. Users will have some key information on a timely basis. Enterprises should not incur significant incremental costs to provide the information because it is based on information that is used internally and therefore already available.

Restatement of Previously Reported Information

100. The Board decided to require restatement of previously reported segment information following a change in the composition of an enterprise's segments unless it is impracticable to do so. Changes in the composition of segments interrupt trends, and trend analysis is important to users of financial statements. Some financial statement issuers have said that their policy is to restate one or more prior years for internal trend analysis. Many reorganizations result in discrete profit centers' being reassigned from one segment to another and lead to relatively simple restatements. However, if an enterprise undergoes a fundamental reorganization, restatement may be very difficult and expensive. The Board concluded that in those situations restatement may be impracticable and, therefore, should not be required. However, if an enterprise does not restate its segment information, the enterprise is required to provide current-period segment information on both the old and new bases of segmentation in the year in which the change occurs unless it is impracticable to do so.

Enterprise-Wide Disclosures

101. Paragraphs 36-39 require disclosure of information about an enterprise's products and services, geographic areas, and major customers, regardless of the enterprise's organization. The required disclosures need be provided only if they are not included

as part of the disclosures about segments. The Exposure Draft proposed requiring additional disclosures about products and services and geographic areas *by segment*. Many respondents said that that proposal would have resulted in disclosure of excessive amounts of information. Some enterprises providing a variety of products and services throughout many countries, for example, would have been required to present a large quantity of information that would have been time-consuming to prepare and of questionable benefit to most financial statement users. The Board decided that additional disclosures provided on an enterprise-wide basis rather than on a segment basis would be appropriate and not unduly burdensome. The Board also agreed that those enterprise-wide disclosures are appropriate for all enterprises including those that have a single operating segment if the enterprise offers a range of products and services, derives revenues from customers in more than one country, or both.

102. Based on reviews of published information about public enterprises, discussions with constituents, and a field test of the Exposure Draft, the Board believes that most enterprises are organized by products and services or by geography and will report one or both of those types of information in their reportable operating segment disclosures. However, some enterprises will be required by paragraphs 36-39 to report additional information because the enterprise-wide disclosures are required for all enterprises, even those that have a single reportable segment.

Information about Products and Services

103. This Statement requires that enterprises report revenues from external customers for each product and service or each group of similar products and services for the enterprise as a whole. Analysts said that an analysis of trends in revenues from products and services is important in assessing both past performance and prospects for future growth. Those trends can be compared to benchmarks such as industry statistics or information reported by competitors. Information about the assets that are used to produce specific products and deliver specific services also might be useful. However, in many enterprises, assets are not dedicated to specific products and services and reporting assets by products and services would require arbitrary allocations.

Information about Geographic Areas

104. This Statement requires disclosure of information about both revenues and assets by geographic area. Analysts said that information about revenues from customers in different geographic areas assists them in understanding concentrations of risks due to negative changes in economic conditions and prospects for growth due to positive economic changes. They said that information about assets located in different areas assists them in understanding concentrations of risks (for example, political risks such as expropriation).

105. Statement 14 requires disclosure of geographic information by geographic region, whereas this Statement requires disclosure of individually material countries as well as information for the enterprise's country of domicile and all foreign countries in the aggregate. This Statement's approach has two significant benefits. First, it will reduce the burden on preparers of financial statements because most enterprises are likely to have material operations in only a few countries or perhaps only in their country of domicile. Second, and more important, it will provide information that is more useful in assessing the impact of concentrations of risk. Information disclosed by country is more useful because it is easier to interpret. Countries in contiguous areas often experience different rates of growth and other differences in economic conditions. Under the requirements of Statement 14, enterprises often reported information about broad geographic areas that included groupings such as Europe, Africa, and the Middle East. Analysts and others have questioned the usefulness of that type of broad disclosure.

106. Respondents to the Exposure Draft questioned how revenues should be allocated to individual countries. For example, guidance was requested for situations in which products are shipped to one location but the customer resides in another location. The Board decided to provide flexibility concerning the basis on which enterprises attribute revenues to individual countries rather than requiring that revenues be attributed to countries according to the location of customers. The Board also decided to require that enterprises disclose the basis they have adopted for attributing revenues to countries to permit financial statement users to understand the geographic information provided.

107. As a result of its decision to require geographic information on an enterprise-wide basis, the Board decided not to require disclosure of capital expenditures on certain long-lived assets by geographic area. Such information on an enterprise-wide basis is not necessarily helpful in forecasting future cash flows of operating segments.

Information about Major Customers

108. The Board decided to retain the requirement in Statement 14, as amended by FASB Statement No. 30, *Disclosure of Information about Major Customers,* to report information about major customers because major customers of an enterprise represent a significant concentration of risk. The 10 percent threshold is arbitrary; however, it has been accepted practice since Statement 14 was issued, and few have suggested changing it.

Competitive Harm

109. A number of respondents to the Exposure Draft noted the potential for competitive harm as a result of disclosing segment information in accordance with this Statement. The Board considered adopting special provisions to reduce the potential for competitive harm from certain segment information but decided against it. In the Invitation to Comment, the Tentative Conclusions, and the Exposure Draft, the Board asked constituents for specific illustrations of competitive harm that has resulted from disclosing segment information. Some respondents said that public enterprises may be at a disadvantage to nonpublic enterprises or foreign competitors that do not have to disclose segment information. Other respondents suggested that information about narrowly defined segments may put an enterprise at a disadvantage in price negotiations with customers or in competitive bid situations.

110. Some respondents said that if a competitive disadvantage exists, it is a consequence of an obligation that enterprises have accepted to gain greater access to capital markets, which gives them certain advantages over nonpublic enterprises and many foreign enterprises. Other respondents said that enterprises are not likely to suffer competitive harm because most competitors have other sources of more detailed information about an enterprise than that disclosed in the financial statements. In addition, the information that is required to be disclosed about an operating segment is no more detailed or specific than the information typically provided by a smaller enterprise with a single operation.

111. The Board was sympathetic to specific concerns raised by certain constituents; however, it decided that a competitive-harm exemption was inappropriate because it would provide a means for broad noncompliance with this Statement. Some form of relief for single-product or single-service segments

was explored; however, there are many enterprises that produce a single product or a single service that are required to issue general-purpose financial statements. Those statements would include the same information that would be reported by single-product or single-service segments of an enterprise. The Board concluded that it was not necessary to provide an exemption for single-product or single-service segments because enterprises that produce a single product or service that are required to issue general-purpose financial statements have that same exposure to competitive harm. The Board noted that concerns about competitive harm were addressed to the extent feasible by four changes made during redeliberations: (a) modifying the aggregation criteria, (b) adding quantitative materiality thresholds for identifying reportable segments, (c) eliminating the requirements to disclose research and development expense and liabilities by segment, and (d) changing the second-level disclosure requirements about products and services and geography from a segment basis to an enterprise-wide basis.

Cost-Benefit Considerations

112. One of the precepts of the Board's mission is to promulgate standards only if the expected benefits of the resulting information exceed the perceived costs. The Board strives to determine that a proposed standard will fill a significant need and that the costs incurred to satisfy that need, as compared with other alternatives, are justified in relation to the overall benefits of the resulting information. The Board concluded that the benefits that will result from this Statement will exceed the related costs.

113. The Board believes that the primary benefits of this Statement are that enterprises will report segment information in interim financial reports, some enterprises will report a greater number of segments, most enterprises will report more items of information about each segment, enterprises will report segments that correspond to internal management reports, and enterprises will report segment information that will be more consistent with other parts of their annual reports.

114. This Statement will reduce the cost of providing disaggregated information for many enterprises. Statement 14 required that enterprises define segments by both industry and by geographical area, ways that often did not match the way that information was used internally. Even if the reported segments aligned with the internal organization, the information required was often created solely for

external reporting because Statement 14 required certain allocations of costs, prohibited other cost allocations, and required allocations of assets to segments. This Statement requires that information about operating segments be provided on the same basis that it is used internally. The Board believes that most of the enterprise-wide disclosures in this Statement about products and services, geography, and major customers typically are provided in current financial statements or can be prepared with minimal incremental cost.

Applicability to Nonpublic Enterprises and Not-for-Profit Organizations

115. The Board decided to continue to exempt nonpublic enterprises from the requirement to report segment information. Few users of nonpublic enterprises' financial statements have requested that the Board require that those enterprises provide segment information.

116. At the time the Board began considering improvements to disclosures about segment information, FASB Statement No. 117, *Financial Statements of Not-for-Profit Organizations,* had not been issued and there were no effective standards for consolidated financial statements of not-for-profit organizations. Most not-for-profit organizations provided financial information for each of their funds, which is a form of disaggregated information. The situation in Canada was similar. Thus, when the two boards agreed to pursue a joint project, they decided to limit the scope to public business enterprises.

117. The Board provided for a limited form of disaggregated information in paragraph 26 of Statement 117, which requires disclosure of expense by functional classification. However, the Board acknowledges that the application of that Statement may increase the need for disaggregated information about not-for-profit organizations. A final Statement expected to result from the FASB Exposure Draft, *Consolidated Financial Statements: Policy and Procedures,* also may increase that need by requiring aggregation of information about more entities in the financial statements of not-for-profit organizations.

118. The general approach of providing information based on the structure of an enterprise's internal organization may be appropriate for not-for-profit organizations. However, the Board decided not to add not-for-profit organizations to the scope of this Statement. Users of financial statements of not-for-profit organizations have not urged the Board to include those organizations, perhaps because they have not yet seen the effects of Statement 117 and the Exposure Draft on consolidations. Furthermore, the term *not-for-profit organizations* applies to a wide variety of entities, some of which are similar to business enterprises and some of which are very different. There are likely to be unique characteristics of some of those entities or special user needs that require special provisions, which the Board has not studied. In addition, the AcSB has recently adopted standards for reporting by not-for-profit organizations that are different from Statement 117. In the interest of completing this joint project in a timely manner, the Board decided not to undertake the research and deliberations that would be necessary to adapt the requirements of this Statement to not-for-profit organizations at this time. Few respondents to the Exposure Draft disagreed with the Board's position.

Effective Date and Transition

119. The Board concluded that this Statement should be effective for financial statements issued for fiscal years beginning after December 15, 1997. In developing the Exposure Draft, the Board had decided on an effective date of December 15, 1996. The Board believed that that time frame was reasonable because almost all of the information that this Statement requires is generated by systems already in place within an enterprise and a final Statement was expected to be issued before the end of 1996. However, respondents said that some enterprises may need more time to comply with the requirements of this Statement than would have been provided under the Exposure Draft.

120. The Board also decided not to require that segment information be reported in financial statements for interim periods in the initial year of application. Some of the information that is required to be reported for interim periods is based on information that would have been reported in the most recent annual financial statements. Without a full set of segment information to use as a comparison and to provide an understanding of the basis on which it is provided, interim information would not be as meaningful.

Appendix B

ILLUSTRATIVE GUIDANCE

121. This appendix provides specific examples that illustrate the disclosures that are required by this Statement and provides a diagram for identifying reportable operating segments. The formats in the illustrations are not requirements. The Board encourages a format that provides the information in the most understandable manner in the specific circumstances. The following illustrations are for a single hypothetical enterprise referred to as Diversified Company.

122. The following is an illustration of the disclosure of descriptive information about an enterprise's reportable segments. (References to paragraphs in which the relevant requirements appear are given in parentheses.)

Description of the types of products and services from which each reportable segment derives its revenues (paragraph 26(b))

Diversified Company has five reportable segments: auto parts, motor vessels, software, electronics, and finance. The auto parts segment produces replacement parts for sale to auto parts retailers. The motor vessels segment produces small motor vessels to serve the offshore oil industry and similar businesses. The software segment produces application software for sale to computer manufacturers and retailers. The electronics segment produces integrated circuits and related products for sale to computer manufacturers. The finance segment is responsible for portions of the company's financial operations including financing customer purchases of products from other segments and real estate lending operations in several states.

Measurement of segment profit or loss and segment assets (paragraph 31)

The accounting policies of the segments are the same as those described in the summary of significant accounting policies except that pension expense for each segment is recognized and measured on the basis of cash payments to the pension plan. Diversified Company evaluates performance based on profit or loss from operations before income taxes not including nonrecurring gains and losses and foreign exchange gains and losses.

Diversified Company accounts for intersegment sales and transfers as if the sales or transfers were to third parties, that is, at current market prices.

Factors management used to identify the enterprise's reportable segments (paragraph 26(a))

Diversified Company's reportable segments are strategic business units that offer different products and services. They are managed separately because each business requires different technology and marketing strategies. Most of the businesses were acquired as a unit, and the management at the time of the acquisition was retained.

123. The following table illustrates a suggested format for presenting information about reported segment profit or loss and segment assets (paragraphs 27 and 28). The same type of information is required for each year for which an income statement is presented. Diversified Company does not allocate income taxes or unusual items to segments. In addition, not all segments have significant noncash items other than depreciation and amortization in reported profit or loss. The amounts in this illustration are assumed to be the amounts in reports used by the chief operating decision maker.

	Auto Parts	Motor Vessels	Software	Electronics	Finance	All Other	Totals
Revenues from external customers	$3,000	$5,000	$9,500	$12,000	$ 5,000	$1,000[a]	$35,500
Intersegment revenues	—	—	3,000	1,500	—	—	4,500
Interest revenue	450	800	1,000	1,500	—	—	3,750
Interest expense	350	600	700	1,100	—	—	2,750
Net interest revenue[b]	—	—	—	—	1,000	—	1,000
Depreciation and amortization	200	100	50	1,500	1,100	—	2,950
Segment profit	200	70	900	2,300	500	100	4,070
Other significant noncash items:							
Cost in excess of billings on long-term contracts	—	200	—	—	—	—	200
Segment assets	2,000	5,000	3,000	12,000	57,000	2,000	81,000
Expenditures for segment assets	300	700	500	800	600	—	2,900

[a]Revenue from segments below the quantitative thresholds are attributable to four operating segments of Diversified Company. Those segments include a small real estate business, an electronics equipment rental business, a software consulting practice, and a warehouse leasing operation. None of those segments has ever met any of the quantitative thresholds for determining reportable segments.

[b]The finance segment derives a majority of its revenue from interest. In addition, management primarily relies on net interest revenue, not the gross revenue and expense amounts, in managing that segment. Therefore, as permitted by paragraph 27, only the net amount is disclosed.

124. The following are illustrations of reconciliations of reportable segment revenues, profit or loss, and assets, to the enterprise's consolidated totals (paragraphs 32(a), 32(b), and 32(c)). Reconciliations also are required to be shown for every other significant item of information disclosed (paragraph 32(d)). For example, if Diversified Company disclosed segment liabilities, they are required to be reconciled to total consolidated liabilities. The enterprise's financial statements are assumed not to include discontinued operations or the cumulative effect of a change in accounting principles.

As discussed in the illustration in paragraph 122, the enterprise recognizes and measures pension expense of its segments based on cash payments to the pension plan, and it does not allocate certain items to its segments.

Revenues

Total revenues for reportable segments	$39,000
Other revenues	1,000
Elimination of intersegment revenues	(4,500)
Total consolidated revenues	$35,500

Profit or Loss

Total profit or loss for reportable segments	$3,970
Other profit or loss	100
Elimination of intersegment profits	(500)
Unallocated amounts:	
Litigation settlement received	500
Other corporate expenses	(750)
Adjustment to pension expense in consolidation	(250)
Income before income taxes and extraordinary items	$3,070

Assets

Total assets for reportable segments	$79,000
Other assets	2,000
Elimination of receivables from corporate headquarters	(1,000)
Goodwill not allocated to segments	4,000
Other unallocated amounts	1,000
Consolidated total	$85,000

Other Significant Items

	Segment Totals	Adjustments	Consolidated Totals
Interest revenue	$3,750	$ 75	$3,825
Interest expense	2,750	(50)	2,700
Net interest revenue (finance segment only)	1,000	—	1,000
Expenditures for assets	2,900	1,000	3,900
Depreciation and amortization	2,950	—	2,950
Cost in excess of billing on long-term contracts	200	—	200

The reconciling item to adjust expenditures for assets is the amount of expenses incurred for the corporate headquarters building, which is not included in segment information. None of the other adjustments are significant.

Disclosures about Segments of an Enterprise   **FAS131**
and Related Information

125. The following illustrates the geographic information required by paragraph 38. (Because Diversified Company's segments are based on differences in products and services, no additional disclosures of revenue information about products and services are required (paragraph 37)).

Geographic Information

	Revenues[a]	Long-Lived Assets
United States	$19,000	$11,000
Canada	4,200	—
Taiwan	3,400	6,500
Japan	2,900	3,500
Other foreign countries	6,000	3,000
Total	$35,500	$24,000

[a]Revenues are attributed to countries based on location of customer.

126. The following is an illustration of the information about major customers required by paragraph 39. Neither the identity of the customer nor the amount of revenues for each operating segment is required.

Revenues from one customer of Diversified Company's software and electronics segments represents approximately $5,000 of the company's consolidated revenues.

Diagram for Identifying Reportable Operating Segments

127. The following diagram illustrates how to apply the main provisions for identifying reportable operating segments as defined in this Statement. The diagram is a visual supplement to the written standards section. It should not be interpreted to alter any requirements of this Statement nor should it be considered a substitute for the requirements.

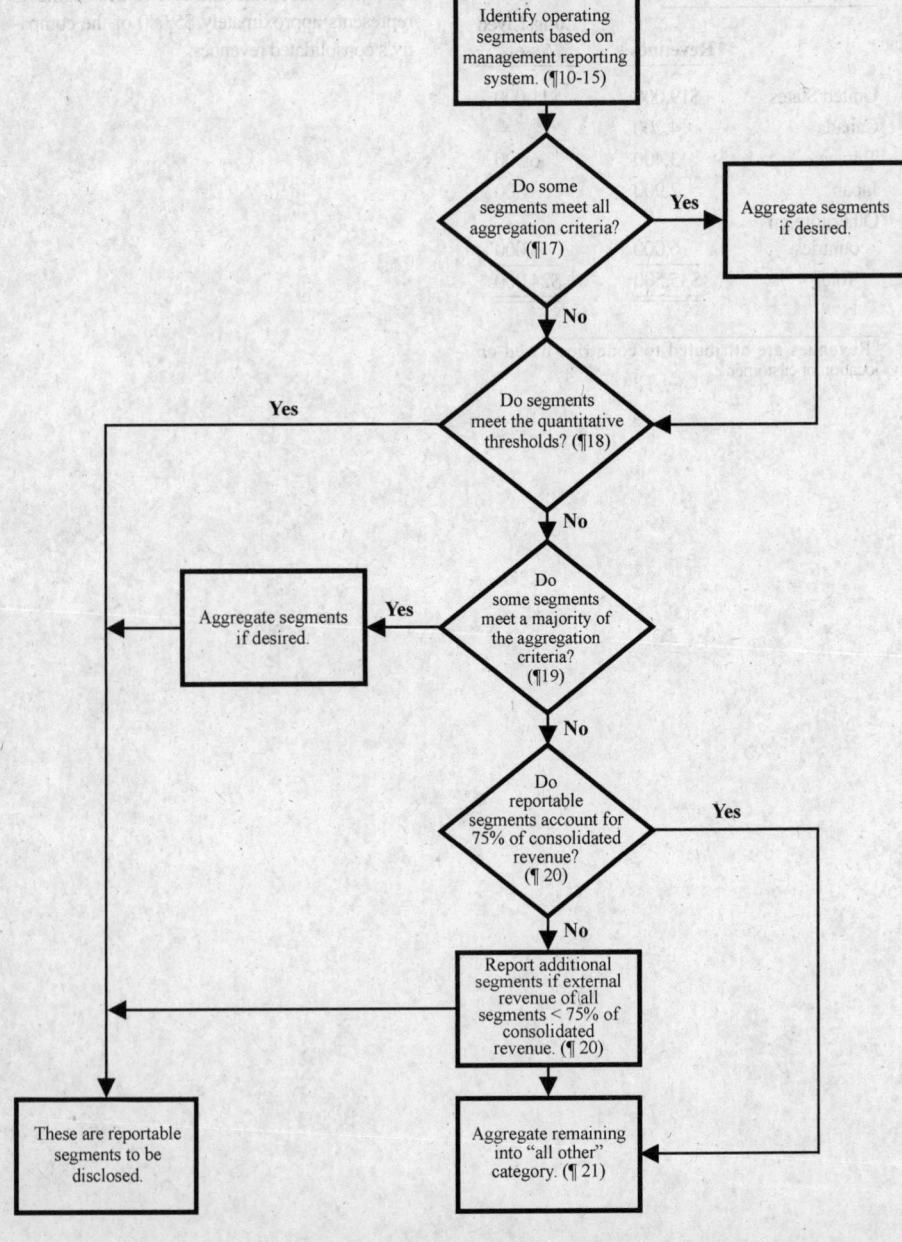

Appendix C

**AMENDMENTS TO EXISTING
PRONOUNCEMENTS**

128. This Statement supersedes the following
pronouncements:

a. FASB Statement No. 14, *Financial Reporting for
Segments of a Business Enterprise*
b. FASB Statement No. 18, *Financial Reporting for
Segments of a Business Enterprise—Interim Financial Statements*
c. FASB Statement No. 21, *Suspension of the Reporting of Earnings per Share and Segment Information by Nonpublic Enterprises*
d. FASB Statement No. 24, *Reporting Segment
Information in Financial Statements That Are
Presented in Another Enterprise's Financial
Report*
e. FASB Statement No. 30, *Disclosure of Information about Major Customers*
f. FASB Technical Bulletin No. 79-8, *Applicability
of FASB Statements 21 and 33 to Certain Brokers
and Dealers in Securities.*

129. ARB No. 43, Chapter 12, "Foreign Operations
and Foreign Exchange," is amended as follows:

a. The following is added at the end of paragraph 5:

FASB Statement No. 131, *Disclosures about
Segments of an Enterprise and Related Information,* discusses the requirements for reporting
revenues from foreign operations.

b. Paragraph 6 is replaced by the following:

Statement 131 discusses the requirements for
reporting assets located outside the United
States.

130. Paragraph 19 of ARB No. 51, *Consolidated
Financial Statements,* as amended by FASB State-
ment No. 94, *Consolidation of All Majority-Owned
Subsidiaries,* is deleted.

131. The following is added to the listing in paragraph 30 of APB Opinion No. 28, *Interim Financial
Reporting:*

i. The following information about reportable
operating segments determined according to
the provisions of FASB Statement No. 131,
*Disclosures about Segments of an Enterprise
and Related Information,* including provisions
related to restatement of segment information
in previously issued financial statements:

(1) Revenues from external customers
(2) Intersegment revenues
(3) A measure of segment profit or loss
(4) Total assets for which there has been a
material change from the amount disclosed in the last annual report
(5) A description of differences from the last
annual report in the basis of segmentation
or in the measurement of segment profit
or loss
(6) A reconciliation of the total of the reportable segments' measures of profit or loss
to the enterprise's consolidated income
before income taxes, extraordinary items,
discontinued operations, and the cumulative effect of changes in accounting
principles.* However, if, for example,
an enterprise allocates items such as income taxes and extraordinary items to
segments, the enterprise may choose to
reconcile the total of the segments' measures of profit or loss to consolidated income after those items. Significant reconciling items shall be separately identified
and described in that reconciliation.

---

*After the effective date of FASB Statement No. 154, *Ac-
counting Changes and Error Corrections,* voluntary
changes in accounting principle will no longer be reported
via a cumulative-effect adjustment through the income
statement of the period of change.

132. In footnote 3 to paragraph 5 of FASB Statement No. 51, *Financial Reporting by Cable Television Companies,* the reference to Statement 14 is replaced by a reference to FASB Statement No. 131, *Disclosures about Segments of an Enterprise and Related Information.*

133. FASB Statement No. 69, *Disclosures about Oil and Gas Producing Activities,* is amended as follows:

a. Footnote 4 to paragraph 8(a) is replaced by the following:

> For purposes of this Statement, an industry segment is a component of an enterprise engaged in providing a product or service or a group of related products or services primarily to external customers (that is, customers outside the enterprise) for a profit.

b. Paragraph 8(c) is replaced by the following:

> The identifiable assets of oil- and gas-producing activities (tangible and intangible enterprise assets that are used by oil- and gas-producing activities, including an allocated portion of assets used jointly with other operations) are 10 percent or more of the assets of the enterprise, excluding assets used exclusively for general corporate purposes.

c. The second sentence of footnote 7 to paragraph 24 is replaced by the following:

> If oil- and gas-producing activities constitute an operating segment, as discussed in paragraphs 10-24 of FASB Statement No. 131,

Disclosures about Segments of an Enterprise and Related Information, information about the results of operations required by paragraphs 24–29 of this Statement may be included with segment information disclosed elsewhere in the financial report.

134. Paragraph 14 of Statement 94 is deleted.

135. FASB Technical Bulletin No. 79-4, *Segment Reporting of Puerto Rican Operations,* is amended as follows:

a. In paragraph 1, *paragraphs 31-38 of Statement 14* is replaced by *paragraph 38 of FASB Statement No. 131, Disclosures about Segments of an Enterprise and Related Information.*

b. Paragraph 2 is replaced by the following:

> Paragraph 38 of Statement 131 requires that certain enterprises disclose information about an enterprise's revenues from customers outside their country of domicile and assets located outside their country of domicile.

c. In paragraph 3, the first sentence and the phrase *Based on those guidelines* in the second sentence are deleted.

136. In FASB Technical Bulletin No. 79-5, *Meaning of the Term "Customer" as It Applies to Health Care Facilities under FASB Statement No. 14,* references to paragraph 39 of Statement 14 are replaced by references to paragraph 39 of FASB Statement No. 131, *Disclosures about Segments of an Enterprise and Related Information.*

Statement of Financial Accounting Standards No. 132
Employers' Disclosures about Pensions and Other Postretirement Benefits

an amendment of FASB Statements No. 87, 88, and 106

STATUS

Issued: February 1998

Effective Date: For fiscal years beginning after December 15, 1997

Affects: Replaces FAS 87, paragraphs 54, 56, 65, and 69
Replaces FAS 87, Illustration 6 (paragraph 261)
Replaces FAS 88, paragraph 17
Replaces FAS 106, paragraphs 74, 77, 78, 82, and 106
Replaces FAS 106, paragraphs 479 through 483

Affected by: Paragraphs 12(b) and 63 amended by FAS 135, paragraph 4(y)
Paragraphs 12(d) and 14(e) deleted by FAS 135, paragraph 4(y)
Superseded by FAS 132(R), paragraph 14

Statement of Financial Accounting Standards No. 132 (revised 2003)
Employers' Disclosures about Pensions and Other Postretirement Benefits

an amendment of FASB Statements No. 87, 88, and 106

STATUS

Issued: December 2003

Effective Date: For domestic plans, for all new provisions except for estimated future benefit payments disclosures, effective for fiscal years ending after December 15, 2003; for foreign plans and nonpublic entities, for all new provisions, and for estimated future benefit payments disclosures for all entities, effective for fiscal years ending after June 15, 2004; and for interim-period disclosures, effective for quarters beginning after December 15, 2003

Affects: Amends APB 28, paragraph 30
Effectively amends FAS 87, paragraphs 49 and 66
Replaces FAS 87, paragraphs 54, 56, 65, and 69
Replaces FAS 87, Illustration 6 (paragraph 261)
Replaces FAS 88, paragraph 17
Effectively amends FAS 106, paragraphs 65, 107, 417, and 461
Replaces FAS 106, paragraphs 74, 77, 78, 82, and 106
Replaces FAS 106, paragraphs 479 through 483
Supersedes FAS 132

Affected by: Paragraphs 3, 5(c), 5(h), 5(o), 6, 8(g), 9, and C3 amended by FAS 158, paragraphs E1(a),
E1(c), E1(d), E1(h), E1(k), E1(m), E1(s), and E1(u), respectively
Paragraph 5 amended by FAS 158, paragraphs E1(b), E1(f), E1(i), and E1(j)
Paragraphs 5(i) and 8(h) replaced by FAS 158, paragraphs E1(e) and E1(n), respectively
Paragraphs 5(k) and 8(j) deleted by FAS 158, paragraphs E1(g) and E1(p), respectively
Paragraph 8 amended by FAS 158, paragraphs E1(l), E1(o), E1(q), and E1(r)
Paragraphs 10A through 10D added by FAS 158, paragraph E1(t)
Paragraph E1 amended by FSP FAS 126-1, paragraph A7

Issues Discussed by FASB Emerging Issues Task Force (EITF)

Affects: No EITF Issues

Interpreted by: No EITF Issues

Related Issues: EITF Issues No. 92-12, 92-13, and 03-2

SUMMARY

This Statement revises employers' disclosures about pension plans and other postretirement benefit plans. It does not change the measurement or recognition of those plans required by FASB Statements No. 87, *Employers' Accounting for Pensions,* No. 88, *Employers' Accounting for Settlements and Curtailments of Defined Benefit Pension Plans and for Termination Benefits,* and No. 106, *Employers' Accounting for Postretirement Benefits Other Than Pensions.* This Statement retains the disclosure requirements contained in FASB Statement No. 132, *Employers' Disclosures about Pensions and Other Postretirement Benefits,* which it replaces. It requires additional disclosures to those in the original Statement 132 about the assets, obligations, cash flows, and net periodic benefit cost of defined benefit pension plans and other defined benefit postretirement plans. The required information should be provided separately for pension plans and for other postretirement benefit plans.

Reasons for Issuing This Statement

This Statement was developed in response to concerns expressed by users of financial statements about their need for more information about pension plan assets, obligations, benefit payments, contributions, and net benefit cost. Users of financial statements cited the significance of pensions for many entities and the need for more information about economic resources and obligations related to pension plans as reasons for requesting this additional information. In light of certain similarities between defined benefit pension arrangements and arrangements for other postretirement benefits, this Statement requires similar disclosures about postretirement benefits other than pensions.

Differences between This Statement and Statement 132

This Statement retains the disclosures required by Statement 132, which standardized the disclosure requirements for pensions and other postretirement benefits to the extent practicable and required additional information on changes in the benefit obligations and fair values of plan assets. Additional disclosures have been added in response to concerns expressed by users of financial statements; those disclosures include information describing the types of plan assets, investment strategy, measurement date(s), plan obligations, cash flows, and components of net periodic benefit cost recognized during interim periods. This Statement retains reduced disclosure requirements for nonpublic entities from Statement 132, and it includes reduced disclosures for certain of the new requirements.

How the Changes in This Statement Improve Financial Reporting and How the Conclusions in This Statement Relate to the Conceptual Framework

FASB Concepts Statement No. 1, *Objectives of Financial Reporting by Business Enterprises,* states that financial reporting should provide information about economic resources of an enterprise, claims to those resources, and the effects of transactions, events, and circumstances that change its resources and claims to those resources. This Statement, including the manner of presentation illustrated in Appendix C, results in more complete information about pension and other postretirement benefit plan assets, obligations, cash flows, and net cost and, thereby, assists users of financial statements in assessing the market risk of plan assets, the amount and timing of cash flows, and reported earnings.

FASB Concepts Statement No. 2, *Qualitative Characteristics of Accounting Information,* identifies relevance and reliability as the characteristics of financial information that make it useful. This Statement enhances disclosures of relevant accounting information by providing more information about the plan assets available to finance benefit payments, the obligations to pay benefits, and an entity's obligation to fund the plan, thus improving the information's predictive value. Reliability of accounting information will be improved by providing more complete and precise information about postretirement benefit resources and obligations.

Benefits and Costs

Entities that prepare financial statements in conformity with generally accepted accounting principles already compile and aggregate information about pension plans and other postretirement benefit plans, including information about plan assets, benefit obligations, and net cost. Information about equity securities, debt securities, real estate, and other assets is likely to be available from asset management records. Reporting of information about pension plans and other postretirement benefit plans required by this Statement may require some additional effort and cost, including amounts that may be paid to entities' auditors and actuaries; however, that information is already essential in complying with Statements 87, 106, and 132 and therefore should be available to, and understood by, preparers of financial statements. Additional costs to compile, analyze, and audit the additional disclosures required by this Statement are believed to be modest in relation to the benefits to be derived by users of financial statements.

Effective Date and Transition

The provisions of Statement 132 remain in effect until the provisions of this Statement are adopted. Except as noted below, this Statement is effective for financial statements with fiscal years ending after December 15, 2003. The interim-period disclosures required by this Statement are effective for interim periods beginning after December 15, 2003.

Disclosure of information about foreign plans required by paragraphs 5(d), 5(e), 5(g), and 5(k) of this Statement is effective for fiscal years ending after June 15, 2004.

Disclosure of estimated future benefit payments required by paragraph 5(f) of this Statement is effective for fiscal years ending after June 15, 2004.

Disclosure of information for nonpublic entities required by paragraphs 8(c)–(f) and 8(j) of this Statement is effective for fiscal years ending after June 15, 2004.

Until this Statement is fully adopted, financial statements that exclude foreign plans from (a) the actual allocation of assets, (b) the description of investment strategies, (c) the basis used to determine the expected long-term rate-of-return-on-assets assumption, or (d) the amount of accumulated benefit obligation should include, separately for domestic plans, the total fair value of plan assets as of the measurement date(s) used for the latest statement of financial position presented and the overall expected long-term rate of return on assets for the latest period for which a statement of income is presented.

The disclosures for earlier annual periods presented for comparative purposes should be restated for (a) the percentages of each major category of plan assets held, (b) the accumulated benefit obligation, and (c) the assumptions used in the accounting for the plans. The disclosures for earlier interim periods presented for comparative purposes should be restated for the components of net benefit cost. However, if obtaining this information relating to earlier periods is not practicable, the notes to the financial statements should include all available information and identify the information not available.

Early application of the disclosure provisions of this Statement is encouraged.

Statement of Financial Accounting Standards No. 132 (revised 2003)

Employers' Disclosures about Pensions and Other Postretirement Benefits

an amendment of FASB Statements No. 87, 88, and 106

CONTENTS

INTRODUCTION

1. The Board added a project on pension disclosures to its technical agenda in March 2003 in response to concerns about insufficient information in employers' financial statements about their defined benefit pension plan assets, obligations, cash flows, and net pension costs.[1] The project's objective was to (a) improve the content and organization of annual disclosures about defined benefit pension plans, (b) determine what, if any, disclosures would be required for interim-period financial reports, and (c) determine whether the disclosures to be required for defined benefit pension plans also would be required for other postretirement benefit plans.

2. Despite extensive disclosure requirements for pension plans and other postretirement benefit plans, many users of financial statements told the Board that the information provided for defined benefit pension plans was not adequate. Users of financial statements requested additional information that would assist them in (a) evaluating plan assets and the expected long-term rate of return used in determining net pension cost, (b) evaluating the employer's obligations under pension plans and the effects of those obligations on the employer's future cash flows, and (c) estimating the potential impact of net pension cost on future net income. The Board concluded that disclosures about pensions could be improved to provide information that would better serve users' needs.

3. This Statement incorporates all of the disclosure requirements of FASB Statement No. 132, *Employers' Disclosures about Pensions and Other Postretirement Benefits*. This Statement amends APB Opinion No. 28, *Interim Financial Report-*

---

[1]The terms *net pension cost, net benefit cost, net cost,* or other similar terms include net pension income and other postretirement benefit income.

ing, to require interim-period disclosure of the components of net periodic benefit cost and, if significantly different from previously disclosed amounts, the amounts of contributions and projected contributions to fund pension plans and other postretirement benefit plans. Information required to be disclosed about pension plans should not be combined with information required to be disclosed about other postretirement benefit plans except as permitted by paragraph 12 of this Statement. Public and nonpublic entities shall provide the disclosures required in paragraphs 5–9, as applicable. Paragraphs 10A–10D describe how those requirements shall be applied to not-for-profit organizations and other entities that do not report other comprehensive income. Appendix A provides background information and the basis for the Board's conclusions in this Statement. Appendix B provides background information and the basis for the Board's conclusions as originally contained in Statement 132. Appendix C provides illustrations of the required disclosures. Appendix D provides information about the impact of this Statement on the consensuses reached on EITF Issues relating to disclosures about pension plans and other postretirement benefit plans. Appendix E provides a glossary of terms that are used in this Statement.

STANDARDS OF FINANCIAL ACCOUNTING AND REPORTING

Scope

4. This Statement replaces the disclosure requirements in FASB Statements No. 87, *Employers' Accounting for Pensions,* No. 88, *Employers' Accounting for Settlements and Curtailments of Defined Benefit Pension Plans and for Termination Benefits,* and No. 106, *Employers' Accounting for Postretirement Benefits Other Than Pensions.* This Statement retains the disclosure requirements in Statement 132 and contains additional requirements.[2] This Statement addresses disclosure only; it does not address measurement or recognition.

Disclosures about Pension Plans and Other Postretirement Benefit Plans

5. Certain terms used in this Statement, such as **projected benefit obligation,**[3] **accumulated benefit obligation, accumulated postretirement benefit obligation,** and *net pension cost,* are defined in Statements 87 and 106. An employer that sponsors one or more defined benefit pension plans or one or more other defined benefit postretirement plans shall provide the following information, separately for pension plans and other postretirement benefit plans. Amounts related to the employer's results of operations shall be disclosed for each period for which a statement of income is presented. Amounts related to the employer's statement of financial position shall be disclosed as of the date of each statement of financial position presented.

a.　A reconciliation of beginning and ending balances of the benefit obligation[4] showing separately, if applicable, the effects during the period attributable to each of the following: service cost, interest cost, contributions by plan participants, actuarial gains and losses, foreign currency exchange rate changes,[5] benefits paid, plan amendments, business combinations, divestitures, curtailments, settlements, and special termination benefits.

b.　A reconciliation of beginning and ending balances of the fair value of plan assets showing separately, if applicable, the effects during the period attributable to each of the following: actual return on plan assets, foreign currency exchange rate changes,[6] contributions by the employer, contributions by plan participants, benefits paid, business combinations, divestitures, and settlements.

c.　The funded status of the plans and the amounts recognized in the statement of financial position, showing separately the assets and current and noncurrent liabilities recognized.

---

[2]Disclosures required by paragraphs 5–11 of Statement 132 are carried forward and included with the new disclosure requirements in paragraphs 5–8 and 11–13 of this Statement.

[3]Terms defined in Appendix E are set in **boldface type** the first time they appear.

[4]For defined benefit pension plans, the benefit obligation is the projected benefit obligation. For defined benefit postretirement plans, the benefit obligation is the accumulated postretirement benefit obligation.

[5]The effects of foreign currency exchange rate changes that are to be disclosed are those applicable to plans of a foreign operation whose functional currency is not the reporting currency pursuant to FASB Statement No. 52, *Foreign Currency Translation.*

[6]Refer to footnote 5.

d. Information about plan assets:

(1) For each major category of plan assets, which shall include, but is not limited to, **equity securities, debt securities,** real estate, and all other assets, the percentage of the fair value of total plan assets held as of the measurement date used for each statement of financial position presented.

(2) A narrative description of investment policies and strategies, including target allocation percentages or range of percentages for each major category of plan assets presented on a weighted-average basis as of the measurement date(s) of the latest statement of financial position presented, if applicable, and other factors that are pertinent to an understanding of the policies or strategies such as investment goals, risk management practices, permitted and prohibited investments including the use of derivatives, diversification, and the relationship between plan assets and benefit obligations.

(3) A narrative description of the basis used to determine the overall expected long-term rate-of-return-on-assets assumption, such as the general approach used, the extent to which the overall rate-of-return-on-assets assumption was based on historical returns, the extent to which adjustments were made to those historical returns in order to reflect expectations of future returns, and how those adjustments were determined.

(4) Disclosure of additional asset categories and additional information about specific assets within a category is encouraged if that information is expected to be useful in understanding the risks associated with each asset category and the overall expected long-term rate of return on assets.

e. For defined benefit pension plans, the accumulated benefit obligation.

f. The benefits (as of the date of the latest statement of financial position presented) expected to be paid in each of the next five fiscal years, and in the aggregate for the five fiscal years thereafter. The expected benefits should be estimated based on the same assumptions used to measure the company's benefit obligation at the end of the year and should include benefits attributable to estimated future employee service.

g. The employer's best estimate, as soon as it can reasonably be determined, of contributions expected to be paid to the plan during the next fiscal year beginning after the date of the latest statement of financial position presented. Estimated contributions may be presented in the aggregate combining (1) contributions required by funding regulations or laws, (2) discretionary contributions, and (3) noncash contributions.

h. The amount of net periodic benefit cost recognized, showing separately the service cost component, the interest cost component, the expected return on plan assets for the period, the gain or loss component, the prior service cost or credit component, the transition asset or obligation component, and the gain or loss recognized due to settlements or curtailments.

i. Separately the net gain or loss and net prior service cost or credit recognized in other comprehensive income for the period pursuant to paragraphs 25 and 29 of Statement 87 and paragraphs 52 and 56 of Statement 106, as amended, and reclassification adjustments of other comprehensive income for the period, as those amounts, including amortization of the net transition asset or obligation, are recognized as components of net periodic benefit cost.

ii. The amounts in accumulated other comprehensive income that have not yet been recognized as components of net periodic benefit cost, showing separately the net gain or loss, net prior service cost or credit, and net transition asset or obligation.

j. On a weighted-average basis, the following assumptions used in the accounting for the plans: assumed discount rates, rates of compensation increase (for pay-related plans), and expected long-term rates of return on plan assets specifying, in a tabular format, the assumptions used to determine the benefit obligation and the assumptions used to determine net benefit cost.

k. [This subparagraph has been deleted. See Status page.]

l. The assumed health care cost trend rate(s) for the next year used to measure the expected cost of benefits covered by the plan (gross eligible charges), and a general description of the direction and pattern of change in the assumed trend rates thereafter, together with the ultimate trend rate(s) and when that rate is expected to be achieved.

m. The effect of a one-percentage-point increase and the effect of a one-percentage- point decrease in the assumed health care cost trend rates on (1) the aggregate of the service and interest cost components of net periodic postretirement health care benefit costs and (2) the accumulated postretirement benefit obligation for health care benefits. (For purposes of this disclosure, all other assumptions shall be held constant, and the effects shall be measured based on the substantive plan that is the basis for the accounting.)

n. If applicable, the amounts and types of securities of the employer and related parties included in plan assets, the approximate amount of future annual benefits of plan participants covered by insurance contracts issued by the employer or related parties, and any significant transactions between the employer or related parties and the plan during the period.

o. If applicable, any alternative method used to amortize prior service amounts or net gains and losses pursuant to paragraphs 26 and 33 of Statement 87 or paragraphs 53 and 60 of Statement 106.

p. If applicable, any substantive commitment, such as past practice or a history of regular benefit increases, used as the basis for accounting for the benefit obligation.

q. If applicable, the cost of providing special or contractual termination benefits recognized during the period and a description of the nature of the event.

r. An explanation of any significant change in the benefit obligation or plan assets not otherwise apparent in the other disclosures required by this Statement.

s. The amounts in accumulated other comprehensive income expected to be recognized as components of net periodic benefit cost over the fiscal year that follows the most recent annual statement of financial position presented, showing separately the net gain or loss, net prior service cost or credit, and net transition asset or obligation.

t. The amount and timing of any plan assets expected to be returned to the employer during the 12-month period, or operating cycle if longer, that follows the most recent annual statement of financial position presented.

Employers with Two or More Plans

6. The disclosures required by this Statement shall be aggregated for all of an employer's defined benefit pension plans and for all of an employer's other defined benefit postretirement plans unless disaggregating in groups is considered to provide useful information or is otherwise required by this paragraph and paragraph 7 of this Statement. Disclosures shall be as of the date of each statement of financial position presented. Disclosures about pension plans with assets in excess of the accumulated benefit obligation generally may be aggregated with disclosures about pension plans with accumulated benefit obligations in excess of assets. The same aggregation is permitted for other postretirement benefit plans. If aggregate disclosures are presented, an employer shall disclose:

a. The aggregate benefit obligation and aggregate fair value of plan assets for plans with benefit obligations in excess of plan assets as of the measurement date of each statement of financial position presented

b. The aggregate pension accumulated benefit obligation and aggregate fair value of plan assets for pension plans with accumulated benefit obligations in excess of plan assets.

7. A U.S. reporting entity may combine disclosures about pension plans or other postretirement benefit plans outside the United States with those for U.S. plans unless the benefit obligations of the plans outside the United States are significant relative to the total benefit obligation and those plans use significantly different assumptions. A foreign reporting entity that prepares financial statements in conformity with U.S. generally accepted accounting principles (GAAP) shall apply the preceding guidance to its domestic and foreign plans.

Reduced Disclosure Requirements for Nonpublic Entities

8. A **nonpublic entity** is not required to disclose the information required by paragraphs 5(a)–(c), 5(h), 5(m), and 5(o)–(r) of this Statement. A nonpublic entity that sponsors one or more defined benefit pension plans or one or more other defined benefit postretirement plans shall provide the following information, separately for pension plans and other postretirement benefit plans. Amounts related to the employer's results of operations shall be disclosed for each period for which a statement of income is presented. Amounts related to the employer's statement of financial position shall be disclosed as of the date of each statement of financial position presented.

a. The benefit obligation, fair value of plan assets, and funded status of the plan.

b. Employer contributions, participant contributions, and benefits paid.
c. Information about plan assets:
   (1) For each major category of plan assets which shall include, but is not limited to, equity securities, debt securities, real estate, and all other assets, the percentage of the fair value of total plan assets held as of the measurement date used for each statement of financial position presented.
   (2) A narrative description of investment policies and strategies, including target allocation percentages or range of percentages for each major category of plan assets presented on a weighted-average basis as of the measurement date(s) of the latest statement of financial position presented, if applicable, and other factors that are pertinent to an understanding of the policies or strategies such as investment goals, risk management practices, permitted and prohibited investments including the use of derivatives, diversification, and the relationship between plan assets and benefit obligations.
   (3) A narrative description of the basis used to determine the overall expected long-term rate-of-return-on-assets assumption, such as the general approach used, the extent to which the overall rate-of-return-on-assets assumption was based on historical returns, the extent to which adjustments were made to those historical returns in order to reflect expectations of future returns, and how those adjustments were determined.
   (4) Disclosure of additional asset categories and additional information about specific assets within a category is encouraged if that information is expected to be useful in understanding the risks associated with each asset category and the overall expected long-term rate of return on assets.
d. For defined benefit pension plans, the accumulated benefit obligation.
e. The benefits (as of the date of the latest statement of financial position presented) expected to be paid in each of the next five fiscal years, and in the aggregate for the five fiscal years thereafter. The expected benefits should be estimated based on the same assumptions used to measure the company's benefit obligation at the end of the year and should include benefits attributable to estimated future employee service.

f. The employer's best estimate, as soon as it can reasonably be determined, of contributions expected to be paid to the plan during the next fiscal year beginning after the date of the latest statement of financial position presented. Estimated contributions may be presented in the aggregate combining (1) contributions required by funding regulations or laws, (2) discretionary contributions, and (3) noncash contributions.
g. The amounts recognized in the statements of financial position, showing separately the postretirement benefit assets and current and noncurrent postretirement benefit liabilities.
h. Separately, the net gain or loss and net prior service cost or credit recognized in other comprehensive income for the period pursuant to paragraphs 25 and 29 of Statement 87 and paragraphs 52 and 56 of Statement 106, as amended, and reclassification adjustments of other comprehensive income for the period, as those amounts, including amortization of the net transition asset or obligation, are recognized as components of net periodic benefit cost.
hh. The amounts in accumulated other comprehensive income that have not yet been recognized as components of net periodic benefit cost, showing separately the net gain or loss, net prior service cost or credit, and net transition asset or obligation.
i. On a weighted-average basis, the following assumptions used in the accounting for the plans: assumed discount rates, rates of compensation increase (for pay-related plans), and expected long-term rates of return on plan assets specifying, in a tabular format, the assumptions used to determine the benefit obligation and the assumptions used to determine net benefit cost.
j. [This subparagraph has been deleted. See Status page.]
k. The assumed health care cost trend rate(s) for the next year used to measure the expected cost of benefits covered by the plan (gross eligible charges), and a general description of the direction and pattern of change in the assumed trend rates thereafter, together with the ultimate trend rate(s) and when that rate is expected to be achieved.
l. If applicable, the amounts and types of securities of the employer and related parties included in

plan assets, the approximate amount of future annual benefits of plan participants covered by insurance contracts issued by the employer or related parties, and any significant transactions between the employer or related parties and the plan during the period.

m. The nature and effect of significant nonroutine events, such as amendments, combinations, divestitures, curtailments, and settlements.

n. The amounts in accumulated other comprehensive income expected to be recognized as components of net periodic benefit cost over the fiscal year that follows the most recent annual statement of financial position presented, showing separately the net gain or loss, net prior service cost or credit, and net transition asset or obligation.

o. The amount and timing of any plan assets expected to be returned to the employer during the 12-month period, or operating cycle if longer, that follows the most recent annual statement of financial position presented.

Disclosures in Interim Financial Reports

9. A **publicly traded entity** shall disclose the following information in its interim financial statements that include a statement of income:

a. The amount of net periodic benefit cost recognized, for each period for which a statement of income is presented, showing separately the service cost component, the interest cost component, the expected return on plan assets for the period, the gain or loss component, the prior service cost or credit component, the transition asset or obligation component, and the gain or loss recognized due to a settlement or curtailment

b. The total amount of the employer's contributions paid, and expected to be paid, during the current fiscal year, if significantly different from amounts previously disclosed pursuant to paragraph 5(g) of this Statement. Estimated contributions may be presented in the aggregate combining (1) contributions required by funding regulations or laws, (2) discretionary contributions, and (3) noncash contributions.

10. A nonpublic entity shall disclose in interim periods, for which a complete set of financial statements is presented, the total amount of the employer's contributions paid, and expected to be paid, during the current fiscal year, if significantly different from amounts previously disclosed pursuant to paragraph 8(f) of this Statement. Estimated contributions

may be presented in the aggregate combining (a) contributions required by funding regulations or laws, (b) discretionary contributions, and (c) noncash contributions.

Not-for-Profit Organizations and Other Entities That Do Not Report Other Comprehensive Income

10A. For not-for-profit employers and other employers that do not report other comprehensive income in accordance with FASB Statement No. 130, *Reporting Comprehensive Income,* the references to the net gain or loss, net prior service cost or credit, and net transition asset or obligation recognized in other comprehensive income in paragraphs 5(i) and 8(h) of this Statement shall instead be to such amounts recognized as changes in unrestricted net assets arising from a defined benefit plan but not yet included in net periodic benefit cost.

10B. For those employers, the references to reclassification adjustments of other comprehensive income in paragraphs 5(i) and 8(h) of this Statement shall instead be to reclassifications to net periodic benefit cost of amounts previously recognized as changes in unrestricted net assets arising from a defined benefit plan but not included in net periodic benefit cost when they arose.

10C. For those employers, the references to the net gain or loss, net prior service cost or credit, and net transition asset or obligation recognized in accumulated other comprehensive income in paragraphs 5(ii), 5(s), 8(hh), and 8(n) of this Statement shall instead be to such amounts that have been recognized as changes in unrestricted net assets arising from a defined benefit plan but not yet reclassified as components of net periodic benefit cost.

10D. For those employers, the references to results of operations (including items of other comprehensive income) in paragraphs 5 and 8 shall instead be to changes in unrestricted net assets and the references to a statement of income in those paragraphs shall instead be to a statement of activities.

Defined Contribution Plans

11. An employer shall disclose the amount of cost recognized for defined contribution pension plans and for other defined contribution postretirement benefit plans for all periods presented separately from the amount of cost recognized for defined benefit plans. The disclosures shall include a description

of the nature and effect of any significant changes during the period affecting comparability, such as a change in the rate of employer contributions, a business combination, or a divestiture.

Multiemployer Plans

12. An employer shall disclose the amount of contributions to multiemployer plans for each annual period for which a statement of income is presented. An employer may disclose total contributions to multiemployer plans without disaggregating the amounts attributable to pension plans and other postretirement benefit plans. The disclosures shall include a description of the nature and effect of any changes affecting comparability, such as a change in the rate of employer contributions, a business combination, or a divestiture.

13. In some situations, withdrawal from a multiemployer plan may result in an employer having an obligation to the plan for a portion of the unfunded benefit obligation of the pension plans and other postretirement benefit plans. If withdrawal under circumstances that would give rise to an obligation is either probable or reasonably possible, the provisions of FASB Statement No. 5, *Accounting for Contingencies,* shall apply (Statement 87, paragraph 70). If it is either probable or reasonably possible that (a) an employer would withdraw from the plan under circumstances that would give rise to an obligation or (b) an employer's contribution to the fund would be increased during the remainder of the contract period to make up a shortfall in the funds necessary to maintain the negotiated level of benefit coverage (a "maintenance of benefits" clause), the employer shall apply the provisions of Statement 5 (Statement 106, paragraph 83).

Amendments to Existing Pronouncements

14. Statement 132 is superseded by this Statement.

15. The following is added to the list of disclosures in paragraph 30 of Opinion 28:

    k. The following information about defined benefit pension plans and other defined benefit postretirement benefit plans, disclosed for all periods presented pursuant to the provisions of FASB Statement No. 132 (revised 2003), *Employers' Disclosures about Pensions and Other Postretirement Benefits:*

       (1) The amount of net periodic benefit cost

recognized, for each period for which a statement of income is presented, showing separately the service cost component, the interest cost component, the expected return on plan assets for the period, the amortization of the unrecognized transition obligation or transition asset, the amount of recognized gains or losses, the amount of prior service cost recognized, and the amount of gain or loss recognized due to a settlement or curtailment.*

    (2) The total amount of the employer's contributions paid, and expected to be paid, during the current fiscal year, if significantly different from amounts previously disclosed pursuant to paragraph 5(g) of Statement 132(R). Estimated contributions may be presented in the aggregate combining (a) contributions required by funding regulations or laws, (b) discretionary contributions, and (c) noncash contributions.*

Amendments Made by Statement 132 Carried Forward in This Statement with Minor Changes

16. Statement 87 is amended as follows:

a. Paragraph 54 is replaced by the following:

    Refer to paragraphs 5 and 8 of FASB Statement No. 132 (revised 2003), *Employers' Disclosures about Pensions and Other Postretirement Benefits.*

b. Paragraph 56 is replaced by the following:

    Refer to paragraphs 6 and 7 of Statement 132(R).

c. Paragraph 65 is replaced by the following:

    Refer to paragraph 11 of Statement 132(R).

d. Paragraph 69 is replaced by the following:

    Refer to paragraph 12 of Statement 132(R).

17. Paragraph 17 of Statement 88 is replaced by the following:

    Refer to paragraphs 5(a), 5(b), 5(h), 5(q), and 8(m) of FASB Statement No. 132 (revised 2003), *Employers' Disclosures about Pensions and Other Postretirement Benefits.*

18. Statement 106 is amended as follows:

a. Paragraph 74 is replaced by the following:

Refer to paragraphs 5 and 8 of FASB Statement No. 132 (revised 2003), *Employers' Disclosures about Pensions and Other Postretirement Benefits.*

b. Paragraphs 77 and 78 are replaced by the following:

Refer to paragraphs 6 and 7 of Statement 132(R).

c. Paragraph 82 is replaced by the following:

Refer to paragraph 12 of Statement 132(R).

d. Paragraph 106 is replaced by the following:

Refer to paragraph 11 of Statement 132(R).

Effective Date and Transition

19. The provisions of Statement 132 remain in effect until the provisions of this Statement are adopted. Except as noted below, this Statement shall be effective for fiscal years ending after December 15, 2003. The interim-period disclosures required by this Statement shall be effective for interim periods beginning after December 15, 2003.

a. Disclosure of information about foreign plans required by paragraphs 5(d), 5(e), 5(g), and 5(k) of this Statement shall be effective for fiscal years ending after June 15, 2004.

b. Estimated future benefit payments required by paragraph 5(f) of this Statement shall be effective for fiscal years ending after June 15, 2004.

c. Disclosure of information for nonpublic entities required by paragraphs 8(c)–(f) and 8(j) of this Statement shall be effective for fiscal years ending after June 15, 2004.

Until this Statement is fully adopted, financial statements that exclude foreign plans from (a) the actual allocation of assets, (b) the description of investment strategies, (c) the basis used to determine the expected long-term rate-of-return-on-assets assumption, or (d) the amount of accumulated benefit obligation shall include, separately for domestic plans, the total fair value of plan assets as of the measurement date(s) used for the latest statement of financial position presented and the overall expected long-term rate of return on assets for the latest period for which a statement of income is presented.

20. The disclosures for earlier annual periods presented for comparative purposes shall be restated for (a) the percentages of each major category of plan assets held, (b) the accumulated benefit obligation, and (c) the assumptions used in the accounting for the plans. The disclosures for earlier interim periods presented for comparative purposes shall be restated for the components of net benefit cost. However, if obtaining this information relating to earlier periods is not practicable, the notes to the financial statements shall include all available information and identify the information not available. Early application of the disclosure provisions of this Statement is encouraged.

> **The provisions of this Statement need not be applied to immaterial items.**

This Statement was adopted by the unanimous vote of the seven members of the Financial Accounting Standards Board:

Robert H. Herz,
Chairman
George J. Batavick

G. Michael Crooch
Gary S. Schieneman
Katherine Schipper

Leslie F. Seidman
Edward W. Trott

Appendix A

STATEMENT 132(R): BACKGROUND INFORMATION AND BASIS FOR CONCLUSIONS

CONTENTS

Appendix A

STATEMENT 132(R): BACKGROUND INFORMATION AND BASIS FOR CONCLUSIONS

Introduction

A1. This appendix summarizes considerations that Board members deemed significant in reaching the conclusions in this Statement. It includes reasons for accepting certain views and rejecting others. Individual Board members gave greater weight to some factors than to others.

Objectives of Disclosure

A2. In considering existing and proposed disclosures about pension plans and other postretirement benefit plans, the Board noted that disclosures should provide (a) qualitative information about the items in the financial statements, such as measurement and recognition policies and principles, (b) quantitative information about items recognized or disclosed in the financial statements, such as disaggregated data, (c) information that enables users of financial statements to assess the effect that pension plans and other postretirement benefit plans have on entities' results of operations, and (d) information to facilitate assessments of future earnings and cash flows, including the effects of benefit obligations on long-term liquidity and strategic decisions.

Background

A3. Discussions with users of financial statements indicated that the disclosures required by FASB Statement No. 132, *Employers' Disclosures about Pensions and Other Postretirement Benefits,* although extensive, do not provide sufficient information to users of financial statements in their analysis and understanding of entities' pension plans and other postretirement benefit plans.

A4. The Board identified four types of information sought by users of financial statements that would facilitate analyses of the plans' financial condition, net periodic cost, and cash flows: information about (a) plan assets, (b) benefit obligations, (c) cash flows for both benefit payments to retirees and contributions by the plan sponsor to investment trusts, and (d) net benefit costs. This Statement is intended to improve disclosures about those four aspects of defined benefit pension plans and other defined benefit postretirement benefit plans.

A5. On September 12, 2003, the Board issued an Exposure Draft, *Employers' Disclosures about Pensions and Other Postretirement Benefits.* The Board received 97 letters commenting on the Exposure Draft and redeliberated the issues raised in those comment letters in November 2003, in some cases reaffirming its prior decisions and in other cases revising or eliminating the proposed disclosure requirements.

A6. This Statement continues the standardization of the disclosure requirements of FASB Statements No. 87, *Employers' Accounting for Pensions,* and No. 106, *Employers' Accounting for Postretirement Benefits Other Than Pensions,* to the extent practicable, so that the required information will be easier to prepare and understand. This Statement also continues to require the parallel format for presenting information about pension plans and other postretirement benefit plans.

Benefits and Costs

A7. The mission of the FASB is to establish and improve standards of financial accounting and reporting for the guidance and education of the public, including preparers, auditors, and users of financial information. In fulfilling that mission, the Board endeavors to determine that a proposed standard will fill a significant need and that the costs imposed to meet that standard, as compared with other alternatives, are justified in relation to the overall benefits of the resulting information. Although the costs to implement a new standard may not be borne evenly, investors and creditors—both present and future—and other users of financial information benefit from improvements in financial reporting, thereby facilitating the functioning of markets for capital and credit and the efficient allocation of resources in the economy.

A8. The Board's assessment of the benefits and costs of providing these additional disclosures was based on discussions with certain users of financial statements, preparers of financial statements, and actuaries. Benefits to users of financial statements include information that will facilitate assessments of market risk and cash flows. Costs to preparers of financial statements include time and resources to incorporate the new information needed into existing processes and to validate the data, audit fees for independent verification of the disclosures, and actuarial fees. Some information, such as benefit payments, may require greater effort to obtain. Many, if not most, of the new disclosures represent either disaggregation of information already disclosed, such as the fair value of plan assets, or information already used in the determination of disclosed amounts.

A9. As most of the information required by this Statement is already essential in complying with Statements 87, 106, and 132, and is used by most preparers to monitor funding, it should be available to preparers of financial statements. The Board considered the availability of data in establishing the effective date and transition provisions of this Statement. Additional costs to compile, analyze, and audit the proposed additional disclosures are believed to be modest in relation to the benefits to be derived by users of financial statements.

International Accounting Standards

A10. The International Accounting Standards Board's (IASB's) IAS 19, *Employee Benefits,* establishes recognition, measurement, and disclosure requirements for financial statements prepared in conformity with international accounting standards. The disclosure requirements of IAS 19 are similar to the requirements of Statement 132, as both require information that describes activity during the period and certain key assumptions used to determine benefit obligations and net periodic benefit cost. The IASB is proposing an amendment of IAS 19. One disclosure being considered for the proposed amendment that is similar to the requirements of this Statement is information about the major categories of plan assets. Other disclosures are dissimilar based on differing assessments by the FASB and IASB regarding users' needs and differences in the recognition and measurement principles applied to pension and other postretirement benefits.

Disclosure Requirements

Plan Assets

A11. The Board concluded in Statements 87 and 132 that disclosure of the fair value of plan assets is essential to understanding the economics of the employer's benefit plans and useful in assessing management's stewardship responsibilities for efficient use of those assets.

A12. In Statement 132, as described in paragraphs B33 and B34 of this Statement, the Board did not require disclosure of the composition of plan assets. The Board noted that the information required to enable users of financial statements to identify and assess concentrations of risk would be extensive and add significant complexity to the disclosure. However, in recent years, users of financial statements have indicated that information about plan assets, in the aggregate, is not adequate for assessing investment risk. This Statement requires disclosure of the major types of plan assets including, but not limited to, equity securities, debt securities, real estate, and all other assets. For each major category of assets, annual disclosures would include the percentage of the fair value of total plan assets held as of the measurement date used for each statement of financial position presented. The Board believes that such information would be useful to users of financial statements in evaluating the plans' exposure to market risk and potential cash flow demands on the sponsor. In addition, it would enable users to better understand and evaluate management's selection of its expected long-term rate-of-return-on-assets assumption.

A13. In its discussion of asset categories to be disclosed separately, the Board considered requiring narrower categories but decided that the cost of doing so would outweigh the benefits. Those categories included public and nonpublic equity securities, domestic and international equity and debt securities, and government and corporate debt securities. In addition, the Board considered requiring identification of equity securities by expected returns and volatility. The Board concluded that those additional categories would not provide enough incremental benefit to justify the costs of compliance. For example, the Board concluded that disclosure of the amounts invested in international equity and debt securities would not adequately capture the particular market, credit, and exchange risks that exist in each country. The Board intends for the major asset categories to be the minimum level of detail to be provided by plan sponsors. If plan sponsors determine that additional categories and additional information about specific assets within a category would enhance financial statements users' understanding of investment risk or

the expected long-term rates of return, they are encouraged to provide additional detail.

A14. Most respondents to the Exposure Draft agreed that information about the allocation of assets would enable users of financial statements to better understand management's investment policies and strategies and allow these users to better assess investment risk and the potential for future volatility in the fair value of assets and the overall expected long-term rate of return on assets. Some asked for additional guidance describing how individual securities should be classified into the major asset categories. The Board decided that the classification would be left to the judgment of the plan sponsor, based on the specific characteristics of each investment and existing accounting literature.

A15. In addition, the Board decided to require all entities that sponsor defined benefit pension plans and other defined benefit postretirement benefit plans to provide a narrative description of the investment strategies employed for those plans. The Board has not identified the specific information to be included in those descriptions because investment strategies are not uniform from plan to plan. Information that might be included in this disclosure is described in paragraph 5(d)(2) of this Statement. Information should be included in the description if it is an important element of the entity's investment strategy.

A16. The Exposure Draft would have required annual disclosure of the target allocation percentage, or range of percentages, for each major category of plan assets, presented on a weighted-average basis as of the measurement date used for the latest statement of financial position presented. The Board believed that that information would be useful to users of financial statements in understanding and assessing investment strategies as well as market risk and would enable those users to better understand and evaluate management's expected long-term rate-of-return-on-assets assumption by indicating the likely mix of plan assets over time. The Board acknowledged that asset allocation targets are subject to revision, should be based on management's expectations, and should be revised in subsequent annual disclosures as those expectations change. The target asset allocation percentages would be calculated on a weighted-average basis so that the average target percentage, or range of percentages, reflects the relative size of each plan. In its redeliberations, the Board noted that some entities may not use target allocations as part of their investment policies or strategies. The Board decided that entities that do not use target allocations would not be required to create them. All other entities should include target asset allocations within their description of investment policies and strategies.

A17. The Exposure Draft would have required the disclosure of the expected long-term rate of return on assets, presented on a weighted-average basis, by individual asset class, for the latest period for which a statement of income is presented. Respondents who disagreed with the proposal noted that management often derives its overall rate-of-return assumption from its analysis of the portfolio as a whole and not from the sum of individual asset categories (a "building block" method). They pointed out that the "building block" method is only one of several acceptable methods for developing the expected long-term rate-of-return-on-assets assumption and that the disclosure requirement would lead users to expect that this method should be applied. Those expectations might cause some plan sponsors to change to the "building block" method or to perform an allocation solely for purposes of that disclosure. Respondents also indicated that the proposed disclosure (a) represented forward-looking information that should not be included in the financial statements, (b) would change frequently, because most plans are actively managed, (c) would be of limited usefulness because it represents the aggregation of multiple plans and jurisdictions, and (d) would not add sufficiently to the insights users of financial statements would derive from the disclosure of the actual asset allocations. After considering respondents' comments, the Board decided not to require disclosure of the expected long-term rate of return by individual asset category.

A18. A number of respondents favored disclosure of the basis used to determine the overall expected long-term rate-of-return-on-assets assumption. They indicated that this would be a preferable alternative to the disclosure of the expected rate of return by individual asset category. The Board concluded that this information would assist users in assessing management's long-term rate-of-return-on-assets assumption. A description of the basis used to determine the overall expected long-term rate of return on plan assets should reflect significant factors considered, which may vary from plan sponsor to plan sponsor. Therefore, the Board has not specified the information to be included. The disclosure should describe important considerations such as the general approach used, the extent to which the expected long-term rate of return is based on historical returns, the extent to which adjustments were made to those historical re-

turns in order to reflect expectations of future returns, and how those adjustments were determined.

A19. The Exposure Draft would have required disclosure of information about the maturities of debt securities. The Board believed that that information, when matched with information about expected future benefit payments, would help users of financial statements assess the degree to which investment cash flows are aligned with benefit payments. Numerous respondents asked the Board to eliminate the requirement, noting that debt instruments typically represent only a small proportion of plan assets and, often, are not held to maturity. The Board agreed with respondents' comments and decided not to require that disclosure.

Obligations

A20. The Board discussed two obligations associated with pension plans. The first is the plan sponsor's obligation to contribute cash or other assets to fund the pension plan. For U.S. plans, those assets are set aside in accordance with standards established by the Employee Retirement Income Security Act of 1974 (ERISA) and are used to pay pension benefits to retirees. The second obligation is to pay pension benefits to retirees out of the assets in the pension plan. The Board received requests from users of financial statements for enhanced disclosures about both kinds of obligations. Paragraphs A21–A32 describe the Board's conclusions about those disclosures.

Disclosures about obligations not required by the Board

A21. Some users of financial statements and other respondents suggested requiring disclosure of the pension obligation on an ERISA funding basis and on a Pension Benefit Guaranty Corporation (PBGC) termination funding basis. Those definitions of the pension obligation, they noted, are relevant because they determine entities' funding obligations.

A22. The Board decided not to require disclosures of the obligation measured on an ERISA or other regulatory funding basis because introducing additional measures of the obligation would increase complexity and because the ERISA or other regulatory measures, by themselves, would not convey useful information about funding. To be useful, those disclosures would have to be supplemented with information about minimum and maximum funding amounts, excess funding credits available to reduce current-period minimum funding requirements, and management's intent regarding voluntary contributions.

A23. The Board decided that pension obligations measured on a PBGC termination funding basis (or similar statutory termination obligation outside the United States) should not be disclosed because that measurement basis is relevant only if a plan will be terminated or partially terminated and because that basis is not consistent with the concept of a going concern. Also, obligations determined on a termination funding basis are not routinely computed by plan actuaries, and disclosure would, therefore, impose additional implementation costs. Respondents who commented on this issue generally agreed with the Board's conclusions.

A24. Prior to issuing the Exposure Draft, the Board considered requests for additional disclosures that would enable users of financial statements to better understand the amounts and timing of benefit payments and to assess the time horizon over which benefit payments would be made. The Board considered requiring the disclosure of the number of plan participants by group (for example, active, terminated-vested, and retired) or the weighted-average duration and amount of the benefit obligation, both stratified by active, terminated-vested, and retired plan participants. The intent of that requirement would be to assist users of financial statements in assessing how well asset maturities align with the duration of the benefit obligation. Users indicated that that information could be compared to plan asset maturities to understand the entity's strategy for investing in plan assets and would enable them to assess the potential effects of changes in certain key assumptions.

A25. The Board excluded these requirements from the Exposure Draft but invited comments on these issues. Some respondents requested that duration information be required because it would facilitate sensitivity analysis. The Board considered that request but decided to exclude the disclosure of duration information from this Statement, concluding that it and the other proposed disclosures would provide minimal information about the amounts and timing of benefit payments. The Board was concerned that information about the weighted-average duration of benefit obligations would not enable users of financial statements to reliably assess the degree to which plan asset and benefit obligation cash flows are

aligned, noting that two sets of cash flows could have similar durations but significantly different amounts and timing.

A26. The Board considered requiring additional disclosures about multiemployer pension plans. Among the disclosures considered were (a) a description of the plan, including the number of employees and employee groups covered, (b) the basis on which costs are charged and the cost rate, (c) contributions expected to be made for the next fiscal year, (d) the funded status of the plan, together with the entity's workforce as a percentage of the total participants in the plan, and (e) the name of each multiemployer plan. Respondents who addressed this issue expressed varying views about whether these disclosures should be required. The Board decided not to require any of those disclosures, concluding that the costs of providing such information would exceed the benefits to users of financial statements.

Disclosures about obligations required by the Board

A27. The Exposure Draft would have required the disclosure of future benefit payments included in the determination of the projected benefit obligation. The Board concluded that that information would assist users of financial statements in understanding the cash flow requirements of benefit payments to retirees. Respondents noted that a measure of benefit payments based on employees' past service does not accurately represent the benefits that are actually paid. In addition, respondents noted that information about benefit payments determined on that basis is not readily available to financial statement preparers or actuaries. Discussions with actuaries confirmed that significant cost and effort would be involved in obtaining that information. Respondents suggested that the Board require the disclosure of benefit payments based on amounts that consider benefits attributable to expected future service. Some actuaries refer to those amounts as "expected benefit payments." Respondents also indicated that information systems often are able to provide estimated benefit payments that include benefits attributable to expected future employee service. Plan sponsors often use those estimated benefit payments for cash budgeting purposes.

A28. During its redeliberations, the Board acknowledged that significant cost and effort would be involved in obtaining estimates of benefit payments based on the projected benefit obligation. The Board reaffirmed its view that such estimates are relevant to users of financial statements and decided to adopt respondents' suggestions to require disclosure of estimated future benefits that include benefits attributable to estimated future employee service, recognizing that that information is more readily available from existing actuarial systems. That information would be presented as of the date of the latest statement of financial position presented, for each of the next five fiscal years, and in the aggregate for the five fiscal years thereafter.

A29. Estimated future benefit payments need not be separated between benefit payments made from plan assets and direct payments from the plan sponsor to plan participants (for example, for unfunded plans). Respondents noted that this aggregation impairs the ability to assess the alignment between asset maturities and benefit payments. The Board concluded that this aggregation should be permitted because of cost and benefit considerations and in the interest of consistency with other provisions of this Statement that permit the combining of individual plans.

A30. The Board decided to require disclosure of the employer's best estimate of the contributions expected to be paid to fund pension plans and other postretirement benefit plans during the next fiscal year beginning after the date of the latest statement of financial position presented, as soon as those amounts can be reasonably determined. Users of financial statements indicated that that information would be useful in analyzing future cash flows between the plan sponsor and its plans. They noted that because of the complexities of funding regulations and the significance of voluntary contributions, disclosure by the employer is the most reliable source of contribution information for users of financial statements. As proposed in the Exposure Draft, that disclosure would have separately identified the required minimum and any additional discretionary funding amounts and the aggregate amount and description of any noncash contributions. Respondents expressed concern that because of the complexities of funding regulations and the uncertain distinction between required and voluntary contributions and cash and noncash contributions, separately identifying those amounts would involve significant judgment and period-to-period volatility. During redeliberations, the Board acknowledged those concerns and decided to require disclosure of management's best estimate, once the information can reasonably be determined, of only the aggregate amount of all contributions expected to be made during the next fiscal year.

A31. An *additional minimum liability* must be recognized if the accumulated benefit obligation exceeds the fair value of plan assets. Recognition of an additional minimum liability may result in the recognition of an intangible asset, a charge to other comprehensive income, or a combination of both, in accordance with paragraphs 36 and 37 of Statement 87. In Statement 132, as described in paragraphs B36 and B37 of this Statement, the Board did not require disclosure of the accumulated benefit obligation for pension plans with assets in excess of the accumulated benefit obligation. The Board reasoned that the accumulated benefit obligation is not used to forecast pension costs or obligations and, therefore, had limited relevance to users of financial statements. The Board did require disclosure of the accumulated benefit obligation for plans with assets less than the accumulated benefit obligation because the accumulated benefit obligation is used to determine the minimum liability. Users of financial statements noted that the accumulated benefit obligation is an input to their analysis of whether plan sponsors are close to recognizing an additional minimum liability. Acknowledging that concern, the Board decided to require annual disclosure of the accumulated benefit obligation for all defined benefit pension plans. That disclosure will enable users of financial statements to monitor the funded status of the plans, determined in the aggregate, using the accumulated benefit obligation as the measure of the benefit obligation.

A32. Respondents who supported annual disclosure of the accumulated benefit obligation noted that the accumulated benefit obligation is an important factor in the recognition of an additional minimum liability when the accumulated benefit obligation exceeds the fair value of plan assets. A few respondents expressed concern that the disclosure would represent the aggregate accumulated benefit obligation for multiple plans while recognition of an additional minimum liability is determined on a plan-by-plan basis. The Board reaffirmed its previous decision to require disclosure of the accumulated benefit obligation, noting that disclosure of aggregate information for multiple plans is not unique to the accumulated benefit obligation.

Net Benefit Cost or Income

A33. Several types of events and consequences affecting pension plans and other postretirement benefit plans are combined and recognized as net benefit cost. This approach aggregates items that might be reported separately for other parts of an employer's operations, including service cost (representing compensation), interest cost resulting from deferred payment, and the results of investing in plan assets. Users of financial statements have indicated that they want information that will facilitate cost and margin analysis, either over time for a particular entity or comparatively between a reporting entity and other entities. Users of financial statements have stated that they wish to analyze operating results absent the financing elements of pension plans and other postretirement benefit plans and to compare costs and margins across entities with and without those plans or alternative benefit plans or with different actuarial assumptions.

A34. Periodic variation in net benefit cost will affect operating cost trends. Users of financial statements have said that additional disclosures about the effects of net benefit cost on line items of the statement of income will facilitate trend analysis by highlighting the degree to which those costs influence cost trends. Users of financial statements also have said that the additional disclosures would assist them in identifying the effect on operating results of financing elements of net benefit cost, such as expected long-term investment returns. Displaying the net benefit cost by income statement line item would enable users to better identify the effects of pension plans and other postretirement benefit plans on results, including both from a trend and a competitive standpoint.

A35. The Board decided not to include in the Exposure Draft a requirement to disclose the income statement classification of net benefit costs and invited respondents' comments on this issue. Some respondents favored the inclusion of that requirement in this Statement. They reasoned that the information would be useful for performing trend analyses and competitive comparisons. Other respondents expressed concern about the cost of obtaining that information. The Board decided not to require that disclosure, reasoning that existing disclosures adequately convey the operating and financing elements of net benefit cost, and the aggregate amounts of net periodic benefit costs are, for many reporting entities, generally relatively insignificant in relation to individual income statement line items.

Assumptions

A36. The Board observed that disclosures about certain key assumptions would be more useful if those disclosures followed consistent conventions. For example, some entities' disclosures under Statement 132 indicate that the disclosed key assumptions are as of the latest measurement date even though the expected long-term rate-of-return-on-assets assumption is as of an earlier date used to determine current-period assumed investment earnings. In the Exposure Draft, the Board decided to require a tabular format for the disclosure of certain assumptions and to improve clarity about the period and measure to which those assumptions relate by separately disclosing the assumptions used to determine benefit obligations and the assumptions used to determine net benefit cost. Respondents generally supported the Board's decision to improve clarity about key assumptions. Some stated that a standard format for disclosing key assumptions would facilitate financial statement users' analysis, interpretation, and comparisons among the disclosures of different entities.

Measurement Date(s)

A37. The Board discussed the provisions of Statements 87 and 106 that permit measuring plan assets and obligations as of the date of the financial statements presented or as of a date not more than three months prior to that date, as long as the earlier date is used consistently. The Board noted that events that occur after the measurement date but prior to fiscal year-end would affect, but might not be reflected in, plan assets, benefit obligations, and net periodic cost. Examples of such events are changes in equity returns and changes in interest rates.

A38. In the Exposure Draft, the Board proposed that disclosure of the measurement date(s) used to measure pension plans and other postretirement benefit plans be required when an economic event occurs, or economic conditions change, after the measurement date(s) but before the fiscal year-end if those changes would have had a significant effect on reported amounts for plan assets and obligations had the fiscal year-end date been used as the measurement date. The Exposure Draft also required that the nature of the significant changes be described.

A39. Respondents agreed that the disclosure of the plan measurement date(s) would better enable users of financial statements to understand the key assumptions selected. Most respondents who supported disclosure of the measurement date(s) stated that it should be required at all times; requiring contingent disclosure, they noted, would penalize preparers who use a measurement date other than the fiscal year-end by requiring them to assess the significance of economic events occurring between the measurement date(s) and fiscal year-end. During its redeliberations, the Board agreed with respondents and decided to require disclosure, in all cases, of the measurement date(s) used to determine pension and other postretirement benefit measurements for the plans that make up at least the majority of plan assets and benefit obligations.

Reduced Disclosure Requirements for Nonpublic Entities

A40. This Statement retains the reduced disclosure requirements for nonpublic entities provided in Statement 132. The Board considered but rejected the establishment of a materiality threshold that would determine when nonpublic entities would be required to provide pension and other postretirement benefits disclosures. In reaching its decision, the Board acknowledged that Statement 132 contained no such threshold. Nonpublic entities are exempt from the requirements of paragraphs 5(a)–(c), 5(h), 5(m), and 5(o)–(r) of this Statement and from the requirement to present interim-period disclosure of the separate components of net periodic benefit cost recognized. Users of financial statements have observed that when analyzing the financial statements of nonpublic entities, they rely on information about the benefit obligation, assets, and cash flows, but they do not require that same level of detail about benefit costs and net income as is provided by publicly traded entities.

A41. Few respondents addressed disclosure requirements for nonpublic entities. Of those that did, most agreed with the Board's decision, indicating that nonpublic entities do not have special circumstances that should exempt them from most of the disclosure requirements. Respondents who disagreed expressed concern about the cost and burden those requirements would impose on small and nonpublic entities. One respondent noted that many nonpublic entities do not perform annual measurements of costs and obligations and that incremental costs of providing some of the new disclosures could be significant. After considering all comments, the Board decided to reaffirm its previous decision to require the same information for nonpublic entities as for publicly traded entities except as described in paragraph A40. The Board concluded that the disclosures are not inappropriately burdensome and that nonpublic entities should perform measurements of costs and obligations as appropriate to provide reliable information.

Sensitivity Information

A42. The Board considered the requests of users of financial statements for sensitivity information about the effects of hypothetical changes in certain assumptions used in accounting for pension plans and other postretirement benefit plans. The Board was concerned that providing sensitivity information for individual assumptions, while holding all other assumptions constant, may be misunderstood. The effects of hypothetical changes in assumptions determined in this way may not be a reasonable representation of future results. Economic factors and conditions often affect multiple assumptions simultaneously, and the effects of changes in key assumptions are not linear.

A43. In the Exposure Draft, the Board decided not to require disclosure of sensitivity information about hypothetical changes in discount rates, expected long-term rates of return on assets, or rates of future compensation increase; however, the Exposure Draft requested respondents' views on these issues. In addition, the Board retained the requirement to provide the effect of a one-percentage-point increase and the effect of a one-percentage-point decrease in the assumed health care cost trend rates for the reasons identified in Statement 132, including the statement in paragraph B30 of this Statement that ". . . the effects of a one-percentage-point change in a plan's assumed health care cost trend rate would be difficult to assess because the way in which health care cost assumptions interact with caps, cost-sharing provisions, and other factors in the plan precludes reasonable estimates of the effects of those changes. The effects of changes in other assumptions, such as the weighted-average discount rate, can be more easily approximated."

A44. Most respondents supported the Board's decision not to require the disclosure of sensitivity information. Those who disagreed noted that sensitivity information about hypothetical changes in key assumptions would facilitate forecasts of the effects of changes in assumptions and would enable financial statement users to better compare similar companies that use different assumptions. Respondents expressed the most interest in sensitivity information about changes in discount rates and rates of future compensation increase. They expressed less interest in sensitivity information about changes in the expected long-term rate of return on plan assets. The Board considered those comments and reaffirmed its decision not to require disclosure of sensitivity information about changes in key assumptions. The

Board reasoned that sensitivity information may be misunderstood by investors and may not adequately take into account the interdependency of certain assumptions.

Reconsideration of Certain Statement 132 Disclosures

A45. The Board recognizes that pension and other postretirement benefit disclosures are substantial and that the benefits derived by users of financial statements should exceed the costs of compliance. To balance the addition of numerous disclosures in this project, the Board considered eliminating certain disclosures required by Statement 132. Specifically, the Board considered eliminating the reconciliations of beginning and ending balances of the fair value of plan assets and benefit obligations and replacing those reconciliations with disclosures of ending balances and key categories of activity not disclosed elsewhere, such as actual investment returns, benefit payments, employer contributions, and participant contributions.

A46. The Board's tentative decision to eliminate the reconciliations was included in the Exposure Draft. Most respondents disagreed with the Board's decision. They indicated that, absent that presentation, some users of financial statements might try to reconstruct the reconciliations. They also noted that preparers already have processes in place to provide the reconciliations and that auditors likely would continue to include the reconciliations in their reviews. After considering those comments, the Board decided to retain the Statement 132 requirements to provide a reconciliation of the beginning and ending balances of the fair value of plan assets and benefit obligations.

A47. The Board also considered eliminating the requirement to disclose the amounts and types of securities of the employer and its related parties included in plan assets. Holdings of related-party securities, while limited by ERISA, may not be limited in all jurisdictions and represent important information about plan assets. Therefore, the Board decided to retain that requirement of Statement 132.

Disclosures in Interim Financial Reports

A48. Some users of financial statements asked for the same disclosures in interim financial reports as in annual financial statements, reasoning that pension plans are often significant to enterprises and are sub-

ject to the volatility of equity markets and interest rates. However, the Board concluded that requiring all of those disclosures in interim-period financial statements would be overly burdensome to preparers of financial statements. The Board recognized that pension plans are long-term in nature and that many of the elements of net periodic cost are determined on an annual basis. The Board also was concerned about requiring interim-period disclosure of only certain aspects of pension plans. For example, interim-period disclosure of the fair value of plan assets, without an updated projected benefit obligation, would not provide enough information for users of financial statements to assess changes in the funded status.

A49. The Exposure Draft required interim-period disclosure of the components of net pension and other postretirement benefit costs. Although net benefit cost would not be expected to vary significantly from quarter to quarter because quarterly amounts would be based on the annual measurements, the amount of net benefit cost based on the most recent annual measurements would otherwise not be disclosed until year-end. Interim-period disclosure would better inform users about the effects of the most recent measurements on net benefit cost and would be useful to users in analyzing interim-period results.

A50. Many respondents disagreed with the interim-period disclosure of the components of net benefit cost. They reasoned that the accounting for pensions and other postretirement benefits is based on annual measurements and that certain interim-period amounts are often based on estimates. In addition, they noted that the nature of those benefits is long-term and that short-term information is therefore less meaningful. Finally, they noted that interim-period disclosure of the components of net benefit cost might imply that the disclosed cost was based on quarterly measurements of costs and obligations. During its redeliberations, the Board considered respondents' views and reaffirmed its previous decision to require interim-period disclosure of the components of net pension and other postretirement benefit cost. The Board acknowledged that interim-period financial statements often are based on estimates but concluded that this is not a sufficient reason not to disclose relevant information about amounts recognized.

Materiality

A51. The Board considered whether this Statement should require disclosures only for pension plans and other postretirement benefit plans that are material. The Board considered several possible bases for a materiality threshold including (a) plan assets as a percentage of total assets of the reporting entity, (b) benefit obligations as a percentage of total liabilities of the reporting entity, (c) net periodic benefit cost as a percentage of total income before taxes of the reporting entity, and (d) plan assets as a percentage of plan obligations. The Board decided that no general basis for a materiality threshold could be developed that would take into account all the considerations entering into a judgment about the materiality of pension plans and other postretirement benefit plans. In addition, the Board observed that a quantitative threshold based on net periodic benefit cost and reported income was not practicable because of the volatility of both net periodic benefit cost and reported income, and a threshold based on plan assets or obligations could result in inconsistent year-to-year designations. Based on those conclusions, the Board decided not to include a materiality threshold but noted that this decision does not imply that the provisions of this Statement should be applied to immaterial amounts.

Effective Date and Transition

A52. The Board believes that application of this Statement should not impose significant costs on most preparers of financial statements because the systems and processes necessary to provide most, if not all, of the required disclosures are already in place. Preparers of financial statements who comply with Statements 87, 106, and 132 have processes in place to compile information about plan assets. In addition, the annual measurements used to determine the benefit obligation are based on expected benefit payment cash flows, which actuaries have indicated should not require excessive effort to provide. For those reasons, the Board anticipates that most entities should have little difficulty providing the disclosures required by this Statement, including comparable prior-year information.

A53. The Board decided to make this Statement effective shortly after issuance for the new disclosures that it understood would be readily available in existing information systems, such as information about domestic plan assets, the accumulated benefit obligation, measurement date(s), estimated contributions, and assumptions. The Board believes that those disclosures are important to users of financial statements and that the data needed is readily available to preparers of financial statements. The Board decided that the other new disclosures might be more difficult to compile quickly, such as the information about benefit payments, along with all of the new disclosure requirements for foreign plans and nonpublic entities; therefore, those disclosures would be effective for fiscal years ending after June 15, 2004.

A54. The Board understands that some plan sponsors disclose aggregate amounts for domestic and foreign plans and that the usefulness of certain disclosures for domestic plans required for years ending after December 15, 2003, will therefore be limited. As a result, the Board decided that sponsors who adopt this Statement for years ending after December 15, 2003, only for domestic plans are also required to provide only domestic information for the fair value of plan assets and the expected long-term rate of return on assets. The Board concluded that the staggered effective date and transition provisions provide entities with adequate time to accumulate and develop the information required by this Statement.

Appendix B

STATEMENT 132: BACKGROUND INFORMATION AND BASIS FOR CONCLUSIONS

CONTENTS

Appendix B

STATEMENT 132: BACKGROUND INFORMATION AND BASIS FOR CONCLUSIONS (Note: *Paragraph numbering has been changed from original Statement.*)

Introduction

B1. This appendix summarizes considerations that were deemed significant by Board members in reaching the conclusions in this Statement. It includes reasons for accepting certain approaches and rejecting others. Individual Board members gave greater weight to some factors than to others. The Board concluded that it could reach an informed decision on the basis of existing information without a public hearing.

B2. The AICPA Special Committee on Financial Reporting (Special Committee) issued a report, *Improving Business Reporting—A Customer Focus,* in December 1994. In that report, the Special Committee recommended that "standard setters should search for and eliminate less relevant disclosures." The Special Committee also noted that many users indicated that "they would be willing to give up less important disclosures to make room for more important information."

B3. Disclosure effectiveness has been a concern of the Board for some time. FASB documents that have addressed this issue include the 1980 Invitation to Comment, *Financial Statements and Other Means of Financial Reporting,* and the 1981 Exposure Draft, *Reporting Income, Cash Flows, and Financial Position of Business Enterprises.* Board members and FASB staff have written numerous articles on the topic. In addition, disclosure effectiveness was discussed at an April 1995 Financial Accounting Standards Advisory Council (FASAC) meeting and at several liaison meetings during 1995.

B4. The Board issued a Prospectus, *Disclosure Effectiveness,* in July 1995. The Prospectus asked readers to consider possible changes to disclosure requirements consistent with one or both of two objectives: to reduce the cost of preparing and disseminating disclosures while providing users with information they need and to eliminate disclosures that are not useful for decision making. The Prospectus also encouraged further research and discussion on improving the effectiveness of financial reporting.

B5. The Board received 71 letters in response to the Prospectus. Respondents generally supported a project to improve disclosure effectiveness, and many respondents suggested that pensions, other postretirement benefits, income taxes, and leases were topics that required specific attention. Several respondents suggested that the Board develop a framework for disclosure.

B6. At the January 1996 FASAC meeting, several Council members suggested that the Board take an inductive approach to disclosure effectiveness, beginning by evaluating the requirements for disclosure about pensions and other postretirement benefits. A working group of FASAC members was formed to follow up on that suggestion. That group prepared a proposal that was discussed at the July 1996 FASAC meeting and in August 1996 at a public Board meeting with representatives of the Financial Executives Institute, the Association for Investment Management and Research, and other interested parties.

A Conceptual Framework for Disclosure

B7. Some participants in the August 1996 meeting did not favor proceeding with a project before defining the general objectives of disclosure. The Board considered developing a framework for disclosure based on FASB Concepts Statement No. 1, *Objectives of Financial Reporting by Business Enterprises,* and a review of published studies but concluded that not enough information was available to formulate a

framework at that time. In October 1996, the Board decided to proceed with an inductive approach to disclosure by initiating a project to examine pensions and other postretirement benefits to determine whether disclosures in that specific area could be improved, and, if so, whether any of the approaches undertaken could be applied to other accounting topics.

B8. In June 1997, the Board issued an Exposure Draft, *Employers' Disclosures about Pensions and Other Postretirement Benefits.* The Board received 90 comment letters in response to that Exposure Draft. Most respondents supported the Board's goal of improving disclosure effectiveness and generally stated that the revised disclosures proposed in the Exposure Draft were an improvement over those required by Statements 87 and 106. A few respondents noted that they were able to easily apply the requirements of the Exposure Draft to their prior year's pension and other postretirement benefits note disclosures and that the requirements resulted in more understandable disclosure.

General Considerations

B9. Discussions with certain users of financial statements indicated that the disclosures required by Statements 87 and 106, although extensive, did not provide sufficient information to understand the changes in the benefit obligation or to analyze the quality of earnings. This Statement is intended to enhance the utility of the information disclosed.

B10. As a result of those discussions, the Board identified two distinct sets of information used by analysts. Some requested information that enabled them to analyze the benefit obligation, fair value of plan assets, and changes in both during the period, including unrecognized gains and losses. The Board stated in Statement 87 that it believed that "it would be conceptually appropriate and preferable to recognize a net pension liability or asset measured as the difference between the projected benefit obligation and plan assets, either with no delay in recognition of gains and losses, or perhaps with gains and losses reported currently in comprehensive income but not in earnings" (paragraph 107). However, because Statement 87 did not require that accounting, the Board decided that this Statement should require disclosure of additional information about the changes in the benefit obligation and the fair value of plan assets during the period, including unrecognized gains and losses.

B11. The second set of information was most often requested by those analysts who follow publicly traded companies. Those users stated that they needed information about the quality of current earnings, including recognized and unrecognized amounts, that is useful in forecasting earnings for future periods in an effective and efficient manner.

B12. This Statement standardizes the disclosure requirements of Statements 87 and 106 to the extent practicable so that the required information should be easier to prepare and easier to understand. This Statement also suggests a parallel format for presenting information about pensions and other postretirement benefits in a more understandable manner.

Benefits and Costs

B13. Most or all of the additional information required by this Statement should be already available in actuarial or accounting calculations used to account for an employer's pension and other postretirement benefit plans. The Board believes that standardizing the format of the disclosures and eliminating some of the current requirements may reduce preparation time. The benefits to users are in the form of additional relevant amounts and reduced time and effort required to read and understand the pension and other postretirement benefit notes to the financial statements.

Specific Disclosure Requirements

Benefit Obligation and Fair Value of Plan Assets

B14. The Board concluded in Statements 87 and 106 that disclosure of the benefit obligation and fair value of plan assets is essential to an understanding of the economics of the employer's benefit plans and that disclosure of the fair value of plan assets is useful in assessing management's stewardship responsibilities for efficient use of those assets.

B15. Because the obligation and plan assets are offset in determining the amounts recognized in the statement of financial position and offsetting of assets and liabilities generally is not appropriate unless a right of offset exists,[7] disclosure of the amounts offset provides essential information about future economic benefits and sacrifices.

Explanation of the Changes in the Benefit Obligation and the Fair Value of Plan Assets

B16. This Statement amends Statements 87 and 106 to include disclosure of the changes in the benefit obligation and plan assets during the period, including the effects of economic events during the period (including amendments, combinations, divestitures, curtailments, and settlements). Statement 87 required disclosure of the nature and effect of significant matters affecting comparability of information for all periods presented. Statement 106 required the same disclosure but specifically referred to business combinations or divestitures. In practice, those requirements have not resulted in the anticipated level of disclosure. The Board believes that an explanation of the changes in the benefit obligation and fair value of plan assets in the form of a reconciliation of the beginning and ending balances will provide a format for more complete disclosure that also should be more understandable to users of financial statements.

B17. Disclosure of the benefit obligation, fair value of plan assets, and changes in them during the period is consistent with the Board's conceptual framework, which states that "financial reporting should provide information about the economic resources of an enterprise, the claims to those resources (obligations of the enterprise to transfer resources to other entities and owners' equity), and the effects of transactions, events, and circumstances that change resources and claims to those resources" (Concepts Statement 1, paragraph 40; footnote reference omitted).

Reconciliation of the Funded Status with the Amounts Recognized in the Financial Statements

B18. Both Statement 87 and Statement 106 require a reconciliation of the funded status of the plan with the amounts recognized in the financial statements. The Board considered eliminating those requirements but decided to retain them in this Statement after financial analysts commented that information about unamortized balances of prior service cost and transition amounts is useful in assessing current earnings and forecasting future amortization. The Board also concluded, as it did in Statement 87, that the amount recognized in the financial statements as a net benefit liability or asset does not reflect fully the underlying financial status of the plan and that a reconciliation of the amounts is essential to an

---

[7]Refer to APB Opinion No. 10, *Omnibus Opinion—1966*, paragraph 7.

understanding of the relationship between the accounting methodology and the funded status of the plan. For those reasons the Board decided to retain disclosure of the unrecognized amounts, including unamortized prior service cost, unamortized transition amounts, and unrecognized gains and losses.

B19. If an additional minimum liability is recognized, the reconciliation includes disclosure of any amount recognized as an intangible asset or included in accumulated other comprehensive income. The format recommended in Statement 87 disclosed those amounts as an additional minimum liability. The format that is illustrated in this Statement includes all amounts recognized.

Components of Net Periodic Benefit Cost

B20. The Exposure Draft proposed eliminating the requirement in Statements 87 and 106 to disclose the components of net periodic benefit cost. Several respondents suggested that that disclosure be retained to provide greater visibility of the amounts included in the employer's results of operations. In addition, certain users, primarily equity analysts, stated that information included in that disclosure was useful in forecasting an employer's net income. In response to those concerns, the Board decided to retain the requirement in Statements 87 and 106 to disclose the components of net periodic benefit cost and to add disclosures about the expected return on plan assets, the amortization of the transition obligation or asset, and the recognition of gains and losses.

Employers with Two or More Plans

B21. Both Statement 87 and Statement 106 required additional disclosure of certain benefit plan information if an employer has plans with benefit obligations in excess of plan assets and plans with assets in excess of benefit obligations. Statement 87 required separate schedules reconciling the funded status of the plan with amounts reported in the employer's statement of financial position for plans with assets in excess of accumulated pension benefit obligations and plans with accumulated pension benefit obligations in excess of plan assets. Statement 106 required separate disclosure of the aggregate plan assets and the aggregate benefit obligation of underfunded plans. The Board decided to change the requirements for pension plans to parallel those for other postretirement benefit plans because those requirements are less complex and provide satisfactory information about the financial position of an em-

ployer's plans. The Board decided to retain disclosure of the accumulated pension benefit obligation for pension plans with accumulated benefit obligations in excess of plan assets because that disclosure is useful to regulators and other users of financial information. The Board included a requirement to disclose separately amounts recognized as prepaid benefit costs and accrued benefit costs so that users could determine the amounts included in the statement of financial position.

B22. Some respondents to the Exposure Draft, including preparers, disagreed with the Board's decision to permit aggregation of disclosures about plans with different characteristics. They stated that users of financial statements could draw incorrect conclusions about an employer's funding policies or that employers would be able to offset underfunded plans with well-funded plans. The Board decided that permitting the aggregation of disclosures about multiple plans will simplify disclosure and will conform disclosures about pensions to those about other postretirement plans while continuing to provide users with sufficient information about the employer's plans. The Board also noted that, while aggregation of disclosures about plans is permitted by this Statement, an employer may disclose additional disaggregated information if the employer believes doing so provides more meaningful information.

Foreign Plans

B23. Statement 87 specified that disclosures about plans outside the United States should not be combined with those about U.S. plans unless those plans use similar assumptions. Statement 106 required separate presentation for foreign plans if the benefit obligations are significant relative to the total benefit obligation for all plans. The Board decided to harmonize those disclosures with this Statement. Accordingly, the Board decided that disclosures about U.S. plans may be combined with those about foreign plans unless the benefit obligations of the foreign plans are significant relative to the employer's total benefit obligation and those plans use significantly different assumptions.

B24. Some respondents to the Exposure Draft noted that some foreign plans typically are not funded because there are no tax advantages to funding plans in those jurisdictions. Those respondents suggested that the benefit obligation related to foreign plans be disclosed separately because combining disclosures about foreign and U.S. plans might be misleading.

The Board believes that the requirements of paragraph 6 of this Statement will adequately inform users about the presence of underfunded plans. The Board also decided that whether aggregation of disclosures about underfunded plans was appropriate should not depend on whether the plans are located within the United States or abroad.

Assumed Health Care Cost Trend Rates

B25. Statement 106 requires disclosure of the assumed health care cost trend rate for the next year used to measure the expected cost of benefits covered by the plan (gross eligible charges) and a general description of the direction and pattern of change in assumed trend rates thereafter, together with the ultimate trend rate and when that rate was expected to be achieved. All other requirements for disclosure of plan assumptions in Statements 87 and 106 call for disclosure of weighted-average rates. The Exposure Draft that led to Statement 106 proposed disclosure of a weighted average of the assumed health care cost trend rates, but in its deliberations the Board decided that a weighted-average rate can mask differences in an employer's assumptions about year-by-year health care cost trend rates. In the Exposure Draft that led to this Statement, the Board reconsidered the disclosure requirement for assumed health care cost trend rates and decided that disclosure of a weighted-average rate would provide for better comparability among entities and with other assumptions that are disclosed on a weighted-average basis.

B26. Some respondents to the Exposure Draft stated that the cost of calculating that disclosure could be significant and argued that the increased cost was not justified in the circumstances. Others reiterated the comments made prior to the issuance of Statement 106 about the potential for the use of a weighted-average rate to mask differences in year-by-year health care cost assumptions. Although some Board members continue to believe that disclosure of the weighted-average rate is more effective, the Board ultimately decided that the disclosures about health care cost trend rate assumptions in Statement 106 provide satisfactory information and that disclosure of a weighted-average measure should not be required, primarily because of respondents' assertions about the incremental cost to provide that information.

The Effects of a One-Percentage-Point Change in the Assumed Health Care Cost Trend Rates

B27. Statement 106 requires disclosure of the effects of a one-percentage-point increase in the assumed health care cost trend rates for each future year on (a) the aggregate of the service and interest cost components of net periodic postretirement health care benefit cost and (b) the accumulated postretirement benefit obligation for health care benefits. The Board decided to retain the sensitivity analysis disclosure in Statement 106 and, in addition, to require disclosure of the effects of a one-percentage-point decrease in the assumed health care cost trend rates on (a) the aggregate of the service and interest cost components of net periodic postretirement health care benefit cost and (b) the accumulated postretirement benefit obligation for health care benefits. Most respondents to the Exposure Draft commented on that additional disclosure requirement. The majority stated that the effects of a one-percentage-point decrease should not be required, and many respondents opposed any sensitivity information.

B28. Some Board members questioned the usefulness of a disclosure that focuses on the effects of a change in a single assumption underlying the calculation of the benefit obligation. They noted that calculating the accumulated postretirement benefit obligation requires numerous assumptions and estimates. Changes in certain of those assumptions and estimates may have a much more significant effect on the employer's obligation than changes in the assumed heath care cost trend rates. Moreover, those Board members noted that many assumptions and estimates underlie an entity's financial statements and that one should not focus on the change in a single factor to the exclusion of others that may be equally or more important. Those Board members advocated eliminating the sensitivity analysis as described in the Exposure Draft in favor of examining outside of this project the broader issue of disclosures about risks and uncertainties.

B29. Those Board members also noted that the disclosure of a one-percentage-point increase required by Statement 106 was included in that Statement because, at the time, ". . . users [were] considerably less familiar with postretirement health care measurements than with pension measurements and with the subjectivity of the health care cost trend rate and the significant effect that assumption may have on measurement of the postretirement health care obligation" (paragraph 355). Those Board members believe that users are now sufficiently familiar with the effects of changes in health care trend rates on the postretirement health care obligation and, therefore, this disclosure is no longer useful. Accordingly, they expressed strong reservations about retaining it in this Statement.

B30. However, a majority of the Board concluded that disclosure of the effects of a one-percentage-point increase and a one-percentage-point decrease in the assumed health care cost trend rate provides useful information to users of financial statements. As previously stated in Statement 106, requiring ". . . sensitivity information will assist users in assessing the comparability of information reported by different employers as well as the extent to which future changes in assumptions or actual experience different from that assumed may affect the measurement of the obligation and cost. In addition, the sensitivity information may assist users in understanding the relative significance of an employer's cost-sharing policy as encompassed by the employer's substantive plan" (paragraph 354). The Board concluded that those considerations remain relevant today. It noted that sensitivity disclosures are consistent with the recommendations of the AICPA Special Committee for improved disclosure about the uncertainty inherent in the measurement of certain assets and liabilities. Some Board members also noted that the effects of a one-percentage-point change in a plan's assumed health care cost trend rate would be difficult to assess because the way in which health care cost assumptions interact with caps, cost-sharing provisions, and other factors in the plan precludes reasonable estimates of the effects of those changes. The effects of changes in other assumptions, such as the weighted-average discount rate, can be more easily approximated.

B31. The Board decided to retain the requirement to disclose the effects of both an increase and a decrease in the assumed health care cost trend rates because the effects of an increase and a decrease are not necessarily symmetrical for a plan due to the way in which health care cost assumptions interact with caps or other cost-sharing provisions and for other reasons. In addition, because the growth in the rate of health care costs has decreased for many plans since the issuance of Statement 106, disclosure of the effects of a decrease in the assumed health care cost

trend rates may provide more relevant information than the effects of an increase.

Related Party Transactions

B32. Both Statement 87 and Statement 106 required disclosure of the amounts and types of securities of the employer and related parties included in plan assets and the approximate amount of future annual benefits of plan participants covered by insurance contracts issued by the employer or related parties. The Board decided to retain those disclosure requirements in this Statement. The Board also decided to require added disclosures about any significant transactions between the plan and the employer during the period, including noncash transactions, because of the relevance of information about related party transactions, as described in the basis for conclusions to FASB Statement No. 57, *Related Party Disclosures.*

Other Disclosures Considered

Concentrations of Market Risk

B33. The Board considered whether an employer should disclose concentrations of market risk in plan assets. FASB Statement No. 124, *Accounting for Certain Investments Held by Not-for-Profit Organizations,* requires disclosure of the nature of and carrying amount for each individual investment or group of investments that represents a significant concentration of market risk. The Board concluded that disclosures needed about plan assets differ from those about investments held by not-for-profit organizations because trustees of benefit plans are usually constrained to follow policies for the sole benefit of the plan beneficiaries, whereas fund managers of not-for-profit organizations may be constrained only by donor restrictions. Also, provisions of the Employee Retirement Income Security Act generally require that plan trustees diversify plan investments. Consequently, the usefulness of that disclosure requirement for U.S. plans could be limited.

B34. Several respondents to the Exposure Draft asked that the Board also consider requiring disclosure of the composition of plan assets as a means of enabling users to assess concentrations of risk in the plan's portfolio. The Board noted that disclosure of the type of information about plan assets that would be required to enable the user to identify and assess concentrations of risk would be extensive, in certain circumstances requiring disclosure about individual securities. The Board decided that requiring extensive disclosures about the composition of plan assets in the employer's financial statements would add significant complexity to the disclosure and was generally inconsistent with its objective of promoting more effective disclosure.

Components of the Benefit Obligation

B35. Statements 87 and 106 required disclosure of several components of the benefit obligation. Statement 87 required disclosure of the accumulated pension benefit obligation and the vested pension benefit obligation. Statement 106 required disclosure of the portions of the plan obligation attributable to retirees, other fully eligible plan participants, and other active plan participants.

B36. Disclosure of the accumulated pension benefit obligation and vested pension benefit obligation was considered relevant when Statement 87 was issued because there was less agreement at that time as to the best measure of the pension benefit obligation. Some respondents to the Exposure Draft that led to Statement 87 would have limited the recognized liability to the vested pension benefit obligation. In the deliberations preceding the issuance of Statement 87, the Board considered a minimum liability based on the vested pension benefit obligation but concluded that the time at which benefits vest should not be the primary point for recognition of either cost or liabilities. The disclosure requirements of Statement 106 for the portion attributable to retirees, other fully eligible plan participants, and other active plan participants are proxies for disclosure of the vested and nonvested benefit obligation for other postretirement benefit obligations.

B37. The Board decided to eliminate the requirement to disclose (a) accumulated pension benefit obligations for plans with assets that exceed that amount, (b) vested pension benefit obligations, and (c) the portions of other postretirement benefit plan obligations attributable to retirees, other fully eligible plan participants, and other active plan participants. None of those amounts are used to forecast pension or other postretirement benefit costs or obligations, and, therefore, those amounts have limited relevance to users of financial statements. The Board decided to retain disclosure of the accumulated pension benefit obligation for plans with accumulated pension benefit obligations in excess of plan assets because that component is used to determine the minimum liability and may be relevant to users of financial statements.

General Descriptive Information

B38. Both Statement 87 and Statement 106 required disclosure of general descriptive information about the employer's benefit plans, including employee groups covered, type of benefit formula, funding policy, types of assets held, and significant nonbenefit liabilities, if any. This Statement does not require that disclosure because the Board believes it provides only limited useful information to users of financial statements due to the general nature of the information provided, particularly after aggregating information about multiple plans with different characteristics. In lieu of that disclosure, this Statement requires disclosure of significant events occurring during the period that are otherwise not apparent in the disclosures, as that information is more relevant to users of financial statements. Several respondents to the Exposure Draft stated that the description of the plan required by Statements 87 and 106 can provide useful information about the plan. The Board therefore encourages an employer to provide a description of its plans if such a description would provide meaningful information, such as when the employer sponsors only a single plan.

Materiality

B39. The Board considered whether this Statement should include a materiality threshold for requiring certain disclosures about pension and other postretirement benefit plans. Materiality and relevance are both defined in terms of what influences or makes a difference to a decision maker. The Board's position is that "no general standards of materiality could be formulated to take into account all the considerations that enter into an experienced human judgment," but that quantitative materiality criteria may be given by the Board in specific standards, as appropriate (FASB Concepts Statement No. 2, *Qualitative Characteristics of Accounting Information,* paragraph 131).

B40. The Board considered implementing materiality thresholds for pension and other postretirement benefit disclosures, including thresholds based on the gross obligations for plan benefits and the employer's assets, equity, revenues, or net income. Each measure had disadvantages. Because a materiality threshold should take into account the information most likely to influence or make a difference to a decision maker, net income appeared to be the most relevant element for publicly traded companies. Some analysts use information about current benefit costs and the funded status of the plan to assess the quality of current earnings and the employer's financial condition. They also use that information to prepare their forecasts of future earnings, measuring the impact on net income as precisely as possible. The Board concluded that a precise threshold in terms of net income was not practicable because of the natural volatility of net income and the resulting difficulty in making materiality judgments with a relatively simple materiality rule. Therefore, this Statement does not include a materiality threshold. However, that does not imply that the provisions of this Statement must be applied to immaterial items. Some entities may determine that some or all pension or other postretirement benefit disclosures are not material after evaluation of all the relevant facts and circumstances.

Nonpublic Entities

B41. The *Report of the Committee on Generally Accepted Accounting Principles for Smaller and/or Closely Held Businesses,* issued by the AICPA in August 1976, observed that some disclosures merely provide additional or analytical data and may not be appropriate for all entities. The Committee also observed, however, that analytical data may be appropriate in certain circumstances for certain types of entities.

B42. Before issuing the Exposure Draft, the Board had asked certain users of financial statements of nonpublic entities to comment on the usefulness of current and proposed disclosure requirements. Those users observed that they did not require the same level of precision in assessing benefit costs and net income when analyzing the financial statements of nonpublic entities but that they did rely on information about the benefit obligations, assets, and cash flows. Based on the input of those users, the Board concluded that a reduced disclosure set would be appropriate for nonpublic entities. The Board determined that a nonpublic entity should, at a minimum, provide the same information about the benefit obligations, plan assets, recognized assets or liabilities, cash flows, benefit costs, actuarial assumptions, and related party transactions as required for a public entity.

B43. The Exposure Draft would have required that a nonpublic entity disclose all of the information in paragraph 5 if total unrecognized pension and other postretirement benefit amounts exceeded 5 percent of equity (or unrestricted net assets). Many respondents objected to that provision out of concern that it might be viewed as the establishment of a materiality standard that could be applied in other circumstances. The Board decided not to require that disclosure but, rather, to provide for reduced disclosures for all nonpublic entities. The Board concluded that introducing a specific threshold was therefore unnecessary.

B44. However, because nonpublic entities are not required to provide a reconciliation of the benefit obligation or the fair value of plan assets under the provisions of this Statement, the Board decided to require disclosure of information about the effects of significant nonroutine events during the period, such as amendments, combinations, divestitures, curtailments, and settlements, whenever those events occur. The Board believes that that disclosure is necessary for users of financial statements to understand the effects of those changes that otherwise might not be apparent. Even though this Statement permits reduced disclosures for nonpublic entities, the Board concluded that the incremental information required by paragraph 5 improves understanding and, therefore, encourages those entities to disclose that information.

Effective Date and Transition

B45. This Statement is effective for fiscal years beginning after December 15, 1997. Earlier application is encouraged. The Board decided that the disclosures required by this Statement should be provided for earlier periods presented for comparative purposes, unless that information is not readily available. The Board believes that application of this Statement should not impose a hardship on most preparers of financial statements because the systems necessary to provide most, if not all, of the required disclosures are already in place. For that reason, disclosure of comparable prior-year information should not be difficult for most entities.

Appendix C

ILLUSTRATIONS

C1. This appendix illustrates the following pension and other postretirement benefit disclosures:

a. Illustration 1—Disclosures about Pension and Other Postretirement Benefit Plans in the Annual Financial Statements of a Publicly Traded Entity
b. Illustration 2—Interim-Period Disclosures of a Publicly Traded Entity
c. Illustration 3—Interim-Period Disclosures of a Nonpublic Entity in a Complete Set of Financial Statements.

The financial statements of a nonpublic entity would be similarly presented but would not be required to include the information contained in paragraphs 5(a)–(c), 5(h), 5(m), and 5(o)–(r) of this Statement. The items presented in these examples have been included for illustrative purposes. Certain assumptions have been made to simplify the computations and focus on the disclosure requirements. Illustration 1 replaces Illustrations 1, 2, and 3 in Statement 132, which superseded Illustration 6 in Statement 87 and Illustration 7 in Statement 106.

Illustration 1—Disclosures about Pension and Other Postretirement Benefit Plans in the Annual Financial Statements of a Publicly Traded Entity

C2. The following illustrates the fiscal 20X3 financial statement disclosures for an employer (Company A) with multiple defined benefit pension plans and other postretirement benefit plans. Narrative descriptions of the basis used to determine the overall expected long-term rate-of-return-on-assets assumption (paragraph 5(d)(3)) and investment policies and

strategies for plan assets (paragraph 5(d)(2)) are not included in this illustration. These narrative descriptions are meant to be entity-specific and should reflect an entity's basis for selecting the expected long-term rate-of-return-on-assets assumption and the most important investment policies and strategies.

C3. During 20X3, Company A acquired FV Industries and amended its plans.

Notes to Financial Statements

Pension and Other Postretirement Benefit Plans

Company A has both funded and unfunded noncontributory defined benefit pension plans that together cover substantially all of its employees. The plans provide defined benefits based on years of service and final average salary.

Company A also has other postretirement benefit plans covering substantially all of its employees. The health care plans are contributory with participants' contributions adjusted annually; the life insurance plans are noncontributory. The accounting for the health care plans anticipates future cost-sharing changes to the written plans that are consistent with the company's expressed intent to increase retiree contributions each year by 50 percent of health care cost increases in excess of 6 percent. The postretirement health care plans include a limit on the company's share of costs for recent and future retirees.

Company A acquired FV Industries on December 27, 20X3, including its pension plans and other postretirement benefit plans. Amendments made at the end of 20X3 to Company A's plans increased the pension benefit obligations by $70 and reduced the other postretirement benefit obligations by $75.

Obligations and Funded Status

At December 31

	Pension Benefits		Other Benefits	
	20X3	20X2	20X3	20X2
Change in benefit obligation				
Benefit obligation at beginning of year	$1,246	$1,200	$ 742	$ 712
Service cost	76	72	36	32
Interest cost	90	88	55	55
Plan participants' contributions			20	13
Amendments	70		(75)	
Actuarial loss	20		25	
Acquisition	900		600	
Benefits paid	(125)	(114)	(90)	(70)
Benefit obligation at end of year	2,277	1,246	1,313	742
Change in plan assets				
Fair value of plan assets at beginning of year	1,068	894	206	87
Actual return on plan assets	29	188	5	24
Acquisition	1,000		25	
Employer contribution	75	100	137	152
Plan participants' contributions			20	13
Benefits paid	(125)	(114)	(90)	(70)
Fair value of plan assets at end of year	2,047	1,068	303	206
Funded status at end of year	$ (230)	$ (178)	$(1,010)	$ (536)

Note: Nonpublic entities are not required to provide information in the above tables; they are required to disclose the employer's contributions, participants' contributions, benefit payments, and the funded status.

Amounts recognized in the statement of financial position consist of:

	Pension Benefits		Other Benefits	
	20X3	20X2	20X3	20X2
Noncurrent assets	$ 227	$ 127	$ 0	$ 0
Current liabilities	(125)	(125)	(150)	(150)
Noncurrent liabilities	(332)	(180)	(860)	(386)
	$ (230)	$ (178)	$(1,010)	$ (536)

Amounts recognized in accumulated other comprehensive income consist of:

	Pension Benefits		Other Benefits	
	20X3	20X2	20X3	20X2
Net loss (gain)	$ 94	$ 18	$ (11)	$ (48)
Prior service cost (credit)	210	160	(92)	(22)
	$ 304	$ 178	$ (103)	$ (70)

The accumulated benefit obligation for all defined benefit pension plans was $1,300 and $850 at December 31, 20X3, and 20X2, respectively.

**Information for pension plans with an
 accumulated benefit obligation in excess
 of plan assets**

	December 31	
	20X3	**20X2**
Projected benefit obligation	$263	$247
Accumulated benefit obligation	237	222
Fair value of plan assets	84	95

**Components of Net Periodic Benefit Cost and
 Other Amounts Recognized in Other
 Comprehensive Income**

	Pension Benefits		Other Benefits	
Net Periodic Benefit Cost	**20X3**	**20X2**	**20X3**	**20X2**
Service cost	$ 76	$ 72	$ 36	$32
Interest cost	90	88	55	55
Expected return on plan assets	(85)	(76)	(17)	(8)
Amortization of prior service cost	20	16	(5)	(5)
Amortization of net (gain) loss	0	0	0	0
Net periodic benefit cost	$101	$100	$ 69	$74

**Other Changes in Plan Assets and Benefit
 Obligations Recognized in Other
 Comprehensive Income**

Net loss (gain)	$ 76	$112	$ 37	$(48)
Prior service cost (credit)	70	0	(75)	(27)
Amortization of prior service cost	(20)	(16)	5	5
Total recognized in other comprehensive income	126	96	(33)	(70)
Total recognized in net periodic benefit cost and other comprehensive income	$227	$196	$ 36	$ 4

The estimated net loss and prior service cost for the defined benefit pension plans that will be amortized from accumulated other comprehensive income into net periodic benefit cost over the next fiscal year are $4 and $27, respectively. The estimated prior service credit for the other defined benefit postretirement plans that will be amortized from accumulated other comprehensive income into net periodic benefit cost over the next fiscal year is $10.

Note: Nonpublic entities are not required to separately disclose components of net periodic benefit cost.

Assumptions

**Weighted-average assumptions used
to determine benefit obligations at
December 31**

	Pension Benefits		Other Benefits	
	20X3	20X2	20X3	20X2
Discount rate	6.75%	7.25%	7.00%	7.50%
Rate of compensation increase	4.25	4.50		

**Weighted-average assumptions used
to determine net periodic benefit cost
for years ended December 31**

	Pension Benefits		Other Benefits	
	20X3	20X2	20X3	20X2
Discount rate	7.25%	7.50%	7.50%	7.75%
Expected long-term return on plan assets	8.00	8.50	8.10	8.75
Rate of compensation increase	4.50	4.75		

(Entity-specific narrative description of the basis used to determine the overall expected long-term rate of return on assets, as described in paragraph 5(d)(3) would be included here.)

**Assumed health care cost trend rates at
December 31**

	20X3	20X2
Health care cost trend rate assumed for next year	12%	12.5%
Rate to which the cost trend rate is assumed to decline (the ultimate trend rate)	6%	5%
Year that the rate reaches the ultimate trend rate	20X9	20X9

Assumed health care cost trend rates have a significant effect on the amounts reported for the health care plans. A one-percentage-point change in assumed health care cost trend rates would have the following effects:

	1-Percentage-Point Increase	1-Percentage-Point Decrease
Effect on total of service and interest cost	$ 22	$ (20)
Effect on postretirement benefit obligation	173	(156)

Note: Nonpublic entities are not required to provide the above information about the impact of a one-percentage-point increase and one-percentage-point decrease in the assumed health care cost trend rates.

Plan Assets

Company A's pension plan weighted-average asset allocations at December 31, 20X3, and 20X2, by asset category are as follows:

Asset Category	Plan Assets at December 31	
	20X3	20X2
Equity securities	50%	48%
Debt securities	30	31
Real estate	10	12
Other	10	9
Total	100%	100%

(Entity specific narrative description of investment policies and strategies for plan assets, including weighted-average target asset allocations [if used as part of those policies and strategies] as described in paragraph 5(d)(2) would be included here.)

Equity securities include Company A common stock in the amounts of $80 million (4 percent of total plan assets) and $64 million (6 percent of total plan assets) at December 31, 20X3, and 20X2, respectively.

Company A's other postretirement benefit plan weighted-average asset allocations at December 31, 20X3, and 20X2, by asset category are as follows:

Asset Category	Plan Assets at December 31	
	20X3	20X2
Equity securities	60%	52%
Debt securities	30	27
Real estate	5	13
Other	5	8
Total	100%	100%

Equity securities include Company A common stock in the amounts of $12 million (4 percent of total plan assets) and $8 million (4 percent of total plan assets) at December 31, 20X3, and 20X2, respectively.

Cash Flows

Contributions

Company A expects to contribute $125 million to its pension plan and $150 million to its other postretirement benefit plan in 20X4.

Estimated Future Benefit Payments

The following benefit payments, which reflect expected future service, as appropriate, are expected to be paid:

	Pension Benefits	Other Benefits
20X4	$ 200	$150
20X5	208	155
20X6	215	160
20X7	225	165
20X8	235	170
Years 20X9–20Y3	1,352	984

Illustration 2—Interim-Period Disclosures of a Publicly Traded Entity

C4. The following illustrates the disclosures of a publicly traded entity for the first fiscal quarter beginning after December 15, 20X3.

Components of Net Periodic Benefit Cost

Three months ended March 31

	Pension Benefits		Other Benefits	
	20X4	20X3	20X4	20X3
Service cost	$ 35	$ 19	$ 16	$ 9
Interest cost	38	23	23	14
Expected return on plan assets	(41)	(21)	(6)	(4)
Amortization of prior service cost	7	5	(3)	(1)
Amortization of net (gain) loss	2	0	0	0
Net periodic benefit cost	$ 41	$ 26	$ 30	$ 18

Employer Contributions

Company A previously disclosed in its financial statements for the year ended December 31, 20X3, that it expected to contribute $125 million to its pension plan in 20X4. As of March 31, 20X4, $20 million of contributions have been made. Company A presently anticipates contributing an additional $120 million to fund its pension plan in 20X4 for a total of $140 million.

Illustration 3—Interim-Period Disclosures of a Nonpublic Entity in a Complete Set of Financial Statements

C5. The following illustrates the disclosures for a nonpublic entity (Entity A) for the first fiscal quarter beginning after December 15, 20X3.

Entity A previously disclosed in its financial statements for the year ended December 31, 20X3, that it expected to contribute $125 million to its pension plan in 20X4. As of March 31, 20X4, $20 million of contributions have been made. Entity A presently anticipates contributing an additional $120 million to fund its pension plan in 20X4 for a total of $140 million.

Appendix D

IMPACT ON RELATED LITERATURE

D1. This appendix addresses the impact of this Statement on the consensuses reached on EITF Issues relating to disclosures about pension and other postretirement benefits. This appendix does not address the impact of this Statement on other authoritative accounting literature included in categories (b), (c), and (d) in the GAAP hierarchy discussed in AICPA Statement on Auditing Standards No. 69, *The Meaning of "Present Fairly in Conformity with Generally Accepted Accounting Principles" in the Independent Auditor's Report.*

EITF Consensuses

D2. The following table lists EITF Issues and Topics relating to employers' disclosures about pension plans and other postretirement benefit plans and indicates (a) the status of that literature after issuance of this Statement and (b) the impact of this Statement on that literature (if any) or the reasons that the literature is beyond the scope of this Statement.

Status Legend

N/A   Guidance is either outside the scope of this Statement or unaffected by this Statement.

EITF Issue No.	Title	Status	Commentary	Status Section Update
92-12	Accounting for OPEB Costs by Rate-Regulated Enterprises	N/A	The consensus in Issue 92-12 states that a rate-regulated enterprise should disclose a description of the regulatory treatment of OPEB costs, the status of any pending regulatory action, the amount of any Statement 106 costs deferred, and the period over which the deferred amounts are expected to be recovered in rates.	This Statement does not affect the guidance provided by the EITF on the OPEB disclosures for rate-regulated enterprises.
92-13	Accounting for Estimated Payments in Connection with the Coal Industry Retiree Health Benefit Act of 1992	N/A	The consensus in Issue 92-13 states that enterprises should disclose the impact of the Act, including the estimated amount of their total obligation and the method of accounting adopted.	This Statement does not affect the guidance provided by the EITF on the required disclosures from the Coal Industry Retiree Health Benefit Act of 1992.
03-2	Accounting for the Transfer to the Japanese Government of the Substitutional Portion of Employee Pension Fund Liabilities	N/A	The consensus in Issue 03-2 states that the difference between the obligation settled and assets transferred to the government should be disclosed separately as a subsidy from the government.	This Statement does not affect the guidance provided by the EITF on the disclosure of the transfer to the Japanese government of the substitutional portion of employee pension fund liabilities.

Appendix E

GLOSSARY

E1. This appendix contains definitions of certain terms used in this Statement.

Accumulated benefit obligation

The actuarial present value of pension benefits (whether vested or unvested) attributed to employee service rendered before a specified date and based on employee service and compensation (if applicable) prior to that date. The accumulated benefit obligation differs from the projected benefit obligation in that it includes no assumption about future compensation levels. For plans with flat-benefit or non-pay-related pension benefit formulas, the accumulated benefit obligation and the projected benefit obligation are the same.

Accumulated postretirement benefit obligation

The actuarial present value of benefits attributed to employee service rendered to a particular date. Prior to an employee's full eligibility date, the accumulated postretirement benefit obligation as of a particular date for an employee is the portion of the expected postretirement benefit obligation attributed to that employee's service rendered to that date; on and after the full eligibility date, the accumulated and expected postretirement benefit obligations for an employee are the same.

Debt security

Any security representing a creditor relationship with an enterprise. It also includes (a) preferred stock that by its terms either must be redeemed by the issuing enterprise or is redeemable at the option of the investor and (b) a collateralized mortgage obligation (CMO) (or other instrument) that is issued in equity form but is required to be accounted for as a nonequity instrument regardless of how that instrument is classified (that is, whether equity or debt) in the issuer's statement of financial position. However, it excludes option contracts, financial futures contracts, forward contracts, and lease contracts. Thus, the term *debt security* includes, among other items, U.S. Treasury securities, U.S. government agency securities, municipal securities, corporate bonds, convertible debt, commercial paper, all securitized debt instruments, such as CMOs and real estate mortgage investment conduits (REMICs), and interest-only and principal-only strips. Trade accounts receivable arising from sales on credit by industrial or commercial enterprises and loans receivable arising from consumer, commercial, and real estate lending activities of financial institutions are examples of receivables that do not meet the definition of *security;* thus, those receivables are not debt securities (unless they have been securitized, in which case they would meet the definition).

Equity security

Any security representing an ownership interest in an enterprise (for example, common, preferred, or other capital stock) or the right to acquire (for example, warrants, rights, and call options) or dispose of (for example, put options) an ownership interest in an enterprise at fixed or determinable prices. However, the term does not include convertible debt or preferred stock that by its terms either must be redeemed by the issuing enterprise or is redeemable at the option of the investor.

Nonpublic entity

Any entity other than one (a) whose debt or equity securities trade in a public market either on a stock exchange (domestic or foreign) or in the over-the-counter market, including securities quoted only locally or regionally, (b) that is a conduit bond obligor for conduit debt securities that are traded in a public market (a domestic or foreign stock exchange or an over-the-counter market, including local or regional markets), (c) that makes a filing with a regulatory agency in preparation for the sale of any class of debt or equity securities in a public market, or (d) that is controlled by an entity covered by (a), (b), or (c).

Conduit debt securities refers to certain limited-obligation revenue bonds, certificates of participation, or similar debt instruments issued by a state or local governmental entity for the express purpose of providing financing for a specific third party (the conduit bond obligor) that is not a part of the state or local government's financial reporting entity. Although conduit debt securities bear the name of the governmental entity that issues them, the governmental entity often has no obligation for such debt beyond the resources provided by a lease or loan agreement with the third party on whose behalf the securities are issued. Further, the conduit bond obligor is responsible for any future financial reporting requirements.

Projected benefit obligation

The actuarial present value as of a date of all benefits attributed by the pension benefit formula to employee service rendered prior to that date. The projected benefit obligation is measured using assumptions as to future compensation levels if the pension benefit formula is based on those future compensation levels (pay-related, final-pay, final-average-pay, or career-average-pay plans).

Publicly traded entity

Any entity that does not meet the definition of a *nonpublic entity.*

Statement of Financial Accounting Standards No. 133
Accounting for Derivative Instruments and Hedging Activities

STATUS

Issued: June 1998

Effective Date: For all fiscal quarters of all fiscal years beginning after June 15, 1999 (Deferred to all fiscal quarters of all fiscal years beginning after June 15, 2000 by FAS 137)

Affects: Amends ARB 43, Chapter 4, paragraph 8
Amends FAS 52 by adding paragraph 14A
Amends FAS 52, paragraphs 15, 16, 30, 31(b), and 162
Deletes FAS 52, paragraphs 17 through 19
Replaces FAS 52, paragraph 21
Amends FAS 60, paragraphs 46 and 50
Amends FAS 65, paragraphs 4 and 9(a)
Deletes FAS 65, paragraph 9(b)(1)
Supersedes FAS 80
Amends FAS 95, footnote 4
Supersedes FAS 105
Deletes FAS 107, paragraph 4
Amends FAS 107, paragraphs 10 and 31
Replaces FAS 107, paragraph added after paragraph 13 by FAS 119
Amends FAS 107 by adding paragraphs 15A through 15D
Amends FAS 113, paragraph 28
Amends FAS 115, paragraphs 4, 13, 15(b), 16, 19 through 22, 115, and 137
Supersedes FAS 119
Amends FAS 124, paragraphs 3, 5, 6, and 112 and footnote 6
Amends FAS 125, paragraphs 4, 14, 31, and 243
Replaces FAS 126, paragraph 2(c)
Replaces FTB 79-19, paragraph 6

Affected by: Paragraphs 6 through 8 amended by FAS 149, paragraphs 3 through 5, respectively
Paragraph 9(a) amended by FAS 149, paragraph 6
Paragraph 10 amended by FAS 149, paragraphs 7(d) and 7(e), and FSP EITF 00-19-2, paragraph 13
Paragraph 10(a) replaced by FAS 149, paragraph 7(a)
Paragraph 10(b) replaced by FAS 138, paragraph 4(a), and FAS 149, paragraph 7(b)
Paragraph 10(d) replaced by FAS 149, paragraph 7(c)
Paragraph 10(f) amended by FAS 140, paragraph 353(a)
Paragraph 10(g) amended by FSP FTB 85-4-1, paragraph 21
Paragraph 10(h) amended by FSP AAG INV-1/SOP 94-4-1, paragraph B3
Paragraph 11 amended by FAS 150, paragraph C2(a)
Paragraph 11(b) amended by FAS 123(R), paragraph D15, and FSP FAS 123(R)-1
Paragraph 11(c) amended by FAS 141, paragraph E18(a)
Paragraph 12 amended by FAS 138, paragraph 4(p)
Paragraph 12(c) amended by FAS 150, paragraph C2(b)
Paragraph 13(a) amended by FAS 149, paragraph 8(a)
Paragraph 13(b) replaced by FAS 149, paragraph 8(b)
Paragraph 14 amended by FAS 155, paragraph 4(a)
Paragraphs 14A and 14B added by FAS 155, paragraph 4(b)
Paragraph 15 amended by FAS 149, paragraph 9
Paragraph 16 amended by FAS 155, paragraph 4(c)
Paragraph 16A added by FAS 155, paragraph 4(d), and deleted by FAS 157, paragraph E18(a)

Paragraph 17 amended by FAS 149, paragraph 10, and FAS 157, paragraph E18(b)
Paragraph 19 deleted by FAS 149, paragraph 11
Paragraph 20(c) amended by FAS 149, paragraph 12
Paragraph 21(a)(2)(c) amended by FAS 149, paragraph 14
Paragraph 21(c)(1) amended by FAS 138, paragraph 4(f)
Paragraphs 21(d), 21(f), and 21(f)(2) through 21(f)(4) amended by FAS 138, paragraph 4(b)
Paragraphs 27, 34, 64, 65(c), 94, 96, 97, 99, and 143 amended by FAS 149, paragraph 15
Paragraph 28(c) amended by FAS 149, paragraph 16
Paragraph 29(d) amended by FAS 138, paragraph 4(g)
Paragraphs 29(e), 29(h), and 29(h)(1) through 29(h)(4) amended by FAS 138, paragraph 4(c)
Paragraph 29(f) amended by FAS 141, paragraph E18(b)
Paragraph 29(g)(2) amended by FAS 138, paragraph 4(h)
Paragraph 30 amended by FAS 138, paragraph 4(i)
Paragraph 30(d) replaced by FAS 149, paragraph 17
Paragraph 33 replaced by FAS 138, paragraph 4(q)
Paragraph 36 amended by FAS 138, paragraphs 4(j) and 4(n)
Paragraph 36(a) amended by FAS 138, paragraph 4(j)
Paragraph 36(b) replaced by FAS 138, paragraph 4(j)
Paragraph 36A, paragraph 37A, and paragraphs 40A through 40C added by FAS 138,
  paragraphs 4(k), 4(l), and 4(o), respectively
Paragraphs 37 and 38 amended by FAS 138, paragraphs 4(s) and 4(t), respectively
Paragraph 40 amended by FAS 138, paragraph 4(m)
Paragraph 40(a) replaced by FAS 138, paragraph 4(v)
Paragraph 40(b) amended by FAS 138, paragraph 4(v)
Paragraph 42 amended by FAS 138, paragraph 4(u), and FAS 159, paragraph C7(a)
Paragraph 44A added by FAS 155, paragraph 4(e), and amended by FAS 159, paragraph C7(b)
Paragraph 44B added by FAS 155, paragraph 4(e)
Paragraph 45(b)(4) amended by FAS 138, paragraph 4(r)
Paragraph 45A added by FAS 149, paragraph 18
Paragraph 48 amended by FAS 137, paragraph 3(a)
Paragraph 49 amended by FAS 149, paragraph 19
Paragraph 50 replaced by FAS 137, paragraph 3(b)
Paragraph 52(b) replaced by FAS 138, paragraph 4(w)
Paragraph 54 and footnote 14 amended by FAS 138, paragraph 4(d)
Paragraph 56 amended by FAS 140, paragraph 353(c), and FAS 156, paragraph 5(b)
Paragraphs 57(c)(2) and 57(c)(3) amended by FAS 149, paragraphs 20 and 21, respectively
Paragraph 58(a) amended by FAS 149, paragraph 22(a)
Paragraph 58(b) amended by FAS 138, paragraph 4(x), and FAS 149, paragraph 22(b)
Paragraph 58(c)(2) amended by FAS 138, paragraph 4(x)
Paragraph 59(a) replaced by FAS 149, paragraph 23(a)
Paragraph 59(c) amended by FAS 149, paragraph 23(b)
Paragraph 59(d) amended by FAS 149, paragraph 23(c)
Paragraph 59(e) amended by FAS 140, paragraph 353(d), and FAS 145, paragraph 9(j)
Paragraph 61(a) amended by FAS 149, paragraph 24(a)
Paragraph 61(d) amended by FAS 138, paragraph 4(y), and FAS 149, paragraph 24(b)
Paragraph 61(e) amended by FAS 138, paragraph 4(y), and FAS 149, paragraph 24(c)
Paragraph 61(f) replaced by FAS 149, paragraph 24(d)
Paragraph 61(g) amended by FAS 149, paragraph 24(e)
Paragraph 68 amended by FAS 138, paragraph 4(z), and FAS 149, paragraph 25(a)
Paragraph 68(a) amended by FAS 149, paragraph 25(b)
Paragraph 68(b) amended by FAS 138, paragraph 4(z)
Paragraph 68(b) replaced by FAS 149, paragraph 25(c)
Paragraph 68(d) amended by FAS 138, paragraph 4(z), and FAS 149, paragraph 25(d)
Paragraph 68(g) amended by FAS 149, paragraph 25(e)
Paragraph 68(l) deleted by FAS 138, paragraph 4(z)
Paragraph 90 amended by FAS 138, paragraph 4(e)
Paragraph 95 amended by FAS 149, paragraph 26
Paragraph 115 amended by FAS 138, paragraph 4(bb)
Paragraphs 120A through 120D added by FAS 138, paragraph 4(cc)

Paragraph 134 amended by FAS 138, paragraph 4(dd)
Paragraph 154 amended by FAS 149, paragraph 27
Paragraph 155 replaced by FAS 138, paragraph 4(ee)
Paragraph 161 amended by FAS 138, paragraph 4(ff)
Paragraph 169 amended by FAS 138, paragraph 4(gg)
Paragraph 176 replaced by FAS 149, paragraph 28
Paragraph 197 replaced by FAS 138, paragraph 4(hh)
Paragraph 200 amended by FAS 138, paragraph 4(ii)
Paragraphs 200A through 200D added by FAS 155, paragraph 4(f)
Paragraph 539 effectively amended by FAS 149, paragraphs 10(b), 10(g), 10(h), and 10(i)
Paragraph 540 amended by FAS 138, paragraph 4(jj); FAS 149, paragraph 29; and FAS 157,
   paragraph E18(c)
Footnote 6(c) added by FAS 149, paragraph 10, and deleted by FAS 157, paragraph E18(b)
Footnotes 8 and 16 amended by FAS 149, paragraphs 13 and 22(a), respectively
Footnote 9 amended by FAS 140, paragraph 353(b), and FAS 156, paragraph 5(a)
Footnotes 9b, 10b, 18a, 18b, 20a through 20e, and 24a added by FAS 149, paragraph 15, and
   effectively deleted by FAS 157, paragraph E18(b)
Footnote 17 deleted by FAS 138, paragraph 4(x)
Footnote 19 amended by FAS 138, paragraph 4(aa)

AICPA Accounting Standards Executive Committee (AcSEC)

Related Pronouncements: SOP 94-6
                         SOP 02-2

Issues Discussed by FASB Emerging Issues Task Force (EITF)

Affects: Nullifies EITF Issues No. 84-14, 84-36, 86-34, 87-2, 87-26, 91-1, and 95-2 and Topics No. D-16,
   D-22, and D-64
   Partially nullifies EITF Issues No. 84-4, 84-5, 84-7, 85-9, 85-20, 85-25, 85-27, 85-29, 86-15,
   86-21, 86-28, 88-8, 88-9, 88-18, 89-11, 90-17, 90-19, 91-6, 92-2, 96-11, 96-12, 96-15, 96-17,
   97-7, 98-5, and 98-10 and Topic No. D-50
   Resolves EITF Issues No. 84-31, 86-26, 87-1, 91-4, 93-10, and 95-11
   Partially resolves EITF Issues No. 84-7, 84-20, 85-9, 85-23, 86-28, 88-8, and 90-22

Interpreted by: Paragraph 11(a) interpreted by EITF Issues No. 99-1 and 01-6
   Paragraph 12 interpreted by EITF Issue No. 06-7 and Topic No. D-109
   Paragraphs 20(a), 28(a), 30(b), and 62 interpreted by EITF Topic No. D-102
   Paragraph 60 interpreted by EITF Topic No. D-109
   Paragraph 61(l) interpreted by EITF Issue No. 05-2

Related Issues: EITF Issues No. 86-25, 97-8, 97-15, 99-2, 99-7, 99-8, 99-9, 00-4, 00-6, 00-8, 00-9, 00-18,
   00-19, 01-12, 02-2, 02-3, 02-8, 03-11, 03-14, 05-4, 06-6, and 07-2 and Topics No. D-51,
   D-71, and D-98

SUMMARY

This Statement establishes accounting and reporting standards for derivative instruments, including certain derivative instruments embedded in other contracts, (collectively referred to as derivatives) and for hedging activities. It requires that an entity recognize all derivatives as either assets or liabilities in the statement of financial position and measure those instruments at fair value. If certain conditions are met, a derivative may be specifically designated as (a) a hedge of the exposure to changes in the fair value of a recognized asset or liability or an unrecognized firm commitment, (b) a hedge of the exposure to variable cash flows of a forecasted transaction, or (c) a hedge of the foreign currency exposure of a net investment in a foreign operation, an unrecognized firm commitment, an available-for-sale security, or a foreign-currency-denominated forecasted transaction.

The accounting for changes in the fair value of a derivative (that is, gains and losses) depends on the intended use of the derivative and the resulting designation.

- For a derivative designated as hedging the exposure to changes in the fair value of a recognized asset or liability or a firm commitment (referred to as a fair value hedge), the gain or loss is recognized in earnings in the period of change together with the offsetting loss or gain on the hedged item attributable to the risk being hedged. The effect of that accounting is to reflect in earnings the extent to which the hedge is not effective in achieving offsetting changes in fair value.
- For a derivative designated as hedging the exposure to variable cash flows of a forecasted transaction (referred to as a cash flow hedge), the effective portion of the derivative's gain or loss is initially reported as a component of other comprehensive income (outside earnings) and subsequently reclassified into earnings when the forecasted transaction affects earnings. The ineffective portion of the gain or loss is reported in earnings immediately.
- For a derivative designated as hedging the foreign currency exposure of a net investment in a foreign operation, the gain or loss is reported in other comprehensive income (outside earnings) as part of the cumulative translation adjustment. The accounting for a fair value hedge described above applies to a derivative designated as a hedge of the foreign currency exposure of an unrecognized firm commitment or an available-for-sale security. Similarly, the accounting for a cash flow hedge described above applies to a derivative designated as a hedge of the foreign currency exposure of a foreign-currency-denominated forecasted transaction.
- For a derivative not designated as a hedging instrument, the gain or loss is recognized in earnings in the period of change.

Under this Statement, an entity that elects to apply hedge accounting is required to establish at the inception of the hedge the method it will use for assessing the effectiveness of the hedging derivative and the measurement approach for determining the ineffective aspect of the hedge. Those methods must be consistent with the entity's approach to managing risk.

This Statement applies to all entities. A not-for-profit organization should recognize the change in fair value of all derivatives as a change in net assets in the period of change. In a fair value hedge, the changes in the fair value of the hedged item attributable to the risk being hedged also are recognized. However, because of the format of their statement of financial performance, not-for-profit organizations are not permitted special hedge accounting for derivatives used to hedge forecasted transactions. This Statement does not address how a not-for-profit organization should determine the components of an operating measure if one is presented.

This Statement precludes designating a nonderivative financial instrument as a hedge of an asset, liability, unrecognized firm commitment, or forecasted transaction except that a nonderivative instrument denominated in a foreign currency may be designated as a hedge of the foreign currency exposure of an unrecognized firm commitment denominated in a foreign currency or a net investment in a foreign operation.

This Statement amends FASB Statement No. 52, *Foreign Currency Translation,* to permit special accounting for a hedge of a foreign currency forecasted transaction with a derivative. It supersedes FASB Statements No. 80, *Accounting for Futures Contracts,* No. 105, *Disclosure of Information about Financial Instruments with Off-Balance-Sheet Risk and Financial Instruments with Concentrations of Credit Risk,* and No. 119, *Disclosure about Derivative Financial Instruments and Fair Value of Financial Instruments.* It amends FASB Statement No. 107, *Disclosures about Fair Value of Financial Instruments,* to include in Statement 107 the disclosure provisions about concentrations of credit risk from Statement 105. This Statement also nullifies or modifies the consensuses reached in a number of issues addressed by the Emerging Issues Task Force.

This Statement is effective for all fiscal quarters of fiscal years beginning after June 15, 1999. Initial application of this Statement should be as of the beginning of an entity's fiscal quarter; on that date, hedging relationships must be designated anew and documented pursuant to the provisions of this Statement. Earlier application of all of the provisions of this Statement is encouraged, but it is permitted only as of the beginning of any fiscal quarter that begins after issuance of this Statement. This Statement should not be applied retroactively to financial statements of prior periods.

Statement of Financial Accounting Standards No. 133

Accounting for Derivative Instruments and Hedging Activities

CONTENTS

INTRODUCTION

1. This Statement addresses the accounting for **derivative instruments,**[1] including certain derivative instruments embedded in other contracts, and hedging activities.

2. Prior to this Statement, hedging activities related to changes in foreign exchange rates were addressed in FASB Statement No. 52, *Foreign Currency Translation.* FASB Statement No. 80, *Accounting for Futures Contracts,* addressed the use of futures contracts in other hedging activities. Those Statements addressed only certain derivative instruments and differed in the criteria required for hedge accounting. In addition, the Emerging Issues Task Force (EITF) addressed the accounting for various hedging activities in a number of issues.

3. In developing the standards in this Statement, the Board concluded that the following four fundamental decisions should serve as cornerstones underlying those standards:

a. Derivative instruments represent rights or obligations that meet the definitions of assets or liabilities and should be reported in financial statements.
b. Fair value is the most relevant measure for **financial instruments** and the only relevant measure for derivative instruments. Derivative instruments should be measured at fair value, and adjustments to the carrying amount of hedged items should reflect changes in their fair value (that is, gains or losses) that are attributable to the risk being hedged and that arise while the hedge is in effect.
c. Only items that are assets or liabilities should be reported as such in financial statements.
d. Special accounting for items designated as being hedged should be provided only for qualifying items. One aspect of qualification should be an assessment of the expectation of effective offsetting changes in fair values or cash flows during the term of the hedge for the risk being hedged.

Those fundamental decisions are discussed individually in paragraphs 217–231 of Appendix C.

4. This Statement standardizes the accounting for derivative instruments, including certain derivative instruments embedded in other contracts, by requiring that an entity recognize those items as assets or liabilities in the statement of financial position and measure them at fair value. If certain conditions are met, an entity may elect to designate a derivative instrument as follows:

a. A hedge of the exposure to changes in the fair value of a recognized asset or liability, or of an unrecognized **firm commitment,**[2] that are attributable to a particular risk (referred to as a fair value hedge)
b. A hedge of the exposure to variability in the cash flows of a recognized asset or liability, or of a forecasted transaction, that is attributable to a particular risk (referred to as a cash flow hedge)
c. A hedge of the foreign currency exposure of (1) an unrecognized firm commitment (a foreign currency fair value hedge), (2) an available-for-sale security (a foreign currency fair value hedge), (3) a forecasted transaction (a foreign currency cash flow hedge), or (4) a net investment in a foreign operation.

This Statement generally provides for matching the timing of gain or loss recognition on the hedging instrument with the recognition of (a) the changes in the fair value of the hedged asset or liability that are attributable to the hedged risk or (b) the earnings effect of the hedged forecasted transaction. Appendix A provides guidance on identifying derivative instruments subject to the scope of this Statement and on assessing hedge effectiveness and is an integral part of the standards provided in this Statement. Appendix B contains examples that illustrate application of this Statement. Appendix C contains background information and the basis for the Board's conclusions. Appendix D lists the accounting pronouncements superseded or amended by this Statement. Appendix E provides a diagram for determining whether a contract is a freestanding derivative subject to the scope of this Statement.

---

[1] Words defined in Appendix F, the glossary, are set in **boldface type** the first time they appear.

[2] An unrecognized firm commitment can be viewed as an executory contract that represents both a right and an obligation. When a previously unrecognized firm commitment that is designated as a hedged item is accounted for in accordance with this Statement, an asset or a liability is recognized and reported in the statement of financial position related to the recognition of the gain or loss on the firm commitment. Consequently, subsequent references to an asset or a liability in this Statement include a firm commitment.

STANDARDS OF FINANCIAL ACCOUNTING AND REPORTING

Scope and Definition

5. This Statement applies to all entities. Some entities, such as not-for-profit organizations and defined benefit pension plans, do not report earnings as a separate caption in a statement of financial performance. The application of this Statement to those entities is set forth in paragraph 43.

Derivative Instruments

6. A derivative instrument is a financial instrument or other contract with all three of the following characteristics:

a. It has (1) one or more **underlyings** and (2) one or more **notional amounts**[3] or payment provisions or both. Those terms determine the amount of the settlement or settlements, and, in some cases, whether or not a settlement is required.[4]
b. It requires no initial net investment or an initial net investment that is smaller than would be required for other types of contracts that would be expected to have a similar response to changes in market factors.
c. Its terms require or permit net settlement, it can readily be settled net by a means outside the contract, or it provides for delivery of an asset that puts the recipient in a position not substantially different from net settlement.

Notwithstanding the above characteristics, loan commitments that relate to the origination of mortgage loans that will be held for sale, as discussed in paragraph 21 of FASB Statement No. 65, *Accounting for Certain Mortgage Banking Activities* (as amended), shall be accounted for as derivative instruments by the issuer of the loan commitment (that is, the potential lender). Paragraph 10(i) provides a scope exception for the accounting for loan commitments by issuers of certain commitments to originate loans and all holders of commitments to originate loans (that is, the potential borrowers).

7. *Underlying, notional amount, and payment provision.* An underlying is a specified interest rate, security price, commodity price, foreign exchange rate, index of prices or rates, or other variable (including the occurrence or nonoccurrence of a specified event such as a scheduled payment under a contract). An underlying may be a price or rate of an asset or liability but is not the asset or liability itself. A notional amount is a number of currency units, shares, bushels, pounds, or other units specified in the contract. The settlement of a derivative instrument with a notional amount is determined by interaction of that notional amount with the underlying. The interaction may be simple multiplication, or it may involve a formula with leverage factors or other constants. A payment provision specifies a fixed or determinable settlement to be made if the underlying behaves in a specified manner.

8. *Initial net investment.* Many derivative instruments require no initial net investment. Some require an initial net investment as compensation for time value (for example, a premium on an option) or for terms that are more or less favorable than market conditions (for example, a premium on a forward purchase contract with a price less than the current forward price). Others require a mutual exchange of currencies or other assets at inception, in which case the net investment is the difference in the fair values of the assets exchanged. A derivative instrument does not require an initial net investment in the contract that is equal to the notional amount (or the notional amount plus a premium or minus a discount) or that is determined by applying the notional amount to the underlying. If the initial net investment in the contract (after adjustment for the time value of money) is less, by more than a nominal amount, than the initial net investment that would be commensurate with the amount that would be exchanged either to acquire the asset related to the underlying or to incur the obligation related to the underlying, the characteristic in paragraph 6(b) is met. The amount of that asset acquired or liability incurred should be comparable to the effective notional amount[4a] of the contract.

9. *Net settlement.* A contract fits the description in paragraph 6(c) if its settlement provisions meet one of the following criteria:

a. Neither party is required to deliver an asset that is associated with the underlying and that has a

---

[3]Sometimes other names are used. For example, the notional amount is called a face amount in some contracts.

[4]The terms *underlying, notional amount, payment provision, and settlement* are intended to include the plural forms in the remainder of this Statement. Including both the singular and plural forms used in this paragraph is more accurate but much more awkward and impairs the readability.

[4a]The effective notional amount is the stated notional amount adjusted for any leverage factor.

principal amount, stated amount, face value, number of shares, or other denomination that is equal to the notional amount (or the notional amount plus a premium or minus a discount). For example, most interest rate swaps do not require that either party deliver interest-bearing assets with a principal amount equal to the notional amount of the contract.

b. One of the parties is required to deliver an asset of the type described in paragraph 9(a), but there is a market mechanism that facilitates net settlement, for example, an exchange that offers a ready opportunity to sell the contract or to enter into an offsetting contract.

c. One of the parties is required to deliver an asset of the type described in paragraph 9(a), but that asset is readily convertible to cash[5] or is itself a derivative instrument. An example of that type of contract is a forward contract that requires delivery of an exchange-traded equity security. Even though the number of shares to be delivered is the same as the notional amount of the contract and the price of the shares is the underlying, an exchange-traded security is readily convertible to cash. Another example is a swaption—an option to require delivery of a swap contract, which is a derivative.

Derivative instruments embedded in other contracts are addressed in paragraphs 12–16.

10. Notwithstanding the conditions in paragraphs 6–9, the following contracts are not subject to the requirements of this Statement:

a. *"Regular-way" security trades.* Regular-way security trades are contracts that provide for delivery of a security within the time generally established by regulations or conventions in the marketplace or exchange in which the transaction is being executed. However, a contract for an existing security does not qualify for the regular-way security trades exception if it requires or permits net settlement (as discussed in paragraphs 9(a) and 57(c)(1)) or if a market mechanism to facilitate net settlement of that contract (as discussed in paragraphs 9(b) and 57(c)(2)) exists, except as provided in the following sentence.

If an entity is required to account for a contract to purchase or sell an existing security on a trade-date basis, rather than a settlement-date basis, and thus recognizes the acquisition (or disposition) of the security at the inception of the contract, then the entity shall apply the regular-way security trades exception to that contract. A contract for the purchase or sale of *when-issued* securities or other securities that do not yet exist is addressed in paragraph 59(a).

b. *Normal purchases and normal sales.* Normal purchases and normal sales are contracts that provide for the purchase or sale of something other than a financial instrument or derivative instrument that will be delivered in quantities expected to be used or sold by the reporting entity over a reasonable period in the normal course of business. The following guidance should be considered in determining whether a specific type of contract qualifies for the normal purchases and normal sales exception:

(1) *Forward contracts (non-option-based contracts).* Forward contracts are eligible to qualify for the normal purchases and normal sales exception. However, forward contracts that contain net settlement provisions as described in either paragraph 9(a) or paragraph 9(b) are not eligible for the normal purchases and normal sales exception unless it is probable at inception and throughout the term of the individual contract that the contract will not settle net and will result in physical delivery.[5a] Net settlement (as described in paragraphs 9(a) and 9(b)) of contracts in a group of contracts similarly designated as normal purchases and normal sales would call into question the classification of all such contracts as normal purchases or normal sales. Contracts that require cash settlements of gains or losses or are otherwise settled net on a periodic basis, including individual contracts that are part of a series of sequential contracts intended to accomplish ultimate acquisition or sale of a commodity, do not qualify for this exception.

---

[5]FASB Concepts Statement No. 5, *Recognition and Measurement in Financial Statements of Business Enterprises,* states that assets that are readily convertible to cash "have (i) interchangeable (fungible) units and (ii) quoted prices available in an active market that can rapidly absorb the quantity held by the entity without significantly affecting the price" (paragraph 83(a)). For contracts that involve multiple deliveries of the asset, the phrase *in an active market that can rapidly absorb the quantity held by the entity* should be applied separately to the expected quantity in each delivery.

[5a]Contracts that are subject to unplanned netting (referred to as a "bookout" in the electric utility industry) do not qualify for this exception except as specified in paragraph 58(b).

(2) *Freestanding option contracts.* Option contracts that would require delivery of the related asset at an established price under the contract only if exercised are not eligible to qualify for the normal purchases and normal sales exception, except as indicated in paragraph 10(b)(4) below.

(3) *Forward contracts that contain optionality features.* Forward contracts that contain optionality features that do not modify the quantity of the asset to be delivered under the contract are eligible to qualify for the normal purchases and normal sales exception. Except for power purchase or sales agreements addressed in paragraph 10(b)(4), if an option component permits modification of the quantity of the assets to be delivered, the contract is not eligible for the normal purchases and normal sales exception, unless the option component permits the holder only to purchase or sell additional quantities at the market price at the date of delivery. In order for forward contracts that contain optionality features to qualify for the normal purchases and normal sales exception, the criteria discussed in paragraph 10(b)(1) must be met.

(4) *Power purchase or sales agreements.* Notwithstanding the criteria in paragraphs 10(b)(1) and 10(b)(3), a power purchase or sales agreement (whether a forward contract, option contract, or a combination of both) that is a **capacity contract** also qualifies for the normal purchases and normal sales exception if it meets the criteria in paragraph 58(b).

However, contracts that have a price based on an underlying that is not clearly and closely related to the asset being sold or purchased (such as a price in a contract for the sale of a grain commodity based in part on changes in the S&P index) or that are denominated in a foreign currency that meets none of the criteria in paragraphs 15(a)–15(d) shall not be considered normal purchases and normal sales. For contracts that qualify for the normal purchases and normal sales exception, the entity shall document the designation of the contract as a normal purchase or normal sale. For contracts that qualify for the normal purchases and normal sales exception under paragraphs 10(b)(1) and 10(b)(3), the entity shall document the basis for concluding that it is probable that the contract will not settle net and

will result in physical delivery. For contracts that qualify for the normal purchases and normal sales exception under paragraph 10(b)(4), the entity shall document the basis for concluding that the agreement meets the criteria in paragraph 58(b). The documentation requirements can be applied either to groups of similarly designated contracts or to each individual contract. Failure to comply with the documentation requirements precludes application of the normal purchases and normal sales exception to contracts that would otherwise qualify for that exception.

c. *Certain insurance contracts.* Generally, contracts of the type that are within the scope of FASB Statements No. 60, *Accounting and Reporting by Insurance Enterprises,* No. 97, *Accounting and Reporting by Insurance Enterprises for Certain Long-Duration Contracts and for Realized Gains and Losses from the Sale of Investments,* and No. 113, *Accounting and Reporting for Reinsurance of Short-Duration and Long-Duration Contracts,* are not subject to the requirements of this Statement whether or not they are written by insurance enterprises. That is, a contract is not subject to the requirements of this Statement if it entitles the holder to be compensated only if, as a result of an identifiable insurable event (other than a change in price), the holder incurs a liability or there is an adverse change in the value of a specific asset or liability for which the holder is at risk. The following types of contracts written by insurance enterprises or held by the insureds are not subject to the requirements of this Statement for the reasons given:

(1) *Traditional life insurance contracts.* The payment of death benefits is the result of an identifiable insurable event (death of the insured) instead of changes in a variable.

(2) *Traditional property and casualty contracts.* The payment of benefits is the result of an identifiable insurable event (for example, theft or fire) instead of changes in a variable.

However, insurance enterprises enter into other types of contracts that may be subject to the provisions of this Statement. In addition, some contracts with insurance or other enterprises combine derivative instruments, as defined in this Statement, with other insurance products or nonderivative contracts, for example, indexed annuity contracts, variable life insurance contracts, and property and casualty contracts that combine traditional coverages with foreign currency options. Contracts that consist of both derivative portions and nonderivative portions are addressed in paragraph 12.

d. *Financial guarantee contracts.* Financial guarantee contracts are not subject to this Statement only if:

  (1) They provide for payments to be made solely to reimburse the guaranteed party for failure of the debtor to satisfy its required payment obligations under a nonderivative contract, either at pre-specified payment dates or accelerated payment dates as a result of the occurrence of an event of default (as defined in the financial obligation covered by the guarantee contract) or notice of acceleration being made to the debtor by the creditor.

  (2) Payment under the financial guarantee contract is made only if the debtor's obligation to make payments as a result of conditions as described in (1) above is past due.

  (3) The guaranteed party is, as a precondition in the contract (or in the back-to-back arrangement, if applicable) for receiving payment of any claim under the guarantee, exposed to the risk of nonpayment both at inception of the financial guarantee contract and throughout its term either through direct legal ownership of the guaranteed obligation or through a back-to-back arrangement with another party that is required by the back-to-back arrangement to maintain direct ownership of the guaranteed obligation.

In contrast, financial guarantee contracts are subject to this Statement if they do not meet all of the above three criteria, for example, if they provide for payments to be made in response to changes in another underlying such as a decrease in a specified debtor's creditworthiness.

e. *Certain contracts that are not traded on an exchange.* Contracts that are not exchange-traded are not subject to the requirements of this Statement if the underlying on which the settlement is based is one of the following:

  (1) A climatic or geological variable or other physical variable

  (2) The price or value of (a) a nonfinancial asset of one of the parties to the contract provided that the asset is not readily convertible to cash or (b) a nonfinancial liability of one of the parties to the contract provided that the liability does not require delivery of an asset that is readily convertible to cash

  (3) Specified volumes of sales or service revenues of one of the parties to the contract.

If a contract has more than one underlying and some, but not all, of them qualify for one of the exceptions in paragraphs 10(e)(1), 10(e)(2), and 10(e)(3), the application of this Statement to that contract depends on its predominant characteristics. That is, the contract is subject to the requirements of this Statement if all of its underlyings, considered in combination, behave in a manner that is highly correlated with the behavior of any of the component variables that do not qualify for an exception.

f. *Derivatives that serve as impediments to sales accounting.* A derivative instrument (whether freestanding or embedded in another contract) whose existence serves as an impediment to recognizing a related contract as a sale by one party or a purchase by the counterparty is not subject to this Statement. For example, the existence of a guarantee of the residual value of a leased asset by the lessor may be an impediment to treating a contract as a sales-type lease, in which case the contract would be treated by the lessor as an operating lease. Another example is the existence of a call option enabling a transferor to repurchase transferred assets that is an impediment to sales accounting under FASB Statement No. 140, *Accounting for Transfers and Servicing of Financial Assets and Extinguishments of Liabilities.*

g. *Investments in life insurance.* A policyholder's investment in a life insurance contract that is accounted for under FASB Technical Bulletin No. 85-4, *Accounting for Purchases of Life Insurance,* or FASB Staff Position FTB 85-4-1, "Accounting for Life Settlement Contracts by Third-Party Investors," is not subject to this Statement. This does not affect the accounting by the issuer of the life insurance contract.

h. *Certain investment contracts.* A contract that is accounted for under either paragraph 4 of FASB Statement No. 110, *Reporting by Defined Benefit Pension Plans of Investment Contracts,* or paragraph 12 of FASB Statement No. 35, *Accounting and Reporting by Defined Benefit Pension Plans,* as amended by Statement 110, is not subject to this Statement. This exception applies only to the party that accounts for the contract under Statement 35 or Statement 110.

i. *Loan commitments.* The holder of any commitment to originate a loan (that is, the potential borrower) is not subject to the requirements of this Statement. Issuers of commitments to originate mortgage loans that will be held for investment purposes, as discussed in paragraphs 21 and 25 of Statement 65, are not subject to this Statement. In addition, issuers of loan commitments to originate other types of loans (that is, other than mortgage loans) are not subject to the requirements of this Statement.

j. *Registration payment arrangements.* Registration payment arrangements within the scope of FSP EITF 00-19-2, "Accounting for Registration Payment Arrangements," are not subject to the requirements of this Statement. The exception in this subparagraph applies to both (a) the issuer that accounts for the arrangement pursuant to FSP EITF 00-19-2 and (b) the counterparty.

11. Notwithstanding the conditions of paragraphs 6–10, the reporting entity shall *not* consider the following contracts to be derivative instruments for purposes of this Statement:

a. Contracts issued or held by that reporting entity that are both (1) indexed to its own stock and (2) classified in stockholders' equity in its statement of financial position.

b. Contracts issued by the entity that are subject to FASB Statement No. 123 (revised 2004), *Share-Based Payment.* If any such contract ceases to be subject to Statement 123(R) in accordance with paragraph A231 of that Statement, the terms of that contract shall then be analyzed to determine whether the contract is subject to this Statement.

c. Contracts issued by the entity as contingent consideration from a business combination. The accounting for contingent consideration issued in a business combination is addressed in FASB Statement No. 141, *Business Combinations.* In applying this paragraph, the issuer is considered to be the entity that is accounting for the combination using the purchase method.

d. Forward contracts that require settlement by the reporting entity's delivery of cash in exchange for the acquisition of a fixed number of its equity shares (forward purchase contracts for the reporting entity's shares that require physical settlement) that are accounted for under paragraphs 21 and 22 of FASB Statement No. 150, *Accounting for Certain Financial Instruments with Characteristics of both Liabilities and Equity.*

In contrast, the above exceptions do not apply to the counterparty in those contracts. In addition, a contract that an entity either can or must settle by issuing its own equity instruments but that is indexed in part or in full to something other than its own stock can be a derivative instrument for the issuer under paragraphs 6–10, in which case it would be accounted for as a liability or an asset in accordance with the requirements of this Statement.

Embedded Derivative Instruments

12. Contracts that do not in their entirety meet the definition of a derivative instrument (refer to paragraphs 6–9), such as bonds, insurance policies, and leases, may contain "embedded" derivative instruments—implicit or explicit terms that affect some or all of the cash flows or the value of other exchanges required by the contract in a manner similar to a derivative instrument. The effect of embedding a derivative instrument in another type of contract ("the host contract") is that some or all of the cash flows or other exchanges that otherwise would be required by the host contract, whether unconditional or contingent upon the occurrence of a specified event, will be modified based on one or more underlyings. An embedded derivative instrument shall be separated from the host contract and accounted for as a derivative instrument pursuant to this Statement if and only if all of the following criteria are met:

a. The economic characteristics and risks of the embedded derivative instrument are not clearly and closely related to the economic characteristics and risks of the host contract. Additional guidance on applying this criterion to various contracts containing embedded derivative instruments is included in Appendix A of this Statement.

b. The contract ("the hybrid instrument") that embodies both the embedded derivative instrument and the host contract is not remeasured at fair value under otherwise applicable generally accepted accounting principles with changes in fair value reported in earnings as they occur.

c. A separate instrument with the same terms as the embedded derivative instrument would, pursuant to paragraphs 6–11, be a derivative instrument subject to the requirements of this Statement. (The initial net investment for the hybrid instrument shall not be considered to be the initial net investment for the embedded derivative.) However, this criterion is not met if the separate instrument with the same terms as the embedded derivative instrument would be classified as a liability (or an asset in some circumstances) under the provisions of Statement 150 *but* would be classified in stockholders' equity absent the provisions in Statement 150.[5b]

13. For purposes of applying the provisions of paragraph 12, an embedded derivative instrument in which the underlying is an interest rate or interest rate index[6] that alters net interest payments that otherwise would be paid or received on an interest-bearing host contract is considered to be clearly and closely related to the host contract unless either of the following conditions exist:

a. The hybrid instrument can contractually be settled in a such a way that the investor (holder) would not recover *substantially all* of its initial recorded investment.[6a]

b. The embedded derivative meets both of the following conditions:

   (1) There is a possible future interest rate scenario (even though it may be remote) under which the embedded derivative would at least double the investor's initial rate of return on the host contract.

   (2) For each of the possible interest rate scenarios under which the investor's initial rate of return on the host contract would be doubled (as discussed under paragraph 13(b)(1)), the embedded derivative would at the same time result in a rate of return that is at least twice what otherwise would be the then-current market return (under each of those future interest rate scenarios) for a contract that has the same terms as the host contract and that involves a debtor with a credit quality similar to the issuer's credit quality at inception.

Even though the above conditions focus on the investor's rate of return and the investor's recovery of its investment, the existence of either of those conditions would result in the embedded derivative instrument not being considered clearly and closely related to the host contract by both parties to the hybrid instrument. Because the existence of those conditions is assessed at the date that the hybrid instrument is acquired (or incurred) by the reporting entity, the acquirer of a hybrid instrument in the secondary market could potentially reach a different conclusion than could the issuer of the hybrid instrument due to applying the conditions in this paragraph at different points in time.

14. However, interest-only strips and principal-only strips are not subject to the requirements of this Statement provided those strips (a) represent the right to receive only a specified proportion of the contractual interest cash flows of a specific debt instrument or a specified proportion of the contractual principal cash flows of that debt instrument and (b) do not incorporate any terms not present in the original debt instrument. An allocation of a portion of the interest or principal cash flows of a specific debt instrument as reasonable compensation for stripping the instrument or to provide adequate compensation to a servicer (as defined in Statement 140) would meet the intended narrow scope of the exception provided in this paragraph. However, an allocation of a portion of the interest or principal cash flows of a specific debt instrument to provide for a guarantee of payments, for servicing in excess of adequate compensation, or for any other purpose would not meet the intended narrow scope of the exception.

14A. The holder of an interest in securitized financial assets (other than those identified in paragraph 14) shall determine whether the interest is a freestanding derivative or contains an embedded derivative that under paragraphs 12 and 13 would be required to be separated from the host contract and accounted for separately. That determination shall be based on an analysis of the contractual terms of the interest in securitized financial assets, which requires understanding the nature and amount of assets, liabilities, and other financial instruments that compose the entire securitization transaction. A holder of an interest in securitized financial assets should obtain sufficient information about the payoff structure and the payment priority of the interest to determine whether an embedded derivative exists.

14B. Changes in cash flows attributable to changes in the creditworthiness of an interest resulting from

---

[5b]For purposes of analyzing the application of paragraph 11(a) of this Statement to an embedded derivative instrument as though it were a separate instrument, paragraphs 9–12 of Statement 150 should be disregarded. Those embedded features are analyzed by applying other applicable guidance.

[6]Examples are an interest rate cap or an interest rate collar. An embedded derivative instrument that alters net interest payments based on changes in a stock price index (or another non-interest-rate index) is not addressed in paragraph 13.

[6a]The condition in paragraph 13(a) does not apply to a situation in which the terms of a hybrid instrument permit, but do not require, the investor to settle the hybrid instrument in a manner that causes it not to recover substantially all of its initial recorded investment, provided that the issuer does not have the contractual right to demand a settlement that causes the investor not to recover substantially all of its initial net investment.

securitized financial assets and liabilities (including derivative contracts) that represent the assets or liabilities that are held by the issuing entity shall not be considered an embedded derivative under this Statement. The concentration of credit risk in the form of subordination of one financial instrument to another shall not be considered an embedded derivative under this Statement.

15. An embedded foreign currency derivative instrument shall *not* be separated from the host contract and considered a derivative instrument under paragraph 12 if the host contract is not a financial instrument and it requires payment(s) denominated in (a) the functional currency of any substantial party to that contract, (b) the currency in which the price of the related good or service that is acquired or delivered is routinely denominated in international commerce (for example, the U.S. dollar for crude oil transactions),[6b] (c) the local currency of any substantial party to the contract, or (d) the currency used by a substantial party to the contract as if it were the functional currency because the primary economic environment in which the party operates is highly inflationary (as discussed in paragraph 11 of Statement 52). The evaluation of whether a contract qualifies for the exception in this paragraph should be performed only at inception of the contract. Unsettled foreign currency transactions, including financial instruments, that are monetary items and have their principal payments, interest payments, or both denominated in a foreign currency are subject to the requirement in Statement 52 to recognize any foreign currency transaction gain or loss in earnings and shall not be considered to contain embedded foreign currency derivative instruments under this Statement. The same proscription applies to available-for-sale or trading securities that have cash flows denominated in a foreign currency.

16. In subsequent provisions of this Statement, both (a) a derivative instrument included within the scope of this Statement by paragraphs 6–11 and (b) an embedded derivative instrument that has been separated from a host contract as required by paragraph 12 are collectively referred to as derivative instruments. If an embedded derivative instrument is separated from its host contract, the host contract shall be accounted for based on generally accepted accounting principles applicable to instruments of that type that do not contain embedded derivative instruments. If an entity cannot reliably identify and measure the embedded derivative instrument that paragraph 12 requires be separated from the host contract, the entire contract shall be measured at fair value with gain or loss recognized in earnings, but it may not be designated as a hedging instrument pursuant to this Statement. An entity that initially recognizes a hybrid financial instrument that under paragraph 12 would be required to be separated into a host contract and a derivative instrument may irrevocably elect to initially and subsequently measure that hybrid financial instrument[6bb] in its entirety at fair value (with changes in fair value recognized in earnings). The fair value election shall be supported by concurrent documentation or a preexisting documented policy for automatic election. That recognized hybrid financial instrument could be an asset or a liability and it could be acquired or issued by the entity. That election is also available when a previously recognized financial instrument is subject to a remeasurement (new basis) event[6bbb] and the separate recognition of an embedded derivative. However, that recognized hybrid financial instrument may not be designated as a hedging instrument pursuant to this Statement. This election may be made on an instrument-by-instrument basis.

16A. [This paragraph has been deleted. See Status page.]

[6b]If similar transactions for a certain product or service are routinely denominated in international commerce in various different currencies, the transaction does not qualify for the exception.

[6bb]This election shall not be applied to the hybrid instruments described in paragraph 8 of FASB Statement No. 107, *Disclosures about Fair Value of Financial Instruments.*

[6bbb]For purposes of this Statement, a remeasurement (new basis) event is an event identified in other authoritative accounting literature, other than the recognition of an other-than-temporary impairment, that requires a financial instrument to be remeasured to its fair value at the time of the event but does not require that instrument to be reported at fair value on a continuous basis with the change in fair value recognized in earnings. Examples of remeasurement events are business combinations and significant modifications of debt as defined in EITF Issue No. 96-19, "Debtor's Accounting for a Modification or Exchange of Debt Instruments."

Recognition of Derivatives and Measurement of Derivatives and Hedged Items

17. An entity shall recognize all of its derivative instruments in its statement of financial position as either assets or liabilities depending on the rights or obligations under the contracts. All derivative instruments shall be measured at fair value.

18. The accounting for changes in the fair value (that is, gains or losses) of a derivative depends on whether it has been designated and qualifies as part of a hedging relationship and, if so, on the reason for holding it. Either all or a proportion of a derivative may be designated as the hedging instrument. The proportion must be expressed as a percentage of the entire derivative so that the profile of risk exposures in the hedging portion of the derivative is the same as that in the entire derivative. (Thus, an entity is prohibited from separating a compound derivative into components representing different risks and designating any such component as the hedging instrument, except as permitted at the date of initial application by the transition provisions in paragraph 49.) Subsequent references in this Statement to a derivative as a hedging instrument include the use of only a proportion of a derivative as a hedging instrument. Two or more derivatives, or proportions thereof, may also be viewed in combination and jointly designated as the hedging instrument. Gains and losses on derivative instruments are accounted for as follows:

a. *No hedging designation.* The gain or loss on a derivative instrument not designated as a hedging instrument shall be recognized currently in earnings.
b. *Fair value hedge.* The gain or loss on a derivative instrument designated and qualifying as a fair value hedging instrument as well as the offsetting loss or gain on the hedged item attributable to the hedged risk shall be recognized currently in earnings in the same accounting period, as provided in paragraphs 22 and 23.
c. *Cash flow hedge.* The effective portion of the gain or loss on a derivative instrument designated and qualifying as a cash flow hedging instrument shall be reported as a component of other **comprehensive income** (outside earnings) and reclassified into earnings in the same period or periods during which the hedged forecasted transaction affects earnings, as provided in

paragraphs 30 and 31. The remaining gain or loss on the derivative instrument, if any, shall be recognized currently in earnings, as provided in paragraph 30.
d. *Foreign currency hedge.* The gain or loss on a derivative instrument or nonderivative financial instrument designated and qualifying as a foreign currency hedging instrument shall be accounted for as follows:
  (1) The gain or loss on the hedging derivative or nonderivative instrument in a hedge of a foreign-currency-denominated firm commitment and the offsetting loss or gain on the hedged firm commitment shall be recognized currently in earnings in the same accounting period, as provided in paragraph 37.
  (2) The gain or loss on the hedging derivative instrument in a hedge of an available-for-sale security and the offsetting loss or gain on the hedged available-for-sale security shall be recognized currently in earnings in the same accounting period, as provided in paragraph 38.
  (3) The effective portion of the gain or loss on the hedging derivative instrument in a hedge of a forecasted foreign-currency-denominated transaction shall be reported as a component of other comprehensive income (outside earnings) and reclassified into earnings in the same period or periods during which the hedged forecasted transaction affects earnings, as provided in paragraph 41. The remaining gain or loss on the hedging instrument shall be recognized currently in earnings.
  (4) The gain or loss on the hedging derivative or nonderivative instrument in a hedge of a net investment in a foreign operation shall be reported in other comprehensive income (outside earnings) as part of the cumulative translation adjustment to the extent it is effective as a hedge, as provided in paragraph 42.

19. [This paragraph has been deleted. See Status page.]

Fair Value Hedges

General

20. An entity may designate a derivative instrument as hedging the exposure to changes in the fair value

---

6c[This footnote has been deleted. See Status page.]

of an asset or a liability or an identified portion thereof ("hedged item") that is attributable to a particular risk. Designated hedging instruments and hedged items qualify for fair value hedge accounting if all of the following criteria and those in paragraph 21 are met:

a. At inception of the hedge, there is formal documentation of the hedging relationship and the entity's risk management objective and strategy for undertaking the hedge, including identification of the hedging instrument, the hedged item, the nature of the risk being hedged, and how the hedging instrument's effectiveness in offsetting the exposure to changes in the hedged item's fair value attributable to the hedged risk will be assessed. There must be a reasonable basis for how the entity plans to assess the hedging instrument's effectiveness.

   (1) For a fair value hedge of a firm commitment, the entity's formal documentation at the inception of the hedge must include a reasonable method for recognizing in earnings the asset or liability representing the gain or loss on the hedged firm commitment.

   (2) An entity's defined risk management strategy for a particular hedging relationship may exclude certain components of a specific hedging derivative's change in fair value, such as time value, from the assessment of hedge effectiveness, as discussed in paragraph 63 in Section 2 of Appendix A.

b. Both at inception of the hedge and on an ongoing basis, the hedging relationship is expected to be highly effective in achieving offsetting changes in fair value attributable to the hedged risk during the period that the hedge is designated. An assessment of effectiveness is required whenever financial statements or earnings are reported, and at least every three months. If the hedging instrument (such as an at-the-money option contract) provides only one-sided offset of the hedged risk, the increases (or decreases) in the fair value of the hedging instrument must be expected to be highly effective in offsetting the decreases (or increases) in the fair value of the hedged item. All assessments of effectiveness shall be consistent with the risk management strategy documented for that particular hedging relationship (in accordance with paragraph 20(a) above).

c. If a written option is designated as hedging a recognized asset or liability or an unrecognized firm commitment, the combination of the hedged item and the written option provides at least as much potential for gains as a result of a favorable change in the fair value of the combined instruments[7] as exposure to losses from an unfavorable change in their combined fair value. That test is met if all possible percentage favorable changes in the underlying (from zero percent to 100 percent) would provide at least as much gain as the loss that would be incurred from an unfavorable change in the underlying of the same percentage.

   (1) A combination of options (for example, an interest rate collar) entered into contemporaneously shall be considered a written option if either at inception or over the life of the contracts a net premium is received in cash or as a favorable rate or other term. (Thus, a collar can be designated as a hedging instrument in a fair value hedge without regard to the test in paragraph 20(c) unless a net premium is received.) Furthermore, a derivative instrument that results from combining a written option and any other nonoption derivative shall be considered a written option.

A nonderivative instrument, such as a Treasury note, shall not be designated as a hedging instrument, except as provided in paragraphs 37 and 42 of this Statement.

The hedged item

21. An asset or a liability is eligible for designation as a hedged item in a fair value hedge if all of the following criteria are met:

a. The hedged item is specifically identified as either all or a specific portion of a recognized asset

---

[7]The reference to *combined instruments* refers to the written option and the hedged item, such as an embedded purchased option.

or liability or of an unrecognized firm commitment.[8] The hedged item is a single asset or liability (or a specific portion thereof) or is a portfolio of similar assets or a portfolio of similar liabilities (or a specific portion thereof).

(1) If similar assets or similar liabilities are aggregated and hedged as a portfolio, the individual assets or individual liabilities must share the risk exposure for which they are designated as being hedged. The change in fair value attributable to the hedged risk for each individual item in a hedged portfolio must be expected to respond in a generally proportionate manner to the overall change in fair value of the aggregate portfolio attributable to the hedged risk. That is, if the change in fair value of a hedged portfolio attributable to the hedged risk was 10 percent during a reporting period, the change in the fair values attributable to the hedged risk for each item constituting the portfolio should be expected to be within a fairly narrow range, such as 9 percent to 11 percent. In contrast, an expectation that the change in fair value attributable to the hedged risk for individual items in the portfolio would range from 7 percent to 13 percent would be inconsistent with this provision. In aggregating loans in a portfolio to be hedged, an entity may choose to consider some of the following characteristics, as appropriate: loan type, loan size, nature and location of collateral, interest rate type (fixed or variable) and the coupon interest rate (if fixed), scheduled maturity, prepayment history of the loans (if seasoned), and expected prepayment performance in varying interest rate scenarios.[9]

(2) If the hedged item is a specific portion of an asset or liability (or of a portfolio of similar assets or a portfolio of similar liabilities), the hedged item is one of the following:

(a) A percentage of the entire asset or liability (or of the entire portfolio)

(b) One or more selected contractual cash flows (such as the portion of the asset or liability representing the present value of the interest payments in the first two years of a four-year debt instrument)

(c) A put option or call option (including an interest rate or price cap or an interest rate or price floor) embedded in an existing asset or liability that is not an embedded derivative accounted for separately pursuant to paragraph 12 of this Statement

(d) The residual value in a lessor's net investment in a direct financing or sales-type lease.

If the entire asset or liability is an instrument with variable cash flows, the hedged item cannot be deemed to be an implicit fixed-to-variable swap (or similar instrument) perceived to be embedded in a host contract with fixed cash flows.

b. The hedged item presents an exposure to changes in fair value attributable to the hedged risk that could affect reported earnings. The reference to affecting reported earnings does not apply to an entity that does not report earnings as a separate caption in a statement of financial performance, such as a not-for-profit organization, as discussed in paragraph 43.

c. The hedged item is not (1) an asset or liability that is remeasured with the changes in fair value attributable to the hedged risk reported currently in earnings, (2) an investment accounted for by the equity method in accordance with the requirements of APB Opinion No. 18, *The Equity*

---

[8]A firm commitment (as defined in paragraph 540) that represents an asset or liability that a specific accounting standard prohibits recognizing (such as a noncancelable operating lease or an unrecognized mortgage servicing right) may nevertheless be designated as the hedged item in a fair value hedge. A mortgage banker's unrecognized "interest rate lock commitment" (IRLC) does not qualify as a firm commitment (because as an option it does not obligate both parties) and thus is not eligible for fair value hedge accounting as the hedged item. (However, a mortgage banker's "forward sale commitments," which are derivatives that lock in the prices at which the mortgage loans will be sold to investors, may qualify as hedging instruments in cash flow hedges of the forecasted sales of mortgage loans.) A supply contract for which the contract price is fixed only in certain circumstances (such as when the selling price is above an embedded price cap or below an embedded price floor) meets the definition of a firm commitment for purposes of designating the hedged item in a fair value hedge. Provided the embedded price cap or floor is considered clearly and closely related to the host contract and therefore is not accounted for separately under paragraph 12, either party to the supply contract can hedge the fair value exposure arising from the cap or floor.

[9]Mortgage bankers and other servicers of financial assets that designate a hedged portfolio by aggregating servicing rights within one or more risk strata used under paragraph 63(f) of Statement 140 would not necessarily comply with the requirement in this paragraph for portfolios of similar assets. The risk strata under paragraph 63(f) of Statement 140 can be based on any predominant risk characteristic, including date of origination or geographic location.

Method of Accounting for Investments in Common Stock, (3) a minority interest in one or more consolidated subsidiaries, (4) an equity investment in a consolidated subsidiary, (5) a firm commitment either to enter into a business combination or to acquire or dispose of a subsidiary, a minority interest, or an equity method investee, or (6) an equity instrument issued by the entity and classified in stockholders' equity in the statement of financial position.

d. If the hedged item is all or a portion of a debt security (or a portfolio of similar debt securities) that is classified as held-to-maturity in accordance with FASB Statement No. 115, *Accounting for Certain Investments in Debt and Equity Securities,* the designated risk being hedged is the risk of changes in its fair value attributable to credit risk, foreign exchange risk, or both. If the hedged item is an option component of a held-to-maturity security that permits its prepayment, the designated risk being hedged is the risk of changes in the entire fair value of that option component. (The designated hedged risk for a held-to-maturity security may not be the risk of changes in its fair value attributable to interest rate risk. If the hedged item is other than an option component that permits its prepayment, the designated hedged risk also may not be the risk of changes in its overall fair value.)

e. If the hedged item is a nonfinancial asset or liability (other than a recognized loan servicing right or a nonfinancial firm commitment with financial components), the designated risk being hedged is the risk of changes in the fair value of the entire hedged asset or liability (reflecting its actual location if a physical asset). That is, the price risk of a similar asset in a different location or of a major ingredient may not be the hedged risk. Thus, in hedging the exposure to changes in the fair value of gasoline, an entity may not designate the risk of changes in the price of crude oil as the risk being hedged for purposes of determining effectiveness of the fair value hedge of gasoline.

f. If the hedged item is a financial asset or liability, a recognized loan servicing right, or a nonfinancial firm commitment with financial components, the designated risk being hedged is:
 (1) The risk of changes in the overall fair value of the entire hedged item,

(2) The risk of changes in its fair value attributable to changes in the **designated benchmark interest rate** (referred to as interest rate risk),
(3) The risk of changes in its fair value attributable to changes in the related foreign currency exchange rates (referred to as foreign exchange risk) (refer to paragraphs 37, 37A, and 38), or
(4) The risk of changes in its fair value attributable to both changes in the obligor's creditworthiness and changes in the spread over the benchmark interest rate with respect to the hedged item's credit sector at inception of the hedge (referred to as credit risk).

If the risk designated as being hedged is not the risk in paragraph 21(f)(1) above, two or more of the other risks (interest rate risk, foreign currency exchange risk, and credit risk) may simultaneously be designated as being hedged. The benchmark interest rate being hedged in a hedge of interest rate risk must be specifically identified as part of the designation and documentation at the inception of the hedging relationship. Ordinarily, an entity should designate the same benchmark interest rate as the risk being hedged for similar hedges, consistent with paragraph 62; the use of different benchmark interest rates for similar hedges should be rare and must be justified. In calculating the change in the hedged item's fair value attributable to changes in the benchmark interest rate, the estimated cash flows used in calculating fair value must be based on all of the contractual cash flows of the entire hedged item. Excluding some of the hedged item's contractual cash flows (for example, the portion of the interest coupon in excess of the benchmark interest rate) from the calculation is not permitted.[9a] An entity may not simply designate prepayment risk as the risk being hedged for a financial asset. However, it can designate the option component of a prepayable instrument as the hedged item in a fair value hedge of the entity's exposure to changes in the overall fair value of that "prepayment" option, perhaps thereby achieving the objective of its desire to hedge prepayment risk. The effect of an embedded derivative of the same risk

[9a]The first sentence of paragraph 21(a) that specifically permits the hedged item to be identified as either all or a specific portion of a recognized asset or liability or of an unrecognized firm commitment is not affected by the provisions in this subparagraph.

class must be considered in designating a hedge of an individual risk. For example, the effect of an embedded prepayment option must be considered in designating a hedge of interest rate risk.

22. Gains and losses on a qualifying fair value hedge shall be accounted for as follows:

a. The gain or loss on the hedging instrument shall be recognized currently in earnings.
b. The gain or loss (that is, the change in fair value) on the hedged item attributable to the hedged risk shall adjust the carrying amount of the hedged item and be recognized currently in earnings.

If the fair value hedge is fully effective, the gain or loss on the hedging instrument, adjusted for the component, if any, of that gain or loss that is excluded from the assessment of effectiveness under the entity's defined risk management strategy for that particular hedging relationship (as discussed in paragraph 63 in Section 2 of Appendix A), would exactly offset the loss or gain on the hedged item attributable to the hedged risk. Any difference that does arise would be the effect of hedge ineffectiveness, which consequently is recognized currently in earnings. The measurement of hedge ineffectiveness for a particular hedging relationship shall be consistent with the entity's risk management strategy and the method of assessing hedge effectiveness that was documented at the inception of the hedging relationship, as discussed in paragraph 20(a). Nevertheless, the amount of hedge ineffectiveness recognized in earnings is based on the extent to which exact offset is not achieved. Although a hedging relationship must comply with an entity's established policy range of what is considered "highly effective" pursuant to paragraph 20(b) in order for that relationship to qualify for hedge accounting, that compliance does not assure zero ineffectiveness. Section 2 of Appendix A illustrates assessing hedge effectiveness and measuring hedge ineffectiveness. Any hedge ineffectiveness directly affects earnings because there will be no offsetting adjustment of a hedged item's carrying amount for the ineffective aspect of the gain or loss on the related hedging instrument.

23. If a hedged item is otherwise measured at fair value with changes in fair value reported in other comprehensive income (such as an available-for-sale security), the adjustment of the hedged item's carrying amount discussed in paragraph 22 shall be recognized in earnings rather than in other comprehensive income in order to offset the gain or loss on the hedging instrument.

24. The adjustment of the carrying amount of a hedged asset or liability required by paragraph 22 shall be accounted for in the same manner as other components of the carrying amount of that asset or liability. For example, an adjustment of the carrying amount of a hedged asset held for sale (such as inventory) would remain part of the carrying amount of that asset until the asset is sold, at which point the entire carrying amount of the hedged asset would be recognized as the cost of the item sold in determining earnings. An adjustment of the carrying amount of a hedged interest-bearing financial instrument shall be amortized to earnings; amortization shall begin no later than when the hedged item ceases to be adjusted for changes in its fair value attributable to the risk being hedged.

25. An entity shall discontinue prospectively the accounting specified in paragraphs 22 and 23 for an existing hedge if any one of the following occurs:

a. Any criterion in paragraphs 20 and 21 is no longer met.
b. The derivative expires or is sold, terminated, or exercised.
c. The entity removes the designation of the fair value hedge.

In those circumstances, the entity may elect to designate prospectively a new hedging relationship with a different hedging instrument or, in the circumstances described in paragraphs 25(a) and 25(c) above, a different hedged item or a hedged transaction if the hedging relationship meets the criteria specified in paragraphs 20 and 21 for a fair value hedge or paragraphs 28 and 29 for a cash flow hedge.

26. In general, if a periodic assessment indicates noncompliance with the effectiveness criterion in paragraph 20(b), an entity shall not recognize the adjustment of the carrying amount of the hedged item described in paragraphs 22 and 23 after the last date on which compliance with the effectiveness criterion was established. However, if the event or change in circumstances that caused the hedging relationship to fail the effectiveness criterion can be identified, the entity shall recognize in earnings the changes in the hedged item's fair value attributable to the risk being hedged that occurred prior to that event or change in circumstances. If a fair value hedge of a firm commitment is discontinued because the hedged item no longer meets the definition of a firm commitment,

the entity shall derecognize any asset or liability previously recognized pursuant to paragraph 22 (as a result of an adjustment to the carrying amount for the firm commitment) and recognize a corresponding loss or gain currently in earnings.

Impairment

27. An asset or liability that has been designated as being hedged and accounted for pursuant to paragraphs 22–24 remains subject to the applicable requirements in generally accepted accounting principles for assessing impairment for that type of asset or for recognizing an increased obligation for that type of liability. Those impairment requirements shall be applied after hedge accounting has been applied for the period and the carrying amount of the hedged asset or liability has been adjusted pursuant to paragraph 22 of this Statement. Because the hedging instrument is recognized separately as an asset or liability, its fair value or expected cash flows shall not be considered in applying those impairment requirements to the hedged asset or liability.

Cash Flow Hedges

General

28. An entity may designate a derivative instrument as hedging the exposure to variability in expected future cash flows that is attributable to a particular risk. That exposure may be associated with an existing recognized asset or liability (such as all or certain future interest payments on variable-rate debt) or a forecasted transaction (such as a forecasted purchase or sale).[10] Designated hedging instruments and hedged items or transactions qualify for cash flow hedge accounting if all of the following criteria and those in paragraph 29 are met:

a. At inception of the hedge, there is formal documentation of the hedging relationship and the entity's risk management objective and strategy for undertaking the hedge, including identification of the hedging instrument, the hedged transaction, the nature of the risk being hedged, and how the hedging instrument's effectiveness in hedging the exposure to the hedged transaction's variability in cash flows attributable to the hedged risk will be assessed. There must be a reasonable basis for how the entity plans to assess the hedging instrument's effectiveness.

(1) An entity's defined risk management strategy for a particular hedging relationship may exclude certain components of a specific hedging derivative's change in fair value from the assessment of hedge effectiveness, as discussed in paragraph 63 in Section 2 of Appendix A.

(2) Documentation shall include all relevant details, including the date on or period within which the forecasted transaction is expected to occur, the specific nature of asset or liability involved (if any), and the expected currency amount or quantity of the forecasted transaction.

(a) The phrase *expected currency amount* refers to hedges of foreign currency exchange risk and requires specification of the exact amount of foreign currency being hedged.

(b) The phrase *expected . . . quantity* refers to hedges of other risks and requires specification of the physical quantity (that is, the number of items or units of measure) encompassed by the hedged forecasted transaction. If a forecasted sale or purchase is being hedged for price risk, the hedged transaction cannot be specified solely in terms of expected currency amounts, nor can it be specified as a percentage of sales or purchases during a period. The current price of a forecasted transaction also should be identified to satisfy the criterion in paragraph 28(b) for offsetting cash flows.

The hedged forecasted transaction shall be described with sufficient specificity so that when a transaction occurs, it is clear whether that transaction is or is not the hedged transaction. Thus, the forecasted transaction could be identified as the sale of either the first 15,000 units of a specific product sold during a specified 3-month period or the first 5,000 units of a specific product sold in each of

---

[9b][This footnote has been deleted. See Status page.]

[10]For purposes of paragraphs 28–35, the individual cash flows related to a recognized asset or liability and the cash flows related to a forecasted transaction are both referred to as a *forecasted transaction* or *hedged transaction*.

3 specific months, but it could not be identified as the sale of the last 15,000 units of that product sold during a 3-month period (because the last 15,000 units cannot be identified when they occur, but only when the period has ended).

b. Both at inception of the hedge and on an ongoing basis, the hedging relationship is expected to be highly effective in achieving offsetting cash flows attributable to the hedged risk during the term of the hedge, except as indicated in paragraph 28(d) below. An assessment of effectiveness is required whenever financial statements or earnings are reported, and at least every three months. If the hedging instrument, such as an at-the-money option contract, provides only one-sided offset against the hedged risk, the cash inflows (outflows) from the hedging instrument must be expected to be highly effective in offsetting the corresponding change in the cash outflows or inflows of the hedged transaction. All assessments of effectiveness shall be consistent with the originally documented risk management strategy for that particular hedging relationship.

c. If a written option is designated as hedging the variability in cash flows for a recognized asset or liability or an unrecognized firm commitment, the combination of the hedged item and the written option provides at least as much potential for favorable cash flows as exposure to unfavorable cash flows. That test is met if all possible percentage favorable changes in the underlying (from zero percent to 100 percent) would provide at least as much favorable cash flows as the unfavorable cash flows that would be incurred from an unfavorable change in the underlying of the same percentage. (Refer to paragraph 20(c)(1).)

d. If a hedging instrument is used to modify the interest receipts or payments associated with a recognized financial asset or liability from one variable rate to another variable rate, the hedging instrument must be a link between an existing designated asset (or group of similar assets) with variable cash flows and an existing designated liability (or group of similar liabilities) with variable cash flows and be highly effective at achieving offsetting cash flows. A link exists if the basis (that is, the rate index on which the interest rate is based) of one leg of an interest rate swap is the same as the basis of the interest receipts for the designated asset and the basis of the other leg of the swap is the same as the basis of the interest payments for the designated liability. In this situa-

tion, the criterion in the first sentence in paragraph 29(a) is applied separately to the designated asset and the designated liability.

A nonderivative instrument, such as a Treasury note, shall not be designated as a hedging instrument for a cash flow hedge.

The hedged forecasted transaction

29. A forecasted transaction is eligible for designation as a hedged transaction in a cash flow hedge if all of the following additional criteria are met:

a. The forecasted transaction is specifically identified as a single transaction or a group of individual transactions. If the hedged transaction is a group of individual transactions, those individual transactions must share the same risk exposure for which they are designated as being hedged. Thus, a forecasted purchase and a forecasted sale cannot both be included in the same group of individual transactions that constitute the hedged transaction.

b. The occurrence of the forecasted transaction is probable.

c. The forecasted transaction is a transaction with a party external to the reporting entity (except as permitted by paragraph 40) and presents an exposure to variations in cash flows for the hedged risk that could affect reported earnings.

d. The forecasted transaction is not the acquisition of an asset or incurrence of a liability that will subsequently be remeasured with changes in fair value attributable to the hedged risk reported currently in earnings. If the forecasted transaction relates to a recognized asset or liability, the asset or liability is not remeasured with changes in fair value attributable to the hedged risk reported currently in earnings.

e. If the variable cash flows of the forecasted transaction relate to a debt security that is classified as held-to-maturity under Statement 115, the risk being hedged is the risk of changes in its cash flows attributable to credit risk, foreign exchange risk, or both. For those variable cash flows, the risk being hedged cannot be the risk of changes in its cash flows attributable to interest rate risk.

f. The forecasted transaction does not involve a business combination subject to the provisions of Statement 141 and is not a transaction (such as a forecasted purchase, sale, or dividend) involving (1) a parent company's interests in consolidated subsidiaries, (2) a minority interest in a consolidated subsidiary, (3) an equity-method investment, or (4) an entity's own equity instruments.

g. If the hedged transaction is the forecasted purchase or sale of a nonfinancial asset, the designated risk being hedged is (1) the risk of changes in the functional-currency-equivalent cash flows attributable to changes in the related foreign currency exchange rates or (2) the risk of changes in the cash flows relating to all changes in the purchase price or sales price of the asset reflecting its actual location if a physical asset (regardless of whether that price and the related cash flows are stated in the entity's functional currency or a foreign currency), not the risk of changes in the cash flows relating to the purchase or sale of a similar asset in a different location or of a major ingredient. Thus, for example, in hedging the exposure to changes in the cash flows relating to the purchase of its bronze bar inventory, an entity may not designate the risk of changes in the cash flows relating to purchasing the copper component in bronze as the risk being hedged for purposes of assessing offset as required by paragraph 28(b).

h. If the hedged transaction is the forecasted purchase or sale of a financial asset or liability (or the interest payments on that financial asset or liability) or the variable cash inflow or outflow of an existing financial asset or liability, the designated risk being hedged is:
   (1) The risk of overall changes in the hedged cash flows related to the asset or liability, such as those relating to all changes in the purchase price or sales price (regardless of whether that price and the related cash flows are stated in the entity's functional currency or a foreign currency),
   (2) The risk of changes in its cash flows attributable to changes in the designated benchmark interest rate (referred to as interest rate risk),
   (3) The risk of changes in the functional-currency-equivalent cash flows attributable to changes in the related foreign currency exchange rates (referred to as foreign exchange risk) (refer to paragraphs 40, 40A, 40B, and 40C), or
   (4) The risk of changes in its cash flows attributable to default, changes in the obligor's creditworthiness, and changes in the spread over the benchmark interest rate with respect to the hedged item's credit sector at inception of the hedge (referred to as credit risk).

Two or more of the above risks may be designated simultaneously as being hedged. The benchmark interest rate being hedged in a hedge of interest rate risk must be specifically identified as part of the designation and documentation at the inception of the hedging relationship. Ordinarily, an entity should designate the same benchmark interest rate as the risk being hedged for similar hedges, consistent with paragraph 62; the use of different benchmark interest rates for similar hedges should be rare and must be justified. In a cash flow hedge of a variable-rate financial asset or liability, either existing or forecasted, the designated risk being hedged cannot be the risk of changes in its cash flows attributable to changes in the specifically identified benchmark interest rate if the cash flows of the hedged transaction are explicitly based on a different index, for example, based on a specific bank's prime rate, which cannot qualify as the benchmark rate. However, the risk designated as being hedged could potentially be the risk of overall changes in the hedged cash flows related to the asset or liability, provided that the other criteria for a cash flow hedge have been met. An entity may not designate prepayment risk as the risk being hedged (refer to paragraph 21(f)).

30. The effective portion of the gain or loss on a derivative designated as a cash flow hedge is reported in other comprehensive income, and the ineffective portion is reported in earnings. More specifically, a qualifying cash flow hedge shall be accounted for as follows:

a. If an entity's defined risk management strategy for a particular hedging relationship excludes a specific component of the gain or loss, or related cash flows, on the hedging derivative from the assessment of hedge effectiveness (as discussed in paragraph 63 in Section 2 of Appendix A), that excluded component of the gain or loss shall be recognized currently in earnings. For example, if the effectiveness of a hedge with an option contract is assessed based on changes in the option's intrinsic value, the changes in the option's time value would be recognized in earnings. Time value is equal to the fair value of the option less its intrinsic value.

b. Accumulated other comprehensive income associated with the hedged transaction shall be adjusted to a balance that reflects the *lesser* of the following (in absolute amounts):

(1) The cumulative gain or loss on the derivative from inception of the hedge less (a) the excluded component discussed in paragraph 30(a) above and (b) the derivative's gains or losses previously reclassified from accumulated other comprehensive income into earnings pursuant to paragraph 31.

(2) The portion of the cumulative gain or loss on the derivative necessary to offset the cumulative change in expected future cash flows on the hedged transaction from inception of the hedge less the derivative's gains or losses previously reclassified from accumulated other comprehensive income into earnings pursuant to paragraph 31.

That adjustment of accumulated other comprehensive income shall incorporate recognition in other comprehensive income of part or all of the gain or loss on the hedging derivative, as necessary.

c. A gain or loss shall be recognized in earnings, as necessary, for any remaining gain or loss on the hedging derivative or to adjust other comprehensive income to the balance specified in paragraph 30(b) above.

d. If a non-option-based contract is the hedging instrument in a cash flow hedge of the variability of the functional-currency-equivalent cash flows for a recognized foreign-currency-denominated asset or liability that is remeasured at spot exchange rates under paragraph 15 of Statement 52, an amount that will offset the related transaction gain or loss arising from that remeasurement shall be reclassified each period from other comprehensive income to earnings if the assessment of effectiveness and measurement of ineffectiveness are based on total changes in the non-option-based instrument's cash flows. If an option contract is used as the hedging instrument in a cash flow hedge of the variability of the functional-currency-equivalent cash flows for a recognized foreign-currency-denominated asset or liability that is remeasured at spot exchange rates under paragraph 15 of Statement 52 to provide only one-sided offset against the hedged foreign exchange risk, an amount shall be reclassified each period to or from other comprehensive income with respect to the changes in the underlying that result in a change in the hedging option's intrinsic value. In addition, if the assessment of effectiveness and measurement of ineffectiveness are also based on total changes in the option's cash flows (that is, the assessment will include the hedging instrument's entire change in fair value—its entire gain or loss), an amount that adjusts earnings for the amortization of the cost of the option on a rational basis shall be reclassified each period from other comprehensive income to earnings.[10a]

Section 2 of Appendix A illustrates assessing hedge effectiveness and measuring hedge ineffectiveness. Examples 6 and 9 of Section 1 of Appendix B illustrate the application of this paragraph.

31. Amounts in accumulated other comprehensive income shall be reclassified into earnings in the same period or periods during which the hedged forecasted transaction affects earnings (for example, when a forecasted sale actually occurs). If the hedged transaction results in the acquisition of an asset or the incurrence of a liability, the gains and losses in accumulated other comprehensive income shall be reclassified into earnings in the same period or periods during which the asset acquired or liability incurred affects earnings (such as in the periods that depreciation expense, interest expense, or cost of sales is recognized). However, if an entity expects at any time that continued reporting of a loss in accumulated other comprehensive income would lead to recognizing a net loss on the combination of the hedging instrument and the hedged transaction (and related asset acquired or liability incurred) in one or more future periods, a loss shall be reclassified immediately into earnings for the amount that is not expected to be recovered. For example, a loss shall be reported in earnings for a derivative that is designated as hedging the forecasted purchase of inventory to the extent that the cost basis of the inventory plus the related amount reported in accumulated other comprehensive income exceeds the amount expected to be recovered through sales of that inventory. (Impairment guidance is provided in paragraphs 34 and 35.)

[10a]The guidance in this subparagraph is limited to foreign currency hedging relationships because of their unique attributes. That accounting guidance is an exception for foreign currency hedging relationships.

32. An entity shall discontinue prospectively the accounting specified in paragraphs 30 and 31 for an existing hedge if any one of the following occurs:

a. Any criterion in paragraphs 28 and 29 is no longer met.
b. The derivative expires or is sold, terminated, or exercised.
c. The entity removes the designation of the cash flow hedge.

In those circumstances, the net gain or loss shall remain in accumulated other comprehensive income and be reclassified into earnings as specified in paragraph 31. Furthermore, the entity may elect to designate prospectively a new hedging relationship with a different hedging instrument or, in the circumstances described in paragraphs 32(a) and 32(c), a different hedged transaction or a hedged item if the hedging relationship meets the criteria specified in paragraphs 28 and 29 for a cash flow hedge or paragraphs 20 and 21 for a fair value hedge.

33. The net derivative gain or loss related to a discontinued cash flow hedge shall continue to be reported in accumulated other comprehensive income unless it is probable that the forecasted transaction will *not* occur by the end of the originally specified time period (as documented at the inception of the hedging relationship) or within an additional two-month period of time thereafter, except as indicated in the following sentence. In rare cases, the existence of extenuating circumstances that are related to the nature of the forecasted transaction and are outside the control or influence of the reporting entity may cause the forecasted transaction to be probable of occurring on a date that is beyond the additional two-month period of time, in which case the net derivative gain or loss related to the discontinued cash flow hedge shall continue to be reported in accumulated other comprehensive income until it is reclassified into earnings pursuant to paragraph 31. If it is probable that the hedged forecasted transaction will not occur either by the end of the originally specified time period or within the additional two-month period of time and the hedged forecasted transaction also does not qualify for the exception described in the preceding sentence, that derivative gain or loss reported in accumulated other comprehensive income shall be reclassified into earnings immediately.

34. Existing requirements in generally accepted accounting principles for assessing asset impairment or recognizing an increased obligation apply to an asset or liability that gives rise to variable cash flows (such as a variable-rate financial instrument), for which the variable cash flows (the forecasted transactions) have been designated as being hedged and accounted for pursuant to paragraphs 30 and 31. Those impairment requirements shall be applied each period after hedge accounting has been applied for the period, pursuant to paragraphs 30 and 31 of this Statement. The fair value or expected cash flows of a hedging instrument shall not be considered in applying those requirements. The gain or loss on the hedging instrument in accumulated other comprehensive income shall, however, be accounted for as discussed in paragraph 31.

35. If, under existing requirements in generally accepted accounting principles, an impairment loss is recognized on an asset or an additional obligation is recognized on a liability to which a hedged forecasted transaction relates, any offsetting net gain related to that transaction in accumulated other comprehensive income shall be reclassified immediately into earnings. Similarly, if a recovery is recognized on the asset or liability to which the forecasted transaction relates, any offsetting net loss that has been accumulated in other comprehensive income shall be reclassified immediately into earnings.

Foreign Currency Hedges

36. If the hedged item is denominated in a foreign currency, an entity may designate the following types of hedges of foreign currency exposure, as specified in paragraphs 37–42:

a. A fair value hedge of an unrecognized firm commitment or a recognized asset or liability (including an available-for-sale security)
b. A cash flow hedge of a forecasted transaction, an unrecognized firm commitment, the forecasted functional-currency-equivalent cash flows associated with a recognized asset or liability, or a forecasted intercompany transaction
c. A hedge of a net investment in a foreign operation.

The recognition in earnings of the foreign currency transaction gain or loss on a foreign-currency-denominated asset or liability based on changes in

---

[10b][This footnote has been deleted. See Status page.]

the foreign currency spot rate is not considered to be the remeasurement of that asset or liability with changes in fair value attributable to foreign exchange risk recognized in earnings, which is discussed in the criteria in paragraphs 21(c)(1) and 29(d). Thus, those criteria are not impediments to either a foreign currency fair value or cash flow hedge of such a foreign-currency-denominated asset or liability or a foreign currency cash flow hedge of the forecasted acquisition or incurrence of a foreign-currency-denominated asset or liability whose carrying amount will be remeasured at spot exchange rates under paragraph 15 of Statement 52. A foreign currency derivative instrument that has been entered into with another member of a consolidated group can be a hedging instrument in a fair value hedge or in a cash flow hedge of a recognized foreign-currency-denominated asset or liability or in a net investment hedge in the consolidated financial statements only if that other member has entered into an offsetting contract with an unrelated third party to hedge the exposure it acquired from issuing the derivative instrument to the affiliate that initiated the hedge.

36A. The provisions in paragraph 36 that permit a recognized foreign-currency-denominated asset or liability to be the hedged item in a fair value or cash flow hedge of foreign currency exposure also pertain to a recognized foreign-currency-denominated receivable or payable that results from a hedged forecasted foreign-currency-denominated sale or purchase on credit. An entity may choose to designate a single cash flow hedge that encompasses the variability of functional currency cash flows attributable to foreign exchange risk related to the settlement of the foreign-currency-denominated receivable or payable resulting from a forecasted sale or purchase on credit. Alternatively, an entity may choose to designate a cash flow hedge of the variability of functional currency cash flows attributable to foreign exchange risk related to a forecasted foreign-currency-denominated sale or purchase on credit and then separately designate a foreign currency fair value hedge of the resulting recognized foreign-currency-denominated receivable or payable. In that case, the cash flow hedge would terminate (be dedesignated) when the hedged sale or purchase occurs and the foreign-currency-denominated receivable or payable is recognized. The use of the same foreign currency derivative instrument for both the cash flow hedge and the fair value hedge is not prohibited though some ineffectiveness may result.

Foreign currency fair value hedges

37. *Unrecognized firm commitment.* A derivative instrument or a nonderivative financial instrument[11] that may give rise to a foreign currency transaction gain or loss under Statement 52 can be designated as hedging changes in the fair value of an unrecognized firm commitment, or a specific portion thereof, attributable to foreign currency exchange rates. The designated hedging relationship qualifies for the accounting specified in paragraphs 22–27 if all the fair value hedge criteria in paragraphs 20 and 21 and the conditions in paragraphs 40(a) and 40(b) are met.

37A. *Recognized asset or liability.* A nonderivative financial instrument shall not be designated as the hedging instrument in a fair value hedge of the foreign currency exposure of a recognized asset or liability. A derivative instrument can be designated as hedging the changes in the fair value of a recognized asset or liability (or a specific portion thereof) for which a foreign currency transaction gain or loss is recognized in earnings under the provisions of paragraph 15 of Statement 52. All recognized foreign-currency-denominated assets or liabilities for which a foreign currency transaction gain or loss is recorded in earnings may qualify for the accounting specified in paragraphs 22–27 if all the fair value hedge criteria in paragraphs 20 and 21 and the conditions in paragraphs 40(a) and 40(b) are met.

38. *Available-for-sale security.* A nonderivative financial instrument shall not be designated as the hedging instrument in a fair value hedge of the foreign currency exposure of an available-for-sale security. A derivative instrument can be designated as hedging the changes in the fair value of an available-for-sale *debt* security (or a specific portion thereof) attributable to changes in foreign currency exchange rates. The designated hedging relationship qualifies for the accounting specified in paragraphs 22–27 if all the fair value hedge criteria in paragraphs 20 and 21 and the conditions in paragraphs 40(a) and 40(b) are met. An available-for-sale *equity* security can be hedged for changes in the fair value attributable to changes in foreign currency exchange rates

---

[11]The carrying basis for a nonderivative financial instrument that gives rise to a foreign currency transaction gain or loss under Statement 52 is not addressed by this Statement.

and qualify for the accounting specified in paragraphs 22–27 only if the fair value hedge criteria in paragraphs 20 and 21 are met and the following two conditions are satisfied:

a. The security is not traded on an exchange (or other established marketplace) on which trades are denominated in the investor's functional currency.
b. Dividends or other cash flows to holders of the security are all denominated in the same foreign currency as the currency expected to be received upon sale of the security.

The change in fair value of the hedged available-for-sale equity security attributable to foreign exchange risk is reported in earnings pursuant to paragraph 23 and not in other comprehensive income.

39. Gains and losses on a qualifying foreign currency fair value hedge shall be accounted for as specified in paragraphs 22–27. The gain or loss on a nonderivative hedging instrument attributable to foreign currency risk is the foreign currency transaction gain or loss as determined under Statement 52.[12] That foreign currency transaction gain or loss shall be recognized currently in earnings along with the change in the carrying amount of the hedged firm commitment.

Foreign currency cash flow hedges

40. A nonderivative financial instrument shall not be designated as a hedging instrument in a foreign currency cash flow hedge. A derivative instrument designated as hedging the foreign currency exposure to variability in the functional-currency-equivalent cash flows associated with a forecasted transaction (for example, a forecasted export sale to an unaffiliated entity with the price to be denominated in a foreign currency), a recognized asset or liability, an unrecognized firm commitment, or a forecasted intercompany transaction (for example, a forecasted sale to a foreign subsidiary or a forecasted royalty from a foreign subsidiary) qualifies for hedge accounting if all the following criteria are met:

a. For consolidated financial statements, either (1) the operating unit that has the foreign currency exposure is a party to the hedging instrument or (2) another member of the consolidated group that has the same functional currency as that operating unit (subject to the restrictions in this subparagraph and related footnote) is a party to the hedging instrument. To qualify for applying the guidance in (2) above, there may be no intervening subsidiary with a different functional currency.[12a] (Refer to paragraphs 36, 40A, and 40B for conditions for which an intercompany foreign currency derivative can be the hedging instrument in a cash flow hedge of foreign exchange risk.)
b. The hedged transaction is denominated in a currency other than the hedging unit's functional currency.
c. All of the criteria in paragraphs 28 and 29 are met, except for the criterion in paragraph 29(c) that requires that the forecasted transaction be with a party external to the reporting entity.
d. If the hedged transaction is a group of individual forecasted foreign-currency-denominated transactions, a forecasted inflow of a foreign currency and a forecasted outflow of the foreign currency cannot both be included in the same group.
e. If the hedged item is a recognized foreign-currency-denominated asset or liability, all the variability in the hedged item's functional-currency-equivalent cash flows must be eliminated by the effect of the hedge. (For example, a cash flow hedge cannot be used with a variable-rate foreign-currency-denominated asset or liability and a derivative based solely on changes in exchange rates because the derivative does not eliminate all the variability in the functional currency cash flows.)

40A. *Internal derivative.* A foreign currency derivative contract that has been entered into with another member of a consolidated group (such as a treasury center) can be a hedging instrument in a foreign currency cash flow hedge of a forecasted borrowing,

---

[12]The foreign currency transaction gain or loss on a hedging instrument is determined, consistent with paragraph 15 of Statement 52, as the increase or decrease in functional currency cash flows attributable to the change in spot exchange rates between the functional currency and the currency in which the hedging instrument is denominated.

[12a]For example, if a dollar-functional, second-tier subsidiary has a Euro exposure, the dollar-functional consolidated parent company could designate its U.S. dollar–Euro derivative as a hedge of the second-tier subsidiary's exposure provided that the functional currency of the intervening first-tier subsidiary (that is, the parent of the second-tier subsidiary) is also the U.S. dollar. In contrast, if the functional currency of the intervening first-tier subsidiary was the Japanese yen (thus requiring the financial statements of the second-tier subsidiary to be translated into yen before the yen-denominated financial statements of the first-tier subsidiary are translated into U.S. dollars for consolidation), the consolidated parent company could not designate its U.S. dollar–Euro derivative as a hedge of the second-tier subsidiary's exposure.

purchase, or sale or an unrecognized firm commitment in the consolidated financial statements only if the following two conditions are satisfied. (That foreign currency derivative instrument is hereafter in this section referred to as an *internal derivative*.)

a. From the perspective of the member of the consolidated group using the derivative as a hedging instrument (hereafter in this section referred to as the *hedging affiliate*), the criteria for foreign currency cash flow hedge accounting in paragraph 40 must be satisfied.

b. The member of the consolidated group not using the derivative as a hedging instrument (hereafter in this section referred to as the *issuing affiliate*) must either (1) enter into a derivative contract with an unrelated third party to offset the exposure that results from that internal derivative or (2) if the conditions in paragraph 40B are met, enter into derivative contracts with unrelated third parties that would offset, on a net basis for each foreign currency, the foreign exchange risk arising from multiple internal derivative contracts.

40B. *Offsetting net exposures.* If an issuing affiliate chooses to offset exposure arising from multiple internal derivative contracts on an aggregate or net basis, the derivatives issued to hedging affiliates may qualify as cash flow hedges in the consolidated financial statements only if all of the following conditions are satisfied:

a. The issuing affiliate enters into a derivative contract with an unrelated third party to offset, on a net basis for each foreign currency, the foreign exchange risk arising from multiple internal derivative contracts, and the derivative contract with the unrelated third party generates equal or closely approximating gains and losses when compared with the aggregate or net losses and gains generated by the derivative contracts issued to affiliates.

b. Internal derivatives that are not designated as hedging instruments are excluded from the determination of the foreign currency exposure on a net basis that is offset by the third-party derivative. In addition, nonderivative contracts may not be used as hedging instruments to offset exposures arising from internal derivative contracts.

c. Foreign currency exposure that is offset by a single net third-party contract arises from internal derivative contracts that mature within the same 31-day period and that involve the same currency

exposure as the net third-party derivative. The offsetting net third-party derivative related to that group of contracts must offset the aggregate or net exposure to that currency, must mature within the same 31-day period, and must be entered into within 3 business days after the designation of the internal derivatives as hedging instruments.

d. The issuing affiliate tracks the exposure that it acquires from each hedging affiliate and maintains documentation supporting linkage of each internal derivative contract and the offsetting aggregate or net derivative contract with an unrelated third party.

e. The issuing affiliate does not alter or terminate the offsetting derivative with an unrelated third party unless the hedging affiliate initiates that action. If the issuing affiliate does alter or terminate the offsetting third-party derivative (which should be rare), the hedging affiliate must prospectively cease hedge accounting for the internal derivatives that are offset by that third-party derivative.

40C. A member of a consolidated group is not permitted to offset exposures arising from multiple internal derivative contracts on a net basis for foreign currency cash flow exposures related to recognized foreign-currency-denominated assets or liabilities. That prohibition includes situations in which a recognized foreign-currency-denominated asset or liability in a fair value hedge or cash flow hedge results from the occurrence of a specifically identified forecasted transaction initially designated as a cash flow hedge.

41. A qualifying foreign currency cash flow hedge shall be accounted for as specified in paragraphs 30–35.

Hedges of the foreign currency exposure of a net investment in a foreign operation

42. A derivative instrument or a nonderivative financial instrument that may give rise to a foreign currency transaction gain or loss under Statement 52 can be designated as hedging the foreign currency exposure of a net investment in a foreign operation provided the conditions in paragraphs 40(a) and 40(b) are met. (A nonderivative financial instrument that is reported at fair value does not give rise to a foreign currency transaction gain or loss under Statement 52 and, thus, cannot be designated as hedging the foreign currency exposure of a net investment in a foreign operation.) The gain or loss on a hedging derivative instrument (or the foreign currency transaction

gain or loss on the nonderivative hedging instrument) that is designated as, and is effective as, an economic hedge of the net investment in a foreign operation shall be reported in the same manner as a translation adjustment to the extent it is effective as a hedge. The hedged net investment shall be accounted for consistent with Statement 52; the provisions of this Statement for recognizing the gain or loss on assets designated as being hedged in a fair value hedge do not apply to the hedge of a net investment in a foreign operation.

Accounting by Not-for-Profit Organizations and Other Entities That Do Not Report Earnings

43. An entity that does not report earnings as a separate caption in a statement of financial performance (for example, a not-for-profit organization or a defined benefit pension plan) shall recognize the gain or loss on a hedging instrument and a nonhedging derivative instrument as a change in net assets in the period of change unless the hedging instrument is designated as a hedge of the foreign currency exposure of a net investment in a foreign operation. In that case, the provisions of paragraph 42 of this Statement shall be applied. Entities that do not report earnings shall recognize the changes in the carrying amount of the hedged item pursuant to paragraph 22 in a fair value hedge as a change in net assets in the period of change. Those entities are not permitted to use cash flow hedge accounting because they do not report earnings separately. Consistent with the provisions of FASB Statement No. 117, *Financial Statements of Not-for-Profit Organizations,* this Statement does not prescribe how a not-for-profit organization should determine the components of an operating measure, if one is presented.

Disclosures

44. An entity that holds or issues derivative instruments (or nonderivative instruments that are designated and qualify as hedging instruments pursuant to paragraphs 37 and 42) shall disclose its objectives for holding or issuing those instruments, the context needed to understand those objectives, and its strategies for achieving those objectives. The description shall distinguish between derivative instruments (and nonderivative instruments) designated as fair value hedging instruments, derivative instruments designated as cash flow hedging instruments, derivative instruments (and nonderivative instruments) designated as hedging instruments for hedges of the foreign currency exposure of a net investment in a for-

eign operation, and all other derivatives. The description also shall indicate the entity's risk management policy for each of those types of hedges, including a description of the items or transactions for which risks are hedged. For derivative instruments not designated as hedging instruments, the description shall indicate the purpose of the derivative activity. Qualitative disclosures about an entity's objectives and strategies for using derivative instruments may be more meaningful if such objectives and strategies are described in the context of an entity's overall risk management profile. If appropriate, an entity is encouraged, but not required, to provide such additional qualitative disclosures.

44A. In each statement of financial position presented, an entity shall report hybrid financial instruments measured at fair value under the election and under the practicability exception in paragraph 16 of this Statement in a manner that separates those reported fair values from the carrying amounts of assets and liabilities subsequently measured using another measurement attribute on the face of the statement of financial position. To accomplish that separate reporting, an entity may either (a) display separate line items for the fair value and non-fair-value carrying amounts or (b) present the aggregate of those fair value and non-fair-value amounts and parenthetically disclose the amount of fair value included in the aggregate amount. For those hybrid financial instruments measured at fair value under the election and under the practicability exception in paragraph 16, an entity shall also disclose the information specified in paragraphs 18–22 of FASB Statement No. 159, *The Fair Value Option for Financial Assets and Financial Liabilities.*

44B. An entity shall provide information that will allow users to understand the effect of changes in the fair value of hybrid financial instruments measured at fair value under the election and under the practicability exception in paragraph 16 on earnings (or other performance indicators for entities that do not report earnings).

45. An entity's disclosures for every reporting period for which a complete set of financial statements is presented also shall include the following:

Fair value hedges

a. For derivative instruments, as well as nonderivative instruments that may give rise to foreign currency transaction gains or losses under Statement 52, that have been designated and have qualified as fair value hedging instruments and for the related hedged items:

(1) The net gain or loss recognized in earnings during the reporting period representing (a) the amount of the hedges' ineffectiveness and (b) the component of the derivative instruments' gain or loss, if any, excluded from the assessment of hedge effectiveness, and a description of where the net gain or loss is reported in the statement of income or other statement of financial performance.

(2) The amount of net gain or loss recognized in earnings when a hedged firm commitment no longer qualifies as a fair value hedge.

Cash flow hedges

b. For derivative instruments that have been designated and have qualified as cash flow hedging instruments and for the related hedged transactions:

(1) The net gain or loss recognized in earnings during the reporting period representing (a) the amount of the hedges' ineffectiveness and (b) the component of the derivative instruments' gain or loss, if any, excluded from the assessment of hedge effectiveness, and a description of where the net gain or loss is reported in the statement of income or other statement of financial performance.

(2) A description of the transactions or other events that will result in the reclassification into earnings of gains and losses that are reported in accumulated other comprehensive income, and the estimated net amount of the existing gains or losses at the reporting date that is expected to be reclassified into earnings within the next 12 months.

(3) The maximum length of time over which the entity is hedging its exposure to the variability in future cash flows for forecasted transactions excluding those forecasted transactions related to the payment of variable interest on existing financial instruments.

(4) The amount of gains and losses reclassified into earnings as a result of the discontinuance

of cash flow hedges because it is probable that the original forecasted transactions will not occur by the end of the originally specified time period or within the additional period of time discussed in paragraph 33.

Hedges of the net investment in a foreign operation

c. For derivative instruments, as well as nonderivative instruments that may give rise to foreign currency transaction gains or losses under Statement 52, that have been designated and have qualified as hedging instruments for hedges of the foreign currency exposure of a net investment in a foreign operation, the net amount of gains or losses included in the cumulative translation adjustment during the reporting period.

The quantitative disclosures about derivative instruments may be more useful, and less likely to be perceived to be out of context or otherwise misunderstood, if similar information is disclosed about other financial instruments or nonfinancial assets and liabilities to which the derivative instruments are related by activity. Accordingly, in those situations, an entity is encouraged, but not required, to present a more complete picture of its activities by disclosing that information.

Reporting Cash Flows of Derivative Instruments That Contain Financing Elements

45A. An instrument accounted for as a derivative under this Statement that at its inception includes off-market terms, or requires an up-front cash payment, or both often contains a financing element. Identifying a financing element within a derivative instrument is a matter of judgment that depends on facts and circumstances. If an other-than-insignificant financing element is present at inception, other than a financing element inherently included in an at-the-market derivative instrument with no prepayments (that is, the forward points in an at-the-money forward contract),[12b] then the borrower shall report all

---

[12b]An at-the-money plain-vanilla interest rate swap that involves no payments between the parties at inception would not be considered as having a financing element present at inception even though, due to the implicit forward rates derived from the yield curve, the parties to the contract have an expectation that the comparison of the fixed and floating legs will result in payments being made by one party in the earlier periods and being made by the counterparty in the later periods of the swap's term. If a derivative instrument is an at-the-money or out-of-the-money option contract or contains an at-the-money or out-of-the-money option contract, a payment made at inception to the writer of the option for the option's time value by the counterparty should not be viewed as evidence that the derivative instrument contains a financing element. In contrast, if the contractual terms of a derivative have been structured to *ensure* that net payments will be made by one party in the earlier periods and subsequently returned by the counterparty in the later periods of the derivative's term, that derivative instrument should be viewed as containing a financing element even if the derivative has a fair value of zero at inception.

cash inflows and outflows associated with that derivative instrument in a manner consistent with financing activities as described in paragraphs 18–20 of FASB Statement No. 95, *Statement of Cash Flows.*

Reporting Changes in the Components of Comprehensive Income

46. An entity shall display as a separate classification within other comprehensive income the net gain or loss on derivative instruments designated and qualifying as cash flow hedging instruments that are reported in comprehensive income pursuant to paragraphs 30 and 41.

47. As part of the disclosures of accumulated other comprehensive income, pursuant to paragraph 26 of FASB Statement No. 130, *Reporting Comprehensive Income,* an entity shall separately disclose the beginning and ending accumulated derivative gain or loss, the related net change associated with current period hedging transactions, and the net amount of any reclassification into earnings.

Effective Date and Transition

48. This Statement shall be effective for all fiscal quarters of all fiscal years beginning after June 15, 2000. Initial application of this Statement shall be as of the beginning of an entity's fiscal quarter; on that date, hedging relationships shall be designated anew and documented pursuant to the provisions of this Statement. Earlier application of all of the provisions of this Statement is encouraged but is permitted only as of the beginning of any fiscal quarter that begins after issuance of this Statement. Earlier application of selected provisions of this Statement is not permitted. This Statement shall not be applied retroactively to financial statements of prior periods.

49. At the date of initial application, an entity shall recognize all freestanding derivative instruments (that is, derivative instruments other than embedded derivative instruments) in the statement of financial position as either assets or liabilities and measure them at fair value, pursuant to paragraph 17.[13] The difference between a derivative's previous carrying amount and its fair value shall be reported as a transition adjustment, as discussed in paragraph 52. The entity also shall recognize offsetting gains and losses on hedged assets, liabilities, and firm commitments by adjusting their carrying amounts at that date, as discussed in paragraph 52(b). Any gains or losses on derivative instruments that are reported independently as deferred gains or losses (that is, liabilities or assets) in the statement of financial position at the date of initial application shall be derecognized from that statement; that derecognition also shall be reported as transition adjustments as indicated in paragraph 52. Any gains or losses on derivative instruments reported in other comprehensive income at the date of initial application because the derivative instruments were hedging the fair value exposure of available-for-sale securities also shall be reported as transition adjustments; the offsetting losses and gains on the securities shall be accounted for pursuant to paragraph 52(b). Any gain or loss on a derivative instrument reported in accumulated other comprehensive income at the date of initial application because the derivative instrument was hedging the *variable cash flow exposure* of a forecasted (anticipated) transaction related to an available-for-sale security shall remain in accumulated other comprehensive income and shall *not* be reported as a transition adjustment. The accounting for any gains and losses on derivative instruments that arose prior to the initial application of the Statement and that were previously added to the carrying amount of recognized hedged assets or liabilities is not affected by this Statement. Those gains and losses shall not be included in the transition adjustment.[13a]

50. At the date of initial application, an entity shall choose to either (a) recognize as an asset or liability in the statement of financial position all embedded

---

[13]For a compound derivative that has a foreign currency exchange risk component (such as a foreign currency interest rate swap), an entity is permitted at the date of initial application to separate the compound derivative into two parts: the foreign currency derivative and the remaining derivative. Each of them would thereafter be accounted for at fair value, with an overall limit that the sum of their fair values could not exceed the fair value of the compound derivative. An entity may not separate a compound derivative into components representing different risks after the date of initial application.

[13a]If immediately prior to the application of Statement 133 an entity has a fair value or cash flow hedging relationship in which an intercompany interest rate swap is the hedging instrument and if that relationship would have qualified for the shortcut method under the criteria in paragraph 68 had that swap not been an intercompany transaction, that entity may qualify for applying the shortcut method to a newly designated hedging relationship that is effectively the continuation of the preexisting hedging relationship provided that (a) the post–Statement 133 hedging relationship is hedging the same exposure to interest rate risk (that is, exposure to changes in fair value of the same hedged item or exposure to changes in variable cash flows for the same forecasted transaction) and (b) the hedging instrument is a third-party interest rate swap whose terms exactly match the terms of the intercompany swap with respect to its remaining cash flows. In that case, if the shortcut method is applied to the new hedging relationship upon adoption of Statement 133, the transition adjustment should include the appropriate adjustments at the date of adoption to reflect the retroactive application of the shortcut method.

derivative instruments that are required pursuant to paragraphs 12–16 to be separated from their host contracts or (b) select either January 1, 1998 or January 1, 1999 as a transition date for embedded derivatives. If the entity chooses to select a transition date, it shall recognize as separate assets and liabilities (pursuant to paragraphs 12–16) only those derivatives embedded in hybrid instruments issued, acquired, or substantively modified by the entity on or after the selected transition date. That choice is not permitted to be applied to only some of an entity's individual hybrid instruments and must be applied on an all-or-none basis.

51. If an embedded derivative instrument is to be separated from its host contract in conjunction with the initial application of this Statement, the entity shall consider the following in determining the related transition adjustment:

a. The carrying amount of the host contract at the date of initial application shall be based on its fair value on the date that the hybrid instrument was issued or acquired by the entity and shall reflect appropriate adjustments for subsequent activity, such as subsequent cash receipts or payments and the amortization of any premium or discount on the host contract arising from the separation of the embedded derivative.

b. The carrying amount of the embedded derivative instrument at the date of initial application shall be its fair value.

c. The transition adjustment shall be the difference at the date of initial application between (1) the previous carrying amount of the hybrid instrument and (2) the sum of the new net carrying amount of the host contract and the fair value of the embedded derivative instrument. The entity shall not retroactively designate a hedging relationship that could have been made had the embedded derivative instrument initially been accounted for separate from the host contract.

52. The transition adjustments resulting from adopting this Statement shall be reported in net income or other comprehensive income, as appropriate, as the effect of a change in accounting principle and presented in a manner similar to the cumulative effect of a change in accounting principle as described in paragraph 20 of APB Opinion No. 20, *Accounting Changes.* Whether a transition adjustment related to a specific derivative instrument is reported in net income, reported in other comprehensive income, or allocated between both is based on the hedging relationships, if any, that had existed for that derivative

instrument and that were the basis for accounting under generally accepted accounting principles before the date of initial application of this Statement.

a. If the transition adjustment relates to a derivative instrument that had been designated in a hedging relationship that addressed the variable cash flow exposure of a forecasted (anticipated) transaction, the transition adjustment shall be reported as a cumulative-effect-type adjustment of accumulated other comprehensive income.

b. If the transition adjustment relates to a derivative instrument that had been designated in a hedging relationship that addressed the fair value exposure of an asset, a liability, or a firm commitment, the transition adjustment for the derivative shall be reported as a cumulative-effect-type adjustment of net income. Concurrently, any gain or loss on the hedged item shall be recognized as an adjustment of the hedged item's carrying amount at the date of initial application, but only to the extent of an offsetting transition adjustment for the derivative. Only for purposes of applying the preceding sentence in determining the hedged item's transition adjustment, the gain or loss on the hedged item may be either (1) the overall gain or loss on the hedged item determined as the difference between the hedged item's fair value and its carrying amount on the date of initial application (that is, not limited to the portion attributable to the hedged risk nor limited to the gain or loss occurring during the period of the preexisting hedging relationship) or (2) the gain or loss on the hedged item attributable to the hedged risk (limited to the hedged risks that can be designated under paragraph 21 of this Statement) during the period of the preexisting hedging relationship. That adjustment of the hedged item's carrying amount shall also be reported as a cumulative-effect-type adjustment of net income. The transition adjustment related to the gain or loss reported in accumulated other comprehensive income on a derivative instrument that hedged an available-for-sale security, together with the loss or gain on the related security (to the extent of an offsetting transition adjustment for the derivative instrument), shall be reclassified to earnings as a cumulative-effect-type adjustment of both net income and accumulated other comprehensive income.

c. If a derivative instrument had been designated in multiple hedging relationships that addressed both the fair value exposure of an asset or a liability and the variable cash flow exposure of a forecasted (anticipated) transaction, the transition adjustment for the derivative shall be allocated between the cumulative-effect-type adjustment of net income and the cumulative-effect-type adjustment of accumulated other comprehensive income and shall be reported as discussed in paragraphs 52(a) and 52(b) above. Concurrently, any gain or loss on the hedged item shall be accounted for at the date of initial application as discussed in paragraph 52(b) above.

d. Other transition adjustments not encompassed by paragraphs 52(a), 52(b), and 52(c) above shall be reported as part of the cumulative-effect-type adjustment of net income.

53. Any transition adjustment reported as a cumulative-effect-type adjustment of accumulated other comprehensive income shall be subsequently reclassified into earnings in a manner consistent with paragraph 31. For those amounts, an entity shall disclose separately in the year of initial application the amount of gains and losses reported in accumulated other comprehensive income and associated with the transition adjustment that are being reclassified into earnings during the 12 months following the date of initial application.

54. At the date of initial application, an entity may transfer any held-to-maturity security into the available-for-sale category or the trading category. An entity will then be able in the future to designate a security transferred into the available-for-sale category as the hedged item, or its variable interest payments as the cash flow hedged transactions, in a hedge of the exposure to changes in the designated benchmark interest rate or changes in its overall fair value. (Paragraph 21(d) precludes a held-to-maturity security from being designated as the hedged item in a fair value hedge of interest rate risk or the risk of changes in its overall fair value. Paragraph 29(e) similarly precludes the variable cash flows of a held-to-maturity security from being designated as the hedged transaction in a cash flow hedge of interest rate risk.) The unrealized holding gain or loss on a held-to-maturity security transferred to another category at the date of initial application shall be reported in net income or accumulated other comprehensive income consistent with the requirements of paragraphs 15(b) and 15(c) of Statement 115 and reported with the other transition adjustments discussed in paragraph 52 of this Statement. Such transfers from the held-to-maturity category at the date of initial adoption shall not call into question an entity's intent to hold other debt securities to maturity in the future.[14]

55. At the date of initial application, an entity may transfer any available-for-sale security into the trading category. After any related transition adjustments from initially applying this Statement have been recognized, the unrealized holding gain or loss remaining in accumulated other comprehensive income for any transferred security at the date of initial application shall be reclassified into earnings (but not reported as part of the cumulative-effect-type adjustment for the transition adjustments), consistent with paragraph 15(b) of Statement 115. If a derivative instrument had been hedging the variable cash flow exposure of a forecasted transaction related to an available-for-sale security that is transferred into the trading category at the date of initial application and the entity had reported a gain or loss on that derivative instrument in other comprehensive income (consistent with paragraph 115 of Statement 115), the entity also shall reclassify those derivative gains and losses into earnings (but not report them as part of the cumulative-effect-type adjustment for the transition adjustments).

56. At the date of initial application, mortgage bankers and other servicers of financial assets may choose to restratify their servicing rights pursuant to paragraph 63(f) of Statement 140 in a manner that would enable individual strata to comply with the requirements of this Statement regarding what constitutes "a portfolio of similar assets." As noted in footnote 9 of this Statement, mortgage bankers and other servicers of financial assets that designate a hedged portfolio by aggregating servicing rights within one or more risk strata used under paragraph 63(f) of Statement 140 would not necessarily comply with the requirement in paragraph 21(a) of this Statement for

---

[14]EITF Topic No. D-51, "The Applicability of FASB Statement No. 115 to Desecuritizations of Financial Assets," indicates that certain financial assets received or retained in a desecuritization must be held to maturity to avoid calling into question the entity's intent to hold other debt securities to maturity in the future. In conjunction with the initial adoption of this Statement, the held-to-maturity restriction on those financial assets held on the date of initial application is removed, and those financial assets that had been received or retained in a previous desecuritization are available in the future to be designated as the hedged item, or their variable interest payments as the hedged transaction, in a hedge of the exposure to changes in interest rate risk. Consequently, the sale of those financial assets before maturity would not call into question the entity's intent to hold other debt securities to maturity in the future.

portfolios of similar assets, since the risk stratum under paragraph 63(f) of Statement 140 can be based on any predominant risk characteristic, including date of origination or geographic location. The restratification of servicing rights is a change in the application of an accounting principle, and the effect of that change as of the initial application of this Statement shall be reported as part of the cumulative-effect-type adjustment for the transition adjustments.

> **The provisions of this Statement need not be applied to immaterial items.**

This Statement was adopted by the unanimous vote of the seven members of the Financial Accounting Standards Board:

Edmund L. Jenkins,	Anthony T. Cope	James J. Leisenring
Chairman	John M. Foster	Gerhard G. Mueller
Joseh V. Anania	Gaylen N. Larson	

Appendix A

IMPLEMENTATION GUIDANCE

Section 1: Scope and Definition

Application of Paragraphs 6–11

57. The following discussion further explains the three characteristics of a derivative instrument discussed in paragraphs 6–9.

a. *Underlying.* An underlying is a variable that, along with either a notional amount or a payment provision, determines the settlement of a derivative. An underlying usually is one or a combination of the following:
   (1) A security price or security price index
   (2) A commodity price or commodity price index
   (3) An interest rate or interest rate index
   (4) A credit rating or credit index
   (5) An exchange rate or exchange rate index
   (6) An insurance index or catastrophe loss index
   (7) A climatic or geological condition (such as temperature, earthquake severity, or rainfall), another physical variable, or a related index.
   However, an underlying may be any variable whose changes are observable or otherwise objectively verifiable. Paragraph 10(e) specifically excludes a contract with settlement based on certain variables unless the contract is exchange-traded. A contract based on any variable that is not specifically excluded is subject to the requirements of this Statement if it has the other two characteristics identified in paragraph 6 (which also are discussed in paragraph 57(b) and paragraph 57(c) below).

b. *Initial net investment.* A derivative requires no initial net investment or a smaller initial net investment than other types of contracts that have a similar response to changes in market factors. For example, entering into a commodity futures contract generally requires no net investment, while purchasing the same commodity requires an initial net investment equal to its market price. However, both contracts reflect changes in the price of the commodity in the same way (that is, similar gains or losses will be incurred). A swap or forward contract also generally does not require an initial net investment unless the terms favor one party over the other. An option generally requires that one party make an initial net investment (a premium) because that party has the rights under the contract and the other party has the obligations. The phrase *initial net investment* is stated from the perspective of only one party to the contract, but it determines the application of the Statement for both parties.[15]

c. *Net settlement.* A contract that meets any one of the following criteria has the characteristic described as net settlement:
   (1) Its terms implicitly or explicitly require or permit net settlement. For example, a penalty

---

[15]Even though a contract may be a derivative as described in paragraphs 6–10 for both parties, the exceptions in paragraph 11 apply only to the issuer of the contract and will result in different reporting by the two parties. The exception in paragraph 10(b) also may apply to one of the parties but not the other.

for nonperformance in a purchase order is a net settlement provision if the amount of the penalty is based on changes in the price of the items that are the subject of the contract. Net settlement may be made in cash or by delivery of any other asset, whether or not it is readily convertible to cash. A fixed penalty for nonperformance is not a net settlement provision.

(2) There is an established market mechanism that facilitates net settlement outside the contract. The term *market mechanism* is to be interpreted broadly. Any institutional arrangement or other agreement that enables either party to be relieved of all rights and obligations under the contract and to liquidate its net position without incurring a significant transaction cost is considered net settlement. The evaluation of whether a market mechanism exists and whether items to be delivered under a contract are readily convertible to cash must be performed at inception and on an ongoing basis throughout a contract's life.

(3) It requires delivery of an asset that is readily convertible to cash.[15a] The definition of *readily convertible to cash* in FASB Concepts Statement No. 5, *Recognition and Measurement in Financial Statements of Business Enterprises,* includes, for example, a security or commodity traded in an active market and a unit of foreign currency that is readily convertible into the functional currency of the reporting entity. A security that is publicly traded but for which the market is not very active is readily convertible to cash if the number of shares or other units of the security to be exchanged is small relative to the daily transaction volume. That same security would not be readily convertible if the number of shares to be exchanged is large relative to the daily transaction volume. The ability to use a security that is not publicly traded or an agricultural or mineral product without an active market as collateral in a borrowing does not, in and of itself, mean that the security or the commodity is readily convertible to cash. Shares of stock in a publicly traded company to be received upon the exercise of a stock

purchase warrant do not meet the characteristic of being readily convertible to cash if both of the following conditions exist: (a) the stock purchase warrant is issued by an entity for only its own stock (or stock of its consolidated subsidiaries) and (b) the sale or transfer of the issued shares is restricted (other than in connection with being pledged as collateral) for a period of 32 days or more from the date the stock purchase warrant is exercised. In contrast, restrictions imposed by a stock purchase warrant on the sale or transfer of shares of stock that are received from the exercise of that warrant issued by an entity for *other* than its own stock (whether those restrictions are for more or less than 32 days) do not affect the determination of whether those shares are readily convertible to cash. The accounting for restricted stock to be received upon exercise of a stock purchase warrant should not be analogized to any other type of contract.

58. The following discussion further explains some of the exceptions discussed in paragraph 10.

a. *"Regular-way" security trades.* The exception in paragraph 10(a) applies only to a contract that requires delivery of securities that are readily convertible to cash[16] except (1) as provided in paragraph 59(a) for a contract for the purchase or sale of when-issued securities or other securities that do not yet exist and (2) for contracts that are required to be accounted for on a trade-date basis by the reporting entity. To qualify, a contract must require delivery of such a security within the period of time after the trade date that is customary in the market in which the trade takes place. For example, a contract to purchase or sell a publicly traded equity security in the United States customarily requires settlement within three business days. If a contract for purchase of that type of security requires settlement in three business days, the regular-way security trades exception applies, but if the contract requires settlement in five days, the regular-way security trades exception does not apply unless the reporting entity is required to account for the contract on a trade-date basis. This Statement does not change whether an entity

---

[15a]The evaluation of *readily convertible to cash* shall be applied to a contract throughout its life.

[16]Contracts that require delivery of securities that are not readily convertible to cash (and thus do not permit net settlement) are not subject to the requirements of this Statement unless there is a market mechanism outside the contract to facilitate net settlement (as described in paragraphs 9(b) and 57(c)(2)).

recognizes regular-way security trades on the trade date or the settlement date.

b. *Normal purchases and normal sales.* The exception in paragraph 10(b) applies only to a contract that involves future delivery of assets (other than financial instruments or derivative instruments). To qualify for the exception, a contract's terms also must be consistent with the terms of an entity's normal purchases or normal sales, that is, the quantity purchased or sold must be reasonable in relation to the entity's business needs. Determining whether or not the terms are consistent will require judgment. In making those judgments, an entity should consider all relevant factors, such as (1) the quantities provided under the contract and the entity's need for the related assets, (2) the locations to which delivery of the items will be made, (3) the period of time between entering into the contract and delivery, and (4) the entity's prior practices with regard to such contracts. Evidence such as past trends, expected future demand, other contracts for delivery of similar items, an entity's and industry's customs for acquiring and storing the related commodities, and an entity's operating locations should help in identifying contracts that qualify as normal purchases or normal sales. Also, in order for a contract that meets the net settlement provisions of paragraphs 9(a) and 57(c)(1) and the market mechanism provisions of paragraphs 9(b) and 57(c)(2) to qualify for the exception, it must be probable at inception and throughout the term of the individual contract that the contract will not settle net and will result in physical delivery. Power purchase or sales agreements (whether a forward contract, an option contract, or a combination of both) for the purchase or sale of electricity qualify for the normal purchases and normal sales exception in paragraph 10(b)(4) if all of the following applicable criteria are met:

(1) For both parties to the contract:

    (a) The terms of the contract require physical delivery of electricity. That is, the contract does not permit net settlement, as described in paragraphs 9(a) and 57(c)(1). For an option contract, physical delivery is required if the option contract is exercised.

    (b) The power purchase or sales agreement is a capacity contract.[17a] Differentiating be-

tween a capacity contract and a traditional option contract (that is, a financial option on electricity) is a matter of judgment that depends on the facts and circumstances.

(2) For the seller of electricity: The electricity that would be deliverable under the contract involves quantities that are expected to be sold by the reporting entity in the normal course of business.

(3) For the buyer of electricity:

    (a) The electricity that would be deliverable under the contract involves quantities that are expected to be used or sold by the reporting entity in the normal course of business.

    (b) The buyer of the electricity under the power purchase or sales agreement is an entity that is engaged in selling electricity to retail or wholesale customers and is statutorily or otherwise contractually obligated to maintain sufficient capacity to meet electricity needs of its customer base.

    (c) The contracts are entered into to meet the buyer's obligation to maintain a sufficient capacity, including a reasonable reserve margin established by or based on a regulatory commission, local standards, regional reliability councils, or regional transmission organizations.

Power purchase or sales agreements that meet only the above applicable criteria in paragraph 58(b) qualify for the normal purchases and normal sales exception even if they are subject to being booked out or are scheduled to be booked out. Forward contracts for the purchase or sale of electricity that do not meet the above applicable criteria are nevertheless eligible to qualify for the normal purchases and normal sales exception by meeting the criteria in paragraph 10(b) other than paragraph 10(b)(4).

c. *Certain contracts that are not traded on an exchange.* A contract that is not traded on an exchange is not subject to the requirements of this Statement if the underlying is:

(1) A climatic or geological variable or other physical variable. Climatic, geological, and other physical variables include things like the number of inches of rainfall or snow in a

---

[17][This footnote has been deleted. See Status page.]

[17a]As defined in paragraph 540.

particular area and the severity of an earthquake as measured by the Richter scale.

(2) The price or value of (a) a nonfinancial asset of one of the parties to the contract unless that asset is readily convertible to cash or (b) a nonfinancial liability of one of the parties to the contract unless that liability requires delivery of an asset that is readily convertible to cash. This exception applies only to nonfinancial assets that are unique and only if a nonfinancial asset related to the underlying is owned by the party that would *not* benefit *under the contract* from an increase in the price or value of the nonfinancial asset. If the contract is a call option contract, the exception applies only if that nonfinancial asset is owned by the party that would not benefit under the contract from an increase in the price or value of the nonfinancial asset above the option's strike price.

(3) Specified volumes of sales or service revenues by one of the parties. That exception is intended to apply to contracts with settlements based on the volume of items sold or services rendered, for example, royalty agreements. It is not intended to apply to contracts based on changes in sales or revenues due to changes in market prices.

If a contract's underlying is the combination of two or more variables, and one or more would not qualify for one of the exceptions above, the application of this Statement to that contract depends on the predominant characteristics of the combined variable. The contract is subject to the requirements of this Statement if the changes in its combined underlying are highly correlated with changes in one of the component variables that would not qualify for an exception.

59. The following discussion illustrates the application of paragraphs 6–11 in several situations.

a. *Forward purchases or sales of when-issued securities or other securities that do not yet exist.* Contracts for the purchase or sale of when-issued securities or other securities that do not yet exist are excluded from the requirements of this Statement as a regular-way security trade only if (1) there is no other way to purchase or sell that security, (2) delivery of that security and settlement will occur within the shortest period possible for that type of security, and (3) it is probable at inception and throughout the term of the individual contract that the contract will not settle net and will result in physical delivery of a security when it is issued. A contract for the purchase or sale of when-issued securities or other securities that do not yet exist is eligible to qualify for the regular-way security trades exception even though that contract permits net settlement (as discussed in paragraphs 9(a) and 57(c)(1)) or a market mechanism to facilitate net settlement of that contract (as discussed in paragraphs 9(b) and 57(c)(2)) exists. The entity shall document the basis for concluding that it is probable that the contract will not settle net and will result in physical delivery. Net settlement (as described in paragraphs 9(a) and 9(b)) of contracts in a group of contracts similarly designated as regular-way security trades would call into question the continued exemption of such contracts. In addition, if an entity is required to account for a contract for the purchase or sale of when-issued securities or other securities that do not yet exist on a trade-date basis, rather than a settlement-date basis, and thus recognizes the acquisition or disposition of the securities at the inception of the contract, that entity shall apply the regular-way security trades exception to those contracts.

b. *Credit-indexed contracts (often referred to as credit derivatives).* Many different types of contracts are indexed to the creditworthiness of a specified entity or group of entities, but not all of them are derivative instruments. Credit-indexed contracts that have certain characteristics described in paragraph 10(d) are guarantees and are not subject to the requirements of this Statement. Credit-indexed contracts that do not have the characteristics necessary to qualify for the exception in paragraph 10(d) are subject to the requirements of this Statement. One example of the latter is a credit-indexed contract that requires a payment due to changes in the creditworthiness of a specified entity even if neither party incurs a loss due to the change (other than a loss caused by the payment under the credit-indexed contract).

c. *Take-or-pay contracts.* Under a take-or-pay contract, an entity agrees to pay a specified price for a specified quantity of a product whether or not it takes delivery. Whether a take-or-pay contract is subject to this Statement depends on its terms.[17b] For example, if the product to be delivered is not readily convertible to cash and there is no net settlement option, the contract fails to meet the criterion in paragraph 6(c) and is not subject to the requirements of this Statement. However, a contract that meets all of the following conditions is subject to the requirements of this Statement: (1) the product to be delivered is readily convertible to cash, (2) the contract does not qualify for the normal purchases and normal sales exception in paragraph 10(b), and (3) the contract requires no initial net investment or an initial net investment that is smaller by more than a nominal amount than would be required for other types of contracts that would be expected to have a similar response to changes in market factors. (Refer to paragraph 8.)

d. *Short sales (sales of borrowed securities).*[18] Short sales typically involve the following activities:

   (1) Selling a security (by the short seller to the purchaser)
   (2) Borrowing a security (by the short seller from the lender)
   (3) Delivering the borrowed security (by the short seller to the purchaser)
   (4) Purchasing a security (by the short seller from the market)
   (5) Delivering the purchased security (by the short seller to the lender).

Those five activities involve three separate contracts. A contract that distinguishes a short sale involves activities (2) and (5), borrowing a security and replacing it by delivering an identical security. Such a contract has two of the three characteristics of a derivative instrument. The settlement is based on an underlying (the price of the security) and a notional amount (the face amount of the security or the number of shares), and the settlement is made by delivery of a security that is readily convertible to cash. However, the other characteristic, no initial net investment or an initial net investment that is smaller by more than a nominal amount than would be required for other types of contracts that would be expected to have a similar response to changes in market factors, is not present. (Refer to paragraph 8.) The bor-

rowed security is the lender's initial net investment in the contract. Consequently, the contract relating to activities (2) and (5) is not a derivative instrument. The other two contracts (one for activities (1) and (3) and the other for activity (4)) are routine and do not generally involve derivative instruments. However, if a forward purchase or sale is involved, and the contract does not qualify for the exception in paragraph 10(a), it is subject to the requirements of this Statement.

e. *Repurchase agreements and "wash sales"* (accounted for as sales as described in paragraphs 98 and 99 of Statement 140). A transfer of financial assets accounted for as a sale under Statement 140 in which the transferor is both obligated and entitled to repurchase the transferred asset at a fixed or determinable price contains two separate features, one of which may be a derivative. The initial exchange of financial assets for cash is a sale-purchase transaction—generally not a transaction that involves a derivative instrument. However, the accompanying forward contract that gives the transferor the right and obligation to repurchase the transferred asset involves an underlying and a notional amount (the price of the security and its denomination), and it does not require an initial net investment in the contract. Consequently, if the forward contract requires delivery of a security that is readily convertible to cash or otherwise meets the net settlement criterion in paragraph 9, it is subject to the requirements of this Statement.

Application of the Clearly-and-Closely-Related Criterion in Paragraphs 12–16

60. In discussing whether a hybrid instrument contains an embedded derivative instrument (also simply referred to as an *embedded derivative*) that warrants separate accounting, paragraph 12 focuses on whether the economic characteristics and risks of the embedded derivative are clearly and closely related to the economic characteristics and risks of the host contract. If the host contract encompasses a residual interest in an entity, then its economic characteristics and risks should be considered that of an equity instrument and an embedded derivative would need to possess principally equity characteristics (related to the same entity) to be considered clearly and closely

---

[17b]In certain circumstances, a take-or-pay contract may represent or contain a lease that should be accounted for in accordance with FASB Statement No. 13, *Accounting for Leases.*

[18]This discussion applies only to short sales with the characteristics described here. Some groups of transactions that are referred to as short sales may have different characteristics. If so, a different analysis would be appropriate, and other derivative instruments may be involved.

related to the host contract. However, most commonly, a financial instrument host contract will not embody a claim to the residual interest in an entity and, thus, the economic characteristics and risks of the host contract should be considered that of a debt instrument. For example, even though the overall hybrid instrument that provides for repayment of principal may include a return based on the market price (the underlying as defined in this Statement) of XYZ Corporation common stock, the host contract does not involve any existing or potential residual interest rights (that is, rights of ownership) and thus would not be an equity instrument. The host contract would instead be considered a debt instrument, and the embedded derivative that incorporates the equity-based return would not be clearly and closely related to the host contract. If the embedded derivative is considered *not* to be clearly and closely related to the host contract, the embedded derivative must be separated from the host contract and accounted for as a derivative instrument *by both parties* to the hybrid instrument, except as provided by paragraph 11(a).

61. The following guidance is relevant in deciding whether the economic characteristics and risks of the embedded derivative are clearly and closely related to the economic characteristics and risks of the host contract.

a. *Interest rate indexes.* An embedded derivative in which the underlying is an interest rate or interest rate index and a host contract that is considered a debt instrument are considered to be clearly and closely related unless, as discussed in paragraph 13, the embedded derivative contains a provision that (1) permits any possibility whatsoever that the investor's (or creditor's) undiscounted net cash inflows over the life of the instrument would not recover substantially all of its initial recorded investment in the hybrid instrument under its contractual terms or (2) could under any possibility whatsoever at least double the investor's initial rate of return on the host contract and at the same time result in a rate of return that is at least twice what otherwise would be the then-current market return for a contract that has the same terms as the host contract and that involves a debtor with a similar credit quality. The requirement to separate the embedded derivative from the host contract applies to *both parties* to the hybrid instrument even though the above tests focus on the investor's net cash inflows. Plain-vanilla servicing rights, which involve an obligation to perform servicing and the right to receive

fees for performing that servicing, do not contain an embedded derivative that would be separated from those servicing rights and accounted for as a derivative.

b. *Inflation-indexed interest payments.* The interest rate and the rate of inflation in the economic environment for the currency in which a debt instrument is denominated are considered to be clearly and closely related. Thus, nonleveraged inflation-indexed contracts (debt instruments, capitalized lease obligations, pension obligations, and so forth) would *not* have the inflation-related embedded derivative separated from the host contract.

c. *Credit-sensitive payments.* The creditworthiness of the debtor and the interest rate on a debt instrument are considered to be clearly and closely related. Thus, for debt instruments that have the interest rate reset in the event of (1) default (such as violation of a credit-risk-related covenant), (2) a change in the debtor's published credit rating, or (3) a change in the debtor's creditworthiness indicated by a change in its spread over Treasury bonds, the related embedded derivative would *not* be separated from the host contract.

d. *Calls and puts on debt instruments.* Call options (or put options) that can accelerate the repayment of principal on a debt instrument are considered to be clearly and closely related to a debt instrument that requires principal repayments unless both (1) the debt involves a substantial premium or discount (which is common with zero-coupon bonds) and (2) the put or call option is only contingently exercisable, provided the call options (or put options) are also considered to be clearly and closely related to the debt host contract under paragraph 13. Thus, if a substantial premium or discount is not involved, embedded calls and puts (including contingent call or put options that are not exercisable unless an event of default occurs) would *not* be separated from the host contract. However, for contingently exercisable calls and puts to be considered clearly and closely related, they can be indexed only to interest rates or credit risk, not some extraneous event or factor. In contrast, call options (or put options) that do not accelerate the repayment of principal on a debt instrument but instead require a cash settlement that is equal to the price of the option at the date of exercise would *not* be considered to be clearly and closely related to the debt instrument in which it is embedded.

e. *Calls and puts on equity instruments.* A put option that enables the holder to require the issuer of an equity instrument to reacquire that equity instrument for cash or other assets is *not* clearly and closely related to that equity instrument. Thus, such a put option embedded in a publicly traded equity instrument to which it relates should be separated from the host contract by the holder of the equity instrument if the criteria in paragraphs 12(b) and 12(c) are also met. That put option also should be separated from the host contract by the issuer of the equity instrument except in those cases in which the put option is not considered to be a derivative instrument pursuant to paragraph 11(a) because it is classified in stockholders' equity. A purchased call option that enables the issuer of an equity instrument (such as common stock) to reacquire that equity instrument would not be considered to be a derivative instrument by the issuer of the equity instrument pursuant to paragraph 11(a). Thus, if the call option were embedded in the related equity instrument, it would not be separated from the host contract by the issuer. However, for the holder of the related equity instrument, the embedded written call option would *not* be considered to be clearly and closely related to the equity instrument and, if the criteria in paragraphs 12(b) and 12(c) were met, should be separated from the host contract.

f. *Interest rate floors, caps, and collars.* Floors or caps (or collars, which are combinations of caps and floors) on interest rates and the interest rate on a debt instrument are considered to be clearly and closely related unless the conditions in either paragraph 13(a) or paragraph 13(b) are met, in which case the floors or the caps are not considered to be clearly and closely related.

g. *Term-extending options.* An embedded derivative provision that either (1) unilaterally enables one party to extend significantly the remaining term to maturity or (2) automatically extends significantly the remaining term triggered by specific events or conditions is *not* clearly and closely related to the interest rate on a debt instrument unless the interest rate is concurrently reset to the approximate current market rate for the extended term and the debt instrument initially involved no significant discount. Thus, if there is no reset of interest rates, the embedded derivative is not clearly and closely related to the host contract. That is, a term-extending option cannot be used to circumvent the restriction in paragraph 61(a)

regarding the investor's not recovering substantially all of its initial recorded investment.

h. *Equity-indexed interest payments.* The changes in fair value of an equity interest and the interest yield on a debt instrument are *not* clearly and closely related. Thus, an equity-related derivative embedded in an equity-indexed debt instrument (whether based on the price of a specific common stock or on an index that is based on a basket of equity instruments) must be separated from the host contract and accounted for as a derivative instrument.

i. *Commodity-indexed interest or principal payments.* The changes in fair value of a commodity (or other asset) and the interest yield on a debt instrument are *not* clearly and closely related. Thus, a commodity-related derivative embedded in a commodity-indexed debt instrument must be separated from the noncommodity host contract and accounted for as a derivative instrument.

j. *Indexed rentals:*

 (1) *Inflation-indexed rentals.* Rentals for the use of leased assets and adjustments for inflation on similar property are considered to be clearly and closely related. Thus, unless a significant leverage factor is involved, the inflation-related derivative embedded in an inflation-indexed lease contract would *not* be separated from the host contract.

 (2) *Contingent rentals based on related sales.* Lease contracts that include contingent rentals based on certain sales of the lessee would *not* have the contingent-rental-related embedded derivative separated from the host contract because, under paragraph 10(e)(3), a non-exchange-traded contract whose underlying is specified volumes of sales by one of the parties to the contract would not be subject to the requirements of this Statement.

 (3) *Contingent rentals based on a variable interest rate.* The obligation to make future payments for the use of leased assets and the adjustment of those payments to reflect changes in a variable-interest-rate index are considered to be clearly and closely related. Thus, lease contracts that include contingent rentals based on changes in the prime rate would *not* have the contingent-rental-related embedded derivative separated from the host contract.

k. *Convertible debt.* The changes in fair value of an equity interest and the interest rates on a debt instrument are not clearly and closely related. Thus, for a debt security that is convertible into a specified number of shares of the debtor's common stock or another entity's common stock, the embedded derivative (that is, the conversion option) must be separated from the debt host contract and accounted for as a derivative instrument provided that the conversion option would, as a freestanding instrument, be a derivative instrument subject to the requirements of this Statement. (For example, if the common stock was not readily convertible to cash, a conversion option that requires purchase of the common stock would not be accounted for as a derivative.) That accounting applies only to the holder (investor) if the debt is convertible to the debtor's common stock because, under paragraph 11(a), a separate option with the same terms would not be considered to be a derivative for the issuer.

l. *Convertible preferred stock.* Because the changes in fair value of an equity interest and interest rates on a debt instrument are not clearly and closely related, the terms of the preferred stock (other than the conversion option) must be analyzed to determine whether the preferred stock (and thus the potential host contract) is more akin to an equity instrument or a debt instrument. A typical cumulative fixed-rate preferred stock that has a mandatory redemption feature is more akin to debt, whereas cumulative participating perpetual preferred stock is more akin to an equity instrument.

Section 2: Assessment of Hedge Effectiveness

Hedge Effectiveness Requirements of This Statement

62. This Statement requires that an entity define at the time it designates a hedging relationship the method it will use to assess the hedge's effectiveness in achieving offsetting changes in fair value or offsetting cash flows attributable to the risk being hedged. It also requires that an entity use that defined method consistently throughout the hedge period (a) to assess at inception of the hedge and on an ongoing basis whether it expects the hedging relationship to be highly effective in achieving offset and (b) to measure the ineffective part of the hedge. If the entity identifies an improved method and wants to apply that method prospectively, it must discontinue the existing hedging relationship and designate the relationship anew using the improved method. This Statement does not specify a single method for either assessing whether a hedge is expected to be highly

effective or measuring hedge ineffectiveness. The appropriateness of a given method of assessing hedge effectiveness can depend on the nature of the risk being hedged and the type of hedging instrument used. Ordinarily, however, an entity should assess effectiveness for similar hedges in a similar manner; use of different methods for similar hedges should be justified.

63. In defining how hedge effectiveness will be assessed, an entity must specify whether it will include in that assessment all of the gain or loss on a hedging instrument. This Statement permits (but does not require) an entity to exclude all or a part of the hedging instrument's time value from the assessment of hedge effectiveness, as follows:

a. If the effectiveness of a hedge with an option contract is assessed based on changes in the option's intrinsic value, the change in the time value of the contract would be excluded from the assessment of hedge effectiveness.
b. If the effectiveness of a hedge with an option contract is assessed based on changes in the option's minimum value, that is, its intrinsic value plus the effect of discounting, the change in the volatility value of the contract would be excluded from the assessment of hedge effectiveness.
c. If the effectiveness of a hedge with a forward or futures contract is assessed based on changes in fair value attributable to changes in spot prices, the change in the fair value of the contract related to the changes in the difference between the spot price and the forward or futures price would be excluded from the assessment of hedge effectiveness.

In each circumstance above, changes in the excluded component would be included currently in earnings, together with any ineffectiveness that results under the defined method of assessing ineffectiveness. As noted in paragraph 62, the effectiveness of similar hedges generally should be assessed similarly; that includes whether a component of the gain or loss on a derivative is excluded in assessing effectiveness. No other components of a gain or loss on the designated hedging instrument may be excluded from the assessment of hedge effectiveness.

64. In assessing the effectiveness of a cash flow hedge, an entity generally will need to consider the time value of money if significant in the circumstances. Considering the effect of the time value of money is especially important if the hedging instrument involves periodic cash settlements. An example

of a situation in which an entity likely would reflect the time value of money is a tailing strategy with futures contracts. When using a tailing strategy, an entity adjusts the size or contract amount of futures contracts used in a hedge so that earnings (or expense) from reinvestment (or funding) of daily settlement gains (or losses) on the futures do not distort the results of the hedge. To assess offset of expected cash flows when a tailing strategy has been used, an entity could reflect the time value of money, perhaps by comparing the present value of the hedged forecasted cash flow with the results of the hedging instrument.

65. Whether a hedging relationship qualifies as highly effective sometimes will be easy to assess, and there will be no ineffectiveness to recognize in earnings during the term of the hedge. If the critical terms of the hedging instrument and of the entire hedged asset or liability (as opposed to selected cash flows) or hedged forecasted transaction are the same, the entity could conclude that changes in fair value or cash flows attributable to the risk being hedged are expected to completely offset at inception and on an ongoing basis. For example, an entity may assume that a hedge of a forecasted purchase of a commodity with a forward contract will be highly effective and that there will be no ineffectiveness to be recognized in earnings if:

a. The forward contract is for purchase of the same quantity of the same commodity at the same time and location as the hedged forecasted purchase.
b. The fair value of the forward contract at inception is zero.
c. Either the change in the discount or premium on the forward contract is excluded from the assessment of effectiveness and included directly in earnings pursuant to paragraph 63 or the change in expected cash flows on the forecasted transaction is based on the forward price for the commodity.

66. Assessing hedge effectiveness and measuring the ineffective part of the hedge, however, can be more complex. For example, hedge ineffectiveness would result from the following circumstances, among others:

a. A difference between the basis of the hedging instrument and the hedged item or hedged transaction (such as a Deutsche mark–based hedging instrument and Dutch guilder–based hedged item), to the extent that those bases do not move in tandem
b. Differences in critical terms of the hedging instrument and hedged item or hedged transaction, such as differences in notional amounts, maturities, quantity, location, or delivery dates.

Ineffectiveness also would result if part of the change in the fair value of a derivative is attributable to a change in the counterparty's creditworthiness.

67. A hedge that meets the effectiveness test specified in paragraphs 20(b) and 28(b) (that is, both at inception and on an ongoing basis, the entity expects the hedge to be highly effective at achieving offsetting changes in fair values or cash flows) also must meet the other hedge accounting criteria to qualify for hedge accounting. If the hedge initially qualifies for hedge accounting, the entity would continue to assess whether the hedge meets the effectiveness test and also would measure any ineffectiveness during the hedge period. If the hedge fails the effectiveness test at any time (that is, if the entity does not expect the hedge to be highly effective at achieving offsetting changes in fair values or cash flows), the hedge ceases to qualify for hedge accounting. The discussions of measuring hedge ineffectiveness in the examples in the remainder of this section of Appendix A assume that the hedge satisfied all of the criteria for hedge accounting at inception.

Assuming no ineffectiveness in a hedge with an interest rate swap

68. An assumption of no ineffectiveness is especially important in a hedging relationship involving an interest-bearing financial instrument and an interest rate swap because it significantly simplifies the computations necessary to make the accounting entries. An entity may assume no ineffectiveness in a hedging relationship of interest rate risk involving a recognized interest-bearing asset or liability and an

---

interest rate swap (or a compound hedging instrument composed of an interest rate swap and a mirror-image call or put option as discussed in paragraph 68(d) below) if all of the applicable conditions in the following list are met:

Conditions applicable to both fair value hedges and cash flow hedges

a. The notional amount of the swap matches the principal amount of the interest-bearing asset or liability being hedged.
b. If the hedging instrument is solely an interest rate swap, the fair value of that swap at the inception of the hedging relationship is zero. If the hedging instrument is a compound derivative composed of an interest rate swap and mirror-image call or put option as discussed in paragraph 68(d), the premium for the mirror-image call or put option must be paid or received in the same manner as the premium on the call or put option embedded in the hedged item. That is, the reporting entity must determine whether the implicit premium for the purchased call or written put option embedded in the hedged item was principally paid at inception-acquisition (through an original issue discount or premium) or is being paid over the life of the hedged item (through an adjustment of the interest rate). If the implicit premium for the call or put option embedded in the hedged item was principally paid at inception-acquisition, the fair value of the hedging instrument at the inception of the hedging relationship must be equal to the fair value of the mirror-image call or put option. In contrast, if the implicit premium for the call or put option embedded in the hedged item is principally being paid over the life of the hedged item, fair value of the hedging instrument at the inception of the hedging relationship must be zero.
c. The formula for computing net settlements under the interest rate swap is the same for each net settlement. (That is, the fixed rate is the same throughout the term, and the variable rate is based on the same index and includes the same constant adjustment or no adjustment.)
d. The interest-bearing asset or liability is not prepayable (that is, able to be settled by either party prior to its scheduled maturity), except as indicated in the following sentences. This criterion does not apply to an interest-bearing asset or liability that is prepayable solely due to an embedded call option provided that the hedging instrument is a compound derivative composed of an interest rate swap and a mirror-image call option. The call option is considered a mirror image of the call option embedded in the hedged item if (1) the terms of the two call options match (including matching maturities, strike price, related notional amounts, timing and frequency of payments, and dates on which the instruments may be called) and (2) the entity is the writer of one call option and the holder (or purchaser) of the other call option. Similarly, this criterion does not apply to an interest-bearing asset or liability that is prepayable solely due to an embedded put option provided that the hedging instrument is a compound derivative composed of an interest rate swap and a mirror-image put option.

dd. The index on which the variable leg of the swap is based matches the benchmark interest rate designated as the interest rate risk being hedged for that hedging relationship.[18c]
e. Any other terms in the interest-bearing financial instruments or interest rate swaps are typical of those instruments and do not invalidate the assumption of no ineffectiveness.

Conditions applicable to fair value hedges only

f. The expiration date of the swap matches the maturity date of the interest-bearing asset or liability.
g. There is no floor or cap on the variable interest rate of the swap.
h. The interval between repricings of the variable interest rate in the swap is frequent enough to justify an assumption that the variable payment or receipt is at a market rate (generally three to six months or less).

Conditions applicable to cash flow hedges only

i. All interest receipts or payments on the variable-rate asset or liability during the term of the swap are designated as hedged, and no interest payments beyond the term of the swap are designated as hedged.
j. There is no floor or cap on the variable interest rate of the swap unless the variable-rate asset or liability has a floor or cap. In that case, the swap

---

[18c]For cash flow hedge situations in which the cash flows of the hedged item and the hedging instrument are based on the same index but that index is not the benchmark interest rate, the shortcut method is not permitted. However, the entity may obtain results similar to results obtained if the shortcut method was permitted.

must have a floor or cap on the variable interest rate that is comparable to the floor or cap on the variable-rate asset or liability. (For this purpose, comparable does not necessarily mean equal. For example, if a swap's variable rate is LIBOR and an asset's variable rate is LIBOR plus 2 percent, a 10 percent cap on the swap would be comparable to a 12 percent cap on the asset.)

k. The repricing dates match those of the variable-rate asset or liability.

l. [This subparagraph has been deleted. See Status page.]

69. The fixed rate on a hedged item need not exactly match the fixed rate on a swap designated as a fair value hedge. Nor does the variable rate on an interest-bearing asset or liability need to be the same as the variable rate on a swap designated as a cash flow hedge. A swap's fair value comes from its net settlements. The fixed and variable rates on a swap can be changed without affecting the net settlement if both are changed by the same amount. That is, a swap with a payment based on LIBOR and a receipt based on a fixed rate of 5 percent has the same net settlements and fair value as a swap with a payment based on LIBOR plus 1 percent and a receipt based on a fixed rate of 6 percent.

70. Comparable credit risk at inception is not a condition for assuming no ineffectiveness even though actually achieving perfect offset would require that the same discount rate be used to determine the fair value of the swap and of the hedged item or hedged transaction. To justify using the same discount rate, the credit risk related to both parties to the swap as well as to the debtor on the hedged interest-bearing asset (in a fair value hedge) or the variable-rate asset on which the interest payments are hedged (in a cash flow hedge) would have to be the same. However, because that complication is caused by the interaction of interest rate risk and credit risk, which are not easily separable, comparable creditworthiness is not considered a necessary condition to assume no ineffectiveness in a hedge of interest rate risk.

After-tax hedging of foreign currency risk

71. Statement 52 permitted hedging of foreign currency risk on an after-tax basis. The portion of the gain or loss on the hedging instrument that exceeded the loss or gain on the hedged item was required to be included as an offset to the related tax effects in the period in which those tax effects are recognized. This Statement continues those provisions.

Illustrations of Assessing Effectiveness and Measuring Ineffectiveness

72. The following examples illustrate some ways in which an entity may assess hedge effectiveness and measures hedge ineffectiveness for specific strategies. The examples are not intended to imply that other reasonable methods are precluded. However, not all possible methods are reasonable or consistent with this Statement. This section also discusses some methods of assessing hedge effectiveness and determining hedge ineffectiveness that are not consistent with this Statement and thus may not be used.

Example 1: Fair value hedge of natural gas inventory with futures contracts

73. Company A has 20,000 MMBTU's of natural gas stored at its location in West Texas. To hedge the fair value exposure of the natural gas, the company sells the equivalent of 20,000 MMBTU's of natural gas futures contracts on a national mercantile exchange. The futures prices are based on delivery of natural gas at the Henry Hub gas collection point in Louisiana.

Assessing the hedge's expected effectiveness

74. The price of Company A's natural gas inventory in West Texas and the price of the natural gas that is the underlying for the futures it sold will differ as a result of regional factors (such as location, pipeline transmission costs, and supply and demand).[19] Company A therefore may not automatically assume that the hedge will be highly effective at achieving offsetting changes in fair value, and it cannot assess effectiveness by looking solely to the change in the price of natural gas delivered to the Henry Hub.

75. Both at inception of the hedge and on an ongoing basis, Company A might assess the hedge's expected effectiveness based on the extent of correlation in recent years for periods similar to the spot

---

[19]The use of a hedging instrument with a different underlying basis than the item or transaction being hedged is generally referred to as a *cross-hedge*. The principles for cross-hedges illustrated in this example also apply to hedges involving other risks. For example, the effectiveness of a hedge of interest rate risk in which one interest rate is used as a surrogate for another interest rate would be evaluated in the same way as the natural gas cross-hedge in this example.

prices term of the futures contracts between the spot prices of natural gas in West Texas and at the Henry Hub.[20] If those prices have been and are expected to continue to be highly correlated, Company A might reasonably expect the changes in the fair value of the futures contracts attributable to changes in the spot price of natural gas at the Henry Hub to be highly effective in offsetting the changes in the fair value of its natural gas inventory. In assessing effectiveness during the term of the hedge, Company A must take into account actual changes in spot prices in West Texas and at the Henry Hub.

76. Company A may not assume that the change in the spot price of natural gas located at Henry Hub, Louisiana, is the same as the change in fair value of its West Texas inventory. The physical hedged item is natural gas in West Texas, not natural gas at the Henry Hub. In identifying the price risk that is being hedged, the company also may not assume that its natural gas in West Texas has a Louisiana natural gas "component." Use of a price for natural gas located somewhere other than West Texas to assess the effectiveness of a fair value hedge of natural gas in West Texas would be inconsistent with this Statement and could result in an assumption that a hedge was highly effective when it was not. If the price of natural gas in West Texas is not readily available, Company A might use a price for natural gas located elsewhere as a base for estimating the price of natural gas in West Texas. However, that base price must be adjusted to reflect the effects of factors, such as location, transmission costs, and supply and demand, that would cause the price of natural gas in West Texas to differ from the base price.

Measuring hedge ineffectiveness

77. Consistent with the company's method of assessing whether the hedge is expected to be highly effective, the hedge would be ineffective to the extent that (a) the actual change in the fair value of the futures contracts attributable to changes in the spot price of natural gas at the Henry Hub did not offset (b) the actual change in the spot price of natural gas in West Texas per MMBTU multiplied by 20,000. That method excludes the change in the fair value of the futures contracts attributable to changes in the difference between the spot price and the forward price of natural gas at the Henry Hub in determining ineffectiveness. The excluded amount would be reported directly in earnings.

Example 2: Fair value hedge of tire inventory with a forward contract

78. Company B manufactures tires. The production of those tires incorporates a variety of physical components, of which rubber and steel are the most significant, as well as labor and overhead. The company hedges its exposure to changes in the fair value of its inventory of 8,000 steel-belted radial tires by entering into a forward contract to sell rubber at a fixed price.

Assessing the hedge's expected effectiveness

79. Company B decides to base its assessment of hedge effectiveness on changes in the fair value of the forward contract attributable to changes in the spot price of rubber. To determine whether the forward contract is expected to be highly effective at offsetting the change in fair value of the tire inventory, Company B could estimate and compare such changes in the fair value of the forward contract and changes in the fair value of the tires (computed as the market price per tire multiplied by 8,000 tires) for different rubber and tire prices. Company B also should consider the extent to which past changes in the spot prices of rubber and tires have been correlated. Because tires are a nonfinancial asset and rubber is only an ingredient in manufacturing them, Company B may not assess hedge effectiveness by looking to the change in the fair value of only the rubber component of the steel-belted radial tires (paragraph 21(e)). Both at inception of the hedge and during its term, the company must base its assessment of hedge effectiveness on changes in the market price of steel-belted radial tires and changes in the fair value of the forward contract attributable to changes in the spot price of rubber.

Measuring hedge ineffectiveness

80. It is unlikely that this transaction would be highly effective in achieving offsetting changes in fair value. However, if Company B concludes that the hedge will be highly effective and the hedge otherwise qualifies for hedge accounting, the ineffective part of the hedge would be measured consistent with the company's method of assessing whether the

---

[20]The period of time over which correlation of prices should be assessed would be based on management's judgment in the particular circumstance.

hedge is expected to be highly effective. Based on that method, the hedge would be ineffective to the extent that the actual changes in (a) the fair value of the forward contract attributable to the change in the spot price of rubber and (b) the market price of steel-belted radials multiplied by the number of tires in inventory did not offset. Because Company B bases its assessment of effectiveness on changes in spot prices, the change in the fair value of the forward contract attributable to changes in the difference between the spot and forward price of rubber would be excluded from the measure of effectiveness and reported directly in earnings.

Example 3: Fair value hedge of growing wheat with futures contracts

81. Company C has a tract of land on which it is growing wheat. Historically, Company C has harvested at least 40,000 bushels of wheat from that tract of land. Two months before its expected harvest, the company sells 2-month futures contracts for 40,000 bushels of wheat, which it wants to designate as a fair value hedge of its growing wheat, rather than as a cash flow hedge of the projected sale of the wheat after harvest.

Assessing the hedge's expected effectiveness and measuring ineffectiveness

82. Even though the futures contracts are for the same type of wheat that Company C expects to harvest in two months, the futures contracts and hedged wheat have different bases because the futures contracts are based on fully grown, harvested wheat, while the hedged item is unharvested wheat with two months left in its growing cycle. The company therefore may not automatically assume that the hedge will be highly effective in achieving offsetting changes in fair value.

83. To determine whether the futures contracts are expected to be highly effective in providing offsetting changes in fair value for the growing wheat, Company C would need to estimate and compare the fair value of its growing wheat and of the futures contracts for different levels of wheat prices. Company C may not base its estimate of the value of its growing wheat solely on the current price of wheat because that price is for grown, harvested wheat. The company might, however, use the current price of harvested wheat together with other relevant factors,

such as additional production and harvesting costs and the physical condition of the growing wheat, to estimate the current fair value of its growing wheat crop.

84. It is unlikely that wheat futures would be highly effective in offsetting the changes in value of growing wheat. However, if Company C concludes that the hedge qualifies as highly effective, it would use the same method for measuring actual hedge effectiveness that it uses initially and on an ongoing basis to assess whether the hedge is expected to be highly effective. The hedge would be ineffective to the extent that the actual changes in fair value of the futures contract and of the growing wheat crop did not offset.

Example 4: Fair value hedge of equity securities with option contracts

85. Company D holds 10,000 shares of XYZ stock. It purchases put option contracts on 20,000 shares of XYZ stock with a strike price equal to the current price of the stock to hedge its exposure to changes in the fair value of its investment position attributable to changes in the price of XYZ stock. Company D manages the position using a "delta-neutral" strategy. That is, it monitors the option's "delta"—the ratio of changes in the option's price to changes in the price of XYZ stock. As the delta ratio changes, Company D buys or sells put options so that the next change in the fair value of all of the options held can be expected to counterbalance the next change in the value of its investment in XYZ stock. For put options, the delta ratio moves closer to one as the share price of the stock falls and moves closer to zero as the share price rises. The delta ratio also changes as the exercise period decreases, as interest rates change, and as expected volatility changes. Company D designates the put options as a fair value hedge of its investment in XYZ stock.

Assessing the hedge's expected effectiveness and measuring ineffectiveness

86. Because Company D plans to change the number of options that it holds to the extent necessary to maintain a delta-neutral position, it may not automatically assume that the hedge will be highly effective at achieving offsetting changes in fair value. Also, because the "delta-neutral" hedging strategy is based on expected changes in the option's fair value, the company may not assess effectiveness based on changes in the option's intrinsic value. Instead, Company D would estimate (a) the gain or loss on the option position that would result from various decreases

or increases in the market price of XYZ stock and (b) the loss or gain on its investment in XYZ stock for the same market price changes. To assess the effectiveness of the hedge both at inception and on an ongoing basis, the company could compare the respective gains and losses from different market price changes. The ongoing assessment of effectiveness also must consider the actual changes in the fair value of the put options held and of the investment in XYZ stock during the hedge period.

87. Consistent with the company's method of assessing effectiveness, the hedge would be ineffective to the extent that the actual realized and unrealized gains or losses from changes in the fair value of the options held is greater or less than the change in value of the investment in XYZ stock. The underlying for the put option contracts is the market price of XYZ stock. Therefore, if Company D continually monitors the delta ratio and adjusts the number of options held accordingly, the changes in the fair value of the options and of the hedged item may almost completely offset, resulting in only a small amount of ineffectiveness to be recognized in earnings.

Example 5: Fair value hedge of a treasury bond with a put option contract

88. Company E owns a Treasury bond and wants to protect itself against the fair value exposure to declines in the price of the bond. The company purchases an at-the-money put option on a Treasury security with the same terms (remaining maturity, notional amount, and interest rate) as the Treasury bond held and designates the option as a hedge of the fair value exposure of the Treasury bond. Company E plans to hold the put option until it expires.

Assessing the hedge's expected effectiveness and measuring ineffectiveness

89. Because Company E plans to hold the put option (a static hedge) rather than manage the position with a delta-neutral strategy, it could assess whether it expects the hedge to be highly effective at achieving offsetting changes in fair value by calculating and comparing the changes in the intrinsic value of the option and changes in the price (fair value) of the Treasury bond for different possible market prices. In assessing the expectation of effectiveness on an ongoing basis, the company also must consider the actual changes in the fair value of the Treasury bond and in the intrinsic value of the option during the hedge period.

90. However, because the pertinent critical terms of the option and the bond are the same in this example, the company could expect the changes in value of the bond attributable to changes in interest rates and changes in the intrinsic value of the option to offset completely during the period that the option is in the money. That is, there will be no ineffectiveness because the company has chosen to exclude changes in the option's time value from the effectiveness test. Because of that choice, Company E must recognize changes in the time value of the option directly in earnings.

Example 6: Fair value hedge of an embedded purchased option with a written option

91. Company F issues five-year, fixed-rate debt with an embedded (purchased) call option and, with a different counterparty, writes a call option to neutralize the call feature in the debt. The embedded call option and the written call option have the same effective notional amount, underlying fixed interest rate, and strike price. (The strike price of the option in the debt usually is referred to as the call price.) The embedded option also can be exercised at the same times as the written option. Company F designates the written option as a fair value hedge of the embedded prepayment option component of the fixed-rate debt.

Assessing the hedge's expected effectiveness and measuring ineffectiveness

92. To assess whether the hedge is expected to be highly effective in achieving offsetting changes in fair value, Company F could estimate and compare the changes in fair values of the two options for different market interest rates. Because this Statement does not permit derivatives, including embedded derivatives whether or not they are required to be accounted for separately, to be separated into components, Company F can only designate a hedge of the entire change in fair value of the embedded purchased call option. The resulting changes in fair value will be included currently in earnings. Changes in the fair value of the written option also will be included currently in earnings; any ineffectiveness thus will be automatically reflected in earnings. (The hedge is likely to have some ineffectiveness because the premium for the written call option is unlikely to be the same as the premium for the embedded purchased call option.)

Example 7: Cash flow hedge of a forecasted purchase of inventory with a forward contract

93. Company G forecasts the purchase of 500,000 pounds of Brazilian coffee for U.S. dollars in 6 months. It wants to hedge the cash flow exposure associated with changes in the U.S. dollar price of Brazilian coffee. Rather than acquire a derivative based on Brazilian coffee, the company enters into a 6-month forward contract to purchase 500,000 pounds of Colombian coffee for U.S. dollars and designates the forward contract as a cash flow hedge of its forecasted purchase of Brazilian coffee. All other terms of the forward contract and the forecasted purchase, such as delivery locations, are the same.

Assessing the hedge's expected effectiveness and measuring ineffectiveness

94. Company G bases its assessment of hedge effectiveness and measure of ineffectiveness on changes in forward prices, with the resulting gain or loss discounted to reflect the time value of money. Because of the difference in the bases of the forecasted transaction (Brazilian coffee) and forward contract (Colombian coffee), Company G may not assume that the hedge will automatically be highly effective in achieving offsetting cash flows. Both at inception and on an ongoing basis, Company G could assess the effectiveness of the hedge by comparing changes in the expected cash flows from the Colombian coffee forward contract with the expected net change in cash outflows for purchasing the Brazilian coffee for different market prices. (A simpler method that should produce the same results would consider the expected future correlation of the prices of Brazilian and Colombian coffee, based on the correlation of those prices over past six-month periods.)

95. In assessing hedge effectiveness on an ongoing basis, Company G also must consider the extent of offset between the change in expected cash flows on its Colombian coffee forward contract and the expected net change in expected cash flows for the forecasted purchase of Brazilian coffee. Both changes would be measured on a cumulative basis for actual changes in the forward price of the respective coffees during the hedge period.

96. Because the only difference between the forward contract and forecasted purchase relates to the type of coffee (Colombian versus Brazilian), Company G could consider the changes in the cash flows on a forward contract for Brazilian coffee to be a measure of perfectly offsetting changes in cash flows for its forecasted purchase of Brazilian coffee. For example, for given changes in the U.S. dollar prices of six-month and three-month Brazilian and Colombian contracts, Company G could compute the effect of a change in the price of coffee on the expected cash flows of its forward contract on Colombian coffee and of a forward contract for Brazilian coffee as follows:

Estimate of Change in Cash Flows

	Hedging Instrument: Forward Contract on Colombian Coffee	Estimate of Forecasted Transaction: Forward Contract on Brazilian Coffee
Forward price of Colombian and Brazilian coffee:		
At hedge inception—6-month price	$ 2.54	$ 2.43
3 months later—3-month price	2.63	2.53
Cumulative change in price—gain	$ .09	$ .10
× 500,000 pounds of coffee	× 500,000	× 500,000
Estimate of change in cash flows	$ 45,000	$ 50,000

[20a–20c][These footnotes have been deleted. See Status page.]

97. Using the above amounts, Company G could evaluate effectiveness 3 months into the hedge by comparing the $45,000 change on its Colombian coffee contract with what would have been a perfectly offsetting change in cash flow for its forecasted purchase—the $50,000 change on an otherwise identical forward contract for Brazilian coffee. The hedge would be ineffective to the extent that there was a difference between the changes in the present value of the expected cash flows on (a) the company's Colombian coffee contract and (b) a comparable forward contract for Brazilian coffee (the equivalent of the present value of $5,000 in the numerical example).

Example 8: Cash flow hedge with a basis swap

98. Company H has a 5-year, $100,000 variable-rate asset and a 7-year, $150,000 variable-rate liability. The interest on the asset is payable by the counterparty at the end of each month based on the prime rate as of the first of the month. The interest on the liability is payable by Company H at the end of each month based on LIBOR as of the tenth day of the month (the liability's anniversary date). The company enters into a 5-year interest rate swap to pay interest at the prime rate and receive interest at LIBOR at the end of each month based on a notional amount of $100,000. Both rates are determined as of the first of the month. Company H designates the swap as a hedge of 5 years of interest receipts on the $100,000 variable-rate asset and the first 5 years of interest payments on $100,000 of the variable-rate liability.

Assessing the hedge's expected effectiveness and measuring ineffectiveness

99. Company H may not automatically assume that the hedge always will be highly effective at achieving offsetting changes in cash flows because the reset date on the receive leg of the swap differs from the reset date on the corresponding variable-rate liability. Both at hedge inception and on an ongoing basis, the company's assessment of expected effectiveness could be based on the extent to which changes in LIBOR have occurred during comparable 10-day periods in the past. Company H's ongoing assessment of expected effectiveness and measurement of actual ineffectiveness would be on a cumulative basis and would incorporate the actual interest rate changes to date. The hedge would be ineffective to the extent

that the cumulative change in cash flows on the prime leg of the swap did not offset the cumulative change in expected cash flows on the asset, *and* the cumulative change in cash flows on the LIBOR leg of the swap did not offset the change in expected cash flows on the hedged portion of the liability. The terms of the swap, the asset, and the portion of the liability that is hedged are the same, with the exception of the reset dates on the liability and the receive leg of the swap. Thus, the hedge will only be ineffective to the extent that LIBOR has changed between the first of the month (the reset date for the swap) and the tenth of the month (the reset date for the liability).

Example 9: Cash flow hedge of forecasted sale with a forward contract

100. Company I, a U.S. dollar functional currency company, forecasts the sale of 10,000 units of its principal product in 6 months to French customers for FF500,000 (French francs). The company wants to hedge the cash flow exposure of the French franc sale related to changes in the US$-FF exchange rate. It enters into a 6-month forward contract to exchange the FF500,000 it expects to receive in the forecasted sale for the U.S. dollar equivalent specified in the forward contract and designates the forward contract as a cash flow hedge of the forecasted sale.

Assessing the hedge's expected effectiveness and measuring ineffectiveness

101. Company I chooses to assess hedge effectiveness at inception and during the term of the hedge based on (a) changes in the fair value of the forward contract attributable to changes in the US$-FF spot rate and (b) changes in the present value of the current U.S. dollar equivalent of the forecasted receipt of FF500,000. Because the critical terms of the forward contract and the forecasted transaction are the same, presumably there would be no ineffectiveness unless there is a reduction in the expected sales proceeds from the forecasted sales. Because Company I is assessing effectiveness based on spot rates, it would exclude the change in the fair value of the forward contract attributable to changes in the difference between the forward rate and spot rate from the measure of hedge ineffectiveness and report it directly in earnings.

20d–20e[These footnotes have been deleted. See Status page.]

Example 10: Attempted hedge of a forecasted sale with a written call option

102. Company J forecasts the sale in 9 months of 100 units of product with a current market price of $95 per unit. The company's objective is to sell the upside potential associated with the forecasted sale by writing a call option for a premium. The company plans to use the premium from the call option as an offset to decreases in future cash inflows from the forecasted sale that will occur if the market price of the product decreases below $95. Accordingly, Company J sells an at-the-money call option on 100 units of product with a strike price of $95 for a premium. The premium represents only the time value of the option. The option is exercisable at any time within nine months.

103. Company J's objective of using the premium from the written call option as an offset to any decrease in future cash inflows would not meet the notion of effectiveness in this Statement. Future changes in the market price of the company's product will not affect the premium that Company J received, which is all related to time value in this example and thus is the maximum amount by which Company J can benefit. That is, the company could not expect the cash flows on the option to increase so that, at different price levels, a decrease in cash flows from the forecasted sale would be offset by an increase in cash flows on the option.

Appendix B

EXAMPLES ILLUSTRATING APPLICATION OF THIS STATEMENT

Section 1: Hedging Relationships

104. This appendix presents examples that illustrate the application of this Statement. The examples do not address all possible uses of derivatives as hedging instruments. For simplicity, commissions and most other transaction costs, initial margin, and income taxes are ignored unless otherwise stated in an example. It is also assumed in each example that there are no changes in creditworthiness that would alter the effectiveness of any of the hedging relationships.

Example 1: Fair Value Hedge of a Commodity Inventory

105. This example illustrates the accounting for a fair value hedge of a commodity inventory. In the first scenario, the terms of the hedging derivative have been negotiated to produce no ineffectiveness in the hedging relationship. In the second scenario, there is ineffectiveness in the hedging relationship. To simplify the illustration and focus on basic concepts, the derivative in these two scenarios is assumed to have no time value. In practice, a derivative used for a fair value hedge of a commodity would have a time value that would change over the term of the hedging relationship. The changes in that time value would be recognized in earnings as they occur, either because they represent ineffectiveness or because they are excluded from the assessment of effectiveness (as discussed in paragraph 63). Other examples in this section illustrate accounting for the time value component of a derivative.

Scenario 1—No ineffectiveness in the hedging relationship

106. ABC Company decides to hedge the risk of changes during the period in the overall fair value of its entire inventory of Commodity A by entering into a derivative contract, Derivative Z. On the first day of period 1, ABC enters into Derivative Z and neither receives nor pays a premium (that is, the fair value at inception is zero). ABC designates the derivative as a hedge of the changes in fair value of the inventory due to changes in the price of Commodity A during period 1. The hedging relationship qualifies for fair value hedge accounting. ABC will assess effectiveness by comparing the entire change in fair value of Derivative Z with the change in the market price of the hedged commodity inventory. ABC expects no ineffectiveness because (a) the notional amount of Derivative Z matches the amount of the hedged inventory (that is, Derivative Z is based on the same number of bushels as the number of bushels of the commodity that ABC designated as hedged) and (b) the underlying of Derivative Z is the price of the same variety and grade of Commodity A as the inventory at the same location.

107. At inception of the hedge, Derivative Z has a fair value of zero and the hedged inventory has a carrying amount of $1,000,000 and a fair value of $1,100,000. On the last day of period 1, the fair value of Derivative Z has increased by $25,000, and the fair value of the inventory has decreased by $25,000. The inventory is sold, and Derivative Z is settled on the last day of period 1. The following table illustrates the accounting for the situation described above.

	Debit (Credit)			
	Cash	Derivative	Inventory	Earnings
Period 1				
Recognize change in fair value of derivative		$ 25,000		$ (25,000)
Recognize change in fair value of inventory			$ (25,000)	25,000
Recognize revenue from sale	$1,075,000			(1,075,000)
Recognize cost of sale of inventory			(975,000)	975,000
Recognize settlement of derivative	25,000	(25,000)		
Total	$1,100,000	$ 0	$(1,000,000)	$ (100,000)

108. If ABC had sold the hedged inventory at the inception of the hedge, its gross profit on that sale would have been $100,000. The above example illustrates that, by hedging the risk of changes in the overall fair value of its inventory, ABC recognized the same gross profit at the end of the hedge period even though the fair value of its inventory decreased by $25,000.

Scenario 2—Ineffectiveness in the hedging relationship

109. No ineffectiveness was recognized in earnings in the above situation because the gain on Derivative Z exactly offsets the loss on the inventory. However, if the terms of Derivative Z did not perfectly match the inventory and its fair value had increased by $22,500 as compared with the decline in fair value of the inventory of $25,000, then ineffectiveness of $2,500 would have been recognized in earnings. The following table illustrates that situation (all other facts are assumed to be the same as in Scenario 1).

	Debit (Credit)			
	Cash	Derivative	Inventory	Earnings
Period 1				
Recognize change in fair value of derivative		$ 22,500		$ (22,500)
Recognize change in fair value of inventory			$ (25,000)	25,000
Recognize revenue from sale	$1,075,000			(1,075,000)
Recognize cost of sale of inventory			(975,000)	975,000
Recognize settlement of derivative	22,500	(22,500)		
Total	$1,097,500	$ 0	$(1,000,000)	$ (97,500)

110. The difference between the effect on earnings in this scenario and the effect on earnings in Scenario 1 is the $2,500 of hedge ineffectiveness.

Example 2: Fair Value Hedge of Fixed-Rate Interest-Bearing Debt

Purpose of the example

111. This example demonstrates the mechanics of reporting an interest rate swap used as a fair value hedge of an interest-bearing liability. It is not intended to demonstrate how to compute the fair value of an interest rate swap or an interest-bearing liability. This example has been simplified by assuming that the interest rate applicable to a payment due at any future date is the same as the rate for a payment due at any other date (that is, the yield curve is flat). Although that is an unrealistic assumption, it makes the amounts used in the example easier to understand without detracting from the purpose of the example.

112. The fair values of the swap in this example are determined using the "zero-coupon method." That method involves computing and summing the present value of each future net settlement that would be required by the contract terms if future spot interest rates match the forward rates implied by the current yield curve. The discount rates used are the spot interest rates implied by the current yield curve for

hypothetical zero coupon bonds due on the date of each future net settlement on the swap. The zero-coupon method is not the only acceptable method. Explanations of other acceptable methods of determining the fair value of an interest rate swap can be obtained from various published sources. Fair values also may be available from dealers in interest rate swaps and other derivatives.

113. In this example, the term and notional amount of the interest rate swap match the term and principal amount of the interest-bearing liability being hedged. The fixed and variable interest rates used to determine the net settlements on the swap match the current yield curve, and the sum of the present values of the expected net settlements is zero at inception. Thus, paragraph 68 of this Statement permits the reporting entity to assume that there will be no ineffectiveness. Assessment of effectiveness at one of the swap's repricing dates would confirm the validity of that assumption.

114. A shortcut method can be used to produce the same reporting results as the method illustrated in this example. This shortcut is only appropriate for a fair value hedge of a fixed-rate asset or liability using an interest rate swap and only if the assumption of no ineffectiveness is appropriate.[21] The steps in the shortcut method are as follows:

a. Determine the difference between the fixed rate to be received on the swap and the fixed rate to be paid on the bonds.
b. Combine that difference with the variable rate to be paid on the swap.

c. Compute and recognize interest expense using that combined rate and the fixed-rate liability's principal amount. (Amortization of any purchase premium or discount on the liability also must be considered, although that complication is not incorporated in this example.)
d. Determine the fair value of the interest rate swap.
e. Adjust the carrying amount of the swap to its fair value and adjust the carrying amount of the liability by an offsetting amount.

Amounts determined using the shortcut method and the facts in this example will match the amounts in paragraph 117 even though the shortcut does not involve explicitly amortizing the hedge accounting adjustments on the debt. That is, the quarterly adjustments of the debt and explicit amortization of previous adjustments will have the same net effect on earnings as the shortcut method.

Assumptions

115. On July 1, 20X1, ABC Company borrows $1,000,000 to be repaid on June 30, 20X3. On that same date, ABC also enters into a two-year receive-fixed, pay-variable interest rate swap. ABC designates the interest rate swap as a hedge of the changes in the fair value of the fixed-rate debt attributable to changes in the designated benchmark interest rate. ABC designates changes in **LIBOR swap rates** as the benchmark interest rate in hedging interest rate risk. The terms of the interest rate swap and the debt are as follows:

	Interest Rate Swap	**Fixed-Rate Debt**
Trade date and borrowing date*	July 1, 20X1	July 1, 20X1
Termination date and maturity date	June 30, 20X3	June 30, 20X3
Notional amount and principal amount	$1,000,000	$1,000,000
Fixed interest rate*	6.41%	6.41%
Variable interest rate	3-month US$ LIBOR	Not applicable
Settlement dates and interest payment dates*	End of each calendar quarter	End of each calendar quarter
Reset dates	End of each calendar quarter through March 31, 20X3	Not applicable

---

[21]A slightly different shortcut method for interest rate swaps used as cash flow hedges is illustrated in Example 5.

*These terms need not match for the assumption of no ineffectiveness to be appropriate. (Refer to paragraphs 68 and 69.)

116. The US$ LIBOR rates that are in effect at inception of the hedging relationship and at each of the quarterly reset dates are assumed to be as follows:

Reset Date	3-Month LIBOR Rate
7/1/X1	6.41%
9/30/X1	6.48%
12/31/X1	6.41%
3/31/X2	6.32%
6/30/X2	7.60%
9/30/X2	7.71%
12/31/X2	7.82%
3/31/X3	7.42%

Amounts to be reported

117. The following table summarizes the fair values of the debt and the swap at each quarter end, the details of the changes in the fair values during each quarter (including accrual and payment of interest, the effect of changes in rates, and level-yield amortization of hedge accounting adjustments), the expense for each quarter, and the net cash payments for each quarter. The calculations of fair value of both the debt and the swap are made using LIBOR. (A discussion of the appropriate discount rate appears in paragraph 70.)

	Fixed-Rate Debt	Interest Rate Swap	Expense	Net Payment
July 1, 20X1	$(1,000,000)	$ 0		
Interest accrued	(16,025)	0	$(16,025)	
Payments (receipts)	16,025	0		$ 16,025
Effect of change in rates	1,149	(1,149)	0	
September 30, 20X1	(998,851)	(1,149)	$(16,025)	$ 16,025
Interest accrued	(16,025)	(19)	$(16,044)	
Payments (receipts)	16,025	175		$ 16,200
Amortization of basis adjustments	(156)	0	(156)	
Effect of change in rates	(993)	993	0	
December 31, 20X1	(1,000,000)	0	$(16,200)	$ 16,200
Interest accrued	(16,025)	0	$(16,025)	
Payments (receipts)	16,025	0		$ 16,025
Amortization of basis adjustments	0	0	0	
Effect of change in rates	(1,074)	1,074	0	
March 31, 20X2	(1,001,074)	1,074	$(16,025)	$ 16,025
Interest accrued	(16,025)	17	$(16,008)	
Payments (receipts)	16,025	(225)		$ 15,800
Amortization of basis adjustments	208	0	208	
Effect of change in rates	12,221	(12,221)	0	
June 30, 20X2	(988,645)	(11,355)	$(15,800)	$ 15,800
Interest accrued	(16,025)	(216)	$(16,241)	
Payments (receipts)	16,025	2,975		$ 19,000
Amortization of basis adjustments	(2,759)	0	(2,759)	
Effect of change in rates	789	(789)	0	
September 30, 20X2	(990,615)	(9,385)	$(19,000)	$ 19,000
Interest accrued	(16,025)	(181)	$(16,206)	
Payments (receipts)	16,025	3,250		$ 19,275
Amortization of basis adjustments	(3,069)	0	(3,069)	
Effect of change in rates	532	(532)	0	
December 31, 20X2	(993,152)	(6,848)	$(19,275)	$ 19,275
Interest accrued	(16,025)	(134)	$(16,159)	
Payments (receipts)	16,025	3,525		$ 19,550
Amortization of basis adjustments	(3,391)	0	(3,391)	
Effect of change in rates	(978)	978	0	
March 31, 20X3	(997,521)	(2,479)	$(19,550)	$ 19,550
Interest accrued	(16,025)	(46)	$(16,071)	
Payments (receipts)	1,016,025	2,525		$1,018,550
Amortization of basis adjustments	(2,479)	0	(2,479)	
June 30, 20X3	$ 0	$ 0	$(18,550)	$1,018,550

118. The table demonstrates two important points that explain why the shortcut method described in paragraph 114 produces the same results as the computation in the above table when there is no ineffectiveness in the hedging relationship.

a. In every quarter, the effect of changes in rates on the swap completely offsets the effect of changes in rates on the debt. That is as expected because there is no ineffectiveness.

b. In every quarter except the last when the principal is repaid, the expense equals the cash payment.

119. The following table illustrates the computation of interest expense using the shortcut method described in paragraph 114. The results are the same as the results computed in the above table.

Quarter Ended	(a) Difference between Fixed Rates	(b) Variable Rate on Swap	(c) Sum (a) + (b)	(d) Debt's Principal Amount	(e) Interest Expense ((c) × (d))/4
September 30, 20X1	0.00%	6.41%	6.41%	$1,000,000	$16,025
December 31, 20X1	0.00%	6.48%	6.48%	1,000,000	16,200
March 31, 20X2	0.00%	6.41%	6.41%	1,000,000	16,025
June 30, 20X2	0.00%	6.32%	6.32%	1,000,000	15,800
September 30, 20X2	0.00%	7.60%	7.60%	1,000,000	19,000
December 31, 20X2	0.00%	7.71%	7.71%	1,000,000	19,275
March 31, 20X3	0.00%	7.82%	7.82%	1,000,000	19,550
June 30, 20X3	0.00%	7.42%	7.42%	1,000,000	18,550

120. As stated in the introduction to this example, a flat yield curve is assumed for simplicity. An upward-sloping yield curve would have made the computations more complex. Paragraph 116 would have shown different interest rates for each quarterly repricing date, and the present value of each future payment would have been computed using a different rate (as described in paragraph 112). However, the basic principles are the same. As long as there is no ineffectiveness in the hedging relationship, the shortcut method is appropriate.

Example 2A: Fair Value Hedge of the LIBOR Swap Rate in a $100,000 BBB-Quality 5-Year Fixed-Rate Noncallable Note

120A. This example illustrates one method that could be used in determining the hedged item's change in fair value attributable to changes in the benchmark interest rate. Other methods could be used in determining the hedged item's change in fair value attributable to changes in the benchmark interest rate as long as those methods meet the criteria in paragraph 21(f).

120B. On January 1, 20X0, GHI Company issues at par a $100,000 BBB-quality 5-year fixed-rate noncallable debt instrument with an annual 10 percent interest coupon. On that date, the issuer enters into a 5-year interest rate swap based on the LIBOR swap rate and designates it as the hedging instrument in a fair value hedge of the $100,000 liability. Under the terms of the swap, GHI will receive fixed interest at 7 percent and pay variable interest at LIBOR. The variable leg of the swap resets each year on December 31 for the payments due the following year. This example has been simplified by assuming that the interest rate applicable to a payment due at any future date is the same as the rate for a payment at any other date (that is, the yield curve is flat). During the hedge period, the gain or loss on the swap will be recorded in earnings. The example assumes that immediately before the interest rate on the variable leg resets on December 31, 20X0, the LIBOR swap rate increased by 50 basis points to 7.50 percent, and the change in fair value of the swap for the period from January 1 to December 31, 20X0 is a loss in value of $1,675.

Changes in the fair value of the hedged item attributable to the changes in the benchmark interest rate for a specific period

120C. Under this method, the change in a hedged item's fair value attributable to changes in the benchmark interest rate for a specific period is determined as the difference between two present value calculations as of the end of the period that exclude or include, respectively, the effect of the changes in the benchmark interest rate during the period. The discount rates used for those present value calculations would be, respectively, (a) the discount rate equal to the market interest rate for that hedged item at the inception of the hedge adjusted (up or down) for changes in the benchmark rate (designated as the interest rate risk being hedged) from the inception of the hedge to the beginning date of the period for which the change in fair value is being calculated[21a] and (b) the discount rate equal to the market interest rate for that hedged item at the inception of the hedge adjusted (up or down) for changes in the designated benchmark rate from the inception of the hedge to the ending date of the period for which the change in fair value is being calculated. Both present value calculations are computed using the estimated future cash flows for the hedged item (which typically would be its remaining contractual cash flows).

120D. In GHI's quarterly assessments of hedge effectiveness for each of the first three quarters of year 20X0 in this example, there was zero change in the hedged item's fair value attributable to changes in the benchmark interest rate because there was no change in the LIBOR swap rate. However, in the assessment for the fourth quarter 20X0, the discount rate for the beginning of the period is 10 percent (the hedged item's original market interest rate with an adjustment of zero), and the discount rate for the end of the period is 10.50 percent (the hedged item's original market interest rate adjusted for the change during the period in the LIBOR swap rate [+ 0.50 percent]).

December 31, 20X0

Calculate the present value using the beginning-of-period discount rate of 10 percent:

$10,000pmt, 10%i, 4n, PV =	$ 31,699 (interest payments)
$100,000fv, 10%i, 4n, PV =	$ 68,301 (principal payment)
Total present value	$100,000

Calculate the present value using the end-of-period discount rate of 10.50 percent (that is, the beginning-of-period discount rate adjusted for the change during the period in the LIBOR swap rate of 50 basis points):

$10,000pmt, 10.50%i, 4n, PV =	$31,359 (interest payments)
$100,000fv, 10.50%i, 4n, PV =	$67,073 (principal payment)
Total present value	$98,432

The change in fair value of the hedged item attributable to the change in the benchmark interest rate is $100,000 – $98,432 = $1,568 (the fair value decrease in the liability is a gain on debt).

When the change in fair value of the hedged item ($1,568 gain) attributable to the risk being hedged is compared with the change in fair value of the hedging instrument ($1,675 loss), ineffectiveness of $107 results. That ineffectiveness will be reported in earnings, because both changes in fair value are recorded in earnings.

Example 3: Fair Value Hedge—Using a Forward Contract to Purchase Foreign Currency to Hedge a Firm Commitment Denominated in a Different Foreign Currency

121. This example illustrates a fair value hedge of a firm commitment to purchase an asset for a price denominated in a foreign currency. In this example, the hedging instrument and the firm commitment are denominated in different foreign currencies. Consequently, the hedge is not perfectly effective, and ineffectiveness is recognized immediately in earnings.

[21a]This Statement does not provide specific guidance on the discount rate that must be used in the calculation. However, the method chosen by GHI and described in this illustration requires that the discount rate be based on the market interest rate for the hedged item at the inception of the hedging relationship.

(The entity in the example could have designed a hedge with no ineffectiveness by using a hedging instrument denominated in the same foreign currency as the firm commitment with terms that match the appropriate terms in the firm commitment.)

122. MNO Company's functional currency is the U.S. dollar. On February 3, 20X7, MNO enters into a firm commitment to purchase a machine for delivery on May 1, 20X7. The price of the machine will be 270,000 Dutch guilders (Dfl270,000). Also on February 3, 20X7, MNO enters into a forward contract to purchase 240,000 Deutsche marks (DM240,000) on May 1, 20X7. MNO will pay $0.6125 per DM1 (a total of $147,000), which is the current forward rate for an exchange on May 1, 20X7. MNO designates the forward contract as a hedge of its risk of changes in the fair value of the firm commitment resulting from changes in the U.S. dollar–Dutch guilder forward exchange rate.

123. MNO will assess effectiveness by comparing the overall changes in the fair value of the forward contract to the changes in fair value in U.S. dollars of the firm commitment due to changes in U.S. dollar–Dutch guilder forward exchange rates. MNO expects

the forward contract to be highly effective as a hedge because:

a. DM240,000 is approximately equal to Dfl270,000 at the May 1, 20X1 forward exchange rate in effect on February 3, 20X7.
b. Settlement of the forward contract and the firm commitment will occur on the same date.
c. In recent years, changes in the value in U.S. dollars of Deutsche marks over three-month periods have been highly correlated with changes in the value in U.S. dollars of Dutch guilders over those same periods.

Ineffectiveness will result from the difference between changes in the U.S. dollar equivalent of DM240,000 (the notional amount of the forward contract) and changes in the U.S. dollar equivalent of Dfl270,000 (the amount to be paid for the machine). The difference between the spot rate and the forward exchange rate is not excluded from the hedging relationship because changes in the fair value of the firm commitment are being measured using forward exchange rates.[22]

124. The forward exchange rates in effect on certain key dates are assumed to be as follows:

Date	$-DM Forward Exchange Rate for Settlement on 5/1/X7	$-Dfl Forward Exchange Rate for Settlement on 5/1/X7
Inception of the hedge—2/3/X7	$0.6125 = DM1	$0.5454 = Dfl1
Quarter end—3/31/X7	$0.5983 = DM1	$0.5317 = Dfl1
Machine purchase—5/1/X7	$0.5777 = DM1	$0.5137 = Dfl1

---

[22]If the hedged item were a foreign-currency-denominated available-for-sale security instead of a firm commitment, Statement 52 would have required its carrying value to be measured using the spot exchange rate. Therefore, the spot-forward difference would have been recognized immediately in earnings either because it represented ineffectiveness or because it was excluded from the assessment of effectiveness.

125. The U.S. dollar equivalent and changes in the U.S. dollar equivalent of the forward contract and the firm commitment, the changes in fair value of the forward contract and the firm commitment, and the ineffectiveness of the hedge on those same key dates are shown in the following table. A 6 percent discount rate is used in this example.

	2/3/X7	3/31/X7	5/1/X7
Forward contract			
$-DM forward exchange rate for settlement on May 1, 20X7	$ 0.6125	$ 0.5983	$ 0.5777
Units of currency (DM)	× 240,000	× 240,000	× 240,000
Forward price of DM240,000 in dollars	147,000	143,592	138,648
Contract price in dollars	(147,000)	(147,000)	(147,000)
Difference	$ 0	$ (3,408)	$ (8,352)
Fair value (present value of the difference)	$ 0	$ (3,391)	$ (8,352)
Change in fair value during the period		$ (3,391)	$ (4,961)
Firm commitment			
$-Dfl forward exchange rate for settlement on May 1, 20X7	$ 0.5454	$ 0.5317	$ 0.5137
Units of currency (Dfl)	× 270,000	× 270,000	× 270,000
Forward price of Dfl270,000 in dollars	(147,258)	(143,559)	(138,699)
Initial forward price in dollars	147,258	147,258	147,258
Difference	$ 0	$ 3,699	$ 8,559
Fair value (present value of the difference)	$ 0	$ 3,681	$ 8,559
Change in fair value during the period		$ 3,681	$ 4,878
Hedge ineffectiveness (difference between changes in fair values of the forward contract denominated in Deutsche marks and the firm commitment denominated in Dutch guilders)		$ 290	$ (83)

This Statement requires that MNO recognize immediately in earnings all changes in fair values of the forward contract. Because MNO is hedging the risk of changes in fair value of the firm commitment attributable to changes in the forward exchange rates, this Statement also requires recognizing those changes immediately in earnings.

126. On May 1, 20X7, MNO fulfills the firm commitment to purchase the machine and settles the forward contract. The entries illustrating fair value hedge accounting for the hedging relationship and the purchase of the machine are summarized below.

		Debit (Credit)			
	Cash	**Firm Commitment**	**Forward Contract**	**Machine**	**Earnings**
March 31, 20X7					
Recognize change in fair value of firm commitment		$ 3,681			$(3,681)
Recognize change in fair value of forward contract			$(3,391)		3,391
					(290)
April 30, 20X7					
Recognize change in fair value of firm commitment		4,878			(4,878)
Recognize change in fair value of forward contract			(4,961)		4,961
					83
May 1, 20X7					
Recognize settlement of forward contract	$ (8,352)		8,352		
Recognize purchase of machine	(138,699)	(8,559)		$147,258	
Total	$(147,051)	$ 0	$ 0	$147,258	$ (207)

Note: To simplify this example and focus on the effects of the hedging relationship, other amounts that would be involved in the purchase of the machine by MNO (for example, shipping costs and installation costs) have been ignored.

The effect of the hedge is to recognize the machine at its price in Dutch guilders (Dfl270,000) translated at the forward rate in effect at the inception of the hedge ($0 .5454 per Dfl1).

Example 4: Cash Flow Hedge of the Forecasted Sale of a Commodity Inventory

127. This example illustrates the accounting for a cash flow hedge of a forecasted sale of a commodity. The terms of the hedging derivative have been negotiated to match the terms of the forecasted transaction. Thus, there is no ineffectiveness. The assumptions in this example are similar to those in Example 1, including the assumption that there is no time value in the derivative. However, the entity has chosen to hedge the variability of the cash flows from the forecasted sale of the commodity instead of the changes in its fair value.

128. ABC Company decides to hedge the risk of changes in its cash flows relating to a forecasted sale of 100,000 bushels of Commodity A by entering into a derivative contract, Derivative Z. ABC expects to sell the 100,000 bushels of Commodity A on the last day of period 1. On the first day of period 1, ABC enters into Derivative Z and designates it as a cash flow hedge of the forecasted sale. ABC neither pays nor receives a premium on Derivative Z (that is, its fair value is zero). The hedging relationship qualifies for cash flow hedge accounting. ABC expects that there will be no ineffectiveness from the hedge because (a) the notional amount of Derivative Z is 100,000 bushels and the forecasted sale is for 100,000 bushels, (b) the underlying of Derivative Z is the price of the same variety and grade of Commodity A that ABC expects to sell (assuming delivery to ABC's selling point), and (c) the settlement date of Derivative Z is the last day of period 1 and the forecasted sale is expected to occur on the last day of period 1.

129. At inception of the hedge, the expected sales price of 100,000 bushels of Commodity A is $1,100,000. On the last day of period 1, the fair value of Derivative Z has increased by $25,000, and the expected sales price of 100,000 bushels of Commodity A has decreased by $25,000. Both the sale of 100,000 bushels of Commodity A and the settlement of Derivative Z occur on the last day of period 1. The following table illustrates the accounting, including the net impact on earnings and other comprehensive income (OCI), for the situation described above.

	Debit (Credit)			
	Cash	Derivative	OCI	Earnings
Recognize change in fair value of derivative		$ 25,000	$(25,000)	
Recognize revenue from sale	$1,075,000			$(1,075,000)
Recognize settlement of derivative	25,000	(25,000)		
Reclassify change in fair value of derivative to earnings			25,000	(25,000)
Total	$1,100,000	$ 0	$ 0	$(1,100,000)

130. At the inception of the hedge, ABC anticipated that it would receive $1,100,000 from the sale of 100,000 bushels of Commodity A. The above example illustrates that by hedging the risk of changes in its cash flows relating to the forecasted sale of 100,000 bushels of Commodity A, ABC still received a total of $1,100,000 in cash flows even though the sales price of Commodity A declined during the period.

Example 5: Cash Flow Hedge of Variable-Rate Interest-Bearing Asset

Purpose of the example

131. This example demonstrates the mechanics of accounting for an interest rate swap used as a cash flow hedge of variable interest receipts. It is not intended to demonstrate how to compute the fair value of an interest rate swap. As in Example 2, the zero-coupon method[23] is used to determine the fair values. (Unlike Example 2, the yield curve in this example is assumed to be upward sloping, that is, interest rates are higher for payments due further into the future). In this example, the term, notional amount, and repricing date of the interest rate swap match the term, repricing date, and principal amount of the interest-bearing asset on which the hedged interest receipts are due. The swap terms are "at the market" (as described in paragraphs 68 and 69), so it has a zero value at inception. Thus, the reporting entity is permitted to assume that there will be no ineffectiveness.

132. A shortcut method can be used to produce the same reporting results as the method illustrated in this example. This shortcut is only appropriate if the assumption of no ineffectiveness applies for an interest rate swap used as a cash flow hedge of interest receipts on a variable-rate asset (or interest payments on a variable-rate liability). The steps in the shortcut method are as follows:[24]

a. Determine the difference between the variable rate to be paid on the swap and the variable rate to be received on the bonds.
b. Combine that difference with the fixed rate to be received on the swap.
c. Compute and recognize interest income using that combined rate and the variable-rate asset's principal amount. (Amortization of any purchase premium or discount on the asset must also be considered, although that complication is not incorporated in this example.)
d. Determine the fair value of the interest rate swap.
e. Adjust the carrying amount of the swap to its fair value and adjust other comprehensive income by an offsetting amount.

---

[23]Paragraph 112 discusses the zero-coupon method.

[24]A slightly different shortcut method for interest rate swaps used as fair value hedges is illustrated in Example 2.

Background and assumptions

133. On July 1, 20X1, XYZ Company invests $10,000,000 in variable-rate corporate bonds that pay interest quarterly at a rate equal to the 3-month US$ LIBOR rate plus 2.25 percent. The $10,000,000 principal will be repaid on June 30, 20X3.

134. Also on July 1, 20X1, XYZ enters into a two-year receive-fixed, pay-variable interest rate swap and designates it as a cash flow hedge of the variable-rate interest receipts on the corporate bonds. The risk designated as being hedged is the risk of changes in cash flows attributable to changes in the designated benchmark interest rate. XYZ designates changes in LIBOR swap rates as the benchmark interest rate in hedging interest rate risk. The terms of the interest rate swap and the corporate bonds are shown below.

	Interest Rate Swap	Corporate Bonds
Trade date and borrowing date*	July 1, 20X1	July 1, 20X1
Termination date	June 30, 20X3	June 30, 20X3
Notional amount	$10,000,000	$10,000,000
Fixed interest rate	6.65%	Not applicable
Variable interest rate[†]	3-month US$ LIBOR	3-month US$ LIBOR + 2.25%
Settlement dates and interest payment dates*	End of each calendar quarter	End of each calendar quarter
Reset dates	End of each calendar quarter through March 31, 20X3	End of each calendar quarter through March 31, 20X3

---

*These terms need not match for the assumption of no ineffectiveness to be appropriate. (Refer to paragraphs 68 and 69.)

†Only the interest rate basis (for example, LIBOR) must match. The spread over LIBOR does not invalidate the assumption of no ineffectiveness.

135. Because the conditions described in paragraph 68 are met, XYZ is permitted to assume that there is no ineffectiveness in the hedging relationship and to recognize in other comprehensive income the entire change in the fair value of the swap.

136. The three-month US$ LIBOR rates in effect at the inception of the hedging relationship and at each of the quarterly reset dates are assumed to be as follows:

Reset Date	3-Month LIBOR Rate
7/1/X1	5.56%
9/30/X1	5.63%
12/31/X1	5.56%
3/31/X2	5.47%
6/30/X2	6.75%
9/30/X2	6.86%
12/31/X2	6.97%
3/31/X3	6.57%

Amounts to be reported

137. XYZ must reclassify to earnings the amount in accumulated other comprehensive income as each interest receipt affects earnings. In determining the amounts to reclassify each quarter, it is important to recognize that the interest rate swap does not hedge the bonds. Instead, it hedges the eight variable interest payments to be received. That is, each of the eight quarterly settlements on the swap is associated with an interest payment to be received on the bonds. Under the zero-coupon method discussed in paragraph 131, the present value of each quarterly settlement is computed separately. Because each payment occurs at a different point on the yield curve, a different interest rate must be used to determine its present value. As each individual interest receipt on the bonds is recognized in earnings, the fair value of the related quarterly settlement on the swap is reclassified

to earnings. The fair values and changes in fair values of the interest rate swap and the effects on earnings and other comprehensive income (OCI) for each quarter are as follows:

	Swap Debit (Credit)	OCI Debit (Credit)	Earnings Debit (Credit)	Cash Debit (Credit)
July 1, 20X1	$ 0			
Interest accrued	0			
Payment (receipt)	(27,250)			$27,250
Effect of change in rates	52,100	$ (52,100)		
Reclassification to earnings		27,250	$(27,250)	
September 30, 20X1	24,850	(24,850)	$(27,250)	$27,250
Interest accrued	330	(330)		
Payment (receipt)	(25,500)			$25,500
Effect of change in rates	74,120	(74,120)		
Reclassification to earnings		25,500	$(25,500)	
December 31, 20X1	73,800	(73,800)	$(25,500)	$25,500
Interest accrued	1,210	(1,210)		
Payment (receipt)	(27,250)			$27,250
Effect of change in rates	38,150	(38,150)		
Reclassification to earnings		27,250	$(27,250)	
March 31, 20X2	85,910	(85,910)	$(27,250)	$27,250
Interest accrued	1,380	(1,380)		
Payment (receipt)	(29,500)			$29,500
Effect of change in rates	(100,610)	100,610		
Reclassification to earnings		29,500	$(29,500)	
June 30, 20X2	(42,820)	42,820	$(29,500)	$29,500
Interest accrued	(870)	870		
Payment (receipt)	2,500			$ (2,500)
Effect of change in rates	8,030	(8,030)		
Reclassification to earnings		(2,500)	$ 2,500	
September 30, 20X2	(33,160)	33,160	$ 2,500	$ (2,500)
Interest accrued	(670)	670		
Payment (receipt)	5,250			$ (5,250)
Effect of change in rates	6,730	(6,730)		
Reclassification to earnings		(5,250)	$ 5,250	
December 31, 20X2	(21,850)	21,850	$ 5,250	$ (5,250)
Interest accrued	(440)	440		
Payment (receipt)	8,000			$ (8,000)
Effect of change in rates	16,250	(16,250)		
Reclassification to earnings		(8,000)	$ 8,000	
March 31, 20X3	1,960	(1,960)	$ 8,000	$ (8,000)
Interest accrued	40	(40)		
Payment (receipt)	(2,000)			$ 2,000
Reclassification to earnings		2,000	$ (2,000)	
June 30, 20X3	$ 0	$ 0	$ (2,000)	$ 2,000

138. The table shows that, in each quarter, the net cash receipt or payment on the swap equals the income or expense to be recorded. The net effect on earnings of the interest on the bonds and the reclassification of gains or losses on the swap is shown below.

For the Quarter Ending		Earnings	
	Interest on Bonds	Gains (Losses) Reclassified from OCI	Net Effect
9/30/X1	$ 195,250	$27,250	$ 222,500
12/31/X1	197,000	25,500	222,500
3/31/X2	195,250	27,250	222,500
6/30/X2	193,000	29,500	222,500
9/30/X2	225,000	(2,500)	222,500
12/31/X2	227,750	(5,250)	222,500
3/31/X3	230,500	(8,000)	222,500
6/30/X3	220,500	2,000	222,500
Totals	$1,684,250	$95,750	$1,780,000

139. In this example, the shortcut method described in paragraph 132 works as follows. The difference between the variable rate on the swap and the variable rate on the asset is a net receipt of 2.25 percent. That rate combined with the 6.65 percent fixed rate received on the swap is 8.9 percent. The computed interest income is $890,000 per year or $222,500 per quarter, which is the same as the amount in the table in paragraph 138.

Example 6: Accounting for a Derivative's Gain or Loss in a Cash Flow Hedge—Effectiveness Based on the Entire Change in the Derivative's Fair Value

140. This example has been designed to illustrate application of the guidance for cash flow hedges described in paragraph 30 of this Statement. At the beginning of period 1, XYZ Company enters into a qualifying cash flow hedge of a transaction forecasted to occur early in period 6. XYZ's documented policy is to assess hedge effectiveness by comparing the changes in present value of the expected future cash flows on the forecasted transaction to all of the hedging derivative's gain or loss (that is, no time value component will be excluded as discussed in paragraph 63). In this hedging relationship, XYZ has designated changes in cash flows related to the forecasted transaction attributable to any cause as the hedged risk.

141. The following table includes the assumptions for this example and details the steps necessary to account for a cash flow hedge that is not perfectly effective.

	Fair Value of Derivative Increase (Decrease)		Present Value of Expected Future Cash Flows on Hedged Transaction Increase (Decrease)			
	(A)	(B)	(C)	(D)	(E)	(F)
Period	Change during the Period	Cumulative Change	Change during the Period	Cumulative Change	Lesser of the Two Cumulative Changes	Adjustment to OCI
1	$ 100	$100	$ (96)	$ (96)	$ 96	$ 96
2	94	194	(101)	(197)	194	98
3	(162)	32	160	(37)	32	(162)
4	(101)	(69)	103	66	(66)	(98)
5	30	(39)	(32)	34	(34)	32

Step 1: Determine the change in fair value of the derivative and the change in present value of the cash flows on the hedged transaction (columns A and C).

Step 2: Determine the cumulative changes in fair value of the derivative and the cumulative changes in present value of the cash flows on the hedged transaction (columns B and D).

Step 3: Determine the lesser of the absolute values of the two amounts in Step 2 (column E).

Step 4: Determine the change during the period in the lesser of the absolute values (column F).

Step 5: Adjust the derivative to reflect its change in fair value and adjust other comprehensive income by the amount determined in Step 4. Balance the entry, if necessary, with an adjustment to earnings.

142. The following are the entries required to account for the above cash flow hedge.

		Debit (Credit)		
Period	Description	Derivative	Earnings	OCI
1	Adjust derivative to fair value and OCI by the calculated amount	$ 100	$(4)	$ (96)
2	Adjust derivative to fair value and OCI by the calculated amount	94	4	(98)
3	Adjust derivative to fair value and OCI by the calculated amount	(162)	0	162
4	Adjust derivative to fair value and OCI by the calculated amount	(101)	3	98
5	Adjust derivative to fair value and OCI by the calculated amount	30	2	(32)

143. The following table reconciles the beginning and ending balances in accumulated other comprehensive income.

	Accumulated Other Comprehensive Income—Debit (Credit)			
Period	Beginning Balance	Change in Fair Value	Reclassification	Ending Balance
1	$ 0	$ (96)	$ 0	$ (96)
2	(96)	(94)	(4)	(194)
3	(194)	162	0	(32)
4	(32)	98	0	66
5	66	(30)	(2)	34

The reclassification column relates to reclassifications between earnings and other comprehensive income. In period 2, the $(4) in that column relates to the prior period's derivative gain that was previously recognized in earnings. That amount is reclassified to other comprehensive income in period 2 because the cumulative gain on the derivative is less than the amount necessary to offset the cumulative change in the present value of expected future cash flows on the hedged transaction. In period 5, the $(2) in the reclassification column relates to the derivative loss that was recognized in other comprehensive income in a prior period. At the end of period 4, the derivative's cumulative loss of $69 was greater in absolute terms than the $66 increase in the present value of expected future cash flows on the hedged transaction. That $3 excess had been recognized in earnings during period 4. In period 5, the value of the derivative increased (and reduced the cumulative loss) by $30. The present value of the expected cash flows on the hedged transaction decreased (and reduced the cumulative increase) by $32. The gain on the derivative in period 5 was $2 smaller, in absolute terms, than the decrease in the present value of the expected cash flows on the hedged transaction. Consequently, the entire gain on the derivative is recognized in other comprehensive income. In addition, in absolute terms, the $3 cumulative excess of the loss on the derivative over the increase in the present value of the expected cash flows on the hedged transaction (which had previously been recognized in earnings) increased to $5. As a result, $2 is reclassified from other comprehensive income to earnings so that the $5 cumulative excess has been recognized in earnings.

Example 7: Designation and Discontinuance of a Cash Flow Hedge of the Forecasted Purchase of Inventory

144. This example illustrates the effect on earnings and other comprehensive income of discontinuing a cash flow hedge by dedesignating the hedging derivative before the variability of the cash flows from the hedged forecasted transaction has been eliminated. It also discusses the effect that the location of a physical asset has on the effectiveness of a hedging relationship.

145. On February 3, 20X1, JKL Company forecasts the purchase of 100,000 bushels of corn on May 20, 20X1. It expects to sell finished products produced from the corn on May 31, 20X1. On February 3, 20X1, JKL enters into 20 futures contracts, each for the purchase of 5,000 bushels of corn on May 20, 20X1 (100,000 in total) and immediately designates those contracts as a hedge of the forecasted purchase of corn.

146. JKL chooses to assess effectiveness by comparing the entire change in fair value of the futures contracts to changes in the cash flows on the forecasted transaction. JKL estimates its cash flows on the forecasted transaction based on the futures price of corn adjusted for the difference between the cost of corn delivered to Chicago and the cost of corn delivered to Minneapolis. JKL does not choose to use a tailing strategy (as described in paragraph 64). JKL expects changes in fair value of the futures contracts to be highly effective at offsetting changes in the expected cash outflows for the forecasted purchase of corn because (a) the futures contracts are for the same variety and grade of corn that JKL plans to purchase and

---

[24a][This footnote has been deleted. See Status page.]

(b) on May 20, 20X1, the futures price for delivery on May 20, 20X1 will be equal to the spot price (because futures prices and spot prices converge as the delivery date approaches). However, the hedge may not be perfectly effective. JKL will purchase corn for delivery to its production facilities in Minneapolis, but the price of the futures contracts is based on delivery of corn to Chicago. If the difference between the price of corn delivered to Chicago and the price of corn delivered to Minneapolis changes during the period of the hedge, the effect of that change will be included currently in earnings according to the provisions of paragraph 30 of this Statement.

147. On February 3, 20X1, the futures price of corn for delivery to Chicago on May 20, 20X1 is $2.6875 per bushel resulting in a total price of $268,750 for 100,000 bushels.

148. On May 1, 20X1, JKL dedesignates the related futures contracts and closes them out by entering into offsetting contracts on the same exchange. As of that date, JKL had recognized in accumulated other comprehensive income gains on the futures contracts of $26,250. JKL still plans to purchase 100,000 bushels of corn on May 20, 20X1. Consequently, the gains that occurred prior to dedesignation will remain in other comprehensive income until the finished product is sold. If JKL had not closed out the futures contracts when it dedesignated them, any further gains or losses would have been recognized in earnings.

149. On May 20, 20X1, JKL purchases 100,000 bushels of corn, and on May 31, 20X1, JKL sells the finished product.

150. The futures prices of corn that are in effect on key dates are assumed to be as follows:

Date	Futures Price per Bushel for Delivery to Chicago on May 20, 20X1	Futures Price Adjusted for Delivery to Minneapolis on May 20, 20X1
Inception of hedging relationship—February 3, 20X1	$2.6875	$2.7375
End of quarter—March 31, 20X1	3.1000	3.1500
Discontinue hedge—May 1, 20X1	2.9500	3.0000
Purchase of corn—May 20, 20X1	2.8500	2.9000

151. The changes in fair value of the futures contracts between inception (February 3, 20X1) and discontinuation (May 1, 20X1) of the hedge are as follows:

	February 3– March 31, 20X1	April 1– May 1, 20X1
Futures price at beginning of period	$ 2.6875	$ 3.1000
Futures price at end of period	3.1000	2.9500
Change in price per bushel	0.4125	(0.1500)
Bushels under contract (20 contracts @ 5,000 bushels each)	× 100,000	× 100,000
Change in fair value—gain (loss)	$ 41,250	$ (15,000)

152. The following table displays the entries to recognize the effects of (a) entering into futures contracts as a hedge of the forecasted purchase of corn, (b) dedesignating and closing out the futures contracts, (c) completing the forecasted purchase of corn, and (d) selling the finished products produced from the corn. Because the difference in prices between corn delivered to Chicago and corn delivered to Minneapolis ($.05 per bushel, as illustrated in paragraph 150) did not change during the period of the hedge, no ineffectiveness is recognized in earnings. If that difference had changed, the resulting ineffectiveness would have been recognized immediately in earnings.

	Debit (Credit)			
	Cash	Inventory	OCI	Earnings
March 31, 20X1 (end of quarter)				
Recognize change in fair value of futures contracts	$ 41,250		$(41,250)	
May 1, 20X1 (discontinue hedge)				
Recognize change in fair value of futures contracts	(15,000)		15,000	
May 20, 20X1				
Recognize purchase of corn	(290,000)	$ 290,000		
May 31, 20X1				
Recognize cost of sale of product		(290,000)		$290,000
Reclassify changes in fair value of futures contracts to earnings			26,250	(26,250)
Total	$(263,750)	$ 0	$ 0	$263,750

Note: To simplify this example and focus on the effects of the hedging relationship, the margin account with the clearinghouse and certain amounts that would be involved in a sale of JKL's inventory (for example, additional costs of production, selling costs, and sales revenue) have been ignored.

The effect of the hedging strategy is that the cost of the corn recognized in earnings when the finished product was sold was $263,750. If the hedging relationship had not been discontinued early, the cost recognized in earnings would have been $273,750, which was the futures price of the corn, adjusted for delivery to Minneapolis, at the inception of the hedge. Without the strategy, JKL would have recognized $290,000, which was the price of corn delivered to Minneapolis at the time it was purchased.

Example 8: Changes in a Cash Flow Hedge of Forecasted Interest Payments with an Interest Rate Swap

Background

153. This example describes the effects on earnings and other comprehensive income of certain changes in a cash flow hedging relationship. It presents two different scenarios. In the first, the variability of the hedged interest payments is eliminated before the hedging derivative expires. In the second, the interest rate index that is the basis for the hedged interest payments is changed to a different index before the hedging derivative expires.

154. MNO Company enters into an interest rate swap (Swap 1) and designates it as a hedge of the variable quarterly interest payments on the company's 5-year $5 million borrowing program, initially expected to be accomplished by a series of $5 million notes with 90-day terms. MNO plans to continue issuing new 90-day notes over the next five years as each outstanding note matures. The interest on each note will be determined based on LIBOR at the time each note is issued. Swap 1 requires a settlement every 90 days, and the variable interest rate is reset immediately following each payment. MNO pays a fixed rate of interest (6.5 percent) and receives interest at LIBOR. MNO neither pays nor receives a premium at the inception of Swap 1. The notional amount of the contract is $5 million, and it expires in 5 years.

155. Because Swap 1 and the hedged forecasted interest payments are based on the same notional amount, have the same reset dates, and are based on the same benchmark interest rate designated under paragraph 29(h), MNO may conclude that there will be no ineffectiveness in the hedging relationship (absent a default by the swap counterparty).

Scenario 1—Two undesignated interest rate swaps

156. At the end of the second year of the 5-year hedging relationship, MNO discontinues its practice of issuing 90-day notes. Instead, MNO issues a 3-year, $5 million note with a fixed rate of interest (7.25 percent). Because the interest rate on the three-year note is fixed, the variability of the future interest payments has been eliminated. Thus, Swap 1 no longer qualifies for cash flow hedge accounting. However, the net gain or loss on Swap 1 in accumulated other comprehensive income is not reclassified to earnings immediately. Immediate reclassification is required (and permitted) only if it becomes probable that the hedged transactions (future interest payments) will not occur. The variability of the payments has been eliminated, but it still is probable that they will occur. Thus, those gains or losses will continue to be reclassified from accumulated other comprehensive income to earnings as the interest payments affect earnings (as required by paragraph 31).[25]

157. Rather than liquidate the pay-fixed, receive-variable Swap 1, MNO enters into a pay-variable, receive-fixed interest rate swap (Swap 2) with a 3-year term and a notional amount of $5 million. MNO neither pays nor receives a premium. Like Swap 1, Swap 2 requires a settlement every 90 days and reprices immediately following each settlement. The relationship between 90-day interest rates and longer term rates has changed since MNO entered into Swap 1 (that is, the shape of the yield curve is different). As a result, Swap 2 has different terms and its settlements do not exactly offset the settlements on Swap 1. Under the terms of Swap 2, MNO will receive a fixed rate of 7.25 percent and pay interest at LIBOR.

158. The two swaps are not designated as hedging instruments and are reported at fair value. The changes in fair value are reported immediately in earnings and offset each other to a significant degree.

Scenario 2—Two interest rate swaps designated as a hedge of future variable interest payments

159. At the end of the second year of the 5-year hedging relationship, MNO discontinues its practice of issuing 90-day notes and issues a 3-year, $5 million note with a rate of interest that adjusts every 90 days to the prime rate quoted on that day. Swap 1 is no longer effective as a cash flow hedge because the receive-variable rate on the swap is LIBOR, and the prime rate and LIBOR are expected to change differently. Thus, the cash flows from the swap will not effectively offset changes in cash flows from the three-year note.

160. The net gain or loss on Swap 1 in accumulated other comprehensive income as of the date MNO issues the three-year note is not reclassified into earnings immediately. Immediate reclassification would be required only if it becomes probable that the hedged transactions (future interest payments) will not occur. The expected amounts of those payments have changed (because they will be based on prime instead of LIBOR, as originally expected), but it still is probable that the payments will occur. Thus, those gains or losses will continue to be reclassified to earnings as the interest payments affect earnings.

161. Rather than liquidate Swap 1 and obtain a separate derivative to hedge the variability of the prime-rate-based interest payments, MNO enters into a pay-LIBOR, receive-prime basis swap. The basis swap has a $5 million notional amount and a 3-year term and requires a settlement every 90 days. MNO designates Swap 1 and the basis swap in combination as the hedging instrument in a cash flow hedge of the variable interest payments on the three-year note. On the three-year note, MNO pays interest at prime. On the basis swap, MNO receives interest at prime and pays interest at LIBOR. On Swap 1, MNO receives interest at LIBOR and pays interest at 6.5 percent. Together, the cash flows from the two derivatives are effective at offsetting changes in the interest payments on the three-year note. Changes in fair values of the two swaps are recognized in other comprehensive income and are reclassified to earnings when the hedged forecasted transactions (the variable interest payments) affect earnings (as required by paragraph 31).

---

[25]If the term of the fixed rate note had been longer than three years, the amounts in accumulated other comprehensive income still would have been reclassified into earnings over the next three years, which was the term of the designated hedging relationship.

Example 9: Accounting for a Derivative's Gain or Loss in a Cash Flow Hedge—Effectiveness Based on Changes in Intrinsic Value

162. This example illustrates application of the accounting guidance for cash flow hedges described in paragraph 30 of this Statement. At the beginning of period 1, XYZ Company purchases for $9.25 an at-the-money call option on 1 unit of Commodity X with a strike price of $125.00 to hedge a purchase of 1 unit of that commodity projected to occur early in period 5. XYZ's documented policy is to assess hedge effectiveness by comparing changes in cash flows on the hedged transaction (based on changes in the spot price) with changes in the option contract's intrinsic value. Because the hedging instrument is a purchased call option, its intrinsic value cannot be less than zero. If the price of the commodity is less than the option's strike price, the option is out-of-the-money. Its intrinsic value cannot decrease further regardless of how far the commodity price falls, and the intrinsic value will not increase until the commodity price increases to exceed the strike price. Thus, changes in cash flows from the option due to changes in its intrinsic value will offset changes in cash flows on the forecasted purchase only when the option is in-the-money or at-the-money. That phenomenon is demonstrated in period 3 in the following table when the commodity price declines by $1.25. Because the commodity price is $.75 below the option's strike price, the option's intrinsic value declines by only $.50 (to zero). The effect reverses in period 4 when the commodity price increases by $6.50 and the option's intrinsic value increases by $5.75.

	Period 1	Period 2	Period 3	Period 4
Assumptions				
Ending market price of Commodity X	$127.25	$125.50	$124.25	$130.75
Ending fair value of option:				
Time value	$ 7.50	$ 5.50	$ 3.00	$ 0.00
Intrinsic value	2.25	0.50	0.00	5.75
Total	$ 9.75	$ 6.00	$ 3.00	$ 5.75
Change in time value	$ (1.75)	$ (2.00)	$ (2.50)	$ (3.00)
Change in intrinsic value	2.25	(1.75)	(0.50)	5.75
Total current-period gain (loss) on derivative	$ 0.50	$ (3.75)	$ (3.00)	$ 2.75
Gain (loss) on derivative, adjusted to remove the component excluded from effectiveness test:				
For the current period	$ 2.25	$ (1.75)	$ (0.50)	$ 5.75
Cumulative	2.25	0.50	0.00	5.75
Change in expected future cash flows on hedged transaction:				
For the current period	(2.25)	1.75	1.25	(6.50)
Cumulative	(2.25)	(0.50)	0.75	(5.75)
Balance to be reflected in accumulated other comprehensive income (paragraph 30(b))				
Lesser (in absolute amounts) of derivative's cumulative gain (loss) or amount necessary to offset the cumulative change in expected future cash flows on hedged transaction	$ 2.25	$ 0.50	$ 0.00	$ 5.75

163. The following are the entries required to account for the above cash flow hedge. The steps involved in determining the amounts are the same as in Example 6.

Period	Description	Debit (Credit)		
		Derivative	Earnings	OCI
1	Adjust derivative to fair value and OCI by the calculated amount	$ 0.50	$1.75	$(2.25)
2	Adjust derivative to fair value and OCI by the calculated amount	(3.75)	2.00	1.75
3	Adjust derivative to fair value and OCI by the calculated amount	(3.00)	2.50	0.50
4	Adjust derivative to fair value and OCI by the calculated amount	2.75	3.00	(5.75)

164. The following table reconciles the beginning and ending balances in accumulated other comprehensive income.

	Accumulated Other Comprehensive Income—Debit (Credit)		
Period	Beginning Balance	Change in Intrinsic Value	Ending Balance
1	$ 0.00	$(2.25)	$(2.25)
2	(2.25)	1.75	(0.50)
3	(0.50)	0.50	0.00
4	0.00	(5.75)	(5.75)

The amount reflected in earnings relates to the component excluded from the effectiveness test, that is, the time value component. No reclassifications between other comprehensive income and earnings of the type illustrated in Example 6 are required because no hedge ineffectiveness is illustrated in this example. (The change in cash flows from the hedged transaction was not fully offset in period 3. However, that is not considered ineffectiveness. As described in paragraph 20(b), a purchased call option is considered effective if it provides one-sided offset.)

Example 10: Cash Flow Hedge of the Foreign Currency Exposure in a Royalty Arrangement

165. This example illustrates the accounting for a hedging relationship involving a single hedging derivative and three separate forecasted transactions. The three transactions occur on three separate dates, but the payment on receivables related to all three occurs on the same date. The settlement of the hedging derivative will occur on the date the receivable is paid.

166. DEF Company's functional currency is the U.S. dollar. ZYX's functional currency is the Deutsche mark (DM). Effective January 1, 20X1, DEF enters into a royalty agreement with ZYX Company that gives ZYX the right to use DEF's technology in manufacturing Product X. On April 30, 20X1, ZYX will pay DEF a royalty of DM1 million for each unit of Product X sold by that date. DEF expects ZYX to sell one unit of Product X on January 31, one on February 28, and one on March 31. The forecasted royalty is probable because ZYX has identified a demand for Product X and no other supplier has the capacity to fill that demand.

167. Also on January 1, 20X1, DEF enters into a forward contract to sell DM3 million on April 30, 20X1 for a price equal to the forward price of $0.6057 per Deutsche mark. DEF designates the forward contract as a hedge of the risk of changes in its functional-currency-equivalent cash flows attributable to changes in the Deutsche mark–U.S. dollar exchange rates related to the forecasted receipt of DM3 million from the royalty agreement. The spot price and forward price of Deutsche marks at January 1, 20X1 and the U.S. dollar equivalent of DM3 million at those prices are assumed to be as follows:

Prices at January 1, 20X1	$ per DM	$ Equivalent of DM3 Million
Spot price	$0.6019	$1,805,700
4-month forward price	0.6057	1,817,100

168. DEF will exclude from its assessment of effectiveness the portion of the fair value of the forward contract attributable to the spot-forward difference (the difference between the spot exchange rate and the forward exchange rate). That is, DEF will recognize changes in that portion of the derivative's fair value in earnings but will not consider those changes to represent ineffectiveness. DEF will estimate the cash flows on the forecasted transactions based on the current spot exchange rate and will discount that amount. Thus, DEF will assess effectiveness by comparing (a) changes in the fair value of the forward contract attributable to changes in the dollar spot price of Deutsche marks and (b) changes in the present value of the forecasted cash flows based on the current spot exchange rate. Those two changes will exactly offset because the currency and the notional amount of the forward contract match the currency and the total of the expected foreign currency amounts of the forecasted transactions. Thus, if DEF dedesignates a proportion of the forward contract each time a royalty is earned (as described in the following paragraph), the hedging relationship will meet the "highly effective" criterion.

169. As each royalty is earned, DEF recognizes a receivable and royalty income. The forecasted transaction (the earning of royalty income) has occurred. The receivable is an asset, not a forecasted transaction, and would separately be eligible to be designated as a fair value hedge of foreign exchange risk or continue to be eligible as a cash flow hedge of foreign exchange risk. Consequently, if the variability of the functional currency cash flows related to the royalty receivable is not being hedged, DEF will dedesignate a proportion of the hedging instrument in the original hedge relationship with respect to the proportion of the forward contract corresponding to the earned royalty. As the royalty is recognized in earnings and each proportion of the derivative is dedesignated, the related derivative gain or loss in accumulated other comprehensive income is reclassified into earnings. After that date, any gain or loss on the dedesignated proportion of the derivative and any transaction loss or gain on the royalty receivable[26] will be recognized in earnings and may substantially offset each other.

170. The spot prices and forward prices for settlement on April 30, 20X1 in effect at inception of the hedge (January 1, 20X1) and at the end of each month between inception and April 30, 20X1 are assumed to be as follows:

| | **$ per DM** | |
	Spot Price	Forward Price for Settlement on 4/30/X1
January 1	$0.6019	$0.6057
January 31	0.5970	0.6000
February 28	0.5909	0.5926
March 31	0.5847	0.5855
April 30	0.5729	0.5729

---

[26]Statement 52 requires immediate recognition in earnings of any foreign currency transaction gain or loss on a foreign-currency-denominated receivable that is not designated as a hedging instrument. Therefore, the effect of changes in spot prices on the royalty receivable must be recognized immediately in earnings.

171. The changes in fair value of the forward contract that are recognized each month in earnings and other comprehensive income are shown in the following table. The fair value of the forward is the present value of the difference between the U.S. dollars to be received on the forward ($1,817,100) and the U.S. dollar equivalent of DM3 million based on the current forward rate. A 6 percent discount rate is used in this example.

	Debit (Credit)		
	Forward Contract	Earnings	OCI
Fair value on January 1	$ 0		
Period ended January 31:			
Change in spot-forward difference	2,364	$ (2,364)	
Change in fair value of dedesignated proportion	0	0	
Change in fair value of designated proportion	14,482		$(14,482)
Reclassification of gain	0	(4,827)	4,827
Fair value on January 31	16,846		
Period ended February 28:			
Change in spot-forward difference	3,873	(3,873)	
Change in fair value of dedesignated proportion	6,063	(6,063)	
Change in fair value of designated proportion	12,127		(12,127)
Reclassification of gain	0	(10,891)	10,891
Fair value on February 28	38,909		
Period ended March 31:			
Change in spot-forward difference	2,718	(2,718)	
Change in fair value of dedesignated proportion	12,458	(12,458)	
Change in fair value of designated proportion	6,213		(6,213)
Reclassification of gain	0	(17,104)	17,104
Fair value on March 31	60,298		
Period ended April 30:			
Change in spot-forward difference	2,445	(2,445)	
Change in fair value of dedesignated proportion	35,657	(35,657)	
Change in fair value of designated proportion	0		0
Fair value on April 30	$98,400		
Cumulative effect		$(98,400)	$ 0

172. The effect on earnings of the royalty agreement and hedging relationship illustrated in this example is summarized by month in the following table.

	Amounts Recognized in Earnings Related to					
	Receivable		Forward Contract			
Period Ended	$ Equivalent of DM1 Million Royalty	Foreign Currency Transaction Gain (Loss)	Amount Attributable to the Dedesignated Proportion	Reclassifications from OCI	Amount Attributable to the Difference between the Spot and Forward Rates	Total Amount Reported in Earnings
January 31	$ 597,000	$　0	$　0	$ 4,827	$ 2,364	$ 604,191
February 28	590,900	(6,100)	6,063	10,891	3,873	605,627
March 31	584,700	(12,400)	12,458	17,104	2,718	604,580
April 30	0	(35,400)	35,657	0	2,445	2,702
	$1,772,600	$(53,900)	$54,178	$32,822	$11,400	$1,817,100

$98,400

Example 11: Reporting Cash Flow Hedges in Comprehensive Income and Accumulated Other Comprehensive Income

173. TUV Company's cash flow hedge transactions following adoption of this Statement through the end of 20X4 are as follows:

a. It continually purchases pork belly futures contracts to hedge its anticipated purchases of pork belly inventory.

b. In 20X2, it entered into a Deutsche mark forward exchange contract to hedge the foreign currency risk associated with the expected purchase of a pork belly processing machine with a five-year life that it bought from a vendor in Germany at the end of 20X2.

c. In 20X2, it entered into a 10-year interest rate swap concurrent with the issuance of 10-year variable rate debt (cash flow hedge of future variable interest payments).

d. In January 20X4, it entered into a two-year French franc forward exchange contract to hedge a forecasted export sale (denominated in French francs, expected to occur in December 20X5) of hot dogs to a large customer in France. In June 20X4, it closed the forward contract, but the forecasted transaction is still expected to occur.

174. The following table reconciles the beginning and ending accumulated other comprehensive income balances for 20X4. It supports the comprehensive income display and disclosures that are required under Statement 130, as amended by this Statement. It is assumed that there are no other amounts in accumulated other comprehensive income. The after-tax amounts assume a 30 percent effective tax rate.

	Other Comprehensive Income—Debit (Credit)			
	Accumulated Other Comprehensive Income as of 1/1/X4	Changes in Fair Value Recognized in 20X4	Reclassification Adjustments	Accumulated Other Comprehensive Income as of 12/31/X4
Derivatives designated as hedges of:				
Inventory purchases	$230	$ 85	$(270)	$ 45
Equipment purchase	120		(30)	90
Variable interest rate payments	(40)	10	5	(25)
Export sale	0	(50)	0	(50)
Before-tax totals	$310	$ 45	$(295)	$ 60
After-tax totals	$217	$ 32	$(207)	$ 42

175. The following table illustrates an acceptable method, under the provisions of Statement 130 as amended by this Statement, of reporting the transactions described in paragraphs 173 and 174 in earnings, comprehensive income, and shareholders' equity.

Effect of Selected Items on Earnings and Comprehensive Income
Year Ended December 31, 20X4

	Debit (Credit)
Effect on earnings before taxes:	
Cost of goods sold	$ 270
Depreciation	30
Interest	(5)
Total	295
Income tax effect	(88)*
Effect on earnings after taxes	$ 207
Other comprehensive income, net of tax:	
Cash flow hedges:	
Net derivative losses, net of tax effect of $13	32
Reclassification adjustments, net of tax effect of $88	(207)
Net change	(175)
Effect on total comprehensive income	$ 32

---

*This example assumes that it is appropriate under the circumstances, in accordance with FASB Statement No. 109, *Accounting for Income Taxes,* to recognize the related income tax benefit in the current year.

Effect of Selected Items on Shareholders' Equity
Year Ended December 31, 20X4
Debit (Credit)

Accumulated other comprehensive income:	
Balance on December 31, 20X3	$ 217
Net change during the year related to cash flow hedges	(175)
Balance on December 31, 20X4	$ 42

Section 2: Examples Illustrating Application of the Clearly-and-Closely-Related Criterion to Derivative Instruments Embedded in Hybrid Instruments

176. The following examples in Section 2 discuss instruments that contain a variety of embedded derivative instruments. They illustrate how the provisions of paragraphs 12–16 of this Statement would be applied to contracts with the described terms. If the terms of a contract are different from the described terms, the application of this Statement by either party to the contract may be affected. Furthermore, if any contract of the types discussed in Section 2 meets the definition of a derivative instrument in its entirety under paragraphs 6–9 and related paragraphs, the guidance in this section for the application of the provisions of paragraphs 12–16 to embedded derivative instruments does not apply. The illustrative instruments and related assumptions in Examples 12–27 are based on examples in Exhibit 96-12A of EITF Issue No. 96-12, "Recognition of Interest Income and Balance Sheet Classification of Structured Notes."

177. Specifically, each example (a) provides a brief discussion of the terms of an instrument that contains an embedded derivative and (b) analyzes the instrument (as of the date of inception) in relation to the provisions of paragraphs 12–16 that require an embedded derivative to be accounted for according to this Statement if it is not clearly and closely related to the host contract. Unless otherwise stated, the examples are based on the assumptions (1) that if the embedded derivative and host portions of the contract are not clearly and closely related, a separate instrument with the same terms as the embedded derivative would meet the scope requirements in paragraphs 6–11 and (2) that the contract is not remeasured at fair value under otherwise applicable generally accepted accounting principles with changes in fair value currently included in earnings.

178. **Example 12: Inverse Floater.** A bond with a coupon rate of interest that varies inversely with changes in specified general interest rate levels or indexes (for example, LIBOR).

Example: Coupon = 5.25 percent for 3 months to July 1994; thereafter at 8.75 percent – 6-month US$ LIBOR to January 1995. "Stepping" option allows for spread and caps to step semiannually to maturity.

Scope Application: An inverse floater contains an embedded derivative (a fixed-for-floating interest rate swap) that is referenced to an interest rate index (in this example, LIBOR) that alters net interest payments that otherwise would be paid by the debtor or received by the investor on an interest-bearing host contract. If the embedded derivative could potentially result in the investor's not recovering substantially all of its initial recorded investment in the bond (that is, if the inverse floater contains no floor to prevent any erosion of principal due to a negative interest rate), the embedded derivative is not considered to be clearly and closely related to the host contract (refer to paragraph 13(a)). In that case, the embedded derivative should be separated from the host contract and accounted for by both parties pursuant to the provisions of this Statement. (In this example, there appears to be no possibility of the embedded derivative increasing the investor's rate of return on the host contract to an amount that is at least double the initial rate of return on the host contract [refer to paragraph 13(b)].) In contrast, if the embedded derivative could not potentially result in the investor's failing to recover substantially all of its initial recorded investment in the bond, the embedded derivative is considered to be clearly and closely related to the host contract and separate accounting for the derivative is neither required nor permitted.

179. **Example 13: Levered Inverse Floater.** A bond with a coupon that varies indirectly with

changes in general interest rate levels and applies a multiplier (greater than 1.00) to the specified index in its calculation of interest.

Example: Accrues at 6 percent to June 1994; thereafter at 14.55 percent – (2.5 × 3-month US$ LIBOR).

Scope Application: A levered inverse floater can be viewed as an inverse floater in which the embedded interest rate swap is leveraged. Similar to Example 12, the embedded derivative would not be clearly and closely related to the host contract if it potentially could result in the investor's not recovering substantially all of its initial recorded investment in the bond (refer to paragraph 13(a)) because there is no floor to the interest rate. In that case, the embedded derivative (the leveraged interest rate swap) should be separated from the host contract and accounted for by both parties pursuant to the provisions of this Statement. In contrast, if an embedded derivative could not potentially result in the investor's failing to recover substantially all of its initial recorded investment in the bond and if there was no possibility of the embedded derivative increasing the investor's rate of return on the host contract to an amount that is at least double the initial rate of return on the host contract (refer to paragraph 13(b)), the embedded derivative is considered to be clearly and closely related to the host contract and no separate accounting for the derivative is required or permitted.

180. **Example 14: Delevered Floater.** A bond with a coupon rate of interest that lags overall movements in specified general interest rate levels or indices.

Example: Coupon = (.5 × 10-year constant maturity treasuries (CMT)) + 1.25 percent.

Scope Application: A delevered floater may be viewed as containing an embedded derivative (a deleveraged swap or a series of forward agreements) that is referenced to an interest rate index (for example, 50 percent of 10-year CMT) that alters net interest payments that otherwise would be paid or received on an interest-bearing host contract but could not potentially result in the investor's failing to recover substantially all of its initial recorded investment in the bond (refer to paragraph 13(a)). (In this example, there appears to be no possibility of the embedded derivative increasing the investor's rate of return on the host

contract to an amount that is at least double the initial rate of return on the host contract [refer to paragraph 13(b)].) The embedded derivative is considered to be clearly and closely related to the host contract as described in paragraph 13 of this Statement. Therefore, the embedded derivative should *not* be separated from the host contract.

181. **Example 15: Range Floater.** A bond with a coupon that depends on the *number of days* that a reference rate stays within a preestablished collar; otherwise, the bond pays either zero percent interest or a below-market rate.

Example: Standard range floater—The investor receives 5.5 percent on *each day* that 3-month US$ LIBOR is between 3 percent and 4 percent, with the upper limit increasing annually after a specified date. The coupon will be equal to zero percent for each day that 3-month US$ LIBOR is *outside* that range.

Scope Application: A range floater may be viewed as containing embedded derivatives (two written conditional exchange option contracts with notional amounts equal to the par value of the fixed-rate instrument) that are referenced to an interest rate index (in this example, LIBOR) that alter net interest payments that otherwise would be paid by the debtor or received by the investor on an interest-bearing host contract but could not potentially result in the investor's failing to recover substantially all of its initial recorded investment in the bond (refer to paragraph 13(a)). In this example, there appears to be no possibility of increasing the investor's rate of return on the host contract to an amount that is at least double the initial rate of return on the host contract (refer to paragraph 13(b)). The embedded derivatives are considered to be clearly and closely related to the host contract as described in paragraph 13 of this Statement. Therefore, the embedded derivatives should *not* be separated from the host contract.

182. **Example 16: Ratchet Floater.** A bond that pays a floating rate of interest and has an adjustable cap, adjustable floor, or both that move in sync with each new reset rate.

Example: Coupon = 3-month US$ LIBOR + 50 basis points. In addition to having a lifetime cap of 7.25 percent, the coupon will be collared each period between the previous coupon and the previous coupon plus 25 basis points.

Scope Application: A ratchet floater may be viewed as containing embedded derivatives (combinations of purchased and written options that create changing caps and floors) that are referenced to an interest rate index (in this example, LIBOR) that alter net interest payments that otherwise would be paid by the debtor or received by the investor on an interest-bearing host contract but could not potentially result in the investor's failing to recover substantially all of its initial recorded investment in the bond (refer to paragraph 13(a)). In this example, there appears to be no possibility of increasing the investor's rate of return on the host contract to an amount that is at least double the initial rate of return on the host contract (refer to paragraph 13(b)). The embedded derivatives are considered to be clearly and closely related to the host contract as described in paragraph 13 of this Statement. Therefore, the embedded derivatives should *not* be separated from the host contract.

183. **Example 17: Fixed-to-Floating Note.** A bond that pays a varying coupon (first-year coupon is fixed; second- and third-year coupons are based on LIBOR, Treasury bills, or prime rate).

Scope Application: A fixed-to-floating note may be viewed as containing an embedded derivative (a forward-starting interest rate swap) that is referenced to an interest rate index (such as LIBOR) that alters net interest payments that otherwise would be paid by the debtor or received by the investor on an interest-bearing host instrument but could not potentially result in the investor's failing to recover substantially all of its initial recorded investment in the bond (refer to paragraph 13(a)). Likewise, there is no possibility of increasing the investor's rate of return on the host contract to an amount that is both at least double the initial rate of return on the host contract and at least twice what otherwise would be the market return for a contract that has the same terms as the host contract and that involves a debtor with a similar credit quality (refer to paragraph 13(b)). The embedded derivative is considered to be clearly and closely related to the host contract as described in paragraph 13 of this Statement. Therefore, the embedded derivative should *not* be separated from the host contract.

184. **Example 18: Indexed Amortizing Note.** A bond that repays principal based on a predetermined amortization schedule or target value. The amortiza-

tion is linked to changes in a specific mortgage-backed security index or interest rate index. The maturity of the bond changes as the related index changes. This instrument includes a varying maturity. (It is assumed for this example that the bond's terms could not potentially result in the investor's failing to recover substantially all of its initial recorded investment in the bond [refer to paragraph 13(a)] nor is there the possibility of increasing the investor's rate of return on the host contract to an amount that is both at least double the initial rate of return on the host contract and at least twice what otherwise would be the market return for a contract that has the same terms as the host contract and that involves a debtor with a similar credit quality [refer to paragraph 13(b)].)

Scope Application: An indexed amortizing note can be viewed as a fixed-rate amortizing note combined with a conditional exchange option contract that requires partial or total "early" payment of the note based on changes in a specific mortgage-backed security index or a specified change in an interest rate index. Because the requirement to prepay is ultimately tied to changing interest rates, the embedded derivative is considered to be clearly and closely related to a fixed-rate note. Therefore, the embedded derivative should *not* be separated from the host contract.

185. **Example 19: Equity-Indexed Note.** A bond for which the return of interest, principal, or both is tied to a specified equity security or index (for example, the Standard and Poor's 500 [S&P 500] index). This instrument may contain a fixed or varying coupon rate and may place all or a portion of principal at risk.

Scope Application: An equity-indexed note essentially combines an interest-bearing instrument with a series of forward exchange contracts or option contracts. Often, a portion of the coupon interest rate is, in effect, used to purchase options that provide some form of floor on the potential loss of principal that would result from a decline in the referenced equity index. Because forward or option contracts for which the underlying is an equity index are not clearly and closely related to an investment in an interest-bearing note, those embedded derivatives should be separated from the host contract and accounted for by both parties pursuant to the provisions of this Statement.

186. **Example 20: Variable Principal Redemption Bond.** A bond whose principal redemption value at

maturity depends on the change in an underlying index over a predetermined observation period. A typical example would be a bond that guarantees a minimum par redemption value of 100 percent and provides the potential for a supplemental principal payment at maturity as compensation for the below-market rate of interest offered with the instrument.

Example: A supplemental principal payment will be paid to the investor, at maturity, if the final S&P 500 closing value (determined at a specified date) is less than its initial value at date of issuance *and* the 10-year CMT is greater than 2 percent as of a specified date. In all cases, the minimum principal redemption will be 100 percent of par.

Scope Application: A variable principal redemption bond essentially combines an interest-bearing investment with an option that is purchased with a portion of the bond's coupon interest payments. Because the embedded option entitling the investor to an additional return is partially contingent on the S&P 500 index closing above a specified amount, it is not clearly and closely related to an investment in a debt instrument. Therefore, the embedded option should be separated from the host contract and accounted for by both parties pursuant to the provisions of this Statement.

187. **Example 21: Crude Oil Knock-in Note.** A bond that has a 1 percent coupon and guarantees repayment of principal with upside potential based on the strength of the oil market.

Scope Application: A crude oil knock-in note essentially combines an interest-bearing instrument with a series of option contracts. A significant portion of the coupon interest rate is, in effect, used to purchase options that provide the investor with potential gains resulting from increases in specified crude oil prices. Because the option contracts are indexed to the price of crude oil, they are not clearly and closely related to an investment in an interest-bearing note. Therefore, the embedded option contract should be separated from the host contract and accounted for by both parties pursuant to the provisions of this Statement.

188. **Example 22: Gold-Linked Bull Note.** A bond that has a fixed 3 percent coupon and guarantees repayment of principal with upside potential if the price of gold increases.

Scope Application: A gold-linked bull note can be viewed as combining an interest-bearing instrument with a series of option contracts. A portion of the coupon interest rate is, in effect, used to purchase call options that provide the investor with potential gains resulting from increases in gold prices. Because the option contracts are indexed to the price of gold, they are not clearly and closely related to an investment in an interest-bearing note. Therefore, the embedded option contracts should be separated from the host contract and accounted for by both parties pursuant to the provisions of this Statement.

189. **Example 23: Step-up Bond.** A bond that provides an introductory above-market yield and steps up to a new coupon, which will be below then-current market rates or, alternatively, the bond may be called in lieu of the step-up in the coupon rate.

Scope Application: A step-up bond can be viewed as a fixed-rate bond with an embedded call option and a changing interest rate feature. The bond pays an initial above-market interest rate to compensate for the call option and the future below-market rate (that is, below the forward yield curve, as determined at issuance based on the existing upward-sloping yield curve). Because the call option is related to changes in interest rates, it is clearly and closely related to an investment in a fixed-rate bond. Therefore, the embedded derivatives should *not* be separated from the host contract.

190. **Example 24: Credit-Sensitive Bond.** A bond that has a coupon rate of interest that resets based on changes in the issuer's credit rating.

Scope Application: A credit-sensitive bond can be viewed as combining a fixed-rate bond with a conditional exchange contract (or an option) that entitles the investor to a higher rate of interest if the credit rating of the issuer declines. Because the creditworthiness of the debtor and the interest rate on a debt instrument are clearly and closely related, the embedded derivative should *not* be separated from the host contract.

191. **Example 25: Inflation Bond.** A bond with a contractual principal amount that is indexed to the inflation rate but cannot decrease below par; the coupon rate is typically below that of traditional bonds of similar maturity.

Scope Application: An inflation bond can be viewed as a fixed-rate bond for which a portion of the coupon interest rate has been exchanged for a conditional exchange contract (or option) indexed to the consumer price index, or other index of inflation in the economic environment for the currency in which the bond is denominated, that entitles the investor to payment of additional principal based on increases in the referenced index. Such rates of inflation and interest rates on the debt instrument are considered to be clearly and closely related. Therefore, the embedded derivative should *not* be separated from the host contract.

192. **Example 26: Disaster Bond.** A bond that pays a coupon above that of an otherwise comparable traditional bond; however, all or a substantial portion of the principal amount is subject to loss if a specified disaster experience occurs.

Scope Application: A disaster bond can be viewed as a fixed-rate bond combined with a conditional exchange contract (an option). The investor receives an additional coupon interest payment in return for giving the issuer an option indexed to industry loss experience on a specified disaster. Because the option contract is indexed to the specified disaster experience, it cannot be viewed as being clearly and closely related to an investment in a fixed-rate bond. Therefore, the embedded derivative should be separated from the host contract and accounted for by both parties pursuant to the provisions of this Statement.

However, if the "embedded derivative" entitles the holder of the option (that is, the issuer of the disaster bond) to be compensated only for changes in the value of specified assets or liabilities for which the holder is at risk (including the liability for insurance claims payable due to the specified disaster) as a result of an identified insurable event (refer to paragraph 10(c)(2)), a separate instrument with the same terms as the "embedded derivative" would *not* meet the Statement's definition of a derivative in paragraphs 6–11. In that circumstance, because the criterion in paragraph 12(c) would not be met, there is no embedded derivative to be separated from the host contract, and the disaster bond would not be subject to the requirements of this Statement. The investor is essentially providing a form of insurance or reinsurance coverage to the issuer.

193. **Example 27: Specific Equity-Linked Bond.** A bond that pays a coupon slightly below that of tra-

ditional bonds of similar maturity; however, the principal amount is linked to the stock market performance of an equity investee of the issuer. The issuer may settle the obligation by delivering the shares of the equity investee or may deliver the equivalent fair value in cash.

Scope Application: A specific equity-linked bond can be viewed as combining an interest-bearing instrument with, depending on its terms, a series of forward exchange contracts or option contracts based on an equity instrument. Often, a portion of the coupon interest rate is used to purchase options that provide some form of floor on the loss of principal due to a decline in the price of the referenced equity instrument. The forward or option contracts do not qualify for the exception in paragraph 10(e)(2) because the shares in the equity investee owned by the issuer meet the definition of a *financial instrument*. Because forward or option contracts for which the underlying is the price of a specific equity instrument are not clearly and closely related to an investment in an interest-bearing note, the embedded derivative should be separated from the host contract and accounted for by both parties pursuant to the provisions of this Statement.

194. **Example 28: Dual Currency Bond.** A bond providing for repayment of principal in U.S. dollars and periodic interest payments denominated in a foreign currency. In this example, a U.S. entity with the dollar as its functional currency is borrowing funds from an independent party with those repayment terms as described.

Scope Application: Because the portion of this instrument relating to the periodic interest payments denominated in a foreign currency is subject to the requirement in Statement 52 to recognize the foreign currency transaction gain or loss in earnings, the instrument should not be considered as containing an embedded foreign currency derivative instrument pursuant to paragraph 15 of this Statement. In this example, the U.S. entity has the dollar as the functional currency and is making interest payments in a foreign currency. Remeasurement of the liability is required using future equivalent dollar interest payments determined by the current spot exchange rate and discounted at the historical effective interest rate.

195. **Example 29: Short-Term Loan with a Foreign Currency Option.** A U.S. lender issues a loan

at an above-market interest rate. The loan is made in U.S. dollars, the borrower's functional currency, and the borrower has the option to repay the loan in U.S. dollars or in a fixed amount of a specified foreign currency.

Scope Application: This instrument can be viewed as combining a loan at prevailing market interest rates and a foreign currency option. The lender has written a foreign currency option exposing it to changes in foreign currency exchange rates during the outstanding period of the loan. The premium for the option has been paid as part of the interest rate. Because the borrower has the option to repay the loan in U.S. dollars or in a fixed amount of a specified foreign currency, the provisions of paragraph 15 are not relevant to this example. Paragraph 15 addresses foreign-currency-denominated interest or principal payments but does not apply to foreign currency options. Because a foreign currency option is not clearly and closely related to issuing a loan, the embedded option should be separated from the host contract and accounted for by both parties pursuant to the provisions of this Statement. In contrast, if both the principal payment and the interest payments on the loan had been payable only in a fixed amount of a specified foreign currency, there would be no embedded foreign currency derivative pursuant to this Statement.

196. **Example 30: Lease Payment in Foreign Currency.** A U.S. company's operating lease with a Japanese lessor is payable in yen. The functional currency of the U.S. company is the U.S. dollar.

Scope Application: Paragraph 15(a) provides that contracts, other than financial instruments, that specify payments denominated in the currency of the primary economic environment in which any substantial party to that contract operates shall *not* be separated from the host contract and considered a derivative instrument for purposes of this Statement. Using available information about the lessor and its operations, the U.S. company may decide it is reasonable to conclude that the yen would be the currency of the primary economic environment in which the Japanese lessor operates, consistent with the functional currency notion in Statement 52. (That decision can be based on available information and reasonable assumptions about the counterparty; representations from the counterparty are not required.) Thus, the lease should *not* be viewed as

containing an embedded swap converting U.S. dollar lease payments to yen. Alternatively, if the lease payments are specified in a currency seemingly unrelated to each party's functional currency, such as drachmas (assuming the leased property is not in Greece), the embedded foreign currency swap should be separated from the host contract and accounted for as a derivative for purposes of this Statement because the provisions of paragraph 15 would not apply and a separate instrument with the same terms would meet the definition of a derivative instrument in paragraphs 6–11.

197. **Example 31: Certain Purchases in a Foreign Currency.** A U.S. company enters into a contract to purchase corn from a local American supplier in six months for a fixed amount of Japanese yen; the yen is the functional currency of neither party to the transaction. The corn is expected to be delivered and used over a reasonable period in the normal course of business.

Scope Application: Paragraph 10(b) excludes contracts that require future delivery of commodities that are readily convertible to cash from the accounting for derivatives if the commodities will be delivered in quantities expected to be used or sold by the reporting entity over a reasonable period in the normal course of business. However, that paragraph also states that contracts that are denominated in a foreign currency that meets neither of the criteria in paragraphs 15(a) and 15(b) shall not be considered normal purchases and normal sales. Because the Japanese yen is not the functional currency of either party to the contract and the purchase of corn is transacted internationally in many different currencies, the contract does not qualify for the normal purchases and normal sales exception. The contract is a compound derivative comprising a U.S. dollar-denominated forward contract for the purchase of corn and an embedded foreign currency swap from the purchaser's functional currency (the U.S. dollar) to yen. Consistent with the last sentence of footnote 13 to paragraph 49, the compound derivative cannot be separated into its components (representing the foreign currency derivative and the forward commodity contract) and accounted for separately under this Statement.

198. **Example 32: Participating Mortgage.** A mortgage in which the investor receives a below-market interest rate and is entitled to participate in the

appreciation in the market value of the project that is financed by the mortgage upon sale of the project, at a deemed sale date, or at the maturity or refinancing of the loan. The mortgagor must continue to own the project over the term of the mortgage.

Scope Application: This instrument has a provision that entitles the investor to participate in the appreciation of the referenced real estate (the "project"). However, a separate contract with the same terms would be excluded by the exception in paragraph 10(e)(2) because settlement is based on the value of a nonfinancial asset of one of the parties that is not readily convertible to cash. (This Statement does not modify the guidance in AICPA Statement of Position 97-1, *Accounting by Participating Mortgage Loan Borrowers*.)

199. **Example 33: Convertible Debt.** An investor receives a below-market interest rate and receives the option to convert its debt instrument into the equity of the issuer at an established conversion rate. The terms of the conversion require that the issuer deliver shares of stock to the investor.

Scope Application: This instrument essentially contains a call option on the issuer's stock. Under the provisions of this Statement, the accounting by the issuer and investor can differ. The issuer's accounting depends on whether a separate instrument with the same terms as the embedded written option would be a derivative instrument pursuant to paragraphs 6–11 of this Statement. Because the option is indexed to the issuer's own stock and a separate instrument with the same terms would be classified in stockholders' equity in the statement of financial position, the written option is not considered to be a derivative instrument for the issuer under paragraph 11(a) and should *not* be separated from the host contract.

In contrast, if the terms of the conversion allow for a cash settlement rather than delivery of the issuer's shares at the investor's option, the exception in paragraph 11(a) for the issuer does not apply because the contract would not be classified in stockholders' equity in the issuer's statement of financial position. In that case, the issuer should separate the embedded derivative from the host contract and account for it pursuant to the provisions of this Statement because (a) an option based on the entity's stock price is not clearly and closely related to an interest-bearing debt instrument and (b) the option would not be considered an equity instrument of the issuer.

Similarly, if the convertible debt is indexed to another entity's publicly traded common stock, the issuer should separate the embedded derivative from the host contract and account for it pursuant to the provisions of this Statement because (a) an option based on another entity's stock price is not clearly and closely related to an investment in an interest-bearing note and (b) the option would not be considered an equity instrument of the issuer.

The exception in paragraph 11 does not apply to the investor's accounting. Therefore, in both cases described above, the investor should separate the embedded option contract from the host contract and account for the embedded option contract pursuant to the provisions of this Statement because the option contract is based on the price of another entity's equity instrument and thus is not clearly and closely related to an investment in an interest-bearing note. However, if the terms of conversion do not allow for a cash settlement and if the common stock delivered upon conversion is privately held (that is, is not readily convertible to cash), the embedded derivative would not be separated from the host contract because it would not meet the criteria in paragraph 9.

200. **Example 34: Variable Annuity Products.** These products are investment contracts as contemplated in Statements 60 and 97. Similar to variable life insurance products, policyholders direct their investment account asset mix among a variety of mutual funds composed of equities, bonds, or both, and assume the risks and rewards of investment performance. The funds are generally maintained in separate accounts by the insurance company. Contract terms provide that if the policyholder dies, the greater of the account market value or a minimum death benefit guarantee will be paid. The minimum death benefit guarantee is generally limited to a return of premium plus a minimum return (such as 3 or 4 percent); this life insurance feature represents the fundamental difference from the life insurance contracts that include significant (rather than minimal) levels of life insurance. The investment account may have various payment alternatives at the end of the accumulation period. One alternative is the right to purchase a life annuity at a fixed price determined at the initiation of the contract.

Scope Application: Variable annuity product structures as contemplated in Statement 97 are generally not subject to the scope of this Statement (except for payment options at the end of the accumulation period), as follows:

- *Death benefit component.* Paragraph 10(c)(1) excludes a death benefit from the scope of this Statement because the payment of the death benefit is the result of an identifiable insurable event instead of changes in an underlying. The death benefit in this example is limited to the floor guarantee of the investment account, calculated as the premiums paid into the investment account plus a guaranteed rate of return, less the account market value. Statement 60 remains the applicable guidance for the insurance-related liability accounting.
- *Investment component.* The policyholder directs certain premium investments in the investment account that includes equities, bonds, or both, which are held in separate accounts that are distinct from the insurer's general account assets. This component is not considered a derivative because of the unique attributes of traditional variable annuity contracts issued by insurance companies. Furthermore, any embedded derivatives within those investments should not be separated from the host contract by the insurer because the separate account assets are already marked-to-market under Statement 60. In contrast, if the product were an equity-index-based interest annuity (rather than a traditional variable annuity), the investment component would contain an embedded derivative (the equity index-based derivative) that meets all the requirements of paragraph 12 of this Statement for separate accounting: (a) the economic characteristics and risks of the embedded derivative would not be clearly and closely related to the economic characteristics and risks of the host contract (that is, the host contract is a debt instrument and the embedded option is equity-indexed), (b) the hybrid instrument would not be remeasured at fair value with changes in fair value reported in earnings as they occur under GAAP, and (c) a separate instrument with the same terms as the embedded derivative instrument would be a derivative instrument pursuant to paragraphs 6–11 of this Statement.
- *Investment account surrender right at market value.* Because this right is exercised only at

the fund market value (without the insurer's floor guarantee) and relates to a traditional variable annuity contract issued by an insurance company, this right is not within the scope of this Statement.
- *Payment alternatives at the end of the accumulation period.* Payment alternatives are options subject to the requirements of this Statement if interest rates or other underlying variables affect the value.

The guidance in the second and third bullets above is an exception for traditional variable annuity contracts issued by insurance companies. In determining the accounting for other seemingly similar structures, it would be inappropriate to analogize to the above guidance due to the unique attributes of traditional variable annuity contracts.

Section 2A: Examples Illustrating Application of Paragraphs 14A and 14B Relating to Embedded Derivatives in Securitized Financial Assets

200A. **Example 35: A Dollar-Denominated Floating-Rate Interest Issued by an SPE That Holds Yen-Denominated Floating-Rate Bonds and a Cross-Currency Swap to Pay Yen and Receive Dollars.** If the floating rate reflects a current market rate and the notional amounts of the bonds and the swap correspond to the notional amount of the interests issued, the dollar-denominated floating-rate interest would *not* have an embedded derivative requiring bifurcation because the terms of the beneficial interest do not indicate an embedded derivative and the financial instruments held by the entity provide the necessary cash flows.

200B. **Example 36: A Variable-Rate Interest Issued by an SPE That Holds Fixed-Rate Bonds and a Pay-Fixed, Receive-Variable Interest Rate Swap.** The variable-rate interest would *not* have an embedded derivative requiring bifurcation because the terms of the beneficial interest do not indicate an embedded derivative and the financial instruments held by the entity provide the necessary cash flows. However, if the notional amounts of the fixed-rate bonds and the variable interest rate swap do not match, the variable-rate interest would have to be evaluated for an embedded derivative under paragraph 13 because the financial instruments held by the entity might not provide the necessary cash flows.

200C. **Example 37: A Securitization Involving Subordination.** An SPE that holds fixed-rate bonds issues (a) a senior, floating-rate financial instrument,

(b) a subordinated financial instrument that is entitled to 90 percent of the difference between the fixed rate received and the floating rate paid to the senior financial instrument, and (c) a residual financial instrument that is entitled to the remainder of the fixed-rate payment from the bonds after any credit losses. The subordinated financial instrument could be a hybrid financial instrument with an embedded interest rate derivative requiring bifurcation because the terms are floating rate, but the entity does not hold assets that bear a floating rate. This analysis considers the structure as a whole including the related liabilities. Therefore, there could be a shortfall of cash flow after the senior interest holders are paid, due to adverse changes in interest rates, and the investor in the subordinated interest might not recover substantially all of its initial recorded investment in the interest (see

paragraph 13(a)). The residual financial instrument would not have an embedded derivative for the concentration of credit risk as discussed in paragraph 14B, because the concentration of credit risk relates to the financial instruments held by the entity, but the residual instrument would have an embedded interest rate derivative.

200D. **Example 38: A Securitization That Introduces New Credit Risk.** An entity holds a credit derivative referenced to Company A and high-quality bonds but issues beneficial interests explicitly referenced to Company B. The beneficial interests would be a hybrid financial instrument with an embedded derivative because the cash flows relating to changes in the credit risk of Company B are not present in the financial instruments held by the entity.

Section 3: Examples Illustrating Application of the Transition Provisions

201. Assume that at December 31, 1999, a calendar-year entity has the following derivatives and hedging relationships in place (for simplicity, income tax effects are ignored):

(a) Item	Before Transition Adjustment—December 31, 1999		(d) GAAP Classification prior to Transition	(e) Previous Hedge Resembles	(f) Assumed Post-Transition-Date Accounting under This Statement
	Asset (Liability)				
	(b) Carrying Amount	(c) Fair Value			
A.					
Forward contract	$ 0	$(1,500)	Hedges existing inventory (though fair value changes have not been recognized)	Fair value hedge	Fair value hedge of inventory
Inventory	5,000	6,400	Hedged by forward contract		
B.					
Interest rate swap	0	180	Hedges fixed-rate bond	Fair value hedge	Would not qualify as a hedge of the held-to-maturity security—account for swap as a nonhedging derivative*
Fixed-rate bond (classified as held-to-maturity)	1,000	800	Hedged by interest rate swap		

*Prior to the effective date of Statement 133, generally accepted accounting principles did not prohibit hedge accounting for a hedge of the interest rate risk in a held-to-maturity security. Thus, transition adjustments may be necessary for hedges of that type because that type of hedging relationship will no longer qualify for hedge accounting under the provisions of this Statement. At the date of initial application, an entity may reclassify any held-to-maturity security into the available-for-sale or trading category (refer to paragraph 54).

Before Transition Adjustment—December 31, 1999 (continued)

| (a) Item | Asset (Liability) | | (d) GAAP Classification prior to Transition | (e) Previous Hedge Resembles | (f) Assumed Post-Transition-Date Accounting under This Statement |
	(b) Carrying Amount	(c) Fair Value			
C.					
Interest rate swap	0	(350)	Hedges fixed-rate bond	Fair value hedge	Fair value hedge of the fixed-rate bond
Fixed-rate bond (classified as available-for-sale)	1,000	1,000	Hedged by interest rate swap (cost basis is $650; unrealized holding gain is $350)		
Other comprehensive income (Statement 115)	(350)	N/A			
D.					
Foreign currency forward contract	1,000	1,200	Hedges firm purchase commitment	Fair value hedge	Fair value hedge of the firm commitment
Deferred credit	(1,000)	N/A	Deferred gain related to foreign currency forward contract		
Firm commitment to pay foreign currency to purchase machinery	0	(1,200)	Hedged by foreign currency forward contract		

E. Swap (no longer held)					
Deferred credit	(1,000)	N/A	Swap that was hedging a probable forecasted transaction was terminated prior to 12/31/99 and the related gain was deferred	Cash flow hedge	Since the swap is no longer held, there is no new designation
F. 2-year forward contract	0	1,000	Hedges a probable forecasted transaction projected to occur in 1 year	Cash flow hedge	Forward could possibly qualify as a hedging instrument
G. 6-month futures contract (cash settled daily)	0	0	Hedges a probable forecasted transaction projected to occur in 6 months	Cash flow hedge	Cash flow hedge
Deferred debit	500	N/A	Deferred loss related to futures contract		N/A

202. To determine transition accounting, existing hedge relationships must be identified as either a fair value *type* of hedge or a cash flow *type* of hedge as identified pursuant to this Statement. They do not have to meet the hedge criteria of this Statement. That identification is indicated in column (e) of the above table.

203. At transition, an entity has an opportunity to redesignate hedging relationships. This example makes certain assumptions regarding post-transition-date accounting pursuant to this Statement as indicated in column (f) of the above table that cannot necessarily be determined from the information provided in this example. The appropriate conditions in this Statement must be met to continue hedge accounting for periods subsequent to transition. However, determining whether a potential hedging relationship meets the conditions of this Statement does not impact the transition accounting. For purposes of determining transition adjustments, existing hedging relationships are categorized as fair value or cash flow hedges based on their general characteristics, without assessing whether all of the applicable conditions would be met.

204. After applying the transition provisions, the above items would be reflected in the financial statements as follows:

After Transition Adjustment—January 1, 2000

Item	Statement of Financial Position		Income Statement	Explanation of Accounting at Transition
	Asset (Liability)	Other Comprehensive Income	Transition Adjustment Gain (Loss)	
A.				
Forward contract	$(1,500)	N/A	$(1,500)	Adjust to fair value by recognizing $1,500 loss as a transition adjustment
Inventory	6,400	N/A	1,400	Recognize offsetting $1,400 gain as a transition adjustment*
Net impact			$ (100)	
B.				
Interest rate swap	180	N/A	$ 180	Adjust to fair value by recognizing $180 gain as a transition adjustment
Fixed-rate bond (classified as held-to-maturity)	820	N/A	(180)	Recognize offsetting $180 loss as a transition adjustment
Net impact			$ 0	

*The transition adjustment for the gain on the hedged inventory is limited to the amount that is offset by the loss on the hedging derivative. The entire $1,400 gain is recognized in this example because it is less than the $1,500 loss on the derivative. If the inventory gain had been more than $1,500, only $1,500 would have been recognized as a transition adjustment.

C.	Interest rate swap	(350)	N/A	$ (350)	Adjust to fair value by recognizing a $350 loss as a transition adjustment
	Fixed-rate bond (classified as available-for-sale)	1,000	N/A	—	Remove offsetting $350 gain previously reported in OCI (Statement 115) and recognize as a transition adjustment
	Other comprehensive income (OCI)	N/A	—	350	
	Net impact			$ 0	
D.	Foreign currency forward contract	1,200	N/A	$ 200	Adjust to fair value by recognizing $200 gain as a transition adjustment
	Deferred credit	0	N/A	1,000	Remove deferred credit and recognize as a transition adjustment
	Firm commitment to pay foreign currency to purchase machinery	(1,200)	N/A	(1,200)	Recognize offsetting $1,200 loss as a transition adjustment
	Net impact			$ 0	
E.	Terminated swap	—	—	$ —	No asset exists for the terminated swap
	Deferred credit	—	N/A	—	Remove the deferred credit and recognize in OCI—to be reclassified into earnings consistent with the earnings effect of the hedged forecasted transaction
	OCI	N/A	$(1,000)	—	
	Net impact			$ 0	

After Transition Adjustment—January 1, 2000 (continued)

Item	Statement of Financial Position		Income Statement	Explanation of Accounting at Transition
	Asset (Liability)	Other Comprehensive Income	Transition Adjustment Gain (Loss)	
F.				
Forward contract	1,000	(1,000)	$ 0	Adjust to fair value by recognizing $1,000 gain in OCI—to be reclassified into earnings consistent with the earnings effect of the hedged forecasted transaction
G.				
Futures contract	0	N/A	—	Asset already reported at fair value—no adjustment necessary
Deferred debit	—	N/A	—	Remove deferred debit and recognize in OCI—to be reclassified into earnings consistent with the earnings effect of the hedged forecasted transaction
OCI	N/A	500	—	
Net impact			$ 0	

205. In the initial year of application, an entity would also disclose the amounts of deferred gains and losses included in other comprehensive income that are expected to be reclassified into earnings within the next 12 months.

Appendix C

BACKGROUND INFORMATION AND BASIS FOR CONCLUSIONS

CONTENTS

Appendix C

BACKGROUND INFORMATION AND BASIS FOR CONCLUSIONS

Introduction

206. This appendix summarizes considerations that Board members deemed significant in reaching the conclusions in this Statement. It includes reasons for accepting certain views and rejecting others. Individual Board members gave greater weight to some factors than to others.

Background Information

207. The Board is addressing the accounting for derivative instruments[27] and hedging activities as part of its broad project on financial instruments. That project was added to the Board's agenda in 1986 to address financial reporting issues that were arising, or that were given a new sense of urgency, as a result of financial innovation. The project initially focused on disclosures and resulted in the issuance of FASB Statements No. 105, *Disclosure of Information about Financial Instruments with Off-Balance-Sheet Risk and Financial Instruments with Concentrations of Credit Risk,* in March 1990, and No. 107, *Disclosures about Fair Value of Financial Instruments,* in December 1991. This Statement supersedes Statement 105 and amends Statement 107.

208. An FASB staff-authored Research Report, *Hedge Accounting: An Exploratory Study of the Underlying Issues,* was published in September 1991.[28] An FASB Discussion Memorandum, *Recognition and Measurement of Financial Instruments,* was issued in November 1991 as a basis for considering the financial accounting and reporting issues of recognition and measurement raised by financial instruments. The recognition and measurement phase of the financial instruments project, which began with the issuance of that Discussion Memorandum, resulted in the issuance of FASB Statements No. 114, *Accounting by Creditors for Impairment of a Loan,* and No. 115, *Accounting for Certain Investments in Debt and Equity Securities,* in May 1993, FASB Statement No. 118, *Accounting by Creditors for Impairment of a Loan—Income Recognition and Disclosures,* in October 1994, and FASB Statement No. 125, *Accounting for Transfers and Servicing of Financial Assets and Extinguishments of Liabilities,* in June 1996.

209. Concern about financial reporting for derivative instruments and hedging activities is an international phenomenon. In October 1995, an FASB staff-authored Special Report, *Major Issues Related to Hedge Accounting,* was published jointly with representatives of the accounting standards-setting bodies of the United Kingdom, Canada, and Australia and the International Accounting Standards Committee.[29] That Special Report discusses many of the issues that needed to be resolved in developing a hedge accounting model.

---

[27]The terms *derivative instrument* and *derivative* are used interchangeably in this appendix.

[28]Harold Bierman, Jr., L. Todd Johnson, and D. Scott Peterson, FASB Research Report, *Hedge Accounting: An Exploratory Study of the Underlying Issues.*

[29]Jane B. Adams and Corliss J. Montesi, FASB Special Report, *Major Issues Related to Hedge Accounting.*

210. The Board began deliberating issues relating to derivatives and hedging activities in January 1992. From then until June 1996, the Board held 100 public meetings to discuss various issues and proposed accounting approaches, including 74 Board meetings, 10 meetings with members of the Financial Accounting Standards Advisory Council, 7 meetings with members of the Financial Instruments Task Force and its subgroup on hedging, and 9 meetings with outside representatives. In addition, individual Board members and staff visited numerous companies in a variety of fields and participated in meetings with different representational groups, both nationally and internationally, to explore how different entities manage risk and how those risk management activities should be accounted for.

211. In June 1993, the Board issued a report, "A Report on Deliberations, Including Tentative Conclusions on Certain Issues, related to Accounting for Hedging and Other Risk-adjusting Activities." That report included background information about the Board's deliberations and some tentative conclusions on accounting for derivatives and hedging activities. It also solicited comments from constituents and provided the basis for two public meetings in September 1993.

212. Concern has grown about the accounting and disclosure requirements for derivatives and hedging activities as the extent of use and the complexity of derivatives and hedging activities have rapidly increased in recent years. Changes in global financial markets and related financial innovations have led to the development of new derivatives used to manage exposures to risk, including interest rate, foreign exchange, price, and credit risks. Many believe that accounting standards have not kept pace with those changes. Derivatives can be useful risk management tools, and some believe that the inadequacy of financial reporting may have discouraged their use by contributing to an atmosphere of uncertainty. Concern about inadequate financial reporting also was heightened by the publicity surrounding large derivative losses at a few companies. As a result, the Securities and Exchange Commission, members of Congress, and others urged the Board to deal expeditiously with reporting problems in this area. For example, a report of the General Accounting Office prepared for Congress in 1994 recommended, among other things, that the FASB "proceed expeditiously to develop and

issue an exposure draft that provides comprehensive, consistent accounting rules for derivative products. . . ."[30] In addition, some users of financial statements asked for improved disclosures and accounting for derivatives and hedging. For example, one of the recommendations in the December 1994 report published by the AICPA Special Committee on Financial Reporting, *Improving Business Reporting—A Customer Focus,* was to address the disclosures and accounting for innovative financial instruments.

213. Because of the urgency of improved financial information about derivatives and related activities, the Board decided, in December 1993, to redirect some of its efforts toward enhanced disclosures and, in October 1994, issued FASB Statement No. 119, *Disclosure about Derivative Financial Instruments and Fair Value of Financial Instruments.* This Statement supersedes Statement 119.

214. In June 1996, the Board issued an Exposure Draft, *Accounting for Derivative and Similar Financial Instruments and for Hedging Activities.* Approximately 300 organizations and individuals responded to the Exposure Draft, some with multiple letters. In November 1996, 36 individuals and organizations presented their views at 4 days of public hearings. In addition, six enterprises participated in a limited field test of the provisions of the Exposure Draft. In December 1996, the Board's Financial Instruments Task Force met to discuss the issues raised during the comment letter process and during the public hearings. The Board considered the comments and field test results during its redeliberations of the issues addressed by the Exposure Draft in 21 public meetings in the first 7 months of 1997. The Financial Instruments Task Force met again with the Board in April 1997 and discussed, among other things, proposed changes to the Exposure Draft reflected in a draft of a Statement. As a consequence of the comments received, the Board made certain changes to the proposals in the Exposure Draft.

215. In August 1997, a draft of the standards section of this Statement and related examples was made available to the Financial Instruments Task Force and other interested parties for comment on its clarity and operationality. The Board received approximately 150 comment letters on that draft and discussed those

---

[30]United States General Accounting Office, Report to Congressional Requesters, *Financial Derivatives: Actions Needed to Protect the Financial System,* May 1994, 16.

comments in 10 open Board meetings. Those comments also led to changes to the requirements, intended to make the Statement clearer and more operational.

216. This Statement is an additional step in the Board's project on financial instruments and is intended to address the immediate problems about the recognition and measurement of derivatives while the Board's vision of having all financial instruments measured at fair value in the statement of financial position is pursued. Certain provisions of this Statement will be reconsidered as the Board continues to address the issues in its broad project on financial instruments.

Fundamental Decisions Underlying the Statement

217. The Board made four fundamental decisions about how to account for derivatives and hedging activities; those decisions became the cornerstones of this Statement:

a. Derivative instruments represent rights or obligations that meet the definitions of assets or liabilities and should be reported in financial statements.
b. Fair value is the most relevant measure for financial instruments and the only relevant measure for derivative instruments. Derivative instruments should be measured at fair value, and adjustments to the carrying amounts of hedged items should reflect changes in their fair value (that is, gains or losses) that are attributable to the risk being hedged and that arise while the hedge is in effect.
c. Only items that are assets or liabilities should be reported as such in financial statements.
d. Special accounting for items designated as being hedged should be provided only for qualifying items. One aspect of qualification should be an assessment of the expectation of effective offsetting changes in fair values or cash flows during the term of the hedge for the risk being hedged.

218. *Derivative instruments represent rights or obligations that meet the definitions of assets or liabilities and should be reported in financial statements.* Derivatives are assets or liabilities because they represent rights or obligations. FASB Concepts Statement No. 6, *Elements of Financial Statements,* describes the characteristics of assets and liabilities as follows:

An asset has three essential characteristics: (a) it embodies a probable future benefit that involves a capacity, singly or in combination with other assets, to contribute directly or indirectly to future net cash inflows, (b) a particular entity can obtain the benefit and control others' access to it, and (c) the transaction or other event giving rise to the entity's right to or control of the benefit has already occurred. . . .

A liability has three essential characteristics: (a) it embodies a present duty or responsibility to one or more other entities that entails settlement by probable future transfer or use of assets at a specified or determinable date, on occurrence of a specified event, or on demand, (b) the duty or responsibility obligates a particular entity, leaving it little or no discretion to avoid the future sacrifice, and (c) the transaction or other event obligating the entity has already happened. [paragraphs 26 and 36]

219. The ability to settle a derivative in a gain position by receiving cash, another financial asset, or a nonfinancial asset is evidence of a right to a future economic benefit and is compelling evidence that the instrument is an asset. Similarly, the payment of cash, a financial asset, or a nonfinancial asset that is required to settle a derivative in a loss position is evidence of a duty to sacrifice assets in the future and indicates that the instrument is a liability. The Board believes that recognizing those assets and liabilities will make financial statements more complete and more informative. Before the issuance of this Statement, many derivatives were "off-balance-sheet" because, unlike conventional financial instruments such as stocks, bonds, and loans, derivatives often reflect at their inception only a mutual exchange of promises with little or no transfer of tangible consideration.

220. *Fair value is the most relevant measure for financial instruments and the only relevant measure for derivative instruments. Derivative instruments should be measured at fair value, and adjustments to the carrying amounts of hedged items should reflect changes in their fair value (that is, gains or losses) that are attributable to the risk being hedged and that arise while the hedge is in effect.* In 1991, with the issuance of Statement 107, the Board concluded that disclosure of fair value information about financial instruments is useful to present and potential investors, creditors, and other users of financial statements

in making rational investment, credit, and other decisions. Statement 107 describes the Board's rationale:

> Fair values of financial instruments depict the market's assessment of the present value of net future cash flows directly or indirectly embodied in them, discounted to reflect both current interest rates and the market's assessment of the risk that the cash flows will not occur. Investors and creditors are interested in predicting the amount, timing, and uncertainty of future net cash inflows to an entity, as those are the primary sources of future cash flows from the entity to them. Periodic information about the fair value of an entity's financial instruments under current conditions and expectations should help those users both in making their own predictions and in confirming or correcting their earlier expectations.
>
> Information about fair value better enables investors, creditors, and other users to assess the consequences of an entity's investment and financing strategies, that is, to assess its performance. For example, information about fair value shows the effects of a decision to borrow using fixed-rate rather than floating-rate financial instruments or of a decision to invest in long-term rather than short-term instruments. Also, in a dynamic economy, information about fair value permits continuous reassessment of earlier decisions in light of current circumstances. [paragraphs 40 and 41]

221. The Board believes fair values for financial assets and liabilities provide more relevant and understandable information than cost or cost-based measures. In particular, the Board believes that fair value is more relevant to financial statement users than cost for assessing the liquidity or solvency of an entity because fair value reflects the current cash equivalent of the entity's financial instruments rather than the price of a past transaction. With the passage of time, historical prices become irrelevant in assessing present liquidity or solvency.

222. The Board also believes fair value measurement is practical for most financial assets and liabilities. Fair value measurements can be observed in markets or estimated by reference to markets for similar instruments. If market information is not available, fair value can be estimated using other measurement techniques, such as discounted cash flow analyses and option or other pricing models, among others.

223. The Board believes fair value is the *only* relevant measurement attribute for derivatives. Amortized cost is not a relevant measure for derivatives because the historical cost of a derivative often is zero, yet a derivative generally can be settled or sold at any time for an amount equivalent to its fair value. Statement 115 provides reasoning for the belief that amortized cost may be relevant for debt securities that will be held to maturity. In the absence of default, that cost will be realized at maturity, and any interim unrealized gains or losses will reverse. That reasoning does not hold for derivatives or for other financial instruments. The volatility of derivatives' fair values and the irrelevance of amortized cost for derivatives convinced the Board that fair value is the only relevant measure for derivatives and that all derivatives should be reported in financial statements at fair value. (The latter part of the Board's second fundamental decision, which deals with the mechanics of hedge accounting, is discussed in paragraphs 362 and 363.)

224. Some of the Board's constituents contend that reporting derivatives at fair value will not result in more useful information than results from present practice. Some also say that reporting derivatives at fair value will result in reported gains or losses and increases or decreases in reported equity that are "artificial" because they do not reflect economic benefits or detriments. Some of those concerns are based in part on concerns about using different measurement attributes for derivatives and for other financial instruments. The Board agrees that financial statements would be even more useful if all financial instruments were reported at fair value, and that is its long-term goal. However, some of the arguments against reporting derivatives at fair value are made in the context of assertions that fair value measurements do not provide useful information for either derivatives or other instruments. The following simple example illustrates why the Board does not agree with that view.

225. Bank A and Bank B have identical financial positions at December 31, 20X1, as follows:

Loans	$10 billion	Liabilities	$9 billion
		Equity	1 billion
Total assets	$10 billion	Total liabilities and equity	$10 billion

Both banks' assets consist entirely of variable-rate loans. Both also have fixed-rate debt at 9 percent.

226. In January of 20X2, Bank A becomes concerned that market interest rates will fall below the current level of 10 percent, and it therefore enters into a pay-variable, receive-fixed-at-10-percent interest rate swap. Bank B, on the other hand, chooses not to hedge its variable-rate loans. Bank A's swap will reprice every three months, beginning on April 15, 20X2. By March 31, 20X2, interest rates have fallen significantly, and the fair value of Bank A's swap is $1 billion.

227. For simplicity, the example assumes that each bank's interest income for the first quarter of 20X2 was exactly offset by expenses so that both had earnings of zero. The effects of deferred taxes also are ignored. Thus, if the change in fair value of Bank A's interest rate swap is excluded from its financial statements, as was general practice before this Statement, both banks' balance sheets at March 31, 20X2 would continue to appear as presented in paragraph 225. However, the two banks are not in the same economic position—Bank A has a $1 billion asset that Bank B does not.

228. The following statement of financial position, which reflects the requirements of this Statement if Bank A accounts for the swap as a cash flow hedge, better reflects Bank A's economic position at March 31, 20X2:

Loans	$10 billion	Liabilities	$ 9 billion
		Equity:	
Interest rate swap	1 billion	Beginning equity	1 billion
		Gain on swap	1 billion
		Total equity	2 billion
Total assets	$11 billion	Total liabilities and equity	$11 billion

Bank A's statement of comprehensive income for the quarter ending March 31, 20X2 will report a gain of $1 billion. Bank B's comprehensive income for the same period will be reported as zero. Under previous accounting for swaps, Bank A would only accrue periodic cash receipts or payments on the swap as the swap reprices and those receipts or payments become due. In contrast, the financial statements of Banks A and B at March 31, 20X2 presented in accordance with this Statement signal to investors and creditors that the future reported earnings and cash flows of the banks will be different. If interest rates remain below 10 percent during the remainder of the term of the loans, Bank A will report higher earnings and will receive higher cash inflows than Bank B. Indeed, whatever happens to interest rates in the future, the two banks are likely to be affected differently. Under previous reporting practices for interest rate swaps and many other derivatives, Bank A and Bank B would have looked exactly alike at March 31, 20X2. However, the two banks are not in the same economic position at March 31, 20X2, and Bank A's increase in reported equity reflects the real difference in the position of the two banks. That increase in equity is by no means "artificial."

229. *Only items that are assets or liabilities should be reported as such in financial statements.* Derivatives are assets or liabilities, and the Board decided that they should be reported in financial statements (fundamental decision 1) and measured at fair value (fundamental decision 2). If derivatives are measured at fair value, the losses or gains that result from changes in their fair values must be reported in the financial statements. However, those losses or gains are not separate assets or liabilities because they have

none of the essential characteristics of assets or liabilities as described in paragraph 218. The act of designating a derivative as a hedging instrument does not convert a subsequent loss or gain into an asset or a liability. A loss is not an asset because no future economic benefit is associated with it. The loss cannot be exchanged for cash, a financial asset, or a nonfinancial asset used to produce something of value, or used to settle liabilities. Similarly, a gain is not a liability because no obligation exists to sacrifice assets in the future. Consequently, the Board concluded that losses or gains on derivatives should not be reported as assets or liabilities in a statement of financial position.

230. *Special accounting for items designated as being hedged should be provided only for qualifying items. One aspect of qualification should be an assessment of the expectation of effective offsetting changes in fair values or cash flows during the term of the hedge for the risk being hedged.* Because hedge accounting is elective and relies on management's intent, it should be limited to transactions that meet reasonable criteria. The Board concluded that hedge accounting should not be permitted in all cases in which an entity might assert that a relationship exists between items or transactions. A primary purpose of hedge accounting is to link items or transactions whose changes in fair values or cash flows are expected to offset each other. The Board therefore decided that one of the criteria for qualification for hedge accounting should focus on the extent to which offsetting changes in fair values or cash flows on the derivative and the hedged item or transaction during the term of the hedge are expected and ultimately achieved.

231. The offset criterion precludes hedge accounting for certain risk management techniques, such as hedges of strategic risk. For example, a U.S. manufacturer, with no export business, that designates a forward contract to buy U.S. dollars for Japanese yen as a hedge of its U.S. dollar sales would fail the requirement that the cash flows of the derivative are expected to be highly effective in achieving offsetting cash flows on the hedged transaction. A weakened yen might allow a competitor to sell goods imported from Japan more cheaply, undercutting the domestic manufacturer's prices and reducing its sales volume and revenues. However, it would be difficult for the U.S. manufacturer to expect a high degree of offset between a decline in U.S. sales revenue due to increased competition and cash inflows on a foreign currency derivative. Any relationship between the

exposure and the "hedging" derivative typically would be quite indirect, would depend on price elasticities, and would be only one of many factors influencing future results. In addition, the risk that a desired or expected number of transactions will not occur, that is, the potential absence of a transaction, is not a hedgeable risk under this Statement. Hedge accounting in this Statement is limited to the direct effects of price changes of various kinds (commodity prices, interest rates, and so on) on fair values of assets and liabilities and the cash flows from transactions, including qualifying forecasted transactions.

Benefits and Costs of This Statement

232. In accomplishing its mission, the Board follows certain precepts, including the precept to promulgate standards only when the expected benefits of the information exceed the perceived cost. The Board works to determine that a proposed standard will fill a significant need and that the costs imposed to meet the standard, as compared to other alternatives, are justified in relation to the overall benefits of the resulting information.

Problems with Previous Accounting and Reporting Practices

233. The first step in considering whether the benefits of a new accounting standard will justify the related costs is to identify the problems in the existing accounting guidance that a new standard seeks to resolve. The problems with previous accounting and reporting practices for derivatives and hedging activities are discussed below.

234. *The effects of derivatives were not transparent in the basic financial statements.* Under the varied accounting practices that existed before the issuance of this Statement, some derivatives were recognized in financial statements, others were not. If recognized in financial statements, some realized and unrealized gains and losses on derivatives were deferred from earnings recognition and reported as part of the carrying amount (or "basis") of a related item or as if they were freestanding assets and liabilities. Users of financial statements found it difficult to determine what an entity had or had not done with derivatives and the related effects because the basic financial statements often did not report the rights or obligations associated with derivative instruments.

235. *The accounting guidance for derivative instruments and hedging activities was incomplete.* Before the issuance of this Statement, accounting standards

specifically addressed only a few types of derivatives. Statement 52 addressed foreign exchange forward contracts, and Statement 80 addressed exchange-traded futures contracts. Only those two Statements specifically provided for "hedge accounting." That is, only those Statements provided special accounting to permit a gain or loss on a derivative to be deferred beyond the period in which it otherwise would be recognized in earnings because it was designated as a hedging instrument. The EITF addressed the accounting for some derivatives and for some hedging activities not covered in either Statement 52 or Statement 80. However, that effort was on an ad hoc basis and gaps remained in the authoritative literature. Accounting practice filled some gaps on specific issues, such as with "synthetic instrument accounting" as described in paragraph 349, but without commonly understood limitations on the appropriate use of that accounting. The result was that (a) many derivative instruments were carried "off-balance-sheet" regardless of whether they were formally part of a hedging strategy, (b) practices were inconsistent among entities, and (c) users of financial reports had inadequate information.

236. *The accounting guidance for derivative instruments and hedging activities was inconsistent.* Under previous accounting guidance, the required accounting treatment differed depending on the type of instrument used in a hedge and the type of risk being hedged. For example, an instrument hedging an anticipated transaction may have qualified for special accounting if it was a purchased option with certain characteristics or an interest rate futures contract, but not if it was a foreign currency forward or futures contract. Derivatives also were measured differently under previous standards—futures contracts were reported at fair value, foreign currency forward contracts were reported at amounts that reflected changes in foreign exchange spot rates but not changes in forward rates and that were not discounted for the time value of money, and other derivatives often were unrecognized or were reported at nominal amounts not closely related to the fair value of the derivatives (for example, reported at the net cash due that period). Accounting standards also were inconsistent on whether qualification for hedge accounting was based on risk assessment at an entity-wide or an individual-transaction level.

237. *The accounting guidance for derivatives and hedging was difficult to apply.* The lack of a single, comprehensive approach to accounting for derivatives and hedging made the accounting guidance difficult to apply. The incompleteness of FASB Statements on derivatives and hedging forced entities to look to a variety of different sources, including the numerous EITF issues and nonauthoritative literature, to determine how to account for specific instruments or transactions. Because there often was nothing directly on point, entities analogized to other existing guidance. Different sources of analogy often conflicted, and a wide range of answers sometimes was deemed supportable, but those answers often were subject to later challenge.

This Statement Mitigates Those Problems

238. This Statement mitigates those four problems. It increases the visibility, comparability, and understandability of the risks associated with derivatives by requiring that all derivatives be reported as assets or liabilities and measured at fair value. It reduces the inconsistency, incompleteness, and difficulty of applying previous accounting guidance and practice by providing comprehensive guidance for all derivatives and hedging activities. The comprehensive guidance in this Statement also eliminates some accounting practices, such as "synthetic instrument accounting," that had evolved beyond the authoritative literature.

239. In addition to mitigating the previous problems, this Statement accommodates a range of hedge accounting practices by (a) permitting hedge accounting for most derivative instruments, (b) permitting hedge accounting for cash flow hedges of forecasted transactions for specified risks, and (c) eliminating the requirement in Statement 80 that an entity demonstrate risk reduction on an entity-wide basis to qualify for hedge accounting. The combination of accommodating a range of hedge accounting practices and removing the uncertainty about the accounting requirements for certain strategies should facilitate, and may actually increase, entities' use of derivatives to manage risks.

240. The benefits of improving financial reporting for derivatives and hedging activities come at a cost. Even though much of the information needed to implement this Statement is substantially the same as was required for prior accounting standards for many hedges, and therefore should be available, many entities will incur one-time costs for requisite systems changes. But the benefits of more credible and more understandable information will be ongoing.

241. The Board believes that accounting requirements should be neutral and should not encourage or discourage the use of particular types of contracts.

That desire for neutrality must be balanced with the need to reflect substantive economic differences between different instruments. This Statement is the product of a series of many compromises made by the Board to improve financial reporting for derivatives and hedging activities while giving consideration to cost-benefit issues, as well as current practice. The Board believes that most hedging strategies for which hedge accounting is available in current practice have been reasonably accommodated. The Board recognizes that this Statement does not provide special accounting that accommodates some risk management strategies that certain entities wish to use, such as hedging a portfolio of dissimilar items. However, this Statement clarifies and accommodates hedge accounting for more types of derivatives and different views of risk, and provides more consistent accounting for hedges of forecasted transactions than did the limited guidance that existed before this Statement.

242. Some constituents have said that the requirements of this Statement are more complex than existing guidance. The Board disagrees. It believes that compliance with previous guidance was more complex because the lack of a single, comprehensive framework forced entities to analogize to different and often conflicting sources of guidance. The Board also believes that some constituents' assertions about increased complexity may have been influenced by some entities' relatively lax compliance with previous guidance. For example, the Board understands that not all entities complied with Statement 80's entity-wide risk reduction criterion to qualify for hedge accounting, and that also may have been true for requirements for hedging a portfolio of dissimilar items. The Board also notes that some of the more complex requirements of this Statement, such as reporting the gain or loss on a cash flow hedge in earnings in the periods in which the hedged transaction affects earnings, are a direct result of the Board's efforts to accommodate respondents' wishes.

243. The Board took several steps to minimize the incremental costs of the accounting and disclosure requirements of this Statement. For example, this Statement relies on the valuation guidance provided in Statement 107, which most entities have been applying for several years. The Board also decided not to continue the previously required assessment of risk at an entity-wide level, which constituents said is very difficult and costly to make. This Statement also reduces the disclosure requirements that previously were required for derivatives. Some of the previous

disclosure requirements for derivatives were intended to partially compensate for inadequate accounting; improving the information provided in the basic financial statements makes possible a reduction in such disclosures.

Scope and Definition

244. As already discussed, the Board decided that derivative instruments should be measured at fair value. The Board also decided that accounting for gains or losses that result from measuring derivatives at fair value should depend on whether or not the derivative instrument is designated and qualifies as a hedging instrument. Those decisions require that the Board clearly identify (a) those instruments to which this Statement applies and (b) the criteria that must be met for a relationship to qualify for hedge accounting.

245. The Board decided that this Statement should apply to many, but not all, instruments that are often described as derivatives. In reaching that decision, the Board observed that prior accounting standards did not clearly distinguish derivative instruments from other financial and nonfinancial instruments. Financial statement preparers, users, and other interested parties often have trouble clearly distinguishing between instruments that are commonly considered derivatives and other instruments. Accordingly, they often do not agree on whether certain instruments are derivatives. This Statement defines derivative instruments based on their characteristics; the resulting definition may not always coincide with what some market participants consider to be derivatives.

Why Hedging Instruments Are Limited to Derivatives

246. This Statement limits hedge accounting to those relationships in which derivative instruments and certain foreign-currency-denominated nonderivative instruments are designated as hedging instruments and the necessary qualifying criteria are met. The Board recognizes that there may be valid reasons for entering into transactions intended to be hedges using nonderivative instruments, but the Board continues to believe that permitting nonderivative instruments to be designated as hedging instruments would be inappropriate.

247. Achieving the Board's long-term objective of having all financial instruments—both derivative and nonderivative—measured at fair value would eliminate the need for hedge accounting for the risks inherent in existing financial instruments. Both the

hedging instrument and the hedged item would be measured at fair value. Accounting for the gains and losses on each in the same way would leave no measurement anomalies to which to apply hedge accounting. As further discussed in paragraphs 326 and 327, the Board considers hedge accounting for forecasted transactions to be inappropriate from a conceptual perspective. In practice, hedge accounting for forecasted (anticipated) transactions has been limited to derivatives, and the Board does not think it would be appropriate to extend hedge accounting for what is not a conceptually defensible practice to nonderivative instruments. To include nonderivative financial instruments, other than in circumstances already permitted by existing accounting pronouncements, as hedging instruments also would add complexity and delay issuing guidance on accounting for derivative instruments. The Board therefore decided to limit hedge accounting to derivatives. Consequently, items such as securities, trade receivables and payables, and deposit liabilities at banks may not be designated as hedging instruments except that, consistent with existing provisions in Statement 52, nonderivative instruments that give rise to transaction gains or losses may be designated as hedges of certain foreign currency exposures.

Defining Characteristics of a Derivative Instrument

248. The Board considered defining a *derivative instrument* in this Statement by merely referencing those instruments commonly understood to be derivatives. That would be similar to the method used in paragraph 5 of Statement 119, which said that "... a *derivative financial instrument* is a futures, forward, swap, or option contract, or other financial instrument with similar characteristics." However, the expansion of financial markets and continued development of innovative financial instruments and other contracts could ultimately render obsolete a definition based solely on examples. Currently, contracts often referred to as derivatives have characteristics similar to other contracts that often are *not* considered to be derivative instruments. For example, purchase orders for certain raw materials have many similarities to forward contracts that are referenced to those same raw materials. The Board is concerned that the existing distinctions between many types of contracts are likely to become even more blurred as new innovative instruments are developed. Therefore, to distinguish between similar contracts and to deal with new instruments that may be developed in the future, this Statement provides a definition of de-

rivative instruments based on distinguishing characteristics rather than merely referring to classes of instruments or titles used to describe them.

249. For purposes of this Statement, a derivative instrument is a financial instrument or other contract that has all three of the following characteristics:

a. It has (1) one or more underlyings and (2) one or more notional amounts or payment provisions or both.
b. It requires no initial net investment or an initial net investment that is smaller than would be required for other types of contracts that would be expected to have a similar response to changes in market factors.
c. Its terms require or permit net settlement, it can readily be settled net by a means outside the contract, or it provides for delivery of an asset that puts the recipient in a position not substantially different from net settlement.

The Board believes those three characteristics capture the essence of instruments, such as futures and options, that have long been considered derivatives and instruments that are sufficiently similar to those traditional derivatives that they should be accounted for similarly. The following paragraphs discuss each characteristic in more depth. Section 1 of Appendix A provides additional discussion of the three characteristics of a derivative instrument.

Underlyings and notional amounts or payment provisions

250. Derivative instruments typically permit the parties to participate in some or all of the effects of changes in a referenced price, rate, or other variable, which is referred to as the *underlying,* for example, an interest rate or equity index or the price of a specific security, commodity, or currency. As the term is used in this Statement, a referenced asset or liability, if any, is not itself the *underlying* of a derivative contract. Instead, the *price* or *rate* of the associated asset or liability, which is used to determine the settlement amount of the derivative instrument, is the underlying.

251. By itself, an underlying cannot determine the value or settlement of a derivative. Most derivatives also refer to a *notional amount,* which is a number of units specified in the contract. The multiplication or other arithmetical interaction of the notional amount and the underlying determines the settlement of the derivative. However, rather than referring to a notional amount, some derivatives instead contain a

payment provision that requires settlement if an underlying changes in a specified way. For example, a derivative might require a specified payment if a referenced interest rate increases by 300 basis points. Reference to either a notional amount or a payment provision is needed to compute the contract's periodic settlements and resulting changes in fair value.

252. In concept, any observable variable, including physical as well as financial variables, may be the underlying for a derivative instrument. For example, a contract might specify a payment to be made if it rains more than one inch on a specified day. However, throughout the project that led to this Statement, discussion focused on more traditional derivatives for which the underlying is some form of price, including an interest rate or exchange rate. For example, paragraph 6 of the Exposure Draft referred to "a rate, an index of prices, or another market indicator" in describing an underlying. Relatively late in the process that led to this Statement, the Board considered expanding its scope to include all derivatives based on physical variables but decided not to do so. It was concerned that constituents had not had sufficient opportunity to consider the implications and potential measurement difficulties of including contracts based on physical variables. The Board believes many contracts for which the underlying is a physical variable are currently accounted for as insurance contracts, and it considers that accounting to be adequate for now. However, the Board decided that any derivative instrument that is traded on an exchange, including one based on a physical variable, should be subject to the requirements of this Statement. Accordingly, any derivative based on a physical variable that eventually becomes exchange traded will automatically become subject to the requirements of this Statement. The Board does not believe that measurement or other implementation problems exist for exchange-traded instruments.

253. This Statement also excludes from its scope a derivative instrument for which the underlying is the price or value of a nonfinancial asset of one of the parties to the contract provided that the asset is not readily convertible to cash. Similarly excluded is a derivative instrument for which the underlying is the price or value of a nonfinancial liability of one of the parties to the contract provided that the liability does not require delivery of an asset that is not readily convertible to cash. A contract for which the underlying is specified volumes of sales or service revenues by one of the parties also is excluded. Many such contracts are insurance contracts. An example is a contract based on the condition or value of a building. Others contain an element of compensation for service or for use of another entity's asset. An example is a royalty agreement based on sales of a particular product.

254. Because a derivative may have an underlying that is a combination of variables, the Board added a requirement to clarify the application of paragraph 10(e). Some of the variables in an underlying that is a combination of variables may be subject to the exceptions in paragraph 10(e) and others may not. The Board did not intend for all contracts with those types of underlyings to be excluded automatically from the scope of this Statement. A contract with a combined underlying is subject to the requirements of this Statement if its settlement is expected to change in a way that is highly correlated with the way it would change if it was based on an underlying that would not be eligible for one of the exceptions in paragraph 10(e).

Initial investment in the contract

255. The second characteristic of a derivative instrument refers to the relative amount of the initial net investment in the contract. Providing the opportunity to participate in the price changes of an underlying without actually having to own an associated asset or owe an associated liability is the basic feature that distinguishes most traditional derivative instruments from nonderivative instruments. Therefore, the Board decided that a contract that at inception requires the holder or writer to invest or receive an amount approximating the notional amount of the contract is not a derivative instrument. The following example illustrates that fundamental difference between a derivative instrument and a nonderivative instrument.

256. A party that wishes to participate in the changes in the fair value of 10,000 shares of a specific marketable equity security can, of course, do so by purchasing 10,000 shares of that security. Alternatively, the party may enter into a forward purchase contract with a notional amount of 10,000 shares of that security and an underlying that is the price of that security. Purchasing the shares would require an initial investment equal to the current price for 10,000 shares and would result in benefits such as the receipt of dividends (if any) and the ability to vote the shares. A simple forward contract entered into at the current

forward price for 10,000 shares of the equity instrument would not require an initial investment equal to the notional amount but would offer the same opportunity to benefit or lose from changes in the price of that security.

257. Some respondents to the Exposure Draft suggested that the definition of a derivative instrument should include contracts that require gross exchanges of currencies (for example, currency swaps that require an exchange of different currencies at both inception and maturity). They noted that those contracts are commonly viewed as derivatives, are used in the same manner as derivatives, and therefore should be included in the definition of a derivative instrument. The Board agreed and notes that this Statement's definition of a derivative instrument, as revised from the Exposure Draft, explicitly includes such currency swaps. The Board observes that the initial exchange of currencies of equal fair values in those arrangements does not constitute an initial net *investment* in the contract. Instead, it is the exchange of one kind of *cash* for another kind of *cash* of equal value. The balance of the agreement, a forward contract that obligates and entitles both parties to exchange specified currencies, on specified dates, at specified prices, is a derivative instrument.

258. Paragraphs 6–11 of this Statement address only those contracts that in their entirety are derivative instruments. A contract that requires a relatively large initial net investment may include one or more embedded derivative instruments. The Board's conclusions on embedded derivatives are discussed in paragraphs 293–311.

Net settlement

259. The third distinguishing characteristic of a derivative instrument as defined in this Statement is that it can be readily settled with only a net delivery of assets. Therefore, a derivative contract must meet one of the following criteria:

a. It does not require either party to deliver an asset that is associated with its underlying or that has a principal amount, stated amount, face value, number of shares, or other denomination that is equal to the notional amount (or the notional amount plus a premium or minus a discount).
b. It requires one of the parties to deliver such an asset, but there is a market mechanism that facilitates net settlement.

c. It requires one of the parties to deliver such an asset, but that asset either is readily convertible to cash or is itself a derivative instrument.

260. The Exposure Draft proposed that derivative instruments be distinguished from other instruments by determining whether (a) the holder could settle the contract with only a net cash payment, either by its contractual terms or by custom, and (b) the net payment was determined by reference to changes in the underlying.[31] Under the Exposure Draft, a contract that required ownership or delivery of an asset associated with the underlying would have been a derivative instrument if a mechanism existed in the market to enter into a closing contract with only a net settlement or if the contract was customarily settled with only a net cash payment based on changes in the underlying. The Board focused in the Exposure Draft on whether there is a mechanism in the market for net settlement because it observed that many derivative instruments are actively traded and can be closed or settled before the contract's expiration or maturity by net settlement in active markets. The Board included the requirement for customary settlement in the Exposure Draft for two reasons: (a) to prevent circumvention of the requirements of this Statement by including nonsubstantive delivery provisions in a contract that otherwise would be considered a derivative and (b) to include in the definition of a derivative all contracts that are typically settled net even if the ability to settle net is not an explicit feature of the contract.

261. Several respondents to the Exposure Draft requested clarification of its net settlement provisions. Respondents observed that the phrase *mechanism in the market* was unclear and could lead to different interpretations in practice. They asked whether *only* an organized exchange would constitute the type of market mechanism that the Board had in mind, or whether a willingness of market participants to enter into such a contract in the over-the-counter or other markets would require that the contract be viewed as a derivative instrument. This Statement responds to those questions by indicating in paragraph 57(c)(2) that the Board intends *market mechanism* to be interpreted broadly to include any institutional arrangement or side agreement that permits either party to be relieved of all rights and obligations under the contract and to liquidate its net position without incurring a significant transaction cost.

---

[31]The term *underlying* as used in the Exposure Draft encompassed the asset or liability, the price of which was the underlying for the contract.

262. Respondents also questioned whether *customary* referred to the customs of the reporting entity or the customs of the marketplace. They said that it would be difficult to discern the custom of the marketplace for a non-exchange-traded instrument for which settlement information is not publicly available. They also observed that market customs vary by industry and over time. A criterion based on such customs therefore might lead to different answers at different points in time (for example, customs that currently require gross settlement might subsequently change) and for different participants to the contracts (for example, a bank might customarily settle a certain type of contract with only a net payment of cash, while a manufacturing entity might customarily settle the same type of contract by delivering the assets associated with the underlying). The definition of a derivative in this Statement does not refer to customary settlement. The Board decided that the provisions of paragraph 9 would achieve the objective of the Exposure Draft.

263. During its redeliberations, the Board discussed whether the definition of a derivative instrument should depend on whether net settlement occurs in cash or for another asset. The Board also discussed whether this Statement should apply to a derivative instrument in which at least one of the items to be exchanged in the future is something other than a financial instrument. The Board decided that the medium of exchange used in the net settlement of a derivative contract should not determine whether the instrument is within the scope of this Statement. A contract that can readily be settled net, whether the settlement is for cash or another asset, should be within the scope of this Statement. As a result of that decision, the Board also decided to delete *financial* from the term *derivative financial instruments* in describing the instruments that are within the scope of this Statement.

Assets that are readily convertible to cash

264. The Board decided that a contract that requires delivery of an asset associated with the underlying in a denomination equal to the notional amount should qualify as a derivative instrument if the asset is readily convertible to cash. (Paragraphs 271 and 272 and 275 and 276, respectively, discuss two exceptions to that provision.) As indicated in footnote 5, the term *readily convertible to cash* refers to assets that "have (i) interchangeable (fungible) units and (ii) quoted prices available in an active market that can rapidly absorb the quantity held by the entity without significantly affecting the price."

265. Net settlement is an important characteristic that distinguishes a derivative from a nonderivative because it permits a contract to be settled without either party's accepting the risks and costs customarily associated with owning and delivering the asset associated with the underlying (for example, storage, maintenance, and resale). However, if the assets to be exchanged or delivered are themselves readily convertible to cash, those risks are minimal or nonexistent. Thus, the parties generally should be indifferent as to whether they exchange cash or the assets associated with the underlying. The Board recognizes that determining whether assets are readily convertible to cash will require judgment and sometimes will lead to different applications in practice. However, the Board believes that the use of *readily convertible to cash* permits an appropriate amount of flexibility and describes an important characteristic of the derivative instruments addressed by this Statement.

266. The Board considered using the idea of *readily obtainable elsewhere* as is used in Statement 125 to determine whether a derivative instrument that requires that the holder or writer own or deliver the asset or liability that is associated with the underlying is within the scope of this Statement. However, the Board noted that readily obtainable elsewhere relates to the availability of an asset; not necessarily its liquidity. The Board decided that *readily convertible to cash* is the appropriate criterion because it addresses whether the asset can be converted to cash with little effort, not just whether the asset is readily available in the marketplace.

Commodity Contracts

267. Statements 105, 107, and 119 did not address commodity-based contracts because those contracts require or permit future delivery of an item that is not a financial instrument. Statement 105 explained that for a commodity-based contract ". . . the future economic benefit is receipt of goods or services instead of a right to receive cash or an ownership interest in an entity and the economic sacrifice is delivery of goods or services instead of an obligation to deliver cash or an ownership interest in an entity" (paragraph 32). Some respondents to the Exposure Draft that preceded Statement 119 suggested that the scope be expanded to include commodity-based contracts. The Board decided not to expand the scope at that time principally because of that project's accelerated timetable.

268. The Exposure Draft proposed that the definition of *derivative* include only *financial instruments*.

Nevertheless, the Exposure Draft would have included certain commodity contracts because they often have many of the same characteristics as other derivative contracts. They often are used interchangeably with other derivatives, and they present risks similar to other derivatives. The Board initially proposed to resolve that apparent conflict by amending the definition of *financial instrument* in Statement 107 to include contracts that permit a choice of settlement by delivering either a commodity or cash. As discussed in paragraph 263, the Board decided to change the scope of this Statement to address the accounting for *derivative instruments* rather than just derivative *financial* instruments. Therefore, it was not necessary to amend the definition of a financial instrument in Statement 107 to include certain commodity-based contracts in the scope of this Statement.

269. Changing the scope of this Statement from derivative *financial* instruments to derivative instruments results in including some contracts that settle net for a commodity or other nonfinancial asset. The Board believes that including commodity-based contracts with the essential characteristics of a derivative instrument within the scope of this Statement will help to avoid accounting anomalies that result from measuring similar contracts differently. The Board also believes that including those commodity-based contracts in this Statement will provide worthwhile information to financial statement users and will resolve concerns raised by some respondents to the Exposure Drafts that preceded Statements 107 and 119.

270. The Exposure Draft would have included only commodity-based contracts that permitted net cash settlement, either by their contractual terms or by custom. For the reasons discussed in paragraphs 264–266, the Board decided, instead, to include a contract that requires delivery of an asset associated with the underlying if that asset is readily convertible to cash (for example, gold, silver, corn, and wheat). Different accounting will result depending on whether or not the assets associated with the underlying for a contract are readily convertible to cash. The Board considers that difference to be appropriate because contracts that settle net or by delivering assets readily convertible to cash provide different benefits and pose different risks than those that require exchange of cash or other assets for an asset that is not readily convertible to cash.

Normal purchases and normal sales

271. The Board decided that contracts that require delivery of nonfinancial assets that are readily convertible to cash need not be accounted for as derivative instruments under this Statement if the assets constitute *normal purchases* or *normal sales* of the reporting entity unless those contracts can readily be settled net. The Board believes contracts for the acquisition of assets in quantities that the entity expects to use or sell over a reasonable period in the normal course of business are not unlike binding purchase orders or other similar contracts to which this Statement does not apply. The Board notes that the normal purchases and normal sales exemption is necessary only for contracts based on assets that are readily convertible to cash.

272. The Board understands that the normal purchases and normal sales provision sometimes will result in different parties to a contract reaching different conclusions about whether the contract is required to be accounted for as a derivative instrument. For example, the contract may be for ordinary sales by one party (and therefore not a derivative instrument) but not for ordinary purchases by the counterparty (and therefore a derivative instrument). The Board considered requiring both parties to account for a contract as a derivative instrument if the purchases or sales by either party were other than ordinary in the normal course of business. However, that approach would have required that one party to the contract determine the circumstances of the other party to that same contract. Although the Board believes that the accounting by both parties to a contract generally should be symmetrical, it decided that symmetry would be impractical in this instance and that a potential asymmetrical result is acceptable.

Financial Instruments

273. Some contracts require the holder or writer to deliver a financial asset or liability that is associated with the underlying and that has a denomination equal to the notional amount of the contract. Determining whether those contracts are derivative instruments depends, at least in part, on whether the related financial assets or liabilities are readily convertible to cash.

Trade date versus settlement date accounting

274. Existing accounting practice is inconsistent about the timing of recognition of transfers of various financial instruments. Some transfers of securities are

recognized as of the date of trade (often referred to as trade date accounting). Other transfers are recognized as of the date the financial instrument is actually transferred and the transaction is settled (often referred to as settlement date accounting). During the period between trade and settlement dates, the parties essentially have entered into a forward contract that might meet the definition of a derivative if the financial instrument is readily convertible to cash. Requiring that all forward contracts for purchases and sales of financial instruments that are readily convertible to cash be accounted for as derivatives would effectively require settlement date accounting for all such transactions. Resolving the issue of trade date versus settlement date accounting was not an objective of the project that led to this Statement. Therefore, the Board decided to explicitly exclude forward contracts for "regular-way" security trades from the scope of this Statement.

Regular-way security trades

275. Regular-way security trades are those that are completed (or settled) within the time period generally established by regulations and conventions in the marketplace or by the exchange on which the transaction is being executed. The notion of a regular-way security trade is based on marketplace regulations or conventions rather than on the normal practices of an individual entity. For example, if it is either required or customary for certain securities on a specified exchange to settle within three days, a contract that requires settlement in more than three days is not a regular-way security trade even if the entity customarily enters into contracts to purchase such securities more than three days forward. The Board considered other approaches that focused on reasonable settlement periods or customary settlement periods for the specific parties to a transfer. The Board decided that those approaches were inferior because they lacked the consistency and discipline that are provided by focusing on regular-way security trades. The Board also believes that participants can reasonably determine settlement periods required by the regulations or conventions of an active marketplace. Regulations or conventions may be more difficult to determine for foreign or less active exchanges. However, the provisions in paragraph 10(a) apply only if the holder or writer of the contract is required to deliver assets that are readily convertible to cash. Therefore, the regulations or conventions of the marketplace should be reasonably apparent because the related market must be active enough to rapidly absorb the quantities involved without significantly affecting the price.

276. The Board considered limiting the exclusion for regular-way security trades to purchases or sales of *existing* securities. A forward contract for a regular-way trade of an existing security entitles the purchaser to receive and requires the seller to deliver a specific security. The delay is a matter of market regulations and conventions for delivery. In contrast, a forward contract for a when-issued or other security that does not yet exist does not entitle or obligate the parties to exchange a specific security. Instead, it entitles the issuer and holder to participate in price changes that occur before the security is issued. For that reason, the Board would have preferred that a forward contract on a security that does not yet exist be subject to the requirements of this Statement. However, the Board was concerned that including, for example, to-be-announced (TBA) Government National Mortgage Association (GNMA) forward contracts and other forward contracts for when-issued securities within the scope of this Statement might subject some entities to potentially burdensome regulatory requirements for transactions in derivatives. On balance, the Board decided to extend the regular-way exemption to purchases and sales of when-issued and TBA securities. However, the exemption applies only if (a) there is no other way to purchase or sell the security and (b) the trade will settle within the shortest period permitted for the security.

Insurance contracts

277. The Exposure Draft explicitly excluded insurance contracts, as defined in Statements 60, 97, and 113, from its definition of a derivative financial instrument. The insurance contracts described in those Statements also were excluded from the scope of Statement 107, which states:

> The Board concluded that disclosures about fair value should not be required for insurance contracts. . . . The Board believes that definitional and valuation difficulties are present to a certain extent in those contracts and obligations, and that further consideration is required before decisions can be made about whether to apply the definition to components of those contracts and whether to require disclosures about fair value for the financial components. [paragraph 74]

278. During the deliberations before issuance of the Exposure Draft, the Board decided to specifically preclude an insurance contract from qualifying as a

derivative because it believed definitional and valuation difficulties still existed. The Exposure Draft observed that the insurance industry and the accounting and actuarial professions have not reached a common understanding about how to estimate the fair value of insurance contracts. Developing measurement guidance for them might have delayed the issuance of guidance on accounting for derivatives. The Board intends to reconsider the accounting for insurance contracts in other phases of its financial instruments project.

279. Although the term *insurance contract* is frequently used in Statements 60, 97, and 113, it is not clearly defined in those or other accounting pronouncements. As a result, the Exposure Draft's provision that insurance contracts and reinsurance contracts generally are not derivative instruments may not have been workable. The Board was concerned that the phrase *insurance contracts* might be interpreted quite broadly to encompass most agreements or contracts issued by insurance enterprises as part of their ongoing operations.

280. The accounting provisions for insurance contracts in Statements 60, 97, and 113 are significantly different from the accounting provisions for derivative instruments in this Statement. The Board was concerned that contracts that are substantially the same as other derivative instruments might, instead, be accounted for as insurance contracts. The Board therefore decided to eliminate the Exposure Draft's proposed scope exclusion for insurance contracts and, instead, require that those contracts be included in or excluded from the scope of this Statement based on their characteristics.

281. Insurance contracts often have some of the same characteristics as derivative instruments that are within the scope of this Statement. Often, however, they lack one or more of those characteristics. As a result, most traditional insurance contracts will not be derivative instruments as defined in this Statement. They will be excluded from that definition because they entitle the holder to compensation only if, as a result of an identifiable insurable event (other than a change in price), the holder incurs a liability or there is an adverse change in the value of a specific asset or liability for which the holder is at risk. However, contracts that in their entirety meet this Statement's definition of a derivative instrument, whether issued by an insurance enterprise or another type of enterprise,

must be accounted for as such. The Board does not believe that a decision on whether a contract must be accounted for as a derivative should depend on the identity of the issuer. To help in applying the provisions of this Statement, paragraph 10(c) provides some examples illustrating the application of the definition to insurance contracts.

282. The Board acknowledges that many of the problems with determining the fair value of traditional insurance liabilities are still unresolved. The Board notes, however, that many of the issues of how to measure the fair value of insurance contracts do not apply to instruments issued by insurance enterprises that, in their entirety, qualify as derivative instruments under this Statement. Instead, the methods for estimating the fair values of those contracts should be similar to the methods used for derivative instruments with similar characteristics issued by other types of enterprises.

283. Although many contracts issued by insurance enterprises will not, in their entirety, meet the definition of a derivative instrument, some may include embedded derivatives that are required by this Statement to be accounted for separately from the host contract. Contracts that may include embedded derivatives include, but are not limited to, annuity contracts that promise the policyholder a return based on selected changes in the S&P 500 index, variable life and annuity contracts, and property and casualty contracts that combine protection for property damage and changes in foreign currency exchange rates. Section 2 of Appendix B provides additional guidance on insurance contracts with embedded derivative instruments.

Exception for derivatives that serve as impediments to recognition of a sale

284. The existence of certain derivatives affects the accounting for the transfer of an asset or a pool of assets. For example, a call option that enables a transferor to repurchase transferred financial assets that are not readily available would prevent accounting for that transfer as a sale. The consequence is that to recognize the call option would be to count the same thing twice. The holder of the option already recognizes in its financial statements the assets that it has the option to purchase. Thus those types of derivatives are excluded from the scope of this Statement.

Exception for instruments classified in stockholders' equity

285. As noted in paragraph 3(a) of this Statement, derivative instruments are assets or liabilities. Consequently, items appropriately classified in stockholders' equity in an entity's statement of financial position are not within the scope of this Statement. The Board decided to clarify that point by explicitly excluding from the scope of this Statement the accounting for such equity instruments.

286. The Board considered whether this Statement also should exclude instruments that an entity either can or must settle by issuing its own stock but that are indexed to something else. For example, the Board discussed whether an instrument that requires settlement in the issuer's or holder's common stock but that is indexed to changes in the S&P 500 index should be excluded from the scope of this Statement. The Board currently has a project on its agenda that considers whether certain instruments are equity or liabilities. That project will address the issue of whether instruments to be settled in the entity's stock but indexed to something other than its stock are liabilities or equity. The Board will reconsider the application of this Statement to such contracts as necessary when that project is completed. Until that time, contracts that provide for settlement in shares of an entity's stock but that are indexed in part or in full to something other than the entity's stock are to be accounted for as derivative instruments if the contracts satisfy the criteria in paragraphs 6–10 of this Statement. Those contracts are to be classified as assets or liabilities and not as part of stockholders' equity.

Stock-based compensation contracts

287. Paragraph 11(b) of this Statement excludes the issuer's accounting for derivative instruments issued in connection with stock-based compensation arrangements addressed in FASB Statement No. 123, *Accounting for Stock-Based Compensation*. Many such instruments would be excluded by paragraph 11(a) because they are classified in stockholders' equity. However, Statement 123 also addresses stock-based compensation arrangements that are derivatives and that qualify as a liability of the issuer. The Board decided that the issuer's accounting for those contracts is adequately addressed by Statement 123. As with the other exclusions in paragraph 11, the holder's accounting for a derivative instrument in a compensation arrangement addressed by Statement 123 is subject to this Statement.

Contingent consideration in a business combination

288. Opinion 16 addresses the purchaser's (issuer's) accounting for contingent consideration provided in a purchase business combination. The effect of a contingent consideration arrangement on the accounting for a business combination often is significant and depends on the terms and conditions of both the business combination and the contingent consideration arrangement. Although contingent consideration arrangements may share at least some of the characteristics of derivative instruments addressed by this Statement, the Board decided that without further study it would be inappropriate to change the accounting for them by the entity that accounts for the business combination. The Board currently has a project on its agenda to reconsider the accounting for business combinations. It will consider this issue as part of that project.

289. This Statement does apply to contracts that are similar to, but not accounted for as, contingent consideration under the provisions of Opinion 16 if those contracts satisfy the scope provisions either for a derivative instrument (paragraphs 6–10) or for a contract with an embedded derivative instrument (paragraphs 12–16). In addition, this Statement applies to a seller's (holder's) accounting for contingent consideration that meets its definition of a derivative. For example, assume that a purchaser of a business issues to the seller a freestanding financial instrument (as addressed in EITF Issue No. 97-8, "Accounting for Contingent Consideration Issued in a Purchase Business Combination") that provides contingent consideration in a purchase business combination under Opinion 16. That freestanding instrument is assumed to meet this Statement's definition of a derivative instrument. The purchaser's accounting for the instrument is explicitly excluded from the scope of this Statement, but the seller who receives the instrument must account for it according to the requirements of this Statement.

Application to specific contracts

290. Several respondents to the Exposure Draft asked the Board for specific guidance about whether some contracts meet the definition of a derivative instrument, including sales of securities not yet owned ("short sales"), take-or-pay contracts, and contracts with liquidating damages or other termination clauses. The Board cannot definitively state whether those types of contracts will always (or never) meet

the definition because their terms and related customary practices vary. In addition, the terms of the contracts or customary practices may change over time, thereby affecting the determination of whether a particular type of contract meets the definition of a derivative instrument. Appendix A provides examples illustrating how the definition of a derivative instrument applies to certain specific situations.

The Scope of Statement 119

291. This Statement's definition of derivative contracts excludes certain contracts that were included in the scope of Statement 119. For example, a loan commitment would be excluded if it (a) requires the holder to deliver a promissory note that would not be readily convertible to cash and (b) cannot readily be settled net. Other conditional and executory contracts that were included in the scope of Statement 119 may not qualify as derivative instruments under the definition in this Statement. The Board decided that some change in scope from Statement 119 is an appropriate consequence of defining derivative instruments based on their primary characteristics.

292. This Statement supersedes Statement 119. Therefore, one result of excluding instruments that were included in the scope of Statement 119 from the scope of this Statement is that some disclosures previously required for those excluded contracts will no longer be required. The Board considers that result to be acceptable. Moreover, Statement 107 continues to require disclosure of the fair value of all financial instruments by the entities to which it applies.

Embedded Derivatives

293. The Board considers it important that an entity not be able to avoid the recognition and measurement requirements of this Statement merely by embedding a derivative instrument in a nonderivative financial instrument or other contract. Therefore, certain embedded derivatives are included in the scope of this Statement if they would be subject to the Statement on a freestanding basis. However, the Board also decided that some derivatives embedded in host contracts, such as many of the prepayment or call options frequently included as part of mortgage loans and other debt instruments, should be excluded from the scope of this Statement.

Approaches considered

294. The Board considered a number of approaches for determining which contracts with embedded derivatives should be included in the scope of this Statement. Some approaches focused either on an instrument's yield or on its predominant characteristics. The Board decided that those approaches would likely include callable or prepayable debt and perhaps other instruments that often are not thought of as including an embedded derivative, even though they do. The Board also was concerned about the operationality of those approaches.

295. The scope of the Exposure Draft included a contract with both nonderivative and derivative characteristics if some or all of its contractually required cash flows were determined by reference to changes in one or more underlyings in a manner that multiplied or otherwise exacerbated the effect of those changes. That scope was intended to incorporate embedded forwards, swaps, and options with a notional amount that was greater than the face value of the "host" contract or that otherwise "leveraged" the effect of changes in one or more underlyings. Numerous respondents to the Exposure Draft asked for clarification of the phrase *multiplies or otherwise exacerbates* and said that they did not understand why certain instruments were included in the scope of the Exposure Draft while others were not.

296. The Board agreed with respondents that the approach in the Exposure Draft was difficult to apply in a consistent manner. The Board also concluded that the Exposure Draft inappropriately excluded some instruments from its scope and inappropriately included others. For example, an instrument that paid a simple multiple of a market interest rate (for example, 120 percent of U.S. dollar LIBOR) might be considered to have an embedded derivative that requires separate accounting. In contrast, a structured note that paid a return based on 100 percent of the appreciation in the fair value of an equity instrument would not be considered to have an embedded derivative that requires separate accounting.

297. Some respondents to the Exposure Draft suggested that all financial instruments with embedded derivatives be excluded from the scope of this Statement because existing accounting standards for nonderivative instruments provide adequate guidance for those compound financial instruments. The Board rejected that suggestion for three reasons. First, applying existing accounting standards for nonderivative instruments would not necessarily achieve the Board's goal of increasing the transparency of derivatives in the financial statements. For example, existing guidance for the issuer's accounting for indexed debt instruments is incomplete and would not

necessarily result in recognition of changes in the fair value of the embedded derivative in either the balance sheet or the income statement. Second, a derivative can be embedded in a contract other than a financial instrument, such as a purchase order. The existing accounting pronouncements for such contracts do not adequately address the accounting for embedded derivatives in those contracts. Third, excluding all compound instruments from its scope would make it possible to circumvent the provisions of this Statement. One apparent reason that structured notes have become prevalent is that combining various features of derivative and nonderivative instruments produces different accounting results than accounting for each component separately, and participants in transactions involving structured notes sometimes considered the accounting results attractive. Excluding all instruments that embed derivative instruments in nonderivative host contracts from the scope of this Statement would likely increase the incentive to combine those instruments to avoid accounting for derivative instruments according to the provisions of this Statement.

298. Under the approach in the Exposure Draft, contracts designed to result in a rate of return that differs in a nontrivial way from the change in price that would be realized from a direct investment (or obligation) in the referenced asset(s) or other item(s) of an amount comparable to the notional amount or par value of the contract would have been accounted for as derivative instruments. Clarifying the phrase *multiplies or otherwise exacerbates* would have addressed some of the problems raised by respondents to the Exposure Draft, but it still would have focused solely on whether the derivative feature resulted in a meaningful amount of positive or negative leverage. It would not have addressed whether the derivative component and host contract are of the type generally expected to be combined. The results still seemed counterintuitive in that an instrument that paid interest of 120 percent of LIBOR (assuming that 120 percent was not deemed to be a trivial amount of leverage) would be accounted for as a derivative instrument, but a note indexed to 100 percent of the S&P 500 index would not.

Accounting for embedded derivatives separately from the host contract

299. The Exposure Draft would have required that both a host contract and an embedded derivative feature, *together,* be accounted for as a derivative instrument if prescribed criteria were met. As a result,

some contracts with embedded derivative features would have been accounted for like derivatives and could have been designated as hedging instruments. Some respondents to the Exposure Draft were concerned that its approach would permit an entity to use a cash instrument as a hedging instrument, which was generally precluded by the Exposure Draft, simply by embedding an insignificant leverage factor in the interest formula. The Board agreed with those respondents and decided that (a) it was inappropriate to treat instruments that include both nonderivative and derivative components entirely as derivative instruments and (b) nonderivative instruments should only be eligible as hedging instruments in selected circumstances.

300. For several reasons, the Board decided to change the accounting for instruments with embedded derivatives. Most importantly, accounting for the entire instrument as a derivative or nonderivative is inconsistent with the accounting for hedged items required by this Statement. For a fair value hedge, the Exposure Draft would have required that all or a proportionate part of the total changes in fair value of a hedged item be recognized. However, this Statement requires recognizing at its fair value only the portion or proportion of a hedged item attributable to the risk being hedged. That change to a "separation-by-risk" approach is consistent with accounting for a derivative separately from the host contract in which it is embedded. Accounting for the derivative separately from the host contract also is more consistent with the objective of measuring derivative instruments at fair value and does not result in measuring derivative instruments differently simply because they are combined with other instruments.

301. The Board recognizes that there may be circumstances in which an embedded derivative cannot be reliably identified and measured for separation from the host contract. In those circumstances, this Statement requires that the entire contract, including both its derivative and nonderivative portions, be measured at fair value with changes in fair value recognized currently in earnings. The Board expects that an entity that enters into sophisticated investment and funding strategies such as structured notes or other contracts with embedded derivatives will be able to obtain the information necessary to reliably identify and measure the separate components. Accordingly, the Board believes it should be unusual that an entity would conclude that it cannot reliably separate an embedded derivative from its host contract.

302: Instruments that include embedded derivatives that are not accounted for separately from the host contract because the entity is unable to reliably identify and measure the derivative may not be designated as hedging instruments. That prohibition applies to the entire contract, as well as any portion of it, and addresses some of respondents' concerns about designating nonderivative instruments as hedging instruments. Prohibiting an entire contract with an embedded derivative from being designated as a hedging instrument will avoid the inappropriate use of nonderivative instruments as hedging instruments. It also should serve as an incentive to identify and separate derivative features from their host contracts.

303. Measuring an embedded derivative separately from its host contract will require judgment, and sometimes such measurements may be difficult. The Board considered providing specific guidelines for making such measurements but decided that such guidance could be unduly restrictive and could not address all relevant concerns. Instead, the Board decided only to clarify that the objective is to estimate the fair value of the derivative features separately from the fair value of the nonderivative portions of the contract. Estimates of fair value should reflect all relevant features of each component and their effect on a current exchange between willing parties. For example, an embedded purchased option that expires if the contract in which it is embedded is prepaid would have a different value than an option whose term is a specified period that is not subject to truncation.

The clearly-and-closely-related approach

304. This Statement requires that an embedded derivative be accounted for separately from a nonderivative host contract if (a) the derivative, considered on a freestanding basis, would be accounted for as a derivative instrument under this Statement and (b) the economic characteristics of the derivative and the host contract are not *clearly and closely related* to one another. The first of those criteria ensures that only derivative instruments as defined by, and subject to the requirements of, this Statement are accounted for separately. For example, the issuer would not account separately for an option embedded in a hybrid instrument if, on a freestanding basis, that option would be an equity instrument of the entity that is properly classified in stockholders' equity.

Whether the issuer should account separately for an equity instrument embedded in an asset or a liability is an issue in the Board's project on liabilities and equity.

305. The second criterion listed in paragraph 304 focuses on whether an embedded derivative bears a close economic relationship to the host contract. As a practical matter, the Board decided that not all embedded derivative features should be required to be accounted for separately from the host contract. Many hybrid instruments with embedded derivatives that bear a close economic relationship to the host contract were developed many years ago, for reasons that clearly were not based on achieving a desired accounting result. Prepayable mortgages and other prepayable debt instruments are examples of such familiar compound instruments with embedded derivatives. The accounting for those types of hybrid instruments is well established and generally has not been questioned. However, other embedded derivatives, such as an equity- or commodity-linked return included in a debt instrument that may cause the value of the instrument to vary inversely with changes in interest rates, do not bear a close economic relationship to the host contract. Even though conceptually all embedded derivatives should be accounted for separately, the Board decided, as a practical accommodation, that only an embedded derivative that is not considered to be clearly and closely related to its host contract should be accounted for separately.

306. The Board expects the clearly-and-closely-related approach to affect a significant number and wide variety of structured notes and other contracts that include embedded derivatives. Applying the approach will require judgment, which may lead to different accounting for similar instruments. To reduce that possibility, Appendix B provides examples illustrating how to apply the approach.

307. The clearly-and-closely-related approach sometimes will result in different accounting by the parties to a contract. For example, the issuer of convertible debt would not account for the embedded derivative feature separately from the host contract if the derivative component, on a freestanding basis, would not be subject to the requirements of this Statement because of the exclusion in paragraph 11(a). However, an investor in the convertible debt instrument would not be afforded that exclusion and would be required to account for the conversion feature separately from the host contract if the criteria in paragraph 12 are met.

308. The holder and issuer of an equity instrument with an embedded put, such as puttable common stock, would not, however, necessarily treat the embedded derivative differently. A put option embedded in an equity security has the potential to convert the equity security to cash or another asset, and conversion to cash according to the terms of the instrument is not a usual characteristic of an equity security. Accordingly, a put option embedded in an equity security is not clearly and closely related to the host contract if exercise of the put option would result in the payment of cash or delivery of another asset by the issuer of a security (except in those circumstances in which the put option is not considered to be a derivative pursuant to paragraph 11(a) because it is classified in shareholders' equity). Because the embedded put is more closely related to a liability than an equity security, both the issuer and the holder would account for it separately if the criteria in paragraph 12 are met. However, if exercise of the put would result in the issuance of additional equity instruments rather than paying cash or delivering another asset, the put is considered to be clearly and closely related to the equity security.

309. Paragraphs 13–15 of this Statement discuss some common relationships between interest rate features and host contracts, and foreign currency exchange rate features and host contracts. That guidance is provided to simplify the analysis of whether some of the more common types of contracts include embedded derivatives that require separate accounting. Paragraph 13 clarifies that most interest-bearing instruments that include derivative features that serve only to alter net interest payments that otherwise would be made on an interest-bearing host contract are considered to be clearly and closely related to the host contract. However, an embedded derivative that affects interest rates in such a way that the investor might not recover substantially all of its initial recorded investment is not considered to be clearly and closely related to the host contract and therefore should be accounted for separately. Similarly, an embedded derivative that could at least double the investor's initial rate of return on the host contract and also could result in a rate of return that is at least twice what otherwise would be the market return for a contract that has the same terms as the host contract and that involves a debtor with similar credit quality is not considered to be clearly and closely related and should be accounted for separately. The test for separate accounting pursuant to paragraph 13 should be applied based on what is possible under the contractual terms and not on a probability basis. For ex-

ample, an embedded derivative that could under any circumstances result in the hybrid instrument's being settled in such a way that the holder does not recover substantially all of its initial recorded investment would not be considered to be clearly and closely related to the host contract even though the possibility that such a situation would occur is remote.

310. The Board recognizes that the provisions of paragraph 13(a) might raise the question of whether an interest-only strip is subject to the provisions of this Statement because the holder of an interest-only strip may not recover substantially all of its initial recorded investment. The Board notes that accounting for interest-only and principal-only strips is related to issues concerning accounting for retained interests in securitizations that the Board is currently reconsidering in conjunction with the implementation of Statement 125. Accordingly, the Board decided to exclude from the scope of this Statement interest-only and principal-only strips that meet the criteria in paragraph 14 and further consider the accounting for them in conjunction with its consideration of accounting for retained interests in securitizations.

311. Paragraph 15 provides that an embedded foreign currency derivative is not to be separated from the host contract and considered a derivative pursuant to paragraph 12 if the host contract is not a financial instrument and specifies payments denominated in either of the following currencies:

a. The currency of the primary economic environment in which any substantial party to the contract operates (that is, its functional currency)
b. The currency in which the price of the related good or service is routinely denominated in international commerce (such as the U.S. dollar for crude oil transactions).

For example, a lease of U.S. real estate with payments denominated in Deutsche marks contains an embedded derivative that should be viewed as clearly and closely related to the host lease contract and thus does not require separate accounting if the Deutsche mark is the functional currency of at least one substantial party to the lease. The Board decided that it was important that the payments be denominated in the functional currency of at least one *substantial* party to the transaction to ensure that the foreign currency is integral to the arrangement and thus considered to be clearly and closely related to the terms of the lease. A contract with payments denominated in a currency that is not the functional currency of any substantial party to that contract includes an embedded derivative that is not considered to be clearly and closely related to the host contract and should be accounted for separately under the provisions of this Statement. The second exclusion in paragraph 15 also permits contractual payments to be denominated in the currency in which the price of the related commodity or service is routinely stated in international commerce without requiring separate accounting for an embedded derivative. The Board decided that it would be appropriate to consider the currency in which contracts for a given commodity are routinely denominated to be clearly and closely related to those contracts, regardless of the functional currency of the parties to that contract.

Fair Value Measurement Guidance

312. The definition of fair value in this Statement is derived from paragraphs 42–44 of Statement 125. The definition originated in paragraphs 5, 6, and 18–29 of Statement 107.

313. This Statement refers to Statement 107 for guidance in applying the definition of fair value. Some respondents to the Exposure Draft asked either for additional guidance on estimating the fair value of financial instruments or for amendments of part of the guidance in Statement 107. They said that the guidance in Statement 107 is not robust enough for recognition purposes (as opposed to disclosure) and allows too much variability in the estimates of fair value, especially for items not traded on a public exchange. The Board decided for several reasons to retain the guidance provided by Statement 107. Statement 107 has been in effect for several years, and entities are familiar with its measurement guidance. In addition, Board members were concerned that reevaluating and making the fair value guidance more prescriptive would significantly delay issuance of this Statement. On balance, the Board decided that the measurement guidance in Statement 107 is sufficient for use in applying this Statement. The Board will consider measurement issues and likely provide additional guidance or change Statement 107's guidance in some areas, perhaps including the areas discussed in the following paragraphs in the course of its project on the fair value measurement of financial instruments.

314. Respondents to the Exposure Draft also provided comments on specific measurement issues, focusing on the following three areas: (a) consideration of a discount or premium in the valuation of a large

position, (b) consideration of changes in creditworthiness in valuing a debtor's liabilities, and (c) the valuation of deposit liabilities. Those areas are discussed below.

Consideration of a Discount or Premium in the Valuation of a Large Position

315. Consistent with Statement 107, the definition of fair value in this Statement precludes an entity from using a "blockage" factor (that is, a premium or discount based on the relative size of the position held, such as a large proportion of the total trading units of an instrument) in determining the fair value of a large block of financial instruments. The definition of fair value requires that fair value be determined as the product of the number of trading units of an asset times a quoted market price if available. Statement 107 further clarifies the issue:

> Under the definition of fair value in paragraph 5, the quoted price for a single trading unit in the most active market is the basis for determining market price and reporting fair value. This is the case even if placing orders to sell all of an entity's holdings of an asset or to buy back all of a liability might affect the price, or if a market's normal volume for one day might not be sufficient to absorb the quantity held or owed by an entity. [paragraph 6]

Some respondents to the Exposure Draft indicated that the guidance in Statement 107 (and implicitly the definition of *fair value* in this Statement) should be revised to require or permit consideration of a discount in valuing a large asset position. They asserted that an entity that holds a relatively large amount (compared with average trading volume) of a traded asset and liquidates the entire amount at one time likely would receive an amount less than the quoted market price. Although respondents generally focused on a discount, holding a relatively large amount of an asset might sometimes result in a premium over the market price for a single trading unit. The Board currently believes that the use of a blockage factor would lessen the reliability and comparability of reported estimates of fair value.

Valuation of Liabilities

316. Some respondents to the Exposure Draft noted that Statement 107 permits an entity to choose whether to consider changes in its own creditworthiness in determining the fair value of its debt and

asked for further guidance on that issue. The definition of fair value in Statement 125 says that in measuring liabilities at fair value by discounting estimated future cash flows, an objective is to use discount rates at which those liabilities could be settled in an arm's-length transaction. However, the FASB's pronouncements to date have not broadly addressed whether changes in a debtor's creditworthiness after incurrence of a liability should be reflected in measuring its fair value. Pending resolution of the broad issue of the effect of a debtor's creditworthiness on the fair value of its liabilities, the Board decided to use the definition in Statement 125 but not to provide additional guidance on reflecting the effects of changes in creditworthiness.

Valuation of deposit liabilities

317. The guidance in Statement 107 precludes an entity from reflecting a long-term relationship with depositors, commonly known as a core deposit intangible, in determining the fair value of a deposit liability. Paragraph 12 of Statement 107 states, in part:

> In estimating the fair value of deposit liabilities, a financial entity shall not take into account the value of its long-term relationships with depositors, commonly known as core deposit intangibles, which are separate intangible assets, not financial instruments. For deposit liabilities with no defined maturities, the fair value to be disclosed under this Statement is the amount payable on demand at the reporting date.

Some respondents to the Exposure Draft requested that this Statement permit the fair value of deposit liabilities to reflect the effect of the core deposit intangible. The Board decided to make no change to the guidance in Statement 107 on that issue because it will be addressed as part of the Board's current project on measuring financial instruments at fair value. Issues of whether the fair values of certain liabilities (or assets) should reflect their values as if they were settled immediately or whether they should be based on their expected settlement dates, as well as issues of whether or when it would be appropriate to measure portfolios of assets or liabilities rather than individual items in those portfolios, are central to that project.

Other Fair Value Measurement Guidance

318. Statement 107 requires disclosure of the fair value of financial instruments "for which it is *practi-*

cable to estimate that value" (emphasis added). Unlike Statement 107, this Statement provides no *practicability* exception that would permit an entity to avoid the required fair value measurements. The Board believes that prudent risk management generally would require an entity to measure the fair value of any derivative that it holds as well as any item (or the portion of the item attributable to the identified risk) designated as being hedged in a fair value hedge.

319. This Statement requires that in measuring the change in fair value of a forward contract by discounting future cash flows, the estimate of future cash flows be based on changes in forward rates rather than spot rates. Thus, the gain or loss on, for example, a foreign currency forward contract would be based on the change in the forward rate, discounted to reflect the time value of money until the settlement date. The Board notes that the accounting literature in effect before the issuance of this Statement discusses different methods of estimating the value of a foreign currency forward contract. The Board decided that the valuation of a foreign currency forward contract should consider that (a) currencies will be exchanged at a future date, (b) relative interest rates determine the difference between spot and forward rates, and (c) valuation is affected by the time value of money. The net present value technique is the only method that considers all three items as well as the current settlement of present gains or losses that arise from changes in the spot rate.

Demand for Hedge Accounting

320. The Report on Deliberations describes hedge accounting as a "special accounting treatment that alters the normal accounting for one or more components of a hedge so that counterbalancing changes in the fair values of hedged items and hedging instruments, from the date the hedge is established, are not included in earnings in different periods" (paragraph 28). Demand for special accounting for hedges of the fair value exposure associated with assets and liabilities arises, in part, because of accounting anomalies—that is, differences in the way hedged items and hedging instruments are recognized and measured. Recognition anomalies arise because some assets and liabilities are recognized in the statement of financial position, while others, such as many firm commitments, are not. Measurement anomalies arise because existing accounting standards use different measurement attributes for different assets and liabilities. Some assets and liabilities

are measured based on historical costs, others are measured based on current values, and still others are measured at the lower of cost or market value, which is a combination of historical costs and current values. Accounting recognition and measurement decisions generally have been made independently for each kind of asset or liability without considering relationships with other assets or liabilities. Hedge accounting for assets and liabilities initially arose as a means of compensating for situations in which measurement anomalies between a hedged item and hedging instrument result in recognizing offsetting gains and losses in earnings in different periods.

Hedges of Fair Value Exposures

321. For hedges of fair value exposures, this Statement provides for certain gains and losses on designated assets and liabilities to be recognized in earnings in the same period as the losses and gains on the related derivative hedging instrument. Accounting for all financial instruments at fair value with all changes in fair value recognized similarly, such as in earnings, would eliminate the need for special accounting to accommodate the current mixed-attribute measurement model for fair value hedges of financial assets and liabilities. Fair value accounting for all financial instruments would not, however, affect either the perceived need for special accounting for fair value hedges of nonfinancial assets and liabilities or constituents' desire for special accounting for cash flow hedges of forecasted transactions.

Hedges of Cash Flow Exposures

322. Although accounting anomalies do not exist for cash flow hedges of forecasted transactions, many constituents want special accounting for transactions designed to manage cash flow risk associated with forecasted transactions. Entities often hedge the cash flow risk of forecasted transactions by using a derivative to "lock in" or "fix" the price of the future transaction, or to mitigate the cash flow risk for a certain period of time. They want to recognize the gain or loss on the derivative hedging instrument in earnings in the period or periods in which the forecasted transaction will affect earnings. If the hedging instrument is held until the forecasted transaction occurs, that accounting would base the earnings effect of the transaction on the "fixed price."

323. Some constituents suggested that there is little distinction between forecasted transactions and firm commitments and, consequently, that hedges of forecasted transactions should be accounted for in the same way as hedges of firm commitments. They said that (a) some forecasted transactions may be as probable as, if not more probable than, some firm commitments, (b) it is often difficult to distinguish between forecasted transactions and firm commitments, and (c) entities do not view forecasted transactions and firm commitments separately for risk management purposes.

324. The Board believes there are several differences between firm commitments and forecasted transactions, irrespective of the probability of occurrence, that make it possible to distinguish between them. Firm commitments and forecasted transactions create different exposures to risk. Firm commitments are fixed-price contracts that expose an entity to a risk of a change in fair value. For example, an increase in the market price of a commodity will not affect the cash to be paid to purchase that commodity under a firmly committed contract; however, it will affect the value of that contract. In contrast, forecasted transactions do not have a fixed price and do expose an entity to a risk of a change in the cash to be paid to purchase the commodity in the future. Because firm commitments and forecasted transactions give rise to different exposures, different hedging strategies must be used. For example, an entity that hedges a firm commitment to purchase an item (a long position) would generally enter into a derivative to "undo" that fixed price (such as an offsetting short position). In contrast, an entity that hedges a forecasted purchase of an item would generally enter into a derivative (such as a contract to purchase the item—a long position) to "fix" the price.

325. Although many firm commitments are not recognized in financial statements, they qualify as assets or liabilities with determinable values, which makes them different from forecasted transactions. The value of a firm commitment is equal to the unrealized gain or loss on the commitment. In contrast, a forecasted transaction has no value and cannot give rise to a gain or loss. Regardless of their probability of occurrence, forecasted transactions are not present rights or obligations of the entity.

326. The Board recognizes that hedging is used to cope with uncertainty about the future and that the risks associated with forecasted transactions may appear to be similar to those associated with assets and liabilities, including firm commitments. However, the fundamental purpose of financial statements is to present relevant measures of *existing* assets and liabilities and changes in them. The Board believes

there is no conceptual justification for providing special accounting for the effects of transactions that have already occurred based solely on management's assertions about other transactions expected to occur in the future. The Board believes it would be conceptually preferable to provide descriptive information about intended links between current and forecasted future transactions in accompanying notes than to let those intended links directly affect the financial statements. As indicated by the Board's third fundamental decision, deferring a derivative gain or loss as a separate asset or liability in the statement of financial position is conceptually inappropriate because the gain or loss neither is itself a liability or an asset nor is it associated with the measurement of another existing asset or liability.

327. To the extent that hedge accounting is justifiable conceptually, it is for the purpose of dealing with anomalies caused by the mixed-attribute accounting model. The lack of an associated asset, liability, gain, or loss to be recognized in the financial statements means that there are no measurement anomalies for a forecasted transaction. Gains and losses on derivative instruments designated as hedges of forecasted transactions can be distinguished from gains and losses on other derivatives only on the basis of management intent. That makes hedge accounting for forecasted transactions problematic from a practical, as well as a conceptual, perspective. Furthermore, it generally is more difficult to assess the effectiveness of a hedge of a forecasted transaction than of a hedge of an existing asset or liability, because a forecasted transaction reflects expectations and intent, not measurable present rights or obligations.

328. Regardless of those conceptual and practical questions, the Board decided to accommodate certain hedges of forecasted transactions because of the current widespread use of and demand for special accounting for forecasted transactions. However, because the Board does not consider hedge accounting for forecasted transactions to be conceptually supportable, the Board chose to impose limits on that accounting, as discussed further in paragraphs 382 and 383.

329. This Statement provides for gains and losses on derivatives designated as cash flow hedges of forecasted transactions to be initially recognized in other comprehensive income and reclassified into earnings in the period(s) that the forecasted transaction affects earnings. As the Board pursues its long-term objective of measuring all financial instruments at fair value in the statement of financial position, it will reconsider whether special accounting for hedges of forecasted transactions should continue to be permitted. Special accounting for hedges of forecasted financial instrument transactions would serve no purpose if all financial instruments were measured at fair value both at initial recognition and subsequently, with changes in fair value reported in earnings. This Statement consequently prohibits hedge accounting for the acquisition or incurrence of financial instruments that will be subsequently measured at fair value, with changes in fair value reported in earnings.

Hedge Accounting Approaches Considered

330. Over its six years of deliberations, the Board considered four broad approaches, and combinations of those approaches, in addition to the one proposed in the Exposure Draft, as a way to resolve issues related to hedge accounting. Those four broad approaches are discussed below. The hedge accounting approach proposed in the Exposure Draft is discussed in conjunction with the hedge accounting adopted in this Statement (which is discussed beginning at paragraph 351).

Measure All Financial Instruments at Fair Value

331. Consistent with its conclusion that fair value is the most relevant measure for all financial instruments, the Board considered measuring all financial instruments at fair value. Using that single measurement attribute for initial recognition and subsequent measurement would have resolved problems caused by the current mixed-attribute measurement model, at least for financial instruments, and would have been relatively simple and more readily understandable to financial statement users. It also would have increased comparability for identical balance sheet positions between entities, and it would have obviated the need for special accounting for hedges of financial instruments.

332. Several respondents to the Exposure Draft said that fair value measurement should be expanded to all financial instruments, and a few respondents suggested expanding fair value measurement to all assets and liabilities. Some respondents said that it is inconsistent or inappropriate to expand fair value measurement to derivatives before it is expanded to all financial instruments. Other respondents said that fair value measurement for all financial instruments is not a desirable goal.

333. The Board believes changing the accounting model so that all financial instruments are measured

at fair value in the statement of financial position is the superior conceptual solution to hedging issues. However, the Board decided that it was not appropriate at this time to require fair value measurement for all financial instruments. Board members decided that they must first deliberate and reach agreement on conceptual and practical issues related to the valuation of certain financial instruments, including liabilities, and portfolios of financial instruments. The Board is pursuing issues related to fair value measurement of all financial assets and liabilities in a separate project.

334. The Board is committed to work diligently toward resolving, in a timely manner, the conceptual and practical issues related to determining the fair values of financial instruments and portfolios of financial instruments. Techniques for refining the measurement of the fair values of all financial instruments continue to develop at a rapid pace, and the Board believes that all financial instruments should be carried in the statement of financial position at fair value when the conceptual and measurement issues are resolved. For now, the Board believes it is a significant improvement in financial reporting that this Statement requires that all derivatives be measured at fair value in the statement of financial position.

Mark-to-Fair-Value Hedge Accounting

335. Having concluded that its long-term objective of measuring all financial instruments at fair value was not attainable at this time, the Board decided that it needed to permit some form of hedge accounting. One alternative, termed mark-to-fair-value hedge accounting, would have required that an entity measure both the derivative and the hedged item at fair value and report the changes in the fair value of both items in earnings as they occur. Similar to measuring all financial instruments at fair value, that approach would have accommodated a wide variety of risk management strategies and would have overcome the problems attributable to the mixed-attribute measurement model by using a common measurement attribute for both the derivative and the hedged item. Additionally, that approach would have been relatively easy for entities to apply and for financial statement users to understand because hedged items would be reported at fair value and the net ineffectiveness of a hedge would be reported in earnings. There would have been no need to specify which risks could be separately hedged or how to reflect basis risk. However, like measuring all financial instruments at fair

value, mark-to-fair-value hedge accounting would not have addressed constituents' desire for special accounting for cash flow hedges of forecasted transactions.

336. Although the Board liked the idea of extending fair value measurement by marking hedged items to fair value with changes in fair value reported in earnings, it ultimately decided not to adopt mark-to-fair-value hedge accounting for two main reasons. First, measuring hedged items at fair value would have recognized, at the inception of a hedge, unrealized gains and losses on the hedged item that occurred before the hedge period ("preexisting" gains and losses). The Board believes that preexisting gains and losses on the hedged item are unrelated to the hedge and should not provide earnings offset for derivative gains and losses (consistent with its second fundamental decision [paragraphs 220–228]). Recognizing those gains and losses at the inception of a hedge would result in recognizing a gain or loss simply because the hedged item was designated as part of a hedge. That ability to selectively recognize preexisting gains and losses caused some Board members to reject the mark-to-fair-value approach.

337. Another reason the Board rejected that approach is that constituents objected to its effect on earnings—that is, earnings would have reflected changes in the fair value of a hedged item unrelated to the risk being hedged. For example, a hedge of one risk (such as interest rate risk) could have caused recognition in earnings of gains and losses from another risk (such as credit risk) because the mark-to-fair-value approach would have required recognition of the full change in fair value of the hedged item, including the changes in fair value attributable to risk components *not* being hedged. The hedge accounting approach proposed in the Exposure Draft also could have resulted in recognition of the change in fair value of a hedged item attributable to risk components not being hedged. However, the approach in the Exposure Draft would have (a) limited how much of those fair value changes were recognized in earnings and (b) prevented the change in the fair value of the hedged item that is not offset by the change in fair value on the hedging instrument from being recognized in earnings.

Comprehensive Income Approach

338. The Board considered another hedge accounting approach, referred to as the comprehensive income approach, that would have required that derivatives be measured at fair value and classified in one

of two categories, *trading* or *risk management.* Gains and losses on derivatives classified as trading would be recognized in earnings in the periods in which they occur. Unrealized gains and losses on risk management derivatives would be reported as a component of other comprehensive income until realized. Realized gains and losses on risk management derivatives would be reported in earnings.

339. That approach would have been relatively easy to apply, it would have made derivatives and related risks transparent, and it would have accommodated some risk management strategies. Hedges of assets, liabilities, and some forecasted transactions would have been accommodated if the duration of the derivative was structured by management to achieve recognition, in the desired period, of any realized gains or losses. Also, because the approach would not have permitted deferral of derivative gains or losses as liabilities or assets, it would not have violated the fundamental decision that only assets and liabilities should be reported as such.

340. The Board rejected the comprehensive income approach for three main reasons. First, the Board does not believe that the distinction between realized and unrealized gains and losses that is the basis for the comprehensive income approach is relevant for financial instruments. The Board acknowledges that the current accounting model often distinguishes between realized and unrealized gains and losses. That distinction, however, is inappropriate for financial instruments. The occurrence of gains and losses on financial instruments—not the act of selling or settling them—affects an entity's economic position and thus should affect its reported financial performance. The Board is concerned that the comprehensive income approach would provide an opportunity for an entity to manage its reported earnings, per-share amounts, and other comprehensive income. Financial instruments generally are liquid, and an entity can easily sell or settle a financial instrument, realize a gain or loss, and maintain the same economic position as before the sale by reacquiring the same or a similar instrument.

341. Second, under the comprehensive income approach, offsetting gains and losses often would not have been reported in earnings at the same time. For example, if an entity used a series of short-term derivatives as a fair value hedge of a long-term fixed-rate loan, the gains and losses on the derivatives would have been recognized in earnings over the life of the loan each time an individual derivative expired

or was terminated. However, the offsetting unrealized losses and gains on the loan would not have been recognized in those same periods. Similarly, offsetting gains and losses on a derivative and a nonfinancial asset or liability would have been recognized together in earnings only if both transactions were specially structured to be realized in the same period. The Board decided on the approach in this Statement, in part, because off-setting gains and losses on fair value hedges would be recognized in earnings in the same period.

342. The third reason the Board did not adopt the comprehensive income approach is that all unrealized gains and losses on derivatives classified as risk management would have been reported in other comprehensive income without offsetting losses or gains, if any, on the hedged item. Thus, the resulting other comprehensive income could have implied a change in net assets when net assets did not change or when they changed in the opposite direction. For example, a $1,000 increase in the fair value of a derivative would have increased other comprehensive income and the carrying amount of the derivative by $1,000. If there was also an offsetting $1,000 loss on the hedged asset or liability, which would not have been reflected in other comprehensive income, the change in other comprehensive income would have implied that net assets had increased by $1,000 when there had been no real change.

343. The hedge accounting approach in this Statement also may result in reporting some derivative gains and losses in other comprehensive income. However, the Board notes that the approach in this Statement limits the amounts reported in other comprehensive income to gains and losses on derivatives designated as hedges of cash flow exposures. The transactions that will give rise to cash flow exposures do not provide offsetting changes in fair value when the related price or rate changes. Consequently, the gains and losses reported in other comprehensive income under this Statement are a faithful representation of the actual volatility of comprehensive income. The Board's reasoning for recognizing in other comprehensive income gains and losses on derivatives designated as hedges of cash flow exposures is further discussed in paragraph 377.

344. Only a few respondents to the Exposure Draft advocated the comprehensive income approach. Although they did not specifically comment on that approach, many respondents objected to recognizing derivative gains and losses in earnings in a period

other than the one in which the hedged item affects earnings. Some opposed reporting derivative gains and losses in other comprehensive income because of the potential for volatility in reported stockholders' equity or net assets, which they considered undesirable.

Full-Deferral Hedge Accounting

345. The Board considered maintaining the approach outlined in Statement 80. Statement 80 permitted deferral of the entire change in the fair value of a derivative used as a hedging instrument by adjusting the basis of a hedged asset or liability, or by recognizing a separate liability or asset associated with a hedge of an unrecognized firm commitment or a forecasted transaction, if the appropriate hedge criteria were met. Many respondents to the Exposure Draft advocated a full-deferral approach. They noted that a full-deferral approach would have been familiar to entities that have applied hedge accounting in the past. That approach also would have provided a mechanism to moderate the earnings "mismatch" that is attributable to the mixed-attribute measurement model. By deferring the earnings recognition of a derivative's gain or loss until the loss or gain on the hedged item has been recognized, offsetting gains or losses on the derivative and hedged item would be recognized in earnings at the same time.

346. However, the full-deferral approach goes beyond correcting for the anomalies created by using different attributes to measure assets and liabilities. The Board rejected that approach for three reasons. First, full-deferral hedge accounting inappropriately permits gains or losses on derivatives designated as hedging the cash flow exposure of forecasted transactions to be reported as separate liabilities or assets in the statement of financial position. Those gains and losses do not represent probable future sacrifices or benefits, which are necessary characteristics of liabilities and assets. Thus, reporting deferred gains or losses as separate liabilities or assets is inconsistent with the Board's conceptual framework.

347. Second, a full-deferral approach is inconsistent with the Board's long-term goal of reporting all financial instruments at fair value in the statement of financial position. For fair value hedges, a full-deferral approach could only have been described as deferring the derivative gain or loss as an adjustment of the basis of the hedged item. For a cash flow hedge of a forecasted purchase of an asset or incurrence of an obligation, a full-deferral approach would have resulted in systematically adjusting the initial carrying amount of the acquired asset or incurred liability away from its fair value.

348. Finally, the full-deferral approach permits a derivative's gain or loss for a period to be deferred regardless of whether there is a completely offsetting decrease or increase in the fair value of the hedged item for that period. The Board believes it is inappropriate to treat that portion of a hedge that does not achieve its objective as if it had been effective.

Synthetic Instrument Accounting

349. A number of respondents to the Exposure Draft suggested that a different kind of special accounting be provided for "synthetic instrument" strategies. Synthetic instrument accounting, which evolved in practice, views two or more distinct financial instruments (generally a cash instrument and a derivative instrument) as having synthetically created another single cash instrument. The objective of synthetic instrument accounting is to present those multiple instruments in the financial statements as if they were the single instrument that the entity sought to create. Some respondents to the Exposure Draft advocated a synthetic instrument accounting approach for interest rate swaps that are used to modify the interest receipts or payments associated with a hedged financial instrument. That approach, which its advocates also refer to as "the accrual approach," would require the accrual of only the most imminent net cash settlement on the swap. It would not require recognition of the swap itself in the financial statements.

350. The Board decided not to allow synthetic instrument accounting because to do so would be inconsistent with (a) the fundamental decision to report all derivatives in the financial statements, (b) the fundamental decision to measure all derivatives at fair value, (c) the Board's objective to increase the transparency of derivatives and derivative activities, and (d) the Board's objective of providing consistent accounting for all derivative instruments and for all hedging strategies. Synthetic instrument accounting also is not conceptually defensible because it results in netting assets against liabilities (or vice versa) for no reason other than an asserted "connection" between the netted items.

Hedge Accounting in This Statement

351. The hedge accounting approach in this Statement combines elements from each of the approaches considered by the Board. The Board believes the approach in this Statement is consistent

with all four of its fundamental decisions and is a significant improvement in financial reporting. It is also more consistent than the approach in the Exposure Draft with what many respondents said was necessary to accommodate their risk management strategies.

352. Some respondents suggested that the financial statement results of applying this Statement will not reflect what they perceive to be the economics of certain hedging and risk management activities. However, there is little agreement about just what the "economics" of hedging and risk management activities are. Because entities have different and often conflicting views of risk and manage risk differently, the Board does not think that a single approach to hedge accounting could fully reflect the hedging and risk management strategies of all entities. The Board also believes that some aspects of "risk management" are hard to distinguish from speculation or "position taking" and that speculative activities should not be afforded special accounting. Thus, providing hedge accounting to the whole range of activities undertaken by some under the broad heading of "risk management" would be inconsistent with improving the usefulness and understandability of financial reporting.

Exposures to Changes in Fair Value or Changes in Cash Flow

353. The accounting prescribed by this Statement is based on two types of risk exposures. One reflects the possibility that a change in price will result in a change in the fair value of a particular asset or liability—a *fair value exposure*. The other reflects the possibility that a change in price will result in variability in expected future cash flows—a *cash flow exposure*.

354. Fair value exposures arise from existing assets or liabilities, including firm commitments. Fixed-rate financial assets and liabilities, for example, have a fair value exposure to changes in market rates of interest and changes in credit quality. Nonfinancial assets and liabilities, on the other hand, have a fair value exposure to changes in the market price of a particular item or commodity. Some assets and liabilities have fair value exposures arising from more than one type of risk.

355. Some cash flow exposures relate to forecasted transactions. For example, a change in the market price of an asset will change the expected cash out-

flows for a future purchase of the asset and may affect the subsequent earnings impact from its use or sale. Similarly, a change in market interest rates will change the expected cash flows for the future interest payments resulting from the forecasted issuance of fixed-rate debt (for which the interest rate has not yet been fixed). Other cash flow exposures relate to existing assets and liabilities. For example, a change in market interest rates will affect the future cash receipts or payments associated with a variable-rate financial asset or liability.

356. Fair value exposures and cash flow exposures often are mutually exclusive, and hedging to reduce one exposure generally increases the other. For example, hedging the variability of interest receipts on a variable-rate loan with a receive-fixed, pay-variable swap "fixes" the interest receipts on the loan and eliminates the exposure to risk of a change in cash flows, but it creates an exposure to the risk of a change in the fair value of the swap. The net cash flows on the loan and the swap will not change (or will change minimally) with market rates of interest, but the combined fair value of the loan and the swap will fluctuate. Additionally, the changes in the fair value of an asset or liability are inseparable from its expected cash flows because those cash flows are a major factor in determining fair value.

Hedge Accounting in This Statement and Risk Reduction

357. The Board believes that entity-wide risk reduction should be a criterion for hedge accounting; it therefore would have preferred to require an entity to demonstrate that a derivative reduces the risk to the entity as a criterion for hedge accounting. However, requiring that a derivative contribute to entity-wide risk reduction would necessitate a single, restrictive definition of risk, such as *either* fair value risk *or* cash flow risk. Actions to mitigate the risk of a change in fair value generally exacerbate the variability of cash flows. Likewise, actions to mitigate the variability of cash flows of existing assets and liabilities necessitate "fixing" cash flows, which in turn generally exacerbates an entity's exposure to changes in fair value. Because this Statement provides hedge accounting for both fair value risk and cash flow risk, an objective assessment of entity-wide risk reduction would be mechanically impossible in most situations. Therefore, the Board did not continue the requirement in Statement 80 that a hedging transaction must contribute to reducing risk at the entity-wide level to qualify for hedge accounting.

358. As discussed in paragraph 322, a hedge of a forecasted transaction can be described as "fixing" the price of the item involved in the transaction if the hedging instrument is held until the hedged transaction occurs. "Fixing" the price of an expected future transaction is a form of risk management on an individual-transaction basis. The Exposure Draft would have provided cash flow hedge accounting only for derivative instruments with a contractual maturity or repricing date that was on or about the date of the hedged forecasted transaction. However, as discussed further in paragraph 468, the Board removed that criterion for cash flow hedge accounting principally because of respondents' objections to it. This Statement also places no limitations on an entity's ability to prospectively designate, dedesignate, and redesignate a qualifying hedge of the same forecasted transaction. The result of those provisions is that this Statement permits an entity to exclude derivative gains or losses from earnings and recognize them in other comprehensive income even if its objective is to achieve a desired level of risk based on its view of the market rather than to reduce risk. If an entity enters into and then discontinues a derivative transaction designated as a hedge of a forecasted transaction for which the exposure has not changed, one of those actions—either the hedge or the discontinuance of it—must increase, rather than reduce, risk.

359. The considerations just discussed, together with the intense focus on the part of many investors on earnings as a measure of entity performance, lead some Board members to prefer that the gain or loss on a derivative designated as a hedge of a forecasted transaction but not intended to be held until the transaction occurs be recognized directly in earnings. However, those Board members also consider comprehensive income to be a measure of an entity's financial performance that is at least as, if not more, important as earnings. Consequently, those Board members found it acceptable to recognize in other comprehensive income the gain or loss on a derivative designated as a hedge of a forecasted transaction, regardless of whether that derivative is held until the hedged transaction occurs. Those Board members observe, however, that recognizing such gains and losses in other comprehensive income rather than in earnings creates additional pressure concerning the method and prominence of the display of both the items in other comprehensive income and total comprehensive income.

A Compound Derivative May Not Be Separated into Risk Components

360. The Exposure Draft would have prohibited separating a derivative into either separate *proportions* or separate *portions* and designating any component as a hedging instrument or designating different components as hedges of different exposures. Some respondents objected to both prohibitions. They said that either a pro rata part of a derivative, such as 60 percent, or a portion of a derivative, such as the portion of the change in value of a combined interest rate and currency swap deemed to be attributable to changes in interest rates, should qualify for separate designation as a hedging instrument. The Board decided to permit designation of a pro rata part of a derivative as a hedge. Example 10 in Appendix B illustrates that situation.

361. The Board decided to retain the prohibition against separating a compound derivative into components representing different risks. This Statement permits separation of a hedged item or transaction by risk and also places the burden on management to design an appropriate effectiveness test, including a means of measuring the change in fair value or cash flows attributable to the risk being hedged. In view of those requirements, the Board decided that it was especially important that, to the extent possible, the gain or loss on the derivative be an objectively determined market-based amount rather than an amount "separated out" of an overall gain or loss on the derivative as a whole. Otherwise, even for a derivative for which a quoted price is available, the effectiveness test would compare two computed amounts of gain or loss deemed to be "attributable to the risk being hedged" with no tie to a total gain or loss separately observable in the market, which would make the effectiveness test less meaningful. To permit that would have required that the Board provide guidance on how to compute the fair value of the "synthetic" derivative that is separated out of a compound derivative, both at inception and during the term of the hedge. That would have added complexity to the requirements in this Statement without, in the Board's view, adding offsetting benefits to justify the additional complexity. However, the Board decided to permit separation of the foreign currency component of a compound derivative at the date of initial application of this Statement, as discussed in paragraph 524.

Fair Value Hedges

362. As discussed in paragraph 320, the demand for special accounting for hedges of existing assets and liabilities, including unrecognized firm commitments, arises because of differences in the way derivatives and hedged assets and liabilities are measured. This Statement requires derivatives designated as part of a fair value hedge to be measured at fair value with changes in fair value reported in earnings as they occur. Without special accounting, the gain or loss on a derivative that hedges an item not measured at fair value would be reported in earnings without also reporting the potentially offsetting loss or gain on the item being hedged. Those who engage in hedging transactions do not consider that result to appropriately reflect the relationship between a derivative and hedged item or how they manage risk. Accordingly, this Statement permits gains and losses on designated assets and liabilities to be recognized in earnings in the same period as the losses and gains on related derivative hedging instruments.

Accelerated recognition of the gain or loss on a hedged item

363. Similar to the Exposure Draft, this Statement (a) requires that the gains or losses on a derivative used as a fair value hedging instrument be recognized in earnings as they occur and (b) permits earnings offset by accelerating the recognition of the offsetting losses or gains attributable to the risk being hedged and adjusting the carrying amount of the hedged item accordingly. That notion is consistent with part of the Board's second fundamental decision, namely, that adjustments to the carrying amount of hedged items should reflect offsetting changes in their fair value arising while the hedge is in effect. This Statement modifies the proposals in the Exposure Draft for recognizing the gains and losses on the hedged item in two ways, which are explained below.

Attributable to the risk being hedged

364. The Exposure Draft proposed that the gain or loss on the hedged item that would be recognized under fair value hedge accounting incorporate all risk factors and, therefore, reflect the full change in fair value of the hedged item to the extent of an offsetting gain or loss on the hedging instrument. That focus was intended to prevent a hedged asset or liability from being adjusted farther away from its fair value than it was at inception of the hedge. For example, if the fair value of a hedged asset increased due to a

change in interest rates but simultaneously decreased due to a change in credit quality, the Exposure Draft would have prevented an entity that was hedging only interest rate risk from accelerating recognition of the interest rate gain without also effectively accelerating the credit quality loss. Accelerating only the interest rate gain would adjust the hedged asset away from its fair value.

365. Respondents to the Exposure Draft opposed the proposed approach for the very reason that the Board originally favored it—the approach would not have segregated the sources of the change in a hedged item's fair value. Respondents focused on the earnings impact and expressed concern about recognizing in earnings the fair value changes on the hedged item related to an unhedged risk. They said that recognizing the changes in fair value of the hedged item attributable to all risks would cause unrepresentative earnings volatility and would be misleading in reflecting the results of the entity's hedging activities.

366. The Board believes that the earnings effect of the approach proposed in the Exposure Draft would have reflected an exacerbation of the mixed-attribute measurement model, rather than "unrepresentative earnings volatility." However, because of the concerns expressed by respondents, the Board reconsidered the proposed requirements. The Board generally focuses on the appropriate recognition and measurement of assets and liabilities in developing accounting standards. However, the principal purpose of providing special accounting for hedging activities is to mitigate the effects on earnings of different existing recognition and measurement attributes. Consequently, in this instance, the Board found the focus of respondents on the earnings impact of the approach to hedge accounting to be persuasive and decided to modify the Exposure Draft to focus on the risk being hedged. The Board decided to adopt an approach that accelerates the earnings recognition of the portion of the hedged item's gain or loss attributable to the risk being hedged for the following reasons:

a. It provides the matching of gains and losses on the hedging instrument and the hedged item that respondents desire.

b. It accounts for all or a portion of the change in fair value of the hedged item, and, consequently, it is not inconsistent with the Board's long-term objective of measuring all financial instruments at fair value.

Entire gain or loss attributable to risk being hedged

367. The Exposure Draft proposed that the gain or loss on the hedged item be recognized in earnings only to the extent that it provided offset for the loss or gain on the hedging instrument. Under that proposal, earnings would have reflected hedge ineffectiveness to the extent that the derivative gain or loss exceeded an offsetting loss or gain on the hedged item. It would not have reflected hedge ineffectiveness to the extent that the gain or loss on the derivative was less than the loss or gain on the hedged item. For example, ineffectiveness of $10 would have been recognized if the gain on the derivative was $100 and the corresponding loss on the hedged item was $90, but not if the gain on the derivative was $90 and the loss on the hedged item was $100. The Board would have preferred to reflect all hedge ineffectiveness in earnings. However, the Exposure Draft did not propose that the excess gain or loss on the hedged item be reflected in earnings because that could have resulted in reporting in earnings a gain or loss on the hedged item attributable to changes in unhedged risks.

368. When the Board modified the Exposure Draft to focus only on the gain or loss on the hedged item attributable to the risk being hedged, it decided to report all hedge ineffectiveness in earnings. Recognizing the hedged item's gain or loss due only to the hedged risk will not result in earnings recognition of gains or losses related to unhedged risks.

Measurement of hedged item's gain or loss

369. In this Statement, the gain or loss on the hedged item that is accelerated and recognized in earnings is the portion of the gain or loss that is attributable to the risk being hedged. Although the Board considered several approaches to measuring the gain or loss attributable to the risk being hedged, it decided not to provide detailed guidance on how that gain or loss should be measured. The Board believes that the appropriate measurement of the gain or loss on a hedged item may depend on how an entity manages the hedged risk. Consistent with its decision to require an entity to define at inception how it will assess hedge effectiveness, the Board decided that an entity also should define at inception how it will measure the gain or loss on a hedged item attributable to the risk being hedged. The measurement of that gain or loss should be consistent with the entity's approach to managing risk, assessing hedge effectiveness, and determining hedge ineffectiveness. It

follows that the gain or loss on the hedged item attributable to the risk being hedged can be based on the loss or gain on the derivative, adjusted in certain ways that will be identified during the assessment of hedge effectiveness. Both Section 2 of Appendix A and Appendix B discuss and illustrate situations in which the gain or loss on a hedging derivative must be adjusted to measure the loss or gain on the hedged item.

The Exposure Draft's exception for certain firm commitments

370. The Exposure Draft proposed a specific exception for a derivative that hedges the foreign currency exposure of a firm commitment to purchase a nonfinancial asset for a fixed amount of foreign currency. That exception would have permitted an entity to consider separately the financial aspect and the nonfinancial aspect of the firm commitment for purposes of designating the hedged item and thus to record the purchased asset at a fixed-dollar (or other functional currency) equivalent of the foreign currency price. The exception is no longer necessary because this Statement permits separate consideration of financial and nonfinancial risks for all fair value hedges of firm commitments.

Cash Flow Hedges

371. As discussed in paragraphs 322–329, the Board decided to permit hedge accounting for certain hedges of forecasted transactions because of the widespread use of and demand for that accounting. The "need" for special accounting for cash flow hedges arises because the hedged transactions are recognized in periods after the one in which a change in the fair value of the derivative occurs and is recognized. Without special accounting, gains and losses on derivatives would be reported in a period different from the earnings impact of the hedged transaction or the related asset acquired or liability incurred.

372. In developing a hedge accounting approach for hedges of cash flow exposures, the Board identified four objectives: (a) to avoid the recognition of the gain or loss on a derivative hedging instrument as a liability or an asset, (b) to make gains and losses not yet recognized in earnings visible, (c) to reflect hedge ineffectiveness, and (d) to limit the use of hedge accounting for cash flow hedges.

First two objectives—avoid conceptual difficulties and increase visibility

373. The Board believes that recognizing gains or losses on derivatives in other comprehensive income, rather than as liabilities or assets, best meets the first two objectives. Many respondents to the Exposure Draft objected to that approach because of the potential for volatility in reported equity. Instead, they advocated reporting a derivative's gain or loss as a freestanding liability or asset. The Board did not change its decision for several reasons. First, the Board believes that reporting a derivative's gain or loss as a liability or an asset is inappropriate and misleading because a gain is not a liability and a loss is not an asset. Second, the Board believes the volatility in other comprehensive income that results from gains and losses on derivatives that hedge cash flow exposures properly reflects what occurred during the hedge period. There are no gains or losses to offset the losses or gains on the derivatives that are reported in other comprehensive income because the hedged transaction has not yet occurred. Third, the Board believes the advantages of reporting all derivatives at fair value, together with recognizing gains and losses on derivatives that hedge cash flow exposures in other comprehensive income, outweigh any perceived disadvantages of potential equity volatility.

Third and fourth objectives—reflect ineffectiveness and impose limitations

374. The Board proposed in the Exposure Draft that the best way to meet the last two objectives (reflect ineffectiveness and impose limitations) would be to reclassify a gain or loss on a derivative designated as a hedging instrument into earnings on the projected date of the hedged forecasted transaction. Effectiveness thus would have been reflected at the date the forecasted transaction was projected to occur. In addition, there would have been little, if any, opportunity for earnings management because gains and losses would not have been reclassified into earnings when realized, when a forecasted transaction actually occurs, or when a forecasted transaction's occurrence is no longer considered probable. The Exposure Draft explained that requiring recognition at the date the forecasted transaction is initially expected to occur emphasizes the importance of carefully evaluating and forecasting future transactions before designating them as being hedged with specific derivatives.

375. Respondents generally opposed the approach in the Exposure Draft because it often would not have

matched the derivative gain or loss with the earnings effect of the forecasted transaction, thereby making earnings appear volatile. Respondents generally advocated recognizing a derivative gain or loss in earnings in the same period or periods as the earnings effect of (a) the forecasted transaction (such as a forecasted sale) or (b) the subsequent accounting for the asset acquired or liability incurred in conjunction with the forecasted transaction. To accomplish that result, many respondents advocated deferring the gain or loss on the derivative beyond the date of the forecasted transaction as an adjustment of the basis of the asset acquired or liability incurred in the forecasted transaction.

376. The Board considered two approaches that would have provided basis adjustment for assets acquired or liabilities incurred in conjunction with a forecasted transaction. One approach would have initially deferred a derivative gain or loss as a separate (freestanding) liability or asset and later reported it as an adjustment of the basis of the acquired asset or incurred liability when it was recorded. The Board rejected that approach because a deferred loss is not an asset and a deferred gain is not a liability; reporting them as if they were would be misleading. The other approach would have initially recognized the derivative gain or loss in other comprehensive income and later reported it as an adjustment of the basis of the acquired asset or incurred liability when it was recorded. The Board rejected that approach because it would have distorted reported periodic comprehensive income. For example, removing a gain from other comprehensive income and reporting it as an adjustment of the basis of an acquired asset would result in a decrease in periodic comprehensive income (and total stockholders' equity) caused simply by the acquisition of an asset at its fair value—a transaction that should have no effect on comprehensive income. Additionally, both approaches would have systematically measured the acquired asset or incurred liability at an amount other than fair value at the date of initial recognition. That is, the adjustment would have moved the initial carrying amount of the acquired asset or incurred liability away from its fair value.

377. The Board decided to require that the gain or loss on a derivative be reported initially in other comprehensive income and reclassified into earnings when the forecasted transaction affects earnings. That requirement avoids the problems caused by adjusting the basis of an acquired asset or incurred liability and provides the same earnings impact. The approach in

this Statement, for example, provides for (a) recognizing the gain or loss on a derivative that hedged a forecasted purchase of a machine in the same periods as the depreciation expense on the machine and (b) recognizing the gain or loss on a derivative that hedged a forecasted purchase of inventory when the cost of that inventory is reflected in cost of sales.

378. The Board was concerned that recognizing all derivative gains and losses in other comprehensive income and reclassifying them into earnings in the future, perhaps spread out over a number of years, would not meet its third objective of reflecting hedge ineffectiveness, if any. The Board therefore decided to require that, in general, the ineffective part of a cash flow hedge be immediately recognized in earnings.

Measure of hedge ineffectiveness

379. The Board believes that, in principle, earnings should reflect (a) the component of a derivative gain or loss that is excluded from the defined assessment of hedge effectiveness and (b) any hedge ineffectiveness. However, the Board had concerns about the effect of that approach on other comprehensive income and earnings for a period in which the change in the present value of the future expected cash flows on the hedged transaction exceeds the change in the present value of the expected cash flows on the derivative. In that circumstance, the result would be to defer in other comprehensive income a nonexistent gain or loss on the derivative and to recognize in earnings an offsetting nonexistent loss or gain. For example, if the derivative hedging instrument had a $50 loss for a period in which the change in the present value of the expected cash flows on the hedged transaction was a $55 gain, an approach that reflected all hedge ineffectiveness in earnings would result in reflecting a $55 loss in other comprehensive income and reporting a $5 gain in earnings.

380. To avoid that result, the Board decided that only ineffectiveness due to excess expected cash flows on the derivative should be reflected in earnings. The Board discussed whether that approach should be applied period by period or cumulatively and decided that the ineffectiveness of a cash flow hedge should be determined on a cumulative basis since the inception of the hedge.

381. To illustrate the difference between the period-by-period and cumulative approaches, consider a derivative that had gains (expected cash inflows) of $75 in period 1 and $70 in period 2. The derivative hedges a forecasted transaction for which expected cash outflows increased by $70 and $75 in the same periods, respectively. At the end of period 2, the changes in expected cash flows on the hedge are completely offsetting on a cumulative basis. That is, the derivative has expected cash inflows of $145 and the hedged transaction has an offsetting increase in expected cash outflows of $145. If hedge ineffectiveness is measured and accounted for on a cumulative basis, the $5 excess derivative gain reported in earnings in period 1 would be reversed in period 2. At the end of period 2, retained earnings would reflect zero gain or loss, and comprehensive income would reflect $145 of derivative gain. However, measuring and accounting for hedge ineffectiveness on a period-by-period basis would give a different result because earnings and comprehensive income would be affected for the $5 excess derivative gain in period 1 but not the $5 excess hedged transaction loss in period 2. As a result, at the end of period 2, retained earnings would reflect a $5 gain, even though actual ineffectiveness since hedge inception was a zero gain or loss. Other comprehensive income would reflect a gain of $140, even though the derivative's actual effectiveness since the inception of the hedge was a gain of $145. Thus, in a situation like the one illustrated, retained earnings under the cumulative approach will more accurately reflect total hedge ineffectiveness since the inception of the hedge, and comprehensive income will more accurately reflect total hedge effectiveness for the hedge period. The Board rejected a period-by-period approach because, under that approach, retained earnings would not reflect total hedge ineffectiveness, and comprehensive income would not reflect total hedge effectiveness. Section 2 of Appendix A provides some examples of how the ineffective portion of a derivative gain or loss might be estimated, and Section 1 of Appendix B further illustrates application of the cumulative approach.

Limitations on cash flow hedges

382. Because hedge accounting for forecasted transactions is not conceptually supportable and is not necessary to compensate for recognition or measurement anomalies, the Board decided that this Statement should provide only limited hedge accounting for hedges of forecasted transactions (the Board's fourth objective). In the Exposure Draft, the Board concluded that the best way to limit hedge accounting for a hedge of a forecasted transaction was to require that the gain or loss on a derivative that hedges a forecasted transaction be reclassified into earnings

on the projected date of the forecasted transaction and to limit hedge accounting to the life of the hedging instrument. In formulating this Statement, the Board decided that, because of current practice, it was acceptable to provide for an earnings effect that is more consistent with the entity's objective in entering into a hedge. Consequently, the Board decided to provide limitations on hedges of forecasted transactions through the criteria for qualification for cash flow hedge accounting. The Board believes the criteria discussed in paragraphs 458–473 provide sufficient limitations.

383. The Board also considered limiting hedge accounting for hedges of cash flow exposures based on pragmatic, but arbitrary, limitations. The pragmatic approaches that were considered included limitations based on the length of time until the expected occurrence of the forecasted transaction, the amount of the gain or loss reflected in other comprehensive income, and specific linkage to existing assets or liabilities. For example, a limitation might have required that cash flows occur within five years to qualify as hedgeable. The Board decided that it was more appropriate to rely on specified criteria for cash flow hedges than to apply arbitrary, pragmatic limitations.

General Criteria to Qualify for Designation as a Hedge

384. This Statement requires that certain criteria be met for a hedge to qualify for hedge accounting. The criteria are intended to ensure that hedge accounting is used in a reasonably consistent manner for transactions and exposures that qualify as hedgeable pursuant to this Statement. The criteria discussed in this section are required for both fair value hedges and cash flow hedges. Criteria that are unique to either fair value hedges or cash flow hedges are discussed separately.

Designation, Documentation, and Risk Management

385. The Board decided that concurrent designation and documentation of a hedge is critical; without it, an entity could retroactively identify a hedged item, a hedged transaction, or a method of measuring effectiveness to achieve a desired accounting result. The Board also decided that identifying the nature of the risk being hedged and using a hedging derivative consistent with an entity's established policy for risk management are essential components of risk management and are necessary to add verifiability to the hedge accounting model.

Highly Effective in Achieving Offsetting Changes in Fair Values or Cash Flows

386. To qualify for hedge accounting, this Statement requires that an entity must expect a hedging relationship to be highly effective in achieving offsetting changes in fair value or cash flows for the risk being hedged. That requirement is consistent with the Board's fourth fundamental decision, which is that one aspect of qualification for special hedge accounting should be an assessment of the effectiveness of a derivative in offsetting the entity's exposure to changes in fair value or variability of cash flows. This Statement does not specify how effectiveness should be assessed; assessment of effectiveness should be based on the objective of management's risk management strategy. However, this Statement does require that the method of assessing effectiveness be reasonable and that the same method be used for similar hedges unless different methods are explicitly justified. The Board considers it essential that an entity document at the inception of the hedge how effectiveness will be assessed for each hedge and then apply that effectiveness test on a consistent basis for the duration of the designated hedge. However, if an entity identifies an improved method for assessing effectiveness, it may discontinue the existing hedging relationship and then designate and document a new hedging relationship using the improved method prospectively.

387. In formulating this Statement, the Board would have preferred specific effectiveness tests for fair value hedges and for cash flow hedges to (a) provide limitations on hedge accounting, (b) result in consistent application of hedge accounting guidance, and (c) increase the comparability of financial statements. The Exposure Draft therefore proposed specific effectiveness tests that would have required an expectation that the changes in fair value or net cash flows of the derivative would "offset substantially all" of the changes in fair value of the hedged item or the variability of cash flows of the hedged transaction attributable to the risk being hedged. Those proposed offset tests were intended to be similar to, though more stringent than, the related requirements of Statement 80:

At the inception of the hedge and throughout the hedge period, high correlation of changes in (1) the market value of the futures contract(s) and (2) the fair value of, or interest income or expense associated with, the hedged item(s) shall be probable so that the results of the futures contract(s) will substantially offset the effects of price or interest rate changes on the exposed item(s). [Paragraph 4(b); footnote reference omitted.]

388. Respondents to the Exposure Draft commented that the proposed effectiveness tests for fair value and cash flow hedges would have precluded certain risk management strategies from qualifying for hedge accounting because those tests were based on singular objectives for fair value and cash flow hedges. For example, the effectiveness tests in the Exposure Draft would have prohibited delta-neutral hedging strategies, partial-term hedging strategies, rollover hedging strategies, and hedging based on changes in the intrinsic value of options. Respondents also noted that risk management objectives and strategies differ between entities as well as between different types of hedges within an entity. Based on those concerns, the Board reconsidered the effectiveness tests proposed in the Exposure Draft.

389. The Board attempted to develop a workable effectiveness test that would appropriately deal with the variety of risk management objectives and strategies that exist in practice. It ultimately decided to remove the specific effectiveness tests and, instead, to require that a hedge be expected to be highly effective in achieving offsetting changes in either fair value or cash flows, consistent with an entity's documented risk management objectives and strategy. The Board intends "highly effective" to be essentially the same as the notion of "high correlation" in Statement 80.

390. Because that modification places more emphasis on each entity's approach to risk management, the Board decided to require an expanded description and documentation of an entity's risk management objectives and strategy, including how a derivative's effectiveness in hedging an exposure will be assessed. It also decided that the description of how an entity plans to assess effectiveness must (a) include identification of whether all of the gain or loss on the derivative hedging instrument will be included in the assessment and (b) have a reasonable basis. Those limitations, along with examples of different ways to assess hedge effectiveness in a variety of circumstances, are discussed in Section 2 of Appendix A. The Board may need to revisit the idea of more specific effectiveness tests if an evaluation of the application of this Statement indicates either too great a disparity in the techniques used for assessing effectiveness or widespread abuse of the flexibility provided.

Basis swaps

391. Basis swaps are derivative instruments that are used to modify the receipts or payments associated with a recognized, variable-rate asset or liability from one variable amount to another variable amount. They do not eliminate the variability of cash flows; instead, they change the basis or index of variability. The Exposure Draft would have required that an entity expect the net cash flows of a derivative to "offset substantially all" of the variability of cash flows associated with the asset or liability to qualify for cash flow hedge accounting. That requirement would have precluded basis swaps from qualifying as hedging instruments.

392. Some respondents to the Exposure Draft criticized its prohibition of hedge accounting for basis swaps. They commented that it should not matter whether an interest rate swap, for example, is used to change the interest receipts or payments associated with a hedged asset or liability from fixed to variable, variable to fixed, or variable to variable. They noted that the fair value and cash flow criteria accommodated only fixed-to-variable and variable-to-fixed swaps. Additionally, some respondents commented that basis swaps should be eligible for hedge accounting treatment because they are an effective means of creating comparable asset-liability positions. For example, if an entity holds a variable-rate, LIBOR-based asset and a variable-rate, prime-based liability, an easy way to match that asset and liability position is to "swap" either the LIBOR asset to prime or the prime liability to LIBOR.

393. Many respondents advocating the use of basis swaps as hedging instruments suggested accommodating basis swaps by accounting for all swaps on a synthetic instrument basis. For the reasons discussed in paragraphs 349 and 350, the Board decided not to provide special accounting based on the creation of synthetic instruments. The Board recognizes, however, that basis swaps can provide offsetting cash flows when they are used to hedge a combined asset-liability position in which the asset and liability have different rate bases. For that reason, this Statement provides an exception for a basis swap that is highly effective as a link between an asset (or group of similar assets) with variable cash flows and a liability (or a group of similar liabilities) with variable cash flows.

394. Some respondents to the Task Force Draft objected to what they saw as stricter requirements for a basis swap to qualify for hedge accounting than for

other derivatives. They noted that to qualify for hedge accounting, other strategies need not link an asset and a liability. The Board notes that the requirement that a basis swap link the cash flows of an asset and a liability is necessary for a basis swap to qualify under the general criterion that a derivative must provide offsetting cash flows to an exposure to qualify for cash flow hedge accounting. That is, one leg of the basis swap that links an asset and a liability will provide offsetting cash flows for the asset, and the other leg will provide offsetting cash flows for the liability. Thus, the criteria for basis swaps are essentially the same as—not stricter than—the criteria for other strategies to qualify for hedge accounting.

395. To ensure that a basis swap does, in fact, result in offsetting cash flows, this Statement also requires that the basis of one leg of the swap be the same as the basis of the identified asset and that the basis of the other leg of the swap be the same as the basis of the identified liability. Some respondents to the Task Force Draft suggested that the only requirement should be that one leg of the basis swap be highly effective in offsetting the variable cash flows of the asset and the other leg be highly effective in offsetting the variable cash flows of the liability. The Board noted that such a provision could have an additive effect if neither leg is entirely effective. The sum of the two amounts of ineffectiveness might not satisfy the effectiveness test that other derivatives must meet to qualify for hedge accounting. The Board therefore decided to retain the requirement that the basis of one leg of the basis swap be the same as that of a recognized asset and that the basis of the other leg be the same as that of a recognized liability. Section 2 of Appendix A provides an example of assessing the effectiveness of a hedge with a basis swap.

Written options

396. A written option exposes its writer to the possibility of unlimited loss but limits the gain to the amount of premium received. The Board is concerned about permitting written options to be designated as hedging instruments because a written option serves only to reduce the potential for gain in the hedged item or hedged transaction. It leaves the potential for loss on the hedged item or hedged transaction unchanged except for the amount of premium received on the written option. Consequently, on a net basis, an entity may be worse off as a result of trying to hedge with a written option. Because of those concerns, the Exposure Draft proposed prohibiting a written option from being eligible for designation as a hedging instrument.

397. Respondents to the Exposure Draft objected to categorically prohibiting written options from being designated as hedging instruments. A number of respondents specifically referred to the use of a written option to hedge the call option feature in a debt instrument. They explained that it may be more cost-effective to issue fixed-rate, callable debt and simultaneously enter into a receive-fixed, pay-variable interest rate swap with an embedded written call option than to directly issue variable-rate, noncallable debt. The Board agreed that hedge accounting should be available for that use of written options. Consequently, this Statement permits designation of a written option as hedging the purchased option embedded in a financial instrument. The Board notes that if the option features in both instruments are exactly opposite, any gains or losses on the two options generally will offset. Section 2 of Appendix A includes an example illustrating such a strategy.

398. The requirements in this Statement for hedge accounting for strategies that use written options are based on symmetry of the gain and loss potential of the combined hedged position. To qualify for hedge accounting, either the upside and downside potential of the net position must be symmetrical or the upside potential must be greater than the downside potential. That is, the combination of the hedged item and the written option must result in a position that provides at least as much potential for gains (or favorable cash flows) as exposure to losses (or unfavorable cash flows). Evaluation of the combined position's relative potential for gains and losses is based on the effect of a favorable or unfavorable change in price of a given percentage. For example, a 25 percent favorable change in the fair value of the hedged item must provide a gain on the combined position that is at least as large as the loss on that combined position that would result from a 25 percent unfavorable change in the fair value of the hedged item.

399. This Statement does not permit hedge accounting for "covered call" strategies—strategies in which an entity writes an option on an asset that it owns (unless that asset is a call option that is embedded in another instrument). In that strategy, any loss on the written option will be covered by the gain on the owned asset. However, a covered call strategy will not qualify for hedge accounting because the risk profile of the combined position is asymmetrical (the

exposure to losses is greater than the potential for gains). In contrast, the risk profile of the asset alone is "symmetrical or better" (the potential for gains is at least as great as the exposure to losses).

400. The symmetry requirement for hedges with written options described in paragraph 398 is intended to preclude a written option that is used to sell a portion of the gain potential on an asset or liability from being eligible for hedge accounting. For example, assume that an entity has an investment in equity securities that have a current fair value of $150 per share. To sell some, but not all, of the upside potential of those securities, the entity writes a call option contract to sell the securities for $150 per share and purchases a call option contract to buy the same securities at $160 per share. On a net basis, the entity still has *unlimited* upside potential because there are infinite possible outcomes above $160 per share, but its downside risk is limited to $150 per share. Without the requirement to compare increases and decreases of comparable percentages, an entity could assert that its written option strategy warrants hedge accounting because, after entering into the written and purchased option contracts, there is still more potential for gains than for losses from its combined position in the equity securities and option contracts. The Board decided that hedge accounting should not be available for a transaction that merely "sells" part of the potential for gain from an existing asset.

401. This Statement does not require that a written option be entered into at the same time the hedged item is issued or acquired because the combined position is the same regardless of when the position originated (assuming, of course, that the price of the hedged item is the same as the underlying for the option at the time the hedge is entered into). In addition, the Board decided not to limit the items that may be hedged with written options to financial instruments. The Board decided that this Statement's provisions for hedging with written options should accommodate similar risk management strategies regardless of the nature of the asset or liability that is the hedged item.

Exposures to Changes in Fair Value or Cash Flows That Could Affect Reported Earnings

402. This Statement requires that a hedged item or hedged forecasted transaction embody an exposure to changes in fair value or variations in cash flow, for the risk being hedged, that could affect reported earnings. That is, a change in the fair value of a hedged item or variation in the cash flow of a hedged forecasted transaction attributable to the risk being hedged must have the potential to change the amount that could be recognized in earnings. For example, the future sale of an asset or settlement of a liability that exposes an entity to the risk of a change in fair value may result in recognizing a gain or loss in earnings when the sale or settlement occurs. Changes in market price could change the amount for which the asset or liability could be sold or settled and, consequently, change the amount of gain or loss recognized. Forecasted transactions that expose an entity to cash flow risk have the potential to affect reported earnings because the amount of related revenue or expense may differ depending on the price eventually paid or received. Thus, an entity could designate the forecasted sale of a product at the market price at the date of sale as a hedged transaction because revenue will be recorded at that future sales price.

403. Some respondents to the Exposure Draft asked the Board to permit some transactions that create an exposure to variability in cash flows to qualify as hedgeable transactions even though they could not affect reported earnings. They asserted that hedges of those transactions successfully reduce an entity's cash flow exposure. The Board decided to retain the criterion of an earnings exposure because the objective of hedge accounting is to allow the gain or loss on a hedging instrument and the loss or gain on a designated hedged item or transaction to be recognized in earnings at the same time. Moreover, without an earnings exposure, there would be no way to determine the period in which the derivative gain or loss should be included in earnings to comply with this Statement.

404. The earnings exposure criterion specifically precludes hedge accounting for derivatives used to hedge (a) transactions with stockholders as stockholders, such as projected purchases of treasury stock or payments of dividends, (b) intercompany transactions (except for foreign-currency-denominated forecasted intercompany transactions, which are discussed in paragraphs 482–487) between entities included in consolidated financial statements, and (c) the price of stock expected to be issued pursuant to a stock option plan for which recognized compensation expense is not based on changes in stock prices after the date of grant. However, intercompany transactions may present an earnings exposure for a

subsidiary in its freestanding financial statements; a hedge of an intercompany transaction would be eligible for hedge accounting for purposes of those statements.

The Hedged Item or Transaction Is Not Remeasured through Earnings for the Hedged Risk

405. Special hedge accounting is not necessary if both the hedged item and the hedging instrument are measured at fair value with changes in fair value reported in earnings as they occur because offsetting gains and losses will be recognized in earnings together. The Board therefore decided to specifically prohibit hedge accounting if the related asset or liability is, or will be, measured at fair value, with changes in fair value reported in earnings when they occur. That prohibition results from the Board's belief that a standard on hedge accounting should not provide the opportunity to change the accounting for an asset or liability that would otherwise be reported at fair value with changes in fair value reported in earnings. Thus, for a fair value hedge, the prohibition is intended to prevent an entity from recognizing only the change in fair value of the hedged item attributable to the risk being hedged rather than its entire change in fair value. For a cash flow hedge, the prohibition is intended to prevent an entity from reflecting a derivative's gain or loss in accumulated other comprehensive income when the related asset or liability will be measured at fair value upon acquisition or incurrence.

406. The Exposure Draft would have excluded from its scope all of the assets and liabilities of an entity that follows specialized industry practice under which it measures substantially all of its assets at fair value and recognizes changes in those fair values in earnings. That exclusion was aimed at preventing those entities from avoiding fair value accounting. Respondents to the Exposure Draft noted that exclusion also would have prohibited those entities from applying hedge accounting to hedged assets or liabilities that are not measured at fair value, such as long-term debt. The Board decided to remove the exclusion and instead focus on assets and liabilities that are reported at fair value because that approach would (a) be consistent with the notion that eligibility for hedge accounting should be based on the criteria in this Statement, (b) provide consistent fair value accounting for all derivatives, and (c) be responsive to the concerns of constituents.

407. The criteria in this Statement also preclude hedge accounting for an asset or a liability that is remeasured for changes in price attributable to the risk being hedged, with those changes in value reported currently in earnings. The criteria therefore preclude fair value or cash flow hedge accounting for foreign currency risk associated with any asset or liability that is denominated in a foreign currency and remeasured into the functional currency under Statement 52. The Board believes that special accounting is neither appropriate nor necessary in that situation because the transaction gain or loss on the foreign-currency-denominated asset or liability will be reported in earnings along with the gain or loss on the undesignated derivative. The criteria also preclude a cash flow hedge of the forecasted acquisition or incurrence of an item that will be denominated in a foreign currency and remeasured into the functional currency each period after acquisition or incurrence. However, the criteria do not preclude a cash flow hedge of the foreign currency exposure associated with the forecasted purchase of a nonmonetary item for a foreign currency, even if the purchase will be on credit, because nonmonetary items are not subsequently remeasured into an entity's functional currency. Nor do the criteria preclude hedging the forecasted sale of a nonmonetary asset for a foreign currency, even if the sale will be on credit.

Risks That May Be Designated as Being Hedged

408. The Board recognizes that entities are commonly exposed to a variety of risks in the course of their activities, including interest rate, foreign exchange, market price, credit, liquidity, theft, weather, health, catastrophe, competitive, and business cycle risks. The Exposure Draft did not propose detailed guidance on what risks could be designated as being hedged, other than to note in the basis for conclusions that special hedge accounting for certain risk management transactions, such as hedges of strategic risk, would be precluded. In redeliberating the issue of risk, the Board reaffirmed that hedge accounting cannot be provided for all possible risks and decided to be more specific about the risks for which hedge accounting is available.

409. Because this Statement, unlike the Exposure Draft, bases the accounting for a hedged item in a fair value hedge on changes in fair value attributable to the risk being hedged, the Board decided that it needed to limit the types of risks that could be designated as being hedged. The absence of limits could make meaningless the notion of hedge effectiveness

by ignoring the consequence of basis or other differences between the hedged item or transaction and the hedging instrument in assessing the initial and continuing qualification for hedge accounting.

410. For example, an entity using a LIBOR-based interest rate futures contract as a hedge of a prime-based asset might assert that the risk being hedged is the fair value exposure of the prime-based asset to changes in LIBOR. Because that designation would ignore the basis difference between the prime-based hedged asset and the LIBOR-based derivative hedging instrument, it could result in asserted "automatic" compliance with the effectiveness criterion. That type of designation might also lead an entity to assert that the amount of the change in the hedged item's fair value attributable to the hedged risk corresponds to the change in the fair value of the hedging derivative and, therefore, to erroneously conclude that the derivative's change in fair value could be used as a surrogate for changes in the fair value of the hedged item attributable to the hedged risk. Such a designation also would remove any possibility that actual ineffectiveness of a hedge would be measured and reflected in earnings in the period in which it occurs.

Financial assets and liabilities

411. For financial instruments, this Statement specifies that hedge accounting is permitted for hedges of changes in fair value or variability of future cash flows that result from changes in four types of risk. As indicated in paragraph 21(f), those four risks also apply to fair value hedges of firm commitments with financial components.

a. *Market price risk.* A fair value hedge focuses on the exposure to changes in the fair value of the entire hedged item. The definition of *fair value* requires that the fair value of a hedged item be based on a quoted market price in an active market, if available. Similarly, a cash flow hedge focuses on variations in cash flows, for example, the cash flows stemming from the purchase or sale of an asset, which obviously are affected by changes in the market price of the item. The Board therefore concluded that the market price risk of the entire hedged item (that is, the risk of changes in the fair value of the entire hedged item) should be eligible for designation as the hedged risk in a fair value hedge. Likewise, variable cash flows stemming from changes in the market price of the entire item are eligible for designation as the hedged risk in a cash flow hedge.

b. *Market interest rate risk.* For financial assets and liabilities, changes in market interest rates may affect the right to receive (or obligation to pay or transfer) cash or other financial instruments in the future or the fair value of that right (or obligation). The time value of money is a broadly accepted concept that is incorporated in generally accepted accounting principles (for example, in APB Opinion No. 21, *Interest on Receivables and Payables,* and FASB Statement No. 91, *Accounting for Nonrefundable Fees and Costs Associated with Originating or Acquiring Loans and Initial Direct Costs of Leases*). Because the marketplace has developed techniques to delineate and extract interest rate risk from financial instruments, the Board decided that the risk that changes in market interest rates will affect the fair value or cash flows of the hedged item warrants being identified as a risk that may be designated as being hedged.

c. *Foreign exchange risk.* The fair value (expressed in the entity's functional currency) of an asset such as a foreign debt or equity security that is classified as available for sale, as well as the fair value of the financial component of a firm commitment that is denominated in a currency other than the entity's functional currency, generally is exposed to changes in foreign exchange rates. Similarly, the cash flows of a forecasted transaction generally are exposed to changes in foreign exchange rates if the transaction will be denominated in a foreign currency. Statement 52 specifies special accounting for reflecting the effects of changes in foreign exchange rates, and this Statement continues much of that accounting. The Board therefore decided that the risk of changes in foreign exchange rates on the fair value of certain hedged items and on the cash flows of hedged transactions warrants being identified as a risk that may be designated as being hedged.

d. *Default (credit) risk.* A financial asset embodies a right to receive cash or another financial instrument from a counterparty. A financial asset thus embodies a risk that the counterparty will fail to perform according to the terms of the contract; that risk generally is referred to as credit risk. Because that risk affects the fair value of a financial asset, as well as the related cash flows, the Board decided that the risk of the counterparty's default on its obligation is a risk that may be designated as being hedged.

Focusing on those four risks is consistent with the belief that the largest amount of present hedging activity is aimed at protecting against market price, credit, foreign exchange, or interest rate risk. Those also were the risks generally accommodated by special hedge accounting before this Statement. Focusing on those four risks also is consistent with responses to the Exposure Draft. Although the notice for recipients did not ask respondents to comment on the type of risks that should be eligible for hedge accounting, respondents generally discussed hedging transactions in terms of those four risks.

412. This Statement also focuses on those four specified risks because a change in the price associated with one of those risks ordinarily will directly affect the fair value of an asset or liability or the cash flows of a future transaction in a determinable or predictable manner. Price changes associated with other risks may not be as direct. For example, price changes associated with "strategic risk" exposures do not have a direct impact on the fair value of a hedged item or cash flow of a forecasted transaction and thus may not be designated as the risk being hedged. Strategic hedges are described in paragraph 231.

413. This Statement does not permit designating a subcomponent of market price, market interest rate, foreign exchange, or credit risk as the risk being hedged. However, some of those subcomponents may be embodied in a separable portion of a financial instrument. For example, prepayment risk is a subcomponent of market interest rate risk, but the prepayment risk in a financial asset stems from the embedded written call option. An entity may hedge prepayment risk by separately designating a hedge of the embedded call option. Even though this Statement does not require an embedded prepayment option to be accounted for separately because it is deemed to be clearly and closely related to the host contract, that embedded call option still is a derivative. Because this Statement does not permit a compound derivative to be separated into risk components for hedge accounting purposes, only the market price risk of the entire option qualifies as the hedged risk. Hedge effectiveness therefore must be measured based on changes in the fair value of the option.

414. Measuring the effectiveness of a fair value hedge requires determining whether a gain or loss on

a hedging derivative offsets the loss or gain in the value of the hedged item that is attributable to the risk being hedged. Once the change in the value of a hedged item attributable to a particular risk has been offset by the change in value of a hedging derivative, a second, identical derivative cannot also be an effective hedge of that same risk. Similarly, an embedded derivative in a hedged item will modify the nature of the risk to which that item is exposed. Thus, all embedded derivatives relating to the same risk class (that is, market prices, market interest rates, foreign exchange rates, or credit) in a hedged item must be considered together in assessing the effectiveness of an additional (freestanding) derivative as the hedging instrument.

415. For example, an entity might enter into a firm commitment to purchase an asset for 1,000,000 Deutsche marks (DM), with a provision that caps the U.S. dollar equivalent price at $600,000. A hedge of the foreign currency risk in that commitment cannot be effective unless it takes into account the effect of the cap. Similarly, a hedge of the effect on the holder of changes in market interest rates on the unconditional receivable component of a prepayable bond cannot ignore the effect of the embedded prepayment option. To disregard the effects of embedded derivatives related to the same risk class could result in a designated hedge that is not effective at achieving offsetting changes in fair value attributable to the risk being hedged.

Nonfinancial assets and liabilities

416. The Board decided to limit fair value and cash flow hedge accounting for hedges of nonfinancial assets and liabilities (other than recognized loan servicing rights and nonfinancial firm commitments with financial components) to hedges of the risk of changes in the market price of the *entire* hedged item in a fair value hedge or the *entire* asset to be acquired or sold in a hedged forecasted transaction, with one exception. The risk of changes in the functional-currency-equivalent cash flows attributable to changes in foreign exchange rates may be separately hedged in a cash flow hedge of the forecasted purchase or sale of a nonfinancial item. The Board decided not to permit the market price risk of only a principal ingredient or other component of a nonfinancial hedged item to be designated as the risk being hedged because changes in the price of an ingredient or component of a nonfinancial item generally

do not have a predictable, separately measurable effect on the price of the item that is comparable to the effect of, say, a change in market interest rates on the price of a bond.

417. For example, if an entity wishes to enter into a cash flow hedge of the variability in cash inflows from selling tires, the market price risk of rubber alone could not be designated as the risk being hedged. There is no mechanism in the market for tires to directly relate the amount or quality of rubber in a tire to the price of the tire. Similarly, if a derivative is used in a fair value hedge to hedge the exposure to changes in the fair value of tires held in inventory, the entity could not designate the market price of rubber as the hedged risk even though rubber is a component of the tires. The fair value of the tire inventory is based on the market price of tires, not rubber, even though the price of rubber may have an effect on the fair value of the tires. Permitting an entity to designate the market price of rubber as the risk being hedged would ignore other components of the price of the tires, such as steel and labor. It also could result in automatic compliance with the effectiveness test even though the price of rubber may not be highly correlated with the market price of tires. As discussed in the effectiveness examples in Section 2 of Appendix A, the use of a rubber-based derivative as a fair value hedge of the tire inventory or a cash flow hedge of its sale or purchase may qualify for hedge accounting. To do so, however, the entire change in the fair value of the derivative and the entire change in the fair value of the hedged item must be expected to be highly effective at offsetting each other, and all of the remaining hedge criteria must be met. Any ineffectiveness must be included currently in earnings.

418. Some respondents to the Task Force Draft objected to this Statement's different provisions about risks that may be hedged in financial versus nonfinancial items. They asserted that an entity also should be permitted to separate a nonfinancial item into its principal components for hedge accounting purposes. The Board considers those differing requirements to be an appropriate consequence of the nature of the items being hedged.

419. For example, the effect of changes in market interest rates qualifies for designation as the hedged risk in a financial item but not in a nonfinancial item. An increase in market interest rates will result in a decrease in the fair value of a fixed-rate financial asset because the market rate of interest directly affects the

present value computation of the item's future cash flows. Similarly, an increase in market interest rates will result in an increase in the cash flows of a variable-rate financial asset. For both fixed- and variable-rate financial assets, the effect of a change in market interest rates is not only direct but also predictable and separately determinable. For instance, holding factors like credit risk constant, it is relatively easy to calculate the effect of a 100-basis-point increase in market interest rates on the market price of a fixed-rate bond with a specified interest rate and specified time to maturity. It is even easier to determine the effect of a 100-basis-point increase in interest rates on the cash flows stemming from a variable-rate bond. In contrast, although an increase of 100 basis points in market interest rates may affect the market price of a residential building, techniques do not currently exist to isolate and predict that effect.

420. The effect of changes in interest rates on the market price of residential real estate is much less direct than the effect of interest rate changes on financial items. Interest rates may indirectly affect the market price of a single-family house because of the effect of a change in market interest rates on consumer buying behavior or rental rates. For example, an increase in market interest rates may lead to decreased consumer demand for real estate mortgage loans and, in turn, for real estate purchases. Enticing consumers to purchase real estate in a higher interest-rate environment may necessitate lower prices. However, a myriad of other factors may affect the price of residential real estate, and any effect of interest rates is not predictable, immediate, or subject to isolation.

421. Unlike a change in market interest rates, it may be possible to isolate the effect of a change in foreign exchange rates on the functional currency cash flows stemming from a nonfinancial item. For example, an entity with a U.S. dollar functional currency owns residential real estate located in France with a market price of FF5,000,000. If the price of residential real estate in France and the U.S. dollar–French franc exchange rate are not correlated, an increase of $0.01 in the value of the franc will increase the U.S. dollar equivalent of the sales price of the real estate by $50,000 (FF5,000,000 × 0.01). This Statement thus permits the effect of changes in foreign exchange rates to be designated as the hedged risk in a cash flow hedge of a forecasted transaction involving a nonfinancial item.

Simultaneous Hedges of Fair Value and Cash Flow Exposures

422. The Exposure Draft would have prohibited the simultaneous designation of an asset or liability as a fair value hedged item and that asset's or liability's cash flows as a hedged forecasted transaction. The Board had previously concluded that, in certain circumstances, if an entity were permitted to apply hedge accounting at the same time for hedges of both the fair value and the cash flow variability of a single item, the results would be questionable because the entity may be hedging some (if not all) of the same cash flows twice. For example, simultaneous hedging of both the fair value of 1,000 barrels of existing crude oil inventory in a fair value hedge and the forecasted sale of refined oil from those 1,000 barrels of oil in a cash flow hedge would change the nature of the entity's exposure to oil price movements. The two hedges would take the entity from a net long position to a net short position; together they would not necessarily neutralize risk.

423. The Board decided to remove the restriction on simultaneous fair value and cash flow hedges. That change was made, in part, because of the change to base both the assessment of hedge effectiveness and hedge accounting on the change in fair value or cash flows attributable to the risk being hedged. The Board believes this Statement can accommodate simultaneous fair value and cash flow hedging in certain situations if different risk exposures are being hedged because hedge accounting in this Statement accounts for each risk exposure separately. For example, an entity might designate both a cash flow hedge of the interest rate risk associated with a variable-rate financial asset and a fair value hedge of the credit risk on that asset.

424. Removing the restriction on simultaneous fair value and cash flow hedges is not, however, intended to permit simultaneous hedges of the same risk, such as credit risk or market price risk, with both a fair value hedge and a cash flow hedge. For example, the Board does not consider the simultaneous hedge of the fair value of crude oil and the cash flows from selling a product made from that oil described in paragraph 422 to be consistent with the requirements of this Statement because the crude oil and the refined product do not present separate earnings exposures. The entity cannot sell both the crude oil and a refined product made from the same oil—it can only do one or the other. Regardless of how it intends to use the crude oil, the entity can choose to hedge its

exposure to changes in the price of a specific amount of crude oil as either a fair value exposure or a cash flow exposure, but not as both.

425. Some respondents to the Exposure Draft opposed the prohibition on simultaneous hedges because it would preclude swapping foreign-currency-denominated variable-rate debt to U.S. dollar fixed-rate debt. That strategy was not eligible for hedge accounting under the Exposure Draft because the variable interest rate exposure is a cash flow exposure and the foreign currency exposure was deemed to be a fair value exposure. Even though this Statement no longer includes a restriction on simultaneous hedges, the foreign currency aspect of that strategy is not hedgeable under this Statement because the debt will be remeasured into the entity's functional currency under Statement 52, with the related transaction gain or loss reported in earnings. An entity might, however, be able to achieve income statement results similar to hedge accounting using separate interest rate and foreign currency derivatives and designating only the interest rate derivative as a hedging instrument. Income statement offset would be achieved for the foreign currency aspect because the change in fair value of the undesignated foreign currency derivatives will flow through earnings along with the remeasurement of the debt into the functional currency.

Prohibition against Hedge Accounting for Hedges of Interest Rate Risk of Debt Securities Classified as Held-to-Maturity

426. This Statement prohibits hedge accounting for a fair value or cash flow hedge of the interest rate risk associated with a debt security classified as held-to-maturity pursuant to Statement 115. During the deliberations that preceded issuance of Statement 115, the Board considered whether such a debt security could be designated as being hedged for hedge accounting purposes. Although the Board's view at that time was that hedging debt securities classified as held-to-maturity is inconsistent with the basis for that classification, Statement 115 did not restrict hedge accounting of those securities because constituents argued that the appropriateness of such restrictions should be considered in the Board's project on hedging.

427. The Exposure Draft proposed prohibiting a held-to-maturity debt security from being designated as a hedged item, regardless of the risk being hedged. The Exposure Draft explained the Board's belief that

designating a derivative as a hedge of the changes in fair value, or variations in cash flow, of a debt security that is classified as held-to-maturity contradicts the notion of that classification. Respondents to the Exposure Draft objected to the proposed exclusion, asserting the following: (a) hedging a held-to-maturity security does not conflict with an asserted intent to hold that security to maturity, (b) a held-to-maturity security contributes to interest rate risk if it is funded with shorter term liabilities, and (c) prohibiting hedge accounting for a hedge of a held-to-maturity security is inconsistent with permitting hedge accounting for other fixed-rate assets and liabilities that are being held to maturity.

428. The Board continues to believe that providing hedge accounting for a held-to-maturity security conflicts with the notion underlying the held-to-maturity classification in Statement 115 if the risk being hedged is the risk of changes in the fair value of the entire hedged item or is otherwise related to interest rate risk. The Board believes an entity's decision to classify a security as held-to-maturity implies that future decisions about continuing to hold that security will not be affected by changes in market interest rates. The decision to classify a security as held-to-maturity is consistent with the view that a change in fair value or cash flow stemming from a change in market interest rates is not relevant for that security. In addition, fair value hedge accounting effectively alters the traditional income recognition pattern for that debt security by accelerating gains and losses on the security during the term of the hedge into earnings, with subsequent amortization of the related premium or discount over the period until maturity. That accounting changes the measurement attribute of the security away from amortized historical cost. The Board also notes that the rollover of a shorter term liability that funds a held-to-maturity security may be eligible for hedge accounting. The Board therefore decided to prohibit both a fixed-rate held-to-maturity debt security from being designated as a hedged item in a fair value hedge and the variable interest receipts on a variable-rate held-to-maturity security from being designated as hedged forecasted transactions in a cash flow hedge if the risk being hedged includes changes in market interest rates.

429. The Board does not consider it inconsistent to prohibit hedge accounting for a hedge of market interest rate risk in a held-to-maturity debt security while permitting it for hedges of other items that an entity may be holding to maturity. Only held-to-maturity debt securities receive special accounting

(that is, being measured at amortized cost when they otherwise would be required to be measured at fair value) as a result of an asserted intent to hold them to maturity.

430. The Board modified the Exposure Draft to permit hedge accounting for hedges of credit risk on held-to-maturity debt securities. It decided that hedging the credit risk of a held-to-maturity debt security is not inconsistent with Statement 115 because that Statement allows a sale or transfer of a held-to-maturity debt security in response to a significant deterioration in credit quality.

431. Some respondents to the Task Force Draft said that a hedge of the prepayment risk in a held-to-maturity debt security should be permitted because it does not contradict the entity's stated intention to hold the instrument to maturity. The Board agreed that in designating a security as held-to-maturity, an entity declares its intention not to voluntarily sell the security as a result of changes in market interest rates, and "selling" a security in response to the exercise of a call option is not a voluntary sale. Accordingly, the Board decided to permit designating the embedded written prepayment option in a held-to-maturity security as the hedged item. Although prepayment risk is a subcomponent of market interest rate risk, the Board notes that prepayments, especially of mortgages, occur for reasons other than changes in interest rates. The Board therefore does not consider it inconsistent to permit hedging of prepayment risk but not interest rate risk in a held-to-maturity security.

Additional Qualifying Criteria for Fair Value Hedges

Specific Identification

432. This Statement requires specific identification of the hedged item. The hedged item must be (a) an entire recognized asset or liability, or an unrecognized firm commitment, (b) a portfolio of similar assets or similar liabilities, or (c) a specific portion of a recognized asset or liability, unrecognized firm commitment, or portfolio of similar items. If an entity hedges a specified portion of a portfolio of similar assets or similar liabilities, that portion should relate to every item in the portfolio. If an entity wishes to hedge only certain similar items in a portfolio, it should first identify a smaller portfolio of only the items to be hedged.

433. The Exposure Draft would not have permitted designation of a portion of an asset or a liability as a

hedged item. Under the Exposure Draft, those items could only have been hedged in their entirety or on a percentage basis. Some respondents to the Exposure Draft objected to that limitation because it precluded identification of only selected contractual cash flows as the item being hedged (referred to as partial-term hedging for a debt security). For example, it would have prohibited identification of the interest payments for the first two years of a four-year fixed-rate debt instrument as the hedged item and, therefore, would have precluded hedge accounting for a hedge of that debt with a two-year interest rate swap.

434. The Board was reluctant to permit identification of a selected portion (rather than proportion) of an asset or liability as the hedged item because it believes that, in many cases, partial-term hedge transactions would fail to meet the offset requirement. For example, the changes in the fair value of a two-year interest rate swap cannot be expected to offset the changes in fair value attributable to changes in market interest rates of a four-year fixed-rate debt instrument. For offset to be expected, a principal repayment on the debt (equal to the notional amount on the swap) would need to be expected at the end of year two. The Board decided to remove the prohibition against partial-term hedging and other designations of a portion of an asset or liability to be consistent with the modification to the Exposure Draft to require an entity to define how the expectation of offsetting changes in fair value or cash flows would be assessed. However, removal of that criterion does not necessarily result in qualification for hedge accounting for partial-term or other hedges of part of an asset or a liability.

435. The criterion in paragraph 21(a) that permits a hedged item in a fair value hedge to be a designated portion of an asset or liability (or a portfolio of similar assets or similar liabilities) makes the following eligible for designation as a hedged item:

a. A percentage of the entire asset or liability (or of the entire portfolio)
b. One or more selected contractual cash flows (such as the asset or liability representing the interest payments in the first two years of a four-year debt instrument)[32]
c. A put option, a call option, an interest rate cap, or an interest rate floor embedded in an existing asset or liability that is not an embedded derivative accounted for separately under this Statement

d. The residual value in a lessor's net investment in a direct-financing or sales-type lease.

If the entire asset or liability is a variable-rate instrument, the hedged item cannot be a fixed-to-variable interest rate swap (or similar instrument) perceived to be embedded in a fixed-rate host contract. The Board does not intend for an entity to be able to use the provision that a hedged item may be a portion of an asset or liability to justify hedging a contractual provision that creates variability in future cash flows as a fair value hedge rather than as a cash flow hedge. In addition, all other criteria, including the criterion that requires a hedge to be expected to be highly effective at achieving offset, must still be met for items such as the above to be designated and to qualify for hedge accounting.

436. As discussed in paragraphs 414 and 415, in designating a hedge of a component of an asset or liability, an entity must consider the effect of any derivatives embedded in that asset or liability related to the same risk class. To disregard the effects of an embedded derivative related to the same risk class could result in a designated hedge that is not effective at achieving offsetting changes in fair value or cash flows. The same unacceptable result would occur if a freestanding derivative that was accounted for as hedging a particular item was ignored in considering whether another derivative would qualify as a hedge of the same risk in that item.

Recognized Asset or Liability or Unrecognized Firm Commitment

437. This Statement requires that the item designated as hedged in a fair value hedge be a recognized asset or liability or an unrecognized firm commitment. The Board decided that an unrecognized asset or liability that does not embody a firm commitment should not be eligible for designation as a hedged item because applying fair value hedge accounting to such an unrecognized asset or liability would result in recognizing a portion of it. For example, fair value hedge accounting for an unrecognized intangible asset, such as an internally generated core deposit intangible, would have the effect of recognizing the change in the present value of the intangible asset. The Board believes a change to require or permit recognition of certain intangible assets or potential liabilities that are not now recognized should be made

---

[32]However, as noted in paragraph 434, it likely will be difficult to find a derivative that will be effective as a fair value hedge of selected cash flows.

only after careful consideration of the related conceptual and practical issues rather than being a by-product of hedge accounting.

438. This Statement permits an unrecognized firm commitment, including one that is embodied in an unrecognized asset or liability such as an operating lease with substantial cancellation penalties, to be designated as the hedged item in a fair value hedge. The Board recognizes that permitting certain such firm commitments to be designated as hedged items may be viewed as inconsistent with not permitting other unrecognized assets and liabilities to be hedged items. The Board considered limiting the firm commitments that can be hedged items, for example, to those for which there is no explicit authoritative accounting requirement that precludes recognition of the related asset or liability. However, the Board was unable to identify a specific limitation that would be both workable and equitable. Moreover, the Board notes that a firm commitment as defined in this Statement must have a fixed price and a disincentive for nonperformance sufficiently large to make performance probable (discussed further in paragraphs 440 and 441), which makes hedging a firm commitment less problematic than hedging an unrecognized item such as an internally generated intangible asset. Accordingly, with the limited exceptions discussed in paragraphs 455 and 456, the Board decided to permit all firm commitments as defined in this Statement to qualify as hedged items in fair value hedges.

439. This Statement requires that hedge accounting adjustments to the carrying amount of hedged assets and liabilities be subsequently reported in earnings in the same manner as other adjustments of the carrying amount of the hedged item. For example, gains and losses on an interest-bearing debt instrument that are attributable to interest rate risk generally would be amortized over the life of the instrument as a yield adjustment. For some unrecognized firm commitments, such as a firm commitment to purchase inventory, the nature of the hedged item will clearly specify a basis for recognizing hedge accounting adjustments in income. For others, such as the operating lease discussed in paragraph 438, there will be no obvious pattern of income recognition for hedge accounting adjustments. This Statement requires that an entity specify as part of its initial hedge designation how hedge accounting adjustments will be subsequently recognized in income. The Board believes

that such designation at inception of a hedge is consistent with other provisions in this Statement that prohibit retroactive decisions after the results of a hedge are known.

Definition of a firm commitment

440. Because this Statement provides fair value hedge accounting for hedges of unrecognized firm commitments, a definition of *firm commitment* is necessary. For purposes of this Statement, a firm commitment is defined as:

> An agreement with an unrelated party, binding on both parties and usually legally enforceable, with the following characteristics:
>
> a. The agreement specifies all significant terms, including the quantity to be exchanged, the fixed price, and the timing of the transaction. The fixed price may be expressed as a specified amount of an entity's functional currency or of a foreign currency. It also may be expressed as a specified interest rate or specified effective yield.
> b. The agreement includes a disincentive for nonperformance that is sufficiently large to make performance probable.

That definition is based on the definition of a firm commitment in Statements 52 and 80.

441. Some respondents to the Exposure Draft focused more on the "probability" aspect of the definition than on the requirements that the agreement be binding on both parties and that it specify the significant terms of the transaction, including the price. For example, some respondents wanted to treat as a firm commitment for hedge accounting purposes a group of contracts that are binding on one party but not on the other. They said that if the entity is a party to a sufficient number of those contracts, sufficient evidence would be available to permit a reasonable estimate of the number of transactions that would be consummated under the agreements. The Board notes that an agreement that is binding on one party but not on the other is an option rather than a firm commitment. In developing hedge accounting requirements, the Board believes that the fundamental nature of a financial instrument should not be ignored.

442. The definition of a firm commitment in this Statement requires that the fixed price be specified in

terms of a currency (or an interest rate) rather than an index or in terms of the price or a number of units of an asset other than a currency, such as ounces of gold. A price that varies with the market price of the item that is the subject of the firm commitment cannot qualify as a "fixed" price. For example, a price that is specified in terms of ounces of gold would not be a fixed price if the market price of the item to be purchased or sold under the firm commitment varied with the price of gold. To avoid such a situation, the Board decided that it was necessary to require that the fixed price in a firm commitment be specified in terms of a currency or a rate. A similar situation can exist for a firm commitment that is denominated in a foreign currency if the price of the item to be purchased or sold varies with changes in exchange rates. The Board accepted that possibility because it had been accepted under Statement 52, and it did not want to undertake a complete reconsideration of the hedging provisions of that Statement at this time. Therefore, the price may be specified in any currency—it need not be in the entity's functional currency.

Single Asset or Liability or a Portfolio of Similar Assets or Similar Liabilities

443. This Statement retains the provision from the Exposure Draft that prohibits a portfolio of dissimilar items from being designated as a hedged item. Many respondents said that hedge accounting should be extended to hedges of portfolios of dissimilar items (often called *macro hedges*) because macro hedging is an effective and efficient way to manage risk. To qualify for designation as a hedged item on an aggregate rather than individual basis, the Exposure Draft would have required that individual items in a portfolio of similar assets or liabilities be expected to respond to changes in a market variable in an equivalent way. The Exposure Draft also included a list of specific characteristics to be considered in determining whether items were sufficiently similar to qualify for hedging as a portfolio. Respondents said that, taken together, the list of characteristics and the "equivalent way" requirement would have meant that individual items could qualify as "similar" only if they were virtually identical.

444. To deal with the concerns of respondents, the Board modified the Exposure Draft in two ways. First, the Board deleted the requirement that the value of all items in a portfolio respond in an equivalent way to changes in a market variable. Instead, this Statement requires that the items in a portfolio share

the risk exposure for which they are designated as being hedged and that the fair values of individual items attributable to the hedged risk be expected to respond proportionately to the total change in fair value of the hedged portfolio. The Board intends *proportionately* to be interpreted strictly, but the term does not mean *identically*. For example, a group of assets would not be considered to respond proportionately to a change in interest rates if a 100-basis-point increase in interest rates is expected to result in percentage decreases in the fair values of the individual items ranging from 7 percent to 13 percent. However, percentage decreases within a range of 9 percent to 11 percent could be considered proportionate if that change in interest rates reduced the fair value of the portfolio by 10 percent.

445. The second way in which the Board modified the Exposure Draft was to delete the requirement to consider all specified risk characteristics of the items in a portfolio. The Board considered completely deleting the list of risk characteristics included in the Exposure Draft, and the Task Force Draft did not include that list. However, respondents to that draft asked for additional guidance on how to determine whether individual assets or liabilities qualify as "similar." In response to those requests, the Board decided to reinstate the list of characteristics from the Exposure Draft. The Board intends the list to be only an indication of factors that an entity may find helpful.

446. Those two changes are consistent with other changes to the Exposure Draft to focus on the risk being hedged and to rely on management to define how effectiveness will be assessed. It is the responsibility of management to appropriately assess the similarity of hedged items and to determine whether the derivative and a group of hedged items will be highly effective at achieving offset. Those changes to the Exposure Draft do not, however, permit aggregation of dissimilar items. Although the Board recognizes that certain entities are increasingly disposed toward managing specific risks within portfolios of assets and liabilities, it decided to retain the prohibition of hedge accounting for a hedge of a portfolio of dissimilar items for the reasons discussed in the following paragraphs.

447. Hedge accounting adjustments that result from application of this Statement must be allocated to individual items in a hedged portfolio to determine the carrying amount of an individual item in various circumstances, including (a) upon sale or settlement of

the item (to compute the gain or loss), (b) upon discontinuance of a hedging relationship (to determine the new carrying amount that will be the basis for subsequent accounting), and (c) when other generally accepted accounting principles require assessing that item for impairment. The Board decided that a hedge accounting approach that adjusts the basis of the hedged item could not accommodate a portfolio of dissimilar items (macro hedging) because of the difficulties of allocating hedge accounting adjustments to dissimilar hedged items. It would be difficult, if not impossible, to allocate derivative gains and losses to a group of items if their values respond differently (both in direction and in amount) to a change in the risk being hedged, such as market interest rate risk. For example, some components of a portfolio of dissimilar items may increase in value while other components decrease in value as a result of a given price change. Those allocation difficulties are exacerbated if the items to be hedged represent different exposures, that is, a fair value risk and a cash flow risk, because a single exposure to risk must be chosen to provide a basis on which to allocate a net amount to multiple hedged items.

448. The Board considered alternative approaches that would require amortizing the hedge accounting adjustments to earnings based on the average holding period, average maturity or duration of the items in the hedged portfolio, or in some other manner that would not allocate adjustments to the individual items in the hedged portfolio. The Board rejected those approaches because determining the carrying amount for an individual item when it is (a) impaired or (b) sold, settled, or otherwise removed from the hedged portfolio would ignore its related hedge accounting adjustment, if any. Additionally, it was not clear how those approaches would work for certain portfolios, such as a portfolio of equity securities.

449. Advocates of macro hedging generally believe that it is a more effective and efficient way of managing an entity's risk than hedging on an individual-item basis. Macro hedging seems to imply a notion of entity-wide risk reduction. The Board also believes that permitting hedge accounting for a portfolio of dissimilar items would be appropriate only if risk were required to be assessed on an entity-wide basis. As discussed in paragraph 357, the Board decided not to include entity-wide risk reduction as a criterion for hedge accounting.

450. Although this Statement does not accommodate designating a portfolio of dissimilar items as a hedged item, the Board believes that its requirements

are consistent with (a) the hedge accounting guidance that was in Statements 52 and 80, (b) what the Board generally understands to have been current practice in accounting for hedges not addressed by those Statements, and (c) what has been required by the SEC staff. The Board's ultimate goal of requiring that all financial instruments be measured at fair value when the conceptual and measurement issues are resolved would better accommodate risk management for those items on a portfolio basis. Measuring all financial instruments at fair value with all gains or losses recognized in earnings would, without accounting complexity, faithfully represent the results of operations of entities using sophisticated risk management techniques for hedging on a portfolio basis.

Items the Exposure Draft Prohibited from Designation as Hedged Items in Fair Value Hedges

451. The Exposure Draft proposed to prohibit the following from being designated as a hedged item in a fair value hedge:

a. Oil or gas that has not yet been produced, unmined mineral ore, an agricultural product in process of growing, and similar items
b. An intangible asset
c. An investment accounted for by the equity method
d. Mortgage servicing rights not recognized as assets in accordance with FASB Statement No. 122, *Accounting for Mortgage Servicing Rights*
e. A lease, as defined in FASB Statement No. 13, *Accounting for Leases*
f. A liability for insurance contracts written, as defined and discussed in FASB Statements No. 60, *Accounting and Reporting by Insurance Enterprises*, No. 97, *Accounting and Reporting by Insurance Enterprises for Certain Long-Duration Contracts and for Realized Gains and Losses from the Sale of Investments*, and No. 113, *Accounting and Reporting for Reinsurance of Short-Duration and Long-Duration Contracts*, except for a financial guarantee.

The Board proposed those exclusions, in part, because of concerns about the reliability of available measures of fair values for those items. However, this Statement focuses on changes in the fair value of a hedged item attributable to the risk being hedged, rather than the entire change in the fair value of a hedged item. That shift in focus somewhat mitigated the Board's concerns about determining changes in fair value for those hedged items. The Board agrees with respondents to the Exposure Draft that eligibility for designation as a hedged item should rely on the fair value hedge criteria. Consequently, the Board decided to remove the prohibitions proposed in the Exposure Draft, some of which are discussed further in the following paragraphs. The Board notes, however, that some intangible assets would fail to qualify for hedge accounting because they are neither recognized assets nor firm commitments and would not meet the criterion that requires that the hedged item embody an exposure that could affect reported earnings.

Oil or gas that has not been produced and similar items

452. The Board decided to permit designating as a hedged item in a fair value hedge oil or gas that has not been produced, unmined mineral ore, agricultural products in process of growing, and similar items. In reconsidering whether to specifically prohibit such items from hedge accounting, the Board addressed issues such as (a) whether the costs capitalized to extract, harvest, or mine those items would qualify as a "recognized" asset (one of the criteria for a fair value hedge), (b) whether the amounts recognized for those items bear a close relationship to their fair values, and (c) whether the offset test could ever be met because, for example, extracting and otherwise turning unproduced oil or gas into a salable product would require significant costs. The unproduced oil or gas thus is a different asset from the product upon which a forward sales contract would be based. The Board also considered limiting qualification as a "recognized asset or liability" to those assets and liabilities whose initial recorded amounts represent their fair value at acquisition or incurrence.

453. The Board ultimately decided that hedge accounting qualification for oil or gas that has not been produced, unmined mineral ore, agricultural products in process of growing, and similar items should be consistent—that is, all of them should be either eligible or ineligible for designation as a hedged item. It decided that such items should be eligible for designation, subject to the other criteria for hedge accounting. However, the Board has significant reservations about how the fair value of such items would be determined and how the effectiveness of a fair value hedge of such items would be assessed. It notes that oil or gas that has not yet been produced, unmined mineral ore, agricultural products in the process of growing, and similar items are not final, salable prod-

ucts. Consequently, a derivative based on a final, salable product has a different basis than the hedged item and may not be highly effective at providing offsetting changes in fair value. It would be more likely that such a derivative would be highly effective at providing offsetting cash flows for the forecasted sale of a product made from oil in the ground, for example. Section 2 of Appendix A provides additional discussion and examples on assessing offset for agricultural products in the process of growing and similar items.

Leases

454. In developing the Exposure Draft, the Board had concerns about the consistency of permitting fair value hedge accounting of a specific risk inherent in a lessor's net investment in a direct financing, sales-type, or leveraged lease (for example, the interest rate risk associated with the minimum lease payments but not the unguaranteed residual value). Under Statement 13, the unguaranteed residual value is viewed simply as a final payment on which income is earned during the lease term. The Board ultimately decided to make all recognized assets and liabilities and unrecognized firm commitments related to leases eligible for designation as hedged items in fair value hedges because it believes that the modification to the Exposure Draft to permit designation of a portion of an item as being hedged would enable a lessor to split out the residual value from its net investment in identifying the hedged item. However, an entity may not designate an operating lease that does not qualify under this Statement's definition of a firm commitment as a hedged item in a fair value hedge because a hedged item must be either a recognized asset or liability or a firm commitment as defined in this Statement.

Investment accounted for by the equity method

455. The Board decided to retain the prohibition in the Exposure Draft from designating an investment accounted for by the equity method as a hedged item to avoid conflicts with the existing accounting requirements for that item. Providing fair value hedge accounting for an equity method investment conflicts with the notion underlying APB Opinion No. 18, *The Equity Method of Accounting for Investments in Common Stock*. Opinion 18 requires an investor in common stock and corporate joint ventures to apply the equity method of accounting when the investor has the ability to exercise significant influence over the operating and financial policies of the investee.

Under the equity method of accounting, the investor generally records its share of the investee's earnings or losses from its investment. It does not account for changes in the price of the common stock, which would become part of the basis of an equity method investment under fair value hedge accounting. Changes in the earnings of an equity method investee presumably would affect the fair value of its common stock. Applying fair value hedge accounting to an equity method investment thus could result in some amount of double counting of the investor's share of the investee's earnings. The Board believes that result would be inappropriate. In addition to those conceptual issues, the Board was concerned that it would be difficult to develop a method of implementing fair value hedge accounting, including measuring hedge ineffectiveness, for equity method investments and that the results of any method would be difficult to understand. For similar reasons, this Statement also prohibits fair value hedge accounting for an unrecognized firm commitment to acquire or dispose of an investment accounted for by the equity method.

Other exclusions

456. For reasons similar to those discussed above, the Board also decided to specifically prohibit designation of (a) a minority interest in one or more consolidated subsidiaries and (b) an equity investment in a consolidated subsidiary as the hedged item in a fair value hedge. Those assets do not qualify for designation as a hedged item in a fair value hedge, and a forecasted transaction to acquire or sell them does not qualify as a hedged transaction in a cash flow hedge. Thus, a firm commitment to acquire or sell one of them also does not qualify as a hedged item in a fair value hedge. For the same reason, a firm commitment to enter into a business combination does not qualify as a hedged item in a fair value hedge.

457. This Statement also specifically prohibits an equity instrument classified by an entity in its stockholders' equity in the statement of financial position from being designated as a hedged item. That prohibition is consistent with the requirements that (a) a hedged item be a recognized asset or liability and (b) the hedged item present an exposure to changes in fair value that could affect reported earnings. That prohibition does not, of course, apply to the holder of an equity instrument. Paragraph 286 discusses the application of this Statement to obligations (or rights) that may be settled in an entity's own stock but that are indexed to something other than that stock.

Additional Qualifying Criteria for Cash Flow Hedges

Specific Identification

458. To qualify for cash flow hedge accounting, this Statement requires that an entity specifically identify the forecasted transaction that gives rise to the cash flow exposure. That information is necessary to (a) assess the likelihood that the transaction will occur, (b) determine if the cumulative cash flows of the designated derivative are expected to be highly effective at offsetting the change in expected cash flow of the forecasted transaction attributable to the risk being hedged, and (c) assess the hedge's effectiveness on an ongoing basis. The expected market price of the transaction, both at inception of the hedge and subsequently, is necessary information to determine the change in expected cash flows. Because the circumstances of each entity and transaction are different, the information needed to assess the expected offset may vary.

Single Transaction or Group of Individual Transactions

459. The Exposure Draft would have required that an entity be able to predict the date on which a forecasted transaction will occur for it to qualify for cash flow hedge accounting. The Exposure Draft also would have required the gain or loss on a derivative that hedges a forecasted transaction to be reclassified into earnings on the date that the forecasted transaction was expected to occur. This Statement instead requires the gain or loss on a hedge of a forecasted transaction to be reclassified into earnings in the same period(s) that the hedged transaction affects earnings. That change makes it less important for an entity to be able to predict the exact date on which a hedged forecasted transaction will occur. The Board decided to require an entity to identify the hedged forecasted transaction with sufficient specificity to make it clear whether a particular transaction is a hedged transaction when it occurs. An entity should not be able to choose when to reclassify into earnings a gain or loss on a hedging instrument in accumulated other comprehensive income after the gain or loss has occurred by asserting that the instrument hedges a transaction that has or has not yet occurred. However, the Board does not consider it necessary to require that an entity be able to specify at the time of entering into a hedge the date on which the hedged forecasted transaction will occur to prevent such after-the-fact designation.

FAS133 *FASB Statement of Standards*

460. The following example illustrates the requirement for specific identification of the hedged transaction. Company A determines with a high degree of probability that it will issue $5,000,000 of fixed-rate bonds with a 5-year maturity sometime during the next 6 months, but it cannot predict exactly when the debt issuance will occur. That situation might occur, for example, if the funds from the debt issuance are needed to finance a major project to which Company A is already committed but the precise timing of which has not yet been determined. To qualify for cash flow hedge accounting, Company A might identify the hedged forecasted transaction as, for example, the first issuance of five-year, fixed-rate bonds that occurs during the next six months.

461. The Board understands that it sometimes will be impractical (perhaps impossible) and not cost-effective for an entity to identify each individual transaction that is being hedged. An example is a group of sales or purchases over a period of time to or from one or more parties. The Board decided that an entity should be permitted to aggregate individual forecasted transactions for hedging purposes in some circumstances. As for a hedge of a single forecasted transaction, an entity must identify the hedged transactions with sufficient specificity that it is possible to determine which transactions are hedged transactions when they occur. For example, an entity that expects to sell at least 300,000 units of a particular product in its next fiscal quarter might designate the sales of the first 300,000 units as the hedged transactions. Alternatively, it might designate the first 100,000 sales in each month as the hedged transactions. It could not, however, simply designate any sales of 300,000 units during the quarter as the hedged transaction because it then would be impossible to determine whether the first sales transaction of the quarter was a hedged transaction. Similarly, an entity could not designate the last 300,000 sales of the quarter as the hedged transaction because it would not be possible to determine whether sales early in the quarter were hedged or not.

462. To qualify for hedging as a group rather than individually, the aggregated transactions must share the risk exposure for which they are being hedged. If a forecasted transaction does not share the risk exposure for which the group of items is being hedged, it should not be part of the group being hedged. The Board considers that requirement to be necessary to ensure that a single derivative will be effective as a hedge of the aggregated transactions. To illustrate, under the guidance in this Statement, a single derivative of appropriate size could be designated as hedging a given amount of aggregated forecasted transactions such as the following:

a. Forecasted sales of a particular product to numerous customers within a specified time period, such as a month, a quarter, or a year
b. Forecasted purchases of a particular product from the same or different vendors at different dates within a specified time period
c. Forecasted interest payments on several variable-rate debt instruments within a specified time period.

However, the transactions in each group must share the risk exposure for which they are being hedged. For example, the interest payments in group (c) above must vary with the same index to qualify for hedging with a single derivative. In addition, a forecasted purchase and a forecasted sale cannot both be included in the same group of individual transactions. Although they may be based on the same underlying, they have opposite exposures.

Probability of a Forecasted Transaction

463. The Board concluded that, similar to Statement 80, changes in the fair value of a derivative should be excluded from current earnings only if the related forecasted transaction is probable. An assessment of the likelihood that a forecasted transaction will take place should not be based solely on management's intent because intent is not verifiable. The transaction's probability should be supported by observable facts and the attendant circumstances. Consideration should be given to the following circumstances in assessing the likelihood that a transaction will occur:

a. The frequency of similar past transactions
b. The financial and operational ability of the entity to carry out the transaction
c. Substantial commitments of resources to a particular activity (for example, a manufacturing facility that can be used in the short run only to process a particular type of commodity)
d. The extent of loss or disruption of operations that could result if the transaction does not occur
e. The likelihood that transactions with substantially different characteristics might be used to achieve the same business purpose (for example, an entity that intends to raise cash may have several ways of doing so, ranging from a short-term bank loan to a common stock offering).

464. The term *probable* is used in this Statement consistent with its use in paragraph 3 of FASB Statement No. 5, *Accounting for Contingencies,* which defines *probable* as an area within a range of the likelihood that a future event or events will occur confirming the fact of the loss. That range is from probable to remote, as follows:

> *Probable.* The future event or events are likely to occur.
> *Reasonably possible.* The chance of the future event or events occurring is more than remote but less than likely.
> *Remote.* The chance of the future event or events occurring is slight.

The term *probable* requires a significantly greater likelihood of occurrence than the phrase *more likely than not.*

465. In addition, the Board believes that both the length of time until a forecasted transaction is projected to occur and the quantity of the forecasted transaction are considerations in determining probability. Other factors being equal, the more distant a forecasted transaction is, the less likely it is that the transaction would be considered probable and the stronger the evidence that would be needed to support an assertion that it is probable. For example, a transaction forecasted to occur in five years may be less likely than a transaction forecasted to occur in one year. However, forecasted interest payments for the next 20 years on variable-rate debt typically would be probable if supported by an existing contract. Additionally, other factors being equal, the greater the physical quantity or future value of a forecasted transaction, the less likely it is that the transaction would be considered probable and the stronger the evidence that would be required to support an assertion that it is probable. For example, less evidence generally would be needed to support forecasted sales of 100,000 units in a particular month than would be needed to support forecasted sales of 950,000 units in that month by an entity, even if its sales have averaged 950,000 units per month for the past 3 months.

Contractual Maturity

466. When an entity enters into a hedge that uses a derivative with a maturity that extends approximately to the date the forecasted transaction is expected to occur, the derivative "locks in" a price or rate for the entire term of the hedge, provided that the hedging instrument is held to its maturity. Consistent with that view, the Exposure Draft proposed that, to qualify for hedge accounting, the contractual maturity or repricing date of the derivative must be on or about the same date as the projected date of the hedged forecasted transaction.

467. Respondents to the Exposure Draft objected to that requirement because it would have precluded rollover strategies and hedges of a portion of the term of a forecasted transaction from qualifying for hedge accounting. A rollover strategy involves establishing over time a series of short-term futures, options, or both in consecutive contract months to hedge a forecasted transaction. In a rollover strategy, the complete series of derivatives is not acquired at the inception of the hedge; rather, short-term derivatives are initially acquired as part of a plan to replace maturing derivatives with successive new short-term hedging derivatives. The Exposure Draft explained the Board's belief that, even though an entity may ultimately achieve the same or similar result with a series of short-term contracts, a single short-term derivative by itself does not lock in a price or rate for the period until the forecasted transaction is expected to occur.

468. The Board decided to remove the maturity criterion and thus to permit hedge accounting for rollover strategies. Respondents asserted that those strategies are a common, cost-effective, risk management practice that may achieve results similar to the results of using a single long-term derivative as the hedging instrument. Although the Board notes that a rollover strategy or other hedge using a derivative that does not extend to the transaction date does not necessarily "fix" the price of a forecasted transaction, it decided to accede to respondents' requests to permit hedge accounting for rollover strategies. The Board also decided that removing the maturity criterion was acceptable because it makes the qualifying requirements for fair value and cash flow hedge accounting more consistent. Prohibiting hedges of a portion of a forecasted transaction term from qualifying for cash flow hedge accounting would have been inconsistent with permitting fair value hedge accounting for hedges of a portion of the life of a hedged asset or liability.

Transaction with External Third Party

469. The Exposure Draft proposed that, to qualify for hedge accounting, a hedged forecasted exposure must be a *transaction,* which Concepts Statement 6 defines as an external event involving transfer of

something of value (future economic benefit) between two (or more) entities. That definition was intended to clearly distinguish a transaction from an internal cost allocation or an event that happens within an entity. The Exposure Draft explained that the Board considers hedge accounting to be appropriate only when there is a hedgeable risk arising from a transaction with an external party. Accounting allocations and intercompany transactions, in and of themselves, do not give rise to economic exposure.

470. A number of respondents to the Exposure Draft objected to the requirement that a hedgeable transaction be with an external party because it prohibited an intercompany transaction, including one denominated in a foreign currency, from being designated as a forecasted transaction and afforded hedge accounting.

471. Although the requirements of this Statement are not described in terms of the Concepts Statement 6 definition of a *transaction,* the requirements for hedges of other than foreign currency risk are the same as in the Exposure Draft. As discussed in paragraphs 482–487, the Board decided to accommodate cash flow hedges of the foreign currency risk in forecasted intercompany foreign currency transactions. However, for other than foreign currency hedges, this Statement requires that a forecasted transaction be with a party external to the reporting entity to qualify as a hedged transaction, which is consistent with the Exposure Draft. Therefore, depreciation expense, cost of sales, and similar internal accounting allocations do not qualify as hedgeable forecasted transactions. Forecasted transactions between members of a consolidated entity, except for intercompany transactions denominated in a foreign currency, are not hedgeable transactions except for purposes of separate stand-alone subsidiary financial statements. Thus, a consolidated entity cannot apply hedge accounting to forecasted intercompany transactions, unless the risk being hedged is a foreign currency exposure. A subsidiary could, however, apply hedge accounting to a hedge of a forecasted intercompany transaction in its separate, stand-alone financial statements because those transactions are with a party "external to" the reporting entity in those stand-alone statements.

Forecasted Transactions Prohibited from Designation as the Hedged Item in a Cash Flow Hedge

472. This Statement prohibits cash flow hedge accounting for forecasted transactions involving (a) an entity's interests in consolidated subsidiaries, (b) minority interests in consolidated subsidiaries, (c) investments accounted for by the equity method, or (d) an entity's own equity instruments classified in stockholders' equity. The reasons for those prohibitions are similar to those for prohibiting the same items from being hedged items in fair value hedges, as discussed in paragraphs 455–457. In addition, the Board noted that implementing cash flow hedge accounting for those items could present significant practical and conceptual problems, such as determining when to transfer to earnings amounts accumulated in other comprehensive income. Finally, certain of those items, such as issuances and repurchases of an entity's own equity instruments, would not qualify for hedge accounting because they do not present a cash flow risk that could affect earnings.

473. Prohibiting the forecasted purchase of a consolidated subsidiary from being the hedged item in a cash flow hedge effectively prohibits cash flow hedge accounting for a forecasted business combination to be accounted for as a purchase, and paragraph 29(f) of this Statement makes that prohibition explicit. The Board noted that the current accounting for a business combination is based on considering the combination as a discrete event at the consummation date. Applying cash flow hedge accounting to a forecasted business combination would be inconsistent with that current accounting. It also would be, at best, difficult to determine when to reclassify the gain or loss on the hedging derivative to earnings.

Foreign Currency Hedges

474. The Board's objectives in providing hedge accounting for hedges of foreign currency exposures are the following:

a. To continue to permit hedge accounting for the types of hedged items and hedging instruments that were permitted hedge accounting under Statement 52
b. To increase the consistency of hedge accounting guidance for foreign currency hedges and other types of hedges by broadening the scope of foreign currency hedges that are eligible for hedge accounting, as necessary.

Carried Forward from Statement 52

475. Because the scope of this project did not include a comprehensive reconsideration of accounting for foreign currency translation, this Statement makes two exceptions to retain certain provisions of

Statement 52. The Board decided to make those exceptions to the hedge accounting requirements in this Statement because of the accounting anomalies that otherwise would be created by this Statement and the existing guidance in Statement 52.

476. Although the Board decided not to extend hedge accounting to nonderivative instruments used as hedging instruments, as discussed in paragraphs 246 and 247, it decided to permit an entity to designate a nonderivative financial instrument denominated in a foreign currency as a hedge of a firm commitment. It did so for practical reasons. The Board understands that such hedges are extensively used in practice, and it does not think constituents would understand why that practice should be prohibited now, given the acceptance of it in Statement 52.

477. This Statement also makes an exception to permit an entity to designate a financial instrument denominated in a foreign currency (derivative or nonderivative) as a hedge of the foreign currency exposure of a net investment in a foreign operation. Net investment hedges are subject only to the criteria in paragraph 20 of Statement 52. The net investment in a foreign operation can be viewed as a portfolio of dissimilar assets and liabilities that would not meet the criterion in this Statement that the hedged item be a single item or a group of similar items. Alternatively, it can be viewed as part of the fair value of the parent's investment account. Under either view, without a specific exception, the net investment in a foreign operation would not qualify for hedging under this Statement. The Board decided, however, that it was acceptable to retain the current provisions of Statement 52 in that area. The Board also notes that, unlike other hedges of portfolios of dissimilar items, hedge accounting for the net investment in a foreign operation has been explicitly permitted by the authoritative literature.

478. The Exposure Draft would have retained the approach required by paragraph 20 of Statement 52 for measuring the effective portion of a foreign currency forward contract that is designated as a hedge of the net investment in a foreign operation. The resulting difference between the effective portion and the change in fair value of the hedging derivative would have been reported currently in earnings. The approach in Statement 52 was appropriate given how forward contracts were measured under that Statement. Unlike Statement 52, this Statement requires that forward contracts be measured, at fair value,

which incorporates discounting future cash flows. Accordingly, the Exposure Draft's requirements would have always produced an amount to be recognized in earnings that would have been of opposite sign to the effective portion recognized in the cumulative translation adjustment component of other comprehensive income. That amount could have been explained only in terms of the arithmetic process that produced it. The Board therefore decided that the effective portion of a forward contract that is a hedge of a net investment should be determined not by looking only to changes in spot rates but should include the effects of discounting in the same way as for forward contracts used in other foreign currency hedges.

*Fair value hedges of foreign currency risk in
available-for-sale securities*

479. This Statement permits the portion of the change in value of foreign-currency-denominated debt securities and certain foreign marketable equity securities classified as available-for-sale that is attributable to foreign exchange risk to qualify for fair value hedge accounting. The requirements of this Statement in that area are generally consistent with the provisions of EITF Issues No. 96-15, "Accounting for the Effects of Changes in Foreign Currency Exchange Rates on Foreign-Currency-Denominated Available-for-Sale Debt Securities," and No. 97-7, "Accounting for Hedges of the Foreign Currency Risk Inherent in an Available-for-Sale Marketable Equity Security." However, unlike those EITF Issues, this Statement does not permit a nonderivative instrument to be used as the hedging instrument in a hedge of an available-for-sale security.

480. Foreign available-for-sale debt securities give rise to hedgeable foreign exchange risk because they embody cash flows denominated in a foreign currency. The cash flows embodied in an investment in a marketable equity security, on the other hand, are not inherently "denominated" in a particular currency. Therefore, both the EITF and the Board concluded that a marketable equity security has hedgeable foreign exchange risk only if both of the following criteria are met:

a. The marketable equity security (or an instrument that represents an interest in it, such as an American Depository Receipt) is not traded on an exchange (or other established marketplace) on which trades are denominated in the investor's functional currency.

b. The dividends or other cash flows to be received by the investor are all denominated in the same foreign currency as the currency expected to be received upon sale of the security.

Regardless of the country in which the issuer of an equity security is domiciled, that security presents no discernible foreign exchange risk to a holder who may trade the security for a price denominated in its functional currency. For example, for an investor with a U.S. dollar functional currency, its foreign exchange risk related to the equity securities of a multinational company domiciled in Italy that trade on a U.S. exchange is essentially the same as its foreign exchange risk in the equity securities of a U.S. company with significant foreign operations in Italy. In both situations, the investor's foreign exchange risk is indirect and not reliably measurable. The operations of the issuer rather than the prices in which trades in its equity securities are denominated are the source of the investor's foreign exchange risk.

Broadening of Statement 52

481. Unlike Statement 52, this Statement permits hedge accounting for hedges of forecasted foreign currency transactions, including intercompany transactions. Because this Statement permits hedge accounting for hedges of forecasted interest rate, credit, and market price exposures, the Board considered it appropriate to include foreign currency exposures as well. Forecasted intercompany foreign currency transactions are discussed in the following paragraphs.

Forecasted intercompany foreign currency transactions

482. This Statement permits an entity to designate the foreign currency exposure of a forecasted foreign-currency-denominated intercompany transaction as a hedged transaction in a cash flow hedge. The Exposure Draft proposed that, in general, forecasted transactions between members of a consolidated group would not qualify as hedgeable exposures in the consolidated financial statements. However, if costs are incurred in one currency and the third-party revenues for recovering those costs are generated in another currency, the Exposure Draft would have permitted the entity that incurred the costs to designate the forecasted third-party revenues as a hedged transaction. The Exposure Draft would have required a direct, substantive relationship between the costs incurred and the recovery of those

costs from the outside third party. For example, the Exposure Draft would have permitted an English subsidiary that incurs manufacturing costs in pounds sterling to hedge the ultimate sale of that product for French francs by its affiliated French subsidiary to an unrelated third party. The Board proposed that exception because it considered those transactions to be, in substance, direct foreign export sales.

483. A number of respondents said that the guidance provided in the Exposure Draft was unduly restrictive because forecasted intercompany royalties and licensing fees, which are based on third-party sales and remitted from foreign subsidiaries to a parent company, would not be afforded cash flow hedge accounting. Respondents also took exception to the requirement that there be a "direct, substantive relationship" between costs incurred and recovery of those costs.

484. The Board decided to remove the restrictions on hedge accounting for hedges of forecasted intercompany foreign currency transactions because, pursuant to Statement 52 as amended by this Statement, an intercompany transaction that is denominated in a currency other than the entity's functional currency gives rise to a transaction gain or loss if exchange rates change. A forecasted intercompany transaction that is expected to be denominated in a foreign currency can be viewed as giving rise to the same kind of foreign currency risk. Therefore, pursuant to this Statement, a forecasted intercompany transaction that presents an exposure to foreign currency risk and that otherwise satisfies the criteria for a foreign currency cash flow hedge is eligible for designation as a hedged transaction.

485. As with other hedges of forecasted transactions, amounts accumulated in other comprehensive income for a forecasted foreign currency transaction are to be recognized in earnings in the same period or periods that the hedged transaction affects earnings. Because an intercompany dividend does not affect earnings, a forecasted intercompany dividend cannot qualify as a hedgeable forecasted transaction. In essence, a hedge of a forecasted intercompany dividend expected to be paid from future earnings is a hedge of those future earnings. This Statement prohibits hedge accounting for hedges of future earnings.

486. The Board also made an exception for forecasted intercompany foreign currency transactions because hedging foreign currency intercompany cash flows with foreign currency options is a common practice among multinational companies—a practice

that was permitted in specified circumstances under EITF Issue No. 91-1, "Hedging Intercompany Foreign Currency Risks." This Statement modifies Issue 91-1 to permit hedge accounting for intercompany transactions using other derivatives, such as forward contracts, as the hedging instrument and expands the situations in which hedge accounting may be applied because the Board believes the accounting for all derivative instruments should be the same.

487. For a hedge of a forecasted foreign currency transaction to qualify for hedge accounting, this Statement requires that the component of the entity that has the foreign currency exposure be a party to the hedging transaction. That requirement is necessary because, under the functional currency approach in Statement 52, all foreign currency exposures exist only in relation to an entity's functional currency. Thus, for example, a U.S. parent company cannot directly hedge the foreign currency risk in its French franc subsidiary's U.S.-dollar-denominated export sales because the U.S. parent has no exposure to exchange risk for dollar-denominated sales. However, one component of a consolidated entity, such as a central treasury operation, can effectively take on another component's exchange risk by means of an intercompany transaction. For example, the U.S. parent (or a centralized treasury operation with a U.S. dollar functional currency) might enter into a forward contract to buy dollars from its French subsidiary in exchange for francs. The French subsidiary could designate that intercompany forward contract (in which the French subsidiary sells dollars for francs) as a hedge of its forecasted U.S.-dollar-denominated sales. The U.S. parent then would enter into a sell dollars–buy francs forward contract with an unaffiliated third party to offset its foreign exchange risk on the intercompany forward contract. That third-party transaction is required for the previous intercompany arrangement to qualify in the consolidated financial statements as a hedge of the French subsidiary's forecasted dollar sales. (As noted in paragraph 471, a parent company is a "third party" in a subsidiary's separate financial statements. Thus, the French subsidiary could designate the intercompany derivative as a hedge of its U.S. dollar sales in its stand-alone financial statements regardless of whether the parent has entered into an offsetting contract with an outside party.)

Discontinuing Hedge Accounting

488. This Statement requires that an entity discontinue hedge accounting prospectively if the qualifying criteria are no longer met; if a derivative expires or is sold, terminated, or exercised; or if the entity removes the designation of the hedge. The Board believes hedge accounting is no longer appropriate in those circumstances. This Statement also requires certain modifications to hedge accounting for the interim reporting period in which a discontinuance occurs in circumstances discussed below.

Discontinuing Fair Value Hedge Accounting

489. The Board is concerned that a fair value hedge that no longer qualifies as being highly effective at achieving offsetting changes in fair value for the risk being hedged may continue to receive hedge accounting simply because an entity fails to assess compliance with that effectiveness criterion on a sufficiently frequent basis. If an entity determines at the end of a period that a hedge is no longer effective, it is likely that it was also ineffective during a portion of that period. To minimize the possibility of providing hedge accounting for hedges that do not qualify as highly effective, the Board decided that fair value hedge accounting should not be provided from the point at which the hedge ceased to qualify. It believes that an entity will be able to determine the point at which a hedge became ineffective if it assesses compliance with the effectiveness criterion at the inception of the hedge, on a recurring basis, and whenever something happens that could affect the hedging relationship. The Board believes that immediate evaluation of the effect of relevant changes in circumstances on a hedge's qualification for hedge accounting should be an integral aspect of an ongoing assessment of compliance.

490. The Board expects that entities entering into hedging transactions that do not qualify for an assumption of automatic effectiveness and zero ineffectiveness under the criteria discussed in Appendix A will monitor hedge effectiveness frequently—often daily. However, the Board recognizes that it may not be cost-effective for some entities to assess compliance with the effectiveness criterion on a daily or weekly basis. It therefore decided that compliance should be assessed no less frequently than quarterly. However, if the event or change in circumstances that caused the hedging relationship to cease to qualify cannot be identified, the entity is prohibited from applying hedge accounting from the date at which compliance was last assessed and satisfied. Otherwise, a hedging relationship that does not satisfy the conditions for fair value hedge accounting might nevertheless receive such accounting.

491. For hedges of firm commitments, the Board decided that if hedge accounting is discontinued because the hedged item no longer meets the definition of a firm commitment, an entity should derecognize any previously recognized asset or liability and recognize a corresponding loss or gain in earnings. That accounting is appropriate because the asset or liability that represented the value of the firm commitment no longer exists if the hedged transaction no longer qualifies as a firm commitment, for example, because performance is no longer probable. The Board believes those circumstances should be rare. A pattern of discontinuing hedge accounting and derecognizing firm commitments would call into question the "firmness" of future hedged firm commitments and the entity's accounting for future hedges of firm commitments.

Discontinuing Cash Flow Hedge Accounting

492. The Exposure Draft proposed that if cash flow hedge accounting is discontinued, the derivative gain or loss accumulated in other comprehensive income to the date of discontinuance would be recognized in earnings on the originally projected date of the hedged forecasted transaction. That proposed requirement was intended to instill discipline in the accounting for cash flow hedges and reduce the possibility for managing earnings. Respondents to the Exposure Draft disagreed with that provision as it related to discontinuances that resulted from a change in probability. They said that gains and losses previously recognized in other comprehensive income should be reclassified into earnings on the date it is decided that the forecasted transaction is no longer considered probable.

493. The Board considers it inappropriate to defer a gain or loss on a derivative that arises after a hedged forecasted transaction is deemed no longer probable. However, if the occurrence of the forecasted transaction is still reasonably possible, the Board considers it appropriate to continue to include in accumulated other comprehensive income the gain or loss that arose before the date the forecasted transaction is deemed no longer probable. The Board also was concerned that requiring a gain or loss in accumulated other comprehensive income to be reported in earnings when a forecasted transaction is no longer probable but still is reasonably possible (paragraph 464 describes the range of probability) would provide an entity with the opportunity to manage earnings by changing its estimate of probability. For those reasons, the Board decided to require earnings recogni-

tion of a related gain or loss in accumulated other comprehensive income only when an entity determines it is probable that the transaction will *not* occur.

494. A pattern of determining that hedged forecasted transactions probably will not occur would call into question both an entity's ability to accurately predict forecasted transactions and the propriety of using hedge accounting in the future for similar forecasted transactions.

Interaction with Standards on Impairment

495. A hedged item may be reported at fair value as a consequence of applying the provisions of this Statement. That would occur if the carrying amount of the hedged item equaled its fair value at the inception of a hedge and all changes in the fair value of a hedged item were recognized as a result of hedge accounting. However, that is not the same as continuous measurement at fair value. Therefore, accounting for changes in the fair value of a hedged item attributable to the risk being hedged does not exempt the hedged item from accounting provisions of other Statements that apply to assets or liabilities that are not measured at fair value. For example, a loan that is designated as a hedged item but is not otherwise measured at fair value or lower of cost or market value is subject to the impairment provisions of Statement 114.

496. Respondents to the Exposure Draft questioned whether the carrying amount of a derivative should be considered in assessing impairment of a related asset or liability, if any. (In this Statement, the term *impairment* includes the recognition of an increase in a liability as well as a decrease in an asset.) The related asset or liability would be either an existing asset or liability or an asset or liability that was acquired or incurred as a result of a hedged forecasted transaction.

497. The Board decided that it would be inappropriate to consider the carrying amount of a derivative hedging instrument in an assessment of impairment of a related asset or liability in either a fair value hedge or a cash flow hedge. To do so would be inconsistent with the fact that the derivative is a separate asset or liability.

498. This Statement provides that a derivative gain or loss recognized in accumulated other comprehensive income as a hedge of a variable cash flow on a

forecasted transaction is to be reclassified into earnings in the same period or periods as the offsetting loss or gain on the hedged item. For example, a derivative gain that arose from a cash flow hedge of a purchase of equipment used in operations is to be included in earnings in the same periods that depreciation on the equipment is recognized. The net effect on earnings should be the same as if the derivative gain or loss had been included in the basis of the asset or liability to which the hedged forecasted transaction relates. To be consistent with that provision, the Board decided that a derivative gain that offsets part or all of an impairment loss on a related asset or liability should be reclassified into earnings in the period that an impairment loss is recognized. Similarly, a related derivative loss, if any, in accumulated other comprehensive income should be reclassified into earnings in the same period that a recovery of a previous impairment loss is recognized. The Board decided that the reason that a loss or gain on a hedged asset or liability is recognized in income—for example, whether through an ordinary depreciation charge or an impairment write-down—should not affect the reclassification into earnings of a related offsetting gain or loss in accumulated other comprehensive income.

Current Earnings Recognition of Certain Derivative Losses

499. The Board sees no justification for delaying recognition in earnings of a derivative loss that the entity does not expect to recover through revenues related to the hedged transaction. Accordingly, this Statement prohibits continuing to report a loss in accumulated other comprehensive income if the entity expects that doing so would lead to recognizing a net loss on the combined hedging instrument and the hedged transaction in a future period(s). For example, a loss on a derivative designated as a hedge of the forecasted purchase of inventory should be recognized in earnings immediately to the extent that the loss is not expected to be recovered through future sales of the inventory. Statements 52 and 80 included the same requirement.

Accounting by Not-for-Profit Organizations and Other Entities That Do Not Report Earnings

500. This Statement applies to all entities, including not-for-profit organizations, defined benefit pension plans, and other entities that do not report earnings as a separate caption in a statement of financial performance. For example, a not-for-profit entity reports the total change in net assets during a period, which is analogous to total comprehensive income for a business enterprise. The Exposure Draft indicated that cash flow hedge accounting would not be available to an entity that does not report earnings. A few respondents objected to what they interpreted as the Exposure Draft's unequal treatment of not-for-profit and other entities that do not report earnings. They did not consider it fair to deny those entities access to hedge accounting for hedges of forecasted transactions.

501. The effect of cash flow hedge accounting is to report a derivative gain or loss in other comprehensive income—that is, outside earnings—in the period in which it occurs and then to reclassify that gain or loss into earnings in a later period. It thus would be mechanically impossible for an entity that only reports an amount comparable to total comprehensive income to apply cash flow hedge accounting. For this Statement to permit a not-for-profit entity, for example, to apply cash flow hedge accounting, the Board would first have to define a subcomponent of the total change in net assets during a period that would be analogous to earnings for a business enterprise. Neither Concepts Statement 6 nor Statement 117 defines such a measure of operating performance for a not-for-profit entity, and an attempt to define that measure was beyond the scope of the project that led to this Statement. Accordingly, the Board decided to retain the provision that cash flow hedge accounting is not available to a not-for-profit or other entity that does not report earnings as a separate caption in a statement of financial performance.

Disclosures

502. This Statement supersedes Statements 105 and 119, both of which provided disclosure guidance for derivatives and financial instruments. Consistent with its objective of making the guidance on financial reporting related to derivatives easier to use, the Board decided that this Statement should provide comprehensive disclosure guidance, as well as recognition and measurement guidance, for derivatives. This Statement therefore carries forward from Statement 119 the requirement for disclosure of a description of the objectives, context, and strategies for holding or issuing derivatives. The purpose of that disclosure is to "help investors and creditors understand what an entity is trying to accomplish with its derivatives" (Statement 119, paragraph 58). The Board also decided to require additional qualitative disclosures describing an entity's risk management

policy and the items or transactions and the risks being hedged for each type of hedge. The Board believes the qualitative disclosures are necessary to assist investors, creditors, and other users of financial statements in understanding the nature of an entity's derivative activities and in evaluating the success of those activities, their importance to the entity, and their effect on the entity's financial statements. Many respondents to the Exposure Draft supported the qualitative disclosures.

503. This Statement modifies some of the disclosure requirements from the Exposure Draft, mostly as a result of changes to the accounting requirements proposed in the Exposure Draft. Notwithstanding the modifications, the Board decided to retain many of the disclosure requirements in the Exposure Draft given the extent of use and complexity of derivatives and hedging activities and because many users of financial statements have asked for improved disclosures.

504. A few respondents to the Task Force Draft suggested that both the qualitative and the quantitative disclosures should distinguish between derivatives used for risk management based on the type of risk (for example, interest rate risk, foreign currency risk, or credit risk) being hedged rather than based on accounting designations (for example, fair value hedges versus cash flow hedges). Those respondents said that disclosures organized in that manner, perhaps including even narrower distinctions such as the type of asset or liability that is hedged, would better aid the financial statement user in understanding an entity's success in managing the different types of risk that it encounters.

505. The Board agreed that disclosures presented in a manner that distinguishes between the nature of the risk being hedged would provide useful information that would help users understand management's risk management strategies. However, the Board decided not to require that disclosures about derivative instruments be organized in the manner suggested by those respondents. The Board made that decision somewhat reluctantly, based primarily on its concern that it could not require such disclosures without additional study and that such a requirement would necessitate a greater level of detail than the disclosures required by this Statement. Distinguishing between derivatives based on their accounting designation, as this Statement requires, helps users understand the information provided in the financial statements. Information about derivatives used in fair value hedges, cash flow

hedges, hedges of the net investment in a foreign operation, and for other purposes likely would be needed even if the disclosures distinguished between derivatives based on the type of risk being hedged. The result could be a rather complicated multilevel set of disclosures. The Board also notes that this Statement requires disclosures about the risks that management hedges with derivatives as part of the description of the "context needed" to understand the entity's objectives for holding or issuing those instruments. The Board encourages companies to experiment with ways in which disclosures about derivative instruments, including how the gains and losses on them relate to other exposures of the entity, might be presented to make them more understandable and useful.

506. In response to comments about the volume of the proposed disclosure requirements in both the Exposure Draft and the Task Force Draft, the Board reconsidered the costs and benefits of the proposed disclosures. In reconsidering the proposed disclosures, the Board concluded that by eliminating certain of the requirements, it could reduce the cost of applying the Statement without a significant reduction in the benefits to users. Consequently, the following proposed disclosures were eliminated:

a. Amount of gains and losses on hedged items and on related derivatives recognized in earnings for fair value hedges

b. Description of where in the financial statements hedged items and the gains and losses on those hedged items are reported

c. Cumulative net unamortized amount of gains and losses included in the carrying amount of hedged items

d. Separate amounts for the reporting period of hedging gains and hedging losses on derivatives not recognized in earnings for cash flow hedges

e. Description of where derivatives related to cash flow hedges are reported in the statement of financial position

f. Separate amounts for the reporting period of gains and losses on the cash flow hedging instrument

g. Amount of gains and losses recognized during the period on derivatives not designated as hedges

h. Beginning and ending balances in accumulated other comprehensive income for accumulated derivative gains and losses, and the related current period changes, separately for the following two categories: (1) gains and losses related to forecasted transactions for which the variability of hedged future cash flows has ceased and (2) gains and losses related to forecasted transactions for which that variability has not ceased

i. Description of where gains and losses on derivatives not designated as hedges are reported in the statement of income or other statement of financial performance.

In addition, the Board replaced some of the remaining proposed disclosures requiring separate amounts of *gains and losses* with disclosures requiring the amount of *net gain or loss*.

507. The Board also modified the disclosure requirements as a result of changes to the accounting for fair value and cash flow hedges. Those modifications include:

Modification to Hedge Accounting	Resulting Modification to Disclosure
a. Require an entity to determine how to assess hedge effectiveness and to report all hedge ineffectiveness in earnings.	Add a requirement to disclose the net amount of hedge ineffectiveness recognized in earnings and the component of the derivative's gain or loss excluded from the assessment of hedge effectiveness and included directly in earnings.
b. Require gains and losses included in accumulated other comprehensive income to be reclassified into earnings when the forecasted transaction affects earnings.	Replace proposed disclosure of designated reporting periods in which forecasted transactions are expected to occur and the amounts to be reclassified into earnings in those periods with a description of the transactions or other events that will result in reclassification into earnings of gains and losses that are reported in accumulated other comprehensive income and the estimated net amount of existing gains or losses at the reporting date that is expected to be reclassified into earnings within the next 12 months.
c. Require gain or loss included in accumulated other comprehensive income to be reclassified into earnings when it is probable that a hedged forecasted transaction will not occur.	Require disclosure of gross gains and losses reclassified into earnings as a result of the discontinuance of cash flow hedges because it is probable that the forecasted transactions will not occur.

508. Certain respondents were concerned that some of the cash flow hedge disclosures would reveal proprietary information that could be used by competitors and market participants, putting the disclosing entity at a competitive disadvantage. The Board carefully considered those concerns and decided that the ability of traders and competitors to use the cash flow hedge disclosures to determine an entity's competitively sensitive positions would be significantly limited by an entity's ability to designate and dedesignate derivative instruments as cash flow hedges during the reporting period, the aggregate nature of the cash flow hedging disclosures, and the timing and frequency of those disclosures. Notwithstanding that conclusion, the Board notes that the following modifications to the disclosures proposed in the Exposure Draft and the Task Force Draft are directly respon-

sive to the competitive harm concerns raised by some respondents:

a. Elimination of the proposed disclosure of the separate amounts for the reporting period of hedging gains and hedging losses on the derivatives not recognized in earnings

b. Replacement of the proposed disclosure of the designated reporting periods in which the forecasted transactions are expected to occur and the amounts of gains and losses to be reclassified to earnings in those periods with a description of the transactions or other events that will result in the reclassification into earnings of gains and losses that are reported in accumulated other comprehensive income, and the estimated net amount of the existing gains or losses at the reporting date that is expected to be reclassified into earnings within the next 12 months

c. Elimination of the proposed disclosure of the separate amounts for the reporting period of gains and losses on the cash flow hedging instruments

d. Elimination of the proposed disclosure of the beginning and ending balances in accumulated other comprehensive income for accumulated derivative gains and losses, and the related current period changes, separately for the following two categories: gains and losses related to forecasted transactions for which the variability of hedged future cash flows has ceased and gains and losses related to forecasted transactions for which the variability of hedged future cash flows has not ceased

e. Replacement of some of the remaining proposed disclosures of separate amounts of *gains and losses* with disclosure of the amount of *net gain or loss*.

The Board believes the required cash flow hedge disclosures, as modified, provide necessary information in helping financial statement users assess the effect on the financial statements of an entity's cash flow hedge strategies.

509. This Statement also amends Statement 107 to carry forward the provision in Statement 119 that encourages disclosure of quantitative information about market risk. That provision has been revised to clarify that it applies to all financial instruments—not just to derivatives. The Board believes that disclosure will provide useful information to users of financial statements about the overall market risk of an entity's financial instruments. The Board is encouraging, rather than requiring, that information because it continues to believe that ". . . the continuing evolution of approaches to risk management limits the ability to clearly define the most useful approach to disclosing quantitative information about market risks" (Statement 119, paragraph 72). The Board observes that the SEC issued final rules[33] in January 1997 that require certain registrants to make quantitative disclosures of market risk similar to those encouraged by Statement 119.

510. The Board decided that disclosures about concentrations of credit risk previously included in Statement 105 should continue to be required because a number of constituents, including some regulators, have commented on their usefulness. The purpose of those disclosures is to allow "investors, creditors, and other users to make their own assessments of the credit risk associated with the area of concentration" (Statement 105, paragraph 100). The Board decided to modify the disclosure about concentrations of credit risk to require that the amount disclosed be based on the gross fair value of the financial instruments rather than the "amount of the accounting loss" (described in Statement 105, paragraph 20(b)). Preparers found "the amount of the accounting loss" to be confusing, and users of financial statements have stated that fair value information provides a better indication of the credit exposure arising from financial instruments. The disclosure was also modified to require information about an entity's master netting arrangements and their effect on the maximum amount of loss due to credit risk. The Board believes that information provides users with important insight into the potential impact of those arrangements on concentrations of credit risk of an entity.

511. The Board considered either leaving the disclosures about concentrations of credit risk in Statement 105 or including them in this Statement. The Board decided not to retain them in Statement 105 because this Statement supersedes all other guidance in that Statement. The Board decided not to include those disclosures in this Statement because they refer to all financial instruments and this Statement addresses derivative instruments. The Board decided instead to amend Statement 107 to include those disclosures so that all disclosure requirements that apply to all financial instruments will be available in one place.

512. Certain other requirements from Statements 105 and 119 have been deleted, including disclosure of the "face or contract amount" for all derivative financial instruments held at the balance sheet date (Statement 105, paragraph 17, and Statement 119, paragraph 8). The Board originally required that disclosure, in part, to provide users with "information [that] conveys some of the same information provided by amounts recognized for on-balance-sheet instruments" (Statement 105, paragraph 89). That disclosure also provided an indication "of the volume of derivative activity"

---

[33]SEC Final Rules, *Disclosure of Accounting Policies for Derivative Financial Instruments and Derivative Commodity Instruments and Disclosure of Quantitative and Qualitative Information about Market Risk Inherent in Derivative Financial Instruments, Other Financial Instruments, and Derivative Commodity Instruments.*

(Statement 119, paragraph 79). This Statement's requirement that all derivatives be recognized in the statement of financial position at fair value lessens the usefulness of the disclosure of the face or contract amount. For example, reporting all derivatives as assets or liabilities in the statement of financial position will provide an indication of the use of derivatives. More important, although the face or contract amount of derivative instruments held provides some indication of derivatives activity, their usefulness for that purpose may be suspect given that some derivatives are commonly neutralized either by canceling the original derivative—which lowers the reported amount—or by acquiring or issuing an offsetting derivative—which increases the reported amount. The Exposure Draft would have required the disclosure only when necessary to enable investors and creditors to understand what an entity is trying to accomplish with its derivatives. Some respondents were concerned that provision would not have been operational. The Board agreed and decided that disclosure of the face or contract amount should no longer be required.

513. Also deleted is the requirement to disclose the average fair value of derivative financial instruments held for trading purposes (Statement 119, paragraph 10(a)). The Board originally required that disclosure to provide users "with a better indication of the level of risk assumed by an entity when holding or issuing derivative financial instruments for _trading purposes_" (Statement 119, paragraph 50). The Board had noted that "trading positions typically fluctuate, and the ending balance may not always be representative of the range of balances and related risks that an entity has assumed during a period" (Statement 119, paragraph 50). The Board had also indicated that it did not extend the disclosure to derivatives used for other than trading purposes because "the necessary data may be less likely to be available for derivative financial instruments held or issued for purposes other than trading" (Statement 119, paragraph 54). Because this Statement eliminates the distinction between derivatives held for _trading purposes_ and those held for _purposes other than trading_ and because of the Board's continuing concerns about the availability of that information, particularly for nonfinancial entities, the Board decided to eliminate that disclosure.

Effective Date and Transition

514. This Statement is effective for fiscal years beginning after June 15, 1999. Recognizing derivatives as assets and liabilities and measuring them at fair value is a primary objective of this Statement, and the Board considers it important to achieve the objective as early as is reasonably possible following the issuance of this Statement. However, many respondents indicated that they would need more than a year following the issuance of this Statement to make the systems changes necessary to implement it. The Board notes that an effective date of years beginning after June 15, 1999 will provide an implementation period of at least a year for all entities. That should be adequate time for entities to assimilate and develop the information required by this Statement. The Board also decided to permit an entity to adopt the provisions of this Statement as of the beginning of any fiscal quarter that begins after issuance of this Statement. The Board recognizes that the financial statements of an entity that adopts this Statement during a fiscal year will be based on differing measurement principles and hedge accounting requirements for derivative instruments. The Board decided that the urgency of providing improved information about derivatives outweighed concerns about the resulting potential lack of consistency within that year's financial statements.

515. Because hedge accounting is based on an entity's intent at the time a hedging relationship is established, the Board decided that retroactive application of the provisions of this Statement was not appropriate. Accordingly, changes in the fair value of derivatives that arose before initial application of this Statement and were previously recognized in net income, added to the carrying amount of hedged assets or liabilities, or included in other comprehensive income as part of a hedge of a net investment in a foreign entity are not to be included in transition adjustments. However, the Board decided that hedging relationships that existed before the date of initial application are relevant in determining other transition adjustments. Basing the transition adjustments on past hedging relationships also should prevent an entity from selectively affecting the transition adjustments by changing previously designated hedging relationships.

516. The Board considered whether past changes in the fair values of derivatives that were deferred as separate assets or liabilities in the statement of financial position rather than being added to the carrying amount of hedged assets or liabilities, such as those related to hedged forecasted transactions, should continue to be deferred at the date of initial application. Continued deferral of those gains and losses would

be consistent with the continued deferral of amounts that were previously added to the carrying amount of hedged assets or liabilities. However, separately deferred losses and gains do not represent assets or liabilities and thus are different from amounts that adjusted the basis of an asset or liability or otherwise represent assets or liabilities. Continuing to report them in the statement of financial position would be inconsistent with the Board's fundamental decision to recognize in the statement of financial position only items that are assets or liabilities (paragraph 229). The Board concluded that gains and losses separately characterized as liabilities and assets in the statement of financial position should be removed and reported in a manner consistent with the requirements of this Statement.

517. The adjustments to recognize all derivatives as assets or liabilities at fair value and to reverse certain deferred gains and losses will affect net income or other comprehensive income at the date of initial application. Consequently, the Board decided also to require that an entity recognize concurrently the effect of any preexisting offsetting differences between the carrying amount and the fair value of hedged items; that is, differences that arose before the date of initial application. The Board noted that reporting offsetting unrealized gains and losses on hedged items is consistent with the notion in this Statement of accelerating gains and losses on hedged items to provide income statement offset.

Transition Provisions for Embedded Derivatives

518. Paragraphs 12–16 of this Statement require that certain embedded derivatives be separated from their host contracts and accounted for as derivative instruments under this Statement. The Board considered how that requirement for separate accounting should apply to hybrid instruments outstanding at the date of initial application of this Statement. In considering that issue, the Board first considered two alternative ways in which an embedded derivative could be separated from the host contract after the date of acquisition or issuance:

a. Based on the fair values of the embedded derivative and the host contract at the date of initial application
b. Based on the fair values of the embedded derivative and the host contract at the date of initial acquisition or issuance.

The choice between those two methods determines the carrying amount of the host contract after separa-

tion of the embedded derivative. It also significantly affects the difficulty of obtaining the necessary information needed to separate an embedded derivative from the host contract after the date of initial acquisition or incurrence.

519. Separating a hybrid instrument into its host contract and its embedded derivative based on fair values at the date of initial adoption would be the simpler method. Under that method, the fair value of all of an entity's host contracts and embedded derivatives would be determined as of the same date, based on information current as of that date. In contrast, basing the separation of an embedded derivative on fair values at the date a hybrid instrument was acquired or incurred would necessitate calculations as of multiple past dates. For an entity with many hybrid instruments, some of which may have been initiated a decade or more in the past, separation based on fair values at dates of acquisition or incurrence could be a significant effort.

520. Although separation based on fair values at the date of initial application of this Statement would be the easier method, its results could be questionable. Many host contracts will be interest-bearing financial instruments, and separating the value of their embedded derivatives will affect both the carrying amounts of the host contracts and their effective interest rates. Determining the carrying amount of such a host contract based on the value of an embedded derivative at a date significantly later than acquisition or issuance of the instrument could result in a substantial discount or premium to be amortized as an adjustment of interest income or expense. For example, several years before it adopts this Statement, an entity might have purchased an equity-indexed note in which the principal is linked to the S&P 500 index. If the S&P 500 index is, say, 60 percent higher on July 1, 1999 when the entity adopts this Statement than it was at the date the note was acquired and the embedded derivative is separated on that basis, the carrying amount of the host contract would be artificially low, resulting in an artificially high reported interest yield. In contrast, separation based on fair values at the date the equity-indexed note was acquired would result in carrying amounts for both components that are determined on the same basis, and the carrying amount for the host contract need not compensate for subsequent changes in the value of the embedded derivative.

521. For the reasons just discussed, the Board decided that separation of a hybrid instrument into its host contract and embedded derivative instrument

should be based on fair values at the date the instrument was acquired or issued. Having made that decision, the Board decided it was not feasible to require entities to apply the requirements of paragraphs 12–16 of this Statement to all hybrid instruments held or owed at the date of initial adoption. However, the Board also did not want to provide an entity with the opportunity to embed numerous derivatives in hybrid instruments during the year or two before the effective date of this Statement for the purpose of avoiding its requirements. Therefore, this Statement requires that a hybrid instrument acquired or issued after December 31, 1997 be separated into its host contract and embedded derivative. For instruments acquired or issued after that date, separation on the basis of fair values at the date of acquisition or issuance should not be unduly burdensome.

522. The Board also considered whether an entity should be permitted to separate hybrid instruments acquired or issued before January 1, 1998 into their host contracts and derivative components if it wishes to do so. That alternative might be provided on either an individual instrument or an entity-wide basis. The Board recognizes that an entity might wish to separate the embedded derivative from a hybrid instrument and designate it as a hedging instrument. However, the Board was concerned that providing a choice on an instrument-by-instrument basis might have unintended consequences, such as separate accounting only for those embedded derivatives that are in a loss position at the date of initial adoption. The Board therefore decided to provide an entity the choice of separating out the embedded derivatives of existing hybrid instruments, but only on an all-or-none basis. The Board also believes that providing the choice only on an entity-wide basis will make it easier for users of financial statements to understand the effects of an entity's choices in transition and the resulting financial information.

Transition Provisions for Compound Derivatives

523. This Statement prohibits separation of a compound derivative instrument into its components for hedge accounting purposes (paragraph 18). The Board does not consider that prohibition to be unduly burdensome on an ongoing basis. To qualify for hedge accounting, an entity will simply need to obtain separate derivative instruments in some situations in which compound derivatives may have been used in the past. However, the Board recognizes that an entity may have entered into long-term derivative instruments combining, for example, foreign exchange and interest rate components before it knew that only separate derivatives would qualify for hedge accounting. The Board therefore considered whether this Statement should include special transition provisions for compound derivatives entered into before the date of initial adoption.

524. The Board understands that many hedging relationships in which compound derivatives were used involved hybrid instruments. For example, an entity may have entered into an interest rate swap with an embedded equity option to hedge outstanding debt with an embedded equity feature, such as a bond whose principal amount increases with specified percentage increases in the S&P 500 index. The Board believes that its decision not to require separate accounting for the derivative features of hybrid instruments acquired or issued before January 1, 1998 significantly reduces the need to permit compound derivatives outstanding at the date of initial adoption to be separated into dissimilar components. However, this Statement prohibits hedge accounting for the foreign exchange risk in instruments that are remeasured with changes in carrying amounts attributable to changes in foreign exchange rates included currently in earnings. A similar prohibition applies to cash flow hedges of the future acquisition or incurrence of instruments that will be remeasured with changes in carrying value attributable to changes in foreign exchange rates included in current earnings. Thus, a compound derivative that includes a foreign exchange component rarely will qualify for use as a hedging instrument under this Statement. The Board therefore decided to permit only the foreign exchange component of a compound derivative entered into before this Statement is adopted to be separated for accounting purposes. Thus, for example, a derivative that combines a foreign currency forward contract with an interest rate swap may be separated into its components at the date of initial adoption based on the fair values of the components at that date. In contrast, a combined interest rate swap and equity option may not be separated into its components.

Appendix D

AMENDMENTS TO EXISTING PRONOUNCEMENTS

525. This Statement supersedes the following pronouncements:

a. FASB Statement No. 80, *Accounting for Futures Contracts*

b. FASB Statement No. 105, *Disclosure of Information about Financial Instruments with Off-Balance-Sheet Risk and Financial Instruments with Concentrations of Credit Risk*

c. FASB Statement No. 119, *Disclosure about Derivative Financial Instruments and Fair Value of Financial Instruments.*

526. In paragraph 8 of Chapter 4, "Inventory Pricing," of ARB No. 43, *Restatement and Revision of Accounting Research Bulletins,* the following is inserted after the fourth sentence:

> (If inventory has been the hedged item in a fair value hedge, the inventory's "cost" basis used in the cost-or-market-whichever-is-lower accounting shall reflect the effect of the adjustments of its carrying amount made pursuant to paragraph 22(b) of FASB Statement No. 133, *Accounting for Derivative Instruments and Hedging Activities.*)

527. FASB Statement No. 52, *Foreign Currency Translation,* is amended as follows:

a. The following paragraph is inserted after the heading *Foreign Currency Transactions* and before paragraph 15:

> 14A. FASB Statement No. 133, *Accounting for Derivative Instruments and Hedging Activities,* addresses the accounting for freestanding foreign currency derivatives and certain foreign currency derivatives embedded in other instruments. This Statement does not address the accounting for derivative instruments.

b. In the last sentence of paragraph 15, *paragraphs 20 and 21* is replaced by *paragraph 20* and *and foreign currency commitments* is deleted.

c. In the first sentence of paragraph 16, *forward exchange contracts (paragraphs 17–19)* is replaced by *derivative instruments (Statement 133).*

d. Paragraphs 17–19 and the heading preceding paragraph 17 are deleted.

e. Paragraph 21 is replaced by the following:

Hedges of Firm Commitments

The accounting for a gain or loss on a foreign currency transaction that is intended to hedge

an identifiable foreign currency commitment (for example, an agreement to purchase or sell equipment) is addressed by paragraph 37 of Statement 133.

f. In the second sentence of paragraph 30, *forward contracts determined in conformity with the requirements of paragraphs 18 and 19 shall be considered transaction gains or losses* is replaced by *derivative instruments shall comply with paragraph 45 of Statement 133.*

g. The following sentence is added at the end of paragraph 31(b):

> (Paragraph 45(c) of Statement 133 specifies additional disclosures for instruments designated as hedges of the foreign currency exposure of a net investment in a foreign operation.)

h. The definitions of *currency swaps, discount or premium on a forward contract, forward exchange contract,* and *forward rate* in paragraph 162, the glossary, are deleted.

528. FASB Statement No. 60, *Accounting and Reporting by Insurance Enterprises,* is amended as follows:

a. Paragraph 46, as amended by FASB Statements No. 115, *Accounting for Certain Investments in Debt and Equity Securities,* and No. 124, *Accounting for Certain Investments Held by Not-for-Profit Organizations,* is amended as follows:

(1) The phrase *except as indicated in the following sentence* is added to the end of the second sentence.

(2) The following sentence is added after the second sentence:

> All or a portion of the unrealized gain or loss of a security that is designated as being hedged in a fair value hedge shall be recognized in earnings during the period of the hedge, pursuant to paragraph 22 of FASB Statement No. 133, *Accounting for Derivative Instruments and Hedging Activities.*

b. In the first sentence of paragraph 50, as amended by FASB Statement No. 97, *Accounting and Reporting by Insurance Enterprises for Certain*

Long-Duration Contracts and for Realized Gains and Losses from the Sale of Investments, and Statement 115, *as hedges as described in FASB Statements No. 52, Foreign Currency Translation, and No. 80, Accounting for Futures Contracts* is replaced by *as either hedges of net investments in foreign operations or cash flow hedges as described in Statement 133.*

529. FASB Statement No. 65, *Accounting for Certain Mortgage Banking Activities,* is amended as follows:

a. The following sentence is added after the first sentence of paragraph 4, as amended by Statements 115 and 124:

> If a mortgage loan has been the hedged item in a fair value hedge, the loan's "cost" basis used in lower-of-cost-or-market accounting shall reflect the effect of the adjustments of its carrying amount made pursuant to paragraph 22(b) of FASB Statement No. 133, *Accounting for Derivative Instruments and Hedging Activities.*

b. In the first sentence of paragraph 9(a), as amended by Statement 115 and FASB Statement No. 125, *Accounting for Transfers and Servicing of Financial Assets and Extinguishments of Liabilities,* the phrase *commitment prices* is replaced by *fair values.*

c. The last sentence of paragraph 9(a), which was added by Statement 115, is deleted.

d. Paragraph 9(b)(1) is deleted.

530. In the third sentence of footnote 4 of FASB Statement No. 95, *Statement of Cash Flows,* as amended by FASB Statement No. 104, *Statement of Cash Flows—Net Reporting of Certain Cash Receipts and Cash Payments and Classification of Cash Flows from Hedging Transactions,* the phrase *futures contracts, forward contracts, option contracts, or swap contracts that are accounted for as hedges of identifiable transactions or events (for example, a cash payment from a futures contract that hedges a purchase or sale of inventory), including anticipatory hedges,* is replaced by *derivative instruments that are accounted for as fair value hedges or cash flow hedges under FASB Statement No. 133, Accounting for Derivative Instruments and Hedging Activities.* In the last sentence of footnote 4, *identifiable transaction or event* is replaced by *asset, liability, firm commitment, or forecasted transaction.*

531. FASB Statement No. 107, *Disclosures about Fair Value of Financial Instruments,* is amended as follows:

a. Paragraph 4 is deleted.

b. The last sentence of paragraph 10, which was added by Statement 119, is deleted.

c. The paragraph added by Statement 119 after paragraph 13 is replaced by the following; the related footnote is deleted:

> In disclosing the fair value of a financial instrument, an entity shall not net that fair value with the fair value of other financial instruments—even if those financial instruments are of the same class or are otherwise considered to be related, for example, by a risk management strategy—except to the extent that the offsetting of carrying amounts in the statement of financial position is permitted under the general principle in paragraphs 5 and 6 of FASB Interpretation No. 39, *Offsetting of Amounts Related to Certain Contracts,* or the exceptions for master netting arrangements in paragraph 10 of Interpretation 39 and for amounts related to certain repurchase and reverse repurchase agreements in paragraphs 3 and 4 of FASB Interpretation No. 41, *Offsetting of Amounts Related to Certain Repurchase and Reverse Repurchase Agreements.*

d. The following paragraphs, with related headings and footnotes, are added after paragraph 15:

Disclosure about Concentrations of Credit Risk of All Financial Instruments

15A. Except as indicated in paragraph 15B, an entity shall disclose all significant concentrations of credit risk arising from *all* financial instruments, whether from an individual counterparty or groups of counterparties. *Group concentrations* of credit risk exist if a number of counterparties are engaged in similar activities and have similar economic characteristics that would cause their ability to meet contractual obligations to be similarly affected by changes in economic or other conditions. The following shall be disclosed about each significant concentration:

a. Information about the (shared) activity, region, or economic characteristic that identifies the concentration

b. The maximum amount of loss due to credit risk that, based on the gross fair value of the financial instrument, the entity would incur if parties to the financial instruments that make up the concentration failed completely to perform according to the terms of the contracts and the collateral or other security, if any, for the amount due proved to be of no value to the entity

c. The entity's policy of requiring collateral or other security to support financial instruments subject to credit risk, information about the entity's access to that collateral or other security, and the nature and a brief description of the collateral or other security supporting those financial instruments

d. The entity's policy of entering into master netting arrangements to mitigate the credit risk of financial instruments, information about the arrangements for which the entity is a party, and a brief description of the terms of those arrangements, including the extent to which they would reduce the entity's maximum amount of loss due to credit risk.

15B. The requirements of the preceding paragraph do not apply to the following financial instruments, whether written or held:

a. Financial instruments of a pension plan, including plan assets, when subject to the accounting and reporting requirements of Statement 87*

b. The financial instruments described in paragraphs 8(a), 8(c), 8(e), and 8(f) of this Statement, as amended by FASB Statements No. 112, *Employers' Accounting for Postemployment Benefits,* No. 123, *Accounting for Stock-Based Compensation,* and 125, except for reinsurance receivables and prepaid reinsurance premiums.

---

*Financial instruments of a pension plan, other than the obligations for pension benefits, when subject to the accounting and reporting requirements of FASB Statement No. 35, *Accounting and Reporting by Defined Benefit Pension Plans,* are subject to the requirements of paragraph 15A.

Encouraged Disclosure about Market Risk of All Financial Instruments

15C. An entity is encouraged, but not required, to disclose quantitative information about the market risks of financial instruments that is consistent with the way it manages or adjusts those risks.

15D. Appropriate ways of reporting the quantitative information encouraged in paragraph 15C will differ for different entities and will likely evolve over time as management approaches and measurement techniques evolve. Possibilities include disclosing (a) more details about current positions and perhaps activity during the period, (b) the hypothetical effects on comprehensive income (or net assets), or annual income, of several possible changes in market prices, (c) a gap analysis of interest rate repricing or maturity dates, (d) the duration of the financial instruments, or (e) the entity's value at risk from derivatives and from other positions at the end of the reporting period and the average value at risk during the year. This list is not exhaustive, and an entity is encouraged to develop other ways of reporting quantitative information.

e. Example 1 in paragraph 31 is amended as follows:

(1) The following heading and sentence are deleted from illustrative Note V:

Interest rate swap agreements

The fair value of interest rate swaps (used for hedging purposes) is the estimated amount that the Bank would receive or pay to terminate the swap agreements at the reporting date, taking into account current interest rates and the current creditworthiness of the swap counterparties.

(2) In the table, the subheading *Interest rate swaps* and the two following related lines (*In a net receivable position* and *In a net payable position*) are deleted. In the second sentence of the related footnote *, Interest rate swaps and* is deleted.

532. This Statement carries forward the following amendments that Statement 119 made to Statement 107:

a. In paragraph 10, the following footnote is added after *either in the body of the financial statements or in the accompanying notes*:

> *If disclosed in more than a single note, one of the notes shall include a summary table. The summary table shall contain the fair value and related carrying amounts and cross-references to the location(s) of the remaining disclosures required by this Statement, as amended.

b. In paragraph 10, the following is added after the first sentence:

> Fair value disclosed in the notes shall be presented together with the related carrying amount in a form that makes it clear whether the fair value and carrying amount represent assets or liabilities and how the carrying amounts relate to what is reported in the statement of financial position.

533. In paragraph 28 of FASB Statement No. 113, *Accounting and Reporting for Reinsurance of Short-Duration and Long-Duration Contracts,* the phrase *FASB Statement No. 105, Disclosure of Information about Financial Instruments with Off-Balance-Sheet Risk and Financial Instruments with Concentrations of Credit Risk* is replaced by *paragraph 15A of FASB Statement No. 107, Disclosures about Fair Value of Financial Instruments, as amended by FASB Statement No. 133, Accounting for Derivative Instruments and Hedging Activities.*

534. FASB Statement No. 115, *Accounting for Certain Investments in Debt and Equity Securities,* is amended as follows:

a. The following sentence is added at the end of paragraph 4, as amended by Statement 124:

> This Statement does not apply to investments in derivative instruments that are subject to the requirements of FASB Statement No. 133, *Accounting for Derivative Instruments and Hedging Activities.* If an investment would otherwise be in the scope of this Statement and it has within it an embedded derivative that is subject to Statement 133, the host instrument (as described in State-

ment 133) remains within the scope of this Statement. A transaction gain or loss on a held-to-maturity foreign-currency-denominated debt security shall be accounted for pursuant to FASB Statement No. 52, *Foreign Currency Translation.*

b. Paragraph 13, as amended by FASB Statement No. 130, *Reporting Comprehensive Income,* is amended as follows:

(1) The phrase *until realized except as indicated in the following sentence* is added to the end of the second sentence.

(2) The following sentence is added after the second sentence:

> All or a portion of the unrealized holding gain and loss of an available-for-sale security that is designated as being hedged in a fair value hedge shall be recognized in earnings during the period of the hedge, pursuant to paragraph 22 of Statement 133.

c. In paragraph 15(b), *portion of the* is inserted before *unrealized,* and *that has not been previously recognized in earnings* is added after *transfer.*

d. In paragraph 16, the following is inserted after the first sentence:

> (If a security has been the hedged item in a fair value hedge, the security's "amortized cost basis" shall reflect the effect of the adjustments of its carrying amount made pursuant to paragraph 22(b) of Statement 133.)

e. The first sentence of paragraph 19 is replaced by the following two sentences:

> For securities classified as available-for-sale, all reporting enterprises shall disclose the aggregate fair value, the total gains for securities with net gains in accumulated other comprehensive income, and the total losses for securities with net losses in accumulated other comprehensive income, by major security type as of each date for which a statement of financial position is presented. For securities classified as held-to-maturity, all reporting enterprises shall disclose the aggregate fair value, gross unrecognized holding gains, gross unrecognized holding losses, the net carrying amount, and the gross gains and

losses in accumulated other comprehensive income for any derivatives that hedged the forecasted acquisition of the held-to-maturity securities, by major security type as of each date for which a statement of financial position is presented.

f. In the third sentence in paragraph 20, *amortized cost* is replaced by *net carrying amount (if different from fair value).*

g. Paragraph 21 is amended as follows:

(1) In paragraph 21(a), *on those sales* is replaced by *that have been included in earnings as a result of those sales*

(2) In paragraph 21(b), *cost was determined in computing realized gain or loss* is replaced by *the cost of a security sold or the amount reclassified out of accumulated other comprehensive income into earnings was determined*

(3) Paragraph 21(d) is replaced by the following:

The amount of the net unrealized holding gain or loss on available-for-sale securities for the period that has been included in accumulated other comprehensive income and the amount of gains and losses reclassified out of accumulated other comprehensive income into earnings for the period

(4) Paragraph 21(e) is replaced by *The portion of trading gains and losses for the period that relates to trading securities still held at the reporting date.*

h. In the first sentence of paragraph 22, *amortized cost* is replaced by *net carrying* and *the net gain or loss in accumulated other comprehensive income for any derivative that hedged the forecasted acquisition of the held-to-maturity security,* is added immediately preceding *the related realized.*

i. The last four sentences of paragraph 115 are deleted.

j. The definition of *fair value* in paragraph 137, the glossary, is replaced by the following:

The amount at which an asset could be bought or sold in a current transaction be-

tween willing parties, that is, other than in a forced or liquidation sale. Quoted market prices in active markets are the best evidence of fair value and should be used as the basis for the measurement, if available. If a quoted market price is available, the fair value is the product of the number of trading units times that market price. If a quoted market price is not available, the estimate of fair value should be based on the best information available in the circumstances. The estimate of fair value should consider prices for similar assets and the results of valuation techniques to the extent available in the circumstances. Examples of valuation techniques include the present value of estimated expected future cash flows using a discount rate commensurate with the risks involved, option-pricing models, matrix pricing, option-adjusted spread models, and fundamental analysis. Valuation techniques for measuring assets should be consistent with the objective of measuring fair value. Those techniques should incorporate assumptions that market participants would use in their estimates of values, including assumptions about interest rates, default, prepayment, and volatility.

535. FASB Statement No. 124, *Accounting for Certain Investments Held by Not-for-Profit Organizations,* is amended as follows:

a. In paragraph 3, *except as noted in paragraph 5* is added to the end of the first sentence.

b. The following is added to the end of paragraph 5:

This Statement also does not apply to investments in derivative instruments that are subject to the requirements of FASB Statement No. 133, *Accounting for Derivative Instruments and Hedging Activities.* If an investment would otherwise be in the scope of this Statement and it has within it an embedded derivative that is subject to Statement 133, the host instrument (as described in Statement 133) remains within the scope of this Statement.

c. In the second sentence of paragraph 6, *No. 105, Disclosure of Information about Financial Instruments with Off-Balance-Sheet Risk and Financial Instruments with Concentrations of Credit Risk,* and *No. 119, Disclosure about Derivative Financial Instruments and Fair Value of*

Financial Instruments are deleted and *No. 133, Accounting for Derivative Instruments and Hedging Activities,* is added to the end of the sentence.

d. In footnote 6 of paragraph 16, *Paragraph 20 of Statement 105* is replaced by *Paragraph 15A of Statement 107, as amended by Statement 133.*

e. The definition of *fair value* in paragraph 112, the glossary, is replaced by the following:

> The amount at which an asset could be bought or sold in a current transaction between willing parties, that is, other than in a forced or liquidation sale. Quoted market prices in active markets are the best evidence of fair value and should be used as the basis for the measurement, if available. If a quoted market price is available, the fair value is the product of the number of trading units times that market price. If a quoted market price is not available, the estimate of fair value should be based on the best information available in the circumstances. The estimate of fair value should consider prices for similar assets and the results of valuation techniques to the extent available in the circumstances. Examples of valuation techniques include the present value of estimated expected future cash flows using a discount rate commensurate with the risks involved, option-pricing models, matrix pricing, option-adjusted spread models, and fundamental analysis. Valuation techniques for measuring assets should be consistent with the objective of measuring fair value. Those techniques should incorporate assumptions that market participants would use in their estimates of values, including assumptions about interest rates, default, prepayment, and volatility.

536. FASB Statement No. 125, *Accounting for Transfers and Servicing of Financial Assets and Extinguishments of Liabilities,* is amended as follows:

a. In paragraph 4, *and that are not within the scope of FASB Statement No. 133, Accounting for Derivative Instruments and Hedging Activities* is added to the end of the second sentence.

b. In paragraph 14, *Except for instruments that are within the scope of Statement 133* is added to the beginning of the first sentence.

c. In the fourth sentence of paragraph 31, **derivative financial instrument** is replaced by **derivative instrument.**

d. In paragraph 243, the glossary, the definition of *derivative financial instrument* is replaced by:

> **Derivative instrument**
> Refer to paragraphs 6–9 in FASB Statement No. 133, *Accounting for Derivative Instruments and Hedging Activities.*

537. Paragraph 2(c) of FASB Statement No. 126, *Exemption from Certain Required Disclosures about Financial Instruments for Certain Nonpublic Entities,* is replaced by the following:

> The entity has no instrument that, in whole or in part, is accounted for as a derivative instrument under FASB Statement No. 133, *Accounting for Derivative Instruments and Hedging Activities,* during the reporting period.

538. Paragraph 6 of FASB Technical Bulletin No. 79-19, *Investor's Accounting for Unrealized Losses on Marketable Securities Owned by an Equity Method Investee,* as amended by FASB Statement No. 115, *Accounting for Certain Investments in Debt and Equity Securities,* is replaced by the following:

> If an investee that is accounted for by the equity method is required to include unrealized holding gains and losses on investments in debt and equity securities in other comprehensive income pursuant to the provisions of FASB Statement No. 115, *Accounting for Certain Investments in Debt and Equity Securities,* as amended by FASB Statement No. 133, *Accounting for Derivative Instruments and Hedging Activities,* the investor shall adjust its investment in that investee by its proportionate share of the unrealized gains and losses and a like amount shall be included in its other comprehensive income.

Appendix E

DIAGRAM FOR DETERMINING WHETHER A CONTRACT IS A FREESTANDING DERIVATIVE SUBJECT TO THE SCOPE OF THIS STATEMENT

539. The following diagram depicts the process for determining whether a freestanding contract is within the scope of this Statement. The diagram is a visual supplement to the written standards section. It should not be interpreted to alter any requirements of this Statement nor should it be considered a substitute for the requirements. The relevant paragraphs in the standards section and Appendix A are identified in the parenthetical note after the question.

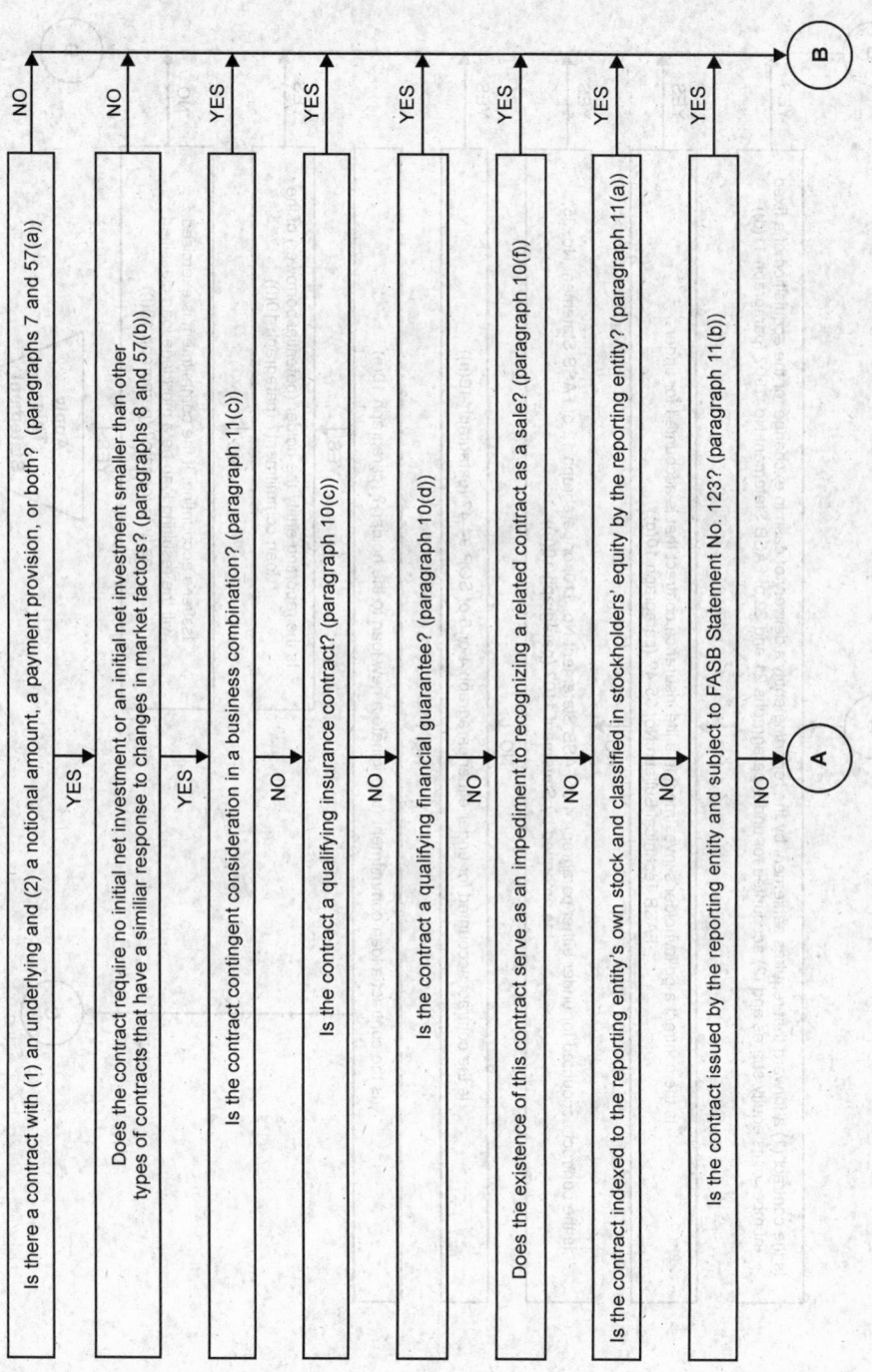

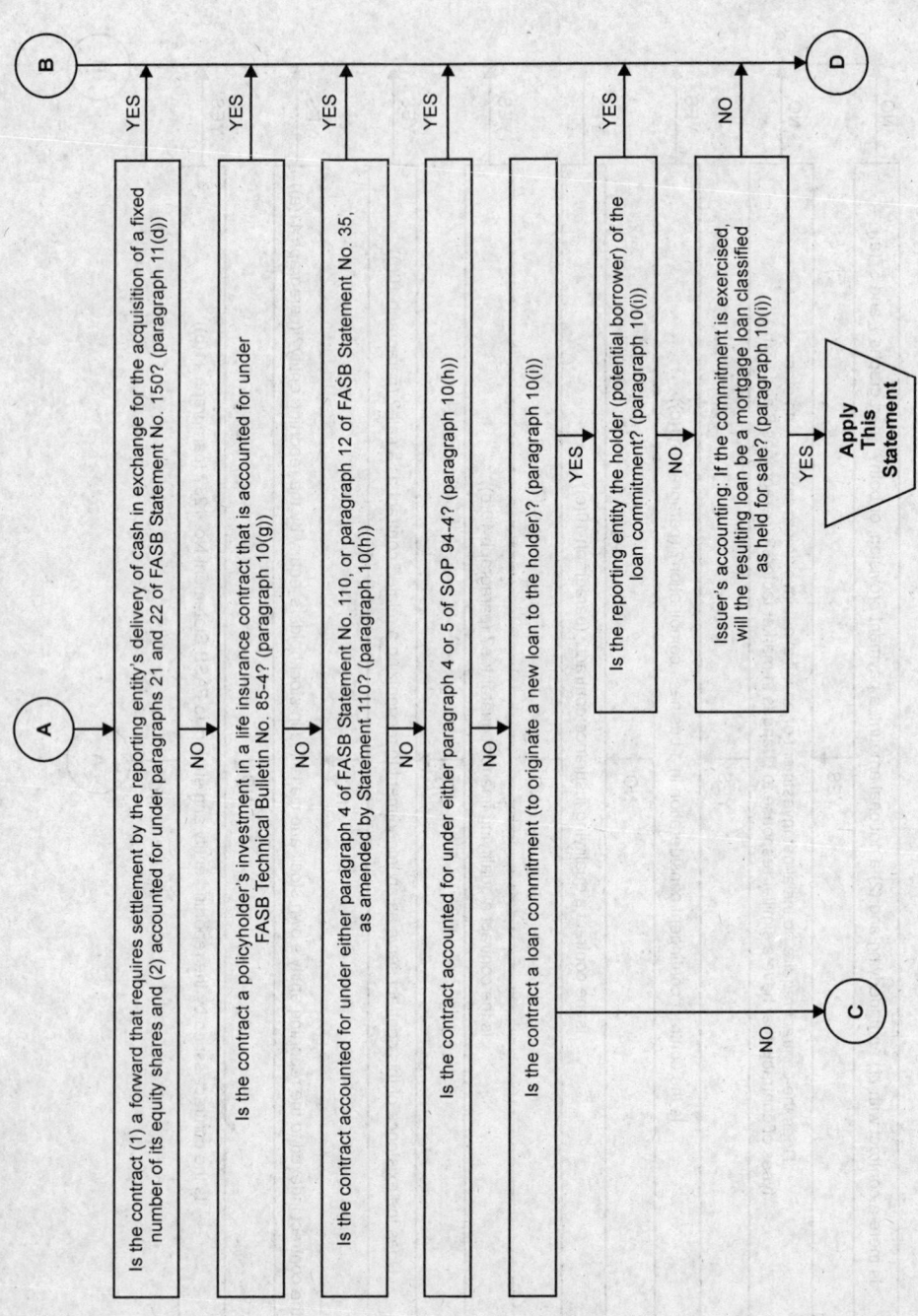

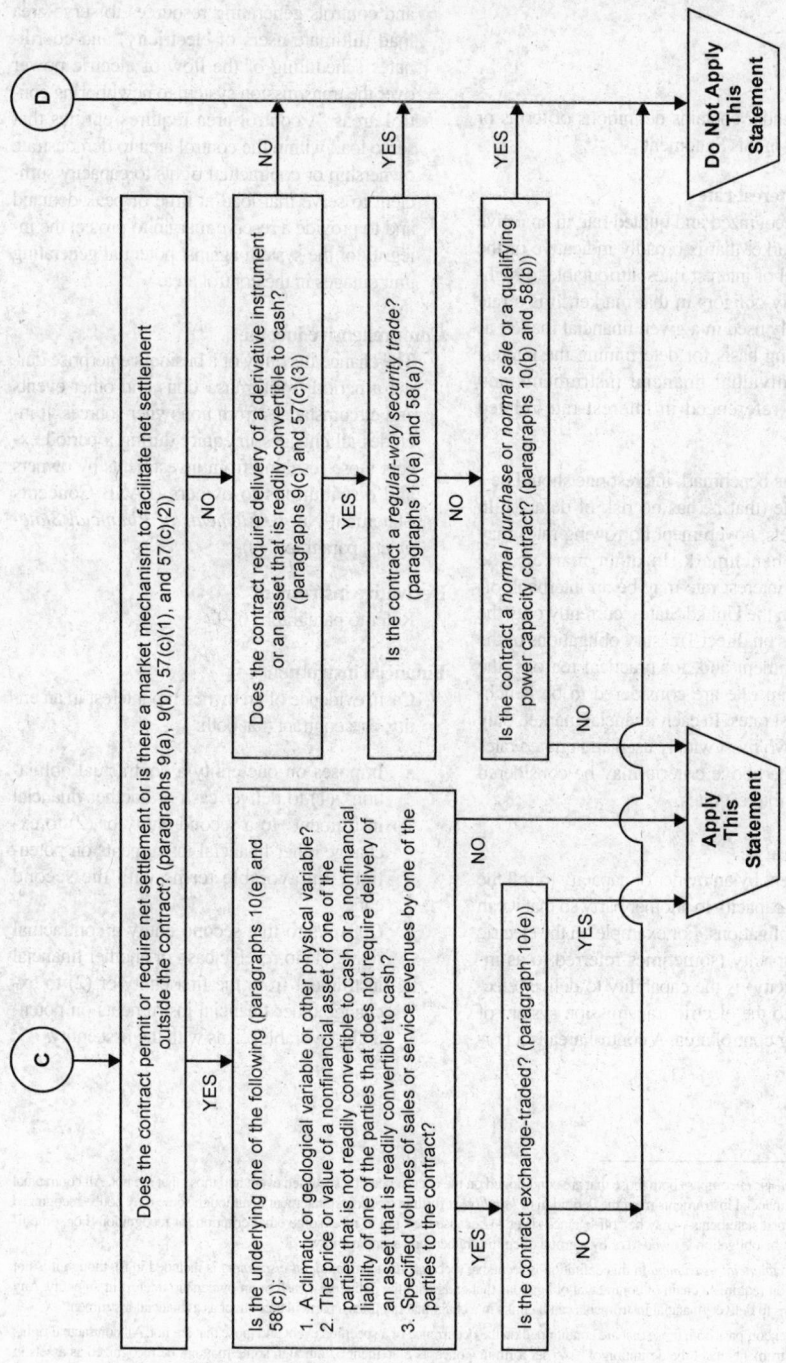

Appendix F

GLOSSARY

540. This appendix contains definitions of terms or phrases as used in this Statement.

Benchmark interest rate

A widely recognized and quoted rate in an active financial market that is broadly indicative of the overall level of interest rates attributable to high-credit-quality obligors in that market. It is a rate that is widely used in a given financial market as an underlying basis for determining the interest rates of individual financial instruments and commonly referenced in interest-rate-related transactions.

In theory, the benchmark interest rate should be a risk-free rate (that is, has no risk of default). In some markets, government borrowing rates may serve as a benchmark. In other markets, the benchmark interest rate may be an interbank offered rate. In the United States, currently only the interest rates on direct Treasury obligations of the U.S. government and, for practical reasons, the LIBOR swap rate are considered to be benchmark interest rates. In each financial market, only the one or two most widely used and quoted rates that meet the above criteria may be considered benchmark interest rates.

Capacity contract

An agreement by an owner of capacity to sell the right to that capacity to another party so that it can satisfy its obligations. For example, in the electric industry, capacity (sometimes referred to as installed capacity) is the capability to deliver electric power to the electric transmission system of an operating control area. A control area is a portion of the electric grid that schedules, dispatches, and controls generating resources to serve area load (ultimate users of electricity) and coordinates scheduling of the flow of electric power over the transmission system to neighboring control areas. A control area requires entities that serve load within the control area to demonstrate ownership or contractual rights to capacity sufficient to serve that load at time of peak demand and to provide a reserve margin to protect the integrity of the system against potential generating unit outages in the control area.

Comprehensive income

The change in equity of a business enterprise during a period from transactions and other events and circumstances from nonowner sources. It includes all changes in equity during a period except those resulting from investments by owners and distributions to owners (FASB Concepts Statement No. 6, *Elements of Financial Statements,* paragraph 70).

Derivative instrument

Refer to paragraphs 6–9.

Financial instrument

Cash, evidence of an ownership interest in an entity, or a contract that both:

a. Imposes on one entity a contractual obligation* (1) to deliver cash or another financial instrument[†] to a second entity or (2) to exchange other financial instruments on potentially unfavorable terms with the second entity
b. Conveys to that second entity a contractual right[‡] (1) to receive cash or another financial instrument from the first entity or (2) to exchange other financial instruments on potentially favorable terms with the first entity.

Contractual obligations encompass both those that are conditioned on the occurrence of a specified event and those that are not. All contractual obligations that are financial instruments meet the definition of *liability* set forth in Concepts Statement 6, although some may not be recognized as liabilities in financial statements—may be "off-balance-sheet"—because they fail to meet some other criterion for recognition. For some financial instruments, the obligation is owed to or by a group of entities rather than a single entity.

[†]The use of the term *financial instrument* in this definition is recursive (because the term *financial instrument* is included in it), though it is not circular. The definition requires a chain of contractual obligations that ends with the delivery of cash or an ownership interest in an entity. Any number of obligations to deliver financial instruments can be links in a chain that qualifies a particular contract as a financial instrument.

[‡]*Contractual rights* encompass both those that are conditioned on the occurrence of a specified event and those that are not. All contractual rights that are financial instruments meet the definition of *asset* set forth in Concepts Statement 6, although some may not be recognized as assets in financial statements—may be "off-balance-sheet"—because they fail to meet some other criterion for recognition. For some financial instruments, the right is held by or the obligation is due from a group of entities rather than a single entity.

Firm commitment

An agreement with an unrelated party, binding on both parties and usually legally enforceable, with the following characteristics:

a. The agreement specifies all significant terms, including the quantity to be exchanged, the fixed price, and the timing of the transaction. The fixed price may be expressed as a specified amount of an entity's functional currency or of a foreign currency. It may also be expressed as a specified interest rate or specified effective yield.

b. The agreement includes a disincentive for nonperformance that is sufficiently large to make performance probable.

Forecasted transaction

A transaction that is expected to occur for which there is no firm commitment. Because no transaction or event has yet occurred and the transaction or event when it occurs will be at the prevailing market price, a forecasted transaction does not give an entity any present rights to future benefits or a present obligation for future sacrifices.

LIBOR swap rate

The fixed rate on a single-currency, constant-notional interest rate swap that has its floating-rate leg referenced to the London Interbank Offered Rate (LIBOR) with no additional spread over LIBOR on that floating-rate leg. That fixed rate is the derived rate that would result in the swap having a zero fair value at inception because the present value of fixed cash flows, based on that rate, equate to the present value of the floating cash flows.

Notional amount

A number of currency units, shares, bushels, pounds, or other units specified in a derivative instrument.

Underlying

A specified interest rate, security price, commodity price, foreign exchange rate, index of prices or rates, or other variable (including the occurrence or nonoccurrence of a specified event such as a scheduled payment under a contract). An underlying may be a price or rate of an asset or liability but is not the asset or liability itself.

Statement of Financial Accounting Standards No. 134
Accounting for Mortgage-Backed Securities Retained after the Securitization of Mortgage Loans Held for Sale by a Mortgage Banking Enterprise

an amendment of FASB Statement No. 65

STATUS

Issued: October 1998

Effective Date: For the first fiscal quarter beginning after December 15, 1998

Affects: Amends FAS 65, paragraphs 4 and 6
Amends FAS 115, paragraphs 12(a) and 128(a)

Affected by: No other pronouncements

AICPA Accounting Standards Executive Committee (AcSEC)

Related Pronouncement: PB 6

Statement of Financial Accounting Standards No. 134

Accounting for Mortgage-Backed Securities Retained after the Securitization of Mortgage Loans Held for Sale by a Mortgage Banking Enterprise

an amendment of FASB Statement No. 65

CONTENTS

INTRODUCTION

1. FASB Statement No. 65, *Accounting for Certain Mortgage Banking Activities,* establishes accounting and reporting standards for certain activities of mortgage banking enterprises and other enterprises that conduct operations that are substantially similar to the primary operations of a mortgage banking enterprise.

2. Statement 65, as amended by FASB Statements No. 115, *Accounting for Certain Investments in Debt and Equity Securities,* and No. 125, *Accounting for Transfers and Servicing of Financial Assets and Extinguishments of Liabilities,* requires that after the securitization of a mortgage loan held for sale, an entity engaged in mortgage banking activities classify the resulting mortgage-backed security as a trading security. This Statement further amends Statement 65 to require that after the securitization of mortgage loans held for sale, an entity engaged in mortgage banking activities classify the resulting mortgage-backed securities or other retained interests based on its ability and intent to sell or hold those investments. This Statement conforms the subsequent accounting for securities retained after the securitization of mortgage loans by a mortgage banking enterprise with the subsequent accounting for securities retained after the securitization of other types of assets by a non-mortgage banking enterprise.

STANDARDS OF FINANCIAL ACCOUNTING AND REPORTING

Amendment to Statement 65

3. The second sentence of paragraph 6 of Statement 65, which was added by Statement 115 and amended by Statement 125, is deleted. The following is added to the end of paragraph 6:

> After the securitization of a mortgage loan held for sale, any retained mortgage-backed securities shall be classified in accordance with the provisions of Statement 115. However, a mortgage banking enterprise must classify as trading any retained mortgage-backed securities that it commits to sell before or during the securitization process.

4. The fifth sentence of paragraph 4 of Statement 65, as amended by Statement 115, FASB Statement No. 124, *Accounting for Certain Investments Held by Not-for-Profit Organizations,* and FASB Statement No. 133, *Accounting for Derivative Instruments and Hedging Activities,* is deleted.

Amendment to Statement 115

5. The third and fourth sentences of paragraph 12(a) of Statement 115 are deleted.

Effective Date and Transition

6. This Statement shall be effective for the first fiscal quarter beginning after December 15, 1998. Early application is encouraged and is permitted as of the issuance of this Statement. On the date this Statement is initially applied, an enterprise may reclassify mortgage-backed securities and other beneficial interests retained after the securitization of mortgage loans held for sale from the trading category, except for those with sales commitments in place.[1] Those securities and other interests shall be classified based on the entity's ability and intent, on the date this Statement is initially applied, to hold those investments. Transfers from the trading category that result from implementing this Statement shall be accounted for in accordance with paragraph 15(a) of Statement 115.

The provisions of this Statement need not be applied to immaterial items.

This Statement was adopted by the unanimous vote of the seven members of the Financial Accounting Standards Board:

Edmund L. Jenkins,
Chairman
Joseph V. Anania

Anthony T. Cope
John M. Foster
Gaylen N. Larson

James J. Leisenring
Gerhard G. Mueller

Appendix

BACKGROUND INFORMATION AND BASIS FOR CONCLUSIONS

Background Information

7. Prior to its amendment by Statements 115 and 125, Statement 65 required that mortgage loans and mortgage-backed securities be classified as either held for sale or long-term investments. Mortgage loans and mortgage-backed securities held for sale were reported at the lower of cost or market value. Statement 65 permitted an enterprise to transfer loans or mortgage-backed securities from a held-for-sale to a long-term investment category if the enterprise had both the ability and the intent to hold those loans or securities for the foreseeable future or until maturity.

8. Statement 115 did not allow for debt or marketable equity securities to be measured at the lower of cost or market and amended Statement 65 to require that "the securitization of a mortgage loan held for sale shall be accounted for as the sale of the mortgage loan and the purchase of a mortgage-backed security classified as a trading security at fair value" (para-graph 128(c)). Statement 125 amended Statement 115 and required that "after the securitization of a mortgage loan held for sale, the mortgage-backed security shall be classified as a trading security" (paragraph 237(a)). As a result, Statement 65, as amended, required that an enterprise engaged in mortgage banking activities classify all mortgage-backed securities retained after the securitization of mortgage loans held for sale as trading under Statement 115, regardless of whether the enterprise intended to sell those securities or hold them as long-term investments. Therefore, all unrealized gains or losses on those securities were recognized currently in earnings.

Decision to Amend Statement 65

9. In March 1997, the Mortgage Bankers Association of America (MBAA) asked the Board to reconsider the accounting for securities retained after the securitization of mortgage loans held for sale. The MBAA explained that an enterprise engaged in mortgage banking activities was required to classify those securities exclusively as trading. The MBAA observed that a nonmortgage banking enterprise engaged in the securitization of other types of assets

---

[1] Mortgage-backed securities and other beneficial interests may be reclassified from the trading category when initially applying this Statement without regard for the provisions in paragraph 15 of Statement 115, which states that "given the nature of a trading security, transfers into or from the trading category . . . should be rare."

was able to classify the retained securities as trading, available-for-sale, or held-to-maturity under Statement 115.

10. The Board believes that the fair value of financial assets and liabilities provides more relevant and understandable information than cost or cost-based measures and has a project on its agenda to consider measuring all financial instruments at fair value. The Board, therefore, considered rejecting the MBAA's request to amend Statement 65 and, instead, addressing the issues as part of its fair value project. However, because the requirements for entities engaged in mortgage banking activities were more stringent than for other entities and it is expected to be several years before a standard addressing the fair value of all financial instruments is effective, the Board decided to address the concerns of the MBAA through an amendment of Statement 65. The Board decided that Statement 65 should be amended to require that an enterprise engaged in mortgage banking activities classify mortgage-backed securities retained after the securitization of mortgage loans held for sale based on its ability and intent to sell or hold those investments. The Board based its decision on several factors, including the concerns of the MBAA.

11. First, an enterprise engaged in mortgage banking activities frequently does not plan to sell all securities or other retained interests resulting from the securitization of mortgage loans held for sale. The enterprise may retain some of those beneficial interests as long-term investments because they are illiquid and difficult to sell. Those beneficial interests also may be retained because the enterprise decides, for a variety of reasons, to maintain a financial interest in the mortgage loans that it originates.

12. Second, some enterprises do not engage in mortgage banking but their activities are similar to those of a mortgage banking enterprise. Because the receivables they originate, transfer, and service are not *mortgages,* their activities are not within the scope of Statement 65. Those enterprises, unlike mortgage banking enterprises, are not required to classify securities retained after the securitization of their receivables as trading. They may, instead, choose to classify their retained securities as available-for-sale and, in some cases, held-to-maturity under Statement 115. The Board considered requiring that those enterprises classify securities retained after securitizing nonmortgage receivables as trading. While that approach would result in greater consistency among enter-

prises engaged in similar activities, it would require that the scope of this project be expanded significantly. The Board decided against that approach and chose, instead, to amend Statement 65. This approach provides a "level playing field" among enterprises engaged in similar activities while addressing only mortgage banking activities at this time.

13. Third, allowing an enterprise to classify retained securities based on its ability and intent to sell or hold those investments is consistent with the approach in Statement 115. While Statement 115 restricts the ability to classify debt securities as held-to-maturity, it permits an enterprise to choose the appropriate classification based on the enterprise's ability and intent to sell or hold the securities. This Statement allows an enterprise engaged in mortgage banking activities an opportunity to choose the appropriate classification for its retained securities, rather than requiring a trading classification in all cases.

14. In April 1998, the Board issued an Exposure Draft, *Accounting for Mortgage-Backed Securities and Certain Other Interests Retained after the Securitization of Mortgage Loans Held for Sale by a Mortgage Banking Enterprise,* for a 45-day comment period. Twenty-five organizations and individuals responded to the Exposure Draft. In August 1998, the Board discussed the issues raised in the comment letters in a public Board meeting. The Board concluded that it could reach an informed decision on the basis of existing information without a public hearing.

The Approach in This Statement

15. The Exposure Draft proposed that an enterprise decide whether securities and other beneficial interests that are retained after the securitization of mortgage loans held for sale would, themselves, be held for sale to determine their proper classification. Retained securities that the enterprise holds for sale would have been classified in the trading category, with changes in their fair value recognized currently in earnings. Other retained nonsecurity beneficial interests that the enterprise holds for sale would have been accounted for like securities and also classified as trading. The Board reasoned that a mortgage banking enterprise should use the same criteria to identify retained securities intended to be sold as it uses to identify loans intended to be sold. That approach would primarily ensure that losses on retained securities and other beneficial interests intended to be sold would be recognized currently in earnings.

Accounting for Mortgage-Backed Securities Retained   **FAS134**
after the Securitization of Mortgage Loans Held for Sale
by a Mortgage Banking Enterprise

Accounting for Retained Securities

16. Many respondents commented that the approach in the Exposure Draft was complex and did not completely level the playing field between a mortgage banking enterprise and a nonmortgage banking enterprise engaged in securitization activities. Those respondents indicated that the accounting for securities retained after the securitization of mortgage loans should be the same as the accounting for securities retained after the securitization of other types of assets. The Board agreed with those respondents and decided to require that retained securities be accounted for in accordance with Statement 115.

17. The Board was concerned that because the term *trading* is not defined precisely in Statement 115, a mortgage banking enterprise could avoid a trading classification for retained securities it had committed to sell. That might occur because the settlement periods for the retained securities of a mortgage banking enterprise may be longer than the typical settlement periods for other types of securities classified as trading in paragraph 12(a) of Statement 115. The Board decided to require a trading classification for any retained securities that a mortgage banking enterprise commits to sell before or during the securitization process.

Accounting for Other Beneficial Interests

18. Statement 115's amendment of Statement 65 addressed only the accounting for *securities* that are retained as beneficial interests. The Exposure Draft proposed that retained nonsecurity interests that are held for sale also be classified as trading. Several respondents to the Exposure Draft observed that paragraph 4 of Statement 65 provides applicable guidance for those other beneficial interests and that other enterprises that securitize loans are not required to classify nonsecurity interests as trading. Because the objective of this project was to conform, as nearly as possible, the accounting for all securitizations of loans, the Board agreed and deleted that requirement. This Statement also does not address the accounting for other beneficial interests that are not held for sale. The Board observes that paragraph 6 of Statement 65 provides applicable guidance. Some of those other retained beneficial interests, however, are subject to the provisions of paragraph 14 of Statement 125 and, therefore, must be measured like investments in debt securities classified as available-for-sale or trading under Statement 115.

Classifying Retained Securities as Held-to-Maturity

19. The Board considered restricting the potential categories to trading or available-for-sale for retained securities but decided that that restriction was unjustified. Some observed that permitting an enterprise engaged in mortgage banking activities to classify retained securities as held-to-maturity was undesirable and incompatible with the Board's project to consider measuring all financial instruments at fair value. However, others observed that nonmortgage banking enterprises may choose to classify debt securities as held-to-maturity if all of the necessary provisions of Statement 115 are met. The Board decided that it is beyond the scope of this Statement to reconsider whether Statement 115 should continue to permit historical cost accounting for some securities. Therefore, the Board decided to permit an enterprise engaged in mortgage banking activities to apply the same intent-based accounting that is applied by other enterprises. Therefore, any sales or transfers of retained securities that are classified as held-to-maturity for reasons other than those in paragraphs 8 and 11 of Statement 115 would call into question an enterprise's ability and intent to hold other debt securities to maturity in the future.

20. The Board expects that many mortgage-backed securities retained after the securitization of mortgage loans held for sale would not be classified as held-to-maturity under Statement 115, as amended by Statement 125. Specifically, the Board notes that paragraph 7 of Statement 115 was amended by Statement 125 to require that "a security may not be classified as held-to-maturity if that security can contractually be prepaid or otherwise settled in such a way that the holder of the security would not recover substantially all of its recorded investment." Likewise, paragraph 14 of Statement 125 requires that "interest-only strips, loans, other receivables, or retained interests in securitizations that can contractually be prepaid or otherwise settled in such a way that the holder would not recover substantially all of its recorded investment shall be subsequently measured like investments in debt securities classified as available-for-sale or trading under Statement 115, as amended by this Statement" (references omitted). However, retained beneficial interests that meet the definition of a derivative or that contain embedded derivative instruments must be accounted for in accordance with Statement 133 upon its adoption. Paragraph 14 of Statement 133 provides an exception for certain interest-only and principal-only strips.

Transition

21. The Board decided to permit an enterprise a one-time opportunity to reclassify mortgage-backed securities and other beneficial interests from the trading category, without regard to the restriction in paragraph 15 of Statement 115. That opportunity is available only on the date that this Statement is initially applied. Transfers from the trading category that result from implementing this Statement should be accounted for in accordance with paragraph 15(a) of Statement 115, that is, the unrealized gain or loss at the date of transfer will have already been recognized in earnings and should not be reversed. While this Statement does not address the accounting for other retained beneficial interests, some mortgage banking enterprises may have classified all of the interests that were measured like securities in accordance with paragraph 14 of Statement 125 as trading. Accordingly, some of those other retained beneficial interests may be eligible for transfer into the available-for-sale category when implementing this Statement. An enterprise engaged in mortgage banking activities often holds other securities unrelated to those retained after the securitization of mortgage loans previously held for sale by that enterprise. Statement 65 did *not* require that those securities be classified as trading, and they should already be classified in one of the three categories required by Statement 115. Therefore, the transition provisions of this Statement do *not* apply to those investments.

Statement of Financial Accounting Standards No. 135
Rescission of FASB Statement No. 75
and Technical Corrections

STATUS

Issued: February 1999

Effective Date: For financial statements issued for fiscal years ending after February 15, 1999

Affects: Deletes ARB 43, Chapter 1A, paragraph 4
  Amends ARB 43, Chapter 1B, paragraph 7
  Amends ARB 43, Chapter 3A, paragraph 9
  Amends APB 6, paragraph 12(b)
  Amends APB 16, paragraph 88(a)
  Amends APB 17, paragraph 31
  Amends APB 28, paragraphs 30, 31, and 33
  Amends AIN-APB 30, Interpretation No. 1
  Amends FAS 3, paragraph 14
  Replaces FAS 13, paragraph 20
  Amends FAS 15, paragraph 4
  Amends FAS 35, paragraphs 2 and 30
  Amends FAS 43, paragraph 2
  Amends FAS 52, paragraphs 24, 26, 31, 34, and 46
  Amends FAS 60, paragraph 46
  Amends FAS 66, footnote 34
  Replaces FAS 71, footnote 3
  Supersedes FAS 75
  Amends FAS 87, paragraphs 49 and 66 and Illustration 4
  Deletes FAS 87, footnote 13
  Amends FAS 89, paragraph 8(b)
  Amends FAS 93, footnote 1
  Amends FAS 102, footnote 3
  Amends FAS 106, paragraphs 65, 103, 107, 392, 417, and 461
  Replaces FAS 106, paragraphs 464 and 467
  Deletes FAS 106, paragraph 471 and footnote 23
  Amends FAS 109, paragraph 276
  Amends FAS 115, paragraph 7 and footnote 4
  Replaces FAS 115, paragraph 17
  Amends FAS 123, paragraphs 49, 358, and 359
  Amends FAS 128, paragraph 28
  Amends FAS 130, paragraph 27
  Amends FAS 131, paragraphs 18, 25, 27, 28, 33, and 123
  Amends FAS 132, paragraphs 12(b) and 63
  Deletes FAS 132, paragraphs 12(d) and 14(e)
  Amends FIN 18, footnote 8
  Deletes FIN 27, footnote 3
  Amends FIN 39, paragraph 7
  Amends FIN 40, paragraph 5
  Amends FTB 79-5, paragraph 3

Affected by: Paragraphs 4(p)(1), 4(p)(7), and 4(r)(2)(a) deleted by FAS 145, paragraph 9(k)

SUMMARY

This Statement rescinds FASB Statement No. 75, *Deferral of the Effective Date of Certain Accounting Requirements for Pension Plans of State and Local Governmental Units.* GASB Statement No. 25, *Financial Reporting for Defined Benefit Pension Plans and Note Disclosures for Defined Contribution Plans,* was issued November 1994, and establishes financial reporting standards for defined benefit pension plans and for the notes to the financial statements of defined contribution plans of state and local governmental entities. Statement 75 is, therefore, no longer needed. This Statement also amends FASB Statement No. 35, *Accounting and Reporting by Defined Benefit Pension Plans,* to exclude from its scope plans that are sponsored by and provide benefits for the employees of one or more state or local governmental units.

This Statement also amends other existing authoritative literature to make various technical corrections, clarify meanings, or describe applicability under changed conditions.

This Statement is effective for financial statements issued for fiscal years ending after February 15, 1999. Earlier application is encouraged.

Statement of Financial Accounting Standards No. 135

Rescission of FASB Statement No. 75 and Technical Corrections

CONTENTS

INTRODUCTION

Rescission of Statement 75

1. FASB Statement No. 75, *Deferral of the Effective Date of Certain Accounting Requirements for Pension Plans of State and Local Governmental Units,* indefinitely deferred the effective date of FASB Statement No. 35, *Accounting and Reporting by Defined Benefit Pension Plans,* for plans that are sponsored by and provide benefits for the employees of one or more state or local governmental units. In November 1994, the Governmental Accounting Standards Board issued GASB Statement No. 25, *Financial Reporting for Defined Benefit Pension Plans and Note Disclosures for Defined Contribution Plans,* which establishes financial reporting standards for defined benefit pension plans and for the notes to the financial statements of defined contribution plans of state and local governmental entities. With the issuance of GASB Statement 25, the provisions of Statement 35, as deferred indefinitely by Statement 75, are no longer applicable for plans that are sponsored by and provide benefits for the employees of one or more state or local governmental units.

Technical Corrections

2. When the Board issues a pronouncement that contains amendments to prior pronouncements, the proposed amendments are reviewed by the Board and exposed for comment as part of the due process procedures. Over the years, the FASB staff and various constituents have identified instances where additional amendments should have been made explicit in certain pronouncements. Although, in general, those "effective" amendments have been appro-priately indicated in the various editions of the FASB's *Original Pronouncements* and *Current Text* publications, those effective amendments were not subjected to the Board's review and due process procedures. This Statement identifies those effective amendments and establishes them as Board-approved amendments. In addition, this Statement amends existing authoritative literature to (a) correct references to AICPA guidance that has been revised or superseded since the issuance of that literature, (b) extend certain provisions to reflect established practice, and (c) eliminate inconsistencies in existing pronouncements.

STANDARDS OF FINANCIAL ACCOUNTING AND REPORTING

Rescission of Statement 75

3. This Statement rescinds FASB Statement No. 75, *Deferral of the Effective Date of Certain Accounting Requirements for Pension Plans of State and Local Governmental Units.*

Technical Corrections

4. This Statement amends the following pronouncements to make technical corrections to existing authoritative literature:

a. Accounting Research Bulletin No. 43, *Restatement and Revision of Accounting Research Bulletins.*

  (1) Paragraph 4 of Chapter 1A, "Prior Opinions—Rules Adopted by Membership," is deleted (to reflect current established prac-

tice that it is no longer acceptable to show stock of a corporation held in its own treasury as an asset).

(2) Paragraph 9 of Chapter 3A, "Working Capital—Current Assets and Current Liabilities," is amended as follows (effectively amended by FASB Statement No. 115, *Accounting for Certain Investments in Debt and Equity Securities*):

(a) In the third sentence, *marketable securities and* is deleted.

(b) The fourth sentence is deleted.

(c) In the sixth sentence, *for temporary investments, their market value at the balance-sheet date, and* is deleted.

b. APB Opinion No. 6, *Status of Accounting Research Bulletins.* In the first sentence of paragraph 12(b), *,or in some circumstances may be shown as an asset in accordance with paragraph 4 of Chapter 1A of ARB 43* is deleted (to reflect current established practice that it is no longer acceptable to show stock of a corporation held in its own treasury as an asset).

c. APB Opinion No. 16, *Business Combinations.* In paragraph 88(a), *net realizable values* is replaced by *fair values* (effectively amended by Statement 115).

d. APB Opinion No. 17, *Intangible Assets.* In the third sentence of paragraph 31, *(APB Opinion No. 9, paragraph 21)* is deleted, and in the fourth and fifth sentences of paragraph 31, *extraordinary* is replaced by *unusual* (effectively amended by APB Opinion No. 30, *Reporting the Results of Operations—Reporting the Effects of Disposal of a Segment of a Business, and Extraordinary, Unusual and Infrequently Occurring Events and Transactions*).

e. APB Opinion No. 28, *Interim Financial Reporting.* The following changes are made to clarify the requirements for interim reporting:

(1) In the first and fourth sentences of paragraph 30, *to their securityholders* is deleted.

(2) In the second sentence of paragraph 30, *securityholders with* is deleted.

(3) In the first sentence of paragraph 31, *securityholders* is replaced by *users of the interim financial information.*

(4) In the first sentence of paragraph 33, *securityholders* is replaced by *users of the interim financial information.*

f. AICPA Accounting Interpretation 1, "Illustration of the Application of APB Opinion No. 30." Example (12) is deleted (effectively superseded by Statement 115).

g. FASB Statement No. 3, *Reporting Accounting Changes in Interim Financial Statements.* In paragraph 14, *to its securityholders* is deleted (to clarify the requirements for interim reporting).

h. FASB Statement No. 13, *Accounting for Leases.* Paragraph 20, as amended by FASB Statement No. 77, *Reporting by Transferors for Transfers of Receivables with Recourse,* FASB Statement No. 125, *Accounting for Transfers and Servicing of Financial Assets and Extinguishments of Liabilities,* and Statement 135 is replaced by the following (to revise the amendment made by Statement 125):

The sale or assignment of a lease or of property subject to a lease that was accounted for as a sales-type lease or direct financing lease shall not negate the original accounting treatment accorded the lease. Any transfer of minimum lease payments or guaranteed residual values subject to a sales-type lease or direct financing lease shall be accounted for in accordance with FASB Statement No. 125, *Accounting for Transfers and Servicing of Financial Assets and Extinguishments of Liabilities.* However, transfers of unguaranteed residual values are not subject to the provisions of Statement 125.

i. FASB Statement No. 15, *Accounting by Debtors and Creditors for Troubled Debt Restructurings.* In the second sentence of paragraph 4, *investing in debt securities that were previously issued,* is deleted (effectively amended by Statement 115).

j. FASB Statement No. 35, *Accounting and Reporting by Defined Benefit Pension Plans.* In the first sentence of paragraph 2, *,including state and local governments,* is deleted (to amend the scope of Statement 35 to reflect the issuance of GASB Statement 25).

k. FASB Statement No. 43, *Accounting for Compensated Absences,* as amended by FASB Statement No. 112, *Employers' Accounting for Postemployment Benefits.* In the last sentence of paragraph 2, *or a portion of a line of business* is deleted (effectively amended by FASB Statement No. 121, *Accounting for the Impairment of Long-Lived Assets and for Long-Lived Assets to Be Disposed Of*).

l. FASB Statement No. 52, *Foreign Currency Translation.*

(1) In paragraph 24, *a separate component of equity* in the second sentence and *that separate component of equity* in the last sentence are replaced by *other comprehensive income* (effectively amended by FASB Statement No. 130, *Reporting Comprehensive Income*).

(2) In the last sentence of paragraph 26, *(ARB 43, Chapter 12, paragraph 8)* is deleted (effectively amended by paragraph 16 of FASB Statement No. 94, *Consolidation of All Majority-Owned Subsidiaries,* which deleted ARB 43, Chapter 12, paragraph 8).

(3) In the first sentence of paragraph 31, *separate component of equity for cumulative* is replaced by *accumulated amount of* and *reported in equity* is inserted after *translation adjustments* (effectively amended by Statement 130).

(4) In the first sentence of paragraph 34, *as the opening balance of the cumulative translation adjustments component of equity* is replaced by *in other comprehensive income* (effectively amended by Statement 130).

(5) In the last sentence of paragraph 46, *the cumulative translation adjustments component of equity* is replaced by *other comprehensive income* (effectively amended by Statement 130).

m. FASB Statement No. 60, *Accounting and Reporting by Insurance Enterprises.* In the second sentence of paragraph 46, as amended by Statement 115 and FASB Statement No. 124, *Accounting for Certain Investments Held by Not-for-Profit Organizations,* the phrase *a separate component of equity* is replaced by *other comprehensive income* (effectively amended by Statement 130).

n. FASB Statement No. 66, *Accounting for Sales of Real Estate.* In footnote 34 to paragraph 101, letter *(a)* and *or (b) a right-to-use time-sharing interest that is a sales-type lease as defined in Statement 13, as amended and interpreted* are deleted (to reflect amendments made to Statement 13 by FASB Statement No. 98, *Accounting for Leases;* Statement 98 amends Statement 13 to prohibit a lease involving real estate from being classified as a sales-type lease unless the lease transfers ownership of the property to the lessee by the end of the lease term; therefore, a right-to-use time-sharing interest would not meet this requirement).

o. FASB Statement No. 71, *Accounting for the Effects of Certain Types of Regulation.* Footnote 3 to paragraph 5(a) is replaced by the following (to update the scope of Statement 71 to reflect both the existence of the GASB as well as the appropriate literature to be followed):

> GASB Statement No. 20, *Accounting and Financial Reporting for Proprietary Funds and Other Governmental Entities That Use Proprietary Fund Accounting,* paragraph 9, provides that state and local proprietary activities that meet the criteria of paragraph 5 may apply this FASB Statement and related pronouncements (including FASB Statements No. 90, *Regulated Enterprises—Accounting for Abandonments and Disallowances of Plant Costs,* No. 92, *Regulated Enterprises—Accounting for Phase-in Plans,* and No. 101, *Regulated Enterprises—Accounting for the Discontinuation of Application of FASB Statement No. 71*) that were issued on or before November 30, 1989. Amendments of FASB pronouncements related to regulated operations issued after that date are subject to the provisions of GASB Statement 20, paragraph 7.

p. FASB Statement No. 87, *Employers' Accounting for Pensions.* The following changes are made to revise the amendments made by FASB Statement No. 132, *Employers' Disclosures about Pensions and Other Postretirement Benefits:*

(1) [This subparagraph has been deleted. See Status page.]

(2) In the first sentence of paragraph 49, *paragraph 54* is replaced by *paragraphs 5 and 8 of FASB Statement No. 132, Employers' Disclosures about Pensions and Other Postretirement Benefits.*

(3) Footnote 13 to paragraph 54(b) is deleted.

(4) Paragraph 55, deleted by Statement 132, is reinstated.

(5) Paragraph 66, deleted by Statement 132, is reinstated. In the last sentence of that paragraph, *and disclosure requirements shall be determined in accordance with the provisions of this Statement applicable to a defined benefit plan* is replaced by *requirements shall be determined in accordance with the provisions of this Statement applicable to a defined benefit plan and the disclosure requirements shall be determined in accordance with the provisions of paragraphs 5 and 8 of Statement 132.*

(6) In Illustration 4 in paragraph 261, the disclosures for the years 1987, 1988, and 1989 and the related footnotes are deleted. (Appendix B of Statement 132 provides examples that illustrate the revised required disclosures.)

(7) [This subparagraph has been deleted. See Status page.]

q. FASB Statement No. 89, *Financial Reporting and Changing Prices.* In paragraph 8(b), *(currently 1967)* is replaced by *(currently 1982–1984)* (to bring the measurement guidance up to date).

r. FASB Statement No. 106, *Employers' Accounting for Postretirement Benefits Other Than Pensions.*

(1) In the first sentence of paragraph 103, *or a portion of a line of business* is deleted (effectively amended by Statement 121).

(2) The following changes are made to revise the amendments made by Statement 132:

    (a) [This subparagraph has been deleted. See Status page.]

    (b) In the first sentence of paragraph 65, *paragraph 74* is replaced by *paragraphs 5 and 8 of FASB Statement No. 132, Employers' Disclosures about Pensions and Other Postretirement Benefits.*

    (c) Footnote 23 to paragraph 74(b) is deleted.

    (d) Paragraph 107, deleted by Statement 132, is reinstated. In the last sentence of that paragraph *and disclosure requirements shall be determined in accordance with the provisions of this Statement applicable to a defined benefit plan* is replaced by *requirements shall be determined in accordance with the provisions of this Statement applicable to a defined benefit plan and the disclosure requirements shall be determined in accordance with the provisions of paragraphs 5 and 8 of Statement 132.*

    (e) The fourth sentence of paragraph 392 is deleted.

    (f) In the third sentence of paragraph 417, *paragraph 74(c)* is replaced by *paragraph 5(c) of Statement 132.*

    (g) In the first sentence of paragraph 461, *paragraph 74(b)* is replaced by *paragraph 5(d) of Statement 132.*

(h) Paragraph 464 and the related footnotes are replaced by the following:

The 1994 financial statements include the following disclosure of the components of net periodic postretirement benefit cost:

Service cost	$ 320,000
Interest cost	630,000
Expected return on plan assets	(87,000)
Amortization of transition obligation	300,000
Recognized net actuarial loss	5,000
Net periodic postretirement benefit cost	$1,168,000

(i) Paragraph 467 and the related footnotes are replaced by the following:

The 1995 financial statements include the following disclosure of the components of net periodic postretirement benefit cost:

Service cost	$ 360,000
Interest cost	652,500
Expected return on plan assets	(193,700)
Amortization of transition obligation	300,000
Net periodic postretirement benefit cost	$1,118,800

(j) Paragraph 471, its heading, and the related footnotes are deleted.

s. FASB Statement No. 109, *Accounting for Income Taxes.* Paragraph 276 is amended as follows (effectively amended by Statement 130):

(1) In the first sentence, *or to other comprehensive income* is inserted after *equity.*

(2) In the second sentence, *directly to shareholders' equity* is replaced by *to other comprehensive income.*

(3) In subparagraph (c), *charged to the cumulative translation adjustment account* is replaced by *reported in other comprehensive income and accumulated.*

(4) In subparagraph (f), *credited directly to the cumulative translation adjustment account* is replaced by *reported in other comprehensive income and accumulated.*

t. FASB Statement No. 115, *Accounting for Certain Investments in Debt and Equity Securities.*

(1) The following sentence is added to the end of paragraph 7, as amended by FASB Statement 125 (effectively amended by FASB Statement No. 133, *Accounting for Derivative Instruments and Hedging Activities*):

A debt security with those characteristics should be evaluated in accordance with paragraphs 12–16 of Statement 133 to determine whether it contains an embedded derivative that must be accounted for separately.

(2) Paragraph 17 is replaced by the following (to supersede the requirement that all trading securities be classified as current assets):

An enterprise that presents a classified statement of financial position shall report individual held-to-maturity securities, individual available-for-sale securities, and individual trading securities as either current or noncurrent, as appropriate, under the provisions of ARB No. 43, Chapter 3A, "Working Capital—Current Assets and Current Liabilities."[5]

u. FASB Statement No. 123, *Accounting for Stock-Based Compensation.* The following changes are made to clarify the amendments made by FASB Statement No. 128, *Earnings per Share:*

(1) In the last sentence of paragraph 49, as amended by Statement 128, *or forfeited* is inserted after *granted.*

(2) The following is inserted at the beginning of paragraph 358, as amended by Statement 128:

> Under paragraph 28 of this Statement, an entity has the choice of estimating forfeitures in advance or recognizing forfeitures as they occur. However, the weighted-average number of options outstanding, rather than the number of options expected to vest, would be used in computing diluted EPS. In addition, the average net unrecognized compensation cost would include the options not expected to vest.

(3) In paragraph 359, as amended by Statement 128, *all* is replaced by *the weighted-average number of.*

v.   FASB Statement No. 128, *Earnings per Share.* In paragraph 28, the first sentence is replaced by the following (to clarify the effect of dilutive securities):

> Dilutive securities that are issued during a period and dilutive convertible securities for which conversion options lapse, for which preferred stock is redeemed, or for which related debt is extinguished during a period shall be included in the denominator of diluted EPS for the period that they were outstanding.

w.   FASB Statement No. 130, *Reporting Comprehensive Income.* In the last sentence of paragraph 27, *issued to shareholders* is deleted (to clarify the requirements for interim reporting).

x.   FASB Statement No. 131, *Disclosures about Segments of an Enterprise and Related Information.*

(1) In paragraph 18:

(a) In subparagraph (a), *reported* preceding *operating segments* is deleted (to clarify

that the test is applied to the total revenues of all operating segments).

(b) The last sentence is replaced with the following (to clarify the requirements for reporting operating segments):

> Operating segments that do not meet any of the quantitative thresholds may be considered reportable, and separately disclosed, if management believes that information about the segment would be useful to readers of the financial statements.

(2) In paragraph 25 (to clarify the requirements for periods for which segment information is required):

(a) In the first sentence, *for each period for which an income statement is presented* is inserted after *following.*

(b) The penultimate sentence of that paragraph is replaced with the following:

> However, reconciliations of balance sheet amounts for reportable segments to consolidated balance sheet amounts are required only for each year for which a balance sheet is presented.

(3) In the second sentence of paragraph 27, *(a)* is inserted after *specified amounts* and *or (b) are otherwise regularly provided to the chief operating decision maker, even if not included in that measure of segment profit or loss* is inserted before the colon (to clarify the circumstances under which the items identified by that paragraph are required to be disclosed).

(4) In the first sentence of paragraph 28, *(a)* is inserted after *specified amounts* and *or (b) are otherwise regularly provided to the chief operating decision maker, even if not included in the determination of segment assets* is inserted before the colon (to clarify the circumstances under which the items identified by that paragraph are required to be disclosed).

(5) In the first sentence of paragraph 33, *issued to shareholders* is deleted (to clarify the requirements for interim reporting).

(6) In the second sentence of paragraph 123, *a complete set of financial statements* is replaced by *an income statement* (to clarify the requirements for periods for which segment information is required).

y. FASB Statement No. 132, *Employers' Disclosures about Pensions and Other Postretirement Benefits.* The following changes are made to revise the amendments made by Statement 132:

(1) In paragraph 12(b), *Paragraphs 55 and 56 are* is replaced by *Paragraph 56 is.*

(2) Paragraphs 12(d) and 14(e) are deleted.

(3) In the third bullet of paragraph 63, *transition obligation* is replaced by *prior service cost.*

z. FASB Interpretation No. 18, *Accounting for Income Taxes in Interim Periods.* In footnote 8 to paragraph 9, *realization of the tax benefit is not assured* is replaced by *it is more likely than not that the tax benefit will not be realized* (effectively amended by Statement 109).

aa. FASB Interpretation No. 27, *Accounting for a Loss on a Sublease.* Footnote 3 to paragraph 3 is deleted (effectively superseded by Statement 121).

bb. FASB Interpretation No. 40, *Applicability of Generally Accepted Accounting Principles to Mutual Life Insurance and Other Enterprises.* The last sentence of paragraph 5 is deleted (effectively amended by paragraph 4 of FASB Statement No. 120, *Accounting and Reporting by Mutual Life Insurance Enterprises and by Insurance Enterprises for Certain Long-Duration Participating Contracts).*

cc. FASB Technical Bulletin No. 79-5, *Meaning of the Term "Customer" as It Applies to Health Care Facilities under FASB Statement No. 14.* In the first sentence of paragraph 3, *Statement 14* is replaced by *Statement 131* (effectively amended by Statement 131, which supersedes FASB Statement No. 14, *Financial Reporting for Segments of a Business Enterprise).*

5. This Statement amends the following pronouncements to delete or amend references to AICPA pronouncements that have been revised or superseded:

a. FASB Statement No. 93, *Recognition of Depreciation by Not-for-Profit Organizations.* In footnote 1 to paragraph 1, *Hospital Audit Guide (1972), Audits of Colleges and Universities (1973), Audits of Voluntary Health and Welfare Organizations (1974), and Statement of Position 78-10, Accounting Principles and Reporting Practices for Certain Nonprofit Organizations (1978)* is replaced by *Health Care Organizations and Not-for-Profit Organizations.*

b. FASB Statement No. 102, *Statement of Cash Flows—Exemption of Certain Enterprises and Classification of Cash Flows from Certain Securities Acquired for Resale.* In footnote 3 to paragraph 8, *Industry Audit Guide, Audits of Banks* is replaced by *Audit and Accounting Guide, Banks and Savings Institutions.*

c. FASB Statement No. 115, *Accounting for Certain Investments in Debt and Equity Securities.* In footnote 4 to paragraph 16, *AICPA Auditing Interpretation, Evidential Matter for the Carrying Amount of Marketable Securities, which was issued in 1975 and incorporated in Statement on Auditing Standards No. 1, Codification of Auditing Standards and Procedures, as Interpretation 20* is replaced by *AICPA Statement on Auditing Standards No. 81, Auditing Investments.*

d. FASB Interpretation No. 39, *Offsetting of Amounts Related to Certain Contracts.* In paragraph 7, *Industry Audit Guide, Audits of Banks* is replaced by *Audit and Accounting Guide, Banks and Savings Institutions.*

Effective Date and Transition

6. This Statement is effective for financial statements issued for fiscal years ending after February 15, 1999. Earlier application is encouraged.

> **The provisions of this Statement need
> not be applied to immaterial items.**

*This Statement was adopted by the unanimous vote of the seven members of the Financial Accounting
Standards Board:*

Edmund L. Jenkins,	Anthony T. Cope	James J. Leisenring
Chairman	John M. Foster	Gerhard G. Mueller
Joseph V. Anania	Gaylen N. Larson	

Appendix

BACKGROUND INFORMATION AND
BASIS FOR CONCLUSIONS

Rescission of Statement 75

7. Statement 35 was issued in March 1980 and defines generally accepted accounting principles for general-purpose external financial reports of defined benefit pension plans. It was intended to apply both to plans in the private sector and to plans sponsored by state and local governmental units. As originally issued, Statement 35 was to be effective for plan years beginning after December 15, 1980.

8. In April 1982, the Board issued FASB Statement No. 59, *Deferral of the Effective Date of Certain Accounting Requirements for Pension Plans of State and Local Governmental Units.* That Statement amended Statement 35 by deferring its applicability until plan years beginning after June 15, 1982, for plans that are sponsored by and provide benefits for the employees of one or more state or local governmental units.

9. In November 1982, the Financial Accounting Foundation (FAF) reached agreement with the Municipal Finance Officers Association, the National Association of State Auditors, Comptrollers and Treasurers, and the American Institute of Certified Public Accountants regarding the establishment of a Governmental Accounting Standards Board (GASB).

10. In November 1983, the Board issued Statement 75. Statement 75 indefinitely deferred the effective date of Statement 35 for plans that are sponsored by and provide benefits for the employees of one or more state or local governmental units. The Board

believed that while discussions relating to the formation and operation of the GASB were in progress, those efforts should not be impaired by the imposition of a new standard (that is, Statement 35) or by the existence of differing standards issued by different bodies.

11. The GASB was organized in 1984 by the FAF to establish standards of financial accounting and reporting for state and local governmental entities. Its standards guide the preparation of external financial reports of those entities.

12. In June 1984, the GASB placed on its agenda a project on pension accounting and financial reporting for plans and participating employers. In July 1984, the GASB issued GASB Statement No. 1, *Authoritative Status of NCGA Pronouncements and AICPA Industry Audit Guide.* In that Statement, the GASB identified three pronouncements (one of which was Statement 35) as sources of acceptable accounting and reporting principles for pension plans and employers, pending issuance of a GASB Statement or Statements on pensions.

13. In November 1986, the GASB issued GASB Statement No. 5, *Disclosure of Pension Information by Public Employee Retirement Systems and State and Local Governmental Employers.* GASB Statement 5 superseded all previous authoritative guidance on pension note disclosures but continued to recognize the pronouncements, as amended, previously identified (including Statement 35) as sources of guidance for pension recognition, measurement, and display, pending issuance of a future GASB Statement or Statements.

14. In July 1990, the GASB began deliberations on pension plan reporting issues. An Exposure Draft, *Financial Reporting for Defined Benefit Pension Plans and Note Disclosures for Defined Contribution*

Plans, was released for comment in 1994, and the final Statement (GASB Statement 25) was issued in November 1994.

15. GASB Statement 25 establishes financial reporting standards for defined benefit pension plans and for the notes to the financial statements of defined contribution plans of state and local governmental entities. Financial reporting standards for postemployment healthcare plans administered by defined benefit pension plans and for the pension expenditure/expense of employers are included, respectively, in GASB Statements No. 26, *Financial Reporting for Postemployment Healthcare Plans Administered by Defined Benefit Pension Plans,* and No. 27, *Accounting for Pensions by State and Local Governmental Employers.* The requirements of GASB Statement 25 are effective for periods beginning after June 15, 1996. Accordingly, Statement 75 is no longer necessary.

Technical Corrections

16. At the time a pronouncement is developed by the Board, part of the process requires that a determination be made of the effect this new guidance will have on existing authoritative accounting pronouncements. If there is an effect, then the new pronouncement should amend or supersede the existing authoritative literature in detail so that there is (a) no doubt about what the amendment changes and (b) no conflict between the requirements of prior pronouncements and the requirements of the new pronouncement.

17. However, sometimes certain detailed amendments that could have been explicitly made to the authoritative literature were omitted because, for example, they were overlooked when the new pronouncement was prepared. As those omissions were discovered by the FASB staff or members of the accounting profession, corrections were made to the various editions of the FASB's *Current Text* through effective amendments, and the locations of those amendments were appropriately indicated in the *Original Pronouncements.* However, those effective technical amendments have not been subjected to the Board's usual due process procedures. The Board decided to take this opportunity to identify those effective amendments and issue them as Board-approved amendments.

18. When the Board first issued a standard to make technical corrections (FASB Statement No. 111, *Rescission of FASB Statement No. 32 and Technical*

Corrections, in November 1992) the Board considered what parts of previously issued pronouncements to amend and decided that only the official guidance sections should be amended. The Board continues to believe that only the official guidance sections should be amended. In other words, the Board believes that the introduction, background information, and basis for conclusions paragraphs provide historical information that should not be amended or superseded unless the entire pronouncement is superseded. Those paragraphs are considered historical because they document the circumstances surrounding the development of a pronouncement. For example, they record (a) the reasons why the accounting requirements were considered to be necessary at that time, (b) what alternative guidance was considered, and (c) what the public comments were regarding the proposed requirements and how those comments were resolved.

19. In addition to the accounting guidance and historical paragraphs, a pronouncement sometimes contains other paragraphs or appendixes. Those paragraphs or appendixes are ones that (a) state the scope of the pronouncement, (b) indicate substantive amendments to other existing pronouncements, (c) present examples or illustrations of application of the requirements of the pronouncement, and (d) present a glossary of the terms used in the pronouncement. The Board believes that the content of those various paragraphs and appendixes does provide part of the accounting guidance of the pronouncement and should be amended if the pronouncement is amended by a subsequent pronouncement. The Board has further decided that when a pronouncement is superseded, the amendments made by that superseded pronouncement remain in effect unless they are explicitly amended. Thus, if a paragraph (or part of one) is deleted without any replacement text, the deletion would still stand. If the Board decides to undo the deletion, then the new (superseding) Statement must explicitly add back the deleted text. However, if a superseded document either (a) has superseded text in a previous standard by replacing it with new text or (b) has added text to a previous standard, the new (superseding) Statement must either (1) explicitly repeat the amendment from the superseded document that added text or replaced text (for example, refer to paragraph 238 of Statement 125 and paragraph 532 of Statement 133) or (2) explicitly delete text that was added or replaced by the superseded document (for example, refer to paragraph 237(h) of Statement 125 and paragraph 531(b) of Statement 133).

20. Some of the technical corrections in this Statement are not the direct result of effective amendments by new standards. That is, some amendments have been made to extend certain provisions to reflect established practice or clarify inconsistencies in existing pronouncements. For example:

a. Prior to being superseded by the Accounting Principles Board, the Committee on Accounting Procedure and the Committee on Terminology of the AICPA issued a series of Accounting Research Bulletins between 1939 and 1953. In 1953, the Committee on Accounting Procedure restated and revised the first 42 Bulletins. The purpose of the restatement (codified into ARB 43) was to eliminate what was no longer applicable, to condense and clarify required revisions, and to arrange the retained material by subjects rather than in the order of issuance. In 1953, practice permitted the accounting, in some circumstances, for stock of a corporation held in its own treasury as an asset. In EITF Issue No. 97-14, "Accounting for Deferred Compensation Arrangements Where Amounts Earned Are Held in a Rabbi Trust and Invested," the Emerging Issues Task Force reached a consensus that company shares held by a rabbi trust should be treated as treasury stock in the employer's financial statements. In connection with that Issue, the staff of the Securities and Exchange Commission (SEC) nullified its previously stated position that asset classification may be appropriate if the shares repurchased are expected to be reissued promptly (within one year) under existing stock plans. The Board also believes that it is no longer acceptable to show stock of a corporation held in its own treasury as an asset. One constituent notified the Board that that position may conflict with a provision in paragraph 13 of Opinion 6, which states:

> Laws of some states govern the circumstances under which a corporation may acquire its own stock and prescribe the accounting treatment therefor. Where such requirements are at variance with paragraph 12, the accounting should conform to the applicable law.

The Board considered the point and observed that that reference is not specific to classifying treasury stock as an asset. Furthermore, several Board members expressed concern about that sentence being applied too broadly.

b. Paragraph 21 of APB Opinion No. 9, *Reporting the Results of Operations,* provided criteria for the determination of extraordinary items. Examples of extraordinary items included "the write-off of goodwill due to unusual events or developments within the period." Paragraph 31 of Opinion 17 provides that a loss resulting from a reduction in the unamortized cost of intangible assets does "not necessarily justify an extraordinary charge to income" and that "the reason for an extraordinary deduction should be disclosed." In June 1973 (three years after Opinion 17 was issued), Opinion 30 was issued which supersedes the criteria in Opinion 9 for the determination of extraordinary items. Paragraph 23 of Opinion 30 states that "certain gains and losses should not be reported as extraordinary items because they are usual in nature or may be expected to recur as a consequence of customary and continuing business activities. Examples include: (a) write-down or write-off of . . . other intangible assets." Paragraph 26 of Opinion 30, however, provides the following guidance on disclosure of unusual or infrequently occurring items: "A material event or transaction that is unusual in nature or occurs infrequently but not both, and therefore does not meet both criteria for classification as an extraordinary item, should be reported as a separate component of income from continuing operations." The Board observes that Opinion 17 was never amended to reflect the provisions of Opinion 9 that were superseded by Opinion 30 in that the write-down or write-off of intangibles may be an unusual item but may not be an extraordinary item. Accordingly, that change is being made at this time.

c. Paragraph 1 of Opinion 28 states that "the purpose of this Opinion is to clarify the application of accounting principles and reporting practices to interim financial information, including interim financial statements and summarized interim financial data of publicly traded companies issued for external reporting purposes." The specific requirements for interim disclosures found in Opinion 28 and various other pronouncements refer to the applicability of such requirements to financial information *issued to an enterprise's shareholders or securityholders.* Some have suggested that the interim disclosure requirements of those standards are not applicable to quarterly financial information reported pursuant to the Securities Exchange Act of 1934 on Forms 10-Q or

10-QSB, which generally are not issued to shareholders or securityholders. The interim disclosure requirements have been amended to clarify that the requirements are intended to be applied to interim financial reporting, including interim financial statements and summarized interim financial data of publicly traded companies issued for external reporting purposes.

d. Example (12) of the Accounting Interpretation of Opinion 30, provides as an example of a transaction that would meet both criteria of being unusual in nature and infrequent of occurrence a situation in which a company sells a block of common stock of a publicly traded company. The block of shares, which represents less than 10 percent of the publicly held company, is the only security investment the company has ever owned. The Board acknowledges that it would be a very rare situation for an entity to ever own (and intend to ever own) just one security investment. However, were that situation to arise, the Board believes that in accordance with Statement 115, it would no longer be acceptable to report the realized gain or loss on the sale of such a security as an extraordinary item when the unrealized gains or losses are reported in other comprehensive income or income from operations, as applicable.

e. The SEC, in Regulation S-X, requires that for public companies segment information required by Statement 14 must be provided for each year for which an audited statement of income is presented. As originally issued, Statement 131 requires segment information to be provided for each year for which a complete set of financial statements is presented. Because Statement 131 is applicable to only public companies, and the SEC will continue to require that segment information be presented for each year for which an audited statement of income is presented, the Board believes that amending Statement 131 to conform the reporting requirements is appropriate.

f. Paragraphs 27 and 28 of Statement 131 require disclosure of certain specified amounts relating to segment profit or loss and assets. The introductory language of those paragraphs states that disclosure of the specified amounts is required if the specified amounts are included in the measure of segment profit or loss (or in the determination of segment assets) reviewed by the chief operating decision maker. The first sentence of paragraph 29 further states that "the amount of each

segment item reported shall be the measure reported to the chief operating decision maker for purposes of making decisions about allocating resources to the segment and assessing its performance." In May 1998, the FASB staff made an announcement at an EITF meeting (refer to EITF Topic No. D-70, "Questions Related to the Implementation of FASB Statement No. 131") that indicates the staff response to a technical inquiry relating to the requirements of paragraph 27. Specifically, the staff responded that if the items specified in paragraph 27 (and in paragraph 28) are provided to the chief operating decision maker for purposes of evaluating segment performance, then disclosure of such items is required even if such items are not included in the measure of segment profit or loss (or in the determination of segment assets) that is reviewed by the chief operating decision maker. The Board agreed with the staff's conclusion that the introductory language of paragraphs 27 and 28 should be considered together with the measurement guidance provided in paragraphs 29–31 and that as part of this project to make technical corrections, the introductory language of paragraphs 27 and 28 should be amended.

Comments on Exposure Draft

21. The Board issued an Exposure Draft, *Amendment to FASB Statement No. 66, Rescission of FASB Statement No. 75, and Technical Corrections,* for comment on October 13, 1998, and received nine letters of comment. Many of the respondents expressed concern about an amendment to Statement 66 that was proposed in the Exposure Draft. Subsequent to the issuance of the Exposure Draft, the Board decided to exclude that proposed amendment from this project because of the complexity of some of the issues that were raised in the comment letters. That issue will be addressed separately by the Board.

22. A majority of respondents agreed with the technical corrections proposed in the Exposure Draft. Several respondents indicated support for the practice of making needed technical corrections when they are identified and then formally issuing those corrections as Board-approved amendments after due process. A few respondents had suggestions for additional amendments and technical corrections. Some of those suggested amendments are included in this Statement.

Statement of Financial Accounting Standards No. 136
Transfers of Assets to a Not-for-Profit Organization or Charitable Trust That Raises or Holds Contributions for Others

STATUS

Issued: June 1999

Effective Date: For financial statements issued for fiscal periods beginning after December 15, 1999; paragraph 12 continues to be effective for fiscal years ending after September 15, 1996

Affects: Supersedes FIN 42

Affected by: Summary, paragraphs 15 and 36 amended by FAS 157, paragraph E19
Footnote 5 amended by FAS 140, paragraph 354

SUMMARY

This Statement establishes standards for transactions in which an entity—the *donor*—makes a contribution by transferring assets to a not-for-profit organization or charitable trust—the *recipient organization*—that accepts the assets from the donor and agrees to use those assets on behalf of or transfer those assets, the return on investment of those assets, or both to another entity—the *beneficiary*—that is specified by the donor. It also establishes standards for transactions that take place in a similar manner but are not contributions because the transfers are revocable, repayable, or reciprocal.

This Statement requires a recipient organization that accepts cash or other financial assets from a donor and agrees to use those assets on behalf of or transfer those assets, the return on investment of those assets, or both to a specified unaffiliated beneficiary to recognize the fair value of those assets as a liability to the specified beneficiary concurrent with recognition of the assets received from the donor. However, if the donor explicitly grants the recipient organization variance power or if the recipient organization and the specified beneficiary are financially interrelated organizations, the recipient organization is required to recognize the fair value of any assets it receives as a contribution received. Not-for-profit organizations are financially interrelated if (a) one organization has the ability to influence the operating and financial decisions of the other and (b) one organization has an ongoing economic interest in the net assets of the other.

This Statement does not establish standards for a trustee's reporting of assets held on behalf of specified beneficiaries, but it does establish standards for a beneficiary's reporting of its rights to assets held in a charitable trust.

This Statement requires that a specified beneficiary recognize its rights to the assets held by a recipient organization as an asset unless the donor has explicitly granted the recipient organization variance power. Those rights are either an interest in the net assets of the recipient organization, a beneficial interest, or a receivable. If the beneficiary and the recipient organization are financially interrelated organizations, the beneficiary is required to recognize its interest in the net assets of the recipient organization and adjust that interest for its share of the change in net assets of the recipient organization. If the beneficiary has an unconditional right to receive all or a portion of the specified cash flows from a charitable trust or other identifiable pool of assets, the beneficiary is required to recognize that beneficial interest, measuring and subsequently remeasuring it at fair value. If the recipient organization is explicitly granted variance power, the specified beneficiary does not recognize its potential for future distributions from the assets held by the recipient organization. In all other cases, a beneficiary recognizes its rights as a receivable.

This Statement describes four circumstances in which a transfer of assets to a recipient organization is accounted for as a liability by the recipient organization and as an asset by the resource provider because the transfer is revocable or reciprocal. Those four circumstances are if (a) the transfer is subject to the resource provider's unilateral right to redirect the use of the assets to another beneficiary, (b) the transfer is accompanied by the resource provider's conditional promise to give or is otherwise revocable or repayable, (c) the resource provider controls the recipient organization and specifies an unaffiliated beneficiary, or (d) the resource provider specifies itself or its affiliate as the beneficiary and the transfer is not an equity transaction. If the transfer is an equity transaction and the resource provider specifies itself as beneficiary, it records an interest in the net assets of the recipient organization (or an increase in a previously recognized interest). If the resource provider specifies an affiliate as beneficiary, the resource provider records an equity transaction as a separate line item in its statement of activities, and the affiliate named as beneficiary records an interest in the net assets of the recipient organization. The recipient organization records an equity transaction as a separate line item in its statement of activities.

This Statement requires certain disclosures if a not-for-profit organization transfers assets to a recipient organization and specifies itself or its affiliate as the beneficiary or if it includes in its financial statements a ratio of fundraising expenses to amounts raised.

This Statement incorporates without reconsideration the guidance in FASB Interpretation No. 42, *Accounting for Transfers of Assets in Which a Not-for-Profit Organization Is Granted Variance Power,* and supersedes that Interpretation.

This Statement is effective for financial statements issued for fiscal periods beginning after December 15, 1999, except for the provisions incorporated from Interpretation 42, which continue to be effective for fiscal years ending after September 15, 1996. Earlier application is encouraged. This Statement may be applied either by restating the financial statements of all years presented or by recognizing the cumulative effect of the change in accounting principle in the year of the change.

Transfers of Assets to a Not-for-Profit
Organization or Charitable Trust That Raises
or Holds Contributions for Others

FAS136

Statement of Financial Accounting Standards No. 136

Transfers of Assets to a Not-for-Profit Organization or Charitable Trust That Raises or Holds Contributions for Others

CONTENTS

INTRODUCTION

1. Paragraph 4 of FASB Statement No. 116, *Accounting for Contributions Received and Contributions Made,* states, "This Statement does not apply to transfers of assets in which the reporting entity acts as an agent, trustee, or intermediary, rather than as a donor or donee." The Board was asked how to differentiate situations in which a not-for-profit organization acts as an agent, trustee, or intermediary from situations in which a not-for-profit organization acts as a donor and a donee. The Board was told that those determinations are especially difficult if, as part of its charitable mission, an organization solicits and collects cash, products, or services and distributes those assets, the return on investment of those assets, or both to other organizations.

2. The Board also was asked how an organization that has that mission should report receipts and disbursements of assets if those transfers are not its contributions as defined in Statement 116. Additionally, some organizations asked whether a beneficiary should report its rights to the assets held by a recipient organization and, if so, how those rights should be reported.

STANDARDS OF FINANCIAL ACCOUNTING AND REPORTING

Scope

3. Paragraphs 8–16 of this Statement apply to transactions in which an entity—the *donor*—makes a contribution by transferring assets to a not-for-profit organization or charitable trust—the *recipient organization*—that accepts the assets from the donor and agrees to use those assets on behalf of or transfer those assets, the return on investment of those assets,

or both to an unaffiliated[1] entity—the *beneficiary*—that is specified by the donor.[2]

4. Paragraphs 17–19 of this Statement apply to transactions that take place in a similar manner but are not contributions for one of the following reasons:

a. The entity that transfers the assets to the recipient organization—the *resource provider*[3]—is related to the beneficiary in a way that causes the transfer to be reciprocal.

b. Conditions imposed by the resource provider or the relationships between the parties make the transfer of assets to the recipient organization revocable or repayable.

5. Paragraph 20 of this Statement applies to all not-for-profit organizations that disclose a ratio of fund-raising expenses to amounts raised, including organizations that are not involved in transfers of the types described in paragraphs 3 and 4.

6. This Statement applies to transfers of cash and other assets, including the assets described in paragraph 5 of Statement 116: "securities, land, buildings, use of facilities or utilities, materials and supplies, intangible assets, services, and unconditional promises to give those items in the future."

7. This Statement supersedes FASB Interpretation No. 42, *Accounting for Transfers of Assets in Which a Not-for-Profit Organization Is Granted Variance Power*. Paragraph 2 of Interpretation 42 is carried forward without reconsideration in paragraph 12 of this Statement.

Intermediary

8. Although in general usage the term *intermediary* encompasses a broad range of situations in which an organization acts between two or more other parties, use of the term in paragraph 4 of Statement 116 is more narrow and specific. The term is used to refer to situations in which a recipient organization acts as a facilitator for the transfer of assets between a potential donor and a potential beneficiary (donee) but is neither an agent or trustee nor a donee and donor as contemplated by Statement 116.[4] If an intermediary receives cash or other financial assets,[5] it shall recognize its liability to the specified beneficiary concurrent with its recognition of the assets received from the donor. Both the liability and the assets shall be measured at the fair value of the assets received. If an intermediary receives nonfinancial assets, it is permitted, but not required, to recognize its liability and those assets provided that the intermediary reports consistently from period to period and discloses its accounting policy.

Trustee

9. A recipient organization acts as a *trustee* if it has a duty to hold and manage assets for the benefit of a specified beneficiary in accordance with a charitable trust agreement. This Statement does not establish standards for a trustee's reporting of assets held on behalf of a specified beneficiary, but paragraphs 15 and 16 establish standards for the beneficiary's reporting of its rights to trust assets—its beneficial interest in the charitable trust.

Agent

10. An *agent* acts for and on behalf of another. Although the term *agency* has a legal definition, the term is used in this Statement with a broader meaning to encompass not only legal agency, but also the relationships described in this Statement. A recipient organization acts as an agent for and on behalf of a donor if it receives assets from the donor and agrees

---

[1]FASB Statement No. 57, *Related Party Disclosures,* defines *affiliate* as "a party that, directly or indirectly through one or more intermediaries, controls, is controlled by, or is under common control with an enterprise" (paragraph 24(a)). Thus, an *unaffiliated* beneficiary is a beneficiary other than the donor or its affiliate.

[2]In some cases, the donor, recipient organization, or beneficiary is a governmental entity. This Statement and other pronouncements of the Financial Accounting Standards Board do not apply to governmental entities unless the Governmental Accounting Standards Board issues a pronouncement that makes them applicable.

[3]If the transfer of assets is not a contribution or not yet a contribution, this Statement uses the term resource provider rather than the term donor to refer to the entity that transfers the assets to the recipient organization.

[4]Example 4 of Statement 116 (paragraph 180) illustrates the use of the term intermediary. In that example, the organization facilitates a contribution between a potential donor, a lawyer willing to provide free legal services, and a potential donee, an individual in need of free legal services. The organization is not itself a donee and donor, nor is it a recipient of the services provided by the donor (lawyer) to the donee (individual).

[5]FASB Statement No. 140, *Accounting for Transfers and Servicing of Financial Assets and Extinguishments of Liabilities,* defines *financial asset* as "cash, evidence of an ownership interest in an entity, or a contract that conveys to a second entity a contractual right (a) to receive cash or another financial instrument from a first entity or (b) to exchange other financial instruments on potentially favorable terms with the first entity" (paragraph 364).

Transfers of Assets to a Not-for-Profit Organization or Charitable Trust That Raises or Holds Contributions for Others

FAS136

to use those assets on behalf of or transfer those assets, the return on investment of those assets, or both to a specified beneficiary. A recipient organization acts as an agent for and on behalf of a beneficiary if it agrees to solicit assets from potential donors specifically for the beneficiary's use and to distribute those assets to the beneficiary. A recipient organization also acts as an agent if a beneficiary can compel the organization to make distributions to it or on its behalf.

11. Except as described in paragraphs 12 and 14 of this Statement, a recipient organization that accepts assets from a donor and agrees to use those assets on behalf of or transfer those assets, the return on investment of those assets, or both to a specified beneficiary is not a donee. It shall recognize its liability to the specified beneficiary concurrent with its recognition of cash or other financial assets received from the donor. Both the liability and the assets shall be measured at the fair value of the assets received. Except as described in paragraphs 12 and 14 of this Statement, a recipient organization that receives non-financial assets is permitted, but not required, to recognize its liability and those assets provided that the organization reports consistently from period to period and discloses its accounting policy.

12. A recipient organization that is directed by a donor to distribute the transferred assets, the return on investment of those assets, or both to a specified unaffiliated beneficiary acts as a donee, rather than an agent, trustee, or intermediary, if the donor explicitly grants the recipient organization variance power—that is, the unilateral power to redirect the use of the transferred assets to another beneficiary. In that situation, *explicitly grants* means that the recipient organization's unilateral power to redirect the use of the assets is explicitly referred to in the instrument transferring the assets, and *unilateral power* means that the recipient organization can override the donor's instructions without approval from the donor, specified beneficiary, or any other interested party.

Financially Interrelated Organizations

13. The recipient organization and the specified beneficiary are *financially interrelated organizations* if the relationship between them has both of the following characteristics:

a. One organization has the ability to influence the operating and financial decisions of the other. The ability to exercise that influence may be demonstrated in several ways:

(1) The organizations are affiliates.
(2) One organization has considerable representation on the governing board of the other organization.
(3) The charter or bylaws of one organization limit its activities to those that are beneficial to the other organization.
(4) An agreement between the organizations allows one organization to actively participate in policymaking processes of the other, such as setting organizational priorities, budgets, and management compensation.

b. One organization has an ongoing economic interest in the net assets of the other. If the specified beneficiary has an ongoing economic interest in the net assets of the recipient organization, the beneficiary's rights to the assets held by the recipient organization are residual rights; that is, the value of those rights increases or decreases as a result of the investment, fundraising, operating, and other activities of the recipient organization. Alternatively, but less common, a recipient organization may have an ongoing economic interest in the net assets of the specified beneficiary. If so, the recipient organization's rights are residual rights, and their value changes as a result of the operations of the beneficiary.

14. If a recipient organization and a specified beneficiary are financially interrelated organizations and the recipient organization is not a trustee, the recipient organization shall recognize a contribution received when it receives assets (financial or nonfinancial) from the donor that are specified for the beneficiary. For example, a foundation that exists to raise, hold, and invest assets for the specified beneficiary or for a group of affiliates of which the specified beneficiary is a member generally is financially interrelated with the organization or organizations it supports and recognizes contribution revenue when it receives assets from the donor.

Beneficiary

15. A specified beneficiary shall recognize its rights to the assets (financial or nonfinancial) held by a recipient organization as an asset unless the recipient organization is explicitly granted variance power. Those rights are either an interest in the net assets of the recipient organization, a beneficial interest, or a receivable. If the beneficiary and the recipient organization are financially interrelated organizations, the beneficiary shall recognize its interest in the net

assets of the recipient organization and adjust that interest for its share of the change in net assets of the recipient organization.[6] If the beneficiary has an unconditional right to receive all or a portion of the specified cash flows from a charitable trust or other identifiable pool of assets, the beneficiary shall recognize that beneficial interest, measuring and subsequently remeasuring it at fair value. In all other cases, a beneficiary shall recognize its rights to the assets held by a recipient organization as a receivable and contribution revenue in accordance with the provisions of Statement 116 for unconditional promises to give.[7]

16. If the donor explicitly grants a recipient organization variance power, the specified unaffiliated beneficiary shall not recognize its potential for future distributions from the assets held by the recipient organization.

Transfers of Assets That Are Not Contributions

17. A transfer of assets to a recipient organization is not a contribution and shall be accounted for as an asset by the resource provider and as a liability by the recipient organization if one or more of the following conditions is present:

a. The transfer is subject to the resource provider's unilateral right to redirect the use of the assets to another beneficiary.
b. The transfer is accompanied by the resource provider's conditional promise to give or is otherwise revocable or repayable.
c. The resource provider controls the recipient organization and specifies an unaffiliated beneficiary.
d. The resource provider specifies itself or its affiliate as the beneficiary and the transfer is not an equity transaction (paragraph 18).

18. A transfer of assets to a recipient organization is an equity transaction if all of the following conditions are present:

a. The resource provider specifies itself or its affiliate as the beneficiary.
b. The resource provider and the recipient organization are financially interrelated organizations.
c. Neither the resource provider nor its affiliate expects payment of the transferred assets, although payment of investment return on the transferred assets may be expected.

If a resource provider specifies itself as beneficiary, it shall report an equity transaction as an interest in the net assets of the recipient organization (or as an increase in a previously recognized interest). If a resource provider specifies an affiliate as beneficiary, the resource provider shall report an equity transaction as a separate line in its statement of activities, and the affiliate named as beneficiary shall report an interest in the net assets of the recipient organization. A recipient organization shall report an equity transaction as a separate line item in its statement of activities.

Disclosures

19. If a not-for-profit organization transfers assets to a recipient organization and specifies itself or its affiliate as the beneficiary, it shall disclose the following information for each period for which a statement of financial position is presented:

a. The identity of the recipient organization to which the transfer was made
b. Whether variance power was granted to the recipient organization and, if so, a description of the terms of the variance power
c. The terms under which amounts will be distributed to the resource provider or its affiliate
d. The aggregate amount recognized in the statement of financial position for those transfers and

---

[6]Recognizing an interest in the net assets of the recipient organization and adjusting that interest for a share of the change in net assets of the recipient organization is similar to the equity method, which is described in APB Opinion No. 18, *The Equity Method of Accounting for Investments in Common Stock.* If the beneficiary and the recipient organization are included in consolidated financial statements, the beneficiary's interest in the net assets of the recipient organization would be eliminated in accordance with paragraph 6 of Accounting Research Bulletin No. 51, *Consolidated Financial Statements.*

[7]For an unconditional promise to give to be recognized in financial statements, paragraph 6 of Statement 116 states, "... there must be sufficient evidence in the form of verifiable documentation that a promise was made and received." Paragraph 15 of Statement 116 states, "Receipts of unconditional promises to give with payments due in future periods shall be reported as restricted support unless explicit donor stipulations or circumstances surrounding the receipt of a promise make clear that the donor intended it to be used to support activities of the current period." Paragraph 20 of Statement 116 states, "The present value of estimated future cash flows using a discount rate commensurate with the risks involved is an appropriate measure of fair value of unconditional promises to give cash" (footnote reference omitted).

Transfers of Assets to a Not-for-Profit
Organization or Charitable Trust That Raises
or Holds Contributions for Others

FAS136

whether that amount is recorded as an interest in the net assets of the recipient organization or as another asset (for example, as a beneficial interest in assets held by others or a refundable advance).

20. If a not-for-profit organization discloses in its financial statements a ratio of fundraising expenses to amounts raised, it also shall disclose how it computes that ratio.

EFFECTIVE DATE AND TRANSITION

21. Except for the provisions of paragraph 12, the provisions of this Statement shall be effective for financial statements issued for fiscal periods beginning after December 15, 1999. Earlier application is encouraged. The provisions of paragraph 12, which are carried forward from Interpretation 42, shall continue to be effective for fiscal years ending after September 15, 1996. Unless this Statement is applied retroactively under the provisions of paragraph 22, the effect of initially applying this Statement shall be reported as the effect of a change in accounting principle in a manner similar to the cumulative effect of a change in accounting principle (APB Opinion No. 20, *Accounting Changes,* paragraph 19). The amount of cumulative effect shall be based on a retroactive computation.

22. This Statement may be applied retroactively by restating opening net assets for the earliest year presented or for the year in which this Statement is first applied if no prior years are presented. In the period in which this Statement is first applied, an entity shall disclose the nature of any restatement and its effect on the change in net assets and each class of net assets for each period presented.

> **The provisions of this Statement need
> not be applied to immaterial items.**

This Statement was adopted by the unanimous vote of the seven members of the Financial Accounting Standards Board:

Edmund L. Jenkins,	Anthony T. Cope	James J. Leisenring
Chairman	John M. Foster	Gerhard G. Mueller
Joseph V. Anania	Gaylen N. Larson	

Appendix A

ILLUSTRATIVE GUIDANCE

Introduction

23. This appendix provides a diagram to assist entities in the application of this Statement and examples that illustrate the application of the standards in specific situations. The diagram is a visual supplement to the written standards section. It should not be interpreted to alter any requirements of this Statement, nor should it be considered a substitute for those requirements. The relevant paragraphs of the standards section of this Statement and of FASB Statement No. 116, *Accounting for Contributions Received and Contributions Made,* are identified in the parenthetical notes. The examples do not address all possible situations or applications of this Statement.

Diagram

24. The diagram depicts the process for determining the appropriate accounting for a transfer of assets from a donor to a recipient organization that accepts the assets and agrees to use those assets on behalf of a beneficiary specified by the donor or transfer those assets, the return on investment of those assets, or both to a beneficiary specified by the donor. (For additional information about how a beneficiary is specified, refer to paragraphs 68 and 69.) The diagram also depicts the process for determining the appropriate accounting for a transfer from a resource provider that takes place in a similar manner but is not a contribution because the transfer is revocable, repayable, or reciprocal.

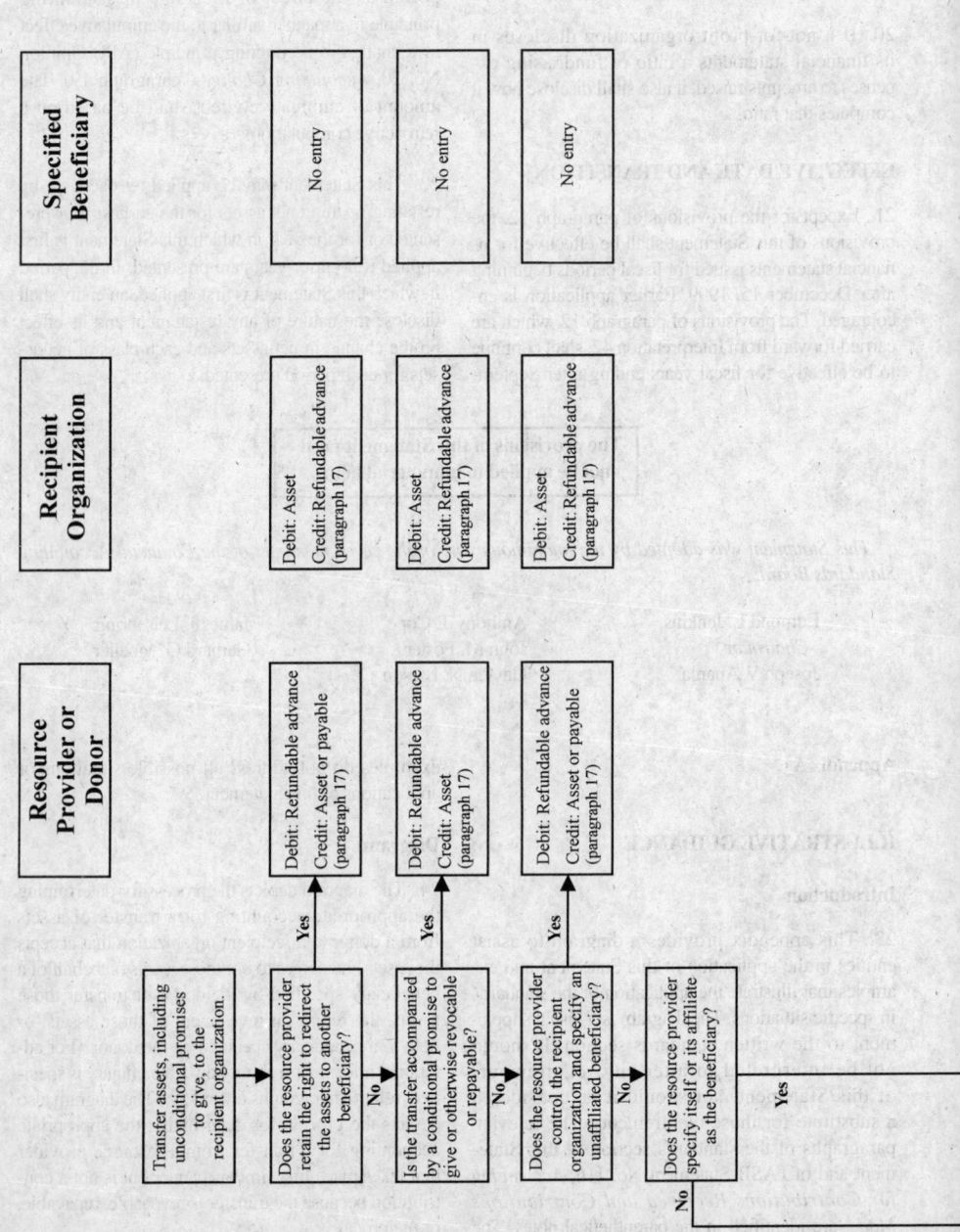

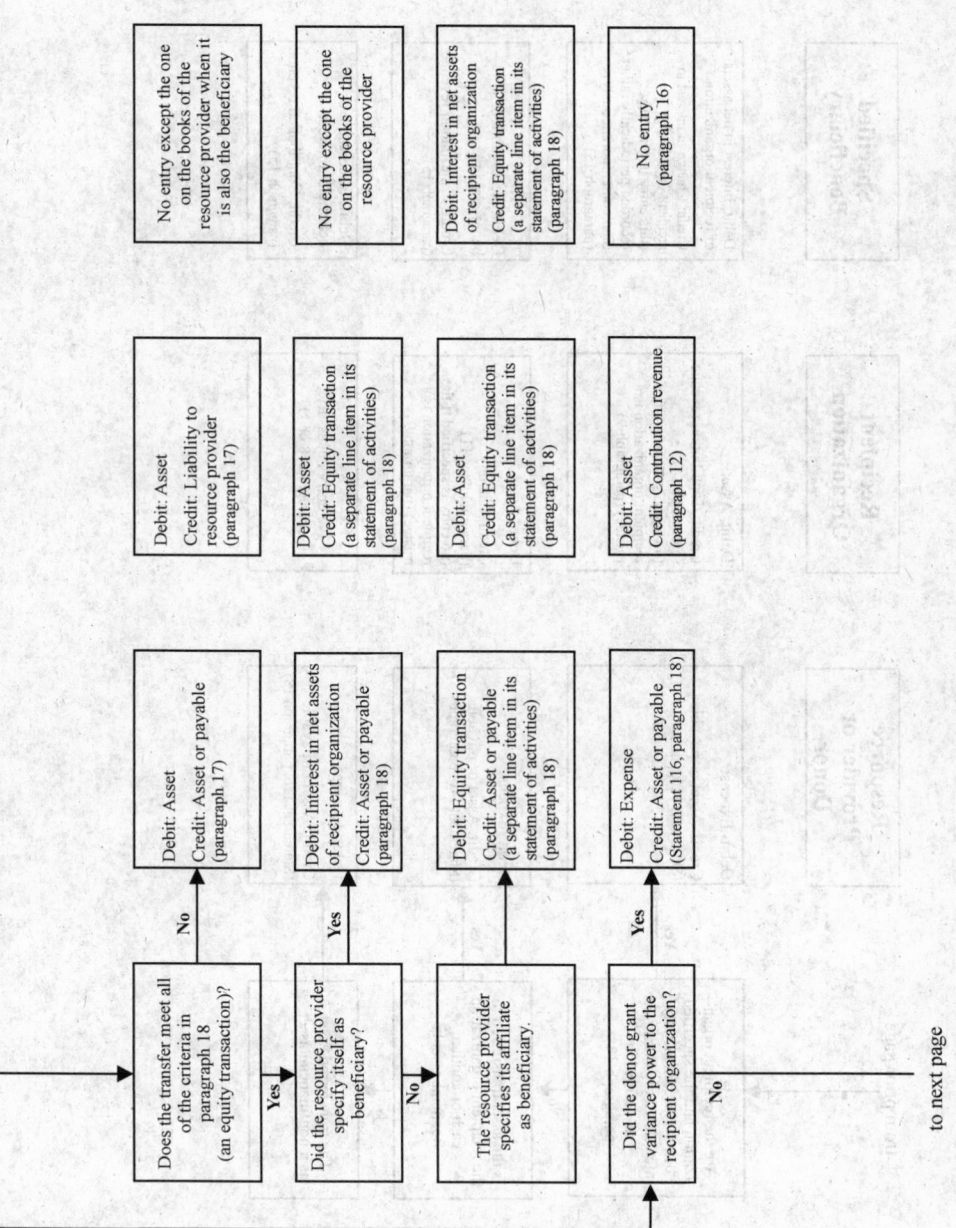

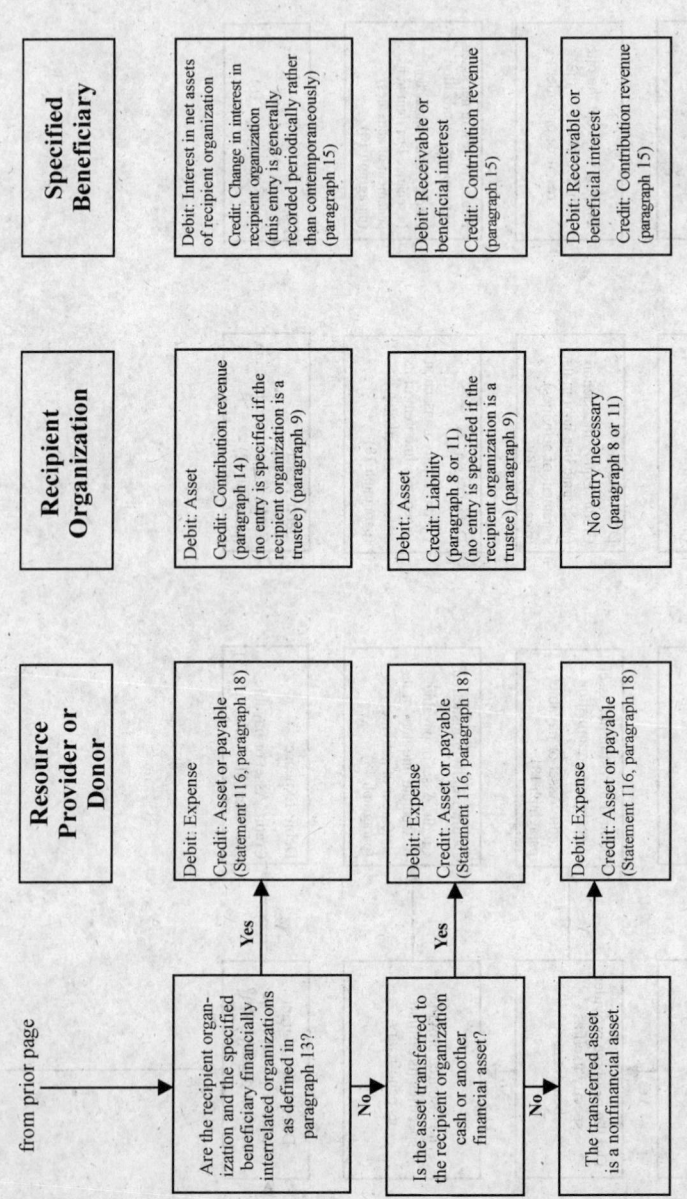

Transfers of Assets to a Not-for-Profit **FAS136**
Organization or Charitable Trust That Raises
or Holds Contributions for Others

Example 1—Gifts to a Federated Fundraising Organization

25. Federated Fundraising Organization provides three choices to donors in its annual workplace campaign. Donors can give without restriction, direct their gifts to one of four community needs identified by Federated Fundraising Organization, or specify that their gifts be transferred to an organization of their choice. The campaign literature informs donors that if they choose to specify an organization to which their gift should be transferred, the organization must be a social welfare organization within the community that has tax-exempt status under Internal Revenue Code Section 501(c)(3). The campaign literature also provides a schedule of the administrative fees that will be deducted from all gifts that are to be transferred to the donor's chosen organization.

26. Federated Fundraising Organization would recognize the fair values of the unrestricted gifts as contribution revenue that increases unrestricted net assets. It would recognize the fair values of the gifts targeted to the four specified community needs as contribution revenue that increases temporarily restricted net assets. It would recognize the fair values of gifts that are to be transferred to organizations chosen by the donors as increases in its assets and as liabilities to those specified beneficiaries (paragraph 11). However, if some of the gifts that are intended for specified beneficiaries are gifts of nonfinancial assets, Federated Fundraising Organization would recognize those nonfinancial assets and its liability to transfer them to the specified beneficiaries if that were its policy; otherwise, it would recognize neither the nonfinancial assets nor a liability (paragraph 11). Federated Fundraising Organization would recognize as revenue the administrative fees withheld from amounts to be transferred to the donors' chosen organizations.

27. The organizations chosen by the donors would recognize the fair value of the transferred assets as contribution revenue in accordance with the provisions of Statement 116 for unconditional promises to give (paragraph 15). Thus, the revenue would increase temporarily restricted net assets unless the donor specified a permanent restriction or it was clear that the donor intended the gift to support activities of the current period (Statement 116, paragraph 15). In accordance with paragraph 24 of FASB Statement No. 117, *Financial Statements of Not-for-Profit Organizations,* the beneficiaries would report the gross amounts of the gifts as contribution revenue and the administrative fees withheld by Federated Fundraising Organization as expenses. The net amount would be recognized as a receivable (paragraph 15).

28. Instead of conducting the campaign as described above, Federated Fundraising Organization's campaign literature, including the form that donors use to specify a beneficiary, clearly states that if donors choose to give and specify a beneficiary, the allocation committee has the authority to redirect their gifts if the committee perceives needs elsewhere in the community that are greater. By giving under those terms, donors explicitly grant Federated Fundraising Organization variance power. Thus, Federated Fundraising Organization would recognize an unrestricted contribution (paragraph 12), and the specified beneficiaries would be precluded from recognizing their potential for future distributions from the assets (paragraph 16).

Example 2—Gifts to a Community Foundation for the Benefit of a Not-for-Profit Organization

29. The governing board of City Botanical Society decides to raise funds to build an endowment. The governing board signs an agreement to establish a fund at Community Foundation. Community Foundation and City Botanical Society are not financially interrelated organizations. City Botanical Society solicits gifts to the fund. The campaign materials inform donors that the endowment will be owned and held by Community Foundation. The materials explain that the gifts will be invested and that the return from their investment will be distributed to City Botanical Society, subject to Community Foundation's spending policy and to Community Foundation's right to redirect the return to another beneficiary without the approval of the donor, City Botanical Society, or any other party if distributions to City Botanical Society become unnecessary, impossible, or inconsistent with the needs of the community. The donor-response card also clearly describes Community Foundation's right to redirect the return of the fund. The campaign materials indicate that donors should send their contributions to Community Foundation using a preaddressed envelope included for that purpose.

30. Community Foundation would recognize the fair value of gifts received as assets and as contribution revenue. The donors explicitly granted variance power by using a donor-response card that clearly states that gifts are subject to Community Foundation's unilateral power to redirect the return to another beneficiary (paragraph 12).

31. City Botanical Society is precluded from recognizing its potential rights to the assets held by Community Foundation because the donors explicitly granted variance power (paragraph 16). City Botanical Society would recognize only its annual grants from Community Foundation as contributions.

32. Whether a donor intended to make a contribution to Community Foundation may not be clear if the donor responds to the campaign materials by sending a contribution and the donor-response card directly to City Botanical Society. City Botanical Society could resolve the ambiguity by a review of the facts and circumstances surrounding the gift, communications with the donor, or both. If it is ultimately determined that the donor intended to make a gift to the fund owned and held by Community Foundation and to explicitly grant variance power, City Botanical Society would be an agent responsible for transferring that gift to Community Foundation (paragraph 11).

Example 3—Cash Transfer from a Not-for-Profit Organization to Another Not-for-Profit Organization for the Benefit of an Individual

33. Local Church transfers cash to Seminary and instructs Seminary to use the money to grant a scholarship to Individual, who is a parishioner of Local Church.

34. Seminary would recognize the cash and a liability to Individual in the same amount because it merely is facilitating the cash transfer from Local Church to Individual (paragraph 8).

Example 4—Assets Transferred from an Individual to a Bank to Establish a Charitable Trust for the Benefit of a Not-for-Profit Organization

35. Individual transfers assets to National Bank to establish an irrevocable charitable trust for the sole benefit of Museum. National Bank will serve as trustee. Individual sets forth in the trust agreement the policies that direct the economic activities of the trust. The trust term is five years. Each year, the income received on the investments of the trust will be distributed to Museum. At the end of year 5, the corpus of the trust (original assets and net appreciation on those assets) will be paid to Museum.

36. This Statement does not establish standards for the trustee, National Bank (paragraph 9). Because Museum is unable to influence the operating or fi-

nancial decisions of the trustee, Museum and National Bank are not financially interrelated organizations (paragraph 13(a)). Therefore, Museum would recognize its asset (a beneficial interest in the trust) and contribution revenue that increases temporarily restricted net assets (paragraph 15). Museum would measure its beneficial interest at fair value. That value generally can be measured by the fair value of the assets contributed to the trust.

Example 5—Gift of Nonfinancial Assets to an Institutionally Related Foundation

37. Corporation sends dental supplies to University Foundation to be used by students in University's dental clinic. University Foundation's bylaws state that it is organized for the purpose of stimulating voluntary financial support from alumni and other donors for the benefit of University, especially for addressing the long-term academic priorities of University. As with most gifts it receives, University Foundation can choose the timing of the distribution to University and can place additional limitations on the distribution if those limitations are consistent with Corporation's restrictions. University does not control University Foundation.

38. University Foundation recognizes the fair value of the dental supplies (nonfinancial assets) as an increase in assets and as contribution revenue that increases temporarily restricted net assets because University and University Foundation are financially interrelated organizations (paragraph 14). University can influence the financial and operating decisions of University Foundation because the bylaws of University Foundation limit its activities to those that benefit University (paragraph 13(a)). University has an ongoing economic interest in the net assets of University Foundation because the results of University Foundation's activities accrue to the benefit of University (paragraph 13(b)). When University Foundation distributes the dental supplies to University, it reduces its assets and recognizes an expense and the expiration of the restriction.

39. Periodically, in conjunction with preparing its financial statements, University recognizes the change in its interest in the net assets of University Foundation, which would include the gift of nonfinancial assets received by the foundation (paragraph 15). Because payments from University Foundation are due in future periods, the increase (or decrease) in University's interest would be classified as a change in temporarily restricted net assets unless donors placed

Transfers of Assets to a Not-for-Profit **FAS136**
Organization or Charitable Trust That Raises
or Holds Contributions for Others

permanent restrictions on their gifts (footnote 6 to paragraph 15). When the dental supplies and other assets are distributed to it, University would recognize the assets received and decrease its interest in the net assets of University Foundation.[8]

40. If, instead, University controlled University Foundation, University would be able to access at will any assets held by University Foundation. Implying a time restriction on the gifts held by University Foundation would be inappropriate. When recognizing the change in its interest in University Foundation, University would report the resulting net assets in the same net asset classifications as University Foundation.

Example 6—Cash Gift to a Healthcare Foundation That Supports Three Affiliated Organizations

41. Corporation transfers cash to Healthcare Foundation and requests that Healthcare Foundation use the gift to provide healthcare benefits to the community. Healthcare Foundation's bylaws state that it is organized for the purpose of stimulating voluntary financial support from donors for the benefit of Hospital, Nursing Home, and Walk-in Clinic, all of which are located in the community. Hospital, Nursing Home, Walk-in Clinic, and Healthcare Foundation are affiliates that are controlled by Healthcare System.

42. Healthcare Foundation would recognize cash and contribution revenue that increases unrestricted net assets because Corporation did not specify a beneficiary for its gift. Healthcare Foundation can choose how to distribute the gift among the three affiliates (paragraph 69).

43. Periodically, in conjunction with preparing their financial statements, Hospital, Nursing Home, and Walk-in Clinic recognize the changes in their interests in the net assets of Healthcare Foundation (paragraph 15). When measuring its interest in Healthcare Foundation, each affiliate would include only the net assets of Healthcare Foundation that are restricted to that affiliate's use. None of them would include in

their individual interest the net assets resulting from the gift received from Corporation because Healthcare Foundation can choose how to distribute the gift among the three affiliates. Healthcare System would include the net assets resulting from the gift received from Corporation, as well as other changes in the net assets of Healthcare Foundation, in its interest in the net assets of the foundation.[9]

44. If Healthcare Foundation, Hospital, Nursing Home, and Walk-in Clinic entered into an agreement that specified how unrestricted gifts to Healthcare Foundation should be divided, each affiliate would also include its share of Healthcare Foundation's unrestricted net assets, computed in accordance with that agreement, when it measured its interest in Healthcare Foundation. Similarly, if Healthcare System directed that unrestricted gifts to Healthcare Foundation be distributed to the three affiliates in accordance with a specified formula, each affiliate would include its share of unrestricted net assets, computed in accordance with that formula, when it measured its interest in Healthcare Foundation.

45. If Corporation had specified that its gift be used for the benefit of Walk-in Clinic rather than giving without restriction, Healthcare Foundation would recognize contribution revenue that increases temporarily restricted net assets because Hospital, Nursing Home, Walk-in Clinic, and Healthcare Foundation are financially interrelated organizations (paragraph 14). Their relationship meets both requirements of paragraph 13. Hospital, Nursing Home, and Walk-in Clinic can influence the financial and operating decisions of Healthcare Foundation because all four organizations are under common control and the bylaws of Healthcare Foundation limit its activities to support of its three affiliates (paragraph 13(a)). Hospital, Nursing Home, and Walk-in Clinic each have an ongoing economic interest in the net assets of Healthcare Foundation because their rights to the assets held by Healthcare Foundation are residual rights in an ongoing relationship (paragraph 13(b)). Walk-in Clinic would include the net assets resulting from the gift received from Corporation in its interest in the net assets of Healthcare Foundation.

---

[8]The provisions of this Statement do not apply to University if University is a governmental entity. The Governmental Accounting Standards Board sets standards for those entities.

[9]An interest in the net assets of an affiliate would be eliminated if that affiliate were included in the consolidated financial statements of the interest holder.

Example 7—Cash Gift to a Foundation That Supports Two Unaffiliated Not-for-Profit Organizations

46. Individual transfers cash to Arts Foundation and specifies that the money be used to support the expenses of the ballet. Arts Foundation's bylaws state that it is organized for the purpose of stimulating voluntary financial support from donors for the benefit of Community Ballet and Community Theater. At the time Arts Foundation was created, the three organizations entered into an agreement that specifies that if a donor does not specify the organization to which the gift should be transferred, the gift will be split equally between Community Ballet and Community Theater. The agreement also specifies that (a) representatives from the three organizations will meet annually and determine campaign priorities for the next year and (b) the costs of operating Arts Foundation will be equally split between Community Ballet and Community Theater. Arts Foundation is not controlled by Community Ballet, Community Theater, or Individual.

47. Arts Foundation would report assets and contribution revenue that increases temporarily restricted net assets because Community Ballet and Arts Foundation are financially interrelated organizations (paragraph 14). Community Ballet has the ability to influence the operating and financial decisions of Arts Foundation because the agreement allows Community Ballet to participate in the policymaking processes of Arts Foundation (paragraph 13(a)). The agreement also establishes Community Ballet's rights as residual rights because it specifies how the revenues and expenses of Arts Foundation will be shared (paragraph 13(b)). When Arts Foundation distributes assets to Community Ballet, it reduces its assets and recognizes an expense.

48. Periodically, in conjunction with preparing their financial statements, Community Ballet and Community Theater recognize the changes in their interests in the net assets of Arts Foundation (paragraph 15). Community Ballet would include the net assets resulting from the gift received from Individual in its interest in the net assets of Arts Foundation because Individual specified that the gift be used to support the ballet and Arts Foundation's bylaws limit it to supporting Community Ballet. Community Ballet would also include in its interest all other gifts restricted to its benefit and its share of unrestricted net assets. Because payments from Arts Foundation are due in future periods, the increase (or decrease) in

Community Ballet's interest would be classified as a change in temporarily restricted net assets unless donors placed permanent restrictions on their gifts (footnote 6 to paragraph 15). When assets are distributed to Community Ballet, it recognizes the assets received and decreases its interest in the net assets of Arts Foundation.

49. In contrast to this example, some foundations and associations raise contributions for a large number of unaffiliated not-for-profit organizations (often referred to as member organizations). By virtue of their numbers, those member organizations generally do not individually influence the operating and financial decisions of the foundation (or association). Thus, any one member organization and the foundation (or association) are not financially interrelated organizations (paragraph 13(a)). Because the organizations are not financially interrelated, the foundation (or association) recognizes a liability if a donor to the foundation (or association) specifies that the gift should be transferred to a particular member organization (paragraph 11). The specified member organization would recognize a receivable and contribution revenue that increases temporarily restricted net assets unless the donor specified a permanent restriction or it was clear that the donor intended the gift to support activities of the current period (paragraph 15 and footnote 6).

Example 8—Gift of a Nonfinancial Asset to a Federated Fundraising Organization for Transfer to Another Not-for-Profit Organization

50. Individual transfers a car to Federated Fundraising Organization and requests that the car be transferred to Local Daycare Center. Individual specifies that Federated Fundraising Organization may use the car for one year before transferring it to Local Daycare Center. Local Daycare Center is a member organization of Federated Fundraising Organization, but that status does not confer any ability to actively participate in the policymaking processes of Federated Fundraising Organization.

51. Because Federated Fundraising Organization and Local Daycare Center are not financially interrelated organizations, Federated Fundraising Organization would recognize the car as an asset and a liability to Local Daycare Center if its policy were to recognize nonfinancial assets; otherwise, it would recognize neither the nonfinancial assets nor a liability (paragraph 11). If, instead of refusing the gift of the use of the car, Federated Fundraising Organization decides to use it for a year before transfer-

Transfers of Assets to a Not-for-Profit   **FAS136**
Organization or Charitable Trust That Raises
or Holds Contributions for Others

ring it to Local Daycare Center, Federated Fundraising Organization would recognize the fair value of the gift of one-year's use of the car in accordance with paragraph 8 of Statement 116. (The use of a car is a contributed asset and not a contributed service.)

52. Local Daycare Center would recognize a receivable and contribution revenue that increases temporarily restricted net assets (paragraph 15). It would measure the contribution received at the fair value of the car; however, if Federated Fundraising Organization chooses to use the car for a year before transferring it, the fair value would be reduced accordingly.

Example 9—Transfer of Assets from a Not-for-Profit Organization to a Community Foundation to Establish an Endowment for the Benefit of the Not-for-Profit Organization

53. Symphony Orchestra receives a large unrestricted gift of securities from Individual. Because it has no investment expertise, Symphony Orchestra transfers the securities to Community Foundation to establish an endowment fund. The agreement between Symphony Orchestra and Community Foundation states that the transfer is irrevocable and that the transferred assets will not be returned to Symphony Orchestra. However, Community Foundation will make annual distributions of the income earned on the endowment fund, subject to Community Foundation's spending policy. The agreement also permits Community Foundation to substitute another beneficiary in the place of Symphony Orchestra if Symphony Orchestra ceases to exist or if the governing board of Community Foundation votes that support of Symphony Orchestra (a) is no longer necessary or (b) is inconsistent with the needs of the community. (That is, Symphony Orchestra explicitly grants variance power to Community Foundation.) The agreement does not permit either organization to appoint members to the other organization's governing board or otherwise participate in the policy-making processes of the other.

54. Community Foundation would recognize the fair value of the transferred securities as an increase in investments and a liability to Symphony Orchestra because Symphony Orchestra transferred assets to Community Foundation and specified itself as beneficiary (paragraph 17(d)). The transfer is not an equity transaction because Community Foundation and Symphony Orchestra are not financially interrelated organizations (paragraph 18(b)). Sym-

phony Orchestra is unable to influence the operating or financial decisions of Community Foundation (paragraph 13(a)).

55. Symphony Orchestra would recognize the fair value of the gift of securities from Individual as contribution revenue. When it transfers the securities to Community Foundation, it would recognize the transfer as a decrease in investments and an increase in an asset, for example, as a beneficial interest in assets held by Community Foundation (paragraph 17(d)). Also, Symphony Orchestra would disclose in its financial statements the identity of Community Foundation, the terms under which Community Foundation will distribute amounts to Symphony Orchestra, a description of the variance power granted to Community Foundation, and the aggregate amount reported in the statement of financial position and how that amount is described (paragraph 19).

56. In this example, Symphony Orchestra would recognize an asset and Community Foundation would recognize a liability because the transaction is deemed to be reciprocal (paragraph 96). Symphony Orchestra transfers its securities to Community Foundation in exchange for future distributions. Community Foundation, by its acceptance of the transfer, agrees that at the time of the transfer distributions to Symphony Orchestra are capable of fulfillment and consistent with the foundation's mission. Although the value of those future distributions may not be commensurate with the value of the securities given up (because Symphony Orchestra is at risk of cessation of the distributions), the transaction is accounted for as though those values are commensurate. In comparison, the donors to Community Foundation in Example 2 explicitly grant variance power to Community Foundation in a nonreciprocal transfer. In that example, it is clear that the donors have made a contribution because they retain no beneficial interests in the transferred assets. Because the donors in Example 2 explicitly grant variance power to Community Foundation, it, rather than City Botanical Society, is the recipient of that contribution.

Example 10—Transfer of Investments from a Not-for-Profit Organization to a Foundation It Creates to Hold Those Assets

57. The governing board of Private Elementary School creates a foundation to hold and manage the school's investments. It transfers its investment portfolio to the newly created PES Foundation. An agreement between Private Elementary School and PES

Foundation allows the school to request distributions from both the original investments and the return on those investments, subject to approval by the governing board of PES Foundation, which will not be unreasonably withheld. The agreement also permits Private Elementary School to transfer additional investments in the future.

58. PES Foundation would recognize the fair value of the investments as assets and a liability to Private Elementary School because Private Elementary School transferred assets to PES Foundation and specified itself as beneficiary (paragraph 17(d)). The transfer of assets is not an equity transaction because Private Elementary School expects repayment of the transferred assets, and thus the transaction does not meet the criterion in paragraph 18(c).

59. Private Elementary School would decrease its investments and recognize another asset, for example, a beneficial interest in assets held by PES Foundation (paragraph 17(d)). Also, Private Elementary School would disclose in its financial statements the identity of PES Foundation, the terms of the agreement under which it can receive future distributions, including the fact that the distributions are not subject to variance power, and the aggregate amount reported in the statement of financial position and how that amount is described (paragraph 19).

Appendix B

BACKGROUND INFORMATION AND BASIS FOR CONCLUSIONS

CONTENTS

Transfers of Assets to a Not-for-Profit **FAS136**
Organization or Charitable Trust That Raises
or Holds Contributions for Others

Appendix B

BACKGROUND INFORMATION AND BASIS FOR CONCLUSIONS

Introduction

60. This appendix summarizes considerations that Board members deemed significant in reaching the conclusions in this Statement. It includes reasons for accepting certain approaches and rejecting others. Individual Board members gave greater weight to some factors than to others.

Background Information

61. The Board issued FASB Statement No. 116, *Accounting for Contributions Received and Contributions Made,* in June 1993. In May 1995, at the request of several community foundations and other interested parties, the Board decided to provide an interpretation of paragraph 4 of Statement 116 to address whether a transfer of assets from a donor to a community foundation is a contribution received by the community foundation if the donor (a) directs the foundation to distribute the transferred assets, the return on investment of those assets, or both to a specified beneficiary and (b) grants the foundation variance power to redirect the use of the transferred assets away from the specified beneficiary.

62. Subsequently, other not-for-profit organizations, including federated fundraising organizations and institutionally related foundations, asked the Board to expand the scope of the project to describe the circumstances in which they could report contributions received for transfers of assets that ultimately would be transferred to another organization. Some organizations, particularly federated fundraising organizations and institutionally related foundations, said that if paragraph 4 of Statement 116 were interpreted in a broad way, many or most of their current activities no longer would be accounted for as contributions received and contributions made. They asserted that recording only some of their fundraising activities as contributions received would understate the amounts raised, result in misleading financial statements, and render meaningless many key financial ratios used in the industry. The Board considered the concerns expressed by those organizations and decided to address the applicability of paragraph 4 of Statement 116 for all not-for-profit organizations that receive and distribute assets for charitable purposes.

63. In December 1995, the Board issued an Exposure Draft of a proposed Interpretation, *Transfers of Assets in Which a Not-for-Profit Organization Acts as an Agent, Trustee, or Intermediary.* That Exposure Draft would have clarified the use of the terms *agent, trustee,* and *intermediary* in Statement 116. The Board received 115 comment letters on the Exposure Draft. The Board considered the concerns raised by respondents at several public meetings. In September 1996, the Board issued FASB Interpretation No. 42, *Accounting for Transfers of Assets in Which a Notfor-Profit Organization Is Granted Variance Power,* which had a narrower scope than that of the Exposure Draft. Interpretation 42 clarified that an organization that receives assets acts as a donee and a donor, rather than as an agent, trustee, or intermediary, if the donor specifies an unaffiliated beneficiary or beneficiaries and explicitly grants the recipient organization variance power, that is, grants the unilateral power to redirect the use of the assets away from the specified beneficiary or beneficiaries. With only minor editorial changes, the guidance in that Interpretation is incorporated in paragraph 12 of this Statement.

64. Concurrent with its decision to issue Interpretation 42, the Board also agreed to consider the following three situations in a second phase of the project: (a) accounting by a recipient organization that is not granted variance power, (b) accounting by a beneficiary if a donor transfers assets to a recipient organization and specifies that the assets must be conveyed to the beneficiary or used for its benefit, and (c) accounting for transfers in which the resource provider and the beneficiary are the same party.

65. In July 1998, the Board issued an Exposure Draft of a proposed Statement, *Transfers of Assets involving a Not-for-Profit Organization That Raises or Holds Contributions for Others.* The Board received over 450 comment letters from representatives of over 280 entities. Most respondents commented only on the issue of accounting by agents and intermediaries; the majority of them were federated fundraising organizations. The concerns raised by respondents were considered by the Board at four public meetings. The redeliberation of the issues addressed by this Statement did not result in substantive changes in the proposed requirements; however, disclosure requirements, clarifications, and illustrative guidance were added. The Board concluded that it could reach an informed decision on the basis of existing information without a public hearing.

Basis for Conclusions

66. Paragraph 4 of Statement 116 states that that Statement does not apply in situations in which an organization acts as an agent, trustee, or intermediary between two or more other parties but is not itself a donee and donor. Paragraphs 52–54 and 175 of Statement 116, as well as Examples 2–5 in paragraphs 177–181 of Statement 116, indicate the Board's intentions. Those examples focus on an organization that is both a trustee and a donee (Example 2), an organization that is an agent for the receipt of goods (Example 3), an organization that facilitates a transfer of assets between other parties and is neither a donee nor a donor (Example 4), and an organization that is an intermediary in processing a transfer payment between other parties (Example 5).

Recipient Organizations

Intermediary

67. In general usage, the term intermediary encompasses a broad range of situations in which an organization acts between two or more other parties. In some of those situations, the organization may be both a donee (when it receives a gift) and a donor (when it makes a gift to a beneficiary). In other situations, the organization does not itself receive or make a gift, but it may be a facilitator, conduit, agent, or trustee between a donor and a donee. The use of the term intermediary in paragraph 4 of Statement 116 is not intended to preclude charitable and other not-for-profit organizations from accounting for transfers of assets they receive and transfers of assets they make as contributions if they are donees and donors. Instead, the use of the term intermediary in Statement 116 is narrow and specific and refers to situations in which an organization facilitates the transfer of assets but does not itself receive or make a gift.

Agent and trustee

68. In some agency and some trustee arrangements, a resource provider has not made a gift because it can derive future economic benefit from the transferred assets. In other cases, it is clear that the resource provider is a donor and has made a gift; however, it may not be clear who the donee is because the donor transfers the assets to the recipient organization but specifies another entity as beneficiary of the gift. A donor may specify the beneficiary (a) by name, (b) by stating that all entities that meet a set of donor-defined criteria are beneficiaries, or (c) by actions surrounding the transfer that make clear the identity of the beneficiary, such as by responding to a request from an organization that exists to raise assets for the beneficiary. Because paragraph 53 of Statement 116 states that "the recipient of assets who is an agent or trustee has *little or no discretion* in determining how the assets transferred will be used" (emphasis added), the Board considered whether a recipient organization can recognize a contribution received if its discretion is limited by the donor's specification of a beneficiary.

69. By contrasting three situations, paragraphs 53 and 54 of Statement 116 indicate the Board's view that an organization has discretion sufficient to recognize a contribution received if it can choose the beneficiaries of the assets. Paragraph 53 describes two situations that may be agency transactions: (a) a recipient organization that receives cash that it must disburse to all that meet guidelines specified by the resource provider or return the cash and (b) a recipient organization that receives cash that it must disburse to individuals identified by the resource provider or return the cash. Paragraph 54 contrasts those two situations to a situation in which ". . . the resource provider allows the recipient to establish, define, and carry out the programs that disburse the cash, products, or services to the recipient's beneficiaries. . . ." In that latter situation, Statement 116 specifies that ". . . the recipient generally is involved in receiving and making contributions" (paragraph 54). Thus, if a donor uses broad generalizations to describe beneficiaries or to indicate a field of interest, such as Midwestern flood victims, homeless individuals, or teenaged children, the recipient organization has the ability to choose the beneficiaries of the assets and is a donee.

70. Similarly, the recipient organization has the ability to choose the beneficiaries if neither the language used by the donor nor the representations of the recipient organization cause the donor to believe that it can direct the gift to a specified beneficiary. For example, a recipient organization might request that a donor indicate an organization that best serves the needs of the community and tell the donor that the information will be considered by the allocation committee when it makes its distributions to community organizations. If that request is conveyed in a manner that leads a donor to reasonably conclude that its role is merely to propose a possible allocation, the recipient organization has the discretion to choose the beneficiary of the assets.

Transfers of Assets to a Not-for-Profit **FAS136**
Organization or Charitable Trust That Raises
or Holds Contributions for Others

71. Conversely, if that request is conveyed in a manner that creates a donor's reasonable expectation that the gift will be used for the benefit of or will be transferred to the indicated beneficiary, the recipient organization does not have discretion to choose the beneficiary unless the donor explicitly grants variance power. Paragraph 2 of Interpretation 42 stated that "a recipient organization that is directed by a resource provider to distribute the transferred assets . . . to a specified third-party beneficiary acts as a donee and a donor . . . if the resource provider explicitly grants the recipient organization the unilateral power to redirect the use of the transferred assets to another beneficiary" (footnote reference omitted).

72. The Board considered whether discretion to determine the timing of the distribution to the specified beneficiary, by itself, gives the recipient organization discretion sufficient to recognize a contribution. The Board concluded that that limited discretion is not sufficient. The ability to choose a payment date does not relieve an entity from its obligation to pay.

Meeting the definition of a liability

73. To qualify as a liability of a recipient organization, an agreement to transfer assets to the beneficiary specified by the donor must obligate the recipient organization, leaving it little or no discretion to avoid a future sacrifice of assets without significant penalty. FASB Concepts Statement No. 6, *Elements of Financial Statements,* states, "Liabilities are probable future sacrifices of economic benefits arising from present obligations of a particular entity to transfer assets or provide services to other entities in the future as a result of past transactions or events" (paragraph 35; footnote references omitted).

74. The Board concluded that when a recipient organization accepts assets from a donor and agrees to use them on behalf of or transfer them to a beneficiary specified by the donor, the recipient organization assumes an obligation that meets the definition of a liability unless the donor explicitly grants variance power. The recipient organization represents to the donor that it will deliver the assets, the return on investment of those assets, or both to the beneficiary specified by the donor. The donor relies on that representation and expects the recipient organization to carry out its duties in due course or at the time specified by the donor. Thus, unless the recipient organization explicitly reserves a right to do so, it cannot, at its own discretion, avoid its transfer to the specified beneficiary or make the transfer to a different beneficiary.

The donor has a right to expect that the assets will be transferred to the specified beneficiary in the future, and the recipient organization has a social and moral obligation, and most likely a legal obligation, to make the transfer. Consequently, if it is the donor's understanding that the recipient organization will transfer the contributed assets to its intended beneficiary, that beneficiary, not the recipient organization, has received the contribution.

75. The Board concluded that a representation made to a donor to transfer assets to a specified beneficiary differs from other representations made to donors when accepting gifts, such as representations to use assets in a particular program or to buy a fixed asset. That second type of representation (a donor-imposed restriction) is a fiduciary responsibility, and ". . . a not-for-profit organization's fiduciary responsibility to use assets to provide services to beneficiaries does not itself create a duty of the organization to pay cash, transfer other assets, or provide services to one or more creditors" (Concepts Statement 6, paragraph 57). The donor's identification of a specific beneficiary to which the assets must be transferred differentiates the transaction from time- and purpose-restricted contributions and makes the recipient organization's representation to the donor one that constitutes a present obligation of the recipient organization to another entity.

Meeting the definition of an asset

76. To qualify as an asset of the recipient organization, an asset received from a donor must provide a recipient organization with a future economic benefit that it can control. Concepts Statement 6 states, "Assets are probable future economic benefits obtained or controlled by a particular entity as a result of past transactions or events" (paragraph 25; footnote reference omitted).

77. The Board concluded that a recipient organization should recognize an asset because it has the ability to obtain and control the future economic benefits of the assets transferred to it, albeit temporarily. The recipient organization has an asset because, until it must transfer cash to the beneficiary, it can invest the cash received, use it to pay other liabilities or to purchase goods or services, or otherwise use the cash for its own purposes. Similarly, most financial assets received also can be temporarily used for the recipient organization's own purposes. Those assets should be recognized in the financial statements along with the liability to transfer the assets to the specified beneficiary.

78. However, the nature of nonfinancial assets (for example, land, buildings, use of facilities or utilities, materials and supplies, intangible assets, or services) usually limits the ability of an intermediary or agent to use the assets for its own benefit before it transfers them to the beneficiary. For example, fiduciary responsibilities of the intermediary or agent prevent it from using the assets if they are of a type that could be used up or would diminish in value if used. Also, if the assets are nonfinancial assets, the intermediary or agent is likely to deliver to the beneficiary the same assets that it received from the donor. Thus, any changes in the value of those assets during the holding period would accrue to the beneficiary (rather than the intermediary or agent). Additionally, excluding nonfinancial assets from the recognition requirement also has the practical effect of relieving an intermediary or agent from the burden of obtaining fair values for food, supplies, and similar items that it holds only for a short time.

79. The Board decided to permit, but not require, the recipient organizations described in paragraphs 8 and 11 of this Statement to recognize transferred nonfinancial assets and the liability to transfer those nonfinancial assets to the specified beneficiary. Several respondents to the Exposure Draft commented on reporting nonfinancial assets; half of them agreed with the Board's conclusions. The majority of the respondents that disagreed said that recipient organizations should recognize all nonfinancial assets that they hold. The Board acknowledges that a standard that permits, but does not require, the recognition of nonfinancial assets may result in reporting that excludes some items from the statement of financial position even though they are assets of the recipient organization because it can temporarily obtain some economic benefits from those items. However, a standard that requires recognition of all nonfinancial assets might result in inclusion of items in the statement of financial position that do not meet the definition of an asset in Concepts Statement 6 because the recipient organization does not control any economic benefits from those items; thus, that standard, also, would arguably be flawed. The Board was not convinced that requiring recognition of all nonfinancial assets would be preferable, and it decided to retain the conclusions of the Exposure Draft.

80. The Board considered whether recipient organizations that are trustees of charitable trusts should recognize an asset and a liability for trust assets but decided that this Statement should not establish standards for accounting by trustees. The Board specified two reasons for that decision. First, a recipient organization that is a trustee may not have an asset because a trustee's ability to obtain the benefits of trust assets is usually significantly limited by its fiduciary responsibilities and by the trust agreement. For example, the trust agreement often requires separate identification of trust property, defines permissible investments, and describes allocation of investment return. Second, current financial reporting requirements for trustees that are banks differ from requirements for trustees that are not-for-profit organizations,[10] primarily in the area of whether the trustees include the assets and liabilities of trusts in their own financial statements. A separate project on consolidated financial statements is expected to provide guidance for determining when, if ever, a trustee controls a trust and should include the assets and liabilities of the trust in its consolidated financial statements.

81. Only a few respondents to the Exposure Draft commented on the exclusion of standards for trustees, and none of those respondents indicated that the existing guidance needed improvement. One respondent asked whether the Board intended to exclude certain not-for-profit organizations from the scope of this Statement by its decision to exclude standards for trustees. That respondent explained that in some states not-for-profit organizations are organized under trust law rather than as corporations. Those organizations are not trustees as described in paragraph 9 of this Statement because, under those statutes, they hold assets "in trust" for the community or some other broadly described group, rather than for a specific beneficiary. Thus, those organizations are included within the scope of this Statement.

Transfers in which the donor grants variance power

82. This Statement supersedes Interpretation 42 and incorporates its conclusions without reconsideration. Paragraphs 12–15 of the basis for conclusions of that Interpretation are also incorporated as paragraphs 83–86 of this Statement.

83. The Board concluded that an organization that receives assets has discretion sufficient to recognize a

---

[10]Chapter 6 of the AICPA Audit and Accounting Guide, *Not-for-Profit Organizations,* describes those requirements.

Transfers of Assets to a Not-for-Profit
Organization or Charitable Trust That Raises
or Holds Contributions for Others

FAS136

contribution received if it can choose the beneficiary of the assets. For example, if a donor instructs a recipient organization to use the assets only within a particular field of interest, the recipient organization has discretion to choose a specific beneficiary and, accordingly, has received a contribution. In interpreting the application of Statement 116 to situations in which a donor specifies an unaffiliated beneficiary, the Board concluded that a recipient organization can choose the beneficiary if the donor explicitly grants the recipient organization variance power, that is, the power to override the donor's instructions without approval by another party.

84. A recipient organization may obtain the power to redirect the use of assets transferred to it through various means, including standard provisions in donor-choice forms or explicit donor stipulation in gift instruments. For example, community foundations may obtain the unilateral power to redirect the use of assets transferred to them through explicit reference to the variance power granted to them by donors in written gift instruments. The variance power may be explicitly referred to in the terms of the gift instrument and further explained in the community foundation's declaration of trust, articles of incorporation, or governing instruments. Variance power, required by the U.S. Treasury Regulations for trust-form community foundations, is described in those Regulations as the power to

> . . . modify any restriction or condition on the distribution of funds for any specified charitable purposes or to specified organizations if in the sole judgment of the governing body (without the necessity of the approval of any participating trustee, custodian, or agent), such restriction or condition becomes, in effect, unnecessary, incapable of fulfillment, or inconsistent with the charitable needs of the community or area served. [1.170A–9(e)(11)(v)(B)(1)]

85. Some say that variance power, as described in the U.S. Treasury Regulations, is conditional. They say that until a change in circumstances occurs and the recipient organization exercises its power to redirect the use of the assets transferred by the donor, the recipient organization should not recognize a contribution (or revenue) because it does not control the future economic benefits of the transferred assets. Some also say that organizations use variance power infrequently because use of that power is typically conditioned on a change in circumstances.

86. The Board believes that while variance power, as described in the U.S. Treasury Regulations, has the appearance of being conditional, the asserted "condition" is not effective because (a) the condition can be substantially met solely by a declaration of the governing board of the recipient organization that states that a distribution to a specified beneficiary is unnecessary, incapable of fulfillment, or inconsistent with the charitable needs of the community or organizations being served and (b) the variance power is unilateral—exercise of the power does not require approval from the donor, beneficiary, or any other interested party. The Board concluded that an organization that is explicitly granted variance power has the ability to use assets it receives to further its own purpose—meeting community needs—from the date it accepts the assets. In that situation, the recipient organization should account for receipt of funds by recognizing an asset and corresponding contribution revenue. Respondents to the December 1995 Exposure Draft generally agreed with the Board's conclusion that an organization that is explicitly granted variance power has sufficient discretion to recognize assets and contribution revenue.

87. The Board's conclusions about transactions in which a resource provider grants variance power but specifies itself or its affiliate, rather than a third party, as beneficiary are discussed in paragraph 96.

Beneficiaries

88. The Board considered whether a beneficiary's rights to the assets transferred to a recipient organization should be recognized as an asset of the beneficiary. The Board concluded that the beneficiary should recognize those rights as an asset if the recipient organization is not explicitly granted variance power. Clearly, unless the donor grants variance power, the recipient organization's representation to the donor that it will transfer the assets to the specified beneficiary is evidence of a probable future benefit to that beneficiary. The donor expects that the recipient organization will deliver and that the specified beneficiary will receive the assets it transferred. In addition, the recipient organization has a social and moral obligation, and most likely a legal obligation, to deliver the assets to the beneficiary. That obligation provides the beneficiary with the ability to obtain the future benefit of the assets. (An obligation may not exist if the recipient organization and the specified beneficiary are financially interrelated organizations. Refer to paragraphs 98–104.) Finally, unless

the recipient organization is explicitly granted variance power, the event that gives rise to the beneficiary's rights (the acceptance of the assets from the donor and the representation that they will be transferred to the specified beneficiary) has already occurred.

89. In contrast, the Board concluded that if the recipient organization is explicitly granted variance power, the specified beneficiary does not have a right that meets the criteria for recognition in financial statements. Because variance power is defined as a unilateral power, another beneficiary can be substituted without the permission of the donor, the specified beneficiary, or any other interested party. Thus, the specified beneficiary is unable to control others' access to the future economic benefits of the assets held by the recipient organization. Further, because the recipient organization can change the beneficiary at will, no past event giving rise to a beneficiary's right has occurred and none will occur until the recipient organization promises to give the transferred assets to the specified beneficiary. Thus, the specified beneficiary's potential for future distributions from the assets held by the recipient organization does not meet the definition of an asset.

90. Most respondents to the Exposure Draft that commented about beneficiary reporting agreed with the Board's conclusions. However, several of those that disagreed expressed concerns about the administrative burdens of identifying assets that are held by recipient organizations for the beneficiary. In addition, many respondents that act as recipient organizations expressed concerns about the burden of notifying beneficiaries of the amounts of assets they hold. The Board believes that in most instances recipient organizations tend to raise resources on an ongoing basis for a select group of beneficiaries. Thus, specified beneficiaries generally are aware of the efforts of recipient organizations, and the ongoing relationships between the organizations usually enable the beneficiaries to request and receive the information that they need for the preparation of their annual (or quarterly) financial statements. Although systems may need to be enhanced to gather or provide information on a more timely basis, the Board believes that the basic systems generally are in place.

Relationships between Resource Providers, Recipient Organizations, and Beneficiaries

91. Relationships between two or more of the parties—resource provider (or donor), recipient or-

ganization, and beneficiary—may indicate that a recipient organization's role differs from that of an agent (paragraph 10). The Board decided that to ensure comparable accounting between similar organizations, it was necessary to consider the three specific situations that are discussed in paragraphs 92–104.

Relationship between a resource provider and a recipient organization

92. If a resource provider transfers assets to a recipient organization that it controls and directs that recipient organization to transfer the assets to a specified beneficiary, the resource provider, by virtue of its control over the recipient organization, has the ability to revoke the transfer or to substitute another beneficiary or another purpose for the transferred assets. Because the resource provider retains control of the transferred assets, it has not made a contribution. The Board concluded that until the transferred assets are beyond the control of the resource provider, the transaction should be reported as an asset by the resource provider and a liability by the recipient organization (for example, as a refundable advance).

93. Some respondents to the Exposure Draft asked the Board to provide a definition of control. The Board declined to do so in this Statement. Several definitions of control exist. For the purposes of FASB Statement No. 57, *Related Party Disclosures,* control is defined as "the possession, direct or indirect, of the power to direct or cause the direction of the management and policies of an enterprise through ownership, by contract, or otherwise" (paragraph 24(b)). AICPA Statement of Position 94-3, *Reporting of Related Entities by Not-for-Profit Organizations,* has a similar definition; it defines control as "the direct or indirect ability to determine the direction of management and policies through ownership, contract, or otherwise" (glossary). The guidance in those documents should be considered when determining whether one entity controls another. In February 1999, the Board issued an Exposure Draft, *Consolidated Financial Statements: Purpose and Policy,* which defines control as "the ability of an entity to direct the policies and management that guide the ongoing activities of another entity so as to increase its benefits and limit its losses from that other entity's activities" (paragraph 6(a)). If the provisions of that Exposure Draft are adopted, its definition of control will supersede those in Statement 57 and SOP 94-3.

Transfers of Assets to a Not-for-Profit **FAS136**
Organization or Charitable Trust That Raises
or Holds Contributions for Others

Relationship between a resource provider and a
beneficiary

94. The Board decided that if a resource provider and a specified beneficiary are one and the same or if they are affiliates (as defined in Statement 57, paragraph 24(a)), the transfer of assets to the recipient organization differs from one in which a resource provider specifies an unaffiliated beneficiary. If a resource provider and a beneficiary are neither the same nor affiliated, the resource provider retains no future economic benefit in the assets transferred and a contribution has been made. However, if a resource provider specifies itself or its affiliate as the beneficiary, it retains a future economic benefit in the transferred assets. Because the transfer of assets is not a nonreciprocal transfer,[11] a contribution neither has been made by the resource provider nor has been received by the beneficiary. The Board concluded that the transfer should be reported as an exchange of an asset for another asset by the resource provider and as an asset and a liability by the recipient organization or as an equity transaction by both entities.

95. The Exposure Draft used the term *equity transfer* rather than *equity transaction.* Some respondents found the use of that term confusing because the AICPA Audit and Accounting Guide, *Health Care Organizations,* uses the term equity transfer to describe another type of transaction—one in which the transferor receives nothing of immediate economic value; for example, the transferor does not receive a financial interest or ownership. The transaction described in the healthcare organizations Guide may not meet the second of the three criteria in paragraph 18 of this Statement—the requirement that the resource provider and the recipient organization be financially interrelated organizations. Although the organizations meet the first requirement of paragraph 13 of this Statement (because the healthcare organizations Guide requires that the transferor and the transferee be affiliates), they may not meet the second requirement of that paragraph. To avoid confusion, the term in this Statement was changed from equity transfer to equity transaction.

96. If a resource provider transfers assets to a recipient organization and specifies itself or its affiliate as the beneficiary, the Board believes that a presump-

tion that the transfer is reciprocal, and therefore not a contribution, is necessary even if the resource provider explicitly grants the recipient organization variance power. At the time of the transfer, the resource provider expects to receive future distributions because it specifies itself or its affiliate as a beneficiary, and, by its acceptance of the transfer, the recipient organization agrees that distributions to the resource provider or its affiliate are capable of fulfillment and consistent with the recipient organization's mission. The value of those future distributions, however, may not be commensurate with the value of the transferred assets because the resource provider is at risk of cessation of the distributions as a result of its grant of variance power. If the values exchanged are not commensurate, in concept, the transfer is in part a contribution (paragraphs 3 and 51 of Statement 116). The Board decided that presuming that the entire transfer is reciprocal is preferable to requiring that a resource provider compute the contribution portion because that computation would require measuring the risk that the variance power would be exercised. Further, it is not clear whether a not-for-profit organization (resource provider) can grant a recipient organization the legally valid power to redirect the use of the transferred assets to another beneficiary if the not-for-profit organization originally received those assets with donors' restrictions on their use. The recipient organization might redirect the use of the assets in a way that could violate the resource provider's fiduciary responsibilities to its own donors. The Board decided that it is necessary to presume that the resource provider has retained the future economic benefits of the transferred assets.

97. Some respondents also asked about other transfers to affiliates that did not meet the criteria of either paragraph 17 or 18 of this Statement. The answers to those questions are beyond the scope of this Statement. This Statement sets standards only for transfers to a recipient organization that is not the beneficiary of the transferred assets.

Relationship between a recipient organization and
a beneficiary

98. The Board decided that if a beneficiary and a recipient organization are financially interrelated organizations, the recipient organization may not have

---

[11]Statement 116 defines *contribution* as "an unconditional transfer of cash or other assets to an entity or a settlement or cancellation of its liabilities in a voluntary nonreciprocal transfer by another entity acting other than as an owner" (paragraph 209). Statement 116 defines *nonreciprocal transfer* as "a transaction in which an entity incurs a liability or transfers an asset to another entity (or receives an asset or cancellation of a liability) without directly receiving (or giving) value in exchange" (paragraph 209).

a liability to deliver the transferred assets, the return on investment of those assets, or both to the beneficiary. Some respondents disagreed and said that a recipient organization should report a liability regardless of its relationship to the beneficiary. The Board concluded that because the beneficiary can influence the operating and financial decisions of the related recipient organization (or alternatively, the recipient organization can influence the operating and financial decisions of the beneficiary), their relationship differs from that of most debtors and creditors. In the absence of a donor's instruction to do otherwise, a related recipient organization often has the discretion to decide whether to transfer the assets to the beneficiary, to invest them and transfer only the investment return, or to spend them for a purpose that directly or indirectly benefits the beneficiary (including payment of the recipient organization's operating expenses). Further, the beneficiary generally does not attempt to compel delivery of the transferred assets if the recipient organization chooses to hold them. The beneficiary and its related recipient organization often have a collective mission—to best provide the philanthropic services of the beneficiary. They cooperate because they are more effective in achieving their missions when they work harmoniously. Thus, the nature of the relationship between the recipient organization and the beneficiary may permit the recipient organization to avoid the delivery of the transferred assets without significant penalty. If that is so, there is no present obligation to transfer assets or provide services in the future and no liability exists.

99. The Board attempted to define a set of criteria for agents, trustees, and intermediaries that would distinguish transactions that create liabilities from those that increase net assets (contribution revenue). It decided that the criteria being developed were overly complex and not operational. Instead, the Board decided that if a recipient organization and a beneficiary are financially interrelated organizations and the recipient organization is not a trustee, the recipient organization should recognize a contribution received, and the beneficiary should recognize its interest in the net assets of the recipient organization and subsequent changes in the value of that interest.

100. In some cases, the relationship between a beneficiary and a recipient organization is characterized by control in addition to an ongoing economic interest in net assets. If existing standards required consolidation whenever there is a control relationship,[12] then a contribution to either the beneficiary or the recipient organization would be a contribution to the consolidated entity and would be reflected in the consolidated financial statements. If the entities were consolidated, the question of whether the contribution should be recognized by the recipient organization or the beneficiary would be relevant only to separately issued financial statements of the controlled entity. The lack of standards requiring consolidation when a control relationship exists was a factor in the Board's decision to specifically address the relationship between the recipient organization and the beneficiary. Several respondents to the Exposure Draft said that the Board should defer establishing standards for financially interrelated organizations until after the completion of the Board's consolidations project. Because the guidance developed in this project is consistent with the proposed guidance in the consolidations project, the Board saw no compelling reason to delay the issuance of this Statement.

101. The Board considered whether special accounting should apply only to relationships between recipient organizations and beneficiaries that are characterized by control but determined that it would be inappropriate to base the approach on a definition of control that is currently under examination in the Board's project on consolidations. Some respondents to the Exposure Draft suggested that the Board could use *significant influence* rather than control as the basis for its approach. However, significant influence is described in APB Opinion No. 18, *The Equity Method of Accounting for Investments in Common Stock,* in terms of ownership of voting shares. Thus, it could not be applied easily and on a consistent basis to relationships between not-for-profit organizations. Instead, the Board chose to describe relationships that demonstrate one organization's ability to influence the operating and financial decisions of the other.

102. The Board also focused on relationships in which a beneficiary's rights to the assets held by the recipient organization are residual rights; that is, the value of those rights increases or decreases as a result of the investment, fundraising, operating, and other

---

[12]Paragraph 12 of SOP 94-3 and Chapter 11 of the healthcare organizations Guide permit but do not require consolidation if a not-for-profit organization controls another organization in which it has an economic interest and its control takes a form other than majority ownership or voting interest. Consolidation of related entities is required only in the circumstances described in paragraphs 10 and 11 of SOP 94-3 and in Chapter 11 of the healthcare organizations Guide.

Transfers of Assets to a Not-for-Profit
Organization or Charitable Trust That Raises
or Holds Contributions for Others

FAS136

activities of the recipient organization. Although the beneficiary may not have control of the recipient organization, its interest is essentially equivalent to a parent's residual interest in a subsidiary or an investor's residual interest if the investor has significant influence over the investee's operating and financial policies. In contrast, if a relationship between a beneficiary and a recipient organization is not characterized by an ongoing economic interest of a residual nature, the rights of a beneficiary are fixed or determinable and similar to those of a creditor.

103. The Board concluded that it is appropriate to use a method of accounting that, like the equity method of accounting, recognizes increases or decreases in the economic resources underlying the beneficiary's interest in the periods in which those changes are reflected in the accounts of the recipient organization. That method is appropriate because the cooperative relationship with the recipient organization allows the beneficiary to influence the operating or financial decisions of the recipient organization, and "The equity method tends to be most appropriate if an investment enables the investor to influence the operating or financial decisions of the investee" (Opinion 18, paragraph 12).

104. The Board noted that SOP 94-3 defines and provides examples of economic interest. Chapter 11 of the healthcare organizations Guide has the same definition and examples. Although most of the relationships described in that definition are potentially ongoing economic interests in the net assets, some do not meet the criterion in paragraph 13(b) of this Statement. Only economic interests that are both ongoing and residual interests in the net assets are ongoing economic interests in the net assets.

Disclosures

105. A few respondents to the Exposure Draft suggested that the Board require organizations to disclose the ratio of fundraising expenses to amounts raised. They expressed concern that a recipient organization might appear less efficient if the ratio was computed using contributions rather than total amounts raised as the denominator. The Board observed that not-for-profit organizations do not agree on how fundraising ratios should be computed or whether they should be required in financial statements. Rather than requiring a ratio and prescribing one method of computing it, which might appear to be an endorsement of that ratio as the best measure of fundraising efficiency, the Board decided

that if an organization chooses to include on the face of its statement of activities or in the notes to its financial statements a ratio of fundraising expenses to total amounts raised, it must describe how it computes that ratio.

106. Other respondents to the Exposure Draft suggested that specified beneficiaries should disclose information about legal or donor-imposed restrictions on the availability of assets held for them by recipient organizations. In most cases, the disclosures required by paragraphs 11 and 14 of FASB Statement No. 117, *Financial Statements of Not-for-Profit Organizations,* are sufficient. However, if an organization transfers assets to another and specifies itself or its affiliate as the beneficiary, the users of its financial statements might not be aware of additional limitations imposed by the terms of the agreement with the recipient organization. The Board believes that the disclosures specified in paragraph 19 of this Statement provide information that is useful in assessing management's stewardship and the organization's liquidity and exposure to risk.

107. A few respondents asked whether the disclosure requirements of paragraph 20 of Opinion 18 apply to beneficiaries that report their interests in the net assets of the recipient organization using a method similar to the equity method. The specific terms of those requirements are not particularly relevant because they are expressed in terms of the ownership of common stock of another entity. The Board decided that the disclosure requirements of SOP 94-3 are sufficient to provide the information that users of financial statements are likely to need.

Reporting Results of Fundraising Efforts in the Financial Statements

108. Recipient organizations that solicit and collect cash, products, or services and distribute those assets for charitable purposes have expressed concern that reporting less than 100 percent of the results of their fundraising efforts as contribution revenue would understate the magnitude of their central operations. The Board acknowledges the desire of those organizations to report the results of total campaign efforts to the users of financial statements. However, the Board believes that if a recipient organization is acting as an agent, trustee, or intermediary, the assets received are not its revenue. Although the receipt of the transferred assets is an inflow of assets from activities that constitute the entity's ongoing major or central

operations (and, thus, might seem to meet the definition of revenue in paragraph 78 of Concepts Statement 6), that inflow is accompanied by an offsetting liability to the specified beneficiary. Consequently, the receipt of the transferred assets is not revenue, just as a deposit to an escrow account (which is also an inflow of assets from activities that constitute the entity's major or central operations) is not revenue to the real estate agency that receives it.

109. To the extent that an organization's activities include raising and distributing cash, the total amounts raised and distributed may be evident from a statement of cash flows prepared using the direct method for reporting operating cash flows. In addition, generally accepted accounting principles do not preclude entities from providing supplementary information or additional disclosures. An organization may provide a schedule reflecting fundraising efforts or campaign accomplishments or may disclose total amounts raised on the statement of activities, provided that amounts raised in an agent, trustee, or intermediary capacity are not shown as revenues. The following illustration provides three possible methods of displaying fundraising efforts in the revenue section of the statement of activities. Methods 2 and 3 display the total amounts raised.

An organization raises $6,000 of contributions, $100 of other support, and $4,000 accounted for as agent, trustee, or intermediary transactions because donors have specified beneficiaries without granting variance power. Of the $4,000 accounted for as agent, trustee, or intermediary transactions, the organization pays out $3,600 to specified beneficiaries and retains $400 as its administrative fee.

Method 1

Contributions	$ 6,000
Other support	100
Total support	6,100
Administrative fees retained on amounts	
designated by donors for specific organizations	400
Total support and revenue	$ 6,500

Method 2

Contributions		$ 6,000
Other support		100
Total support		6,100
Other revenue:		
Amounts designated by donors for specific organizations	$4,000	
Less: Amounts held for or remitted to those organizations	3,600	
Administrative fees retained on amounts designated		
by donors for specific organizations		400
Total support and revenue		$ 6,500

Method 3

Total amounts raised*	$10,000
Less: Amounts designated by donors for specific organizations	4,000
Total contributions	6,000
Other revenue:	
Other support	100
Administrative fees retained on amounts designated by donors	
for specific organizations	400
Total support and revenue	$ 6,500

---

*Other terms, such as *campaign results* or *campaign efforts,* may be used.

Transfers of Assets to a Not-for-Profit   **FAS136**
Organization or Charitable Trust That Raises
or Holds Contributions for Others

The Board concluded that each of the methods reports the recipient organization's revenues ($6,500) in a way that is both easily understood by users of the financial statements and representationally faithful.

Effective Date and Transition

110. The Board decided that this Statement should be effective for financial statements issued for fiscal periods beginning after December 15, 1999, except for the provisions of paragraph 12, which already are effective because they are incorporated from Interpretation 42. A few respondents to the Exposure Draft said that organizations might have difficulty implementing this Statement by its proposed effective date, which was for fiscal years beginning after June 15, 1999. The Board believes that the revised effective date provides adequate time for entities to implement this Statement's provisions and for users of financial statements to understand how those provisions affect their analyses. Although the provisions of this Statement must be applied retroactively to appropriately reflect the interests of specified beneficiaries in endowment gifts held on their behalf by recipient organizations, the Board decided that the effect of applying the provisions could be reported either as a cumulative effect of a change in accounting principle or by restatement of prior years' information. The Board encourages earlier application of this Statement.

Statement of Financial Accounting Standards No. 137
Accounting for Derivative Instruments and
Hedging Activities—Deferral of the Effective Date
of FASB Statement No. 133

an amendment of FASB Statement No. 133

STATUS

Issued: June 1999

Effective Date: June 1999

Affects: Amends FAS 133, paragraph 48
Replaces FAS 133, paragraph 50

Affected by: No other pronouncements

Statement of Financial Accounting Standards No. 137

Accounting for Derivative Instruments and Hedging Activities— Deferral of the Effective Date of FASB Statement No. 133

an amendment of FASB Statement No. 133

CONTENTS

INTRODUCTION

1. FASB Statement No. 133, *Accounting for Derivative Instruments and Hedging Activities,* was issued in June 1998. It establishes accounting and reporting standards for derivative instruments, including certain derivative instruments embedded in other contracts (collectively referred to as derivatives), and for hedging activities. As issued, Statement 133 is effective for all fiscal quarters of all fiscal years beginning after June 15, 1999, with earlier application encouraged.

2. The Board received requests to consider delaying the effective date of Statement 133. Entities and their auditors requested more time to study, understand, and implement the provisions of that Statement as they apply to entities' transactions and circumstances. Entities also requested more time to complete information system modifications. The Board concluded that, for the reasons presented in the appendix to this Statement, it is appropriate to defer the effective date of Statement 133. However, the Board continues to encourage early application of Statement 133.

STANDARDS OF FINANCIAL ACCOUNTING AND REPORTING

Amendments to Statement 133

3. Statement 133 is amended as follows:

a. The first sentence of paragraph 48 is replaced by the following:

> This Statement shall be effective for all fiscal quarters of all fiscal years beginning after June 15, 2000.

b. Paragraph 50 is replaced by the following:

> At the date of initial application, an entity shall choose to either (a) recognize as an asset or liability in the statement of financial position all embedded derivative instruments that are required pursuant to paragraphs 12–16 to be separated from their host contracts or (b) select either January 1, 1998 or January 1, 1999 as a transition date for embedded derivatives. If the entity chooses to select a

Accounting for Derivative Instruments and Hedging Activities—Deferral of the Effective Date of FASB Statement No. 133

FAS137

transition date, it shall recognize as separate assets and liabilities (pursuant to paragraphs 12–16) only those derivatives embedded in hybrid instruments issued, acquired, or substantively modified by the entity on or after the selected transition date. That choice is not permitted to be applied to only some of an entity's individual hybrid instruments and must be applied on an all-or-none basis.

Effective Date

4. This Statement is effective upon issuance. An entity that has already applied the provisions of Statement 133 and has issued interim or annual financial statements reflecting that application may not revert to a previous method of accounting for derivative instruments and hedging activities.

The provisions of this Statement need not be applied to immaterial items.

This Statement was adopted by the affirmative votes of five members of the Financial Accounting Standards Board. Messrs. Cope and Foster dissented.

Messrs. Cope and Foster dissent from the issuance of this Statement. They disagree with the conclusion that the benefits of delay outweigh the advantages of prompt implementation. They are concerned that users of financial statements will continue to be deprived of information that has long been recognized as critical to the investment decision-making process. Lack of transparent recognition and consistent accounting for derivatives and hedging transactions has already led to substantial investor losses that could have been avoided had there been proper accounting and disclosures. As the number and variety of derivative transactions expand, and considering increased market volatility, they believe that, without appropriate accounting and disclosure, the risk of investors and creditors incurring unanticipated losses in the future remains high. Users of financial statements need to know what risk exposures exist or do not exist. The implementation of Statement 133 will contribute significantly toward meeting that need, and Messrs. Cope and Foster believe that its implementation should not be delayed.

Mr. Cope also believes that, although the provisions of paragraph 3(b) are a logical extension of a decision to defer implementation of the entire standard, the result is a complication and extension of the transition period during which it will be even more difficult for investors to make valid comparisons between entities. That transitional problem would be avoided if the Statement was not deferred.

Mr. Foster also believes that the change in the transition requirements set out in paragraph 3(b) is inappropriate. The Board's constituents have known since June 1998 when Statement 133 was issued that they would be required to account separately for derivatives embedded in complex financial instruments entered into on or after January 1, 1998. Mr. Foster sees no reason to grandfather the accounting for any more embedded derivatives than those that were originally grandfathered by Statement 133.

Members of the Financial Accounting Standards Board:

Edmund L. Jenkins,	Anthony T. Cope	James J. Leisenring
Chairman	John M. Foster	Gerhard G. Mueller
Joseph V. Anania	Gaylen N. Larson	

Appendix

BACKGROUND INFORMATION AND BASIS FOR CONCLUSIONS

5. At the time Statement 133 was issued in June 1998, the Board was aware of the complexities associated with transactions involving derivative instruments and their prevalent use as hedging instruments. Because of that, even before Statement 133 was issued, the Board established the Derivatives Implementation Group (DIG) to assist the FASB in answering questions that companies might face as they began implementing the Statement. Additionally, early on, the FASB developed an educational course on implementing Statement 133, which has been widely used.

6. Despite the anticipatory effort extended by the Board to address implementation issues, some preparers of financial statements and auditors expressed concern about certain challenges they face in applying Statement 133. Those challenges include organization-wide educational efforts and information system modifications.

7. The educational challenges relate mainly to the scope of the Statement and the new approach to recognizing and measuring hedge effectiveness. Statement 133 has a potentially pervasive effect that requires an understanding of technical issues that span several functional areas in some organizations. Constituents expressed concern that they simply have not had enough time to master the new accounting requirements and their implications for derivative and hedging transactions throughout their organizations. In many cases, there may be an unanticipated need to modify existing contracts that currently include embedded derivatives.

8. The Board was informed that the ability to modify or develop information systems in response to Statement 133 is hindered by the level of effort required to modify and test those systems to ensure their proper operation in the year 2000. Constituents reported that those required information systems modifications consumed more resources than expected. In turn, information systems resources were unavailable to ensure compliance with Statement 133. Many companies have imposed moratoriums on information systems changes during the third and fourth quarters of 1999 that will extend through the first quarter of 2000. That has created obstacles that were unantici-pated by the Board and constituents when the original effective date of the Statement was selected.

9. The Board believes that the issues identified by constituents regarding the difficulties associated with implementation will prevent many of them from achieving a sound and consistent implementation of Statement 133. The Board was requested to consider different types of deferrals that included rolling effective dates for DIG conclusions and deferring selected provisions of Statement 133 that were of particular concern to some constituents. The Board decided that the simplest and most effective alternative was a complete deferral for a period of one year.

10. With a delayed effective date, the Board remains concerned that users of financial statements will be deprived of information that the Board continues to believe is critical. Nonetheless, the Board believes that the disadvantages associated with immediate implementation, particularly inconsistent application of the standard caused by lack of adequate information systems, outweigh the benefits of requiring immediate implementation. A one-year deferral will allow constituents to overcome the educational and information systems challenges they currently face. The Board believes that the deferral of the effective date of Statement 133 will not only facilitate its adoption but also enhance consistent application of its provisions for the ultimate benefit of users.

11. On May 20, 1999, the Board issued an Exposure Draft, *Accounting for Derivative Instruments and Hedging Activities—Deferral of the Effective Date of FASB Statement No. 133,* which proposed deferring the effective date of Statement 133 for one year. The Board received 77 letters of comment from respondents. There was overwhelming support for the Board's decision to defer the effective date of Statement 133. Two respondents requested that the Board consider deferring the date that differentiates which hybrid instruments in existence at the date of initial application must be analyzed to determine whether the related embedded derivatives are required to be separated from host contracts. The Board concluded that was a reasonable request given the change in the effective date of Statement 133. The Board concluded that it could reach an informed decision on the basis of existing information without a public hearing and that the effective date specified in paragraph 4 is advisable in the circumstances.

Statement of Financial Accounting Standards No. 138
Accounting for Certain Derivative Instruments and Certain Hedging Activities

an amendment of FASB Statement No. 133

STATUS

Issued: June 2000

Effective Date: For all fiscal quarters of all fiscal years beginning after June 15, 2000

Affects: Replaces FAS 133, paragraphs 10(b), 33, 36(b), 40(a), 52(b), 68(l), 155, and 197
Amends FAS 133, paragraphs 12, 21(c)(1), 21(d), 21(f), 21(f)(2) through 21(f)(4), 29(d), 29(e), 29(g)(2), 29(h), 29(h)(1) through 29(h)(4), 30, 36, 36(a), 37, 38, 40, 40(b), 42, 45(b)(4), 54, 58(b), 58(c)(2), 61(d), 61(e), 68, 68(b), 68(d), 90, 115, 134, 161, 169, 200, and 540 and footnotes 14 and 19
Amends FAS 133 by adding paragraphs 36A, 37A, 40A through 40C, and 120A through 120D
Deletes FAS 133, paragraph 68(l) and footnote 17

Affected by: No other pronouncements

Statement of Financial Accounting Standards No. 138

Accounting for Certain Derivative Instruments and Certain Hedging Activities

an amendment of FASB Statement No. 133

CONTENTS

INTRODUCTION

1. FASB Statement No. 133, *Accounting for Derivative Instruments and Hedging Activities,* establishes accounting and reporting standards for derivative instruments, including certain derivative instruments embedded in other contracts, (collectively referred to as derivatives) and for hedging activities. This Statement addresses a limited number of issues causing implementation difficulties for numerous entities that apply Statement 133.

2. This Statement amends the accounting and reporting standards of Statement 133 for certain derivative instruments and certain hedging activities as indicated below.

a. The normal purchases and normal sales exception in paragraph 10(b) may be applied to contracts that implicitly or explicitly permit net settlement, as discussed in paragraphs 9(a) and 57(c)(1), and contracts that have a market mechanism to facilitate net settlement, as discussed in paragraphs 9(b) and 57(c)(2).

b. The specific risks that can be identified as the hedged risk are redefined so that in a hedge of interest rate risk, the risk of changes in the benchmark interest rate[1] would be the hedged risk.

c. Recognized foreign-currency-denominated assets and liabilities for which a foreign currency transaction gain or loss is recognized in earnings under the provisions of paragraph 15 of FASB Statement No. 52, *Foreign Currency Translation,* may be the hedged item in fair value hedges or cash flow hedges.

d. Certain intercompany derivatives may be designated as the hedging instruments in cash flow hedges of foreign currency risk in the consolidated financial statements if those intercompany derivatives are offset by unrelated third-party contracts on a net basis.

3. This Statement also amends Statement 133 for decisions made by the Board relating to the Derivatives Implementation Group (DIG) process. Certain decisions arising from the DIG process that required specific amendments to Statement 133 are incorporated in this Statement.

---

[1]Benchmark interest rate is defined in paragraph 4(jj) of this Statement.

STANDARDS OF FINANCIAL ACCOUNTING AND REPORTING

Amendments to Statement 133

4. Statement 133 is amended as follows:

Amendment Related to Normal Purchases and Normal Sales

a. Paragraph 10(b) is replaced by the following:

> *Normal purchases and normal sales.* Normal purchases and normal sales are contracts that provide for the purchase or sale of something other than a financial instrument or derivative instrument that will be delivered in quantities expected to be used or sold by the reporting entity over a reasonable period in the normal course of business. However, contracts that have a price based on an underlying that is not clearly and closely related to the asset being sold or purchased (such as a price in a contract for the sale of a grain commodity based in part on changes in the S&P index) or that are denominated in a foreign currency that meets neither of the criteria in paragraphs 15(a) and 15(b) shall not be considered normal purchases and normal sales. Contracts that contain net settlement provisions as described in paragraphs 9(a) and 9(b) may qualify for the normal purchases and normal sales exception if it is probable at inception and throughout the term of the individual contract that the contract will not settle net and will result in physical delivery. Net settlement (as described in paragraphs 9(a) and 9(b)) of contracts in a group of contracts similarly designated as normal purchases and normal sales would call into question the classification of all such contracts as normal purchases or normal sales. Contracts that require cash settlements of gains or losses or are otherwise settled net on a periodic basis, including individual contracts that are part of a series of sequential contracts intended to accomplish ultimate acquisition or sale of a commodity, do not qualify for this exception. For contracts that qualify for the normal purchases and normal sales exception, the entity shall document the basis for concluding that it is probable that the contract will result in physical delivery. The documentation re-

quirements can be applied either to groups of similarly designated contracts or to each individual contract.

Amendments to Redefine Interest Rate Risk

b. Paragraph 21 is amended as follows:

(1) The first sentence of subparagraph (d) is replaced by the following:

> If the hedged item is all or a portion of a debt security (or a portfolio of similar debt securities) that is classified as held-to-maturity in accordance with FASB Statement No. 115, *Accounting for Certain Investments in Debt and Equity Securities,* the designated risk being hedged is the risk of changes in its fair value attributable to credit risk, foreign exchange risk, or both. If the hedged item is an option component of a held-to-maturity security that permits its prepayment, the designated risk being hedged is the risk of changes in the entire fair value of that option component.

(2) In the first parenthetical sentence of subparagraph (d), *changes in market interest rates or foreign exchange rates* is replaced by *interest rate risk.*

(3) In subparagraph (f)(2), *market interest rates* is replaced by *the designated **benchmark interest rate** (referred to as interest rate risk).*

(4) In subparagraph (f)(3), *(refer to paragraphs 37 and 38)* is replaced by *(referred to as foreign exchange risk) (refer to paragraphs 37, 37A, and 38).*

(5) In subparagraph (f)(4), *both* is inserted between *to* and *changes* and *the obligor's creditworthiness* is replaced by *the obligor's creditworthiness and changes in the spread over the benchmark interest rate with respect to the hedged item's credit sector at inception of the hedge (referred to as credit risk).*

(6) In the second sentence of subparagraph (f), *market* is deleted.

(7) In subparagraph (f), the following sentences and footnote are added after the second sentence:

The benchmark interest rate being hedged in a hedge of interest rate risk must be specifically identified as part of the designation and documentation at the inception of the hedging relationship. Ordinarily, an entity should designate the same benchmark interest rate as the risk being hedged for similar hedges, consistent with paragraph 62; the use of different benchmark interest rates for similar hedges should be rare and must be justified. In calculating the change in the hedged item's fair value attributable to changes in the benchmark interest rate, the estimated cash flows used in calculating fair value must be based on all of the contractual cash flows of the entire hedged item. Excluding some of the hedged item's contractual cash flows (for example, the portion of the interest coupon in excess of the benchmark interest rate) from the calculation is not permitted.*

---

*The first sentence of paragraph 21(a) that specifically permits the hedged item to be identified as either all or a specific portion of a recognized asset or liability or of an unrecognized firm commitment is not affected by the provisions in this subparagraph.

(8) In the fourth sentence of subparagraph (f), *overall* is inserted between *exposure to changes in the* and *fair value of that.*

(9) In the last sentence of subparagraph (f), *market* is deleted.

c. Paragraph 29 is amended as follows:

(1) In the first sentence of subparagraph (e), *default or changes in the obligor's creditworthiness* is replaced by *credit risk, foreign exchange risk, or both.*

(2) In the last sentence of subparagraph (e), *changes in market interest rates* is replaced by *interest rate risk.*

(3) In the first sentence of subparagraph (h), *(or the interest payments on that financial asset or liability)* is added after *sale of a financial asset or liability.*

(4) In subparagraph (h)(1), *the risk of changes in the cash flows of the entire asset or liability* is replaced by *the risk of overall changes in the hedged cash flows related to the asset or liability.*

(5) In subparagraph (h)(2), *market interest rates* is replaced by *the designated benchmark interest rate (referred to as interest rate risk).*

(6) In subparagraph (h)(3), *(refer to paragraph 40)* is replaced by *(referred to as foreign exchange risk) (refer to paragraphs 40, 40A, 40B, and 40C).*

(7) In subparagraph (h)(4), *default or changes in the obligor's creditworthiness* is replaced by *default, changes in the obligor's creditworthiness, and changes in the spread over the benchmark interest rate with respect to the hedged item's credit sector at inception of the hedge (referred to as credit risk).*

(8) In subparagraph (h), the following sentences are added after the second sentence:

The benchmark interest rate being hedged in a hedge of interest rate risk must be specifically identified as part of the designation and documentation at the inception of the hedging relationship. Ordinarily, an entity should designate the same benchmark interest rate as the risk being hedged for similar hedges, consistent with paragraph 62; the use of different benchmark interest rates for similar hedges should be rare and must be justified. In a cash flow hedge of a variable-rate financial asset or liability, either existing or forecasted, the designated risk being hedged cannot be the risk of changes in its cash flows attributable to changes in the specifically identified benchmark interest rate if the cash flows of the hedged transaction are explicitly based on a different index, for example, based on a specific bank's prime rate, which cannot qualify as the benchmark rate. However, the risk designated as being hedged could potentially be the risk of overall changes in the hedged cash flows related to the asset or liability, provided that the other criteria for a cash flow hedge have been met.

d. Paragraph 54 is amended as follows:

(1) In the second sentence, *market interest rates, changes in foreign currency exchange rates,* is replaced by *the designated benchmark interest rate.*

(2) In the third and fourth (parenthetical) sentences, *market* is deleted.

(3) In the penultimate sentence of footnote 14, *market interest rates* is replaced by *interest rate risk.*

e. In the first sentence of paragraph 90, *market* is deleted.

Amendments Related to Hedging Recognized Foreign-Currency-Denominated Assets and Liabilities

f. In paragraph 21(c)(1), *(for example, if foreign exchange risk is hedged, a foreign-currency-denominated asset for which a foreign currency transaction gain or loss is recognized in earnings)* is deleted.

g. Paragraph 29(d) is amended as follows:

  (1) In the first sentence, *(for example, if foreign exchange risk is hedged, the forecasted acquisition of a foreign-currency-denominated asset for which a foreign currency transaction gain or loss will be recognized in earnings)* is deleted.

  (2) The second sentence is deleted.

h. In paragraph 29(g)(2), *(reflecting its actual location if a physical asset)* is replaced by *reflecting its actual location if a physical asset (regardless of whether that price and the related cash flows are stated in the entity's functional currency or a foreign currency).*

i. The following subparagraph is added after subparagraph (c) of paragraph 30:

  d. In a cash flow hedge of the variability of the functional-currency-equivalent cash flows for a recognized foreign-currency-denominated asset or liability that is remeasured at spot exchange rates under paragraph 15 of Statement 52, an amount that will offset the related transaction gain or loss arising from the remeasurement and adjust earnings for the cost to the purchaser (income to the seller) of the hedging instrument shall be reclassified each period from other comprehensive income to earnings.

j. Paragraph 36 is amended as follows:

  (1) In the first sentence, *Consistent with the functional currency concept in Statement 52* is replaced by *If the hedged item is denominated in a foreign currency.*

  (2) In subparagraph (a), *an available-for-sale security* is replaced by *a recognized asset or liability (including an available-for-sale security).*

  (3) Subparagraph (b) is replaced by the following:

  A cash flow hedge of a forecasted transaction, an unrecognized firm commitment, the forecasted functional-currency-equivalent cash flows associated with a recognized asset or liability, or a forecasted intercompany transaction.

  (4) The first two sentences following subparagraph (c) are replaced by the following:

  The recognition in earnings of the foreign currency transaction gain or loss on a foreign-currency-denominated asset or liability based on changes in the foreign currency spot rate is not considered to be the remeasurement of that asset or liability with changes in fair value attributable to foreign exchange risk recognized in earnings, which is discussed in the criteria in paragraphs 21(c)(1) and 29(d). Thus, those criteria are not impediments to either a foreign currency fair value or cash flow hedge of such a foreign-currency-denominated asset or liability or a foreign currency cash flow hedge of the forecasted acquisition or incurrence of a foreign-currency-denominated asset or liability whose carrying amount will be remeasured at spot exchange rates under paragraph 15 of Statement 52.

k. The following paragraph is added after paragraph 36:

  36A. The provisions in paragraph 36 that permit a recognized foreign-currency-denominated asset or liability to be the hedged item in a fair value or cash flow hedge of foreign currency exposure also pertain to a recognized foreign-currency-denominated receivable or payable that results from a hedged forecasted foreign-currency-denominated sale or purchase on credit. An entity may choose to designate a single cash flow hedge that encompasses the variability of functional currency cash flows attributable to foreign exchange risk related to the settlement of the foreign-currency-denominated receivable or payable resulting from a forecasted sale or purchase on credit. Alternatively, an entity may choose to designate a cash flow hedge of the variability of functional currency cash flows attributable to foreign exchange risk related to a forecasted foreign-currency-denominated sale or purchase on credit and then separately designate a foreign currency fair value hedge of the resulting recognized foreign-currency-denominated receivable or payable. In that case, the cash flow hedge would terminate (be dedesignated) when the hedged sale or purchase occurs and the foreign-currency-denominated receivable or payable is recognized. The use of the same foreign currency derivative instrument for both the cash flow hedge and the fair value hedge is not prohibited though some ineffectiveness may result.

l.   The following paragraph is added after paragraph 37:

37A. *Recognized asset or liability.* A non-derivative financial instrument shall not be designated as the hedging instrument in a fair value hedge of the foreign currency exposure of a recognized asset or liability. A derivative instrument can be designated as hedging the changes in the fair value of a recognized asset or liability (or a specific portion thereof) for which a foreign currency transaction gain or loss is recognized in earnings under the provisions of paragraph 15 of Statement 52. All recognized foreign-currency-denominated assets or liabilities for which a foreign currency transaction gain or loss is recorded in earnings may qualify for the accounting specified in paragraphs 22–27 if all the fair value hedge criteria in paragraphs 20 and 21 and the conditions in paragraphs 40(a) and 40(b) are met.

m. Paragraph 40 is amended as follows:

(1) The second sentence is replaced by the following:

A derivative instrument designated as hedging the foreign currency exposure to variability in the functional-currency-equivalent cash flows associated with a forecasted transaction (for example, a forecasted export sale to an unaffiliated entity with the price to be denominated in a foreign currency), a recognized asset or liability, an unrecognized firm commitment, or a forecasted intercompany transaction (for example, a forecasted sale to a foreign subsidiary or a forecasted royalty from a foreign subsidiary) qualifies for hedge accounting if all the following criteria are met:

(2) The following subparagraph is added:

e. If the hedged item is a recognized foreign-currency-denominated asset or liability, all the variability in the hedged item's functional-currency-equivalent cash flows must be eliminated by the effect of the hedge. (For example, a cash flow hedge cannot be used with a variable-rate foreign-currency-denominated asset or liability and a derivative based solely on changes in exchange rates because the derivative does not eliminate all the variability in the functional currency cash flows.)

Amendments Related to Intercompany Derivatives

n. In the last sentence of paragraph 36, *in a fair value hedge or in a cash flow hedge of a recognized foreign-currency-denominated asset or liability or in a net investment hedge* is added after *can be a hedging instrument.*

o. The following paragraphs are added after paragraph 40:

40A. *Internal derivative.* A foreign currency derivative contract that has been entered into with another member of a consolidated group (such as a treasury center) can be a hedging instrument in a foreign currency cash flow hedge of a forecasted borrowing, purchase, or sale or an unrecognized firm commitment in the consolidated financial statements only if the following two conditions are satisfied. (That foreign currency derivative instrument is hereafter in this section referred to as an *internal derivative.*)

a. From the perspective of the member of the consolidated group using the derivative as a hedging instrument (hereafter in this section referred to as the *hedging affiliate*), the criteria for foreign currency cash flow hedge accounting in paragraph 40 must be satisfied.

b. The member of the consolidated group not using the derivative as a hedging instrument (hereafter in this section referred to as the *issuing affiliate*) must either (1) enter into a derivative contract with an unrelated third party to offset the exposure that results from that internal derivative or (2) if the conditions in paragraph 40B are met, enter into derivative contracts with unrelated third parties that would offset, on a net basis for each foreign currency, the foreign exchange risk arising from multiple internal derivative contracts.

40B. *Offsetting net exposures.* If an issuing affiliate chooses to offset exposure arising from multiple internal derivative contracts on an aggregate or net basis, the derivatives issued to hedging affiliates may qualify as cash flow hedges in the consolidated financial statements only if all of the following conditions are satisfied:

a. The issuing affiliate enters into a derivative contract with an unrelated third party to offset, on a net basis for each foreign currency, the foreign exchange risk arising from multiple internal derivative contracts, and the derivative contract with the unrelated third party generates equal or

closely approximating gains and losses when compared with the aggregate or net losses and gains generated by the derivative contracts issued to affiliates.

b. Internal derivatives that are not designated as hedging instruments are excluded from the determination of the foreign currency exposure on a net basis that is offset by the third-party derivative. In addition, nonderivative contracts may not be used as hedging instruments to offset exposures arising from internal derivative contracts.

c. Foreign currency exposure that is offset by a single net third-party contract arises from internal derivative contracts that mature within the same 31-day period and that involve the same currency exposure as the net third-party derivative. The offsetting net third-party derivative related to that group of contracts must offset the aggregate or net exposure to that currency, must mature within the same 31-day period, and must be entered into within 3 business days after the designation of the internal derivatives as hedging instruments.

d. The issuing affiliate tracks the exposure that it acquires from each hedging affiliate and maintains documentation supporting linkage of each internal derivative contract and the offsetting aggregate or net derivative contract with an unrelated third party.

e. The issuing affiliate does not alter or terminate the offsetting derivative with an unrelated third party unless the hedging affiliate initiates that action. If the issuing affiliate does alter or terminate any offsetting third-party derivative (which should be rare), the hedging affiliate must prospectively cease hedge accounting for the internal derivatives that are offset by that third-party derivative.

40C. A member of a consolidated group is not permitted to offset exposures arising from multiple internal derivative contracts on a net basis for foreign currency cash flow exposures related to recognized foreign-currency-denominated assets or liabilities. That prohibition includes situations in which a recognized foreign-currency-denominated asset or liability in a fair value hedge or cash flow hedge results from the occurrence of a specifically identified forecasted transaction initially designated as a cash flow hedge.

Amendments for Certain Interpretations of Statement 133 Cleared by the Board Relating to the Derivatives Implementation Group Process

p. In the second sentence of paragraph 12, *host* is inserted between *would be required by the* and *contract, whether unconditional.*

Amendments to Implement Guidance in Implementation Issue No. G3, "Discontinuation of a Cash Flow Hedge"

q. Paragraph 33 is replaced by the following:

> The net derivative gain or loss related to a discontinued cash flow hedge shall continue to be reported in accumulated other comprehensive income unless it is probable that the forecasted transaction will *not* occur by the end of the originally specified time period (as documented at the inception of the hedging relationship) or within an additional two-month period of time thereafter, except as indicated in the following sentence. In rare cases, the existence of extenuating circumstances that are related to the nature of the forecasted transaction and are outside the control or influence of the reporting entity may cause the forecasted transaction to be probable of occurring on a date that is beyond the additional two-month period of time, in which case the net derivative gain or loss related to the discontinued cash flow hedge shall continue to be reported in accumulated other comprehensive income until it is reclassified into earnings pursuant to paragraph 31. If it is probable that the hedged forecasted transaction will not occur either by the end of the originally specified time period or within the additional two-month period of time and the hedged forecasted transaction also does not qualify for the exception described in the preceding sentence, that derivative gain or loss reported in accumulated other comprehensive income shall be reclassified into earnings immediately.

r. The following is added at the end of paragraph 45(b)(4):

> by the end of the originally specified time period or within the additional period of time discussed in paragraph 33.

Amendments to Implement Guidance in Implementation Issue No. H1, "Hedging at the Operating Unit Level"

s. In the last sentence of paragraph 37, *and the conditions in paragraphs 40(a) and 40(b)* is added between *paragraphs 20 and 21* and *are met.*

t. In the third sentence of paragraph 38, *and the conditions in paragraphs 40(a) and 40(b)* is added between *paragraphs 20 and 21* and *are met.*

u. In paragraph 42, *provided the conditions in paragraphs 40(a) and 40(b) are met* is added to the end of the first sentence.

Amendments to Implement Guidance in Implementation Issue No. H2, "Requirement That the Unit with the Exposure Must Be a Party to the Hedge"

v. Paragraph 40 is amended as follows:

> (1) Subparagraph (a) is replaced by the following:

> > For consolidated financial statements, either (1) the operating unit that has the foreign currency exposure is a party to the hedging instrument or (2) another member of the consolidated group that has the same functional currency as that operating unit (subject to the restrictions in this subparagraph and related footnote) is a party to the hedging instrument. To qualify for applying the guidance in (2) above, there may be no intervening subsidiary with a different functional

currency.* (Refer to paragraphs 36, 40A, and 40B for conditions for which an intercompany foreign currency derivative can be the hedging instrument in a cash flow hedge of foreign exchange risk.)

---

*For example, if a dollar-functional, second-tier subsidiary has a Euro exposure, the dollar-functional consolidated parent company could designate its U.S. dollar–Euro derivative as a hedge of the second-tier subsidiary's exposure provided that the functional currency of the intervening first-tier subsidiary (that is, the parent of the second-tier subsidiary) is also the U.S. dollar. In contrast, if the functional currency of the intervening first-tier subsidiary was the Japanese yen (thus requiring the financial statements of the second-tier subsidiary to be translated into yen before the yen-denominated financial statements of the first-tier subsidiary are translated into U.S. dollars for consolidation), the consolidated parent company could not designate its U.S. dollar–Euro derivative as a hedge of the second-tier subsidiary's exposure.

(2) In subparagraph (b), *that* is replaced by *the hedging*.

Amendments to the Transition Guidance, the Implementation Guidance in Appendix A of Statement 133, and the Examples in Appendix B of Statement 133

w. Paragraph 52(b) is replaced by the following:

If the transition adjustment relates to a derivative instrument that had been designated in a hedging relationship that addressed the fair value exposure of an asset, a liability, or a firm commitment, the transition adjustment for the derivative shall be reported as a cumulative-effect-type adjustment of net income. Concurrently, any gain or loss on the hedged item shall be recognized as an adjustment of the hedged item's carrying amount at the date of initial application, but only to the extent of an offsetting transition adjustment for the derivative. Only for purposes of applying the preceding sentence in determining the hedged item's transition adjustment, the gain or loss on the hedged item may be either (1) the overall gain or loss on the hedged item determined as the difference between the hedged item's fair value and its carrying amount on the date of initial application (that is, not limited to the portion attributable to the hedged risk nor limited to the gain or loss occurring during the period of the preexisting hedging relationship) or (2) the gain or loss on the hedged item attributable to the hedged

risk (limited to the hedged risks that can be designated under paragraph 21 of this Statement) during the period of the preexisting hedging relationship. That adjustment of the hedged item's carrying amount shall also be reported as a cumulative-effect-type adjustment of net income. The transition adjustment related to the gain or loss reported in accumulated other comprehensive income on a derivative instrument that hedged an available-for-sale security, together with the loss or gain on the related security (to the extent of an offsetting transition adjustment for the derivative instrument), shall be reclassified to earnings as a cumulative-effect-type adjustment of both net income and accumulated other comprehensive income.

x. Paragraph 58 is amended as follows:

(1) In the first sentence of subparagraph (b), *requires* is replaced by *involves* and *that are readily convertible to cash*[17] *and only if there is no market mechanism to facilitate net settlement outside the contract* and footnote 17 are deleted.

(2) The following sentence is added at the end of subparagraph (b):

Also, in order for a contract that meets the net settlement provisions of paragraphs 9(a) and 57(c)(1) and the market mechanism provisions of paragraphs 9(b) and 57(c)(2) to qualify for the exception, it must be probable at inception and throughout the term of the individual contract that the contract will not settle net and will result in physical delivery.

(3) The following two sentences are added at the end of subparagraph (c)(2):

This exception applies only to nonfinancial assets that are unique and only if a nonfinancial asset related to the underlying is owned by the party that would *not* benefit *under the contract* from an increase in the price or value of the nonfinancial asset. If the contract is a call option contract, the exception applies only if that nonfinancial asset is owned by the party that would not benefit under the contract from an increase in the price or value of the nonfinancial asset above the option's strike price.

y. Paragraph 61 is amended as follows:

(1) The last two sentences of subparagraph (d) are deleted.

(2) In the second sentence of subparagraph (e), *the equity instrument* is replaced by *a publicly traded equity instrument.*

z. Paragraph 68 is amended as follows:

(1) In the second sentence, *an interest-bearing asset or liability* is replaced by *a recognized interest-bearing asset or liability.*

(2) In subparagraph (b), *its inception* is replaced by *the inception of the hedging relationship.*

(3) In subparagraph (d), the following is added at the end of the sentence:

(that is, able to be settled by either party prior to its scheduled maturity), except as indicated in the following sentences. This criterion does not apply to an interest-bearing asset or liability that is prepayable solely due to an embedded call option provided that the hedging interest rate swap contains an embedded mirror-image call option. The call option embedded in the swap is considered a mirror image of the call option embedded in the hedged item if (1) the terms of the two call options match (including matching maturities, strike price, related notional amounts, timing and frequency of payments, and dates on which the instruments may be called) and (2) the entity is the writer of one call option and the holder (or purchaser) of the other call option. Similarly, this criterion does not apply to an interest-bearing asset or liability that is prepayable solely due to an embedded put option provided that the hedging interest rate swap contains an embedded mirror-image put option.

(4) The following subparagraph and footnote are added after subparagraph (d):

dd. The index on which the variable leg of the swap is based matches the benchmark interest rate designated as the interest rate risk being hedged for that hedging relationship.*

---

*For cash flow hedge situations in which the cash flows of the hedged item and the hedging instrument are based on the same index but that index is not the benchmark interest rate, the shortcut method is not permitted. However, the entity may obtain results similar to results obtained if the shortcut method was permitted.

(5) Subparagraph (l) is deleted.

aa. In the third sentence of footnote 19 to paragraph 74, *market* is deleted.

bb. Paragraph 115 is amended as follows:

(1) In the third sentence, *market interest rates* is replaced by *the designated benchmark interest rate.*

(2) The following sentence is added after the third sentence:

ABC designates changes in LIBOR swap rates as the benchmark interest rate in hedging interest rate risk.

cc. The following example is added after paragraph 120 and before Example 3:

Example 2A: Fair Value Hedge of the LIBOR Swap Rate in a $100,000 BBB-Quality 5-Year Fixed-Rate Noncallable Note

120A. This example illustrates one method that could be used in determining the hedged item's change in fair value attributable to changes in the benchmark interest rate. Other methods could be used in determining the hedged item's change in fair value attributable to changes in the benchmark interest rate as long as those methods meet the criteria in paragraph 21(f).

120B. On January 1, 20X0, GHI Company issues at par a $100,000 BBB-quality 5-year fixed-rate noncallable debt instrument with an annual 10 percent interest coupon. On that date, the issuer enters into a 5-year interest rate swap based on the LIBOR swap rate and designates it as the hedging instrument in a fair value hedge of the $100,000 liability. Under the terms of the swap, GHI will receive fixed interest at 7 percent and pay variable interest at LIBOR. The variable leg of the swap resets each year on December 31 for the payments due the following year. This example has been simplified by assuming that the interest rate applicable to a payment due at any future date is the same as the rate for a payment at any other date (that is, the yield curve is flat). During the hedge period, the gain or loss on the swap will be recorded in earnings. The example assumes that immediately before the interest rate on the variable leg resets on December 31, 20X0, the LIBOR swap rate increased by 50 basis points to 7.50 percent, and the change in fair value of the swap for the period from January 1 to December 31, 20X0 is a loss in value of $1,675.

Changes in the fair value of the hedged item attributable to the changes in the benchmark interest rate for a specific period

120C. Under this method, the change in a hedged item's fair value attributable to changes in the benchmark interest rate for a specific period is determined as the difference between two present value calculations as of the end of the period that exclude or include, respectively, the effect of the changes in the benchmark interest rate during the period. The discount rates used for those present value calculations would be, respectively, (a) the discount rate equal to the market interest rate for that hedged item at the inception

of the hedge adjusted (up or down) for changes in the benchmark rate (designated as the interest rate risk being hedged) from the inception of the hedge to the beginning date of the period for which the change in fair value is being calculated* and (b) the discount rate equal to the market interest rate for that hedged item at the inception of the hedge adjusted (up or down) for changes in the designated benchmark rate from the inception of the hedge to the ending date of the period for which the change in fair value is being calculated. Both present value calculations are computed using the estimated future cash flows for the hedged item (which typically would be its remaining contractual cash flows).

120D. In GHI's quarterly assessments of hedge effectiveness for each of the first three quarters of year 20X0 in this example, there was zero change in the hedged item's fair value attributable to changes in the benchmark interest rate because there was no change in the LIBOR swap rate. However, in the assessment for the fourth quarter 20X0, the discount rate for the beginning of the period is 10 percent (the hedged item's original market interest rate with an adjustment of zero), and the discount rate for the end of the period is 10.50 percent (the hedged item's original market interest rate adjusted for the change during the period in the LIBOR swap rate [+0.50 percent]).

December 31, 20X0

Calculate the present value using the beginning-of-period discount rate of 10 percent:

$10,000pmt, 10%i, 4n, PV =	$ 31,699	(interest payments)
$100,000fv, 10%i, 4n, PV =	68,301	(principal payment)
Total present value	$100,000	

Calculate the present value using the end-of-period discount rate of 10.50 percent (that is, the beginning-of-period discount rate adjusted for the change during the period in the LIBOR swap rate of 50 basis points):

$10,000pmt, 10.50%i, 4n, PV =	$31,359	(interest payments)
$100,000fv, 10.50%i, 4n, PV =	67,073	(principal payment)
Total present value	$98,432	

The change in fair value of the hedged item attributable to the change in the benchmark interest rate is $100,000 − $98,432 = $1,568 (the fair value decrease in the liability is a gain on debt).

When the change in fair value of the hedged item ($1,568 gain) attributable to the risk being hedged is compared with the change in fair value of the hedging instrument ($1,675 loss), ineffectiveness of $107 results. That ineffectiveness will be reported in earnings, because both changes in fair value are recorded in earnings.

---

*This Statement does not provide specific guidance on the discount rate that must be used in the calculation. However, the method chosen by GHI and described in this illustration requires that the discount rate be based on the market interest rate for the hedged item at the inception of the hedging relationship.

dd. Paragraph 134 is amended as follows:

(1) In the second sentence, *market interest rates* is replaced by *the designated benchmark interest rate.*

(2) The following sentence is added after the second sentence:

XYZ designates changes in LIBOR swap rates as the benchmark interest rate in hedging interest rate risk.

ee. Paragraph 155 is replaced by the following:

Because Swap 1 and the hedged forecasted interest payments are based on the same notional amount, have the same reset dates, and are based on the same benchmark interest rate designated under paragraph 29(h), MNO may conclude that there will be no ineffectiveness in the hedging relationship (absent a default by the swap counterparty).

ff. The last sentence of paragraph 161 is deleted.

gg. Paragraph 169 is amended as follows:

(1) In the third sentence, *is not eligible for cash flow hedge accounting* is replaced by *would separately be eligible to be designated as a fair value hedge of foreign exchange risk or continue to be eligible as a cash flow hedge of foreign exchange risk.*

(2) The fourth sentence and the fifth (parenthetical) sentence are deleted.

(3) The sixth sentence is replaced by the following:

Consequently, if the variability of the functional currency cash flows related to the royalty receivable is not being hedged, DEF will dedesignate a proportion of the hedging instrument in the original hedge relationship with respect to the proportion of the forward contract corresponding to the earned royalty.

(4) In the last sentence, *will substantially offset* is replaced by *may substantially offset.*

hh. Paragraph 197 is replaced by the following:

> **Example 31: Certain Purchases in a Foreign Currency.** A U.S. company enters into a contract to purchase corn from a local American supplier in six months for a fixed amount of Japanese yen; the yen is the functional currency of neither party to the transaction. The corn is expected to be delivered and used over a reasonable period in the normal course of business.
>
> > *Scope Application:* Paragraph 10(b) excludes contracts that require future delivery of commodities that are readily convertible to cash from the accounting for derivatives if the commodities will be delivered in quantities expected to be used or sold by the reporting entity over a reasonable period in the normal course of business. However, that paragraph also states that contracts that are denominated in a foreign currency that meets neither of the criteria in paragraphs 15(a) and 15(b) shall not be considered normal purchases and normal sales. Because the Japanese yen is not the functional currency of either party to the contract and the purchase of corn is transacted internationally in many different currencies, the contract does not qualify for the normal purchases and normal sales exception. The contract is a compound derivative comprising a U.S. dollar-denominated forward contract for the purchase of corn and an embedded foreign currency swap from the purchaser's functional currency (the U.S. dollar) to yen. Consistent with the last sentence of footnote 13 to paragraph 49, the compound derivative cannot be separated into its components (representing the foreign currency derivative and the forward commodity contract) and accounted for separately under this Statement.

ii. Paragraph 200 is amended as follows:

(1) The second bullet is amended as follows:

(a) In the first sentence, *owned by the policyholder and separate* is replaced by *distinct*.

(b) The second sentence is deleted.

(c) In the third sentence, *considered* is inserted between *not* and *a derivative,* and *the policyholder has invested the premiums in acquiring those investments* is replaced by *of the unique attributes of traditional variable annuity contracts issued by insurance companies.*

(d) In the penultimate sentence, *traditional* is inserted between *rather than a* and *variable annuity* in the parenthetical phrase, and *not be viewed as a direct investment because the policyholder does not own those investments, which are assets recorded in the general account of the insurance company* is replaced by *contain an embedded derivative (the equity index-based derivative) that meets all the requirements of paragraph 12 of this Statement for separate accounting: (a) the economic characteristics and risks of the embedded derivative would not be clearly and closely related to the economic characteristics and risks of the host contract (that is, the host contract is a debt instrument and the embedded option is equity-indexed), (b) the hybrid instrument would not be remeasured at fair value with changes in fair value reported in earnings as they occur under GAAP, and (c) a separate instrument with the same terms as the embedded derivative instrument would be a derivative instrument pursuant to paragraphs 6–11 of this Statement.*

(e) The last sentence is deleted.

(2) In the third bullet, *an investment owned by the insured* is replaced by *a traditional variable annuity contract issued by an insurance company.*

(3) The following sentences are added to the end of the paragraph after the last bullet:

> The guidance in the second and third bullets above is an exception for traditional variable annuity contracts issued by insurance companies. In determining the accounting for other seemingly similar structures, it would be inappropriate to analogize to the above guidance due to the unique attributes of traditional variable annuity contracts.

Amendments to the Glossary of Statement 133

jj. The following terms and definitions are added to paragraph 540:

Benchmark interest rate

A widely recognized and quoted rate in an active financial market that is broadly indicative of the overall level of interest rates attributable to high-credit-quality obligors in that market. It is a rate that is widely used in a given financial market as an underlying basis for determining the interest rates of individual financial instruments and commonly referenced in interest-rate-related transactions.

In theory, the benchmark interest rate should be a risk-free rate (that is, has no risk of default). In some markets, government borrowing rates may serve as a benchmark. In other markets, the benchmark interest rate may be an interbank offered rate. In the United States, currently only the interest rates on direct Treasury obligations of the U.S. government and, for practical reasons, the LIBOR swap rate are considered to be benchmark interest rates. In each financial market, only the one or two most widely used and quoted rates that meet the above criteria may be considered benchmark interest rates.

LIBOR swap rate

The fixed rate on a single-currency, constant-notional interest rate swap that has its floating-rate leg referenced to the London Interbank Offered Rate (LIBOR) with no additional spread over LIBOR on that floating-rate leg. That fixed rate is the derived rate that would result in the swap having a zero fair value at inception because the present value of fixed cash flows, based on that rate, equate to the present value of the floating cash flows.

Effective Date and Transition

5. For an entity that has not adopted Statement 133 before June 15, 2000, this Statement shall be adopted concurrently with Statement 133 according to the provisions of paragraph 48 of Statement 133.

6. For an entity that has adopted Statement 133 prior to June 15, 2000, this Statement shall be effective for all fiscal quarters beginning after June 15, 2000, in accordance with the following transition provisions.

a. At the date of initial application, an entity may elect to derecognize in the balance sheet any derivative instrument that would qualify under this Statement as a normal purchases or normal sales contract and record a cumulative effect of a change in accounting principle as described in paragraph 20 of APB Opinion No. 20, *Accounting Changes*. The election to derecognize may not be applied to only some of an entity's normal purchases and normal sales contracts and must be applied on an all-or-none basis. That election to derecognize a derivative instrument may be applied retroactively to the beginning of any fiscal quarter for which interim financial information or financial statements have not been issued.

b. At the date of initial application, an entity must dedesignate the market interest rate as the hedged risk in a hedge of interest rate risk. An entity is permitted to designate anew the benchmark interest rate as the hedged risk in a hedge of interest rate risk.

c. At the date of initial application, an entity may designate a recognized foreign-currency-denominated asset or liability as the hedged item in a hedge of foreign exchange risk pursuant to paragraphs 21 and 29 of Statement 133, as amended by this Statement. An entity may also designate intercompany derivatives that meet the requirements in paragraph 4(l) of this Statement (paragraphs 40A and 40B of Statement 133) as hedging instruments in cash flow hedges of foreign exchange risk when those intercompany derivatives have been offset on only a net basis with third-party derivatives. Any designations permitted by this subparagraph shall be made on a prospective basis.

The provisions of this Statement need not be applied to immaterial items.

This Statement was adopted by the affirmative votes of five members of the Financial Accounting Standards Board. Messrs. Foster and Leisenring dissented.

Messrs. Foster and Leisenring dissent from the issuance of this Statement because they believe this Statement does not represent an improvement in financial reporting. The Board concluded in Statement 133, because of anomalies created by a mixed-attribute accounting model, that hedge accounting was appropriate in certain limited circumstances. At the same time, however, it concluded that hedge accounting was appropriate only to the extent that the hedging instrument was effective in offsetting changes in the fair value of the hedged item or the variability of cash flows of the hedged transaction and that any ineffectiveness in achieving that offset should be reflected in earnings. While Statement 133 gave wide latitude to management in determining the method for measuring effectiveness, it is clear that the hedged risk is limited to (a) the risk of changes in the entire hedged item, (b) the risk attributable to changes in market interest rates, (c) the risk attributable to changes in foreign currency exchange rates, and (d) the risk attributable to changes in the obligor's creditworthiness. Those limitations were designed to limit an entity's ability to define the risk being hedged in such a manner as to eliminate or minimize ineffectiveness for accounting purposes. The effect of the provisions in this amendment relating to (1) the interest rate that is permitted to be designated as the hedged risk and (2) permitting the foreign currency risk of foreign-currency-denominated assets and liabilities to be designated as hedges will be to substantially reduce or, in some circumstances, eliminate the amount of hedge ineffectiveness that would otherwise be reflected in earnings. For example, permitting an entity to designate the risk of changes in the LIBOR swap rate curve as the risk being hedged in a fair value hedge when the interest rate of the instrument being hedged is not based on the LIBOR swap rate curve ignores certain effects of basis risk, which, prior to this amendment, would have been appropriately required to be recognized in earnings. Messrs. Foster and Leisenring believe that retreat from Statement 133 is a modification to the basic model of Statement 133, which requires that ineffectiveness of hedging relationships be measured and reported in earnings.

In Statement 133, the Board stated its vision for all financial instruments ultimately to be measured at fair value. If all financial instruments were measured at fair value with changes in fair value recorded currently in earnings, the need for hedge accounting for the risks inherent in existing financial instruments would be eliminated because both the hedging instrument and the hedged item would be measured at fair value. Recognizing and measuring the changes in fair value of all financial instruments using the same criteria and measurement attributes would leave no anomalies related to financial instruments. Consequently, the Board has tentatively concluded in its project on measuring all financial instruments at fair value that all changes in fair value be reflected in earnings. Statement 133 is a step toward achieving the Board's vision because it requires recognizing currently in earnings the amounts for which a hedging instrument is ineffective in offsetting the changes in the fair value of the hedged item or the variability of cash flows of the hedged transaction. Messrs. Foster and Leisenring believe the amendments to Statement 133 referred to in the paragraph above represent steps backward from achieving the Board's vision of reporting all financial instruments at fair value because the result of those amendments is to report the effects of hedging instruments that are not fully effective in offsetting the changes in fair value attributable to the risk being hedged as if they were.

Messrs. Foster and Leisenring believe that even if one accepts the exception that a benchmark interest rate that clearly is not a risk-free rate can be considered to be a risk-free rate, the extension of that exception to permit the benchmark interest rate to be the hedged risk in a financial instrument for which the interest rate is less than the benchmark rate is inappropriate. There can be no risk to an entity for that portion of the credit spread of the benchmark interest rate that is in excess of the credit spread of the hedged item. Yet that exception requires the change in that portion of the credit spread to be recognized in the basis adjustment of the hedged item, so that the ineffectiveness attributable to the portion of the derivative that hedges a nonexistent risk is not recognized. For example, if there is a change during a period in the value of the portion of the credit spread of the LIBOR swap rate (designated hedged risk) that is in excess of the credit spread of the hedged item, under no circumstances could that change affect the fair value of the hedged item. This Statement, however, mandates that in those circumstances an artificial change in fair value be recognized in the basis of the hedged item.

In this regard, Messrs. Foster and Leisenring observe that permitting the benchmark interest rate to be the hedged risk in a financial instrument that has an interest rate that is less than the benchmark rate creates an anomaly related to the shortcut method. In hedges in which a portion of the derivative is designated as hedging a nonexistent risk (the excess of the benchmark interest rate over the actual interest rate of the hedged item), no ineffectiveness will be recognized when using the shortcut method even though the hedging relationship is clearly not effective. But in certain hedges where there is likely to be little ineffectiveness because the interest rate indexes of the hedged item and the hedging instrument are the same, the shortcut method, in which no ineffectiveness is assumed, is not available.

Members of the Financial Accounting Standards Board:

Edmund L. Jenkins,	John M. Foster	Gerhard G. Mueller
Chairman	Gaylen N. Larson	Edward W. Trott
Anthony T. Cope	James J. Leisenring	

Appendix A

BACKGROUND INFORMATION AND BASIS FOR CONCLUSIONS

CONTENTS

Appendix A

BACKGROUND INFORMATION AND BASIS FOR CONCLUSIONS

Introduction

7. This appendix summarizes considerations that Board members deemed significant in reaching the conclusions in this Statement. It includes reasons for accepting certain views and rejecting others. Individual Board members gave greater weight to some factors than to others.

Background Information

8. The Board received numerous requests to amend Statement 133. The requests focused mainly on guidance related to specific issues that, if amended, would ease implementation difficulties for a large number of entities. In reviewing those requests, the Board did not discover any new significant information suggesting that the framework of Statement 133 was inappropriate or that major changes should be made. However, after meeting with members of the Derivatives Implementation Group (DIG) in an open meeting, the Board decided to analyze six specific issues, and it developed the following criteria to help in de-

termining which issues, if any, to consider for a possible amendment of Statement 133:

a. Implementation difficulties would be eased for a large number of entities.
b. There would be no conflict with or modifications to the basic model of Statement 133.
c. There would be no delay in the effective date of Statement 133.

9. Of the six issues, the Board determined that it would be appropriate to amend Statement 133 for four of those issues (identified as the normal purchases and normal sales exception, hedging the benchmark interest rate, hedging recognized foreign-currency-denominated debt instruments, and hedging with intercompany derivatives). The Board determined that amending Statement 133 for the remaining two issues (identified as partial-term hedging and purchased option hedges) would conflict with the basic model of Statement 133. The Board also concluded that additional amendments to Statement 133 were warranted to clarify certain provisions of the Statement related to implementation guidance arising from the DIG process and cleared by the Board and posted on its web site.

10. In March 2000, the Board issued an Exposure Draft, *Accounting for Certain Derivative Instruments*

and Certain Hedging Activities, for a 31-day comment period. Eighty-two organizations and individuals responded to the Exposure Draft. The Board considered the comments received during its redeliberations of the issues addressed by the Exposure Draft in three public meetings during April and May 2000. The Board concluded that it could reach informed decisions on the basis of existing information without a public hearing.

Amendments to Statement 133

Normal Purchases and Normal Sales Exception

11. This Statement amends Statement 133 to permit the normal purchases and normal sales exception in paragraph 10(b) of Statement 133 to be applied to certain contracts that meet the net settlement provisions discussed in paragraphs 9(a) and 57(c)(1) and the market mechanism provisions discussed in paragraphs 9(b) and 57(c)(2). The Board received comments that certain contracts, such as purchase orders for which physical delivery was intended and expected in the normal course of business, met the definition of a derivative because of the net settlement provisions in paragraphs 9(a) and 57(c)(1) and the market mechanism provisions in paragraphs 9(b) and 57(c)(2). The Board decided that contracts that require delivery of nonfinancial assets need not be accounted for as derivative instruments under this Statement if the assets constitute normal purchases or normal sales of the reporting entity and the criteria identified in paragraph 4(a) of this Statement were met.

12. The Board believes that the normal purchases and normal sales exception should not be permitted to be applied to contracts that require cash settlements of gains or losses or otherwise settle gains or losses on a periodic basis because those settlements are net settlements. The Board observed that an entity may designate those contracts as a hedged item in an all-in-one hedge, pursuant to Statement 133 Implementation Issue No. G2, "Hedged Transactions That Arise from Gross Settlement of a Derivative ('All in One' Hedges)."

13. Some respondents to the Exposure Draft suggested that a planned series of contracts used in the normal course of business consistent with recognized industry practice should qualify for the normal purchases and normal sales exception. Some respondents in the electric utility industry suggested that the unplanned netting of transactions with the same counterparty (referred to as a "bookout") should also qualify for the normal purchases and normal sales exception. They also noted that because of changes in circumstances, the bookout procedure is common in the electric utility industry as a scheduling convenience when two utilities happen to have offsetting transactions. The Board rejected both notions because those transactions result in a net settlement of the contract. The normal purchases and normal sales exception only relates to a contract that results in gross delivery of the commodity under that contract.

Hedging the Benchmark Interest Rate

14. This Statement amends Statement 133 to permit a *benchmark interest rate* to be designated as the hedged risk in a hedge of interest rate risk. Statement 133 Implementation Issue No. E1, "Hedging the Risk-Free Interest Rate," provided implementation guidance for Statement 133 that indicated that the hedged risk in a hedge of interest rate risk would be the hedged item's *market interest rate,* defined as the risk-free rate plus the credit sector spread appropriate for that hedged item at the inception of the hedge. Comments received by the Board on Implementation Issue E1 indicated (a) that the concept of market interest rate risk as set forth in Statement 133 differed from the common understanding of interest rate risk by market participants, (b) that the guidance in the Implementation Issue was inconsistent with present hedging activities, and (c) that measuring the change in fair value of the hedged item attributable to changes in credit sector spreads would be difficult because consistent sector spread data are not readily available in the market.

15. The Board decided that, with respect to the separation of interest rate risk and credit risk, the risk of changes in credit sector spread and any credit spread attributable to a specific borrower should be encompassed in credit risk rather than interest rate risk. Under that approach, an entity would be permitted to designate the risk of changes in the risk-free rate as the hedged risk, and any spread above that rate would be deemed to reflect credit risk. The Board concluded that considering all the effects of credit risk together was more understandable and more operational than the distinction between interest rate risk and credit risk in Implementation Issue E1.

16. The Board decided that, in the United States, the interest rate on direct Treasury obligations of the U.S. government provides the best measure of the risk-free rate. Thus, the Board considered defining interest

rate risk based only on Treasury rates in the United States. However, the Board decided to make an exception and extend the definition of interest rate risk to include interest rate swap rates based on the London Interbank Offered Rate (LIBOR). The Board had been informed that

a. LIBOR-based interest rate swaps are the most commonly used hedging instruments in the U.S. financial markets in hedges of interest rate risk.
b. There are technical factors (such as supply and demand) that may affect the rates on direct obligations of any single issuer, even the U.S. government.
c. Financial markets consider LIBOR rates as inherently liquid, stable, and a reliable indicator of interest rates and, if the rate for hedging interest rate risk was limited to U.S. Treasury rates, many common hedging relationships using LIBOR-based swaps might not qualify for hedge accounting.

Because the Board decided to permit a rate that is not fully risk-free to be the designated risk in a hedge of interest rate risk, it developed the general notion of *benchmark interest rate* to encompass both risk-free rates and rates based on the LIBOR swap curve in the United States.

17. In deliberations leading up to the Exposure Draft and in response to comments on the Exposure Draft, the Board considered whether other rates, such as the commercial paper rate and the Fed Funds rate, in the U.S. financial markets should be included in the definition of benchmark interest rate and whether those rates should be permitted to be designated as the hedged risk in a hedge of interest rate risk. The Board also considered the notion of defining the benchmark interest rate as the portion of an instrument's overall rate that is used as the underlying basis for pricing a financial instrument. (For example, numerous indexes such as the Fed Funds rate, the Prime rate, the FNMA Par Mortgage rate, and the BMA index are used as the underlying basis for pricing a financial instrument.) The Board rejected both notions and decided that allowing more than two benchmark rates to define interest rate risk was unnecessary and would make the resulting financial statements more difficult to understand. Therefore, other such indexes may not be used as the benchmark interest rate in the United States.

18. The Board considered the operationality of the definition of the benchmark interest rate in global financial markets. The Board acknowledged that, in some foreign markets, the rate of interest on sovereign debt is considered the benchmark interest rate; that is, market participants consider that rate free of credit risk. However, in other markets, the relevant interbank offered rate may be the best reflection of the benchmark interest rate.

19. The Board determined that any definition of the benchmark interest rate that may be hedged should be flexible enough to withstand potential future developments in financial markets. For example, the Board decided that the current definition would result in the ability to replace the LIBOR swap rate with a more relevant benchmark interest rate should changes in the financial markets render the use of LIBOR swap rates obsolete.

20. Respondents to the Exposure Draft indicated that the Board should revise the proposed amendments to paragraphs 21(f) and 29(h) that stated that the benchmark interest rate being hedged in a hedge of interest rate risk should not reflect greater credit risk than is inherent in the hedged item. They said that many financial instruments are priced based on a positive or negative credit spread to the benchmark rate and that interest rate risk is managed based on the benchmark rate, regardless of whether the rate inherent in the instrument is above or below the benchmark rate. The Board rejected the notion of the existence of negative credit risk, but on an exception basis it decided to remove the prohibition that the benchmark interest rate being hedged in a hedge of interest rate risk should not reflect greater credit risk than is inherent in the hedged item. Thus, the benchmark interest rate can be the designated hedged risk in a hedge of interest rate risk regardless of the credit risk inherent in the hedged item (for example, the LIBOR swap rate could be the designated hedged risk in an AAA-rated security even if the overall market interest rate of the instrument is less than the LIBOR swap rate).

21. This Statement requires that in a cash flow hedge of a variable-rate financial asset or liability, either existing or forecasted, the designated risk being hedged cannot be the risk of changes in its cash flows attributable to changes in the benchmark interest rate if the cash flows of the hedged transaction are explicitly based on a different index. The effectiveness of a cash flow hedge of the variability in interest payments of a variable-rate financial asset or liability, either existing or forecasted, is affected by the interest rate index on which the variability is based and the extent to which the hedging instrument provides offset. Changes in credit sector spreads embodied

within the interest rate index on which the variability is based do not affect the assessment and measurement of hedge effectiveness if both the cash flows on the hedging instrument and the hedged cash flows of the existing financial asset or liability or the variable-rate financial asset or liability that is forecasted to be acquired or issued are based on the same index. However, if the cash flows on the hedging instrument and the hedged cash flows of the existing financial asset or liability or the variable-rate financial asset or liability that is forecasted to be acquired or issued are based on different indexes, the basis difference between those indexes would affect the assessment and measurement of hedge effectiveness.

Shortcut method

22. Because the shortcut method applies to hedges of interest rate risk with the use of an interest rate swap, the decision to redefine interest rate risk necessitated that the Board address the effect on the shortcut method for fair value hedges and cash flow hedges. For fair value hedges, an assumption of no ineffectiveness, an important premise of the shortcut method, is invalidated when the interest rate index embodied in the variable leg of the interest rate swap is different from the benchmark interest rate being hedged. In situations in which the interest rate index embodied in the variable leg of the swap has greater credit risk than that embodied in the benchmark interest rate, the effect of the change in the swap's credit sector spread over that in the benchmark interest rate would represent hedge ineffectiveness because it relates to an *unhedged* risk (credit risk) rather than to the hedged risk (interest rate risk). In situations in which the interest rate index embodied in the variable leg of the swap has less credit risk than that embodied in the benchmark interest rate, the effect of the change in a certain portion of the hedged item's spread over the swap interest rate would also represent hedge ineffectiveness. The Board decided that in order for an entity to comply with an assumption of no ineffectiveness, the index on which the variable leg of the swap is based should match the benchmark interest rate designated as the interest rate risk being hedged for the hedging relationship.

23. For cash flow hedges of an existing variable-rate financial asset or liability, the designated risk being hedged cannot be the risk of changes in its cash flows attributable to changes in the benchmark interest rate if the cash flows of the hedged item are explicitly based on a different index. In those situations, because the risk of changes in the benchmark interest

rate (that is, interest rate risk) cannot be the designated risk being hedged, the shortcut method cannot be applied. The Board's decision to require that the index on which the variable leg of the swap is based match the benchmark interest rate designated as the interest rate risk being hedged for the hedging relationship also ensures that the shortcut method is applied only to interest rate risk hedges. The Board's decision precludes use of the shortcut method in situations in which the cash flows of the hedged item and the hedging instrument are based on the same index but that index is not the designated benchmark interest rate. The Board noted, however, that in some of those situations, an entity easily could determine that the hedge is perfectly effective. The shortcut method would be permitted for cash flow hedges in situations in which the cash flows of the hedged item and the hedging instrument are based on the same index and that index is the designated benchmark interest rate.

Determining the change in a hedged item's fair value attributable to changes in the benchmark interest rate

24. This Statement provides limited guidance on how the change in a hedged item's fair value attributable to changes in the designated benchmark interest rate should be determined. The Board decided that in calculating the change in the hedged item's fair value attributable to changes in the designated benchmark interest rate, the estimated cash flows used must be based on all of the contractual cash flows of the entire hedged item. That guidance does not mandate the use of any one method, but it precludes the use of a method that excludes some of the hedged item's contractual cash flows (such as the portion of interest payments attributable to the obligor's credit risk above the benchmark rate) from the calculation. The Board concluded that excluding some of the hedged item's contractual cash flows would introduce a new approach to bifurcation of a hedged item that does not currently exist in the Statement 133 hedging model.

Hedging Recognized Foreign-Currency-Denominated Assets or Liabilities

25. This Statement amends Statement 133 to allow a recognized foreign-currency-denominated asset or liability to be the hedged item in a fair value or cash flow hedge. Statement 133 precluded hedge accounting for an asset or liability that is remeasured for changes in price attributable to the risk being hedged when those changes are reported currently in earnings. Statement 133 also precluded fair value or cash

flow hedge accounting for foreign currency risk associated with any asset or liability that is denominated in a foreign currency and remeasured into the functional currency under FASB Statement No. 52, *Foreign Currency Translation*. The Board received requests to remove the preclusion for any asset or liability denominated in a foreign currency because, even though the transaction gain or loss on the undesignated asset or liability and the change in fair value of the undesignated derivative were reported currently in earnings, different measurement criteria were used for each instrument, which created volatility in earnings.

26. The Exposure Draft proposed an exception to the general principle to permit both fair value hedges and cash flow hedges of foreign-currency-denominated debt instruments. The exception was applicable to foreign-currency-denominated debt instruments that were either held (assets) or owed (liabilities) and included instruments such as bonds, loans, receivables, and payables. The Board initially decided to limit the hedged items to debt instruments because of uncertainty related to the types of instruments that could possibly be included in the scope if all recognized foreign-currency-denominated assets or liabilities were permitted to be hedged. Respondents to the Exposure Draft requested that the Board expand the scope of the allowable hedged items beyond debt instruments. They noted that the concerns expressed by the Board could be mitigated if the determination of the eligibility of a hedged item was based on whether the item gives rise to a transaction gain or loss under paragraph 15 of Statement 52. The Board concluded that basing the eligibility of the hedged item on the guidance in paragraph 15 of Statement 52 would mitigate the scope concerns. Therefore, the Board decided to permit all recognized foreign-currency-denominated assets and liabilities for which a foreign currency transaction gain or loss is recognized in earnings to be hedged items.

27. Designated hedging instruments and hedged items qualify for fair value hedge accounting and cash flow hedge accounting under this Statement only if all of the criteria in Statement 133 for fair value hedge accounting and cash flow hedge accounting are met. The Board concluded that fair value hedges could be used for all recognized foreign-currency-denominated asset or liability hedging situations and that cash flow hedges could be used for recognized foreign-currency-denominated asset or liability hedging situations in which all of the variability in the functional-currency-equivalent cash flows are eliminated by the effect of the hedge. Remeasurement of the foreign-currency-denominated assets and liabilities will continue to be based on the guidance in Statement 52, which requires remeasurement based on spot exchange rates, regardless of whether a fair value hedging relationship or a cash flow hedging relationship exists.

28. The Board decided to permit cash flow hedge accounting for recognized foreign-currency-denominated assets and liabilities because it believes that the effects on earnings related to the use of different measurement criteria for the hedged transaction and the hedging instrument will be eliminated. The transaction gain or loss arising from the remeasurement of the foreign-currency-denominated asset or liability would be offset by a related amount reclassified each period from other comprehensive income to earnings. The Board believes that is consistent with the principal purpose of providing special hedge accounting to mitigate the effects on earnings of different existing measurement criteria.

29. The Board's decision to permit fair value hedge accounting for assets and liabilities denominated in a foreign currency relates to the ability of an entity to designate a compound derivative as a hedging instrument in a hedge of both interest rate risk and foreign exchange rate risk. An entity's ability to use a compound derivative would achieve the same result that would be achieved prior to this amendment with the use of an interest rate derivative as a qualifying hedging instrument to hedge interest rate risk and an undesignated foreign currency derivative to hedge exchange rate risk. Permitting use of a compound derivative in a fair value hedge of interest rate risk and foreign exchange risk would result in the value of the foreign currency asset or liability being adjusted for changes in fair value attributable to changes in foreign interest rates before remeasurement at the spot exchange rate. The ability to adjust the foreign currency asset or liability for changes in foreign interest rates effectively eliminates any difference recognized currently in earnings related to the use of different measurement criteria for the hedged item and the hedging instrument. The Board concluded that in the situations in which fair value hedges would be used, remeasurement of the foreign-currency-denominated asset or liability based on the spot exchange rate would result in the same functional currency value that would result if the instrument was remeasured based on the forward exchange rate.

Hedging with Intercompany Derivatives

30. Paragraph 36 of Statement 133 permits a derivative instrument entered into with another member of the consolidated group to qualify as a foreign currency hedging instrument in the consolidated financial statements only if the member of the consolidated group has entered into an individual offsetting derivative contract with an unrelated third party. Constituents requested that Statement 133 be amended to permit derivative instruments entered into with a member of the consolidated group to qualify as hedging instruments in the consolidated financial statements if those internal derivatives are offset by unrelated third-party contracts on a net basis.

31. Constituents requested that those amendments continue to reflect the practice employed by many organizations of managing risk on a centralized basis. That practice involves transferring risk exposures assumed by various affiliates to a treasury center through internal derivative contracts, which are designated as hedging instruments by the affiliates. The risk exposures assumed by the treasury center by issuing internal derivative contracts to affiliates are offset on a net basis, rather than individually, by contracts with unrelated third parties. In the original deliberations leading to the issuance of Statement 133, the Board determined that the functional currency concepts of Statement 52 necessitated that the operating unit that has exposure to foreign exchange risk be a party to the hedging instrument. That foreign exchange risk exists because the currency in which a transaction is denominated is different from the operating unit's functional currency. The Board also recognized the prevalent use of treasury center operations to centrally manage foreign exchange risk. Because of those factors, the Board decided in its original deliberations of Statement 133 to permit the designation of a derivative issued by a member of the consolidated group as a foreign currency hedging instrument in the consolidated financial statements, provided that the internal derivative was offset on a one-to-one basis with a third party. Constituents said that while paragraph 36 of Statement 133 permits both the designation of internal derivatives as hedges of foreign exchange risk and the use of a treasury center, the requirement to individually offset each internal derivative with a third-party contract negates the efficiency and cost savings provided by a treasury center.

32. In considering the requests for amendment, the Board observed that a fundamental justification for the application of hedge accounting to internal derivative contracts in consolidated financial statements under paragraph 36 of Statement 133 is the existence of an individual offsetting third-party derivative contract that supports each internal derivative. Further, the practice of offsetting multiple internal derivatives with a net third-party contract appears to portray the nonderivative hedged items in various affiliates functioning as hedges of one another. The Board also observed that applying hedge accounting to internal derivatives that are offset on a net basis by a third-party derivative contract could be viewed as macro hedging—using a single derivative to hedge a dissimilar portfolio of assets *and* liabilities—which is not permitted under Statement 133. However, the Board acknowledged that this practice differs from macro hedging because internal derivative contracts establish individual hedging relationships that can be linked to the net third-party contract.

33. In addition, the Board concluded that applying hedge accounting in the consolidated financial statements under Statement 133 to internal derivatives that are offset on a net basis by third-party contracts would conflict with basic consolidation procedures required by paragraph 6 of ARB No. 51, *Consolidated Financial Statements.* The Board determined that such a conflict exists because certain effects related to intercompany balances arising from the application of hedge accounting to internal derivative contracts would not be eliminated in consolidation. For example, for fair value hedges, the adjustment to the carrying amount of the hedged item, as determined by the change in fair value of the hedged item attributable to the hedged risk, results from applying hedge accounting to internal derivatives and would not be eliminated in consolidation. For cash flow hedges, amounts recorded in other comprehensive income, and the timing of reclassification of those amounts into earnings, similarly result from applying hedge accounting to internal derivatives and would not be eliminated in consolidation. For those reasons, the Board determined that, as a general rule, derivatives entered into with a member of the consolidated group should not qualify as hedging instruments in the consolidated financial statements if those internal derivatives are not offset by unrelated third-party contracts on an individual basis.

34. Notwithstanding, the Board decided to permit a limited exception for internal derivatives designated as foreign currency cash flow hedges of forecasted borrowings, purchases, or sales denominated in foreign currency or unrecognized firm commitments,

subject to meeting certain criteria. For foreign currency cash flow hedges of those items, the Board decided to permit internal derivatives designated as hedging instruments to be offset on a net basis, rather than individually, by third-party derivative contracts. The Board believes that exception for those foreign currency cash flow hedges is not sufficiently different from the accounting for certain foreign currency items provided for in existing accounting literature.

35. The Board decided that that exception should not be extended to internal derivatives designated either as foreign currency fair value hedges or foreign currency cash flow hedges of recognized foreign-currency-denominated assets or liabilities (as permitted by paragraphs 36(a) and 36(b) of Statement 133, as amended by this Statement). That is, in order to apply hedge accounting to internal derivatives designated as hedges of those hedged items in the consolidated financial statements, the internal derivatives must be offset by third-party contracts on an individual basis rather than on a net basis. In reaching that conclusion, the Board reasoned that permitting internal derivatives that hedge recognized foreign-currency-denominated assets or liabilities in foreign currency fair value or cash flow hedges to be offset on a net basis would result in the consolidated financial statements reflecting those nonderivative hedged items effectively functioning as hedging instruments in hedges of other foreign-currency-denominated assets or liabilities, forecasted borrowings, purchases, or sales or unrecognized firm commitments in various affiliates. The Board decided not to change the prohibition against using a nonderivative instrument as the hedging instrument in a foreign currency cash flow hedge.

36. The Board also decided not to permit internal derivative contracts to be designated as hedging instruments in the consolidated financial statements in fair value or cash flow hedges of interest rate risk, credit risk, or the risk of changes in overall fair value or cash flows. The Board observed that the requirement that the operating unit that has exposure to risk be a party to the hedging instrument exists only for hedges of foreign exchange risk but not for hedges of risks other than foreign exchange risk. Further, even if internal derivative contracts were permitted to be designated as hedging instruments in the consolidated financial statements in a hedge of interest rate risk, credit risk, or the risk of

changes in overall fair value or cash flows, permitting those internal derivatives to be offset on a net basis by a third-party derivative would create a new anomaly with respect to the application of consolidation procedures. However, in hedging interest rate risk, credit risk, or the risk of changes in overall fair value or cash flows, an entity may use internal derivatives as hedging instruments in separate company financial statements.

Amendments to the Transition Provisions and the Examples in Appendix B

37. This Statement amends the transition provisions in paragraph 52(b) of Statement 133 for determining the transition adjustment for the hedged item designated in a preexisting fair-value-type hedging relationship. The Board received comments that the requirements that the overall gain or loss on the hedged item determined based on the difference between the hedged item's fair value and its carrying amount on the date of initial application could result in recognizing the effect of unhedged risks in that transition adjustment. As a result, the Board decided to also allow the determination of the hedged item's transition adjustment to be based on the change in the hedged item's fair value attributable to the hedged risk (limited to the hedged risks that can be designated under paragraph 21 of Statement 133) during the period of the preexisting hedging relationship.

38. This Statement also deletes the last sentence of paragraph 161 because the hedging instrument in Example 8 does not meet the criterion in paragraph 68(b) to qualify for the shortcut method. The hedging instrument does not have fair value of zero at inception of the hedging relationship.

39. Paragraph 155 is also amended because Swap 1 in Example 8 does not qualify for the shortcut method. The swap is designated in a hedge of a series of forecasted interest payments, only one of which relates to a recognized interest-bearing liability; the remainder relate to a forecasted borrowing. The shortcut method is limited to either a fair value or cash flow hedging relationship of interest rate risk involving an existing recognized interest-bearing asset or liability and an interest rate swap. Thus, a cash flow hedge of the variability in interest on a probable forecasted lending or borrowing is not eligible for the shortcut method.

Appendix B

AMENDED PARAGRAPHS OF STATEMENT 133 MARKED TO SHOW CHANGES MADE BY THIS STATEMENT

40. This appendix contains paragraphs of Statement 133 marked to integrate changes from this amendment. The Board plans to issue an amended version of Statement 133 that includes the standards section, the implementation guidance (including examples), and the glossary.

> 10b. *Normal purchases and normal sales.* Normal purchases and normal sales are contracts that provide for the purchase or sale of something other than a financial instrument or derivative instrument that will be delivered in quantities expected to be used or sold by the reporting entity over a reasonable period in the normal course of business. However, contracts that have a price based on an underlying that is not clearly and closely related to the asset being sold or purchased (such as a price in a contract for the sale of a grain commodity based in part on changes in the S&P index) or that are denominated in a foreign currency that meets neither of the criteria in paragraphs 15(a) and 15(b) shall not be considered normal purchases and normal sales. Contracts that contain net settlement provisions as described in paragraphs 9(a) and 9(b) may qualify for the normal purchases and normal sales exception if it is probable at inception and throughout the term of the individual contract that the contract will not settle net and will result in physical delivery. Net settlement (as described in paragraphs 9(a) and 9(b)) of contracts in a group of contracts similarly designated as normal purchases and normal sales would call into question the classification of all such contracts as normal purchases or normal sales. Contracts that require cash settlements of gains or losses or are otherwise settled net on a periodic basis, including individual contracts that are part of a series of sequential contracts intended to accomplish ultimate acquisition or sale of a commodity, do not qualify for this exception. For contracts that qualify for the normal purchases and normal sales exception, the entity shall document the basis for concluding that it is probable that the contract will result in physical delivery. The documentation requirements can be applied either to groups of similarly designated contracts or to each individual contract.~~with no net settlement provision and no market mechanism to facilitate net settlement (as described in paragraphs 9(a) and 9(b)). They provide for the purchase or sale of something other than a financial instrument or derivative instrument that will be delivered in quantities expected to be used or sold by the reporting entity over a reasonable period in the normal course of business.~~

12. Contracts that do not in their entirety meet the definition of a derivative instrument (refer to paragraphs 6–9), such as bonds, insurance policies, and leases, may contain "embedded" derivative instruments—implicit or explicit terms that affect some or all of the cash flows or the value of other exchanges required by the contract in a manner similar to a derivative instrument. The effect of embedding a derivative instrument in another type of contract ("the host contract") is that some or all of the cash flows or other exchanges that otherwise would be required by the host contract, whether unconditional or contingent upon the occurrence of a specified event, will be modified based on one or more underlyings. An embedded derivative instrument shall be separated from the host contract and accounted for as a derivative instrument pursuant to this Statement if and only if all of the following criteria are met:

a. The economic characteristics and risks of the embedded derivative instrument are not clearly and closely related to the economic characteristics and risks of the host contract. Additional guidance on applying this criterion to various contracts containing embedded derivative instruments is included in Appendix A of this Statement.

b. The contract ("the hybrid instrument") that embodies both the embedded derivative instrument and the host contract is not remeasured at fair value under otherwise applicable generally accepted accounting principles with changes in fair value reported in earnings as they occur.

c. A separate instrument with the same terms as the embedded derivative instrument would, pursuant to paragraphs 6–11, be a derivative instrument subject to the requirements of this Statement. (The initial net investment for the hybrid instrument shall not be considered to be the initial net investment for the embedded derivative.)

Fair Value Hedges

The hedged item

21(c). The hedged item is not (1) an asset or liability that is remeasured with the changes in fair value attributable to the hedged risk reported currently in earnings ~~(for example, if foreign exchange risk is hedged, a foreign-currency-denominated asset for which a foreign currency transaction gain or loss is recognized in earnings)~~, (2) an investment accounted for by the equity method in accordance with the requirements of APB Opinion No. 18, *The Equity Method of Accounting for Investments in Common Stock,* (3) a minority interest in one or more consolidated subsidiaries, (4) an equity investment in a consolidated subsidiary, (5) a firm commitment either to enter into a business combination or to acquire or dispose of a subsidiary, a minority interest, or an equity method investee, or (6) an equity instrument issued by the entity and classified in stockholders' equity in the statement of financial position.

21(d). If the hedged item is all or a portion of a debt security (or a portfolio of similar debt securities) that is classified as held-to-maturity in accordance with FASB Statement No. 115, *Accounting for Certain Investments in Debt and Equity Securities,* the designated risk being hedged is the risk of changes in its fair value attributable to credit risk, foreign exchange risk, or both. If the hedged item is an option component of a held-to-maturity security that permits its prepayment, the designated risk being hedged is the risk of changes in the entire fair value of that option component.~~the risk of changes in its fair value attributable to changes in the obligor's creditworthiness or if the hedged item is an option component of a held-to-maturity security that permits its prepayment, the designated risk being hedged is the risk of changes in the entire fair value of that option component.~~ (The designated hedged risk for a held-to-maturity security may not be the risk of changes in its fair value attributable to interest rate risk~~changes in market interest rates or foreign exchange rates~~. If the hedged item is other than an option component that permits its prepayment, the designated hedged risk also may not be the risk of changes in its overall fair value.)

21(f). If the hedged item is a financial asset or liability, a recognized loan servicing right, or a nonfinancial firm commitment with financial components, the designated risk being hedged is

    (1) the risk of changes in the overall fair value of the entire hedged item,

    (2) the risk of changes in its fair value attributable to changes in the designated benchmark interest rate (referred to as interest rate risk)~~market interest rates~~,

    (3) the risk of changes in its fair value attributable to changes in the related foreign currency exchange rates (referred to as foreign exchange risk) (refer to paragraphs 37, 37A, and 38)~~(refer to paragraphs 37 and 38)~~, or

    (4) the risk of changes in its fair value attributable to both changes in the obligor's creditworthiness and changes in the spread over the benchmark interest rate with respect to the hedged item's credit sector at inception of the hedge (referred to as credit risk)~~the obligor's creditworthiness~~.

If the risk designated as being hedged is not the risk in paragraph 21(f)(1) above, two or more of the other risks (~~market~~ interest rate risk, foreign currency exchange risk, and credit risk) may simultaneously be designated as being hedged. The benchmark interest rate being hedged in a hedge of interest rate risk must be specifically identified as part of the designation and documentation at the inception of the hedging relationship. Ordinarily, an entity should designate the same benchmark interest rate as the risk being hedged for similar hedges, consistent with paragraph 62; the use of different benchmark interest rates for similar hedges should be rare and must be justified. In calculating the change in the hedged item's fair value attributable to changes in the benchmark interest rate, the estimated cash flows used in calculating fair value must be based on all of the contractual cash flows of the entire hedged item. Excluding some of the hedged item's contractual cash flows (for example, the portion of the interest coupon in excess of the benchmark interest rate) from the calculation is not permitted.* An entity may not simply designate prepayment risk as the risk being hedged for a financial asset. However, it can designate the option component of a prepayable instrument as the hedged item in a fair value hedge of the entity's exposure to changes in the overall fair value of that "prepayment" option, perhaps thereby achieving the objective of its desire to hedge prepayment risk. The effect of an embedded derivative of the same risk class must be considered in designating a hedge of an individual risk. For example, the effect of an embedded prepayment option must be considered in designating a hedge of ~~market~~ interest rate risk.

---

*The first sentence of paragraph 21(a) that specifically permits the hedged item to be identified as either all or a specific portion of a recognized asset or liability or of an unrecognized firm commitment is not affected by the provisions in this subparagraph.

Cash Flow Hedges

The hedged forecasted transaction

29(d). The forecasted transaction is not the acquisition of an asset or incurrence of a liability that will subsequently be remeasured with changes in fair value attributable to the hedged risk reported currently in earnings ~~(for example, if foreign exchange risk is hedged, the forecasted acquisition of a foreign-currency-denominated asset for which a foreign currency transaction gain or loss will be recognized in earnings). However, forecasted sales on credit and the forecasted accrual of royalties on probable future sales by third-party licensees are not considered the forecasted acquisition of a receivable~~. If the forecasted transaction relates to a recognized asset or liability, the asset or liability is not remeasured with changes in fair value attributable to the hedged risk reported currently in earnings.

29(e). If the variable cash flows of the forecasted transaction relate to a debt security that is classified as held-to-maturity under Statement 115, the risk being hedged is the risk of changes in its cash flows attributable to credit risk, foreign exchange risk, or both~~default or changes in the obligor's creditworthiness~~. For those variable cash flows, the risk being hedged cannot be the risk of changes in its cash flows attributable to interest rate risk~~changes in market interest rates~~.

29(g)(2). the risk of changes in the cash flows relating to all changes in the purchase price or sales price of the asset ~~(reflecting its actual location if a physical asset)~~ (regardless of whether that price and the related cash flows are stated in the entity's functional currency or a foreign currency), not the risk of changes in the cash flows relating to the purchase or sale of a similar asset in a different location or of a major ingredient. Thus, for example, in hedging the exposure to changes in the cash flows relating to the purchase of its bronze bar inventory, an entity may not designate the risk of changes in the cash flows relating to purchasing the copper component in bronze as the risk being hedged for purposes of assessing offset as required by paragraph 28(b).

29(h). If the hedged transaction is the forecasted purchase or sale of a financial asset or liability (or the interest payments on that financial asset or liability) or the variable cash inflow or outflow of an existing financial asset or liability, the designated risk being hedged is
    (1) the risk of overall changes in the hedged cash flows ~~of~~related to the ~~entire~~ asset or liability, such as those relating to all changes in the purchase price or sales price (regardless of whether that price and the related cash flows are stated in the entity's functional currency or a foreign currency),
    (2) the risk of changes in its cash flows attributable to changes in the designated benchmark interest rate (referred to as interest rate risk)~~market interest rates~~,

(3) the risk of changes in the functional-currency-equivalent cash flows attributable to changes in the related foreign currency exchange rates (referred to as foreign exchange risk) (refer to paragraphs 40, 40A, 40B, and 40C)~~(refer to paragraph 40)~~, or

(4) the risk of changes in its cash flows attributable to default, changes in the obligor's credit-worthiness, and changes in the spread over the benchmark interest rate with respect to the hedged item's credit sector at inception of the hedge (referred to as credit risk)~~default or changes in the obligor's creditworthiness~~.

Two or more of the above risks may be designated simultaneously as being hedged. The benchmark interest rate being hedged in a hedge of interest rate risk must be specifically identified as part of the designation and documentation at the inception of the hedging relationship. Ordinarily, an entity should designate the same benchmark interest rate as the risk being hedged for similar hedges, consistent with paragraph 62; the use of different benchmark interest rates for similar hedges should be rare and must be justified. In a cash flow hedge of a variable-rate financial asset or liability, either existing or forecasted, the designated risk being hedged cannot be the risk of changes in its cash flows attributable to changes in the specifically identified benchmark interest rate if the cash flows of the hedged transaction are explicitly based on a different index, for example, based on a specific bank's prime rate, which cannot qualify as the benchmark rate. However, the risk designated as being hedged could potentially be the risk of overall changes in the hedged cash flows related to the asset or liability, provided that the other criteria for a cash flow hedge have been met. An entity may not designate prepayment risk as the risk being hedged (refer to paragraph 21(f)).

30. The effective portion of the gain or loss on a derivative designated as a cash flow hedge is reported in other comprehensive income, and the ineffective portion is reported in earnings. More specifically, a qualifying cash flow hedge shall be accounted for as follows:

a. If an entity's defined risk management strategy for a particular hedging relationship excludes a specific component of the gain or loss, or related cash flows, on the hedging derivative from the assessment of hedge effectiveness (as discussed in paragraph 63 in Section 2 of Appendix A), that excluded component of the gain or loss shall be recognized currently in earnings. For example, if the effectiveness of a hedge with an option contract is assessed based on changes in the option's intrinsic value, the changes in the option's time value would be recognized in earnings. Time value is equal to the fair value of the option less its intrinsic value.

b. Accumulated other comprehensive income associated with the hedged transaction shall be adjusted to a balance that reflects the *lesser* of the following (in absolute amounts):

(1) The cumulative gain or loss on the derivative from inception of the hedge less (a) the excluded component discussed in paragraph 30(a) above and (b) the derivative's gains or losses previously reclassified from accumulated other comprehensive income into earnings pursuant to paragraph 31

(2) The portion of the cumulative gain or loss on the derivative necessary to offset the cumulative change in expected future cash flows on the hedged transaction from inception of the hedge less the derivative's gains or losses previously reclassified from accumulated other comprehensive income into earnings pursuant to paragraph 31.

That adjustment of accumulated other comprehensive income shall incorporate recognition in other comprehensive income of part or all of the gain or loss on the hedging derivative, as necessary.

c. A gain or loss shall be recognized in earnings, as necessary, for any remaining gain or loss on the hedging derivative or to adjust other comprehensive income to the balance specified in paragraph 30(b) above.

d. In a cash flow hedge of the variability of the functional-currency-equivalent cash flows for a recognized foreign-currency-denominated asset or liability that is remeasured at spot exchange rates under paragraph 15 of Statement 52, an amount that will offset the related transaction gain or loss arising from the remeasurement and adjust earnings for the cost to the purchaser (income to the seller) of the hedging instrument shall be reclassified each period from other comprehensive income to earnings.

Section 2 of Appendix A illustrates assessing hedge effectiveness and measuring hedge ineffectiveness. Examples 6 and 9 of Section 1 of Appendix B illustrate the application of this paragraph.

33. The net derivative gain or loss related to a discontinued cash flow hedge shall continue to be reported in accumulated other comprehensive income unless it is probable that the forecasted transaction will *not* occur by the end of the originally specified time period (as documented at the inception of the hedging relationship) or within an additional two-month period of time thereafter, except as indicated in the following sentence. In rare cases, the existence of extenuating circumstances that are related to the nature of the forecasted transaction and are outside the control or influence of the reporting entity may cause the forecasted transaction to be probable of occurring on a date that is beyond the additional two-month period of time, in which case the net derivative gain or loss related to the discontinued cash flow hedge shall continue to be reported in accumulated other comprehensive income until it is reclassified into earnings pursuant to paragraph 31. If it is probable that the hedged forecasted transaction will not occur either by the end of the originally specified time period or within the additional two-month period of time and the hedged forecasted transaction also does not qualify for the exception described in the preceding sentence, that derivative gain or loss reported in accumulated other comprehensive income shall be reclassified into earnings immediately.~~If a cash flow hedge is discontinued because it is probable that the original forecasted transaction will not occur, the net gain or loss in accumulated other comprehensive income shall be immediately reclassified into earnings.~~

Foreign Currency Hedges

36. ~~Consistent with the functional currency concept in Statement 52~~If the hedged item is denominated in a foreign currency, an entity may designate the following types of hedges of foreign currency exposure, as specified in paragraphs 37–42:

a. A fair value hedge of an unrecognized firm commitment or a recognized asset or liability (including an available-for-sale security)

b. A cash flow hedge of a forecasted ~~foreign-currency-denominated~~ transaction, an unrecognized firm commitment, the forecasted functional-currency-equivalent cash flows associated with a recognized asset or liability, or a forecasted intercompany ~~foreign-currency-denominated~~ transaction

c. A hedge of a net investment in a foreign operation.

The recognition in earnings of the foreign currency transaction gain or loss on a foreign-currency-denominated asset or liability based on changes in the foreign currency spot rate is not considered to be the remeasurement of that asset or liability with changes in fair value attributable to foreign exchange risk recognized in earnings, which is discussed in the criteria~~The criterion~~ in paragraphs 21(c)(1) and 29(d).~~requires that a recognized asset or liability that may give rise to a foreign currency transaction gain or loss under Statement 52 (such as a foreign-currency-denominated receivable or payable) not be the hedged item in a foreign currency fair value or cash flow hedge because it is remeasured with the changes in the carrying amount attributable to what would be the hedged risk (an exchange rate change) reported currently in earnings.~~ Thus, those criteria are not impediments to either a foreign currency fair value or cash flow hedge of such a foreign-currency-denominated asset or liability or a foreign currency cash flow hedge of the forecasted acquisition or incurrence of a foreign-currency-denominated asset or liability whose carrying amount will be remeasured at spot exchange rates under paragraph 15 of Statement 52.~~Similarly, the criterion in paragraph 29(d) requires that the forecasted acquisition of an asset or the incurrence of a liability that may give rise to a foreign currency transaction gain or loss under Statement 52 not be the hedged item in a foreign currency cash flow hedge because, subsequent to acquisition or incurrence, the asset or liability will be remeasured with changes in the carrying amount attributable to what would be the hedged risk reported currently in earnings.~~ A foreign currency derivative instrument that has been entered into with another member of a consolidated group can be a hedging instrument in a fair value hedge or in a cash flow hedge of a recognized foreign-currency-denominated asset or liability or in a net investment hedge in the consolidated financial statements only if that other member has entered into an offsetting contract with an unrelated third party to hedge the exposure it acquired from issuing the derivative instrument to the affiliate that initiated the hedge.

36A. The provisions in paragraph 36 that permit a recognized foreign-currency-denominated asset or liability to be the hedged item in a fair value or cash flow hedge of foreign currency exposure also pertain to a recognized foreign-currency-denominated receivable or payable that results from a hedged forecasted foreign-currency-denominated sale or purchase on credit. An entity may choose to designate a single cash flow hedge that encompasses the variability of functional currency cash flows attributable to foreign exchange risk related to the settlement of the foreign-currency-denominated receivable or payable resulting from a forecasted sale or purchase on credit. Alternatively, an entity may choose to designate a cash flow hedge of the variability of functional currency cash flows attributable to foreign exchange risk related to a forecasted foreign-currency-denominated sale or purchase on credit and then separately designate a foreign currency fair value hedge of the resulting recognized foreign-currency-denominated receivable or payable. In that case, the cash flow hedge would terminate (be dedesignated) when the hedged sale or purchase occurs and the foreign-currency-denominated receivable or payable is recognized. The use of the same foreign currency derivative instrument for both the cash flow hedge and the fair value hedge is not prohibited though some ineffectiveness may result.

Foreign currency fair value hedges

37. *Unrecognized firm commitment.* A derivative instrument or a nonderivative financial instrument[11] that may give rise to a foreign currency transaction gain or loss under Statement 52 can be designated as hedging changes in the fair value of an unrecognized firm commitment, or a specific portion thereof, attributable to foreign currency exchange rates. The designated hedging relationship qualifies for the accounting specified in paragraphs 22–27 if all the fair value hedge criteria in paragraphs 20 and 21 and the conditions in paragraphs 40(a) and 40(b) are met.

37A. *Recognized asset or liability.* A nonderivative financial instrument shall not be designated as the hedging instrument in a fair value hedge of the foreign currency exposure of a recognized asset or liability. A derivative instrument can be designated as hedging the changes in the fair value of a recognized asset or liability (or a specific portion thereof) for which a foreign currency transaction gain or loss is recognized in earnings under the provisions of paragraph 15 of Statement 52. All recognized foreign-currency-denominated assets or liabilities for which a foreign currency transaction gain or loss is recorded in earnings may qualify for the accounting specified in paragraphs 22–27 if all the fair value hedge criteria in paragraphs 20 and 21 and the conditions in paragraphs 40(a) and 40(b) are met.

38. *Available-for-sale security.* A nonderivative financial instrument shall not be designated as the hedging instrument in a fair value hedge of the foreign currency exposure of an available-for-sale security. A derivative instrument can be designated as hedging the changes in the fair value of an available-for-sale *debt* security (or a specific portion thereof) attributable to changes in foreign currency exchange rates. The designated hedging relationship qualifies for the accounting specified in paragraphs 22–27 if all the fair value hedge criteria in paragraphs 20 and 21 and the conditions in paragraphs 40(a) and 40(b) are met. An available-for-sale *equity* security can be hedged for changes in the fair value attributable to changes in foreign currency exchange rates and qualify for the accounting specified in paragraphs 22–27 only if the fair value hedge criteria in paragraphs 20 and 21 are met and the following two conditions are satisfied:

a. The security is not traded on an exchange (or other established marketplace) on which trades are denominated in the investor's functional currency.
b. Dividends or other cash flows to holders of the security are all denominated in the same foreign currency as the currency expected to be received upon sale of the security.

The change in fair value of the hedged available-for-sale equity security attributable to foreign exchange risk is reported in earnings pursuant to paragraph 23 and not in other comprehensive income.

Foreign currency cash flow hedges

40. A nonderivative financial instrument shall not be designated as a hedging instrument in a foreign currency cash flow hedge. A derivative instrument designated as hedging the foreign currency exposure to variability in the functional-currency-equivalent cash flows associated with ~~either~~ a forecasted ~~foreign-currency-denominated~~ transaction (for example, a forecasted export sale to an unaffiliated entity with the price to be denominated in a foreign currency), a recognized asset or liability, an unrecognized firm commitment, or a forecasted intercompany ~~foreign-currency-denominated~~ transaction (for example, a forecasted sale to a foreign subsidiary or a forecasted royalty from a foreign subsidiary) qualifies for hedge accounting if all ~~of~~ the following criteria are met:

a. For consolidated financial statements, either (1) the operating unit that has the foreign currency exposure is a party to the hedging instrument or (2) another member of the consolidated group that has the same functional currency as that operating unit (subject to the restrictions in this subparagraph and related footnote) is a party to the hedging instrument. To qualify for applying the guidance in (2) above, there may be no intervening subsidiary with a different functional currency.* (Refer to paragraphs 36, 40A, and 40B for conditions for which an intercompany foreign currency derivative can be the hedging instrument in a cash flow hedge of foreign exchange risk.)~~The operating unit that has the foreign currency exposure is a party to the hedging instrument (which can be an instrument between a parent company and its subsidiary—refer to paragraph 36).~~

b. ~~The hedged transaction is denominated in a currency other than that~~the hedging unit's functional currency.

c. All of the criteria in paragraphs 28 and 29 are met, except for the criterion in paragraph 29(c) that requires that the forecasted transaction be with a party external to the reporting entity.

d. If the hedged transaction is a group of individual forecasted foreign-currency-denominated transactions, a forecasted inflow of a foreign currency and a forecasted outflow of the foreign currency cannot both be included in the same group.

e. If the hedged item is a recognized foreign-currency-denominated asset or liability, all the variability in the hedged item's functional-currency-equivalent cash flows must be eliminated by the effect of the hedge. (For example, a cash flow hedge cannot be used with a variable-rate foreign-currency-denominated asset or liability and a derivative based solely on changes in exchange rates because the derivative does not eliminate all the variability in the functional currency cash flows.)

40A. *Internal derivative.* A foreign currency derivative contract that has been entered into with another member of a consolidated group (such as a treasury center) can be a hedging instrument in a foreign currency cash flow hedge of a forecasted borrowing, purchase, or sale or an unrecognized firm commitment in the consolidated financial statements only if the following two conditions are satisfied. (That foreign currency derivative instrument is hereafter in this section referred to as an *internal derivative.*)

a. From the perspective of the member of the consolidated group using the derivative as a hedging instrument (hereafter in this section referred to as the *hedging affiliate*), the criteria for foreign currency cash flow hedge accounting in paragraph 40 must be satisfied.

---

*For example, if a dollar-functional, second-tier subsidiary has a Euro exposure, the dollar-functional consolidated parent company could designate its U.S. dollar–Euro derivative as a hedge of the second-tier subsidiary's exposure provided that the functional currency of the intervening first-tier subsidiary (that is, the parent of the second-tier subsidiary) is also the U.S. dollar. In contrast, if the functional currency of the intervening first-tier subsidiary was the Japanese yen (thus requiring the financial statements of the second-tier subsidiary to be translated into yen before the yen-denominated financial statements of the first-tier subsidiary are translated into U.S. dollars for consolidation), the consolidated parent company could not designate its U.S. dollar–Euro derivative as a hedge of the second-tier subsidiary's exposure.

b. The member of the consolidated group not using the derivative as a hedging instrument (hereafter in this section referred to as the *issuing affiliate*) must either (1) enter into a derivative contract with an unrelated third party to offset the exposure that results from that internal derivative or (2) if the conditions in paragraph 40B are met, enter into derivative contracts with unrelated third parties that would offset, on a net basis for each foreign currency, the foreign exchange risk arising from multiple internal derivative contracts.

40B. *Offsetting net exposures.* If an issuing affiliate chooses to offset exposure arising from multiple internal derivative contracts on an aggregate or net basis, the derivatives issued to hedging affiliates may qualify as cash flow hedges in the consolidated financial statements only if all of the following conditions are satisfied:

a. The issuing affiliate enters into a derivative contract with an unrelated third party to offset, on a net basis for each foreign currency, the foreign exchange risk arising from multiple internal derivative contracts, and the derivative contract with the unrelated third party generates equal or closely approximating gains and losses when compared with the aggregate or net losses and gains generated by the derivative contracts issued to affiliates.
b. Internal derivatives that are not designated as hedging instruments are excluded from the determination of the foreign currency exposure on a net basis that is offset by the third-party derivative. In addition, nonderivative contracts may not be used as hedging instruments to offset exposures arising from internal derivative contracts.
c. Foreign currency exposure that is offset by a single net third-party contract arises from internal derivative contracts that mature within the same 31-day period and that involve the same currency exposure as the net third-party derivative. The offsetting net third-party derivative related to that group of contracts must offset the aggregate or net exposure to that currency, must mature within the same 31-day period, and must be entered into within 3 business days after the designation of the internal derivatives as hedging instruments.
d. The issuing affiliate tracks the exposure that it acquires from each hedging affiliate and maintains documentation supporting linkage of each internal derivative contract and the offsetting aggregate or net derivative contract with an unrelated third party.
e. The issuing affiliate does not alter or terminate the offsetting derivative with an unrelated third party unless the hedging affiliate initiates that action. If the issuing affiliate does alter or terminate the offsetting third-party derivative (which should be rare), the hedging affiliate must prospectively cease hedge accounting for the internal derivatives that are offset by that third-party derivative.

40C. A member of a consolidated group is not permitted to offset exposures arising from multiple internal derivative contracts on a net basis for foreign currency cash flow exposures related to recognized foreign-currency-denominated assets or liabilities. That prohibition includes situations in which a recognized foreign-currency-denominated asset or liability in a fair value hedge or cash flow hedge results from the occurrence of a specifically identified forecasted transaction initially designated as a cash flow hedge.

42. A derivative instrument or a nonderivative financial instrument that may give rise to a foreign currency transaction gain or loss under Statement 52 can be designated as hedging the foreign currency exposure of a net investment in a foreign operation provided the conditions in paragraphs 40(a) and 40(b) are met. The gain or loss on a hedging derivative instrument (or the foreign currency transaction gain or loss on the nonderivative hedging instrument) that is designated as, and is effective as, an economic hedge of the net investment in a foreign operation shall be reported in the same manner as a translation adjustment to the extent it is effective as a hedge. The hedged net investment shall be accounted for consistent with Statement 52; the provisions of this Statement for recognizing the gain or loss on assets designated as being hedged in a fair value hedge do not apply to the hedge of a net investment in a foreign operation.

45. An entity's disclosures for every reporting period for which a complete set of financial statements is presented also shall include the following: . . .

Cash flow hedges

b. For derivative instruments that have been designated and have qualified as cash flow hedging instruments and for the related hedged transactions:

   (1) The net gain or loss recognized in earnings during the reporting period representing (a) the amount of the hedges' ineffectiveness and (b) the component of the derivative instruments' gain or loss, if any, excluded from the assessment of hedge effectiveness, and a description of where the net gain or loss is reported in the statement of income or other statement of financial performance

   (2) A description of the transactions or other events that will result in the reclassification into earnings of gains and losses that are reported in accumulated other comprehensive income, and the estimated net amount of the existing gains or losses at the reporting date that is expected to be reclassified into earnings within the next 12 months

   (3) The maximum length of time over which the entity is hedging its exposure to the variability in future cash flows for forecasted transactions excluding those forecasted transactions related to the payment of variable interest on existing financial instruments

   (4) The amount of gains and losses reclassified into earnings as a result of the discontinuance of cash flow hedges because it is probable that the original forecasted transactions will not occur by the end of the originally specified time period or within the additional period of time discussed in paragraph 33.

Effective Date and Transition

52(b). If the transition adjustment relates to a derivative instrument that had been designated in a hedging relationship that addressed the fair value exposure of an asset, a liability, or a firm commitment, the transition adjustment for the derivative shall be reported as a cumulative-effect-type adjustment of net income. Concurrently, any gain or loss on the hedged item ~~(that is, difference between the hedged item's fair value and its carrying amount)~~ shall be recognized as an adjustment of the hedged item's carrying amount at the date of initial application, but only to the extent of an offsetting transition adjustment for the derivative. Only for purposes of applying the preceding sentence in determining the hedged item's transition adjustment, the gain or loss on the hedged item may be either (1) the overall gain or loss on the hedged item determined as the difference between the hedged item's fair value and its carrying amount on the date of initial application (that is, not limited to the portion attributable to the hedged risk nor limited to the gain or loss occurring during the period of the preexisting hedging relationship) or (2) the gain or loss on the hedged item attributable to the hedged risk (limited to the hedged risks that can be designated under paragraph 21 of this Statement) during the period of the preexisting hedging relationship. That adjustment of the hedged item's carrying amount shall also be reported as a cumulative-effect-type adjustment of net income. The transition adjustment related to the gain or loss reported in accumulated other comprehensive income on a derivative instrument that hedged an available-for-sale security, together with the loss or gain on the related security (to the extent of an offsetting transition adjustment for the derivative instrument), shall be reclassified to earnings as a cumulative-effect-type adjustment of both net income and accumulated other comprehensive income.

54. At the date of initial application, an entity may transfer any held-to-maturity security into the available-for-sale category or the trading category. An entity will then be able in the future to designate a security transferred into the available-for-sale category as the hedged item, or its variable interest payments as the cash flow hedged transactions, in a hedge of the exposure to changes in the designated benchmark interest rate~~market interest rates, changes in foreign currency exchange rates~~, or changes in its overall fair value. (Paragraph 21(d) precludes a held-to-maturity security from being designated as the hedged item in a fair value hedge of ~~market~~ interest rate risk or the risk of changes in its overall fair value. Paragraph 29(e) similarly precludes the variable cash flows of a held-to-maturity security from being designated as the hedged transaction in a cash flow hedge of ~~market~~ interest rate risk.) The unrealized holding gain or loss on a held-to-maturity security transferred to another category at the date of

initial application shall be reported in net income or accumulated other comprehensive income consistent with the requirements of paragraphs 15(b) and 15(c) of Statement 115 and reported with the other transition adjustments discussed in paragraph 52 of this Statement. Such transfers from the held-to-maturity category at the date of initial adoption shall not call into question an entity's intent to hold other debt securities to maturity in the future.[14]

---

[14] EITF Topic No. D-51, "The Applicability of FASB Statement No. 115 to Desecuritizations of Financial Assets," indicates that certain financial assets received or retained in a desecuritization must be held to maturity to avoid calling into question the entity's intent to hold other debt securities to maturity in the future. In conjunction with the initial adoption of this Statement, the held-to-maturity restriction on those financial assets held on the date of initial application is removed, and those financial assets that had been received or retained in a previous desecuritization are available in the future to be designated as the hedged item, or their variable interest payments as the hedged transaction, in a hedge of the exposure to changes in interest rate risk~~market interest rates~~. Consequently, the sale of those financial assets before maturity would not call into question the entity's intent to hold other debt securities to maturity in the future.

Appendix A—Implementation Guidance

58. The following discussion further explains some of the exceptions discussed in paragraph 10.

a. *"Regular-way" security trades.* The exception in paragraph 10(a) applies only to a contract that requires delivery of securities that are readily convertible to cash.[16] To qualify, a contract must require delivery of such a security within the period of time after the trade date that is customary in the market in which the trade takes place. For example, a contract to purchase or sell a publicly traded equity security in the United States customarily requires settlement within three business days. If a contract for purchase of that type of security requires settlement in three business days, the regular-way exception applies, but if the contract requires settlement in five days, the regular-way exception does not apply. This Statement does not change whether an entity recognizes regular-way security trades on the trade date or the settlement date. However, trades that do not qualify for the regular-way exception are subject to the requirements of this Statement regardless of the method an entity uses to report its security trades.

b. *Normal purchases and normal sales.* The exception in paragraph 10(b) applies only to a contract that ~~requires~~involves future delivery of assets (other than financial instruments or derivative instruments)~~ that are readily convertible to cash~~[17] ~~and only if there is no market mechanism to facilitate net settlement outside the contract~~. To qualify for the exception, a contract's terms also must be consistent with the terms of an entity's normal purchases or normal sales, that is, the quantity purchased or sold must be reasonable in relation to the entity's business needs. Determining whether or not the terms are consistent will require judgment. In making those judgments, an entity should consider all relevant factors, such as (1) the quantities provided under the contract and the entity's need for the related assets, (2) the locations to which delivery of the items will be made, (3) the period of time between entering into the contract and delivery, and (4) the entity's prior practices with regard to such contracts. Evidence such as past trends, expected future demand, other contracts for delivery of similar items, an entity's and industry's customs for acquiring and storing the related commodities, and an entity's operating locations should help in identifying contracts that qualify as normal purchases or normal sales. Also, in order for a contract that meets the net settlement provisions of paragraphs 9(a) and 57(c)(1) and the market mechanism provisions of paragraphs 9(b) and 57(c)(2) to qualify for the exception, it must be probable at inception and throughout the term of the individual contract that the contract will not settle net and will result in physical delivery.

c. *Certain contracts that are not traded on an exchange.* A contract that is not traded on an exchange is not subject to the requirements of this Statement if the underlying is:

   (1) A climatic or geological variable or other physical variable. Climatic, geological, and other physical variables include things like the number of inches of rainfall or snow in a particular area and the severity of an earthquake as measured by the Richter scale.

---

[17] ~~Contracts that require delivery of assets that are not readily convertible to cash are not subject to the requirements of this Statement unless there is a market mechanism outside the contract to facilitate net settlement.~~

(2) The price or value of (a) a nonfinancial asset of one of the parties to the contract unless that asset is readily convertible to cash or (b) a nonfinancial liability of one of the parties to the contract unless that liability requires delivery of an asset that is readily convertible to cash. This exception applies only to nonfinancial assets that are unique and only if a nonfinancial asset related to the underlying is owned by the party that would *not* benefit *under the contract* from an increase in the price or value of the nonfinancial asset. If the contract is a call option contract, the exception applies only if that nonfinancial asset is owned by the party that would not benefit under the contract from an increase in the price or value of the nonfinancial asset above the option's strike price.

(3) Specified volumes of sales or service revenues by one of the parties. That exception is intended to apply to contracts with settlements based on the volume of items sold or services rendered, for example, royalty agreements. It is not intended to apply to contracts based on changes in sales or revenues due to changes in market prices.

If a contract's underlying is the combination of two or more variables, and one or more would not qualify for one of the exceptions above, the application of this Statement to that contract depends on the predominant characteristics of the combined variable. The contract is subject to the requirements of this Statement if the changes in its combined underlying are highly correlated with changes in one of the component variables that would not qualify for an exception.

61(d).   *Calls and puts on debt instruments.* Call options (or put options) that can accelerate the repayment of principal on a debt instrument are considered to be clearly and closely related to a debt instrument that requires principal repayments unless both (1) the debt involves a substantial premium or discount (which is common with zero-coupon bonds) and (2) the put or call option is only contingently exercisable. Thus, if a substantial premium or discount is not involved, embedded calls and puts (including contingent call or put options that are not exercisable unless an event of default occurs) would *not* be separated from the host contract. However, for contingently exercisable calls and puts to be considered clearly and closely related, they can be indexed only to interest rates or credit risk, not some extraneous event or factor. In contrast, call options (or put options) that do not accelerate the repayment of principal on a debt instrument but instead require a cash settlement that is equal to the price of the option at the date of exercise would *not* be considered to be clearly and closely related to the debt instrument in which it is embedded and would be separated from the host contract. ~~In certain unusual situations, a put or call option may have been subsequently added to a debt instrument in a manner that causes the investor (creditor) to be exposed to performance risk (default risk) by different parties for the embedded option and the host debt instrument, respectively. In those unusual situations, the embedded option and the host debt instrument are *not* clearly and closely related.~~

61(e).   *Calls and puts on equity instruments.* A put option that enables the holder to require the issuer of an equity instrument to reacquire that equity instrument for cash or other assets is *not* clearly and closely related to that equity instrument. Thus, such a put option embedded in a publicly traded ~~the~~ equity instrument to which it relates should be separated from the host contract by the holder of the equity instrument. That put option also should be separated from the host contract by the issuer of the equity instrument except in those cases in which the put option is not considered to be a derivative instrument pursuant to paragraph 11(a) because it is classified in stockholders' equity. A purchased call option that enables the issuer of an equity instrument (such as common stock) to reacquire that equity instrument would not be considered to be a derivative instrument by the issuer of the equity instrument pursuant to paragraph 11(a). Thus, if the call option were embedded in the related equity instrument, it would not be separated from the host contract by the issuer. However, for the holder of the related equity instrument, the embedded written call option would *not* be considered to be clearly and closely related to the equity instrument and should be separated from the host contract.

68.   An assumption of no ineffectiveness is especially important in a hedging relationship involving an interest-bearing financial instrument and an interest rate swap because it significantly simplifies the computations necessary to make the accounting entries. An entity may assume no ineffectiveness in a

hedging relationship of interest rate risk involving a recognizedan interest-bearing asset or liability and an interest rate swap if all of the applicable conditions in the following list are met:

Conditions applicable to both fair value hedges and cash flow hedges

a. The notional amount of the swap matches the principal amount of the interest-bearing asset or liability.

b. The fair value of the swap at the inception of the hedging relationshipits inception is zero.

c. The formula for computing net settlements under the interest rate swap is the same for each net settlement. (That is, the fixed rate is the same throughout the term, and the variable rate is based on the same index and includes the same constant adjustment or no adjustment.)

d. The interest-bearing asset or liability is not prepayable (that is, able to be settled by either party prior to its scheduled maturity), except as indicated in the following sentences. This criterion does not apply to an interest-bearing asset or liability that is prepayable solely due to an embedded call option provided that the hedging interest rate swap contains an embedded mirror-image call option. The call option embedded in the swap is considered a mirror image of the call option embedded in the hedged item if (1) the terms of the two call options match (including matching maturities, strike price, related notional amounts, timing and frequency of payments, and dates on which the instruments may be called) and (2) the entity is the writer of one call option and the holder (or purchaser) of the other call option. Similarly, this criterion does not apply to an interest-bearing asset or liability that is prepayable solely due to an embedded put option provided that the hedging interest rate swap contains an embedded mirror-image put option.

dd. The index on which the variable leg of the swap is based matches the benchmark interest rate designated as the interest rate risk being hedged for that hedging relationship.*

e. Any other terms in the interest-bearing financial instruments or interest rate swaps are typical of those instruments and do not invalidate the assumption of no ineffectiveness.

Conditions applicable to fair value hedges only

f. The expiration date of the swap matches the maturity date of the interest-bearing asset or liability.

g. There is no floor or ceiling on the variable interest rate of the swap.

h. The interval between repricings of the variable interest rate in the swap is frequent enough to justify an assumption that the variable payment or receipt is at a market rate (generally three to six months or less).

Conditions applicable to cash flow hedges only

i. All interest receipts or payments on the variable-rate asset or liability during the term of the swap are designated as hedged, and no interest payments beyond the term of the swap are designated as hedged.

j. There is no floor or cap on the variable interest rate of the swap unless the variable-rate asset or liability has a floor or cap. In that case, the swap must have a floor or cap on the variable interest rate that is comparable to the floor or cap on the variable-rate asset or liability. (For this purpose, comparable does not necessarily mean equal. For example, if a swap's variable rate is LIBOR and an asset's variable rate is LIBOR plus 2 percent, a 10 percent cap on the swap would be comparable to a 12 percent cap on the asset.)

k. The repricing dates match those of the variable-rate asset or liability.

l. The index on which the variable rate is based matches the index on which the asset or liability's variable rate is based.

---

*For cash flow hedge situations in which the cash flows of the hedged item and the hedging instrument are based on the same index but that index is not the benchmark interest rate, the shortcut method is not permitted. However, the entity may obtain results similar to results obtained if the shortcut method was permitted.

[19]The use of a hedging instrument with a different underlying basis than the item or transaction being hedged is generally referred to as a *cross-hedge*. The principles for cross-hedges illustrated in this example also apply to hedges involving other risks. For example, the effectiveness of a hedge of market interest rate risk in which one interest rate is used as a surrogate for another interest rate would be evaluated in the same way as the natural gas cross-hedge in this example.

[Paragraph 74 to which this footnote relates has not been amended by this Statement.]

90. However, because the pertinent critical terms of the option and the bond are the same in this example, the company could expect the changes in value of the bond attributable to changes in ~~market~~ interest rates and changes in the intrinsic value of the option to offset completely during the period that the option is in the money. That is, there will be no ineffectiveness because the company has chosen to exclude changes in the option's time value from the effectiveness test. Because of that choice, Company E must recognize changes in the time value of the option directly in earnings.

Appendix B—Examples

115. On July 1, 20X1, ABC Company borrows $1,000,000 to be repaid on June 30, 20X3. On that same date, ABC also enters into a two-year receive-fixed, pay-variable interest rate swap. ABC designates the interest rate swap as a hedge of the changes in the fair value of the fixed-rate debt attributable to changes in the designated benchmark interest rate~~market interest rates~~. ABC designates changes in LIBOR swap rates as the benchmark interest rate in hedging interest rate risk. The terms of the interest rate swap and the debt are as follows:

	Interest Rate Swap	Fixed-Rate Debt
Trade date and borrowing date*	July 1, 20X1	July 1, 20X1
Termination date and maturity date	June 30, 20X3	June 30, 20X3
Notional amount and principal amount	$1,000,000	$1,000,000
Fixed interest rate*	6.41%	6.41%
Variable interest rate	3-month US$ LIBOR	Not applicable
Settlement dates and interest payment dates*	End of each calendar quarter	End of each calendar quarter
Reset dates	End of each calendar quarter through March 31, 20X3	Not applicable

---

*These terms need not match for the assumption of no ineffectiveness to be appropriate. (Refer to paragraphs 68 and 69.)

Example 2A: Fair Value Hedge of the LIBOR Swap Rate in a $100,000 BBB-Quality 5-Year Fixed-Rate Noncallable Note

120A. This example illustrates one method that could be used in determining the hedged item's change in fair value attributable to changes in the benchmark interest rate. Other methods could be used in determining the hedged item's change in fair value attributable to changes in the benchmark interest rate as long as those methods meet the criteria in paragraph 21(f).

120B. On January 1, 20X0, GHI Company issues at par a $100,000 BBB-quality 5-year fixed-rate noncallable debt instrument with an annual 10 percent interest coupon. On that date, the issuer enters into a 5-year interest rate swap based on the LIBOR swap rate and designates it as the hedging instrument in a fair value hedge of the $100,000 liability. Under the terms of the swap, GHI will receive fixed interest at 7 percent and pay variable interest at LIBOR. The variable leg of the swap resets each year on December 31 for the payments due the following year. This example has been simplified by assuming that the interest rate applicable to a payment due at any future date is the same as the rate for a payment at any other date (that is, the yield curve is flat). During the hedge period, the gain or loss on the swap will be recorded in earnings. The example assumes that immediately before the interest rate on the variable leg resets on December 31, 20X0, the LIBOR swap rate increased by 50 basis points to 7.50 percent, and the change in fair value of the swap for the period from January 1 to December 31, 20X0 is a loss in value of $1,675.

Changes in the fair value of the hedged item attributable to the changes in the benchmark interest rate for a specific period

120C. Under this method, the change in a hedged item's fair value attributable to changes in the benchmark interest rate for a specific period is determined as the difference between two present value calculations as of the end of the period that exclude or include, respectively, the effect of the changes in the benchmark interest rate during the period. The discount rates used for those present value calculations would be, respectively, (a) the discount rate equal to the market interest rate for that hedged item at the inception of the hedge adjusted (up or down) for changes in the benchmark rate (designated as the interest rate risk being hedged) from the inception of the hedge to the beginning date of the period for which the change in fair value is being calculated* and (b) the discount rate equal to the market interest rate for that hedged item at the inception of the hedge adjusted (up or down) for changes in the designated benchmark rate from the inception of the hedge to the ending date of the period for which the change in fair value is being calculated. Both present value calculations are computed using the estimated future cash flows for the hedged item (which typically would be its remaining contractual cash flows).

120D. In GHI's quarterly assessments of hedge effectiveness for each of the first three quarters of year 20X0 in this example, there was zero change in the hedged item's fair value attributable to changes in the benchmark interest rate because there was no change in the LIBOR swap rate. However, in the assessment for the fourth quarter 20X0, the discount rate for the beginning of the period is 10 percent (the hedged item's original market interest rate with an adjustment of zero), and the discount rate for the end of the period is 10.50 percent (the hedged item's original market interest rate adjusted for the change during the period in the LIBOR swap rate [+0.50 percent]).

December 31, 20X0

Calculate the present value using the beginning-of-period discount rate of 10 percent:

$10,000pmt, 10%i, 4n, PV =	$ 31,699	(interest payments)
$100,000fv, 10%i, 4n, PV =	$ 68,301	(principal payment)
Total present value	$100,000	

Calculate the present value using the end-of-period discount rate of 10.50 percent (that is, the beginning-of-period discount rate adjusted for the change during the period in the LIBOR swap rate of 50 basis points):

$10,000pmt, 10.50%i, 4n, PV =	$31,359	(interest payments)
$100,000fv, 10.50%i, 4n, PV =	$67,073	(principal payment)
Total present value	$98,432	

The change in fair value of the hedged item attributable to the change in the benchmark interest rate is $100,000 − $98,432 = $1,568 (the fair value decrease in the liability is a gain on debt).

---

*This Statement does not provide specific guidance on the discount rate that must be used in the calculation. However, the method chosen by GHI and described in this illustration requires that the discount rate be based on the market interest rate for the hedged item at the inception of the hedging relationship.

When the change in fair value of the hedged item ($1,568 gain) attributable to the risk being hedged is compared with the change in fair value of the hedging instrument ($1,675 loss), ineffectiveness of $107 results. That ineffectiveness will be reported in earnings, because both changes in fair value are recorded in earnings.

134. Also on July 1, 20X1, XYZ enters into a two-year receive-fixed, pay-variable interest rate swap and designates it as a cash flow hedge of the variable-rate interest receipts on the corporate bonds. The risk designated as being hedged is the risk of changes in cash flows attributable to changes in the designated benchmark interest rate~~market interest rates~~. XYZ designates changes in LIBOR swap rates as the benchmark interest rate in hedging interest rate risk. The terms of the interest rate swap and the corporate bonds are shown below.

	Interest Rate Swap	Corporate Bonds
Trade date and borrowing date*	July 1, 20X1	July 1, 20X1
Termination date	June 30, 20X3	June 30, 20X3
Notional amount	$10,000,000	$10,000,000
Fixed interest rate	6.65%	Not applicable
Variable interest rate[†]	3-month US$ LIBOR	3-month US$ LIBOR + 2.25%
Settlement dates and interest payment dates*	End of each calendar quarter	End of each calendar quarter
Reset dates	End of each calendar quarter through March 31, 20X3	End of each calendar quarter through March 31, 20X3

*These terms need not match for the assumption of no ineffectiveness to be appropriate. (Refer to paragraphs 68 and 69.)

[†]Only the interest rate basis (for example, LIBOR) must match. The spread over LIBOR does not invalidate the assumption of no ineffectiveness.

155. Because Swap 1 and the hedged forecasted interest payments are based on the same notional amount, have the same reset dates, and are based on the same benchmark interest rate designated under paragraph 29(h)~~meets all of the conditions discussed in paragraph 68~~, MNO may conclude~~is permitted to assume~~ that there will be no ineffectiveness in the hedging relationship ~~and to use the shortcut method illustrated in Example 2~~(absent a default by the swap counterparty).

161. Rather than liquidate Swap 1 and obtain a separate derivative to hedge the variability of the prime-rate-based interest payments, MNO enters into a pay-LIBOR, receive-prime basis swap. The basis swap has a $5 million notional amount and a 3-year term and requires a settlement every 90 days. MNO designates Swap 1 and the basis swap in combination as the hedging instrument in a cash flow hedge of the variable interest payments on the three-year note. On the three-year note, MNO pays interest at prime. On the basis swap, MNO receives interest at prime and pays interest at LIBOR. On Swap 1, MNO receives interest at LIBOR and pays interest at 6.5 percent. Together, the cash flows from the two derivatives are effective at offsetting changes in the interest payments on the three-year note. Changes in fair values of the two swaps are recognized in other comprehensive income and are reclassified to earnings when the hedged forecasted transactions (the variable interest payments) affect earnings (as required by paragraph 31). ~~Because the two swaps in combination meet the conditions discussed in paragraph 68, MNO is permitted to assume no ineffectiveness and use the shortcut method illustrated in Example 5.~~

169. As each royalty is earned, DEF recognizes a receivable and royalty income. The forecasted transaction (the earning of royalty income) has occurred. The receivable is an asset, not a forecasted transaction, and would separately be eligible to be designated as a fair value hedge of foreign exchange risk or

continue to be eligible as a cash flow hedge of foreign exchange risk~~is not eligible for cash flow hedge accounting. Nor is it eligible for fair value hedge accounting of the foreign exchange risk because changes in the receivable's fair value due to exchange rate changes are recognized immediately in earnings. (Paragraph 21(c) prohibits hedge accounting in that situation.)~~ Consequently, <u>if the variability of the functional currency cash flows related to the royalty receivable is not being hedged,</u> DEF will dedesignate a proportion of <u>the hedging instrument in the original hedge relationship with respect to the proportion of the</u> forward contract corresponding to the earned royalty. As the royalty is recognized in earnings and each proportion of the derivative is dedesignated, the related derivative gain or loss in accumulated other comprehensive income is reclassified into earnings. After that date, any gain or loss on the dedesignated proportion of the derivative and any transaction loss or gain on the royalty receivable[26] will be recognized in earnings and <u>may</u>~~will~~ substantially offset each other.

197. **Example 31: Certain Purchases in a Foreign Currency.** A U.S. company enters into a contract to purchase corn from a local American supplier in six months for <u>a fixed amount of Japanese yen;</u> the yen is the functional currency of neither party to the transaction. The corn is expected to be delivered and used over a reasonable period in the normal course of business.

> *Scope Application:* Paragraph 10(b) excludes contracts that require future delivery of commodities that are readily convertible to cash from the accounting for derivatives if the commodities will be delivered in quantities expected to be used or sold by the reporting entity over a reasonable period in the normal course of business. However, <u>that paragraph also states that contracts that are denominated in a foreign currency that meets neither of the criteria in paragraphs 15(a) and 15(b) shall not be considered normal purchases and normal sales.</u>~~the corn purchase contract must be examined to determine whether it contains an embedded derivative that warrants separate accounting.~~ <u>Because the Japanese yen is not the functional currency of either party to the contract and the purchase of corn is transacted internationally in many different currencies, the contract does not qualify for the normal purchases and normal sales exception. The contract is a compound derivative comprising</u>~~The corn purchase contract can be viewed as~~ a U.S. dollar-denominated forward contract for the purchase of corn and an embedded foreign currency swap from the purchaser's functional currency (the U.S. dollar) to yen. <u>Consistent with the last sentence of footnote 13 to paragraph 49, the compound derivative cannot be separated into its components (representing the foreign currency derivative and the forward commodity contract) and accounted for separately under this Statement.</u>~~Because the yen is the functional currency of neither party to the transaction and the purchase of corn is transacted internationally in many different currencies, the contract does not qualify for the exception in paragraph 15 that precludes separating the embedded foreign currency derivative from the host contract. The embedded foreign currency swap should be separated from the host contract and accounted for as a derivative for purposes of this Statement because a separate instrument with the same terms would meet the definition of a derivative instrument in paragraphs 6–11.~~

200. **Example 34: Variable Annuity Products.** These products are investment contracts as contemplated in Statements 60 and 97. Similar to variable life insurance products, policyholders direct their investment account asset mix among a variety of mutual funds composed of equities, bonds, or both, and assume the risks and rewards of investment performance. The funds are generally maintained in separate accounts by the insurance company. Contract terms provide that if the policyholder dies, the greater of the account market value or a minimum death benefit guarantee will be paid. The minimum death benefit guarantee is generally limited to a return of premium plus a minimum return (such as 3 or 4 percent); this life insurance feature represents the fundamental difference from the life insurance contracts that include significant (rather than minimal) levels of life insurance. The investment account may have various payment alternatives at the end of the accumulation period. One alternative is the right to purchase a life annuity at a fixed price determined at the initiation of the contract.

> *Scope Application:* Variable annuity product structures as contemplated in Statement 97 are generally not subject to the scope of this Statement (except for payment options at the end of the accumulation period), as follows:

- *Death benefit component.* Paragraph 10(c)(1) excludes a death benefit from the scope of this Statement because the payment of the death benefit is the result of an identifiable insurable event instead of changes in an underlying. The death benefit in this example is limited to the floor guarantee of the investment account, calculated as the premiums paid into the investment account plus a guaranteed rate of return, less the account market value. Statement 60 remains the applicable guidance for the insurance-related liability accounting.
- *Investment component.* The policyholder directs certain premium investments in the investment account that includes equities, bonds, or both, which are held in separate accounts that are distinct~~owned by the policyholder and separate~~ from the insurer's general account assets. ~~This component is viewed as a direct investment because the policyholder directs and owns these investments.~~ This component is not considered a derivative because of the unique attributes of traditional variable annuity contracts issued by insurance companies~~the policyholder has invested the premiums in acquiring those investments~~. Furthermore, any embedded derivatives within those investments should not be separated from the host contract by the insurer because the separate account assets are already marked-to-market under Statement 60. In contrast, if the product were an equity-index-based interest annuity (rather than a traditional variable annuity), the investment component would contain an embedded derivative (the equity index-based derivative) that meets all the requirements of paragraph 12 of this Statement for separate accounting: (a) the economic characteristics and risks of the embedded derivative would not be clearly and closely related to the economic characteristics and risks of the host contract (that is, the host contract is a debt instrument and the embedded option is equity-indexed), (b) the hybrid instrument would not be remeasured at fair value with changes in fair value reported in earnings as they occur under GAAP, and (c) a separate instrument with the same terms as the embedded derivative instrument would be a derivative instrument pursuant to paragraphs 6–11 of this Statement.~~not be viewed as a direct investment because the policyholder does not own those investments, which are assets recorded in the general account of the insurance company. As a result, the host contract would be a debt instrument, and the equity-index-based derivative should be separated and accounted for as a derivative instrument.~~
- *Investment account surrender right at market value.* Because this right is exercised only at the fund market value (without the insurer's floor guarantee) and relates to a traditional variable annuity contract issued by an insurance company~~an investment owned by the insured~~, this right is not within the scope of this Statement.
- *Payment alternatives at the end of the accumulation period.* Payment alternatives are options subject to the requirements of this Statement if interest rates or other underlying variables affect the value.

The guidance in the second and third bullets above is an exception for traditional variable annuity contracts issued by insurance companies. In determining the accounting for other seemingly similar structures, it would be inappropriate to analogize to the above guidance due to the unique attributes of traditional variable annuity contracts.

Appendix F—Glossary

540. This appendix contains definitions of terms or phrases as used in this Statement.

Benchmark interest rate

A widely recognized and quoted rate in an active financial market that is broadly indicative of the overall level of interest rates attributable to high-credit-quality obligors in that market. It is a rate that is widely used in a given financial market as an underlying basis for determining the interest rates of individual financial instruments and commonly referenced in interest-rate-related transactions.

In theory, the benchmark interest rate should be a risk-free rate (that is, has no risk of default). In some markets, government borrowing rates may serve as a benchmark. In other markets, the benchmark interest rate may be an interbank offered rate. In the United States, currently only the interest rates on direct Treasury obligations of the U.S. government and, for practical reasons, the LIBOR swap rate are considered to be benchmark interest rates. In each financial market, only the one or two most widely used and quoted rates that meet the above criteria may be considered benchmark interest rates.

Comprehensive income

The change in equity of a business enterprise during a period from transactions and other events and circumstances from nonowner sources. It includes all changes in equity during a period except those resulting from investments by owners and distributions to owners (FASB Concepts Statement No. 6, *Elements of Financial Statements,* paragraph 70).

Derivative instrument

Refer to paragraphs 6–9.

Fair value

The amount at which an asset (liability) could be bought (incurred) or sold (settled) in a current transaction between willing parties, that is, other than in a forced or liquidation sale. Quoted market prices in active markets are the best evidence of fair value and should be used as the basis for the measurement, if available. If a quoted market price is available, the fair value is the product of the number of trading units times that market price. If a quoted market price is not available, the estimate of fair value should be based on the best information available in the circumstances. The estimate of fair value should consider prices for similar assets or similar liabilities and the results of valuation techniques to the extent available in the circumstances. Examples of valuation techniques include the present value of estimated expected future cash flows using discount rates commensurate with the risks involved, option-pricing models, matrix pricing, option-adjusted spread models, and fundamental analysis. Valuation techniques for measuring assets and liabilities should be consistent with the objective of measuring fair value. Those techniques should incorporate assumptions that market participants would use in their estimates of values, future revenues, and future expenses, including assumptions about interest rates, default, prepayment, and volatility. In measuring forward contracts, such as foreign currency forward contracts, at fair value by discounting estimated future cash flows, an entity should base the estimate of future cash flows on the changes in the forward rate (rather than the spot rate). In measuring financial liabilities and nonfinancial derivatives that are liabilities at fair value by discounting estimated future cash flows (or equivalent outflows of other assets), an objective is to use discount rates at which those liabilities could be settled in an arm's-length transaction.

Financial instrument

Cash, evidence of an ownership interest in an entity, or a contract that both:

a. Imposes on one entity a contractual obligation* (1) to deliver cash or another financial instrument[†] to a second entity or (2) to exchange other financial instruments on potentially unfavorable terms with the second entity

b. Conveys to that second entity a contractual right[‡] (1) to receive cash or another financial instrument from the first entity or (2) to exchange other financial instruments on potentially favorable terms with the first entity.

Firm commitment

An agreement with an unrelated party, binding on both parties and usually legally enforceable, with the following characteristics:

a. The agreement specifies all significant terms, including the quantity to be exchanged, the fixed price, and the timing of the transaction. The fixed price may be expressed as a specified amount of an entity's functional currency or of a foreign currency. It may also be expressed as a specified interest rate or specified effective yield.

b. The agreement includes a disincentive for nonperformance that is sufficiently large to make performance probable.

Forecasted transaction

A transaction that is expected to occur for which there is no firm commitment. Because no transaction or event has yet occurred and the transaction or event when it occurs will be at the prevailing market price, a forecasted transaction does not give an entity any present rights to future benefits or a present obligation for future sacrifices.

LIBOR swap rate

The fixed rate on a single-currency, constant-notional interest rate swap that has its floating-rate leg referenced to the London Interbank Offered Rate (LIBOR) with no additional spread over LIBOR on that floating-rate leg. That fixed rate is the derived rate that would result in the swap having a zero fair value at inception because the present value of fixed cash flows, based on that rate, equate to the present value of the floating cash flows.

Notional amount

A number of currency units, shares, bushels, pounds, or other units specified in a derivative instrument.

Underlying

A specified interest rate, security price, commodity price, foreign exchange rate, index of prices or rates, or other variable. An underlying may be a price or rate of an asset or liability but is not the asset or liability itself.

Contractual obligations encompass both those that are conditioned on the occurrence of a specified event and those that are not. All contractual obligations that are financial instruments meet the definition of *liability* set forth in Concepts Statement 6, although some may not be recognized as liabilities in financial statements—may be "off-balance-sheet"—because they fail to meet some other criterion for recognition. For some financial instruments, the obligation is owed to or by a group of entities rather than a single entity.

[†]The use of the term *financial instrument* in this definition is recursive (because the term *financial instrument* is included in it), though it is not circular. The definition requires a chain of contractual obligations that ends with the delivery of cash or an ownership interest in an entity. Any number of obligations to deliver financial instruments can be links in a chain that qualifies a particular contract as a financial instrument.

[‡]*Contractual rights* encompass both those that are conditioned on the occurrence of a specified event and those that are not. All contractual rights that are financial instruments meet the definition of *asset* set forth in Concepts Statement 6, although some may not be recognized as assets in financial statements—may be "off-balance-sheet"—because they fail to meet some other criterion for recognition. For some financial instruments, the right is held by or the obligation is due from a group of entities rather than a single entity.

Statement of Financial Accounting Standards No. 139
Rescission of FASB Statement No. 53 and amendments to FASB Statements No. 63, 89, and 121

STATUS

Issued: June 2000

Effective Date: For financial statements for fiscal years beginning after December 15, 2000

Affects: Supersedes FAS 53
    Amends FAS 63, paragraph 1
    Amends FAS 63 by adding paragraph 1A
    Amends FAS 89, paragraph 44
    Replaces FAS 121, paragraph 3(b)
    Amends FAS 121, paragraph 147

Affected by: No other pronouncements

AICPA Accounting Standards Executive Committee (AcSEC)

Related Pronouncement: SOP 00-2

SUMMARY

This Statement rescinds FASB Statement No. 53, *Financial Reporting by Producers and Distributors of Motion Picture Films.* An entity that previously was subject to the requirements of Statement 53 shall follow the guidance in AICPA Statement of Position 00-2, *Accounting by Producers or Distributors of Films.* This Statement also amends FASB Statements No. 63, *Financial Reporting by Broadcasters,* No. 89, *Financial Reporting and Changing Prices,* and No. 121, *Accounting for the Impairment of Long-Lived Assets and for Long-Lived Assets to Be Disposed Of.*

This Statement is effective for financial statements for fiscal years beginning after December 15, 2000. Earlier application is permitted only upon early adoption of the Statement of Position.

Statement of Financial Accounting Standards No. 139

Rescission of FASB Statement No. 53 and amendments to FASB Statements No. 63, 89, and 121

CONTENTS

INTRODUCTION

1. FASB Statement No. 53, *Financial Reporting by Producers and Distributors of Motion Picture Films,* was issued in 1981. Statement 53 extracted specialized accounting and reporting principles and practices from the AICPA Industry Accounting Guide, *Accounting for Motion Picture Films,* and AICPA Statement of Position 79-4, *Accounting for Motion Picture Films.* It also established financial accounting and reporting standards for producers or distributors of motion picture films.

2. Since the issuance of Statement 53, extensive changes have occurred in the film industry. Through 1981, the majority of a film's revenue resulted from distribution to movie theaters and free television. Since that time, numerous additional forms of exploitation (such as home video, satellite and cable television, and pay-per-view television) have come into existence, and international revenue has increased in significance. Concurrent with those changes, significant variations in the application of Statement 53 arose.

3. In 1995, in response to concerns raised by constituents, the Board asked the Accounting Standards Executive Committee (AcSEC) of the AICPA to develop a Statement of Position providing guidance on the accounting and reporting requirements for producers or distributors of motion picture films. In response to that request, AcSEC developed AICPA

Statement of Position 00-2, *Accounting by Producers or Distributors of Films.* An entity that is a producer or distributor of films and that previously applied Statement 53 is now required to follow the guidance in SOP 00-2. This Statement and SOP 00-2 are effective for fiscal years beginning after December 15, 2000.

STANDARDS OF FINANCIAL ACCOUNTING AND REPORTING

Rescission of Statement 53

4. This Statement rescinds FASB Statement No. 53, *Financial Reporting by Producers and Distributors of Motion Picture Films.*

Amendments to Existing Pronouncements

5. FASB Statement No. 63, *Financial Reporting by Broadcasters,* is amended as follows:

a. The following is inserted before the last sentence of paragraph 1:

> In June 2000, AICPA Statement of Position 00-2, *Accounting by Producers or Distributors of Films,* was issued and is applicable to all producers or distributors that own or hold rights to distribute or exploit films.

b. The following paragraph is added after the caption *Standards of Financial Accounting and Reporting* and before the caption *License Agreements for Program Material:*

> A broadcaster shall apply the guidance in SOP 00-2 if it owns the film (program material) that is shown on its cable, network, or local television outlets.

6. In paragraph 44 of FASB Statement No. 89, *Financial Reporting and Changing Prices,* the definition of *motion picture films* is replaced by the following:

> All types of film, including feature films, television specials, television series, or similar products (including animated films and television programming) that are sold, licensed, or exhibited, whether produced on film, video tape, digital, or other video recording format.

7. FASB Statement No. 121, *Accounting for the Impairment of Long-Lived Assets and for Long-Lived Assets to Be Disposed Of,* is amended as follows:

a. Paragraph 3(b) is replaced by *AICPA Statement of Position 00-2, Accounting by Producers or Distributors of Films.*

b. In the table following paragraph 147, the reference to Statement 53 is deleted and the following is added to the table.

> FASB Statement No. 139, *Rescission of FASB Statement 53 and amendments to FASB Statements No. 63, 89, and 121**

---

*In June 2000, AICPA Statement of Position 00-2, *Accounting by Producers or Distributors of Films,* was issued. Motion picture films are subject to the impairment guidance in paragraphs 43–47 of SOP 00-2.

EFFECTIVE DATE AND TRANSITION

8. This Statement shall be effective for financial statements for fiscal years beginning after December 15, 2000. Earlier application is permitted only upon early adoption of SOP 00-2.

> **The provisions of this Statement need not be applied to immaterial items.**

This Statement was adopted by the unanimous vote of the seven members of the Financial Accounting Standards Board:

Edmund L. Jenkins,	John M. Foster	Gerhard G. Mueller
Chairman	Gaylen N. Larson	Edward W. Trott
Anthony T. Cope	James J. Leisenring	

Appendix

BACKGROUND INFORMATION AND BASIS FOR CONCLUSIONS

9. This appendix summarizes considerations that Board members deemed significant in reaching the conclusions in this Statement.

10. Statement 53 was issued in December 1981 as part of the process of extracting specialized accounting and reporting principles and practices from AICPA Statements of Position and Guides on accounting and auditing matters and issuing them in

FASB Statements after appropriate due process. Statement 53 established the financial accounting and reporting standards for producers or distributors of motion picture films.

11. The Entertainment and Sports Industry Committee of the California Society of Certified Public Accountants (the Committee) submitted a letter dated September 15, 1994, to the FASB requesting that the Board reconsider certain provisions of Statement 53. The Committee's letter included a White Paper containing the recommendations of the Committee's FAS 53 Task Force to revise Statement 53. The Committee's request was endorsed by AcSEC in a letter dated September 27, 1994, to the FASB.

12. According to the September 15, 1994 letter, the Committee formed the FAS 53 Task Force because of concerns relating to the following issues:

a. Statement 53 did not address the extensive changes that have occurred in the industry since its issuance. When Statement 53 was issued, most of a film's revenue came from distribution to U.S. movie theaters. At present, the industry has additional forms of distribution (videocassettes, satellite and cable television, CD-ROM, laser and digital video discs [DVD], and pay-per-view television, plus licensing revenues from products tied to the film) that did not exist or were not significant when Statement 53 was issued. The industry now also distributes to new emerging international markets (for example, eastern Europe and China).

b. Application of Statement 53 varied significantly within the industry.

c. The validity and accuracy of financial statements issued by companies in the motion picture industry were questioned after certain business failures.

13. In response to those concerns, the Board requested in July 1995 that AcSEC undertake a project to reconsider the accounting and financial reporting for the motion picture industry. The Board considered adding the project to its own agenda because certain Board members at that time believed that "maintenance" of an FASB Statement was the Board's responsibility. However, the Board ultimately decided that AcSEC was better suited to address the needs of that specific industry. The Board indicated that it would either amend or rescind Statement 53 depending on the outcome of AcSEC's project.

14. The Board concluded that it should rescind Statement 53 based on the results of the AcSEC project to develop guidance on the accounting and financial reporting requirements for producers or distributors of motion picture films. The Board believes that (a) there is a need for the guidance, (b) the guidance will improve practice, and (c) the benefits will exceed the cost of implementation.

Comments on Exposure Drafts

15. The FASB Exposure Draft, *Rescission of FASB Statement No. 53,* and the Exposure Draft of the proposed AICPA Statement of Position, *Accounting by Producers and Distributors of Films,* were issued for comment on October 16, 1998. Twenty-eight organizations commented on those Exposure Drafts. The notice to respondents of the proposed SOP indicated that it was only necessary to send one letter to the AICPA commenting on both of the Exposure Drafts. However, 10 of those 28 organizations sent separate letters to the FASB, and those additional letters were primarily from respondents that did not support the issuance of the proposed SOP. As a result, many of those letters did not support the Board's rescinding Statement 53. The basis for conclusions in SOP 00-2 discusses AcSEC's resolution of matters raised in the comment letters. The Board held two public meetings with representatives of AcSEC and reviewed the issues raised in the comment letters. The Board believes that AcSEC responded to those issues in an acceptable manner.

Amendment of Statement 63

16. The Board decided to amend FASB Statement No. 63, *Financial Reporting by Broadcasters,* to clarify that the requirements of SOP 00-2 apply to a film owned by a broadcaster. Previously, Statement 63 only addressed licensing agreements.

Statement of Financial Accounting Standards No. 140
Accounting for Transfers and Servicing of
Financial Assets and Extinguishments of Liabilities

a replacement of FASB Statement No. 125

STATUS

Issued: September 2000

Effective Date: For transfers and servicing of financial assets and extinguishments of liabilities occurring after March 31, 2001, and for disclosures relating to securitization transactions and collateral for fiscal years after December 15, 2000 (but amended, for certain provisions, by FASB Technical Bulletin No. 01-1, *Effective Date for Certain Financial Institutions of Certain Provisions of Statement 140 Related to the Isolation of Transferred Financial Assets,* for certain banks and other financial institutions and for voluntary transfers to certain transferees. See FTB 01-1 for details.)

Affects: Replaces APB 26, paragraph 3(a)
Replaces FAS 13, paragraph 20
Amends FAS 22, footnote 1
Amends FAS 65, paragraphs 1, 9(a), 10, 15, 34
Deletes FAS 65, paragraphs 8, 11, 16 through 19, 30, and the paragraphs added after paragraph 30 by FAS 122 and footnotes 4 and 6
Supersedes FAS 76
Supersedes FAS 77
Replaces FAS 107, paragraph 8(b)
Amends FAS 107, paragraph 28
Amends FAS 115, paragraph 7
Supersedes FAS 122
Supersedes FAS 125
Supersedes FAS 127
Amends FAS 133, paragraphs 10(f), 56, 59(e), and footnote 9
Amends FAS 136, footnote 5
Amends FIN 43, footnote 2
Supersedes FTB 84-4
Supersedes FTB 85-2
Replaces FTB 86-2, paragraph 12
Deletes FTB 87-3, paragraphs 1 through 7
Replaces FTB 87-3, paragraph 9

Affected by: Paragraph 4 amended by FAS 153, paragraph 4, and FAS 156, paragraph 4(a)
Paragraphs 5, 10, and 11 amended by FAS 156, paragraphs 4(b) through 4(d), respectively
Paragraph 11(c) amended by FAS 157, paragraph E20(a)
Paragraph 13 replaced by FAS 156, paragraph 4(e)
Paragraphs 13A and 13B added by FAS 156, paragraph 4(f)
Paragraph 14 amended by FAS 156, paragraph 4(g)
Paragraph 17 amended by FAS 156, paragraph 4(h), and FAS 157, paragraphs E20(b) and E20(c)

Paragraph 19 amended by FTB 01-1, paragraph 5

Paragraph 24 replaced by FTB 01-1, paragraph 8

Paragraphs 35(c)(2) and 40 amended by FAS 155, paragraph 5

Paragraphs 56 through 62 amended by FAS 156, paragraphs 4(j) through 4(p), respectively

Paragraph 62A added by FAS 156, paragraph 4(q)

Paragraphs 63 and 65 through 67 amended by FAS 156, paragraphs 4(r) through 4(u), respectively

Paragraph 63(b) amended by FAS 156, paragraph 4(r), and FAS 157, paragraph E20(d)

Paragraphs 68 through 70 deleted by FAS 157, paragraph E20(e)

Paragraphs 72, 76, 82, 83(b), 87(a), and 343 through 349 amended by FAS 156, paragraphs 4(w) through 4(hh), respectively

Paragraph 349A added by FAS 156, paragraph 4(ii)

Paragraph 364 amended by FAS 157, paragraph E20(f), and effectively amended by FAS 159, paragraph A44

Footnote 17 amended by FAS 156, paragraph 4(i)

Footnotes 20 and 21 amended by FAS 156, paragraph 4(v)

Footnotes 20 and 21 deleted by FAS 157, paragraph E20(e)

Other Interpretive Pronouncement: FTB 01-1

Other Interpretive Releases: FASB Special Report, *A Guide to Implementation of Statement 140 on Accounting for Transfers and Servicing of Financial Assets and Extinguishments of Liabilities: Questions and Answers* (in *Current Text* Sections F35, F39, and L35)

FASB Staff Positions FAS 140-1 and FAS 140-2

AICPA Accounting Standards Executive Committee (AcSEC)

Related Pronouncements: SOP 90-3
SOP 90-7
SOP 01-6
PB 4
PB 6

Issues Discussed by FASB Emerging Issues Task Force (EITF)

Affects: Nullifies EITF Issues No. 86-24, 86-39, 90-2, 94-9, 96-20, and 97-6 and Topics No. D-13, D-48, and D-75

Partially nullifies EITF Issues No. 84-5, 85-25, 85-40, 86-38, 87-30, 88-17, 88-22, 89-2, 89-4, 92-2, and 96-10

Resolves EITF Issues No. 84-21, 84-26, 85-26, 85-30, 85-34, 87-25, and 94-4 and Topic No. D-67

Partially resolves EITF Issues No. 84-20, 84-30, 87-18, 87-20, 87-30, 88-11, and 92-2 and Topic No. D-14

Interpreted by: Paragraph 9 interpreted by EITF Topics No. D-51 and D-65

Paragraph 9(a) interpreted by EITF Topic No. D-94

Paragraph 10 interpreted by EITF Issue No. 98-15

Paragraph 11 interpreted by EITF Topic No. D-69

Paragraph 16 interpreted by EITF Issues No. 96-19 and 98-14

Paragraph 17 interpreted by EITF Topic No. D-65

Paragraph 17(e)(2) interpreted by EITF Topic No. D-69

Paragraphs 47 and 49 interpreted by EITF Topic No. D-65

Paragraph 55 interpreted by EITF Issue No. 02-9

Paragraph 69 interpreted by EITF Topic No. D-69

Related Issues: EITF Issues No. 84-15, 85-13, 86-8, 86-36, 87-34, 88-18, 88-20, 90-18, 90-19, 90-21, 95-5, 97-3, 97-14, 98-8, 99-8, 99-20, 00-9, 01-2, 02-2, 02-12, and 06-6 and Topic No. D-66

SUMMARY

This Statement replaces FASB Statement No. 125, *Accounting for Transfers and Servicing of Financial Assets and Extinguishments of Liabilities*. It revises the standards for accounting for securitizations and other transfers of financial assets and collateral and requires certain disclosures, but it carries over most of Statement 125's provisions without reconsideration.

This Statement provides accounting and reporting standards for transfers and servicing of financial assets and extinguishments of liabilities. Those standards are based on consistent application of a *financial-components approach* that focuses on control. Under that approach, after a transfer of financial assets, an entity recognizes the financial and servicing assets it controls and the liabilities it has incurred, derecognizes financial assets when control has been surrendered, and derecognizes liabilities when extinguished. This Statement provides consistent standards for distinguishing transfers of financial assets that are sales from transfers that are secured borrowings.

A transfer of financial assets in which the transferor surrenders control over those assets is accounted for as a sale to the extent that consideration other than beneficial interests in the transferred assets is received in exchange. The transferor has surrendered control over transferred assets if and only if all of the following conditions are met:

a. The transferred assets have been isolated from the transferor—put presumptively beyond the reach of the transferor and its creditors, even in bankruptcy or other receivership.
b. Each transferee (or, if the transferee is a qualifying special-purpose entity (SPE), each holder of its beneficial interests) has the right to pledge or exchange the assets (or beneficial interests) it received, and no condition both constrains the transferee (or holder) from taking advantage of its right to pledge or exchange and provides more than a trivial benefit to the transferor.
c. The transferor does not maintain effective control over the transferred assets through either (1) an agreement that both entitles and obligates the transferor to repurchase or redeem them before their maturity or (2) the ability to unilaterally cause the holder to return specific assets, other than through a cleanup call.

This Statement requires that liabilities and derivatives incurred or obtained by transferors as part of a transfer of financial assets be initially measured at fair value, if practicable. It also requires that servicing assets and other retained interests in the transferred assets be measured by allocating the previous carrying amount between the assets sold, if any, and retained interests, if any, based on their relative fair values at the date of the transfer.

This Statement requires that servicing assets and liabilities be subsequently measured by (a) amortization in proportion to and over the period of estimated net servicing income or loss and (b) assessment for asset impairment or increased obligation based on their fair values.

This Statement requires that a liability be derecognized if and only if either (a) the debtor pays the creditor and is relieved of its obligation for the liability or (b) the debtor is legally released from being the primary obligor under the liability either judicially or by the creditor. Therefore, a liability is not considered extinguished by an in-substance defeasance.

This Statement provides implementation guidance for assessing isolation of transferred assets, conditions that constrain a transferee, conditions for an entity to be a qualifying SPE, accounting for transfers of partial interests, measurement of retained interests, servicing of financial assets, securitizations, transfers of sales-type and direct financing lease receivables, securities lending transactions, repurchase agreements including "dollar rolls," "wash sales," loan syndications and participations, risk participations in banker's acceptances, factoring arrangements, transfers of receivables with recourse, and extinguishments of liabilities. This Statement also provides guidance about whether a transferor has retained effective control over assets transferred to qualifying SPEs through removal-of-accounts provisions, liquidation provisions, or other arrangements.

This Statement requires a debtor to (a) reclassify financial assets pledged as collateral and report those assets in its statement of financial position separately from other assets not so encumbered if the secured party has the right by contract or custom to sell or repledge the collateral and (b) disclose assets pledged as collateral that have not been reclassified and separately reported in the statement of financial position. This Statement also requires a secured party to disclose information about collateral that it has accepted and is permitted by contract or custom to sell or repledge. The required disclosure includes the fair value at the end of the period of that collateral, and of the portion of that collateral that it has sold or repledged, and information about the sources and uses of that collateral.

This Statement requires an entity that has securitized financial assets to disclose information about accounting policies, volume, cash flows, key assumptions made in determining fair values of retained interests, and sensitivity of those fair values to changes in key assumptions. It also requires that entities that securitize assets disclose for the securitized assets and any other financial assets it manages together with them (a) the total principal amount outstanding, the portion that has been derecognized, and the portion that continues to be recognized in each category reported in the statement of financial position, at the end of the period; (b) delinquencies at the end of the period; and (c) credit losses during the period.

In addition to replacing Statement 125 and rescinding FASB Statement No. 127, *Deferral of the Effective Date of Certain Provisions of FASB Statement No. 125,* this Statement carries forward the actions taken by Statement 125. Statement 125 superseded FASB Statements No. 76, *Extinguishment of Debt,* and No. 77, *Reporting by Transferors for Transfers of Receivables with Recourse.* Statement 125 amended FASB Statement No. 115, *Accounting for Certain Investments in Debt and Equity Securities,* to clarify that a debt security may not be classified as held-to-maturity if it can be prepaid or otherwise settled in such a way that the holder of the security would not recover substantially all of its recorded investment. Statement 125 amended and extended to all servicing assets and liabilities the accounting standards for mortgage servicing rights now in FASB Statement No. 65, *Accounting for Certain Mortgage Banking Activities,* and superseded FASB Statement No. 122, *Accounting for Mortgage Servicing Rights.* Statement 125 also superseded FASB Technical Bulletins No. 84-4, *In-Substance Defeasance of Debt,* and No. 85-2, *Accounting for Collateralized Mortgage Obligations (CMOs),* and amended FASB Technical Bulletin No. 87-3, *Accounting for Mortgage Servicing Fees and Rights.*

Statement 125 was effective for transfers and servicing of financial assets and extinguishments of liabilities occurring after December 31, 1996, and on or before March 31, 2001, except for certain provisions. Statement 127 deferred until December 31, 1997, the effective date (a) of paragraph 15 of Statement 125 and (b) for repurchase agreement, dollar-roll, securities lending, and similar transactions, of paragraphs 9–12 and 237(b) of Statement 125.

This Statement is effective for transfers and servicing of financial assets and extinguishments of liabilities occurring after March 31, 2001. This Statement is effective for recognition and reclassification of collateral and for disclosures relating to securitization transactions and collateral for fiscal years ending after December 15, 2000. Disclosures about securitization and collateral accepted need not be reported for periods ending on or before December 15, 2000, for which financial statements are presented for comparative purposes.

This Statement is to be applied prospectively with certain exceptions. Other than those exceptions, earlier or retroactive application of its accounting provisions is not permitted.

Statement of Financial Accounting Standards No. 140

Accounting for Transfers and Servicing of Financial Assets and Extinguishments of Liabilities

a replacement of FASB Statement No. 125

CONTENTS

INTRODUCTION AND SCOPE

1. The Board added a project on financial instruments and off-balance-sheet financing to its agenda in May 1986. The project is intended to develop standards to aid in resolving existing financial accounting and reporting issues and other issues likely to arise in the future about various financial instruments and related transactions. The November 1991 FASB Discussion Memorandum, *Recognition and Measurement of Financial Instruments,* describes the issues to be considered. This Statement focuses on the issues of accounting for **transfers**[1] and servicing of **financial assets** and extinguishments of liabilities.

2. Transfers of financial assets take many forms. Accounting for transfers in which the **transferor** has no continuing involvement with the transferred assets or with the **transferee** has not been controversial. However, transfers of financial assets often occur in which the transferor has some continuing involve-

ment either with the assets transferred or with the transferee. Examples of continuing involvement are **recourse,** servicing, agreements to reacquire, options written or held, and pledges of **collateral.** Transfers of financial assets with continuing involvement raise issues about the circumstances under which the transfers should be considered as sales of all or part of the assets or as secured borrowings and about how transferors and transferees should account for sales and secured borrowings. This Statement establishes standards for resolving those issues.

3. An entity may settle a liability by transferring assets to the creditor or otherwise obtaining an unconditional release. Alternatively, an entity may enter into other arrangements designed to set aside assets dedicated to eventually settling a liability. Accounting for those arrangements has raised issues about when a liability should be considered extinguished. This Statement establishes standards for resolving those issues.

---

[1]Terms defined in Appendix E, the glossary, are set in **boldface type** the first time they appear.

4. This Statement does not address transfers of custody of financial assets for safekeeping, contributions,[2] transfers of ownership interests that are in substance sales of real estate, or investments by owners or distributions to owners of a business enterprise. This Statement does not address subsequent measurement of assets and liabilities, except for (a) **servicing assets** and **servicing liabilities** and (b) **interest-only strips**, securities, interests that continue to be held by a transferor in securitizations, loans, other receivables, or other financial assets that can contractually be prepaid or otherwise settled in such a way that the holder would not recover substantially all of its recorded investment and that are not within the scope of FASB Statement No. 133, *Accounting for Derivative Instruments and Hedging Activities.* This Statement does not change the accounting for employee benefits subject to the provisions of FASB Statement No. 87, *Employers' Accounting for Pensions,* No. 88, *Employers' Accounting for Settlements and Curtailments of Defined Benefit Pension Plans and for Termination Benefits,* or No. 106, *Employers' Accounting for Postretirement Benefits Other Than Pensions.* This Statement does not change the provisions relating to leveraged leases in FASB Statement No. 13, *Accounting for Leases,* or money-over-money and wrap lease transactions involving nonrecourse debt subject to the provisions of FASB Technical Bulletin No. 88-1, *Issues Relating to Accounting for Leases.* This Statement does not address transfers of nonfinancial assets, for example, servicing assets, or transfers of unrecognized financial assets, for example, minimum lease payments to be received under operating leases.

5. The Board concluded that an objective in accounting for transfers of financial assets is for each entity that is a party to the transaction to recognize only assets it controls and liabilities it has incurred, to **derecognize** assets only when control has been surrendered, and to derecognize liabilities only when they have been extinguished. Sales and other transfers frequently result in a disaggregation of financial assets and liabilities into components, which become separate assets and liabilities. For example, if an entity sells a portion of a financial asset it owns, the portion that continues to be held by a transferor becomes an asset separate from the portion sold and from the assets obtained in exchange.

6. The Board concluded that another objective is that recognition of financial assets and liabilities should not be affected by the sequence of transactions that result in their acquisition or incurrence unless the effect of those transactions is to maintain effective control over a transferred financial asset. For example, if a transferor sells financial assets it owns and at the same time writes an "at-the-money" put option (such as a guarantee or recourse obligation) on those assets, it should recognize the put obligation in the same manner as would another unrelated entity that writes an identical put option on assets it never owned. Similarly, a creditor may release a debtor on the condition that a third party assumes the obligation and that the original debtor becomes secondarily liable. In those circumstances, the original debtor becomes a guarantor and should recognize a guarantee obligation in the same manner as would a third-party guarantor that had never been primarily liable to that creditor, whether or not explicit consideration was paid for that guarantee. However, certain agreements to repurchase or redeem transferred assets maintain effective control over those assets and should therefore be accounted for differently than agreements to acquire assets never owned.

7. Before FASB Statement No. 125, *Accounting for Transfers and Servicing of Financial Assets and Extinguishments of Liabilities,* accounting standards generally required that a transferor account for financial assets transferred as an inseparable unit that had been either entirely sold or entirely retained. Those standards were difficult to apply and produced inconsistent and arbitrary results. For example, whether a transfer "purported to be a sale" was sufficient to determine whether the transfer was accounted for and reported as a sale of receivables under one accounting standard or as a secured borrowing under another. After studying many of the complex developments that have occurred in financial markets during recent years, the Board concluded that previous approaches that viewed each financial asset as an indivisible unit do not provide an appropriate basis for developing consistent and operational standards for dealing with transfers and servicing of financial assets and extinguishments of liabilities. To address those issues adequately and consistently, the Board decided to adopt as the basis for this Statement a *financial-components approach* that focuses on control and recognizes that

---

[2]Contributions—unconditional nonreciprocal transfers of assets—are addressed in FASB Statement No. 116, *Accounting for Contributions Received and Contributions Made.*

financial assets and liabilities can be divided into a variety of components.

8. The Board issued Statement 125 in June 1996. After the issuance of that Statement, several parties called for reconsideration or clarification of certain provisions. Matters the Board was asked to reconsider or clarify included:

a. Circumstances in which a special-purpose entity (SPE) can be considered qualifying
b. Circumstances in which the assets held by a qualifying SPE should appear in the consolidated financial statements of the transferor
c. Whether sale accounting is precluded if the transferor holds a right to repurchase transferred assets that is attached to, is embedded in, or is otherwise transferable with the financial assets
d. Circumstances in which sale accounting is precluded if transferred financial assets can be removed from an SPE by the transferor (for example, under a removal-of-accounts provision (ROAP))
e. Whether arrangements that obligate, but do not entitle, a transferor to repurchase or redeem transferred financial assets should affect the accounting for those transfers
f. The impact of the powers of the Federal Deposit Insurance Corporation (FDIC) on isolation of assets transferred by financial institutions
g. Whether transfers of financial assets measured using the equity method of accounting should continue to be included in the scope of Statement 125
h. Whether disclosures should be enhanced to provide more information about assumptions used to determine the fair value of retained interests and the gain or loss on financial assets sold in securitizations
i. The accounting for and disclosure about collateral that can be sold or repledged.

The Board concluded that those requests to reconsider certain provisions of Statement 125 were appropriate and added a project to amend Statement 125 to its agenda in March 1997. This Statement is the result. To present the amended accounting standards for transfers of financial assets more clearly, this Statement replaces Statement 125. However, most of the provisions of Statement 125 have been carried forward without reconsideration.

STANDARDS OF FINANCIAL ACCOUNTING AND REPORTING

Accounting for Transfers and Servicing of Financial Assets

9. A transfer of financial assets (or all or a portion of a financial asset) in which the transferor surrenders control over those financial assets shall be accounted for as a sale to the extent that consideration other than **beneficial interests** in the transferred assets is received in exchange. The transferor has surrendered control over transferred assets if and only if *all of the following conditions* are met:

a. The transferred assets have been isolated from the transferor—put presumptively beyond the reach of the transferor and its creditors, even in bankruptcy or other receivership (paragraphs 27 and 28).
b. Each transferee (or, if the transferee is a qualifying SPE (paragraph 35), each holder of its beneficial interests) has the right to pledge or exchange the assets (or beneficial interests) it received, and no condition both constrains the transferee (or holder) from taking advantage of its right to pledge or exchange and provides more than a trivial benefit to the transferor (paragraphs 29–34).
c. The transferor does not maintain effective control over the transferred assets through either (1) an agreement that both entitles and obligates the transferor to repurchase or redeem them before their maturity (paragraphs 47–49) or (2) the ability to unilaterally cause the holder to return specific assets, other than through a **cleanup call** (paragraphs 50–54).

10. Upon completion of any transfer of financial assets, the transferor shall:

a. Initially recognize and measure at fair value, if practicable (paragraph 71), servicing assets and servicing liabilities that require recognition under the provisions of paragraph 13
b. Allocate the previous carrying amount between the assets sold, if any, and the interests that continue to be held by the transferor, if any, based on their relative fair values at the date of transfer (paragraphs 56–60)

c. Continue to carry in its statement of financial position any interest it continues to hold in the transferred assets, including, if applicable, beneficial interests in assets transferred to a qualifying SPE in a **securitization** (paragraphs 73–84), and any **undivided interests** (paragraphs 58 and 59).

11. Upon completion[3] of a transfer of financial assets that satisfies the conditions to be accounted for as a sale (paragraph 9), the transferor (**seller**) shall:

a. Derecognize all assets sold
b. Recognize all assets obtained and liabilities incurred in consideration as **proceeds** of the sale, including cash, put or call options held or written (for example, guarantee or recourse obligations), forward commitments (for example, commitments to deliver additional receivables during the revolving periods of some securitizations), swaps (for example, provisions that convert interest rates from fixed to variable), and servicing assets and servicing liabilities, if applicable (paragraphs 56, 57, and 61–67)
c. Initially measure at fair value assets obtained and liabilities incurred in a sale or, if it is not practicable to estimate the fair value of an asset or a liability, apply alternative measures (paragraphs 71 and 72)
d. Recognize in earnings any gain or loss on the sale.

The transferee shall recognize all assets obtained and any liabilities incurred and initially measure them at fair value (in aggregate, presumptively the price paid).

12. If a transfer of financial assets in exchange for cash or other consideration (other than beneficial interests in the transferred assets) does not meet the criteria for a sale in paragraph 9, the transferor and transferee shall account for the transfer as a secured borrowing with pledge of collateral (paragraph 15).

Recognition and Measurement of Servicing Assets and Servicing Liabilities

13. An entity shall recognize and initially measure at fair value, if practicable, a servicing asset or servicing liability each time it undertakes an obligation to

service a financial asset by entering into a servicing contract in any of the following situations:

a. A transfer of the servicer's financial assets that meets the requirements for sale accounting
b. A transfer of the servicer's financial assets to a qualifying SPE in a **guaranteed mortgage securitization** in which the transferor retains all of the resulting securities and classifies them as either available-for-sale securities or trading securities in accordance with FASB Statement No. 115, *Accounting for Certain Investments in Debt and Equity Securities*
c. An acquisition or assumption of a servicing obligation that does not relate to financial assets of the servicer or its consolidated affiliates.

An entity that transfers its financial assets to a qualifying SPE in a guaranteed mortgage securitization in which the transferor retains all of the resulting securities and classifies them as debt securities held-to-maturity in accordance with Statement 115 may either separately recognize its servicing assets or servicing liabilities or report those servicing assets or servicing liabilities together with the asset being serviced.

13A. An entity shall subsequently measure each class of servicing assets and servicing liabilities using one of the following methods:

a. *Amortization method:* Amortize servicing assets or servicing liabilities in proportion to and over the period of estimated net servicing income (if servicing revenues exceed servicing costs) or net servicing loss (if servicing costs exceed servicing revenues), and assess servicing assets or servicing liabilities for impairment or increased obligation based on fair value at each reporting date
b. *Fair value measurement method:* Measure servicing assets or servicing liabilities at fair value at each reporting date and report changes in fair value of servicing assets and servicing liabilities in earnings in the period in which the changes occur.

The election described in this paragraph shall be made separately for each class of servicing assets and servicing liabilities. An entity shall apply the same subsequent measurement method to each servicing

---

[3]Although a transfer of securities may not be considered to have reached completion until the settlement date, this Statement does not modify other generally accepted accounting principles, including FASB Statement No. 35, *Accounting and Reporting by Defined Benefit Pension Plans,* and AICPA Statements of Position and audit and accounting Guides for certain industries, that require accounting at the trade date for certain contracts to purchase or sell securities.

asset and servicing liability in a class. Classes of servicing assets and servicing liabilities shall be identified based on (a) the availability of market inputs used in determining the fair value of servicing assets or servicing liabilities, (b) an entity's method for managing the risks of its servicing assets or servicing liabilities, or (c) both. Once an entity elects the fair value measurement method for a class of servicing assets and servicing liabilities, that election shall not be reversed (paragraph 63). If it is not practicable to initially measure a servicing asset or servicing liability at fair value, an entity shall initially recognize the servicing asset or servicing liability in accordance with paragraph 71 and shall include it in a class subsequently measured using the amortization method.

13B. An entity shall report recognized servicing assets and servicing liabilities that are subsequently measured using the fair value measurement method in a manner that separates those carrying amounts on the face of the statement of financial position from the carrying amounts for separately recognized servicing assets and servicing liabilities that are subsequently measured using the amortization method. To accomplish that separate reporting, an entity may either (a) display separate line items for the amounts that are subsequently measured using the fair value measurement method and amounts that are subsequently measured using the amortization method or (b) present the aggregate of those amounts that are subsequently measured at fair value and those amounts that are subsequently measured using the amortization method (paragraph 63) and disclose parenthetically the amount that is subsequently measured at fair value that is included in the aggregate amount.

Financial Assets Subject to Prepayment

14. Interest-only strips, other interests that continue to be held by a transferor in securitizations, loans, other receivables, or other financial assets that can contractually be prepaid or otherwise settled in such a way that the holder would not recover substantially all of its recorded investment, except for instruments that are within the scope of Statement 133, shall be

subsequently measured like investments in debt securities classified as available-for-sale or trading under Statement 115, as amended (paragraph 362).

Secured Borrowings and Collateral

15. A debtor may grant a **security interest** in certain assets to a lender (the secured party) to serve as collateral for its obligation under a borrowing, with or without recourse to other assets of the debtor. An obligor under other kinds of current or potential obligations, for example, interest rate swaps, also may grant a security interest in certain assets to a secured party. If collateral is transferred to the secured party, the custodial arrangement is commonly referred to as a pledge. Secured parties sometimes are permitted to sell or repledge (or otherwise transfer) collateral held under a pledge. The same relationships occur, under different names, in transfers documented as sales that are accounted for as secured borrowings (paragraph 12). The accounting for noncash[4] collateral by the debtor (or obligor) and the secured party depends on whether the secured party has the right to sell or repledge the collateral and on whether the debtor has defaulted.

a. If the secured party (transferee) has the right by contract or custom to sell or repledge the collateral, then the debtor (transferor) shall reclassify that asset and report that asset in its statement of financial position separately (for example, as security pledged to creditors) from other assets not so encumbered.

b. If the secured party (transferee) sells collateral pledged to it, it shall recognize the proceeds from the sale and its obligation to return the collateral. The sale of the collateral is a transfer subject to the provisions of this Statement.

c. If the debtor (transferor) defaults under the terms of the secured contract and is no longer entitled to redeem the pledged asset, it shall derecognize the pledged asset, and the secured party (transferee) shall recognize the collateral as its asset initially measured at fair value or, if it has already sold the collateral, derecognize its obligation to return the collateral.

---

[4]Cash "collateral," sometimes used, for example, in securities lending transactions (paragraphs 91–95), shall be derecognized by the payer and recognized by the recipient, not as collateral, but rather as proceeds of either a sale or a borrowing.

d. Except as provided in paragraph 15(c), the debtor (transferor) shall continue to carry the collateral as its asset, and the secured party (transferee) shall not recognize the pledged asset.

Extinguishments of Liabilities

16. A debtor shall derecognize a liability if and only if it has been extinguished. A liability has been extinguished if either of the following conditions is met:

a. The debtor pays the creditor and is relieved of its obligation for the liability. Paying the creditor includes delivery of cash, other financial assets, goods, or services or reacquisition by the debtor of its outstanding debt securities whether the securities are canceled or held as so-called treasury bonds.
b. The debtor is legally released[5] from being the primary obligor under the liability, either judicially or by the creditor.

Disclosures

17. An entity shall disclose the following:

a. For collateral:
   (1) If the entity has entered into repurchase agreements or securities lending transactions, its policy for requiring collateral or other security
   (2) If the entity has pledged any of its assets as collateral that are not reclassified and separately reported in the statement of financial position pursuant to paragraph 15(a), the carrying amount and classification of those assets as of the date of the latest statement of financial position presented
   (3) If the entity has accepted collateral that it is permitted by contract or custom to sell or repledge, the fair value as of the date of each statement of financial position presented of that collateral and of the portion of that collateral that it has sold or repledged, and information about the sources and uses of that collateral.
b. If debt was considered to be extinguished by in-substance defeasance under the provisions of FASB Statement No. 76, *Extinguishment of Debt,* prior to the effective date of Statement 125,[6] a general description of the transaction and the amount of debt that is considered extinguished at the end of the period so long as that debt remains outstanding.
c. If assets are set aside after the effective date of Statement 125 solely for satisfying scheduled payments of a specific obligation, a description of the nature of restrictions placed on those assets.
d. If it is not practicable to estimate the fair value of certain assets obtained or liabilities incurred in transfers of financial assets during the period, a description of those items and the reasons why it is not practicable to estimate their fair value.
e. For all servicing assets and servicing liabilities:
   (1) Management's basis for determining its classes of servicing assets and servicing liabilities (paragraph 13A).
   (2) A description of the risks inherent in servicing assets and servicing liabilities and, if applicable, the instruments used to mitigate the income statement effect of changes in fair value of the servicing assets and servicing liabilities. (Disclosure of quantitative information about the instruments used to manage the risks inherent in servicing assets and servicing liabilities, including the fair value of those instruments at the beginning and end of the period, is encouraged but not required.)
   (3) The amount of contractually specified servicing fees (as defined in the glossary), late fees, and ancillary fees earned for each period for which results of operations are presented, including a description of where each amount is reported in the statement of income.
f. For servicing assets and servicing liabilities subsequently measured at fair value:
   (1) For each class of servicing assets and servicing liabilities, the activity in the balance of servicing assets and the activity in the balance of servicing liabilities (including a description of where changes in fair value are reported in the statement of income for each period for which results of operations are presented), including, but not limited to, the following:
      (a) The beginning and ending balances

---

[5] If nonrecourse debt (such as certain mortgage loans) is assumed by a third party in conjunction with the sale of an asset that serves as sole collateral for that debt, the sale and related assumption effectively accomplish a legal release of the seller-debtor for purposes of applying this Statement.

[6] Refer to footnote 11 to paragraph 19.

Accounting for Transfers and Servicing of
Financial Assets and Extinguishments of Liabilities
FAS140

(b) Additions (through purchases of servicing assets, assumptions of servicing obligations, and servicing obligations that result from transfers of financial assets)

(c) Disposals

(d) Changes in fair value during the period resulting from:

  (i) Changes in valuation inputs or assumptions used in the valuation model

  (ii) Other changes in fair value and a description of those changes

(e) Other changes that affect the balance and a description of those changes

(2) A description of the valuation techniques or other methods used to estimate the fair value of servicing assets and servicing liabilities. If a valuation model is used, the description shall include the methodology and model validation procedures, as well as quantitative and qualitative information about the assumptions used in the valuation model (for example, discount rates and prepayment speeds). (An entity that provides quantitative information about the instruments used to manage the risks inherent in the servicing assets and servicing liabilities, as encouraged by paragraph 17(e)(2), is also encouraged, but not required, to disclose a description of the valuation techniques, as well as quantitative and qualitative information about the assumptions used to estimate the fair value of those instruments.)

g. For servicing assets and servicing liabilities subsequently amortized in proportion to and over the period of estimated net servicing income or loss and assessed for impairment or increased obligation:

(1) For each class of servicing assets and servicing liabilities, the activity in the balance of servicing assets and the activity in the balance of servicing liabilities (including a description of where changes in the carrying amount are reported in the statement of income for each period for which results of operations are presented), including, but not limited to, the following:

(a) The beginning and ending balances

(b) Additions (through purchases of servicing assets, assumption of servicing obligations, and servicing obligations that result from transfers of financial assets)

(c) Disposals

(d) Amortization

(e) Application of valuation allowance to adjust carrying value of servicing assets

(f) Other-than-temporary impairments

(g) Other changes that affect the balance and a description of those changes.

(2) For each class of servicing assets and servicing liabilities, the fair value of recognized servicing assets and servicing liabilities at the beginning and end of the period if it is practicable to estimate the value.

(3) A description of the valuation techniques or other methods used to estimate fair value of the servicing assets and servicing liabilities. If a valuation model is used, the description shall include the methodology and model validation procedures, as well as quantitative and qualitative information about the assumptions used in the valuation model (for example, discount rates and prepayment speeds). (An entity that provides quantitative information about the instruments used to manage the risks inherent in the servicing assets and servicing liabilities, as encouraged by paragraph 17(e)(2), is also encouraged, but not required, to disclose a description of the valuation techniques as well as quantitative and qualitative information about the assumptions used to estimate the fair value of those instruments.)

(4) The risk characteristics of the underlying financial assets used to stratify recognized servicing assets for purposes of measuring impairment in accordance with paragraph 63.

(5) The activity by class in any valuation allowance for impairment of recognized servicing assets—including beginning and ending balances, aggregate additions charged and recoveries credited to operations, and aggregate write-downs charged against the allowance—for each period for which results of operations are presented.

h. If the entity has securitized financial assets during any period presented and accounts for that transfer as a sale, for each major asset type (for example, mortgage loans, credit card receivables, and automobile loans):

(1) Its accounting policies for initially measuring the interests that continue to be held by the transferor, if any, and servicing assets or servicing liabilities, if any, including the methodology (whether quoted market price, prices based on sales of similar assets and liabilities,

or prices based on valuation techniques) used in determining their fair value

(2) The characteristics of securitizations (a description of the transferor's continuing involvement with the transferred assets, including, but not limited to, servicing, recourse, and restrictions on interests that continue to be held by the transferor) and the gain or loss from sale of financial assets in securitizations

(3) The key assumptions[7] used in measuring the fair value of interests that continue to be held by the transferor and servicing assets or servicing liabilities, if any, at the time of securitization (including, at a minimum, quantitative information about discount rates, expected prepayments including the expected weighted-average life of prepayable financial assets,[8] and anticipated credit losses, if applicable)

(4) Cash flows between the securitization SPE and the transferor, unless reported separately elsewhere in the financial statements or notes (including proceeds from new securitizations, proceeds from collections reinvested in revolving-period securitizations, purchases of delinquent or foreclosed loans, servicing fees, and cash flows received on interests that continue to be held by the transferor).

i. If the entity has interests that continue to be held by the transferor in financial assets that it has securitized or servicing assets or servicing liabilities relating to assets that it has securitized, at the date of the latest statement of financial position presented, for each major asset type (for example, mortgage loans, credit card receivables, and automobile loans):

(1) Its accounting policies for subsequently measuring those interests, including the methodology (whether quoted market price, prices based on sales of similar assets and li-

abilities, or prices based on valuation techniques) used in determining their fair value

(2) The key assumptions used in subsequently measuring the fair value of those interests (including, at a minimum, quantitative information about discount rates, expected prepayments including the expected weighted-average life of prepayable financial assets, and anticipated credit losses, including expected static pool losses,[9] if applicable)[9a]

(3) A sensitivity analysis or stress test showing the hypothetical effect on the fair value of those interests (including any servicing assets or servicing liabilities) of two or more unfavorable variations from the expected levels for each key assumption that is reported under (2) above independently from any change in another key assumption, and a description of the objectives, methodology, and limitations of the sensitivity analysis or stress test

(4) For the securitized assets and any other financial assets that it manages together with them:[10]

(a) The total principal amount outstanding, the portion that has been derecognized, and the portion that continues to be recognized in each category reported in the statement of financial position, at the end of the period

(b) Delinquencies at the end of the period

(c) Credit losses, net of recoveries, during the period.

(Disclosure of average balances during the period is encouraged, but not required.)

Implementation Guidance

18. Appendix A describes certain provisions of this Statement in more detail and describes their application to certain types of transactions. Appendix A is an integral part of the standards provided in this Statement.

---

[7]If an entity has made multiple securitizations of the same major asset type during a period, it may disclose the range of assumptions.

[8]The weighted-average life of prepayable assets in periods (for example, months or years) can be calculated by multiplying the principal collections expected in each future period by the number of periods until that future period, summing those products, and dividing the sum by the initial principal balance.

[9]Expected static pool losses can be calculated by summing the actual and projected future credit losses and dividing the sum by the original balance of the pool of assets.

[9a]The timing and amount of future cash flows for retained interests in securitizations are commonly uncertain, especially if those interests are subordinate to more senior beneficial interests. Thus, estimates of future cash flows used for a fair value measurement depend heavily on assumptions about default and prepayment of all the assets securitized, because of the implicit credit or prepayment risk enhancement arising from the subordination.

[10]Excluding securitized assets that an entity continues to service but with which it has no other continuing involvement.

Effective Date and Transition

19. This Statement shall be effective for transfers and servicing of financial assets and extinguishments of liablilities occurring after March 31, 2001, except as provided in paragraphs 20–25 and except that for banks and other financial institutions subject to possible receivership under the FDIC (and for other affected entities that have previously considered their transfers of financial assets in "single-step" securitizations to have isolated those assets in circumstances similar to those of entities subject to possible FDIC receivership), paragraphs 9(a), 27, 28, and 80–84 shall be effective for transfers of financial assets occurring after December 31, 2001. This Statement shall be applied prospectively,[11] except as provided in paragraphs 20, 21, 23, and 24. Earlier or retroactive application of this Statement is not permitted.

20. For each servicing contract in existence before January 1, 1997, previously recognized servicing rights and "excess servicing" receivables that do not exceed **contractually specified servicing fees** shall be combined, net of any previously recognized servicing obligations under that contract, as a servicing asset or liability. Previously recognized servicing receivables that exceed contractually specified servicing fees shall be reclassified as interest-only strips receivable. Thereafter, the subsequent measurement provisions of this Statement shall be applied to the servicing assets or liabilities for those servicing contracts (paragraph 63) and to the interest-only strips receivable (paragraph 14).

21. The provisions of paragraph 14 and the amendment to Statement 115 (paragraph 362) shall be effective for financial assets held on or acquired after January 1, 1997.

22. Paragraphs 17(f) and 17(g) shall be effective for financial statements for fiscal years ending after December 15, 2000. The information required to be disclosed about securitizations of financial assets during the period that are accounted for as sales need not be reported for periods ending on or before December 15, 2000, for which an income statement is presented for comparative purposes.

23. Collateral previously recognized in financial statements in accordance with the requirements of paragraphs 15(a)(ii) and 15(b) of Statement 125 that is no longer to be recognized in accordance with paragraph 15 of this Statement shall no longer be recognized in financial statements for fiscal years ending after December 15, 2000, and financial statements for previous periods presented for comparative purposes shall be restated accordingly. The requirements for reclassification of certain assets in paragraph 15(a) of this Statement and for disclosure about collateral pledged and accepted in paragraphs 17(a)(2) and 17(a)(3) shall be effective for financial statements for fiscal years ending after December 15, 2000; that information need not be reported for periods ending on or before December 15, 2000, for which a statement of financial position is presented for comparative purposes.

24. Assets transferred on or before the effective date of this Statement for transfers of financial assets (paragraph 19) and transfer of assets after that date required by commitments made before that date to transferees or beneficial interest holders (BIHs) other than the transferor, its affiliates,[12] or its **agents** shall continue to be accounted for under the previous accounting standards for transfers of assets that applied when the transferor made or committed to those transfers. Also, transfers during an additional transition period[12a] that are constrained under certain contractual arrangements shall continue to be accounted for under the previous accounting standards for transfer of assets that applied when the transferor entered into those constraining contractual arrangements.

---

[11]Statement 125 applies to transfers and servicing of financial assets and extinguishments of liabilities occurring after December 31, 1996 (after December 31, 1997, for transfers affected by FASB Statement No. 127, *Deferral of the Effective Date of Certain Provisions of FASB Statement No. 125*) and on or before March 31, 2001. Statement 127 deferred until December 31, 1997, the effective date (a) of paragraph 15 of Statement 125 and (b) for repurchase agreement, dollar-roll, securities lending, and similar transactions, of paragraphs 9–12 and 237(b) of Statement 125.

[12]In this Statement, the term *affiliate* is used in the same sense as it is used in FASB Statement No. 57, *Related Party Disclosures.*

[12a]The additional transition period applies to voluntary transfers that under prior contractual arrangements with qualifying SPE BIHs other than the transferor, its affiliates, or its agents, are constrained to be made in such a way that the transfer cannot meet all the requirements for sale accounting in paragraphs 9(a), 27, 28, and 80–84 of this Statement. That additional transition period is available only for such transfers by banks and other financial institutions subject to possible receivership under the FDIC (and for other affected entities that have previously considered their transfers of financial assets in "single-step" securitizations to have isolated those assets in circumstances similar to those of entities subject to possible FDIC receivership). The additional transition period is available only if all beneficial interests issued by the qualifying SPE after the publication of FASB Technical Bulletin No. 01-1, *Effective Date for Certain Financial Institutions of Certain Provisions of Statement 140 Related to the Isolation of Transferred Financial Assets,* permit the necessary changes in structure. The additional transition period ends three months after the earliest date at which sufficient approvals to permit the necessary changes can be obtained from BIHs and any other persons whose approvals are required by the terms of the prior contractual arrangement, but in no event later than June 30, 2006.

Transfers of assets after the effective date, unless required by commitments made before that date to transferees or BIHs other than the transferor, its affiliates, or its agents or constrained during the additional transition period, shall be subject to all the provisions of this Statement.

25. A formerly qualifying SPE that fails to meet one or more conditions for being a qualifying SPE under this Statement shall continue to be considered a qualifying SPE if it maintains its qualifying status under previous accounting standards, does not issue new beneficial interests after the effective date, and does not receive assets it was not committed to receive (through a commitment to BIHs unrelated to the transferor) before the effective date. Otherwise, the formerly qualifying SPE and assets transferred to it shall be subject to other consolidation policy standards and guidance and to all the provisions of this Statement.

**The provisions of this Statement need
not be applied to immaterial items.**

This Statement was adopted by the affirmative votes of five members of the Financial Accounting Standards Board. Mr. Crooch abstained. Mr. Foster dissented.

Mr. Foster dissents from the issuance of this Statement *[Statement 140]* because he believes its amendments to Statement 125 negate the rationale in that Statement *[Statement 125]* that underlies the accounting for transfers of financial assets to certain qualifying SPEs. Furthermore, he believes the amendments made by this Statement to the accounting for collateral conflict with the underlying concept that an entity recognizes assets that it controls.

A principal requirement for transfers of financial assets to be accounted for as sales pursuant to Statement 125 is that the transferor surrenders control of those assets. The Board reasoned that in most situations, excepting transactions involving repurchase agreements and similarly structured arrangements, the transferor had not surrendered control unless the transferee had unconstrained rights to pledge or exchange the transferred assets. However, if that criterion was applied to securitization transactions, very few would be accounted for as sales, because, in those transactions, SPEs to which the financial assets have been transferred are generally limited by their governing documents in their ability to pledge or exchange the transferred assets. The Board believes that many securitization transactions are, in substance, sales. Consequently, the Board developed a separate rationale for determining which transfers to SPEs (which are primarily securitization transactions) could qualify as sales.

In securitization transactions, assets are transferred to an SPE, which holds the assets on behalf of the BIHs. As discussed in paragraph 173 of this Statement, the Board developed a notion that in a qualifying SPE, the BIHs are the ultimate holders of the transferred assets. That notion is based on the premise that because the powers of a qualifying SPE are essentially limited to holding the transferred assets and collecting and distributing the cash flows that arise from the transferred assets, the BIHs effectively have undivided interests in the transferred assets. The Board observed that "the effect of establishing the qualifying SPE is to merge the contractual rights in the transferred assets and to *allocate undivided interests in them*—the beneficial interests" (Statement 125, paragraph 127; paragraph 173 of this Statement; emphasis added). Accordingly, the Board concluded that if the BIHs can pledge or exchange their beneficial interests without constraint (and if the other criteria in paragraph 9 are met), the transferor has surrendered control over the transferred assets.

Mr. Foster believes it is clear that if an SPE can pledge or exchange its assets, the BIHs do not have undivided interests in the assets initially transferred to that SPE. Rather, they have undivided interests in an undefined pool of assets, and having the ability to freely pledge or exchange their beneficial interests is not tantamount to being able to transfer undivided interests in those assets that were transferred to the SPE. It is the ability to pledge or exchange undivided interests in the transferred assets that underlies the conclusion that transfers of financial assets to qualifying SPEs be accounted for as sales. For that conclusion to be valid, Mr. Foster believes qualifying SPEs should not be permitted to pledge or exchange assets under any circumstances and particularly so when the exchanges occur at the behest and on behalf of the transferor/servicer. When transferred assets can be pledged or exchanged by the SPE, the ability of BIHs to transfer their beneficial interests in the SPE has no bearing on whether the transferor has surrendered control over those assets. Yet, this Statement offers no other rationale for why control over assets transferred to an SPE having the expanded powers provided by this amendment is considered to be surrendered.

Mr. Foster dissented from the issuance of Statement 125 (see previous dissent included below) in part because he believes that in securitizations having a revolving-period agreement, effective control over the assets has not been surrendered. He believes the existence of and the need for ROAPs that enable the transferor to reclaim specific transferred receivables in securitizations having a revolving-period agreement are further evidence that the receivables transferred in those securitizations continue to be effectively controlled by the transferor and that those securitization transactions are, therefore, secured borrowings. (He notes that, in addition to the transferor's ability to reclaim specific receivables from the SPE, the transferor generally continues to collect the cash from the transferred receivables, commingles that cash with its own cash, invests the cash for its own benefit, and uses the cash to buy additional receivables from itself that it selects. Furthermore, the transferor, within fairly wide latitude, has the power to change the interest rate on already transferred receivables.)

Statement 125, prior to amendment by this Statement, provides that for a sale to occur a transferor of financial assets to a qualifying SPE cannot maintain effective control over those assets. That notion that a transferor cannot recognize a sale if it maintains effective control through an option to reclaim the transferred assets is carried forward in this Statement in paragraph 9(c)(2). However, the notion is modified in this Statement to make a distinction between call options that are unilaterally exercisable by the transferor and options for which the exercise by the transferor is conditioned upon an event outside its control. The effect of this modification is that if the transferor can only reclaim the receivable upon the occurrence of an event outside its control, it is not considered to have retained effective control. Mr.

Foster believes that effective control is maintained by any option to reclaim transferred assets that is held by the transferor, but even more so in the case where the transferor holds a call on a specific receivable transferred to an SPE for which it has previously issued a call on that same receivable to another party (such as in the case of an affinity relationship described in paragraph 87(c)). In that case, the transferor has already promised that if that other party calls the receivable, it will deliver it. Consequently, if it transfers the receivable, it must control it through a ROAP that enables it to reclaim it—the transferor cannot surrender control of the receivable because it would be unable to perform in the event that specific receivable is called by that other party. Mr. Foster does not understand why control is deemed to have been surrendered in circumstances that *require* that a transferor have the ability to reclaim a transferred receivable when control is deemed not to have been surrendered in circumstances that enable a transferor to reclaim transferred receivables at its discretion.

A fundamental tenet of Statement 125 is that a transferor has surrendered control over an asset only if the transferee can exchange or pledge that transferred asset. The transferee then can control the asset, because it is free to sell, pledge, or do anything else it desires with the asset.[13] An entity that holds collateral in the form of a financial asset that it can pledge or exchange likewise can control that collateral. Statement 125, prior to amendment by this Statement, required that an entity that holds collateral that can be sold or repledged recognize that collateral as its asset unless the transferor can redeem the pledged collateral on short notice. This Statement amends Statement 125 to require that collateral not be recognized by the entity that holds it, even in circumstances in which it can be sold or repledged. Only after cash is received in exchange for collateral that is subsequently sold is the fact that the holder of the collateral had an asset acknowledged. Mr. Foster believes that the amendment related to collateral also is inconsistent with the concepts underlying Statement 125.

---

[13]The Board crafted an exception to this principle so that repurchase agreements, securities lending transactions, and similarly structured transactions would not be accounted for as sales.

Statement 125 was adopted in June 1996 by the affirmative votes of six members of the Financial Accounting Standards Board. Mr. Foster dissented.

Mr. Foster dissents from the issuance of Statement 125 because he believes that the notion of effective control that is applied to repurchase agreements, including dollar rolls, and securities lending transactions should be applied consistently to other transfers of financial assets, including securitization transactions. Furthermore, he believes that in those instances where the financial-components approach is applied, all rights (assets) and obligations (liabilities) that are recognized by the transferor after a sale or securitization has occurred should be measured at fair value.

Under paragraphs 9(a) and 9(b) of Statement 125, control is deemed to have been surrendered if the transferred assets have been legally isolated from the transferor and the transferee has the right to pledge or exchange the transferred assets. That notion of control is the cornerstone of the financial-components approach. However, the Board considered that approach inappropriate to account for certain transactions, such as those involving repurchase agreements, including dollar rolls, and securities lending transactions, where legal control over the assets has been surrendered, but where the Board believes that effective control still exists. For those transactions, paragraph 9(c) of Statement 125 was specifically crafted to override the criteria for transfers of legal control in paragraphs 9(a) and 9(b) of Statement 125. Paragraph 9(c), however, was designed to provide an exception only for certain transactions resulting in inconsistent application of the control notion: one set of transfers of financial assets—securitizations—is accounted for using a narrow, legal definition of control while others are accounted for using a broad notion of effective control. Mr. Foster favors an approach that encompasses the broader notion of effective control. He questions why, if the financial-components approach is inappropriate to account for all transfers of financial assets, it is appropriate to apply it to securitizations. He believes that if the entirety of the arrangement is considered, certain securitization transactions, such as those having a revolving-period agreement, also result in effective control being retained by the transferor and accordingly those transactions should be accounted for as secured borrowings.

In securitizations having a revolving-period agreement, which are described in paragraphs 130–133 of Statement 125 [paragraphs 192–195 of this State-

ment], the transferor generally continues to collect the cash from the transferred receivables, commingles that cash with its own cash, invests the cash for its own benefit, and uses the cash to buy additional receivables from itself that it selects. As a result of those features, the future benefits of the receivables (the cash flows to be received from them) that inure to the transferor are little different, if at all, from the future benefits that the transferor would obtain from receivables that it holds for its own account. Mr. Foster believes that in those transactions effective control of the receivables has not been surrendered and that the transferred receivables continue to be assets of the transferor.

Paragraph 26 of FASB Concepts Statement No. 6, *Elements of Financial Statements,* states, "An asset has three essential characteristics: (a) it embodies a probable future benefit that involves a capacity, singly or in combination with other assets, to contribute directly or indirectly to future net cash inflows, (b) a particular entity can obtain the benefit and control others' access to it, and (c) the transaction or other event giving rise to the entity's right to or control of the benefit has already occurred." Mr. Foster believes that in securitizations having revolving-period agreements, the transferred receivables meet each of those criteria from the perspective of the transferor. The transferred receivables directly or indirectly contribute to the transferor's cash inflows—it generally receives and retains all of the cash inflows during the term of the arrangement subject only to payment of what amounts to interest on the investment of the holders of beneficial interests—and the transferor can and does obtain and control others' access to both the receivables and the cash inflows by its structuring of the transaction and retention of most of the cash flows until termination of the arrangement. Paragraph 131 of Statement 125 [paragraph 193 of this Statement] asserts that the cash obtained by the transferor in those securitizations is received in exchange for new receivables and is not obtained as a benefit attributable to its previous ownership of the transferred receivables. In substance, however, the transfer of new receivables is little different from the substitution of collateral prevalent in many secured loan arrangements. In short, the transferred receivables have all of the attributes of assets controlled by the transferor.

As described below, the principal criteria cited in the basis for conclusions for treating repurchase agreements and securities lending transactions as secured borrowings apply equally to many securitizations, particularly those having a revolving-period agreement.

The inability of the transferor in a transfer with a revolving-period agreement to sell new receivables elsewhere because it has contracted to sell those new receivables on prearranged terms at times that it does not determine or have much influence over is asserted to be significant in paragraph 131 of Statement 125 [paragraph 193 of this Statement]. However, within fairly wide latitude, the transferor in those circumstances has retained the right to change the interest rate (the price) on both the previously transferred receivables and receivables to be transferred in the future. Mr. Foster believes that that right substantially diminishes any disadvantage of not being able to sell the receivables elsewhere and substantially negates any effect, favorable or onerous, on the transferor as a result of changes in market conditions as asserted in paragraph 50 of Statement 125 [paragraph 76 of this Statement]. In fact, any effects on the transferor result solely from having financed the receivables at whatever rate is paid the beneficial owners of the securities. Furthermore, the transferor of assets transferred under repurchase agreements or in securities lending transactions cannot sell those assets elsewhere.

Two reasons advanced in support of the treatment of repurchase agreements and securities lending transactions as secured borrowings are that (a) those transactions are difficult to characterize because they have attributes of both borrowings and sales and (b) supporting arguments can be found for accounting for those transactions as borrowings or sales. Those two reasons are equally applicable to securitization transactions having a revolving-period agreement—they are treated as sales for purposes of marketing to investors and as borrowings for tax purposes, and legal opinions and the prospectuses for those transactions acknowledge that their treatment as sales may not be sustained in a legal dispute.

The only supporting arguments cited for the treatment of repurchase agreements and securities lending transactions as secured borrowings that are not equally applicable to certain securitizations are that (a) forward contracts that are fully secured should be treated differently than those that are unsecured and (b) making a change in existing accounting practice would have a substantial impact on the reported financial position of certain entities and on the markets in which they participate. Mr. Foster does not believe that the existence of security in support of a transaction should determine its accounting treatment and notes that extension of the reasoning in paragraph 141 of Statement 125 [paragraph 207 of this Statement] would lead to lenders not recognizing loans receivable that are unsecured. While it may be necessary to consider prior accounting treatment and the effect a change in accounting practice would have on certain entities, Mr. Foster believes that those factors should carry relatively little weight in determining what is an appropriate accounting standard.

Paragraph 18 of Opinion 29 states, "The Board concludes that in general accounting for nonmonetary transactions should be based on the fair values of the assets (or services) involved which is the same basis as that used in monetary transactions. Thus, the cost of a nonmonetary asset acquired in exchange for another nonmonetary asset is the fair value of the asset surrendered to obtain it . . ." (footnote reference omitted). The conclusion embodied in that language is that the accounting for both monetary and nonmonetary transactions acquired in an exchange should be based on the fair values of the assets (or services) involved. Mr. Foster believes that in securitization transactions in which control is deemed under this Statement to be surrendered and in partial sales of financial assets, assets (or rights) are surrendered in exchange for cash and other rights and obligations, all of which are new.[14] The new assets (rights) received are part of the proceeds of the exchange, and any liabilities (obligations) incurred are a reduction of the proceeds. As such, those new assets and liabilities should be measured at their fair values as they are in all other exchange transactions.

Statement 125 contends that in those transactions certain components of the original assets have not been exchanged. If that is one's view, however, it is clear that a transaction of sufficient significance to result in the derecognition of assets has occurred. Furthermore, the event of securitization results in a change in the form and value of assets—securities are generally more easily sold or used as collateral and thus are more valuable than receivables. Mr. Foster believes that a securitization transaction, like the initial recognition of an asset or liability and derecognition of assets and liabilities where it is clear an exchange has occurred, is also sufficiently significant

---

[14]In the case of a partial sale of a financial asset, the transferor generally has reduced the marketability of the asset because it can no longer sell the entire asset—it can only sell part of that asset. Consequently, the partial interest in the original asset has different rights and privileges than those embodied in the original asset and, therefore, is a new asset—different from the original asset.

that the resulting, or remaining components of, assets and liabilities should be recorded at fair value.

Mr. Foster also notes, as described in paragraphs 182–184 of Statement 125 [paragraphs 271–273 of this Statement], that the distinctions made in paragraphs 10 and 11 between (a) assets retained and (b) assets obtained and liabilities incurred are arbitrary. For example, one could easily argue that beneficial interests acquired in a transfer of receivables have different rights and obligations than the receivables and accordingly should be accounted for not as retained assets, but as new and different assets, and, arguably, the rights inherent in derivatives arising in a securitization transaction, which are considered new rights (assets) in Statement 125, were embedded, albeit in an obscure form, in the transferred assets and could be as readily identified as retained portions of them. That the Board needed to make those distinctions arbitrarily begs for a consistent measurement attribute—fair value—for all of the rights and obligations held by the transferor subsequent to the transfer.

Members of the Financial Accounting Standards Board, June 1996:

Dennis R. Beresford,	Anthony T. Cope	Robert H. Northcutt
Chairman	John M. Foster	Robert J. Swieringa
Joseph V. Anania	James J. Leisenring	

Appendix A

IMPLEMENTATION GUIDANCE

CONTENTS

Appendix A

IMPLEMENTATION GUIDANCE

Introduction

26. This appendix describes certain provisions of this Statement in more detail and describes how they apply to certain types of transactions. This appendix discusses generalized situations. Facts and circumstances and specific contracts need to be considered carefully in applying this Statement. This appendix is an integral part of the standards provided in this Statement.

Isolation beyond the Reach of the Transferor and Its Creditors

27. The nature and extent of supporting evidence required for an assertion in financial statements that transferred financial assets have been isolated—put presumptively beyond the reach of the transferor and its creditors, either by a single transaction or a series of transactions taken as a whole—depend on the facts and circumstances. All available evidence that either supports or questions an assertion shall be considered. That consideration includes making judgments about whether the contract or circumstances permit the transferor to revoke the transfer. It also

may include making judgments about the kind of bankruptcy or other receivership into which a transferor or SPE might be placed, whether a transfer of financial assets would likely be deemed a true sale at law, whether the transferor is affiliated with the transferee, and other factors pertinent under applicable law. Derecognition of transferred assets is appropriate only if the available evidence provides reasonable assurance that the transferred assets would be beyond the reach of the powers of a bankruptcy trustee or other receiver for the transferor or any **consolidated affiliate of the transferor** that is not a special-purpose corporation or other entity designed to make remote the possibility that it would enter bankruptcy or other receivership (paragraph 83(c)).

28. Whether securitizations isolate transferred assets may depend on such factors as whether the securitization is accomplished in one step or two steps (paragraphs 80–84). Many common financial transactions, for example, typical repurchase agreements and securities lending transactions, isolate transferred assets from the transferor, although they may not meet the other criteria for surrender of control.

Conditions That Constrain a Transferee

29. Sale accounting is allowed under paragraph 9(b) only if each transferee has the right to pledge, or the right to exchange, the transferred assets or beneficial

interests it received, but constraints on that right also matter. Many transferor-imposed or other conditions on a transferee's right to pledge or exchange a transferred asset both constrain a transferee from pledging or exchanging the transferred assets and, through that constraint, provide more than a trivial benefit to the transferor. For example, a provision in the transfer contract that prohibits selling or pledging a transferred loan receivable not only constrains the transferee but also provides the transferor with the more-than-trivial benefits of knowing who has the asset, a prerequisite to repurchasing the asset, and of being able to block the asset from finding its way into the hands of a competitor for the loan customer's business or someone that the loan customer might consider an undesirable creditor. Transferor-imposed contractual constraints that narrowly limit timing or terms, for example, allowing a transferee to pledge only on the day assets are obtained or only on terms agreed with the transferor, also constrain the transferee and presumptively provide the transferor with more-than-trivial benefits.

30. However, some conditions do not constrain a transferee from pledging or exchanging the asset and therefore do not preclude a transfer subject to such a condition from being accounted for as a sale. For example, a transferor's right of first refusal on the occurrence of a bona fide offer to the transferee from a third party presumptively would not constrain a transferee, because that right in itself does not enable the transferor to compel the transferee to sell the assets and the transferee would be in a position to receive the sum offered by exchanging the asset, albeit possibly from the transferor rather than the third party. Further examples of conditions that presumptively would not constrain a transferee include (a) a requirement to obtain the transferor's permission to sell or pledge that is not to be unreasonably withheld, (b) a prohibition on sale to the transferor's competitor if other potential willing buyers exist, (c) a regulatory limitation such as on the number or nature of eligible transferees (as in the case of securities issued under Securities Act Rule 144A or debt placed privately), and (d) illiquidity, for example, the absence of an active market. Judgment is required to assess the significance of some conditions. For example, a prohibition on sale to the transferor's competitor would be a significant constraint if that competitor were the only potential willing buyer other than the transferor.

31. A condition imposed by a transferor that constrains the transferee presumptively provides more than a trivial benefit to the transferor. A condition *not* imposed by the transferor that constrains the transferee may or may not provide more than a trivial benefit to the transferor. For example, if the transferor refrains from imposing its usual contractual constraint on a specific transfer because it knows an equivalent constraint is already imposed on the transferee by a third party, it presumptively benefits more than trivially from that constraint. However, the transferor cannot benefit from a constraint if it is unaware at the time of the transfer that the transferee is constrained.

Transferor's Rights or Obligations to Reacquire Transferred Assets

32. Some rights or obligations to reacquire transferred assets both constrain the transferee and provide more than a trivial benefit to the transferor, thus precluding sale accounting under paragraph 9(b). For example, a **freestanding call** option written by a transferee to the transferor benefits the transferor and, if the transferred assets are not readily obtainable in the marketplace, is likely to constrain a transferee because it might have to default if the call was exercised and it had exchanged or pledged the assets. A freestanding forward purchase-sale contract between the transferor and the transferee on transferred assets not readily obtainable in the marketplace would benefit the transferor and is likely to constrain a transferee in much the same manner. Judgment is necessary to assess constraint and benefit. For example, put options written to the transferee generally do not constrain it, but a put option on a not-readily-obtainable asset may benefit the transferor and effectively constrain the transferee if the option is sufficiently deep-in-the-money when it is written that it is probable that the transferee will exercise it and the transferor will reacquire the transferred asset. In contrast, a sufficiently out-of-the-money call option held by the transferor may not constrain a transferee if it is probable when the option is written that it will not be exercised. Freestanding rights to reacquire transferred assets that are readily obtainable presumptively do not constrain the transferee from exchanging or pledging them and thus do not preclude sale accounting under paragraph 9(b).

33. Other rights or obligations to reacquire transferred assets, regardless of whether they constrain the transferee, may result in the transferor's maintaining

effective control over the transferred assets, as discussed in paragraphs 50–54, thus precluding sale accounting under paragraph 9(c)(2).[15]

Conditions That Constrain a Holder of Beneficial Interests in a Qualifying SPE

34. The considerations in paragraphs 29–32, about conditions that may or may not constrain a transferee that is not a qualifying SPE from pledging or exchanging the transferred assets, also extend to conditions that may or may not constrain a BIH from pledging or exchanging its beneficial interests in assets transferred to a qualifying SPE. For example, if BIHs agree to sell their beneficial interests in a qualifying SPE back to the transferor upon request at the price paid plus a stated return, that arrangement clearly conveys more than a trivial benefit to the transferor; sale accounting for the transfer to the qualifying SPE would be precluded if that agreement constrained a BIH from exchanging or pledging its beneficial interest.

Qualifying SPE

35. A qualifying SPE[16] is a trust or other legal vehicle that meets *all* of the following conditions:

a. It is demonstrably distinct from the transferor (paragraph 36).
b. Its permitted activities (1) are significantly limited, (2) were entirely specified in the legal documents that established the SPE or created the beneficial interests in the transferred assets that it holds, and (3) may be significantly changed only with the approval of the holders of at least a majority of the beneficial interests held by entities other than any transferor, its affiliates, and its agents (paragraphs 37 and 38).
c. It may hold only:
   (1) Financial assets transferred to it that are passive in nature (paragraph 39)
   (2) Passive **derivative financial instruments** that pertain to beneficial interests issued or sold to parties other than the transferor, its affiliates, or its agents (paragraphs 39 and 40)
   (3) Financial assets (for example, guarantees or rights to collateral) that would reimburse it if

others were to fail to adequately service financial assets transferred to it or to timely pay obligations due to it and that it entered into when it was established, when assets were transferred to it, or when beneficial interests (other than derivative financial instruments) were issued by the SPE
   (4) Servicing rights related to financial assets that it holds
   (5) Temporarily, nonfinancial assets obtained in connection with the collection of financial assets that it holds (paragraph 41)
   (6) Cash collected from assets that it holds and investments purchased with that cash pending distribution to holders of beneficial interests that are appropriate for that purpose (that is, money-market or other relatively risk-free instruments without options and with maturities no later than the expected distribution date).
d. If it can sell or otherwise dispose of noncash financial assets, it can do so only in automatic response to one of the following conditions:
   (1) Occurrence of an event or circumstance that (a) is specified in the legal documents that established the SPE or created the beneficial interests in the transferred assets that it holds; (b) is outside the control of the transferor, its affiliates, or its agents; and (c) causes, or is expected at the date of transfer to cause, the fair value of those financial assets to decline by a specified degree below the fair value of those assets when the SPE obtained them (paragraphs 42 and 43)
   (2) Exercise by a BIH (other than the transferor, its affiliates, or its agents) of a right to put that holder's beneficial interest back to the SPE (paragraph 44)
   (3) Exercise by the transferor of a call or ROAP specified in the legal documents that established the SPE, transferred assets to the SPE, or created the beneficial interests in the transferred assets that it holds (paragraphs 51–54 and 85–88)

---

[15]And it is necessary to consider the overall effect of related rights and obligations in assessing such matters as whether a transferee is constrained or a transferor has maintained effective control. For example, if the transferor or its affiliate or agent is the servicer for the transferred asset and is empowered to decide to put the asset up for sale, and has the right of first refusal, that combination would place the transferor in position to unilaterally cause the return of a specific transferred asset and thus maintain the transferor's effective control of the transferred asset as discussed in paragraphs 9(c)(2) and 50.

[16]The description of a qualifying SPE is restrictive. The accounting for qualifying SPEs and transfers of financial assets to them should not be extended to any entity that does not currently satisfy all of the conditions articulated in this paragraph.

(4) Termination of the SPE or maturity of the beneficial interests in those financial assets on a fixed or determinable date that is specified at inception (paragraph 45).

Need to Be Demonstrably Distinct from the Transferor

36. A qualifying SPE is demonstrably distinct from the transferor only if it cannot be unilaterally dissolved by any transferor, its affiliates, or its agents and either (a) at least 10 percent of the fair value of its beneficial interests is held by parties other than any transferor, its affiliates, or its agents or (b) the transfer is a guaranteed mortgage securitization.[17] An ability to unilaterally dissolve an SPE can take many forms, including but not limited to holding sufficient beneficial interests to demand that the trustee dissolve the SPE, the right to call all the assets transferred to the SPE, and a right to call or a prepayment privilege on the beneficial interests held by other parties.

Limits on Permitted Activities

37. The powers of the SPE must be limited to those activities allowed by paragraph 35 for it to be a qualifying SPE. Many kinds of entities are not so limited. For example, any bank, insurance company, pension plan, or investment company has powers that cannot be sufficiently limited for it to be a qualifying SPE.

38. The BIHs other than any transferor, its affiliates, or its agents may have the ability to change the powers of a qualifying SPE. If the powers of a previously qualifying SPE are changed so that the SPE is no longer qualifying, unless the conditions in paragraph 9(b) are then met by the SPE itself and the conditions in paragraphs 9(a) and 9(c) continue to be met, that change would bring the transferred assets held in the SPE back under the control of the transferor (paragraph 55).

Limits on What a Qualifying SPE May Hold

39. A financial asset or derivative financial instrument is passive only if holding the asset or instrument does not involve its holder in making decisions other than the decisions inherent in servicing (paragraph 61). An equity instrument is not passive if the qualifying SPE can exercise the voting rights and is permitted to choose how to vote. Investments are not passive if through them, either in themselves or in combination with other investments or rights, the SPE or any related entity, such as the transferor, its affiliates, or its agents, is able to exercise control or significant influence (as defined in generally accepted accounting principles for consolidation policy and for the equity method, respectively) over the investee. A derivative financial instrument is not passive if, for example, it includes an option allowing the SPE to choose to call or put other financial instruments; but other derivative financial instruments can be passive, for example, interest rate caps and swaps and forward contracts. Derivative financial instruments that result in liabilities, like other liabilities of a qualifying SPE, are a kind of beneficial interest in the qualifying SPE's assets.

40. A derivative financial instrument pertains to beneficial interests issued only if it:

a. Is entered into (1) when the beneficial interests are issued by the qualifying SPE to parties other than the transferor, its affiliates, or its agents or sold to such other parties after being issued by the qualifying SPE to the transferor, its affiliates, or its agents or (2) when a passive derivative financial instrument needs to be replaced upon occurrence of an event or circumstance (specified in the legal documents that established the SPE or created the beneficial interests in the transferred assets that it holds) outside the control of the transferor, its affiliates, or its agents, for example, when the counterparty to the derivative defaults or is downgraded below a specified threshold

b. Has a notional amount that does not initially exceed the amount of those beneficial interests and is not expected to exceed them subsequently

c. Has characteristics that relate to, and partly or fully but not excessively counteract, some risk associated with those beneficial interests or the related transferred assets.

41. A qualifying SPE may hold nonfinancial assets other than servicing rights only temporarily and only if those nonfinancial assets result from collecting the transferred financial assets. For example, a qualifying SPE could be permitted to temporarily hold foreclosed nonfinancial collateral. In contrast, an entity cannot be a qualifying SPE if, for

---

[17]An effect of that provision, in conjunction with paragraph 46, is that mortgage-backed securities that continue to be held by a transferor in a guaranteed mortgage securitization in which the SPE meets all conditions for being a qualifying SPE are classified in the financial statements of the transferor as securities that are subsequently measured under Statement 115.

example, it receives from a transferor significant secured financial assets likely to default with the expectation that it will foreclose on and profitably manage the securing nonfinancial assets. A qualifying SPE also may hold the residual value of a sales-type or a direct financing lease only to the extent that it is guaranteed at the inception of the lease either by the lessee or by a third party financially capable of discharging the obligations that may arise from the guarantee (paragraph 89).

Limits on Sales or Other Dispositions of Assets

42. Examples of requirements to sell, exchange, put, or distribute (hereinafter referred to collectively as dispose of) noncash financial assets that *are* permitted activities of a qualifying SPE—because they respond automatically to the occurrence of an event or circumstance that (a) is specified in the legal documents that established the SPE or created the beneficial interests in the transferred assets that it holds; (b) is outside the control of the transferor, its affiliates, or its agents; and (c) causes, or is expected to cause, the fair value of those assets to decline by a specified degree below the fair value of those assets when the qualifying SPE obtained them—include requirements to dispose of transferred assets in response to:

a. A failure to properly service transferred assets that could result in the loss of a substantial third-party credit guarantee
b. A default by the obligor
c. A downgrade by a major rating agency of the transferred assets or of the underlying obligor to a rating below a specified minimum rating
d. The involuntary insolvency of the transferor
e. A decline in the fair value of the transferred assets to a specified value less than their fair value at the time they were transferred to the SPE.

43. The following are examples of powers or requirements to dispose of noncash financial assets that *are not* permitted activities of a qualifying SPE, because they do not respond automatically to the occurrence of a specified event or circumstance outside the control of the transferor, its affiliates, or its agents that causes, or is expected to cause, the fair value of those transferred assets to decline by a specified degree below the fair value of those assets when the SPE obtained them:

a. A power that allows an SPE to choose to either dispose of transferred assets or hold them in response to a default, a downgrade, a decline in fair value, or a servicing failure
b. A requirement to dispose of marketable equity securities upon a specified decline from their "highest fair value" if that power could result in disposing of the asset in exchange for an amount that is more than the fair value of those assets at the time they were transferred to the SPE
c. A requirement to dispose of transferred assets in response to the violation of a nonsubstantive contractual provision (that is, a provision for which there is not a sufficiently large disincentive to ensure performance).

44. A qualifying SPE may dispose of transferred assets automatically to the extent necessary to comply with the exercise by a BIH (other than the transferor, its affiliates, or its agents) of its right to put beneficial interests back to the SPE in exchange for:

a. A full or partial distribution of those assets
b. Cash (which may require that the SPE dispose of those assets or issue beneficial interests to generate cash to fund settlement of the put)
c. New beneficial interests in those assets.

45. A qualifying SPE may have the power to dispose of assets to a party other than the transferor, its affiliate, or its agent on termination of the SPE or maturity of the beneficial interests, but only automatically on fixed or determinable dates that are specified at inception. For example, if an SPE is required to dispose of long-term mortgage loans and terminate itself at the earlier of (a) the specified maturity of beneficial interests in those mortgage loans or (b) the date of prepayment of a specified amount of the transferred mortgage loans, the termination date is a fixed or determinable date that was specified at inception. In contrast, if that SPE has the power to dispose of transferred assets on two specified dates and the SPE can decide which transferred assets to sell on each date, the termination date is *not* a fixed or determinable date that was specified at inception.

Qualifying SPEs and Consolidated Financial Statements

46. A qualifying SPE shall not be consolidated in the financial statements of a transferor or its affiliates.

Maintaining Effective Control over Transferred Assets

Agreement to Repurchase or Redeem Transferred Assets

47. An agreement that both entitles and obligates the transferor to repurchase or redeem transferred assets from the transferee maintains the transferor's effective control over those assets under paragraph 9(c)(1), and the transfer is therefore to be accounted for as a secured borrowing, if and only if all of the following conditions are met:

a. The assets to be repurchased or redeemed are the same or substantially the same as those transferred (paragraph 48).
b. The transferor is able to repurchase or redeem them on substantially the agreed terms, even in the event of default by the transferee (paragraph 49).
c. The agreement is to repurchase or redeem them before maturity, at a fixed or determinable price.
d. The agreement is entered into concurrently with the transfer.

48. To be substantially the same,[18] the asset that was transferred and the asset that is to be repurchased or redeemed need to have all of the following characteristics:

a. The same primary obligor (except for debt guaranteed by a sovereign government, central bank, government-sponsored enterprise or agency thereof, in which case the guarantor and the terms of the guarantee must be the same)
b. Identical form and type so as to provide the same risks and rights
c. The same maturity (or in the case of mortgage-backed pass-through and pay-through securities, similar remaining weighted-average maturities that result in approximately the same market yield)
d. Identical contractual interest rates
e. Similar assets as collateral
f. The same aggregate unpaid principal amount or principal amounts within accepted "good delivery" standards for the type of security involved.

49. To be able to repurchase or redeem assets on substantially the agreed terms, even in the event of default by the transferee, a transferor must at all times during the contract term have obtained cash or other collateral sufficient to fund substantially all of the cost of purchasing replacement assets from others.

Ability to Unilaterally Cause the Return of Specific Transferred Assets

50. Some rights to reacquire transferred assets (or to acquire beneficial interests in transferred assets held by a qualifying SPE), regardless of whether they constrain the transferee, may result in the transferor's maintaining effective control over the transferred assets through the **unilateral ability** to cause the return of specific transferred assets. Such rights preclude sale accounting under paragraph 9(c)(2). For example, an **attached call** in itself would not constrain a transferee who is able, by exchanging or pledging the asset subject to that call, to obtain substantially all of its economic benefits. An attached call could result, however, in the transferor's maintaining effective control over the transferred asset(s) because the attached call gives the transferor the ability to unilaterally cause whoever holds that specific asset to return it. In contrast, transfers of financial assets subject to calls embedded by the issuers of the financial instruments, for example, callable bonds or prepayable mortgage loans, do not preclude sale accounting. Such an **embedded call** does not result in the transferor's maintaining effective control, because it is the issuer rather than the transferor who holds the call.

51. If the transferee is a qualifying SPE, it has met the conditions in paragraph 35(d) and therefore must be constrained from choosing to exchange or pledge the transferred assets. In that circumstance, any call held by the transferor is effectively attached to the assets and could—depending on the price and other terms of the call—maintain the transferor's effective control over transferred assets through the ability to unilaterally cause the transferee to return specific assets. For example, a transferor's unilateral ability to cause a qualifying SPE to return to the transferor or otherwise dispose of specific transferred assets at will or, for example, in response to its decision to exit a market or a particular activity, could provide the transferor with effective control over the transferred assets.

---

[18]In this Statement, the term *substantially the same* is used consistently with the usage of that term in the AICPA Statement of Position 90-3, *Definition of the Term Substantially the Same for Holders of Debt Instruments, as Used in Certain Audit Guides and a Statement of Position.*

52. A call that is attached to transferred assets maintains the transferor's effective control over those assets if, under its price and other terms, the call conveys more than a trivial benefit to the transferor. Similarly, any unilateral right to reclaim specific assets transferred to a qualifying SPE maintains the transferor's effective control over those assets if the right conveys more than a trivial benefit to the transferor. A call or other right conveys more than a trivial benefit if the price to be paid is fixed, determinable, or otherwise potentially advantageous, unless because that price is so far out of the money or for other reasons it is probable when the option is written that the transferor will not exercise it. Thus, for example, a call on specific assets transferred to a qualifying SPE at a price fixed at their principal amount maintains the transferor's effective control over the assets subject to that call. Effective control over transferred assets can be present even if the right to reclaim is indirect. For example, if an embedded call allows a transferor to buy back the beneficial interests of a qualifying SPE at a fixed price, then the transferor remains in effective control of the assets underlying those beneficial interests. A cleanup call, however, is permitted as an exception to that general principle.

53. A right to reclaim specific transferred assets by paying their fair value when reclaimed generally does not maintain effective control, because it does not convey a more than trivial benefit to the transferor. However, a transferor has maintained effective control if it has such a right and also holds the residual interest in the transferred assets. For example, if a transferor can reclaim such assets at termination of the qualifying SPE by purchasing them in an auction, and thus at what might appear to be fair value, then sale accounting for the assets it can reclaim would be precluded. Such circumstances provide the transferor with a more than trivial benefit and effective control over the assets, because it can pay any price it chooses in the auction and recover any excess paid over fair value through its residual interest.

54. A transferor that has a right to reacquire transferred assets from a qualifying SPE does not maintain effective control if the reclaimed assets would be randomly selected and the amount of the assets reacquired is sufficiently limited (paragraph 87(a)), because that would not be a right to reacquire *specific* assets. Nor does a transferor maintain effective control through an obligation to reacquire transferred assets from a qualifying SPE if the transfer could occur only after a specified failure of the servicer to properly service the transferred assets that could result in

the loss of a third-party guarantee (paragraph 42(a)) or only after a BIH other than the transferor, its affiliate, or its agent requires a qualifying SPE to repurchase that beneficial interest (paragraph 44(b)), because the transferor could not cause that reacquisition *unilaterally*.

Changes That Result in the Transferor's Regaining Control of Assets Sold

55. A change in law, status of the transferee as a qualifying SPE, or other circumstance may result in the transferor's regaining control of assets previously accounted for appropriately as having been sold, because one or more of the conditions in paragraph 9 are no longer met. Such a change, unless it arises solely from either the initial application of this Statement or a change in market prices (for example, an increase in price that moves into-the-money a freestanding call that was originally sufficiently out-of-the-money that it was judged not to constrain the transferee), is accounted for in the same manner as a purchase of the assets from the former transferee(s) in exchange for liabilities assumed (paragraph 11). After that change, the transferor recognizes in its financial statements those assets together with liabilities to the former transferee(s) or BIHs in those assets (paragraph 38). The transferor initially measures those assets and liabilities at fair value on the date of the change, as if the transferor purchased the assets and assumed the liabilities on that date. The former transferee would derecognize the assets on that date, as if it had sold the assets in exchange for a receivable from the transferor.

Measurement of Interests Held after a Transfer of Financial Assets

Assets Obtained and Liabilities Incurred as Proceeds

56. The proceeds from a sale of financial assets consist of the cash and any other assets obtained, including separately recognized servicing assets, in the transfer less any liabilities incurred, including separately recognized servicing liabilities. Any asset obtained that is not an interest in the transferred asset is part of the proceeds from the sale. Any liability incurred, even if it is related to the transferred assets, is a reduction of the proceeds. Any derivative financial instrument entered into concurrently with a transfer of financial assets is either an asset obtained

or a liability incurred and part of the proceeds received in the transfer. All proceeds and reductions of proceeds from a sale shall be initially measured at fair value, if practicable.

Illustration—Recording Transfers with Proceeds of Cash, Derivatives, and Other Liabilities

57. Company A sells loans with a fair value of $1,100 and a carrying amount of $1,000. Company A undertakes no servicing responsibilities but obtains an option to purchase from the transferee loans similar to the loans sold (which are readily obtainable in the marketplace) and assumes a limited recourse obligation to repurchase delinquent loans.

Company A agrees to provide the transferee a return at a floating rate of interest even though the contractual terms of the loan are fixed rate in nature (that provision is effectively an interest rate swap).

Fair Values

Cash proceeds	$1,050
Interest rate swap	40
Call option	70
Recourse obligation	60

Net Proceeds

Cash received	$1,050
Plus: Call option	70
Interest rate swap	40
Less: Recourse obligation	(60)
Net proceeds	$1,100

Gain on Sale

Net proceeds	$1,100
Carrying amount of loans sold	1,000
Gain on sale	$ 100

Journal Entry

Cash	1,050	
Interest rate swap	40	
Call option	70	
Loans		1,000
Recourse obligation		60
Gain on sale		100
To record transfer		

Interests That Contine to Be Held by a Transferor

58. Other interests in transferred assets—those that are not part of the proceeds of the transfer—are interests that continue to be held by a transferor over which the transferor has not relinquished control. Interests that continue to held by a transferor shall be measured at the date of the transfer by allocating the previous carrying amount between the assets sold, if any, and the interests that continue to be held by a transferor, based on their relative fair values. Allocation procedures shall be applied to all transfers in which interests continue to be held by a transferor, even those that do not qualify as sales. Examples of interests that continue to be held by a transferor include securities backed by the transferred assets, undivided interests, and cash reserve accounts and residual interests in securitization trusts. If a transferor cannot determine whether an asset is an interest that continues to be held by a transferor or proceeds from the sale, the asset shall be treated as proceeds from the sale and accounted for in accordance with paragraph 56.

59. If the interests that continue to be held by a transferor are subordinate to more senior interests held by

others, that subordination may concentrate most of the risks inherent in the transferred assets into the interests that continue to be held by a transferor and shall be taken into consideration in estimating the fair value of those interests. For example, if the amount of the gain recognized, after allocation, on a securitization with a subordinated interest that continues to be held by a transferor is greater than the gain that would have been recognized had the entire asset been sold, the transferor needs to be able to identify why that can occur. Otherwise, it is likely that the effect of subordination to a senior interest has not been adequately considered in the determination of the fair

value of the subordinated interest that continues to be held by a transferor.

Illustration—Recording Transfers of Partial Interests

60. Company B sells a pro rata nine-tenths interest in loans with a fair value of $1,100 and a carrying amount of $1,000. There is no servicing asset or liability, because Company B estimates that the **benefits of servicing** are just adequate to compensate it for its servicing responsibilities.

Fair Values

Cash proceeds for nine-tenths interest sold	$990
One-tenth interest that continues to be held by a transferor [($990 ÷ $\frac{9}{10}$) × $\frac{1}{10}$]	110

Carrying Amount Based on Relative Fair Values

	Fair Value	Percentage of Total Fair Value	Allocated Carrying Amount
Nine-tenths interest sold	$ 990	90	$ 900
One-tenth interest that continues to be held by a transferor	110	10	100
Total	$1,100	100	$1,000

Gain on Sale

Net proceeds	$990
Carrying amount of loans sold	900
Gain on sale	$ 90

Journal Entry

Cash	990	
Loans		900
Gain on sale		90
To record transfer		

Servicing Assets and Liabilities

61. Servicing of mortgage loans, credit card receivables, or other financial assets commonly includes, but is not limited to, collecting principal, interest, and escrow payments from borrowers; paying taxes and insurance from escrowed funds; monitoring delinquencies; executing foreclosure if necessary; tempo-

rarily investing funds pending distribution; remitting fees to guarantors, trustees, and others providing services; and accounting for and remitting principal and interest payments to the holders of beneficial interests in the financial assets. Servicing is inherent in all financial assets; it becomes a distinct asset or liability for accounting purposes only in the circumstances described in paragraph 62.

62. An entity that undertakes a contract to service financial assets shall recognize either a servicing asset or a servicing liability, each time it undertakes an obligation to service a financial asset that (a) results from a transfer of the servicer's financial assets that meets the requirements for sale accounting, (b) results from a transfer of the servicer's financial assets to a qualifying SPE in a guaranteed mortgage securitization in which the transferor retains all of the resulting securities and classifies them as either available-for-sale securities or trading securities in accordance with Statement 115, or (c) is acquired or assumed and the servicing obligation does not relate to financial assets of the servicer or its consolidated affiliates. However, if the transferor transfers the assets in a guaranteed mortgage securitization, retains all of the resulting securities, and classifies them as debt securities held-to-maturity in accordance with Statement 115, the servicing asset or servicing liability may be reported together with the asset being serviced and not recognized separately. A servicer of financial assets commonly receives the benefits of servicing—revenues from contractually specified servicing fees, a portion of the interest from the financial assets, late charges, and other ancillary sources, including "float," all of which it is entitled to receive only if it performs the servicing—and incurs the costs of servicing the assets. Typically, the benefits of servicing are expected to be more than **adequate compensation** to a servicer for performing the servicing, and the contract results in a servicing asset. However, if the benefits of servicing are not expected to adequately compensate a servicer for performing the servicing, the contract results in a servicing liability. (A servicing asset may become a servicing liability, or vice versa, if circumstances change, and the initial measure for servicing may be zero if the benefits of servicing are just adequate to compensate the servicer for its servicing responsibilities.) A servicer would account for its servicing contract that qualifies for separate recognition as a servicing asset or a servicing liability initially measured at its fair value regardless of whether explicit consideration was exchanged.

62A. A servicer that transfers or securitizes financial assets in a transaction that does not meet the requirements for sale accounting and is accounted for as a secured borrowing with the underlying assets remaining on the transferor's balance sheet shall not recognize a servicing asset or a servicing liability. However, if a transferor enters into a servicing contract when the transferor transfers mortgage loans in a guaranteed mortgage securitization, retains all the resulting securities, and classifies those securities as either available-for-sale securities or trading securities in accordance with Statement 115, the transferor shall separately recognize a servicing asset or a servicing liability.

63. A servicer that recognizes a servicing asset or servicing liability shall account for the contract to service financial assets separately from those financial assets, as follows:

a. Report servicing assets separately from servicing liabilities in the statement of financial position (paragraph 13B).

b. Initially measure servicing assets and servicing liabilities at fair value, if practicable (paragraphs 10, 11(b), 11(c), 71, and 72).

c. Account separately for rights to future interest income from the serviced assets that exceed contractually specified servicing fees. Those rights are not servicing assets; they are financial assets, effectively interest-only strips to be accounted for in accordance with paragraph 14 of this Statement.

d. Identify classes of servicing assets and servicing liabilities based on (1) the availability of market inputs used in determining the fair value of servicing assets and servicing liabilities, (2) an entity's method for managing the risks of its servicing assets and servicing liabilities, or (3) both.

e. Subsequently measure each class of separately recognized servicing assets and servicing liabilities either at fair value or by amortizing the amount recognized in proportion to and over the period of estimated net servicing income for assets (the excess of servicing revenues over servicing costs) or the period of estimated net servicing loss for servicing liabilities (the excess of servicing costs over servicing revenues). Different elections can be made for different classes of servicing assets and servicing liabilities. An entity may make an irrevocable decision to subsequently measure a class of servicing assets and servicing liabilities at fair value at the beginning of any fiscal year. Once a servicing asset or a servicing liability is reported in a class of servicing assets and servicing liabilities that an entity elects to subsequently measure at fair value, that servicing asset or servicing liability cannot be placed in a class of servicing assets and servicing liabilities that is subsequently measured using the amortization method. Changes in fair value should be reported in earnings for servicing assets and servicing liabilities subsequently measured at fair value (paragraph 13A(b)).

f. Subsequently evaluate and measure impairment of each class of separately recognized servicing assets that are subsequently measured using the amortization method described in paragraph 13A(a) as follows:

(1) Stratify servicing assets within a class based on one or more of the predominant risk characteristics of the underlying financial assets. Those characteristics may include financial asset type,[19] size, interest rate, date of origination, term, and geographic location.

(2) Recognize impairment through a valuation allowance for an individual stratum. The amount of impairment recognized separately shall be the amount by which the carrying amount of servicing assets for a stratum exceeds their fair value. The fair value of servicing assets that have not been recognized shall not be used in the evaluation of impairment.

(3) Adjust the valuation allowance to reflect changes in the measurement of impairment subsequent to the initial measurement of impairment. Fair value in excess of the carrying amount of servicing assets for that stratum, however, shall not be recognized. This Statement does not address when an entity should record a direct write-down of recognized servicing assets.

g. For servicing liabilities subsequently measured using the amortization method, if subsequent events have increased the fair value of the liability above the carrying amount, for example, because of significant changes in the amount or timing of actual or expected future cash flows relative to the cash flows previously projected, the servicer shall revise its earlier estimates and recognize the increased obligation as a loss in earnings (paragraph 13).

64. As indicated above, transferors sometimes agree to take on servicing responsibilities when the future benefits of servicing are not expected to adequately compensate them for performing that servicing. In that circumstance, the result is a servicing liability rather than a servicing asset. For example, if in the transaction illustrated in paragraph 57 the transferor had agreed to service the loans without explicit compensation and it estimated the fair value of that servicing obligation at $50, net proceeds would be reduced to $1,050, gain on sale would be reduced to $50, and the transferor would report a servicing liability of $50.

Illustration—Sale of Receivables with Servicing Obtained

65. Company C originates $1,000 of loans that yield 10 percent interest income for their estimated lives of 9 years. Company C sells the $1,000 principal plus the right to receive interest income of 8 percent to another entity for $1,000. Company C will continue to service the loans, and the contract stipulates that its compensation for performing the servicing is the right to receive half of the interest income not sold. The remaining half of the interest income not sold is considered an interest-only strip receivable that Company C classifies as an available-for-sale security. At the date of the transfer, the fair value of the loans is $1,100. The fair values of the servicing asset and the interest-only strip receivable are $40 and $60, respectively.

Fair Values	
Cash proceeds	$1,000
Servicing asset	40
Interest-only strip receivable	60
Net Proceeds	
Cash proceeds	$1,000
Servicing asset	40
Net proceeds	$1,040

---

[19]For example, for mortgage loans, financial asset type refers to the various conventional or government guaranteed or insured mortgage loans and adjustable-rate or fixed-rate mortgage loans.

Carrying Amount Based on Relative Fair Values

	Fair Value	Percentage of Total Fair Value	Allocated Carrying Amount
Loans sold	$1,040	94.55	$ 945.50
Interest-only strip receivable	60	5.45	54.50
Total	$1,100	100.00	$1,000.00

Gain on Sale

Net proceeds	$1,040.00
Less: Carrying amount of loans sold	945.50
Gain on sale	$ 94.50

Journal Entries

Cash	1,000.00	
Interest-only strip receivable	54.50	
Servicing asset	40.00	
Loans		1,000.00
Gain on sale		94.50

To record transfer and to recognize interest-only strip receivable and servicing asset

Interest-only strip receivable	5.50	
Other comprehensive income		5.50

To begin to subsequently measure interest-only strip receivable like an available-for-sale security (paragraph 14)

66. The previous illustration demonstrates how a transferor would account for a simple sale in which servicing is obtained. Company C might instead transfer the financial assets to a corporation or a trust that is a qualifying SPE. The qualifying SPE then securitizes the loans by selling beneficial interests to the public. The qualifying SPE pays the cash proceeds to the original transferor, which accounts for the transfer as a sale and derecognizes the financial assets assuming that the criteria in paragraph 9 are met. Securitizations often combine the elements shown in paragraphs 57, 60, and 65, as illustrated below.

Illustration—Recording Transfers of Partial Interests with Proceeds of Cash, Derivatives, Other Liabilities, and Servicing

67. Company D originates $1,000 of prepayable loans that yield 10 percent interest income for their 9-year expected lives. Company D sells nine-tenths of the principal plus interest of 8 percent to another entity. Company D will continue to service the loans, and the contract stipulates that its compensation for performing the servicing is the 2 percent of the interest income not sold. Company D obtains an option to purchase from the transferee loans similar to the loans sold (which are readily obtainable in the marketplace) and incurs a limited recourse obligation to repurchase delinquent loans. At the date of transfer, the fair value of the loans is $1,100.

Fair Values

Cash proceeds	$ 900
Call option	70
Recourse obligation	(60)
Servicing asset	90
One-tenth interest that continues to be held by the transferor	100

Net Proceeds

Cash received	$ 900
Plus: Servicing asset	90
Plus: Call option	70
Less: Recourse obligation	(60)
Net proceeds	$1,000

Carrying Amount Based on Relative Fair Values

	Fair Value	Percentage of Total Fair Value	Allocated Carrying Amount
Interest sold	$1,000	90.9	$ 909
One-tenth interest that continues to be held by the transferor	100	9.1	91
Total	$1,100	100.0	$1,000

Gain on Sale

Net proceeds	$1,000
Less: Carrying amount of loans sold	(909)
Gain on sale	$ 91

Loans Sold

Carrying amount of loans	$1,000
Less: Allocated carrying amount of interest that continues to be held by the transferor	(91)
Loans sold	$ 909

Journal Entries

Cash	900	
Call option	70	
Servicing asset	90	
Loans		909
Recourse obligation		60
Gain on sale		91

To record transfer and to recognize servicing asset, call option, and recourse obligation

68–70. [These paragraphs have been deleted. See Status page.]

If It Is Not Practicable to Estimate Fair Values

71. If it is not practicable to estimate the fair values of assets, the transferor shall record those assets at zero. If it is not practicable to estimate the fair values of liabilities, the transferor shall recognize no gain on the transaction and shall record those liabilities at the greater of:

a. The excess, if any, of (1) the fair values of assets obtained less the fair values of other liabilities incurred, over (2) the sum of the carrying values of the assets transferred

b. The amount that would be recognized in accordance with FASB Statement No. 5, *Accounting for Contingencies,* as interpreted by FASB Interpretation No. 14, *Reasonable Estimation of the Amount of a Loss.*

Illustration—Recording Transfers If It Is Not Practicable to Estimate a Fair Value

72. Company E sells loans with a carrying amount of $1,000 to another entity for cash proceeds of $1,050 plus a call option to purchase loans similar to the loans sold (which are readily obtainable in the marketplace) and incurs a limited recourse obligation to repurchase any delinquent loans. Company E undertakes an obligation to service the transferred assets for the other entity. In Case 1, Company E finds it impracticable to estimate the fair value of the servicing contract, although it is confident that servicing revenues will be more than adequate compensation for performing the servicing. In Case 2, Company E finds it impracticable to estimate the fair value of the recourse obligation.

20–21[These footnotes have been deleted. See Status page.]

Fair Values	Case 1	Case 2
Cash proceeds	$1,050	$1,050
Servicing asset	XX*	40
Call option	70	70
Recourse obligation	(60)	XX*
Fair value of loans transferred	1,100	1,100

*Not practicable to estimate fair value.

Net Proceeds	Case 1	Case 2
Cash received	$1,050	$1,050
Plus: Servicing asset	XX*	40
Plus: Call option	70	70
Less: Recourse obligation	(60)	XX†
Net proceeds	$1,060	$1,160

Gain on Sale	Case 1	Case 2
Net proceeds	$1,060	$1,160
Carrying amount of loans	1,000	1,000
Less: Recourse obligation	0	(160)†
Gain on sale	$ 60	$ 0

Journal Entries	Case 1		Case 2	
Cash	1,050		1,050	
Servicing asset	0*		40	
Call option	70		70	
Loans		1,000		1,000
Recourse obligation		60		160†
Gain on sale		60		0
To record transfer				

*Assets shall be recorded at zero if an estimate of the fair value of the assets is not practicable.

†The amount recorded as a liability in this example equals the sum of the known assets less the fair value of the known liabilities, that is, the amount that results in no gain or loss.

Securitizations

73. Financial assets such as mortgage loans, automobile loans, trade receivables, credit card receivables, and other revolving charge accounts are assets commonly transferred in securitizations. Securitizations of mortgage loans may include pools of single-family residential mortgages or other types of real estate mortgage loans, for example, multifamily residential mortgages and commercial property mortgages. Securitizations of loans secured by chattel mortgages on automotive vehicles as well as other equipment (including direct financing or sales-type leases) also are common. Both financial and nonfinancial assets can be securitized; life insurance policy loans, patent and copyright royalties, and even taxi medallions also have been securitized. But securitizations of nonfinancial assets are outside the scope of this Statement.

74. An originator of a typical securitization (the transferor) transfers a portfolio of financial assets to an SPE, commonly a trust. In "pass-through" and "pay-through" securitizations, receivables are transferred to the SPE at the inception of the securitization, and no further transfers are made; all cash collections are paid to the holders of beneficial interests in the SPE. In "revolving-period" securitizations, receivables are transferred at the inception and also periodically (daily or monthly) thereafter for a defined period (commonly three to eight years), referred to as the revolving period. During the revolving period, the SPE uses most of the cash collections to purchase additional receivables from the transferor on prearranged terms.

75. Beneficial interests in the SPE are sold to investors and the proceeds are used to pay the transferor for the assets transferred. Those beneficial interests may comprise either a single class having equity characteristics or multiple classes of interests, some having debt characteristics and others having equity characteristics. The cash collected from the portfolio is distributed to the investors and others as specified by the legal documents that established the SPE.

76. Pass-through, pay-through, and revolving-period securitizations that meet the criteria in paragraph 9 qualify for sale accounting under this Statement. All financial assets obtained or that continue to be held by a transferor and liabilities incurred by the originator of a securitization that qualifies as a sale shall be recognized and measured as provided in paragraphs 10 and 11; that includes the implicit forward contract to sell new receivables during a revolving period, which may become valuable or onerous to the transferor as interest rates and other market conditions change.

Revolving-Period Securitizations

77. The value of the forward contract implicit in a revolving-period securitization arises from the difference between the agreed-upon rate of return to investors on their beneficial interests in the trust and current market rates of return on similar investments. For example, if the agreed-upon annual rate of return to investors in a trust is 6 percent, and later market rates of return for those investments increased to 7 percent, the forward contract's value to the transferor (and burden to the investors) would approximate the present value of 1 percent of the amount of the investment for each year remaining in the revolving structure after the receivables already transferred have been collected. If a forward contract to sell receivables is entered into at the market rate, its value at inception may be zero. Changes in the fair value of the forward contract are likely to be greater if the investors receive a fixed rate than if the investors receive a rate that varies based on changes in market rates.

78. Gain or loss recognition for revolving-period receivables sold to a securitization trust is limited to receivables that exist and have been sold. Recognition of servicing assets or liabilities for revolving-period receivables is similarly limited to the servicing for the receivables that exist and have been transferred. As new receivables are sold, rights to service them become assets or liabilities and are recognized.

79. Revolving-period securitizations may use either a discrete trust, used for a single securitization, or a master trust, used for many securitizations. To achieve another securitization using an existing master trust, a transferor first transfers additional receivables to the trust and then sells additional ownership interests in the trust to investors. Adding receivables to a master trust, in itself, is neither a sale nor a secured borrowing under paragraph 9, because that transfer only increases the transferor's beneficial interest in the trust's assets. A sale or secured borrowing does not occur until the transferor receives consideration other than beneficial interests in the transferred assets. Transfers that result in an exchange of cash, that is, either transfers that in essence replace previously transferred receivables that have been collected or sales of beneficial interests to outside investors, are transfers in exchange for consideration other

than beneficial interests in the transferred assets and thus are accounted for as sales (if they satisfy all the criteria in paragraph 9) or as secured borrowings.

Isolation of Transferred Assets in Securitizations

80. A securitization carried out in one transfer or a series of transfers may or may not isolate the transferred assets beyond the reach of the transferor and its creditors. Whether it does depends on the structure of the securitization transaction taken as a whole, considering such factors as the type and extent of further involvement in arrangements to protect investors from credit and interest rate risks, the availability of other assets, and the powers of bankruptcy courts or other receivers.

81. In certain securitizations, a corporation that, if it failed, would be subject to the U.S. Bankruptcy Code transfers financial assets to a special-purpose trust in exchange for cash. The trust raises that cash by issuing to investors beneficial interests that pass through all cash received from the financial assets, and the transferor has no further involvement with the trust or the transferred assets. The Board understands that those securitizations generally would be judged as having isolated the assets, because in the absence of any continuing involvement there would be reasonable assurance that the transfer would be found to be a true sale at law that places the assets beyond the reach of the transferor and its creditors, even in bankruptcy or other receivership.

82. In other securitizations, a similar corporation transfers financial assets to an SPE in exchange for cash and beneficial interests in the transferred assets. That entity raises the cash by issuing to investors commercial paper that gives them a senior interest in cash received from the financial assets. The beneficial interests that continue to be held by the transferring corporation represent a junior interest to be reduced by any credit losses on the financial assets in trust. The commercial paper interests are highly rated by credit rating agencies only if both (a) the credit enhancement from the junior interest is sufficient and (b) the transferor is highly rated. Depending on facts and circumstances, the Board understands that those "single-step" securitizations often would be judged in the United States as not having isolated the assets, because the nature of the continuing involvement may make it difficult to obtain reasonable assurance that the transfer would be found to be a true sale at law that places the assets beyond the reach of the transferor and its creditors in U.S. bankruptcy (para-

graph 113). If the transferor fell into bankruptcy and the transfer was found not to be a true sale at law, investors in the transferred assets might be subjected to an automatic stay that would delay payments due them, and they might have to share in bankruptcy expenses and suffer further losses if the transfer was recharacterized as a secured loan.

83. Still other securitizations use two transfers intended to isolate transferred assets beyond the reach of the transferor and its creditors, even in bankruptcy. In those "two-step" structures:

a. First, the corporation transfers financial assets to a special-purpose corporation that, although wholly owned, is so designed that the possibility that the transferor or its creditors could reclaim the assets is remote. This first transfer is designed to be judged to be a true sale at law, in part because the transferor does not provide "excessive" credit or yield protection to the special-purpose corporation, and the Board understands that transferred assets are likely to be judged beyond the reach of the transferor or the transferor's creditors even in bankruptcy.

b. Second, the special-purpose corporation transfers the assets to a trust or other legal vehicle with a sufficient increase in the credit or yield protection on the second transfer (provided by a junior beneficial interest that continues to be held by the transferor or other means) to merit the high credit rating sought by third-party investors who buy senior beneficial interests in the trust. Because of that aspect of its design, that second transfer might not be judged to be a true sale at law and, thus, the transferred assets could at least in theory be reached by a bankruptcy trustee for the special-purpose corporation.

c. However, the special-purpose corporation is designed to make remote the possibility that it would enter bankruptcy, either by itself or by substantive consolidation into a bankruptcy of its parent should that occur. For example, its charter forbids it from undertaking any other business or incurring any liabilities, so that there can be no creditors to petition to place it in bankruptcy. Furthermore, its dedication to a single purpose is intended to make it extremely unlikely, even if it somehow entered bankruptcy, that a receiver under the U.S. Bankruptcy Code could reclaim the transferred assets because it has no other assets to substitute for the transferred assets.

The Board understands that the "two-step" securitizations described above, taken as a whole, generally would be judged under present U.S. law as having isolated the assets beyond the reach of the transferor and its creditors, even in bankruptcy or other receivership.

84. The powers of receivers for entities not subject to the U.S. Bankruptcy Code (for example, banks subject to receivership by the FDIC) vary considerably, and therefore some receivers may be able to reach financial assets transferred under a particular arrangement and others may not. A securitization may isolate transferred assets from a transferor subject to such a receiver and its creditors even though it is accomplished by only one transfer directly to an SPE that issues beneficial interests to investors and the transferor provides credit or yield protection. For entities that are subject to other possible bankruptcy, conservatorship, or other receivership procedures in the United States or other jurisdictions, judgments about whether transferred assets have been isolated need to be made in relation to the powers of bankruptcy courts or trustees, conservators, or receivers in those jurisdictions.

Removal-of-Accounts Provisions

85. Many transfers of financial assets in securitizations empower the transferor to reclaim assets subject to certain restrictions. Such a power is sometimes called a removal-of-accounts provision (ROAP). Whether a ROAP precludes sale accounting depends on whether the ROAP results in the transferor's maintaining effective control over specific transferred assets (paragraphs 9(c)(2) and 51–54).

86. The following are examples of ROAPs that preclude transfers from being accounted for as sales:

a. An unconditional ROAP or repurchase agreement that allows the transferor to specify the assets that may be removed, because such a provision allows the transferor unilaterally to remove specific assets

b. A ROAP conditioned on a transferor's decision to exit some portion of its business, because whether it can be triggered by canceling an affinity relationship, spinning off a business segment, or accepting a third party's bid to purchase a specified (for example, geographic) portion of the transferor's business, such a provision allows the transferor unilaterally to remove specific assets.

87. The following are examples of ROAPs that *do not* preclude transfers from being accounted for as sales:

a. A ROAP for random removal of excess assets, if the ROAP is sufficiently limited so that the transferor cannot remove specific transferred assets, for example, by limiting removals to the amount of the interests that continue to be held by the transferor and to one removal per month

b. A ROAP for defaulted receivables, because the removal would be allowed only after a third party's action (default) and could not be caused unilaterally by the transferor

c. A ROAP conditioned on a third-party cancellation, or expiration without renewal, of an affinity or private-label arrangement, because the removal would be allowed only after a third party's action (cancellation) or decision not to act (expiration) and could not be caused unilaterally by the transferor.

88. A ROAP that can be exercised only in response to a third party's action that has not yet occurred does not maintain the transferor's effective control over assets potentially subject to that ROAP. However, when a third party's action (such as default or cancellation) or decision not to act (expiration) occurs that allows removal of assets to be initiated solely by the transferor, the transferor must recognize any assets subject to the ROAP, whether the ROAP is exercised or not. If the ROAP is exercised, the assets are recognized because the transferor has reclaimed the assets. If the ROAP is not exercised, the assets are recognized because the transferor now can unilaterally cause the qualifying SPE to return those specific assets and, therefore, the transferor once again has effective control over those transferred assets (paragraph 55).

Sales-Type and Direct Financing Lease Receivables

89. Sales-type and direct financing receivables secured by leased equipment, referred to as gross investment in lease receivables, are made up of two components: minimum lease payments and residual values. Minimum lease payments are requirements for lessees to pay cash to lessors and meet the definition of a financial asset. Thus, transfers of minimum lease payments are subject to the requirements of this Statement. Residual values represent the lessor's estimate of the "salvage" value of the leased equipment at the end of the lease term and may be either guaranteed or unguaranteed; residual values meet the definition of financial assets *to the extent that they are guaranteed at the inception of the lease.* Thus, transfers of residual values guaranteed at inception also

Accounting for Transfers and Servicing of
Financial Assets and Extinguishments of Liabilities
FAS140

are subject to the requirements of this Statement. Unguaranteed residual values do not meet the definition of financial assets, nor do residual values guaranteed after inception, and transfers of them are not subject to the requirements of this Statement. Transfers of residual values not guaranteed at inception continue to be subject to Statement 13, as amended. Because residual values guaranteed at inception are financial assets, increases to their estimated value over the life of the related lease are recognized. Entities selling or securitizing lease financing receivables shall allocate the gross investment in receivables between minimum lease payments, residual values guaranteed at inception, and residual values not guaranteed at inception using the individual carrying amounts of those components at the date of transfer. Those entities also shall record a servicing asset or liability in accordance with paragraphs 10 and 13, if appropriate.

Illustration—Recording Transfers of Lease Financing Receivables with Residual Values

90. At the beginning of the second year in a 10-year sales-type lease, Company F sells for $505 a nine-tenths interest in the minimum lease payments and retains a one-tenth interest in the minimum lease payments and a 100 percent interest in the unguaranteed residual value of leased equipment. Company F receives no explicit compensation for servicing, but it estimates that the other benefits of servicing are just adequate to compensate it for its servicing responsibilities and hence initially records no servicing asset or liability. The carrying amounts and related gain computation are as follows:

Carrying Amounts

Minimum lease payments		$ 540
Unearned income related to minimum lease payments		370
Gross investment in minimum lease payments		910
Unguaranteed residual value	$ 30	
Unearned income related to residual value	60	
Gross investment in residual value		90
Total gross investment in financing lease receivable		$1,000

Gain on Sale

Cash received		$ 505
Nine-tenths of carrying amount of gross investment in minimum lease payments	$819	
Nine-tenths of carrying amount of unearned income related to minimum lease payments	333	
Net carrying amount of minimum lease payments sold		486
Gain on sale		$ 19

Journal Entry

Cash	505	
Unearned income	333	
Lease receivable		819
Gain on sale		19

To record sale of nine-tenths of the minimum lease payments at the beginning of year 2

Securities Lending Transactions

91. Securities lending transactions are initiated by broker-dealers and other financial institutions that need specific securities to cover a short sale or a customer's failure to deliver securities sold. Transferees ("borrowers") of securities generally are required to provide "collateral" to the transferor ("lender") of securities, commonly cash but sometimes other securities or standby letters of credit, with a value slightly higher than that of the securities "borrowed." If the "collateral" is cash, the transferor typically earns a return by investing that cash at rates higher than the rate paid or "rebated" to the transferee. If the "collateral" is other than cash, the transferor typically receives a fee. Securities custodians or other agents commonly carry out securities lending activities on behalf of clients. Because of the protection of "collateral" (typically valued daily and adjusted frequently for changes in the market price of the securities transferred) and the short terms of the transactions, most securities lending transactions in themselves do not impose significant credit risks on either party. Other risks arise from what the parties to the transaction do with the assets they receive. For example, investments made with cash "collateral" impose market and credit risks on the transferor.

92. In some securities lending transactions, the criteria in paragraph 9 are met, including the effective control criterion in paragraph 9(c), and consideration other than beneficial interests in the transferred assets is received. Those transactions shall be accounted for (a) by the transferor as a sale of the "loaned" securities for proceeds consisting of the cash "collateral"[22] and a forward repurchase commitment and (b) by the transferee as a purchase of the "borrowed" securities in exchange for the "collateral" and a forward resale commitment. During the term of that agreement, the transferor has surrendered control over the securities transferred and the transferee has obtained control over those securities with the ability to sell or transfer them at will. In that case, creditors of the transferor have a claim only to the "collateral" and the forward repurchase commitment.

93. However, many securities lending transactions are accompanied by an agreement that entitles and obligates the transferor to repurchase or redeem the transferred assets before their maturity under which the transferor maintains effective control over those assets (paragraphs 47–49). Those transactions shall be accounted for as secured borrowings, in which cash (or securities that the holder is permitted by contract or custom to sell or repledge) received as "collateral" is considered the amount borrowed, the securities "loaned" are considered pledged as collateral against the cash borrowed and reclassified as set forth in paragraph 15(a), and any "rebate" paid to the transferee of securities is interest on the cash the transferor is considered to have borrowed.

94. The transferor of securities being "loaned" accounts for cash received in the same way whether the transfer is accounted for as a sale or a secured borrowing. The cash received shall be recognized as the transferor's asset—as shall investments made with that cash, even if made by agents or in pools with other securities lenders—along with the obligation to return the cash. If securities that may be sold or repledged are received, the transferor of the securities being "loaned" accounts for those securities in the same way as it would account for cash received.

---

[22]If the "collateral" in a transaction that meets the criteria in paragraph 9 is a financial asset that the holder is permitted by contract or custom to sell or repledge, that financial asset is proceeds of the sale of the "loaned" securities. To the extent that the "collateral" consists of letters of credit or other financial instruments that the holder is not permitted by contract or custom to sell or repledge, a securities lending transaction does not satisfy the sale criteria and is accounted for as a loan of securities by the transferor to the transferee.

Illustration—Securities Lending Transaction Treated as a Secured Borrowing

95. The following example illustrates the accounting for a securities lending transaction treated as a secured borrowing, in which the securities borrower sells the securities upon receipt and later buys similar securities to return to the securities lender:

Facts

Transferor's carrying amount and fair value of security loaned	$1,000
Cash "collateral"	1,020
Transferor's return from investing cash collateral at a 5 percent annual rate	5
Transferor's rebate to the securities borrower at a 4 percent annual rate	4

For simplicity, the fair value of the security is assumed not to change during the 35-day term of the transaction.

Journal Entries for the Transferor

At inception:

Cash	1,020	
Payable under securities loan agreements		1,020
To record the receipt of cash collateral		

Securities pledged to creditors	1,000	
Securities		1,000
To reclassify loaned securities that the secured party has the right to sell or repledge		

Money market instrument	1,020	
Cash		1,020
To record investment of cash collateral		

At conclusion:

Cash	1,025	
Interest		5
Money market instrument		1,020
To record results of investment		

Securities	1,000	
Securities pledged to creditors		1,000
To record return of security		

Payable under securities loan agreements	1,020	
Interest ("rebate")	4	
Cash		1,024
To record repayment of cash collateral plus interest		

Journal Entries for the Transferee

At inception:

Receivable under securities loan agreements	1,020	
Cash		1,020
To record transfer of cash collateral		

Cash	1,000	
Obligation to return borrowed securities		1,000
To record sale of borrowed securities to a third party and the resulting obligation to return securities that it no longer holds		

At conclusion:

Obligation to return borrowed securities	1,000	
Cash		1,000
To record the repurchase of securities borrowed		

Cash	1,024	
Receivable under securities loan agreements		1,020
Interest revenue ("rebate")		4
To record the receipt of cash collateral and rebate interest		

Repurchase Agreements and "Wash Sales"

96. Government securities dealers, banks, other financial institutions, and corporate investors commonly use repurchase agreements to obtain or use short-term funds. Under those agreements, the transferor ("repo party") transfers a security to a transferee ("repo counterparty" or "reverse party") in exchange for cash[23] and concurrently agrees to reacquire that security at a future date for an amount equal to the cash exchanged plus a stipulated "interest" factor.

97. Repurchase agreements can be effected in a variety of ways. Some repurchase agreements are similar to securities lending transactions in that the transferee has the right to sell or repledge the securities to a third party during the term of the repurchase agreement. In other repurchase agreements, the transferee does not have the right to sell or repledge the securities during the term of the repurchase agreement. For example, in a tri-party repurchase agreement, the transferor transfers securities to an independent third-party custodian that holds the securities during the term of the repurchase agreement. Also, many repurchase agreements are for short terms, often overnight, or have indefinite terms that allow either party to terminate the arrangement on short notice. However, other repurchase agreements are for longer terms, sometimes until the maturity of the transferred asset. Some repurchase agreements call for repurchase of securities that need not be identical to the securities transferred.

98. If the criteria in paragraph 9 are met, including the criterion in paragraph 9(c)(1), the transferor shall account for the repurchase agreement as a sale of financial assets and a forward repurchase commitment, and the transferee shall account for the agreement as a purchase of financial assets and a forward resale commitment. Other transfers that are accompanied by an agreement to repurchase the transferred assets that shall be accounted for as sales include transfers with agreements to repurchase at maturity and transfers with repurchase agreements in which the [transferor] has not obtained collateral sufficient to fund substantially all of the cost of purchasing replacement assets.

---

[23]Instead of cash, other securities or letters of credit sometimes are exchanged. Those transactions are accounted for in the same manner as securities lending transactions (paragraphs 92–94).

99. Furthermore, "wash sales" that previously were not recognized if the same financial asset was purchased soon before or after the sale shall be accounted for as sales under this Statement. Unless there is a concurrent contract to repurchase or redeem the transferred financial assets from the transferee, the transferor does not maintain effective control over the transferred assets.

100. As with securities lending transactions, under many agreements to repurchase transferred assets before their maturity the transferor maintains effective control over those assets. Repurchase agreements that do not meet all the criteria in paragraph 9 shall be treated as secured borrowings. Fixed-coupon and dollar-roll repurchase agreements, and other contracts under which the securities to be repurchased need not be the same as the securities sold, qualify as borrowings if the return of substantially the same (paragraph 48) securities as those concurrently transferred is assured. Therefore, those transactions shall be accounted for as secured borrowings by both parties to the transfer.

101. If a transferor has transferred securities to an independent third-party custodian, or to a transferee, under conditions that preclude the transferee from selling or repledging the assets during the term of the repurchase agreement (as in most tri-party repurchase agreements), the transferor has not surrendered control over those assets.

Loan Syndications

102. Borrowers often borrow amounts greater than any one lender is willing to lend. Therefore, it is common for groups of lenders to jointly fund those loans. That may be accomplished by a syndication under which several lenders share in lending to a single borrower, but each lender loans a specific amount to the borrower and has the right to repayment from the borrower.

103. A loan syndication is not a transfer of financial assets. Each lender in the syndication shall account for the amounts it is owed by the borrower. Repayments by the borrower may be made to a lead lender that then distributes the collections to the other lenders of the syndicate. In those circumstances, the lead lender is simply functioning as a servicer and, therefore, shall not recognize the aggregate loan as an asset.

Loan Participations

104. Groups of banks or other entities also may jointly fund large borrowings through loan participations in which a single lender makes a large loan to a borrower and subsequently transfers undivided interests in the loan to other entities.

105. Transfers by the originating lender may take the legal form of either assignments or participations. The transfers are usually on a nonrecourse basis, and the transferor ("originating lender") continues to service the loan. The transferee ("participating entity") may or may not have the right to sell or transfer its participation during the term of the loan, depending upon the terms of the participation agreement.

106. If the loan participation agreement gives the transferee the right to pledge or exchange those participations and the other criteria in paragraph 9 are met, the transfers to the transferee shall be accounted for by the transferor as sales of financial assets. A transferor's right of first refusal on a bona fide offer from a third party, a requirement to obtain the transferor's permission that shall not be unreasonably withheld, or a prohibition on sale to the transferor's competitor if other potential willing buyers exist is a limitation on the transferee's rights but presumptively does not constrain a transferee from exercising its right to pledge or exchange. However, if the loan participation agreement constrains the transferees from pledging or exchanging their participations, the transferor presumptively receives a more than trivial benefit, has not relinquished control over the loan, and shall account for the transfers as secured borrowings.

Banker's Acceptances and Risk Participations in Them

107. Banker's acceptances provide a way for a bank to finance a customer's purchase of goods from a vendor for periods usually not exceeding six months. Under an agreement between the bank, the customer, and the vendor, the bank agrees to pay the customer's liability to the vendor upon presentation of specified documents that provide evidence of delivery and acceptance of the purchased goods. The principal document is a draft or bill of exchange drawn by the customer that the bank stamps to signify its "acceptance" of the liability to make payment on the draft on its due date.

108. Once the bank accepts a draft, the customer is liable to repay the bank at the time the draft matures. The bank recognizes a receivable from the customer and a liability for the acceptance it has issued to the

vendor. The accepted draft becomes a negotiable financial instrument. The vendor typically sells the accepted draft at a discount either to the accepting bank or in the marketplace.

109. A risk participation is a contract between the accepting bank and a participating bank in which the participating bank agrees, in exchange for a fee, to reimburse the accepting bank in the event that the accepting bank's customer fails to honor its liability to the accepting bank in connection with the banker's acceptance. The participating bank becomes a guarantor of the credit of the accepting bank's customer.

110. An accepting bank that obtains a risk participation shall not derecognize the liability for the banker's acceptance, because the accepting bank is still primarily liable to the holder of the banker's accept-

ance even though it benefits from a guarantee of reimbursement by a participating bank. The accepting bank shall not derecognize the receivable from the customer because it has not transferred the receivable: it controls the benefits inherent in that receivable and it is still entitled to receive payment from the customer. The accepting bank shall, however, record the guarantee purchased, and the participating bank shall record a liability for the guarantee issued.

Illustration—Banker's Acceptance with a Risk Participation

111. An accepting bank assumes a liability to pay a customer's vendor and obtains a risk participation from another bank. The details of the banker's acceptance are provided below:

Facts

Face value of the draft provided to vendor	$1,000
Term of the draft provided to vendor	90 days
Commission with an annual rate of 10 percent	25
Fee paid for risk participation	10

Journal Entries for Accepting Bank

At issuance of acceptance:

Receivable from customer	1,000	
Cash	25	
Time draft payable to vendor		1,000
Deferred acceptance commission revenue		25

At purchase of risk participation from a participating bank:

Guarantee purchased	10	
Cash		10

Upon presentation of the accepted time draft:

Time draft payable to vendor	1,000	
Deferred acceptance commission revenue	25	
Cash		1,000
Acceptance commission revenue		25

Upon collection from the customer (or the participating bank, if the customer defaults):

Cash	1,000	
Guarantee expense	10	
Receivable from customer		1,000
Guarantee purchased		10

Journal Entries for Participating Bank

Upon issuing the risk participation:

Cash	10	
Guarantee liability		10

Upon payment by the customer to the accepting bank:

Guarantee liability	10	
Guarantee revenue		10

OR:

In the event of total default by the customer:

Guarantee loss	990	
Guarantee liability	10	
Cash (paid to accepting bank)		1,000

Factoring Arrangements

112. Factoring arrangements are a means of discounting accounts receivable on a nonrecourse, notification basis. Accounts receivable are sold outright, usually to a transferee (the factor) that assumes the full risk of collection, without recourse to the transferor in the event of a loss. Debtors are directed to send payments to the transferee. Factoring arrangements that meet the criteria in paragraph 9 shall be accounted for as sales of financial assets because the transferor surrenders control over the receivables to the factor.

Transfers of Receivables with Recourse

113. In a transfer of receivables with recourse, the transferor provides the transferee with full or limited recourse. The transferor is obligated under the terms of the recourse provision to make payments to the transferee or to repurchase receivables sold under certain circumstances, typically for defaults up to a specified percentage. The effect of a recourse provision on the application of paragraph 9 may vary by jurisdiction. In some jurisdictions, transfers with full recourse may not place transferred assets beyond the reach of the transferor and its creditors, but transfers with limited recourse may. A transfer of receivables with recourse shall be accounted for as a sale, with the proceeds of the sale reduced by the fair value of the recourse obligation, if the criteria in paragraph 9 are met. Otherwise, a transfer of receivables with recourse shall be accounted for as a secured borrowing.

Extinguishments of Liabilities

114. If a creditor releases a debtor from primary obligation on the condition that a third party assumes the obligation and that the original debtor becomes secondarily liable, that release extinguishes the original debtor's liability. However, in those circumstances, whether or not explicit consideration was paid for that guarantee, the original debtor becomes a guarantor. As a guarantor, it shall recognize a guarantee obligation in the same manner as would a guarantor that had never been primarily liable to that creditor, with due regard for the likelihood that the third party will carry out its obligations. The guarantee obligation shall be initially measured at fair value, and that amount reduces the gain or increases the loss recognized on extinguishment.

Appendix B

BACKGROUND INFORMATION AND BASIS FOR CONCLUSIONS

CONTENTS

Appendix B

BACKGROUND INFORMATION AND BASIS FOR CONCLUSIONS

Introduction

115. This appendix summarizes considerations that were deemed significant by Board members in reaching the conclusions in this Statement. It also summarizes the considerations that were deemed significant by Board members in reaching the conclusions in Statement 125. Most of those conclusions and considerations are carried forward without reconsideration. It includes reasons for accepting certain approaches and rejecting others. Individual Board members gave greater weight to some factors than to others.

Background to Statement 125

116. In recent years, transfers of financial assets in which the transferor has some continuing involvement with the transferred assets or with the transferee have grown in volume, variety, and complexity. Those transfers raise the issues of whether transferred financial assets should be considered to be sold and a related gain or loss recorded, whether the assets should be considered to be collateral for borrowings, or whether the transfer should not be recognized.

117. A transferor may sell financial assets and receive in exchange cash or other assets that are unrelated to the assets sold so that the transferor has no continuing involvement with the assets sold. Alternatively, an entity may borrow money and pledge financial assets as collateral, or a transferor may engage in any of a variety of transactions that transfer financial assets to another entity with the transferor having some continuing involvement with the assets transferred. Examples of continuing involvement are recourse or guarantee obligations, servicing, agreements to repurchase or redeem, retained subordinated interests, and put or call options on the assets transferred.

118. Many transactions disaggregate financial assets into separate components by creating undivided interests in pools of financial assets that frequently reflect multiple participations (often referred to as tranches) in a single pool. The components created may later be recombined to restore the original assets or may be combined with other financial assets to create still different assets.

119. An entity also may enter into transactions that change the characteristics of an asset that the entity

continues to hold. An entity may sell part of an asset, or an undivided interest in the asset, and retain part of the asset. In some cases, it was not always clear what the accounting should have been.

120. An entity may settle a liability by transferring assets to a creditor and obtaining an unconditional release from the obligation. Alternatively, an entity may arrange for others to settle or set aside assets to settle a liability later. Those alternative arrangements have raised issues about when a liability is extinguished.

121. The Board previously provided guidance for two specific types of transfers of financial assets in FASB Statement No. 77, *Reporting by Transferors for Transfers of Receivables with Recourse,* and in FASB Technical Bulletin No. 85-2, *Accounting for Collateralized Mortgage Obligations (CMOs).* Confusion and inconsistency in accounting practices developed because the provisions of those two pronouncements provided seemingly conflicting guidance. In practice, if an entity sold financial assets to an SPE that issued debt securities, the guidance under Technical Bulletin 85-2 would be applied, and if any of those securities were obtained by the seller, the transaction would be accounted for as a borrowing. However, if the interests issued by the SPE were designated as participations instead of debt securities, the guidance in Statement 77 would be applied, and the transaction would be accounted for as a sale even if the seller retained recourse on some of the participations. Further, accounting for other types of transfers, whether developed by analogy to Statement 77 or Technical Bulletin 85-2, in industry practices codified in various AICPA audit and accounting Guides, in consensuses of the Emerging Issues Task Force (EITF), or in other ways, added to the confusion and inconsistency.

122. FASB Statement No. 76, *Extinguishment of Debt,* established accounting practices that (a) treat liabilities that are not fully settled as if they had been extinguished and (b) derecognize assets transferred to a trust even though the assets continue to benefit the transferor. Some criticized Statement 76 as being inconsistent with Statement 77; others disagreed.

123. The Board decided that it was necessary to reconsider Statements 76 and 77, Technical Bulletin 85-2, and other guidance and to develop new standards for transfers of financial assets and extinguishments of liabilities.

124. The Board added a project to its agenda in May 1986 to address those and other problems in accounting for financial instruments and off-balance-sheet financing. Statement 125 and this Statement, as part of that project, focus on accounting for transfers and servicing of financial assets and extinguishments of liabilities. The Financial Instruments Task Force, which was formed in January 1989, assisted in the preparation of a Discussion Memorandum on those issues and advised the Board in its deliberations. The FASB Discussion Memorandum, *Recognition and Measurement of Financial Instruments,* was issued in November 1991. The Board received 96 comment letters on the Discussion Memorandum. During 1994 and 1995, the Board discussed issues about transfers and servicing of financial assets and extinguishments of liabilities at numerous public meetings. The Financial Instruments Task Force reviewed drafts of the proposed Statement and discussed it with the Board at a public meeting in February 1995. The Financial Accounting Standards Advisory Council discussed a draft of the proposed Statement and advised the Board at public meetings. The Board also received requests from constituents to discuss issues about credit card securitizations and securities lending transactions and repurchase agreements. The Board met with constituents interested in those issues at public meetings in November 1994 and April 1995.

125. In October 1995, the Board issued an Exposure Draft, *Accounting for Transfers and Servicing of Financial Assets and Extinguishments of Liabilities.* The Board received 112 comment letters on the Exposure Draft, and 24 individuals and organizations presented their views at a public hearing held in February 1996. In addition, 10 enterprises participated in limited field-testing of the provisions of the Exposure Draft. The comments and test results were considered by the Board during its redeliberations of the issues addressed by the Exposure Draft in public meetings in 1996. The Financial Instruments Task Force reviewed a draft of the final Statement. Statement 125 was a result of those Board meetings and deliberations.

Background to This Statement

126. Statement 125 was issued in June 1996 and as issued was effective for transfers and servicing of financial assets and extinguishments of liabilities occurring after December 31, 1996. In December 1996, the Board considered constituents' concerns about their ability to apply certain provisions of Statement 125 by that date, including (a) making the changes to information and accounting systems

needed to apply the newly established accounting requirements and (b) effectively tracking supporting data. The Board noted those concerns and issued Statement 127 to defer for one year the effective date of paragraph 15 (addressing secured borrowings and collateral) for all transactions and paragraphs 9–12 (addressing transfers of financial assets) only for transfers of financial assets that are part of repurchase agreement, dollar-roll, securities lending, and similar transactions.

127. In December 1996, after considering other constituent concerns, the Board added to its agenda a project to interpret or possibly amend Statement 125. The project initially focused on the effect of EITF Issue No. 90-18, "Effect of a 'Removal of Accounts' Provision on the Accounting for a Credit Card Securitization," on accounting for credit card securitizations under Statement 125 and whether a removal-of-accounts provision (ROAP) maintains a transferor's effective control over transferred assets by entitling it to repurchase or redeem transferred assets that are not readily obtainable. The Board subsequently decided that the project also should consider several other issues concerning whether transfers of financial assets are accounted for as sales, including (a) the impact on isolation of transferred assets of the powers of the FDIC as receiver for a failed institution, (b) a transferee's right to sell or pledge transferred assets and the effect of conditions that constrain the transferee, (c) circumstances in which an SPE with some ability to sell transferred financial assets can be considered qualifying under the criteria in paragraph 26 of Statement 125, (d) the conditions for deciding whether assets transferred to a qualifying SPE and beneficial interests in those assets should appear in the consolidated financial statements of the transferor, and (e) a transferor's right to call a transferred financial asset that is not readily obtainable. In response to other concerns expressed by constituents, the Board also decided to consider (1) possible changes to the collateral provisions of paragraph 15 of Statement 125, (2) possible enhanced disclosures for securitizations involving financial assets, and (3) possible exclusion of transfers of financial assets measured using the equity method of accounting from the scope of Statement 125. The Board concluded that resolution of those issues would require an amendment, rather than an interpretation, of Statement 125.

128. In June 1999, the Board issued an Exposure Draft, *Accounting for Transfers of Financial Assets.* The Board received 40 comment letters on the Expo-

sure Draft. In addition, four enterprises and members of the Bond Market Association participated in limited field-testing of certain provisions of the Exposure Draft. The comment letters and test results were considered by the Board during its redeliberations of the issues addressed by the Exposure Draft in 16 public meetings in 1999 and 2000. The Board concluded that it could reach an informed decision on the basis of existing information without a public hearing. The Board decided to issue a final Statement that replaces, rather than amends, Statement 125 after some commentators suggested that that would improve the readability and usefulness of the Statement. The Financial Instruments Task Force and other interested parties reviewed a draft of the final Statement for clarity and operationality. This Statement is a result of those Board meetings and deliberations.

Benefits and Costs

129. The Board's mission statement charges the Board to determine that a proposed standard will fill a significant need and that the costs it imposes will be justified in relation to the overall benefits.

130. Previous practices in accounting for transfers of financial assets were inconsistent about the circumstances that distinguish sales from secured borrowings. The result was confusion on the part of both users and preparers of financial statements. Statement 125 and this Statement eliminate that inconsistency and reduce that confusion by distinguishing sales from secured borrowings based on the underlying contractual commitments and customs that determine substance. Much of the information needed to implement the accounting required by Statement 125 and carried forward without reconsideration in this Statement is substantially the same as that required for previous accounting and, therefore, should be available. Some of the information may not have been collected in accounting systems but is commonly obtained by sellers and buyers for use in negotiating transactions. Although there will be one-time costs for systems changes needed to apply the accounting required by this Statement, the benefits in terms of more credible, consistent, and understandable information will be ongoing.

131. In addition, in developing Statement 125 and this Statement, the Board considered how the costs incurred to implement their requirements could be minimized by, for example, (a) not requiring retroactive application of the initial measurement provisions of Statement 125 to existing servicing rights and excess servicing receivables, (b) carrying over without

change the subsequent measurement (amortization and impairment) provisions of FASB Statement No. 122, *Accounting for Mortgage Servicing Rights,*(c) not requiring allocation of previous carrying amounts of assets partially sold based on relative fair values at acquisition, but rather at the date of transfer, and (d) eliminating the requirement to recognize collateral because the limited benefits do not justify the burden of preparing the information. This Statement requires additional disclosures for securitizations, because events since the issuance of Statement 125 convinced the Board that the need of investors and creditors for better information justifies the costs other entities will incur in developing and reporting that information. Furthermore, many of those disclosures are already being made voluntarily by some entities. The Board is confident that the benefits derived from the accounting and disclosure required by Statement 125 and this Statement will outweigh the costs of implementation.

Approaches Considered in Developing Statement 125

132. The Board noted that the most difficult questions about accounting for transfers of financial assets concern the circumstances in which it is appropriate to remove previously recognized financial assets from the statement of financial position and to recognize gain or loss. One familiar approach to those questions views each financial asset as a unit that should not be derecognized until the risks and rewards that are embodied in that asset have been surrendered. Variations on that approach attempt to choose which risks and rewards are most critical and whether all or some major portion of those risks and rewards must be surrendered to allow derecognition.

133. In addition to reviewing U.S. accounting literature, the Board reviewed the approach described by the International Accounting Standards Committee (IASC) in its proposed International Accounting Standard, *Financial Instruments,* Exposure Draft E40 (1992), later revised as Exposure Draft E48 (1994). In E40, derecognition of financial assets and liabilities would have been permitted only upon the transfer to others of the underlying risks and rewards, presumably all risks and rewards. That approach could have resulted in an entity's continuing to recognize assets even though it had surrendered control over the assets to a successor entity. The approach in E40 was similar to that taken in Technical Bulletin 85-2. The Board conc ⌐d that the approaches proposed in E40 and provided in Technical Bulletin 85-2

were unsatisfactory because the result does not faithfully represent the effects of the transfer of assets and because of the potential for inconsistencies.

134. In response to comments received on E40, the IASC proposal was revised in E48 to require the transfer of *substantially all* risks and rewards. That modification did not overcome the inconsistency noted in paragraphs 130 and 133 of this Statement and would have added the prospect of difficulties in application because of the need to identify, measure, and weigh in the balance each of possibly many and varied risks and rewards embodied in a particular financial asset. The number of different risks and rewards would have varied depending on the definitions used. Questions would have arisen about whether each identified risk and reward should be substantially surrendered to allow derecognition, whether all risks should be aggregated separately from all rewards, and whether risks and rewards should somehow be offset and then combined for evaluation. That modification also might have led to wide variations in practice depending on how various entities interpreted *substantially all* in the necessarily subjective evaluation of the aggregated, offset, and combined risks and rewards. Moreover, viewing each financial asset as an indivisible unit is contrary to the growing practice in financial markets of disaggregating individual financial assets or pools of financial assets into components. The IASC was still studying that issue in its financial instruments project when Statement 125 was issued.

135. In March 1997, the IASC issued jointly with the Canadian Institute of Chartered Accountants a comprehensive Discussion Paper, *Accounting for Financial Assets and Financial Liabilities*. Later in 1997, the IASC Board decided to pursue its financial instruments project along two paths. It joined with national standard setters, including the FASB, in a Joint Working Group to develop, integrate, and harmonize international accounting standards on financial instruments, building on the March 1997 Joint Discussion Paper. At the same time, the IASC decided to complete an interim international standard to serve until the integrated comprehensive standard is completed. In December 1998, the IASC issued that interim standard, IAS 39, *Financial Instruments: Recognition and Measurement*. The provisions for derecognition of a financial asset in that interim standard continue to focus on whether the transferor has retained, or the transferee has taken on, substantially all of the risks and rewards of ownership. The

Joint Working Group has reached tentative conclusions on issues about transfers of financial assets that resemble the conclusions in Statement 125 in some respects, with less focus on risks and rewards, but that differ significantly in other respects. However, that group has yet to reach conclusions on certain issues and its work is still in progress. The tentative conclusions have not yet been exposed for public comment. Because (a) the comprehensive international project is still in that early stage, (b) the project has a broad scope including many other issues likely to prove controversial, and (c) the FASB project to amend Statement 125 was limited in scope and urgently needed, the Board did not consider in this project whether to replace the fundamental principles of Statement 125 with the principles being developed internationally. The Board plans to join the other members of the Joint Working Group in circulating that group's document for public comment, after which the Board expects to consider what further steps it should take.

136. In developing Statement 125, the Board noted that application of a risks-and-rewards approach for derecognizing financial assets would be highly dependent on the sequence of transactions leading to their acquisition. For example, if Entity A initially acquired an undivided subordinated interest in a pool of financial assets, it would recognize that subordinated interest as a single asset. If, on the other hand, Entity B initially acquired a pool of financial assets identical to the pool in which Entity A participates, then sold a senior interest in the pool and continued to hold a subordinated interest identical to the undivided interest held by Entity A, Entity B might be judged under a risks-and-rewards approach to have retained substantially all the risks of the entire pool. Thus, Entity B would carry in its statement of financial position the entire pool of financial assets as well as an obligation equal to the proceeds from the sale of the undivided senior interest, while Entity A would report its identical position quite differently. Those accounting results would disregard one of the fundamental tenets of the Board's conceptual framework; that is, ". . . accountants must not disguise real differences nor create false differences."[24]

137. The Board also considered the approach required by the United Kingdom's Accounting Standards Board in Financial Reporting Standard No. 5, *Reporting the Substance of Transactions,* a variation of the risks-and-rewards approach that requires the surrender of substantially all risks and rewards for derecognition of financial assets but permits, in limited circumstances, the use of a *linked presentation.* Use of the linked presentation is restricted to circumstances in which an entity borrows funds to be repaid from the proceeds of pledged financial assets, any excess proceeds go to the borrower, and the lender has no recourse to other assets of the borrower. In those circumstances, the pledged assets remain on the borrower's statement of financial position, but the unpaid borrowing is reported as a deduction from the pledged assets rather than as a liability; no gain or loss is recognized. That approach had some appeal to the Board because it would have highlighted significant information about transactions that many believe have characteristics of both sales and secured borrowings. The Board observed, however, that the linked presentation would not have dealt with many of the problems created by the risks-and-rewards approach. Further, the Board concluded that it is not appropriate for an entity to offset restricted assets against a liability or to derecognize a liability merely because assets are dedicated to its repayment, as discussed in paragraphs 309–312.

138. Statement 77 based the determination of whether to derecognize receivables on transfer of control instead of on evaluation of risks and rewards. Statement 125 and this Statement take a similar approach. However, Statement 77 was narrowly focused on sales of receivables with recourse and did not address other transfers of financial assets. Also, the derecognition of receivables under that Statement could depend on the sequence of transactions that led to their acquisition or on whether any options were involved. The Board concluded that simply superseding Technical Bulletin 85-2 and allowing Statement 77 to remain in effect would not have dealt adequately with the issues about transfers of financial assets.

139. Statement 76 followed a risks-and-rewards approach in requiring that (a) it be probable that a debtor would not be required to make future payments with respect to the debt under any guarantees and (b) an in-substance defeasance trust be restricted to owning only monetary assets that are risk free with cash flows that approximately coincide, as to timing and amount, with the scheduled interest and principal payments on the debt being extinguished. The Board concluded that that approach was inconsistent with the financial-components approach that focuses on

---

[24]FASB Concepts Statement No. 2, *Qualitative Characteristics of Accounting Information,* par. 119.

control developed in this Statement (paragraphs 309–312). As a result, the Board decided to supersede Statement 76 but to carry forward those of its criteria that could be modified to conform to the financial-components approach.

140. The considerations discussed in paragraphs 132–139 led the Board to seek an alternative to the risks-and-rewards approach and variations to that approach.

Objectives of the Financial-Components Approach

141. The Board concluded in Statement 125 that it was necessary to develop an approach that would be responsive to current developments in the financial markets to achieve consistent accounting for transfers and servicing of financial assets and extinguishments of liabilities. That approach—the financial-components approach—is designed to:

a. Be consistent with the way participants in the financial markets deal with financial assets, including the combination and separation of components of those assets
b. Reflect the economic consequences of contractual provisions underlying financial assets and liabilities
c. Conform to the FASB conceptual framework.

142. The approach analyzes a transfer of a financial asset by examining the component assets (controlled economic benefits) and liabilities (present obligations for probable future sacrifices of economic benefits) that exist after the transfer. Each party to the transfer recognizes the assets and liabilities that it controls after the transfer and no longer recognizes the assets and liabilities that were surrendered or extinguished in the transfer. That approach has some antecedents in existing accounting guidance, for example, in EITF Issue No. 88-11, "Allocation of Recorded Investment When a Loan or Part of a Loan Is Sold." The Board identified the concepts set forth in paragraphs 143–145 as an appropriate basis for the financial-components approach.

Conceptual Basis for the Financial-Components Approach

143. FASB Concepts Statement No. 6, *Elements of Financial Statements,* states the following about assets:

Assets are probable future economic benefits obtained or controlled by a particular entity as a result of past transactions or events. [Paragraph 25, footnote reference omitted.]

Every asset is an asset of some entity; moreover, no asset can simultaneously be an asset of more than one entity, although a particular physical thing or other agent [for example, contractual rights and obligations] that provides future economic benefit may provide separate benefits to two or more entities at the same time. . . . To have an asset, an entity must control future economic benefit to the extent that it can benefit from the asset and generally can deny or regulate access to that benefit by others, for example, by permitting access only at a price.

Thus, *an asset of an entity is the future economic benefit that the entity can control and thus can, within limits set by the nature of the benefit or the entity's right to it, use as it pleases.* The entity having an asset is the one that can exchange it, use it to produce goods or services, exact a price for others' use of it, use it to settle liabilities, hold it, or perhaps distribute it to owners.

The definition of assets focuses primarily on the future economic benefit to which an entity has access and only secondarily on the physical things and other agents that provide future economic benefits. *Many physical things and other agents are in effect bundles of future economic benefits that can be unbundled in various ways, and two or more entities may have different future economic benefits from the same agent at the same time or the same continuing future economic benefit at different times.* For example, two or more entities may have undivided interests in a parcel of land. Each has a right to future economic benefit that may qualify as an asset under the definition in paragraph 25, even though the right of each is subject at least to some extent to the rights of the other(s). Or, one entity may have the right to the interest from an investment, while another has the right to the principal. [Paragraphs 183–185; emphasis added.]

144. Concepts Statement 6 states the following about liabilities:

> Liabilities are probable future sacrifices of economic benefits arising from present obligations of a particular entity to transfer assets or provide services to other entities in the future as a result of past transactions or events. [Paragraph 35, footnote references omitted.]
>
> Most liabilities are obligations of only one entity at a time. Some liabilities are shared—for example, two or more entities may be "jointly and severally liable" for a debt or for the unsatisfied liabilities of a partnership. But most liabilities bind a single entity, and those that bind two or more entities are commonly ranked rather than shared. For example, *a primary debtor and a guarantor may both be obligated for a debt, but they do not have the same obligation—the guarantor must pay only if the primary debtor defaults and thus has a contingent or secondary obligation,* which ranks lower than that of the primary debtor.
>
> Secondary, and perhaps even lower ranked, obligations may qualify as liabilities under the definition in paragraph 35, but recognition considerations are highly significant in deciding whether they should formally be included in financial statements because of the effects of uncertainty (paragraphs 44–48). For example, the probability that a secondary or lower ranked obligation will actually have to be paid must be assessed to apply the definition. [Paragraphs 204 and 205; emphasis added.]

145. Financial assets and liabilities are assets and liabilities that qualify as financial instruments as defined in paragraph 3 of FASB Statement No. 107, *Disclosures about Fair Value of Financial Instruments:*

> A financial instrument is defined as cash, evidence of an ownership interest in an entity, or a contract that both:
>
> a. Imposes on one entity a contractual obligation (1) to deliver cash or another financial instrument to a second entity or (2) to exchange other financial instruments on potentially unfavorable terms with the second entity

> b. Conveys to that second entity a contractual right (1) to receive cash or another financial instrument from the first entity or (2) to exchange other financial instruments on potentially favorable terms with the first entity. [Footnote references omitted.]

146. Based on the concepts and definitions cited in paragraphs 143–145, the Board concluded that the key to applying the financial-components approach can be summarized as follows:

a. The economic benefits provided by a financial asset (generally, the right to future cash flows) are derived from the contractual provisions that underlie that asset, and the entity that controls those benefits should recognize them as its asset.
b. A financial asset should be considered sold and therefore should be derecognized if it is transferred and control is surrendered.
c. A transferred financial asset should be considered pledged as collateral to secure an obligation of the transferor (and therefore should not be derecognized) if the transferor has not surrendered control of the financial asset.
d. Each liability should be recognized by the entity that is primarily liable and, accordingly, an entity that guarantees another entity's obligation should recognize only its obligation to perform on the guarantee.
e. The recognition of financial assets and liabilities should not be affected by the sequence of transactions that led to their existence unless as a result of those transactions the transferor maintains effective control over a transferred asset.
f. Transferors and transferees should account symmetrically for transfers of financial assets.

147. Most respondents to the Exposure Draft of Statement 125 generally supported the financial-components approach, especially as it applies to securitization transactions.

148. The concepts underlying the financial-components approach could be applied by analogy to accounting for transfers of nonfinancial assets and thus could result in accounting that differs significantly from that required by existing standards and practices. However, the Board believes that financial and nonfinancial assets have significantly different characteristics, and it is not clear to what extent the financial-components approach is applicable to nonfinancial assets. Nonfinancial assets have a variety of

operational uses, and management skill plays a considerable role in obtaining the greatest value from those assets. In contrast, financial assets have no operational use. They may facilitate operations, and financial assets may be the principal "product" offered by some entities. However, the promise embodied in a financial asset is governed by contract. Once the contract is established, management skill plays a limited role in the entity's ability to realize the value of the instrument. Furthermore, the Board believes that attempting to extend Statement 125 and this Statement to transfers of nonfinancial assets would unduly delay resolving the issues for transfers of financial assets, because of the significant differences between financial assets and nonfinancial assets and because of the significant unresolved recognition and measurement issues posed by those differences. For those reasons, the Board concluded that existing accounting practices for transfers of nonfinancial assets should not be changed at this time. The Board further concluded that transfers of servicing assets and transfers of property subject to operating leases are not within the scope of Statement 125 and this Statement because they are nonfinancial assets.

149. The following paragraphs discuss the application of the concepts and principles described in paragraphs 143–148, both as the concepts and principles were applied initially in Statement 125 and as they are, in some cases, applied differently in this Statement. First, circumstances that require derecognition of transferred assets and recognition of assets and liabilities received in exchange are discussed in the paragraphs about sales of financial assets, transfers to SPEs, and other transfers (paragraphs 150–264). Then, the measurement of assets controlled and liabilities incurred (paragraphs 265–305) and subsequent measurement (paragraphs 306–308) are discussed. Finally, extinguishments of liabilities are discussed (paragraphs 309–315).

Sales of Financial Assets

150. If an entity transfers financial assets, surrenders control of those assets to a successor entity, and has no continuing involvement with those assets, accounting for the transaction as a sale and derecognizing the assets and recognizing the related gain or loss is not controversial. However, accounting for transfers of financial assets has been controversial and inconsistent in circumstances in which an entity transfers only a partial interest in a financial asset or has some other continuing involvement with the transferred asset or the transferee.

151. Under the financial-components approach, the accounting for a transfer is based on whether a transferor surrenders control of financial assets. Paragraph 3 of Statement 77 states, "This Statement establishes standards of financial accounting and reporting by transferors for transfers of receivables with recourse that *purport to be sales* of receivables" (emphasis added). The Board believes that, while it may have some significance at law, a more exacting test than whether a transaction purports to be a sale is needed to conclude that control has been surrendered in a manner that is consistent with the definitions in Concepts Statement 6. The Board concluded that a sale occurs only if control has been surrendered to another entity or group of entities and that surrender of control depends on whether (a) transferred assets have been isolated from the transferor, (b) transferees have obtained the right to pledge or exchange either the transferred assets or beneficial interests in the transferred assets, and (c) the transferor does not maintain effective control over the transferred assets through an agreement to repurchase or redeem them before their maturity or through the ability to unilaterally cause the holder to return specific assets.

Isolation beyond the Reach of the Transferor, Even in Bankruptcy or Other Receivership

152. The Board developed its criterion that transferred assets must be isolated—put presumptively beyond the reach of the transferor and its creditors, even in bankruptcy or other receivership (paragraph 9(a))—in large part with reference to securitization practices. Credit rating agencies and investors in securitized assets pay close attention to (a) the possibility of bankruptcy or other receivership of the transferor, its affiliates, or the SPE, even though that possibility may seem unlikely given the present credit standing of the transferor, and (b) what might happen in such a receivership, because those are major areas of risk for them. If certain receivers can reclaim securitized assets, investors will suffer a delay in payments due them and may be forced to accept a pro rata settlement. Credit rating agencies and investors commonly demand transaction structures that minimize those possibilities and sometimes seek assurances from attorneys about whether entities can be forced into receivership, what the powers of a receiver might be, and whether the transaction structure would withstand receivers' attempts to reach the securitized assets in ways that would harm investors.

Unsatisfactory structures or assurances commonly result in credit ratings that are no higher than those for the transferor's liabilities and in lower prices for transferred assets.

153. Because legal isolation of transferred assets has substance, the Board decided that it could and should serve as an important part of the basis for determining whether a sale should be recognized. Some constituents expressed concern about the feasibility of an accounting standard based on those legal considerations, but the Board concluded that having to consider only the evidence available should make that requirement workable.

154. Respondents to the Exposure Draft of Statement 125 raised several questions about the application of the isolation criterion in paragraph 9(a) to existing securitization structures. The questions included whether it was necessary to consider separately the accounting by the first-tier SPE, whose transfer to the second-tier trust taken by itself might not satisfy the isolation test. After considering those comments and consulting with respondents who specialize in the structure of securitization transactions, the Board concluded that related language in Appendix A should be revised to explain that that criterion can be satisfied either by a single transaction or by a series of transactions considered as a whole. As discussed in paragraphs 80–84, the Board understands that the series of transactions in a typical two-tier structure taken as a whole may satisfy the isolation test because the design of the structure achieves isolation.

155. The Board understands that a one-tier structure with significant continuing involvement by a transferor subject to the U.S. Bankruptcy Code might not satisfy the isolation test, because a trustee in bankruptcy has substantial powers that could alter amounts that investors might receive and thus it may be difficult to conclude that control has been relinquished. Some respondents argued that a one-tier structure with continuing involvement generally should be adequate if the transferor's credit rating is sufficiently high that the chance of sudden bankruptcy is remote. The Board did not accept that view because isolation should not depend on the credit standing of the transferor.

156. Some constituents questioned whether the term *affiliates* was used in Statement 125 in the same sense as it was used in FASB Statement No. 57, *Related Party Disclosures,* or more narrowly. Their concerns included, for example, how the meaning of that term might affect whether a transfer from a subsidiary to a sister subsidiary, which would be eliminated in the consolidated financial statements of their common parent, could ever qualify as a sale in the separate financial statements of the transferring subsidiary. The Board chose to clarify that matter by (a) revising the discussion in paragraph 27 of this Statement to emphasize that whether a transfer has isolated the transferred assets can depend on which financial statements are being presented and (b) introducing the term *consolidated affiliate of the transferor* where the Board intended a narrower sense than *affiliate* as used in Statement 57.

If the FDIC is receiver

157. During the deliberations leading up to the issuance of Statement 125, constituents asked the Board to explain how the criterion in paragraph 9(a) applied to transfers by institutions subject to possible receivership by the FDIC, in view of the limited, special powers of the FDIC to repudiate certain contracts. The Board's understanding at the time Statement 125 was issued was that financial assets transferred by a U.S. bank were not subject to an automatic stay under FDIC receivership and that the receiver could only obtain those assets if it makes the investors whole, that is, by paying them compensation equivalent to all the economic benefits embodied in the transferred assets (principal and interest earned to date). Based on that understanding, the Board concluded, as explained in paragraphs 58 and 121 of Statement 125, that those limited powers appeared insufficient to place transferred assets within reach of the receiver and, therefore, assets transferred subject to those powers could be considered isolated from their transferor.

158. In implementing Statement 125, the Board's earlier understanding of the powers of the FDIC, as explained in paragraphs 58 and 121 of Statement 125, was called into question. During 1998, the Board learned the following from attorneys specializing in FDIC matters and from members of the FDIC staff:

a. The FDIC's practice in repudiating contracts has most often been to pay principal and interest *to date of payment,* unless the assets have been fraudulently conveyed or conveyed to an affiliate under improper circumstances. However, the FDIC has the power to repudiate contracts that it characterizes as secured borrowings and, thereby, reclaim transferred assets by paying principal and interest *to the date of receivership,* which may be as many as 180 days before the date of payment.

b. Relevant statutes require, in the case of certain repurchase agreements and similar contracts characterized as *qualified financial contracts,* that the FDIC pay all reasonably expected damages to repudiate those contracts. Therefore, the FDIC has to pay at least principal and interest to *date of payment* on those contracts.

c. Attorneys generally have been unable to provide opinions sufficient to satisfy preparers and auditors that many kinds of transfers of financial assets by financial institutions subject to the powers of the FDIC have isolated those assets. It is unclear in which circumstances attorneys might be able to provide such opinions for certain other transfers of financial assets by those institutions.

159. Based on that new information, the Board decided that this issue required reconsideration. The Board considered whether the FDIC's powers to reclaim transferred assets by paying principal and interest to date of receivership were still limited enough that transferred assets potentially subject to those powers could be considered isolated. The Board rejected the possibility of modifying the observations in paragraphs 58 and 121 of Statement 125 to indicate that a receiver's right to reclaim transferred assets by paying principal and interest *to date of receivership* does not preclude sale accounting because that would selectively weaken the standard of isolation and impair comparability across industries. Instead, the Board decided that any discussion about the FDIC's powers should simply reiterate, perhaps more clearly, that transferred financial assets subject to the limited power of a receiver to reclaim them could be considered isolated only if the receiver would have to pay at least principal and interest *to date of payment.*

160. After that decision, representatives of the FDIC, the Auditing Standards Board of the AICPA, banks, and the securities bar discussed what actions, if any, the FDIC could take that would alleviate those legal, auditing, and accounting difficulties. In July 2000, the FDIC adopted, after public comment and other due process, a final rule, *Treatment by the Federal Deposit Insurance Corporation as Conservator or Receiver of Financial Assets Transferred by an Insured Depository Institution in Connection with a Securitization or Participation.* That final rule modifies the FDIC's powers so that, subject to certain conditions, it shall not recover, reclaim, or recharacterize as property of the institution or the re-

ceivership any financial assets transferred by an insured depository institution in connection with a securitization or participation. The final rule also states that the FDIC may repeal or amend that final rule but that any such repeal or amendment would not apply to any transfers of financial assets made in connection with a securitization or participation that was in effect before such repeal or amendment. In view of that final rule and after consultation with other affected parties, the Board concluded that specific guidance about the effect of the FDIC's powers as receiver on the isolation of transferred assets would no longer be needed. Therefore, this Statement removes that specific guidance.

Transferee's Rights to Pledge or Exchange

161. The second criterion (paragraph 9(b)) for a transfer to be a sale focuses on whether the transferee has the right to pledge or exchange the transferred assets. That criterion is consistent with the idea that the entity that has an asset is the one that can use it in the various ways set forth in Concepts Statement 6, paragraph 184 (quoted in paragraph 143 of this Statement). A transferee may be able to use a transferred asset in some of those ways but not in others. Therefore, establishing criteria for determining whether control has been relinquished to a transferee necessarily depends in part on identifying which ways of using the kind of asset transferred are the decisive ones. In the case of transfers of financial assets, the transferee holds the assets, but that is not necessarily decisive because the economic benefits of financial assets consist primarily of future cash inflows. The Board concluded that the ways of using assets that are important in determining whether a transferee holding a financial asset controls it are the ability to exchange it or pledge it as collateral and thus obtain all or most of the cash inflows that are the primary economic benefits of financial assets. As discussed in paragraph 173, if the transferee is a qualifying SPE, the ultimate holders of the assets are the beneficial interest holders (BIHs), and the important rights concern their ability to exchange or pledge their interests.

162. The Exposure Draft of Statement 125 proposed that a transferee be required to have the right—free of transferor-imposed conditions—to pledge or exchange the transferred assets for a transfer to qualify as a sale. Respondents to the Exposure Draft observed that some transferor-imposed conditions may not indicate that the transferor retains control over the assets transferred. The respondents suggested that

some conditions are imposed for business or competitive purposes, not to keep control over future economic benefits of the transferred assets, and that those conditions should not preclude a transfer from being accounted for as a sale. Other respondents noted that not all conditions that might limit a transferee's ability to take advantage of a right to pledge or exchange transferred assets were necessarily imposed by the transferor. The Board decided that the criterion should not be restricted to being transferor imposed and that some conditions, described in paragraph 25 of Statement 125, should not disqualify a transaction, so long as those conditions do not constrain the transferee from taking advantage of its right to pledge or exchange the transferred assets.

163. In implementing Statement 125, two issues emerged relating to its second criterion for recognizing a transfer of financial assets as a sale (paragraph 9(b)(1) of Statement 125). The first issue was what types of constraints on the transferee's right to pledge or exchange transferred assets preclude sale accounting. The second issue was whether a transferee must obtain *either* the right to pledge transferred assets *or* the right to exchange them or whether a transferee must obtain *both* rights for the transfer to qualify for sale accounting.

164. The Board questioned whether sale accounting should be precluded because of a constraint on the transferee's ability to sell or pledge that does not benefit the transferor. The Board concluded that unless the constraint provides more than a trivial benefit to the transferor, it does not affect whether the transferor has surrendered control and, therefore, there is little reason for the transferor to continue recognizing the transferred asset. Consequently, such constraints should not preclude sale accounting.

165. Whether a constraint is of more than trivial benefit to the transferor may not always be clear. The Board reasoned that transferors incur costs if they impose constraints, since transferees presumably pay less than they would pay to obtain the asset without constraint. Transferors presumably incur those costs for good reasons. The Board therefore concluded that, absent evidence to the contrary, imposition of a constraint by a transferor results in a more than trivial benefit to the transferor.

166. However, it is not so clear whether conditions not imposed by the transferor constrain the transferee *and* benefit the transferor. The Board considered four possibilities. First, Statement 125 could have been

left unchanged, and therefore it would have continued to preclude sale accounting if any condition constrained the transferee, even if the transferor did not somehow benefit. The Board rejected that first possibility because transferred assets from which the transferor can obtain no further benefits are no longer its assets and should be removed from its statement of financial position. Second, the Board could have returned to the provisions proposed in the Exposure Draft of Statement 125, under which conditions not imposed by the transferor that constrain the transferee have no effect on the accounting. The Board rejected that second possibility because it would have excluded from the transferor's statement of financial position some assets from which, through the constraint, it still can obtain future benefits. Third, the Board could have precluded sale accounting for conditions not imposed by the transferor that constrain the transferee, unless the transferor has no continuing involvement with the transferred assets. The Board rejected that third possibility, even though it avoided the problems of the first two possibilities, because it seemed in conflict with the financial-components approach and would have required resolving numerous issues including whether some types of continuing involvement are so minor that they should not preclude sale accounting. The fourth possibility, which the Board adopted because it avoided the problems of the other three possibilities, was to preclude sale accounting for conditions not imposed by the transferor that constrain the transferee only if the constraint is known to the transferor and it is evident that the transferor, directly or indirectly, obtains a more than trivial benefit from those constraints. While some respondents to the Exposure Draft for this Statement raised issues about the difficulty in making judgments about whether a transferor is aware of a constraint and whether a benefit to the transferor is more than trivial, the Board concluded that the fourth possibility is nonetheless the best of the alternatives and reaffirmed that conclusion.

167. As discussed in paragraphs 32 and 33, assessing whether an option to reacquire a transferred asset constrains a transferee's apparent right to pledge or exchange transferred assets requires judgment. Despite the challenges of making such judgments in practice, the Board concluded that some options do constrain a transferee and benefit a transferor so that a transferor remained in control, and others do not. Whether they do or do not can only be assessed after considering all the relevant facts and circumstances. The Board reasoned that if, for example, a call option is sufficiently deep-in-the-money, the transferee

would be more likely to have to hold the assets to comply with a potential exercise of the call. Conversely, even though it technically conveys no right to a transferor, a put option written by the transferor to the transferee on assets not readily obtainable elsewhere might constrain a transferee if, for example, it is sufficiently deep-in-the-money that it would be imprudent for the transferee to sell the assets for the market price rather than holding it to get the much higher put price from the transferor. The Board concluded that that assessment of whether an option constrains a transferee need only be made at the date of transfer because it was impractical to require that the transferor reevaluate the written call or put option after the transfer date, and if prices changed sufficiently that a call that did not initially constrain the transferee subsequently went into-the-money, it might not matter because the transferee might already have sold the transferred assets.

168. Paragraph 9(b)(1) of Statement 125 established a criterion that, for sale treatment, the transferee be able to pledge *or* exchange the transferred assets. Some constituents found that criterion ambiguous for (a) certain transfers after which transferees have the right to pledge the transferred assets but not to exchange them and (b) other transfers after which the transferees are permitted to exchange transferred assets but not to pledge them. Some constituents contended that because the implementation guidance in paragraph 25 of Statement 125 included no mention of pledging in its examples of when a transferee is constrained, the Board must have meant that the test of paragraph 9(b)(1) could be failed exclusively by lack of the unconstrained right to exchange the asset, implying that the transferee must have both the right to pledge and the right to exchange to qualify for sale treatment under that criterion. The Board intended that the *or* in that test should be inclusive, indicating in paragraph 122 of Statement 125 (and carried forward in paragraph 161 of this Statement) that the ability to obtain all or most of the cash inflows that are the primary economic benefits of a financial asset, whether by exchanging it or pledging it as collateral, is what is important in determining whether a transferee controls a financial asset.

169. The Board revisited the "exchange *or* pledge" question and again in developing this Statement concluded that the criterion in paragraph 9(b) is inclusive: it is the ability to obtain all or most of the cash inflows, *either* by exchanging the transferred asset *or* by pledging it as collateral. The Board was concerned that requiring both the ability to pledge

and the ability to exchange would, for example, permit some transferors to opt out of sale accounting by simply adding a prohibition—unimportant to that transferee—against pledging the asset.

Settlement Date and Trade Date Accounting

170. Many transfers of financial assets have been recognized at the settlement date. During its redeliberations of Statement 125, the Board discussed the implications of that Statement on trade date accounting for certain securities transactions and concluded that Statement 125 did not set out to address that issue. Therefore, the Board decided that Statement 125 should not modify generally accepted accounting principles, including FASB Statement No. 35, *Accounting and Reporting by Defined Benefit Pension Plans,* and AICPA Statements of Position and audit and accounting Guides for certain industries, that require accounting at the trade date for certain contracts to purchase or sell securities. That decision is carried forward without reconsideration in this Statement.

Transfers to Qualifying SPEs, including Securitizations

171. Many transfers of financial assets are to qualifying SPEs of the type described in paragraph 26 of Statement 125 (paragraph 35 of this Statement). After those transfers, the qualifying SPE holds legal title to the transferred assets but does not have the right to pledge or exchange the transferred assets free of constraints. Rather, the activities of the qualifying SPE are limited to carrying out the provisions of the legal documents that established it. One significant purpose of those limitations on activities often is to make remote the possibility that a qualifying SPE could enter bankruptcy or other receivership, even if the transferor were to enter receivership.

172. Some commentators asked whether the qualifying SPE criteria apply to entities formed for purposes other than transfers of financial assets. The Board decided that the description of a qualifying SPE in paragraph 26 of Statement 125 should be restrictive. Transfers to entities that meet all of the conditions in paragraph 26 of Statement 125 may qualify for sale accounting under paragraph 9 of Statement 125. Other entities with some similar characteristics also might be broadly described as "special-purpose." For example, an entity might be formed for the purpose of holding specific nonfinancial assets and liabilities or carrying on particular commercial activities. The Board decided that those entities are

not qualifying SPEs under Statement 125 nor under this Statement and that the accounting for transfers of financial assets to SPEs should not be extended to transfers to any entity that does not satisfy all of the conditions in paragraph 26 of Statement 125 (paragraph 35 of this Statement).

173. Qualifying SPEs issue beneficial interests of various kinds—variously characterized as debt, participations, residual interests, and otherwise—as required by the provisions of those agreements. Holders of beneficial interests in the qualifying SPE have the right to pledge or exchange those interests but do not control the individual assets held by the qualifying SPE. The effect of establishing the qualifying SPE is to merge the contractual rights in the transferred assets and to allocate undivided interests in them—the beneficial interests. Therefore, the right of holders to pledge or exchange those beneficial interests is the counterpart of the right of a transferee to pledge or exchange the transferred assets themselves.

174. Sometimes financial assets, especially mortgage loans, are securitized and the transferor retains all of the beneficial interests in the qualifying SPE as securities. The objective is to increase financial flexibility because securities are more liquid and can more readily be sold or pledged as collateral to secure borrowings. In some cases, securitization may reduce regulatory capital requirements. The Board concluded that transfers of financial assets to a qualifying SPE, including securitizations, should qualify as sales only to the extent that consideration other than beneficial interests in the transferred assets is received.

The Conditions for a Qualifying SPE

175. One condition for sale accounting in Statement 125 was that the transferee must obtain "the right—free of conditions that constrain it from taking advantage of that right . . .—to pledge or exchange the transferred assets" (Statement 125, paragraph 9(b)(1)). In developing that criterion, the Board reasoned that the transferee's ability to control the transferred financial assets provides strong evidence that the transferor has surrendered control. However, one principal objective of Statement 125 was to address the accounting for securitization transactions; the Board recognized that often the transferee in a securitization is a trust, corporation, or other legal vehicle (an SPE) that can engage in only limited activities and, therefore, is typically constrained from pledging or exchanging the transferred asset. The

Board decided that some transfers to SPEs should qualify for sale accounting and, therefore, developed in Statement 125 the idea of a qualifying SPE.

176. Under Statement 125, a trust, corporation, or other legal vehicle that has a standing at law distinct from the transferor and whose activities are permanently limited by the legal documents establishing it to those identified in paragraph 26 of Statement 125 (and reconsidered in this Statement in paragraph 35) is a qualifying SPE. The Board observed that "the effect of establishing the qualifying special-purpose entity is to merge the contractual rights in the transferred assets and to allocate undivided interests in them—the beneficial interests" (Statement 125, paragraph 127). The Board reached that conclusion in part because a qualifying SPE "does not have the right to pledge or exchange the transferred assets" (paragraph 125 of Statement 125, reconsidered in this Statement in paragraph 171), a right that would involve its acting as an operating entity. Therefore, the Board observed that if the transferee is a qualifying SPE, the assets are legally owned by the trustee on behalf of those parties having a beneficial interest in the assets, and the right of those BIHs to pledge or exchange their beneficial interests is the counterpart of the right of an ordinary transferee (for example, an entity other than a qualifying SPE) to pledge or exchange the transferred assets themselves.

177. When Statement 125 was issued, the Board's understanding was that the activities of most SPEs used in securitization transactions were limited to those identified in paragraph 26 of Statement 125. After Statement 125 was issued, commentators expressed concern that many SPEs that are transferees in securitization transactions have more and different powers than those described in that paragraph.

178. In response to that concern, the FASB staff developed an announcement issued as EITF Topic No. D-66, "Effect of a Special-Purpose Entity's Powers to Sell, Exchange, Repledge, or Distribute Transferred Financial Assets under FASB Statement No. 125," in January 1998. While the FASB staff was developing that announcement, it became apparent that some SPEs engage in activities such as selling transferred assets and refinancing or reselling the rights to transferred financial assets. While the Board did not object to the issuance of Topic D-66 as an interim step, the Board recognized that it raised significant issues that warranted consideration as part of its project to amend Statement 125.

179. In 1998 and 1999, the Board reconsidered how it could better distinguish between qualifying SPEs,

transfers to which fell under paragraph 9(b)(2) of Statement 125, and other entities, transfers to which fell under paragraph 9(b)(1) of Statement 125. The Board reviewed the various powers held and activities engaged in by SPEs whose primary purpose is limited to passively holding financial assets on behalf of BIHs in those assets. The Board concluded that some powers and activities are appropriate or even necessary to support that primary purpose, while other powers and activities are unnecessary or even inappropriate for that purpose. The Board developed a revised notion of *qualifying SPE* based on that conclusion. The Board identified four conditions necessary for an SPE to be a qualifying SPE under this Statement. Those conditions must be present in order for it to be appropriate to look through the qualifying SPE to the BIHs and their ability to pledge or exchange their interests to determine sale accounting.

Need to be demonstrably distinct from the transferor

180. The first condition is that a qualifying SPE must be demonstrably distinct from the transferor. One of the original conditions for being a qualifying SPE in Statement 125, carried over in the Exposure Draft for this Statement, required a qualifying SPE to have distinct standing at law. Commentators urged the Board to replace that notion with the requirement that the transferor not be able to unilaterally dissolve an SPE as a condition for qualifying status. Those commentators argued that (a) *distinct standing at law* does not seem to have a uniform meaning that could be an acceptable basis upon which to build a standard, (b) distinct standing at law is possible without a third-party investor and could be achieved in some cases by simply pledging collateral, (c) a standard that enables accountants to determine, through analyzing the provisions of a trust agreement, whether or not the termination and dissolution of the trust are within the control of the transferor would be preferable, and (d) attorneys cannot opine on the concept of "distinct standing at law" by using case law or legal references because it is not an established legal concept. In lieu of *distinct standing at law,* some commentators suggested that the Board develop a notion based on the premise that no accounting recognition should be given to a transaction with an SPE unless a third party is involved. A number of constituents went further to suggest that there be some minimum level of outside beneficial interests.

181. The Board considered those suggestions and concluded that requiring that a qualifying SPE have a minimum level of outside beneficial interests is a useful concept. The Board reasoned that a required minimum outside beneficial interest is consistent with the idea that an ownership interest has been transferred and gave substance to the qualifying SPE's limitations in that another party is relying on those limitations. But to be operational, it was necessary to determine the minimum percentage of outside beneficial interests. After considering the characteristics of common securitization SPEs, the Board chose not to set a high minimum percentage, in part because, while most common securitization SPEs have outside interests in excess of two-thirds much of the time, they do not maintain that level during ramp-up and wind-down phases or, in some cases, during seasonal variations in the levels of assets in the trust. The Board concluded that its objective in requiring a minimum outside beneficial interest is to establish that the qualifying SPE is demonstrably distinct from the transferor. The Board decided that if at least 10 percent of the interests in the transferred assets (or 10 percent of the interests in a series in the master trust) were currently held by third parties and if the transferor could not unilaterally dissolve the SPE, that is sufficient evidence to demonstrate that the SPE is demonstrably distinct from the transferor, its affiliates, or its agents. The Board settled on the 10 percent level, not because it was grounded in any particular literature, but because it appeared sufficient to demonstrate that the transferee is distinct from the transferor.

182. In connection with its discussion of minimum outside beneficial interest, the Board was asked whether a guarantee, if it is the only outside beneficial interest and worth less than 10 percent of the total value of the securitization, was sufficient to demonstrate that an SPE was distinct from the transferor. Some commentators mentioned "swap-and-hold" securitizations, in which the transferor takes back and retains all the mortgage-backed securities. The Board decided to make an exception to the 10 percent minimum for what this Statement refers to as a *guaranteed mortgage securitization,* a securitization of mortgage loans that is within the scope of FASB Statement No. 65, *Accounting for Certain Mortgage Banking Activities,* as amended, and includes a substantive guarantee by a third party. While a substantive guarantee by a third party clearly can have significant impact on the value and liquidity of the interests retained in guaranteed mortgage securitizations, which is consistent with the conclusion that the SPE is demonstrably distinct from the transferor, that impact is not the primary reason for

Accounting for Transfers and Servicing of
Financial Assets and Extinguishments of Liabilities
FAS140

this exception. Instead, the Board made that exception primarily in view of the long history of specialized accounting for mortgage banking activities, including its recent reconsideration of the measurement of retained mortgage-backed securities in FASB Statement No. 134, *Accounting for Mortgage-Backed Securities Retained after the Securitization of Mortgage Loans Held for Sale by a Mortgage Banking Enterprise.*

183. The Board considered extending that exception to other kinds of securitizations, for example, securitizations using nonqualifying SPEs or securitizations of assets that do not arise from mortgage banking activities, but decided that that exception should not be extended, even by analogy in practice. That resolves an issue that was the subject of proposed FASB Technical Bulletin 99-a, *Classification and Measurement of Financial Assets Securitized Using a Special-Purpose Entity,* issued for comment on August 11, 1999, but not issued in final form.

Limits on permitted activities

184. The second condition is that the permitted activities of a qualifying SPE are significantly limited, were entirely specified in the legal documents that established the SPE or that created the beneficial interests in the transferred assets that it holds, and may be significantly changed only with the approval of at least a majority of the beneficial interests held by entities other than the transferor, its affiliates, or its agents. In Statement 125, the Board required that a qualifying SPE's powers be permanently limited, in part so that a transferor could not treat as sold assets it had seemingly relinquished if it could still control them by changing the SPE's rules specifying required or permitted activities. However, the Board later learned that limitations on entities in certain forms, including many corporation or partnership forms sometimes used for SPEs, cannot be permanent. Rather than effectively precluding sale treatment for transfers to such SPEs, the Board instead chose to modify this condition to allow for the impermanence of limitations but still limit the ability of the transferor to modify the structure. Consequently, the second condition allows changes to the structure only with the approval of a majority of third-party BIHs that, presumably, would be reluctant to make changes that would adversely affect their interests.

Limits on the assets it can hold

185. The third condition is that a qualifying SPE must be limited as to the assets it can hold. That is in keeping with the Board's view that a qualifying SPE is not an ordinary business but rather a vehicle for indirect ownership by the BIHs of the assets held by the qualifying SPE. The principal type of assets that a qualifying SPE can hold are financial assets transferred to it. The Board concluded that it would be inconsistent with a qualifying SPE's limited purpose for it to actively purchase its principal assets in the marketplace; instead, the SPE should passively accept those assets transferred to it. The Board also concluded that it would be inconsistent for a qualifying SPE to hold assets that are not passive, because holding nonpassive assets involves making decisions and decision-making is not consistent with the notion of only having passive custody of assets for the benefit of BIHs. Thus, the Board did not allow a qualifying SPE to hold investments large enough either in themselves or in combination with other investments to enable it or any related entity to exercise control or significant influence over an investee. For the same reasons, the Board did not allow a qualifying SPE to hold equity securities that have voting rights attached unless the SPE has no ability to exercise the voting rights or choose how to vote.

186. The Exposure Draft of this Statement proposed that in addition to financial assets transferred to it, a qualifying SPE be permitted to hold five other types of assets: (a) derivative instruments entered into at the same time that financial assets were transferred to the SPE or beneficial interests (other than derivatives) were created, (b) rights to service its financial assets, (c) financial assets that would reimburse it if others were to fail to adequately service its financial assets or to timely pay obligations due on those financial assets, (d) temporarily, nonfinancial assets received in connection with collection of its financial assets, and (e) cash collected from its financial instruments and certain investments purchased with that cash pending distribution. Constituents pointed out that SPEs used in securitizations were commonly permitted to hold those types of assets. The Board decided to permit a qualifying SPE to hold those types of assets because they are inherent in financial assets, are necessary in connection with fiduciary responsibilities to BIHs, or are held only temporarily as a result of collecting or attempting to collect some of the financial assets the qualifying SPE previously held. The Board decided that only those types of assets can be held because holding other types of assets is inconsistent with the qualifying SPE's principal purpose of passively conveying indirect ownership of transferred financial assets to BIHs.

187. The concerns of respondents to the Exposure Draft of this Statement as to the types of assets that a qualifying SPE can hold focused on the proposed limitations on derivative instruments. Specifically, respondents were concerned whether allowing a qualifying SPE to enter into a derivative instrument avoids accounting requirements under FASB Statement No. 133, *Accounting for Derivative Instruments and Hedging Activities,* and whether a large derivative, instrument could be put into or entered into by a qualifying SPE that held only a small amount of other financial assets. They also were concerned that some derivative instruments require too many decision-making abilities to be held by a qualifying SPE. The Board decided to limit the notional amount of derivative instruments that a qualifying SPE could enter into. The Board decided that the limit should comprehend only derivative instruments that pertain to outside beneficial interests—those issued by the qualifying SPE to parties other than the transferor, its affiliates, or its agents or sold to such other parties after being issued by the qualifying SPE to the transferor, its affiliates, or its agents. The Board noted that if the transferor wanted to enter into derivative instruments pertaining to the beneficial interests it holds, it could accomplish that by entering into such derivative instruments on its own behalf, which would be accounted for under Statement 133.

188. Several other issues arose concerning derivative instruments in qualifying SPEs. The Board considered requiring that the derivative instruments qualify as a fair value or cash flow hedge of the qualifying SPE's assets or beneficial interests under Statement 133. The Board rejected that approach after considering the various purposes for which securitizations and other qualifying SPE activities are formed. The Board, however, still wanted to ensure that the derivative instrument *pertains* to outside beneficial interests. Therefore, the Board decided that for a qualifying SPE, a derivative instrument should have a notional amount not exceeding the amount of those beneficial interests. Because leverage can make a derivative instrument more powerful than its notional amount indicates, the Board decided that a derivative instrument should have characteristics that relate to and partly or fully (but not excessively) counteract some risk associated with those beneficial interests or the related transferred assets. The Board also decided, consistent with its decisions on equity instruments, that qualifying SPEs should hold only

derivative instruments that do not require active decisions. The Board further decided, in keeping with limiting qualifying SPEs to holding financial assets, that the only derivative instruments they can hold are those that are financial instruments—*derivative financial instruments.*

Limits on sales or other dispositions of assets

189. The fourth condition is that if a qualifying SPE has powers to sell or otherwise dispose of[25] its assets those powers must be limited in specified ways. After considering what the FASB staff had learned in developing its announcement on Topic D-66, the Board concluded, in contrast to its conclusion in Statement 125, that a qualifying SPE should not be entirely prohibited from disposing of assets. The Board considered that, in many securitizations, the trustee or management of the SPE (under fiduciary duties to protect the interests of *all* parties to the structure) is required to dispose of assets in response to adverse events specified in the legal documents that established the SPE or created its beneficial interests in the transferred assets, that are outside the control of the transferor, its affiliates, or its agents. Also, in some securitizations, the SPE is required to dispose of assets, if necessary, to repurchase or redeem beneficial interests at the option of BIHs other than the transferor and its affiliates. In other securitizations, the transferor has the right to remove assets from the SPE under ROAPs or call provisions (discussed further in paragraphs 231–236). And in some securitizations, the SPE is required to liquidate itself or otherwise dispose of its assets on a date set at inception. The Board reasoned that in all four of those situations, the disposal is forced on the SPE. That is, in none of those situations does the SPE or its agents have the power to choose whether the SPE disposes of specific assets or when that disposal occurs. The Board therefore concluded that a qualifying SPE's powers to dispose of assets should be limited to those four narrowly defined circumstances. Constituents generally supported allowing disposal of assets in those circumstances, although some suggested that disposal of transferred assets also be allowed in response to a specified adverse event, without having to wait for it to cause a specified decline in fair value, if it is the type of event that would reasonably be expected at the outset to cause such a decline and that event is identified in the documents establishing the SPE. The Board adopted that suggestion.

---

[25]The term *dispose of* is used to collectively refer to the SPE's ability to sell, exchange, put, or distribute its assets.

190. The Board reasoned that an SPE that has the power to choose whether to dispose of its assets, even in limited circumstances, has much of the same ability to manage its assets as an ordinary entity. In those situations, the Board concluded that the SPE is not simply acting like a custodian, passively holding assets on behalf of the BIHs, and consequently it should not be a qualifying SPE. Some constituents argued that a qualifying SPE or its servicer should be allowed to exercise at least what constituents termed a *commercially reasonable and customary amount of discretion* in deciding whether to dispose of assets in the specified circumstances. Some constituents argued that allowing a qualifying SPE only to have provisions that require disposal without choice raises the risks of forcing a disposal at a bad time or that allowing no discretion conflicts with the fiduciary duties of the SPE's trustee or servicer. The Board acknowledged the concerns that underlie those views but did not change that provision, reasoning that a qualifying SPE with that flexibility should not be considered to be a passive conduit through which its BIHs own portions of its assets, as opposed to owning shares or obligations in an ordinary business enterprise.

191. The Board considered but rejected a general condition that would permit a qualifying SPE to sell assets as long as the sales were made "to avoid losses." Such a condition would have allowed an SPE to have powers to sell as long as the primary objective was not to realize gains or maximize return, a concept introduced in Topic D-66. The Board rejected it because it would have given the trustee, servicer, or transferor considerable discretion in choosing whether or not the SPE should sell if a loss was threatened. Such discretion is more in keeping with being an ordinary business that manages its own assets than with being a passive repository of assets on behalf of others. The Board did, however, choose to retain some notion of selling to avoid losses in paragraph 42 of this Statement. That paragraph describes circumstances specified at the inception of the qualifying SPE in which the qualifying SPE is required to sell transferred assets that have declined (or are expected to decline) below their fair value at the date of transfer into the qualifying SPE. The Board also considered but rejected requiring that a qualifying SPE derive no more than an insignificant value from collecting or otherwise preserving the assets it holds. The Board reasoned that while some financial assets need more servicing efforts than do others, the amount of effort expended in servicing an asset does not justify different accounting.

Securitizations with Revolving-Period Features

192. As noted in paragraph 74, in some securitizations, short-term receivables are transferred to an SPE, and the SPE then issues long-term beneficial interests. Collections from transferred receivables are used to purchase additional receivables during a defined period called the revolving period. Thereafter, the collections are used to redeem beneficial interests in due course. Some have questioned the propriety of sales treatment in those securitizations because much of the cash collected during the revolving period is returned to the transferor. The Board decided that sales treatment is appropriate for transfers with revolving-period features because the transferor surrenders control of the assets transferred. While the revolving-period agreement requires that the transferor sell receivables to the trust in exchange for cash on prearranged terms, sales of additional receivables during the revolving period are separate transactions from the original sale.

193. The transferor in a transfer with a revolving-period agreement, such as a credit card securitization, must sell receivables to the securitization trust on prearranged terms. The transferor can perhaps predict the timing of transfers, but the actual timing depends primarily on borrower behavior. If not bound by that contract, the transferor could sell its new receivables elsewhere, possibly on better terms. The transferor obtains the cash as proceeds in exchange for new receivables transferred under the revolving-period agreement, not as benefits from its previous ownership of the receivables or its residual interest in the securitization trust.

194. The revolving-period agreement is an implicit forward contract, with rights and obligations on both sides. The transferor has little or no discretion to avoid its obligations under the revolving-period agreement and would suffer adverse consequences for failure to deliver receivables to the trust during the revolving period. For example, if the transferor were to take deliberate actions to avoid its obligations to sell receivables by triggering the agreement's "early amortization" provisions, the transferor would be exposed to litigation for not honoring its commitment. The transferor also could suffer if it later tried to sell its receivables in the securitization market: the transferor would probably have to offer wary investors a higher return. Deliberate early termination by the transferor is rare in practice because of those adverse consequences. Similarly, the securitization trust and investors cannot avoid the obligation to purchase

additional receivables. For those reasons, the revolving-period agreement does not provide control over receivables previously sold but rather is an implicit forward contract for future sales of receivables.

195. Some respondents to the Exposure Draft of Statement 125 proposed that existing revolving-period securitizations should continue to apply previous accounting standards for all transfers into an existing trust after the effective date of Statement 125. Several respondents asked about the effect of the provisions of Statement 125 on transfers into a master trust that is used for a series of securitizations. They pointed out that it would be difficult to change the present structure of those trusts in response to new accounting standards. Others observed that because master trusts have very long or indefinite lives, "grandfathering" transfers to existing trusts would result in noncomparable financial statements for a long time to come. After considering those arguments, the Board decided to retain the proposed requirement that Statement 125 apply to all transfers of assets after its effective date, in order to minimize the noncomparability caused by the transition. For similar reasons, the Board adopted the same requirement in this Statement. (Paragraph 341 discusses transition provisions relating to qualifying SPEs that would no longer qualify under current guidance in this Statement.) Separately, in response to constituents' questions, the Board also clarified in paragraph 79 that a transfer into a master trust in exchange for beneficial interests is neither a sale nor a secured borrowing under the provisions of paragraph 9.

Qualifying SPEs and Consolidated Financial Statements

196. Statement 125 did not address whether a transferor should consolidate a qualifying SPE. In that Statement, the Board acknowledged that consolidation of SPEs was an issue that merited further consideration and that it would deliberate that issue in its current project on consolidated financial statements. Because the Board had not yet issued a new Statement on consolidation policy,[26] constituents were concerned about whether assets sold to a qualifying SPE might still be shown in the consolidated financial statements of the transferor and requested additional guidance on that issue. In September 1996, the EITF discussed Issue No. 96-20, "Impact of FASB Statement No. 125 on Consolidation of Special-

Purpose Entities." The EITF reached a consensus that the Statement 125 definition of control should be applied in assessing whether an SPE should be consolidated, but only if all assets in the qualifying SPE are financial assets and are not the result of a structured transaction that has the effect of converting nonfinancial assets into financial assets or recognizing previously unrecognized financial assets. In all other circumstances, the EITF stated that the transferor should continue to apply the criteria of EITF Topic No. D-14, "Transactions involving Special-Purpose Entities," and EITF Issue No. 90-15, "Impact of Nonsubstantive Lessors, Residual Value Guarantees, and Other Provisions in Leasing Transactions," as appropriate. The Board indicated at that time that it planned to include further guidance on consolidating qualifying SPEs either in the Statement on consolidation policy or in this Statement.

197. The Board considered resolving the qualifying SPE consolidation issue by making an exception to present and perhaps future consolidation standards to exempt from ordinary consolidation policies entities whose assets are all or almost all financial assets. That exception arguably could be justified because financial assets are different from other assets and entities that hold little else should be treated differently. While that alternative would have resolved the immediate issue, the Board rejected it because it would have prejudged a significant issue in the separate project on consolidation policy, without having sufficiently examined the ramifications of an exception to consolidation.

198. Instead, the Board reasoned that the event that warrants derecognition of assets transferred to a qualifying SPE is the issuance of beneficial interests in the transferred assets to third-party BIHs in exchange for cash or other assets. That reasoning is consistent with paragraphs 9 and 79 of this Statement (paragraphs 9 and 53 of Statement 125). Paragraph 9 states that "a transfer of financial assets . . . in which the transferor surrenders control over those financial assets shall be accounted for as a sale *to the extent that consideration other than beneficial interests in the transferred assets* is received in exchange" (emphasis added). Paragraph 79 states that "adding receivables to a master trust, in itself, is neither a sale nor a secured borrowing under paragraph 9, because that transfer only increases the transferor's beneficial

---

[26]An Exposure Draft, *Consolidated Financial Statements: Purpose and Policy,* was issued in February 1999, with a comment period that ended May 24, 1999. That Exposure Draft has not yet resulted in a final Statement.

interest in the trust's assets. A sale or secured borrowing does not occur *until the transferor receives consideration other than beneficial interests in the transferred assets*" (emphasis added). Once beneficial interests are issued to BIHs other than the transferor or its affiliates in exchange for consideration, the economic benefits of all the assets held in a qualifying SPE are divided among and controlled by the BIHs, not by the transferor whose assets they once were and not by the qualifying SPE or the trustee that may be the legal owner. Once the assets are legally isolated and beneficial interests in those assets are issued, the qualifying SPE is in the position of a custodian holding the underlying assets for the BIHs. Assets held in a qualifying SPE are therefore effectively the assets of its BIHs. Accordingly, the Board proposed in the Exposure Draft of this Statement that assets sold to a qualifying SPE should not be recognized as assets and that related beneficial interests should not be recognized as liabilities in consolidated or other financial statements of a transferor, servicer, or sponsor of the SPE.

199. Constituents urged the Board to retain that provision. They argued that it would be unreasonable to grant sale treatment to a transferor for a transfer of assets to a qualifying SPE and issuance of beneficial interests to third-party BIHs, which acknowledges that such assets have been effectively sold to third parties, and then to require that a qualifying SPE be consolidated in the financial statements of the transferor with the sale effectively eliminated in consolidation. The Board accepted that reasoning, in view of the criteria for sale treatment in paragraph 9 and the characteristics of entities that meet the conditions established by this Statement to be qualifying SPEs. However, the Board concluded that this Statement's special guidance for consolidation of qualifying SPEs should focus only on the consolidated financial statements of the transferor and its affiliates because, unless it is an affiliate of the transferor, a servicer, sponsor, agent, or other BIH of a qualifying SPE did not transfer the assets and record a sale. This Statement therefore provides that a qualifying SPE should not be consolidated in the financial statements of a transferor and its affiliates. The Board has tentatively decided that the scope of the planned Statement on consolidation policy will exclude that issue; however, any entity that is not a transferor of assets to a qualifying SPE, or an affiliate of the transferor, needs to consider other existing or future generally accepted accounting principles on consolidation policy to determine whether it is required to consolidate a qualifying SPE in the financial statements being presented.

Arrangements That Arguably Maintain a Transferor's Effective Control over Transferred Assets

Repurchase Agreements and Securities Lending Transactions

200. The Exposure Draft of Statement 125 proposed that transfers of financial assets with repurchase commitments, such as repurchase agreements and securities lending transactions, should qualify as secured borrowings only if the transfer was *assuredly temporary*—the period until repurchase is less than three months or the period is indefinite but the contracts are repriced daily at overnight market rates and can be terminated by either party on short notice. It also proposed that the assets to be repurchased had to be the same (for example, U.S. securities having the same CUSIP number) as those transferred. Respondents generally disagreed with those provisions of the Exposure Draft of Statement 125 about those transactions, and the Board changed the provisions in its redeliberations.

Legal and economic ambiguity of these transactions

201. Repurchase agreements and securities lending transactions are difficult to characterize because those transactions are ambiguous: they have attributes of both sales and secured borrowings. Repurchase agreements typically are documented as sales with forward purchase contracts and generally are treated as sales in bankruptcy law and receivers' procedures, but as borrowings in tax law, under court decisions that cite numerous economic and other factors. Repurchase agreements are commonly characterized by market participants as secured borrowings, even though one reason that repurchase agreements arose is that selling and then buying back securities, rather than borrowing with those securities as collateral, allow many government agencies, banks, and other active participants in the repurchase agreement market to stay "within investment and borrowing parameters that delineate what they may or may not do."[27] Securities loans are commonly documented as loans of securities collateralized by cash or by other securities or

---

[27]Marcia Stigum, *The Repo and Reverse Markets* (Homewood, Ill.: Dow Jones-Irwin, 1989), 313.

by letters of credit, but the "borrowed" securities are invariably sold, free of any conditions, by the "borrowers," to fulfill obligations under short sales or customers' failure to deliver securities they have sold; securities loans are generally treated as sales under U.S. bankruptcy and tax laws (but only as they relate to income distributions).

202. Previous accounting practice generally has treated repurchase agreements as secured borrowings, although "repos-to-maturity" and certain other longer term repurchase agreements have been treated as sales. Previous accounting practice has not recognized some securities lending transactions, because the transactions were executed by an entity's custodian or other agent, and has treated others as secured borrowings. Supporting arguments exist for accounting for both kinds of transactions as borrowings, both kinds as sales, or some as borrowings and others as sales.

203. The American Law Institute[28] describes the legal status of a securities lending transaction as follows:

> The securities lender does not retain any property interest in the securities that are delivered to the borrower. The transaction is an outright transfer in which the borrower obtains full title . . . the borrower needs the securities to transfer them to someone else . . . if the securities borrower defaults on its redelivery obligation, the securities lender has no property interest in the original securities that could be asserted against any person to whom the securities borrower may have transferred them. . . . The securities lender's protection is its right to foreclose on the collateral given to secure the borrower's redelivery obligation. Perhaps the best way to understand securities lending is to note that the word "loan" in securities lending transactions is used in the sense it carries in loans of money, as distinguished from loans of specific identifiable chattels. Someone who lends money does not retain any property interest in the money that is handed over to the borrower.

204. While that description focuses on securities lending, much of it appears applicable to repurchase agreements as well. If judged by the criteria in paragraphs 9(a) and 9(b) and the legal reasoning in paragraph 203, financial assets transferred under typical repurchase or securities lending agreements would qualify for derecognition as having been sold for proceeds consisting of cash and a forward purchase contract. During the term of the agreement, the transferred assets are isolated from the transferor, are placed in the hands of a transferee that can—and typically does—obtain their benefits by selling or pledging them, and are readily obtainable in the market.

205. The Board considered requiring sales treatment for all of those transactions. The Board also considered an approach that would have recognized the effects of the transaction in the statement of financial position (recognizing the proceeds received as cash or securities and a forward purchase contract) without characterizing the transaction as a sale. The Board ultimately decided, for both conceptual and practical reasons, that secured borrowing treatment should be retained for most of those transactions.

206. In concept, having a forward purchase contract—a right and obligation to buy an asset—is not the same as owning that asset. Dividends or interest on securities are paid by the issuer to the current security holder, that is, to whoever may now hold the securities transferred in the repurchase agreement or loan, while the transferor has at most only the contractual right to receive—from the transferee—payments in lieu of dividends or interest. In addition, the voting rights reside not with the transferor but with the current security holder, because those rights generally cannot be contractually released.

207. However, the commitments entered into in a repurchase or securities lending agreement are more extensive than a common forward purchase contract. The transferor has agreed to repurchase the security, often in as little as a day, at a fixed price that differs from the sale price by an amount that is essentially interest on the cash transferred. The transferor also commonly receives payments in lieu of interest or dividends and has protection of collateral that is valued daily and adjusted frequently for changes in the market value of the transferred asset—collateral that the transferor is entitled to use to purchase replacement securities should the transferee default, even in

---

[28]*Uniform Commercial Code, Revised Article 8, Investment Securities,* Proposed Final Draft (Philadelphia: American Law Institute, 1994), 18 and 19.

the event of bankruptcy or other receivership. Those arrangements are not typical of forward purchase contracts and suggest that having a repurchase agreement or securities lending contract to repurchase a transferred asset before its maturity is much like still owning that asset.

208. Practically, participants in the very large markets for repurchase agreements and securities lending transactions are, for the most part, unaccustomed to treating those transactions as sales, and a change to sale treatment would have a substantial impact on their reported financial position. Given the difficulty in characterizing those ambiguous transactions, the decision to treat all of those transactions as sales would be a close call, and the Board was not convinced that the benefits of a change based on that close call would justify the costs.

209. The Exposure Draft of Statement 125 proposed that transfers of financial assets with repurchase commitments, such as repurchase agreements and securities lending transactions, should be accounted for as secured borrowings if the transfers were assuredly temporary, and as sales if the transfers were not assuredly temporary. As proposed, to be assuredly temporary, the period until repurchase would have had to be short enough not to diminish assurance that the contract and arrangements backing it up would prove effective, that is, with maturities either under three months or indefinite and terminable by either party on short notice. Also, to be assuredly temporary, the entity would have had to be entitled and obligated to repurchase the same assets. After considering comment letters and testimony at the public hearing, the Board decided to change both of those proposed requirements.

The period until repurchase

210. The Exposure Draft of Statement 125 proposed that transfers of financial assets should qualify as borrowings if the period until repurchase is less than three months or the period is indefinite but the contracts are repriced daily at overnight market rates and can be terminated by either party on short notice. A three-month limit was arbitrary, but based on its initial inquiries, the Board tentatively concluded that three months would be a clear and workable time limit that should not present difficulty, because it understood that most repurchase agreements and securities loans are for periods much shorter than three months or are indefinite, and almost all of the others are for periods much longer than three months.

211. Respondents generally disagreed with that provision of the Exposure Draft of Statement 125. They argued that the arbitrary three-month limit would not be effective and that entities could alter the accounting for a transfer by adding or subtracting one or two days to or from the term of the agreement. While some offered other arbitrary time limits, many respondents argued that all transfers accompanied by a forward contract to repurchase the transferred assets before maturity should be accounted for as secured borrowings. In their view, most repurchase agreements represent a temporary transfer of only some elements of control over the transferred assets.

212. After considering those comments, the Board decided to remove the proposed requirement that the period until repurchase be less than three months. Board members concluded that any distinction based on the specified time until repurchase would not be workable. As outlined in paragraph 207, the elements of control by the transferee over assets obtained in a typical securities lending or repurchase agreement are both temporary and limited. The Board concluded that the contractual obligation and right to repurchase an asset before its maturity effectively bind the asset transferred back to the transferor.

213. Some respondents suggested a distinction based on a different time period, or on the proportion of the life of the asset transferred, but the Board rejected those possibilities. Any other time period would have the same faults as the three-month limit proposed in that Exposure Draft: it would be arbitrary, with no meaningful distinction between transactions just on one side of the limit and those just on the other side. Similarly, the Board concluded that the only meaningful distinction based on required repurchase at some proportion of the life of the assets transferred is between a "repo-to-maturity," in which the typical settlement is a net cash payment, and a repurchase before maturity, in which the portion of the asset that remains outstanding is indeed reacquired in an exchange.

Substantially the same assets

214. The Exposure Draft of Statement 125 proposed that a repurchase agreement would have to require return of the same asset (for example, U.S. securities having the same CUSIP number) for the transfer to be treated as a borrowing. In that Exposure Draft, the Board reasoned that agreements to acquire securities that—while perhaps similar—are not the same as those transferred do not maintain any kind of control

over the transferred securities. Most repurchase agreements require return of the same asset. Some are less rigid. For example, some mortgage-backed instruments are transferred in a class of repurchase agreements known as *dollar rolls*. There are several procedural differences between dollar-roll transactions and ordinary repurchase agreements. However, the most significant difference is the agreement that assets returned need not be the same as those transferred. Instead, the transferor agrees to accept back assets with characteristics that are substantially the same within limits established by the market.

215. While a few respondents supported the reasoning in the Exposure Draft of Statement 125, most did not. Respondents argued that the economic differences between the assets initially transferred and assets to be reacquired under a dollar-roll transaction that meets the existing accounting criteria for being substantially the same are, as the term implies, not substantial and should not result in an accounting difference. They argued that existing accounting guidance found in AICPA Statement of Position 90-3, *Definition of the Term Substantially the Same for Holders of Debt Instruments, as Used in Certain Audit Guides and a Statement of Position,* has proven adequate to constrain the characteristics of assets that are to be reacquired. After redeliberation, the Board accepted those arguments and decided that if the assets to be repurchased are the same or substantially the same as those concurrently transferred, the transaction should be accounted for as a secured borrowing. The Board also decided to incorporate the definition in SOP 90-3 in this Statement (carried forward without reconsideration). The Board noted that not all contracts in the dollar-roll market require that the securities involved have all of the characteristics of "substantially the same." If the contract does not require that, the transferor does not maintain effective control.

The importance of the right and obligation to repurchase, collateral, and symmetry

216. The Board based its decisions about agreements that maintain effective control over transferred assets in part on observation of contracts and practices that prevail in the repurchase agreement and securities lending markets. Concerns of market participants about risk of default by the parties to the contract, rights at law in the event of default, and credit risk of transferred assets, among other factors, have led to several contractual features intended to assure that the transferors indeed maintain effective control.

217. The Board decided that to maintain effective control, the transferor must have *both* the contractual right *and* the contractual obligation to reacquire securities that are identical to or substantially the same as those concurrently transferred. Transfers that include only the right to reacquire, at the option of the transferor or upon certain conditions, or only the obligation to reacquire, at the option of the transferee or upon certain conditions, generally do not maintain the transferor's control, because the option might not be exercised or the conditions might not occur. Similarly, expectations of reacquiring the same securities without any contractual commitments, as in "wash sales," provide no control over the transferred securities.

218. The Board also decided that the transferor's right to repurchase is not assured unless it is protected by obtaining collateral sufficient to fund substantially all of the cost of purchasing identical replacement securities during the term of the contract so that it has received the means to replace the assets even if the transferee defaults. Judgment is needed to interpret the term *substantially all* and other aspects of the criterion that the terms of a repurchase agreement do not maintain effective control over the transferred asset. However, arrangements to repurchase or lend readily obtainable securities, typically with as much as 98 percent collateralization (for entities agreeing to repurchase) or as little as 102 percent overcollateralization (for securities lenders), valued daily and adjusted up or down frequently for changes in the market price of the security transferred and with clear powers to use that collateral quickly in the event of default, typically fall clearly within that guideline. The Board believes that other collateral arrangements typically fall well outside that guideline.

219. Some commentators argued for a continuation of previous asymmetrical practices in accounting for dollar rolls. In previous practice, transferors have accounted for dollar-roll agreements as borrowing transactions, while dealers who receive the transferred assets have accounted for them as purchases. The Board observed that the same transaction cannot in concept or simple logic be a borrowing-lending arrangement to the transferor and a purchase-sale transaction to the transferee. The Exposure Draft of Statement 125 would have resolved that asymmetry by

requiring that transferors account for the transactions as sales. In response to commentators' concerns about transferors' accounting, Statement 125 and this Statement instead call for transferors to account for qualifying dollar-roll transactions as secured borrowings and requires that dealers account for the same transactions as secured loans.

Other Arrangements to Reclaim Transferred Assets

220. The Board considered whether to allow sale treatment if a transferor of financial assets concurrently acquires from the transferee a call option on the assets sold. Some questioned under what conditions the transferor that holds a call option has surrendered control of the assets to the transferee. Some believe that an entity that holds an option to acquire a financial asset controls that asset. However, the holder of a call option does not receive interest or dividends generated by the asset, cannot exercise any voting rights inherent in the asset, may not be aware of the location or present custody of the asset, and is not able to sell the asset and deliver it without first exercising the call. And it may never exercise the call. If an entity that holds a call option on an asset controls that asset, then it follows that the entity should recognize the asset under the call option at the time the call option is acquired. However, two parties would then recognize the same asset—the entity that holds the call option and either the writer of the call option or the party from whom the writer plans to acquire the asset if the call is exercised. Therefore, others believe that a call option never conveys effective control over a transferred asset. The Board concluded that whether a transferor maintains effective control over a transferred asset through an option to reacquire it depends on the nature of the asset and the terms of that option.

221. The Board concluded in Statement 125 that sale treatment should not be precluded in instances in which the transferor simultaneously obtains a call option on the asset sold, provided that the asset is readily obtainable. The writer of a call option on a financial asset may choose not to own the asset under the call option if it is readily obtainable; it may instead plan to acquire that asset if the call is exercised and delivery is demanded. In those circumstances, it is realistic to assume that the transferee can sell or repledge the asset to a third party and, at the same time, in good faith write a call option on that asset.

222. The Board concluded in Statement 125 that a sale should not be recognized in instances in which the transferor simultaneously obtains a call on a transferred asset that is not readily obtainable. The resulting accounting treatment of an option on a not-readily-obtainable asset that is obtained as part of a transfer of financial assets is different from the accounting treatment generally accorded to the same option that is purchased for cash. From the transferor's viewpoint, that difference in accounting treatment between an option purchased and an option obtained as part of a transfer of assets conflicts with the principle that the recognition of financial assets and liabilities should not be affected by the sequence of transactions that led to their existence. However, as noted in paragraph 25 of Statement 125, if the option is a component of a transfer of financial assets, and it does not constrain the transferee from selling or repledging the asset, that should not preclude the transfer from being accounted for as a sale. If the existence of an option constrains the transferee from selling or repledging the transferred asset (because the asset is not readily obtainable to satisfy the option if exercised), then the transferor has not relinquished effective control over the asset and thus should not derecognize it.

223. The Board reached a somewhat different conclusion in this Statement. The Board began its work on this Statement by considering the impact of Statement 125 on Issue 90-18. In particular, the concern was whether certain ROAPs maintain the transferor's effective control over the transferred assets through an agreement to repurchase or redeem transferred financial assets that are not readily obtainable and thus preclude sale treatment under paragraph 9(c)(2) of Statement 125. Initial Board discussions focused on the various circumstances under which transferors can remove transferred assets from securitization trusts and on the nature of the assets in question.

224. In those discussions, the Board noted that assets substantially the same as the credit card receivables in a particular securitization trust are readily obtainable only from within the trust itself or from the transferor, arguably indicating that such transfers fail to satisfy the criterion for sale treatment in paragraph 9(c)(2) of Statement 125 and therefore should be accounted for as secured borrowings. In developing this Statement, the Board concluded that after a securitization that isolates assets transferred into a qualifying SPE, the assets being accounted for in a securitization are not the underlying transferred assets but rather the beneficial interests in those assets that were sold to third-party investors or retained by the transferor. Therefore, for qualifying SPEs, the pertinent criterion is whether the transferor has a right

to redeem the beneficial interests that constrain the BIHs from exchanging or pledging those interests, a matter already dealt with in a separate criterion (paragraph 9(b) of this Statement).

225. The Board concluded in this Statement that whether the transferor maintains control over assets transferred to a qualifying SPE does not depend entirely on whether those assets were readily obtainable. Rather, whether the transferor maintains control depends on whether it can unilaterally cause the return of specific transferred assets (for example, an asset with a certain certificate number) held in the qualifying SPE. That led to the criterion in paragraph 9(c) of this Statement, as discussed in paragraphs 231–236.

Rights to repurchase or redeem assets from transferees that are not qualifying SPEs

226. The Board also discussed in developing this Statement whether it should continue to include an explicit criterion, like that in paragraph 9(c)(2) of Statement 125, that would preclude sale treatment for transfers of not-readily-obtainable assets to transferees that are *not* qualifying SPEs if the transferor has the right to repurchase or redeem those assets. Some constituents suggested that transfers in which the transferor has a call provision entitling it to repurchase the transferred assets should not be accounted for as sales, particularly if the assets are not readily obtainable, because the transferor is able to use the call to get back the same assets it transferred or similar assets. Those constituents argue that the transferee's ability or inability to exchange or pledge the assets should not determine whether the transfer is a sale.

227. The Board reviewed its reasoning in Statement 125, paragraph 156, and again concluded that a call provision or other right to repurchase or redeem should preclude sale accounting if (a) the existence of that right constrains the transferee from exchanging or pledging the assets or (b) the rights to reacquire transferred assets result in the transferor's maintaining effective control over the transferred assets. The Board continues to support the fundamental principle of symmetry in Statement 125: for a transfer to be a sale, the transferor must relinquish control and the transferee must be in control, so that the criteria need to look to the position of both parties.

228. The Board reasoned that if the transferee is able, notwithstanding the transferor's right to repurchase or redeem, to pledge or exchange the trans-

ferred assets and thereby obtain substantially all of the cash flows embodied in them, then the transferor's right to repurchase or redeem does not give it effective control over the assets and should not preclude sale accounting, except in the circumstances described in paragraph 9(c) of Statement 125 and this Statement. The Board agreed that a transferee is not constrained if it can subsequently pledge or exchange transferred assets subject to an attached or embedded call, even if the assets are not readily obtainable. The Board also agreed that the transferee is not constrained by a freestanding call if it can redeem or repurchase the assets it has sold or repledged from the subsequent transferee or obtain them elsewhere when the call is exercised. In light of that set of decisions, the Exposure Draft to this Statement concluded that the condition in paragraph 9(c)(2) of Statement 125 should no longer be required because (a) it is redundant for transfers to entities other than qualifying SPEs and (b) it is unnecessary for transfers to qualifying SPEs as discussed in paragraphs 224 and 225.

229. Some respondents to the Exposure Draft of this Statement suggested that the Board reconsider whether a call on not-readily-obtainable assets should preclude sale accounting, expressing particular concern about the accounting for attached calls. They argued that the transferor is in the same economic position and therefore indifferent to whether the call is freestanding or attached, because it can reassume control over the assets in either case. In redeliberations, the Board concluded that a freestanding call leaves both the transferor and the transferee in a different economic position than does an attached call. A freestanding call may constrain the transferee from disposing of a transferred asset, out of concern that it could not be replaced should the transferor exercise its call. If the transferee is constrained, the transferor's control over the asset is maintained because the transferee is not only obligated to deliver the asset but has on hand the very asset that was transferred. However, if the transferee is not constrained by a freestanding call (for example, because the asset is readily obtainable), the call gives the transferor no remaining connection with the transferred asset. The transferor's only asset under a nonconstraining freestanding call is the transferee's promise to find an asset sufficiently like the transferred asset to satisfy the transferor should it exercise its call. In contrast, a call attached to the asset does not constrain the transferee from disposing of the asset, subject to that call, even if the asset is not readily obtainable. However, an attached call maintains the

Accounting for Transfers and Servicing of
Financial Assets and Extinguishments of Liabilities
FAS140

transferor's connection with the transferred asset, because exercise of the call brings back that very asset from whoever now holds it. The Board concluded that those different economic positions call for different accounting.

230. The Board considered two approaches for resolving this difficulty. The first would have reinstated the wording in paragraph 9(c)(2) of Statement 125. The Board rejected that approach because some calls on not-readily-obtainable assets (for example, certain conditional calls or out-of-the-money calls) do not necessarily constrain transferees or benefit transferors, making it difficult to conclude that they give a transferor effective control over the assets, and because that approach would be difficult to reconcile with the accounting for ROAPs (paragraphs 231–236). The other approach, which the Board adopted because it avoided those difficulties, was to revise paragraph 9(c)(2) to preclude sale accounting if the transferor maintains effective control through a call option or other right that gives it the ability to unilaterally cause the transferee to return specific transferred assets, and to clarify in paragraphs 50–54 the kinds of rights that do and do not maintain effective control. The Board continues to believe that an option to acquire assets, even assets previously owned, is not the same as owning those assets, unless that option conveys effective control over the assets.

Rights to unilaterally reclaim specific assets transferred to qualifying SPEs

231. The Board concluded in Statement 125 that sale treatment is inappropriate for transfers to a qualifying SPE of assets that the transferor is in a position to reclaim. The Board did not change its view in developing this Statement. However, the Board decided to change the way that view is carried out in the standards. Statement 125 excluded the ability to return assets to the transferor from the list of activities that a qualifying SPE was permitted to engage in. Therefore, an SPE that was permitted to return assets to the transferor could not be a qualifying SPE under Statement 125 as originally interpreted. (The staff announcement in Topic D-66 later did permit qualifying SPEs to have certain powers to return assets to the transferor, its affiliates, or its agents.) Rather than disqualify SPEs because the transferor has the unilateral ability to cause the SPE to return specified assets, this Statement instead provides that transfers of assets to qualifying SPEs are not sales if the transferor through that ability retains effective control over specific transferred assets.

232. The Board chose to preclude sale accounting if the transferor has any ability to unilaterally reclaim specific transferred assets from a qualifying SPE on terms that are potentially advantageous to the transferor—whether through a ROAP, the ability to cause the liquidation of the entity, a call option, forward purchase contract, or other means—because, in those circumstances, the transferor would effectively control the transferred assets. The transferor maintains effective control by being able to initiate action to reclaim specific assets with the knowledge that the qualifying SPE cannot sell or distribute the assets because of restrictions placed on it.

233. The Board's decision precludes sale accounting for transfers of financial assets subject to an unconditional ROAP or repurchase agreement that allows the transferor to specify the assets removed. It also precludes sale accounting for transfers of financial assets subject to a ROAP in response to a transferor's decision to exit some portion of its business. The Board reached that conclusion because such provisions allow the transferor to unilaterally remove specified assets from the qualifying SPE, which demonstrates that the transferor retains effective control over the assets.

234. The Board did decide to allow sale accounting for transfers subject to certain other types of ROAPs that are commonly found in securitization structures. For example, it permitted sale treatment for transfers subject to a ROAP that allows the transferor to remove specific financial assets after a third-party cancellation, or expiration without renewal, of an affinity or private-label arrangement on the grounds that the removal would be allowed only after a third party's action (cancellation) or decision not to act (expiration) and could not be initiated *unilaterally* by the transferor. In reaching that conclusion, the Board acknowledged that the transferor may, through its action or inaction, sometimes instigate the third-party cancellation or expiration of an affinity or private-label arrangement but noted that it would be unworkable to base the accounting on identifying which entity was the main instigator and unreasonable to deny sale treatment just because removal of accounts could be required by a cancellation or nonrenewal that the transferor was powerless to avoid. The Board's decision also does not preclude sale accounting because of a ROAP that allows the transferor to

randomly remove transferred assets at its discretion, but only if the ROAP is sufficiently limited so that it does not allow the transferor to remove *specific* transferred assets.

235. This Statement also precludes sale accounting if the transferor of financial assets to a qualifying SPE has the ability to unilaterally take back specific transferred assets through the liquidation of the entity, a call option, forward purchase contract, or other means. The Board's reasoning behind this more general principle is the same as for ROAPs. For example, the Board concluded that a transferor has maintained effective control over specific transferred assets if (a) the transferor or its affiliates may reclaim the transferred assets, for example, at termination of the qualifying SPE or at maturity or redemption of the beneficial interests *and* (b) either the price the transferor is to pay is fixed or determinable or the transferor holds the residual interest in the transferred assets, because those abilities provide the transferor with effective control over the assets. In the latter circumstance, the transferor that holds the residual interest could pay any price it wished to buy back the assets in a public auction, for example, because it would get back any excess paid over fair value via its residual interest.

236. For the same practical reasons as those in Statement 125, the Board chose to continue to allow a cleanup call and, in response to constituents' requests, changed the definition of *cleanup call* to allow the servicer, which may be the transferor, to hold a cleanup call as Statement 77 had done. In reaching this decision, the Board considered but rejected the notion that parties other than the servicer could hold the option, because only the servicer is burdened when the amount of outstanding assets falls to a level at which the cost of servicing the assets becomes burdensome—the defining condition of a cleanup call—and any other party would be motivated by some other incentive in exercising a call. The Board permitted a cleanup call on beneficial interests in the transferred assets because the same sort of burdensome costs in relation to benefits may arise when the remaining assets or beneficial interests fall to a small portion of their original level.

Collateral

Accounting for Collateral under Statement 125

237. The Exposure Draft of Statement 125 proposed that for transactions involving collateral, including securities lending transactions and repurchase agreements, secured parties should recognize all cash collateral received as well as all other financial instruments received as collateral that they have the ability by contract or custom to sell or repledge prior to the debtor's default, because they have important rights over that collateral. Secured parties in those positions are entitled and able to use the cash received as collateral, or the cash they can obtain by selling or repledging other collateral, for their own purposes. Therefore, in the Exposure Draft of Statement 125, the Board concluded that that collateral is the secured party's asset, along with an obligation to return the collateral that is the secured party's liability, and reasoned that if that collateral was permitted to be excluded from the statement of financial position, assets that secured parties can use to generate income would not be recognized. Reporting income but not the assets that generate it could understate a secured party's assets (and liabilities) as well as overstate its return on assets. In contrast, noncash collateral that secured parties are not able to sell or repledge cannot be used to generate cash or otherwise benefit the secured party (other than by reducing the credit risk on the financial asset it secures, an effect already recognized in measuring that financial asset) and is not the secured party's asset.

238. The Board noted that the accounting proposed was consistent with Governmental Accounting Standards Board (GASB) Statement No. 28, *Accounting and Financial Reporting for Securities Lending Transactions,* which was issued in May 1995. GASB Statement 28 also requires, for reasons similar to those noted in Statement 125, that securities lenders record noncash collateral if the contract specifically allows the governmental entity to pledge or sell the collateral before a debtor defaults.

239. Many respondents to the Exposure Draft of Statement 125 objected to recognition of collateral because they contended that the proposed accounting would result in the same asset being recognized by two entities. As discussed in paragraph 259 of this Statement (carried forward from paragraph 172 of Statement 125), while the secured party reports the security as its asset, the transferor reports a different asset, a receivable for the return of the collateral from the secured party. Respondents also argued that recognizing the collateral implies that the secured party expects all the benefits of that asset, whereas it typically is not entitled to retain dividends, interest, or benefits from appreciation. Respondents who objected to recognizing collateral generally preferred that secured parties disclose collateral received.

Other respondents suggested that it was not clear that the proposed collateral provisions applied not only to a secured borrowing but also to collateral pledged in all other kinds of transactions.

240. The Board reconsidered the provisions of the Exposure Draft of Statement 125 in light of those comments. To improve clarity and refine its conclusions, the Board focused on four types of collateral that a secured party arguably should recognize as its assets: (a) cash collateral, (b) collateral securing obligations in default, (c) other collateral that the secured party has sold or repledged, and (d) other collateral that the secured party can sell or repledge.

Cash collateral

241. Some respondents objected to recording any asset received as collateral, even cash, on the grounds that it remains the asset of the party posting it as collateral and is therefore not the secured party's asset. Other respondents agreed that cash collateral should be recognized because transfers of financial assets in exchange for cash collateral cannot be distinguished from borrowing cash and because cash is fungible. It is therefore impossible to determine whether it has been used by the secured party. The Board concluded for the latter reason that all cash collateral should be recorded as an asset by the party receiving it, together with a liability for the obligation to return it to the payer, whose asset is a receivable.

Collateral securing obligations in default

242. Many respondents pointed out that collateral securing an obligation becomes the property of the secured party upon default on the secured obligation. A respondent argued differently, maintaining that a defaulting debtor does not relinquish control over the collateral until it no longer has an opportunity to redeem the collateral by curing the default. The Board agreed in Statement 125 that the secured party should recognize collateral, to the extent it has not already recognized the collateral, if the debtor defaults and is no longer entitled to redeem it.

Other collateral that the secured party has sold or repledged

243. Some respondents to the Exposure Draft of Statement 125 who agreed that cash collateral should be recognized argued that the secured party should not recognize other collateral unless the debtor had defaulted, no matter what powers it has over that collateral, again because in their view the transferred assets remain the assets of the transferor. Others argued that while it may make sense for the secured party to recognize an obligation if collateral is sold, as is common practice in some industries, it is not common practice for broker-dealers and others to recognize an asset and a liability when they repledge collateral. Respondents from the broker-dealer community noted that they regularly repledge substantial amounts of collateral in conjunction with loans secured by customer margin balances and "borrow versus pledge" matched securities transactions and that that collateral activity has not been recognized under previous practice, although it has been disclosed. After considering those arguments, the Board concluded that collateral should be considered for recognition when it is sold or repledged, because the ability to pledge or exchange an asset is the benefit that the Board determined constitutes control over a financial asset, as set forth in paragraph 9(b) and discussed in paragraphs 161 and 162 of this Statement.

244. One respondent observed that the documentation supporting some transactions preserves the transferor's legal right to redeem its collateral, even though the transferee has repledged the assets to a third entity. In those instances, should the transferee default, the transferor has rights to redeem its collateral directly from the third entity to which the initial transferee repledged it. The respondent argued that a transferee with that right has not surrendered control over the assets. The Board agreed with that reasoning and adopted it. Because the status of the right to redeem may not always be clear, the Board chose to implement it by requiring recognition of collateral by the secured party if it sells or repledges collateral on terms that do not enable it to repurchase or redeem the collateral from the transferor on short notice. One result is that broker-dealers and others who obtain financial assets in reverse repurchase agreements, securities loans, or as collateral for loans and then sell or repledge those assets will in some cases recognize under Statement 125 assets and liabilities that previously went unrecognized. The Board noted that obligations to return to the transferor assets borrowed and then sold have sometimes been effectively recognized as part of a liability for securities sold but not yet purchased, and it did not require any change in that practice.

Other collateral that the secured party can sell or repledge

245. The Exposure Draft of Statement 125 called for recognition of collateral that the secured party can repledge or exchange but has not yet used. Some argued that secured parties should not be required to recognize any unused collateral, reasoning that the collateral and related obligation do not meet the definition of an asset or a liability of the secured party. They contended that to be considered an asset of the secured party the collateral must embody a probable future economic benefit that contributes directly or indirectly to future net cash inflows and that in the case of many kinds of collateral, there is only a possible benefit that has not been realized until that collateral is sold or repledged. The Board disagreed, noting that collateral that can be sold or repledged has a capacity to contribute directly to future cash inflows—from a sale or secured borrowing—and that the obligation to return the collateral when reclaimed will require a future economic sacrifice—the relinquishing of control. The Board also observed that broker-dealers and others are able to benefit from collateral in various ways and that the right to benefit from the use of a financial asset is, in itself, an asset.

246. A respondent to the Exposure Draft of Statement 125 pointed out that the right to repledge or exchange is significantly constrained if the transferor has the right and ability to redeem the collateral on short notice, for example, by substituting other collateral or terminating the contract on short notice, and thereby demand the return of the particular security pledged as collateral. The Board agreed, reasoning that a transferor that can redeem its pledged collateral on short notice has not surrendered control of the transferred assets. The transferee would be able to use the transferred assets in certain ways to earn a return during the period of the agreement, but the value of its asset may be very limited because of the transferor's rights to substitute or cancel.

247. In developing the Exposure Draft of Statement 125, the Board considered an approach that would have recorded only the net value of the specific rights that the secured party has over the collateral. That approach might have been consistent with the financial-components approach, and several respondents asked the Board to consider it. However, no one, including the Board, was able to identify a method that the Board judged to be sound for separating the collateral into components.

248. Another possibility considered would have been to recognize the transfer of control over the collateral and for the two parties each to report their mutual rights and obligations under the contract net, that is, for the debtor to net its receivable for the transferred security against its obligation under the secured borrowing and for the secured creditor to net its obligation to return the security against its secured loan receivable. The only change to the statement of financial position would have been the difference in carrying amounts, if any, with a note disclosing the details. That approach is different from present practice in its details but would have produced similar total assets and liabilities. It arguably would have been more consistent with the financial-components approach that focuses on control and would have simplified the accounting. While this approach appealed to some Board members, the Board ultimately rejected it. The approach would have been inconsistent with other pronouncements that govern offsetting, because in this case there is no intent to settle net.

249. After considering comments and testimony on those matters, the Board decided in Statement 125 that financial assets transferred as collateral in a secured borrowing should be recognized by the secured party as an asset with a corresponding liability for the obligation to return the collateral if the secured party was permitted by contract or custom to sell or repledge the collateral and the transferor did not have the right and ability to redeem the collateral on short notice, for example, by substituting other collateral or terminating the contract.

Accounting for Collateral under This Statement

250. After the issuance of Statement 125, implementation issues emerged in applying the requirements for accounting for collateral in paragraph 15 of that Statement. Those issues focused on whether the secured party is constrained from taking advantage of the right to sell or repledge collateral. The notion of constraint was expressed in paragraph 15(a)(2) of Statement 125, which required determining whether the debtor has the right and ability to redeem the collateral on short notice, for example, by substituting other collateral or terminating the contract. In developing Statement 125, the Board assumed that the debtor's right to redeem the collateral on short notice would significantly constrain the secured party from realizing a substantial portion of the value from the collateral and that that constraint would benefit the debtor. While a secured party subject to that constraint might use the collateral in certain ways to earn

a return during the period of the agreement, the value of its asset seemed to be very limited because of the debtor's right to demand the return of the particular security pledged as collateral on short notice.

251. However, the Board learned that paragraph 15 had been interpreted by constituents to indicate that collateral is not required to be recorded as an asset by a secured party if the debtor has the right to substitute other collateral or terminate the agreement on short notice, even if that right to substitute or terminate does not constrain the secured party from selling or repledging the collateral and therefore realizing all or most of its value. Because paragraph 15 did not explicitly require the secured party to consider factors beyond the existence of the debtor's right to substitute the collateral or terminate the contract on short notice in determining whether the ability of a secured party to obtain a benefit from the collateral is significantly constrained, some secured parties may not have recognized as assets collateral pledged under contracts even if the debtor's right may not have imposed a significant constraint. The result of those differing interpretations was lack of comparability between entities.

252. The Board decided to address this issue by reconsidering the accounting model for transfers of collateral. The Board proposed in the Exposure Draft of this Statement to require that the secured party record the fair value of the right to sell or repledge collateral in all transactions in which the secured party receives that right. The fair value of that right would have been symmetrically derecognized by the debtor.

253. Under that approach, the nature of the right to sell or repledge would have been viewed as the secured party's opportunity to use that asset to generate income during the period that it is available to the secured party. That right represents only a portion of the rights associated with the collateral. Not recording the full value of the collateral is consistent with the Board's conclusion that the secured party does not obtain enough control to cause the transferor to derecognize the assets but that the secured party does obtain some rights to the collateral.

254. The Board also decided at that time that if a secured party has exercised its right to sell or repledge the collateral, it has and should recognize a liability to the transferor. The Board concluded that if the secured party has sold another entity's asset, the best measure of that liability is what it would have to sacrifice now to settle the liability—by obtaining a similar asset in the market to deliver to the debtor—which is the fair value of the pledged asset. Extending that reasoning, the Board concluded in the Exposure Draft of this Statement that the best measure of the secured party's liability if it has repledged the collateral is what it would have to sacrifice now to settle its obligation—either by redeeming the repledged asset early or by borrowing in the market a similar asset to deliver to the debtor—which is the fair value of the right to sell or repledge.

255. Constituents expressed concern about whether the approach proposed in the Exposure Draft of this Statement was operational. Some members of the Bond Market Association also questioned the operationality of the approach and conducted a limited field test. At a Board meeting to discuss the results of the field test, representatives of that association voiced three concerns about the "value-of-the-rights" approach. First, the value of the right was not priced in the marketplace, so it was necessary to estimate the fair value of the right indirectly by measuring the difference between the unsecured rate and the secured rate for each transaction category multiplied by the duration and the notional amount. Second, there were a number of ways to calculate that estimate. Third, it was necessary to assume durations for open transactions, because there is no termination date on open transactions, and there was little evidence to support the assumptions as to how long the transaction would be open. Participants in the field test argued that subsequent accounting at fair value would be difficult but that disclosure of the gross amount of the collateral instead would convey useful information that would be less difficult to obtain.

256. After considering the results of that field test and other comments, the Board decided that while the value-of-the-rights approach was conceptually the best of the alternatives it had discussed, the cost of measuring the value of the right to use collateral outweighed the benefit of the generally immaterial result of the measurement. In addition, some Board members expressed concern that the right under consideration (the financial component of the asset no longer held by the debtor) in that approach was not the same as the debtor's right to reclaim the pledged asset.

257. The Board adopted an alternative approach that requires the debtor to reclassify, in its statement of financial position, financial assets pledged that the secured party has the right to sell or repledge. That alternative carries over, and extends, a requirement in

Statement 125 that applied only to collateral that the debtor did not have the right to redeem on short notice. The Board considers separate classification of pledged receivables in the statement of financial position to be necessary once those assets are pledged to a party who has the right to, and commonly does, sell or repledge them, because those financial assets pledged are effectively only receivables from the secured party and should not be reported in a way that suggests that the debtor still holds them. The Board considered requiring that the secured party recognize all such collateral as its assets but concluded that was inappropriate for the reasons cited in developing the value-of-the-rights approach. The Board carried over the requirement in Statement 125 that the secured party recognize its obligation to return collateral that it has sold to other parties, which had not been questioned by commentators. The Board also carried over, in paragraphs 92–94 of this Statement, the requirement to recognize cash "collateral" or securities received as "collateral" that a securities lender is permitted to sell or repledge, because the Board considers them to be, not collateral, but the proceeds of either a sale of the "loaned" securities or a borrowing secured by them.

Security Interests, Custodial Arrangements, Contributions, and Other Transfers That Do Not Qualify as Sales

258. The Board concluded that a borrower that grants a security interest in financial assets should not derecognize the financial assets during the term of the secured obligation. Although the borrower's rights to those assets are restricted because it cannot sell them until the borrowing is repaid, it has not surrendered control if the lender cannot sell or repledge the assets unless the borrower defaults. That assets subject to a security interest have been pledged, and are therefore collateral in the possession of the lender or the lender's agent, does not affect recognition by the debtor because effective control over those assets remains with the debtor in the absence of default under the terms of the borrowing.

259. To maintain symmetry in the accounting of secured parties and debtors (paragraphs 237–257), the Board decided that debtors should reclassify in their statements of financial position collateral that has been put into the hands of a secured party that is permitted by contract or custom to sell or repledge it.

That reclassification avoids a situation in which two or more entities report the same assets as if both held them (as could occur under previous accounting practices).

260. Under previous practice, financial assets transferred to another party for safekeeping or custody continue to be carried as assets by the transferor. The only consideration exchanged in those transfers is, perhaps, payment of a fee by the transferor to the custodian for the custodial services. The custodian does not control the assets but must follow the transferor's instructions. The Board concluded that existing practice should continue and that this Statement need not deal with transfers of custody for safekeeping.

261. Some transfers of financial assets are unconditional nonreciprocal transfers that are contributions. The Board did not address them in Statement 125 and this Statement because accounting for contributions is addressed in FASB Statement No. 116, *Accounting for Contributions Received and Contributions Made.*

262. Some transfers of financial assets will fail to meet the criteria specified in paragraph 9 to be accounted for as sales even though they might be structured as and purport to be sales. The Board concluded that those transfers should be accounted for as secured borrowings.

Scope and Definition

263. In developing this Statement, the Board chose to exclude from its scope transfers of investments in financial assets that are in substance the sale of real estate and exchanges of equity method investments for similar productive assets. Those transactions were excluded because, as the EITF noted in its Issues No. 98-7, "Accounting for Exchanges of Similar Equity Method Investments," and No. 98-8, "Accounting for Transfers of Investments That Are in Substance Real Estate," there were inadvertent overlaps in scope between Statement 125 and other accounting standards issued previously. Under APB Opinion No. 29, *Accounting for Nonmonetary Transactions,* exchanges of similar productive assets, including equity investments accounted for under the equity method, are accounted for based on the recorded amount of the asset relinquished. Under FASB Statement No. 66, *Accounting for Sales of Real Estate,* the sale of stock in enterprises with substantial real estate or of interests in certain partnerships are examples of transactions that are in substance the sale of real estate, and sales of real estate are accounted for differently from the accounting for transfers of financial

assets under Statement 125. The Board's decision affirms the consensuses in Issues 98-7 and 98-8. The Board also considered removing from the scope of this Statement all other transfers of equity interests accounted for under the equity method but decided against that because no other pronouncements of the FASB or its predecessors provide accounting standards for such transactions.

264. Statement 125 amended earlier leasing pronouncements to require the residual value of an asset leased in a sales-type or direct financing lease to be classified as a financial asset, and the increase in its estimated value to be recognized over the remaining lease term, *to the extent that the residual value is guaranteed* by any party. In response to a constituent's comment that practice in interpreting that guidance was diverse, the Board decided to amend that guidance, in paragraphs 89 and 352 of this Statement, to clarify that a residual value of a leased asset is a financial asset only to the extent of a guarantee obtained (whether from a third party or the lessee) *at inception of the lease*. The Board considered several alternatives. It rejected financial instrument classification for all guaranteed residual values (whether guaranteed at inception or later) because the Board views a guarantee obtained after lease inception as a contract separate from the lease. The Board rejected restricting that classification only to residual values guaranteed by the lessee because it was convinced by constituents that it did not matter who guaranteed the residual value and that securitizations of leases commonly involve a third-party guarantee. The Board also accepted that it was important for securitization purposes to allow a guarantee at inception to change the nature of a residual value to a financial asset so that it could be held by a qualifying SPE. Constituents noted that unless the qualifying SPE holds the residual interests as well as the guarantee and the lease receivables, concern may arise that the party holding the residual interests could nullify the lease contract in receivership.

Measurement under the Financial-Components Approach

265. Following a transfer of financial assets that qualifies as a sale, assets retained or obtained and liabilities incurred by the transferor could at first be measured at either (a) fair value at the date of the transfer or (b) an allocated portion of the transferor's carrying amount for the assets transferred.

266. The usual initial measure of assets and liabilities is the price in an exchange transaction or the equivalent fair value. Paragraph 88 of FASB Concepts Statement No. 5, *Recognition and Measurement in Financial Statements of Business Enterprises,* states:

> Initial recognition of assets acquired and liabilities incurred generally involves measurement based on current exchange prices at the date of recognition. Once an asset or a liability is recognized, it continues to be measured at the amount initially recognized until an event that changes the asset or liability or its amount occurs and meets the recognition criteria.

267. In Opinion 29, the Accounting Principles Board, in prescribing the basis for measurement of assets received in nonmonetary exchanges, states:

> . . . in general accounting for nonmonetary transactions should be based on the fair values of the assets (or services) involved which is the same basis as that used in monetary transactions. [Paragraph 18, footnote reference omitted.]

268. The Board believes that those concepts should be applied to new interests obtained or incurred in transfers of financial assets. At issue is whether the financial assets controlled and liabilities incurred in a transfer of financial assets that qualifies as a sale are new to the transferor and thus are part of the proceeds from the transfer, subject to initial measurement using the concepts summarized in paragraphs 266 and 267, or instead are retained beneficial interests over which the transferor has not surrendered control that need not be subject to new measurement under those concepts. The Board concluded that the answer depends on the type of financial instrument or other interest held or incurred.

269. The Board decided that a distinction can and should be made between new assets and liabilities that are part of the proceeds from the transfer and continuing interests in retained assets held in a new form. Cash received as proceeds for assets sold has no continuing connection with those assets and is clearly a new asset. Unrelated assets obtained also are clearly new assets, for example, a government bond received in exchange for transferred accounts receivable. Any asset received that is not an interest in the transferred asset is new to the transferor and thus is part of the proceeds from the sale. Any liability incurred, even if it is related to the transferred assets, is an obligation that is new to the transferor and

thus a reduction of proceeds. Therefore, all of those new assets and liabilities should be initially measured at fair value. The issue becomes more challenging for assets controlled after a sale that are related to the assets sold.

Measuring Liabilities and Derivative Financial Instruments Related to Assets Sold at Fair Value

270. An entity that sells a financial asset may incur liabilities that are related to the assets sold. A common example of a liability incurred by the transferor is a recourse or guarantee obligation. Certain risks, such as recourse or guarantees, are inherent in the original financial asset before it is transferred, which might seem to support carrying over the prior carrying amount. However, before the transfer, the transferor has no obligation to another party; after the transfer, it does. The Board concluded that liabilities incurred in a transfer of financial assets are therefore new and should be initially measured at fair value.

271. An entity that sells a financial asset may enter into derivative financial instrument contracts that are related to the assets sold, for example, options, forwards, or swaps. One example is an option that allows purchasers of receivables to put them back to the transferor, which is similar to a recourse obligation. Another example is a repurchase commitment held by the seller in a repurchase agreement that is accounted for as a sale,[29] which is a kind of forward contract. A third example is an agreement similar to an interest rate swap in which the transferor receives from a securitization trust the fixed interest amounts due on securitized receivables and pays the trust variable amounts based on a floating interest rate index. A party to an option or a forward purchase or sale commitment generally does not recognize the acquisition or disposition of the underlying assets referenced in the contract until and unless delivery occurs. A party to a swap recognizes the net present value of amounts receivable or payable under the swap rather than the full notional amount of the contract. Options, forward commitments, swaps, and other derivative contracts are financial assets or liabilities separate and distinct from the underlying asset. For that reason and because of the practical need to make a workable distinction, the Board concluded that derivative financial instruments entered into by a seller in an exchange for a financial asset are newly created

in the transaction and should be considered part of the proceeds and initially measured at fair value at the date of exchange.

272. Respondents to the Exposure Draft of Statement 125 asked the Board to provide more detailed guidance on how they should differentiate between an asset or liability that is part of the proceeds of a transfer and a retained interest in transferred assets. The Board acknowledges that, at the margin, it may be difficult to distinguish between a retained interest in the asset transferred and a newly created asset. The Board believes that it is impractical to provide detailed guidance that would cover all possibilities. A careful examination of cash flows, risks, and other provisions should provide a basis for resolving most questions. However, the Board agreed that it would be helpful to provide guidance if an entity cannot determine how to classify an instrument and decided that in that case the instrument should be considered to be a new asset and thus part of the proceeds of the sale initially measured at fair value.

Measuring Retained Interests in Assets Sold at Allocated Previous Carrying Amount

273. The Board decided that all other interests in the transferred financial assets held after a securitization or other transfer of financial assets should be measured at their previous carrying amount, allocated between the assets sold, if any, and the retained interests, if any, based on their relative fair values at the date of the transfer. Retained interests in the transferred assets continue to be assets of the transferor, albeit assets of a different kind, because they never left the possession of the transferor and, thus, a surrender of control cannot have occurred. Therefore, the retained interests should continue to be carried at their allocated previous carrying amount, with no gain or loss recognized. Defining this category as the residual set of interests in transferred instruments held after the transfer (those interests that are neither derivatives nor liabilities of the transferor) establishes a clearer distinction between assets and liabilities that are part of the proceeds of the transfer and retained interests.

Other Alternatives Considered

274. In developing the Exposure Draft of Statement 125, the Board considered several alternative measurement approaches including (a) measuring all

---

[29]Accounting for repurchase agreements is discussed in paragraphs 96–101.

assets held after a securitization or sale of a partial undivided interest (either a pro rata interest or a nonproportional interest) initially at fair value, (b) measuring interests held after a securitization at fair value and measuring retained undivided interests at allocated previous carrying amounts, and (c) measuring all interests in transferred financial assets held after a transfer at their allocated previous carrying amounts. Some respondents to that Exposure Draft supported each of those approaches. However, most respondents agreed with the Board's reasoning that a retained interest in a transferred asset represents continuing control over a previous asset, albeit in different form, and thus should not be remeasured at fair value. Most respondents also accepted the approach proposed in the Exposure Draft of Statement 125 as workable.

275. Another possibility that was rejected by the Board was to allocate the carrying amount between the portion of an asset sold and the portion of an asset retained based on relative fair values at the date the receivable was originated or acquired by the transferor, adjusted for payments and other activity from the date of acquisition to the date of transfer. The consensus reached in EITF Issue No. 88-11, "Allocation of Recorded Investment When a Loan or Part of a Loan Is Sold," required use of that acquisition date method unless it is not practical, in which case the allocation should be based on relative fair values at the date of sale. In its deliberations of Statement 125 and this Statement, the Board decided to require allocation based on fair values at the date of sale or securitization because it is more representative of the asset's value, and the cost of re-creating the information from the date of acquisition would exceed the perceived benefits. The Board decided that the acquisition date method was not clearly superior in concept to an allocation based on fair values at the date of sale or securitization and, based in part on practices under that consensus, that that method was so often impractical because of recordkeeping difficulties that it was not useful as a general principle. No other possible methods of allocation appeared likely to produce results that were significantly more relevant.

Servicing Assets and Servicing Liabilities

276. Previously, net "mortgage servicing rights" were recognized as assets, and those rights were accounted for in accordance with FASB Statements No. 65, *Accounting for Certain Mortgage Banking Activities,* No. 91, *Accounting for Nonrefundable Fees and Costs Associated with Originating or Acquiring Loans and Initial Direct Costs of Leases,* No. 115, *Accounting for Certain Investments in Debt and Equity Securities,* and No. 122, *Accounting for Mortgage Servicing Rights.* The amount recognized as net mortgage servicing rights was based on the fair value of certain expected cash inflows net of expected cash outflows. The expected cash inflows—future servicing revenues—included a normal servicing fee,[30] expected late charges, and other ancillary revenues. The expected cash outflows—future servicing costs—included various costs of performing the servicing. A separate "excess servicing fee receivable" was recognized if the servicer expected to receive cash flows in excess of a normal servicing fee, and a liability was recognized if the servicer expected to receive less than a normal servicing fee or if the entity's servicing costs were expected to exceed normal costs. The servicing rights asset was subsequently measured by amortization and assessment for impairment based on its fair value. That set of procedures has been called the mortgage servicing method.

277. Servicing assets and obligations for other assets sold or securitized were either accounted for like mortgage servicing or, more commonly, remained unrecognized until amounts were received and services were provided. Attempts have been made in practice to extend the mortgage servicing method to the servicing of other financial assets. However, identifying a normal servicing fee and other aspects of the mortgage servicing method have been difficult and disparate practices have resulted. The Board concluded it was necessary to address in this project accounting for servicing of all kinds of financial assets.

278. In October 1993, the Board decided to reconsider the accounting for mortgage servicing activities established in Statement 65. The primary thrust of that project was to resolve differences in the accounting for purchased versus originated mortgage servicing. Statement 122 was the result of that effort. In February 1995, the Board decided that accounting for excess mortgage servicing receivables and other servicing issues should be dealt with, to the extent necessary, not in that project but rather in this one,

---

[30]Statement 65 defined a current (normal) servicing fee rate as "a servicing fee rate that is representative of servicing fee rates most commonly used in comparable servicing agreements covering similar types of mortgage loans." FASB Technical Bulletin No. 87-3, *Accounting for Mortgage Servicing Fees and Rights,* clarified what rate a seller-servicer should use as a servicing fee rate as described in Statement 65.

because those issues largely arise in transfers of financial assets and possible answers are necessarily interrelated. The Board considered alternative methods of accounting for servicing (the mortgage servicing method required by Statement 65, as amended by Statement 122, as well as a gross method and a right or obligation method) and chose a method that combines the best features of the mortgage servicing method and other possible methods.

Alternatives to the Mortgage Servicing Method

279. The mortgage servicing method described in paragraph 276 was required by Statement 65, as amended by Statement 122, for mortgage servicing rights. While that method was familiar to mortgage servicers and had certain advantages over other methods, the distinction between normal and excess servicing and other complexities of the method made it difficult to apply for some other kinds of servicing.

280. The Board considered a gross method that would have required that a servicer recognize both a servicing receivable asset consisting of expected future servicing revenues and a servicing obligation liability for the servicing work to be performed. The Board decided that it was questionable whether a receivable for servicing not yet rendered met the definition of an asset and that, given the conceptual questions, that method did not merit the large change in practice that it would have required.

281. The Board also considered a right or obligation method that would have recognized a single item, commonly an asset but occasionally a liability, for each servicing contract. That asset or liability would have been the net of the gross asset and liability that would have been reported separately under the gross approach. The resulting asset would have been subsequently measured like an interest-only strip, that is, at fair value with unrealized gains and losses recognized in equity if available-for-sale. Some respondents suggested that servicing rights should be subsequently measured in that way, because reporting servicing rights at fair value would be more useful to investors and other financial statement users than the historical cost amortization and impairment methods of the mortgage servicing approach. Furthermore, under an approach like that in Statement 115, unrealized gains and losses would not have been recognized in earnings, but rather in a separate component of shareholders' equity.

282. The Board considered the right or obligation method well suited in several respects to the range of mortgage and other servicing contracts that now exist or might arise. However, the Board did not choose that method in part for the practical reason of avoiding an early change from the recently adopted provisions of Statement 122. Instead, the Board chose to combine the best features of that method—the simplicity of reporting only a single asset or liability for each servicing contract and not having to distinguish between normal and excess servicing—with the best features of the mortgage servicing method.

Recognition and Measurement of Servicing Assets and Servicing Liabilities

283. The method adopted in Statement 125 carries forward the amortization and impairment provisions that were required under the mortgage servicing method in Statements 65 and 122 and that method was not reconsidered in this Statement. The Board considers those subsequent measurement provisions workable. However, changes to the mortgage servicing method are necessary to adapt the accounting for mortgage servicing to all servicing assets and servicing liabilities, to reduce complexities for financial statement preparers and users, and to be compatible with the other recognition and initial measurement principles in Statement 125 and this Statement.

284. One change is the elimination of the distinction between normal and excess servicing. The Board decided that that distinction has been too difficult to make except in markets as liquid as the market for residential mortgage servicing. The Board considered two ways in which normal and excess servicing might be retained in accounting for those liquid markets.

285. One way would have been to leave in place the accounting for servicing of mortgages as required in Statement 65, as amended by Statement 122, while using a different method that was not dependent on determining a normal servicing fee for all other servicing. However, the Board concluded that comparability of financial statements would have suffered if the accounting for essentially similar servicing activities differed depending on the type of asset serviced. Another way would have been to revise the definition of normal servicing fee rates so that servicers could determine a normal servicing fee rate in the absence of a developed secondary market for servicing. That change would have provided servicers of other types of loans or receivables (such as auto loans and credit card balances) with an opportunity to establish normal servicing rates and apply the mortgage servicing

method to other servicing rights, rather than be subject to recognizing less gain or more loss on the sale of receivables because normal servicing was unknown. The Board considered that method but concluded that that alternative might result in continuing questions about what are normal servicing fees for different types of servicing.

286. The Board also noted that the distinction between normal and excess servicing, even in liquid markets, is no longer relevant for financial reporting because under current market practices, excess and normal servicing assets, which arise from a single contract, generally cannot be sold separately after the sale or securitization of the underlying financial assets. The excess servicing receivable, like normal servicing, will be collected only if the servicing work is performed satisfactorily. In addition, accounting based on that distinction is unduly complex and often results in several assets and liabilities being recognized for one servicing contract. While excess servicing continues to resemble an interest-only strip in some respects, the Board concluded in light of the lessened distinction between normal and excess servicing that it is more useful to account for all servicing assets and servicing liabilities in a similar manner.

287. The Board chose instead to distinguish only between the benefits of servicing—amounts that will be received only if the servicing work is performed to the satisfaction of the assets' owner or trustee—and other amounts retained after a securitization or other transfer of financial assets. A consequence of that method is that interest-only strips retained in securitizations, which do not depend on the servicing work being performed satisfactorily, are subsequently measured differently from servicing assets that arise from the same securitizations. That difference in accounting could lead transferors that retain an interest in transferred assets to select a stated servicing fee that results in larger servicing assets and lower retained interests (or vice versa) with an eye to subsequent accounting. The Board believes, however, that the potential accounting incentives for selecting a higher or lower stated servicing fee largely will counterbalance each other.

288. Most respondents agreed with the Board's decision to eliminate the distinction between excess and normal servicing. Some respondents to the Exposure Draft of Statement 125 asked for further explanation of the new terms it used for accounting for servicing and about how they differed from the terminology of the mortgage servicing approach used in prior pronouncements. In response, Statement 125 defines the terms *adequate compensation* for servicing, *benefits of servicing,* and *contractually specified servicing fees.* Those definitions and the discussion of them are carried forward without reconsideration in the glossary and in paragraphs 61–64 of this Statement.

289. The Exposure Draft of Statement 125 proposed that an entity account for all servicing assets in the same manner because rights to service financial assets, while they may differ in the particulars of the servicing, in the extent of compensation, and in liquidity, are in essence the same. As with other retained interests in transferred assets, valid arguments can be made for measuring servicing assets either at allocated previous carrying amount or at fair value. However, the Board saw no reason to treat retained servicing assets differently than other retained interests and therefore decided that they should be initially measured at allocated previous carrying amount.

290. For similar reasons, the Board viewed servicing liabilities as new obligations arising from a transfer and decided to account for them like other liabilities incurred upon sale or securitization, at fair value.

291. Some respondents questioned how to apply the transition provisions to servicing rights and excess servicing receivables in existence as of the effective date of Statement 125. The Board retained paragraph 20 of Statement 125 without reconsideration in this Statement. Paragraph 25 does not permit retroactive application of Statement 125 to (a) ensure comparability between entities and (b) clarify how Statement 125 should be applied to previous balances.

Financial Assets Subject to Prepayment

292. Paragraph 362 of this Statement carries forward without reconsideration from Statement 125 the amendment to Statement 115 to eliminate the use of the *held-to-maturity* category for securities subject to substantial prepayment risk, thereby requiring that they be classified as either available-for-sale or trading and subsequently measured at fair value. Paragraph 14 extends that measurement principle to interest-only strips, loans, other receivables, and retained interests in securitizations subject to substantial prepayment risk.

293. The justification for using historical-cost-based measurement for debt securities classified as held-to-maturity is that no matter how market interest rates

fluctuate, the holder will recover its recorded investment and thus realize no gains or losses when the issuer pays the amount promised at maturity. The same argument is used to justify historical-cost-based measurement for other receivables not held for sale. That justification does not extend to receivables purchased at a substantial premium over the amount at which they can be prepaid, and it does not apply to instruments whose payments derive from prepayable receivables but have no principal balance, as demonstrated by large losses realized in recent years by many holders of interest-only strips and other mortgage derivatives. As a result, the Board concluded that those receivables must be subsequently measured at fair value with gains or losses being recognized either in earnings (if classified as trading) or in a separate component of shareholders' equity (if classified as available-for-sale). The Board, by deciding that a receivable may not be classified as held-to-maturity if it can be prepaid or otherwise settled in such a way that the holder of the asset would not recover *substantially all* of its recorded investment, left room for judgment, so that investments in mortgage-backed securities or callable securities purchased at an insubstantial premium, for example, are not necessarily disallowed from being classified as held-to-maturity.

294. Some respondents to the Exposure Draft of Statement 125 agreed with the Board's conclusions about financial assets subject to prepayment when applied to interest-only strips but questioned the application of those conclusions to loans, other receivables, and retained interests in securitizations. They maintained that the nature of the instrument and management's intent should govern classification rather than actions that a borrower might take under the contract.

295. The Board did not agree with those arguments. A lender that holds a portfolio of prepayable loans or bonds at par will realize the carrying amount of its investment if the borrowers prepay. However, if the lender originated or acquired those loans or bonds at a substantial premium to par, it may lose some or all of that premium and thus not recover a substantial portion of its recorded investment if borrowers prepay. The potential loss is less drastic for premium loans or bonds than for interest-only strips, but it can still be substantial. The Board concluded that the rationale outlined in paragraph 293 extends to any situation in which a lender would not recover substantially all of its recorded investment if borrowers were to exercise prepayment or other rights granted to them under the contracts. The Board also concluded that the provisions of paragraph 14 do not apply to situations in which events that are not the result of contractual provisions, for example, borrower default or changes in the value of an instrument's denominated currency relative to the entity's functional currency, cause the holder not to recover substantially all of its recorded investment.

296. Other respondents asked that the Board clarify the term *substantially all.* Some suggested that the Board use the 90 percent test found in APB Opinion No. 16, *Business Combinations.* Although applying the term *substantially all* requires judgment about how close to 100 percent is close enough, the Board decided to leave the language of paragraphs 14 and 362 unchanged rather than to require a specific percentage test that would be inherently arbitrary.

Fair Value

297. The Board decided to include an approach for measuring fair value that would be broadly applicable. The definition of fair value in paragraphs 68–70 is consistent with that included in other recent Statements.[31] The Board found no compelling reason to redefine *fair value* under the financial-components approach.

298. Many of the assets and liabilities held after a sale by a transferor with continuing involvement are not traded regularly. Because quoted market values would not be available for those assets and liabilities, fair values would need to be determined by other means in applying the financial-components approach. There was concern that, in some cases, the best estimate of fair value would not be sufficiently reliable to justify recognition in earnings of a gain following a sale of financial assets with continuing involvement, because errors in the estimate of asset value or liability value might result in recording a nonexistent gain. The Board considered requiring that fair value be verifiable to achieve a higher degree of reliability to justify recognition in earnings of a gain following a sale of financial assets with continuing involvement. However, to promote

---

[31]FASB Statement No. 121, *Accounting for the Impairment of Long-Lived Assets and for Long-Lived Assets to Be Disposed Of,* par. 7, Statement 122, par. 3(f), and Statement No. 133, *Accounting for Derivative Instruments and Hedging Activities,* par. 540.

consistency between its Statements, the Board decided not to introduce a new notion of fair value based on reliability.

299. The Exposure Draft of Statement 125 proposed that gain recognition following a sale with continuing involvement should be allowed only to the extent that it is practicable to estimate fair values for assets obtained and liabilities incurred in sales with continuing involvement. To accomplish that, the Board concluded that if it is not practicable to estimate their fair values, assets should be measured at zero and liabilities at the greater of the amount called for under FASB Statement No. 5, *Accounting for Contingencies,* as interpreted by FASB Interpretation No. 14, *Reasonable Estimation of the Amount of a Loss,* or the excess, if any, of the fair value of the assets obtained less the fair value of the other liabilities incurred over the sum of the carrying values of the assets transferred. That requirement was intended to prevent recognition of nonexistent gains through underestimating liabilities. The Board considered whether the practicability exception should be extended to the transferee's accounting and decided not to allow such an exception. The Board concluded that because the transferee is the purchaser of the assets, it should be able to value all assets and any liabilities it purchased or incurred, presumptively based on the purchase price paid. In addition, because the transferee recognizes no gain or loss on the transfer, there is no possibility of recognizing a nonexistent gain.

300. Respondents to the Exposure Draft of Statement 125 asked the Board to clarify the meaning of the term *practicable,* especially in relation to the use of the same term in Statement 107. The comment letters also revealed a considerable range of interpretation of that provision among respondents. Some suggested that the provision would apply to all but the most common transactions. Others suggested that the provision would seldom apply and alluded to the relatively few entities that have used the practicability exception in Statement 107.

301. Because no practicability exception is used, for example, in Statement 133, the Board considered whether to expand the discussion of practicability, or to remove it from Statement 125 and this Statement. The Board ultimately concluded that the practicability provisions should remain unchanged in this Statement for the reasons noted in paragraphs 298 and 299.

302. Other respondents to the Exposure Draft of Statement 125 suggested that there should be a limit on the amount of gain that can be recognized in a transfer of financial assets. Several suggested the limitation found in Issue 88-11. In that Issue, the task force reached a consensus that "the amount of any gain recognized when a portion of a loan is sold should not exceed the gain that would be recognized if the entire loan was sold." Respondents maintained that a limitation would meet the Board's objective of preventing recognition of nonexistent gains through underestimating liabilities.

303. The Board rejected the suggested limitation for several reasons. First, it was not clear that the limitation in Issue 88-11 could have been applied across a wide range of transactions. The limitation presumes that a market price exists for transfers of whole assets, but one reason that securitization transactions take place is because sometimes no market exists for the whole assets being securitized. Second, the limitation would have required that accountants ignore the added value that many maintain is created when assets are divided into their several parts. Third, the use of relative fair values at the date of transfer, rather than relative fair values on initial acquisition as in Issue 88-11, would have mitigated many of the concerns that appear to have prompted the task force to adopt a limitation. Finally, the Board was concerned that a gain limitation might have obscured the need to consider whether the transaction gives rise to a loss.

304. In its deliberations of this Statement, the Board considered constituents' concerns that retained interests were not being appropriately valued in certain securitizations. One constituent suggested that, under the relative-fair-value allocation method required by paragraph 10 of Statement 125, transferors were allocating too much to the relatively low-risk senior interests that have been sold, whereas the bulk of the profit from lending and selling loans ought to be attributed to realizing the value of the high-risk subordinated interests, which typically have not yet been sold. The Board again considered limiting the amount of the gain, as discussed prior to Statement 125, but rejected that limitation for the same reasons cited in paragraph 303.

305. The Board recognizes that risk assumed in connection with subordinated retained interests will affect the expected cash flows or discount rate used to value the retained interests and agreed with constituents' concern that risk has not always been adequately taken into account. To the extent that risk is not adequately taken into account, subordinated retained interests are overvalued and consequently the

gain calculated is higher (or loss is lower) than it should be. However, the Board does not believe that concerns about failure to reasonably estimate the fair value of the various items created in a securitization can be eliminated by an arbitrary ceiling. Instead, the Board believes those responsible for financial statements need to exercise care in applying this Statement, and, as discussed in paragraph 59, should be able to identify the reasons for gains on securitization. For the same reasons, as discussed in paragraphs 323–332, the Board also decided in this Statement to require disclosure about the key assumptions made in valuing retained interests.

Subsequent Measurement

306. The provisions of Statement 125 that were carried forward without reconsideration in this Statement focus principally on the initial recognition and measurement of assets and liabilities that result from transfers of financial assets. This Statement does not address subsequent measurement except for servicing assets and servicing liabilities and financial assets subject to prepayment that were also addressed in Statement 125.

307. Several respondents to the Exposure Draft of Statement 125 also asked the Board to include guidance about subsequent measurement. They observed that the financial-components approach leads to recognition of assets and liabilities that were not recognized under previous standards. They also observed that accountants who draw analogies to existing accounting practices may find a variety of equally plausible approaches to subsequent measurement.

308. The Board is sensitive to concerns about subsequent measurement, especially to the possibility of emerging diversity in practice. However, attempting to address subsequent measurement would have expanded significantly the scope of this project. In addition, any guidance on subsequent measurement in this project would have applied only to assets and liabilities that emerge from a transfer of financial assets. Accounting for similar assets and liabilities not connected with a transfer of financial assets would have continued to follow existing practice; if so, diversity would have continued to exist. On balance,

the Board concluded that it was better to complete this project without providing guidance on subsequent measurement and leave reconsideration of existing standards and practices for subsequent measurement for future segments of the Board's financial instruments project or other projects.

Extinguishments of Liabilities

309. Statement 76 required that a debtor treat a liability as if extinguished if it completed an in-substance defeasance. Under that Statement, a debtor derecognized a liability if it transferred essentially risk-free assets to an irrevocable defeasance trust and the cash flows from those assets approximated the scheduled interest and principal payments of the debt that was being extinguished. Under that Statement, the debtor also derecognized the assets that were set aside in the trust.

310. Derecognition of liabilities after an in-substance defeasance has been controversial. A number of respondents to the Exposure Drafts that led to Statement 76 and subsequent Board requests for comment have criticized the transactions as having insufficient economic substance to justify derecognition or gain recognition. Researchers and analysts have demonstrated that in-substance defeasance transactions conducted after interest rates have risen, which resulted in an accounting gain under Statement 76, have economic impact; those transactions constitute an economic loss to shareholders.[32] That research and analysis suggest that derecognition of liabilities and recognition of a gain in those circumstances may not be representationally faithful.

311. Under the financial-components approach, an in-substance defeasance transaction does not meet the derecognition criteria for either the liability or the asset. The transaction lacks the following critical characteristics:

a. The debtor is not released from the debt by putting assets in the trust; if the assets in the trust prove insufficient, for example, because a default by the debtor accelerates its debt, the debtor must make up the difference.

---

[32]The research referred to includes John R. M. Hand, Patricia J. Hughes, and Stephan E. Sefcik, "In-Substance Defeasances: Security Price Reactions and Motivations," *Journal of Accounting and Economics* (May 1990): 47–89; Judy Beckman, J. Ralph Byington, and Paul Munter, "Extinguishment of Debt by In-Substance Defeasance: Managerial Perspectives," *Journal of Corporate Accounting and Finance* (Winter 1989/90): 167–174; Bruce R. Gaumnitz and Joel E. Thompson, "In-Substance Defeasance: Costs, Yes; Benefits, No," *Journal of Accountancy* (March 1987): 102–105; and Abraham M. Stanger, "Accounting Developments: In-Substance Defeasance—Reality or Illusion?" *The Corporation Law Review* (Summer 1984): 274–277.

b. The lender is not limited to the cash flows from the assets in trust.
c. The lender does not have the ability to dispose of the assets at will or to terminate the trust.
d. If the assets in the trust exceed what is necessary to meet scheduled principal and interest payments, the transferor can remove the assets.
e. Neither the lender nor any of its representatives is a contractual party to establishing the defeasance trust, as holders of interests in a qualifying SPE or their representatives would be.
f. The debtor does not surrender control of the benefits of the assets because those assets are still being used for the debtor's benefit, to extinguish its debt, and because no asset can be an asset of more than one entity, those benefits must still be the debtor's assets.

312. The Board concluded that the previous treatment of in-substance defeasance was inconsistent with the derecognition criteria of the financial-components approach and that the provisions on in-substance defeasance in Statement 76 should be superseded by Statement 125. Respondents to the Exposure Draft of Statement 125 generally accepted that change, although some disagreed, citing arguments similar to those made in Statement 76 and refuted, in the Board's view, by the critical characteristics cited in paragraph 311.

313. Paragraph 3(a) of Statement 76 required derecognition of the transferred assets and the liability by the debtor if a debtor transfers assets to its creditor in exchange for a release from all further obligation under the liability. That provision has not been controversial and is consistent with the financial-components approach. Accordingly, paragraph 3(a) of Statement 76 was incorporated substantially unchanged as paragraph 16(a) of this Statement.

314. Paragraph 3(b) of Statement 76 stated, "The debtor is legally released from being the primary obligor under the debt either judicially or by the creditor *and it is probable that the debtor will not be required to make future payments with respect to that debt under any guarantees*" (emphasis added; footnote references omitted). Except for the italicized portion, paragraph 3(b) was carried forward without reconsideration as paragraph 16(b) of this Statement. Some respondents to the Exposure Draft of Statement 125 disagreed with that change, arguing that the revised provision was too lenient in that it might allow, for example, derecognition of liabilities and inappropriate gain recognition when entities are

replaced as primary obligor by entities with little economic substance. However, the italicized phrase is omitted from Statement 125 and this Statement because it is contrary to the financial-components approach. If an entity is released from being a primary obligor and becomes a secondary obligor and thus effectively a guarantor of that liability, it should recognize that guarantee in the same manner as a third-party guarantor that was never the primary obligor. The Board noted, however, that concerns about inappropriate gains are unwarranted: if an entity with little substance were to become a primary obligor, a guarantor of that obligation would have to recognize a liability almost as great as if it were the primary obligor. To emphasize those matters, the Board included a discussion of the secondary obligor's liability in Appendix A.

315. The Board concluded that the basic principle that liabilities should be derecognized only if the debtor pays the creditor or is legally released from its obligation applies not just to debt securities but to all liabilities. Accordingly, Statement 125 and this Statement broaden the scope of paragraphs 3(a) and 3(b) of Statement 76 to include all liabilities not excluded from Statement 125 and this Statement's scope by paragraph 4 and to delete the reference to sales in the public market.

Disclosures

316. The Board decided that Statement 125 should continue to require disclosure of debt defeased in accordance with Statement 76 before the effective date of Statement 125 because Statement 125 does not change the accounting for those defeasance transactions. The Board also decided to require that an entity disclose assets restricted to the repayment of particular debt obligations, for example, in in-substance defeasance transactions after Statement 125 becomes effective, because while that restriction is insufficient cause to derecognize the assets, that information is useful in determining what resources are unavailable to general creditors and for general operations. The Board decided that an entity should disclose its policies for requiring collateral or other securities in repurchase agreements and securities lending transactions accounted for as borrowings. The Board believes that that information is useful for assessing the amount of risk that an entity assumes in repurchase agreements and securities lending transactions, which appears to vary considerably in practice.

317. The Board also decided to carry forward the disclosures required by Statement 122 and extend

them to all servicing rights, because those disclosures provide information financial statement users need to make independent judgments about the value of servicing rights and obligations and the related risks.

318. In addition, the Board decided to require that an entity describe items for which it is impracticable to measure their fair value and disclose why the fair value of an asset obtained or liability incurred could not be estimated, despite the concerns of some Board members that this requirement was unnecessary and might lead to uninformative disclosures.

Disclosures about Collateral

319. In connection with the issuance of Statement 125, the Board decided to require entities to disclose their policies for requiring collateral or other security for securities lending transactions and repurchase agreements to inform users about the credit risk that entities assume in those transactions, because there appeared to be significant variation in practice. Commentators did not object to that disclosure, which is carried forward without substantial change in this Statement.

320. After it decided to remove certain of Statement 125's recognition requirements for collateral, the Board decided that further disclosures about the value of collateral are appropriate. It chose to require disclosure of (a) the fair value of collateral accepted that could be sold or repledged and (b) the portion of that collateral that had been sold or repledged. The Board considers that information relevant for investors and creditors who wish to understand the scale of collateralized transactions, the extent to which that collateral is used, or the relationship between income from use of collateral and the amount of collateral used and available for use. In considering the costs of preparing that information, the Board determined that similar information is already maintained for other purposes by entities that accept large amounts of collateral. The Board believes that that information could be developed by other entities at a moderate cost well justified by the value of the information. Commentators generally favored that disclosure instead of the proposal to account for the value of rights to use collateral. After the Board decided in its redeliberations that collateral should not be accounted for under the value-of-the-rights approach or recognized as an asset by secured parties, it concluded that those disclosures are necessary to indicate the extent of collateral available to the secured party and the usage of that resource, and required them in this Statement.

321. In the Exposure Draft of Statement 125, the Board did not propose additional disclosures by entities that pledge their assets, largely because disclosure of assets pledged as security is already required under paragraphs 18 and 19 of Statement 5. After the Board decided in its redeliberations that collateral should not be accounted for under the value-of-the-rights approach, as discussed in paragraphs 255 and 256, it chose to refine the general requirement from Statement 5, to avoid redundant information. Specifically, this Statement requires an entity that pledges any assets as collateral that the secured party *cannot* sell or repledge to disclose the carrying amount and classification of those assets. Collateral that a secured party can sell or repledge is already reclassified and separately reported in the statement of financial position pursuant to paragraph 15(a).

322. In the redeliberations of this Statement, the Board considered two other alternatives for disclosing collateral. The first alternative was to require disclosure of the value of the right to use collateral, in place of recognition of that value in the financial statements. The Board concluded, based in part on the results of the informal field test, that the cost of computing and disclosing the value of the right to use the collateral would exceed its benefits. The second alternative would have required the disclosure of earnings generated by secured parties from the use of pledged collateral. Additional research on the feasibility of that alternative uncovered a potential for inconsistency in disclosures across firms that could result in lack of comparability. In addition, the Board accepted arguments that information about earnings generated from the use of collateral is not currently isolated for management or reporting purposes and therefore new systems would have been needed to be developed by the larger firms to generate that information for disclosure. Because it appeared doubtful that the value of this information would justify the cost of extensive systems changes, the Board rejected that alternative.

Disclosures about Securitizations

323. During the deliberations leading to Statement 125, the Board considered whether additional disclosures were necessary in the context of that Statement or whether current standards provide adequate disclosure of interests retained in a transfer of financial assets. The Board concluded then that sufficient requirements were in place (for example, in FASB Statement No. 95, *Statement of Cash Flows,*

and other pronouncements) for transfers and servicing of financial assets, extinguishments of liabilities, and the resulting components of those transfers and extinguishments and that the potential benefits of requiring additional disclosures did not appear to justify the costs involved.

324. Since Statement 125 became effective, however, a number of entities that securitize financial assets have materially restated gains recognized in earlier financial statements or have materially changed estimates of the fair value of their retained interests. Those restatements led some to contend that gain or loss recognition should not be permitted for securitizations in which significant interests are retained by the transferor and others to demand additional disclosures. The Board rejected suggestions that gain or loss recognition is inappropriate for transfers of financial assets that qualify as sales, though it observed that Statement 125 and this Statement do have procedures to be followed if it is impracticable to measure the fair value of retained interests. However, the Board did agree to consider whether, in light of those developments, the benefits of further disclosure might indeed justify the costs involved.

325. Members of the Board and staff met with analysts, investors, and preparers during 1998 to learn more about the type of information that financial statement users need to adequately assess the amounts of risks involved in securitization transactions and the availability of that information. Some analysts and investors called for increased disclosure about key assumptions because they believe that the current disclosures are inadequate and sometimes misleading. They contend that assumptions about interest rates, prepayments, and losses are especially important in assessing whether the projected future earnings of an entity are attainable and whether write-downs of retained interests or other unfavorable events will occur.

326. Based on those discussions and the concerns voiced, the Board concluded that disclosures about securitization transactions needed to be enhanced. Preparers of financial statements from the financial services industry told Board members and staff that they already prepare and disclose much of the information that financial statement users want, in documents required to be filed with the SEC, in electronic information media in connection with publicly offered securitizations, or in data voluntarily provided on an entity-wide basis. They suggested that summary disclosures (disaggregated on a product-by-

product basis) provided in financial statements or in the management discussion and analysis (MD&A) could offer investors and analysts the information that they need to assess both the level of risk and the impact that securitizations have on an entity's overall earnings.

327. The Board decided that enhanced disclosures should focus on two aspects of securitizations: the results of securitization transactions entered into during the period and the valuation of retained interests in past securitizations that are still outstanding at the end of the period.

328. The Board concluded that, at a minimum, financial statements should provide, for all securitizations entered into during the period, a description of (a) the transferor's accounting policies for initially measuring interests retained in a securitization; (b) the characteristics of securitizations entered into, and gain or loss from securitizations of financial assets during the year by major type of asset; (c) quantitative information about key assumptions used to value interests retained at the time of securitization that affect the amount of income recognized during the period; and (d) cash flows between the securitization SPE and the transferor. The Board concluded that under those requirements, financial statement users would receive information that would assist them in assessing the effect of securitization transactions on the results of operations and cash flows and be useful in assessing the valuation of interest-only strips, subordinated tranches, servicing, cash reserve accounts, and other interests retained in the securitization. The Board chose to require disclosures by major class of asset securitized because prepayment, credit loss, and interest rates vary so widely between major classes that aggregating data across those classes would obscure useful information. The Board decided to require information about weighted-average life so that disclosures of prepayment assumptions would be more comparable if different companies use different calculation methods. While other disclosures were suggested, the Board concluded that the problems associated with restatements and inappropriate assumptions could be best highlighted by the disclosures it selected and that the cost of further disclosures might outweigh the benefits of requiring those disclosures.

329. Some commentators suggested that certain of the proposed required disclosures about cash flows between the securitization SPE and the transferor might be redundant with information already disclosed elsewhere; for example, the proceeds from securitization might already be reported in cash flow

statements. Other constituents pointed out that that information is not always apparent in cash flow statements, perhaps because it is aggregated with other in-·formation. The Board agreed with both groups. To avoid requiring any redundancy, the Board revised its proposed requirement to require disclosure of cash flows between the securitization SPE and the transferor, unless that information is reported separately elsewhere in the financial statements or notes.

330. For retained interests outstanding at the end of the period, the Board concluded that three types of disclosures would be useful in assessing their valuation. Those disclosures include (a) the accounting policies for measuring retained interests at the end of the period being reported on, including the methodology used in determining or estimating their fair value; (b) quantitative information about key assumptions used in valuing those retained interests; and (c) a sensitivity analysis or stress test that would quantify the effect that unfavorable variations from the expected levels of interest rates, prepayment patterns, credit losses, or other key assumptions would have on the estimates of fair value of the retained interests. The Board decided to require static pool information so that disclosures of credit loss assumptions would be more comparable if different entities use different calculation methods. The Board concluded that sensitivity information would provide users of financial statements with a means of comparing their estimates of the market's performance with the entity's estimates, seeing the pro forma effects of changes in assumptions on the financial statements, and assessing the potential effect of a future change in market conditions on the value of the entity's retained interests. The Board chose to require disclosure of the impact of two or more pessimistic variations for each key assumption so that the results would indicate whether the valuation had a linear relationship to the assumption. The Board chose not to specify any particular changes in assumptions so that companies could select the changes that best portray the sensitivity of estimates of fair value.

331. Some commentators supported the proposed disclosures and asked for additional information. One request that the Board adopted was to require disclosure of the total financial assets managed by securitizers from loans sold as well as those that remain on the statement of financial position, with the goal of highlighting a source of risks (and benefits) to securitizers through their retained interests. The Board chose to specifically exclude from this disclosure securitized assets that an entity continues to service but

with which it has no other continuing involvement. The Board reasoned that a disclosure of the total financial assets managed by securitizers, including loans sold as well as those that remain on the statement of financial position, would not only be useful but would also be economical for many securitizers to produce because many already report that in the MD&A or in voluntary disclosures. The Board discussed, but decided against, requiring disclosure of average balances of managed assets outstanding for the year, partly because current GAAP does not require disclosures of other average balances; it decided to encourage that disclosure, however, in part, because it provides a useful base for comparison of credit losses for the year.

332. Some commentators suggested that this Statement include a specific materiality threshold below which certain disclosures for securitization transactions would not be required. The Board chose not to do that. Materiality and relevance are both defined in terms of what influences or makes a difference to a decision maker. The Board's position is that " . . . no general standards of materiality could be formulated to take into account all the considerations that enter into an experienced human judgment," but that quantitative materiality criteria may be given by the Board in specific standards, as appropriate (FASB Concepts Statement No. 2, *Qualitative Characteristics of Accounting Information,* paragraph 131). The Board has only rarely given quantitative materiality criteria in specific standards. The one recent example is the 10 percent threshold for reported segments in FASB Statement No. 131, *Disclosures about Segments of an Enterprise and Related Information,* which the Board retained from an earlier Statement "because it can be objectively applied and because preparers and users of financial statements already understand it" (paragraph 76). The latter reason does not apply in this Statement, and the Board identified no persuasive reason to take its place. Therefore, this Statement does not include a materiality threshold. However, that conclusion does not imply that the provisions of this Statement must be applied to immaterial items. Some entities may determine that some or all disclosures about securitization transactions are not material after an evaluation of all the relevant facts and circumstances.

Effective Date and Transition for Statement 125

333. The Board proposed that Statement 125 should be effective for transfers and servicing of financial assets and extinguishments of liabilities occurring after

December 31, 1996, and the Board did not change that effective date in the final Statement. While many respondents accepted and some even urged adoption on that date, some respondents expressed concern about the ability to carry out certain of Statement 125's provisions by that date, including systems changes needed to keep track of supporting data efficiently. The Board concluded that some of those concerns should be ameliorated by the effects of changes from the Exposure Draft on the accounting for repurchase agreements, securities lending, loan participations, and collateral, and that in other cases data adequate for external financial reporting could be obtained in other ways while systems changes were being completed. After Statement 125 was issued, representatives from various enterprises, particularly those representing brokers and dealers in securities, continued to express to the Board concerns about the effective date of Statement 125 for those types of transactions (repurchase agreements, securities lending, loan participations, and collateral). Those representatives convinced the Board that for those types of transactions, substantial changes to information systems and accounting processes were essential for brokers and dealers in securities and other enterprises to comply with Statement 125 and that those changes would make it extremely difficult, if not impossible, for affected enterprises to account for those transfers of financial assets and apply the secured borrowing and collateral provisions of Statement 125 as soon as January 1, 1997. The Board appreciated the concerns expressed by those enterprises that attempting to account for those types of transactions manually until appropriate modifications could be made to information systems and accounting processes might lead to a significant temporary deterioration in the financial controls and quality of financial information of the affected enterprises. In November 1996, the Board decided to defer for one year the effective date (a) of paragraph 15 and (b) for repurchase agreement, dollar-roll, securities lending, and similar transactions, of paragraphs 9–12 and 237(b) of Statement 125. For those types of transfers, Statement 125 became effective for transfers occurring after December 31, 1997.

334. The Exposure Draft of Statement 125 proposed that the Statement should be applied prospectively to achieve consistency in accounting for transfers of financial assets. That requirement was also meant to ensure that all entities entering into a given transaction report that transaction under the same guidance. If entities were permitted to implement early or implement at the beginning of fiscal years that did not coincide, opportunities might arise to structure transactions in ways that result in the same assets and liabilities being reported in the financial statements of both parties or in the financial statements of neither party. The Board found that possibility undesirable. Most respondents to the Exposure Draft of Statement 125 generally accepted that conclusion.

335. The Board also decided that retroactive implementation for all entities was not feasible and that allowing voluntary retroactive implementation was unwise because it would impair comparability of financial statements by permitting disparate accounting treatment for similar transactions reported in previous periods. The Board concluded that those considerations outweighed the lack of consistency within an entity's financial statements for transactions occurring before and after the effective date of Statement 125. In addition, the Board concluded that the benefits of retroactive application of the provisions of Statement 125 would not justify the considerable cost of doing that. Respondents generally accepted that conclusion.

Effective Date and Transition for This Statement

336. The Board decided that the accounting provisions of this Statement that are changed from or in addition to those in Statement 125 should be applied prospectively to transfers of financial assets occurring after March 31, 2001, except for the provisions relating to collateral. That transaction-based prospective approach is the same as that used in Statement 125 and was adopted in this Statement for the same reason: to achieve consistency in accounting for transfers of financial assets and to ensure that all entities entering into a given transaction report that transaction under the same guidance. Retroactive implementation for all entities was not feasible, and allowing voluntary retroactive implementation was unwise because it would impair comparability of financial statements by permitting disparate accounting treatment for similar transactions reported in previous periods.

337. The Board initially considered making this Statement effective for transfers occurring after December 31, 2000. Adopting the accounting provisions of this Statement at the beginning of a calendar year would simplify the transition for preparers and users of the financial statements of a majority of larger U.S. enterprises, which use the calendar year as their fiscal year. However, after considering constituents' comments, the Board concluded that an effective date that soon would be inappropriate. The

Board also concluded that a one-year postponement in effective date would unduly delay necessary improvements in financial reporting. Instead, the Board decided that entities would be in a better position to implement this Statement if it were effective for transfers occurring after March 31, 2001, six months after issuance. The Board concluded that that interval should allow constituents the time needed to assess the standards, consider the effect of EITF issues and other implementation guidance, negotiate new contractual arrangements, and revise their accounting systems to conform to the amendment.

338. The Board believes that the disclosure requirements of this Statement for securitization transactions should be implemented as early as possible, in view of concerns that markets for securitized assets and other securities of the issuers of securitized assets have been adversely affected by the lack of sufficient and comparable information. In addition, constituents informed the Board that many entities that securitize assets use the kind of information required to be disclosed under this Statement to manage internally. Therefore, for many entities, the cost and time to aggregate the data for disclosure in financial statements should be minimal. For those reasons, the Board concluded that securitization disclosures mandated by this Statement could be required for financial statements for fiscal years ending after December 15, 2000. The Board also decided that disclosures required for securitization transactions that have occurred during the period that are accounted for as sales should be made for each year for which an income statement is presented for comparative purposes, so that investors and creditors can better understand the effects of the key assumptions on those income statements. However, in response to comments from constituents, the Board chose not to require that those disclosures be reported for periods ending on or before December 15, 2000, for which an income statement is presented for comparative purposes. The Board reasoned that those disclosures should be required only prospectively because they might be difficult to develop for prior years, especially if securitzations are not the company's core business.

339. For the reasons cited above, the Board decided that disclosures about the assumptions used in valuing the retained interests remaining at the end of the period and the sensitivity of those assumptions need not be required for earlier periods in comparative financial statements, as that information is relevant primarily as of the latest statement of financial position.

340. In light of the Board's decision not to require that collateral be accounted for under the value-of-the-rights approach, the Board decided that collateral that was previously recognized by secured parties in accordance with paragraphs 15(a)(ii) and 15(b) of Statement 125 should not continue to be recognized in financial statements for fiscal years ending after December 15, 2000, and that financial statements for earlier periods presented for comparative purposes should be restated accordingly. The Board concluded that (a) to do so would improve comparability between entities and consistency between periods in recognized amounts and (b) the amount of collateral that would be reported on future statements of financial position would soon become minimal given the short average time that much pledged collateral is held. The Board had originally proposed in the Exposure Draft of this Statement that disclosure requirements for collateral should first be required in financial statements prepared for fiscal years ending after December 15, 2001, because of the relationship between the disclosures about collateral and the proposed accounting provisions that would not have been effective until January 1, 2001. However, in keeping with its decision to require that the asset and liability accounts currently being reported for collateral be removed from the statement of financial position for fiscal years ending after December 15, 2000, the Board decided to require the same effective date for disclosures about collateral. The Board reasoned that those disclosures should be required only prospectively because they might be difficult to develop for prior years.

341. The Board also considered the effect of applying this Statement on previously transferred assets and previously qualifying SPEs in light of constituents' arguments that changing the requirements for a qualifying SPE without some transition relief would result in (a) assets that were previously recorded as having been sold to previously qualifying SPEs suddenly reappearing in the financial statements of the transferor solely because the SPEs could not meet the revised standards for qualifying SPEs and (b) future transfers that were required under previous commitments to unrelated transferees or BIHs having to be accounted for as secured borrowings. The Board discussed the validity of constituents' concerns that changes in the requirements would (1) cause an unexpected build-up of assets on the transferor's balance sheet, (2) conflict with transition guidance in paragraph 55 of this Statement, (3) result in significant costs to restructure existing qualifying SPEs if

that could be done at all, (4) result in partial consolidation of transferred assets, and (5) cause certain transfers subject to the new conditions for ROAPs to no longer be accounted for as sales. The Board decided to ameliorate what it judged to be the more onerous of those concerns by permitting formerly qualifying SPEs to continue to apply the requirements of Statement 125 but limiting that "grandfathering" to entities just carrying out previous commitments made to unrelated BIHs, and at the same time complying with previous standards. The Board did not extend that transition relief to SPEs that engage in new transactions, such as taking in new assets not already committed to or issuing new beneficial interests, because the Board wanted to minimize the length of the period of noncomparability that that transition provision will cause.

Appendix C

ILLUSTRATIVE GUIDANCE

342. This appendix provides specific examples that illustrate the disclosures that are required by this Statement. The formats in the illustrations are not required by the Statement. The Board encourages entities to use a format that displays the information in the most understandable manner in the specific circumstances. References to paragraphs of this Statement in which the relevant requirements appear are given in parentheses.

343. The first example illustrates the disclosure of accounting policies for interests that continue to be held by the transferor. In particular, it describes the accounting policies for (a) initial measurement (paragraph 17(h)(1)) and (b) subsequent measurement (paragraph 17(i)(1)), including determination of fair value.

NOTE X—SUMMARY OF SIGNIFICANT ACCOUNTING POLICIES

Receivable Sales

When the Company sells receivables in securitizations of automobile loans, credit card loans, and residential mortgage loans, it may hold interest-only strips, one or more subordinated tranches, and in some cases a cash reserve account, all of which are interests that continue to be held by the transferor in the securitized receivables. It may also obtain servicing assets or assume servicing liabilities that are initially measured at fair value. Gain or loss on sale of the receivables depends in part on both (a) the previous carrying amount of the financial assets involved in the transfer, allocated between the assets sold and the interests that continue to be held by the transferor based on their relative fair value at the date of transfer, and (b) the proceeds received. To obtain fair values, quoted market prices are used if available. However, quotes are generally not available for interests that continue to be held by the transferor, so the Company generally estimates fair value based on the present value of future expected cash flows estimated using management's best estimates of the key assumptions—credit losses, prepayment speeds, forward yield curves, and discount rates commensurate with the risks involved.

344. In addition to the disclosure of assumptions used in determining the values of interests that continue to be held by the transferor at the time of securitization that are presented in paragraph 343, this Statement also requires similar disclosures at the end of the latest period being presented. The following example illustrates disclosures about the characteristics of securitizations and gain or loss from securitizations and other sales by major type of asset (paragraph 17(h)(2)).

NOTE Y—SALES OF RECEIVABLES

During 20X2 and 20X1, the Company sold automobile loans, residential mortgage loans, and credit card loans in securitization transactions. In all those securitizations, the Company obtained servicing responsibilities and subordinated interests. The Company receives annual servicing fees approximating 0.5 percent (for mortgage loans), 2 percent (for credit card loans), and 1.5 percent (for automobile loans) of the outstanding balance and rights to future cash flows arising after the investors in the securitization trust have received the return for which they contracted. The investors and the securitization trusts have no recourse to the Company's other assets for failure of debtors to pay when due. The interests that continue to be held by the Company are subordinate to investor's interests. Their value is subject to credit, prepayment, and interest rate risks on the transferred financial assets.

In 20X2, the Company recognized pretax gains of $22.3 million on the securitization of the automobile loans, $30.2 million on the securitization of credit card loans, and $25.6 million on the securitization of residential mortgage loans.

In 20X1, the Company recognized pretax gains of $16.9, $21.4, and $15.0 million on the securitization of the automobile loans, credit card loans, and residential mortgage loans, respectively.

345. The following is an illustration of the quantitative information about key assumptions used in measuring interests that continue to be held by the transferor at the date of sale or securitization for each financial period presented (paragraph 17(h)(3)).

Key economic assumptions used in measuring the interests that continue to be held by the transferor at the date of securitization resulting from securitizations completed during the year were as follows (rates* per annum):

| | 20X2 | | | | 20X1 | | | |
| | | | Residential Mortgage Loans | | | | Residential Mortgage Loans | |
	Automobile Loans	Credit Card Loans	Fixed-Rate	Adjustable[†]	Automobile Loans	Credit Card Loans	Fixed-Rate	Adjustable[†]
Prepayment speed	1.00%	15.0%	10.00%	8.0%	1.00%	12.85%	8.00%	6.00%
Weighted-average life (in years)[33]	1.8	0.4	7.2	6.5	1.8	0.4	8.5	7.2
Expected credit losses	3.10–3.40%	6.10%	1.25%	1.30%	3.50–3.80%	5.30%	1.25%	2.10%
Residual cash flows discounted at	12.0–13.0%	12.00%	10.00%	8.50%	13.00–13.50%	13.00%	11.75%	11.00%
Variable returns to transferees	Forward Eurodollar curve plus contractual spread over LIBOR ranging from 30 to 80 basis points		Not applicable		Forward Eurodollar yield curve plus contractual spread over LIBOR ranging from 28 to 70 basis points		Not applicable	

Notes:

*Weighted-average rates for securitizations entered into during the period for securitizations of loans with similar characteristics.

[†]Rates for these loans are adjusted based on an index (for most loans, the 1-year Treasury note rate plus 2.75 percent). Contract terms vary, but for most loans, the rate is adjusted every 12 months by no more than 2 percent.

[33]The weighted-average life in periods (for example, months or years) of prepayable assets is calculated by summing the product of (a) the sum of the principal collections expected in each future period times (b) the number of periods until collection, and then dividing that total by (c) the initial principal balance.

346. The following is an illustration that combines disclosure of the key assumptions used in valuing interests that continue to be held by the transferor at the end of the latest period (paragraph 17(i)(2)) and the hypothetical effect on current fair value of two or more pessimistic variations from the expected levels for each of the key assumptions (paragraph 17(i)(3)).

At December 31, 20X2, key economic assumptions and the sensitivity of the current fair value of residual cash flows to immediate 10 percent and 20 percent adverse changes in those assumptions are as follows ($ in millions):

	Automobile Loans	Credit Card Loans	Residential Mortgage Loans	
			Fixed-Rate	Adjustable
Carrying amount/fair value of interests that continue to be held by the transferor	$15.6	$21.25	$12.0	$13.3
Weighted-average life (in years)[34]	1.7	0.4	6.5	6.1
Prepayment speed assumption (annual rate)	**1.3%**	**15.0%**	**11.5%**	**9.3%**
Impact on fair value of 10% adverse change	*$0.3*	*$1.6*	*$3.3*	*$2.6*
Impact on fair value of 20% adverse change	*$0.7*	*$3.0*	*$7.8*	*$6.0*
Expected credit losses (annual rate)	**3.0%**	**6.1%**	**0.9%**	**1.8%**
Impact on fair value of 10% adverse change	*$4.2*	*$3.2*	*$1.1*	*$1.2*
Impact on fair value of 20% adverse change	*$8.4*	*$6.5*	*$2.2*	*$3.0*
Residual cash flows discount rate (annual)	**14.0%**	**14.0%**	**12.0%**	**9.0%**
Impact on fair value of 10% adverse change	*$1.0*	*$0.1*	*$0.6*	*$0.5*
Impact on fair value of 20% adverse change	*$1.8*	*$0.1*	*$0.9*	*$0.9*
Interest rates on variable and adjustable contracts	Forward Eurodollar yield curve plus contracted spread			
Impact on fair value of 10% adverse change	*$1.5*	*$4.0*	*$0.4*	*$1.5*
Impact on fair value of 20% adverse change	*$2.5*	*$8.1*	*$0.7*	*$3.8*

These sensitivities are hypothetical and should be used with caution. As the figures indicate, changes in fair value based on a 10 percent variation in assumptions generally cannot be extrapolated because the relationship of the change in assumption to the change in fair value may not be linear. Also, in this table, the effect of a variation in a particular assumption on the fair value of the interest that continues to be held by the transferor is calculated without changing any other assumption; in reality, changes in one factor may result in changes in another (for example, increases in market interest rates may result in lower prepayments and increased credit losses), which might magnify or counteract the sensitivities.

[34]Footnote 8, paragraph 17(h)(3), describes how weighted-average life can be calculated.

347. The following is an illustration of disclosure of expected static pool credit losses (paragraph 17(i)(2)).

Actual and Projected Credit Losses (%) as of:	Automobile Loans Securitized in		
	20X0	**20X1**	**20X2**
December 31, 20X2	5.0	5.9	5.1
December 31, 20X1	5.1	5.0	
December 31, 20X0	4.5		

Note: Static pool losses are calculated by summing the actual and projected future credit losses and dividing them by the original balance of each pool of assets. The amount shown here for each year is a weighted average for all securitizations during the period.

348. The following is an illustration of the disclosure of cash flows between the securitization SPE and the transferor (paragraph 17(h)(4)).

The table below summarizes certain cash flows received from and paid to securitization trusts ($ in millions):

	Year Ended December 31	
	20X2	**20X1**
Proceeds from new securitizations	$1,413	$ 971
Proceeds from collections reinvested in previous credit card securitizations	3,150	2,565
Servicing fees received	23	19
Other cash flows received on interests that continue to be held by the transferor*	81	52
Purchases of delinquent or foreclosed assets	(45)	(25)
Servicing advances	(102)	(73)
Repayments of servicing advances	90	63

Note:

*This amount represents total cash flows received from interests that continue to be held by the transferor. Other cash flows include, for example, all cash flows from interest-only strips and cash above the minimum required level in cash collateral accounts.

349. The following illustration presents quantitative information about delinquencies, net credit losses, and components of securitized financial assets and other assets managed together with them ($ in millions):

| Type of Loan | Total Principal Amount of Loans | | Principal Amount of Loans 60 Days or More Past Due* | | Average Balances[35] | | Net Credit Losses[†] | |
| | At December 31 | | At December 31 | | During the Year | | During the Year | |
	20X2	20X1	20X2	20X1	20X2	20X1	20X2	20X1
Automobile loans	$ 830	$ 488	$42.3	$26.8	$ 720	$ 370	$21.6	$12.6
Residential mortgage loans (fixed-rate)	482	302	5.8	3.6	470	270	5.6	3.2
Residential mortgage loans (adjustable)	544	341	7.1	6.8	520	300	6.2	6.0
Credit card loans	300	250	15	12.5	350	300	16	15
Total loans managed or securitized‡	2,156	1,381	$70.2	$49.7	2,060	1,240	$49.4	$36.8
Less:								
Loans securitized§	1,485	905			1,368	752		
Loans held for sale or securitization	19	11			17	9		
Loans held in portfolio[36]	$ 652	$ 465			$ 675	$ 479		

Notes:

*Loans 60 days or more past due are based on end of period total loans.

†Net credit losses are charge-offs and are based on total loans outstanding.

‡Owned and securitized loans are customer loans, credit card loans, mortgage loans, auto loans, and other loans, as applicable, in which the transferor retains a subordinate interest or retains any risk of loss (for example, 10 percent recourse).

§Represents the principal amount of the loan. Interest-only strips (or other interests that continue to be held by a transferor) and servicing assets and servicing liabilities held for securitized assets are excluded from this table because they are recognized separately.

---

[35]This disclosure is optional.

[36]Loans held in portfolio are reported separately from loans held for securitization because they are measured differently.

349A. The following is an illustration of disclosures related to the activity in the balance of servicing assets and servicing liabilities by class (paragraphs 17(f)(1) and 17(g)(1)):

**Tabular Disclosure of Changes in Servicing Assets and Servicing
Liabilities Subsequently Measured Using the Fair Value Measurement Method**

Balance Sheet Disclosures	Class 1		Class 2		Reference
	Servicing Asset	Servicing Liability	Servicing Asset	Servicing Liability	
Fair value as of the beginning of the period	XX	XX	XX	XX	17(f)(1)(a)
Additions:					17(f)(1)(b)
Purchases of servicing assets	XX	N/A	XX	N/A	
Assumption of servicing obligations	XX	XX	XX	XX	
Servicing obligations that result from transfers of financial assets	XX	XX	XX	XX	
Subtractions:					
Disposals	(XX)	(XX)	(XX)	(XX)	17(f)(1)(c)
Changes in fair value:					17(f)(1)(d)
Due to change in valuation inputs or assumptions used in the valuation model	XX/(XX)	XX/(XX)	XX/(XX)	XX/(XX)	
Other changes in fair value	XX/(XX)	XX/(XX)	XX/(XX)	XX/(XX)	
Other changes that affect the balance	XX/(XX)	XX/(XX)	XX/(XX)	XX/(XX)	17(f)(1)(e)
Fair value as of the end of the period	XX	XX	XX	XX	17(f)(1)(a)

Tabular Disclosure of Changes in Servicing Assets and Servicing
Liabilities Subsequently Measured Using the Amortization Method

Balance Sheet Disclosures	Class 3		Class 4		Reference
	Servicing Asset	Servicing Liability	Servicing Asset	Servicing Liability	
Carrying amount as of the beginning of the period	XX	XX	XX	XX	17(g)(1)(a)
Additions:					17(g)(1)(b)
Purchases of servicing assets	XX	N/A	XX	N/A	
Assumption of servicing obligations	XX	XX	XX	XX	
Servicing obligations that result from transfers of financial assets	XX	XX	XX	XX	
Subtractions:					
Disposals	(XX)	(XX)	(XX)	(XX)	17(g)(1)(c)
Amortization	(XX)	(XX)	(XX)	(XX)	17(g)(1)(d)
Application of valuation allowance to adjust carrying values of servicing assets	XX/(XX)	N/A	XX/(XX)	N/A	17(g)(1)(e)
Other-then-temporary impairments	(XX)	(XX)	(XX)	(XX)	17(g)(1)(f)
Other changes that affect the balance	XX/(XX)	XX/(XX)	XX/(XX)	XX/(XX)	17(g)(1)(g)
Carrying amount before valuation allowance	XX	XX	XX	XX	
Valuation allowance for servicing assets:					17(g)(5)
Beginning balance	XX	N/A	XX	N/A	
Provisions/recoveries	XX/(XX)	N/A	XX/(XX)	N/A	
Other-than-temporary impairments	(XX)	N/A	(XX)	N/A	17(g)(1)(f)
Sales and disposals	(XX)	N/A	(XX)	N/A	
Ending balance	XX/(XX)	N/A	XX/(XX)	N/A	
Carrying amount as of the end of the period	XX	XX	XX	XX	17(g)(1)(a)
Fair Value Disclosures					
Fair value as of the beginning of the period	XX	XX	XX	XX	17(g)(2)
Fair value as of the end of the period	XX	XX	XX	XX	17(g)(2)

Appendix D

AMENDMENTS TO EXISTING PRONOUNCEMENTS

350. This Statement replaces FASB Statement No. 125, *Accounting for Transfers and Servicing of Financial Assets and Extinguishments of Liabilities,* and rescinds FASB Statement No. 127, *Deferral of the Effective Date of Certain Provisions of FASB Statement No. 125.*

351. This Statement also carries forward the following supersessions that were made by Statement 125:

a. FASB Statement No. 76, *Extinguishment of Debt*
b. FASB Statement No. 77, *Reporting by Transferors for Transfers of Receivables with Recourse*
c. FASB Statement No. 122, *Accounting for Mortgage Servicing Rights*
d. FASB Technical Bulletin No. 84-4, *In-Substance Defeasance of Debt*
e. FASB Technical Bulletin No. 85-2, *Accounting for Collateralized Mortgage Obligations (CMOs).*

352. Paragraph 20 of FASB Statement No. 13, *Accounting for Leases,* as amended by Statements 77 and 125, and FASB Statement No. 135, *Rescission of FASB Statement No. 75 and Technical Corrections,* is replaced by the following:

> The sale or assignment of a lease or of property subject to a lease that was accounted for as a sales-type lease or direct financing lease shall not negate the original accounting treatment accorded the lease. Any transfer of minimum lease payments under, or residual values that are guaranteed at the inception of, a sales-type lease or direct financing lease shall be accounted for in accordance with FASB Statement No. 140, *Accounting for Transfers and Servicing of Financial Assets and Extinguishments of Liabilities.* However, transfers of unguaranteed residual values and residual values that are guaranteed after the inception of the lease are not subject to the provisions of Statement 140.

353. FASB Statement No. 133, *Accounting for Derivative Instruments and Hedging Activities,* is amended as follows:

a. In the last sentence of paragraph 10(f), *FASB Statement No. 125, Accounting for Transfers and Servicing of Financial Assets and Extinguishments of Liabilities* is replaced by *FASB Statement No. 140, Accounting for Transfers and Servicing of Financial Assets and Extinguishments of Liabilities.*

b. In both sentences of footnote 9 to paragraph 21, *paragraph 37(g) of Statement 125* is replaced by *paragraph 63(g) of Statement 140.*

c. In the first and second sentences of paragraph 56, *paragraph 37(g) of Statement 125* is replaced by *paragraph 63(g) of Statement 140.*

d. In the first sentence of paragraph 59(e), *paragraphs 68 and 69 of Statement 125* is replaced by *paragraphs 98 and 99 of Statement 140.*

354. In footnote 5 to paragraph 8 of FASB Statement No. 136, *Transfers of Assets to a Not-for-Profit Organization or Charitable Trust That Raises or Holds Contributions for Others,* the reference to *FASB Statement No. 125, Accounting for Transfers and Servicing of Financial Assets and Extinguishments of Liabilities* is replaced by *FASB Statement No. 140, Accounting for Transfers and Servicing of Financial Assets and Extinguishments of Liabilities* and *(paragraph 243)* is replaced by *(paragraph 364).*

355. In footnote 2 to paragraph 3 of FASB Interpretation No. 43, *Real Estate Sales,* the reference to *FASB Statement No. 125, Accounting for Transfers and Servicing of Financial Assets and Extinguishments of Liabilities* is replaced by *FASB Statement No. 140, Accounting for Transfers and Servicing of Financial Assets and Extinguishments of Liabilities.*

356. Paragraph 12 of FASB Technical Bulletin No. 86-2, *Accounting for an Interest in the Residual Value of a Leased Asset: Acquired by a Third Party or Retained by a Lessor That Sells the Related Minimum Rental Payments,* as amended by Statement 125, is replaced by the following:

> Yes. A residual value of a leased asset is a financial asset to the extent guaranteed at the inception of the lease. Accordingly, increases to its estimated value over the remaining lease term should be recognized.

Amendments and Deletions Made by Statement 125 Carried Forward in This Statement with Minor Changes

357. Paragraph 3(a) of APB Opinion No. 26, *Early Extinguishment of Debt,* as amended by Statement 76, is replaced by the following:

> *Extinguishment of liabilities.* FASB Statement No. 140, *Accounting for Transfers and Servicing of Financial Assets and Extinguishments of Liabilities,* defines transactions that the debtor shall recognize as an extinguishment of a liability.

358. The last sentence of footnote 1 to paragraph 1 of FASB Statement No. 22, *Changes in the Provisions of Lease Agreements Resulting from Refundings of Tax-Exempt Debt,* as amended by Statement 76 is deleted.

359. FASB Statement No. 65, *Accounting for Certain Mortgage Banking Activities,* is amended as follows:

a. Paragraph 8, as amended by FASB Statement No. 115, *Accounting for Certain Investments in Debt and Equity Securities,* is deleted.

b. The last sentence of paragraph 9(a) prior to the amendment by Statement 115 is deleted.

c. In paragraph 10, *(paragraphs 16 through 19)* is deleted and replaced by *(paragraph 13 of FASB Statement No. 140, Accounting for Transfers and Servicing of Financial Assets and Extinguishments of Liabilities).*

d. Paragraph 11 and footnote 4 are deleted.

e. In paragraph 15, the reference to paragraph 18 (as amended by FASB Statement No. 122, *Accounting for Mortgage Servicing Rights*) is deleted, and the following is added to the end of paragraph 15 replacing the sentence added by Statement 122:

> The rate used to determine the present value shall be an appropriate long-term interest rate. For this purpose, estimates of future servicing revenue shall include expected late charges and other ancillary revenue. Estimates of expected future servicing costs shall include direct costs associated with performing the servicing function and appropriate al-

locations of other costs. Estimated future servicing costs may be determined on an incremental cost basis. The amount capitalized shall be amortized in proportion to, and over the period of, estimated net servicing income—the excess of servicing revenues over servicing costs.

f. Paragraphs 16–19 and 30 and footnote 6, as amended by Statement 122, are deleted.

g. The three paragraphs added by Statement 122 after paragraph 30 are deleted.

h. In paragraph 34, the terms *current (normal) servicing fee rate* and *servicing* and their definitions are deleted.

360. This Statement carries forward the following amendments that Statement 122 made to Statement 65:

a. In the first sentence of paragraph 1, *origination or acquisition* is replaced by *purchase or acquisition.*

b. In the first sentence of paragraph 10, *of existing* is replaced by *or origination of.*

361. FASB Statement No. 107, *Disclosures about Fair Value of Financial Instruments,* is amended as follows:

a. Paragraph 8(b) is replaced by the following:

> Substantively extinguished debt subject to the disclosure requirements of FASB Statement No. 140, *Accounting for Transfers and Servicing of Financial Assets and Extinguishments of Liabilities*

b. In the last sentence of paragraph 28, , *or the rate that an entity would have to pay to acquire essentially risk-free assets to extinguish the obligation in accordance with the requirements of Statement 76* is deleted.

362. The following sentence is added after the first sentence of paragraph 7 of Statement 115 as amended by FASB Statement No. 135, *Rescission of FASB Statement No. 75 and Technical Corrections:*

> A security may not be classified as held-to-maturity if that security can contractually be prepaid or otherwise settled in such a way that the holder of the security would not recover substantially all of its recorded investment.

363. FASB Technical Bulletin No. 87-3, *Accounting for Mortgage Servicing Fees and Rights,* is amended as follows:

a. Paragraphs 1–7 are deleted.

b. Paragraph 9, as amended by Statement 122, is replaced by the following:

> An enterprise may acquire servicing assets or liabilities by purchasing or originating financial assets with servicing rights retained or by purchasing the servicing rights separately. Servicing assets and liabilities are amortized in proportion to, and over the period of, estimated net servicing income—the excess of servicing revenues over servicing costs.

Appendix E

GLOSSARY

364. This appendix defines terms used in this Statement.

Adequate compensation
The amount of benefits of servicing that would fairly compensate a substitute servicer should one be required, which includes the profit that would be demanded in the marketplace.

Agent
A party that acts for and on behalf of another party. For example, a third-party intermediary is an agent of the transferor if it acts on behalf of the transferor.

Attached call
A call option held by the transferor of a financial asset that becomes part of and is traded with the underlying instrument. Rather than being an obligation of the transferee, an attached call is traded with and diminishes the value of the underlying instrument transferred subject to that call.

Beneficial interests
Rights to receive all or portions of specified cash inflows to a trust or other entity, including senior and subordinated shares of interest, principal, or other cash inflows to be "passed-through" or "paid-through," premiums due to guarantors, commercial paper obligations, and residual interests, whether in the form of debt or equity.

Benefits of servicing
Revenues from contractually specified servicing fees, late charges, and other ancillary sources, including "float."

Cleanup call
An option held by the servicer or its affiliate, which may be the transferor, to purchase the remaining transferred financial assets, or the remaining beneficial interests not held by the transferor, its affiliates, or its agents in a qualifying SPE (or in a series of beneficial interests in transferred assets within a qualifying SPE), if the amount of outstanding assets or beneficial interests falls to a level at which the cost of servicing those assets or beneficial interests becomes burdensome in relation to the benefits of servicing.

Collateral
Personal or real property in which a security interest has been given.

Consolidated affiliate of the transferor
An entity whose assets and liabilities are included with those of the transferor in the consolidated, combined, or other financial statements being presented.

Contractually specified servicing fees
All amounts that, per contract, are due to the servicer in exchange for servicing the financial asset and would no longer be received by a servicer if the beneficial owners of the serviced assets (or their trustees or agents) were to exercise their actual or potential authority under the contract to shift the servicing to another servicer. Depending on the servicing contract, those fees may include some or all of the difference between the interest rate collectible on the asset being serviced and the rate to be paid to the beneficial owners of those assets.

Derecognize
Remove previously recognized assets or liabilities from the statement of financial position.

Derivative financial instrument
A derivative instrument (as defined in Statement 133) that is a financial instrument (refer to Statement 107, paragraph 3).

Embedded call

A call option held by the issuer of a financial instrument that is part of and trades with the underlying instrument. For example, a bond may allow the issuer to call it by posting a public notice well before its stated maturity that asks the current holder to submit it for early redemption and provides that interest ceases to accrue on the bond after the early redemption date. Rather than being an obligation of the initial purchaser of the bond, an embedded call trades with and diminishes the value of the underlying bond.

Financial asset

Cash, evidence of an ownership interest in an entity, or a contract that conveys to [one] entity a right (a) to receive cash or another financial instrument from a [second] entity or (b) to exchange other financial instruments on potentially favorable terms with the [second] entity.

Financial liability

A contract that imposes on one entity [an] obligation (a) to deliver cash or another financial instrument to a second entity or (b) to exchange other financial instruments on potentially unfavorable terms with the second entity.

Freestanding call

A call that is neither embedded in nor attached to an asset subject to that call.

Guaranteed mortgage securitization

A securitization of mortgage loans that is within the scope of FASB Statement No. 65, *Accounting for Certain Mortgage Banking Activities,* as amended, and includes a substantive guarantee by a third party.

Interest-only strip

A contractual right to receive some or all of the interest due on a bond, mortgage loan, collateralized mortgage obligation, or other interest-bearing financial asset.

Proceeds

Cash, derivatives, or other assets that are obtained in a transfer of financial assets, less any liabilities incurred.

Recourse

The right of a transferee of receivables to receive payment from the transferor of those receivables for (a) failure of debtors to pay when due, (b) the effects of prepayments, or (c) adjustments resulting from defects in the eligibility of the transferred receivables.

Securitization

The process by which financial assets are transformed into securities.

Security interest

A form of interest in property that provides that upon default of the obligation for which the security interest is given, the property may be sold in order to satisfy that obligation.

Seller

A transferor that relinquishes control over financial assets by transferring them to a transferee in exchange for consideration.

Servicing asset

A contract to service financial assets under which the estimated future revenues from contractually specified servicing fees, late charges, and other ancillary revenues are expected to more than adequately compensate the servicer for performing the servicing. A servicing contract is either (a) undertaken in conjunction with selling or securitizing the financial assets being serviced or (b) purchased or assumed separately.

Servicing liability

A contract to service financial assets under which the estimated future revenues from contractually specified servicing fees, late charges, and other ancillary revenues are not expected to adequately compensate the servicer for performing the servicing.

Transfer

The conveyance of a noncash financial asset by and to someone other than the issuer of that financial asset. Thus, a transfer includes selling a receivable, putting it into a securitization trust, or posting it as collateral but excludes the origination of that receivable, the settlement of that receivable, or the restructuring of that receivable into a security in a troubled debt restructuring.

Transferee

An entity that receives a financial asset, a portion of a financial asset, or a group of financial assets from a transferor.

Transferor

An entity that transfers a financial asset, a portion of a financial asset, or a group of financial assets that it controls to another entity.

Undivided interest

Partial legal or beneficial ownership of an asset as a tenant in common with others. The proportion owned may be pro rata, for example, the right to receive 50 percent of all cash flows from a security, or non–pro rata, for example, the right to receive the interest from a security while another has the right to the principal.

Unilateral ability

A capacity for action not dependent on the actions (or failure to act) of any other party.

Statement of Financial Accounting Standards No. 141
Business Combinations

STATUS

Issued: June 2001

Effective Date: For all business combinations initiated after June 30, 2001

Affects: Supersedes APB 16
Amends APB 20, paragraphs 12 and 35
Amends APB 28, paragraph 21
Amends APB 29, paragraph 4(a)
Amends APB 30, paragraphs 7 and 20
Supersedes AIN-APB 16, Interpretations No. 1 through 39
Supersedes FAS 10
Amends FAS 15, footnotes 5, 6, and 16
Amends FAS 16, footnote 6
Supersedes FAS 38
Amends FAS 44, paragraph 4
Amends FAS 45, paragraph 19
Effectively amends FAS 52, paragraph 101
Amends FAS 72, paragraphs 4, 8, and 9
Supersedes FAS 79
Amends FAS 87, paragraph 74 and Illustration 7
Amends FAS 95, paragraph 134(g)
Amends FAS 106, paragraphs 86 and 444
Amends FAS 109, paragraphs 11(h), 13, 30, 36(d), 259, and 270
Amends FAS 123, paragraphs 8 and 36
Amends FAS 128, paragraph 59
Amends FAS 133, paragraphs 11(c) and 29(f)
Amends FIN 4, paragraph 4
Amends FIN 21, paragraphs 13, 15, 16, and 19 and footnote 4
Deletes FIN 21, paragraph 14
Deletes FIN 44, paragraphs 81 and 82
Amends FIN 44, paragraphs 83 and 84
Amends FTB 84-1, paragraph 6
Amends FTB 85-5, paragraphs 1 through 4, 6, and 7
Deletes FTB 85-5, paragraphs 13 through 24

Affected by: Paragraph 46 and footnote 25 amended by FAS 145, paragraph 9(l)
Paragraphs 55 and 58(b) amended by FAS 154, paragraph C19(f)
Paragraph 61(b) amended by FAS 147, paragraph B2(a)
Paragraph A3(e) effectively deleted by FAS 123(R), paragraph D7(d)
Paragraph A14 amended by FSP FAS 141-1/142-1
Paragraph E10 deleted by FAS 145, paragraph 9(l)
Paragraph E20 deleted by FAS 147, paragraph B2(b)
Paragraph F1 amended by FAS 157, paragraph E21, and FSP FAS 126-1, paragraph A8, and
effectively amended by FAS 159, paragraph A44
Footnote 18 deleted by FAS 144, paragraph C16

Other Interpretive Release: FASB Staff Position FAS 141-1/142-1

AICPA Accounting Standards Executive Committee (AcSEC)

Related Pronouncements: SOP 90-7
SOP 94-6
SOP 96-1
PB 4
PB 14

Issues Discussed by FASB Emerging Issues Task Force (EITF)

Affects: Nullifies EITF Issues No. 85-14, 86-10, 86-31, 87-15, 87-16, 87-27, 88-26, 88-27, 95-12, 96-8, 97-9, 99-6, and 99-18 and Topics No. D-19, D-40, and D-59
Partially nullifies EITF Issues No. 87-21, 91-5, 95-14, 97-2, 99-7, and 00-23
Resolves EITF Issues No. 84-22, 90-10, 93-2, and 96-23
Partially resolves EITF Issue No. 98-3

Interpreted by: Paragraphs 4 through 7 and 16 through 18 interpreted by EITF Issue No. 90-13
Paragraph 11 interpreted by EITF Issue No. 02-5
Paragraph 20 interpreted by EITF Issues No. 88-16 and 95-3
Paragraph 21 interpreted by EITF Issue No. 88-16
Paragraph 22 interpreted by EITF Issues No. 88-16 and 99-12
Paragraphs 23 and 24 interpreted by EITF Issue No. 88-16
Paragraphs 25 through 27 interpreted by EITF Issues No. 97-8 and 97-15
Paragraph 28 interpreted by EITF Issues No. 95-8 and 97-15
Paragraphs 29 through 31 interpreted by EITF Issue No. 97-15
Paragraph 34 interpreted by EITF Issue No. 95-8
Paragraph 35 interpreted by EITF Issue No. 04-3
Paragraph 36 interpreted by EITF Issues No. 85-41, 90-12, 95-3, and 98-1
Paragraph 37 interpreted by EITF Issues No. 85-41, 88-19, 90-12, 95-3, and 98-1
Paragraph 37(e) interpreted by EITF Topic No. D-108
Paragraph 37(j) interpreted by EITF Issue No. 85-45
Paragraph 40 interpreted by EITF Issue No. 93-7
Paragraph 49 interpreted by EITF Topic No. D-87
Paragraph 61(b) interpreted by EITF Topic No. D-100
Paragraph A14 interpreted by EITF Issue No. 04-2
Paragraphs A19, A20, and A24 interpreted by EITF Issue No. 02-17
Paragraph D12 interpreted by EITF Issue No. 02-5
Paragraph F1 interpreted by EITF Issue No. 95-3

Related Issues: EITF Issues No. 84-35, 85-8, 85-42, 85-46, 86-9, 86-14, 90-5, 92-9, 94-2, 95-7, 96-5, 96-7, 96-17, 98-4, 98-11, 99-15, 00-6, 01-2, 01-3, 03-9, 03-17, 04-1, 04-11, and 05-6 and Topics No. D-54, D-84, and D-97

SUMMARY

This Statement addresses financial accounting and reporting for business combinations and supersedes APB Opinion No. 16, *Business Combinations,* and FASB Statement No. 38, *Accounting for Preacquisition Contingencies of Purchased Enterprises.* All business combinations in the scope of this Statement are to be accounted for using one method—the purchase method.

Reasons for Issuing This Statement

Under Opinion 16, business combinations were accounted for using one of two methods, the pooling-of-interests method (pooling method) or the purchase method. Use of the pooling method was required whenever 12 criteria were met; otherwise, the purchase method was to be used. Because those 12 criteria did not distinguish economically dissimilar transactions, similar business combinations were accounted for using different methods that produced dramatically different financial statement results. Consequently:

- Analysts and other users of financial statements indicated that it was difficult to compare the financial results of entities because different methods of accounting for business combinations were used.
- Users of financial statements also indicated a need for better information about intangible assets because those assets are an increasingly important economic resource for many entities and are an increasing proportion of the assets acquired in many business combinations. While the purchase method recognizes all intangible assets acquired in a business combination (either separately or as goodwill), only those intangible assets previously recorded by the acquired entity are recognized when the pooling method is used.

- Company managements indicated that the differences between the pooling and purchase methods of accounting for business combinations affected competition in markets for mergers and acquisitions.

Differences between This Statement and Opinion 16

The provisions of this Statement reflect a fundamentally different approach to accounting for business combinations than was taken in Opinion 16. The single-method approach used in this Statement reflects the conclusion that virtually all business combinations are acquisitions and, thus, all business combinations should be accounted for in the same way that other asset acquisitions are accounted for—based on the values exchanged.

This Statement changes the accounting for business combinations in Opinion 16 in the following significant respects:

- This Statement requires that all business combinations be accounted for by a single method—the purchase method.
- In contrast to Opinion 16, which required separate recognition of intangible assets that can be identified and named, this Statement requires that they be recognized as assets apart from goodwill if they meet one of two criteria—the contractual-legal criterion or the separability criterion. To assist in identifying acquired intangible assets, this Statement also provides an illustrative list of intangible assets that meet either of those criteria.
- In addition to the disclosure requirements in Opinion 16, this Statement requires disclosure of the primary reasons for a business combination and the allocation of the purchase price paid to the assets acquired and liabilities assumed by major balance sheet caption. When the amounts of goodwill and intangible assets acquired are significant in relation to the purchase price paid, disclosure of other information about those assets is required, such as the amount of goodwill by reportable segment and the amount of the purchase price assigned to each major intangible asset class.

This Statement does not change many of the provisions of Opinion 16 and Statement 38 related to the application of the purchase method. For example, this Statement does not fundamentally change the guidance for determining the cost of an acquired entity and allocating that cost to the assets acquired and liabilities assumed, the accounting for contingent consideration, and the accounting for preacquisition contingencies. That guidance is carried forward in this Statement (but was not reconsidered by the Board). Also, this Statement does not change the requirement to write off certain research and development assets acquired in a business combination as required by FASB Interpretation No. 4, *Applicability of FASB Statement No. 2 to Business Combinations Accounted for by the Purchase Method.*

How the Changes in This Statement Improve Financial Reporting

The changes to accounting for business combinations required by this Statement improve financial reporting because the financial statements of entities that engage in business combinations will better reflect the underlying economics of those transactions. In particular, application of this Statement will result in financial statements that:

- *Better reflect the investment made in an acquired entity*—the purchase method records a business combination based on the values exchanged, thus, users are provided information about the total purchase price paid to acquire another entity, which allows for more meaningful evaluation of the subsequent performance of that investment. Similar information is not provided when the pooling method is used.
- *Improve the comparability of reported financial information*—all business combinations are accounted for using a single method, thus, users are able to compare the financial results of entities that engage in business combinations on an apples-to-apples basis. That is because the assets acquired and liabilities assumed in all business combinations are recognized and measured in the same way regardless of the nature of the consideration exchanged for them.
- *Provide more complete financial information*—the explicit criteria for recognition of intangible assets apart from goodwill and the expanded disclosure requirements of this Statement provide more information about the assets acquired and liabilities assumed in business combinations. That additional information should, among other things, provide users with a better understanding of the resources acquired and improve their ability to assess future profitability and cash flows.

Requiring one method of accounting reduces the costs of accounting for business combinations. For example, it eliminates the costs incurred by entities in positioning themselves to meet the criteria for using the pooling method, such as the monetary and nonmonetary costs of taking actions they might not otherwise have taken or refraining from actions they might otherwise have taken.

How the Conclusions in This Statement Relate to the Conceptual Framework

The Board concluded that because virtually all business combinations are acquisitions, requiring one method of accounting for economically similar transactions is consistent with the concepts of representational faithfulness and comparability as discussed in FASB Concepts Statement No. 2, *Qualitative Characteristics of Accounting Information.* In developing this Statement, the Board also concluded that goodwill should be recognized as an asset because it meets the assets definition in FASB Concepts Statement No. 6, *Elements of Financial Statements,* and the asset recognition criteria in FASB Concepts Statement No. 5, *Recognition and Measurement in Financial Statements of Business Enterprises.*

The Board also noted that FASB Concepts Statement No. 1, *Objectives of Financial Reporting by Business Enterprises,* states that financial reporting should provide information that helps in assessing the amounts, timing, and uncertainty of prospective net cash inflows to an entity. The Board noted that because the purchase method records the net assets acquired in a business combination at their fair values, the information provided by that method is more useful in assessing the cash-generating abilities of the net assets acquired than the information provided by the pooling method.

Some of the Board's constituents indicated that the pooling method should be retained for public policy reasons. For example, some argued that eliminating the pooling method would impede consolidation of certain industries, reduce the amount of capital flowing into certain industries, and slow the development of new technology. Concepts Statement 2 states that a necessary and important characteristic of accounting information is neutrality. In the context of business combinations, neutrality means that the accounting standards should neither encourage nor discourage business combinations but rather, provide information about those combinations that is fair and evenhanded. The Board concluded that its public policy goal is to issue accounting standards that result in neutral and representationally faithful financial information and that eliminating the pooling method is consistent with that goal.

The Effective Date of This Statement

The provisions of this Statement apply to all business combinations initiated after June 30, 2001. This Statement also applies to all business combinations accounted for using the purchase method for which the date of acquisition is July 1, 2001, or later.

This Statement does not apply, however, to combinations of two or more not-for-profit organizations, the acquisition of a for-profit business entity by a not-for-profit organization, and combinations of two or more mutual enterprises.

Statement of Financial Accounting Standards No. 141

Business Combinations

CONTENTS

INTRODUCTION

1. This Statement addresses financial accounting and reporting for business combinations. This Statement supersedes APB Opinion No. 16, *Business Combinations,* and amends or supersedes a number of interpretations of that Opinion. However, this Statement carries forward without reconsideration the guidance in Opinion 16 and certain of its amendments and interpretations related to the application of

the purchase method of accounting, including (a) guidance in Opinion 16 described as the principles of historical-cost accounting (refer to paragraphs 3–8), (b) determining the cost of an acquired entity (refer to paragraphs 20–34), (c) allocation of the cost of an acquired entity to assets acquired and liabilities assumed (refer to paragraphs 36–38), and (d) determining the date of acquisition (refer to paragraphs 48 and 49). This Statement also supersedes FASB Statement No. 38, *Accounting for Preacquisition Contingencies of Purchased Enterprises,* but carries forward the guidance from that Statement without reconsideration (refer to paragraphs 40 and 41). The guidance carried forward from Opinion 16 and Statement 38 has been quoted, paraphrased, or rephrased as necessary so that it can be understood in the context of this Statement. The original source of that guidance has been noted parenthetically. The Board intends to reconsider some or all of that guidance (as well as related Emerging Issues Task Force [EITF] issues) in another project.

2. Appendix A to this Statement provides implementation guidance on the application of the purchase method of accounting for a business combination and is an integral part of the standards provided in this Statement. Appendix B provides background information and the basis for the Board's conclusions. Appendix C provides illustrations of some of the financial statement disclosures that this Statement requires. Appendix D carries forward without reconsideration certain provisions of Opinion 16 and its interpretations that have been deleted or superseded by this Statement but that continue to be relevant to past transactions that were accounted for using the **pooling-of-interests method.**[1] This Statement amends or supersedes other accounting pronouncements listed in Appendix E, but it does not change the status of the EITF Issues that provide guidance on applying the purchase method. Appendix F provides a glossary of terms as used in this Statement.

STANDARDS OF FINANCIAL ACCOUNTING AND REPORTING

Accounting for Asset Acquisitions— General Concepts

3. The accounting for a business combination follows the concepts normally applicable to the initial recognition and measurement of assets acquired, liabilities assumed or incurred, and equity shares issued, as well as to the subsequent accounting for those items. Those concepts are set forth in paragraphs 4–8. The standards of accounting and reporting for a business combination by the purchase method, which are based on those concepts, are set forth in paragraphs 9–58 (Opinion 16, paragraph 66).

4. *Initial recognition.* Assets are commonly acquired in exchange transactions that trigger the initial recognition of the assets acquired and any liabilities assumed. If the consideration given in exchange for the asset (or net assets) acquired is in the form of assets surrendered (such as cash), the assets surrendered are derecognized at the date of acquisition. If the consideration given is in the form of liabilities incurred or equity interests issued, the liabilities incurred and equity interests issued are initially recognized at the date of acquisition (Opinion 16, paragraph 67).

5. *Initial measurement.* Like other exchange transactions generally, acquisitions are measured on the basis of the fair values exchanged. In exchange transactions, the fair values of the net assets acquired and the consideration paid are assumed to be equal, absent evidence to the contrary. Thus, the "cost"[2] of an acquisition to the acquiring entity is equal to the fair values exchanged and no gain or loss is generally recognized. Exceptions to that general condition include (a) the gain or loss that is recognized if the fair value of noncash assets given as consideration differs from their carrying amounts on the acquiring entity's books and (b) the extraordinary gain that is sometimes recognized by the acquiring entity if the fair value of the net assets acquired in a business combination exceeds the cost of the acquired entity (refer to paragraphs 45 and 46) (Opinion 16, paragraph 67).

---

[1]Terms defined in Appendix F, the glossary, are set forth in **boldface type** the first time they appear.

[2]Cost is a term that is often used to refer to the amount at which an entity initially recognizes an asset at the date it is acquired, whatever the manner of acquisition.

6. Exchange transactions in which the consideration given is cash are measured by the amount of cash paid. However, if the consideration given is not in the form of cash (that is, in the form of noncash assets, liabilities incurred, or equity interests issued), measurement is based on the fair value of the consideration given or the fair value of the asset (or net assets) acquired, whichever is more clearly evident and, thus, more reliably measurable (Opinion 16, paragraph 67).

7. *Allocating cost.* Acquiring assets in groups requires not only ascertaining the cost of the asset (or net asset) group but also allocating that cost to the individual assets (or individual assets and liabilities) that make up the group. The cost of such a group is determined using the concepts described in paragraphs 5 and 6. A portion of the cost of the group is then assigned to each individual asset (or individual assets and liabilities) acquired on the basis of its fair value. In a business combination, an excess of the cost of the group over the sum of the amounts assigned to the tangible assets, **financial assets,** and separately recognized **intangible assets** acquired less liabilities assumed is evidence of an unidentified intangible asset or assets (Opinion 16, paragraph 68).

8. *Accounting after acquisition.* The nature of an asset and not the manner of its acquisition determines an acquiring entity's subsequent accounting for the asset. The basis for measuring the asset acquired— whether the amount of cash paid, the fair value of an asset received or given up, the fair value of a liability incurred, or the fair value of equity shares issued— has no effect on the subsequent accounting for the asset (Opinion 16, paragraph 69).

Standards of Accounting for Business Combinations

Scope

9. For purposes of applying this Statement, a *business combination* occurs when an entity[3] acquires net assets that constitute a business[4] or acquires equity interests of one or more other entities and obtains control[5] over that entity or entities. This Statement does not address transactions in which control is obtained through means other than an acquisition of net assets or equity interests. For purposes of this Statement, the formation of a joint venture is not a business combination.[6]

10. This Statement applies to combinations involving either incorporated or unincorporated entities. The provisions of this Statement apply equally to a business combination in which (a) one or more entities are merged or become subsidiaries, (b) one entity transfers net assets or its owners transfer their equity interests to another, or (c) all entities transfer net assets or the owners of those entities transfer their equity interests to a newly formed entity (some of which are referred to as roll-up or put-together transactions). All those transactions are business combinations regardless of whether the form of consideration given is cash, other assets, a business or a subsidiary of the entity, debt, common or preferred shares or other equity interests, or a combination of those forms and regardless of whether the former owners of one of the combining entities as a group retain or receive a majority of the voting rights of the combined entity. An exchange of a business for a business also is a business combination.

11. The acquisition of some or all of the noncontrolling interests in a subsidiary is not a business combination. However, paragraph 14 of this Statement specifies the method of accounting for those transactions. The term business combination as used in this Statement also excludes transfers of net assets or exchanges of equity interests between entities under common control. Paragraphs D11–D18 of Appendix D provide examples of those transactions and accounting guidance for them.

12. This Statement does not apply to combinations between **not-for-profit organizations,** nor does it

---

[3]This Statement applies to a business enterprise, a new entity formed to complete a business combination, or a **mutual enterprise**, each of which is referred to herein as an *entity*. That term can refer to any of the various forms in which the participants in a business combination may exist. However, a new entity formed to complete a business combination would not necessarily be the acquiring entity (refer to paragraph 19).

[4]EITF Issue No. 98-3, "Determining Whether a Nonmonetary Transaction Involves Receipt of Productive Assets or of a Business," provides guidance on determining whether an asset group constitutes a business.

[5]Control is generally indicated by "ownership by one company, directly or indirectly, of over fifty percent of the outstanding voting shares of another company" (ARB No. 51, *Consolidated Financial Statements,* paragraph 2, as amended by FASB Statement No. 94, *Consolidation of All Majority-owned Subsidiaries*), although control may exist in other circumstances.

[6]The Board intends to address the accounting for other events or transactions that are similar to a business combination but do not meet this Statement's definition of a business combination and the accounting for joint venture formations in another project.

apply to the acquisition of a for-profit business entity by a not-for-profit organization.[7]

Method of Accounting

13. All business combinations in the scope of this Statement shall be accounted for using the purchase method as described in this Statement and other pronouncements (refer to paragraph A3 of Appendix A).

14. The acquisition of some or all of the noncontrolling interests in a subsidiary—whether acquired by the parent, the subsidiary itself, or another affiliate—shall be accounted for using the purchase method. Paragraphs A5–A7 of Appendix A provide additional accounting guidance for those transactions.[8]

Application of the Purchase Method

Identifying the acquiring entity

15. Application of the purchase method requires the identification of the acquiring entity. All business combinations in the scope of this Statement shall be accounted for using the purchase method. Thus, the acquiring entity shall be identified in all business combinations.

16. In a business combination effected solely through the distribution of cash or other assets or by incurring liabilities, the entity that distributes cash or other assets or incurs liabilities is generally the acquiring entity.

17. In a business combination effected through an exchange of equity interests, the entity that issues the equity interests is generally the acquiring entity. In some business combinations (commonly referred to as reverse acquisitions), however, the acquired entity issues the equity interests. Commonly, the acquiring entity is the larger entity. However, the facts and circumstances surrounding a business combination sometimes indicate that a smaller entity acquires a larger one. In some business combinations, the combined entity assumes the name of the acquired entity.

Thus, in identifying the acquiring entity in a combination effected through an exchange of equity interests, all pertinent facts and circumstances shall be considered, in particular:

a. The relative voting rights in the combined entity after the combination—all else being equal, the acquiring entity is the combining entity whose owners as a group retained or received the larger portion of the voting rights in the combined entity. In determining which group of owners retained or received the larger portion of the voting rights, consideration shall be given to the existence of any unusual or special voting arrangements and options, warrants, or convertible securities.

b. The existence of a large minority voting interest in the combined entity when no other owner or organized group of owners has a significant voting interest—all else being equal, the acquiring entity is the combining entity whose single owner or organized group of owners holds the large minority voting interest in the combined entity.

c. The composition of the governing body of the combined entity—all else being equal, the acquiring entity is the combining entity whose owners or governing body has the ability to elect or appoint a voting majority of the governing body of the combined entity.

d. The composition of the senior management of the combined entity—all else being equal, the acquiring entity is the combining entity whose senior management dominates that of the combined entity. Senior management generally consists of the chairman of the board, chief executive officer, chief operating officer, chief financial officer, and those divisional heads reporting directly to them, or the executive committee if one exists.

e. The terms of the exchange of equity securities—all else being equal, the acquiring entity is the combining entity that pays a premium over the market value of the equity securities of the other combining entity or entities.[9]

---

[7]The Board intends to address issues related to the accounting for combinations between not-for-profit organizations and issues related to the accounting for the acquisition of a for-profit business entity by a not-for-profit organization in another project.

[8]The October 2000 FASB Exposure Draft, *Accounting for Financial Instruments with Characteristics of Liabilities, Equity, or Both,* proposes that a noncontrolling interest in a subsidiary be reported in consolidated financial statements as a separate component of equity and that distributions to holders of those noncontrolling interests be recognized as equity distributions. If those proposed provisions are affirmed, the Board will consider those provisions when it reconsiders the accounting for the acquisition of noncontrolling interests in a subsidiary, in particular whether the acquisition of those interests should be accounted for as an equity distribution rather than by the purchase method.

[9]This criterion shall apply only if the equity securities exchanged in a business combination are traded in a public market on either (a) a stock exchange (domestic or foreign) or (b) in an over-the-counter market (including securities quoted only locally or regionally).

18. Some business combinations involve more than two entities. In identifying the acquiring entity in those cases, consideration also shall be given to which combining entity initiated the combination and whether the assets, revenues, and earnings of one of the combining entities significantly exceed those of the others.

19. If a new entity is formed to issue equity interests to effect a business combination, one of the existing combining entities shall be determined to be the acquiring entity on the basis of the evidence available. The guidance in paragraphs 16–18 shall be used in making that determination.

Determining the cost of the acquired entity

20. The same accounting principles shall apply in determining the cost of assets acquired individually, those acquired in a group, and those acquired in a business combination. A cash payment by an acquiring entity shall be used to measure the cost of an acquired entity. Similarly, the fair values of other assets distributed as consideration, such as marketable securities or properties, and the fair values of liabilities incurred by an acquiring entity shall be used to measure the cost of an acquired entity (Opinion 16, paragraph 72).

21. The distinctive characteristics of preferred shares make some preferred share issues similar to debt securities, while others are similar to common shares, with many gradations in between. Those characteristics may affect the determination of the cost of an acquired entity. For example, the fair value of nonvoting, nonconvertible preferred shares that lack characteristics of common shares may be determined by comparing the specified dividend and redemption terms with those of comparable securities and by assessing market factors. Thus, although the principle of recording the fair value of consideration received for shares issued applies to all equity securities, senior as well as common shares, the cost of an entity acquired by issuing senior equity securities may be determined in practice on the same basis as for debt securities (Opinion 16, paragraph 73).

22. The fair value of securities traded in the market is generally more clearly evident than the fair value of an acquired entity (paragraph 6). Thus, the quoted market price of an equity security issued to effect a business combination generally should be used to estimate the fair value of an acquired entity after recognizing possible effects of price fluctuations, quanti-

ties traded, issue costs, and the like. The market price for a reasonable period before and after the date that the terms of the acquisition are agreed to and announced shall be considered in determining the fair value of securities issued (Opinion 16, paragraph 74).

23. If the quoted market price is not the fair value of the equity securities, either preferred or common, the consideration received shall be estimated even though measuring directly the fair values of net assets received is difficult. Both the net assets received, including **goodwill,** and the extent of the adjustment of the quoted market price of the shares issued shall be weighed to determine the amount to be recorded. All aspects of the acquisition, including the negotiations, shall be studied, and independent appraisals may be used as an aid in determining the fair value of securities issued. Consideration other than equity securities distributed to effect an acquisition may provide evidence of the total fair value received (Opinion 16, paragraph 75).

Costs of the business combination

24. The cost of an entity acquired in a business combination includes the direct costs of the business combination. Costs of registering and issuing equity securities shall be recognized as a reduction of the otherwise determinable fair value of the securities. However, indirect and general expenses related to business combinations shall be expensed as incurred (Opinion 16, paragraph 76).

Contingent consideration

25. A business combination agreement may provide for the issuance of additional shares of a security or the transfer of cash or other consideration contingent on specified events or transactions in the future. Some agreements provide that a portion of the consideration be placed in escrow to be distributed or returned to the transferor when specified events occur. Either debt or equity securities may be placed in escrow, and amounts equal to interest or dividends on the securities during the contingency period may be paid to the escrow agent or to the potential security holder (Opinion 16, paragraph 77).

26. Cash and other assets distributed, securities issued unconditionally, and amounts of contingent consideration that are determinable at the date of acquisition shall be included in determining the cost of an acquired entity and recorded at that date. Consideration that is issued or issuable at the expiration of

the contingency period or that is held in escrow pending the outcome of the contingency shall be disclosed but not recorded as a liability or shown as outstanding securities unless the outcome of the contingency is determinable beyond a reasonable doubt (Opinion 16, paragraph 78).

27. The contingent consideration usually should be recorded when the contingency is resolved and consideration is issued or becomes issuable. In general, the issuance of additional securities or distribution of other consideration at resolution of contingencies based on earnings shall result in an additional element of cost of an acquired entity. In contrast, the issuance of additional securities or distribution of other consideration at resolution of contingencies based on security prices shall not change the recorded cost of an acquired entity (Opinion 16, paragraph 79).

Contingency based on earnings

28. Additional consideration may be contingent on maintaining or achieving specified earnings levels in future periods. When the contingency is resolved and additional consideration is distributable, the acquiring entity shall record the fair value of the consideration issued or issuable as an additional cost of the acquired entity[10] (Opinion 16, paragraph 80).

Contingency based on security prices

29. Additional consideration may be contingent on the market price of a specified security issued to effect a business combination. Unless the price of the security at least equals the specified amount on a specified date or dates, the acquiring entity is required to issue additional equity or debt securities or transfer cash or other assets sufficient to make the current value of the total consideration equal to the specified amount. The securities issued unconditionally at the date the combination is consummated shall be recorded at that date at the specified amount (Opinion 16, paragraph 81).

30. The issuance of additional securities or distribution of other consideration upon resolution of a contingency based on security prices shall not affect the cost of the acquired entity, regardless of whether the amount specified is a security price to be maintained or a higher security price to be achieved. When the contingency is resolved and additional consideration is distributable, the acquiring entity shall record the current fair value of the additional consideration issued or issuable. However, the amount previously recorded for securities issued at the date of acquisition shall be simultaneously reduced to the lower current value of those securities. Reducing the value of debt securities previously issued to their later fair value results in recording a discount on debt securities. That discount shall be amortized from the date the additional securities are issued (Opinion 16, paragraph 82).

31. Accounting for contingent consideration based on conditions other than those described shall be inferred from the procedures outlined. For example, if the consideration contingently issuable depends on both future earnings and future security prices, an additional cost of the acquired entity shall be recorded for the additional consideration contingent on earnings, and previously recorded consideration shall be reduced to the current value of the consideration contingent on security prices. Similarly, if the consideration contingently issuable depends on later settlement of a contingency, an increase in the cost of acquired assets, if any, shall be amortized, if applicable, over the remaining useful lives of the assets[11] (Opinion 16, paragraph 83).

Interest or dividends during contingency period

32. Amounts paid to an escrow agent representing interest and dividends on securities held in escrow shall be accounted for according to the accounting for the securities. That is, until the disposition of the securities in escrow is resolved, payments to the escrow agent shall not be recorded as interest expense or dividend distributions. An amount equal to interest and dividends later distributed by the escrow agent to the former shareholders shall be added to the cost of the acquired assets at the date distributed (Opinion 16, paragraph 84).

Tax effect of imputed interest

33. A tax reduction resulting from imputed interest on contingently issuable shares reduces the fair value

---

[10]Paragraph 46 provides guidance on accounting for contingent consideration in a business combination if the fair value of the net assets acquired exceeds the cost of the acquired entity.

[11]Whether an increase in the cost of the acquired assets will be amortized depends on the nature of the asset. Guidance on the subsequent accounting for goodwill and other intangible assets acquired in a business combination is provided in FASB Statement No. 142, *Goodwill and Other Intangible Assets.*

recorded for contingent consideration based on earnings and increases additional capital recorded for contingent consideration based on security prices (Opinion 16, paragraph 85).

Compensation in contingent agreements

34. If the substance of the agreement for contingent consideration is to provide compensation for services or use of property or profit sharing, the additional consideration given shall be recognized as an expense of the appropriate periods (Opinion 16, paragraph 86).

Allocating the cost of an acquired entity to assets acquired and liabilities assumed

35. Following the process described in paragraphs 36–46 (commonly referred to as the purchase price allocation), an acquiring entity shall allocate the cost of an acquired entity to the assets acquired and liabilities assumed based on their estimated fair values at date of acquisition (refer to paragraph 48). Prior to that allocation, the acquiring entity shall (a) review the purchase consideration if other than cash to ensure that it has been valued in accordance with the requirements in paragraphs 20–23 and (b) identify all of the assets acquired and liabilities assumed, including intangible assets that meet the recognition criteria in paragraph 39, regardless of whether they had been recorded in the financial statements of the acquired entity.

36. Among other sources of relevant information, independent appraisals and actuarial or other valuations may be used as an aid in determining the estimated fair values of assets acquired and liabilities assumed. The tax basis of an asset or liability shall not be a factor in determining its estimated fair value (Opinion 16, paragraph 87).

Assets acquired and liabilities assumed, except goodwill

37. The following is general guidance for assigning amounts to assets acquired and liabilities assumed, except goodwill:

a. Marketable securities at fair values
b. Receivables at present values of amounts to be received determined at appropriate current interest rates, less allowances for uncollectibility and collection costs, if necessary

c. Inventories
  (1) Finished goods and merchandise at estimated selling prices less the sum of (a) costs of disposal and (b) a reasonable profit allowance for the selling effort of the acquiring entity
  (2) Work in process at estimated selling prices of finished goods less the sum of (a) costs to complete, (b) costs of disposal, and (c) a reasonable profit allowance for the completing and selling effort of the acquiring entity based on profit for similar finished goods
  (3) Raw materials at current replacement costs
d. Plant and equipment
  (1) To be used, at the current replacement cost for similar capacity[12] unless the expected future use of the assets indicates a lower value to the acquiring entity
  (2) To be sold, at fair value less cost to sell
e. Intangible assets that meet the criteria in paragraph 39 at estimated fair values
f. Other assets, including land, natural resources, and nonmarketable securities, at appraised values
g. Accounts and notes payable, long-term debt, and other claims payable, at present values of amounts to be paid determined at appropriate current interest rates
h. A liability for the projected benefit obligation in excess of plan assets or an asset for plan assets in excess of the projected benefit obligation of a single-employer defined benefit pension plan, at amounts determined in accordance with paragraph 74 of FASB Statement No. 87, *Employers' Accounting for Pensions*
i. A liability for the accumulated postretirement benefit obligation in excess of the fair value of plan assets or an asset for the fair value of the plan assets in excess of the accumulated postretirement benefit obligation of a single-employer defined benefit postretirement plan at amounts determined in accordance with paragraphs 86–88 of FASB Statement No. 106, *Employers' Accounting for Postretirement Benefits Other Than Pensions*
j. Liabilities and accruals—such as accruals for warranties, vacation pay, and deferred compensation—at present values of amounts to be paid determined at appropriate current interest rates
k. Other liabilities and commitments—such as unfavorable leases, contracts, and commitments and plant closing expense incident to the acquisi-

---

[12]Replacement cost may be determined directly if a used-asset market exists for the assets acquired. Otherwise, the replacement cost should be estimated from the replacement cost new less estimated accumulated depreciation.

tion—at present values of amounts to be paid determined at appropriate current interest rates

l. **Preacquisition contingencies** at amounts determined in accordance with paragraph 40 of this Statement (Opinion 16, paragraph 88).

38. An acquiring entity shall not recognize the goodwill previously recorded by an acquired entity, nor shall it recognize the deferred income taxes recorded by an acquired entity before its acquisition. A deferred tax liability or asset shall be recognized for differences between the assigned values and the tax bases of the recognized assets acquired and liabilities assumed in a business combination in accordance with paragraph 30 of FASB Statement No. 109, *Accounting for Income Taxes* (Opinion 16, paragraph 88).

Intangible assets

39. An intangible asset shall be recognized as an asset apart from goodwill if it arises from contractual or other legal rights (regardless of whether those rights are transferable or separable from the acquired entity or from other rights and obligations). If an intangible asset does not arise from contractual or other legal rights, it shall be recognized as an asset apart from goodwill only if it is separable, that is, it is capable of being separated or divided from the acquired entity and sold, transferred, licensed, rented, or exchanged (regardless of whether there is an intent to do so). For purposes of this Statement, however, an intangible asset that cannot be sold, transferred, licensed, rented, or exchanged individually is considered separable if it can be sold, transferred, licensed, rented, or exchanged in combination with a related contract, asset, or liability. For purposes of this Statement, an assembled workforce shall not be recognized as an intangible asset apart from goodwill. Appendix A provides additional guidance relating to the recognition of acquired intangible assets apart from goodwill, including an illustrative list of intangible assets that meet the recognition criteria in this paragraph.

Preacquisition contingencies

40. A preacquisition contingency other than the potential tax effects of (a) temporary differences and carryforwards of an acquired entity that exist at the acquisition date and (b) income tax uncertainties related to the acquisition (for example, an uncertainty related to the tax basis of an acquired asset that will ultimately be agreed to by the taxing authority)[13] shall be included in the purchase price allocation based on an amount determined as follows:

a. If the fair value of the preacquisition contingency can be determined during the **allocation period,** that preacquisition contingency shall be included in the allocation of the purchase price based on that fair value.[14]

b. If the fair value of the preacquisition contingency cannot be determined during the allocation period, that preacquisition contingency shall be included in the allocation of the purchase price based on an amount determined in accordance with the following criteria:

(1) Information available prior to the end of the allocation period indicates that it is probable that an asset existed, a liability had been incurred, or an asset had been impaired at the consummation of the business combination. It is implicit in this condition that it must be probable that one or more future events will occur confirming the existence of the asset, liability, or impairment.

(2) The amount of the asset or liability can be reasonably estimated.

The criteria of this subparagraph shall be applied using the guidance provided in FASB Statement No. 5, *Accounting for Contingencies,* and related FASB Interpretation No. 14, *Reasonable Estimation of the Amount of a Loss,* for application of the similar criteria of paragraph 8 of Statement 5[15] (Statement 38, paragraph 5).

---

[13]Those potential income tax effects shall be accounted for in accordance with the provisions of Statement 109.

[14]For example, if it can be demonstrated that the parties to a business combination agreed to adjust the total consideration by an amount because of a contingency, that amount would be a determined fair value of that contingency.

[15]Interpretation 14 specifies the amount to be accrued if the reasonable estimate of the amount is a range. If some amount within the range appears at the time to be a better estimate than any other amount within the range, that amount is accrued. If no amount within the range is a better estimate than any other amount, however, the minimum amount in the range is accrued.

41. After the end of the allocation period, an adjustment that results from a preacquisition contingency other than a loss carryforward[16] shall be included in the determination of net income in the period in which the adjustment is determined (Statement 38, paragraph 6).

Research and development assets

42. This Statement does not change the requirement in paragraph 5 of FASB Interpretation No. 4, *Applicability of FASB Statement No. 2 to Business Combinations Accounted for by the Purchase Method,* that the amounts assigned to tangible and intangible assets to be used in a particular research and development project that *have no alternative future use* shall be charged to expense at the acquisition date.

Excess of cost over the fair value of acquired net assets (goodwill)

43. The excess of the cost of an acquired entity over the net of the amounts assigned to assets acquired and liabilities assumed shall be recognized as an asset referred to as goodwill. An acquired intangible asset that does not meet the criteria in paragraph 39 shall be included in the amount recognized as goodwill.

Excess of fair value of acquired net assets over cost

44. In some cases, the sum of the amounts assigned to assets acquired and liabilities assumed will exceed the cost of the acquired entity *(excess over cost* or *excess).* That excess shall be allocated as a pro rata reduction of the amounts that otherwise would have been assigned to all of the acquired assets[17] except (a) financial assets other than investments accounted for by the equity method, (b) assets to be disposed of by sale, (c) deferred tax assets, (d) prepaid assets relating to pension or other postretirement benefit plans, and (e) any other current assets.[19]

45. If any excess remains after reducing to zero the amounts that otherwise would have been assigned to those assets, that remaining excess shall be recog-

nized as an extraordinary gain as described in paragraph 11 of APB Opinion No. 30, *Reporting the Results of Operations—Reporting the Effects of Disposal of a Segment of a Business, and Extraordinary, Unusual and Infrequently Occurring Events and Transactions.* The extraordinary gain shall be recognized in the period in which the business combination is completed unless the combination involves contingent consideration that, if paid or issued, would be recognized as an additional element of cost of the acquired entity (refer to paragraph 46). If an extraordinary gain is recognized before the end of the allocation period, any subsequent adjustments to that extraordinary gain that result from changes to the purchase price allocation shall be recognized as an extraordinary item.

46. If a business combination involves a contingent consideration agreement that might result in recognition of an additional element of cost of the acquired entity when the contingency is resolved (a contingency based on earnings), an amount equal to the lesser of the maximum amount of contingent consideration or the excess prior to the pro rata allocation required by paragraph 44 shall be recognized as if it was a liability. When the contingency is resolved and the consideration is issued or becomes issuable, any excess of the fair value of the contingent consideration issued or issuable over the amount that was recognized as if it was a liability shall be recognized as an additional cost of the acquired entity. If the amount initially recognized as if it was a liability exceeds the fair value of the consideration issued or issuable, that excess shall be allocated as a pro rata reduction of the amounts assigned to assets acquired in accordance with paragraph 44. Any amount that remains after reducing those assets to zero shall be recognized as an extraordinary gain in accordance with paragraph 45.

Accounting for goodwill and other intangible assets acquired

47. After initial recognition, goodwill and other intangible assets acquired in a business combination

---

[16]Refer to footnote 13.

[17]The acquired assets include research and development assets acquired and charged to expense in accordance with paragraph 5 of Interpretation 4 (refer to paragraph 42).

[18][This footnote has been deleted. See Status page.]

[19]Prior to allocation of the excess, if any, the acquiring entity shall reassess whether all acquired assets and assumed liabilities have been identified and recognized and perform remeasurements to verify that the consideration paid, assets acquired, and liabilities assumed have been properly valued (refer to paragraph 35).

shall be accounted for in accordance with the provisions of FASB Statement No. 142, *Goodwill and Other Intangible Assets.*[20]

Date of acquisition

48. The date of acquisition (also referred to as the acquisition date) ordinarily is the date assets are received and other assets are given, liabilities are assumed or incurred, or equity interests are issued. However, the parties may, for convenience, designate as the effective date the end of an accounting period between the dates a business combination is initiated and consummated. The designated date should ordinarily be the acquisition date for accounting purposes if a written agreement provides that effective control of the acquired entity is transferred to the acquiring entity on that date without restrictions except those required to protect the shareholders or other owners of the acquired entity, such as restrictions on significant changes in the operations, permission to pay dividends equal to those regularly paid before the effective date, and the like. Designating an effective date other than the date assets or equity interests are transferred or liabilities are assumed or incurred requires adjusting the cost of an acquired entity and net income otherwise reported to compensate for recognizing income before consideration is transferred. The cost of an acquired entity and net income shall therefore be reduced by imputed interest at an appropriate current rate on assets given, liabilities assumed or incurred, or preferred shares distributed as of the transfer date to acquire the entity (Opinion 16, paragraph 93).

49. The cost of an acquired entity and the amounts assigned to the assets acquired and liabilities assumed shall be determined as of the date of acquisition. The statement of income of an acquiring entity for the period in which a business combination occurs shall include the income of the acquired entity after the date of acquisition by including the revenue and expenses of the acquired entity based on the cost to the acquiring entity (Opinion 16, paragraph 94).

Documentation at date of acquisition

50. The provisions of Statement 142 require that the assets acquired and liabilities assumed in a business combination that meet certain criteria, including goodwill, be assigned to a **reporting unit** as of the

date of acquisition. For use in making those assignments, the basis for and method of determining the purchase price of an acquired entity and other related factors (such as the underlying reasons for the acquisition and management's expectations related to dilution, synergies, and other financial measurements) shall be documented at the date of acquisition.

Disclosures in Financial Statements

51. The notes to the financial statements of a combined entity shall disclose the following information in the period in which a material business combination is completed:

a. The name and a brief description of the acquired entity and the percentage of voting equity interests acquired

b. The primary reasons for the acquisition, including a description of the factors that contributed to a purchase price that results in recognition of goodwill

c. The period for which the results of operations of the acquired entity are included in the income statement of the combined entity

d. The cost of the acquired entity and, if applicable, the number of shares of equity interests (such as common shares, preferred shares, or partnership interests) issued or issuable, the value assigned to those interests, and the basis for determining that value

e. A condensed balance sheet disclosing the amount assigned to each major asset and liability caption of the acquired entity at the acquisition date

f. Contingent payments, options, or commitments specified in the acquisition agreement and the accounting treatment that will be followed should any such contingency occur

g. The amount of purchased research and development assets acquired and written off in the period (refer to paragraph 42) and the line item in the income statement in which the amounts written off are aggregated

h. For any purchase price allocation that has not been finalized, that fact and the reasons therefor. In subsequent periods, the nature and amount of any material adjustments made to the initial allocation of the purchase price shall be disclosed.

52. The notes to the financial statements also shall disclose the following information in the period in

---

[20]As stated in paragraph 8 of Statement 142, the accounting for some acquired intangible assets after initial recognition is prescribed by pronouncements other than Statement 142.

which a material business combination is completed if the amounts assigned to goodwill or to other intangible assets acquired are significant in relation to the total cost of the acquired entity:

a. For intangible assets subject to amortization:[21]
   (1) The total amount assigned and the amount assigned to any major **intangible asset class**
   (2) The amount of any significant **residual value,** in total and by major intangible asset class
   (3) The weighted-average amortization period, in total and by major intangible asset class
b. For intangible assets *not* subject to amortization,[22] the total amount assigned and the amount assigned to any major intangible asset class
c. For goodwill:
   (1) The total amount of goodwill and the amount that is expected to be deductible for tax purposes
   (2) The amount of goodwill by reportable segment (if the combined entity is required to disclose segment information in accordance with FASB Statement No. 131, *Disclosures about Segments of an Enterprise and Related Information*), unless not practicable.[23]

An example of the disclosure requirements in this paragraph and paragraph 51 is provided in illustration 1 in Appendix C.

53. The notes to the financial statements shall disclose the following information if a series of individually immaterial business combinations completed during the period are material in the aggregate:

a. The number of entities acquired and a brief description of those entities
b. The aggregate cost of the acquired entities, the number of equity interests (such as common shares, preferred shares, or partnership interests) issued or issuable, and the value assigned to those interests
c. The aggregate amount of any contingent payments, options, or commitments and the accounting treatment that will be followed should any such contingency occur (if potentially significant in relation to the aggregate cost of the acquired entities)

d. The information described in paragraph 52 if the aggregate amount assigned to goodwill or to other intangible assets acquired is significant in relation to the aggregate cost of the acquired entities.

An example of those disclosure requirements is provided in illustration 2 in Appendix C.

54. If the combined entity is a **public business enterprise,** the notes to the financial statements shall include the following supplemental information on a pro forma basis for the period in which a material business combination occurs (or for the period in which a series of individually immaterial business combinations occur that are material in the aggregate):

a. Results of operations for the current period as though the business combination or combinations had been completed at the beginning of the period, unless the acquisition was at or near the beginning of the period
b. Results of operations for the comparable prior period as though the business combination or combinations had been completed at the beginning of that period if comparative financial statements are presented.

55. At a minimum, the supplemental pro forma information shall display revenue, income before extraordinary items, net income, and earnings per share. In determining the pro forma amounts, income taxes, interest expense, preferred share dividends, and depreciation and amortization of assets shall be adjusted to the accounting base recognized for each in recording the combination. Pro forma information related to results of operations of periods prior to the combination shall be limited to the results of operations for the immediately preceding period. Disclosure also shall be made of the nature and amount of any material, nonrecurring items included in the reported pro forma results of operations.

56. In the period in which an extraordinary gain is recognized related to a business combination (paragraphs 45 and 46), the notes to the financial statements shall disclose the information required by paragraph 11 of Opinion 30.

---

[21]Statement 142 provides guidance for determining whether an intangible asset is subject to amortization.

[22]Refer to footnote 21.

[23]For example, it would not be practicable to disclose this information if the assignment of goodwill to reporting units (as required by Statement 142) has not been completed as of the date the financial statements are issued.

[23a][This footnote has been deleted because the effective date of FASB Statement No. 154, *Accounting Changes and Error Corrections,* has passed.]

57. The notes to the financial statements also shall disclose the information required by paragraphs 51 and 52 if a material business combination is completed after the balance sheet date but before the financial statements are issued (unless not practicable).

Disclosures in Interim Financial Information

58. The summarized interim financial information of a public business enterprise shall disclose the following information if a material business combination is completed during the current year up to the date of the most recent interim statement of financial position presented:

a. The information described in paragraph 51(a)–(d).
b. Supplemental pro forma information that discloses the results of operations for the current interim period and the current year up to the date of the most recent interim statement of financial position presented (and for the corresponding periods in the preceding year) as though the business combination had been completed as of the beginning of the period being reported on. That pro forma information shall display, at a minimum, revenue, income before extraordinary items (including those on an interim basis), net income, and earnings per share.
c. The nature and amount of any material, nonrecurring items included in the reported pro forma results of operations.

Effective Date and Transition

59. Except for combinations between two or more mutual enterprises, this Statement shall be effective as follows:

a. The provisions of this Statement shall apply to all business combinations initiated after June 30, 2001. Use of the pooling-of-interests method for those business combinations is prohibited.
b. The provisions of this Statement also shall apply to all business combinations accounted for by the purchase method for which the date of acquisition is July 1, 2001, or later.

The following definition of *initiated* from paragraph 46 of Opinion 16 shall be used in determining the effective date of this Statement:

A plan of combination is initiated on the earlier of (1) the date that the major terms of a plan, including the ratio of exchange of stock, are announced publicly or otherwise formally made known to the stockholders of any one of the combining companies or (2) the date that stockholders of a combining company are notified in writing of an exchange offer. Therefore, a plan of combination is often initiated even though consummation is subject to the approval of stockholders and others.

Paragraphs D4–D8 of Appendix D provide additional guidance relating to that definition. Any alteration in the terms of the exchange in a plan of combination constitutes initiation of a new plan of combination. Therefore, if the terms of the exchange in a plan of combination initiated on or before June 30, 2001, and in process on June 30, 2001, are altered after that date, the combination shall be accounted for by the purchase method in accordance with this Statement.

60. For combinations between two or more mutual enterprises, this Statement shall not be effective until interpretative guidance related to the application of the purchase method to those transactions is issued.[24]

61. The following transition provisions apply to business combinations for which the acquisition date was before July 1, 2001, that were accounted for using the purchase method:

a. The carrying amount of acquired intangible assets that do not meet the criteria in paragraph 39 for recognition apart from goodwill (and any related deferred tax liabilities if the intangible asset amortization is not deductible for tax purposes) shall be reclassified as goodwill as of the date Statement 142 is initially applied in its entirety.
b. The carrying amount of (1) any recognized intangible assets that meet the recognition criteria in paragraph 39 or (2) any unidentifiable intangible assets recognized in accordance with paragraph 5 of FASB Statement No. 72, *Accounting for Certain Acquisitions of Banking or Thrift Institutions,* and required to be amortized in accordance with paragraph 8 of FASB Statement No. 147, *Acquisitions of Certain Financial Institutions,*

[23b][This footnote has been deleted because the effective date of Statement 154 has passed.]

[24]The Board intends to consider issues related to the application of the purchase method to combinations between two or more mutual enterprises in a separate project.

that have been included in the amount reported as goodwill (or as goodwill and intangible assets) shall be reclassified and accounted for as an asset apart from goodwill as of the date Statement 142 is initially applied in its entirety.[25]

c. Other than as set forth in (a) and (b), an entity shall not change the amount of the purchase price assigned to the assets acquired and liabilities assumed in a business combination for which the acquisition date was before July 1, 2001.[26]

62. As of the earlier of the first day of the fiscal year beginning after December 15, 2001, or the date Statement 142 is initially applied in its entirety, the amount of any unamortized deferred credit related to an excess over cost arising from (a) a business combination for which the acquisition date was before July 1, 2001, or (b) an investment accounted for by the equity method acquired before July 1, 2001, shall be written off and recognized as the effect of a change in accounting principle. The effect of the accounting change and related income tax effects shall be presented in the income statement between the captions *extraordinary items* and *net income.* The per-share information presented in the income statement shall include the per-share effect of the accounting change.

> **The provisions of this Statement need not be applied to immaterial items.**

This Statement was adopted by the unanimous vote of the six members of the Financial Accounting Standards Board:

Edmund L. Jenkins, *Chairman*	G. Michael Crooch John M. Foster Gaylen N. Larsen	Gerhard G. Mueller Edward W. Trott

Appendix A

IMPLEMENTATION GUIDANCE

Introduction

A1. This appendix provides guidance to assist entities in the application of certain provisions of this Statement and is therefore an integral part of the standards provided in this Statement. This appendix discusses generalized situations. The facts and circumstances of each business combination should be considered carefully in applying this Statement.

A2. This Statement requires that all business combinations be accounted for using the purchase method. As stated in paragraph 1, this Statement carries forward without reconsideration portions of APB Opin-

ion No. 16, *Business Combinations,* that provide guidance related to the application of the purchase method. While this Statement supersedes all of the AICPA Accounting Interpretations of Opinion 16, guidance in several of those interpretations continues to be relevant in applying certain of the provisions of Opinion 16 that are carried forward in this Statement. Therefore, the guidance in those interpretations has been carried forward without reconsideration in paragraphs A5–A9 of this appendix. Because that guidance has been quoted, paraphrased, or rephrased so that it can be understood in the context of this Statement, the original source of the guidance has been noted parenthetically. The Board intends to reconsider some of that guidance in another of its business combinations projects.

A3. This Statement does not supersede other pronouncements that provide guidance on accounting

---

[25]For example, when a business combination was initially recorded, a portion of the cost of the acquired entity was assigned to intangible assets that meet the recognition criteria in paragraph 39. Those intangible assets have been included in the amount reported on the statement of financial position as goodwill (or as goodwill and other intangible assets). However, separate general ledger or other accounting records have been maintained for those assets.

[26]This transition provision does not, however, affect the requirement to change the amounts assigned to the assets acquired in a business combination due to (a) the resolution of a consideration contingency based on earnings (paragraph 28) or (b) changes to the purchase price allocation prior to the end of the allocation period (paragraph 40).

for a business combination using the purchase method. Guidance in those pronouncements, which are listed below, shall be considered when applying the provisions of this Statement.

a. FASB Statement No. 72, *Accounting for Certain Acquisitions of Banking or Thrift Institutions*
b. FASB Interpretation No. 4, *Applicability of FASB Statement No. 2 to Business Combinations Accounted for by the Purchase Method*
c. FASB Interpretation No. 9, *Applying APB Opinions No. 16 and 17 When a Savings and Loan Association or a Similar Institution Is Acquired in a Business Combination Accounted for by the Purchase Method*
d. FASB Interpretation No. 21, *Accounting for Leases in a Business Combination*
e. [This subparagraph has been deleted. See Status page.]
f. FASB Technical Bulletin No. 85-5, *Issues Relating to Accounting for Business Combinations.*

A4. This Statement requires that intangible assets that meet the criteria in paragraph 39 be recognized as assets apart from goodwill. Paragraphs A10–A13 provide examples that illustrate how the guidance in paragraph 39 should be applied to certain generalized situations. Paragraph A14 includes a noninclusive list of intangible assets that meet the criteria for recognition apart from goodwill.[27] Paragraphs A15–A28 describe some of the intangible assets included on that list and explain how the criteria in paragraph 39 generally apply to them.

Application of Paragraph 14—Accounting for the Acquisition of Some or All of the Noncontrolling Interests in a Subsidiary

A5. Paragraph 14 continues the practice established by Opinion 16 of accounting for the acquisition of noncontrolling interests of a subsidiary (commonly referred to as a minority interest) using the purchase method. Several interpretations of Opinion 16 provide guidance on the accounting for those transactions, and that guidance has been carried forward in paragraphs A6 and A7. The interpretative guidance in Technical Bulletin 85-5 also shall be considered when accounting for those transactions.

A6. Examples of the types of transactions that constitute the acquisition of a minority interest include the following: (a) a parent exchanges its common stock or assets or debt for common stock held by minority stockholders of its subsidiary, (b) the subsidiary buys as treasury stock the common stock held by minority stockholders, or (c) another subsidiary of the parent exchanges its common stock or assets or debt for common stock held by the minority stockholders of an affiliated subsidiary.

A7. Another type of transaction that constitutes the acquisition of a minority interest is a transaction in which a subsidiary exchanges its common stock for the outstanding voting common stock of its parent (usually referred to as a downstream merger). Those transactions shall be accounted for as if the parent had exchanged its common stock for common stock held by minority stockholders of its subsidiary. Whether a parent acquires the minority or a subsidiary acquires its parent, the result is a single stockholder group, including the former minority stockholders, owning the consolidated net assets. The same would be true if a new corporation exchanged its common stock for the common stock of the parent and the common stock of the subsidiary held by minority stockholders (AICPA Accounting Interpretation 26, "Acquisition of Minority Interest," of Opinion 16).

Application of Paragraph 24—Costs of the Business Combination

A8. Paragraph 24 states that the cost of an acquired entity includes the direct costs of the business combination. Those direct costs include "out-of-pocket" or incremental costs directly related to a business combination such as a finder's fee and fees paid to outside consultants for accounting, legal, or engineering investigations or for appraisals. Internal costs associated with a business combination (whether one-time costs or recurring in nature) shall be expensed as incurred. In addition, costs related to unsuccessful negotiations also shall be expensed as incurred (AICPA Accounting Interpretation 33, "Costs of Maintaining an 'Acquisitions' Department," of Opinion 16).

A9. Paragraph 24 also states that costs of registering and issuing equity securities shall be recognized as a reduction of the otherwise determinable fair value of the securities. A publicly held company issuing *unregistered* equity securities in a business combination

---

[27]As described in paragraph A18, some of the intangible assets identified on that list as meeting the separability criterion should not be recognized apart from goodwill if terms of confidentiality or other agreements prohibit the acquiring entity from selling, leasing, or otherwise exchanging the asset.

with an agreement for subsequent registration shall record those securities at the fair value of its registered securities less an estimate of the related registration costs. A liability shall be recognized at the date of acquisition in the amount of the present value of the estimated costs of registration. Any difference between the actual costs of registration and the recorded liability (including imputed interest) shall be recognized as an adjustment to the carrying amount of goodwill. If the securities issued in the business combination are to be included in the registration of a planned future offering of other securities (piggyback registration), only the incremental costs of registering the equity securities issued shall be recognized as a liability at the acquisition date (AICPA Accounting Interpretation 35, "Registration Costs in a Purchase," of Opinion 16).

Application of Paragraph 39—Recognition of Intangible Assets Apart from Goodwill

A10. Paragraph 39 states that an acquired intangible asset shall be recognized as an asset apart from goodwill if it arises from contractual or other legal rights (the contractual-legal criterion). Intangible assets that meet that criterion shall be recognized apart from goodwill even if the asset is not transferable or separable from the acquired entity or from other rights and obligations. For example:

a. An acquired entity leases a manufacturing facility under an operating lease that has terms that are favorable relative to market prices.[28] The lease terms explicitly prohibit transfer of the lease (through either sale or sublease). The value arising from that operating lease contract is an intangible asset that meets the contractual-legal criterion for recognition apart from goodwill, even though the lease contract cannot be sold or otherwise transferred.

b. An acquired entity owns and operates a nuclear power plant. The license to operate that power plant is an intangible asset that meets the contractual-legal criterion for recognition apart from goodwill, even if it cannot be sold or transferred apart from the acquired power plant. This Statement does not preclude an acquiring entity from recognizing the fair value of the operating license and the fair value of the power plant as a single asset for financial reporting purposes if the useful lives of those assets are similar.

c. An acquired entity owns a technology patent. It has licensed that patent to others for their exclusive use outside the United States in exchange for which the entity receives a specified percentage of future non-U.S. revenue. Both the technology patent and the related license agreement meet the contractual-legal criterion for recognition apart from goodwill even if it would not be practical to sell or exchange the patent and the related license agreement apart from one another.

A11. If an acquired intangible asset does *not* arise from contractual or other legal rights, paragraph 39 requires that it be recognized as an asset apart from goodwill only if it is separable—that is, it is capable of being separated or divided from the acquired entity and sold, transferred, licensed, rented, or exchanged (the separability criterion). Exchange transactions provide evidence that an intangible asset is separable from the acquired entity and might provide information that can be used to estimate its fair value. An acquired intangible asset meets the separability criterion if there is evidence of exchange transactions for that type of asset or an asset of a similar type (even if those exchange transactions are infrequent and regardless of whether the acquiring entity is involved in them). For example, customer and subscriber lists are frequently leased and thus meet the separability criterion. Even if an entity believes its customer lists have different characteristics than other customer lists, the fact that customer lists are frequently leased generally means that the acquired entity's customer list meets the separability criterion. Title plant assets also are bought and sold in exchange transactions (either in whole or in part) or are leased, although less frequently than customer lists. Title plant assets also would meet the separability criterion.

A12. An intangible asset that meets the separability criterion shall be recognized apart from goodwill even if the acquiring entity does not intend to sell, lease, or otherwise exchange that asset. The separability criterion is met because the asset is capable of being separated from the acquired entity and sold, transferred, licensed, rented, or otherwise exchanged for something else of value. For example, because an acquired customer list is generally capable of being rented, it meets the separability criterion regardless of whether the acquiring entity intends to rent it.

---

[28]In some cases, the terms of an operating lease might be unfavorable relative to market prices. Paragraph 37(k) of this Statement states that a portion of the purchase price should be assigned to liabilities such as unfavorable leases.

A13. As stated in paragraph 39, an intangible asset that is not separable from the entity individually still meets the separability criterion if it is separable from the acquired entity in combination with a related contract, asset, or liability. For example:

a. Deposit liabilities and related depositor relationship intangible assets are exchanged in observable exchange transactions. Therefore, the depositor relationship intangible asset shall be recognized apart from goodwill.

b. An acquired entity owns a registered trademark, a related secret formula, and unpatented technical expertise used to manufacture the trademarked product. To transfer ownership of a trademark in the United States, the owner is also required to transfer everything else necessary for the new owner to produce a product or service indistinguishable from that produced by the former owner. Because the unpatented technical expertise must be separated from the entity and sold if the related trademark is sold, it meets the separability criterion.

Examples of Intangible Assets That Meet the Criteria for Recognition Apart from Goodwill

A14. The following are examples of intangible assets that meet the criteria for recognition as an asset apart from goodwill. The following illustrative list is not intended to be all-inclusive, thus, an acquired intangible asset might meet the recognition criteria of this Statement but not be included on that list. Assets designated by the symbol (†) are those that would be recognized apart from goodwill because they meet the contractual-legal criterion.[29] Assets designated by the symbol (▲) do not arise from contractual or other legal rights, but shall nonetheless be recognized apart from goodwill because they meet the separability criterion. The determination of whether a specific acquired intangible asset meets the criteria in this Statement for recognition apart from goodwill shall be based on the facts and circumstances of each individual business combination.

a. Marketing-related intangible assets
   (1) Trademarks, tradenames[†]
   (2) Service marks, collective marks, certification marks[†]
   (3) Trade dress (unique color, shape, or package design)[†]
   (4) Newspaper mastheads[†]
   (5) Internet domain names[†]
   (6) Noncompetition agreements[†]

b. Customer-related intangible assets
   (1) Customer lists[▲]
   (2) Order or production backlog[†]
   (3) Customer contracts and related **customer relationships**[†]
   (4) Noncontractual customer relationships[▲]

c. Artistic-related intangible assets
   (1) Plays, operas, ballets[†]
   (2) Books, magazines, newspapers, other literary works[†]
   (3) Musical works such as compositions, song lyrics, advertising jingles[†]
   (4) Pictures, photographs[†]
   (5) Video and audiovisual material, including motion pictures, music videos, television programs[†]

d. Contract-based intangible assets
   (1) Licensing, royalty, standstill agreements[†]
   (2) Advertising, construction, management, service or supply contracts[†]
   (3) Lease agreements[†]
   (4) Construction permits[†]
   (5) Franchise agreements[†]
   (6) Operating and broadcast rights[†]
   (7) Use rights such as drilling, water, air, mineral, timber cutting, and route authorities[†, 29a]
   (8) Servicing contracts such as mortgage servicing contracts[†]
   (9) Employment contracts[†]

e. Technology-based intangible assets
   (1) Patented technology[†]
   (2) Computer software and mask works[†]
   (3) Unpatented technology[▲]
   (4) Databases, including title plants[▲]
   (5) Trade secrets, such as secret formulas, processes, recipes.[†]

Marketing-related intangible assets

A15. Marketing-related intangible assets are those assets that are primarily used in the marketing or promotion of products or services. Trademarks are words, names, symbols, or other devices used in trade to indicate the source of the product and to distinguish it from the products of others. A service

---

[29]The intangible assets designated by the symbol (†) also might meet the separability criterion. However, separability is not a necessary condition for an asset to meet the contractual-legal criterion.

[29a]Certain use rights may have characteristics of assets other than intangible assets. For example, certain mineral rights are considered tangible assets based on the consensus in EITF Issue No. 04-2, "Whether Mineral Rights Are Tangible or Intangible Assets." Accordingly, use rights should be accounted for based on their substance.

mark identifies and distinguishes the source of a service rather than a product. Collective marks are used to identify the goods or services of members of a group, and certification marks are used to certify the geographic origin or other characteristics of a good or service. In the United States and other countries, trademarks, service marks, collective marks, and certification marks may be protected legally through registration with governmental agencies, continuous use in commerce, or by other means. If registered or otherwise provided legal protection, a trademark or other mark is an intangible asset that meets the contractual-legal criterion for recognition apart from goodwill. Otherwise, a trademark or other mark shall be recognized apart from goodwill only if the separability criterion is met, which would normally be the case.

A16. The terms *brand* and *brand name* often are used as synonyms for trademarks and tradenames. However, the former are general marketing terms that are typically used to refer to a group of complementary assets such as the trademark (or service mark) and its related tradename, formulas, recipes, and technological expertise (which may or may not be patented). This Statement does not preclude an entity from recognizing, as a single asset apart from goodwill, a group of complementary intangible assets commonly referred to as a brand if the assets that make up that group have similar useful lives.

A17. An Internet domain name is a unique alphanumeric name that is used to identify a particular numeric Internet address. Registration of a domain name associates the name with a designated computer on the Internet for the period the registration is in effect. Those registrations are renewable. Registered domain names shall be recognized as an intangible asset apart from goodwill because they meet the contractual-legal criterion.

Customer-related intangible assets

Customer lists

A18. A customer list consists of information about customers such as their name and contact information. A customer list also may be in the form of a database that includes other information about the customers such as their order history and demographic information. A customer list does not generally arise from contractual or other legal rights. However, customer lists are valuable and are frequently leased or exchanged. Therefore, an acquired customer list would meet the separability criterion for recognition

apart from goodwill. An acquired customer list would *not* meet that criterion, however, if the terms of confidentiality or other agreements prohibit an entity from selling, leasing, or otherwise exchanging information about its customers.

Order or production backlog

A19. If an acquired order or production backlog arises from contracts such as purchase or sales orders, it meets the contractual-legal criterion for recognition apart from goodwill (even if the purchase or sales orders were cancelable).

Customer contracts and related customer relationships

A20. If an entity establishes relationships with its customers through contracts, those customer relationships would arise from contractual rights. Therefore, customer contracts and the related customer relationships are intangible assets that meet the contractual-legal criterion. This Statement requires that those intangible assets be recognized as assets apart from goodwill even if confidentiality or other contractual terms prohibit the sale or transfer of the contract separately from the acquired entity.

Noncontractual customer relationships

A21. If a customer relationship does not arise from a contract, this Statement requires that the relationship be recognized as an intangible asset apart from goodwill if it meets the separability criterion. Exchange transactions for the same asset or a similar type of asset provide evidence of separability of a noncontractual customer relationship and might also provide information about exchange prices that should be considered when estimating its fair value. For example, relationships with depositors are frequently exchanged with the related deposits and, thus, meet the criteria for recognition as an intangible asset apart from goodwill.

Artistic-related intangible assets

A22. Artistic-related intangible assets meet the criteria for recognition apart from goodwill if the assets arise from contractual rights or legal rights such as those provided by copyright. In the United States for example, copyrights are granted by the government for the life of the creator plus 50 years. Copyrights can be transferred either in whole through assignments or in part through licensing agreements. In determining the fair value of a copyright intangible asset, consideration shall be given to the existence of any assignments or licenses of the acquired copyright. This Statement does not preclude an acquiring entity from recognizing a copyright intangible asset and any related assignments or license agreements as a single intangible asset for financial reporting purposes if their useful lives are similar.

Contract-based intangible assets

A23. Contract-based intangible assets represent the value of rights that arise from contractual arrangements. Customer contracts (refer to paragraph A20) are one particular type of contract-based intangible asset. Contracts to service financial assets are another. While servicing is inherent in all financial assets, it becomes a distinct asset or liability only when (a) contractually separated from the underlying financial assets by sale or securitization of the assets with servicing retained or (b) through the separate purchase and assumption of the servicing. If mortgage loans, credit card receivables, or other financial assets are acquired in a business combination with servicing retained, this Statement does not require recognition of the inherent servicing rights as an intangible asset because the fair value of the servicing intangible asset is considered in the measurement of the fair value of the acquired financial asset. However, a contract representing an acquired **servicing asset** is an intangible asset that shall be recognized apart from goodwill.

A24. If the terms of a contract give rise to a liability or commitment (which might be the case if the terms of an operating lease or customer contract are unfavorable relative to market prices), that liability or commitment shall be recognized as required by paragraph 37(k) of this Statement.

Technology-based intangible assets

A25. Technology-based intangible assets relate to innovations or technological advances. As stated in paragraphs A26–A28, the future economic benefits of those assets are often protected through contractual or other legal rights. Thus, many technology-based intangible assets meet the contractual-legal criterion for recognition apart from goodwill.

Computer software and mask works

A26. If computer software and program formats are protected legally such as by patent or copyright, they meet the contractual-legal criterion for recognition apart from goodwill. Mask works are software permanently stored on a read-only memory chip as a series of stencils or integrated circuitry. Mask works may be provided legal protection; for example, in the United States mask works qualify for protection under the Semiconductor Chip Protection Act of 1984. Acquired mask works protected under the provisions of that Act or other similar laws or regulations also meet the contractual-legal criterion for recognition apart from goodwill.

Databases, including title plants

A27. Databases are collections of information, often stored in electronic form (such as on computer disks or files). An acquired database that includes original works of authorship is entitled to copyright protection and, if so protected, meets the contractual-legal criterion for recognition apart from goodwill. However, a database often includes information created as a consequence of an entity's normal operations, such as a customer list or specialized information such as a title plant, scientific data, and credit information. Databases that are not protected by copyright can be (and often are) exchanged in their entirety or in part. Alternatively, they can be (and often are) licensed or leased to others. Thus, even if the future economic benefit of a database does not arise from legal rights, it meets the separability criterion for recognition as an asset apart from goodwill.

Trade secrets, such as secret formulas, processes, recipes

A28. A trade secret is "information, including a formula, pattern, compilation, program, device, method, technique, or process, that (1) derives independent economic value, actual or potential, from not being generally known ... and (2) is the subject of efforts that are reasonable under the circumstances to maintain its secrecy."[30] If the future economic benefit of an acquired trade secret is protected legally, such as by the Uniform Trade Secrets Act or other laws and regulations, that asset meets the contractual-legal criterion for recognition as an asset apart from goodwill. Otherwise, a trade secret would be recognized as an asset apart from goodwill only if the separability criterion was met, which is likely to be the case.

---

[30]Melvin Simensky and Lanning Bryer, *The New Role of Intellectual Property in Commercial Transactions* (New York: John Wiley & Sons, 1998), page 293.

APPENDIX B

BACKGROUND INFORMATION AND BASIS FOR CONCLUSIONS

CONTENTS

Appendix B

**BACKGROUND INFORMATION AND BASIS
FOR CONCLUSIONS**

Introduction

B1. This appendix summarizes considerations that Board members deemed significant in reaching the conclusions in this Statement. It includes reasons for accepting certain approaches and rejecting others. Individual Board members gave greater weight to some factors than to others. It also summarizes the considerations that were deemed significant in reach-

ing the conclusions in FASB Statement No. 38, *Accounting for Preacquisition Contingencies of Purchased Enterprises*. Those conclusions and considerations are carried forward in this Statement without reconsideration.

Background Information

B2. Prior to the issuance of this Statement, the guidance on accounting for business combinations was provided by APB Opinion No. 16, *Business Combinations,* which the Accounting Principles Board (APB) of the American Institute of Certified Public Accountants (AICPA) issued in 1970. Opinion 16 provided for two methods of accounting for business combinations, the pooling-of-interests method (pooling method) and the purchase method. Those methods were not alternatives or substitutes for one another. Opinion 16 required that the pooling method be used if a business combination met 12 specified conditions; otherwise, the purchase method was to be used.

B3. During the 1970s, the FASB had an active project on its agenda to reconsider the accounting for business combinations and purchased intangible assets. However, the Board later decided to defer consideration of the issues in that project until after it had completed development of its conceptual framework for accounting and reporting. In 1981, the Board removed the inactive business combinations project from its agenda to focus on higher priority projects.

B4. In August 1996, the Board added the current project on accounting for business combinations to its agenda. The objective of this project was to improve the transparency of accounting and reporting of business combinations including the accounting for goodwill and other intangible assets by reconsidering the requirements of Opinion 16 and APB Opinion No. 17, *Intangible Assets* (which also was issued in 1970). In 1999, the Board decided that that objective would best be achieved through several projects focused on specific issues. In the first of those projects, which ended with the concurrent issuance of this Statement and FASB Statement No. 142, *Goodwill and Other Intangible Assets,* the Board reconsidered the methods of accounting for business combinations and the accounting for goodwill and other intangible assets. Another project will address issues associated with the accounting for combinations between not-for-profit organizations, the acquisition of a for-profit entity by a not-for-profit organization, and combinations between mutual enterprises. The Board intends to consider issues related to the accounting for the formation of joint ventures and other new entities, push-down accounting (including spinoffs), and common control transactions in another project. In still another project the Board intends to consider issues related to the provisions of Opinion 16 and Statement 38 that are carried forward in this Statement without reconsideration and other issues related to the application of the purchase method, such as the accounting for step acquisitions.[31]

Reasons the FASB Took on the Project

B5. A principal reason for taking on this project in 1996 was the increase in merger and acquisition activity that brought greater attention to the fact that two transactions that are economically similar may be accounted for by different methods that produce dramatically different financial statement results. Consequently, both the representational faithfulness and the comparability of those financial statements suffer.

B6. Another reason that the Board decided to undertake this project was that many perceived the differences in the pooling and purchase methods to have affected competition in markets for mergers and acquisitions. Entities that could not meet all of the conditions for applying the pooling method believed that they faced an unlevel playing field in competing for targets with entities that could apply that method. That perception and the resulting attempts to expand the application of the pooling method placed considerable tension on the interpretation and application of the provisions of Opinion 16. The volume of inquiries fielded by the staffs of the FASB and Securities and Exchange Commission (SEC) and the auditing profession was evidence of that tension.

B7. The unlevel playing field that was perceived to stem from the application of the pooling and purchase methods extended internationally as well. Cross-border differences in accounting standards for business combinations and the rapidly accelerating movement of capital flows globally heightened the need for accounting standards to be comparable internationally. Promoting international comparability in accounting standards is part of the Board's mission, and many members of the Financial Accounting Standards Advisory Council (FASAC) cited the opportunity to promote greater international comparability in the standards for business combinations as a reason for adding this project to the Board's agenda. (FASAC had consistently ranked a possible project on business combinations as a high priority for a number of years.)

International Cooperation

B8. Largely because of concerns about the perception of an unlevel cross-border playing field with the

---

[31]For example, AICPA Accounting Interpretation 2, "Goodwill in a Step Acquisition," of Opinion 17, stated that when an entity acquires another entity or an investment accounted for by the equity method through a series of purchases (commonly referred to as a step acquisition), the entity should identify the cost of each investment, the fair value of the underlying assets acquired, and the goodwill for each step acquisition.

United States in the accounting standards for business combinations, the Accounting Standards Board (AcSB) of the Canadian Institute of Chartered Accountants (CICA) conducted a business combinations project concurrently with the FASB's project. The goal of that concurrent effort was to establish common standards on business combinations and intangible assets.

B9. The FASB also worked with other members of an international organization of standard-setting bodies with the aim of achieving convergence internationally with respect to the methods of accounting for business combinations. That organization, known as the "Group of 4 plus 1" (G4+1), consisted of the Australian Accounting Standards Board (AASB), the New Zealand Financial Reporting Standards Board (FRSB), the United Kingdom Accounting Standards Board (UK ASB), the AcSB, the FASB, and an observer, the International Accounting Standards Committee (IASC).

Conduct of the FASB's Project

B10. The Board formed a business combinations task force comprising individuals from a number of organizations representing a wide range of the Board's constituents. The first meeting of that task force was held in February 1997. Relevant academic research was reviewed, and the meeting discussion centered on a background paper that addressed the project's scope, the direction the project should take, and how the project should be conducted.

B11. The June 1997 FASB Special Report, *Issues Associated with the FASB Project on Business Combinations,* was based on that background paper and indicated some of the Board's initial decisions about the project's scope, direction, and conduct. The 54 comment letters received in response to that Special Report generally expressed agreement with those decisions.

B12. In 1998, the FASB participated in the development of a G4+1 Position Paper, *Recommendations for Achieving Convergence on the Methods of Accounting for Business Combinations.* That Position Paper considered the pooling method, the purchase

method, and the fresh-start method,[32] and concluded that only the purchase method should be used to account for business combinations.

B13. The Board issued the Position Paper as an FASB Invitation to Comment, *Methods of Accounting for Business Combinations: Recommendations of the G4+1 for Achieving Convergence,* in December 1998, the same date on which other G4+1 member organizations issued similar documents for comment. The FASB received 148 comment letters, the AcSB received 40 letters, the UK ASB received 35 letters, the IASC received 35 letters, the AASB received 5 letters, and the FRSB received 4 letters.

B14. After considering the recommendations of the G4+1 and the responses to the Invitation to Comment, the Board decided that only the purchase method should be used to account for business combinations. The Board also decided that certain changes should be made in how the purchase method should be applied, particularly in the accounting for and financial statement presentation of goodwill and other intangible assets. Those changes were proposed in the September 1999 FASB Exposure Draft, *Business Combinations and Intangible Assets* (1999 Exposure Draft). The Board received 210 comment letters in response to the 1999 Exposure Draft. In February 2000, the Board held 4 days of public hearings, 2 days in San Francisco and 2 days in New York City, at which 43 individuals or organizations presented their views on the 1999 Exposure Draft.

B15. In redeliberating the proposals in the 1999 Exposure Draft, the Board considered changes suggested by various constituents, in particular those related to the accounting for goodwill. During October and November 2000, Board and staff members explored the suggested changes to the accounting for goodwill in field visits with 14 companies. The Board's deliberations resulted in significant changes to the proposed requirements related to goodwill but not to other issues addressed in the 1999 Exposure Draft. In particular, the Board decided that goodwill should no longer be amortized and should be tested for impairment in a manner different from how other assets are tested for impairment. The Board also affirmed the proposal that only the purchase method

---

[32]Under the fresh-start method, the assets and liabilities of the combining entities (regardless of whether they had been recognized in the statements of financial position of those entities) are recognized in the statement of financial position of the combined entity at fair value. The combined entity is treated as a new entity as of the date of the combination and its history commences on that date. The fresh-start method is currently used in practice to account for certain corporate reorganization transactions. As with the purchase method, the fresh-start method can be applied to business combinations that are effected by cash, other assets, debt, equity shares, or a combination thereof.

should be used to account for business combinations. In February 2001, the Board issued a revised Exposure Draft, *Business Combinations and Intangible Assets—Accounting for Goodwill* (2001 Exposure Draft), that proposed changes to the 1999 Exposure Draft with regard to the accounting for goodwill and the initial recognition of intangible assets other than goodwill. The Board received 211 comment letters on the 2001 Exposure Draft.

B16. The Board decided to separate the guidance for business combinations from that for goodwill and other intangible assets and issue that guidance in two final documents, this Statement and Statement 142. Those two Statements parallel and supersede Opinions 16 and 17, respectively. Statement 142 was issued concurrently with this Statement.

B17. The Board also decided that this Statement should supersede Statement 38 and carry forward without reconsideration portions of the guidance in Opinion 16 and that Statement related to the application of the purchase method.

Basis for Conclusions

Definition and Scope

B18. In developing the 1999 Exposure Draft, the Board concluded that because this project is primarily focused on the methods of accounting for business combinations, this Statement should generally retain the definition and scope of Opinion 16. The Board affirmed that conclusion in its redeliberations of the 1999 Exposure Draft.

B19. The 1999 Exposure Draft proposed certain changes to the Opinion 16 definition of a business combination to reflect the Board's conclusion that all two-party business combinations and virtually all other business combinations (other than joint venture formations) are acquisitions. Specifically, the 1999 Exposure Draft proposed that a *business combination* be defined as occurring when one entity acquires all or a portion of the net assets that constitutes a business or equity interests of one or more entities and obtains control over the entity or entities.

B20. Respondents to the 1999 Exposure Draft were asked to comment on that proposed definition, in particular whether it would appear to include or exclude business combinations that were not similarly covered by the Opinion 16 definition. The principal concern expressed by respondents that commented on

that issue related to the proposal that a business combination be defined as occurring when one entity acquires equity interests of another entity and obtains control over that entity. Many of those respondents said that that definition would exclude certain transactions covered by Opinion 16 from the scope of the 1999 Exposure Draft, in particular, transactions in which none of the former shareholder groups of the combining entities obtain control over the combined entity (such as roll-ups, put-togethers, and so-called mergers of equals). During its redeliberations of the 1999 Exposure Draft, the Board concluded that those transactions should be included in the definition of a business combination and in the scope of this Statement. Therefore, paragraph 10 explicitly states that the provisions of this Statement also apply to business combinations in which none of the owners of the combining entities as a group retain or receive a majority of the voting rights of the combined entity. However, the Board acknowledges that some of those business combinations might not be acquisitions, and it intends to consider in another project whether business combinations that are not acquisitions should be accounted for using the fresh-start method rather than the purchase method.

B21. Respondents to the 1999 Exposure Draft suggested that because joint venture formations were to be excluded from the scope of that proposed Statement, the Board should define *joint venture*. The Board concluded that this Statement should not provide that definition. The Board noted that constituents consider the guidance in paragraph 3(d) of APB Opinion No. 18, *The Equity Method of Accounting for Investments in Common Stock,* in assessing whether an entity is a joint venture, and it decided not to change that practice at this time. The Board intends to develop a definition of joint venture as part of its project on accounting for joint venture and other new entity formations.

B22. Respondents to the 1999 Exposure Draft also said that the Board should define the term *business.* The Board observed that in EITF Issue No. 98-3, "Determining Whether a Nonmonetary Transaction Involves Receipt of Productive Assets or of a Business," the EITF reached a consensus on guidance for determining whether a business has been received in an exchange transaction. That guidance discusses the characteristics of a business. The Board concluded that while it was not necessary to define *business* for purposes of this Statement, this Statement should refer to the guidance provided in Issue 98-3.

B23. The Board affirmed the decision it made in developing the 1999 Exposure Draft that this Statement would not address transactions, events, or circumstances that result in one entity obtaining control over another entity through means other than the acquisition of net assets or equity interests. Therefore, this Statement does not change current accounting practice with respect to those transactions. For example, if a previously unconsolidated majority-owned entity is consolidated as a result of control being obtained by the lapse or elimination of participating veto rights that were held by minority stockholders, a new basis for the investment's total carrying amount is not recognized under current practice. Instead, only the display of the majority-owned investment in the consolidated financial statements is changed. The majority-owned entity is consolidated rather than reported as a single investment accounted for by the equity method. That treatment is consistent with the practice for accounting for step acquisitions, in which a parent obtains control of a subsidiary through two or more purchases of the investee-subsidiary's stock. In addition, this Statement does not change the consensuses reached in EITF Issue No. 97-2, "Application of FASB Statement No. 94 and APB Opinion No. 16 to Physician Practice Management Entities and Certain Other Entities with Contractual Management Arrangements." The Board intends to consider the accounting for transactions in which control of an entity is obtained through means other than the acquisition of net assets or equity interests in another project.

B24. The Board acknowledged, as it did prior to issuing the 1999 Exposure Draft, that this Statement does not address many current practice issues, such as accounting for recapitalization transactions or joint venture and other new entity formations and transactions between entities under common control. Those are among the issues that the Board intends to consider in another project.

Methods of Accounting for Business Combinations

B25. In deliberating the methods of accounting for business combinations, the Board carefully considered the analyses of the issues in the G4+1 Position Paper, as well as the conclusions and recommendations that were based on those analyses. The Board also carefully considered the views expressed by respondents to the Invitation to Comment, as well as those of respondents to the corresponding documents of other G4+1 member organizations. In later redeliberating the proposals made in the 1999 Exposure

Draft, the Board also carefully considered the views expressed by respondents to that Exposure Draft, most of which reiterated views expressed by respondents to the Invitation to Comment.

B26. Like the G4+1, the Board considered three possible methods of accounting for business combinations—the pooling method, the purchase method, and the fresh-start method. Also like the G4+1, the Board observed that neither the pooling method nor the fresh-start method could be appropriately used for all business combinations.

B27. In assessing those methods, the Board was mindful of the disadvantages of having more than one method of accounting for business combinations, as evidenced by the experience with Opinion 16 over the past three decades. Among those disadvantages are the incentives for accounting arbitrage that inevitably exist when different methods produce dramatically different financial statement results for economically similar transactions. Another disadvantage is the difficulty in drawing unambiguous and nonarbitrary boundaries between the transactions to which the different accounting methods would apply. Still others include the difficulties and costs associated with applying, auditing, and enforcing the resulting standards. Yet others relate to difficulties with analyzing the information provided by different methods because users commonly do not have the means available to convert from the information provided by one method to that provided by another.

B28. The Board concluded that having more than one method could be justified only if the alternative method (or methods) could be demonstrated to produce information that is more decision useful and if unambiguous and nonarbitrary boundaries could be established that unequivocally distinguish when one method is to be applied rather than another.

Reasons for adopting the purchase method

B29. The Board concluded that the purchase method is the appropriate method of accounting for all business combinations that are acquisitions, as did the G4+1. The purchase method is consistent with how the historical-cost accounting model generally accounts for transactions in which assets are acquired and liabilities are assumed or incurred, and it therefore produces information that is comparable to other accounting information. Under the purchase method, one of the combining entities is viewed as surviving the transaction and is considered the acquiring entity.

The other combining entities that do not survive the combination as independent entities are considered the acquired entities. The purchase method recognizes and measures assets and liabilities in the same way regardless of the nature of the consideration that is exchanged for them. Consequently, users of financial statements are better able to assess the initial costs of the investments made and the subsequent performance of those investments and compare them with the performance of other entities. Moreover, the purchase method is familiar to preparers, auditors, regulators, and users of financial statements.

B30. Respondents to both the Invitation to Comment and the 1999 Exposure Draft generally agreed that most business combinations are acquisitions, and many stated that all combinations involving only two entities are acquisitions. Respondents also agreed that the purchase method is the appropriate method of accounting for business combinations that are acquisitions. However, some qualified their support for the purchase method contingent upon the Board's decisions about certain aspects of applying that method, particularly the accounting for goodwill.

B31. Because the purchase method is the only appropriate method of accounting for business combinations that are acquisitions, the question considered by the Board was whether any combinations are not acquisitions and, if so, whether the pooling method or the fresh-start method should be used to account for them. The Board generally agreed with the analyses and conclusions in the G4+1 Position Paper and concluded that all two-party business combinations other than joint venture formations are acquisitions. Accordingly, the Board decided that one method, the purchase method, should be used to account for all two-party business combinations except joint venture formations.

B32. The Board also concluded that most business combinations involving three or more entities (multiparty combinations) are acquisitions. The Board acknowledged that some multi-party combinations (in particular, those that are commonly referred to as roll-up or put-together transactions) might not be acquisitions; however, it noted that presently those transactions are generally accounted for by the purchase method. The Board decided not to change that practice at this time. Consequently, this Statement requires that the purchase method be used to account for all multi-party combinations, including those that some might not consider to be acquisitions. As discussed in paragraph B4, however, the Board

intends to consider whether joint venture formations and multi-party business combinations that are not acquisitions should be accounted for by the fresh-start method rather than the purchase method.

B33. The Board noted that requiring the use of the purchase method will bring the accounting for business combinations in the United States more in step with how those combinations are accounted for in other jurisdictions because that method is widely or exclusively used in those jurisdictions.

B34. The Board also concluded that identifying the acquiring entity is practicable in all cases, although doing so may be difficult in some instances. In that regard, some respondents to the 1999 Exposure Draft noted that even though identifying an acquirer might sometimes be difficult, an acquirer nonetheless must be identified for U.S. federal income tax purposes.

B35. Paragraphs B36–B85 discuss the bases for the Board's decision to reaffirm its proposal in the 1999 Exposure Draft to reject the pooling method and fresh-start method in favor of the purchase method.

Reasons for rejecting the pooling method

Mergers and acquisitions are similar economically

B36. Many respondents to the Invitation to Comment and the 1999 Exposure Draft argued that mergers (business combinations in which the consideration is in the form of equity interests) should be accounted for differently than acquisitions. They stated that, in mergers, ownership interests are completely or substantially continued, no new capital is invested and no assets are distributed, postcombination ownership interests are proportional to those prior to the combination, and the intention is to have a uniting of commercial strategies going forward. Moreover, no change in control of the entity's assets or liabilities occurs and no earnings process culminates. Those respondents said that a merger should be accounted for in terms of the carrying amounts of the assets and liabilities of the combining entities because unlike acquisitions, in which only the acquiring entity survives the combination, all of the combining entities effectively survive a merger.

B37. A few respondents urged that the pooling method be applied to all business combinations, regardless of the nature of the consideration, and a few others urged that it be applied to all mergers. The

Board is not aware of any jurisdiction in which *all* business combinations are or may be accounted for by the pooling method. In most jurisdictions, use of that method has been limited to mergers. The Board also is not aware of any jurisdiction in which all *mergers* are accounted for by the pooling method. In most jurisdictions that permit use of the pooling method for mergers, many mergers are accounted for by the purchase method. Thus, adoption of the suggestions to broaden the application of the pooling method would move away from rather than toward greater convergence of accounting standards internationally for business combinations. Furthermore, the Board does not believe that the nature of the consideration tendered—equity interests in the case of mergers—should dictate how the net assets acquired should be recorded.

B38. Most respondents that favored retaining the pooling method urged that its application be limited. Some stated that application of the pooling method should be limited to those combinations that meet certain conditions, either the same as those in Opinion 16 or a simpler set. However, many stated that its application should be more restricted than under Opinion 16. They generally urged that its application be limited to "true mergers" or "mergers of equals," which they described as combinations of entities of approximately equal size or those in which an acquirer could not be readily identified. Some added that the combining businesses should be complementary in nature and that the risks and rewards associated with the assets obtained should be similar to those associated with assets given up. Several respondents stated that true mergers or mergers of equals might be accounted for by either the pooling method or the fresh-start method but did not suggest which of those methods might be more appropriate or what the criteria should be for determining which method to apply.

B39. The Board noted that mergers are not transactions between owners as asserted by proponents of the pooling method, but rather that the combining entities themselves are deeply involved in those transactions. The issuance of shares is an investment by owners from the issuing entity's perspective. The net assets of one entity are transferred to another, which issues its shares in exchange, and that transaction should be accounted for on the same basis that would be used to record an investment by owners in the form of cash—that is, on a fair value basis. From the perspective of the acquired entity's shareholders, that transaction is an exchange transaction, a sale on their part and a purchase on the part of the surviving entity. In that regard, the Board observed that the shareholders of the acquired entity typically receive a premium for their shares, which is consistent with being sellers. Furthermore, the acquired entity's shareholders often become relatively more liquid following the exchange by virtue of receiving shares that are more widely and deeply traded than those they gave up (particularly if their shares had been privately held or closely held), which also is consistent with the usual outcome for sellers.

B40. Many respondents agreed with the Board's conclusion that although ownership interests are continued in a merger, they are not the same interests as before the combination. That is because control over precombination assets is reduced by sharing, and shared control over other assets is gained. Thus, not only does control change but also what is controlled changes. Furthermore, the risks and rewards associated with the assets obtained may or may not be similar to those given up, and the combination itself may have either increased or decreased risks and the potential for rewards. Finally, even though "intent" in the form of a uniting of commercial strategies going forward is sometimes cited as a feature of mergers, the Board believes that all business combinations entail some bringing together of commercial strategies and, thus, that feature is not unique to mergers.

B41. Some respondents stated that mergers are virtually identical to acquisitions economically, making them in-substance acquisitions. In that regard, some noted that shares could have been issued for cash and that cash then used to effect the combination, with the end result being the same economically as if shares had been used to effect the combination.

B42. The Board concluded that "true mergers" or "mergers of equals" are nonexistent or so rare as to be virtually nonexistent, and many respondents agreed. Other respondents stated that even if a true merger or merger of equals did occur, it would be so rare that a separate accounting treatment is not warranted. They also stated that developing the criteria necessary to identify those transactions simply would be a continuation of the same problems and potential for abuse evidenced by Opinion 16. The Board agreed, observing that even in those standards set by others that restrict use of the pooling method to true mergers or mergers of equals (such as the AcSB, the UK ASB, and the IASC), there are differences not only in the criteria themselves but in how they are interpreted and applied. The Board further observed that respondents and other constituents were unable to suggest an unambiguous and nonarbitrary boundary for distinguishing true mergers or mergers of equals from other two-party business combinations and concluded that developing such an operational boundary would not be feasible. Moreover, even if those mergers could feasibly be distinguished from other combinations, the Board concluded that it does not follow that such combinations should be accounted for on a carry-over basis. If they were to be accounted for using a method other than the purchase method, the Board believes that a better method would be the fresh-start method.

Information provided is not decision useful

B43. Some proponents of the pooling method argued that the information it provides for some business combinations is more decision useful. They argued that the information is more reliable, in particular, more representationally faithful, than the information that the purchase method would provide if it were applied to those combinations. However, other respondents countered, stating that the information provided by the purchase method is more revealing than that provided by the pooling method. Respondents also noted that the pooling method does not hold management accountable for the investment made and the subsequent performance of that investment. In contrast, the accountability that results from applying the purchase method forces management to examine business combination deals carefully to see that they make sense economically.

B44. The Board observed that an important facet of decision-useful information is information about cash-generating abilities and cash flows generated. As FASB Concepts Statement No. 1, *Objectives of Financial Reporting by Business Enterprises,* states, "... financial reporting should provide information to help investors, creditors, and others assess the amounts, timing, and uncertainty of prospective net cash inflows to the related enterprise" (paragraph 37; footnote reference omitted). The Board noted that neither the cash-generating abilities of the combined entity nor its future cash flows generally are affected by the method used to account for the combination. However, fair values reflect the expected cash flows associated with acquired assets and assumed liabilities. Because the pooling method records the net assets acquired at their carrying amounts rather than at

their fair values, the information that the pooling method provides about the cash-generating abilities of those net assets is less useful than that provided by other methods.

B45. The Board also concluded that the information provided by the pooling method is less relevant in terms of completeness, predictive value, and feedback value than the information that is provided by other methods. It also is less reliable because, for example, by recording assets and liabilities at the carrying amounts of predecessor entities, postcombination revenues may be overstated (and expenses understated) as the result of embedded gains that were generated by predecessor entities but not recognized by them. Furthermore, because of variations in when the pooling method is applied, similar combinations may be accounted for by different methods, adversely affecting both representational faithfulness and comparability.

B46. Comparability is another important facet of information that is decision useful. As FASB Concepts Statement No. 2, *Qualitative Characteristics of Accounting Information,* states, "The purpose of comparison is to detect and explain similarities and differences" (paragraph 113). It also notes that "the difficulty in making financial comparisons among enterprises because of the use of different accounting methods has been accepted for many years as the principal reason for the development of accounting standards" (paragraph 112).

B47. Most of the respondents to the Invitation to Comment agreed that differences in the methods of accounting for business combinations and when they are applied make it difficult to compare financial statements.

B48. Respondents to the 1999 Exposure Draft expressed mixed views. Some proponents of the pooling method argued that eliminating it would hinder comparability, describing the purchase method as an "apples and oranges approach" because it measures the net assets of the acquired entity at fair value and those of the acquiring entity at historical cost. However, opponents of the pooling method stated that the purchase method produces results that are comparable with those of entities that grow by acquiring similar assets in a number of smaller purchases that are not business combinations. The Board agreed with those who stated that the purchase method is consistent with how other asset acquisitions are accounted for, and it disagreed with those who described it as an apples-and-oranges approach.

B49. Proponents of the pooling method also argued that the pooling method enhances the comparability of the financial statements of entities that grow though acquisition (a "buy strategy") with those of entities that grow internally (a "build strategy"). They asserted that the pooling method enhances comparability because it avoids recognizing assets on the statement of financial position and related charges to the income statement that the purchase method requires. The Board concluded that comparability between entities that "buy" and those that "build" is a false comparability because the outlays that are made for the assets in question are never accounted for under the pooling method, whereas they are accounted for when the assets are developed internally.

B50. Opponents of the pooling method stated that eliminating that method would enhance the comparability of financial statements of entities that grow by means of acquisitions. After considering all of the views expressed by respondents, the Board agreed with those that stated that comparability of financial information reported by entities that engage in business combinations would be enhanced by eliminating the pooling method.

Inconsistencies across jurisdictions and over time

B51. The Board observed that there are inconsistencies internationally with regard to whether and when the pooling method is applied. In some jurisdictions, its use is prohibited, and in those jurisdictions where its use is not prohibited, it is applied to some—but not all—business combinations in which the consideration is in the form of equity interests, with the particulars varying from jurisdiction to jurisdiction.

B52. The Board also observed that because accounting standards for business combinations in the United States have changed over time, there has been variation over time as to which business combinations qualify for application of the pooling method. For example, Opinion 16 was designed to narrow the application of the pooling method to only those combinations that met 12 stated conditions.

B53. The Board noted that if the pooling method were based on a sound underlying conceptual foundation, there would not be inconsistencies in how that method is applied internationally, nor would there have been changes over time in the transactions that qualify for use of that method in the United States.

B54. The Board observed that the pooling method is used today to account for transactions that are quite different from those it was originally intended to account for. As discussed in the Invitation to Comment's appendix entitled "The History of the Pooling-of-Interests Method in the Jurisdictions of G4+1 Member Organizations," the pooling method in the United States

> . . . has its roots in an approach developed for combinations in which a strong degree of affiliation existed between the combining companies prior to the combination. That approach was gradually extended to a quite different set of combinations, namely those in which the combining companies had not been part of the same "family" and whose existing relationships—if any—had simply been incident to normal business activities, such as those with suppliers or customers. [page 26]

B55. The Board also observed that early uses of the pooling method occurred in certain regulated industries in which the rates that regulated entities could charge their customers were based on the cost of their assets. Rather than permit those entities to charge higher rates as a result of business combinations, particularly between entities that had been so closely related that the presence of arm's-length bargaining was open to question, regulators held that no new values should be assigned to the assets being combined. That was because no change in substance had occurred from the rate payers' perspective—the net assets being employed before and after the combination were the same. Accordingly, rate regulation issues expanded the use of the pooling method, even to combinations in which the consideration was not in the form of stock.

B56. Although use of the pooling method has spread considerably in the years since its inception, the Board observed that the criteria for its application today bear little or no resemblance to those that would be consistent with its roots.

Inconsistent with historical-cost accounting model

B57. The Board observed that the pooling method is an exception to the general concept that exchange transactions are accounted for in terms of the fair values of the items exchanged. Because the pooling method records the combination in terms of the carrying amounts of the parties to the transaction, it fails to record the investment made in the combination and fails to hold management accountable for that investment and its subsequent performance.

B58. Some proponents of the pooling method asserted that use of that method is consistent with the historical-cost model and that eliminating it would be another step down the road toward a fair value model. They argued that before eliminating the pooling method, the Board should resolve the broad issue of whether to adopt a fair value model in place of the historical-cost model. In the Board's view, regardless of the merits of a fair value model, the pooling method is an aberration that is inconsistent with the historical-cost model. The reason relates to the fundamental role of transactions in accounting.

B59. The Board observed that although the historical-cost model is frequently described as being "transaction based," the fair value model also records all transactions. In both models, the transactions are recorded at the same amounts. The main difference between those models does not relate to whether transactions that the entity engages in are recorded; it lies in what is recorded between transactions.

B60. Under the fair value model, a "truing up" takes place between transactions that involves recognizing nontransactional events and circumstances that affect the entity's assets and liabilities. That "truing up" also involves making end-of-period adjustments that are needed to update the fair values of those assets and liabilities in order to prepare financial statements.

B61. In contrast, under the historical-cost model, entries that are recorded between transactions are not generally aimed at truing-up the measures of the entity's assets and liabilities but rather at allocating or assigning costs to particular accounting periods. To the extent that any truing-up takes place, it generally is limited to recognizing such events as calamities, decreases in the market value of inventories below their cost, and impairments of long-lived assets. Thus, the truing-up is largely left to subsequent transactions that the entity engages in. Therefore, those transactions provide the "reality check" that is needed to validate the historical-cost model, without which its outputs would be suspect. Stated another way, transactions are the essential part of the historical-cost model that provide the reckoning that otherwise might not occur.

B62. The pooling method effectively sidesteps the reckoning that comes with business combination transactions by assuming that those transactions are exchanges between the owners of the combining entities rather than between the entities themselves. That method does not recognize the values exchanged in the records of the combined entity, only the carrying amounts of the predecessor entities. The failure to record those values can adversely affect the reliability of the combined entity's financial statements for years—and even decades—to come. For those reasons, the Board concluded that the pooling method is inconsistent with the historical-cost model.

Consistency with other standards

B63. A few respondents noted that FASB Statement No. 140, *Accounting for Transfers and Servicing of Financial Assets and Extinguishments of Liabilities,* precludes sale accounting for transfers of financial assets when there is continuing involvement of the transferor (such as retaining an ownership interest in the asset purported to be sold). Those respondents argued that if owners of both combining entities in a business combination have a significant degree of continuing involvement in the combined entity, neither owner has "sold" their entity. Therefore, the use of the purchase method for all business combinations may be inconsistent with accounting for certain securitization transactions as set forth in Statement 140. The Board observed, however, that Statement 140 addresses transfers of financial assets and that those transactions are fundamentally different from business combinations. Moreover, the provisions of Statement 140 preclude recognition of a transfer of assets as a sale if the transferor does not surrender control over those assets. In contrast, in a business combination that is effected by cash, control over the net assets of the acquired entity *is* transferred, and in those affected by stock, control over precombination net assets *is* reduced and shared.

Disclosure not an adequate response

B64. In urging that the pooling method be retained, a few respondents to the Invitation to Comment and the 1999 Exposure Draft stated that any perceived problems with having two methods of accounting could be addressed by enhanced disclosures in the notes to the financial statements. However, they generally did not specify what those disclosures should be and how they would help overcome the comparability problems that inevitably result from having two methods.

B65. In developing the 1999 Exposure Draft, the Board considered the matter of enhanced disclosures but doubted the usefulness of almost any disclosures short of disclosing what the results would have been had the purchase method been used to account for the business combination. Even so, providing disclosures that would enable users of financial statements to determine what the results would have been had the transaction been accounted for by the purchase method would be a costly solution that begs the question of why the purchase method was not used to account for the transaction in the first place. Since the respondents to the 1999 Exposure Draft that raised that issue did not provide any information that the Board had not already considered, the Board rejected the addition of enhanced disclosures as a viable alternative.

Not cost beneficial

B66. Some respondents cited cost-benefit considerations as a reason for retaining the pooling method. They argued that the pooling method is a quicker and less expensive way to account for a business combination because it does not require an entity to hire outside appraisers to value assets for accounting purposes.

B67. Other respondents favored eliminating the pooling method for cost-benefit reasons. Some argued that the pooling method causes preparers of financial statements, auditors, regulators, and others to spend unproductive time dealing with what they described as the detailed and somewhat illogical criteria required by Opinion 16 in attempts to have certain business combinations qualify for application of the pooling method. Others noted that using the purchase method of accounting for all business combinations would eliminate the enormous amount of interpretive guidance necessary to accommodate the pooling method. They also stated that the benefits derived from the purchase method as the only method of accounting for business combinations would significantly outweigh any issues that might arise from accounting for the very rare true merger or merger of equals by the purchase method.

B68. The Board addressed cost-benefit considerations in developing the 1999 Exposure Draft and concluded that a single method of accounting is preferable in light of those considerations because having more than one method would lead to higher costs associated with applying, auditing, enforcing, and analyzing the information produced by them. Cost-benefit considerations were thoroughly analyzed at that time and are discussed in paragraphs B225–B234. The Board concluded that those that favor retaining the pooling method on the basis of cost-benefit considerations did not provide any additional information that the Board did not consider previously.

Public policy not served by retention

B69. A number of respondents to the Invitation to Comment and the 1999 Exposure Draft argued that public policy considerations should dominate the Board's decisions. Some argued that eliminating the pooling method would require some investors to adjust to different measures of performance, potentially affecting market valuations adversely in certain industries during the transition period. Others argued that it would impede desirable consolidation in certain industries, reduce the amount of capital flowing into those industries, slow the development of new technology, and adversely affect entrepreneurial culture. Still others argued that eliminating the pooling method would remove a competitive advantage that U.S. companies have in competing with foreign companies for acquisitions and could impose a competitive disadvantage on them. Yet others argued that it would reduce the options available to certain regulatory agencies and possibly require regulated entities to maintain a second set of books. A few argued that elimination of the pooling method, by imposing an accounting hurdle on business combinations, would hinder obtaining the economic advantages afforded by the recently enacted Financial Services Reform Act in the United States that reforms the Glass-Steagall Act of 1933.

B70. Other respondents did not share those views. Some stated that because business combinations are driven by their underlying economics and not accounting considerations, economically sound deals would be completed regardless of the method used to account for them. Others noted that the financial community values business combinations in terms of their fair values rather than book values and, therefore, those transactions should initially be recognized in the financial statements at fair value.

B71. The Board has long held that accounting standards should not be slanted to favor one set of economic interests over another. For example, if accounting standards result in information that favors sellers in capital markets, those standards simultaneously disfavor buyers in those markets. If accounting standards were slanted, they would not be neutral, and the information that they produce would not be neutral. Consequently, financial reporting would not be fair and evenhanded and thus would lose its credibility.

B72. The Board noted that Concepts Statement 2 states that "neutrality means that either in formulating or implementing standards, the primary concern should be the relevance and reliability of the information that results, not the effect that the new rule may have on a particular interest" (paragraph 98). It goes on to explain that:

> Neutrality does not mean "without purpose," nor does it mean that accounting should be without influence on human behavior. Accounting information cannot avoid affecting behavior, nor should it. If it were otherwise, the information would be valueless—by definition, irrelevant—and the effort to produce it would be futile. It is, above all, the predetermination of a desired result, and the consequential selection of information to induce that result, that is the negation of neutrality in accounting. To be neutral, accounting information must report economic activity as faithfully as possible, without coloring the image it communicates for the purpose of influencing behavior in *some particular direction.* [Paragraph 100, emphasis in original.]

B73. Concepts Statement 2 acknowledges the argument that has been made against neutrality in accounting standards—that it may inhibit the FASB from working toward achieving public policy goals. However, the Board noted that that argument raises several issues. One is that there would have to be agreement on what those goals should be. Another is that since goals change with changes in government, questions would arise about the desirability or feasibility of changing accounting standards every time public policy changes. Moreover, to the extent that accounting standards become a means of facilitating or implementing public policy, the ability of those standards to help guide policy and measure its results is unavoidably diminished. For those reasons, the Board concluded that accounting standards should be neutral.

B74. Neutrality is also an essential component of the precepts that the Board follows in the conduct of its activities. One of those precepts, as stated in the FASB's mission statement, is as follows:

> *To be objective in its decision making* and to ensure, insofar as possible, the neutrality of

information resulting from its standards. To be neutral, information must report economic activity as faithfully as possible without coloring the image it communicates for the purpose of influencing behavior in any particular direction. [FASB *Rules of Procedure,* page 3]

B75. In the final analysis, the Board concluded that the accounting standards for business combinations should not seek to encourage or discourage business combinations. Instead, those standards should produce information about those combinations that is fair and evenhanded to those having opposing economic interests. The Board also concluded that those who argue for the pooling method on the basis that they believe that it fosters more combinations are not seeking to have neutral, evenhanded information disseminated.

B76. The Board carefully studied the responses to the 1999 Exposure Draft including those of respondents that favored retaining the pooling method on the basis of what they asserted to be public policy reasons. The information provided by those respondents did not cause the Board to change its view that its public policy goal is to issue accounting standards that result in neutral and representationally faithful financial information and that eliminating the pooling method is consistent with that goal.

Purchase method flaws remedied

B77. A number of respondents to the Invitation to Comment and the 1999 Exposure Draft indicated that the pooling method should be retained because of problems associated with the purchase method, particularly the requirement to recognize goodwill and subsequently amortize it in determining net income. Some argued that goodwill is not an asset and should not be recognized (and thus not amortized). Others argued that goodwill is an asset but not a wasting asset and thus should not be amortized. Still others argued that goodwill may be a wasting asset but that estimates of its useful life are inherently subjective. They argued that goodwill should be written off immediately in determining net income, other comprehensive income, or equity or, alternatively, that it should be assigned an arbitrary life that is both short and uniform and then amortized in determining net income, other comprehensive income, or equity. Yet others noted that reported earnings might be drastically affected by additional noncash charges for depreciation, depletion, and amortization that result from accounting for a business combination by the purchase method. However, most focused on the effects of goodwill amortization.

B78. The Board concluded that the concerns cited about the purchase method did not justify retaining the pooling method, as some had urged, and it affirmed its decision that the pooling method was so fundamentally flawed as to not warrant retention.

B79. For the reasons cited in paragraphs B36–B78, the Board concluded that the pooling method should not be used to account for any business combination.

Reasons for rejecting the fresh-start method

B80. Few of the respondents to the Invitation to Comment and the 1999 Exposure Draft that commented on the fresh-start method supported its use to account for any business combination. And, as noted previously, several respondents to that Exposure Draft stated that mergers of equals could be accounted for by either the pooling method or the fresh-start method but did not indicate which would be more appropriate or suggest criteria for making that determination.

B81. The Board acknowledged that a case can be made for using the fresh-start method to account for business combinations that are not acquisitions, which might be defined as transactions in which an acquiring entity cannot be identified or one in which the acquiring entity is substantially modified by the transaction. Under the fresh-start method, none of the combining entities are viewed as having survived the combination as an independent reporting entity. Rather, the combination is viewed as the transfer of the net assets of the combining entities to a new entity that assumes control over them, and the history of that new entity, by definition, begins with the combination.

B82. The Board noted that under the fresh-start method, the new entity has no history against which to compare itself and it is difficult to compare the results of the new entity with those of its predecessors for periods before the combination. Furthermore, new accounting guidance would have to be developed for implementing the method, and many unsettled aspects (such as whether goodwill should be recognized and how it should be measured) would have to be addressed before it could be applied.

B83. The Board noted that if the fresh-start method were to be applied only to those two-party combina-

tions in which an acquiring entity cannot be identified or the combining entities were equal in all respects, such combinations would be so rare—if they occurred at all—as to not justify the need for a new and separate method. The Board also noted that if the method also were to be applied to two-party combinations in which the acquiring entity is substantially modified, *substantially modified* would have to be defined, which would likely prove to be difficult to do in an unambiguous and nonarbitrary way. Moreover, those two-party combinations would be relatively few in number. Furthermore, the method may offer the potential for accounting arbitrage because the financial statement results it produces are apt to differ significantly from those that the purchase method produces.

B84. The Board concluded that the advantages of using the fresh-start method for two-party combinations such as those discussed in paragraph B81 (primarily enhanced representational faithfulness) were outweighed by the disadvantages of having two methods of accounting (particularly the potential for accounting arbitrage but also the difficulties of drawing unambiguous and nonarbitrary boundaries between the methods). The Board further concluded that an alternative to the purchase method of accounting for those combinations was not needed because it is possible to apply the purchase method to them.

B85. The Board observed that the fresh-start method might be appropriate for certain multi-party combinations. However, as discussed in paragraph B32, the Board noted that those transactions are generally accounted for by the purchase method and it decided not to change that practice at this time. Also as discussed in paragraph B32, the Board intends to consider whether joint venture formations and multi-party business combinations that are not acquisitions should be accounted for by the fresh-start method rather than by the purchase method.

Acquisition of Noncontrolling Interests in a Subsidiary

B86. As it did prior to issuing the 1999 Exposure Draft, the Board concluded that this Statement should continue the practice established in Opinion 16 of accounting for the acquisition of noncontrolling interests in a subsidiary (commonly referred to as minority interests) using the purchase method. The Board intends to consider the accounting for those transactions in another project. The

Board also noted that those deliberations might be affected by conclusions reached in its liabilities and equity project. In the development of the October 2000 FASB Exposure Draft, *Accounting for Financial Instruments with Characteristics of Liabilities, Equity, or Both,* the Board concluded that (a) noncontrolling interests in a subsidiary should be reported in consolidated financial statements as a separate component of equity and (b) distributions to holders of instruments that are classified as equity should be recognized as equity distributions. If the Board affirms those provisions in its redeliberations of that Exposure Draft, it will consider whether the acquisition of a minority interest should be accounted for as an equity distribution rather than by the purchase method.

Application of the Purchase Method

Accounting for asset acquisitions—general concepts

B87. In reaching the conclusion that the purchase method should be used to account for all business combinations, the Board affirmed the basic principles of historical-cost accounting included in paragraphs 66–69 of Opinion 16. Specifically, the Board affirmed that an asset acquisition should be measured on the basis of the values exchanged and that measurement of the values exchanged should be based on the fair value of the consideration given or the fair value of the net assets acquired, whichever is more reliably measurable. The Board also affirmed that when groups of assets are acquired, the value of the asset (or net asset) group as a whole should be allocated to the individual assets (or assets and liabilities) that make up the group on the basis of their fair values. Accordingly, this Statement carries forward from Opinion 16 those general principles; however, those principles have been rephrased as general concepts so that they can be understood in the context of this Statement.

Identifying the acquiring entity

B88. The Board's decision that all business combinations in the scope of this Statement should be accounted for by the purchase method means that the acquiring entity must be identified in every business combination. One of the issues raised in the Invitation to Comment focused on situations in which identifying the acquiring entity is difficult. Most of the respondents that commented on that issue suggested that the Board develop additional criteria for identifying the acquiring entity.

B89. In developing the 1999 Exposure Draft, the Board affirmed the guidance in Opinion 16 that states that in a business combination effected solely through the distribution of cash or other assets or by incurring liabilities, the entity that distributes cash or other assets or assumes or incurs liabilities is the acquiring entity. The Board considered a variety of suggestions made by respondents to the Invitation to Comment on factors that should be considered in applying the purchase method to situations in which the acquiring entity cannot be as readily identified. The guidance proposed in the 1999 Exposure Draft reflected the Board's conclusion that all pertinent facts and circumstances should be considered when identifying the acquiring entity, particularly the relative voting rights in the combined entity after the combination. That proposed guidance stated that in determining which shareholder group retained or received the larger portion of the voting rights in the combined entity, the existence of any unusual or special voting arrangements, and options, warrants, or convertible securities should be considered. The proposed guidance also reflected the Board's conclusion that consideration also should be given to factors related to the composition of the board of directors and senior management of the combined entity and that those factors should be weighted equally with the factors related to voting rights.

B90. The respondents to the 1999 Exposure Draft that commented on the proposed criteria for identifying the acquiring entity generally agreed that they were appropriate. Some of those respondents said that the guidance proposed in that Exposure Draft was an improvement over Opinion 16 because it provided additional factors to consider in determining which shareholder group retained or received the larger share of the voting rights in the combined entity. However, many of the respondents suggested improvements to the proposed criteria and some suggested that the Board consider other criteria.

B91. Several respondents to the 1999 Exposure Draft suggested that the Board retain the presumptive approach in Opinion 16 for identifying the acquiring entity in transactions effected through an exchange of equity interests. That approach presumes that absent evidence to the contrary, the acquiring entity is the combining entity whose owners as a group retain or receive the larger share of the voting rights in the combined entity. Other respondents suggested that the factors to be considered in identifying the acquiring entity should be provided in the form of a hierarchy. Some of those respondents also suggested that the Board provide additional guidance explaining how factors relating to voting rights (unusual special voting arrangements and options, warrants, or convertible securities) would affect the determination of the acquiring entity.

B92. The Board carefully considered those suggestions. However, the Board observed, as it did in developing the 1999 Exposure Draft, that each business combination is unique and, therefore, the facts and circumstances relevant to identifying the acquiring entity in one combination may be less relevant in another. The Board affirmed its conclusion that this Statement should not retain the presumptive approach in Opinion 16 nor provide hierarchical guidance. The Board concluded that doing so would imply that some factors are more important in identifying the acquiring entity than others. However, as suggested by respondents, the Board decided to modify the guidance proposed in the 1999 Exposure Draft to explain how some of the factors influence the identification of the acquiring entity.

B93. In developing the 1999 Exposure Draft, the Board decided not to require consideration of the payment of a premium over the market value of the equity securities acquired as evidence of the identity of the acquiring entity. The Board observed that while that criterion would be a useful indicator, it would be difficult to evaluate when quoted market prices are not available for the equity securities exchanged. A number of respondents to the 1999 Exposure Draft said that the payment of a premium is a strong indicator of the identity of the acquirer. Upon reconsideration, the Board decided that this Statement would include the payment of a premium as a criterion to be considered in identifying the acquirer, but only when the equity securities exchanged in a business combination are traded in a public market.

B94. Some respondents to the Invitation to Comment and the 1999 Exposure Draft suggested that the relative market capitalizations and relative net asset sizes of the combining entities also should be considered when identifying the acquiring entity. The Board noted, however, that entities could engage in various transactions in contemplation of a business combination, such as asset dispositions and treasury stock transactions. Those transactions would result in different market capitalizations and net asset sizes than those that existed before the combination was con-

templated. The Board also noted that assessing relative net assets on the basis of precombination carrying amounts would be inappropriate, while assessing them on the basis of fair values could entail significant cost. Thus, although those factors may in some cases provide evidence as to which entity is the acquiring entity, the Board concluded that consideration of those factors should not be required in all combinations.

B95. In developing the 1999 Exposure Draft, the Board observed that identifying the acquirer might be difficult in some multi-party business combinations, particularly those combinations that might not be acquisitions but are to be accounted for as such under this Statement. In the basis for conclusions to that Exposure Draft, the Board noted that in those circumstances it might be helpful to consider additional factors such as which of the entities initiated the combination and whether the reported amounts of assets, revenues, and earnings of one of the combining entities significantly exceed those of the others. In response to suggestions made by respondents to the 1999 Exposure Draft, the Board decided to include that guidance in the standards section of this Statement.

B96. In addition, as suggested by respondents, the Board decided that this Statement should explicitly state that in some business combinations, such as those described as "reverse acquisitions," the entity that issues the equity interests may not be the acquiring entity for financial reporting purposes.

Determining the cost of the acquired entity and date of acquisition

B97. The Board decided that this Statement would carry forward without reconsideration the provisions of Opinion 16 related to determining the cost of the acquired entity and the date of acquisition. The Board intends to reconsider some or all of that guidance in its separate project focused on issues related to the application of the purchase method.

B98. The Board recognizes that this Statement carries forward from Opinion 16 contradictory guidance about the date that should be used to value equity interests issued to effect a business combination. Paragraph 74 of Opinion 16, carried forward in paragraph 22, states that the market price for a reasonable period before and after the date the terms of the acquisition are agreed to and announced should be considered in determining the fair value of the securities issued. However, paragraph 94 of Opinion 16, carried forward in paragraph 49, states that the cost of an acquired entity should be determined as of the date of acquisition. Paragraph 48 defines that date as the date that assets are received and other assets are given, liabilities are assumed or incurred, or equity interests are issued. The Board decided to defer resolution of that apparent contradiction to its project on issues related to the application of the purchase method. Therefore, this Statement does not change the status of the guidance in EITF Issue No. 99-12, "Determination of the Measurement Date for the Market Price of Acquirer Securities Issued in a Purchase Business Combination," or EITF Topic No. D-87, "Determination of the Measurement Date for Consideration Given by the Acquirer in a Business Combination When That Consideration is Securities Other Than Those Issued by the Acquirer." This Statement also does not change the status of the guidance of other EITF issues interpreting the provisions of Opinion 16 related to determining the cost of the acquired entity.

Allocating the cost of the acquired entity

B99. In developing this Statement, the Board affirmed the basic principle set forth in Opinion 16 that the cost of an asset group should be allocated to the individual assets (or assets and liabilities) that make up the group on the basis of their fair values. However, the Board decided that this project would reconsider several aspects of the Opinion 16 guidance related to the allocation of the cost of an acquired entity in a business combination. As described in paragraphs B101–B146, the Board affirmed the requirement in Opinion 16 that the excess of the cost of an acquired entity over the net of the amounts assigned to assets acquired and liabilities assumed should be recognized as an asset referred to as goodwill. The Board decided to change the requirements in Opinion 16 for determining whether an acquired intangible asset should be recognized as an asset apart from goodwill (refer to paragraphs B147–B170). The Board also reconsidered and decided to change the guidance in Opinion 16 related to the accounting for the excess of the fair value of net assets acquired over the cost of an acquired entity (commonly referred to as negative goodwill) (refer to paragraphs B187–B193).

B100. The Board decided that this Statement should carry forward, without reconsideration, the general guidance in Opinion 16 for assigning amounts to assets acquired and liabilities assumed (paragraph 88 of that Opinion). The Board recognizes that some of that guidance may be inconsistent with the term *fair value* as defined in this Statement. For example, uncertainties about the collectibility of accounts or loans receivable would affect their fair value. If accounts or loans receivable were assigned an amount equal to their fair value, there would be no need to separately recognize an allowance for uncollectible accounts as stated in paragraph 37(b). The Board decided, however, that it would consider those inconsistencies in a separate project on issues related to the application of the purchase method.

Excess of cost over the fair value of acquired net assets (goodwill)

B101. For the reasons described in paragraphs B102–B139, the Board affirmed the conclusion expressed in both the 1999 Exposure Draft and the 2001 Exposure Draft that goodwill meets the assets definition in FASB Concepts Statement No. 6, *Elements of Financial Statements,* and the asset recognition criteria in FASB Concepts Statement No. 5, *Recognition and Measurement in Financial Statements of Business Enterprises.* Most respondents to those Exposure Drafts agreed with that conclusion. Generally, those in agreement said that goodwill is an asset because future benefits are expected from it in conjunction with the future benefits expected from other assets and that the consideration paid is evidence of the existence of that asset. Many of those respondents referred to goodwill as a special type of asset—one that cannot be separated from the other net assets of an entity.

The nature of goodwill

B102. As described in the 1999 Exposure Draft and the 2001 Exposure Draft, the amount that in practice has been recognized as goodwill includes the following six components:

- Component 1—The excess of the fair values over the book values of the acquired entity's net assets at the date of acquisition.
- Component 2—The fair values of other net assets that had not been recognized by the acquired entity at the date of acquisition. They may not have been recognized because they failed to meet the recognition criteria (perhaps because of measurement difficulties), because of a requirement that prohibited their recognition, or because the entity concluded that the costs of recognizing them separately were not justified by the benefits.

- Component 3—The fair value of the "going-concern" element of the acquired entity's existing business. The going-concern element represents the ability of the established business to earn a higher rate of return on an assembled collection of net assets than would be expected if those net assets had to be acquired separately. That value stems from the synergies of the net assets of the business, as well as from other benefits (such as factors related to market imperfections, including the ability to earn monopoly profits and barriers to market entry—either legal or because of transaction costs—by potential competitors).
- Component 4—The fair value of the expected synergies and other benefits from combining the acquiring entity's and acquired entity's net assets and businesses. Those synergies and other benefits are unique to each combination, and different combinations would produce different synergies and, hence, different values.
- Component 5—Overvaluation of the consideration paid by the acquiring entity stemming from errors in valuing the consideration tendered. Although the purchase price in an all-cash transaction would not be subject to measurement error, the same may not necessarily be said of a transaction involving the acquiring entity's equity interests. For example, if the number of common shares being traded daily is small relative to the number of shares issued in the combination, imputing the current market price to all of the shares issued to effect the combination may produce a higher value than those shares would produce if they were sold for cash and the cash then used to effect the combination.
- Component 6—Overpayment or underpayment by the acquiring entity. Overpayment might occur, for example, if the price is driven up in the course of bidding for the acquired entity, while underpayment may occur in the case of a distress sale or fire sale.

B103. The Board continues to believe that the following analysis of those components is useful in understanding the nature of goodwill. The first two components, both of which relate to the acquired entity, conceptually are not part of goodwill. The first component is not an asset in and of itself but instead reflects gains that were not recognized by the acquired entity on its net assets. As such, that component is part of those assets rather than part of goodwill. The second component also is not part of goodwill conceptually; it primarily reflects intangible assets that might be recognized as individual assets.

B104. The fifth and sixth components, both of which relate to the acquiring entity, also are not conceptually part of goodwill. The fifth component is not an asset in and of itself or even part of an asset but, rather, is a measurement error. The sixth component also is not an asset; conceptually it represents a loss (in the case of overpayment) or a gain (in the case of underpayment) to the acquiring entity. Thus, neither of those components is conceptually part of goodwill.

B105. As the Board noted in both the 1999 Exposure Draft and the 2001 Exposure Draft, the third and fourth components *are* conceptually part of goodwill. The third component relates to the acquired entity and reflects the excess assembled value of the acquired entity's net assets. It represents the preexisting goodwill that was either internally generated by the acquired entity or acquired by it in prior business combinations. The fourth component relates to the acquired entity and acquiring entity jointly and reflects the excess assembled value that is created by the combination—the synergies that are expected from combining those businesses. The Board described the third and fourth components collectively as "core goodwill."

B106. Consistent with both the 1999 Exposure Draft and the 2001 Exposure Draft, this Statement calls for efforts to avoid subsuming the first, second, and fifth components of goodwill into the amount initially recognized as goodwill. Specifically, an acquiring entity is required to make every effort to (a) measure the purchase consideration accurately (eliminating or reducing component 5), (b) record the net assets acquired at their fair values rather than their carrying amounts (eliminating or reducing component 1), and (c) recognize all acquired intangible assets meeting the criteria in paragraph 39 of this Statement so that they are not subsumed into the amount initially recognized as goodwill (reducing component 2).

Whether goodwill meets the assets definition

B107. Opinion 16 defined goodwill as the "excess of the cost of the acquired company over the sum of the amounts assigned to identifiable assets acquired less liabilities assumed" (paragraph 87). That definition describes how the cost of goodwill should be calculated rather than explaining what goodwill is or what it represents. As such, it confuses the substance of goodwill with how goodwill is to be measured.

B108. Opinion 16 was adopted in August 1970, at a time when the APB was developing its own definition of assets. However, that definition has been replaced by the FASB's definition, which is the benchmark against which goodwill should be judged.

B109. According to Concepts Statement 6:

> Assets are probable future economic benefits obtained or controlled by a particular entity as a result of past transactions or events. [Paragraph 25; footnote reference omitted.]

The footnote to that paragraph points out that "*probable* is used with its usual general meaning, rather than in a specific accounting or technical sense (such as that in FASB Statement No. 5, *Accounting for Contingencies,* par. 3), and refers to that which can reasonably be expected or believed on the basis of available evidence or logic but is neither certain nor proved. . . ."

B110. Concepts Statement 6 further explains that:

> An asset has three essential characteristics: (a) it embodies a probable future benefit that involves a capacity, singly or in combination with other assets, to contribute directly or indirectly to future net cash inflows, (b) a particular entity can obtain the benefit and control others' access to it, and (c) the transaction or other event giving rise to the entity's right to or control of the benefit has already occurred. [paragraph 26]

Because the question of whether goodwill meets the assets definition depends on whether core goodwill possesses each of those three essential characteristics, the Board considered it in the context of each of those characteristics.

Future Economic Benefit

B111. Concepts Statement 6 states that:

> Future economic benefit is the essence of an asset. . . . An asset has the capacity to serve the entity by being exchanged for something else of value to the entity, by being used to produce something of value to the entity, or by being used to settle its liabilities. [paragraph 172]

The Board noted that goodwill cannot be exchanged for something else of value to the entity, nor can it be used to settle the entity's liabilities. Goodwill also lacks the capacity singly to produce future net cash inflows, although it can—in combination with other assets—produce cash flows. As a result, the future benefit associated with goodwill generally is more nebulous and may be less certain than the benefit that is associated with most other assets.

B112. Concepts Statement 6 states that "the most obvious evidence of future economic benefit is a market price" (paragraph 173). Because goodwill does not have the capacity to contribute directly to future net cash inflows, it is not priced separately in the marketplace, but rather is priced in combination with other assets with which it produces future net cash inflows. That capacity is reflected by the premium that an entity as a whole commands in comparison to the sum of the fair values of its component parts.

B113. The Board concluded that although goodwill is not priced separately, that does not preclude it from having future economic benefit. In that regard, Concepts Statement 6 states that "anything that is commonly bought and sold has future economic benefit, including the individual items that a buyer obtains and is willing to pay for in a 'basket purchase' of several items or in a business combination" (paragraph 173).

B114. The Board observed that the premium associated with goodwill may be reflected in several ways. One way is based on the market capitalization of the acquired entity as a stand-alone entity, with the premium over the sum of the fair values of the identifiable net assets reflecting the "going concern" element of the business. Another way is by the takeover premium, the price that the acquired entity as a whole commands as a target, which often is considerably higher than its market capitalization on a stand-alone basis, and reflects the synergies arising out of the combination.

Control

B115. In addition to having future economic benefit, there must be control over that benefit if goodwill is to meet the definition of assets. The Board concluded that control is provided by means of the acquiring entity's ability to direct the policies and management of the acquired entity.

Past Transaction or Event

B116. The control over future economic benefit must also result from a past transaction or event if goodwill is to meet the definition of assets. The Board concluded that the past transaction or event is the transaction in which the controlling interest was obtained by the acquiring entity.

Opposing Views

B117. Some respondents to the 1999 Exposure Draft and the 2001 Exposure Draft expressed opposing views about whether goodwill meets the assets definition. Some argued that goodwill is not an asset because that conclusion would equate costs with assets. Concepts Statement 6 states that "although an entity normally incurs costs to acquire or use assets, costs incurred are not themselves assets. The essence of an asset is its future economic benefit rather than whether or not it was acquired at a cost" (paragraph 179). It further states that ". . . since an entity commonly obtains assets by incurring costs, incurrence of a cost may be evidence that an entity has acquired one or more assets, but it is not conclusive evidence. . . . The ultimate evidence of the existence of assets is the future economic benefit, not the costs incurred" (paragraph 180). Thus, the Board rejected that argument because it concluded that goodwill has future economic benefit.

B118. Other respondents argued that goodwill does not meet the assets definition because it cannot be sold apart from the business. Under that view, assets that are not cash or contractual claims to cash or services must be capable of being sold separately for cash, and thus exchangeability is an essential characteristic. In that regard, the Board noted that Concepts Statement 6 expressly considers the matter of exchangeability, noting that, in addition to the three essential characteristics described above:

> Assets commonly have other features that help identify them—for example, assets may be acquired at a cost and they may be tangible, exchangeable, or legally enforceable. However, those features are not essential characteristics of assets. Their absence, by itself, is not sufficient to preclude an item's qualifying as an asset. That is, assets may be acquired without cost, they may be intangible, and although not exchangeable they may be usable by the entity in producing or distributing other goods or services. [Paragraph 26; footnote reference omitted.]

B119. Concepts Statement 6 noted that absence of exchangeability of an asset may create recognition

and measurement problems, "but it in no way negates future economic benefit that can be obtained . . ." (footnote 62). Thus, exchangeability is expressly ruled out as an element of the assets definition, and so the Board rejected that argument.

Initial recognition of goodwill as an asset

B120. Paragraph 63 of Concepts Statement 5 contains four fundamental recognition criteria that apply to all recognition decisions:

a. Definitions—The item meets the definition of an element of financial statements.
b. Measurability—It has a relevant attribute measurable with sufficient reliability.
c. Relevance—The information about it has the potential to make a difference in user decisions.
d. Reliability—The information is representationally faithful, verifiable, and neutral.

An item meeting those criteria should be recognized in the financial statements, subject to a cost-benefit constraint and a materiality threshold.

Definition

B121. Based on its analysis, the Board concluded that core goodwill meets the assets definition in Concepts Statement 6, thereby leaving the criteria of measurability, relevance, and reliability to be considered.

Measurability

B122. Because the scope of the business combinations project focuses only on goodwill that is acquired in conjunction with a business combination, the Board noted that the cost incurred in the combination transaction provides the basis for initially measuring goodwill.

B123. The Board questioned whether goodwill should be initially recognized as an asset because of concerns about its measurability, since it is not exchangeable separate from other assets of the entity. The Board's concerns focused on the ability to measure goodwill both initially, based on the combination transaction, and subsequent to that transaction. However, the Board acknowledged that exchangeability is not a criterion of the assets definition in Concepts Statement 6 and that even though assets like goodwill may be more difficult to measure than other assets, measurement would be possible.

B124. The Board also noted that the measurement of goodwill is complicated by the potential that some or all of components 1, 2, 5, or 6 (identified in paragraph B102) might be included. However, the Board concluded that including those components in the measurement of goodwill is preferable to not recording goodwill at all.

B125. The Board further noted that measuring goodwill subsequent to its initial recognition is complicated by difficulties in determining its consumption or decline in value. However, the Board concluded that such difficulties are not unique to goodwill.

B126. The Board concluded that the measurability criterion is met, although not as readily as with many other assets, particularly with respect to measurement after initial recognition.

Relevance

B127. In assessing whether information about goodwill is relevant, the Board considered the views of users as reported by the AICPA Special Committee[33] and as expressed by the Financial Accounting Policy Committee (FAPC) of the Association for Investment Management and Research (AIMR) in its 1993 position paper, *Financial Reporting in the 1990s and Beyond.* The Board observed that users have mixed views about whether goodwill should be recognized as an asset. While some are troubled by the lack of comparability between internally generated goodwill and acquired goodwill that results under present standards, others do not appear to be particularly bothered by it. However, users appear to be reluctant to give up information about the cost of goodwill that is acquired in conjunction with a business combination and measured as part of the transaction price. In the view of the AICPA Special Committee, users want to retain the option of being able to use that information. Similarly, the FAPC stated that the amount paid for goodwill should be reported.

B128. The Board also considered the growing use of "economic value added" (EVA)[34] and similar measures, which increasingly are being employed as means of assessing performance. The Board observed that such measures commonly incorporate goodwill, and in the case of business combinations that are accounted for by the pooling method, an adjustment is commonly made to incorporate a measure of the goodwill that would not be recognized under that method. As a result, the aggregate amount of goodwill is included in the base that is subject to a capital charge that is part of the EVA measure, and management is held accountable for the total investment in the acquired entities.

B129. The Board also considered evidence about the relevance of goodwill that has been provided by a number of recent research studies that empirically examined the relationship between goodwill and the market value of business entities.[35] Those studies generally found a positive relationship between the reported goodwill of entities and their market values, thereby indicating that investors in the markets behave as if they view goodwill as an asset. For those reasons, the Board concluded that the relevance criterion is met.

Reliability

B130. According to Concepts Statement 2, to be reliable, information about an item must be representationally faithful, verifiable, and neutral. It must also be sufficiently faithful in its representation of the underlying resource and sufficiently free of error and bias to be useful to investors, creditors, and others in making decisions. Thus, for an asset to be recognized, information about the existence and amount of an asset must be reliable.

B131. Concepts Statement 2 states that "representational faithfulness is correspondence or agreement between a measure or description and the phenomenon it purports to represent" (paragraph 63). Thus, to the extent that recorded goodwill consists of the

---

[33]AICPA Special Committee on Financial Reporting, *Improving Business Reporting—A Customer Focus* (New York: AICPA, 1994).

[34]EVA was developed by the consulting firm of Stern Stewart & Company (and is a registered trademark of Stern Stewart) as a financial performance measure that improves management's ability to make decisions that enhance shareholder value.

[35]Refer to, for example, Eli Amir, Trevor S. Harris, and Elizabeth K. Venuti, "A Comparison of the Value-Relevance of U.S. versus Non-U.S. GAAP Accounting Measures Using Form 20-F Reconciliations," *Journal of Accounting Research,* Supplement (1993): 230–264; Mary Barth and Greg Clinch, "International Accounting Differences and Their Relation to Share Prices: Evidence from U.K., Australian and Canadian Firms," *Contemporary Accounting Research* (spring 1996): 135–170; Keith W. Chauvin and Mark Hirschey, "Goodwill, Profitability, and the Market Value of the Firm," *Journal of Accounting and Public Policy* (summer 1994): 159–180; Ross Jennings, John Robinson, Robert B. Thompson, and Linda Duvall, "The Relation between Accounting Goodwill Numbers and Equity Values," *Journal of Business Finance and Accounting* (June 1996): 513–533; and Mark G. McCarthy and Douglas K. Schneider, "Market Perception of Goodwill: Some Empirical Evidence," *Accounting and Business Research* (winter 1995): 69–81.

excess of fair values over book values of the acquired entity's net assets (component 1) or the fair values of unrecorded net assets of the acquired entity (component 2), it is not representationally faithful. However, the Board observed that this Statement contains guidance aimed at minimizing the inclusion of those components in the amount recorded for goodwill. Moreover, any problem that would result from their inclusion is limited to mislabeling items that are all assets of some kind, which is not as serious as labeling expenses or losses as assets, in which case the amount reported for total assets would not be representationally faithful.

B132. Alternatively, recorded goodwill might include overvaluation of the consideration paid by the acquiring entity (component 5) or overpayment by the acquiring entity (component 6). To the extent that goodwill includes those components, it is including items that are not assets at all. Thus, including them in the asset described as goodwill would not be representationally faithful, nor would the amount reported for total assets be representationally faithful because it would include amounts that are not assets. The Board noted that that would constitute a more serious breach of representational faithfulness than would including components 1 or 2.

B133. However, the Board observed that it may be difficult to determine the cost attributable to each item in a basket purchase and that the acquisition cost may be difficult to determine if equity interests were used to acquire the basket of assets. The problem thus is not unique to the accounting for goodwill in conjunction with business combinations, but arises in many other situations as well. That indicates that representational faithfulness or reliability of measurement in accounting is often not an absolute, but rather one of degree.

B134. While there may be difficulties of representational faithfulness in recognizing most or all of an acquisition premium as an asset labeled goodwill for the reasons cited above, the Board observed that there are corresponding difficulties in the alternative of writing it off immediately as an expense or loss. That is because, to the extent that recorded goodwill consists of what conceptually is goodwill (components 3 and 4) and other assets (components 1 and 2), depicting those assets as expenses or losses is not representationally faithful either.

B135. Indeed, to the extent that recorded goodwill consists primarily of core goodwill and other assets, the Board observed that writing it off as an expense

or loss would be less representationally faithful than recognizing it as an asset, particularly at the date of the business combination. Treating an item that primarily is an asset as an expense or loss may be said to reflect bias, which Concepts Statement 2 described as "the tendency of a measure to fall more often on one side than the other of what it represents instead of being equally likely to fall on either side. Bias in accounting measures means a tendency to be consistently too high or too low" (paragraph 77). Accordingly, the Board concluded that the reliability criterion is met.

Opposing Views

B136. Some of the respondents to the 1999 Exposure Draft and the 2001 Exposure Draft argued that goodwill should be written off immediately to earnings, other comprehensive income, or equity on the basis that goodwill does not meet the assets definition or the other criteria for initial recognition. Others argued that writing goodwill off immediately would eliminate much of the difference between the financial statements of entities that grow by acquisitions and those that grow internally and would be preferable to the alternative of capitalizing internally generated goodwill. The Board observed those views in reaching its tentative decision that goodwill should be recognized as an asset and again in certain of the responses to the Invitation to Comment that expressed disagreement with that tentative decision.

B137. In its redeliberations of the 1999 Exposure Draft, the Board affirmed its observation that goodwill does meet the assets definition and the other criteria for initial recognition and, therefore, writing it off immediately to earnings or other comprehensive income would not be representationally faithful. The Board also affirmed its observation that charging it off to equity directly without flowing through earnings or other comprehensive income could only be interpreted conceptually as a distribution to owners.

B138. The Board acknowledged that recognizing only goodwill acquired in a business combination and not goodwill that is generated internally results in differences in financial statements that make comparison more difficult. However, as it did in developing the 1999 Exposure Draft and the 2001 Exposure Draft, the Board concluded that the differences in accounting between acquired goodwill and internally generated goodwill are not unique as they also arise between other assets that are acquired and those that are internally generated.

B139. The Board also observed the potential for accounting arbitrage that might accompany a requirement that goodwill be written off immediately while other components of the acquisition premium could not be similarly written off. That sharply different treatment would provide incentives for entities to allocate more of the premium to goodwill and less to other assets in order to enhance future earnings by avoiding the future charges against earnings related to those assets.

Initial measurement of goodwill

B140. In developing the 1999 Exposure Draft, the Board observed that because goodwill cannot be purchased separately but only as part of business combination transactions, those transactions are necessarily the basis for initially measuring it. As such, difficulties associated with measuring the acquisition cost in those transactions can have a direct effect on the measurement of goodwill.

B141. Difficulties in measuring acquisition costs in a business combination relate largely to the nature of the consideration tendered. Concepts Statement 2 acknowledged that, stating, "The acquisition cost may also be difficult to determine if assets are acquired . . . by issuing stock . . ." (paragraph 65). Although the acquisition costs in all-cash transactions are not difficult to measure, the Board noted the potential for overvaluation (component 5) when the consideration consists wholly or partially of shares of the acquiring entity's stock.

B142. The Board also noted that that difficulty is not unique to the measurement of goodwill, however, and extends to all the net assets acquired in a business combination in which the consideration involves equity interests of the acquiring entity. It also is not unique to business combinations and extends to any transaction in which assets or groups of assets are acquired in exchange for equity interests of the acquiring entity. However, the Board acknowledged that the effects of those difficulties would be more pronounced for goodwill than for other assets and liabilities, since it is measured as a residual of the acquisition cost incurred.

B143. The Board also observed that even if the acquisition cost can be measured without difficulty, difficulties may arise in assigning that cost to the individual net assets acquired in the "basket purchase," including goodwill. Although measuring some items acquired in a basket purchase is less difficult than measuring other items, particularly if they are exchangeable and traded regularly in the marketplace (or otherwise routinely obtained in transactions other than a business combination), that is not the case with goodwill, since it is not exchangeable. However, many other assets acquired in a business combination—especially many intangible assets—are not traded regularly or otherwise routinely obtained in other transactions. As a result, assigning a portion of the cost of the acquisition to goodwill is not necessarily more difficult than it is for those other assets.

B144. Despite those difficulties, the Board believes that knowledgeable users of financial statements can and do understand the limitations inherent in accounting for goodwill. The Board also believes that users are generally familiar with and understand the present requirements in Opinion 16 for initially measuring purchased goodwill.

B145. The Board therefore concluded that the approach to initial measurement of goodwill that is taken in Opinion 16 is appropriate and that no other alternative identified would be a significant improvement. The Board expressed concern about measuring goodwill as a residual but acknowledged that there is no other real measurement alternative, since goodwill is not separable from the entity or exchangeable.

B146. Accordingly, the 1999 Exposure Draft and the 2001 Exposure Draft proposed that goodwill should be measured initially as the excess of the cost of the acquired entity over the fair value of the net assets acquired, consistent with the requirements of Opinion 16. In that regard, the Board noted that acquiring entities should make every effort (a) to measure the purchase consideration accurately, (b) to record the fair values rather than the book values of net assets acquired, and (c) to ensure that all intangible assets not previously recorded are recorded so that those items are not included in what is recognized as goodwill. Few respondents to those Exposure Drafts commented on that requirement or suggested alternative measurement approaches. The Board affirmed that requirement in its redeliberations.

Initial recognition and measurement of intangible assets other than goodwill

Definition of intangible assets

B147. In the deliberations that led to the 1999 Exposure Draft, the Board concluded that the characteristics that distinguish intangible assets from other assets are that they are (a) without physical substance, (b) not financial instruments, and (c) not current assets. The 1999 Exposure Draft defined intangible assets in terms of those characteristics. Several respondents to that Exposure Draft noted that some intangible assets (such as order or production backlogs) are current assets. They observed that some might interpret the proposed definition in the 1999 Exposure Draft as prohibiting recognition of those intangible assets apart from goodwill, which they believed was not the Board's intent. The Board agreed with those respondents and decided that this Statement should define intangible assets more broadly, that is, as assets (not including financial assets) that lack physical substance.

Distinguishing intangible assets from goodwill

B148. At the inception of this project, the Board observed that intangible assets make up an increasing proportion of the assets of many (if not most) entities. The Board also observed that intangible assets acquired in a business combination often were included in the amount recognized as goodwill, despite the provisions in Opinion 16 that required they be recognized apart from goodwill.

B149. For two primary reasons, the Board concluded that this Statement should provide explicit criteria for determining whether an acquired intangible asset should be recognized apart from goodwill. First, the Board affirmed the conclusion it reached prior to issuance of the 1999 Exposure Draft that the decision usefulness of financial statements would be enhanced if intangible assets acquired in a business combination were distinguished from goodwill. As stated in Concepts Statement 5:

> Classification in financial statements facilitates analysis by grouping items with essentially similar characteristics and separating items with essentially different characteristics. Analysis aimed at objectives such as predicting amounts, timing, and uncertainty of future cash flows requires financial information segregated into reasonably homog-

enous groups. For example, components of financial statements that consist of items that have similar characteristics in one or more respects, such as continuity or recurrence, stability, risk, and reliability, are likely to have more predictive value than if their characteristics are dissimilar. [paragraph 20]

B150. Second, for several Board members, having explicit criteria that determine whether an acquired intangible asset should be recognized apart from goodwill was important to their decision that goodwill is an indefinite-lived asset that should no longer be amortized. Absent such criteria, many more finite-lived intangible assets would be included in the amount recognized as goodwill.

B151. In developing the 1999 Exposure Draft, the Board considered various characteristics that might distinguish other intangible assets from goodwill. Based on the Board's conclusion that identifiability is the characteristic that conceptually distinguishes other intangible assets from goodwill, the 1999 Exposure Draft proposed that intangible assets that are identifiable and reliably measurable should be recognized as assets apart from goodwill. Most respondents to the 1999 Exposure Draft agreed that many intangible assets are identifiable and that various intangible assets are reliably measurable. Many of those respondents generally agreed that the proposed recognition criteria would improve the transparency of financial reporting for business combinations—a primary objective of this project. However, respondents' views on the proposed recognition criteria varied. Many of those respondents suggested alternative recognition criteria and many urged the Board to clarify the term *reliably measurable.*

B152. The Board considered those suggestions and decided to modify the proposed recognition criteria to provide a clearer distinction between intangible assets that should be recognized apart from goodwill and those that should be subsumed into goodwill. The 2001 Exposure Draft reflected the Board's conclusion that an intangible asset should be recognized apart from goodwill if it meets the asset recognition criteria in Concepts Statement 5 and if either (a) control over the future economic benefits of the asset results from contractual or other legal rights (the contractual-legal criterion) or (b) the intangible asset is capable of being separated or divided and sold, transferred, licensed, rented, or exchanged (either separately or as part of a group of assets) (the separability criterion). The Board concluded that sufficient information should exist to reliably measure the fair value of that asset if an asset has an underlying contractual or legal basis or if it is capable of being separated from the entity. Thus, the change in the recognition criteria eliminated the need to explicitly include reliably measurable as a recognition criterion or to clarify the meaning of that term.

B153. In developing those recognition criteria, the Board acknowledged that they would result in some finite-lived intangible assets being subsumed into the amount initially recognized as goodwill. The Board concluded, however, that the advantages of the revised criteria (in particular, greater consistency in their application) outweighed the disadvantages of recognizing some finite-lived intangible assets as part of goodwill.

B154. Most of the respondents to the 2001 Exposure Draft that commented on the revised recognition criteria agreed that they were an improvement over the recognition criteria proposed in the 1999 Exposure Draft. However, some of those respondents suggested alternative recognition criteria or made other suggestions. Many of those alternative recognition criteria were similar to the suggestions made by respondents to the 1999 Exposure Draft. Paragraphs B155–B164 describe the Board's reasons for accepting some suggestions made by respondents and rejecting others.

B155. The 2001 Exposure Draft proposed that an intangible asset would need to meet the asset recognition criteria in Concepts Statement 5 in order to be recognized apart from goodwill. Several respondents to that Exposure Draft said that inclusion of that criterion was inconsistent with the Board's stated presumption that an intangible asset that meets the contractual-legal criterion or the separability criterion also would meet the asset recognition criteria. The Board agreed with those respondents that it was not necessary to explicitly state that an intangible asset that meets the recognition criteria in paragraph 39 also meets the asset recognition criteria in Statement 5.

Reasons for the contractual-legal criterion

B156. In considering alternative recognition criteria, the Board observed that in contrast to goodwill, the values of many intangible assets arise from rights conveyed legally by contract, statute, or similar means. For example, franchises are granted to automobile dealers, fast-food outlets, and professional sports teams. Trademarks and service marks may be registered with the government. Contracts are often negotiated with customers or suppliers. Technological innovations are often protected by patent. In contrast, the value of goodwill arises from the collection of assembled assets that make up an acquired entity or the value created by assembling a collection of assets through a business combination, such as the synergies that are expected to result from combining one or more businesses. In developing the 2001 Exposure Draft, the Board concluded that the fact that an intangible asset arises from contractual or other legal rights is an important characteristic that distinguishes many intangible assets from goodwill and, therefore, acquired intangible assets with that characteristic should be recognized as an asset apart from goodwill. The Board affirmed that conclusion in its redeliberations of the 2001 Exposure Draft.

Reasons for the separability criterion

B157. In reconsidering the recognition criteria proposed in the 1999 Exposure Draft, the Board also noted that although some intangible assets do not arise from rights conveyed by contract or other legal means, they are nonetheless capable of being separated from the acquired entity and exchanged for something else of value. Others, like goodwill, cannot be separated from an entity and sold or otherwise transferred. The Board concluded that separability is another important characteristic that distinguishes many intangible assets from goodwill and, therefore, acquired intangible assets with that characteristic should be recognized as assets apart from goodwill. The Board affirmed that conclusion in its redeliberations of the 2001 Exposure Draft.

B158. The 2001 Exposure Draft proposed that an intangible asset that was not separable individually would meet the separability criterion if it could be sold, transferred, licensed, rented, or exchanged along with a group of related assets or liabilities. Some respondents to that Exposure Draft suggested that the Board eliminate that requirement, arguing that unless the asset is separable individually it should be included in the amount recognized as goodwill. Others suggested the Board clarify the meaning of the term *group of related assets,* noting that even goodwill can be separated from the acquired entity if the asset group sold constitutes a business.

B159. As it did prior to issuing the 2001 Exposure Draft, the Board noted that some intangible assets are so closely related to another asset or liability that they are usually sold as a "package" (as is the case with deposit liabilities and the related depositor relationship intangible asset). The Board concluded that if those intangible assets were subsumed into goodwill, gains might be inappropriately recognized if the intangible asset was later sold along with the related asset or obligation. However, the Board agreed that the proposed requirement to recognize an intangible asset separately from goodwill if it could be sold or transferred as part of an asset group was a broader criterion than it had intended. For those reasons, this Statement states that an intangible asset that is not separable individually meets the separability criterion if it can be separated and divided from the entity and sold, transferred, licensed, rented, or exchanged in combination with a related contract, other asset, or liability.

B160. At the suggestion of some respondents to the 2001 Exposure Draft, the Board considered explicitly limiting the separability criterion to intangible assets that are separable *and* that trade in observable exchange transactions. While the Board agreed that exchange transactions provide evidence of an asset's separability, it concluded that those transactions were not necessarily the only evidence of separability. Therefore, the Board concluded that it should not limit the recognition of intangible assets that meet the separability criterion to only those that are traded in observable exchange transactions.

B161. Several respondents to the 2001 Exposure Draft suggested that the separability criterion be modified to require recognition of an intangible asset apart from goodwill only if management of the entity *intends* to sell, lease, or otherwise exchange the asset. The Board rejected that suggestion because it does not believe that the intent to sell or otherwise exchange the asset is the relevant factor that distinguishes some intangible assets from goodwill. Rather, it is the asset's *capability* of being separated from the entity and exchanged for something else of value that is the distinction requiring that it be accounted for separately from goodwill.

Reasons for rejecting other suggested recognition criteria

B162. Some respondents to both the 1999 Exposure Draft and the 2001 Exposure Draft suggested that the Board eliminate the requirement to recognize intangible assets apart from goodwill. Others suggested that all intangible assets with characteristics similar

to goodwill should be included in the amount recorded as goodwill. The Board rejected those suggestions because they would diminish rather than improve the decision usefulness of reported financial information.

B163. Some respondents to the 1999 Exposure Draft and the 2001 Exposure Draft doubted their ability to reliably measure the fair values of many intangible assets. They suggested, therefore, that the only intangible assets that should be recognized apart from goodwill are those that have direct cash flows and those that are bought and sold in observable exchange transactions. The Board rejected that suggestion. The Board noted that in a business combination, the fair value of the asset acquired—the acquired entity—is established through a bargained exchange transaction. This Statement requires allocation of that fair value to individual assets acquired, including financial assets, tangible assets, and intangible assets based on their fair values. During redeliberations of the 2001 Exposure Draft, the Board affirmed its belief that the fair value estimates for intangible assets that meet the recognition criteria in this Statement will be sufficiently reliable for the purpose of that purchase price allocation. The Board acknowledged that the fair value estimates for some intangible assets that meet the recognition criteria might lack the precision of the fair value measurements for other assets. However, the Board also concluded that the financial information that will be provided by recognizing intangible assets at their estimated fair values is more representationally faithful than that which would be provided if those intangible assets were subsumed into goodwill on the basis of measurement difficulties. Moreover, including finite-lived intangible assets in goodwill that is not being amortized would further diminish the representational faithfulness of financial statements.

B164. Some of the Board's constituents believe that an item is not an asset if it is not separable. As it did prior to issuance of the 1999 Exposure Draft and the 2001 Exposure Draft, the Board noted that the assets definition in Concepts Statement 6 does not include separability as a necessary characteristic. Thus, although certain intangible assets meeting the contractual-legal criterion might not be separable, they do meet the assets definition.

Illustrative list of intangible assets

B165. Appendix A of the 1999 Exposure Draft included an illustrative list of identifiable intangible assets that might be acquired in a business combination (some of which did not meet the recognition criteria proposed in the 1999 Exposure Draft). The Board agreed with the respondents to the 2001 Exposure Draft that urged the Board to retain such a list in this Statement. However, because the Board changed the criteria for recognizing intangible assets apart from goodwill and decided to include on the list intangible assets meeting the recognition criteria in this Statement, the list of intangible assets in Appendix A of this Statement differs from the proposed list in the 1999 Exposure Draft. For example, the list in the Exposure Draft included customer base as an identifiable intangible asset. The Board views a customer base as a group of customers that are not known or identifiable to the entity (such as customers of a fast-food franchise). The Board concluded that a customer base does not meet the criteria for recognition apart from goodwill and, therefore, customer base is not included on the list in paragraph A14. The Board similarly concluded that other intangible assets listed in Appendix A of the 1999 Exposure Draft would not generally meet the recognition criteria in this Statement and, thus, those assets also have been excluded from the list in paragraph A14. Examples of those intangible assets include customer service capability, presence in geographic markets or locations, non-union status or strong labor relations, ongoing training or recruiting programs, outstanding credit ratings and access to capital markets, and favorable government relations.

B166. The Board also removed some of the items included on the proposed list in the 1999 Exposure Draft because they represent asset categories that might include both tangible and intangible assets. For example, many different types of assets might be included in the broad category of research and development assets. Whether a specific research and development asset is an intangible asset depends on the nature of the asset.

B167. The Board noted that the list in paragraph A14 is not all-inclusive. The fact that an intangible asset that was included on the proposed list in the 1999 Exposure Draft is not listed in paragraph A14 does not mean that the intangible asset does not meet the recognition criteria in paragraph 39. The nature of each acquired intangible asset needs to be considered in determining whether the recognition criteria of this Statement are met.

Exceptions to the recognition criteria

Assembled workforce

B168. The Board recognizes that the intellectual capital of an assembled workforce is an important resource of many entities. The Board therefore decided that this Statement should address whether an assembled workforce of at-will employees should be recognized as an intangible asset apart from goodwill.

B169. Some constituents believe there are circumstances under which an assembled workforce could be viewed as meeting either the contractual-legal criterion or the separability criterion for recognition as an asset apart from goodwill. However, the Board decided not to explicitly consider whether and in what circumstances an assembled workforce would meet those criteria. The Board observed that even if an assembled workforce met the criteria for recognition as an intangible asset apart from goodwill, the technique often used to measure the fair value of that asset is replacement cost—the cost to hire and train a comparable assembled workforce. The Board believes that replacement cost is not a representationally faithful measurement of the fair value of the intellectual capital acquired in a business combination. The Board concluded that techniques to measure the value of an assembled workforce and the related intellectual capital with sufficient reliability are not currently available. Consequently, it decided to make an exception to the recognition criteria and require that the fair value of an assembled workforce acquired be included in the amount initially recorded as goodwill, regardless of whether it meets the recognition criteria in paragraph 39.

Acquired research and development assets

B170. The Board also considered whether this Statement should address issues related to the accounting for research and development assets acquired in business combinations. During development of the 1999 Exposure Draft, the Board noted that some of the issues associated with acquired research and development assets are unique to those assets and not directly related to other business combinations issues. The Board concluded that it was not possible to address those issues without considering the issues associated with accounting for research and development costs generally. Consequently, the Board decided not to address them in this Statement. Therefore, neither the 1999 Exposure Draft nor the 2001 Exposure Draft proposed any change to the requirement in paragraph 5 of FASB Interpretation No. 4, *Applicability of FASB Statement No. 2 to Business Combinations Accounted for by the Purchase Method,* that the amounts assigned to tangible and intangible assets to be used in a particular research and development project that *have no alternative future use* be charged to expense at the acquisition date. A few respondents to the 2001 Exposure Draft suggested that the amount of acquired research and development assets be subsumed into the amount recognized as goodwill. In its redeliberations, the Board affirmed its conclusion not to reconsider the guidance in Interpretation 4 at this time. The Board concluded that intangible assets in the scope of that Interpretation should be charged to expense at the acquisition date regardless of whether they meet the criteria in paragraph 39 for recognition apart from goodwill.

Initial measurement of intangible assets

B171. As proposed in the 1999 Exposure Draft and consistent with the requirements of Opinion 16, intangible assets acquired in a business combination and recognized in accordance with paragraph 39 of this Statement should initially be assigned an amount based on their fair values. As noted in paragraph 7 of FASB Concepts Statement No. 7, *Using Cash Flow Information and Present Value in Accounting Measurements,* in recent years the Board has identified fair value as the objective for most measurements at initial recognition. None of the respondents to the 1999 Exposure Draft suggested alternative measurement approaches.

B172. The Board noted that an intangible asset arising from a contractual or other legal rights represents the future cash flows that are expected to result from ownership of that contract or legal right. Its fair value represents the amount at which it could be bought or sold in a current transaction between willing parties, that is, other than in a forced or liquidation sale. For example, the fair value of an order backlog would represent the amount a buyer would be willing to pay to acquire the future cash flows expected to arise from that order backlog.

B173. The Board recognizes that the requirements in this Statement might change current practice with respect to the amounts assigned to some intangible assets, in particular those that arise from contractual

or other legal rights. For example, the Board has been informed that in current practice, the amount assigned to acquired operating lease contracts (when the acquired entity is the lessor) and customer contracts often is based on the amount by which the contract terms are favorable relative to market prices at the date of acquisition. Thus, in some cases, no amount is assigned to lease and other contracts that are "at the money"—that is, when the contract terms reflect market prices at the date of acquisition. The Board observed, however, that such "at the money" contracts are bought and sold in exchange transactions—the purchase and sale of airport gates (an operating lease) within the airline industry and customer contracts in the home security industry are two examples of those exchange transactions. The Board believes that those transactions provide evidence that a contract may have value for reasons other than terms that are favorable relative to market prices. The Board therefore concluded that the amount by which the terms of a contract are favorable relative to market prices would not necessarily represent the fair value of that contract.

B174. Several respondents noted that a present value technique might often be the best available technique with which to estimate the fair value of an acquired intangible asset. Some of those respondents asked whether the estimated cash flows used in applying that technique should be limited to the cash flows expected over the remaining legal or contractual term of the acquired asset. The Board noted that judgment is required in estimating the period and amount of expected cash flows. Those estimates should be consistent with the objective of measuring fair value and, thus, should incorporate assumptions that marketplace participants would use in making estimates of fair value, such as assumptions about future contract renewals and other benefits such as those that might result from acquisition-related synergies. The Board noted that if such information is not available without undue cost and effort, an entity should use its own assumptions. The Board also noted that while many contracts or other rights (including customer contracts) are fixed in duration, past history (and industry practice) often provides evidence that the contracts or rights are generally renewed without substantial cost and effort. For example, although contracts to manage investments of mutual funds are often short-term contracts (one year or less), the Board has been informed that in many (if not most) cases those contracts are continuously renewed. The Board has also been informed that while some legal rights such as trademarks and broadcast licenses have finite legal lives, those rights are renewable and are often renewed without challenge. In cases such as those, the Board believes that estimates of future cash flows used in measuring the fair value of the acquired intangible asset likely would reflect cash flows for periods that extend beyond the remaining term of the acquired contract or legal right. The Board noted that Concepts Statement 7 discusses the essential elements of a present value measurement (paragraph 23), provides examples of circumstances in which an entity's expected cash flows might differ from the market expected cash flows (paragraph 32), and discusses the use of present value techniques in measuring the fair value of an asset or liability (paragraphs 39–54 and 75–88).

Preacquisition contingencies

B175. This Statement carries forward without reconsideration the provisions in Statement 38, as amended, that relate to the accounting for preacquisition contingencies of purchased entities. Specifically, paragraph 40 of this Statement carries forward the requirement in paragraph 5 of Statement 38 that the amount paid for the contingent asset or liability be estimated. Paragraph 41 of this Statement carries forward the requirement in paragraph 6 that after the end of the allocation period, an adjustment that results from a preacquisition contingency other than an income tax loss carryforward should be included in the determination of net income in the period in which the adjustment is determined. Paragraphs 19–21 of the basis for conclusions of Statement 38 explain the approach the Board used in developing that guidance:

> This Statement distinguishes between (a) an amount deemed to have been paid for an item that includes an element of risk and (b) the gain or loss that results from the risk assumed.
>
> Paragraph 5 [carried forward in paragraph 40 of this Statement] requires that the amount paid for the contingent asset or liability be estimated. If its fair value can be determined, that fair value is used as the basis for recording the asset or liability. Otherwise, an amount determined on the basis of criteria drawn from Statement 5 is used as the best available estimate of fair value. In accordance with the rationale of Opinion 16 (which requires that all assets and liabilities of the acquired enterprise, whether recorded or unrecorded, be identified and recorded by the

acquiring enterprise and that only the residual purchase price that cannot be allocated to specific assets and liabilities be allocated to goodwill) this Statement allows a period of time (the "allocation period") for discovery and quantification of preacquisition contingencies.

> Paragraph 6 [carried forward in paragraph 41 of this Statement] requires that subsequent adjustments of the amounts recorded as a part of the purchase allocation be included in the determination of net income in the period in which the adjustments are determined. In contrast to the amounts deemed paid for the asset or liability, those subsequent adjustments are gains or losses that result from the uncertainties and related risks assumed in the purchase.

B176. Paragraph 22 of the basis for conclusions of Statement 38 also explains the differences between the accounting for contingent consideration and the accounting for preacquisition contingencies, as follows.

> The following examples illustrate the relationship of the accounting for contingent consideration to the nature of the agreement and contrast the nature of each agreement with the nature of a preacquisition contingency:
>
> a. If the contingent consideration is based on subsequent earnings, the additional consideration, when determinable, increases the purchase price because the increased value that was purchased has been demonstrated. Additional goodwill was proven to exist by the achievement of the specified level of earnings. In contrast, when an enterprise changes its estimate of a preacquisition contingent liability, there is nothing to indicate that additional value has been created. A payment is expected to be required, but the payment does not demonstrate that an asset exists or is more valuable than before the payment was anticipated.
> b. If the contingent consideration represents payment of amounts withheld to insure against the existence of contingencies, neither the payment of the contingent consideration nor the payment of a liability that results from the contingency with the

funds withheld affects the acquiring enterprise's accounting for the business combination. The escrow is a way of protecting the buyer against risk. The buyer has agreed to pay the amount either to the seller or to a third-party claimant; and thus, the only uncertainty to the buyer is the identity of the payee. The amount of the agreed consideration that is withheld would be recorded as part of the purchase price in the original allocation. In contrast, a change in an estimate of a preacquisition contingency for which the acquiring enterprise assumed responsibility represents a change in the total amount that will be paid out or received by the acquiring enterprise. The buyer assumed the risk and is subject to the results of that risk.

B177. In developing Statement 38, the Board concluded that the provisions of that Statement should not be applied to contingencies that arise from the acquisition and that did not exist prior to the acquisition (such as contingencies related to litigation over the acquisition and the tax effect of the purchase). Paragraph 23 of Statement 38 explains the basis for that conclusion:

A number of respondents to the Exposure Draft questioned whether this Statement should be applied to contingencies that arise from the acquisition and that did not exist prior to the acquisition. Examples provided included litigation over the acquisition and the tax effect of the purchase. The Board concluded that such contingencies are the acquiring enterprise's contingencies, rather than preacquisition contingencies of the acquired enterprise. Accordingly, Statement 16 applies to those contingencies after the initial purchase allocation.

B178. Also in developing Statement 38, the Board considered and rejected an approach that would have made a distinction based on whether contingencies were known to the acquiring entity at the date of the purchase. As was explained in paragraphs 24 and 25 of Statement 38:

Some believe that a distinction should be made based on whether contingencies were known to the acquiring enterprise at the date of the purchase. In their opinion, the initial recorded estimate for contingencies that were identified at the date of the purchase should be an adjustment of the purchase price and its allocation regardless of when that estimate becomes determinable. The acquiring enterprise agreed to assume those identified contingencies as a condition of the purchase, and presumably that assessment was considered directly in arriving at the purchase price; accordingly, they should be accounted for as part of the purchase. On the other hand, the discovery of contingent assets or liabilities that were *not* identified at the date of the purchase should not affect the allocation of a purchase price because unknown contingencies could not enter directly in the determination of the purchase price and discovery of unexpected assets or liabilities should not affect cost assigned to the other assets and liabilities acquired.

The Board rejected the approach outlined in paragraph 24 for a number of reasons, including the following:

a. An approach that would base the allocation of the purchase price on whether an item was known to the acquiring enterprise at the date of the purchase would conflict with the requirements of Opinion 16 for allocation of the cost of an enterprise accounted for by the purchase method. Paragraph 87 of Opinion 16 [carried forward without reconsideration in paragraph 36 of this Statement] requires the acquiring enterprise to assign "a portion of the cost of the acquired company" to "all identifiable assets acquired . . . and liabilities assumed . . . , whether or not shown in the financial statements of the acquired company." The reference to "identifiable" does not indicate an intent to limit the allocation to items that were known at the date of the purchase.

b. A distinction based on whether contingencies were known to the acquiring enterprise at the date of the purchase could be viewed as only partially reflecting the economics of many purchase combinations. Many factors affect the purchase price in a business combination. Known contingencies would be one of those factors. Other factors might include amounts of earnings, demonstrated growth in earnings, and unknown preacquisition contingencies, the potential existence of which would never-theless enter into an assessment of risk and affect the purchase price.

c. If all preacquisition contingencies that re-sult from a cause that was identified at the date of the purchase were considered part of the purchase consideration, the distinc-tion between an identified contingency and one that was not identified would be vague.

d. A requirement that initial recorded esti-mates for some contingencies be recorded as adjustments of the purchase allocation could discourage an enterprise from recording timely estimates.

B179. In Statement 38, the Board also considered and rejected an approach that would exclude from in-come of the acquiring entity all adjustments that re-sult from preacquisition contingencies. Paragraph 27 of Statement 38 cited the following as the Board's reasons for rejecting that approach:

a. The usual practice in the current accounting environment is for irregularly occurring costs that result from risks assumed by the enterprise to be reflected in income when they occur. The Board did not believe that it should differentiate be-tween risks assumed by purchase and other business risks.

b. The distinction between an adjustment related to a preacquisition contingency and an adjustment that results from current events is not always clear. For example, an enterprise may settle litiga-tion because the cost of a successful defense would exceed the cost of the settlement. The opinion of counsel may be that the case can be successfully defended. In that case, whether the cost of the settlement relates to the preacquisition event that is the stated cause of the litigation or to the current litigious environment is not clear.

B180. As was explained in paragraph 28 of Statement 38, the Board also considered whether all adjustments related to preacquisition contingen-cies should be included in income of the acquired entity in the period in which the adjustments are determined:

> [Some] note that Statement 16 requires ac-cruals of estimated losses from loss contin-gencies to be included in income in the period in which they are determined, and they be-lieve that contingencies assumed through

purchase should be accounted for the same as other contingencies. Although the Board gen-erally agreed, it concluded that an "allocation period" was needed to permit adequate time to make reasonable estimates for the purchase allocation required by Opinion 16.

Criteria for amount to be included in purchase allocation

B181. In developing Statement 38, the Board noted that a requirement to recognize contingent assets in the allocation of the purchase price could be viewed as inconsistent with the practice described in para-graph 17(a) of Statement 5 that "contingencies that might result in gains usually are not reflected in the accounts since to do so might be to recognize rev-enue prior to its realization." As discussed in para-graph 30 of Statement 38, "The Board concluded that this usual practice is not applicable to a purchase allo-cation because revenue does not result from such an allocation; rather, the question is whether to allocate amounts paid to identifiable assets that have value or to goodwill."

B182. During the development of Statement 38, the Board considered comments made by constituents that the fair value of a preacquisition contingency can sometimes be determined and that that fair value might not equal the amount determined in accord-ance with the criteria in Statement 5. As explained in paragraphs 32 and 33 of Statement 38, the Board de-cided to permit recording a preacquisition contin-gency based on its fair value if that fair value can be determined:

> The Board did not intend to modify the general requirement of paragraph 87 of Opin-ion 16 . . . that the purchase allocation be based on the fair value of the assets acquired and the liabilities assumed. Rather, the crite-ria were provided because fair value of a pre-acquisition contingency usually would not be determinable. Accordingly, the Board added paragraph 5(a) to this Statement, to permit re-cording a preacquisition contingency based on its fair value if that fair value can be deter-mined. Otherwise, paragraph 5(b) requires that the amount recorded be based on the cri-teria included in the Exposure Draft.
>
> Some respondents to the Exposure Draft inquired whether it would be appropriate to base the amount recorded on the present

value of the amount determined in accordance with the criteria in paragraph 5(b) because the nature of the resulting amount would be a monetary asset or liability. The Board concluded that it should not specify such a requirement because the timing of payment or receipt of a contingent item seldom would be sufficiently determinable to permit the use of a present value technique on a reasonable basis. However, this Statement does not prohibit the use of a present value if appropriate.

Allocation period

B183. Paragraphs 34–38 of Statement 38 explain the Board's reasons for specifying a time period, referred to as the allocation period, during which estimates of preacquisition contingencies could be included in the purchase price allocation:

> Opinion 16 provides the general principles of accounting for a business combination by the purchase method. The acquiring enterprise determines the value of the consideration given to the sellers, the present value of the liabilities assumed, and the value of the assets acquired. The total value of the consideration given and the liabilities assumed is then allocated among the identifiable assets acquired based on their value; and the balance, if any, is allocated to "goodwill."
>
> The Board recognizes that completion of the allocation process that is required by Opinion 16 may sometimes require an extended period of time. For example, appraisals might be required to determine replacement cost of plant and equipment acquired, a discovery period may be needed to identify and value intangible assets acquired, and an actuarial determination may be required to determine the pension liability to be accrued.
>
> If a business combination is consummated toward the end of an acquiring enterprise's fiscal year or the acquired enterprise is very large or unusually complex, the acquiring enterprise may not be able to obtain some of the data required to complete the allocation of the cost of the purchased enterprise for inclusion in its next annual financial report. In that case, a tentative allocation might be made using the values that have been determined and preliminary estimates of the values that have not

yet been determined. The portions of the allocation that relate to the data that were not available subsequently are adjusted to reflect the finally determined amounts, usually by adjusting the preliminary amount with a corresponding adjustment of goodwill.

> The Board considered specifying a time period during which estimates of preacquisition contingencies could be recorded as part of the purchase allocation. The Board concluded that it should relate the recording of preacquisition contingencies in the purchase allocation to the nature and process of the allocation, rather than to an arbitrary time limit. However, to indicate the Board's intent that the defined "allocation period" should not be unreasonably extended, paragraph 4(b) notes that the existence of a preacquisition contingency for which an amount cannot be estimated does not, of itself, extend the "allocation period." For example, the existence of litigation for which no estimate can be made in advance of the disposition by a court does not extend the "allocation period." That paragraph also notes that the "allocation period" should usually not exceed one year from the consummation date.
>
> The "allocation period" is intended to differentiate between amounts that are determined as a result of the identification and valuation process required by Opinion 16 for all assets acquired and liabilities assumed and amounts that are determined because information that was not previously obtainable becomes obtainable. Thus, the "allocation period" would continue while the acquiring enterprise's counsel was making an evaluation of a claim, but it would not continue if the counsel's evaluation were complete and resulted in the conclusion that no estimate could be made pending further negotiations with the claimant.

Preacquisition net operating loss carryforwards

B184. Also during development of Statement 38, the Board noted the similarity of preacquisition net operating tax loss carryforwards to the other types of preacquisition contingencies. The Board decided that the accounting for net operating loss carryforwards should not be conformed to the accounting for preacquisition contingencies for those contingencies in the scope of Statement 38.

Recognition of deferred taxes

B185. As proposed in the 2001 Exposure Draft, Statement 142 does not permit amortization of either goodwill or intangible assets with indefinite useful lives. Several respondents to the 2001 Exposure Draft suggested that the Board consider permitting nonrecognition of deferred taxes for the differences between the carrying amount and the tax bases of goodwill and intangible assets that are not amortized (whether those differences exist at the date the assets are initially recognized or arise in future periods). Some of those respondents noted that if goodwill or other intangible assets are not amortized, the related deferred tax liability will remain on the balance sheet until the asset is sold, completely impaired, or otherwise disposed of. In that case, settlement of that deferred tax liability could take an extremely long time. Others argued that the proposed nonrecognition of deferred tax liabilities related to goodwill and intangible assets with indefinite useful lives is analogous to two exceptions to the comprehensive recognition of deferred taxes required by FASB Statement No. 109, *Accounting for Income Taxes*— nonrecognition of deferred U.S. tax liabilities for foreign unremitted earnings and nonrecognition of a deferred tax liability for nondeductible goodwill.

B186. The Board acknowledged that its decision not to amortize goodwill and certain intangible assets creates a situation that did not exist when the Board deliberated Statement 109. However, the same arguments made by respondents to the 2001 Exposure Draft for nonrecognition of deferred tax liabilities related to goodwill and intangible assets with indefinite useful lives also were made at the time Statement 109 was developed. Those arguments were extensively studied and debated, and in the end the Board decided that Statement 109 would require comprehensive recognition of deferred taxes subject only to the limited number of exceptions identified in paragraph 9 of that Statement. In its redeliberations of the 2001 Exposure Draft, the Board concluded that this Statement should not amend Statement 109 to provide more exceptions to comprehensive recognition of deferred taxes.

Excess of the fair value of acquired net assets over cost

B187. In some business combinations, the amounts assigned to the acquired net assets exceed their cost. That excess (commonly referred to as negative goodwill) is referred to herein as the *excess over cost* or *excess*. The Board affirmed its belief expressed in both the 1999 Exposure Draft and the 2001 Exposure Draft that substantially all business combinations are exchange transactions in which each party receives and sacrifices commensurate value. Accordingly, an excess rarely would remain if the valuations inherent in the purchase price allocation process were properly performed. The Board affirmed the requirement proposed in both the 1999 Exposure Draft and the 2001 Exposure Draft that if an excess remains after the initial allocation of the purchase price, the acquiring entity shall reassess whether all acquired assets and liabilities assumed have been identified and recognized. In addition, accurate and thorough remeasurements should be performed to verify that the consideration paid and the assets acquired and liabilities assumed have been properly valued.

B188. As expressed in both the 1999 Exposure Draft and the 2001 Exposure Draft, Board members believe that, in most cases, the excess is due to measurement errors in the purchase price allocation. Therefore, the Board affirmed its conclusion that the excess should be used to adjust the amounts initially assigned to certain assets. Based on suggestions made by respondents to the 1999 Exposure Draft and the 2001 Exposure Draft, the Board concluded that the excess should be allocated on a pro rata basis to all acquired assets *except* financial assets other than investments accounted for by the equity method, assets to be disposed of by sale, deferred tax assets, prepaid assets relating to pension or other postretirement benefit plans, and any other current assets. The Board concluded that those assets should be excluded from the allocation of the excess because (with the exception of equity method investments and deferred tax assets) their fair values are generally more certain than those of other assets. The Board also observed that not excluding those assets potentially would result in ordinary gain recognition in the near term as those assets are realized.

B189. As it did prior to issuing the 1999 Exposure Draft and the 2001 Exposure Draft, the Board concluded that any excess remaining after those assets had been reduced to zero should be recognized as an extraordinary gain.

B190. Respondents to both the 1999 Exposure Draft and the 2001 Exposure Draft offered little support for the proposed treatment of the excess—particularly the requirement to record an extraordinary gain (if an excess remained after reducing the amount assigned to certain assets to zero). Respondents asserted that recognizing any gain on a purchase transaction cannot be justified conceptually. They generally favored recognizing the remaining excess as a deferred credit that would be amortized in some manner—as is done in current practice.

B191. A number of respondents also disagreed with the proposed requirement to allocate the excess to specified acquired assets—especially given the emphasis in both Exposure Drafts on initially recording assets and liabilities at their fair value. Most of those respondents suggested that the entire excess should be recognized as a deferred credit. However, a few respondents suggested that the excess should be recognized as a component of equity or as a contingent liability.

B192. While the Board acknowledged the views expressed by those respondents, it affirmed its conclusion that accounting for the excess as an unrecognizable obligation would require recognition of a credit balance that does not meet the definition of a liability in Concepts Statement 6. Moreover, if that credit balance was treated as if it was a liability, that credit balance would be reduced only when, if ever, it was determined that the related outlays had been incurred. Because of the inherent difficulties in making those determinations and because entities would not be permitted to recognize such obligations in other circumstances, the Board affirmed its conclusion that the only practical approach would be to recognize the excess as an extraordinary gain. The Board noted that extraordinary treatment is appropriate to highlight the fact that an excess exists and to reflect the unusual nature and infrequent occurrence of the item. The Board also noted that regardless of how the excess is accounted for, it results in recognition of a gain as a result of the purchase transaction. The only issue is when that gain is recognized—immediately or in future periods.

B193. In developing the 2001 Exposure Draft the Board decided that recognition of the excess as a reduction in the amounts that would otherwise have been assigned to the assets acquired or as an extraordinary gain should be delayed in combinations involving contingent consideration. That is because, while the initial purchase price (excluding the contingent amount) could be below the fair value of the net assets acquired prior to resolution of the contingency (giving rise to an excess over cost), resolution resulting in additional consideration could significantly change that result. Thus, recognizing an extraordinary gain related to that excess when the business

combination is recognized initially could result in recognition of an extraordinary gain that perhaps should not have been recognized and that may be reversed (partially or fully) if and when the contingent consideration is paid or issued. None of the respondents to the 2001 Exposure Draft specifically objected to that view and the Board affirmed it during redeliberations. Thus, this Statement requires that if a business combination involves a consideration contingency that might result in additional cost of the acquired entity, an amount equal to the lesser of the excess or the maximum amount of contingent consideration is to be recognized as if it was a liability until the consideration contingency is resolved.

Documentation at date of acquisition

B194. Statement 142 requires that acquiring entities assign acquired assets (including goodwill) and liabilities to reporting units. In developing the 2001 Exposure Draft, the Board concluded that entities should be required to document certain facts and circumstances surrounding the business combination for use in making those assignments. The proposed documentation requirements included the basis for and method of determining the purchase price and other information such as the reasons for the acquisition and management's expectations related to dilution, synergies, and other financial measurements. None of the respondents to that Exposure Draft commented on those requirements. The Board concluded that those documentation requirements should be retained in this Statement.

Disclosures in Financial Statements

B195. Because a business combination often results in a significant change to an entity's operations, the nature and extent of the information disclosed about the transaction bear on users' abilities to assess the effects of such changes on postacquisition earnings and cash flows. Accordingly, the Board decided that as part of this project, it would assess the usefulness of the disclosure requirements in Opinion 16 for entities that apply the purchase method. As part of that assessment, the Board solicited input from analysts and other users of financial statements on ways to improve the disclosure requirements in Opinion 16. As it did prior to issuing the 1999 Exposure Draft, the Board concluded that the disclosure requirements in Opinion 16 should be retained. The Board then considered whether other information should be disclosed to supplement the information provided under the disclosure requirements in Opinion 16.

B196. In developing the 1999 Exposure Draft the Board concluded that additional disclosures should be required to provide decision-useful information about the net assets acquired in a business combination. Specifically, the Board concluded that additional information should be provided relating to (a) the allocation of the purchase price to assets acquired and liabilities assumed, (b) the nature and amount of intangible assets acquired, and (c) the amount of goodwill recognized.

Disclosure of information about the purchase price allocation and pro forma sales and earnings

B197. In developing the 1999 Exposure Draft, the Board decided to require disclosure of information about the purchase price allocation, specifically, information about the amount of the step-up in assets acquired and liabilities assumed. That Exposure Draft would have required tabular disclosure of the fair values allocated to each of the major balance sheet captions and the related carrying amounts as recognized in the statement of financial position of the acquired entity immediately before its acquisition. Based on input received from analysts, the Board concluded that that information would provide users with a powerful tool for assessing the postacquisition earnings and cash flows of acquiring entities. That input also led the Board to conclude that information about the step-up in the basis of assets acquired and liabilities assumed would be more useful in assessing those postacquisition earnings and cash flows than the pro forma sales and earnings disclosures required by Opinion 16. Consequently, the 1999 Exposure Draft proposed that the pro forma disclosure requirement in Opinion 16 be eliminated.

B198. Respondents' views on the proposed requirement to disclose information about the purchase price allocation were mixed. About half of the respondents that commented on that proposed requirement agreed that the information it would provide would be useful in assessing postacquisition earnings and cash flow of the acquiring entity. The respondents that disagreed with that proposed requirement were primarily opposed to disclosure of information about the carrying amounts of assets acquired and liabilities assumed. They questioned the usefulness of that information, particularly if the financial statements of the acquired entity were not audited or if they were prepared on a basis other than U.S. generally accepted accounting principles. After considering those views, the Board affirmed its conclusion that information about the allocation of the purchase price to major balance sheet captions would be useful in assessing the amount and timing of future cash flows. However, it agreed with those respondents that information about the related carrying amounts might be of limited usefulness. Thus, this Statement requires disclosure of information about the allocation of the purchase price to each major balance sheet caption of the acquired entity but not their related carrying amounts.

B199. Respondents also expressed mixed views about the proposal to eliminate the pro forma sales and earnings disclosures required by Opinion 16. Many of the respondents supported elimination of those disclosure requirements. Those respondents said that the information provided has little value because it is based on hypothetical assumptions and mechanical computations. Respondents that favored retaining those disclosures said that the pro forma information is useful for measuring growth and in assessing whether the synergies expected to result from the combination have been achieved. After considering respondents' views, the Board concluded that the pro forma disclosure requirements in Opinion 16 should be retained in this Statement.

B200. Several users suggested that the Board require disclosure of pro forma sales and earnings information at the reportable segment level because that information would be useful in assessing the amount and timing of future goodwill impairment losses. The Board rejected that suggestion because it concluded that the costs of preparing and disclosing that information would exceed the benefits derived from its use.

B201. The Board noted that FASB Statement No. 79, *Elimination of Certain Disclosures for Business Combinations by Nonpublic Enterprises,* exempts nonpublic entities from the Opinion 16 requirement to disclose supplemental pro forma information. Preparers and attestors of financial statements of nonpublic entities urged the Board to continue that exemption, arguing that the costs of preparing the pro forma information exceed the benefit of providing it. After considering those views, the Board concluded that nonpublic entities should continue to be exempt from the pro forma disclosure requirements of this Statement.

Disclosures related to goodwill

B202. The 1999 Exposure Draft proposed that in the year of acquisition, the notes to financial statements should include a description of the elements that underlie goodwill, the useful life of goodwill and how it was determined, and the amortization method. As a consequence of its decision that goodwill should not be amortized, the Board decided to eliminate the requirement to disclose the useful life of goodwill and the amortization method because they are not applicable under a nonamortization approach. The Board also decided to eliminate the requirement to disclose a description of the elements that underlie goodwill because its purpose was to provide a basis for assessing the appropriateness of the goodwill amortization period.

B203. The Board concluded, however, that information about the amount of goodwill, in particular the amount of goodwill by reportable segment, would be useful in assessing the amount and timing of potential goodwill impairment charges. After considering input from analysts and other users of financial statements, the Board decided that for each material business combination, the notes to the financial statements should disclose (a) the reasons for the acquisition including a description of the factors that led to the payment of a purchase price that resulted in goodwill and (b) the amount of goodwill assigned to each reportable segment.

B204. The Board acknowledged, however, that information about the amount of goodwill by reportable segment is only useful if users also are provided information about performance at that level. The Board decided, therefore, that the requirement to disclose the amount of goodwill by reportable segment should be limited to those entities that are within the scope of FASB Statement No. 131, *Disclosures about Segments of an Enterprise and Related Information.*

B205. Based on input received from analysts and other users, the Board also concluded that information about the amount of goodwill that is expected to be deducted for tax purposes is useful in assessing the amount and timing of future cash flows of the combined entity. The Board therefore decided to require disclosure of that amount if the goodwill initially recognized in a material business combination is significant in relation to the total cost of the acquired entity.

B206. Several respondents to the 2001 Exposure Draft commented on the proposed requirement to disclose goodwill by reportable segment. Half of those respondents agreed with the requirement and half suggested it be eliminated. The Board affirmed

its conclusion that disclosure of that information is useful in estimating the amount and timing of future impairment losses and, thus, concluded that the disclosure requirement should be retained.

B207. Several respondents to the 2001 Exposure Draft suggested that entities be required to provide information about the methods and key assumptions that would be used in measuring the fair value of a reporting unit and the types of events that would likely give rise to a goodwill impairment test. They argued that that information is needed to make informed judgments about the timing and amount of potential future impairment losses. The Board considered similar suggestions during development of the 2001 Exposure Draft. The Board concluded that without access to management's cash flow projections and its methods of estimating those future cash flows, and information about past cash flows or earnings at the reporting unit level, the suggested disclosures would be of little benefit to users in making those judgments. In addition, the Board noted that information about methods and assumptions could be useful only if changes to those methods and assumptions are disclosed almost continuously. The Board affirmed its initial conclusions in its redeliberations of the 2001 Exposure Draft and, therefore, this Statement does not require disclosure of that information.

Disclosure of information about intangible assets other than goodwill

B208. The 1999 Exposure Draft proposed that certain information be disclosed in the notes to the financial statements for each major intangible asset class. The information that would have been required to be disclosed included (a) a description of the assets and the amounts assigned to them at the acquisition date, (b) the key assumptions and methodologies used to determine those amounts, (c) a description of the amortization method, and (d) the weighted-average amortization period. Many respondents to that Exposure Draft commented on the proposed disclosure requirements. Most agreed that additional information about intangible assets acquired would be useful, but many urged the Board to consider reducing the extent of the disclosure requirements. They argued that the cost of providing the information, particularly for entities that complete multiple acquisitions in a single period, would exceed the benefits derived from that information.

B209. After considering the suggestions made by those respondents, the Board affirmed its conclusion that financial statements should provide additional information about acquired intangible assets other than goodwill. However, in view of the changes made to the proposed accounting for intangible assets and the comments made by respondents, the Board revised the disclosure requirements related to acquired intangible assets.

B210. The Board concluded that if the amount assigned to intangible assets is significant in relation to the total cost of an acquired entity, the following information should be disclosed because it is useful in assessing the amount and timing of future cash flows: (a) the total amount assigned to intangible assets subject to amortization and the total amount assigned to those that are not subject to amortization, (b) the amount assigned to each major intangible asset class, and (c) for intangible assets subject to amortization, the weighted-average amortization period in total and for each major intangible asset class. The Board also concluded that disclosure should be made, both in total and for each major intangible asset class, of the amount of any significant residual value assumed.

B211. Although not proposed in the 1999 Exposure Draft, at the suggestion of respondents the Board also decided to require disclosure of the amount of research and development assets acquired and written off at the date of acquisition in accordance with Interpretation 4, as well as the line item in which those write-offs are aggregated.

Other disclosure requirements

B212. The 1999 Exposure Draft proposed disclosure of certain information (as provided for in paragraph 53) if a series of immaterial business combinations were completed in a reporting period that are material in the aggregate. The Board affirmed that requirement, noting that it is consistent with Opinion 16.

B213. In addition, the 1999 Exposure Draft proposed that the information required to be disclosed for a completed business combination would also be disclosed for a material business combination completed after the balance sheet date but before the financial statements are issued (unless disclosure of such information is not practicable). The Board concluded that that disclosure requirement should be retained in this Statement, noting that none of the respondents to the 1999 Exposure Draft commented on that disclosure requirement and that the requirement is consistent with subsequent-events literature within the auditing standards.

Disclosures in Interim Financial Information

B214. Several analysts and other users recommended that the Board consider requiring disclosure of supplemental pro forma sales and earnings information in interim financial information. They argued that that information would be more useful if it was available on a timelier basis. Board members noted that APB Opinion No. 28, *Interim Financial Reporting,* requires disclosures about completed business combinations but does not specify what those disclosures should be. The Board agreed with the suggestion that it amend Opinion 28 to require disclosure of pro forma sales and earnings information in interim financial information.

Effective Date and Transition

Method of accounting for business combinations

B215. The 1999 Exposure Draft proposed that the requirements of this Statement would be effective for business combinations initiated after the date this Statement is issued. A number of respondents to that Exposure Draft suggested the Board consider deferring the effective date for three to six months after issuance to provide time for analysis, interpretation, and implementation of this Statement. The Board affirmed its conclusion that deferral of the effective date would not be necessary because its constituents will have had sufficient time to consider the implications of the Board's decision on planned transactions and because application of the purchase method to all business combinations will not create significant new implementation issues. Thus, the Board concluded that the requirements of this Statement should be applied to business combinations initiated after June 30, 2001. As with the 1999 Exposure Draft, this Statement uses the Opinion 16 definition of initiation date. According to that definition, a business combination is initiated on the earlier of (a) the date that the major terms of a plan are announced publicly or otherwise formally made known or (b) the date that stockholders of a combining entity are notified in writing of an exchange offer.

B216. In reaching its decision on the effective date, the Board noted that business combinations generally are undertaken for strategic and economic considerations that are largely independent of accounting standards. However, the effect of the proposed transaction on postcombination reported earnings commonly is considered by entities in planning and negotiating those transactions. Prospective application for transactions initiated after this Statement is issued therefore avoids situations in which transactions are planned using one accounting standard and accounted for using another.

B217. In developing the 1999 Exposure Draft, the Board concluded that business combinations recorded prior to the issuance of this Statement and business combinations in process when this Statement is issued should be "grandfathered" under Opinion 16. The Board noted that retroactive application of the purchase method to business combinations previously accounted for by the pooling method would have resulted in more comparable financial statements. However, retroactive application would be impractical or burdensome for many entities because the information needed to apply the purchase method may not exist or may no longer be obtainable. Respondents to the 1999 Exposure Draft that addressed that issue supported that decision, and the Board affirmed it in the course of its redeliberations. Several respondents to the 1999 Exposure Draft raised questions related to how the purchase method should be applied to combinations between mutual enterprises. The Board decided to defer the effective date of this Statement with respect to those transactions until interpretative guidance addressing those questions is issued.

Provisions related to the application of the purchase method

B218. This Statement changes certain requirements in Opinion 16 related to the application of the purchase method. Under the transition provisions included in the 1999 Exposure Draft, similar proposed changes would have been effective for business combinations *initiated* after the date that a final Statement was issued. Because amortization of all goodwill will cease upon initial application of Statement 142, Board members concluded that the effective date for the provisions of this Statement related to the application of the purchase method, in particular the criteria for recognition of intangible assets apart from goodwill, should be changed. Therefore, the Board concluded that this Statement should be effective for all business combinations accounted for by the purchase method for which the date of acquisition is July 1, 2001, or later.

Transition

Excess of the fair value of acquired net assets over cost

B219. In developing the 1999 Exposure Draft, the Board concluded that the provisions related to the excess of the fair values of acquired net assets over cost should be applied on a prospective basis because of the operational difficulties that retroactive application would present. The Board reconsidered that decision in developing the 2001 Exposure Draft and decided that as of the beginning of the first fiscal quarter after the date the final Statement is issued, the amount of such excess that is recorded in the statement of financial position as a deferred credit as required by Opinion 16 should be recognized as an extraordinary gain. As suggested by respondents to the 2001 Exposure Draft, the Board concluded that the amount of any excess over cost that is recorded in the statement of financial position as a deferred credit as required by Opinion 16 should be recognized as the effect of a change in accounting principle as of the earlier of either the first day of the fiscal year beginning after December 15, 2001, or the date that Statement 142 is initially applied in its entirety.

Goodwill and other intangible assets

B220. Because this Statement changes the criteria for recognizing intangible assets apart from goodwill, the Board considered whether entities should be required to reassess the intangible assets currently recognized separately in the statement of financial position and possibly reclassify intangible assets that do not meet the new recognition criteria as goodwill and vice versa. For example, some entities may have an assembled workforce recognized as a separate intangible asset, which is not permitted by this Statement. Conversely, some entities may have subsumed into goodwill acquired intangible assets that would be recognized separately under the criteria in this Statement.[36] The Board noted that it would be fairly straightforward to determine whether recognized intangible assets meet the new criteria for recognition apart from goodwill but that it would not be so straightforward to identify intangible assets that meet those criteria that were previously subsumed in goodwill. In developing the 2001 Exposure Draft,

---

[36]Entities might not have adhered strictly to the purchase price allocation requirements in Opinion 16 because Opinion 17 required amortization of all acquired intangible assets and limited the maximum amortization for both goodwill and other intangible assets to 40 years.

the Board concluded that it would not be appropriate to require the reassessment in one direction but not the other.

B221. Several respondents to the 2001 Exposure Draft urged the Board to reconsider those proposed transition provisions, in particular the prohibition against reclassification as goodwill those recognized intangible assets that do not meet the recognition criteria in this Statement. They argued that permitting such reclassifications would improve the comparability of financial statements.

B222. The basis for conclusions to the 2001 Exposure Draft stated that if an entity had aggregated goodwill and intangible assets as one amount for reporting purposes and information exists on how the purchase price was initially allocated between goodwill and other intangible assets, that entity would be required to disaggregate existing intangible assets that meet the recognition criteria in paragraph 39 and report them separately in subsequent statements of financial position. The Board agreed that it should not require disaggregation of that type while prohibiting reclassification of recognized intangible assets that do not meet the criteria for recognition apart from goodwill. Accordingly, the Board decided to retain the disaggregation requirement proposed in the 2001 Exposure Draft and require that entities reclassify as goodwill any recognized intangible assets that do not meet the recognition criteria in paragraph 39.

B223. The Board considered whether the requirement to disaggregate existing intangible assets that meet the recognition criteria from the amount reported as goodwill would affect the recorded deferred tax balances. The Board noted that Statement 109 requires that deferred taxes be provided for differences between the book and tax bases of intangible assets acquired in a business combination. Only goodwill that is not deductible for tax purposes is exempt from that requirement. The Board concluded that the requirement to disaggregate existing intangible assets that were previously included in the amount reported as goodwill would not affect the amount of recorded deferred tax balances, as deferred taxes would have been provided for any differences between the book and tax bases of those assets.

B224. The Board then considered the consequences of reclassifying existing intangible assets as goodwill on recorded deferred tax balances. The Board concluded that when an existing intangible asset is re-

classified as goodwill (because it does not meet the recognition criteria in this Statement), it should be considered goodwill for purposes of accounting for income taxes. Thus, if an intangible asset reclassified as goodwill is an asset for which amortization is not deductible for tax purposes, that asset should be considered as nondeductible goodwill that Statement 109 exempts from the requirements for deferred tax recognition. The Board concluded that any deferred tax liabilities associated with those intangible assets should be eliminated through a corresponding reduction in the carrying amount of goodwill. The Board concluded that if an intangible asset that is deductible for tax purposes is reclassified as goodwill under the transition provisions of this Statement, it should be deemed to be deductible goodwill for which recognition of deferred taxes is required. Thus, reclassification of that asset as goodwill would not affect the recorded deferred tax balances.

Benefits and Costs

B225. The mission of the FASB is to establish and improve standards of financial accounting and reporting for the guidance and education of the public, including preparers, auditors, and users of financial information. In fulfilling that mission, the Board endeavors to determine that a proposed standard will fill a significant need and that the costs imposed to meet that standard, as compared with other alternatives, are justified in relation to the overall benefits of the resulting information. Although the costs to implement a new standard may not be borne evenly, investors and creditors—both present and potential—as well as others benefit from improvements in financial reporting, thereby facilitating the functioning of markets for capital and credit and the efficient allocation of resources in the economy.

B226. The Board believes that this Statement will remedy certain significant deficiencies and fill certain significant voids in financial reporting. The requirement to account for all business combinations by the purchase method will provide users of financial statements with information about the cost of those transactions that the pooling method does not provide because that method does not reflect the values exchanged in the business combination transaction. Therefore, users of financial statements will be better able to assess the initial costs of those investments. They also will be better able to assess the subsequent performance of those investments.

B227. Information about assets and liabilities also will be more complete and comparable. Assets acquired and liabilities assumed that were not previously recorded by predecessor entities will be recorded, as they would be if they had been obtained outside a business combination. Moreover, assets and liabilities that are acquired in a business combination will be measured in the same way as those assets and liabilities that are acquired by other means, either individually or in groups. Consequently, financial statement comparability will be enhanced.

B228. The Board observed that intangible assets constitute a growing share of assets for entities generally and are, in fact, most of the assets of some individual entities. However, information about the intangible assets owned by those entities is often incomplete and inadequate. The Board believes that the changes in the criteria for initial recognition of goodwill and other intangible assets acquired in business combinations will result in more information about those assets than was the case previously.

B229. This Statement also will bring the accounting for business combinations in the United States more in step with how those combinations are accounted for outside the United States. The Board observed that widespread use of the pooling method is largely a phenomenon in the United States and that use of that method in other countries around the world is rare in many jurisdictions and prohibited in others. Consequently, investors will be better able to compare the financial statements of U.S. entities that enter business combinations with those of foreign entities that have engaged in business combinations. Furthermore, this Statement will be an important step in the process of achieving greater convergence of cross-border accounting requirements generally, consistent with the Board's mission statement. That, in turn, will reduce costs now borne by preparers, auditors, and users of financial statements alike, as well as facilitate the efficient allocation of capital globally.

B230. The Board believes that preparers and auditors of financial statements domestically also will benefit from this Statement. The existence of two methods of accounting for similar business combinations that produce such dramatically different financial statement results often puts preparers of financial statements under pressure to obtain the accounting treatment that is deemed to have the more favorable effect on the earnings that are reported postcombination. As a result, the Board has been informed that the ability or inability to use the pooling method is per-

ceived by many to affect competition for mergers and acquisitions, including whether those transactions are entered into and the prices that are negotiated for them. However, there are often uncertainties about whether entities can qualify to use the favored method, and those uncertainties can lead to conflicts between preparers, auditors, and regulators in interpreting and applying those qualifying criteria. This Statement removes those uncertainties.

B231. The Board observed that business entities often incur significant costs in seeking to use the pooling method. Those costs are both monetary and nonmonetary as entities try to position themselves to meet the criteria to qualify for use of that method and sometimes take actions that those entities might not otherwise take or refrain from taking actions that they might otherwise take. This Statement removes the need to incur those costs.

B232. The Board believes that the guidance in this Statement is not overly complex. Indeed, it eliminates guidance that many have found to be complex, costly, and arbitrary, and that has been the source of considerable uncertainties and costs in the marketplace. Moreover, this Statement does not introduce a new method of accounting but rather expands the use of an existing method that is familiar, has been widely used, and for which there is a substantial base of experience.

B233. Some argue that the pooling method is less costly to apply than the purchase method and thus a requirement to use only the purchase method will impose costs on preparers. However, as noted above, preparers of financial statements often incur significant costs in attempting to qualify to use the pooling method, and those costs may be greater than the costs incurred in applying the purchase method. Moreover, the use of two methods that produce such dramatically different financial statement outcomes makes it difficult or impossible for users to compare the financial statements of entities that have accounted for their business combinations by different methods. Use of the pooling method also makes it difficult or impossible for users to compare the financial statements of entities that acquire their assets in business combinations accounted for by that method with the financial statements of entities that purchase their assets individually or in groups rather than by means of business combinations. Therefore, the Board believes that this Statement will not impose aggregate costs greater than those that have been borne previously and instead should reduce some costs significantly.

B234. The Board has sought to reduce the costs of applying this Statement and facilitate transition to its requirements by making its provisions with respect to the method to be used to account for business combinations prospective rather than retroactive.

Appendix C

ILLUSTRATIONS

Introduction

C1. This appendix provides illustrations of some of the disclosure requirements of this Statement. The information is presented for illustrative purposes only and, therefore, may not be representative of actual transactions.

Illustration 1—Disclosure of a Material Business Combination in the Year of Acquisition

C2. The following illustrates the disclosures required if a material business combination is completed during the reporting period (paragraphs 51 and 52).

Footnote C: Acquisitions (dollars in thousands)

On June 30, 20X2, Alpha acquired 100 percent of the outstanding common shares of Beta. The results of Beta's operations have been included in the consolidated financial statements since that date. Beta is a provider of data networking products and services in Canada and Mexico. As a result of the acquisition, Alpha is expected to be the leading provider of data networking products and services in those markets. It also expects to reduce costs through economies of scale.

The aggregate purchase price was $9,400, including $7,000 of cash and common stock valued at $2,400. The value of the 100,000 common shares issued was determined based on the average market price of Alpha's common shares over the 2-day period before and after the terms of the acquisition were agreed to and announced.

The following table summarizes the estimated fair values of the assets acquired and liabilities assumed at the date of acquisition. Alpha is in the process of obtaining third-party valuations of certain intangible assets; thus, the allocation of the purchase price is subject to refinement.

At June 30, 20X2 ($000s)	
Current assets	$ 2,400
Property, plant, and equipment	1,500
Intangible assets	4,900
Goodwill	2,200
Total assets acquired	11,000
Current liabilities	(500)
Long-term debt	(1,100)
Total liabilities assumed	(1,600)
Net assets acquired	$ 9,400

Of the $4,900 of acquired intangible assets, $1,400 was assigned to registered trademarks that are not subject to amortization and $1,000 was assigned to research and development assets that were written off at the date of acquisition in accordance with FASB Interpretation No. 4, *Applicability of FASB Statement No. 2 to Business Combinations Accounted for by the Purchase Method.* Those write-offs are included in general and administrative expenses. The remaining $2,500 of acquired intangible assets have a weighted-average useful life of approximately 4 years. The intangible assets that make up that amount include computer software of $1,500 (3-year weighted-average useful life), patents of $800 (7-year weighted-average useful life), and other assets of $200 (5-year weighted-average useful life).

The $2,200 of goodwill was assigned to the technology and communications segments in the amounts of $1,300 and $900, respectively. Of that total amount, $250 is expected to be deductible for tax purposes.

Illustration 2—Disclosures in Year of Acquisition of Several Individually Immaterial Business Combinations That Are Material in the Aggregate

C3. The following illustrates the disclosures required if a series of individually immaterial business combinations are completed during a period that are material in the aggregate (paragraph 53). The illustration assumes that Alpha completed four business combinations, one during each quarter of its fiscal year ending December 31, 20X3.

Footnote C: Acquisitions (dollars in thousands)

In 20X3, Alpha acquired the following 4 entities for a total cost of $1,000, which was paid primarily in cash:

- Omega Consulting, based in Zurich, Switzerland, a leading provider of telecommunications consulting services
- Nittany Systems, based in Toronto, Canada, a producer of digital networking technology
- Sherman Communications, Inc., based in Portland, Oregon, a start-up data networking company
- Blue and White Networks, Inc., based in Atlanta, Georgia, a designer and manufacturer of wireless communications networks.

Goodwill recognized in those transactions amounted to $300, and that amount is expected to be fully deductible for tax purposes. Goodwill was assigned to the communication and technology segments in the amounts of $120 and $180, respectively.

Appendix D

CONTINUING AUTHORITATIVE GUIDANCE

Introduction

D1. APB Opinion No. 16, *Business Combinations,* required that the pooling-of-interests method (pooling method) be used if a business combination met certain criteria. This Statement prohibits the use of the pooling method for business combinations initiated after June 30, 2001. This Statement supersedes Opinion 16 and the AICPA Accounting Interpretations of that Opinion that provide guidance on applying the pooling method. This appendix carries forward, without reconsideration, guidance in Opinion 16 and its interpretations that may be helpful in applying the transition provisions of this Statement and in accounting for past transactions to which the pooling method was applied (paragraphs D4–D10).

D2. Consistent with the provisions of Opinion 16, the provisions of this Statement do not apply to transfers of net assets or exchanges of shares between entities under common control. Guidance in Opinion 16 and an interpretation of that Opinion that has been used in past practice to account for those transactions also is carried forward without reconsideration in this appendix (paragraphs D11–D18).

D3. The following guidance has been quoted, paraphrased, or modified as necessary so that it can be understood in the context of this Statement. The original source of the guidance is noted parenthetically or otherwise. Some of that guidance may be reconsidered by the Board in another project.

Initiation Date of a Business Combination

D4. Paragraph 59 of this Statement carries forward the Opinion 16 definition of *initiated* as it relates to a business combination. Paragraphs D5–D8 carry forward without reconsideration the interpretations of Opinion 16 that provide guidance relating to that definition. That guidance should be considered in applying the transition provisions of this Statement.

D5. A business combination is not initiated until the major terms are set and announced publicly or formally communicated to the shareholders who will tender their shares to the issuing corporation. A corporation may communicate to its own shareholders its intent to make a tender offer or to negotiate the terms of a proposed business combination with another company. However, intent to tender or to negotiate does not constitute "initiation." A business combination is not initiated until the major terms are "set" and announced publicly or formally communicated to shareholders. Paragraph 59 of this Statement defines initiation in terms of two dates. The first date is for the announcement of an exchange offer negotiated between representatives of two (or more) corporations. The second date is for a tender offer made by a corporation directly or by newspaper advertisement to the shareholders of another company. In the second date specified for initiation, a *combining company* refers to the company whose shareholders will tender their shares to the issuing corporation. An *exchange offer* refers to the major terms of a plan including the ratio of exchange (or formula to determine that ratio). A corporation may communicate to its *own* shareholders its intent to make a tender offer or to negotiate the terms of a proposed business combination with another company. However, intent to tender or to negotiate does not constitute initiation (AICPA Accounting Interpretation 2, "Notification to Stockholders," of Opinion 16).

D6. To constitute initiation of a business combination, the actual exchange ratio (1 for 1, 2 for 1, and so forth) of shares need not be known provided that the ratio of exchange is absolutely determinable by objective means in the future. A formula would usually provide such a determination. A formula to determine the exchange ratio might include factors such as earnings for a period of time, market prices of shares at a particular date, average market prices for a period of time, and appraised valuations. The formula may include upper limits, lower limits, or both for the exchange ratio, and the limits may provide for adjustments based on appraised valuations, audits of the financial statements, and so forth. However, to constitute initiation of a business combination, the formula must be announced or communicated to shareholders. Any subsequent changes in the terms of a formula used to initiate a business combination constitute a new plan of combination. That new plan of combination would be accounted for in accordance with the provisions of this Statement (AICPA Accounting Interpretation 1, "Ratio of Exchange," of Opinion 16).

D7. A business combination also may be initiated at the date the shareholders of a closely held company grant an option to exchange shares at a future date to another company. The terms of the grant must require unilateral performance by either party or bilateral performance by both parties in order to constitute initiation of a business combination. Thus, if one company is required to issue shares upon the tendering of shares by the shareholders of another company, or if the shareholders are required to tender their shares upon demand, the date the option is granted is the initiation date. However, an agreement that grants only the right of first refusal *does not* constitute initiation of a business combination. For example, if the shareholders of a closely held company decide to consider entering into a business combination in the future and the shareholders agree to negotiate with one company before negotiating with any other company, a business combination has not been initiated. Neither party may be obligated to perform or to pay damages in the absence of performance (AICPA Accounting Interpretation 29, "Option May Initiate Combination," of Opinion 16).

D8. Termination of a plan of combination prior to shareholder approval has an effect on the initiation date of a business combination. If negotiations of a plan of combination are formally terminated and then are subsequently resumed, the subsequent resumption always constitutes a new plan. Formal announcement of the major terms of the new plan constitutes a new initiation date, even if the terms are the same as the terms of the previously terminated plan. In such circumstances, if the new initiation date falls after June 30, 2001, that combination should be accounted for in accordance with the provisions of this Statement (AICPA Accounting Interpretation 10, "Effect of Termination," of Opinion 16).

Disposition of Assets after a Combination Accounted for Using the Pooling Method

D9. Following a business combination accounted for by the pooling method, the combined entity might dispose of assets of the previously separate entities. Unless those disposals are part of customary business activities of the combined entity, any gain or loss recognized resulting from that disposition might require recognition as an extraordinary item. Recognition as an extraordinary item is warranted because the pooling method of accounting would have been inappropriate if the combined entity had made a commitment or had planned to dispose of a significant part of the assets of one of the combining entities.

D10. The combined entity should recognize the gain or loss resulting from the disposal of a significant part of the assets or a separable segment of the previously separate entities, less applicable income tax effect, as an extraordinary item if (a) the gain or loss is material in relation to the net income of the combined entity and (b) the disposition is within two years after the combination is consummated (Opinion 16, paragraph 60).

Transactions between Entities under Common Control

D11. Consistent with the provisions of Opinion 16, paragraph 11 of this Statement states that the term *business combination* excludes transfers of net assets or exchanges of shares between entities under common control. The following are examples of those types of transactions:

a. An entity charters a newly formed entity and then transfers some or all of its net assets to that newly chartered entity.
b. A parent company transfers the net assets of a wholly owned subsidiary into the parent company and liquidates the subsidiary. That transaction is a change in legal organization but not a change in the reporting entity.
c. A parent company transfers its interest in several partially owned subsidiaries to a new wholly

owned subsidiary. That also is a change in legal organization but not in the reporting entity.

d. A parent company exchanges its ownership interests or the net assets of a wholly owned subsidiary for additional shares issued by the parent's partially owned subsidiary, thereby increasing the parent's percentage of ownership in the partially owned subsidiary but leaving all of the existing minority interest outstanding.

D12. When accounting for a transfer of assets or exchange of shares between entities under common control, the entity that receives the net assets or the equity interests shall initially recognize the assets and liabilities transferred at their carrying amounts in the accounts of the transferring entity at the date of transfer.

D13. The purchase method of accounting shall be applied if the effect of the transfer or exchange described in paragraph D11 is the acquisition of all or a part of the noncontrolling equity interests in a subsidiary (refer to paragraph 14).

Procedural Guidance

D14. Some transfers of net assets or exchanges of shares between entities under common control result in a change in the reporting entity. In practice, the method that many entities have used to account for those transactions is similar to the pooling method. Certain provisions in Opinion 16 relating to application of the pooling method provide a source of continuing guidance on the accounting for transactions between entities under common control. Paragraphs D15–D18 provide procedural guidance that should be considered when preparing financial statements and related disclosures for the entity that receives the net assets.

D15. In some instances, the entity that receives the net assets or equity interests (the receiving entity) and the entity that transferred the net assets or equity interests (the transferring entity) may account for similar assets and liabilities using different accounting methods. In such circumstances, the carrying values of the assets and liabilities transferred may be adjusted to the basis of accounting used by the receiving entity if the change would otherwise have been

appropriate. Any such change in accounting method should be applied retroactively, and financial statements presented for prior periods should be restated (Opinion 16, paragraph 52).

D16. The financial statements of the receiving entity should report results of operations for the period in which the transfer occurs as though the transfer of net assets or exchange of equity interests had occurred at the beginning of the period. Results of operations for that period will thus comprise those of the previously separate entities combined from the beginning of the period to the date the transfer is completed and those of the combined operations from that date to the end of the period. By eliminating the effects of intercompany transactions in determining the results of operations for the period before the combination, those results will be on substantially the same basis as the results of operations for the period after the date of combination. The effects of intercompany transactions on current assets, current liabilities, revenue, and cost of sales for periods presented and on retained earnings at the beginning of the periods presented should be eliminated to the extent possible. The nature of and effects on earnings per share of nonrecurring intercompany transactions involving long-term assets and liabilities need not be eliminated but should be disclosed (Opinion 16, paragraph 56).

D17. Similarly, the receiving entity should present the statement of financial position and other financial information as of the beginning of the period as though the assets and liabilities had been transferred at that date. Financial statements and financial information presented for prior years should also be restated to furnish comparative information. All restated financial statements and financial summaries should indicate clearly that financial data of previously separate entities are combined (Opinion 16, paragraph 57).

D18. Notes to financial statements of the receiving entity should disclose the following for the period in which the transfer of assets and liabilities or exchange of equity interests occurred:

a. The name and brief description of the entity included in the reporting entity as a result of the net asset transfer or exchange of equity interests

b. The method of accounting for the transfer of net assets or exchange of equity interests.

Appendix E

AMENDMENTS TO EXISTING PRONOUNCEMENTS

E1. This Statement supersedes the following pronouncements:

a. APB Opinion No. 16, *Business Combinations*
b. All of the AICPA Accounting Interpretations of Opinion 16
c. FASB Statement No. 10, *Extension of "Grandfather" Provisions for Business Combinations*
d. FASB Statement No. 38, *Accounting for Preacquisition Contingencies of Purchased Enterprises*
e. FASB Statement No. 79, *Elimination of Certain Disclosures for Business Combinations by Nonpublic Enterprises.*

E2. APB Opinion No. 20, *Accounting Changes,* is amended as follows:

a. The last sentence of paragraph 12 is deleted.

b. In the last sentence of paragraph 35, *Paragraphs 56 to 65 and 93 to 96 of APB Opinion No. 16, Business Combinations* is replaced by *Paragraphs 51–58 of FASB Statement No. 141, Business Combinations.*

E3. The fourth sentence of paragraph 21 of APB Opinion No. 28, *Interim Financial Reporting,* is amended as follows:

a. The phrase *, business combinations treated for accounting purposes as poolings of interests and acquisition of a significant business* is replaced by *and business combinations.*

b. The following footnote is added to the end of that sentence:

Disclosures required in interim financial information related to a business combination are set forth in paragraph 58 of FASB Statement No. 141, Business Combinations.

E4. In paragraph 4(a) of APB Opinion No. 29, *Accounting for Nonmonetary Transactions,* the phrase *APB Opinion No. 16, Business Combinations,* is re-

placed by *FASB Statement No. 141, Business Combinations,* and the following footnote is added to the end of that paragraph:

*Paragraph 10 of Statement 141 states that an exchange of a business for a business is a business combination.

E5. APB Opinion No. 30, *Reporting the Results of Operations—Reporting the Effects of Disposal of a Segment of a Business, and Extraordinary, Unusual and Infrequently Occurring Events and Transactions,* is amended as follows:

a. In the third sentence of paragraph 7, *or of APB Opinion No. 16, Business Combinations, paragraph 60,* is deleted.

b. The following sentence is added at the end of paragraph 20:

However, the following items shall be recognized as extraordinary items regardless of whether those criteria are met:

(1) Classifications of gains or losses from extinguishment of debt pursuant to paragraph 8 of FASB Statement No. 4, *Reporting Gains and Losses from Extinguishment of Debt*
(2) The net effect of discontinuing the application of FASB Statement No. 71, *Accounting for the Effects of Certain Types of Regulation,* pursuant to paragraph 6 of FASB Statement No. 101, *Regulated Enterprises—Accounting for the Discontinuation of Application of FASB Statement No. 71*
(3) The remaining excess of fair value of acquired net assets over cost pursuant to paragraphs 45 and 46 of FASB Statement No. 141, *Business Combinations.*

E6. FASB Statement No. 15, *Accounting by Debtors and Creditors for Troubled Debt Restructurings,* is amended as follows:

a. In footnote 5 to paragraph 13, *(See paragraph 67 of APB Opinion No. 16, "Business Combinations.")* is replaced by *(See paragraph 6 of FASB Statement No. 141, Business Combinations.).*

b. In footnote 6 to paragraph 13, *paragraphs 88 and 89 of APB Opinion No. 16* is replaced by *paragraphs 37 and 38 of Statement 141.*

c. In footnote 16 to paragraph 28, *(See paragraph 67 of APB Opinion No. 16.)* is replaced by *(See paragraph 6 of Statement 141.).*

E7. In the first sentence of footnote 6 to paragraph 12 of FASB Statement No. 16, *Prior Period Adjustments,* the phrase *a change in accounting method permitted by paragraph 52 of APB Opinion No. 16,* is deleted.

E8. In the first sentence of paragraph 4 of FASB Statement No. 44, *Accounting for Intangible Assets of Motor Carriers,* the following footnote is added after *APB Opinion No. 16, Business Combinations*:

> *FASB Statement No. 141, *Business Combinations,* supersedes Opinion 16. However, the guidance from paragraph 88 of Opinion 16 is carried forward in paragraphs 37 and 38 of Statement 141.

E9. Paragraph 19 of FASB Statement No. 45, *Accounting for Franchise Fee Revenue,* is amended as follows:

a. In the first sentence, *APB Opinion No. 16, Business Combinations,* is replaced by *FASB Statement No. 141, Business Combinations,* .

b. The second and third sentences are deleted.

E10. [This paragraph has been deleted. See Status page.]

E11. FASB Statement No. 72, *Accounting for Certain Acquisitions of Banking or Thrift Institutions,* is amended as follows:

a. The first sentence of paragraph 4 is replaced by the following:

> In a business combination involving the acquisition of a banking or thrift institution, intangible assets acquired that meet the criteria in paragraph 39 of FASB Statement No. 141, *Business Combinations,* shall be recognized as assets apart from goodwill.

b. In the second sentence of paragraph 8, *(paragraphs 87 and 88 of Opinion 16)* is replaced by *(paragraphs 35–39 of Statement 141).*

c. In the first sentence of paragraph 9, *accounted for by the purchase method* is deleted.

E12. FASB Statement No. 87, *Employers' Accounting for Pensions,* is amended as follows:

a. In the first sentence of paragraph 74, *that is accounted for by the purchase method under Opinion 16* is deleted.

b. In the first sentence of Illustration 7—Accounting for a Business Combination, in paragraph 261, *accounted for as a purchase* is deleted.

E13. Paragraph 134(g) of FASB Statement No. 95, *Statement of Cash Flows,* is amended as follows:

a. At the end of the first sentence, *in a business combination* is added.

b. The second sentence is deleted.

E14. FASB Statement No. 106, *Employers' Accounting for Postretirement Benefits Other Than Pensions,* is amended as follows:

a. In the first sentence of paragraph 86, *that is accounted for by the purchase method under Opinion 16* is deleted.

b. In the first sentence of paragraph 444, *and accounts for the business combination as a purchase pursuant to APB Opinion No. 16, Business Combinations* is replaced by *in a business combination.*

E15. FASB Statement No. 109, *Accounting for Income Taxes,* is amended as follows:

a. In the heading to paragraph 11(h), *accounted for by the purchase method* is deleted.

b. In the first sentence of paragraph 11(h), *accounted for as a purchase under APB Opinion No. 16, Business Combinations* is deleted.

c. In the last sentence of paragraph 13, *accounted for by the purchase method* is deleted.

d. In the first sentence of paragraph 30, *"negative goodwill"* is replaced by *excess over cost (also referred to as negative goodwill).*

e. In paragraph 36(d), the following footnote is added to *pooling of interests*:

> *FASB Statement No. 141, *Business Combinations,* prohibits the use of the pooling-of-interests method for all business combinations initiated after June 30, 2001.

f. In the first sentence of paragraph 259, *accounted for as a purchase under Opinion 16* is deleted.

g. In paragraph 270, the following footnote is added to the end of the first sentence:

*Statement 141 prohibits the use of the pooling-of-interests method for all business combinations initiated after June 30, 2001.

E16. FASB Statement No. 123, *Accounting for Stock-Based Compensation,* is amended as follows:

a. In the last sentence of paragraph 8, *purchase* is deleted.

b. In the first sentence of paragraph 36, *, except for those made to reflect the terms of the exchange of shares in a business combination accounted for as a pooling of interests,* is deleted.

E17. Paragraph 59 of FASB Statement No. 128, *Earnings per Share,* is amended as follows:

a. In the first sentence, *transaction accounted for as a purchase* is deleted.

b. The second sentence is deleted.

E18. FASB Statement No. 133, *Accounting for Derivative Instruments and Hedging Activities,* is amended as follows:

a. In the second sentence of paragraph 11(c), *APB Opinion No. 16* is replaced by *FASB Statement No. 141.*

b. In paragraph 29(f), *Opinion 16* is replaced by *Statement 141.*

E19. The following footnote is added to the end of the first sentence of paragraph 4 of FASB Interpretation No. 4, *Applicability of FASB Statement No. 2 to Business Combinations Accounted for by the Purchase Method:*

*Opinion 16 was superseded by FASB Statement No. 141, *Business Combinations.* However, Statement 141 (paragraph 42) does not change the requirement in paragraph 5 of this Interpretation that the amounts assigned to acquired tangible and intangible assets to be used in a particular research and development project that have no alternative future use be charged to expense at the date of acquisition.

E20. [This paragraph has been deleted. See Status page.]

E21. FASB Interpretation No. 21, *Accounting for Leases in a Business Combination,* is amended as follows:

a. In the first sentence of paragraph 13, *, whether accounted for by the purchase method or by the pooling of interests method,* is deleted.

b. Paragraph 14 and the heading preceding it are deleted.

c. Paragraph 15 is amended as follows:

(1) In the first sentence, *that is accounted for by the purchase method* is deleted.

(2) In the second sentence, *paragraph 88 of APB Opinion No. 16* is replaced by *paragraphs 36–39 of FASB Statement No. 141, Business Combinations.*

(3) In the third sentence, *Opinion No. 16* is replaced by *Statement 141.*

d. Paragraph 16 is amended as follows:

(1) In the first sentence, *that is accounted for by the purchase method* is deleted.

(2) In the third sentence, *paragraph 88 of APB Opinion No. 16* is replaced by *paragraphs 37 and 38 of Statement 141.*

e. In footnote 4 to paragraph 18, *paragraph 46(a) of APB Opinion No. 16* is replaced by *paragraph 59 of Statement 141.*

f. In the heading above paragraph 19, *PURCHASE* is replaced by *BUSINESS.*

g. In the first sentence of paragraph 19, *accounted for by the purchase method* is deleted.

E22. FASB Interpretation No. 44, *Accounting for Certain Transactions involving Stock Compensation,* is amended as follows:

a. Paragraphs 81 and 82 are deleted.

b. In the first sentence of paragraph 83, *purchase* is deleted and *APB Opinion No. 16* is replaced by *FASB Statement No. 141.*

c. In the first sentence of paragraph 84, *purchase* is deleted and *Opinion 16* is replaced by *Statement 141.*

E23. In paragraph 6 of FASB Technical Bulletin No. 84-1, *Accounting for Stock Issued to Acquire the*

Results of a Research and Development Arrangement, the phrase *paragraph 67 of Opinion 16* is replaced by *paragraphs 4–6 of FASB Statement No. 141, Business Combinations.*

E24. FASB Technical Bulletin No. 85-5, *Issues Relating to Accounting for Business Combinations,* is amended as follows:

a. In paragraph 1, *accounted for by the purchase method* is deleted.

b. Paragraph 2 is amended as follows:

   (1) In the first sentence, *accounted for by the purchase method* is deleted.

   (2) In the second sentence, *purchase* is deleted.

c. The first sentence of paragraph 3 is replaced by the following:

   Paragraph 24 of FASB Statement No. 141, *Business Combinations,* states that:

   The cost of an entity acquired in a business combination includes the direct costs of the business combination. . . . However, indirect and general expenses related to business combinations shall be expensed as incurred.

d. Paragraph 4 is amended as follows:

   (1) In the fifth sentence, *Paragraph 88 of Opinion 16 provides* is replaced by *Paragraphs 37 and 38 of Statement 141 provide.*

   (2) In the sixth sentence, *Paragraph 88(i)* is replaced by *Paragraph 37(k).*

   (3) In the eighth sentence, *paragraph 88(i)* is replaced by *paragraph 37(k).*

e. In the second sentence of paragraph 6, *paragraph 43 of Opinion 16* is replaced by *paragraph 14 of Statement 141.*

f. In the last sentence of paragraph 7, *Accounting Interpretation 39 of Opinion 16* is replaced by *Paragraph D12 of Statement 141.*

g. Paragraphs 13–24 and the related headings are deleted.

Appendix F

GLOSSARY

F1. This appendix contains definitions of certain terms used in this Statement.

Allocation period
   The period that is required to identify and measure the fair value of the assets acquired and the liabilities assumed in a business combination. The allocation period ends when the acquiring entity is no longer waiting for information that it has arranged to obtain and that is known to be available or obtainable. Thus, the existence of a preacquisition contingency for which an asset, a liability, or an impairment of an asset cannot be estimated does not, of itself, extend the allocation period. Although the time required will vary with circumstances, the allocation period should usually not exceed one year from the consummation of a business combination (FASB Statement No. 38, *Accounting for Preacquisition Contingencies of Purchased Enterprises,* paragraph 4(b)).

Customer relationship
   For purposes of this Statement, a customer relationship exists between an entity and its customer if (a) the entity has information about the customer and has regular contact with the customer and (b) the customer has the ability to make direct contact with the entity. Relationships may arise from contracts (such as supplier contracts and service contracts). However, customer relationships may arise through means other than contracts, such as through regular contact by sales or service representatives.

Financial asset
   Cash, evidence of an ownership interest in an entity, or a contract that conveys to [one] entity a right (a) to receive cash or another financial instrument from a [second] entity or (b) to exchange other financial instruments on potentially favorable terms with the [second] entity.

Goodwill
   The excess of the cost of an acquired entity over the net of the amounts assigned to assets acquired and liabilities assumed. The amount recognized as goodwill includes acquired intangible assets that do not meet the criteria in paragraph 39 for recognition as assets apart from goodwill.

Intangible assets

Assets (not including financial assets) that lack physical substance.

Intangible asset class

A group of intangible assets that are similar, either by their nature or by their use in the operations of an entity.

Mutual enterprise

An entity other than an investor-owned entity that provides dividends, lower costs, or other economic benefits directly and proportionately to its owners, members, or participants. Mutual insurance companies, credit unions, and farm and rural electric cooperatives are examples of mutual enterprises (FASB Concepts Statement No. 4, *Objectives of Financial Reporting by Non-business Organizations,* paragraph 7).

Not-for-profit organization

An entity that possesses the following characteristics that distinguish it from a business enterprise: (a) contributions of significant amounts of resources from resource providers who do not expect commensurate or proportionate pecuniary return, (b) operating purposes other than to provide goods or services at a profit, and (c) absence of ownership interests like those of business enterprises. Not-for-profit organizations have those characteristics in varying degrees (Concepts Statement 4, paragraph 6). Entities that clearly fall outside this definition include all investor-owned entities and mutual enterprises.

Pooling-of-interests method

A method of accounting for business combinations that was required to be used in certain circumstances by APB Opinion No. 16, *Business Combinations.* Under the pooling-of-interests method, the carrying amount of assets and liabilities recognized in the statements of financial position of each combining entity are carried forward to the statement of financial position of the combined entity. No other assets or liabilities are recognized as a result of the combination, and thus the excess of the purchase price over the book value of the net assets acquired (the purchase premium) is not recognized. The income statement of the combined entity for the year of the combination is presented as if the entities had been combined for the full year; all comparative financial statements are presented as if the entities had previously been combined.

Preacquisition contingency

A contingency of an entity that is acquired in a business combination that is in existence before the consummation of the combination. A preacquisition contingency can be a contingent asset, a contingent liability, or a contingent impairment of an asset (Statement 38, paragraph 4(a)).

Public business enterprise

An enterprise that has issued debt or equity securities or is a conduit bond obligor for conduit debt securities that are traded in a public market (a domestic or foreign stock exchange or an over-the-counter market, including local or regional markets), that is required to file financial statements with the Securities and Exchange Commission, or that provides financial statements for the purpose of issuing any class of securities in a public market.

Conduit debt securities refers to certain limited-obligation revenue bonds, certificates of participation, or similar debt instruments issued by a state or local governmental entity for the express purpose of providing financing for a specific third party (the conduit bond obligor) that is not a part of the state or local government's financial reporting entity. Although conduit debt securities bear the name of the governmental entity that issues them, the governmental entity often has no obligation for such debt beyond the resources provided by a lease or loan agreement with the third party on whose behalf the securities are issued (FASB Statement No. 131, *Disclosures about Segments of an Enterprise and Related Information,* paragraph 9). Further, the conduit bond obligor is responsible for any future financial reporting requirements.

Reporting unit

The level of reporting at which goodwill is tested for impairment. A reporting unit is an operating segment or one level below an operating segment (as that term is defined in paragraph 10 of Statement 131) (FASB Statement No. 142, *Goodwill and Other Intangible Assets,* paragraph F1).

Residual value

The estimated fair value of an intangible asset at the end of its useful life to the entity, less any disposal costs.

Servicing asset

A contract to service financial assets under which the estimated future revenues from contractually specified servicing fees, late charges, and other ancillary revenues are expected to more than adequately compensate the servicer for performing the servicing. A servicing contract is either (a) undertaken in conjunction with selling or securitizing the financial assets being serviced or (b) purchased or assumed separately (FASB Statement No. 140, *Accounting for Transfers and Servicing of Financial Assets and Extinguishments of Liabilities,* paragraph 364).

Statement of Financial Accounting Standards No. 142
Goodwill and Other Intangible Assets

STATUS

Issued: June 2001

Effective Date: For fiscal years beginning after December 31, 2001; goodwill acquired in business combinations after June 30, 2001, shall not be amortized

Affects: Deletes ARB 43, Chapter 5
Supersedes APB 17
Amends APB 18, paragraphs 19(m) and 19(n)
Replaces APB 18, footnote 9
Deletes APB 18, footnote 12
Supersedes AIN-APB 17, Interpretations No. 1 and 2
Amends FAS 2, paragraph 11(c)
Amends FAS 44, paragraphs 3, 4, and 7
Amends FAS 51, paragraphs 13 and 14
Amends FAS 52, paragraph 48
Amends FAS 68, footnote 3
Replaces FAS 71, paragraphs 29 and 30
Amends FAS 72, paragraphs 4, 6, and 7
Deletes FAS 72, footnotes 5 and 6
Amends FAS 121, paragraphs 3, 4, 6, 27, and 147
Deletes FAS 121, paragraph 12

Affected by: Paragraph 3 amended by FAS 157, paragraph E22(a)
Paragraph 7 and footnote 22 deleted by FAS 144, paragraphs C17(a) and C17(f), respectively
Paragraphs 8, 8(i), and 35 amended by FAS 145, paragraph 9(m)
Paragraph 8(c) effectively deleted by FAS 145, paragraph 6
Paragraph 11 amended by FSP FAS 141-1/142-1
Paragraphs 15, 17, 28(f), 29, and Appendix A (Examples 1 through 3, 5, and 9) amended by FAS 144, paragraphs C17(b) through C17(e) and C17(g), respectively
Paragraphs 19, 23, and F1 amended by FAS 157, paragraphs E22(c), E22(d), and E22(g), respectively
Paragraphs 24 and E1 through E3 deleted by FAS 157, paragraphs E22(e) and E22(f), respectively
Paragraph 49(b) amended by FAS 147, paragraph B3(a)
Paragraph D9(a) effectively deleted by FAS 147, paragraph 5
Paragraph D11 deleted by FAS 147, paragraph B3(b)
Paragraph D11(a)(2) deleted by FAS 145, paragraph 9(m)
Footnotes 12 and 16 deleted by FAS 157, paragraphs E22(b) and E22(d), respectively

Other Interpretive Releases: FASB Staff Positions FAS 141-1/142-1 and FAS 142-2

AICPA Accounting Standards Executive Committee (AcSEC)

Related Pronouncements: SOP 88-1
SOP 90-7
SOP 93-7
SOP 94-6

Issues Discussed by FASB Emerging Issues Task Force (EITF)

Affects: Partially nullifies EITF Issues No. 85-8, 85-42, 88-20, and 90-6

Interpreted by: Paragraph 10 interpreted by EITF Issue No. 97-13
Paragraph 17 interpreted by EITF Issue No. 02-7
Paragraph 19 interpreted by EITF Issue No. 02-13
Paragraph 20 interpreted by EITF Issues No. 02-7 and 02-13
Paragraph 21 interpreted by EITF Issue No. 02-13 and Topic No. D-10
Paragraph 30 interpreted by EITF Topic No. D-101
Paragraph 32 interpreted by EITF Issue No. 02-13
Paragraph 49(b) interpreted by EITF Topic No. D-100

Related Issues: EITF Issues No. 85-41, 88-19, 89-19, 92-9, 93-1, 98-11, 02-17, 03-9, 03-14, 03-17, 04-1,
04-2, and 04-4

SUMMARY

This Statement addresses financial accounting and reporting for acquired goodwill and other intangible assets and supersedes APB Opinion No. 17, *Intangible Assets*. It addresses how intangible assets that are acquired individually or with a group of other assets (but not those acquired in a business combination) should be accounted for in financial statements upon their acquisition. This Statement also addresses how goodwill and other intangible assets should be accounted for after they have been initially recognized in the financial statements.

Reasons for Issuing This Statement

Analysts and other users of financial statements, as well as company managements, noted that intangible assets are an increasingly important economic resource for many entities and are an increasing proportion of the assets acquired in many transactions. As a result, better information about intangible assets was needed. Financial statement users also indicated that they did not regard goodwill amortization expense as being useful information in analyzing investments.

Differences between This Statement and Opinion 17

This Statement changes the unit of account for goodwill and takes a very different approach to how goodwill and other intangible assets are accounted for subsequent to their initial recognition. Because goodwill and some intangible assets will no longer be amortized, the reported amounts of goodwill and intangible assets (as well as total assets) will not decrease at the same time and in the same manner as under previous standards. There may be more volatility in reported income than under previous standards because impairment losses are likely to occur irregularly and in varying amounts.

This Statement changes the subsequent accounting for goodwill and other intangible assets in the following significant respects:

- Acquiring entities usually integrate acquired entities into their operations, and thus the acquirers' expectations of benefits from the resulting synergies usually are reflected in the premium that they pay to acquire those entities. However, the transaction-based approach to accounting for goodwill under Opinion 17 treated the acquired entity as if it remained a stand-alone entity rather than being integrated with the acquiring entity; as a result, the portion of the premium related to expected synergies (goodwill) was not accounted for appropriately. This Statement adopts a more aggregate view of goodwill and bases the accounting for goodwill on the units of the combined entity into which an acquired entity is integrated (those units are referred to as reporting units).

- Opinion 17 presumed that goodwill and all other intangible assets were wasting assets (that is, finite lived), and thus the amounts assigned to them should be amortized in determining net income; Opinion 17 also mandated an arbitrary ceiling of 40 years for that amortization. This Statement does not presume that those assets are wasting assets. Instead, goodwill and intangible assets that have indefinite useful lives will not be amortized but rather will be tested at least annually for impairment. Intangible assets that have finite useful lives will continue to be amortized over their useful lives, but without the constraint of an arbitrary ceiling.
- Previous standards provided little guidance about how to determine and measure goodwill impairment; as a result, the accounting for goodwill impairments was not consistent and not comparable and yielded information of questionable usefulness. This Statement provides specific guidance for testing goodwill for impairment. Goodwill will be tested for impairment at least annually using a two-step process that begins with an estimation of the fair value of a reporting unit. The first step is a screen for potential impairment, and the second step measures the amount of impairment, if any. However, if certain criteria are met, the requirement to test goodwill for impairment annually can be satisfied without a remeasurement of the fair value of a reporting unit.
- In addition, this Statement provides specific guidance on testing intangible assets that will not be amortized for impairment and thus removes those intangible assets from the scope of other impairment guidance. Intangible assets that are not amortized will be tested for impairment at least annually by comparing the fair values of those assets with their recorded amounts.
- This Statement requires disclosure of information about goodwill and other intangible assets in the years subsequent to their acquisition that was not previously required. Required disclosures include information about the changes in the carrying amount of goodwill from period to period (in the aggregate and by reportable segment), the carrying amount of intangible assets by major intangible asset class for those assets subject to amortization and for those not subject to amortization, and the estimated intangible asset amortization expense for the next five years.

This Statement carries forward without reconsideration the provisions of Opinion 17 related to the accounting for internally developed intangible assets. This Statement also does not change the requirement to expense the cost of certain acquired research and development assets at the date of acquisition as required by FASB Statement No. 2, *Accounting for Research and Development Costs,* and FASB Interpretation No. 4, *Applicability of FASB Statement No. 2 to Business Combinations Accounted for by the Purchase Method.*

How the Changes in This Statement Improve Financial Reporting

The changes included in this Statement will improve financial reporting because the financial statements of entities that acquire goodwill and other intangible assets will better reflect the underlying economics of those assets. As a result, financial statement users will be better able to understand the investments made in those assets and the subsequent performance of those investments. The enhanced disclosures about goodwill and intangible assets subsequent to their acquisition also will provide users with a better understanding of the expectations about and changes in those assets over time, thereby improving their ability to assess future profitability and cash flows.

How the Conclusions in This Statement Relate to the Conceptual Framework

The Board concluded that amortization of goodwill was not consistent with the concept of representational faithfulness, as discussed in FASB Concepts Statement No. 2, *Qualitative Characteristics of Accounting Information.* The Board concluded that nonamortization of goodwill coupled with impairment testing *is* consistent with that concept. The appropriate balance of both relevance and reliability and costs and benefits also was central to the Board's conclusion that this Statement will improve financial reporting.

This Statement utilizes the guidance in FASB Concepts Statement No. 7, *Using Cash Flow Information and Present Value in Accounting Measurements,* for estimating the fair values used in testing both goodwill and other intangible assets that are not being amortized for impairment.

The Effective Date of This Statement

The provisions of this Statement are required to be applied starting with fiscal years beginning after December 15, 2001. Early application is permitted for entities with fiscal years beginning after March 15, 2001, provided that the first interim financial statements have not previously been issued. This Statement is required to be applied at the beginning of an entity's fiscal year and to be applied to all goodwill and other intangible assets recognized in its financial statements at that date. Impairment losses for goodwill and indefinite-lived intangible assets that arise due to the initial application of this Statement (resulting from a transitional impairment test) are to be reported as resulting from a change in accounting principle.

There are two exceptions to the date at which this Statement becomes effective:

- Goodwill and intangible assets acquired after June 30, 2001, will be subject immediately to the nonamortization and amortization provisions of this Statement.
- The provisions of this Statement will not be applicable to goodwill and other intangible assets arising from combinations between mutual enterprises or to not-for-profit organizations until the Board completes its deliberations with respect to application of the purchase method by those entities.

Statement of Financial Accounting Standards No. 142

Goodwill and Other Intangible Assets

CONTENTS

INTRODUCTION

1. This Statement addresses financial accounting and reporting for intangible assets acquired individually or with a group of other assets (but not those acquired in a business combination) at acquisition. This Statement also addresses financial accounting and reporting for goodwill and other intangible assets subsequent to their acquisition. FASB Statement No. 141, *Business Combinations,* addresses financial accounting and reporting for goodwill and other intangible assets acquired in a business combination at acquisition.[1]

2. This Statement supersedes APB Opinion No. 17, *Intangible Assets;* however, it carries forward without reconsideration the provisions in Opinion 17 related to internally developed intangible assets. The Board did not reconsider those provisions because they were outside the scope of its project on business combinations and acquired intangible assets. The guidance carried forward from Opinion 17 has been quoted, paraphrased, or rephrased as necessary so that it can be understood in the context of this Statement. The original source of that guidance has been noted parenthetically.

3. Appendix A to this Statement provides implementation guidance on how intangible assets should be accounted for in accordance with this Statement. Appendix A is an integral part of the standards provided in this Statement. Appendix B provides background information and the basis for the Board's conclusions. Appendix C provides illustrations of some of the financial statement disclosures that this Statement requires. Appendix D lists other accounting pronouncements superseded or amended by this Statement. Appendix F provides a glossary of terms used in this Statement.

STANDARDS OF FINANCIAL ACCOUNTING AND REPORTING

Scope

4. The initial recognition and measurement provisions of this Statement apply to **intangible assets**[2] acquired individually or with a group of other assets (but not those acquired in a business combination).[3] The remaining provisions of this Statement apply to **goodwill** that an entity[4] recognizes in accordance with Statement 141 and to other intangible assets that an entity acquires, whether individually, with a group of other assets, or in a business combination. While goodwill is an intangible asset, the term *intangible asset* is used in this Statement to refer to an intangible asset other than goodwill.

5. This Statement applies to costs of internally developing goodwill and other unidentifiable intangible assets with indeterminate lives. Some entities capitalize costs incurred to develop identifiable intangible assets, while others expense those costs as incurred. This Statement also applies to costs of internally developing identifiable intangible assets that an entity recognizes as assets (Opinion 17, paragraphs 5 and 6).

6. This Statement applies to goodwill and other intangible assets recognized on the acquisition of some or all of the noncontrolling interests in a subsidiary—whether acquired by the parent, the subsidiary itself, or another affiliate.[5] This Statement, including its transition provisions, applies to amounts recognized as goodwill in applying the equity method of accounting and to the excess reorganization value recognized by entities that adopt fresh-start reporting in accordance with AICPA Statement of Position 90-7, *Financial Reporting by Entities in Reorganization Under the Bankruptcy Code.* That excess reorganization value shall be reported as goodwill and accounted for in the same manner as goodwill.

---

[1]Statement 141 was issued concurrently with this Statement and addresses financial accounting and reporting for business combinations. It supersedes APB Opinion No. 16, *Business Combinations,* and FASB Statement No. 38, *Accounting for Preacquisition Contingencies of Purchased Enterprises.*

[2]Terms defined in Appendix F, the glossary, are set forth in **boldface** type the first time they are used.

[3]Statement 141 addresses the initial recognition and measurement of intangible assets acquired in a business combination.

[4]This Statement applies to a business enterprise, a **mutual enterprise,** and a **not-for-profit organization,** each of which is referred to herein as an *entity.*

[5]Statement 141 requires that the acquisition of some or all of the noncontrolling interests in a subsidiary be accounted for using the purchase method.

7. [This paragraph has been deleted. See Status page.]

8. Except as described in Appendix D, this Statement does not change the accounting prescribed in the following pronouncements:

a. FASB Statement No. 2, *Accounting for Research and Development Costs*
b. FASB Statement No. 19, *Financial Accounting and Reporting by Oil and Gas Producing Companies*
c. [This subparagraph has been deleted. See Status page.]
d. FASB Statement No. 50, *Financial Reporting in the Record and Music Industry*
e. FASB Statement No. 61, *Accounting for Title Plant*
f. FASB Statement No. 63, *Financial Reporting by Broadcasters*
g. FASB Statement No. 71, *Accounting for the Effects of Certain Types of Regulation* (paragraphs 29 and 30)
h. FASB Statement No. 72, *Accounting for Certain Acquisitions of Banking or Thrift Institutions* (paragraphs 4–7)
i. FASB Statement No. 86, *Accounting for the Costs of Computer Software to Be Sold, Leased, or Otherwise Marketed*
j. FASB Statement No. 109, *Accounting for Income Taxes* (a deferred tax asset)
k. FASB Statement No. 140, *Accounting for Transfers and Servicing of Financial Assets and Extinguishments of Liabilities* (a servicing asset or liability)
l. FASB Interpretation No. 4, *Applicability of FASB Statement No. 2 to Business Combinations Accounted for by the Purchase Method.*
m. FASB Interpretation No. 9, *Applying APB Opinions No. 16 and 17 When a Savings and Loan Association or a Similar Institution Is Acquired in a Business Combination Accounted for by the Purchase Method.*

Initial Recognition and Measurement of Intangible Assets

9. An intangible asset that is acquired either individually or with a group of other assets (but not those acquired in a business combination) shall be initially recognized and measured based on its fair value. General concepts related to the initial measurement of assets acquired in exchange transactions, including intangible assets, are provided in paragraphs 5–7 of Statement 141.[6] The cost of a group of assets acquired in a transaction other than a business combination shall be allocated to the individual assets acquired based on their relative fair values and shall not give rise to goodwill.[7] Intangible assets acquired in a business combination are initially recognized and measured in accordance with Statement 141.[8]

Internally Developed Intangible Assets

10. Costs of internally developing, maintaining, or restoring intangible assets (including goodwill) that are not specifically identifiable, that have indeterminate lives, or that are inherent in a continuing business and related to an entity as a whole, shall be recognized as an expense when incurred (Opinion 17, paragraph 24).

Accounting for Intangible Assets

Determining the Useful Life of an Intangible Asset

11. The accounting for a recognized intangible asset is based on its **useful life** to the reporting entity. An intangible asset with a finite useful life is amortized; an intangible asset with an indefinite useful life is not amortized. The useful life of an intangible asset to an entity is the period over which the asset is expected to contribute directly or indirectly to the future cash

---

[6]Although those paragraphs refer to determining the cost of the assets acquired, both paragraph 6 of Statement 141 and paragraph 18 of APB Opinion No. 29, *Accounting for Nonmonetary Transactions*, note that, in general, cost should be measured based on the fair value of the consideration given or the fair value of the net assets acquired, whichever is more reliably measurable.

[7]Statement 141 requires intangible assets acquired in a business combination that do not meet certain criteria to be included in the amount initially recognized as goodwill. Those recognition criteria do not apply to intangible assets acquired in transactions other than business combinations.

[8]Statement 2 and Interpretation 4 require amounts assigned to acquired intangible assets that are to be used in a particular research and development project and that *have no alternative future use* to be charged to expense at the acquisition date. Statement 141 does not change that requirement, nor does this Statement.

flows of that entity.[9] The estimate of the useful life of an intangible asset to an entity shall be based on an analysis of all pertinent factors, in particular:

a. The expected use of the asset by the entity
b. The expected useful life of another asset or a group of assets to which the useful life of the intangible asset may relate
c. Any legal, regulatory, or contractual provisions that may limit the useful life
d. Any legal, regulatory, or contractual provisions that enable renewal or extension of the asset's legal or contractual life without substantial cost (provided there is evidence to support renewal or extension and renewal or extension can be accomplished without material modifications of the existing terms and conditions)
e. The effects of obsolescence, demand, competition, and other economic factors (such as the stability of the industry, known technological advances, legislative action that results in an uncertain or changing regulatory environment, and expected changes in distribution channels)
f. The level of maintenance expenditures required to obtain the expected future cash flows from the asset (for example, a material level of required maintenance in relation to the carrying amount of the asset may suggest a very limited useful life).[10]

If no legal, regulatory, contractual, competitive, economic, or other factors limit the useful life of an intangible asset to the reporting entity, the useful life of the asset shall be considered to be indefinite. The term *indefinite* does not mean infinite. Appendix A includes illustrative examples of different intangible assets and how they should be accounted for in accordance with this Statement, including determining whether the useful life of an intangible asset is indefinite.

Intangible Assets Subject to Amortization

12. A recognized intangible asset shall be amortized over its useful life to the reporting entity unless that life is determined to be indefinite. If an intangible asset has a finite useful life, but the precise length of that life is not known, that intangible asset shall be

amortized over the best estimate of its useful life. The method of amortization shall reflect the pattern in which the economic benefits of the intangible asset are consumed or otherwise used up. If that pattern cannot be reliably determined, a straight-line amortization method shall be used. An intangible asset shall not be written down or off in the period of acquisition unless it becomes impaired during that period.[11]

13. The amount of an intangible asset to be amortized shall be the amount initially assigned to that asset less any **residual value.** The residual value of an intangible asset shall be assumed to be zero unless at the end of its useful life to the reporting entity the asset is expected to continue to have a useful life to another entity and (a) the reporting entity has a commitment from a third party to purchase the asset at the end of its useful life or (b) the residual value can be determined by reference to an exchange transaction in an existing market for that asset and that market is expected to exist at the end of the asset's useful life.

14. An entity shall evaluate the remaining useful life of an intangible asset that is being amortized each reporting period to determine whether events and circumstances warrant a revision to the remaining period of amortization. If the estimate of an intangible asset's remaining useful life is changed, the remaining carrying amount of the intangible asset shall be amortized prospectively over that revised remaining useful life. If an intangible asset that is being amortized is subsequently determined to have an indefinite useful life, the asset shall be tested for impairment in accordance with paragraph 17. That intangible asset shall no longer be amortized and shall be accounted for in the same manner as other intangible assets that are not subject to amortization.

Recognition and measurement of an impairment loss

15. An intangible asset that is subject to amortization shall be reviewed for impairment in accordance with FASB Statement No. 144, *Accounting for the Impairment or Disposal of Long-Lived Assets,* by applying the recognition and measurement provisions in paragraphs 7–24 of that Statement. In accordance with Statement 144, an impairment loss shall be recognized if the carrying amount of an intangible asset is

[9]The useful life of an intangible asset shall reflect the period over which it will contribute to the cash flows of the reporting entity, not the period of time that it would take that entity to internally develop an intangible asset that would provide similar benefits.

[10]As in determining the useful life of depreciable tangible assets, regular maintenance may be assumed but enhancements may not.

[11]However, both Statement 2 and Interpretation 4 require amounts assigned to acquired intangible assets that are to be used in a particular research and development project and that have no alternative future use to be charged to expense at the acquisition date.

not recoverable and its carrying amount exceeds its fair value. After an impairment loss is recognized, the adjusted carrying amount of the intangible asset shall be its new accounting basis. Subsequent reversal of a previously recognized impairment loss is prohibited.

Intangible Assets Not Subject to Amortization

16. If an intangible asset is determined to have an indefinite useful life, it shall not be amortized until its useful life is determined to be no longer indefinite. An entity shall evaluate the remaining useful life of an intangible asset that is not being amortized each reporting period to determine whether events and circumstances continue to support an indefinite useful life. If an intangible asset that is not being amortized is subsequently determined to have a finite useful life, the asset shall be tested for impairment in accordance with paragraph 17. That intangible asset shall then be amortized prospectively over its estimated remaining useful life and accounted for in the same manner as other intangible assets that are subject to amortization.

Recognition and measurement of an impairment loss

17. An intangible asset that is not subject to amortization shall be tested for impairment annually, or more frequently if events or changes in circumstances indicate that the asset might be impaired. (Paragraph 8 of Statement 144 includes examples of impairment indicators.) The impairment test shall consist of a comparison of the fair value of an intangible asset with its carrying amount. If the carrying amount of an intangible asset exceeds its fair value, an impairment loss shall be recognized in an amount equal to that excess. After an impairment loss is recognized, the adjusted carrying amount of the intangible asset shall be its new accounting basis. Subsequent reversal of a previously recognized impairment loss is prohibited.

Accounting for Goodwill

18. Goodwill shall not be amortized. Goodwill shall be tested for impairment at a level of reporting referred to as a **reporting unit**. (Paragraphs 30–36 provide guidance on determining reporting units.) Im-

pairment is the condition that exists when the carrying amount of goodwill exceeds its implied fair value.[13] The two-step impairment test discussed in paragraphs 19–22 shall be used to identify potential goodwill impairment and measure the amount of a goodwill impairment loss to be recognized (if any).

Recognition and Measurement of an Impairment Loss

19. The first step of the goodwill impairment test, used to identify potential impairment, compares the fair value of a reporting unit with its carrying amount, including goodwill. The guidance in paragraphs 23 and 25 shall be considered in determining the fair value of a reporting unit. If the fair value of a reporting unit exceeds its carrying amount, goodwill of the reporting unit is considered not impaired, thus the second step of the impairment test is unnecessary. If the carrying amount of a reporting unit exceeds its fair value, the second step of the goodwill impairment test shall be performed to measure the amount of impairment loss, if any.

20. The second step of the goodwill impairment test, used to measure the amount of impairment loss, compares the implied fair value of reporting unit goodwill with the carrying amount of that goodwill. The guidance in paragraph 21 shall be used to estimate the implied fair value of goodwill. If the carrying amount of reporting unit goodwill exceeds the implied fair value of that goodwill, an impairment loss shall be recognized in an amount equal to that excess. The loss recognized cannot exceed the carrying amount of goodwill. After a goodwill impairment loss is recognized, the adjusted carrying amount of goodwill shall be its new accounting basis. Subsequent reversal of a previously recognized goodwill impairment loss is prohibited once the measurement of that loss is completed.

21. The implied fair value of goodwill shall be determined in the same manner as the amount of goodwill recognized in a business combination is determined. That is, an entity shall allocate the fair value of a reporting unit to all of the assets and liabilities of that unit (including any unrecognized intangible assets) as if the reporting unit had been acquired in a business combination and the fair value of the reporting

---

[12][This footnote has been deleted. See Status page.]

[13]The fair value of goodwill can be measured only as a residual and cannot be measured directly. Therefore, this Statement includes a methodology to determine an amount that achieves a reasonable estimate of the value of goodwill for purposes of measuring an impairment loss. That estimate is referred to herein as the *implied fair value of goodwill*.

unit was the price paid to acquire the reporting unit.[14] The excess of the fair value of a reporting unit over the amounts assigned to its assets and liabilities is the implied fair value of goodwill. That allocation process shall be performed only for purposes of testing goodwill for impairment; an entity shall not write up or write down a recognized asset or liability, nor should it recognize a previously unrecognized intangible asset as a result of that allocation process.

22. If the second step of the goodwill impairment test is not complete before the financial statements are issued and a goodwill impairment loss is probable and can be reasonably estimated, the best estimate of that loss shall be recognized in those financial statements.[15] Paragraph 47(c) requires disclosure of the fact that the measurement of the impairment loss is an estimate. Any adjustment to that estimated loss based on the completion of the measurement of the impairment loss shall be recognized in the subsequent reporting period.

Fair value measurements

23. The fair value of a reporting unit refers to the price that would be received to sell the unit as a whole in an orderly transaction between market participants at the measurement date. Quoted market prices in active markets are the best evidence of fair value and shall be used as the basis for the measurement, if available. However, the market price of an individual equity security (and thus the market capitalization of a reporting unit with publicly traded equity securities) may not be representative of the fair value of the reporting unit as a whole. Substantial value may arise from the ability to take advantage of synergies and other benefits that flow from control over another entity. Consequently, measuring the fair value of a collection of assets and liabilities that operate together in a controlled entity is different from measuring the fair value of that entity's individual equity securities. An acquiring entity often is willing to pay more for equity securities that give it a controlling interest than an investor would pay for a number of equity securities representing less than a controlling interest. That control premium may cause the fair value of a reporting unit to exceed its market

capitalization. The quoted market price of an individual equity security, therefore, need not be the sole measurement basis of the fair value of a reporting unit.

24. [This paragraph has been deleted. See Status page.]

25. In estimating the fair value of a reporting unit, a valuation technique based on multiples of earnings or revenue or a similar performance measure may be used if that technique is consistent with the objective of measuring fair value. Use of multiples of earnings or revenue in determining the fair value of a reporting unit may be appropriate, for example, when the fair value of an entity that has comparable operations and economic characteristics is observable and the relevant multiples of the comparable entity are known. Conversely, use of multiples would not be appropriate in situations in which the operations or activities of an entity for which the multiples are known are not of a comparable nature, scope, or size as the reporting unit for which fair value is being estimated.

When to test goodwill for impairment

26. Goodwill of a reporting unit shall be tested for impairment on an annual basis and between annual tests in certain circumstances (refer to paragraph 28). The annual goodwill impairment test may be performed any time during the fiscal year provided the test is performed at the same time every year. Different reporting units may be tested for impairment at different times.

27. A detailed determination of the fair value of a reporting unit may be carried forward from one year to the next if all of the following criteria have been met:

a. The assets and liabilities that make up the reporting unit have not changed significantly since the most recent fair value determination. (A recent significant acquisition or a reorganization of an entity's segment reporting structure is an example of an event that might significantly change the composition of a reporting unit.)

---

[14]The relevant guidance in paragraphs 35–38 of Statement 141 shall be used in determining how to allocate the fair value of a reporting unit to the assets and liabilities of that unit. Included in that allocation would be research and development assets that meet the criteria in paragraph 32 of this Statement even if Statement 2 or Interpretation 4 would require those assets to be written off to earnings when acquired.

[15]Refer to FASB Statement No. 5, *Accounting for Contingencies.*

[16][This footnote has been deleted. See Status page.]

b. The most recent fair value determination resulted in an amount that exceeded the carrying amount of the reporting unit by a substantial margin.

c. Based on an analysis of events that have occurred and circumstances that have changed since the most recent fair value determination, the likelihood that a current fair value determination would be less than the current carrying amount of the reporting unit is remote.

28. Goodwill of a reporting unit shall be tested for impairment between annual tests if an event occurs or circumstances change that would more likely than not reduce the fair value of a reporting unit below its carrying amount. Examples of such events or circumstances include:

a. A significant adverse change in legal factors or in the business climate

b. An adverse action or assessment by a regulator

c. Unanticipated competition

d. A loss of key personnel

e. A more-likely-than-not expectation that a reporting unit or a significant portion of a reporting unit will be sold or otherwise disposed of

f. The testing for recoverability under Statement 144 of a significant asset group within a reporting unit

g. Recognition of a goodwill impairment loss in the financial statements of a subsidiary that is a component of a reporting unit.

In addition, paragraph 39 requires that goodwill be tested for impairment after a portion of goodwill has been allocated to a business to be disposed of.

29. If goodwill and another asset (or asset group) of a reporting unit are tested for impairment at the same time, the other asset (or asset group) shall be tested for impairment before goodwill. For example, if a significant asset group is to be tested for impairment under Statement 144 (thus potentially requiring a goodwill impairment test), the impairment test for the significant asset group would be performed before the goodwill impairment test. If the asset group was impaired, the impairment loss would be recognized prior to goodwill being tested for impairment.

Reporting unit

30. A reporting unit is an operating segment or one level below an operating segment (referred to as a component).[17] A component of an operating segment is a reporting unit if the component constitutes a business[18] for which discrete financial information is available and segment management[19] regularly reviews the operating results of that component. However, two or more components of an operating segment shall be aggregated and deemed a single reporting unit if the components have similar economic characteristics.[20] An operating segment shall be deemed to be a reporting unit if all of its components are similar, if none of its components is a reporting unit, or if it comprises only a single component. The relevant provisions of Statement 131 and related interpretive literature shall be used to determine the reporting units of an entity.

31. An entity that is not required to report segment information in accordance with Statement 131 is nonetheless required to test goodwill for impairment at the reporting unit level. That entity shall use the guidance in paragraphs 10–15 of Statement 131 to determine its operating segments for purposes of determining its reporting units.

Assigning acquired assets and assumed liabilities to reporting units

32. For the purpose of testing goodwill for impairment, acquired assets and assumed liabilities shall be assigned to a reporting unit as of the acquisition date if both of the following criteria are met:

a. The asset will be employed in or the liability relates to the operations of a reporting unit.

b. The asset or liability will be considered in determining the fair value of the reporting unit.

Assets or liabilities that an entity considers part of its corporate assets or liabilities shall also be assigned to a reporting unit if both of the above criteria are met. Examples of corporate items that may meet those criteria and therefore would be assigned to a reporting

---

[17]For purposes of determining reporting units, an operating segment is as defined in paragraph 10 of FASB Statement No. 131, *Disclosures about Segments of an Enterprise and Related Information.*

[18]Emerging Issues Task Force Issue No. 98-3, "Determining Whether a Nonmonetary Transaction Involves Receipt of Productive Assets or of a Business," includes guidance on determining whether an asset group constitutes a business.

[19]Segment management consists of one or more segment managers, as that term is defined in paragraph 14 of Statement 131.

[20]Paragraph 17 of Statement 131 shall be considered in determining if the components of an operating segment have similar economic characteristics.

unit are environmental liabilities that relate to an existing operating facility of the reporting unit and a pension obligation that would be included in the determination of the fair value of the reporting unit. This provision applies to assets acquired and liabilities assumed in a business combination and to those acquired or assumed individually or with a group of other assets.

33. Some assets or liabilities may be employed in or relate to the operations of multiple reporting units. The methodology used to determine the amount of those assets or liabilities to assign to a reporting unit shall be reasonable and supportable and shall be applied in a consistent manner. For example, assets and liabilities not directly related to a specific reporting unit, but from which the reporting unit benefits, could be allocated according to the benefit received by the different reporting units (or based on the relative fair values of the different reporting units). In the case of pension items, for example, a pro rata allocation based on payroll expense might be used.

Assigning goodwill to reporting units

34. For the purpose of testing goodwill for impairment, *all* goodwill acquired in a business combination shall be assigned to one or more reporting units as of the acquisition date. Goodwill shall be assigned to reporting units of the acquiring entity that are expected to benefit from the synergies of the combination even though other assets or liabilities of the acquired entity may not be assigned to that reporting unit. The total amount of acquired goodwill may be divided among a number of reporting units. The methodology used to determine the amount of goodwill to assign to a reporting unit shall be reasonable and supportable and shall be applied in a consistent manner. In addition, that methodology shall be consistent with the objectives of the process of assigning goodwill to reporting units described in paragraph 35.

35. In concept, the amount of goodwill assigned to a reporting unit would be determined in a manner similar to how the amount of goodwill recognized in a business combination is determined. An entity would determine the fair value of the acquired business (or portion thereof) to be included in a reporting unit—in essence a "purchase price" for that business. The entity would then allocate that purchase price to

the individual assets acquired and liabilities assumed related to that acquired business (or portion thereof).[21] Any excess purchase price is the amount of goodwill assigned to that reporting unit. However, if goodwill is to be assigned to a reporting unit that has not been assigned any of the assets acquired or liabilities assumed in that acquisition, the amount of goodwill to be assigned to that unit might be determined by applying a "with and without" computation. That is, the difference between the fair value of that reporting unit before the acquisition and its fair value after the acquisition represents the amount of goodwill to be assigned to that reporting unit.

Reorganization of reporting structure

36. When an entity reorganizes its reporting structure in a manner that changes the composition of one or more of its reporting units, the guidance in paragraphs 32 and 33 shall be used to reassign assets and liabilities to the reporting units affected. However, goodwill shall be reassigned to the reporting units affected using a relative fair value allocation approach similar to that used when a portion of a reporting unit is to be disposed of (refer to paragraph 39). For example, if existing reporting unit A is to be integrated with reporting units B, C, and D, goodwill in reporting unit A would be assigned to units B, C, and D based on the relative fair values of the three portions of reporting unit A prior to those portions being integrated with reporting units B, C, and D.

Goodwill impairment testing by a subsidiary

37. All goodwill recognized by a public or nonpublic subsidiary (subsidiary goodwill) in its separate financial statements that are prepared in accordance with generally accepted accounting principles shall be accounted for in accordance with this Statement. Subsidiary goodwill shall be tested for impairment at the subsidiary level using the subsidiary's reporting units. If a goodwill impairment loss is recognized at the subsidiary level, goodwill of the reporting unit or units (at the higher consolidated level) in which the subsidiary's reporting unit with impaired goodwill resides must be tested for impairment if the event that gave rise to the loss at the subsidiary level would more likely than not reduce the fair value of the reporting unit (at the higher consolidated level) below its carrying amount (refer to

---

[21]Paragraphs 35–38 of Statement 141 provide guidance on allocating the purchase price to the assets acquired and liabilities assumed in a business combination.

paragraph 28(g)). Only if goodwill of that higher-level reporting unit is impaired would a goodwill impairment loss be recognized at the consolidated level.

Goodwill impairment testing when a noncontrolling interest exists

38. Goodwill arising from a business combination with a continuing noncontrolling interest shall be tested for impairment using an approach consistent with the approach used to measure the noncontrolling interest at the acquisition date. (A noncontrolling interest is sometimes referred to as a minority interest.) For example, if goodwill is initially recognized based only on the controlling interest of the parent, the fair value of the reporting unit used in the impairment test should be based on that controlling interest and should not reflect the portion of fair value attributable to the noncontrolling interest. Similarly, the implied fair value of goodwill that is determined in the second step of the impairment test and used to measure the impairment loss should reflect only the parent company's interest in that goodwill.

Disposal of All or a Portion of a Reporting Unit

39. When a reporting unit is to be disposed of in its entirety, goodwill of that reporting unit shall be included in the carrying amount of the reporting unit in determining the gain or loss on disposal. When a portion of a reporting unit that constitutes a business[23] is to be disposed of, goodwill associated with that business shall be included in the carrying amount of the business in determining the gain or loss on disposal. The amount of goodwill to be included in that carrying amount shall be based on the relative fair values of the business to be disposed of and the portion of the reporting unit that will be retained. For example, if a business is being sold for $100 and the fair value of the reporting unit excluding the business being sold is $300, 25 percent of the goodwill residing in the reporting unit would be included in the carrying amount of the business to be sold. However, if the business to be disposed of was never integrated into the reporting unit after its acquisition and thus the benefits of the acquired goodwill were never realized by the rest of the reporting unit, the current carrying amount of that acquired goodwill shall be included in the carrying amount of the business to be disposed of. That situation might occur when the acquired business is operated as a stand-alone entity or when the business is to be disposed of shortly after it is acquired. When only a portion of goodwill is allocated to a business to be disposed of, the goodwill remaining in the portion of the reporting unit to be retained shall be tested for impairment in accordance with paragraphs 19–22 (using its adjusted carrying amount).

Equity Method Investments

40. The portion of the difference between the cost of an investment and the amount of underlying equity in net assets of an equity method investee that is recognized as goodwill in accordance with paragraph 19(b) of APB Opinion No. 18, *The Equity Method of Accounting for Investments in Common Stock* (equity method goodwill) shall not be amortized. However, equity method goodwill shall not be tested for impairment in accordance with this Statement. Equity method investments shall continue to be reviewed for impairment in accordance with paragraph 19(h) of Opinion 18.

Deferred Income Taxes

41. Paragraph 30 of Statement 109 states that deferred income taxes are not recognized for any portion of goodwill for which amortization is not deductible for income tax purposes. Paragraphs 261 and 262 of that Statement provide additional guidance for recognition of deferred income taxes related to goodwill when amortization of goodwill is deductible for tax purposes. This Statement does not change the requirements in Statement 109 for recognition of deferred income taxes related to goodwill and intangible assets.

Financial Statement Presentation

Intangible Assets

42. At a minimum, all intangible assets shall be aggregated and presented as a separate line item in the statement of financial position. However, that requirement does not preclude presentation of individual intangible assets or classes of intangible assets as separate line items. The amortization expense and impairment losses for intangible assets shall be presented in income statement line items within continuing operations as deemed appropriate for each entity.

---

[22][This footnote has been deleted. See Status page.]
[23]Refer to footnote 18.

Paragraphs 14 and 16 require that an intangible asset be tested for impairment when it is determined that the asset should no longer be amortized or should begin to be amortized due to a reassessment of its remaining useful life. An impairment loss resulting from that impairment test shall *not* be recognized as a change in accounting principle.

Goodwill

43. The aggregate amount of goodwill shall be presented as a separate line item in the statement of financial position. The aggregate amount of goodwill impairment losses shall be presented as a separate line item in the income statement before the subtotal *income from continuing operations* (or similar caption) unless a goodwill impairment loss is associated with a discontinued operation. A goodwill impairment loss associated with a discontinued operation shall be included (on a net-of-tax basis) within the results of discontinued operations.

Disclosures

44. For intangible assets acquired either individually or with a group of assets, the following information shall be disclosed in the notes to the financial statements in the period of acquisition:

a. For intangible assets subject to amortization:
   (1) The total amount assigned and the amount assigned to any major **intangible asset class**
   (2) The amount of any significant residual value, in total and by major intangible asset class
   (3) The weighted-average amortization period, in total and by major intangible asset class
b. For intangible assets *not* subject to amortization, the total amount assigned and the amount assigned to any major intangible asset class
c. The amount of research and development assets acquired and written off in the period and the line item in the income statement in which the amounts written off are aggregated.

45. The following information shall be disclosed in the financial statements or the notes to the financial statements for each period for which a statement of financial position is presented:

a. For intangible assets subject to amortization:
   (1) The gross carrying amount and accumulated amortization, in total and by major intangible asset class
   (2) The aggregate amortization expense for the period

   (3) The estimated aggregate amortization expense for each of the five succeeding fiscal years
b. For intangible assets *not* subject to amortization, the total carrying amount and the carrying amount for each major intangible asset class
c. The changes in the carrying amount of goodwill during the period including:
   (1) The aggregate amount of goodwill acquired
   (2) The aggregate amount of impairment losses recognized
   (3) The amount of goodwill included in the gain or loss on disposal of all or a portion of a reporting unit.

Entities that report segment information in accordance with Statement 131 shall provide the above information about goodwill in total and for each reportable segment and shall disclose any significant changes in the allocation of goodwill by reportable segment. If any portion of goodwill has not yet been allocated to a reporting unit at the date the financial statements are issued, that unallocated amount and the reasons for not allocating that amount shall be disclosed.

Illustration 1 in Appendix C provides an example of those disclosure requirements.

46. For each impairment loss recognized related to an intangible asset, the following information shall be disclosed in the notes to the financial statements that include the period in which the impairment loss is recognized:

a. A description of the impaired intangible asset and the facts and circumstances leading to the impairment
b. The amount of the impairment loss and the method for determining fair value
c. The caption in the income statement or the statement of activities in which the impairment loss is aggregated
d. If applicable, the segment in which the impaired intangible asset is reported under Statement 131.

47. For each goodwill impairment loss recognized, the following information shall be disclosed in the notes to the financial statements that include the period in which the impairment loss is recognized:

a. A description of the facts and circumstances leading to the impairment
b. The amount of the impairment loss and the method of determining the fair value of the associated reporting unit (whether based on quoted market prices, prices of comparable businesses, a

present value or other valuation technique, or a combination thereof)

c. If a recognized impairment loss is an estimate that has not yet been finalized (refer to paragraph 22), that fact and the reasons therefor and, in subsequent periods, the nature and amount of any significant adjustments made to the initial estimate of the impairment loss.

Illustration 1 in Appendix C provides an example of those disclosure requirements.

Effective Date and Transition

48. This Statement shall be effective as follows:

a. All of the provisions of this Statement shall be applied in fiscal years beginning after December 15, 2001, to all goodwill and other intangible assets recognized in an entity's statement of financial position at the beginning of that fiscal year, regardless of when those previously recognized assets were initially recognized. Early application is permitted for entities with fiscal years beginning after March 15, 2001, provided that the first interim financial statements have not been issued previously. In all cases, the provisions of this Statement shall be initially applied at the beginning of a fiscal year. Retroactive application is not permitted. (Refer to paragraphs 53–61 for additional transition provisions.)

b. As described in paragraphs 50 and 51, certain provisions of this Statement shall be applied to goodwill and other acquired intangible assets for which the acquisition date is after June 30, 2001, even if an entity has not adopted this Statement in its entirety.

c. This Statement shall not be applied to previously recognized goodwill and intangible assets acquired in a combination between two or more mutual enterprises, acquired in a combination between not-for-profit organizations, or arising from the acquisition of a for-profit business entity by a not-for-profit organization until interpretive

guidance related to the application of the purchase method to those transactions is issued (refer to paragraph 52).[24]

49. Paragraph 61 of Statement 141 includes the following transition provisions related to goodwill and intangible assets acquired in business combinations for which the acquisition date was before July 1, 2001, that were accounted for by the purchase method.

a. The carrying amount of acquired intangible assets that do not meet the criteria in paragraph 39 of Statement 141 for recognition apart from goodwill (and any related deferred tax liabilities if the intangible asset amortization is not deductible for tax purposes) shall be reclassified as goodwill as of the date this Statement is initially applied in its entirety.

b. The carrying amount of (1) any recognized intangible assets that meet the recognition criteria in paragraph 39 of Statement 141 or (2) any unidentifiable intangible assets recognized in accordance with paragraph 5 of Statement 72 and required to be amortized in accordance with paragraph 8 of FASB Statement No. 147, *Acquisitions of Certain Financial Institutions,* that have been included in the amount reported as goodwill (or as goodwill and intangible assets) shall be reclassified and accounted for as an asset apart from goodwill as of the date this Statement is initially applied in its entirety.[25]

Goodwill and Intangible Assets Acquired after June 30, 2001

50. Goodwill acquired in a business combination for which the acquisition date is after June 30, 2001, shall not be amortized. For example, an entity with a December 31, 2001 fiscal year-end would be required to initially apply the provisions of this Statement on January 1, 2002; if that entity completed a business combination on October 15, 2001, that gave rise to goodwill, it would not amortize the goodwill acquired in that business combination even though it would continue to amortize until January 1, 2002,

---

[24]The Board plans to consider issues related to the application of the purchase method to combinations between two or more mutual enterprises, combinations between not-for-profit organizations, and the acquisition of a for-profit business entity by a not-for-profit organization in a separate project.

[25]For example, when a business combination was initially recorded, a portion of the acquired entity was assigned to intangible assets that meet the recognition criteria in paragraph 39 of Statement 141. Those intangible assets have been included in the amount reported on the statement of financial position as goodwill (or as goodwill and other intangible assets). However, separate general ledger or other accounting records have been maintained for those assets.

goodwill that arose from any business combination completed before July 1, 2001. Intangible assets other than goodwill acquired in a business combination or other transaction for which the date of acquisition is after June 30, 2001, shall be amortized or not amortized in accordance with paragraphs 11–14 and 16 of this Statement.

51. Goodwill and intangible assets acquired in a transaction for which the acquisition date is after June 30, 2001, but before the date that this Statement is applied in its entirety (refer to paragraph 48(a)), shall be reviewed for impairment in accordance with Opinion 17 or Statement 121 (as appropriate) until the date that this Statement is applied in its entirety. Similarly, the financial statement presentation and disclosure provisions of this Statement shall not be applied to those assets until this Statement is applied in its entirety.

52. Goodwill and intangible assets acquired in a combination between two or more mutual enterprises, acquired in a combination between not-for-profit organizations, or arising from the acquisition of a for-profit business entity by a not-for-profit organization for which the acquisition date is after June 30, 2001, shall continue to be accounted for in accordance with Opinion 17 (refer to footnote 24).

Previously Recognized Intangible Assets

53. To apply this Statement to intangible assets acquired in a transaction for which the acquisition date is on or before June 30, 2001, the useful lives of those previously recognized intangible assets shall be reassessed using the guidance in paragraph 11 and the remaining amortization periods adjusted accordingly.[26] That reassessment shall be completed prior to the end of the first interim period of the fiscal year in which this Statement is initially applied. Previously recognized intangible assets deemed to have indefinite useful lives shall be tested for impairment as of the beginning of the fiscal year in which this Statement is initially applied (in accordance with paragraph 17). That transitional intangible asset impairment test shall be completed in the first interim period in which this Statement is initially applied, and any resulting impairment loss shall be recognized as the effect of a change in accounting principle. The effect of the accounting change and related income tax effects shall be presented in the income

statement between the captions *extraordinary items* and *net income*. The per-share information presented in the income statement shall include the per-share effect of the accounting change.

Previously Recognized Goodwill

54. At the date this Statement is initially applied, an entity shall establish its reporting units based on its reporting structure at that date and the guidance in paragraphs 30 and 31. Recognized net assets, excluding goodwill, shall be assigned to those reporting units using the guidance in paragraphs 32 and 33. Recognized assets and liabilities that do not relate to a reporting unit, such as an environmental liability for an operation previously disposed of, need not be assigned to a reporting unit. *All* goodwill recognized in an entity's statement of financial position at the date this Statement is initially applied shall be assigned to one or more reporting units. Goodwill shall be assigned in a reasonable and supportable manner. The sources of previously recognized goodwill shall be considered in making that initial assignment as well as the reporting units to which the related acquired net assets were assigned. The guidance in paragraphs 34 and 35 may be useful in assigning goodwill to reporting units upon initial application of this Statement.

55. Goodwill in each reporting unit shall be tested for impairment as of the beginning of the fiscal year in which this Statement is initially applied in its entirety (in accordance with paragraphs 19–21). An entity has six months from the date it initially applies this Statement to complete the first step of that transitional goodwill impairment test. However, the amounts used in the transitional goodwill impairment test shall be measured as of the beginning of the year of initial application. If the carrying amount of the net assets of a reporting unit (including goodwill) exceeds the fair value of that reporting unit, the second step of the transitional goodwill impairment test must be completed as soon as possible, but no later than the end of the year of initial application.

56. An impairment loss recognized as a result of a transitional goodwill impairment test shall be recognized as the effect of a change in accounting principle. The effect of the accounting change and related income tax effects shall be presented in the income statement between the captions *extraordinary items*

---

[26]For example, the amortization period for a previously recognized intangible asset might be increased if its original useful life was estimated to be longer than the 40-year maximum amortization period allowed by Opinion 17.

and *net income*. The per-share information presented in the income statement shall include the per-share effect of the accounting change. Although a transitional impairment loss for goodwill may be measured in other than the first interim reporting period, it shall be recognized in the first interim period irrespective of the period in which it is measured, consistent with paragraph 10 of FASB Statement No. 3, *Reporting Accounting Changes in Interim Financial Statements*. The financial information for the interim periods of the fiscal year that precede the period in which the transitional goodwill impairment loss is measured shall be restated to reflect the accounting change in those periods. The aggregate amount of the accounting change shall be included in restated net income of the first interim period of the year of initial application (and in any year-to-date or last-12-months-to-date financial reports that include the first interim period). Whenever financial information is presented that includes the periods that precede the period in which the transitional goodwill impairment loss is measured, that financial information shall be presented on the restated basis.

57. If events or changes in circumstances indicate that goodwill of a reporting unit might be impaired before completion of the transitional goodwill impairment test, goodwill shall be tested for impairment when the impairment indicator arises (refer to paragraph 28). A goodwill impairment loss that does *not* result from a transitional goodwill impairment test shall not be recognized as the effect of a change in accounting principle; rather it shall be recognized in accordance with paragraph 43.

58. In addition to the transitional goodwill impairment test, an entity shall perform the required annual goodwill impairment test in the year that this Statement is initially applied in its entirety. That is, the transitional goodwill impairment test may not be considered the initial year's annual test unless an entity designates the beginning of its fiscal year as the date for its annual goodwill impairment test.

Equity Method Goodwill

59. Upon initial application of this Statement, the portion of the excess of cost over the underlying eq-

uity in net assets of an investee accounted for using the equity method that has been recognized as goodwill shall cease being amortized. However, equity method goodwill shall not be tested for impairment in accordance with this Statement (refer to paragraph 40).

Transitional Disclosures

60. Upon completion of the first step of the transitional goodwill impairment test, the reportable segment or segments in which an impairment loss might have to be recognized and the period in which that potential loss will be measured shall be disclosed in any interim financial information.

61. In the period of initial application and thereafter until goodwill and all other intangible assets have been accounted for in accordance with this Statement in all periods presented, the following information shall be displayed either on the face of the income statement or in the notes to the financial statements: income before extraordinary items and net income for all periods presented adjusted to exclude amortization expense (including any related tax effects) recognized in those periods related to goodwill, intangible assets that are no longer being amortized, any deferred credit related to an excess over cost (amortized in accordance with Opinion 16), and equity method goodwill. The adjusted income before extraordinary items and net income also shall reflect any adjustments for changes in amortization periods for intangible assets that will continue to be amortized as a result of initially applying this Statement (including any related tax effects). In addition, the notes to the financial statements shall disclose a reconciliation of reported net income to the adjusted net income. Similarly adjusted earnings-per-share amounts for all periods presented may be presented either on the face of the income statement or in the notes to the financial statements. Illustration 2 in Appendix C provides an example of those transitional disclosure requirements.

The provisions of this Statement need not be applied to immaterial items.

This Statement was adopted by the unanimous vote of the six members of the Financial Accounting Standards Board:

Edmund L. Jenkins,
Chairman

G. Michael Crooch
John M. Foster
Gaylen N. Larsen

Gerhard G. Mueller
Edward W. Trott

Appendix A

IMPLEMENTATION GUIDANCE ON INTANGIBLE ASSETS

A1. This appendix provides guidance on how intangible assets should be accounted for in accordance with paragraphs 11–17 of this Statement and is an integral part of the standards of this Statement. Each of the following examples describes an acquired intangible asset and the facts and circumstances surrounding the determination of its useful life and the subsequent accounting based on that determination. The facts and circumstances unique to each acquired intangible asset need to be considered in making similar determinations.

Example 1

An acquired customer list. A direct-mail marketing company acquired the customer list and expects that it will be able to derive benefit from the information on the acquired customer list for at least one year but for no more than three years.

The customer list would be amortized over 18 months, management's best estimate of its useful life, following the pattern in which the expected benefits will be consumed or otherwise used up. Although the acquiring entity may intend to add customer names and other information to the list in the future, the expected benefits of the acquired customer list relate only to the customers on that list at the date of acquisition (a closed-group notion). The customer list would be reviewed for impairment under Statement 144.

Example 2

An acquired patent that expires in 15 years. The product protected by the patented technology is expected to be a source of cash flows for at least 15 years. The reporting entity has a commitment from a third party to purchase that patent in 5 years for 60 percent of the fair value of the patent at the date it was acquired, and the entity intends to sell the patent in 5 years.

The patent would be amortized over its five-year useful life to the reporting entity following the pattern in which the expected benefits will be consumed or otherwise used up. The amount to be amortized is 40 percent of the patent's fair value at the acquisition date (residual value is 60 percent). The patent would be reviewed for impairment under Statement 144.

Example 3

An acquired copyright that has a remaining legal life of 50 years. An analysis of consumer habits and market trends provides evidence that the copyrighted material will generate cash flows for approximately 30 more years.

The copyright would be amortized over its 30-year estimated useful life following the pattern in which the expected benefits will be consumed or otherwise used up and reviewed for impairment under Statement 144.

Example 4

An acquired broadcast license that expires in five years. The broadcast license is renewable every 10 years if the company provides at least an average level of service to its customers and complies with the applicable Federal Communications Commission (FCC) rules and policies and the FCC Communications Act of 1934. The license may be renewed indefinitely at little cost and was renewed twice prior to its recent acquisition. The acquiring entity intends to renew the license indefinitely, and evidence supports its ability to do so. Historically, there has been no compelling challenge to the license renewal. The technology used in broadcasting is not expected to be replaced by another technology any time in the foreseeable future. Therefore, the cash flows from that license are expected to continue indefinitely.

The broadcast license would be deemed to have an indefinite useful life because cash flows are expected to continue indefinitely. Therefore, the license would not be amortized until its useful life is deemed to be no longer indefinite. The license would be tested for impairment in accordance with paragraph 17 of this Statement.

Example 5

The broadcast license in Example 4. The FCC subsequently decides that it will no longer renew broadcast licenses, but rather will auction those licenses. At the time the FCC decision is made, the broadcast license has three years until it expires. The cash flows from that license are expected to continue until the license expires.

Because the broadcast license can no longer be renewed, its useful life is no longer indefinite. Thus, the acquired license would be tested for impairment in accordance with paragraph 17 of this Statement. The license would then be amortized over its remaining three-year useful life following the pattern in which the expected benefits will be consumed or otherwise used up. Because the license will be subject to amortization, in the future it would be reviewed for impairment under Statement 144.

Example 6

An acquired airline route authority from the United States to the United Kingdom that expires in three years. The route authority may be renewed every five years, and the acquiring entity intends to comply with the applicable rules and regulations surrounding renewal. Route authority renewals are routinely granted at a minimal cost and have historically been renewed when the airline has complied with the applicable rules and regulations. The acquiring entity expects to provide service to the United Kingdom from its hub airports indefinitely and expects that the related supporting infrastructure (airport gates, slots, and terminal facility leases) will remain in place at those airports for as long as it has the route authority. An analysis of demand and cash flows supports those assumptions.

Because the facts and circumstances support the acquiring entity's ability to continue providing air service to the United Kingdom from its U.S. hub airports indefinitely, the intangible asset related to the route authority is considered to have an indefinite useful life. Therefore, the route authority would not be amortized until its useful life is deemed to be no longer indefinite and would be tested for impairment in accordance with paragraph 17 of this Statement.

Example 7

An acquired trademark that is used to identify and distinguish a leading consumer product that has been a market-share leader for the past eight years. The trademark has a remaining legal life of 5 years but is renewable every 10 years at little cost. The acquiring entity intends to continuously renew the trademark, and evidence supports its ability to do so. An analysis of product life cycle studies; market, competitive, and environmental trends; and brand extension opportunities provides evidence that the trademarked product will generate cash flows for the acquiring entity for an indefinite period of time.

The trademark would be deemed to have an indefinite useful life because it is expected to contribute to cash flows indefinitely. Therefore, the trademark would not be amortized until its useful life is no longer indefinite. The trademark would be tested for impairment in accordance with paragraph 17 of this Statement.

Example 8

A trademark that distinguished a leading consumer product that was acquired 10 years ago. When it was acquired, the trademark was considered to have an indefinite useful life because the product was expected to generate cash flows indefinitely. During the annual impairment test of the intangible asset, the entity determines that unexpected competition has entered the market that will reduce future sales of the product. Management estimates that cash flows generated by that consumer product will be 20 percent less for the foreseeable future; however, management expects that the product will continue to generate cash flows indefinitely at those reduced amounts.

As a result of the projected decrease in future cash flows, the entity determines that the estimated fair value of the trademark is less than its carrying amount, and an impairment loss is recognized. Because it is still deemed to have an indefinite useful life, the trademark would continue to not be amortized and would continue to be tested for impairment in accordance with paragraph 17 of this Statement.

Example 9

A trademark for a line of automobiles that was acquired several years ago in an acquisition of an automobile company. The line of automobiles had been produced by the acquired entity for 35 years with numerous new models developed under the trademark. At the acquisition date, the acquiring entity expected to continue to produce that line of automobiles, and an analysis of various economic factors indicated there was no limit to the period of time the trademark would contribute to cash flows. Because cash flows were expected to continue indefinitely, the trademark was not amortized. Management recently decided to phase out production of that automobile line over the next four years.

Because the useful life of that acquired trademark is no longer deemed to be indefinite, the trademark would be tested for impairment in accordance with paragraph 17 of this Statement. The carrying amount

of the trademark after adjustment, if any, would then be amortized over its remaining four-year useful life following the pattern in which the expected benefits will be consumed or otherwise used up. Because the trademark will be subject to amortization, in the future it would be reviewed for impairment under Statement 144.

Appendix B

BACKGROUND INFORMATION AND BASIS FOR CONCLUSIONS

CONTENTS

Appendix B

BACKGROUND INFORMATION AND BASIS FOR CONCLUSIONS

Introduction

B1. This appendix summarizes considerations that Board members deemed significant in reaching the conclusions in this Statement. It includes reasons for accepting certain approaches and rejecting others. Individual Board members gave greater weight to some factors than to others.

Background Information

B2. Prior to the issuance of this Statement, the guidance on accounting for goodwill and other intangible assets was provided by APB Opinion No. 17, *Intangible Assets,* which the Accounting Principles Board (APB) of the American Institute of Certified Public Accountants (AICPA) issued in 1970. Opinion 17 required that intangible assets that are acquired in business combination transactions or other transactions be recognized as assets in the financial statements of acquiring entities and that the costs incurred to develop intangible assets that are not specifically identifiable be recognized as expenses in the financial statements of entities incurring those costs. It also required that goodwill and other intangible assets be amortized by systematic charges over the period expected to be benefited by those assets, not to exceed 40 years.

B3. During the 1970s, the FASB had an active project on its agenda to reconsider the accounting for business combinations and purchased intangible assets. However, the Board later decided to defer consideration of the issues in that project until after it completed development of its conceptual framework for accounting and reporting. In 1981, the Board removed the inactive business combinations project from its agenda to focus on higher priority projects.

B4. In August 1996, the Board added the current project on accounting for business combinations to its agenda. The objective of this project was to improve the transparency of accounting and reporting of business combinations, including the accounting for goodwill and other intangible assets, by reconsidering the requirements of Opinion 17 and APB Opinion No. 16, *Business Combinations* (which also was issued in 1970). In 1999, the Board decided that that objective would best be achieved through several projects focused on specific issues. In the first of those projects, which ended with the concurrent issuance of this Statement and FASB Statement No. 141, *Business Combinations,* the Board reconsidered the accounting for goodwill and other intangible assets and the methods of accounting for business combinations. Another project will address issues associated with the accounting for combinations between not-for-profit organizations, the acquisition of a for-profit entity by a not-for-profit organization, and combinations between mutual enterprises. The Board intends to consider issues related to the accounting for the formation of joint ventures and other new entities, push-down accounting (including spinoffs), and common control transactions in another project. In still another project, the Board intends to consider issues related to the provisions of Opinion 16 and FASB Statement No. 38, *Accounting for Preacquisition Contingencies of Purchased Enterprises,* that were carried forward in Statement 141 without reconsideration, and other issues related to the application of the purchase method, such as the accounting for step acquisitions.[27]

Reasons the FASB Took on the Project

B5. A principal reason for taking on this project in 1996 was the increase in merger and acquisition activity that brought greater attention to the fact that two transactions that are economically similar may be accounted for by different methods that produce dramatically different financial statement results. Consequently, both the representational faithfulness and the comparability of those financial statements suffer.

B6. Another reason that the Board decided to undertake this project was that many perceived the differences in the pooling-of-interests method (pooling method) and purchase method to have affected competition in markets for mergers and acquisitions. Entities that could not meet all of the conditions for applying the pooling method believed that they faced an unlevel playing field in competing for targets with entities that could apply that method. That perception and the resulting attempts to expand the application of the pooling method placed considerable tension on the interpretation and application of the provisions of Opinion 16. The volume of inquiries fielded by the staffs of the FASB and Securities and Exchange Commission (SEC) and the auditing profession was evidence of that tension.

B7. The unlevel playing field that was perceived to stem from the application of the pooling and purchase methods extended internationally as well. Cross-border differences in accounting standards for business combinations and the rapidly accelerating movement of capital flows globally heightened the need for accounting standards to be comparable internationally. Promoting international comparability in accounting standards is part of the Board's mission, and many members of the Financial Accounting Standards Advisory Council (FASAC) cited the opportunity to promote greater international comparability in the standards for business combinations as a reason for adding this project to the Board's agenda. (FASAC had consistently ranked a possible project on business combinations as a high priority for a number of years.)

International Cooperation

B8. Largely because of concerns about the perception of an unlevel cross-border playing field with the United States in the accounting standards for business combinations, the Accounting Standards Board (AcSB) of the Canadian Institute of Chartered Accountants conducted a business combinations project

---

[27]For example, AICPA Accounting Interpretation 2, "Goodwill in a Step Acquisition," of Opinion 17 stated that when an entity acquires another entity or an investment accounted for by the equity method through a series of purchases (commonly referred to as a step acquisition), the entity should identify the cost of each investment, the fair value of the underlying assets acquired, and the goodwill for each step acquisition.

concurrently with the FASB's project. The goal of that concurrent effort was to establish common standards on business combinations and intangible assets.

B9. The FASB also worked with other members of an international organization of standard-setting bodies with the aim of achieving convergence internationally with respect to the methods of accounting for business combinations. That organization, known as the "Group of 4 plus 1" (G4+1), consisted of the Australian Accounting Standards Board, the New Zealand Financial Reporting Standards Board, the United Kingdom Accounting Standards Board (UK ASB), the AcSB, the FASB, and an observer, the International Accounting Standards Committee (IASC).

Conduct of the FASB's Project

B10. The Board formed a business combinations task force comprising individuals from a number of organizations representing a wide range of the Board's constituents. The first meeting of that task force was held in February 1997. Relevant academic research was reviewed, and the meeting discussion centered on a background paper that addressed the project's scope, the direction the project should take, and how the project should be conducted.

B11. The June 1997 FASB Special Report, *Issues Associated with the FASB Project on Business Combinations,* was based on that background paper and indicated some of the Board's initial decisions about the project's scope, direction, and conduct. The 54 comment letters received in response to that Special Report generally expressed agreement with those decisions.

B12. In 1998, the FASB participated in the development of a G4+1 Position Paper, *Recommendations for Achieving Convergence on the Methods of Accounting for Business Combinations.* The Board issued the Position Paper as an FASB Invitation to Comment, *Methods of Accounting for Business Combinations: Recommendations of the G4+1 for Achieving Convergence,* in December 1998, the same date on which other G4+1 member organizations issued similar documents for comment.

B13. After considering the recommendations of the G4+1 and the responses to the Invitation to Comment, the Board decided that only the purchase method should be used to account for business com-

binations. The Board also decided that certain changes should be made in how the purchase method should be applied, particularly in the accounting for and financial statement presentation of goodwill and other intangible assets. Those changes included limiting the maximum amortization period for goodwill to 20 years, presenting goodwill amortization expense on a net-of-tax basis in the income statement, and not amortizing certain intangible assets. Those changes were proposed in the September 1999 FASB Exposure Draft, *Business Combinations and Intangible Assets* (1999 Exposure Draft). The Board received 210 comment letters in response to that Exposure Draft. In February 2000, the Board held 4 days of public hearings, 2 days in San Francisco and 2 days in New York City, at which 43 individuals or organizations presented their views on the 1999 Exposure Draft.

B14. In redeliberating the proposals in the 1999 Exposure Draft, the Board considered changes suggested by various constituents, in particular those related to the accounting for goodwill. During October and November 2000, Board and staff members explored the suggested changes to the accounting for goodwill in field visits with 14 companies. The Board's deliberations resulted in significant changes to the proposed requirements related to goodwill but not to other issues addressed in the 1999 Exposure Draft. In particular, the Board decided that goodwill should no longer be amortized and should be tested for impairment in a manner different from other assets. The Board also affirmed the proposal that only the purchase method should be used to account for business combinations. In February 2001, the Board issued a revised Exposure Draft, *Business Combinations and Intangible Assets—Accounting for Goodwill* (2001 Exposure Draft), that proposed changes to the 1999 Exposure Draft with regard to the accounting for goodwill and the initial recognition of intangible assets other than goodwill. The Board received 211 comment letters on the 2001 Exposure Draft.

B15. The Board decided to separate the guidance for goodwill and other intangible assets from that for business combinations and issue that guidance in two final documents, this Statement and Statement 141. Those two Statements parallel and supersede Opinions 17 and 16, respectively. Statement 141 was issued concurrently with this Statement.

Scope

B16. This Statement applies to all entities, including mutual enterprises and not-for-profit organizations.

The 2001 Exposure Draft excluded from its scope goodwill and other intangible assets acquired in combinations between two or more not-for-profit organizations and goodwill acquired in an acquisition of a for-profit entity by a not-for-profit organization. Rather than exclude goodwill and other intangible assets acquired in those transactions from the scope of this Statement, the Board concluded that it would be more appropriate to include those assets in the scope of this Statement. However, the Board agreed to delay the effective date of this Statement as it applies to not-for-profit organizations and combinations between two or more mutual enterprises until it completes the project on its agenda addressing issues related to combinations of those entities. The Board noted that goodwill and intangible assets acquired in those types of combinations would be accounted for in the same manner as goodwill and intangible assets acquired in business combinations unless distinguishing characteristics or circumstances are identified justifying a different accounting treatment.

B17. This Statement applies to excess reorganization value recognized in accordance with AICPA Statement of Position (SOP) 90-7, *Financial Reporting by Entities in Reorganization Under the Bankruptcy Code.* SOP 90-7 states that the excess reorganization value resulting from reorganization under the Bankruptcy Code is an intangible asset that should be amortized in accordance with Opinion 17, generally over a period substantially less than 40 years. Because this Statement supersedes Opinion 17, respondents to the 2001 Exposure Draft requested that the Board address whether excess reorganization value should be accounted for like goodwill and not be amortized or accounted for like an intangible asset and thus possibly continue to be amortized.

B18. Most respondents stated that excess reorganization value is similar to goodwill and therefore should be accounted for in the same manner as goodwill. The Board agreed with those respondents and concluded that excess reorganization value recognized in accordance with SOP 90-7 should be accounted for as goodwill in accordance with this Statement. The Board decided that the transition provisions in this Statement should apply to previously recognized excess reorganization value that is being accounted for in accordance with Opinion 17.

B19. The Board decided that this Statement should not change the accounting for an unidentifiable intangible asset recognized in an acquisition of a bank or thrift institution that is prescribed in FASB Statement No. 72, *Accounting for Certain Acquisitions of Banking or Thrift Institutions.* The Board noted that Statement 72 does not refer to the unidentifiable intangible asset as goodwill and concluded that it would not be appropriate to account for that intangible asset as if it were goodwill without a full reconsideration of the issues associated with that industry, which is beyond the issues addressed in this Statement.

Intangible Assets

Scope and Definition

B20. The Board initially decided that the focus of this project with respect to intangible assets should be limited to those intangible assets acquired in a business combination. However, the Board acknowledged in the Special Report that it would consider the need to expand the scope to other intangible assets as the project progressed.

B21. The Board observed that the scope of Opinion 17 is not limited to intangible assets acquired in a business combination but rather encompasses intangible assets generally. Other standards, such as Financial Reporting Standard (FRS) 10, *Goodwill and Intangible Assets,* issued by the UK ASB, and International Accounting Standard (IAS) 38, *Intangible Assets,* issued by the IASC, also apply to intangible assets generally.

B22. The Board considered whether to include in the scope of this project all acquired intangible assets rather than only those acquired in a business combination. The Board noted that doing so would have the advantage of treating all acquired intangible assets similarly regardless of whether they were acquired in a business combination or in another transaction. The Board also noted that it might result in greater convergence with the requirements in standards outside the United States.

B23. The Board noted, however, that the guidance in Opinion 17 does not specify how the costs of internally developing specifically identifiable intangible assets that have limited lives should be treated. As a result, those costs may be either recognized as assets and amortized or expensed as incurred. The only provisions of Opinion 17 that relate to such assets are those concerning amortization, which relate to other intangible assets as well. The Board further noted that guidance for certain types of intangible assets, such as computer software, is provided in other standards and that the Board's intent generally was not to amend those standards as part of the business combinations project.

B24. Internally developed intangible assets raise many accounting issues that have little to do with business combinations, so the Board decided not to address them in the business combinations project.[28] However, the Board concluded that the accounting issues associated with intangible assets acquired in transactions other than business combinations are sufficiently similar to those associated with such assets acquired in business combinations and thus decided to address them in this project.

B25. The Board also noted that research and development costs are excluded from the scope of Opinion 17 by FASB Interpretation No. 4, *Applicability of FASB Statement No. 2 to Business Combinations Accounted for by the Purchase Method,* but not from the scope of Opinion 16. The Board therefore considered issues related to the accounting for research and development assets acquired in business combinations. During the development of the 1999 Exposure Draft, the Board noted that some of the issues associated with research and development assets are unique to those assets and not directly related to other business combinations issues. The Board concluded that it was not possible to address those issues without considering the issues associated with accounting for research and development costs generally. Consequently, the Board decided not to address issues associated with research and development assets in this project.

B26. Statement 141, which supersedes Opinion 16, addresses the initial recognition and measurement of intangible assets, including goodwill, that are acquired in a business combination. This Statement addresses the initial recognition and measurement of intangible assets acquired in transactions other than business combinations, as well as the subsequent recognition and measurement of intangible assets generally.

B27. In the deliberations that led to the 1999 Exposure Draft, the Board concluded that the characteristics that distinguish intangible assets from other assets are that they are (a) without physical substance, (b) not financial instruments, and (c) not current assets. The 1999 Exposure Draft defined intangible assets in terms of those characteristics. Several respondents to that Exposure Draft noted that some intangible assets (such as order or production backlogs) are current assets. They observed that some might interpret that proposed definition as prohibiting recognition of those intangible assets as intangible assets, which they believed was not the Board's intent. The Board agreed with those respondents and decided that this Statement should define intangible assets more broadly, that is, as assets (not including financial assets) that lack physical substance.

Initial Recognition of Intangible Assets Acquired in Transactions Other Than Business Combinations

B28. At the inception of this project, the Board observed that intangible assets make up an increasing proportion of the assets of many (if not most) entities, but despite their importance, those assets often are not recognized as such. Accordingly, the Board concluded in the 1999 Exposure Draft that the decision usefulness of financial statements would be enhanced by the recognition of more intangible assets. The Board affirmed that view in its redeliberations.

B29. The Board noted that, to be recognized, intangible assets acquired in transactions other than business combinations must meet the four fundamental recognition criteria for assets in paragraph 63 of FASB Concepts Statement No. 5, *Recognition and Measurement in Financial Statements of Business Enterprises.* Those criteria are that the item meets the assets definition, it has an attribute that is measurable with sufficient reliability, the information about it is capable of making a difference in user decisions, and the information is representationally faithful, verifiable, and neutral.

B30. The Board observed that bargained exchange transactions that are conducted at arm's length provide reliable evidence about the existence and fair value of acquired intangible assets. Accordingly, the Board concluded that those transactions provide a basis for recognizing those assets in the financial statements of the acquiring entities. The Board also observed that similarly reliable evidence about the existence and fair value of intangible assets that are developed internally is not generally available.

---

[28]Because this Statement supersedes all of Opinion 17, this Statement carries forward the provisions in that Opinion related to internally developed intangible assets. As noted in paragraph 2, the Board has not reconsidered those provisions as they are outside the project's scope.

B31. The Board also considered how to distinguish intangible assets from each other. The Board observed that, conceptually, the main reason for distinguishing intangible assets from each other is to enhance the decision usefulness of financial statements. As stated in Concepts Statement 5:

> Classification in financial statements facilitates analysis by grouping items with essentially similar characteristics and separating items with essentially different characteristics. Analysis aimed at objectives such as predicting amounts, timing, and uncertainty of future cash flows requires financial information segregated into reasonably homogenous groups. For example, components of financial statements that consist of items that have similar characteristics in one or more respects, such as continuity or recurrence, stability, risk, and reliability, are likely to have more predictive value than if their characteristics are dissimilar. [paragraph 20]

B32. In the 1999 Exposure Draft, the Board observed that many intangible assets are based on rights that are conveyed legally by contract, statute, or similar means. It also noted that many such assets are exchangeable, as are other intangible assets that are not based on such rights. The Board noted that intangible assets span a spectrum, with intangible assets that are readily exchangeable at one end and others that are "goodwill like" at the other end. In that regard, it noted that exchangeability is a useful basis for distinguishing different types of intangible assets because those that are capable of being sold or otherwise transferred constitute a potential source of funds.

B33. In considering responses to the 1999 Exposure Draft, the Board reconsidered the guidance proposed for the recognition of intangible assets apart from goodwill. As a result, Statement 141 requires that an intangible asset be recognized apart from goodwill if it meets either of two criteria.

B34. Statement 141 requires that an intangible asset be recognized apart from goodwill if it arises from contractual or other legal rights, regardless of whether those rights are transferable or separable from the entity or from other rights and obligations

(the contractual-legal criterion). In that regard, the Board observed that the values of many intangible assets arise from rights conveyed legally by contract, statute, or similar means. For example, franchises are granted to automobile dealers, fast-food outlets, and professional sports teams. Trademarks and service marks may be registered with the government. Contracts often are negotiated with customers or suppliers. Technological innovations are often protected by patents. The Board concluded that the fact that an intangible asset arises from contractual or other legal rights is an important characteristic and intangible assets with that characteristic should be recognized apart from goodwill.

B35. Statement 141 also requires that an acquired intangible asset be recognized apart from goodwill if the intangible asset is separable, that is, it is capable of being separated or divided from the entity and sold, transferred, licensed, rented, or exchanged, regardless of whether there is an intent to do so (the separability criterion). The Board noted that some acquired intangible assets may have been developed internally by the acquired entity. The Board noted that although some intangible assets do not arise from rights conveyed by contract or other legal means, they are nonetheless capable of being separated and exchanged for something else of value. Other intangible assets cannot be separated and sold or otherwise transferred. The Board concluded that separability is another important characteristic and, therefore, intangible assets with that characteristic should be recognized apart from goodwill.[29]

B36. The Board observed that the contractual-legal criterion and the separability criterion are the basis for distinguishing between intangible assets and goodwill acquired in business combination transactions and are not applicable to other transactions in which intangible assets are acquired (because goodwill arises only in business combinations or in transactions accounted for like business combinations). However, the Board observed that those criteria may constitute a useful basis for distinguishing between different types of recognized intangible assets that are acquired in other transactions, thereby enhancing the decision usefulness of the financial statements, consistent with paragraph 20 of Concepts Statement 5.

---

[29]As it did prior to issuing the 2001 Exposure Draft, the Board noted that some intangible assets are so closely related to another asset or liability that they usually are sold as a "package" (as is the case with deposit liabilities and the related depositor relationship intangible asset). The Board concluded that an intangible asset that does not meet the separability criterion individually meets the separability criterion if it can be separated and divided from the entity and sold, transferred, licensed, rented, or exchanged with a related contract, asset, or liability.

B37. The Board also noted that Statement 141 contains a presumption that an intangible asset that meets the contractual-legal criterion or the separability criterion also would meet the asset recognition criteria in Concepts Statement 5.[30] The Board observed that intangible assets that are acquired individually or with a group of assets in a transaction other than a business combination also may meet the asset recognition criteria in Concepts Statement 5 even though they do not meet either the contractual-legal criterion or the separability criterion (for example, specially-trained employees or a unique manufacturing process related to an acquired manufacturing plant). Such transactions commonly are bargained exchange transactions that are conducted at arm's length, which the Board concluded provides reliable evidence about the existence and fair value of those assets. Thus, those assets should be recognized as intangible assets.

Initial Measurement of Intangible Assets Acquired in Transactions Other Than Business Combinations

B38. Both Statement 141 and this Statement require that acquired intangible assets initially be assigned an amount based on their fair values, which is consistent with the requirements of Opinions 16 and 17 and the proposals of the 1999 Exposure Draft. As noted in paragraph 7 of FASB Concepts Statement No. 7, *Using Cash Flow Information and Present Value in Accounting Measurements,* in recent years the Board has identified fair value as the objective for most measurements at initial recognition. None of the respondents to the 1999 Exposure Draft suggested alternative measurement approaches.

B39. In Statement 141 the Board affirmed the basic principles of historical-cost accounting included in paragraphs 66–69 of Opinion 16. Specifically, the Board affirmed that an asset acquisition should be measured on the basis of the values exchanged and that measurement of the values exchanged should be based on the fair value of the consideration given or the fair value of the net assets acquired, whichever is more reliably measurable. For similar reasons, the Board concluded in this Statement that acquired intangible assets should be initially measured based on

their fair values. The Board also agreed that when groups of assets are acquired, the value of the asset (or net asset) group as a whole should be allocated to the individual assets (or assets and liabilities) that make up the group on the basis of their relative fair values.

B40. The Board noted that an intangible asset arising from a contractual or other legal right represents the future cash flows that are expected to result from ownership of that contract or legal right. Fair value represents the amount at which that asset could be bought or sold in a current transaction between willing parties, that is, in other than a forced or liquidation sale. For example, the fair value of an order backlog would represent the amount a buyer would be willing to pay to acquire the future cash flows expected to arise from that order backlog.

B41. The Board recognizes that the requirements of this Statement might change current practice with respect to the amounts assigned to some intangible assets, in particular those that arise from contractual or other legal rights. For example, the Board has been informed that in current practice the amount assigned to acquired operating lease contracts (from the lessor's perspective) and customer contracts often is based on the amount by which the contract terms are favorable relative to market prices at the date of acquisition. Thus, no amount is typically assigned to lease and other contracts that are "at the money"—that is, when the contract terms reflect market prices at the date of acquisition. The Board observed, however, that such "at the money" contracts are bought and sold in exchange transactions—the purchase and sale of airport gates (an operating lease) within the airline industry and customer contracts in the home security industry are two examples of those exchange transactions. The Board believes that those transactions provide evidence that a contract may have value for reasons other than terms that are favorable relative to market prices. The Board therefore concluded that the amount by which the terms of a contract are favorable relative to market prices would not always represent the fair value of that contract.

B42. Several respondents noted that a present value technique might often be the best available technique

---

[30]Some respondents to both Exposure Drafts doubted their ability to reliably measure the fair values of many intangible assets, particularly those acquired in groups with other assets. The Board noted that the fair values of the assets acquired are established through bargained exchange transactions. The Board acknowledged that the fair value estimates for some intangible assets that meet the recognition criteria might lack the precision of the fair value measurements for other assets. However, the Board also concluded that the financial information that will be provided by recognizing intangible assets at their estimated fair values is more representationally faithful than that which would be provided if those intangible assets were not recognized as intangible assets on the basis of measurement difficulties.

with which to estimate the fair value of an acquired intangible asset. Some of those respondents asked whether the estimated cash flows used in applying that technique should be limited to the cash flows expected over the remaining legal or contractual term of the acquired asset. The Board noted that judgment is required in estimating the period of expected cash flows. Those estimates should be consistent with the objective of measuring fair value and, thus, should incorporate assumptions that marketplace participants would use in estimating fair value, such as assumptions about contract renewals and other benefits, such as those that might result from acquisition-related synergies.

B43. The Board noted that if such information is not available without undue cost and effort, an entity should use its own assumptions. The Board also noted that while many contracts or other rights (including customer contracts) are fixed in duration, past history (and industry practice) often provides evidence that the contracts or rights generally are renewed without substantial cost and effort. For example, although contracts to manage investments of mutual funds are often short-term contracts (one-year term or less), the Board has been informed that in many (if not most) cases those contracts are continuously renewed. The Board has also been informed that while some legal rights such as trademarks and broadcast licenses have finite legal lives, those rights are renewable and are often renewed without challenge. In those cases, the Board believes that estimates of future cash flows used in measuring the fair value of the acquired intangible asset would reflect cash flows for periods that extend beyond the remaining term of the acquired contract or legal right. The Board noted that Concepts Statement 7 discusses the essential elements of a present value measurement (paragraph 23), provides examples of circumstances in which an entity's expected cash flows might differ from the market cash flows (paragraph 32), and discusses the use of present value techniques in measuring the fair value of an asset or liability (paragraphs 39–54 and 75–88).

Subsequent Recognition and Measurement

Useful lives of intangible assets

B44. The Board observed that the useful lives of intangible assets are related to the expected cash inflows that are associated with those assets. Accordingly, the Board concluded that the amortization periods for intangible assets should generally reflect

those useful lives and, by extension, the cash flow streams associated with them. The Board noted that the useful lives and amortization periods of intangible assets should reflect the periods over which those assets will contribute to cash flows, not the period of time that would be required to internally develop those assets.

B45. The Board agreed that the useful life of an intangible asset is indefinite if that life extends beyond the foreseeable horizon—that is, there is no foreseeable limit on the period of time over which it is expected to contribute to the cash flows of the reporting entity. The Board concluded that if an entity performs an analysis of all of the pertinent factors that should be considered in determining the useful life of an intangible asset (such as those in paragraph 11) and finds that there is no limit on the useful life of an intangible asset, that asset should be deemed to have an indefinite useful life.

B46. The Board noted that the cash flows and useful lives of intangible assets that are based on legal rights are constrained by the duration of those legal rights. Thus, the useful lives of such intangible assets cannot extend beyond the length of their legal rights and may be shorter. Accordingly, the Board concluded that in determining the useful lives of those intangible assets, consideration should be given to the periods that the intangible assets contribute to cash flows, which are subject to the expiration of the legal rights.

B47. The Board observed that legal rights often are conveyed for limited terms that may be renewed, and therefore it considered whether renewals should be assumed in establishing useful lives for those intangible assets. The Board noted that some types of licenses are initially issued for finite periods but renewals are routinely granted with little cost, provided that licensees have complied with the applicable rules and regulations. Such licenses trade at prices that reflect more than the remaining term, thereby indicating that renewal at minimal cost is the general expectation, and thus their useful lives may be indefinite. However, renewals are not assured for other types of licenses, and even if they are renewed, substantial costs may be incurred for their renewal. Because the useful lives of certain intangible assets depend on renewal and on the associated costs, the Board concluded that the useful lives assigned to those assets may reflect renewal only if there is evidence to support renewal without substantial cost.

B48. The Board observed that renewals could result in some of those intangible assets having long or indefinite useful lives. The Board also observed that some assets are based on legal rights that are conveyed in perpetuity rather than for finite terms. As such, those assets may have cash flows associated with them that may be expected to continue for many years or even indefinitely. If the cash flows are expected to continue for a finite period, then the useful life of the asset is limited to that finite period. However, if the cash flows are expected to continue indefinitely, the useful life may be indefinite rather than finite. The Board also observed that intangible assets that are not based on legal rights also may have long or indefinite useful lives. Such assets, for example, may be ones that can be and are bought and sold, thereby providing evidence of their continued existence. Those markets also provide evidence of the fair values of those assets, either directly from transactions in which those assets are exchanged, or indirectly, utilizing models that incorporate transaction prices for similar assets as inputs.

Amortization

Amortization period

B49. The Board observed that Opinion 17 required intangible assets to be amortized over their expected useful lives; however, amortization periods were limited to 40 years. The Board noted that standards elsewhere that address intangible assets are generally similar. However, in some cases, the maximum amortization period is less than 40 years, with 20 years frequently being the presumed or absolute maximum. The Board noted that both FRS 10 and IAS 38 have presumptive maximums of 20 years. However, FRS 10 permits some intangible assets not to be amortized at all, provided that (a) the durability of the asset can be demonstrated[31] and justifies an amortization period longer than 20 years and (b) the asset is capable of continued measurement so that annual impairment reviews can be conducted. IAS 38 requires all intangible assets to be amortized but does not specify a maximum amortization period.

B50. Because of the potential for at least some intangible assets to have long or indefinite useful lives, the Board initially considered whether a maximum amortization period of 20 years should be applied to all of those assets, as it initially had decided with respect to goodwill (in developing the 1999 Exposure Draft). The Board observed that reducing the maximum amortization period for those assets from 40 years to 20 years would be a significant change from the requirements of Opinion 17.

B51. The Board noted in the 1999 Exposure Draft that having the same maximum amortization periods for intangible assets as for goodwill might discourage entities from recognizing more intangible assets apart from goodwill. Not independently recognizing those intangible assets when they exist and can be reliably measured adversely affects the relevance and representational faithfulness of the financial statements. Accordingly, the Board concluded in the 1999 Exposure Draft that setting a maximum amortization period of 20 years for all intangible assets would not have been appropriate.

B52. The Board observed, however, that a 20-year limitation constituted a useful benchmark or hurdle and concluded that it should be a presumptive maximum. Accordingly, the Board concluded in the 1999 Exposure Draft that intangible assets that have useful lives exceeding 20 years could be amortized over periods exceeding 20 years if they generate clearly identifiable cash flows that are expected to continue for more than 20 years. Support for that amortization period would have been provided by a legal life exceeding 20 years or exchangeability of the asset.

B53. Responses to the 1999 Exposure Draft varied. Some respondents stated that no intangible assets should be amortized; others stated that a presumption about the length of the amortization period was not necessary, nor was a maximum. The Board reaffirmed in this Statement that intangible assets with finite useful lives should be amortized. The Board noted that the revised criteria for an intangible asset to be recognized apart from goodwill (contractual-legal and separability) are similar to the criteria in the 1999 Exposure Draft for overcoming the 20-year useful life presumption. (The 1999 Exposure Draft would have required an intangible asset to have clearly identifiable cash flows in order to overcome that presumption.) The Board noted that the useful life of an intangible asset is defined in this Statement as the period over which an asset is expected to contribute directly or indirectly to future cash flows.

---

[31]Paragraph 20 of FRS 10 notes that durability depends on a number of factors such as the nature of the business, the stability of the industry in which the acquired business operates, typical lifespans of the products to which the goodwill attaches, the extent to which the acquisition overcomes market entry barriers that will continue to exist, and the expected future impact of competition on the business.

The Board therefore concluded that a recognized intangible asset should be amortized over its useful life to the reporting entity and that there should be no limit, presumed or maximum, on that amortization period. However, the Board agreed that an entity is required to periodically evaluate the remaining useful lives of intangible assets and revise the amortization period of an intangible asset if it is determined that the useful life of the asset is longer or shorter than originally estimated.

Amortization method

B54. In considering the methods of amortization, the Board noted that Opinion 17 required that a straight-line method be used to amortize intangible assets unless another method was demonstrated to be more appropriate. However, the Board also noted that circumstances may exist in which another method may be more appropriate, such as in the case of a license that entitles the holder to produce a finite quantity of product. The Board therefore concluded that the amortization method adopted should reflect the pattern in which the asset is consumed if that pattern can be reliably determined, with the straight-line method being used as a default.

Amortizable amount and residual value

B55. The Board noted that some intangible assets could have residual values at the ends of their useful lives to the entity that acquired them. Opinion 17 was silent about the role of residual values in determining the amortizable amount; however, both FRS 10 and IAS 38 address residual values. Thus, the Board concluded that explicit mention should be made of the use of residual values in determining amortizable amounts. Specifically, the Board decided that the residual value of an intangible asset should be assumed to be zero unless the asset's useful life to the reporting entity is less than its useful life generally and reliable evidence is available concerning the residual value. Such evidence should be in the form of either a commitment by a third party to purchase the asset at the end of its useful life or an existing market for the asset that is expected to exist at the end of the asset's useful life. During its redeliberations of the 1999 Exposure Draft, the Board clarified that the residual value is the net amount that an entity expects to obtain for an intangible asset at the end of its useful life to that entity—not at the end of its useful life in general. The Board also clarified that the residual value should be determined net of any costs to dispose of the intangible asset.

Nonamortization

B56. In developing the 1999 Exposure Draft, the Board observed that certain intangible assets may have useful lives that are indefinite and amortizing those assets would not be representationally faithful. However, because most intangible assets have finite useful lives, the Board noted that an assertion of an indefinite useful life should have to meet a high hurdle in terms of evidence to justify nonamortization. In the 1999 Exposure Draft, the Board concluded that the only evidence that would be sufficient to overcome such a hurdle would be that the intangible asset generates cash flows indefinitely and that there is an observable market for it. Examples of such intangible assets might be airport route authorities, certain trademarks, and taxicab medallions.

B57. Respondents to the 1999 Exposure Draft generally supported nonamortization of certain intangible assets; however, some respondents suggested that all intangible assets be amortized (over a maximum of 20 years). Some respondents noted that the existence of an observable market is not pertinent to the decision as to whether an asset's useful life is finite or indefinite; therefore, an observable market should not be a criterion for nonamortization of intangible assets. The Board affirmed its decision that intangible assets with indefinite useful lives should not be amortized and reconsidered the need for an observable market criterion. The Board observed that in light of the revised criteria for determining which intangible assets are to be recognized apart from goodwill, an observable market might not be necessary to support nonamortization of intangible assets deemed to have indefinite useful lives.

B58. The Board reasoned that an intangible asset that is separable or is subject to contractual or legal-based rights will have an observable market or will have identifiable cash flows associated with it. The Board noted that Concepts Statement 7 (issued after issuance of the 1999 Exposure Draft) provides guidance for using cash flows to determine the fair value of an asset in the absence of an observable market. Because there are different ways to determine fair value, the Board concluded that it was not necessary that there be an observable market for an intangible asset in order for that asset not to be amortized. Therefore, any intangible asset that is determined to have an indefinite useful life should not be amortized until that life is determined to be no longer indefinite.

B59. The Board observed that an indefinite useful life is not necessarily an infinite useful life. As noted in paragraph B45, the useful life of an intangible asset is indefinite if no limit is placed on the end of its useful life to the reporting entity. The Board also observed that indefinite does not mean the same as indeterminate. Thus, even if the precise useful life of a finite-lived intangible asset is not determinable, the intangible asset still would have to be amortized, and the amortization period would reflect the best estimate of the useful life of that asset.

B60. The Board affirmed that an intangible asset like a taxicab medallion may be considered to have an indefinite useful life because the right associated with that asset can be renewed indefinitely at little or no cost. The Board observed that paragraph 11(d) requires an entity to consider the ability to renew or extend a specified limit on an intangible asset's legal or contractual life in determining the length of its useful life to the reporting entity if evidence supports renewal or extension without substantial cost. The Board noted that whether the cost of renewal is substantial should be determined based on the relationship of the renewal cost to the fair value of the intangible asset at the time it is acquired.

B61. As noted previously, the Board agreed that an entity should periodically evaluate the remaining useful lives of intangible assets. The Board affirmed that when an intangible asset's useful life is no longer considered to be indefinite, such as when unanticipated competition enters the market, the intangible asset must be amortized over the remaining period that it is expected to contribute to cash flows. Similarly, the Board agreed that an intangible asset that initially is deemed to have a finite useful life should cease being amortized if it is subsequently determined to have an indefinite useful life, for example, due to a change in legal requirements.

Reviews for impairment

B62. The Board concluded that intangible assets that are being amortized should continue to be reviewed for impairment in accordance with FASB Statement No. 121, *Accounting for the Impairment of Long-Lived Assets and for Long-Lived Assets to Be Disposed Of.* However, the Board noted that a different approach to impairment reviews was needed for intangible assets that are not being amortized. As the Board observed in conjunction with its consideration of goodwill impairment, nonamortization places heavy reliance on the reviews for impairment. Because the cash flows associated with intangible assets having indefinite useful lives would extend into the

future indefinitely, those assets might never fail the undiscounted cash flows recoverability test in Statement 121, even if those cash flows were expected to decrease over time.

B63. Accordingly, the Board decided that the recognition of impairment losses on intangible assets with indefinite useful lives should be based on the fair values of those assets without performing the recoverability test, noting that that would be an exception to Statement 121. However, the impairment losses would be measured as the excess of the carrying amount over fair value, which is consistent with Statement 121.

B64. Because the Board eliminated the observable market criterion for nonamortization of intangible assets, the Board addressed how fair value should be determined for impairment purposes in the absence of an observable market price. When it agreed to eliminate the observable market criterion, the Board noted that Concepts Statement 7 provides guidance for using cash flows to determine the fair value of an asset in the absence of an observable market. The Board concluded that the fair value measurement guidance included in this Statement that is based on Concepts Statement 7 should be used to determine the fair value of intangible assets for impairment purposes.

B65. The 1999 Exposure Draft required that the fair value of an intangible asset not being amortized be tested for impairment on an annual basis. The Board reaffirmed that requirement after it decided that goodwill should be tested for impairment on an annual basis. The Board also concluded that an intangible asset not being amortized should be tested for impairment whenever events occur or circumstances change between annual tests indicating that the asset might be impaired. The Board agreed that the examples of impairment indicators in paragraph 5 of Statement 121 were appropriate for intangible assets not being amortized.

B66. The Board agreed that when the estimate of the remaining useful life of an intangible asset changes from finite to indefinite or vice versa, the asset should be tested for impairment (in accordance with paragraph 17) prior to the change in the method of accounting for that intangible asset. The Board observed that any resulting impairment loss would be due to a change in accounting estimate and thus, consistent with APB Opinion No. 20, *Accounting*

Changes, should be recognized as a change in estimate, not as a change in accounting principle. Therefore, that loss would be presented in the income statement in the same manner as other impairment losses (except a transitional impairment loss).

Goodwill

Initial Recognition and Measurement

B67. Statement 141 addresses the initial recognition and measurement of acquired goodwill. In that Statement, the Board concluded that acquired goodwill meets the assets definition in FASB Concepts Statement No. 6, *Elements of Financial Statements,* and the asset recognition criteria in Concepts Statement 5. In addition, the Board concluded that goodwill should be measured as the excess of the cost of an acquired entity over the sum of the amounts assigned to assets acquired and liabilities assumed. This Statement addresses the recognition and measurement of goodwill subsequent to its acquisition.

Subsequent Recognition and Measurement

B68. The Board considered the following alternatives for accounting for goodwill after it has been initially recognized: (a) write off all or a portion of goodwill immediately, (b) report goodwill as an asset that is amortized over its useful life, (c) report goodwill as an asset that is not amortized but is reviewed for impairment, or (d) report goodwill as an asset, a portion of which is amortized and a portion of which is not amortized (a mixed approach).

Immediate write-off

B69. As explained in Statement 141, the Board concluded that goodwill meets the criteria for recognition of an asset and therefore should not be written off at the date of an acquisition. In discussing whether goodwill should be written off immediately subsequent to its initial recognition, the Board noted that it would be difficult to explain why goodwill is written off immediately after having just been recognized as an asset. If goodwill had been worthless on the date of acquisition, it would not have met the assets definition and would not have been recognized. However, if goodwill had value initially, virtually no event other than a catastrophe could subsequently occur in which it instantaneously became worthless.

B70. Some respondents to both Exposure Drafts argued that goodwill should be written off immediately because of the uncertainties associated with goodwill

subsequent to its initial recognition. The Board noted that if the uncertainties associated with goodwill were so great as to mandate its write-off immediately following initial recognition, those same uncertainties should have been present when it was acquired and would have been reflected in the purchase price of the acquired entity. Furthermore, the Board questioned whether an informational purpose would be served if goodwill were to be recognized only momentarily as an asset unless it were in fact only momentarily an asset. The Board additionally noted that difficulties arise in determining the diminution in value of goodwill in subsequent periods but observed that such difficulties are not unique to goodwill. The Board accordingly concluded that immediate write-off subsequent to initial recognition was not justifiable.

A mixture of amortization and nonamortization

B71. Early in the project, the Board concluded that at least part of goodwill may be a nonwasting asset and thus may have an indefinite useful life. To the extent that recognized goodwill is a composite of several "discernible elements" having different useful lives, the Board concluded that goodwill should in concept be accounted for in such a way as to reflect those lives. That is, ideally, the portion of goodwill that has an indefinite useful life would not be amortized, and the portion of goodwill that has a finite useful life would be amortized over that life. Accordingly, the Board considered what it described as the "discernible-elements approach" as the basis for determining the portion of goodwill that should not be amortized and the amortization period for the portion of goodwill that should be amortized.

B72. The discernible-elements approach may be described broadly as follows. At acquisition, the reasons for paying a premium over the fair value of the acquired entity's identifiable net assets would be identified and documented, with that analysis supporting and justifying the amount of goodwill recorded. The recorded amount of goodwill would be allocated to each of its discernible elements based on that analysis. Those elements would be assessed to determine whether they had finite or indefinite useful lives, based on the length of time that they were expected to contribute to cash flows. The lengths of the finite useful lives also would be determined. The portion of goodwill with a finite useful life would then be amortized over the weighted-average useful life of the discernible elements. The portion of goodwill with an indefinite useful life would not be amortized but would be subject to impairment reviews (if an appropriate impairment test could be developed).

B73. The Board acknowledged, however, that such an approach would involve numerous subjective judgments on the part of entities in identifying discernible elements, allocating the purchase premium to them, and assessing their useful lives. As a result, the Board conducted a field test of its proposed approach in mid-1998. Participants supported the approach conceptually but expressed concerns about the subjective judgments required to apply it and noted that it affords opportunities for manipulation of reported amounts in financial statements. Moreover, comparisons of how those participants applied the approach to prior business combinations demonstrated significant differences, thereby underscoring concerns about its operationality. The Board concluded that the discernible-elements approach was not sufficiently operational to require its use in amortizing goodwill. Because the Board concluded that segregating the parts of goodwill that are wasting and nonwasting is not feasible, it proposed in the 1999 Exposure Draft that all goodwill should continue to be amortized.

Amortization

B74. The 1999 Exposure Draft proposed that goodwill would be amortized over its useful life and that the amortization period would not exceed 20 years. At the time, the Board observed that one argument for amortizing goodwill was that goodwill should be allocated to achieve a proper allocation of its costs to future operations. Another argument was that acquired goodwill is an asset that is consumed and replaced with internally generated goodwill and that the acquired goodwill therefore must be amortized (even though the internally generated goodwill that is replacing it cannot be recognized as an asset). Another argument was that the useful life of goodwill cannot be predicted with a satisfactory level of reliability, nor can the pattern in which goodwill diminishes be known. Hence, in the 1999 Exposure Draft the Board concluded that amortization over an arbitrary period of time was the only practical solution to an intractable problem and was preferable to the alternative of writing off goodwill immediately because that would be even less representationally faithful.

B75. The Board acknowledged that achieving an acceptable level of reliability in the form of representational faithfulness was one of the primary challenges it faced in deliberating the accounting for goodwill. The useful life of goodwill and the pattern in which it diminishes are both difficult to predict, yet its amortization depends on such predictions. As a result, the Board acknowledged that the amount amortized in any given period can be described as only a rough estimate of the decrease in goodwill during that period. However, the Board noted that users of financial statements can be expected to understand such limitations of goodwill amortization.

B76. To assist users in understanding those limitations, the Board concluded in the 1999 Exposure Draft that goodwill amortization expense should be separated from other items on the income statement to make it more transparent. In reaching that conclusion, the Board noted the anomalous accounting between acquired goodwill and internally generated goodwill and that goodwill is different from other assets. The Board concluded that those differences justified displaying charges associated with goodwill (amortization expense and impairment losses) differently, particularly because goodwill may be a nonwasting asset in part and because measures of its amortization and impairment may be less precise than other measures of income items.

B77. The Board further acknowledged constituents' assertions that many users assess goodwill charges differently than other income items, in some cases eliminating them from their analysis of earnings per share. The Board therefore concluded that a more transparent display would facilitate the analyses of those users but would not impair the analyses of users that do not assess those charges differently. Thus, the 1999 Exposure Draft proposed that goodwill charges be presented on a net-of-tax basis as a separate line item in the income statement. That line item would have been immediately preceded by a required subtotal of income after taxes but before goodwill charges and would have been immediately followed by an appropriately titled subtotal.

B78. Respondents' views on the requirements proposed in the 1999 Exposure Draft varied. Some respondents agreed with the Board that goodwill should be amortized like other assets; others favored not amortizing goodwill but testing it for impairment; still others suggested that goodwill be written off immediately. Many respondents that expressed support for the requirement to amortize goodwill stated that although amortization was not necessarily their first preference, they were willing to accept the proposed requirement given the method proposed in the 1999

Exposure Draft of displaying goodwill amortization in the income statement. Many respondents, however, did not agree with the proposal to place an arbitrary limit of 20 years on the goodwill amortization period. Others expressed the view that 20 years was too long.

Reconsideration of a nonamortization approach

B79. When it issued the 1999 Exposure Draft, the Board acknowledged that not all goodwill declines in value and that goodwill that does decline in value rarely does so on a straight-line basis. Because the Board agreed with respondents who stated that straight-line amortization of goodwill over an arbitrary period does not reflect economic reality and thus does not provide useful information, the Board reconsidered its decision to require amortization of goodwill. The Board reaffirmed its belief that immediate write-off of goodwill was not appropriate and thus focused its reconsideration on nonamortization of goodwill.

B80. As part of its reconsideration of the 1999 Exposure Draft, the Board sought additional input from its constituents. Two groups of constituents met with the Board to discuss their proposed approaches to accounting for goodwill, under which goodwill would not be amortized but would be tested for impairment. Based on those presentations, informal discussion with Board members, and additional research, a general approach to testing goodwill for impairment (general impairment approach) was developed.

B81. During October and November 2000, the Board discussed that general impairment approach with 14 companies in a variety of industries to gather input on how it might be implemented. Those field visits also included a discussion of the methods currently used by companies to value potential acquisitions, analyze the subsequent performance of an acquired business, test goodwill for impairment, and determine the amount of goodwill to write off when an acquired business is subsequently sold or disposed of. Field visit participants offered suggestions to change and improve the general impairment approach. After contemplating and summarizing the findings from those field visits, the Board reconsidered its reasons for concluding in the 1999 Exposure Draft that a nonamortization approach was *not* appropriate for goodwill.

Some portion of goodwill is a wasting asset

B82. The 1999 Exposure Draft noted that, conceptually, at least part of what is recognized as goodwill may have an indefinite useful life that could last as long as the business is considered a going concern. However, the Board concluded that some of what is recognized as goodwill might have a finite useful life partly because goodwill is measured as a residual and may include components (representing assets or components of assets) that are wasting assets and therefore should be amortized. As discussed previously, prior to issuing the 1999 Exposure Draft, the Board considered the discernible-elements approach that would have required amortization of the wasting portion of goodwill and nonamortization of the nonwasting portion (that is, the portion with an indefinite useful life). However, the Board concluded that segregating the portion of recognized goodwill that might not be a wasting asset from the portion that is a wasting asset would not be practicable.

B83. The 1999 Exposure Draft proposed that an intangible asset that could not be reliably measured should be recognized as part of goodwill. The Board decided to change that proposed treatment to require that only intangible assets that do not have an underlying contractual or other legal basis or are not capable of being separated and sold, transferred, licensed, rented, or exchanged be recognized as part of goodwill. The Board believes that application of those criteria should result in more recognition and reporting uniformity in the intangible assets that are recognized apart from goodwill. In addition, the intangible assets that would be recognized as part of goodwill using the revised criteria generally would be "goodwill like" in nature. The Board concluded that by revising the criteria for separating intangible assets from goodwill, the portion of recognized goodwill that might be wasting would be smaller than it might have been using the criteria in the 1999 Exposure Draft. Thus, Board members viewed nonamortization of all goodwill as more appropriate than it would have been under the 1999 Exposure Draft. However, the Board still needed to overcome its concerns with testing goodwill for impairment and develop an operational impairment test.

Concerns with testing goodwill for impairment

Internally generated goodwill

B84. Unlike many other assets that are tested for impairment, goodwill does not have a set of cash flows uniquely associated with it. Instead, the cash flows associated with acquired goodwill usually are intermingled with those associated with internally generated goodwill and other assets because entities generally enter into business combinations to reduce costs and achieve synergies, which entails integrating the acquired entity with the acquiring entity.

B85. In its reconsideration of the goodwill impairment issue, the Board assessed to what extent it would be appropriate to allow the accounting model to compensate for the fact that acquired goodwill might be replaced by internally generated goodwill. Many respondents noted that the current accounting model does not permit recognition of internally generated intangible assets, including goodwill. They also noted that a good portion of an entity's value may be related to those unrecognized intangible assets. Respondents mentioned the growing disparity between the market capitalization of many entities and their book values as strong evidence of that unrecognized value. Board members concluded that it is appropriate to assume that acquired goodwill is being replaced by internally generated goodwill provided that an entity is able to maintain the overall value of goodwill (for example, by expending resources on advertising and customer service).

Integration of an acquired entity

B86. Prior to issuing the 1999 Exposure Draft, the Board's discussions of goodwill impairment tests generally centered on testing goodwill specific to an acquisition. The Board concluded that keeping track of acquisition-specific goodwill for impairment purposes would be almost impossible once an acquired entity was integrated with the acquiring entity. The Board considered the alternative of testing goodwill at the combined entity (total company) level to be unacceptable. The Board learned in its field visits that synergies occur below the combined entity level and that management is often held accountable for acquisitions at a lower level. In addition, Board members noted that the higher the level of review, the more difficult it would be to develop a robust impairment test and the less confident investors would be with the results of the impairment tests. The Board considered further the fact that an acquired entity often is integrated with a part of the acquiring entity and concluded that, in those cases, goodwill should be tested for impairment in conjunction with more than just the net assets of the acquired entity. The Board concluded that, in most cases, it is appropriate to test goodwill for impairment in the aggregate at a level higher than that of the acquired entity and lower than

that of the combined entity. Thus, the 2001 Exposure Draft proposed that goodwill be tested for impairment at a level referred to as a reporting unit. The Board envisioned that a reporting unit generally would be at a level somewhere between a reportable operating segment (as defined in FASB Statement No. 131, *Disclosures about Segments of an Enterprise and Related Information*) and an asset group (as that term is used in Statement 121). (Paragraphs B101–B112 discuss the reporting unit in more detail.)

B87. The Board noted that the anomalies that result from the differences in how acquired goodwill and internally generated goodwill are accounted for also justify a departure from the current model of accounting for goodwill on an acquisition-specific basis subsequent to an acquisition. The Board observed that an entity often has internally generated goodwill and goodwill-like assets that are not recognized on its balance sheet. Thus, it would be infrequent that the value of the actual (recognized and unrecognized) goodwill and goodwill-like assets of an entity would be less than the amount portrayed as goodwill in its balance sheet even if the value of the goodwill associated with a specific acquisition declined subsequent to its acquisition. This point was significant to some Board members in agreeing to accept a nonamortization approach and depart from the normal acquisition-specific model for testing goodwill for impairment.

Undiscounted cash flows

B88. Prior to issuing the 1999 Exposure Draft, the Board discussed testing goodwill for impairment using an undiscounted cash flow method similar to that required for long-lived assets in Statement 121. The Board concluded at that time that a similar method would not be appropriate for goodwill because the cash flows in question could continue for many years—longer than most other assets.

B89. Another reason the Board ultimately decided against using an undiscounted cash flow method to test goodwill for impairment was that constituents generally agreed with the 1999 Exposure Draft proposal that intangible assets that are not being amortized should not be tested for impairment in accordance with Statement 121 and thus should be excluded from the scope of that Statement. The 1999 Exposure Draft would have required that an intangible asset not being amortized be tested for impairment on an annual basis and that an impairment loss be recognized if the carrying amount of the intangible asset exceeded its fair value. That proposed fair value impairment test would have differed from the impairment test used for all other assets. Thus, the Board decided to continue to pursue an approach that would exclude nonamortized intangible assets—including goodwill—from the scope of Statement 121 and to test for impairment using a fair-value-based approach.

Decision usefulness

B90. During its field visits, the Board learned that, in addition to the many analysts that ignore goodwill amortization expense in their analyses, many entities ignore goodwill amortization expense in measuring operating performance for internal reporting purposes; rather, they hold management responsible for the amount invested in an acquired entity (including goodwill). A number of field visit participants noted, for example, that in measuring return on net assets, management would include goodwill in the denominator (asset base) but would exclude the amortization expense from the numerator (operating earnings). Thus, Board members acknowledged that not only do many users of financial statements ignore goodwill amortization expense in making investment and credit decisions, entities often do not consider goodwill amortization expense in evaluating the performance of management.

B91. In addition, Board members noted that reported earnings often increase in the period following the final amortization expense of goodwill even though operations may not have changed significantly. Some Board members believe that result is not representationally faithful because that earnings increase arises from the cessation of prior "doubling-up" of expenses related to goodwill, which occurs when the income statement is charged for expiring goodwill (amortization of past outlays for acquired goodwill) at the same time it is charged for current outlays to create goodwill (internally generated goodwill). As a result, reported earnings in those prior periods were decreased in such a way that they did not faithfully reflect the economic changes that occurred in those periods.

Nonamortization in some or all cases

B92. Upon reconsideration of all of those issues, the Board concluded that an acceptable impairment test could be developed based on aggregate goodwill rather than only acquired goodwill and that nonamor-tization of goodwill coupled with a fair-value-based impairment test would result in more representationally faithful and decision-useful financial information. The Board then considered whether it was appropriate to permit entities to amortize acquired goodwill in certain circumstances, noting that impairment issues would have to be considered regardless of whether goodwill was being amortized.

B93. The Board was doubtful that it could develop operational criteria to identify the circumstances in which goodwill should be amortized. The Board noted that if it were to permit both nonamortization and amortization of goodwill (a variation of the mixed approach), entities effectively would have a free choice as to which method to use to account for goodwill, resulting in a significant potential for noncomparable financial reporting among entities. More important, because the Board concluded that its approach would result in more representationally faithful financial information, to permit goodwill to be amortized would be inappropriate.

B94. The Board also concluded that not amortizing goodwill in all circumstances would provide information that is more useful to investors than adopting a mixed approach under which goodwill would be permitted to be amortized in some circumstances. The Board observed that adopting a nonamortization approach for all goodwill would not mean that goodwill would never be written down or that it would only be written down occasionally in large amounts. Board members noted that if the carrying amount of goodwill of a reporting unit cannot be maintained, the impairment test would accommodate both periodic and irregular write-downs of goodwill to reflect that decline in value. For example, an entity might acquire a mature business that is considered a "cash cow" and is not expected to grow. Specifically, the acquired business is expected to generate cash flows for a limited period of time as it winds down its operations and eventually ceases to operate. The Board acknowledged that if that acquired business were to be operated as a separate reporting unit, that reporting unit would recognize goodwill impairment losses on a regular basis until its goodwill is reduced to zero, presumably when operations cease. Thus, the Board concluded in the 2001 Exposure Draft to depart from the prior view that all goodwill should be amortized and adopted a nonamortization approach for all goodwill.

Nonamortization of goodwill and related impairment tests

B95. Most respondents to the 2001 Exposure Draft agreed with the Board's conclusions on the fundamental aspects of the proposed nonamortization approach. They said that nonamortization of goodwill, coupled with impairment testing and appropriate disclosure, promotes transparency in financial reporting and thus provides useful information to those who rely on financial statements. In addition, respondents noted that not amortizing goodwill is consistent with both how an entity manages its business and how investors view goodwill.

B96. Most respondents that disagreed with the Board's conclusions did so because they consider goodwill to be a wasting asset or because the proposed nonamortization approach in essence allows acquisitive entities to capitalize internally generated goodwill. Respondents argued that effectively capitalizing internally generated goodwill is inconsistent with the general accounting model and introduces an unlevel playing field favoring entities that grow by acquisition rather than internally. Most respondents who disagreed with nonamortization of goodwill suggested that goodwill be amortized over a life of up to 20 years with "below-the-line" income statement presentation, as proposed in the 1999 Exposure Draft.

B97. The Board acknowledged that the proposed impairment test would ensure only that the carrying amount of goodwill of a reporting unit does not exceed the total goodwill (acquired and internally generated) of that unit and thus could be viewed as effectively capitalizing internally generated goodwill. However, acquired goodwill cannot be isolated from internally generated goodwill after the acquired business is integrated with a larger part of the acquiring entity. Moreover, acquired goodwill and goodwill created subsequent to the acquisition cannot be separately identified even if the acquired business is not integrated with other parts of the acquiring entity.

B98. Without the ability to measure internally generated goodwill and factor that measure into the impairment test, the carrying amount of goodwill that is tested for impairment always will be shielded by goodwill internally generated both before and after the acquisition. Thus, the Board was unable to determine a way to apply a nonamortization approach coupled with impairment testing and avoid the possibility of what some describe as "backdoor" capitali-

zation of internally generated goodwill. The Board noted that some consider amortization of goodwill to be unfair to entities whose growth comes largely from acquisitions rather than from internal sources because of the "doubling-up" of expenses that occurs within a specific reporting period as the result of expensing current outlays that generate goodwill (such as advertising and research and development outlays) and concurrently amortizing acquired goodwill. Thus, the Board did not consider it possible to develop a method of accounting for acquired goodwill that all would agree established a level playing field in all circumstances. Accordingly, the Board focused on which method better reflects the economic impact of goodwill on an entity.

B99. The Board reaffirmed its decision that nonamortization of goodwill combined with an adequate impairment test will provide financial information that more faithfully reflects the economic impact of acquired goodwill on the value of an entity than does amortization of goodwill. The Board concluded that the goodwill impairment test prescribed by this Statement will adequately capture goodwill impairment. It thus concluded that nonamortization of goodwill will result in the most useful financial information within the constraints of the current accounting model and available valuation techniques.

B100. Some respondents to the 2001 Exposure Draft stated that while their preference is an impairment-only (nonamortization) model for goodwill, it would be appropriate to amortize goodwill in certain circumstances. Examples include acquisition of a business that is a cash cow, a small business that is unable to devote resources to the impairment test, and acquisitions of high-tech companies. In developing the 2001 Exposure Draft, the Board considered whether a mixed model would be more appropriate than an impairment-only model. At that time, the Board was concerned that unless operational criteria could be developed that would limit amortization of goodwill to specific circumstances, preparers might interpret this Statement as allowing free choice in accounting for goodwill. In addition, the Board was not confident that operational criteria could be developed that would distinguish those circumstances in which amortization would be appropriate from those in which it would *not* be appropriate. The Board noted that allowing some entities to amortize goodwill might impair comparability in financial reporting. For those same reasons, the Board concluded that amortization of goodwill should not be permitted in any circumstance, noting that the impairment test will capture steadily declining goodwill provided that the level of testing is low enough.

Reporting unit

B101. The 2001 Exposure Draft proposed that goodwill be tested for impairment at the reporting unit level. A reporting unit was defined in that Exposure Draft as the lowest level of an entity that is a business and that can be distinguished, physically and operationally and for internal reporting purposes, from the other activities, operations, and assets of the entity. As defined, a reporting unit could be no higher than a reportable operating segment (segment) and would generally be lower than that level of reporting. However, the Board acknowledged that for some entities, a reporting unit would be the same as a segment and that for narrowly focused entities, the entity as a whole might be one reporting unit.

B102. The Board initially considered testing goodwill at the segment level in all cases, based on the presumption that that level generally is the lowest reporting level that captures all of the goodwill of a specific acquisition. However, field visit participants informed the Board that they often allocate goodwill below the segment level—for example, to operating or business unit levels. After considering the views of field visit participants and others, the Board concluded that the Statement should permit some flexibility in the level at which goodwill is tested for impairment and that it should allow the level to differ as appropriate from entity to entity and industry to industry. Board members noted that goodwill by its nature will be associated with the operations of an entity at different levels—possibly different levels within the same overall entity. The Board's intent was that a reporting unit would be the level of internal reporting that reflects the way an entity manages its business or operations and to which goodwill naturally would be associated.

B103. It was important to the Board that the impairment test be performed at a level at which information about the operations of an entity and the assets and liabilities that support those operations are documented for internal reporting purposes (as well as possibly for external reporting purposes). That approach reflects the Board's belief that the information an entity reports for internal use will reflect the way the overall entity is managed. Therefore, the Board did not intend the concept of a reporting unit and the requirement to test goodwill for impairment at that

level to create a new internal reporting level. The Board believed that information entities currently generate about their operations, such as cash flows by business unit for planning purposes, would be used in measuring the fair value of a reporting unit. Similarly, information about the underlying assets and liabilities currently reported by an entity, such as a balance sheet for each division, would be used to identify the net assets of a reporting unit.

B104. However, many respondents to the 2001 Exposure Draft interpreted the reporting unit to be a level much lower than the level the Board had intended. Some respondents asserted that an entity could have hundreds or possibly thousands of reporting units. Also, there were differences of opinion about whether the reporting unit as defined in the 2001 Exposure Draft allowed for the flexibility that the Board had intended. Many respondents asserted that they would be required to test goodwill for impairment at a level that had no bearing on how the acquisition was integrated into the acquiring entity or how the overall combined entity was managed.

B105. Most respondents who disagreed with using the reporting unit as defined in the 2001 Exposure Draft suggested that goodwill be tested at the reportable segment level or at the operating segment level (both as defined in Statement 131). Respondents stated that testing goodwill for impairment at a level based on Statement 131 would be more operational and more consistently applied. Respondents observed that public entities currently apply the operating segment concept for financial reporting purposes and have processes in place to identify and accumulate information about operating segments. Thus, the operating segment concept is more easily understood than the proposed reporting unit concept and also takes advantage of the processes currently in place. In addition, respondents noted that segments would be a more manageable level for impairment testing because segments are changed far less often than lower level units. It was also observed that because financial statement users are more familiar with Statement 131, testing goodwill for impairment at the segment level would provide information that financial statement users can relate to other segment information provided in the financial statements.

B106. However, many respondents who suggested that goodwill be tested for impairment at the segment level also suggested that entities be permitted to test goodwill for impairment at a lower "reporting unit" level as long as the entity documented its policy for doing so and applied that policy on a consistent basis. The Board reaffirmed its belief that there should be a common methodology for determining the unit of account (the reporting unit) and that permitting exceptions would raise comparability and unlevel playing field issues.

B107. Because it did not intend the requirement to test goodwill for impairment at the reporting unit level to create a new level of reporting and because of concerns about inconsistent application, the Board reconsidered the definition of a reporting unit proposed in the 2001 Exposure Draft. The Board considered and rejected attempting to revise the reporting unit definition to better describe what the Board originally intended. While revising the definition would allow for the most flexibility in determining the appropriate level at which to test goodwill for impairment, Board members did not think it would be possible to devise a definition that would be interpreted and applied in a consistent manner.

B108. The Board agreed with respondents who suggested that the level of impairment testing should relate to the segment reporting requirements of Statement 131. The Board thus considered requiring goodwill to be tested for impairment at the operating segment level in all instances. An operating segment is defined in Statement 131 (paragraph 10) as a component of an enterprise:

   (a) That engages in business activities from which it may earn revenues and incur expenses (including revenues and expenses relating to transactions with other components of the same enterprise),

   (b) Whose operating results are regularly reviewed by the enterprise's chief operating decision maker to make decisions about resources to be allocated to the segment and assess its performance, and

   (c) For which discrete financial information is available.

B109. The Board concluded that in many cases the operating segment level may be too high a level at which to perform the goodwill impairment test. That conclusion was based on the requests of respondents that the Statement permit entities to test goodwill for impairment below the operating segment level if the entity is able to do so.

B110. Consequently, the Board considered defining a reporting unit to be one reporting level below the operating segment level, which would be the business units or components of an operating segment whose operating results are regularly reviewed by the segment manager. (As described in Statement 131, segment managers are the direct reports of the chief operating decision maker.) Under that approach, reporting units would align with how operating results are regularly reviewed by the segment manager to make decisions about resource allocation and to assess segment performance. That definition also would be similar to what the Board intended the proposed definition of a reporting unit to capture.

B111. The Board concluded that this Statement should retain the term *reporting unit* but should redefine the term using the concepts in Statement 131 so that the concept would be familiar to both preparers and users. However, the Board wanted to retain some flexibility in application of the reporting unit definition such that a reporting unit could vary somewhat from entity to entity and even within an entity, as appropriate under the circumstances. Thus, as defined in this Statement, a component of an operating segment is a reporting unit if the component is a business for which discrete financial information is available and segment management regularly reviews the operating results of that component. However, the Board acknowledged that even though segment management might review the operating results of a number of business units (components of an operating segment), components with similar economic characteristics should be aggregated into one reporting unit. The Board reasoned that the benefits of goodwill would be shared by components of an operating segment that have similar economic characteristics and that requiring goodwill to be allocated among components with similar economic characteristics would be arbitrary and unnecessary for purposes of impairment testing. Consider an operating segment that consists of four components. Segment management reviews the operating results of each component, all of which are businesses for which discrete financial information is available. If three of those components share similar economic characteristics, the operating segment would consist of two reporting units. The component that has economic characteristics dissimilar from the other components of the operating segment would be its own reporting unit, and the three components with similar economic characteristics would constitute one reporting unit.

B112. Therefore, reporting units will vary depending on the level at which performance of the segment is reviewed, how many businesses the operating segment includes, and the similarity of those businesses. Thus, as in the 2001 Exposure Draft, a reporting unit could be the same as an operating segment, which could be the same as a reportable segment, which could be the same as the entity as a whole (entity level). Board members observed that the revised definition of a reporting unit will yield the same results for many entities as was intended by the reporting unit definition proposed in the 2001 Exposure Draft.

Nonpublic entities

B113. Having decided that the determination of reporting units should be linked to segment reporting in Statement 131, the Board considered whether to make an exception or provide additional guidance for entities that are not required to apply Statement 131. The Board concluded that although nonpublic entities are not required to follow the segment disclosure requirements in Statement 131, those entities should *not* be exempt from testing goodwill for impairment at the reporting unit level. The Board noted that many nonpublic entities have internal reporting systems that currently gather or are capable of gathering the data necessary to test goodwill for impairment at a level below the entity level. As with public entities, the reporting unit level for many nonpublic entities may be the same as the entity level. Thus, nonpublic entities would not be precluded from testing for impairment at the entity level—if in fact that level meets the definition of a reporting unit. The Board believes that the guidance in this Statement and Statement 131 is sufficient for nonpublic entities with more than one reporting unit to test goodwill for impairment at the reporting unit level.

Assigning acquired assets and assumed liabilities to reporting units

B114. The 2001 Exposure Draft proposed that for purposes of testing goodwill for impairment, the assets and liabilities of an acquired entity (including goodwill) that would be used in the operations of a reporting unit or that relate to those operations would have to be assigned to that reporting unit as of the acquisition date. The Board concluded that assigning assets and liabilities to reporting units would be necessary to make the goodwill impairment test that incorporates the values of those net assets operational. The Board noted that to the extent corporate assets or liabilities related to a reporting unit (such as pension and environmental liabilities), those assets and liabilities should be assigned as well.

B115. Respondents to the 2001 Exposure Draft expressed concerns with the requirement to assign goodwill and other assets and liabilities to reporting units. Respondents were particularly concerned with the requirement to assign corporate assets and liabilities to reporting units because of the difficulty, cost, inconsistency of application, and loss of synergies in making what they viewed as subjective and arbitrary allocation decisions. Other respondents disagreed with that requirement, noting that many businesses are best managed with the evaluation and responsibility of corporate assets and liabilities occurring at the overall entity level. Some respondents noted that their concerns would be minimized if goodwill were to be tested for impairment at the segment level instead of the proposed reporting unit level.

B116. The Board noted that the 2001 Exposure Draft would not have required *all* acquired assets and assumed liabilities to be assigned to reporting units, only those that would be employed in or were related to the operations of a unit. The Board concluded that the objective of the assignment process should be to ensure that the assets and liabilities that are assigned to a reporting unit are the same net assets that are considered in determining the fair value of that unit—an "apples-to-apples" comparison. Therefore, to the extent corporate items are reflected in the value of a reporting unit, they should be assigned to the reporting unit. For example, pension liabilities related to active employees would normally be assumed when acquiring a business; thus, that type of liability generally would be considered in determining the fair value of a reporting unit.

B117. The Board agreed that this Statement should clarify that an asset or liability should be assigned to a reporting unit only if it would be considered in determining the fair value of the unit. To do otherwise would not result in an apples-to-apples comparison. The Board confirmed that another objective of the exercise is to assign to a reporting unit all of the assets and liabilities that would be necessary for that reporting unit to operate as a business. Board members noted that it is those net assets that will generate the cash flows used to determine the fair value of a reporting unit.

B118. The Board agreed to retain the general guidance proposed in the 2001 Exposure Draft for determining how to assign assets and liabilities to reporting units. That is, the methodology used to assign assets and liabilities to reporting units should be reasonable, supportable, and applied in a consistent manner. Board members observed that it is possible for a reasonable allocation method to be very general.

Assigning goodwill to reporting units

B119. The 2001 Exposure Draft included limited guidance on how to assign acquired goodwill to reporting units. Respondents to the 2001 Exposure Draft questioned whether an entity would be required to assign goodwill only to the reporting units where the net assets acquired have been assigned and whether it would be possible to have overall "enterprise" goodwill that would not be assigned to any reporting unit. Respondents suggested that enterprise goodwill could be tested for impairment at the total entity level.

B120. The Board affirmed that all goodwill should be allocated to reporting units. Board members observed that if some portion of goodwill is deemed to relate to the entity as a whole, that portion of goodwill should be assigned to all of the reporting units of the entity in a reasonable and supportable manner. The Board also concluded that goodwill should be assigned to the reporting units of the acquiring entity that are expected to benefit from the synergies of the combination even though those units may not be assigned any other assets or any liabilities of the acquired entity.

B121. The Board acknowledged that the requirement in this Statement to assign what some view as corporate assets and liabilities to reporting units could be considered inconsistent with the requirements in Statement 131. For purposes of reporting information about assets by segment, entities are required by Statement 131 to include in reported segment assets only those assets that are included in the measure of the segment's assets that is used by the chief operating decision maker. Thus, goodwill and other assets and liabilities may not be included in reported segment assets. This Statement does not require that goodwill and all other related assets and liabilities assigned to reporting units for purposes of testing goodwill for impairment be reflected in the entity's reported segments. However, even though an asset may not be included in reported segment assets, the asset (or liability) should be allocated to a reporting unit for purposes of testing for impairment if it meets the criteria in paragraph 32 of this Statement. This Statement also requires that the amount of goodwill in each segment be disclosed in the notes to the financial statements.

Reorganization of reporting structure

B122. The 2001 Exposure Draft did not address how goodwill and the other assets and liabilities that make up a reporting unit should be reassigned when an entity reorganizes its reporting structure. The Board concluded that the guidance provided in the Statement for assigning acquired assets and assumed liabilities should be used to reassign assets and liabilities of reporting units that are reorganized. However, this Statement requires goodwill to be reassigned to reorganized reporting units using a relative fair value allocation method similar to that used to determine the amount of goodwill to allocate to a business being disposed of. The Board concluded that reorganizing a reporting unit is similar to selling off a business within that reporting unit; thus, the same allocation methodology should be used.

Recognition and measurement of an impairment loss

B123. In the 2001 Exposure Draft, the Board concluded that a fair-value-based impairment test should estimate the implied fair value of goodwill, which would be compared with the carrying amount of goodwill to determine whether goodwill is impaired. The Board acknowledged that it is not possible to directly measure the fair value of goodwill, noting that goodwill is measured as a residual amount at acquisition. The Board concluded that a method similar to the method of allocating the purchase price to the net assets acquired could be used to measure the value of goodwill subsequent to its initial recognition. Thus, the Board decided that some measure of net assets of a reporting unit should be subtracted from the fair value of a reporting unit to determine the implied fair value of that reporting unit's goodwill.

B124. The Board then considered how to measure the value of net assets that will be subtracted from the fair value of a reporting unit to determine the implied fair value of goodwill. The Board considered the following alternatives: (a) the fair value of recognized net assets (excluding goodwill), (b) the fair value of *both* recognized *and* unrecognized net assets (excluding goodwill), (c) the book value of recognized net assets (excluding goodwill), and (d) the book value of recognized net assets (excluding goodwill) adjusted for any known differences between book value and fair value. The Board concluded that subtracting the fair value of *both* recognized *and* unrecognized net assets would result in an estimate closest to the implied fair value of goodwill. However, the

Board concluded that the cost of identifying the un-recognized net assets and determining their fair values in addition to the costs of determining the fair values of the recognized net assets outweighed the benefits of that alternative.

B125. The Board acknowledged that subtracting the fair value of only *recognized* net assets (excluding goodwill) from the fair value of a reporting unit generally would result in a residual amount that includes more than acquired goodwill. That is, the residual amount also would include the fair value of unrecognized goodwill and other intangible assets that were internally generated both before and after an acquisition and the fair value of any unrecognized goodwill and other intangible assets that were acquired in prior business combinations accounted for by the pooling method, as well as asset "step-ups" in basis that were not recognized. The Board referred to the above amounts as adding "cushion" to the estimate of the implied fair value of goodwill. The Board was not as concerned about the cushion resulting from unrecognized internally generated goodwill as it was about the cushion arising from other unrecognized assets of the reporting unit because the latter confuses different types of assets while the former does not. The Board noted that if the *book value* of recognized net assets was subtracted, the cushion also would include the unrecognized increase (or decrease) in the fair value of the reporting unit's recognized net assets.

B126. The Board concluded that subtracting the fair value of recognized net assets (excluding goodwill) would result in the next best estimate of the implied fair value of goodwill, even though it would include an additional cushion attributable to the fair value of the *unrecognized* net assets. Even though that choice had its associated costs, after considering the remaining two choices—subtracting the book value or adjusted book value of recognized net assets—both of which generally would include even more cushion, the Board decided that subtracting the fair value of recognized net assets would strike an acceptable balance between costs and benefits. Thus, the 2001 Exposure Draft proposed that the implied fair value of reporting unit goodwill be estimated by subtracting the fair value of the recognized net assets of a reporting unit from the fair value of the reporting unit as a whole. If the resulting implied fair value of goodwill were less than the carrying amount of that goodwill, an impairment loss equal to that difference should have been recognized.

B127. While a few respondents to the 2001 Exposure Draft supported the proposed impairment test, most respondents asserted that the proposed test would not be cost-effective. Their concerns related primarily to the requirement to determine the fair value of recognized net assets (in order to estimate the implied fair value of goodwill). Most respondents said that the costs related to estimating the fair value of recognized net assets did not outweigh the benefits associated with having a better estimate of the implied fair value of goodwill to use in the impairment test. Respondents noted that a goodwill impairment test by its very nature will include some level of imprecision.

B128. Respondents suggested a variety of approaches to test goodwill for impairment, including using an approach similar to that in Statement 121 (and the June 2000 FASB Exposure Draft, *Accounting for the Impairment or Disposal of Long-Lived Assets and for Obligations Associated with Disposal Activities,* which would amend Statement 121). Some respondents argued for a Statement 121 approach on the basis of familiarity, reliability, practicality, and consistency. However, the recoverability test in Statement 121 uses undiscounted cash flows, and the Board again rejected that approach because it results in an unacceptably large cushion in the impairment test.

B129. Very few respondents to the 2001 Exposure Draft took exception to using the fair value of a reporting unit as the starting point for the impairment test or with the conceptual soundness of basing the impairment test on the implied fair value of goodwill. Thus, the Board agreed that it would consider only an approach that began with a determination of the fair value of a reporting unit, and it reaffirmed its conclusion that a fair-value-based impairment model should be used for goodwill. The Board thus sought to develop an approach that would lessen the cost of performing the impairment test.

B130. The suggestion that was provided most often by respondents to reduce the cost of the impairment test was to compare the fair value of a reporting unit with its carrying amount, including goodwill (carrying amount approach). Respondents observed that carrying amounts may be a reasonable proxy for fair values. Under that approach, if the carrying amount of a reporting unit exceeds its fair value, goodwill would be considered impaired, and an impairment loss would be recognized equal to that excess. The carrying amount approach is the least costly of all the suggested approaches because it requires only an estimate of the reporting unit's fair value and not of the fair value of its associated assets and liabilities.

B131. The Board decided not to adopt the carrying amount approach for the dual purpose of (a) identifying situations in which goodwill is impaired and (b) measuring the amount of impairment in the situations identified. The Board noted that comparing the carrying amount of a reporting unit, including goodwill, with the fair value of that unit could not be said to be an estimate of the implied fair value of goodwill. The difference generally would include too much cushion, and that approach also would be inconsistent with the way in which impairments of other assets and asset groups are measured under Statement 121.

B132. Some respondents suggested that the Board adopt a two-step approach if it found the measure of impairment under a carrying amount approach unacceptable. They noted that the comparison of the carrying amount with the fair value of a reporting unit could be the first step—a screen to identify potential goodwill impairment. If the carrying amount of a reporting unit exceeded its fair value, the actual amount of impairment loss could be measured on a different basis.

B133. The Board considered the extent to which adding the carrying amount comparison as a screen to identify potential goodwill impairment would allow possibly significant impairments to go unrecognized. The Board noted that use of that screen would add a cushion to the impairment test proposed in the 2001 Exposure Draft equal to the difference between the carrying amounts of tangible and intangible assets and their fair values—with the greater disparity likely to be in the intangible assets. That cushion would exist, however, only if the value of the intangible assets is being maintained or increased. In that situation, the value of goodwill is most likely also being maintained. That is, the Board observed that the appreciation of intangible assets and the appreciation of goodwill likely are correlated to some extent. The Board observed that the converse is likely also to be true—if the value of goodwill is *not* being maintained, the value of intangible assets probably also is not being maintained, and the value of recognized intangible assets would provide little or no cushion to the impairment test. Thus, using a carrying amount comparison as a screen for potential goodwill impairment likely would not allow as many impairments to go unrecognized as it might at first appear to do.

B134. Thus, the Board concluded that adding a carrying amount comparison to the impairment test would reduce the costs of applying the goodwill impairment test without unduly compromising the integrity of the model. Having decided that a two-step test would be a reasonable response to the cost-benefit challenge posed by its constituents, the Board considered whether to retain the measure of impairment proposed in the 2001 Exposure Draft or whether an improved measure would be feasible.

B135. As noted in paragraph B124, in developing the 2001 Exposure Draft, the Board observed that the best estimate of goodwill impairment would be based on a purchase price allocation approach in which the fair value of both recognized and unrecognized net assets is subtracted from the fair value of a reporting unit to determine the implied fair value of goodwill. Because that method is the same method by which goodwill is initially measured, the resulting reported amount of goodwill (after the impairment charge) would be the best available estimate consistent with the initial measurement of goodwill upon its acquisition. The Board rejected that approach in its deliberations of the 2001 Exposure Draft because it considered the process of identifying unrecognized net assets and determining their fair values to be too costly to require on a relatively frequent basis. However, the Board reasoned that if the measurement of goodwill impairment was preceded by a less costly screen for potential impairment, the cost of measuring goodwill impairment using a purchase price allocation process would be justifiable. The measurement process would be required relatively infrequently, and it would produce better information in those situations in which there was potential goodwill impairment. Therefore, this Statement requires goodwill impairment to be measured using a purchase price allocation process. That is, if the first step of the goodwill impairment test indicates potential impairment, then the implied fair value of goodwill would be estimated by allocating the already estimated fair value of the reporting unit to all the assets and liabilities associated with that unit, including unrecognized intangible assets.

B136. The Board concluded that this Statement should require that the allocation of the total fair value of the reporting unit to its net assets follow the purchase price allocation guidance in Statement 141. That process is familiar to all entities that would be testing goodwill for impairment because it is the same process the entity would have used to initially measure the goodwill recognized in its financial statements.

When to test goodwill for impairment

B137. After discussions with field visit participants, the Board proposed in the 2001 Exposure Draft that goodwill be tested for impairment whenever events occur or circumstances change indicating potential impairment (an events-and-circumstances approach) and not on an annual basis. The Board acknowledged that management often reviews the operating performance of reporting units on a regular basis; therefore, a requirement for an annual impairment test might be redundant and thus might involve unnecessary time and expense.

B138. The 1999 Exposure Draft included examples of events and circumstances that would give rise to a goodwill impairment test (in addition to the examples in Statement 121). The Board revised those examples to reflect its decision that goodwill should be tested for impairment at the reporting unit level. The 2001 Exposure Draft included the revised examples of events or circumstances that would require an entity to test goodwill in one or more reporting units for impairment (impairment indicators). The Board affirmed that the list of impairment indicators is not meant to be exhaustive and that an individual event, as well as a series of events, might give rise to the need for an impairment test.

B139. Most respondents agreed with the Board's conclusion in the 2001 Exposure Draft to test goodwill for impairment using an events-and-circumstances approach. Most of those respondents stated that such an approach would be cost-effective because it would generally result in testing goodwill for impairment less frequently than once a year and because the fair value of each reporting unit would not have to be determined annually. However, respondents expressed concern that because the proposed list of impairment indicators included events that occur often in the common course of business, goodwill impairment tests would be required more frequently than is feasible. Respondents offered a number of suggestions for ways to reduce the frequency of an impairment test under an events-and-circumstances approach, including requiring the impairment test only if two or more indicators are present and using the indicators as a guide for testing instead of as a mandatory requirement to test for impairment.

B140. Some respondents disagreed with the proposal that goodwill be tested for impairment using only an events-and-circumstances approach, preferring that goodwill be tested for impairment annually. Attestors noted that under an annual approach, they would be able to provide positive assurance about whether goodwill is impaired, rather than negative assurance that no event occurred or circumstance changed that would require an impairment test. Other respondents noted that an annual approach would result in more consistent application and comparable financial statements and would reduce the subjectivity of and second-guessing about the timing of an impairment charge.

B141. The Board noted that although most respondents supported the proposed events-and-circumstances approach, the concerns that were expressed with the list of impairment indicators suggest that such an approach might not be operational. That is, even if the list of impairment indicators was revised, the revised list still might not be applied or interpreted consistently—thereby undermining the integrity of the impairment model itself. Furthermore, if goodwill was tested for impairment on an annual basis, the recognition of an impairment loss would be less dependent on the subjective interpretation of the performance of reporting units. In addition, Board members observed that goodwill impairments generally do not occur suddenly but occur as a result of a series of events that might not be captured by a list of impairment indicators. An annual test would provide a safety net for impairments that arise as the result of a series of events.

B142. A principal reason that the Board concluded not to propose an annual test in the 2001 Exposure Draft was the cost associated with the proposed impairment test. Having decided to reduce the cost of the impairment test by adding a screen for potential impairment and also to decrease in many cases the number of reporting units, the Board observed that the cost of an annual impairment test would be lower than under the 2001 Exposure Draft, thereby making an annual approach more feasible.

B143. The Board acknowledged that an annual test would entail some cost to preparers because fair value determinations will have to be made for each reporting unit. However, for most entities, the most labor-intensive and potentially expensive part of the process relates to assigning goodwill and net assets to reporting units and establishing the model and key assumptions that will be used to measure the fair value of each reporting unit. Board members observed that those costs will be incurred whether goodwill is tested for impairment annually or on an events-and-circumstances basis. Thus, once the initial fair value of each reporting unit has been determined, the incremental costs associated with annual testing generally will be much lower than those one-time costs.

B144. The Board concluded that the incremental cost of an annual impairment test can be justified because of the benefit to users of financial statements in the form of positive assurance that the carrying amount of goodwill is not overstated. Annual testing would also enhance comparability between entities, since every entity would be testing goodwill for impairment with the same frequency.

B145. Integral to the Board's decision that goodwill should be tested for impairment annually was the view that an annual requirement should not call for a "fresh start" effort in determining the fair value of each reporting unit every year. That is, many entities should be able to conclude that the fair value of a reporting unit is greater than its carrying amount without actually recomputing the fair value of the reporting unit. That conclusion could be supported if the last fair value determination exceeded the carrying amount by a substantial margin and nothing had happened since the last fair value determination that would make the likelihood that the current fair value of the reporting unit would be less than its current carrying amount remote. However, if a recent acquisition, divestiture, or reorganization affected a reporting unit, the fair value of the reporting unit would need to be remeasured for purposes of impairment testing.

B146. The Board noted that testing annually for goodwill impairment would not negate the need for management to be aware of events occurring or circumstances changing between annual tests indicating potential impairment. Should there be such an event or circumstance, an entity would be required to test goodwill for impairment at that time and not wait until the next annual test. Board members observed that when an impairment indicator arises toward the end of an interim reporting period, an entity might not be able to complete the goodwill impairment test before its financial statements are issued. The Board concluded that it would be appropriate for an entity to recognize its best estimate of that impairment loss in those circumstances.

Benchmark assessment

B147. The 2001 Exposure Draft proposed that a benchmark assessment be performed in conjunction with most significant acquisitions and in conjunction with a reorganization of an entity's reporting structure. As proposed, a benchmark assessment involved identifying and documenting the goodwill and net assets associated with a reporting unit, the expectations related to the performance of the unit, and the valuation model and key assumptions to be used in measuring the fair value of the reporting unit. In addition, an entity would have been required to measure the fair value of the reporting unit, compare the fair value of the reporting unit with its carrying amount, and possibly test goodwill for impairment. The purpose of the benchmark assessment was to establish a starting point for future goodwill impairment tests.

B148. Most respondents to the 2001 Exposure Draft disagreed with the specific steps of the benchmark assessment, stating that the assessment would be time-consuming, costly to implement and comply with, and in excess of what is necessary to establish a baseline for performing future impairment tests. Most respondents agreed that entities should be required to document expectations, assumptions, and valuation models after an acquisition. However, respondents stated that a determination of the fair value of the unit should not be required unless an impairment indicator is present.

B149. The Board concluded that a requirement to perform a benchmark assessment was no longer necessary because goodwill would be tested for impairment annually and because the first step of the impairment test would be a comparison of the fair value of a reporting unit with its carrying amount. Board members observed that most of the identification and documentation steps inherent in the benchmark assessment would have to be performed subsequent to an acquisition or reorganization and prior to any impairment test regardless of whether this Statement required performance of those steps. However, this Statement does not require that the groundwork for performing an impairment test be completed within a set time period, other than that necessary to perform the transitional goodwill impairment test.

Fair value of a reporting unit

B150. Prior to issuing the 2001 Exposure Draft, the Board considered various valuation methods that could be used in testing goodwill for impairment, including methods based on market capitalization, discounted cash flow, residual income valuation, cash flow return on investment, and economic value added. Board members generally agreed that each of those methods could be used to determine the fair value of a reporting unit and that entities should be permitted to use a valuation method with which they are familiar, providing that the result is consistent with the objective of fair value.

B151. Some respondents to the 2001 Exposure Draft stated that because of the subjectivity inherent in measuring the fair value of a reporting unit, the Board should provide more guidance in this Statement on using present value techniques to estimate fair value. In particular, respondents requested that this Statement provide guidance on how to use cash flows to measure the fair value of a reporting unit. Some respondents suggested that this Statement incorporate the guidance from FRS 11, *Impairment of Fixed Assets and Goodwill,* including growth rate assumptions used in estimating cash flows.

B152. The Board observed that the goodwill impairment test in FRS 11 is focused on acquisition-specific goodwill. Thus, the unit of account in FRS 11 is inconsistent with the use of the reporting unit in this Statement as the unit of account for goodwill impairment testing. The Board concluded that because the restrictions on growth assumptions in FRS 11 could be inconsistent with the requirement to measure the reporting unit at fair value, similar assumptions should *not* be included in this Statement. However, Board members observed that when cash flows are used to estimate fair value, those cash flows should be consistent with the most recent budgets and plans approved by management. As noted previously, one of the reasons the Board decided to test goodwill for impairment at the reporting unit level is that it is generally the level at which information about cash flows is generated for planning purposes. Board members also observed that in estimating cash flows for purposes of determining the fair value of a reporting unit, some consideration should be given to industry trends.

B153. The Board noted that addressing the various issues raised by respondents would require the Board to develop "how to" guidance (including valuation guidance) on using present value techniques to estimate fair value that is beyond the scope of this Statement. The Board reaffirmed that this Statement should explain the objective of the fair value measurement exercise and allow preparers latitude in applying that objective to their specific circumstances based on the guidance in Concepts Statement 7. To assist preparers in applying that guidance, the Board decided to include in Appendix E of this Statement excerpts from Concepts Statement 7 that discuss present value techniques (both expected and traditional) and when those techniques should be used.

B154. The Board reaffirmed its conclusion that if a reporting unit has publicly traded equity securities, the ability of a controlling shareholder to benefit from synergies and other intangible assets that arise from control might cause the fair value of a reporting unit as a whole to exceed its market capitalization. Therefore, in those few instances in which a reporting unit has publicly traded equity securities, the fair value measurement need not be based solely on the quoted market price of an individual share of that security. The Board acknowledges that the assertion in paragraph 23 that the market capitalization of a reporting unit with publicly traded equity securities may not be representative of the fair value of the reporting unit as a whole can be viewed as inconsistent with the definition of fair value in FASB Statements No. 115, *Accounting for Certain Investments in Debt and Equity Securities,* and No. 133, *Accounting for Derivative Instruments and Hedging Activities.* Those Statements maintain that "if a quoted market price is available, the fair value is the product of the number of trading units times that market price." However, the Board decided that measuring the fair value of an entity with a collection of assets and liabilities that operate together to produce cash flows is different from measuring the fair value of that entity's individual equity securities. That decision is supported by the fact that an entity often is willing to pay more for equity securities that give it a controlling interest than an investor would pay for a number of equity securities that represent less than a controlling interest. Thus, consideration of the impact of a control premium when control is known to exist in measuring the fair value of a reporting unit is appropriate, whereas it is not for a noncontrolling position in equity interests.

B155. The Board noted that in most instances quoted market prices for a reporting unit would not be available and thus would not be used to measure the fair value of a reporting unit. The Board concluded that absent a quoted market price, a present value technique might be the best available technique to measure the fair value of a reporting unit. However, the Board agreed that this Statement should not preclude use of valuation techniques other than a present value technique, as long as the resulting measurement is consistent with the objective of fair value. That is, the valuation technique used should capture the five elements outlined in paragraph 23 of

Concepts Statement 7 and should result in a valuation that yields results similar to a discounted cash flows method. The Board also noted that, consistent with Concepts Statement 7, the fair value measurement should reflect estimates and expectations that marketplace participants would use in their estimates of fair value whenever that information is available without undue cost and effort. This Statement, like Concepts Statement 7, does not preclude the use of an entity's own estimates, as long as there is no information indicating that marketplace participants would use different assumptions. If such information exists, the entity must adjust its assumptions to incorporate that market information. The Board clarified that use of a valuation technique based on multiples of earnings or revenues or similar performance measures should not be precluded so long as the resulting measurement is consistent with a fair value objective. Use of such multiples may be appropriate when both the fair value and multiple of a comparable entity are available. The Board also agreed that if an acquired entity is a significant portion of a reporting unit (or a reporting unit itself) and the technique used to value the acquisition (determine the purchase price) is consistent with the objective of measuring fair value, the assumptions underlying that valuation should be used in measuring the fair value of the reporting unit. Board members noted that a valuation technique similar to that used to value the acquisition would most likely be used by the entity to determine the fair value of the reporting unit. For example, if the purchase price were based on an expected cash flow model, that cash flow model and related assumptions would be used to measure the fair value of the reporting unit.

Goodwill impairment testing by a subsidiary

B156. Some respondents to the 2001 Exposure Draft raised issues about how goodwill should be tested for impairment when the reporting entity has one or more subsidiaries that prepare separate financial statements in accordance with generally accepted accounting principles (separate GAAP financial statements). They questioned whether goodwill that is reported in the separate GAAP financial statements of a subsidiary (subsidiary goodwill) should be tested for impairment at the subsidiary level (that is, at the level of the subsidiary's reporting units) or at the higher consolidated level (that is, at the level of the parent's reporting unit or units that encompass the subsidiary).

B157. The Board noted that subsidiary goodwill might arise from (a) acquisitions that a subsidiary made prior to its being acquired by the parent, (b) acquisitions that a subsidiary made subsequent to its being acquired by the parent, and (c) goodwill arising from the business combination in which a subsidiary was acquired that the parent company pushed down to the subsidiary's financial statements. Some respondents urged that subsidiary goodwill be tested for impairment only at the reporting units at the higher consolidated level, with any impairment losses recognized being pushed down to the subsidiary. Other respondents urged that subsidiary goodwill be tested for impairment at the subsidiary level, and some also urged that any impairment losses recognized at the subsidiary level also be recognized at (pushed up to) the consolidated level.

B158. Some respondents asked that a distinction be made between the requirements for subsidiaries that are public entities and those that are nonpublic entities. Those respondents suggested that goodwill of a public subsidiary be tested for impairment at the subsidiary level but that goodwill of a nonpublic subsidiary be tested only at the consolidated level, with any impairment losses recognized at the consolidation level being allocated to the subsidiaries. The Board observed that subsidiaries prepare separate GAAP financial statements largely because the information needs of minority stockholders, creditors, and regulators of those subsidiaries cannot be filled by the GAAP financial statements of the consolidated group. Information that pertains to the consolidated group is not relevant to them because their interests are limited to the subsidiary. Users of subsidiary financial statements therefore should be entitled to expect that the same accounting requirements have been applied regardless of whether the reporting entity in question is a subsidiary of another reporting entity. The Board accordingly concluded that goodwill that is reported on the separate GAAP financial statements of a subsidiary should be tested for impairment at the subsidiary level.

B159. The Board observed that if goodwill impairment testing is performed at the subsidiary level, the question of whether to push down impairment losses from the consolidated level is not pertinent. However, it noted that an impairment loss that is recognized at the subsidiary level may indicate potential goodwill impairment in the reporting unit or units at the consolidated level at which the subsidiary resides. The Board therefore concluded that if an impairment loss is recognized at the subsidiary level, that loss should not be recognized at (pushed up to) the consolidated level; rather, an entity should consider whether an interim impairment test should be performed on goodwill in the reporting unit or units of the parent company in which the subsidiary resides. (Paragraph 28 addresses when an entity should test goodwill for impairment between annual tests.) If testing at the consolidated level leads to an impairment loss, that loss should be recognized at that level separately from the subsidiary's loss. The Board further concluded that the requirements for testing goodwill should be the same for both public and nonpublic subsidiaries because the needs of the users of those subsidiaries' separate GAAP financial statements are the same.

Disposal of all or a portion of a reporting unit

B160. The 1999 Exposure Draft proposed that when goodwill is associated with assets to be sold or otherwise disposed of, some amount of goodwill should be included in the cost of the assets disposed of. The June 2000 impairment Exposure Draft proposed guidance for associating assets to be disposed of with related goodwill. That Exposure Draft proposed that goodwill generally should be allocated to assets to be disposed of on a pro rata basis using the relative fair values of the acquired long-lived assets and intangible assets at the acquisition date. In developing the 2001 Exposure Draft, the Board observed that the guidance proposed in the June 2000 impairment Exposure Draft was based on the current acquisition-specific model of accounting for goodwill subsequent to an acquisition. Thus, the Board considered whether that guidance was appropriate given its fundamental decision to move to a model that considers the reporting unit to be the unit of account for goodwill after an acquisition.

B161. The Board concluded that because the reporting unit is the unit of account for goodwill, goodwill cannot be identified or associated with an asset group at a level lower than the reporting unit, other than in an arbitrary manner. However, the Board realized that when a significant portion of a reporting unit is to be disposed of, it is necessary to determine whether the net assets of the reporting unit that remain after the disposition can support the carrying amount of goodwill. Thus, the 2001 Exposure Draft would have required that goodwill be tested for impairment in those circumstances; however, the assets to be disposed of would not have been included in that test. In that Exposure Draft, if the implied fair value of the reporting unit's goodwill were determined to be less than its carrying amount, the excess of the carrying amount of goodwill over its implied fair value would

have been included in the carrying amount of the net assets to be disposed of. The 2001 Exposure Draft also proposed that when a reporting unit is to be disposed of in its entirety, all of that reporting unit's goodwill would be included in the carrying amount of its net assets.

B162. Many respondents to the 2001 Exposure Draft did not agree with the proposed accounting for disposal of a significant portion of a reporting unit because it might distort the calculation of the gain or loss to be recognized on disposal. Those respondents noted that because the proposed goodwill impairment approach may result in capitalization of internally generated goodwill and other unrecognized assets, goodwill associated with the net assets disposed of might not be included in the gain or loss calculation, thus exaggerating any gain or minimizing any loss. Some respondents suggested that some amount of goodwill should always be allocated to the portion of a reporting unit that is sold.

B163. Having redefined the reporting unit to be generally a higher level than that proposed in the 2001 Exposure Draft, the Board assessed whether it would be possible for goodwill to be meaningfully allocated below the reporting unit level. For example, the Board considered how frequently a reporting unit would consist of one or more businesses. The Board acknowledged that if this Statement were to permit or require allocation of goodwill below the reporting unit for disposal accounting purposes, it would be nearly impossible to limit how low that allocation could go.

B164. The Board concluded that it would not be possible to describe the circumstances in which goodwill should be allocated to a portion of a reporting unit being disposed of with sufficient rigor that the guidance would be interpreted and applied consistently. However, the Board acknowledged that when a business is being disposed of, it would be appropriate to presume that some amount of goodwill is associated with that business. Thus, the Board concluded that an allocation should be required only when the net assets being disposed of constitute a business. The Board noted that that would be consistent with recognizing goodwill when a business is acquired.

B165. The Board considered various allocation approaches, recognizing that any allocation approach would be arbitrary. The Board agreed that this Statement should prescribe use of a specific allocation method such that the amount of goodwill allocated to a business to be disposed of would be determined consistently from entity to entity. The Board concluded that a relative-fair-value allocation method would result in a reasonable estimation of the amount of goodwill that might be associated with a business being disposed of and would not be overly complex to apply. Therefore, this Statement requires that when a portion of a reporting unit being disposed of constitutes a business, the amount of goodwill assigned to that business should be based on the relative fair values of the business to be disposed of and the remaining portion of the reporting unit. However, due to the imprecision of any allocation approach, the Board concluded that the goodwill remaining with the reporting unit should be tested for impairment after goodwill has been allocated to the business being sold.

B166. The Board observed that when an acquired business is being disposed of and the benefits of goodwill acquired with that business have not been realized by any portion of the reporting unit other than the acquired business, the carrying amount of that acquired goodwill should be included in the net assets disposed of. Therefore, this Statement requires that the relative-fair-value allocation method *not* be used to allocate goodwill to a business being disposed of if that business was not integrated into the reporting unit after its acquisition. Board members noted that those situations (such as when the acquired business is operated as a stand-alone entity) would be infrequent because some amount of integration generally occurs after an acquisition.

Amendment of Statement 121

B167. This Statement amends Statement 121 to eliminate the requirement that the carrying amount of goodwill associated with a long-lived asset be combined with that asset's carrying value when testing that long-lived asset (or group of assets) for impairment. Goodwill is to be tested for impairment only in accordance with this Statement. The 2001 Exposure Draft proposed that when an asset group being tested for impairment is also a reporting unit, goodwill would be tested for impairment (and any impairment loss recognized) *before* the other long-lived assets are tested for impairment. The Board reconsidered that proposal given its decision to add a step to the impairment test that is based on the carrying amounts of the assets and liabilities of the reporting unit. Board members considered it important that the carrying amount used to identify potential impairment reflect

amounts that have already been adjusted for impairment. Thus, this Statement requires goodwill to be tested for impairment *after* all other assets have been tested for impairment when more than one impairment test is required at the same time. The Board clarified that that requirement applies to all assets that are tested for impairment, not just those included in the scope of Statement 121.

B168. The Board observed that in situations in which a reporting unit consists of multiple lower-level asset groups, an event might occur that requires an impairment test of some, but not all, of those asset groups. That same event might or might not require an impairment test of reporting unit goodwill. The Board concluded that because the reporting unit is the unit of account for goodwill, the reporting unit *is* the lowest level with which goodwill can be associated; therefore, goodwill is not associated with a lower-level asset group. Based on that view, the Board decided that reporting unit goodwill should not be allocated to or otherwise associated with a lower-level asset group as previously required by Statement 121. This Statement amends Statement 121 to eliminate that requirement.

Equity method investments

B169. Under APB Opinion No. 18, *The Equity Method of Accounting for Investments in Common Stock,* an investor is required to apply the equity method of accounting if its investment in voting stock gives it the ability to exercise significant influence over operating and financial policies of the investee. The investor's cost and the underlying equity in net assets of the investee often differ, and Opinion 18 requires that that difference be accounted for as if the investee were a consolidated subsidiary. An investor is therefore required to complete a purchase price allocation, which often results in identification of part of the difference as goodwill. (However, that amount is not reported as goodwill in the investor's statement of financial position.) The Board reasoned that goodwill associated with equity method investments (equity method goodwill) should be accounted for in the same manner as goodwill arising from a business combination. Thus, the 2001 Exposure Draft proposed that equity method goodwill should not be amortized.

B170. Equity method investments are reviewed for impairment in accordance with Opinion 18, and it is the equity investment as a whole that is reviewed for impairment, not the underlying net assets. The Board concluded that because equity method goodwill is not separable from the related investment, that goodwill should not be tested for impairment in accordance with this Statement. Thus, the 2001 Exposure Draft proposed that equity method goodwill be exempt from the impairment provisions of this Statement. Respondents generally agreed with the Board's conclusions related to equity method goodwill, and the Board reaffirmed those conclusions.

Deferred Income Taxes

B171. The 2001 Exposure Draft proposed that the requirement in Statement 109, *Accounting for Income Taxes* (paragraphs 30, 262, and 263), to recognize deferred taxes related to goodwill when amortization of goodwill is deductible for tax purposes not be changed. Some respondents to that Exposure Draft, however, objected to recognition of a deferred tax liability related to tax-deductible goodwill.

B172. In a taxable business combination, the purchase price is allocated to the acquired assets and liabilities for tax purposes similarly to the way it is allocated for financial reporting (book) purposes. Because usually there is no temporary difference created at the date of acquisition, no deferred tax liability related to goodwill is recognized at that date. However, taxable temporary differences will arise in the future as goodwill is amortized for tax purposes but not for book purposes. In those circumstances, an excess of the book basis over the tax basis of goodwill is a taxable temporary difference for which a deferred tax liability must be recognized under Statement 109. This issue does not arise for nontaxable business combinations because Statement 109 prohibits recognition of a deferred tax liability related to goodwill when amortization is not deductible for tax purposes.

B173. Respondents to the 2001 Exposure Draft noted that a deferred tax liability would not be settled until some indefinite future period when goodwill is impaired, sold, or otherwise disposed of—all of which are future events that respondents asserted are unlikely to occur. They requested that this Statement amend Statement 109 to require recognition of a deferred tax liability related to tax-deductible goodwill only at such time as a goodwill impairment loss is recognized or goodwill is assigned to a business that is sold or otherwise disposed of.

B174. Board members observed that similar issues exist for intangible assets other than goodwill, because they also could have a book basis with little or no tax basis. Statement 109 requires recognition of a deferred tax liability related to other intangible assets. Like goodwill, absent amortization, the deferred tax liability will remain on the balance sheet until such time as the intangible asset is impaired, sold, or otherwise disposed of.

B175. The Board acknowledged that nonamortization of goodwill and intangible assets with indefinite useful lives was not contemplated when the Board deliberated Statement 109. However, the arguments used by respondents to the 2001 Exposure Draft for nonrecognition of deferred tax liabilities related to goodwill and intangible assets with indefinite useful lives were made at that time and were extensively debated. Statement 109 requires comprehensive recognition of deferred taxes subject only to a limited number of exceptions. Statement 109 continues exceptions for some of the areas addressed by APB Opinion No. 23, *Accounting for Income Taxes—Special Areas,* but prohibits nonrecognition of a deferred tax liability for all analogous types of taxable temporary differences. Therefore, the Board reconfirmed that Statement 109 should not be amended for the purposes of permitting additional exceptions to comprehensive recognition of deferred income taxes.

Financial Statement Presentation

Presentation in Statement of Financial Position

B176. The Board observed that Opinion 17 did not require that goodwill be displayed separately in the statement of financial position and that, in practice, goodwill has been displayed together with other intangible assets. However, the Board agreed that goodwill is unique among assets and that different users of financial statements may assess it differently in their analyses. The Board therefore concluded that goodwill differed sufficiently from other assets and other intangible assets to justify being displayed separately in the statement of financial position.

B177. The Board further observed that intangible assets other than goodwill also differ significantly from other assets and therefore concluded that they also should be displayed in the aggregate separately in the statement of financial position. The Board noted that such a requirement would not preclude separately displaying individual intangible assets or classes of those assets that are material. The Board clarified that an entity should continue to display intangible assets in their proper classification whether that be as a current asset or a noncurrent asset.

B178. The 1999 Exposure Draft proposed that both goodwill and other intangible assets be displayed in the aggregate separately in the statement of financial position, and the 2001 Exposure Draft (which focused only on goodwill) affirmed that display for goodwill. Respondents agreed that separate presentations of those items provide useful information. The Board therefore decided to retain those presentation requirements in this Statement, noting that separating goodwill from other assets in the statement of financial position is even more important under a nonamortization model.

Presentation in the Income Statement

B179. The Board observed that amortization and impairment charges for goodwill and other intangible assets traditionally have been displayed in the income statement among those expenses that are presented on a pretax basis. Moreover, in practice, those charges often have been commingled with other expenses, such as depreciation and amortization or selling and administrative expenses. The Board noted concerns that such commingling can make the analysis of financial statements more difficult. Some respondents urged that the charges for goodwill and other intangible assets be separated from charges for other items, as well as from each other.

B180. Under the 1999 Exposure Draft, goodwill impairment losses would have been combined with goodwill amortization expense and presented on a net-of-tax basis as a separate line item in the income statement. The Board noted that the special income statement treatment proposed in the 1999 Exposure Draft was aimed at making goodwill amortization expense more transparent. Therefore, the special display provisions were designed primarily for goodwill amortization expense—not goodwill impairment losses. The 1999 Exposure Draft also proposed that charges for the amortization or impairment of intangible assets continue to be displayed on a pretax basis in line items as deemed appropriate by the reporting entity, as they traditionally had been displayed.

B181. Some respondents to that Exposure Draft suggested that all of the charges related to the entire premium of the purchase price of an entity over the book value of its net assets (including charges related to the step-up in basis of recorded net assets and the recognition of previously unrecognized assets and liabilities) be afforded a special presentation, similar to that proposed in the 1999 Exposure Draft for goodwill charges. They argued that such a presentation would

facilitate the analysis of earnings trends related to the combining entities following the business combination. They also argued that those charges should be accorded similar presentation because (a) goodwill is an intangible asset, (b) the amount recognized as goodwill may include certain intangible assets that cannot be recognized apart from goodwill, and (c) some intangible assets are "goodwill like."

B182. The Board observed that there may have been cases in practice in which much or all of the premium over book value had been assigned to goodwill and thus the amortization charge for goodwill would have included much or all of the charges relating to that premium. However, the Board noted that accounting standards have consistently differentiated goodwill from the premium over book values. Moreover, the Board noted that such a presentation would be akin to those produced by the pooling method, which would conflict with the Board's decision to eliminate that method. The Board further noted that its subsequent adoption of the contractual-legal criterion and separability criterion sharpened the differences between what would be recognized as goodwill and what would be recognized as other intangible assets. The Board therefore rejected suggestions that other charges related to the purchase premium (other than goodwill charges) should be afforded a special presentation.

B183. In developing the 2001 Exposure Draft, the Board discussed whether goodwill impairment losses should be presented in the income statement in the same manner as any other impairment loss (as a component of pretax operating income) or in accordance with the special display provisions proposed in the 1999 Exposure Draft. The 2001 Exposure Draft proposed that a goodwill impairment loss recognized under a nonamortization model be reported in the same manner as an impairment loss recognized on other assets. Respondents to the 2001 Exposure Draft agreed with that proposal. The Board therefore reaffirmed its conclusion that a goodwill impairment loss (other than a transitional goodwill impairment loss) should be reported as a component of income from operations (before income taxes) unless the goodwill impairment loss is associated with a discontinued operation—in which case it would be included within the results of the discontinued operation.

B184. Consistent with its decision that the impairment charges for goodwill should be displayed on a pretax basis like that for charges related to other intangible assets, the Board reaffirmed its conclusion in the 1999 Exposure Draft that the charges related to other intangible assets should continue to be displayed on a pretax basis as a component of income from continuing operations. As noted in paragraph B66, the Board concluded that an impairment loss recognized as the result of a change in the estimate of the remaining useful life of an intangible asset should not be recognized as the effect of a change in accounting principle.

Disclosures

Information about Intangible Assets in the Year of Acquisition

B185. The 1999 Exposure Draft proposed that certain information be disclosed in the notes to the financial statements for each class of intangible asset. The information that would have been required to be disclosed included (a) a description of the intangible assets and the amounts assigned to them at the acquisition date, (b) the key assumptions and methodologies used to determine those amounts, (c) a description of the amortization method, and (d) the weighted-average amortization period. Many respondents to that Exposure Draft commented on the proposed disclosure requirements. Most agreed that additional information about acquired intangible assets would be useful, but many urged the Board to consider reducing the extent of the disclosure requirements. They argued that the cost of providing the information would exceed the benefits derived from it.

B186. After considering the suggestions made by those respondents, the Board reaffirmed its conclusion that financial statements should provide additional information about acquired intangible assets other than goodwill. However, the Board agreed that eliminating certain proposed disclosures would not significantly diminish the decision usefulness of the information provided.

B187. The Board concluded that the following information should be disclosed for use in assessing the amount and timing of future cash inflows: (a) the total amounts assigned to intangible assets subject to amortization and those that are not subject to amortization, (b) the amount assigned to each major class of intangible asset, and (c) the weighted-average amortization period in total and for each major class of asset. The Board also concluded that disclosure should

be made of the amount of any significant residual values assumed both in total and for each major class of intangible asset. Although not proposed in the 1999 Exposure Draft, the Board also decided that when an entity acquires research and development assets and writes off those assets at the date of acquisition, it should be required to disclose the amount written off as well as the line item in which that write-off is aggregated.

Information about Intangible Assets Subsequent to an Acquisition

B188. The Board decided to require disclosure of certain information for each class of intangible asset subject to amortization in periods following the acquisition. That information includes the gross carrying amount, amortization method, accumulated amortization, current-period amortization expense, and the estimated aggregate amortization expense for each of the five succeeding fiscal years. The Board noted that presenting that information in tabular form would be a concise way to meet the disclosure requirement. The Board concluded that that disclosure requirement was appropriate, given its decision to permit entities to aggregate the presentation of intangible assets in the statement of financial position.

B189. In addition, the Board concluded that in the years subsequent to an acquisition, entities should disclose by major class information about the total carrying amount of those intangible assets not subject to amortization. That information is useful because those intangible assets are tested for impairment on an annual basis.

Information about Goodwill Subsequent to an Acquisition

B190. In its redeliberations of the 1999 Exposure Draft, the Board reconsidered all of the proposed goodwill disclosure requirements because they were based on a model that would have required amortization of goodwill. The Board consulted with a group of financial statement users before deciding what information about goodwill should be disclosed in the notes to the financial statements if goodwill is to be tested for impairment rather than amortized. The 2001 Exposure Draft proposed that in the years subsequent to an acquisition, entities should disclose information about changes in the carrying amount of goodwill and the reasons for those changes. The

Board observed that that information might be concisely disclosed in a tabular format. The 2001 Exposure Draft also proposed that entities presenting segment information in accordance with Statement 131 should disclose information about the changes in the carrying amount of goodwill by segment.

B191. Some respondents stated that the requirement to disclose the changes in the carrying amount of goodwill is not necessary because that information is presented elsewhere in the financial statements. In addition, respondents questioned why the 2001 Exposure Draft would require disclosure of goodwill information at the segment level when Statement 131 does not require disclosure of that information. The Board agreed that if the required information about goodwill is disclosed elsewhere in the financial statements, it would not need to be repeated in the notes. In addition, the Board decided to retain the requirement to disclose information about goodwill by segment, noting that the unit of account used for impairment testing (the reporting unit) is based on the segment reporting structure.

B192. In its discussions about what information should be disclosed when a goodwill impairment loss is recognized, the Board considered the disclosures required by Statement 121 when an impairment loss is recognized for a long-lived asset or group of assets. The 2001 Exposure Draft proposed disclosure of similar information when a goodwill impairment loss is recognized—including the facts and circumstances leading to the impairment of goodwill, such as the events or series of events that gave rise to the impairment test. The Board agreed to retain that requirement in this Statement, noting that it is important for users to understand whether an impairment loss is due to external factors or events that should have been within management's control and whether the loss is related to a recently acquired entity.

B193. The 2001 Exposure Draft proposed that when an impairment loss is recognized, information should be disclosed at the reporting unit level. That information would have included a description of the reporting unit for which the loss is recognized, the adjusted carrying amount of reporting unit goodwill, and the amount of the impairment loss. The Board observed that when an impairment loss is recognized, disclosure of information about goodwill at the reporting unit level would be helpful both in assessing the magnitude of the loss recognized and in assessing the amount of potential future impairment losses.

B194. Most respondents disagreed with that requirement, noting that no other information is provided at the reporting unit level and that disclosing only one piece of information at that level would be both confusing and useless. The Board agreed, further noting that based on the revised definition of a reporting unit, information provided to users about impairment losses at a level below the segment level would not be significantly different from the information available at the segment level. Therefore, the Board concluded that disclosure of general information about an impairment loss and of the segment to which the impaired goodwill relates would be sufficient.

Effective Date and Transition

B195. The 2001 Exposure Draft proposed that all entities initially apply this Statement at the beginning of the first fiscal quarter following its issuance. Based on that proposed effective date, it was estimated that an entity with a fiscal year ending on December 31, 2001, would initially apply this Statement on July 1, 2001. That proposed effective date was based on the Board's conclusion that because nonamortization of goodwill results in financial statements that are more representationally faithful, it would be important for this Statement to become effective as soon as possible after issuance. The Board also noted that for comparability reasons, amortization of all previously recognized goodwill should stop within the same interim (three month) reporting period following issuance of this Statement.

B196. A number of respondents to the 2001 Exposure Draft indicated a preference for applying this Statement as of the beginning of a fiscal year. Those respondents noted that mid-year implementation of this Statement would hinder comparability of financial statements and cause confusion for financial statement users. Most respondents who suggested changing the effective date to the beginning of a fiscal year suggested that this Statement be effective for fiscal years beginning after its issuance date. Others preferred allowing entities some lead time and suggested that this Statement be effective for fiscal years beginning after December 15, 2001. The Board noted that under either approach the vast majority of entities would be required to initially apply this Statement on or after January 1, 2002—at least six months after the proposed effective date.

Previously Recognized Goodwill

B197. The 2001 Exposure Draft proposed that this Statement apply to goodwill already recognized in an entity's financial statements at the date an entity initially applies this Statement (previously recognized goodwill) as well as to goodwill recognized in its financial statements after that date. Respondents agreed that previously recognized goodwill should no longer be amortized upon initial application of this Statement. The Board reaffirmed that provision, noting that if amortization of previously recognized goodwill were to continue after an entity initially applies this Statement, financial statements would suffer from the noncomparability the Board was concerned about in discussing whether to adopt a mixed approach to account for goodwill. In addition, the Board noted that to be operational the goodwill impairment provisions in this Statement must apply to previously recognized goodwill as well as to goodwill recognized in the future. Most important, the Board concluded that nonamortization of goodwill in conjunction with testing for impairment is the most representationally faithful method of accounting for goodwill and that a nonamortization approach should be applied in all circumstances.

B198. Board members concluded that, for the reasons provided by respondents, this Statement should be applied as of the beginning of a fiscal year and that entities should be provided additional time to prepare for its initial application. Therefore, this Statement is to be applied to previously recognized goodwill and other intangible assets in fiscal years beginning after December 15, 2001, and is to be applied at the beginning of the year of initial application. Retroactive application of this Statement is not permitted. However, the Board did not want to preclude an entity that was prepared to initially apply this Statement sooner than the required effective date from being able to initially apply it earlier than that date. Thus, an entity with a fiscal year beginning after March 15, 2001, may initially apply this Statement as of the beginning of that fiscal year provided its first interim financial statements have not been issued.

B199. However, mutual enterprises and not-for-profit organizations may not apply this Statement until interpretive guidance related to the application of the purchase method by those entities is issued. The Board plans to consider issues related to the application of the purchase method to combinations between two or more mutual enterprises, combinations between not-for-profit organizations, and the acquisition of a for-profit business entity by a not-for-profit organization in a separate project. In the interim, Opinions 16 and 17 continue to apply to those transactions.

B200. Upon initial application of this Statement, an entity will have to establish its reporting units and as-

sign recognized assets and liabilities that meet the criteria in paragraph 32 to those reporting units. The Board concluded that the guidance in this Statement on assigning acquired assets and assumed liabilities to reporting units should be used to make the initial assignment of assets and liabilities to reporting units. Board members noted that recognized assets and liabilities that do not relate to a reporting unit (such as an environmental liability for an operation previously disposed of) should not be allocated to a reporting unit.

B201. Once those reporting units are established, all previously recognized goodwill will have to be assigned to those units—no matter how long ago it was acquired. However, because of the difficulties in reconstructing conditions that existed when past acquisitions were made, the Board concluded that previously recognized goodwill should be assigned based on the current reporting unit structure and not the structure that existed when the goodwill was acquired. However, the Board observed that in making that assignment, an entity should consider the source of previously recognized goodwill and the reporting units to which the related acquired net assets were assigned. Board members noted that the guidance provided in paragraphs 34 and 35 might also be helpful in assigning previously recognized goodwill to reporting units.

Transitional goodwill impairment test

B202. Having decided that previously recognized goodwill should no longer be amortized upon initial application of this Statement, the Board addressed whether previously recognized goodwill should be tested for impairment concurrent with the cessation of amortization. The Board observed that previously recognized goodwill is currently subject to the limited impairment guidance in Opinion 17 and ARB 43, Chapter 5, "Intangible Assets." Many entities currently test goodwill for impairment on an undiscounted cash flow basis, similar to the method that Statement 121 requires to test long-lived assets for recoverability. Thus, it is possible that previously recognized goodwill that is not considered impaired under current U.S. GAAP would be determined to be impaired if the impairment provisions in this Statement were applied to goodwill at the date an entity initially applied this Statement.

B203. In developing the 2001 Exposure Draft, Board members observed that requiring goodwill in each reporting unit to be tested for impairment upon initial application of this Statement—particularly determining the fair value of the underlying net assets of each reporting unit—would be both costly and difficult. Thus, for cost-benefit reasons the 2001 Exposure Draft proposed that, absent an impairment indicator, previously recognized goodwill should not be tested for impairment upon initial application of this Statement. However, an entity would have been required to perform a transitional benchmark assessment within six months of the date it initially applied this Statement. As part of that transitional benchmark assessment, an entity would have been required to compare the fair value of each reporting unit having goodwill with the carrying amount of its net assets (including goodwill). If the carrying amount of the reporting unit exceeded its fair value, goodwill of that reporting unit would have been required to be tested for impairment.

B204. Most respondents to the 2001 Exposure Draft agreed with the proposed requirement to perform a benchmark assessment on previously recognized goodwill upon initial application of this Statement rather than a full impairment test. However, those respondents stated that entities would need more than the proposed six months to complete the transitional benchmark assessment. Respondents suggested that it would take up to one year for an entity to complete all of the steps of the transitional benchmark assessment.

B205. Recognizing that the step added to the goodwill impairment test to identify potential impairment is the same as the last step of the proposed benchmark assessment (a comparison of the fair value of a reporting unit with its carrying amount), the Board reconsidered its prior decision to not require previously recognized goodwill to be tested for impairment upon initial application of this Statement. Because of the revisions made to the reporting unit definition and goodwill impairment test during its redeliberations of the 2001 Exposure Draft, the Board believes that the revised impairment test will not be as costly or as difficult to apply as the proposed impairment test. Therefore, the Board concluded that previously recognized goodwill *should* be tested for impairment upon initial application of this Statement.

B206. The 2001 Exposure Draft proposed that a goodwill impairment loss recognized as the result of a transitional benchmark assessment (a transitional impairment loss) should be presented as a component of operating income, not as a change in accounting principle. That proposed requirement was based on the Board's belief that it would not be possible to determine the amount of a transitional impairment loss related to current and past reporting periods.

B207. Most respondents disagreed with the Board's conclusion that transitional impairment losses should be recognized in the same manner as all other impairment losses. Those respondents observed that the majority of transitional impairment losses would relate to adoption of the new impairment method and that few, if any, of the losses would relate to current-period losses. Accordingly, respondents asserted that it would be more representationally faithful to depict any transitional impairment losses as stemming from changes in accounting principles rather than as occurring in the current period.

B208. The Board acknowledged that the preponderance of any transitional impairment losses recognized are likely to result from the change in methods and that treating those losses as stemming from changes in accounting principles would be more representationally faithful than treating them as ordinary impairment losses. Therefore, the Board concluded that a transitional impairment loss should be recognized as the effect of a change in accounting principle.

B209. Because the transitional impairment loss is to be reported as a change in accounting principle, the Board considered whether it was necessary to place any parameters around the transitional goodwill impairment test. For example, without parameters, an entity would be permitted to wait until the end of the year of initial application to complete the transitional goodwill impairment test and still report any resulting impairment loss as a change in accounting principle. Board members observed that the reason they decided that a transitional impairment loss should be reported as a change in accounting principle was because most losses would relate primarily to the change in methodology used to test goodwill for impairment. Thus, ideally, the transitional goodwill impairment test should apply to reporting unit goodwill as of the date this Statement is initially applied—not as of any date in the year of initial application.

B210. To address those concerns, the Board concluded that this Statement should require the first step of the transitional goodwill impairment test to be performed within six months of the date the Statement is initially applied. Board members observed that that requirement is similar to the proposed requirement to complete the transitional benchmark assessment within six months of initial application. The purpose of that first step is to identify potential goodwill impairment. The Board noted that because this Statement is not required to be initially applied until at least six months after the date proposed in the 2001 Exposure Draft, entities will have the additional time that respondents to the 2001 Exposure Draft requested to establish reporting units and measure the fair value of those reporting units. The Board concluded that, given the change in the effective date and the change in the definition of a reporting unit, six months is adequate time for preparers to establish their reporting units and develop systems for testing goodwill for impairment at the reporting unit level.

B211. The Board concluded that the fair value of a reporting unit used to identify any potential impairment existing upon initial application of this Statement should be measured as of the beginning of the year in which this Statement is initially applied. Therefore, this Statement requires the amounts used to identify potential impairment (the fair value of a reporting unit and its corresponding carrying amount) to be measured *as of* the first of the year of initial application. The Board noted that specifying an initial measurement date would ensure that transitional goodwill impairment losses would be measured on a consistent basis.

B212. This Statement requires that if the first step of the transitional goodwill impairment test identifies potential impairment, the second step of the impairment test should be completed as soon as possible, but no later than the end of the year of initial application. Regardless of the interim period in which a transitional goodwill impairment loss is measured, the resulting accounting change should be reflected as of the beginning of an entity's fiscal year. The Board observed that this is consistent with the requirements in FASB Statement No. 3, *Reporting Accounting Changes in Interim Financial Statements.*

B213. The Board concluded that because any transitional goodwill impairment loss would be measured as of the first of the year of initial application, an entity should perform the required annual impairment test also in the year of initial application. Otherwise, depending on the measurement date chosen for future annual tests, almost two years could elapse between the transitional goodwill impairment test and the next goodwill impairment test. Notwithstanding the requirement to perform the required annual test in addition to the transitional impairment test, Board

members observed that given the provisions in paragraph 27 governing when a detailed determination of the fair value of a reporting unit might not be necessary, it is likely that an entity will not have to recompute the fair value of all its reporting units in the year this Statement is initially applied.

Previously Recognized Intangible Assets

B214. This Statement applies to intangible assets already recognized in an entity's financial statements at the date it initially applies this Statement (previously recognized intangible assets) as well as to intangible assets recognized in its financial statements after that date. The Board concluded that the most representationally faithful method of accounting for intangible assets is to amortize an intangible asset over its useful life with no limit on that amortization period and to not amortize an intangible asset that is deemed to have an indefinite useful life. Thus, upon initial application of this Statement an entity is required to reassess the useful lives of its previously recognized intangible assets using the factors in paragraph 11. As a result of that reassessment, the remaining amortization period for an intangible asset might need to be adjusted. In addition, a previously recognized intangible asset that is deemed to have an indefinite useful life would cease being amortized.

B215. The Board agreed that recognition of an impairment loss related to an intangible asset that will cease being amortized upon initial application of this Statement should be treated in a manner similar to a transitional goodwill impairment loss. Like goodwill, those intangible assets will be tested for impairment using a different method than had been previously applied to those assets. The Board therefore concluded that an intangible asset that is deemed to have an indefinite useful life should be tested for impairment upon initial application of this Statement and any resulting impairment loss recognized as the effect of a change in accounting principle. The Board clarified that, unlike goodwill, the measurement of that transitional intangible asset impairment loss should be completed in the first interim period in which this Statement is initially applied.

Equity Method Goodwill

B216. In considering the impact this Statement would have on the accounting for equity method investments, Board members noted that Opinion 18 requires entities to allocate the excess of cost over the underlying equity in net assets of an investee accounted for using the equity method to specific accounts of the investee (including intangible assets) and that only the amount remaining after that allocation should be recognized as goodwill (equity method goodwill). The Board clarified that upon initial application of this Statement, the amount previously recognized as equity method goodwill should also cease being amortized.

Transitional Disclosures

B217. As proposed in the 2001 Exposure Draft, many entities would have initially applied this Statement in the middle of their fiscal year. Thus, that Exposure Draft would have required disclosure of income before extraordinary items and net income on a pro forma basis; that is, what those amounts would have been if the amortization and nonamortization provisions for goodwill and other intangible assets had been applied in all periods presented. However, that pro forma information would not have reflected the impact the impairment provisions might have had on prior-period information. The Board reasoned that requiring entities to determine the impact of the impairment provisions on prior periods would not be cost beneficial.

B218. Respondents to the 2001 Exposure Draft were generally supportive of the proposal to present pro forma information, noting that that information would be important for preparing trend analyses and providing comparable information. However, some respondents stated that because a prior-period impairment loss would *not* be adjusted to reflect what it would have been if goodwill had not been amortized, financial statement users will not have a complete picture of what an entity's pattern of goodwill charges would have been under a nonamortization approach. Those respondents suggested that because of that lack of information, pro forma information should *not* be presented in the financial statements.

B219. The Board acknowledged those concerns but concluded that the lack of certain information is an insufficient reason *not* to provide information about what prior earnings may have been if goodwill had not been amortized. However, Board members observed that describing the information to be disclosed as pro forma information might be misleading, since the adjustment to earnings is not all-inclusive. The Board agreed that this Statement should not refer to information as pro forma if in fact it is not. Therefore, this Statement retains the proposed requirements to

present (a) prior-period income before extraordinary items and net income adjusted to exclude, among other things, amortization expense related to goodwill and intangible assets that will no longer be amortized and (b) a reconciliation of reported net income to the adjusted net income; however, those adjusted amounts are not to be labeled "pro forma."

Goodwill and Intangible Assets Acquired after June 30, 2001

B220. Because this Statement will not be effective immediately after it is issued as proposed in the 2001 Exposure Draft, the Board considered how an entity should account for goodwill and other intangible assets acquired in transactions completed after this Statement is issued but before an entity initially applies this Statement to previously recognized goodwill and intangible assets. The Board agreed that it was not appropriate to require such goodwill and intangible assets to be accounted for under the current accounting literature. Thus, the Board concluded that goodwill acquired in a business combination completed after June 30, 2001, but before the acquiring entity initially applies this Statement to previously recognized goodwill should not be amortized. However, the Board observed that because this Statement requires goodwill to be tested for impairment at the reporting unit level, the impairment provisions in this Statement cannot be applied to acquisition-specific goodwill. Therefore, an entity may not apply the goodwill impairment provisions to goodwill acquired in a business combination completed after June 30, 2001, until the date that an entity initially applies this Statement to its previously recognized goodwill and intangible assets. For example, an entity with a December 31, 2001 fiscal year-end is required to initially apply this Statement on January 1, 2002, to its previously recognized goodwill. If that entity completed a business combination on October 15, 2001, that gave rise to goodwill, it would not amortize that goodwill even though it would continue to amortize until January 1, 2002, goodwill that arose from business combinations completed before July 1, 2001. The recently acquired goodwill would not be tested for impairment in accordance with this Statement until January 1, 2002. In the interim, the recently acquired goodwill would be tested for impairment in the same manner as previously recognized goodwill.

B221. Similarly, the Board concluded that an intangible asset acquired in a transaction completed after June 30, 2001, but before the acquiring entity initially applies this Statement to previously recognized intangible assets should be accounted for in accordance with the amortization and nonamortization provisions in this Statement related to intangible assets. The impairment provisions in this Statement for intangible assets that are not being amortized differ from the impairment provisions in Chapter 5 of ARB 43, Opinion 17, and Statement 121. Thus, for consistency purposes, the Board concluded that the impairment provisions in this Statement should not apply to intangible assets acquired in a transaction completed after June 30, 2001, until the date that an entity initially applies this Statement to previously recognized goodwill and intangible assets.

Benefits and Costs

B222. The mission of the FASB is to establish and improve standards of financial accounting and reporting for the guidance and education of the public, including preparers, auditors, and users of financial information. In fulfilling that mission, the Board endeavors to determine that a proposed standard will fill a significant need and that the costs imposed to meet that standard, as compared with other alternatives, are justified in relation to the overall benefits of the resulting information. Although the costs to implement a new standard may not be borne evenly, investors and creditors—both present and potential—as well as others, benefit from improvements in financial reporting, thereby facilitating the functioning of markets for capital and credit and the efficient allocation of resources in the economy.

B223. The Board believes that the requirements in this Statement will result in improved financial reporting. The Board observed that intangible assets constitute a growing share of assets for entities generally and are, in fact, most of the assets of some individual entities. However, information about the intangible assets owned by those entities is often incomplete and inadequate. This Statement should lead to the provision of more information about those assets. The Board also believes that the changes in how goodwill and other intangible assets are accounted for subsequent to their acquisition will provide investors with greater transparency with respect to the economic value of goodwill and other acquired intangible assets and the amount and timing of their impact on earnings.

B224. The Board concluded that the benefits of recognizing goodwill charges in the income statement only when goodwill is impaired rather than on a systematic basis over an arbitrary period of time exceed the costs associated with the impairment test required by this Statement. The Board reached several conclusions related to the goodwill impairment test after weighing the costs and benefits of the possible choices. For example, the Board adopted a two-step impairment test that will be less costly to apply than the one-step impairment test proposed in the 2001 Exposure Draft. The step added to the impairment test serves as a screen to identify potential goodwill impairment. If the fair value of a reporting unit exceeds its carrying amount, goodwill is not considered impaired; thus, the more costly step of estimating the implied fair value of goodwill and the amount of impairment loss, if any, is not required. In addition, the Board agreed to revise the definition of a reporting unit proposed in the 2001 Exposure Draft such that it is defined using terminology similar to that in Statement 131—terminology familiar to both preparers and users. Based on that revised definition, an entity may have fewer reporting units than it would have had under the proposed definition.

B225. The Board observed that entities were required to test goodwill for impairment under Opinion 17 and Chapter 5 of ARB 43 and that costs were associated with those impairment tests. Because Opinion 17 and Chapter 5 of ARB 43 included little guidance on how to test goodwill for impairment, entities differed as to how they tested goodwill for impairment. In addition, some or a portion of goodwill was required to be tested for impairment in conjunction with related assets in accordance with Statement 121. Therefore, in some instances goodwill was being tested for impairment under more than one method. This Statement requires that all entities test goodwill for impairment only in accordance with the provisions of this Statement, which will result in financial statements that are more comparable.

B226. Finally, the requirement in this Statement to test previously recognized goodwill for impairment upon initial application of this Statement is similar to the requirement in the 2001 Exposure Draft to perform a transitional benchmark assessment. However, the Board agreed to defer the effective date of this Statement with respect to previously recognized goodwill and intangible assets, thus providing an entity with more time to perform the transitional impairment test than it would have had to perform the transitional benchmark assessment. While this Statement requires goodwill to be tested for impairment on an annual basis beginning with the year in which this Statement is initially applied, the Board agreed that this Statement should provide entities with some relief from having to recompute the fair value of each reporting unit every year.

Appendix C

DISCLOSURE ILLUSTRATIONS

Introduction

C1. This appendix provides illustrations of the financial statement disclosure requirements of this Statement. The information presented in the following examples has been included for illustrative purposes only and, therefore, may not be representative of actual transactions. For simplicity, the illustrative disclosures do not provide all of the background information that would be necessary to arrive at the disclosed information.

Illustration 1—Disclosure Requirements in Periods Subsequent to a Business Combination

C2. In accordance with paragraphs 45 and 47, the following disclosures would be made by Theta Company in its December 31, 20X3 financial statements relating to acquired intangible assets and goodwill. Theta Company has two reporting units with goodwill—Technology and Communications—which also are reportable segments.

Note B: Acquired Intangible Assets

($000s)	As of December 31, 20X3	
	Gross Carrying Amount	**Accumulated Amortization**
Amortized intangible assets		
Trademark	$1,078	$ (66)
Unpatented technology	475	(380)
Other	90	(30)
Total	$1,643	$(476)
Unamortized intangible assets		
Broadcast licenses	$1,400	
Trademark	600	
Total	$2,000	

Aggregate Amortization Expense:

For year ended 12/31/X3	$319

Estimated Amortization Expense:

For year ended 12/31/X4	$199
For year ended 12/31/X5	$ 74
For year ended 12/31/X6	$ 74
For year ended 12/31/X7	$ 64
For year ended 12/31/X8	$ 54

Note C: Goodwill

The changes in the carrying amount of goodwill for the year ended December 31, 20X3, are as follows:

($000s)	Technology Segment	Communications Segment	Total
Balance as of January 1, 20X3	$1,413	$904	$2,317
Goodwill acquired during year	189	115	304
Impairment losses	—	(46)	(46)
Goodwill written off related to sale of business unit	(484)	—	(484)
Balance as of December 31, 20X3	$1,118	$973	$2,091

The Communications segment is tested for impairment in the third quarter, after the annual forecasting process. Due to an increase in competition in the Texas and Louisiana cable industry, operating profits and cash flows were lower than expected in the fourth quarter of 20X2 and the first and second quarters of 20X3. Based on that trend, the earnings forecast for the next five years was revised. In September 20X3, a goodwill impairment loss of $46 was recognized in the Communications reporting unit. The fair value of that reporting unit was estimated using the expected present value of future cash flows.

Illustration 2—Transitional Disclosures

C3. Paragraph 61 requires disclosure of what reported income before extraordinary items and net income would have been in all periods presented exclusive of amortization expense (including any related tax effects) recognized in those periods related to goodwill, intangible assets that are no longer being amortized, any deferred credit related to an excess over cost, equity method goodwill, and changes in amortization periods for intangible assets that will continue to be amortized (including any related tax effects). Similarly adjusted per-share amounts also are required to be disclosed for all periods presented. Omega Corporation initially applies this Statement on January 1, 2002. The amortization expense and net income of Omega Corporation for the year of initial application and prior two years follow (Omega Corporation recognized no extraordinary items in those years):

	For the Year Ended December 31,		
	20X2	20X1	20X0
Goodwill amortization	$	$ (40)	$ (40)
Trademark amortization	$	$ (20)	$ (20)
Copyright amortization	$ (9)	$ (12)	$ (12)
Net income	$1,223	$1,450	$1,360

C4. The copyright and the trademark were purchased on January 1, 19X9, and are being amortized on a straight-line basis over 40 years (maximum permitted by APB Opinion No. 17, *Intangible Assets*). Upon initial application of this Statement, Omega Corporation reassesses the useful lives of its intangible assets and determines that the copyright has a remaining useful life of 47 years. Omega Corporation will amortize the remaining balance of $444

related to the copyright over 47 years. The trademark is deemed to have an indefinite useful life because it is expected to generate cash flows indefinitely. Thus, Omega Corporation ceases amortizing the trademark on January 1, 2002.

C5. The following disclosure would be made by Omega Corporation in its December 31, 20X2 financial statements.

Footnote D: Goodwill and Other Intangible Assets—Adoption of Statement 142

	For the Year Ended December 31,		
($000s except for earnings-per-share amounts)	**20X2**	**20X1**	**20X0**
Reported net income	$1,223	$1,450	$1,360
Add back: Goodwill amortization		40	40
Add back: Trademark amortization		20	20
Adjust: Copyright amortization		3	3
Adjusted net income	$1,223	$1,513	$1,423
Basic earnings per share:			
Reported net income	$ 2.45	$ 2.90	$ 2.72
Goodwill amortization		0.08	0.08
Trademark amortization		0.04	0.04
Copyright amortization		0.01	0.01
Adjusted net income	$ 2.45	$ 3.03	$ 2.85
Diluted earnings per share:			
Reported net income	$ 2.23	$ 2.64	$ 2.47
Goodwill amortization		0.07	0.07
Trademark amortization		0.04	0.04
Copyright amortization		0.01	0.01
Adjusted net income	$ 2.23	$ 2.76	$ 2.59

Appendix D

AMENDMENTS TO EXISTING PRONOUNCEMENTS

D1. This Statement supersedes the following pronouncements:

a. APB Opinion No. 17, *Intangible Assets*
b. Both AICPA Accounting Interpretations of Opinion 17
c. ARB No. 43, Chapter 5, "Intangible Assets."

D2. APB Opinion No. 18, *The Equity Method of Accounting for Investments in Common Stock,* is amended as follows:

a. Footnote 9 to paragraph 19(b) is replaced by the following:

> Investors shall not amortize goodwill associated with equity method investments after the date FASB Statement No. 142, *Goodwill and Other Intangible Assets,* is initially applied by the entity in its entirety.

b. The following sentence is added to the end of paragraph 19(m):

> If that retroactive adjustment is made on or after the date Statement 142 is initially applied in its entirety, the goodwill related to that investment (including goodwill related to step purchases made prior to the initial application of Statement 142) shall not be amortized in determining the amount of the adjustment.

c. The last sentence of paragraph 19(n) is replaced by the following:

> However, if the investor is unable to relate the difference to specific accounts of the investee, the difference shall be recognized as goodwill and not be amortized in accordance with Statement 142.

d. Footnote 12 is deleted.

D3. The heading and first sentence of paragraph 11(c) of FASB Statement No. 2, *Accounting for Research and Development Costs,* are replaced by the following:

> *Intangible assets purchased from others.* The costs of intangible assets that are purchased from

others for use in research and development activities and that have alternative future uses (in research and development projects or otherwise) shall be accounted for in accordance with FASB Statement No. 142, *Goodwill and Other Intangible Assets.*

D4. FASB Statement No. 44, *Accounting for Intangible Assets of Motor Carriers,* is amended as follows:

a. In the last sentence of paragraph 3, the two references to *identifiable intangible assets* are replaced by *recognized intangible assets.*

b. Paragraph 4 is amended as follows:

> (1) In the first sentence, *identifiable intangible assets* is replaced by *recognized intangible assets* and *paragraphs 24–26 of APB Opinion No. 17, Intangible Assets* is replaced by *paragraphs 9 and 10 of FASB Statement No. 142, Goodwill and Other Intangible Assets.*
>
> (2) In the third sentence, the two references to *identifiable intangibles* are replaced by *recognized intangible assets.*
>
> (3) The last sentence is deleted.

c. The first sentence of paragraph 7 is replaced by the following:

> Other recognized intangible assets and goodwill relating to motor carrier operations shall be accounted for in accordance with Statement 142.

D5. FASB Statement No. 51, *Financial Reporting by Cable Television Companies,* is amended as follows:

a. In the first sentence of paragraph 13, *APB Opinion No. 17, Intangible Assets* is replaced by *FASB Statement No. 142, Goodwill and Other Intangible Assets.*

b. Paragraph 14, as amended by FASB Statement No. 121, *Accounting for the Impairment of Long-Lived Assets and Long-Lived Assets to Be Disposed Of,* is amended as follows:

> (1) In the first sentence, which was added by Statement 121, *identifiable* is deleted.

(2) The following sentence is added after the first sentence:

> Other intangible assets are subject to the provisions of Statement 142.

D6. In the table in paragraph 48 of FASB Statement No. 52, *Foreign Currency Translation,* under the subheading "Examples of revenues and expenses related to nonmonetary items:" *goodwill* is deleted from the line item "Amortization of intangible items such as goodwill, patents, licenses, etc."

D7. The last sentence of footnote 3 to paragraph 11 of FASB Statement No. 68, *Research and Development Arrangements,* is replaced by the following:

> The accounting for other recognized intangible assets acquired by the enterprise is specified in FASB Statement No. 142, *Goodwill and Other Intangible Assets.*

D8. FASB Statement No. 71, *Accounting for the Effects of Certain Types of Regulation,* is amended as follows:

a. Paragraph 29 and the heading before it are replaced by the following:

> **Goodwill**
>
> FASB Statement No. 142, *Goodwill and Other Intangible Assets,* states that goodwill shall not be amortized and shall be tested for impairment in accordance with that Statement. For rate-making purposes, a regulator may permit an enterprise to amortize purchased goodwill over a specified period. In other cases, a regulator may direct an enterprise not to amortize goodwill or to write off goodwill.

b. Paragraph 30 is replaced by the following:

> If the regulator permits all or a portion of goodwill to be amortized over a specific time period as an allowable cost for rate-making purposes, the regulator's action provides reasonable assurance of the existence of a regulatory asset (paragraph 9). That regulatory asset would then be amortized for financial reporting purposes over the period during which it will be allowed for rate-making purposes. Otherwise, goodwill shall not be amortized and shall be accounted for in accordance with Statement 142.

D9. FASB Statement No. 72, *Accounting for Certain Acquisitions of Banking or Thrift Institutions,* is amended as follows:

a. [This subparagraph has been deleted. See Status page.]

b. The following sentences are added after the last sentence of paragraph 4:

> An enterprise shall evaluate the periods of amortization continually to determine whether later events and circumstances warrant revised estimates of useful lives. If estimates are changed, the unamortized cost shall be allocated to the increased or reduced number of remaining periods in the revised useful life but not to exceed 40 years after acquisition. Estimation of value and future benefits of an intangible asset may indicate that the unamortized cost should be reduced significantly. However, a single loss year or even a few loss years together do not necessarily justify an unusual charge to income for all or a large part of the unamortized cost of intangible assets. The reason for an unusual deduction shall be disclosed.

c. The first sentence of paragraph 6 is replaced by the following:

> Paragraph 14 of Statement 142 specifies that an entity should evaluate the remaining useful life of an intangible asset that is being amortized each reporting period to determine whether events and circumstances warrant a revision to the remaining period of amortization.

d. In the first sentence of paragraph 7, *For purposes of applying paragraph 32 of Opinion 17,* and related footnote are deleted.

e. Footnote 6 is deleted.

D10. FASB Statement No 121, *Accounting for the Impairment of Long-Lived Assets and for Long-Lived Assets to Be Disposed Of,* is amended as follows:

a. The first sentence of paragraph 3 is replaced by the following:

> This Statement applies to long-lived assets and certain recognized intangible assets (except those not being amortized) to be held

and used, and to long-lived assets and certain recognized intangible assets (including those not being amortized) to be disposed of.

b. In paragraph 4, *identifiable intangibles* is replaced by *recognized intangible assets.*

c. In the last sentence of paragraph 6, *and amortization periods* is added after *policies.*

d. Paragraph 12 and the heading before it are deleted.

e. In the table in paragraph 147, the section relating to APB Opinion No. 17 is deleted.

D11. [This paragraph has been deleted. See Status page.]

E1–E3. [These paragraphs have been deleted. See Status page.]

Appendix F

GLOSSARY

F1. This appendix contains definitions of certain terms used in this Statement.

Goodwill
The excess of the cost of an acquired entity over the net of the amounts assigned to assets acquired and liabilities assumed. The amount recognized as goodwill includes acquired intangible assets that do not meet the criteria in FASB Statement No. 141, *Business Combinations,* for recognition as an asset apart from goodwill.

Intangible assets
Assets (not including financial assets) that lack physical substance. (The term *intangible assets* is used in this Statement to refer to intangible assets other than goodwill.)

Intangible asset class
A group of intangible assets that are similar, ei-

ther by their nature or by their use in the operations of an entity.

Mutual enterprise
An entity other than an investor-owned entity that provides dividends, lower costs, or other economic benefits directly and proportionately to its owners, members, or participants. Mutual insurance companies, credit unions, and farm and rural electric cooperatives are examples of mutual enterprises (FASB Concepts Statement No. 4, *Objectives of Financial Reporting by Nonbusiness Organizations,* paragraph 7).

Not-for-profit organization
An entity that possesses the following characteristics that distinguish it from a business enterprise: (a) contributions of significant amounts of resources from resource providers who do not expect commensurate or proportionate pecuniary return, (b) operating purposes other than to provide goods or services at a profit, and (c) absence of ownership interests like those of business enterprises. Not-for-profit organizations have those characteristics in varying degrees (Concepts Statement 4, paragraph 6). Entities that clearly fall outside this definition include all investor-owned entities and mutual enterprises.

Reporting unit
The level of reporting at which goodwill is tested for impairment. A reporting unit is an operating segment or one level below an operating segment (as that term is defined in paragraph 10 of FASB Statement No. 131, *Disclosures about Segments of an Enterprise and Related Information*).

Residual value
The estimated fair value of an intangible asset at the end of its useful life to an entity, less any disposal costs.

Useful life
The period over which an asset is expected to contribute directly or indirectly to future cash flows.

Statement of Financial Accounting Standards No. 143
Accounting for Asset Retirement Obligations

STATUS

Issued: June 2001

Effective Date: For financial statements for fiscal years beginning after June 15, 2002

Affects: Replaces FAS 19, paragraph 37

Affected by: Paragraphs 2 and 12 amended by FAS 144, paragraph C18
  Paragraphs 6, 7, and 9 deleted by FAS 157, paragraphs E23(a) and E23(c), respectively
  Paragraph 8 amended by FAS 157, paragraph E23(b)
  Paragraph 15 amended by FAS 154, paragraph C14
  Paragraphs A19 and F1 through F4 deleted by FAS 157, paragraphs E23(e) and E23(r), respectively
  Paragraphs A20, A21, A26, C1, C3(d), C4, C6 through C9, C11, and C12 amended by FAS 157, paragraphs E23(f) through E23(q), respectively
  Footnotes 5 through 8, 17, and 19 deleted by FAS 157, paragraphs E23(a) through E23(c), E23(f), and E23(g), respectively
  Footnote 11 deleted by FAS 144, paragraph C18(b)
  Footnotes 12 and 18 amended by FAS 157, paragraphs E23(d) and E23(g), respectively

Other Interpretive Pronouncement: FIN 47

Other Interpretive Release: FASB Staff Position FAS 143-1

AICPA Accounting Standards Executive Committee (AcSEC)

  Related Pronouncements: SOP 94-6
                          SOP 96-1

Issues Discussed by FASB Emerging Issues Task Force (EITF)

  Affects: No EITF Issues

  Interpreted by: No EITF Issues

  Related Issues: EITF Issues No. 89-13, 90-8, 95-23, and 02-6

SUMMARY

This Statement addresses financial accounting and reporting for obligations associated with the retirement of tangible long-lived assets and the associated asset retirement costs. This Statement applies to all entities. It applies to legal obligations associated with the retirement of long-lived assets that result from the acquisition, construction, development and (or) the normal operation of a long-lived asset, except for certain obligations of lessees. As used in this Statement, a legal obligation is an obligation that a party is required to settle as a result of an existing or enacted law, statute, ordinance, or written or oral contract or by legal construction of a contract under the doctrine of promissory estoppel. This Statement amends FASB Statement No. 19, *Financial Accounting and Reporting by Oil and Gas Producing Companies.*

Reasons for Issuing This Statement

The Board decided to address the accounting and reporting for asset retirement obligations because:

- Users of financial statements indicated that the diverse accounting practices that have developed for obligations associated with the retirement of tangible long-lived assets make it difficult to compare the financial position and results of operations of companies that have similar obligations but account for them differently.
- Obligations that meet the definition of a liability were not being recognized when those liabilities were incurred or the recognized liabilty was not consistently measured or presented.

Differences between This Statement, Statement 19, and Existing Practice

This Statement requires that the fair value of a liability for an asset retirement obligation be recognized in the period in which it is incurred if a reasonable estimate of fair value can be made. The associated asset retirement costs are capitalized as part of the carrying amount of the long-lived asset. This Statement differs from Statement 19 and current practice in several significant respects.

- Under Statement 19 and most current practice, an amount for an asset retirement obligation was recognized using a cost-accumulation measurement approach. Under this Statement, the amount initially recognized is measured at fair value.
- Under Statement 19 and most current practice, amounts for retirement obligations were not discounted and therefore no accretion expense was recorded in subsequent periods. Under this Statement, the liability is discounted and accretion expense is recognized using the credit-adjusted risk-free interest rate in effect when the liability was initially recognized.
- Under Statement 19, dismantlement and restoration costs were taken into account in determining amortization and depreciation rates. Consequently, many entities recognized asset retirement obligations as a contra-asset. Under this Statement, those obligations are recognized as a liability. Also, under Statement 19 the obligation was recognized over the useful life of the related asset. Under this Statement, the obligation is recognized when the liability is incurred.

Some current practice views a retirement obligation as a contingent liability and applies FASB Statement No. 5, *Accounting for Contingencies,* in determining when to recognize a liability. The measurement objective in this Statement is fair value, which is not compatible with a Statement 5 approach. A fair value measurement accommodates uncertainty in the amount and timing of settlement of the liability, whereas under Statement 5 the recognition decision is based on the level of uncertainty.

This Statement contains disclosure requirements that provide descriptions of asset retirement obligations and reconciliations of changes in the components of those obligations.

How the Changes in This Statement Improve Financial Reporting

Because all asset retirement obligations that fall within the scope of this Statement and their related asset retirement cost will be accounted for consistently, financial statements of different entities will be more comparable. Also,

- Retirement obligations will be recognized when they are incurred and displayed as liabilities. Thus, more information about future cash outflows, leverage, and liquidity will be provided. Also, an initial measurement at fair value will provide relevant information about the liability.
- Because the asset retirement cost is capitalized as part of the asset's carrying amount and subsequently allocated to expense over the asset's useful life, information about the gross investment in long-lived assets will be provided.

- Disclosure requirements contained in this Statement will provide more information about asset retirement obligations.

How the Statement Generally Changes Financial Statements

Because of diverse practice in current accounting for asset retirement obligations, various industries and entities will be affected differently. This Statement will likely have the following effects on current accounting practice:

- Total liabilities generally will increase because more retirement obligations will be recognized. For some entities, obligations will be recognized earlier, and they will be displayed as liabilities rather than as contra-assets. In certain cases, the amount of a recognized liability may be lower than that recognized in current practice because a fair value measurement entails discounting.
- The recognized cost of assets will increase because asset retirement costs will be added to the carrying amount of the long-lived asset. Assets also will increase because assets acquired with an existing retirement obligation will be displayed on a gross rather than on a net basis.
- The amount of expense (accretion expense plus depreciation expense) will be higher in the later years of an asset's life than in earlier years.

How the Conclusions in the Statement Relate to the Conceptual Framework

The Board concluded that all retirement obligations within the scope of this Statement that meet the definition of a liability in FASB Concepts Statement No. 6, *Elements of Financial Statements,* should be recognized as a liability when the recognition criteria in FASB Concepts Statement No. 5, *Recognition and Measurement in Financial Statements of Business Enterprises,* are met.

The Board also decided that the liability for an asset retirement obligation should be initially recognized at its estimated fair value as discussed in FASB Concepts Statement No. 7, *Using Cash Flow Information and Present Value in Accounting Measurements.*

Effective Date

This Statement is effective for financial statements issued for fiscal years beginning after June 15, 2002. Earlier application is encouraged.

Statement of Financial Accounting Standards No. 143

Accounting for Asset Retirement Obligations

CONTENTS

INTRODUCTION

1. Diverse accounting practices have developed for obligations associated with the retirement of tangible long-lived assets. Some entities accrue those obligations ratably over the useful life of the related asset, either as an element of depreciation expense (and accumulated depreciation) or as a liability. Other entities do not recognize liabilities for those obligations until an asset is retired. This Statement establishes accounting standards for recognition and measurement of a liability for an asset retirement obligation and the associated asset retirement cost.[1]

STANDARDS OF FINANCIAL ACCOUNTING AND REPORTING

Scope

2. This Statement applies to all entities. This Statement applies to legal obligations associated with the *retirement*[2] of a tangible long-lived asset that result from the acquisition, construction, or development and (or) the normal operation of a long-lived asset, except as explained in paragraph 17 for certain obligations of lessees. As used in this Statement, a legal obligation is an obligation that a party is required to

---

[1] The term *asset retirement obligation* refers to an obligation associated with the retirement of a tangible long-lived asset. The term *asset retirement cost* refers to the amount capitalized that increases the carrying amount of the long-lived asset when a liability for an asset retirement obligation is recognized.

[2] In this Statement, the term *retirement* is defined as the other-than-temporary removal of a long-lived asset from service. That term encompasses sale, abandonment, recycling, or disposal in some other manner. However, it does not encompass the temporary idling of a long-lived asset.

settle as a result of an existing or enacted law, statute, ordinance, or written or oral contract or by legal construction of a contract under the doctrine of promissory estoppel.[3] This Statement does not apply to obligations that arise solely from a plan to sell or otherwise dispose of a long-lived asset covered by FASB Statement No. 144, *Accounting for the Impairment or Disposal of Long-Lived Assets.* An obligation that results from the improper operation of an asset also is not within the scope of this Statement but may be subject to the provisions of AICPA Statement of Position 96-1, *Environmental Remediation Liabilities.*

Initial Recognition and Measurement of a Liability for an Asset Retirement Obligation

3. An entity shall recognize the fair value of a liability for an asset retirement obligation in the period in which it is incurred if a reasonable estimate of fair value can be made.[4] If a reasonable estimate of fair value cannot be made in the period the asset retirement obligation is incurred, the liability shall be recognized when a reasonable estimate of fair value can be made.

4. Paragraph 35 of FASB Concepts Statement No. 6, *Elements of Financial Statements,* defines a liability as follows:

> Liabilities are probable[21] future sacrifices of economic benefits arising from present obligations of a particular entity to transfer assets or provide services to other entities in the future as a result of past transactions or events. [Footnote 22 omitted.]

---

[21]*Probable* is used with its usual general meaning, rather than in a specific accounting or technical sense (such as that in Statement 5, par. 3), and refers to that which can reasonably be expected or believed on the basis of

available evidence or logic but is neither certain nor proved (*Webster's New World Dictionary,* p. 1132). Its inclusion in the definition is intended to acknowledge that business and other economic activities occur in an environment characterized by uncertainty in which few outcomes are certain (pars. 44–48).

5. As stated in the above footnote, the definition of a liability in Concepts Statement 6 uses the term *probable* in a different sense than it is used in FASB Statement No. 5, *Accounting for Contingencies.* As used in Statement 5, probable requires a high degree of expectation. The term probable in the definition of a liability, however, is intended to acknowledge that business and other economic activities occur in an environment in which few outcomes are certain.

6–7. [These paragraphs have been deleted. See Status page.]

8. An expected present value technique will usually be the only appropriate technique with which to estimate the fair value of a liability for an asset retirement obligation.[6a] An entity, when using that technique, shall discount the expected cash flows using a credit-adjusted risk-free rate. Thus, the effect of an entity's credit standing is reflected in the discount rate rather than in the expected cash flows.

9. [This paragraph has been deleted. See Status page.]

10. A liability for an asset retirement obligation may be incurred over more than one reporting period if the events that create the obligation occur over more than one reporting period. Any incremental liability incurred in a subsequent reporting period shall be considered to be an additional layer of the original liability. Each layer shall be initially measured at fair value. For example, the liability for decommissioning a nuclear power plant is incurred as contamination occurs. Each period, as contamination increases, a separate layer shall be measured and recognized.

---

[3]*Black's Law Dictionary,* seventh edition, defines *promissory estoppel* as, "The principle that a promise made without consideration may nonetheless be enforced to prevent injustice if the promisor should have reasonably expected the promisee to rely on the promise and if the promisee did actually rely on the promise to his or her detriment."

[4]If a tangible long-lived asset with an existing asset retirement obligation is acquired, a liability for that obligation shall be recognized at the asset's acquisition date as if that obligation were incurred on that date.

[5–6][These footnotes have been deleted. See Status page.]

[6a]Proper application of a discount rate adjustment technique entails analysis of at least two liabilities—the liability that exists in the marketplace and has an observable interest rate and the liability being measured. The appropriate rate of interest for the cash flows being measured must be inferred from the observable rate of interest of some other liability, and to draw that inference the characteristics of the cash flows must be similar to those of the liability being measured. Rarely, if ever, would there be an observable rate of interest for a liability that has cash flows similar to an asset retirement obligation being measured. In addition, an asset retirement obligation usually will have uncertainties in both timing and amount. In that circumstance, employing a discount rate adjustment technique, where uncertainty is incorporated into the rate, will be difficult, if not impossible.

[7–8][These footnotes have been deleted. See Status page.]

Recognition and Allocation of an Asset Retirement Cost

11. Upon initial recognition of a liability for an asset retirement obligation, an entity shall capitalize an asset retirement cost by increasing the carrying amount of the related long-lived asset by the same amount as the liability.[9] An entity shall subsequently allocate that asset retirement cost to expense using a systematic and rational method over its useful life. Application of a systematic and rational allocation method does not preclude an entity from capitalizing an amount of asset retirement cost and allocating an equal amount to expense in the same accounting period.[10]

Asset Impairment

12. In applying the provisions of Statement 144, the carrying amount of the asset being tested for impairment shall include amounts of capitalized asset retirement costs. Estimated future cash flows related to the liability for an asset retirement obligation that has been recognized in the financial statements shall be excluded from (a) the undiscounted cash flows used to test the asset for recoverability and (b) the discounted cash flows used to measure the asset's fair value. If the fair value of the asset is based on a quoted market price and that price considers the costs that will be incurred in retiring that asset, the quoted market price shall be increased by the fair value of the asset retirement obligation for purposes of measuring impairment.

Subsequent Recognition and Measurement

13. In periods subsequent to initial measurement, an entity shall recognize period-to-period changes in the liability for an asset retirement obligation resulting from (a) the passage of time and (b) revisions to either the timing or the amount of the original estimate of undiscounted cash flows. An entity shall measure and incorporate changes due to the passage of time into the carrying amount of the liability before measuring changes resulting from a revision to either the timing or the amount of estimated cash flows.

14. An entity shall measure changes in the liability for an asset retirement obligation due to passage of time by applying an interest method of allocation to the amount of the liability at the beginning of the period.[12] The interest rate used to measure that change shall be the credit-adjusted risk-free rate that existed when the liability, or portion thereof, was initially measured. That amount shall be recognized as an increase in the carrying amount of the liability and as an expense classified as an operating item in the statement of income, hereinafter referred to as *accretion expense*.[13] Accretion expense shall not be considered to be interest cost for purposes of applying FASB Statement No. 34, *Capitalization of Interest Cost.*

15. Changes resulting from revisions to the timing or the amount of the original estimate of undiscounted cash flows shall be recognized as an increase or a decrease in (a) the carrying amount of the liability for an asset retirement obligation and (b) the related asset retirement cost capitalized as part of the carrying amount of the related long-lived asset. Upward revisions in the amount of undiscounted estimated cash flows shall be discounted using the current credit-adjusted risk-free rate. Downward revisions in the amount of undiscounted estimated cash flows shall be discounted using the credit-adjusted risk-free rate that existed when the original liability was recognized. If an entity cannot identify the prior period to which the downward revision relates, it may use a weighted-average credit-adjusted risk-free rate to discount the downward revision to estimated future cash flows. When asset retirement costs change as a result of a revision to estimated cash flows, an entity shall adjust the amount of asset retirement cost allocated to expense in the period of change if the change affects

---

[9]Capitalized asset retirement costs do not qualify as *expenditures* for purposes of paragraph 16 of FASB Statement No. 34, *Capitalization of Interest Cost.*

[10]For example, assume an entity acquires a long-lived asset with an estimated life of 10 years. As that asset is operated, the entity incurs one-tenth of the liability for an asset retirement obligation each year. Application of a systematic and rational allocation method would not preclude that entity from capitalizing and then expensing one-tenth of the asset retirement costs each year.

[11][This footnote has been deleted. See Status page.]

[12]The subsequent measurement provisions require an entity to identify undiscounted estimated cash flows associated with the initial measurement of a liability. Therefore, an entity that obtains an initial measurement of fair value from a market price or from a technique other than an expected present value technique must determine the undiscounted cash flows and estimated timing of those cash flows that are embodied in that fair value amount for purposes of applying the subsequent measurement provisions. Appendix E includes an example of the subsequent measurement of a liability that is initially obtained from a market price.

[13]An entity may use any descriptor for accretion expense so long as it conveys the underlying nature of the expense.

that period only or in the period of change and future periods if the change affects more than one period as required by FASB Statement No. 154, *Accounting Changes and Error Corrections,* (paragraphs 19–22), for a change in estimate.

Effects of Funding and Assurance Provisions

16. Providing assurance that an entity will be able to satisfy its asset retirement obligation does not satisfy or extinguish the related liability. Methods of providing assurance include surety bonds, insurance policies, letters of credit, guarantees by other entities, and establishment of trust funds or identification of other assets dedicated to satisfy the asset retirement obligation. The existence of funding and assurance provisions may affect the determination of the credit-adjusted risk-free rate. For a previously recognized asset retirement obligation, changes in funding and assurance provisions have no effect on the initial measurement or accretion of that liability, but may affect the credit-adjusted risk-free rate used to discount upward revisions in undiscounted cash flows for that obligation. Costs associated with complying with funding or assurance provisions are accounted for separately from the asset retirement obligation.

Leasing Transactions

17. This Statement does not apply to obligations of a lessee in connection with leased property, whether imposed by a lease agreement or by a party other than the lessor, that meet the definition of either minimum lease payments or contingent rentals in paragraph 5 of FASB Statement No. 13, *Accounting for Leases.*[14] Those obligations shall be accounted for by the lessee in accordance with the requirements of Statement 13 (as amended). However, if obligations of a lessee in connection with leased property, whether imposed by a lease agreement or by a party other than the lessor, meet the provisions in paragraph 2 of this Statement but do not meet the definition of either minimum lease payments or contingent rentals in paragraph 5 of Statement 13, those obligations shall be accounted for by the lessee in accordance with the requirements of this Statement.

18. Obligations of a lessor in connection with leased property that meet the provisions in paragraph 2 of this Statement shall be accounted for by the lessor in accordance with the requirements of this Statement.

Rate-Regulated Entities

19. This Statement applies to rate-regulated entities that meet the criteria for application of FASB Statement No. 71, *Accounting for the Effects of Certain Types of Regulation,* as provided in paragraph 5 of that Statement. Paragraphs 9 and 11 of Statement 71 provide specific conditions that must be met to recognize a regulatory asset and a regulatory liability, respectively.

20. Many rate-regulated entities currently provide for the costs related to the retirement of certain long-lived assets in their financial statements and recover those amounts in rates charged to their customers. Some of those costs result from asset retirement obligations within the scope of this Statement; others result from costs that are not within the scope of this Statement. The amounts charged to customers for the costs related to the retirement of long-lived assets may differ from the period costs recognized in accordance with this Statement and, therefore, may result in a difference in the timing of recognition of period costs for financial reporting and rate-making purposes. An additional recognition timing difference may exist when the costs related to the retirement of long-lived assets are included in amounts charged to customers but liabilities are not recognized in the financial statements. If the requirements of Statement 71 are met, a regulated entity also shall recognize a regulatory asset or liability for differences in the timing of recognition of the period costs associated with asset retirement obligations for financial reporting pursuant to this Statement and rate-making purposes.

21. The capitalized amount of an asset retirement cost shall be included in the assessment of impairment of long-lived assets of a rate-regulated entity just as that cost is included in the assessment of impairment of long-lived assets of any other entity. FASB Statement No. 90, *Regulated Enterprises— Accounting for Abandonments and Disallowances of Plant Costs,* applies to the asset retirement cost related to a long-lived asset of a rate-regulated entity that has been closed or abandoned.

---

[14]Paragraph 1 of Statement 13 provides that Statement 13 does not apply to lease agreements concerning the rights to explore for or to exploit natural resources such as oil, gas, minerals, and timber.

Disclosures

22. An entity shall disclose the following information about its asset retirement obligations:

a. A general description of the asset retirement obligations and the associated long-lived assets
b. The fair value of assets that are legally restricted for purposes of settling asset retirement obligations
c. A reconciliation of the beginning and ending aggregate carrying amount of asset retirement obligations showing separately the changes attributable to (1) liabilities incurred in the current period, (2) liabilities settled in the current period, (3) accretion expense, and (4) revisions in estimated cash flows, whenever there is a significant change in one or more of those four components during the reporting period.

If the fair value of an asset retirement obligation cannot be reasonably estimated, that fact and the reasons therefor shall be disclosed.

Amendment to Existing Pronouncement

23. Paragraph 37 of FASB Statement No. 19, *Financial Accounting and Reporting by Oil and Gas Producing Companies,* is replaced by the following:

Obligations for dismantlement, restoration, and abandonment costs shall be accounted for in accordance with the provisions of FASB Statement No. 143, *Accounting for Asset Retirement Obligations.* Estimated residual salvage values shall be taken into account in determining amortization and depreciation rates.

Effective Date and Transition

24. This Statement shall be effective for financial statements issued for fiscal years beginning after June 15, 2002. Earlier application is encouraged. Initial application of this Statement shall be as of the beginning of an entity's fiscal year. If this Statement is adopted prior to the effective date and during an interim period other than the first interim period of a fiscal year, all prior interim periods of that fiscal year shall be restated.

25. Upon initial application of this Statement, an entity shall recognize the following items in its statement of financial position: (a) a liability for any existing asset retirement obligations adjusted for cumulative accretion to the date of adoption of this Statement, (b) an asset retirement cost capitalized as an increase to the carrying amount of the associated long-lived asset, and (c) accumulated depreciation on that capitalized cost. Amounts resulting from initial application of this Statement shall be measured using current (that is, as of the date of adoption of this Statement) information, current assumptions, and current interest rates. The amount recognized as an asset retirement cost shall be measured as of the date the asset retirement obligation was incurred. Cumulative accretion and accumulated depreciation shall be measured for the time period from the date the liability would have been recognized had the provisions of this Statement been in effect to the date of adoption of this Statement. Appendix D provides examples that illustrate application of the transition provisions of this Statement.

26. An entity shall recognize the cumulative effect of initially applying this Statement as a change in accounting principle as described in paragraph 20 of Opinion 20. The amount to be reported as a cumulative-effect adjustment in the statement of operations is the difference between the amounts, if any, recognized in the statement of financial position prior to the application of this Statement (for example, under the provisions of Statement 19) and the net amount that is recognized in the statement of financial position pursuant to paragraph 25.

27. In addition to disclosures required by paragraphs 19(c), 19(d), and 21 of Opinion 20,[15] an entity shall compute on a pro forma basis and disclose in the footnotes to the financial statements for the beginning of the earliest year presented and at the end of all years presented the amount of the liability for asset retirement obligations as if this Statement had been applied during all periods affected. The pro forma amounts of that liability shall be measured using current (that is, as of the date of adoption of this Statement) information, current assumptions, and current interest rates.

28. Lease classification tests performed in accordance with the requirements of Statement 13 at, or subsequent to, the date of initial application of this

---

[15]Opinion 20 requires an entity to disclose the effect of adopting a new accounting principle on income before extraordinary items and on net income (and on the related per-share amounts) of the period of the change. In addition, it requires an entity to compute on a pro forma basis and disclose on the face of the income statements for all periods presented income before extraordinary items and net income (and the related per-share amounts) as if the newly adopted accounting principle had been applied during all periods affected.

Statement shall incorporate the requirements of this Statement to the extent applicable.[16] However, leases existing at the date of initial application of this Statement shall not be reclassified to reflect the effects of the requirements of this Statement on the lease classification tests previously performed in accordance with the requirements of Statement 13.

> **The provisions of this Statement need not be applied to immaterial items.**

This Statement was adopted by the unanimous vote of the six members of the Financial Accounting Standards Board.

Edmund L. Jenkins,	G. Michael Crooch	Gerhard G. Mueller
Chairman	John M. Foster	Edward W. Trott
	Gaylen N. Larsen	

Appendix A

IMPLEMENTATION GUIDANCE

CONTENTS

---

[16]For example, the recorded cost of an asset leased by a lessor may be affected by the requirements of this Statement and would potentially affect the application of the classification criterion in paragraph 7(d) of Statement 13.

Appendix A

IMPLEMENTATION GUIDANCE

Introduction

A1. This appendix describes certain provisions of this Statement in more detail and explains how they apply to certain situations. Facts and circumstances need to be considered carefully in applying this Statement. This appendix is an integral part of the standards of this Statement.

Scope

Legal Obligation

A2. This Statement applies to legal obligations associated with the retirement of a tangible long-lived asset. For purposes of this Statement, a legal obligation can result from (a) a government action, such as a law, statute, or ordinance, (b) an agreement between entities, such as a written or oral contract, or (c) a promise conveyed to a third party that imposes a reasonable expectation of performance upon the promisor under the doctrine of promissory estoppel. *Black's Law Dictionary,* seventh edition, defines *promissory estoppel* as, "The principle that a promise made without consideration may nonetheless be enforced to prevent injustice if the promisor should have reasonably expected the promisee to rely on the promise and if the promisee did actually rely on the promise to his or her detriment."

A3. In most cases involving an asset retirement obligation, the determination of whether a legal obligation exists should be unambiguous. However, in situations in which no law, statute, ordinance, or contract exists but an entity makes a promise to a third party (which may include the public at large) about its intention to perform retirement activities, facts and circumstances need to be considered carefully in determining whether that promise has imposed a legal obligation upon the promisor under the doctrine of promissory estoppel. A legal obligation may exist even though no party has taken any formal action. In assessing whether a legal obligation exists, an entity is not permitted to forecast changes in the law or changes in the interpretation of existing laws and regulations. Preparers and their legal advisors are required to evaluate current circumstances to determine whether a legal obligation exists.

A4. For example, assume a company operates a manufacturing facility and has plans to retire it within five years. Members of the local press have begun to publicize the fact that when the company ceases operations at the plant, it plans to abandon the site without demolishing the building and restoring the underlying land. Due to the significant negative publicity and demands by the public that the company commit to dismantling the plant upon retirement, the company's chief executive officer holds a press conference at city hall to announce that the company will demolish the building and restore the underlying land when the company ceases operations at the plant. Although no law, statute, ordinance, or written contract exists requiring the company to perform any demolition or restoration activities, the promise made by the company's chief executive officer may have created a legal obligation under the doctrine of promissory estoppel. In that circumstance, the company's management (and legal counsel, if necessary) would have to evaluate the particular facts and circumstances to determine whether a legal obligation exists.

A5. Contracts between entities may contain an option or a provision that requires one party to the contract to perform retirement activities when an asset is retired. The other party may decide in the future not to exercise the option or to waive the provision to perform retirement activities, or that party may have a history of waiving similar provisions in other contracts. Even if there is an expectation of a waiver or nonenforcement, the contract still imposes a legal obligation. That obligation is included in the scope of this Statement. The likelihood of a waiver or nonenforcement will affect the measurement of the liability.

Issues Associated with the Retirement of a Tangible Long-Lived Asset

A6. In this Statement, the term *retirement* is defined as the other-than-temporary removal of a long-lived asset from service. As used in this Statement, that term encompasses sale, abandonment, or disposal in some other manner. However, it does not encompass the temporary idling of a long-lived asset. After an entity retires an asset, that asset is no longer under the control of that entity, no longer in existence, or no longer capable of being used in the manner for which the asset was originally acquired, constructed, or developed. Activities necessary to prepare an asset for an alternative use are not associated with the retirement of the asset and are not within the scope of this Statement.

A7. Typically, settlement of an asset retirement obligation is not required until the associated asset is retired. However, certain circumstances may exist in which partial settlement of an asset retirement obligation is required or performed before the asset is fully retired. The fact that partial settlement of an obligation is required or performed prior to full retirement of an asset does not remove that obligation from the scope of this Statement.

A8. For example, consider an entity that owns and operates a landfill. Regulations require that that entity perform capping, closure, and post-closure activities. Capping activities involve covering the land with topsoil and planting vegetation. Closure activities include drainage, engineering, and demolition and must be performed prior to commencing the post-closure activities. Post-closure activities, the final retirement activities, include maintaining the landfill once final certification of closure has been received and monitoring the ground and surface water, gas emissions, and air quality. Closure and post-closure activities are performed after the entire landfill ceases receiving waste (that is, after the landfill is retired). However, capping activities are performed as sections of the landfill become full and are effectively retired. The fact that some of the capping activities are performed while the landfill continues to accept waste does not remove the obligation to perform those intermediate capping activities from the scope of this Statement.

A9. Obligations associated with maintenance, rather than retirement, of a long-lived asset are excluded from the scope of this Statement. The cost of a replacement part that is a component of a long-lived asset is not within the scope of this Statement. Any legal obligations that require disposal of the replaced part are within the scope of this Statement.

Obligations Resulting from the Acquisition, Construction, or Development and (or) Normal Operation of an Asset

A10. Paragraph 2 of this Statement limits its scope to those legal obligations that result from the acquisition, construction, or development and (or) the normal operation of a long-lived asset.

A11. Whether an obligation results from the acquisition, construction, or development of a long-lived asset should, in most circumstances, be clear. For example, if an entity acquires a landfill that is already in operation, an obligation to perform capping, closure,

and post-closure activities results from the acquisition and assumption of obligations related to past normal operations of the landfill. Additional obligations will be incurred as a result of future operations of the landfill.

A12. Whether an obligation results from the normal operation of a long-lived asset may require judgment. Obligations that result from the normal operation of an asset should be predictable and likely of occurring. For example, consider a company that owns and operates a nuclear power plant. That company has a legal obligation to perform decontamination activities when the plant ceases operations. Contamination, which gives rise to the obligation, is predictable and likely of occurring and is unavoidable as a result of operating the plant. Therefore, the obligation to perform decontamination activities at that plant results from the normal operation of the plant.

A13. An environmental remediation liability that results from the improper operation of a long-lived asset does not fall within the scope of this Statement. Obligations resulting from improper operations do not represent costs that are an integral part of the tangible long-lived asset and therefore should not be accounted for as part of the cost basis of the asset. For example, a certain amount of spillage may be inherent in the normal operations of a fuel storage facility, but a catastrophic accident caused by noncompliance with a company's safety procedures is not. The obligation to clean up after the catastrophic accident does not result from the normal operation of the facility and is not within the scope of this Statement. An environmental remediation liability that results from the normal operation of a long-lived asset and that is associated with the retirement of that asset shall be accounted for under the provisions of this Statement.

Asset Retirement Obligations with Indeterminate Settlement Dates

A14. An asset retirement obligation may result from the acquisition, construction, or development and (or) normal operation of a long-lived asset that has an indeterminate useful life and thereby an indeterminate settlement date for the asset retirement obligation. Uncertainty about the timing of settlement of the asset retirement obligation does not remove that obligation from the scope of this Statement but will affect the measurement of a liability for that obligation (refer to paragraph A16).

Asset Retirement Obligations Related to Component Parts of Larger Systems

A15. An asset retirement obligation may exist for component parts of a larger system. In some circumstances, the retirement of the component parts may be required before the retirement of the larger system to which the component parts belong. For example, consider an aluminum smelter that owns and operates several kilns lined with a special type of brick. The kilns have a long useful life, but the bricks wear out after approximately five years of use and are replaced on a periodic basis to maintain optimal efficiency of the kilns. Because the bricks become contaminated with hazardous chemicals while in the kiln, a state law requires that when the bricks are removed, they must be disposed of at a special hazardous waste site. The obligation to dispose of those bricks is within the scope of this Statement. The cost of the replacement bricks and their installation are not part of that obligation.

Liability Recognition—Asset Retirement Obligations with Indeterminate Settlement Dates

A16. Instances may occur in which insufficient information to estimate the fair value of an asset retirement obligation is available. For example, if an asset has an indeterminate useful life, sufficient information to estimate a range of potential settlement dates for the obligation might not be available. In such cases, the liability would be initially recognized in the period in which sufficient information exists to estimate a range of potential settlement dates that is needed to employ a present value technique to estimate fair value.

Liability Recognition—Conditional Obligations

A17. A conditional obligation to perform a retirement activity is within the scope of this Statement. For example, if a governmental unit retains the right (an option) to decide whether to require a retirement activity, there is some uncertainty about whether those retirement activities will be required or waived. Regardless of the uncertainty attributable to the option, a legal obligation to stand ready to perform retirement activities still exists, and the governmental unit might require them to be performed. Uncertainty about whether performance will be required does not defer the recognition of a retirement obligation; rather, that uncertainty is factored into the measure-

ment of the fair value of the liability through assignment of probabilities to cash flows. Uncertainty about performance of conditional obligations shall not prevent the determination of a reasonable estimate of fair value.

A18. A past history of nonenforcement of an unambiguous obligation does not defer recognition of a liability, but its measurement is affected by the uncertainty over the requirement to perform retirement activities. Uncertainty about the requirement to perform retirement activities shall not prevent the determination of a reasonable estimate of fair value. Guidance on how to estimate a liability in the presence of uncertainty about a requirement to perform retirement activities is provided in Appendix C.

Initial Measurement of a Liability for an Asset Retirement Obligation

A19. [This paragraph has been deleted. See Status page.]

A20. In estimating the fair value of a liability for an asset retirement obligation using an expected present value technique, an entity shall begin by estimating the expected cash flows that reflect, to the extent possible, a marketplace assessment of the cost and timing of performing the required retirement activities. Considerations in estimating those expected cash flows include developing and incorporating explicit assumptions, to the extent possible, about all of the following:

a. The costs that a third party would incur in performing the tasks necessary to retire the asset
b. Other amounts that a third party would include in determining the price of the transfer, including, for example, inflation, overhead, equipment charges, profit margin, and advances in technology
c. The extent to which the amount of a third party's costs or the timing of its costs would vary under different future scenarios and the relative probabilities of those scenarios
d. The price that a third party would demand and could expect to receive for bearing the uncertainties and unforeseeable circumstances inherent in the obligation, sometimes referred to as a market-risk premium.

It is expected that uncertainties about the amount and timing of future cash flows can be accommodated by

---

[17][This footnote has been deleted. See Status page.]

using the expected present value technique and therefore will not prevent the determination of a reasonable estimate of fair value.

A21. An entity shall discount expected cash flows using an interest rate that equates to a risk-free interest rate adjusted for the effect of its credit standing (a credit-adjusted risk-free rate).[18] Adjustments for default risk can be reflected in either the discount rate or the expected cash flows. The Board believes that in most situations, an entity will know the adjustment required to the risk-free interest rate to reflect its credit standing. Consequently, it would be easier and less complex to reflect that adjustment in the discount rate. In addition, because of the requirements in paragraph 15 relating to upward and downward adjustments in expected cash flows, it is essential to the operationality of this Statement that the credit standing of the entity be reflected in the discount rate. For those reasons, the Board chose to require that the risk-free rate be adjusted for the credit standing of the entity to determine the discount rate.

A22. Where assets with asset retirement obligations are components of a larger group of assets (for example, a number of oil wells that make up an entire oil field operation), aggregation techniques may be necessary to derive a collective asset retirement obligation. This Statement does not preclude the use of estimates and computational shortcuts that are consistent with the fair value measurement objective when computing an aggregate asset retirement obligation for assets that are components of a larger group of assets.

A23. This Statement requires recognition of the fair value of a conditional asset retirement obligation before the event that either requires or waives performance occurs. Uncertainty surrounding conditional performance of the retirement obligation is factored into its measurement by assessing the likelihood that performance will be required. In situations in which the conditional aspect has only 2 outcomes and there is no information about which outcome is more probable, a 50 percent likelihood for each outcome shall be used until additional information is available. As the time for notification approaches, more information and a better perspective about the ultimate outcome will likely be obtained. Consequently, reassessment of the timing, amount, and probabilities

associated with the expected cash flows may change the amount of the liability recognized. If, as time progresses, it becomes apparent that retirement activities will not be required, the liability and the remaining unamortized asset retirement cost are reduced to zero.

A24. In summary, an unambiguous requirement that gives rise to an asset retirement obligation coupled with a low likelihood of required performance still requires recognition of a liability. Uncertainty about the conditional outcome of the obligation is incorporated into the measurement of the fair value of that liability, not the recognition decision.

Subsequent Recognition and Measurement

A25. In periods subsequent to initial measurement, an entity recognizes the effect of the passage of time on the amount of a liability for an asset retirement obligation. A period-to-period increase in the carrying amount of the liability shall be recognized as an operating item (accretion expense) in the statement of income. An equivalent amount is added to the carrying amount of the liability. To calculate accretion expense, an entity shall multiply the beginning of the period liability balance by the credit-adjusted risk-free rate that existed when the liability was initially measured. The liability shall be adjusted for accretion prior to adjusting for revisions in estimated cash flows.

A26. Revisions to a previously recorded asset retirement obligation will result from changes in the assumptions used to estimate the expected cash flows required to settle the asset retirement obligation, including changes in estimated probabilities, amounts, and timing of the settlement of the asset retirement obligation, as well as changes in the legal requirements of an obligation. Any changes that result in upward revisions to the expected cash flows shall be treated as a new liability and discounted at the current rate. Any downward revisions to the expected cash flows will result in a reduction of the asset retirement obligation. For downward revisions, the amount of the liability to be removed from the existing accrual shall be discounted at the credit-adjusted risk-free rate that was used at the time the obligation to which

---

[18]In determining the adjustment for the effect of its credit standing, an entity should consider the effects of all terms, collateral, and existing guarantees on the fair value of the liability.

[19][This footnote has been deleted. See Status page.]

the downward revision relates was originally re-corded (or the historical weighted-average rate if the year(s) to which the downward revision applies cannot be determined).

A27. Revisions to the asset retirement obligation result in adjustments of capitalized asset retirement

costs and will affect subsequent depreciation of the related asset. Such adjustments are depreciated on a prospective basis.

Appendix B

BACKGROUND INFORMATION AND BASIS FOR CONCLUSIONS

CONTENTS

Appendix B

BACKGROUND INFORMATION AND BASIS FOR CONCLUSIONS

Introduction

B1. This appendix summarizes considerations that Board members deemed significant in reaching the conclusions in this Statement. It includes reasons for accepting certain approaches and rejecting others. Individual Board members gave greater weight to some factors than to others.

Background Information

B2. In February 1994, the Edison Electric Institute (EEI) requested that the Board add a project to its agenda to address accounting for removal costs, including the costs of nuclear decommissioning as well as similar costs incurred in other industries. At its April 1994 meeting, the Financial Accounting Standards Advisory Council (FASAC) discussed the advisability of the Board's adding to its agenda a project limited to accounting for the costs of nuclear decommissioning, a broader project on accounting for removal costs including nuclear decommissioning, or an even broader project on environmental costs. At that time, most FASAC members suggested that the Board undertake either a project on accounting for removal costs or a broader project on environmental costs. In June 1994, the Board also met with representatives from the EEI, the oil and gas industry, the mining industry, and the AICPA Environmental Task Force to discuss the EEI's request.

B3. In June 1994, the Board added a project to its agenda on accounting for the costs of nuclear decommissioning. Shortly thereafter, the Board expanded the scope of the project to include similar closure or removal-type costs in other industries. An FASB Exposure Draft, *Accounting for Certain Liabilities Related to Closure or Removal of Long-Lived Assets* (initial Exposure Draft), was issued on February 7, 1996. The Board received 123 letters of comment.

B4. In October 1997, the Board decided to continue with the closure or removal project by proceeding toward a revised Exposure Draft. The Board decided to change the title of the project to accounting for obligations associated with the retirement of long-lived assets and the project became subsequently known as the asset retirement obligations project. The Board issued a revised Exposure Draft, *Accounting for Obli-gations Associated with the Retirement of Long-Lived Assets,* in February 2000 and received 50 letters of comment. The Board concluded that it could reach an informed decision on the basis of existing information without a public hearing.

B5. The major objective of the asset retirement obligations project was to provide accounting requirements for the recognition and measurement of liabilities for obligations associated with the retirement of long-lived assets. Another objective was to provide accounting requirements with respect to the recognition of asset retirement costs as well as guidance for the periodic allocation of those costs to results of operations. The key differences between the initial Exposure Draft and the revised Exposure Draft were in the scope and the requirements for initial measurement of a liability for an asset retirement obligation. Specifically, the revised Exposure Draft (a) broadened the scope of the initial Exposure Draft beyond obligations incurred in the acquisition, construction, development, or early operation of a long-lived asset to asset retirement obligations incurred any time during the life of an asset and (b) roposed that an asset retirement obligation be initially measured at fair value. The initial Exposure Draft would have required an initial measurement that reflected the present value of the estimated future cash flows required to satisfy the closure or removal obligation. One key difference between this Statement and the revised Exposure Draft is in the Statement's scope. This Statement applies only to existing legal obligations, including those for which no formal legal action has been taken but that would be considered legal obligations under the doctrine of promissory estoppel.

Benefits and Costs

B6. The mission of the Board is to establish and improve standards of financial accounting and reporting for the guidance and education of the public, including issuers, auditors, and users of financial information. In fulfilling that mission, the Board must determine that a proposed standard will fill a significant need and that the costs it imposes, compared with possible alternatives, will be justified in relation to the overall benefits of the resulting information. The Board's assessment of the costs and benefits of issuing an accounting standard is unavoidably subjective because there is no method to measure objectively the costs to implement an accounting standard or to quantify the value of improved information in financial statements.

B7. Existing accounting practices for asset retirement obligations were inconsistent in the criteria used for recognition, the measurement objective, and the presentation of those obligations in the financial statements. Some entities did not recognize any asset retirement obligations. Some entities that recognized asset retirement obligations displayed them as a contra-asset. As a result, information that was conveyed in the financial statements about those obligations was inconsistent. This Statement eliminates those inconsistencies and requires disclosure of additional relevant information about those obligations in financial statements.

B8. One of the principal costs of applying this Statement is the cost of implementing the requirement to initially measure the liability for an asset retirement obligation using a fair value measurement objective. Most entities will meet that requirement by using an expected present value technique that incorporates various estimates of expected cash flows. The basis for and procedures necessary to perform that type of calculation can be found in FASB Concepts Statement No. 7, *Using Cash Flow Information and Present Value in Accounting Measurements.* Although many entities have developed information to estimate amounts for asset retirement obligations based on some notion of "cost accumulation," that information probably is not consistent with the requirements of this Statement. Some entities may not have developed any information about asset retirement obligations because, prior to this Statement, they were not required to account for that type of obligation in their financial statements. The Board believes that the benefits resulting from the improvements in financial reporting that result from the application of the requirements of this Statement outweigh the costs of implementing it.

Basis for Conclusions

Scope

B9. The scope of the initial Exposure Draft applied to all entities and to obligations for the closure or removal of long-lived assets that possessed all of the following characteristics:

a. The obligation is incurred in the acquisition, construction, development, or early operation of a long-lived asset.
b. The obligation is related to the closure or removal of a long-lived asset and cannot be satisfied until the current operation or use of the asset ceases.
c. The obligation cannot be realistically avoided if the asset is operated for its intended use.

B10. The objective of those characteristics was to limit the obligations included in the scope to those that were similar in nature to nuclear decommissioning costs and that could, therefore, be recognized and measured according to the accounting model that was proposed for decommissioning obligations.[20] Through educational sessions and the comment letters, the Board learned that, in some industries, closure or removal obligations[21] are not incurred in the same pattern as those for decommissioning. Respondents expressed concern that those characteristics could be interpreted to allow many types of closure or removal obligations to fall outside the scope of the initial Exposure Draft.

B11. Many comments related to the intended meaning of *early operation* as used in the first characteristic in paragraph B9. Many respondents indicated that it was unclear whether that phrase could be interpreted to mean that obligations incurred ratably over the operating life of a long-lived asset were not within the scope of the initial Exposure Draft. Others said that that phrase was ambiguous and, therefore, could result in entities within the same industry accounting for the same type of obligation differently depending on how they interpreted the phrase for their particular situation. Some respondents indicated that the Board should define *early operation* by using bright-line conditions or describe that phrase by using specific examples from various industries.

B12. In deliberations leading to the revised Exposure Draft, the Board decided to eliminate the first characteristic, thereby broadening the scope of the project to asset retirement obligations incurred any time during the life of an asset. In making that decision, the Board emphasized that the determination of whether to recognize a liability should be based on

---

[20]In general, that model required (a) recognition of the amount of a decommissioning obligation as a liability when incurred, (b) measurement of that liability based on discounted future cash flows using a cost-accumulation approach, and (c) capitalization of the decommissioning costs (the offsetting debit) by increasing the cost of the nuclear facility.

[21]Although the nature of *closure or removal obligations* is similar to the nature of *asset retirement obligations,* the former is used to refer to the obligations that were within the scope of the initial Exposure Draft, and the latter is used to refer to the obligations that are within the broader scope of this Statement.

the characteristics of the obligation instead of when that obligation arose. Therefore, the Board agreed that it was unnecessary to limit the scope to obligations that were similar in nature to decommissioning obligations. It also decided that the scope should be equally applicable to asset retirement obligations incurred during the operating life of a long-lived asset. In addition, the Board decided that the requirements for (a) a discounted liability measurement and (b) the capitalization of asset retirement costs were applicable regardless of when in the life of an asset a liability is incurred.

B13. Respondents to the initial Exposure Draft indicated that the second characteristic in paragraph B9 was subject to ambiguous interpretation, especially for an obligation that could be partially satisfied over the useful life of a long-lived asset even though it would not be completely satisfied until operation of that asset ceased. Specifically, in that case, one interpretation of the second characteristic is that the portion of the obligation that could be satisfied before the current operation or use of the asset ceases would not fall within the scope of this Statement, while the remaining portion of the obligation would be considered within the scope. An alternative interpretation is that the entire obligation would be considered to be outside the scope of this Statement.

B14. In deliberations leading to the revised Exposure Draft, the Board decided to eliminate the second characteristic. It observed that the nature of asset retirement obligations in various industries is such that the obligations are not necessarily satisfied when the current operation or use of the asset ceases and, in fact, can be settled during operation of the asset or after the operations cease. The Board agreed that the timing of the ultimate settlement of a liability was unrelated to and should not affect its initial recognition in the financial statements provided the obligation is associated with the retirement of a tangible long-lived asset.

B15. The Board retained the essence of the third characteristic in paragraph B9 that limited the obligations included within the scope to those that cannot be realistically avoided if the asset is operated for its intended use. Specifically, paragraph 2 of this Statement limits the obligations included within the scope to those that are unavoidable by an entity as a result

of the acquisition, construction, or development and (or) the normal operation of a long-lived asset, except for certain obligations of lessees.

B16. The initial and revised Exposure Drafts included in their scope both legal and constructive obligations. In the basis for conclusions of the initial Exposure Draft, the Board stressed that the identification of constructive obligations will be more difficult than the identification of legal obligations. It noted that judgment would be required to determine if constructive obligations exist. Many respondents to the initial Exposure Draft indicated that more guidance was needed with respect to the identification of constructive obligations. Therefore, in the revised Exposure Draft, the Board focused on the three characteristics of a liability in paragraph 36 of FASB Concepts Statement No. 6, *Elements of Financial Statements,* rather than on the distinction between a legal obligation and a constructive obligation. Nevertheless, many respondents to the revised Exposure Draft addressed the notion of constructive obligations. Many of those respondents stated that without improved guidance for determining whether a constructive obligation exists, inconsistent application of this Statement would likely result. In deliberations of the revised Exposure Draft, the Board conceded that determining when a constructive obligation exists is very subjective. To achieve more consistent application of this Statement, the Board decided that only existing legal obligations, including legal obligations under the doctrine of promissory estoppel, should be included in the scope. Legal obligations, as used in this Statement, encompass both legally enforceable obligations and constructive obligations, as those terms are used in Concepts Statement 6.

B17. In addition to comments about scope-limiting characteristics, respondents expressed uncertainty about whether the scope of the initial Exposure Draft applied to closure and removal obligations for interim property retirements and replacements for component parts of larger systems.[22] The Board believes that there is no conceptual difference between interim property retirements and replacements and those retirements that occur in circumstances in which the retired asset is not replaced. Therefore, any

---

[22]Examples of interim property retirements and replacements for component parts of larger systems are components of transmission and distribution systems (utility poles), railroad ties, a single oil well that is part of a larger oil field, and aircraft engines. The assets in those examples may or may not have associated retirement obligations.

asset retirement obligation associated with the retirement of or the retirement and replacement of a component part of a larger system qualifies for recognition provided that the obligation meets the definition of a liability. The cost of replacement components is excluded.

B18. Some respondents questioned whether asset retirement obligations with indeterminate settlement dates, such as for an oil refinery, were within the scope of the initial Exposure Draft. They suggested that it would be difficult to estimate a retirement obligation because of uncertainty about the timing of retirement.

B19. The Board decided that asset retirement obligations with indeterminate settlement dates should be included within the scope of this Statement. Uncertainty about the timing of the settlement date does not change the fact that an entity has a legal obligation. The Board acknowledged that although there is an obligation, measurement of that obligation might not be possible if literally no information exists about the timing of settlement. However, some information about the timing of the settlement of a retirement obligation will become available as time goes by. The Board decided that an entity should measure and recognize the fair value of an obligation at the point in time when some information is available to develop various assumptions about the potential timing of cash flows.

B20. The Board also clarified the scope of this Statement relative to the scope of AICPA Statement of Position 96-1, *Environmental Remediation Liabilities.* This Statement applies to legal obligations associated with asset retirements. Legal obligations exist as a result of existing or enacted law, statute, ordinance, or written or oral contract or by legal construction of a contract under the doctrine of promissory estoppel. SOP 96-1 applies to environmental remediation liabilities that relate to pollution arising from some past act, generally as a result of the provisions of Superfund, the corrective-action provisions of the Resource Conservation and Recovery Act of 1976, or analogous state and non-U.S. laws and regulations. An environmental remediation liability that results from the normal operation of a long-lived asset and that is associated with the retirement of that asset shall be accounted for under the provisions of this Statement. An environmental remediation liability that results from other than the normal operation of a long-lived asset probably falls within the scope of SOP 96-1.

Recognition of a Liability for an Asset Retirement Obligation

B21. Prior to this Statement, the objective of many accounting practices was not to recognize and measure obligations associated with the retirement of long-lived assets. Rather, the objective was to achieve a particular expense recognition pattern for those obligations over the operating life of the associated long-lived asset. Using that objective, some entities followed an approach whereby they estimated an amount that would satisfy the costs of retiring the asset and accrued a portion of that amount each period as an expense and as a liability. Other entities used that objective and the provision in paragraph 37 of FASB Statement No. 19, *Financial Accounting and Reporting by Oil and Gas Producing Companies,* that allows them to increase periodic depreciation expense by increasing the depreciable base of a long-lived asset for an amount representing estimated asset retirement costs. Under either of those approaches, the amount of liability or accumulated depreciation recognized in a statement of financial position usually differs from the amount of obligation that an entity actually has incurred. In effect, by focusing on an objective of achieving a particular expense recognition pattern, accounting practices developed that disregarded or circumvented the recognition and measurement requirements of FASB Concepts Statements.

B22. Paragraph 37 of Statement 19 states that "estimated dismantlement, restoration, and abandonment costs . . . shall be taken into account in determining amortization and depreciation rates." Application of that paragraph has the effect of accruing an expense irrespective of the requirements for liability recognition in the FASB Concepts Statements. In doing so, it results in recognition of accumulated depreciation that can exceed the historical cost of a long-lived asset. The Board concluded that an entity should be precluded from including an amount for an asset retirement obligation in the depreciable base of a long-lived asset unless that amount also meets the recognition criteria in this Statement. When an entity recognizes a liability for an asset retirement obligation, it also will recognize an increase in the carrying amount of the related long-lived asset. Consequently, depreciation of that asset will not result in the recognition of accumulated depreciation in excess of the historical cost of a long-lived asset.

B23. This Statement applies to legal obligations associated with the retirement of a tangible long-lived asset that result from the acquisition, construction, or development and (or) the normal operation of a long-lived asset, except for certain obligations of lessees. As used in this Statement, a legal obligation is an obligation that a party is required to settle as a result of existing or enacted law, statute, ordinance, written or oral contract or by legal construction under the doctrine of promissory estoppel. The Board believes that using legal obligations as a scope characteristic includes appropriate constructive obligations. An asset retirement obligation encompasses the three characteristics of a liability set forth in paragraphs 36–40 of Concepts Statement as discussed below. Those characteristics are interrelated; however, each characteristic must be present to meet the definition of a liability.

Duty or responsibility

B24. The first characteristic of a liability is that an entity has "a present duty or responsibility to one or more other entities that entails settlement by probable future transfer or use of assets at a specified or determinable date, on occurrence of a specified event, or on demand." A duty or responsibility becomes a *present* duty or responsibility when an obligating event occurs that leaves the entity little or no discretion to avoid a future transfer or use of assets. A present duty or responsibility does not mean that the obligation must be satisfied immediately. Rather, if events or circumstances have occurred that, as discussed below, give an entity little or no discretion to avoid a future transfer or use of assets, that entity has a present duty or responsibility. If an entity is required by current laws, regulations, or contracts to settle an asset retirement obligation upon retirement of the asset, that requirement is a present duty.

B25. In general, a duty or responsibility is created by an entity's promise, on which others are justified in relying, to take a particular course of action (to perform). That performance will entail the future transfer or use of assets. An entity's promise may be:

a. Unconditional or conditional on the occurrence of a specified future event that is or is not within the entity's control
b. Stated in words, either oral or written, or inferred from the entity's past practice, which, absent evidence to the contrary, others can presume that the entity will continue.

B26. Others are justified in relying on an entity to perform as promised if:

a. They or their representatives are the recipient of the entity's promise.
b. They can reasonably expect the entity to perform (that is, the entity's promise is credible).
c. They either will benefit from the entity's performance or will suffer loss or harm from the entity's nonperformance.

B27. In other situations, a duty or responsibility is created by circumstances in which, absent a promise, an entity finds itself bound to perform, and others are justified in relying on the entity to perform.[23] In those circumstances, others are justified in relying on an entity to perform if:

a. They can reasonably expect the entity to perform.
b. They either will benefit from the entity's performance or will suffer loss or harm from the entity's nonperformance.

B28. The reasonable expectation that the entity will perform is inferred from the particular circumstances, and those circumstances bind the entity to the same degree that it would have been bound had it made a promise.

B29. The assessment of whether there is a legal duty or responsibility for an asset retirement obligation is usually quite clear. However, the assessment of whether there is a duty or responsibility resulting, for example, from a past practice or a representation made to another entity, including the public at large, will require judgment, especially with respect to whether others are justified in relying on the entity to perform as promised. Those judgments should be made within the framework of the doctrine of promissory estoppel (refer to paragraph A3). Once an entity determines that a duty or responsibility exists, it will then need to assess whether an obligating event has occurred that leaves it little or no discretion to avoid the future transfer or use of assets. If such an obligating event has occurred, an asset retirement obligation meets the definition of a liability and qualifies for recognition in the financial statements. However, if an obligating event that leaves an entity little or no discretion to avoid the future transfer or

---

[23]For example, an entity that has recently commenced operations in a particular industry may find itself bound to perform by practice that is predominant in that industry. Absent evidence to the contrary, others are justified in relying on the entity to follow that practice.

use of assets has not occurred, an asset retirement obligation does not meet the definition of a liability and, therefore, should not be recognized in the financial statements.

Little or no discretion to avoid a future transfer or use of assets

B30. The second characteristic of a liability is that ". . . the duty or responsibility obligates a particular entity, leaving it little or no discretion to avoid the future sacrifice." Paragraph 203 of Concepts Statement 6 elaborates on that characteristic by indicating that an entity is not obligated to transfer or use assets in the future if it can avoid that transfer or use of assets at its discretion without significant penalty.

Obligating event

B31. The third characteristic of a liability is that ". . . the transaction or other event obligating the entity has already happened." The definition of a liability distinguishes between present obligations and future obligations of an entity. Only present obligations are liabilities under the definition, and they are liabilities of a particular entity as a result of the occurrence of transactions or other events or circumstances affecting the entity. Identifying the obligating event is often difficult, especially in situations that involve the occurrence of a series of transactions or other events or circumstances affecting the entity. For example, in the case of an asset retirement obligation, a law or an entity's promise may create a duty or responsibility, but that law or promise in and of itself may not be the obligating event that results in an entity's having little or no discretion to avoid a future transfer or use of assets. An entity must look to the nature of the duty or responsibility to assess whether the obligating event has occurred. For example, in the case of a nuclear power facility, an entity assumes responsibility for decontamination of that facility upon receipt of the license to operate it. However, no obligation to decontaminate exists until the facility is operated and contamination occurs. Therefore, the contamination, not the receipt of the license, constitutes the obligating event.

Initial Recognition and Measurement of a Liability

B32. The initial Exposure Draft would have required that a liability for an asset retirement obligation be initially measured at an amount that reflected the present value of the estimated future cash flows required to satisfy the closure or removal obligation.

Subsequent to the issuance of the initial Exposure Draft, the Board issued Concepts Statement 7. In that Concepts Statement, the Board concluded that "the only objective of present value, when used in accounting measurements at initial recognition and fresh-start measurements, is to estimate fair value" (paragraph 25). Consequently, in its deliberations leading to the revised Exposure Draft, the Board concluded that the objective for the initial measurement of a liability for an asset retirement obligation is fair value, which is the amount that an entity would be required to pay in an active market to settle the asset retirement obligation in a current transaction in circumstances other than a forced settlement. In that context, fair value represents the amount that a willing third party of comparable credit standing would demand and could expect to receive to assume all of the duties, uncertainties, and risks inherent in the entity's obligation.

B33. The revised Exposure Draft proposed that an entity should recognize a liability for an asset retirement obligation in the period in which all of the following criteria are met:

a. The obligation meets the definition of a liability in paragraph 35 of Concepts Statement 6.
b. A future transfer of assets associated with the obligation is probable.
c. The amount of the liability can be reasonably estimated.

B34. The definition of a liability in Concepts Statement 6 uses the term *probable* in a different sense than it is used in FASB Statement No. 5, *Accounting for Contingencies*. As used in Statement 5, probable requires a high degree of expectation. The term probable in the definition of a liability is intended to acknowledge that business and other economic activities occur in an environment characterized by uncertainty in which few outcomes are certain.

B35. Statement 5 and Concepts Statement deal with uncertainty in different ways. Statement 5 deals with uncertainty about whether a loss has been incurred by setting forth criteria to determine when to *recognize* a loss contingency. Concepts Statement 7, on the other hand, addresses measurement of liabilities and provides a *measurement* technique to deal with uncertainty about the amount and timing of the future cash flows necessary to settle the liability. Because of the Board's decision to incorporate probability into the measurement of an asset retirement obligation, the guidance in Statement 5 and FASB Interpretation No. 14, *Reasonable Estimation of the Amount of a Loss,* is not applicable.

B36. The objective of recognizing the fair value of an asset retirement obligation will result in recognition of some asset retirement obligations for which the likelihood of future settlement, although more than zero, is less than probable from a Statement 5 perspective.[24] A third party would charge a price to assume an uncertain liability even though the likelihood of a future sacrifice is less than probable. Similarly, when the likelihood of a future sacrifice is probable, the price a third party would charge to assume an obligation incorporates expectations about some future events that are less than probable. Thus, this Statement does not retain the criterion (paragraph B33(b)) that a future transfer of assets associated with the obligation is probable for recognition purposes. This Statement does retain the criteria concerning the existence of a liability (paragraph B33(a)) and the ability to make a reasonable estimate of the amount (paragraph B33(c)).

B37. The Board considered two alternatives to fair value for initial measurement of the liability associated with an asset retirement obligation. One alternative was an entity-specific measurement that would attempt to value the liability in the context of a particular entity. An entity-specific measurement is different from a fair value measurement because it substitutes the entity's assumptions for those that marketplace participants make. Therefore, the assumptions used in an entity-specific measurement of a liability would reflect the entity's expected settlement of the liability and the role of the entity's proprietary skills in that settlement.

B38. Another alternative was a cost-accumulation measurement that would attempt to capture the costs (for example, incremental costs) that an entity anticipates it will incur in settling the liability over its expected term. A cost-accumulation measurement is different from an entity-specific measurement because it excludes assumptions related to a risk premium and may exclude overhead and other internal costs. It is different from a fair value measurement because it excludes those assumptions as well as any

additional assumptions market participants would make about estimated cash flows, such as a market-based profit margin.

B39. Most respondents to the revised Exposure Draft disagreed with the Board's decision to require that a liability for an asset retirement obligation be initially measured at fair value. In general, those respondents stated that in most cases an entity settles an asset retirement obligation with internal resources rather than by contracting with a third party and, therefore, a fair value measurement objective would not provide a reasonable estimate of the costs that an entity expects to incur to settle an asset retirement obligation. Additionally, those respondents stated that a fair value measurement objective would overstate an entity's assets and liabilities and result in a gain being reported upon the settlement of the obligation. For those reasons, most of those respondents stated that the Board should adopt a cost-accumulation approach.

B40. The Board considered a cost-accumulation approach[25] in its deliberations of Concepts Statement 7. However, the Board observed there were several problems with that approach.

- Cost-accumulation measurements are accounting conventions, not attempts to replicate market transactions. Consequently, it may be difficult to discern the objective of the measurement. For example, is the "cost" based on direct, incremental expenditures or is it a "full-cost" computation that includes an allocation of overhead and fixed costs? Which costs are included in the overhead pool? Lacking a clear measurement objective, any cost accumulation method would inevitably have to be based on rules that are essentially arbitrary.

- Cost-accumulation measurements are inherently intent-driven and thus lack comparability. One entity might expect to settle all of its asset retirement obligations using internal resources. Another might expect to use internal and outsourced resources. Still another might expect to outsource the settlement of all its obligations. All three could describe the resulting measurement as "cost accumulation," but the results would hardly be comparable—each entity would have a different measurement objective for the same liability.

---

[24]Recognition at fair value of an obligation for which the likelihood of future settlement is less than probable is consistent with the criteria described in FASB Concepts Statement No. 5, *Recognition and Measurement in Financial Statements of Business Enterprises.*

[25]A cost-accumulation approach is a measurement that includes some of the costs an entity would incur to construct an asset or settle a liability.

- Cost-accumulation measurements present a "value" on the balance sheet that an entity would not accept in an exchange transaction. A third party would not willingly assume an asset retirement obligation at a price equal to the cost-accumulation measure. That party would include a margin for the risk involved and a profit margin for performing the service.

Of overriding importance, Board members were concerned that identical liabilities (assuming equivalent credit standing) would be measured at different amounts by different entities. The Board believes that the *value* of a liability is the same regardless of how an entity intends to settle the liability (unless the entities have different credit standing) and that the relative efficiency of an entity in settling a liability using internal resources (that is, the entity's profit margin) should be reflected over the course of its settlement and not before.

B41. If an entity elects to settle an asset retirement obligation using its internal resources, the total cash outflows—no more, no less—required to settle the obligation will, at some time, be included in operating results. The *timing* of when those cash outflows are recognized will affect the profitability of different periods, but when all of the costs of settling the liability have been incurred, the cumulative profitability from that transaction over all periods will be determined only by the total of those cash outflows. The real issue is which period or periods should reflect the efficiencies of incurring lower costs than the costs that would be required by the market to settle the liability. The Board believes it is those periods in which the activities necessary to settle the liability are incurred. If the measurement of the liability does not include the full amount of the costs required by the market to settle it, including a normal profit margin, the "profits" will be recognized prematurely.

Recognition and Allocation of Asset Retirement Costs

B42. This Statement requires that upon initial recognition of a liability, an entity capitalizes an asset retirement cost by increasing the carrying amount of the related long-lived asset. The Board believes that asset retirement costs are integral to or are a prerequisite for operating the long-lived asset and noted that current accounting practice includes in the historical-cost basis of an asset all costs that are necessary to prepare the asset for its intended use. Capitalized asset retirement costs are not a separate asset because there is no specific and separate future eco-

nomic benefit that results from those costs. In other words, the future economic benefit of those costs lies in the productive asset that is used in the entity's operations.

B43. The Board considered whether asset retirement costs should be recognized as a separately identifiable intangible asset. The Board acknowledges that in certain situations an intangible asset, such as the right to operate a long-lived asset, may be acquired when obligations for asset retirement costs are incurred. However, the intangible asset is not separable from the long-lived asset, and similar intangible assets, such as building and zoning permits, are generally included in the historical cost of the long-lived asset that is acquired or constructed. Furthermore, the acquisition of an intangible asset in exchange for the agreement to incur asset retirement costs does not occur in all situations.

B44. A majority of respondents to the revised Exposure Draft agreed with the requirement to recognize an amount as an increase in the carrying amount of an asset upon initial recognition of a liability for an asset retirement obligation. However, some respondents indicated that the capitalized amount should be separately classified as an intangible asset because, for example, property taxes might increase if it was classified as a plant cost. For the reasons discussed in paragraph B43, the Board decided that such a concern did not warrant special consideration for classification of an asset retirement cost as an intangible asset.

B45. Because the scope of this Statement includes some obligations incurred more or less ratably over the entire life of a long-lived asset, the Board considered whether asset retirement costs associated with those types of obligations should be recognized as an expense of the period rather than capitalized.

B46. The Board could not develop any rationale for distinguishing between which asset retirement costs should be capitalized and which should be recognized as an expense of the period. The Board concluded that whether a cost is incurred upon acquisition or incurred ratably over the life of an asset does not change its underlying nature and its association with the asset. Therefore, the Board decided that an entity should capitalize all asset retirement costs by increasing the carrying amount of the related long-lived asset. The Board decided to couple that provision with a requirement that an entity allocate that cost to expense using a systematic and rational method over periods in which the related asset is expected to provide benefits. Application of a systematic and rational method does not preclude an entity from using an allocation method that would have the effect of capitalizing an amount of cost and allocating an equal amount to expense in the same accounting period. The Board concluded that a requirement for capitalization of an asset retirement cost along with a requirement for the systematic and rational allocation of it to expense achieves the objectives of (a) obtaining a measure of cost that more closely reflects the entity's total investment in the asset and (b) permitting the allocation of that cost, or portions thereof, to expense in the periods in which the related asset is expected to provide benefits.

B47. The Board noted that if the asset for which there is an associated asset retirement obligation were to be sold, the price a buyer would consent to pay for that asset would reflect an estimate of the fair value of the asset retirement obligation. Because that asset retirement obligation meets the definition of a liability, however, the Board believes that reporting it as a liability with a corresponding increase in the carrying amount of the asset for the asset retirement costs, which has the same net effect as incorporating the fair value of the costs to settle the liability in the valuation of the asset, is more representationally faithful and in concert with Concepts Statement 6.

Subsequent Measurement

B48. The Board considered whether to require a *fresh-start approach* or an *interest method of allocation* for subsequent measurement of the liability for an asset retirement obligation. Using a fresh-start approach, the liability would be remeasured at fair value each period, and all changes in that fair value, including those associated with changes in interest rates, would be recognized in the financial statements. Using an interest method of allocation, the liability would not be remeasured at fair value each period. Instead, an accounting convention would be employed to measure period-to-period changes in the liability resulting from the passage of time and revisions to cash flow estimates. Those changes would then be incorporated into a remeasurement of the liability. That convention would not include changes in interest rates in that remeasurement.

B49. The major advantage of a fresh-start approach over an interest method of allocation is that the fresh-start approach results in the liability being carried in the financial statements at fair value at each reporting period. To preserve the advantages of a fair value measurement objective, the Board concluded in Concepts Statement 7 that fair value should be the objective of fresh-start measurements. The major disadvantage of a fair value objective is that it results in a more volatile expense recognition pattern than an interest method of allocation primarily due to the recognition of changes in fair value resulting from period-to-period changes in interest rates. For entities that incur a liability ratably over the life of an asset, a fresh-start approach may be less burdensome to apply than an interest method of allocation because total expected cash flows are all discounted at a current interest rate. While a fresh-start approach and an interest method of allocation both require revised estimates of expected cash flows each period, under a fresh-start approach the estimated cash flows would all be discounted at the current rate. Alternatively, an interest method of allocation requires maintenance of detailed records of expected cash flows because each layer of the liability is discounted by employing a predetermined interest amortization scheme.

B50. In May 1999, some Board members and staff met with industry representatives to discuss the advantages and disadvantages of a fresh-start approach versus an interest method of allocation for subsequent measurement of a liability for an asset retirement obligation. The industry representatives were asked to prepare examples that were used as a basis for providing input to the Board about the accounting results obtained under the two approaches and the complexity or simplicity of one approach compared with the other.

B51. The industry representatives agreed that the major advantages of a fresh-start approach are that it (a) results in the liability for an asset retirement obligation being carried in the financial statements at fair value and (b) is somewhat less burdensome to apply than an interest method of allocation. However, they emphasized that those advantages do not outweigh the overwhelming disadvantage resulting from the volatile expense recognition pattern created by the requirement under the fresh-start approach to recognize period-to-period changes in interest rates through accretion expense. In fact, they stressed that a fresh-start approach could create negative expense recognition in periods of increasing interest rates and that the effects of significant changes in interest rates during a period could, in certain circumstances, result in gains or losses attributable to the change in the measurement of the asset retirement obligation that would overwhelm income from continuing operations.

B52. The Board agreed that, conceptually, a fresh-start approach is preferable to an interest method of allocation for subsequent measurement of a liability for an asset retirement obligation. However, it acknowledged the perceived disadvantage of the volatile expense recognition pattern resulting from the use of the fresh-start approach. The Board decided that it could justify a departure from the conclusions in Concepts Statement 7, in this instance, because of the volatility a fair value measurement would entail and because the capitalized amount of the associated asset retirement cost would not be measured at fair value in subsequent periods. Until fair value is required for subsequent measurement of more (or all) liabilities, the Board decided that it may be premature to require that type of measurement in this Statement. For those reasons, the Board decided to require an interest method of allocation for subsequent measurement of a liability for an asset retirement obligation.

B53. Subsequent measurement using an interest method of allocation requires that an entity identify undiscounted estimated cash flows associated with the initial fair value measurement of the liability. Therefore, an entity that obtains the initial fair value of a liability for an asset retirement obligation from, for example, a market price, must nonetheless determine the undiscounted cash flows and estimated timing of those cash flows that are embodied in that fair value amount in order to apply the subsequent measurement requirements of this Statement. Appendix E of this Statement includes an example that illustrates a procedure to impute undiscounted cash flows from market prices.

Measurement of changes resulting from revisions to cash flow estimates

B54. The Board considered situations that might give rise to a change in cash flow estimates. Some situations might occur when a new law is enacted that gives rise to previously unrecognized asset retirement obligations. Another situation might be a *change* in a law that changes the expected cash outflows required to settle an asset retirement obligation. Still other situations might arise as a result of changes in technology or inflation assumptions. The Board considered the appropriate discount rate to apply in each of those circumstances. One possible answer would be to apply the current discount rate to a new obligation and use historical discount rates when there is a modification to the previous cash flow estimates. In the course of its discussion, however, the Board realized that it might be difficult to distinguish

the changes in cash flows that arise from a new liability from those attributable to a modification to an estimate for an existing liability. For practical reasons, the Board decided that upward revisions in the undiscounted cash flows related to an asset retirement obligation should be discounted at the current credit-adjusted risk-free rate and that downward revisions in the undiscounted cash flows should be discounted using historical discount rates. If an entity cannot identify the period in which the original cash flows were estimated, it may use a weighted-average credit-adjusted risk-free rate to measure a change in the liability resulting from a downward revision to estimated cash flows.

B55. The Board concluded that revisions in estimates of cash flows are refinements of the amount of the asset retirement obligation, and as such are also refinements of the estimated asset retirement costs that result in adjustments to the carrying amounts of the related asset. Therefore, the Board noted that it was not necessary to distinguish revisions in cash flow estimates that arise from changes in assumptions from those revisions that arise from a new liability—both adjust the carrying amount of the related asset.

Measurement of changes in the liability due to the passage of time (accretion expense)

B56. Also for practical reasons, the Board decided that an entity should be required to measure accretion expense on the carrying amount of the liability by using the same credit-adjusted risk-free rate or rates used to initially measure the liability at fair value.

B57. The Board discussed whether it should specify how the amount representing a change in the liability due to the passage of time should be classified in the statement of operations. The revised Exposure Draft proposed that such a change was most appropriately described as interest expense and that, therefore, an entity should be required to classify it as such in its statement of operations. Respondents expressed concern about the classification as interest expense. Some respondents stated that financial statement users view interest expense as a financing cost arising from borrowing and lending transactions. They also stated that classifying the accretion of the liability as interest expense would distort certain financial ratios, hindering some entities' ability to satisfy current debt covenants and to obtain future borrowings. In response to those concerns, the Board decided that the only requirement should be that the period-to-period change in the liability be classified as a separate item in the operating portion of the income statement.

B58. The Board also discussed whether accretion expense on the liability for an asset retirement obligation should qualify for the pool of interest eligible for capitalization under the provisions of paragraph 12 of FASB Statement No. 34, *Capitalization of Interest Cost.* Specifically, paragraph 12 states that "the amount of interest cost to be capitalized for qualifying assets is intended to be that portion of the interest cost incurred during the assets' acquisition periods that theoretically could have been avoided . . . if expenditures for the assets had not been made." Paragraph 1 of Statement 34 states that "for the purposes of this Statement, *interest cost* includes interest recognized on obligations having explicit interest rates, interest imputed on certain types of payables in accordance with APB Opinion No. 21, *Interest on Receivables and Payables,* and interest related to a capital lease determined in accordance with FASB Statement No. 13, *Accounting for Leases*" (footnote reference omitted). The Board decided that accretion expense on the liability for an asset retirement obligation should not qualify for interest capitalization because it does not qualify as *interest cost* under the provisions of paragraph 1 of Statement 34.

Funding and Assurance Provisions

B59. In some circumstances, an entity is legally required to provide assurance that it will be able to satisfy its asset retirement obligations. That assurance may be accomplished by demonstrating that the financial resources and financial condition of the entity are sufficient to assure that it can meet those obligations. Other commonly used methods of providing assurance include surety bonds, insurance policies, letters of credit, guarantees by other entities, and establishment of trust funds or identification of other funds for satisfying the asset retirement obligations.

B60. The effect of surety bonds, letters of credit, and guarantees is to provide assurance that third parties will provide amounts to satisfy the asset retirement obligations if the entity that has primary responsibility (the obligor) to do so cannot or does not fulfill its obligations. The possibility that a third party will satisfy the asset retirement obligations does not relieve the obligor from its primary responsibility for those obligations. If a third party is required to satisfy asset retirement obligations due to the failure or inability of the obligor to do so directly, the obligor would then

have a liability to the third party. Established generally accepted accounting principles require that the entity's financial statements reflect its obligations even if it has obtained surety bonds, letters of credit, or guarantees by others. However, as discussed in paragraph 16 of this Statement, the effects of those provisions should be considered in adjusting the risk-free interest rate for the effect of the entity's credit standing to arrive at the credit-adjusted risk-free rate.

B61. The option of prepaying an asset retirement obligation may exist; however, it would rarely, if ever, be exercised because prepayment would not relieve the entity of its liability for future changes in its asset retirement obligations. Obtaining insurance for asset retirement obligations is currently as rare as prepayment of those obligations. Because of the limited instances, if any, in which prepayment of asset retirement obligations is made or insurance is acquired, the Board decided to address neither topic. However, the Board noted that even if insurance was obtained, the liability would continue to exist.

B62. In evaluating what effect, if any, assets identified to satisfy asset retirement obligations should have on the accounting and reporting of liabilities, the Board considered two approaches that would have resulted in reporting less than the amount of the present liability for an asset retirement obligation. Under one approach, any assets dedicated to satisfy the asset retirement obligation would, for financial reporting purposes, be offset against the liability. Under the other approach, those dedicated assets could be viewed as an extinguishment of the liability in whole or in part.

B63. Paragraph 7 of APB Opinion No. 10, *Omnibus Opinion—1966,* and FASB Interpretation No. 39, *Offsetting of Amounts Related to Certain Contracts,* establish the general criteria for offsetting of amounts in the statement of financial position. Paragraph 50 of Interpretation 39 discusses offsetting of trust funds established for nuclear decommissioning, which is one of the asset retirement obligations within the scope of this Statement. Those trust funds cannot be offset because the right of offset is not enforceable at law and the payees for costs of asset retirement obligations generally have not been identified at the reporting date.

B64. Some have suggested that trust funds established to meet obligations for pensions and other postretirement benefits are similar to the trust funds established for nuclear decommissioning. In FASB

Statements No. 87, *Employers' Accounting for Pensions,* and No. 106, *Employers' Accounting for Postretirement Benefits Other Than Pensions,* the Board provided specific requirements to allow offsetting of plan assets in trust funds established for pension benefits and for other postretirement benefits against the related liabilities of those plans. The Board noted that the offsetting provisions in Statements 87 and 106 are exceptions influenced, in part, by then-existing practice. In addition, the offsetting allowed in Statements 87 and 106 is one part of an accounting model that also allows for delayed recognition in financial statements of the changes in the values of the plan assets and liabilities. This Statement provides for immediate recognition of changes in estimated cash flows related to asset retirement obligations. Changes in certain assets dedicated to satisfy those obligations that are subject to the provisions of FASB Statement No. 115, *Accounting for Certain Investments in Debt and Equity Securities,* would also be recognized immediately. The Board decided that it should not provide an exception to the general principle for offsetting in this Statement.

B65. FASB Statement No. 140, *Accounting for Transfers and Servicing of Financial Assets and Extinguishments of Liabilities,* requires that a liability be derecognized if and only if either the debtor pays the creditor and is relieved of its obligation for the liability or the debtor is legally released from being the primary obligor under the liability. Therefore, a liability is not considered extinguished by an in-substance defeasance.

Leasing Transactions

B66. The Board considered whether to amend FASB Statement No. 13, *Accounting for Leases,* and related leasing literature to address asset retirement obligations associated with leased property. However, the Board chose not to amend the existing leasing literature for a number of reasons. When the Board undertook this project, it did not have as an objective a revision of the accounting requirements for leasing transactions. The Board realized that a revision of the existing leasing literature to incorporate the requirements of this Statement would be difficult to accomplish in a limited-scope amendment because of the requirements of the leasing literature with respect to present value measurements and certain concepts concerning how payments for the leased property and residual values affect the criteria for lease classification. Because those aspects of the leasing literature are interrelated and fundamental to the

lease accounting model, the Board concluded that a wholesale amendment of the existing leasing literature would likely be required in order to conform the pertinent aspects of the lease accounting model to the accounting model in this Statement. The Board agreed that any substantial revision of the existing leasing literature should be addressed in a separate project. The Board also recognized that Statement 13 (as amended) already contains guidance for lessees with respect to certain obligations that meet the provisions in paragraph 2 of this Statement. The Board concluded that by including in the scope of this Statement all lessor obligations in connection with leased property that meet the provisions in paragraph 2 of this Statement and those lessee obligations in connection with leased property that meet the provisions in paragraph 2 of this Statement but do not meet the definition of either minimum lease payments or contingent rentals in paragraph 5 of Statement 13, it could retain substantially the same scope as it originally contemplated for this project without an amendment of the existing leasing literature.

Rate-Regulated Entities

B67. The Board considered how existing rate-making practices for entities subject to FASB Statement No. 71, *Accounting for the Effects of Certain Types of Regulation,* would affect the accounting by those entities for costs related to asset retirement obligations. The way in which those costs are treated for financial reporting purposes and the way in which they are treated for rate-making purposes often differ. The most common differences arise from different estimates by the entity and its regulator of the future cost of asset retirement activities. Those differences may relate to the estimates of the cost of performing asset retirement activities or the assumptions necessary to develop the estimated future cash flows required to satisfy those obligations. In addition, an entity may make revisions to its estimate of the obligation before a regulator considers those revisions in setting the entity's rates.

B68. Statement 71 requires, subject to meeting certain criteria, that the timing of recognition of certain revenues and expenses for financial reporting purposes conform to decisions or probable decisions of regulators responsible for setting the entity's rates. Because the practices of those regulators for allowing costs related to asset retirement activities are well established, the Board did not consider any future changes in those practices. The Board considered specific issues arising from current rate-making practices about the recognition of regulatory assets or liabilities for differences, if any, in the timing of recognition of costs for financial reporting and rate-making purposes. The Board also considered the appropriate method for recognition and measurement of impairment of the capitalized amount of an asset retirement cost for an asset subject to Statement 71.

B69. An entity is responsible for developing timely and reasonably accurate estimates of the cash flows related to asset retirement obligations. That responsibility is inherent in the preparation of external financial statements and may be a part of the entity's reporting to others in connection with its asset retirement obligations. The regulator that sets the entity's rates has a responsibility to both the entity and its customers to establish rates that are just and reasonable. Sometimes the responsibilities of the regulator and those of the regulated entity conflict, producing differences in the estimated costs related to asset retirement obligations as discussed in paragraph B67. Statement 71, as amended, specifies the general criteria for the recognition of regulatory assets and liabilities that result from differences, if any, in the timing of recognition of costs for financial reporting and rate-making purposes. FASB Statement No. 92, *Regulated Enterprises—Accounting for Phase-in Plans,* establishes more restrictive criteria for the recognition of regulatory assets in certain situations.

B70. The Board considered whether the general principles of Statement 71 should apply or whether specific criteria similar to those in Statement 92 should apply to the recognition of regulatory assets and liabilities that result from the circumstances described in paragraph B67. The Board concluded that judgment would be required in recognizing regulatory assets and liabilities because of the many reasons for differences between the obligations and costs related to asset retirement obligations recognized for financial reporting and those considered for rate-making purposes. Therefore, the Board decided that the general principles in Statement 71 should be applied in recognizing regulatory assets and liabilities for those differences.

B71. The Board also considered the appropriate method for recognition and measurement of impairment of assets that include capitalized asset retirement costs for entities subject to Statement 71. In FASB Statement No. 121, *Accounting for the Impairment of Long-Lived Assets and for Long-Lived Assets*

to Be Disposed Of, the Board considered the issues of recognition and measurement of impairment of long-lived assets of rate-regulated entities. The Board concluded that no additional guidance was needed for recognition and impairment of capitalized assets that include capitalized retirement costs for rate-regulated entities.

B72. Paragraph 12 of this Statement requires that capitalized asset retirement costs be included in the assessment of impairment of long-lived assets. In recent years, several nuclear power plants have ceased operations, and the method and timing of their nuclear decommissioning are being considered. Some of those plants reached the end of their expected useful lives, and others closed prior to the end of their expected useful lives. The actual decommissioning may begin immediately after plant closure or it may be deferred until some future time. In either case, the Board decided that FASB Statement No. 90, *Regulated Enterprises—Accounting for Abandonments and Disallowances of Plant Costs,* should apply to asset retirement costs recognized under the provisions of this Statement in the same way that it applies to other costs of closed or abandoned facilities of rate-regulated entities.

B73. Many rate-regulated entities currently provide for the costs related to asset retirement obligations in their financial statements and recover those amounts in rates charged to their customers. Some of those costs relate to asset retirement obligations within the scope of this Statement; others are not within the scope of this Statement and, therefore, cannot be recognized as liabilities under its provisions. The objective of including those amounts in rates currently charged to customers is to allocate costs to customers over the lives of those assets. The amount charged to customers is adjusted periodically to reflect the excess or deficiency of the amounts charged over the amounts incurred for the retirement of long-lived assets. The Board concluded that if asset retirement costs are charged to customers of rate-regulated entities but no liability is recognized, a regulatory liability should be recognized if the requirements of Statement 71 are met.

Disclosures

B74. The Board believes that the financial statement disclosures required by this Statement will provide information that will be useful in understanding the effects of a liability for an asset retirement obligation on a particular entity and that those disclosures can be prepared without encountering undue complexities or significant incremental costs. The Board decided that information about the general nature of an asset retirement obligation and the related long-lived asset is a fundamental and necessary disclosure.

B75. The Board believes that information about assets that are legally restricted for purposes of settling asset retirement obligations is important to financial statement users and should be disclosed.

B76. The Board considered whether it should require disclosure of other measures of a liability for an asset retirement obligation (for example, current cost, future cost, undiscounted expected cash flows, or entity-specific value). Because the Board decided to require the initial measurement of the liability at fair value, it decided that disclosure of other amounts based on other measurement objectives are inappropriate.

B77. The Board believes that a reconciliation showing the changes in the aggregate carrying amount of the asset retirement obligation would sometimes be useful. Components of the change include (a) liabilities incurred in the current period, (b) liabilities settled in the current period, (c) accretion expense, and (d) revisions resulting from changes in expected cash flows. To reduce the burden on preparers, the Board concluded that a reconciliation showing the changes in the asset retirement obligation would be required only when a significant change occurs in one or more of those components during the reporting period.

B78. Some of the disclosures required by this Statement were proposed by the EEI in its request that the Board consider adding a project on removal costs to its agenda. The Board also received input from some users of financial statements indicating that the disclosures required by this Statement would be useful in understanding the asset retirement obligations of an entity.

Effective Date

B79. This Statement is effective for financial statements issued for fiscal years beginning after June 15, 2002. The Board believes that the effective date provides adequate time for an entity that previously had not reported information about an asset retirement obligation to determine whether any such obligation exists. Furthermore, the Board believes that the effective date provides adequate time for all entities with

asset retirement obligations to develop the necessary information to apply the requirements of this Statement. The Board encourages early application of this Statement.

Transition

B80. The transition provisions in the initial Exposure Draft would have required an entity to recognize balance sheet amounts for (a) a closure or removal liability adjusted for the cumulative period costs caused by changes in the present value of that liability due to the passage of time, (b) the capitalized costs of closure or removal, and (c) the related accumulated depreciation of the capitalized costs. The difference between those amounts and the amount recognized in the statement of financial position under present practice would have been recognized as a cumulative-effect adjustment in the period in which the Statement was adopted. The initial Exposure Draft would have required that an entity measure transition amounts by applying its provisions as if the initial Exposure Draft had been in effect when the closure or removal obligation was incurred and without the benefit of hindsight. However, if an entity could not make a reasonable approximation of those amounts based solely on information known in previous periods, it could measure those amounts using current information.

B81. Many respondents to the initial Exposure Draft agreed with its recognition provisions (for example, a cumulative-effect adjustment) but disagreed with the requirement to use information from previous periods to measure transition amounts. They stressed that such a requirement was overly complex and unjustified because it would require an entity to use old cost studies, update the asset calculation with newer studies, and use interest rates in effect when the obligations were incurred. Some respondents further indicated that a requirement to use information from previous periods would only result in the *appearance* of accuracy.

Measurement of transition amounts

B82. The Board discussed whether it should retain in this Statement the requirement in the initial Exposure Draft to measure transition amounts by applying the provisions of this Statement based on information available when an obligation was incurred. That requirement would have entailed retroactively measuring the initial fair value of a liability for an asset retirement obligation and using that same amount as a basis for recognizing the amount to be capitalized as part of the cost of the long-lived asset. Those amounts would then have been used to calculate depreciation related to the long-lived asset and accretion expense on the liability. To measure those amounts retroactively, an entity would have been required to determine historical data and assumptions about the economic environment that would have been considered at the date or dates that (a) a liability for an asset retirement obligation was incurred and (b) any subsequent revisions to cash flow estimates were made.

B83. The Board reasoned that although some entities may have data and assumptions in their historical records related to measurements that were already being made (for example, under the provisions of Statement 19), those records may not include sufficient information to retroactively employ the fair value measurement approach required by this Statement. Furthermore, the Board acknowledged that many entities that are required to apply the provisions of this Statement have not been accounting for asset retirement obligations in present practice because they were not required to do so. The Board concluded that it would not only be costly, but also difficult if not impossible, to reconstruct historical data and assumptions without incorporating the benefit of hindsight.

B84. The Board decided that, at transition, an entity should measure the fair value of a liability for an asset retirement obligation and the corresponding capitalized cost at the date the liability was initially incurred using current (that is, as of the date of adoption of this Statement) information, current assumptions, and current interest rates. That initial fair value of the liability and initial capitalized cost should be used as the basis for measuring depreciation expense and accretion expense for the time period from the date the liability was incurred to the date of adoption of this Statement.

Recognition of transition amounts

B85. The Board considered requiring the changes in accounting that result from the application of this Statement to be recognized (a) as the cumulative effect, based on a retroactive computation, of initially applying a new accounting principle, (b) by restating the financial statements of prior periods, or (c) prospectively, for example, over the remaining life of the long-lived asset. The Board also considered two simplified approaches to recognizing the changes in accounting that result from the application of this Statement.

B86. A cumulative-effect approach results in the immediate recognition and measurement of liability, asset, and accumulated depreciation amounts consistent with the provisions of this Statement. The difference between those amounts and any amounts that had been recognized in the statement of financial position prior to application of this Statement are reported as a cumulative-effect adjustment in the income statement of the period in which this Statement is initially applied. Consistent with paragraph 21 of APB Opinion No. 20, *Accounting Changes,* an entity is required to disclose the pro forma effects of retroactive application for income before extraordinary items and net income (and the related per-share amounts) for all periods presented.

B87. Restatement, like a cumulative-effect approach, results in the immediate recognition and measurement of liability, asset, and accumulated depreciation amounts consistent with the provisions of this Statement. However, restatement differs from a cumulative-effect approach because prior-period financial statements would be restated to conform to the provisions of this Statement. Therefore, in financial statements presented for comparative purposes, financial statement users would be able to assess the impact of this Statement on income statement and balance sheet amounts.

B88. A prospective approach would result in the delayed recognition or adjustment of a liability for an asset retirement obligation as well as corresponding amounts to the long-lived asset and accumulated depreciation measured under the provisions of this Statement. Under a prospective approach, an entity would neither recognize a cumulative-effect adjustment in the income statement of the period in which this Statement is initially applied nor restate financial statements of previous periods affected by this Statement. Instead, all of the income statement effects related to initial application of this Statement would be recognized in future accounting periods.

B89. When compared with either a cumulative-effect approach or restatement, the Board decided that a prospective approach to transition provides the least useful financial statement information because asset retirement obligations that existed prior to the adoption of this Statement would not be reflected in the financial statements upon adoption of this Statement. For that reason, the Board decided against a prospective approach to transition.

B90. The Board discussed whether a cumulative-effect approach and restatement provide equally useful financial statement information. It acknowledged that restatement would provide more useful information because prior-period balance sheet amounts and prior-period income statement amounts would be restated to reflect the provisions of this Statement. However, some rate-regulated entities expressed concern that if restatement resulted in recognition of additional expenses in prior periods, those expenses might not be recovered in current or future rates. The Board decided that a cumulative-effect approach would provide sufficient information if, in addition to disclosure of the pro forma income statement amounts required by paragraphs 19(c), 19(d), and 21 of Opinion 20, an entity also disclosed on a pro forma basis for the beginning of the earliest year presented and for the ends of all years presented the balance sheet amounts for the liability for asset retirement obligations as if this Statement had been applied during all periods affected. Therefore, the Board decided to require a cumulative-effect approach as described in Opinion 20 with additional prior-period balance sheet disclosures.

B91. The Board also considered, but rejected, two simplified approaches to recognition of transition amounts. Both approaches would have required that an entity recognize a liability for an asset retirement obligation at fair value upon initial application of the provisions of this Statement. The difference between the fair value of the obligation and any amount presently recognized in the balance sheet for that obligation would have been recognized as either (a) an increase or a decrease in the associated long-lived asset or (b) a cumulative-effect adjustment in the income statement of the period of initial application of this Statement. Neither of those approaches would have resulted in the recognition of an amount of accumulated depreciation related to an asset retirement cost.

B92. The Board decided that even though the simplified approaches would have been easier to apply than either a cumulative-effect approach or restatement, except for recognition of a liability for an asset retirement obligation at fair value, they would not have provided financial statement information that is consistent with the provisions of this Statement. Furthermore, both of the simplified approaches would have resulted in an arbitrary amount being recognized as either an asset or a cumulative-effect adjustment. The Board agreed that the simplified approaches would have provided less useful financial statement information than either the cumulative-effect approach or restatement.

Appendix C

ILLUSTRATIVE EXAMPLES—RECOGNITION AND MEASUREMENT PROVISIONS

C1. This appendix includes four examples that illustrate the recognition and measurement provisions of this Statement. Example 1 illustrates (a) initial measurement of a liability for an asset retirement obligation using an expected present value technique, (b) subsequent measurement assuming that there are no changes in expected cash flows, and (c) settlement of the asset retirement obligation liability (ARO liability) at the end of its term. Example 2 is similar to Example 1. However, Example 2 illustrates subsequent measurement of an ARO liability after a change in expected cash flows. Example 3 highlights the recognition and measurement provisions of this Statement for an ARO liability that is incurred over more than one reporting period. Example 4 illustrates accounting for asset retirement obligations that are conditional and that have a low likelihood of enforcement.

C2. The examples in this appendix and those in Appendixes D and E incorporate simplified assumptions to provide guidance in implementing this Statement. For instance, Examples 1 and 2 relate to the asset retirement obligation associated with an offshore production platform that also would likely have individual wells and production facilities that would have separate asset retirement obligations. Those examples also assume straight-line depreciation, even though, in practice, depreciation would likely be applied using a units-of-production method. Other simplifying assumptions are used throughout the examples.

Example 1

C3. Example 1 depicts an entity that completes construction of and places into service an offshore oil platform on January 1, 2003. The entity is legally required to dismantle and remove the platform at the end of its useful life, which is estimated to be 10 years. Based on the requirements of this Statement, on January 1, 2003, the entity recognizes a liability for an asset retirement obligation and capitalizes an amount for an asset retirement cost. The entity estimates the initial fair value of the liability using an expected present value technique. The significant assumptions used in that estimate of fair value are as follows:

a. Labor costs are based on current marketplace wages required to hire contractors to dismantle and remove offshore oil platforms. The entity assigns probability assessments to a range of cash flow estimates as follows:

Cash Flow Estimate	Probability Assessment	Expected Cash Flows
$100,000	25%	$ 25,000
125,000	50	62,500
175,000	25	43,750
		$131,250

b. The entity estimates allocated overhead and equipment charges using the rate it applies to labor costs for transfer pricing (80 percent). The entity has no reason to believe that its overhead rate differs from those used by contractors in the industry.
c. A contractor typically adds a markup on labor and allocated internal costs to provide a profit margin on the job. The rate used (20 percent) represents the entity's understanding of the profit that contractors in the industry generally earn to dismantle and remove offshore oil platforms.
d. A contractor would typically demand and receive a premium (market risk premium) for bearing the uncertainty and unforeseeable circumstances inherent in "locking in" today's price for a project that will not occur for 10 years. The entity estimates the amount of that premium to be 5 percent of the expected cash flows adjusted for inflation.
e. The risk-free rate of interest on January 1, 2003, is 5 percent. The entity adjusts that rate by 3.5 percent to reflect the effect of its credit standing. Therefore, the credit-adjusted risk-free rate used to compute expected present value is 8.5 percent.
f. The entity assumes a rate of inflation of 4 percent over the 10-year period.

Example 1 (continued)

C4. On December 31, 2012, the entity settles its asset retirement obligation by using its internal workforce at a cost of $351,000. Assuming no changes during the 10-year period in the expected cash flows used to estimate the obligation, the entity would recognize a gain of $89,619 on settlement of the obligation:

Labor	$195,000
Allocated overhead and equipment charges (80 percent of labor)	156,000
Total costs incurred	351,000
ARO liability	440,619
Gain on settlement of obligation	$ 89,619

Initial Measurement of the ARO Liability at January 1, 2003

	Expected Cash Flows 1/1/03
Expected labor costs	$131,250
Allocated overhead and equipment charges (.80 × $131,250)	105,000
Contractor's markup [.20 × ($131,250 + $105,000)]	47,250
Expected cash flows before inflation adjustment	283,500
Inflation factor assuming 4 percent rate for 10 years	1.4802
Expected cash flows adjusted for inflation	419,637
Market-risk premium (.05 × $419,637)	20,982
Expected cash flows adjusted for market risk	$440,619
Expected present value using credit-adjusted risk-free rate of 8.5 percent for 10 years	$194,879

Interest Method of Allocation

Year	Liability Balance 1/1	Accretion	Liability Balance 12/31
2003	$194,879	$16,565	$211,444
2004	211,444	17,973	229,417
2005	229,417	19,500	248,917
2006	248,917	21,158	270,075
2007	270,075	22,956	293,031
2008	293,031	24,908	317,939
2009	317,939	27,025	344,964
2010	344,964	29,322	374,286
2011	374,286	31,814	406,100
2012	406,100	34,519	440,619

Example 1 (continued)

Schedule of Expenses

Year-End	Accretion Expense	Depreciation Expense	Total Expense
2003	$16,565	$19,488	$36,053
2004	17,973	19,488	37,461
2005	19,500	19,488	38,988
2006	21,158	19,488	40,646
2007	22,956	19,488	42,444
2008	24,908	19,488	44,396
2009	27,025	19,488	46,513
2010	29,322	19,488	48,810
2011	31,814	19,488	51,302
2012	34,519	19,488	54,007

Journal Entries

January 1, 2003:

Long-lived asset (asset retirement cost)	194,879	
ARO liability		194,879
To record the initial fair value of the ARO liability		

December 31, 2003–2012:

Depreciation expense (asset retirement cost)	19,488	
Accumulated depreciation		19,488
To record straight-line depreciation on the asset retirement cost		
Accretion expense	Per schedule	
ARO liability		Per schedule
To record accretion expense on the ARO liability		

December 31, 2012:

ARO liability	440,619	
Wages payable		195,000
Allocated overhead and equipment charges (.80 × $195,000)		156,000
Gain on settlement of ARO liability		89,619
To record settlement of the ARO liability		

Example 2

C5. Example 2 is the same as Example 1 with respect to initial measurement of the ARO liability. In this example, the entity's credit standing improves over time, causing the credit-adjusted risk-free rate to decrease by .5 percent to 8 percent at December 31, 2004.

C6. On December 31, 2004, the entity revises its estimate of labor costs to reflect an increase of 10 percent in the marketplace. In addition, it revises the probability assessments related to those labor costs. The change in labor costs results in an upward revision to the expected cash flows; consequently, the incremental expected cash flows are discounted at the current credit-adjusted risk-free rate of 8 percent. All other assumptions remain unchanged. The revised estimate of expected cash flows for labor costs is as follows:

Cash Flow Estimate	Probability Assessment	Expected Cash Flows
$110,000	30%	$ 33,000
137,500	45	61,875
192,500	25	48,125
		$143,000

C7. On December 31, 2012, the entity settles its asset retirement obligation by using an outside contractor. It incurs costs of $463,000, resulting in the recognition of a $14,091 gain on settlement of the obligation:

ARO liability	$477,091
Outside contractor	463,000
Gain on settlement of obligation	$ 14,091

Initial Measurement of the ARO Liability at January 1, 2003

	Expected Cash Flows 1/1/03
Expected labor costs	$131,250
Allocated overhead and equipment charges (.80 × $131,250)	105,000
Contractor's markup [.20 × ($131,250 + $105,000)]	47,250
Expected cash flows before inflation adjustment	283,500
Inflation factor assuming 4 percent rate for 10 years	1.4802
Expected cash flows adjusted for inflation	419,637
Market-risk premium (.05 × $419,637)	20,982
Expected cash flows adjusted for market risk	$440,619
Present value using credit-adjusted risk-free rate of 8.5 percent for 10 years	$194,879

Example 2 (continued)

Subsequent Measurement of the ARO Liability Reflecting a Change in Labor Cost Estimate as of December 31, 2004

	Incremental Expected Cash Flows 12/31/04
Incremental expected labor costs ($143,000 – $131,250)	$11,750
Allocated overhead and equipment charges (.80 × $11,750)	9,400
Contractor's markup [.20 × ($11,750 + $9,400)]	4,230
Expected cash flows before inflation adjustment	25,380
Inflation factor assuming 4 percent rate for 8 years	1.3686
Expected cash flows adjusted for inflation	34,735
Market-risk premium (.05 × $34,735)	1,737
Expected cash flows adjusted for market risk	$36,472
Expected present value of incremental liability using credit-adjusted risk-free rate of 8 percent for 8 years	$19,704

Interest Method of Allocation

Year	Liability Balance 1/1	Accretion	Change in Cash Flow Estimate	Liability Balance 12/31
2003	$194,879	$16,565		$211,444
2004	211,444	17,973	$19,704	249,121*
2005	249,121	21,078		270,199
2006	270,199	22,862		293,061
2007	293,061	24,796		317,857
2008	317,857	26,894		344,751
2009	344,751	29,170		373,921
2010	373,921	31,638		405,559
2011	405,559	34,315		439,874
2012	439,874	37,217		477,091

*The remainder of this table is an aggregation of two layers: the original liability, which is accreted at a rate of 8.5%, and the new incremental liability, which is accreted at a rate of 8.0%.

Schedule of Expenses

Year-End	Accretion Expense	Depreciation Expense	Total Expense
2003	$16,565	$19,488	$36,053
2004	17,973	19,488	37,461
2005	21,078	21,951	43,029
2006	22,862	21,951	44,813
2007	24,796	21,951	46,747
2008	26,894	21,951	48,845
2009	29,170	21,951	51,121
2010	31,638	21,951	53,589
2011	34,315	21,951	56,266
2012	37,217	21,951	59,168

Example 2 (continued)

Journal Entries

January 1, 2003:

Long-lived asset (asset retirement cost)	194,879	
ARO liability		194,879
To record the initial fair value of the ARO liability		

December 31, 2003:

Depreciation expense (asset retirement cost)	19,488	
Accumulated depreciation		19,488
To record straight-line depreciation on the asset retirement cost		
Accretion expense	16,565	
ARO liability		16,565
To record accretion expense on the ARO liability		

December 31, 2004:

Depreciation expense (asset retirement cost)	19,488	
Accumulated depreciation		19,488
To record straight-line depreciation on the asset retirement cost		
Accretion expense	17,973	
ARO liability		17,973
To record accretion expense on the ARO liability		
Long-lived asset (asset retirement cost)	19,704	
ARO liability		19,704
To record the change in estimated cash flows		

December 31, 2005–2012:

Depreciation expense (asset retirement cost)	21,951	
Accumulated depreciation		21,951
To record straight-line depreciation on the asset retirement cost adjusted for the change in cash flow estimate		
Accretion expense	Per schedule	
ARO liability		Per schedule
To record accretion expense on the ARO liability		

December 31, 2012:

ARO liability	477,091	
Gain on settlement of ARO liability		14,091
Accounts payable (outside contractor)		463,000
To record settlement of the ARO liability		

Example 3

C8. Example 3 depicts an entity that places a nuclear utility plant into service on December 31, 2003. The entity is legally required to decommission the plant at the end of its useful life, which is estimated to be 20 years. Based on the requirements of this Statement, the entity recognizes a liability for an asset retirement obligation and capitalizes an amount for an asset retirement cost over the life of the plant as contamination occurs. The following schedule reflects the expected cash flows and respective credit-adjusted risk-free rates used to measure each portion of the liability through December 31, 2005, at which time the plant is 90 percent contaminated.

Date	Expected Cash Flows	Credit-Adjusted Risk-Free Rate
12/31/03	$23,000	9.0%
12/31/04	1,150	8.5
12/31/05	1,900	9.2

C9. On December 31, 2005, the entity increases by 10 percent its estimate of expected cash flows that were used to measure those portions of the liability recognized on December 31, 2003, and December 31, 2004, which results in an upward revision to the expected cash flows. Accordingly, the incremental expected cash flows of $2,415 [$2,300 (10 percent of $23,000) plus $115 (10 percent of $1,150)] are discounted at the then-current credit-adjusted risk-free rate of 9.2 percent and recorded as a liability on December 31, 2005.

	Date Incurred		
	12/31/03	**12/31/04**	**12/31/05**
Initial measurement of the ARO liability:			
Expected cash flows adjusted for market risk	$23,000	$1,150	$1,900
Credit-adjusted risk-free rate	9.00%	8.50%	9.20%
Discount period in years	20	19	18
Expected present value	$4,104	$244	$390
Measurement of incremental expected cash flows occurring on December 31, 2005:			
Incremental expected cash flows (increase of 10 percent)			$2,415
Credit-adjusted risk-free rate at December 31, 2005			9.20%
Discount period remaining in years			18
Expected present value			$495

Example 3 (continued)

Carrying Amount of Liability Incurred in 2003

Year	Liability Balance 1/1	Accretion (9.0%)	New Liability	Liability Balance 12/31
2003			$4,104	$4,104
2004	$4,104	$369		4,473
2005	4,473	403		4,876

Carrying Amount of Liability Incurred in 2004

Year	Liability Balance 1/1	Accretion (8.5%)	New Liability	Liability Balance 12/31
2004			$ 244	$ 244
2005	$ 244	$21		265

Carrying Amount of Liability Incurred in 2005
Plus Effect of Change in Expected Cash Flows

Year	Liability Balance 1/1	Accretion (9.2%)	Change in Estimate	New Liability	Liability Balance 12/31
2005			$495	$390	$885

Carrying Amount of Total Liability

Year	Liability Balance 1/1	Accretion	Change in Estimate	New Liability	Total Carrying Amount 12/31
2003				$4,104	$4,104
2004	$4,104	$369		244	4,717
2005	4,717	424	$495	390	6,026

Example 3 (continued)

Journal Entries

December 31, 2003:

Long-lived asset (asset retirement cost)	4,104	
ARO liability		4,104

  To record the initial fair value of the ARO
  liability incurred this period

December 31, 2004:

Depreciation expense ($4,104 ÷ 20)	205	
Accumulated depreciation		205

  To record straight-line depreciation on the
  asset retirement cost

Accretion expense	369	
ARO liability		369

  To record accretion expense on the ARO liability

Long-lived asset (asset retirement cost)	244	
ARO liability		244

  To record the initial fair value of the ARO
  liability incurred this period

December 31, 2005:

Depreciation expense [($4,104 ÷ 20) + ($244 ÷ 19)]	218	
Accumulated depreciation		218

  To record straight-line depreciation on the
  asset retirement cost

Accretion expense	424	
ARO liability		424

  To record accretion expense on the ARO liability

Long-lived asset (asset retirement cost)	495	
ARO liability		495

  To record the change in liability resulting
  from a revision in expected cash flows

Long-lived asset (asset retirement cost)	390	
ARO liability		390

  To record the initial fair value of the ARO
  liability incurred this period

Example 4

C10. Example 4 illustrates a timber lease[26] wherein the lessor has an option to require the lessee to settle an asset retirement obligation. Assume an entity enters into a five-year lease agreement that grants it the right to harvest timber on a tract of land and that agreement grants the lessor an option to require that the lessee reforest the underlying land at the end of the lease term. Based on past history, the lessee believes that the likelihood that the lessor will exercise that option is low. Rather, at the end of the lease, the lessor will likely accept the land without requiring reforestation. The lessee estimates that there is only a 10 percent probability that the lessor will elect to enforce reforestation.

C11. At the end of the first year, 20 percent of the timber has been harvested. The lessee estimates that the possible cash flows associated with performing reforestation activities in 4 years for the portion of the land that has been harvested will be $300,000. When estimating the fair value of the ARO liability to be recorded (using an expected present value technique), the lessee incorporates the probability that the restoration provisions will not be enforced:

Possible Cash Flows	Probability Assessment	Expected Cash Flows
$300,000	10%	$30,000
0	90	0
		$30,000

Expected present value using credit-adjusted risk-free rate of 8.5 percent for 4 years	$21,647

C12. During the term of the lease, the lessee should reassess the likelihood that the lessor will require reforestation. For example, if the lessee subsequently determines that the likelihood of the lessor electing the reforestation option has increased, that change will result in a change in the expected cash flows and be accounted for as illustrated in Example 2.

Appendix D

ILLUSTRATIVE EXAMPLES— TRANSITION PROVISIONS

D1. This appendix includes four examples that illustrate application of the transition provisions assuming that this Statement is adopted on January 1, 2003 (calendar-year-ends 2001 and 2002 are shown for illustration purposes). Therefore, for measurement purposes, the examples use information and assumptions to derive cash flow estimates related to asset retirement obligations at January 1, 2003. Additionally, the January 1, 2003, risk-free rate adjusted for the effect of the entity's credit standing is 8.5 percent.

Example 1

D2. Example 1 depicts an entity that has not been recognizing amounts related to an asset retirement obligation because no requirement existed. Therefore, in Example 1, prior to adoption of this Statement, no amounts are recognized for an asset retirement obligation in the statement of financial position.

D3. In addition to the assumptions described in paragraph D1, other significant assumptions in Example 1 are as follows:

a. The long-lived asset to which the asset retirement obligation relates was acquired on January 1, 1993, and is estimated to have a useful life of 15 years.
b. 100 percent of the asset retirement obligation occurred at acquisition.
c. The entity uses straight-line depreciation.
d. At January 1, 2003, undiscounted expected cash flows that will be required to satisfy the ARO liability in 2008 are $3 million. Discounting at an 8.5 percent credit-adjusted risk-free rate, the present value of the ARO liability at January 1, 1993, is $882,000.

D4. The interest allocation table, amounts measured under the provisions of this Statement, and journal entries to record the transition amounts are shown below (in thousands).

---

[26]FASB Statement No. 13, *Accounting for Leases,* excludes from its scope "lease agreements concerning the rights to explore for or to exploit natural resources such as oil, gas, minerals, and timber" (paragraph 1).

Example 1 (continued)

Interest Allocation Table
(8.5% Credit-Adjusted Risk-Free Rate)

Year	Liability Balance 1/1	Accretion	Liability Balance 12/31
1993	$ 882	$ 75	$ 957
1994	957	81	1,038
1995	1,038	88	1,126
1996	1,126	96	1,222
1997	1,222	104	1,326
1998	1,326	113	1,439
1999	1,439	122	1,561
2000	1,561	133	1,694
2001	1,694	144	1,838
2002	1,838	156	1,994
2003	1,994	170	2,164
2004	2,164	184	2,348
2005	2,348	200	2,548
2006	2,548	217	2,765
2007	2,765	235	3,000

Transition Amounts Required by the Provisions of ARO Statement

	1/1/93–12/31/00	2001	2002
Liability 1/1	$ 882	$1,694	$1,838
Accretion	812	144	156
Liability 12/31	$1,694	$1,838	$1,994
Asset		$ 882	$ 882
Amount capitalized	$ 882	—	—
Asset 12/31	$ 882	$ 882	$ 882
Accumulated depreciation 1/1		$ 472	$ 531
Depreciation expense ($882 ÷ 15)	$ 472*	59	59
Accumulated depreciation 12/31	$ 472	$ 531	$ 590

---

*$59 × 8 = $472

Journal Entry Required at Transition (1/1/03)

Cumulative-effect adjustment	1,702	
Long-lived asset	882	
Accumulated depreciation		590
Liability for an asset retirement obligation		1,994

Example 2

D5. Example 2 depicts an entity that has been recognizing amounts related to an asset retirement obligation under the provisions of Statement 19. Prior to adoption of this Statement, amounts have been recognized in the statement of financial position as accumulated depreciation. The entity would have previously recognized expense in the income statement under the provisions of Statement 19.

D6. Significant assumptions in Example 2 are as follows:

a. The long-lived asset to which the asset retirement obligation relates was acquired on January 1, 1999, and is estimated to have a useful life of 15 years.
b. 100 percent of the asset retirement obligation occurs at acquisition.
c. The entity uses straight-line depreciation.
d. At January 1, 2003, undiscounted expected cash flows that will be required to satisfy the ARO liability in 2014 are $75 million. Discounting at an 8.5 percent credit-adjusted risk-free rate, the present value of the ARO liability at January 1, 1999, is $22.060 million. That is also the amount that would have been capitalized as an increase to the carrying amount of the long-lived asset at acquisition.
e. The estimated (undiscounted) retirement obligation under the provisions of Statement 19 was $67 million. The entity had been accruing that amount on a straight-line basis over 15 years by recognizing an expense and a credit to accumulated depreciation in the amount of $4.467 million per year.

D7. The interest allocation table, amounts measured under the provisions of this Statement, amounts recognized and measured under the provisions of Statement 19, and journal entries to record the transition amounts are shown below (in thousands).

Interest Allocation Table
(8.5% Credit-Adjusted Risk-Free Rate)

Year	Liability Balance 1/1	Accretion	Liability Balance 12/31
1999	$22,060	$1,875	$23,935
2000	23,935	2,035	25,970
2001	25,970	2,207	28,177
2002	28,177	2,395	30,572
2003	30,572	2,599	33,171
2004	33,171	2,820	35,991
2005	35,991	3,059	39,050
2006	39,050	3,319	42,369
2007	42,369	3,601	45,970
2008	45,970	3,907	49,877
2009	49,877	4,240	54,117
2010	54,117	4,600	58,717
2011	58,717	4,991	63,708
2012	63,708	5,415	69,123
2013	69,123	5,877	75,000

Example 2 (continued)

Transition Amounts Required by the Provisions of ARO Statement

	1999	2000	2001	2002
Liability 1/1		$23,935	$25,970	$28,177
Accretion	$ 1,875	2,035	2,207	2,395
Liability incurred	22,060	—	—	—
Liability 12/31	$23,935	$25,970	$28,177	$30,572
Asset 1/1		$22,060	$22,060	$22,060
Amount capitalized	$22,060	—	—	—
Asset 12/31	$22,060	$22,060	$22,060	$22,060
Accumulated depreciation 1/1		$ 1,471	$ 2,942	$ 4,413
Depreciation expense ($22,060 ÷ 15)	$ 1,471	1,471	1,471	1,471
Accumulated depreciation 12/31	$ 1,471	$ 2,942	$ 4,413	$ 5,884

Amounts Recorded under the Provisions of Statement 19

	1999	2000	2001	2002
Accumulated depreciation 1/1		$ 4,467	$ 8,934	$13,401
Accrued expense (estimated costs of $67 million)	$4,467	4,467	4,467	4,467
Accumulated depreciation 12/31	$4,467	$ 8,934	$13,401	$17,868

Journal Entry Required at Transition (1/1/03)

Accumulated depreciation (Statement 19)	17,868	
Long-lived asset (Statement 143)	22,060	
Accumulated depreciation (Statement 143)		5,884
Liability for an asset retirement obligation (Statement 143)		30,572
Cumulative-effect adjustment		3,472

Example 3

D8. Example 3 depicts an entity that has been recognizing amounts related to an asset retirement obligation under the provisions of Statement 19. The entity incurs 90 percent, 8 percent, and 2 percent of the asset retirement obligation over the first 3 years of the life of the asset, respectively. In Example 2, the entity incurred 100 percent of the asset retirement obligation upon acquisition.

D9. Significant assumptions in Example 3 are as follows:

a. The long-lived asset to which the asset retirement obligation relates was acquired on January 1, 1986, and is estimated to have a useful life of 20 years.

Example 3 (continued)

b. Upon transition to this Statement, the entity has incurred 100 percent of the asset retirement obligation. However, as discussed in paragraph D8, that obligation was incurred over the first three years of the life of the asset.

c. The entity uses straight-line depreciation.

d. At January 1, 2003, undiscounted expected cash flows that will be required to satisfy the ARO liability in 2006 are $250 million. Discounting at an 8.5 percent credit-adjusted risk-free rate, the present value of the ARO liability at January 1, 2003, is $195.726 million.

e. The total estimated (undiscounted) retirement obligation under the provisions of Statement 19 was $220 million. As of January 1, 2003, $186.785 million of that amount had been accrued.

D10. The following table shows (by year) the undiscounted expected cash flows incurred under the provisions of this Statement and the amounts estimated under the provisions of Statement 19 (in thousands).

		ARO Statement	Statement 19
Date	Percentage of Total Costs Incurred	Undiscounted Expected Cash Flows	Estimated Retirement Costs
1/1/86	90%	$225,000	$198,000
1/1/87	8	20,000	17,600
1/1/88	2	5,000	4,400
	100%	$250,000	$220,000

D11. The interest allocation table, amounts measured under the provisions of this Statement, amounts recognized and measured under the provisions of Statement 19, and journal entries to record the transition amounts are shown below (in thousands).

Interest Allocation Table
(8.5% Credit-Adjusted Risk-Free Rate)

Year	Liability Balance 1/1	Accretion	Liability Balance 12/31
2000	$153,236*	$13,025	$166,261
2001	166,261	14,132	180,393
2002	180,393	15,333	195,726
2003	195,726	16,637	212,363
2004	212,363	18,051	230,414
2005	230,414	19,586	250,000

*$153,236 = present value of $250,000, 8.5%, 6 years.

Example 3 (continued)

Transition Amounts Required by the Provisions of ARO Statement

	2000	2001	2002
Liability 1/1	$153,236	$166,261	$180,393
Accretion	13,025	14,132	15,333
Liability 12/31	$166,261	$180,393	$195,726
Asset 1/1:			
Capitalized 1/1/86 (PV of $225,000, 8.5%, 20 yrs.)	$ 44,014	$ 44,014	$ 44,014
Capitalized 1/1/87 (PV of $20,000, 8.5%, 19 yrs.)	4,245	4,245	4,245
Capitalized 1/1/88 (PV of $5,000, 8.5%, 18 yrs.)	1,151	1,151	1,151
Asset 12/31	$ 49,410	$ 49,410	$ 49,410
Accumulated depreciation 1/1:		$ 36,970	$ 39,458
Capitalized 1/1/86 [($44,014 ÷ 20) × 14]	$ 30,810		
Capitalized 1/1/87 [($4,245 ÷ 19) × 13]	2,904		
Capitalized 1/1/88 [($1,151 ÷ 18) × 12]	768		
Depreciation expense			
[($44,014 ÷ 20) + ($4,245 ÷ 19) + ($1,151 ÷ 18)]	2,488	2,488	2,488
Accumulated depreciation 12/31	$ 36,970	$ 39,458	$ 41,946

Amounts Recorded under the Provisions of Statement 19

	2000	2001	2002
Accumulated depreciation 1/1:		$164,645	$175,715
1/1/86 accrual [($198,000 ÷ 20) × 14]	$138,600		
1/1/87 accrual [($17,600 ÷ 19) × 13]	12,042		
1/1/88 accrual [($4,400 ÷ 18) × 12]	2,933		
Accrued expense			
[($198,000 ÷ 20) + ($17,600 ÷ 19) + ($4,400 ÷ 18)]	11,070	11,070	11,070
Accumulated depreciation 12/31	$164,645	$175,715	$186,785

Journal Entry Required at Transition (1/1/03)

Cumulative-effect adjustment	1,477	
Accumulated depreciation (Statement 19)	186,785	
Long-lived asset (Statement 143)	49,410	
Accumulated depreciation (Statement 143)		41,946
Liability for an asset retirement obligation (Statement 143)		195,726

Example 4

D12. Example 4 illustrates transition accounting for an oil field composed of numerous individual wells that has been in production for several years before adoption of this Statement. In periods prior to the adoption of this Statement, the entity had been recognizing amounts related to an asset retirement obligation under the provisions of Statement 19. Those amounts have been recognized on the balance sheet as a liability.

D13. Additional assumptions related to this example are as follows:

a. The oil field was discovered in 1990. Production started in 1993.
b. The producing platform is a concrete structure that supports 35 individual wells.
c. The estimated reserves at the time of discovery was 465 millions of barrels of oil equivalent (mmboe) with an expected production life of 20 years.

d. At the time of adoption of this Statement, cumulative production at the site is 300 mmboe, and remaining reserves are estimated to be 250 mboe. (The increase in reserves is due to enhanced recovery methods.)
e. The amount of ARO liability accrued under Statement 19 at the time of adoption of this Statement on January 1, 2003, was $750,000.[27]
f. The estimated undiscounted cash flows for the asset retirement obligation at the estimated date of retirement in 2013 is $1.5 million.

Discounting at an 8.5 percent credit-adjusted risk-free rate, the present value of the asset retirement obligation for the entire operation is $663,428 at January 1, 2003. The discounted amount in 1993 when the field started production is $293,425. That is the amount that would have been capitalized as part of the oil field cost. The amount of that cost that would have been expensed to date using a units-of-production method is computed as follows:

$$(\text{Cumulative production} \div \text{estimated total production}) \times \$293,425 =$$

$$[300 \div (300 + 250)] \times \$293,425 = \underline{\$160,050}$$

The reduction in the liability to be recognized upon transition is ($750,000 − $663,428) $86,572.

Journal Entry Required at Transition (1/1/03)

Liability (Statement 19)	750,000	
Long-lived asset (Statement 143)	293,425	
Cumulative effect adjustment		219,947
Accumulated depreciation (Statement 143)		160,050
Liability for ARO (Statement 143)		663,428

Appendix E

ILLUSTRATIVE EXAMPLE— SUBSEQUENT MEASUREMENT OF A LIABILITY OBTAINED FROM A MARKET PRICE

E1. Subsequent to initial measurement, an entity is required to recognize period-to-period changes in an

ARO liability resulting from (a) the passage of time (accretion expense) and (b) revisions in cash flow estimates. To apply the subsequent measurement provisions of this Statement, an entity must identify undiscounted cash flows related to an ARO liability irrespective of how the liability was initially measured. Therefore, if an entity obtains the initial fair value from a market price, it must impute undiscounted cash flows from that price.

E2. This appendix includes an example that illustrates the subsequent measurement of a liability in

---

[27]Because of changes in estimates of both total reserves and retirement costs during the life of the field, the amount of estimated costs to retire an asset that may have been previously recognized in accumulated depreciation may not be determinable using cumulative production data. However, in the absence of more complete information, a shortcut approach that bases an estimate of that amount on cumulative production to date, current reserve estimates, or similar data and the current estimate of the asset retirement obligation is appropriate.

situations where the initial liability is based on a market price. The example assumes that the liability is initially recognized at the end of period 0 when the market price is $300,000 and the entity's credit-adjusted risk-free rate is 8 percent. As required by this Statement, revisions in the timing or the amount of estimated cash flows are assumed to occur at the end of the period after accretion on the beginning balance of the liability is calculated. At the end of each period, the following procedure is used to impute cash flows from the end of period market price, compute the change in that price attributable to revisions in estimated cash flows, and calculate accretion expense.

a. The market price and the credit-adjusted risk-free interest rate are used to impute the undiscounted cash flows embedded in the market price.

b. The undiscounted cash flows from (a) are discounted at the initial credit-adjusted risk-free rate of 8 percent to arrive at the ending balance of the ARO liability per the provisions of this Statement.

c. The beginning balance of the ARO liability is multiplied by the initial credit-adjusted risk-free rate of 8 percent to arrive at the amount of accretion expense per the provisions of this Statement.

d. The difference between the undiscounted cash flows at the beginning of the period and the undiscounted cash flows at the end of the period represents the revision in cash flow estimates that occurred during the period. If that change is an upward revision to the undiscounted estimated cash flows, it is discounted at the current credit-adjusted risk-free rate. If that change is a downward revision, it is discounted at the historical weighted-average rate because it is not practicable to separately identify the period to which the downward revision relates.

Subsequent Measurement of an ARO Liability
Obtained from a Market Price

	End of Period			
	0	1	2	3
Market assumptions:				
Market price (includes market risk premium)	$ 300,000	$400,000	$ 350,000	$380,000
Current risk-free rate adjusted for entity's credit standing	8.00%	7.00%	7.50%	7.50%
Time period remaining	3	2	1	0
Imputed undiscounted cash flows (market price discounted at market rate)	$ 377,914	$457,960	$ 376,250	$380,000
Change in undiscounted cash flows	377,914	80,046	(81,710)	3,750
Discount rate:				
Current credit-adjusted risk-free rate (for upward revisions)	8.00%	7.00%		
Historical weighted-average credit-adjusted risk-free rate (for downward revisions)			7.83%	
Change in undiscounted cash flows discounted at credit-adjusted risk-free rate (current rate for upward revisions and historical rate for downward revisions)	$300,000	$69,916	$(75,777)	$3,750

Measurement of Liability under Provisions of ARO Statement

Period	Beginning Balance	Accretion (8.0%)	Change in Cash Flows	Ending Balance
0			$300,000	$300,000
1	$300,000	$24,000		324,000
2	324,000	25,920		349,920
3	349,920	27,994		377,914

Period	Beginning Balance	Accretion (7.0%)	Change in Cash Flows	Ending Balance
0				
1			$69,916	$69,916
2	$69,916	$4,894		74,810
3	74,810	5,236		80,046

Period	Beginning Balance	Accretion (7.83%)	Change in Cash Flows	Ending Balance
0				
1				
2			$(75,777)	$(75,777)
3	$(75,777)	$(5,933)		(81,710)

Period	Beginning Balance	Accretion	Change in Cash Flows	Ending Balance
0				
1				
2				
3			$3,750	$3,750

Total

Period	Beginning Balance	Accretion Expense	Change in Cash Flows	Ending Balance
0			$300,000	$300,000
1	$300,000	$24,000	69,916	393,916
2	393,916	30,814	(75,777)	348,953
3	348,953	27,297	3,750	380,000

F1–F4. [These paragraphs have been deleted. See Status page.]

Statement of Financial Accounting Standards No. 144
Accounting for the Impairment or Disposal of
Long-Lived Assets

STATUS

Issued: August 2001

Effective Date: For financial statements issued for fiscal years beginning after December 15, 2001 and interim
periods within those fiscal years

Affects: Amends ARB 51, paragraph 2
Deletes ARB 51, paragraph 12
Amends APB 18, paragraph 19(h)
Amends APB 28, paragraphs 21, 30(e), and 31
Amends APB 29, paragraphs 21 and 23
Amends APB 30, paragraphs 3, 11, 23, and 25
Deletes APB 30, paragraphs 8, 9, and 13 through 18 and footnotes 2 and 5 through 7
Amends AIN-APB 30, Interpretation No. 1
Amends FAS 15, paragraphs 28 and 33
Replaces FAS 19, paragraph 44(a)
Replaces FAS 19, paragraph after paragraph 62 added by FAS 121
Amends FAS 34, paragraph 19
Amends FAS 43, paragraph 2
Amends FAS 51, paragraph 14
Amends FAS 60, paragraph 48
Amends FAS 61, paragraph 6
Amends FAS 66, paragraph 65
Replaces FAS 66, footnote 5
Amends FAS 67, paragraphs 3, 24, and 28
Deletes FAS 67, paragraph 16
Replaces FAS 67, paragraph 25
Amends FAS 71, paragraphs 9 and 10 and by adding paragraph after paragraph 10
Amends FAS 88, paragraphs 6(a) and 57 (Example 3A)
Deletes FAS 88, paragraphs 8 and 16
Amends FAS 101, paragraph 6
Amends FAS 106, paragraph 96(a)
Deletes FAS 106, paragraph 103
Amends FAS 115, paragraph 8(c)
Amends FAS 117, paragraph 164
Supersedes FAS 121
Amends FAS 123, paragraph 9
Deletes FAS 141, footnote 18
Deletes FAS 142, paragraph 7 and footnote 22
Amends FAS 142, paragraphs 15, 17, 28(f), 29, and Appendix A (Examples 1 through 3, 5, and 9)
Amends FAS 143, paragraphs 2 and 12
Deletes FAS 143, footnote 11
Amends FIN 18, paragraphs 19, 35, and 71
Replaces FIN 18, footnotes 1 and 20
Deletes FIN 27, paragraph 3
Amends FIN 39, paragraph 7

Affected by: Paragraphs 5 and D1 amended by FAS 145, paragraphs 7(d) and 9(n), and FAS 147, paragraph B4

                    Paragraphs 9 and 28 amended by FAS 154, paragraphs C15(a) and C15(b), respectively

                    Paragraphs 22 and 24 deleted by FAS 157, paragraphs E24(a) and E24(c), respectively

                    Paragraph 23 amended by FAS 157, paragraph E24(b)

                    Paragraphs 27 and 29 and footnote 17 amended by FAS 153, paragraph 5

                    Paragraph 43 amended by FAS 154, paragraph C19(g)

                    Paragraph 45 amended by FAS 145, paragraph 9(n)

                    Paragraph A3 amended by FAS 151, paragraph 3

                    Paragraphs A6 through A8, A11, A13, and A14 amended by FAS 157, paragraphs E24(d) through E24(g), E24(i), and E24(j), respectively

                    Paragraphs A12 and E1 through E3 deleted by FAS 157, paragraphs E24(h) and E24(k), respectively

                    Footnotes 7 and 24 amended by FAS 154, paragraphs C15(a) and C15(c), respectively

                    Footnotes 12 through 14, 28, and 29 deleted by FAS 157, paragraphs E24(a) through E24(c), E24(g), and E24(h), respectively

Other Interpretive Release: FASB Staff Position FAS 144-1

AICPA Accounting Standards Executive Committee (AcSEC)

  Related Pronouncements: SOP 85-3
                             SOP 90-7

Issues Discussed by FASB Emerging Issues Task Force (EITF)

  Affects: Nullifies EITF Issues No. 85-36, 87-11, 90-6, 90-16, 95-18, and Topic No. D-45
          Partially nullifies EITF Issue No. 93-4
          Resolves EITF Issues No. 84-28 and 95-21
          Partially resolves EITF Issue No. 01-2

  Interpreted by: Paragraphs 8 through 16 interpreted by EITF Issue No. 95-23
                 Paragraphs 17 through 21 interpreted by EITF Issues No. 95-23 and 04-3
                 Paragraphs 29, 41, and 42 interpreted by EITF Issue No. 02-11
                 Paragraph 34 interpreted by EITF Issue No. 01-5
                 Paragraph 43 interpreted by EITF Issues No. 87-24, 93-17, and 02-11
                 Paragraph 44 interpreted by EITF Issue No. 02-11
                 Paragraph 51 interpreted by EITF Topic No. D-104

  Related Issues: EITF Issues No. 86-22, 87-4, 87-18, 87-24, 89-13, 93-11, 97-4, 99-14, 00-26, 01-2, and 03-13

SUMMARY

    This Statement addresses financial accounting and reporting for the impairment or disposal of long-lived assets. This Statement supersedes FASB Statement No. 121, *Accounting for the Impairment of Long-Lived Assets and for Long-Lived Assets to Be Disposed Of,* and the accounting and reporting provisions of APB Opinion No. 30, *Reporting the Results of Operations—Reporting the Effects of Disposal of a Segment of a Business, and Extraordinary, Unusual and Infrequently Occurring Events and Transactions,* for the disposal of a *segment of a business* (as previously defined in that Opinion). This Statement also amends ARB No. 51, *Consolidated Financial Statements,* to eliminate the exception to consolidation for a subsidiary for which control is likely to be temporary.

Reasons for Issuing This Statement

    Because Statement 121 did not address the accounting for a segment of a business accounted for as a discontinued operation under Opinion 30, two accounting models existed for long-lived assets to be disposed of. The Board decided to establish a single accounting model, based on the framework established in Statement 121, for long-lived assets to be disposed of by sale. The Board also decided to resolve significant implementation issues related to Statement 121.

Differences between This Statement, Statement 121, and Opinion 30 and Additional Implementation Guidance

Long-Lived Assets to Be Held and Used

This Statement retains the requirements of Statement 121 to (a) recognize an impairment loss only if the carrying amount of a long-lived asset is not recoverable from its undiscounted cash flows and (b) measure an impairment loss as the difference between the carrying amount and fair value of the asset. To resolve implementation issues, this Statement:

- Removes goodwill from its scope and, therefore, eliminates the requirement of Statement 121 to allocate goodwill to long-lived assets to be tested for impairment
- Describes a probability-weighted cash flow estimation approach to deal with situations in which alternative courses of action to recover the carrying amount of a long-lived asset are under consideration or a range is estimated for the amount of possible future cash flows
- Establishes a "primary-asset" approach to determine the cash flow estimation period for a group of assets and liabilities that represents the unit of accounting for a long-lived asset to be held and used.

Long-Lived Assets to Be Disposed Of Other Than by Sale

This Statement requires that a long-lived asset to be abandoned, exchanged for a similar productive asset, or distributed to owners in a spinoff be considered held and used until it is disposed of. To resolve implementation issues, this Statement:

- Requires that the depreciable life of a long-lived asset to be abandoned be revised in accordance with APB Opinion No. 20, *Accounting Changes*
- Amends APB Opinion No. 29, *Accounting for Nonmonetary Transactions,* to require that an impairment loss be recognized at the date a long-lived asset is exchanged for a similar productive asset or distributed to owners in a spinoff if the carrying amount of the asset exceeds its fair value.

Long-Lived Assets to Be Disposed Of by Sale

The accounting model for long-lived assets to be disposed of by sale is used for all long-lived assets, whether previously held and used or newly acquired. That accounting model retains the requirement of Statement 121 to measure a long-lived asset classified as held for sale at the lower of its carrying amount or fair value less cost to sell and to cease depreciation (amortization). Therefore, discontinued operations are no longer measured on a net realizable value basis, and future operating losses are no longer recognized before they occur.

This Statement retains the basic provisions of Opinion 30 for the presentation of discontinued operations in the income statement but broadens that presentation to include a component of an entity (rather than a segment of a business). A component of an entity comprises operations and cash flows that can be clearly distinguished, operationally and for financial reporting purposes, from the rest of the entity. A component of an entity that is classified as held for sale or that has been disposed of is presented as a discontinued operation if the operations and cash flows of the component will be (or have been) eliminated from the ongoing operations of the entity and the entity will not have any significant continuing involvement in the operations of the component.

To resolve implementation issues, this Statement:

- Establishes criteria beyond that previously specified in Statement 121 to determine when a long-lived asset is held for sale, including a group of assets and liabilities that represents the unit of accounting for a long-lived asset classified as held for sale. Among other things, those criteria specify that (a) the asset must be available for immediate sale in its present condition subject only to terms that are usual and customary for sales of such assets and (b) the sale of the asset must be probable, and its transfer expected to qualify for recognition as a completed sale, within one year, with certain exceptions.

- Provides guidance on the accounting for a long-lived asset if the criteria for classification as held for sale are met after the balance sheet date but before issuance of the financial statements. That guidance prohibits retroactive reclassification of the asset as held for sale at the balance sheet date. Therefore, the guidance in EITF Issue No. 95-18, "Accounting and Reporting for a Discontinued Business Segment When the Measurement Date Occurs after the Balance Sheet Date but before the Issuance of Financial Statements," is superseded.
- Provides guidance on the accounting for a long-lived asset classified as held for sale if the asset is reclassified as held and used. The reclassified asset is measured at the lower of its (a) carrying amount before being classified as held for sale, adjusted for any depreciation (amortization) expense that would have been recognized had the asset been continuously classified as held and used, or (b) fair value at the date the asset is reclassified as held and used.

How the Changes in This Statement Improve Financial Reporting

The changes in this Statement improve financial reporting by requiring that one accounting model be used for long-lived assets to be disposed of by sale, whether previously held and used or newly acquired, and by broadening the presentation of discontinued operations to include more disposal transactions. Therefore, the accounting for similar events and circumstances will be the same. Additionally, the information value of reported financial information will be improved. Finally, resolving significant implementation issues will improve compliance with the requirements of this Statement and, therefore, comparability among entities and the representational faithfulness of reported financial information.

How the Conclusions in This Statement Relate to the Conceptual Framework

In reconsidering the use of a measurement approach based on net realizable value, and the accrual of future operating losses required under that approach, the Board used the definition of a liability in FASB Concepts Statement No. 6, *Elements of Financial Statements.* The Board determined that future operating losses do not meet the definition of a liability.

In considering changes to Statement 121, the Board focused on the qualitative characteristics discussed in FASB Concepts Statement No. 2, *Qualitative Characteristics of Accounting Information.* In particular, the Board determined that:

- Broadening the presentation of discontinued operations to include more disposal transactions provides investors, creditors, and others with decision-useful information that is relevant in assessing the effects of disposal transactions on the ongoing operations of an entity
- Eliminating inconsistencies from having two accounting models for long-lived assets to be disposed of by sale improves comparability in financial reporting among entities, enabling users to identify similarities in and differences between two sets of economic events.

This Statement also incorporates the guidance in FASB Concepts Statement No. 7, *Using Cash Flow Information and Present Value in Accounting Measurements,* for using present value techniques to measure fair value.

The Effective Date of This Statement

The provisions of this Statement are effective for financial statements issued for fiscal years beginning after December 15, 2001, and interim periods within those fiscal years, with early application encouraged. The provisions of this Statement generally are to be applied prospectively.

Statement of Financial Accounting Standards No. 144

Accounting for the Impairment or Disposal of Long-Lived Assets

CONTENTS

INTRODUCTION

1. This Statement addresses financial accounting and reporting for the impairment of long-lived assets and for long-lived assets to be disposed of. This Statement supersedes FASB Statement No. 121, *Accounting for the Impairment of Long-Lived Assets and for Long-Lived Assets to Be Disposed Of.* However, this Statement retains the fundamental provisions of Statement 121 for (a) recognition and measurement of the impairment of long-lived assets to be held and used and (b) measurement of long-lived assets to be disposed of by sale.

2. This Statement supersedes the accounting and reporting provisions of APB Opinion No. 30, *Reporting the Results of Operations—Reporting the Effects of Disposal of a Segment of a Business, and Extraordinary, Unusual and Infrequently Occurring Events and Transactions,* for segments of a business to be

disposed of. However, this Statement retains the requirement of Opinion 30 to report discontinued operations separately from continuing operations and extends that reporting to a component of an entity that either has been disposed of (by sale, by abandonment, or in a distribution to owners) or is classified as held for sale. This Statement also amends ARB No. 51, *Consolidated Financial Statements,* to eliminate the exception to consolidation for a temporarily controlled subsidiary.

STANDARDS OF FINANCIAL ACCOUNTING AND REPORTING

Scope

3. Except as indicated in paragraphs 4 and 5, this Statement applies to recognized long-lived assets of an *entity*[1] to be held and used or to be disposed of, including (a) capital leases of lessees, (b) long-lived assets of lessors subject to operating leases, (c) proved oil and gas properties that are being accounted for using the successful-efforts method of accounting,[2] and (d) long-term prepaid assets.[3]

4. If a long-lived asset (or assets) is part of a group that includes other assets and liabilities not covered by this Statement, this Statement applies to the group. In those situations, the unit of accounting for the long-lived asset is its group. For a long-lived asset or assets to be held and used, that group (hereinafter referred to as an *asset group*) represents the lowest level for which identifiable cash flows are largely independent of the cash flows of other groups of assets and liabilities. For a long-lived asset or assets to be disposed of by sale or otherwise, that group (hereinafter referred to as a *disposal group*) represents assets to be disposed of together as a group in a single trans-

action and liabilities directly associated with those assets that will be transferred in the transaction.[4] This Statement does not change generally accepted accounting principles applicable to those other individual assets (such as accounts receivable and inventory) and liabilities (such as accounts payable, long-term debt, and asset retirement obligations) not covered by this Statement that are included in such groups.

5. This Statement does not apply to (a) goodwill, (b) intangible assets not being amortized that are to be held and used, (c) servicing assets, (d) financial instruments, including investments in equity securities accounted for under the cost or equity method, (e) deferred policy acquisition costs, (f) deferred tax assets, and (g) unproved oil and gas properties that are being accounted for using the successful-efforts method of accounting. This Statement also does not apply to long-lived assets for which the accounting is prescribed by:

- FASB Statement No. 50, *Financial Reporting in the Record and Music Industry*
- FASB Statement No. 63, *Financial Reporting by Broadcasters*
- FASB Statement No. 86, *Accounting for the Costs of Computer Software to Be Sold, Leased, or Otherwise Marketed*
- FASB Statement No. 90, *Regulated Enterprises—Accounting for Abandonments and Disallowances of Plant Costs.*

6. Appendix C lists the accounting pronouncements affected by this Statement. Appendix D shows the status of FASB and Accounting Principles Board (APB) pronouncements that refer to impairment of long-lived assets, including those pronouncements that remain authoritative.[5]

---

[1]This Statement applies to a business enterprise and a not-for-profit organization, each of which is referred to herein as an *entity*.

[2]Accounting requirements for oil and gas properties that are accounted for using the full-cost method of accounting are prescribed by the Securities and Exchange Commission (Regulation S-X, Rule 4-10, "Financial Accounting and Reporting for Oil and Gas Producing Activities Pursuant to the Federal Securities Laws and the Energy Policy and Conservation Act of 1975").

[3]In this Statement, all references to a *long-lived asset* refer to a long-lived asset covered by this Statement.

[4]Examples of such liabilities include, but are not limited to, legal obligations that transfer with a long-lived asset, such as certain environmental obligations, and obligations that, for business reasons, a potential buyer would prefer to settle when assumed as part of a group, such as warranty obligations that relate to an acquired customer base.

[5]This Statement amends only pronouncements of the FASB, the APB, and the Committee on Accounting Procedure. Conforming changes to other literature, including consensuses of the FASB's Emerging Issues Task Force and pronouncements of the American Institute of Certified Public Accountants, may be made subsequently.

Long-Lived Assets to Be Held and Used

*Recognition and Measurement of an
Impairment Loss*

7. For purposes of this Statement, *impairment* is the condition that exists when the carrying amount of a long-lived asset (asset group) exceeds its fair value. An impairment loss shall be recognized only if the carrying amount of a long-lived asset (asset group) is not recoverable and exceeds its fair value. The carrying amount of a long-lived asset (asset group) is not recoverable if it exceeds the sum of the undiscounted cash flows expected to result from the use and eventual disposition of the asset (asset group). That assessment shall be based on the carrying amount of the asset (asset group) at the date it is tested for recoverability, whether in use (paragraph 19) or under development (paragraph 20). An impairment loss shall be measured as the amount by which the carrying amount of a long-lived asset (asset group) exceeds its fair value.

When to test a long-lived asset for recoverability

8. A long-lived asset (asset group) shall be tested for recoverability whenever events or changes in circumstances indicate that its carrying amount may not be recoverable. The following are examples of such events or changes in circumstances:

a. A significant decrease in the market price of a long-lived asset (asset group)

b. A significant adverse change in the extent or manner in which a long-lived asset (asset group) is being used or in its physical condition

c. A significant adverse change in legal factors or in the business climate that could affect the value of a long-lived asset (asset group), including an adverse action or assessment by a regulator

d. An accumulation of costs significantly in excess of the amount originally expected for the acquisition or construction of a long-lived asset (asset group)

e. A current-period operating or cash flow loss combined with a history of operating or cash flow losses or a projection or forecast that demon-

strates continuing losses associated with the use of a long-lived asset (asset group)

f. A current expectation that, *more likely than not,*[6] a long-lived asset (asset group) will be sold or otherwise disposed of significantly before the end of its previously estimated useful life.

9. When a long-lived asset (asset group) is tested for recoverability, it also may be necessary to review depreciation estimates and method as required by FASB Statement No. 154, *Accounting Changes and Error Corrections,* or the amortization period as required by FASB Statement No. 142, *Goodwill and Other Intangible Assets.*[7] Any revision to the remaining useful life of a long-lived asset resulting from that review also shall be considered in developing estimates of future cash flows used to test the asset (asset group) for recoverability (paragraph 18). However, any change in the accounting method for the asset resulting from that review shall be made only after applying this Statement.

Grouping long-lived assets to be held and used

10. For purposes of recognition and measurement of an impairment loss, a long-lived asset or assets shall be grouped with other assets and liabilities at the lowest level for which identifiable cash flows are largely independent of the cash flows of other assets and liabilities. However, an impairment loss, if any, that results from applying this Statement shall reduce only the carrying amount of a long-lived asset or assets of the group in accordance with paragraph 14.

11. In limited circumstances, a long-lived asset (for example, a corporate headquarters facility) may not have identifiable cash flows that are largely independent of the cash flows of other assets and liabilities and of other asset groups. In those circumstances, the asset group for that long-lived asset shall include all assets and liabilities of the entity.

12. Goodwill shall be included in an asset group to be tested for impairment under this Statement only if the asset group is or includes a *reporting unit.*[8] Goodwill shall not be included in a lower-level asset group that includes only part of a reporting unit. Estimates

---

[6]The term *more likely than not* refers to a level of likelihood that is more than 50 percent.

[7]Paragraphs 19–22 of Statement 154 address the accounting for changes in estimates, including changes in the method of depreciation, amortization, and depletion. Paragraph 11 of Statement 142 addresses the determination of the useful life of an intangible asset.

[8]The term *reporting unit* is defined in Statement 142 as the same level as or one level below an operating segment (as that term is defined in paragraph 10 of FASB Statement No. 131, *Disclosures about Segments of an Enterprise and Related Information*). Statement 142 requires that goodwill be tested for impairment at the reporting unit level.

of future cash flows used to test that lower-level asset group for recoverability shall not be adjusted for the effect of excluding goodwill from the group.

13. Other than goodwill, the carrying amounts of any assets (such as accounts receivable and inventory) and liabilities (such as accounts payable, long-term debt, and asset retirement obligations) not covered by this Statement that are included in an asset group shall be adjusted in accordance with other applicable generally accepted accounting principles prior to testing the asset group for recoverability.[9]

14. An impairment loss for an asset group shall reduce only the carrying amounts of a long-lived asset or assets of the group. The loss shall be allocated to the long-lived assets of the group on a pro rata basis using the relative carrying amounts of those assets, except that the loss allocated to an individual long-lived asset of the group shall not reduce the carrying amount of that asset below its fair value whenever that fair value is determinable without undue cost and effort. (Example 1 of Appendix A illustrates the allocation of an impairment loss for an asset group.)

New cost basis

15. If an impairment loss is recognized, the adjusted carrying amount of a long-lived asset shall be its new cost basis. For a depreciable long-lived asset, the new cost basis shall be depreciated (amortized) over the remaining useful life of that asset. Restoration of a previously recognized impairment loss is prohibited.

Estimates of future cash flows used to test a long-lived asset for recoverability

16. Estimates of future cash flows used to test the recoverability of a long-lived asset (asset group) shall include only the future cash flows (cash inflows less associated cash outflows) that are directly associated with and that are expected to arise as a direct result of the use and eventual disposition of the asset (asset group). Those estimates shall exclude interest charges that will be recognized as an expense when incurred.

17. Estimates of future cash flows used to test the recoverability of a long-lived asset (asset group) shall

incorporate the entity's own assumptions about its use of the asset (asset group) and shall consider all available evidence. The assumptions used in developing those estimates shall be reasonable in relation to the assumptions used in developing other information used by the entity for comparable periods, such as internal budgets and projections, accruals related to incentive compensation plans, or information communicated to others. However, if alternative courses of action to recover the carrying amount of a long-lived asset (asset group) are under consideration or if a range is estimated for the amount of possible future cash flows associated with the likely course of action, the likelihood of those possible outcomes shall be considered. A probability-weighted approach may be useful in considering the likelihood of those possible outcomes. (Example 2 of Appendix A illustrates the use of that approach when alternative courses of action are under consideration.)

18. Estimates of future cash flows used to test the recoverability of a long-lived asset (asset group) shall be made for the remaining useful life of the asset (asset group) to the entity. The remaining useful life of an asset group shall be based on the remaining useful life of the primary asset of the group. For purposes of this Statement, the *primary asset* is the principal long-lived tangible asset being depreciated or intangible asset being amortized that is the most significant component asset from which the asset group derives its cash-flow-generating capacity.[10] Factors that an entity generally should consider in determining whether a long-lived asset is the primary asset of an asset group include the following: (a) whether other assets of the group would have been acquired by the entity without the asset, (b) the level of investment that would be required to replace the asset, and (c) the remaining useful life of the asset relative to other assets of the group. If the primary asset is not the asset of the group with the longest remaining useful life, estimates of future cash flows for the group should assume the sale of the group at the end of the remaining useful life of the primary asset.

19. Estimates of future cash flows used to test the recoverability of a long-lived asset (asset group) that is in use, including a long-lived asset (asset group) for which development is substantially complete, shall be based on the existing service potential of the asset

---

[9]Paragraph 29 of Statement 142 requires that goodwill be tested for impairment only after the carrying amounts of the other assets of the reporting unit, including the long-lived assets covered by this Statement, have been tested for impairment under other applicable accounting pronouncements.

[10]The primary asset of an asset group therefore cannot be land or an intangible asset not being amortized.

(asset group) at the date it is tested. The service potential of a long-lived asset (asset group) encompasses its remaining useful life, cash-flow-generating capacity, and for tangible assets, physical output capacity. Those estimates shall include cash flows associated with future expenditures necessary to maintain the existing service potential of a long-lived asset (asset group), including those that replace the service potential of component parts of a long-lived asset (for example, the roof of a building) and component assets other than the primary asset of an asset group. Those estimates shall exclude cash flows associated with future capital expenditures that would increase the service potential of a long-lived asset (asset group).

20. Estimates of future cash flows used to test the recoverability of a long-lived asset (asset group) that is under development shall be based on the expected service potential of the asset (group) when development is substantially complete. Those estimates shall include cash flows associated with all future expenditures necessary to develop a long-lived asset (asset group), including interest payments that will be capitalized as part of the cost of the asset (asset group).[11]

21. If a long-lived asset that is under development is part of an asset group that is in use, estimates of future cash flows used to test the recoverability of that group shall include the cash flows associated with future expenditures necessary to maintain the existing service potential of the group (paragraph 19) as well as the cash flows associated with all future expenditures necessary to substantially complete the asset that is under development (paragraph 20). (Example 3 of Appendix A illustrates that situation.)

Fair value

22. [This paragraph has been deleted. See Status page.]

23. For long-lived assets (asset groups) that have uncertainties both in timing and amount, an expected present value technique will often be the appropriate technique with which to estimate fair value. (Example 4 of Appendix A illustrates the use of that technique.)

24. [This paragraph has been deleted. See Status page.]

Reporting and Disclosure

25. An impairment loss recognized for a long-lived asset (asset group) to be held and used shall be included in income from continuing operations before income taxes in the income statement of a business enterprise and in income from continuing operations in the statement of activities of a not-for-profit organization. If a subtotal such as "income from operations" is presented, it shall include the amount of that loss.

26. The following information shall be disclosed in the notes to the financial statements that include the period in which an impairment loss is recognized:

a. A description of the impaired long-lived asset (asset group) and the facts and circumstances leading to the impairment

b. If not separately presented on the face of the statement, the amount of the impairment loss and the caption in the income statement or the statement of activities that includes that loss

c. The method or methods for determining fair value (whether based on a quoted market price, prices for similar assets, or another valuation technique)

d. If applicable, the segment in which the impaired long-lived asset (asset group) is reported under FASB Statement No. 131, *Disclosures about Segments of an Enterprise and Related Information.*

Long-Lived Assets to Be Disposed Of Other Than by Sale

27. A long-lived asset to be disposed of other than by sale (for example, by abandonment, in an exchange measured based on the recorded amount of the nonmonetary asset relinquished, or in a distribution to owners in a spinoff) shall continue to be classified as held and used until it is disposed of. Paragraphs 7–26 shall apply while the asset is classified as held and used. If a long-lived asset is to be abandoned or distributed to owners in a spinoff together with other assets (and liabilities) as a group and that disposal group is a *component of an entity,*[15] paragraphs 41–44 shall apply to the disposal group at the date it is disposed of.

---

[11]FASB Statement No. 34, *Capitalization of Interest Cost,* states, "The capitalization period shall end when the asset is substantially complete and ready for its intended use" (paragraph 18).

[12–14][These footnotes have been deleted. See Status page.]

[15]A *component of an entity* is defined in paragraph 41 of this Statement as comprising operations and cash flows that can be clearly distinguished, operationally and for financial reporting purposes, from the rest of the entity.

Long-Lived Asset to Be Abandoned

28. For purposes of this Statement, a long-lived asset to be abandoned is disposed of when it ceases to be used. If an entity commits to a plan to abandon a long-lived asset before the end of its previously estimated useful life, depreciation estimates shall be revised in accordance with paragraphs 19–22 of Statement 154 to reflect the use of the asset over its shortened useful life (refer to paragraph 9).[16] A long-lived asset that has been temporarily idled shall not be accounted for as if abandoned.

Long-Lived Asset to Be Exchanged or to Be Distributed to Owners in a Spinoff

29. For purposes of this Statement, a long-lived asset to be disposed of in an exchange measured based on the recorded amount of the nonmonetary asset relinquished or to be distributed to owners in a spinoff is disposed of when it is exchanged or distributed. If the asset (asset group) is tested for recoverability while it is classified as held and used, the estimates of future cash flows used in that test shall be based on the use of the asset for its remaining useful life, assuming that the disposal transaction will not occur. In addition to any impairment losses required to be recognized while the asset is classified as held and used, an impairment loss, if any, shall be recognized when the asset is disposed of if the carrying amount of the asset (disposal group) exceeds its fair value.[17]

Long-Lived Assets to Be Disposed Of by Sale

Recognition

30. A long-lived asset (disposal group) to be sold shall be classified as held for sale in the period in which all of the following criteria are met:

a. Management, having the authority to approve the action, commits to a plan to sell the asset (disposal group).

b. The asset (disposal group) is available for immediate sale in its present condition subject only to terms that are usual and customary for sales of such assets (disposal groups). (Examples 5–7 of Appendix A illustrate when that criterion would be met.)

c. An active program to locate a buyer and other actions required to complete the plan to sell the asset (disposal group) have been initiated.

d. The sale of the asset (disposal group) is probable,[18] and transfer of the asset (disposal group) is expected to qualify for recognition as a completed sale, within one year, except as permitted by paragraph 31. (Example 8 of Appendix A illustrates when that criterion would be met.)

e. The asset (disposal group) is being actively marketed for sale at a price that is reasonable in relation to its current fair value.

f. Actions required to complete the plan indicate that it is unlikely that significant changes to the plan will be made or that the plan will be withdrawn.

If at any time the criteria in this paragraph are no longer met (except as permitted by paragraph 31), a long-lived asset (disposal group) classified as held for sale shall be reclassified as held and used in accordance with paragraph 38.

31. Events or circumstances beyond an entity's control may extend the period required to complete the sale of a long-lived asset (disposal group) beyond one year. An exception to the one-year requirement in paragraph 30(d) shall apply in the following situations in which such events or circumstances arise:

a. If at the date an entity commits to a plan to sell a long-lived asset (disposal group) the entity reasonably expects that others (not a buyer) will impose conditions on the transfer of the asset (group) that will extend the period required to

---

[16]Because the continued use of a long-lived asset demonstrates the presence of service potential, only in unusual situations would the fair value of a long-lived asset to be abandoned be zero while it is being used. When a long-lived asset ceases to be used, the carrying amount of the asset should equal its salvage value, if any. The salvage value of the asset should not be reduced to an amount less than zero.

[17]The provisions of this paragraph apply to nonmonetary exchanges that are not recorded at fair value under the provisions of APB Opinion No. 29, *Accounting for Nonmonetary Transactions,* as amended.

[18]The term *probable* is used consistent with the meaning associated with it in paragraph 3(a) of FASB Statement No. 5, *Accounting for Contingencies,* and refers to a future sale that is "likely to occur."

complete the sale and (1) actions necessary to respond to those conditions cannot be initiated until after a _firm purchase commitment_[19] is obtained and (2) a firm purchase commitment is probable within one year. (Example 9 of Appendix A illustrates that situation.)

b. If an entity obtains a firm purchase commitment and, as a result, a buyer or others unexpectedly impose conditions on the transfer of a long-lived asset (disposal group) previously classified as held for sale that will extend the period required to complete the sale and (1) actions necessary to respond to the conditions have been or will be timely initiated and (2) a favorable resolution of the delaying factors is expected. (Example 10 of Appendix A illustrates that situation.)

c. If during the initial one-year period, circumstances arise that previously were considered unlikely and, as a result, a long-lived asset (disposal group) previously classified as held for sale is not sold by the end of that period and (1) during the initial one-year period the entity initiated actions necessary to respond to the change in circumstances, (2) the asset (group) is being actively marketed at a price that is reasonable given the change in circumstances, and (3) the criteria in paragraph 30 are met. (Example 11 of Appendix A illustrates that situation.)

32. A long-lived asset (disposal group) that is newly acquired and that will be sold rather than held and used shall be classified as held for sale at the acquisition date only if the one-year requirement in paragraph 30(d) is met (except as permitted by paragraph 31) and any other criteria in paragraph 30 that are not met at that date are probable of being met within a short period following the acquisition (usually within three months).

33. If the criteria in paragraph 30 are met after the balance sheet date but before issuance of the financial statements, a long-lived asset shall continue to be classified as held and used in those financial statements when issued.[20] The information required by paragraph 47(a) shall be disclosed in the notes to the financial statements. If the asset (asset group) is tested for recoverability (on a held-and-used basis) as of the balance sheet date, the estimates of future cash flows used in that test shall consider the likelihood of possible outcomes that existed at the balance sheet date, including the assessment of the likelihood of the future sale of the asset. That assessment made as of the balance sheet date shall not be revised for a decision to sell the asset after the balance sheet date.[21] An impairment loss, if any, to be recognized shall be measured as the amount by which the carrying amount of the asset (asset group) exceeds its fair value at the balance sheet date.

Measurement

34. A long-lived asset (disposal group) classified as held for sale shall be measured at the lower of its carrying amount or fair value less cost to sell. If the asset (disposal group) is newly acquired, the carrying amount of the asset (disposal group) shall be established based on its fair value less cost to sell at the acquisition date. A long-lived asset shall not be depreciated (amortized) while it is classified as held for sale. Interest and other expenses attributable to the liabilities of a disposal group classified as held for sale shall continue to be accrued.

35. Costs to sell are the incremental direct costs to transact a sale, that is, the costs that result directly from and are essential to a sale transaction and that would not have been incurred by the entity had the decision to sell not been made. Those costs include broker commissions, legal and title transfer fees, and closing costs that must be incurred before legal title can be transferred. Those costs exclude expected future losses associated with the operations of a long-lived asset (disposal group) while it is classified as held for sale.[22] If the sale is expected to occur beyond one year as permitted in limited situations by paragraph 31, the cost to sell shall be discounted.

---

[19]A _firm purchase commitment_ is an agreement with an unrelated party, binding on both parties and usually legally enforceable, that (a) specifies all significant terms, including the price and timing of the transaction, and (b) includes a disincentive for nonperformance that is sufficiently large to make performance probable.

[20]Refer to AICPA Statement on Auditing Standards No. 1, _Codification of Auditing Standards and Procedures,_ Section 560, "Subsequent Events."

[21]Because it is difficult to separate the benefit of hindsight when assessing conditions that existed at a prior date, it is important that judgments about those conditions, the need to test an asset for recoverability, and the application of a recoverability test be made and documented together with supporting evidence on a timely basis.

[22]Expected future operating losses that marketplace participants would not similarly consider in their estimates of the fair value less cost to sell of a long-lived asset (disposal group) classified as held for sale shall not be indirectly recognized as part of an expected loss on the sale by reducing the carrying amount of the asset (disposal group) to an amount less than its current fair value less cost to sell.

36. The carrying amounts of any assets that are not covered by this Statement, including goodwill, that are included in a disposal group classified as held for sale shall be adjusted in accordance with other applicable generally accepted accounting principles prior to measuring the fair value less cost to sell of the disposal group.[23]

37. A loss shall be recognized for any initial or subsequent write-down to fair value less cost to sell. A gain shall be recognized for any subsequent increase in fair value less cost to sell, but not in excess of the cumulative loss previously recognized (for a write-down to fair value less cost to sell). The loss or gain shall adjust only the carrying amount of a long-lived asset, whether classified as held for sale individually or as part of a disposal group. A gain or loss not previously recognized that results from the sale of a long-lived asset (disposal group) shall be recognized at the date of sale.

Changes to a Plan of Sale

38. If circumstances arise that previously were considered unlikely and, as a result, an entity decides not to sell a long-lived asset (disposal group) previously classified as held for sale, the asset (disposal group) shall be reclassified as held and used. A long-lived asset that is reclassified shall be measured individually at the lower of its (a) carrying amount before the asset (disposal group) was classified as held for sale, adjusted for any depreciation (amortization) expense that would have been recognized had the asset (disposal group) been continuously classified as held and used, or (b) fair value at the date of the subsequent decision not to sell.

39. Any required adjustment to the carrying amount of a long-lived asset that is reclassified as held and used shall be included in income from continuing operations in the period of the subsequent decision not to sell. That adjustment shall be reported in the same income statement caption used to report a loss, if any, recognized in accordance with paragraph 45. If a component of an entity is reclassified as held and used, the results of operations of the component previously reported in discontinued operations in accordance with paragraph 43 shall be reclassified and included in income from continuing operations for all periods presented.

40. If an entity removes an individual asset or liability from a disposal group previously classified as held for sale, the remaining assets and liabilities of the disposal group to be sold shall continue to be measured as a group only if the criteria in paragraph 30 are met. Otherwise, the remaining long-lived assets of the group shall be measured individually at the lower of their carrying amounts or fair values less cost to sell at that date. Any long-lived assets that will not be sold shall be reclassified as held and used in accordance with paragraph 38.

Reporting Long-Lived Assets and Disposal Groups to Be Disposed Of

Reporting Discontinued Operations

41. For purposes of this Statement, a *component of an entity* comprises operations and cash flows that can be clearly distinguished, operationally and for financial reporting purposes, from the rest of the entity. A component of an entity may be a reportable segment or an operating segment (as those terms are defined in paragraph 10 of Statement 131), a reporting unit (as that term is defined in Statement 142), a subsidiary, or an asset group (as that term is defined in paragraph 4).

42. The results of operations of a component of an entity that either has been disposed of or is classified as held for sale shall be reported in discontinued operations in accordance with paragraph 43 if both of the following conditions are met: (a) the operations and cash flows of the component have been (or will be) eliminated from the ongoing operations of the entity as a result of the disposal transaction and (b) the entity will not have any significant continuing involvement in the operations of the component after the disposal transaction. (Examples 12–15 of Appendix A illustrate disposal activities that do or do not qualify for reporting as discontinued operations.)

43. In a period in which a component of an entity either has been disposed of or is classified as held for sale, the income statement of a business enterprise (or statement of activities of a not-for-profit organization) for current and prior periods shall report the results of operations of the component, including any gain or loss recognized in accordance with paragraph 37, in discontinued operations. The results of operations of a component classified as held for sale

---

[23]Paragraph 39 of Statement 142 provides guidance for allocating goodwill to a lower-level asset group to be disposed of that is part of a reporting unit and that constitutes a business. Goodwill is not included in a lower-level asset group to be disposed of that is part of a reporting unit if it does not constitute a business.

shall be reported in discontinued operations in the period(s) in which they occur. The results of discontinued operations, less applicable income taxes (benefit), shall be reported as a separate component of income before extraordinary items (if applicable). For example, the results of discontinued operations may be reported in the income statement of a business enterprise as follows:

Income from continuing operations before income taxes	$XXXX
Income taxes	XXX
Income from continuing operations[24]	$XXXX
Discontinued operations (Note X)	
Loss from operations of discontinued Component X (including loss on disposal of $XXX)	XXXX
Income tax benefit	XXXX
Loss on discontinued operations	XXXX
Net income	$XXXX

A gain or loss recognized on the disposal shall be disclosed either on the face of the income statement or in the notes to the financial statements (paragraph 47(b)).

44. Adjustments to amounts previously reported in discontinued operations that are directly related to the disposal of a component of an entity in a prior period shall be classified separately in the current period in discontinued operations. The nature and amount of such adjustments shall be disclosed. Examples of circumstances in which those types of adjustments may arise include the following:

a. The resolution of contingencies that arise pursuant to the terms of the disposal transaction, such as the resolution of purchase price adjustments and indemnification issues with the purchaser
b. The resolution of contingencies that arise from and that are directly related to the operations of the component prior to its disposal, such as environmental and product warranty obligations retained by the seller
c. The settlement of employee benefit plan obligations (pension, postemployment benefits other than pensions, and other postemployment benefits), provided that the settlement is directly related to the disposal transaction.[25]

Reporting Disposal Gains or Losses in Continuing Operations

45. A gain or loss recognized on the sale of a long-lived asset (disposal group) that is not a component of an entity shall be included in income from continuing operations before income taxes in the income statement of a business enterprise and in income from continuing operations in the statement of activities of a not-for-profit organization. If a subtotal such as "income from operations" is presented, it shall include the amounts of those gains or losses.

Reporting a Long-Lived Asset or Disposal Group Classified as Held for Sale

46. A long-lived asset classified as held for sale shall be presented separately in the statement of financial position. The assets and liabilities of a disposal group classified as held for sale shall be presented separately in the asset and liability sections, respectively, of the statement of financial position. Those assets and liabilities shall not be offset and presented as a single amount. The major classes of assets and liabilities classified as held for sale shall be separately disclosed either on the face of the statement of financial position or in the notes to financial statements (paragraph 47(a)).

[23a][This footnote has been deleted because the effective date of FASB Statement No. 154, *Accounting Changes and Error Corrections*, has passed.]

[24]This caption shall be modified appropriately when an entity reports an extraordinary item. If applicable, the presentation of per-share data will need similar modification.

[25]Paragraph 3 of FASB Statement No. 88, *Employers' Accounting for Settlements and Curtailments of Defined Benefit Pension Plans and for Termination Benefits,* defines *settlement* as "a transaction that (a) is an irrevocable action, (b) relieves the employer (or the plan) of primary responsibility for a pension benefit obligation, and (c) eliminates significant risks related to the obligation and the assets used to effect the settlement." A settlement is directly related to the disposal transaction if there is a demonstrated direct cause-and-effect relationship and the settlement occurs no later than one year following the disposal transaction, unless it is delayed by events or circumstances beyond an entity's control (refer to paragraph 31).

Disclosure

47. The following information shall be disclosed in the notes to the financial statements that cover the period in which a long-lived asset (disposal group) either has been sold or is classified as held for sale:

a. A description of the facts and circumstances leading to the expected disposal, the expected manner and timing of that disposal, and, if not separately presented on the face of the statement, the carrying amount(s) of the major classes of assets and liabilities included as part of a disposal group
b. The gain or loss recognized in accordance with paragraph 37 and if not separately presented on the face of the income statement, the caption in the income statement or the statement of activities that includes that gain or loss
c. If applicable, amounts of revenue and pretax profit or loss reported in discontinued operations
d. If applicable, the segment in which the long-lived asset (disposal group) is reported under Statement 131.

48. If either paragraph 38 or paragraph 40 applies, a description of the facts and circumstances leading to the decision to change the plan to sell the long-lived asset (disposal group) and its effect on the results of operations for the period and any prior periods presented shall be disclosed in the notes to financial statements that include the period of that decision.

Effective Date and Transition

49. Except as specified in paragraphs 50 and 51, the provisions of this Statement shall be effective for financial statements issued for fiscal years beginning after December 15, 2001, and interim periods within those fiscal years. Early application is encouraged. Initial application of this Statement shall be as of the beginning of an entity's fiscal year. That is, if the Statement is initially applied prior to the effective date and during an interim period other than the first interim period, all prior interim periods of that fiscal year shall be restated. Restatement of previously issued annual financial statements is not permitted.[26] However, previously issued statements of financial position presented for comparative purposes shall be reclassified to reflect application of the provisions of paragraph 46 of this Statement for reporting disposal groups classified as held for sale.

50. The provisions of this Statement for long-lived assets (disposal groups) to be disposed of by sale or otherwise (paragraphs 27–45 and paragraphs 47 and 48) shall be effective for disposal activities initiated by an entity's commitment to a plan after the effective date of this Statement or after it is initially applied.

51. Except as provided in the following sentence, long-lived assets (disposal groups) classified as held for disposal as a result of disposal activities that were initiated prior to this Statement's initial application shall continue to be accounted for in accordance with the prior pronouncement (Statement 121 or Opinion 30) applicable for that disposal. If the criteria in paragraph 30 of this Statement are not met by the end of the fiscal year in which this Statement is initially applied, the related long-lived assets shall be reclassified as held and used in accordance with paragraph 38 of this Statement.

---

[26]Paragraph 43 requires that when a component of an entity is reported as a discontinued operation, the income statements of prior periods be reclassified to report the results of operations of the component separately. This transition provision does not affect that requirement.

> **The provisions of this Statement need
> not be applied to immaterial items.**

This Statement was adopted by the unanimous vote of the six members of the Financial Accounting Standards Board:

Edmund L. Jenkins,	G. Michael Crooch	Edward W. Trott
Chairman	John M. Foster	John K. Wulff
	Gary S. Schieneman	

Appendix A

IMPLEMENTATION GUIDANCE

Introduction

A1. This appendix illustrates application of some of the provisions of this Statement in certain specific situations. The relevant paragraphs of this Statement are identified in the parenthetical notes. The examples do not address all possible situations or applications of this Statement. This appendix is an integral part of the standards provided in this Statement.

Example 1—Allocating an Impairment Loss

A2. This example illustrates the allocation of an impairment loss to the long-lived assets of an asset group (paragraph 14).

A3. An entity owns a manufacturing facility that together with other assets is tested for recoverability as a group. In addition to long-lived assets (Assets A–D), the asset group includes inventory, which is reported at the lower of cost or market in accordance with ARB No. 43, Chapter 4, "Inventory Pricing," as amended by FASB Statements No. 133, *Accounting for Derivative Instruments and Hedging Activities,* and No. 151, *Inventory Costs,* and other current assets and liabilities that are not covered by this Statement. The $2.75 million aggregate carrying amount of the asset group is not recoverable and exceeds its fair value by $600,000. In accordance with paragraph 14, the impairment loss of $600,000 would be allocated as shown below to the long-lived assets of the group.

Asset Group	Carrying Amount	Pro Rata Allocation Factor	Allocation of Impairment (Loss)	Adjusted Carrying Amount
	(in $ 000s)			
Current assets	$ 400	—	—	$ 400
Liabilities	(150)	—	—	(150)
Long-lived assets:				
Asset A	590	24%	$(144)	446
Asset B	780	31	(186)	594
Asset C	950	38	(228)	722
Asset D	180	7	(42)	138
Subtotal—long-lived assets	2,500	100	(600)	1,900
Total	$2,750	100%	$(600)	$2,150

A4. If the fair value of an individual long-lived asset of an asset group is determinable without undue cost and effort and exceeds the adjusted carrying amount of that asset after an impairment loss is allocated initially, the excess impairment loss initially allocated to that asset would be reallocated to the other long-lived assets of the group. For example, if the fair value of Asset C is $822,000, the excess impairment loss of $100,000 initially allocated to that asset (based on its adjusted carrying amount of $722,000) would be reallocated as shown below to the other long-lived assets of the group on a pro rata basis using the relative adjusted carrying amounts of those assets.

Long-Lived Assets of Asset Group	Adjusted Carrying Amount	Pro Rata Reallocation Factor	Reallocation of Excess Impairment (Loss)	Adjusted Carrying Amount after Reallocation
		(in $ 000s)		
Asset A	$ 446	38%	$ (38)	$ 408
Asset B	594	50	(50)	544
Asset D	138	12	(12)	126
Subtotal	1,178	100%	(100)	1,078
Asset C	722		100	822
Total—long-lived assets	$1,900		$ 0	$1,900

Example 2—Probability-Weighted Cash Flows

A5. This example illustrates the use of a probability-weighted approach for developing estimates of future cash flows used to test a long-lived asset for recoverability when alternative courses of action are under consideration (paragraph 17).

A6. At December 31, 20X2, a manufacturing facility with a carrying amount of $48 million is tested for recoverability. At that date, 2 courses of action to recover the carrying amount of the facility are under consideration—sell in 2 years or sell in 10 years (at the end of its remaining useful life).

A7. As indicated in the following table, the possible cash flows associated with each of those courses of action are $41 million and $48.7 million, respectively. They are developed based on entity-specific assumptions about future sales (volume and price) and costs in varying scenarios that consider the likelihood that existing customer relationships will continue, changes in economic (market) conditions, and other relevant factors.

Course of Action	Cash Flows (Use)	Cash Flows (Disposition)	Cash Flows (Total)	Probability Assessment	Possible Cash Flows (Probability-Weighted)
		(in $ millions)			
Sell in 2 years	$ 8	$30	$38	20%	$ 7.6
	11	30	41	50	20.5
	13	30	43	30	12.9
					$41.0

Course of Action	Cash Flows (Use)	Cash Flows (Disposition)	Cash Flows (Total)	Probability Assessment	Possible Cash Flows (Probability-Weighted)
			(in $ millions)		
Sell in 10 years	36	1	37	20%	$ 7.4
	48	1	49	50	24.5
	55	1	56	30	16.8
					$48.7

A8. As further indicated in the following table, there is a 60 percent probability that the facility will be sold in 2 years and a 40 percent probability that the facility will be sold in 10 years.[27] As shown, the expected cash flows are $44.1 million (undiscounted). Therefore, the carrying amount of the facility of $48 million would not be recoverable.

Course of Action	Possible Cash Flows (Probability-Weighted)	Probability Assessment (Course of Action)	Expected Cash Flows (Undiscounted)
		(in $ millions)	
Sell in 2 years	$41.0	60%	$24.6
Sell in 10 years	48.7	40	19.5
			$44.1

Example 3—Estimates of Future Cash Flows Used to Test an Asset Group for Recoverability

A9. A long-lived asset that is under development may be part of an asset group that is in use. In that situation, estimates of future cash flows used to test the recoverability of that group shall include the cash flows associated with future expenditures necessary to maintain the existing service potential of the group as well as the cash flows associated with future expenditures necessary to substantially complete the asset that is under development (paragraph 21).

A10. An entity engaged in mining and selling phosphate estimates future cash flows from its commercially minable phosphate deposits in order to test the recoverability of the asset group that includes the mine and related long-lived assets (plant and equipment). Deposits from the mined rock must be processed in order to extract the phosphate. As the active mining area expands along the geological structure of the mine, a new processing plant is constructed near the production area. Depending on the size of the mine, extracting the minable deposits may require building numerous processing plants over the life of the mine. In testing the recoverability of the mine and related long-lived assets, the estimates of future cash flows from its commercially minable phosphate deposits would include cash flows associated with future expenditures necessary to build all of the required processing plants.

---

[27]The alternatives of whether to sell or use an asset are not necessarily independent of each other. In many situations, after estimating the possible future cash flows relating to those potential courses of action, an entity might select the course of action that results in a significantly higher estimate of possible future cash flows. In that situation, the entity generally would use the estimates of possible future cash flows relating only to that course of action in computing future cash flows.

Example 4—Expected Present Value Technique

A11. This example illustrates the application of an expected present value technique to estimate the fair value of a long-lived asset in an impairment situation. It is based on the facts provided for the manufacturing facility in Example 2.

A12. [This paragraph has been deleted. See Status page.]

A13. The following table shows by year the computation of the expected cash flows used in the measurement. They reflect the possible cash flows (probability-weighted) used to test the manufacturing facility for recoverability in Example 2, adjusted for relevant marketplace assumptions, which increases the possible cash flows in total by approximately 15 percent.

Year	Possible Cash Flows (Market)	Probability Assessment	Expected Cash Flows (Undiscounted)
	(in $ millions)		
1	$4.6	20%	$ .9
	6.3	50	3.2
	7.5	30	2.3
			$6.4
2	$4.6	20%	$ .9
	6.3	50	3.2
	7.5	30	2.3
			$6.4
3	$4.3	20%	$ .9
	5.8	50	2.9
	6.7	30	2.0
			$5.8
4	$4.3	20%	$ .9
	5.8	50	2.9
	6.7	30	2.0
			$5.8
5	$4.0	20%	$ .8
	5.4	50	2.7
	6.4	30	1.9
			$5.4
6	$4.0	20%	$ .8
	5.4	50	2.7
	6.4	30	1.9
			$5.4
7	$3.9	20%	$ .8
	5.1	50	2.6
	5.6	30	1.7
			$5.1

[28–29][These footnotes have been deleted. See Status page.]

Year	Possible Cash Flows (Market)	Probability Assessment	Expected Cash Flows (Undiscounted)
	(in $ millions)		
8	$3.9	20%	$ .8
	5.1	50	2.6
	5.6	30	1.7
			$5.1
9	$3.9	20%	$ .8
	5.0	50	2.5
	5.5	30	1.7
			$5.0
10	$4.9	20%	$1.0
	6.0	50	3.0
	6.5	30	2.0
			$6.0

A14. The following table shows the computation of the expected present value; that is, the sum of the present values of the expected cash flows by year, each discounted at a risk-free interest rate determined from the yield curve for U.S. Treasury instruments.[29a] As shown, the expected present value is $42.3 million, which is less than the carrying amount of $48 million. In accordance with paragraph 7, the entity would recognize an impairment loss of $5.7 million.

Year	Expected Cash Flows (Undiscounted)	Risk-Free Rate of Interest	Expected Present Value
	(in $ millions)		
1	$ 6.4	5.0%	$ 6.1
2	6.4	5.1	5.8
3	5.8	5.2	5.0
4	5.8	5.4	4.7
5	5.4	5.6	4.1
6	5.4	5.8	3.9
7	5.1	6.0	3.4
8	5.1	6.2	3.2
9	5.0	6.4	2.9
10	6.0	6.6	3.2
	$56.4		$42.3

[29a]In this example, a market risk premium is included in the expected cash flows; that is, the cash flows are certainty equivalent cash flows.

Examples 5–7—Plan-of-Sale Criterion 30(b)

A15. To qualify for classification as held for sale, a long-lived asset (disposal group) must be available for immediate sale in its present condition subject only to terms that are usual and customary for sales of such assets (disposal groups) (paragraph 30(b)). A long-lived asset (disposal group) is available for immediate sale if an entity currently has the intent and ability to transfer the asset (disposal group) to a buyer in its present condition. Examples 5–7 illustrate situations in which the criterion in paragraph 30(b) would or would not be met.

Example 5

A16. An entity commits to a plan to sell its headquarters building and has initiated actions to locate a buyer.

a. The entity intends to transfer the building to a buyer after it vacates the building. The time necessary to vacate the building is usual and customary for sales of such assets. The criterion in paragraph 30(b) would be met at the plan commitment date.

b. The entity will continue to use the building until construction of a new headquarters building is completed. The entity does not intend to transfer the existing building to a buyer until after construction of the new building is completed (and it vacates the existing building). The delay in the timing of the transfer of the existing building imposed by the entity (seller) demonstrates that the building is not available for immediate sale. The criterion in paragraph 30(b) would not be met until construction of the new building is completed, even if a firm purchase commitment for the future transfer of the existing building is obtained earlier.

Example 6

A17. An entity commits to a plan to sell a manufacturing facility and has initiated actions to locate a buyer. At the plan commitment date, there is a backlog of uncompleted customer orders.

a. The entity intends to sell the manufacturing facility with its operations. Any uncompleted customer orders at the sale date would transfer to the buyer. The transfer of uncompleted customer orders at the sale date will not affect the timing of the transfer of the facility. The criterion in paragraph 30(b) would be met at the plan commitment date.

b. The entity intends to sell the manufacturing facility, but without its operations. The entity does not intend to transfer the facility to a buyer until after it ceases all operations of the facility and eliminates the backlog of uncompleted customer orders. The delay in the timing of the transfer of the facility imposed by the entity (seller) demonstrates that the facility is not available for immediate sale. The criterion in paragraph 30(b) would not be met until the operations of the facility cease, even if a firm purchase commitment for the future transfer of the facility is obtained earlier.

Example 7

A18. An entity acquires through foreclosure a real estate property that it intends to sell.

a. The entity does not intend to transfer the property to a buyer until after it completes renovations to increase its sales value. The delay in the timing of the transfer of the property imposed by the entity (seller) demonstrates that the property is not available for immediate sale. The criterion in paragraph 30(b) would not be met until the renovations are completed.

b. After the renovations are completed and the property is classified as held for sale but before a firm purchase commitment is obtained, the entity becomes aware of environmental damage requiring remediation. The entity still intends to sell the property. However, the entity does not have the ability to transfer the property to a buyer until after the remediation is completed. The delay in the timing of the transfer of the property imposed by others before a firm purchase commitment is obtained demonstrates that the property is not available for immediate sale. The criterion in paragraph 30(b) would not continue to be met. The property would be reclassified as held and used in accordance with paragraph 39.

Example 8—Plan-of-Sale Criterion 30(d)

A19. To qualify for classification as held for sale, the sale of a long-lived asset (disposal group) must be probable, and transfer of the asset (disposal group) must be expected to qualify for recognition as a completed sale, within one year (paragraph 30(d)). That criterion would not be met if, for example:

a. An entity that is a commercial leasing and finance company is holding for sale or lease equipment that has recently come off lease and the ultimate form of a future transaction (sale or lease) has not yet been determined.

b. An entity commits to a plan to "sell" a property that is in use, and the transfer of the property will be accounted for as a sale-leaseback through which the seller-lessee will retain more than a minor portion of the use of the property. The property would continue to be classified as held and used and paragraphs 7–26 would apply.[30]

Examples 9–11—Exceptions to Plan-of-Sale Criterion 30(d)

A20. An exception to the one-year requirement in paragraph 30(d) applies in limited situations in which the period required to complete the sale of a long-lived asset (disposal group) will be (or has been) extended by events or circumstances beyond an entity's control and certain conditions are met (paragraph 31). Examples 9–11 illustrate those situations.

Example 9

A21. An entity in the utility industry commits to a plan to sell a disposal group that represents a significant portion of its regulated operations. The sale will require regulatory approval, which could extend the period required to complete the sale beyond one year. Actions necessary to obtain that approval cannot be initiated until after a buyer is known and a firm purchase commitment is obtained. However, a firm purchase commitment is probable within one year. In that situation, the conditions in paragraph 31(a) for an exception to the one-year requirement in paragraph 30(d) would be met.

Example 10

A22. An entity commits to a plan to sell a manufacturing facility in its present condition and classifies the facility as held for sale at that date. After a firm purchase commitment is obtained, the buyer's inspection of the property identifies environmental damage not previously known to exist. The entity is required by the buyer to remediate the damage, which will extend the period required to complete the sale beyond one year. However, the entity has initiated actions to remediate the damage, and satisfactory remediation of the damage is probable. In that situation, the conditions in paragraph 31(b) for an exception to the one-year requirement in paragraph 30(d) would be met.

Example 11

A23. An entity commits to a plan to sell a long-lived asset and classifies the asset as held for sale at that date.

a. During the initial one-year period, the market conditions that existed at the date the asset was classified initially as held for sale deteriorate and, as a result, the asset is not sold by the end of that period. During that period, the entity actively solicited but did not receive any reasonable offers to purchase the asset and, in response, reduced the price. The asset continues to be actively marketed at a price that is reasonable given the change in market conditions, and the criteria in paragraph 30 are met. In that situation, the conditions in paragraph 31(c) for an exception to the one-year requirement in paragraph 30(d) would be met. At the end of the initial one-year period, the asset would continue to be classified as held for sale.

b. During the following one-year period, market conditions deteriorate further, and the asset is not sold by the end of that period. The entity believes that the market conditions will improve and has not further reduced the price of the asset. The asset continues to be held for sale, but at a price in excess of its current fair value. In that situation, the absence of a price reduction demonstrates that

---

[30]If at the date of the sale-leaseback the fair value of the property is less than its undepreciated cost, a loss would be recognized immediately up to the amount of the difference between undepreciated cost and fair value in accordance with paragraph 3(c) of FASB Statement No. 28, *Accounting for Sales with Leasebacks.*

the asset is not available for immediate sale as required by the criterion in paragraph 30(b). In addition, the criterion in paragraph 30(e) requires that an asset be marketed at a price that is reasonable in relation to its current fair value. Therefore, the conditions in paragraph 31(c) for an exception to the one-year requirement in paragraph 30(d) would not be met. The asset would be reclassified as held and used in accordance with paragraph 38.

Examples 12–15—Reporting Discontinued Operations

A24. The results of operations of a component of an entity that either has been disposed of or is classified as held for sale shall be reported in discontinued operations if (a) the operations and cash flows of the component have been (or will be) eliminated from the ongoing operations of the entity as a result of the disposal transaction and (b) the entity will not have any significant continuing involvement in the operations of the component after the disposal transaction (paragraph 42). Examples 12–15 illustrate disposal activities that do or do not qualify for reporting as discontinued operations.

Example 12

A25. An entity that manufactures and sells consumer products has several product groups, each with different product lines and brands. For that entity, a product group is the lowest level at which the operations and cash flows can be clearly distinguished, operationally and for financial reporting purposes, from the rest of the entity. Therefore, each product group is a component of the entity.

A26. The entity has experienced losses associated with certain brands in its beauty care products group.

a. The entity decides to exit the beauty care business and commits to a plan to sell the product group with its operations. The product group is classified as held for sale at that date. The operations and cash flows of the product group will be eliminated from the ongoing operations of the entity as a result of the sale transaction, and the entity will not have any continuing involvement in the operations of the product group after it is sold. In that situation, the conditions in paragraph 42 for reporting in discontinued operations the op-

erations of the product group while it is classified as held for sale would be met.

b. The entity decides to remain in the beauty care business but will discontinue the brands with which the losses are associated. Because the brands are part of a larger cash-flow-generating product group and, in the aggregate, do not represent a group that on its own is a component of the entity, the conditions in paragraph 42 for reporting in discontinued operations the losses associated with the brands that are discontinued would not be met.

Example 13

A27. An entity that is a franchiser in the quick-service restaurant business also operates company-owned restaurants. For that entity, an individual company-owned restaurant is the lowest level at which the operations and cash flows can be clearly distinguished, operationally and for financial reporting purposes, from the rest of the entity. Therefore, each company-owned restaurant is a component of the entity.

a. The entity has experienced losses on its company-owned restaurants in one region. The entity decides to exit the quick-service restaurant business in that region and commits to a plan to sell the restaurants in that region. The restaurants are classified as held for sale at that date. The operations and cash flows of the restaurants in that region will be eliminated from the ongoing operations of the entity as a result of the sale transaction, and the entity will not have any continuing involvement in the operations of the restaurants after they are sold. In that situation, the conditions in paragraph 42 for reporting in discontinued operations the operations of the restaurants while they are classified as held for sale would be met.

b. Based on its evaluation of the ownership mix of its system-wide restaurants in certain markets, the entity commits to a plan to sell its company-owned restaurants in one region to an existing franchisee. The restaurants are classified as held for sale at that date. Although each company-owned restaurant, on its own, is a component of the entity, through the franchise agreement, the entity will (1) receive franchise fees determined, in part, based on the future revenues of the restaurants and (2) have significant continuing involvement in the operations of the restaurants after they are sold. In that situation, the conditions in paragraph 42 for reporting in discontinued operations the operations of the restaurants would not be met.

Example 14

A28. An entity that manufactures sporting goods has a bicycle division that designs, manufactures, markets, and distributes bicycles. For that entity, the bicycle division is the lowest level at which the operations and cash flows can be clearly distinguished, operationally and for financial reporting purposes, from the rest of the entity. Therefore, the bicycle division is a component of the entity.

A29. The entity has experienced losses in its bicycle division resulting from an increase in manufacturing costs (principally labor costs).

a. The entity decides to exit the bicycle business and commits to a plan to sell the division with its operations. The bicycle division is classified as held for sale at that date. The operations and cash flows of the division will be eliminated from the ongoing operations of the entity as a result of the sale transaction, and the entity will not have any continuing involvement in the operations of the division after it is sold. In that situation, the conditions in paragraph 42 for reporting in discontinued operations the operations of the division while it is classified as held for sale would be met.
b. The entity decides to remain in the bicycle business but will outsource the manufacturing operations and commits to a plan to sell the related

manufacturing facility. The facility is classified as held for sale at that date. Because the manufacturing facility is part of a larger cash-flow-generating group (the bicycle division), and on its own is not a component of the entity, the conditions in paragraph 42 for reporting in discontinued operations the operations (losses) of the manufacturing facility would not be met. (Those conditions also would not be met if the manufacturing facility on its own was a component of the entity because the decision to outsource the manufacturing operations of the division will not eliminate the operations and cash flows of the division [and its bicycle business] from the ongoing operations of the entity.)

Example 15

A30. An entity owns and operates retail stores that sell household goods. For that entity, each store is the lowest level at which the operations and cash flows can be clearly distinguished, operationally and for financial reporting purposes, from the rest of the entity. Therefore, each store is a component of the entity.

A31. To expand its retail store operations in one region, the entity decides to close two of its retail stores and open a new "superstore" in that region. The new superstore will continue to sell the household goods previously sold through the two retail stores as well as other related products not previously sold. Although each retail store on its own is a component of the entity, the operations and cash flows from the sale of household goods previously sold through the two retail stores in that region will not be eliminated from the ongoing operations of the entity. In that situation, the conditions in paragraph 42 for reporting in discontinued operations the operations of the stores would not be met.

Appendix B

BACKGROUND INFORMATION AND BASIS FOR CONCLUSIONS

CONTENTS

Appendix B

BACKGROUND INFORMATION AND BASIS FOR CONCLUSIONS

Introduction

B1. This appendix summarizes considerations that Board members deemed significant in reaching the conclusions in this Statement. It includes the reasons for accepting certain approaches and rejecting others. Individual Board members gave greater weight to some factors than to others. This appendix also summarizes the considerations that Board members deemed significant in reaching the conclusions in FASB Statement No. 121, *Accounting for the Impairment of Long-Lived Assets and for Long-Lived Assets to Be Disposed Of,* that are still relevant.

Background

B2. Statement 121, which was issued in 1995, established accounting standards for the impairment of long-lived assets to be held and used, including certain identifiable intangibles and goodwill related to those assets. It also established accounting standards for long-lived assets to be disposed of, including certain identifiable intangibles, that were not covered by APB Opinion No. 30, *Reporting the Results of Operations—Reporting the Effects of Disposal of a Segment of a Business, and Extraordinary, Unusual and Infrequently Occurring Events and Transactions.* Opinion 30 established, among other things, accounting and reporting standards for segments of a business to be disposed of. Paragraph 13 of Opinion 30 defined a segment of a business as "a component of an entity whose activities represent a separate major line of business or class of customer."

B3. After the issuance of Statement 121, significant differences existed in the accounting for long-lived assets to be disposed of covered by that Statement and by Opinion 30. The principal differences related to measurement and presentation.

B4. Under Statement 121, a long-lived asset classified as held for disposal was measured at the lower of its carrying amount or fair value less cost to sell, which excludes expected future operating losses that marketplace participants would not similarly consider in their estimates of the fair value less cost to sell of a long-lived asset classified as held for disposal. The gain or loss recognized on the disposal and any related results of operations were reported in continuing operations and separately disclosed in the notes to the financial statements.

B5. Under Opinion 30, a segment of a business to be disposed of was measured at the lower of its carrying amount or net realizable value, adjusted for expected future operating losses of the segment held for disposal. The accrual of future operating losses as previously required under Opinion 30 generally is inappropriate under the Board's conceptual framework, which was developed after the issuance of Opinion 30. The gain or loss recognized on the disposal and the related results of operations were reported in discontinued operations, separately from continuing operations. Under other accounting pronouncements, the measurement but not reporting requirements of Opinion 30 were extended to certain other disposal transactions.

B6. In Statement 121, the Board acknowledged that inconsistency in accounting for long-lived assets to be disposed of. However, at that time, the Board decided not to expand the scope of that Statement to reconsider the requirements of Opinion 30.

B7. Soon after the issuance of Statement 121, the Emerging Issues Task Force (EITF) and others identified significant issues related to the implementation of that Statement. They asked the Board to address those issues, including:

a. How to apply the provisions for long-lived assets to be held and used to a long-lived asset that an entity expects to sell or otherwise dispose of if the entity has not yet committed to a plan to sell or otherwise dispose of the asset

b. How to determine an "indicated impairment of value" of a long-lived asset to be exchanged for a similar productive long-lived asset or to be distributed to owners

c. What criteria must be met to classify a long-lived asset as held for sale and how to account for the asset if those criteria are met after the balance sheet date but before issuance of the financial statements

d. How to account for a long-lived asset classified as held for sale if the plan to sell the asset changes

e. How to display in the income statement the results of operations while a long-lived asset or a group of long-lived assets with separately identifiable operations is classified as held for sale

f. How to display in the statement of financial position a long-lived asset or a group of long-lived assets and liabilities classified as held for sale.

B8. In August 1996, the Board added this project to its agenda to (a) develop a single accounting model, based on the framework established in Statement 121, for long-lived assets to be disposed of by sale and (b) address significant implementation issues.

B9. In June 2000, the Board issued an Exposure Draft of a proposed Statement, *Accounting for the Impairment or Disposal of Long-Lived Assets and for Obligations Associated with Disposal Activities.* The Board received comment letters from 53 respondents to the Exposure Draft. In January 2001, the Board held a public roundtable meeting with some of those respondents to discuss significant issues raised in comment letters. The Board considered respondents' comments during its redeliberations of the issues addressed by the Exposure Draft in public meetings in 2001.

Scope

B10. Except as discussed in paragraphs B11–B14, this Statement applies to recognized long-lived assets to be held and used or to be disposed of. If a long-lived asset is part of a group that includes other assets and liabilities not covered by this Statement, this Statement applies to its asset group or disposal group, as discussed in paragraph 4 of this Statement.

B11. Long-lived assets excluded from the scope of Statement 121 also are excluded from the scope of this Statement. The Board concluded that the objectives of this project could be achieved without reconsidering the accounting for the impairment or disposal of those long-lived assets. Accordingly, this Statement does not apply to (a) financial assets, (b) long-lived assets for which the accounting is prescribed in other broadly applicable accounting pronouncements (such as deferred tax assets), and (c) long-lived assets for which the accounting is prescribed in accounting pronouncements that apply to certain specialized industries (including the record and music, motion picture, broadcasting, software, and insurance industries).

B12. The scope of Statement 121 included goodwill related to an asset group but not goodwill related to a disposal group. Goodwill not covered by Statement 121 was covered by APB Opinion No. 17, *Intangible Assets.* The Exposure Draft would have included in its scope goodwill related to an asset group, and would have amended Opinion 17 to also include in its scope goodwill related to a disposal group. However, after issuance of the Exposure Draft, the Board decided to reconsider the accounting for goodwill and intangible assets in its project on accounting for business combinations. In that project, the Board decided that goodwill and certain other intangible assets should no longer be amortized and should be tested for impairment in a manner different from how the long-lived assets covered by this Statement are tested for impairment. FASB Statement No. 142, *Goodwill and Other Intangible Assets,* addresses the accounting for the impairment of those assets. It also addresses the allocation of goodwill to a disposal group that constitutes a business. Accordingly, this Statement does not apply to goodwill or to intangible assets not being amortized.

B13. Statement 121 did not address the accounting for obligations associated with the disposal of a long-lived asset (disposal group) or for the results of operations during the holding period of the asset (disposal group). Instead, Statement 121 referred to EITF Issue No. 94-3, "Liability Recognition for Certain Employee Termination Benefits and Other Costs to Exit an Activity (including Certain Costs Incurred in a Restructuring)." Issue 94-3 provides guidance on recognition of liabilities for costs associated with restructuring and related disposal activities, including certain employee termination benefits and lease termination costs. During its deliberations of the Exposure Draft, the Board noted that liabilities are recognized under Issue 94-3 even though some of those items might not meet the definition of a liability set forth in the Board's conceptual framework. Because the types of costs covered by Issue 94-3 often are associated with the disposal of long-lived assets, the Board decided to reconsider the guidance in Issue 94-3 and include obligations associated with a disposal activity in the scope of this project.

B14. The Exposure Draft proposed significant changes to the guidance in Issue 94-3. Many respondents to the Exposure Draft disagreed with those proposed changes. Some of those respondents noted potential inconsistencies between the accounting requirements proposed in the Exposure Draft and the accounting requirements of other existing accounting pronouncements. Other respondents said that the Board should not reconsider the guidance in Issue 94-3 until after it undertakes a full conceptual reconsideration of all liabilities. Yet other respondents said that the Board should not reconsider that guidance at all, noting that SEC Staff Accounting Bulletin No. 100, *Restructuring and Impairment Charges,* now provides additional guidance for applying Issue 94-3. To avoid delaying the issuance of guidance on the accounting for the impairment or disposal of long-lived assets to address those issues, the Board decided to remove obligations associated with a disposal activity from the scope of this Statement. The Board plans to redeliberate those issues addressed by the Exposure Draft in a separate project.

Long-Lived Assets to Be Held and Used

Recognition of an Impairment Loss

B15. This Statement retains the requirement of Statement 121 to recognize an impairment loss only if the carrying amount of a long-lived asset (asset group) is not recoverable from its undiscounted cash flows and exceeds its fair value. In Statement 121, the Board decided for practical reasons to require an undiscounted cash flows recoverability test. In reaching that decision, the Board considered but rejected alternative criteria for recognition of an impairment loss. Specifically, the Board considered (a) an economic (fair value) criterion, (b) a permanence criterion, and (c) a probability criterion. Those criteria were discussed in paragraphs 60–62 of Statement 121:

The economic criterion calls for loss recognition whenever the carrying amount of an asset exceeds the asset's fair value. It is an approach that would require continuous evaluation for impairment of long-lived assets similar to the ongoing lower-of-cost-or-market measurement of inventory. The economic criterion is based on the measurement of the asset. Using the same measure for recognition and measurement assures consistent outcomes for identical fact situations. However, the economic criterion presupposes that a fair value is available for every asset on an ongoing basis. Otherwise, an event or change in circumstance would be needed to determine which assets needed to be measured and in which period. Some respondents to the Discussion Memorandum indicated that the results of a measurement should not be sufficient reason to trigger recognition of an impairment loss. They favored using either the permanence or probability criterion to avoid recognition of write-downs that might result from measurements reflecting only temporary market fluctuations.

The permanence criterion calls for loss recognition when the carrying amount of an asset exceeds the asset's fair value and the condition is judged to be permanent. Some respondents to the Discussion Memorandum indicated that a loss must be permanent rather than temporary before recognition should occur. In their view, a high hurdle for recognition of an impairment loss is necessary to prevent premature write-offs of productive assets. Others stated that requiring the impairment loss to be permanent makes the criterion too restrictive and virtually impossible to apply with any reliability. Still others noted that the permanence criterion is not practical to implement; in their view, requiring management to assess whether a loss is permanent goes beyond management's ability to apply judgment and becomes a requirement for management to predict future events with certainty.

The probability criterion, initially presented in the Issues Paper, calls for loss recognition based on the approach taken in FASB Statement No. 5, *Accounting for Contingencies.* Using that approach, an impairment loss would be recognized when it is deemed probable that the carrying amount of an asset cannot be fully recovered. Some respondents to the Discussion Memorandum stated that assessing the probability that an impairment loss has occurred is preferable to other recognition alternatives because it is already required by Statement 5. Most respondents to the Discussion Memorandum supported the probability criterion because, in their view, it best provides for management judgment.

When to test a long-lived asset for recoverability

B16. This Statement retains the requirement of Statement 121 to test a long-lived asset (asset group) for recoverability whenever events or changes in circumstances indicate that its carrying amount may not be recoverable. Paragraph 57 of Statement 121 discussed the basis for the Board's conclusion:

> The Board concluded . . . that management has the responsibility to consider whether an asset is impaired but that to test each asset each period would be too costly. Existing information and analyses developed for management review of the entity and its operations generally will be the principal evidence needed to determine when an impairment exists. Indicators of impairment, therefore, are useful examples of events or changes in circumstances that suggest that the recoverability of the carrying amount of an asset should be assessed.

B17. Statement 121 provided examples of such events or changes in circumstances. The Board decided to expand those examples, carried forward in paragraph 8 of this Statement, to also refer to a current expectation that a long-lived asset (asset group) will be disposed of significantly before the end of its previously estimated useful life (paragraph 8(f)). The Board reasoned that a current expectation that a long-lived asset (asset group) will be disposed of significantly before the end of its previously estimated useful life might indicate that the carrying amount of the asset (group) is not recoverable.

Estimates of future cash flows used to test a long-lived asset for recoverability

B18. Statement 121 provided general guidance for developing estimates of future cash flows used to estimate the fair value of a long-lived asset (asset group) in the absence of an observable market price.

However, it did not specify whether that guidance also should apply for developing estimates of future cash flows used to test a long-lived asset (asset group) for recoverability. Consequently, in implementing Statement 121, questions emerged about how to develop those estimates.

B19. In considering that issue, the Board noted that in contrast to an objective of measuring fair value, the objective of the undiscounted cash flows recoverability test is to assess the recoverability of a long-lived asset (asset group) in the context of a particular entity. The Board decided that because the objectives of measuring fair value and testing a long-lived asset (asset group) for recoverability are different, this Statement should provide guidance for developing estimates of future cash flows used to test for recoverability. The Board acknowledges that significant judgment is required in developing estimates of future cash flows. However, the Board believes that the level of guidance provided by this Statement is sufficient for meeting the objective of an undiscounted cash flows recoverability test.

B20. The guidance provided by this Statement focuses on (a) the cash flow estimation approach, (b) the cash flow estimation period, and (c) the types of asset-related expenditures that should be considered in developing estimates of future cash flows.

Cash flow estimation approach

B21. The guidance in Statement 121 permitted the use of either a probability-weighted approach or a best-estimate approach in developing estimates of future cash flows used to test for recoverability. Both of those cash flow estimation approaches are discussed in FASB Concepts Statement No. 7, *Using Cash Flow Information and Present Value in Accounting Measurements,* issued in February 2000. A probability-weighted approach refers to the sum of probability-weighted amounts in a range of possible estimated amounts. A best-estimate approach refers to the single most-likely amount in a range of possible estimated amounts. During its deliberations leading to the Exposure Draft, the Board reasoned that because the probability-weighted approach discussed in Concepts Statement 7 incorporates uncertainty in estimates of future cash flows, it would provide a more complete and disciplined estimate of future cash flows than would a best-estimate approach. Therefore, the Exposure Draft would have required, rather than permitted, the use of that approach in developing estimates of future cash flows used to test for recoverability.

B22. Several respondents to the Exposure Draft disagreed with that proposed requirement, stating that, for many entities, a probability-weighted approach would not be practical or cost-beneficial in developing estimates of future cash flows used to test for recoverability. The principal concern expressed by respondents was that in many cases, reliable information about the likelihood of possible outcomes would not be available. They said that the Board should permit the use of either a best-estimate approach or a probability-weighted approach in developing those estimates, as under Statement 121. During its redeliberations of the Exposure Draft, the Board decided not to require the probability-weighted approach in Concepts Statement 7 in developing estimates of future cash flows used to test for recoverability. The Board noted that Concepts Statement 7 expresses a preference for a probability-weighted approach, but that preference is discussed in the context of developing estimates of future cash flows that provide the basis for an accounting measurement (fair value). The Board concluded that because estimates of future cash flows used to test for recoverability, in and of themselves, do not provide the basis for an accounting measurement, the preference for a probability-weighted approach in Concepts Statement 7 need not be extended to those estimates. However, the Board agreed that in situations in which alternative courses of action to recover the carrying amount of a long-lived asset (asset group) are under consideration or in which a range is estimated for the amount of possible future cash flows associated with the likely course of action, a probability-weighted approach may be useful in considering the likelihood of those possible outcomes.

Cash flow estimation period

B23. Statement 121 did not specify the cash flow estimation period for estimates of future cash flows used to test for recoverability. The Board decided that the cash flow estimation period should correspond to the period that a long-lived asset (asset group) is expected to provide service potential to the entity. Accordingly, the cash flow estimation period for a long-lived asset is based on its remaining useful life to the entity. If long-lived assets having different remaining useful lives are grouped, the cash flow estimation period for the asset group is based on the remaining useful life of the primary asset of the group to the en-

tity. The definition of a primary asset proposed in the Exposure Draft limited that asset to a tangible long-lived asset. Several respondents to the Exposure Draft agreed with the primary asset approach for determining the cash flow estimation period for an asset group. However, many said that because intangible assets often are more significant than tangible assets, the Board should expand the definition of a primary asset to include those assets.

B24. The Board initially decided to limit the primary asset to a tangible long-lived asset principally to prohibit an entity from arbitrarily designating as the primary asset goodwill associated with the group. The Board's decision was influenced by the then-existing requirement to amortize goodwill over a period of up to 40 years. However, in view of its subsequent decision in Statement 142 that goodwill should no longer be amortized, the Board decided to broaden the definition of a primary asset to include either a recognized tangible asset being depreciated or an intangible asset being amortized. The Board concluded that because there needs to be some boundaries on the cash flow estimation period for an asset group, indefinite-lived assets, such as land and intangible assets not being amortized, are not eligible to be primary assets. The Board affirmed its conclusion in the Exposure Draft that, for many asset groups, the primary asset will be readily identifiable and that the remaining useful life of that asset to the entity is a reasonable basis for consistently determining the cash flow estimation period for an asset group.

B25. During its deliberations leading to the Exposure Draft, the Board considered but rejected alternative approaches for determining the cash flow estimation period for an asset group. One approach would have limited the estimation period to the shorter of (a) the remaining useful life of the primary asset of the group or (b) 10 years and would have assumed the sale of the group at the end of that shortened period (limited estimation approach). The Board observed that because a limited estimation approach would include estimated disposal values (fair values) in estimates of future cash flows used to test for recoverability, the effect of that approach would be to discount some portion of those cash flows. The Board concluded that a limited estimation approach would be inconsistent with the requirement of this Statement to recognize an impairment loss only if the carrying amount of a long-lived asset (asset group) is not recoverable from its undiscounted future cash flows.

B26. Another approach for determining the cash flow estimation period for an asset group would have used the average of the remaining useful lives of the long-lived assets of the group, weighted based on the relative carrying amounts of those assets (weighted-average approach). The Board acknowledged that for some asset groups, a weighted-average approach could avoid difficulties in identifying the primary asset, but it concluded that for many entities, that approach could be unduly burdensome and result in little, if any, incremental benefit. Some respondents to the Exposure Draft suggested that the Board reconsider a weighted-average approach for entities that use a group composite depreciation method. However, the Board noted that the cost-capitalization approach proposed in the Exposure Draft of a proposed AICPA Statement of Position, *Accounting for Certain Costs and Activities Related to Property, Plant, and Equipment,* issued in June 2001, would effectively eliminate that depreciation method. The Board also believes that the approach for determining the cash flow estimation period should be the same for all entities with long-lived assets covered by this Statement.

Asset-related expenditures for a long-lived asset in use

B27. Statement 121 did not identify the types of asset-related expenditures that should be considered in estimates of future cash flows used to test a long-lived asset (asset group) for recoverability. During its deliberations leading to the Exposure Draft, the Board observed that, as a result, an entity could avoid the write-down of a long-lived asset that is in use by including in those estimates the cash flows (cash outflows and cash inflows) associated with all possible improvements that would be capitalized in future periods. In that case, the recoverability of the long-lived asset (asset group) would be assessed based on its expected future service potential ("as improved"), rather than on its existing service potential ("as is").

B28. The Board decided that a long-lived asset (asset group) that is in use, including a long-lived asset (asset group) for which development is substantially complete, should be tested for recoverability based on its existing service potential at the date of that test. Therefore, estimates of future cash flows used in that test should exclude the cash flows associated with asset-related expenditures that would enhance the existing service potential of a long-lived asset (asset group) that is in use.

B29. The Board decided that estimates of future cash flows used to test for recoverability should include cash flows (including estimated salvage values) associated with asset-related expenditures that replace (a) component parts of a long-lived asset or (b) component assets (other than the primary asset) of an asset group, whether those expenditures would be recognized as an expense or capitalized in future periods. The Board considered an alternative approach that would have excluded the cash flows associated with those expenditures. However, the Board observed that because an asset group could not continue to be used without replacing the component assets of the group, there would be an assumption that the asset of the group would be sold at the end of the remaining useful life of the primary asset. By including the estimated disposal values of those assets (fair values) in estimates of future cash flows used to test for recoverability, the effect of that approach would be to discount some portion of the cash flows. As discussed in paragraph B25, such an approach would be inconsistent with the requirement of this Statement to recognize an impairment loss only if the carrying amount of a long-lived asset (asset group) is not recoverable from its undiscounted future cash flows.

B30. Some respondents to the Exposure Draft noted that if an entity has a plan to improve a long-lived asset (asset group) that is in use, the entity could be required to write down the carrying amount of the asset (asset group) even if it would be recoverable after it is improved. They suggested that the Board permit an exception to the existing service potential requirement for a long-lived asset (asset group) that is in use in that situation. During its redeliberations of the Exposure Draft, the Board decided not to make that exception for the reason discussed in paragraph B27. However, the Board observed that in measuring fair value, if marketplace participants would assume the same improvements to the asset as the entity, the estimates of future cash flows used to measure fair value would include the cash flows (cash outflows and cash inflows) associated with those improvements. Consequently, it is possible that although the carrying amount of the asset (asset group) is not recoverable in its present condition, the fair value of the asset (asset group) could exceed its carrying amount and no impairment would exist.

Asset-related expenditures for a long-lived asset under development

B31. The Board observed that in contrast to a long-lived asset (asset group) that is in use, a long-lived asset (asset group) that is under development will not provide service potential until development is substantially complete. The Board decided that such an asset (asset group) should be tested for recoverability based on its expected service potential. Therefore, estimates of future cash flows used in that test should include the cash flows (cash outflows and cash inflows) associated with all future asset-related expenditures necessary to develop the asset (asset group), whether those expenditures would be recognized as an expense or capitalized in future periods.

B32. In Statement 121, the Board decided that estimates of future cash flows used to test a long-lived asset (asset group) for recoverability should exclude all future interest payments, whether those payments would be recognized as an expense or capitalized in future periods. In this Statement, the Board reconsidered that decision, noting that for a long-lived asset (asset group) that is under development, interest payments during the development period would be capitalized in accordance with paragraph 6 of FASB Statement No. 34, *Capitalization of Interest Cost,* which states:

> The historical cost of acquiring an asset includes the costs necessarily incurred to bring it to the condition and location necessary for its intended use. If an asset requires a period of time in which to carry out the activities necessary to bring it to that condition and location, the interest cost incurred during that period as a result of expenditures for the asset is a part of the historical cost of acquiring the asset. [Footnote references omitted.]

The Board reasoned that for a long-lived asset (asset group) that is under development, there is no difference between interest payments and other asset-related expenditures that would be capitalized in future periods. Therefore, the Board decided that estimates of future cash flows used to test a long-lived asset (asset group) for recoverability should exclude only those interest payments that would be recognized as an expense when incurred.

B33. Some respondents to the Exposure Draft asked the Board to clarify how the service potential requirements of this Statement would apply if a long-lived asset that is under development is part of an asset group that includes other assets that are in use. This Statement clarifies that the estimates of future cash flows used to test such an asset group for recoverability should include the cash flows (cash outflows and cash inflows) associated with (a) future asset-related expenditures necessary to complete the asset that is under development and (b) future asset-related expenditures necessary to maintain the existing service potential of the other assets that are in use.

Measurement of an Impairment Loss

B34. This Statement retains the requirement of Statement 121 to measure an impairment loss for a long-lived asset, including an asset that is subject to nonrecourse debt, as the amount by which the carrying amount of the asset (asset group) exceeds its fair value. Paragraphs 69–72 and 103 and 104 of Statement 121 discussed the basis for the Board's conclusion:

> The Board concluded that a decision to continue to operate rather than sell an impaired asset is economically similar to a decision to invest in that asset and, therefore, the impaired asset should be measured at its fair value. The amount of the impairment loss should be the amount by which the carrying amount of the impaired asset exceeds the fair value of the asset. That fair value then becomes the asset's new cost basis.
>
> When an entity determines that expected future cash flows from using an asset will not result in the recovery of the asset's carrying amount, it must decide whether to sell the asset and use the proceeds for an alternative purpose or to continue to use the impaired asset in its operations. The decision presumably is based on a comparison of expected future cash flows from those alternative courses of action and is essentially a capital investment decision. In either alternative, proceeds from the sale of the impaired asset are considered in the capital investment decision. Consequently, a decision to continue to use the impaired asset is equivalent to a new asset purchase decision, and a new basis of fair value is appropriate.
>
> . . . The Board . . . concluded that the fair value of an impaired asset is the best measure of the cost of continuing to use that asset because it is consistent with management's decision process. Presumably, no entity would

decide to continue to use an asset unless that alternative was expected to produce more in terms of expected future cash flows or service potential than the alternative of selling it and reinvesting the proceeds. The Board also believes that using fair value to measure the amount of an impairment loss is not a departure from the historical cost principle. Rather, it is a consistent application of principles practiced elsewhere in the current system of accounting whenever a cost basis for a newly acquired asset must be determined.

The Board believes that fair value is an easily understood notion. It is the amount at which an asset could be bought or sold in a current transaction between willing parties. The fair value measure is basic to economic theory and is grounded in the reality of the marketplace. Fair value estimates are readily available in published form for many assets, especially machinery and equipment. For some assets, multiple, on-line database services provide up-to-date market price information. Estimates of fair value also are subject to periodic verification whenever assets are exchanged in transactions between willing parties.

The Board considered requests for a limited exception to the fair value measurement for impaired long-lived assets that are subject to nonrecourse debt. Some believe that the nonrecourse provision is effectively a put option for which the borrower has paid a premium. They believe that the impairment loss on an asset subject entirely to nonrecourse debt should be limited to the loss that would occur if the asset were put back to the lender.

The Board decided not to provide an exception for assets subject to nonrecourse debt. The recognition of an impairment loss and the recognition of a gain on the extinguishment of debt are separate events, and each event should be recognized in the period in which it occurs. The Board believes that the recognition of an impairment loss should be based on the measurement of the asset at its fair value and that the existence of nonrecourse debt should not influence that measurement.

Alternative measures of an impairment loss

B35. In Statement 121, the Board considered but rejected measures other than fair value for measuring an impairment loss that could have been achieved within the historical cost framework. Specifically, the Board considered (a) a recoverable cost measure, (b) a recoverable cost including interest measure, and (c) different measures for different impairment losses.

B36. Paragraphs 77–81 of Statement 121 discussed a recoverable cost measure:

Recoverable cost is measured as the sum of the undiscounted future cash flows expected to be generated over the life of an asset. For example, if an asset has a carrying amount of $1,000,000, a remaining useful life of 5 years, and expected future cash flows over the 5 years of $180,000 per year, the recoverable cost would be $900,000 (5 × $180,000), and the impairment loss would be $100,000 ($1,000,000 − $900,000).

The Board did not adopt recoverable cost as the measure of an impairment loss. Proponents of the recoverable cost measure believe that impairment is the result of the inability to recover the carrying amount of an asset. They do not view the decision to retain an impaired asset as an investment decision; rather, they view the recognition of an impairment loss as an adjustment to the historical cost of the asset. They contend that recoverable cost measured by the sum of the undiscounted expected future cash flows is the appropriate carrying amount for an impaired asset and the amount on which the impairment loss should be determined.

Proponents of the recoverable cost measure do not believe that the fair value of an asset is a relevant measure unless a transaction or other event justifies a new basis for the asset at fair value. They do not view impairment to be such an event.

Some proponents of the recoverable cost measure assert that measuring an impaired asset at either fair value or a discounted present value results in an inappropriate understatement of net income in the period of the impairment and an overstatement of net income in subsequent periods. The Board did not agree with that view. Board members noted that measuring an impaired asset at recoverable cost could result in reported losses in future periods if the entity had incurred debt directly associated with the asset.

Proponents of the recoverable cost measure view interest cost as a period cost that should not be included as part of an impairment loss regardless of whether the interest is an accrual of actual debt costs or the result of discounting expected future cash flows using a debt rate.

B37. Paragraphs 82–85 of Statement 121 discussed a recoverable cost including interest measure:

Recoverable cost including interest generally is measured as either (a) the sum of the undiscounted expected future cash flows including interest costs on actual debt or (b) the present value of expected future cash flows discounted at some annual rate such as a debt rate. For example, if an asset has a carrying value of $1,000,000, a remaining useful life of 5 years, expected future cash flows (excluding interest) over the 5 years of $180,000 per year, and a debt rate of 6 percent, recoverable cost including interest would be $758,225 (4.21236 × $180,000), and the impairment loss would be $241,775 ($1,000,000 – $758,225).

The Board did not adopt recoverable cost including interest as an appropriate measure of an impairment loss. Proponents of the recoverable cost including interest measure agree that the time value of money should be considered in the measure, but they view the time value of money as an element of cost recovery rather than as an element of fair value. Proponents believe that the measurement objective for an impaired asset should be recoverable cost and not fair value. However, they believe that interest should be included as a carrying cost in determining the recoverable cost. To them, the objective is to recognize the costs (including the time value of money) that are not recoverable as an impairment loss and to measure an impaired asset at the costs that are recoverable.

Because of the difficulties in attempting to associate actual debt with individual assets, proponents of the recoverable cost including interest measure believe that the present value of expected future cash flows using a debt rate such as an incremental borrowing rate is a practical means of achieving their measurement objective. They recognize that an entity that has no debt may be required to discount expected future cash flows. They believe that the initial investment decision would have included consideration of the debt or equity cost of funds.

The Board believes that use of the recoverable cost including interest measure would result in different carrying amounts for essentially the same impaired assets because they are owned by different entities that have different debt capacities. The Board does not believe that discounting expected future cash flows using a debt rate is an appropriate measure for determining the value of those assets.

B38. Paragraph 86 of Statement 121 discussed different measures for different impairment losses:

The Board also considered but did not adopt an alternative approach that would require different measures for different impairments. At one extreme, an asset might be impaired because depreciation assumptions were not adjusted appropriately. At the other extreme, an asset might be impaired because of a major change in its use. Some believe that the first situation is similar to a depreciation "catch-up" adjustment and that an undiscounted measure should be used. They believe that the second situation is similar to a new investment in an asset with the same intended use and that a fair value measure should be used. The Board was unable to develop a workable distinction between the first and second situations that would support the use of different measures.

Fair value

B39. This Statement retains the hierarchy in Statement 121 for measuring fair value. Because quoted market prices in active markets are the best evidence of fair value, they should be used, if available. Otherwise, the estimate of fair value should be based on the best information available in the circumstances, including prices for similar assets (asset groups) and the results of using other valuation techniques.

B40. The Board acknowledges that in many instances, quoted market prices in active markets will not be available for the long-lived assets (asset groups) covered by this Statement. The Board concluded that for those long-lived assets (asset groups), a present value technique is often the best available valuation technique with which to estimate fair value.

Paragraphs 39–54 of Concepts Statement 7, which are incorporated in Appendix E, discuss the use of two present value techniques—expected present value and traditional present value. During its deliberations leading to the Exposure Draft, the Board concluded that an expected present value technique is superior to a traditional present value technique, especially in situations in which the timing or amount of estimated future cash flows is uncertain. Because such situations often arise for the long-lived assets (asset groups) covered by this Statement, the Exposure Draft set forth the Board's expectation that when using a present value technique, most entities would use expected present value.

B41. Several respondents to the Exposure Draft suggested that the Board provide clearer guidance on whether and, if so, when entities are required to use an expected present value technique versus a traditional present value technique to minimize confusion and inconsistent application of this Statement. During its redeliberations of the Exposure Draft, the Board decided not to specify a requirement for either present value technique. The Board decided that preparers should determine the present value technique best suited to their specific circumstances based on the guidance in Concepts Statement 7. However, the Board noted that a traditional present value technique cannot accommodate uncertainties in the timing of future cash flows. Further, for nonfinancial assets, such as those covered by this Statement, paragraph 44 of Concepts Statement 7 explains:

> The traditional approach is useful for many measurements, especially those in which comparable assets and liabilities can be observed in the marketplace. However, the Board found that the traditional approach does not provide the tools needed to address some complex measurement problems, including the measurement of nonfinancial assets and liabilities for which no market for the item or a comparable item exists. The traditional approach places most of the emphasis on selection of an interest rate. A proper search for "the rate commensurate with the risk" requires analysis of at least two items—one asset or liability that exists in the marketplace and has an observed interest rate and the asset or liability being measured. The appropriate rate of interest for the cash flows being measured must be inferred from the observable rate of interest in some other asset or liability and, to draw that inference, the characteristics of the cash flows must be similar to those of the asset being measured.

B42. In this Statement, the Board clarified that consistent with the objective of measuring fair value, assumptions that marketplace participants would use in their estimates of fair value should be incorporated in estimates of future cash flows whenever that information is available without undue cost and effort. The Exposure Draft provided examples of circumstances in which an entity's assumptions might differ from marketplace assumptions. During its redeliberations of the Exposure Draft, the Board decided that it was not necessary to include those examples in this Statement, noting that related guidance is provided in paragraphs 23 and 32 of Concepts Statement 7, which are incorporated in Appendix E.

B43. The Board recognizes that there may be practical problems in determining the fair value of certain types of long-lived assets (asset groups) covered by this Statement that do not have observable market prices. Because precise information about the relevant attributes of those assets (asset groups) seldom will be available, judgments, estimates, and projections will be required for estimating fair value. Although the objective of using a present value or other valuation technique is to determine fair value, the Board acknowledges that, in some circumstances, the only information available to estimate fair value without undue cost and effort will be the entity's estimates of future cash flows. Paragraph 38 of Concepts Statement 7 explains:

> As a practical matter, an entity that uses cash flows in accounting measurements often has little or no information about some or all of the assumptions that marketplace participants would use in assessing the fair value of an asset or a liability. In those situations, the entity must necessarily use the information that is available without undue cost and effort in developing cash flow estimates. The use of an entity's own assumptions about future cash flows is compatible with an estimate of fair value, as long as there are no contrary data indicating that marketplace participants would use different assumptions. If such data exist, the entity must adjust its assumptions to incorporate that market information.

Grouping Long-Lived Assets to Be Held and Used

B44. For purposes of recognition and measurement of an impairment loss, this Statement retains the requirement of Statement 121 to group a long-lived asset or assets with other assets and liabilities at the lowest level for which identifiable cash flows are largely independent of the cash flows of other assets and liabilities. In Statement 121, the Board acknowledged that the primary issue underlying the grouping of long-lived assets is when, if ever, it is appropriate to offset unrealized losses on some assets by unrealized gains on other assets. However, the Board concluded that such offsetting is appropriate when a long-lived asset that is not an individual source of cash flows is part of a group of assets that are used together to generate joint cash flows. The Board affirmed that conclusion in this Statement. This Statement establishes that an asset group is the unit of accounting for a long-lived asset while it is classified as held and used.

B45. In Statement 121, the Board also acknowledged that grouping long-lived assets requires significant judgment. In that regard, the Board reviewed a series of cases that demonstrated the subjectivity of grouping issues. Paragraphs 96–98 of Statement 121 stated:

> Varying facts and circumstances introduced in the cases inevitably justified different groupings. Although most respondents to the Discussion Memorandum generally favored grouping at the lowest level for which there are identifiable cash flows for recognition and measurement of an impairment loss, determining that lowest level requires considerable judgment.
>
> The Board considered a case that illustrated the need for judgment in grouping assets for impairment. In that case, an entity operated a bus company that provided service under contract with a municipality that required minimum service on each of five separate routes. Assets devoted to serving each route and the cash flows from each route were discrete. One of the routes operated at a significant deficit that resulted in the inability to recover the carrying amounts of the dedicated assets. The Board concluded that the five bus routes would be an appropriate level at which to group assets to test for and measure impairment because the entity did not have the option to curtail any one bus route.

The Board concluded that the grouping issue requires significant management judgment within certain parameters. Those parameters are that the assets should be grouped at the lowest level for which there are cash flows that are identifiable and that those cash flows should be largely independent of the cash flows of other groupings of assets.

B46. In this Statement, as in Statement 121, the Board acknowledges that in limited circumstances, an asset group will include all assets and liabilities of the entity. Paragraphs 99 and 100 of Statement 121 explained:

> Not-for-profit organizations that rely in part on contributions to maintain their assets may need to consider those contributions in determining the appropriate cash flows to compare with the carrying amount of an asset. Some respondents to the Exposure Draft stated that the recognition criteria in paragraph 6 would be problematic for many not-for-profit organizations because it may be difficult, if not impossible, for them to identify expected future cash flows with specific assets or asset groupings. In other cases, expected future cash flows can be identified with asset groups. However, if future unrestricted contributions to the organization as a whole are not considered, the sum of the expected future cash flows may be negative, or positive but less than the carrying amount of the asset. For example, the costs of administering a museum may exceed the admission fees charged, but the organization may fund the cash flow deficit with unrestricted contributions.
>
> Other respondents indicated that similar difficulties would be experienced by business enterprises. For example, the cost of operating assets such as corporate headquarters or centralized research facilities may be funded by revenue-producing activities at lower levels of the enterprise. Accordingly, in limited circumstances, the lowest level of identifiable cash flows that are largely independent of other asset groups may be the entity level. The Board concluded that the recoverability test in paragraph 6 should be performed at the entity level if an asset does not have identifiable cash flows lower than the entity level. The cash flows used in the recoverability test should be reduced by the carrying amounts of

the entity's other assets that are covered by this Statement to arrive at the cash flows expected to contribute to the recoverability of the asset being tested. Not-for-profit organizations should include unrestricted contributions to the organization as a whole that are a source of funds for the operation of the asset.

B47. Based on the Board's previous decisions discussed in paragraph 100 of Statement 121, the Exposure Draft would have required that estimates of future cash flows for an asset group be adjusted to exclude the portion of those cash flows necessary to recover the carrying amounts of the assets and liabilities of the group not covered by this Statement. However, during its redeliberations of the Exposure Draft, the Board decided to eliminate that requirement, noting that because the unit of accounting for a long-lived asset to be held and used is its asset group, such adjustments are unnecessary.

Goodwill

B48. In Statement 142, the Board decided that because goodwill should no longer be amortized, it should be tested for impairment in a manner different from how the long-lived assets covered by this Statement are tested for impairment. In developing the guidance in Statement 142, the Board decided that the reporting unit (as defined in that Statement) is the unit of measure for goodwill and that all goodwill should be tested for impairment at that level. The Board therefore decided to eliminate the requirement of Statement 121 to include goodwill in an asset group previously acquired in a business combination to be tested for impairment, which the Exposure Draft would have retained. The Board decided that goodwill should be included in such an asset group only if it is or includes a reporting unit. Goodwill should be excluded from such an asset group if it is only part of a reporting unit.

B49. During its redeliberations of the Exposure Draft, the Board considered the effect of excluding goodwill from an asset group that is only part of a reporting unit. The Board observed that although the carrying amount of the asset group would exclude goodwill, the estimates of future cash flows used to test the group for recoverability could include cash flows attributable to goodwill. However, the Board decided that those estimates of future cash flows should not be adjusted for the effect of excluding goodwill. The Board reasoned that because any adjustment likely would be arbitrary, adjusted estimates

of future cash flows would not necessarily provide a better estimate of the cash flows expected to contribute to the recoverability of the group. Further, an additional requirement to determine a goodwill adjustment under this Statement would not be cost beneficial.

Allocation of an impairment loss

B50. Paragraph 12 of Statement 121 specified that "in instances where goodwill is identified with assets that are subject to an impairment loss, the carrying amount of the identified goodwill shall be eliminated before making any reduction of the carrying amounts of impaired long-lived assets and identifiable intangibles." However, it did not specify how the excess, if any, should be allocated to the other assets of the group. The Board observed that if long-lived assets having different depreciable lives are grouped, the method used to allocate the excess impairment loss, if any, to the assets of the group can affect the pattern of income recognition over the succeeding years. To improve the consistency and comparability of reported financial information over time and among entities, the Board decided that this Statement should specify an allocation method.

B51. The Board decided that because other accounting requirements prescribe the accounting for assets and liabilities not covered by this Statement that are included in an asset group, an impairment loss that is determined based on the carrying amount and fair value of an asset group should reduce only the carrying amounts of the long-lived assets of the group. Paragraph 14 of this Statement requires that an impairment loss be allocated to those long-lived assets on a pro rata basis using their relative carrying amounts, provided that the carrying amount of an individual long-lived asset of the group is not reduced to an amount less than its fair value whenever that fair value is determinable without undue cost and effort. The Board concluded that it would be inappropriate to reduce the carrying amount of a long-lived asset to an amount below its fair value. The Board believes that the allocation method for an impairment loss provides a consistent basis for adjusting the carrying amounts of the long-lived assets of an asset group.

Depreciation

B52. This Statement retains the requirement of Statement 121 to consider the need to review depreciation estimates and method for a long-lived asset in accordance with APB Opinion No. 20, *Accounting Changes,* if a long-lived asset is tested for recoverability. This Statement clarifies that any revision to the remaining useful life of a long-lived asset resulting from that review should be considered in developing estimates of future cash flows used to test for recoverability but that any change in the method of accounting for the asset should be made only after applying this Statement. In Statement 121, the Board decided not to expand the scope of that Statement to address depreciation issues. The Board affirmed its initial decisions in Statement 121 and, therefore, this Statement does not prescribe the basis for revisions to depreciation estimates or method, or otherwise address depreciation issues.

Restoration of an Impairment Loss

B53. This Statement retains the prohibition in Statement 121 on the restoration of a previously recognized impairment loss. Paragraph 105 of Statement 121 discussed the basis for the Board's conclusion:

> The Board considered whether to prohibit or require restoration of previously recognized impairment losses. It decided that an impairment loss should result in a new cost basis for the impaired asset. That new cost basis puts the asset on an equal basis with other assets that are not impaired. In the Board's view, the new cost basis should not be adjusted subsequently other than as provided under the current accounting model for prospective changes in the depreciation estimates and method and for further impairment losses. Most respondents to the Exposure Draft agreed with the Board's decision that restoration should be prohibited.

Reporting and Disclosure

B54. Paragraph 25 of this Statement retains the requirements of Statement 121 for reporting an impairment loss recognized for a long-lived asset to be held and used. Paragraph 108 of Statement 121 discussed the basis for the Board's conclusion:

> The Board considered the alternative ways described in the Discussion Memorandum for reporting an impairment loss: reporting the loss as a component of continuing operations, reporting the loss as a special item outside continuing operations, or separate re-

porting of the loss without specifying the classification in the statement of operations. The Board concluded that an impairment loss should be reported as a component of income from continuing operations before income taxes for entities that present an income statement and in the statement of activities of a not-for-profit organization. If no impairment had occurred, an amount equal to the impairment loss would have been charged to operations over time through the allocation of depreciation or amortization. That depreciation or amortization charge would have been reported as part of continuing operations of a business enterprise or as an expense in the statement of activities of a not-for-profit organization. Further, an asset that is subject to a reduction in its carrying amount due to an impairment loss will continue to be used in operations. The Board concluded that an impairment loss does not have characteristics that warrant special treatment, for instance, as an extraordinary item.

B55. Paragraph 26 of this Statement retains the disclosure requirements of Statement 121 relating to impairment losses. Paragraphs 109 and 94 of Statement 121 discussed the basis for the Board's conclusion:

> The Board believes that financial statements should include information on impairment losses that would be most useful to users. After considering responses to the Exposure Draft, the Board concluded that an entity that recognizes an impairment loss should describe the assets impaired and the facts and circumstances leading to the impairment; disclose the amount of the loss and how fair value was determined; disclose the caption in the income statement or the statement of activities in which the loss is aggregated unless that loss has been presented as a separate caption or reported parenthetically on the face of the statement; and, if applicable, disclose the business segment(s) affected. The Board decided not to require further disclosures, such as the assumptions used to estimate expected future cash flows and the discount rate used when fair value is estimated by discounting expected future cash flows.

> Several respondents to the Exposure Draft said that disclosure of the discount rate used

to determine the present value of the estimated expected future cash flows should not be required. The Board decided that disclosure of the discount rate without disclosure of the other assumptions used in estimating expected future cash flows generally would not be meaningful to financial statement users. Therefore, this Statement does not require disclosure of the discount rate.

B56. A few respondents to the Exposure Draft suggested that the Board reconsider its decision in Statement 121 not to require disclosure of the discount rate and other assumptions used in measuring fair value. They said that such disclosures would provide useful information for evaluating impairment write-downs. However, the Board concluded that without access to management's cash flow projections and its methods of estimating those cash flows, the suggested disclosures would not necessarily be useful to users in evaluating impairment write-downs. The Board affirmed its initial conclusions in Statement 121 and, therefore, this Statement does not require disclosure of that information.

Early warning disclosures

B57. This Statement, like Statement 121, does not require early warning disclosures. Paragraphs 110 and 111 of Statement 121 discussed the basis for the Board's conclusion:

> In 1985, the AICPA established a task force to consider the need for improved disclosures about risks and uncertainties that affect companies and the manner in which they do business. In July 1987, the task force published *Report of the Task Force on Risks and Uncertainties,* which concluded that companies should make early warning disclosures in their financial statements. In December 1994, AcSEC issued AICPA Statement of Position 94-6, *Disclosure of Certain Significant Risks and Uncertainties.* That SOP requires entities to include in their financial statements disclosures about (a) the nature of operations, (b) the use of estimates in the preparation of financial statements, (c) certain significant estimates, and (d) current vulnerability due to certain concentrations.
>
> The Board observed that early warning disclosures would be useful for certain potential impairments. However, most respondents to the Exposure Draft said that the

Statement should not require early warning disclosures. The Board observed that SOP 94-6 uses essentially the same events or changes in circumstances as those in paragraph 5 of this Statement to illustrate when disclosures of certain significant estimates should be made for long-lived assets. Therefore, the Board concluded that it was not necessary for this Statement to require early warning disclosures.

Amendment to Statement 15

B58. This Statement carries forward the amendment made by Statement 121 to FASB Statement No. 15, *Accounting by Debtors and Creditors for Troubled Debt Restructurings,* discussed in paragraphs 136–138 of Statement 121:

> In May 1993, the Board issued FASB Statement No. 114, *Accounting by Creditors for Impairment of a Loan,* which requires certain impaired loans to be measured based on the present value of expected future cash flows, discounted at the loan's effective interest rate, or as a practical expedient, at the loan's observable market price or the fair value of the collateral if the impaired loan is collateral dependent. Regardless of the measurement method, a creditor should measure impairment based on the fair value of the collateral when the creditor determines that foreclosure is probable. A creditor should consider estimated costs to sell, on a discounted basis, in the measure of impairment if those costs are expected to reduce the cash flows available to repay or otherwise satisfy the loan.
>
> As suggested by one commentator to the Exposure Draft, the Board decided to amend Statement 15 to make the measurement of long-lived assets that are received in full satisfaction of a receivable and that will be sold consistent with the measurement of other long-lived assets under this Statement. The amendment requires that those assets be measured at fair value less cost to sell. The Board considered amending Statement 15 to address shares of stock or equity interests in long-lived assets that are received in full satisfaction of a receivable and that will be sold, but it determined that those items are outside the scope of this Statement.
>
> Loans and long-lived assets are similar in that both are cash-generating assets that are

subject to impairment. However, inherent differences between monetary and nonmonetary assets have resulted in different accounting treatments for them under the current reporting model.

Amendment to Statement 71

B59. This Statement carries forward the amendment made by Statement 121 to FASB Statement No. 71, *Accounting for the Effects of Certain Types of Regulation,* to apply the provisions of this Statement for long-lived assets to be held and used to all assets of a regulated enterprise except (a) regulatory assets that meet the criteria of paragraph 9 of Statement 71 and (b) costs of recently completed plants that are covered by paragraph 7 of FASB Statement No. 90, *Regulated Enterprises—Accounting for Abandonments and Disallowances of Plant Costs.* Therefore, regulatory assets capitalized as a result of paragraph 9 of Statement 71 should be tested for impairment whenever the criteria of that paragraph are no longer met. Paragraphs 127 and 128 of Statement 121 explained:

FASB Statement No. 71, *Accounting for the Effects of Certain Types of Regulation,* establishes the accounting model for certain rate-regulated enterprises. Because the rates of rate-regulated enterprises generally are designed to recover the costs of providing regulated services or products, those enterprises are usually able to recover the carrying amounts of their assets. Paragraph 10 of Statement 71 states that when a regulator excludes a cost from rates, "the carrying amount of any related asset shall be reduced to the extent that the asset has been impaired. Whether the asset has been impaired shall be judged the same as for enterprises in general" (footnote reference omitted). Statement 71 does not provide any guidance about when an impairment has, in fact, occurred or about how to measure the amount of the impairment.

The Board considered whether the accounting for the impairment of long-lived assets and identifiable intangibles by rate-regulated enterprises that meet the criteria for applying Statement 71 should be the same as for enterprises in general. In March 1993, the EITF discussed incurred costs capitalized pursuant to the criteria of paragraph 9 of Statement 71. The EITF reached a consensus in EITF Issue No. 93-4, "Accounting for

Regulatory Assets," that a cost that does not meet the asset recognition criteria in paragraph 9 of Statement 71 at the date the cost is incurred should be recognized as a regulatory asset when it does meet those criteria at a later date. The EITF also reached a consensus that the carrying amount of a regulatory asset should be reduced to the extent that the asset has been impaired with impairment judged the same as for enterprises in general; the provisions of [Statement 121] nullify that consensus.

B60. Paragraphs 129–134 of Statement 121 discussed approaches considered and the basis for the Board's conclusion:

The Board considered several approaches to recognizing and measuring the impairment of long-lived assets and identifiable intangibles of rate-regulated enterprises. One approach the Board considered was to apply paragraph 7 of FASB Statement No. 90, *Regulated Enterprises—Accounting for Abandonments and Disallowances of Plant Costs,* to all assets of a regulated enterprise and not just to costs of recently completed plants. That paragraph requires that an impairment loss be recognized when a disallowance is probable and the amount can be reasonably estimated. If a regulator explicitly disallows a certain dollar amount of plant costs, an impairment loss should be recognized for that amount. If a regulator explicitly but indirectly disallows plant costs (for example, by excluding a return on investment on a portion of plant costs), an impairment loss should be recognized for the effective disallowance by estimating the expected future cash flows that have been disallowed as a result of the regulator's action and then computing the present value of those cash flows. That approach would recognize a probable disallowance as an impairment loss, the amount of the loss would be the discounted value of the expected future cash flows disallowed, and the discount rate would be the same as the rate of return used to estimate the expected future cash flows.

A second approach the Board considered was to supersede paragraph 7 of Statement 90 and apply this Statement's requirements to all plant costs. A disallowance would result in costs being excluded from the rate base. The recognition and measurement requirements of this Statement would be applied to determine whether an impairment loss would be recognized for financial reporting purposes.

A third approach the Board considered was to apply the general impairment provisions of this Statement to all assets of a regulated enterprise except for disallowances of costs of recently completed plants, which would continue to be covered by paragraph 7 of Statement 90. A disallowance would result in the exclusion of costs from the rate base. That disallowance would result in an impairment loss for financial reporting purposes if the costs disallowed relate to a recently completed plant. If the costs disallowed do not relate to a recently completed plant, the recognition and measurement requirements of this Statement would be applied to determine whether and how much of an impairment loss would be recognized for financial reporting purposes.

A fourth approach the Board considered was to apply the general impairment standard to all assets of a regulated enterprise except (a) regulatory assets that meet the criteria of paragraph 9 of Statement 71 and (b) costs of recently completed plants that are covered by paragraph 7 of Statement 90. Impairment of regulatory assets capitalized as a result of paragraph 9 of Statement 71 would be recognized whenever the criteria of that paragraph are no longer met.

The Board decided that the fourth approach should be used in accounting for the impairment of all assets of a rate-regulated enterprise. The Board amended paragraph 9 of Statement 71 to provide that a rate-regulated enterprise should charge a regulatory asset to earnings if and when that asset no longer meets the criteria in paragraph 9(a) and (b) of that Statement. The Board also amended paragraph 10 of Statement 71 to require that a rate-regulated enterprise recognize an impairment for the amount of costs excluded when a regulator excludes all or part of a cost from rates, even if the regulator allows the rate-regulated enterprise to earn a return on the remaining costs allowed.

The Board believes that because a rate-regulated enterprise is allowed to capitalize costs that enterprises in general would otherwise have charged to expense, the impairment criteria for those assets should be different from enterprises in general. The Board believes that symmetry should exist between the recognition of those assets and the subsequent impairment of those assets. The Board could see no reason that an asset created as a result of regulatory action could not be impaired by the actions of the same regulator. Other assets that are not regulatory assets covered by Statement 71 or recently completed plant costs covered by Statement 90, such as older plants or other nonregulatory assets of a rate-regulated enterprise, would be covered by the general provisions of this Statement.

B61. Paragraph 135 of Statement 121 further clarified the accounting for previously disallowed costs that are subsequently allowed by a regulator:

> The Board decided that previously disallowed costs that are subsequently allowed by a regulator should be recorded as an asset, consistent with the classification that would have resulted had those costs initially been included in allowable costs. Thus, plant costs subsequently allowed should be classified as plant assets, whereas other costs (expenses) subsequently allowed should be classified as regulatory assets. The Board amended Statement 71 to reflect this decision. The Board decided to restore the original classification because there is no economic change to the asset—it is as if the regulator never had disallowed the cost. The Board determined that restoration of cost is allowed for rate-regulated enterprises in this situation, in contrast to other impairment situations, because the event requiring recognition of the impairment resulted from actions of an independent party and not management's own judgment or determination of recoverability.

Long-Lived Assets to Be Disposed Of Other Than by Sale

B62. In Statement 121, the Board decided that the provisions for long-lived assets to be disposed of, including the requirement to cease depreciating (amortizing) a long-lived asset when it is classified as held for disposal, should be applied to all long-lived assets to be disposed of, whether by sale or abandonment. During its deliberations leading to the Exposure Draft, the Board reconsidered that decision, noting that its rationale for not depreciating (amortizing) a long-lived asset to be disposed of by sale does not apply to a long-lived asset to be disposed of other than by sale. Such transactions include the abandonment of a long-lived asset, as well as the exchange of a long-lived asset for a similar productive long-lived asset and the distribution of a long-lived asset to owners in a spinoff (including a pro rata distribution to owners of shares of a subsidiary or other investee company that has been or is being consolidated or that has been or is being accounted for under the equity method) or other form of reorganization or liquidation or in a plan that is in substance the rescission of a prior business combination covered by APB Opinion No. 29, *Accounting for Nonmonetary Transactions.*

B63. Specifically, the Board observed that to the extent the carrying amount of a long-lived asset to be disposed of by abandonment is recoverable, it will be recovered principally through operations, rather than through the disposal transaction. Additionally, the accounting guidance in Opinion 29 for the exchange of a similar productive long-lived asset and for the distribution of a long-lived asset to owners in a spinoff is based on the carrying amount of the asset exchanged or distributed. The Board concluded that the Opinion 29 guidance is more consistent with the accounting for a long-lived asset to be held and used than for a long-lived asset to be sold. Thus, the Board decided that a long-lived asset to be disposed of other than by sale should continue to be classified as held and used and depreciated (amortized) until it is abandoned, exchanged, or distributed.

B64. Some respondents to the Exposure Draft said that there is no conceptual difference between sale and other disposal transactions and that the provisions of this Statement for long-lived assets to be disposed of by sale should be applied to other disposal transactions. During its redeliberations of the Exposure Draft, the Board affirmed its conclusion that a long-lived asset to be disposed of other than by sale should continue to be classified as held and used and depreciated (amortized) until disposed of for the reasons discussed in paragraph B63. Accordingly, paragraphs 7–26 of this Statement, except as modified by paragraph 29, apply to that asset or its asset group as previously determined on a held-and-used basis until it is disposed of. If that asset will be disposed of together with other assets and liabilities as a group and the group is a component of an entity, paragraphs 41–44 of this Statement apply to that disposal group when it is disposed of.

Long-Lived Asset to Be Abandoned

B65. The Board decided that if a long-lived asset that is being used is to be abandoned before the end of its previously estimated useful life, depreciation estimates should be revised in accordance with Opinion 20 to reflect the use of the asset over that shortened period. The Board reasoned that because the continued use of a long-lived asset demonstrates the presence of service potential, the immediate writedown of the asset to zero generally is inappropriate. A few respondents to the Exposure Draft suggested that the Board provide additional guidance for revising those depreciation estimates under Opinion 20. However, the Board decided not to address that issue because depreciation issues are beyond the scope of this Statement.

Long-Lived Asset to Be Exchanged for a Similar Productive Long-Lived Asset or to Be Distributed to Owners in a Spinoff

B66. Under Opinion 29 the accounting for the exchange of a long-lived asset for a similar productive long-lived asset and the distribution of a long-lived asset to owners in a spinoff, is based on the recorded amount, "after reduction, if appropriate, for an indicated impairment of value" of the asset exchanged (paragraph 21) or distributed (paragraph 23). After Statement 121 was issued, questions emerged on how to determine "an indicated impairment of value" of the asset exchanged or distributed. The primary issue was whether to apply an undiscounted cash flows recoverability test and, if so, at what level. The EITF discussed the issue in Issue No. 96-2, "Impairment Recognition When a Nonmonetary Asset Is Exchanged or Is Distributed to Owners and Is Accounted for at the Asset's Recorded Amount," but did not reach a consensus.

B67. The Board did not redeliberate the Opinion 29 guidance for exchanges of similar productive assets or spinoffs. This Statement, however, resolves Issue 96-2 by requiring that an indicated impairment of value of a long-lived asset that is exchanged for a similar productive long-lived asset or distributed to owners in a spinoff be recognized if the carrying amount of the asset (disposal group) exceeds its fair value at the disposal date. The accounting guidance in Opinion 29 for an exchange of similar productive assets and for a distribution to owners in a spinoff is based on recorded amounts and not fair value. The Board concluded that using recorded amounts is more consistent with the accounting for a long-lived asset to be held and used than for a long-lived asset to be sold. For that reason, the Board believes that an undiscounted cash flows recoverability test should apply prior to the disposal date. The estimates of future cash flows used in that test are based on the use of the asset for its remaining useful life, assuming that the disposal transaction will not occur.

B68. The Board acknowledges the view of some respondents to the Exposure Draft that because the exchange of a long-lived asset for a similar productive long-lived asset does not culminate an earning process, an undiscounted cash flows recoverability test should apply up through the disposal date. The Board observed that the distribution of a long-lived asset to owners also does not culminate an earning process. However, the Board concluded that those disposal transactions are significant economic events that should result in recognition of an impairment loss if the carrying amount of the asset (disposal group) exceeds its fair value at the disposal date. The Board decided that because the fair value of the asset (disposal group) will be determined in connection with the decision to dispose, the practical expedient of an undiscounted cash flows recoverability test should not apply at the disposal date.

B69. This Statement amends Opinion 29 to require that an indicated impairment of value of a long-lived asset that is exchanged for a similar productive long-lived asset or distributed to owners in a spinoff be recognized if the carrying amount of the asset (disposal group) exceeds its fair value at the disposal date. It also amends paragraph 44(a) of FASB Statement No. 19, *Financial Accounting and Reporting by Oil and Gas Producing Companies,* to extend that requirement to transactions involving the exchange of proved oil- and gas-producing assets that are being accounted for by the successful-efforts method of accounting.

Long-Lived Assets to Be Disposed Of by Sale

Recognition

Plan-of-sale criteria

B70. As a basis for determining when to classify a long-lived asset (disposal group) as held for sale, Statement 121 required a commitment to a plan to sell the asset (disposal group) but did not specify factors beyond that commitment that should be considered. Consequently, in implementing Statement 121, questions emerged about when to classify a long-

lived asset (disposal group) as held for sale. Because a long-lived asset is not depreciated (amortized) while it is classified as held for sale, those questions raised concerns that an entity could improve its operating results by asserting a commitment to a plan to sell a long-lived asset (disposal group) at a future date. Because of those concerns, the Board decided that this Statement should specify criteria for determining when an entity's commitment to a plan to sell a long-lived asset (disposal group) is sufficient for purposes of classifying the asset (disposal group) as held for sale.

B71. The Board decided that a long-lived asset (disposal group) should be classified as held for sale in the period in which all of the criteria in paragraph 30 are met, except as permitted in limited situations by paragraphs 31 and 32. In developing those criteria, the Board considered the criteria established by Opinion 30 for a measurement date and by Issue 94-3 for a commitment date. Certain of those criteria are incorporated in paragraphs 30(a), (c), and (f) of this Statement. Additional criteria established by this Statement are incorporated in paragraphs 30(b), (d), and (e). The Board concluded, and many respondents agreed, that those criteria should enable entities to determine consistently when to classify assets (disposal groups) as held for sale.

Available for immediate sale

B72. Paragraph 30(b) of this Statement establishes a criterion that to qualify for classification as held for sale, a long-lived asset (disposal group) must be available for immediate sale in its present condition. The Board concluded that an asset (disposal group) is available for immediate sale if an entity currently has the intent and ability to transfer the asset (disposal group) to a buyer in its present condition within a period that is usual and customary for sales of such assets. In developing that criterion, the Board decided not to preclude a long-lived asset (disposal group) from being classified as held for sale while it is being used. The Board reasoned that if a long-lived asset (disposal group) is available for immediate sale, the remaining use of the asset (disposal group) is incidental to its recovery through sale and that the carrying amount of the asset (disposal group) will be recovered principally through sale. The Board also decided not to require a binding agreement for a future sale. The Board concluded that such a requirement would unduly delay reporting the effects of a commitment to a plan to sell a long-lived asset (disposal group).

Maximum one-year holding period

B73. In Statement 121, the Board decided not to limit the holding period for a long-lived asset (disposal group) classified as held for sale, principally to allow for situations in which environmental concerns extend the period required to complete a sale beyond one year. In this Statement, the Board reconsidered that decision, noting that in some other situations, a long-lived asset could, as a result, be inappropriately classified as held for sale and not depreciated (amortized) for an extended period. Consequently, paragraph 30(d) of this Statement establishes a maximum one-year holding period for a long-lived asset (disposal group) classified as held for sale. The Board concluded that for a long-lived asset (disposal group) covered by this Statement, a one-year period is a reasonable period within which to assess the probability of a future sale, noting that the APB previously reached a similar conclusion in Opinion 30 for the disposal of a segment.[31]

B74. Because in some situations events or circumstances might extend the period required to complete the sale of a long-lived asset (disposal group) beyond one year, the Board considered whether and, if so, when to permit an exception to the one-year requirement. The Board decided that a delay in the period required to complete a sale should not preclude a long-lived asset (disposal group) from being classified as held for sale if the delay is caused by events or circumstances beyond an entity's control and there is sufficient evidence that the entity remains committed to its plan to sell the asset (disposal group). The Board decided to permit an exception in such situations. The Board concluded that the usefulness and clarity of financial statements would not be improved by having long-lived assets (disposal groups) moving in and out of the held-for-sale classification.

B75. A few respondents to the Exposure Draft suggested that the Board permit an exception to the one-year requirement in all situations in which a long-lived asset is acquired through foreclosure by incorporating in this Statement the held-for-sale presumption in paragraph 10 of AICPA Statement of Position 92-3, *Accounting for Foreclosed Assets*, which stated:

> Most enterprises do not intend to hold foreclosed assets for the production of income but intend to sell them; in fact, some laws and regulations applicable to financial institutions require the sale of foreclosed assets. Therefore, under this SOP, it is presumed that foreclosed assets are held for sale and not for the production of income.

Those respondents said that in situations in which an entity acquires a long-lived asset through foreclosure, circumstances attendant to the foreclosure often extend the period required to complete the sale beyond one year. The Board concluded that this Statement sufficiently addresses the need for an exception to the one-year requirement for all long-lived assets (disposal groups) covered by this Statement, whether previously held and used or newly acquired. To be consistent with an objective of developing a single accounting model for long-lived assets to be disposed of by sale, the Board decided not to incorporate the held-for-sale presumption in SOP 92-3.

Market price reasonable in relation to current fair value

B76. Paragraph 30(e) of this Statement establishes a criterion that to qualify for classification as held for sale, an entity must be actively marketing a long-lived asset (disposal group) at a price that is reasonable in relation to its current fair value. The Board believes that the price at which a long-lived asset (disposal group) is being marketed is indicative of whether the entity currently has the intent and ability to sell the asset (disposal group). A market price that is reasonable in relation to fair value indicates that the asset (disposal group) is available for immediate sale, whereas a market price in excess of fair value indicates that the asset (disposal group) is not available for immediate sale.

Commitment to a plan to sell a long-lived asset after the balance sheet date but before issuance of financial statements

B77. In implementing Statement 121, questions emerged about the required accounting if an entity commits to a plan to sell a long-lived asset after the balance sheet date but before issuance of the financial statements. Prior to this Statement, Opinion 30 and EITF Issue No. 95-18, "Accounting and Reporting for a Discontinued Business Segment When the Measurement Date Occurs after the Balance Sheet

---

[31]Paragraph 15 of Opinion 30 stated that "in the usual circumstance, it would be expected that the plan of disposal would be carried out within a period of one year from the measurement date. . . ."

Date but before the Issuance of Financial Statements," provided related guidance for a segment of a business (as defined in that Opinion). In an expected loss situation, Opinion 30 required that the financial statements be adjusted if the loss "provides evidence of conditions that existed at the date of such statements and affects estimates inherent in the process of preparing them" (footnote 5). Issue 95-18 later incorporated the presumption that an expected loss is evidence of a loss existing at the balance sheet date, unless the subsequent decision to dispose of the segment results from a discrete and identifiable event that occurs unexpectedly after the balance sheet date.

B78. The Board decided that if an entity commits to a plan to sell a long-lived asset after the balance sheet date but before issuance of the financial statements, the asset should continue to be classified as held and used. The Board concluded that retroactively classifying the asset as held for sale would be inconsistent with having specified criteria for determining when an entity's commitment to a plan to sell a long-lived asset (disposal group) is sufficient for purposes of classifying the asset (disposal group) as held for sale. Similarly, the Board concluded that if the asset (asset group) is tested for recoverability on a held-and-used basis as of the balance sheet date, the estimates of future cash flows used in that test should consider the likelihood of possible outcomes that existed at the balance sheet date, including the assessment of the likelihood of the future sale of the asset. That assessment made as of the balance sheet date should not be revised for a decision to sell the asset after the balance sheet date. Therefore, this Statement nullifies Issue 95-18.

B79. The Board considered the view of some respondents to the Exposure Draft that in an expected loss situation, a requirement to classify the asset as held and used could unduly delay recognition of a loss that existed at the balance sheet date. The Board concluded that, on balance, the benefits of having well-defined criteria for when to classify a long-lived asset as held for sale outweigh that concern, noting that the situation referred to by respondents can arise whenever a long-lived asset is expected to be sold but there is no commitment to a plan of sale. The Board observed that if the plan-of-sale criteria are met after the balance sheet date but before issuance of the financial statements, the entity could be required to perform a recoverability test in accordance with paragraph 8(f). In that situation, application of the recoverability test as well as any fair value assessment would be based on facts and circumstances existing

at the balance sheet date and could result in an impairment adjustment as of the balance sheet date. The Board agreed that if prior to meeting the plan-of-sale criteria the entity had previously tested the asset (asset group) for impairment on a held-and-used basis at the balance sheet date, it would be inappropriate to undertake a new recoverability test.

Measurement

Lower of carrying amount or fair value less cost to sell

B80. This Statement retains the requirement of Statement 121 to measure a long-lived asset (disposal group) classified as held for sale at the lower of its carrying amount or fair value less cost to sell. In contrast to a long-lived asset (asset group) to be held and used, a long-lived asset (disposal group) classified as held for sale will be recovered principally through sale rather than through operations. Therefore, accounting for that asset (disposal group) is a process of valuation rather than allocation. The asset (disposal group) is reported at the lower of its carrying amount or fair value less cost to sell, and fair value less cost to sell is evaluated each period to determine if it has changed. Losses (and gains, as permitted by paragraph 37) are reported as adjustments to the carrying amount of a long-lived asset while it is classified as held for sale.

Cost to sell

B81. The Exposure Draft proposed to retain the requirements of Statement 121 for determining cost to sell. Those requirements were discussed in paragraph 116 of Statement 121, which stated:

> The Board concluded that the cost to sell an asset to be disposed of generally includes the incremental direct costs to transact the sale of the asset. Cost to sell is deducted from the fair value of an asset to be disposed of to arrive at the current value of the estimated net proceeds to be received from the asset's future sale. The Board decided that costs incurred during the holding period to protect or maintain an asset to be disposed of generally are excluded from the cost to sell an asset because those costs usually are not required to be incurred in order to sell the asset. However, the Board believes that costs required to be incurred under the terms of a contract for an asset's sale as a condition of the buyer's

consummation of the sale should be included in determining the cost to sell an asset to be disposed of.

B82. Some respondents to the Exposure Draft noted that those requirements for determining cost to sell did not limit cost to sell to the incremental direct costs to transact a sale. They said that, as a result, cost to sell could be interpreted as including normal operating costs (losses) expected to be incurred while a long-lived asset (disposal group) is classified as held for sale, which they did not believe was consistent with the Board's intent. To convey its intent more clearly, the Board decided to revise those requirements to limit cost to sell in all circumstances to the incremental direct costs to transact the sale. Accordingly, costs that are "required to be incurred under the terms of a contract for an asset's sale as a condition of the buyer's consummation of the sale," as referred to in paragraph 116 of Statement 121, would be excluded. In addition, expected future operating losses that marketplace participants would not similarly consider in their estimates of the fair value less cost to sell of a long-lived asset (disposal group) classified as held for sale also would be excluded. In this Statement, the Board clarified that such losses should not be indirectly recognized as part of an expected loss on sale by reducing the carrying amount of the asset (disposal group) to an amount less than its current fair value less cost to sell. Excluding such losses from the measurement of a long-lived asset (disposal group) classified as held for sale supersedes the net realizable value measurement approach previously required under Opinion 30.

Ceasing depreciation (amortization)

B83. This Statement retains the requirement of Statement 121 to cease depreciating (amortizing) a long-lived asset when it is classified as held for sale and measured at the lower of its carrying amount or fair value less cost to sell. Some respondents disagreed with that requirement as also proposed in the Exposure Draft. They said that not depreciating (amortizing) a long-lived asset that is being used is inconsistent with the basic principle that the cost of a long-lived asset should be allocated over the period during which benefits are obtained from its use. The Board considered that view but affirmed its conclusion in Statement 121 that depreciation accounting is inconsistent with the use of a lower of carrying amount or

fair value measure for a long-lived asset classified as held for sale because, as previously stated, accounting for that asset is a process of valuation rather than allocation.

B84. Some respondents also said that not depreciating (amortizing) a long-lived asset that is being used while it is classified as held for sale hinders the comparability of operating results during that period. They said that the comparability of operating results (reported in both continuing operations and in discontinued operations) between periods is more important than the valuation of the asset while it is classified as held for sale. The Board also considered those concerns but observed that in situations where the carrying amount of the asset (disposal group) is written down to its fair value less cost to sell, continuing to depreciate (amortize) the asset reduces its carrying amount below its fair value less cost to sell. The Board concluded that it would be inappropriate to reduce the carrying amount of the asset to an amount below its fair value. The Board further observed that because fair value less cost to sell is required to be evaluated each period, a subsequent decline in the fair value of the asset while it is classified as held for sale will be appropriately reflected in the period of decline.

Long-lived asset acquired in a purchase business combination

B85. Prior to the issuance of Statement 121, EITF Issue No. 87-11, "Allocation of Purchase Price to Assets to Be Sold," provided guidance on the accounting for a disposal group to be sold that was newly acquired in a purchase business combination, including, but not limited to, a segment of a business covered by Opinion 30. The guidance in Issue 87-11 extended the measurement provisions of Opinion 30 in determining the purchase price allocation under Opinion 16. Accordingly, the disposal group was measured at the lower of its carrying amount or net realizable value, adjusted for future operating losses.

B86. Statement 121 subsequently required that a long-lived asset (disposal group) to be sold other than a segment of a business covered by Opinion 30 be measured at the lower of its carrying amount or fair value less cost to sell. However, it did not nullify Issue 87-11 to reflect that change for a long-lived asset (disposal group) to be sold that was newly acquired in a purchase business combination. Consequently, in implementing Statement 121, questions emerged about the impact of that Statement on Issue 87-11. The primary issue was whether and, if so, how the measurement guidance provided by Issue 87-11 should be applied to a long-lived asset (disposal group) that was newly acquired in a purchase business combination. A related issue was how to account for the results of operations of the asset (disposal group) while it was classified as held for sale and whether future operating losses could be considered in measuring the fair value less cost to sell of the asset (disposal group). The EITF discussed that issue in Issue No. 95-21, "Accounting for Assets to Be Disposed Of Acquired in a Purchase Business Combination," but did not reach a consensus.

B87. This Statement resolves Issue 95-21 by requiring that a long-lived asset (disposal group) classified as held for sale be measured at the lower of its carrying amount or fair value less cost to sell, whether previously held and used or newly acquired. This Statement also requires that the results of operations of a long-lived asset (disposal group) classified as held for sale be recognized in the period in which those operations occur, whether reported in continuing operations or in discontinued operations. Therefore, this Statement nullifies Issue 87-11.

Grouping Assets and Liabilities to Be Sold

B88. During its deliberations leading to the Exposure Draft, the Board noted that long-lived assets often are sold together with other assets and liabilities as a group. The Board observed that, as is the case for long-lived assets to be held and used, measuring assets and liabilities classified as held for sale as a group raises the issue of when, if ever, it is appropriate to offset unrealized losses on some assets (liabilities) with unrealized gains on other assets (liabilities). In addition, because liabilities often can be settled separately from the sale of assets, measuring assets and liabilities classified as held for sale as a group also could permit an entity to achieve a desired result by selectively designating the liabilities to be included in a disposal group. To prevent grouping from being used inappropriately to offset unrealized losses with unrealized gains, the Board initially decided that the plan-of-sale criteria should address when assets and liabilities should be classified as held for sale and measured as a group.

B89. The Exposure Draft proposed a criterion that, to classify assets and liabilities as held for sale as a group, the estimated proceeds expected to result from the sale of the group must exceed those that would result from the sale of the assets of the group individually. The Board reasoned that because estimated

proceeds reflect the underlying economics of an expected sale transaction, that criterion would provide evidence of an entity's commitment to a plan to sell assets (and liabilities) as a group. Several respondents to the Exposure Draft disagreed with a criterion based on estimated net proceeds, stating that proceeds alone do not necessarily reflect the total (direct and indirect) economic benefit that may result from the sale of assets (and liabilities) as a group. They said that in many situations, valid reasons may exist to sell assets and liabilities as a group even though the estimated net proceeds expected to result from the sale of that group may be less than those that would result from the sale of the assets individually. They also said that in other situations, particularly those in which several assets are to be sold as a group, a requirement to estimate the net proceeds that would result from the sale of assets individually would be unduly burdensome and costly.

B90. Upon reconsideration, the Board decided to eliminate a criterion based on estimated net proceeds. Instead, the Board decided that assets and liabilities should be classified as held for sale as a group if (a) the assets will be sold as a group in a single transaction and (b) the liabilities are directly related to the assets and will be transferred in that transaction. The Board concluded that if assets and liabilities will be sold as a group in a single transaction, accounting for those assets and liabilities as held for sale as a group is appropriate.

Allocation of a loss

B91. During its deliberations leading to the Exposure Draft, the Board decided that this Statement should provide guidance for allocating a loss recognized for a disposal group classified as held for sale that includes assets and liabilities, principally to facilitate the requirement of this Statement to present those assets and liabilities separately in the asset and liability sections of the statement of financial position. The Exposure Draft proposed that a loss be allocated, first, by adjusting the carrying amounts of the liabilities of the group to their fair values and, then, by adjusting the carrying amounts of the long-lived assets of the group by the remaining amount, if any. The Board reasoned that the fair values of the liabilities included in a disposal group generally would be determinable and that the presentation of those liabilities at their fair values would improve the usefulness of the information provided by the statement of financial position.

B92. Upon further consideration, the Board subsequently decided not to retain that allocation method. Instead, the Board decided that because other accounting pronouncements prescribe the accounting for assets and liabilities not covered by this Statement that are included in a disposal group, a loss recognized for a disposal group classified as held for sale should reduce only the carrying amounts of the long-lived assets of the group. The Board concluded that the allocation method for a loss recognized for a disposal group classified as held for sale provides a reasonable basis for reporting both the assets and liabilities of the disposal group in the statement of financial position.

Changes to a Plan of Sale

Reversal of a decision to sell a long-lived asset classified as held for sale

B93. In implementing Statement 121, questions emerged about the required accounting if an entity subsequently decides not to sell a long-lived asset classified as held for sale. Prior to this Statement, other accounting pronouncements provided related guidance, but only for certain assets. If the asset previously was acquired through foreclosure, SOP 92-3 required that the asset be reclassified as held and used and measured at what would have been its carrying amount had the asset been continuously classified as held and used since the time of foreclosure. If the asset previously was acquired in a purchase business combination, EITF Issue No. 90-6, "Accounting for Certain Events Not Addressed in Issue No. 87-11 Relating to an Acquired Operating Unit to Be Sold," required that the asset be reclassified as held and used and measured as under SOP 92-3 if the subsequent decision not to sell was made within one year. If the asset was a segment accounted for as a discontinued operation under Opinion 30, EITF Issue No. 90-16, "Accounting for Discontinued Operations Subsequently Retained," provided guidance on the reclassification to continuing operations of amounts previously reported in discontinued operations.

B94. The Board decided that a long-lived asset to be reclassified as held and used should be measured at the lower of (a) its fair value at the date of the subsequent decision not to sell or (b) its carrying amount on a held-and-used basis at the date of the decision to sell, adjusted for any depreciation (amortization) expense that would have been recognized had the asset been continuously classified as held and used. Therefore, this Statement nullifies Issues 90-6 and 90-16.

B95. The Board considered but rejected an approach that, based on the guidance in SOP 92-3 and Issue 90-6, would have measured a long-lived asset to be reclassified as held and used at what would have been its carrying amount had the asset been continuously classified as held and used (held-and-used approach). The Board observed that a held-and-used approach could measure an asset previously written down to its fair value less cost to sell at an amount greater than its fair value at the date of the subsequent decision not to sell. That would be the case if, for example, the adjusted carrying amount of the asset is recoverable at the date of the subsequent decision not to sell. The Board concluded that it would be inappropriate to write up the carrying amount of a long-lived asset to an amount greater than its fair value based solely on an undiscounted cash flows recoverability test.

B96. Some respondents to the Exposure Draft suggested that the Board reconsider a held-and-used approach. They said that if the adjusted carrying amount of the asset is recoverable at the date of the subsequent decision not to sell, measuring the asset at its fair value would be inconsistent with the requirements of this Statement for other assets to be held and used, in particular, the requirement to write down the carrying amount of a long-lived asset (asset group) only if it is not recoverable. During its redeliberations of the Exposure Draft, the Board considered that inconsistency but again rejected that approach for the reason discussed in paragraph B95.

Removal of an individual asset or liability from disposal group

B97. In view of its decision that assets and liabilities classified as held for sale should be measured as a group, the Board decided that this Statement should address the accounting if an entity subsequently removes an individual asset or liability from a disposal group previously classified as held for sale. The Board considered situations in which an entity decides not to sell an individual asset of the group, decides to sell an individual asset separately from the group, or settles before its maturity an individual liability of the group.

B98. The Exposure Draft would have required that the remaining long-lived assets of the disposal group be measured individually at the lower of their carrying amounts or fair values less cost to sell whenever an individual asset or liability is removed from the group. Several respondents to the Exposure Draft disagreed with that proposed requirement. They said that in many situations, valid reasons may exist for removing an individual asset or liability from a disposal group that have no bearing on an entity's intent and ability to sell the remaining assets and liabilities as a group. They also said that in other situations, particularly those in which several long-lived assets are included in a disposal group, a requirement to measure those assets individually would be unduly burdensome and costly.

B99. The Board considered those concerns raised by respondents. The Board decided that the remaining long-lived assets of the disposal group should be measured individually at the lower of their fair values less cost to sell only if the plan-of-sale criteria in paragraph 30 are no longer met for that group. The Board concluded that those criteria provide sufficient evidence of a commitment to a plan to sell the remaining assets and liabilities as a group and that continuing to account for those assets and liabilities as held for sale as a group is appropriate. In addition, the Board observed that for some disposal groups, there may not be significant offsetting issues.

Reporting and Disclosure of Long-Lived Assets (Disposal Groups) to Be Disposed Of

Reporting Discontinued Operations

B100. Prior to this Statement, guidance on reporting discontinued operations was provided by Opinion 30, which limited that reporting to the results of operations of a segment of a business to be disposed of. Paragraph 13 of Opinion 30 defined a segment of a business as a "component of an entity whose activities represent a separate major line of business or class of customer." Opinion 30 required that the results of operations of a segment to be disposed of be reported in discontinued operations, separately from continuing operations, in the period in which the measurement date occurred and in prior periods presented.

B101. During its deliberations leading to the Exposure Draft, the Board concluded that reporting discontinued operations separately from continuing operations provides investors, creditors, and others with information that is relevant in assessing the effects of disposal transactions on the ongoing operations of an entity. FASB Concepts Statement No. 1, *Objectives of Financial Reporting by Business Enterprises,* states, "... financial reporting should provide information to help investors, creditors, and others assess the amounts, timing, and uncertainty of prospective

net cash inflows to the related enterprise" (paragraph 37; footnote reference omitted). FASB Concepts Statement No. 5, *Recognition and Measurement in Financial Statements of Business Enterprises,* further states:

> Classification in financial statements facilitates analysis by grouping items with essentially similar characteristics and separating items with essentially different characteristics. Analysis aimed at objectives such as predicting amounts, timing, and uncertainty of future cash flows requires financial information segregated into reasonably homogenous groups. For example, components of financial statements that consist of items that have similar characteristics in one or more respects, such as continuity or recurrence, stability, risk, and reliability, are likely to have more predictive value than if their characteristics are dissimilar. [paragraph 20]

B102. The Board observed that the Opinion 30 definition of a segment of a business has been effective in distinguishing disposal transactions that are likely to have a significant effect on the ongoing operations of the entity. However, the Board also observed that the disposal of other disposal groups that are not reported separately in discontinued operations because they are not segments of a business covered by Opinion 30 also might have a significant effect on the ongoing operations of the entity. To improve the usefulness of the information provided to users, the Board decided to broaden the reporting of discontinued operations, consistent with the recommendation made by the AICPA Special Committee on Financial Reporting in its 1994 report, *Improving Business Reporting—A Customer Focus,* which states:

> Discontinued operations is defined in current practice as a component of a company whose activities represent a separate major line of business or class of customer. That definition should be broadened to include all significant discontinued operations whose assets and results of operations and activities can be distinguished physically and operationally and for business-reporting purposes. [page 138]

B103. The Exposure Draft proposed to broaden the reporting of discontinued operations to include the results of operations of a significant component of an entity, which was defined as a disposal group with operations and assets that can be clearly distinguished physically, operationally, and for financial reporting purposes from the rest of the entity. However, the Board chose not to define the term *significant* to allow for judgment in determining whether, based on facts and circumstances unique to a particular entity, a disposal transaction should be reported in discontinued operations.

B104. Nearly all of the respondents to the Exposure Draft that commented on the proposed requirements for reporting discontinued operations agreed with the Board's decision to broaden the reporting of discontinued operations. However, many of those respondents said that to promote consistent application of the Statement, the Board should provide additional guidance for determining the significance of a component of an entity. Many respondents also referred to the interaction of the significance notion proposed in the Exposure Draft with the materiality concept discussed in SEC Staff Accounting Bulletin No. 99, *Materiality*. Those respondents asked the Board to clarify whether the criteria for assessing materiality in SAB 99 also should apply in assessing significance.

B105. During its redeliberations of the Exposure Draft, the Board decided to eliminate the significance notion from the definition of a component of an entity. The Board concluded that the requirements for reporting discontinued operations should not focus on whether a component of an entity is significant or otherwise incorporate a quantitative criterion. Instead, the Board concluded that those requirements should focus on whether a component of an entity has operations and cash flows that can be clearly distinguished from the rest of the entity, consistent with its objective of broadening the reporting of discontinued operations.

B106. The Board also decided to eliminate the requirement proposed in the Exposure Draft that assets be eliminated in a disposal transaction as a condition for reporting discontinued operations. The Board observed that the emphasis on assets would preclude a component of an entity from being reported as a discontinued operation unless the disposal transaction involved all of the assets of the component—even if the component is a separate business and was an operating segment under FASB Statement No. 131, *Disclosures about Segments of an Enterprise and Related Information*. The Board also decided to eliminate the Exposure Draft's reference to disposal activities that are incident to the evolution of an entity's business, which would have prohibited those disposal activities from being reported as discontinued operations. As noted by some respondents, many disposal transactions could be viewed as incident to the evolution of an entity's business.

B107. As revised, the requirements for reporting discontinued operations focus on whether a component of an entity has operations and cash flows that can be clearly distinguished from the rest of the entity and whether those operations and cash flows have been (or will be) eliminated from the ongoing operations of the entity in the disposal transaction. Given the emphasis on operations, the Board decided to incorporate as a condition for reporting discontinued operations the requirement that an entity have no significant continuing involvement in the operations of a component after it is disposed of. The Board concluded that it would be inappropriate to report a disposal transaction as a discontinued operation in circumstances in which an entity will have significant continuing involvement in the operations of a component after it is disposed of.

B108. During its deliberations of this Statement, the Board considered but rejected other approaches that would have reported in discontinued operations the results of operations of other asset groups as defined in other existing accounting pronouncements. One approach would have used the definition of an *operating segment* in paragraph 10 of Statement 131. Another approach would have used the definition of a *reporting unit* in Statement 142. Yet another approach would have used the definition of a *business* in EITF Issue No. 98-3, "Determining Whether a Nonmonetary Transaction Involves Receipt of Productive Assets or of a Business." The Board concluded that those approaches would not necessarily broaden the reporting of discontinued operations beyond that previously permitted by Opinion 30.

B109. The Board acknowledges that judgment will be required in distinguishing components of an entity from other disposal groups. However, the Board affirmed its conclusion in the Exposure Draft that, on balance, the advantages of broadening the presentation of discontinued operations (primarily enhanced decision usefulness) outweigh the disadvantages of broadening that presentation (primarily the possibility that the use of inconsistent judgments will affect the comparability of information reported about disposal transactions).

Subsequent adjustments to discontinued operations

B110. This Statement specifies requirements for reporting in discontinued operations adjustments in the current period that are related to the disposal of a component of an entity in a prior period. Those requirements carry forward certain of the provisions of other accounting pronouncements relating to the disposal of an Opinion 30 segment that are still relevant.

B111. Paragraphs 44(a) and (b) of this Statement refer to adjustments relating to the resolution of contingencies that arise pursuant to the terms of the disposal transaction, as well as to those that arise from, and that are directly related to, the operations of a component of an entity prior to its disposal. Paragraph 25 of Opinion 30 specified requirements for reporting in discontinued operations adjustments related to the disposal of a segment of a business that was reported in a prior period. It did not, however, specify the types of adjustments to which that reporting was intended to apply. Paragraph 25 of Opinion 30, as amended by FASB Statement No. 16, *Prior Period Adjustments,* stated:

> Circumstances attendant to disposals of a segment of a business and extraordinary items frequently require estimates, for example, of associated costs and occasionally of associated revenue, based on judgment and evaluation of the facts known at the time of first accounting for the event. Each adjustment in the current period of a loss on disposal of a business segment or of an element of an extraordinary item that was reported in a prior period should be separately disclosed as to year of origin, nature, and amount and classified separately in the current period in the same manner as the original item. If the adjustment is the correction of an error, the provisions of APB Opinion No. 20, *Accounting Changes,* paragraphs 36 and 37 should be applied.

B112. SEC Staff Accounting Bulletin No. 93, *Accounting and Disclosures Relating to Discontinued Operations,* clarified for public enterprises the reporting required by paragraph 25 of Opinion 30 as follows:

> The [SEC] staff believes that the provisions of paragraph 25 apply only to adjustments that are necessary to reflect new information about events that have occurred that

becomes available prior to disposal of the business, to reflect the actual timing and terms of the disposal when it is consummated, and to reflect the resolution of contingencies associated with that business, such as warranties and environmental liabilities retained by the seller.

B113. Paragraph 44(c) of this Statement refers to adjustments (gains or losses) associated with the settlement of employee benefit plan obligations (pension, postemployment benefits other than pensions, and other postemployment benefits). Paragraph 3 of FASB Statement No. 88, *Employers' Accounting for Settlements and Curtailments of Defined Benefit Pension Plans and for Termination Benefits,* defines *settlement* as:

> . . . a transaction that (a) is an irrevocable action, (b) relieves the employer (or the plan) of primary responsibility for a pension benefit obligation, and (c) eliminates significant risks related to the obligation and the assets used to effect the settlement.

B114. In accordance with FASB Statement No. 43, *Accounting for Compensated Absences,* Statement 88, and FASB Statement No. 106, *Employers' Accounting for Postretirement Benefits Other Than Pensions,* as amended by this Statement, settlement gains or losses should be recognized in the period in which the settlement occurs. Such gains or losses should be reported in discontinued operations if the settlement is directly related to the disposal of a component of an entity. The Board concluded that a settlement is directly related to the disposal of a component of an entity if (a) there is a demonstrated cause-and-effect relationship and (b) the settlement occurs no later than one year following the disposal transaction, unless it is delayed by events or circumstances beyond an entity's control.

B115. The requirement that a demonstrated cause-and-effect relationship exist incorporates guidance from Statement 88 related to the disposal of a segment of a business previously covered by Opinion 30. Specifically, the answer to Question 37 in the FASB Special Report, *A Guide to Implementation of Statement 88 on Employers' Accounting for Settlements and Curtailments of Defined Benefit Pension Plans and for Termination Benefits,* clarifies that a cause-and-effect relationship can be demonstrated if, for example, settlement of a pension benefit obligation for those employees affected by the sale is a necessary condition of the sale. It further clarified that "in a disposal of all or a portion of a line of business, the timing of a settlement may be at the discretion of the employer. If the employer simply chooses to settle a pension benefit obligation at the time of the sale, the resulting coincidence of events is not, in and of itself, an indication of a cause-and-effect relationship. . . ." In addition, the Board reasoned that a decision to settle later than one year after the disposal date is unlikely to be a direct consequence of the disposal transaction unless that decision is delayed beyond one year by events and circumstances beyond an entity's control.

Reporting Disposal Gains or Losses in Continuing Operations

B116. This Statement retains the requirements of Statement 121 to report gains or losses recognized on long-lived assets (disposal groups) to be sold that are not components of an entity presented in discontinued operations as a component of income from continuing operations. In Statement 121, the Board concluded that the requirements for reporting gains or losses recognized on long-lived assets (disposal groups) to be sold should be consistent with the requirements for reporting impairment losses recognized on long-lived assets (asset groups) to be held and used. The Board affirmed that conclusion in this Statement.

Reporting Long-Lived Assets (Disposal Groups) Classified as Held for Sale

B117. Under Opinion 30, the assets and liabilities of a segment of a business accounted for as a discontinued operation were permitted to be offset and reported in the statement of financial position "net." Footnote 7 of paragraph 18(d) of Opinion 30 explained:

> Consideration should be given to disclosing this information by segregation in the balance sheet of the net assets and liabilities (current and noncurrent) of the discontinued segment. Only liabilities which will be assumed by others should be designated as liabilities of the discontinued segment.

B118. The Board noted that the reporting previously permitted under Opinion 30 is an exception to the general rule that assets and liabilities should not be offset. Assets and liabilities that an entity expects to transfer to a buyer in connection with the sale of assets do not meet the conditions for offsetting in FASB

Interpretation No. 39, *Offsetting of Amounts Related to Certain Contracts*. Paragraph 5 of Interpretation 39 carries forward from APB Opinion No. 10, *Omnibus Opinion—1966*, the general principle that ". . . the offsetting of assets and liabilities in the balance sheet is improper except where a right of setoff exists." In addition, liabilities that an entity expects to transfer to a potential buyer in a disposal transaction do not qualify for derecognition prior to being assumed by a purchaser (or otherwise settled). Paragraph 42 of Concepts Statement 6 states, "Once incurred, a liability continues as a liability of the entity until the entity settles it, or another event or circumstance discharges it or removes the entity's responsibility to settle it."

B119. The Board decided that the assets and liabilities of a disposal group classified as held for sale should not be offset in the statement of financial position. Accordingly, this Statement eliminates the exception to consolidation for a subsidiary for which control is likely to be temporary in paragraph 2 of ARB No. 51, *Consolidated Financial Statements,* as amended by FASB Statement No. 94, *Consolidation of All Majority-Owned Subsidiaries.* The Board concluded that for any disposal group, information about the nature of both the assets and the liabilities of an asset group classified as held for sale is useful to users. Separately presenting those items in the statement of financial position provides information that is relevant and faithfully reports an entity's assets and its liabilities. Also, it segregates (a) those assets that have been measured at the lower of carrying amount or fair value less cost to sell and are not being depreciated from (b) those assets that are measured on a cost basis and are being depreciated. Therefore, this Statement requires that those assets and liabilities be presented separately in the asset and liability sections of the statement of financial position.

B120. The Board decided not to specify whether assets and liabilities held for sale should be classified as current or noncurrent in the statement of financial position. The Board concluded that because requirements for classifying assets and liabilities as current or noncurrent are provided by other accounting pronouncements, including ARB No. 43, Chapter 3, "Working Capital," further guidance in this Statement is not needed.

Disclosure

B121. The Board concluded that the financial statement disclosures previously required by paragraph 19 of Statement 121 and by paragraph 18 of

Opinion 30 provide information that is useful in understanding the effects of the disposal of a long-lived asset (disposal group), including a component of an entity. In the Exposure Draft, the Board decided to retain those disclosures that were still relevant, including the requirement of Opinion 30 to disclose the proceeds from a disposal transaction. Some respondents to the Exposure Draft stated that disclosure of proceeds is of little value, noting that information about cash proceeds is now provided in the statement of cash flows. The Board agreed and decided to eliminate that requirement.

Amendment to Statement 67

B122. Statement 121 amended FASB Statement No. 67, *Accounting for Costs and Initial Rental Operations of Real Estate Projects,* to apply (a) its provisions for long-lived assets to be held and used to land to be developed and projects under development and (b) its provisions for long-lived assets to be disposed of to all completed real estate projects. At that time, the Board believed that assets under development were similar to long-lived assets to be held and used and that all completed projects were "clearly assets to be disposed of." Paragraphs 124–126 of Statement 121 explained:

The Exposure Draft proposed amending FASB Statements No. 66, *Accounting for Sales of Real Estate,* and No. 67, *Accounting for Costs and Initial Rental Operations of Real Estate Projects,* to change the lower of carrying amount or net realizable value measure to the lower of carrying amount or fair value less cost to sell measure. The Board initially decided to amend those Statements to conform the measurement of assets subject to those Statements with the measurement of assets to be disposed of.

Some real estate development organizations objected to the proposed amendments in the Exposure Draft. They questioned why the scope of a project on long-lived assets included real estate development. They argued that real estate development assets are more like inventory and, therefore, the lower of carrying amount or net realizable value measure is more relevant. They did not address, however, why that measure would be more appropriate for real estate inventory than the lower of cost or market measure required for inventory under paragraph 4 of ARB No. 43, Chapter 4, "Inventory Pricing."

Others disagreed with the inventory argument, asserting that although real estate development assets will eventually be disposed of, the provisions of the Exposure Draft would have required long-term real estate projects to recognize impairments far too frequently. They said that nearly all long-term projects, regardless of their overall profitability, would become subject to write-downs in their early stages of development, only to be reversed later in the life of the project due to revised estimates of fair value less cost to sell. The Board considered alternative approaches to measuring those real estate assets. The Board decided to apply the provisions of paragraphs 4–7 to land to be developed and projects under development and to apply paragraphs 15–17 to completed projects. The Board believes that assets under development are similar to assets held for use, whereas completed projects are clearly assets to be disposed of.

B123. In this Statement, the Board reconsidered the amendment to Statement 67, noting that a completed real estate project might be held available for occupancy (either for rental or for use in the entity's operations), in which case the asset would be similar to a long-lived asset to be held and used. The Board concluded that the provisions of this Statement for long-lived assets to be held and used should be applied to those real estate assets. Therefore, this Statement revises the previous amendment to Statement 67. The provisions of this Statement for long-lived assets to be held and used should be applied to completed real estate projects to be held available for occupancy. The provisions of this Statement for long-lived assets to be disposed of by sale should be applied to completed real estate projects to be sold.

B124. In implementing Statement 121, questions also emerged about the application of its impairment provisions to rental real estate property to be held and used. The primary issue was whether property-related assets should be grouped together with the real estate property in determining whether to recognize, and in measuring, an impairment loss. Such property-related assets include accrued rent and deferred leasing costs recognized for operating leases in accordance with FASB Statement No. 13, *Accounting for Leases* (paragraph 19 and paragraph 5(m), as amended by FASB Statement No. 91, *Accounting for Nonrefundable Fees and Costs Associated with Originating or Acquiring Loans and Initial Direct*

Costs of Leases), and FASB Technical Bulletin No. 85-3, *Accounting for Operating Leases with Scheduled Rent Increases.* The Board concluded that the provisions of paragraphs 10–14 of this Statement for grouping long-lived assets to be held and used should be applied to those real estate assets.

Benefits and Costs

B125. The mission of the FASB is to establish and improve standards of financial accounting and reporting for the guidance and education of the public, including preparers, auditors, and users of financial information. In fulfilling that mission, the Board endeavors to determine that a proposed standard will fill a significant need and that the costs imposed to meet that standard, as compared with other alternatives, are justified in relation to the overall benefits of the resulting information. Although the costs to implement a new standard may not be borne evenly, investors and creditors—both present and potential—as well as others, benefit from improvements in financial reporting, thereby facilitating the functioning of markets for capital and credit and the efficient allocation of resources in the economy.

B126. The Board determined that the requirements in this Statement will result in improved financial reporting. In Statement 121, the Board determined that the information provided to users of financial statements about long-lived assets could be improved by eliminating inconsistencies in the accounting and reporting of the impairment of those assets, thereby improving comparability in financial reporting. In this Statement, the Board determined that the information provided to users of financial statements about long-lived assets could be further improved by eliminating inconsistencies in the accounting and reporting of the disposal of those assets. As discussed in FASB Concepts Statement No. 2, *Qualitative Characteristics of Accounting Information,* providing comparable financial information enables users to identify similarities in and differences between two sets of economic events.

B127. The Board believes that the incremental costs of implementing this Statement have been minimized principally by retaining certain of the fundamental provisions of Statement 121 that are already in effect, in particular, its recognition and measurement provisions for the impairment of long-lived assets to be held and used and its measurement provisions for long-lived assets classified as held for sale. In addition, the Board decided to eliminate from this Statement certain of the proposals in the Exposure Draft that would have changed those existing requirements. Further, the provisions of this Statement generally are to be applied prospectively. Although there may be one-time costs for changes needed to apply the accounting requirements of this Statement, the benefits from more consistent, comparable, and reliable information will be ongoing. The Board believes that the benefits of this Statement outweigh the costs of implementing it.

Effective Date and Transition

B128. The Board decided, except as follows, to require that this Statement be effective for financial statements issued for fiscal years beginning after December 15, 2001, and interim periods within those fiscal years. The Board decided that the provisions relating to disposal transactions should be effective for disposal transactions initiated by a commitment to a plan after the earlier of the effective date of this Statement or the entity's initial application of this Statement. The Board believes that that effective date provides sufficient time for entities and their auditors to analyze, interpret, and prepare for implementation of the provisions of this Statement.

B129. This Statement requires that impairment losses resulting from the initial application of its provisions for long-lived assets to be held and used be reported in the period in which the recognition criteria are initially applied and met based on facts and circumstances existing at that date. This Statement, like Statement 121, requires consideration of the continuing effect of events or changes in circumstances that occurred prior to the Statement's initial application. The Board recognizes the benefits of comparative financial statements but questions the ability of entities to reconstruct estimates of future cash flows based on assessments of events and circumstances as they existed in prior periods and without the use of hindsight.

B130. This Statement requires prospective application of its provisions for disposal transactions, including its provisions for the presentation of discontinued operations, and prohibits retroactive application.[32] The Board concluded that obtaining or developing the information necessary to apply this Statement retroactively could be burdensome for many entities. In addition, the Board observed that information about disposal transactions generally is disclosed by public enterprises (for example, in management's discussion and analysis and in press releases). Disposal transactions involving a component of an entity that are "grandfathered" under Statement 121 would continue to be reported in continuing operations, while disposal transactions involving a segment of a business that are "grandfathered" under Opinion 30 would continue to be reported in discontinued operations. The Board noted that segregating those disposal transactions would mitigate the effect of having different measurement approaches under Statement 121 and Opinion 30—one based on the fair value less cost to sell and the other based on net realizable value. The Board concluded that prospective application for disposal transactions is the most reasonable and practical transition approach when considered together with the need for consistent transition provisions for disposal transactions and the cost associated with retroactive application.

B131. The Board observed that for long-lived assets (disposal groups) to be sold that meet the criteria for a qualifying plan of sale when this Statement is initially applied, a cumulative-effect adjustment would not require an entity to retroactively derive fair values for those assets to be disposed of. Rather, the adjustment would be based on fair values at the date this Statement is initially applied. The Board concluded, however, that it would be inappropriate to require retroactive application for some, but not all, of the provisions for disposal transactions. The Board expects that, based on the requirements of previous accounting pronouncements that address the accounting for disposal transactions, many disposal transactions that are in process when this Statement is initially applied will be completed within one year. Therefore, prospective application should not have a significant, continuing impact on the comparability and consistency of the financial statements.

B132. The Board observed, however, that in some cases assets that are classified as held for disposal when this Statement is initially applied may not meet the criteria in paragraph 30 by the end of the fiscal year in which the Statement is initially applied. The

Board concluded that it would be inappropriate to allow the accounting for those assets to be "grandfathered" indefinitely. Doing so could impair the comparability and consistency of the financial statements and extend the provisions of Opinion 30 that require the accrual of future operating losses for several reporting periods. Therefore, for a long-lived asset (disposal group) classified as held for disposal when this Statement is initially applied, the asset (disposal group) must be reclassified as held and used in accordance with paragraph 38 if the criteria in paragraph 30 are not met by the end of the fiscal year in which this Statement is initially applied.

B133. This Statement requires reclassification of previously issued statements of financial position included for comparative purposes to reflect application of the reporting provisions in paragraph 46 for long-lived assets and disposal groups, including a temporarily controlled subsidiary, classified as held for sale under Statement 121 (that is, the prohibition of offsetting assets and liabilities). The Board believes that requiring reclassification will improve the comparability of those financial statements. Moreover, because that reporting affects only how the assets and liabilities of disposal groups previously classified as held for sale are displayed, the Board concluded that the information necessary to disaggregate and separately report those assets and liabilities would be available.

Appendix C

AMENDMENTS TO EXISTING PRONOUNCEMENTS

C1. This Statement supersedes FASB Statement No. 121, *Accounting for the Impairment of Long-Lived Assets and for Long-Lived Assets to Be Disposed Of.*

C2. Accounting Research Bulletin No. 51, *Consolidated Financial Statements,* is amended as follows:

a. In the last sentence of paragraph 2, as amended by FASB Statement No. 94, *Consolidation of All Majority-Owned Subsidiaries,* the phrase *is likely to be temporary or if it* is deleted.

b. Paragraph 12 is deleted.

---

[32]The prohibition on retroactive application does not extend to the provisions of this Statement for reporting discontinued operations after this Statement is initially applied.

C3. In paragraphs 21 and the heading preceding it, 30(e), and 31 of APB Opinion No. 28, *Interim Financial Reporting,* all references to *segment of a business* or *segments of a business* are replaced by *component of an entity* or *components of an entity,* respectively.

C4. APB Opinion No. 29, *Accounting for Nonmonetary Transactions,* is amended as follows:

a. The following footnote is added to the end of the first sentence of paragraph 21 and to the first sentence of paragraph 23 after the parenthetical phrase:

>*An indicated impairment of value of a long-lived asset covered by FASB Statement No. 144, *Accounting for the Impairment or Disposal of Long-Lived Assets,* shall be determined in accordance with paragraph 29 of that Statement.

C5. APB Opinion No. 30, *Reporting the Results of Operations—Reporting the Effects of Disposal of a Segment of a Business, and Extraordinary, Unusual and Infrequently Occurring Events and Transactions,* is amended as follows:

a. In paragraph 3, *to specify the accounting and reporting for disposal of a segment of a business, (4)* is deleted.

b. Paragraphs 8 and 9 and footnote 2 are deleted.

c. Paragraph 11 is amended as follows:

(1) The following footnote is added to the first sentence immediately following *discontinued operations*:

>*Paragraphs 41–44 of Statement 144 address the reporting of discontinued operations.

(2) In the second sentence, *segment of a business* is replaced by *component of an entity.*

d. Paragraphs 13–18 and the heading preceding those paragraphs are deleted.

e. Footnotes 5–7 are deleted.

f. Paragraph 23 is amended as follows:

(1) The references to *segment of a business* are replaced by *component of an entity.*

(2) The last sentence is replaced by the following:

>Disposals of a component of an entity shall be accounted for and presented in the income statement in accordance with Statement 144 even though the circumstances of the disposal meet the criteria specified in paragraph 20.

g. Paragraph 25 is amended as follows:

(1) In the first sentence, *disposals of a segment of a business and* is deleted.

(2) In the second sentence, *of a loss on disposal of a business segment or* is deleted.

C6. AICPA Accounting Interpretation 1, "Illustration of the Application of APB Opinion No. 30," is amended as follows:

a. The first question and its interpretation are amended as follows:

(1) The interpretation and first discussion are deleted.

(2) The following interpretation is inserted before the second discussion:

>*Interpretation*—The criteria for extraordinary items classification should be considered. That is:

>Does the event or transaction meet both criteria of *unusual nature* and *infrequency of occurrence?*

b. The second question and its interpretation are superseded.

C7. In FASB Statement No. 19, *Financial Accounting and Reporting by Oil and Gas Producing Companies,* paragraph 44(a) is replaced by the following:

a. A transfer of assets used in oil and gas producing activities related to unproved properties in exchange for other assets also used in oil and gas producing activities.*

---

*If assets used in oil and gas producing activities related to proved properties are transferred in exchange for other assets also used in oil and gas producing activities, a loss, if any, shall be recognized in accordance with paragraph 29 of FASB Statement No. 144, *Accounting for the Impairment or Disposal of Long-Lived Assets.*

C8. In FASB Statement No. 43, *Accounting for Compensated Absences,* the last sentence of paragraph 2, as added by FASB Statement No. 112, *Employers' Accounting for Postemployment Benefits,* is deleted.

C9. In FASB Statement No. 66, *Accounting for Sales of Real Estate,* the following is added to the end of the second sentence of paragraph 65:

> unless the property has been classified as held for sale in accordance with paragraph 30 of FASB Statement No. 144, *Accounting for the Impairment or Disposal of Long-Lived Assets.*

C10. In FASB Statement No. 67, *Accounting for Costs and Initial Rental Operations of Real Estate Projects,* the first and second sentences of paragraph 24 are replaced by the following:

> The provisions in Statement 144 for long-lived assets to be disposed of by sale shall apply to a real estate project, or parts thereof, that is substantially completed and that is to be sold. The provisions in that Statement for long-lived assets to be held and used shall apply to real estate held for development, including property to be developed in the future as well as that currently under development, and to a real estate project, or parts thereof, that is substantially completed and that is to be held and used (for example, for rental). Determining whether the carrying amounts of real estate projects require recognition of an impairment loss shall be based on an evaluation of individual projects.

C11. FASB Statement No. 88, *Employers' Accounting for Settlements and Curtailments of Defined Benefit Pension Plans and for Termination Benefits,* is amended as follows:

a. In paragraph 6(a), *segment of a business* is replaced by *component of an entity.*

b. Paragraphs 8 and 16 and the heading preceding paragraph 16 are deleted.

c. Paragraph 57 is amended as follows:

   (1) In the title of Example 3A, *segment* is replaced by *component.*

   (2) In Example 3A, the reference to *segment of its business* is replaced by *component of the entity.*

   (3) Footnote d to Example 3A is deleted.

C12. FASB Statement No. 106, *Employers' Accounting for Postretirement Benefits Other Than Pensions,* is amended as follows:

a. In paragraph 96(a), *segment of a business* is replaced by *component of an entity.*

b. Paragraph 103 and the heading preceding it are deleted.

C13. In paragraph 8(c) of FASB Statement No. 115, *Accounting for Certain Investments in Debt and Equity Securities,* the reference to *segment* is replaced by *component of an entity.*

C14. In the last sentence of paragraph 164 of FASB Statement No. 117, *Financial Statements of Not-for-Profit Organizations,* the reference to *a discontinued operating segment* is replaced by *reporting discontinued operations.*

C15. Paragraph 9 of FASB Statement No. 123, *Accounting for Stock-Based Compensation,* is amended as follows:

a. In the first sentence, *with the same meaning as in FASB Statement No. 121, Accounting for the Impairment of Long-Lived Assets and for Long-Lived Assets to Be Disposed Of.* is replaced by *to refer to.*

b. In the second sentence, *Statement 121 says that the fair value of an asset is . . .* is deleted.

c. The reference to *[paragraph 7]* at the end of the quotation is deleted.

C16. Footnote 18 to paragraph 44 of FASB Statement No. 141, *Business Combinations,* is deleted.

C17. FASB Statement No. 142, *Goodwill and Other Intangible Assets,* is amended as follows:

a. Paragraph 7 is deleted.

b. Paragraph 15 is amended as follows:

   (1) In the first sentence, *Statement 121* is replaced by *FASB Statement No. 144, Accounting for the Impairment or Disposal of Long-Lived Assets,* and *paragraphs 4–11* are replaced by *paragraphs 7–24.*

   (2) In the second sentence, *Statement 121* is replaced by *Statement 144.*

c. The second (parenthetical) sentence of paragraph 17 is replaced by *(Paragraph 8 of Statement 144 includes examples of impairment indicators.).*

d. In paragraph 28(f), *Statement 121* is replaced by *Statement 144.*

e. In the second sentence of paragraph 29, *Statement 121* is replaced by *Statement 144.*

f. Footnote 22 to paragraph 39 is deleted.

g. Appendix A is amended as follows:

   (1) In the last sentence of Example 1, *FASB Statement No. 121, Accounting for the Impairment of Long-Lived Assets and for Long-Lived Assets to Be Disposed Of* is replaced by *FASB Statement No. 144, Accounting for the Impairment or Disposal of Long-Lived Assets.*

   (2) In Examples 2, 3, 5, and 9, all references to *Statement 121* are replaced by *Statement 144.*

C18. FASB Statement No. 143, *Accounting for Asset Retirement Obligations,* is amended as follows:

a. The fourth sentence of paragraph 2 is replaced by:

> This Statement does not apply to obligations that arise solely from a plan to sell or otherwise dispose of a long-lived asset covered by FASB Statement No. 144, *Accounting for the Impairment or Disposal of Long-Lived Assets.*

b. Paragraph 12 is amended as follows:

   (1) In the first sentence, *Statement 121* is replaced by *Statement 144.*

   (2) Footnote 11 is deleted.

C19. FASB Interpretation No. 18, *Accounting for Income Taxes in Interim Periods,* is amended as follows:

a. Footnote 1 to paragraph 5 is replaced by the following:

> The terms used in this definition are described in APB Opinion No. 20, *Accounting Changes,* in APB Opinion No. 30, *Reporting the Results of Operations—Reporting the Effects of Disposal of a Segment of a Business, and Extraordinary, Unusual and Infrequently Occurring Events and Transactions,* and in FASB Statement No. 144, *Accounting for the Impairment or Disposal of Long-Lived Assets.* See paragraph 10 of Opinion 30 for *extraordinary items* and paragraph 26 for *unusual items* and *infrequently occurring items.* See paragraph 20 of Opinion 20 for *cumula-*

tive effects of changes in accounting principles. See paragraphs 41–44 of Statement 144 for *discontinued operations.*

b. Paragraph 19 is amended as follows:

   (1) All references to *measurement date* are replaced by *date on which the criteria in paragraph 30 of Statement 144 are met.*

   (2) In the first sentence, *both (a)* and *and (b) the gain (or loss) on disposal of discontinued operations (including any provision for operating loss subsequent to the measurement date)* are deleted.

   (3) All references to *discontinued segment* are replaced by *discontinued component.*

   (4) Footnote 20 is replaced by the following:

> The term *discontinued component* refers to the disposal of a component of an entity as described in paragraph 41 of Statement 144.

c. In paragraph 35, the references to *segment of a business* are replaced by *component of an entity.*

d. In paragraph 71, under Discontinued operations, *Division* is replaced by *Component* and *Income (loss) on disposal of Division X, including provision of $XXXX for operating losses during phase-out period (less applicable income taxes of $XXXX)* is deleted.

C20. Paragraph 3 of FASB Interpretation No. 27, *Accounting for a Loss on a Sublease,* is deleted.

C21. In paragraph 7 of FASB Interpretation No. 39, *Offsetting of Amounts Related to Certain Contracts,* the reference to *APB Opinion No. 30, Reporting the Results of Operations—Reporting the Effects of Disposal of a Segment of a Business, and Extraordinary, Unusual and Infrequently Occurring Events and Transactions (reporting of discontinued operations)* is deleted.

AMENDMENTS MADE BY STATEMENT 121 CARRIED FORWARD IN THIS STATEMENT WITH MINOR CHANGES

C22. In the first sentence of paragraph 19(h) of APB Opinion No. 18, *The Equity Method of Accounting for Investments in Common Stock,* the phrase *the same as a loss in value of other long-term assets* is deleted.

C23. The last question and its interpretation of AICPA Accounting Interpretation 1, "Illustration of the Application of APB Opinion No. 30," are superseded.

C24. FASB Statement No. 15, *Accounting by Debtors and Creditors for Troubled Debt Restructurings,* is amended as follows:

a. The following sentence is added after the first sentence of paragraph 28:

> A creditor that receives long-lived assets that will be sold from a debtor in full satisfaction of a receivable shall account for those assets at their fair value less cost to sell, as that term is used in paragraph 34 of FASB Statement No. 144, *Accounting for the Impairment or Disposal of Long-Lived Assets.*

b. The last sentence of paragraph 28 is replaced by the following:

> The excess of (i) the recorded investment in the receivable[17] satisfied over (ii) the fair value of assets received (less cost to sell, if required above) is a loss to be recognized. For purposes of this paragraph, losses, to the extent they are not offset against allowances for uncollectible amounts or other valuation accounts, shall be included in measuring net income for the period.

c. In the second sentence of paragraph 33, *at their fair values* is deleted and *less cost to sell* is inserted after *reduced by the fair value.*

C25. The following new heading and paragraph are added after paragraph 62 of FASB Statement No. 19, *Financial Accounting and Reporting by Oil and Gas Producing Companies:*

Impairment Test for Proved Properties and Capitalized Exploration and Development Cost

The provisions of FASB Statement No. 144, *Accounting for the Impairment or Disposal of Long-Lived Assets,* are applicable to the costs of an enterprise's wells and related equipment and facilities and the costs of the related proved properties. The impairment provisions relating to unproved properties referred to in paragraphs 12, 27–29, 31(b), 33, 40, 47(g), and 47(h) of this Statement remain applicable to unproved properties.

C26. The following sentence is added to the end of paragraph 19 of FASB Statement No. 34, *Capitalization of Interest Cost:*

> The provisions of FASB Statement No. 144, *Accounting for the Impairment or Disposal of Long-Lived Assets,* apply in recognizing impairment of long-lived assets held for use.

C27. The first two sentences of paragraph 14 of FASB Statement No. 51, *Financial Reporting by Cable Television Companies,* are replaced by the following: **[Note: This amendment does not affect the amendment made by paragraph D5(2) of Statement 142 to refer to other intangible assets subject to the provisions of that Statement.]**

> Capitalized plant and certain intangible assets are subject to the provisions of FASB Statement No. 144, *Accounting for the Impairment or Disposal of Long-Lived Assets.*

C28. Paragraph 48 of FASB Statement No. 60, *Accounting and Reporting by Insurance Enterprises,* is amended as follows:

a. In the first sentence, *and an allowance for any impairment in value* is deleted.

b. In the last sentence, *Changes in the allowance for any impairment in value relating to real estate investments* is replaced by *Reductions in the carrying amount of real estate investments resulting from the application of FASB Statement No. 144, Accounting for the Impairment or Disposal of Long-Lived Assets,.*

C29. FASB Statement No. 61, *Accounting for Title Plant,* is amended as follows:

a. In the first and second sentences of paragraph 6, *value* is replaced by *carrying amount.*

b. The last sentence of paragraph 6 is replaced by the following:

> Those events or changes in circumstances, in addition to the examples in paragraph 8 of FASB Statement No. 144, *Accounting for the Impairment or Disposal of Long-Lived Assets,* indicate that the carrying amount of the capitalized costs may not be recoverable. Accordingly, the provisions of Statement 144 apply.

C30. Footnote 5 to paragraph 21 of FASB Statement No. 66, *Accounting for Sales of Real Estate,* is replaced by the following:

Paragraph 24 of FASB Statement No. 67, *Accounting for Costs and Initial Rental Operations of Real Estate Projects,* as amended by FASB Statement No. 144, *Accounting for the Impairment or Disposal of Long-Lived Assets,* specifies the accounting for property that is substantially completed and that is to be sold.

C31. FASB Statement No. 67, *Accounting for Costs and Initial Rental Operations of Real Estate Projects,* is amended as follows:

a. In paragraph 3, *costs in excess of estimated net realizable value* is replaced by *reductions in the carrying amounts of real estate assets prescribed by FASB Statement No. 144, Accounting for the Impairment or Disposal of Long-Lived Assets.*

b. Paragraph 16 is deleted.

c. Paragraph 25 is replaced by the following:

Paragraph 8 of Statement 144 provides examples of events or changes in circumstances that indicate that the recoverability of the carrying amount of a long-lived asset should be assessed. Insufficient rental demand for a rental project currently under construction is an additional example that indicates that the recoverability of the real estate project should be assessed in accordance with the provisions of Statement 144.

d. In paragraph 28, the term *net realizable value* and its definition are deleted.

C32. FASB Statement No. 71, *Accounting for the Effects of Certain Types of Regulation,* is amended as follows:

a. The following sentence is added to the end of paragraph 9:

If at any time the incurred cost no longer meets the above criteria, that cost shall be charged to earnings.

b. Paragraph 10 is amended as follows:

(1) The second and third sentences are replaced by:

If a regulator excludes all or part of a cost from allowable costs, the carrying amount of any asset recognized pursuant to paragraph 9 of this Statement shall be reduced to the extent of the excluded cost.

(2) In the fourth sentence, *the asset has* is replaced by *other assets have* and *and FASB Statement No. 144, Accounting for the Impairment or Disposal of Long-Lived Assets, shall apply* is added to the end of that sentence after the footnote added by FASB Statement No. 90, *Regulated Enterprises—Accounting for Abandonments and Disallowances of Plant Costs.*

c. The following new paragraph is added after paragraph 10:

If a regulator allows recovery through rates of costs previously excluded from allowable costs, that action shall result in recognition of a new asset. The classification of that asset shall be consistent with the classification that would have resulted had those costs been initially included in allowable costs.

C33. The following phrase is added to the end of the third sentence of paragraph 6 of FASB Statement No. 101, *Regulated Enterprises—Accounting for the Discontinuation of Application of FASB Statement No. 71:*

, and FASB Statement No. 144, *Accounting for the Impairment or Disposal of Long-Lived Assets,* shall apply, except for the provisions for income statement reporting in paragraphs 25 and 26 of that Statement.

Appendix D

REFERENCES TO PRONOUNCEMENTS

D1. There are many references in the existing authoritative literature to impairment of assets. Appendix C indicates the amendments to pronouncements existing at the date of this Statement. The following table lists FASB and APB pronouncements that refer to impairment of long-lived assets and indicates which of those pronouncements will apply the applicable requirements of this Statement and which will continue to apply some other applicable existing requirement.

Existing Pronouncement	Title	Apply Requirement in This Statement	Apply Existing Requirement	Existing Requirement Paragraph Number
APB Opinion No. 18	*The Equity Method of Accounting for Investments in Common Stock*		X	19(h) (as amended by this Statement)
FASB Statement No. 7	*Accounting and Reporting by Development Stage Enterprises*	X		
FASB Statement No. 13	*Accounting for Leases*			
	• Capital leases of lessees	X		
	• Assets of lessors subject to operating leases	X		
	• Sales-type, direct financing, and leveraged leases of lessors		X	17
FASB Statement No. 19	*Financial Accounting and Reporting by Oil and Gas Producing Companies*			
	• Unproved properties	X		
	• Proved properties, wells, and related equipment and facilities accounted for using the successful-efforts method of accounting		X	12, 27–29, 31, 33, 34, 40, 47(g), 47(h)

Existing Pronouncement	Title	Apply Requirement in This Statement	Apply Existing Requirement	Existing Requirement Paragraph Number
FASB Statement No. 28	*Accounting for Sales with Leasebacks*		X	3(c)
FASB Statement No. 34	*Capitalization of Interest Cost*	X		
FASB Statement No. 50	*Financial Reporting in the Record and Music Industry*		X	11, 15
FASB Statement No. 51	*Financial Reporting by Cable Television Companies*			
	• Assets that are being depreciated (amortized)	X		
	• Other intangible assets		X	14
FASB Statement No. 60	*Accounting and Reporting by Insurance Enterprises*			
	• Real estate investments	X		
	• Deferred policy acquisition costs		X	32–37
FASB Statement No. 61	*Accounting for Title Plant*	X		
FASB Statement No. 63	*Financial Reporting by Broadcasters*		X	7

Existing Pronouncement	Title	Apply Requirement in This Statement	Apply Existing Requirement	Existing Requirement Paragraph Number
FASB Statement No. 65	*Accounting for Certain Mortgage Banking Activities*		X	7
FASB Statement No. 67	*Accounting for Costs and Initial Rental Operations of Real Estate Projects*	X		
FASB Statement No. 71	*Accounting for the Effects of Certain Types of Regulation*			
	• Rate-regulated assets		X	9, 10 (as amended by this Statement)
	• Other assets	X		
FASB Statement No. 86	*Accounting for the Costs of Computer Software to Be Sold, Leased, or Otherwise Marketed*		X	10
FASB Statement No. 90	*Regulated Enterprises—Accounting for Abandonments and Disallowances of Plant Costs*		X	7
FASB Statement No. 97	*Accounting and Reporting by Insurance Enterprises for Certain Long-Duration Contracts and for Realized Gains and Losses from the Sale of Investments*		X	25, 27

Existing Pronouncement	Title	Apply Requirement in This Statement	Apply Existing Requirement	Existing Requirement Paragraph Number
FASB Statement No. 101	*Regulated Enterprises—Accounting for the Discontinuation of Application of FASB Statement No. 71*	X		
FASB Statement No. 109	*Accounting for Income Taxes*		X	20–26
FASB Statement No. 114	*Accounting by Creditors for Impairment of a Loan*		X	8–16
FASB Statement No. 115	*Accounting for Certain Investments in Debt and Equity Securities*		X	16
FASB Statement No. 140	*Accounting for Transfers and Servicing of Financial Assets and Extinguishments of Liabilities*		X	13, 63(g)
FASB Statement No. 142	*Goodwill and Other Intangible Assets*			
	• Goodwill and intangible assets not being amortized	X		
	• Intangible assets being amortized		X	17, 19–22
FASB Statement No. 147	*Acquisitions of Certain Financial Institutions*			
	• Depositor- and borrower-relationship intangible assets	X		
	• Credit cardholder intangible assets	X		

E1–E3. [These paragraphs have been deleted. See Status page.]

Statement of Financial Accounting Standards No. 145
Rescission of FASB Statements No. 4, 44, and 64,
Amendment of FASB Statement No. 13,
and Technical Corrections

STATUS

Issued: April 2002

Effective Date: For financial statements issued on or after May 15, 2002

Affects: Amends APB 28, paragraph 21
Amends APB 30, paragraphs 20 and 26
Supersedes FAS 4
Amends FAS 13, paragraph 14(a)
Replaces FAS 13, paragraph 38
Amends FAS 15, paragraphs 13, 15, 17, 25(b), and 25(d)
Deletes FAS 15, paragraph 21
Replaces FAS 19, paragraph 44
Amends FAS 22, paragraphs 12(a)(i) and 17
Supersedes FAS 44
Deletes FAS 60, paragraph 12
Supersedes FAS 64
Amends FAS 95, paragraphs 15, 16(a), 16(b), 17(a), 17(b), footnote 5, and footnotes added to
    paragraphs 22(a) and 23(a) by FAS 102
Amends FAS 102, paragraph 8
Amends FAS 115, footnote 4
Amends FAS 128, paragraph 171
Amends FAS 133, paragraph 59(e)
Deletes FAS 135, paragraphs 4(p)(1), 4(p)(7), and 4(r)(2)(a)
Amends FAS 141, paragraph 46 and footnote 25
Deletes FAS 141, paragraph E10
Amends FAS 142, paragraphs 8, 8(i), and 35
Effectively deletes FAS 142, paragraph 8(c)
Deletes FAS 142, paragraph D11(a)(2)
Amends FAS 144, paragraphs 5, 45, and D1
Amends FIN 21, paragraph 15
Amends FTB 80-1, paragraphs 3 and 4
Amends FTB 82-1, paragraph 6

Affected by: No other pronouncements

Issues Discussed by FASB Emerging Issues Task Force (EITF)

Affects: Partially nullifies EITF Issues No. 90-19 and 00-9

Interpreted by: No EITF Issues

Related Issues: EITF Issues No. 86-15, 91-2, 96-19, 98-5, and 01-2

SUMMARY

This Statement rescinds FASB Statement No. 4, *Reporting Gains and Losses from Extinguishment of Debt,* and an amendment of that Statement, FASB Statement No. 64, *Extinguishments of Debt Made to Satisfy Sinking-Fund Requirements.* This Statement also rescinds FASB Statement No. 44, *Accounting for Intangible Assets of Motor Carriers.* This Statement amends FASB Statement No. 13, *Accounting for Leases,* to eliminate an inconsistency between the required accounting for sale-leaseback transactions and the required accounting for certain lease modifications that have economic effects that are similar to sale-leaseback transactions. This Statement also amends other existing authoritative pronouncements to make various technical corrections, clarify meanings, or describe their applicability under changed conditions.

Reasons for Issuing This Statement

When Statement 4 was issued in 1975, the Board noted that the provisions of that Statement represented a "practical and reasonable solution to the question regarding income statement classification of gains or losses from extinguishment of debt until such time as the broader issues involved can be addressed" (paragraph 15). Since the issuance of Statement 4, the use of debt extinguishment has become part of the risk management strategy of many companies, particularly those operating in the secondary lending market. Debt extinguishments used as part of an entity's risk management strategy represent one example of debt extinguishments that do not meet the criteria for classification as extraordinary items in APB Opinion No. 30, *Reporting the Results of Operations—Reporting the Effects of Disposal of a Segment of a Business, and Extraordinary, Unusual and Infrequently Occurring Events and Transactions,* and therefore, should not be classified as extraordinary. Statement 64 amended Statement 4 and is no longer necessary because Statement 4 has been rescinded.

Statement 44 was issued to establish accounting requirements for the effects of transition to the provisions of the Motor Carrier Act of 1980 (Public Law 96-296, 96th Congress, July 1, 1980). Those transitions are completed; therefore, Statement 44 is no longer necessary.

This Statement also amends Statement 13 to require sale-leaseback accounting for certain lease modifications that have economic effects that are similar to sale-leaseback transactions. This Statement also makes various technical corrections to existing pronouncements. Those corrections are not substantive in nature.

How the Changes in This Statement Improve Financial Reporting

Under Statement 4, all gains and losses from extinguishment of debt were required to be aggregated and, if material, classified as an extraordinary item, net of related income tax effect. This Statement eliminates Statement 4 and, thus, the exception to applying Opinion 30 to all gains and losses related to extinguishments of debt (other than extinguishments of debt to satisfy sinking-fund requirements—the exception to application of Statement 4 noted in Statement 64). As a result, gains and losses from extinguishment of debt should be classified as extraordinary items only if they meet the criteria in Opinion 30. Applying the provisions of Opinion 30 will distinguish transactions that are part of an entity's recurring operations from those that are unusual or infrequent or that meet the criteria for classification as an extraordinary item.

Under Statement 13, the required accounting treatment of certain lease modifications that have economic effects similar to sale-leaseback transactions was inconsistent with the required accounting treatment for sale-leaseback transactions. This Statement amends paragraph 14(a) of Statement 13 to require that those lease modifications be accounted for in the same manner as sale-leaseback transactions. This amendment is in accordance with the Board's goal of requiring similar accounting treatment for transactions that have similar economic effects.

Statement of Financial Accounting Standards No. 145

Rescission of FASB Statements No. 4, 44, and 64, Amendment of FASB Statement No. 13, and Technical Corrections

CONTENTS

INTRODUCTION

Statements 4 and 64

1. FASB Statement No. 4, *Reporting Gains and Losses from Extinguishment of Debt,* was issued in 1975. Statement 4 required that gains and losses from extinguishment of debt that were included in the determination of net income be aggregated and, if material, classified as an extraordinary item, net of related income tax effect. Statement 4 also required certain disclosures for those items. At the time Statement 4 was issued, the Board concluded that classifying gains and losses from extinguishment of debt as extraordinary items represented a practical and reasonable solution to the issues regarding income statement classification of those gains or losses. However, the Board indicated that that solution was not intended to be permanent.

2. FASB Statement No. 64, *Extinguishments of Debt Made to Satisfy Sinking-Fund Requirements,* was issued in 1982. That Statement made an exception to the provisions of Statement 4 for certain debt extinguishment transactions.

Statement 44

3. FASB Statement No. 44, *Accounting for Intangible Assets of Motor Carriers,* was issued to establish accounting requirements for the effects of transition to the provisions of the Motor Carrier Act of 1980 (Public Law 96-296, 96th Congress, July 1, 1980). Statement 44 also contained a provision that in the event that intrastate operating rights were to be deregulated, the accounting requirements for the effects of transition to those laws would be in accordance with the provisions of Statement 44. All intrastate operating rights have since been deregulated, and the transition to the provisions of those laws is complete.

Amendment of Statement 13

4. Paragraph 14(a) of FASB Statement No. 13, *Accounting for Leases,* describes the accounting by a lessee for certain lease modifications. If a capital lease is modified in such a way that the change in the lease provisions gives rise to a new agreement classified as an operating lease, paragraph 14(a) requires that the asset and obligation under the lease be

removed, a gain or loss be recognized for the difference, and the new lease agreement thereafter be accounted for as any other operating lease. Several constituents advised the Board that, in their view, if a capital lease is modified as described above, the modification has economic effects that are similar to a sale-leaseback transaction. However, Statement 13 does not require the lessee to account for those lease modifications as sale-leaseback transactions. This Statement requires that capital leases that are modified so that the resulting lease agreement is classified as an operating lease be accounted for under the sale-leaseback provisions of FASB Statement No. 98, *Accounting for Leases: Sale-Leaseback Transactions Involving Real Estate; Sales-Type Leases of Real Estate; Definition of the Lease Term; Initial Direct Costs of Direct Financing Leases,* or paragraphs 2 and 3 of FASB Statement No. 28, *Accounting for Sales with Leasebacks,* as applicable.

Technical Corrections

5. Before the Board issues a pronouncement that contains amendments to existing pronouncements, those amendments are reviewed by the Board. This Statement identifies amendments that should have been made to previously existing pronouncements and formally amends the appropriate pronouncements. In addition, this Statement amends existing authoritative pronouncements to (a) correct references to guidance issued by the American Institute of Certified Public Accountants (AICPA) or the FASB that has been revised or superseded since the issuance of the pronouncement and (b) eliminate inconsistencies in existing pronouncements.

STANDARDS OF FINANCIAL ACCOUNTING AND REPORTING

Rescission of Statements 4, 44, and 64

6. This Statement rescinds the following pronouncements:

a. FASB Statement No. 4, *Reporting Gains and Losses from Extinguishment of Debt*
b. FASB Statement No. 44, *Accounting for Intangible Assets of Motor Carriers*
c. FASB Statement No. 64, *Extinguishments of Debt Made to Satisfy Sinking-Fund Requirements.*

Amendments to Existing Pronouncements to Reflect Rescission of Statements 4, 44, and 64

7. This Statement amends the following pronouncements to reflect the rescission of Statements 4, 44, and 64:

a. APB Opinion No. 30, *Reporting the Results of Operations—Reporting the Effects of Disposal of a Segment of a Business, and Extraordinary, Unusual and Infrequently Occurring Events and Transactions.* In the last sentence of paragraph 20, as amended by FASB Statement No. 141, *Business Combinations,* the phrase *(1) Classifications of gains or losses from extinguishment of debt pursuant to paragraph 8 of FASB Statement No. 4, Reporting Gains and Losses from Extinguishment of Debt* is deleted.

b. FASB Statement No. 15, *Accounting by Debtors and Creditors for Troubled Debt Restructurings.*

   (1) In paragraphs 13, 15, and 17, *(see paragraph 21)* is deleted.

   (2) Paragraph 21 is deleted.

   (3) In paragraph 25(b), *and the related income tax effect (paragraph 21)* is deleted.

   (4) In paragraph 25(d), *, net of related income tax effect* is deleted.

c. FASB Statement No. 22, *Changes in the Provisions of Lease Agreements Resulting from Refundings of Tax-Exempt Debt.*

   (1) The last sentence of paragraph 12(a)(i) is deleted.

   (2) In the last sentence of the example of lessee accounting in paragraph 17, *(The loss shall be classified in accordance with FASB Statement No. 4.)* is deleted.

d. FASB Statement No. 144, *Accounting for the Impairment or Disposal of Long-Lived Assets.*

   (1) In the last sentence of paragraph 5, the following is deleted:

   • FASB Statement No. 44, *Accounting for Intangible Assets of Motor Carriers*

Rescission of FASB Statements No. 4, 44, and 64,
Amendment of FASB Statement No. 13,
and Technical Corrections

FAS145

(2) In the table in paragraph D1, the reference to Statement 44 is deleted.

e. FASB Technical Bulletin No. 80-1, *Early Extinguishment of Debt through Exchange for Common or Preferred Stock.* The third sentence of paragraph 4 is deleted.

Amendment of Statement 13

8. FASB Statement No. 13, *Accounting for Leases.* The last sentence of paragraph 14(a) is replaced by the following:

> If the change in the lease provisions gives rise to a new agreement classified as an operating lease, the transaction shall be accounted for under the sale-leaseback requirements of FASB Statement No. 98, *Accounting for Leases: Sale-Leaseback Transactions Involving Real Estate; Sales-Type Leases of Real Estate; Definition of the Lease Term; Initial Direct Costs of Direct Financing Leases,* or paragraphs 2 and 3 of FASB Statement No. 28, *Accounting for Sales with Leasebacks,* as applicable.

Technical Corrections

9. This Statement amends the following pronouncements to make technical corrections to existing authoritative pronouncements:

a. APB Opinion No. 28, *Interim Financial Reporting.* In the fourth sentence of paragraph 21, as amended by FASB Statement No. 141, *Business Combinations,* the phrase *in a purchase* is deleted.

b. APB Opinion No. 30, *Reporting the Results of Operations—Reporting the Effects of Disposal of a Segment of a Business, and Extraordinary, Unusual and Infrequently Occurring Events and Transactions.* In the fourth sentence of paragraph 26, *or in any manner inconsistent with the provisions of paragraphs 8 and 11 of this Opinion* is deleted.

c. FASB Statement No. 13, *Accounting for Leases.* Paragraph 38 is replaced by the following:

> If the nature of the transaction is such that the original lessee is relieved of the primary obligation under the original lease, as would be the case in transactions of the type described in paragraphs 35(b) and 35(c), the termination of the original lease agreement shall be accounted for as follows:

a. If the original lease was a capital lease of property other than real estate (including integral equipment), the asset and obligation representing the original lease shall be removed from the accounts, a gain or loss shall be recognized for the difference, and, if the original lessee is secondarily liable, the guarantee obligation shall be recognized in accordance with paragraph 114 of FASB Statement No. 140, *Accounting for Transfers and Servicing of Financial Assets and Extinguishments of Liabilities.* Any consideration paid or received upon termination shall be included in the determination of gain or loss to be recognized.

b. If the original lease was a capital lease of real estate (including integral equipment), the determination as to whether the asset held under the capital lease and the related obligation may be removed from the balance sheet shall be made in accordance with the requirements of FASB Statement No. 66, *Accounting for Sales of Real Estate.* If the criteria for recognition of a sale in Statement 66 are met, the asset and obligation representing the original lease shall be removed from the accounts and any consideration paid or received upon termination and any guarantee obligation shall be recognized in accordance with the requirements above for property other than real estate. If the transaction results in a gain, that gain may be recognized if the criteria in Statement 66 for recognition of profit by the full accrual method are met. Otherwise, the gain shall be recognized in accordance with one of the other profit recognition methods discussed in Statement 66. Any loss on the transaction shall be recognized immediately.

c. If the original lease was an operating lease and the original lessee is secondarily liable, the guarantee obligation shall be recognized in accordance with paragraph 114 of Statement 140.

d. FASB Statement No. 19, *Financial Accounting and Reporting by Oil and Gas Producing Companies.* Paragraph 44, as amended by FASB Statement No. 144, *Accounting for the Impairment or Disposal of Long-Lived Assets,* is replaced by the following:

In the following types of conveyances, gain or loss shall not be recognized at the time of the conveyance, except as otherwise provided:

a. A transfer of assets used in oil and gas producing activities (including either proved or unproved properties) in exchange for other assets also used in oil and gas producing activities. However, when proved properties are transferred in exchange for other assets also used in oil and gas producing activities, if an impairment loss is indicated under the provisions of FASB Statement No. 144, *Accounting for the Impairment or Disposal of Long-Lived Assets,* it shall be recognized in accordance with paragraph 29 of Statement 144.

b. A pooling of assets in a joint undertaking intended to find, develop, or produce oil or gas from a particular property or group of properties.

e. FASB Statement No. 60, *Accounting and Reporting by Insurance Enterprises.* Paragraph 12 is deleted.

f. FASB Statement No. 95, *Statement of Cash Flows.*

(1) In the last sentence of paragraph 15, as amended by FASB Statement No. 102, *Statement of Cash Flows—Exemption of Certain Enterprises and Classification of Cash Flows from Certain Securities Acquired for Resale,* the phrase *, and securities that are classified as trading securities as discussed in FASB Statement No. 115, Accounting for Certain Investments in Debt and Equity Securities* is added after *Statement 102.*

(2) The parenthetical comment in paragraphs 16(a) and 17(a), as amended by Statement 102, is replaced by the following:

(other than cash equivalents, certain debt instruments that are acquired specifically for resale as discussed in Statement 102, and securities classified as trading securities as discussed in Statement 115)

(3) The parenthetical comment in paragraphs 16(b) and 17(b), as amended by Statement 102, is replaced by the following:

(other than certain equity instruments carried in a trading account as described in Statement 102 and certain securities classified as trading securities as discussed in Statement 115)

(4) In footnote 5, the following parenthetical comment is added after *debt or equity instruments*:

(other than cash equivalents, certain debt instruments that are acquired specifically for resale as discussed in Statement 102, and securities classified as trading securities as discussed in Statement 115)

(5) In the footnote after *goods* in paragraphs 22(a) and 23(a), added by Statement 102, *, and securities that are classified as trading securities as discussed in Statement 115* is added after *Statement 102.*

g. FASB Statement No. 102, *Statement of Cash Flows—Exemption of Certain Enterprises and Classification of Cash Flows from Certain Securities Acquired for Resale.* Paragraph 8 is amended as follows:

(1) The following sentence is added after the first sentence:

Cash receipts and cash payments resulting from purchases and sales of securities classified as trading securities as discussed in FASB Statement No. 115, *Accounting for Certain Investments in Debt and Equity Securities,* shall be classified as operating cash flows.

(2) In the second sentence, *other* is added before *securities.*

h. FASB Statement No. 115, *Accounting for Certain Investments in Debt and Equity Securities.* In footnote 4 to paragraph 16, as amended by FASB Statement No. 135, *Rescission of FASB Statement No. 75 and Technical Corrections,* the phrase *AICPA Statement on Auditing Standards No. 81, Auditing Investments*, is replaced by *AICPA Statement on Auditing Standards No. 92, Auditing Derivative Instruments, Hedging Activities, and Investments in Securities.*

i. FASB Statement No. 128, *Earnings per Share.* In the first sentence of the definition of *contingent stock agreement* in paragraph 171, *accounted for by the purchase method* is deleted.

j. FASB Statement No. 133, *Accounting for Derivative Instruments and Hedging Activities.* In the second sentence of paragraph 59(e), *Statement 125* is replaced by *Statement 140.*

k. FASB Statement No. 135, *Rescission of FASB Statement No. 75 and Technical Corrections.* Paragraphs 4(p)(1), 4(p)(7), and 4(r)(2)(a) are deleted.

l. FASB Statement No. 141, *Business Combinations.*

   (1) In the first sentence of paragraph 46, *prior to the pro rata allocation required by paragraph 44* is added after *excess.*

   (2) In the first sentence of footnote 25, *cost of the* is added before *acquired.*

   (3) Paragraph E10 is deleted.

m. FASB Statement No. 142, *Goodwill and Other Intangible Assets.*

   (1) In paragraph 8(i), *(paragraph 7)* is deleted.

   (2) The following is added to the end of paragraph 8:

       m. FASB Interpretation No. 9, *Applying APB Opinions No. 16 and 17 When a Savings and Loan Association or a Similar Institution Is Acquired in a Business Combination Accounted for by the Purchase Method.*

   (3) The second and third sentences of paragraph 35 are replaced by the following:

       An entity would determine the fair value of the acquired business (or portion thereof) to be included in a reporting unit—in essence a "purchase price" for that business. The entity would then allocate that purchase price to the individual assets acquired and liabilities assumed related to that acquired business (or portion

thereof).[21] Any excess purchase price is the amount of goodwill assigned to that reporting unit.

   (4) Paragraph D11(a)(2) is deleted.

n. FASB Statement No. 144, *Accounting for the Impairment or Disposal of Long-Lived Assets.*

   (1) In the first sentence of paragraph 5, *that are to be held and used* is added after *amortized.*

   (2) In the first sentence of paragraph 45, *for a long-lived asset (disposal group) classified as held for sale* is replaced by *on the sale of a long-lived asset (disposal group).*

   (3) Under the column "Existing Requirement Paragraph Number" in the section of the table in paragraph D1 relating to FASB Statement No. 19, *Financial Accounting and Reporting by Oil and Gas Producing Companies,* the numbers *31(b), 33* are replaced by *31, 33, 34.*

o. FASB Interpretation No. 21, *Accounting for Leases in a Business Combination.* In the heading before paragraph 15, **Purchase** is replaced by **Business.**

p. FASB Technical Bulletin No. 80-1, *Early Extinguishment of Debt through Exchange for Common or Preferred Stock.* In the first sentence of paragraph 3, *Statement 15 or Opinion 26* is replaced by *Statement 15, as amended by FASB Statement No. 145, Rescission of FASB Statements No. 4, 44, and 64, Amendment of FASB Statement No. 13, and Technical Corrections; Opinion 26; or APB Opinion No. 30, Reporting the Results of Operations—Reporting the Effects of Disposal of a Segment of a Business, and Extraordinary, Unusual and Infrequently Occurring Events and Transactions.*

q. FASB Technical Bulletin No. 82-1, *Disclosure of the Sale or Purchase of Tax Benefits through Tax Leases.* In the first sentence of paragraph 6, , *as amended by FASB Statement No. 145, Rescission of FASB Statements No. 4, 44, and 64, Amendment of FASB Statement No. 13, and Technical Corrections,* is added after *Opinion 30.*

Effective Date and Transition

10. The provisions of this Statement related to the rescission of Statement 4 shall be applied in fiscal years beginning after May 15, 2002. Any gain or loss on extinguishment of debt that was classified as an extraordinary item in prior periods presented that does not meet the criteria in Opinion 30 for classification as an extraordinary item shall be reclassified. Early application of the provisions of this Statement related to the rescission of Statement 4 is encouraged.

11. The provisions in paragraphs 8 and 9(c) of this Statement related to Statement 13 shall be effective for transactions occurring after May 15, 2002, with early application encouraged. All other provisions of this Statement shall be effective for financial statements issued on or after May 15, 2002, with early application encouraged.

12. Early application of the provisions of this Statement may be as of the beginning of the fiscal year or as of the beginning of the interim period in which this Statement is issued.

> **The provisions of this Statement need not be applied to immaterial items.**

This Statement was adopted by the unanimous vote of the seven members of the Financial Accounting Standards Board:

Edmund L. Jenkins,	John M. Foster	Edward W. Trott
Chairman	Gary S. Schieneman	John K. Wulff
G. Michael Crooch	Katherine A. Schipper	

Appendix

BACKGROUND INFORMATION AND BASIS FOR CONCLUSIONS

Introduction

A1. This appendix summarizes considerations that Board members deemed significant in reaching the conclusions in this Statement. It includes reasons for accepting certain approaches and rejecting others. Individual Board members gave greater weight to some factors than to others.

A2. In August 2001, in response to constituent requests, the Board undertook a project to rescind Statement 4. As part of that project, the Board decided to take the opportunity to make various technical corrections to other pronouncements. In November 2001, the Board issued the Exposure Draft, *Rescission of FASB Statements No. 4, 44, and 64 and Technical Corrections.* The Board received 30 letters in response to that Exposure Draft.

A3. In redeliberating the proposed technical corrections of the 2001 Exposure Draft, the Board considered additional amendments and technical corrections suggested by various respondents to the

Exposure Draft. The Board decided to include one substantive amendment of Statement 13 and several technical corrections that were suggested by respondents and FASB staff members. In February 2002, the Board issued a limited revised Exposure Draft, *Rescission of FASB Statements No. 4, 44, and 64 and Technical Corrections—Amendment of FASB Statement No. 13,* that proposed that the substantive amendment to Statement 13 be included in this Statement. The Board received 10 letters in response to the 2002 Exposure Draft. The Board concluded that on the basis of existing information it could make an informed decision on the matters addressed in this Statement without a public hearing.

Rescission of Statements 4 and 64

A4. The Board noted that at the time Statement 4 was issued, its requirement to classify all gains and losses associated with extinguishment of debt as extraordinary items was intended to be a temporary measure and that application of the criteria in Opinion 30 would seldom, if ever, require that resulting gains and losses be classified as extraordinary items. The Board noted that Statement 4 dictated the classification of gains and losses from extinguishment of debt and, thus, did not permit a conceptual consideration under the provisions of Opinion 30 of whether an extinguishment of debt is extraordinary in nature.

The Board concurred that debt extinguishments are often routine, recurring transactions and concluded that classifying the associated gains and losses as extraordinary items in all cases is inconsistent with the criteria in Opinion 30. Furthermore, such classification may not provide the most useful information to users of financial statements.

A5. The Board observed that the rescission of Statement 4 would not preclude gains and losses from extinguishment of debt that meet the criteria in Opinion 30 from being classified as extraordinary items. The Board noted that Opinion 30 requires disclosures about material gains and losses associated with debt extinguishments that are unusual or infrequent in nature. Thus, applying the provisions of Opinion 30 would distinguish transactions that are part of an entity's recurring operations from those that are unusual or infrequent or that meet the criteria for classification as extraordinary items. The Board concluded that the rescission of Statement 4 would improve financial reporting by eliminating a requirement to classify a normal and important part of many entities' ongoing activities to manage interest rate risk as an extraordinary item.

A6. Some respondents to the 2001 Exposure Draft suggested that the Statement should prohibit classification of gains and losses associated with the extinguishment of debt as extraordinary items. The Board concurred with the observation made at the time Statement 4 was issued that application of the criteria of Opinion 30 to debt extinguishment transactions would seldom, if ever, result in extraordinary item classification of the resulting gains and losses. However, the Board noted that *prohibiting* extraordinary item classification of gains and losses associated with the extinguishment of debt also would not permit a conceptual consideration under the provisions of Opinion 30 of whether an extinguishment of debt is extraordinary in nature. Thus, the Board decided not to prohibit extraordinary item classification of gains and losses related to the extinguishment of debt.

A7. Some respondents suggested that the Board reconsider the criteria in Opinion 30 for extraordinary item classification. Those respondents noted that the recent consensus reached on EITF Issue No. 01-10, "Accounting for the Impact of the Terrorist Attacks of September 11, 2001," raises questions about the appropriateness of those criteria and of the need for extraordinary item classification in general. The Board decided that reconsideration of the extraordi-

nary item classification criteria is beyond the scope of this project. However, the Board is considering matters of financial statement display in its performance reporting project.

A8. Statement 64 amended Statement 4 to require that gains and losses from extinguishments of debt made to satisfy future sinking-fund requirements meet the criteria in paragraph 20 of Opinion 30 in order to qualify for extraordinary item classification. Because Statement 4 is rescinded, Statement 64 is no longer necessary.

Rescission of Statement 44

A9. The Board noted that Statement 44 was issued to establish accounting requirements for the effects of transition to the provisions of the Motor Carrier Act of 1980. The Board concluded that Statement 44 is no longer needed because transition to the provisions of the Motor Carrier Act of 1980 is complete.

Amendment of Statement 13

A10. Several respondents to the 2001 Exposure Draft suggested that Statement 13 be amended to eliminate an inconsistency between the accounting by lessees for certain lease modification transactions that would require reclassification of a capital lease as an operating lease and the accounting for sale-leaseback transactions required by Statement 28 or 98. The Board concluded that the former transactions have economic effects that are similar to sale-leaseback transactions and that it would be appropriate to amend paragraph 14(a) of Statement 13 to eliminate that inconsistency. However, the Board concluded that that particular amendment is not a technical correction because it is substantive in nature. Because a substantive amendment must be subjected to the Board's due process, the Board decided to issue a limited revised Exposure Draft that would amend paragraph 14(a) of Statement 13.

A11. Most respondents to the 2002 Exposure Draft agreed with the Board's conclusions and the provisions of the proposed Statement. No respondents raised compelling arguments opposing the provisions of the 2002 Exposure Draft; therefore, the Board decided to include its provisions in this Statement.

Technical Corrections

A12. At the time a pronouncement is developed, the Board's due process procedures require determination of the effect of the new standard on existing authoritative accounting pronouncements. The existing authoritative pronouncements should be amended for any such effects thereby eliminating doubt as to what is amended and eliminating conflicts between the requirements of prior pronouncements and the requirements of the new pronouncement. When changes that should have been made as a result of that process are subsequently discovered, those changes are made to the various editions of the FASB's *Current Text,* and those editorial corrections are appropriately indicated in its *Original Pronouncements.* The Board decided to formalize those technical corrections by amending the appropriate pronouncements.

A13. A technical correction is a nonsubstantive amendment to an authoritative pronouncement. The Board concluded that an amendment is not substantive if there is evidence in existing authoritative pronouncements that at the time the pronouncement was issued, the issue addressed by the technical correction had been considered by the Board and the Board had reached a conclusion on the issue. A technical correction reflects the Board's intent on decisions that were previously subjected to the Board's due process but that were overlooked or were not clearly stated at the time a pronouncement was issued. The Board observed that some technical corrections may change current practice.

A14. In November 1992, when the Board first issued a standard to make technical corrections (FASB Statement No. 111, *Rescission of FASB Statement No. 32 and Technical Corrections*), the Board considered what parts of previously issued pronouncements to amend and decided that only the official guidance sections should be amended. The Board continues to believe that only those sections should be amended. In other words, the Board believes that the introduction, background information, and basis for conclusions paragraphs provide historical information that should not be amended or superseded unless the entire pronouncement is superseded. Those paragraphs are considered historical because they document the circumstances surrounding the development of a pronouncement. For example, they record (a) the reasons why the accounting requirements were considered to be necessary at that time, (b) the alternative guidance considered, and (c) public comments on the proposed requirements and how those comments were addressed.

A15. In addition to the accounting guidance and historical paragraphs, a pronouncement sometimes contains other paragraphs or appendixes that (a) state the scope of the pronouncement, (b) indicate substantive

amendments to other existing pronouncements, (c) present examples or illustrations of application of the requirements of the pronouncement, or (d) present a glossary of the terms used in the pronouncement. The Board believes that the content of those various paragraphs and appendixes provides part of the accounting guidance of the pronouncement and should be amended if the pronouncement is amended by a subsequent pronouncement.

A16. Most respondents to the 2001 Exposure Draft agreed that the proposed technical corrections represent nonsubstantive amendments to existing authoritative pronouncements. Several respondents suggested additional technical corrections. The Board considered those suggestions and decided to include in this Statement those that met the criteria established for a technical correction.

Effective Date and Transition

A17. The Board noted that the rescission of Statement 4 represents a change in practice relating to the classification of gains and losses from extinguishment of debt. The 2001 Exposure Draft proposed that the provisions of the Statement related to the rescission of Statement 4 be applied as of the beginning of the fiscal year in which the Statement is issued. The Board reasoned that if the provisions of this Statement related to the rescission of Statement 4 were required to be applied from the beginning of an entity's fiscal year, the financial statements for that year would present the debt extinguishment transactions in that year consistently. Further, the Board noted that it would not be onerous for preparers to determine whether debt extinguishments completed prior to the issuance of this Statement meet the criteria for extraordinary item classification.

A18. Several respondents to the 2001 Exposure Draft commented that the requirement to apply those provisions retroactively to the beginning of the fiscal year could have a negative effect on certain debt covenants. The Board considered those comments and decided to require that entities apply the provisions of this Statement related to the rescission of Statement 4 in fiscal years beginning after the Statement is issued. However, the Board decided to encourage early application of those provisions. In addition, the Board decided to require reclassification of the gains and losses related to debt extinguishments that do not meet the criteria in Opinion 30 for extraordinary item treatment for all prior periods presented in comparative financial statements.

A19. The Board decided that the provisions in paragraphs 8 and 9(c) of this Statement that amend Statement 13 should be applied for transactions entered into after issuance of this Statement, with early application encouraged.

A20. The amendments to make technical corrections to existing pronouncements represent codification of items the Board intended to include within accounting pronouncements that are already in effect. The 2001 Exposure Draft proposed that the provisions of this Statement not related to Statement 4 should be effective upon issuance of the Statement. Respondents asked for clarification of whether those provisions should be effective for financial statements issued after the Statement is issued or for transactions occurring after issuance of the final Statement. The Board decided that, except for the provisions discussed in paragraphs A18 and A19, all provisions of this Statement should be effective for financial statements issued after this Statement is issued, with early application encouraged.

Benefits and Costs

A21. The Board's mission statement charges the Board to determine that a proposed standard will fill a significant need and that the costs it imposes will be justified in relation to the overall benefits. The rescis-

sion of Statements 4 and 64 eliminates an exception to general practice relating to how to determine whether certain items should be classified as extraordinary. The criteria for extraordinary item classification are outlined in paragraph 20 of Opinion 30, and entities have been successfully applying those criteria for almost 30 years. The Board believes that the benefits of consistent application of the criteria for extraordinary item classification outweigh any effort required on the part of preparers to apply the criteria of Opinion 30 to debt extinguishment transactions. The rescission of Statement 44 removes a no longer relevant standard from the authoritative literature.

A22. The amendment of Statement 13 affects the accounting by the lessee for certain lease modifications that have economic effects similar to sale-leaseback transactions. The Board believes that that amendment improves financial accounting because similar transactions should be accounted for in a similar manner. Further, the Board believes that applying sale-leaseback accounting to the lease modifications addressed in this Statement would not be costly.

A23. The Board believes that financial reporting is both simplified and improved by eliminating the inconsistent and obsolete reporting requirements of Statements 4, 44, and 64 and by incorporating the amendments and technical corrections in this Statement.

Statement of Financial Accounting Standards No. 146
Accounting for Costs Associated with Exit or Disposal Activities

STATUS

Issued: June 2002

Effective Date: For exit or disposal activities initiated after December 31, 2002

Affects: No other pronouncements

Affected by: Paragraphs 5, A4, and A5 and footnotes 13 through 16 deleted by FAS 157, paragraph E25
Paragraph A2 amended by FAS 157, paragraph E25(b)

Other Interpretive Release: FASB Staff Position FAS 146-1

Issues Discussed by FASB Emerging Issues Task Force (EITF)

Affects: Nullifies EITF Issues No. 88-10, 94-3, and 95-14

Interpreted by: No EITF Issues

Related Issues: EITF Issues No. 86-22, 87-4, 95-3, 95-17, 96-5, 96-9, 97-13, 99-14, 00-26, and 01-10

SUMMARY

This Statement addresses financial accounting and reporting for costs associated with exit or disposal activities and nullifies Emerging Issues Task Force (EITF) Issue No. 94-3, "Liability Recognition for Certain Employee Termination Benefits and Other Costs to Exit an Activity (including Certain Costs Incurred in a Restructuring)."

Reasons for Issuing This Statement

The Board decided to address the accounting and reporting for costs associated with exit or disposal activities because entities increasingly are engaging in exit and disposal activities and certain costs associated with those activities were recognized as liabilities at a plan (commitment) date under Issue 94-3 that did not meet the definition of a liability in FASB Concepts Statement No. 6, *Elements of Financial Statements*.

Differences between This Statement and Issue 94-3

The principal difference between this Statement and Issue 94-3 relates to its requirements for recognition of a liability for a cost associated with an exit or disposal activity. This Statement requires that a liability for a cost associated with an exit or disposal activity be recognized when the liability is incurred. Under Issue 94-3, a liability for an exit cost as defined in Issue 94-3 was recognized at the date of an entity's commitment to an exit plan. A fundamental conclusion reached by the Board in this Statement is that an entity's commitment to a plan, by itself, does not create a present obligation to others that meets the definition of a liability. Therefore, this Statement eliminates the definition and requirements for recognition of exit costs in Issue 94-3. This Statement also establishes that fair value is the objective for initial measurement of the liability.

How the Changes in This Statement Improve Financial Reporting

This Statement improves financial reporting by requiring that a liability for a cost associated with an exit or disposal activity be recognized and measured initially at fair value only when the liability is incurred. The accounting for similar events and circumstances will be the same, thereby improving the comparability and representational faithfulness of reported financial information.

How the Conclusions in This Statement Relate to the Conceptual Framework

This Statement specifies that a liability for a cost associated with an exit or disposal activity is incurred when the definition of a liability in Concepts Statement 6 is met.

This Statement affirms the Board's view that a fair value measurement is the most relevant and faithful representation of the underlying economics of a transaction. As discussed in FASB Concepts Statement No. 7, *Using Cash Flow Information and Present Value in Accounting Measurements,* fair value is the objective for initial measurements that are developed using present value techniques.

This Statement considers the qualitative characteristics discussed in FASB Concepts Statement No. 2, *Qualitative Characteristics of Accounting Information,* specifically, that providing comparable financial information enables investors, creditors, and other users of financial statements to identify similarities in and differences between two sets of economic events. Ultimately, that financial information facilitates their investment, credit, and other resource allocation decisions and contributes to the efficient functioning of the capital markets.

The Effective Date of This Statement

The provisions of this Statement are effective for exit or disposal activities that are initiated after December 31, 2002, with early application encouraged.

Statement of Financial Accounting Standards No. 146

Accounting for Costs Associated with Exit or Disposal Activities

CONTENTS

INTRODUCTION

1. This Statement addresses financial accounting and reporting for costs associated with exit or disposal activities and nullifies Emerging Issues Task Force (EITF) Issue No. 94-3, "Liability Recognition for Certain Employee Termination Benefits and Other Costs to Exit an Activity (including Certain Costs Incurred in a Restructuring)." Appendix A provides additional guidance on the application of certain provisions of this Statement and is an integral part of the standards provided in this Statement.

STANDARDS OF FINANCIAL ACCOUNTING AND REPORTING

Scope

2. This Statement applies to costs associated with an *exit activity*[1] that does not involve an entity newly acquired in a business combination[2] or with a disposal activity covered by FASB Statement No. 144, *Accounting for the Impairment or Disposal of Long-Lived Assets*.[3] Those costs include, but are not limited to, the following:

---

[1]For purposes of this Statement, an *exit activity* includes but is not limited to a *restructuring* as that term is defined in IAS 37, *Provisions, Contingent Liabilities and Contingent Assets*. Paragraph 10 of IAS 37 defines a restructuring as "a programme that is planned and controlled by management, and materially changes either: (a) the scope of a business undertaken by an enterprise; or (b) the manner in which that business is conducted." A restructuring covered by IAS 37 (paragraph 70) includes the sale or termination of a line of business, the closure of business activities in a particular location, the relocation of business activities from one location to another, changes in management structure, and a fundamental reorganization that affects the nature and focus of operations.

[2]EITF Issue No. 95-3, "Recognition of Liabilities in Connection with a Purchase Business Combination," provides guidance on the accounting for costs associated with an exit activity that involves a company newly acquired in a business combination. The Board is reconsidering that guidance in its project on business combinations—purchase method procedures.

[3]Statement 144 addresses the accounting for the impairment of long-lived assets and for long-lived assets and disposal groups to be disposed of, including components of an entity that are discontinued operations.

a. Termination benefits provided to current employees that are involuntarily terminated under the terms of a benefit arrangement that, in substance, is not an ongoing benefit arrangement or an individual deferred compensation contract (hereinafter referred to as *one-time termination benefits*)[4]

b. Costs to terminate a contract that is not a capital lease[5]

c. Costs to consolidate facilities or relocate employees.

This Statement does not apply to costs associated with the retirement of a long-lived asset covered by FASB Statement No. 143, *Accounting for Asset Retirement Obligations.*

Recognition and Measurement

3. A liability for a cost associated with an exit or disposal activity shall be recognized and measured initially at its fair value in the period in which the liability is incurred, except as indicated in paragraph 11 (for a liability for one-time termination benefits that is incurred over time). In the unusual circumstance in which fair value cannot be reasonably estimated, the liability shall be recognized initially in the period in which fair value can be reasonably estimated.

4. A liability for a cost associated with an exit or disposal activity is incurred when the definition of a liability is met. Paragraph 35 of FASB Concepts Statement No. 6, *Elements of Financial Statements,* defines liabilities as follows:

> Liabilities are probable[21] future sacrifices of economic benefits arising from present obligations[22] of a particular entity to transfer assets or provide services to other entities in the future as a result of past transactions or events.

---

[21]*Probable* is used with its usual general meaning, rather than in a specific accounting or technical sense (such as that in Statement 5, par. 3), and refers to that which can reasonably be expected or believed on the basis of available evidence or logic but is neither certain nor proved (*Webster's New World Dictionary,* p. 1132). Its inclusion in the definition is intended to acknowledge that business and other economic activities occur in an environment characterized by uncertainty in which few outcomes are certain (pars. 44-48).

[22]*Obligations* in the definition is broader than *legal obligations.* It is used with its usual general meaning to refer to duties imposed legally or socially; to that which one is bound to do by contract, promise, moral responsibility, and so forth (*Webster's New World Dictionary,* p. 981). It includes equitable and constructive obligations as well as legal obligations (pars. 37-40).

Only present obligations to others are liabilities under the definition. An obligation becomes a present obligation when a transaction or event occurs that leaves an entity little or no discretion to avoid the future transfer or use of assets to settle the liability. An exit or disposal plan, by itself, does not create a present obligation to others for costs expected to be incurred under the plan; thus, an entity's commitment to an exit or disposal plan, by itself, is not the requisite past transaction or event for recognition of a liability.

5. [This paragraph has been deleted. See Status page.]

6. In periods subsequent to initial measurement, changes to the liability shall be measured using the credit-adjusted risk-free rate that was used to measure the liability initially. The cumulative effect of a change resulting from a revision to either the timing or the amount of estimated cash flows shall be recognized as an adjustment to the liability in the period of the change and reported in the same line item(s) in the income statement (statement of activities) used when the related costs were recognized initially. Changes due to the passage of time shall be recognized as an increase in the carrying amount of the liability and as an expense (for example, accretion expense).[6]

Recognition and Measurement of Certain Costs

7. Paragraphs 8–17 provide additional guidance for applying the recognition and measurement provisions of this Statement to certain costs that often are associated with an exit or disposal activity.

---

[4]FASB Statements No. 87, *Employers' Accounting for Pensions,* No. 88, *Employers' Accounting for Settlements and Curtailments of Defined Benefit Pension Plans and for Termination Benefits,* No. 106, *Employers' Accounting for Postretirement Benefits Other Than Pensions,* and No. 112, *Employers' Accounting for Postemployment Benefits,* address the accounting for other employee benefits. APB Opinion No. 12, *Omnibus Opinion—1967,* as amended by Statement 106, addresses the accounting for deferred compensation contracts with individual employees. This Statement does not change the accounting for termination benefits, including one-time termination benefits granted in the form of an enhancement to an ongoing benefit arrangement, covered by those accounting pronouncements.

[5]FASB Statement No. 13, *Accounting for Leases,* addresses the accounting for the termination of a capital lease (paragraph 14(c)).

[6]Accretion expense shall not be considered interest cost for purposes of applying FASB Statement No. 34, *Capitalization of Interest Cost,* or for purposes of classification in the income statement (statement of activities).

One-Time Termination Benefits

8. As indicated in paragraph 2(a), one-time termination benefits are benefits provided to current employees that are involuntarily terminated under the terms of a one-time benefit arrangement. A one-time benefit arrangement is an arrangement established by a plan of termination that applies for a specified termination event or for a specified future period.[7] A one-time benefit arrangement exists at the date the plan of termination meets all of the following criteria and has been communicated to employees (hereinafter referred to as the *communication date*):

a. Management, having the authority to approve the action, commits to a plan of termination.

b. The plan identifies the number of employees to be terminated, their job classifications or functions and their locations, and the expected completion date.

c. The plan establishes the terms of the benefit arrangement, including the benefits that employees will receive upon termination (including but not limited to cash payments), in sufficient detail to enable employees to determine the type and amount of benefits they will receive if they are involuntarily terminated.

d. Actions required to complete the plan indicate that it is unlikely that significant changes to the plan will be made or that the plan will be withdrawn.

9. The timing of recognition and related measurement of a liability for one-time termination benefits depends on whether employees are required to render service until they are terminated in order to receive the termination benefits and, if so, whether employees will be retained to render service beyond a minimum retention period. The minimum retention period shall not exceed the *legal notification period,*[8] or in the absence of a legal notification requirement, 60 days.

10. If employees are not required to render service until they are terminated in order to receive the termination benefits (that is, if employees are entitled to receive the termination benefits regardless of when they leave) or if employees will not be retained to render service beyond the minimum retention period, a liability for the termination benefits shall be recognized and measured at its fair value at the communication date. The provisions of paragraph 6 shall apply in periods subsequent to the communication date. (Example 1 of Appendix A illustrates that situation.)

11. If employees are required to render service until they are terminated in order to receive the termination benefits and will be retained to render service beyond the minimum retention period, a liability for the termination benefits shall be measured initially at the communication date based on the fair value of the liability as of the termination date. The liability shall be recognized ratably over the future service period. A change resulting from a revision to either the timing or the amount of estimated cash flows over the future service period shall be measured using the credit-adjusted risk-free rate that was used to measure the liability initially. The cumulative effect of the change shall be recognized as an adjustment to the liability in the period of the change. The provisions of paragraph 6 shall apply in periods subsequent to the termination date. (Example 2 of Appendix A illustrates that situation.)

12. If a plan of termination changes and employees that were expected to be terminated within the minimum retention period are retained to render service beyond that period, a liability previously recognized at the communication date shall be adjusted to the amount that would have been recognized if the provisions of paragraph 11 had been applied in all periods subsequent to the communication date. The cumulative effect of the change shall be recognized as an adjustment to the liability in the period of the change. The provisions of paragraph 11 shall apply in subsequent periods.

13. If a plan of termination that meets the criteria in paragraph 8 includes both involuntary termination benefits and termination benefits offered for a short period of time in exchange for employees' voluntary termination of service, a liability for the involuntary termination benefits shall be recognized in accordance with this Statement. A liability for the incremental voluntary termination benefits (the excess of the

---

[7]Absent evidence to the contrary, an ongoing benefit arrangement is presumed to exist if an entity has a past practice of providing similar termination benefits.

[8]*Legal notification period* refers to the notification period that an entity is required to provide to employees in advance of a specified termination event as a result of an existing law, statute, or contract. For example, in the United States, the Worker Adjustment and Retraining Notification Act requires entities with 100 or more employees to notify employees 60 days in advance of covered plant closings and mass layoffs, unless otherwise specified. Collective bargaining or other labor contracts may require different notification periods.

voluntary termination benefit amount over the involuntary termination benefit amount) shall be recognized in accordance with FASB Statement No. 88, *Employers' Accounting for Settlements and Curtailments of Defined Benefit Pension Plans and for Termination Benefits.*[9] (Example 3 of Appendix A illustrates that situation.)

Contract Termination Costs

14. For purposes of this Statement, costs to terminate an operating lease or other contract are (a) costs to terminate the contract before the end of its term or (b) costs that will continue to be incurred under the contract for its remaining term without economic benefit to the entity.

15. A liability for costs to terminate a contract before the end of its term shall be recognized and measured at its fair value when the entity terminates the contract in accordance with the contract terms (for example, when the entity gives written notice to the counterparty within the notification period specified by the contract or has otherwise negotiated a termination with the counterparty). The provisions of paragraph 6 shall apply in periods subsequent to that date.

16. A liability for costs that will continue to be incurred under a contract for its remaining term without economic benefit to the entity shall be recognized and measured at its fair value when the entity ceases using the right conveyed by the contract, for example, the right to use a leased property or to receive future goods or services (hereinafter referred to as the *cease-use date*).[10] If the contract is an operating lease, the fair value of the liability at the cease-use date shall be determined based on the remaining lease rentals,[11] reduced by estimated sublease rentals that could be reasonably obtained for the property, even if the entity does not intend to enter into a sublease. Remaining lease rentals shall not be reduced to an amount less than zero. The provisions of paragraph 6 shall apply in periods subsequent to the cease-use date. (Example 4 of Appendix A illustrates that situation.)

Other Associated Costs

17. Other costs associated with an exit or disposal activity include, but are not limited to, costs to consolidate or close facilities and relocate employees. A liability for other costs associated with an exit or disposal activity shall be recognized and measured at its fair value in the period in which the liability is incurred (generally, when goods or services associated with the activity are received). The liability shall not be recognized before it is incurred, even if the costs are incremental to other operating costs and will be incurred as a direct result of a plan.

Reporting

18. Costs associated with an exit or disposal activity that does not involve a discontinued operation shall be included in income from continuing operations before income taxes in the income statement of a business enterprise and in income from continuing operations in the statement of activities of a not-for-profit organization. If a subtotal such as "income from operations" is presented, it shall include the amounts of those costs. Costs associated with an exit or disposal activity that involves a discontinued operation shall be included in the results of discontinued operations.[12]

19. If an event or circumstance occurs that discharges or removes an entity's responsibility to settle a liability for a cost associated with an exit or disposal activity recognized in a prior period, the liability shall be reversed. The related costs shall be reversed through the same line item(s) in the income statement (statement of activities) used when those costs were recognized initially.

Disclosure

20. The following information shall be disclosed in notes to financial statements that include the period in which an exit or disposal activity is initiated (refer to paragraph 21) and any subsequent period until the activity is completed:

a. A description of the exit or disposal activity, including the facts and circumstances leading to the

---

[9]Paragraph 15 of Statement 88 states, "An employer that offers special termination benefits to employees shall recognize a liability and a loss when the employees accept the offer and the amount can be reasonably estimated."

[10]This Statement does not address impairment of an unrecognized asset while it is being used. The EITF is addressing related issues in Issues No. 99-14, "Recognition by a Purchaser of Losses on Firmly Committed Executory Contracts," and No. 00-26, "Recognition by a Seller of Losses on Firmly Committed Executory Contracts."

[11]The remaining lease rentals should be adjusted for the effects of any prepaid or deferred items recognized under the lease.

[12]Paragraphs 41–44 of Statement 144 address the reporting of discontinued operations.

expected activity and the expected completion date

b. For each major type of cost associated with the activity (for example, one-time termination benefits, contract termination costs, and other associated costs):

(1) The total amount expected to be incurred in connection with the activity, the amount incurred in the period, and the cumulative amount incurred to date

(2) A reconciliation of the beginning and ending liability balances showing separately the changes during the period attributable to costs incurred and charged to expense, costs paid or otherwise settled, and any adjustments to the liability with an explanation of the reason(s) therefor

c. The line item(s) in the income statement or the statement of activities in which the costs in (b) above are aggregated

d. For each reportable segment, the total amount of costs expected to be incurred in connection with the activity, the amount incurred in the period, and the cumulative amount incurred to date, net

of any adjustments to the liability with an explanation of the reason(s) therefor

e. If a liability for a cost associated with the activity is not recognized because fair value cannot be reasonably estimated, that fact and the reasons therefor.

Effective Date and Transition

21. The provisions of this Statement shall be effective for exit or disposal activities initiated after December 31, 2002. Early application is encouraged. Previously issued financial statements shall not be restated. For purposes of this Statement, an exit or disposal activity is initiated when management, having the authority to approve the action, commits to an exit or disposal plan or otherwise disposes of a long-lived asset (disposal group) and, if the activity involves the termination of employees, the criteria for a plan of termination in paragraph 8 of this Statement are met. The provisions of Issue 94-3 shall continue to apply for an exit activity initiated under an exit plan that met the criteria of Issue 94-3 prior to this Statement's initial application.

> **The provisions of this Statement need not be applied to immaterial items.**

This Statement was adopted by the affirmative votes of six members of the Financial Accounting Standards Board. Mr. Foster dissented.

Mr. Foster dissents from the issuance of this Statement because he disagrees with the Board's conclusions on (1) subsequent measurement of liabilities for property leased under operating leases that will not be used in future operations, (2) permitting the time value of money to be ignored in measuring liabilities for one-time termination benefits that are granted in the form of an enhancement to an existing post-employment benefit plan for which obligations are not recognized by the employer on a discounted basis, as permitted by FASB Statement No. 112, *Employers' Accounting for Postemployment Benefits,* and (3) using the employee benefits model to account for one-time termination benefits.

The cash flows used in measuring liabilities for leases of property that will not be used in future operations must be reassessed each period for market changes in lease rates. Consequently, when there is a change in the expected cash flows, the new carrying amount is unrelated to previous amounts and accounting conventions and is a fresh-start measure-

ment as that term is defined in FASB Concepts Statement No. 7, *Using Cash Flow Information and Present Value in Accounting Measurements.* In that Concepts Statement, the Board concluded that the only objective of using present value, when used in accounting measurements at initial recognition and fresh-start measurements, is to estimate fair value. Mr. Foster believes the Board should adhere to its conceptual framework and require that the objective of subsequent measurements of liabilities for leases of property that will not be used in future operations, which are fresh-start measurements, be fair value. He observes that the difference between measuring such liabilities at fair value and the method adopted by the Board is solely which interest rate is used to discount the estimated cash flows. Furthermore, the current risk-free rate is always easily observable. Thus, there are no incremental costs involved in estimating fair value, and Mr. Foster believes fair value is clearly a more relevant measurement of the liability than that resulting from the method required by this Statement.

This Statement does not amend Statement 112 to require that all one-time termination benefits that are granted in the form of enhancements to existing postemployment benefit plans be accounted for in accordance with the requirements for other one-time termination benefits under this Statement—specifically, that liabilities for those termination benefits be discounted, consistent with Concepts Statement 7. Mr. Foster believes there is trivial effort involved in discounting liabilities for the time value of money and that the benefits to users of financial statements of doing so are significant.

While Mr. Foster acknowledges that paragraph 207 of Concepts Statement 6 sanctions the employee service model, he believes that the require-ment of this Statement that liabilities should be recognized initially when incurred is a more appropriate method for accounting for one-time termination benefits. He prefers the approach described in paragraph B33 that would delay recognition of a liability for those termination benefits until the entity has little or no discretion to avoid a transfer of assets—the termination date. He notes that the entity has discretion to avoid payment of the termination benefits at all times during the period in which an employee is to render service by not terminating the employee. It is only when the employee is terminated that the employee becomes entitled to receive the termination benefits, and termination is the event that causes the obligation to become a present obligation.

Members of the Financial Accounting Standards Board:

Edmund L. Jenkins,	John M. Foster	Edward W. Trott
Chairman	Gary S. Schieneman	John K. Wulff
G. Michael Crooch	Katherine Schipper	

Appendix A

IMPLEMENTATION GUIDANCE

Introduction

A1. This appendix describes certain provisions of this Statement in more detail. This appendix also provides examples that incorporate simplified assumptions to illustrate how certain provisions of this Statement apply in certain specific situations. The examples do not address all possible situations or applications of this Statement. This appendix is an integral part of the standards provided in this Statement.

Fair Value

A2. The objective of initial measurement of a liability for a cost associated with an exit or disposal activity is fair value (paragraph 3). A present value technique is often the best available valuation technique with which to estimate the fair value of a liability for a cost associated with an exit or disposal activity. For a liability that has uncertainties both in timing and amount, an expected present value technique generally will be the appropriate technique.

A3. Quoted market prices are the best representation of fair value. However, for many of the liabilities covered by this Statement, quoted market prices will not be available. Consequently, in those circumstances fair value will be estimated using some other valuation technique.

A4–A5. [These paragraphs have been deleted. See Status page.]

A6. In some situations, a fair value measurement for a liability associated with an exit or disposal activity obtained using a valuation technique other than a present value technique may not be materially different from a fair value measurement obtained using a present value technique. In those situations, this Statement does not preclude the use of estimates and computational shortcuts that are consistent with a fair value measurement objective.

13–16[These footnotes have been deleted. See Status page.]

Examples 1–3—One-Time Termination Benefits

A7. Examples 1–3 illustrate the application of the recognition and measurement provisions of this Statement to one-time termination benefits. Each example assumes that an entity has a one-time benefit arrangement established by a plan of termination that meets the criteria of paragraph 8 and has been communicated to employees.

Example 1

A8. An entity plans to cease operations in a particular location and determines that it no longer needs the 100 employees that currently work in that location. The entity notifies the employees that they will be terminated in 90 days. Each employee will receive as a termination benefit a cash payment of $6,000, which will be paid at the date an employee ceases rendering service during the 90-day period. In accordance with paragraph 10, a liability would be recognized at the communication date and measured at its fair value. In this case, because of the short discount period, $600,000 may not be materially different from the fair value of the liability at the communication date.

Example 2

A9. An entity plans to shut down a manufacturing facility in 16 months and, at that time, terminate all of the remaining employees at the facility. To induce employees to stay until the facility is shut down, the entity establishes a one-time stay bonus arrangement. Each employee that stays and renders service for the full 16-month period will receive as a termination benefit a cash payment of $10,000, which will be paid 6 months after the termination date. An employee that leaves voluntarily before the facility is shut down will not be entitled to receive any portion of the termination benefit. In accordance with paragraph 11, a liability for the termination benefits would be measured initially at the communication date based on the fair value of the liability as of the termination date and recognized ratably over the future service period (as illustrated in (a) below). The fair value of the liability as of the termination date would be adjusted cumulatively for changes resulting from revisions to estimated cash flows over the future service period, measured using the credit-adjusted risk-free rate that was used to measure the liability initially (as illustrated in (b) below).

a. The fair value of the liability as of the termination date is $962,240, estimated at the communication date using an expected present value technique. The expected cash flows of $1 million (to be paid 6 months after the termination date), which consider the likelihood that some employees will leave voluntarily before the facility is shut down, are discounted for 6 months at the credit-adjusted risk-free rate of 8 percent.[17] Thus, a liability of $60,140 would be recognized in each month during the future service period (16 months).

b. After eight months, more employees than originally estimated leave voluntarily. The entity adjusts the fair value of the liability as of the termination date to $769,792 to reflect the revised expected cash flows of $800,000 (to be paid 6 months after the termination date), discounted for 6 months at the credit-adjusted risk-free rate that was used to measure the liability initially (8 percent). Based on that revised estimate, a liability (expense) of $48,112 would have been recognized in each month during the future service period. Thus, the liability recognized to date of $481,120 ($60,140 × 8) would be reduced to $384,896 ($48,112 × 8) to reflect the cumulative effect of that change (of $96,224). A liability of $48,112 would be recognized in each month during the remaining future service period (8 months). Accretion expense would be recognized after the termination date in accordance with paragraph 6.

Example 3

A10. An entity initiates changes to streamline operations in a particular location and determines that, as a result, it no longer needs 100 of the employees that currently work in that location. The plan of termination provides for both voluntary and involuntary termination benefits (in the form of cash payments). Specifically, the entity offers each employee (up to 100 employees) that voluntarily terminates within 30 days a voluntary termination benefit of $10,000 to be paid at the separation date. Each employee that is involuntarily terminated thereafter (to reach the target of 100) will receive an involuntary termination benefit of $6,000 to be paid at the termination date. The entity expects all 100 employees to

---

[17]In this case, a risk premium is not considered in the present value measurement. Because the amounts of the cash flows will be fixed and certain as of the termination date, marketplace participants would not demand a risk premium.

leave (voluntarily or involuntarily) within the minimum retention period. In accordance with paragraphs 9 and 10, a liability for the involuntary termination benefit (of $6,000 per employee) would be recognized at the communication date and measured at its fair value. In this case, because of the short discount period, $600,000 may not be materially different from the fair value of the liability at the communication date. As noted in paragraph 13, a liability for the incremental voluntary termination benefit (of $4,000 per employee) would be recognized in accordance with FASB Statement No. 88, *Employers' Accounting for Settlements and Curtailments of Defined Benefit Pension Plans and for Termination Benefits* (that is, when employees accept the offer).

Example 4—Costs to Terminate an Operating Lease

A11. An entity leases a facility under an operating lease that requires the entity to pay lease rentals of $100,000 per year for 10 years. After using the facility for five years, the entity commits to an exit plan. In connection with that plan, the entity will cease using the facility in 1 year (after using the facility for 6 years), at which time the remaining lease rentals will be $400,000 ($100,000 per year for the remaining term of 4 years). In accordance with paragraph 16, a liability for the remaining lease rentals, reduced by actual (or estimated) sublease rentals, would be recognized and measured at its fair value at the cease-use date (as illustrated in (a) below). In accordance with paragraph 6, the liability would be adjusted for changes, if any, resulting from revisions to estimated cash flows after the cease-use date, measured using the credit-adjusted risk-free rate that was used to measure the liability initially (as illustrated in (b) below).

a. Based on market rentals for similar leased property, the entity determines that if it desired, it could sublease the facility and receive sublease rentals of $300,000 ($75,000 per year for the remaining lease term of 4 years). However, for competitive reasons, the entity decides not to sublease the facility (or otherwise terminate the lease) at the cease-use date. The fair value of the liability at the cease-use date is $89,427, estimated using an expected present value technique. The expected net cash flows of $100,000 ($25,000 per year for the remaining lease term of 4 years) are discounted using a credit-adjusted risk-free rate of 8 percent.[18] Thus, a liability (expense) of $89,427 would be recognized at the cease-use date. Accretion expense would be recognized after the cease-use date in accordance with paragraph 6. (The entity will recognize the impact of deciding not to sublease the property over the period the property is not subleased. For example, in the first year after the cease-use date, an expense of $75,000 would be recognized as the impact of not subleasing the property, which reflects the annual lease payment of $100,000 net of the liability extinguishment of $25,000.)

b. At the end of one year, the competitive factors referred to above are no longer present. The entity decides to sublease the facility and enters into a sublease. The entity will receive sublease rentals of $250,000 ($83,333 per year for the remaining lease term of 3 years), negotiated based on market rentals for similar leased property at the sublease date. The entity adjusts the carrying amount of the liability at the sublease date to $46,388 to reflect the revised expected net cash flows of $50,000 ($16,667 per year for the remaining lease term of 3 years), which are discounted at the credit-adjusted risk-free rate that was used to measure the liability initially (8 percent). Accretion expense would be recognized after the sublease date in accordance with paragraph 6.

---

[18]In this case, a risk premium is not considered in the present value measurement. Because the lease rentals are fixed by contract and the estimated sublease rentals are based on market prices for similar leased property for other entities having similar credit standing as the entity, there is little uncertainty in the amount and timing of the expected cash flows used in estimating fair value at the cease-use date and any risk premium would be insignificant. In other circumstances, a risk premium would be appropriate if it is significant.

Appendix B

BACKGROUND INFORMATION AND BASIS FOR CONCLUSIONS

CONTENTS

Appendix B

BACKGROUND INFORMATION AND BASIS FOR CONCLUSIONS

Introduction

B1. This appendix summarizes considerations that Board members deemed significant in reaching the conclusions in this Statement. It includes the reasons for accepting certain approaches and rejecting others. Individual Board members gave greater weight to some factors than to others.

Background Information

B2. APB Opinion No. 30, *Reporting the Results of Operations—Reporting the Effects of Disposal of a Segment of a Business, and Extraordinary, Unusual and Infrequently Occurring Events and Transactions,* was issued in 1973. Opinion 30 addressed the accounting for the operations of a *segment of a business* to be disposed of, as previously defined in that Opinion. Under Opinion 30, a segment of a business to be disposed of was measured at the lower of its carrying amount or net realizable value, adjusted for expected future operating losses and costs associated with the disposal, at a plan (measurement) date. If a loss on disposal was expected, those items (expected future operating losses and costs associated with the disposal) were recognized (as liabilities) as part of the loss at that date so that they would not affect earnings reported in future periods.[19]

B3. The definition of a liability subsequently set forth in FASB Concepts Statement No. 6, *Elements of Financial Statements* (paragraph 35), incorporates the view that assets and liabilities are the fundamental elements of financial statements. An essential characteristic of that definition is that a liability is a present obligation to others. In its discussions leading to this Statement, the Board observed that because a plan merely reflects an entity's intended actions, it does not, by itself, create a present obligation to others for the costs expected to be incurred under the plan. Thus, some costs were recognized as liabilities at a plan (measurement) date under Opinion 30 that did not meet the definition of a liability.

B4. FASB Statement No. 121, *Accounting for the Impairment of Long-Lived Assets and for Long-Lived Assets to Be Disposed Of,* was issued in 1995. Among other things, Statement 121 addressed the accounting for long-lived assets to be disposed of that were not covered by Opinion 30. Under Statement 121, a long-lived asset to be disposed of was measured at the lower of its carrying amount or fair value less cost to sell, which excludes expected future operating losses and costs associated with the disposal that marketplace participants would not similarly consider in their estimates of fair value less cost to sell. However, Statement 121 did not address the accounting for expected future operating losses or recognition of liabilities for other costs. Instead, Statement 121 referred to the guidance in EITF Issue No. 94-3, "Liability Recognition for Certain Employee Termination Benefits and Other Costs to Exit an Activity (including Certain Costs Incurred in a Restructuring)."

B5. Issue 94-3, which was completed in 1995, addressed the recognition of liabilities for costs associated with an exit activity not covered by Opinion 30. Under Issue 94-3, only costs that met its definition of exit costs were recognized as liabilities at a plan (commitment) date. The definition of exit costs in

Issue 94-3 excluded expected future operating losses. However, in its discussions leading to this Statement, the Board observed that because Issue 94-3 retained the plan date notion in Opinion 30, some costs continued to be recognized as liabilities at a plan (commitment) date under Issue 94-3 that did not meet the definition of a liability.

B6. In August 1996, the Board added to its agenda a project related to Statement 121. The principal objectives of that project were to address (a) differences in the accounting for long-lived assets and operations (segments) to be disposed of under Statement 121 and Opinion 30 and (b) the accounting for costs associated with asset disposal activities and other similar activities, including exit activities under Issue 94-3.

B7. In June 2000, the Board issued an Exposure Draft, *Accounting for the Impairment or Disposal of Long-Lived Assets and for Obligations Associated with Disposal Activities.* The Board received comment letters from 53 respondents to the Exposure Draft. In January 2001, the Board held a public roundtable meeting with some of those respondents to discuss significant issues raised in the comment letters. During its redeliberations of those issues, the Board decided to complete the project in two phases to avoid delaying the issuance of guidance on the accounting for long-lived assets and operations to be disposed of.

B8. The first phase of the project was completed in August 2001 with the issuance of FASB Statement No. 144, *Accounting for the Impairment or Disposal of Long-Lived Assets.* Statement 144 establishes an accounting model based on the framework in Statement 121 for long-lived assets and disposal groups to be disposed of, including operations (components of an entity), and supersedes Statement 121 in its entirety and Opinion 30 as it relates to operations (segments) to be disposed of.

B9. This Statement represents the second and final phase of the project. It establishes an accounting model based on the FASB's conceptual framework for recognition and measurement of a liability for a cost associated with an exit or disposal activity and nullifies Issue 94-3. The fundamental conclusion

---

[19]At that time, the definition of a liability in paragraph 132 of APB Statement No. 4, *Basic Concepts and Accounting Principles Underlying Financial Statements of Business Enterprises,* incorporated the view that the matching of costs and revenues to avoid "distortions" in reporting of income was the central function of financial accounting. In addition to economic obligations of an enterprise, the Accounting Principles Board's definition of a liability included "certain deferred credits that are not obligations but that are recognized and measured in conformity with generally accepted accounting principles" (footnote references omitted).

reached by the Board in developing that accounting model is that a liability for a cost associated with an exit or disposal activity should be recognized and measured initially at its fair value when it is incurred. A liability is incurred when the definition of a liability in paragraph 35 of Concepts Statement 6 is met.

Basis for Conclusions

Scope

B10. This Statement applies to costs associated with an exit activity or with a disposal activity covered by Statement 144. As indicated in paragraph 2, costs excluded from the scope of this Statement include costs associated with an exit activity that involves an entity newly acquired in a business combination (which the Board is reconsidering in its project on business combinations—purchase method procedures), termination benefits provided to employees that are involuntarily or voluntarily terminated covered by the other accounting pronouncements listed in footnote 4 to paragraph 2, and costs to terminate a capital lease. The Board concluded that the objectives of this project could be achieved without reconsidering the accounting for those costs in this Statement.

B11. The Exposure Draft proposed to exclude costs to terminate a contract other than an operating lease. At that time, the Board concluded that addressing all contract termination costs included in the scope of Issue 94-3 could require it to address issues on the accounting for other executory contracts that are beyond the scope of this Statement. For that reason, the Board initially decided that the guidance in Issue 94-3 should continue to apply for those contract termination costs. However, some respondents to the Exposure Draft said that allowing the guidance in Issue 94-3 to continue to apply only for those contract termination costs would be confusing. The Board subsequently decided to reconsider the guidance in Issue 94-3 in its entirety and include in the scope of this Statement the contract termination costs previously included in the scope of Issue 94-3.

Recognition and Measurement

B12. During its deliberations leading to the Exposure Draft, the Board decided that the requirements of this Statement for recognition of a liability for a cost associated with an exit or disposal activity should incorporate the guidance in FASB Statement No. 5, *Accounting for Contingencies.* Accordingly, the Exposure Draft would have required that the liability be recognized initially when the likelihood of future settlement is probable, as that term is used in Statement 5,[20] and the amount can be reasonably estimated—the transaction or other event obligating the entity having occurred previously. The Board also decided that fair value should be the objective for initial measurement of the liability.

Fair value

B13. During its redeliberations of the Exposure Draft, the Board affirmed that fair value is the objective for initial measurement of a liability for a cost associated with an exit or disposal activity. The Board believes that fair value is the most relevant and faithful representation of the underlying economics of a transaction—it is basic to economic theory and is grounded in the reality of the marketplace. FASB Concepts Statement No. 7, *Using Cash Flow Information and Present Value in Accounting Measurements,* establishes fair value as the objective for both initial measurements and fresh-start measurements in subsequent periods that are developed using present value techniques. Accordingly, the Board considered whether to require a fresh-start approach for subsequent measurements of a liability for a cost associated with an exit or disposal activity covered by this Statement or to limit the fair value objective to initial measurement.[21]

B14. The Board agreed that, conceptually, subsequent measurements of the liabilities covered by this Statement are fresh-start measurements that should be measured at fair value. For some of those liabilities, in particular, liabilities related to a leased property under an operating lease that will not be used in

---

[20]Statement 5 uses the term *probable* in a different sense than the term is used in the definition of a liability. In Statement 5, probable refers to a high degree of expectation. In the definition of a liability, probable is intended to acknowledge that business and other economic activities occur in an environment in which few outcomes are certain.

[21]Concepts Statement 7 does not specify when fresh-start measurements are appropriate. Paragraph 14 of Concepts Statement 7 clarifies that the Board expects to decide whether a particular situation requires a fresh-start measurement or some other accounting response on a project-by-project basis.

future operations, measurements are based on estimates that are revised to incorporate current information as new facts and circumstances become known. Moreover, most of those liabilities often will be settled in cash, similar to financial instruments, which the Board believes should be measured at fair value.

B15. However, the Board decided, as it did in FASB Statement No. 143, *Accounting for Asset Retirement Obligations,* not to require a fresh-start approach for the liabilities covered by this Statement. The Board concluded that until issues related to determining the fair values of financial instruments are resolved and fair value is required for subsequent measurement of more (or all) liabilities, it would be premature to require that type of ongoing measurement in this Statement.[22] Instead, the Board decided to require an approach that holds interest rates constant, thereby measuring changes, if any, resulting from revisions to either the timing or the amount of estimated cash flows using the credit-adjusted risk-free rate that was used to measure the liability initially.

Statement 5 probability criterion

B16. In view of its decision that fair value is the objective for initial measurement of a liability for a cost associated with an exit or disposal activity, the Board reconsidered its decision that the recognition requirements of this Statement should incorporate the guidance in Statement 5. The Board subsequently concluded, as it did in Statement 143, that because Statement 5 and Concepts Statement 7 deal with uncertainty differently, the recognition guidance in Statement 5 is inconsistent with an objective of measuring fair value. Statement 5 deals with uncertainty by requiring a probability threshold for *recognition* of a loss contingency. Concepts Statement 7 deals with uncertainty in the amount and timing of the future cash flows necessary to settle a liability by requiring that the likelihood of possible outcomes be incorporated into the *measurement* of the fair value of the liability.[23]

B17. To resolve that inconsistency, the Board decided that a liability for a cost associated with an exit or disposal activity should be recognized initially when the liability is incurred. Thus, in determining whether to recognize a liability for a cost associated

with an exit or disposal activity, and in measuring its fair value, the guidance in Statement 5 and FASB Interpretation No. 14, *Reasonable Estimation of the Amount of a Loss,* does not apply.

Definition and essential characteristics of a liability

B18. This Statement specifies that a liability for a cost associated with an exit or disposal activity is incurred when the definition of a liability is met. Paragraph 35 of Concepts Statement 6 states:

> Liabilities are probable future sacrifices of economic benefits arising from present obligations of a particular entity to transfer assets or provide services to other entities in the future as a result of past transactions or events. [Footnote references omitted.]

Paragraph 36 of Concepts Statement 6 identifies three essential characteristics of a liability, all of which must be present to meet the definition of a liability. In this Statement, the Board clarifies those essential characteristics of a liability as they apply to a cost associated with an exit or disposal activity covered by this Statement.

B19. The first essential characteristic of a liability is that an entity has "a present duty or responsibility to one or more other entities that entails settlement by probable future transfer or use of assets at a specified or determinable date, on occurrence of a specified event, or on demand." In general, an obligation is created by an entity's promise, on which others are justified in relying, to take a particular course of action (perform) that will entail the future transfer or use of assets. In that context:

a. An entity's promise may be (1) unconditional or conditional upon the occurrence of a specified future event that is or is not within the entity's control, (2) stated in words, either oral or written, or (3) inferred from the entity's past practice, which, absent evidence to the contrary, others can presume that the entity will continue.

b. Others are justified in relying on an entity's promise if (1) they, or their representatives, are the recipients of the promise, (2) they can reasonably expect the entity to perform (that is, the

---

[22]As noted in paragraph 2 of FASB Concepts Statement No. 5, *Recognition and Measurement in Financial Statements of Business Enterprises,* "the Board intends future change [in practice] to occur in the gradual, evolutionary way that has characterized past change."

[23]Paragraphs 55–61 of Concepts Statement 7 discuss the relations between the fair value measurement objective discussed in Concepts Statement 7 and accounting for contingencies under Statement 5.

promise is credible), and (3) they either will benefit from the entity's performance or will suffer loss or harm from the entity's nonperformance.

B20. The second essential characteristic of a liability is that "... the duty or responsibility obligates a particular entity, leaving it little or no discretion to avoid the future sacrifice." Paragraph 203 of Concepts Statement 6 elaborates on that characteristic, stating that an entity is not obligated to others if it can avoid the future transfer or use of assets at its discretion without significant penalty.

B21. The third essential characteristic of a liability is that "... the transaction or other event obligating the entity has already happened." Paragraph 206 of Concepts Statement 6 states:

> The definition of liabilities in paragraph 35 distinguishes between present and future obligations of an entity. Only present obligations are liabilities under the definition, and they are liabilities of a particular entity as a result of the occurrence of transactions or other events or circumstances affecting the entity.

The Board concluded that because an exit or disposal plan merely reflects an entity's intended actions and, by itself, does not create a present obligation to others for the costs expected to be incurred under the plan, an entity's commitment to such a plan, by itself, is not the requisite past transaction or event for recognition of a liability.[24]

B22. The Board acknowledges that identifying the requisite past transaction or event for recognition of a liability requires judgment, especially in situations that involve a series of transactions or other events or circumstances affecting the entity over time. The Board decided that this Statement should provide additional guidance for applying its recognition and measurement provisions to certain costs that often are associated with an exit or disposal activity. That additional guidance focuses principally on one-time termination benefits and contract termination costs.

One-time termination benefits

B23. This Statement applies to one-time termination benefits provided to current employees that are involuntarily terminated under the terms of a one-time benefit arrangement, that is, a benefit arrangement established by a plan of termination that applies for a specified termination event or for a specified future period. A one-time benefit arrangement exists at the date the plan of termination meets all of the criteria in paragraph 8 and has been communicated to employees. This Statement refers to that date as the *communication date*. The Board concluded that an entity's communication of a promise to provide one-time termination benefits is a promise that, as discussed in paragraph B19, creates an obligation at the communication date to provide the termination benefits if employees are terminated.

Future service requirement

B24. During its deliberations leading to the Exposure Draft, the Board decided that the recognition approach for an obligation to provide one-time termination benefits should be based on whether the benefit arrangement requires employees to render future service and, in substance, is a "stay bonus" arrangement, as discussed in Issue 94-3.

B25. Under Issue 94-3, the determination of whether employees were required to render future service was based on facts and circumstances that, while largely unspecified, included the benefit formula used to calculate an employee's termination benefit. Issue 94-3 stated that "... facts and circumstances would have to be evaluated to determine if, in substance, all or some portion of those benefits should be accounted for prospectively as payments for future services rather than recognized currently as benefits for termination." The Board concluded that because a one-time benefit arrangement does not exist until a plan of termination meets all of the criteria in paragraph 8 and has been communicated to employees, a benefit formula should not be used as a basis for determining whether the future services of employees are required (as discussed in paragraph B28). Also, the Board observed that numerous facts and circumstances affect an entity's decision to provide termination benefits and that the judgment applied in assessing those facts and circumstances is necessarily

---

[24]For a recognized asset (or liability), the definition of an asset (or liability) having been met previously, an entity's commitment to a plan may be relevant in determining whether to reclassify and, in certain circumstances, remeasure the asset (or liability)—as is the case for a long-lived asset (disposal group) to be disposed of under Statement 144. However, reclassification and remeasurement issues are fundamentally different from initial recognition issues. An entity's commitment to a plan, by itself, is not sufficient for initial recognition of an asset (or liability).

subjective. Largely for those reasons, the Board concluded that the facts-and-circumstances approach in Issue 94-3 could result in differences in accounting for one-time termination benefits that are substantively identical.

B26. The Board decided that the determination of whether employees are required to render future service should be based on when employees are entitled to receive the termination benefits, without regard to other facts and circumstances. In reaching that decision, the Board reasoned that an entity would not communicate a promise to provide one-time termination benefits in advance of termination unless the entity had a need for employees to render future service. Thus, the Exposure Draft specified that employees are required to render future service if they are not entitled to receive the termination benefits until they are terminated. The Board decided that if employees are required to render future service until they are terminated in order to receive the termination benefits, a liability for the termination benefits should be recognized over the future service period. Otherwise, a liability for the termination benefits should be recognized at the communication date.

B27. Several respondents to the Exposure Draft disagreed with that approach. They said that there may be valid reasons, other than the need for employees to render future service, for communicating a promise to provide one-time termination benefits in advance of termination. Some respondents said that the termination benefits are "rewards" for past service, that is, service rendered prior to the communication date, especially when the benefit formula used to calculate an employee's termination benefit is based on length of service. Other respondents said that an entity may be legally obligated to notify employees of a termination decision in advance or, for some other reason, may decide to provide a transition period for employees that are to be terminated. A few respondents said that even if there is a need for employees to render future service, for example, to wind down operations, the future service period often is relatively short. Respondents indicated that in those situations, a requirement to recognize a liability for the termination benefits over the future service period would, among other things, result in "excessive" compensation expense during that period.

B28. During its redeliberations of the Exposure Draft, the Board acknowledged that in some situations, the benefit formula used to calculate an employee's termination benefit may attribute some (or all) of the termination benefits to past service. However, as previously noted (in paragraph B25), the Board concluded that in those situations, the benefit formula, in and of itself, does not render one-time termination benefits a "reward" for past service. The Board observed that an objective of providing a "reward" for past service could be accomplished by granting immediately vested benefits. In that case, the benefit arrangement could be structured so that employees are entitled to receive the termination benefits regardless of whether they choose to render future service.

B29. The Board acknowledged that an entity may communicate a promise to provide one-time termination benefits in advance of termination for reasons other than the need for employees to render future service, including the need to identify and notify individual employees that are to be terminated and to provide a transition period for those employees, which also may be required by law. For example, in the United States, the Worker Adjustment and Retraining Notification Act (WARN) requires entities with 100 or more employees to notify employees 60 days in advance of covered plant closings and mass layoffs, except as specified. Similar advance notification requirements exist in countries outside the United States but vary with respect to the requisite notification periods. Thus, the Board decided for practical reasons to modify the recognition approach to allow for those situations by referring to a minimum retention period determined based on the legal notification period, that is, the notification period that an entity is required to provide to employees in advance of a specified termination event as a result of an existing law, statute, or contract. In the absence of a legal notification requirement, that period is limited to 60 days, consistent with the minimum notification period of WARN.

Recognition and measurement

B30. This Statement specifies that employees are required to render future service if they are required to render service until they are terminated in order to receive the termination benefits (as proposed in the Exposure Draft) and will be retained to render service beyond the minimum retention period (as modified). The Board affirmed that if employees are required to render future service, the entity's communication of a promise to provide one-time termination benefits forms the basis for an exchange transaction between the entity and its employees. In exchange for the future services of employees who may be terminated, the entity promises to provide, in addition to current wages and other benefits, additional compensation in the form of one-time termination benefits.

B31. A similar exchange notion forms the basis for the conclusions reached by the Board in developing the accounting model for other employee benefits that, like those one-time termination benefits, "vest" and are payable at a future date (pensions and other postemployment benefits). A principal conclusion reached by the Board in developing that accounting model is that an employer's obligation for the additional compensation (in the form of benefits) is incurred and, therefore, should be recognized as employees render services necessary to earn the benefits. Paragraph 163 of FASB Statement No. 106, *Employers' Accounting for Postretirement Benefits Other Than Pensions,* states:

> The Board concluded that the obligation to provide postretirement benefits meets the definition of a liability (paragraphs 152-158), is representationally faithful, is relevant to financial statement users, and can be measured with sufficient reliability at a justifiable cost. To imply by a failure to accrue that no obligation exists prior to the payment of benefits is not a faithful representation of what the financial statements purport to represent. The Board concluded that failure to recognize the existence of the obligation significantly impairs the usefulness and credibility of the employer's financial statements.

B32. The Board decided that the recognition approach for one-time termination benefits should conform to the accounting model for other employee benefits if employees are required to render future service, noting that Concepts Statement 6 supports accruing for employee service as an exchange transaction. Paragraph 207 of Concepts Statement 6 states that "most liabilities result from exchange transactions in which an entity borrows funds or acquires goods or services and agrees . . . to pay for goods or services received. For example, using employees' services obligates an entity to pay wages or salaries and usually fringe benefits." Thus, this Statement requires that a liability for those one-time termination benefits be recognized as employees render service over the future service period.

B33. In reaching that decision, the Board considered and rejected an alternative approach that would have required that a liability for one-time termination ben-efits be recognized at the termination date if employees are required to render future service. That approach is based on the view that an entity does not have a present obligation that meets the definition of a liability until the termination date because, prior to that date, the entity has the discretion to reverse a decision to terminate employees without significant penalty. The Board concluded that such an approach, if adopted, would conflict with the accounting model for other employee benefits, noting that it had considered and rejected a similar approach when developing that accounting model. The Board decided that changes to that accounting model should be addressed in a separate project.

B34. Because the liability for those one-time termination benefits is incurred over time prior to the termination date, that is, over a future service period, the Board decided for practical reasons to modify the fair value measurement date. Specifically, the Board decided that a liability for those one-time termination benefits should be measured initially at the communication date based on the fair value of the liability *as of* the termination date and accrued ratably over the future service period. If the liability is not settled at the termination date, accretion expense should be recognized in accordance with paragraph 6 after that date.

B35. The Board clarified that the fair value of the liability as of the termination date should be adjusted for changes resulting from revisions to either the timing or the amount of estimated cash flows over the future service period using the catch-up approach discussed in Concepts Statement 7. That approach adjusts the carrying amount of the liability to the present value of the revised estimated cash flows, discounted at the credit-adjusted risk-free rate that was used to measure the liability initially. Paragraph 98 of Concepts Statement 7 states:

> The Board considers the catch-up approach to be preferable to other techniques for reporting changes in estimated cash flows because it is consistent with the present value relationships portrayed by the interest method and can be implemented at a reasonable cost. Under the catch-up approach, the recorded amount of an asset or liability, as long as estimated cash flows do not change, is the present value of the estimated future cash flows discounted at the original effective interest rate. If a change in estimate is effected through the catch-up approach, the measurement basis after the change will be the same

as the measurement basis for the same asset or liability before the change in estimate (estimated cash flows discounted at the original effective rate).

B36. This Statement specifies that employees are not required to render future service if employees are entitled to receive termination benefits covered by this Statement regardless of when they leave or if employees will not be retained to render service beyond the minimum retention period (regardless of when they are entitled to receive the termination benefits). The Board affirmed that if employees are not required to render future service, the entity's communication of a promise to provide one-time termination benefits creates an obligation at that date to provide the termination benefits. Absent an exchange for the future services of employees who may be terminated, that obligation is a present obligation that is incurred and, thus, meets the definition of a liability at the communication date. In that situation, a liability for the termination benefits should be recognized and measured at its fair value at the communication date, even though in some cases employees may be retained to render service for some future period (not to exceed the minimum retention period).

B37. During its redeliberations of the Exposure Draft, the Board decided to incorporate guidance, similar to the guidance previously included in Issue 94-3, clarifying the application of the requirements of this Statement for one-time involuntary termination benefits together with the requirements of FASB Statement No. 88, *Employers' Accounting for Settlements and Curtailments of Defined Benefit Pension Plans and for Termination Benefits,* for special voluntary termination benefits. In that situation, a liability for the incremental voluntary termination benefit amount should be recognized in accordance with Statement 88 (that is, when the employee accepts the offer of special voluntary termination benefits), as previously required by Issue 94-3. The Board concluded that it was not necessary to reconsider that guidance in this Statement.

Differences between this Statement and Statement 112

B38. The Board acknowledges, as it did in the Exposure Draft, that the accounting for termination benefits will differ depending on whether the benefits are provided under a one-time benefit arrangement covered by this Statement or an ongoing benefit arrangement covered by FASB Statement No. 112, *Employ-*

ers' Accounting for Postemployment Benefits. Statement 112 requires that a liability for certain termination benefits provided under an ongoing benefit arrangement covered by that Statement be recognized when the likelihood of future settlement is probable, as that term is used in Statement 5. Thus, termination benefits that, based on the benefit formula, are attributable to past service may be recognized initially at a plan date if at that date it becomes probable that employees will be terminated and receive termination benefits under the benefit arrangement (the benefit arrangement having been communicated to employees previously, for example, at the date of hire). Further, Statement 112 permits, but does not require, discounting in measuring postemployment benefit obligations covered by that Statement.

B39. During its deliberations leading to the Exposure Draft, the Board decided to address certain of those differences. Specifically, because not discounting is inconsistent with Concepts Statement 7, the Exposure Draft proposed to amend Statement 112 to preclude that alternative to the extent one-time termination benefits are granted in the form of enhancements to a postemployment benefit plan covered by that Statement. The Exposure Draft also proposed additional guidance for one-time termination benefits that are granted in the form of enhancements to an ongoing benefit arrangement consistent with that amendment. However, upon reconsideration, the Board concluded that those proposals, if retained, would create conflicts with how other postemployment benefits are accounted for and, in addition, could add unnecessary complexity in applying this Statement. The Board believes that, conceptually, liabilities for one-time termination benefit enhancements should be discounted. However, given its decision that changes to the accounting model for employee benefits should be addressed in a separate project, the Board decided not to address any of those differences in this Statement. Thus, this Statement does not retain the proposed amendment to Statement 112 or the additional guidance proposed in the Exposure Draft for one-time termination benefit enhancements to an ongoing benefit arrangement.

Contract termination costs

B40. This Statement applies to costs to terminate an operating lease or other contract that are (a) costs to terminate the contract before the end of its term or

(b) costs that will continue to be incurred under the contract for its remaining term without economic benefit to the entity.

B41. Under Issue 94-3, a liability for costs to terminate a contract in situations involving an exit activity was recognized at the commitment date. For an operating lease, other accounting pronouncements addressed the accounting for similar costs to terminate the lease in other situations. For example, EITF Issue No. 88-10, "Costs Associated with Lease Modification or Termination," referred to the situation in which an entity (lessee) ceases using a property that is leased under an operating lease before the end of its term and enters into a replacement lease with a different lessor. Under Issue 88-10, a liability for the lease termination costs (including remaining lease rentals, reduced by actual or probable sublease rentals) was recognized when the leased property had "no substantive future use or benefit to the lessee." Issue 88-10 permitted, but did not require, discounting in measuring that liability.

B42. During its deliberations leading to the Exposure Draft, the Board reasoned that lease termination costs, in substance, are adjustments to the rentals specified by the lease (the agreed-upon exchange price at the inception of the lease) attributable to the total utilization period. The Board decided that, in contrast to Issue 94-3 and other accounting pronouncements, the recognition approach for lease termination costs should conform to the accounting model for operating leases, which requires that rental expense be allocated on a straight-line basis over the total utilization period as the entity uses the leased property. Thus, the Exposure Draft specified that if an entity's commitment to a plan makes it probable that the entity will cease using the leased property, lease termination costs should be allocated (accrued) over the total utilization period at the commitment date. A liability for the portion of those costs allocable to the past utilization period would be recognized at the commitment date, and a liability for the portion of those costs allocable to the future utilization period would be recognized (ratably) over that future period.

B43. Several respondents to the Exposure Draft disagreed with that approach. They indicated that allocating lease termination costs over the total utilization period would, among other things, result in "excessive" rental expense during the future utilization period, noting that the entity likely will receive reduced benefit from its use of the leased property during that period. Some respondents also said that

the proposed method of allocation, based on the ratio of the past and future utilization periods to the total utilization period, would represent a significant change in current practice that would not improve financial reporting and, in some cases, would be unnecessarily complex.

B44. During its redeliberations of the Exposure Draft, the Board reconsidered the recognition approach for lease termination costs. The Board observed that those costs arise from the rights and obligations conveyed by an operating lease. The Board agreed that, conceptually, those rights and obligations give rise to assets and liabilities at the inception of the lease and that recognition of some (or all) of those rights and obligations at that time would be consistent with the recognition requirements of this Statement (paragraph 3). However, the Board observed that because the rights and obligations under an operating lease are not recognized as assets and liabilities in the financial statements of an entity (lessee), applying those recognition requirements to an operating lease that is included in the scope of this Statement would conflict with the accounting model for operating leases. The Board decided that changes to that accounting model should be addressed in a separate project. In view of that decision, the Board decided for practical reasons that this Statement should specify the event for recognition of a liability for costs to terminate an operating lease and, further, that the same event should apply for recognition of a liability for costs to terminate the other contracts included in the scope of this Statement.

B45. The Board considered and rejected an approach that would have required that a liability for contract termination costs be recognized at the date of an entity's commitment to an exit or disposal plan—a commitment date approach similar to the approach in Issue 94-3. The Board concluded that a commitment date approach, based on the intended actions of an entity at a plan (commitment) date, would be discretionary. In addition, that approach raises issues that are beyond the scope of this Statement about the accounting for impairment losses on firmly committed executory contracts (including operating leases).

B46. The Board decided that a liability for costs to terminate a contract before the end of its term should be recognized and measured at its fair value when an entity terminates the contract in accordance with the contract terms (for example, when the entity gives written notice to the counterparty within the notification period specified by the contract or has otherwise negotiated a termination with the counterparty). The Board concluded that having exercised its option to terminate a contract by communicating that decision to the counterparty, an entity has a legal obligation under the contract for the penalty or other costs specified by the contract.

B47. The Board decided that a liability for other costs that will continue to be incurred under a contract for its remaining term without economic benefit to an entity should be recognized and measured at its fair value when the entity ceases using the right conveyed by the contract (for example, the right to use a leased property or to receive future goods or services)—a cease-use date approach similar to the recognition approach in Issue 88-10. The Board concluded that a cease-use date approach is less discretionary than a commitment date approach because it does not rely on an entity's intended actions at a plan (commitment) date. The Board also observed that a cease-use date approach can be applied consistently, regardless of whether the termination involves an operating lease or other contract. Because the measurement approach in Issue 88-10 permits but does not require discounting, the Board decided that this Statement's cease-use date approach and its requirement for a fair value measurement at that date should apply for a liability for costs to terminate an operating lease in the situation referred to in Issue 88-10. Thus, this Statement substantially nullifies Issue 88-10.

B48. The Board acknowledged that for an operating lease, a cease-use date approach might not eliminate discretion if an entity does not give up its right to use the leased property by terminating the lease or entering into a sublease. For example, the entity could, at its discretion, place the property back in use after having recognized a liability for the future lease rentals (rental expense) otherwise allocable to that future utilization period. However, the Board decided not to modify or otherwise reconsider the cease-use date approach to address that situation. The Board reasoned that if sublease rentals could be reasonably obtained for the property, an entity likely would enter into a sublease. Alternatively, if sublease rentals could not be reasonably obtained for the property, or if the entity chooses for other reasons not to enter into a sublease, the fact that the entity has ceased using the property generally would provide evidence that the entity will not use the property for the remaining lease term.

B49. If an operating lease is not terminated, this Statement requires that measurement of the fair value of the liability at the cease-use date be determined based on the remaining lease rentals, reduced by estimated sublease rentals that could be reasonably obtained for the property, regardless of whether the entity intends to enter into a sublease. The Exposure Draft proposed a similar requirement, with which some respondents disagreed. They said that there may be valid reasons for deciding not to sublease a leased property and that, in those situations, it would be inappropriate to reduce the liability for the remaining lease rentals by "unexpected and hypothetical" sublease rentals.

B50. In response to those concerns, this Statement clarifies that, absent a decision to sublease a leased property, measurement of the fair value of the liability should consider estimated sublease rentals only to the extent that such sublease rentals could be *reasonably* obtained for the property. The Board affirmed that because fair value is a market-based measure, a liability (loss) should be recognized at the cease-use date only if the terms of an operating lease are unfavorable relative to the terms of a new lease for a similar property. Also, the Board observed, as it did in the Exposure Draft, that although an operating lease may be noncancellable by its terms, if a lessee breaches its lease agreement, the lessor may be required by law to mitigate its damages (for example, by taking reasonable steps to locate a new tenant). Thus, if the leased property can be subleased, reducing the remaining lease rentals by estimated sublease rentals would measure the entity's (lessee's) obligation under the lease agreement as the amount of its potential damages in the event of a breach.

Other associated costs

B51. This Statement also applies to other costs associated with an exit or disposal activity. Under Issue 94-3, a liability for exit costs as defined in Issue 94-3 (such as costs to consolidate or close facilities) was recognized at the commitment date. A liability for other costs that were not exit costs (such as costs to relocate employees) was recognized in the period in which the liability was incurred. This Statement eliminates that difference, requiring that a liability for a cost associated with an exit or disposal activity be recognized in the period in which the liability is incurred, for example, when goods or services related to an exit or disposal activity are received. Paragraph 194 of Concepts Statement 6 clarifies:

> The most obvious evidence of liabilities are contracts or other agreements resulting

from exchange transactions and laws or governmental regulations that require expending assets to comply. Although receipt of proceeds is not conclusive evidence that a liability has been incurred (paragraph 198), receipt of cash, other assets, or services without an accompanying cash payment is often evidence that a liability has been incurred.

B52. This Statement similarly requires that future operating losses expected to be incurred in connection with an exit or disposal activity be recognized in the period(s) in which they are incurred. During its deliberations of this Statement, the Board clarified that because future operating losses are the summation of individual items of revenue and expense that result from changes in assets and liabilities, those expected losses, in and of themselves, do not meet the definition of a liability. In Statement 144, the Board clarified that future operating losses expected to be incurred in connection with the sale of a long-lived asset or disposal group, including a component of an entity that is a discontinued operation, should not otherwise be recognized by including those losses in the measurement of the asset or disposal group. As discussed in footnote 22 to paragraph 35 of Statement 144:

> Expected future operating losses that marketplace participants would not similarly consider in their estimates of the fair value less cost to sell of a long-lived asset (disposal group) classified as held for sale shall not be indirectly recognized as part of an expected loss on the sale by reducing the carrying amount of the asset (disposal group) to an amount less than its current fair value less cost to sell.

Reporting and Disclosure

B53. Issue 94-3 provided guidance for reporting costs associated with an exit activity in the income statement, requiring that those costs be included in continuing operations (before income taxes). During its redeliberations of the Exposure Draft, the Board decided that similar reporting requirements should apply for costs associated with an exit or disposal activity covered by this Statement that does not involve a discontinued operation. The Board decided not to prohibit separate presentation of those costs in the income statement. However, because neither an exit activity nor a disposal activity is both unusual and infrequent, the Board decided to prohibit those costs

from being presented in the income statement net of income taxes or in any manner that implies they are similar to an extraordinary item, as defined in Opinion 30. If an exit or disposal activity involves a discontinued operation, costs associated with that activity should be included within the results of discontinued operations in accordance with Statement 144.

B54. Issue 94-3 also set forth disclosure requirements for costs associated with an exit activity. During its redeliberations of the Exposure Draft, the Board affirmed its decision that similar disclosure requirements should apply for costs associated with an exit or disposal activity covered by this Statement. The Board concluded that because those disclosure requirements focus on the major types of costs associated with an exit or disposal activity, they provide information that is useful to investors, creditors, and other users in assessing the overall effects of that activity on an entity's ongoing operations. The Board concluded that the principal focus of the required disclosures for one-time termination benefits should be on the amounts to be paid. Accordingly, this Statement eliminates the requirement of Issue 94-3 to disclose information about the number of employees to be (or actually) terminated. However, it does not prohibit disclosure of that or other information about an exit or disposal activity.

B55. Few respondents to the Exposure Draft commented specifically on the proposed disclosure requirements for costs associated with an exit or disposal activity. However, during its redeliberations of the Exposure Draft, the Board decided that the disclosures previously required by Issue 94-3 and retained in this Statement should be presented as a reconciliation of the beginning and ending liability balances for each major type of cost associated with the activity and should include an explanation of the reasons for adjustments, if material. The Board concluded that a reconciliation format would improve the comparability of information provided about exit and disposal activities and aid users in assessing the effects of such activities over time, including the related cash flow implications. Also, given the importance of segment information, the Board decided that entities that are within the scope of FASB Statement No. 131, *Disclosures about Segments of an Enterprise and Related Information,* should disclose, by reportable segment, the amount of costs incurred in connection with those activities in the current period and the cumulative amount to date.

B56. During its deliberations leading to the Exposure Draft, the Board observed that certain costs that were recognized as liabilities at a plan (commitment) date under Issue 94-3 would be recognized as liabilities at a later date under this Statement. The Board concluded that information about the costs the entity expects to incur in connection with an exit or disposal activity is useful in assessing the effects of the activity initially and over time. For that reason, the Board decided to require disclosure of the major types of costs expected to be incurred in connection with the exit or disposal activity at the date an entity initiates a plan, whether or not a liability for those costs is recognized at that date. The Board affirmed that decision in this Statement.

Effective Date and Transition

B57. The Board decided that this Statement should be effective for exit or disposal activities initiated after December 31, 2002. The Board believes that that effective date provides sufficient time for entities and their auditors to analyze, interpret, and prepare for implementation of the provisions of this Statement. The Board encourages early application of this Statement. Retroactive application of this Statement is prohibited.

B58. During its deliberations leading to the Exposure Draft, the Board decided that the provisions of the Exposure Draft for all disposal activities should be applied prospectively. In this Statement, the Board affirmed prospective application for costs associated with asset disposal activities and other similar activities, including exit activities under Issue 94-3. The Board believes that using the date that management, having the authority to approve the action, commits to an exit or disposal plan as a basis for applying the provisions of this Statement initially will facilitate transition to the provisions of this Statement.

B59. The Board recognizes the benefits of comparative financial statements. However, the Board observed that applying this Statement retroactively would require entities to (a) reverse liabilities recognized in prior periods and (b) determine fair value measurements for liabilities that would continue to be recognized in those prior periods under this Statement. The Board concluded that obtaining or deriving the information necessary to apply this Statement retroactively could be costly and unduly burdensome for many entities. In particular, the Board questions the ability of entities to retroactively assess when the recognition criteria in this Statement would otherwise have been met in those prior periods based on facts and circumstances as they existed at that time and without the benefit of hindsight. Further, the Board observed that in many cases the related exit or disposal activity will have been completed and the liabilities settled before this Statement is initially applied. In other cases in which the exit or disposal activity is in process at the date this Statement is initially applied, information about that activity would have been disclosed and communicated to users in a prior period. The Board concluded that applying this Statement retroactively generally would not provide users with sufficiently useful additional information to justify the related costs. Moreover, because liabilities associated with an exit or disposal activity generally are short-lived, prospective application should not have a significant, continuing impact on the comparability and consistency of the financial statements.

International Accounting Standards

B60. The International Accounting Standard for costs associated with a restructuring other than employee termination benefits is IAS 37, *Provisions, Contingent Liabilities and Contingent Assets* (1998). Paragraph 13 of IAS 37 defines a *restructuring* as a "programme that is planned and controlled by management, and materially changes either: (a) the scope of a business undertaken by an enterprise; or (b) the manner in which that business is conducted." The International Accounting Standard for employee termination benefits is IAS 19, *Employee Benefits* (revised 2000).

B61. For costs associated with a restructuring other than employee termination benefits, the recognition guidance in IAS 37 is similar to that previously included in Issue 94-3 for exit costs and, in addition, requires public announcement (or implementation) of an exit plan. Because this Statement does not retain the definition or requirements for recognition of exit costs, the timing of recognition of a liability for similar costs under IAS 37 and this Statement will differ. For purposes of measurement, IAS 37 refers to settlement of the present obligation at the balance sheet date, which is similar to fair value. However, the extent to which initial measurements under IAS 37 and this Statement will be similar will depend on, among other things, how the measurement objective of IAS 37 is interpreted and the specific measurement approaches used to achieve that objective under IAS 37.

B62. Paragraph 132 of IAS 19 states that the accounting model for employee benefits does not apply to employee termination benefits because "the event which gives rise to an obligation is the termination rather than employee service." Paragraph 137 of IAS 19 explains that because employee termination benefits do not provide an enterprise with future economic benefits, they are recognized as an expense immediately. In this Statement, the accounting model for employee benefits is used for one-time termination benefits that, in substance, are stay bonuses provided by an entity in exchange for the employees' rendering of service over a future period. Thus, the accounting for certain employee termination benefits under IAS 19 and this Statement will differ, even though the benefit arrangements may be similar. However, the Board believes that the accounting model for employee benefits more faithfully represents the underlying economics of stay bonus arrangements.

B63. In developing this Statement, the Board acknowledged those differences, noting that they arise from linking the recognition and measurement requirements for costs associated with an exit or disposal activity to fundamental concepts in the Board's conceptual framework. The Board concluded that, at this time, the benefits resulting from the improvements to financial reporting under this Statement outweigh the costs resulting from the lack of convergence with those International Accounting Standards.

Benefits and Costs

B64. The mission of the Board is to establish and improve standards of financial accounting and reporting for the guidance and education of the public, including preparers, auditors, and users of financial information. In fulfilling that mission, the Board endeavors to determine that a proposed standard will fill a significant need and that the costs imposed to meet that standard, as compared with other alternatives, are justified in relation to the overall benefits of the resulting information. Although the costs to implement a new standard may not be borne evenly, investors and creditors—both present and potential —as well as others, benefit from improvements in financial reporting, thereby facilitating the functioning of markets for capital and credit and the efficient allocation of resources in the economy.

B65. The Board determined that the requirements in this Statement will result in a significant improvement to financial reporting. Prior to this Statement, the liability recognized for some costs associated with an exit or disposal activity did not meet the definition of a liability set forth in the Board's conceptual framework. Moreover, Issue 94-3 and other accounting pronouncements did not require that a liability be measured initially at its fair value. This Statement addresses those differences, requiring that a liability for a cost associated with an exit or disposal activity be recognized when the liability is incurred and setting forth a fair value objective for initial measurement of the liability, thereby improving comparability in financial reporting. As discussed in FASB Concepts Statement No. 2, *Qualitative Characteristics of Accounting Information,* providing comparable financial information enables users to identify similarities in and differences between two sets of economic events.

B66. The principal cost of applying this Statement is the cost of measuring the fair value of a liability for a cost associated with an exit or disposal activity at initial recognition. Other accounting pronouncements require fair value measurements, and techniques for developing those measurements, including the expected present value technique discussed in Concepts Statement 7, are currently being applied. As a practical matter, however, in many cases, the related liability will be relatively short-lived, mitigating the need to apply complex valuation techniques in order to derive the fair value measurements required by this Statement. In addition, the Board believes that prospective application with a delayed effective date further reduces the costs of implementing this Statement. While some entities may incur one-time costs to apply this Statement, in particular, for changes needed to apply present value and other valuation techniques to liabilities, the benefits from more comparable information will be ongoing. The Board believes that the benefits of this Statement outweigh the costs of implementing it.

Statement of Financial Accounting Standards No. 147
Acquisitions of Certain Financial Institutions

an amendment of FASB Statements No. 72 and 144 and FASB Interpretation No. 9

STATUS

Issued: October 2002

Effective Date: For acquisitions on or after October 1, 2002

Affects: Amends FAS 72, paragraphs 2, 4, and 5
Deletes FAS 72, paragraphs 3 and 7 through 11
Amends FAS 141, paragraph 61(b)
Deletes FAS 141, paragraph E20
Amends FAS 142, paragraph 49(b)
Effectively deletes FAS 142, paragraph D9(a)
Deletes FAS 142, paragraph D11
Amends FAS 144, paragraphs 5 and D1
Replaces FIN 9, footnote 1

Affected by: No other pronouncements

Issues Discussed by FASB Emerging Issues Task Force (EITF)

Affects: Partially nullifies EITF Issue No. 88-19

Interpreted by: Paragraph 9 interpreted by EITF Topic No. D-100

Related Issues: EITF Issues No. 85-8, 85-41, 85-42, and 89-19 and Topic No. D-78

SUMMARY

FASB Statement No. 72, *Accounting for Certain Acquisitions of Banking or Thrift Institutions,* and FASB Interpretation No. 9, *Applying APB Opinions No. 16 and 17 When a Savings and Loan Association or a Similar Institution Is Acquired in a Business Combination Accounted for by the Purchase Method,* provided interpretive guidance on the application of the purchase method to acquisitions of financial institutions. Except for transactions between two or more mutual enterprises, this Statement removes acquisitions of financial institutions from the scope of both Statement 72 and Interpretation 9 and requires that those transactions be accounted for in accordance with FASB Statements No. 141, *Business Combinations,* and No. 142, *Goodwill and Other Intangible Assets.* Thus, the requirement in paragraph 5 of Statement 72 to recognize (and subsequently amortize) any excess of the fair value of liabilities assumed over the fair value of tangible and identifiable intangible assets acquired as an unidentifiable intangible asset no longer applies to acquisitions within the scope of this Statement. In addition, this Statement amends FASB Statement No. 144, *Accounting for the Impairment or Disposal of Long-Lived Assets,* to include in its scope long-term customer-relationship intangible assets of financial institutions such as depositor- and borrower-relationship intangible assets and credit cardholder intangible assets. Consequently, those intangible assets are subject to the same undiscounted cash flow recoverability test and impairment loss recognition and measurement provisions that Statement 144 requires for other long-lived assets that are held and used.

Scope of This Statement

The provisions of this Statement that relate to the application of the purchase method of accounting apply to all acquisitions of financial institutions, except transactions between two or more mutual enterprises. The provisions of this Statement that relate to the application of Statement 144 apply to certain long-term customer-relationship intangible assets recognized in an acquisition of a financial institution, including those acquired in transactions between mutual enterprises.

Reasons for Issuing This Statement

Following the issuance of Statements 141 and 142, constituents asked the Board to reconsider the need for the guidance in Statement 72 and Interpretation 9; in particular, the special accounting for the unidentifiable intangible asset recognized under paragraph 5 of Statement 72. In developing this Statement, the Board concluded that the guidance in Statement 72 and Interpretation 9 is no longer necessary because:

a. For a transaction that is a business combination, the unidentifiable intangible asset that is required to be recognized under paragraph 5 of Statement 72 represents goodwill that should be accounted for under Statement 142.
b. Statement 141 provides sufficient guidance for assigning amounts to assets acquired and liabilities assumed; therefore, the specialized industry guidance in Interpretation 9 and paragraph 4 of Statement 72 is no longer necessary.

In addition, constituents asked the Board to clarify whether the acquisition of a less-than-whole financial institution (often referred to as a branch acquisition) should be accounted for as a business combination or in some other manner. This Statement clarifies that a branch acquisition that meets the definition of a business should be accounted for as a business combination, otherwise the transaction should be accounted for as an acquisition of net assets that does not result in the recognition of goodwill.

How the Changes in This Statement Improve Financial Reporting

The industry-specific guidance in Statement 72 will no longer apply to transactions in the scope of this Statement. Therefore, comparability of financial reporting will improve because Statement 141 will be used to account for financial institution acquisitions except transactions between mutual enterprises.

The Effective Date of This Statement

Paragraph 5 of this Statement, which relates to the application of the purchase method of accounting, is effective for acquisitions for which the date of acquisition is on or after October 1, 2002. The provisions in paragraph 6 related to accounting for the impairment or disposal of certain long-term customer-relationship intangible assets are effective on October 1, 2002. Transition provisions for previously recognized unidentifiable intangible assets in paragraphs 8–14 are effective on October 1, 2002, with earlier application permitted.

Statement of Financial Accounting Standards No. 147

Acquisitions of Certain Financial Institutions

an amendment of FASB Statements No. 72 and 144 and FASB Interpretation No. 9

CONTENTS

INTRODUCTION

1. This Statement addresses the financial accounting and reporting for the acquisition of all or part of a financial institution,[1] except for a transaction between two or more **mutual enterprises**.[2] This Statement removes acquisitions of financial institutions, other than transactions between two or more mutual enterprises, from the scope of FASB Statement No. 72, *Accounting for Certain Acquisitions of Banking or Thrift Institutions,* and FASB Interpretation No. 9, *Applying APB Opinions No. 16 and 17 When a Savings and Loan Association or a Similar Institution Is Acquired in a Business Combination Accounted for by the Purchase Method.* This State-ment also provides guidance on the accounting for the impairment or disposal of acquired long-term customer-relationship intangible assets (such as depositor- and borrower-relationship intangible assets and credit cardholder intangible assets), including those acquired in transactions between two or more mutual enterprises.

2. The provisions of Statement 72, as amended by this Statement, and those of Interpretation 9 continue to apply to transactions between financial institutions that are mutual enterprises. The Board intends to provide guidance on the accounting and reporting for those transactions in a separate Statement, and that

---

[1]Hereafter, the term *financial institution* as used in this Statement includes *all or part of* a commercial bank, a savings and loan association, a credit union, or other depository institution having assets and liabilities of the same types as those institutions.

[2]Terms defined in Appendix C, the glossary, are set forth in **boldface** type the first time they are used.

Statement may further amend or rescind Statement 72 and Interpretation 9.

3. Appendix A to this Statement provides background information and the basis for the Board's conclusions. Appendix B lists other pronouncements that are amended by this Statement. Appendix C provides a glossary of terms as used in this Statement.

STANDARDS OF FINANCIAL ACCOUNTING AND REPORTING

Scope

4. Paragraph 5 of this Statement applies to the acquisition of all or part[3] of a financial institution, except for a transaction between two or more mutual enterprises. Paragraph 6 of this Statement applies to certain long-term customer-relationship intangible assets recognized in an acquisition of a financial institution, including a transaction between mutual enterprises.

Method of Accounting

5. Statement 72 and Interpretation 9 shall not apply to acquisitions in the scope of this Statement. The acquisition of all or part of a financial institution that meets the definition of a business combination shall be accounted for by the purchase method in accordance with FASB Statement No. 141, *Business Combinations*. If the acquisition is not a business combination[4] because the transferred net assets and activities do not constitute a business,[5] that transaction shall be accounted for in accordance with paragraphs 4–8 of Statement 141. As discussed in paragraph 9 of FASB Statement No. 142, *Goodwill and Other Intangible Assets*, such transactions do not give rise to **goodwill.**

Impairment and Disposal Accounting for Certain Acquired Long-Term Customer-Relationship Intangible Assets

6. The provisions of FASB Statement No. 144, *Accounting for the Impairment or Disposal of Long-Lived Assets*, apply to long-term customer-relationship intangible assets, except for servicing assets,[6] recognized in the acquisition of a financial institution.

Effective Date

7. The provisions in paragraph 5 of this Statement shall be effective for acquisitions for which the date of acquisition[7] is on or after October 1, 2002. The provisions in paragraph 6 shall be effective on October 1, 2002. Transition provisions for previously recognized **unidentifiable intangible assets** in paragraphs 8–14 are effective on October 1, 2002, with earlier application permitted.

Transition

Previously Recognized Unidentifiable Intangible Assets

8. The carrying amount of an unidentifiable intangible asset shall continue to be amortized as set forth in paragraph 5 of Statement 72 after October 1, 2002, unless the transaction in which that asset arose was a business combination.

9. If the transaction that gave rise to the unidentifiable intangible asset was a business combination, the carrying amount of that asset shall be reclassified to goodwill[8] (reclassified goodwill) as of the later of the

---

[3]Some transactions involve the acquisition of a less-than-whole, or part of a, financial institution. Those transactions are sometimes referred to as branch acquisitions.

[4]Refer to paragraph 9 of Statement 141 for determining when an acquisition is a business combination.

[5]EITF Issue No. 98-3, "Determining Whether a Nonmonetary Transaction Involves Receipt of Productive Assets or of a Business," provides guidance on determining whether an asset group constitutes a business.

[6]Examples of long-term customer-relationship intangible assets include depositor- and borrower-relationship intangible assets, credit cardholder intangible assets, and servicing assets. Servicing assets, however, are tested for impairment under FASB Statement No. 140, *Accounting for Transfers and Servicing of Financial Assets and Extinguishments of Liabilities*.

[7]Refer to paragraph 48 of Statement 141 for guidance on determining the date of acquisition.

[8]If the amortization of the unidentifiable intangible asset is not deductible for tax purposes, any deferred tax liabilities related to that asset also shall be reclassified to goodwill.

date of acquisition or the date Statement 142 is applied in its entirety[9] (Statement 142 application date). The carrying amounts of any recognized intangible assets that meet the recognition criteria in paragraph 39 of Statement 141 that have been included in the amount reported as an unidentifiable intangible asset and for which separate accounting records have been maintained (as discussed in footnote 25 of Statement 141) shall be reclassified and accounted for as assets apart from the unidentifiable intangible asset and shall not be reclassified to goodwill.

10. The reclassified goodwill shall be accounted for and reported prospectively as goodwill under Statement 142. In addition:

a. If the Statement 142 application date preceded October 1, 2002, any previously issued interim or annual financial statements that reflect amortization of the unidentifiable intangible asset subsequent to the Statement 142 application date shall be restated to remove that amortization expense. When financial information is presented that includes those periods, that financial information shall be presented on the restated basis.
b. If the Statement 142 application date falls after October 1, 2002, the unidentifiable intangible asset shall continue to be amortized in accordance with paragraph 5 of Statement 72 until the Statement 142 application date.

Transitional Impairment Testing for Reclassified Goodwill

11. As described in paragraphs 12–14 of this Statement, reclassified goodwill shall be tested for impairment as of the Statement 142 application date. Paragraphs 12–14 apply only to reclassified goodwill for which the date of acquisition precedes the Statement 142 application date.

12. If an entity has no goodwill other than reclassified goodwill, the transitional impairment testing provisions in paragraphs 54–58 of Statement 142 shall be completed for the reclassified goodwill by the end of the fiscal year in which the transition provisions of this Statement are applied.

13. If an entity has other goodwill in addition to reclassified goodwill, and it has not completed the transitional impairment testing provisions in paragraphs 54–58 of Statement 142 as of October 1, 2002, the reclassified goodwill shall be combined with other goodwill in applying those transition provisions.

14. If an entity has other goodwill in addition to reclassified goodwill, and it has completed the transitional impairment testing provisions in paragraphs 54–58 of Statement 142 as of October 1, 2002, the following transition provisions shall be applied for each reporting unit that includes reclassified goodwill:

a. If the fair value of the reporting unit exceeded its carrying amount (including the unidentifiable intangible asset) at the Statement 142 application date,[10] additional impairment testing related to the reclassified goodwill is not required.
b. If the first step of the transitional goodwill impairment test indicated a potential impairment of goodwill at the Statement 142 application date, the amount of the goodwill impairment loss (if any) shall be remeasured based on the revised carrying amount of goodwill.[11] The revised carrying amount of goodwill used in remeasuring the loss equals the amount of previously recognized goodwill and the amount of any unidentifiable intangible asset reclassified as goodwill under the transition provisions of this Statement. Any adjustment to the impairment loss shall be recognized as the effect of a change in accounting principle in accordance with paragraph 56 of Statement 142.

Transition for Impairment Accounting for Certain Acquired Long-Term Customer-Relationship Intangible Assets to Be Held and Used

15. Impairment losses resulting from the application of Statement 144 to acquired long-term customer-relationship intangible assets to be held and used shall be reported in the period in which the impairment loss recognition criteria in that Statement are first applied and met and shall not be reported as a cumulative effect of a change in accounting principle.

---

[9]Statement 142 applies in its entirety in fiscal years beginning after December 15, 2001. However, early application was permitted for entities with fiscal years beginning after March 15, 2001, in certain circumstances, as indicated in paragraph 48(a) of Statement 142.

[10]That is, the first step of the transitional goodwill impairment test indicated no impairment.

[11]The fair value of the reporting unit and related assets and liabilities used in calculating the implied fair value of goodwill shall not be remeasured for purposes of applying this transition provision.

Transitional Disclosures for Reclassified Goodwill

16. In the period that the transition provisions are first applied, an entity shall disclose the following in the notes to the financial statements:

a. The carrying amount of previously recognized unidentifiable intangible assets reclassified as goodwill
b. The effect of any restatement on net income for each period for which restated financial statements are presented pursuant to paragraph 10(a)

c. The amount of any adjustment to the previously recognized goodwill impairment loss recognized pursuant to paragraph 14(b).

17. For each period presented that precedes the Statement 142 application date, the amount of amortization expense related to reclassified goodwill shall be disclosed, either separately or as part of the transitional disclosure requirements of Statement 142 (paragraph 61).

> **The provisions of this Statement need not be applied to immaterial items.**

This Statement was adopted by the unanimous vote of the seven members of the Financial Accounting Standards Board.

Robert H. Herz,	John M. Foster	Edward W. Trott
Chairman	Gary S. Schieneman	John K. Wulff
G. Michael Crooch	Katherine Schipper	

Appendix A

BACKGROUND INFORMATION AND BASIS FOR CONCLUSIONS

CONTENTS

Appendix A

BACKGROUND INFORMATION AND BASIS FOR CONCLUSIONS

Introduction

A1. This appendix summarizes considerations that Board members deemed significant in reaching the conclusions in this Statement. It includes reasons for accepting certain approaches and rejecting others. Individual Board members gave greater weight to some factors than to others.

Background

A2. FASB Statement No. 72, *Accounting for Certain Acquisitions of Banking or Thrift Institutions,* and FASB Interpretation No. 9, *Applying APB Opinions No. 16 and 17 When a Savings and Loan Association or a Similar Institution Is Acquired in a Business Combination Accounted for by the Purchase Method,* provided interpretive guidance related to the application of the purchase method to the acquisition of a financial institution. In the deliberations that led to FASB Statements No. 141, *Business Combinations,* and No. 142, *Goodwill and Other Intangible Assets,* the Board decided that reconsideration of that specialized industry guidance was beyond the scope of those Statements. Thus, the provisions of Statement 72 and Interpretation 9 were largely unaffected by the issuance of Statements 141 and 142.

A3. After Statements 141 and 142 were issued, constituents asked the Board to reconsider the guidance in Statement 72, in particular, the requirement to amortize the unidentifiable intangible asset recognized pursuant to paragraph 5 of that Statement. Those constituents expressed the belief that the unidentifiable intangible asset represents goodwill and, therefore, should be accounted for as goodwill under Statement 142 (that is, by a nonamortization approach). In response to those requests, the Board decided to reconsider the guidance in Statement 72 and Interpretation 9. In May 2002, the Board issued an Exposure Draft, *Acquisitions of Certain Financial Institutions.* The Board received 24 comment letters on the Exposure Draft. The Board concluded that on the basis of existing information, it could reach an informed decision on the matters addressed in this Statement without a public hearing.

Basis for Conclusions

Scope

A4. The scope of Statement 72 included the acquisition of any financial institution, whether investor-owned or organized as a mutual enterprise (such as a savings bank or a credit union). Because the Board has a separate project on its agenda to provide guidance on the accounting and reporting for transactions between mutual enterprises, the Board decided to reconsider the guidance in Statement 72 and Interpretation 9 as it applies to transactions between mutual enterprises in that separate project. As a result, the Exposure Draft proposed that the guidance in this Statement related to the application of the purchase method (paragraph 5) should apply to all acquisitions of financial institutions, except for transactions between two or more mutual enterprises.

A5. In developing the Exposure Draft, the Board noted, however, that transactions between mutual enterprises may give rise to recognition of long-term customer-relationship intangible assets. The scope of the Board's project on acquisitions of mutual enterprises does not include consideration of impairment and disposal guidance for those assets. Therefore, the Exposure Draft proposed that the guidance in paragraph 6 of this Statement related to the impairment and disposal accounting for certain acquired long-term customer-relationship intangible assets should apply to all such assets of financial institutions, including those acquired in transactions between mutual enterprises.

A6. Respondents agreed with the scope of the Exposure Draft, and the Board affirmed that scope in its redeliberations.

Reconsideration of Statement 72 and Interpretation 9

A7. In the deliberations that led to the Exposure Draft, the Board concluded (for the reasons discussed in paragraphs A8–A23) that the guidance in Statement 72 and Interpretation 9 should not apply to transactions in the scope of this Statement. Respondents to the Exposure Draft generally agreed with that conclusion and the reasons for it. Accordingly, this Statement removes those transactions from the scope of both Statement 72 and Interpretation 9.

Reconsideration of Statement 72

A8. Statement 72 was developed and issued in the early 1980s when economic and competitive conditions were adversely affecting financial institutions. That Statement provided a pragmatic resolution of specific reporting issues that arose when applying the purchase method to the acquisition of a financial institution when the fair value of liabilities assumed exceeded the fair value of assets acquired.[12] Statement 72 required that excess to be recognized as an unidentifiable intangible asset other than goodwill and also required that asset to be amortized over a specified period.

Method of accounting

A9. Statement 72 applied to acquisitions of all financial institutions, including acquisitions of less-than-whole financial institutions (such as the acquisition of a branch). During the development of the Exposure Draft, constituents asked the Board to clarify whether acquisitions of less-than-whole financial institutions should be accounted for as business combinations or in some other manner. This Statement clarifies that acquisitions of financial institutions, including branch acquisitions that meet the definition of a business combination, should be accounted for by the purchase method under Statement 141. In the deliberations that led to this Statement, some Board members expressed their belief, however, that for those acquisitions, proper application of the provisions of Statement 141 will often result in a relatively small amount of goodwill. As did the Exposure Draft, this Statement also clarifies that an acquisition that does not meet the definition of a business combination because the transferred net assets and activities do not constitute a business is an acquisition of net assets. Those acquisitions should be accounted for in the same manner as any other net asset acquisition and do not give rise to goodwill.

A10. For an acquisition to meet the definition of a business combination, the transferred net assets and activities must constitute a business. Statement 141 refers to EITF Issue No. 98-3, "Determining Whether a Nonmonetary Transaction Involves Receipt of Productive Assets or of a Business," for guidance in making that determination. During the development of the Exposure Draft, constituents suggested that the Board supplement the guidance in Issue 98-3 to identify specific elements to be considered in evaluating whether the net assets and activities transferred in the acquisition of a financial institution are a business. For example, some constituents noted that a financial institution cannot conduct business without a charter and deposit insurance coverage. Those constituents suggested that the Board clarify whether an acquisition of net assets that did not include the transfer of the charter or deposit insurance coverage would be considered the acquisition of a business.

A11. The Board observed that determining whether the transferred net assets and activities constitute a business under Issue 98-3 requires analysis of all facts and circumstances and the exercise of professional judgment. Board members concluded that reconsideration of Issue 98-3 was beyond the scope of this Statement. Thus, as it did in developing the Exposure Draft, the Board concluded that this Statement should not provide supplemental guidance for determining whether transferred net assets and activities constitute a business. The Board noted, however, that deposit insurance coverage is not transferable. In addition, the Board indicated that in evaluating whether the net assets transferred in the acquisition of a financial institution represent a business, neither the presence nor the absence of a charter should be the sole deciding factor; all facts and circumstances need to be considered in applying Issue 98-3.

An unidentifiable intangible asset

A12. In developing this Statement, the Board considered whether an excess of the fair value of liabilities assumed over the fair value of assets acquired (an unidentifiable excess) should continue to be recognized as an unidentifiable intangible asset other than goodwill and amortized as required by paragraph 5 of Statement 72.

A13. The Board noted that the condition giving rise to the recognition of an unidentifiable intangible asset in Statement 72—an unidentifiable excess of the fair value of liabilities assumed over the fair value of assets acquired—is not unique to acquisitions of financial institutions. The Board noted that when business combinations involving entities other than financial institutions are accounted for under Statement 141, an unidentifiable excess would be included in the amount recognized as goodwill. During the deliberations that led to this Statement, the Board did not identify any differences between acquisitions of financial institutions and acquisitions of other types of

---

[12]The assets acquired may include financial assets, tangible assets, or identifiable intangible assets.

entities that would justify the different accounting treatment for the unidentifiable excess required by paragraph 5 of Statement 72. Therefore, this Statement requires that for the acquisition of a financial institution that meets the definition of a business combination, the amount of any unidentifiable excess should be recognized and accounted for as goodwill.

A14. Some respondents to the Exposure Draft suggested that the Board provide guidance on accounting for the impairment and disposal of an unidentifiable intangible asset that is not reclassified as goodwill upon adoption of this Statement. The Board concluded that such guidance is not necessary because that unidentifiable intangible asset is included in the scope of FASB Statement No. 144, *Accounting for the Impairment or Disposal of Long-Lived Assets.*

Identifiable intangible assets

A15. Paragraph 4 of Statement 72 required that separately identifiable intangible assets acquired be assigned a portion of the total cost of the acquired entity and cited depositor- and borrower-relationship intangible assets as examples of such identifiable intangible assets. The Board noted that removing certain acquisitions of financial institutions from the scope of Statement 72 would mean that that guidance would no longer apply to those transactions. The Board noted, however, that paragraph 39 of Statement 141 requires that intangible assets that meet certain criteria be recognized separately from goodwill. In addition, paragraph A21 of that Statement cites depositor-relationship intangible assets as an example of an intangible asset that meets the criteria for recognition apart from goodwill. The Board noted that borrower-relationship and credit cardholder intangible assets are other examples of finite-lived intangible assets that meet the criteria for recognition apart from goodwill. Therefore, the Board affirmed its previous decision that because Statement 141 provides the necessary guidance for determining the acquired intangible assets to be recognized separate from goodwill, the specialized industry guidance in paragraph 4 of Statement 72 is no longer needed.

Impairment and disposal accounting for certain acquired long-term customer-relationship intangible assets

A16. Paragraph 5 of Statement 144 excluded long-term customer relationships of financial institutions, such as depositor- and borrower-relationship intangible assets and credit cardholder intangible assets, from that Statement's scope because "they have characteristics that make their measurements similar to measurements that are used for financial instruments."[13] Paragraph 4 of Statement 72, as amended by Statement 142, provided some limited impairment guidance for those assets.

A17. Because the Exposure Draft proposed removing certain acquisitions of financial institutions from the scope of Statement 72, the Board considered the appropriate impairment guidance for acquired long-term customer-relationship intangible assets. The Board noted that (a) the impairment guidance for long-term customer-relationship intangible assets was incomplete, (b) the measurement of those relationship assets is similar to that of financial assets, and (c) measuring financial assets at fair value is a longer-term project of the Board. For those reasons, and in the interest of simplifying the accounting guidance, the Exposure Draft proposed that Statement 144 should be amended to include in its scope depositor- and borrower-relationship intangible assets and credit cardholder intangible assets. Respondents to the Exposure Draft agreed with the proposed amendment to Statement 144, and the Board affirmed that amendment during its redeliberations.

Regulatory-assisted transactions

A18. The Board noted that by removing acquisitions of certain financial institutions from the scope of Statement 72, existing guidance on the accounting for regulatory assistance would no longer apply to those transactions. Therefore, the Exposure Draft proposed that, except for changes related to the issuance of FASB Statement No. 133, *Accounting for Derivative Instruments and Hedging Activities,* this

---

[13]Refer to paragraph 50 of FASB Statement No. 121, *Accounting for the Impairment of Long-Lived Assets and for Long-Lived Assets to Be Disposed Of.* Statement 144 supersedes Statement 121; however, Statement 144 retains the fundamental provisions of Statement 121 for (a) recognition and measurement of the impairment of long-lived assets to be held and used and (b) measurement of long-lived assets to be disposed of by sale.

Statement would carry forward without reconsideration the provisions in Statement 72 related to regulatory-assisted acquisitions.

A19. After considering respondents' comments to the Exposure Draft, the Board decided to amend Statement 72 to delete the guidance on accounting for regulatory assistance. The Board concluded that this guidance is not needed because the types of regulatory-assistance agreements addressed by Statement 72 are not used in current transactions. Also, the Board noted that the business combinations–purchase method procedures project may provide sufficient guidance for regulatory-assistance agreements that might be included in future transactions.

Reconsideration of Interpretation 9

A20. Consistent with the Exposure Draft, this Statement reflects the Board's conclusion that the guidance in Interpretation 9 should no longer apply to transactions in the scope of this Statement. Most respondents agreed with that conclusion.

A21. Interpretation 9, issued in 1976, provided specific guidance related to the application of the purchase method to acquisitions of financial institutions. The primary purpose for issuing Interpretation 9 was to resolve a practice question about whether the net-spread method[14] or the separate-valuation method was appropriate for determining the amounts assigned to assets and liabilities of acquired financial institutions. That Interpretation clarified that the net-spread method should *not* be used and provided limited guidance on how to allocate the purchase price to a portfolio of acquired loans and assumed deposit liabilities.

A22. The Board observed that the net-spread method continues to be inappropriate. However, the Board noted that Statement 141 requires that assets acquired and liabilities assumed in a business combination be measured at their fair values. Thus, the clarifying guidance in paragraphs 2–7 of Interpretation 9 (which stipulates the use of the separate-valuation method) is no longer needed for transactions in the scope of this Statement.

A23. Interpretation 9 also included interpretive guidance related to the requirement in APB Opinion No. 16, *Business Combinations,* to recognize acquired intangible assets separately from goodwill. Specifically, paragraph 8 of Interpretation 9 listed several identifiable intangible assets that, if acquired, may meet the recognition criteria in that Opinion. During development of the Exposure Draft, the Board noted that Statement 141 superseded the provisions of Opinion 16 related to the recognition of acquired intangible assets. The Board concluded that in light of the recognition criteria provided in Statement 141, the interpretive guidance in paragraph 8 of Interpretation 9 is not needed for transactions in the scope of this Statement.

Effective Date and Transition

A24. The Board noted that the principal change resulting from this Statement's issuance is the requirement to recognize an unidentifiable excess in a business combination as goodwill rather than as a separate unidentifiable intangible asset and that this change would not create any significant implementation issues. Thus, the Exposure Draft proposed that the provisions in paragraph 5 of this Statement should be effective for acquisitions for which the date of acquisition is on or after the date this Statement is issued. It also proposed that the provisions in paragraph 6 related to the impairment and disposal accounting for certain acquired long-term customer-relationship intangible assets be effective immediately upon issuance. Respondents to the Exposure Draft were generally supportive of the proposed effective dates, and the Board affirmed those dates during its redeliberations.

A25. The Exposure Draft proposed that the unidentifiable intangible asset recognized in a past transaction should be reclassified as goodwill and accounted for in accordance with Statement 142 prospectively, if both of the following criteria were met: (a) the transaction in which the unidentifiable intangible asset arose was a business combination and (b) intangible assets acquired in that business combination that met the criteria in paragraph 39 of Statement 141 (in particular, long-term customer-relationship intangible assets) were recognized and accounted for apart from the unidentifiable intangible asset following the date of acquisition.

---

[14]Under the net-spread method, the acquisition of a financial institution was viewed as the acquisition of a leveraged whole rather than the acquisition of the separate assets and liabilities of the institution. Therefore, if the spread between the rates of interest received on mortgage loans and the rates of interest paid on savings accounts was normal for the particular market area, then the acquired mortgage loan portfolio and savings accounts were brought forward at the carrying amounts shown in the financial statements of the acquired institution. Application of that method is not consistent with the requirements of Statement 141.

A26. In developing Statement 142, the Board concluded that goodwill arises only in a business combination. Thus, during deliberations that led to the Exposure Draft, the Board concluded that an unidentifiable intangible asset recognized in a past transaction that was not a business combination is not goodwill and should not be reclassified as goodwill upon adoption of this Statement. The Board noted that because an asset acquisition that is not a business combination does not give rise to goodwill, the unidentifiable intangible asset recognized in that transaction represents finite-lived identifiable intangible assets that were not separately recognized, errors in measuring the fair values of recognized assets acquired and liabilities assumed, or both. Therefore, the Exposure Draft required that the unidentifiable intangible asset continue to be amortized if the transaction that gave rise to the asset was not a business combination. Respondents to the Exposure Draft were generally supportive of this requirement, and the Board affirmed the requirement during its redeliberations.

A27. During development of the Exposure Draft, the Board noted that the unidentifiable intangible asset arises only in combinations in which the fair value of liabilities assumed exceeds the fair value of the assets acquired. Board members stated that in such transactions, a primary motivation is often to acquire identifiable intangible assets such as long-term customer-relationship intangible assets. Therefore, except in those cases in which identifiable intangible assets were separately recognized, the unidentifiable intangible asset likely represents an identifiable, finite-lived asset that should be amortized. Accordingly, the Exposure Draft proposed that amortization of the unidentifiable intangible asset should continue after the date this Statement is adopted unless the other finite-lived intangible assets acquired in the transaction had been recognized apart from the unidentifiable intangible asset (separate recognition criterion).

A28. Most of the respondents disagreed with the proposed separate recognition criterion, mainly because they disagreed that the motivation for a business combination in the scope of Statement 72 was to acquire intangible assets other than goodwill. Many of those respondents commented that a business combination in the scope of Statement 72 is undertaken for the same reasons as any other business combination and, therefore, often gives rise to goodwill.

A29. Some of those respondents suggested that the Board eliminate the separate recognition criterion so that the transition provisions in this Statement would be consistent with the transition provisions of Statements 141 and 142. Those respondents commented that upon adoption of Statements 141 and 142, entities were required to cease amortization of the amount recorded as goodwill *regardless* of whether they had separately recognized all acquired intangible assets. During the development of Statements 141 and 142, the Board noted that some entities had included acquired intangible assets in the amount recognized as goodwill and subsequently amortized that asset over a period reflecting its composite useful life.[15] Those entities concluded that their financial statements were fairly presented in accordance with U.S. generally accepted accounting principles because the goodwill amortization expense recorded under that approach was not materially different from the amount that would have been recognized had the acquired intangible assets been separately recognized. The Board decided not to require entities to disaggregate existing intangible assets from goodwill in those circumstances unless separate accounting records were maintained for those assets.

A30. In their comment letters, respondents noted that for that same reason, many financial institutions had recognized acquired intangible assets in the amount recorded as an unidentifiable intangible asset. Moreover, respondents noted that for acquisitions of financial institutions, the staff of the Securities and Exchange Commission (SEC) did not object to the practice of recognizing the core deposit intangible asset and the unidentifiable intangible asset as a composite asset as long as the useful life assigned to that asset did not exceed 15 years.[16] For those reasons, those respondents indicated that the transition provisions in this Statement should be similar to the transition provisions in Statements 141 and 142. That is,

---

[15]Entities might not have adhered strictly to the purchase price allocation requirements in Opinion 16 because APB Opinion No. 17, *Intangible Assets,* required amortization of all acquired intangible assets and limited the maximum amortization for both goodwill and other intangible assets to 40 years.

[16]As SEC Staff Accounting Bulletin Topic 2.A.3, "Acquisitions Involving Financial Institutions," states, "The allocation to goodwill of significant amounts of the purchase price, which appeared to be the result of a failure to properly identify and quantify all intangible assets purchased, was often a factor which influenced these decisions."

the carrying amount of the unidentifiable intangible asset should be reclassified as goodwill (and amortization should cease) upon adoption of this Statement even if entities had included acquired intangible assets in that amount. Upon consideration of those respondents' comments, the Board decided to eliminate the separate recognition criterion.

A31. During redeliberations of the Exposure Draft, the Board also considered and rejected another alternative to transition suggested by some respondents. Under that alternative, entities would be allowed to retroactively determine the portion of the unidentifiable intangible asset that represents goodwill and reclassify that amount as goodwill upon adoption of the final Statement. The Board concluded, as it did in the deliberations that led to the Exposure Draft, that that alternative would be impractical or burdensome for many enterprises to apply, principally because the information needed to identify those intangible assets may not exist or may no longer be obtainable.

A32. The Board decided during development of the Exposure Draft that comparability would be improved if amortization of previously recognized unidentifiable intangible assets reclassified as goodwill ceased as of the date that Statement 142 was applied in its entirety. In addition, the Exposure Draft proposed that reclassified goodwill should be tested for impairment under the transition provisions of Statement 142. Respondents to the Exposure Draft supported those provisions, and the Board affirmed the provisions during its redeliberations.

A33. Consistent with the Exposure Draft, this Statement does not require a transitional impairment test for acquired long-term customer-relationship intangible assets of financial institutions that, effective with the issuance of this Statement, are included in the scope of Statement 144. The Board noted that if those intangible assets had originally been within the scope of FASB Statement No. 121, *Accounting for the Impairment of Long-Lived Assets and for Long-Lived Assets to Be Disposed Of,*[17] a transitional impairment test would not have been required when Statement 121 was adopted. None of the respondents to the Exposure Draft disagreed with this provision, and the Board affirmed the provision during its redeliberations.

Benefits and Costs

A34. The Board's mission statement charges the Board to determine that a standard will fill a significant need and that the costs it imposes will be justified in relation to the overall benefits. The Board concluded that the changes made by this Statement will not impose significant costs on preparers or auditors and that the removal of certain financial institutions from the scope of Statement 72 and Interpretation 9 simplifies the accounting literature. The Board concluded that the changes required by this Statement are consistent with its goal of improving the usefulness of financial reporting by focusing on the primary characteristics of relevance and reliability and on the qualities of comparability and consistency.

International Accounting Standards

A35. The International Accounting Standard, IAS 22, *Business Combinations,* does not provide industry-specific guidance for acquisitions in which the fair value of liabilities assumed exceeds the fair value of tangible and identifiable intangible assets acquired. At the time this Statement was developed, IAS 22 was under reconsideration; however, it seemed unlikely that industry-specific guidance like that provided in Statement 72 would be added to the new international business combinations standard. Therefore, the elimination of paragraphs 5 and 6 of Statement 72 for acquisitions of financial institutions in the scope of this Statement broadly promotes international convergence.

Appendix B

AMENDMENTS TO EXISTING PRONOUNCEMENTS

B1. FASB Statement No. 72, *Accounting for Certain Acquisitions of Banking or Thrift Institutions,* is amended as follows:

a. Paragraph 2 is amended as follows:

  (1) The first sentence is replaced by the following:

      As of October 1, 2002, this Statement applies only to acquisitions between two or more mutual enterprises that are financial institutions.

---

[17]Refer to footnote 13.

(2) The last sentence is replaced by the following:

> The provisions of paragraph 4 apply to all transactions within the scope of this Statement.

b. Paragraph 3 is deleted.

c. The first sentence of paragraph 4, as amended by FASB Statement No. 141, *Business Combinations,* is replaced by the following:

> In a business combination accounted for by the purchase method, intangible assets acquired that can be separately identified shall be assigned a portion of the total cost of the acquired enterprise if the fair values of those assets can be reliably[1] determined.

d. The last three sentences of paragraph 4, which were added by FASB Statement No. 142, *Goodwill and Other Intangible Assets,* are replaced by the following:

> Identified intangible assets shall be reviewed for impairment in accordance with FASB Statement No. 144, *Accounting for the Impairment or Disposal of Long-Lived Assets.*

e. In the penultimate sentence of paragraph 5, *paragraphs 6 and 7* is replaced by *paragraph 6.*

f. Paragraph 7, as amended by Statement 142, is deleted.

g. Paragraphs 8 and 9, as amended by Statement 141, and paragraphs 10 and 11 are deleted.

B2. FASB Statement No. 141, *Business Combinations,* is amended as follows:

a. In item (2) of paragraph 61(b), *and required to be amortized in accordance with paragraph 8 of FASB Statement No. 147, Acquisitions of Certain Financial Institutions,* is added after *FASB Statement No. 72, Accounting for Certain Acquisitions of Banking or Thrift Institutions.*

b. Paragraph E20 is deleted.

B3. FASB Statement No. 142, *Goodwill and Other Intangible Assets,* is amended as follows:

a. In item (2) of paragraph 49(b), *and required to be amortized in accordance with paragraph 8 of FASB Statement No. 147, Acquisitions of Certain Financial Institutions,* is added after *in accordance with paragraph 5 of Statement 72.*

b. Paragraph D11 is deleted.

B4. FASB Statement No. 144, *Accounting for the Impairment or Disposal of Long-Lived Assets,* is amended as follows:

a. In item (c) of paragraph 5, *long-term customer relationships of a financial institution, such as core deposit intangibles, credit cardholder intangibles, and* is deleted.

b. Appendix D is amended as follows:

(1) The reference to Statement 72 is deleted.

(2) The following is added to the table:

		Apply Requirement in This Statement
FASB Statement No. 147	*Acquisitions of Certain Financial Institutions*	
	• Depositor- and borrower-relationship intangible assets	X
	• Credit cardholder intangible assets	X

B5. Footnote 1 of FASB Interpretation No. 9, *Applying APB Opinions No. 16 and 17 When a Savings and Loan Association or a Similar Institution Is Acquired in a Business Combination Accounted for by the Purchase Method,* is replaced by the following:

> As of October 1, 2002, this Interpretation applies only to acquisitions between two or more mutual enterprises that are financial institutions.

Appendix C

GLOSSARY

C1. This appendix contains definitions of certain terms used in this Statement.

Goodwill
> The excess of the cost of an acquired entity over the net of the amounts assigned to assets acquired and liabilities assumed. The amount recognized as goodwill includes acquired intangible assets that do not meet the criteria in FASB Statement No. 141, *Business Combinations,* for recognition as assets apart from goodwill.

Mutual enterprise

An entity other than an investor-owned entity that provides dividends, lower costs, or other economic benefits directly and proportionately to its owners, members, or participants. Credit unions are an example of a mutual enterprise (FASB Concepts Statement No. 4, *Objectives of Financial Reporting by Nonbusiness Organizations,* paragraph 7).

Unidentifiable intangible asset

The amount by which the fair value of liabilities assumed exceeds the fair value of tangible and identified intangible assets acquired (FASB Statement No. 72, *Accounting for Certain Acquisitions of Banking or Thrift Institutions,* paragraph 5).

Statement of Financial Accounting Standards No. 148
Accounting for Stock-Based Compensation—
Transition and Disclosure

an amendment of FASB Statement No. 123

STATUS

Issued: December 2002

Effective Date: For fiscal years ending after December 15, 2002, for transition guidance and annual disclosure provisions; for financial reports containing financial statements for interim periods beginning after December 15, 2002, for interim disclosure provisions

Affects: Amends APB 28, paragraph 30
Amends FAS 123, paragraphs 44 and 53 and by adding paragraphs 52A and 52B
Replaces FAS 123, paragraphs 45 and 52

Affected by: Superseded by FAS123(R), paragraph D8

SUMMARY

This Statement amends FASB Statement No. 123, *Accounting for Stock-Based Compensation,* to provide alternative methods of transition for a voluntary change to the fair value based method of accounting for stock-based employee compensation. In addition, this Statement amends the disclosure requirements of Statement 123 to require prominent disclosures in both annual and interim financial statements about the method of accounting for stock-based employee compensation and the effect of the method used on reported results.

Reasons for Issuing This Statement

Statement 123 required prospective application of the fair value recognition provisions to new awards granted after the beginning of the period of adoption. When Statement 123 was issued in 1995, the Board recognized the potential for misleading implications caused by the "ramp-up" effect on reported compensation cost from prospective application of the fair value based method of accounting for stock-based employee compensation to only new grants after the date of adoption. However, the Board was concerned that retroactive application would be excessively burdensome to financial statement preparers because the historical assumptions required to determine the fair value of awards of stock-based compensation for periods prior to the issuance of Statement 123 were not readily available. Because Statement 123 requires disclosure of the pro forma effect of applying the fair value based method of accounting for those entities that continue to use the intrinsic value method of accounting, historical information about the fair value of awards granted since the original effective date of Statement 123 is readily available.

A number of companies have recently adopted or announced their intention to adopt the fair value based method of accounting for stock-based employee compensation. To respond to concerns raised by constituents, including financial statement preparers' concerns about the ramp-up effect arising from the transition method prescribed by Statement 123 and financial statement users' concerns about the lack of consistency and comparability in reported results caused by that transition method, this Statement requires new disclosures about the effect of stock-based employee compensation on reported results. This Statement also requires that those effects be disclosed more prominently by specifying the form, content, and location of those disclosures.

How the Changes in This Statement Improve Financial Reporting

This Statement permits two additional transition methods for entities that adopt the preferable method of accounting for stock-based employee compensation. Both of those methods avoid the ramp-up effect arising from prospective application of the fair value based method. In addition, to address concerns raised by some constituents about the lack of comparability caused by multiple transition methods, this Statement does not permit the use of the original Statement 123 prospective method of transition for changes to the fair value based method made in fiscal years beginning after December 15, 2003.

Also, in the absence of a single accounting method for stock-based employee compensation, this Statement requires disclosure of comparable information for all companies regardless of whether, when, or how an entity adopts the preferable, fair value based method of accounting. This Statement improves the prominence and clarity of the pro forma disclosures required by Statement 123 by prescribing a specific tabular format and by requiring disclosure in the "Summary of Significant Accounting Policies" or its equivalent. In addition, this Statement improves the timeliness of those disclosures by requiring their inclusion in financial reports for interim periods.

International Convergence

The Board did not reconsider the recognition and measurement provisions of Statement 123 in this Statement because of the ongoing International Accounting Standards Board (IASB) project on share-based payment. The IASB concluded its deliberations on the accounting for share-based payments, including employee stock options, and issued an exposure draft for public comment in November 2002. That proposal would require companies using IASB standards to recognize as an expense, starting in 2004, the fair value of employee stock options granted. While there are some important differences between the recognition and measurement provisions in the IASB proposal and those contained in Statement 123, the basic approach is the same—fair value measurement of stock-based employee compensation at the date of grant with expense recognition over the vesting period.

The Board has been actively working with the IASB and other major national standard setters to bring about convergence of accounting standards across the major world capital markets. In particular, the Board and the FASB staff have been monitoring the IASB's deliberations on share-based payments and, in November 2002, issued an Invitation to Comment summarizing the IASB's proposal and explaining the key similarities of and differences between its provisions and current U.S. accounting standards. In the near future, the Board plans to consider whether it should propose changes to the U.S. standards on accounting for stock-based compensation.

Statement of Financial Accounting Standards No. 148

Accounting for Stock-Based Compensation—Transition and Disclosure

an amendment of FASB Statement No. 123

CONTENTS

INTRODUCTION

1. This Statement amends FASB Statement No. 123, *Accounting for Stock-Based Compensation,* to provide alternative methods of transition for an entity that voluntarily changes to the fair value based method of accounting for stock-based employee compensation. It also amends the disclosure provisions of that Statement to require prominent disclosure about the effects on reported net income of an entity's accounting policy decisions with respect to stock-based employee compensation. Finally, this Statement amends APB Opinion No. 28, *Interim Financial Reporting,* to require disclosure about those effects in interim financial information.

STANDARDS OF FINANCIAL ACCOUNTING AND REPORTING

Amendments to Statement 123

2. Statement 123 is amended as follows:

Amendments to Transition Provisions

a. Paragraph 52 is replaced by the following:

> If an entity elects to adopt the recognition provisions of this Statement for stock-based employee compensation in a fiscal year beginning before December 16, 2003, that change in accounting principle shall be reported using any one of the following methods:

> a. *Prospective method.* Apply the recognition provisions to all employee awards granted, modified, or settled after the beginning of the fiscal year in which the recognition provisions are first applied.

> b. *Modified prospective method.* Recognize stock-based employee compensation cost from the beginning of the fiscal year in which the recognition provisions are first applied as if the fair value based accounting method in this Statement had been used to account for all employee awards granted, modified, or settled in fiscal years beginning after December 15, 1994.

> c. *Retroactive restatement method.* Restate all periods presented to reflect stock-based employee compensation cost under the fair value based accounting method in this Statement for all employee awards granted, modified, or settled in fiscal years beginning after December 15, 1994. Restatement of periods prior to those presented is permitted but not required. The

restated net income and earnings per share of prior periods shall be determined in a manner consistent with the requirements of paragraphs 12, 13, and 45 of this Statement.

Accounting for modifications and settlements of awards initially accounted for in accordance with Opinion 25 is discussed and illustrated in Appendix B. Awards are considered to be accounted for under Opinion 25 only if they were issued in fiscal periods beginning before December 15, 1994 (that is, the grant date fair value of the awards was never required to be measured under this Statement).

b. The following new paragraph 52A is inserted after paragraph 52:

If an entity elects to adopt the recognition provisions of this Statement for stock-based employee compensation in fiscal years beginning after December 15, 2003, that change in accounting must be reported using either the method described in paragraph 52(b) or the method described in paragraph 52(c).

c. The following new paragraph 52B is inserted after paragraph 52A:

An entity that elects the transition method described in paragraph 52(b) or 52(c) may need to report an adjustment to additional paid-in capital as of the beginning of the first period for which stock-based employee compensation cost is accounted for in accordance with the fair value based method. For awards that are unvested or, in the case of certain variable awards, unexercised as of the beginning of that period, that adjustment shall be determined as follows:

  a. The carrying amounts of unearned or deferred compensation (contra-equity accounts), stock-based compensation liabilities, and the related deferred tax balances recognized under Opinion 25, if any, shall be reversed.
  b. The stock-based compensation liabilities and related deferred tax balances determined under this Statement shall be recognized.
  c. The difference between the amounts reversed in (a) and the amounts recognized in (b) shall be reported as an adjustment

to additional paid-in capital as of the beginning of the period. No cumulative effect of a change in accounting principle shall be presented.

Examples of determining and recording that adjustment are included in Appendix B of Statement 148. For those entities that elect retroactive restatement, any effect on additional paid-in capital or retained earnings arising from the restatement of periods subsequent to the period of initial application of the fair value based method but prior to the earliest period for which an income statement is presented should be reported as an adjustment to those accounts as of the beginning of the earliest period for which an income statement is presented. The transition adjustment as well as the effect of restatement of intervening periods, if any, should be disclosed in the year of adoption.

d. The following sentence is added to the end of paragraph 44:

If an entity that continued to apply Opinion 25 subsequently adopts the fair value based method in this Statement, only the additional paid-in capital recognized from excess tax deductions for awards accounted for under the fair value based method pursuant to the transition provisions of paragraph 52 is available to absorb any such write-offs.

Amendments to Disclosure Provisions

e. Paragraph 45 of Statement 123 is replaced by the following:

Regardless of the method used to account for stock-based employee compensation arrangements, the financial statements of an entity shall include the disclosures specified in paragraphs 46–48. All entities shall disclose the following information in the "Summary of Significant Accounting Policies" or its equivalent:*

  a. The method used—either the intrinsic value method or the fair value based method—to account for stock-based employee compensation in each period presented
  b. For an entity that adopts the fair value recognition provisions of this Statement, for all financial statements in which the

period of adoption is presented, a description of the method of reporting the change in accounting principle

c. If awards of stock-based employee compensation were outstanding and accounted for under the intrinsic value method of Opinion 25 for any period for which an income statement is presented, a tabular presentation of the following information for all periods presented:

   (1) Net income and basic and diluted earnings per share as reported

   (2) The stock-based employee compensation cost, net of related tax effects, included in the determination of net income as reported

   (3) The stock-based employee compensation cost, net of related tax effects, that would have been included in the determination of net income if the fair value based method had been applied to all awards[†]

   (4) Pro forma net income as if the fair value based method had been applied to all awards

   (5) Pro forma basic and diluted earnings per share as if the fair value based method had been applied to all awards.

The required pro forma amounts shall reflect the difference in stock-based employee compensation cost, if any, included in net income and the total cost measured by the fair value based method, as well as additional tax effects, if any, that would have been recognized in the income statement if the fair value based method had been applied to all awards. The required pro forma per share amounts shall reflect the change in the denominator of the diluted earnings per share calculation as if the assumed proceeds under the treasury stock method, including measured but unrecognized compensation cost and the excess tax benefits credited to additional paid-in capital, were determined under the fair value based method. Examples of the required tabular presentation are included in Appendix B of FASB Statement No. 148, *Accounting for Stock-Based Compensation—Transition and Disclosure.*

---

*APB Opinion No. 22, *Disclosure of Accounting Policies*, paragraph 15, introduces the term *Summary of Significant Accounting Policies* and expresses a preference for disclosure of accounting policies preceding the notes to financial statements or as the initial note.

[†]For purposes of applying the guidance in this Statement, *all awards* refers to awards granted, modified, or settled in fiscal periods beginning after December 15, 1994—that is, awards for which the grant date fair value was required to be measured under this Statement.

f. The second sentence of paragraph 53 is deleted.

Amendment to Opinion 28

3. The following is added to the list of disclosures in paragraph 30 of Opinion 28:

   j. The following information about stock-based employee compensation costs, disclosed prominently and in tabular form for all periods presented pursuant to the provisions of FASB Statement No. 148, *Accounting for Stock-Based Compensation—Transition and Disclosure,* if awards of stock-based employee compensation were outstanding and accounted for under the intrinsic value method of Opinion 25 for any period for which an income statement is presented:

   (1) Net income and basic and diluted earnings per share as reported

   (2) The stock-based employee compensation cost, net of related tax effects, included in the determination of net income as reported

   (3) The stock-based employee compensation cost, net of related tax effects, that would have been included in the determination of net income if the fair value based method had been applied to all awards*

   (4) Pro forma net income as if the fair value based method had been applied to all awards

   (5) Pro forma basic and diluted earnings per share as if the fair value based method had been applied to all awards.

---

*For purposes of applying the guidance in this subparagraph, *all awards* refers to awards granted, modified, or settled in fiscal periods beginning after December 15, 1994—that is, awards for which the grant date fair value was required to be measured under FASB Statement No. 123, *Accounting for Stock-Based Compensation.*

Effective Dates

4. The amendments to Statement 123 in paragraphs 2(a)–2(e) of this Statement shall be effective

for financial statements for fiscal years ending after December 15, 2002. Earlier application of the transition provisions in paragraphs 2(a)–2(d) is permitted for entities with a fiscal year ending prior to December 15, 2002, provided that financial statements for the 2002 fiscal year have not been issued as of the date this Statement is issued. Early application of the disclosure provisions in paragraph 2(e) is encouraged.

5. The amendment to Statement 123 in paragraph 2(f) of this Statement and the amendment to Opinion 28 in paragraph 3 shall be effective for financial reports containing condensed financial statements for interim periods beginning after December 15, 2002. Early application is encouraged.

> **The provisions of this Statement need not be applied to immaterial items.**

This Statement was adopted by the unaimous vote of the seven members of the Financial Accounting Standards Board.

Robert H. Herz,
  Chairman
G. Michael Crooch

John M. Foster
Gary S. Schieneman
Katherine Schipper

Edward W. Trott
John K. Wulff

Appendix A

BACKGROUND INFORMATION AND BASIS FOR CONCLUSIONS

CONTENTS

Appendix A

BACKGROUND INFORMATION AND BASIS FOR CONCLUSIONS

Introduction

A1. This appendix summarizes considerations that Board members deemed significant in reaching the conclusions in this Statement. It includes the reasons for accepting certain approaches and rejecting others. Individual Board members gave greater weight to some factors than to others.

Background Information

A2. Statement 123 was issued in 1995. In the deliberations that led to that Statement, the Board concluded that the fair value based method of recognizing stock-based compensation expense was the preferable method of accounting, but, in an effort to end an extremely divisive debate between the Board and its constituents, the Board decided to permit the continued use of the intrinsic value method of accounting under APB Opinion No. 25, *Accounting for Stock Issued to Employees*. However, the Board decided to require companies to disclose the pro forma effect of applying the fair value based method of accounting for stock-based employee compensation. Following the issuance of Statement 123, most companies continued to account for stock-based employee compensation using the intrinsic value method of accounting under Opinion 25.

A3. Prior to the issuance of Statement 123, companies had not been gathering the necessary information or making the necessary assumptions to measure the fair value of employee stock options. Therefore, although the Board acknowledged that the "ramp-up" effect[1] created by the prospective transition method was undesirable, the Board decided to require prospective application because retroactive application would have required preparers of financial statements to make numerous assumptions in order to estimate the grant date fair value of previously issued stock-based awards.[2] In 2002, however, seven

years after the issuance of Statement 123, historical information necessary for retroactive application of the recognition provisions of Statement 123 is available.

A4. A number of companies have recently elected to adopt the fair value recognition provisions of Statement 123 for stock-based employee compensation awards. In conjunction with those decisions, a number of companies, as well as financial statement users, expressed concern to the Board about the lack of comparability and consistency of reported results between periods caused by the ramp-up effect inherent in the requirement to adopt the fair value based method prospectively.

A5. In August 2002, the Board decided to add a limited-scope project to its agenda to reconsider the transition and disclosure provisions of Statement 123. The principal objective of that project was to address the concerns of preparers and users about the comparability and consistency of reported results in light of the increased number of entities electing to adopt the fair value based method of accounting for stock-based employee compensation. Because of the Board's commitment to international convergence of accounting standards and the ongoing International Accounting Standards Board project on share-based payment, the Board decided not to reconsider the recognition and measurement provisions of Statement 123, including the optional use of the intrinsic value method, in the context of this limited-scope project. Reconsideration of the accounting for stock-based compensation has been deferred pending receipt of feedback from constituents on the November 2002 Invitation to Comment, *Accounting for Stock-Based Compensation: A Comparison of FASB Statement No. 123*, Accounting for Stock-Based Compensation, *and Its Related Interpretations, and IASB Proposed IFRS*, Share-based Payment.

A6. In October 2002, the Board issued an Exposure Draft, *Accounting for Stock-Based Compensation—Transition and Disclosure*, for a 30-day comment period. The Board received 70 comment letters on the Exposure Draft. In November 2002, the Board redeliberated the issues identified in the Exposure Draft and concluded that on the basis of

---

[1] As Statement 123, paragraph 269, states, "Some respondents were concerned about the inherent 'ramp-up' effect on compensation cost as additional awards are granted and the first awards to which the new method applies move through their vesting periods."

[2] Statement 123, paragraph 270, states, "The Board recognizes the potential for misleading implications caused by the ramp-up effect of prospective application of a new accounting or pro forma disclosure requirement for a recurring transaction. . . . The Board decided that requiring retroactive application would be excessively burdensome."

existing information, it could reach an informed decision on the matters addressed in this Statement without a public hearing.

Basis for Conclusions

Transition Alternatives

A7. In its deliberations leading to the issuance of the Exposure Draft, the Board considered three possible transition methods in addition to prospective application to new awards[3] (the "prospective" method) prescribed by Statement 123:

a. Cumulative effect of a change in accounting principle under APB Opinion No. 20, *Accounting Changes*
b. Retroactive restatement
c. Prospective recognition for unvested awards and new awards (the "modified prospective" method).

Cumulative effect of a change in accounting principle

A8. During the deliberations leading to the Exposure Draft, the Board rejected the cumulative effect of a change in accounting principle method primarily because the cumulative effect, in the case of a change from the intrinsic value method to the fair value based method, would be the cumulative effect only from the original effective date of Statement 123 and, therefore, would not represent a meaningful amount. In addition, some preparers and users of financial statements expressed concern over the confusion often created by including the cumulative effect of a change in accounting principle in the determination of current period net income. The Board also noted that the cumulative effect from this particular accounting change generally would result in a reduction in retained earnings offset by an increase in additional paid-in capital. A number of respondents were concerned about the implications for future voluntary accounting changes of the Board's rejection of the cumulative effect transition method prescribed by Opinion 20. The Board's rejection of that method, however, stems from the unique characteristics of this particular accounting change and is not intended to imply that the Board has reconsidered the appropriateness of that method for voluntary accounting changes in general.

Retroactive restatement

A9. The retroactive restatement method, as used in this Statement, refers to the restatement of prior periods' reported net income to give effect to the fair value based method of accounting for awards granted, modified, or settled in fiscal years beginning after December 15, 1994, on a basis consistent with the pro forma disclosures required by Statement 123. Retroactive application to awards made in periods beginning before that date involves the problems cited by the Board in originally rejecting retroactive application and would likely result in restated amounts different from those pro forma amounts previously disclosed in financial statements.

A10. During the deliberations leading to the Exposure Draft, the Board considered the views of some financial statement users who suggested that the Board require retroactive restatement for reporting this change in accounting. Board members agreed that retroactive application maximizes consistency between periods and comparability among companies. The Board also considered the views of some preparers who echoed the Accounting Principles Board's concerns expressed in Opinion 20 that the restatement of prior-period results detracts from the credibility of reported results.

Modified prospective method

A11. Some preparers suggested that both the ramp-up effect of prospective application and the perceived credibility issue of retroactive restatement could be avoided by prospectively applying the fair value recognition provisions of Statement 123 to the unvested portion of previously issued awards and unvested variable awards as well as new awards. Under that approach, the stock-based employee compensation cost recognized in the year of adoption would be the same as that which would be recognized if the company had applied the retroactive restatement method.

Multiple transition methods

A12. The Exposure Draft reflected the Board's decision to allow multiple transition methods. The majority of respondents disagreed with that decision, citing the arguments considered by the Board in the deliberations leading to the Exposure Draft, but were divided as to which of the proposed transition methods

---

[3]For purposes of the discussion in the basis for conclusions, *new awards* refers to awards granted, modified, or settled in periods subsequent to adoption of the fair value based method of Statement 123.

they preferred. The Board acknowledges the arguments cited by respondents, which confirm that preparers' and users' concerns are primarily related to the lack of comparability and consistency arising from (a) the ramp-up effect resulting from prospective application and (b) the existence of multiple transition methods. However, because a choice of accounting methods for stock-based employee compensation continues to exist—intrinsic value or fair value—comparability is impaired currently. As stated in paragraph A19, the Board believes that the new disclosures required by this Statement mitigate those concerns about comparability by providing information that enables users of financial statements to make comparisons.

A13. Although information is now available to facilitate retroactive application, the Board notes that the guidance in Statement 123 is unambiguous—it requires prospective application to awards granted, modified, or settled after the beginning of the period of adoption. Therefore, in the deliberations leading to the Exposure Draft, the Board decided that it would be inappropriate to preclude the existing Statement 123 transition method, particularly for those companies that previously had decided to adopt the preferable method of accounting in accordance with that Statement. However, the Board was persuaded by respondents' comments that the practical argument for retaining the prospective method no longer exists. Therefore, the Board decided that the prospective method would no longer be permitted for those entities adopting the fair value based method of accounting for stock-based employee compensation in fiscal years beginning after December 15, 2003.

A14. During its redeliberations, the Board affirmed its decision to permit both the retroactive restatement method and the modified prospective method because (a) both methods address the ramp-up effect and (b) the reported amount of stock-based compensation cost determined under either method will be the same in the period of adoption and all subsequent periods. The Board decided not to *require* restatement for an entity that *voluntarily* adopts the preferable accounting method because, for the reasons cited in paragraph A12, concerns about comparability and consistency continue to exist. The Board believes that the amended disclosures, which are required for all companies except those that adopt the fair value based method using the retroactive restate-

ment method of transition, provide information that will mitigate any additional comparability concerns caused by the decision to permit multiple transition methods.

Accumulated Opinion 25 Balances

A15. The modified prospective method and the retroactive restatement method (if fewer than all of the periods since the original effective date of Statement 123 are restated) raise the issue of accounting for the accumulated deferred compensation, if any, and related deferred income tax balances that arose from the application of Opinion 25. In the deliberations leading to the Exposure Draft, the Board concluded that the carrying amounts of those items should be reversed and that any required beginning balances under Statement 123 relating to unvested awards should be recorded with the effect recognized in additional paid-in capital. The Opinion 25 balances and Statement 123 balances both ultimately increase additional paid-in capital for the value of the employee services received. However, because the two accounting models under which those balances arise are fundamentally different, the Board decided not to require reclassifications between retained earnings (either directly or through the income statement) and additional paid-in capital because doing so would be tantamount to reporting the cumulative effect of a change in accounting principle, which, as described in paragraph A8, the Board believes would not provide useful information to financial statement users about the change from the intrinsic value method to the fair value based method. Of those respondents that addressed the accounting for the transition effect, most agreed with the Board's decision, and the Board affirmed that decision during redeliberations.

Accounting for Excess Tax Benefits

A16. Under Statement 123, the write-off of deferred tax assets recognized in excess of the tax benefit ultimately realized from the exercise of employee stock options reduces net income unless there are accumulated balances in additional paid-in capital related to previous excess tax benefits related to awards accounted for under the fair value based method of Statement 123. In that case, the write-off of those excess deferred tax assets reduces additional paid-in capital. In developing the Exposure Draft, the Board decided that the determination of whether sufficient excess tax benefits are accumulated in additional paid-in capital should be based on the excess tax benefits that are recorded in additional paid-in capital after adoption of the fair value based method and that relate only to awards accounted for under the fair value based method. Although only a few respondents addressed that decision, those respondents generally agreed with the Board's decision, and it was affirmed during redeliberations. As a result of that decision, under either the prospective method or the modified prospective method, no excess tax benefits from the exercise of awards accounted for under the fair value based method will be accumulated in additional paid-in capital as of the beginning of the period of initial application.

Prominence of Disclosures

A17. During the Board's deliberations leading to the Exposure Draft, a number of users of financial statements raised concerns about the consistency and comparability of reported results arising from the choice between the intrinsic value method and the fair value based method of accounting for stock-based employee compensation. The Board decided to address those concerns in the context of this limited-scope project by improving the required disclosures about the effects on reported results of accounting policy decisions related to stock-based employee compensation.

A18. The Board considered whether the pro forma disclosures required by paragraph 45 of Statement 123 should be presented on the face of the income statement. The Board considered existing FASB literature and other financial reporting guidance governing pro forma financial information (for example, the rules and regulations of securities regulators) and the proliferation of "pro forma" language in various public reports of financial performance. The Exposure Draft reflected the Board's decision not to require disclosure of the Statement 123 pro forma amounts on the face of the income statement. The Board noted that all financial statement disclosures required under generally accepted accounting principles are integral to the financial statements and necessary for a proper understanding of reported results, financial position, and cash flows.

A19. However, in the deliberations leading to the Exposure Draft, the Board acknowledged constituents' concerns about the possible lack of comparability and concluded that all companies should be required to provide comparable information about stock-based employee compensation cost. Although the Board continues to believe that disclosure is not an adequate substitute for recognition of items that

qualify for recognition in financial statements, the Board believes that the disclosures required by this Statement will mitigate the disadvantages of permitting multiple transition methods by providing information to enable users of financial statements to make comparisons among entities while a choice between the intrinsic value and fair value based methods continues to exist. Therefore, the Exposure Draft reflected the Board's decision that the disclosures required by paragraph 2(e) of this Statement should be included in the financial statements of all entities that cover periods in which all or a portion of the cost of stock-based awards was determined under Opinion 25.

A20. Also, during the deliberations leading to the Exposure Draft, the Board observed that the effects of some stock-based compensation arrangements accounted for under Opinion 25 continue to appear in the financial statements of companies that voluntarily adopt the fair value recognition provisions of Statement 123. The Exposure Draft reflected the Board's decision that the disclosure requirements of paragraphs 2(e) and 3 of this Statement should, therefore, apply to those companies as well until the fair value based method applies to all stock-based employee compensation that affects all periods presented. However, entities that elect the retroactive restatement method will have no need to provide those pro forma disclosures. Respondents generally agreed that the required disclosures, overall, represent an improvement over the existing requirements, and the Board affirmed that decision during redeliberations.

A21. Because the disclosures required by paragraph 2(e) are intended to provide information to enable users of financial statements to make comparisons among companies, the Exposure Draft reflected the Board's conclusion that those disclosures should be displayed prominently. Specifically, the Board decided to require (a) that those disclosures be presented in the "Summary of Significant Accounting Policies" or its equivalent and (b) that the pro forma information be disclosed in tabular form. The Board acknowledged, however, that some companies may not have adopted the preferable method of disclosing accounting policies as expressed in paragraph 15 of APB Opinion No. 22, *Disclosure of Accounting Policies,* which states:

The Board recognizes the need for flexibility in matters of format (including the location) of disclosure of accounting policies provided that the reporting entity identifies and describes its significant accounting policies as an integral part of its financial statements in accordance with the foregoing guides in this Opinion. The Board believes that the disclosure is particularly useful if given in a separate *Summary of Significant Accounting Policies* preceding the notes to financial statements or as the initial note. Accordingly, it expresses its preference for that format under the same or a similar title.

The Board decided that companies must disclose prominently the information required by this Statement. The Board also believes that companies may wish to reconsider the method of disclosing accounting policies in light of the guidance in Opinion 22.

A22. Respondents generally agreed with the Board's decision to require a tabular presentation of the pro forma disclosures. However, a number of respondents stated that the tabular, quantitative disclosures required by this Statement are inconsistent with the narrative, descriptive, or qualitative disclosures contemplated by Opinion 22 and that it is highly unusual for the Board to prescribe a specific format and location for financial statement disclosures. The Board believes, however, that as long as the choice between the intrinsic value method and the fair value based method continues to exist, the decision about which accounting method to apply to stock-based employee compensation has a material, permanent effect on reported results for many companies. Therefore, that particular accounting policy decision warrants amplification through quantification in the "Summary of Significant Accounting Policies" or its equivalent. That accounting policy decision is further distinguished from most other accounting policy decisions that generally affect the timing of recognition of revenues or expenses because it permanently includes or excludes an item from the determination of income. Therefore, the Board affirmed its decision to require tabular presentation of the pro forma information in the "Summary of Significant Accounting Policies" or its equivalent.

Interim Disclosures

A23. Paragraph 106 of Statement 123 states, in part:

> If a need for pro forma disclosures on a quarterly basis becomes apparent, the Board will consider at a later date whether to require those disclosures.

Based on concerns expressed by investors and creditors and on research demonstrating the importance of interim financial reporting to timely decision making by investors, the Exposure Draft reflected the Board's conclusion that the pro forma disclosures required under Statement 123 should be provided on a quarterly basis. Although quarterly financial information is not required to, and generally does not, include a "Summary of Significant Accounting Policies," the Board decided that the pro forma information required by this Statement should be disclosed prominently in financial reports containing condensed financial statements for interim periods.

A24. Respondents generally agreed with the Board's decision to require more frequent disclosures of the effects of stock-based employee compensation, and the Board affirmed that decision during redeliberations.

Effective Dates

A25. The Exposure Draft reflected the Board's decision that the alternative transition methods permitted by this Statement should be effective for fiscal years ending after December 15, 2002, with earlier application permitted to the extent that, upon issuance of this Statement, a company has not already issued annual financial statements reflecting this change in accounting. Because one objective of this Statement is to respond to the concerns of preparers about the lack of consistency arising from the ramp-up effect, the Board concluded that immediate availability of this guidance and the transition methods it allows is appropriate. Respondents generally agreed with that decision, and the Board affirmed it during redeliberations.

A26. The Exposure Draft proposed that the annual disclosures required by this Statement be effective for financial statements for fiscal years ending after December 15, 2002. The Board believes that those disclosures are important to financial statement users and that the data needed to make those disclosures are readily available to preparers. Earlier application is encouraged for entities with fiscal years that end prior to December 16, 2002, but that upon issuance of this Statement, have not yet issued financial statements for the 2002 fiscal year. Respondents generally agreed with that decision, and the Board affirmed it during redeliberations.

A27. The Exposure Draft reflected the Board's decision that the disclosure provisions for interim financial information would be effective for all periods presented in financial reports containing condensed financial statements for interim periods beginning after December 15, 2002. The Board considered the incremental cost of providing those disclosures and concluded that the benefit of those disclosures to investors and creditors outweighs that cost. Respondents generally agreed with that decision, and the Board affirmed it during redeliberations.

Appendix B

ILLUSTRATIVE GUIDANCE

Transition Provisions

B1. The following illustrations provide examples of how to determine the transition effect (described in paragraph 2(c) of this Statement) arising at the beginning of the period of initial application of the fair value based method of accounting for stock-based employee compensation. One example illustrates the retroactive restatement method, and the other illustrates the modified prospective method. The retroactive restatement example also illustrates the accounting for forfeitures in periods subsequent to adoption as well as the impact of recognized deferred tax assets upon exercise of the awards.

Illustration 1—Fixed Stock Option Award: Retroactive Restatement Method

B2. On January 1, 1999, ABC Company grants its employees options to purchase 100,000 shares of ABC Company common stock at $10 per share, the market price on January 1, 1999. All of the options vest five years from the grant date. ABC Company elects to adopt the fair value based method of accounting for stock-based employee compensation on January 1, 2003. ABC Company elects the retroactive restatement method of transition. The earliest year for which an income statement will be presented in ABC Company's 2003 financial statements is 2001, and ABC Company elects not to restate earlier periods. Because the intrinsic value of the awards was zero at the grant date (also the measurement date in this case) no compensation cost or deferred tax benefit was recognized by ABC Company related to those awards under Opinion 25.

B3. The fair value of the stock options on the grant date was $6 per share, or $600,000. Had ABC Company applied the fair value based method from the grant date, it would have recognized the following

amounts related to the January 1, 1999 grant as of January 1, 2001, the date of initial application of the fair value based method:

	1999	2000
Compensation cost	$120,000	$120,000
Deferred tax benefit @ 50%	$60,000	$60,000

When ABC Company adopts the fair value based method, it will record the following adjustment to the beginning balances as of January 1, 2001:

| Deferred tax asset | 120,000 | |
| Additional paid-in capital | | 120,000 |

Because ABC Company elected not to restate periods prior to 2001, the transition effect is determined as of the beginning of 2001 and is reported as an adjustment to additional paid-in capital pursuant to the requirements of this Statement. If ABC Company had elected to restate earlier periods, the transition effect would be determined as of the beginning of the period of initial application, and the effect on retained earnings of restating subsequent periods would have been reported as an adjustment to retained earnings as of the beginning of 2001.

B4. ABC Company will then restate its reported results for 2001 and 2002 to reflect the compensation cost determined under the fair value based method of $120,000 in each period, with a corresponding increase to additional paid-in capital. In addition, ABC Company will record the deferred tax benefit of $60,000 each year, with a corresponding increase in the deferred tax asset of $60,000.

Forfeitures

B5. For its previous pro forma disclosures under Statement 123 and upon adoption of the recognition provisions of that Statement, ABC Company followed an accounting policy of recognizing employee forfeitures as they occur, and no compensation cost was capitalized as part of the cost of producing inventory or other self-produced assets. During the first quarter of 2003, ABC Company's stock price declines to $2. Twenty-five percent of the work force leaves to pursue more attractive employment opportunities, and another 25 percent is terminated in connection with a strategic reorganization. For purposes of this illustration, no forfeitures occurred prior to January 1, 2003. To account for the forfeiture of the related awards, ABC Company records the following journal entries:

Additional paid-in capital	240,000	
Deferred tax expense	120,000	
Deferred tax asset		120,000
Compensation expense		240,000

Under the provisions of this Statement, 50 percent of the $480,000 ($240,000) of cumulative compensation expense that would have been recognized had the recognition provisions of Statement 123 been applied from its original effective date is reversed during the period even though only $120,000 (50 percent of the $240,000 in cumulative cost recognized in 2001 and 2002) of that amount was recognized cumulatively in income.

Tax effects

B6. In 2005, ABC Company's stock price increases to $12 per share, and all of the outstanding options are exercised. Based on the exercise date intrinsic value of $2 per share, ABC Company realizes an aggregate tax deduction of $100,000 and a tax benefit of $50,000. On a cumulative basis, ABC Company had recognized a deferred tax asset of $150,000. The $100,000 excess deferred tax asset that is not realized is recognized as tax expense during 2005 because ABC Company has no accumulated "excess tax benefits" in additional paid-in capital from prior stock option exercises. For purposes of this illustration, no employee options were exercised subsequent to January 1, 2001, that both (a) were accounted for under the fair value based method and (b) resulted in a tax benefit upon exercise that was greater than the previously recognized deferred tax asset.

Illustration 2—Stock Appreciation Rights: Modified Prospective Method

B7. XYZ Company granted stock appreciation rights (SARs) to certain employees on January 1, 2001, based on 100,000 shares. The stated price of $10 per share was equal to the fair market value of the stock on that date. The SARs provide the employees with the right to receive, at the date the rights are exercised, shares having a then-current market value equal to the market appreciation since the grant date. The employees do not have the ability to receive a cash payment. All of the rights vest at the end of three years and must be exercised no later than the end of the fifth year. XYZ Company uses a calendar year for financial reporting purposes and elects on January 1, 2003, to adopt the fair value based method for recog-

nizing stock-based employee compensation cost. XYZ Company elects the modified prospective method of transition.

B8. The underlying stock price, compensation cost recognized, and related deferred tax benefit recognized under the intrinsic value method of Opinion 25 are as follows:

	2001	2002
Stock price at December 31	$12	$14
Compensation cost	$66,667	$200,000
Deferred tax benefit @ 50%	$33,333	$100,000

As of December 31, 2002, XYZ Company has recognized a deferred tax asset of $133,333 and has increased additional paid-in capital by $266,667.

B9. The fair value of the SAR on the grant date was $2.10 per share, or $210,000. Had XYZ Company applied the fair value based method from the grant date it would have recognized the following amounts related to the January 1, 2001 grant:

	2001	2002
Compensation cost	$70,000	$70,000
Deferred tax benefit @ 50%	$35,000	$35,000

Under the fair value based method, XYZ Company would have recognized a deferred tax asset at December 31, 2002, of $70,000 and an increase in additional paid-in capital of $140,000.

B10. As of January 1, 2003, when XYZ Company adopts the fair value based method, it will record the following transition adjustment:

Additional paid-in capital	63,333	
Deferred tax asset		63,333

Because this Statement requires that the transition effect be recorded as an adjustment to additional paid-in capital rather than retained earnings, the net reduction in additional paid-in capital in the entry above reflects the change in net assets arising from transition. To the extent that contra-equity balances had been recorded related to an entity's stock-based compensation arrangements, those balances also would be charged against additional paid-in capital. Under paragraph 30 of Statement 123, neither deferred (prepaid) compensation (a contra-equity account) nor additional paid-in capital is recognized on the grant date. Additional paid-in capital is increased as compensation cost is recognized.

Disclosure Provisions

B11. The following illustrations provide examples of the disclosures required under paragraphs 2(e) and 3 of this Statement. Three examples illustrate the disclosures required under the various transition methods permitted under this Statement, one example illustrates the amended disclosures required for a company that continues to apply the Opinion 25 intrinsic value method, and one example illustrates the disclosures required by this Statement in financial reports for interim periods.

B12. The disclosures required by paragraphs 46–48 of Statement 123 are unaffected by this Statement. Examples of the disclosures required under those paragraphs are provided in Appendix B of Statement 123.

Illustration 3—Prospective Method

B13. The following disclosures for the financial statements for the year ended December 31, 2003, assume that the company has adopted in 2002 the fair value based method of accounting for stock-based employee compensation using the prospective method of transition. For simplicity, this illustration also assumes that all previous awards were fixed stock options with no intrinsic value at the date of grant.

At December 31, 2003, the company has four stock-based employee compensation plans, which are described more fully in Note XX.[4] Prior to 2002, the company accounted for those plans under the recognition and measurement provisions of APB Opinion No. 25, *Accounting for Stock Issued to Employees,* and related Interpretations. No stock-based employee compensation cost is reflected in 2001 net income, as all options granted under those plans had an exercise price equal to the market value of the underlying common stock on the date of grant. Effective January 1, 2002, the company adopted the fair value recognition provisions of FASB Statement No. 123, *Accounting for Stock-Based Compensation,* prospectively to all employee awards granted, modified, or settled after January 1, 2002. Awards under the company's plans vest over periods ranging from three to five years. Therefore, the cost related to stock-based employee compensation included in the determination of net income for 2002 and 2003 is less than that which would have been recognized if the fair value based method had been applied to all awards since the original effective date of Statement 123. The following table illustrates the effect on net income and earnings per share if the fair value based method had been applied to all outstanding and unvested awards in each period.

	Year Ended December 31		
	2003	**2002**	**2001**
Net income, as reported	$471,387	$404,113	$347,790
Add: Stock-based employee compensation expense included in reported net income, net of related tax effects	7,913	3,187	—
Deduct: Total stock-based employee compensation expense determined under fair value based method for all awards,[5] net of related tax effects	(18,902)	(12,747)	(10,962)
Pro forma net income	$460,398	$394,553	$336,828
Earnings per share:			
Basic—as reported	$ 2.62	$ 2.27	$ 1.97
Basic—pro forma	$ 2.56	$ 2.22	$ 1.91
Diluted—as reported	$ 1.99	$ 1.72	$ 1.49
Diluted—pro forma	$ 1.94	$ 1.68	$ 1.44

---

[4]Note XX would include the disclosures required by paragraphs 46–48 of Statement 123.

[5]*All awards* refers to awards granted, modified, or settled in fiscal periods beginning after December 15, 1994—that is, awards for which the fair value was required to be measured under Statement 123.

Illustration 4—Modified Prospective Method

B14. The following disclosures for the financial statements for the year ended December 31, 2003, assume that the company has adopted in 2003 the fair value based method of accounting for stock-based employee compensation using the modified prospective method of transition. For simplicity, this illustration also assumes that all previous awards were fixed stock options with no intrinsic value at the date of grant.

At December 31, 2003, the company has four stock-based employee compensation plans, which are described more fully in Note XX. Prior to 2003, the company accounted for those plans under the recognition and measurement provisions of APB Opinion No. 25, *Accounting for Stock Issued to Employees,* and related Interpretations. No stock-based employee compensation cost was reflected in 2001 or 2002 net income, as all options granted under those plans had an exercise price equal to the market value of the underlying common stock on the date of grant. Effective January 1, 2003, the company adopted the fair value recognition provisions of FASB Statement No. 123, *Accounting for Stock-Based Compensation.* Under the modified prospective method of adoption selected by the company under the provisions of FASB Statement No. 148, *Accounting for Stock-Based Compensation— Transition and Disclosure,* compensation cost recognized in 2003 is the same as that which would have been recognized had the recognition provisions of Statement 123 been applied from its original effective date. Results for prior years have not been restated. The following table illustrates the effect on net income and earnings per share if the fair value based method had been applied to all outstanding and unvested awards in each period.

	Year Ended December 31		
	2003	**2002**	**2001**
Net income, as reported	$460,398	$407,300	$347,790
Add: Stock-based employee compensation expense included in reported net income, net of related tax effects	18,902	—	—
Deduct: Total stock-based employee compensation expense determined under fair value based method for all awards,[6] net of related tax effects	(18,902)	(12,747)	(10,962)
Pro forma net income	$460,398	$394,553	$336,828
Earnings per share:			
Basic—as reported	$ 2.56	$ 2.29	$ 1.97
Basic—pro forma	$ 2.56	$ 2.22	$ 1.91
Diluted—as reported	$ 1.94	$ 1.73	$ 1.49
Diluted—pro forma	$ 1.94	$ 1.68	$ 1.44

Illustration 5—Retroactive Restatement

B15. The following disclosures for the financial statements for the year ended December 31, 2003, assume that the company has adopted in 2003 the fair value based method of accounting for stock-based employee compensation using the retroactive restatement method of transition. For simplicity, this illus-

---

[6]Refer to footnote 5 to this Statement.

tration also assumes that all previous awards were fixed stock options with no intrinsic value at the date of grant.

At December 31, 2003, the company has four stock-based employee compensation plans, which are described more fully in Note XX. Prior to 2003, the company accounted for those plans under the recognition and measurement provisions of APB Opinion No. 25, *Accounting for Stock Issued to Employees,* and related Interpretations. No stock-based employee compensation cost was reflected in previously reported results, as all options granted under those plans had an exercise price equal to the market value of the underlying common stock on the date of grant. Effective January 1, 2003, the company adopted the fair value recognition provisions of FASB Statement No. 123, *Accounting for Stock-Based Compensation,* for stock-based employee compensation. All prior periods presented have been restated to reflect the compensation cost that would have been recognized had the recognition provisions of Statement 123 been applied to all awards granted to employees after January 1, 1995.

Illustration 6—Continued Accounting under Opinion 25

B16. The following disclosures for the financial statements for the year ended December 31, 2003, assume that the company continues to account for stock-based employee compensation using the intrinsic value method under Opinion 25. For simplicity, this illustration also assumes that all previous awards were fixed stock options with no intrinsic value at the date of grant.

At December 31, 2003, the company has four stock-based employee compensation plans, which are described more fully in Note XX. The company accounts for those plans under the recognition and measurement principles of APB Opinion No. 25, *Accounting for Stock Issued to Employees,* and related Interpretations. No stock-based employee compensation cost is reflected in net income, as all options granted under those plans had an exercise price equal to the market value of the underlying common stock on the date of grant. The following table illustrates the effect on net income and earnings per share if the company had applied the fair value recognition provisions of FASB Statement No. 123, *Accounting for Stock-Based Compensation,* to stock-based employee compensation.

	Year Ended December 31		
	2003	**2002**	**2001**
Net income, as reported	$479,300	$407,300	$347,790
Deduct: Total stock-based employee compensation expense determined under fair value based method for all awards,[7] net of related tax effects	(18,902)	(12,747)	(10,962)
Pro forma net income	$460,398	$394,553	$336,828
Earnings per share:			
Basic—as reported	$ 2.66	$ 2.29	$ 1.97
Basic—pro forma	$ 2.56	$ 2.22	$ 1.91
Diluted—as reported	$ 2.02	$ 1.73	$ 1.49
Diluted—pro forma	$ 1.94	$ 1.68	$ 1.44

[7]Refer to footnote 5 to this Statement.

Illustration 7—Interim Disclosures

B17. The following disclosures for the interim financial information for the three-month and nine-month periods ended June 30, 2003, assume that during the third quarter of its fiscal 2003, a company with a September 30 year-end adopts the fair value based method of accounting for stock-based employee compensation as of the beginning of fiscal 2003 using the modified prospective method of transition. For simplicity, this illustration also assumes that all previous awards were fixed stock options with no intrinsic value at the date of grant.

During the third quarter of fiscal 2003, the company adopted the fair value recognition provisions of FASB Statement No. 123, *Accounting for Stock-Based Compensation,* for stock-based employee compensation, effective as of the beginning of the fiscal year. Under the modified prospective method of adoption selected by the company, stock-based employee compensation cost recognized in 2003 is the same as that which would have been recognized had the fair value recognition provisions of Statement 123 been applied to all awards granted after October 1, 1995. The following table illustrates the effect on net income and earnings per share as if the fair value based method had been applied to all outstanding and unvested awards in each period.

	3 Months Ended June 30		9 Months Ended June 30	
	2003	**2002**	**2003**	**2002**
Net income, as reported	$115,100	$101,825	$345,299	$305,475
Add: Stock-based employee compensation expense included in reported net income, net of related tax effects	4,725	—	14,177	—
Deduct: Total stock-based employee compensation expense determined under fair value based method for all awards,[8] net of related tax effects	(4,725)	(3,187)	(14,177)	(9,560)
Pro forma net income	$115,100	$ 98,638	$345,299	$295,915
Earnings per share:				
Basic—as reported	$ 0.64	$ 0.57	$ 1.92	$ 1.72
Basic—pro forma	$ 0.64	$ 0.55	$ 1.92	$ 1.66
Diluted—as reported	$ 0.49	$ 0.43	$ 1.45	$ 1.29
Diluted—pro forma	$ 0.49	$ 0.42	$ 1.45	$ 1.25

---

[8]Refer to footnote 5 to this Statement.

Statement of Financial Accounting Standards No. 149
Amendment of Statement 133 on Derivative Instruments and Hedging Activities

STATUS

Issued: April 2003

Effective Date: For contracts entered into or modified after June 30, 2003; for hedging relationships designated after June 30, 2003; for provisions that relate to Statement 133 Implementation Issues that have been effective for fiscal quarters that began prior to June 15, 2003, apply in accordance with their respective effective dates; for paragraphs 7(a) and 23(a), apply to both existing contracts and new contracts entered into after June 30, 2003

Affects: Amends FAS 15, paragraph 13
   Amends FAS 35, paragraph 11
   Amends FAS 60, paragraph 19
   Amends FAS 65, paragraph 3
   Amends FAS 87, paragraph 49
   Amends FAS 91, paragraph 3
   Amends FAS 95, paragraphs 19, 20, and 24
   Replaces FAS 95, footnote 4
   Amends FAS 106, paragraph 65
   Amends FAS 126, paragraph 2(c)
   Amends FAS 133, paragraphs 6 through 8, 9(a), 10, 13(a), 15, 17, 20(c), 21(a)(2)(c), 27, 28(c), 34, 49, 57(c)(2), 57(c)(3), 58(a), 58(b), 59(c), 59(d), 61(a), 61(d), 61(e), 61(g), 64, 65(c), 68, 68(a), 68(d), 68(g), 94 through 97, 99, 143, 154, and 540 and footnotes 8 and 16
   Amends FAS 133 by adding paragraph 45A
   Replaces FAS 133, paragraphs 10(a), 10(b), 10(d), 13(b), 30(d), 59(a), 61(f), 68(b), and 176
   Deletes FAS 133, paragraph 19
   Effectively amends FAS 133, paragraph 539

Affected by: No other pronouncements

SUMMARY

This Statement amends and clarifies financial accounting and reporting for derivative instruments, including certain derivative instruments embedded in other contracts (collectively referred to as derivatives) and for hedging activities under FASB Statement No. 133, *Accounting for Derivative Instruments and Hedging Activities*.

Reasons for Issuing This Statement

This Statement amends Statement 133 for decisions made (1) as part of the Derivatives Implementation Group process that effectively required amendments to Statement 133, (2) in connection with other Board projects dealing with financial instruments, and (3) in connection with implementation issues raised in relation to the application of the definition of a derivative, in particular, the meaning of *an initial net investment that is smaller than would be required for other types of contracts that would be expected to have a similar response to changes in market factors,* the meaning of *underlying,* and the characteristics of a derivative that contains financing components.

How the Changes in This Statement Improve Financial Reporting

The changes in this Statement improve financial reporting by requiring that contracts with comparable characteristics be accounted for similarly. In particular, this Statement (1) clarifies under what circumstances a contract with an initial net investment meets the characteristic of a derivative discussed in paragraph 6(b) of Statement 133, (2) clarifies when a derivative contains a financing component, (3) amends the definition of an underlying to conform it to language used in FASB Interpretation No. 45, *Guarantor's Accounting and Disclosure Requirements for Guarantees, Including Indirect Guarantees of Indebtedness of Others,* and (4) amends certain other existing pronouncements. Those changes will result in more consistent reporting of contracts as either derivatives or hybrid instruments.

The Effective Date of This Statement

This Statement is effective for contracts entered into or modified after June 30, 2003, except as stated below and for hedging relationships designated after June 30, 2003. In addition, except as stated below, all provisions of this Statement should be applied prospectively.

The provisions of this Statement that relate to Statement 133 Implementation Issues that have been effective for fiscal quarters that began prior to June 15, 2003, should continue to be applied in accordance with their respective effective dates. In addition, paragraphs 7(a) and 23(a), which relate to forward purchases or sales of *when-issued* securities or other securities that do not yet exist, should be applied to both existing contracts and new contracts entered into after June 30, 2003.

Statement of Financial Accounting Standards No. 149

Amendment of Statement 133 on Derivative Instruments and Hedging Activities

CONTENTS

INTRODUCTION

1. FASB Statements No. 133, *Accounting for Derivative Instruments and Hedging Activities,* and No. 138, *Accounting for Certain Derivative Instruments and Certain Hedging Activities,* establish accounting and reporting standards for derivative instruments including derivatives embedded in other contracts (collectively referred to as derivatives) and for hedging activities.

2. This Statement amends Statement 133 for certain decisions made by the Board as part of the Derivatives Implementation Group (DIG) process. For those amendments that relate to Statement 133 implementation guidance, the specific Statement 133 Implementation Issue necessitating the amendment is identified. If the amendment relates to a cleared issue, the clearance date also is noted. This Statement also amends Statement 133 to incorporate clarifications of the definition of a derivative. This Statement contains amendments relating to FASB Concepts Statement No. 7, *Using Cash Flow Information and Present Value in Accounting Measurements,* and FASB Statements No. 65, *Accounting for Certain Mortgage Banking Activities,* No. 91, *Accounting for Nonrefundable Fees and Costs Associated with Originating* or *Acquiring Loans and Initial Direct Costs of Leases,* No. 95, *Statement of Cash Flows,* and No. 126, *Exemption from Certain Required Disclosures about Financial Instruments for Certain Nonpublic Entities.*

STANDARDS OF FINANCIAL ACCOUNTING AND REPORTING

Amendments to Statement 133

3. The following is added to paragraph 6 after subparagraph (c):

Notwithstanding the above characteristics, loan commitments that relate to the origination of mortgage loans that will be held for sale, as discussed in paragraph 21 of FASB Statement No. 65, *Accounting for Mortgage Banking Activities* (as amended), shall be accounted for as derivative instruments by the issuer of the loan commitment (that is, the potential lender). Paragraph 10(i) provides a scope exception for the accounting for loan commitments by issuers of certain commitments to originate loans and all holders of commitments to originate loans (that is, the potential borrowers).

4. The phrase *(including the occurrence or nonoccurrence of a specified event such as a scheduled payment under a contract)* is added at the end of the first sentence in paragraph 7.

[FASB Interpretation No. 45, Guarantor's Accounting and Disclosure Requirements for Guarantees, Including Indirect Guarantees of Indebtedness of Others]

5. The following sentence and footnote are added at the end of paragraph 8:

> If the initial net investment in the contract (after adjustment for the time value of money) is less, by more than a nominal amount, than the initial net investment that would be commensurate with the amount that would be exchanged either to acquire the asset related to the underlying or to incur the obligation related to the underlying, the characteristic in paragraph 6(b) is met. The amount of that asset acquired or liability incurred should be comparable to the effective notional amount* of the contract.

> ---
> *The effective notional amount is the stated notional amount adjusted for any leverage factor.

6. In the first sentence of paragraph 9(a), *or* is replaced by *and* between *that is associated with the underlying* and *that has a principal amount.*

[Statement 133 Implementation Issue No. A17, "Contracts That Provide for Net Share Settlement," cleared March 21, 2001]

7. Paragraph 10 is amended as follows:

a. Subparagraph (a) is replaced by the following:

> *"Regular-way" security trades.* Regular-way security trades are contracts that provide for delivery of a security within the time generally established by regulations or conventions in the marketplace or exchange in which the transaction is being executed. However, a contract for an existing security does not qualify for the regular-way security trades exception if it requires or permits net settlement (as discussed in paragraphs 9(a) and 57(c)(1)) or if a market mechanism to facilitate net settlement of that contract (as discussed in paragraphs 9(b) and 57(c)(2)) exists, except as provided in the following sentence. If an entity is required to account for a contract to purchase or sell an existing security on a trade-date basis, rather than a settlement-date

basis, and thus recognizes the acquisition (or disposition) of the security at the inception of the contract, then the entity shall apply the regular-way security trades exception to that contract. A contract for the purchase or sale of *when-issued* securities or other securities that do not yet exist is addressed in paragraph 59(a).

[Statement 133 Implementation Issue No. C18, "Shortest Period Criterion for Applying the Regular-Way Security Trades Exception to When-Issued Securities"]

b. Subparagraph (b), as amended by Statement 138, is replaced by the following:

> *Normal purchases and normal sales.* Normal purchases and normal sales are contracts that provide for the purchase or sale of something other than a financial instrument or derivative instrument that will be delivered in quantities expected to be used or sold by the reporting entity over a reasonable period in the normal course of business. The following guidance should be considered in determining whether a specific type of contract qualifies for the normal purchases and normal sales exception:

> (1) *Forward contracts (non-option-based contracts).* Forward contracts are eligible to qualify for the normal purchases and normal sales exception. However, forward contracts that contain net settlement provisions as described in either paragraph 9(a) or paragraph 9(b) are not eligible for the normal purchases and normal sales exception unless it is probable at inception and throughout the term of the individual contract that the contract will not settle net and will result in physical delivery.* Net settlement (as described in paragraphs 9(a) and 9(b)) of contracts in a group of contracts similarly designated as normal purchases and normal sales would call into question the classification of all such contracts as normal purchases or normal sales. Contracts that require cash settlements of gains or losses or are otherwise settled net on a periodic basis, including individual contracts that are part of a series of sequential contracts intended to accomplish ultimate acquisition or sale of a commodity, do not qualify for this exception.

(2) *Freestanding option contracts.* Option contracts that would require delivery of the related asset at an established price under the contract only if exercised are not eligible to qualify for the normal purchases and normal sales exception, except as indicated in paragraph 10(b)(4) below.

(3) *Forward contracts that contain optionality features.* Forward contracts that contain optionality features that do not modify the quantity of the asset to be delivered under the contract are eligible to qualify for the normal purchases and normal sales exception. Except for power purchase or sales agreements addressed in paragraph 10(b)(4), if an option component permits modification of the quantity of the assets to be delivered, the contract is not eligible for the normal purchases and normal sales exception, unless the option component permits the holder only to purchase or sell additional quantities at the market price at the date of delivery. In order for forward contracts that contain optionality features to qualify for the normal purchases and normal sales exception, the criteria discussed in paragraph 10(b)(1) must be met.

(4) *Power purchase or sales agreements.* Notwithstanding the criteria in paragraphs 10(b)(1) and 10(b)(3), a power purchase or sales agreement (whether a forward contract, option contract, or a combination of both) that is a **capacity contract** also qualifies for the normal purchases and normal sales exception if it meets the criteria in paragraph 58(b).

However, contracts that have a price based on an underlying that is not clearly and closely related to the asset being sold or purchased (such as a price in a contract for the sale of a grain commodity based in part on changes in the S&P index) or that are denominated in a foreign currency that meets none of the criteria in paragraphs 15(a)–15(d) shall not be considered normal purchases and normal sales. For contracts that qualify for the normal purchases and normal sales exception, the entity shall document the designation of the contract as a normal purchase or normal sale. For contracts that qualify for the normal purchases and normal sales exception under

paragraphs 10(b)(1) and 10(b)(3), the entity shall document the basis for concluding that it is probable that the contract will not settle net and will result in physical delivery. For contracts that qualify for the normal purchases and normal sales exception under paragraph 10(b)(4), the entity shall document the basis for concluding that the agreement meets the criteria in paragraph 58(b). The documentation requirements can be applied either to groups of similarly designated contracts or to each individual contract. Failure to comply with the documentation requirements precludes application of the normal purchases and normal sales exception to contracts that would otherwise qualify for that exception.

---

*Contracts that are subject to unplanned netting (referred to as a "book out" in the electric utility industry) do not qualify for this exception except as specified in paragraph 58(b).

[Statement 133 Implementation Issue No. C10, "Can Option Contracts and Forward Contracts with Optionality Features Qualify for the Normal Purchases and Normal Sales Exception," cleared March 21, 2001, revised June 27, 2001; Statement 133 Implementation Issue No. C15, "Normal Purchases and Normal Sales Exception for Certain Option-Type Contracts and Forward Contracts in Electricity," cleared June 27, 2001, revised December 19, 2001; and Statement 133 Implementation Issue No. C16, "Applying the Normal Purchases and Normal Sales Exception to Contracts That Combine a Forward Contract and a Purchased Option Contract," cleared September 19, 2001, revised December 19, 2001]

c. Subparagraph (d) is replaced by the following:

  Financial guarantee contracts. Financial guarantee contracts are not subject to this Statement only if:

  (1) They provide for payments to be made solely to reimburse the guaranteed party for failure of the debtor to satisfy its required payment obligations under a nonderivative contract, either at pre-specified payment dates or accelerated payment dates as a result of the occurrence of an event of default (as defined in the financial obligation covered by the guarantee contract) or notice of acceleration being made to the debtor by the creditor.

(2) Payment under the financial guarantee contract is made only if the debtor's obligation to make payments as a result of conditions as described in (1) above is past due.

(3) The guaranteed party is, as a precondition in the contract (or in the back-to-back arrangement, if applicable) for receiving payment of any claim under the guarantee, exposed to the risk of nonpayment both at inception of the financial guarantee contract and throughout its term either through direct legal ownership of the guaranteed obligation or through a back-to-back arrangement with another party that is required by the back-to-back arrangement to maintain direct ownership of the guaranteed obligation.

In contrast, financial guarantee contracts are subject to this Statement if they do not meet all of the above three criteria, for example, if they provide for payments to be made in response to changes in another underlying such as a decrease in a specified debtor's creditworthiness.

d. The following subparagraph is added after subparagraph (f):

g. *Investments in life insurance.* A policyholder's investment in a life insurance contract that is accounted for under FASB Technical Bulletin No. 85-4, *Accounting for Purchases of Life Insurance,* is not subject to this Statement. The exception in this subparagraph affects only the accounting by the policyholder; it does not affect the accounting by the issuer of the life insurance contract.

[Statement 133 Implementation Issue No. B31, "Accounting for Purchases of Life Insurance," cleared July 11, 2001]

e. The following subparagraphs are added after subparagraph (g):

h. *Certain investment contracts.* A contract that is accounted for under either paragraph 4 of FASB Statement No. 110, *Reporting by Defined Benefit Pension Plans of Investment Contracts,* or paragraph 12 of FASB Statement No. 35, *Accounting and Reporting by Defined Benefit Pen-*

sion Plans, as amended by Statement 110, is not subject to this Statement. Similarly, a contract that is accounted for under either paragraph 4 or paragraph 5 of AICPA Statement of Position 94-4, *Reporting of Investment Contracts Held by Health and Welfare Benefit Plans and Defined-Contribution Pension Plans,* is not subject to this Statement. Those exceptions apply only to the party that accounts for the contract under Statement 35, Statement 110, or SOP 94-4.

[Statement 133 Implementation Issue No. C19, "Contracts Subject to Statement 35, Statement 110, or Statement of Position 94-4"]

i. *Loan commitments.* The holder of any commitment to originate a loan (that is, the potential borrower) is not subject to the requirements of this Statement. Issuers of commitments to originate mortgage loans that will be held for investment purposes, as discussed in paragraphs 21 and 25 of Statement 65, are not subject to this Statement. In addition, issuers of loan commitments to originate other types of loans (that is, other than mortgage loans) are not subject to the requirements of this Statement.

[Statement 133 Implementation Issue No. C13, "When a Loan Commitment Is Included in the Scope of Statement 133," guidance previously cleared on March 13, 2002, and subsequently revised by the Board]

8. Paragraph 13 is amended as follows:

a. The following footnote is added at the end of subparagraph (a):

*The condition in paragraph 13(a) does not apply to a situation in which the terms of a hybrid instrument permit, but do not require, the investor to settle the hybrid instrument in a manner that causes it not to recover substantially all of its initial recorded investment, provided that the issuer does not have the contractual right to demand a settlement that causes the investor not to recover substantially all of its initial net investment.

[Statement 133 Implementation Issue No. B5, "Investor Permitted, but Not Forced, to Settle without Recovering Substantially All of the Initial Net Investment," cleared July 28, 1999]

b. Subparagraph (b) is replaced by the following:

> The embedded derivative meets both of the following conditions:
>
> (1) There is a possible future interest rate scenario (even though it may be remote) under which the embedded derivative would at least double the investor's initial rate of return on the host contract.
>
> (2) For each of the possible interest rate scenarios under which the investor's initial rate of return on the host contract would be doubled (as discussed under paragraph 13(b)(1)), the embedded derivative would at the same time result in a rate of return that is at least twice what otherwise would be the then-current market return (under each of those future interest rate scenarios) for a contract that has the same terms as the host contract and that involves a debtor with a credit quality similar to the issuer's credit quality at inception.

9. Paragraph 15 is amended as follows:

a. In item (a) of the first sentence, *functional* is inserted between *the* and *currency* and *the primary economic environment in which* and *operates (that is, its functional currency) or* are deleted.

b. In item (b) of the first sentence, the following footnote is added after *(for example, the U.S. dollar for crude oil transactions)*:

> *If similar transactions for a certain product or service are routinely denominated in international commerce in various different currencies, the transaction does not qualify for the exception.

c. The following is added at the end of the first sentence:

> , (c) the local currency of any substantial party to the contract, or (d) the currency used by a substantial party to the contract as if it were the functional currency because the primary economic environment in which the party operates is highly inflationary (as discussed in paragraph 11 of Statement 52). The evaluation of whether a contract qualifies for the exception in this paragraph should be performed only at inception of the contract.

[Statement 133 Implementation Issue No. B21, "When Embedded Foreign Currency Derivatives Warrant Separate Accounting," cleared June 28, 2000]

10. In the fourth sentence of paragraph 17, the following footnote is added after *expected cash flows*:

> *This Statement was issued prior to FASB Concepts Statement No. 7, *Using Cash Flow Information and Present Value in Accounting Measurements,* and therefore the term *expected cash flows* does not necessarily have the same meaning as that term does in Concepts Statement 7.

11. Paragraph 19 is deleted.

12. In the first sentence of paragraph 20(c), *or an unrecognized firm commitment* is added after *a recognized asset or liability.*

13. Footnote 8 to paragraph 21 is amended as follows:

a. In the first sentence, *(as defined in paragraph 540)* is added after *A firm commitment.*

b. The following sentence is added at the end of the footnote:

> A supply contract for which the contract price is fixed only in certain circumstances (such as when the selling price is above an embedded price cap or below an embedded price floor) meets the definition of a firm commitment for purposes of designating the hedged item in a fair value hedge. Provided the embedded price cap or floor is considered clearly and closely related to the host contract and therefore is not accounted for separately under paragraph 12, either party to the supply contract can hedge the fair value exposure arising from the cap or floor.

[Statement 133 Implementation Issue No. F10, "Definition of Firm Commitment in Relation to Long-Term Supply Contracts with Embedded Price Caps or Floors," cleared June 27, 2001]

14. In paragraph 21(a)(2)(c), *A put option, a call option, an interest rate cap, or an interest rate floor* is replaced by *A put option or call option (including an interest rate or price cap or an interest rate or price floor).*

[Implementation Issue F10]

15. In paragraphs 27, 34, 64, 65(c), 94, 96, and 97, the following footnote is added after *expected cash flows*, and in paragraphs 95, 99, and 143, the following footnote is added after the first mention of *expected cash flows*:

> †Refer to footnote* to paragraph 17 of Statement 133.

16. In the first sentence of paragraph 28(c), *or an unrecognized firm commitment* is added after *recognized asset or liability*.

17. Paragraph 30(d), which was added by Statement 138, is replaced by the following:

> If a non-option-based contract is the hedging instrument in a cash flow hedge of the variability of the functional-currency-equivalent cash flows for a recognized foreign-currency-denominated asset or liability that is remeasured at spot exchange rates under paragraph 15 of Statement 52, an amount that will offset the related transaction gain or loss arising from that remeasurement shall be reclassified each period from other comprehensive income to earnings if the assessment of effectiveness and measurement of ineffectiveness are based on total changes in the non-option-based instrument's cash flows. If an option contract is used as the hedging instrument in a cash flow hedge of the variability of the functional-currency-equivalent cash flows for a recognized foreign-currency-denominated asset or liability that is remeasured at spot exchange rates under paragraph 15 of Statement 52 to provide only one-sided offset against the hedged foreign exchange risk, an amount shall be reclassified each period to or from other comprehensive income with respect to the changes in the underlying that result in a change in the hedging option's intrinsic value. In addition, if the assessment of effectiveness and measurement of ineffectiveness are also based on total changes in the option's cash flows (that is, the assessment will include the hedging instrument's entire change in fair value—its entire gain or loss), an amount that adjusts earnings for the amortization of the cost of the option on a rational basis shall be reclassified each period from other comprehensive income to earnings.*

---

*The guidance in this subparagraph is limited to foreign currency hedging relationships because of their unique attributes. That accounting guidance is an exception for foreign currency hedging relationships.

[Statement 133 Implementation Issue No. G20, "Assessing and Measuring the Effectiveness of a Purchased Option Used in a Cash Flow Hedge," cleared June 27, 2001; Implementation Issue G20 is still in effect for the non-foreign-currency situations discussed therein.]

18. The following heading and paragraph are added after paragraph 45:

Reporting Cash Flows of Derivative Instruments That Contain Financing Elements

45A. An instrument accounted for as a derivative under this Statement that at its inception includes off-market terms, or requires an up-front cash payment, or both often contains a financing element. Identifying a financing element within a derivative is a matter of judgment that depends on facts and circumstances. If an other-than-insignificant financing element is present at inception, other than a financing element inherently included in an at-the-market derivative instrument with no prepayments (that is, the forward points in an at-the-money forward contract),* then the borrower shall report all cash inflows and outflows associated with that derivative instrument in a manner consistent with financing activities as described in paragraphs 18–20 of FASB Statement No. 95, *Statement of Cash Flows.*

---

*An at-the-money plain-vanilla interest rate swap that involves no payments between the parties at inception would not be considered as having a financing element present at inception even though, due to the implicit forward rates derived from the yield curve, the parties to the contract have an expectation that the comparison of the fixed and floating legs will result in payments being made by one party in the earlier periods and being made by the counterparty in the later periods of the swap's term. If a derivative instrument is an at-the-money or out-of-the-money option contract or contains an at-the-money or out-of-the-money option contract, a payment made at inception to the writer of the option for the option's time value by the counterparty should not be viewed as evidence that the derivative instrument contains a financing element. In contrast, if the contractual terms of a derivative have been structured to *ensure* that net payments will be made by one party in the earlier periods and subsequently returned by the counterparty in the later periods of the derivative's term, that derivative instrument should be viewed as containing a financing element even if the derivative has a fair value of zero at inception.

19. The following footnote is added at the end of paragraph 49:

> *If immediately prior to the application of Statement 133 an entity has a fair value or cash flow hedging relationship in which an intercompany interest rate swap is the hedging instrument and if that relationship would have qualified for the shortcut method under the criteria in paragraph 68 had that swap not been an intercompany transaction, that entity may qualify for applying the shortcut method to a newly designated hedging relationship that is effectively the continuation of the pre-existing hedging relationship provided that (a) the post-Statement 133 hedging relationship is hedging the same exposure to interest rate risk (that is, exposure to changes in fair value of the same hedged item or exposure to changes in variable cash flows for the same forecasted transaction) and (b) the hedging instrument is a third-party interest rate swap whose terms exactly match the terms of the intercompany swap with respect to its remaining cash flows. In that case, if the shortcut method is applied to the new hedging relationship upon adoption of Statement 133, the transition adjustment should include the appropriate adjustments at the date of adoption to reflect the retroactive application of the shortcut method.

[Statement 133 Implementation Issue No. J12, "Intercompany Derivatives and the Shortcut Method," cleared June 28, 2000]

20. The following sentence is added at the end of paragraph 57(c)(2):

> The evaluation of whether a market mechanism exists and whether items to be delivered under a contract are readily convertible to cash must be performed at inception and on an ongoing basis throughout a contract's life.

21. Paragraph 57(c)(3) is amended as follows:

a. The following footnote is added at the end of the first sentence:

> *The evaluation of *readily convertible to cash* shall be applied to a contract throughout its life.

b. The following is added at the end of the paragraph:

> Shares of stock in a publicly traded company to be received upon the exercise of a stock purchase warrant do not meet the characteristic of being readily convertible to cash if both of the following conditions exist: (a) the stock purchase warrant is issued by an entity for only its own stock (or stock of its consolidated subsidiaries) and (b) the sale or transfer of the issued shares is restricted (other than in connection with being pledged as collateral) for a period of 32 days or more from the date the stock purchase warrant is exercised. In contrast, restrictions imposed by a stock purchase warrant on the sale or transfer of shares of stock that are received from the exercise of that warrant issued by an entity for *other* than its own stock (whether those restrictions are for more or less than 32 days) do not affect the determination of whether those shares are readily convertible to cash. The accounting for restricted stock to be received upon exercise of a stock purchase warrant should not be analogized to any other type of contract.

[Statement 133 Implementation Issue No. A14, "Derivative Treatment of Stock Purchase Warrants Issued by a Company for Its Own Shares of Stock Where the Subsequent Sale or Transfer Is Restricted," cleared December 6, 2000, and revised May 8, 2002]

22. Paragraph 58 is amended as follows:

a. Subparagraph (a) is amended as follows:

> (1) At the end of the first sentence after the reference to footnote 16, *except (1) as provided in paragraph 59(a) for a contract for the purchase or sale of when-issued securities or other securities that do not yet exist and (2) for contracts that are required to be accounted for on a trade-date basis by the reporting entity* is added.

> (2) In the fourth sentence, both references to *regular-way exception* are replaced by *regular-way security trades exception,* and *unless the reporting entity is required to account for the contract on a trade-date basis* is added at the end of that sentence.

(3) The last sentence is deleted.

(4) Footnote 16 is amended as follows:

    (a) The parenthetical phrase *(and thus do not permit net settlement)* is added after *not readily convertible to cash.*

    (b) The parenthetical phrase *(as described in paragraphs 9(b) and 57(c)(2))* is added at the end of the sentence.

b. The following is added at the end of subparagraph (b) (as amended by Statement 138):

Power purchase or sales agreements (whether a forward contract, an option contract, or a combination of both) for the purchase or sale of electricity qualify for the normal purchases and normal sales exception in paragraph 10(b)(4) if all of the following applicable criteria are met:

    (1) For both parties to the contract:

        (a) The terms of the contract require physical delivery of electricity. That is, the contract does not permit net settlement, as described in paragraphs 9(a) and 57(c)(1). For an option contract, physical delivery is required if the option contract is exercised.

        (b) The power purchase or sales agreement is a capacity contract.* Differentiating between a capacity contract and a traditional option contract (that is, a financial option on electricity) is a matter of judgment that depends on the facts and circumstances.

    (2) For the seller of electricity: The electricity that would be deliverable under the contract involves quantities that are expected to be sold by the reporting entity in the normal course of business.

    (3) For the buyer of electricity:

        (a) The electricity that would be deliverable under the contract involves quantities that are expected to be used or sold by the reporting entity in the normal course of business.

        (b) The buyer of the electricity under the power purchase or sales agreement is an entity that is engaged in selling electricity to retail or wholesale customers and is statutorily or otherwise contractually obligated to maintain sufficient capacity to meet electricity needs of its customer base.

        (c) The contracts are entered into to meet the buyer's obligation to maintain a sufficient capacity, including a reasonable reserve margin established by or based on a regulatory commission, local standards, regional reliability councils, or regional transmission organizations.

Power purchase or sales agreements that meet only the above applicable criteria in paragraph 58(b) qualify for the normal purchases and normal sales exception even if they are subject to being booked out or are scheduled to be booked out. Forward contracts for the purchase or sale of electricity that do not meet the above applicable criteria are nevertheless eligible to qualify for the normal purchases and normal sales exception by meeting the criteria in paragraph 10(b) other than paragraph 10(b)(4).

---

*As defined in paragraph 540.

[Implementation Issues C10, C15, and C16, cleared March 21, 2001; June 27, 2001; and September 19, 2001, respectively]

23. Paragraph 59 is amended as follows:

a. Subparagraph (a) is replaced by the following:

    a. *Forward purchases or sales of when-issued securities or other securities that do not yet exist.* Contracts for the purchase or sale of when-issued securities or other securities that do not yet exist are excluded from the requirements of this Statement as a regular-way security trade only if (1) there is no other way to purchase or sell that security, (2) delivery of that security and settlement will occur within the shortest period possible for that type of security, and (3) it is probable at inception and throughout the term of the individual contract that the contract will not settle net and will result in physical delivery of a security when it is issued. A contract for the purchase or sale of when-issued securities or other securities that do not yet exist is eligible to qualify for the regular-way security trades exception even though that contract permits net settlement (as discussed in paragraphs 9(a) and 57(c)(1)) or a market mechanism to facilitate net settlement of that contract (as discussed in paragraphs 9(b) and 57(c)(2)) exists. The entity shall document the basis for concluding that it is probable that the contract will not settle net and will result in physical delivery. Net settlement (as described in paragraphs 9(a) and 9(b)) of contracts in a group of contracts similarly designated as regular-way security trades would call into question the continued exemption of such contracts. In addition, if an entity is required to account for a contract for the purchase or sale of when-issued securities or other securities that do not yet exist on a trade-date basis, rather than a settlement-date basis, and thus recognizes the acquisition or disposition of the securities at the inception of the contract, that entity shall apply the regular-way security trades exception to those contracts.

b.　Subparagraph (c) is amended as follows:

(1)　The following footnote is added at the end of the second sentence:

*In certain circumstances, a take-or-pay contract may represent or contain a lease that should be accounted for in accordance with FASB Statement No. 13, *Accounting for Leases.*

(2)　In the fourth sentence, item (3) *little or no initial net investment in the contract is required* is replaced by *the contract requires no initial net investment or an initial net investment that is smaller by more than a nominal amount than would be required for other types of contracts that would be expected to have a similar response to changes in market factors. (Refer to paragraph 8.)*

c.　In the fifth sentence following the list in subparagraph (d), *little or no initial net investment, is not present* is replaced by *no initial net investment or an initial net investment that is smaller by more than a nominal amount than would be required*

for other types of contracts that would be expected to have a similar response to changes in market factors, is not present. (Refer to paragraph 8.)

24.　Paragraph 61 is amended as follows:

a.　In item 2 of subparagraph (a), *also* is replaced by *at the same time* and *then-current* is inserted between *would be the* and *market return.*

b.　Subparagraph (d) is amended as follows:

(1)　At the end of the first sentence, *provided the call options (or put options) are also considered to be clearly and closely related to the debt host contract under paragraph 13* is added.

(2)　In the last sentence, after the amendment by Statement 138, *and would be separated from the host contract* is deleted.

c.　Subparagraph (e) is amended as follows:

(1)　At the end of the second sentence, *if the criteria in paragraphs 12(b) and 12(c) are also met* is added.

(2)　In the last sentence, , *if the criteria in paragraphs 12(b) and 12(c) were met,* is inserted between *equity instrument and* and *should be separated.*

d.　Subparagraph (f) is replaced by the following:

Interest rate floors, caps, and collars. Floors or caps (or collars, which are combinations of caps and floors) on interest rates and the interest rate on a debt instrument are considered to be clearly and closely related unless the conditions in either paragraph 13(a) or paragraph 13(b) are met, in which case the floors or the caps are not considered to be clearly and closely related.

e.　In the second sentence of subparagraph (g), *must be separated from the host contract and accounted for as a derivative instrument* is replaced by *is not clearly and closely related to the host contract.*

25.　Paragraph 68 is amended as follows:

a.　In the second sentence, as amended by Statement 138, *(or a compound hedging instrument* composed of an interest rate swap and a mirror-image call or put option as discussed in paragraph 68(d) below) is inserted between *interest rate swap* and *if all of the applicable.*

b. In subparagraph (a), *being hedged* is added at the end of the sentence.

[Statement 133 Implementation Issue No. E10, "Application of the Shortcut Method to Hedges of a Portion of an Interest-Bearing Asset or Liability (or Its Related Interest) or a Portfolio of Similar Interest-Bearing Assets or Liabilities," cleared June 28, 2000, and revised September 25, 2000]

c. Subparagraph (b), as amended by Statement 138, is replaced by the following:

If the hedging instrument is solely an interest rate swap, the fair value of that swap at the inception of the hedging relationship is zero. If the hedging instrument is a compound derivative composed of an interest rate swap and mirror-image call or put option as discussed in paragraph 68(d), the premium for the mirror-image call or put option must be paid or received in the same manner as the premium on the call or put option embedded in the hedged item. That is, the reporting entity must determine whether the implicit premium for the purchased call or written put option embedded in the hedged item was principally paid at inception-acquisition (through an original issue discount or premium) or is being paid over the life of the hedged item (through an adjustment of the interest rate). If the implicit premium for the call or put option embedded in the hedged item was principally paid at inception-acquisition, the fair value of the hedging instrument at the inception of the hedging relationship must be equal to the fair value of the mirror-image call or put option. In contrast, if the implicit premium for the call or put option embedded in the hedged item is principally being paid over the life of the hedged item, fair value of the hedging instrument at the inception of the hedging relationship must be zero.

d. Subparagraph (d), as amended by Statement 138, is amended as follows:

(1) In the second sentence, *the hedging interest rate swap contains an embedded mirror-image call option* is replaced by *the hedging instrument is a compound derivative composed of an interest rate swap and a mirror-image call option.*

(2) In the third sentence, *embedded in the swap* is deleted.

(3) In the last sentence, *the hedging interest rate swap contains an embedded mirror-image put option* is replaced by *the hedging instrument is a compound derivative composed of an interest rate swap and a mirror-image put option.*

e. In subparagraph (g), *ceiling* is replaced by *cap.*

26. The first sentence of paragraph 95 is replaced by the following:

In assessing hedge effectiveness on an ongoing basis, Company G also must consider the extent of offset between the change in expected cash flows[†] on its Colombian coffee forward contract and the expected net change in expected cash flows for the forecasted purchase of Brazilian coffee.

[†]Refer to footnote* to paragraph 17 of Statement 133.

27. In the first sentence of paragraph 154, *interest payments on* is replaced by *quarterly interest payments on the company's 5-year $5 million borrowing program, initially expected to be accomplished by.*

28. Paragraph 176 is replaced by the following:

The following examples in Section 2 discuss instruments that contain a variety of embedded derivative instruments. They illustrate how the provisions of paragraphs 12–16 of this Statement would be applied to contracts with the described terms. If the terms of a contract are different from the described terms, the application of this Statement by either party to the contract may be affected. Furthermore, if any contract of the types discussed in Section 2 meets the definition of a derivative instrument in its entirety under paragraphs 6–9 and related paragraphs, the guidance in this section for the application of the provisions of paragraphs 12–16 to embedded derivative instruments does not apply. The illustrative instruments and related assumptions in Examples 12–27 are based on examples in Exhibit 96-12A of EITF Issue No. 96-12, "Recognition of Interest Income and Balance Sheet Classification of Structured Notes."

29. Paragraph 540 is amended as follows:

a. The following definition is added to the glossary:

Capacity contract
An agreement by an owner of capacity to sell the right to that capacity to another party so that it can satisfy its obligations. For example, in the electric industry, capacity (sometimes referred to as installed capacity) is the capability to deliver electric power to the electric transmission system of an operating control area. A control area is a portion of the electric grid that schedules, dispatches, and controls generating resources to serve area load (ultimate users of electricity) and coordinates scheduling of the flow of electric power over the transmission system to neighboring control areas. A control area requires entities that serve load within the control area to demonstrate ownership or contractual rights to capacity sufficient to serve that load at time of peak demand and to provide a reserve margin to protect the integrity of the system against potential generating unit outages in the control area.

b. The phrase *(including the occurrence or nonoccurrence of a specified event such as a scheduled payment under a contract)* is added at the end of the first sentence under the definition of *underlying.*

Amendments to Existing Pronouncements Relating to the Definition of *Expected Cash Flows* in FASB Concepts Statement No. 7, *Using Cash Flow Information and Present Value in Accounting Measurements*

30. FASB Statement No. 15, *Accounting by Debtors and Creditors for Troubled Debt Restructurings.* In the last sentence of paragraph 13, the following footnote is added after the first mention of *expected cash flows*:

*This pronouncement was issued prior to FASB Concepts Statement No. 7, *Using*

Cash Flow Information and Present Value in Accounting Measurements, and therefore the term *expected cash flows* does not necessarily have the same meaning as that term in Concepts Statement 7.

31. FASB Statement No. 35, *Accounting and Reporting by Defined Benefit Pension Plans.* In the last sentence of paragraph 11, the following footnote is added after the first mention of *expected cash flows*:

*This pronouncement was issued prior to FASB Concepts Statement No. 7, *Using Cash Flow Information and Present Value in Accounting Measurements,* and therefore the term *expected cash flows* does not necessarily have the same meaning as that term in Concepts Statement 7.

32. FASB Statement No. 60, *Accounting and Reporting by Insurance Enterprises.* In the second sentence of paragraph 19, the following footnote is added after the first mention of *expected cash flows*:

*This pronouncement was issued prior to FASB Concepts Statement No. 7, *Using Cash Flow Information and Present Value in Accounting Measurements,* and therefore the term *expected cash flows* does not necessarily have the same meaning as that term in Concepts Statement 7.

33. FASB Statement No. 87, *Employers' Accounting for Pensions.* In the last sentence of paragraph 49, the following footnote is added after the first mention of *expected cash flows*:

*This pronouncement was issued prior to FASB Concepts Statement No. 7, *Using Cash Flow Information and Present Value in Accounting Measurements,* and therefore the term *expected cash flows* does not necessarily have the same meaning as that term in Concepts Statement 7.

34. FASB Statement No. 106, *Employers' Accounting for Postretirement Benefits Other Than Pensions.* In the last sentence of paragraph 65, the following footnote is added after the first mention of *expected cash flows*:

*This pronouncement was issued prior to FASB Concepts Statement No. 7, *Using Cash Flow Information and Present Value in Accounting Measurements,* and therefore the term *expected cash flows* does not necessarily have the same meaning as that term in Concepts Statement 7.

Amendments to Other Existing Pronouncements

35. FASB Statement No. 65, *Accounting for Certain Mortgage Banking Activities.* The following sentence is added at the end of paragraph 3:

> In addition, this Statement does not apply to commitments related to the origination of mortgage loans to be held for sale, or fees and costs related to commitments to sell or purchase loans that are accounted for as derivatives under FASB Statement No. 133, *Accounting for Derivative Instruments and Hedging Activities.*

36. FASB Statement No. 91, *Accounting for Nonrefundable Fees and Costs Associated with Originating or Acquiring Loans and Initial Direct Costs of Leases.* The following sentence is added at the end of paragraph 3:

> In addition, this Statement does not apply to fees and costs related to commitments to originate, sell, or purchase loans that are accounted for as derivatives under FASB Statement No. 133, *Accounting for Derivatives Instruments and Hedging Activities.*

37. FASB Statement No. 95, *Statement of Cash Flows,* is amended as follows:

a. Footnote 4 of paragraph 14, as amended by Statements 104 and 133, is replaced by the following:

> Generally, each cash receipt or payment is to be classified according to its nature without regard to whether it stems from an item intended as a hedge of another item. For example, the proceeds of a borrowing are a financing cash inflow even though the debt is intended as a hedge of an investment, and the purchase or sale of a futures contract is an investing activity even though the contract is intended as a hedge of a firm commitment to purchase inventory. However, cash flows from a derivative instrument that is accounted for as a fair value hedge or cash flow hedge may be classified in the same category as the cash flows from the items being hedged provided that the derivative instrument does not include an other-than-insignificant financing element at inception, other than a financing element inherently included in an at-the-market derivative instrument with no prepayments (that is, the forward points in an at-the-money forward contract) and that the accounting policy is disclosed. If the derivative instrument includes an other-than-insignificant financing element at inception, all cash inflows and outflows of the derivative instrument shall be considered cash flows from financing activities by the borrower. If for any reason hedge accounting for an instrument that hedges an identifiable transaction or event is discontinued, then any cash flows subsequent to the date of discontinuance shall be classified consistent with the nature of the instrument.

b. The following is added after paragraph 19(c), as added by FASB Statement No. 117, *Financial Statements of Not-for-Profit Organizations:*

> d. Proceeds received* from derivative instruments that include financing elements[†] at inception.

---

*Whether at inception or over the term of the derivative instrument.

[†]Other than a financing element inherently included in an at-the-market derivative instrument with no prepayments.

c. The following is added after paragraph 20(c):

> d. Distributions* to counterparties of derivative instruments that include financing elements[†] at inception.

---

*Whether at inception or over the term of the derivative instrument.

[†]Other than a financing element inherently included in an at-the-market derivative instrument with no prepayments.

d. The following sentences are added at the end of paragraph 24:

> Another example where cash receipts and payments include more than one class of cash flows involves a derivative instrument that includes a financing element[†] at inception because the borrower's cash flows are associated with both the financing element and the derivative. For that derivative instrument, all cash inflows and outflows shall be considered cash flows from financing activities by the borrower.

[†]Other than a financing element inherently included in an at-the-market derivative instrument with no prepayments.

38. FASB Statement No. 126, *Exemption from Certain Required Disclosures about Financial Instruments for Certain Nonpublic Entities.* In paragraph 2(c), as amended by Statement 133, *other than commitments related to the origination of mortgage loans to be held for sale* is added before *during the reporting period.*

Effective Dates and Transition

39. This Statement shall be effective for contracts entered into or modified after June 30, 2003, except as stated in paragraph 40. This Statement also is effective for hedging relationships designated after June 30, 2003, except as stated in paragraph 40. Except as stated below, all provisions of this Statement shall be applied prospectively.

Effective Date and Transition for Other Amendments to Statement 133 That Resulted Principally from the Derivatives Implementation Group Process

40. Paragraphs 6, 7(b), 7(d), 8(a), 9, 13, 14, 17, 19, 21(b), 22(b), and 25(b) of this Statement, which relate to guidance in Statement 133 Implementation Issues that have been cleared by the Board and have been effective for fiscal quarters that began prior to June 15, 2003, shall continue to be applied in accordance with their respective effective dates. Because Implementation Issues C7 and C13 have been modified in accordance with the decisions made as part of the amendment process, entities should apply the guidance in those Issues as revised in this amendment prospectively to contracts entered into after June 30, 2003. In addition, paragraphs 7(a) and 23(a), which relate to forward purchases or sales of when-issued or other securities that do not yet exist, shall be applied to both existing contracts and new contracts entered into after June 30, 2003.

> The provisions of this Statement need
> not be applied to immaterial items.

This Statement was adopted by the unanimous vote of the seven members of the Financial Accounting Standards Board.

Robert H. Herz,	John M. Foster	Edward W. Trott
Chairman	Gary S. Schieneman	John K. Wulff
G. Michael Crooch	Katherine Schipper	

Appendix A

BACKGROUND INFORMATION AND BASIS FOR CONCLUSIONS

CONTENTS

Appendix A

BACKGROUND INFORMATION AND BASIS FOR CONCLUSIONS

Introduction

A1. This appendix summarizes considerations that Board members deemed significant in reaching the conclusions in this Statement. It includes reasons for accepting certain views and rejecting others. Individual Board members gave greater weight to some factors than to others.

Background Information

A2. Statement 133 was issued in June 1998. It has been amended by FASB Statements No. 137, *Accounting for Derivative Instruments and Hedging Activities—Deferral of the Effective Date of FASB Statement No. 133,* and No. 138, *Accounting for Certain Derivative Instruments and Certain Hedging Activities.* After Statement 133's issuance, the Derivatives Implementation Group (DIG) was formed to consider a number of implementation issues. Many of the amendments in this standard are derived from Statement 133 Implementation Issues that were cleared by the Board during the derivatives implementation process, after soliciting public comment on tentative guidance posted on the FASB website.

A3. In May 2002, the Board issued an Exposure Draft, *Amendment of Statement 133 on Derivative Instruments and Hedging Activities,* for a 60-day comment period. Forty organizations and individuals responded to the Exposure Draft. The Board considered the comments received in its redeliberations of the issues raised by the Exposure Draft during the fourth quarter of 2002. The Board concluded that it could reach an informed decision on the basis of existing information without a public hearing.

A4. The Board initially concluded that paragraph 6 of Statement 133 should be amended to resolve issues raised in connection with the definition of a derivative. Those issues were identified in Statement 133 Implementation Issue No. D1, "Application of Statement 133 to Beneficial Interests in Securitized Financial Assets." Paragraph 6 of Statement 133 sets forth a characteristic-based definition of a derivative. For certain types of instruments, the meaning of the characteristic in paragraph 6(b)—the instrument has an initial net investment that is smaller than would be required for other types of contracts that would be expected to have a similar response to changes in market factors—is especially important in determining whether the instrument meets the definition of a derivative in its entirety. Constituents indicated that without further clarification, they would have difficulty determining whether an instrument is a hybrid instrument that contains an embedded derivative or a derivative in its entirety.

A5. In the Exposure Draft of this Statement, the Board proposed amending paragraph 6(b) of Statement 133 to require that entities consider a financial instrument or other contract as meeting that paragraph's criteria if (a) the contract was option-based and had an initial net investment that was equal to the fair value of the option component or (b) the contract was non-option-based and had an initial net investment of less than 5 percent of the fully prepaid amount. The Board also proposed amending paragraph 12 to permit entities that held a contract that, in its entirety, met the definition of a derivative but was non-option-based and required an initial net investment that was less than 5 percent of the fully prepaid amount to account for the contract as either a derivative in its entirety or a hybrid instrument that must be bifurcated into a debt host and a derivative with a fair value of zero at acquisition of the hybrid instrument.

Those proposed amendments would have resulted in fewer instruments meeting the definition of a derivative in its entirety.

A6. A number of respondents to the Exposure Draft, both those that were involved with accounting for beneficial interests in securitizations and those that were not, expressed concerns that the proposed changes to the definition had far-reaching consequences for all parties subject to Statement 133. Respondents cited increased cost, complexity, adverse consequences (such as constituents misreading the language for option-based contracts or arbitrarily using 5 percent as a precedent for defining materiality under Statement 133), and lack of comparability as reasons why the definition of a derivative should not be amended.

A7. The Board reconsidered its decision to amend the definition of a derivative because it concluded that doing so would not clarify the basic issue—the amount of initial net investment that distinguishes a hybrid instrument from a derivative—and would create issues for certain derivative instruments that are not beneficial interests. After reviewing constituents' requests not to amend paragraph 6(b), the Board concluded that it would not amend the current definition of a derivative but would (a) clarify the meaning of *an initial net investment that is smaller than would be required for other types of contracts that would be expected to have a similar response to changes in market factors* in paragraph 6(b) of Statement 133 and (b) develop guidance to ensure the transparency of financing or debt elements embedded in derivatives at inception. For those reasons, and the reasons cited in paragraphs A11 and A12 of this Statement, the Board concluded that the definition of a derivative should be clarified, not amended.

Benefits and Costs

A8. The Board's mission statement charges the Board to determine that a proposed standard will fill a significant need and that the costs it imposes will be justified in relation to the overall benefits.

A9. The amendments to Statement 133 fall principally into three categories: amendments related to Statement 133 Implementation Issues that were previously cleared by the Board during the DIG process, amendments clarifying the definition of a derivative, and amendments relating to the definition of *expected cash flows* in FASB Concepts Statement

No. 7, *Using Cash Flow Information and Present Value in Accounting Measurements*. The Board believes that the incremental costs of implementing the amendments to this Statement are minimal given that most are simply clarifications of existing literature. The Board decided that the amendments that are not already effective should be applied prospectively and that retroactive application of those amendments was not appropriate given that they are to be applied to contracts or hedging relationships. The Board also evaluated whether to apply retroactively the requirement to report cash flows of derivatives with an other-than-insignificant financing element at inception as cash flows from financing activities in the statement of cash flows. The Board decided that the amount of time needed and costs incurred to collect that information would exceed the benefits of retroactively reporting that financing element as a cash flow from financing activities and that prospective application was the most appropriate transition.

Amendments to Statement 133

A10. This Statement amends paragraphs 10(a) and 59(a) of Statement 133 to remove from the scope of Statement 133 contracts for the purchase or sale of securities referred to as *when-issued* securities or other securities that do not yet exist if the contracts meet all three criteria in paragraph 59(a) of Statement 133. The Board decided to provide that scope exception to eliminate the potential burden associated with accounting for those contracts as derivatives. The amendments of those paragraphs similarly remove from the scope of that Statement contracts for the purchase or sale of when-issued securities or other securities that do not yet exist for which the acquisition or disposition of securities is required by the entity to be accounted for on a trade-date basis. Language relating to trade-date accounting was added to clarify that if an entity is required to account for a contract under trade-date accounting and thus already recognizes the acquisition or disposition of the securities at inception of the contract, that contract is not included within the scope of Statement 133. This Statement also adds new scope exceptions in paragraphs 10(g)–10(i). In addition, this Statement amends paragraph 10(b) to clarify when the normal purchases and normal sales exception can be applied to option-type contracts and forward contracts on electricity and paragraph 10(d) to clarify which financial guarantee contracts are within that scope exception. In each case, the Board decided to provide a scope exception for practical reasons.

Amendments Relating to the Definition of a Derivative

A11. The Board decided not to establish a quantitative threshold for evaluating when a contract meets the criterion in paragraph 6(b) that the contract "requires no initial net investment or an initial net investment that is smaller than would be required for other types of contracts that would be expected to have a similar response to changes in market factors." The Board concluded that broader qualitative guidance would (a) result in more consistent accounting for economically similar contracts and (b) provide a means of clarifying when derivatives contain financing elements. The Board added qualitative guidance to paragraph 8 of Statement 133 related to when an initial net investment is considered to be an initial net investment that "is smaller than would be required for other types of contracts that would be expected to have a similar response to changes in market factors." That guidance indicates that a contract meets the criterion in paragraph 6(b) if the initial net investment is less, by more than a nominal amount, than the initial net investment that would be commensurate with the amount that would be exchanged either to acquire the asset related to the underlying or to incur the obligation related to the underlying. The Board did not intend that guidance to imply that a slightly off-market contract cannot be a derivative in its entirety. That determination is a matter of facts and circumstances and should be evaluated on a case-by-case basis.

A12. The Board also amended paragraph 7 of Statement 133 to reflect its decision in FASB Interpretation No. 45, *Guarantor's Accounting and Disclosure Requirements for Guarantees, Including Indirect Guarantees of Indebtedness of Others,* to clarify the definition of an underlying. In that Interpretation, the Board clarifies how the definition of an underlying in Statement 133 applies to a guarantee contract. The Board added the phrase *(including the occurrence or nonoccurrence of a specified event such as a scheduled payment under a contract)* to explain what was meant by the phrase *or other variable* in the first sentence of paragraph 7 of Statement 133. Footnote 2 of Interpretation 45 states, "The occurrence or nonoccurrence of a specified event (such as a scheduled payment under a contract) is a variable that is considered an underlying under [the] definition [in Statement 133]. . ."; therefore, the clarification's inclusion in this amendment does not require further due process. However, because that clarification was included in an Interpretation involving guarantor's accounting and disclosure requirements for guarantees, constituents may not have focused on the clarification. Therefore, the Board decided that the clarification should be applied prospectively for contracts entered into after June 30, 2003.

Amendment of Paragraph 10

A13. As a result of issues addressed as part of the DIG process and various other Statement 133 Implementation Issues raised by constituents, the Board amended paragraph 10 of Statement 133 as discussed below.

Securities referred to as when-issued securities or other securities that do not yet exist

A14. The Board concluded in paragraph 276 of Statement 133 that the regular-way security trades exception in paragraph 10(a) should be extended to securities referred to as when-issued securities or other securities that do not yet exist "only if (a) there is no other way to purchase or sell the security and (b) the trade will settle within the shortest period permitted for the security." Paragraph 10(a) indicates that contracts are eligible for that exception only if they have no net settlement provision and there is no market mechanism to facilitate net settlement. Paragraph 59(a) of Statement 133 discusses the application of that scope exception to when-issued securities or other securities that do not yet exist. Constituents questioned whether that exception was applicable to when-issued securities or other securities that do not yet exist if a market mechanism exists, which is the case for GNMA to-be-announced forward contracts. If that exception is not applicable when a market mechanism exists, constituents asked that a special exception be made for when-issued securities or other securities that do not yet exist.

A15. The Board considered constituents' comments and decided that the regular-way security trades exception in paragraph 10(a) should apply to certain securities referred to as when-issued securities or other securities that do not yet exist, even if they have net settlement provisions or a market mechanism exists if it is probable at inception and throughout the term that the contract will not settle net and will result in physical delivery. The Board reasoned that requiring when-issued securities or other securities that do not yet exist to be accounted for as derivatives if there is no intention to net settle the contract would not be cost beneficial. Accordingly, this Statement amends paragraphs 10(a) and 59(a) to indicate that the

regular-way security trades exception may be applied to securities referred to as when-issued securities or other securities that do not yet exist even though a market mechanism exists. Paragraph 59(a) also is amended to include the additional requirement that it be probable at inception and throughout the term of the individual contract that the contract will not settle net and will result in physical delivery of a security when it is issued.

Power purchase or sales agreements

A16. This Statement amends Statement 133 to permit a scope exception for a power purchase or sales agreement if specific criteria are met. Under Statement 133 Implementation Issue No. C10, "Can Option Contracts and Forward Contracts with Optionality Features Qualify for the Normal Purchases and Normal Sales Exception," option and forward contracts that contain optionality features that can modify the quantity of the asset to be delivered under the contract cannot qualify for the normal purchases and normal sales exception in paragraph 10(b). Companies in the electric industry enter into contracts, which frequently provide optionality about the quantity to be delivered, that permit, but do not require, one party to purchase electricity (also referred to as "power").

A17. The Board decided that certain unique characteristics of the electric industry justify extending the scope exception in paragraph 10(b) to certain power purchase or sales agreements. The Board understands that deregulation has influenced the way contracts to buy and sell power are structured. A unique characteristic of the industry is that electricity cannot be readily stored in significant quantities. Another unique characteristic is that many suppliers are statutorily or contractually obligated to maintain a specified level of electricity supply to meet demand. Therefore, suppliers must maintain access to an additional supply of electricity (through generation or purchase) to meet spikes in demand. As a result, some contracts to buy and sell electricity permit the buyer some flexibility in determining when to take electricity and in what quantities in order to match power to fluctuating demand.

A18. The Board understands that another important characteristic of the industry is that fixed costs are a very high percentage of the total cost of producing power. To provide for recovery of fixed costs, power contracts typically include a specified charge (sometimes referred to as the capacity or demand charge) to provide for recovery of the cost of the plant (or, in some cases, recovery of the market-based value of the plant) and related financing. Generally, contracts also will include a variable charge to recover, among other things, the variable cost of producing power (the energy charge). For the regulated electric industry, regulators set rates in order to recover plant fixed costs and variable costs plus a reasonable return. Tariffs are established that generally separate the capacity charge and the energy charges, among other charges. Some contracts to buy and sell power of independent power producers, which are not regulated, also include capacity charges and energy charges, which, in the past, were generally established by regulators. The intent to physically deliver power at rates that will recover the plant fixed costs and variable cost to produce power while giving the buyer the ability to have some control over when and in what quantity power is delivered is a consistent characteristic of these contracts.

A19. The Board decided to permit the normal purchases and normal sales exception to be applied to a power purchase or sales agreement if certain criteria are met, regardless of whether the agreement includes optionality features that can modify the quantity of the asset to be delivered. Those criteria are outlined in paragraph 58(b) of Statement 133 as amended by this Statement.

Financial guarantee contracts

A20. This Statement amends Statement 133 to clarify the types of financial guarantee contracts that are included in the scope exception in paragraph 10(d). Constituents questioned whether this scope exception was intended to encompass financial guarantee contracts acquired by entities to obtain protection against events of default that are stipulated in the legal documents used to consummate a credit agreement. Financial guarantee contracts typically provide for payment upon several default events (as specified in the underlying credit agreement) and not just the single triggering event described in paragraph 10(d)—that is, failure to pay when payment is due. The events of default specified in credit agreements may be either "payment-based" (for example, payment of principal or interest when due) or "non-payment-based" (for example, violation of a covenant or a change in control). Constituents questioned whether a guarantee contract that mirrors exactly the events of default covered by the original loan agreement and permits the guaranteed party to deliver the loan to the guarantor upon the occurrence

of a non-payment-based event of default (such as a change in control of the debtor) would qualify for the scope exception. Under that scenario, the guaranteed party would receive payment under the contract even though the debtor did not literally fail to pay when payment was due.

A21. In considering this issue, the Board discussed two possible alternatives:(a) amend paragraph 10(d) to permit financial guarantee contracts that provide protection to a guaranteed party in any event of default to qualify for the scope exception or (b) clarify paragraph 10(d) to emphasize the need for the guaranteed party to demand payment prior to collecting any payment from the guarantor in order for a guarantee contract to be eligible for the scope exception. Both alternatives contemplate that, as part of the financial guarantee arrangement, the guarantor receives either the rights to any payments subsequently advanced to the guaranteed party or delivery of the defaulted receivable upon an event of default.

A22. The Board selected the second alternative, because it is more consistent with the Board's original intent in Statement 133. The Board concluded that the intent of the scope exception for guarantee contracts in paragraph 10(d) of Statement 133 was to more closely align that exception with the scope exception for traditional insurance contracts addressed in paragraph 10(c). The Board reasoned that guarantees eligible for the scope exception are similar to insurance contracts in that they entitle the holder to compensation only if, as a result of an insurable event (other than a change in price), the holder incurs a liability or there is an adverse change in the value of a specific asset or liability for which the holder is at risk. Accordingly, the Board determined that, in order for a financial guarantee contract to qualify for the scope exception in paragraph 10(d), the guaranteed party must demand payment from the debtor and that once it is determined that the required obligation will not be satisfied by the debtor, the guaranteed party must relinquish to the guarantor its rights to receive payment from the debtor in order to receive payment from the guarantor. The Board also concluded that the language in paragraph 10(d) should be clarified to eliminate use of the term *loss incurred* and instead focus on amounts due to the guaranteed party but not paid by the debtor.

A23. In addition, the Board decided that the concepts in Statement 133 Implementation Issue No. C7, "Certain Financial Guarantee Contracts," are critical to differentiating guarantee contracts covered by the scope exception in paragraph 10(d) from credit derivatives that provide payments in response to a change in credit rating or credit spreads of a reference credit. The amended language in paragraph 7(c) of this Statement was written to include financial guarantees with all of the following characteristics: (a) the guaranteed party's direct exposure on the referenced asset must be present both at the inception of the contract and throughout its life; (b) to be paid under the financial guarantee, the guaranteed party has an amount that is due from the debtor (at either pre-specified payment dates or accelerated payment dates as a result of the occurrence of an event of default, as defined in the guarantee contract, or notice of acceleration to the debtor by the creditor) and that amount is past due; and (c) the compensation paid to the guaranteed party under the contract does not exceed the direct exposure of the guaranteed party relating to the referenced asset either from owning the referenced asset or from back-to-back arrangements with another party that is required by the back-to-back arrangement to maintain direct ownership of the guaranteed obligation.

Investments in life insurance

A24. If a hybrid instrument is remeasured at fair value with changes in fair value reported in earnings as they occur, the hybrid instrument does not satisfy the criterion in paragraph 12(b) of Statement 133 and, thus, the embedded derivative instrument is not separated from the host contract. Certain life insurance policies (for example, corporate-owned life insurance, business-owned life insurance, or key-man insurance subject to FASB Technical Bulletin No. 85-4, *Accounting for Purchases of Life Insurance*) that contain embedded derivatives satisfy the criterion in paragraph 12(b). While Technical Bulletin 85-4 requires that those contracts be measured at cash surrender value or contract value with changes in value recognized in the income statement during the contract period, contract value may not equal the fair value of the insurance policy. In those instances, policyholders otherwise would be required to separate the embedded derivative from the host contract and account for the host contract under generally accepted accounting principles. However, because the policyholder would not have a table of cash surrender values that relate only to the host contract, application of existing guidance in Technical Bulletin 85-4 for only the host contract is not feasible. For that reason, the Board decided that the policyholder should not separate the embedded derivative from the host contract and should continue to account for

those policies in accordance with Technical Bulletin 85-4. A new scope exception has been added as paragraph 10(g).

Contracts held by benefit plans

A25. Constituents identified conflicts between the requirements of Statement 133 and both FASB Statement No. 110, *Reporting by Defined Benefit Pension Plans of Investment Contracts* (which amends FASB Statement No. 35, *Accounting and Reporting by Defined Benefit Pension Plans*), and AICPA Statement of Position 94-4, *Reporting of Investment Contracts Held by Health and Welfare Benefit Plans and Defined-Contribution Pension Plans*. Paragraph 7(b) of Statement 110 requires a defined benefit plan to report insurance contracts "in the same manner as specified in the annual report filed by the plan with certain governmental agencies pursuant to ERISA; that is, either at fair value or at amounts determined by the insurance enterprise (contract value)," while Statement 133 requires that the embedded derivative in some insurance contracts be bifurcated. In addition, SOP 94-4 indicates that a fully benefit-responsive investment contract (such as a guaranteed investment contract [GIC] that is subject to SOP 94-4) should be reported at contract value. However, Statement 133 Implementation Issue No. A16, "Synthetic Guaranteed Investment Contracts," concludes that synthetic GICs meet Statement 133's definition of a derivative. Statement 133 does not contain an exception for synthetic GICs held by reporting entities subject to SOP 94-4. Due to the limited scope of those identified conflicts, the Board decided to exclude contracts that are subject to Statements 35 and 110 or SOP 94-4 from the scope of Statement 133 for the party that accounts for those contracts under those pronouncements.

Loan commitments

A26. Paragraph 291 of Statement 133 addresses loan commitments. Under that paragraph, a loan commitment would be excluded from the scope of Statement 133 "if it (a) requires the holder to deliver a promissory note that would not be readily convertible to cash and (b) cannot readily be settled net." Constituents questioned whether any loan commitments are subject to Statement 133 and, if so, which types of loan commitments meet the definition of a derivative. Constituents noted that if a loan commitment is subject to Statement 133, an overlap exists between a requirement to account for that arrangement as a derivative and the existing accounting guidance for commitment fees and costs in FASB Statements No. 65, *Accounting for Certain Mortgage Banking Activities,* and No. 91, *Accounting for Nonrefundable Fees and Costs Associated with Originating or Acquiring Loans and Initial Direct Costs of Leases,* as amended. Statements 65 and 91 were not amended by Statement 133.

A27. As reflected in paragraph 291, the Board believed that the characteristic of net settlement in paragraph 6(c) determines whether a loan commitment meets the definition of a derivative and that loan commitments generally meet the characteristics of a derivative described in paragraphs 6(a) and 6(b) of Statement 133. That is, a loan commitment contains an underlying (the specified interest rate) and a notional amount (the maximum amount of the borrowing), and the initial net investment in the contract is similar to a premium on other option-type contracts. In considering the net settlement characteristic, the Board had understood that most loan commitments are not contractually required or permitted to be net settled as discussed in paragraph 9(a) of Statement 133. While the Board acknowledged that a loan commitment may meet the characteristic of net settlement either because there is a market mechanism that facilitates net settlement (under paragraph 9(b)) or because the underlying asset that will be delivered under the contract (the loan) is readily convertible to cash (under paragraph 9(c)), during the development of Statement 133, the Board was under the impression that most loan commitments would not meet the net settlement characteristic. The Board subsequently was informed that certain types of loan commitments meet the net settlement characteristic and, therefore, meet the definition of a derivative.

A28. In an effort to resolve the scope overlap of Statement 133 and Statements 65 and 91, in December 2000, the FASB issued tentative guidance on the application of Statement 133 to loan commitments in Statement 133 Implementation Issue No. C13, "When a Loan Commitment Is Included in the Scope of Statement 133." That tentative guidance provided that only loan commitments that relate to the origination or acquisition of mortgage loans held for resale under Statement 65 would be accounted for as derivatives under Statement 133. However, Statement 65 would continue to apply to loan commitments that relate to the origination or acquisition of mortgage loans held for investment. Also, Statement 91 would continue to apply to all commitments that relate to the origination of loans that are not mortgage loans (for example, loan commitments is-

sued to commercial and industrial enterprises). The Board recognized that the approach in Implementation Issue C13 could have included in the scope of Statement 133 certain loan commitments that technically do not meet the definition of a derivative. For example, commitments that relate to mortgage loans classified as held for sale under Statement 65 would be considered derivatives under that guidance, even if the underlying loans did not meet the definition of *readily convertible to cash* under paragraph 9(c) of Statement 133.

A29. Because of concerns about the possible outcomes under Implementation Issue C13, the Board studied several alternatives for accounting for loan commitments. Those alternatives included (a) requiring the characteristic-based definition of a derivative to be applied to loan commitments and (b) providing a scope exception for some or all loan commitments. The Board consulted with members of the DIG and other constituents. Constituents highlighted the unique considerations surrounding the application of the definition of a derivative to different types of loan commitments. Many constituents indicated that additional guidance would be needed to assist in the application of the net settlement characteristic, including how to determine whether a market mechanism exists for commercial loan commitments and when a loan is considered readily convertible to cash. Constituents highlighted the operational burden of applying the characteristic-based definition of a derivative to various types of loan commitments.

A30. During the deliberations leading up to the Exposure Draft, the Board decided to clear the guidance in Implementation Issue C13 and include that guidance in the Exposure Draft, rather than going forward with a characteristic-based approach previously identified. The Board observed that requiring an evaluation of loan commitments under the characteristic-based definition of a derivative in Statement 133 would impose a significant operational burden on entities, for example, by requiring an evaluation of some types of loan commitments on a contract-by-contract basis. In addition, the Board was persuaded by constituents that there would be significant disagreement as to whether a given loan had a market mechanism or was readily convertible to cash. Consequently, the Board was concerned that requiring entities to determine whether either of those requirements was met would result in both diversity of practice and ongoing requests for implementation guidance. Because of those concerns, the Board believed that if that requirement was imposed, the costs that entities could incur would exceed the incremental improvement to financial reporting for banks' lending activities. The Board also observed that the approach in Implementation Issue C13 would limit the need for ongoing implementation guidance because many entities had already developed procedures for its implementation.

A31. During redeliberations, the Board discovered that Implementation Issue C13's use of the phrase *loan commitments that relate to the origination or acquisition of mortgage loans,* specifically the inclusion of the phrase *or acquisition,* caused confusion. That language had been carried forward from Statements 65 and 91. The Exposure Draft and Implementation Issue C13 included the phrase *or acquisition* simply to be consistent with those Statements. However, that phrase was not meant to include commitments to purchase or sell existing loans in the scope exception of paragraph 10(i).

A32. The Board affirmed its intent that commitments to purchase or sell existing loans are not included in the new paragraph 10(i) scope exception and that the definition of a derivative in Statement 133 should be applied to those commitments to determine if they are subject to the provisions of Statement 133. The Board noted that both parties to those contracts need to evaluate the commitment. To clarify this point, the Board decided to remove the references to *acquiring loans* that were in the proposed amendment to Statement 133 and Implementation Issue C13 and amend Statements 65 and 91 to indicate that those Statements should not be applied to fees and costs related to commitments to purchase or sell loans that are accounted for as derivatives under Statement 133. The Board also affirmed that commitments to originate nonmortgage loans are exempt from Statement 133 and that the accounting by the issuer of a commitment to issue nonmortgage loans should not be analogized to in the accounting for mortgage loans because that accounting was based on specialized accounting and reporting principles that were developed specifically for mortgage banking activities.

A33. Paragraph 10(i) of Statement 133 therefore provides a scope exception for holders (the potential borrowers) of all commitments to originate loans, issuers of commitments to originate other than mortgage loans, and issuers of commitments to originate mortgage loans that will be held for investment. However, with respect to issuers of commitments to originate loans that will be held for resale under

Statement 65, the Board concluded that those commitments should be accounted for by issuers as derivatives under Statement 133. Paragraph 35 of this Statement amends Statement 65 to exclude from the scope of that Statement any loan commitments that are required to be accounted for as derivatives by the issuer (that is, the potential lender) under Statement 133. Paragraph 36 of this Statement amends Statement 91 to exclude from the scope of that Statement any fees and costs related to commitments to sell or purchase loans that are accounted for as derivatives under Statement 133. In addition, paragraph 38 of this Statement amends FASB Statement No. 126, *Exemption from Certain Required Disclosures about Financial Instruments for Certain Nonpublic Entities,* to indicate that certain disclosures about the fair value of financial instruments would continue to be optional for a nonpublic entity that holds loan commitments to originate mortgage loans to be held for sale that are considered derivatives under Statement 133.

Amendment of Paragraphs 13(b) and 61(f)

A34. Paragraph 61(f) of Statement 133 states that interest rate caps that are at or above the current market price (or rate) and interest rate floors that are at or below the current market price (or rate) at issuance of an instrument are considered to be clearly and closely related to the debt host. The last sentence of that paragraph references paragraph 13(b) of Statement 133 and states that the derivative embedded in a variable-rate debt instrument that has a floor on the interest rate would not be separated from the host contract and accounted for separately even though, in a falling interest rate environment, the debt instrument may have a return to the investor that is significantly above the market return of a debt instrument without a floor provision. Constituents' views differed on the application of paragraph 61(f). Some constituents said that any embedded floor or cap that is in-the-money must be accounted for separately. Other constituents said that an embedded floor would never be accounted for separately.

A35. To clarify this issue, the Board decided to modify paragraph 61(f) to indicate that interest rate floors and caps are typically considered clearly and closely related to a debt host. However, determining whether any floor or cap is considered clearly and closely related depends on the analysis required in paragraph 13 for embedded derivative instruments in which the underlying is an interest rate or interest rate index that alters net interest payments that otherwise would be paid or received on an interest-bearing host contract.

A36. Constituents' views differed on the application of paragraph 13(b) in the context of an interest rate cap or an interest rate floor. Prior to this amendment, paragraph 13(b) indicated that if an embedded derivative could at least double the investor's initial rate of return on the host contract *and* could also result in a rate of return that is at least twice what otherwise would be the *market return* for a contract that has the same terms as the host contract and that involves a debtor with a similar credit quality, the embedded derivative would not be clearly and closely related to the host contract. Some constituents interpreted paragraph 13(b) to indicate that the two conditions in that paragraph were identical.

A37. As a result of constituent concerns, the Board decided to clarify paragraph 13(b) to indicate that if an embedded derivative could at least double the investor's initial rate of return on the host contract and at the same time result in a rate of return that is at least twice what otherwise would be the *then-current market return* for a contract that has the same terms as the host contract and that involves a debtor with a credit quality similar to the issuer's credit quality at inception, the embedded derivative is not clearly and closely related to the debt host contract. In other words, application of paragraph 13(b) requires first that the embedded derivative could, considering all possible interest rate scenarios, at least double the investor's initial rate of return on a contract that did not contain the embedded derivative. When that condition is met, the embedded derivative is not considered clearly and closely related if, for any of those possible scenarios in which the investor's initial rate of return is at least doubled, the rate of return the investor will obtain in the future on the host contract is at least twice the then-current market return for that contract.

Amendments Relating to Reporting Cash Flows

A38. This Statement adds a requirement to report all cash flows associated with a derivative that contains an other-than-insignificant financing element at inception, other than a financing element inherently included in an at-the-market derivative instrument with no prepayments (that is, the forward points in an at-the-money forward contract), as cash flows from financing activities in the statement of cash flows as opposed to reporting only the cash flows related to a

financing element of a derivative as a financing activity. The Board acknowledged that a derivative containing an other-than-insignificant financing element is already shown on the balance sheet. Even so, the Board believes that transparency would be improved by focusing on the cash flows associated with those derivatives.

A39. Two characteristics often are associated with a derivative that contains a financing element—upfront cash payments and off-market terms (for example, terms, rates, or prices that are not consistent with the current market for that type of contract). The Board agreed that those characteristics indicate that the derivative contains a financing element at inception. However, the Board chose not to establish a specific criterion for when a derivative does or does not contain a financing element because of the unlimited ways to structure those arrangements. Rather, identification of a financing element should be based on the specific facts and circumstances. The Board decided that the presence of only an insignificant financing element at inception does not warrant modifying the entity's cash flow reporting. However, when an other-than-insignificant financing element is present at inception, the borrower in the arrangement should report all of the derivative's cash inflows and outflows as a financing activity in the statement of cash flows. The Board noted that while it may be conceptually preferable to report only those cash flows associated with the financing element as a financing activity in the statement of cash flows, identifying those cash flows would be difficult. Therefore, because of cost-benefit concerns, the Board decided to require in those circumstances that all cash inflows and outflows associated with derivatives that contain an other-than-insignificant financing element at inception be reported as cash flows from financing activities. As a result, the Board also amended FASB Statement No. 95, *Statement of Cash Flows.* The Board considered whether it should require entities to revise their statements of cash flows retroactively for this change in reporting but decided that retroactive application would be overly burdensome and would not be cost beneficial.

Other Amendments and Clarifications

Amendment to paragraph 19

A40. Paragraph 19 of Statement 133 was deleted because the guidance in that paragraph was considered unnecessary. For example, it should be readily apparent that the notion of a hedging derivative's change in fair value (gain or loss) for a period is not merely the difference between the beginning fair value and the ending fair value when payments under that derivative have been received or made during the period. In addition, it contained guidance that was not appropriate in all instances. For example, the guidance in paragraph 19 would preclude the changes in a derivative's fair value due to the passage of time from being reported in other comprehensive income when it is used in a cash flow hedge. That consequence was not intended in Statement 133.

Amendment to paragraph 57(c)(3)

A41. In connection with Statement 133 Implementation Issue No. A14, "Derivative Treatment of Stock Purchase Warrants Issued by a Company for Its Own Shares of Stock Where the Subsequent Sale or Transfer Is Restricted," the Board chose to clarify in paragraph 57(c)(3) that restrictions (whether temporary or permanent) imposed by either party on the sale or transfer of the assets that are received upon exercise of the contract do not affect the determination of whether those assets are readily convertible to cash except as indicated in the following sentence. Stock that is traded in an active market and is to be delivered under a stock purchase warrant is not considered to be readily convertible to cash when both of the following conditions exist: (a) the contract is a stock purchase warrant issued by an entity for its own stock (or stock of its consolidated subsidiaries) and (b) the sale or transfer of the issued shares is restricted (other than in connection with being pledged as collateral) by the issuer for a period of 32 days or more from the date the stock purchase warrant is exercised.

Clarification of the notion of **clearly and closely related** *used in paragraphs 10(b), 12(a), and 60*

A42. The use of the phrase *clearly and closely related* in the normal purchases and normal sales exception in paragraph 10(b) has a different meaning than it does in paragraphs 12(a) and 60 of Statement 133 that address the relationship between an embedded derivative and the host contract. In that context (paragraphs 12(a) and 60), the phrase focuses on the *economic characteristics and risks* of the embedded derivative and the host contract. In the context of the assessment of whether a contract qualifies for the normal purchase and normal sales exception, the phrase *clearly and closely related* focuses on whether a price adjustment within the contract is clearly and closely related to the asset being sold or purchased.

Amendments Relating to the Definition of Expected Cash Flows in Concepts Statement 7

A43. The Board concluded that it was necessary to add footnotes to the term *expected cash flows* in Statements No. 15, *Accounting by Debtors and Creditors for Troubled Debt Restructurings,* No. 60, *Accounting and Reporting by Insurance Enterprises,* No. 87, *Employers' Accounting for Pensions,* No. 106, *Employers' Accounting for Postretirement Benefits Other Than Pensions,* and Statements 35 and 133 because the use of that term in those Statements is not consistent with the definition of *expected cash flows* in the glossary to Concepts Statement 7. In addition to the footnotes added to Statement 133, paragraphs 30–34 of this Statement amend other pronouncements to reflect the fact that because those pronouncements were issued prior to Concepts Statement 7, the term *expected cash flows* does not necessarily have the same meaning as it does in Concepts Statement 7.

Effective Dates and Transition

A44. The Board decided that, except as stated in paragraph A45, this Statement should be effective for contracts entered into or modified after June 30, 2003, and for hedging relationships designated after June 30, 2003. In addition, except as stated in paragraph A45, all provisions of this Statement should be applied prospectively. The Board decided not to require retroactive application of this Statement because it concluded that obtaining or developing the information necessary to apply this Statement retroactively could be burdensome for many entities.

A45. The Board chose not to readdress the effective dates of the Statement 133 Implementation Issues referenced in the provisions of paragraphs 6, 7(b), 7(d), 8(a), 9, 13, 14, 17, 19, 21(b), 22(b), and 25(b) of this Statement. It concluded that those effective dates should remain unchanged from those noted in the respective Statement 133 Implementation Issues that were cleared by the Board. However, because Implementation Issues C7 and C13 have been modified in accordance with the decisions made as part of the amendment process, the Board decided that entities should apply the guidance in those issues as revised in this amendment prospectively to contracts entered into after June 30, 2003. In addition, the Board decided that paragraphs 7(a) and 23(a), which relate to forward purchases or sales of when-issued or other securities that do not yet exist, should be applied to both existing contracts and new contracts entered into after June 30, 2003, in order to allow entities that would now meet the regular-way security trades exception to discontinue accounting for those transactions as derivatives.

Appendix B

AMENDED PARAGRAPHS OF STATEMENT 133 MARKED TO SHOW CHANGES MADE BY THIS STATEMENT

B1. This appendix contains paragraphs of Statement 133, as amended by Statements 138, 140, 141, and 145 marked to integrate changes from this amendment. The Board plans to issue an amended version of Statement 133 that includes the standards section, the implementation guidance (including examples), and the glossary.

STANDARDS OF FINANCIAL ACCOUNTING AND REPORTING

Derivative Instruments

6. A derivative instrument is a financial instrument or other contract with all three of the following characteristics:

a. It has (1) one or more **underlyings** and (2) one or more **notional amounts**[3] or payment provisions or both. Those terms determine the amount of the settlement or settlements, and, in some cases, whether or not a settlement is required.[4]
b. It requires no initial net investment or an initial net investment that is smaller than would be required for other types of contracts that would be expected to have a similar response to changes in market factors.
c. Its terms require or permit net settlement, it can readily be settled net by a means outside the contract, or it provides for delivery of an asset that puts the recipient in a position not substantially different from net settlement.

Notwithstanding the above characteristics, loan commitments that relate to the origination of mortgage loans that will be held for sale, as discussed in paragraph 21 of FASB Statement No. 65, *Accounting for Mortgage Banking Activities* (as amended), shall be accounted for as derivative instruments by the issuer of the loan commitment (that is, the potential lender). Paragraph 10(i) provides a scope exception for the accounting for loan commitments by issuers of certain commitments to originate loans and all holders of commitments to originate loans (that is, the potential borrowers).

7. *Underlying, notional amount, and payment provision.* An underlying is a specified interest rate, security price, commodity price, foreign exchange rate, index of prices or rates, or other variable (including the occurrence or nonoccurrence of a specified event such as a scheduled payment under a contract). An underlying may be a price or rate of an asset or liability but is not the asset or liability itself. A notional amount is a number of currency units, shares, bushels, pounds, or other units specified in the contract. The settlement of a derivative instrument with a notional amount is determined by interaction of that notional amount with the underlying. The interaction may be simple multiplication, or it may involve a formula with leverage factors or other constants. A payment provision specifies a fixed or determinable settlement to be made if the underlying behaves in a specified manner.

8. *Initial net investment.* Many derivative instruments require no initial net investment. Some require an initial net investment as compensation for time value (for example, a premium on an option) or for terms that are more or less favorable than market conditions (for example, a premium on a forward purchase contract with a price less than the current forward price). Others require a mutual exchange of currencies or other assets at inception, in which case the net investment is the difference in the fair values of the assets exchanged. A derivative instrument does not require an initial net investment in the contract that is equal to the notional amount (or the notional amount plus a premium or minus a discount) or that is determined by applying the notional amount to the underlying. If the initial net investment in the contract (after adjustment for the time value of money) is less, by more than a nominal amount, than the initial net investment that would be commensurate with the amount that would be exchanged either to acquire the

---

[3]Sometimes other names are used. For example, the notional amount is called a face amount in some contracts.

[4]The terms *underlying, notional amount, payments provision,* and *settlement* are intended to include the plural forms in the remainder of this Statement. Including both the singular and plural forms used in this paragraph is more accurate but much more awkward and impairs the readability.

asset related to the underlying or to incur the obligation related to the underlying, the characteristic in paragraph 6(b) is met. The amount of that asset acquired or liability incurred should be comparable to the effective notional amount* of the contract.

9. *Net settlement.* A contract fits the description in paragraph 6(c) if its settlement provisions meet one of the following criteria:

a. Neither party is required to deliver an asset that is associated with the underlying ~~or~~and that has a principal amount, stated amount, face value, number of shares, or other denomination that is equal to the notional amount (or the notional amount plus a premium or minus a discount). For example, most interest rate swaps do not require that either party deliver interest-bearing assets with a principal amount equal to the notional amount of the contract.

b. One of the parties is required to deliver an asset of the type described in paragraph 9(a), but there is a market mechanism that facilitates net settlement, for example, an exchange that offers a ready opportunity to sell the contract or to enter into an offsetting contract.

c. One of the parties is required to deliver an asset of the type described in paragraph 9(a), but that asset is readily convertible to cash[5] or is itself a derivative instrument. An example of that type of contract is a forward contract that requires delivery of an exchange-traded equity security. Even though the number of shares to be delivered is the same as the notional amount of the contract and the price of the shares is the underlying, an exchange-traded security is readily convertible to cash. Another example is a swaption—an option to require delivery of a swap contract, which is a derivative.

Derivative instruments embedded in other contracts are addressed in paragraphs 12–16.

10. Notwithstanding the conditions in paragraphs 6–9, the following contracts are not subject to the requirements of this Statement:

a. *"Regular-way" security trades.* Regular-way security trades are contracts ~~with no net settlement provision and no market mechanism to facilitate~~ ~~net settlement (as described in paragraphs 9(a) and 9(b)). They~~ that provide for delivery of a security within the time generally established by regulations or conventions in the marketplace or exchange in which the transaction is being executed. However, a contract for an existing security does not qualify for the regular-way security trades exception if it requires or permits net settlement (as discussed in paragraphs 9(a) and 57(c)(1)) or if a market mechanism to facilitate net settlement of that contract (as discussed in paragraphs 9(b) and 57(c)(2)) exists, except as provided in the following sentence. If an entity is required to account for a contract to purchase or sell an existing security on a trade-date basis, rather than a settlement-date basis, and thus recognizes the acquisition (or disposition) of the security at the inception of the contract, then the entity shall apply the regular-way security trades exception to that contract. A contract for the purchase or sale of *when-issued* securities or other securities that do not yet exist is addressed in paragraph 59(a).

b. *Normal purchases and normal sales.* Normal purchases and normal sales are contracts that provide for the purchase or sale of something other than a financial instrument or derivative instrument that will be delivered in quantities expected to be used or sold by the reporting entity over a reasonable period in the normal course of business. ~~However, contracts that have a price based on an underlying that is not clearly and closely related to the asset being sold or purchased (such as a price in a contract for the sale of a grain commodity based in part on changes in the S&P index) or that are denominated in a foreign currency that meets neither of the criteria in paragraphs 15(a) and 15(b) shall not be considered normal purchases and normal sales.~~ The following guidance should be considered in determining whether a specific type of contract qualifies for the normal purchases and normal sales exception:

(1) *Forward contracts (non-option-based contracts).* Forward contracts are eligible to qualify for the normal purchases and normal sales exception. However, forward ~~c~~con-

---

*The effective notional amount is the stated notional amount adjusted for any leverage factor.

[5]FASB Concepts Statement No. 5, *Recognition and Measurement in Financial Statements of Business Enterprises,* states that assets that are readily convertible to cash "have (i) interchangeable (fungible) units and (ii) quoted prices available in an active market that can rapidly absorb the quantity held by the entity without significantly affecting the price" (paragraph 83(a)). For contracts that involve multiple deliveries of the asset, the phrase *in an active market that can rapidly absorb the quantity held by the entity* should be applied separately to the expected quantity in each delivery.

tracts that contain net settlement provisions as described in either paragraphs 9(a) ~~and~~or paragraph 9(b) are not eligible ~~may qualify~~ for the normal purchases and normal sales exception ~~unless~~if it is probable at inception and throughout the term of the individual contract that the contract will not settle net and will result in physical delivery.* Net settlement (as described in paragraphs 9(a) and 9(b)) of contracts in a group of contracts similarly designated as normal purchases and normal sales would call into question the classification of all such contracts as normal purchases or normal sales. Contracts that require cash settlements of gains or losses or are otherwise settled net on a periodic basis, including individual contracts that are part of a series of sequential contracts intended to accomplish ultimate acquisition or sale of a commodity, do not qualify for this exception.

(2) *Freestanding option contracts.* Option contracts that would require delivery of the related asset at an established price under the contract only if exercised are not eligible to qualify for the normal purchases and normal sales exception, except as indicated in paragraph 10(b)(4) below.

(3) *Forward contracts that contain optionality features.* Forward contracts that contain optionality features that do not modify the quantity of the asset to be delivered under the contract are eligible to qualify for the normal purchases and normal sales exception. Except for power purchase or sales agreements addressed in paragraph 10(b)(4), if an option component permits modification of the quantity of the assets to be delivered, the contract is not eligible for the normal purchases and normal sales exception, unless the option component permits the holder only to purchase or sell additional quantities at the market price at the date of delivery. In order for forward contracts that contain optionality features to qualify for the normal purchases and normal sales exception, the criteria discussed in paragraph 10(b)(1) must be met.

(4) *Power purchase or sales agreements.* Notwithstanding the criteria in paragraphs 10(b)(1) and 10(b)(3), a power purchase or sales agreement (whether a forward contract, option contract, or a combination of both) that is a **capacity contract** also qualifies for the normal purchases and normal sales exception if it meets the criteria in paragraph 58(b).

However, contracts that have a price based on an underlying that is not clearly and closely related to the asset being sold or purchased (such as a price in a contract for the sale of a grain commodity based in part on changes in the S&P index) or that are denominated in a foreign currency that meets ~~neither~~none of the criteria in paragraphs 15(a) ~~and 15(b)~~–15(d) shall not be considered normal purchases and normal sales. For contracts that qualify for the normal purchases and normal sales exception, the entity shall document the designation of the contract as a normal purchase or normal sale. For contracts that qualify for the normal purchases and normal sales exception under paragraphs 10(b)(1) and 10(b)(3), the entity shall document the basis for concluding that it is probable that the contract will not settle net and will result in physical delivery. For contracts that qualify for the normal purchases and normal sales exception under paragraph 10(b)(4), the entity shall document the basis for concluding that the agreement meets the criteria in paragraph 58(b). The documentation requirements can be applied either to groups of similarly designated contracts or to each individual contract. Failure to comply with the documentation requirements precludes application of the normal purchases and normal sales exception to contracts that would otherwise qualify for that exception.

c. *Certain insurance contracts.* Generally, contracts of the type that are within the scope of FASB Statements No. 60, *Accounting and Reporting by Insurance Enterprises,* No. 97, *Accounting and Reporting by Insurance Enterprises for Certain Long-Duration Contracts and for Realized Gains and Losses from the Sale of Investments,* and No. 113, *Accounting and Reporting for Reinsurance of Short-Duration and Long-Duration Contracts,* are not subject to the requirements of this Statement whether or not they are written by insurance enterprises. That is, a contract is not subject to the requirements of this Statement if it entitles the holder to be compensated only if, as a result of an identifiable insurable event (other

---

*Contracts that are subject to unplanned netting (referred to as a "book out" in the electricity utility industry) do not qualify for this exception except as specified in paragraph 58(b).

than a change in price), the holder incurs a liability or there is an adverse change in the value of a specific asset or liability for which the holder is at risk. The following types of contracts written by insurance enterprises or held by the insureds are not subject to the requirements of this Statement for the reasons given:

(1) *Traditional life insurance contracts.* The payment of death benefits is the result of an identifiable insurable event (death of the insured) instead of changes in a variable.

(2) *Traditional property and casualty contracts.* The payment of benefits is the result of an identifiable insurable event (for example, theft or fire) instead of changes in a variable.

However, insurance enterprises enter into other types of contracts that may be subject to the provisions of this Statement. In addition, some contracts with insurance or other enterprises combine derivative instruments, as defined in this Statement, with other insurance products or nonderivative contracts, for example, indexed annuity contracts, variable life insurance contracts, and property and casualty contracts that combine traditional coverages with foreign currency options. Contracts that consist of both derivative portions and nonderivative portions are addressed in paragraph 12.

d. ~~Certain~~ Financial guarantee contracts. Financial guarantee contracts are not subject to this Statement only if:

(1) ~~t~~They provide for payments to be made ~~only~~ solely to reimburse the guaranteed party for failure of the debtor to satisfy its required payment obligations under a nonderivative contract, either at pre-specified payment dates or accelerated payment dates as a result of the occurrence of an event of default (as defined in the financial obligation covered by the guarantee contract) or notice of acceleration being made to the debtor by the creditor.

(2) Payment under the financial guarantee contract is made only if the debtor's obligation to make payments as a result of conditions as described in (1) above is past due.

(3) The guaranteed party is, as a precondition in the contract (or in the back-to-back arrangement, if applicable) for receiving payment of any claim under the guarantee, exposed to the risk of nonpayment both at inception of the financial guarantee contract and throughout its term either through direct legal ownership of the guaranteed obligation or through a back-to-back arrangement with another party that is required by the back-to-back arrangement to maintain direct ownership of the guaranteed obligation.~~a loss incurred because the debtor fails to pay when payment is due, which is an identifiable insurable event.~~

In contrast, financial guarantee contracts are subject to this Statement if they do not meet all of the above three criteria, for example, if they provide for payments to be made in response to changes in another underlying ~~(for example,~~ such as a decrease in a specified debtor's creditworthiness~~)~~.

e. *Certain contracts that are not traded on an exchange.* Contracts that are not exchange-traded are not subject to the requirements of this Statement if the underlying on which the settlement is based is one of the following:

(1) A climatic or geological variable or other physical variable

(2) The price or value of (a) a nonfinancial asset of one of the parties to the contract provided that the asset is not readily convertible to cash or (b) a nonfinancial liability of one of the parties to the contract provided that the liability does not require delivery of an asset that is readily convertible to cash

(3) Specified volumes of sales or service revenues of one of the parties to the contract.

If a contract has more than one underlying and some, but not all, of them qualify for one of the exceptions in paragraphs 10(e)(1), 10(e)(2), and 10(e)(3), the application of this Statement to that contract depends on its predominant characteristics. That is, the contract is subject to the requirements of this Statement if all of its underlyings, considered in combination, behave in a manner that is highly correlated with the behavior of any of the component variables that do not qualify for an exception.

f. *Derivatives that serve as impediments to sales accounting.* A derivative instrument (whether freestanding or embedded in another contract) whose existence serves as an impediment to recognizing a related contract as a sale by one party or a purchase by the counterparty is not subject to this Statement. For example, the existence of a guarantee of the residual value of a leased asset by the lessor may be an impediment to treating a contract as a sales-type lease, in which case the contract would be treated by the lessor as an operating lease. Another example is the existence of a call option enabling a transferor to repurchase transferred assets that is an impediment to sales accounting under FASB Statement No. 140, *Accounting for Transfers and Servicing of Financial Assets and Extinguishments of Liabilities.*

g. *Investments in life insurance.* A policyholder's investment in a life insurance contract that is accounted for under FASB Technical Bulletin No. 85-4, *Accounting for Purchases of Life Insurance,* is not subject to this Statement. The exception in this subparagraph affects only the accounting by the policyholder; it does not affect the accounting by the issuer of the life insurance contract.

h. *Certain investment contracts.* A contract that is accounted for under either paragraph 4 of FASB Statement No. 110, *Reporting by Defined Benefit Pension Plans of Investment Contracts,* or paragraph 12 of FASB Statement No. 35, *Accounting and Reporting by Defined Benefit Pension Plans,* as amended by Statement 110, is not subject to this Statement. Similarly, a contract that is accounted for under either paragraph 4 or paragraph 5 of AICPA Statement of Position 94-4, *Reporting of Investment Contracts Held by Health and Welfare Benefit Plans and Defined-Contribution Pension Plans,* is not subject to this Statement. Those exceptions apply only to the party that accounts for the contract under Statement 35, Statement 110, or SOP 94-4.

i. *Loan commitments.* The holder of any commitment to originate a loan (that is, the potential borrower) is not subject to the requirements of this Statement. Issuers of commitments to originate mortgage loans that will be held for investment purposes, as discussed in paragraphs 21 and 25 of Statement 65, are not subject to this Statement. In addition, issuers of loan commitments to originate other types of loans (that is, other than mortgage loans) are not subject to the requirements of this Statement.

13. For purposes of applying the provisions of paragraph 12, an embedded derivative instrument in which the underlying is an interest rate or interest rate index[6] that alters net interest payments that otherwise

would be paid or received on an interest-bearing host contract is considered to be clearly and closely related to the host contract unless either of the following conditions exist:

a. The hybrid instrument can contractually be settled in such a way that the investor (holder) would not recover *substantially all* of its initial recorded investment.[*]

b. The embedded derivative meets both of the following conditions:

(1) There is a possible future interest rate scenario (even though it may be remote) under which the embedded derivative would~~could~~ at least double the investor's initial rate of return on the host contract.

(2) For each of the possible interest rate scenarios under which the investor's initial rate of return on the host contract would be doubled (as discussed under paragraph 13(b)(1)), the embedded derivative would at the same time~~and could also~~ result in a rate of return that is at least twice what otherwise would be the then-current market return (under each of those future interest rate scenarios) for a contract that has the same terms as the host contract and that involves a debtor with a ~~similar~~ credit quality similar to the issuer's credit quality at inception.

Even though the above conditions focus on the investor's rate of return and the investor's recovery of its investment, the existence of either of those conditions would result in the embedded derivative instrument not being considered clearly and closely related to the host contract by both parties to the hybrid instrument. Because the existence of those conditions is assessed at the date that the hybrid instrument is acquired (or incurred) by the reporting entity, the acquirer of a hybrid instrument in the secondary market could potentially reach a different conclusion than could the issuer of the hybrid instrument due to applying the conditions in this paragraph at different points in time.

15. An embedded foreign currency derivative instrument shall *not* be separated from the host contract

---

[6]Examples are an interest rate cap or an interest rate collar. An embedded derivative instrument that alters net interest payments based on changes in a stock price index (or another non-interest-rate index) is not addressed in paragraph 13.

[*]The condition in paragraph 13(a) does not apply to a situation in which the terms of a hybrid instrument permit, but do not require, the investor to settle the hybrid instrument in a manner that causes it not to recover substantially all of its initial recorded investment, provided that the issuer does not have the contractual right to demand a settlement that causes the investor not to recover substantially all of its initial net investment.

and considered a derivative instrument under paragraph 12 if the host contract is not a financial instrument and it requires payment(s) denominated in (a) the functional currency of ~~the primary economic environment in which~~ any substantial party to that contract, ~~operates (that is, its functional currency) or~~ (b) the currency in which the price of the related good or service that is acquired or delivered is routinely denominated in international commerce (for example, the U.S. dollar for crude oil transactions),* (c) the local currency of any substantial party to the contract, or (d) the currency used by a substantial party to the contract as if it were the functional currency because the primary economic environment in which the party operates is highly inflationary (as discussed in paragraph 11 of Statement 52). The evaluation of whether a contract qualifies for the exception in this paragraph should be performed only at inception of the contract. Unsettled foreign currency transactions, including financial instruments, that are monetary items and have their principal payments, interest payments, or both denominated in a foreign currency are subject to the requirement in Statement 52 to recognize any foreign currency transaction gain or loss in earnings and shall not be considered to contain embedded foreign currency derivative instruments under this Statement. The same proscription applies to available-for-sale or trading securities that have cash flows denominated in a foreign currency.

Recognition of Derivatives and Measurement of Derivatives and Hedged Items

17. An entity shall recognize all of its derivative instruments in its statement of financial position as either assets or liabilities depending on the rights or obligations under the contracts. All derivative instruments shall be measured at fair value. The guidance in FASB Statement No. 107, *Disclosures about Fair Value of Financial Instruments,* as amended, shall apply in determining the fair value of a financial instrument (derivative or hedged item). If expected future cash flows are used to estimate fair value, those expected cash flows[†] shall be the best estimate based on reasonable and supportable assumptions and projections. All available evidence shall be considered in developing estimates of expected future cash flows. The weight given to the evidence shall be

commensurate with the extent to which the evidence can be verified objectively. If a range is estimated for either the amount or the timing of possible cash flows, the likelihood of possible outcomes shall be considered in determining the best estimate of future cash flows.

~~19. In this Statement, the *change in the fair value* of an entire financial asset or liability for a period refers to the difference between its fair value at the beginning of the period (or acquisition date) and the end of the period adjusted to exclude (a) changes in fair value due to the passage of time and (b) changes in fair value related to any payments received or made, such as in partially recovering the asset or partially settling the liability.~~

Fair Value Hedges

General

20. An entity may designate a derivative instrument as hedging the exposure to changes in the fair value of an asset or a liability or an identified portion thereof ("hedged item") that is attributable to a particular risk. Designated hedging instruments and hedged items qualify for fair value hedge accounting if all of the following criteria and those in paragraph 21 are met:

a. At inception of the hedge, there is formal documentation of the hedging relationship and the entity's risk management objective and strategy for undertaking the hedge, including identification of the hedging instrument, the hedged item, the nature of the risk being hedged, and how the hedging instrument's effectiveness in offsetting the exposure to changes in the hedged item's fair value attributable to the hedged risk will be assessed. There must be a reasonable basis for how the entity plans to assess the hedging instrument's effectiveness.
   (1) For a fair value hedge of a firm commitment, the entity's formal documentation at the inception of the hedge must include a reasonable method for recognizing in earnings the asset or liability representing the gain or loss on the hedged firm commitment.

---

*If similar transactions for a certain product or service are routinely denominated in international commerce in various different currencies, the transaction does not qualify for the exception.

[†]This Statement was issued prior to FASB Concepts Statement No. 7, *Using Cash Flow Information and Present Value in Accounting Measurements,* and therefore the term *expected cash flows* does not necessarily have the same meaning as that term does in Concepts Statement 7.

(2) An entity's defined risk management strategy for a particular hedging relationship may exclude certain components of a specific hedging derivative's change in fair value, such as time value, from the assessment of hedge effectiveness, as discussed in paragraph 63 in Section 2 of Appendix A.

b. Both at inception of the hedge and on an ongoing basis, the hedging relationship is expected to be highly effective in achieving offsetting changes in fair value attributable to the hedged risk during the period that the hedge is designated. An assessment of effectiveness is required whenever financial statements or earnings are reported, and at least every three months. If the hedging instrument (such as an at-the-money option contract) provides only one-sided offset of the hedged risk, the increases (or decreases) in the fair value of the hedging instrument must be expected to be highly effective in offsetting the decreases (or increases) in the fair value of the hedged item. All assessments of effectiveness shall be consistent with the risk management strategy documented for that particular hedging relationship (in accordance with paragraph 20(a) above).

c. If a written option is designated as hedging a recognized asset or liability or an unrecognized firm commitment, the combination of the hedged item and the written option provides at least as much potential for gains as a result of a favorable change in the fair value of the combined instruments[7] as exposure to losses from an unfavorable change in their combined fair value. That test is met if all possible percentage favorable changes in the underlying (from zero percent to 100 percent) would provide at least as much gain as the loss that would be incurred from an unfavorable change in the underlying of the same percentage.

(1) A combination of options (for example, an interest rate collar) entered into contemporaneously shall be considered a written option if either at inception or over the life of the contracts a net premium is received in cash or as a favorable rate or other term. (Thus, a collar can be designated as a hedging instrument in a fair value hedge without regard to the test in paragraph 20(c) unless a net premium is received.) Furthermore, a derivative instrument that results from combining a written option and any other nonoption derivative shall be considered a written option.

A nonderivative instrument, such as a Treasury note, shall not be designated as a hedging instrument, except as provided in paragraphs 37 and 42 of this Statement.

The hedged item

21. An asset or a liability is eligible for designation as a hedged item in a fair value hedge if all of the following criteria are met:

a. The hedged item is specifically identified as either all or a specific portion of a recognized asset or liability or of an unrecognized firm commitment.[8] The hedged item is a single asset or liability (or a specific portion thereof) or is a portfolio of similar assets or a portfolio of similar liabilities (or a specific portion thereof).

(1) If similar assets or similar liabilities are aggregated and hedged as a portfolio, the individual assets or individual liabilities must share the risk exposure for which they are designated as being hedged. The change in fair value attributable to the hedged risk for each individual item in a hedged portfolio must be expected to respond in a generally proportionate manner to the overall change in fair value of the aggregate portfolio attributable to the hedged risk. That is, if the change in fair value of a hedged portfolio attributable to the hedged risk was 10 percent during a reporting period, the change in the fair values attributable to the hedged risk for each item constituting the portfolio should be expected to be within a fairly narrow range, such as 9 percent to 11 percent. In contrast, an expec-

---

[7]The reference to *combined instruments* refers to the written option and the hedged item, such as an embedded purchased option.

[8]A firm commitment (as defined in paragraph 540) that represents an asset or liability that a specific accounting standard prohibits recognizing (such as a noncancelable operating lease or an unrecognized mortgage servicing right) may nevertheless be designated as the hedged item in a fair value hedge. A mortgage banker's unrecognized "interest rate lock commitment" (IRLC) does not qualify as a firm commitment (because as an option it does not obligate both parties) and thus is not eligible for fair value hedge accounting as the hedged item. (However, a mortgage banker's "forward sale commitments," which are derivatives that lock in the prices at which the mortgage loans will be sold to investors, may qualify as hedging instruments in cash flow hedges of the forecasted sales of mortgage loans.) A supply contract for which the contract price is fixed only in certain circumstances (such as when the selling price is above an embedded price cap or below an embedded price floor) meets the definition of a firm commitment for purposes of designating the hedged item in a fair value hedge. Provided the embedded price cap or floor is considered clearly and closely related to the host contract and therefore is not accounted for separately under paragraph 12, either party to the supply contract can hedge the fair value exposure arising from the cap or floor.

tation that the change in fair value attributable to the hedged risk for individual items in the portfolio would range from 7 percent to 13 percent would be inconsistent with this provision. In aggregating loans in a portfolio to be hedged, an entity may choose to consider some of the following characteristics, as appropriate: loan type, loan size, nature and location of collateral, interest rate type (fixed or variable) and the coupon interest rate (if fixed), scheduled maturity, prepayment history of the loans (if seasoned), and expected prepayment performance in varying interest rate scenarios.[9]

(2) If the hedged item is a specific portion of an asset or liability (or of a portfolio of similar assets or a portfolio of similar liabilities), the hedged item is one of the following:

(a) A percentage of the entire asset or liability (or of the entire portfolio)

(b) One or more selected contractual cash flows (such as the portion of the asset or liability representing the present value of the interest payments in the first two years of a four-year debt instrument)

(c) A put option; or a call option; (including an interest rate or price cap; or an interest rate or price floor) embedded in an existing asset or liability that is not an embedded derivative accounted for separately pursuant to paragraph 12 of this Statement

(d) The residual value in a lessor's net investment in a direct financing or sales-type lease.

If the entire asset or liability is an instrument with variable cash flows, the hedged item cannot be deemed to be an implicit fixed-to-variable swap (or similar instrument) perceived to be embedded in a host contract with fixed cash flows.

b. The hedged item presents an exposure to changes in fair value attributable to the hedged risk that could affect reported earnings. The reference to affecting reported earnings does not apply to an entity that does not report earnings as a separate caption in a statement of financial performance, such as a not-for-profit organization, as discussed in paragraph 43.

c. The hedged item is not (1) an asset or liability that is remeasured with the changes in fair value attributable to the hedged risk reported currently in earnings, (2) an investment accounted for by the equity method in accordance with the requirements of APB Opinion No. 18, *The Equity Method of Accounting for Investments in Common Stock,* (3) a minority interest in one or more consolidated subsidiaries, (4) an equity investment in a consolidated subsidiary, (5) a firm commitment either to enter into a business combination or to acquire or dispose of a subsidiary, a minority interest, or an equity method investee, or (6) an equity instrument issued by the entity and classified in stockholders' equity in the statement of financial position.

d. If the hedged item is all or a portion of a debt security (or a portfolio of similar debt securities) that is classified as held-to-maturity in accordance with FASB Statement No. 115, *Accounting for Certain Investments in Debt and Equity Securities,* the designated risk being hedged is the risk of changes in its fair value attributable to credit risk, foreign exchange risk, or both. If the hedged item is an option component of a held-to-maturity security that permits its prepayment, the designated risk being hedged is the risk of changes in the entire fair value of that option component. (The designated hedged risk for a held-to-maturity security may not be the risk of changes in its fair value attributable to interest rate risk. If the hedged item is other than an option component that permits its prepayment, the designated hedged risk also may not be the risk of changes in its overall fair value.)

e. If the hedged item is a nonfinancial asset or liability (other than a recognized loan servicing right or a nonfinancial firm commitment with financial components), the designated risk being hedged is the risk of changes in the fair value of the entire hedged asset or liability (reflecting its actual location if a physical asset). That is, the price risk of a similar asset in a different location or of a major ingredient may not be the hedged risk. Thus, in hedging the exposure to changes in the fair value of gasoline, an entity may not designate the risk of changes in the price of crude oil as the risk being hedged for purposes of determining effectiveness of the fair value hedge of gasoline.

---

[9]Mortgage bankers and other servicers of financial assets that designate a hedged portfolio by aggregating servicing rights within one or more risk strata used under paragraph 63(g) of Statement 140 would not necessarily comply with the requirement in this paragraph for portfolios of similar assets. The risk stratum under paragraph 63(g) of Statement 140 can be based on any predominant risk characteristic, including date of origination or geographic location.

f. If the hedged item is a financial asset or liability, a recognized loan servicing right, or a nonfinancial firm commitment with financial components, the designated risk being hedged is:

    (1) The risk of changes in the overall fair value of the entire hedged item,

    (2) The risk of changes in its fair value attributable to changes in the **designated benchmark interest rate** (referred to as interest rate risk),

    (3) The risk of changes in its fair value attributable to changes in the related foreign currency exchange rates (referred to as foreign exchange risk) (refer to paragraphs 37, 37A, and 38), or

    (4) The risk of changes in its fair value attributable to both changes in the obligor's creditworthiness and changes in the spread over the benchmark interest rate with respect to the hedged item's credit sector at inception of the hedge (referred to as credit risk).

If the risk designated as being hedged is not the risk in paragraph 21(f)(1) above, two or more of the other risks (interest rate risk, foreign currency exchange risk, and credit risk) may simultaneously be designated as being hedged. The benchmark interest rate being hedged in a hedge of interest rate risk must be specifically identified as part of the designation and documentation at the inception of the hedging relationship. Ordinarily, an entity should designate the same benchmark interest rate as the risk being hedged for similar hedges, consistent with paragraph 62; the use of different benchmark interest rates for similar hedges should be rare and must be justified. In calculating the change in the hedged item's fair value attributable to changes in the benchmark interest rate, the estimated cash flows used in calculating fair value must be based on all of the contractual cash flows of the entire hedged item. Excluding some of the hedged item's contractual cash flows (for example, the portion of the interest coupon in excess of the benchmark interest rate) from the calculation is not permitted.* An entity may not simply designate prepayment risk as the risk being hedged for a financial asset. However, it can designate the option component

of a prepayable instrument as the hedged item in a fair value hedge of the entity's exposure to changes in the overall fair value of that "prepayment" option, perhaps thereby achieving the objective of its desire to hedge prepayment risk. The effect of an embedded derivative of the same risk class must be considered in designating a hedge of an individual risk. For example, the effect of an embedded prepayment option must be considered in designating a hedge of interest rate risk.

Impairment

27. An asset or liability that has been designated as being hedged and accounted for pursuant to paragraphs 22–24 remains subject to the applicable requirements in generally accepted accounting principles for assessing impairment for that type of asset or for recognizing an increased obligation for that type of liability. Those impairment requirements shall be applied after hedge accounting has been applied for the period and the carrying amount of the hedged asset or liability has been adjusted pursuant to paragraph 22 of this Statement. Because the hedging instrument is recognized separately as an asset or liability, its fair value or expected cash flows† shall not be considered in applying those impairment requirements to the hedged asset or liability.

Cash Flow Hedges

General

28. An entity may designate a derivative instrument as hedging the exposure to variability in expected future cash flows that is attributable to a particular risk. That exposure may be associated with an existing recognized asset or liability (such as all or certain future interest payments on variable-rate debt) or a forecasted transaction (such as a forecasted purchase or sale).[10] Designated hedging instruments and hedged items or transactions qualify for cash flow hedge accounting if all of the following criteria and those in paragraph 29 are met:

a. At inception of the hedge, there is formal documentation of the hedging relationship and the entity's risk management objective and strategy for

---

*The first sentence of paragraph 21(a) that specifically permits the hedged item to be identified as either all or a specific portion of a recognized asset or liability or of an unrecognized firm commitment is not affected by the provisions in this subparagraph.

†Refer to footnote* to paragraph 17 of Statement 133.

[10]For purposes of paragraphs 28–35, the individual cash flows related to a recognized asset or liability and the cash flows related to a forecasted transaction are both referred to as a *forecasted transaction* or *hedged transaction*.

undertaking the hedge, including identification of the hedging instrument, the hedged transaction, the nature of the risk being hedged, and how the hedging instrument's effectiveness in hedging the exposure to the hedged transaction's variability in cash flows attributable to the hedged risk will be assessed. There must be a reasonable basis for how the entity plans to assess the hedging instrument's effectiveness.

(1) An entity's defined risk management strategy for a particular hedging relationship may exclude certain components of a specific hedging derivative's change in fair value from the assessment of hedge effectiveness, as discussed in paragraph 63 in Section 2 of Appendix A.

(2) Documentation shall include all relevant details, including the date on or period within which the forecasted transaction is expected to occur, the specific nature of asset or liability involved (if any), and the expected currency amount or quantity of the forecasted transaction.

   (a) The phrase *expected currency amount* refers to hedges of foreign currency exchange risk and requires specification of the exact amount of foreign currency being hedged.

   (b) The phrase *expected . . . quantity* refers to hedges of other risks and requires specification of the physical quantity (that is, the number of items or units of measure) encompassed by the hedged forecasted transaction. If a forecasted sale or purchase is being hedged for price risk, the hedged transaction cannot be specified solely in terms of expected currency amounts, nor can it be specified as a percentage of sales or purchases during a period. The current price of a forecasted transaction also should be identified to satisfy the criterion in paragraph 28(b) for offsetting cash flows.

The hedged forecasted transaction shall be described with sufficient specificity so that when a transaction occurs, it is clear whether that transaction is or is not the hedged transaction. Thus, the forecasted transaction could be identified as the sale of either the first 15,000 units of a specific product sold during a specified 3-month period or the first 5,000 units of a specific product sold in each of 3 specific months, but it could not be identi-

fied as the sale of the last 15,000 units of that product sold during a 3-month period (because the last 15,000 units cannot be identified when they occur, but only when the period has ended).

b. Both at inception of the hedge and on an ongoing basis, the hedging relationship is expected to be highly effective in achieving offsetting cash flows attributable to the hedged risk during the term of the hedge, except as indicated in paragraph 28(d) below. An assessment of effectiveness is required whenever financial statements or earnings are reported, and at least every three months. If the hedging instrument, such as an at-the-money option contract, provides only one-sided offset against the hedged risk, the cash inflows (outflows) from the hedging instrument must be expected to be highly effective in offsetting the corresponding change in the cash outflows or inflows of the hedged transaction. All assessments of effectiveness shall be consistent with the originally documented risk management strategy for that particular hedging relationship.

c. If a written option is designated as hedging the variability in cash flows for a recognized asset or liability or an unrecognized firm commitment, the combination of the hedged item and the written option provides at least as much potential for favorable cash flows as exposure to unfavorable cash flows. That test is met if all possible percentage favorable changes in the underlying (from zero percent to 100 percent) would provide at least as much favorable cash flows as the unfavorable cash flows that would be incurred from an unfavorable change in the underlying of the same percentage. (Refer to paragraph 20(c)(1).)

d. If a hedging instrument is used to modify the interest receipts or payments associated with a recognized financial asset or liability from one variable rate to another variable rate, the hedging instrument must be a link between an existing designated asset (or group of similar assets) with variable cash flows and an existing designated liability (or group of similar liabilities) with variable cash flows and be highly effective at achieving offsetting cash flows. A link exists if the basis (that is, the rate index on which the interest rate is based) of one leg of an interest rate swap is the same as the basis of the interest receipts for the designated asset and the basis of the other leg of the swap is the same as the basis of the interest payments for the designated liability. In this situation, the criterion in the first sentence in paragraph 29(a) is applied separately to the designated asset and the designated liability.

A nonderivative instrument, such as a Treasury note, shall not be designated as a hedging instrument for a cash flow hedge.

30. The effective portion of the gain or loss on a derivative designated as a cash flow hedge is reported in other comprehensive income, and the ineffective portion is reported in earnings. More specifically, a qualifying cash flow hedge shall be accounted for as follows:

a. If an entity's defined risk management strategy for a particular hedging relationship excludes a specific component of the gain or loss, or related cash flows, on the hedging derivative from the assessment of hedge effectiveness (as discussed in paragraph 63 in Section 2 of Appendix A), that excluded component of the gain or loss shall be recognized currently in earnings. For example, if the effectiveness of a hedge with an option contract is assessed based on changes in the option's intrinsic value, the changes in the option's time value would be recognized in earnings. Time value is equal to the fair value of the option less its intrinsic value.

b. Accumulated other comprehensive income associated with the hedged transaction shall be adjusted to a balance that reflects the *lesser* of the following (in absolute amounts):

  (1) The cumulative gain or loss on the derivative from inception of the hedge less (a) the excluded component discussed in paragraph 30(a) above and (b) the derivative's gains or losses previously reclassified from accumulated other comprehensive income into earnings pursuant to paragraph 31.

  (2) The portion of the cumulative gain or loss on the derivative necessary to offset the cumulative change in expected future cash flows on the hedged transactionfrom inception of the hedge less the derivative's gains or losses previously reclassified from accumulated other comprehensive income into earnings pursuant to paragraph 31.

That adjustment of accumulated other comprehensive income shall incorporate recognition in other comprehensive income of part or all of the gain or loss on the hedging derivative, as necessary.

c. A gain or loss shall be recognized in earnings, as necessary, for any remaining gain or loss on the hedging derivative or to adjust other comprehensive income to the balance specified in paragraph 30(b) above.

d. If a non-option-based contract is the hedging instrument ~~I~~in a cash flow hedge of the variability of the functional-currency-equivalent cash flows for a recognized foreign-currency-denominated asset or liability that is remeasured at spot exchange rates under paragraph 15 of Statement 52, an amount that will offset the related transaction gain or loss arising from ~~the~~that remeasurement ~~and adjust earnings for the cost to the purchaser (income to the seller) of the hedging instrument~~ shall be reclassified each period from other comprehensive income to earnings if the assessment of effectiveness and measurement of ineffectiveness are based on total changes in the non-option-based instrument's cash flows. If an option contract is used as the hedging instrument in a cash flow hedge of the variability of the functional-currency-equivalent cash flows for a recognized foreign-currency-denominated asset or liability that is remeasured at spot exchange rates under paragraph 15 of Statement 52 to provide only one-sided offset against the hedged foreign exchange risk, an amount shall be reclassified each period to or from other comprehensive income with respect to the changes in the underlying that result in a change in the hedging option's intrinsic value. In addition, if the assessment of effectiveness and measurement of ineffectiveness are also based on total changes in the option's cash flows (that is, the assessment will include the hedging instrument's entire change in fair value—its entire gain or loss), an amount that adjusts earnings for the amortization of the cost of the option on a rational basis shall be reclassified each period from other comprehensive income to earnings.*

Section 2 of Appendix A illustrates assessing hedge effectiveness and measuring hedge ineffectiveness. Examples 6 and 9 of Section 1 of Appendix B illustrate the application of this paragraph.

---

*The guidance in this subparagraph is limited to foreign currency hedging relationships because of their unique attributes. That accounting guidance is an exception for foreign currency hedging relationships.

34. Existing requirements in generally accepted accounting principles for assessing asset impairment or recognizing an increased obligation apply to an asset or liability that gives rise to variable cash flows (such as a variable-rate financial instrument), for which the variable cash flows (the forecasted transactions) have been designated as being hedged and accounted for pursuant to paragraphs 30 and 31. Those impairment requirements shall be applied each period after hedge accounting has been applied for the period, pursuant to paragraphs 30 and 31 of this Statement. The fair value or expected cash flows[†] of a hedging instrument shall not be considered in applying those requirements. The gain or loss on the hedging instrument in accumulated other comprehensive income shall, however, be accounted for as discussed in paragraph 31.

Reporting Cash Flows of Derivative Instruments That Contain Financing Elements

45A. An instrument accounted for as a derivative under this Statement that at its inception includes off-market terms, or requires an up-front cash payment, or both often contains a financing element. Identifying a financing element within a derivative instrument is a matter of judgment that depends on facts and circumstances. If an other-than-insignificant financing element is present at inception, other than a financing element inherently included in an at-the-market derivative instrument with no prepayments (that is, the forward points in an at-the-money forward contract),[*] then the borrower shall report all cash inflows and outflows associated with that derivative instrument in a manner consistent with financing activities as described in paragraphs 18–20 of FASB Statement No. 95, *Statement of Cash Flows.*

Effective Date and Transition

49. At the date of initial application, an entity shall recognize all freestanding derivative instruments (that is, derivative instruments other than embedded derivative instruments) in the statement of financial position as either assets or liabilities and measure them at fair value, pursuant to paragraph 17.[13] The difference between a derivative's previous carrying amount and its fair value shall be reported as a transition adjustment, as discussed in paragraph 52. The entity also shall recognize offsetting gains and losses on hedged assets, liabilities, and firm commitments by adjusting their carrying amounts at that date, as discussed in paragraph 52(b). Any gains or losses on derivative instruments that are reported independently as deferred gains or losses (that is, liabilities or assets) in the statement of financial position at the date of initial application shall be derecognized from that statement; that derecognition also shall be reported as transition adjustments as indicated in paragraph 52. Any gains or losses on derivative instruments reported in other comprehensive income at the date of initial application because the derivative instruments were hedging the fair value exposure of available-for-sale securities also shall be reported as transition adjustments; the offsetting losses and gains on the securities shall be accounted for pursuant to paragraph 52(b). Any gain or loss on a derivative instrument reported in accumulated other comprehensive income at the date of initial application because the derivative instrument was hedging the *variable cash flow exposure* of a forecasted (anticipated) transaction related to an available-for-sale security shall remain in accumulated other comprehensive income and shall *not* be reported as a transition adjustment. The accounting for any gains and losses on derivative instruments that arose prior to the initial

---

[†]Refer to footnote* to paragraph 17 of Statement 133.

[*]An at-the-money plain-vanilla interest rate swap that involves no payments between the parties at inception would not be considered as having a financing element present at inception even though, due to the implicit forward rates derived from the yield curve, the parties to the contract have an expectation that the comparison of the fixed and floating legs will result in payments being made by one party in the earlier periods and being made by the counterparty in the later periods of the swap's term. If a derivative instrument is an at-the-money or out-of-the-money option contract or contains an at-the-money or out-of-the-money option contract, a payment made at inception to the writer of the option for the option's time value by the counterparty should not be viewed as evidence that the derivative instrument contains a financing element. In contrast, if the contractual terms of a derivative have been structured to *ensure* that net payments will be made by one party in the earlier periods and subsequently returned by the counterparty in the later periods of the derivative's term, that derivative instrument should be viewed as containing a financing element even if the derivative has a fair value of zero at inception.

[13]For a compound derivative that has a foreign currency exchange risk component (such as a foreign currency interest rate swap), an entity is permitted at the date of initial application to separate the compound derivative into two parts: the foreign currency derivative and the remaining derivative. Each of them would thereafter be accounted for at fair value, with an overall limit that the sum of their fair values could not exceed the fair value of the compound derivative. An entity may not separate a compound derivative into components representing different risks after the date of initial application.

application of the Statement and that were previously added to the carrying amount of recognized hedged assets or liabilities is not affected by this Statement. Those gains and losses shall not be included in the transition adjustment.*

IMPLEMENTATION GUIDANCE

Section 1: Scope and Definition

Application of Paragraphs 6–11

57. The following discussion further explains the three characteristics of a derivative instrument discussed in paragraphs 6–9.

a. *Underlying.* An underlying is a variable that, along with either a notional amount or a payment provision, determines the settlement of a derivative. An underlying usually is one or a combination of the following:

   (1) A security price or security price index
   (2) A commodity price or commodity price index
   (3) An interest rate or interest rate index
   (4) A credit rating or credit index
   (5) An exchange rate or exchange rate index
   (6) An insurance index or catastrophe loss index
   (7) A climatic or geological condition (such as temperature, earthquake severity, or rainfall), another physical variable, or a related index.

   However, an underlying may be any variable whose changes are observable or otherwise objectively verifiable. Paragraph 10(e) specifically excludes a contract with settlement based on certain variables unless the contract is exchange-traded. A contract based on any variable that is not specifically excluded is subject to the requirements of this Statement if it has the other two characteristics identified in paragraph 6 (which also are discussed in paragraph 57(b) and paragraph 57(c) below).

b. *Initial net investment.* A derivative requires no initial net investment or a smaller initial net investment than other types of contracts that have a similar response to changes in market factors. For example, entering into a commodity futures contract generally requires no net investment, while purchasing the same commodity requires an initial net investment equal to its market price. However, both contracts reflect changes in the price of the commodity in the same way (that is, similar gains or losses will be incurred). A swap or forward contract also generally does not require an initial net investment unless the terms favor one party over the other. An option generally requires that one party make an initial net investment (a premium) because that party has the rights under the contract and the other party has the obligations. The phrase *initial net investment* is stated from the perspective of only one party to the contract, but it determines the application of the Statement for both parties.[15]

c. *Net settlement.* A contract that meets any one of the following criteria has the characteristic described as net settlement:

   (1) Its terms implicitly or explicitly require or permit net settlement. For example, a penalty for nonperformance in a purchase order is a net settlement provision if the amount of the penalty is based on changes in the price of the items that are the subject of the contract. Net settlement may be made in cash or by delivery of any other asset, whether or not it is readily convertible to cash. A fixed penalty for nonperformance is not a net settlement provision.

   (2) There is an established market mechanism that facilitates net settlement outside the contract. The term *market mechanism* is to be interpreted broadly. Any institutional arrangement or other agreement that enables either party to be relieved of all rights and obligations under the contract and to liquidate its net

---

*If immediately prior to the application of Statement 133 an entity has a fair value or cash flow hedging relationship in which an intercompany interest rate swap is the hedging instrument and if that relationship would have qualified for the shortcut method under the criteria in paragraph 68 had that swap not been an intercompany transaction, that entity may qualify for applying the shortcut method to a newly designated hedging relationship that is effectively the continuation of the preexisting hedging relationship provided that (a) the post–Statement 133 hedging relationship is hedging the same exposure to interest rate risk (that is, exposure to changes in fair value of the same hedged item or exposure to changes in variable cash flows for the same forecasted transaction) and (b) the hedging instrument is a third-party interest rate swap whose terms exactly match the terms of the intercompany swap with respect to its remaining cash flows. In that case, if the shortcut method is applied to the new hedging relationship upon adoption of Statement 133, the transition adjustment should include the appropriate adjustments at the date of adoption to reflect the retroactive application of the shortcut method.

[15]Even though a contract may be a derivative as described in paragraphs 6–10 for both parties, the exceptions in paragraph 11 apply only to the issuer of the contract and will result in different reporting by the two parties. The exception in paragraph 10(b) also may apply to one of the parties but not the other.

position without incurring a significant transaction cost is considered net settlement. The evaluation of whether a market mechanism exists and whether items to be delivered under a contract are readily convertible to cash must be performed at inception and on an ongoing basis throughout a contract's life.

(3) It requires delivery of an asset that is readily convertible to cash.* The definition of *readily convertible to cash* in FASB Concepts Statement No. 5, *Recognition and Measurement in Financial Statements of Business Enterprises,* includes, for example, a security or commodity traded in an active market and a unit of foreign currency that is readily convertible into the functional currency of the reporting entity. A security that is publicly traded but for which the market is not very active is readily convertible to cash if the number of shares or other units of the security to be exchanged is small relative to the daily transaction volume. That same security would not be readily convertible if the number of shares to be exchanged is large relative to the daily transaction volume. The ability to use a security that is not publicly traded or an agricultural or mineral product without an active market as collateral in a borrowing does not, in and of itself, mean that the security or the commodity is readily convertible to cash. Shares of stock in a publicly traded company to be received upon the exercise of a stock purchase warrant do not meet the characteristic of being readily convertible to cash if both of the following conditions exist: (a) the stock purchase warrant is issued by an entity for only its own stock (or stock of its consolidated subsidiaries) and (b) the sale or transfer of the issued shares is restricted (other than in connection with being pledged as collateral) for a period of 32 days or more from the date the stock purchase warrant is exercised. In contrast, restrictions imposed by a stock purchase warrant on the sale or transfer of shares of stock that are received from the exercise of that warrant issued by an entity for *other* than its own stock (whether those restrictions are for more or less than 32 days) do not affect

the determination of whether those shares are readily convertible to cash. The accounting for restricted stock to be received upon exercise of a stock purchase warrant should not be analogized to any other type of contract.

58. The following discussion further explains some of the exceptions discussed in paragraph 10.

a. *"Regular-way" security trades.* The exception in paragraph 10(a) applies only to a contract that requires delivery of securities that are readily convertible to cash[16] except (1) as provided in paragraph 59(a) for a contract for the purchase or sale of when-issued securities or other securities that do not yet exist and (2) for contracts that are required to be accounted for on a trade-date basis by the reporting entity. To qualify, a contract must require delivery of such a security within the period of time after the trade date that is customary in the market in which the trade takes place. For example, a contract to purchase or sell a publicly traded equity security in the United States customarily requires settlement within three business days. If a contract for purchase of that type of security requires settlement in three business days, the regular-way security trades exception applies, but if the contract requires settlement in five days, the regular-way security trades exception does not apply unless the reporting entity is required to account for the contract on a trade-date basis. This Statement does not change whether an entity recognizes regular-way security trades on the trade date or the settlement date. However, trades that do not qualify for the regular-way exception are subject to the requirements of this Statement regardless of the method an entity uses to report its security trades.

b. *Normal purchases and normal sales.* The exception in paragraph 10(b) applies only to a contract that involves future delivery of assets (other than financial instruments or derivative instruments). To qualify for the exception, a contract's terms also must be consistent with the terms of an entity's normal purchases or normal sales, that is, the quantity purchased or sold must be reasonable in relation to the entity's business needs. Determining whether or not the terms are consistent will require judgment. In making those judgments, an

---

*The evaluation of *readily convertible to cash* shall be applied to a contract throughout its life.

[16]Contracts that require delivery of securities that are not readily convertible to cash (and thus do not permit net settlement) are not subject to the requirements of this Statement unless there is a market mechanism outside the contract to facilitate net settlement (as described in paragraphs 9(b) and 57(c)(2)).

entity should consider all relevant factors, such as (1) the quantities provided under the contract and the entity's need for the related assets, (2) the locations to which delivery of the items will be made, (3) the period of time between entering into the contract and delivery, and (4) the entity's prior practices with regard to such contracts. Evidence such as past trends, expected future demand, other contracts for delivery of similar items, an entity's and industry's customs for acquiring and storing the related commodities, and an entity's operating locations should help in identifying contracts that qualify as normal purchases or normal sales. Also, in order for a contract that meets the net settlement provisions of paragraphs 9(a) and 57(c)(1) and the market mechanism provisions of paragraphs 9(b) and 57(c)(2) to qualify for the exception, it must be probable at inception and throughout the term of the individual contract that the contract will not settle net and will result in physical delivery. Power purchase or sales agreements (whether a forward contract, an option contract, or a combination of both) for the purchase or sale of electricity qualify for the normal purchases and normal sales exception in paragraph 10(b)(4) if all of the following applicable criteria are met:

(1) For both parties to the contract:

    (a) The terms of the contract require physical delivery of electricity. That is, the contract does not permit net settlement, as described in paragraphs 9(a) and 57(c)(1). For an option contract, physical delivery is required if the option contract is exercised.

    (b) The power purchase or sales agreement is a capacity contract.* Differentiating between a capacity contract and a traditional option contract (that is, a financial option on electricity) is a matter of judgment that depends on the facts and circumstances.

(2) For the seller of electricity: The electricity that would be deliverable under the contract involves quantities that are expected to be sold by the reporting entity in the normal course of business.

(3) For the buyer of electricity:

    (a) The electricity that would be deliverable under the contract involves quantities that are expected to be used or sold by the reporting entity in the normal course of business.

    (b) The buyer of the electricity under the power purchase or sales agreement is an entity that is engaged in selling electricity to retail or wholesale customers and is statutorily or otherwise contractually obligated to maintain sufficient capacity to meet electricity needs of its customer base.

    (c) The contracts are entered into to meet the buyer's obligation to maintain a sufficient capacity, including a reasonable reserve margin established by or based on a regulatory commission, local standards, regional reliability councils, or regional transmission organizations.

Power purchase or sales agreements that meet only the above applicable criteria in paragraph 58(b) qualify for the normal purchases and normal sales exception even if they are subject to being booked out or are scheduled to be booked out. Forward contracts for the purchase or sale of electricity that do not meet the above applicable criteria are nevertheless eligible to qualify for the normal purchases and normal sales exception by meeting the criteria in paragraph 10(b) other than paragraph 10(b)(4).

c. *Certain contracts that are not traded on an exchange.* A contract that is not traded on an exchange is not subject to the requirements of this Statement if the underlying is:

(1) A climatic or geological variable or other physical variable. Climatic, geological, and other physical variables include things like the number of inches of rainfall or snow in a particular area and the severity of an earthquake as measured by the Richter scale.

(2) The price or value of (a) a nonfinancial asset of one of the parties to the contract unless that asset is readily convertible to cash or (b) a nonfinancial liability of one of the parties to the contract unless that liability requires delivery of an asset that is readily convertible to cash. This exception applies only to nonfinancial assets that are unique and only if a nonfinancial asset related to the underlying is owned by the party that would *not* benefit *under the contract* from an increase in the price

---

*As defined in paragraph 540.

or value of the nonfinancial asset. If the contract is a call option contract, the exception applies only if that nonfinancial asset is owned by the party that would not benefit under the contract from an increase in the price or value of the nonfinancial asset above the option's strike price.

(3) Specified volumes of sales or service revenues by one of the parties. That exception is intended to apply to contracts with settlements based on the volume of items sold or services rendered, for example, royalty agreements. It is not intended to apply to contracts based on changes in sales or revenues due to changes in market prices.

If a contract's underlying is the combination of two or more variables, and one or more would not qualify for one of the exceptions above, the application of this Statement to that contract depends on the predominant characteristics of the combined variable. The contract is subject to the requirements of this Statement if the changes in its combined underlying are highly correlated with changes in one of the component variables that would not qualify for an exception.

59. The following discussion illustrates the application of paragraphs 6–11 in several situations.

a. *Forward purchases or sales of to-be-announced securities or securities when-issued, as-issued, or if-issuedof when-issued securities or other securities that do not yet exist. A contract for the purchase and sale of a security when, as, or if issued or to be announced is excluded from the requirements of this Statement as a regular-way security trade ifContracts for the purchase or sale of when-issued securities or other securities that do not yet exist are excluded from the requirements of this Statement as a regular-way security trade only if (1) there is no other way to purchase or sell that security, and (2) delivery of that security and settlement will occur within the shortest period possible for that type of security, and (3) it is probable at inception and throughout the term of the individual contract that the contract will not settle net and will result in physical delivery of a security when it is issued. A contract for the purchase or sale of when-issued securities or other securities that do not yet exist is eligible to qualify for the regular-way security trades excep-*tion even though that contract permits net settlement (as discussed in paragraphs 9(a) and 57(c)(1)) or a market mechanism to facilitate net settlement of that contract (as discussed in paragraphs 9(b) and 57(c)(2)) exists. The entity shall document the basis for concluding that it is probable that the contract will not settle net and will result in physical delivery. Net settlement (as described in paragraphs 9(a) and 9(b)) of contracts in a group of contracts similarly designated as regular-way security trades would call into question the continued exemption of such contracts. In addition, if an entity is required to account for a contract for the purchase or sale of when-issued securities or other securities that do not yet exist on a trade-date basis, rather than a settlement-date basis, and thus recognizes the acquisition or disposition of the securities at the inception of the contract, that entity shall apply the regular-way security trades exception to those contracts.

b. *Credit-indexed contracts (often referred to as credit derivatives).* Many different types of contracts are indexed to the creditworthiness of a specified entity or group of entities, but not all of them are derivative instruments. Credit-indexed contracts that have certain characteristics described in paragraph 10(d) are guarantees and are not subject to the requirements of this Statement. Credit-indexed contracts that do not have the characteristics necessary to qualify for the exception in paragraph 10(d) are subject to the requirements of this Statement. One example of the latter is a credit-indexed contract that requires a payment due to changes in the creditworthiness of a specified entity even if neither party incurs a loss due to the change (other than a loss caused by the payment under the credit-indexed contract).

c. *Take-or-pay contracts.* Under a take-or-pay contract, an entity agrees to pay a specified price for a specified quantity of a product whether or not it takes delivery. Whether a take-or-pay contract is subject to this Statement depends on its terms.* For example, if the product to be delivered is not readily convertible to cash and there is no net settlement option, the contract fails to meet the criterion in paragraph 6(c) and is not subject to the requirements of this Statement. However, a contract that meets all of the following conditions

---

*In certain circumstances, a take-or-pay contract may represent or contain a lease that should be accounted for in accordance with FASB Statement No. 13, *Accounting for Leases.*

is subject to the requirements of this Statement: (1) the product to be delivered is readily convertible to cash, (2) the contract does not qualify for the normal purchases and normal sales exception in paragraph 10(b), and (3) ~~little or no initial net investment in the contract is required~~ the contract requires no initial net investment or an initial net investment that is smaller by more than a nominal amount than would be required for other types of contracts that would be expected to have a similar response to changes in market factors. (Refer to paragraph 8.)

d. *Short sales (sales of borrowed securities).*[18] Short sales typically involve the following activities:

(1) Selling a security (by the short seller to the purchaser)

(2) Borrowing a security (by the short seller from the lender)

(3) Delivering the borrowed security (by the short seller to the purchaser)

(4) Purchasing a security (by the short seller from the market)

(5) Delivering the purchased security (by the short seller to the lender).

Those five activities involve three separate contracts. A contract that distinguishes a short sale involves activities (2) and (5), borrowing a security and replacing it by delivering an identical security. Such a contract has two of the three characteristics of a derivative instrument. The settlement is based on an underlying (the price of the security) and a notional amount (the face amount of the security or the number of shares), and the settlement is made by delivery of a security that is readily convertible to cash. However, the other characteristic, ~~little or~~ no initial net investment or an initial net investment that is smaller by more than a nominal amount than would be required for other types of contracts that would be expected to have a similar response to changes in market factors, is not present. (Refer to paragraph 8.) The borrowed security is the lender's initial net investment in the contract. Consequently, the contract relating to activities (2) and (5) is not a derivative instrument. The other two contracts (one for activities (1) and (3) and the other for activity (4)) are routine and do not generally involve derivative instruments. However, if a forward purchase or sale is involved, and the

contract does not qualify for the exception in paragraph 10(a), it is subject to the requirements of this Statement.

e. *Repurchase agreements and "wash sales"* (accounted for as sales as described in paragraphs 98 and 99 of Statement 140). A transfer of financial assets accounted for as a sale under Statement 140 in which the transferor is both obligated and entitled to repurchase the transferred asset at a fixed or determinable price contains two separate features, one of which may be a derivative. The initial exchange of financial assets for cash is a sale-purchase transaction—generally not a transaction that involves a derivative instrument. However, the accompanying forward contract that gives the transferor the right and obligation to repurchase the transferred asset involves an underlying and a notional amount (the price of the security and its denomination), and it does not require an initial net investment in the contract. Consequently, if the forward contract requires delivery of a security that is readily convertible to cash or otherwise meets the net settlement criterion in paragraph 9, it is subject to the requirements of this Statement.

61. The following guidance is relevant in deciding whether the economic characteristics and risks of the embedded derivative are clearly and closely related to the economic characteristics and risks of the host contract.

a. *Interest rate indexes.* An embedded derivative in which the underlying is an interest rate or interest rate index and a host contract that is considered a debt instrument are considered to be clearly and closely related unless, as discussed in paragraph 13, the embedded derivative contains a provision that (1) permits any possibility whatsoever that the investor's (or creditor's) undiscounted net cash inflows over the life of the instrument would not recover substantially all of its initial recorded investment in the hybrid instrument under its contractual terms or (2) could under any possibility whatsoever at least double the investor's initial rate of return on the host contract and ~~also~~at the same time result in a rate of return that is at least twice what otherwise would be the then-current market return for a contract that has the same terms as the host contract and that involves a debtor with a similar credit quality. The

---

[18]This discussion applies only to short sales with the characteristics described here. Some groups of transactions that are referred to as short sales may have different characteristics. If so, a different analysis would be appropriate, and other derivative instruments may be involved.

requirement to separate the embedded derivative from the host contract applies to *both parties* to the hybrid instrument even though the above tests focus on the investor's net cash inflows. Plain-vanilla servicing rights, which involve an obligation to perform servicing and the right to receive fees for performing that servicing, do not contain an embedded derivative that would be separated from those servicing rights and accounted for as a derivative.

b. *Inflation-indexed interest payments.* The interest rate and the rate of inflation in the economic environment for the currency in which a debt instrument is denominated are considered to be clearly and closely related. Thus, nonleveraged inflation-indexed contracts (debt instruments, capitalized lease obligations, pension obligations, and so forth) would *not* have the inflation-related embedded derivative separated from the host contract.

c. *Credit-sensitive payments.* The creditworthiness of the debtor and the interest rate on a debt instrument are considered to be clearly and closely related. Thus, for debt instruments that have the interest rate reset in the event of (1) default (such as violation of a credit-risk-related covenant), (2) a change in the debtor's published credit rating, or (3) a change in the debtor's creditworthiness indicated by a change in its spread over Treasury bonds, the related embedded derivative would *not* be separated from the host contract.

d. *Calls and puts on debt instruments.* Call options (or put options) that can accelerate the repayment of principal on a debt instrument are considered to be clearly and closely related to a debt instrument that requires principal repayments unless both (1) the debt involves a substantial premium or discount (which is common with zero-coupon bonds) and (2) the put or call option is only contingently exercisable, provided the call options (or put options) are also considered to be clearly and closely related to the debt host contract under paragraph 13. Thus, if a substantial premium or discount is not involved, embedded calls and puts (including contingent call or put options that are not exercisable unless an event of default occurs) would *not* be separated from the host contract. However, for contingently exercisable calls and puts to be considered clearly and closely related, they can be indexed only to interest rates or credit risk, not some extraneous event or factor. In contrast, call options (or put options) that do not accelerate the repayment of principal on a debt in-

strument but instead require a cash settlement that is equal to the price of the option at the date of exercise would *not* be considered to be clearly and closely related to the debt instrument in which it is embedded ~~and would be separated from the host contract.~~

e. *Calls and puts on equity instruments.* A put option that enables the holder to require the issuer of an equity instrument to reacquire that equity instrument for cash or other assets is *not* clearly and closely related to that equity instrument. Thus, such a put option embedded in a publicly traded equity instrument to which it relates should be separated from the host contract by the holder of the equity instrument if the criteria in paragraphs 12(b) and 12(c) are also met. That put option also should be separated from the host contract by the issuer of the equity instrument except in those cases in which the put option is not considered to be a derivative instrument pursuant to paragraph 11(a) because it is classified in stockholders' equity. A purchased call option that enables the issuer of an equity instrument (such as common stock) to reacquire that equity instrument would not be considered to be a derivative instrument by the issuer of the equity instrument pursuant to paragraph 11(a). Thus, if the call option were embedded in the related equity instrument, it would not be separated from the host contract by the issuer. However, for the holder of the related equity instrument, the embedded written call option would *not* be considered to be clearly and closely related to the equity instrument and, if the criteria in paragraphs 12(b) and 12(c) were met, should be separated from the host contract.

f. *Interest rate ~~F~~floors, caps, and collars.* Floors or caps (or collars, which are combinations of caps and floors) on interest rates and the interest rate on a debt instrument are considered to be clearly and closely related ~~;~~ unless the conditions in either paragraph 13(a) or paragraph 13(b) are met, in which case the floors or the caps are not considered to be clearly and closely related. ~~provided the cap is at or above the current market price (or rate) and the floor is at or below the current market price (or rate) at issuance of the instrument. Thus, the derivative embedded in a variable-rate debt instrument that has a floor on the interest rate (that is, the floor option) would not be separated from the host contract and accounted for separately even though, in a falling interest rate environment, the debt instrument may have a return~~

to the investor that is a significant amount above the market return of a debt instrument without the floor provision (refer to paragraph 13(b)).

g. *Term-extending options.* An embedded derivative provision that either (1) unilaterally enables one party to extend significantly the remaining term to maturity or (2) automatically extends significantly the remaining term triggered by specific events or conditions is *not* clearly and closely related to the interest rate on a debt instrument unless the interest rate is concurrently reset to the approximate current market rate for the extended term and the debt instrument initially involved no significant discount. Thus, if there is no reset of interest rates, the embedded derivative is not clearly and closely related to must be separated from the host contract and accounted for as a derivative instrument. That is, a term-extending option cannot be used to circumvent the restriction in paragraph 61(a) regarding the investor's not recovering substantially all of its initial recorded investment.

h. *Equity-indexed interest payments.* The changes in fair value of an equity interest and the interest yield on a debt instrument are *not* clearly and closely related. Thus, an equity-related derivative embedded in an equity-indexed debt instrument (whether based on the price of a specific common stock or on an index that is based on a basket of equity instruments) must be separated from the host contract and accounted for as a derivative instrument.

i. *Commodity-indexed interest or principal payments.* The changes in fair value of a commodity (or other asset) and the interest yield on a debt instrument are *not* clearly and closely related. Thus, a commodity-related derivative embedded in a commodity-indexed debt instrument must be separated from the noncommodity host contract and accounted for as a derivative instrument.

j. *Indexed rentals:*
   (1) Inflation-indexed rentals. Rentals for the use of leased assets and adjustments for inflation on similar property are considered to be clearly and closely related. Thus, unless a significant leverage factor is involved, the inflation-related derivative embedded in an inflation-indexed lease contract would *not* be separated from the host contract.

   (2) *Contingent rentals based on related sales.* Lease contracts that include contingent rentals based on certain sales of the lessee would *not* have the contingent-rental-related embedded derivative separated from the host contract because, under paragraph 10(e)(3), a non-exchange-traded contract whose underlying is specified volumes of sales by one of the parties to the contract would not be subject to the requirements of this Statement.

   (3) *Contingent rentals based on a variable interest rate.* The obligation to make future payments for the use of leased assets and the adjustment of those payments to reflect changes in a variable-interest-rate index are considered to be clearly and closely related. Thus, lease contracts that include contingent rentals based on changes in the prime rate would *not* have the contingent-rental-related embedded derivative separated from the host contract.

k. *Convertible debt.* The changes in fair value of an equity interest and the interest rates on a debt instrument are not clearly and closely related. Thus, for a debt security that is convertible into a specified number of shares of the debtor's common stock or another entity's common stock, the embedded derivative (that is, the conversion option) must be separated from the debt host contract and accounted for as a derivative instrument provided that the conversion option would, as a freestanding instrument, be a derivative instrument subject to the requirements of this Statement. (For example, if the common stock was not readily convertible to cash, a conversion option that requires purchase of the common stock would not be accounted for as a derivative.) That accounting applies only to the holder (investor) if the debt is convertible to the debtor's common stock because, under paragraph 11(a), a separate option with the same terms would not be considered to be a derivative for the issuer.

l. *Convertible preferred stock.* Because the changes in fair value of an equity interest and interest rates on a debt instrument are not clearly and closely related, the terms of the preferred stock (other than the conversion option) must be analyzed to determine whether the preferred stock (and thus the potential host contract) is more akin to an equity instrument or a debt instrument. A typical cumulative fixed-rate preferred stock that has a mandatory redemption feature is more akin to debt, whereas cumulative participating perpetual preferred stock is more akin to an equity instrument.

Section 2: Assessment of Hedge Effectiveness

Hedge Effectiveness Requirements of This Statement

64. In assessing the effectiveness of a cash flow hedge, an entity generally will need to consider the time value of money if significant in the circumstances. Considering the effect of the time value of money is especially important if the hedging instrument involves periodic cash settlements. An example of a situation in which an entity likely would reflect the time value of money is a tailing strategy with futures contracts. When using a tailing strategy, an entity adjusts the size or contract amount of futures contracts used in a hedge so that earnings (or expense) from reinvestment (or funding) of daily settlement gains (or losses) on the futures do not distort the results of the hedge. To assess offset of expected cash flows[†] when a tailing strategy has been used, an entity could reflect the time value of money, perhaps by comparing the present value of the hedged forecasted cash flow with the results of the hedging instrument.

65. Whether a hedging relationship qualifies as highly effective sometimes will be easy to assess, and there will be no ineffectiveness to recognize in earnings during the term of the hedge. If the critical terms of the hedging instrument and of the entire hedged asset or liability (as opposed to selected cash flows) or hedged forecasted transaction are the same, the entity could conclude that changes in fair value or cash flows attributable to the risk being hedged are expected to completely offset at inception and on an ongoing basis. For example, an entity may assume that a hedge of a forecasted purchase of a commodity with a forward contract will be highly effective and that there will be no ineffectiveness to be recognized in earnings if:

a. The forward contract is for purchase of the same quantity of the same commodity at the same time and location as the hedged forecasted purchase.
b. The fair value of the forward contract at inception is zero.
c. Either the change in the discount or premium on the forward contract is excluded from the assessment of effectiveness and included directly in

earnings pursuant to paragraph 63 or the change in expected cash flows[†] on the forecasted transaction is based on the forward price for the commodity.

Assuming no ineffectiveness in a hedge with an interest rate swap

68. An assumption of no ineffectiveness is especially important in a hedging relationship involving an interest-bearing financial instrument and an interest rate swap because it significantly simplifies the computations necessary to make the accounting entries. An entity may assume no ineffectiveness in a hedging relationship of interest rate risk involving a recognized interest-bearing asset or liability and an interest rate swap (or a compound hedging instrument composed of an interest rate swap and a mirror-image call or put option as discussed in paragraph 68(d) below) if all of the applicable conditions in the following list are met:

Conditions applicable to both fair value hedges and cash flow hedges

a. The notional amount of the swap matches the principal amount of the interest-bearing asset or liability being hedged.
b. If the hedging instrument is solely an interest rate swap, ~~T~~the fair value of ~~the~~that swap at the inception of the hedging relationship is zero. If the hedging instrument is a compound derivative composed of an interest rate swap and mirror-image call or put option as discussed in paragraph 68(d), the premium for the mirror-image call or put option must be paid or received in the same manner as the premium on the call or put option embedded in the hedged item. That is, the reporting entity must determine whether the implicit premium for the purchased call or written put option embedded in the hedged item was principally paid at inception-acquisition (through an original issue discount or premium) or is being paid over the life of the hedged item (through an adjustment of the interest rate). If the implicit premium for the call or put option embedded in the hedged item was principally paid at inception-acquisition, the fair value of the hedging instrument at the inception of the hedging relationship must be equal to the fair value of the mirror-

---

[†]Refer to footnote* to paragraph 17 of Statement 133.

image call or put option. In contrast, if the implicit premium for the call or put option embedded in the hedged item is principally being paid over the life of the hedged item, fair value of the hedging instrument at the inception of the hedging relationship must be zero.

c. The formula for computing net settlements under the interest rate swap is the same for each net settlement. (That is, the fixed rate is the same throughout the term, and the variable rate is based on the same index and includes the same constant adjustment or no adjustment.)

d. The interest-bearing asset or liability is not prepayable (that is, able to be settled by either party prior to its scheduled maturity), except as indicated in the following sentences. This criterion does not apply to an interest-bearing asset or liability that is prepayable solely due to an embedded call option provided that the hedging instrument is a compound derivative composed of an interest rate swap contains and a embedded mirror-image call option. The call option embedded in the swap is considered a mirror image of the call option embedded in the hedged item if (1) the terms of the two call options match (including matching maturities, strike price, related notional amounts, timing and frequency of payments, and dates on which the instruments may be called) and (2) the entity is the writer of one call option and the holder (or purchaser) of the other call option. Similarly, this criterion does not apply to an interest-bearing asset or liability that is prepayable solely due to an embedded put option provided that the hedging instrument is a compound derivative composed of an interest rate swap contains and a embedded mirror-image put option.

dd. The index on which the variable leg of the swap is based matches the benchmark interest rate designated as the interest rate risk being hedged for that hedging relationship.*

e. Any other terms in the interest-bearing financial instruments or interest rate swaps are typical of those instruments and do not invalidate the assumption of no ineffectiveness.

Conditions applicable to fair value hedges only

f. The expiration date of the swap matches the maturity date of the interest-bearing asset or liability.

g. There is no floor or ceiling cap on the variable interest rate of the swap.

h. The interval between repricings of the variable interest rate in the swap is frequent enough to justify an assumption that the variable payment or receipt is at a market rate (generally three to six months or less).

Conditions applicable to cash flow hedges only

i. All interest receipts or payments on the variable-rate asset or liability during the term of the swap are designated as hedged, and no interest payments beyond the term of the swap are designated as hedged.

j. There is no floor or cap on the variable interest rate of the swap unless the variable-rate asset or liability has a floor or cap. In that case, the swap must have a floor or cap on the variable interest rate that is comparable to the floor or cap on the variable-rate asset or liability. (For this purpose, comparable does not necessarily mean equal. For example, if a swap's variable rate is LIBOR and an asset's variable rate is LIBOR plus 2 percent, a 10 percent cap on the swap would be comparable to a 12 percent cap on the asset.)

k. The repricing dates match those of the variable-rate asset or liability.

Assessing the hedge's expected effectiveness and measuring ineffectiveness

94. Company G bases its assessment of hedge effectiveness and measure of ineffectiveness on changes in forward prices, with the resulting gain or loss discounted to reflect the time value of money. Because of the difference in the bases of the forecasted transaction (Brazilian coffee) and forward contract (Colombian coffee), Company G may not assume that the hedge will automatically be highly effective in achieving offsetting cash flows. Both at inception and on an ongoing basis, Company G could assess the effectiveness of the hedge by comparing changes in the

---

*For cash flow hedge situations in which the cash flows of the hedged item and the hedging instrument are based on the same index but that index is not the benchmark interest rate, the shortcut method is not permitted. However, the entity may obtain results similar to results obtained if the shortcut method was permitted.

expected cash flows[†] from the Colombian coffee forward contract with the expected net change in cash outflows for purchasing the Brazilian coffee for different market prices. (A simpler method that should produce the same results would consider the expected future correlation of the prices of Brazilian and Colombian coffee, based on the correlation of those prices over past six-month periods.)

95. In assessing hedge effectiveness on an ongoing basis, Company G also must consider the extent of offset between the change in expected cash flows[†] on its Colombian coffee <u>forward</u> contract and the <u>expected net</u> change in expected cash flows for the forecasted purchase of Brazilian coffee. Both changes would be measured on a cumulative basis for actual

changes in the forward price of the respective coffees during the hedge period.

96. Because the only difference between the forward contract and forecasted purchase relates to the type of coffee (Colombian versus Brazilian), Company G could consider the changes in the cash flows on a forward contract for Brazilian coffee to be a measure of perfectly offsetting changes in cash flows for its forecasted purchase of Brazilian coffee. For example, for given changes in the U.S. dollar prices of six-month and three-month Brazilian and Colombian contracts, Company G could compute the effect of a change in the price of coffee on the expected cash flows[†] of its forward contract on Colombian coffee and of a forward contract for Brazilian coffee as follows:

Estimate of Change in Cash Flows

	Hedging Instrument: Forward Contract on Colombian Coffee	Estimate of Forecasted Transaction: Forward Contract on Brazilian Coffee
Forward price of Colombian and Brazilian coffee:		
At hedge inception—6-month price	$ 2.54	$ 2.43
3 months later—3-month price	2.63	2.53
Cumulative change in price—gain	$ .09	$ .10
× 500,000 pounds of coffee	× 500,000	× 500,000
Estimate of change in cash flows	$ 45,000	$ 50,000

97. Using the above amounts, Company G could evaluate effectiveness 3 months into the hedge by comparing the $45,000 change on its Colombian coffee contract with what would have been a perfectly offsetting change in cash flow for its forecasted purchase—the $50,000 change on an otherwise identical forward contract for Brazilian coffee. The hedge would be ineffective to the extent that there was a difference between the changes in the present value of the expected cash flows[†] on (a) the company's Colombian coffee contract and (b) a comparable forward contract for Brazilian coffee (the equivalent of the present value of $5,000 in the numerical example).

Assessing the hedge's expected effectiveness and measuring ineffectiveness

99. Company H may not automatically assume that the hedge always will be highly effective at achieving offsetting changes in cash flows because the reset date on the receive leg of the swap differs from the reset date on the corresponding variable-rate liability. Both at hedge inception and on an ongoing basis, the company's assessment of expected effectiveness could be based on the extent to which changes in LIBOR have occurred during comparable 10-day periods in the past. Company H's ongoing assessment of expected effectiveness and measurement of actual

---

[†]Refer to footnote* to paragraph 17 of Statement 133.

ineffectiveness would be on a cumulative basis and would incorporate the actual interest rate changes to date. The hedge would be ineffective to the extent that the cumulative change in cash flows on the prime leg of the swap did not offset the cumulative change in expected cash flows[†] on the asset, *and* the cumulative change in cash flows on the LIBOR leg of the swap did not offset the change in expected cash flows on the hedged portion of the liability. The terms of the swap, the asset, and the portion of the liability that is hedged are the same, with the exception of the reset dates on the liability and the receive leg of the swap. Thus, the hedge will only be ineffective to the extent that LIBOR has changed between the first of the month (the reset date for the swap) and the tenth of the month (the reset date for the liability).

EXAMPLES ILLUSTRATING APPLICATION OF THIS STATEMENT

143. The following table reconciles the beginning and ending balances in accumulated other comprehensive income.

Accumulated Other Comprehensive Income—Debit (Credit)

Period	Beginning Balance	Change in Fair Value	Reclassification	Ending Balance
1	$ 0	$ (96)	$ 0	$ (96)
2	(96)	(94)	(4)	(194)
3	(194)	162	0	(32)
4	(32)	98	0	66
5	66	(30)	(2)	34

The reclassification column relates to reclassifications between earnings and other comprehensive income. In period 2, the $(4) in that column relates to the prior period's derivative gain that was previously recognized in earnings. That amount is reclassified to other comprehensive income in period 2 because the cumulative gain on the derivative is less than the amount necessary to offset the cumulative change in the present value of expected future cash flows on the hedged transaction. In period 5, the $(2) in the reclassification column relates to the derivative loss that was recognized in other comprehensive income in a prior period. At the end of period 4, the derivative's cumulative loss of $69 was greater in absolute terms than the $66 increase in the present value of expected future cash flows on the hedged transaction. That $3 excess had been recognized in earnings during period 4. In period 5, the value of the derivative increased (and reduced the cumulative loss) by $30. The present value of the expected cash flows[†] on the hedged transaction decreased (and reduced the cumulative increase) by $32. The gain on the derivative in period 5 was $2 smaller, in absolute terms, than the decrease in the present value of the expected cash flows on the hedged transaction. Consequently, the entire gain on the derivative is recognized in other comprehensive income. In addition, in absolute terms, the $3 cumulative excess of the loss on the derivative over the increase in the present value of the expected cash flows on the hedged transaction (which had previously been recognized in earnings) increased to $5. As a result, $2 is reclassified from other comprehensive income to earnings so that the $5 cumulative excess has been recognized in earnings.

Example 8: Changes in a Cash Flow Hedge of Forecasted Interest Payments with an Interest Rate Swap

Background

154. MNO Company enters into an interest rate swap (Swap 1) and designates it as a hedge of the variable quarterly interest payments on the company's 5-year $5 million borrowing program, initially expected to be accomplished by a series of $5 million notes with 90-day terms. MNO plans to continue issuing new 90-day notes over the next 5 years as each outstanding note matures. The interest on each note will be determined based on LIBOR at the time each

---

[†]Refer to footnote* to paragraph 17 of Statement 133.

note is issued. Swap 1 requires a settlement every 90 days, and the variable interest rate is reset immediately following each payment. MNO pays a fixed rate of interest (6.5 percent) and receives interest at LIBOR. MNO neither pays nor receives a premium at the inception of Swap 1. The notional amount of the contract is $5 million, and it expires in 5 years.

Section 2: Examples Illustrating Application of the Clearly-and-Closely-Related Criterion to Derivative Instruments Embedded in Hybrid Instruments

176. The following examples in Section 2 discuss instruments that contain a variety of embedded derivative instruments. They illustrate how the provisions of paragraphs 12–16 of this Statement would be applied to contracts with the described terms. If the terms of a contract are different from the described terms, the application of this Statement by either party to the contract may be affected. Furthermore, if any contract of the types discussed in Section 2 meets the definition of a derivative instrument in its entirety under paragraphs 6–9 and related paragraphs, the guidance in this section for the application of the provisions of paragraphs 12–16 to embedded derivative instruments does not apply. The illustrative instruments and related assumptions in Examples 12–27 are based on examples in Exhibit 96-12A of EITF Issue No. 96-12, "Recognition of Interest Income and Balance Sheet Classification of Structured Notes."

GLOSSARY

540. This appendix contains definitions of terms or phrases as used in this Statement.

Benchmark interest rate

A widely recognized and quoted rate in an active financial market that is broadly indicative of the overall level of interest rates attributable to high-credit-quality obligors in that market. It is a rate that is widely used in a given financial market as an underlying basis for determining the interest rates of individual financial instruments and commonly referenced in interest-rate-related transactions.

In theory, the benchmark interest rate should be a risk-free rate (that is, has no risk of default). In some markets, government borrowing rates may serve as a benchmark. In other markets, the benchmark interest rate may be an interbank offered rate. In the United States, currently only the interest rates on direct Treasury obligations of the U.S. government and, for practical reasons, the LIBOR swap rate are considered to be benchmark interest rates. In each financial market, only the one or two most widely used and quoted rates that meet the above criteria may be considered benchmark interest rates.

Capacity contract

An agreement by an owner of capacity to sell the right to that capacity to another party so that it can satisfy its obligations. For example, in the electric industry, capacity (sometimes referred to as installed capacity) is the capability to deliver electric power to the electric transmission system of an operating control area. A control area is a portion of the electric grid that schedules, dispatches, and controls generating resources to serve area load (ultimate users of electricity) and coordinates scheduling of the flow of electric power over the transmission system to neighboring control areas. A control area requires entities that serve load within the control area to demonstrate ownership or contractual rights to capacity sufficient to serve that load at time of peak demand and to provide a reserve margin to protect the integrity of the system against potential generating unit outages in the control area.

Comprehensive income

The change in equity of a business enterprise during a period from transactions and other events and circumstances from nonowner sources. It includes all changes in equity during a period except those resulting from investments by owners and distributions to owners (FASB Concepts Statement No. 6, *Elements of Financial Statements*, paragraph 70).

Derivative instrument

Refer to paragraphs 6–9.

Fair value

The amount at which an asset (liability) could be bought (incurred) or sold (settled) in a current transaction between willing parties, that is, other than in a forced or liquidation sale. Quoted market prices in active markets are the best evidence of fair value and should be used as the basis for the measurement, if available. If a quoted market price is available, the fair value is the product of the number of trading units times that market price. If a quoted market price is not available, the estimate of fair value should be based on the best information available in the circumstances. The estimate of fair value should consider prices for similar assets or similar liabilities and the results of valuation techniques to the extent available in the circumstances. Examples of valuation techniques include the present value of estimated expected future cash flows using discount rates commensurate with the risks involved, option-pricing models, matrix pricing, option-adjusted spread models, and fundamental analysis. Valuation techniques for measuring assets and liabilities should be consistent with the objective of measuring fair value. Those techniques should incorporate assumptions that market participants would use in their estimates of values, future revenues, and future expenses, including assumptions about interest rates, default, prepayment, and volatility. In measuring forward contracts, such as foreign currency forward contracts, at fair value by discounting estimated future cash flows, an entity should base the estimate of future cash flows on the changes in the forward rate (rather than the spot rate). In measuring financial liabilities and nonfinancial derivatives that are liabilities at fair value by discounting estimated future cash flows (or equivalent outflows of other assets), an objective is to use discount rates at which those liabilities could be settled in an arm's-length transaction.

Financial instrument

Cash, evidence of an ownership interest in an entity, or a contract that both:

a. Imposes on one entity a contractual obligation* (1) to deliver cash or another financial instrument[†] to a second entity or (2) to exchange other financial instruments on potentially unfavorable terms with the second entity

b. Conveys to that second entity a contractual right[‡] (1) to receive cash or another financial instrument from the first entity or (2) to exchange other financial instruments on potentially favorable terms with the first entity.

Contractual obligations encompass both those that are conditioned on the occurrence of a specified event and those that are not. All contractual obligations that are financial instruments

meet the definition of *liability* set forth in Concepts Statement 6, although some may not be recognized as liabilities in financial statements—may be "off-balance-sheet"—because they fail to meet some other criterion for recognition. For some financial instruments, the obligation is owed to or by a group of entities rather than a single entity.

[†]The use of the term *financial instrument* in this definition is recursive (because the term *financial instrument* is included in it), though it is not circular. The definition requires a chain of contractual obligations that ends with the delivery of cash or an ownership interest in an entity. Any number of obligations to deliver financial instruments can be links in a chain that qualifies a particular contract as a financial instrument.

[‡]*Contractual rights* encompass both those that are conditioned on the occurrence of a specified event and those that are not. All contractual rights that are financial instruments meet the definition of *asset* set forth in Concepts Statement 6, although some may not be recognized as assets in financial statements—may be "off-balance-sheet"—because they fail to meet some other criterion for recognition. For some financial instruments, the right is held by or the obligation is due from a group of entities rather than a single entity.

Firm commitment

An agreement with an unrelated party, binding on both parties and usually legally enforceable, with the following characteristics:

a. The agreement specifies all significant terms, including the quantity to be exchanged, the fixed price, and the timing of the transaction. The fixed price may be expressed as a specified amount of an entity's functional currency or of a foreign currency. It may also be expressed as a specified interest rate or specified effective yield.

b. The agreement includes a disincentive for nonperformance that is sufficiently large to make performance probable.

Forecasted transaction

A transaction that is expected to occur for which there is no firm commitment. Because no transaction or event has yet occurred and the transaction or event when it occurs will be at the prevailing market price, a forecasted transaction does not give an entity any present rights to future benefits or a present obligation for future sacrifices.

LIBOR swap rate

The fixed rate on a single-currency, constant-notional interest rate swap that has its floating-rate leg referenced to the London Interbank Offered Rate (LIBOR) with no additional spread over LIBOR on that floating-rate leg. That fixed rate is the derived rate that would result in the swap having a zero fair value at inception because the present value of fixed cash flows, based on that rate, equate to the present value of the floating cash flows.

Notional amount

A number of currency units, shares, bushels, pounds, or other units specified in a derivative instrument.

Underlying

A specified interest rate, security price, commodity price, foreign exchange rate, index of prices or rates, or other variable (including the occurrence or non- occurrence of a specified event such as a scheduled payment under a contract). An underlying may be a price or rate of an asset or liability but is not the asset or liability itself.

Statement of Financial Accounting Standards No. 150
Accounting for Certain Financial Instruments
with Characteristics of both Liabilities and Equity

STATUS

Issued: May 2003

Effective Date: For financial instruments entered into or modified after May 31, 2003; otherwise effective at the beginning of the first interim period beginning after June 15, 2003, except for mandatorily redeemable financial instruments of nonpublic entities which are subject to the provisions of this Statement for the first fiscal period beginning after December 15, 2003

Affects: Amends FAS 128, paragraph 24
Amends FAS 133, paragraphs 11 and 12(c)

Affected by: Paragraph 17 amended by FAS 123(R), paragraph D16
Paragraph 17A added by FSP EITF 00-19-2, paragraph 14
Paragraph D1 amended by FAS 123(R), paragraph D16, and FAS 157, paragraph E26

Other Interpretive Releases: FASB Staff Positions FAS 150-1 through FAS 150-5

Issues Discussed by FASB Emerging Issues Task Force (EITF)

Affects: Nullifies EITF Issues No. 98-12 and 00-4
Partially nullifies EITF Issues No. 86-32, 88-9, 89-11, 00-6, 00-19, and 00-27 and Topics
No. D-42, D-72, and D-98
Resolves EITF Issue No. 01-11
Partially resolves EITF Issues No. 84-40 and 02-2

Interpreted by: No EITF Issues

Related Issues: EITF Issues No. 97-8, 97-15, 01-6, 05-4, and 07-2 and Topic No. D-98

SUMMARY

This Statement establishes standards for how an issuer classifies and measures certain financial instruments with characteristics of both liabilities and equity. It requires that an issuer classify a financial instrument that is within its scope as a liability (or an asset in some circumstances). Many of those instruments were previously classified as equity. Some of the provisions of this Statement are consistent with the current definition of liabilities in FASB Concepts Statement No. 6, *Elements of Financial Statements*. The remaining provisions of this Statement are consistent with the Board's proposal to revise that definition to encompass certain obligations that a reporting entity can or must settle by issuing its own equity shares, depending on the nature of the relationship established between the holder and the issuer. While the Board still plans to revise that definition through an amendment to Concepts Statement 6, the Board decided to defer issuing that amendment until it has concluded its deliberations on the next phase of this project. That next phase will deal with certain compound financial instruments including puttable shares, convertible bonds, and dual-indexed financial instruments.

This Statement concludes the first phase of the Board's redeliberations of the Exposure Draft, *Accounting for Financial Instruments with Characteristics of Liabilities, Equity, or Both.*

Scope and Requirements of This Statement

This Statement requires an issuer to classify the following instruments as liabilities (or assets in some circumstances):

- A financial instrument issued in the form of shares that is mandatorily redeemable—that embodies an unconditional obligation requiring the issuer to redeem it by transferring its assets at a specified or determinable date (or dates) or upon an event that is certain to occur
- A financial instrument, other than an outstanding share, that, at inception, embodies an obligation to repurchase the issuer's equity shares, or is indexed to such an obligation, and that requires or may require the issuer to settle the obligation by transferring assets (for example, a forward purchase contract or written put option on the issuer's equity shares that is to be physically settled or net cash settled)
- A financial instrument that embodies an unconditional obligation, or a financial instrument other than an outstanding share that embodies a conditional obligation, that the issuer must or may settle by issuing a variable number of its equity shares, if, at inception, the monetary value of the obligation is based solely or predominantly on any of the following:
  a. A fixed monetary amount known at inception, for example, a payable settleable with a variable number of the issuer's equity shares
  b. Variations in something other than the fair value of the issuer's equity shares, for example, a financial instrument indexed to the S&P 500 and settleable with a variable number of the issuer's equity shares
  c. Variations inversely related to changes in the fair value of the issuer's equity shares, for example, a written put option that could be net share settled.

The requirements of this Statement apply to issuers' classification and measurement of freestanding financial instruments, including those that comprise more than one option or forward contract.

This Statement does not apply to features that are embedded in a financial instrument that is not a derivative in its entirety. For example, it does not change the accounting treatment of conversion features, conditional redemption features, or other features embedded in financial instruments that are not derivatives in their entirety. It also does not affect the classification or measurement of convertible bonds, puttable stock, or other outstanding shares that are conditionally redeemable. This Statement also does not address certain financial instruments indexed partly to the issuer's equity shares and partly, but not predominantly, to something else. Financial instruments with characteristics of both liabilities and equity not addressed in this Statement will be addressed in the next phase of the project. Guidance currently in effect for those instruments continues to apply. In applying the classification provisions of this Statement, nonsubstantive or minimal features are to be disregarded.

Forward contracts to repurchase an issuer's equity shares that require physical settlement in exchange for cash are initially measured at the fair value of the shares at inception, adjusted for any consideration or unstated rights or privileges, which is the same as the amount that would be paid under the conditions specified in the contract if settlement occurred immediately. Those contracts and mandatorily redeemable financial instruments are subsequently measured at the present value of the amount to be paid at settlement (discounted at the rate implicit at inception), if both the amount of cash and the settlement date are fixed, or, otherwise, at the amount that would be paid under the conditions specified in the contract if settlement occurred at the reporting date. Other financial instruments within the scope of this Statement are initially and subsequently measured at fair value, unless required by this Statement or other generally accepted accounting principles to be measured differently. Disclosures are required about the terms of the instruments and settlement alternatives.

Reasons for Issuing This Statement

This Statement was developed in response to concerns expressed by preparers, auditors, regulators, investors, and other users of financial statements about issuers' classification in the statement of financial position of certain financial instruments that have characteristics of both liabilities and equity but that have been presented either entirely as equity or between the liabilities section and the equity section of the statement of financial position. This Statement also addresses questions about the classification of certain financial instruments that embody obligations to issue equity shares. Previously, under Emerging Issues Task Force Issue No. 00-19, "Accounting for Derivative Financial Instruments Indexed to, and Potentially Settled in, a Company's Own Stock," an issuer of a contract to repurchase its equity shares generally accounted for that contract as equity if the issuer must or could settle it by delivering its equity shares (net share settled). Additionally, certain obligations settleable by delivery of the issuer's equity shares but not indexed to the issuer's shares may have been classified as equity. Under this Statement, those obligations are accounted for as liabilities.

How the Changes in This Statement Improve Financial Reporting and How the Conclusions in This Statement Relate to the Conceptual Framework

FASB Concepts Statement No. 1, *Objectives of Financial Reporting by Business Enterprises,* states that financial reporting should provide information that is useful in making business and economic decisions. The changes in this Statement will result in a more complete depiction of an entity's liabilities and equity and will, thereby, assist investors and creditors in assessing the amount, timing, and likelihood of potential future cash outflows and equity share issuances.

FASB Concepts Statement No. 2, *Qualitative Characteristics of Accounting Information,* identifies the characteristics of financial information that make it useful: relevance and reliability and their components. The changes in this Statement will enhance the relevance of accounting information by providing more information about an entity's obligations to transfer assets or issue shares, thus, improving its predictive value to users. Reliability of accounting information will be improved by providing a portrayal of an entity's capital structure that is unbiased, verifiable, and more representationally faithful than information reported prior to issuance of this Statement. Because restatement on transition is prohibited, the initial and ongoing costs of those changes have been minimized. Overall, in the Board's opinion, the benefits of this Statement in terms of improved decision usefulness, relevance, and reliability justify the costs.

Concepts Statement 6 defines liabilities and equity. This Statement requires that certain obligations that require a transfer of assets and that meet the definition of liabilities in Concepts Statement 6 and other recognition criteria in FASB Concepts Statement No. 5, *Recognition and Measurement in Financial Statements of Business Enterprises,* be reported as liabilities. This Statement also requires that certain obligations that could be settled by issuance of an entity's equity but lack other characteristics of equity be reported as liabilities even though the obligation does not meet the definition of liabilities in Concepts Statement 6. The Board expects to amend Concepts Statement 6 to eliminate that inconsistency in the next phase of this project.

The Effective Date of This Statement

This Statement is effective for financial instruments entered into or modified after May 31, 2003, and otherwise is effective at the beginning of the first interim period beginning after June 15, 2003, except for mandatorily redeemable financial instruments of nonpublic entities. It is to be implemented by reporting the cumulative effect of a change in an accounting principle for financial instruments created before the issuance date of the Statement and still existing at the beginning of the interim period of adoption. Restatement is not permitted.

For nonpublic entities, mandatorily redeemable financial instruments are subject to the provisions of this Statement for the first fiscal period beginning after December 15, 2003.

Statement of Financial Accounting Standards No. 150

Accounting for Certain Financial Instruments with Characteristics of both Liabilities and Equity

CONTENTS

INTRODUCTION

1. This Statement establishes standards for how an issuer[1] classifies and measures in its statement of financial position certain financial instruments with characteristics of both liabilities and equity. It requires that an issuer classify a **financial instrument** that is within its scope as a liability (or an asset[2] in some circumstances) because that financial instrument embodies an **obligation** of the issuer.

2. In August 1990, as part of its financial instruments project, the Board issued an FASB Discussion Memorandum, *Distinguishing between Liability and Equity Instruments and Accounting for Instruments with Characteristics of Both*. In October 2000, the Board issued an FASB Exposure Draft, *Accounting for Financial Instruments with Characteristics of Liabilities, Equity, or Both*. That Exposure Draft proposed classification as a liability or as equity based on the nature of the relationship that an instrument or

---

[1]Terms defined in Appendix D are set in **boldface type** the first time they appear.

[2]This Statement does not address instruments that have only characteristics of assets. However, this Statement does apply to instruments having characteristics of both liabilities and equity that, in some circumstances, also have characteristics of assets, for example, a forward contract to purchase the issuer's equity shares that is to be net cash settled.

component of an instrument established between the holder and the issuer. This Statement is the initial result of redeliberations of that Exposure Draft.

Key Terms

3. In this Statement, an *obligation* is a conditional or unconditional duty or responsibility to transfer assets or to issue equity shares. For example, an entity incurs a conditional obligation to transfer assets[3] by issuing (writing) a put option that would, if exercised, require an entity to repurchase its equity shares by **physical settlement.** An entity also incurs a conditional obligation to transfer assets by issuing a similar contract that requires or could require **net cash settlement.** An entity incurs a conditional obligation to issue its equity shares by issuing a similar contract that requires **net share settlement.** In contrast, by issuing shares of stock, an entity generally does not incur an obligation to redeem the shares, and, therefore, that entity does not incur an obligation to transfer assets or issue additional equity shares. However, some issuances of stock (for example, mandatorily redeemable preferred stock) do impose obligations requiring the issuer to transfer assets or issue its equity shares.

4. In this Statement, **monetary value** is what the fair value of the cash, shares, or other instruments that a financial instrument obligates the issuer to convey to the holder would be at the settlement date under specified market conditions. For certain financial instruments, this Statement requires consideration of whether monetary value would remain fixed or would vary in response to changes in market conditions. How the monetary value of a financial instrument varies in response to changes in market conditions depends on the nature of the arrangement, including, in part, the form of settlement. For example, for a financial instrument that embodies an obligation that requires:

a. Settlement either by transfer of $100,000 in cash or by issuance of $100,000 worth of equity shares, the monetary value is fixed at $100,000, even if the share price changes.

b. Physical settlement by transfer of $100,000 in cash in exchange for the issuer's equity shares, the monetary value is fixed at $100,000, even if the fair value of the equity shares changes.

c. Net share settlement by issuance of a variable number of shares based on the change in the fair value of a fixed number of the issuer's equity shares, the monetary value varies based on the number of shares required to be issued to satisfy the obligation. For example, if the exercise price of a net-share-settled written put option entitling the holder to put back 10,000 of the issuer's equity shares is $11, and the fair value of the issuing entity's equity shares on the exercise date decreases from $13 to $10, that change in fair value of the issuer's shares increases the monetary value of that obligation at settlement from $0 to $10,000 ($110,000 minus $100,000), and the option would be settled by issuance of 1,000 shares ($10,000 divided by $10).

d. Net cash settlement based on the change in the fair value of a fixed number of the issuer's equity shares, the monetary value varies in the same manner as in the illustration for net share settlement, but the obligation is settled with cash. In a net-cash-settled variation of the previous example, the option would be settled by delivery of $10,000.

e. Settlement by issuance of a variable number of shares that is based on variations in something other than the issuer's equity shares, the monetary value varies based on changes in the price of another variable. For example, a net-share-settled obligation to deliver the number of shares equal in value at settlement to the change in fair value of 100 ounces of gold has a monetary value that varies based on the price of gold and not on the price of the issuer's equity shares.

5. For purposes of this Statement, three related terms are used in particular ways. *Shares* includes various forms of ownership that may not take the legal form of securities (for example, partnership interests),[4] as well as other interests, including those that are liabilities in substance but not in form. *Equity shares* refers

---

[3]An instrument that requires the issuer to settle its obligation by issuing another instrument (for example, a note payable in cash) ultimately requires settlement by a transfer of assets.

[4]Business enterprises have interest holders that are commonly known by specialized names, such as stockholders, partners, and proprietors, and by more general names, such as investors, but all are encompassed by the descriptive term *owners*. Equity of business enterprises is, thus, commonly known by several names, such as owners' equity, stockholders' equity, ownership, equity capital, partners' capital, and proprietorship. Some enterprises (for example, mutual organizations) do not have stockholders, partners, or proprietors in the usual sense of those terms but do have participants whose interests are essentially ownership interests, residual interests, or both.

only to shares that are accounted for as equity. For financial instruments issued by members of a consolidated group of entities, *issuer's equity shares* includes the equity shares of any entity whose financial statements are included in the consolidated financial statements.

Proposed Amendment to Concepts Statement 6

6. In October 2000, concurrent with the issuance of the Exposure Draft described in paragraph 2, the Board issued an FASB Exposure Draft, *Proposed Amendment to FASB Concepts Statement No. 6 to Revise the Definition of Liabilities*. That Exposure Draft proposed to revise the definition of liabilities so that, depending on the nature of the relationship established between the holder and the issuer, it would encompass certain obligations that a reporting entity can or must settle by issuing its own equity shares. While the Board still plans to issue such an amendment to FASB Concepts Statement No. 6, *Elements of Financial Statements,* the Board decided to defer that amendment until it has concluded its deliberations on the next phase of this project, which will deal with whether and how to separate certain compound financial instruments, including puttable shares, convertible bonds, and dual-indexed financial instruments, into debt and equity components.

Appendixes

7. Appendix A provides implementation guidance and examples of financial instruments that are within the scope of this Statement and are classified as liabilities. That appendix is an integral part of the standards provided in this Statement. Appendix B provides background information and the basis for the Board's conclusions. Appendix C provides amendments to existing accounting pronouncements and discusses the impact of this Statement on EITF Issues and FASB Statement No. 133, *Accounting for Derivative Instruments and Hedging Activities,* Implementation Issues. Appendix D provides a glossary of certain terms that are used in this Statement.

STANDARDS OF FINANCIAL ACCOUNTING AND REPORTING

Scope and Initial Classification

8. The objective of this Statement is to require issuers to classify as liabilities (or assets in some circumstances) three classes of **freestanding financial instruments** that embody obligations for the issuer. In applying this Statement, that objective shall not be circumvented by nonsubstantive or minimal features included in instruments. Any nonsubstantive or minimal features shall be disregarded in applying the classification provisions of this Statement (paragraphs 9–15). Judgment, based on consideration of all the terms of an instrument and other relevant facts and circumstances, is necessary to distinguish substantive, nonminimal features from nonsubstantive or minimal features.

Mandatorily Redeemable Financial Instruments

9. A **mandatorily redeemable financial instrument** shall be classified as a liability unless the redemption is required to occur only upon the liquidation or termination of the reporting entity. A financial instrument issued in the form of shares is mandatorily redeemable if it embodies an unconditional obligation requiring the issuer to redeem the instrument by transferring its assets at a specified or determinable date (or dates) or upon an event certain to occur.[5]

10. A financial instrument that embodies a conditional obligation to redeem the instrument by transferring assets upon an event not certain to occur becomes mandatorily redeemable—and, therefore, becomes a liability—if that event occurs, the condition is resolved, or the event becomes certain to occur.

Obligations to Repurchase the Issuer's Equity Shares by Transferring Assets

11. A financial instrument, other than an outstanding share, that, at inception, (a) embodies an obligation to

---

[5]In determining if an instrument is mandatorily redeemable, all terms within a redeemable instrument shall be considered. A term extension option, a provision that defers redemption until a specified liquidity level is reached, or a similar provision that may delay or accelerate the timing of a mandatory redemption does not affect the classification of a mandatorily redeemable financial instrument as a liability.

repurchase the issuer's equity shares, or is indexed to[6] such an obligation, and (b) requires or may require the issuer to settle the obligation by transferring assets shall be classified as a liability (or an asset in some circumstances[7]). Examples include forward purchase contracts or written put options on the issuer's equity shares that are to be physically settled or net cash settled.

Certain Obligations to Issue a Variable Number of Shares

12. A financial instrument that embodies an unconditional obligation, or a financial instrument other than an outstanding share that embodies a conditional obligation, that the issuer must or may settle by issuing a variable number of its equity shares shall be classified as a liability (or an asset in some circumstances) if, at inception, the monetary value of the obligation is based solely or predominantly on any one of the following:

a. A fixed monetary amount known at inception (for example, a payable settleable with a variable number of the issuer's equity shares)
b. Variations in something other than the fair value of the issuer's equity shares (for example, a financial instrument indexed to the S&P 500 and settleable with a variable number of the issuer's equity shares)
c. Variations inversely related to changes in the fair value of the issuer's equity shares (for example, a written put option that could be net share settled).

Freestanding Financial Instruments

13. This Statement applies to freestanding financial instruments, including those that comprise more than one option or forward contract, and paragraphs 9–12 shall be applied to a freestanding financial instrument in its entirety. For example, an instrument that consists of a written put option for an issuer's equity shares and a purchased call option and nothing else is

a freestanding financial instrument (paragraphs A15 and A16 provide examples of such instruments). That freestanding financial instrument embodies an obligation to repurchase the issuer's equity shares and is subject to the requirements of this Statement.

14. A freestanding financial instrument that is within the scope of this Statement shall not be combined with another freestanding financial instrument in applying paragraphs 9–12, unless combination is required under the provisions of Statement 133 and related guidance. For example, a freestanding written put option that is classified as a liability under this Statement shall not be combined with an outstanding equity share.

Embedded features

15. This Statement does not apply to features embedded in a financial instrument that is not a derivative in its entirety. An example is an option on the issuer's equity shares that is embedded in a nonderivative host contract. For purposes of applying paragraph 11(a) of Statement 133 in analyzing an embedded feature as though it were a separate instrument,[8] paragraphs 9–12 of this Statement shall not be applied to the embedded feature. Embedded features shall be analyzed by applying other applicable guidance.

Scope Limitation

16. This Statement does not affect the timing of recognition of financial instruments issued as contingent consideration in a business combination. The accounting for business combinations is addressed in FASB Statement No. 141, *Business Combinations*.[9] This Statement also does not alter the measurement guidance for contingent consideration set forth in paragraphs 25–36 of Statement 141. However, when recognized, a financial instrument within the scope of this Statement that is issued as consideration (whether contingent or noncontingent) in a business

---

[6]In this Statement, *indexed to* is used interchangeably with *based on variations in the fair value of*.

[7]Certain financial instruments that embody obligations that are liabilities within the scope of this Statement also may contain characteristics of assets but be reported as single items. Some examples include net-cash-settled or net-share-settled forward purchase contracts and certain combined options to repurchase the issuer's shares. Those instruments are classified as assets or liabilities initially or subsequently depending on the instrument's fair value on the reporting date.

[8]Paragraph 12 of Statement 133 requires an entity to identify derivative instruments that are embedded in contracts that do not meet the definition of a derivative instrument in their entirety. That paragraph sets forth criteria for determining whether such embedded derivative instruments are required to be separated from the host contract and accounted for separately as derivative instruments. One of those criteria, in paragraph 12(c) of that Statement, requires an embedded derivative instrument to be analyzed as though it were a separate instrument.

[9]The Board currently is addressing the accounting for contingent consideration issued in a business combination in its project on purchase method procedures.

combination shall be classified pursuant to the requirements of this Statement.

17. This Statement does not apply to obligations under share-based compensation arrangements if those obligations are accounted for under FASB Statement No. 123 (revised 2004), *Share-Based Payment,* AICPA Statement of Position (SOP) 93-6, *Employers' Accounting for Employee Stock Ownership Plans,* or related guidance. However, this Statement does apply to a freestanding financial instrument that was issued under a share-based compensation arrangement but is no longer subject to Statement 123(R), SOP 93-6, or related guidance. For example, this Statement applies to mandatorily redeemable shares issued upon an employee's exercise of an employee share option.

17A. This Statement does not apply to registration payment arrangements within the scope of FSP EITF 00-19-2, "Accounting for Registration Payment Arrangements."

Presentation

18. Items within the scope of this Statement shall be presented as liabilities (or assets in some circumstances). Those items shall not be presented between the liabilities section and the equity section of the statement of financial position.

19. Entities that have no equity instruments outstanding but have financial instruments issued in the form of shares, all of which are mandatorily redeemable financial instruments required to be classified as liabilities, shall describe those instruments as *shares subject to mandatory redemption* in statements of financial position to distinguish those instruments from other liabilities. Similarly, payments to holders of such instruments and related accruals shall be presented separately from payments to and interest due to other creditors in statements of cash flows and income.

Initial and Subsequent Measurement

20. Mandatorily redeemable financial instruments shall be initially measured at fair value.

21. Forward contracts that require physical settlement by repurchase of a fixed number of the issuer's

equity shares in exchange for cash shall be measured initially at the fair value of the shares at inception, adjusted for any consideration or unstated rights or privileges.[10] Equity shall be reduced by an amount equal to the fair value of the shares at inception.

22. Forward contracts that require physical settlement by repurchase of a fixed number of the issuer's equity shares in exchange for cash and mandatorily redeemable financial instruments shall be measured subsequently in one of two ways. If both the amount to be paid and the settlement date are fixed, those instruments shall be measured subsequently at the present value of the amount to be paid at settlement, accruing interest cost using the rate implicit at inception. If either the amount to be paid or the settlement date varies based on specified conditions, those instruments shall be measured subsequently at the amount of cash that would be paid under the conditions specified in the contract if settlement occurred at the reporting date, recognizing the resulting change in that amount from the previous reporting date as interest cost. Any amounts paid or to be paid to holders of those contracts in excess of the initial measurement amount shall be reflected in interest cost.

23. All other financial instruments within the scope of this Statement shall be measured initially at fair value. If a conditionally redeemable instrument becomes mandatorily redeemable, upon reclassification the issuer shall measure that liability initially at fair value and reduce equity by the amount of that initial measure, recognizing no gain or loss.

24. Financial instruments within the scope of Statement 133 shall be measured subsequently as required by the provisions of that Statement. All remaining financial instruments within the scope of this Statement not covered by the guidance in paragraph 22 shall be measured subsequently at fair value with changes in fair value recognized in earnings, unless either this Statement or other accounting guidance specifies another measurement attribute.

Earnings per Share

25. Entities that have issued mandatorily redeemable shares of common stock or entered into forward contracts that require physical settlement by repurchase

---

[10]One way to obtain that amount is by determining the amount of cash that would be paid under the conditions specified in the contract if the shares were repurchased immediately. Another way to obtain the same result is by discounting the settlement amount, at the rate implicit at inception after taking into account any consideration or unstated rights or privileges that may have affected the terms of the transaction.

of a fixed number of the issuer's equity shares of common stock in exchange for cash shall exclude the common shares that are to be redeemed or repurchased in calculating basic and diluted earnings per share. Any amounts, including contractual (accumulated) dividends and participation rights in undistributed earnings, attributable to shares that are to be redeemed or repurchased that have not been recognized as interest costs in accordance with paragraph 22 shall be deducted in computing income available to common shareholders (the numerator of the earnings per share calculation), consistently with the "two-class" method set forth in paragraph 61 of FASB Statement No. 128, *Earnings per Share*.

Disclosures

26. Issuers of financial instruments within the scope of this Statement shall disclose the nature and terms of the financial instruments and the rights and obligations embodied in those instruments. That disclosure shall include information about settlement alternatives, if any, in the contract and identify the entity that controls the settlement alternatives.

27. Additionally, for all outstanding financial instruments within the scope of this Statement and for each settlement alternative, issuers shall disclose:

a. The amount that would be paid, or the number of shares that would be issued and their fair value, determined under the conditions specified in the contract if the settlement were to occur at the reporting date
b. How changes in the fair value of the issuer's equity shares would affect those settlement amounts (for example, "the issuer is obligated to issue an additional x shares or pay an additional y dollars in cash for each $1 decrease in the fair value of one share")
c. The maximum amount that the issuer could be required to pay to redeem the instrument by physical settlement, if applicable
d. The maximum number of shares that could be required to be issued,[11] if applicable
e. That a contract does not limit the amount that the issuer could be required to pay or the number of shares that the issuer could be required to issue, if applicable
f. For a forward contract or an option indexed to the issuer's equity shares, the forward price or option

strike price, the number of issuer's shares to which the contract is indexed, and the settlement date or dates of the contract, as applicable.

28. Some entities have no equity instruments outstanding but have financial instruments in the form of shares, all of which are mandatorily redeemable financial instruments required to be classified as liabilities. Those entities are required under paragraph 19 of this Statement to describe those instruments as *shares subject to mandatory redemption* in statements of financial position to distinguish those instruments from other liabilities. Those entities shall disclose the components of the liability that would otherwise be related to shareholders' interest and other comprehensive income (if any) subject to the redemption feature (for example, par value and other paid-in amounts of mandatorily redeemable instruments shall be disclosed separately from the amount of retained earnings or accumulated deficit).

Effective Date and Transition

29. This Statement shall be effective for financial instruments entered into or modified after May 31, 2003, and otherwise shall be effective at the beginning of the first interim period beginning after June 15, 2003, except for mandatorily redeemable financial instruments of a **nonpublic entity.** For mandatorily redeemable financial instruments of a nonpublic entity, this Statement shall be effective for existing or new contracts for fiscal periods beginning after December 15, 2003. For financial instruments created before the issuance date of this Statement and still existing at the beginning of the interim period of adoption, transition shall be achieved by reporting the cumulative effect of a change in an accounting principle by initially measuring the financial instruments at fair value or other measurement attribute required by this Statement.

30. For mandatorily redeemable financial instruments and physically settled forward purchase contracts subject to the measurement requirements in paragraph 22 of this Statement, "dividends" and other amounts paid or accrued prior to reclassification of the instrument as a liability shall not be reclassified as interest cost upon transition. Reclassification to liabilities of preexisting noncontrolling interests that were recognized in business combinations under

---

[11]Paragraph 5 of FASB Statement No. 129, *Disclosure of Information about Capital Structure,* requires additional disclosures for actual issuances and settlements that occurred during the accounting period.

the purchase method and are mandatorily redeemable shall not result in changes in amounts previously recognized under the purchase method.

31. Restatement of financial statements for earlier years presented is not permitted.

The provisions of this Statement need not be applied to immaterial items.

This Statement was adopted by the affirmative votes of six members of the Financial Accounting Standards Board. Mr. Foster dissented.

Mr. Foster dissents from this Statement because he believes its provisions concerning the accounting for forward purchase contracts on an issuer's equity securities that require physical settlement in exchange for cash are inappropriate. First, the provisions that govern accounting for a forward purchase contract on an issuer's equity securities that requires physical settlement conflict with the accounting for almost all other forward purchase contracts and other executory contracts because this Statement requires a forward purchase contract to be recognized as if the future transaction specified in the contract had already occurred. Specifically, stock that is subject to purchase under the forward purchase contract but that is currently outstanding is accounted for as if it had been retired. This is in marked contrast with the accounting for a forward purchase contract on a commodity or other asset for which the asset and liability governed by the contract are not recognized until the transaction subject to the contract is consummated.

Mr. Foster acknowledges that transactions in an entity's equity securities have different characteristics than other transactions of an entity that sometimes justify different accounting treatment. However, in his view, even if the accounting model permitted other forward contracts and executory contracts to be accounted for on a gross basis (that is, the asset to be acquired under the contract and the liability to settle the contract were both recognized upon execution of the contract), the facts that (1) the equity securities are outstanding until a forward purchase contract on an issuer's equity securities is settled and (2) the holder of the securities retains all the associated rights until settlement would take precedence. To clarify, even if practice was to account for executory contracts on a gross basis, Mr. Foster would not permit the accounting for any forward purchase contracts on an issuer's equity securities to ignore the fact that the equity securities are outstanding.

Second, in reaching its conclusion, the Board likened a forward purchase contract that requires physical settlement in exchange for cash to mandatorily redeemable stock because the terms of the forward purchase contract require that equity securities be purchased. However, there is a significant difference between an instrument that is mandatorily redeemable by its terms and a contract separate from any shares of stock that requires a share (any share) of stock to be purchased. The Board has concluded that mandatorily redeemable financial instruments are liabilities—that is, they are not equity instruments. In contrast, outstanding shares of stock are equity instruments and should be accounted for as such. The Board's view that the combination of an outstanding share of stock and a forward purchase contract on any outstanding share of stock is tantamount to mandatorily redeemable stock is predicated on the view that two distinct and separate financial instruments should be combined and treated as a single contract. Statement 133 generally prohibits combining a derivative with another financial instrument to achieve a synthetic instrument that would result in different accounting for the combined contracts than if they were accounted for individually. For all the reasons set forth in the basis for conclusions of Statement 133, Mr. Foster agrees with that general prohibition and would apply it in these circumstances.

Finally, forward purchase contracts on an entity's equity securities as a result of this Statement meet the definition of a derivative in Statement 133. As such, Mr. Foster believes those contracts should be recognized and accounted for, like other derivatives, at fair value. To achieve the accounting for physically settled forward purchase contracts on an issuer's equity securities that is required by this Statement entails yet another exception to the basic provisions of Statement 133. Mr. Foster believes that an additional exception to the scope of Statement 133 in this circumstance is unwarranted.

Appendix A

IMPLEMENTATION GUIDANCE

CONTENTS

Appendix A

IMPLEMENTATION GUIDANCE

Introduction

A1. For each class of instrument within this Statement's scope, this appendix provides examples showing classification as a liability (or asset in some circumstances) and, for certain financial instruments, initial and subsequent measurement guidance.

Mandatorily Redeemable Financial Instruments

A2. Various financial instruments issued in the form of shares embody unconditional obligations of the issuer to redeem the instruments by transferring its assets at a specified or determinable date or dates or upon an event that is certain to occur. Paragraph 9 of this Statement requires that those mandatorily redeemable instruments be classified as liabilities. Mandatorily redeemable financial instruments include (among other instruments) certain forms of trust-preferred securities (those that are required to be redeemed at specified or determinable dates) and stock that must be redeemed upon the death or termination of the individual who holds it, which is an event that is certain to occur.

A3. Although some mandatorily redeemable instruments are issued in the form of shares, those instruments are classified as liabilities under this Statement because of the embodied obligation on the part of the issuer to transfer its assets.

Example: Trust-Preferred Securities

A4. Mandatorily redeemable preferred stock and trust-preferred securities may be issued in many forms, including those referred to as monthly-income-preferred securities, trust-preferred securities, and trust-originated-preferred securities. Many trust-preferred securities are issued in the following manner. A financial institution establishes a trust or other entity that the financial institution consoli-

dates.[12] The trust issues preferred securities to outside investors and uses the proceeds of the issuance of those securities to purchase from the financial institution an equivalent amount of junior subordinated debentures or other loans having stated maturities. The debentures or other loans are the only assets of the trust. When the financial institution makes its payments of interest on the debentures or other loans, the trust distributes the cash to the holders of the trust-preferred securities. The trust-preferred securities must be redeemed upon maturity of the debentures or other loans.

A5. In the above example, because the trust-preferred securities are mandatorily redeemable and represent obligations to transfer assets to redeem the shares, those instruments are classified as liabilities in the consolidated financial statements of the financial institution,[13] and payments or accruals of "dividends" and other amounts to be paid to holders are reported as interest cost.

Example: Stock to Be Redeemed upon Death of the Holder

A6. An entity may issue shares of stock that are required to be redeemed upon the death of the holder for a proportionate share of the book value of the entity. The death of the holder is an event that is certain to occur. Therefore, the stock is classified as a liability.[14] If the stock represents the only shares in the entity, the entity reports those instruments in the liabilities section of its statement of financial position and describes them as *shares subject to mandatory redemption* so as to distinguish the instruments from other financial statement liabilities. The issuer presents interest cost and payments to holders of such instruments separately, apart from interest and payments to other creditors, in statements of income and cash flows. The entity also discloses that the instruments are mandatorily redeemable upon the death of the holders. The following presentation is an example of the required presentation and disclosure for

---

[12]In this example, assume that the trust is required to be consolidated under the provisions of FASB Interpretation No. 46, *Consolidation of Variable Interest Entities*, and related guidance. However, if it were determined that the trust or other variable interest entity is not consolidated by the financial institution, the financial statements would reflect the liability owed to the variable interest entity.

[13]If redemption is required only upon liquidation or termination of the trust, this Statement does not require the securities to be reported as liabilities in the trust's standalone financial statements. However, this Statement does require the obligation to be reported as a liability in the consolidated financial statements of the financial institution because redemption is required to occur before the liquidation or termination of the reporting entity, that is, of the financial institution.

[14]An insurance contract that would cover the cost of the redemption does not affect the classification of the stock as a liability.

entities that have no equity instruments outstanding but have shares, all of which are mandatorily redeemable financial instruments classified as liabilities:

Statement of Financial Position:

Total assets	$1,800,000
Liabilities other than shares	$1,000,000
Shares subject to mandatory redemption*	800,000
Total liabilities	$1,800,000

Notes to Financial Statements:

*Shares, all subject to mandatory redemption upon death of the holders, consist of:

Common stock—$100 par value, 10,000 shares authorized, 5,000 shares issued and outstanding	$ 500,000
Retained earnings attributable to those shares	320,000
Accumulated other comprehensive income attributable to those shares	(20,000)
	$ 800,000

Example: Reclassification of Stock That Becomes Mandatorily Redeemable

A7. If a financial instrument will be redeemed only upon the occurrence of a conditional event, redemption of that instrument is conditional and, therefore, the instrument does not meet the definition of *mandatorily redeemable financial instrument* in this Statement. However, that financial instrument would be assessed at each reporting period to determine whether circumstances have changed such that the instrument now meets the definition of mandatorily redeemable (that is, the event is no longer conditional). If the event has occurred, the condition is resolved, or the event has become certain to occur, the financial instrument is reclassified as a liability.

A8. For example, an entity may issue equity shares on January 2, 2004, that must be redeemed (not at the option of the holder) six months after a change in control. When issued, the shares are conditionally redeemable and, therefore, do not meet the definition of mandatorily redeemable. On December 30, 2008, there is a change in control, requiring the shares to be redeemed on June 30, 2009. On December 31, 2008, the issuer would treat the shares as mandatorily redeemable and reclassify the shares as liabilities, measured initially at fair value. Additionally, the is-

suer would reduce equity by the amount of that initial measure, recognizing no gain or loss.

A9. For another example of a conditionally redeemable instrument, an entity may issue preferred shares with a stated redemption date 30 years hence that also are convertible at the option of the holders into a fixed number of common shares during the first 10 years. Those instruments are not mandatorily redeemable for the first 10 years because the redemption is conditional, contingent upon the holder's not exercising its option to convert into common shares.[15] However, when the conversion option (the condition) expires, the shares would become mandatorily redeemable and would be reclassified as liabilities, measured initially at fair value.

Obligations to Repurchase an Issuer's Equity Shares That Require a Transfer of Assets

Written Put Options That Require Physical or Net Cash Settlement

A10. Freestanding written put options on the option writer's (issuer's) equity shares that require physical settlement were generally classified, before this Statement, as equity under Emerging Issues Task Force (EITF) Issue No. 00-19, "Accounting for Derivative Financial Instruments Indexed to, and Potentially Settled in, a Company's Own Stock." Under

---

[15]If the conversion option were nonsubstantive, for example, because the conversion price is extremely high in relation to the current share price, it would be disregarded as provided in paragraph 8 of this Statement. If that were the case at inception, those preferred shares would be considered mandatorily redeemable and classified as liabilities with no subsequent reassessment of the nonsubstantive feature.

paragraph 11 of this Statement, written put options that require physical settlement are classified as liabilities because those instruments embody obligations to repurchase the issuer's equity shares that require the issuer to settle by transferring its assets. Written put options that require or permit net cash settlement also are classified as liabilities under paragraph 11 because those instruments are indexed to obligations to repurchase the issuer's equity shares and require the issuer to settle by transferring its assets. Because written put options are classified as liabilities under this Statement, those instruments no longer meet the exception for equity derivatives of the issuer in paragraph 11(a) of FASB Statement No. 133, *Accounting for Derivative Instruments and Hedging Activities.* Consequently, they either are derivative instruments, if they meet other criteria in Statement 133, or are required to be measured initially and subsequently at fair value under paragraphs 23 and 24 of this Statement.

Forward Purchase Contracts That Require Physical or Net Cash Settlement

A11. Freestanding forward contracts to purchase an issuer's equity shares that require physical settlement were generally classified, before this Statement, as equity under Issue 00-19. Under paragraph 11 of this Statement, those forward purchase contracts are classified as liabilities because those instruments embody obligations that require the issuer to settle by transferring its assets. Unlike physically settled written put options, which are initially and measured subsequently at fair value, liabilities arising from forward contracts to repurchase the issuer's equity shares for cash[16] that must be physically settled are measured initially under paragraph 21 of this Statement at the fair value of the shares at inception adjusted for any consideration or unstated rights or privileges. Under paragraph 22 of this Statement, if both the amount of cash and the settlement date are fixed, those contracts are measured subsequently at the present value of the amount to be paid at settlement by accruing interest cost at the rate implicit at inception, resulting in a liability at maturity equal to the forward contract amount. If, under the forward purchase contract, either the amount of cash to be paid or the settlement

date varies based on specified conditions, those instruments are measured subsequently at the amount of cash that would be paid under the conditions specified in the contract if the shares were redeemed or repurchased at the reporting date, recognizing interest cost for the change from the previous reporting date.

Example: Physically Settled Forward Purchase Contract

A12. An entity may enter into a forward contract to repurchase 1 million shares of its common stock from another party 2 years later. At inception, the forward contract price[17] per share is $30, and the current price of the underlying shares is $25. The contract's terms require that the entity pay cash to repurchase the shares (the entity is obligated to transfer $30 million in 2 years). Because the instrument embodies an unconditional obligation to transfer assets, it is a liability under paragraph 11 of this Statement. The entity would recognize a liability and reduce equity by $25 million (which is the present value, at the 9.54 percent rate implicit in the contract, of the $30 million contract amount, and also, in this example, the fair value of the underlying shares at inception). Interest would be accrued over the 2-year period to the forward contract amount of $30 million, using the 9.54 percent rate implicit in the contract. If the underlying shares are expected to pay dividends before the repurchase date and that fact is reflected in the rate implicit in the contract, the present value of the liability and subsequent accrual to the contract amount would reflect that implicit rate. Amounts accrued are recognized as interest cost.

A13. In the example in paragraph A12, no consideration or other rights or privileges changed hands at inception. If the same contract price of $30 per share had been agreed to even though the current price of the issuer's shares was $30, because the issuer had simultaneously sold the counterparty a product at a $5 million discount, that right or privilege unstated in the forward purchase contract would be taken into consideration in arriving at the appropriate implied discount rate—9.54 percent rather than 0 percent—for that contract. That entity would recognize a liability for $25 million, reduce equity by

---

[16]Cash includes foreign currency, so physically settled forward purchase contracts in exchange for foreign currency are to be measured as provided in paragraphs 21 and 22 of this Statement, then remeasured under FASB Statement No. 52, *Foreign Currency Translation.*

[17]Contracts referred to as variable-rate forwards are commonly used to effect equity forward transactions. The contract price on those forward contracts is not fixed at inception but varies based on changes in a specified index (for example, 3-month US LIBOR) during the life of the contract. If such a contract requires physical settlement, a different measurement method is required subsequently, as set forth in paragraph 22 of this Statement.

$30 million, and increase its revenue for the sale of the product by $5 million. Alternatively, if the same contract price of $30 per share had been agreed to even though the current price of the issuer's shares was only $20, because the issuer received a $5 million payment at inception of the contract, the issuer would recognize a liability for $25 million and reduce equity by $20 million. In both examples, interest would be accrued over the 2-year period using the 9.54 percent implicit rate, increasing the liability to the $30 million contract price.

A14. In contrast to forward purchase contracts that require physical settlement in exchange for cash, forward purchase contracts that require or permit net cash settlement, require or permit net share settlement, or require physical settlement in exchange for specified quantities of assets other than cash are measured initially and subsequently at fair value, as provided in paragraphs 23 and 24, and classified as assets or liabilities depending on the fair value of the contracts on the reporting date.

Example: Combination of Written Put Option and Purchased Call Option Issued as a Freestanding Instrument

A15. If a freestanding financial instrument consists solely of a written put option to repurchase the issuer's equity shares and another option, that freestanding financial instrument in its entirety is subjected to paragraphs 9–12 of this Statement to determine if it meets the requirements to be classified as a liability. For example, a company may enter into a contract that requires it to purchase 100 shares of its own stock on a specified date for $20 if the stock price falls below $20 and entitles the company to purchase 100 shares on that date for $21 if the stock price is greater than $21. That contract shall be analyzed as the combination of a written put option and a purchased call option and not as a forward contract. The written put option on 100 shares has a strike price of $20, and the purchased call option on 100 shares has a strike price of $21. If at issuance the fair value of the written put option exceeds the fair value of the purchased call option, the issuer receives cash and the contract is a net written option—a liability. If required to be physically settled, that contract is a liability under the provisions in paragraph 11 of this Statement because it embodies an obligation that may require repurchase of the issuer's equity shares and settlement by a transfer of assets. If the issuer must or can net cash settle the contract, the contract is a liability under the provisions of paragraph 11 of this

Statement because it embodies an obligation that is indexed to an obligation to repurchase the issuer's equity shares and may require settlement by a transfer of assets. If the issuer must or can net share settle the contract, that contract is a liability under the provisions in paragraph 12(c) of this Statement, because the monetary value of the obligation varies inversely in relation to changes in the fair value of the issuer's equity shares.

A16. If, in the example in paragraph A15, the fair value of the purchased call option at issuance exceeds the fair value of the written put option, the issuer pays out cash and the contract is a net purchased option, to be initially classified as an asset under either paragraph 11 or paragraph 12(c) of this Statement. If the fair values of the two options are equal and opposite at issuance, the financial instrument has an initial fair value of zero, and is commonly called a zero-cost collar. Thereafter, if the fair value of the instrument changes, the instrument is classified as an asset or a liability and measured subsequently at fair value.

Certain Obligations to Issue a Variable Number of Shares

A17. Paragraph 12 of this Statement requires liability classification if, at inception, the monetary value of an obligation to issue a variable number of shares is based solely or predominantly on (a) a fixed monetary amount known at inception, (b) variations in something other than the fair value of the issuer's equity shares, or (c) variations inversely related to changes in the fair value of the issuer's equity shares. The following examples illustrate the application of this Statement to such share-settled obligations.

Example: Obligation to Issue Shares with Monetary Value Based on a Fixed Monetary Amount Known at Inception

A18. Certain financial instruments embody obligations that require (or permit at the issuer's discretion) settlement by issuance of a variable number of the issuer's equity shares that have a value equal to a fixed monetary amount. For example, an entity may receive $100,000 in exchange for a promise to issue a sufficient number of its own shares to be worth $110,000 at a future date. The number of shares required to be issued to settle that unconditional obligation is variable, because that number will be determined by the fair value of the issuer's equity shares on the date of settlement. Regardless of the fair value of the shares on the date of settlement, the holder will receive a fixed monetary value of $110,000. Therefore, the instrument is classified as a liability under paragraph 12(a) of this Statement.

A19. Some share-settled obligations of this kind require that the variable number of shares to be issued be based on an average market price for the shares over a stated period of time, such as the average over the last 30 days prior to settlement, instead of the fair value of the issuer's equity shares on the date of settlement. Thus, if the average market price differs from the share price on the date of settlement, the monetary value of the obligation is not entirely fixed at inception and is based, in small part, on variations in the fair value of the issuer's equity shares. Although the monetary amount of the obligation at settlement may differ from the initial monetary value because it is tied to the change in fair value of the issuer's equity shares over the last 30 days prior to settlement, the monetary value of the obligation is predominantly based on a fixed monetary amount known at inception. The obligation is classified as a liability under paragraph 12(a) of this Statement. Upon issuance of the shares to settle the obligation, equity is increased by the amount of the liability and no gain or loss is recognized for the difference between the average and the ending market price.

Example: Obligation to Issue Shares with Monetary Value Based on Something Other Than Changes in the Fair Value of the Issuer's Equity

A20. An entity's guarantee of the value of an asset, liability, or equity security of another entity may require or permit settlement in the entity's equity shares. For example, an entity may guarantee that the value of a counterparty's equity investment in another entity will not fall below a specified level. The guarantee contract requires that the guarantor stand ready to issue a variable number of its shares whose fair value equals the deficiency, if any, on a specified date between the guaranteed value of the investment and its current fair value. Upon issuance, unless the guarantee is accounted for as a derivative, the obligation to stand ready to perform is a liability addressed by FASB Interpretation No. 45, *Guarantor's Accounting and Disclosure Requirements for Guarantees, Including Indirect Guarantees of Indebtedness of Others*. If, during the period the contract is outstanding, the fair value of the guaranteed investment falls below the specified level, absent an increase in value, the guarantor will be required to issue its equity shares. At that point in time, the liability recognized in accordance with Interpretation 45 would be subject to the requirements of FASB Statement No. 5, *Accounting for Contingencies*. This Statement establishes that, even though the loss contingency is settleable in equity shares, the obligation under Statement 5 is a liability under paragraph 12(b) of this Statement until the guarantor settles the obligation by issuing its shares. That is because the guarantor's conditional obligation to issue shares is based on the value of the counterparty's equity investment in another entity and not on changes in the fair value of the guarantor's equity instruments.

A21. If the example in paragraph A20 of this Statement were altered so that the monetary value of the obligation is based on (a) the deficiency on a specified date between the guaranteed value of the investment in another entity and its current fair value plus (b) .005 times the change in value of 100 of the guarantor's equity shares, the monetary value of the obligation would not be *solely* based on variations in something other than the fair value of the issuer's (guarantor's) equity shares. However, the monetary value of the obligation would be *predominantly* based on variations in something other than the fair value of the issuer's (guarantor's) equity shares and, therefore, the obligation would be classified as a liability under paragraph 12(b) of this Statement. That obligation differs in degree from the obligation under a contract that is indexed in part to the issuer's shares and in part (but not predominantly) to something other than the issuer's shares (commonly called a dual-indexed obligation). The latter contract is not within the scope of this Statement. Paragraph 12(b) of this Statement applies only if the monetary value of an obligation to issue equity shares is based *solely* or *predominantly* on variations in something other than the fair value of the issuer's equity shares. For example, an instrument meeting the definition of a derivative that requires delivery of a variable number of the issuer's equity shares with a monetary value equaling changes in the price of a fixed number of the issuer's shares multiplied by the Euro/US$ exchange rate embodies an obligation with a monetary value that is based on variations in both the issuer's share price and the foreign exchange rate and, therefore, is not within the scope of this Statement. (However, that instrument would be a derivative under Statement 133.)[18]

Example: Obligation to Issue Shares with Monetary Value Based on Variations Inversely Related to Changes in the Fair Value of the Issuer's Equity Shares

A22. A freestanding forward purchase contract, a freestanding written put option, or a net written option (otherwise similar to the example in paragraph A15) that must or may be net share settled is a liability under paragraph 12(c) of this Statement, because the monetary value of the obligation to deliver a variable number of shares embodied in the contract varies inversely in relation to changes in the fair value of the issuer's equity shares; when the issuer's share price decreases, the issuer's obligation under those contracts increases. Such a contract is measured initially and subsequently at fair value (with changes in fair value recognized in earnings) and classified as a liability or an asset, depending on the fair value of the contract on the reporting date. A net written or net purchased option or a zero-cost collar similar to the examples in paragraphs A15 and A16 that must or may be net share settled is classified as a liability (or asset) under paragraph 12(c), because the monetary value of the issuer's obligation to deliver a variable number of shares under the written put option varies inversely in relation to changes in the fair value of the issuer's share price. The purchased call option element of that freestanding instrument does not embody an obligation to deliver a variable number of shares and does not affect the classification of the entire instrument when applying paragraph 12(c). In addition, a freestanding purchased call option is not within the scope of this Statement because it does not embody an obligation.

Example: Unconditional Obligation That Must Be either Redeemed for Cash or Settled by Issuing Shares

A23. Some instruments do not require the issuer to transfer assets to settle the obligation but, instead, unconditionally require the issuer to settle the obligation

either by transferring assets or by issuing a variable number of its equity shares. Because those instruments do not require the issuer to settle by transfer of assets, those instruments are not within the scope of paragraph 9. However, those instruments may be classified as liabilities under paragraph 12 of this Statement.

A24. For example, an entity may issue 1 million shares of cumulative preferred stock for cash equal to the stock's liquidation preference of $25 per share. The entity is required either to redeem the shares on the fifth anniversary of issuance for the issuance price plus any accrued but unpaid dividends in cash or to settle by issuing sufficient shares of its common stock to be worth $25 per share. Preferred stockholders are entitled to a mandatory dividend, payable quarterly at a rate of 6 percent per annum based on the $25 per share liquidation preference ($1.50 per share annually). The dividend is cumulative and is payable in cash or in a sufficient number of additional shares of the preferred stock based on the liquidation preference of $25 per share. That obligation does not represent an unconditional obligation to transfer assets and, therefore, is not a mandatorily redeemable financial instrument subject to paragraph 9. But it is still a liability, under paragraph 12(a) of this Statement, because the preferred shares embody an unconditional obligation that the issuer may settle by issuing a variable number of its equity shares with a monetary value that is fixed and known at inception. Because the preferred shares are liabilities, payments to holders are reported as interest cost, and accrued but not-yet-paid payments are part of the liability for the shares.

Freestanding Financial Instruments

A25. Paragraph 13 of this Statement requires that the provisions of paragraphs 9–12 be applied to a freestanding instrument in its entirety. Paragraph 14 requires that a freestanding instrument within the scope of this Statement not be combined with other instruments in applying paragraphs 9–12, unless combination is required under Statement 133 and its related guidance.[19] Paragraph 8 requires that any nonsubstantive or minimal features be disregarded in

---

[18]Paragraph 11(a) of Statement 133 and Statement 133 Implementation Issue No. C8, "Derivatives That Are Indexed to both an Entity's Own Stock and Currency Exchange Rates," address derivative instruments that are dual indexed and require an issuer to report those instruments as derivative liabilities or assets.

[19]This Statement precludes combining freestanding instruments only for purposes of applying this Statement's provisions and only if Statement 133 and related guidance do not require combination. For example, Statement 133 Implementation Issue No. K1, "Determining Whether Separate Transactions Should Be Viewed as a Unit," requires certain separate transactions to be combined.

that application. The following examples illustrate how those provisions apply in four circumstances.

Example 1—Three Freestanding Instruments

A26. An issuer has the following three freestanding instruments with the same counterparty, entered into contemporaneously: (a) a written put option on its equity shares, (b) a purchased call option on its equity shares, and (c) outstanding shares of stock. Under this Statement, those three contracts would be separately evaluated. The written put option is reported as a liability under either paragraph 11 or paragraph 12(c) of this Statement (depending on the form of settlement) and is measured at fair value. The purchased call option does not embody an obligation and, therefore, is not within the scope of this Statement. The outstanding shares of stock also are not within the scope of this Statement, because the shares do not embody an obligation for the issuer. Under paragraph 14, neither the purchased call option nor the shares of stock are to be combined with the written put option in applying paragraphs 9–12 unless otherwise required by Statement 133 and its related guidance.[20]

Example 2—Two Freestanding Instruments

A27. An issuer has the following two freestanding instruments with the same counterparty entered into contemporaneously: (a) a contract that combines a written put option at one strike price and a purchased call option at another strike price on its equity shares and (b) outstanding shares of stock. As required by paragraph 13 of this Statement, paragraphs 9–12 are applied to the entire freestanding instrument that comprises both a put option and a call option. Because the put option element of the contract embodies an obligation to repurchase the issuer's equity shares, the freestanding instrument that comprises a put option and a call option is reported as a liability (or asset), under either paragraph 11 or paragraph 12(c) of this Statement (depending on the form of settlement) and is measured at fair value. Under paragraph 13, that freestanding financial instrument is within the scope of this Statement regardless of whether at current prices it is a net written, net purchased, or zero-cost collar option and regardless of the form of settlement. The outstanding shares of stock are not within the scope of this Statement[21] and, under paragraph 14, are not combined with the freestanding written put and purchased call option.

Example 3—One Freestanding Instrument That Is an Outstanding Share of Stock Containing Multiple Embedded Features

A28. An entity issues a share of stock that is not mandatorily redeemable. However, under its terms the stock is (a) puttable by the holder any time after five years or upon a change in control and is (b) callable by the issuer any time after five years. That instrument is outside the scope of this Statement. The instrument as a whole is not mandatorily redeemable under paragraph 9, because (1) the redemption is optional (conditional) and (2) a written put option and a purchased call option issued together with the same terms differ from a forward purchase contract under this Statement. That combination of embedded features does not render the stock mandatorily redeemable because the options could expire at the money, unexercised, and, thus, the redemption is not unconditional. Because the instrument as a whole is an outstanding share, it is not subject to paragraph 11 of this Statement nor, because the embedded obligation is conditional, is it subject to paragraph 12 of this Statement. As a financial instrument that is not a derivative in its entirety, it is subject to analysis under paragraph 12 of Statement 133 and to related guidance in Issue 00-19 or other applicable literature to determine whether the issuer must account for any embedded feature separately as a derivative. Because of the guidance in paragraph 15 of this Statement, paragraphs 9–12 shall not be applied to any embedded feature for the purposes of that analysis. In applying paragraph 12 of Statement 133, the embedded written put option is evaluated under the previous guidance in Issue 00-19 and would generally be classified in equity. If so, the embedded written put option meets the criterion for exclusion in paragraph 11(a) of Statement 133 and, therefore, is not separated from its host contract. If the written put option was not embedded in the share, but was issued as a freestanding instrument, it would be a liability under this Statement.

---

[20]If Statement 133 and its related guidance required the freestanding written put option and purchased call option to be combined and viewed as a unit, the unit would be accounted for as a combination of options, following the guidance in paragraphs A15 and A16 of this Statement.

[21]Some outstanding shares of stock are within the scope of this Statement, for example, mandatorily redeemable shares or shares subject to a physically settled forward purchase contract in exchange for cash.

Example 4—Option to Redeem Shares Embedded in a Minimal Host

A29. An entity issues one share of preferred stock (with a par amount of $100), paying a small dividend, and embeds in it an option allowing the holder to put the preferred share along with 100,000 shares of the issuer's common stock (currently trading at $50) for a fixed price of $45 per share in cash. The preferred stock host is judged at inception to be minimal and would be disregarded under paragraph 8 in applying the classification provisions of this Statement. Therefore, under either paragraph 11 or paragraph 12(c) of this Statement (depending on the form of settlement), that instrument would be analyzed as a written put option in its entirety, classified as a liability, and measured at fair value.

Examples of Cumulative-Effect Entries upon Transition

A30. The following table illustrates examples of cumulative-effect entries upon transition under paragraphs 29 and 30 of this Statement. The financial instruments in the table are outstanding on July 1, 2003. The liability and transition adjustment columns illustrate the entry made upon transition, with the balance being a reduction to equity.

Item	Previous Carrying Amount (Equity)	New Carrying Amount (Liability)	Transition Adjustment (Gain) Loss[a]	Explanation of Accounting at Transition
Mandatorily Redeemable Shares	$(5,250)	$(5,250)[b]	$0	Recognize liability at present value of redemption amount, using rate implicit in the contract at inception. Do not reclassify prior dividends or accruals.
Physically Settled Forward Purchase Contract	(2,500)[c]	(2,600)[d]	100	Recognize liability at present value of redemption amount, using rate implicit in the contract at inception. Reduce equity by the fair value of the shares at inception (the $2,500 in this example).
Physically Settled Forward Purchase Contract—Unstated Provision[e]	(3,000)[c]	(2,600)[d]	(400)	Recognize liability at present value of the redemption amount, using rate implicit in the contract at inception adjusted for unstated provision (present value of $3,000; rate was adjusted for revenue of $500). Reduce equity by the fair value of the shares at inception (the $3,000 in this example).
Written Put Option	(10)	(100)[f]	90	Recognize liability at fair value at the date of adoption.
Mandatorily Redeemable Noncontrolling Interests[g]	(5,000)	(5,000)[h]	0	Reclassify carrying amount as a liability if not already recognized as such.

[a]The transition adjustment is before tax considerations.

[b]The liability is measured initially at its present value at the date of adoption, using the rate implicit at inception of the contract. Upon transition, a cumulative adjustment is recognized in the statement of income for any difference between the carrying amount and the present value.

[c]The forward contract had a previous carrying amount of $0. Equity represents the fair value at inception of the shares underlying the forward purchase contract.

[d]The liability is measured initially at its present value at the date of adoption, using the rate implicit at inception of the contract adjusted for any consideration or unstated provision. Equity is reduced by the fair value of the shares at inception. Upon transition, a cumulative adjustment is recognized in the statement of income for any difference between those amounts.

[e]In this example, the unstated provision is revenue of $500 attributable to a simultaneous sale to a counterparty at a discount, similar to the example presented in paragraph A13.

[f]The liability (or asset in some circumstances) is measured initially at its fair value at the date of adoption. Upon transition, a cumulative adjustment is recognized in the statement of income for any difference between the carrying amount and the fair value.

[g]Prior to adoption of this Statement, some enterprises classified mandatorily redeemable noncontrolling interest as a liability, and others classified it as equity but reported it between the liabilities section and the equity section of the statement of financial position. The cumulative-effect entry illustrated for that financial instrument is applicable only if the mandatorily redeemable noncontrolling interest was classified as equity and presented between the liabilities section and the equity section and if it arose in a business combination under the purchase method.

[h]The liability is reclassified at its current carrying amount, with no cumulative adjustment recognized in the statement of income upon transition.

Appendix B

BACKGROUND INFORMATION AND BASIS FOR CONCLUSIONS

Appendix B

BACKGROUND INFORMATION AND BASIS FOR CONCLUSIONS

Introduction

B1. This appendix summarizes considerations that Board members deemed significant in reaching the conclusions in this Statement. It includes reasons for accepting certain views and rejecting other views. Individual Board members gave greater weight to some factors than to others.

B2. The Board undertook this project in response to constituents' concerns about classification in the statement of financial position of financial instru-ments with characteristics of liabilities, equity, or both. Financial instruments with characteristics of liabilities were being presented either entirely as equity or between the liabilities section and the equity section of the statement of financial position. Financial instruments with characteristics of equity also were being presented between the liabilities section and the equity section of the statement of financial position. Additionally, certain financial instruments with characteristics of both liabilities and equity were being classified entirely as liabilities or entirely as equity.

B3. The Board also undertook this project to acceler-ate international convergence of accounting stand-ards. The Canadian Institute of Chartered Accoun-tants (CICA), the Australian Accounting Standards Board (AASB), and the International Accounting

Standards Committee (IASC) have addressed the issue of accounting for financial instruments with characteristics of liabilities, equity, or both. The International Accounting Standards Board (IASB) has proposed significant revisions to existing IASC standards for such instruments. Paragraphs B77–B81 discuss how issuance of this Statement contributes to convergence of accounting standards.

Background Information

B4. This Statement is issued as part of the Board's broad project on financial instruments. That project was added to the Board's agenda in 1986 to address financial reporting issues that were arising, or were given a new sense of urgency, as a result of financial innovation. The project initially focused on disclosures and resulted in the issuance of FASB Statements No. 105, *Disclosure of Information about Financial Instruments with Off-Balance-Sheet Risk and Financial Instruments with Concentrations of Credit Risk,* in March 1990, and No. 107, *Disclosures about Fair Value of Financial Instruments,* in December 1991.

B5. In August 1990, the Board issued a Discussion Memorandum, *Distinguishing between Liability and Equity Instruments and Accounting for Instruments with Characteristics of Both.* The issuance of that Discussion Memorandum, combined with the issuance of another Discussion Memorandum in November 1991, *Recognition and Measurement of Financial Instruments,* began the recognition phase of the financial instruments project. That phase of the project has resulted in the issuance of:

- FASB Statement No. 114, *Accounting by Creditors for Impairment of a Loan,* May 1993
- FASB Statement No. 115, *Accounting for Certain Investments in Debt and Equity Securities,* May 1993
- FASB Statement No. 118, *Accounting by Creditors for Impairment of a Loan—Income Recognition and Disclosures,* October 1994
- FASB Statement No. 133, *Accounting for Derivative Instruments and Hedging Activities,* June 1998
- FASB Statement No. 134, *Accounting for Mortgage-Backed Securities Retained after the Securitization of Mortgage Loans Held for Sale by a Mortgage Banking Enterprise,* October 1998
- FASB Statement No. 137, *Accounting for Derivative Instruments and Hedging Activities—*

Deferral of the Effective Date of FASB Statement No. 133, June 1999
- FASB Statement No. 138, *Accounting for Certain Derivative Instruments and Certain Hedging Activities,* June 2000
- FASB Statement No. 140, *Accounting for Transfers and Servicing of Financial Assets and Extinguishments of Liabilities,* September 2000.

B6. The 1990 Discussion Memorandum elicited views on 12 issues. Four of those issues related to interpretation and application of the definitions of liabilities and equity in FASB Concepts Statement No. 6, *Elements of Financial Statements,* and whether the distinction between liabilities and equity should be changed. Two issues related to whether particular instruments should be classified as liabilities or as equity. Three issues related to whether the Board should change the distinction between liabilities and equity, including whether equity should be defined independently of liabilities and assets, whether a third "capital" element should be added to include certain instruments with characteristics of both liabilities and equity, and whether the distinction between liabilities and equity should be eliminated. One issue related to measurement at issuance and repurchases of equity instruments. The two remaining issues addressed accounting by issuers for compound instruments with characteristics of both liabilities and equity. The Board received 104 comment letters in response to that Discussion Memorandum.

B7. The Board held 2 days of public hearings on the 1990 Discussion Memorandum in March 1991, at which representatives from 13 organizations testified. Subsequent to the public hearings, the Board held two public meetings to discuss the conceptual distinctions between liabilities and equity that were pertinent to its project on accounting for stock compensation and whether the conceptual framework should be changed. At those meetings, the Board initially decided not to make fundamental changes to the definitions of liabilities and equity in Concepts Statement 6. After the second of those meetings (held in March 1992), the Board decided to suspend work on the liabilities and equity project to devote its resources to financial instrument issues that were deemed more urgent. The project was inactive until December 1996, at which time it was discussed by the Board's Financial Instruments Task Force. Based on the discussion at that task force meeting, work on the project began again.

B8. After discussing issues related to the liabilities and equity project at 30 Board meetings, as well as

2 additional task force meetings, the Board issued on October 27, 2000, an Exposure Draft of a proposed Statement of Accounting Standards, *Accounting for Financial Instruments with Characteristics of Liabilities, Equity, or Both.* On the same day, the Board issued another Exposure Draft, *Proposed Amendment to FASB Concepts Statement No. 6 to Revise the Definition of Liabilities.*

B9. The Board received 71 letters commenting on those Exposure Drafts. During May, June, and July 2001, Board members and staff met with seven different companies that volunteered to participate in field visits. The objectives of those field visits were to (a) test the understanding of the Exposure Drafts, (b) identify problems related to the implementation of the guidance in the Exposure Drafts, and (c) identify situations that produce results that raise questions about the representational faithfulness of the reporting of instruments or transactions. Board members and staff also met in field visits in November 2001 with various users of financial statements to discuss, from their perspective, the usefulness of the reporting that would result from the proposed change to the definition of liabilities in Concepts Statement 6.

B10. On October 16, 2001, 18 constituents participated in a roundtable discussion focusing on several issues raised in comment letters on the Exposure Drafts. At that roundtable discussion, constituents discussed several aspects of the Exposure Drafts including representational faithfulness, understandability of the proposed reporting, and the appropriateness of classifying certain instruments as liabilities, including mandatorily redeemable stock and certain share-settled obligations.

B11. At 16 public meetings during 2001 and 2002, the Board redeliberated the issues raised in the Exposure Drafts, comment letters, field visits, and the roundtable discussion. At those meetings, the Board affirmed its conclusions that certain freestanding financial instruments should be classified as liabilities: mandatorily redeemable instruments, instruments embodying obligations (or indexed to such obligations) to repurchase an issuer's equity shares by transferring assets, and certain instruments that the issuer must or can choose to settle with equity shares. However, at the end of 2002 the Board had not completed its redeliberations on several other issues, including separation of instruments with characteristics of both liabilities and equity into components, accounting for noncontrolling interests in consolidated subsidiaries, and inclusion of ownership interest concepts in revised definitions of liabilities and equity. During four further public meetings during 2003, the Board decided that issuance of this limited-scope Statement, even though separation and conceptual issues affecting other instruments are not yet resolved, is needed to provide timely and necessary guidance for certain troublesome instruments for which the practice problems are both clear and resolvable without necessarily addressing separation and conceptual issues. The Board plans to continue redeliberating the remaining issues and to issue another Statement at a future date. Moreover, because the Board believes resolution of those issues may affect any modification to the definition of a liability, the Board decided to delay any changes to that definition until those issues are resolved.

Proposed Amendment to Concepts Statement 6

B12. As part of its deliberations on this Statement, the Board discussed the accounting for financial instruments that embody obligations that require (or permit at the issuer's discretion) settlement by issuance of the issuer's equity shares. Those obligations do not require a transfer of assets and, thus, do not meet the current definition of liabilities in Concepts Statement 6. Therefore, those financial instruments have been classified as equity.

B13. However, not all such obligations establish the type of relationship that exists between an entity and its owners. For example, a financial instrument that requires settlement by issuance of $100,000 worth of equity shares establishes something more akin to a debtor-creditor relationship than to an ownership relationship, because it requires that the issuer convey a fixed amount of value to the holder that does not vary with the issuer's equity shares. A share-settled put option on the issuer's equity shares establishes the opposite (inverse) of an ownership relationship, because it requires the issuer to convey value to the holder that *increases* as the value of other owners' interests *decreases*.

B14. The Board considered and rejected the alternative of resolving the accounting issues raised by those financial instruments by applying the original definitions of liabilities and equity in Concepts Statement 6. The Board decided that it would be preferable to reconsider the distinction between liabilities and equity. Otherwise, classification by issuers of financial instruments that embody obligations would be based solely on whether the obligation requires settlement by a transfer of assets or by an issuance of equity instruments. As a result, certain instruments would be classified as equity even though those instruments do not establish the type of relationship that exists between an entity and its owners. Instead, the Board decided that the relevance and representational faithfulness of the reporting of those obligations would be improved if classification were based on the type of relationship established between the issuer and the holder of the instrument as well as the form of settlement.

B15. The Board, therefore, proposed an amendment to Concepts Statement 6 to revise its definition of liabilities.

B16. Commentators on the proposed amendment generally objected to the proposed revision to the definition of liabilities. Many said they saw no need to change the current definition. Some pointed out conceptual and practical concerns with the ramifications of incorporating the concept of ownership relationship into the distinction between liabilities and equity. Others, who agreed that an amendment is needed for the reasons cited by the Board, suggested revisions to the definition of liabilities different from the Board's proposal.

B17. After considering those comments and events since the issuance of the Exposure Drafts, the Board did not agree with the majority of commentators and decided that an amendment to Concepts Statement 6 to revise the definition of liabilities is necessary and that the amendment should incorporate the absence of an ownership relationship into the definition of liabilities. The Board affirmed its conclusions that certain financial instruments that embody obligations to issue shares place the holder of the instrument in a position fundamentally different from the position of a holder of the issuer's equity shares, that such obligations do not result in an ownership relationship, and that an instrument that embodies an obligation that does not establish an ownership relationship should be a liability. However, the Board agreed that the proposed amendment to Concepts Statement 6 needs further refinements and that the refinements could not be completed until the Board has considered, in further detail, certain instruments with liability and equity characteristics that are beyond the scope of this limited-scope Statement. The Board plans to deal with those instruments, including compound financial instruments, puttable shares, and dual-indexed financial instruments, in the next phase of this project.

B18. While the Board expects that the requirements of this Statement will be consistent with the revised definition of liabilities in its planned amendment to Concepts Statement 6, it decided to defer completion and issuance of that amendment until it completes its redeliberations of several remaining issues. The Board also notes that its project on revenue recognition may require other amendments to concepts of liabilities and that the Board and international standards-setting bodies have decided to work toward converging their standards and Concepts Statements. That project and those convergence efforts also may affect the timing of the amendment to the definition of liabilities in Concepts Statement 6.

Scope and Initial Classification

B19. This Statement provides guidance for determining the classification of and accounting for certain financial instruments that embody obligations of the issuing entity and fall within its limited scope. The limited scope includes mandatorily redeemable instruments, freestanding instruments that embody obligations to repurchase (or obligations that are indexed to the repurchase of) an issuer's equity shares by transferring assets, and freestanding instruments that embody certain obligations that the issuer must or can settle by issuing a variable number of its equity shares. The Board plans to provide standards in a later phase of this project for classification of other instruments with characteristics of both liabilities and equity that fall outside the limited scope of this Statement.

Mandatorily Redeemable Financial Instruments

B20. This Statement includes in its scope financial instruments issued in the form of shares that are mandatorily redeemable by transfers of assets because such instruments embody obligations that meet the current definition of liabilities in Concepts Statement 6 and satisfy all other recognition criteria. Mandatorily redeemable instruments, even though they may have the form of shares, (a) embody a present duty that entails settlement by future transfer of assets at a specified or determinable date or on occurrence of a specified event, (b) leave the issuer no discretion to avoid the future sacrifice of assets, and (c) result from a transaction—the issuance of the instrument—that has already happened. Therefore, the obligations under those instruments meet the current definition of liabilities.[22] Liabilities for mandatorily redeemable instruments also satisfy the other recognition criteria set forth in FASB Concepts Statement No. 5, *Recognition and Measurement in Financial Statements of Business Enterprises.* Those liabilities are readily measurable, for example, at fair value by observing market prices for those instruments or by determining the present value of the future cash flows required by the instrument. The measure, and other information about the obligation, is clearly relevant to investors, creditors, and other users of financial statements and has sufficient reliability at issuance for a liability to be recognized.

B21. Commentators on the Exposure Draft generally agreed with that proposal. Those who did not agree did not provide persuasive arguments. Many commentators expressed concern over the effect of transition to that proposed accounting on entities other than public companies (refer to paragraphs B58–B60). One commentator noted that ". . . if the issuing entity must be liquidated and ceases to exist when the mandatory redemption of its shares occurs, then the holders of those shares appear to have an ownership interest similar to the equity owners of the company." The Board agreed and drafted paragraph 9 of this Statement so that if redemption of an equity instrument is required on liquidation or termination of the reporting entity, the instrument is classified as equity.

B22. Some commentators inquired about certain shares that allow the issuer to extend their term, defer redemption until a specified liquidity level is reached, or have similar provisions that may delay or accelerate the timing of a required redemption. The Board concluded that such shares meet the definition of mandatorily redeemable financial instruments and should be classified as liabilities because those kinds of provisions may affect the timing of but do not remove the unconditional requirement for redemption.

B23. In contrast to mandatorily redeemable shares, shares of nonredeemable common stock do not impose on the issuer an obligation to pay dividends or to reacquire the shares. Declaration of dividends is at the discretion of the issuer, as is a decision to reacquire the shares. Similarly, preferred stock that is not redeemable does not impose on the issuer any obliga-

tion either to repurchase the shares or to pay dividends, even though failure to pay dividends may have adverse economic consequences for the issuer. Nonredeemable outstanding shares of both common and preferred stock lack an essential characteristic of a liability.

B24. Some types of preferred stock pay no, or low, dividends during the first few years they are outstanding and then pay dividends at an increasing rate. The Board considered whether an issuer of such "increasing-rate preferred stock" should be deemed to have an obligation to redeem the shares even though it is not legally obligated to do so. The Exposure Draft proposed that to the extent the shares are not mandatorily redeemable and no enforceable obligation to pay dividends exists, increasing-rate preferred stock does not embody an obligation on the part of the issuer and, therefore, should not be classified as a liability. Some commentators proposed that increasing-rate preferred stock be classified as a liability on the grounds that the increasing rate made redemption economically compelling or created an implied mandatory redemption date. The Board reconsidered that issue during its redeliberations but did not resolve it. The Board deferred until the next phase of the project a decision about whether an increasing-rate dividend provision, as well as other forms of economic compulsion, imposes an obligation on the issuer that causes the instrument to be a liability. However, the Board noted that increasing-rate preferred stock that is mandatorily redeemable on (or not later than) a specified date, like other mandatorily redeemable preferred stock, embodies an obligation to transfer assets and, therefore, is classified as a liability under the provisions of this Statement.

B25. Some commentators suggested that shares that the holder can choose to require the issuer to redeem—puttable shares—also should be classified entirely as liabilities. They noted that IAS 32, *Financial Instruments: Disclosure and Presentation,* has such a requirement, based on the characteristic that whether the shares are to be redeemed is outside the issuer's control. In response, the Board considered whether to include within the scope of this Statement shares that *could* be redeemed—mandatorily, at the option of the holder, or upon some contingent event that is outside the control of the issuer and the holder.

---

[22]This Statement also includes in its scope and requires liability classification for financial instruments issued in the form of shares that are mandatorily redeemable by issuance of a variable number of the issuer's equity shares, rather than by transfers of assets. The basis for that conclusion is discussed in paragraphs B30–B49.

However, this Statement limits the meaning of mandatorily redeemable to unconditional obligations to redeem the instrument by transferring assets at a specified or determinable date (or dates) or upon an event certain to occur. The Board decided that puttable and contingently redeemable stock raise issues that should be discussed in the next phase of this project, together with convertible bonds and other compound instruments that raise similar issues.

Obligations to Repurchase the Issuer's Equity Shares by Transferring Assets

B26. This Statement includes in its scope instruments, other than an outstanding share, that, at inception, (a) embody an obligation to repurchase the issuer's equity shares (or instruments that are indexed to such an obligation) and (b) require or may require the issuer to settle the obligation by transferring assets because such instruments meet the current definition of liabilities in Concepts Statement 6 and satisfy the other recognition criteria. The Board views such instruments as resulting in liabilities of two types: unconditional and conditional.

B27. Forward purchase contracts that must be physically settled by delivering cash in exchange for shares embody an unconditional obligation to transfer cash to pay the full repurchase price. The Board considers that situation as more akin to a treasury stock purchase using borrowed funds than to participating in a derivative instrument; put another way, such a forward contract effectively converts the shares that the counterparty must deliver into mandatorily redeemable instruments, which this Statement classifies as liabilities. The Board rejected the view that forward purchase contracts that must be physically settled by delivering cash should be reported like other derivative instruments. The Board concluded that the unconditional obligation should result in recognition of a liability that, like many other liabilities that require cash payments, should be subsequently measured at the present value of the full repurchase price, if the amounts to be paid and the settlement date are fixed, or at the (undiscounted) amounts that would be paid under the conditions specified in the contract if the shares were repurchased at the reporting date if the amounts or settlement date can vary.

B28. In contrast, other kinds of contracts to repurchase the issuer's equity shares embody conditional obligations. Forward purchase contracts that must or can be net cash settled embody obligations that are indexed to a repurchase of the equity shares. Such contracts require the issuer of the underlying shares to transfer assets if the fair value of the forward purchase contract at the settlement date places the issuer in a loss position. If prices instead move in the issuer's favor, the issuer will receive assets and will not have to transfer anything. Conditional purchase contracts also embody obligations that are conditional, whether settled by physical exchange or net cash payment. The issuer might have to transfer assets if, for example, the holder of a put option exercises its option, but the issuer will not have to transfer assets if that put option expires unexercised. The Board reasoned that forward purchase contracts that can be cash settled and contingent purchase contracts are liabilities in themselves and that they are generally derivative instruments under Statement 133. However, because the obligation in those contracts is conditional, the Board reasoned that those instruments should be accounted for differently from forward purchase contracts that must be physically settled for cash. Contracts that embody conditional obligations are not akin to a treasury stock purchase using borrowed funds, and they do not effectively convert the shares that the counterparty might or might not deliver into mandatorily redeemable shares, that is, into liabilities. Therefore, those contracts should not be accounted for as if they did.

B29. Forward purchase contracts that must be physically settled by delivering assets other than cash in exchange for shares—barter contracts—also embody an unconditional obligation. However, the Board did not consider barter contracts akin to a treasury stock purchase using borrowed funds, since no cash is involved. Therefore, it decided that those contracts should be accounted for in the same manner as conditional obligations to purchase the issuer's equity shares.

Obligations to Issue a Variable Number of Shares

B30. Obligations that the issuer can or must settle by issuing its equity shares do not meet the current definition of liabilities in Concepts Statement 6 because, although those instruments embody an obligation that entails settlement, and the obligation arises from a past event, the issuer can avoid having to transfer assets. Because the issuer can or must settle the obligation by issuing its equity shares, under current concepts such instruments have been classified as equity—an ownership interest.

B31. However, certain share-settled obligations establish relationships that, in the Board's view, have little if anything in common with ownership interests. For that reason, the Board proposed to amend Concepts Statement 6 to revise the definition of liabilities to include certain obligations to issue equity shares. However, as discussed in paragraphs B12–B18, the Board decided to defer completion and issuance of that amendment. Instead, the Board decided that this Statement should require certain share-settled obligations to be classified as liabilities rather than as equity, in the expectation that that requirement will be consistent with the revised definition of liabilities in that planned amendment.

B32. This Statement requires that a financial instrument that embodies an unconditional obligation, or a financial instrument other than an outstanding share that embodies a conditional obligation, that the issuer must or may settle by issuing a variable number of its equity shares be classified as a liability (or an asset in some circumstances) if, at inception, the monetary value of the obligation is based solely or predominantly on (a) a fixed monetary amount known at inception, (b) variations in something other than the fair value of the issuer's equity shares, or (c) variations inversely related to changes in the fair value of the issuer's equity shares. The Board's conclusions about the elements of that requirement are discussed in paragraphs B33–B49.

Obligation

B33. Identifying whether a financial instrument embodies an obligation is the starting point in determining the appropriate classification of that instrument. Both the definition of liabilities in paragraph 35 of Concepts Statement 6 and the essential characteristics of a liability listed in paragraph 36 of that Statement include the notion of an obligation being an essential characteristic. A financial instrument that does not embody an obligation cannot be a liability under the current Concepts Statement 6 definition. The Board concluded in the Exposure Draft that the existence of an obligation should continue to be an essential characteristic of a liability.

B34. In this Statement, an *obligation* is a duty or responsibility on the part of the issuer either to transfer assets or to issue its equity shares. That differs from the usage of that term in Concepts Statement 6 in two respects. This Statement omits the Concepts Statement's phrase *to provide services,* because this Statement applies only to financial instruments. This Statement adds to the notion of an obligation a duty or responsibility to issue equity shares. Although an

issuer's equity shares are not assets to the issuer, they become assets to the new holder of the shares. Settling an obligation by issuing shares will adversely affect the interests of the other holders of the issuer's equity shares by diluting their interests in the issuer's assets, just as settling an obligation by transferring assets will adversely affect their interests by reducing the issuer's assets. The duty or responsibility to issue shares leaves an entity little or no discretion to avoid taking an action that it might otherwise wish to avoid. Therefore, the Board concluded that a duty or responsibility to issue shares is an obligation and, potentially, a liability.

B35. Many commentators disagreed with that conclusion. They argued that the current definition of liabilities is appropriate, there are no practice problems related to the current definition, and EITF Issue No. 00-19, "Accounting for Derivative Financial Instruments Indexed to, and Potentially Settled in, a Company's Own Stock," provides adequate guidance based on the concept that *all* contracts that require or permit the issuer to settle in shares are equity instruments. Other commentators supported the Board's conclusion, citing practice problems and the reasoning presented in the Exposure Draft. The Board observed a number of practice problems, some of which were associated with major business failures that occurred between the comment period and the Board's final deliberations on this Statement. The Board decided that its conclusion in the Exposure Draft was appropriate and reaffirmed it.

Monetary value

B36. Obligations that require the issuer to issue its equity shares were classified as equity under the original definitions in Concepts Statement 6. As discussed in paragraphs B12–B18, however, the Board concluded in the Exposure Draft that those obligations should not be classified as equity unless they establish an ownership relationship. To be classified as equity, the Board believes that an obligation must expose the holder of the instrument that embodies that obligation to certain risks and benefits that are similar to those to which an owner (that is, a holder of an outstanding share of the entity's equity) is exposed.

B37. The Board concluded in the Exposure Draft that, in determining whether an owner benefits, it is appropriate to consider whether the owner's investment increases in value, not whether the entity is profitable. The value of an owner's investment changes in response to changes in the fair value of the entity's equity shares. Therefore, the Board concluded that exposure to changes in the fair value of the issuer's equity shares is a characteristic of an ownership relationship, because that fair value reflects the realizable benefits of owners that are within their control. Therefore, for the purpose of classifying an obligation that requires settlement by issuance of the issuer's equity shares, the distinction between obligations that are liabilities and obligations that are equity should be based on the relationship between (a) the value that the holder of the instrument that embodies the obligation is entitled to receive upon settlement of the obligation and (b) the value of the underlying equity shares. In particular, the Board concluded that for an obligation to be classified as equity, any benefits or risks of changes in the obligation must stem directly from changes in the fair value of the issuer's equity shares and be similar to the risks or benefits that would be realized by a holder of an outstanding equity share of the entity.

B38. The Board developed the notion of monetary value to assist in determining whether the risks or benefits from changes in fair value of the issuer's equity shares to which a holder of a financial instrument that embodies an obligation is exposed are similar to those to which a holder of outstanding equity shares is exposed. The Exposure Draft described monetary value as the amount of value measured in units of currency that must be conveyed to the holder upon settlement of an obligation at its maturity, absent a change in current market conditions. Some commentators suggested that the term should be more clearly defined. In response, this Statement further refines the notion of monetary value, defining it as what the fair value of the cash, shares, or other instruments that a financial instrument obligates the issuer to convey to the holder would be at the settlement date under specified market conditions.

B39. The Board concluded that the relationship between changes in the monetary value of an instrument that embodies an obligation and changes in the fair value of the issuer's equity shares during the period the obligation is outstanding would be an effective basic principle to assess whether the holder of the instrument is exposed to risks and benefits that are similar to those to which a holder of a corresponding number of outstanding equity shares (an owner) is exposed.

Variable number of the issuer's equity shares

B40. In applying that basic principle, the Exposure Draft proposed that a financial instrument that em-

bodies an obligation that requires settlement by issuance of a *fixed* number of the issuer's equity shares should be classified as equity, reasoning that changes in the monetary values of such instruments arise from and are equal to changes in the fair value of that fixed number of shares. Commentators generally supported that view. One possibility that arose in subsequent deliberations is that even the interest of a holder of that sort of obligation differs from the interest of a holder of shares and, therefore, perhaps the obligation should not be classified as equity. While a fixed-price physically settled written call option or warrant would, if exercised, require settlement by a fixed number of shares, such an option might never be exercised and so returns to the option holder would differ from returns to a shareholder. The Board did not decide whether to classify such obligations as liabilities in this limited-scope Statement; the Board deferred resolution of that issue until it can be discussed together with related issues in the next phase of this project.

B41. Other financial instruments require settlement by issuance of a *variable* number of shares. For some of those kinds of obligations, the monetary values may arise from, and may change equally to and in the same direction as, changes in the fair value of the issuer's equity shares. Those obligations remain outside the scope of this Statement. However, the monetary values of many kinds of obligations to issue a variable number of shares behave differently. Their monetary values may be fixed, may vary in relation to some factor other than the fair value of the issuer's equity shares, or may vary inversely with changes in the fair value of the issuer's equity shares.

Fixed monetary amount

B42. Some obligations to issue a variable number of shares have contractually fixed monetary values. For example, if an obligation requires settlement by issuance of shares worth $100,000 on the settlement date, the number of shares to be issued varies based on the fair value of those shares at settlement. Regardless of changes in the fair value of the shares, however, the holder is to receive $100,000 of value at settlement— that is, the monetary value of the obligation does not change. The holder of that instrument does not benefit if the fair value of the issuer's equity shares increases and does not bear the risk that the fair value of those shares might decrease. The Board decided that that type of instrument should be classified as a liability because it does not establish an ownership relationship. That is, even though the obligation will be settled by issuance of equity shares, the instrument has more characteristics of a liability than of equity because the holder's return is fixed and, thus, unrelated to changes in the fair value of the issuer's equity shares.

Variations in something other than the fair value of the issuer's equity shares

B43. Some obligations to issue a variable number of shares are indexed or otherwise tied to the value of something other than the issuer's equity shares. One example is a guarantee contract that requires that the guarantor issue a variable number of its shares whose fair value equals the deficiency on a specified date between the guaranteed value of the investment and its current market value. Even though the issuer's equity shares will be issued in settlement of the obligation, that type of contract should be classified as a liability because it does not establish an ownership relationship. That is, even though the obligation will be settled by issuance of equity shares, the component has more characteristics of a liability than of equity because the guaranteed party's return is unrelated to changes in the fair value of the issuer's equity shares.

Variations inversely related to changes in the fair value of the issuer's equity shares

B44. Some obligations to issue a variable number of shares have monetary values that are indexed or otherwise tied to the fair value of the issuer's equity shares, but those monetary values vary inversely with changes in the fair value of the issuer's shares. Examples include forward purchase contracts, written put options, or net written (or purchased or zero-cost) options or collars that require or permit net share settlement. Because the interests of holders of those instruments are diametrically opposed to those of holders of the issuer's equity shares, the Board concluded that the issuer's obligations under those instruments could not be considered equity interests and, therefore, must be liabilities (or assets in some circumstances).

B45. Some commentators argued that written put options on a company's own stock and forward repurchase agreements are often entered into to manage the risk of price fluctuations during the course of stock repurchase programs and, as a result, should be treated as equity. The Board rejected that argument because (a) efforts to manage the risks of stock repurchase programs would merit accounting recognition

only if those efforts met the criteria for hedge accounting, and (b) among its other requirements, Statement 133 permits hedge accounting only if the hedging instrument is a derivative instrument and is classified as a liability or asset, and only if either the hedged item is an asset or liability or the forecasted transaction presents an exposure to variations in cash flows that could affect reported earnings, none of which is the case with stock repurchase programs. Others argued that differentiating between obligations with monetary values that change in the same direction as the fair value of the issuer's shares and those with monetary values that change in the opposite direction would create inconsistency and confusion. The Board rejected that argument because it sees no basis for accounting in the same way for different obligations, one of which comports with the interests of holders of the issuer's equity shares and the other of which is opposed to those interests.

Solely or predominantly based

B46. The scope of this Statement is limited because the Board has not completed its redeliberations on several major issues raised in the liabilities and equity Exposure Draft, one of which is the separation of instruments with characteristics of both liabilities and equity into components. Most issues affecting compound instruments, including dual-indexed share-settled instruments (instruments whose value is tied not only to an issuer's equity shares but also to something else), therefore, are beyond the scope of this Statement. Because of that limitation, the Board initially decided that the requirements of paragraph 12 of this Statement should be limited to instruments that embody obligations, the monetary value of which is based *solely* on (a) a fixed monetary amount known at inception, (b) variations in something other than the fair value of the issuer's equity shares, or (c) variations inversely related to changes in the fair value of the issuer's equity shares.

B47. The Board considered that issue further in light of suggestions that requiring the monetary value to be based solely on those factors might result in instruments constructed to avoid this Statement's scope, for example, by embedding a small amount of monetary value variation in response to changes in the fair value of the issuer's equity shares even though the overall variation would predominantly respond to something else. To avoid that, the Board decided to extend the scope to include share-settled instruments whose monetary value is based solely or *predominantly* on one of the three factors in paragraph 12 of this Statement. The Board acknowledged that judgment will be required to distinguish instruments with monetary values predominantly based on one of those three factors from instruments with monetary values that are indexed both to the issuer's equity shares and to one or more other factors and, thus, are excluded from this Statement's scope.

Must or may settle by issuing equity shares

B48. Certain financial instruments embody obligations that permit the *issuer* to determine whether it will settle the obligation by transferring assets or by issuing equity shares. Because those obligations provide the issuer with discretion to avoid a transfer of assets, the Board concluded that those obligations should be treated like obligations that require settlement by issuance of equity shares. That is, the Board concluded that this Statement should require liability classification of obligations that provide the issuer with the discretion to determine how the obligations will be settled if, and only if, the conditions in paragraph 12 related to changes in monetary value are met.

B49. Other obligations permit the *holder* to determine whether the issuer will be required to transfer assets or issue equity shares to settle the obligation. For that type of obligation, the Exposure Draft proposed that if the monetary values of the two settlement alternatives do not have the potential to differ, the obligation does not establish an ownership relationship, regardless of the settlement provision chosen. Consequently, the Exposure Draft concluded that such an instrument should be classified entirely as a liability. Commentators provided little specific comment on that provision. In its redeliberations, the Board concluded that *all* obligations that permit the holder to require the issuer to transfer assets result in liabilities, regardless of whether the settlement alternatives have the potential to differ. The Board reasoned that such an obligation *could* leave the issuer with no discretion to avoid the future sacrifice of having to transfer assets and, therefore, is a liability under the definition in Concepts Statement 6. That change also makes this Statement more convergent with proposed international accounting standards, although those proposed standards would measure some of those obligations differently (at the full amount that might be paid rather than at the fair value of the option-like conditional obligation).

Freestanding Financial Instruments

B50. The Board decided that, in applying this Statement to freestanding instruments that comprise two or more option or forward contracts, its requirements should be applied to the freestanding instrument in its entirety rather than to separate components in those instruments. The Board also decided that, in applying the classification and measurement provisions of this Statement, freestanding financial instruments that are within the scope of this Statement should not be combined with other freestanding instruments unless combination is required under the requirements of Statement 133 and related guidance. The Board reasoned that those decisions conform to provisions of Statement 133 and related guidance that prohibit separating a compound derivative into risk components or, generally, combining separate freestanding instruments into synthetic instruments for accounting purposes. The Board noted that there are certain circumstances in which Statement 133 and related guidance require separate transactions to be viewed in combination. Those circumstances arise if it is determined that one or more transactions were entered into separately to circumvent the requirements of Statement 133. The Board decided that, in those circumstances, it would be appropriate to retain that guidance.

B51. However, the Board prohibited the combining of instruments within the scope of this Statement to avoid comparability and representational faithfulness problems from inadvertent or planned circumvention of the requirements of this Statement. The Board saw no justification for combining an instrument that in itself is a liability within the scope of this Statement with another freestanding instrument, because that combination might (a) cause a freestanding instrument to be considered to be outside the scope of this Statement, (b) change the reported amount of the liability, or (c) change the required measurement method. For example, combining a freestanding instrument that is a liability under this Statement with a freestanding instrument that is equity under other guidance might have been considered sufficient to change the nature of the instrument such that it would be outside the scope of this Statement and a liability (and any gains or losses resulting from fair value changes of that liability) would not be recognized. Also, permitting freestanding instruments to be combined might have circumvented a requirement to measure those instruments at fair value. For example, combining a written put option and purchased call option might have allowed the combination to be accounted for as a physically settled forward purchase contract. Additionally, the Board noted that allowing or requiring the combining of instruments to create components with differing characteristics might have led to accounting changes that would be reversed in the next phase of this project.

B52. As noted earlier, the scope of this Statement is limited because the Board has not completed its redeliberations on several major issues, one of which is whether and how to separate certain instruments with characteristics of both liabilities and equity into components as proposed in the Exposure Draft. Most issues affecting compound instruments are beyond the scope of this Statement, including how a conversion option or conditional redemption feature embedded in a financial instrument that is not a derivative in its entirety should affect the classification of the instrument in which it is embedded. Those issues will be addressed in the next phase of this project.

B53. The Board considered the related issue of whether the classification requirements of this Statement should be applied to features embedded in a financial instrument that is not a derivative in its entirety, which would have had the effect of requiring separate accounting—bifurcation—for some embedded features now exempt from that accounting because they are considered not to be derivatives under the existing requirements of Statement 133. Concerns arose about the complexity of those requirements, the measurability of certain embedded features, the possibility of a further required change in accounting in the next phase of this project, and the interaction between that potential requirement and the requirements of the SEC to present redeemable preferred stocks between liabilities and equity in registrants' statements of financial position. In view of those concerns, the Board decided not to apply the classification requirements of this Statement to embedded derivatives. However, the Board noted that other standards and guidance (for example, the embedded derivatives provisions of Statement 133) already require certain compound instruments to be analyzed and separated into components and that current guidance will continue to apply to those embedded derivatives. That decision is effected in paragraph 15 of this Statement and in an amendment to paragraph 12(c) of Statement 133. For similar reasons, paragraph 11 of this Statement excludes outstanding shares from its scope, and paragraph 12 of this Statement excludes outstanding shares embodying conditional obligations that the issuer must or

may settle in shares; the Board decided on those scope exclusions so that this Statement does not require outstanding shares in which such derivatives are embedded to be classified entirely as liabilities.

B54. In reaching its conclusion to limit this Statement's classification requirements only to certain freestanding financial instruments, the Board became concerned that a nonsubstantive or minimal feature might be inserted into a financial instrument, which otherwise would be a freestanding financial instrument subject to this Statement, to circumvent the provisions of this Statement. The Board decided to prevent that possibility by providing that any nonsubstantive or minimal features should be disregarded in applying the classification provisions of this Statement. The Board acknowledges that judgment will be required to distinguish nonsubstantive or minimal features from substantive, nonminimal features.

Scope Limitations

B55. The Exposure Draft proposed scope exclusions so as not to affect the timing of recognition of contingent consideration in a business combination and the basic expense recognition criteria for stock compensation arrangements. Commentators did not offer any reasons to change either of those decisions, and the Board excluded both kinds of arrangements from the scope of this Statement. The Board also decided after considering comments on its tentative conclusions in redeliberations to entirely exclude obligations relating to stock compensation from the scope if those obligations are subject to specified guidance for stock compensation arrangements. The Board noted that it expects to revisit the classification, measurement, and expense recognition for stock compensation arrangements that would be classified as liabilities under this Statement either in the next phase of this project or in its project on stock-based compensation, and, therefore, it saw no need to resolve those issues in this Statement. However, the Board decided that freestanding instruments that are no longer subject to specified guidance for stock compensation arrangements should be within the scope of this Statement, for example, a mandatorily redeemable share that was issued upon exercise of an employee stock option.

Presentation between Liabilities and Equity in Statements of Financial Position

B56. Certain financial instruments were presented between the liabilities section and the equity section of the statement of financial position before the issuance of this Statement. Because Concepts Statement 6 does not accommodate classification of items outside the elements of assets, liabilities, and equity, developing a model that would permit that practice would require the Board to define a new element of financial statements. The Board elected not to pursue that course of action, in part because, among other concerns, adding another element would set an undesirable precedent of adding elements whenever new instruments are created that are difficult to classify.

B57. The Board instead elected to develop an approach that would address the issues related to determining the appropriate classification of financial instruments with characteristics of liabilities, equity, or both. Because the Board believes that the provisions of this Statement sufficiently address those issues for the items within its scope, the Board concluded that presentation of those items between the liabilities section and the equity section of the statement of financial position should be prohibited.

Presentation If All Shares Are Mandatorily Redeemable

B58. The Exposure Draft noted that shares issued by some privately held companies must be sold back to the company, for example, upon the holder's termination of his or her employment and that those financial instruments in the form of shares are liabilities because they are mandatorily redeemable upon an event certain to occur. Accounting for those financial instruments in the form of shares as liabilities would reduce or eliminate the equity of those companies. Some commentators suggested that an exception be made to allow such arrangements to continue to be reported as equity. Others suggested that while those instruments were appropriately classified as liabilities, some sort of special reporting was merited, disclosure about those arrangements was necessary for other investors and creditors, and affected companies needed more time to revise debt covenants or make other changes in response to the change in classification.

B59. The Board concluded that those kinds of arrangements meet the definition of mandatorily redeemable financial instruments, that the definition should not be changed to classify them differently from other mandatorily redeemable financial instruments, and that there is no adequate basis for any exception. However, the Board acknowledged the need for special reporting in the most often cited circumstance in which no equity would be reported. Therefore, the Board concluded that entities that have no equity instruments outstanding but have financial instruments in the form of shares, all of which are mandatorily redeemable financial instruments required to be classified as liabilities, should describe those instruments as *shares subject to mandatory redemption* to distinguish them from other liabilities and should separately present payments to and interest due to creditors in statements of cash flows and income.

B60. For entities that have financial instruments in the form of shares that are all mandatorily redeemable, the Board decided that, in addition to separate presentation, a related disclosure is needed that displays the nature and composition of the mandatorily redeemable instruments. For example, such an entity would disclose the event triggering the redemption, the number of shares issued and outstanding, the value associated with those financial instruments, and any retained earnings or accumulated other comprehensive income that would be distributed on redemption (the items that those entities have previously displayed in equity). The Board concluded that for those entities that have financial instruments in the form of shares that are all mandatorily redeemable, disclosure will assist financial statement users in assessing the amount and timing of redemptions.

Initial and Subsequent Measurement

B61. This Statement requires that forward contracts that require settlement by delivery of cash in exchange for a fixed number of the issuer's equity shares (forward purchase contracts for the issuer's equity shares that require physical settlement) be initially measured at the fair value of the shares at inception, adjusted for any consideration or unstated rights or privileges. The Board noted that (a) discounting the settlement amount at the rate implicit in the contract after taking into account any consideration or unstated rights or privileges that may have affected the terms of the transaction and (b) determining the amount of cash that would be paid under the conditions specified in the contract if the shares were repurchased immediately, adjusted for any consideration or unstated rights or privileges, are possible ways to obtain that initial measurement. Those are the common ways of measuring fixed- and floating-rate borrowings, respectively. In the Board's view, such forward contracts are more like a treasury stock purchase using borrowed funds than a derivative instrument. Accounting for this arrangement like a borrowing led the Board to note the need to consider the effect of any unstated rights or privileges, for the same reasons discussed in paragraph 7 of APB Opinion No. 21, *Interest on Receivables and Payables.* The same reasoning also led the Board to decide that those measurement provisions for forward purchase contracts apply only if the issuer will exchange cash for the shares. If the exchange involves barter (for example, specified quantities of gold for shares), the Board saw no reason to reconsider, in this limited-scope project, guidance under Statement 133 under which that forward purchase contract would be accounted for as a derivative at its fair value.

B62. This Statement requires that those forward contracts, and mandatorily redeemable financial instruments, be subsequently measured in one of two ways. If both the amount of cash and the settlement date are fixed, subsequent measurement is at the present value of the amounts to be paid at settlement, with interest accreted using the rate implicit at inception. If either the amount or the date varies based on specified conditions, subsequent measurement is at the amount of cash that would be paid under the conditions specified in the contract if the shares were redeemed or repurchased at the reporting date. The Board chose those methods because they are generally used to subsequently measure liabilities for funds borrowed at fixed and floating rates. Some Board members prefer those methods to subsequently measuring the obligation at its fair value because they do not accept the recognition of gains and losses on transactions involving the issuer's own stock in circumstances in which cash is exchanged for shares and the obligation is unconditional. The Board also decided that accrued dividends (whether or not declared) on underlying shares and any other amounts paid or to be paid to holders of those contracts be reflected as interest cost because that is consistent with the reporting of those shares as liabilities.

B63. This Statement also requires that all remaining financial instruments within its scope be measured initially and subsequently at fair value unless otherwise required by this Statement or other accounting standards. While many, if not most, of those instruments are classified as derivative instruments under Statement 133, the Board took no inventory of such instruments and did not want to leave constituents without guidance for measuring some newly recognized liabilities. The Board reasoned that subsequent measurement of any such liabilities at fair value would provide more relevant information than measures based on historical proceeds.

B64. The Board decided that when a contingently redeemable instrument becomes mandatorily redeemable, that instrument should be reclassified as a liability and should be initially measured at fair value. The Board decided that the issuer should reduce equity by the amount of that initial measure, so as to recognize no gain or loss. The Board sees that decision as consistent with its other initial measurement decisions in this Statement and believes that recognition of a liability to a former owner on removal of a contingency about redemption is, like other distributions to owners, not an occasion for recognizing gain or loss.

Earnings per Share

B65. In its redeliberations related to financial instruments that could be settled by delivery of an issuer's shares and physically settled forward purchase contracts that are measured at the present value of the contract amount with a corresponding reduction to equity, the Board discussed the implications for calculating diluted and basic earnings per share.

B66. The Board considered, but decided against, amending the guidance in paragraph 29 of FASB Statement No. 128, *Earnings per Share,* so that the dilutive earnings per share calculation and numerator adjustments would no longer be based on the intent to settle in shares or in cash. The Board noted that the issue applies to a broader class of contracts than those included within the scope of this Statement and that this issue is not a result of this Statement. The Board noted that it would reconsider amending those provisions of Statement 128 in the next phase of this project.

B67. The Board also considered, but decided against, amending Statement 128 to treat obligations to repurchase an issuer's equity shares that were previously classified as equity but would now be classified as liabilities differently in calculating dilutive earnings per share under the reverse treasury stock method. The Board decided that including the effect of certain instruments previously classified as equity but now classified as liabilities and measured at fair value in the dilutive earnings per share calculation was appropriate even though those instruments might be "out-of-the-money" from the holder's perspective. The Board noted that being "out-of-the-money" is a calculation issue, not a flaw in the dilutive earnings per share model. Additionally, the Board decided not to change the requirement under Statement 128 that any dilutive effects of those contracts be included in calculating dilutive earnings per share.

B68. The Board decided that the number of outstanding shares associated with physically settled forward purchase contracts measured at the present value of the contract amount should be removed from the denominator in computing basic and diluted earnings per share in the same way as required for mandatorily redeemable shares classified as liabilities. The Board reasoned that, because the accounting for physically settled forward contracts reduces equity, even though the shares are still outstanding, they are effectively accounted for as if retired. Like mandatorily redeemable shares accounted for as liabilities, shares subject to physically settled forward contracts should not be treated as outstanding in earnings per share calculations. The Board noted that amounts paid to holders are interest costs reflected in earnings available to common shareholders, the numerator in calculating earnings per share.

B69. The Board noted that some amounts attributable to shares that are to be redeemed or repurchased, for example, amounts associated with participation rights such as a preferred instrument that entitles the holder to participate in 50 percent of all future declared dividends on common shares, are not recognized as interest costs until the dividend is declared under this Statement or other existing standards. The Board concluded that earnings available to common shareholders (the numerator of the earnings per share calculation) should be reduced by amounts attributable to participation rights as those rights are earned, consistently with the "two-class" method required by Statement 128.

Disclosures

B70. The Board concluded that the existing disclosure requirements for liabilities and for equity instruments, notably the requirements in FASB Statement No. 129, *Disclosure of Information about Capital Structure,* provide users of financial statements with information useful in analyzing an entity's liabilities and equity. The Board decided that additional information would be helpful to users in evaluating an entity's economic exposure to financial instruments that could be settled in an entity's shares. The disclosure requirements for instruments that could be settled with an issuer's shares that were established in Issue 00-19 appear to provide that kind of information, and preparers and users of financial statements are familiar with those requirements. Therefore, the Board decided to require, in addition to the requirements in Statement 129, certain of the disclosures required by Issue 00-19 for all contracts within the scope of this Statement.

Effective Date and Transition

B71. The Board decided to make this Statement effective shortly after issuance for contracts created or modified after it is issued and for existing contracts at the beginning of the first interim period beginning after June 15, 2003. The Board concluded that in view of practice problems that have emerged since the Exposure Draft was issued, it is important that most of the provisions of the Statement be adopted without delay. The Board concluded that that effective date provides entities with adequate time to accumulate and develop the information required by this Statement. The Board also concluded that private companies needed more time to adapt to liability classification, in part because many of them are affected significantly by the requirements on mandatorily redeemable shares, and decided to delay the effective date for mandatorily redeemable instruments of a nonpublic company.

B72. In determining the appropriate transition method, the Board considered prospective application, cumulative-effect transition, and retroactive application. The Board concluded that for contracts created before the issuance date of the Statement and existing at the beginning of that interim period, transition is best achieved by reporting the cumulative effect of a change in accounting principle by initially measuring the contract at fair value or as otherwise required by this Statement. The Board concluded that prospective application (that is, application to financial instruments issued after the adoption of this Statement or some other specified date) would diminish both the comparability of financial statements among entities and consistency within an entity that had entered into similar transactions both before and after adoption of this Statement for quite some time given the long lives of certain financial instruments within the scope of this Statement.

B73. In considering the possibilities of retroactive or cumulative-effect transition, the Board noted that some recent standards issued as part of the comprehensive project on financial instruments have prohibited retroactive application for two reasons—reliance on intent and transition costs. Statements 115 and 133 do not permit retroactive application partly because both of those standards rely on the reporting entity's intent. However, the reporting entity's intent is not a factor in this Statement and, therefore, is not a factor that would prohibit restatement.

B74. Statement 140 does not permit retroactive application because of the perceived costs of restatement. Transition costs also are a factor in this Statement. However, in the Exposure Draft for this Statement, the Board stated its belief that to determine the effect of adopting that proposed Statement, an entity would be required to determine the fair value of each financial instrument within its scope and its components at the date the financial instrument was issued. That determination would be required regardless of whether the Board required cumulative-effect transition or restatement. In the Exposure Draft, with its significantly broader scope, the Board concluded, therefore, that requiring restatement would not result in significant additional costs to entities above the costs required for cumulative-effect transition. The Exposure Draft for this Statement noted that retroactive application and restatement would maximize consistency and comparability. Given that, and the belief that the costs of restatement would not be materially greater than the costs of cumulative-effect transition, the Exposure Draft proposed that restatement would be the appropriate transition method.

B75. In this limited-scope Statement, the Board again decided to require a single method to improve comparability. However, the Board chose to require cumulative-effect transition instead of restatement. Some commentators suggested that the options in the transition method proposed in the Exposure Draft would confuse some investors and creditors; the Board agreed. Others objected to the costs of restatement, whatever the scope of the restatement. The Board concluded that a full restatement would often cost more than cumulative-effect presentation and that, given the limited scope of this Statement, those incremental costs are not justified by the incremental benefits to investors and creditors from restatement. Some Board members also believe that because the major impact of this Statement would be on the statement of financial position, the need for full restatement is less compelling.

B76. For practical reasons, the Board decided that for mandatorily redeemable instruments and physically settled forward purchase contracts, accumulated prior interest accruals would not be recognized upon transition. The Board also decided that amounts previously recognized in business combinations under the purchase method should not be changed

when liabilities for existing noncontrolling interests that are mandatorily redeemable are recognized on adoption of this Statement. The Board plans to address the effects of transition for those mandatorily redeemable noncontrolling interests in the transition guidance in the Board's planned Statement on business combination purchase method procedures.

International Accounting Standards

B77. In June 2002, the IASB issued an Exposure Draft, *Amendments to IAS 32, Financial Instruments: Disclosure and Presentation, and IAS 39, Financial Instruments: Recognition and Measurement.* IAS 32 now does, and the proposed amendments would, provide international guidance for financial instruments within the scope of this Statement. Paragraphs B78–B81 summarize the differences between this Statement and that IASB Exposure Draft.

B78. Paragraph 22 of the current unrevised IAS 32 (which would be consistent with the proposed revisions to IAS 32) states, "When a preferred share provides for mandatory redemption by the issuer for a fixed or determinable amount at a fixed or determinable future date or gives the holder the right to require the issuer to redeem the share at or after a particular date for a fixed or determinable amount, the instrument meets the definition of a financial liability and is classified as such." Thus, IAS 32 requires that preferred shares be classified as a liability if the holder can choose to require redemption, even if redemption is uncertain. In contrast, under this Statement, only shares (whether common or preferred) that are mandatorily redeemable (upon a specified date, determinable date, or event certain to occur) are classified as a liability.

B79. IAS 32 requires the same accounting for conditionally redeemable instruments as for mandatorily redeemable instruments. This Statement does not go that far. The Board acknowledges that the conditional obligation embedded in such shares may, if accounted for separately, meet the definition of a liability; however, the accounting for such compound instruments is beyond the scope of this Statement.

B80. Paragraph 29F of the proposed revised IAS 32 would require an entity that enters into a derivative contract (such as a forward repurchase contract or written put option) for its equity shares to recognize a liability measured at the present value of the contract's redemption amount if any of the following is true: (a) the contract requires physical settlement by delivery of cash or other assets, (b) the entity has an unconditional right to require physical settlement, has a past practice of physically settling such contracts, and intends to physically settle the contract, or (c) the counterparty to the contract has the option to require physical settlement of the contract. This Statement requires an entity that enters into a forward purchase contract for its equity shares in exchange for cash to recognize a liability measured at the present value of the redemption amount only if physical settlement is the only settlement method. If physical settlement is not the only settlement method or something other than cash would be exchanged, under this Statement such forward purchase contracts (and *all* written put options) are measured initially at fair value with subsequent changes in fair value recognized in earnings. The difference between IAS 32 as proposed and this Statement is that IAS 32 would define the class of instruments to be measured at the present value of the redemption amount more broadly. The Board views physically settled forward purchase contracts of an entity's own shares in exchange for cash as being similar to financing a stock purchase or a treasury stock transaction and, therefore, would require the recognition of a liability for the future sacrifice of assets, but that view holds only if the obligation to purchase is unconditional and requires physical settlement in exchange for cash.

B81. Paragraphs 22C and 22D of the proposed revised IAS 32 would require a liability to be recognized if an entity has a fixed monetary obligation or one that fluctuates in part or in full in response to changes in a variable other than the issuer's own shares that can be settled with a number of shares that equals that obligation. Those paragraphs are consistent with this Statement except for instruments with monetary values that fluctuate in part based on something other than changes in the fair value of the issuer's shares and that are settled with a variable number of the issuer's equity shares. This Statement excludes from its scope share-settled "dual-indexed" financial instruments that are indexed (or have fair values that fluctuate) in part based on changes in the fair value of the issuer's shares and in part based on one or more additional underlyings. The Board plans to address those dual-indexed financial instruments in the next phase of the project. The Board notes that the accounting required for dual-indexed financial instruments that are within the scope of Statement 133 is consistent with the accounting under the proposed revised IAS 32.

Benefits and Costs

B82. The mission of the FASB is to establish and improve standards of financial accounting and reporting for the guidance and education of the public, including preparers, auditors, and users of financial information. In fulfilling that mission, the Board endeavors to determine that a proposed standard will fill a significant need and that the costs imposed to meet that standard, as compared with other alternatives, are justified in relation to the overall benefits of the resulting information. Although the costs to implement a new standard may not be borne evenly, investors and creditors—both present and potential—and other users of financial information benefit from improvements in financial reporting, thereby facilitating the functioning of markets for capital and credit and the efficient allocation of resources in the economy.

B83. The Board determined that the requirements in this Statement will result in improved financial reporting. In this Statement, certain obligations that require a transfer of assets and that meet the definition of liabilities in Concepts Statement 6 will be reported as liabilities rather than as equity or between the liability and equity sections of the statement of financial position. Also, certain obligations that can be settled by issuance of an entity's equity shares but lack other characteristics of equity will be reported as liabilities, rather than as equity as previously required under Issue 00-19. Those changes result in financial statements that are more representationally faithful and present a more complete depiction of an entity's liabilities that will assist users in assessing the future cash flows and equity share issuances of an entity.

B84. The Board believes that the incremental costs of implementing this Statement have been minimized principally by (a) requiring cumulative-effect transition instead of restatement of financial statements and (b) providing a delayed effective date for mandatorily redeemable financial instruments of nonpublic companies. Although the one-time costs for changes needed to apply the accounting requirements of this Statement may be significant, the benefits from more representationally faithful information will outweigh those one-time implementation costs and will be ongoing.

Appendix C

AMENDMENTS TO EXISTING PRONOUNCEMENTS AND IMPACT ON EITF ISSUES AND STATEMENT 133 IMPLEMENTATION ISSUES

Amendments to Existing Pronouncements

C1. In the first sentence of paragraph 24 of FASB Statement No. 128, *Earnings per Share,* the phrase *other than forward purchase contracts accounted for under paragraphs 21 and 22 of FASB Statement No. 150, Accounting for Certain Financial Instruments with Characteristics of both Liabilities and Equity,* is added after *forward purchase contracts.*

C2. FASB Statement No. 133, *Accounting for Derivative Instruments and Hedging Activities,* is amended as follows:

a. In paragraph 11, the following subparagraph is added after subparagraph 11(c):

  d. Forward contracts that require settlement by the reporting entity's delivery of cash in exchange for the acquisition of a fixed number of its equity shares (forward purchase contracts for the reporting entity's shares that require physical settlement) that are accounted for under paragraphs 21 and 22 of FASB Statement No. 150, *Accounting for Certain Financial Instruments with Characteristics of both Liabilities and Equity.*

b. The following is added to the end of subparagraph 12(c):

  However, this criterion is not met if the separate instrument with the same terms as the embedded derivative instrument would be classified as a liability (or an asset in some circumstances) under the provisions of Statement 150 *but* would be classified in stockholders' equity absent the provisions in Statement 150.*

---

*For purposes of analyzing the application of paragraph 11(a) of this Statement to an embedded derivative instrument as though it were a separate instrument, paragraphs 9–12 of Statement 150 should be disregarded. Those embedded features are analyzed by applying other applicable guidance.

Impact of This Statement on EITF Issues and Statement 133 Implementation Issues

C3. The remainder of this appendix discusses the impact of the provisions of this Statement on the consensuses reached on EITF Issues and the responses to Statement 133 Implementation Issues through March 31, 2003. This appendix does not address the impact of this Statement on other authoritative accounting literature included in categories (b), (c), and (d) in the GAAP hierarchy discussed in AICPA Statement on Auditing Standards No. 69, *The Meaning of "Present Fairly in Conformity with Generally Accepted Accounting Principles" in the Independent Auditor's Report.*

C4. The provisions of this Statement nullify or partially nullify the consensuses (or views) in the following EITF Issues and Topics:

86-32	"Early Extinguishment of a Subsidiary's Mandatorily Redeemable Preferred Stock" (partially nullified)
88-9	"Put Warrants" (nullified)
89-11	"Sponsor's Balance Sheet Classification of Capital Stock with a Put Option Held by an Employee Stock Ownership Plan" (partially nullified)
98-12	"Application of Issue No. 00-19 to Forward Equity Sales Transactions" (nullified)
00-4	"Majority Owner's Accounting for a Transaction in the Shares of a Consolidated Subsidiary and a Derivative Indexed to the Minority Interest in That Subsidiary" (nullified)
00-6	"Accounting for Freestanding Derivative Financial Instruments Indexed to, and Potentially Settled in, the Stock of a Consolidated Subsidiary" (partially nullified)
00-19	"Accounting for Derivative Financial Instruments Indexed to, and Potentially Settled in, a Company's Own Stock" (partially nullified)
00-27	"Application of Issue No. 98-5 to Certain Convertible Instruments" (partially nullified)

D-42   "The Effect on the Calculation of Earnings per Share for the Redemption or Induced Conversion of Preferred Stock" (partially nullified)

D-72   "Effect of Contracts That May Be Settled in Stock or Cash on the Computation of Diluted Earnings per Share" (partially nullified)

D-98   "Classification and Measurement of Redeemable Securities" (partially nullified)

C5. The provisions of this Statement resolve or partially resolve the following EITF Issues:

84-40   "Long-Term Debt Repayable by a Capital Stock Transaction" (partially resolved)

01-11   "Application of Issue No. 00-19 to a Contemporaneous Forward Purchase Contract and Written Put Option" (resolved)

02-2   "When Separate Contracts That Meet the Definition of Financial Instruments Should Be Combined for Accounting Purposes" (partially resolved)

C6. The effect of the issuance of this Statement will be added to the status section of each affected EITF Issue or Topic in *EITF Abstracts*.

C7. Even though the provisions of this Statement do not nullify or partially nullify the consensuses in the following EITF Issues, the status section of each of those Issues in *EITF Abstracts* will include a reference to the requirements of this Statement:

97-8   "Accounting for Contingent Consideration Issued in a Purchase Business Combination"

97-15   "Accounting for Contingency Arrangements Based on Security Prices in a Purchase Business Combination"

01-6   "The Meaning of 'Indexed to a Company's Own Stock'"

C8. Even though the provisions of this Statement do not nullify or partially nullify the responses in the following Statement 133 Implementation Issues, the Implementation Issues will include a reference to the requirements of this Statement:

A18   "Application of Market Mechanism and Readily Convertible to Cash Subsequent to the Inception or Acquisition of a Contract"

C2   "Application of the Exception to Contracts Classified in Temporary Equity"

C9   "Mandatorily Redeemable Preferred Stock Denominated in either a Precious Metal or a Foreign Currency"

G1   "Hedging an SAR Obligation"

K3   "Determination of Whether Combinations of Options with the Same Terms Must Be Viewed as Separate Option Contracts or as a Single Forward Contract"

Appendix D

GLOSSARY

D1. This appendix defines terms used in this Statement.

Financial instrument
Cash, evidence of an ownership interest in an entity, or a contract that both:

a. Imposes on one entity a contractual obligation[*] (1) to deliver cash or another financial instrument[†] to a second entity or (2) to exchange other financial instruments on potentially unfavorable terms with the second entity

b. Conveys to that second entity a contractual right[‡] (1) to receive cash or another financial instrument from the first entity or (2) to exchange other financial instruments on potentially favorable terms with the first entity. [Statement 133, paragraph 540]

---

[*]*Contractual obligations* encompass both those that are conditioned on the occurrence of a specified event and those that are not. All contractual obligations that are financial instruments meet the definition of *liability* set forth in Concepts Statement 6, although some may not be recognized as liabilities in financial statements—may be "off-balance-sheet"—because they fail to meet some other criterion for recognition. For some financial instruments, the obligation is owed to or by a group of entities rather than a single entity.

[†]The use of the term *financial instrument* in this definition is recursive (because the term *financial instrument* is included in it), though it is not circular. The definition requires a chain of contractual obligations that ends with the delivery of cash or an ownership interest in an entity. Any number of obligations to deliver financial instruments can be links in a chain that qualifies a particular contract as a financial instrument.

[‡]*Contractual rights* encompass both those that are conditioned on the occurrence of a specified event and those that are not. All contractual rights that are financial instruments meet the definition of *asset* set forth in Concepts Statement 6, although some may not be recognized as assets in financial statements—may be "off-balance-sheet"—because they fail to meet some other criterion for recognition. For some financial instruments, the right is held by or the obligation is due from a group of entities rather than a single entity.

Freestanding financial instrument
A financial instrument that is entered into separately and apart from any of the entity's other financial instruments or equity transactions, or that

is entered into in conjunction with some other transaction and is legally detachable and separately exercisable.

Issuer
The entity that issued a financial instrument or may be required under the terms of a financial instrument to issue its equity shares.

Mandatorily redeemable financial instrument
Any of various financial instruments issued in the form of shares that embody an unconditional obligation requiring the issuer to redeem the instrument by transferring its assets at a specified or determinable date (or dates) or upon an event that is certain to occur.

Monetary value
What the fair value of the cash, shares, or other instruments that a financial instrument obligates the issuer to convey to the holder would be at the settlement date under specified market conditions.

Net cash settlement
A form of settling a financial instrument under which the party with a loss delivers to the party with a gain cash equal to the gain.

Net share settlement
A form of settling a financial instrument under which the party with a loss delivers to the party with a gain shares of stock with a current fair value equal to the gain.

Nonpublic entity
Any entity other than one (a) whose equity securities trade in a public market either on a stock exchange (domestic or foreign) or in the over-the-counter market, including securities quoted only locally or regionally, (b) that makes a filing with a regulatory agency in preparation for the sale of any class of equity securities in a public market, or (c) that is controlled by an entity covered by (a) or (b). [Statement 123(R), paragraph E1]

Obligation

A conditional or unconditional duty or responsibility to transfer[23] assets or to issue equity shares.[24]

Physical settlement

A form of settling a financial instrument under which (a) the party designated in the contract as the buyer delivers the full stated amount of cash or other financial instruments to the seller and (b) the seller delivers the full stated number of shares of stock or other financial instruments or nonfinancial instruments to the buyer.

---

[23]The term *transfer* is used in this Statement in a broad sense consistent with its use in Concepts Statement 6, rather than in the narrow sense in which it is used in Statement 140.

[24]Because this Statement relates only to financial instruments and not to contracts to provide services and other types of contracts, but includes duties or responsibilities to issue equity shares, this definition of *obligation* differs from the definition found in Concepts Statement 6 and is applicable only for items in the scope of this Statement.

Statement of Financial Accounting Standards No. 151
Inventory Costs

an amendment of ARB No. 43, Chapter 4

STATUS

Issued: November 2004

Effective Date: For inventory costs incurred during fiscal years beginning after June 15, 2005

Affects: Amends ARB 43, Chapter 4, paragraph 5 and footnote 2
Amends FAS 144, paragraph A3

Affected by: No other pronouncements

SUMMARY

This Statement amends the guidance in ARB No. 43, Chapter 4, "Inventory Pricing," to clarify the accounting for abnormal amounts of idle facility expense, freight, handling costs, and wasted material (spoilage). Paragraph 5 of ARB 43, Chapter 4, previously stated that "... under some circumstances, items such as idle facility expense, excessive spoilage, double freight, and rehandling costs may be so abnormal as to require treatment as current period charges...." This Statement requires that those items be recognized as current-period charges regardless of whether they meet the criterion of "so abnormal." In addition, this Statement requires that allocation of fixed production overheads to the costs of conversion be based on the normal capacity of the production facilities.

Reasons for Issuing This Statement

This Statement is the result of a broader effort by the FASB to improve the comparability of cross-border financial reporting by working with the International Accounting Standards Board (IASB) toward development of a single set of high-quality accounting standards. As part of that effort, the FASB and the IASB identified opportunities to improve financial reporting by eliminating certain narrow differences between their existing accounting standards. The accounting for inventory costs, in particular, abnormal amounts of idle facility expense, freight, handling costs, and spoilage, is one such narrow difference that the FASB decided to address by issuing this Statement. As currently worded in ARB 43, Chapter 4, the term *so abnormal* was not defined and its application could lead to unnecessary noncomparability of financial reporting. This Statement eliminates that term.

How the Changes in This Statement Improve Financial Reporting

ARB 43, Chapter 4, and IAS 2, *Inventories,* are based on the principle that the primary basis of accounting for inventory is cost. Both those accounting standards also require that abnormal amounts of idle facility expense, freight, handling costs, and spoilage be recognized as current-period charges; however, differences in the wording of the two standards could lead to inconsistent application of those requirements. This Statement improves financial reporting by amending ARB 43, Chapter 4, to clarify that abnormal amounts of costs should be recognized as period costs. The amending language is similar to that in IAS 2, in order to promote consistent application of those standards.

Statement of Financial Accounting Standards No. 151

Inventory Costs

an amendment of ARB No. 43, Chapter 4

CONTENTS

INTRODUCTION

1. ARB No. 43, Chapter 4, "Inventory Pricing," discusses the general principles applicable to the pricing of inventory. Paragraph 5 of ARB 43, Chapter 4 provides guidance on allocating certain costs to inventory. This Statement amends ARB 43, Chapter 4, to clarify that abnormal amounts of idle facility expense, freight, handling costs, and wasted materials (spoilage) should be recognized as current-period charges. In addition, this Statement requires that allocation of fixed production overheads to the costs of conversion be based on the normal capacity of the production facilities.

STANDARDS OF FINANCIAL ACCOUNTING AND REPORTING

Amendment of ARB No. 43, Chapter 4

2. Paragraph 5 and footnote 2 of ARB 43, Chapter 4, are amended as follows: [Added text is underlined and deleted text is struck out.]

> 5. ~~In keeping with the principle that accounting is primarily based on cost, there is a presumption that inventories should be stated at cost.~~ Inventories are presumed to be stated at cost. The definition of cost as applied to inventories is understood to mean acquisition and production cost,[2] and its determination involves many considerations~~problems~~. Although principles for the determination of inventory costs may be easily stated, their application, particularly to such inventory items as work in process and finished goods, is difficult because of the variety of considerations ~~problems encountered~~ in the allocation of costs and charges. For example, variable production overheads are allocated to each unit of production on the basis of the actual use of the production facilities. However, the allocation of fixed production overheads to the costs of conversion is based on the normal capacity of the production facilities. Normal capacity refers to a range of production levels. Normal capacity is the production expected to be achieved over a number of periods or seasons under normal circumstances, taking into account the loss of capacity resulting from planned maintenance. Some variation in production levels from period to period is expected and establishes the range of normal capacity. The range of normal capacity will vary based on business- and industry-specific factors. Judgment is required to determine when a production level is abnormally low (that is, outside the range of expected variation in production). Examples of factors that might be anticipated to

cause an abnormally low production level include significantly reduced demand, labor and materials shortages, and unplanned facility or equipment downtime. The actual level of production may be used if it approximates normal capacity. In periods of abnormally high production, the amount of fixed overhead allocated to each unit of production is decreased so that inventories are not measured above cost. The amount of fixed overhead allocated to each unit of production is not increased as a consequence of abnormally low production or idle plant.

5A. Unallocated overheads are recognized as an expense in the period in which they are incurred.under some circumstances, Other items such as abnormal idle facility expense, excessive spoilage, double-freight, and rehandling costs, may be so abnormaland amounts of wasted materials (spoilage)as to require treatment as current period charges rather than as a portion of the inventory cost. Also, under most circumstances, general and administrative expenses[2a] should be included as period charges, except for the portion of such expenses that may be clearly related to production and thus constitute a part of inventory costs (product charges). Selling expenses constitute no part of inventory costs. It should also be recognized that tThe exclusion of all overheads from inventory costs does not constitute an accepted accounting procedure. The exercise of judgment in an individual situation involves a consideration of the adequacy of the procedures of the cost accounting system in use, the soundness of the principles thereof, and their consistent application.

---

[2]In the case of goods which have been written down below cost at the close of a fiscal periodyear, such reduced amount is to be considered the cost for subsequent accounting purposes. Paragraph 14 of APB Opinion No. 28, *Interim Financial Reporting,* provides guidance for preparing interim financial statements.

[2a]General and administrative expenses ordinarily should be charged to expense as incurred but may be accounted for as contract costs under the completed-contract method of accounting or, in some circumstances, as indirect contract costs by government contractors.

Other Amendment to Existing Pronouncements

3. Paragraph A3 of FASB Statement No. 144, *Accounting for the Impairment or Disposal of Long-Lived Assets,* is amended as follows:

> An entity owns a manufacturing facility that together with other assets is tested for recoverability as a group. In addition to long-lived assets (Assets A–D), the asset group includes inventory, which is reported at the lower of cost or market in accordance with ARB No. 43, Chapter 4, "Inventory Pricing," as amended by FASB Statements No. 133, *Accounting for Derivative Instruments and Hedging Activities,* and No. 151, *Inventory Costs,* and other current assets and liabilities that are not covered by this Statement. The $2.75 million aggregate carrying amount of the asset group is not recoverable and exceeds its fair value by $600,000. In accordance with paragraph 14, the impairment loss of $600,000 would be allocated as shown below to the long-lived assets of the group. [Table has been omitted here.]

Transitional Disclosures

4. The disclosures required by paragraph 19(c) of APB Opinion No. 20, *Accounting Changes,* are applicable if significant changes to an entity's inventory accounting result from the adoption of this Statement.

Effective Date and Transition

5. The provisions of this Statement shall be effective for inventory costs incurred during fiscal years beginning after June 15, 2005. Earlier application is permitted for inventory costs incurred during fiscal years beginning after the date this Statement is issued. The provisions of this Statement shall be applied prospectively.

> **The provisions of this Statement need not be applied to immaterial items.**

This Statement was adopted by the unanimous vote of the seven members of the Financial Accounting Standards Board:

Robert H. Herz,	G. Michael Crooch	Leslie F. Seidman
Chairman	Gary S. Schieneman	Edward W. Trott
George J. Batavick	Katherine Schipper	

Appendix

BACKGROUND INFORMATION AND BASIS FOR CONCLUSIONS

Introduction

A1. This appendix summarizes considerations that Board members deemed significant in reaching the conclusions in this Statement. It includes reasons for accepting certain approaches and rejecting others. Individual Board members gave greater weight to some factors than to others.

Background Information

A2. In September 2002, the FASB and the International Accounting Standards Board (IASB) (collectively, the Boards) committed to a broad effort to improve international comparability of financial reporting by working toward development of a single set of high-quality accounting standards. As part of that effort, the Boards jointly undertook a short-term project to eliminate certain narrow differences between the accounting pronouncements issued by the IASB and the accounting standards issued by the FASB. Both Boards agreed to limit the scope of the short-term project to issues for which (a) the Boards' respective accounting pronouncements were different; (b) convergence to a high-quality solution would appear to be achievable in the short-term, usually by selecting between the existing standards of either the FASB or the IASB; and (c) the issue was not within the scope of other projects on the current agenda of either Board. The accounting for inventory costs, in particular, the accounting for abnormal amounts of idle facility expense, freight, handling costs, and wasted materials (spoilage), is one such difference that the FASB decided should be addressed in the short-term convergence project. While the Board believes ARB 43, Chapter 4, and IAS 2, *Inventories,* are based on the same principle—that abnormal amounts of such costs should be recognized as current-period

charges—the Board decided that differences in the wording of the two standards could have led to inconsistent application of that principle.

A3. In December 2003, the Board issued an Exposure Draft, *Inventory Costs,* for a 120-day comment period. The Board received 26 comment letters on the Exposure Draft. In August 2004, the Board redeliberated the issues identified in the Exposure Draft and concluded that on the basis of existing information, it could reach an informed decision without a public hearing.

Basis for Conclusions

A4. Paragraph 5 of ARB 43, Chapter 4, previously stated that ". . . under some circumstances, items such as idle facility expense, excessive spoilage, double freight, and rehandling costs may be so abnormal as to require treatment as current period charges. . . ." In the Exposure Draft, the Board proposed amending paragraph 5 to adopt the language of IAS 2. That proposed amendment would have (a) clarified that abnormal amounts of idle facility expense, freight, handling costs, and wasted materials (spoilage) should be recognized as current-period charges, regardless of whether the "so abnormal" criterion is met and (b) incorporated into ARB 43, Chapter 4, guidance for determining whether idle capacity was abnormal. In proposing that amendment, the Board believed that adopting the language used in IAS 2, in this instance, would not substantially change current inventory accounting practice in the United States.

A5. Many respondents to the Exposure Draft disagreed with the Board's conclusion that the proposed amendment would not substantially change current inventory accounting practice. In particular, they noted that incorporating the guidance from IAS 2 that states that fixed production overhead costs should be allocated to inventory based on the "normal capacity" of the production facility would result in recognition of all unfavorable volume variances as a period expense, while favorable variances that are normal would be recognized in inventory. Those respondents noted that under ARB 43, Chapter 4, volume variances are recognized as a period cost only when the "so abnormal" criterion is met. For that reason and others, some respondents urged the Board not to proceed with the proposed changes unless and until a comprehensive project on inventory accounting is undertaken.

A6. In its redeliberations, the Board reaffirmed its decision to amend ARB 43, Chapter 4, to clarify that abnormal amounts of idle facility expense, freight, handling costs, and wasted materials (spoilage) should be recognized as a period expense regardless of whether the "so abnormal" criterion is met. However, to address respondents' concerns, the Board decided that the amendment should include guidance slightly more detailed than that in IAS 2 regarding normal capacity. In particular, the Board decided to add guidance clarifying that normal capacity refers to a range of production levels within which ordinary variations in production levels are expected. The Board believes the amendment to ARB 43, Chapter 4, as modified, will not lead to significant changes in inventory accounting practice.

A7. Some respondents to the Exposure Draft requested that the Board provide definitions of certain terms such as *fixed* and *variable production overheads, low production,* and *idle plant.* The Board considered those requests but decided not to provide those definitions because the terms have been used for many years and, therefore, should be well understood by constituents.

Effective Date and Transition

A8. The Board decided that this Statement should be effective for fiscal years beginning after June 15, 2005. The Board does not anticipate significant changes in financial reporting to result from these clarifications and therefore does not believe that a more significant amount of lead time is required prior to implementation. Further, early application of the provisions of this Statement is permitted. Allowing early adoption will enable entities based in the European Union that report under U.S. generally accepted accounting principles to implement these provisions prior to the requirement to report under international financial reporting standards.

A9. The Exposure Draft reflected the Board's decision that prospective application of the provisions of this Statement would be appropriate because the effects of retrospective application may not be determinable for many entities or because the cost to accomplish retrospective application would be excessive in relation to the benefits to users of the financial statements.

A10. Several respondents to the Exposure Draft asked the Board to clarify whether the provisions of this Statement were intended to be applied to inventory on hand as of the date of adoption. In response, the Board clarified that this Statement applies only to inventory costs incurred during periods beginning after the date of adoption.

Benefits and Costs

A11. The mission of the FASB is to establish and improve standards of financial accounting and reporting for the guidance and education of the public, including preparers, auditors, and users of financial information. In fulfilling that mission, the Board endeavors to determine that a proposed standard will fill a significant need and that the costs imposed to meet that standard, as compared with other alternatives, are justified in relation to the overall benefits of the resulting information. Although the costs to implement a new standard may not be borne evenly, investors and creditors—both present and potential—and other users of financial information benefit from improvements in financial reporting, thereby facilitating the functioning of markets for capital and credit and the efficient allocation of resources in the economy. The Board believes the benefit of reducing the possibility for potential misinterpretation of the principles of inventory pricing outweighs the cost of applying this Statement.

Statement of Financial Accounting Standards No. 152
Accounting for Real Estate Time-Sharing Transactions

an amendment of FASB Statements No. 66 and 67

STATUS

Issued: December 2004

Effective Date: For financial statements for fiscal years beginning after June 15, 2005

Affects: Amends FAS 66, paragraph 2
Amends FAS 67, paragraph 2

Affected by: No other pronouncements

SUMMARY

This Statement amends FASB Statement No. 66, *Accounting for Sales of Real Estate,* to reference the financial accounting and reporting guidance for real estate time-sharing transactions that is provided in AICPA Statement of Position (SOP) 04-2, *Accounting for Real Estate Time-Sharing Transactions.* This Statement also amends FASB Statement No. 67, *Accounting for Costs and Initial Rental Operations of Real Estate Projects,* to state that the guidance for (a) incidental operations and (b) costs incurred to sell real estate projects does not apply to real estate time-sharing transactions. The accounting for those operations and costs is subject to the guidance in SOP 04-2.

This Statement is effective for financial statements for fiscal years beginning after June 15, 2005.

Statement of Financial Accounting Standards No. 152

Accounting for Real Estate Time-Sharing Transactions

an amendment of FASB Statements No. 66 and 67

CONTENTS

INTRODUCTION

1. FASB Statements No. 66, *Accounting for Sales of Real Estate,* and No. 67, *Accounting for Costs and Initial Rental Operations of Real Estate Projects,* were issued in 1982 as part of the process of extracting specialized accounting and reporting principles and practices from AICPA Statements of Position (SOPs) and AICPA Industry Accounting Guides (Guides) and issuing them in FASB Statements after appropriate due process. Statement 66 established the financial accounting and reporting standards for sales of real estate. Statement 67 established the financial accounting and reporting standards for the acquisition, development, construction, selling, rental costs, and initial operations of real estate projects. In its deliberations of Statement 66, the Board acknowledged that sales of time-sharing interests were not addressed in the SOPs and Guides. The Board concluded that the sales of real estate time-sharing interests should be accounted for as sales of real estate using the other-than-retail-land-sales model and that further guidance should not be provided at that time.

2. In the years following the issuance of Statements 66 and 67, changes in the methods used by the real estate time-sharing industry to offer its products resulted in divergent accounting practices including practices associated with revenue recognition, recording of credit losses, and the treatment of selling costs. In response, the AICPA's Accounting Standards Executive Committee developed SOP 04-2, *Accounting for Real Estate Time-Sharing Transactions,* which applies to all real estate time-sharing transactions. This Statement amends Statements 66 and 67 in association with the issuance of SOP 04-2.

STANDARDS OF FINANCIAL ACCOUNTING AND REPORTING

Amendments to Existing Pronouncements

3. FASB Statement No. 66, *Accounting for Sales of Real Estate,* is amended as follows (added text is underlined):

a. Paragraph 2:

> Although this Statement applies to all sales of real estate, many of the extensive provisions were developed over several years to deal with complex transactions that are frequently encountered in enterprises that specialize in real estate transactions. The decision trees in Appendix F highlight the major provisions of the Statement and will help a user of the Statement identify criteria that determine when and how profit is recognized. Those using this Statement to determine the accounting for relatively simple real estate sales transactions will need to apply only limited portions of the Statement. The general requirements for recognizing all of the profit on a nonretail land sale at the date of sale are set forth in paragraphs 3–5 and are highlighted on the first decision tree. Paragraphs 6–18

elaborate on those general provisions. Paragraphs 19–43 provide more detailed guidance for a variety of more complex transactions. Real estate time-sharing transactions should be accounted for as nonretail land sales. AICPA Statement of Position 04-2, *Accounting for Real Estate Time-Sharing Transactions,* provides additional guidance on the accounting for real estate time-sharing transactions.

4. FASB Statement No. 67, *Accounting for Costs and Initial Rental Operations of Real Estate Projects,* is amended as follows:

a. Paragraph 2:

This Statement does not apply to:

   a. Real estate developed by an enterprise for use in its own operations,[1] other than for sale or rental.

   b. "Initial direct costs" of sales-type, operating, and other types of leases, which are defined in FASB Statement No. 91, *Accounting for Nonrefundable Fees and Costs Associated with Originating or Acquiring Loans and Initial Direct Costs of Leases.* The accounting for initial direct costs is prescribed in FASB Statement No. 13, *Accounting for Leases,* as amended by Statement 91 and FASB Statement No. 98, *Accounting for Leases: Sale-Leaseback Transactions Involving Real Estate, Sales-Type Leases of Real Estate, Definition of the Lease Term, and Initial Direct Costs of Direct Financing Leases.*

   c. Costs directly related to manufacturing, merchandising, or service activities as distinguished from real estate activities.

Paragraphs 20–23 of this Statement do not apply to real estate rental activity in which the predominant rental period is less than one month. Paragraphs 10 and 17–19 of this Statement do not apply to real estate time-sharing transactions. AICPA Statement of Position 04-2, *Accounting for Real Estate Time-Sharing Transactions,* provides guidance on the accounting for those transactions.

EFFECTIVE DATE AND TRANSITION

5. This Statement shall be effective for financial statements for fiscal years beginning after June 15, 2005. Restatement of previously issued financial statements is not permitted.

The provisions of this Statement need not be applied to immaterial items.

This Statement was adopted by the unanimous vote of the seven members of the Financial Accounting Standards Board:

Robert H. Herz,   G. Michael Crooch   Leslie F. Seidman
  Chairman   Gary S. Schieneman   Edward W. Trott
George J. Batavick   Katherine Schipper

Appendix

BACKGROUND INFORMATION AND BASIS FOR CONCLUSIONS

A1. This appendix summarizes considerations that Board members deemed significant in reaching the conclusions in this Statement.

A2. FASB Statements No. 66, *Accounting for Sales of Real Estate,* and No. 67, *Accounting for Costs and Initial Rental Operations of Real Estate Projects,* were issued in 1982. Statement 66 adopted the specialized profit recognition principles in the AICPA Industry Accounting Guides, *Accounting for Profit Recognition on Sales of Real Estate,* and *Accounting for Retail Land Sales;* and AICPA Statements of Position (SOPs) 75-6, *Questions Concerning Profit Recognition on Sales of Real Estate,* and 78-4, *Application of the Deposit, Installment, and Cost Recovery Methods in Accounting for Sales of Real Estate.* Statement 67 adopted the specialized principles and practices in AICPA SOPs 80-3, *Accounting for Real Estate Acquisition, Development, and Construction Costs,* and 78-3, *Accounting for Costs to Sell and Rent, and Initial Rental Operations of, Real Estate Projects,* and the AICPA Industry Accounting Guide, *Accounting for Retail Land Sales,* that address the costs of real estate projects. In its deliberations of Statement 66, the Board acknowledged that sales of real estate time-sharing interests were not addressed in the AICPA SOPs and Guides. The Board concluded that sales of real estate time-sharing interests should be accounted for as sales of real estate using the other-than-retail-land-sales model and that further guidance should not be provided at that time.

A3. In the years following the issuance of Statements 66 and 67, changes in the methods used by the real estate time-sharing industry to offer its products resulted in divergent accounting practices including practices associated with revenue recognition, recording of credit losses, and the treatment of selling costs. In response, the Accounting Standards Executive Committee (AcSEC) developed SOP 04-2, *Accounting for Real Estate Time-Sharing Transactions,* which applies to all real estate time-sharing transactions. AcSEC requested that the Board amend Statements 66 and 67 to accommodate the issuance of SOP 04-2, which provides accounting and reporting guidance that differs from the guidance in those Statements.

A4. In February 2003, the Board issued an Exposure Draft, *Accounting for Real Estate Time-Sharing Transactions,* for a 60-day comment period. After the exposure period, the Board concluded that the final SOP should not include revenue recognition guidance for real estate time-sharing transactions. The Board considered a number of factors in arriving at its conclusion including (a) changes to the revenue recognition practices that have occurred since AcSEC originally added this project to its agenda, (b) the Board's revenue recognition project and the potential for requiring preparers to change their revenue recognition practices twice in a short time frame, and (c) the "rules-based" nature of the revenue recognition requirements in the proposed SOP. As a result of the Board's conclusion, SOP 04-2 does not change the revenue recognition guidance in Statement 66 for real estate time-sharing transactions and, accordingly, this Statement does not amend the guidance in Statement 66. However, the Board agreed to amend Statement 66 to include a reference to the guidance in SOP 04-2 for real estate time-sharing transactions. This amendment does not change the financial accounting and reporting standards in Statement 66 for real estate time-sharing transactions.

A5. The Board concluded that it should amend Statement 67 to state that the guidance for (a) incidental operations and (b) costs incurred to sell real estate projects (paragraphs 10 and 17–19 of Statement 67, respectively) does not apply to real estate time-sharing transactions.

A6. The Board concluded that SOP 04-2 would result in an improvement in the accounting and reporting of real estate time-sharing transactions and that, accordingly, it should make the amendments to Statements 66 and 67. The Board believes that there is a need for the guidance and that the benefits will exceed the cost of implementation.

Statement of Financial Accounting Standards No. 153
Exchanges of Nonmonetary Assets

an amendment of APB Opinion No. 29

STATUS

Issued: December 2004

Effective Date: For nonmonetary asset exchanges occurring in fiscal periods beginning after June 15, 2005

Affects: Amends APB 29, paragraphs 3(c) and 4 and footnote 5a
       Replaces APB 29, paragraphs 20 and 21
       Amends APB 29 by adding paragraph 21A
       Deletes APB 29, footnotes 3 and 6
       Amends FAS 19, paragraphs 44 and 47(e)
       Amends FAS 140, paragraph 4
       Amends FAS 144, paragraphs 27 and 29 and footnote 17

Affected by: No other pronouncements

SUMMARY

The guidance in APB Opinion No. 29, *Accounting for Nonmonetary Transactions,* is based on the principle that exchanges of nonmonetary assets should be measured based on the fair value of the assets exchanged. The guidance in that Opinion, however, included certain exceptions to that principle. This Statement amends Opinion 29 to eliminate the exception for nonmonetary exchanges of similar productive assets and replaces it with a general exception for exchanges of nonmonetary assets that do not have commercial substance. A nonmonetary exchange has commercial substance if the future cash flows of the entity are expected to change significantly as a result of the exchange.

Reasons for Issuing This Statement

This Statement is the result of a broader effort by the FASB to improve the comparability of cross-border financial reporting by working with the International Accounting Standards Board (IASB) toward development of a single set of high-quality accounting standards. As part of that effort, the FASB and the IASB identified opportunities to improve financial reporting by eliminating certain narrow differences between their existing accounting standards. The accounting for nonmonetary exchanges was identified as an area in which the U.S. standard could be improved by eliminating certain differences between the measurement guidance in Opinion 29 and that in IAS 16, *Property, Plant and Equipment,* and IAS 38, *Intangible Assets.*

How the Changes in This Statement Improve Financial Reporting

Opinion 29 provided an exception to the basic measurement principle (fair value) for exchanges of similar productive assets. That exception required that some nonmonetary exchanges, although commercially substantive, be recorded on a carryover basis. This Statement eliminates the exception to fair value for exchanges of similar productive assets and replaces it with a general exception for exchange transactions that do not have commercial substance—that is, transactions that are not expected to result in significant changes in the cash flows of the reporting entity. By focusing the exception on exchanges that lack commercial substance, the

Board believes this Statement produces financial reporting that more faithfully represents the economics of the transactions. Moreover, in making that amendment, the Board decided to use language that is similar to that used in IAS 16, noting that doing so would promote more consistent application of the requirements of those standards.

Statement of Financial Accounting Standards No. 153

Exchanges of Nonmonetary Assets

an amendment of APB Opinion No. 29

CONTENTS

INTRODUCTION

1. This Statement addresses the measurement of exchanges of nonmonetary assets. It eliminates the exception from fair value measurement for nonmonetary exchanges of similar productive assets in paragraph 21(b) of APB Opinion No. 29, *Accounting for Nonmonetary Transactions,* and replaces it with an exception for exchanges that do not have commercial substance. This Statement specifies that a nonmonetary exchange has commercial substance if the future cash flows of the entity are expected to change significantly as a result of the exchange.

STANDARDS OF FINANCIAL ACCOUNTING AND REPORTING

Amendments to Opinion 29

2. Opinion 29 is amended as follows: [Added text is underlined and deleted text is struck out.]

a. Paragraph 3(c) and its related footnote 3:

Exchange (or *exchange transaction*) is a reciprocal transfer between an enterprise and another entity that results in the enterprise's acquiring assets or services or satisfying liabilities by surrendering other assets or services or incurring other obligations.[3] A reciprocal transfer of a nonmonetary asset shall be deemed an exchange only if the transferor has no substantial continuing involvement in the transferred asset such that the usual risks and rewards of ownership of the asset are transferred.

---

[3] ~~APB Statement No. 4, *Basic Concepts and Accounting Principles Underlying Financial Statements of Business Enterprises,* paragraphs 180–183, contains a more complete explanation of exchanges and nonreciprocal transfers.~~

b. Paragraph 4, as amended by FASB Statements No. 71, *Accounting for the Effects of Certain Types of Regulation,* and No. 141, *Business Combinations:*

This Opinion does not apply to the following transactions:

a. A business combination accounted for by an enterprise according to the provisions of FASB Statement No. 141, *Business Combinations,*[3a]

b. A transfer of nonmonetary assets solely between companies or persons under common control, such as between a parent company and its subsidiaries or between two subsidiary corporations of the same parent, or between a corporate joint venture and its owners,

c. Acquisition of nonmonetary assets or services on issuance of the capital stock of an enterprise,[4] ~~and~~

d. Stock issued or received in stock dividends and stock splits which are accounted for in accordance with ARB No. 43, Chapter 7B,

e. A transfer of assets to an entity in exchange for an equity interest in that entity,

f. A pooling of assets in a joint undertaking intended to find, develop, or produce oil or gas from a particular property or group of properties, as described in paragraph 44 of FASB Statement No. 19, *Financial Accounting and Reporting by Oil and Gas Producing Companies,* as amended by FASB Statements No. 144, *Accounting for the Impairment or Disposal of Long-Lived Assets,* No. 145, *Rescission of FASB Statements No. 4, 44, and 64, Amendment of FASB Statement No. 13, and Technical Corrections,* and No. 153, *Exchanges of Nonmonetary Assets,*

g. The exchange of a part of an operating interest owned for a part of an operating interest owned by another party that is subject to paragraph 47(e) of Statement 19, and

h. The transfer of a financial asset within the scope of FASB Statement No. 140, *Accounting for Transfers and Servicing of Financial Assets and Extinguishments of Liabilities.*

~~This Opinion amends APB Statement No. 4, Basic Concepts and Accounting Principles Underlying Financial Statements of Business Enterprises, to the extent it relates to measuring transfers of certain nonmonetary assets.~~ Some exchanges of nonmonetary assets involve a small monetary consideration, referred to as "boot," even though the exchange is essentially nonmonetary. This Opinion also applies to those transactions. For purposes of applying this Opinion, events and transactions in which nonmonetary assets are involuntarily converted (for example, as a result of total or partial destruction, theft, seizure, or condemnation) to monetary assets that are then reinvested in other nonmonetary assets—are monetary transactions since the recipient is not obligated to reinvest the monetary consideration in other nonmonetary assets.

c. Paragraph 20:

> ~~Fair Value Not Determinable. Accounting for a nonmonetary transaction should not be based on the fair values of the assets transferred unless those fair values are determinable within reasonable limits (paragraph 25).~~
>
> A nonmonetary exchange shall be measured based on the recorded amount (after reduction, if appropriate, for an indicated impairment of value) of the nonmonetary asset(s) relinquished,[5a] and not on the fair values of the exchanged assets, if any of the following conditions apply:
>
> a. *Fair Value Not Determinable.* The fair value of neither the asset(s) received nor the asset(s) relinquished is determinable within reasonable limits (paragraph 25).
>
> b. *Exchange Transaction to Facilitate Sales to Customers.* The transaction is an exchange of a product or property held for sale in the ordinary course of business for a product or property to be sold in the same line of business to facilitate sales to customers other than the parties to the exchange.
>
> c. *Exchange Transaction That Lacks Commercial Substance.* The transaction lacks commercial substance (paragraph 21).

[5a]An indicated impairment of value of a long-lived asset within the scope of Statement 144 shall be determined in accordance with paragraph 29 of that Statement.

d. Paragraph 21 and its related footnotes 5a and 6:

> ~~Exchanges. If the exchange is not essentially the culmination of an earning process, accounting for an exchange of a nonmonetary asset between an enterprise and another entity should be based on the recorded amount (after reduction, if appropriate, for an indicated impairment of value) of the nonmonetary asset relinquished.[5a] The Board believes that the following two types of nonmonetary exchange transactions do not culminate an earning process:~~
>
> ~~a. An exchange of a product or property held for sale in the ordinary course of business for a product or property to be sold in the same line of business to facilitate sales to customers other than the parties to the exchange, and~~

b. ~~An exchange of a productive asset not held for sale in the ordinary course of business for a similar productive asset or an equivalent interest in the same or similar productive asset (similar productive asset is defined in paragraph 3 and examples are given in paragraph 7).[6]~~

~~[5a]An indicated impairment of value of a long-lived asset covered by FASB Statement No. 144, *Accounting for the Impairment or Disposal of Long-Lived Assets*, shall be determined in accordance with paragraph 29 of that Statement.~~

~~[6]The fact that an exchange of productive assets is not a taxable transaction for tax purposes may be evidence that the assets exchanged are similar for purposes of applying this Opinion.~~

Commercial Substance

21. A nonmonetary exchange has commercial substance if the entity's future cash flows[5b] are expected to significantly change as a result of the exchange. The entity's future cash flows are expected to significantly change if either of the following criteria is met:

a. The configuration (risk, timing, and amount)[5c] of the future cash flows of the asset(s) received differs significantly from the configuration of the future cash flows of the asset(s) transferred.

b. The entity-specific value[5d] of the asset(s) received differs from the entity-specific value of the asset(s) transferred, and the difference is significant in relation to the fair values of the assets exchanged.

A qualitative assessment will, in some cases, be conclusive in determining that the estimated cash flows of the entity are expected to significantly change as a result of the exchange.

[5b]FASB Concepts Statement No. 7, *Using Cash Flow Information and Present Value in Accounting Measurements*, contains guidance that may be useful in evaluating changes in future cash flows.

[5c]The configuration of future cash flows is composed of the risk, timing, and amount of the cash flows. A change in any one of those elements would be a change in configuration.

[5d]An entity-specific value (referred to as an entity-specific measurement in Concepts Statement 7) is different from a fair value measurement. As described in paragraph 24(b) of Concepts Statement 7, an entity-specific value attempts to

capture the value of an asset or liability in the context of a particular entity. For example, an entity computing an entity-specific value of an asset would use its expectations about its use of that asset rather than the use assumed by marketplace participants. If it is determined that the transaction has commercial substance, the exchange would be measured at fair value, rather than at the entity-specific value.

21A. In the United States and some other tax jurisdictions, a transaction is not given effect for tax purposes unless it serves a legitimate business purpose other than tax avoidance. In assessing the commercial substance of an exchange, tax cash flows that arise solely because the tax business purpose is based on achieving a specified financial reporting result shall not be considered.

Amendments to Other Pronouncements

3. FASB Statement No. 19, *Financial Accounting and Reporting by Oil and Gas Producing Companies*, is amended as follows:

a. Paragraph 44, as amended by FASB Statements No. 144, *Accounting for the Impairment or Disposal of Long-Lived Assets*, and No. 145, *Rescission of FASB Statements No. 4, 44, and 64, Amendment of FASB Statement No. 13, and Technical Corrections:*

~~In the following types of conveyances, gain or loss shall not be recognized at the time of the conveyance, except as otherwise provided:~~

~~a. A transfer of assets used in oil and gas producing activities (including either proved or unproved properties) in exchange for other assets also used in oil and gas producing activities. However, when proved properties are transferred in exchange for other assets also used in oil and gas producing activities, if an impairment loss is indicated under the provisions of FASB Statement No. 144, *Accounting for the Impairment or Disposal of Long-Lived Assets*, it shall be recognized in accordance with paragraph 29 of Statement 144.~~

b. ~~A~~In a pooling of assets in a joint undertaking intended to find, develop, or produce oil or gas from a particular property or group of properties, gain or loss shall not be recognized at the time of the conveyance.

b. Paragraph 47(e):

> A part of an operating interest owned may be exchanged for a part of an operating interest owned by another party. The purpose of such an arrangement, commonly called a joint venture in the oil and gas industry, often is to avoid duplication of facilities, diversify risks, and achieve operating efficiencies. ~~Such reciprocal conveyances represent exchanges of similar productive assets, and n~~No gain or loss shall be recognized by either party at the time of the transaction. In some joint ventures which may or may not involve an exchange of interests, the parties may share different elements of costs in different proportions. In such an arrangement a party may acquire an interest in a property or in wells and related equipment that is disproportionate to the share of costs borne by it. As in the case of a carried interest or a free well, each party shall account for its own cost under the provisions of this Statement. No gain shall be recognized for the acquisition of an interest in joint assets, the cost of which may have been paid in whole or in part by another party.

4. FASB Statement No. 140, *Accounting for Transfers and Servicing of Financial Assets and Extinguishments of Liabilities,* is amended as follows:

a. Paragraph 4:

> This Statement does not address transfers of custody of financial assets for safekeeping, contributions,[2] transfers of ownership interests that are in substance sales of real estate, ~~exchanges of equity method investments for similar productive assets,~~ or investments by owners or distributions to owners of a business enterprise. This Statement does not address subsequent measurement of assets and liabilities, except for (a) **servicing assets** and **servicing liabilities** and (b) **interest-only strips,** securities, retained interests in securitizations, loans, other receivables, or other financial assets that can contractually be prepaid or otherwise settled in such a way that the holder would not recover substantially all of its recorded investment and that are not within the scope of FASB Statement No. 133, *Accounting for Derivative Instruments and Hedging Activities.* This Statement does not change the accounting for employee benefits subject to the provisions of FASB Statement No. 87, *Employers' Accounting for Pensions,* No. 88, *Employers' Accounting for Settlements and Curtailments of Defined Benefit Pension Plans and for Termination Benefits,* or No. 106, *Employers' Accounting for Postretirement Benefits Other Than Pensions.* This Statement does not change the provisions relating to leveraged leases in FASB Statement No. 13, *Accounting for Leases,* or money-over-money and wrap lease transactions involving nonrecourse debt subject to the provisions of FASB Technical Bulletin No. 88-1, *Issues Relating to Accounting for Leases.* This Statement does not address transfers of nonfinancial assets, for example, servicing assets, or transfers of unrecognized financial assets, for example, minimum lease payments to be received under operating leases.

5. Statement 144 is amended as follows:

a. Paragraph 27:

> A long-lived asset to be disposed of other than by sale (for example, by abandonment, in an exchange measured based on the recorded amount of the nonmonetary asset relinquished~~for a similar productive long-lived asset~~, or in a distribution to owners in a spinoff) shall continue to be classified as held and used until it is disposed of. Paragraphs 7–26 shall apply while the asset is classified as held and used. If a long-lived asset is to be abandoned or distributed to owners in a spinoff together with other assets (and liabilities) as a group and that disposal group is a *component of an entity,*[15] paragraphs 41–44 shall apply to the disposal group at the date it is disposed of.

b. Paragraph 29 and its related footnote 17 and the heading preceding that paragraph:

> ***Long-lived asset to be exchanged*** ~~***for a similar productive long-lived asset***~~ ***or to be distributed to owners in a spinoff***
>
> For purposes of this Statement, a long-lived asset to be disposed of in an exchange measured based on the recorded amount of the nonmonetary asset relinquished~~exchanged for a similar productive long-lived asset~~ or to be distributed to owners in a spinoff is disposed of when it is exchanged or distributed.

If the asset (asset group) is tested for recoverability while it is classified as held and used, the estimates of future cash flows used in that test shall be based on the use of the asset for its remaining useful life, assuming that the disposal transaction will not occur. In addition to any impairment losses required to be recognized while the asset is classified as held and used, an impairment loss, if any, shall be recognized when the asset is disposed of if the carrying amount of the asset (disposal group) exceeds its fair value.[17]

---

[17]The provisions of this paragraph apply to nonmonetary exchanges that are not recorded at fair value under the provisions ~~those transactions described in paragraphs 21 and 23 of~~ APB Opinion No. 29, *Accounting for Nonmonetary Transactions,* as amended.~~for which the accounting is based on the recorded amount (after reduction, if appropriate, for an indicated impairment of value) of a long-lived asset exchanged or distributed.~~

6. The provisions of this Statement partially nullify the following consensuses of the Emerging Issues Task Force (refer to the status sections of those Issues):

a. EITF Issue No. 01-2, "Interpretations of APB Opinion No. 29"

b. EITF Issue No. 98-3, "Determining Whether a Nonmonetary Transaction Involves Receipt of Productive Assets or of a Business."

Effective Date and Transition

7. The provisions of this Statement shall be effective for nonmonetary asset exchanges occurring in fiscal periods beginning after June 15, 2005. Earlier application is permitted for nonmonetary asset exchanges occurring in fiscal periods beginning after the date this Statement is issued. The provisions of this Statement shall be applied prospectively.

> **The provisions of this Statement need not be applied to immaterial items.**

This Statement was adopted by the unanimous vote of the seven members of the Financial Accounting Standards Board:

Robert H. Herz,	G. Michael Crooch	Leslie F. Seidman
Chairman	Gary S. Schieneman	Edward W. Trott
George J. Batavick	Katherine Schipper	

Appendix

BACKGROUND INFORMATION AND BASIS FOR CONCLUSIONS

Introduction

A1. This appendix summarizes considerations that Board members deemed significant in reaching the conclusions in this Statement. It includes reasons for accepting certain approaches and rejecting others. Individual Board members gave greater weight to some factors than to others.

Background Information

A2. In September 2002, the FASB and the International Accounting Standards Board (IASB) (collectively, the Boards) committed to a broad effort to improve international comparability of financial reporting by working toward development of a single set of high-quality accounting standards. As part of that effort, the Boards jointly undertook a short-term project to eliminate certain narrow differences between the accounting pronouncements issued by the IASB and its predecessor and the accounting pronouncements issued by the FASB and its predecessors. Both Boards agreed to limit the scope of the short-term project to issues for which (a) the Boards' respective accounting pronouncements were different; (b) convergence to a high-quality solution would appear to be achievable in the short-term, usually by selecting between the existing standards of either the FASB or the IASB; and (c) the issue was not within the scope of other projects on the current agendas of either Board. The measurement basis of certain nonmonetary asset exchanges is one such difference that the FASB decided should be addressed in the short-term convergence project.

A3. In May 2002, the IASB issued an Exposure Draft, *Improvements to International Accounting Standards,* which, among other things, proposed changing aspects of the accounting for nonmonetary exchanges of assets in IAS 16, *Property, Plant and Equipment,* and IAS 38, *Intangible Assets.* The guidance in those two accounting standards, as in Opinion 29, is based on the principle that nonmonetary exchanges should be measured on the basis of the fair values of the assets exchanged. Also like Opinion 29, those two standards contained an exception to that basic principle for exchanges of similar productive assets. The IASB's Exposure Draft proposed eliminating the "similar productive assets" exception. After considering comments received from respondents on that Exposure Draft, the IASB affirmed its decision to eliminate that exception with the added proviso that exchanges lacking commercial substance do not qualify for recognition at fair value. In October 2002, the FASB added a project to its agenda to consider whether to amend Opinion 29 to similarly eliminate the exception to fair value measurement for exchanges of similar productive assets.

A4. In December 2003, the Board issued an Exposure Draft, *Exchanges of Productive Assets,* for a 120-day comment period, that proposed eliminating the exception to fair value accounting for nonmonetary exchanges of similar productive assets and replacing it with an exception for exchange transactions that lack commercial substance. The Board received 30 comment letters on the Exposure Draft. In September 2004, the Board redeliberated the issues identified in the Exposure Draft and concluded that on the basis of the existing information, it could reach an informed decision on the matters addressed in this Statement without a public hearing or round-table meeting.

Basis for Conclusions

Replacing the "Similar Productive Assets" Exception

A5. In the deliberations that led to the Exposure Draft, the FASB noted that the guidance in Opinion 29 that previously required a determination of whether a nonmonetary exchange is an exchange of similar productive assets was difficult to apply. For example, EITF Issues 98-3 and 01-2 provided detailed guidance for assessing whether the similar productive assets exception should apply. The Board decided to adopt the IASB's approach, which bases the exception to the fair value measurement principle on an assessment of the commercial substance of the exchange. The Board concluded that the IASB's approach would (a) be more consistent with the fair value measurement principle on which Opinion 29 is based, (b) produce financial information that more faithfully represents the economics of the exchange, and (c) be more easily and consistently applied. Thus, the Board proposed amendments to Opinion 29 that would eliminate the similar productive assets exception and replace it with an exception for exchange transactions that lack commercial substance.

A6. A majority of the respondents to the Exposure Draft supported the proposed replacement of the similar productive assets exception, and the Board affirmed its decision in its redeliberations.

Evaluating Commercial Substance

A7. During the deliberations that led to the Exposure Draft, the FASB worked with the IASB to describe the notion of commercial substance. The Boards identified four perspectives from which a reporting entity could evaluate commercial substance: (a) attributes of the reporting entity making the exchange, (b) attributes of the assets being exchanged, (c) attributes of the counterparty to the exchange, and (d) attributes of the terms of the exchange. The FASB and the IASB both concluded that evaluating commercial substance from the reporting entity's perspective would be the most useful because such an evaluation would focus on significant changes in the economic situation of the reporting entity as a result of the exchange.

A8. Both Boards also concluded that changes to the economics of the reporting entity should be evaluated by assessing whether the entity's future cash flows are expected to significantly change as a result of the exchange—specifically, whether (a) the configuration of the future cash flows underlying the asset(s) received differs significantly from the configuration of those underlying the asset(s) transferred or (b) the entity-specific value of the asset(s) received differs significantly from the entity-specific value of the asset(s) transferred. The Board chose to require cash flow tests to determine whether commercial substance exists because it believes those cash flow tests provide objective evidence of a business purpose for the transaction.

A9. A number of respondents stated that they found the guidance for evaluating commercial substance (paragraph 21 of the Exposure Draft) difficult to apply. Paragraph 21(a) would have required that entities determine whether the configuration of the future cash flows of the asset(s) received differed from the configuration of the future cash flows of the asset(s) transferred and then compare that difference to the fair value of the assets exchanged. Respondents noted that it may not be possible to compare a change in configuration to the fair value of the assets exchanged because the change may not be expressed as a dollar amount (for example, a change in timing of cash flows). The Board agreed with those respondents and revised the guidance to eliminate the required comparison to the fair value of the assets exchanged.

A10. A number of respondents to the Exposure Draft that supported the proposed amendment of Opinion 29 suggested improvements to the proposed guidance for assessing the commercial substance of an exchange. Some suggested that the Board eliminate the cash flow tests and replace them with broader, more principles-based guidance that describes the qualitative characteristics of a transaction with commercial substance. After carefully considering that suggestion, the Board affirmed its decision to evaluate commercial substance using an approach that evaluates the risk, timing, and amounts of future cash flows and the entity-specific values of the exchanged assets. The Board believes that approach is more operational than one relying solely on qualitative assessments. The Board agreed, however, that in some cases a conclusive determination of commercial substance can be made based on a qualitative assessment rather than detailed calculations, and guidance to that effect is included in this Statement.

A11. The Exposure Draft proposed that a transaction would have commercial substance if the entity-specific value of *the portion of the reporting entity's operations affected by the transaction* changes as a result of the exchange. A number of respondents to the Exposure Draft commented on that requirement, noting that it was confusing absent a definition for the phrase *portion of the reporting entity's operations affected by the transaction.* In its redeliberations, the Board concluded that the use of that phrase was unnecessary because an entity-specific value of the asset(s) exchanged would, by definition, include all of the cash flow effects of the transaction on the entire entity. Therefore, the Board eliminated that phrase from this Statement and replaced it with a requirement to compare the entity-specific value of the asset(s) received with that of the asset(s) transferred.

A12. A number of respondents to the Exposure Draft suggested that this Statement include examples of transactions that meet the criteria for commercial substance as well as those that do not. The Board agreed that, in some instances, example transactions can be helpful to implement certain requirements. However, the Board decided not to include examples in this Statement because it believes that the additional guidance related to commercial substance sufficiently clarifies the meaning of that term. Additionally, the Board was concerned that example transactions might be viewed as bright lines and might restrict the appropriate use of judgment.

Tax Cash Flows

A13. The Board understands that the tax rules in the United States and some other tax jurisdictions incorporate a business-purpose doctrine. Under that doctrine, a transaction is not given effect for tax purposes unless it serves a legitimate business purpose other than tax avoidance. The Board noted that the interaction between the commercial-substance exception and the business-purpose doctrine could be viewed as circular if (a) the determination of commercial substance is predicated solely on changes in tax cash flows and (b) the tax business purpose asserted is the achievement of a specified financial reporting result. The Board addressed this potential circularity by prohibiting entities from asserting commercial substance if that assertion is predicated on tax cash flows that arise solely because the tax business purpose is based on achieving a specified financial reporting result.

Changes to the Scope of Opinion 29 and Amendments to Other Pronouncements

A14. *Amendments to Opinion 29.* The Exposure Draft proposed amending Opinion 29 to explicitly exclude from its scope exchange transactions that embody a transfer of assets to an entity in exchange for an interest in that entity. Although a number of respondents to the Exposure Draft recommended that this scope exception be eliminated, the Board affirmed its decision, noting that including those exchanges in the scope of Opinion 29 would presuppose answers to issues being addressed in its project on revenue recognition and in potential future projects on fresh-start measurement (new-basis accounting).

A15. The Board noted that certain transactions that appear to be nonmonetary exchanges are, in fact, not exchanges at all because the transferor does not relinquish control of a transferred asset such that derecognition is appropriate. The Board did not want this Statement to establish a less restrictive standard for gain recognition than the standard for gain recognition that is applicable to similar transactions involving monetary consideration. Therefore, the Exposure Draft proposed amending the term *exchange* as defined in Opinion 29 to clarify that a transfer of a nonmonetary asset is not considered an exchange for the purposes of this Statement unless the transferor has no continuing involvement in the transferred asset. Some respondents to the Exposure Draft stated that the phrase *no continuing involvement* establishes a higher threshold for nonmonetary exchanges than for exchanges involving monetary consideration. In response to those concerns, the Board revised that phrase to require that a transfer of a nonmonetary asset is an exchange only if the transferor has no *substantial* continuing involvement in the transferred asset.

A16. *Financial Accounting and Reporting by Oil- and Gas-Producing Companies.* In developing the Exposure Draft, the Board concluded that the accounting for exchange transactions described in paragraph 44(a) of Statement 19 was based on the accounting principles in Opinion 29. The Board therefore proposed an amendment to Statement 19 clarifying that those exchanges should be accounted for in accordance with Opinion 29, as amended. Several respondents to the Exposure Draft recommended that these transactions be excluded from the scope of this Statement. However, the Board affirmed its decision noting that these transactions are consistent with the description of an exchange of nonmonetary assets and, therefore, are appropriately included in the scope of this Statement.

A17. The Board also noted that the transaction described in paragraph 44(b) of Statement 19 is more

closely analogous to an exchange of an asset for an equity interest in an entity than it is to an exchange of productive assets and, accordingly, decided that those transactions should continue to be accounted for under the provisions of Statement 19.

A18. The Board noted that the transactions discussed in paragraph 47(e) of Statement 19 are described as exchanges of similar productive assets. The Board considered whether to amend that paragraph to require that those transactions be accounted for under the provisions of Opinion 29 as amended by this Statement. The Board decided not to amend that paragraph, noting that it is difficult to distinguish "joint venture" transactions from similar transactions that would be included in the scope of Statement 19 because *joint venture* is not defined robustly in current guidance. The majority of respondents agreed with that decision, and the Board affirmed it in its redeliberations.

A19. *Transfers of Financial Assets.* The Exposure Draft proposed amending both Opinion 29 and Statement 140 to clarify that a transfer of an equity method investment for a similar productive asset should be accounted for in accordance with the provisions of Statement 140. The majority of respondents agreed with that decision, and the Board affirmed it in its redeliberations.

A20. FASB Statement No. 66, *Accounting for Sales of Real Estate,* provides guidance on when to derecognize a real estate asset sold and when to recognize profit on the sale of that asset. Statement 66 states that exchanges of real estate for other real estate should be accounted for under the provisions of Opinion 29. The Board considered whether to eliminate that scope exception in Statement 66 but decided not to do so because that Statement was designed to deal with transactions involving monetary consideration. The Board decided that the model established by this Statement is appropriate for evaluating exchanges of real estate for real estate.

International Convergence of Accounting Standards

A21. Although one objective of issuing this Statement is to further the Board's convergence efforts with the IASB, as discussed below, some differences in accounting for nonmonetary exchanges have not been eliminated by this Statement.

A22. The FASB noted that the exception in Opinion 29 for exchanges in which the fair value is *not determinable within reasonable limits* has the same intent as the IASB's exception for nonmonetary asset exchanges in which the fair value of the assets exchanged is *not reliably measurable*. The Board decided to retain its current terminology pending completion of its project on fair value measurement.

A23. Opinion 29 provides guidance for measuring the effects of exchanges of nonmonetary assets. IAS 16 and IAS 38 provide guidance for assessing the effects of exchanges of property, plant, and equipment and intangible assets. Both Boards acknowledge that those differences will likely result in scope differences between the Boards' standards for nonmonetary exchanges. The FASB and the IASB have agreed to use an iterative process to converge the scope of their guidance for nonmonetary exchanges. Under that process, the IASB issued its standard for nonmonetary asset exchanges with a narrower scope than this Statement. This Statement incorporates improvements in the notion of *commercial substance* as that term is used in IAS 16. The IASB plans to add a project to its agenda to converge its standards, in terms of both scope and content, with that of the FASB. The Board noted that its decision to amend Statement 140 brought the scope of this Statement closer to the scope of the IASB Statements.

Effective Date and Transition

A24. The Board decided that the provisions of this Statement should be effective for nonmonetary asset exchanges occurring in fiscal periods beginning after June 15, 2005. Earlier application of the provisions of this Statement is permitted so that entities based in the European Union that report under U.S. generally accepted accounting principles (GAAP) would have the opportunity to implement its provisions prior to the requirement to report under international financial reporting standards (IFRS).

A25. The Board concluded that prospective application of the provisions of this Statement is appropriate because retrospective application in many cases may be impracticable because it would require significant estimates as of a prior period. In some cases, it may not be possible to objectively distinguish between information that would have been available at the time the affected transactions or events would have been recognized in the financial statements and information that arose subsequent to recognition.

Benefits and Costs

A26. The mission of the FASB is to establish and improve standards of financial accounting and reporting for the guidance and education of the public, including preparers, auditors, and users of financial information. In fulfilling that mission, the Board endeavors to determine that a proposed standard will fill a significant need and that the costs imposed to meet that standard, as compared with other alternatives, are justified in relation to the overall benefits of the resulting information. Although the costs to implement a new standard may not be borne evenly, investors and creditors—both present and potential—and other users of financial information benefit from improvements in financial reporting, thereby facilitating the functioning of markets for capital and credit and the efficient allocation of resources in the economy.

A27. The Board believes that the benefits of a more conceptually based standard for accounting for nonmonetary exchanges should outweigh the effort that would be required on the part of preparers to determine whether a nonmonetary exchange has commercial substance. Further, the Board notes that costs would be reduced for entities that prepare financial statements for use in several jurisdictions, because convergence with international accounting standards will reduce the time and effort necessary to prepare reconciliations between U.S. GAAP and IFRS. The Board believes that financial reporting will be both simplified and improved by eliminating the inconsistencies between U.S. GAAP and IFRS.

Statement of Financial Accounting Standards No. 154
Accounting Changes and Error Corrections

a replacement of APB Opinion No. 20
and FASB Statement No. 3

STATUS

Issued: May 2005

Effective Date: For accounting changes and corrections of errors made in fiscal years beginning after
December 15, 2005

Affects: Amends ARB 43, Chapter 2A, paragraph 3
Supersedes APB 20
Amends APB 22, paragraph 14
Amends APB 25, paragraph 15
Amends APB 28, paragraphs 24, 26, 29, 30(a), and 30(i)
Deletes APB 28, paragraphs 25 and 27 through 27D and footnote 5
Amends APB 30, paragraph 25 and footnote 4
Supersedes FAS 3
Amends FAS 16, footnote 3
Deletes FAS 16, footnote 6
Amends FAS 19, paragraphs 30 and 35
Amends FAS 25, paragraph 4
Deletes FAS 25, footnote 1
Amends FAS 52, paragraph 45
Amends FAS 67, paragraph 12
Amends FAS 71, paragraph 31
Supersedes FAS 73
Amends FAS 123(R), paragraphs 38 and A23
Amends FAS 128, paragraphs 15, 37, 148, and 149
Amends FAS 130, paragraph 131
Amends FAS 131, paragraphs 31 through 33
Amends FAS 141, paragraphs 55 and 58
Amends FAS 143, paragraph 15
Amends FAS 144, paragraphs 9, 28, and 43 and footnotes 7 and 24
Amends FIN 1, paragraphs 1 and 5
Amends FIN 7, paragraph 5
Amends FIN 18, paragraphs 64 and 71 and footnote 1
Deletes FIN 18, paragraph 21
Supersedes FIN 20
Effectively amends FSP FAS 106-2, paragraph 29

Affected by: No other pronouncements

Issues Discussed by FASB Emerging Issues Task Force (EITF)

Affects: No EITF Issues

Interpreted by: No EITF Issues

Related Issues: EITF Issues No. 06-3 and 06-9 and Topic No. D-1

SUMMARY

This Statement replaces APB Opinion No. 20, *Accounting Changes,* and FASB Statement No. 3, *Reporting Accounting Changes in Interim Financial Statements,* and changes the requirements for the accounting for and reporting of a change in accounting principle. This Statement applies to all voluntary changes in accounting principle. It also applies to changes required by an accounting pronouncement in the unusual instance that the pronouncement does not include specific transition provisions. When a pronouncement includes specific transition provisions, those provisions should be followed.

Opinion 20 previously required that most voluntary changes in accounting principle be recognized by including in net income of the period of the change the cumulative effect of changing to the new accounting principle. This Statement requires retrospective application to prior periods' financial statements of changes in accounting principle, unless it is impracticable to determine either the period-specific effects or the cumulative effect of the change. When it is impracticable to determine the period-specific effects of an accounting change on one or more individual prior periods presented, this Statement requires that the new accounting principle be applied to the balances of assets and liabilities as of the beginning of the earliest period for which retrospective application is practicable and that a corresponding adjustment be made to the opening balance of retained earnings (or other appropriate components of equity or net assets in the statement of financial position) for that period rather than being reported in an income statement. When it is impracticable to determine the cumulative effect of applying a change in accounting principle to all prior periods, this Statement requires that the new accounting principle be applied as if it were adopted prospectively from the earliest date practicable.

This Statement defines *retrospective application* as the application of a different accounting principle to prior accounting periods as if that principle had always been used or as the adjustment of previously issued financial statements to reflect a change in the reporting entity. This Statement also redefines *restatement* as the revising of previously issued financial statements to reflect the correction of an error.

This Statement requires that retrospective application of a change in accounting principle be limited to the direct effects of the change. Indirect effects of a change in accounting principle, such as a change in nondiscretionary profit-sharing payments resulting from an accounting change, should be recognized in the period of the accounting change.

This Statement also requires that a change in depreciation, amortization, or depletion method for long-lived, nonfinancial assets be accounted for as a change in accounting estimate effected by a change in accounting principle.

This Statement carries forward without change the guidance contained in Opinion 20 for reporting the correction of an error in previously issued financial statements and a change in accounting estimate. This Statement also carries forward the guidance in Opinion 20 requiring justification of a change in accounting principle on the basis of preferability.

Reasons for Issuing This Statement

This Statement is the result of a broader effort by the FASB to improve the comparability of cross-border financial reporting by working with the International Accounting Standards Board (IASB) toward development of a single set of high-quality accounting standards. As part of that effort, the FASB and the IASB identified opportunities to improve financial reporting by eliminating certain narrow differences between their existing accounting standards. Reporting of accounting changes was identified as an area in which financial reporting in the United States could be improved by eliminating differences between Opinion 20 and IAS 8, *Accounting Policies, Changes in Accounting Estimates and Errors.*

How the Changes in This Statement Improve Financial Reporting

Under the provisions of Opinion 20, most accounting changes were recognized by including in net income of the period of the change the cumulative effect of changing to the newly adopted accounting principle. This Statement improves financial reporting because its requirement to report voluntary changes in accounting principles via retrospective application, unless impracticable, enhances the consistency of financial information between periods. That improved consistency enhances the usefulness of the financial information, especially by facilitating analysis and understanding of comparative accounting data.

Also, in instances in which full retrospective application is impracticable, this Statement improves consistency of financial information between periods by requiring that a new accounting principle be applied as of the earliest date practicable.

This Statement requires that a change in depreciation, amortization, or depletion method for long-lived, nonfinancial assets be accounted for as a change in accounting estimate that is effected by a change in accounting principle. The provisions of this Statement better reflect the fact that an entity should change its depreciation, amortization, or depletion method only in recognition of changes in estimated future benefits of an asset, in the pattern of consumption of those benefits, or in the information available to the entity about those benefits.

A change in accounting principle required by the issuance of an accounting pronouncement was not within the scope of Opinion 20. Including all changes in accounting principle within the scope of this Statement establishes, unless impracticable, retrospective application as the transition method for new accounting standards, but only in the unusual instance that the new accounting pronouncement does not include explicit transition provisions.

Statement of Financial Accounting Standards No. 154

Accounting Changes and Error Corrections

a replacement of APB Opinion No. 20 and FASB Statement No. 3

CONTENTS

INTRODUCTION

1. This Statement provides guidance on the accounting for and reporting of accounting changes and error corrections. It establishes, unless impracticable, retrospective application as the required method for reporting a change in accounting principle in the absence of explicit transition requirements specific to the newly adopted accounting principle. This Statement also provides guidance for determining whether retrospective application of a change in accounting principle is impracticable and for reporting a change when retrospective application is impracticable. The correction of an error in previously issued financial statements is not an accounting change. However, the reporting of an error correction involves adjustments to previously issued financial statements similar to those generally applicable to reporting an accounting change retrospectively. Therefore, the reporting of a correction of an error by restating previously issued financial statements is also addressed by this Statement.

STANDARDS OF FINANCIAL ACCOUNTING AND REPORTING

Definitions

2. The following terms are defined as used in this Statement:

a. **Accounting change**—a change in (1) an accounting principle, (2) an accounting estimate, or (3) the reporting entity. The correction of an error in previously issued financial statements is not an accounting change.

b. **Accounting pronouncement**—a source of generally accepted accounting principles (GAAP) in the United States, including FASB Statements of Financial Accounting Standards, FASB Interpretations, FASB Staff Positions, FASB Statement 133 Implementation Issues, Emerging Issues Task Force Consensuses, other pronouncements of the FASB or other designated bodies, or other forms of GAAP as described in categories (a)–(c) of AICPA Statement on Auditing Standards (SAS) No. 69, *The Meaning of* Present Fairly in Conformity With Generally Accepted Accounting Principles, as codified in the AICPA Codification of Statements on Auditing Standards, AU Section 411, *The Meaning of* Present Fairly in Conformity With Generally Accepted Accounting Principles.[1] AICPA accounting interpretations and implementation guides ("Q & A's") issued by the FASB staff, as described in category (d) of SAS 69, also are considered accounting pronouncements for the purpose of applying this Statement.

c. **Change in accounting principle**—a change from one generally accepted accounting principle to another generally accepted accounting principle when there are two or more generally accepted accounting principles that apply or when the accounting principle formerly used is no longer generally accepted. A change in the *method* of applying an accounting principle also is considered a change in accounting principle.

d. **Change in accounting estimate**—a change that has the effect of adjusting the carrying amount of an existing asset or liability or altering the subsequent accounting for existing or future assets or liabilities. A change in accounting estimate is a necessary consequence of the assessment, in conjunction with the periodic presentation of financial statements, of the present status and expected future benefits and obligations associated with assets and liabilities. Changes in accounting estimates result from new information. Examples of items for which estimates are necessary are uncollectible receivables, inventory obsolescence, service lives and salvage values of depreciable assets, and warranty obligations.

e. **Change in accounting estimate effected by a change in accounting principle**—a change in accounting estimate that is inseparable from the effect of a related change in accounting principle. An example of a change in estimate effected by a change in principle is a change in the method of depreciation, amortization, or depletion for long-lived, nonfinancial assets.

f. **Change in the reporting entity**—a change that results in financial statements that, in effect, are those of a different reporting entity. A change in the reporting entity is limited mainly to (1) presenting consolidated or combined financial statements in place of financial statements of individual entities, (2) changing specific subsidiaries that make up the group of entities for which consolidated financial statements are presented, and (3) changing the entities included in combined financial statements. Neither a business combination accounted for by the purchase method nor the consolidation of a variable interest entity pursuant to FASB Interpretation No. 46 (revised December 2003), *Consolidation of Variable Interest Entities,* is a change in reporting entity.

g. **Direct effects of a change in accounting principle**—those recognized changes in assets or liabilities necessary to effect a change in accounting principle. An example of a direct effect is an adjustment to an inventory balance to effect a change in inventory valuation method. Related changes, such as an effect on deferred income tax assets or liabilities or an impairment adjustment resulting from applying the lower-of-cost-or-market test to the adjusted inventory balance, also are examples of direct effects of a change in accounting principle.

h. **Error in previously issued financial statements**—an error in recognition, measurement, presentation, or disclosure in financial statements resulting from mathematical mistakes, mistakes in the application of GAAP, or oversight or misuse of facts that existed at the time the financial statements were prepared. A change from an accounting principle that is not generally accepted to one that is generally accepted is a correction of an error.

i. **Indirect effects of a change in accounting principle**—any changes to current or future cash flows of an entity that result from making a change in accounting principle that is applied retrospectively. An example of an indirect effect is a change in a nondiscretionary profit sharing or royalty payment that is based on a reported amount such as revenue or net income.

---

[1]The Board's technical agenda includes a project that could result in the issuance of a Statement of Financial Accounting Standards that identifies the sources of accounting principles and the framework for selecting the principles used in the preparation of financial statements of nongovernmental enterprises that are presented in conformity with GAAP. The Board issued an Exposure Draft of that proposed Statement in April 2005.

j. **Restatement**—the process of revising previously issued financial statements to reflect the correction of an error in those financial statements.

k. **Retrospective application**—the application of a different accounting principle to one or more previously issued financial statements, or to the statement of financial position at the beginning of the current period, as if that principle had always been used, or a change to financial statements of prior accounting periods to present the financial statements of a new reporting entity as if it had existed in those prior years.

Scope

3. This Statement applies to financial statements of business enterprises and not-for-profit organizations, both of which are referred to herein as entities. This Statement also applies to historical summaries of information based on primary financial statements that include an accounting period in which an accounting change or error correction is reflected. The guidance in this Statement also may be appropriate in presenting financial information in other forms or for special purposes.

Accounting Changes

Change in Accounting Principle

4. A presumption exists that an accounting principle once adopted shall not be changed in accounting for events and transactions of a similar type. Consistent use of the same accounting principle from one accounting period to another enhances the utility of financial statements for users by facilitating analysis and understanding of comparative accounting data.

5. Neither (a) initial adoption of an accounting principle in recognition of events or transactions occurring for the first time or that previously were immaterial in their effect nor (b) adoption or modification of an accounting principle necessitated by transactions or events that are clearly different in substance from those previously occurring is a change in accounting principle. A reporting entity shall change an accounting principle only if (a) the change is required by a newly issued accounting pronouncement or (b) the entity can justify the use of an allowable alternative accounting principle on the basis that it is preferable.

6. It is expected that accounting pronouncements normally will provide specific transition requirements. However, in the unusual instance that there are no transition requirements specific to a particular accounting pronouncement, a change in accounting principle effected to adopt the requirements of that accounting pronouncement shall be reported in accordance with paragraphs 7–10 of this Statement.[2] Early adoption of an accounting pronouncement, when permitted, shall be effected in a manner consistent with the transition requirements of that pronouncement.

7. An entity shall report a change in accounting principle through retrospective application of the new accounting principle to all prior periods, unless it is impracticable to do so. Retrospective application requires the following:

a. The cumulative effect of the change to the new accounting principle on periods prior to those presented shall be reflected in the carrying amounts of assets and liabilities as of the beginning of the first period presented.

b. An offsetting adjustment, if any, shall be made to the opening balance of retained earnings (or other appropriate components of equity or net assets in the statement of financial position) for that period.

c. Financial statements for each individual prior period presented shall be adjusted to reflect the period-specific effects of applying the new accounting principle.

8. If the cumulative effect of applying a change in accounting principle to all prior periods can be determined, but it is impracticable to determine the period-specific effects of that change on all prior periods presented, the cumulative effect of the change to the new accounting principle shall be applied to the carrying amounts of assets and liabilities as of the beginning of the earliest period to which the new accounting principle can be applied. An offsetting adjustment, if any, shall be made to the opening balance of retained earnings (or other appropriate components of equity or net assets in the statement of financial position) for that period.

9. If it is impracticable to determine the cumulative effect of applying a change in accounting principle to

---

[2]This requirement is not limited to newly issued accounting pronouncements. For example, if an existing pronouncement permits a choice between two or more alternative accounting principles, and provides requirements for changing from one to another, those requirements shall be followed.

any prior period, the new accounting principle shall be applied as if the change was made prospectively as of the earliest date practicable. APB Opinion No. 20, *Accounting Changes,* illustrated that type of change with a change from the first-in, first-out (FIFO) method of inventory valuation to the last-in, first-out (LIFO) method. This Statement carries forward that example (as Illustration 2 in Appendix A) for illustrative purposes without implying that such a change would be considered preferable as required by paragraph 13 of this Statement.

10. Retrospective application shall include only the direct effects of a change in accounting principle, including any related income tax effects. Indirect effects that would have been recognized if the newly adopted accounting principle had been followed in prior periods shall not be included in the retrospective application. If indirect effects are actually incurred and recognized, they shall be reported in the period in which the accounting change is made.

Impracticability

11. It shall be deemed impracticable to apply the effects of a change in accounting principle retrospectively only if any of the following conditions exist:

a. After making every reasonable effort to do so, the entity is unable to apply the requirement.
b. Retrospective application requires assumptions about management's intent in a prior period that cannot be independently substantiated.
c. Retrospective application requires significant estimates of amounts, and it is impossible to distinguish objectively information about those estimates that:
   (1) Provides evidence of circumstances that existed on the date(s) at which those amounts would be recognized, measured, or disclosed under retrospective application, and
   (2) Would have been available when the financial statements for that prior period were issued.[3]

Justification for a change in accounting principle

12. In the preparation of financial statements, once an accounting principle is adopted, it shall be used consistently in accounting for similar events and transactions.

13. An entity may change an accounting principle only if it justifies the use of an allowable alternative accounting principle on the basis that it is preferable. However, a method of accounting that was previously adopted for a type of transaction or event that is being terminated or that was a single, nonrecurring event in the past shall not be changed. For example, the method of accounting shall not be changed for a tax or tax credit that is being discontinued. Additionally, the method of transition elected at the time of adoption of an accounting pronouncement shall not be subsequently changed. However, a change in the estimated period to be benefited by an asset, if justified by the facts, shall be recognized as a change in accounting estimate.

14. The issuance of an accounting pronouncement that requires use of a new accounting principle, interprets an existing principle, expresses a preference for an accounting principle, or rejects a specific principle may require an entity to change an accounting principle. The issuance of such a pronouncement constitutes sufficient support for making such a change provided that the hierarchy established for GAAP is followed. The burden of justifying other changes in accounting principle rests with the entity making the change.

Reporting a change in accounting principle made in an interim period

15. A change in accounting principle made in an interim period shall be reported by retrospective application in accordance with paragraphs 7–10 of this Statement. However, the impracticability exception in paragraph 11 may not be applied to prechange interim periods of the fiscal year in which the change is

---

[3]This Statement requires a determination of whether information currently available to develop significant estimates would have been available when the affected transactions or events would have been recognized in the financial statements. However, it is not necessary to maintain documentation from the time that an affected transaction or event would have been recognized to determine whether information to develop the estimates would have been available at that time.

made. When retrospective application to prechange interim periods is impracticable, the desired change may only be made as of the beginning of a subsequent fiscal year.

16. If a public company that regularly reports interim information makes an accounting change during the fourth quarter of its fiscal year and does not report the data specified by paragraph 30 of APB Opinion No. 28, *Interim Financial Reporting* (as amended), in a separate fourth-quarter report or in its annual report, that entity shall include disclosure of the effects of the accounting change on interim-period results, as required by paragraph 17 of this Statement, in a note to the annual financial statements for the fiscal year in which the change is made.

Disclosures

17. An entity shall disclose the following in the fiscal period in which a change in accounting principle is made:

a. The nature of and reason for the change in accounting principle, including an explanation of why the newly adopted accounting principle is preferable.
b. The method of applying the change, and:
   (1) A description of the prior-period information that has been retrospectively adjusted, if any.
   (2) The effect of the change on income from continuing operations, net income (or other appropriate captions of changes in the applicable net assets or performance indicator), any other affected financial statement line item, and any affected per-share amounts for the current period and any prior periods retrospectively adjusted. Presentation of the effect on financial statement subtotals and totals other than income from continuing operations and net income (or other appropriate captions of changes in the applicable net assets or performance indicator) is not required.
   (3) The cumulative effect of the change on retained earnings or other components of equity or net assets in the statement of financial position as of the beginning of the earliest period presented.

(4) If retrospective application to all prior periods (paragraph 7) is impracticable, disclosure of the reasons therefor, and a description of the alternative method used to report the change (paragraphs 8 and 9).
c. If indirect effects of a change in accounting principle are recognized:
   (1) A description of the indirect effects of a change in accounting principle, including the amounts that have been recognized in the current period, and the related per-share amounts, if applicable.
   (2) Unless impracticable,[4] the amount of the total recognized indirect effects of the accounting change and the related per-share amounts, if applicable, that are attributable to each prior period presented.

Financial statements of subsequent periods[5] need not repeat the disclosures required by this paragraph. If a change in accounting principle has no material effect in the period of change but is reasonably certain to have a material effect in later periods, the disclosures required by paragraph 17(a) shall be provided whenever the financial statements of the period of change are presented.

18. In the fiscal year in which a new accounting principle is adopted, financial information reported for interim periods after the date of adoption shall disclose the effect of the change on income from continuing operations, net income (or other appropriate captions of changes in the applicable net assets or performance indicator), and related per-share amounts, if applicable, for those post-change interim periods.

Change in Accounting Estimate

19. A change in accounting estimate shall be accounted for in (a) the period of change if the change affects that period only or (b) the period of change and future periods if the change affects both. A change in accounting estimate shall not be accounted for by restating or retrospectively adjusting amounts reported in financial statements of prior periods or by reporting pro forma amounts for prior periods.

20. Distinguishing between a change in an accounting principle and a change in an accounting estimate

---

[4]Compliance with this disclosure requirement is practicable unless an entity cannot comply with it after making every reasonable effort to do so.
[5]An entity that issues interim financial statements shall provide the required disclosures in the financial statements of both the interim period of the change and the annual period of the change.

is sometimes difficult. In some cases, a change in accounting estimate is effected by a change in accounting principle. One example of this type of change is a change in method of depreciation, amortization, or depletion for long-lived, nonfinancial assets (hereinafter referred to as depreciation method). The new depreciation method is adopted in partial or complete recognition of a change in the estimated future benefits inherent in the asset, the pattern of consumption of those benefits, or the information available to the entity about those benefits. The effect of the change in accounting principle, or the method of applying it, may be inseparable from the effect of the change in accounting estimate. Changes of that type often are related to the continuing process of obtaining additional information and revising estimates and, therefore, are considered changes in estimates for purposes of applying this Statement.

21.   Like other changes in accounting principle, a change in accounting estimate that is effected by a change in accounting principle may be made only if the new accounting principle is justifiable on the basis that it is preferable. For example, an entity that concludes that the pattern of consumption of the expected benefits of an asset has changed, and determines that a new depreciation method better reflects that pattern, may be justified in making a change in accounting estimate effected by a change in accounting principle.[6] (Refer to paragraph 13.)

Disclosures

22.   The effect on income from continuing operations, net income (or other appropriate captions of changes in the applicable net assets or performance indicator), and any related per-share amounts of the current period shall be disclosed for a change in estimate that affects several future periods, such as a change in service lives of depreciable assets. Disclosure of those effects is not necessary for estimates made each period in the ordinary course of accounting for items such as uncollectible accounts or inventory obsolescence; however, disclosure is required if the effect of a change in the estimate is material.[7] When an entity effects a change in estimate by changing an accounting principle, the disclosures re-

quired by paragraphs 17 and 18 of this Statement also are required. If a change in estimate does not have a material effect in the period of change but is reasonably certain to have a material effect in later periods, a description of that change in estimate shall be disclosed whenever the financial statements of the period of change are presented.

Change in the Reporting Entity

23.   When an accounting change results in financial statements that are, in effect, the statements of a different reporting entity, the change shall be retrospectively applied to the financial statements of all prior periods presented to show financial information for the new reporting entity for those periods. Previously issued interim financial information shall be presented on a retrospective basis. However, the amount of interest cost previously capitalized through application of FASB Statement No. 58, *Capitalization of Interest Cost in Financial Statements That Include Investments Accounted for by the Equity Method,* shall not be changed when retrospectively applying the accounting change to the financial statements of prior periods.

Disclosures

24.   When there has been a change in the reporting entity, the financial statements of the period of the change shall describe the nature of the change and the reason for it. In addition, the effect of the change on income before extraordinary items, net income (or other appropriate captions of changes in the applicable net assets or performance indicator), other comprehensive income, and any related per-share amounts shall be disclosed for all periods presented. Financial statements of subsequent periods need not repeat the disclosures required by this paragraph. If a change in reporting entity does not have a material effect in the period of change but is reasonably certain to have a material effect in later periods, the nature of and reason for the change shall be disclosed whenever the financial statements of the period of change are presented. (Paragraphs 51–58 of FASB

---

[6]However, a change to the straight-line method at a specific point in the service life of an asset may be planned at the time some depreciation methods, such as the modified accelerated cost recovery system, are adopted to fully depreciate the cost over the estimated life of the asset. Consistent application of such a policy does not constitute a change in accounting principle for purposes of applying this Statement.

[7]The requirement to disclose the effects if a change in estimate is material is carried forward from Opinion 20. The Board did not reconsider the need for that requirement in the project that led to issuance of this Statement. Numerous Statements have been issued by the Board subsequent to Opinion 20 that address required changes in estimates. Those Statements also include various disclosure requirements. This Statement is not intended to impose new disclosure requirements or change the existing disclosures that GAAP requires for specific changes in estimate.

Statement No. 141, *Business Combinations,* describe the manner of reporting and the disclosures required for a business combination.)

Correction of an Error in Previously Issued Financial Statements

25. Any error in the financial statements of a prior period discovered subsequent to their issuance shall be reported as a prior-period adjustment by restating the prior-period financial statements. Restatement requires that:

a. The cumulative effect of the error on periods prior to those presented shall be reflected in the carrying amounts of assets and liabilities as of the beginning of the first period presented.
b. An offsetting adjustment, if any, shall be made to the opening balance of retained earnings (or other appropriate components of equity or net assets in the statement of financial position) for that period.
c. Financial statements for each individual prior period presented shall be adjusted to reflect correction of the period-specific effects of the error.

Disclosures

26. When financial statements are restated to correct an error, the entity shall disclose that its previously issued financial statements have been restated, along with a description of the nature of the error. The entity also shall disclose the following:

a. The effect of the correction on each financial statement line item and any per-share amounts affected for each prior period presented
b. The cumulative effect of the change on retained earnings or other appropriate components of equity or net assets in the statement of financial position, as of the beginning of the earliest period presented.

In addition, the entity shall make the disclosures of prior-period adjustments and restatements required by paragraph 26 of APB Opinion No. 9, *Reporting the Results of Operations.* Financial statements of subsequent periods[8] need not repeat the disclosures required by this paragraph.

Effective Date and Transition

27. This Statement shall be effective for accounting changes and corrections of errors made in fiscal years beginning after December 15, 2005. Early adoption is permitted for accounting changes and corrections of errors made in fiscal years beginning after the date this Statement is issued. This Statement does not change the transition provisions of any existing accounting pronouncements, including those that are in a transition phase as of the effective date of this Statement.

The provisions of this Statement need not be applied to immaterial items.

This Statement was adopted by the unanimous vote of the seven members of the Financial Accounting Standards Board:

Robert H. Herz,	G. Michael Crooch	Edward W. Trott
Chairman	Katherine Schipper	Donald M. Young
George J. Batavick	Leslie F. Seidman	

---

[8]Refer to footnote 5.

Appendix A

ILLUSTRATIONS

A1. This appendix presents generalized examples intended to illustrate how to apply certain provisions of this Statement. The examples do not address all possible situations or applications of this Statement, nor do they establish additional requirements.

Illustration 1—Retrospective Application of a Change in Accounting Principle

A2. ABC Company decides at the beginning of 20X7 to adopt the FIFO method of inventory valua-

tion. ABC Company had used the LIFO method for financial and tax reporting since its inception on January 1, 20X5, and had maintained records that are adequate to apply the FIFO method retrospectively. ABC Company concluded that the FIFO method is the preferable inventory valuation method for its inventory. The change in accounting principle is reported through retrospective application as described in paragraph 7 of this Statement.

A3. The effects of the change in accounting principle on inventory and cost of sales are presented in the following table:

| Date | Inventory Determined by | | Cost of Sales Determined by | |
	LIFO Method	FIFO Method	LIFO Method	FIFO Method
1/1/20X5	$ 0	$ 0	$ 0	$ 0
12/31/20X5	100	80	800	820
12/31/20X6	200	240	1,000	940
12/31/20X7	320	390	1,130	1,100

A4. This illustration is based on the following assumptions:

a. For each year presented, sales are $3,000 and selling, general, and administrative costs are $1,000. ABC Company's effective income tax rate for all years is 40 percent, and there are no permanent or temporary differences under FASB Statement No. 109, *Accounting for Income Taxes,* prior to the change.

b. ABC Company has a nondiscretionary profit-sharing agreement in place for all years. Under that agreement, ABC Company is required to contribute 10 percent of its reported income before tax and profit sharing to a profit-sharing pool to be distributed to employees. For simplicity, it is assumed that the profit-sharing contribution is not an inventoriable cost.

c. ABC Company determined that its profit-sharing expense would have decreased by $2 in 20X5 and increased by $6 in 20X6 if it had used the FIFO method to compute its inventory cost since inception. The terms of the profit-sharing agreement do not address whether ABC Company is required to adjust its profit-sharing accrual for the incremental amounts.[9] At the time of the accounting change, ABC Company decides to contribute the additional $6 attributable to 20X6 profit and to make no adjustment related to 20X5 profit. The $6 payment is made in 20X7.

d. Profit sharing and income taxes accrued at each year-end under the LIFO method are paid in cash at the beginning of each following year.

e. ABC Company's annual report to shareholders provides two years of financial results, and ABC Company is not subject to the requirements of FASB Statement No. 128, *Earnings per Share.*

---

[9]In accordance with paragraph 10 of this Statement, recognized indirect effects of a change in accounting principle are recorded in the period of change. That provision applies even if recognition of the indirect effect is explicitly required by the terms of the profit-sharing contract.

A5. ABC Company's income statements as originally reported under the LIFO method are presented below.

Income Statement

	20X6	20X5
Sales	$3,000	$3,000
Cost of goods sold	1,000	800
Selling, general, and administrative expenses	1,000	1,000
Income before profit sharing and income taxes	1,000	1,200
Profit sharing	100	120
Income before income taxes	900	1,080
Income taxes	360	432
Net income	$ 540	$ 648

A6. ABC Company's income statements reflecting the retrospective application of the accounting change from the LIFO method to the FIFO method are presented below.

Income Statement

	20X7	20X6 As Adjusted (Note A)
Sales	$3,000	$3,000
Cost of goods sold	1,100	940
Selling, general, and administrative expenses	1,000	1,000
Income before profit sharing and income taxes	900	1,060
Profit sharing	96	100
Income before income taxes	804	960
Income taxes	322	384
Net income	$ 482	$ 576

A7. ABC Company's disclosure related to the accounting change is presented below.

NOTE A:

Change in Method of Accounting for Inventory Valuation

On January 1, 20X7, ABC Company elected to change its method of valuing its inventory to the FIFO method, whereas in all prior years inventory was valued using the LIFO method. The new method of accounting for inventory was adopted (state justification for change in accounting principle) and comparative financial statements of prior years have been adjusted to apply the new method retrospectively. The following financial statement line items for fiscal years 20X7 and 20X6 were affected by the change in accounting principle.

Income Statement
20X7

	As Computed under LIFO	As Reported under FIFO	Effect of Change
Sales	$3,000	$3,000	$ 0
Cost of goods sold	1,130	1,100	(30)
Selling, general, and administrative expenses	1,000	1,000	0
Income before profit sharing and income taxes	870	900	30
Profit sharing	87	96*	9
Income before income taxes	783	804	21
Income taxes	313	322	9
Net income	$ 470	$ 482	$ 12

---

*This amount includes a $90 profit-sharing payment attributable to 20X7 profits and $6 profit-sharing payment attributable to 20X6 profits, which is an indirect effect of the change in accounting principle. The incremental payment attributable to 20X6 would have been recognized in 20X6 if ABC Company's inventory had originally been accounted for using the FIFO method.

20X6

	As Originally Reported	As Adjusted	Effect of Change
Sales	$3,000	$3,000	$ 0
Cost of goods sold	1,000	940	(60)
Selling, general, and administrative expenses	1,000	1,000	0
Income before profit sharing and income taxes	1,000	1,060	60
Profit sharing	100	100	0
Income before income taxes	900	960	60
Income taxes	360	384	24
Net income	$ 540	$ 576	$ 36

Balance Sheet
12/31/X7

	As Computed under LIFO	As Reported under FIFO	Effect of Change
Cash	$2,738	$2,732	$(6)
Inventory	320	390	70
Total assets	$3,058	$3,122	$64
Accrued profit sharing	87	90	3
Income tax liability	313	338	25
Total liabilities	400	428	28
Paid-in capital	1,000	1,000	0
Retained earnings	1,658	1,694	36
Total stockholders' equity	2,658	2,694	36
Total liabilities and stockholders' equity	$3,058	$3,122	$64

12/31/X6

	As Originally Reported	As Adjusted	Effect of Change
Cash	$2,448	$2,448	$ 0
Inventory	200	240	40
Total assets	$2,648	$2,688	$40
Accrued profit sharing	100	100	0
Income tax liability	360	376	16
Total liabilities	460	476	16
Paid-in capital	1,000	1,000	0
Retained earnings	1,188	1,212	24
Total stockholders' equity	2,188	2,212	24
Total liabilities and stockholders' equity	$2,648	$2,688	$40

As a result of the accounting change, retained earnings as of January 1, 20X6, decreased from $648, as originally reported using the LIFO method, to $636 using the FIFO method.

Statement of Cash Flows
20X7

	As Computed under LIFO	As Reported under FIFO	Effect of Change
Net income	$ 470	$ 482	$ 12
Adjustments to reconcile net income to net cash provided by operating activities			
Increase in inventory	(120)	(150)	(30)
Decrease in accrued profit sharing	(13)	(10)	3
Decrease in income tax liability	(47)	(38)	9
Net cash provided by operating activities	290	284	(6)
Net increase in cash	290	284	(6)
Cash, January 1, 20X7	2,448	2,448	0
Cash, December 31, 20X7	$2,738	$2,732	$ (6)

20X6	As Originally Reported	As Adjusted	Effect of Change
Net income	$ 540	$ 576	$ 36
Adjustments to reconcile net income to net cash provided by operating activities			
Increase in inventory	(100)	(160)	(60)
Decrease in accrued profit sharing	(20)	(20)	0
Decrease in income tax liability	(72)	(48)	24
Net cash provided by operating activities	348	348	0
Net increase in cash	348	348	0
Cash, January 1, 20X6	2,100	2,100	0
Cash, December 31, 20X6	$2,448	$2,448	$ 0

Illustration 2—Reporting an Accounting Change When Determining Cumulative Effect for All Prior Years Is Not Practicable

A8. Assume ABC Company changed its accounting principle for inventory measurement from FIFO to LIFO effective January 1, 20X4. ABC Company reports its financial statements on a calendar year-end basis and had used the FIFO method since its inception. ABC Company determined that it is impracticable to determine the cumulative effect of applying this change retrospectively because records of inventory purchases and sales are no longer available for all prior years. However, ABC Company has all of the information necessary to apply the LIFO method on a prospective basis beginning in 20X1. Therefore, ABC Company should present prior periods as if it had (a) carried forward the 20X0 ending balance in inventory (measured on a FIFO basis) and (b) begun applying the LIFO method to its inventory beginning January 1, 20X1. (The example assumes that ABC Company established that the LIFO method was preferable for ABC Company's inventory. No particular inventory measurement method is necessarily preferable in all instances.)

Appendix B

BACKGROUND INFORMATION AND BASIS FOR CONCLUSIONS

CONTENTS

Appendix B

BACKGROUND INFORMATION AND BASIS FOR CONCLUSIONS

Introduction

B1. This appendix summarizes considerations that Board members deemed significant in reaching the conclusions in this Statement. It includes reasons for accepting certain approaches and rejecting others. Individual Board members gave greater weight to some factors than to others.

B2. In September 2002, the FASB and the International Accounting Standards Board (IASB) (collectively, the Boards) committed to a broad effort to improve international comparability of financial reporting by working toward development of a single set of high-quality accounting standards. As part of that effort, the Boards jointly undertook a project to eliminate certain narrow differences between the accounting pronouncements issued by the IASB and the accounting pronouncements issued by the FASB and its predecessors. Both Boards agreed to limit the scope of the short-term project to issues for which (a)

the Boards' respective accounting pronouncements were different; (b) convergence to a high-quality solution would appear to be achievable in the short term, usually by selecting between the existing standards of either the FASB or the IASB; and (c) the issue was not within the scope of other projects on the current agenda of either Board. The reporting of accounting changes is one such difference that the FASB decided should be addressed in the short-term convergence project.

B3. In May 2002, the IASB issued its Exposure Draft, *Improvements to International Accounting Standards* (Improvements Exposure Draft), which, among other things, proposed changing the accounting for certain changes in accounting principles to require that those changes be reported through retrospective application to prior periods. The Improvements Exposure Draft also proposed classifying a change in depreciation method for a previously recorded asset as a change in estimate and accounting for it prospectively. The IASB affirmed those changes during its redeliberations of the proposed standard. In December 2003, the IASB issued IAS 8, *Accounting Policies, Changes in Accounting Estimates and Errors (Revised 2003).*

B4. In December 2003, the Board issued an Exposure Draft, *Accounting Changes and Error Corrections,* for a 120-day comment period. That Exposure Draft proposed retrospective application for voluntary changes in accounting principle and for changes in accounting principle required by a new accounting pronouncement that does not provide specific transition provisions. The Board received 66 comment letters on the Exposure Draft. In late 2004 and early 2005, the Board redeliberated the issues identified in the Exposure Draft and concluded that on the basis of existing information, it could reach an informed decision on the matters addressed in this Statement without a public hearing or roundtable meeting.

Scope

B5. The Board decided to incorporate the guidance for all accounting changes and error corrections, including changes made in interim periods, into this Statement to facilitate its objective of codification and simplification of U.S. GAAP. Thus, this Statement supersedes FASB Statement No. 3, *Reporting Accounting Changes in Interim Financial Statements,* as well as Opinion 20. The Board noted that FASB Statement No. 117, *Financial Statements of Not-for-Profit Organizations,* requires that not-for-profit organizations apply the disclosure and display provisions required by GAAP for accounting changes; therefore, the Board decided to include not-for-profit financial statements within the scope of this Statement.

B6. Under International Financial Reporting Standards (IFRS), entities are required to apply the general guidance for a change in accounting principle when applying a new standard, unless that standard has other specific transition guidance. The Board concluded that including transition for new accounting pronouncements in the scope of this Statement would establish retrospective application as the presumed transition method for new accounting pronouncements. However, the Board noted that this Statement does not preclude the Board or other standard setters from establishing specific transition provisions in future pronouncements that may differ from the provisions of this Statement. The Board expects to establish transition guidance on a standard-by-standard basis by selecting the transition requirements appropriate for those specific circumstances.

Change in Accounting Principle

B7. During the deliberations that led to the Exposure Draft, the Board concluded that use of the retrospective application approach described in IAS 8 would enhance the interperiod comparability of financial information. Accordingly, the Board proposed converging with the requirements of IAS 8 for reporting a change in an accounting principle. The Board noted that, in addition to the benefit of convergence, retrospective application as if a newly adopted accounting principle had always been used results in greater consistency across periods. The FASB's conceptual framework describes comparability (including consistency) as one of the qualitative characteristics of accounting information. The Board concluded that retrospective application improves financial reporting because it enhances the consistency of financial information between periods. That improved consistency enhances the usefulness of the financial statements, especially by facilitating analysis and understanding of comparative accounting data.

B8. During initial deliberations, the Board noted that in some cases the IASB and the FASB use different terms to describe the same principle. For example, the term *retrospective application* as used by the IASB is synonymous with the term *retroactive restatement* as used in Opinion 20. The Boards believe that whenever possible, it is preferable to use the same terms to reduce the potential for inconsistent application of accounting pronouncements. Thus, the Board proposed using the term *retrospective application* to describe the manner of reporting a change in accounting principle or a change in reporting entity and to use the term *restatement* only to refer to the correction of an error. That change reflects the Board's conclusion that a terminology change would better distinguish changes in amounts reported for prior periods related to a change in accounting principle or a change in the reporting entity from those related to the correction of an error. Most respondents to the Exposure Draft agreed with the Board's decision and it was affirmed in redeliberations.

B9. Many respondents to the Exposure Draft, including many users of financial statements, supported the Board's proposal for requiring retrospective application for voluntary changes and mandated changes in accounting principle in instances where specific transition provisions are not provided in accounting pronouncements. Others disagreed with the Board's proposal generally for the reasons that were cited in Opinion 20, such as a disincentive to change to a preferable accounting principle or the dilution of public confidence in financial reporting. During redeliberations, the Board again considered those reasons and affirmed the retrospective approach because that approach improves consistency of information across fiscal periods and converges with the requirements of IAS 8.

B10. Some respondents to the Exposure Draft expressed concern that the proposed requirements did not adequately differentiate between the terms *retrospective application,* for changes in accounting principle and changes in the reporting entity, and *restatement,* for corrections of errors. Those respondents were concerned that numerous reissuances of financial statements to reflect retrospective application might dilute investor confidence in those financial statements. The Board believes that this Statement adequately differentiates between the two terms and the requirements for each. In addition, the Board will consider transition requirements in new accounting standards on a standard-by-standard basis. The Board believes this should mitigate the concerns raised by respondents. Thus, during redeliberations, the Board decided to retain the terminology as originally proposed.

Exceptions from the General Principle of Retrospective Application

B11. The Board believes that under certain circumstances it would be impracticable for an entity to determine (a) the period-specific effects of an accounting change on all prior periods presented or (b) the cumulative effect of applying a change in accounting principle to all prior periods. In those instances, the Board decided to require a limited form of retrospective application to provide financial statement users with the most consistent financial information practicable. The Board decided that if it is impracticable for an entity to determine the period-specific effects of a change in accounting principle for all prior periods, the cumulative effect of the change to the new accounting principle should be applied to the carrying amounts of assets and liabilities as of the beginning of the earliest period to which the new principle is applied, and an offsetting adjustment should be made to the opening balance of retained earnings (or other appropriate components of equity or net assets in the statement of financial position) for that period. The Board believes that method maximizes consistency across accounting periods for which the necessary information is available, and it also provides better information than a cumulative-effect adjustment in the period of change.

B12. This Statement requires that the cumulative effect of the change in accounting principle be recorded directly in the opening retained earnings balance (or other appropriate components of equity or net assets in the statement of financial position) when it is impracticable to determine the period-specific effects of a change in accounting principle. The Board also considered requiring the cumulative effect of the change to be included in the net income (or other appropriate captions of changes in the applicable net assets or performance indicator) of the period in which the change was made, as was required by Opinion 20. However, the Board rejected that alternative on the basis that the cumulative effect of the change in accounting principle does not relate to the period in which the change was made. Therefore, it would be inappropriate to record the cumulative effects on prior periods in net income of the period of change, since none of the effects relate to that period. The Board believes that the requirements of this Statement recast prior-period financial statements to the extent practicable and therefore affirmed that decision in its redeliberations.

B13. For circumstances for which it is impracticable to determine the cumulative effect of applying a change in accounting principle to all prior periods, this Statement requires that the entity apply the new accounting principle as if it was made prospectively as of the earliest date practicable. The Board decided that adjustment of one or more prior periods provides more consistency across periods than the prospective approach required by Opinion 20 for that type of change.

B14. To enhance consistency of application, the Board decided to provide guidance limiting the use of the impracticability exception. The Exposure Draft contained an exception to retrospective application for circumstances in which the effects of retrospective application are not determinable. Many respondents to the Exposure Draft noted that it might be possible to determine the effects of retrospective application but only at unreasonable cost and effort. Those respondents requested that the Board adopt an exception for cases in which retrospective application would involve "undue cost or effort." Other respondents noted that an impracticability exception similar to "undue cost or effort" appears in certain other FASB Statements. During redeliberations, the Board considered those comments and revised its proposed guidance to indicate that retrospective application is impracticable if an entity cannot apply it after making every reasonable effort to do so. The Board also noted that such language was consistent with a similar exception in IAS 8.

B15. The Board noted that retrospective application also would be impracticable if it would require assumptions about management's intent in a prior period that cannot be independently substantiated. The Board was concerned that retrospective application in that case might require an inappropriate use of hindsight and decided to provide an exception from the general principle of retrospective application in those circumstances.

B16. The Board also discussed whether retrospective application involving significant estimates made as of a prior period would be impracticable. The Board notes that it is frequently necessary to make estimates in order to apply an accounting principle. Estimation is inherently subjective, and estimates are frequently developed for the purpose of preparing financial statements after the close of a fiscal period. The use of estimates in retrospective application of an accounting principle is potentially more difficult because a longer period of time may have passed since a transaction or event occurred. However, in the context of retrospective application, the objective of estimates related to prior periods is the same as the objective of estimates related to current periods. That objective is to make an estimate that reflects the conditions that existed at the date the transaction or event would have been recognized in the financial statements had the newly adopted accounting principle been applied as of that earlier date. Achieving that objective requires differentiating between information that provides additional evidence about conditions that existed when an event or transaction occurred and information about conditions that arose subsequently. For some types of estimates (for example, an estimate of fair value based on inputs that are not derived from observable market sources), it may not be practicable to distinguish the information that would have been available about conditions that previously existed from all other types of information. Therefore, the Board decided, and affirmed its decision during redeliberations, that prospective application from the date of change should be required when retrospective application would involve making a significant estimate for which it is not possible to objectively distinguish information that provides additional evidence about conditions that previously existed from other types of information.

B17. A number of respondents to the Exposure Draft stated that the proposed provisions were unclear as to whether contemporaneous documentation was required to objectively determine whether information used to develop significant estimates would have been available at the time the affected transactions or events would have been recognized in the financial statements. The Board does not believe that contemporaneous documentation is necessary. Therefore, the Board added a footnote to paragraph 11 of this Statement to clarify that point.

B18. The Board agrees with the Accounting Principles Board's conclusion that an entity should not change an accounting principle unless the entity can justify the newly adopted accounting principle on the basis that it is preferable. Thus, the Board decided to retain the requirement of Opinion 20 that the nature and justification for a change in accounting principle be disclosed. Similarly, the Board decided that a change in estimate effected by a change in accounting principle must be justified on the basis that the new method is preferable.

Indirect Effects

B19. Some respondents asked that the Board clarify how to report the indirect effects of a change in accounting principle that is accounted for by retrospective application. The Board considered requiring that the indirect effects of an accounting change be included in the retrospective application. Some Board members draw no distinction between indirect effects and other consequential effects of an accounting change and, therefore, believe that indirect effects should be included as part of the retrospective application of the change that gives rise to them. In addition, they believe that including indirect effects in retrospective application may, in some cases, provide better information to users by showing more consistent trend information related to the items indirectly affected by an accounting change. Other Board members believe that an effect on the cash flows of the entity that is caused by the adoption of an accounting change should be recognized in the period in which that adoption occurs. They believe the accounting change is the necessary "past event" in the definition of an asset or a liability that gives rise to accounting recognition of the indirect effect. They also believe that certain practical issues are more easily resolved by recognizing all such effects in the period the accounting change is adopted. The Board considered the various views and ultimately decided to adopt the latter view. The Board also decided to require disclosure of any indirect effects of an accounting change that have been recognized, and the amount of those effects attributable to each prior period presented unless impracticable.

B20. Some Board members expressed concern about circumstances in which the indirect effects of an accounting change are explicitly governed by a contractual agreement. For example, a royalty agreement may require that the amount due to the counterparty be subsequently adjusted, or "trued up," if the reported reference amount (for example, revenues) is subsequently adjusted to reflect an accounting change. However, the Board believes that such cases are rare and that in those cases, the accounting change is still the necessary past event that gives rise to the indirect effect. Therefore, the Board decided that even when the indirect effect is explicitly required to be recognized, it should be recognized in the period of the accounting change.

Disclosures

B21. The Board noted that it is important to provide financial statement users with information that allows them to distinguish between the effect of a change in accounting principle and other income statement changes. Therefore, the Board proposed continuing to require disclosure of the effects of a change in accounting principle. Generally, those disclosure requirements are consistent with those required by Opinion 20.

B22. Some respondents to the Exposure Draft suggested eliminating certain proposed disclosures, such as the requirement to disclose the impact of retrospective application on each line of the financial statements. Other respondents suggested expanding the disclosures to include, for example, a requirement for those entities that use the impracticability exception to specify the information that is missing and which therefore makes retrospective application impracticable. The Board considered those suggestions in its redeliberations and modified or clarified some of the required disclosures. For example, the Board clarified that the requirement to disclose the effect on each financial statement line item applies only to line items actually affected by the change and that presentation of the effect on financial statement subtotals, other than income from continuing operations and net income, is not required. The Board also decided to add an illustration of the application of this Statement as an appendix to the Statement.

Change in Accounting Estimate

B23. Paragraph 21 of FASB Concepts Statement No. 1, *Objectives of Financial Reporting by Business Enterprises,* states that "estimates resting on expecta-

tions of the future are often needed in financial reporting, but their major use, especially of those formally incorporated in financial statements, is to measure financial effects of past transactions or events or the present status of an asset or liability."

B24. The Board carried forward without reconsideration the general provisions in Opinion 20 related to a change in accounting estimate. Those provisions are consistent with the requirements of IFRS, with the exception that IFRS requires a change in the method of depreciation or amortization for a long-lived, nonfinancial asset to be reported as a change in estimate. The Board noted that the information an entity would need to establish a basis for changing the depreciation, amortization, or depletion method for a long-lived, nonfinancial asset (hereinafter described as a change in depreciation method) would be obtained by continued observation of actual use of the expected benefits of the asset as compared to previous estimations of the pattern of consumption that formed the basis for the initial method. Thus, during initial deliberations, the Board concluded that a change in depreciation method is a change in estimate effected by a change in accounting principle. That decision was affirmed in redeliberations.

B25. The Board noted that because it is a change in estimate, a change in depreciation method should not be accounted for by retrospective application to prior periods. However, appropriate disclosures should be required for the change in accounting principle that effected the change in estimate. Thus, the Board decided that a change in estimate effected by a change in accounting principle should be subject to the same requirement to justify the change in principle on the basis that the new principle is preferable. Most respondents to the Exposure Draft agreed with the Board's initial decision. The Board affirmed the disclosure requirements related to a change in estimate during redeliberations.

B26. Several respondents to the Exposure Draft stated that there may be valid reasons unrelated to the available information about the pattern of consumption of future benefits for deciding that a depreciation method other than the one currently used is preferable. Some respondents stated that a change from one method of depreciation to another can be justified as preferable if the new method is more prevalent in the industry in which the reporting entity operates. The Board noted that the objective of depreciation accounting is to allocate the cost of a capital asset over its expected useful life in a manner that best represents the pattern of consumption of the expected benefits. Therefore, in redeliberations, the Board affirmed that better reflecting the pattern of consumption of the asset being depreciated should be the sole basis in determining the preferable depreciation method.

Change in the Reporting Entity

B27. The Board carried forward without reconsideration the guidance in paragraphs 12, 34, and 35 of Opinion 20 on changes in the reporting entity. Editorial changes have been made to the guidance carried forward to make it easier to read within the context of this Statement. In addition, this Statement classifies the recasting of financial statements for a change in the reporting entity as a retrospective application rather than as a restatement.

Accounting Change in Interim-Period Information

B28. During initial deliberations, the Board decided not to permit voluntary accounting changes made in interim periods if it is impracticable to distinguish between the cumulative effects on prior years and the effects on prior interim periods of the year of change. Statement 3 required an entity to report an accounting change made during an interim period as if it had been adopted at the beginning of the fiscal year. Therefore, an entity making an accounting change in other than the first interim period must have been able to distinguish between the effects on the year of change and the effects on prior years to have met the requirements of Statement 3. The Board expects that accounting changes for which it is impracticable to distinguish between the cumulative effects on prior years and the effects on prior interim periods of the year of change will be rare. Also, the benefit of intraperiod consistency of annual reporting outweighs the hardship placed on enterprises that are unable to make that distinction for a given change. Respondents to the Exposure Draft did not disagree with the Board's initial decision. Therefore, that decision was affirmed during redeliberations.

B29. The Board decided to carry forward the disclosure requirements contained in paragraphs 11(e) and 14 of Statement 3 to this Statement.

Correction of an Error

B30. The Board carried forward without substantive change the provisions for correction of an error from paragraphs 13, 36, and 37 of Opinion 20. Editorial changes have been made to the sections carried forward to make those sections easier to read within the context of this Statement. Also, the Board concluded that when an entity restates its financial statements to correct an error, it should disclose that fact so as to distinguish corrections of errors from accounting changes. In response to concerns of the respondents to the Exposure Draft, the Board decided to limit the use of the term *restatement* in this Statement to refer only to the revising of financial statements to correct an error in those previously reported financial statements.

Convergence of U.S. GAAP and International Financial Reporting Standards

B31. This Statement is the result of a broader effort by the FASB to improve the comparability of cross-border financial reporting by working with the IASB toward development of a single set of high-quality accounting standards. Although convergence is an important objective in this Statement, this Statement and IAS 8 differ in some areas. Those areas include the correction of an error, indirect effects of a change in accounting principle, and certain elements of disclosure.

B32. This Statement and IAS 8 both require restatement to correct an error that exists in previously issued financial statements. However, in this Statement that requirement is absolute, while IAS 8 permits an exception to the restatement requirement in instances in which it is not practicable to determine the effect of the error on any or all prior periods. Under IAS 8, if restatement is impracticable, the correction of an error is effected by restating the opening balances of assets, liabilities, and equity or net assets for the earliest period for which retrospective restatement is practicable (which may be the current interim or annual period). The Board considered permitting a similar exception; however, it rejected that proposal because it would be inconsistent for a reporting entity to state that its financial statements for a prior period are prepared in accordance with GAAP if an error had been discovered that affected those financial statements but was not corrected because it was impracticable to do so.

B33. This Statement explicitly requires that the indirect effects of a change in accounting principle be reported in the period in which those effects are actually incurred. This Statement also requires specific disclosures related to the indirect effects of a change in accounting principle. IAS 8 does not specifically address the accounting for or disclosure of indirect effects of a change in accounting principle.

B34. IAS 8 includes some disclosure requirements that differ from the disclosures required by this Statement. The FASB considered each of the disclosure requirements of IAS 8 as well as other potential requirements and concluded that the requirements in this Statement are appropriate and sufficient.

Effective Date and Transition

B35. The Board decided that the provisions of this Statement should be effective for accounting changes made in fiscal years beginning after December 15, 2005. The Board decided to require prospective application of this Statement because it does not believe the benefits of adjusting previously issued financial statements to retrospectively apply accounting changes that were made before this Statement was issued outweigh the costs of doing so.

B36. The Board noted that there may be some accounting pronouncements that are in the transition phase on the effective date of this Statement and that might require transition provisions that are inconsistent with this Statement. The Board decided that changing the transition provisions of existing pronouncements would not be cost-beneficial. Thus, the Board decided to exclude from the provisions of this Statement transition provisions of any existing pronouncements.

Benefits and Costs

B37. The mission of the FASB is to establish and improve standards of financial accounting and reporting for the guidance and education of the public, including preparers, auditors, and users of financial information. In fulfilling that mission, the Board endeavors to determine that a proposed standard will fill a significant need and that the costs imposed to meet that standard, as compared with other alternatives, are justified in relation to the overall benefits of the resulting information. Although the costs to implement a new standard may not be borne evenly, investors and creditors—both present and potential—and other users of financial information benefit from improvements in financial reporting, thereby facilitating the functioning of markets for capital and credit and the efficient allocation of resources in the economy.

B38. The Board acknowledges that there will be costs involved in retrospective application related to accounting changes beyond those previously required to develop pro forma disclosures of the effects of accounting changes on prior periods. However, the Board believes that the benefits to users of more comparable information in comparative financial statements will outweigh the effort that will be required on the part of preparers. Further, the Board notes that this Statement will reduce the number of reconciling items between U.S. GAAP and IFRS, which should reduce the costs borne by an entity that is required to prepare a reconciliation of its balance sheet and statement of financial performance determined under IFRS to U.S. GAAP.

Appendix C

AMENDMENTS TO EXISTING PRONOUNCEMENTS

C1. This Statement supersedes the following pronouncements:

a. APB Opinion No. 20, *Accounting Changes*
b. FASB Statement No. 3, *Reporting Accounting Changes in Interim Financial Statements*
c. FASB Statement No. 73, *Reporting a Change in Accounting for Railroad Track Structures*
d. FASB Interpretation No. 20, *Reporting Accounting Changes under AICPA Statements of Position.*

C2. ARB No. 43, Chapter 2A, "Form of Statements—Comparative Financial Statements," is amended as follows:

a. Paragraph 3, as amended by Opinion 20:

> It is necessary that prior-year figures shown for comparative purposes be in fact comparable with those shown for the most recent period, or that any exceptions to comparability be clearly brought out as described in FASB Statement No. 154, *Accounting Changes and Error Corrections*APB Opinion No. 20, *Accounting Changes*.

C3. APB Opinion No. 22, *Disclosure of Accounting Policies,* is amended as follows:

a. Paragraph 14:

> Financial statement disclosure of accounting policies should not duplicate details (e.g., composition of inventories or of plant assets) presented elsewhere as part of the financial statements. In some cases, the disclosure of

accounting policies should refer to related details presented elsewhere as part of the financial statements; for example, changes in accounting policies during the period should be described with cross-reference to the disclosure required by FASB Statement No. 154, *Accounting Changes and Error Corrections.*~~APB Opinion No. 20, *Accounting Changes,* of the current effect of the change and of the pro forma effect of retroactive application.~~

C4. APB Opinion No. 25, *Accounting for Stock Issued to Employees,* is amended as follows:

a. Paragraph 15:

Accruing compensation expense may require estimates, and adjustment of those estimates in later periods may be necessary (FASB Statement No. 154, *Accounting Changes and Error Corrections,* paragraphs 19–22)~~APB Opinion No. 20, *Accounting Changes,* paragraphs 31 to 33~~. For example, if a stock option is not exercised (or awarded stock is returned to the corporation) because an employee fails to fulfill an obligation, the estimate of compensation expense recorded in previous periods should be adjusted by decreasing compensation expense in the period of forfeiture.

C5. APB Opinion No. 28, *Interim Financial Reporting,* is amended as follows:

a. Paragraph 24:

Changes in an interim or annual accounting ~~practice or policy~~principle made in an interim period should be reported in the period in which the change is made, in accordance with the provisions of FASB Statement No. 154, *Accounting Changes and Error Corrections*~~APB Opinion No. 20, *Accounting Changes.*~~

b. Paragraph 25:

~~Certain changes in accounting principle, such as those described in paragraphs 4 and 27 of APB Opinion 20, require retroactive restatement of previously issued financial statements. Paragraph 26 of APB Opinion No. 9, *Reporting the Results of Operations,* requires similar treatment for prior period adjustments. Previously issued financial statements must also be restated for a change in the reporting entity (see paragraphs 34–35 of APB Opinion No. 20) and for correction of an error (see paragraphs 36–37 of APB Opinion No. 20). Previously issued interim financial information should be similarly restated. APB Opinion Nos. 9 and 20 specify the required disclosures.~~

c. Paragraph 26:

The effect of a change in an accounting estimate, including a change in the estimated effective annual tax rate, should be accounted for in the period in which the change in estimate is made. No restatement of previously reported interim information should be made for changes in estimates, but the effect on earnings of a change in estimate made in a current interim period should be reported in the current and subsequent interim periods, if material in relation to any period presented and should continue to be reported in the interim financial information of the subsequent year for as many periods as necessary to avoid misleading comparisons. Such disclosure should conform with paragraph 22 of Statement 154.~~paragraph 33 of APB Opinion No. 20.~~

d. Paragraphs 27–27D, footnote 5 to paragraph 27C, and the related headings:

~~**Cumulative Effect Type Accounting Changes Other Than Changes to LIFO**~~

~~27. If a cumulative effect type accounting change is made during the *first* interim period of an enterprise's fiscal year, the cumulative effect of the change on retained earnings at the *beginning of that fiscal year* shall be included in net income of the first interim period (and in last-twelve-months-to-date financial reports that include that first interim period).~~

~~27A. If a cumulative effect type accounting change is made in *other than the first* interim period of an enterprise's fiscal year, *no* cumulative effect of the change shall be included in net income of the period of change. Instead, financial information for the pre-change interim periods of the fiscal year in which the change is made shall be restated by applying the newly adopted accounting principle to those pre-change interim periods. The cumulative effect of the change on retained earnings at *the*~~

beginning of that fiscal year shall be included in restated net income of the first interim period of the fiscal year in which the change is made (and in any year-to-date or last-twelve-months-to-date financial reports that include the first interim period). Whenever financial information that includes those pre-change interim periods is presented, it shall be presented on the restated basis.

27B. The following disclosures about a cumulative-effect type accounting change shall be made in interim financial reports:

a. In financial reports for the interim period in which the new accounting principle is adopted, disclosure shall be made of the nature of and justification for the change.
b. In financial reports for the interim period in which the new accounting principle is adopted, disclosure shall be made of the effect of the change on income from continuing operations, net income, and related per share amounts for the interim period in which the change is made. In addition, when the change is made in other than the first interim period of a fiscal year, financial reports for the period of change shall also disclose (i) the effect of the change on income from continuing operations, net income, and related per share amounts for each pre-change interim period of that fiscal year and (ii) income from continuing operations, net income, and related per share amounts for each pre-change interim period restated in accordance with paragraph 27A of this Opinion.
c. In financial reports for the interim period in which the new accounting principle is adopted, disclosure shall be made of income from continuing operations, net income, and related per share amounts computed on a pro forma basis for (i) the interim period in which the change is made and (ii) any interim periods of prior fiscal years for which financial information is being presented. If no financial information for interim periods of prior fiscal years is being presented, disclosure shall be made, in the period of change, of the actual and pro forma amounts of income from continuing operations, net income, and related

per share amounts for the interim period of the immediately preceding fiscal year that corresponds to the interim period in which the change is made. In all cases, the pro forma amounts shall be computed and presented in conformity with paragraphs 19, 21, 22, and 25 of *APB Opinion No. 20*.
d. In year-to-date and last-twelve-months-to-date financial reports that include the interim period in which the new accounting principle is adopted, the disclosures specified in the first sentence of subparagraph (b) above and in subparagraph (c) above shall be made.
e. In financial reports for a subsequent (post-change) interim period of the fiscal year in which the new accounting principle is adopted, disclosure shall be made of the effect of the change on income from continuing operations, net income, and related per share amounts for that post-change interim period.

Changes to the LIFO Method of Inventory Pricing and Similar Situations

27C. Paragraph 26 of *APB Opinion No. 20* indicates that in rare situations—principally a change to the LIFO method of inventory pricing[5]—neither the cumulative effect of the change on retained earnings at the beginning of the fiscal year in which the change is made nor the pro forma amounts can be computed. In those situations, that paragraph requires an explanation of the reasons for omitting (a) accounting for a cumulative effect and (b) disclosure of pro forma amounts for prior years. If a change of that type is made in the *first* interim period of an enterprise's fiscal year, the disclosures specified in paragraph 27B of this Opinion shall be made (except the pro forma amounts for interim periods of prior fiscal years called for by paragraph 27B(c) of this Opinion will not be disclosed).

27D. If the change is made in *other than* the first interim period of an enterprise's fiscal year, the disclosure specified in paragraph 27B of this Opinion shall be made (except the pro forma amounts for interim periods of prior fiscal years called for by paragraph 27B(c) of

~~this Opinion will not be disclosed) and in addition, financial information for the pre-change interim periods of that fiscal year shall be restated by applying the newly adopted accounting principle to those pre-change interim periods. Whenever financial information that includes those pre-change interim periods is presented, it shall be presented on the restated basis.~~

~~[5]In making disclosures about changes to the LIFO method, enterprises should be aware of the limitations the Internal Revenue Service has placed on such disclosures.~~

C6. APB Opinion No. 30, *Reporting the Results of Operations—Reporting the Effects of Disposal of a Segment of a Business, and Extraordinary, Unusual and Infrequently Occurring Events and Transactions,* is amended as follows:

a. Paragraph 25, as amended by FASB Statements No. 16, *Prior Period Adjustments,* and No. 144, *Accounting for the Impairment or Disposal of Long-Lived Assets:*

> Circumstances attendant to extraordinary items frequently require estimates, for example, of associated costs and occasionally of associated revenue, based on judgment and evaluation of the facts known at the time of first accounting for the event. Each adjustment in the current period of an element of an extraordinary item that was reported in a prior period should be separately disclosed as to year of origin, nature, and amount and classified separately in the current period in the same manner as the original item. If the adjustment is the correction of an error, the provisions of FASB Statement No. 154, *Accounting Changes and Error Corrections,* paragraphs 25 and 26 ~~APB Opinion No. 20, Accounting Changes, paragraphs 36 and 37~~ should be applied.

C7. FASB Statement No. 16, *Prior Period Adjustments,* is amended as follows:

a. Footnote 3, as amended by FASB Statements No. 96, *Accounting for Income Taxes,* and No. 109, *Accounting for Income Taxes:*

> As defined in paragraph 2 of FASB Statement No. 154, *Accounting Changes and Error Corrections* ~~paragraph 13 of APB Opinion No. 20~~. That paragraph also describes the distinction

between a correction of an error and a change in accounting estimate.

b. Footnote 6, as amended by FASB Statement No. 141, *Business Combinations:*

> ~~In addition to transition requirements of these pronouncements, accounting changes resulting in restatement of previously issued financial statements of prior periods include a change in the reporting entity described in paragraph 34 of APB Opinion No. 20, and special changes in accounting principle described in paragraphs 27 and 29 of APB Opinion No. 20. See also footnote 5 to APB Opinion No. 20.~~

C8. FASB Statement No. 19, *Financial Accounting and Reporting by Oil and Gas Producing Companies,* is amended as follows:

a. Paragraph 30, as effectively amended by FASB Statement No. 69, *Disclosures about Oil and Gas Producing Activities:*

> Capitalized acquisition costs of proved properties shall be amortized (depleted) by the unit-of-production method so that each unit produced is assigned a pro rata portion of the unamortized acquisition costs. Under the unit-of-production method, amortization (depletion) may be computed either on a property-by-property basis or on the basis of some reasonable aggregation of properties with a common geological structural feature or stratigraphic condition, such as a reservoir or field. When an enterprise has a relatively large number of royalty interests whose acquisition costs are not individually significant, they may be aggregated, for the purpose of computing amortization, without regard to commonality of geological structural features or stratigraphic conditions; if information is not available to estimate reserve quantities applicable to royalty interests owned (paragraph 59E), a method other than the unit-of-production method may be used to amortize their acquisition costs. The unit cost shall be computed on the basis of the total estimated units of proved oil and gas reserves. (Joint production of both oil and gas is discussed in paragraph 38.) Unit-of-production amortization rates shall be revised whenever there is an indication of the need for revision but at least once a year; those revisions shall be accounted for prospectively as changes in accounting estimates—see paragraphs 19–22 of FASB Statement No. 154, *Accounting*

Changes and Error Corrections. ~~paragraphs 31-33 of APB Opinion No. 20, "Accounting Changes."~~

b. Paragraph 35:

Capitalized costs of exploratory wells and exploratory-type stratigraphic test wells that have found proved reserves and capitalized development costs shall be amortized (depreciated) by the unit-of-production method so that each unit produced is assigned a pro rata portion of the unamortized costs. It may be more appropriate, in some cases, to depreciate natural gas cycling and processing plants by a method other than the unit-of-production method. Under the unit-of-production method, amortization (depreciation) may be computed either on a property-by-property basis or on the basis of some reasonable aggregation of properties with a common geological structural feature or stratigraphic condition, such as a reservoir or field. The unit cost shall be computed on the basis of the total estimated units of proved *developed* reserves, rather than on the basis of all proved reserves, which is the basis for amortizing acquisition costs of proved properties. If significant development costs (such as the cost of an off-shore production platform) are incurred in connection with a planned group of development wells before all of the planned wells have been drilled, it will be necessary to exclude a portion of those development costs in determining the unit-of-production amortization rate until the additional development wells are drilled. Similarly it will be necessary to exclude, in computing the amortization rate, those proved developed reserves that will be produced only after significant additional development costs are incurred, such as for improved recovery systems. However, in no case should future development costs be anticipated in computing the amortization rate. (Joint production of both oil and gas is discussed in paragraph 38.) Unit-of-production amortization rates shall be revised whenever there is an indication of the need for revision but at least once a year; those revisions shall be accounted for prospectively as changes in accounting estimates—see paragraphs 19–22 of Statement 154. ~~paragraphs 31-33 of APB Opinion No. 20.~~

C9. FASB Statement No. 25, *Suspension of Certain Accounting Requirements for Oil and Gas Producing Companies,* is amended as follows:

a. Paragraph 4 and its related footnote 1, as effectively amended by Statement 69:

The effective date for application of paragraphs 11–41, 44–47, and 60 of *FASB Statement No. 19* is suspended insofar as those paragraphs pertain to a *required* form of successful efforts accounting. Those paragraphs are not suspended insofar as they provide definitions of terms in paragraph 11 or provide direction and guidance for financial statement disclosures required by paragraphs 59M–59R. Statement No. 19, including paragraphs 11–47, continues in effect as an accounting pronouncement ~~a Statement issued by the FASB~~ for the purpose of applying paragraphs 12–14 of FASB Statement No. 154, *Accounting Changes and Error Corrections.* ~~paragraph 16 of APB Opinion No. 20, "Accounting Changes."[1]~~

---

[1] ~~Paragraph 16 of APB Opinion No. 20 states in part: "The presumption that an entity should not change an accounting principle may be overcome only if the enterprise justifies the use of an alternative acceptable accounting principle on the basis that it is preferable. . . . The issuance of [a Statement of Financial Accounting Standards] that creates a new accounting principle, that expresses a preference for an accounting principle, or that rejects a specific accounting principle is sufficient support for a change in accounting principle. The burden of justifying other changes rests with the entity proposing the change."~~

C10. FASB Statement No. 52, *Foreign Currency Translation,* is amended as follows:

a. Paragraph 45:

Once a determination of the functional currency is made, that decision shall be consistently used for each foreign entity unless significant changes in economic facts and circumstances indicate clearly that the functional currency has changed. (FASB Statement No. 154, *Accounting Changes and Error Corrections,* paragraph 5 ~~APB Opinion No. 20, Accounting Changes, paragraph 8,~~ states that "adoption or modification of an accounting principle necessitated by transactions or events that are clearly different in substance from those previously occurring" is not a change in accounting principles.)

C11. FASB Statement No. 67, *Accounting for Costs and Initial Rental Operations of Real Estate Projects,* is amended as follows:

a. Paragraph 12:

Estimates and cost allocations shall be reviewed at the end of each financial reporting period until a project is substantially completed and available for sale. Costs shall be revised and reallocated as necessary for material changes on the basis of current estimates.[8] Changes in estimates shall be reported in accordance with <u>paragraphs 19–22 of FASB Statement No. 154, *Accounting Changes and Error Corrections*</u>~~paragraph 31 of APB Opinion No. 20, *Accounting Changes*~~.

C12. FASB Statement No. 71, *Accounting for the Effects of Certain Types of Regulation,* is amended as follows:

a. Paragraph 31:

~~Opinion 20~~<u>FASB Statement No. 154, *Accounting Changes and Error Corrections,*</u> defines various types of accounting changes and establishes guidelines for reporting each type. Other authoritative pronouncements specify the manner of reporting initial application of those pronouncements.

C13. FASB Statement No. 123 (revised December 2004), *Share-Based Payment,* is amended as follows:

a. Paragraph 38:

A nonpublic entity shall make a policy decision of whether to measure all of its liabilities incurred under share-based payment arrangements at fair value or to measure all such liabilities at intrinsic value.[23] Regardless of the method selected, a nonpublic entity shall remeasure its liabilities under share-based payment arrangements at each reporting date until the date of settlement. The fair-value-based method is preferable for purposes of justifying a change in accounting principle under <u>FASB Statement No. 154, *Accounting Changes and Error Corrections*</u>~~APB Opinion No. 20, *Accounting Changes*~~. Illustration 10 (paragraphs A127–A133) provides an example of accounting for an instrument classified as a liability using the fair-value-based method. Illustration 11(c) (paragraphs A143–A148) provides an example of accounting for an instrument classified as a liability using the intrinsic value method.

b. Paragraph A23:

Assumptions used to estimate the fair value of equity and liability instruments granted to employees should be determined in a consistent manner from period to period. For example, an entity might use the closing share price or the share price at another specified time as the "current" share price on the grant date in estimating fair value, but whichever method is selected, it should be used consistently. The valuation technique an entity selects to estimate fair value for a particular type of instrument also should be used consistently and should not be changed unless a different valuation technique is expected to produce a better estimate of fair value. A change in either the valuation technique or the method of determining appropriate assumptions used in a valuation technique is a change in accounting estimate for purposes of applying <u>FASB Statement No. 154, *Accounting Changes and Error Corrections*</u>~~APB Opinion No. 20, *Accounting Changes*~~, and should be applied prospectively to new awards.

C14. FASB Statement No. 143, *Accounting for Asset Retirement Obligations,* is amended as follows:

a. Paragraph 15:

Changes resulting from revisions to the timing or the amount of the original estimate of undiscounted cash flows shall be recognized as an increase or a decrease in (a) the carrying amount of the liability for an asset retirement obligation and (b) the related asset retirement cost capitalized as part of the carrying amount of the related long-lived asset. Upward revisions in the amount of undiscounted estimated cash flows shall be discounted using the current credit-adjusted risk-free rate. Downward revisions in the amount of undiscounted estimated cash flows shall be discounted using the credit-adjusted risk-free rate that existed when the original liability was recognized. If an entity cannot identify the prior period to which the downward revision relates, it may use a weighted-average credit-adjusted risk-free rate to discount the downward revision to estimated future cash flows. When asset retirement costs change as a result of a revision to estimated cash flows, an entity shall adjust the amount of asset retirement cost allocated to expense in the period of change if the change affects that period only or in the period of change and future periods if the change affects more than one period as required by <u>FASB Statement No. 154, *Accounting Changes and Error Corrections* (paragraphs 19–22)</u>~~APB Opinion No. 20, *Accounting Changes* (paragraph 31)~~, for a change in estimate.

C15. FASB Statement No. 144, *Accounting for the Impairment or Disposal of Long-Lived Assets,* is amended as follows:

a. Paragraph 9 and its related footnote 7:

> When a long-lived asset (asset group) is tested for recoverability, it also may be necessary to review depreciation estimates and method as required by FASB Statement No. 154, *Accounting Changes and Error Corrections*APB Opinion No. 20, *Accounting Changes,* or the amortization period as required by FASB Statement No. 142, *Goodwill and Other Intangible Assets.*[7] Any revision to the remaining useful life of a long-lived asset resulting from that review also shall be considered in developing estimates of future cash flows used to test the asset (asset group) for recoverability (paragraph 18). However, any change in the accounting method for the asset resulting from that review shall be made only after applying this Statement.

---

[7]Paragraphs 19–22 of Statement 154 address the accounting for changes in estimates, including changes in the method of depreciation, amortization, and depletion.Paragraphs 10 and 31–33 of Opinion 20 address the accounting for changes in estimates; paragraphs 23 and 24 of Opinion 20 address the accounting for changes in the method of depreciation. Paragraph 11 of Statement 142 addresses the determination of the useful life of an intangible asset.

b. Paragraph 28:

> For purposes of this Statement, a long-lived asset to be abandoned is disposed of when it ceases to be used. If an entity commits to a plan to abandon a long-lived asset before the end of its previously estimated useful life, depreciation estimates shall be revised in accordance with paragraphs 19–22 of Statement 154Opinion 20 to reflect the use of the asset over its shortened useful life (refer to paragraph 9).[16] A long-lived asset that has been temporarily idled shall not be accounted for as if abandoned.

c. Footnote 24:

> This caption shall be modified appropriately when an entity reports an extraordinary item or the cumulative effect of a change in accounting principle or bothin accordance with Opinion 20. If applicable, the presentation of per-share data will need similar modification.

C16. FASB Interpretation No. 1, *Accounting Changes Related to the Cost of Inventory,* is amended as follows:

a. Paragraph 1:

> Accounting Principles Board (APB) Opinion No. 20FASB Statement No. 154, *Accounting Changes and Error Corrections,* specifies how changes in accounting principles should be reported in financial statements and what is required to justify such changes. Under that OpinionStatement, the term *accounting principle* includes "not only accounting principles and practices but also the methods of applying them."

b. Paragraph 5:

> A change in composition of the elements of cost included in inventory is an accounting change. A company which makes such a change for financial reporting shall conform to the requirements of FASB Statement No. 154, *Accounting Changes and Error Corrections*APB Opinion No. 20, including justifying the change on the basis of preferability as specified by paragraphs 12–14 of that Statementparagraph 16 of APB Opinion No. 20. In applying Statement 154APB Opinion No. 20, preferability among accounting principles shall be determined on the basis of whether the new principle constitutes an improvement in financial reporting and not on the basis of the income tax effect alone.

C17. FASB Interpretation No. 7, *Applying FASB Statement No. 7 in Financial Statements of Established Operating Enterprises,* is amended as follows:

a. Paragraph 5:

> Except in the circumstances described in the preceding paragraph, the effect of a development stage subsidiary's change in accounting principle to conform its accounting to the requirements of *Statement No. 7* generally would be reflected in an established operating enterprise's consolidated financial statements that include that subsidiary. When a development stage subsidiary adopts a new accounting principle to conform its accounting to the requirements of *Statement No. 7* and the effect of that subsidiary's accounting change is also reflected in an established operating enterprise's consolidated financial statements that include that subsidiary, the provisions of paragraph 14 of *Statement No. 7* apply. In that situation, the established operating enterprise's consolidated financial statements for periods prior to the period in which

the subsidiary's accounting change is made and financial summaries and other data derived therefrom shall be restated by prior period adjustment. It should be noted that *Statement No. 7* does not address the question of how an established operating enterprise should report accounting changes adopted with respect to the revenue and costs related to activities of the parent company or any subsidiaries that are not in the development stage; that question is covered by FASB Statement No. 154, *Accounting Changes and Error Corrections.*~~APB Opinion No. 20, "Accounting Changes."~~

C18. FASB Interpretation No. 18, *Accounting for Income Taxes in Interim Periods,* is amended as follows:

a. Footnote 1, as replaced by Statement 144:

> The terms used in this definition are described in ~~APB Opinion No. 20, Accounting Changes, in~~ APB Opinion No. 30, *Reporting the Results of Operations—Reporting the Effects of Disposal of a Segment of a Business, and Extraordinary, Unusual and Infrequently Occurring Events and Transactions,* ~~and~~ in FASB Statement No. 144, *Accounting for the Impairment or Disposal of Long-Lived Assets,* and in FASB Statement No. 154, *Accounting Changes and Error Corrections.* See paragraph 10 of Opinion 30 for *extraordinary items* and paragraph 26 for *unusual items* and *infrequently occurring items.* See paragraph 7(a) of Statement 154~~20 of Opinion 20~~ for *cumulative effects of changes in accounting principles.* See paragraphs 41–44 of Statement 144 for *discontinued operations.*

b. Paragraph 21 and the heading preceding it:

> ~~**Cumulative Effects of Changes in Accounting Principles**~~
>
> ~~*FASB Statement No. 3,* "Reporting Accounting Changes in Interim Financial Statements,"~~ specifies that the cumulative effect of a change ~~in accounting principle on retained earnings at the beginning of the year shall be reported in the first interim period of the fiscal year. APB Opinion No. 20, "Accounting Changes," specifies that the related income tax effect of a cumulative effect type accounting change shall be computed as though the new accounting principle had been applied retroactively for all prior periods that would have been affected.~~

c. Paragraph 64:

> When an enterprise makes an ~~cumulative effect type~~ accounting change in other than the first interim period of the enterprise's fiscal year, paragraph 15 of FASB Statement No. 154, *Accounting Changes and Error Corrections,* ~~paragraph 10 of FASB Statement No. 3, "Reporting Accounting Changes in Interim Financial Statements,"~~ requires that financial information for the pre-change interim periods of the fiscal year shall be reported by retrospectively~~restated by~~ applying the newly adopted accounting principle to those pre-change interim periods. The tax (or benefit) applicable to those pre-change interim periods shall be recomputed. The revised~~restated~~ tax (or benefit) shall reflect the year-to-date amounts and annual estimates originally used for the pre-change interim periods, modified only for the effect of the change in accounting principle on those year-to-date and estimated annual amounts.

C19. Many pronouncements issued by the Accounting Principles Board and the FASB contain references to the cumulative effect of a change in accounting principle. All such references appearing in paragraphs that establish standards or illustrate their application are hereby amended to include the following footnote:

> After the effective date of FASB Statement No. 154, *Accounting Changes and Error Corrections,* voluntary changes in accounting principle will no longer be reported via a cumulative-effect adjustment through the income statement of the period of change.

That conclusion requires amendments to the following existing pronouncements:*

a. Opinion 28
b. Opinion 30
c. FASB Statement No. 128, *Earnings per Share*
d. FASB Statement No. 130, *Reporting Comprehensive Income*

e. FASB Statement No. 131, *Disclosures about Segments of an Enterprise and Related Information*
f. Statement 141
g. Statement 144
h. Interpretation 18.

---

*Editor's Note: Due to the passing of the effective date of this Statement, this footnote has been removed from the pronouncements in subparagraphs C19(a) through C19(h).

Statement of Financial Accounting Standards No. 155
Accounting for Certain Hybrid Financial Instruments

an amendment of FASB Statements No. 133 and 140

STATUS

Issued: February 2006

Effective Date: For all financial instruments acquired, issued, or subject to a remeasurement (new basis) event occurring after the beginning of an entity's first fiscal year that begins after September 15, 2006

Affects: Amends FAS 133, paragraphs 14 and 16
Amends FAS 133, by adding paragraphs 14A, 14B, 16A, 44A, 44B, and 200A through 200D
Amends FAS 140, paragraphs 35(c)(2) and 40

Affected by: No other pronouncements

Issues Discussed by FASB Emerging Issues Task Force (EITF)

Affects: No EITF Issues

Interpreted by: No EITF Issues

Related Issues: EITF Issues No. 85-9, 85-29, 86-15, 86-28, 90-19, 96-12, 97-15, 98-5, 99-20, 00-19, and 03-7

SUMMARY

This Statement amends FASB Statements No. 133, *Accounting for Derivative Instruments and Hedging Activities,* and No. 140, *Accounting for Transfers and Servicing of Financial Assets and Extinguishments of Liabilities.* This Statement resolves issues addressed in Statement 133 Implementation Issue No. D1, "Application of Statement 133 to Beneficial Interests in Securitized Financial Assets."

This Statement:

a. Permits fair value remeasurement for any hybrid financial instrument that contains an embedded derivative that otherwise would require bifurcation

b. Clarifies which interest-only strips and principal-only strips are not subject to the requirements of Statement 133

c. Establishes a requirement to evaluate interests in securitized financial assets to identify interests that are freestanding derivatives or that are hybrid financial instruments that contain an embedded derivative requiring bifurcation

d. Clarifies that concentrations of credit risk in the form of subordination are not embedded derivatives

e. Amends Statement 140 to eliminate the prohibition on a qualifying special-purpose entity from holding a derivative financial instrument that pertains to a beneficial interest other than another derivative financial instrument.

Reasons for Issuing This Statement

In January 2004, the Board added this project to its agenda to address what had been characterized as a temporary exemption from the application of the bifurcation requirements of Statement 133 to beneficial interests in securitized financial assets.

Prior to the effective date of Statement 133, the FASB received inquiries on the application of the exception in paragraph 14 of Statement 133 to beneficial interests in securitized financial assets. In response to the inquiries, Implementation Issue D1 indicated that, pending issuance of further guidance, entities may continue to apply the guidance related to accounting for beneficial interests in paragraphs 14 and 362 of Statement 140. Those paragraphs indicate that any security that can be contractually prepaid or otherwise settled in such a way that the holder of the security would not recover substantially all of its recorded investment should be subsequently measured like investments in debt securities classified as available-for-sale or trading under FASB Statement No. 115, *Accounting for Certain Investments in Debt and Equity Securities,* and may not be classified as held-to-maturity. Further, Implementation Issue D1 indicated that holders of beneficial interests in securitized financial assets that are not subject to paragraphs 14 and 362 of Statement 140 are not required to apply Statement 133 to those beneficial interests until further guidance is issued.

How the Changes in This Statement Improve Financial Reporting

This Statement improves financial reporting by eliminating the exemption from applying Statement 133 to interests in securitized financial assets so that similar instruments are accounted for similarly regardless of the form of the instruments. This Statement also improves financial reporting by allowing a preparer to elect fair value measurement at acquisition, at issuance, or when a previously recognized financial instrument is subject to a remeasurement (new basis) event, on an instrument-by-instrument basis, in cases in which a derivative would otherwise have to be bifurcated. Providing a fair value measurement election also results in more financial instruments being measured at what the Board regards as the most relevant attribute for financial instruments, fair value.

Effective Date and Transition

This Statement is effective for all financial instruments acquired or issued after the beginning of an entity's first fiscal year that begins after September 15, 2006. The fair value election provided for in paragraph 4(c) of this Statement may also be applied upon adoption of this Statement for hybrid financial instruments that had been bifurcated under paragraph 12 of Statement 133 prior to the adoption of this Statement. Earlier adoption is permitted as of the beginning of an entity's fiscal year, provided the entity has not yet issued financial statements, including financial statements for any interim period for that fiscal year. Provisions of this Statement may be applied to instruments that an entity holds at the date of adoption on an instrument-by-instrument basis.

At adoption, any difference between the total carrying amount of the individual components of the existing bifurcated hybrid financial instrument and the fair value of the combined hybrid financial instrument should be recognized as a cumulative-effect adjustment to beginning retained earnings. An entity should separately disclose the gross gains and losses that make up the cumulative-effect adjustment, determined on an instrument-by-instrument basis. Prior periods should not be restated.

Statement of Financial Accounting Standards No. 155

Accounting for Certain Hybrid Financial Instruments

an amendment of FASB Statements No. 133 and 140

CONTENTS

OBJECTIVE

1. FASB Statement No. 133, *Accounting for Derivative Instruments and Hedging Activities,* establishes, among other things, the accounting for certain derivatives embedded in other financial instruments. (This combination is referred to as a hybrid financial instrument.)

2. The primary objectives of this Statement with respect to Statement 133 are to:

a. Simplify accounting for certain hybrid financial instruments by permitting fair value remeasurement for any hybrid financial instrument that contains an embedded derivative that otherwise would require bifurcation

b. Eliminate the interim guidance in Statement 133 Implementation Issue No. D1, "Application of Statement 133 to Beneficial Interests in Securitized Financial Assets," which provides that beneficial interests in securitized financial assets are not subject to the provisions of Statement 133.

3. The primary objective of this Statement with respect to FASB Statement No. 140, *Accounting for Transfers and Servicing of Financial Assets and Extinguishments of Liabilities,* is to eliminate a restriction on the passive derivative instruments that a qualifying special-purpose entity (SPE) may hold.

STANDARDS OF FINANCIAL ACCOUNTING AND REPORTING

Amendments to Statement 133

4. Statement 133 is amended as follows: [Added text is underlined and deleted text is struck out.]

a. Paragraph 14:

However, interest-only strips and principal-only strips are not subject to the requirements of this Statement provided those stripsthey (a) initially resulted from separatingrepresent the rights to receive only a specified proportion of the contractual interest cash flows of a specific debt instrument or a specified proportion of the contractual principal cash flows of that debt instrumentof a financial instrument that, in and of itself, did not contain an embedded derivative that otherwise would have been accounted for separately as a derivative pursuant to the provisions of paragraphs 12 and 13 and (b) do not incorporate any terms not present in the original financialdebt instrument described above. An allocation of a portion of the interest or principal cash flows of a specific debt instrument as reasonable compensation for stripping the instrument or to provide adequate compensation to a servicer (as defined in Statement 140) would meet the intended narrow scope of the exception provided in this paragraph. However, an allocation of a portion of the interest or principal cash flows of a specific debt instrument to provide for a guarantee of payments, for servicing in excess of adequate compensation, or for any other purpose would not meet the intended narrow scope of the exception.

b. Paragraphs 14A and 14B are added as follows:

14A. The holder of an interest in securitized financial assets (other than those identified in paragraph 14) shall determine whether the interest is a freestanding derivative or contains an embedded derivative that under paragraphs 12 and 13 would be required to be separated from the host contract and accounted for separately. That determination shall be based on an analysis of the contractual terms of the interest in securitized financial assets, which requires understanding the nature and amount of assets, liabilities, and other financial instruments that compose the entire securitization transaction. A holder of an interest in securitized financial assets should obtain sufficient information about the payoff structure and the payment priority of the interest to determine whether an embedded derivative exists.

14B. Changes in cash flows attributable to changes in the creditworthiness of an interest resulting from securitized financial assets and liabilities (including derivative contracts) that represent the assets or liabilities that are held by the issuing entity shall not be considered an embedded derivative under this Statement. The concentration of credit risk in the form of subordination of one financial instrument to another shall not be considered an embedded derivative under this Statement.

c. Paragraph 16:

In subsequent provisions of this Statement, both (a) a derivative instrument included within the scope of this Statement by paragraphs 6–11 and (b) an embedded derivative instrument that has been separated from a host contract as required by paragraph 12 are collectively referred to as derivative instruments. If an embedded derivative instrument is separated from its host contract, the host contract shall be accounted for based on generally accepted accounting principles applicable to instruments of that type that

do not contain embedded derivative instruments. If an entity cannot reliably identify and measure the embedded derivative instrument that paragraph 12 requires be separated from the host contract, the entire contract shall be measured at fair value with gain or loss recognized in earnings, but it may not be designated as a hedging instrument pursuant to this Statement. An entity that initially recognizes a hybrid financial instrument that under paragraph 12 would be required to be separated into a host contract and a derivative instrument may irrevocably elect to initially and subsequently measure that hybrid financial instrument[6bb] in its entirety at fair value (with changes in fair value recognized in earnings). The fair value election shall be supported by concurrent documentation or a preexisting documented policy for automatic election. That recognized hybrid financial instrument could be an asset or a liability and it could be acquired or issued by the entity. That election is also available when a previously recognized financial instrument is subject to a remeasurement (new basis) event[6bbb] and the separate recognition of an embedded derivative. However, that recognized hybrid financial instrument may not be designated as a hedging instrument pursuant to this Statement. This election may be made on an instrument-by-instrument basis.

[6bb]This election shall not be applied to the hybrid instruments described in paragraph 8 of FASB Statement No. 107, *Disclosures about Fair Value of Financial Instruments.*

[6bbb]For purposes of this Statement, a remeasurement (new basis) event is an event identified in other authoritative accounting literature, other than the recognition of an other-than-temporary impairment, that requires a financial instrument to be remeasured to its fair value at the time of the event but does not require that instrument to be reported at fair value on a continuous basis with the change in fair value recognized in earnings. Examples of remeasurement events are business combinations and significant modifications of debt as defined in EITF Issue No. 96-19, "Debtor's Accounting for a Modification or Exchange of Debt Instruments."

d. Paragraph 16A is added as follows:

Any difference between a transaction price and the estimated fair value at the inception of a hybrid financial instrument for which the fair value election is applied shall not be recognized in earnings unless that estimated fair value is (a) obtained from a quoted market price in an active market, or (b) is evidenced by comparison to other observable current market transactions, or (c) is based on a valuation technique incorporating observable market data.

e. Paragraphs 44A and 44B are added as follows:

44A. In each statement of financial position presented, an entity shall report hybrid financial instruments measured at fair value under the election and under the practicability exception in paragraph 16 of this Statement in a manner that separates those reported fair values from the carrying amounts of assets and liabilities subsequently measured using another measurement attribute on the face of the statement of financial position. To accomplish that separate reporting, an entity may either (a) display separate line items for the fair value and non-fair-value carrying amounts or (b) present the aggregate of those fair value and non-fair-value amounts and parenthetically disclose the amount of fair value included in the aggregate amount.

44B. An entity shall provide information that will allow users to understand the effect of changes in the fair value of hybrid financial instruments measured at fair value under the election and under the practicability exception in paragraph 16 on earnings (or other performance indicators for entities that do not report earnings).

f. Paragraphs 200A–200D and the related heading are added as follows:

Section 2A: Examples Illustrating Application of Paragraphs 14A and 14B Relating to Embedded Derivatives in Securitized Financial Assets

200A. **Example 35: A Dollar-Denominated Floating-Rate Interest Issued by an SPE That Holds Yen-Denominated Floating-Rate Bonds and a Cross-Currency Swap to Pay Yen and Receive Dollars.** If the floating rate reflects a current market rate and the notional amounts of the bonds and the swap correspond to the notional amount of the interests issued, the dollar-denominated floating-rate interest would *not* have an embedded derivative requiring bifurcation because the terms of the beneficial interest do not indicate an embedded derivative and the financial instruments held by the entity provide the necessary cash flows.

200B. **Example 36: A Variable-Rate Interest Issued by an SPE That Holds Fixed-Rate Bonds and a Pay-Fixed, Receive-Variable Interest Rate Swap.** The variable-rate interest would *not* have an embedded derivative requiring bifurcation because the terms of the beneficial interest do not indicate an embedded derivative and the financial instruments held by the entity provide the necessary cash flows. However, if the notional amounts of the fixed-rate bonds and the variable interest rate swap do not match, the variable-rate interest would have to be evaluated for an embedded derivative under paragraph 13 because the financial instruments held by the entity might not provide the necessary cash flows.

200C. **Example 37: A Securitization Involving Subordination.** An SPE that holds fixed-rate bonds issues (a) a senior, floating-rate financial instrument, (b) a subordinated financial instrument that is entitled to 90 percent of the difference between the fixed rate received and the floating rate paid to the senior financial instrument, and (c) a residual financial instrument that is entitled to the remainder of the fixed-rate payment from the bonds after any credit losses. The subordinated financial instrument could be a hybrid financial instrument with an embedded interest rate derivative requiring bifurcation because the terms are floating rate, but the entity does not hold assets that bear a floating rate. This analysis considers the structure as a whole including the related liabilities. Therefore, there could be a shortfall of cash flow after the senior interest holders are paid, due to adverse changes in interest rates, and the investor in the subordinated interest might not recover substantially all of its initial recorded investment in the interest (see paragraph 13(a)). The residual financial instrument would not have an embedded derivative for the concentration of credit risk as discussed in paragraph 14B, because the concentration of credit risk relates to the financial instruments held by the entity, but the residual instrument would have an embedded interest rate derivative.

200D. **Example 38: A Securitization That Introduces New Credit Risk.** An entity holds a credit derivative referenced to Company A and high-quality bonds, but issues beneficial interests explicitly referenced to Company B. The beneficial interests would be a hybrid financial instrument with an embedded derivative because the cash flows relating to changes in the credit risk of Company B are not present in the financial instruments held by the entity.

Amendments to Statement 140

5. Statement 140 is amended as follows:

a. Paragraph 35(c)(2):

Passive **derivative financial instruments** that pertain to beneficial interests (other than another derivative financial instrument) issued or sold to parties other than the transferor, its affiliates, or its agents (paragraphs 39 and 40)

b. Paragraph 40:

A derivative financial instrument pertains to beneficial interests (other than another derivative financial instrument) issued only if it:

a. Is entered into (1) when the beneficial interests are issued by the qualifying SPE to parties other than the transferor, its affiliates, or its agents or sold to such other parties after being issued by the qualifying SPE to the transferor, its affiliates, or its agents or (2) when a passive derivative financial instrument needs to be replaced upon occurrence of an event or circumstance (specified in the legal documents that established the SPE or created the beneficial interests in the transferred assets that it holds) outside the control of the transferor, its affiliates, or its agents, for example, when the counterparty to the derivative defaults or is downgraded below a specified threshold

b. Has a notional amount that does not initially exceed the amount of those beneficial interests and is not expected to exceed them subsequently

c. Has characteristics that relate to, and partly or fully but not excessively counteract, some risk associated with those beneficial interests or the related transferred assets.

Effective Date and Transition

6. This Statement shall be effective for all financial instruments acquired, issued, or subject to a remeasurement (new basis) event occurring after the beginning of an entity's first fiscal year that begins after September 15, 2006. The fair value election provided for in paragraph 4(c) of this Statement may also be applied upon adoption of this Statement for hybrid financial instruments that had been bifurcated under paragraph 12 of Statement 133 prior to the adoption of this Statement. Earlier adoption is permitted as of the beginning of an entity's fiscal year, provided the entity has not yet issued financial statements, including financial statements for any interim period, for that fiscal year.

7. At adoption, any difference between the total carrying amount of the individual components of the existing bifurcated hybrid financial instrument and the fair value of the combined hybrid financial instrument shall be recognized as a cumulative-effect adjustment to beginning retained earnings. An entity shall separately disclose the gross gains and losses that make up the cumulative-effect adjustment, determined on an instrument-by-instrument basis. Prior periods shall not be restated.

The provisions of this Statement need not be applied to immaterial items.

This Statement was adopted by the affirmative votes of six members of the Financial Accounting Standards Board. Ms. Schipper dissented.

Ms. Schipper dissents from the issuance of this Statement because she believes that some of its provisions impair comparability and consistency, two desirable qualitative characteristics of financial information in the Board's conceptual framework, and other provisions increase complexity. She believes that neither the increased complexity nor the impair-

ment of comparability and consistency can be justified by a cost-benefit analysis.

Ms. Schipper disagrees with the Board's decision to permit, on an instrument-by-instrument basis, a fair value election for hybrid financial instruments with embedded derivatives that would otherwise require bifurcation. She agrees with the Board's conclusion, expressed in paragraph A14 (as well as elsewhere in other Statements issued by the Board), that fair value is the most relevant measurement attribute for financial instruments, and she believes that the

Board's conclusion, expressed in paragraph A14, would support a requirement that fair value be the initial and subsequent measurement attribute for instruments that are eligible for the treatment alternative provided in this Statement. Ms. Schipper reasons that the requirement in Statement 133 to evaluate certain hybrid financial instruments to determine if they contain an embedded derivative that should be accounted for separately from the host contract is one approach to addressing the use of different measurement attributes for derivatives (fair value) and host contracts (sometimes fair value, and sometimes another attribute). A different approach, which she believes is preferable, is to eliminate the use of different measurement attributes for financial instruments whenever it is practicable to do so. She believes that the hybrid instruments that are subject to the scope of the Statement represent such a case.

Ms. Schipper believes that treatment alternatives, such as the one provided in this Statement, are inherently undesirable because they are inconsistent with comparability, a desirable qualitative characteristic of financial information in the Board's conceptual framework. The Board acknowledges, in paragraph A17 of this Statement, that comparability between entities will be impaired by permitting free choice between two different measurement attributes. In ad-

dition, because the treatment alternative is applied instrument-by-instrument within an entity, it will probably result in inconsistency, in that different measurement attributes will be applied to economically similar financial instruments within an entity. Ms. Schipper believes that the separate display on the statement of financial position of instruments measured at fair value versus instruments measured using another measurement attribute does little to rectify this inconsistency and noncomparability.

Ms. Schipper also disagrees with the Board's decision to continue to provide an exemption (albeit a narrowed one) from the provisions of Statement 133 for certain interest-only and principal-only strips. She agrees with the Board's reasoning, as described in paragraph A8, that there is no conceptual basis for this exemption and that it impairs comparability because it allows economically similar instruments to be accounted for differently. In addition, the exemption increases complexity because it requires preparers to analyze interest-only and principal-only strips to determine if they qualify for the exemption. The extent of that complexity is illustrated by the fact that the Board found it necessary to include guidance, in paragraph 4(a), with respect to certain instruments that would, and would not, qualify for the exemption.

Members of the Financial Accounting Standards Board:

Appendix A

BACKGROUND INFORMATION AND BASIS FOR CONCLUSIONS

CONTENTS

Appendix A

BACKGROUND INFORMATION AND BASIS FOR CONCLUSIONS

Introduction

A1. This appendix summarizes considerations that Board members deemed significant in reaching the conclusions in this Statement. It includes reasons for accepting certain views and rejecting others. Individual Board members gave greater weight to some factors than to others.

Background Information

A2. Prior to the implementation of Statement 133, constituents questioned the application of that Statement's definition of a derivative and bifurcation requirements to interests in securitized financial assets. In response to those questions, the Board issued Implementation Issue D1 in June 2000. That Issue provides that entities need not evaluate interests in securitized financial assets for embedded derivatives. Rather, entities may continue to apply the measurement guidance related to accounting for financial instruments in paragraphs 14 and 362 of State-

ment 140, until further guidance is issued. The scope of Implementation Issue D1 covers transactions involving both qualifying and nonqualifying SPEs.

A3. The Board reconsidered issues relating to Implementation Issue D1 as part of the Exposure Drafts that led to the issuance of Statement 140 and FASB Statement No. 149, *Amendment of Statement 133 on Derivative Instruments and Hedging Activities.* In both instances, the Board was unable to reach a decision that would have resolved the issues.

A4. In January 2004, the Board decided to add a project to its agenda to reconsider the accounting for interests in securitized financial assets with the objective of replacing the interim guidance in Implementation Issue D1.

A5. The scope of the project was expanded to encompass all hybrid financial instruments (including interests in securitized financial assets) in October 2004.

A6. In August 2005, the Board issued an Exposure Draft, *Accounting for Certain Hybrid Financial Instruments,* for a 60-day comment period. The Board received 24 comment letters on the Exposure Draft. In late 2005, the Board redeliberated the issues identified in the Exposure Draft.

Amendments to Statement 133

Amendments Related to Interest-Only Strips and Principal-Only Strips

A7. This Statement clarifies the scope exception for interest-only strips and principal-only strips provided in paragraph 14 of Statement 133.

A8. The Board considered deleting paragraph 14 of Statement 133 in its entirety, which would have resulted in all interest-only strips and principal-only strips being subject to the requirements of Statement 133, including the embedded derivative provisions. The Board acknowledges that there is no conceptual basis for the exemption provided for interest-only strips and principal-only strips. Some Board members supported deleting paragraph 14 because certain financial instruments whose economic characteristics are similar to those that qualify for the paragraph 14 exemption are ineligible for the exemption because of the form of those financial instruments. Thus, paragraph 14 results in economically similar instruments being accounted for differently.

A9. Rather than deleting paragraph 14 of Statement 133, the Board decided to amend that paragraph to limit its application. The Board acknowledged that paragraph 14 was intended to simplify the application of Statement 133 by exempting from the provisions of that Statement financial instruments that represent the right to receive only a specified proportion of the contractual interest cash flows of a specific debt instrument or a specified proportion of the contractual principal repayment cash flows of that debt instrument. The Board concluded that amending paragraph 14 to apply to a narrow set of financial instruments would retain this simplification.

A10. In deciding to limit the application of the exemption provided in paragraph 14 of Statement 133, the Board also observed that, generally, interest-only strips and principal-only strips in securitized financial assets should not qualify for the exemption from the bifurcation requirements of Statement 133.

A11. During redeliberations, the Board affirmed that it intends the interest-only strip and principal-only strip exemption to apply to only the simplest separations of interest payments from principal payments. The process of separating a debt instrument into its principal and interest components is referred to as stripping an instrument.

A12. The Board acknowledged during its redeliberations that the amendments to paragraph 14 of Statement 133 will result in fewer financial instruments being subject to the scope of FASB Statement No. 134, *Accounting for Mortgage-Backed Securities Retained after the Securitization of Mortgage Loans Held for Sale by a Mortgage Banking Enterprise.*

Amendments Related to Interests in Securitized Financial Assets

A13. In reconsidering the accounting for interests in securitized financial assets and the application of Statement 133 to those interests, the Board considered several alternatives. The Board considered and rejected making the temporary exemption provided by Implementation Issue D1 permanent, because doing so would have resulted in permanent differences in the accounting for a wide range of similar financial instruments merely based on the form of the financial instrument.

A14. The Board considered requiring that all interests in securitized financial assets be accounted for at fair value with changes in fair value recognized in earnings. This alternative would have reduced complexity and would have resulted in more financial instruments being reported at fair value, which the Board considers to be the most relevant measurement attribute for financial instruments. However, this alternative also would have perpetuated dissimilar accounting for similar financial instruments merely based on the form of the financial instrument.

A15. The Board also considered requiring that all interests in securitized financial assets be accounted for at fair value with changes in fair value recognized in other comprehensive income until realized. Board members acknowledged that this alternative would have also perpetuated dissimilar accounting for similar financial instruments based on the form of the financial instrument. In addition, some Board members believe that allowing the changes in fair value of embedded derivatives to be recognized in other comprehensive income rather than in earnings does not improve financial reporting.

A16. The Board decided to eliminate the exemption from Statement 133 for interests in securitized financial assets provided temporarily by Implementation Issue D1 and to require that those interests be evaluated to determine whether they are freestanding derivatives or whether they contain embedded derivatives. Eliminating this exemption addressed the Board's concern that is expressed in paragraph A13.

The Board also decided to permit interests in securitized financial assets that contain embedded derivatives that Statement 133 would otherwise require to be accounted for as a derivative separately from the host contract to be accounted for as a single financial instrument measured at fair value with changes in fair value recognized in earnings. The Board reasoned that this approach results in certain financial instruments being subject to the requirements of Statement 133, regardless of the form of the transaction. This approach also simplifies the accounting for financial instruments for which fair value measurement is elected. Of the alternatives considered by the Board, this approach results in the greatest degree of convergence with International Accounting Standards.

A17. The Board acknowledged that comparability among entities and consistency within an entity will be impaired as a result of permitting free choice, on an instrument-by-instrument basis, between two different accounting treatments for similar or identical financial instruments. The Board also noted that financial instruments for which fair value measurement is elected would not be eligible to be used as hedging instruments that receive special hedge accounting. However an entity may still elect to separately account for an embedded derivative so that it is eligible as a hedging instrument under Statement 133.

A18. The Board considered whether the accounting for interests in securitized financial assets should distinguish between financial instruments acquired and financial instruments retained by the transferor in a securitization transaction. The Board decided that there should be no distinction in the application of the requirements of Statement 133 based on how the holder acquired the interest, that is, whether the holder of an interest in a securitized financial asset is a purchaser of that interest or whether the holder is a transferor that retains the interest in transferred assets in the securitization transaction.

A19. The Board considered how an interest in securitized financial assets should be evaluated for embedded derivatives. The Board decided to require that an evaluation of the terms of the financial instrument be performed and that sufficient evidence be obtained to determine whether the instrument contains an embedded derivative that requires bifurcation. The Board believes sufficient evidence can generally be obtained by analyzing the contractual arrangements that govern the payoff structure and the payment pri-

ority of the financial instrument. The Board believes that analysis will require an understanding of the nature and amount of assets and the nature and amount of liabilities and other financial instruments making up a securitization transaction. In securitizations involving the resecuritization of tranches from previous transactions, the analysis might require an understanding of each securitization making up the resecuritization transaction. The Board further believes that in many cases information available to purchasers of financial instruments will be sufficient to perform the analyses required by paragraphs 12 and 13 of Statement 133 to determine whether financial instruments contain embedded derivatives that would require bifurcation. Summarized information may be sufficient in some cases for that determination. However, if summarized information is insufficient for that determination, a purchaser of a financial instrument would be obligated to obtain sufficient detailed information to determine the existence of derivatives or embedded derivatives.

A20. The evaluation of financial instruments for embedded derivatives will vary in complexity depending on the nature of the financial instrument. For example, a senior financial instrument with a market interest rate may require little investigation, whereas a residual financial instrument that absorbs risk disproportionate to other financial instruments will require additional investigation.

A21. The Board also considered whether concentrations of credit risk in subordinated interests in securitized financial assets should be considered embedded derivatives. Some Board members believe that concentrations of credit risk that are created by subordinating one financial instrument to another financial instrument represent, in effect, credit default swaps embedded in the subordinated financial instrument and that such credit default swaps should be identified as embedded derivatives requiring bifurcation. However, the Board decided not to define concentrations of credit risk as embedded derivatives, regardless of how they arise.

A22. The Board decided not to extend the requirements of paragraph 13(b) of Statement 133 for interest rate leverage factors to credit concentrations. Some Board members reasoned that credit concentrations in subordinated interests should not be recognized as embedded derivatives because there is no obligation on the part of the subordinated financial instrument holder to transfer cash or assets. That is, the subordination functions through a cash allocation mechanism in which cash flows that otherwise would have been allocated to the subordinated financial instrument holder instead are allocated to the senior financial instrument holder, to effectively allocate credit losses from the senior financial instrument holder to the subordinated financial instrument holder.

A23. Other Board members reasoned that the purchase price of a subordinated financial instrument reflects the investor's assessment of the cash flows it expects to receive, including the likelihood of default and, therefore, concentrations of credit risk are reflected in the fair value of the subordinated financial instrument. As the credit risk of the subordinated financial instrument is reflected in its fair value, there is no need for separate recognition of credit concentrations.

A24. The Board noted, however, that other aspects of Statement 133 regarding credit risk and the identification of credit risk as an embedded derivative are not affected by the Board's decision on concentrations of credit risk. For instance, the examples in Statement 133 Implementation Issue No. B36, "Modified Coinsurance Arrangements and Debt Instruments That Incorporate Credit Risk Exposures That Are Unrelated or Only Partially Related to the Creditworthiness of the Obligor under Those Instruments," would continue to represent credit risk that is not clearly and closely related to the host contract.

Amendments Related to the Fair Value Election

A25. Having decided to permit fair value measurement for interests in securitized financial assets that contain embedded derivatives that otherwise would be required to be bifurcated, the Board considered how to establish the scope of financial instruments eligible for this election. Financial instruments acquired by a transferor in a securitization transaction would be readily identifiable as interests in securitized financial assets. However, the Board concluded that the fair value election should not be limited to financial instruments created in a transaction accounted for by the transferor as a sale in accordance with Statement 140. The Board considered and rejected definitions that might have specified what financial instruments would be considered interests in securitized financial assets. Likewise, the Board considered and rejected an approach that would have defined interests in securitized financial assets based on the presence of a defined securitization vehicle.

A26. Although the scope of Implementation Issue D1, and the original scope of instruments that would be eligible for the fair value measurement election, is limited to interests in securitized financial assets, the Board decided to extend that election to any recognized hybrid financial instrument that contains an embedded derivative that Statement 133 otherwise would require to be accounted for as a derivative separately from the host contract. The Board believes that this decision eliminates the need to distinguish between interests in securitized financial assets and other hybrid financial instruments and permits many financial instruments other than interests in securitized financial assets to be measured in their entirety at fair value.

A27. The Exposure Draft proposed elimination of the practicability exception in paragraph 16 of Statement 133 because the Board believed that the option to measure hybrid financial instruments at fair value made that exception unnecessary. Many respondents to the Exposure Draft noted that the practicability exception still would be needed in some circumstances because the financial instruments to which the embedded bifurcation analysis would be newly applied as a result of the elimination of Implementation Issue D1 are particularly complex. Those respondents noted that although the practicability exception had rarely been applied in the past, it may be applied more frequently with the elimination of Implementation Issue D1. The Board decided not to eliminate the practicability exception because one objective of the project was to simplify the application of Statement 133 and eliminating the practicability exception would make application more difficult. The Board noted that a financial instrument must be evaluated to determine that it has an embedded derivative requiring bifurcation before the instrument can become a candidate for the fair value election.

A28. The Board decided to limit the election to measure at fair value to hybrid **financial** instruments because it has not yet identified the most relevant measurement attribute for nonfinancial host contracts. The Board also decided to exclude the types of hosts described in paragraph 8 of FASB Statement No. 107, *Disclosures about Fair Value of Financial Instruments,* even though some of the hosts described in that paragraph might represent financial instruments. Additionally, the Board decided during its redeliberations to limit the election to measure at fair value to recognized financial instruments. The Board noted that consideration of expanding a fair value option to include nonfinancial items and unrecognized financial instruments will be considered as part of the Board's broader fair value option project.

A29. The Board considered requiring that the election to adopt fair value as the measurement attribute for certain hybrid financial instruments be made as an entity-wide policy decision. The Board noted that that requirement would increase comparability for instruments held by a given entity. However, the Board rejected this approach because it seemed likely to limit the number of entities that would elect fair value measurement. The Board also considered requiring that the election be applied on a type-of-instrument basis. The Board rejected that approach because it would require definitions of types of instruments, thereby introducing additional complexity, and because it would limit the use of fair value. The Board decided to permit application of the fair value election on an instrument-by-instrument basis. The Board reasoned that the hedge accounting elections of Statement 133 are applied on an item-by-item basis and that an instrument-by-instrument application of the fair value election is most consistent with other requirements of Statement 133. In addition, the Board reasoned that an instrument-by-instrument election is the best way to encourage fair value measurement. The Board was also willing to accept a reduction in comparability to achieve increased relevance through expanded use of fair value measurement.

A30. The Board decided that the fair value election should be applied irrevocably at initial recognition to impose discipline on an elective accounting method. Otherwise preparers would be able to elect fair value measurement to obtain desired reporting results with the benefit of hindsight.

Amendments Related to Disclosure

A31. During the deliberations that led to the Exposure Draft, the Board decided not to require any additional disclosures for entities electing to measure hybrid financial instruments at fair value pursuant to this Statement. While the Board reasoned that additional disclosures might reduce the effects of noncomparability resulting from the election to measure hybrid financial instruments at fair value, it was sympathetic to constituents' concerns that financial instrument disclosures be developed in a comprehensive rather than a piecemeal manner. Thus, the Exposure Draft did not propose any new disclosures. The Board noted that quantitative and qualitative disclosures about the amounts and methods used to measure financial instruments at fair value under this Statement will be required by the Board's project on fair value measurements. The Board also noted that

other applicable disclosure requirements (such as those in FASB Statement No. 115, *Accounting for Certain Investments in Debt and Equity Securities,* and Statement 140, among others) continue to apply to hybrid financial instruments under this Statement.

A32. During its redeliberations, the Board decided to require separate display, either parenthetically or as a separate line on the face of the statement of financial position, of amounts measured at fair value as a result of electing fair value measurement under this Statement. The Board reasoned that separating items electively measured at fair value from similar items measured in other ways mitigates the effects of using multiple measurement attributes and that the benefits of that information avoid the drawbacks of promulgating piecemeal disclosures. The Board also decided to require information about the effect on earnings of measuring hybrid financial instruments at fair value. The Board noted that the earnings disclosure is not intended to require quantifying the effect on earnings of accounting for a hybrid financial instrument at fair value instead of accounting for a hybrid financial instrument on a bifurcated basis. That is, the Board does not intend that entities would calculate the difference between accounting for the hybrid financial instrument on a bifurcated basis and accounting for the hybrid financial instrument in its entirety at fair value. The Board decided to require earnings-related disclosures in the form of a general principle and not to prescribe specific disclosures.

Amendments to Statement 140

A33. The Board considered the effect on the requirements for qualifying SPEs of eliminating the Implementation Issue D1 exemption from the bifurcation requirements of Statement 133 and requiring the evaluation of beneficial interests in securitized financial assets to obtain sufficient evidence to determine whether an embedded derivative exists. The Board decided to eliminate the prohibition on a qualifying SPE from holding a derivative financial instrument that pertains to a beneficial interest **other than another derivative financial instrument.** That prohibition was included in Statement 140 to preclude a qualifying SPE from holding a derivative that, because of the Implementation Issue D1 exemption, might not be accounted for as a derivative by the qualifying SPE's beneficial interest holders. Because this Statement eliminates the Implementation Issue D1 exemption, the prohibition is no longer necessary.

A34. Some respondents to the Exposure Draft asked whether bifurcation that would be required in the separate financial statements of a qualifying SPE (if any were issued) would cause the SPE not to qualify under paragraph 35(c) of Statement 140. That is, those respondents questioned whether the requirement to bifurcate a hybrid financial instrument that might not have been bifurcated previously because of Implementation Issue D1 would influence the qualified status of the SPE as a result of this Statement's superseding Implementation Issue D1. The Board amended paragraph 35(c) to clarify that bifurcation of issued interests under the provisions of this Statement would not disqualify an otherwise qualifying SPE, regardless of whether those interests are retained by the transferor or held by third parties.

Effective Date and Transition

A35. During the deliberations that led to the Exposure Draft, the Board decided that the effective date for the amendments to Statement 133 should be consistent with the amendments to Statement 140 on the accounting for servicing rights and the requirements of a qualifying SPE. The Board noted that many financial institutions requested the election to subsequently measure hybrid financial instruments and servicing rights at fair value and that the application of the election would not be burdensome. Based on these two factors, the Board believed that the measurement provisions in the three related projects that amend Statement 140 should be effective close to the expected issuance dates of the final Statements. The Board initially decided that the application of the measurement guidance in all three projects would be effective at the earlier of fiscal years beginning after December 15, 2005, or fiscal years that begin during the fiscal quarter in which the final Statement is issued, if applicable. The Exposure Draft provided that if the final Statement is issued between December 1, 2005, and February 28, 2006, calendar-year reporting entities would apply the Statement as of January 1, 2006, and entities with fiscal years ending on November 30, 2005, would apply the Statement as of December 1, 2005. If a reporting entity's fiscal year ends on June 30, the final Statement would have been effective for fiscal years beginning July 1, 2006.

A36. Some respondents to the Exposure Draft expressed concern that the proposed effective date would not have provided a sufficient period for implementation especially with respect to the elimination of Implementation Issue D1. The Board decided that the effective date should be changed to fiscal years beginning after September 15, 2006, with early adoption permitted as of the beginning of an entity's fiscal year, provided the entity has not yet issued financial statements, including financial statements for any interim period, for that fiscal year. Additionally, the Board decided that the issuance of this Statement and the final servicing rights Statement could precede the issuance of the final Statement that will amend Statement 140 with regard to the requirements of a qualifying SPE.

A37. During the deliberations that led to the Exposure Draft, the Board considered whether the election to measure hybrid financial instruments that otherwise would require separation into a host contract and a derivative instrument measured at fair value should be applied on a prospective basis for new instruments or on a prospective basis for new instruments *and* for existing instruments with a cumulative-effect adjustment recorded to reflect the measurement of existing hybrid financial instruments at fair value. Some Board members suggested that an entity be allowed to apply the fair value election to existing hybrid financial instruments that are currently being separated into a derivative and a host contract to ease application of Statement 133. During the deliberations that led to the Exposure Draft, the Board believed that if the fair value election were made applicable to existing hybrid financial instruments, the fair value election should be applied to *all* hybrid financial instruments, rather than to only certain bifurcated hybrid financial instruments selected by the reporting entity. However, the Board concluded that application on an all-or-none basis would not be practical because some derivatives from bifurcated hybrid financial instruments could be hedging instruments under Statement 133, and combining the derivative with the host into a hybrid financial instrument measured at fair value would eliminate the opportunity to use the embedded derivative as a hedging instrument. The Board also rejected that alternative because of complexities associated with recognition of gains or losses on host contracts. The Board also considered requiring application of the requirements of this Statement to all existing instruments. The Board rejected that alternative because it would require preparers to perform a bifurcation evaluation on interests that previously had not been subject to Statement 133 because of the Implementation Issue D1 exemption. Instead, the Board initially decided that the election should be applied on a prospective basis for new instruments and that existing instruments would not be eligible for this election.

A38. Many respondents to the Exposure Draft suggested that the scope of the fair value election be expanded to include all hybrid financial instruments that were previously separated into a derivative and a host contract at initial application. Those respondents noted that financial reporting and operational benefits would be realized from having consistent accounting for similar financial instruments. The Board agreed with these respondents and decided to allow an instrument-by-instrument election for existing bifurcated hybrid financial instruments in which the bifurcated embedded derivative is not being used in a qualifying Statement 133 hedging relationship. The Board further noted similar transition provisions being promulgated as part of the servicing rights and the life settlements projects that also provide a fair value election for existing assets.

A39. Having decided to expand the transition provisions to include existing bifurcated hybrid financial instruments, the Board considered how any difference between the carrying amount of the separate components of the bifurcated hybrid financial instrument and the fair value of the combined hybrid financial instrument should be recognized. The Board considered delaying the effective date of this Statement to coincide with the adoption of the Board's final Statement on fair value measurements and the related FASB Staff Position (FSP) FAS 133-a, "Accounting for Unrealized Gains (Losses) Relating to Derivative Instruments Measured at Fair Value under Statement 133." The Board decided against requiring early adoption of the fair value measurements Statement and the related FSP as part of this Statement. The Board decided that at transition any difference between the carrying amount of the bifurcated hybrid and the fair value of the combined hybrid should be recognized as an adjustment to beginning retained earnings.

A40. For hybrids entered into subsequent to adoption of this Statement for which the fair value measurement attribute is elected, the Board believes that guidance currently exists in EITF Issue No. 02-3, "Issues Involved in Accounting for Derivative Contracts Held for Trading Purposes and Contracts Involved in Energy Trading and Risk Management Activities," that could be utilized in the interim and that a delay in the effective date of this Statement would reduce the benefits to be derived from the simplification offered by this Statement. The Board acknowledges that utilizing Issue 02-3 in this manner effectively expands the scope of footnote 3 in the consensus to include embedded derivatives in hybrid financial instruments

electing the fair value measurement attribute. The Board does not intend that the guidance in footnote 3 of Issue 02-3 be applied to transfers accounted for as sales under the provisions of Statement 140. That is, the Board does not intend that the gain on sale resulting from a securitization transaction be deferred as a result of the existence of an embedded derivative in a retained interest that might not meet the observability criteria of Issue 02-3.

Benefits and Costs

A41. The mission of the FASB is to establish and improve standards of financial accounting and reporting for the guidance and education of the public, including preparers, auditors, and users of financial information. In fulfilling that mission, the Board endeavors to determine that a proposed standard will fill a significant need and that the costs imposed to meet that standard, as compared with other alternatives, are justified in relation to the overall benefits of the resulting information. Although the costs to implement a new standard may not be borne evenly, investors and creditors—both present and potential—and other users of financial information benefit from improvements in financial reporting, thereby facilitating the functioning of markets for capital and credit and the efficient allocation of resources in the economy.

A42. The Board's assessment of the benefits and costs of amending Statements 133 and 140 with respect to the accounting for hybrid financial instruments was based on input received from preparers and users of financial statements.

A43. The Board concluded that a fair value measurement election should be provided for certain hybrid financial instruments that otherwise would require bifurcation. The Board reasoned that providing this election would decrease the burden associated with applying Statement 133 to hybrid financial instruments. The Board concluded that the expected benefits of both improved financial reporting resulting from consistent application of Statement 133 to different financial instruments with similar economic characteristics and simplification in financial reporting achieved through permitting fair value measurement for certain hybrid instruments would outweigh the decreased comparability in financial statements and the costs associated with implementing this Statement. Although fair value measurement is elective under this Statement, the Board concluded that providing a fair value election will expand the use of fair value for financial instruments and that such an expansion is consistent with the Board's belief that fair value is the most relevant measurement attribute for financial instruments.

A44. The Board concluded that eliminating the Implementation Issue D1 exemption would improve financial reporting by requiring all financial instruments, including those in the form of interests in securitized financial assets, to be subject to the Statement 133 bifurcation requirements. As a result of eliminating the Implementation Issue D1 exemption, the Board was able to simplify the qualifying SPE criteria by deleting the parenthetical phrase *other than another derivative financial instrument* in paragraphs 35(c) and 40 of Statement 140. Removing this restriction on qualifying SPEs and eliminating the Implementation Issue D1 exemption will result in increased consistency in the application of the bifurcation requirements of Statement 133 and will result in either the identification of more derivatives in interests in securitized financial assets or accounting for these interests in their entirety at fair value.

Appendix B

IMPACT ON EITF ISSUES AND STATEMENT 133 IMPLEMENTATION ISSUES

B1. This appendix addresses the impact of the provisions of this Statement on the consensuses reached on EITF Issues and the responses to Statement 133 Implementation Issues through December 14, 2005. This appendix does not address the impact of this Statement on other authoritative accounting literature included in categories (b), (c), and (d) in the GAAP hierarchy as discussed in AICPA Statement on Auditing Standards (SAS) No. 69, *The Meaning of* Present Fairly in Conformity With Generally Accepted Accounting Principles.

B2. Even though the provisions of this Statement do not nullify or partially nullify the consensuses in the following EITF Issues, the status section of each of those Issues in *EITF Abstracts* will be updated to state: "Statement 155 amended Statement 133 in February 2006. Statement 155 provides a fair value measurement election for certain hybrid financial instruments with embedded derivatives that otherwise would require bifurcation. Hybrid financial instruments that are elected to be accounted for in their entirety at fair value cannot be used as a hedge instrument in a Statement 133 hedge."

85-9 "Revenue Recognition on Options to Purchase Stock of Another Entity"

85-29 "Convertible Bonds with a 'Premium Put'"

86-15 "Increasing-Rate Debt"

86-28 "Accounting Implications of Indexed Debt Instruments"

90-19 "Convertible Bonds with Issuer Option to Settle for Cash upon Conversion"

96-12 "Recognition of Interest Income and Balance Sheet Classification of Structured Notes"

97-15 "Accounting for Contingency Arrangements Based on Security Prices in a Purchase Business Combination"

98-5 "Accounting for Convertible Securities with Beneficial Conversion Features or Contingently Adjustable Conversion Ratios"

99-20 "Recognition of Interest Income and Impairment on Purchased and Retained Beneficial Interests in Securitized Financial Assets"

00-19 "Accounting for Derivative Financial Instruments Indexed to, and Potentially Settled in, a Company's Own Stock"

03-7 "Accounting for the Settlement of the Equity-Settled Portion of a Convertible Debt Instrument That Permits or Requires the Conversion Spread to Be Settled in Stock (Instrument C of Issue No. 90-19)"

B3. Even though the provisions of this Statement do not nullify or partially nullify the consensuses in the following EITF Issue, the status section of that Issue in *EITF Abstracts* will be updated to state: "Statement 155 amended Statement 133 in February 2006. Statement 155 indicates that interest-only and principal-only strips exempt from the bifurcation requirements of Statement 133 are limited to a narrowly defined set of such instruments."

88-11 "Allocation of Recorded Investment When a Loan or Part of a Loan Is Sold"

B4. The provisions of this Statement nullify the response in Statement 133 Implementation Issue No. C4, "Interest-Only and Principal-Only Strips."

B5. Even though the provisions of this Statement do not nullify or partially nullify the responses in the following Statement 133 Implementation Issues, the Implementation Issues will be updated to indicate in the "Affected by" section the following: "FASB Statement No. 155, *Accounting for Certain Hybrid Financial Instruments*," and a revision date of February 2006. Further, where appropriate in each of the Issues, the following statement has been included in the body of the Implementation Issue: "Note that Statement 155 was issued in February 2006 and allows for a fair value election for hybrid financial instruments that otherwise would require bifurcation. Hybrid financial instruments that are elected to be accounted for in their entirety at fair value cannot be used as a hedge instrument in a Statement 133 hedge."

A1   "Initial Net Investment"

B1   "Separating the Embedded Derivative from the Host Contract"

B2   "Leveraged Embedded Terms"

B4   "Foreign Currency Derivatives"

B5   "Investor Permitted, but Not Forced, to Settle without Recovering Substantially All of the Initial Net Investment"

B6   "Allocating the Basis of a Hybrid Instrument to the Host Contract and the Embedded Derivative"

B10   "Equity-Indexed Life Insurance Contracts"

B11   "Volumetric Production Payments"

B15   "Separate Accounting for Multiple Derivative Features Embedded in a Single Hybrid Instrument"

B17   "Term-Extending Options in Contracts Other Than Debt Hosts"

B20   "Must the Terms of a Separated Non-Option Embedded Derivative Produce a Zero Fair Value at Inception?"

B23   "Terms of a Separated Non-Option Embedded Derivative When the Holder Has Acquired the Hybrid Instrument Subsequent to Its Inception"

B24   "Interaction of the Requirements of EITF Issue No. 86-28 and Statement 133 Related to Structured Notes Containing Embedded Derivatives"

B29   "Equity-Indexed Annuity Contracts with Embedded Derivatives"

B30   "Application of Statement 97 and Statement 133 to Equity-Indexed Annuity Contracts"

B35   "Application of Statement 133 to a Not-for-Profit Organization's Obligation Arising from an Irrevocable Split-Interest Agreement"

B36   "Modified Coinsurance Arrangements and Debt Instruments That Incorporate Credit Risk Exposures That Are Unrelated or Only Partially Related to the Creditworthiness of the Obligor under Those Instruments"

B37   "Mandatorily Redeemable Preferred Stock Denominated in either a Precious Metal or a Foreign Currency"

B6. Statement 133 Implementation Issue No. B39, "Application of Paragraph 13(b) to Call Options That Are Exercisable Only by the Debtor," is amended as follows:

a. The "Comments" section of Example 6 in the chart illustrating the guidance to specific debt instruments:

~~Although the related mortgage loans are prepayable, and thus each contain a separate embedded call option, the MBS itself does not contain an embedded call option. The MBS issuer has the obligation (not the option) to pass through cash flows from the related mortgage loans to the MBS investors.~~While the MBS itself does not contain an embedded call option, the Board decided as part of FASB Statement No. 155, *Accounting for Certain Hybrid Financial Instruments,* that an interest in MBS with underlying assets containing an embedded call feature, for which all of the associated cash flows are proportionately passed through to all the interest holders, will not be subject to the conditions in paragraph 13(b) with respect to that embedded call feature. However, in situations in which the cash flows associated with the embedded call feature are disproportionately allocated to different classes of interest holders, all interests in that MBS would be subject to the conditions in paragraph 13(b) with respect to that embedded call feature.

B7. Statement 133 Implementation Issue No. D1, "Application of Statement 133 to Beneficial Interests in Securitized Financial Assets," is amended as follows:

a. The "Affected by" section:

FASB Statement No. 149, *Amendment of Statement 133 on Derivative Instruments and Hedging Activities* **(Revised July 30, 2003)**FASB Statement No. 155, *Accounting for Certain Hybrid Financial Instruments* **(Revised February 14, 2006)**

b. The "Note" section:

NOTE: FASB Statement No. 149, *Amendment of Statement 133 on Derivative Instruments and Hedging Activities,* issued in April 2003, does not address issues surrounding the evaluation of beneficial interests issued in securitization transactions under Statement 133. Rather, the FASB plans to resolve those issues in a limited scope interpretation of FASB Statement No. 140, *Accounting for Transfers and Servicing of Financial Assets and Extinguishments of Liabilities.* The FASB staff interim guidance in this Implementation Issue remains effective until the FASB issues new guidance superseding this Issue and that guidance becomes effective.

c. The following is added at the end of the Implementation Issue:

EFFECTIVE DATE AND TRANSITION

FASB Statement No. 155, *Accounting for Certain Hybrid Financial Instruments,* issued in February 2006, addresses issues on the evaluation of beneficial interests issued in securitization transactions under Statement 133. The FASB staff interim guidance in this Implementation Issue remains effective for instruments recognized prior to the effective date of Statement 155.

Statement of Financial Accounting Standards No. 156
Accounting for Servicing of Financial Assets
an amendment of FASB Statement No. 140

STATUS

Issued: March 2006

Effective Date: As of the beginning of an entity's first fiscal year that begins after September 15, 2006

Affects: Amends FAS 133, paragraph 56 and footnote 9
Amends FAS 140, paragraphs 4, 5, 10, 11, 14, 17, 56 through 63, 65 through 67, 72, 76, 82, 83(b), 87(a), and 343 through 349 and footnotes 17, 20, and 21
Replaces FAS 140, paragraph 13
Amends FAS 140 by adding paragraphs 13A, 13B, 62A, and 349A
Effectively amends FIN 45, footnote 3
Effectively amends FIN 46(R), paragraph B26
Amends FTB 87-3, paragraphs 9 and 10
Effectively amends FSP FAS 140-1

Affected by: Paragraph 3(c) deleted by FAS 157, paragraph E27

Issues Discussed by FASB Emerging Issues Task Force (EITF)

Affects: Nullifies EITF Issue No. 88-11

Interpreted by: No EITF Issues

Related Issues: EITF Issues No. 85-13, 87-34, 88-22, 89-2, 90-18, 90-21, 92-2, 02-9, and 02-12 and Topic No. D-69

SUMMARY

This Statement amends FASB Statement No. 140, *Accounting for Transfers and Servicing of Financial Assets and Extinguishments of Liabilities,* with respect to the accounting for separately recognized servicing assets and servicing liabilities. This Statement:

1. Requires an entity to recognize a servicing asset or servicing liability each time it undertakes an obligation to service a financial asset by entering into a servicing contract in any of the following situations:
   a. A transfer of the servicer's financial assets that meets the requirements for sale accounting
   b. A transfer of the servicer's financial assets to a qualifying special-purpose entity in a guaranteed mortgage securitization in which the transferor retains all of the resulting securities and classifies them as either available-for-sale securities or trading securities in accordance with FASB Statement No. 115, *Accounting for Certain Investments in Debt and Equity Securities*
   c. An acquisition or assumption of an obligation to service a financial asset that does not relate to financial assets of the servicer or its consolidated affiliates.
2. Requires all separately recognized servicing assets and servicing liabilities to be initially measured at fair value, if practicable.

3. Permits an entity to choose either of the following subsequent measurement methods for each class of separately recognized servicing assets and servicing liabilities:
   a. *Amortization method*—Amortize servicing assets or servicing liabilities in proportion to and over the period of estimated net servicing income or net servicing loss and assess servicing assets or servicing liabilities for impairment or increased obligation based on fair value at each reporting date.
   b. *Fair value measurement method*—Measure servicing assets or servicing liabilities at fair value at each reporting date and report changes in fair value in earnings in the period in which the changes occur.
4. At its initial adoption, permits a one-time reclassification of available-for-sale securities to trading securities by entities with recognized servicing rights, without calling into question the treatment of other available-for-sale securities under Statement 115, provided that the available-for-sale securities are identified in some manner as offsetting the entity's exposure to changes in fair value of servicing assets or servicing liabilities that a servicer elects to subsequently measure at fair value.
5. Requires separate presentation of servicing assets and servicing liabilities subsequently measured at fair value in the statement of financial position and additional disclosures for all separately recognized servicing assets and servicing liabilities.

Reasons for Issuing This Statement

The Board added this project to its agenda because constituents asked the Board to reconsider Statement 140's requirements for accounting for mortgage servicing assets and servicing liabilities. The Board decided to broaden the scope of the project to include all servicing assets and servicing liabilities. Servicing assets and servicing liabilities may be subject to significant interest rate and prepayment risks, and many entities use financial instruments to mitigate those risks. Currently, servicing assets and servicing liabilities are amortized over the expected period of estimated net servicing income or loss and assessed for impairment or increased obligation at each reporting date. The Board acknowledged that the application of the lower of carrying amount or fair value measurement attribute to servicing assets results in asymmetrical recognition of economic events, because it requires recognition of all decreases in fair value but limits recognition of increases in fair value to the original carrying amount.

An entity may use derivative instruments to mitigate the risks inherent in its servicing assets and servicing liabilities. An entity that does not apply hedge accounting to these derivative instruments is exposed to income statement volatility that arises from the use of different measurement attributes for the servicing assets and servicing liabilities and the related derivative instruments. For example, in rising interest rate environments, decreases in the fair value of derivatives are reflected in the income statement, but increases in the fair value of related servicing assets are not reflected in the income statement to the extent that fair value exceeds the amortized carrying amount. Some constituents believe that meeting current hedge accounting criteria is burdensome and unduly restrictive and that the asymmetrical accounting for mortgage servicing assets and servicing liabilities and the related financial instruments used to mitigate the related risks does not appropriately reflect the economics of the hedging techniques employed.

When adding this project to its agenda, the Board also considered the complexity of application of the amortization method, such as the timing and characterization of impairment allowances versus write-downs, as well as the desire to simplify the accounting requirements for servicing assets and servicing liabilities.

How This Statement Improves Financial Reporting

This Statement requires that all separately recognized servicing assets and servicing liabilities be initially measured at fair value, if practicable. The Board concluded that fair value is the most relevant measurement attribute for the initial recognition of all servicing assets and servicing liabilities, because it represents the best measure of future cash flows. This Statement permits, but does not require, the subsequent measurement of servicing assets and servicing liabilities at fair value. An entity that uses derivative instruments to mitigate the risks inherent in servicing assets and servicing liabilities is required to account for those derivative instruments at fair value. Under this Statement, an entity can elect subsequent fair value measurement of its servicing assets and servicing liabilities by class, thus simplifying its accounting and providing for income statement recognition of the potential offsetting changes in fair value of the servicing assets, servicing liabilities, and related derivative instruments. An entity that elects to subsequently measure servicing assets and servicing liabilities at fair value is expected to recognize declines in fair value of the servicing assets and servicing liabilities more consistently than by reporting other-than-temporary impairments.

The Board decided to require additional disclosures and separate presentation in the statement of financial position of the carrying amounts of servicing assets and servicing liabilities that an entity elects to subsequently measure at fair value to address concerns about comparability that may result from the use of elective measurement methods.

Effective Date and Transition

An entity should adopt this Statement as of the beginning of its first fiscal year that begins after September 15, 2006. Earlier adoption is permitted as of the beginning of an entity's fiscal year, provided the entity has not yet issued financial statements, including interim financial statements, for any period of that fiscal year. The effective date of this Statement is the date an entity adopts the requirements of this Statement.

An entity should apply the requirements for recognition and initial measurement of servicing assets and servicing liabilities prospectively to all transactions after the effective date of this Statement.

An entity may elect to subsequently measure a class of separately recognized servicing assets and servicing liabilities at fair value as of the beginning of any fiscal year, beginning with the fiscal year in which the entity adopts this Statement. An entity that elects to subsequently measure a class of separately recognized servicing assets and servicing liabilities at fair value should apply that election prospectively to all new and existing separately recognized servicing assets and servicing liabilities within those classes that a servicer elects to subsequently measure at fair value. The effect of remeasuring an existing class of separately recognized servicing assets and servicing liabilities at fair value should be reported as a cumulative-effect adjustment to retained earnings as of the beginning of the fiscal year and should be separately disclosed.

This Statement permits an entity to reclassify certain available-for-sale securities to trading securities, regardless of the restriction in paragraph 15 of Statement 115, provided that those available-for-sale securities are identified in some manner as offsetting the entity's exposure to changes in fair value of servicing assets or servicing liabilities that a servicer elects to subsequently measure at fair value. This option is available only once, as of the beginning of the fiscal year in which the entity adopts this Statement. Any gains and losses associated with the reclassified securities that are included in accumulated other comprehensive income at the time of the reclassification should be reported as a cumulative-effect adjustment to retained earnings as of the beginning of the fiscal year that an entity adopts this Statement. The carrying amount of reclassified securities and the effect of that reclassification on the cumulative-effect adjustment should be separately disclosed.

Statement of Financial Accounting Standards No. 156

Accounting for Servicing of Financial Assets

an amendment of FASB Statement No. 140

CONTENTS

OBJECTIVE

1. FASB Statement No. 140, *Accounting for Transfers and Servicing of Financial Assets and Extinguishments of Liabilities,* establishes, among other things, the accounting for all separately recognized servicing assets and servicing liabilities. This Statement amends Statement 140 to require that all separately recognized servicing assets and servicing liabilities be initially measured at fair value, if practicable. This Statement permits, but does not require, the subsequent measurement of separately recognized servicing assets and servicing liabilities at fair value. An entity that uses derivative instruments to mitigate the risks inherent in servicing assets and servicing liabilities is required to account for those derivative instruments at fair value. Under this Statement, an entity can elect subsequent fair value measurement to account for its separately recognized servicing assets and servicing liabilities. By electing that option, an entity may simplify its accounting because this Statement permits income statement recognition of the potential offsetting changes in fair value of those servicing assets and servicing liabilities and derivative instruments in the same accounting period.

STANDARDS OF FINANCIAL ACCOUNTING AND REPORTING

Scope

2. An entity shall apply this Statement to all separately recognized servicing assets and servicing liabilities. This Statement requires that an entity separately recognize a servicing asset or servicing liability when it undertakes an obligation to service a financial asset by entering into a servicing contract in connection with any of the following situations:

a. A transfer of the servicer's financial assets that meets the requirements for sale accounting

b. A transfer of the servicer's financial assets to a qualifying special-purpose entity in a guaranteed mortgage securitization in which the transferor retains all of the resulting securities and classifies them as either available-for-sale securities or trading securities in accordance with FASB Statement No. 115, *Accounting for Certain Investments in Debt and Equity Securities*

c. An acquisition or assumption of an obligation to service a financial asset that does not relate to financial assets of the servicer or its consolidated affiliates.

An entity that transfers its financial assets to a qualifying special-purpose entity in a guaranteed mortgage securitization in which the transferor retains all of the resulting securities and classifies them as debt securities held-to-maturity in accordance with Statement 115 may either separately recognize its servicing assets or servicing liabilities or report those servicing assets or servicing liabilities together with the asset being serviced.

Key Terms

3. The following terms are used with the same meanings as in paragraph 364 of Statement 140 and are integral to understanding and applying this Statement.

a. **Adequate compensation**
   The amount of benefits of servicing that would fairly compensate a substitute servicer should one be required, which includes the profit that would be demanded in the marketplace.

b. **Contractually specified servicing fees**
   All amounts that, per contract, are due to the servicer in exchange for servicing the financial asset and would no longer be received by a servicer if the beneficial owners of the serviced assets (or their trustees or agents) were to exercise their actual or potential authority under the contract to shift the servicing to another servicer. Depending on the servicing contract, those fees may include some or all of the difference between the interest rate collectible on the asset being serviced and the rate to be paid to the beneficial owners of those assets.

c. [This subparagraph has been deleted. See Status page.]

d. **Financial asset**
   Cash, evidence of an ownership interest in an entity, or a contract that conveys to a second entity a contractual right (1) to receive cash or another financial instrument from a first entity or (2) to exchange other financial instruments on potentially favorable terms with the first entity (Statement 107, paragraph 3(b)).

e. **Guaranteed mortgage securitization**
   A securitization of mortgage loans that is within the scope of FASB Statement No. 65, *Accounting for Certain Mortgage Banking Activities,* as amended, and includes a substantive guarantee by a third party.

f. **Interest-only strip**
   A contractual right to receive some or all of the interest due on a bond, mortgage loan, collateralized mortgage obligation, or other interest-bearing financial asset.

g. **Proceeds**
   Cash, derivatives, or other assets that are obtained in a transfer of financial assets, less any liabilities incurred.

h. **Securitization**
   The process by which financial assets are transformed into securities.

i. **Seller**
   A transferor that relinquishes control over financial assets by transferring them to a transferee in exchange for consideration.

j. **Servicing asset**
   A contract to service financial assets under which the estimated future revenues from contractually specified servicing fees, late charges, and other ancillary revenues are expected to more than adequately compensate the servicer for performing the servicing. A servicing contract is either (1) undertaken in conjunction with selling or securitizing the financial assets being serviced or (2) purchased or assumed separately.

k. **Servicing liability**
   A contract to service financial assets under which the estimated future revenues from contractually specified servicing fees, late charges, and other ancillary revenues are not

expected to adequately compensate the servicer for performing the servicing.

l. **Transfer**

The conveyance of a noncash financial asset by and to someone other than the issuer of that financial asset. Thus, a transfer includes selling a receivable, putting it into a securitization trust, or posting it as collateral but excludes the origination of that receivable, the settlement of that receivable, or the restructuring of that receivable into a security in a troubled debt restructuring.

m. **Undivided interest**

Partial legal or beneficial ownership of an asset as a tenant in common with others. The proportion owned may be pro rata, for example, the right to receive 50 percent of all cash flows from a security, or non–pro rata, for example, the right to receive the interest from a security while another has the right to the principal.

Amendments to Statement 140

4. Statement 140 is amended as follows: [Added text is underlined and deleted text is struck out.]

a. Paragraph 4, as amended:

This Statement does not address transfers of custody of financial assets for safekeeping, contributions,[2] transfers of ownership interests that are in substance sales of real estate, or investments by owners or distributions to owners of a business enterprise. This Statement does not address subsequent measurement of assets and liabilities, except for (a) **servicing assets** and **servicing liabilities** and (b) **interest-only strips,** securities, retained interests that continue to be held by a transferor in securitizations, loans, other receivables, or other financial assets that can contractually be prepaid or otherwise settled in such a way that the holder would not recover substantially all of its recorded investment and that are not within the scope of FASB Statement No. 133, *Accounting for Derivative Instruments and Hedging Activities.* This Statement does not change the accounting for employee benefits subject to the provisions of FASB Statement No. 87, *Employers' Accounting for Pensions,* No. 88, *Employers' Accounting for Settlements and Curtailments of Defined Benefit Pension*

Plans and for Termination Benefits, or No. 106, *Employers' Accounting for Postretirement Benefits Other Than Pensions.* This Statement does not change the provisions relating to leveraged leases in FASB Statement No. 13, *Accounting for Leases,* or money-over-money and wrap lease transactions involving nonrecourse debt subject to the provisions of FASB Technical Bulletin No. 88-1, *Issues Relating to Accounting for Leases.* This Statement does not address transfers of nonfinancial assets, for example, servicing assets, or transfers of unrecognized financial assets, for example, minimum lease payments to be received under operating leases.

b. Paragraph 5:

The Board concluded that an objective in accounting for transfers of financial assets is for each entity that is a party to the transaction to recognize only assets it controls and liabilities it has incurred, to **derecognize** assets only when control has been surrendered, and to derecognize liabilities only when they have been extinguished. Sales and other transfers frequently result in a disaggregation of financial assets and liabilities into components, which become separate assets and liabilities. For example, if an entity sells a portion of a financial asset it owns, the portion retainedthat continues to be held by a transferor becomes an asset separate from the portion sold and from the assets obtained in exchange.

c. Paragraph 10:

Upon completion of any transfer of financial assets, the transferor shall:

a. Continue to carry in its statement of financial position any retained interest in the transferred assets, including, if applicable, servicing assets (paragraphs 61-67), beneficial interests in assets transferred to a qualifying SPE in a **securitization** (paragraphs 73–84), and retained **undivided interests** (paragraphs 58 and 59)

a. Initially recognize and measure at **fair value,** if practicable (paragraph 71), servicing assets and servicing liabilities that require recognition under the provisions of paragraph 13

b. Allocate the previous carrying amount between the assets sold, if any, and the retained interests that continue to be held by the transferor, if any, based on their relative fair values at the date of transfer (paragraphs 56–60).

c. Continue to carry in its statement of financial position any interest it continues to hold in the transferred assets, including, if applicable, beneficial interests in assets transferred to a qualifying SPE in a **securitization** (paragraphs 73–84), and any **undivided interests** (paragraphs 58 and 59).

d. Paragraph 11:

Upon completion[3] of a transfer of financial assets that satisfies the conditions to be accounted for as a sale (paragraph 9), the transferor (**seller**) shall:

a. Derecognize all assets sold

b. Recognize all assets obtained and liabilities incurred in consideration as **proceeds** of the sale, including cash, put or call options held or written (for example, guarantee or recourse obligations), forward commitments (for example, commitments to deliver additional receivables during the revolving periods of some securitizations), swaps (for example, provisions that convert interest rates from fixed to variable), and servicing assets and servicing liabilities, if applicable (paragraphs 56, 57, and 61–67)

c. Initially measure at fair value assets obtained and liabilities incurred in a sale (paragraphs 68–70) or, if it is not practicable to estimate the fair value of an asset or a liability, apply alternative measures (paragraphs 71 and 72)

d. Recognize in earnings any gain or loss on the sale.

The transferee shall recognize all assets obtained and any liabilities incurred and initially measure them at fair value (in aggregate, presumptively the price paid).

e. Paragraph 13:

~~Each time an entity undertakes an obligation to service financial assets it shall recognize either a servicing asset or a servicing liability for that servicing contract, unless it transfers the assets~~ ~~to a qualifying SPE in a **guaranteed mortgage securitization,** retains all of the resulting securities, and classifies them as debt securities held-to-maturity in accordance with FASB Statement No. 115, *Accounting for Certain Investments in Debt and Equity Securities.* If the servicing asset or liability was purchased or assumed rather than undertaken in a sale or securitization of the financial assets being serviced, it shall be measured initially at its fair value, presumptively the price paid. A servicing asset or liability shall be amortized in proportion to and over the period of estimated net servicing income (if servicing revenues exceed servicing costs) or net servicing loss (if servicing costs exceed servicing revenues). A servicing asset or liability shall be assessed for impairment or increased obligation based on its fair value (paragraphs 61–64).~~

An entity shall recognize and initially measure at fair value, if practicable, a servicing asset or servicing liability each time it undertakes an obligation to service a financial asset by entering into a servicing contract in any of the following situations:

a. A transfer of the servicer's financial assets that meets the requirements for sale accounting

b. A transfer of the servicer's financial assets to a qualifying SPE in a **guaranteed mortgage securitization** in which the transferor retains all of the resulting securities and classifies them as either available-for-sale securities or trading securities in accordance with FASB Statement No. 115, *Accounting for Certain Investments in Debt and Equity Securities*

c. An acquisition or assumption of a servicing obligation that does not relate to financial assets of the servicer or its consolidated affiliates.

An entity that transfers its financial assets to a qualifying SPE in a guaranteed mortgage securitization in which the transferor retains all of the resulting securities and classifies them as debt securities held-to-maturity in accordance with Statement 115 may either separately recognize its servicing assets or servicing liabilities or report those servicing assets or servicing liabilities together with the asset being serviced.

f. Paragraphs 13A and 13B are added as follows:

13A. An entity shall subsequently measure each class of servicing assets and servicing liabilities using one of the following methods:

a. *Amortization method:* Amortize servicing assets or servicing liabilities in proportion to and over the period of estimated net servicing income (if servicing revenues exceed servicing costs) or net servicing loss (if servicing costs exceed servicing revenues), and assess servicing assets or servicing liabilities for impairment or increased obligation based on fair value at each reporting date

b. *Fair value measurement method:* Measure servicing assets or servicing liabilities at fair value at each reporting date and report changes in fair value of servicing assets and servicing liabilities in earnings in the period in which the changes occur.

The election described in this paragraph shall be made separately for each class of servicing assets and servicing liabilities. An entity shall apply the same subsequent measurement method to each servicing asset and servicing liability in a class. Classes of servicing assets and servicing liabilities shall be identified based on (a) the availability of market inputs used in determining the fair value of servicing assets or servicing liabilities, (b) an entity's method for managing the risks of its servicing assets or servicing liabilities, or (c) both. Once an entity elects the fair value measurement method for a class of servicing assets and servicing liabilities, that election shall not be reversed (paragraph 63). If it is not practicable to initially measure a servicing asset or servicing liability at fair value, an entity shall initially recognize the servicing asset or servicing liability in accordance with paragraph 71 and shall include it in a class subsequently measured using the amortization method.

13B. An entity shall report recognized servicing assets and servicing liabilities that are subsequently measured using the fair value measurement method in a manner that separates those carrying amounts on the face of the statement of financial position from the carrying amounts for separately recognized servicing assets and servicing liabilities that are subsequently measured using the amortization method. To accomplish that separate reporting, an entity may either (a) display separate line items for the amounts that are subsequently measured using the fair value measurement method and amounts that are subsequently measured using the amortization method or (b) present the aggregate of those amounts that are subsequently measured at fair value and those amounts that are subsequently measured using the amortization method (paragraph 63) and disclose parenthetically the amount that is subsequently measured at fair value that is included in the aggregate amount.

g. Paragraph 14:

Interest-only strips, ~~other~~retained interests that continue to be held by a transferor in securitizations, loans, other receivables, or other financial assets that can contractually be prepaid or otherwise settled in such a way that the holder would not recover substantially all of its recorded investment, except for instruments that are within the scope of Statement 133, shall be subsequently measured like investments in debt securities classified as available-for-sale or trading under Statement 115, as amended (paragraph 362).

h. Paragraph 17:

An entity shall disclose the following:

a. For collateral:

(1) If the entity has entered into repurchase agreements or securities lending transactions, its policy for requiring collateral or other security

(2) If the entity has pledged any of its assets as collateral that are not reclassified and separately reported in the statement of financial position pursuant to paragraph 15(a), the carrying amount and classification of those assets as of the date of the latest statement of financial position presented

(3) If the entity has accepted collateral that it is permitted by contract or custom to sell or repledge, the fair value as of the date of each statement of financial position presented of that collateral and of the portion of that collateral that it has sold or repledged, and information about the sources and uses of that collateral.

b. If debt was considered to be extinguished by in-substance defeasance under the provisions of FASB Statement No. 76, *Extinguishment of Debt,* prior to the effective date of Statement 125,[6] a general description of the transaction and the amount of debt that is considered extinguished at the end of the period so long as that debt remains outstanding.

c. If assets are set aside after the effective date of Statement 125 solely for satisfying scheduled payments of a specific obligation, a description of the nature of restrictions placed on those assets.

d. If it is not practicable to estimate the fair value of certain assets obtained or liabilities incurred in transfers of financial assets during the period, a description of those items and the reasons why it is not practicable to estimate their fair value.

e. ~~For all servicing assets and servicing liabilities:~~
  ~~(1) The amounts of servicing assets or liabilities recognized and amortized during the period~~
  ~~(2) The fair value of recognized servicing assets and liabilities for which it is practicable to estimate that value and the method and significant assumptions used to estimate the fair value~~
  ~~(3) The risk characteristics of the underlying financial assets used to stratify recognized servicing assets for purposes of measuring impairment in accordance with paragraph 63~~
  ~~(4) The activity in any valuation allowance for impairment of recognized servicing assets—including beginning and ending balances, aggregate additions charged and reductions credited to operations, and aggregate direct write-downs charged against the allowances—for each period for which results of operations are presented.~~

e. For all servicing assets and servicing liabilities:
  (1) Management's basis for determining its classes of servicing assets and servicing liabilities (paragraph 13A).
  (2) A description of the risks inherent in servicing assets and servicing liabilities and, if applicable, the instruments used to mitigate the income statement effect of changes in fair value of the servicing assets and servicing liabilities. (Disclosure of quantitative information about the instruments used to manage the risks inherent in servicing assets and servicing liabilities, including the fair value of those instruments at the beginning and end of the period, is encouraged but not required.)
  (3) The amount of contractually specified servicing fees (as defined in the glossary), late fees, and ancillary fees earned for each period for which results of operations are presented, including a description of where each amount is reported in the statement of income.

f. For servicing assets and servicing liabilities subsequently measured at fair value:
  (1) For each class of servicing assets and servicing liabilities, the activity in the balance of servicing assets and the activity in the balance of servicing liabilities (including a description of where changes in fair value are reported in the statement of income for each period for which results of operations are presented), including, but not limited to, the following:
    (a) The beginning and ending balances
    (b) Additions (through purchases of servicing assets, assumptions of servicing obligations, and servicing obligations that result from transfers of financial assets)
    (c) Disposals
    (d) Changes in fair value during the period resulting from:
      (i) Changes in valuation inputs or assumptions used in the valuation model
      (ii) Other changes in fair value and a description of those changes
    (e) Other changes that affect the balance and a description of those changes
  (2) A description of the valuation techniques or other methods used to estimate the fair value of servicing assets

and servicing liabilities. If a valuation model is used, the description shall include the methodology and model validation procedures, as well as quantitative and qualitative information about the assumptions used in the valuation model (for example, discount rates and prepayment speeds). (An entity that provides quantitative information about the instruments used to manage the risks inherent in the servicing assets and servicing liabilities, as encouraged by paragraph 17(e)(2), is also encouraged, but not required, to disclose a description of the valuation techniques, as well as quantitative and qualitative information about the assumptions used to estimate the fair value of those instruments.)

g. For servicing assets and servicing liabilities subsequently amortized in proportion to and over the period of estimated net servicing income or loss and assessed for impairment or increased obligation:

(1) For each class of servicing assets and servicing liabilities, the activity in the balance of servicing assets and the activity in the balance of servicing liabilities (including a description of where changes in the carrying amount are reported in the statement of income for each period for which results of operations are presented), including, but not limited to, the following:

  (a) The beginning and ending balances

  (b) Additions (through purchases of servicing assets, assumption of servicing obligations, and servicing obligations that result from transfers of financial assets)

  (c) Disposals

  (d) Amortization

  (e) Application of valuation allowance to adjust carrying value of servicing assets

  (f) Other-than-temporary impairments

  (g) Other changes that affect the balance and a description of those changes.

(2) For each class of servicing assets and servicing liabilities, the fair value of recognized servicing assets and servicing liabilities at the beginning and

end of the period if it is practicable to estimate the value.

(3) A description of the valuation techniques or other methods used to estimate fair value of the servicing assets and servicing liabilities. If a valuation model is used, the description shall include the methodology and model validation procedures, as well as quantitative and qualitative information about the assumptions used in the valuation model (for example, discount rates and prepayment speeds). (An entity that provides quantitative information about the instruments used to manage the risks inherent in the servicing assets and servicing liabilities, as encouraged by paragraph 17(e)(2), is also encouraged, but not required, to disclose a description of the valuation techniques as well as quantitative and qualitative information about the assumptions used to estimate the fair value of those instruments.)

(4) The risk characteristics of the underlying financial assets used to stratify recognized servicing assets for purposes of measuring impairment in accordance with paragraph 63.

(5) The activity by class in any valuation allowance for impairment of recognized servicing assets—including beginning and ending balances, aggregate additions charged and recoveries credited to operations, and aggregate write-downs charged against the allowance—for each period for which results of operations are presented.

hf. If the entity has securitized financial assets during any period presented and accounts for that transfer as a sale, for each major asset type (for example, mortgage loans, credit card receivables, and automobile loans):

(1) Its accounting policies for initially measuring the retained interests that continue to be held by the transferor, if any, and servicing assets or servicing liabilities, if any, including the methodology (whether quoted market price, prices based on sales of similar assets and liabilities, or prices based on valuation techniques) used in determining their fair value (paragraphs 68–70)

(2)　The characteristics of securitizations (a description of the transferor's continuing involvement with the transferred assets, including, but not limited to, servicing, recourse, and restrictions on ~~retained~~ interests that continue to be held by the transferor) and the gain or loss from sale of financial assets in securitizations

(3)　The key assumptions[7] used in measuring the fair value of ~~retained~~ interests that continue to be held by the transferor and servicing assets or servicing liabilities, if any, at the time of securitization (including, at a minimum, quantitative information about discount rates, expected prepayments including the expected weighted-average life of prepayable financial assets,[8] and anticipated credit losses, if applicable)

(4)　Cash flows between the securitization SPE and the transferor, unless reported separately elsewhere in the financial statements or notes (including proceeds from new securitizations, proceeds from collections reinvested in revolving-period securitizations, purchases of delinquent or foreclosed loans, servicing fees, and cash flows received on interests that continue to be held by the transferor~~retained~~).

ig.　If the entity has ~~retained~~ interests that continue to be held by the transferor in ~~securitized~~ financial assets that it has securitized or servicing assets or servicing liabilities relating to assets that it has securitized, at the date of the latest statement of financial position presented, for each major asset type (for example, mortgage loans, credit card receivables, and automobile loans):

(1)　Its accounting policies for subsequently measuring those ~~retained~~ interests, including the methodology (whether quoted market price, prices based on sales of similar assets and liabilities, or prices based on valuation techniques) used in determining their fair value (paragraphs 68–70)

(2)　The key assumptions used in subsequently measuring the fair value of those interests (including, at a minimum, quantitative information about discount rates, expected prepayments

including the expected weighted-average life of prepayable financial assets, and anticipated credit losses, including expected static pool losses,[9] if applicable)

(3)　A sensitivity analysis or stress test showing the hypothetical effect on the fair value of those interests (including any servicing assets or servicing liabilities) of two or more unfavorable variations from the expected levels for each key assumption that is reported under (2) above independently from any change in another key assumption, and a description of the objectives, methodology, and limitations of the sensitivity analysis or stress test

(4)　For the securitized assets and any other financial assets that it manages together with them:[10]

(a)　The total principal amount outstanding, the portion that has been derecognized, and the portion that continues to be recognized in each category reported in the statement of financial position, at the end of the period

(b)　Delinquencies at the end of the period

(c)　Credit losses, net of recoveries, during the period.

(Disclosure of average balances during the period is encouraged, but not required.)

i.　Footnote 17 to paragraph 36:

An effect of that provision, in conjunction with paragraph 46, is that mortgage-backed securities ~~retained~~ that continue to be held by a transferor in a guaranteed mortgage securitization in which the SPE meets all conditions for being a qualifying SPE are classified in the financial statements of the transferor as securities that are subsequently measured under Statement 115.

j.　Paragraph 56:

The proceeds from a sale of financial assets consist of the cash and any other assets obtained, including separately recognized servicing assets, in the transfer less any liabilities incurred, including separately recognized servicing liabilities. Any asset obtained that is not an interest in the transferred asset is part of the proceeds from the sale. Any liability incurred, even if it is related to the transferred assets, is a reduction of the proceeds. Any derivative financial instrument entered into concurrently with a transfer of financial assets is either an asset obtained or a liability incurred and part of the proceeds received in the transfer. All proceeds and reductions of proceeds from a sale shall be initially measured at fair value, if practicable.

k. Paragraph 57:

Company A sells loans with a fair value of $1,100 and a carrying amount of $1,000. Company A retainsundertakes no servicing responsibilities but obtains an option to purchase from the transferee loans similar to the loans sold (which are readily obtainable in the marketplace) and assumes a limited recourse obligation to repurchase delinquent loans. Company A agrees to provide the transferee a return at a floating rate of interest even though the contractual terms of the loan are fixed rate in nature (that provision is effectively an interest rate swap).

Note: The table in this illustration is not reproduced here because there are no changes to that portion of this paragraph.

l. Paragraph 58 and the heading preceding it:

Retained-Interests That Continue to Be Held by a Transferor

Other interests in transferred assets—those that are not part of the proceeds of a transfer—are retained-interests that continue to be held by a transferor over which a transferor has not relinquished control. Interests that continue to be held by a transferorThey shall be measured at the date of the transfer by allocating the previous carrying amount between the assets sold, if any, and the retained-interests that continue to be held by a transferor, based on their relative fair values. Allocation procedures shall be applied to all

transfers in which interests arecontinue to be held by a transferor-retained, even those that do not qualify as sales. Examples of retained-interests that continue to be held by a transferor include securities backed by the transferred assets, undivided interests, servicing assets, and cash reserve accounts and residual interests in securitization trusts. If a transferor cannot determine whether an asset is an retained-interest that continues to be held by a transferor or proceeds from the sale, the asset shall be treated as proceeds from the sale and accounted for in accordance with paragraph 56.

m. Paragraph 59:

If the retained-interests that continue to be held by a transferor are subordinated to more senior interests held by others, that subordination may concentrate most of the risks inherent in the transferred assets into the retained-interests that continue to be held by a transferormost of the risks inherent in the transferred assets and shall be taken into consideration in estimating the fair value of thosethe retained interests. For example, if the amount of the gain recognized, after allocation, on a securitization with a subordinated retained-interest that continues to be held by the transferor is greater than the gain that would have been recognized had the entire asset been sold, the transferor needs to be able to identify why that can occur. Otherwise, it is likely that the effectimpact of subordinationthe retained interest being subordinate to a senior interest has not been adequately considered in the determination of the fair value of the subordinated retained-interest that continues to be held by a transferor.

n. Paragraph 60:

Company B sells a pro rata nine-tenths interest in loans with a fair value of $1,100 and a carrying amount of $1,000. There is no servicing asset or liability, because Company B estimates that the **benefits of servicing** are just adequate to compensate it for its servicing responsibilities.

Fair Values

Cash proceeds for nine-tenths interest sold	$990
One-tenth interest ~~retained~~that continues to be held by the transferor [($990 ÷ 9/10) × 1/10]	110

Carrying Amount Based on Relative Fair Values

	Fair Value	Percentage of Total Fair Value	Allocated Carrying Amount
Nine-tenths interest sold	$ 990	90	$ 900
One-tenth interest ~~retained~~that continues to be held by the transferor	110	10	100
Total	$1,100	100	$1,000

Gain on Sale

Net proceeds	$990
Carrying amount of loans sold	900
Gain on sale	$ 90

Journal Entry

Cash	990	
Loans		900
Gain on sale		90
To record transfer		

o. Paragraph 61:

Servicing of mortgage loans, credit card receivables, or other financial assets commonly includes, but is not limited to, collecting principal, interest, and escrow payments from borrowers; paying taxes and insurance from escrowed funds; monitoring delinquencies; executing foreclosure if necessary; temporarily investing funds pending distribution; remitting fees to guarantors, trustees, and others providing services; and accounting for and remitting principal and interest payments to the holders of beneficial interests in the financial assets. Servicing is inherent in all financial assets; it becomes a distinct asset or liability ~~only when contractually separated from the underlying assets by sale or securitization of the assets with servicing re~~tained or separate purchase or assumption of the servicingfor accounting purposes only in the circumstances described in paragraph 62.

p. Paragraph 62:

An entity that undertakes a contract to service financial assets shall recognize either a servicing asset or a servicing liability each time it undertakes an obligation to service a financial asset that (a) results from a transfer of the servicer's financial assets that meets the requirements for sale accounting, (b) results from a transfer of the servicer's financial assets to a qualifying SPE in a guaranteed mortgage securitization in which the transferor retains all of the resulting securities and classifies them as either available-for-sale securities or trading securities in accordance with Statement 115, or (c) is acquired or assumed and the servicing obligation does not relate to financial assets of the servicer or its consolidated affiliates.~~, with only one exception.~~ ~~(That exception is~~ However, if the transferor transfers the assets in a guaranteed mortgage securitization, retains all of the resulting securities, and classifies them as debt securities held-to-maturity in accordance with Statement 115, ~~in which case~~ the servicing asset or servicing liability may be reported together with the asset being serviced and not recognized separately.~~)~~ ~~Each sale or securitization with servicing retained or separate purchase or assumption of servicing results in a servicing contract.~~ A servicer of financial assets commonly receives the benefits of servicing—revenues from contractually specified servicing fees, a portion of the interest from the financial assets, late charges, and other ancillary sources, including "float," all of which it is entitled to receive only if it performs the servicing—and incurs the costs of servicing the assets. ~~Each servicing contract results in a servicing asset or servicing liability.~~ Typically, the benefits of servicing are expected to be more than **adequate compensation** to a servicer for performing the servicing, and the contract results in a servicing asset. However, if the benefits of servicing are not expected to adequately compensate a servicer for performing the servicing, the contract results in a servicing liability. (A servicing asset may become a servicing liability, or vice versa, if circumstances change, and the initial measure for servicing may be zero if the benefits of servicing are just adequate to compensate the servicer for its servicing responsibilities.) A servicer would account for its servicing contract that qualifies for separate recognition as a servicing asset or a servicing liability initially measured at its fair value regardless of whether explicit consideration was exchanged.

q. Paragraph 62A is added as follows:

62A. A servicer that transfers or securitizes financial assets in a transaction that does not meet the requirements for sale accounting and is accounted for as a secured borrowing with the underlying assets remaining on the transferor's balance sheet shall not recognize a servicing asset or a servicing liability. However, if a transferor enters into a servicing contract when the transferor transfers mortgage loans in a guaranteed mortgage securitization, retains all the resulting

securities, and classifies those securities as either available-for-sale securities or trading securities in accordance with Statement 115, the transferor shall separately recognize a servicing asset or a servicing liability.

r. Paragraph 63:

A servicer that recognizes a servicing asset or servicing liability shall account for the contract to service financial assets separately from those financial assets, as follows:

a. Report servicing assets separately from servicing liabilities in the statement of financial position (paragraph 13B).

b. Initially measure servicing assets and servicing liabilities~~retained in a sale or securitization of the assets being serviced~~ at fair value~~their allocated previous carrying amount based on relative fair values~~, if practicable~~, at the date of the sale or securitization~~ (paragraphs 10, 11(b), 11(c), ~~58–60,~~ and 68–72).

~~c. Initially measure servicing assets purchased or servicing liabilities assumed at fair value (paragraph 13).~~

~~d. Initially measure servicing liabilities undertaken in a sale or securitization at fair value, if practicable (paragraphs 11(b), 11(c), and 68–72).~~

ce. Account separately for rights to future interest income from the serviced assets that exceed~~s~~ contractually specified servicing fees. Those rights are not servicing assets; they are financial assets, effectively interest-only strips to be accounted for in accordance with paragraph 14 of this Statement.

d. Identify classes of servicing assets and servicing liabilities based on (1) the availability of market inputs used in determining the fair value of servicing assets and servicing liabilities, (2) an entity's method for managing the risks of its servicing assets and servicing liabilities, or (3) both.

ef. Subsequently measure each class of separately recognized servicing assets and servicing liabilities either at fair value or by amortizing the amount recognized in proportion to and over the period of estimated net servicing income for assets—(the excess of servicing revenues over servicing costs) or the period of estimated net servicing loss for servicing liabilities (the excess of servicing costs over servicing revenues). Different elections can be made for different classes of servicing assets and servicing liabilities. An entity may make an irrevocable decision to subsequently measure a class of servicing assets and servicing liabilities at fair value at the beginning of any fiscal year. Once a servicing asset or a servicing liability is reported in a class of servicing assets and servicing liabilities that an entity elects to subsequently measure at fair value, that servicing asset or servicing liability cannot be placed in a class of servicing assets and servicing liabilities that is subsequently measured using the amortization method. Changes in fair value should be reported in earnings for servicing assets and servicing liabilities subsequently measured at fair value (paragraph 13A(b)).

f̲g̲. Subsequently evaluate and measure impairment of each class of separately recognized servicing assets that are subsequently measured using the amortization method described in paragraph 13A(a) as follows:

(1) Stratify servicing assets within a class based on one or more of the predominant risk characteristics of the underlying financial assets. Those characteristics may include financial asset type,[19] size, interest rate, date of origination, term, and geographic location.

(2) Recognize impairment through a valuation allowance for an individual stratum. The amount of impairment recognized separately shall be the amount by which the carrying amount of servicing assets for a stratum exceeds their fair value. The fair value of servicing assets that have not been recognized shall not be used in the evaluation of impairment.

(3) Adjust the valuation allowance to reflect changes in the measurement of impairment subsequent to the initial measurement of impairment. Fair value in excess of the carrying amount of servicing assets for that stratum, however, shall not be recognized. This Statement does not address when an entity should record a direct write-down of recognized servicing assets (paragraph 13).

g̲h̲. ~~Subsequently measure servicing liabilities by amortizing the amount recognized in proportion to and over the period of estimated net servicing loss—the excess of servicing costs over servicing revenues. However,~~ For servicing liabilities subsequently measured using the amortization method, if subsequent events have increased the fair value of the liability above the carrying amount, for example, because of significant changes in the amount or timing of actual or expected future cash flows ~~from~~ relative to the cash flows previously projected, the servicer shall revise its earlier estimates and recognize the increased obligation as a loss in earnings (paragraph 13).

s. Paragraph 65 and the heading preceding it:

Illustration—Sale of Receivables with Servicing ~~Retained~~Obtained

Company C originates $1,000 of loans that yield 10 percent interest income for their estimated lives of 9 years. Company C sells the $1,000 principal plus the right to receive interest income of 8 percent to another entity for $1,000. Company C will continue to service the loans, and the contract stipulates that its compensation for performing the servicing is the right to receive half of the interest income not sold. The remaining half of the interest income not sold is considered an interest-only strip receivable that Company C classifies as an available-for-sale security. At the date of the transfer, the fair value of the loans~~, including servicing,~~ is $1,100. The fair values of the servicing asset and the interest-only strip receivable are̶i̶s̶ $40 and $60, respectively.

Fair Values

Cash proceeds	$1,000
Servicing asset	40
Interest-only strip receivable	60

Net Proceeds

Cash proceeds	$1,000
Servicing asset	40
Net proceeds	$1,040

Carrying Amount Based on Relative Fair Values

	Fair Value	Percentage of Total Fair Value	Allocated Carrying Amount
Loans sold	$1,000	91.0	$ 910
Servicing asset	40	3.6	36
Interest-only strip receivable	60	5.4	54
Total	$1,100	100.0	$1,000

	Fair Value	Percentage of Total Fair Value	Allocated Carrying Amount
Loans sold	$1,040	94.55	$ 945.50
Interest-only strip receivable	60	5.45	54.50
Total	$1,100	100.00	$1,000.00

Gain on Sale

Net proceeds	$1,040.00 ~~1,000~~
Less: Carrying amount of loans sold	945.50 ~~910~~
Gain on sale	$ 94.50 ~~90~~

Journal Entries

Cash	1,000.00	
Interest-only strip receivable	54.50	
Servicing asset	40.00	
Loans		1,000.00~~910~~
Gain on sale		94.50~~90~~

To record transfer and to recognize
interest-only strip receivable and
servicing asset

~~Servicing asset~~	~~36~~	
~~Interest-only strip receivable~~	~~54~~	
~~Loans~~		~~90~~

~~To record servicing asset and
interest-only strip receivable~~

Interest-only strip receivable	5.506	
~~Equity~~Other comprehensive income		5.506

To begin to subsequently measure
interest-only strip receivable like an
available-for-sale security (paragraph 14)

---

t. Paragraph 66:

The previous illustration demonstrates how a transferor would account for a simple sale ~~or securitization~~ in which servicing is ~~retained~~obtained. Company C might instead transfer the financial assets to a corporation or a trust that is a qualifying SPE. The qualifying SPE then securitizes the loans by selling beneficial interests to the public. The qualifying SPE pays the cash proceeds to the original transferor, which accounts for the transfer as a sale and derecognizes the financial assets assuming that the criteria in paragraph 9 are met. Securitizations often combine the elements shown in paragraphs 57, 60, and 65, as illustrated below.

u. Paragraph 67:

Company D originates $1,000 of prepayable loans that yield 10 percent interest income for their 9-year expected lives. Company D sells nine-tenths of the principal plus interest of 8 percent to another entity. Company D will continue to service the loans, and the contract stipulates that its compensation for performing the servicing is the 2 percent of the interest income not sold. Company D obtains an option to purchase from the transferee loans similar to the loans sold (which are readily obtainable in the marketplace) and incurs a limited recourse obligation to repurchase delinquent loans. At the date of transfer, the fair value of the loans is $1,100.

Fair Values

Cash proceeds	$900
Call option	70
Recourse obligation	(60)
Servicing asset	90
One-tenth interest ~~retained~~that continues to be held by the transferor	100

Net Proceeds

Cash received	$ 900
Plus: Servicing asset	90
Plus: Call option	70
Less: Recourse obligation	(60)
Net proceeds	$1,000~~910~~

Carrying Amount Based on Relative Fair Values

	Fair Value	~~Percentage of Total Fair Value~~	~~Allocated Carrying Amount~~
~~Interest sold~~	~~$ 910~~	~~83~~	~~$ 830~~
~~Servicing asset~~	~~90~~	~~8~~	~~80~~
~~One-tenth interest retained~~	~~100~~	~~9~~	~~90~~
~~Total~~	~~$1,100~~	~~100~~	~~$1,000~~

	Fair Value	Percentage of Total Fair Value	Allocated Carrying Amount
Interest sold	$1,000	90.9	$ 909
One-tenth interest that continues to be held by the transferor	100	9.1	91
Total	$1,100	100.0	$1,000

Gain on Sale

Net proceeds	$1,000 ~~910~~
Less: Carrying amount of loans sold	(909) ~~830~~
Gain on sale	$ 91 ~~80~~

Loans Sold

Carrying amount of loans	$1,000
Less: Allocated carrying amount of interest that continues to be held by the transferor	(91)
Loans sold	$ 909

Journal Entries

Cash	900	
Call option	70	
Servicing asset	90	
Loans		909 ~~830~~
Recourse obligation		60
Gain on sale		91 ~~80~~
To record transfer and to recognize servicing asset, call option, and recourse obligation		

~~Servicing asset~~	~~80~~	
~~Loans~~		~~80~~
~~To record servicing asset~~		

~~At the time of the transfer, Company D reports its one-tenth retained interest in the loans at its allocated carrying amount of $90.~~

v. Footnotes 20 and 21 to paragraph 69:

[20]FASB Concepts Statement No. 7, *Using Cash Flow Information and Present Value in Accounting Measurements,* discusses the use of present value techniques in measuring the fair value of an asset (or liability) in paragraphs 42–54 and 75–88. The Board believes that an expected present value technique is superior to traditional "best estimate" techniques, especially in situations in which the timing or amount of estimated cash flows is uncertain, as is often the case for ~~retained~~ interests that continue to be held by a transferor in transferred financial assets. Concepts Statement 7 also discusses in paragraph 44 the steps needed to complete a proper search for the "rate commensurate with the risk" in applying the traditional technique.

[21]The timing and amount of future cash flows for ~~retained~~ interests in securitizations that continue to be held by a transferor are commonly uncertain, especially if those interests are subordinate to more senior beneficial interests. Applying the present value approach depends heavily on assumptions about default and prepayment of all the assets securitized, because of the implicit credit or prepayment risk enhancement arising from the subordination.

w. Paragraph 72:

Company E sells loans with a carrying amount of $1,000 to another entity for cash proceeds of $1,050 plus a call option to purchase loans similar to the loans sold (which are readily obtainable in the marketplace) and incurs a limited recourse obligation to repurchase any delinquent loans. Company E undertakes an obligation to service the transferred assets for the other entity. In Case 1, Company E finds it impracticable to estimate the fair value of the servicing contract, although it is confident that servicing revenues will be more than adequate compensation for performing the servicing. In Case 2, Company E finds it impracticable to estimate the fair value of the recourse obligation.

Fair Values	Case1	Case2
Cash proceeds	$1,050	$1,050
Servicing asset	XX*	40
Call option	70	70
Recourse obligation	(60)	XX*
Fair value of loans transferred	1,100	1,100

---

*Not practicable to estimate fair value.

Net Proceeds	Case 1	Case 2
Cash received	$1,050	$1,050
Plus: Servicing asset	XX*	40
Plus: Call option	70	70
Less: Recourse obligation	(60)	XX[†]
Net proceeds	$1,060	$1,160~~1,120~~

~~Carrying Amount Based on Relative Fair Values (Case 1)~~

	~~Fair Value~~	~~Percentage of Total Fair Value~~	~~Allocated Carrying Amount~~
~~Loans sold~~	~~$1,060~~	~~100~~	~~$1,000~~
~~Servicing asset~~	~~0~~	~~0~~	~~0~~
~~Total~~	~~$1,060~~	~~100~~	~~$1,000~~

~~**Carrying Amount Based on Relative Fair Values (Case 2)**~~

	~~Fair Value~~	~~Percentage of Total Fair Value~~	~~Allocated Carrying Amount~~
~~Loans sold~~	~~$1,120~~	~~97~~	~~$ 970~~
~~Servicing asset~~	~~40~~	~~3~~	~~30~~
~~Total~~	~~$1,160~~	~~100~~	~~$1,000~~

Gain on Sale	**Case 1**	**Case 2**
Net proceeds	$1,060	$1,160
Carrying amount of loans	1,000	1,000
Less: Recourse obligation	0	(160)†
Gain on sale	$ 60	$ 0

Journal Entries	**Case 1**		**Case 2**	
Cash	1,050		1,050	
Servicing asset	0*		~~40~~30	
Call option	70		70	
Loans		1,000		1,000
Recourse obligation		60		~~160~~150†
Gain on sale		60		0
To record transfer				

---

*Assets shall be recorded at zero if an estimate of the fair value of the assets is not practicable.

†The amount recorded as a liability in this example equals the sum of the known assets less the fair value of the known liabilities, that is, the amount that results in no gain or loss.

x. Paragraph 76:

Pass-through, pay-through, and revolving-period securitizations that meet the criteria in paragraph 9 qualify for sale accounting under this Statement. All financial assets obtained or ~~retained~~that continue to be held by a transferor and liabilities incurred by the originator of a securitization that qualifies as a sale shall be recognized and measured as provided in paragraphs 10 and 11; that includes the implicit forward contract to sell new receivables during a revolving period, which may become valuable or onerous to the transferor as interest rates and other market conditions change.

y. Paragraph 82:

In other securitizations, a similar corporation transfers financial assets to an SPE in exchange for cash and beneficial interests in the transferred assets. That entity raises the cash by issuing to investors commercial paper that gives them a senior interest in cash received from the financial assets. The beneficial interests ~~retained~~that continue to be held by the transferring corporation represent a junior interest to be reduced by any credit losses on the financial assets in trust. The commercial paper interests are highly rated by credit rating agencies only if both (a) the credit enhancement from the junior interest is sufficient and (b) the transferor is highly rated. Depending on facts and circumstances, the Board understands that those "single-step" securitizations often would be judged in the United States as not having isolated the assets, because the nature of the continuing involvement may make it difficult to obtain reasonable assurance that the transfer would be found to be a true sale at law that places the assets beyond the reach of the transferor and its creditors in U.S. bankruptcy (paragraph 113). If the transferor fell into bankruptcy and the transfer was found not to be a true sale at law, investors in the transferred assets might be subjected to an automatic stay that would delay payments due them, and they might have to share in bankruptcy expenses and suffer further losses if the transfer was recharacterized as a secured loan.

z.　Paragraph 83(b):

Second, the special-purpose corporation transfers the assets to a trust or other legal vehicle with a sufficient increase in the credit or yield protection on the second transfer (provided by a junior ~~retained~~ beneficial interest that continues to be held by the transferor or other means) to merit the high credit rating sought by third-party investors who buy senior beneficial interests in the trust. Because of that aspect of its design, that second transfer might not be judged to be a true sale at law and, thus, the transferred assets could at least in theory be reached by a bankruptcy trustee for the special-purpose corporation.

aa.　Paragraph 87(a):

A ROAP for random removal of excess assets, if the ROAP is sufficiently limited so that the transferor cannot remove specific transferred assets, for example, by limiting removals to the amount of the ~~transferor's retained~~ interests that continue to be held by the transferor and to one removal per month

bb.　Paragraph 343:

The first example illustrates the disclosure of accounting policies for ~~retained~~ interests that continue to be held by the transferor. In particular, it describes the accounting policies for (a) initial measurement (paragraph 17(~~fh~~)(1)) and (b) subsequent measurement (paragraph 17(~~gi~~)(1)), including determination of fair value.

NOTE X—SUMMARY OF SIGNIFICANT ACCOUNTING POLICIES

Receivable Sales

When the Company sells receivables in securitizations of automobile loans, credit card loans, and residential mortgage loans, it may hold~~retains~~ interest-only strips, one or more subordinated tranches, ~~servicing rights,~~ and in some cases a cash reserve account, all of which are ~~retained~~ interests that continue to be held by the transferor in the securitized receivables. It may also obtain servicing assets or assume servicing liabilities that are initially measured at fair value. Gain or loss on sale of the receivables depends in part on both (a) the previous carrying amount of the financial assets involved in the transfer, allocated between the assets sold and the ~~retained~~ interests that continue to be held by the transferor based on their relative fair value at the date of transfer, and (b) the proceeds received. To obtain fair values, quoted market prices are used if available. However, quotes are generally not available for ~~retained~~ interests that continue to be held by the transferor, so the Company generally estimates fair value based on the present value of future expected cash flows estimated using management's best estimates of the key assumptions—credit losses, prepayment speeds, forward yield curves, and discount rates commensurate with the risks involved.

cc.　Paragraph 344:

In addition to the disclosure of assumptions used in determining the values of ~~retained~~ interests that continue to be held by the transferor at the time of securitization that are presented in paragraph 343, this Statement also requires similar disclosures at the end of the latest period being presented. The following example illustrates disclosures about the characteristics of securitizations and gain or loss from securitizations and other sales by major type of asset (paragraph 17(~~fh~~)(2)).

NOTE Y—SALES OF RECEIVABLES

During 20X2 and 20X1, the Company sold automobile loans, residential mortgage loans, and credit card loans in securitization transactions. In all those securitizations, the Company ~~retained~~obtained servicing responsibilities and subordinated interests. The Company receives annual servicing fees approximating 0.5 percent (for mortgage loans), 2 percent (for credit card loans), and 1.5 percent (for automobile loans) of the outstanding balance and rights to future cash flows arising after the investors in the securitization trust have received the return for which they contracted. The investors and the securitization trusts have no recourse to the Company's other assets for failure of debtors to pay when due. The ~~Company's retained~~ interests that continue to be held by the Company are subordinate to investor's interests. Their value is subject to credit, prepayment, and interest rate risks on the transferred financial assets.

In 20X2, the Company recognized pretax gains of $22.3 million on the securitization of the automobile loans, $30.2 million on the securitization of credit card loans, and $25.6 million on the securitization of residential mortgage loans.

In 20X1, the Company recognized pretax gains of $16.9, $21.4, and $15.0 million on the securitization of the automobile loans, credit card loans, and residential mortgage loans, respectively.

dd. Paragraph 345:

The following is an illustration of the quantitative information about key assumptions used in measuring ~~retained~~ interests that continue to be held by the transferor at the date of sale or securitization for each financial period presented (paragraph 17(~~f~~h)(3)).

Key economic assumptions used in measuring the ~~retained~~ interests that continue to be held by the transferor at the date of securitization resulting from securitizations completed during the year were as follows (rates* per annum):

Note: The table in this illustration is not reproduced here because there are no changes to that portion of this paragraph.

ee. Paragraph 346 and its related footnote:

The following is an illustration that combines disclosure of the key assumptions used in valuing ~~retained~~ interests that continue to be held by the transferor at the end of the latest period (paragraph 17(~~g~~i)(2)) and the hypothetical effect on current fair value of two or more pessimistic variations from the expected levels for each of the key assumptions (paragraph 17(~~g~~i)(3)).

At December 31, 20X2, key economic assumptions and the sensitivity of the current fair value of residual cash flows to immediate 10 percent and 20 percent adverse changes in those assumptions are as follows ($ in millions):

	Automobile Loans	Credit Card Loans	Residential Mortgage Loans	
			Fixed-Rate	Adjustable
Carrying amount/fair value of retained interests that continue to be held by the transferor[34]	$15.6	$21.25	$12.0	$13.3
Weighted-average life (in years)	1.7	0.4	6.5	6.1
Prepayment speed assumption (annual rate)	1.3%	15.0 %	11.5%	9.3%
Impact on fair value of 10% adverse change	$0.3	$1.6	$3.3	$2.6
Impact on fair value of 20% adverse change	$0.7	$3.0	$7.8	$6.0
Expected credit losses (annual rate)	3.0%	6.1 %	0.9%	1.8%
Impact on fair value of 10% adverse change	$4.2	$3.2	$1.1	$1.2
Impact on fair value of 20% adverse change	$8.4	$6.5	$2.2	$3.0
Residual cash flows discount rate (annual)	14.0%	14.0 %	12.0 %	9.0%
Impact on fair value of 10% adverse change	$1.0	$0.1	$0.6	$0.5
Impact on fair value of 20% adverse change	$1.8	$0.1	$0.9	$0.9
Interest rates on variable and adjustable contracts	Forward Eurodollar yield curve plus contracted spread			
Impact on fair value of 10% adverse change	$1.5	$4.0	$0.4	$1.5
Impact on fair value of 20% adverse change	$2.5	$8.1	$0.7	$3.8

These sensitivities are hypothetical and should be used with caution. As the figures indicate, changes in fair value based on a 10 percent variation in assumptions generally cannot be extrapolated because the relationship of the change in assumption to the change in fair value may not be linear. Also, in this table, the effect of a variation in a particular assumption on the fair value of the retained interest that continues to be held by the transferor is calculated without changing any other assumption; in reality, changes in one factor may result in changes in another (for example, increases in market interest rates may result in lower prepayments and increased credit losses), which might magnify or counteract the sensitivities.

[34]Footnote 8, paragraph 17(4)(b)(3), describes how weighted-average life can be calculated.

ff. Paragraph 347:

The following is an illustration of disclosure of expected static pool credit losses (paragraph 17(gi)(2)).

Note: The table in this illustration is not reproduced here because there are no changes to that portion of this paragraph.

gg. Paragraph 348 and note * to paragraph 348:

The following is an illustration of the disclosure of cash flows between the securitization SPE and the transferor (paragraph 17(fh)(4)).

The table below summarizes certain cash flows received from and paid to securitization trusts ($ in millions):

	Year Ended December 31	
	20X2	20X1
Proceeds from new securitizations	$1,413	$ 971
Proceeds from collections reinvested in previous credit card securitizations	3,150	2,565
Servicing fees received	23	19
Other cash flows received on retained interests that continue to be held by the transferor*	81	52
Purchases of delinquent or foreclosed assets	(45)	(25)
Servicing advances	(102)	(73)
Repayments of servicing advances	90	63

Note:

*This amount represents total cash flows received from retained interests that continue to be held by the transferor other than servicing fees. Other cash flows include, for example, all cash flows from interest-only strips and cash above the minimum required level in cash collateral accounts.

hh. Note § to paragraph 349:

Represents the principal amount of the loan. Interest-only strips (or other interests that continue to be held by a transferor) and servicing assets and servicing liabilitiesrights (or other retained interests) held for securitized assets are excluded from this table because they are recognized separately.

ii. Paragraph 349A is added as follows:

349A. The following is an illustration of disclosures related to the activity in the balance of servicing assets and servicing liabilities by class (paragraphs 17(f)(1) and 17(g)(1)):

(This page intentionally left blank.)

Tabular Disclosure of Changes in Servicing Assets and Servicing Liabilities Subsequently Measured Using the Fair Value Measurement Method

Balance Sheet Disclosures	Class 1 Servicing Asset	Class 1 Servicing Liability	Class 2 Servicing Asset	Class 2 Servicing Liability	Reference
Fair value as of the beginning of the period	XX	XX	XX	XX	17(f)(1)(a)
Additions:					17(f)(1)(b)
Purchases of servicing assets	XX	N/A	XX	N/A	
Assumption of servicing obligations	XX	XX	XX	XX	
Servicing obligations that result from transfers of financial assets	XX	XX	XX	XX	
Subtractions:					
Disposals	(XX)	(XX)	(XX)	(XX)	17(f)(1)(c)
Changes in fair value:					17(f)(1)(d)
Due to change in valuation inputs or assumptions used in the valuation model	XX/(XX)	XX/(XX)	XX/(XX)	XX/(XX)	
Other changes in fair value	XX/(XX)	XX/(XX)	XX/(XX)	XX/(XX)	
Other changes that affect the balance	XX/(XX)	XX/(XX)	XX/(XX)	XX/(XX)	17(f)(1)(e)
Fair value as of the end of the period	XX	XX	XX	XX	17(f)(1)(a)

Tabular Disclosure of Changes in Servicing Assets and Servicing Liabilities Subsequently Measured Using the Amortization Method

Balance Sheet Disclosures	Class 3		Class 4		Reference
	Servicing Asset	Servicing Liability	Servicing Asset	Servicing Liability	
Carrying amount as of the beginning of the period	XX	XX	XX	XX	17(g)(1)(a)
Additions:					
Purchases of servicing assets	XX	N/A	XX	N/A	17(g)(1)(b)
Assumption of servicing obligations	XX	XX	XX	XX	
Servicing obligations that result from transfers of financial assets	XX	XX	XX	XX	
Subtractions:					
Disposals	(XX)	(XX)	(XX)	(XX)	17(g)(1)(c)
Amortization	(XX)	(XX)	(XX)	(XX)	17(g)(1)(d)
Application of valuation allowance to adjust carrying values of servicing assets	XX/(XX)	N/A	XX/(XX)	N/A	17(g)(1)(e)
Other-than-temporary impairments	(XX)	(XX)	(XX)	(XX)	17(g)(1)(f)
Other changes that affect the balance	XX/(XX)	XX/(XX)	XX/(XX)	XX/(XX)	17(g)(1)(g)
Carrying amount before valuation allowance	XX	XX	XX	XX	

					17(g)(5)
Valuation allowance for servicing assets:					
Beginning balance	N/A	XX	N/A	XX	
Provisions/recoveries	N/A	XX/(XX)	N/A	XX/(XX)	
Other-than-temporary impairments	N/A	(XX)	N/A	(XX)	
Sales and disposals	N/A	(XX)	N/A	(XX)	
Ending balance	N/A	XX/(XX)	N/A	XX/(XX)	17(g)(1)(f)
Carrying amount as of the end of the period	XX	XX	XX	XX	17(g)(1)(a)
Fair Value Disclosures					
Fair value as of the beginning of the period	XX	XX	XX	XX	17(g)(2)
Fair value as of the end of the period	XX	XX	XX	XX	17(g)(2)

Amendments to Other Existing Pronouncements

5. FASB Statement No. 133, *Accounting for Derivative Instruments and Hedging Activities,* is amended as follows:

a. Footnote 9 to paragraph 21:

Mortgage bankers and other servicers of financial assets that designate a hedged portfolio by aggregating servicing rights within one or more risk strata used under paragraph 63~~(g)~~(f) of Statement 140 would not necessarily comply with the requirement in this paragraph for portfolios of similar assets. The risk ~~stratum~~strata under paragraph 63~~(g)~~(f) of Statement 140 can be based on any predominant risk characteristic, including date of origination or geographic location.

b. Paragraph 56, as amended:

At the date of initial application, mortgage bankers and other servicers of financial assets may choose to restratify their servicing rights pursuant to paragraph 63~~(g)~~(f) of Statement 140 in a manner that would enable individual strata to comply with the requirements of this Statement regarding what constitutes "a portfolio of similar assets." As noted in footnote 9 of this Statement, mortgage bankers and other servicers of financial assets that designate a hedged portfolio by aggregating servicing rights within one or more risk strata used under paragraph 63~~(g)~~(f) of Statement 140 would not necessarily comply with the requirement in paragraph 21(a) of this Statement for portfolios of similar assets, since the risk stratum under paragraph 63~~(g)~~(f) of Statement 140 can be based on any predominant risk characteristic, including date of origination or geographic location. The restratification of servicing rights is a change in the application of an accounting principle, and the effect of that change as of the initial application of this Statement shall be reported as part of the cumulative-effect-type adjustment for the transition adjustments.

6. FASB Technical Bulletin No. 87-3, *Accounting for Mortgage Servicing Fees and Rights,* is amended as follows:

a. Paragraph 9, as amended:

An enterprise should~~may acquire~~ separately recognize either a servicing asset~~s~~ or a servicing liability~~liabilities~~ each time that it undertakes an obligation to service a financial asset by entering into a servicing contract in any of the following situations:~~by purchasing or originating financial assets with servicing rights retained or by purchasing the servicing rights separately.~~

a. A transfer of the servicer's financial assets that meets the requirements for sale accounting
b. A transfer of the servicer's financial assets to a qualifying special-purpose entity (SPE) in a guaranteed mortgage securitization in which the transferor retains all of the resulting securities and classifies them as either available-for-sale securities or trading securities in accordance with FASB Statement No. 115, *Accounting for Certain Investments in Debt and Equity Securities*
c. An acquisition or assumption of a servicing obligation that does not relate to financial assets of the servicer or its consolidated affiliates.

Servicing assets ~~and liabilities~~that are subsequently measured using the amortization method are amortized in proportion to, and over the period of, estimated net servicing income—the excess of servicing revenues over servicing costs. Servicing liabilities that are subsequently measured using the amortization method are amortized in proportion to, and over the period of, estimated net servicing loss—the excess of servicing costs over servicing revenues. For servicing assets and servicing liabilities that are subsequently measured using the fair value measurement method, changes in fair value of servicing assets and liabilities shall be reported in earnings in the period in which the changes occur. An entity that transfers its financial assets to a qualifying SPE in a guaranteed mortgage securitization in which the transferor retains all of the resulting debt securities and classifies them as held-to-maturity in accordance with Statement 115 either may separately recognize its servicing assets or servicing liabilities or may report those servicing assets or servicing liabilities together with the asset being serviced.

b. Paragraph 10:

No. The mortgage servicing right represents a contractual relationship between the servicer and the investor in the loan, not between the servicer and the borrower. The cost of ~~the~~a mortgage servicing right <u>that is subsequently measured using the amortization method</u> may require adjustment as a result of the refinancing transaction depending on the servicer's assumptions in recording the servicing asset. If the refinancing transaction represents prepayment activity anticipated by the servicer when the servicing asset was recorded, an adjustment would not be necessary. However, if actual prepayments differ from anticipated prepayments, an adjustment to the servicing asset would be required. <u>If the servicing rights (assets or liabilities) are subsequently measured using the fair value measurement method, the entity would recognize any adjustment as a result of the refinancing transaction directly in earnings.</u>

Effective Date and Transition

7. An entity shall adopt this Statement as of the beginning of its first fiscal year that begins after September 15, 2006. Earlier adoption is permitted as of the beginning of an entity's fiscal year, provided the entity has not yet issued financial statements, including interim financial statements, for any period of that fiscal year. The effective date of this Statement is the date that an entity adopts the requirements of this Statement.

Initial Recognition and Measurement of Servicing Assets and Servicing Liabilities

8. The guidance on initial recognition and measurement of servicing assets and servicing liabilities shall be applied prospectively to transactions occurring after the effective date of this Statement. The related disclosure requirements in paragraphs 17(e)–17(g) of Statement 140 shall also be applied prospectively to periods ending after the effective date of this Statement.

Subsequent Measurement at Fair Value upon Adoption of This Statement

9. The option, if elected, to subsequently measure separately recognized servicing assets and servicing liabilities at fair value shall be applied to existing servicing assets and servicing liabilities as of the beginning of the fiscal year that an entity adopts this Statement, provided the entity has not yet issued financial statements, including interim financial statements, for any period of that fiscal year. This Statement enables entities to make an irrevocable election

to subsequently measure each class of separately recognized servicing assets and servicing liabilities at fair value. The subsequent measurement of a class of separately recognized servicing assets and servicing liabilities at fair value shall be applied prospectively to all new and existing separately recognized servicing assets and servicing liabilities within that class. The difference between the fair value and the carrying amount, net of any related valuation allowance, of separately recognized servicing assets and servicing liabilities existing at the date of initial application of the subsequent fair value measurement shall be recorded as a cumulative-effect adjustment to retained earnings as of the beginning of the fiscal year and shall be separately disclosed.

10. Upon adoption of this Statement, an entity with recognized servicing rights may make an irrevocable election to reclassify available-for-sale securities to trading securities as of the beginning of the fiscal year in which it adopts this Statement without regard to the restriction in paragraph 15 of Statement 115, provided that those securities are identified in some manner as offsetting the entity's exposure to changes in fair value of servicing assets or servicing liabilities that the entity elects to subsequently measure at fair value. The amount of gains and losses in accumulated other comprehensive income related to the reclassified securities shall be reported as a separate cumulative-effect adjustment to beginning retained earnings. The carrying amount of reclassified securities and the effect of that reclassification on the cumulative-effect adjustment shall be separately disclosed.

Subsequent Measurement at Fair Value after Adoption of This Statement

11. An entity also may make an irrevocable decision to subsequently measure a class of separately recognized servicing assets and servicing liabilities at fair value as of the beginning of any fiscal year that begins subsequent to the initial adoption of this Statement. Transferring servicing assets and servicing liabilities from a class subsequently measured using the amortization method to a class subsequently measured at fair value is permitted as of the beginning of any fiscal year. The subsequent measurement of servicing assets and servicing liabilities at fair value shall be applied prospectively with a cumulative-effect adjustment to retained earnings as of the beginning of the fiscal year to reflect the difference between the fair value and the carrying amount,

net of any related valuation allowance, of the servicing assets and servicing liabilities that exist at the beginning of the fiscal year in which the entity makes the fair value election. The amount of the cumulative-effect adjustment shall be separately disclosed.

Subsequent Measurement at Fair Value for a New Class of Servicing Assets and Servicing Liabilities

12. If, after the initial adoption of this Statement, an entity recognizes a new class of servicing assets and servicing liabilities, and no servicing assets and servicing liabilities that would belong to this class had previously been recognized by the entity, the entity may elect to subsequently measure that new class of servicing assets and servicing liabilities at fair value at the date of initial recognition of those servicing assets and servicing liabilities.

The provisions of this Statement need not be applied to immaterial items.

This Statement was adopted by the affirmative votes of six members of the Financial Accounting Standards Board. Ms. Schipper dissented.

Ms. Schipper dissents from the issuance of this Statement because, by permitting free choice between two different subsequent measurement attributes for servicing rights, the provisions of this Statement impair comparability and consistency, two desirable qualitative characteristics of financial information in the Board's conceptual framework. She believes that the impairment of comparability and consistency cannot be justified by a cost-benefit analysis. Ms. Schipper agrees with the Board's conclusion, as described in paragraph A10, that fair value is the most relevant measurement attribute for servicing rights because of the similarities between those rights and financial instruments, and the Board's conclusion, as described in paragraph A2, that the lower of fair value or carrying amount is a suboptimal measurement attribute. Therefore, she would require that servicing rights be initially and subsequently measured at fair value in the statement of financial position, with changes in fair value reported in earnings.

Ms. Schipper believes that treatment alternatives, such as the one provided in this Statement, are inherently undesirable because they impair comparability, a desirable qualitative characteristic of financial information in the Board's conceptual framework. The Board acknowledges, in paragraph A20 of this Statement, that comparability between entities will be impaired to the extent that different entities that hold servicing rights apply different measurement attributes. In addition, because the treatment alternative is applied class by class within an entity, it will probably result in different measurement attributes for different classes of servicing rights within an entity.

Ms. Schipper believes that the detailed disclosures that are required by this Statement, with the objective of rectifying the noncomparability in measurements, are not a substitute for consistent and comparable measurement of similar items. The requirement in this Statement that fair values of servicing rights be disclosed, if practicable, by entities that elect not to apply fair value measurement for recognition purposes could imply that the Board believes that disclosure of fair value measurements is a substitute for recognition (that is, initial and subsequent measurement in the financial statements) at fair value, an idea that she rejects.

With regard to the cost-benefit criterion of the Board's conceptual framework, Ms. Schipper notes that the incremental burden that would be imposed on preparers by a requirement to measure all servicing rights initially and subsequently at fair value would not be large, given the requirements of existing accounting guidance and the disclosure requirements of this Statement. Specifically, the existing accounting guidance already requires certain fair value measurements (as part of recording servicing rights at the lower of fair value or carrying amount). Thus, as acknowledged in paragraph A11 of this Statement, the ability to measure servicing rights at fair value should already be in place. Ms. Schipper acknowledges that the existing requirement is less burdensome than a fair value remeasurement at every reporting date, but rejects the idea that the incremental burden would be sufficient to justify the noncomparability permitted by this Statement. With regard to disclosure, this Statement requires that entities that do not elect fair value measurement for recognition purposes shall nonetheless disclose those fair value amounts, if practicable. She believes that compliance with the existing accounting requirements to measure servicing rights at the lower of fair value or carrying amount means that this disclosure would be practicable for entities. Therefore, fair value measurements of servicing rights will have to be prepared by entities for disclosure purposes under the requirements of this Statement (that is, it will be practicable for entities to do so), and there would be no incremental preparation burden imposed by requiring those measurements in the financial statements.

Ms. Schipper acknowledges that some holders of servicing rights use instruments to hedge the risks, such as interest rate risk, inherent in those rights while others do not. She also acknowledges the conclusion in paragraph A12 that some entities do not consider servicing rights to be similar to financial instruments and believe that fair value measurement for those rights would create a new source of earnings volatility that those entities do not view as representationally faithful. However, Ms. Schipper believes that the choice of measurement attributes should be predicated on the nature of the item being measured and not on management intent (in this case, to hedge or not to hedge the risks inherent in those rights) and that, regardless of management's intent in holding servicing rights, changes in fair values of those rights represent economic changes that should be included in earnings.

Members of the Financial Accounting Standards Board:

Appendix A

BACKGROUND INFORMATION AND BASIS FOR CONCLUSIONS

CONTENTS

Appendix A

BACKGROUND INFORMATION AND BASIS FOR CONCLUSIONS

Introduction and Background

A1. This appendix summarizes considerations that Board members deemed significant in reaching the conclusions in this Statement. It includes reasons for accepting certain views and rejecting others. Individual Board members gave greater weight to some factors than to others.

A2. The scarcity of over-the-counter derivative instruments whose changes in fair value closely track the changes in fair value of servicing assets and servicing liabilities makes it difficult for entities that acquire derivative instruments for the purpose of offsetting changes in fair value of servicing assets and servicing liabilities to comply with the hedge effectiveness requirements in FASB Statement No. 133, *Accounting for Derivative Instruments and Hedging Activities*. Because servicing assets and servicing liabilities are not measured at fair value and derivative instruments are, the income statements of some entities reflect volatility that is partly due to those differences in accounting requirements. Constituents requested that the Board permit entities to subsequently measure servicing assets and servicing liabilities at fair value to achieve an income statement presentation that is similar to the application of hedge accounting, without meeting the hedge effectiveness requirements of Statement 133. The Board also considered the lower of fair value or carrying amount as a suboptimal measurement attribute when it decided to add this project to its agenda.

A3. Differences exist in whether and how entities choose to offset risks using derivatives and in whether those entities qualify for and apply special hedge accounting permitted under Statement 133. For example, an entity that applies hedge accounting would typically be able to adjust the balance of servicing assets and servicing liabilities for the changes in fair value associated with the risk being hedged, whereas an entity that does not apply hedge accounting would report servicing assets and servicing liabilities at the lower of allocated carrying amount or fair value. The differences in how entities value, amortize, and assess servicing assets and servicing liabilities for impairment can result in different amounts reflected in the servicing assets' and servicing liabilities' balances at the end of each reporting period. To address those factors that affect comparability, some constituents requested that servicing assets and servicing liabilities be recorded at fair value by all entities.

A4. Although the initial request for the project focused on accounting for mortgage servicing assets and servicing liabilities under Statement 140, this Statement applies to all servicing assets and servicing liabilities that are separately recognized, that is, to servicing assets and servicing liabilities recognized as assets or liabilities apart from the assets being serviced. That scope is clarified in this Statement.

A5. In August 2005, the Board issued the Exposure Draft, *Accounting for Servicing of Financial Assets.* Twenty-six organizations and individuals commented on that Exposure Draft. The majority of those respondents noted that the proposed Statement would improve financial reporting but suggested that certain modifications be made to the final Statement. The Board considered the comments and suggestions provided by respondents during its redeliberations in November and December 2005 on the issues addressed by the Exposure Draft.

A6. Based on comments received on the Exposure Draft, the Board decided to clarify the scope of the servicing assets and servicing liabilities provisions of Statement 140. Respondents asked the Board to provide additional guidance on whether the servicing provisions of Statement 140 should be applied to:

a. A servicing contract that a transferor enters into in a transfer of its financial assets that does not meet the requirements for sale accounting
b. A servicing contract that a servicer enters into that does not involve financial assets that it owned, transferred, or securitized.

Amendments to Statement 140

Amendments Related to the Scope of Servicing Assets and Servicing Liabilities

A7. The Board first considered whether it was appropriate to separately recognize servicing assets and servicing liabilities that arise from transfers or securitizations of the servicer's own assets that do not meet the requirements for sale accounting and that are treated as secured borrowings. The Board decided that transfers that do not give rise to a sale should not create a separately recognized servicing asset or servicing liability. The Board does not believe it is appropriate for a servicer to recognize a servicing asset or servicing liability for a servicing contract that relates only to its own assets. However, Statement 140 permits or requires separate recognition of servicing assets or servicing liabilities in a guaranteed mortgage

securitization (depending on the classification of the resulting securities) because that type of securitization changes the legal form of the assets and may create a servicing asset or servicing liability that should be separately recognized even though the transaction does not qualify for sale accounting under Statement 140. The Board did not amend the exception for servicing assets and servicing liabilities created in a guaranteed mortgage securitization.

A8. The Board also considered whether to clarify whether a servicer should separately recognize a servicing asset or servicing liability if it entered into a servicing contract that did not involve assets that it owned, transferred, or securitized. The Board decided to clarify that a servicer should separately recognize servicing assets and servicing liabilities any time the servicer enters into a servicing contract that does not relate to financial assets of the servicer or its consolidated affiliates.

Amendments Related to Initial Measurement of Servicing Assets and Servicing Liabilities

A9. The current requirements for initial measurement of servicing assets and servicing liabilities vary depending on whether they are purchased separately, assumed, or obtained in a sale or securitization transaction, as well as whether they are assets or liabilities. The Board concluded that recognized servicing assets and servicing liabilities should be accounted for similarly, regardless of how they are obtained.

A10. The Board concluded that all servicing assets and servicing liabilities that are required to be separately recognized should be initially measured at fair value. The Board previously concluded that fair value is the most relevant measurement attribute for financial instruments. Because servicing assets and servicing liabilities have characteristics similar to financial instruments, that conclusion logically applies to them as well. Constituents have told the Board that fair value measurements for servicing assets and servicing liabilities are sufficiently reliable to be used in financial statements and that some entities are currently using those values to manage their daily operations. The Board decided to include separately recognized servicing assets as part of proceeds of a sale to simplify the application of the guidance and provide consistency between servicing assets and servicing liabilities obtained in a transfer of financial assets that meets the requirements for sale accounting. Prior to the issuance of this Statement, separately recognized servicing assets were included as part of retained interests. References to *retained interests* have been changed to *interests that continue to be held by a transferor* to clarify that servicing assets are no longer deemed retained interests.

Amendments Related to Subsequent Measurement of Servicing Assets and Servicing Liabilities

A11. Preparers of financial statements have developed techniques to reliably measure servicing assets and servicing liabilities at fair value to comply with Statement 140, which requires that servicing assets and servicing liabilities be assessed for impairment or increased obligation at each reporting date based on their fair values. Subsequent measurement of servicing assets and servicing liabilities at fair value would improve the representational faithfulness of reporting (a) risk management activities associated with such servicing assets and servicing liabilities and (b) declines in the fair value of servicing assets and servicing liabilities. Subsequent measurement of servicing assets and servicing liabilities at fair value would eliminate the necessity for entities that manage the risks inherent in servicing assets and servicing liabilities with derivatives to qualify for hedge accounting treatment to avoid certain income statement effects that result from the use of accounting standards that require different measurement attributes for derivatives and for servicing assets and servicing liabilities. Subsequent measurement of servicing assets and servicing liabilities at fair value would also eliminate diversity in the characterization of declines in fair value as impairments or direct write-downs, which affects the subsequent accounting for the remaining balance of servicing assets and servicing liabilities.

A12. However, some entities use financial instruments other than derivatives, such as available-for-sale securities, to offset risks inherent in servicing assets and servicing liabilities and to avoid the income statement volatility associated with the use of derivatives. Other entities do not attempt to mitigate the risks inherent in servicing assets and servicing liabilities and do not consider servicing assets and servicing liabilities to be similar to financial instruments but consider servicing assets and servicing liabilities to be contracts to provide services. For those entities, subsequent measurement of servicing assets and servicing liabilities at fair value would result in a new source of income statement volatility, which they view as not representationally faithful of their performance.

A13. The Board decided to permit an entity to elect either fair value measurement with changes in fair value reflected in earnings or the amortization and impairment requirements of Statement 140 for subsequent measurement. The election would be made by class of servicing assets and servicing liabilities and would be made at the beginning of a fiscal year. The Board also decided that if an entity chooses fair value measurement for a class of servicing assets and servicing liabilities, that entity cannot decide later to adopt the amortization method for that class or for any servicing asset or servicing liability in that class.

A14. The Board is aware that entities use financial instruments such as derivatives to offset the risks inherent in only certain classes of servicing assets and servicing liabilities. The Board initially believed that application of the fair value measurement election by broad class of servicing assets and servicing liabilities identified by major asset type, similar to the identification of asset classes in paragraph 17(f) of Statement 140 (now 17(h) of Statement 140 as amended), would improve comparability. Many respondents to the Exposure Draft opposed the Board's initial approach to apply the fair value election based on major asset type for several reasons. One reason is that the availability of market-observable inputs used in determining the fair value of servicing assets and servicing liabilities may vary significantly within a broad asset class. Another reason is that entities manage the risks in servicing assets and servicing liabilities with differing risk characteristics differently within major asset types.

A15. Factors such as the nature of the collateral, fixed or floating interest rates, commercial or consumer loans, credit quality, tenor, expected variation in customer prepayment rates, and other factors affect a servicer's decision as to whether and how it manages its risk exposure for its servicing assets and servicing liabilities. Some respondents to the Exposure Draft supported a more finely disaggregated approach to identify classes and recommended that a servicer be permitted to take into account the different valuation and risk characteristics of the underlying assets within a broad asset class as well as the manner in which an entity manages the economic risks for various groups of servicing assets or servicing liabilities when establishing the classes for the election for subsequent measurement.

A16. The Board decided to require a servicer to define its classes of servicing assets and servicing liabilities for the subsequent measurement election based on one or both of the following:

a. The availability of market inputs used to determine the fair value of servicing assets and servicing liabilities
b. An entity's method for managing the risks of its servicing assets and servicing liabilities.

The Board concluded that the additional disclosures required for each class of servicing assets and servicing liabilities would provide meaningful information to users of financial statements. The Board acknowledges that a servicer may or may not consider the major asset type of the underlying financial asset being serviced when identifying its classes of separately recognized servicing assets and servicing liabilities under this approach. Further, the Board believes that this approach is not analogous to the stratification guidance to determine impairment of servicing assets or servicing liabilities that are subsequently measured using the amortization method. An entity must first identify its classes of separately recognized servicing assets and servicing liabilities under this approach. For any class subsequently measured using the amortization method, an entity must then stratify that class to determine if impairment has occurred.

One-Time Option to Reclassify Available-for-Sale Securities

A17. Many servicers purchase securities to partially offset their exposure to certain risks associated with their servicing assets and servicing liabilities. Servicers often classify those securities as available-for-sale securities, which are reported at fair value with unrealized changes in fair value reported in other comprehensive income in accordance with Statement 115. Servicers sell those securities in periods in which the servicing assets are impaired (or servicing liabilities are assessed for increased obligation) to offset the effect of recognizing impairment or increased obligation in the income statement. If a servicer elects to subsequently measure a servicing asset or servicing liability at fair value upon adoption of this Statement, that election may cause such available-for-sale securities to be subsequently measured at fair value through other comprehensive income, while the related servicing asset or servicing liability would be subsequently measured at fair value through earnings. This is not an issue for new servicing assets and servicing liabilities because the servicer has the option to classify newly purchased securities as trading

securities, which are reported at fair value with changes in fair value reported in earnings consistent with the manner in which the related servicing asset or servicing liability would be reported if fair value is elected. However, for existing available-for-sale securities, paragraph 15 of Statement 115 states that ". . . transfers into or from the trading category also should be rare." Constituents told the Board that as a result of paragraph 15, servicers that hold available-for-sale securities to offset changes in the fair value of existing servicing assets and servicing liabilities would be unlikely to elect to subsequently measure those servicing assets and servicing liabilities at fair value unless they were permitted to reclassify the related available-for-sale securities to trading securities.

A18. The Board agreed with constituent concerns and tentatively decided to permit a one-time election for servicers to reclassify available-for-sale securities to trading securities without questioning the treatment of those securities under Statement 115. Similar special reclassification elections were permitted in other Statements, most recently in Statement 133. However, the Board was concerned about permitting an unrestricted election, because that election could involve a large number of securities that are unrelated to servicing assets or servicing liabilities. The Board asked respondents in the notice for recipients of the Exposure Draft whether a servicer that uses available-for-sale securities to offset the income statement effect of changes in fair value of servicing assets and servicing liabilities would be able to identify specific available-for-sale securities held for that purpose. Respondents stated that servicers that held such available-for-sale securities would generally be able to identify both the securities and the related servicing assets and servicing liabilities. Based on that information, the Board decided to permit a one-time election to reclassify available-for-sale securities to trading securities but limited that election to those available-for-sale securities that are intended to offset the income statement effect of changes in the fair value of servicing assets and servicing liabilities that a servicer elects to subsequently measure at fair value. The Board discussed whether prior documentation of the relationship between each available-for-sale security and specific servicing assets or servicing liabilities would be required to reclassify a particular available-for-sale security in this election. The Board concluded that requiring that a servicer provide specific identification retroactively would be impracticable.

A19. The Board considered whether the effect of the reclassification of securities on accumulated other comprehensive income should be reported through earnings, as described in paragraph 15 of Statement 115, or through retained earnings as a cumulative-effect adjustment. The Board also considered whether the reclassification election should be a one-time election at adoption of this Statement or whether it should be allowed each time a servicer elects to subsequently measure a class of servicing assets and servicing liabilities at fair value. The Board decided to limit the reclassification to a one-time election at adoption of this Statement. It also decided to require that the effect of the reclassification on accumulated other comprehensive income be reported as part of the cumulative-effect adjustment to retained earnings with the effect of the reclassification disclosed separately from the effect of the election to subsequently measure servicing assets and servicing liabilities at fair value. The Board decided to adopt that approach because it believes that approach would provide sufficient information in one place to users of financial statements about the effect of adopting this Statement. The Board decided to permit the one-time reclassification only upon adoption of this Statement because it believes that those who intended to offset the income statement effect of changes in the fair value of their servicing assets and servicing liabilities would elect to use fair value for subsequent measurement more quickly.

Amendments Related to Financial Statement Presentation and Disclosures for Servicing Assets and Servicing Liabilities

A20. The Board was concerned that permitting alternative methods for subsequent measurement would reduce the comparability of financial statements. As a result, the Board considered whether special display guidance for the statement of financial position and additional disclosures would be needed to address the comparability issues that may arise from the use of alternative measurement methods. The Board also considered this issue during its deliberations on the fair value option project in which it tentatively decided to require separate presentation of carrying amounts in the statement of financial position when an entity elects to use fair value measurement for certain assets and liabilities but not for other similar assets and liabilities. The Board decided in this project to require that servicing assets and servicing liabilities subsequently measured at fair value be presented in the statement of financial position separately from servicing assets and servicing liabili-

ties that are subsequently measured using the amortization method. The Board decided that an entity may meet the separate reporting requirement by either:

a. Displaying separate line items for servicing assets or servicing liabilities subsequently measured using the fair value measurement method and those that are subsequently measured using the amortization method; or

b. Presenting the aggregate amounts for both servicing assets or servicing liabilities that are subsequently measured at fair value and those that are subsequently measured using the amortization method provided that the amounts of servicing assets or servicing liabilities that are subsequently measured using the fair value measurement method included in the aggregate amount are disclosed parenthetically on the face of the statement.

A21. The Board also decided to require the additional disclosures described in paragraph 4(h) of this Statement to mitigate concerns about comparability. Those additional disclosures are intended to provide users with information about the classes of servicing assets and servicing liabilities that an entity holds and management's basis for identifying its classes of servicing assets and servicing liabilities.

A22. To enable users to better understand the sources of changes in servicing assets and servicing liabilities during the periods presented, this Statement requires that the activity by class in the balance of servicing assets and in the balance of servicing liabilities be disclosed, regardless of whether the class is subsequently measured at fair value or using the amortization method. To improve comparability among classes of servicing assets and servicing liabilities within an entity as well as among different entities, this Statement requires disclosure of the fair values of servicing assets and the fair values of servicing liabilities by class at the beginning and end of each period presented, including those classes using the amortization method, if it is practicable to do so.

A23. Given the diversity in techniques used to measure servicing assets and servicing liabilities at fair value, the Board decided to require an entity to describe the valuation techniques used to estimate fair values of the servicing assets and servicing liabilities. It also encouraged similar disclosures of the valuation techniques used to estimate fair values for instruments used to manage the risks inherent in servicing assets and servicing liabilities, to the extent that those disclosures are not required under existing generally accepted accounting principles. The Board believes that those disclosures will provide insight into how an entity measures the fair value of servicing assets and servicing liabilities when no market quotes are available.

A24. The Board also decided to require an entity to disclose qualitative information about instruments used to manage the risks inherent in servicing assets and servicing liabilities. The Board decided to encourage, rather than require, quantitative information about those instruments as part of this Statement because such quantitative disclosures are generally not required for those instruments that are used to manage other risks, unless those instruments are subject to special hedge accounting requirements. Those disclosures that are required under other accounting guidance continue to be required.

A25. The Board considered but decided not to require a separate sensitivity analysis for classes of servicing assets and servicing liabilities because the costs to prepare that analysis would outweigh the benefits in most cases. However, servicing assets and servicing liabilities obtained by a transferor in a securitization must be included in the sensitivity analysis required by paragraph 17(i) of Statement 140.

A26. This Statement requires disclosure of the activity in the valuation allowance for impairment of recognized servicing assets, if any, for each class of servicing assets and servicing liabilities using the amortization method. This requirement ensures that users understand the reasons for changes in the valuation allowance account.

Effective Date and Transition

A27. The Board decided that the effective date of this Statement should be consistent with the effective date for FASB Statement No. 155, *Accounting for Certain Hybrid Financial Instruments*. The Board understands that the ability to subsequently measure separately recognized servicing assets and servicing liabilities and certain hybrid financial instruments at fair value was supported by many financial institutions and that the application of fair value would not be burdensome, given the existing requirements of Statement 140. Therefore, the Board permitted early adoption of this Statement as well as Statement 155. An entity must adopt this Statement as of the beginning of its first fiscal year that begins after September 15, 2006, with earlier adoption permitted as of the beginning of an entity's fiscal year, provided that the entity has not yet issued financial statements, including any interim financial statements, for that fiscal year.

A28. The Board decided to clarify the requirements for the initial recognition of separate servicing assets and servicing liabilities. The Board is aware that under previous guidance, servicers may have recognized separate servicing assets or separate servicing liabilities that are no longer permitted to be separately recognized under the requirements of this Statement. The Board decided that any servicing assets or servicing liabilities previously recognized by an entity in a securitization transaction that was accounted for as a financing transaction should continue to be recognized after the adoption of this Statement.

A29. The Board decided to provide transition for the provisions related to initial measurement of servicing assets and servicing liabilities separately from those related to subsequent measurement. The Board decided that the requirement to initially measure servicing assets and servicing liabilities at fair value should be applied on a prospective basis for new servicing assets and servicing liabilities. The Board considered the relative merits of applying this Statement to both new assets and existing assets or applying it retrospectively. The Board acknowledged that the difference between initial measurement at fair value and initial measurement at the allocated carrying amount is likely to be minimal for certain servicing assets and servicing liabilities. The Board also acknowledged that the application of initial fair value to existing servicing assets and servicing liabilities would require modifications to the application of the amortization method from the date the servicing asset or servicing liability was separately recognized through the date of adoption of this Statement. The Board concluded that the comparability that would be achieved from either retrospective application or a cumulative-effect adjustment for existing servicing assets and servicing liabilities would be insufficient to justify the cost.

A30. The Board decided that the irrevocable option to subsequently measure servicing assets and servicing liabilities at fair value should be applied on a prospective basis for each class of servicing assets and servicing liabilities, with a cumulative-effect adjustment to retained earnings recorded to reflect the adjustment for existing servicing assets and servicing liabilities to fair value as of the beginning of the fiscal year that the election is made.

A31. To ensure that all servicing assets and servicing liabilities in a class of servicing assets and servicing liabilities would be measured using the same subsequent measurement attribute, the Board decided to allow existing servicing assets and servicing liabilities to be subsequently measured at fair value along with new servicing assets and servicing liabilities. The Board recognized that a prospective application of the subsequent measurement of existing servicing assets and servicing liabilities at fair value would cause entities electing to subsequently measure servicing assets and servicing liabilities at fair value to reflect the unrealized gain or loss of the servicing assets and servicing liabilities on the date the fair value election is made. The Board determined that recognition of a cumulative-effect adjustment to the beginning balance of the existing servicing assets and servicing liabilities would be appropriate because this adjustment would enable preparers to measure and present all of the servicing assets and servicing liabilities in a class in the same manner. The Board decided not to require retrospective application of this election to existing servicing assets and servicing liabilities because the cost of that requirement would outweigh the limited benefits to users in interpreting this information for prior periods presented.

A32. In analyzing the application of the fair value election at a date subsequent to initial adoption, the Board considered the same factors that it considered in determining the transition requirements for making the election upon adoption, as well as FASB Statement No. 154, *Accounting Changes and Error Corrections.* The Board believes that a subsequent fair value election would be considered a voluntary action by the entity and would require use of the retrospective transition method under Statement 154, unless the Board explicitly provided for a different transition method. In evaluating whether a different transition method should be required in this Statement, the Board reasoned that in the first few years of applying this Statement, the application of the retrospective transition provisions would be impracticable as it would require consideration of prior-period servicing assets and servicing liabilities as part of classes that may not be previously identified. The Board decided that the election to subsequently measure a class of servicing assets and servicing liabilities at fair value could be made only at the beginning of a fiscal year because allowing the election to be made at any other time would require recordkeeping that is

not presently required and would impair consistency. The Board considered all of the disclosures related to accounting changes in Statement 154 and amended the disclosures in paragraph 17 of Statement 140 to include those disclosures that it believes are necessary. The Board decided not to require disclosure of the direct and indirect effects of electing the fair value subsequent measurement method because those disclosures would require an entity to maintain two sets of accounting records.

Benefits and Costs

A33. The mission of the FASB is to establish and improve standards of financial accounting and reporting for the guidance and education of the public, including preparers, auditors, and users of financial information. In fulfilling that mission, the Board endeavors to determine that a proposed standard will fill a significant need and that the costs imposed to meet that standard, as compared with other alternatives, are justified in relation to the overall benefits of the resulting information. Although the costs to implement a new standard may not be borne evenly, investors and creditors—both present and potential—and other users of financial information benefit from improvements in financial reporting, thereby facilitating the functioning of markets for capital and credit and the efficient allocation of resources in the economy.

A34. The Board's assessment of the benefits and costs of amending Statement 140 with respect to the accounting for servicing assets and servicing liabilities was based on discussions with preparers, users, and auditors of financial statements. The Board considered the costs associated with decreased comparability as a result of allowing a choice between the amortization method and the fair value measurement method for separately recognized servicing assets and servicing liabilities. The Board also considered the benefits arising from (a) permitting entities to use the same measurement attribute for both separately recognized servicing assets and servicing liabilities and the derivatives held to manage risks inherent in those rights and (b) reducing diversity among entities that apply the amortization method and recognize impairment on separately recognized servicing assets and servicing liabilities. The Board concluded that the financial reporting benefits would outweigh the costs of noncomparability, particularly since the improved disclosures that are required by this Statement would enable users to compare entities that make different decisions about subsequent measurement of servicing assets and servicing liabilities.

Appendix B

EFFECT ON RELATED AUTHORITATIVE LITERATURE

B1. This appendix addresses the effect of this Statement on authoritative accounting literature included in categories (b)–(d) in the GAAP hierarchy discussed in AICPA Statement on Auditing Standards No. 69, *The Meaning of* Present Fairly in Conformity With Generally Accepted Accounting Principles. Any authoritative literature affected by the issuance

of Statement 156 solely due to the replacement of the term *retained interests* with the term *interests that continue to be held by a transferor* has been excluded from this appendix.

EITF Issues

B2. The following table lists EITF Issues and Topic relating to servicing rights and indicates (a) the status of that literature after issuance of this Statement and (b) the effect of this Statement on that literature (if any) or the reasons that the literature is beyond the scope of this Statement. (**Note:** The *EITF Abstracts* that have been affected by this Statement will be updated on the FASB website upon issuance of this Statement.)

Status Legend	
Language revised by this Statement	References and/or language in this Issue have been revised for amendments to Statement 140 by this Statement.
The guidance in this Issue is unaffected by this Statement	The guidance in this Issue is unaffected by this Statement.
Nullified	This Statement provides guidance on this matter. As a result, this Issue has been nullified.

Issue Number/ Question	Title	Status	Description/Effect of Statement 156
EITF Issues			
Issue 85-13	Sale of Mortgage Service Rights on Mortgages Owned by Others	**The guidance in this Issue is unaffected by this Statement**	**Description**—This Issue addresses whether a gain should be recorded on the sale of mortgage servicing rights when the sale is for a participation in a future interest income stream and, if a gain is recognized, how that gain should be measured. Issue 85-13 states that gain recognition is appropriate at the sale date. **Effect of Statement 156**—This Statement does not modify the consensus reached on this Issue. However, changes in the fair value of servicing assets or servicing liabilities that are subsequently measured at fair value should be included in earnings in the period in which those changes occur, with any additional change in fair value from the last measurement date to the sale date included in earnings at that time.

Issue Number/ Question	Title	Status	Description/Effect of Statement 156
Issue 87-34	Sale of Mortgage Servicing Rights with a Subservicing Agreement	**The guidance in this Issue is unaffected by this Statement**	**Description**—This Issue addresses whether the transfer of mortgage servicing rights and the simultaneous agreement to provide subservicing should be reported by the transferor as a sale or as a financing and, if reported as a sale, how the sale should be recognized. The Task Force reached a consensus on this Issue that income should not be recognized immediately as a result of the transaction and that a loss on the transaction should be recognized currently if the transferor determines that prepayments of the underlying mortgage loans may result in performing the future servicing at a loss.

Effect of Statement 156—This Statement does not modify the consensus reached on this Issue. However, changes in the fair value of servicing assets or servicing liabilities that are subsequently measured at fair value should be included in earnings in the period in which those changes occur, with any additional change in fair value from the last measurement date to the date of the transaction included in earnings at that time. |

Issue 88-11	Allocation of Recorded Investment When a Loan or Part of a Loan Is Sold	Nullified	**Description**—This Issue addresses how an entity's recorded investment in a loan should be allocated between the portion of the loan sold (for purposes of determining the gain or loss on the sale) and the portion retained (for purposes of determining the remaining recorded investment) and states that the allocation should be based on the relative fair values of those portions. **Effect of Statement 156**—Paragraph 10 of Statement 140 (as amended by Statement 156) requires that upon initial recognition, servicing assets and servicing liabilities be measured at fair value. Paragraph 10 also describes the allocation method that the transferor is required to follow upon completion of any transfer of financial assets. Statement 125 and Statement 140 (as amended by Statement 156) nullify Issue 88-11.

Issue Number/ Question	Title	Status	Description/Effect of Statement 156
Issue 90-21	Balance Sheet Treatment of a Sale of Mortgage Servicing Rights with a Subservicing Agreement	**The guidance in this Issue is unaffected by this Statement**	**Description**—This Issue addresses whether a transaction described in Issue 87-34 (discussed above) should be accounted for as a financing or as a sale with the gain deferred. The Task Force reached a consensus on this Issue that a sale of mortgage servicing rights with a subservicing agreement should be treated as a sale with gain deferred if substantially all the risks and rewards inherent in owning the mortgage servicing rights have been effectively transferred to the buyer. The risks and rewards associated with a seller performing purely administrative functions under a subservicing agreement would not necessarily preclude sale accounting treatment. **Effect of Statement 156**—This Statement does not modify the consensus reached on this Issue. However, changes in the fair value of servicing assets or servicing liabilities should be included in earnings in the period in which those changes occur, with any additional change in fair value from the last measurement date to the sale date included in earnings at that time.

| Issue 02-9 | Accounting for Changes That Result in a Transferor Regaining Control of Financial Assets Sold | **Language revised by this Statement** | **Description**—This Issue addresses the application of the guidance in paragraph 55 of Statement 140 when transferred assets previously accounted for as sold are subsequently repurchased by the transferor.

Effect of Statement 156—The Application Section of this Issue has been revised to initially measure separately recognized servicing assets at fair value. |
| Topic D-69 | Gain Recognition on Transfers of Financial Assets under FASB Statement No. 125* | **Language revised by this Statement** | **Description**—Paragraph 1 of Topic D-69 summarizes the requirements in paragraph 11 of Statement 140 for determining gain or loss on a sale of financial assets. Topic D-69 also summarizes guidance to be used when estimating the fair value of interests that continue to be held by a transferor and new interests obtained and requirements to disclose significant assumptions used in estimating the fair value of those interests.

Effect of Statement 156—This Topic has been revised to:
a. Refer to additional disclosures required by Statement 140 (as amended by Statement 156)
b. Update references to relevant guidance in Statement 140 (as amended by Statement 156). |

*Editorial Note: Topic D-69 has been renamed to "Gain Recognition on Transfers of Financial Assets under FASB Statement No. 140."

FASB Special Report, *A Guide to Implementation of Statement 140 on Accounting for Transfers and Servicing of Financial Assets and Extinguishments of Liabilities* **(Q&A)**

B3. The following table lists Q&As relating to servicing assets and servicing liabilities and indicates (a) the status of that literature upon issuance of this Statement and (b) the effect of this Statement on that literature. **Note: Questions 1–57, 59–70, 72, 74–80, 83–89, 91, 93, 98, 102–106, and 108–123 have not** been affected by this Statement and therefore are not included herein. In addition, the actual text of questions and answers are not included in this Statement. The revised text can be found in the FASB Special Report, *A Guide to Implementation of Statement 140 on Accounting for Transfers and Servicing of Financial Assets and Extinguishments of Liabilities.* (Note: The Statement 140 Q&A will be updated on the FASB website upon issuance of this Statement.)

Status Legend	
Modified	Guidance provided by the Statement 140 implementation guide is modified by this Statement.
Language revised by this Statement	References and/or language in this Q&A have been revised for amendments to Statement 140 by this Statement.
Nullified	This question has been nullified because this Statement provides specific guidance that addresses this question.

Issue Number/ Question	Status	Description/Effect of Statement 156
Q&A		
58	**Modified**	**Description**—This question addresses how transferred components of financial assets and interests that continue to be held by a transferor should be accounted for upon completion of a transfer.
		Effect of Statement 156—The answer to this question has been modified to:
		a. Provide the new language in paragraph 10 of Statement 140 (as amended by Statement 156), which, in part, requires that separately recognized servicing assets and servicing liabilities be initially measured at fair value
		b. Note the new language in paragraphs 13 and 13A of Statement 140 (as amended by Statement 156) relating to initial and subsequent measurement of servicing assets and servicing liabilities.

| 71 | **Language revised by this Statement** | **Description**—This question addresses whether an asset or liability for which it is not practicable to estimate the fair value at the date of a transfer should be remeasured at a later date if the transferor can estimate the fair value (that is, it becomes practicable). **Effect of Statement 156**—The answer has not been affected by this Statement. Paragraph 13A of Statement 140 (as amended by Statement 156) requires that if it is not practicable to measure a separately recognized servicing asset or servicing liability at fair value at the time of transfer, an entity shall initially recognize the servicing asset or servicing liability in accordance with paragraph 71 of Statement 140 (as amended by Statement 156) and shall include it in a class subsequently measured using the amortization method. |
| 73 | **Language revised by this Statement** | **Description**—This question addresses disclosures about the assumptions used to estimate fair values of interests that continue to be held by a transferor in securitized financial assets or of assets obtained and liabilities incurred as proceeds in a transfer. **Effect of Statement 156**—This Statement does not amend those disclosure requirements and requires additional disclosures for all servicing rights. Paragraph references have been updated. |

Issue Number/ Question	Status	Description/Effect of Statement 156
81	**Language revised by this Statement**	**Description**—This question addresses how to determine the fair value of the servicing asset. The answer states that the unsolicited bid from the third party represents a quoted market price, which represents the fair value of the servicing asset. **Effect of Statement 156**—While this Statement does not amend the answer noted above, the question and the answer have been revised to reflect this Statement's requirement to initially measure all separately recognized servicing assets and servicing liabilities at fair value (paragraphs 13 and 62).
82	**Language revised by this Statement**	**Description**—This question addresses how to determine the value of a servicing asset. The answer states that an estimate of fair value (that is not a bid) from a single third party in an inactive or shallow market does not constitute a quoted market price but raises questions about the reasonableness of a transferor's estimate of zero for fair value. **Effect of Statement 156**—While this Statement does not amend the answer noted above, the question and the answer have been revised to reflect this Statement's requirement to initially measure all separately recognized servicing assets and servicing liabilities at fair value (paragraphs 13 and 62).

90	Modified	**Description**—This question addresses whether Statement 140 includes any requirement to adjust the recorded servicing asset or servicing liability if market rates for servicing a specific type of asset change subsequent to the initial recognition of a servicing asset or servicing liability.
		Effect of Statement 156—This Statement permits an entity to subsequently measure classes of servicing assets and servicing liabilities using either the fair value measurement method or the amortization method (paragraph 13A). If an entity elects to subsequently measure a class of servicing assets and servicing liabilities using the amortization method, then the answer to the question remains appropriate.
		If an entity elects to subsequently measure a class of servicing assets and servicing liabilities using the fair value measurement method, any change in fair value would be recognized in earnings.
92	Nullified	**Description**—This question addresses whether an entity should recognize a servicing asset or servicing liability when it transfers the assets to a qualifying SPE in a guaranteed mortgage securitization, retains all of the resulting securities, and classifies them as debt securities held-to-maturity in accordance with Statement 115.
		Effect of Statement 156—This question was nullified because this Statement provides specific guidance that addresses this question in paragraph 13 of Statement 140 (as amended by Statement 156).

Issue Number/ Question	Status	Description/Effect of Statement 156
94	**Language revised by this Statement**	**Description**—This question addresses whether a loss should be recognized if a servicing fee that is equal to or greater than adequate compensation is to be received but the servicer's anticipated cost of servicing would exceed the fee. **Effect of Statement 156**—This Statement does not affect the answer to this question. However, the excerpt from paragraph 62 of Statement 140 (as amended by Statement 156) has been modified to reflect changes to that paragraph. References to certain paragraphs have been updated.
95	**Language revised by this Statement**	**Description**—This question addresses whether an entity should recognize a servicing liability when the transferor-servicer will not receive a contractually specified fee. **Effect of Statement 156**—Paragraph 13 requires that all separately recognized servicing assets or servicing liabilities be initially measured at fair value, if practicable. This Statement also changes the requirements for separate recognition of a servicing asset or servicing liability (paragraph 13 of Statement 140 [as amended by Statement 156]).
96	**Language revised by this Statement**	**Description**—This question addresses whether an entity that sells a portion of a loan under a loan participation agreement and continues to service the loan is required to recognize a servicing asset. **Effect of Statement 156**—This Statement does not affect the answer to this question. However, references to certain paragraphs have been updated.

	Language revised by this Statement	
97		**Description**—This question addresses how an entity should account for the obligation to service a financial asset when it subcontracts that obligation to another servicer. **Effect of Statement 156**—This Statement does not affect the answer to this question. However, paragraphs 10 and 11 of Statement 140 (as amended by Statement 156) now require that upon recognition, servicing assets and servicing liabilities should be initially measured at fair value, if practicable.
99	Modified	**Description**—This question addresses whether servicing assets must be stratified based on more than one predominant risk characteristic of the underlying financial assets. **Effect of Statement 156**—This Statement permits an entity to subsequently measure classes of servicing assets and servicing liabilities at fair value (paragraph 13 of Statement 140 [as amended by Statement 156]). Classes subsequently measured at fair value will no longer be separately assessed for impairment or increased obligation. For classes of separately recognized servicing assets and servicing liabilities that an entity elects to subsequently measure using the amortization method, the answer still applies. References to certain paragraphs have been updated.

Issue Number/ Question	Status	Description/Effect of Statement 156
100	Modified	**Description**—This question addresses whether the strata selected by the servicer should be used consistently from period to period when evaluating and measuring impairment of servicing assets. **Effect of Statement 156**—This Statement permits an entity to subsequently measure a class of servicing assets and servicing liabilities at fair value (paragraph 13 of Statement 140 [as amended by Statement 156]). If an entity makes this election for one or more classes of servicing assets and servicing liabilities, those classes subsequently measured at fair value will no longer be separately assessed for impairment or increased obligation, and any changes in fair value would be reported in earnings in the period in which the changes occur. For classes of separately recognized servicing assets and servicing liabilities that an entity elects to subsequently measure using the amortization method, the answer still applies. References to certain paragraphs have been updated.

| 101 | Modified | **Description**—This question addresses how an entity should recognize subsequent increases in a previously recognized servicing liability.

Effect of Statement 156—This Statement permits an entity to subsequently measure a class of servicing assets and servicing liabilities at fair value and requires any changes in fair value to be reported in earnings in the period in which the changes occur. If an entity does make this election for one or more classes of servicing assets and servicing liabilities, those classes subsequently measured at fair value will not be separately assessed for impairment or increased obligation. For classes of separately recognized servicing assets and servicing liabilities that an entity elects to subsequently measure using the amortization method, the answer still applies. References to certain paragraphs have been updated. |
| 107 | Language revised by this Statement | **Description**—This question addresses how to account for the servicing asset or servicing liability when the transferor subcontracts its servicing obligation to a third party.

Effect of Statement 156—This Statement does not affect the answer to this question. However, paragraphs 10 and 11 of Statement 140 (as amended by Statement 156) now require that separately recognized servicing assets and servicing liabilities be initially measured at fair value. |

Statement 133 Implementation Issues

B4. The following table addresses the effect of this Statement on the answers to Statement 133 Implementation Issues relating to servicing rights.

Status Legend

Modified
Guidance provided in the Issue is modified by this Statement.

Issue Number/ Question	Title	Status	Description/Effect of Statement 156
Statement 133 Implementation Issues			
F1	Stratification of Servicing Assets	Modified	**Description**—This Issue addresses whether an entity is permitted to use different stratification criteria for the impairment test for servicing assets and to group similar assets to be designated as a hedged portfolio in a fair value hedge. **Effect of Statement 156**—This Statement permits an entity to subsequently measure classes of servicing assets and servicing liabilities using either the fair value measurement method or the amortization method (paragraph 13A). If an entity elects to subsequently measure a class of servicing assets and servicing liabilities using the amortization method, then the answer to the question remains appropriate. Classes that an entity elects to subsequently measure at fair value will not be separately assessed for impairment or increased obligation. References to certain paragraphs have been updated.

Issue Number/ Question	Title	Status	Description/Effect of Statement 156
F8	Hedging Mortgage Servicing Right Assets Using Preset Hedge Coverage Ratios	Modified	**Description**—This Issue addresses whether, in a fair value hedge of a portion of a recognized servicing asset or servicing liability, an entity may designate the hedged item at the inception of the hedge by initially specifying a series of possible percentages of the servicing asset or servicing liability that each correspond to a specified independent variable. **Effect of Statement 156**—This Statement permits an entity to subsequently measure classes of servicing assets and servicing liabilities at fair value (paragraph 13 of Statement 140 [as amended by Statement 156]). Thus, an entity may mitigate its income statement volatility that arises from the use of different measurement attributes for its servicing assets or servicing liabilities and related derivative instruments without applying hedge accounting to those instruments. Classes of servicing assets and servicing liabilities that are subsequently measured at fair value will no longer be separately assessed for impairment or increased obligation, and any changes in fair value would be reported in earnings. For classes of separately recognized servicing assets and servicing liabilities that an entity elects to subsequently measure using the amortization method, the answer still applies.

AICPA Literature

B5. The following table lists guidance issued by the AICPA or its staff that may be affected by the decisions made by the Board in this Statement. This information is presented for informational purposes only. Decisions about whether to amend AICPA guidance are made by the FASB in conjunction with the AICPA prior to issuing a final pronouncement.

Status Legend

Language revised by this Statement	References and/or language in the Statements of Position/Accounting and Audit Guides have been revised for amendments to Statement 140 by this Statement.

Reference	Title	Status	Description/Effect of Statement 156
AICPA Literature			
SOP 01-06	Accounting by Certain Entities (Including Entities With Trade Receivables) That Lend to or Finance the Activities of Others	**Language revised by this Statement**	**Description**—Paragraph .08(h) states that sales of servicing assets and servicing liabilities relating to loans that are retained should be recognized in income on the date of the sale and the carrying amount should be allocated between the servicing assets and servicing liabilities and the loans retained using the relative fair values of each in a manner consistent with paragraph 10(b) of Statement 140. **Effect of Statement 156**—This Statement revises the guidance in paragraph 10 of Statement 140. This Statement does not address sales of servicing assets or servicing liabilities. As a result, the language in paragraph .08(h) will be revised to remove the reference to paragraph 10(b) of Statement 140 and to specify the amended method for allocating the carrying amount between the retained loans and the sold servicing assets or servicing liabilities.

Reference	Title	Status	Description/Effect of Statement 156
Audit and Accounting Guide	Depository and Lending Institutions: Banks and Savings Institutions, Credit Unions, Finance Companies and Mortgage Companies	**Language revised by this Statement**	**Description**—Paragraphs 7.83–7.85 describe the accounting guidance for transfers of financial assets, specifically quoting paragraphs 9–11 of Statement 140.

Effect of Statement 156—This Statement amends paragraphs 10 and 11 of Statement 140 and makes significant changes to paragraphs 58–59, 61–63, and 65–67. Specifically, this Statement provides new guidance for the disclosure of and accounting for servicing assets and servicing liabilities. Paragraphs 7.83–7.85 will be revised as follows: (a) any reference to servicing assets as retained interests will be removed, (b) the term *retained interests will be replaced with interests that continue to be held by a transferor,* and (c) the language quoted from paragraphs 10 and 11 of Statement 140 (as amended by Statement 156) will be revised accordingly. |

| Audit and Accounting Guide | Depository and Lending Institutions: Banks and Savings Institutions, Credit Unions, Finance Companies and Mortgage Companies | Language revised by this Statement | **Description**—Paragraph 7.87 details the recognition and measurement of servicing assets and servicing liabilities as described in paragraph 13 of Statement 140.

Effect of Statement 156—This Statement amends paragraph 13 of Statement 140 to require that an entity measure a servicing asset or servicing liability initially at fair value if it meets the requirements found therein for recognition. It adds paragraph 13A to require that an entity subsequently measure each class of servicing assets and servicing liabilities using either the fair value measurement method or the amortization method. As a result of the amendments to Statement 140, paragraph 7.87 will be revised to reflect the language in paragraphs 13 and 13A of Statement 140 (as amended by Statement 156). |
| Audit and Accounting Guide | Depository and Lending Institutions: Banks and Savings Institutions, Credit Unions, Finance Companies and Mortgage Companies | Language revised by this Statement | **Description**—Paragraph 7.103 references the required disclosures detailed in paragraph 17 of Statement 140.

Effect of Statement 156—This Statement adds to and amends the required disclosures found in paragraph 17 of Statement 140. As a result of the amendments to Statement 140, paragraph 7.103 will be revised to reflect the language in paragraph 17 of Statement 140 (as amended by Statement 156). |

Reference	Title	Status	Description/Effect of Statement 156
Audit and Accounting Guide	Depository and Lending Institutions: Banks and Savings Institutions, Credit Unions, Finance Companies and Mortgage Companies	**Language revised by this Statement**	**Description**—Paragraph 10.22 references the accounting guidance found in paragraphs 13 and 61–67 of Statement 140. **Effect of Statement 156**—This Statement amends paragraph 13 of Statement 140 to require that an entity initially measure a servicing asset or servicing liability at fair value, if practicable, if it meets the revised requirements found therein for recognition. It adds paragraph 13A to require that an entity subsequently measure each class of servicing assets and servicing liabilities using either the fair value measurement method or the amortization method. As a result of the amendments to Statement 140, paragraph 10.22 will be revised to reflect the language in paragraphs 13 and 13A of Statement 140 (as amended by Statement 156).
Audit and Accounting Guide	Depository and Lending Institutions: Banks and Savings Institutions, Credit Unions, Finance Companies and Mortgage Companies	**Language revised by this Statement**	**Description**—Paragraph 10.23 references paragraphs 61–67 of Statement 140, which specify the accounting for a contract to service financial assets separately from those assets. **Effect of Statement 156**—This Statement amends those referenced paragraphs. As a result of the amendments to Statement 140, paragraph 10.23 will be revised to reflect the language in paragraphs 61–67 of Statement 140 (as amended by Statement 156).

Audit and Accounting Guide	Depository and Lending Institutions: Banks and Savings Institutions, Credit Unions, Finance Companies and Mortgage Companies	Language revised by this Statement
		Description—Paragraphs 10.35 and 10.36 reference the disclosure requirements found in paragraphs 17(d) and 17(e) of Statement 140. **Effect of Statement 156**—This Statement amends those disclosure requirements. Certain references to paragraph 17 will be updated.

Appendix C

STATEMENT 140 MARKED TO SHOW CHANGES THAT WOULD BE MADE BY THE COMBINATION OF FASB STATEMENT NO. 155, *ACCOUNTING FOR CERTAIN HYBRID FINANCIAL INSTRUMENTS*, AND THIS STATEMENT

C1. Statement 140 has been amended by FASB Statement No. 155, *Accounting for Certain Hybrid Financial Instruments,* and this Statement. This appendix contains the following sections of Statement 140 as originally issued, marked to integrate changes from Statement 155 and this amendment: introduction and scope, standard, selected sections of the implementation guidance, and the glossary. It does not contain the summary, Appendix B (background information and basis for conclusions), and Appendix D (amendments to existing pronouncements).

[Added text is underlined and deleted text is struck out.]

INTRODUCTION AND SCOPE

1. The Board added a project on financial instruments and off-balance-sheet financing to its agenda in May 1986. The project is intended to develop standards to aid in resolving existing financial accounting and reporting issues and other issues likely to arise in the future about various financial instruments and related transactions. The November 1991 FASB Discussion Memorandum, *Recognition and Measurement of Financial Instruments,* describes the issues to be considered. This Statement focuses on the issues of accounting for **transfers**[1] and servicing of **financial assets** and extinguishments of liabilities.

2. Transfers of financial assets take many forms. Accounting for transfers in which the **transferor** has no continuing involvement with the transferred assets or with the **transferee** has not been controversial. However, transfers of financial assets often occur in which the transferor has some continuing involvement either with the assets transferred or with the transferee. Examples of continuing involvement are **recourse,**

servicing, agreements to reacquire, options written or held, and pledges of **collateral.** Transfers of financial assets with continuing involvement raise issues about the circumstances under which the transfers should be considered as sales of all or part of the assets or as secured borrowings and about how transferors and transferees should account for sales and secured borrowings. This Statement establishes standards for resolving those issues.

3. An entity may settle a liability by transferring assets to the creditor or otherwise obtaining an unconditional release. Alternatively, an entity may enter into other arrangements designed to set aside assets dedicated to eventually settling a liability. Accounting for those arrangements has raised issues about when a liability should be considered extinguished. This Statement establishes standards for resolving those issues.

4. This Statement does not address transfers of custody of financial assets for safekeeping, contributions,[2] transfers of ownership interests that are in substance sales of real estate, or investments by owners or distributions to owners of a business enterprise. This Statement does not address subsequent measurement of assets and liabilities, except for (a) **servicing assets** and **servicing liabilities** and (b) **interest-only strips,** securities, retained interests that continue to be held by a transferor in securitizations, loans, other receivables, or other financial assets that can contractually be prepaid or otherwise settled in such a way that the holder would not recover substantially all of its recorded investment and that are not within the scope of FASB Statement No. 133, *Accounting for Derivative Instruments and Hedging Activities.* This Statement does not change the accounting for employee benefits subject to the provisions of FASB Statement No. 87, *Employers' Accounting for Pensions,* No. 88, *Employers' Accounting for Settlements and Curtailments of Defined Benefit Pension Plans and for Termination Benefits,* or No. 106, *Employers' Accounting for Postretirement Benefits Other Than Pensions.* This Statement does not change the provisions relating to leveraged leases in FASB Statement No. 13, *Accounting for Leases,* or money-over-money and wrap lease transactions involving nonrecourse debt subject to the provisions of FASB Technical Bulletin No. 88-1, *Issues Relating to Accounting for Leases.* This Statement does not address

---

[1]Terms defined in Appendix E, the glossary, are set in **boldface type** the first time they appear.

[2]Contributions—unconditional nonreciprocal transfers of assets—are addressed in FASB Statement No. 116, *Accounting for Contributions Received and Contributions Made.*

transfers of nonfinancial assets, for example, servicing assets, or transfers of unrecognized financial assets, for example, minimum lease payments to be received under operating leases.

5. The Board concluded that an objective in accounting for transfers of financial assets is for each entity that is a party to the transaction to recognize only assets it controls and liabilities it has incurred, to **derecognize** assets only when control has been surrendered, and to derecognize liabilities only when they have been extinguished. Sales and other transfers frequently result in a disaggregation of financial assets and liabilities into components, which become separate assets and liabilities. For example, if an entity sells a portion of a financial asset it owns, the portion ~~retained~~that continues to be held by a transferor becomes an asset separate from the portion sold and from the assets obtained in exchange.

6. The Board concluded that another objective is that recognition of financial assets and liabilities should not be affected by the sequence of transactions that result in their acquisition or incurrence unless the effect of those transactions is to maintain effective control over a transferred financial asset. For example, if a transferor sells financial assets it owns and at the same time writes an "at-the-money" put option (such as a guarantee or recourse obligation) on those assets, it should recognize the put obligation in the same manner as would another unrelated entity that writes an identical put option on assets it never owned. Similarly, a creditor may release a debtor on the condition that a third party assumes the obligation and that the original debtor becomes secondarily liable. In those circumstances, the original debtor becomes a guarantor and should recognize a guarantee obligation in the same manner as would a third-party guarantor that had never been primarily liable to that creditor, whether or not explicit consideration was paid for that guarantee. However, certain agreements to repurchase or redeem transferred assets maintain effective control over those assets and should therefore be accounted for differently than agreements to acquire assets never owned.

7. Before FASB Statement No. 125, *Accounting for Transfers and Servicing of Financial Assets and Extinguishments of Liabilities,* accounting standards generally required that a transferor account for financial assets transferred as an inseparable unit that had been either entirely sold or entirely retained. Those standards were difficult to apply and produced inconsistent and arbitrary results. For example, whether a transfer "purported to be a sale" was sufficient to determine whether the transfer was accounted for and reported as a sale of receivables under one accounting standard or as a secured borrowing under another. After studying many of the complex developments that have occurred in financial markets during recent years, the Board concluded that previous approaches that viewed each financial asset as an indivisible unit do not provide an appropriate basis for developing consistent and operational standards for dealing with transfers and servicing of financial assets and extinguishments of liabilities. To address those issues adequately and consistently, the Board decided to adopt as the basis for this Statement a *financial-components approach* that focuses on control and recognizes that financial assets and liabilities can be divided into a variety of components.

8. The Board issued Statement 125 in June 1996. After the issuance of that Statement, several parties called for reconsideration or clarification of certain provisions. Matters the Board was asked to reconsider or clarify included:

a. Circumstances in which a special-purpose entity (SPE) can be considered qualifying

b. Circumstances in which the assets held by a qualifying SPE should appear in the consolidated financial statements of the transferor

c. Whether sale accounting is precluded if the transferor holds a right to repurchase transferred assets that is attached to, is embedded in, or is otherwise transferable with the financial assets

d. Circumstances in which sale accounting is precluded if transferred financial assets can be removed from an SPE by the transferor (for example, under a removal-of-accounts provision (ROAP))

e. Whether arrangements that obligate, but do not entitle, a transferor to repurchase or redeem transferred financial assets should affect the accounting for those transfers

f. The impact of the powers of the Federal Deposit Insurance Corporation (FDIC) on isolation of assets transferred by financial institutions

g. Whether transfers of financial assets measured using the equity method of accounting should continue to be included in the scope of Statement 125

h. Whether disclosures should be enhanced to provide more information about assumptions used to determine the fair value of retained interests and the gain or loss on financial assets sold in securitizations

i. The accounting for and disclosure about collateral that can be sold or repledged.

The Board concluded that those requests to reconsider certain provisions of Statement 125 were appropriate and added a project to amend Statement 125 to its agenda in March 1997. This Statement is the result. To present the amended accounting standards for transfers of financial assets more clearly, this Statement replaces Statement 125. However, most of the provisions of Statement 125 have been carried forward without reconsideration.

STANDARDS OF FINANCIAL ACCOUNTING AND REPORTING

Accounting for Transfers and Servicing of Financial Assets

9. A transfer of financial assets (or all or a portion of a financial asset) in which the transferor surrenders control over those financial assets shall be accounted for as a sale to the extent that consideration other than **beneficial interests** in the transferred assets is received in exchange. The transferor has surrendered control over transferred assets if and only if *all of the following conditions* are met:

a. The transferred assets have been isolated from the transferor—put presumptively beyond the reach of the transferor and its creditors, even in bankruptcy or other receivership (paragraphs 27 and 28).
b. Each transferee (or, if the transferee is a qualifying SPE (paragraph 35), each holder of its beneficial interests) has the right to pledge or exchange the assets (or beneficial interests) it received, and no condition both constrains the transferee (or holder) from taking advantage of its right to pledge or exchange and provides more than a trivial benefit to the transferor (paragraphs 29–34).
c. The transferor does not maintain effective control over the transferred assets through either (1) an agreement that both entitles and obligates the transferor to repurchase or redeem them before their maturity (paragraphs 47–49) or (2) the abil-

ity to unilaterally cause the holder to return specific assets, other than through a **cleanup call** (paragraphs 50–54).

10. Upon completion of any transfer of financial assets, the transferor shall:

a. ~~Continue to carry in its statement of financial position any retained interest in the transferred assets, including, if applicable, servicing assets (paragraphs 61–67), beneficial interests in assets transferred to a qualifying SPE in a~~ **securitization** ~~(paragraphs 73–84), and retained~~ **undivided interests** ~~(paragraphs 58 and 59)~~
a. Initially recognize and measure at **fair value,** if practicable (paragraph 71), servicing assets and servicing liabilities that require recognition under the provisions of paragraph 13
b. Allocate the previous carrying amount between the assets sold, if any, and the ~~retained~~ interests that continue to be held by the transferor, if any, based on their relative fair values at the date of transfer (paragraphs 56–60)~~.~~
c. Continue to carry in its statement of financial position any interest it continues to hold in the transferred assets, including, if applicable, beneficial interests in assets transferred to a qualifying SPE in a **securitization** (paragraphs 73–84), and any **undivided interests** (paragraphs 58 and 59).

11. Upon completion[3] of a transfer of financial assets that satisfies the conditions to be accounted for as a sale (paragraph 9), the transferor (**seller**) shall:

a. Derecognize all assets sold
b. Recognize all assets obtained and liabilities incurred in consideration as **proceeds** of the sale, including cash, put or call options held or written (for example, guarantee or recourse obligations), forward commitments (for example, commitments to deliver additional receivables during the revolving periods of some securitizations), swaps (for example, provisions that convert interest rates from fixed to variable), and servicing assets and servicing liabilities, if applicable (paragraphs 56, 57, and 61–67)
c. Initially measure at fair value assets obtained and liabilities incurred in a sale (paragraphs 68–70) or, if it is not practicable to estimate the fair value

---

[3]Although a transfer of securities may not be considered to have reached completion until the settlement date, this Statement does not modify other generally accepted accounting principles, including FASB Statement No. 35, *Accounting and Reporting by Defined Benefit Pension Plans,* and AICPA Statements of Position and audit and accounting Guides for certain industries, that require accounting at the trade date for certain contracts to purchase or sell securities.

of an asset or a liability, apply alternative measures (paragraphs 71 and 72)

d. Recognize in earnings any gain or loss on the sale.

The transferee shall recognize all assets obtained and any liabilities incurred and initially measure them at fair value (in aggregate, presumptively the price paid).

12. If a transfer of financial assets in exchange for cash or other consideration (other than beneficial interests in the transferred assets) does not meet the criteria for a sale in paragraph 9, the transferor and transferee shall account for the transfer as a secured borrowing with pledge of collateral (paragraph 15).

Recognition and Measurement of Servicing Assets and Servicing Liabilities

13. ~~Each time an entity undertakes an obligation to service financial assets it shall recognize either a servicing asset or a servicing liability for that servicing contract, unless it transfers the assets to a qualifying SPE in a~~ **guaranteed mortgage securitization,** ~~retains all of the resulting securities, and classifies them as debt securities held-to-maturity in accordance with FASB Statement No. 115, *Accounting for Certain Investments in Debt and Equity Securities.* If the servicing asset or liability was purchased or assumed rather than undertaken in a sale or securitization of the financial assets being serviced, it shall be measured initially at its fair value, presumptively the price paid. A servicing asset or liability shall be amortized in proportion to and over the period of estimated net servicing income (if servicing revenues exceed servicing costs) or net servicing loss (if servicing costs exceed servicing revenues). A servicing asset or liability shall be assessed for impairment or increased obligation based on its fair value (paragraphs 61–64).~~

An entity shall recognize and initially measure at fair value, if practicable, a servicing asset or servicing liability each time it undertakes an obligation to service a financial asset by entering into a servicing contract in any of the following situations:

a. A transfer of the servicer's financial assets that meets the requirements for sale accounting

b. A transfer of the servicer's financial assets to a qualifying SPE in a **guaranteed mortgage securitization** in which the transferor retains all of the resulting securities and classifies them as either

available-for-sale securities or trading securities in accordance with FASB Statement No. 115, *Accounting for Certain Investments in Debt and Equity Securities*

c. An acquisition or assumption of a servicing obligation that does not relate to financial assets of the servicer or its consolidated affiliates.

An entity that transfers its financial assets to a qualifying SPE in a guaranteed mortgage securitization in which the transferor retains all of the resulting securities and classifies them as debt securities held-to-maturity in accordance with Statement 115 may either separately recognize its servicing assets or servicing liabilities or report those servicing assets or servicing liabilities together with the asset being serviced.

13A. An entity shall subsequently measure each class of servicing assets and servicing liabilities using one of the following methods:

a. *Amortization method:* Amortize servicing assets or servicing liabilities in proportion to and over the period of estimated net servicing income (if servicing revenues exceed servicing costs) or net servicing loss (if servicing costs exceed servicing revenues), and assess servicing assets or servicing liabilities for impairment or increased obligation based on fair value at each reporting date

b. *Fair value measurement method:* Measure servicing assets or servicing liabilities at fair value at each reporting date and report changes in fair value of servicing assets and servicing liabilities in earnings in the period in which the changes occur.

The election described in this paragraph shall be made separately for each class of servicing assets and servicing liabilities. An entity shall apply the same subsequent measurement method to each servicing asset and servicing liability in a class. Classes of servicing assets and servicing liabilities shall be identified based on (a) the availability of market inputs used in determining the fair value of servicing assets or servicing liabilities, (b) an entity's method for managing the risks of its servicing assets or servicing liabilities, or (c) both. Once an entity elects the fair value measurement method for a class of servicing assets and servicing liabilities, that election shall not be reversed (paragraph 63). If it is not practicable to initially measure a servicing asset or servicing liability at fair value, an entity shall initially recognize the servicing asset or servicing liability in accordance with paragraph 71 and shall include it in a class subsequently measured using the amortization method.

13B. An entity shall report recognized servicing assets and servicing liabilities that are subsequently measured using the fair value measurement method in a manner that separates those carrying amounts on the face of the statement of financial position from the carrying amounts for separately recognized servicing assets and servicing liabilities that are subsequently measured using the amortization method. To accomplish that separate reporting, an entity may either (a) display separate line items for the amounts that are subsequently measured using the fair value measurement method and amounts that are subsequently measured using the amortization method or (b) present the aggregate of those amounts that are subsequently measured at fair value and those amounts that are subsequently measured using the amortization method (paragraph 63) and disclose parenthetically the amount that is subsequently measured at fair value that is included in the aggregate amount.

Financial Assets Subject to Prepayment

14. Interest-only strips, other~~retained~~ interests that continue to be held by a transferor in securitizations, loans, other receivables, or other financial assets that can contractually be prepaid or otherwise settled in such a way that the holder would not recover substantially all of its recorded investment, except for instruments that are within the scope of Statement 133, shall be subsequently measured like investments in debt securities classified as available-for-sale or trading under Statement 115, as amended (paragraph 362).

Secured Borrowings and Collateral

15. A debtor may grant a **security interest** in certain assets to a lender (the secured party) to serve as collateral for its obligation under a borrowing, with or without recourse to other assets of the debtor. An obligor under other kinds of current or potential obligations, for example, interest rate swaps, also may grant a security interest in certain assets to a secured party. If collateral is transferred to the secured party, the custodial arrangement is commonly referred to as a pledge. Secured parties sometimes are permitted to sell or repledge (or otherwise transfer) collateral held under a pledge. The same relationships occur, under different names, in transfers documented as sales that are accounted for as secured borrowings (paragraph 12). The accounting for noncash[4] collateral by the debtor (or obligor) and the secured party depends on whether the secured party has the right to sell or repledge the collateral and on whether the debtor has defaulted.

a. If the secured party (transferee) has the right by contract or custom to sell or repledge the collateral, then the debtor (transferor) shall reclassify that asset and report that asset in its statement of financial position separately (for example, as security pledged to creditors) from other assets not so encumbered.

b. If the secured party (transferee) sells collateral pledged to it, it shall recognize the proceeds from the sale and its obligation to return the collateral. The sale of the collateral is a transfer subject to the provisions of this Statement.

c. If the debtor (transferor) defaults under the terms of the secured contract and is no longer entitled to redeem the pledged asset, it shall derecognize the pledged asset, and the secured party (transferee) shall recognize the collateral as its asset initially measured at fair value or, if it has already sold the collateral, derecognize its obligation to return the collateral.

d. Except as provided in paragraph 15(c), the debtor (transferor) shall continue to carry the collateral as its asset, and the secured party (transferee) shall not recognize the pledged asset.

Extinguishments of Liabilities

16. A debtor shall derecognize a liability if and only if it has been extinguished. A liability has been extinguished if either of the following conditions is met:

a. The debtor pays the creditor and is relieved of its obligation for the liability. Paying the creditor includes delivery of cash, other financial assets, goods, or services or reacquisition by the debtor of its outstanding debt securities whether the securities are canceled or held as so-called treasury bonds.

b. The debtor is legally released[5] from being the primary obligor under the liability, either judicially or by the creditor.

---

[4]Cash "collateral," sometimes used, for example, in securities lending transactions (paragraphs 91–95), shall be derecognized by the payer and recognized by the recipient, not as collateral, but rather as proceeds of either a sale or a borrowing.

[5]If nonrecourse debt (such as certain mortgage loans) is assumed by a third party in conjunction with the sale of an asset that serves as sole collateral for that debt, the sale and related assumption effectively accomplish a legal release of the seller-debtor for purposes of applying this Statement.

Disclosures

17. An entity shall disclose the following:

a. For collateral:
   (1) If the entity has entered into repurchase agreements or securities lending transactions, its policy for requiring collateral or other security
   (2) If the entity has pledged any of its assets as collateral that are not reclassified and separately reported in the statement of financial position pursuant to paragraph 15(a), the carrying amount and classification of those assets as of the date of the latest statement of financial position presented
   (3) If the entity has accepted collateral that it is permitted by contract or custom to sell or repledge, the fair value as of the date of each statement of financial position presented of that collateral and of the portion of that collateral that it has sold or repledged, and information about the sources and uses of that collateral

b. If debt was considered to be extinguished by insubstance defeasance under the provisions of FASB Statement No. 76, *Extinguishment of Debt,* prior to the effective date of Statement 125,[6] a general description of the transaction and the amount of debt that is considered extinguished at the end of the period so long as that debt remains outstanding.

c. If assets are set aside after the effective date of Statement 125 solely for satisfying scheduled payments of a specific obligation, a description of the nature of restrictions placed on those assets.

d. If it is not practicable to estimate the fair value of certain assets obtained or liabilities incurred in transfers of financial assets during the period, a description of those items and the reasons why it is not practicable to estimate their fair value.

e. For all servicing assets and servicing liabilities:
   (1) The amounts of servicing assets or liabilities recognized and amortized during the period
   (2) The fair value of recognized servicing assets and liabilities for which it is practicable to estimate that value and the method and significant assumptions used to estimate the fair value
   (3) The risk characteristics of the underlying financial assets used to stratify recognized servicing assets for purposes of measuring impairment in accordance with paragraph 63
   (4) The activity in any valuation allowance for impairment of recognized servicing assets—including beginning and ending balances, aggregate additions charged and reductions credited to operations, and aggregate direct write-downs charged against the allowances—for each period for which results of operations are presented.

e. For all servicing assets and servicing liabilities:
   (1) Management's basis for determining its classes of servicing assets and servicing liabilities (paragraph 13A).
   (2) A description of the risks inherent in servicing assets and servicing liabilities and, if applicable, the instruments used to mitigate the income statement effect of changes in fair value of the servicing assets and servicing liabilities. (Disclosure of quantitative information about the instruments used to manage the risks inherent in servicing assets and servicing liabilities, including the fair value of those instruments at the beginning and end of the period, is encouraged but not required.)
   (3) The amount of contractually specified servicing fees (as defined in the glossary), late fees, and ancillary fees earned for each period for which results of operations are presented, including a description of where each amount is reported in the statement of income.

f. For servicing assets and servicing liabilities subsequently measured at fair value:
   (1) For each class of servicing assets and servicing liabilities, the activity in the balance of servicing assets and the activity in the balance of servicing liabilities (including a description of where changes in fair value are reported in the statement of income for each period for which results of operations are presented), including, but not limited to, the following:
      (a) The beginning and ending balances
      (b) Additions (through purchases of servicing assets, assumptions of servicing obligations, and servicing obligations that result from transfers of financial assets)

---

[6]Refer to footnote 11 to paragraph 19.

(c) Disposals

(d) Changes in fair value during the period resulting from:

  (i) Changes in valuation inputs or assumptions used in the valuation model

  (ii) Other changes in fair value and a description of those changes

(e) Other changes that affect the balance and a description of those changes

(2) A description of the valuation techniques or other methods used to estimate the fair value of servicing assets and servicing liabilities. If a valuation model is used, the description shall include the methodology and model validation procedures, as well as quantitative and qualitative information about the assumptions used in the valuation model (for example, discount rates and prepayment speeds). (An entity that provides quantitative information about the instruments used to manage the risks inherent in the servicing assets and servicing liabilities, as encouraged by paragraph 17(e)(2), is also encouraged, but not required, to disclose a description of the valuation techniques, as well as quantitative and qualitative information about the assumptions used to estimate the fair value of those instruments.)

g. For servicing assets and servicing liabilities subsequently amortized in proportion to and over the period of estimated net servicing income or loss and assessed for impairment or increased obligation:

(1) For each class of servicing assets and servicing liabilities, the activity in the balance of servicing assets and the activity in the balance of servicing liabilities (including a description of where changes in the carrying amount are reported in the statement of income for each period for which results of operations are presented), including, but not limited to, the following:

  (a) The beginning and ending balances

  (b) Additions (through purchases of servicing assets, assumption of servicing obligations, and servicing obligations that result from transfers of financial assets)

  (c) Disposals

  (d) Amortization

  (e) Application of valuation allowance to adjust carrying value of servicing assets

  (f) Other-than-temporary impairments

  (g) Other changes that affect the balance and a description of those changes.

(2) For each class of servicing assets and servicing liabilities, the fair value of recognized servicing assets and servicing liabilities at the beginning and end of the period if it is practicable to estimate the value.

(3) A description of the valuation techniques or other methods used to estimate fair value of the servicing assets and servicing liabilities. If a valuation model is used, the description shall include the methodology and model validation procedures, as well as quantitative and qualitative information about the assumptions used in the valuation model (for example, discount rates and prepayment speeds). (An entity that provides quantitative information about the instruments used to manage the risks inherent in the servicing assets and servicing liabilities, as encouraged by paragraph 17(e)(2), is also encouraged, but not required, to disclose a description of the valuation techniques as well as quantitative and qualitative information about the assumptions used to estimate the fair value of those instruments.)

(4) The risk characteristics of the underlying financial assets used to stratify recognized servicing assets for purposes of measuring impairment in accordance with paragraph 63.

(5) The activity by class in any valuation allowance for impairment of recognized servicing assets—including beginning and ending balances, aggregate additions charged and recoveries credited to operations, and aggregate write-downs charged against the allowance—for each period for which results of operations are presented.

hf. If the entity has securitized financial assets during any period presented and accounts for that transfer as a sale, for each major asset type (for example, mortgage loans, credit card receivables, and automobile loans):

(1) Its accounting policies for initially measuring the ~~retained~~ interests that continue to be held by the transferor, if any, and servicing assets or servicing liabilities, if any, including the methodology (whether quoted market price, prices based on sales of similar assets and liabilities, or prices based on

valuation techniques) used in determining their fair value (paragraphs 68–70)

(2) The characteristics of securitizations (a description of the transferor's continuing involvement with the transferred assets, including, but not limited to, servicing, recourse, and restrictions on ~~retained~~ interests that continue to be held by the transferor) and the gain or loss from sale of financial assets in securitizations

(3) The key assumptions[7] used in measuring the fair value of ~~retained~~ interests that continue to be held by the transferor and servicing assets or servicing liabilities, if any, at the time of securitization (including, at a minimum, quantitative information about discount rates, expected prepayments including the expected weighted-average life of prepayable financial assets,[8] and anticipated credit losses, if applicable)

(4) Cash flows between the securitization SPE and the transferor, unless reported separately elsewhere in the financial statements or notes (including proceeds from new securitizations, proceeds from collections reinvested in revolving-period securitizations, purchases of delinquent or foreclosed loans, servicing fees, and cash flows received on interests that continue to be held by the transferor~~retained~~).

ig. If the entity has ~~retained~~ interests that continue to be held by the transferor in ~~securitized~~ financial assets that it has securitized or servicing assets or servicing liabilities relating to assets that it has securitized, at the date of the latest statement of financial position presented, for each major asset type (for example, mortgage loans, credit card receivables, and automobile loans):

(1) Its accounting policies for subsequently measuring those ~~retained~~ interests, including the methodology (whether quoted market price, prices based on sales of similar assets and liabilities, or prices based on valuation techniques) used in determining their fair value (paragraphs 68–70)

(2) The key assumptions used in subsequently measuring the fair value of those interests (including, at a minimum, quantitative information about discount rates, expected prepayments including the expected weighted-average life of prepayable financial assets, and anticipated credit losses, including expected static pool losses,[9] if applicable)

(3) A sensitivity analysis or stress test showing the hypothetical effect on the fair value of those interests (including any servicing assets or servicing liabilities) of two or more unfavorable variations from the expected levels for each key assumption that is reported under (2) above independently from any change in another key assumption, and a description of the objectives, methodology, and limitations of the sensitivity analysis or stress test

(4) For the securitized assets and any other financial assets that it manages together with them:[10]

(a) The total principal amount outstanding, the portion that has been derecognized, and the portion that continues to be recognized in each category reported in the statement of financial position, at the end of the period

(b) Delinquencies at the end of the period

(c) Credit losses, net of recoveries, during the period.

(Disclosure of average balances during the period is encouraged, but not required.)

Implementation Guidance

18. Appendix A describes certain provisions of this Statement in more detail and describes their application to certain types of transactions. Appendix A is an integral part of the standards provided in this Statement.

Effective Date and Transition

[Paragraphs 19–25 have been omitted because the effective dates of those provisions in Statement 140 have passed. However, in July 2001,

---

[7]If an entity has made multiple securitizations of the same major asset type during a period, it may disclose the range of assumptions.

[8]The weighted-average life of prepayable assets in periods (for example, months or years) can be calculated by multiplying the principal collections expected in each future period by the number of periods until that future period, summing those products, and dividing the sum by the initial principal balance.

[9]Expected static pool losses can be calculated by summing the actual and projected future credit losses and dividing the sum by the original balance of the pool of assets.

[10]Excluding securitized assets that an entity continues to service but with which it has no other continuing involvement.

FASB Technical Bulletin No. 01-1, *Effective Date for Certain Financial Institutions of Certain Provisions of Statement 140 Related to the Isolation of Transferred Financial Assets,* was issued to provide certain financial institutions with an additional transition period to apply Statement 140. That transition period will end June 30, 2006.]

Appendix A

IMPLEMENTATION GUIDANCE

Introduction

26. This appendix describes certain provisions of this Statement in more detail and describes how they apply to certain types of transactions. This appendix discusses generalized situations. Facts and circumstances and specific contracts need to be considered carefully in applying this Statement. This appendix is an integral part of the standards provided in this Statement.

Isolation beyond the Reach of the Transferor and Its Creditors

27. The nature and extent of supporting evidence required for an assertion in financial statements that transferred financial assets have been isolated—put presumptively beyond the reach of the transferor and its creditors, either by a single transaction or a series of transactions taken as a whole—depend on the facts and circumstances. All available evidence that either supports or questions an assertion shall be considered. That consideration includes making judgments about whether the contract or circumstances permit the transferor to revoke the transfer. It also may include making judgments about the kind of bankruptcy or other receivership into which a transferor or SPE might be placed, whether a transfer of financial assets would likely be deemed a true sale at law, whether the transferor is affiliated with the transferee, and other factors pertinent under applicable law. Derecognition of transferred assets is appropriate only if the available evidence provides reasonable assurance that the transferred assets would be beyond the reach of the powers of a bankruptcy trustee or other receiver for the transferor or any **consolidated affiliate of the transferor** that is not a special-purpose corporation or other entity designed to make remote the possibility that it would enter bankruptcy or other receivership (paragraph 83(c)).

28. Whether securitizations isolate transferred assets may depend on such factors as whether the securitization is accomplished in one step or two steps (paragraphs 80–84). Many common financial transactions, for example, typical repurchase agreements and securities lending transactions, isolate transferred assets from the transferor, although they may not meet the other criteria for surrender of control.

Conditions That Constrain a Transferee

29. Sale accounting is allowed under paragraph 9(b) only if each transferee has the right to pledge, or the right to exchange, the transferred assets or beneficial interests it received, but constraints on that right also matter. Many transferor-imposed or other conditions on a transferee's right to pledge or exchange a transferred asset both constrain a transferee from pledging or exchanging the transferred assets and, through that constraint, provide more than a trivial benefit to the transferor. For example, a provision in the transfer contract that prohibits selling or pledging a transferred loan receivable not only constrains the transferee but also provides the transferor with the more-than-trivial benefits of knowing who has the asset, a prerequisite to repurchasing the asset, and of being able to block the asset from finding its way into the hands of a competitor for the loan customer's business or someone that the loan customer might consider an undesirable creditor. Transferor-imposed contractual constraints that narrowly limit timing or terms, for example, allowing a transferee to pledge only on the day assets are obtained or only on terms agreed with the transferor, also constrain the transferee and presumptively provide the transferor with more-than-trivial benefits.

30. However, some conditions do not constrain a transferee from pledging or exchanging the asset and therefore do not preclude a transfer subject to such a condition from being accounted for as a sale. For example, a transferor's right of first refusal on the occurrence of a bona fide offer to the transferee from a third party presumptively would not constrain a transferee, because that right in itself does not enable the transferor to compel the transferee to sell the assets and the transferee would be in a position to receive the sum offered by exchanging the asset, albeit possibly from the transferor rather than the third party. Further examples of conditions that presumptively would not constrain a transferee include (a) a requirement to obtain the transferor's permission to sell or pledge that is not to be unreasonably withheld, (b) a prohibition on sale to the transferor's competitor

if other potential willing buyers exist, (c) a regulatory limitation such as on the number or nature of eligible transferees (as in the case of securities issued under Securities Act Rule 144A or debt placed privately), and (d) illiquidity, for example, the absence of an active market. Judgment is required to assess the significance of some conditions. For example, a prohibition on sale to the transferor's competitor would be a significant constraint if that competitor were the only potential willing buyer other than the transferor.

31. A condition imposed by a transferor that constrains the transferee presumptively provides more than a trivial benefit to the transferor. A condition *not* imposed by the transferor that constrains the transferee may or may not provide more than a trivial benefit to the transferor. For example, if the transferor refrains from imposing its usual contractual constraint on a specific transfer because it knows an equivalent constraint is already imposed on the transferee by a third party, it presumptively benefits more than trivially from that constraint. However, the transferor cannot benefit from a constraint if it is unaware at the time of the transfer that the transferee is constrained.

Transferor's Rights or Obligations to Reacquire Transferred Assets

32. Some rights or obligations to reacquire transferred assets both constrain the transferee and provide more than a trivial benefit to the transferor, thus precluding sale accounting under paragraph 9(b). For example, a **freestanding call** option written by a transferee to the transferor benefits the transferor and, if the transferred assets are not readily obtainable in the marketplace, is likely to constrain a transferee because it might have to default if the call was exercised and it had exchanged or pledged the assets. A freestanding forward purchase-sale contract between the transferor and the transferee on transferred assets not readily obtainable in the marketplace would benefit the transferor and is likely to constrain a transferee in much the same manner. Judgment is necessary to assess constraint and benefit. For example, put options written to the transferee generally do not constrain it, but a put option on a not-readily-obtainable asset may benefit the transferor and effec-

tively constrain the transferee if the option is sufficiently deep-in-the-money when it is written that it is probable that the transferee will exercise it and the transferor will reacquire the transferred asset. In contrast, a sufficiently out-of-the-money call option held by the transferor may not constrain a transferee if it is probable when the option is written that it will not be exercised. Freestanding rights to reacquire transferred assets that are readily obtainable presumptively do not constrain the transferee from exchanging or pledging them and thus do not preclude sale accounting under paragraph 9(b).

33. Other rights or obligations to reacquire transferred assets, regardless of whether they constrain the transferee, may result in the transferor's maintaining effective control over the transferred assets, as discussed in paragraphs 50–54, thus precluding sale accounting under paragraph 9(c)(2).[15]

Conditions That Constrain a Holder of Beneficial Interests in a Qualifying SPE

34. The considerations in paragraphs 29–32, about conditions that may or may not constrain a transferee that is not a qualifying SPE from pledging or exchanging the transferred assets, also extend to conditions that may or may not constrain a BIH from pledging or exchanging its beneficial interests in assets transferred to a qualifying SPE. For example, if BIHs agree to sell their beneficial interests in a qualifying SPE back to the transferor upon request at the price paid plus a stated return, that arrangement clearly conveys more than a trivial benefit to the transferor; sale accounting for the transfer to the qualifying SPE would be precluded if that agreement constrained a BIH from exchanging or pledging its beneficial interest.

Qualifying SPE

35. A qualifying SPE[16] is a trust or other legal vehicle that meets *all* of the following conditions:

a. It is demonstrably distinct from the transferor (paragraph 36).

---

[15]And it is necessary to consider the overall effect of related rights and obligations in assessing such matters as whether a transferee is constrained or a transferor has maintained effective control. For example, if the transferor or its affiliate or agent is the servicer for the transferred asset and is empowered to decide to put the asset up for sale, and has the right of first refusal, that combination would place the transferor in position to unilaterally cause the return of a specific transferred asset and thus maintain the transferor's effective control of the transferred asset as discussed in paragraphs 9(c)(2) and 50.

[16]The description of a qualifying SPE is restrictive. The accounting for qualifying SPEs and transfers of financial assets to them should not be extended to any entity that does not currently satisfy all of the conditions articulated in this paragraph.

b. Its permitted activities (1) are significantly limited, (2) were entirely specified in the legal documents that established the SPE or created the beneficial interests in the transferred assets that it holds, and (3) may be significantly changed only with the approval of the holders of at least a majority of the beneficial interests held by entities other than any transferor, its affiliates, and its agents (paragraphs 37 and 38).

c. It may hold only:

   (1) Financial assets transferred to it that are passive in nature (paragraph 39)

   (2) Passive **derivative financial instruments** that pertain to beneficial interests (other than another derivative financial instrument) issued or sold to parties other than the transferor, its affiliates, or its agents (paragraphs 39 and 40)

   (3) Financial assets (for example, guarantees or rights to collateral) that would reimburse it if others were to fail to adequately service financial assets transferred to it or to timely pay obligations due to it and that it entered into when it was established, when assets were transferred to it, or when beneficial interests (other than derivative financial instruments) were issued by the SPE

   (4) Servicing rights related to financial assets that it holds

   (5) Temporarily, nonfinancial assets obtained in connection with the collection of financial assets that it holds (paragraph 41)

   (6) Cash collected from assets that it holds and investments purchased with that cash pending distribution to holders of beneficial interests that are appropriate for that purpose (that is, money-market or other relatively risk-free instruments without options and with maturities no later than the expected distribution date).

d. If it can sell or otherwise dispose of noncash financial assets, it can do so only in automatic response to one of the following conditions:

   (1) Occurrence of an event or circumstance that (a) is specified in the legal documents that established the SPE or created the beneficial interests in the transferred assets that it holds; (b) is outside the control of the transferor, its affiliates, or its agents; and

   (c) causes, or is expected at the date of transfer to cause, the fair value of those financial assets to decline by a specified degree below the fair value of those assets when the SPE obtained them (paragraphs 42 and 43)

   (2) Exercise by a BIH (other than the transferor, its affiliates, or its agents) of a right to put that holder's beneficial interest back to the SPE (paragraph 44)

   (3) Exercise by the transferor of a call or ROAP specified in the legal documents that established the SPE, transferred assets to the SPE, or created the beneficial interests in the transferred assets that it holds (paragraphs 51–54 and 85–88)

   (4) Termination of the SPE or maturity of the beneficial interests in those financial assets on a fixed or determinable date that is specified at inception (paragraph 45).

Need to Be Demonstrably Distinct from the Transferor

36. A qualifying SPE is demonstrably distinct from the transferor only if it cannot be unilaterally dissolved by any transferor, its affiliates, or its agents and either (a) at least 10 percent of the fair value of its beneficial interests is held by parties other than any transferor, its affiliates, or its agents or (b) the transfer is a guaranteed mortgage securitization.[17] An ability to unilaterally dissolve an SPE can take many forms, including but not limited to holding sufficient beneficial interests to demand that the trustee dissolve the SPE, the right to call all the assets transferred to the SPE, and a right to call or a prepayment privilege on the beneficial interests held by other parties.

Limits on Permitted Activities

37. The powers of the SPE must be limited to those activities allowed by paragraph 35 for it to be a qualifying SPE. Many kinds of entities are not so limited. For example, any bank, insurance company, pension plan, or investment company has powers that cannot be sufficiently limited for it to be a qualifying SPE.

38. The BIHs other than any transferor, its affiliates, or its agents may have the ability to change the powers of a qualifying SPE. If the powers of a previously qualifying SPE are changed so that the SPE is no

---

[17]An effect of that provision, in conjunction with paragraph 46, is that mortgage-backed securities retainedthat continue to be held by a transferor in a guaranteed mortgage securitization in which the SPE meets all conditions for being a qualifying SPE are classified in the financial statements of the transferor as securities that are subsequently measured under Statement 115.

longer qualifying, unless the conditions in paragraph 9(b) are then met by the SPE itself and the conditions in paragraphs 9(a) and 9(c) continue to be met, that change would bring the transferred assets held in the SPE back under the control of the transferor (paragraph 55).

Limits on What a Qualifying SPE May Hold

39. A financial asset or derivative financial instrument is passive only if holding the asset or instrument does not involve its holder in making decisions other than the decisions inherent in servicing (paragraph 61). An equity instrument is not passive if the qualifying SPE can exercise the voting rights and is permitted to choose how to vote. Investments are not passive if through them, either in themselves or in combination with other investments or rights, the SPE or any related entity, such as the transferor, its affiliates, or its agents, is able to exercise control or significant influence (as defined in generally accepted accounting principles for consolidation policy and for the equity method, respectively) over the investee. A derivative financial instrument is not passive if, for example, it includes an option allowing the SPE to choose to call or put other financial instruments; but other derivative financial instruments can be passive, for example, interest rate caps and swaps and forward contracts. Derivative financial instruments that result in liabilities, like other liabilities of a qualifying SPE, are a kind of beneficial interest in the qualifying SPE's assets.

40. A derivative financial instrument pertains to beneficial interests (other than another derivative financial instrument) issued only if it:

a. Is entered into (1) when the beneficial interests are issued by the qualifying SPE to parties other than the transferor, its affiliates, or its agents or sold to such other parties after being issued by the qualifying SPE to the transferor, its affiliates, or its agents or (2) when a passive derivative financial instrument needs to be replaced upon occurrence of an event or circumstance (specified in the legal documents that established the SPE or created the beneficial interests in the transferred assets that it holds) outside the control of the transferor, its affiliates, or its agents, for example, when the counterparty to the derivative defaults or is downgraded below a specified threshold

b. Has a notional amount that does not initially exceed the amount of those beneficial interests and is not expected to exceed them subsequently

c. Has characteristics that relate to, and partly or fully but not excessively counteract, some risk associated with those beneficial interests or the related transferred assets.

41. A qualifying SPE may hold nonfinancial assets other than servicing rights only temporarily and only if those nonfinancial assets result from collecting the transferred financial assets. For example, a qualifying SPE could be permitted to temporarily hold foreclosed nonfinancial collateral. In contrast, an entity cannot be a qualifying SPE if, for example, it receives from a transferor significant secured financial assets likely to default with the expectation that it will foreclose on and profitably manage the securing nonfinancial assets. A qualifying SPE also may hold the residual value of a sales-type or a direct financing lease only to the extent that it is guaranteed at the inception of the lease either by the lessee or by a third party financially capable of discharging the obligations that may arise from the guarantee (paragraph 89).

Limits on Sales or Other Dispositions of Assets

42. Examples of requirements to sell, exchange, put, or distribute (hereinafter referred to collectively as dispose of) noncash financial assets that *are* permitted activities of a qualifying SPE—because they respond automatically to the occurrence of an event or circumstance that (a) is specified in the legal documents that established the SPE or created the beneficial interests in the transferred assets that it holds; (b) is outside the control of the transferor, its affiliates, or its agents; and (c) causes, or is expected to cause, the fair value of those assets to decline by a specified degree below the fair value of those assets when the qualifying SPE obtained them—include requirements to dispose of transferred assets in response to:

a. A failure to properly service transferred assets that could result in the loss of a substantial third-party credit guarantee
b. A default by the obligor
c. A downgrade by a major rating agency of the transferred assets or of the underlying obligor to a rating below a specified minimum rating
d. The involuntary insolvency of the transferor
e. A decline in the fair value of the transferred assets to a specified value less than their fair value at the time they were transferred to the SPE.

43. The following are examples of powers or requirements to dispose of noncash financial assets that

are not permitted activities of a qualifying SPE, because they do not respond automatically to the occurrence of a specified event or circumstance outside the control of the transferor, its affiliates, or its agents that causes, or is expected to cause, the fair value of those transferred assets to decline by a specified degree below the fair value of those assets when the SPE obtained them:

a. A power that allows an SPE to choose to either dispose of transferred assets or hold them in response to a default, a downgrade, a decline in fair value, or a servicing failure
b. A requirement to dispose of marketable equity securities upon a specified decline from their "highest fair value" if that power could result in disposing of the asset in exchange for an amount that is more than the fair value of those assets at the time they were transferred to the SPE
c. A requirement to dispose of transferred assets in response to the violation of a nonsubstantive contractual provision (that is, a provision for which there is not a sufficiently large disincentive to ensure performance).

44. A qualifying SPE may dispose of transferred assets automatically to the extent necessary to comply with the exercise by a BIH (other than the transferor, its affiliates, or its agents) of its right to put beneficial interests back to the SPE in exchange for:

a. A full or partial distribution of those assets
b. Cash (which may require that the SPE dispose of those assets or issue beneficial interests to generate cash to fund settlement of the put)
c. New beneficial interests in those assets.

45. A qualifying SPE may have the power to dispose of assets to a party other than the transferor, its affiliate, or its agent on termination of the SPE or maturity of the beneficial interests, but only automatically on fixed or determinable dates that are specified at inception. For example, if an SPE is required to dispose of long-term mortgage loans and terminate itself at the earlier of (a) the specified maturity of beneficial interests in those mortgage loans or (b) the date of prepayment of a specified amount of the transferred mortgage loans, the termination date is a fixed or determinable date that was specified at inception. In contrast, if that SPE has the power to dispose of transferred assets on two specified dates and the SPE

can decide which transferred assets to sell on each date, the termination date is *not* a fixed or determinable date that was specified at inception.

Qualifying SPEs and Consolidated Financial Statements

46. A qualifying SPE shall not be consolidated in the financial statements of a transferor or its affiliates.

Maintaining Effective Control over Transferred Assets

Agreement to Repurchase or Redeem Transferred Assets

47. An agreement that both entitles and obligates the transferor to repurchase or redeem transferred assets from the transferee maintains the transferor's effective control over those assets under paragraph 9(c)(1), and the transfer is therefore to be accounted for as a secured borrowing, if and only if all of the following conditions are met:

a. The assets to be repurchased or redeemed are the same or substantially the same as those transferred (paragraph 48).
b. The transferor is able to repurchase or redeem them on substantially the agreed terms, even in the event of default by the transferee (paragraph 49).
c. The agreement is to repurchase or redeem them before maturity, at a fixed or determinable price.
d. The agreement is entered into concurrently with the transfer.

48. To be substantially the same,[18] the asset that was transferred and the asset that is to be repurchased or redeemed need to have all of the following characteristics:

a. The same primary obligor (except for debt guaranteed by a sovereign government, central bank, government-sponsored enterprise or agency thereof, in which case the guarantor and the terms of the guarantee must be the same)
b. Identical form and type so as to provide the same risks and rights
c. The same maturity (or in the case of mortgage-backed pass-through and pay-through securities, similar remaining weighted-average maturities

---

[18]In this Statement, the term *substantially the same* is used consistently with the usage of that term in the AICPA Statement of Position 90-3, *Definition of the Term Substantially the Same for Holders of Debt Instruments, as Used in Certain Audit Guides and a Statement of Position.*

that result in approximately the same market yield)

d. Identical contractual interest rates
e. Similar assets as collateral
f. The same aggregate unpaid principal amount or principal amounts within accepted "good delivery" standards for the type of security involved.

49. To be able to repurchase or redeem assets on substantially the agreed terms, even in the event of default by the transferee, a transferor must at all times during the contract term have obtained cash or other collateral sufficient to fund substantially all of the cost of purchasing replacement assets from others.

Ability to Unilaterally Cause the Return of Specific Transferred Assets

50. Some rights to reacquire transferred assets (or to acquire beneficial interests in transferred assets held by a qualifying SPE), regardless of whether they constrain the transferee, may result in the transferor's maintaining effective control over the transferred assets through the **unilateral ability** to cause the return of specific transferred assets. Such rights preclude sale accounting under paragraph 9(c)(2). For example, an **attached call** in itself would not constrain a transferee who is able, by exchanging or pledging the asset subject to that call, to obtain substantially all of its economic benefits. An attached call could result, however, in the transferor's maintaining effective control over the transferred asset(s) because the attached call gives the transferor the ability to unilaterally cause whoever holds that specific asset to return it. In contrast, transfers of financial assets subject to calls embedded by the issuers of the financial instruments, for example, callable bonds or prepayable mortgage loans, do not preclude sale accounting. Such an **embedded call** does not result in the transferor's maintaining effective control, because it is the issuer rather than the transferor who holds the call.

51. If the transferee is a qualifying SPE, it has met the conditions in paragraph 35(d) and therefore must be constrained from choosing to exchange or pledge the transferred assets. In that circumstance, any call held by the transferor is effectively attached to the assets and could—depending on the price and other terms of the call—maintain the transferor's effective control over transferred assets through the ability to unilaterally cause the transferee to return specific assets. For example, a transferor's unilateral ability to cause a qualifying SPE to return to the transferor or otherwise dispose of specific transferred assets at will

or, for example, in response to its decision to exit a market or a particular activity, could provide the transferor with effective control over the transferred assets.

52. A call that is attached to transferred assets maintains the transferor's effective control over those assets if, under its price and other terms, the call conveys more than a trivial benefit to the transferor. Similarly, any unilateral right to reclaim specific assets transferred to a qualifying SPE maintains the transferor's effective control over those assets if the right conveys more than a trivial benefit to the transferor. A call or other right conveys more than a trivial benefit if the price to be paid is fixed, determinable, or otherwise potentially advantageous, unless because that price is so far out of the money or for other reasons it is probable when the option is written that the transferor will not exercise it. Thus, for example, a call on specific assets transferred to a qualifying SPE at a price fixed at their principal amount maintains the transferor's effective control over the assets subject to that call. Effective control over transferred assets can be present even if the right to reclaim is indirect. For example, if an embedded call allows a transferor to buy back the beneficial interests of a qualifying SPE at a fixed price, then the transferor remains in effective control of the assets underlying those beneficial interests. A cleanup call, however, is permitted as an exception to that general principle.

53. A right to reclaim specific transferred assets by paying their fair value when reclaimed generally does not maintain effective control, because it does not convey a more than trivial benefit to the transferor. However, a transferor has maintained effective control if it has such a right and also holds the residual interest in the transferred assets. For example, if a transferor can reclaim such assets at termination of the qualifying SPE by purchasing them in an auction, and thus at what might appear to be fair value, then sale accounting for the assets it can reclaim would be precluded. Such circumstances provide the transferor with a more than trivial benefit and effective control over the assets, because it can pay any price it chooses in the auction and recover any excess paid over fair value through its residual interest.

54. A transferor that has a right to reacquire transferred assets from a qualifying SPE does not maintain effective control if the reclaimed assets would be randomly selected and the amount of the assets reacquired is sufficiently limited (paragraph 87(a)), because that would not be a right to reacquire *specific*

assets. Nor does a transferor maintain effective control through an obligation to reacquire transferred assets from a qualifying SPE if the transfer could occur only after a specified failure of the servicer to properly service the transferred assets that could result in the loss of a third-party guarantee (paragraph 42(a)) or only after a BIH other than the transferor, its affiliate, or its agent requires a qualifying SPE to repurchase that beneficial interest (paragraph 44(b)), because the transferor could not cause that reacquisition *unilaterally.*

Changes That Result in the Transferor's Regaining Control of Assets Sold

55. A change in law, status of the transferee as a qualifying SPE, or other circumstance may result in the transferor's regaining control of assets previously accounted for appropriately as having been sold, because one or more of the conditions in paragraph 9 are no longer met. Such a change, unless it arises solely from either the initial application of this Statement or a change in market prices (for example, an increase in price that moves into-the-money a freestanding call that was originally sufficiently out-of-the-money that it was judged not to constrain the transferee), is accounted for in the same manner as a purchase of the assets from the former transferee(s) in exchange for liabilities assumed (paragraph 11). After that change, the transferor recognizes in its financial statements those assets together with liabilities to the former transferee(s) or BIHs in those assets (paragraph 38). The transferor initially measures those assets and liabilities at fair value on the date of the change, as if the transferor purchased the assets and assumed the liabilities on that date. The former transferee would derecognize the assets on that date, as if it had sold the assets in exchange for a receivable from the transferor.

Measurement of Interests Held after a Transfer of Financial Assets

Assets Obtained and Liabilities Incurred as Proceeds

56. The proceeds from a sale of financial assets consist of the cash and any other assets obtained, including separately recognized servicing assets, in the transfer less any liabilities incurred, including separately recognized servicing liabilities. Any asset obtained that is not an interest in the transferred asset is part of the proceeds from the sale. Any liability incurred, even if it is related to the transferred assets, is a reduction of the proceeds. Any derivative financial instrument entered into concurrently with a transfer of financial assets is either an asset obtained or a liability incurred and part of the proceeds received in the transfer. All proceeds and reductions of proceeds from a sale shall be initially measured at fair value, if practicable.

Illustration—Recording Transfers with Proceeds of Cash, Derivatives, and Other Liabilities

57. Company A sells loans with a fair value of $1,100 and a carrying amount of $1,000. Company A ~~retains~~undertakes no servicing responsibilities but obtains an option to purchase from the transferee loans similar to the loans sold (which are readily obtainable in the marketplace) and assumes a limited recourse obligation to repurchase delinquent loans. Company A agrees to provide the transferee a return at a floating rate of interest even though the contractual terms of the loan are fixed rate in nature (that provision is effectively an interest rate swap).

Fair Values

Cash proceeds	$1,050
Interest rate swap	40
Call option	70
Recourse obligation	60

Net Proceeds

Cash received	$1,050
Plus: Call option	70
Interest rate swap	40
Less: Recourse obligation	(60)
Net proceeds	$1,100

Gain on Sale

Net proceeds	$1,100
Carrying amount of loans sold	1,000
Gain on sale	$ 100

Journal Entry

Cash	1,050	
Interest rate swap	40	
Call option	70	
Loans		1,000
Recourse obligation		60
Gain on sale		100
To record transfer		

~~Retained~~ Interests That Continue to Be Held by a Transferor

58. Other interests in transferred assets—those that are not part of the proceeds of a transfer—are ~~retained~~interests that continue to be held by a transferor over which a transferor has not relinquished control. Interests that continue to be held by a transferor~~They~~ shall be measured at the date of the transfer by allocating the previous carrying amount between the assets sold, if any, and the ~~retained~~interests that continue to be held by a transferor, based on their relative fair values. Allocation procedures shall be applied to all transfers in which interests ~~are~~continue to be held by a transferor~~retained~~, even those that do not qualify as sales. Examples of ~~retained~~interests that continue to be held by a transferor include securities backed by the transferred assets, undivided interests, ~~servicing assets,~~ and cash reserve accounts and residual interests in securitization trusts. If a transferor cannot determine whether an asset is an ~~retained~~interest that continues to be held by a transferor or proceeds from the sale, the asset shall be treated as proceeds from the sale and accounted for in accordance with paragraph 56.

59. If the ~~retained~~interests that continue to be held by a transferor are subordinated to more senior interests held by others, that subordination may concentrate most of the risks inherent in the transferred assets into the ~~retained~~interests that continue to be held by a transferor~~most of the risks inherent in the transferred assets~~ and shall be taken into consideration in estimating the fair value of those~~the retained~~ interests. For example, if the amount of the gain recognized, after allocation, on a securitization with a subordinated ~~retained~~interest that continues to be held by the transferor is greater than the gain that would have been recognized had the entire asset been sold, the transferor needs to be able to identify why that can occur. Otherwise, it is likely that the effect~~impact~~ of subordination~~the retained interest being subordinate~~ to a senior interest has not been adequately considered in the determination of the fair value of the subordinated ~~retained~~interest that continues to be held by a transferor.

Illustration—Recording Transfers of Partial Interests

60. Company B sells a pro rata nine-tenths interest in loans with a fair value of $1,100 and a carrying amount of $1,000. There is no servicing asset or liability, because Company B estimates that the **benefits of servicing** are just adequate to compensate it for its servicing responsibilities.

Fair Values

Cash proceeds for nine-tenths interest sold	$990
One-tenth interest ~~retained~~that continues to be held by the transferor [($990 ÷ 9/10) × 1/10]	110

Carrying Amount Based on Relative Fair Values

	Fair Value	Percentage of Total Fair Value	Allocated Carrying Amount
Nine-tenths interest sold	$ 990	90	$ 900
One-tenth interest ~~retained~~that continues to be held by the transferor	110	10	100
Total	$1,100	100	$1,000

Gain on Sale

Net proceeds	$990
Carrying amount of loans sold	900
Gain on sale	$ 90

Journal Entry

Cash	990	
Loans		900
Gain on sale		90
To record transfer		

Servicing Assets and Liabilities

61. Servicing of mortgage loans, credit card receivables, or other financial assets commonly includes, but is not limited to, collecting principal, interest, and escrow payments from borrowers; paying taxes and insurance from escrowed funds; monitoring delinquencies; executing foreclosure if necessary; temporarily investing funds pending distribution; remitting fees to guarantors, trustees, and others providing services; and accounting for and remitting principal and interest payments to the holders of beneficial interests in the financial assets. Servicing is inherent in all financial assets; it becomes a distinct asset or liability ~~only when contractually separated from the underlying assets by sale or securitization of the assets with servicing retained or separate purchase or assumption of the servicing~~for accounting purposes only in the circumstances described in paragraph 62.

62. An entity that undertakes a contract to service financial assets shall recognize either a servicing asset or a servicing liability each time it undertakes an obligation to service a financial asset that (a) results from a transfer of the servicer's financial assets that meets the requirements for sale accounting, (b) results from a transfer of the servicer's financial assets to a qualifying SPE in a guaranteed mortgage securitization in which the transferor retains all of the resulting securities and classifies them as either available-for-sale securities or trading securities in accordance with Statement 115, or (c) is acquired or assumed and the servicing obligation does not relate to financial assets of the servicer or its consolidated affiliates.~~, with only one exception. (That exception is~~ However, if the transferor transfers the assets in a guaranteed mortgage securitization, retains all of the resulting securities, and classifies them as debt se-

curities held-to-maturity in accordance with Statement 115, ~~in which case~~ the servicing asset or servicing liability may be reported together with the asset being serviced and not recognized separately.~~)~~ ~~Each sale or securitization with servicing retained or separate purchase or assumption of servicing results in a servicing contract.~~ A servicer of financial assets commonly receives the benefits of servicing—revenues from contractually specified servicing fees, a portion of the interest from the financial assets, late charges, and other ancillary sources, including "float," all of which it is entitled to receive only if it performs the servicing—and incurs the costs of servicing the assets. ~~Each servicing contract results in a servicing asset or servicing liability.~~ Typically, the benefits of servicing are expected to be more than **adequate compensation** to a servicer for performing the servicing, and the contract results in a servicing asset. However, if the benefits of servicing are not expected to adequately compensate a servicer for performing the servicing, the contract results in a servicing liability. (A servicing asset may become a servicing liability, or vice versa, if circumstances change, and the initial measure for servicing may be zero if the benefits of servicing are just adequate to compensate the servicer for its servicing responsibilities.) A servicer would account for its servicing contract that qualifies for separate recognition as a servicing asset or a servicing liability initially measured at its fair value regardless of whether explicit consideration was exchanged.

62A. A servicer that transfers or securitizes financial assets in a transaction that does not meet the requirements for sale accounting and is accounted for as a secured borrowing with the underlying assets remaining on the transferor's balance sheet shall not recognize a servicing asset or a servicing liability. However, if a transferor enters into a servicing contract when the transferor transfers mortgage loans in a guaranteed mortgage securitization, retains all the resulting securities, and classifies those securities as either available-for-sale securities or trading securities in accordance with Statement 115, the transferor shall separately recognize a servicing asset or a servicing liability.

63. A servicer that recognizes a servicing asset or servicing liability shall account for the contract to service financial assets separately from those financial assets, as follows:

a. Report servicing assets separately from servicing liabilities in the statement of financial position (paragraph 13B).

b. Initially measure servicing assets and servicing liabilities ~~retained in a sale or securitization of the assets being serviced~~ at fair value ~~their allocated previous carrying amount based on relative fair values, if practicable, at the date of the sale or securitization~~ (paragraphs 10, 11(b), 11(c), ~~58–60,~~ and 68–72).

~~c. Initially measure servicing assets purchased or servicing liabilities assumed at fair value (paragraph 13).~~

~~d. Initially measure servicing liabilities undertaken in a sale or securitization at fair value, if practicable (paragraphs 11(b), 11(c), and 68–72).~~

ce. Account separately for rights to future interest income from the serviced assets that exceeds contractually specified servicing fees. Those rights are not servicing assets; they are financial assets, effectively interest-only strips to be accounted for in accordance with paragraph 14 of this Statement.

d. Identify classes of servicing assets and servicing liabilities based on (1) the availability of market inputs used in determining the fair value of servicing assets and servicing liabilities, (2) an entity's method for managing the risks of its servicing assets and servicing liabilities, or (3) both.

ef. Subsequently measure each class of separately recognized servicing assets and servicing liabilities either at fair value or by amortizing the amount recognized in proportion to and over the period of estimated net servicing income for assets—(the excess of servicing revenues over servicing costs) or the period of estimated net servicing loss for servicing liabilities (the excess of servicing costs over servicing revenues). Different elections can be made for different classes of servicing assets and servicing liabilities. An entity may make an irrevocable decision to subsequently measure a class of servicing assets and servicing liabilities at fair value at the beginning of any fiscal year. Once a servicing asset or a servicing liability is reported in a class of servicing assets and servicing liabilities that an entity elects to subsequently measure at fair value, that servicing asset or servicing liability cannot be placed in a class of servicing assets and servicing liabilities that is subsequently measured using the amortization method. Changes in fair value should be reported in earnings for servicing assets and servicing liabilities subsequently measured at fair value (paragraph 13A(b)).

fg. Subsequently evaluate and measure impairment of each class of separately recognized servicing assets that are subsequently measured using the amortization method described in paragraph 13A(a) as follows:

(1) Stratify servicing assets within a class based on one or more of the predominant risk characteristics of the underlying financial assets. Those characteristics may include financial asset type,[19] size, interest rate, date of origination, term, and geographic location.

(2) Recognize impairment through a valuation allowance for an individual stratum. The amount of impairment recognized separately shall be the amount by which the carrying amount of servicing assets for a stratum exceeds their fair value. The fair value of servicing assets that have not been recognized shall not be used in the evaluation of impairment.

(3) Adjust the valuation allowance to reflect changes in the measurement of impairment subsequent to the initial measurement of impairment. Fair value in excess of the carrying amount of servicing assets for that stratum, however, shall not be recognized. This Statement does not address when an entity should record a direct write-down of recognized servicing assets (paragraph 13).

gh. Subsequently measure servicing liabilities by amortizing the amount recognized in proportion to and over the period of estimated net servicing loss—the excess of servicing costs over servicing revenues. However,For servicing liabilities subsequently measured using the amortization method, if subsequent events have increased the fair value of the liability above the carrying amount, for example, because of significant changes in the amount or timing of actual or expected future cash flows fromrelative to the cash flows previously projected, the servicer shall revise its earlier estimates and recognize the increased obligation as a loss in earnings (paragraph 13).

64. As indicated above, transferors sometimes agree to take on servicing responsibilities when the future benefits of servicing are not expected to adequately compensate them for performing that servicing. In that circumstance, the result is a servicing liability rather than a servicing asset. For example, if in the transaction illustrated in paragraph 57 the transferor had agreed to service the loans without explicit compensation and it estimated the fair value of that servicing obligation at $50, net proceeds would be reduced to $1,050, gain on sale would be reduced to $50, and the transferor would report a servicing liability of $50.

Illustration—Sale of Receivables with Servicing ~~*Retained*~~*Obtained*

65. Company C originates $1,000 of loans that yield 10 percent interest income for their estimated lives of 9 years. Company C sells the $1,000 principal plus the right to receive interest income of 8 percent to another entity for $1,000. Company C will continue to service the loans, and the contract stipulates that its compensation for performing the servicing is the right to receive half of the interest income not sold. The remaining half of the interest income not sold is considered an interest-only strip receivable that Company C classifies as an available-for-sale security. At the date of the transfer, the fair value of the loans, including servicing, is $1,100. The fair values of the servicing asset and the interest-only strip receivable areis $40 and $60, respectively.

Fair Values

Cash proceeds	$1,000
Servicing asset	40
Interest-only strip receivable	60

Net Proceeds

Cash proceeds	$1,000
Servicing asset	40
Net proceeds	$1,040

---

[19]For example, for mortgage loans, financial asset type refers to the various conventional or government guaranteed or insured mortgage loans and adjustable-rate or fixed-rate mortgage loans.

Carrying Amount Based on Relative Fair Values

	Fair Value	Percentage of Total Fair Value	Allocated Carrying Amount
~~Loans sold~~	~~$1,000~~	~~91.0~~	~~$ 910~~
~~Servicing asset~~	~~40~~	~~3.6~~	~~36~~
~~Interest-only strip receivable~~	~~60~~	~~5.4~~	~~54~~
~~Total~~	~~$1,100~~	~~100.00~~	~~$1,000~~

	Fair Value	Percentage of Total Fair Value	Allocated Carrying Amount
Loans sold	$1,040	94.55	$ 945.50
Interest-only strip receivable	60	5.45	54.50
Total	$1,100	100.00	$1,000.00

Gain on Sale

Net proceeds	$1,040.00~~1,000~~
Less: Carrying amount of loans sold	945.50~~910~~
Gain on sale	$ 94.50~~90~~

Journal Entries

Cash	1,000.00	
Interest-only strip receivable	54.50	
Servicing asset	40.00	
Loans		1,000.00~~910~~
Gain on sale		94.50~~90~~
To record transfer and to recognize interest-only strip receivable and servicing asset		

~~Servicing asset~~	~~36~~	
~~Interest-only strip receivable~~	~~54~~	
~~Loans~~		~~90~~
~~To record servicing asset and interest-only strip receivable~~		

Interest-only strip receivable	5.506	
~~Equity~~Other comprehensive income		5.506
To begin to subsequently measure interest-only strip receivable like an available-for-sale security (paragraph 14)		

66. The previous illustration demonstrates how a transferor would account for a simple sale ~~or securitization~~ in which servicing is ~~retained~~obtained. Company C might instead transfer the financial assets to a corporation or a trust that is a qualifying SPE. The qualifying SPE then securitizes the loans by selling beneficial interests to the public. The qualifying SPE pays the cash proceeds to the original transferor, which accounts for the transfer as a sale and derecognizes the financial assets assuming that the criteria in paragraph 9 are met. Securitizations often combine the elements shown in paragraphs 57, 60, and 65, as illustrated below.

Illustration—Recording Transfers of Partial Interests with Proceeds of Cash, Derivatives, Other Liabilities, and Servicing

67. Company D originates $1,000 of prepayable loans that yield 10 percent interest income for their 9-year expected lives. Company D sells nine-tenths of the principal plus interest of 8 percent to another entity. Company D will continue to service the loans, and the contract stipulates that its compensation for performing the servicing is the 2 percent of the interest income not sold. Company D obtains an option to purchase from the transferee loans similar to the loans sold (which are readily obtainable in the marketplace) and incurs a limited recourse obligation to repurchase delinquent loans. At the date of transfer, the fair value of the loans is $1,100.

Fair Values

Cash proceeds	$900
Call option	70
Recourse obligation	(60)
Servicing asset	90
One-tenth interest ~~retained~~that continues to be held by the transferor	100

Net Proceeds

Cash received	$ 900
Plus: Servicing asset	90
Plus: Call option	70
Less: Recourse obligation	(60)
Net proceeds	$1,000~~910~~

Carrying Amount Based on Relative Fair Values

	Fair Value	Percentage of Total Fair Value	Allocated Carrying Amount
~~Interest sold~~	~~$ 910~~	~~83~~	~~$ 830~~
~~Servicing asset~~	~~90~~	~~8~~	~~80~~
~~One-tenth interest retained~~	~~100~~	~~9~~	~~90~~
~~Total~~	~~$1,100~~	~~100~~	~~$1,000~~

	Fair Value	Percentage of Total Fair Value	Allocated Carrying Amount
Interest sold	$1,000	90.9	$ 909
One-tenth interest that continues to be held by the transferor	100	9.1	91
Total	$1,100	100.0	$1,000

Gain on Sale

Net proceeds	$1,000 ~~910~~
Less: Carrying amount of loans sold	(909)~~830~~
Gain on sale	$91 ~~80~~

Loans Sold

Carrying amount of loans	$1,000
Less: Allocated carrying amount of interest that continues to be held by the transferor	(91)
Loans sold	$ 909

Journal Entries

Cash	900	
Call option	70	
Servicing asset	90	
Loans		909~~830~~
Recourse obligation		60
Gain on sale		91~~80~~

To record transfer and to recognize servicing asset, call option, and recourse obligation

~~Servicing asset~~	~~80~~	
~~Loans~~		~~80~~

~~To record servicing asset~~

~~At the time of the transfer, Company D reports its one-tenth retained interest in the loans at its allocated carrying amount of $90.~~

Fair Value

68. The fair value of an asset (or liability) is the amount at which that asset (or liability) could be bought (or incurred) or sold (or settled) in a current transaction between willing parties, that is, other than in a forced or liquidation sale. Quoted market prices in active markets are the best evidence of fair value and shall be used as the basis for the measurement, if available. If a quoted market price is available, the fair value is the product of the number of trading units times that market price.

69. If quoted market prices are not available, the estimate of fair value shall be based on the best information available in the circumstances. The estimate

of fair value shall consider prices for similar assets and liabilities and the results of valuation techniques to the extent available in the circumstances. Examples of valuation techniques include the present value of estimated future cash flows,[20] option-pricing models, matrix pricing, option-adjusted spread models, and fundamental analysis. Valuation techniques for measuring financial assets and liabilities and servicing assets and liabilities shall be consistent with the objective of measuring fair value. Those techniques shall incorporate assumptions that market participants would use in their estimates of values, future revenues, and future expenses, including assumptions about interest rates, default, prepayment, and volatility.[21] In measuring **financial liabilities** and servicing liabilities at fair value, the objective is to estimate the value of the assets required currently to (a) settle the liability with the holder or (b) transfer a liability to an entity of comparable credit standing.

70. Estimates of expected future cash flows, if used to estimate fair value, shall be based on reasonable and supportable assumptions and projections. All available evidence shall be considered in developing estimates of expected future cash flows. The weight given to the evidence shall be commensurate with the extent to which the evidence can be verified objectively. If a range is estimated for either the amount or timing of possible cash flows, the likelihood of possible outcomes shall be considered either directly, if applying an expected cash flow approach, or indirectly through the risk-adjusted discount rate, if determining the best estimate of future cash flows.

If It Is Not Practicable to Estimate Fair Values

71. If it is not practicable to estimate the fair values of assets, the transferor shall record those assets at zero. If it is not practicable to estimate the fair values of liabilities, the transferor shall recognize no gain on the transaction and shall record those liabilities at the greater of:

a. The excess, if any, of (1) the fair values of assets obtained less the fair values of other liabilities incurred, over (2) the sum of the carrying values of the assets transferred

b. The amount that would be recognized in accordance with FASB Statement No. 5, *Accounting for Contingencies,* as interpreted by FASB Interpretation No. 14, *Reasonable Estimation of the Amount of a Loss.*

Illustration—Recording Transfers If It Is Not Practicable to Estimate a Fair Value

72. Company E sells loans with a carrying amount of $1,000 to another entity for cash proceeds of $1,050 plus a call option to purchase loans similar to the loans sold (which are readily obtainable in the marketplace) and incurs a limited recourse obligation to repurchase any delinquent loans. Company E undertakes an obligation to service the transferred assets for the other entity. In Case 1, Company E finds it impracticable to estimate the fair value of the servicing contract, although it is confident that servicing revenues will be more than adequate compensation for performing the servicing. In Case 2, Company E finds it impracticable to estimate the fair value of the recourse obligation.

[20]FASB Concepts Statement No. 7, *Using Cash Flow Information and Present Value in Accounting Measurements,* discusses the use of present value techniques in measuring the fair value of an asset (or liability) in paragraphs 42–54 and 75–88. The Board believes that an expected present value technique is superior to traditional "best estimate" techniques, especially in situations in which the timing or amount of estimated cash flows is uncertain, as is often the case for retained interests that continue to be held by a transferor in transferred financial assets. Concepts Statement 7 also discusses in paragraph 44 the steps needed to complete a proper search for the "rate commensurate with the risk" in applying the traditional technique.

[21]The timing and amount of future cash flows for retained interests in securitizations that continue to be held by a transferor are commonly uncertain, especially if those interests are subordinate to more senior beneficial interests. Applying the present value approach depends heavily on assumptions about default and prepayment of all the assets securitized, because of the implicit credit or prepayment risk enhancement arising from the subordination.

Fair Values	Case 1	Case 2
Cash proceeds	$1,050	$1,050
Servicing asset	XX*	40
Call option	70	70
Recourse obligation	(60)	XX*
Fair value of loans transferred	1,100	1,100

*Not practicable to estimate fair value.

Net Proceeds	Case 1	Case 2
Cash received	$1,050	$1,050
Plus: Servicing asset	XX*	40
Plus: Call option	70	70
Less: Recourse obligation	(60)	XX[†]
Net proceeds	$1,060	$1,160~~1,120~~

Carrying Amount Based on Relative Fair Values (Case 1)

	Fair Value	Percentage of Total Fair Value	Allocated Carrying Amount
~~Loans sold~~	~~$1,060~~	~~100~~	~~$1,000~~
~~Servicing asset~~	~~0~~	~~0~~	~~0~~
~~Total~~	~~$1,060~~	~~100~~	~~$1,000~~

Carrying Amount Based on Relative Fair Values (Case 2)

	Fair Value	Percentage of Total Fair Value	Allocated Carrying Amount
~~Loans sold~~	~~$1,120~~	~~97~~	~~$ 970~~
~~Servicing asset~~	~~40~~	~~3~~	~~30~~
~~Total~~	~~$1,160~~	~~100~~	~~$1,000~~

Gain on Sale	Case 1	Case 2
Net proceeds	$1,060	$1,160
Carrying amount of loans	1,000	1,000
Less: Recourse obligation	0	(160)[†]
Gain on sale	$ 60	$ 0

*Assets shall be recorded at zero if an estimate of the fair value of the assets is not practicable.

[†]The amount recorded as a liability in this example equals the sum of the known assets less the fair value of the known liabilities, that is, the amount that results in no gain or loss.

Journal Entries	Case 1		Case 2	
Cash	1,050		1,050	
Servicing asset	0*		40~~30~~	
Call option	70		70	
Loans		1,000		1,000
Recourse obligation		60		160~~150~~†
Gain on sale		60		0
To record transfer				

---

*Assets shall be recorded at zero if an estimate of the fair value of the assets is not practicable.

†The amount recorded as a liability in this example equals the sum of the known assets less the fair value of the known liabilities, that is, the amount that results in no gain or loss.

Securitizations

73. Financial assets such as mortgage loans, automobile loans, trade receivables, credit card receivables, and other revolving charge accounts are assets commonly transferred in securitizations. Securitizations of mortgage loans may include pools of single-family residential mortgages or other types of real estate mortgage loans, for example, multifamily residential mortgages and commercial property mortgages. Securitizations of loans secured by chattel mortgages on automotive vehicles as well as other equipment (including direct financing or sales-type leases) also are common. Both financial and nonfinancial assets can be securitized; life insurance policy loans, patent and copyright royalties, and even taxi medallions also have been securitized. But securitizations of nonfinancial assets are outside the scope of this Statement.

74. An originator of a typical securitization (the transferor) transfers a portfolio of financial assets to an SPE, commonly a trust. In "pass-through" and "pay-through" securitizations, receivables are transferred to the SPE at the inception of the securitization, and no further transfers are made; all cash collections are paid to the holders of beneficial interests in the SPE. In "revolving-period" securitizations, receivables are transferred at the inception and also periodically (daily or monthly) thereafter for a defined period (commonly three to eight years), referred to as the revolving period. During the revolving period, the SPE uses most of the cash collections to purchase additional receivables from the transferor on prearranged terms.

75. Beneficial interests in the SPE are sold to investors and the proceeds are used to pay the transferor

for the assets transferred. Those beneficial interests may comprise either a single class having equity characteristics or multiple classes of interests, some having debt characteristics and others having equity characteristics. The cash collected from the portfolio is distributed to the investors and others as specified by the legal documents that established the SPE.

76. Pass-through, pay-through, and revolving-period securitizations that meet the criteria in paragraph 9 qualify for sale accounting under this Statement. All financial assets obtained or ~~retained~~that continue to be held by a transferor and liabilities incurred by the originator of a securitization that qualifies as a sale shall be recognized and measured as provided in paragraphs 10 and 11; that includes the implicit forward contract to sell new receivables during a revolving period, which may become valuable or onerous to the transferor as interest rates and other market conditions change.

Revolving-Period Securitizations

77. The value of the forward contract implicit in a revolving-period securitization arises from the difference between the agreed-upon rate of return to investors on their beneficial interests in the trust and current market rates of return on similar investments. For example, if the agreed-upon annual rate of return to investors in a trust is 6 percent, and later market rates of return for those investments increased to 7 percent, the forward contract's value to the transferor (and burden to the investors) would approximate the present value of 1 percent of the amount of the investment for each year remaining in the revolving structure after the receivables already transferred have been collected. If a forward contract to sell receivables is entered into at the market rate, its value at

inception may be zero. Changes in the fair value of the forward contract are likely to be greater if the investors receive a fixed rate than if the investors receive a rate that varies based on changes in market rates.

78. Gain or loss recognition for revolving-period receivables sold to a securitization trust is limited to receivables that exist and have been sold. Recognition of servicing assets or liabilities for revolving-period receivables is similarly limited to the servicing for the receivables that exist and have been transferred. As new receivables are sold, rights to service them become assets or liabilities and are recognized.

79. Revolving-period securitizations may use either a discrete trust, used for a single securitization, or a master trust, used for many securitizations. To achieve another securitization using an existing master trust, a transferor first transfers additional receivables to the trust and then sells additional ownership interests in the trust to investors. Adding receivables to a master trust, in itself, is neither a sale nor a secured borrowing under paragraph 9, because that transfer only increases the transferor's beneficial interest in the trust's assets. A sale or secured borrowing does not occur until the transferor receives consideration other than beneficial interests in the transferred assets. Transfers that result in an exchange of cash, that is, either transfers that in essence replace previously transferred receivables that have been collected or sales of beneficial interests to outside investors, are transfers in exchange for consideration other than beneficial interests in the transferred assets and thus are accounted for as sales (if they satisfy all the criteria in paragraph 9) or as secured borrowings.

Isolation of Transferred Assets in Securitizations

80. A securitization carried out in one transfer or a series of transfers may or may not isolate the transferred assets beyond the reach of the transferor and its creditors. Whether it does depends on the structure of the securitization transaction taken as a whole, considering such factors as the type and extent of further involvement in arrangements to protect investors from credit and interest rate risks, the availability of other assets, and the powers of bankruptcy courts or other receivers.

81. In certain securitizations, a corporation that, if it failed, would be subject to the U.S. Bankruptcy Code transfers financial assets to a special-purpose trust in exchange for cash. The trust raises that cash by issuing to investors beneficial interests that pass through all cash received from the financial assets, and the transferor has no further involvement with the trust or the transferred assets. The Board understands that those securitizations generally would be judged as having isolated the assets, because in the absence of any continuing involvement there would be reasonable assurance that the transfer would be found to be a true sale at law that places the assets beyond the reach of the transferor and its creditors, even in bankruptcy or other receivership.

82. In other securitizations, a similar corporation transfers financial assets to an SPE in exchange for cash and beneficial interests in the transferred assets. That entity raises the cash by issuing to investors commercial paper that gives them a senior interest in cash received from the financial assets. The beneficial interests retained~~retained~~that continue to be held by the transferring corporation represent a junior interest to be reduced by any credit losses on the financial assets in trust. The commercial paper interests are highly rated by credit rating agencies only if both (a) the credit enhancement from the junior interest is sufficient and (b) the transferor is highly rated. Depending on facts and circumstances, the Board understands that those "single-step" securitizations often would be judged in the United States as not having isolated the assets, because the nature of the continuing involvement may make it difficult to obtain reasonable assurance that the transfer would be found to be a true sale at law that places the assets beyond the reach of the transferor and its creditors in U.S. bankruptcy (paragraph 113). If the transferor fell into bankruptcy and the transfer was found not to be a true sale at law, investors in the transferred assets might be subjected to an automatic stay that would delay payments due them, and they might have to share in bankruptcy expenses and suffer further losses if the transfer was recharacterized as a secured loan.

83. Still other securitizations use two transfers intended to isolate transferred assets beyond the reach of the transferor and its creditors, even in bankruptcy. In those "two-step" structures:

a. First, the corporation transfers financial assets to a special-purpose corporation that, although wholly owned, is so designed that the possibility that the transferor or its creditors could reclaim the assets is remote. This first transfer is designed to be judged to be a true sale at law, in part because the transferor does not provide "excessive" credit or yield protection to the special-purpose corporation, and the Board understands that transferred assets are likely to be judged beyond the reach of the transferor or the transferor's creditors even in bankruptcy.

b. Second, the special-purpose corporation transfers the assets to a trust or other legal vehicle with a sufficient increase in the credit or yield protection on the second transfer (provided by a junior ~~retained~~ beneficial interest that continues to be held by the transferor or other means) to merit the high credit rating sought by third-party investors who buy senior beneficial interests in the trust. Because of that aspect of its design, that second transfer might not be judged to be a true sale at law and, thus, the transferred assets could at least in theory be reached by a bankruptcy trustee for the special-purpose corporation.

c. However, the special-purpose corporation is designed to make remote the possibility that it would enter bankruptcy, either by itself or by substantive consolidation into a bankruptcy of its parent should that occur. For example, its charter forbids it from undertaking any other business or incurring any liabilities, so that there can be no creditors to petition to place it in bankruptcy. Furthermore, its dedication to a single purpose is intended to make it extremely unlikely, even if it somehow entered bankruptcy, that a receiver under the U.S. Bankruptcy Code could reclaim the transferred assets because it has no other assets to substitute for the transferred assets.

The Board understands that the "two-step" securitizations described above, taken as a whole, generally would be judged under present U.S. law as having isolated the assets beyond the reach of the transferor and its creditors, even in bankruptcy or other receivership.

84. The powers of receivers for entities not subject to the U.S. Bankruptcy Code (for example, banks subject to receivership by the FDIC) vary considerably, and therefore some receivers may be able to reach financial assets transferred under a particular arrangement and others may not. A securitization may isolate transferred assets from a transferor subject to such a receiver and its creditors even though it is accomplished by only one transfer directly to an SPE that issues beneficial interests to investors and the transferor provides credit or yield protection. For entities that are subject to other possible bankruptcy,

conservatorship, or other receivership procedures in the United States or other jurisdictions, judgments about whether transferred assets have been isolated need to be made in relation to the powers of bankruptcy courts or trustees, conservators, or receivers in those jurisdictions.

Removal-of-Accounts Provisions

85. Many transfers of financial assets in securitizations empower the transferor to reclaim assets subject to certain restrictions. Such a power is sometimes called a removal-of-accounts provision (ROAP). Whether a ROAP precludes sale accounting depends on whether the ROAP results in the transferor's maintaining effective control over specific transferred assets (paragraphs 9(c)(2) and 51–54).

86. The following are examples of ROAPs that preclude transfers from being accounted for as sales:

a. An unconditional ROAP or repurchase agreement that allows the transferor to specify the assets that may be removed, because such a provision allows the transferor unilaterally to remove specific assets

b. A ROAP conditioned on a transferor's decision to exit some portion of its business, because whether it can be triggered by canceling an affinity relationship, spinning off a business segment, or accepting a third party's bid to purchase a specified (for example, geographic) portion of the transferor's business, such a provision allows the transferor unilaterally to remove specific assets.

87. The following are examples of ROAPs that *do not* preclude transfers from being accounted for as sales:

a. A ROAP for random removal of excess assets, if the ROAP is sufficiently limited so that the transferor cannot remove specific transferred assets, for example, by limiting removals to the amount of the ~~transferor's retained~~ interests that continue to be held by the transferor and to one removal per month

b. A ROAP for defaulted receivables, because the removal would be allowed only after a third party's action (default) and could not be caused unilaterally by the transferor

c. A ROAP conditioned on a third-party cancellation, or expiration without renewal, of an affinity or private-label arrangement, because the removal would be allowed only after a third party's action (cancellation) or decision not to act (expiration) and could not be caused unilaterally by the transferor.

88. A ROAP that can be exercised only in response to a third party's action that has not yet occurred does not maintain the transferor's effective control over assets potentially subject to that ROAP. However, when a third party's action (such as default or cancellation) or decision not to act (expiration) occurs that allows removal of assets to be initiated solely by the transferor, the transferor must recognize any assets subject to the ROAP, whether the ROAP is exercised or not. If the ROAP is exercised, the assets are recognized because the transferor has reclaimed the assets. If the ROAP is not exercised, the assets are recognized because the transferor now can unilaterally cause the qualifying SPE to return those specific assets and, therefore, the transferor once again has effective control over those transferred assets (paragraph 55).

Sales-Type and Direct Financing Lease Receivables

89. Sales-type and direct financing receivables secured by leased equipment, referred to as gross investment in lease receivables, are made up of two components: minimum lease payments and residual values. Minimum lease payments are requirements for lessees to pay cash to lessors and meet the definition of a financial asset. Thus, transfers of minimum lease payments are subject to the requirements of this Statement. Residual values represent the lessor's estimate of the "salvage" value of the leased equipment at the end of the lease term and may be either guaranteed or unguaranteed; residual values meet the defini-

tion of financial assets *to the extent that they are guaranteed at the inception of the lease.* Thus, transfers of residual values guaranteed at inception also are subject to the requirements of this Statement. Unguaranteed residual values do not meet the definition of financial assets, nor do residual values guaranteed after inception, and transfers of them are not subject to the requirements of this Statement. Transfers of residual values not guaranteed at inception continue to be subject to Statement 13, as amended. Because residual values guaranteed at inception are financial assets, increases to their estimated value over the life of the related lease are recognized. Entities selling or securitizing lease financing receivables shall allocate the gross investment in receivables between minimum lease payments, residual values guaranteed at inception, and residual values not guaranteed at inception using the individual carrying amounts of those components at the date of transfer. Those entities also shall record a servicing asset or liability in accordance with paragraphs 10 and 13, if appropriate.

Illustration—Recording Transfers of Lease Financing Receivables with Residual Values

90. At the beginning of the second year in a 10-year sales-type lease, Company F sells for $505 a nine-tenths interest in the minimum lease payments and retains a one-tenth interest in the minimum lease payments and a 100 percent interest in the unguaranteed residual value of leased equipment. Company F receives no explicit compensation for servicing, but it estimates that the other benefits of servicing are just adequate to compensate it for its servicing responsibilities and hence initially records no servicing asset or liability. The carrying amounts and related gain computation are as follows:

Carrying Amounts

Minimum lease payments		$ 540
Unearned income related to minimum lease payments		370
Gross investment in minimum lease payments		910
Unguaranteed residual value	$ 30	
Unearned income related to residual value	60	
Gross investment in residual value		90
Total gross investment in financing lease receivable		$1,000

Gain on Sale

Cash received		$ 505
Nine-tenths of carrying amount of gross investment in minimum lease payments	$819	
Nine-tenths of carrying amount of unearned income related to minimum lease payments	333	
Net carrying amount of minimum lease payments sold		486
Gain on sale		$ 19

Journal Entry

Cash	505	
Unearned income	333	
Lease receivable		819
Gain on sale		19

To record sale of nine-tenths of the minimum lease payments at the beginning of year 2

Securities Lending Transactions

91. Securities lending transactions are initiated by broker-dealers and other financial institutions that need specific securities to cover a short sale or a customer's failure to deliver securities sold. Transferees ("borrowers") of securities generally are required to provide "collateral" to the transferor ("lender") of securities, commonly cash but sometimes other securities or standby letters of credit, with a value slightly higher than that of the securities "borrowed." If the "collateral" is cash, the transferor typically earns a return by investing that cash at rates higher than the rate paid or "rebated" to the transferee. If the "collateral" is other than cash, the transferor typically receives a fee. Securities custodians or other agents commonly carry out securities lending activities on behalf of clients. Because of the protection of "collateral" (typically valued daily and adjusted frequently for changes in the market price of the securities transferred) and the short terms of the transactions, most securities lending transactions in themselves do not impose significant credit risks on either party. Other risks arise from what the parties to the transaction do with the assets they receive. For example, investments made with cash "collateral" impose market and credit risks on the transferor.

92. In some securities lending transactions, the criteria in paragraph 9 are met, including the effective control criterion in paragraph 9(c), and consideration other than beneficial interests in the transferred assets is received. Those transactions shall be accounted for (a) by the transferor as a sale of the "loaned" securities for proceeds consisting of the cash "collateral"[22] and a forward repurchase commitment and (b) by the transferee as a purchase of the "borrowed" securities in exchange for the "collateral" and a forward resale commitment. During the term of that agreement, the transferor has surrendered control over the securities transferred and the transferee has obtained control over those securities with the ability to sell or transfer them at will. In that case, creditors of the transferor have a claim only to the "collateral" and the forward repurchase commitment.

93. However, many securities lending transactions are accompanied by an agreement that entitles and obligates the transferor to repurchase or redeem the transferred assets before their maturity under which the transferor maintains effective control over those assets (paragraphs 47–49). Those transactions shall be accounted for as secured borrowings, in which

---

[22]If the "collateral" in a transaction that meets the criteria in paragraph 9 is a financial asset that the holder is permitted by contract or custom to sell or repledge, that financial asset is proceeds of the sale of the "loaned" securities. To the extent that the "collateral" consists of letters of credit or other financial instruments that the holder is not permitted by contract or custom to sell or repledge, a securities lending transaction does not satisfy the sale criteria and is accounted for as a loan of securities by the transferor to the transferee.

cash (or securities that the holder is permitted by contract or custom to sell or repledge) received as "collateral" is considered the amount borrowed, the securities "loaned" are considered pledged as collateral against the cash borrowed and reclassified as set forth in paragraph 15(a), and any "rebate" paid to the transferee of securities is interest on the cash the transferor is considered to have borrowed.

94. The transferor of securities being "loaned" accounts for cash received in the same way whether the transfer is accounted for as a sale or a secured borrowing. The cash received shall be recognized as the transferor's asset—as shall investments made with that cash, even if made by agents or in pools with other securities lenders—along with the obligation to return the cash. If securities that may be sold or repledged are received, the transferor of the securities being "loaned" accounts for those securities in the same way as it would account for cash received.

Illustration—Securities Lending Transaction Treated as a Secured Borrowing

95. The following example illustrates the accounting for a securities lending transaction treated as a secured borrowing, in which the securities borrower sells the securities upon receipt and later buys similar securities to return to the securities lender:

Facts

Transferor's carrying amount and fair value of security loaned	$1,000
Cash "collateral"	1,020
Transferor's return from investing cash collateral at a 5 percent annual rate	5
Transferor's rebate to the securities borrower at a 4 percent annual rate	4

For simplicity, the fair value of the security is assumed not to change during the 35-day term of the transaction.

Journal Entries for the Transferor

At inception:

Cash	1,020	
Payable under securities loan agreements		1,020
To record the receipt of cash collateral		
Securities pledged to creditors	1,000	
Securities		1,000
To reclassify loaned securities that the secured party has the right to sell or repledge		
Money market instrument	1,020	
Cash		1,020
To record investment of cash collateral		

At conclusion:

Cash	1,025	
Interest		5
Money market instrument		1,020
To record results of investment		
Securities	1,000	
Securities pledged to creditors		1,000
To record return of security		
Payable under securities loan agreements	1,020	
Interest ("rebate")	4	
Cash		1,024
To record repayment of cash collateral plus interest		

Journal Entries for the Transferee

At inception:

Receivable under securities loan agreements	1,020	
Cash		1,020

To record transfer of cash collateral

Cash	1,000	
Obligation to return borrowed securities		1,000

To record sale of borrowed securities to a third party and the resulting obligation to
return securities that it no longer holds

At conclusion:

Obligation to return borrowed securities	1,000	
Cash		1,000

To record the repurchase of securities borrowed

Cash	1,024	
Receivable under securities loan agreements		1,020
Interest revenue ("rebate")		4

To record the receipt of cash collateral and rebate interest

Repurchase Agreements and "Wash Sales"

96. Government securities dealers, banks, other financial institutions, and corporate investors commonly use repurchase agreements to obtain or use short-term funds. Under those agreements, the transferor ("repo party") transfers a security to a transferee ("repo counterparty" or "reverse party") in exchange for cash[23] and concurrently agrees to reacquire that security at a future date for an amount equal to the cash exchanged plus a stipulated "interest" factor.

97. Repurchase agreements can be effected in a variety of ways. Some repurchase agreements are similar to securities lending transactions in that the transferee has the right to sell or repledge the securities to a third party during the term of the repurchase agreement. In other repurchase agreements, the transferee does not have the right to sell or repledge the securities during the term of the repurchase agreement. For example, in a tri-party repurchase agreement, the transferor transfers securities to an independent third-party custodian that holds the securities during the term of the

repurchase agreement. Also, many repurchase agreements are for short terms, often overnight, or have indefinite terms that allow either party to terminate the arrangement on short notice. However, other repurchase agreements are for longer terms, sometimes until the maturity of the transferred asset. Some repurchase agreements call for repurchase of securities that need not be identical to the securities transferred.

98. If the criteria in paragraph 9 are met, including the criterion in paragraph 9(c)(1), the transferor shall account for the repurchase agreement as a sale of financial assets and a forward repurchase commitment, and the transferee shall account for the agreement as a purchase of financial assets and a forward resale commitment. Other transfers that are accompanied by an agreement to repurchase the transferred assets that shall be accounted for as sales include transfers with agreements to repurchase at maturity and transfers with repurchase agreements in which the transferee has not obtained collateral sufficient to fund substantially all of the cost of purchasing replacement assets.

---

[23]Instead of cash, other securities or letters of credit sometimes are exchanged. Those transactions are accounted for in the same manner as securities lending transactions (paragraphs 92–94).

99. Furthermore, "wash sales" that previously were not recognized if the same financial asset was purchased soon before or after the sale shall be accounted for as sales under this Statement. Unless there is a concurrent contract to repurchase or redeem the transferred financial assets from the transferee, the transferor does not maintain effective control over the transferred assets.

100. As with securities lending transactions, under many agreements to repurchase transferred assets before their maturity the transferor maintains effective control over those assets. Repurchase agreements that do not meet all the criteria in paragraph 9 shall be treated as secured borrowings. Fixed-coupon and dollar-roll repurchase agreements, and other contracts under which the securities to be repurchased need not be the same as the securities sold, qualify as borrowings if the return of substantially the same (paragraph 48) securities as those concurrently transferred is assured. Therefore, those transactions shall be accounted for as secured borrowings by both parties to the transfer.

101. If a transferor has transferred securities to an independent third-party custodian, or to a transferee, under conditions that preclude the transferee from selling or repledging the assets during the term of the repurchase agreement (as in most tri-party repurchase agreements), the transferor has not surrendered control over those assets.

Loan Syndications

102. Borrowers often borrow amounts greater than any one lender is willing to lend. Therefore, it is common for groups of lenders to jointly fund those loans. That may be accomplished by a syndication under which several lenders share in lending to a single borrower, but each lender loans a specific amount to the borrower and has the right to repayment from the borrower.

103. A loan syndication is not a transfer of financial assets. Each lender in the syndication shall account for the amounts it is owed by the borrower. Repayments by the borrower may be made to a lead lender that then distributes the collections to the other lenders of the syndicate. In those circumstances, the lead lender is simply functioning as a servicer and, therefore, shall not recognize the aggregate loan as an asset.

Loan Participations

104. Groups of banks or other entities also may jointly fund large borrowings through loan participations in which a single lender makes a large loan to a borrower and subsequently transfers undivided interests in the loan to other entities.

105. Transfers by the originating lender may take the legal form of either assignments or participations. The transfers are usually on a nonrecourse basis, and the transferor ("originating lender") continues to service the loan. The transferee ("participating entity") may or may not have the right to sell or transfer its participation during the term of the loan, depending upon the terms of the participation agreement.

106. If the loan participation agreement gives the transferee the right to pledge or exchange those participations and the other criteria in paragraph 9 are met, the transfers to the transferee shall be accounted for by the transferor as sales of financial assets. A transferor's right of first refusal on a bona fide offer from a third party, a requirement to obtain the transferor's permission that shall not be unreasonably withheld, or a prohibition on sale to the transferor's competitor if other potential willing buyers exist is a limitation on the transferee's rights but presumptively does not constrain a transferee from exercising its right to pledge or exchange. However, if the loan participation agreement constrains the transferees from pledging or exchanging their participations, the transferor presumptively receives a more than trivial benefit, has not relinquished control over the loan, and shall account for the transfers as secured borrowings.

Banker's Acceptances and Risk Participations in Them

107. Banker's acceptances provide a way for a bank to finance a customer's purchase of goods from a vendor for periods usually not exceeding six months. Under an agreement between the bank, the customer, and the vendor, the bank agrees to pay the customer's liability to the vendor upon presentation of specified documents that provide evidence of delivery and acceptance of the purchased goods. The principal document is a draft or bill of exchange drawn by the customer that the bank stamps to signify its "acceptance" of the liability to make payment on the draft on its due date.

108. Once the bank accepts a draft, the customer is liable to repay the bank at the time the draft matures.

The bank recognizes a receivable from the customer and a liability for the acceptance it has issued to the vendor. The accepted draft becomes a negotiable financial instrument. The vendor typically sells the accepted draft at a discount either to the accepting bank or in the marketplace.

109. A risk participation is a contract between the accepting bank and a participating bank in which the participating bank agrees, in exchange for a fee, to reimburse the accepting bank in the event that the accepting bank's customer fails to honor its liability to the accepting bank in connection with the banker's acceptance. The participating bank becomes a guarantor of the credit of the accepting bank's customer.

110. An accepting bank that obtains a risk participation shall not derecognize the liability for the banker's acceptance, because the accepting bank is still

primarily liable to the holder of the banker's acceptance even though it benefits from a guarantee of reimbursement by a participating bank. The accepting bank shall not derecognize the receivable from the customer because it has not transferred the receivable: it controls the benefits inherent in that receivable and it is still entitled to receive payment from the customer. The accepting bank shall, however, record the guarantee purchased, and the participating bank shall record a liability for the guarantee issued.

Illustration—Banker's Acceptance with a Risk Participation

111. An accepting bank assumes a liability to pay a customer's vendor and obtains a risk participation from another bank. The details of the banker's acceptance are provided below:

Facts

Face value of the draft provided to vendor	$1,000
Term of the draft provided to vendor	90 days
Commission with an annual rate of 10 percent	25
Fee paid for risk participation	10

Journal Entries for Accepting Bank

At issuance of acceptance:

Receivable from customer	1,000	
Cash	25	
Time draft payable to vendor		1,000
Deferred acceptance commission revenue		25

At purchase of risk participation from a participating bank:

Guarantee purchased	10	
Cash		10

Upon presentation of the accepted time draft:

Time draft payable to vendor	1,000	
Deferred acceptance commission revenue	25	
Cash		1,000
Acceptance commission revenue		25

*Upon collection from the customer (or the participating bank,
  if the customer defaults):*

Cash	1,000	
Guarantee expense	10	
Receivable from customer		1,000
Guarantee purchased		10

Journal Entries for Participating Bank

Upon issuing the risk participation:

Cash	10	
Guarantee liability		10

Upon payment by the customer to the accepting bank:

Guarantee liability	10	
Guarantee revenue		10

OR:

In the event of total default by the customer:

Guarantee loss	990	
Guarantee liability	10	
Cash (paid to accepting bank)		1,000

Factoring Arrangements

112. Factoring arrangements are a means of discounting accounts receivable on a nonrecourse, notification basis. Accounts receivable are sold outright, usually to a transferee (the factor) that assumes the full risk of collection, without recourse to the transferor in the event of a loss. Debtors are directed to send payments to the transferee. Factoring arrangements that meet the criteria in paragraph 9 shall be accounted for as sales of financial assets because the transferor surrenders control over the receivables to the factor.

Transfers of Receivables with Recourse

113. In a transfer of receivables with recourse, the transferor provides the transferee with full or limited recourse. The transferor is obligated under the terms of the recourse provision to make payments to the transferee or to repurchase receivables sold under

certain circumstances, typically for defaults up to a specified percentage. The effect of a recourse provision on the application of paragraph 9 may vary by jurisdiction. In some jurisdictions, transfers with full recourse may not place transferred assets beyond the reach of the transferor and its creditors, but transfers with limited recourse may. A transfer of receivables with recourse shall be accounted for as a sale, with the proceeds of the sale reduced by the fair value of the recourse obligation, if the criteria in paragraph 9 are met. Otherwise, a transfer of receivables with recourse shall be accounted for as a secured borrowing.

Extinguishments of Liabilities

114. If a creditor releases a debtor from primary obligation on the condition that a third party assumes the obligation and that the original debtor becomes secondarily liable, that release extinguishes the original debtor's liability. However, in those circumstances, whether or not explicit consideration was

paid for that guarantee, the original debtor becomes a guarantor. As a guarantor, it shall recognize a guarantee obligation in the same manner as would a guarantor that had never been primarily liable to that creditor, with due regard for the likelihood that the third party will carry out its obligations. The guarantee obligation shall be initially measured at fair value, and that amount reduces the gain or increases the loss recognized on extinguishment.

Appendix C

ILLUSTRATIVE GUIDANCE

342. This appendix provides specific examples that illustrate the disclosures that are required by this Statement. The formats in the illustrations are not required by the Statement. The Board encourages entities to use a format that displays the information in the most understandable manner in the specific circumstances. References to paragraphs of this Statement in which the relevant requirements appear are given in parentheses.

343. The first example illustrates the disclosure of accounting policies for ~~retained~~ interests that continue to be held by the transferor. In particular, it describes the accounting policies for (a) initial measurement (paragraph 17(~~fh~~)(1)) and (b) subsequent measurement (paragraph 17(~~gi~~)(1)), including determination of fair value.

NOTE X—SUMMARY OF SIGNIFICANT ACCOUNTING POLICIES

Receivable Sales

When the Company sells receivables in securitizations of automobile loans, credit card loans, and residential mortgage loans, it may hold ~~retains~~ interest-only strips, one or more subordinated tranches, ~~servicing rights,~~ and in some cases a cash reserve account, all of which are ~~retained~~ interests that continue to be held by the transferor in the securitized receivables. It may also obtain servicing assets or assume servicing liabilities that are initially measured at fair value. Gain or loss on sale of the receivables depends in part on both (a) the previous carrying amount of the financial assets involved in the transfer, allocated between the assets sold and the ~~retained~~ interests that continue to be held by the transferor based on their relative fair value at the date of transfer, and (b) the proceeds received. To obtain fair values, quoted market prices are used if avail-

able. However, quotes are generally not available for ~~retained~~ interests that continue to be held by the transferor, so the Company generally estimates fair value based on the present value of future expected cash flows estimated using management's best estimates of the key assumptions—credit losses, prepayment speeds, forward yield curves, and discount rates commensurate with the risks involved.

344. In addition to the disclosure of assumptions used in determining the values of ~~retained~~ interests that continue to be held by the transferor at the time of securitization that are presented in paragraph 343, this Statement also requires similar disclosures at the end of the latest period being presented. The following example illustrates disclosures about the characteristics of securitizations and gain or loss from securitizations and other sales by major type of asset (paragraph 17(~~fh~~)(2)).

NOTE Y—SALES OF RECEIVABLES

During 20X2 and 20X1, the Company sold automobile loans, residential mortgage loans, and credit card loans in securitization transactions. In all those securitizations, the Company ~~retained~~ obtained servicing responsibilities and subordinated interests. The Company receives annual servicing fees approximating 0.5 percent (for mortgage loans), 2 percent (for credit card loans), and 1.5 percent (for automobile loans) of the outstanding balance and rights to future cash flows arising after the investors in the securitization trust have received the return for which they contracted. The investors and the securitization trusts have no recourse to the Company's other assets for failure of debtors to pay when due. The ~~Company's retained~~ interests that continue to be held by the Company are subordinate to investor's interests. Their value is subject to credit, prepayment, and interest rate risks on the transferred financial assets.

In 20X2, the Company recognized pretax gains of $22.3 million on the securitization of the automobile loans, $30.2 million on the securitization of credit card loans, and $25.6 million on the securitization of residential mortgage loans.

In 20X1, the Company recognized pretax gains of $16.9, $21.4, and $15.0 million on the securitization of the automobile loans, credit card loans, and residential mortgage loans, respectively.

345. The following is an illustration of the quantitative information about key assumptions used in measuring retained interests that continue to be held by the transferor at the date of sale or securitization for each financial period presented (paragraph 17(fh)(3)).

Key economic assumptions used in measuring the retained interests that continue to be held by the transferor at the date of securitization resulting from securitizations completed during the year were as follows (rates* per annum):

20X2

	Automobile Loans	Credit Card Loans	Residential Mortgage Loans	
			Fixed-Rate	Adjustable†
Prepayment speed	1.00%	15.0%	10.00%	8.0%
Weighted-average life (in years)33	1.8	0.4	7.2	6.5
Expected credit losses	3.10–3.40%	6.10%	1.25%	1.30%
Residual cash flows discounted at	12.0–13.0%	12.00%	10.00%	8.50%
Variable returns to transferees	Forward Eurodollar yield curve plus contractual spread over LIBOR ranging from 30 to 80 basis points		Not applicable	

20X1

	Automobile Loans	Credit Card Loans	Residential Mortgage Loans	
			Fixed-Rate	Adjustable†
Prepayment speed	1.00%	12.85%	8.00%	6.00%
Weighted-average life (in years)33	1.8	0.4	8.5	7.2
Expected credit losses	3.50–3.80%	5.30%	1.25%	2.10%
Residual cash flows discounted at	13.00–13.50%	13.00%	11.75%	11.00%
Variable returns to transferees	Forward Eurodollar yield curve plus contractual spread over LIBOR ranging from 28 to 70 basis points		Not applicable	

Notes:

*Weighted-average rates for securitizations entered into during the period for securitizations of loans with similar characteristics.

†Rates for these loans are adjusted based on an index (for most loans, the 1-year Treasury note rate plus 2.75 percent). Contract terms vary, but for most loans, the rate is adjusted every 12 months by no more than 2 percent.

33The weighted-average life in periods (for example, months or years) of prepayable assets is calculated by summing the product of (a) the sum of the principal collections expected in each future period times (b) the number of periods until collection, and then dividing that total by (c) the initial principal balance.

346. The following is an illustration that combines disclosure of the key assumptions used in valuing ~~retained~~ interests that continue to be held by the transferor at the end of the latest period (paragraph 17(g)(2)) and the hypothetical effect on current fair value of two or more pessimistic variations from the expected levels for each of the key assumptions (paragraph 17(g)(3)).

At December 31, 20X2, key economic assumptions and the sensitivity of the current fair value of residual cash flows to immediate 10 percent and 20 percent adverse changes in those assumptions are as follows ($ in millions):

	Automobile Loans	Credit Card Loans	Residential Mortgage Loans Fixed-Rate	Adjustable
Carrying amount/fair value of ~~retained~~ interests that continue to be held by the transferor[34]	$15.6	$21.25	$12.0	$13.3
Weighted-average life (in years)[34]	1.7	0.4	6.5	6.1
Prepayment speed assumption (annual rate)	**1.3%**	**15.0 %**	**11.5%**	**9.3%**
Impact on fair value of 10% adverse change	*$0.3*	*$1.6*	*$3.3*	*$2.6*
Impact on fair value of 20% adverse change	*$0.7*	*$3.0*	*$7.8*	*$6.0*
Expected credit losses (annual rate)	**3.0%**	**6.1 %**	**0.9%**	**1.8%**
Impact on fair value of 10% adverse change	*$4.2*	*$3.2*	*$1.1*	*$1.2*
Impact on fair value of 20% adverse change	*$8.4*	*$6.5*	*$2.2*	*$3.0*
Residual cash flows discount rate (annual)	**14.0%**	**14.0 %**	**12.0%**	**9.0%**
Impact on fair value of 10% adverse change	*$1.0*	*$0.1*	*$0.6*	*$0.5*
Impact on fair value of 20% adverse change	*$1.8*	*$0.1*	*$0.9*	*$0.9*
Interest rates on variable and adjustable contracts	Forward Eurodollar yield curve plus contracted spread			
Impact on fair value of 10% adverse change	*$1.5*	*$4.0*	*$0.4*	*$1.5*
Impact on fair value of 20% adverse change	*$2.5*	*$8.1*	*$0.7*	*$3.8*

---

[34]Footnote 8, paragraph 17(f)b)(3), describes how weighted-average life can be calculated.

These sensitivities are hypothetical and should be used with caution. As the figures indicate, changes in fair value based on a 10 percent variation in assumptions generally cannot be extrapolated because the relationship of the change in assumption to the change in fair value may not be linear. Also, in this table, the effect of a variation in a particular assumption on the fair value of the retained interest that continues to be held by the transferor is calculated without changing any other assumption; in reality, changes in one factor may result in changes in another (for example, increases in market interest rates may result in lower prepayments and increased credit losses), which might magnify or counteract the sensitivities.

347. The following is an illustration of disclosure of expected static pool credit losses (paragraph 17(g)(2)).

	Automobile Loans Securitized in		
Actual and Projected Credit Losses (%) as of:	**20X0**	**20X1**	**20X2**
December 31, 20X2	5.0	5.9	5.1
December 31, 20X1	5.1	5.0	
December 31, 20X0	4.5		

Note: Static pool losses are calculated by summing the actual and projected future credit losses and dividing them by the original balance of each pool of assets. The amount shown here for each year is a weighted average for all securitizations during the period.

348. The following is an illustration of the disclosure of cash flows between the securitization SPE and the transferor (paragraph 17(fh)(4)).

The table below summarizes certain cash flows received from and paid to securitization trusts ($ in millions):

	Year Ended December 31	
	20X2	**20X1**
Proceeds from new securitizations	$1,413	$ 971
Proceeds from collections reinvested in previous credit card securitizations	3,150	2,565
Servicing fees received	23	19
Other cash flows received on retained-interests that continue to be held by the transferor*	81	52
Purchases of delinquent or foreclosed assets	(45)	(25)
Servicing advances	(102)	(73)
Repayments of servicing advances	90	63

Note:

*This amount represents total cash flows received from retained-interests that continue to be held by the transferor other than servicing fees. Other cash flows include, for example, all cash flows from interest-only strips and cash above the minimum required level in cash collateral accounts.

349. The following illustration presents quantitative information about delinquencies, net credit losses, and components of securitized financial assets and other assets managed together with them ($ in millions):

Type of Loan	Total Principal Amount of Loans (At December 31)		Principal Amount of Loans 60 Days or More Past Due* (At December 31)		Average Balances[35] (During the Year)		Net Credit Losses[†] (During the Year)	
	20X2	20X1	20X2	20X1	20X2	20X1	20X2	20X1
Automobile loans	$830	$488	$42.3	$26.8	$720	$370	$21.6	$12.6
Residential mortgage loans (fixed-rate)	482	302	5.8	3.6	470	270	5.6	3.2
Residential mortgage loans (adjustable)	544	341	7.1	6.8	520	300	6.2	6.0
Credit card loans	300	250	15	12.5	350	300	16	15
Total loans managed or securitized ‡	2,156	1,381	$70.2	$49.7	2,060	1,240	$49.4	$36.8
Less:								
Loans securitized§	1,485	905			1,368	752		
Loans held for sale or securitization	19	11			17	9		
Loans held in portfolio[36]	$652	$465			$675	$479		

Notes:

*Loans 60 days or more past due are based on end of period total loans.

†Net credit losses are charge-offs and are based on total loans outstanding.

‡Owned and securitized loans are customer loans, credit card loans, mortgage loans, auto loans, and other loans, as applicable, in which the transferor retains a subordinate interest or retains any risk of loss (for example, 10 percent recourse).

§Represents the principal amount of the loan. Interest-only strips (or other interests that continue to be held by a transferor) and servicing assets and servicing liabilities (or other retained interests) held for securitized assets are excluded from this table because they are recognized separately.

---

[35]This disclosure is optional.

[36]Loans held in portfolio are reported separately from loans held for securitization because they are measured differently.

349A. The following is an illustration of disclosures related to the activity in the balance of servicing assets and servicing liabilities by class (paragraphs 17(f)(1) and 17(g)(1)):

Tabular Disclosure of Changes in Servicing Assets and Servicing Liabilities Subsequently Measured Using the Fair Value Measurement Method

Balance Sheet Disclosures	Class 1		Class 2		Reference
	Servicing Asset	Servicing Liability	Servicing Asset	Servicing Liability	
Fair value as of the beginning of the period	XX	XX	XX	XX	17(f)(1)(a)
Additions:					17(f)(1)(b)
Purchases of servicing assets	XX	N/A	XX	N/A	
Assumption of servicing obligations	XX	XX	XX	XX	
Servicing obligations that result from transfers of financial assets	XX	XX	XX	XX	
Subtractions:					
Disposals	(XX)	(XX)	(XX)	(XX)	17(f)(1)(c)
Changes in fair value:					17(f)(1)(d)
Due to change in valuation inputs or assumptions used in the valuation model	XX/(XX)	XX/(XX)	XX/(XX)	XX/(XX)	
Other changes in fair value	XX/(XX)	XX/(XX)	XX/(XX)	XX/(XX)	
Other changes that affect the balance	XX/(XX)	XX/(XX)	XX/(XX)	XX/(XX)	17(f)(1)(e)
Fair value as of the end of the period	XX	XX	XX	XX	17(f)(1)(a)

(This page intentionally left blank.)

Tabular Disclosure of Changes in Servicing Assets and Servicing Liabilities Subsequently Measured
Using the Amortization Method

Balance Sheet Disclosures	Class 3		Class 4		Reference
	Servicing Asset	Servicing Liability	Servicing Asset	Servicing Liability	
Carrying amount as of the beginning of the period	XX	XX	XX	XX	17(g)(1)(a)
Additions:					17(g)(1)(b)
Purchases of servicing assets	XX	N/A	XX	N/A	
Assumption of servicing obligations	XX	XX	XX	XX	
Servicing obligations that result from transfers of financial assets	XX	XX	XX	XX	
Subtractions:					
Disposals	(XX)	(XX)	(XX)	(XX)	17(g)(1)(c)
Amortization	(XX)	(XX)	(XX)	(XX)	17(g)(1)(d)
Application of valuation allowance to adjust carrying values of servicing assets	XX/(XX)	N/A	XX/(XX)	N/A	17(g)(1)(e)
Other-than-temporary impairments	(XX)	(XX)	(XX)	(XX)	17(g)(1)(f)
Other changes that affect the balance	XX/(XX)	XX/(XX)	XX/(XX)	XX/(XX)	17(g)(1)(g)
Carrying amount before valuation allowance	XX	XX	XX	XX	

	17(g)(5)	17(g)(1)(f)	17(g)(1)(a)	17(g)(2) 17(g)(2)
Valuation allowance for servicing assets:				
Beginning balance	N/A	XX	N/A	XX
Provisions/recoveries	N/A	XX/(XX)	N/A	XX
Other-than-temporary impairments	N/A	(XX)	N/A	XX
Sales and disposals	N/A	(XX)	N/A	XX
Ending balance	N/A	XX/(XX)	N/A	XX
Carrying amount as of the end of the period	XX	XX	XX	XX
Fair Value Disclosures				
Fair value as of the beginning of the period	XX	XX/(XX)	XX	XX
Fair value as of the end of the period	XX	XX/(XX)	XX	XX

Appendix E

GLOSSARY

364. This appendix defines terms used in this Statement.

Adequate compensation

The amount of benefits of servicing that would fairly compensate a substitute servicer should one be required, which includes the profit that would be demanded in the marketplace.

Agent

A party that acts for and on behalf of another party. For example, a third-party intermediary is an agent of the transferor if it acts on behalf of the transferor.

Attached call

A call option held by the transferor of a financial asset that becomes part of and is traded with the underlying instrument. Rather than being an obligation of the transferee, an attached call is traded with and diminishes the value of the underlying instrument transferred subject to that call.

Beneficial interests

Rights to receive all or portions of specified cash inflows to a trust or other entity, including senior and subordinated shares of interest, principal, or other cash inflows to be "passed-through" or "paid-through," premiums due to guarantors, commercial paper obligations, and residual interests, whether in the form of debt or equity.

Benefits of servicing

Revenues from contractually specified servicing fees, late charges, and other ancillary sources, including "float."

Cleanup call

An option held by the servicer or its affiliate, which may be the transferor, to purchase the remaining transferred financial assets, or the remaining beneficial interests not held by the transferor, its affiliates, or its agents in a qualifying SPE (or in a series of beneficial interests in transferred assets within a qualifying SPE), if the amount of outstanding assets or beneficial interests falls to a level at which the cost of servicing those assets or beneficial interests becomes burdensome in relation to the benefits of servicing.

Collateral

Personal or real property in which a security interest has been given.

Consolidated affiliate of the transferor

An entity whose assets and liabilities are included with those of the transferor in the consolidated, combined, or other financial statements being presented.

Contractually specified servicing fees

All amounts that, per contract, are due to the servicer in exchange for servicing the financial asset and would no longer be received by a servicer if the beneficial owners of the serviced assets (or their trustees or agents) were to exercise their actual or potential authority under the contract to shift the servicing to another servicer. Depending on the servicing contract, those fees may include some or all of the difference between the interest rate collectible on the asset being serviced and the rate to be paid to the beneficial owners of those assets.

Derecognize

Remove previously recognized assets or liabilities from the statement of financial position.

Derivative financial instrument

A derivative instrument (as defined in Statement 133) that is a financial instrument (refer to Statement 107, paragraph 3).

Embedded call

A call option held by the issuer of a financial instrument that is part of and trades with the underlying instrument. For example, a bond may allow the issuer to call it by posting a public notice well before its stated maturity that asks the current holder to submit it for early redemption and provides that interest ceases to accrue on the bond after the early redemption date. Rather than being an obligation of the initial purchaser of the bond, an embedded call trades with and diminishes the value of the underlying bond.

Fair value

Refer to paragraphs 68–70.

Financial asset

Cash, evidence of an ownership interest in an entity, or a contract that conveys to a second entity a contractual right (a) to receive cash or another financial instrument from a first entity or

(b) to exchange other financial instruments on potentially favorable terms with the first entity (Statement 107, paragraph 3(b)).

Financial liability

A contract that imposes on one entity a contractual obligation (a) to deliver cash or another financial instrument to a second entity or (b) to exchange other financial instruments on potentially unfavorable terms with the second entity (Statement 107, paragraph 3(a)).

Freestanding call

A call that is neither embedded in nor attached to an asset subject to that call.

Guaranteed mortgage securitization

A securitization of mortgage loans that is within the scope of FASB Statement No. 65, *Accounting for Certain Mortgage Banking Activities,* as amended, and includes a substantive guarantee by a third party.

Interest-only strip

A contractual right to receive some or all of the interest due on a bond, mortgage loan, collateralized mortgage obligation, or other interest-bearing financial asset.

Proceeds

Cash, derivatives, or other assets that are obtained in a transfer of financial assets, less any liabilities incurred.

Recourse

The right of a transferee of receivables to receive payment from the transferor of those receivables for (a) failure of debtors to pay when due, (b) the effects of prepayments, or (c) adjustments resulting from defects in the eligibility of the transferred receivables.

Securitization

The process by which financial assets are transformed into securities.

Security interest

A form of interest in property that provides that upon default of the obligation for which the security interest is given, the property may be sold in order to satisfy that obligation.

Seller

A transferor that relinquishes control over financial assets by transferring them to a transferee in exchange for consideration.

Servicing asset

A contract to service financial assets under which the estimated future revenues from contractually specified servicing fees, late charges, and other ancillary revenues are expected to more than adequately compensate the servicer for performing the servicing. A servicing contract is either (a) undertaken in conjunction with selling or securitizing the financial assets being serviced or (b) purchased or assumed separately.

Servicing liability

A contract to service financial assets under which the estimated future revenues from contractually specified servicing fees, late charges, and other ancillary revenues are not expected to adequately compensate the servicer for performing the servicing.

Transfer

The conveyance of a noncash financial asset by and to someone other than the issuer of that financial asset. Thus, a transfer includes selling a receivable, putting it into a securitization trust, or posting it as collateral but excludes the origination of that receivable, the settlement of that receivable, or the restructuring of that receivable into a security in a troubled debt restructuring.

Transferee

An entity that receives a financial asset, a portion of a financial asset, or a group of financial assets from a transferor.

Transferor

An entity that transfers a financial asset, a portion of a financial asset, or a group of financial assets that it controls to another entity.

Undivided interest

Partial legal or beneficial ownership of an asset as a tenant in common with others. The proportion owned may be pro rata, for example, the right to receive 50 percent of all cash flows from a security, or non–pro rata, for example, the right to receive the interest from a security while another has the right to the principal.

Unilateral ability

A capacity for action not dependent on the actions (or failure to act) of any other party.

Statement of Financial Accounting Standards No. 157
Fair Value Measurements

STATUS

Issued: September 2006

Effective Date: For financial statements issued for fiscal years beginning after November 15, 2007, and interim periods within those fiscal years

Affects: Amends APB 21, paragraphs 13 and 18
    Deletes APB 21, footnote 1
    Amends APB 28, paragraph 30
    Amends APB 29, paragraphs 18 and 20(a)
    Deletes APB 29, paragraph 25 and footnote 5
    Amends FAS 13, paragraph 5(c)
    Amends FAS 15, paragraphs 13 and 28
    Deletes FAS 15, footnotes 2, 5a, and 6
    Amends FAS 19, paragraph 47(l)(i)
    Amends FAS 35, paragraph 11 and footnote 5
    Deletes FAS 35, footnote 4a
    Amends FAS 60, paragraph 19
    Deletes FAS 60, footnote 4a
    Amends FAS 63, paragraphs 4, 8, and 38 through 40
    Amends FAS 65, paragraphs 4, 6, 9, 10, 12, and 29
    Amends FAS 67, paragraphs 8 and 28
    Deletes FAS 67, footnote 6
    Amends FAS 87, paragraphs 49 and 264 and footnote 12
    Deletes FAS 87, footnote 11a
    Amends FAS 106, paragraphs 65 and 518 and footnote 21
    Deletes FAS 106, footnote 20a
    Deletes FAS 107, paragraphs 5, 6, 11, and 18 through 29
    Amends FAS 107, paragraphs 9, 10, 30, and 31
    Amends FAS 115, paragraphs 3(a) and 137
    Replaces FAS 115, footnote 2
    Amends FAS 116, paragraphs 19, 20, 184, 186, and 208
    Deletes FAS 116, footnote 8
    Amends FAS 124, paragraphs 3(a) and 112
    Replaces FAS 124, footnote 3
    Deletes FAS 133, paragraph 16A and footnote 6c
    Amends FAS 133, paragraphs 17 and 540
    Effectively deletes FAS 133, footnotes 9b, 10b, 18a, 18b, 20a through 20e, and 24a
    Amends FAS 136, Summary and paragraphs 15 and 36
    Amends FAS 140, paragraphs 11(c), 17(h), 17(i), 63(b), and 364
    Deletes FAS 140, paragraphs 68 through 70 and footnotes 20 and 21
    Amends FAS 141, paragraph F1
    Amends FAS 142, paragraphs 3, 19, 23, and F1
    Deletes FAS 142, paragraphs 24, E1, and E2 and footnotes 12 and 16
    Deletes FAS 143, paragraphs 6, 7, 9, A19, and F1 through F4 and footnotes 5 through 8, 17, and 19
    Amends FAS 143, paragraphs 8, A20, A21, A26, C1, C3(d), C4, C6 through C9, C11, and C12 and
      footnotes 12 and 18

Deletes FAS 144, paragraphs 22, 24, A12, and E1 through E3 and footnotes 12 through 14, 28, and 29
Amends FAS 144, paragraphs 23, A6 through A8, A11, A13, and A14
Deletes FAS 146, paragraphs 5, A4, and A5 and footnotes 13 through 16
Amends FAS 146, paragraph A2
Amends FAS 150, paragraph D1
Deletes FAS 156, paragraph 3(c)
Amends FIN 45, paragraphs 9(a) and 9(b)

Affected by: No other pronouncements

Issues Discussed by FASB Emerging Issues Task Force (EITF)

Affects: Modifies EITF Issue No. 02-3

Interpreted by: No EITF Issues

Related Issues: No EITF Issues

SUMMARY

This Statement defines fair value, establishes a framework for measuring fair value in generally accepted accounting principles (GAAP), and expands disclosures about fair value measurements. This Statement applies under other accounting pronouncements that require or permit fair value measurements, the Board having previously concluded in those accounting pronouncements that fair value is the relevant measurement attribute. Accordingly, this Statement does not require any new fair value measurements. However, for some entities, the application of this Statement will change current practice.

Reason for Issuing This Statement

Prior to this Statement, there were different definitions of fair value and limited guidance for applying those definitions in GAAP. Moreover, that guidance was dispersed among the many accounting pronouncements that require fair value measurements. Differences in that guidance created inconsistencies that added to the complexity in applying GAAP. In developing this Statement, the Board considered the need for increased consistency and comparability in fair value measurements and for expanded disclosures about fair value measurements.

Differences between This Statement and Current Practice

The changes to current practice resulting from the application of this Statement relate to the definition of fair value, the methods used to measure fair value, and the expanded disclosures about fair value measurements.

The definition of fair value retains the exchange price notion in earlier definitions of fair value. This Statement clarifies that the exchange price is the price in an orderly transaction between market participants to sell the asset or transfer the liability in the market in which the reporting entity would transact for the asset or liability, that is, the principal or most advantageous market for the asset or liability. The transaction to sell the asset or transfer the liability is a hypothetical transaction at the measurement date, considered from the perspective of a market participant that holds the asset or owes the liability. Therefore, the definition focuses on the price that would be received to sell the asset or paid to transfer the liability (an exit price), not the price that would be paid to acquire the asset or received to assume the liability (an entry price).

This Statement emphasizes that fair value is a market-based measurement, not an entity-specific measurement. Therefore, a fair value measurement should be determined based on the assumptions that market participants would use in pricing the asset or liability. As a basis for considering market participant assumptions in fair value measurements, this Statement establishes a fair value hierarchy that distinguishes between (1) market participant assumptions developed based on market data obtained from sources independent of the reporting entity (observable inputs) and (2) the reporting entity's own assumptions about market participant assumptions developed based on the best information available in the circumstances (unobservable inputs). The notion of unobservable inputs is intended to allow for situations in which there is little, if any, market activity for the asset or liability at the measurement date. In those situations, the reporting entity need not undertake all possible efforts to obtain information about market participant assumptions. However, the reporting entity must not ignore information about market participant assumptions that is reasonably available without undue cost and effort.

This Statement clarifies that market participant assumptions include assumptions about risk, for example, the risk inherent in a particular valuation technique used to measure fair value (such as a pricing model) and/or the risk inherent in the inputs to the valuation technique. A fair value measurement should include an adjustment for risk if market participants would include one in pricing the related asset or liability, even if the adjustment is difficult to determine. Therefore, a measurement (for example, a "mark-to-model" measurement) that does not include an adjustment for risk would not represent a fair value measurement if market participants would include one in pricing the related asset or liability.

This Statement clarifies that market participant assumptions also include assumptions about the effect of a restriction on the sale or use of an asset. A fair value measurement for a restricted asset should consider the effect of the restriction if market participants would consider the effect of the restriction in pricing the asset. That guidance applies for stock with restrictions on sale that terminate within one year that is measured at fair value under FASB Statements No. 115, *Accounting for Certain Investments in Debt and Equity Securities,* and No. 124, *Accounting for Certain Investments Held by Not-for-Profit Organizations.*

This Statement clarifies that a fair value measurement for a liability reflects its nonperformance risk (the risk that the obligation will not be fulfilled). Because nonperformance risk includes the reporting entity's credit risk, the reporting entity should consider the effect of its credit risk (credit standing) on the fair value of the liability in all periods in which the liability is measured at fair value under other accounting pronouncements, including FASB Statement No. 133, *Accounting for Derivative Instruments and Hedging Activities.*

This Statement affirms the requirement of other FASB Statements that the fair value of a position in a financial instrument (including a block) that trades in an active market should be measured as the product of the quoted price for the individual instrument times the quantity held (within Level 1 of the fair value hierarchy). The quoted price should not be adjusted because of the size of the position relative to trading volume (blockage factor). This Statement extends that requirement to broker-dealers and investment companies within the scope of the AICPA Audit and Accounting Guides for those industries.

This Statement expands disclosures about the use of fair value to measure assets and liabilities in interim and annual periods subsequent to initial recognition. The disclosures focus on the inputs used to measure fair value and for recurring fair value measurements using significant unobservable inputs (within Level 3 of the fair value hierarchy), the effect of the measurements on earnings (or changes in net assets) for the period. This Statement encourages entities to combine the fair value information disclosed under this Statement with the fair value information disclosed under other accounting pronouncements, including FASB Statement No. 107, *Disclosures about Fair Value of Financial Instruments,* where practicable.

The guidance in this Statement applies for derivatives and other financial instruments measured at fair value under Statement 133 at initial recognition and in all subsequent periods. Therefore, this Statement nullifies the guidance in footnote 3 of EITF Issue No. 02-3, "Issues Involved in Accounting for Derivative Contracts Held for Trading Purposes and Contracts Involved in Energy Trading and Risk Management Activities." This Statement also amends Statement 133 to remove the similar guidance to that in Issue 02-3, which was added by FASB Statement No. 155, *Accounting for Certain Hybrid Financial Instruments.*

How the Conclusions in This Statement Relate to the FASB's Conceptual Framework

The framework for measuring fair value considers the concepts in FASB Concepts Statement No. 2, *Qualitative Characteristics of Accounting Information.* Concepts Statement 2 emphasizes that providing comparable information enables users of financial statements to identify similarities in and differences between two sets of economic events.

The definition of fair value considers the concepts relating to assets and liabilities in FASB Concepts Statement No. 6, *Elements of Financial Statements,* in the context of market participants. A fair value measurement reflects current market participant assumptions about the future inflows associated with an asset (future economic benefits) and the future outflows associated with a liability (future sacrifices of economic benefits).

This Statement incorporates aspects of the guidance in FASB Concepts Statement No. 7, *Using Cash Flow Information and Present Value in Accounting Measurements,* as clarified and/or reconsidered in this Statement. This Statement does not revise Concepts Statement 7. The Board will consider the need to revise Concepts Statement 7 in its conceptual framework project.

The expanded disclosures about the use of fair value to measure assets and liabilities should provide users of financial statements (present and potential investors, creditors, and others) with information that is useful in making investment, credit, and similar decisions—the first objective of financial reporting in FASB Concepts Statement No. 1, *Objectives of Financial Reporting by Business Enterprises.*

How the Changes in This Statement Improve Financial Reporting

A single definition of fair value, together with a framework for measuring fair value, should result in increased consistency and comparability in fair value measurements.

The expanded disclosures about the use of fair value to measure assets and liabilities should provide users of financial statements with better information about the extent to which fair value is used to measure recognized assets and liabilities, the inputs used to develop the measurements, and the effect of certain of the measurements on earnings (or changes in net assets) for the period.

The amendments made by this Statement advance the Board's initiatives to simplify and codify the accounting literature, eliminating differences that have added to the complexity in GAAP.

Costs and Benefits of Applying This Statement

The framework for measuring fair value builds on current practice and requirements. However, some entities will need to make systems and other changes to comply with the requirements of this Statement. Some entities also might incur incremental costs in applying the requirements of this Statement. However, the benefits from increased consistency and comparability in fair value measurements and expanded disclosures about those measurements should be ongoing.

The Effective Date of This Statement

This Statement is effective for financial statements issued for fiscal years beginning after November 15, 2007, and interim periods within those fiscal years. Earlier application is encouraged, provided that the reporting entity has not yet issued financial statements for that fiscal year, including financial statements for an interim period within that fiscal year.

The provisions of this Statement should be applied prospectively as of the beginning of the fiscal year in which this Statement is initially applied, except as follows. The provisions of this Statement should be applied retrospectively to the following financial instruments as of the beginning of the fiscal year in which this Statement is initially applied (a limited form of retrospective application):

a. A position in a financial instrument that trades in an active market held by a broker-dealer or investment company within the scope of the AICPA Audit and Accounting Guides for those industries that was measured at fair value using a blockage factor prior to initial application of this Statement

b. A financial instrument that was measured at fair value at initial recognition under Statement 133 using the transaction price in accordance with the guidance in footnote 3 of Issue 02-3 prior to initial application of this Statement

c. A hybrid financial instrument that was measured at fair value at initial recognition under Statement 133 using the transaction price in accordance with the guidance in Statement 133 (added by Statement 155) prior to initial application of this Statement.

The transition adjustment, measured as the difference between the carrying amounts and the fair values of those financial instruments at the date this Statement is initially applied, should be recognized as a cumulative-effect adjustment to the opening balance of retained earnings (or other appropriate components of equity or net assets in the statement of financial position) for the fiscal year in which this Statement is initially applied.

Statement of Financial Accounting Standards No. 157

Fair Value Measurements

CONTENTS

OBJECTIVE

1. This Statement defines fair value, establishes a framework for measuring fair value, and expands disclosures about fair value measurements. Where applicable, this Statement simplifies and codifies related guidance within generally accepted accounting principles (GAAP).

STANDARDS OF FINANCIAL ACCOUNTING AND REPORTING

Scope

2. This Statement applies under other accounting pronouncements[1] that require or permit fair value measurements, except as follows:

a. This Statement does not apply under accounting pronouncements that address share-based payment transactions: FASB Statement No. 123 (revised 2004), *Share-Based Payment,* and its related interpretive accounting pronouncements that address share-based payment transactions.

b. This Statement does not eliminate the practicability exceptions to fair value measurements in accounting pronouncements within the scope of this Statement.[2]

3. This Statement does not apply under accounting pronouncements that require or permit measurements that are similar to fair value but that are not intended to measure fair value, including the following:

a. Accounting pronouncements that permit measurements that are based on, or otherwise use, vendor-specific objective evidence of fair value[3]

b. ARB No. 43, Chapter 4, "Inventory Pricing."

4. Appendix D lists pronouncements of the Accounting Principles Board (APB) and the FASB existing at the date of this Statement that are within the scope of this Statement. Appendix E lists those APB and FASB pronouncements that are amended by this Statement.

Measurement

Definition of Fair Value

5. Fair value is the price that would be received to sell an asset or paid to transfer a liability in an orderly transaction between market participants at the measurement date.

The asset or liability

6. A fair value measurement is for a particular asset or liability.[4] Therefore, the measurement should consider attributes specific to the asset or liability, for example, the condition and/or location of the asset or liability and restrictions, if any, on the sale or use of the asset at the measurement date. The asset or liability might be a standalone asset or liability (for example, a financial instrument or an operating asset) or a group of assets and/or liabilities (for example, an asset group, a reporting unit, or a business). Whether the asset or liability is a standalone asset or liability or a group of assets and/or liabilities depends on its unit of account. The unit of account determines what is being measured by reference to the level at which the asset or liability is aggregated (or disaggregated) for purposes of applying other accounting pronouncements. The unit of account for the asset or liability should be determined in accordance with the provisions of other accounting pronouncements, except as provided in paragraph 27.

---

[1]This Statement uses the term *accounting pronouncements* consistent with its use in paragraph 2(b) of FASB Statement No. 154, *Accounting Changes and Error Corrections.*

[2]Accounting pronouncements that permit practicability exceptions to fair value measurements in specified circumstances include APB Opinion No. 29, *Accounting for Nonmonetary Transactions,* FASB Statements No. 87, *Employers' Accounting for Pensions,* No. 106, *Employers' Accounting for Postretirement Benefits Other Than Pensions,* No. 107, *Disclosures about Fair Value of Financial Instruments,* No. 116, *Accounting for Contributions Received and Contributions Made,* No. 140, *Accounting for Transfers and Servicing of Financial Assets and Extinguishments of Liabilities,* No. 141, *Business Combinations,* No. 143, *Accounting for Asset Retirement Obligations,* No. 146, *Accounting for Costs Associated with Exit or Disposal Activities,* and No. 153, *Exchanges of Nonmonetary Assets,* and FASB Interpretations No. 45, *Guarantor's Accounting and Disclosure Requirements for Guarantees, Including Indirect Guarantees of Indebtedness of Others,* and No. 47, *Accounting for Conditional Asset Retirement Obligations.* Also included among those pronouncements are AICPA Audit and Accounting Guide, *Not-for-Profit Organizations,* and EITF Issues No. 85-40, "Comprehensive Review of Sales of Marketable Securities with Put Arrangements," and No. 99-17, "Accounting for Advertising Barter Transactions."

[3]Accounting pronouncements that permit measurements that are based on, or otherwise use, vendor-specific objective evidence of fair value include AICPA Statement of Position 97-2, *Software Revenue Recognition,* as modified by AICPA Statement of Position 98-9, *Modification of SOP 97-2, Software Revenue Recognition, With Respect to Certain Transactions.* Also included among those pronouncements are EITF Issues No. 00-3, "Application of AICPA Statement of Position 97-2 to Arrangements That Include the Right to Use Software Stored on Another Entity's Hardware," and No. 00-21, "Revenue Arrangements with Multiple Deliverables."

[4]The definition of fair value focuses on assets and liabilities because they are a primary subject of accounting measurement. However, the definition of fair value also should be applied to instruments measured at fair value that are classified in stockholders' equity.

The price

7. A fair value measurement assumes that the asset or liability is exchanged in an orderly transaction between market participants to sell the asset or transfer the liability at the measurement date. An orderly transaction is a transaction that assumes exposure to the market for a period prior to the measurement date to allow for marketing activities that are usual and customary for transactions involving such assets or liabilities; it is not a forced transaction (for example, a forced liquidation or distress sale). The transaction to sell the asset or transfer the liability is a hypothetical transaction at the measurement date, considered from the perspective of a market participant that holds the asset or owes the liability. Therefore, the objective of a fair value measurement is to determine the price that would be received to sell the asset or paid to transfer the liability at the measurement date (an exit price).

The principal (or most advantageous) market

8. A fair value measurement assumes that the transaction to sell the asset or transfer the liability occurs in the principal market for the asset or liability or, in the absence of a principal market, the most advantageous market for the asset or liability. The principal market is the market in which the reporting entity would sell the asset or transfer the liability with the greatest volume and level of activity for the asset or liability. The most advantageous market is the market in which the reporting entity would sell the asset or transfer the liability with the price that maximizes the amount that would be received for the asset or minimizes the amount that would be paid to transfer the liability, considering transaction costs in the respective market(s). In either case, the principal (or most advantageous) market (and thus, market participants) should be considered from the perspective of the reporting entity, thereby allowing for differences between and among entities with different activities. If there is a principal market for the asset or liability, the fair value measurement shall represent the price in that market (whether that price is directly observable or otherwise determined using a valuation technique), even if the price in a different market is potentially more advantageous at the measurement date.

9. The price in the principal (or most advantageous) market used to measure the fair value of the asset or liability shall not be adjusted for transaction costs.[5] Transaction costs represent the incremental direct costs to sell the asset or transfer the liability in the principal (or most advantageous) market for the asset or liability.[6] Transaction costs are not an attribute of the asset or liability; rather, they are specific to the transaction and will differ depending on how the reporting entity transacts. However, transaction costs do not include the costs that would be incurred to transport the asset or liability to (or from) its principal (or most advantageous) market. If location is an attribute of the asset or liability (as might be the case for a commodity), the price in the principal (or most advantageous) market used to measure the fair value of the asset or liability shall be adjusted for the costs, if any, that would be incurred to transport the asset or liability to (or from) its principal (or most advantageous) market.

Market participants

10. Market participants are buyers and sellers in the principal (or most advantageous) market for the asset or liability that are:

a. Independent of the reporting entity; that is, they are not related parties[7]
b. Knowledgeable, having a reasonable understanding about the asset or liability and the transaction based on all available information, including information that might be obtained through due diligence efforts that are usual and customary
c. Able to transact for the asset or liability
d. Willing to transact for the asset or liability; that is, they are motivated but not forced or otherwise compelled to do so.

11. The fair value of the asset or liability shall be determined based on the assumptions that market participants would use in pricing the asset or liability. In developing those assumptions, the reporting entity need not identify specific market participants. Rather, the reporting entity should identify characteristics that distinguish market participants generally, considering factors specific to (a) the asset or liability,

---

[5]Transaction costs should be accounted for in accordance with the provisions of other accounting pronouncements.

[6]Incremental direct costs to sell the asset or transfer the liability refer to those costs that result directly from and are essential to that transaction and that would not have been incurred by the reporting entity had the decision to sell the asset (or transfer the liability) not been made (similar to cost to sell, as defined in paragraph 35 of FASB Statement No. 144, *Accounting for the Impairment or Disposal of Long-Lived Assets*).

[7]This Statement uses the term *related parties* consistent with its use in FASB Statement No. 57, *Related Party Disclosures*.

(b) the principal (or most advantageous) market for the asset or liability, and (c) market participants with whom the reporting entity would transact in that market.

Application to assets

12. A fair value measurement assumes the highest and best use of the asset by market participants, considering the use of the asset that is physically possible, legally permissible, and financially feasible at the measurement date. In broad terms, highest and best use refers to the use of an asset by market participants that would maximize the value of the asset or the group of assets within which the asset would be used. Highest and best use is determined based on the use of the asset by market participants, even if the intended use of the asset by the reporting entity is different.

13. The highest and best use of the asset establishes the valuation premise used to measure the fair value of the asset. Specifically:

a. *In-use.* The highest and best use of the asset is in-use if the asset would provide maximum value to market participants principally through its use in combination with other assets as a group (as installed or otherwise configured for use). For example, that might be the case for certain nonfinancial assets. If the highest and best use of the asset is in-use, the fair value of the asset shall be measured using an in-use valuation premise. When using an in-use valuation premise, the fair value of the asset is determined based on the price that would be received in a current transaction to sell the asset assuming that the asset would be used with other assets as a group and that those assets would be available to market participants. Generally, assumptions about the highest and best use of the asset should be consistent for all of the assets of the group within which it would be used.

b. *In-exchange.* The highest and best use of the asset is in-exchange if the asset would provide maximum value to market participants principally on a standalone basis. For example, that might be the case for a financial asset. If the highest and best use of the asset is in-exchange, the fair value of the asset shall be measured using an

in-exchange valuation premise. When using an in-exchange valuation premise, the fair value of the asset is determined based on the price that would be received in a current transaction to sell the asset standalone.

14. Because the highest and best use of the asset is determined based on its use by market participants, the fair value measurement considers the assumptions that market participants would use in pricing the asset, whether using an in-use or an in-exchange valuation premise.[8]

Application to liabilities

15. A fair value measurement assumes that the liability is transferred to a market participant at the measurement date (the liability to the counterparty continues; it is not settled) and that the nonperformance risk relating to that liability is the same before and after its transfer. Nonperformance risk refers to the risk that the obligation will not be fulfilled and affects the value at which the liability is transferred. Therefore, the fair value of the liability shall reflect the nonperformance risk relating to that liability. Nonperformance risk includes but may not be limited to the reporting entity's own credit risk. The reporting entity shall consider the effect of its credit risk (credit standing) on the fair value of the liability in all periods in which the liability is measured at fair value. That effect may differ depending on the liability, for example, whether the liability is an obligation to deliver cash (a financial liability) or an obligation to deliver goods or services (a nonfinancial liability), and the terms of credit enhancements related to the liability, if any.

Fair Value at Initial Recognition

16. When an asset is acquired or a liability is assumed in an exchange transaction for that asset or liability, the transaction price represents the price paid to acquire the asset or received to assume the liability (an entry price). In contrast, the fair value of the asset or liability represents the price that would be received to sell the asset or paid to transfer the liability (an exit price). Conceptually, entry prices and exit prices are different. Entities do not necessarily sell assets at the prices paid to acquire them. Similarly, entities do not necessarily transfer liabilities at the prices received to assume them.

---

[8]The fair value of an asset in-use is determined based on the use of the asset together with other assets as a group (consistent with its highest and best use from the perspective of market participants), even if the asset that is the subject of the measurement is aggregated (or disaggregated) at a different level for purposes of applying other accounting pronouncements.

17. In many cases, the transaction price will equal the exit price and, therefore, represent the fair value of the asset or liability at initial recognition. In determining whether a transaction price represents the fair value of the asset or liability at initial recognition, the reporting entity shall consider factors specific to the transaction and the asset or liability. For example, a transaction price might not represent the fair value of an asset or liability at initial recognition if:

a. The transaction is between related parties.
b. The transaction occurs under duress or the seller is forced to accept the price in the transaction. For example, that might be the case if the seller is experiencing financial difficulty.
c. The unit of account represented by the transaction price is different from the unit of account for the asset or liability measured at fair value. For example, that might be the case if the asset or liability measured at fair value is only one of the elements in the transaction, the transaction includes unstated rights and privileges that should be separately measured, or the transaction price includes transaction costs.
d. The market in which the transaction occurs is different from the market in which the reporting entity would sell the asset or transfer the liability, that is, the principal or most advantageous market. For example, those markets might be different if the reporting entity is a securities dealer that transacts in different markets, depending on whether the counterparty is a retail customer (retail market) or another securities dealer (interdealer market).

Valuation Techniques

18. Valuation techniques consistent with the market approach, income approach, and/or cost approach shall be used to measure fair value. Key aspects of those approaches are summarized below:

a. *Market approach.* The market approach uses prices and other relevant information generated by market transactions involving identical or comparable assets or liabilities (including a business). For example, valuation techniques consistent with the market approach often use market multiples derived from a set of comparables.

Multiples might lie in ranges with a different multiple for each comparable. The selection of where within the range the appropriate multiple falls requires judgment, considering factors specific to the measurement (qualitative and quantitative). Valuation techniques consistent with the market approach include matrix pricing. Matrix pricing is a mathematical technique used principally to value debt securities without relying exclusively on quoted prices for the specific securities, but rather by relying on the securities' relationship to other benchmark quoted securities.

b. *Income approach.* The income approach uses valuation techniques to convert future amounts (for example, cash flows or earnings) to a single present amount (discounted). The measurement is based on the value indicated by current market expectations about those future amounts. Those valuation techniques include present value techniques; option-pricing models, such as the Black-Scholes-Merton formula (a closed-form model) and a binomial model (a lattice model), which incorporate present value techniques;[9] and the multiperiod excess earnings method, which is used to measure the fair value of certain intangible assets.[10]

c. *Cost approach.* The cost approach is based on the amount that currently would be required to replace the service capacity of an asset (often referred to as current replacement cost). From the perspective of a market participant (seller), the price that would be received for the asset is determined based on the cost to a market participant (buyer) to acquire or construct a substitute asset of comparable utility, adjusted for obsolescence. Obsolescence encompasses physical deterioration, functional (technological) obsolescence, and economic (external) obsolescence and is broader than depreciation for financial reporting purposes (an allocation of historical cost) or tax purposes (based on specified service lives).

19. Valuation techniques that are appropriate in the circumstances and for which sufficient data are available shall be used to measure fair value. In some cases, a single valuation technique will be appropriate (for example, when valuing an asset or liability using quoted prices in an active market for identical assets or liabilities). In other cases, multiple valuation

---

[9]The guidance in this Statement does not apply for the fair-value-based measurements using option-pricing models under Statement 123(R).

[10]The use of the multiperiod excess earnings method to measure the fair value of in-process research and development is discussed in AICPA Practice Aid, *Assets Acquired in a Business Combination to Be Used in Research and Development Activities: A Focus on Software, Electronic Devices, and Pharmaceutical Industries.*

techniques will be appropriate (for example, as might be the case when valuing a reporting unit). If multiple valuation techniques are used to measure fair value, the results (respective indications of fair value) shall be evaluated and weighted, as appropriate, considering the reasonableness of the range indicated by those results. A fair value measurement is the point within that range that is most representative of fair value in the circumstances.

20. Valuation techniques used to measure fair value shall be consistently applied. However, a change in a valuation technique or its application (for example, a change in its weighting when multiple valuation techniques are used) is appropriate if the change results in a measurement that is equally or more representative of fair value in the circumstances. That might be the case if, for example, new markets develop, new information becomes available, information previously used is no longer available, or valuation techniques improve. Revisions resulting from a change in the valuation technique or its application shall be accounted for as a change in accounting estimate (FASB Statement No. 154, *Accounting Changes and Error Corrections,* paragraph 19). The disclosure provisions of Statement 154 for a change in accounting estimate are not required for revisions resulting from a change in a valuation technique or its application.

Inputs to Valuation Techniques

21. In this Statement, *inputs* refer broadly to the assumptions that market participants would use in pricing the asset or liability, including assumptions about risk, for example, the risk inherent in a particular valuation technique used to measure fair value (such as a pricing model) and/or the risk inherent in the inputs to the valuation technique. Inputs may be observable or unobservable:

a. *Observable inputs* are inputs that reflect the assumptions market participants would use in pricing the asset or liability developed based on market data obtained from sources independent of the reporting entity.
b. *Unobservable inputs* are inputs that reflect the reporting entity's own assumptions about the assumptions market participants would use in pricing the asset or liability developed based on the best information available in the circumstances.

Valuation techniques used to measure fair value shall maximize the use of observable inputs and minimize the use of unobservable inputs.

Fair Value Hierarchy

22. To increase consistency and comparability in fair value measurements and related disclosures, the fair value hierarchy prioritizes the inputs to valuation techniques used to measure fair value into three broad levels. The fair value hierarchy gives the highest priority to quoted prices (unadjusted) in active markets for identical assets or liabilities (Level 1) and the lowest priority to unobservable inputs (Level 3). In some cases, the inputs used to measure fair value might fall in different levels of the fair value hierarchy. The level in the fair value hierarchy within which the fair value measurement in its entirety falls shall be determined based on the lowest level input that is significant to the fair value measurement in its entirety. Assessing the significance of a particular input to the fair value measurement in its entirety requires judgment, considering factors specific to the asset or liability.

23. The availability of inputs relevant to the asset or liability and the relative reliability of the inputs might affect the selection of appropriate valuation techniques. However, the fair value hierarchy prioritizes the inputs to valuation techniques, not the valuation techniques. For example, a fair value measurement using a present value technique might fall within Level 2 or Level 3, depending on the inputs that are significant to the measurement in its entirety and the level in the fair value hierarchy within which those inputs fall.

Level 1 inputs

24. Level 1 inputs are quoted prices (unadjusted) in active markets for identical assets or liabilities that the reporting entity has the ability to access at the measurement date. An active market for the asset or liability is a market in which transactions for the asset or liability occur with sufficient frequency and volume to provide pricing information on an ongoing basis. A quoted price in an active market provides the most reliable evidence of fair value and shall be used to measure fair value whenever available, except as discussed in paragraphs 25 and 26.

25. If the reporting entity holds a large number of similar assets or liabilities (for example, debt securities) that are required to be measured at fair value, a quoted price in an active market might be available but not readily accessible for each of those assets or liabilities individually. In that case, fair value may be measured using an alternative pricing method that

does not rely exclusively on quoted prices (for example, matrix pricing) as a practical expedient. However, the use of an alternative pricing method renders the fair value measurement a lower level measurement.

26. In some situations, a quoted price in an active market might not represent fair value at the measurement date. That might be the case if, for example, significant events (principal-to-principal transactions, brokered trades, or announcements) occur after the close of a market but before the measurement date. The reporting entity should establish and consistently apply a policy for identifying those events that might affect fair value measurements. However, if the quoted price is adjusted for new information, the adjustment renders the fair value measurement a lower level measurement.

27. If the reporting entity holds a position in a single financial instrument (including a block) and the instrument is traded in an active market, the fair value of the position shall be measured within Level 1 as the product of the quoted price for the individual instrument times the quantity held. The quoted price shall not be adjusted because of the size of the position relative to trading volume (blockage factor). The use of a blockage factor is prohibited, even if a market's normal daily trading volume is not sufficient to absorb the quantity held and placing orders to sell the position in a single transaction might affect the quoted price.[11]

Level 2 inputs

28. Level 2 inputs are inputs other than quoted prices included within Level 1 that are observable for the asset or liability, either directly or indirectly. If the asset or liability has a specified (contractual) term, a Level 2 input must be observable for substantially the full term of the asset or liability. Level 2 inputs include the following:

a. Quoted prices for similar assets or liabilities in active markets
b. Quoted prices for identical or similar assets or liabilities in markets that are not active, that is, markets in which there are few transactions for the asset or liability, the prices are not current, or price quotations vary substantially either over time or among market makers (for example, some brokered markets), or in which little infor-

mation is released publicly (for example, a principal-to-principal market)
c. Inputs other than quoted prices that are observable for the asset or liability (for example, interest rates and yield curves observable at commonly quoted intervals, volatilities, prepayment speeds, loss severities, credit risks, and default rates)
d. Inputs that are derived principally from or corroborated by observable market data by correlation or other means (market-corroborated inputs).

29. Adjustments to Level 2 inputs will vary depending on factors specific to the asset or liability. Those factors include the condition and/or location of the asset or liability, the extent to which the inputs relate to items that are comparable to the asset or liability, and the volume and level of activity in the markets within which the inputs are observed. An adjustment that is significant to the fair value measurement in its entirety might render the measurement a Level 3 measurement, depending on the level in the fair value hierarchy within which the inputs used to determine the adjustment fall.

Level 3 inputs

30. Level 3 inputs are unobservable inputs for the asset or liability. Unobservable inputs shall be used to measure fair value to the extent that observable inputs are not available, thereby allowing for situations in which there is little, if any, market activity for the asset or liability at the measurement date. However, the fair value measurement objective remains the same, that is, an exit price from the perspective of a market participant that holds the asset or owes the liability. Therefore, unobservable inputs shall reflect the reporting entity's own assumptions about the assumptions that market participants would use in pricing the asset or liability (including assumptions about risk). Unobservable inputs shall be developed based on the best information available in the circumstances, which might include the reporting entity's own data. In developing unobservable inputs, the reporting entity need not undertake all possible efforts to obtain information about market participant assumptions. However, the reporting entity shall not ignore information about market participant assumptions that is reasonably available without undue cost and effort. Therefore, the reporting entity's own data used to develop unobservable inputs shall be adjusted

---

[11]The guidance in this Statement applies for positions in financial instruments (including blocks) held by all entities, including broker-dealers and investment companies within the scope of the AICPA Audit and Accounting Guides for those industries.

if information is reasonably available without undue cost and effort that indicates that market participants would use different assumptions.

Inputs based on bid and ask prices

31. If an input used to measure fair value is based on bid and ask prices (for example, in a dealer market), the price within the bid-ask spread that is most representative of fair value in the circumstances shall be used to measure fair value, regardless of where in the fair value hierarchy the input falls (Level 1, 2, or 3). This Statement does not preclude the use of mid-market pricing or other pricing conventions as a practical expedient for fair value measurements within a bid-ask spread.

Disclosures

32. For assets and liabilities that are measured at fair value on a recurring basis in periods subsequent to initial recognition (for example, trading securities), the reporting entity shall disclose information that enables users of its financial statements to assess the inputs used to develop those measurements and for recurring fair value measurements using significant unobservable inputs (Level 3), the effect of the measurements on earnings (or changes in net assets) for the period. To meet that objective, the reporting entity shall disclose the following information for each interim and annual period (except as otherwise specified) separately for each major category of assets and liabilities:

a. The fair value measurements at the reporting date
b. The level within the fair value hierarchy in which the fair value measurements in their entirety fall, segregating fair value measurements using quoted prices in active markets for identical assets or liabilities (Level 1), significant other observable inputs (Level 2), and significant unobservable inputs (Level 3)
c. For fair value measurements using significant unobservable inputs (Level 3), a reconciliation of the beginning and ending balances, separately presenting changes during the period attributable to the following:[12]
  (1) Total gains or losses for the period (realized and unrealized), segregating those gains or losses included in earnings (or changes in net assets), and a description of where those

gains or losses included in earnings (or changes in net assets) are reported in the statement of income (or activities)
  (2) Purchases, sales, issuances, and settlements (net)
  (3) Transfers in and/or out of Level 3 (for example, transfers due to changes in the observability of significant inputs)
d. The amount of the total gains or losses for the period in subparagraph (c)(1) above included in earnings (or changes in net assets) that are attributable to the change in unrealized gains or losses relating to those assets and liabilities still held at the reporting date and a description of where those unrealized gains or losses are reported in the statement of income (or activities)
e. In annual periods only, the valuation technique(s) used to measure fair value and a discussion of changes in valuation techniques, if any, during the period.

33. For assets and liabilities that are measured at fair value on a nonrecurring basis in periods subsequent to initial recognition (for example, impaired assets), the reporting entity shall disclose information that enables users of its financial statements to assess the inputs used to develop those measurements. To meet that objective, the reporting entity shall disclose the following information for each interim and annual period (except as otherwise specified) separately for each major category of assets and liabilities:

a. The fair value measurements recorded during the period and the reasons for the measurements
b. The level within the fair value hierarchy in which the fair value measurements in their entirety fall, segregating fair value measurements using quoted prices in active markets for identical assets or liabilities (Level 1), significant other observable inputs (Level 2), and significant unobservable inputs (Level 3)
c. For fair value measurements using significant unobservable inputs (Level 3), a description of the inputs and the information used to develop the inputs
d. In annual periods only, the valuation technique(s) used to measure fair value and a discussion of changes, if any, in the valuation technique(s) used to measure similar assets and/or liabilities in prior periods.

---

[12]For derivative assets and liabilities, the reconciliation disclosure required by paragraph 32(c) may be presented net.

34. The quantitative disclosures required by this Statement shall be presented using a tabular format. (See Appendix A.)

35. The reporting entity is encouraged, but not required, to combine the fair value information disclosed under this Statement with the fair value information disclosed under other accounting pronouncements (for example, FASB Statement No. 107, *Disclosures about Fair Value of Financial Instruments*) in the periods in which those disclosures are required, if practicable. The reporting entity also is encouraged, but not required, to disclose information about other similar measurements (for example, inventories measured at market value under ARB 43, Chapter 4), if practicable.

Effective Date and Transition

36. This Statement shall be effective for financial statements issued for fiscal years beginning after November 15, 2007, and interim periods within those fiscal years. Earlier application is encouraged, provided that the reporting entity has not yet issued financial statements for that fiscal year, including any financial statements for an interim period within that fiscal year.

37. This Statement shall be applied prospectively as of the beginning of the fiscal year in which this Statement is initially applied, except as follows. This Statement shall be applied retrospectively to the following financial instruments as of the beginning of the fiscal year in which this Statement is initially applied (a limited form of retrospective application):

a. A position in a financial instrument that trades in an active market held by a broker-dealer or investment company within the scope of the AICPA Audit and Accounting Guides for those industries that was measured at fair value using a blockage factor prior to initial application of this Statement

b. A financial instrument that was measured at fair value at initial recognition under Statement 133 using the transaction price in accordance with the guidance in footnote 3 of EITF Issue No. 02-3, "Issues Involved in Accounting for Derivative Contracts Held for Trading Purposes and Contracts Involved in Energy Trading and Risk Management Activities," prior to initial application of this Statement

c. A hybrid financial instrument that was measured at fair value at initial recognition under Statement 133 using the transaction price in accordance with the guidance in Statement 133 (added by FASB Statement No. 155, *Accounting for Certain Hybrid Financial Instruments*) prior to initial application of this Statement.

38. At the date this Statement is initially applied to the financial instruments in paragraph 37(a)–37(c), a difference between the carrying amounts and the fair values of those instruments shall be recognized as a cumulative-effect adjustment to the opening balance of retained earnings (or other appropriate components of equity or net assets in the statement of financial position) for that fiscal year, presented separately. The disclosure requirements of Statement 154 for a change in accounting principle do not apply.

39. The disclosure requirements of this Statement (paragraphs 32–35), including those disclosures that are required in annual periods only, shall be applied in the first interim period of the fiscal year in which this Statement is initially applied. The disclosure requirements of this Statement need not be applied for financial statements for periods presented prior to initial application of this Statement.

> **The provisions of this Statement need not be applied to immaterial items.**

This Statement was adopted by the unanimous vote of the seven members of the Financial Accounting Standards Board:

Robert H. Herz,	G. Michael Crooch	Edward W. Trott
Chairman	Thomas J. Linsmeier	Donald M. Young
George J. Batavick	Leslie F. Seidman	

Appendix A

IMPLEMENTATION GUIDANCE

Introduction

A1. This appendix describes in general terms certain provisions of this Statement and provides examples that incorporate simplified assumptions to illustrate the application of those provisions. This Statement sets out a framework for measuring fair value, which refers to certain valuation concepts and practices. However, this Statement is not intended to establish valuation standards.

The Fair Value Measurement Approach

A2. This Statement clarifies fair value in terms of the price in an orderly transaction between market participants to sell an asset or transfer a liability in the principal (or most advantageous) market for the asset or liability. The transaction to sell the asset or transfer the liability is a hypothetical transaction at the measurement date, considered from the perspective of a market participant that holds the asset or owes the liability. Therefore, the objective of a fair value measurement is to determine the price that would be received to sell the asset or paid to transfer the liability at the measurement date (an exit price). Because that exit price objective applies for all assets and liabilities measured at fair value, any fair value measurement requires that the reporting entity determine:

a. The particular asset or liability that is the subject of the measurement (consistent with its unit of account)

b. For an asset, the valuation premise appropriate for the measurement (consistent with its highest and best use)

c. The principal (or most advantageous) market for the asset or liability (for an asset, consistent with its highest and best use)

d. The valuation technique(s) appropriate for the measurement, considering the availability of data with which to develop inputs that represent the assumptions that market participants would use in pricing the asset or liability and the level in the fair value hierarchy within which the inputs fall.

A3. The judgments applied in different valuation situations often will be different. The examples in this appendix illustrate, in qualitative terms, the judgments a reporting entity that measures assets and/or liabilities at fair value might apply in varying valuation situations.

The Valuation Premise

A4. The valuation premise used to measure the fair value of an asset depends on the highest and best use of the asset by market participants. If the asset would provide maximum value to market participants principally through its use in combination with other assets as a group (highest and best use is "in-use"), the asset would be measured using an in-use valuation premise. If the asset would provide maximum value to market participants principally on a standalone basis (highest and best use is "in-exchange"), the asset would be measured using an in-exchange valuation premise.

A5. When measuring the fair value of an asset in-use, the in-use valuation premise can be incorporated in the measurement differently, depending on the circumstances. For example:

a. The fair value of the asset might be the same whether using an in-use or an in-exchange valuation premise. For example, that might be the case if the asset is a business (such as a reporting unit) that market participants would continue to operate. In that case, the transaction would involve the business in its entirety. The use of the assets as a group in the context of an ongoing business would generate synergies that would be available to market participants (market participant synergies).

b. The in-use valuation premise might be incorporated in the fair value of the asset through adjustments to the value of the asset in-exchange. For example, that might be the case if the asset is a machine and the fair value measurement is determined using an observed price for a similar machine (not installed or otherwise configured for use), adjusted for transportation and installation costs so that the fair value measurement reflects the current condition and location of the machine (installed and configured for use).

c. The in-use valuation premise might be incorporated in the fair value of the asset through the market participant assumptions used to measure the fair value of the asset. For example, if the asset is work-in-process inventory that is unique and market participants would complete the inventory into finished goods, the fair value of the inventory would assume that any specialized machinery necessary to complete the inventory into finished goods would be available to market participants. In that case, market participants would have the specialized machinery in place or would acquire the specialized machinery in conjunction with the inventory.

d. The in-use valuation premise might be incorporated in the fair value of the asset through the valuation technique used to measure the fair value of the asset. For example, that might be the case when using the multiperiod excess earnings method to measure the fair value of certain intangible assets because that valuation technique specifically considers the contribution of any complementary assets in the group in which an intangible asset would be used.

e. In more limited situations, the asset might be measured at an amount that approximates its fair value in-use when allocating the fair value of the asset group within which the asset is used to the individual assets of the group. For example, that might be the case if the valuation involves real property and the fair value of improved property (an asset group) is allocated to its component assets (such as land and improvements).

Highest and Best Use

A6. Highest and best use is a valuation concept that refers broadly to the use of an asset that would maximize the value of the asset or the group of assets in which the asset would be used by market participants. For some assets, in particular, nonfinancial assets, application of the highest-and-best-use concept could have a significant effect on the fair value measurement. Examples 1–3 illustrate the application of the highest-and-best-use concept in situations in which nonfinancial assets are newly acquired.

Example 1—asset group

A7. The reporting entity, a strategic buyer, acquires a group of assets (Assets A, B, and C) in a business combination. Asset C is billing software developed by the acquired entity for its own use in conjunction with Assets A and B (related assets). The reporting entity measures the fair value of each of the assets individually, consistent with the specified unit of account for the assets. The reporting entity determines

that each asset would provide maximum value to market participants principally through its use in combination with other assets as a group (highest and best use is in-use).

A8. In this instance, the market in which the reporting entity would sell the assets is the market in which it initially acquired the assets (that is, the "entry" and "exit" markets from the perspective of the reporting entity are the same). Market participant buyers with whom the reporting entity would transact in that market have characteristics that are generally representative of both financial buyers and strategic buyers and include those buyers that initially bid for the assets.[13] As discussed below, differences between the indicated fair values of the individual assets relate principally to the use of the assets by those market participants within different asset groups:

a. *Strategic buyer asset group.* The reporting entity, a strategic buyer, determines that strategic buyers have related assets that would enhance the value of the group within which the assets would be used (market participant synergies). Those assets include a substitute asset for Asset C (the billing software), which would be used for only a limited transition period and could not be sold standalone at the end of that period. Because strategic buyers have substitute assets, Asset C would not be used for its full remaining economic life. The indicated fair values of Assets A, B, and C within the strategic buyer asset group (reflecting the synergies resulting from the use of the assets within that group) are $360, $260, and $30, respectively. The indicated fair value of the assets as a group within the strategic buyer asset group is $650.

b. *Financial buyer asset group.* The reporting entity determines that financial buyers do not have related or substitute assets that would enhance the value of the group within which the assets would be used. Because financial buyers do not have substitute assets, Asset C (the billing software) would be used for its full remaining economic life. The indicated fair values of Assets A, B, and C within the financial buyer asset group are $300, $200, and $100, respectively. The indicated fair value of the assets as a group within the financial buyer asset group is $600.

A9. The fair values of Assets A, B, and C would be determined based on the use of the assets as a group

---

[13]While market participant buyers might be broadly classified as strategic and/or financial buyers, there often will be differences among the market participant buyers within each of those groups, reflecting, for example, different uses for an asset and different operating strategies.

within the strategic buyer group ($360, $260, and $30). Although the use of the assets within the strategic buyer group does not maximize the fair value of each of the assets individually, it maximizes the fair value of the assets as a group ($650).

Example 2—land

A10. The reporting entity acquires land in a business combination. The land is currently developed for industrial use as a site for a manufacturing facility. The current use of land often is presumed to be its highest and best use. However, nearby sites have recently been developed for residential use as sites for high-rise condominiums. Based on that development and recent zoning and other changes to facilitate that development, the reporting entity determines that the land currently used as a site for a manufacturing facility could be developed as a site for residential use (for high-rise condominiums).

A11. In this instance, the highest and best use of the land would be determined by comparing (a) the fair value of the manufacturing operation, which presumes that the land would continue to be used as currently developed for industrial use (in-use) and (b) the value of the land as a vacant site for residential use, considering the demolition and other costs necessary to convert the land to a vacant site (in-exchange). The highest and best use of the land would be determined based on the higher of those values.[14]

Example 3—IPR&D project

A12. The reporting entity acquires an in-process research and development (IPR&D) project in a business combination. The reporting entity does not intend to complete the IPR&D project. If completed, the IPR&D project would compete with one of its own IPR&D projects (to provide the next generation of the reporting entity's commercialized technology). Instead, the reporting entity intends to hold (lock up) the IPR&D project to prevent its competitors from obtaining access to the technology. The IPR&D project is expected to provide defensive value, principally by improving the prospects for the reporting entity's own competing technology. For purposes of measuring the fair value of the IPR&D project at ini-

tial recognition, the highest and best use of the IPR&D project would be determined based on its use by market participants. For example:

a. The highest and best use of the IPR&D project would be in-use if market participants would continue to develop the IPR&D project and that use would maximize the value of the group of assets in which the IPR&D project would be used. That might be the case if market participants do not have similar technology (in development or commercialized). The fair value of the IPR&D project, measured using an in-use valuation premise, would be determined based on the price that would be received in a current transaction to sell the IPR&D project, assuming that the IPR&D would be used with its complementary assets as a group and that those complementary assets would be available to market participants.

b. The highest and best use of the IPR&D project also would be in-use if, for competitive reasons, market participants would lock up the IPR&D project and that use would maximize the value of the group of assets in which the IPR&D project would be used (as a locked-up project). That might be the case if market participants have technology in a more advanced stage of development that would compete with the IPR&D project (if completed) and the IPR&D project would be expected to provide defensive value (if locked up). The fair value of the IPR&D project, measured using an in-use valuation premise, would be determined based on the price that would be received in a current transaction to sell the IPR&D project, assuming that the IPR&D would be used (locked up) with its complementary assets as a group and that those complementary assets would be available to market participants.

c. The highest and best use of the IPR&D project would be in-exchange if market participants would discontinue the development of the IPR&D project. That might be the case if the IPR&D project is not expected to provide a market rate of return (if completed) and would not otherwise provide defensive value (if locked up). The fair value of the IPR&D project, measured using an in-exchange valuation premise, would

---

[14]In situations involving real estate appraisal, the determination of highest and best use in the manner described above also might consider other factors relating to the manufacturing operation, including its assets and liabilities.

be determined based on the price that would be received in a current transaction to sell the IPR&D project standalone (which might be zero).

Valuation Techniques

A13. This Statement emphasizes that valuation techniques consistent with the market approach, income approach, and/or cost approach should be used to measure fair value. In some cases, a single valuation technique will be appropriate. In other cases, multiple valuation techniques will be appropriate. If multiple valuation techniques are used, the reporting entity should evaluate the results (respective indications of fair value), considering the reasonableness of the range indicated by those results. The fair value measurement is the point within that range that is most representative of fair value in the circumstances. Examples 4 and 5 illustrate the use of multiple valuation techniques.

Example 4—machine held and used

A14. The reporting entity tests for impairment an asset group that is held and used in operations. The asset group is impaired. The reporting entity measures the fair value of a machine that is used in the asset group as a basis for allocating the impairment loss to the assets of the group in accordance with FASB Statement No. 144, *Accounting for the Impairment or Disposal of Long-Lived Assets.* The machine, initially purchased from an outside vendor, was subsequently customized by the reporting entity for use in its operations. However, the customization of the machine was not extensive. The reporting entity determines that the asset would provide maximum value to market participants through its use in combination with other assets as a group (as installed or otherwise configured for use). Therefore, the highest and best use of the machine is in-use.

A15. The reporting entity determines that sufficient data are available to apply the cost approach and, because the customization of the machine was not extensive, the market approach. The income approach is not used because the machine does not have a separately identifiable income stream from which to develop reliable estimates of future cash flows. Further, information about short-term and intermediate-term lease rates for similar used machinery that otherwise could be used to project an income stream (lease payments over remaining service lives) is not

available. The market and cost approaches are applied as follows:

a. *Market approach.* The market approach is applied using quoted prices for similar machines adjusted for differences between the machine (as customized) and the similar machines. The measurement reflects the price that would be received for the machine in its current condition (used) and location (installed and configured for use), thereby including installation and transportation costs. The fair value indicated by that approach ranges from $40,000 to $48,000.

b. *Cost approach.* The cost approach is applied by estimating the amount that currently would be required to construct a substitute (customized) machine of comparable utility. The estimate considers the condition of the machine (for example, physical deterioration, functional obsolescence, and economic obsolescence) and includes installation costs. The fair value indicated by that approach ranges from $40,000 to $52,000.

A16. The reporting entity determines that the fair value indicated by the market approach is more representative of fair value than the fair value indicated by the cost approach and, therefore, ascribes more weight to the results of the market approach. That determination is based on the relative reliability of the inputs, considering the degree of comparability between the machine and the similar machines. In particular:

a. The inputs used in the market approach (quoted prices for similar machines) require relatively fewer and less subjective adjustments than the inputs used in the cost approach.

b. The range indicated by the market approach overlaps with, but is narrower than, the range indicated by the cost approach.

c. There are no known unexplained differences (between the machine and the similar machines) within that range.

The reporting entity further determines that the higher end of the range indicated by the market approach is most representative of fair value, largely because the majority of relevant data points in the market approach fall at or near the higher end of the range. Accordingly, the reporting entity determines that the fair value of the machine is $48,000.

Example 5—software asset

A17. The reporting entity acquires a group of assets. The asset group includes an income-producing software asset internally developed for license to customers and its complementary assets (including a related database with which the software asset is used). For purposes of allocating the cost of the group to the individual assets acquired, the reporting entity measures the fair value of the software asset. The reporting entity determines that the software asset would provide maximum value to market participants through its use in combination with other assets (its complementary assets) as a group. Therefore, the highest and best use of the software asset is in-use. (In this instance, the licensing of the software asset, in and of itself, does not render the highest and best use of the software asset in-exchange.)

A18. The reporting entity determines that in addition to the income approach, sufficient data might be available to apply the cost approach but not the market approach. Information about market transactions for comparable software assets is not available. The income and cost approaches are applied as follows:

a. *Income approach.* The income approach is applied using a present value technique. The cash flows used in that technique reflect the income stream expected to result from the software asset (license fees from customers) over its economic life. The fair value indicated by that approach is $15 million.
b. *Cost approach.* The cost approach is applied by estimating the amount that currently would be required to construct a substitute software asset of comparable utility (considering functional, technological, and economic obsolescence). The fair value indicated by that approach is $10 million.

A19. Through its application of the cost approach, the reporting entity determines that market participants would not be able to replicate a substitute software asset of comparable utility. Certain attributes of the software asset are unique, having been developed using proprietary information, and cannot be readily replicated. The reporting entity determines that the fair value of the software asset is $15 million, as indicated by the income approach.

Inputs to Valuation Techniques

A20. This Statement emphasizes that valuation techniques used to measure the fair value of an asset or liability should maximize the use of observable inputs, that is, inputs that reflect the assumptions market participants would use in pricing the asset or liability developed based on market data obtained from sources independent of the reporting entity. Examples of markets in which inputs might be observable for some assets and liabilities (for example, financial instruments) include the following:

a. *Exchange market.* In an active exchange market, closing prices are both readily available and generally representative of fair value. An example of such a market is the New York Stock Exchange.
b. *Dealer market.* In a dealer market, dealers stand ready to trade (either buy or sell for their own account), thereby providing liquidity by using their capital to hold an inventory of the items for which they make a market. Typically, bid and ask prices (representing the price the dealer is willing to pay and the price at which the dealer is willing to sell, respectively) are more readily available than closing prices. Over-the-counter markets (where prices are publicly reported by the National Association of Securities Dealers Automated Quotations systems or by Pink Sheets LLC) are dealer markets. For example, the market for U.S. Treasury securities is a dealer market. Dealer markets also exist for some other assets and liabilities, including other financial instruments, commodities, and physical assets (for example, certain used equipment).
c. *Brokered market.* In a brokered market, brokers attempt to match buyers with sellers but do not stand ready to trade for their own account. In other words, brokers do not use their own capital to hold an inventory of the items for which they make a market. The broker knows the prices bid and asked by the respective parties, but each party is typically unaware of another party's price requirements. Prices of completed transactions are sometimes available. Brokered markets include electronic communication networks, in which buy and sell orders are matched, and commercial and residential real estate markets.
d. *Principal-to-principal market.* Principal-to-principal transactions, both originations and resales, are negotiated independently with no intermediary. Little information about those transactions may be released publicly.

Fair Value Hierarchy

A21. To increase consistency and comparability in fair value measurements and related disclosures, this Statement establishes a fair value hierarchy that prioritizes the inputs to valuation techniques used to measure fair value into three broad levels. The level in the fair value hierarchy within which the fair value measurement in its entirety falls is determined based on the lowest level input that is significant to the measurement in its entirety.

Level 1 inputs

A22. Level 1 inputs are quoted prices (unadjusted) in active markets for identical assets or liabilities that the reporting entity has the ability to access at the measurement date. A Level 1 input will be available for many financial assets and liabilities, some of which might be exchanged in multiple active markets (for example, on different exchanges). Therefore, the emphasis within Level 1 is on determining both of the following:

a. The principal market for the asset or liability or, in the absence of a principal market, the most advantageous market for the asset or liability, considered from the perspective of the reporting entity; and
b. Whether the reporting entity has the ability to access the price in that market for the asset or liability at the measurement date.

Example 6 illustrates the use of Level 1 inputs to measure the fair value of a financial asset that trades in multiple active markets with different prices.

Example 6—Level 1 principal (or most advantageous) market

A23. A financial asset is traded on two different exchanges with different prices. The reporting entity transacts in both markets and has the ability to access the price in those markets for the asset at the measurement date. In Market A, the price that would be received is $26, and transaction costs in that market are $3 (the net amount that would be received is $23). In Market B, the price that would be received is $25, and transaction costs in that market are $1 (the net amount that would be received in Market B is $24).

a. If Market A is the principal market for the asset (the market in which the reporting entity would sell the asset with the greatest volume and level

of activity for the asset), the fair value of the asset would be measured using the price that would be received in that market ($26).
b. If neither market is the principal market for the asset, the fair value of the asset would be measured using the price in the most advantageous market. The most advantageous market is the market in which the reporting entity would sell the asset with the price that maximizes the amount that would be received for the asset, considering transaction costs in the respective markets (that is, the net amount that would be received in the respective markets). Because the price in Market B adjusted for transaction costs would maximize the net amount that would be received for the asset ($24), the fair value of the asset would be measured using the price in that market ($25). Although transaction costs are considered in determining the most advantageous market, the price in that market used to measure the fair value of the asset is not adjusted for those costs.

Level 2 inputs

A24. Level 2 inputs are inputs other than quoted prices included within Level 1 that are observable for the asset or liability, either directly or indirectly through corroboration with observable market data (market-corroborated inputs). If the asset or liability has a specified (contractual) term, a Level 2 input must be observable for substantially the full term of the asset or liability. An adjustment to a Level 2 input that is significant to the fair value measurement in its entirety might render the measurement a Level 3 measurement, depending on the level in the fair value hierarchy within which the inputs used to determine the adjustment fall. Examples of Level 2 inputs for particular assets and liabilities follow.

a. *Receive-fixed, pay-variable interest rate swap based on the LIBOR swap rate.* A Level 2 input would include the LIBOR swap rate if that rate is observable at commonly quoted intervals for the full term of the swap.
b. *Receive-fixed, pay-variable interest rate swap based on a foreign-denominated yield curve.* A Level 2 input would include the swap rate based on a foreign- denominated yield curve that is observable at commonly quoted intervals for substantially the full term of the swap. That would be the case if the term of the swap is 10 years and

that rate is observable at commonly quoted intervals for 9 years, provided that any reasonable extrapolation of the yield curve for year 10 would not be significant to the fair value measurement of the swap in its entirety.

c. *Receive-fixed, pay-variable interest rate swap based on a specific bank's prime rate.* A Level 2 input would include the bank's prime rate derived through extrapolation if the extrapolated values are corroborated by observable market data, for example, by correlation with an interest rate that is observable over substantially the full term of the swap.

d. *Three-year option on exchange-traded shares.* A Level 2 input would include the implied volatility for the shares derived through extrapolation to year 3 if (1) prices for one- and two-year options on the shares are observable and (2) the extrapolated implied volatility of a three-year option is corroborated by observable market data for substantially the full term of the option. In that case, the implied volatility could be derived by extrapolating from the implied volatility of the one- and two-year options on the shares and corroborated by the implied volatility for three-year options on comparable entities' shares, provided that correlation with the one- and two-year implied volatilities is established.

e. *Licensing arrangement.* For a licensing arrangement that is acquired in a business combination and that was recently negotiated with an unrelated party by the acquired entity (the party to the licensing arrangement), a Level 2 input would include the royalty rate at inception of the arrangement.

f. *Finished goods inventory at retail outlet.* For finished goods inventory that is acquired in a business combination, a Level 2 input would include either a price to customers in a retail market or a wholesale price to retailers in a wholesale market, adjusted for differences between the condition and location of the inventory item and the comparable (similar) inventory items so that the fair value measurement reflects the price that would be received in a transaction to sell the inventory to another retailer that would complete the requisite selling efforts. Conceptually, the fair value measurement should be the same, whether adjustments are made to a retail price (downward) or to a wholesale price (upward). Generally, the price that requires the least amount of subjective adjustments should be used for the fair value measurement.

g. *Building held and used.* A Level 2 input would include the price per square foot for the building (a valuation multiple) derived from observable market data, for example, multiples derived from prices in observed transactions involving comparable (similar) buildings in similar locations.

h. *Reporting unit.* A Level 2 input would include a valuation multiple (for example, a multiple of earnings or revenue or a similar performance measure) derived from observable market data, for example, multiples derived from prices in observed transactions involving comparable (similar) businesses, considering operational, market, financial, and nonfinancial factors.

Level 3 inputs

A25. Level 3 inputs are unobservable inputs for the asset or liability, that is, inputs that reflect the reporting entity's own assumptions about the assumptions market participants would use in pricing the asset or liability (including assumptions about risk) developed based on the best information available in the circumstances. Assumptions about risk include the risk inherent in a particular valuation technique used to measure fair value (such as a pricing model) and/or the risk inherent in the inputs to the valuation technique.[15] Examples of Level 3 inputs for particular assets and liabilities follow.

a. *Long-dated currency swap.* A Level 3 input would include interest rates in a specified currency that are not observable and cannot be corroborated by observable market data at commonly quoted intervals or otherwise for substantially the full term of the currency swap. The interest rates in a currency swap are the swap rates calculated from the respective countries' yield curves.

b. *Three-year option on exchange-traded shares.* A Level 3 input would include historical volatility, that is, the volatility for the shares derived from the shares' historical prices. Historical volatility typically does not represent current market participant expectations about future volatility, even if it is the only information available to price an option.

---

[15]A measurement (for example, a "mark-to-model" measurement) that does not include an adjustment for risk would not represent a fair value measurement if market participants would include one in pricing the related asset or liability.

c. *Interest rate swap.* A Level 3 input would include an adjustment to a mid-market consensus (non-binding) price for the swap developed using data that are not directly observable and that cannot otherwise be corroborated by observable market data.

d. *Asset retirement obligation at initial recognition.* A Level 3 input would include expected cash flows (adjusted for risk) developed using the reporting entity's own data if there is no information reasonably available without undue cost and effort that indicates that market participants would use different assumptions. That Level 3 input would be used in a present value technique together with other inputs, for example (1) a risk-free interest rate or (2) a credit-adjusted risk-free rate if the effect of the reporting entity's credit standing on the fair value of the liability is reflected in the discount rate rather than in the expected cash flows.[16]

e. *Reporting unit.* A Level 3 input would include a financial forecast (for example, of cash flows or earnings) developed using the reporting entity's own data if there is no information reasonably available without undue cost and effort that indicates that market participants would use different assumptions.

Transaction Prices and Initial Fair Value Measurements

A26. This Statement clarifies that in many cases the transaction price, that is, the price paid (received) for a particular asset (liability), will represent the fair value of that asset (liability) at initial recognition, but not presumptively.[17] Example 7 illustrates situations in which the price in a transaction involving a derivative instrument might (and might not) represent the fair value of the instrument.

Example 7—interest rate swap at initial recognition

A27. Entity A (a retail counterparty) enters into an interest rate swap in a retail market with Entity B (a securities dealer) for no initial consideration (transac-

tion price is zero). Entity A transacts only in the retail market. Entity B transacts in the retail market (with retail counterparties) and in the inter-dealer market (with securities dealer counterparties).

a. *Entity A (retail counterparty).* From the perspective of Entity A, the retail market in which it initially transacted is the principal market for the swap; if Entity A were to transfer its rights and obligations under the swap, it would do so with a securities dealer counterparty in that market. In that case, the transaction price (zero) would represent the fair value of the swap to Entity A at initial recognition, that is, the price that Entity A would receive (or pay) to sell (or transfer) the swap in a transaction with a securities dealer counterparty in the retail market (an exit price).[18] That price would not be adjusted for any incremental (transaction) costs that would be charged by that securities dealer counterparty.

b. *Entity B (securities dealer).* From the perspective of Entity B, the inter-dealer market (not the retail market in which it initially transacted) is the principal market for the swap; if Entity B were to transfer its rights and obligations under the swap, it would do so with a securities dealer in that market. Because the market in which Entity B initially transacted is different from the principal market for the swap, the transaction price (zero) would not necessarily represent the fair value of the swap to Entity B at initial recognition.

Restricted Assets

A28. The effect on a fair value measurement of a restriction on the sale or use of an asset by a reporting entity will differ depending on whether the restriction would be considered by market participants in pricing the asset. Examples 8 and 9 illustrate the effect of restrictions in determining the fair value of an asset.

Example 8—restriction on sale of security

A29. The reporting entity holds a security of an issuer for which sale is legally restricted for a specified period. (For example, such a restriction could limit

---

[16]FASB Statement No. 143, *Accounting for Asset Retirement Obligations,* illustrates the application of the expected present value technique to an asset retirement obligation measured at fair value at initial recognition under that Statement. (See Appendix C of Statement 143.)

[17]The guidance in this Statement applies for derivatives and other financial instruments that are measured at fair value under FASB Statement No. 133, *Accounting for Derivative Instruments and Hedging Activities,* including hybrid financial instruments. Therefore, this Statement nullifies the guidance in footnote 3 of EITF Issue No. 02-3, "Issues Involved in Accounting for Derivative Contracts Held for Trading Purposes and Contracts Involved in Energy Trading and Risk Management Activities."

[18]If the transaction price represents fair value at initial recognition and a pricing model will be used to measure fair value in subsequent periods, the model should be calibrated so that the model value at initial recognition equals the transaction price.

sale to qualifying investors, as may be the case under Rule 144 or similar rules of the Securities and Exchange Commission.) The restriction is specific to (an attribute of) the security and, therefore, would transfer to market participants. In that case, the fair value of the security would be based on the quoted price for an otherwise identical unrestricted security of the same issuer that trades in a public market, adjusted to reflect the effect of the restriction. The adjustment would reflect the amount market participants would demand because of the risk relating to the inability to access a public market for the security for the specified period.[19] The adjustment will vary depending on the nature and duration of the restriction, the extent to which buyers are limited by the restriction (for example, there might be a large number of qualifying investors), and factors specific to both the security and the issuer (qualitative and quantitative).[20]

Example 9—restrictions on use of asset

A30. A donor contributes land in an otherwise developed residential area to a not-for-profit neighborhood association (Association). The land is currently used as a playground. The donor specifies that the land must continue to be used by the Association as a playground in perpetuity. Upon review of relevant documentation (legal and other), the Association determines that the fiduciary responsibility to meet the donor's restriction would not otherwise transfer to market participants if the asset was to be sold by the Association, that is, the donor restriction on the use of the land is specific to the Association. Absent the restriction on the use of the land by the Association, the land could be used as a site for residential development. In addition, the land has an easement for utility lines on a portion of the property.

a. *Donor restriction on use of land.* Because in this instance the donor restriction on the use of the land is specific to the Association, the restriction would not transfer to market participants. Therefore, the fair value of the land would be based on the higher of its fair value in-use as a playground or fair value in-exchange as a site for residential

development, regardless of the restriction on the use of the land by the Association.[21]

b. *Easement for utility lines.* Because the easement for utility lines is specific to (an attribute of) the land, it would transfer to market participants. Therefore, the fair value measurement of the land would consider the effect of the easement, regardless of whether highest and best use is in-use as a playground or in-exchange as a site for residential development.

Liabilities and Credit Risk

A31. Nonperformance risk relating to a liability includes the reporting entity's credit risk. The reporting entity should consider the effect of its credit risk (credit standing) on the fair value of the liability in all periods in which the liability is measured at fair value because those who might hold the entity's obligations as assets would consider the effect of the entity's credit standing in determining the prices they would be willing to pay. For example, assume that Entity X and Entity Y each enter into a contractual obligation to pay cash ($500) to Entity Z in 5 years. Entity X has a AA credit rating and can borrow at 6 percent, while Entity Y has a BBB credit rating and can borrow at 12 percent. Entity X will receive about $374 in exchange for its promise (the present value of $500 in 5 years at 6 percent). Entity Y will receive about $284 in exchange for its promise (the present value of $500 in 5 years at 12 percent). The fair value of the liability to each entity (the proceeds) incorporates that entity's credit standing. Example 10 illustrates the effect of credit standing on the fair value of a financial liability at initial recognition and in subsequent periods.

Example 10—structured note

A32. On January 1, 2007, Entity A, an investment bank with a AA credit rating, issues a five-year fixed rate note to Entity B. The contractual principal amount to be paid by Entity A at maturity is linked to the S&P 500 index. No credit enhancements are issued in conjunction with or otherwise related to the contract (that is, no collateral is posted and there is no third-party guarantee). Entity A elects to account for

---

[19]The guidance in this Statement applies for equity securities with restrictions that terminate within one year that are measured at fair value under FASB Statements No. 115, *Accounting for Certain Investments in Debt and Equity Securities,* and No. 124, *Accounting for Certain Investments Held by Not-for-Profit Organizations.*

[20]ASR No. 113, *Statement Regarding "Restricted Securities,"* provides related guidance.

[21]The donor restriction, which is legally binding on the Association, would be indicated through classification of the associated net assets (permanently restricted) and disclosure of the nature of the restriction in accordance with paragraphs 12 and 14 of FASB Statement No. 117, *Financial Statements of Not-for-Profit Organizations.*

the entire note at fair value in accordance with FASB Statement No. 155, *Accounting for Certain Hybrid Financial Instruments.* The fair value of the note (the obligation of Entity A) during 2007 is measured using an expected present value technique. Changes in fair value are discussed below.

a. *Fair value at January 1, 2007.* The expected cash flows used in the expected present value technique are discounted at the risk-free rate (using the treasury yield curve at January 1, 2007), plus the current market observable AA corporate bond spread to treasuries adjusted (up or down) for Entity A's specific credit risk (credit-adjusted risk-free rate). Therefore, the fair value of the obligation of Entity A at initial recognition considers nonperformance risk, including that entity's credit risk (presumably, reflected in the proceeds).

b. *Fair value at March 31, 2007.* During March 2007, the credit spread for AA corporate bonds widens, with no changes to the specific credit risk of Entity A. The expected cash flows used in the expected present value technique are discounted at the risk-free rate (using the treasury yield curve at March 31, 2007), plus the current market observable AA corporate bond spread to treasuries, adjusted for Entity A's specific credit risk (credit-adjusted risk-free rate). Entity A's specific credit risk is unchanged from initial recognition. Therefore, the fair value of the obligation of Entity A changes due to changes in credit spreads generally. Changes in credit spreads reflect current market participant assumptions about changes in nonperformance risk generally.

c. *Fair value at June 30, 2007.* As of June 30, 2007, there have been no changes to the AA corporate bond spreads. However, based on structured note issuances corroborated with other qualitative information, Entity A determines that its own specific credit worthiness has strengthened within the AA credit spread. The expected cash flows used in the expected present value technique are discounted at the risk-free rate (using the treasury yield curve at June 30, 2007), plus the current market observable AA corporate bond spread to treasuries (unchanged from March 31, 2007), adjusted for Entity A's specific credit risk (credit-adjusted risk-free rate). Therefore, the fair value of the obligation of Entity A changes due to the change in its own specific credit risk within the AA corporate bond spread.

Fair Value Disclosures

A33. This Statement requires disclosures about the fair value of assets and liabilities recognized in the statement of financial position in periods subsequent to initial recognition, whether the measurements are made on a recurring basis (for example, trading securities) or on a nonrecurring basis (for example, impaired assets). Quantitative disclosures using a tabular format are required in all periods (interim and annual). Qualitative (narrative) disclosures about the valuation techniques used to measure fair value are required in all annual periods. The disclosures required by paragraph 32(a)–(d) and paragraph 33(a) and (b) are illustrated below.

Assets Measured at Fair Value on a Recurring Basis

A34. For assets and liabilities measured at fair value on a recurring basis during the period, this Statement requires quantitative disclosures about the fair value measurements separately for each major category of assets and liabilities (paragraph 32(a) and (b)). For assets, that information might be presented as follows:

($ in 000s)		**Fair Value Measurements at Reporting Date Using**		
Description	**12/31/XX**	**Quoted Prices in Active Markets for Identical Assets (Level 1)**	**Significant Other Observable Inputs (Level 2)**	**Significant Unobservable Inputs (Level 3)**
Trading securities	$115	$105	$10	
Available-for-sale securities	75	75		
Derivatives	60	25	15	$20
Venture capital investments	10			10
Total	$260	$205	$25	$30

(Note: For liabilities, a similar table should be presented.)

Assets Measured at Fair Value on a Recurring Basis Using Significant Unobservable Inputs (Level 3)

A35. For assets and liabilities measured at fair value on a recurring basis using significant unobservable inputs (Level 3) during the period, this Statement requires a reconciliation of the beginning and ending balances, separately for each major category of assets and liabilities, except for derivative assets and liabilities, which may be presented net (paragraph 32(c) and (d)). For assets, the reconciliation might be presented as follows:

($ in 000s)	Fair Value Measurements Using Significant Unobservable Inputs (Level 3)		
	Derivatives	**Venture Capital Investments**	**Total**
Beginning balance	$14	$11	$25
Total gains or losses (realized/unrealized)			
Included in earnings (or changes in net assets)	11	(3)	8
Included in other comprehensive income	4		4
Purchases, issuances, and settlements	(7)	2	(5)
Transfers in and/or out of Level 3	(2)	0	(2)
Ending balance	$20	$10	$30
The amount of total gains or losses for the period included in earnings (or changes in net assets) attributable to the change in unrealized gains or losses relating to assets still held at the reporting date	$ 7	$ 2	$ 9

(Note: For liabilities, a similar table should be presented.)

Gains and losses (realized and unrealized) included in earnings (or changes in net assets) for the period (above) are reported in trading revenues and in other revenues as follows:

	Trading Revenues	**Other Revenues**
Total gains or losses included in earnings (or changes in net assets) for the period (above)	$11	$(3)
Change in unrealized gains or losses relating to assets still held at reporting date	$ 7	$ 2

Assets Measured at Fair Value on a Nonrecurring Basis

A36. For each major category of assets and liabilities measured at fair value on a nonrecurring basis during the period, this Statement requires disclosures about the fair value measurements (paragraph 33(a) and (b)). That information might be presented as follows:

($ in millions)		Fair Value Measurements Using			
Description	Year Ended 12/31/XX	Quoted Prices in Active Markets for Identical Assets (Level 1)	Significant Other Observable Inputs (Level 2)	Significant Unobservable Inputs (Level 3)	Total Gains (Losses)
Long-lived assets held and used	$75		$75		$(25)
Goodwill	30			$30	(35)
Long-lived assets held for sale	26		26		(15)
					$(75)

In accordance with the provisions of Statement 144, long-lived assets held and used with a carrying amount of $100 million were written down to their fair value of $75 million, resulting in an impairment charge of $25 million, which was included in earnings for the period.

In accordance with the provisions of Statement 142, goodwill with a carrying amount of $65 million was written down to its implied fair value of $30 million, resulting in an impairment charge of $35 million, which was included in earnings for the period.

In accordance with the provisions of Statement 144, long-lived assets held for sale with a carrying amount of $35 million were written down to their fair value of $26 million, less cost to sell of $6 million (or $20 million), resulting in a loss of $15 million, which was included in earnings for the period.

Appendix B

PRESENT VALUE TECHNIQUES

Introduction

B1. FASB Concepts Statement No. 7, *Using Cash Flow Information and Present Value in Accounting Measurements,* provides guidance for using present value techniques to measure fair value. That guidance focuses on a traditional or discount rate adjustment technique and an expected cash flow (expected present value) technique. This appendix clarifies that guidance.[22] This appendix neither prescribes the use of one specific present value technique nor limits the use of present value techniques to measure fair value to the techniques discussed herein. The present value technique used to measure fair value will depend on facts and circumstances specific to the asset or liability being measured (for example, whether comparable assets or liabilities can be observed in the market) and the availability of sufficient data.

The Components of a Present Value Measurement

B2. Present value is a tool used to link uncertain future amounts (cash flows or values) to a present amount using a discount rate (an application of the income approach) that is consistent with value maximizing behavior and capital market equilibrium. A fair value measurement of an asset or liability, using present value, should capture the following elements from the perspective of market participants as of the measurement date:

a. An estimate of future cash flows for the asset or liability being measured.
b. Expectations about possible variations in the amount and/or timing of the cash flows representing the uncertainty inherent in the cash flows.

---

[22]That guidance is included or otherwise referred to principally in paragraphs 39–46, 51, 62–71, 114, and 115 of Concepts Statement 7.

c. The time value of money, represented by the rate on risk-free monetary assets that have maturity dates or durations that coincide with the period covered by the cash flows (risk-free interest rate). For present value computations denominated in nominal U.S. dollars, the yield curve for U.S. Treasury securities determines the appropriate risk-free interest rate. U.S. Treasury securities are deemed (default) risk free because they pose neither uncertainty in timing nor risk of default to the holder.

d. The price for bearing the uncertainty inherent in the cash flows (risk premium).

e. Other case-specific factors that would be considered by market participants.

f. In the case of a liability, the nonperformance risk relating to that liability, including the reporting entity's (obligor's) own credit risk.

General Principles

B3. Present value techniques differ in how they capture those elements. However, certain general principles govern the application of any present value technique:

a. Cash flows and discount rates should reflect assumptions that market participants would use in pricing the asset or liability.

b. Cash flows and discount rates should consider only factors attributed to the asset (or liability) being measured.

c. To avoid double counting or omitting the effects of risk factors, discount rates should reflect assumptions that are consistent with those inherent in the cash flows.[23]

d. Assumptions about cash flows and discount rates should be internally consistent. For example, nominal cash flows (that include the effect of inflation) should be discounted at a rate that includes the effect of inflation. The nominal risk-free interest rate includes the effect of inflation. Real cash flows (that exclude the effect of inflation) should be discounted at a rate that excludes the effect of inflation. Similarly, after-tax cash flows should be discounted using an after-tax discount rate. Pretax cash flows should be discounted at a rate consistent with those cash flows (for example, a U.S. Treasury rate is quoted on a

pretax basis, as is a LIBOR rate or a prevailing term loan rate).

e. Discount rates should be consistent with the underlying economic factors of the currency in which the cash flows are denominated.

Risk and Uncertainty

B4. A fair value measurement, using present value, is made under conditions of uncertainty because the cash flows used are estimates rather than known amounts. In many cases, both the amount and timing of the cash flows will be uncertain. Even contractually fixed amounts, like the payments on a loan, will be uncertain if there is risk of default.

B5. Risk-averse market participants generally seek compensation for bearing the uncertainty inherent in the cash flows of an asset or liability (risk premium). A fair value measurement should include a risk premium reflecting the amount market participants would demand because of the risk (uncertainty) in the cash flows. Otherwise, the measurement would not faithfully represent fair value. In some cases, determining the appropriate risk premium might be difficult. However, the degree of difficulty alone is not a sufficient basis on which to exclude a risk adjustment.

B6. Present value techniques differ in how they adjust for risk and in the type of cash flows they use. For example, the discount rate adjustment technique uses a risk-adjusted discount rate and contractual, promised, or most likely cash flows; Method 1 of the expected present value technique uses a risk-free rate and risk-adjusted expected cash flows; and Method 2 of the expected present value technique uses a risk-adjusted discount rate (which is different from the rate used in the discount rate adjustment technique) and expected cash flows. Those present value techniques are discussed below.

Discount Rate Adjustment Technique

B7. The discount rate adjustment technique uses a single set of cash flows from the range of possible estimated amounts, whether contractual or promised (as is the case for a bond) or most likely cash flows. In all cases, those cash flows are conditional upon the

---

[23]For example, a discount rate that reflects expectations about future defaults is appropriate if using contractual cash flows of a loan (discount rate adjustment technique). That same rate would not be used if using expected (probability-weighted) cash flows (expected present value technique) because the expected cash flows already reflect assumptions about future defaults; instead, a discount rate that is commensurate with the risk inherent in the expected cash flows should be used.

occurrence of specified events (for example, contractual or promised cash flows for a bond are conditional on the event of no default by the debtor). The discount rate used in the discount rate adjustment technique is derived from observed rates of return for comparable assets or liabilities that are traded in the market. Accordingly, the contractual, promised, or most likely cash flows are discounted at a rate that corresponds to an observed market rate associated with such conditional cash flows (market rate of return).

B8. The application of the discount rate adjustment technique requires an analysis of market data for comparable assets or liabilities. Comparability is established by considering the nature of the cash flows (for example, whether the cash flows are contractual or noncontractual and are likely to respond similarly to changes in economic conditions), as well as other factors (for example, credit standing, collateral, duration, restrictive covenants, and liquidity). Alternatively, if a single comparable asset or liability does not fairly reflect the risk inherent in the cash flows of the asset or liability being measured, it may be possible to derive a discount rate using data for several comparable assets or liabilities in conjunction with the risk-free yield curve (a "build-up" approach).

B9. To illustrate a build-up approach, assume that Asset A is a contractual right to receive $800 in 1 year (no timing uncertainty). There is an established market for comparable assets, and information about those assets, including price information, is available. Of those comparable assets:

a. Asset B is a contractual right to receive $1,200 in 1 year and has a market price of $1,083. Thus, the implied annual rate of return (1-year market rate of return) is 10.8 percent [($1,200/$1,083) − 1].
b. Asset C is a contractual right to receive $700 in 2 years and has a market price of $566. Thus, the implied annual rate of return (2-year market rate of return) is 11.2 percent [($700/$566)^0.5 − 1].
c. All three assets are comparable with respect to risk (dispersion of possible payoffs and credit).

B10. Based on the timing of the contractual payments to be received relative to Asset A (one year for Asset B versus two years for Asset C), Asset B is deemed more comparable to Asset A. Using the contractual payment to be received for Asset A ($800) and the 1-year market rate derived from Asset B (10.8 percent), the fair value of Asset A is $722 ($800/1.108). Alternatively, in the absence of available market information for Asset B, the one-year market rate could be derived from Asset C using the build-up approach. In that case, the 2-year market rate indicated by Asset C (11.2 percent) would be adjusted to a 1-year market rate based on the term structure of the risk-free yield curve. Additional information and analysis also might be required to determine if the risk premium for one-year and two-year assets is the same. If it is determined that the risk premium for one-year and two-year assets is not the same, the two-year market rate of return would be further adjusted for that effect.

B11. In applying the discount rate adjustment technique to fixed claims, the adjustment for risk inherent in the cash flows of the asset or liability being measured is included in the discount rate. In some applications of the discount rate adjustment technique to cash flows that are other than fixed claims, an adjustment to the cash flows also may be necessary to achieve comparability with the observed asset or liability from which the discount rate is derived.

Expected Present Value Technique

B12. The expected present value technique uses as a starting point a set of cash flows that, in theory, represents the probability-weighted average of all possible cash flows (expected cash flows). The resulting estimate is identical to *expected value,* which, in statistical terms, is the weighted average of a discrete random variable's possible values where the respective probabilities are used as weights. Because all possible cash flows are probability weighted, the resulting expected cash flow is not conditional upon the occurrence of any specified event (as are the cash flows used in the discount rate adjustment technique).

B13. In making an investment decision, risk-averse market participants would consider the risk inherent in the expected cash flows. Portfolio theory distinguishes between two types of risk. The first is risk specific to a particular asset or liability, also referred to as unsystematic (diversifiable) risk. The second is general market risk, also referred to as systematic (nondiversifiable) risk. The systematic or nondiversifiable risk of an asset (or liability) refers to the amount by which the asset (or liability) increases the variance of a diversified portfolio when it is added to that portfolio. Portfolio theory holds that in a market in equilibrium, market participants will be compensated only for bearing the systematic or nondiversifiable risk inherent in the cash flows. (In markets that are inefficient or out of equilibrium, other forms of return or compensation might be available.)

B14. Method 1 of the expected present value technique adjusts the expected cash flows for the systematic (market) risk by subtracting a cash risk premium (risk-adjusted expected cash flows). These risk-adjusted expected cash flows represent a certainty-equivalent cash flow, which is discounted at a risk-free interest rate. A *certainty-equivalent cash flow* refers to an expected cash flow (as defined), adjusted for risk such that one is indifferent to trading a certain cash flow for an expected cash flow. For example, if one were willing to trade an expected cash flow of $1,200 for a certain cash flow of $1,000, the $1,000 is the certainty equivalent of the $1,200 (the $200 would represent the cash risk premium). In that case, one would be indifferent as to the asset held.

B15. In contrast, Method 2 of the expected present value technique adjusts for systematic (market) risk by adding a risk premium to the risk-free interest rate. Accordingly, the expected cash flows are discounted at a rate that corresponds to an expected rate associated with probability-weighted cash flows (expected rate of return). Models used for pricing risky assets, such as the Capital Asset Pricing Model, can be used to estimate the expected rate of return. Because the discount rate used in the discount rate adjustment technique is a rate of return relating to conditional cash flows, it likely will be higher than the discount rate used in Method 2 of the expected present value technique, which is an expected rate of return relating to expected or probability-weighted cash flows.

B16. To illustrate Methods 1 and 2, assume that an asset has expected cash flows of $780 in 1 year based on the possible cash flows and probabilities shown below. The applicable risk-free interest rate for cash flows with a 1-year horizon is 5 percent, and the systematic risk premium is 3 percent.

Possible Cash Flows	Probability	Probability-Weighted Cash Flows
$500	15%	$75
$800	60%	$480
$900	25%	$225
Expected cash flows		$780

B17. In this simple illustration, the expected cash flows ($780) represent the probability-weighted average of the 3 possible outcomes. In more realistic situations, there could be many possible outcomes. However, it is not always necessary to consider distributions of literally all possible cash flows using complex models and techniques to apply the expected present value technique. Rather, it should be possible to develop a limited number of discrete scenarios and probabilities that capture the array of possible cash flows. For example, a reporting entity might use realized cash flows for some relevant past period, adjusted for changes in circumstances occurring subsequently (for example, changes in external factors, including economic or market conditions, industry trends, and competition as well as changes in internal factors impacting the entity more specifically), considering the assumptions of market participants.

B18. In theory, the present value (fair value) of the asset's cash flows is the same ($722) whether determined under Method 1 or Method 2, as indicated below. Specifically:

a. Under Method 1, the expected cash flows are adjusted for systematic (market) risk. In the absence of market data directly indicating the amount of the risk adjustment, such adjustment could be derived from an asset pricing model using the concept of certainty equivalents. For example, the risk adjustment (cash risk premium of $22) could be determined based on the systematic risk premium of 3 percent ($780 − [$780 × (1.05/1.08)]), which results in risk-adjusted expected cash flows of $758 ($780 − $22). The $758 is the certainty equivalent of $780 and is discounted at the risk-free interest rate (5 percent). The present value (fair value) of the asset is $722 ($758/1.05).

b. Under Method 2, the expected cash flows are not adjusted for systematic (market) risk. Rather, the adjustment for that risk is included in the discount rate. Thus, the expected cash flows are discounted at an expected rate of return of 8 percent (the 5 percent risk-free interest rate plus the 3 percent systematic risk premium). The present value (fair value) of the asset is $722 ($780/1.08).

B19. When using an expected present value technique to measure fair value, either Method 1 or Method 2 could be used. The selection of Method 1 or Method 2 will depend on facts and circumstances specific to the asset or liability being measured, the extent to which sufficient data are available, and the judgments applied.

Appendix C

BACKGROUND INFORMATION AND BASIS FOR CONCLUSIONS

CONTENTS

Appendix C

BACKGROUND INFORMATION AND BASIS FOR CONCLUSIONS

Introduction

C1. This appendix summarizes considerations that Board members deemed significant in reaching the conclusions in this Statement. It includes the reasons for accepting certain views and rejecting others. Individual Board members gave greater weight to some factors than to others.

Background Information

C2. In many accounting pronouncements, the Board has concluded that fair value information is relevant, and users of financial statements generally have agreed. Paragraph 47 of FASB Concepts Statement No. 2, *Qualitative Characteristics of Accounting Information,* states, "To be relevant to investors, creditors, and others for investment, credit, and similar decisions, accounting information must be capable of making a difference in a decision by helping users to form predictions about the outcomes of past, present, and future events or to confirm or correct expectations."

C3. Some have expressed concerns about the ability to apply the fair value measurement objective in GAAP, including in response to the FASB Proposal, *Principles-Based Approach to U.S. Standard Setting,* issued in October 2002.[24] In large part, those concerns focus on the reliability of the measurements in the absence of quoted market prices, including concerns about the ability to verify the measurements. Paragraph 59 of Concepts Statement 2 states, "The reliability of a measure rests on the faithfulness with which it represents what it purports to represent, coupled with an assurance for the user, which comes through verification, that it has that representational quality."

C4. The Board believes that, in part, those concerns result because there is limited guidance for applying the fair value measurement objective in GAAP. The guidance that currently exists has evolved piecemeal over time and is dispersed among the accounting pronouncements that require fair value measurements. Differences in that guidance have created inconsistencies that have added to the complexity in GAAP. There also is limited conceptual guidance for addressing measurement issues in the Board's conceptual framework.

C5. In June 2003, the Board added the fair value measurement project to its agenda to address fair value measurement issues broadly.[25] At that time, the Board agreed that, conceptually, the definition of fair value and its application in GAAP should be the same for all assets and liabilities. This Statement is the result of that project. This Statement defines fair value, establishes a framework for measuring fair value, and expands disclosures about fair value measurements. This Statement also simplifies and codifies the related guidance that currently exists for developing fair value measurements, eliminating differences that have added to the complexity in GAAP. This Statement applies under other accounting pronouncements that require or permit fair value measurements, the Board having previously concluded in those pronouncements that fair value is the relevant measurement attribute. This Statement does not require any new fair value measurements.

C6. In June 2004, the Board issued an Exposure Draft, *Fair Value Measurements,* and received comment letters from nearly 100 respondents. In September 2004, the Board held public roundtable meetings with some of those respondents to discuss significant issues raised in the comment letters. In October 2005, the Board issued a proposed FASB Staff Position (FSP) FAS 133-a, "Accounting for Unrealized Gains (Losses) Relating to Derivative Instruments Measured at Fair Value under Statement 133," to address related practice issues under EITF Issue No. 02-3, "Issues Involved in Accounting for Derivative Contracts Held for Trading Purposes and Contracts Involved in Energy Trading and Risk Management Activities," raised by respondents to the Exposure Draft. (See paragraphs C10–C17.) The Board received comment letters from 25 respondents (principally, financial institutions).

C7. In developing this Statement, the Board considered comments from respondents to the Exposure

---

[24]In July 2003, the Securities and Exchange Commission (SEC) published, "Study Pursuant to Section 108(d) of the Sarbanes-Oxley Act of 2002 on the Adoption by the United States Financial Reporting System of a Principles-Based Accounting System," which encouraged a move to more "objectives-oriented" accounting standards.

[25]The Board has a separate project on its agenda to improve its conceptual framework.

Draft and to proposed FSP FAS 133-a, as well as input from the Valuation Resource Group, the Financial Accounting Standards Advisory Council, the User Advisory Council, members of the Investor Task Force, and other interested parties. In response, the Board reconsidered and/or clarified certain aspects of the proposals in the Exposure Draft.

Scope

Share-Based Payment Transactions

C8. Accounting pronouncements that require fair value measurements but that are excluded from the scope of this Statement are limited to FASB Statement No. 123 (revised 2004), *Share-Based Payment,* and its related interpretive accounting pronouncements that address share-based payment transactions. The fair value measurement objective in Statement 123(R) is generally consistent with the fair value measurement objective in this Statement. However, for certain share-based payment transactions with employees, the measurements at the grant date are fair-value-based measurements, not fair value measurements. Although some measurements in Statement 123(R) are fair value measurements, the Board decided for practical reasons to exclude Statement 123(R) in its entirety from the scope of this Statement.

Leasing Transactions

C9. In the Exposure Draft, the Board decided to exclude from the scope of this Statement FASB Statement No. 13, *Accounting for Leases,* and other accounting pronouncements that require fair value measurements for leasing transactions. At that time, the Board was concerned that applying the fair value measurement objective in this Statement to leasing transactions could have unintended consequences when considered together with longstanding valuation practices common within the leasing industry. The Board decided to defer consideration of fair value measurement issues specific to those transactions. However, respondents indicated that the fair value measurement objective for leasing transactions is generally consistent with the fair value measurement objective in this Statement and that the guidance in this Statement should apply for the fair value measurements required for those transactions. Others in the leasing industry subsequently affirmed that view. Based on that input, the Board decided to include those accounting pronouncements in the scope of this Statement.

EITF Issue 02-3

C10. In the Exposure Draft, the Board decided to exclude from the scope of this Statement the guidance in footnote 3 of Issue 02-3, which stated:

> The FASB staff believes that, in the absence of (a) quoted market prices in an active market, (b) observable prices of other current market transactions, or (c) other observable data supporting a valuation technique, the transaction price represents the best information available with which to estimate fair value at the inception of the arrangement. Therefore, in the FASB staff's view an entity should not recognize an unrealized gain or loss at inception of a derivative instrument unless the fair value of that instrument is obtained from a quoted market price in an active market or is otherwise evidenced by comparison to other observable current market transactions or based on a valuation technique incorporating observable market data. For example, a valuation technique that includes extrapolated price curves with little or no observable market inputs for any significant duration of the instrument should not result in an initial fair value estimate that differs from the transaction price for the instrument taken as a whole, because, in this example, the transaction price is the best evidence of the instrument's fair value at that point in time.

C11. The guidance in footnote 3 of Issue 02-3 applied for derivatives (and other) instruments measured at fair value at initial recognition under FASB Statement No. 133, *Accounting for Derivative Instruments and Hedging Activities.* That guidance precluded immediate recognition in earnings of an unrealized gain or loss, measured as the difference between the transaction price and the fair value of the instrument at initial recognition, if the fair value of the instrument was determined using significant unobservable inputs. However, Issue 02-3 did not provide guidance for when to subsequently recognize that unrealized gain or loss in earnings. As a result, practice was diverse with regard to both the method and timing of revenue recognition. For example, some entities recognized the unrealized gain or loss in earnings when the fair value of the instrument was observable (generally, at or near the end of the contract). Other entities amortized the unrealized gain or loss in earnings over the term of the instrument. In the Exposure Draft, the Board acknowledged that issue but decided not to address that issue in this Statement because it raised recognition issues similar to those that were being addressed in its revenue recognition project.

C12. Respondents disagreed with that scope exclusion. They said that for many entities, in particular, financial institutions, Issue 02-3 is significant and that the Board should address related issues in this Statement, focusing on potential inconsistencies between the guidance in footnote 3 of Issue 02-3 and the related guidance proposed in the Exposure Draft. In response, the Board decided to address those issues separately in proposed FSP FAS 133-a.

C13. In proposed FSP FAS 133-a, the Board decided that an instrument should be measured at fair value under Statement 133 using the guidance in this Statement and that an unrealized gain or loss should not be recognized in earnings until a minimum reliability threshold for the measurement is met. In reaching that decision, the Board concluded that for some entities, in particular, securities dealers that transact in different markets with different counterparties, the transaction price (an entry price) might not represent the fair value of the instrument (an exit price) at initial recognition. The Board agreed that, conceptually, an unrealized gain or loss at initial recognition should be immediately recognized in earnings. However, the Board observed that if the fair value of the instrument is measured using significant unobservable inputs, some (or all) of the unrealized gain or loss might represent measurement error, raising concerns about the reliability of the measurement and the effect of the measurement on earnings. Therefore, the minimum reliability threshold would have precluded recognition in earnings of an unrealized gain or loss at initial recognition if the fair value of the instrument is measured using significant unobservable inputs. Instead, the unrealized gain or loss at initial recognition would have been recognized as a deferred credit or debit, separate from the instrument.

C14. Respondents to proposed FSP FAS 133-a generally agreed that the proposed FSP would represent an improvement over the related guidance in Issue 02-3, largely because an instrument would be measured at its fair value at initial recognition and in all subsequent periods. However, many of those respondents expressed concerns that the minimum reliability threshold approach for revenue recognition would add to the complexity in GAAP. They indicated that if the measurement objective is fair value, then financial reporting should reflect that measurement and the consequences of using that measurement.

C15. In response, the Board met with some respondents to develop an alternative approach focusing on expanded disclosures about fair value measurements using significant unobservable inputs and the effect of the measurements on earnings for the period. The Board discussed that alternative disclosure approach with certain users of financial statements, including members of the Investor Task Force that concentrate on the investment banking, energy trading, and insurance industries, and members of the User Advisory Council. Those users generally supported that disclosure approach (over the minimum reliability threshold approach). In particular, they indicated that the expanded disclosures would allow users of financial statements to make more informed judgments and adjustments to their own models.

C16. Based on the input received, the Board decided not to impose the minimum reliability threshold in proposed FSP FAS 133-a. The Board agreed that the fair value measurement objective in this Statement should apply for fair value measurements at initial recognition under Statement 133 (an exit price objective). Consistent with that objective, this Statement clarifies that the measurements should be adjusted for risk, that is, the amount market participants would demand because of the risk (uncertainty) inherent in a particular valuation technique used to measure fair value (such as a pricing model) and/or the risk inherent in the inputs to the valuation technique (a risk premium notion). Accordingly, a measurement (for example, a "mark-to-model" measurement) that does not include an adjustment for risk would not represent a fair value measurement if market participants would include one in pricing the related asset or liability.

C17. To improve transparency in financial reporting, the Board decided to require expanded disclosures about fair value measurements using significant unobservable inputs and the effects of such measurements on earnings. This Statement includes those expanded disclosure requirements (for all assets and liabilities measured at fair value on a recurring basis using significant unobservable inputs) and nullifies the guidance in footnote 3 of Issue 02-3.

Statement 114

C18. In the Exposure Draft, the Board decided to exclude FASB Statement No. 114, *Accounting by*

Creditors for Impairment of a Loan, from the scope of this Statement. The Board clarified that the measurement for impaired loans, determined using a present value technique, is not a fair value measurement. Respondents agreed. However, they noted that the practical expedient in Statement 114 (observable market price or the fair value of collateral if the loan is collateral-dependent) is a fair value measurement. They said that when the practical expedient is used, the guidance in this Statement should apply. The Board agreed and decided to include Statement 114 in the scope of this Statement as it relates to the practical expedient.

Opinion 21

C19. In this Statement, the Board affirmed that the measurement for receivables and payables in APB Opinion No. 21, *Interest on Receivables and Payables,* determined using a present value technique, is a fair value measurement. The discount rate for contractual (promised) cash flows described in that Opinion (rate commensurate with the risk) embodies the same notion as the discount rate used in the traditional approach (or discount rate adjustment technique) described in FASB Concepts Statement No. 7, *Using Cash Flow Information and Present Value in Accounting Measurements,* and clarified in this Statement. Paragraph 13 of Opinion 21 explains:

> The objective is to approximate the rate which would have resulted if an independent borrower and an independent lender had negotiated a similar transaction under comparable terms and conditions with the option to pay the cash price upon purchase or to give a note for the amount of the purchase which bears the prevailing rate of interest to maturity.

C20. Accordingly, the guidance for using present value techniques to measure fair value in this Statement applies for the measurements required under Opinion 21. It also applies for the similar measurements required under other accounting pronouncements.

Practicability Exceptions

C21. The Board observed that some of the accounting pronouncements within the scope of this Statement permit practicability exceptions to fair value measurements in specified circumstances. Those practicability exceptions include the following:

a. The use of a transaction price (an entry price) to measure fair value (an exit price) at initial recognition (guarantees under FASB Interpretation No. 45, *Guarantor's Accounting and Disclosure Requirements for Guarantees, Including Indirect Guarantees of Indebtedness of Others,* and financial assets and liabilities under FASB Statement No. 140, *Accounting for Transfers and Servicing of Financial Assets and Extinguishments of Liabilities*)

b. An exemption to the requirement to measure fair value if it is not practicable to do so (financial instruments under FASB Statement No. 107, *Disclosures about Fair Value of Financial Instruments,* and financial assets obtained and financial liabilities incurred in a sale under Statement 140 and EITF Issue No. 85-40, "Comprehensive Review of Sales of Marketable Securities with Put Arrangements")

c. An exemption to the requirement to measure fair value if fair value is not reasonably determinable (nonmonetary assets under APB Opinion No. 29, *Accounting for Nonmonetary Transactions,* FASB Statement No. 153, *Exchanges of Nonmonetary Assets,* and EITF Issue No. 99-17, "Accounting for Advertising Barter Transactions"; asset retirement obligations under FASB Statement No. 143, *Accounting for Asset Retirement Obligations,* and FASB Interpretation No. 47, *Accounting for Conditional Asset Retirement Obligations;* restructuring obligations under FASB Statement No. 146, *Accounting for Costs Associated with Exit or Disposal Activities;* and participation rights under FASB Statements No. 87, *Employers' Accounting for Pensions,* and No. 106, *Employers' Accounting for Postretirement Benefits Other Than Pensions*)

d. An exemption to the requirement to measure fair value if fair value cannot be measured with sufficient reliability (contributions under FASB Statement No. 116, *Accounting for Contributions Received and Contributions Made,* and AICPA Audit and Accounting Guide, *Not-for-Profit Organizations*)

e. The use of certain of the measurement methods referred to in paragraph 37 of FASB Statement No. 141, *Business Combinations,* that allow measurements other than fair value for certain assets acquired and liabilities assumed in a business combination.

C22. The Board acknowledged the inconsistencies created by those practicability exceptions. However, the Board decided for practical reasons not to address those inconsistencies in this Statement. The Board is addressing issues relating to some practicability exceptions in other agenda projects (for example, its business combinations project). Other practicability exceptions raise issues about what to measure at fair value that are beyond the scope of this Statement.

Other Similar Measurements

C23. This Statement does not apply under accounting pronouncements that permit measurements that are based on, or otherwise use, vendor-specific objective evidence of fair value. Those accounting pronouncements include AICPA Statement of Position 97-2, *Software Revenue Recognition,* as modified by AICPA Statement of Position 98-9, *Modification of SOP 97-2,* Software Revenue Recognition, *With Respect to Certain Transactions,* and EITF Issue No. 00-21, "Revenue Arrangements with Multiple Deliverables." In those accounting pronouncements, vendor-specific objective evidence of fair value refers to the price for a deliverable established by the reporting entity. Issue 00-21 further refers to the price for a deliverable established by a third-party vendor as a practical expedient to vendor-specific objective evidence of fair value. Conceptually, vendor-specific objective evidence of fair value is a measurement determined based on a transaction price (an entry price) that is different from a fair value measurement (an exit price), whether considered from the perspective of the reporting entity or a third-party vendor (as a practical expedient).

C24. This Statement also does not apply for the market value measurement that results when measuring inventories at the lower of cost or market under ARB No. 43, Chapter 4, "Inventory Pricing." ARB 43, Chapter 4, places upper and lower limits on the measurement that may not result in a fair value measurement.

Definition of Fair Value

C25. The definition of fair value in this Statement retains the exchange price notion contained, either explicitly or implicitly, in earlier definitions of fair value. However, this Statement clarifies that the exchange price is the price in an orderly transaction between market participants to sell the asset or transfer the liability in the principal (or most advantageous) market for the asset or liability. The Board affirmed that the transaction to sell the asset or transfer the liability is an orderly transaction, not a forced transaction (for example, if the seller is experiencing financial difficulty), that assumes exposure to the market for a period prior to the measurement date to allow for information dissemination and marketing in order to transact at the most advantageous price for the asset or liability at the measurement date. To convey that notion more clearly, the Board revised the definition of fair value in this Statement to refer to an orderly transaction, as do other definitions used in valuations for purposes other than financial reporting that are similar to fair value (for example, fair market value).

C26. The transaction to sell the asset or transfer the liability is a hypothetical transaction at the measurement date, considered from the perspective of a market participant that holds the asset or owes the liability. Therefore, the objective of a fair value measurement is to determine the price that would be received for the asset or paid to transfer the liability at the measurement date, that is, an exit price. The Board concluded that an exit price objective is appropriate because it embodies current expectations about the future inflows associated with the asset and the future outflows associated with the liability from the perspective of market participants. The emphasis on inflows and outflows is consistent with the definitions of assets and liabilities in FASB Concepts Statement No. 6, *Elements of Financial Statements.* Paragraph 25 of Concepts Statement 6 defines *assets* in terms of future economic benefits (future inflows). Paragraph 35 of Concepts Statement 6 defines *liabilities* in terms of future sacrifices of economic benefits (future outflows).

Principal (or Most Advantageous) Markets

C27. The Exposure Draft emphasized within Level 1 of the fair value hierarchy that the price in the most advantageous market for the asset or liability should be used to measure the fair value of the asset or liability. The most advantageous market is the market in which the reporting entity would sell the asset or transfer the liability with the price that maximizes the amount that would be received for the asset or minimizes the amount that would be paid to transfer the liability, considering transaction costs in the respective markets. The Board concluded that a most advantageous market approach is reasonable based on the assumption that the goal of most entities is to maximize profits or net assets. The most advantageous market approach embodies both the buying side and the selling side of rational economic behavior and is consistent with normal profit motivations.

C28. Respondents generally agreed with that most advantageous market approach. However, some respondents interpreted the related guidance within Level 1 as requiring the use of prices in most advantageous markets over prices in principal markets, referring to possible conflicts with ASR No. 118, *Accounting for Investment Securities by Registered Investment Companies,* and its principal market approach for registered funds. They noted that an approach that prioritizes prices in most advantageous markets over prices in principal markets would not be cost effective because it would require continuous evaluations of prices for multiple assets and liabilities as a basis for determining which of those prices are the most advantageous at the measurement date. The Board agreed that its intent was not to require that entities continuously search across all possible markets in which transactions for the related asset or liability can be observed for the most advantageous price for the asset or liability. To convey its intent more clearly, the Board clarified its view that generally the principal market for an asset or liability (the market in which the reporting entity would sell the asset or transfer the liability with the greatest volume and level of activity for the asset or liability) will represent the most advantageous market for the asset or liability. Accordingly, this Statement specifies that if there is a principal market for the asset or liability (determined under ASR 118 or otherwise), the fair value measurement should represent the price in that market (whether observable or otherwise determined using a valuation technique), even if the price in a different market is potentially more advantageous at the measurement date.

C29. Some respondents further indicated that to achieve consistency in applying the fair value measurement objective in this Statement, the principal (or most advantageous) market approach should not be limited to Level 1; it is a general principle that should apply broadly. The Board agreed and decided to expand the principal (or most advantageous) market approach so that it applies broadly. The Board observed that because different entities (and operating units within those entities) with different activities transact in different markets, the principal (or most advantageous) market for the same asset or liability might be different for different entities. Because financial reporting is from the perspective of the reporting entity, the Board determined that an exit price should be determined based on the interaction of market participants (buyers and sellers) in the principal (or most

advantageous) market considered from the perspective of the reporting entity, thereby allowing for differences between and among entities.

C30. The Board affirmed that the price in the principal (or most advantageous) market used to measure the fair value of an asset or liability should not be adjusted for transaction costs. Transaction costs refer to the incremental direct costs to transact in the principal (or most advantageous) market for the asset or liability, similar to cost to sell as defined in paragraph 35 of FASB Statement No. 144, *Accounting for the Impairment or Disposal of Long-Lived Assets,* and may differ, depending on how the reporting entity transacts. In other words, transaction costs are not an attribute of an asset or liability.

C31. In response to related issues raised by some respondents, the Board clarified that transaction costs are different from transportation costs, that is, the costs that would be incurred to transport the asset or liability to (or from) its principal (or most advantageous) market. This Statement clarifies that if location is an attribute of the asset or liability (for example, a commodity), the price in the principal (or most advantageous) market used to measure the fair value of the asset or liability should be adjusted for those costs.

Market Participants

C32. This Statement emphasizes that a fair value measurement is a market-based measurement, not an entity-specific measurement. Therefore, a fair value measurement should be determined based on the assumptions that market participants—buyers and sellers in the principal (or most advantageous) market for the asset or liability—would use in pricing the asset or liability. Paragraph 26 of Concepts Statement 7 explains:

> Among their many functions, markets are systems that transmit information in the form of prices. Marketplace participants attribute prices to assets and, in doing so, distinguish the risks and rewards of one asset from those of another. Stated differently, the market's pricing mechanism ensures that unlike things do not appear alike and that like things do not appear to be different (a qualitative characteristic of accounting information). An observed market price encompasses the consensus view of all marketplace participants about an asset or liability's utility, future cash flows,

the uncertainties surrounding those cash flows, and the amount that marketplace participants demand for bearing those uncertainties.

C33. To convey more clearly the idea of a measurement that is made from the perspective of market participants, this Statement clarifies the "willing parties" referred to in earlier definitions of fair value in the context of market participants, referring to buyers and sellers in the principal (or most advantageous) market for the asset or liability that are independent of the reporting entity (unrelated), knowledgeable, and both able and willing to transact.

C34. In that context, some respondents questioned the extent to which market participants would be expected to be knowledgeable, referring to markets that are characterized by information asymmetry, where some market participants have information about an asset or liability that is not available to other market participants. The Board agreed that it would be reasonable to presume that a market participant that is both able and willing to transact for the asset or liability would undertake efforts necessary to become sufficiently knowledgeable about the asset or liability based on available information, including information obtained through usual and customary due diligence efforts, and would factor any related risk into the fair value measurement.

Application to Assets

C35. For an asset, a fair value measurement assumes the highest and best use of the asset by market participants.

Highest and best use

C36. Highest and best use is a valuation concept used to value many assets (for example, real estate). In broad terms, the highest and best use of an asset refers to the use of an asset that would maximize the fair value of the asset or the group of assets in which the asset would be used by market participants. Highest and best use is determined based on the use of the asset by market participants, even if the intended use of the asset by the reporting entity is different. Paragraph 32(a) of Concepts Statement 7 explains:

> The entity's managers might intend a different use or settlement than that anticipated by others. For example, they might intend to operate a property as a bowling alley, even

though others in the marketplace consider its highest and best use to be a parking lot.

C37. This Statement incorporates that highest-and-best-use concept as a basis for selecting the valuation premise that should be used to measure the fair value of the asset. If the highest and best use of an asset is in-use, the fair value of the asset would be measured using an in-use valuation premise, reflecting the price that would be received in a current transaction to sell the asset assuming that the asset would be used with other assets as a group and that those assets would be available to market participants. If the highest and best use of an asset is in-exchange, the fair value of the asset would be measured using an in-exchange valuation premise, reflecting the price that would be received in a current transaction to sell the asset standalone.

C38. In the context of the related guidance included in the Exposure Draft, some respondents referred to possible conflicts between the in-use valuation premise and the exchange notion encompassed within the definition of fair value. In this Statement, the Board clarified that the exchange notion applies regardless of the valuation premise used to measure the fair value of an asset. Whether using an in-use or an in-exchange valuation premise, the measurement is a market-based measurement determined based on the use of an asset by market participants, not a value determined based solely on the use of an asset by the reporting entity (a value-in-use or entity-specific measurement).

Application to Liabilities

C39. For a liability, a fair value measurement assumes that the liability is transferred to a market participant at the measurement date and that the nonperformance risk relating to that liability (that is, the risk that the obligation will not be fulfilled) is the same before and after its transfer.

The transfer

C40. Because the liability is transferred to a market participant, the liability continues; it is not settled with the counterparty. The Board acknowledged that in some cases, the reporting entity might not have the intent to transfer the liability to a third party. For example, the reporting entity might have advantages (or disadvantages) relative to the market that would make it more (or less) beneficial for the reporting entity to perform or otherwise settle the liability using its own internal resources. However, the Board agreed that the fair value of the liability from the perspective of a market participant is the same regardless of how the reporting entity intends to settle the liability. Conceptually, a fair value measurement provides a market benchmark to use as a basis for assessing the reporting entity's advantages (or disadvantages) in performance or settlement relative to the market. Specifically, when a liability is measured at fair value, the relative efficiency of the reporting entity in settling the liability using its own internal resources appears in earnings over the course of its settlement, not before.

C41. In the context of both assets and liabilities, paragraph 33 of Concepts Statement 7 explains:

> If the entity measures an asset or liability at fair value, its comparative advantage or disadvantage will appear in earnings as it realizes assets or settles liabilities for amounts different [from] fair value. The effect on earnings appears when the advantage is employed to achieve cost savings or the disadvantage results in excess costs. In contrast, if the entity measures an asset or liability using a measurement other than fair value, its comparative advantage or disadvantage is embedded in the measurement of the asset or liability at initial recognition. If the offsetting entry is to revenue or expense, measurements other than fair value cause the future effects of this comparative advantage or disadvantage to be recognized in earnings at initial measurement.

Nonperformance risk and credit standing

C42. Nonperformance risk includes (but may not be limited to) the reporting entity's own credit risk. In the Exposure Draft, the Board concluded, as it did in Concepts Statement 7, that a fair value measurement for a liability always considers the credit risk of the entity obligated to perform. Those who might hold the reporting entity's obligations as assets would consider the effect of the entity's credit risk in determining the prices they would be willing to pay. Therefore, this Statement clarifies that a fair value measurement for a liability should consider the effect of the reporting entity's own credit risk (credit standing) on the fair value of the liability in all periods in which the liability is measured at fair value.

C43. Respondents agreed that, conceptually, the effect of the reporting entity's own credit standing should be considered in all liability measurements at fair value. However, they expressed concerns about requiring that the reporting entity consider the effect of changes in its credit standing in liability remeasurements at fair value, noting that related issues are not clearly and consistently addressed in GAAP (including Statements 107 and 133).

C44. Paragraph 68 of Statement 107 states:

> The Board acknowledges that, as for assets with no quoted prices, variations in the methods used to estimate the fair value of liabilities with no quoted prices might reduce the comparability of fair value information among entities. Some entities will estimate fair value by using an incremental rate of borrowing that considers changes in an entity's own credit risk, while others will use a settlement rate that ignores at least part of those credit risk changes. However, the Board concluded that it should not, at this time, prescribe a single method to be used for all unquoted liabilities.

C45. Similarly, paragraph 316 of Statement 133 states:

> Some respondents to the Exposure Draft noted that Statement 107 permits an entity to choose whether to consider changes in its own creditworthiness in determining the fair value of its debt and asked for further guidance on that issue. The definition of fair value in Statement 125 says that in measuring liabilities at fair value by discounting estimated future cash flows, an objective is to use discount rates at which those liabilities could be settled in an arm's-length transaction. However, the FASB's pronouncements to date have not broadly addressed whether changes in a debtor's creditworthiness after incurrence of a liability should be reflected in measuring its fair value. Pending resolution of the broad issue of the effect of a debtor's creditworthiness on the fair value of its liabilities, the Board decided to use the definition in Statement 125 but not to provide additional guidance on reflecting the effects of changes in creditworthiness.

C46. Respondents' concerns focused on the counterintuitive and potentially confusing reporting that could result from including the effect of changes in the reporting entity's credit standing in liability re-measurements at fair value ("gains" for credit deterioration and "losses" for credit improvements). Respondents acknowledged that liabilities currently remeasured at fair value on a regular basis are limited largely to derivative liabilities under Statement 133. However, they stated that issues related to credit standing and liability remeasurements will become more pervasive as more liabilities are remeasured at fair value on a regular basis (referring to other agenda projects, including the fair value option project). Respondents urged the Board to address related issues in this Statement.

C47. In its redeliberations, the Board noted that in Concepts Statement 7, it considered issues related to credit standing and liability remeasurements similar to those referred to by respondents. Paragraphs 83–88 of Concepts Statement 7 explain:

> The role of an entity's credit standing in the accounting measurement of its liabilities has been a controversial question among accountants. The entity's credit standing clearly affects the interest rate at which it borrows in the marketplace. The initial proceeds of a loan, therefore, always reflect the entity's credit standing at that time. Similarly, the price at which others buy and sell the entity's loan includes their assessment of the entity's ability to repay. . . . However, some have questioned whether an entity's financial statements should reflect the effect of its credit standing (or changes in credit standing).
>
> Some suggest that the measurement objective for liabilities is fundamentally different from the measurement objective for assets. In their view, financial statement users are better served by liability measurements that focus on the entity's obligation. They suggest a measurement approach in which financial statements would portray the present value of an obligation such that two entities with the same obligation but different credit standing would report the same carrying amount. Some existing accounting pronouncements take this approach, most notably FASB Statements No. 87, *Employers' Accounting for Pensions,* and No. 106, *Employers' Accounting for Postretirement Benefits Other Than Pensions.*
>
> However, there is no convincing rationale for why the initial measurement of some liabilities would necessarily include the effect of credit standing (as in a loan for cash) while others might not (as in a warranty liability or similar item). Similarly, there is no rationale for why, in initial or fresh-start measurement, the recorded amount of a liability should reflect something other than the price that would exist in the marketplace. Consistent with its conclusions on fair value (refer to paragraph 30), the Board found no rationale for taking a different view in subsequent fresh-start measurements of an existing asset or liability than would pertain to measurements at initial recognition.
>
> Some argue that changes in an entity's credit standing are not relevant to users of financial statements. In their view, a fresh-start measurement that reflects changes in credit standing produces accounting results that are confusing. If the measurement includes changes in credit standing, and an entity's credit standing declines, the fresh-start measurement of its liabilities declines. That decline in liabilities is accompanied by an increase in owners' equity, a result that they find counterintuitive. How, they ask, can a bad thing (declining credit standing) produce a good thing (increased owners' equity)?
>
> Like all measurements at fair value, fresh-start measurement of liabilities can produce unfamiliar results when compared with reporting the liabilities on an amortized basis. A change in credit standing represents a change in the relative positions of the two classes of claimants (shareholders and creditors) to an entity's assets. If the credit standing diminishes, the fair value of creditors' claims diminishes. The amount of shareholders' residual claim to the entity's assets may appear to increase, but that increase probably is offset by losses that may have occasioned the decline in credit standing. Because shareholders usually cannot be called on to pay a corporation's liabilities, the amount of their residual claims approaches, and is limited by, zero. Thus, a change in the position of borrowers necessarily alters the position of shareholders, and vice versa.
>
> The failure to include changes in credit standing in the measurement of a liability ignores economic differences between liabilities. Consider the case of an entity that has two classes of borrowing. Class One was transacted when the entity had a strong credit

standing and a correspondingly low interest rate. Class Two is new and was transacted under the entity's current lower credit standing. Both classes trade in the marketplace based on the entity's current credit standing. If the two liabilities are subject to fresh-start measurement, failing to include changes in the entity's credit standing makes the classes of borrowings seem different—even though the marketplace evaluates the quality of their respective cash flows as similar to one another.

C48. The Board further noted that in the amendment to IAS 39, *Financial Instruments: Recognition and Measurement—The Fair Value Option*, the International Accounting Standards Board (IASB) considered similar issues in the context of a financial liability. Paragraph BC89 of the IAS 39 amendment explains that in reaching its decision to include credit risk relating to a financial liability in the measurement of that liability, the IASB noted that ". . . credit risk affects the value at which liabilities could be repurchased or settled. Accordingly, the fair value of a financial liability reflects the credit risk relating to that liability."

C49. In its redeliberations, the Board affirmed that, conceptually, credit standing is an essential component of a fair value measurement. A measurement that does not consider the effect of the reporting entity's credit standing is not a fair value measurement. The Board acknowledged the practical concerns about credit standing and liability remeasurements at fair value expressed by respondents. Some Board members share those concerns, especially considering situations in which the reporting entity is experiencing financial difficulty and reports gains resulting from credit deterioration that cannot be immediately realized. However, the Board agreed that those concerns derive from a threshold issue that relates principally to the selection of the appropriate measurement attribute for liability remeasurements. The Board plans to continue to address the issue of which measurement attribute should be required for liability remeasurements in individual accounting pronouncements on a project-by-project basis.

Interaction between Fair Value and Fair Market Value

C50. The Board agreed that the measurement objective encompassed in the definition of fair value used for financial reporting purposes is generally consistent with similar definitions of fair market value used

for valuation purposes. For example, the definition of fair market value in Internal Revenue Service Revenue Ruling 59-60 (the legal standard of value in many valuation situations) refers to "the price at which property would change hands between a willing buyer and a willing seller when the former is not under any compulsion to buy and the latter is not under any compulsion to sell, both parties having reasonable knowledge of relevant facts." However, the Board observed that the definition of fair market value relates principally to assets (property). Further, the definition has a significant body of interpretive case law, developed in the context of tax regulation. Because such interpretive case law, in the context of financial reporting, may not be relevant, the Board chose not to adopt the definition of fair market value, and its interpretive case law, for financial reporting purposes.

Fair Value at Initial Recognition

C51. Respondents indicated that the guidance in the Exposure Draft was ambiguous about when a price in an actual transaction that involves the reporting entity should be used to measure the fair value of an asset or liability at initial recognition. Many of those respondents referred to related practice issues under Issue 02-3 (and its guidance in footnote 3 for fair value measurements at initial recognition). In its redeliberations, the Board considered that issue largely in the context of the related guidance in paragraphs 7 and 27 of Concepts Statement 7, which state:

> At initial recognition, the cash or equivalent amount paid or received (historical cost or proceeds) is usually assumed to approximate fair value, absent evidence to the contrary.
>
> A transaction in the marketplace—an exchange for cash at or near to the date of the transaction—is the most common trigger for accounting recognition, and accountants typically accept actual exchange prices as fair value in measuring those transactions, absent persuasive evidence to the contrary. Indeed, the usual condition for using a measurement other than the exchange price is a conclusion that the stated price is not representative of fair value. [Footnote reference omitted.]

C52. In this Statement, the Board clarified that in situations in which the reporting entity acquires an asset or assumes a liability in an exchange transaction, the transaction price represents the price paid to acquire the asset or received to assume the liability (an entry price). The fair value of the asset or liability represents the price that would be received to sell the asset or paid to transfer the liability (an exit price). Conceptually, entry and exit prices are different. Entities do not necessarily sell or otherwise dispose of assets at the prices paid to acquire them. Similarly, entities do not necessarily transfer liabilities at the prices paid to assume them. The Board agreed that in many cases the transaction price will equal the exit price and, therefore, represent the fair value of the asset or liability at initial recognition, but not presumptively (a change to Concepts Statement 7). This Statement includes examples of factors the reporting entity should consider in determining whether a transaction price represents the fair value of the asset or liability at initial recognition. The Board plans to consider those factors in assessing the appropriate measurement attribute at initial recognition in individual accounting pronouncements on a project-by-project basis.

Valuation Techniques

C53. This Statement emphasizes that valuation techniques used to measure fair value should be consistent with the market approach, income approach, and/or cost approach. The related guidance in the Exposure Draft contained references to the use of "multiple" valuation techniques consistent with all three valuation approaches whenever the information necessary to apply those techniques is available without undue "cost and effort." In its redeliberations, the Board reconsidered and/or clarified certain aspects of that guidance.

Single versus Multiple Valuation Techniques

C54. Several respondents interpreted the related guidance in the Exposure Draft as requiring the use of multiple valuation techniques in all cases (except as otherwise indicated, for example, when valuing an asset or liability using quoted prices in an active market for identical assets or liabilities). They emphasized that in many cases, multiple valuation techniques would not be appropriate or cost beneficial. The Board affirmed that its intent was not to require the use of multiple valuation techniques. To convey its intent more clearly, the Board clarified that, consistent with existing valuation practice, valuation techniques that are appropriate in the circumstances and for which sufficient data are available should be used to measure fair value. This Statement does not specify the valuation technique that should be used in

any particular circumstances. Determining the appropriateness of valuation techniques in the circumstances requires judgment.

C55. The Exposure Draft referred to the cost and effort involved in obtaining the information used in a particular valuation technique as a basis for determining whether to use that valuation technique. Some respondents pointed out that the most appropriate valuation technique also might be the most costly valuation technique and that cost and effort should not be a basis for determining whether to use that valuation technique. Moreover, a cost-and-effort criterion likely would not be consistently applied. The Board agreed and removed that cost-and-effort criterion from this Statement.

C56. The Board expects that in some cases, a single valuation technique will be used. In other cases, multiple valuation techniques will be used, and the results of those techniques evaluated and weighted, as appropriate, in determining fair value. The Board acknowledged that valuation techniques will differ, depending on the asset or liability and the availability of data. However, in all cases, the objective is to use the valuation technique (or combination of valuation techniques) that is appropriate in the circumstances and for which there are sufficient data.

Consistency Constraint

C57. This Statement emphasizes the need for consistency in the valuation technique(s) used to measure fair value. This Statement does not preclude a change in the valuation technique used to measure fair value or its application (for example, a change in its weighting when multiple valuation techniques are used), provided that the change results in a measurement that is equally or more representative of fair value in the circumstances. The Board decided that absent an error (for example, in the selection and/or application of a valuation technique), revisions resulting from a change in the valuation technique used or its application should be accounted for as a change in accounting estimate in accordance with the provisions of FASB Statement No. 154, *Accounting Changes and Error Corrections*. The Board concluded that in those situations, the disclosure requirements in Statement 154 for a change in accounting estimate would not be cost beneficial. Therefore, those disclosures are not required.

Present Value Techniques

C58. Valuation techniques consistent with the income approach include the present value techniques discussed in Concepts Statement 7, specifically, the (a) traditional approach (or discount rate adjustment technique) and (b) expected cash flow approach (or expected present value technique). In this Statement, the Board clarified aspects of the guidance for applying those present value techniques in Concepts Statement 7.

C59. Those clarifications focus principally on the adjustment for risk (systematic or nondiversifiable risk) when using an expected present value technique. The Board understands that because Concepts Statement 7 refers to the appropriate discount rate for expected cash flows as the risk-free interest rate, the related guidance could be interpreted as requiring that the adjustment for risk be reflected only in the expected cash flows. However, in many valuation situations, the adjustment for risk is reflected in the discount rate, that is, as an adjustment to the risk-free interest rate. The Board agreed that it was not its intent to preclude that approach. To convey its intent more clearly, the Board expanded the guidance in Concepts Statement 7 to clarify that when using an expected present value technique, the adjustment for risk may be reflected in either:

a. The expected cash flows, in which case the risk-adjusted expected cash flows should be discounted at a risk-free interest rate (Method 1); or
b. The discount rate, in which case the unadjusted expected cash flows should be discounted at a risk-adjusted discount rate, that is, the risk-free interest rate, adjusted for risk (Method 2).

C60. In its discussions, the Board acknowledged, as it did in paragraph 68 of Concepts Statement 7, that "... the appropriate risk premium consistent with fair value may be difficult to determine." However, the Board decided that the potential difficulty of determining the appropriate risk premium is not, in and of itself, a sufficient basis for excluding that adjustment (in effect, permitting the use of no risk adjustment). Risk is an essential element of any present value technique. Therefore, a fair value measurement, using present value, should include an adjustment for risk if market participants would include one in pricing the related asset or liability.

C61. This Statement incorporates the related guidance in Concepts Statement 7, as clarified. (See Appendix B.) However, the Board decided not to revise Concepts Statement 7 in this project to reflect conforming changes to that guidance. Some respondents indicated that leaving the conceptual guidance in

Concepts Statement 7 unchanged would create conflicts between the Concepts Statements and Level A GAAP that would be confusing. The Board acknowledged those concerns but concluded that it was not necessary to revise Concepts Statement 7 at this time. The Board will consider the need to revise Concepts Statement 7 in its conceptual framework project.

Multiperiod Excess Earnings Method

C62. In response to questions raised by some respondents, the Board clarified that valuation techniques consistent with the income approach also include the multiperiod excess earnings method discussed in the AICPA Practice Aid, *Assets Acquired in a Business Combination to Be Used in Research and Development Activities: A Focus on Software, Electronic Devices, and Pharmaceutical Industries* (Practice Aid). However, for in-process research and development (IPR&D), the Board observed that the related guidance in the Practice Aid could be interpreted as permitting a fair value measurement using an in-exchange valuation premise (to value the IPR&D standalone) in some situations in which this Statement would require a fair value measurement using an in-use valuation premise (to value the IPR&D within a group of assets). For example, that might be the case if, for competitive reasons, the reporting entity intends to hold (lock up) IPR&D acquired in a business combination that market participants would develop (and use within a group of assets). The Board agreed that the multiperiod excess earnings method should continue to be used under this Statement. However, consistent with the related guidance in this Statement, the valuation premise used for the fair value measurement should be determined based on the use of an asset by market participants, even if the intended use by the reporting entity is different.

Inputs to Valuation Techniques

C63. In this Statement, *inputs* refer broadly to the assumptions that market participants would use in pricing the asset or liability, including assumptions about risk. The Board decided that a necessary input to a valuation technique is an adjustment for risk. The measurement should include an adjustment for risk whenever market participants would include one in pricing the related asset or liability (consistent with the risk premium notion in Concepts Statement 7, reconsidered in this Statement) so that the measurement reflects an exit price for the related asset or liability, that is, the price the reporting entity would receive (or pay) in a transaction to sell (or transfer) the related asset (or liability). In this Statement, the Board focused on the need to adjust for the risk inherent in a particular valuation technique used to measure fair value, such as a pricing model (model risk) and/or the risk inherent in the inputs to the valuation technique (input risk).

Fair Value Hierarchy

C64. To increase consistency and comparability in fair value measurements and related disclosures, this Statement establishes a fair value hierarchy that prioritizes the inputs used to measure fair value into three broad levels, considering the relative reliability of the inputs. The availability of inputs might affect the valuation technique(s) used to measure fair value. However, the fair value hierarchy focuses on the inputs, not the valuation techniques, thereby requiring judgment in the selection and application of valuation techniques.

C65. Many respondents generally agreed that prioritizing the inputs used to measure fair value is important and that the fair value hierarchy provides a useful construct for considering the relative reliability of fair value measurements. However, several respondents urged the Board to revise the fair value hierarchy initially proposed in the Exposure Draft to convey more clearly a continuum of inputs. The principal concerns focused on the use of the fair value hierarchy as a framework for disclosures about fair value measurements. In response, the Board subsequently revised the fair value hierarchy, as discussed below.

Level 1 Inputs

C66. Like the Exposure Draft, this Statement includes within Level 1 quoted prices (unadjusted) in active markets for identical assets or liabilities. The Board affirmed its conclusion in other accounting pronouncements that quoted prices in active markets generally provide the most reliable evidence of fair value and should be used to measure fair value whenever available. For example, paragraph 57 of Statement 107 states:

> The Board concluded that quoted market prices provide the most reliable measure of fair value. Quoted market prices are easy to obtain and are reliable and verifiable. They are used and relied upon regularly and are well understood by investors, creditors, and other users of financial information. In recent

years, new markets have developed and some existing markets have evolved from thin to active markets, thereby increasing the ready availability of reliable fair value information.

C67. The Board also affirmed its decision in the Exposure Draft that a fair value measurement within Level 1 should be based on a quoted price in an active market that the reporting entity has the ability to access for the asset or liability at the measurement date. Because a quoted price, alone, forms the basis for the measurement, the access requirement within Level 1 limits discretion in pricing the asset or liability, including in situations in which there are multiple markets for the asset or liability with different prices and no single market represents a principal market for the asset or liability.

Adjustments to quoted prices in active markets

C68. The Exposure Draft emphasized that a quoted price (unadjusted) in an active market should be used to measure fair value whenever it is available. Some respondents interpreted the related guidance as requiring the use of a quoted price in an active market without regard to whether that price is readily available or representative of fair value. Those respondents referred to possible conflicts with ASR 118, which requires adjustments to a quoted price in those situations (fair value pricing). In its redeliberations, the Board affirmed that its intent was not to preclude adjustments to a quoted price if that price is not readily available or representative of fair value, noting that in those situations, the market for the particular asset or liability might not be active. To convey its intent more clearly, the Board clarified that in those situations, the fair value of the asset or liability should be measured using the quoted price, as adjusted, but within a lower level of the fair value hierarchy.

C69. A few respondents referred to situations in which an entity holds a large number of similar assets and liabilities (for example, debt securities) that are required to be measured at fair value and a quoted price in an active market is not readily accessible for each of those assets and liabilities. They indicated that in those situations, the fair value hierarchy should allow for practical considerations and trade-offs in selecting the valuation technique used to measure fair value within Level 1, considering the number of assets and/or liabilities required to be measured in a financial reporting period and the timing of that reporting. The Board subsequently revised the guidance within Level 1 to allow for the use of an alternative pricing method that does not rely exclusively on quoted prices (for example, matrix pricing) as a practical expedient in the limited situations referred to. However, when the practical expedient within Level 1 is used, the fair value measurement is a lower level measurement.

C70. The Board observed that in some cases, significant events (for example, principal-to-principal transactions, brokered trades, or announcements) might occur after the close of a market but before the measurement date. In those cases, a quoted price in that market might not be representative of fair value at the measurement date. The Board affirmed its view in the Exposure Draft that the reporting entity need not undertake all possible efforts to obtain information about after-hours trading or news events. However, the reporting entity should not ignore information that is available at the reporting date (for example, a large change in the price in another market after the close of the principal market in which the asset or liability trades). The Board agreed that entities should establish and consistently apply a policy for identifying those events that might affect fair value measurements. However, if a quoted price is adjusted for new information, the fair value measurement is a lower level measurement.

Financial instruments

C71. Prior to this Statement, the FASB, the AICPA Accounting Standards Executive Committee (AcSEC), the Securities and Exchange Commission (SEC), and others considered issues relating to fair value measurements involving financial instruments. The threshold issue focused on whether the appropriate unit of account for a block position in an instrument that trades in an active market is (a) the individual trading unit, where the fair value measurement would be determined as the product of the quoted price for the individual instrument times the quantity held (P×Q), or (b) the block, where the fair value measurement would be determined using the quoted price, adjusted because of the size of the position relative to trading volume (blockage factor).

C72. In other FASB Statements (including Statements 107 and 133, and FASB Statements No. 115, *Accounting for Certain Investments in Debt and Equity Securities,* and No. 124, *Accounting for Certain Investments Held by Not-for-Profit Organizations*), the Board decided that for a block, the fair value measurement should be based on the individual trad-

ing unit, determined using P×Q. Therefore, those Statements preclude the use of a blockage factor, even if the normal trading volume for one day is not sufficient to absorb the quantity held and placing orders to sell the position in a single transaction might affect the quoted price.

C73. Paragraph 58 of Statement 107 states:

Although many respondents to the 1990 and 1987 Exposure Drafts agreed with the usefulness of disclosing quoted market prices derived from active markets, some argued that quoted prices from thin markets do not provide relevant measures of fair value, particularly when an entity holds a large amount of a thinly traded financial instrument that could not be absorbed by the market in a single transaction. The Board considered this issue and reiterated its belief that quoted prices, even from thin markets, provide useful information because investors and creditors regularly rely on those prices to make their decisions. The Board noted that providing the liquidation value of a block of financial instruments is not the objective of this Statement. The Board also concluded that requiring the use of available quoted market prices would increase the comparability of the disclosures among entities.

C74. Similarly, paragraph 315 of Statement 133 states:

The definition of fair value requires that fair value be determined as the product of the number of trading units of an asset times a quoted market price if available [as required by Statement 107]. . . . Some respondents to the Exposure Draft indicated that the guidance in Statement 107 (and implicitly the definition of *fair value* in this Statement) should be revised to require or permit consideration of a discount in valuing a large asset position. They asserted that an entity that holds a relatively large amount (compared with average trading volume) of a traded asset and liquidates the entire amount at one time likely would receive an amount less than the quoted market price. Although respondents generally focused on a discount, holding a relatively large amount of an asset might sometimes result in a premium over the market price for a single trading unit. The Board currently believes that the use of a blockage factor would lessen the reliability and comparability of reported estimates of fair value.

C75. For broker-dealers and certain investment companies (investment companies other than registered funds subject to SEC reporting requirements that used blockage factors in financial statements for fiscal years ending on or before May 31, 2000), the AICPA Audit and Accounting Guides for those industries allowed an exception to the requirement of other FASB pronouncements to use P×Q to measure the fair value of a block. Specifically, the Guides permitted a fair value measurement using a blockage factor, where appropriate.

C76. In developing this Statement, the Board decided to address that inconsistency within GAAP. The Board considered the earlier work completed by AcSEC through its Blockage Factor Task Force, which was formed in 2000 to address issues specific to the use of blockage factors (discounts) by broker-dealers and investment companies. Based on its discussions with industry representatives (broker-dealers, mutual funds, and other investment companies) and a review of relevant academic research and market data, the task force affirmed that discounts involving large blocks exist, generally increasing as the size of the block to be traded (expressed as a percentage of the daily trading volume) increases but that the methods for measuring the blockage factors (discounts) vary among entities and are largely subjective.

C77. In the Exposure Draft, the Board acknowledged the diversity in practice with respect to the methods for measuring blockage factors (discounts). However, the Board agreed that for entities that regularly buy and sell securities in blocks, the financial reporting that would result when using P×Q to measure the fair value of a block position would not be representationally faithful of the underlying business activities. In particular, if a block is purchased at a discount to the quoted price, a fair value measurement using P×Q would give the appearance of a gain upon buying the block, followed by a reported loss on subsequently selling the block (at a discount to the quoted price). At that time, the Board understood that for blocks held by broker-dealers, industry practice was to also sell the securities in blocks. In view of that selling practice (in blocks), the Board decided that this Statement should allow the exception to

P×Q in the Guides to continue, thereby permitting the use of blockage factors by broker-dealers and certain investment companies that buy or sell securities in blocks.

C78. Many respondents, in particular, broker-dealers, agreed with that decision. However, during its redeliberations, the Board discussed the need for expanded disclosures about blocks measured using blockage factors with representative preparers (broker-dealers) and users (analysts that follow broker-dealers). Through those discussions, the Board learned that for blocks held by broker-dealers, industry practice is often to sell the securities in multiple transactions involving quantities that might be large but that are not necessarily blocks; that is, the securities could be sold at the quoted price for an individual trading unit. Because of that selling practice, the majority of the Board decided that there was no compelling reason to allow the exception to P×Q in the Guides to continue under this Statement, noting that revised IAS 39 includes similar guidance in paragraph AG72, which states that "the fair value of a portfolio of financial instruments is the product of the number of units of the instrument and its quoted market price."

C79. In reaching that decision, the majority of the Board affirmed its conclusions relating to the prohibition on the use of blockage factors in other FASB Statements. In particular, the Board emphasized that when a quoted price in an active market for a security is available, that price should be used to measure fair value without regard to an entity's intent to transact at that price. Basing the fair value on the quoted price results in comparable reporting. Adjusting the price for the size of the position introduces management intent (to trade in blocks) into the measurement, reducing comparability. Following the reasoning used in Statement 107, the quoted price provides useful information because investors regularly rely on quoted prices for decision making. Also, the decision to exchange a large position in a single transaction at a price lower than the price that would be available if the position were to be exchanged in multiple transactions (in smaller quantities) is a decision whose consequences should be reported when that decision is executed. Until that transaction occurs, the entity that holds the block has the ability to effect the transaction either in the block market or in another market (the principal or more advantageous market for the individual trading unit).

C80. This Statement precludes the use of blockage factors and eliminates the exception to P×Q in the

Guides for a financial instrument that trades in an active market (within Level 1). In other words, the unit of account for an instrument that trades in an active market is the individual trading unit. This Statement amends Statements 107, 115, 124, 133, and 140 to remove the similar unit-of-account guidance in those accounting pronouncements, which referred to a fair value measurement using P×Q for an instrument that trades in any market, including a market that is not active, for example, a thin market (within Level 2). In this Statement, the Board decided not to specify the unit of account for an instrument that trades in a market that is not active. The Board plans to address unit-of-account issues broadly in its conceptual framework project.

Level 2 Inputs

C81. The Exposure Draft limited the inputs within Level 2 to quoted prices in active markets for similar assets or liabilities, adjusted for differences that are objectively determinable. Several respondents indicated that because all adjustments involve some degree of subjective judgment and estimation, Level 2 would be overly restrictive. The Board agreed and decided to broaden Level 2 to include all inputs other than quoted prices included within Level 1 that are observable for the asset or liability.

C82. Observable inputs within Level 2 include inputs that are directly observable for the asset or liability (including quoted prices for similar assets or liabilities) as well as inputs that are not directly observable for the asset or liability but that are derived principally from or corroborated by observable market data through correlation or by other means (market-corroborated inputs). The concept of market-corroborated inputs is intended to incorporate observable market data (such as interest rates and yield curves that are observable at commonly quoted intervals), based on an assessment of factors relevant to the asset or liability. The Board concluded that market-corroborated inputs are observable inputs and that fair value measurements using market-corroborated inputs (within Level 2) should be distinguished from fair value measurements using unobservable inputs (within Level 3).

Level 3 Inputs

C83. The Exposure Draft included within a single level (Level 3) observable inputs other than quoted prices in active markets (for identical or similar assets or liabilities) together with all unobservable inputs (previously referred to as entity inputs). Several respondents observed that fair value measurements reported and disclosed within Level 3 would be overly broad. In particular, they indicated that the measurements would range widely in reliability and that including such a wide range in a single level could be misleading to users of financial statements. Some fair value measurements would be objectively determined (using quoted inputs other than prices), while other fair value measurements would be more subjectively determined (using unobservable inputs). The Board agreed and decided to limit Level 3 inputs to unobservable inputs.

C84. In reaching that decision, the Board affirmed its conclusion in other accounting pronouncements that unobservable inputs should be used to measure fair value to the extent that observable inputs are not available, allowing for situations in which there might be little, if any, market activity for the asset or liability at the measurement date. However, the fair value measurement objective remains the same—an exit price from the perspective of a market participant that holds the asset or owes the liability. Therefore, unobservable inputs should reflect the reporting entity's own assumptions about the assumptions market participants would use in pricing the asset or liability (including assumptions about risk) developed based on the best information available in the circumstances.

C85. The Board agreed that in many cases, the best information available with which to develop unobservable inputs might be the reporting entity's own data. The Board affirmed its view in Concepts Statement 7 (and other existing accounting pronouncements) that the reporting entity may use its own data to develop unobservable inputs, provided that there is no information reasonably available without undue cost and effort that indicates that market participants would use different assumptions in pricing the asset or liability. Paragraph 38 of Concepts Statement 7 explains:

> . . . an entity that uses cash flows in accounting measurements often has little or no information about some or all of the assumptions that marketplace participants would use in assessing the fair value of an asset or a liability. In those situations, the entity must necessarily use the information that is available without undue cost and effort in developing cash flow estimates. The use of an entity's own assumptions about future cash flows is

compatible with an estimate of fair value, as long as there are no contrary data indicating that marketplace participants would use different assumptions. If such data exist, the entity must adjust its assumptions to incorporate that market information.

C86. In this Statement, the Board clarified that the reporting entity need not undertake all possible efforts to obtain information about the assumptions that market participants would use in pricing the asset or liability or otherwise establish the absence of contrary data indicating that market participants would use different assumptions. However, the reporting entity must not ignore information about market participant assumptions that is available within reasonable cost-benefit constraints.

C87. Within Level 3, unobservable inputs relevant to the asset or liability should be used as a basis for replicating the actions of market participants in a hypothetical transaction for the asset or liability at the measurement date. The Board understands that for some, a measurement using a hypothetical construct that relies on unobservable inputs raises concerns about the resulting fair value measurement. In particular, some believe that a hypothetical construct might not faithfully represent an actual economic phenomenon and, as such, would seem to be of questionable relevance to users of financial statements. Some Board members share those concerns. However, the Board agreed that concerns about fair value measurements that are predicated on hypothetical transactions in hypothetical markets derive from a threshold issue that relates principally to the selection of the appropriate measurement attribute, an area of focus in the Board's conceptual framework project. The Board plans to continue to address the issue of which measurement attribute should be required in individual accounting pronouncements on a project-by-project basis.

Inputs Based on Bid and Ask Prices

C88. The Board observed that in some situations, inputs might be determined based on bid and ask prices, for example, in a dealer market where the bid price represents the price the dealer is willing to pay and the ask price represents the price at which the dealer is willing to sell. The related guidance in ASR 118 provides entities (investment companies and broker-dealers) with flexibility in selecting the bid-ask pricing method used to measure fair value. Accordingly, the practice that has evolved under ASR 118 is diverse.

C89. In the Exposure Draft, the Board agreed that a single bid-ask spread pricing method would maximize the consistency and comparability of fair value measurements within Level 1. At that time, the Board decided to require the use of bid prices for long positions (assets) and ask prices for short positions (liabilities), similar to the related guidance in paragraph BC99 of revised IAS 39, which states:

> The Board confirmed the proposal in the Exposure Draft that the appropriate quoted market price for an asset held or liability to be issued is usually the current bid price and, for an asset to be acquired or liability held, the asking price. It concluded that applying mid-market prices to an individual instrument is not appropriate because it would result in entities recognising up-front gains or losses for the difference between the bid-ask price and the mid-market price.

C90. Respondents agreed that a single bid-ask spread pricing method would maximize the consistency and comparability of fair value measurements using bid and ask prices. However, many respondents stated that because different market participants transact at different prices within a bid-ask spread, the resulting measurements would not be relevant in all cases. Some of those respondents emphasized that for entities that enter into derivative instruments to manage risk, the bid-ask spread pricing method would create operational difficulties because many of those instruments are traded in active dealer markets and currently valued using other pricing methods (for example, mid-market prices or prices within a range of observable bid and ask prices). Other respondents indicated that the bid-ask spread pricing method within Level 1 would create inconsistencies between fair value measurements using bid and ask prices within Level 1 and fair value measurements using bid and ask prices within other levels of the fair value hierarchy. Respondents stated that this Statement should allow an approach consistent with the related guidance in ASR 118.

C91. In its redeliberations, the Board reconsidered the required bid-ask spread pricing method within Level 1. The Board decided that the price within the bid-ask spread that is most representative of fair value in the circumstances should be used to measure the fair value of the related asset or liability within all levels of the fair value hierarchy, provided that the price is consistently determined. In reaching that decision, the Board observed that in many situations, bid and ask prices establish the boundaries within which market participants would negotiate the price in the exchange for the related asset or liability. The Board concluded that having clarified the fair value measurement objective in this Statement, entities should use judgment in meeting that objective. Accordingly, bid-ask spread pricing methods appropriate under ASR 118 are appropriate under this Statement. The use of bid prices for long positions (assets) and ask prices for short positions (liabilities) is permitted but not required.

C92. Because the Exposure Draft would have required the use of bid prices for long positions (assets) and ask prices for short positions (liabilities), the Board initially decided to specify the pricing for off-setting positions to preclude recognition of up-front gains or losses. Specifically, the Board decided to require the use of mid-market prices for the matched portion and bid and ask prices for the net open position, as appropriate, similar to the related guidance in paragraph BC100 of revised IAS 39. Because this Statement does not require the use of bid prices for long positions (assets) and ask prices for short positions (liabilities), the Board decided not to include in this Statement the guidance for offsetting positions in the Exposure Draft.

Disclosures

C93. The Board observed that few of the accounting pronouncements that require fair value measurements also require disclosures about those measurements. Further, the required disclosures vary. The Board decided that having established a framework for measuring fair value, this Statement should require expanded disclosures about fair value measurements. Because at initial recognition many assets and liabilities are measured in the statement of financial position at amounts that approximate fair value (for example, in a business combination), the Board decided to limit the disclosures to fair value measurements in periods subsequent to initial recognition, whether the measurements are made on a recurring or nonrecurring basis.

C94. Some respondents disagreed with the Board's decision to include expanded disclosures about fair value measurements in this Statement. They indicated that, instead, the Board should develop a comprehensive disclosure framework and reconsider all related disclosures currently required under existing accounting pronouncements in the context of that framework. Some of those respondents further indi-

cated that the Board should consider disclosures about fair value (and changes in fair value) in its project on financial statement presentation (formerly, financial performance reporting by business enterprises). In the Exposure Draft, the Board considered the interaction between that project and the fair value measurement project. Based on input initially received from members of the User Advisory Council and others, the Board decided that until such time as a final Statement in that project is issued, expanded disclosures about fair value measurements would provide information that is useful to users of financial statements. The Board agreed that the issues raised by respondents indicate the need to reconsider or otherwise clarify some of the disclosure requirements initially proposed in the Exposure Draft, but not eliminate those requirements from this Statement altogether, noting that some entities (in particular, entities in the financial services industry) already are making similar disclosures in SEC filings.

Fair Value Measurements

C95. The Board affirmed that the reporting entity should disclose information that enables users of its financial statements to assess the extent to which fair value is used to measure assets and liabilities in periods subsequent to initial recognition and the inputs used for fair value measurements. In the Exposure Draft, the Board concluded that information about the inputs used for fair value measurements would allow users of financial statements to assess the relative reliability of the measurements. Many respondents generally agreed with those disclosures, subject to clarifications to conform the disclosures to the levels within the fair value hierarchy, as revised. Therefore, the disclosures required by this Statement segregate fair value measurements using quoted prices in active markets for identical assets or liabilities (Level 1), significant other observable inputs (Level 2), and significant unobservable inputs (Level 3), separately for each major category of assets and liabilities. To improve consistency in the fair value measurements disclosed, this Statement specifies that the level within the fair value hierarchy in which a fair value measurement in its entirety falls should be determined based on the lowest level input that is significant to the measurement in its entirety.

Level 3 Reconciliation for Recurring Fair Value Measurements

C96. The Board affirmed that the reporting entity should disclose information that enables users of its financial statements to assess the effects of recurring fair value measurements on earnings (or changes in net assets) for the period. That disclosure is limited to recurring fair value measurements because similar disclosures for nonrecurring fair value measurements (for example, impaired assets) are currently required under other accounting pronouncements.

C97. In the Exposure Draft, the Board decided that the disclosures for recurring fair value measurements should focus principally on earnings (or changes in net assets), separate from other comprehensive income, and the unrealized gains or losses included in earnings (or changes in net assets) for the period. In reaching that decision, the Board concluded that information about unrealized gains or losses included in earnings would allow users to broadly assess the quality of reported earnings. However, some respondents disagreed. They stated that disclosures about unrealized gains or losses, alone, would not be cost beneficial and, in some cases, could be misleading. For example, users of financial statements might conclude that unrealized gains or losses are of a lesser quality than realized gains or losses, which might not be the case. Also, because some entities do not currently capture that information, incremental systems changes (in some cases significant) would be required to comply with the disclosures. Those respondents encouraged the Board to reconsider the disclosures.

C98. Concurrent with its redeliberations of related issues in proposed FSP FAS 133-a, the Board discussed the need for expanded disclosures about fair value measurements with certain users of financial statements, including members of the Investor Task Force that concentrate on the investment banking, energy trading, and insurance industries, and members of the User Advisory Council. Those discussions focused on expanded disclosures about recurring fair value measurements using significant unobservable inputs (within Level 3) and the effect of the measurements on earnings for the period. Those users strongly supported the expanded disclosures. They indicated that the expanded disclosures would allow users of financial statements to make more informed judgments and segregate the effects of fair value measurements that are inherently subjective, enhancing their ability to assess the quality of earnings broadly. Based on that input, the Board concluded that expanded disclosures about recurring fair value measurements and the effect of the measurements on earnings (or changes in net assets) for the period,

separate from other comprehensive income, would provide useful information to users of financial statements and should be required in this Statement.

C99. To balance the needs of users with the concerns of respondents, the Board discussed the expanded disclosures with some respondents (principally, financial institutions). Those respondents indicated that expanded disclosures for recurring fair value measurements within Level 3 could be provided within reasonable cost-benefit constraints if presented in the form of a reconciliation of beginning and ending balances that segregates all changes during the period for each major category of assets and liabilities, except as follows. They stated that because the same derivative can be an asset in one reporting period and a liability in the next reporting period, separate (gross) presentation for derivative assets and liabilities would not be cost beneficial. In particular, systems changes would be needed to track and reconcile the information necessary to separately capture the related earnings effects. In considering that presentation issue, the Board agreed that the information conveyed by those disclosures would be more meaningful if presented separate (gross) rather than net. However, the Board decided that presentation issues for derivatives disclosures should be considered in the context of its current project on derivatives disclosures. The Board decided to allow derivatives to be presented net for purposes of the reconciliation disclosure in this Statement.

C100. The reconciliation of beginning and ending balances of recurring fair value measurements within Level 3 required in this Statement segregates changes from all sources, including total gains or losses recognized in earnings (or changes in net assets) during the period. The Board concluded (and respondents agreed) that disclosure of total gains or losses would provide needed context for disclosure of the change in unrealized gains or losses recognized in earnings (or changes in net assets) during the period relating to the assets and liabilities measured within Level 3 that are still held at the end of the period. The Board further concluded that because subsequent changes in fair value reflect changes in economic conditions without regard to whether an entity has transacted, disclosure of total gains or losses would provide incremental information about changes in shareholder wealth due to changes in economic conditions that would further enable users of financial statements to assess the effects of fair value measurements on earnings (or changes in net assets) for the period.

Other Disclosures

C101. A few respondents stated that this Statement should standardize disclosures of the discount rate and assumptions used in valuation techniques to measure fair value. The Board affirmed its view in the Exposure Draft that standardizing those disclosures for all assets and liabilities measured at fair value (for example, requiring disclosure of assumptions used to measure fair value) would not be practical. By way of example, the Board referred to other accounting pronouncements in which it reached different decisions on whether to require disclosures about significant assumptions. The Board noted that in some cases, an overwhelming volume of information would need to be disclosed for that information to be meaningful. Because sensitivity disclosures rely largely on those assumptions, the Board also decided not to require sensitivity disclosures (for example, market risk disclosures), as further suggested by some respondents. Instead, this Statement establishes broad disclosure objectives, which the Board expects to consider as a basis for requiring more specific disclosures in individual accounting pronouncements that require fair value measurements on a project-by-project basis.

C102. A few respondents also referred to the disclosures about the fair value of financial instruments required by Statement 107. They suggested that the Board consolidate those disclosures with the disclosures in this Statement. The Board disagreed. The disclosures required by Statement 107 are specific to financial instruments, as defined in that Statement, and extend beyond the measurements themselves. Further, those disclosures apply regardless of whether a financial instrument is recognized in the statement of financial position and measured at fair value. The Board agreed that the disclosures required by this Statement should be encouraged for financial instruments disclosed at fair value, including financial instruments recognized in the statement of financial position at amounts other than fair value (for example, loans carried at cost). Therefore, this Statement amends Statement 107 to refer to the related disclosures in this Statement.

C103. A few respondents also referred to possible conflicts and overlap with SEC disclosure requirements within management discussion and analysis, noting that to varying degrees the disclosures required by this Statement would duplicate those and other industry-specific disclosures made outside the basic financial statements. The Board affirmed its view in the Exposure Draft that the disclosures required by this Statement supplement related disclosures made outside the basic financial statements. The disclosures required by this Statement apply for all entities that hold assets and liabilities recognized in the statement of financial position that are measured at fair value. Further, all entities should include those disclosures within the basic financial statements.

C104. The Board emphasized that consistent with its related codification initiatives, the fair value information disclosed under this Statement should be combined and disclosed together with the fair value information disclosed under other pronouncements, including Statement 107 (for example, in a single fair value footnote), where practicable. The Board concluded that having those disclosures available in one place would enhance users' understanding about fair value and the use of fair value in financial reporting.

Amendment to Opinion 28

C105. In the Exposure Draft, the Board decided that the disclosures required by this Statement should be made in all interim periods. Some respondents emphasized that those disclosures in all interim periods would not be cost beneficial. The Board acknowledged those concerns. However, the Board affirmed its conclusion in the Exposure Draft that fair value disclosures in interim periods would provide timely information to users about fair value measurements and factors affecting those measurements during the year. Moreover, increased information about fair value on an ongoing basis would enhance users' understanding of fair value and the use of fair value in financial reporting. Because of respondents' concerns, the Board decided to limit the disclosures that are required in interim periods to quantitative disclosures. To communicate more clearly the information conveyed by those quantitative disclosures, the Board decided to require tabular presentation (in all periods). In reaching that decision, the Board considered related research, which indicates that tabular presentation of financial information is an important communications tool. This Statement amends APB Opinion No. 28, *Interim Financial Reporting,* to require those disclosures in all interim periods. Qualitative disclosures, for example, narrative disclosure about the valuation techniques used to measure fair value, are required only in annual periods.

Effective Date and Transition

C106. The Board decided that this Statement should be effective for financial statements issued for fiscal years beginning after November 15, 2007, and interim periods within those fiscal years. Because this Statement applies under other accounting pronouncements that require fair value measurements and does not require any new fair value measurements, the Board believes that the extended transition period under this Statement provides sufficient time for entities, their auditors, and users of financial statements to prepare for implementation of the provisions of this Statement. The Board encourages earlier application, provided that the reporting entity has not yet issued financial statements for that fiscal year (annual or interim).

C107. The Board agreed, as it did in the Exposure Draft, that because the substantive guidance in this Statement focuses broadly on the methods used to measure fair value, application of that guidance could result in a change in the method of applying an accounting principle. However, because the methods used to measure fair value are referred to generally, for example, in the context of inputs requiring both quantitative and qualitative assessments, the Board concluded that a change in the methods used to measure fair value would be inseparable from a change in the fair value measurements (that is, as new events occur or as new information is obtained, for example, through better insight or improved judgment). Therefore, the Board decided that the guidance in this Statement should be applied prospectively (similar to a change in accounting estimate) as of the beginning of the fiscal year in which this Statement is initially applied, except as discussed below.

C108. For the change in accounting for derivative (or other) instruments under Issue 02-3, the Board concluded that application of the guidance in this Statement would result in a change in the method of applying an accounting principle and that the change in the method would be separable from the change in the fair value measurements. Therefore, the Board decided that the guidance in this Statement should be applied retrospectively (similar to a change in accounting principle), but on a limited basis as of the beginning of the fiscal year in which this Statement is initially applied, considering the practical limitations involved in applying the change in method in all prior periods. Therefore, the difference between the carrying amount and the fair value of a derivative (or other instrument) that was measured at initial recog-

nition using the transaction price in accordance with the guidance in footnote 3 of Issue 02-3 prior to initial application of this Statement should be recognized as a cumulative-effect adjustment to the opening balance of retained earnings (or other appropriate components of equity or net assets in the statement of financial position) for that fiscal year, presented separately.

C109. For the change in accounting for positions in financial instruments (including blocks) held by broker-dealers and certain investment companies, the Board agreed that application of the guidance in this Statement would result in a change in the method of applying an accounting principle that would be separable from the change in fair value measurements. The Board observed that because the information necessary to apply that change in accounting principle retrospectively to all prior periods presented should be available, the guidance in this Statement could be applied retrospectively (similar to a change in accounting principle) in all prior periods. However, the Board decided that three different transition approaches in this Statement (including two different transition approaches for financial instruments) would be unduly burdensome. Therefore, the Board decided for practical reasons that the limited retrospective transition approach for the change in accounting under Issue 02-3 also should apply for the change in accounting for positions in financial instruments (including blocks) held by broker-dealers and investment companies.

C110. To achieve comparability in future periods, all of the disclosures required by this Statement, including disclosures about the valuation techniques used to measure fair value required in annual periods only, are required in the first interim period in which this Statement is initially applied. However, those disclosures need not be presented in periods prior to initial application of this Statement.

Benefits and Costs

C111. The mission of the FASB is to establish and improve standards of financial accounting and reporting to provide information that is useful to users of financial statements (present and potential investors, creditors, donors, and other capital market participants) in making rational investment, credit, and similar resource allocation decisions. In fulfilling that mission, the Board endeavors to determine that a proposed standard will fill a significant need and that the costs imposed to meet that standard, as compared with other alternatives, are justified in relation to the overall benefits of the resulting information. Although the costs to implement a new standard may not be borne evenly, users of financial statements benefit from improvements in financial reporting, thereby facilitating the functioning of markets for capital and credit and the efficient allocation of resources in the economy.

C112. This Statement establishes a single definition of fair value and a framework for measuring fair value in GAAP. A single definition of fair value, together with a framework for measuring fair value, should result in increased consistency in application and, with respect to the resulting fair value measurements, increased comparability. Concepts Statement 2 emphasizes that providing comparable information enables users of financial statements to identify similarities in and differences between two sets of economic events.

C113. This Statement also expands disclosures about fair value measurements, improving the quality of information provided to users of financial statements. Providing information that is useful to users of financial statements in making rational investment, credit, and similar decisions is the first objective of financial reporting in FASB Concepts Statement No. 1, *Objectives of Financial Reporting by Business Enterprises*. In developing the disclosure requirements of this Statement, the Board obtained input from users, preparers, and other interested parties to ensure that the disclosures would be provided within reasonable cost-benefit constraints. This Statement encourages entities to include the fair value information disclosed under this Statement together with the fair value information disclosed under other accounting pronouncements in one place, where practicable. The Board concluded that having that information available in one place would improve the quality of information provided to users of financial

statements about fair value measurements, thereby enhancing users' understanding about fair value and the use of fair value in financial reporting.

C114. In addition, the amendments made by this Statement simplify and, where appropriate, codify the related guidance that currently exists for measuring fair value, eliminating differences that have added to the complexity in GAAP, consistent with the Board's related codification initiatives.

C115. Although the framework for measuring fair value builds on current practice and requirements, the Board acknowledges that for some entities, certain methods required by this Statement may result in a change to practice. Further, some entities will need to make systems and operational changes, thereby incurring incremental costs. Some entities also might incur incremental costs in applying the requirements of this Statement. However, the Board believes that the benefits resulting from increased consistency and comparability of fair value information and improved communication of that information to users of financial statements will be ongoing. On balance, the Board concluded that this Statement will result in improved financial reporting.

International Financial Reporting Standards

C116. Many International Financial Reporting Standards require fair value measurements. Like the FASB, the IASB has previously addressed issues related to fair value largely in the context of financial instruments included in the scope of revised IAS 39. The IASB currently has on its agenda a fair value measurements project to consider fair value measurement broadly, focusing on the definition of fair value and the framework for measuring fair value. As part of that project, the IASB plans to issue this Statement in the form of a preliminary views document for public comment.

Appendix D

REFERENCES TO APB AND FASB PRONOUNCEMENTS

D1. This appendix lists APB and FASB pronouncements existing at the date of this Statement that refer to fair value. Those pronouncements that are amended by this Statement are indicated by an asterisk. (See Appendix E.)

Pronouncement	Title
Opinion 18	The Equity Method of Accounting for Investments in Common Stock
Opinion 21*	Interest on Receivables and Payables
Opinion 28*	Interim Financial Reporting
Opinion 29*	Accounting for Nonmonetary Transactions
Statement 13*	Accounting for Leases
Statement 15*	Accounting by Debtors and Creditors for Troubled Debt Restructurings
Statement 19*	Financial Accounting and Reporting by Oil and Gas Producing Companies
Statement 23	Inception of the Lease
Statement 28	Accounting for Sales with Leasebacks
Statement 35*	Accounting and Reporting by Defined Benefit Pension Plans
Statement 45	Accounting for Franchise Fee Revenue
Statement 60*	Accounting and Reporting by Insurance Enterprises
Statement 61	Accounting for Title Plant
Statement 63*	Financial Reporting by Broadcasters
Statement 65*	Accounting for Certain Mortgage Banking Activities
Statement 66	Accounting for Sales of Real Estate
Statement 67*	Accounting for Costs and Initial Rental Operations of Real Estate Projects
Statement 68	Research and Development Arrangements
Statement 84	Induced Conversions of Convertible Debt
Statement 87*	Employers' Accounting for Pensions
Statement 98	Accounting for Leases
Statement 106*	Employers' Accounting for Postretirement Benefits Other Than Pensions
Statement 107*	Disclosures about Fair Value of Financial Instruments

Pronouncement	Title
Statement 114	Accounting by Creditors for Impairment of a Loan
Statement 115*	Accounting for Certain Investments in Debt and Equity Securities
Statement 116*	Accounting for Contributions Received and Contributions Made
Statement 124*	Accounting for Certain Investments Held by Not-for-Profit Organizations
Statement 126	Exemption from Certain Required Disclosures about Financial Instruments for Certain Nonpublic Entities
Statement 133*	Accounting for Derivative Instruments and Hedging Activities
Statement 136*	Transfers of Assets to a Not-for-Profit Organization or Charitable Trust That Raises or Holds Contributions for Others
Statement 138	Accounting for Certain Derivative Instruments and Certain Hedging Activities
Statement 140*	Accounting for Transfers and Servicing of Financial Assets and Extinguishments of Liabilities
Statement 141 *	Business Combinations
Statement 142*	Goodwill and Other Intangible Assets
Statement 143*	Accounting for Asset Retirement Obligations
Statement 144*	Accounting for the Impairment or Disposal of Long-Lived Assets
Statement 146*	Accounting for Costs Associated with Exit or Disposal Activities
Statement 149	Amendment of Statement 133 on Derivative Instruments and Hedging Activities
Statement 150*	Accounting for Certain Financial Instruments with Characteristics of both Liabilities and Equity
Statement 153	Exchanges of Nonmonetary Assets
Statement 156*	Accounting for Servicing of Financial Assets
Interpretation 9	Applying APB Opinions No. 16 and 17 When a Savings and Loan Association or a Similar Institution Is Acquired in a Business Combination Accounted for by the Purchase Method
Interpretation 23	Leases of Certain Property Owned by a Governmental Unit or Authority
Interpretation 24	Leases Involving Only Part of a Building
Interpretation 45*	Guarantor's Accounting and Disclosure Requirements for Guarantees, Including Indirect Guarantees of Indebtedness of Others
Interpretation 46 (revised December 2003)	Consolidation of Variable Interest Entities

Pronouncement	Title
Interpretation 47	Accounting for Conditional Asset Retirement Obligations
Technical Bulletin 84-1	Accounting for Stock Issued to Acquire the Results of a Research and Development Arrangement
Technical Bulletin 85-1	Accounting for the Receipt of Federal Home Loan Mortgage Corporation Participating Preferred Stock
Technical Bulletin 85-5	Issues Relating to Accounting for Business Combinations
Technical Bulletin 85-6	Accounting for a Purchase of Treasury Shares at a Price Significantly in Excess of the Current Market Price of the Shares and the Income Statement Classification of Costs Incurred in Defending against a Takeover Attempt
Technical Bulletin 86-2	Accounting for an Interest in the Residual Value of a Leased Asset
Technical Bulletin 88-1	Issues Relating to Accounting for Leases
FSP FAS 115-1 and 124-1	The Meaning of Other-Than-Temporary Impairment and Its Application to Certain Investments
FSP FAS 143-1	Accounting for Electronic Equipment Waste Obligations
FSP FAS 144-1	Determination of Cost Basis for Foreclosed Assets under FASB Statement No. 15 and the Measurement of Cumulative Losses Previously Recognized under Paragraph 37 of FASB Statement No. 144
FSP FAS 150-1	Issuer's Accounting for Freestanding Financial Instruments Composed of More Than One Option or Forward Contract Embodying Obligations under FASB Statement No. 150
FSP FAS 150-2	Accounting for Mandatorily Redeemable Shares Requiring Redemption by Payment of an Amount That Differs from the Book Value of Those Shares under FASB Statement No. 150
FSP FAS 150-3	Effective Date, Disclosures, and Transition for Mandatorily Redeemable Financial Instruments of Certain Nonpublic Entities and Certain Mandatorily Redeemable Noncontrolling Interests under FASB Statement No. 150
FSP FAS 150-4	Issuers' Accounting for Employee Stock Ownership Plans under FASB Statement No. 150
FSP FIN 45-2	Whether FASB Interpretation No. 45 Provides Support for Subsequently Accounting for a Guarantor's Liability at Fair Value
FSP FIN 46(R)-2	Calculation of Expected Losses under FASB Interpretation No. 46(R)
FSP FIN 46(R)-3	Evaluating Whether as a Group the Holders of the Equity Investment at Risk Lack the Direct or Indirect Ability to Make Decisions about an Entity's Activities through Voting Rights or Similar Rights under FASB Interpretation No. 46(R)
FSP FIN 46(R)-5	Implicit Variable Interests under FASB Interpretation No. 46(R)

Pronouncement	Title
FSP FIN 46(R)-6	Determining the Variability to Be Considered in Applying FASB Interpretation No. 46(R)
FSP FTB 85-4-1	Accounting for Life Settlement Contracts by Third-Party Investors
FSP AAG INV-1 and SOP 94-4-1	Reporting of Fully Benefit-Responsive Investment Contracts Held by Certain Investment Companies Subject to the AICPA Investment Company Guide and Defined-Contribution Health and Welfare and Pension Plans

Appendix E

AMENDMENTS TO APB AND FASB PRONOUNCEMENTS

E1. APB Opinion No. 21, *Interest on Receivables and Payables,* is amended as follows: [Added text is underlined and deleted text is struck out.]

a. Footnote 1 to paragraph 1:

> *Present value* is the sum of the future payments discounted to the present date at an appropriate rate of interest. The Appendix contains a description of the valuation process.

b. Paragraph 13:

> *Determining an appropriate interest rate.* The variety of transactions encountered precludes any specific interest rate from being applicable in all circumstances. However, some general guides may be stated. The choice of a rate may be affected by the credit standing of the issuer, restrictive covenants, the collateral, payment and other terms pertaining to the debt, and, if appropriate, the tax consequences to the buyer and seller. The prevailing rates for similar instruments of issuers with similar credit ratings will normally help determine the appropriate interest rate for determining the present value of a specific note at its date of issuance. In any event, the rate used for valuation purposes will normally be at least equal to should be the rate at which the debtor can obtain financing of a similar nature from other sources at the date of the transaction. For purposes of this Opinion, Tthe objective is to approximate the rate which would have resulted if an independent borrower and an inde-

pendent lender had negotiated a similar transaction under comparable terms and conditions with the option to pay the cash price upon purchase or to give a note for the amount of the purchase which bears the prevailing rate of interest to maturity.

c. Paragraph 18:

> *Present value concepts—discount rate adjustment technique.* Upon issuance of a note or bond, the issuer customarily records as a liability the face or principal amount of the obligation. Ordinarily, the recorded liability also represents the amount which is to be repaid upon maturity of the obligation. The value recorded in the liability account, however, may be different from the proceeds received or the present value of the obligation at issuance if the market rate of interest differs from the coupon rate of interest. For example, consider the issuance of a $1,000, 20-year bond which bears interest at 10% annually. If we assume that 10% is an appropriate market rate of interest for such a bond, the proceeds at issuance will be $1,000. The bond payable would be recorded at $1,000 which represents the amount repayable at maturity and also the present value at issuance which is equal to the proceeds. However, under similar circumstances, if the prevailing market rate were more (less) than 10%, a 20-year 10% bond with a face amount of $1,000 would usually have a value at issuance and provide cash proceeds of less (more) than $1,000. The significant point is that, upon issuance, a bond is valued at (1) the present value of the future coupon interest payments *plus* (2) the present value of the future principal payments (face amount). These two sets of future cash payments are discounted at the prevailing market rate of interest (for an equivalent se-

curity) at the date of issuance of the debt. As the 8% and 12% columns show, premium or dis-count arises when the prevailing market rate of interest differs from the coupon rate:

	Assume prevailing market rate of		
	10%	*8%*	*12%*
1. Present value of annual interest payments of $100 (the coupon rate of 10% of $1,000) for 20 years	$ 851	$ 982	$747
2. Present value of payment of the face amount of $1,000 at the end of year 20	149	215	104
Present value and proceeds at date of issuance	$1,000	$1,197	$851

E2. APB Opinion No. 28, *Interim Financial Reporting,* is amended as follows:

a. Paragraph 30(l) is added as follows:

The information about the use of fair value to measure assets and liabilities recognized in the statement of financial position pursuant to paragraphs 32 and 33 of FASB Statement No. 157, *Fair Value Measurements.*

E3. APB Opinion No. 29, *Accounting for Nonmonetary Transactions,* is amended as follows:

a. Paragraph 18 and its related footnote 5:

The Board concludes that in general accounting for nonmonetary transactions should be based on the fair values[5] of the assets (or services) involved which is the same basis as that used in monetary transactions. Thus, the cost of a nonmonetary asset acquired in exchange for another nonmonetary asset is the fair value of the asset surrendered to obtain it, and a gain or loss should be recognized on the exchange. The fair value of the asset received should be used to measure the cost if it is more clearly evident than the fair value of the asset surrendered. Similarly, a nonmonetary asset received in a nonreciprocal transfer should be recorded at the fair value of the asset received. A transfer of a nonmonetary asset to a stockholder or to another entity in a nonreciprocal transfer should be recorded at the fair value of the asset transferred, and a gain or loss should be recognized on the disposition of the asset. The fair value of an entity's own stock reacquired may be a more clearly evident measure of the fair value of the asset distributed in a nonreciprocal transfer if the transaction involves distribution of a nonmonetary asset to eliminate a disproportionate part of owners' interests (that

is, to acquire stock for the treasury or for retirement). If one of the parties in a nonmonetary transaction could have elected to receive cash instead of the nonmonetary asset, the amount of cash that could have been received may be evidence of the fair value of the nonmonetary assets exchanged.

[5]~~See paragraph 25 for determination of fair value.~~

b. Paragraph 20(a), as amended:

Fair Value Not Determinable. The fair value of neither the asset(s) received nor the asset(s) relinquished is determinable within reasonable limits ~~(paragraph 25)~~.

c. Paragraph 25:

~~Fair value of a nonmonetary asset transferred to or from an enterprise in a nonmonetary transaction should be determined by referring to estimated realizable values in cash transactions of the same or similar assets, quoted market prices, independent appraisals, estimated fair values of assets or services received in exchange, and other available evidence. If one of the parties in a nonmonetary transaction could have elected to receive cash instead of the nonmonetary asset, the amount of cash that could have been received may be evidence of the fair value of the nonmonetary assets exchanged.~~

E4. FASB Statement No. 13, *Accounting for Leases,* is amended as follows:

a. Paragraph 5(c):

Fair value of the leased property. ~~The price for which the property could be sold in an arm's length transaction between unrelated parties.~~The price that would be received to sell the property in an orderly transaction between market participants at the measurement date. Market participants are buyers and sellers that are independent of the reporting entity, that is, they are not related parties at the measurement date. (See definition of related parties in leasing transactions in paragraph 5(a).) The following are examples of the determination of fair value:

[For ease of use, the remainder of this subparagraph, which is unaffected by this Statement, has been omitted.]

E5. FASB Statement No. 15, *Accounting by Debtors and Creditors for Troubled Debt Restructurings,* is amended as follows:

a. Footnote 2 to paragraph 7:

~~Defined in paragraph 13.~~

b. Paragraph 13 and its related footnote 6, as amended, and footnote 5a, as added previously:

A debtor that transfers its receivables from third parties, real estate, or other assets to a creditor to settle fully a payable shall recognize a gain on restructuring of payables. The gain shall be measured by the excess of (i) the carrying amount of the payable settled (the face amount increased or decreased by applicable accrued interest and applicable unamortized premium, discount, finance charges, or issue costs) over (ii) the fair value of the assets transferred to the creditor.[5] ~~The fair value of the assets transferred is the amount that the debtor could reasonably expect to receive for them in a current sale between a willing buyer and a willing seller, that is, other than in a forced or liquidation sale. Fair value of assets shall be measured by their market value if an active market for them exists. If no active market exists for the assets transferred but exists for similar assets, the selling prices in that market may be helpful in estimating the fair value of the assets transferred. If no market price is available, a forecast of expected cash flows[5a] may aid in estimating the fair value of assets transferred, provided the expected cash flows are discounted at a rate commensurate with the risk involved.[6]~~

---

[5]Paragraphs 13, 15, and 19 indicate that the fair value of assets transferred or the fair value of an equity interest granted shall be used in accounting for a settlement of a payable in a troubled debt restructuring. That guidance is not intended to preclude using the fair value of the payable settled if more clearly evident than the fair value of the assets transferred or of the equity interest granted in a full settlement of a payable (paragraphs 13 and 15). (See paragraph 6 of FASB Statement No. 141, *Business Combinations.*) However, in a partial settlement of a payable (paragraph 19), the fair value of the assets transferred or of the equity interest granted shall be used in all cases to avoid the need to allocate the fair value of the payable between the part settled and the part still outstanding.

[5a]~~This pronouncement was issued prior to FASB Concepts Statement No. 7, *Using Cash Flow Information and Present Value in Accounting Measurements,* and therefore the term expected cash flows does not necessarily have the same meaning as that term in Concepts Statement 7.~~

[6]~~Some factors that may be relevant in estimating the fair value of various kinds of assets are described in paragraphs 37 and 38 of Statement 141, paragraphs 12–14 of APB Opinion No. 21, "Interest on Receivables and Payables," and paragraph 25 of APB Opinion No. 29, "Accounting for Nonmonetary Transactions."~~

c. Paragraph 28, as amended:

A creditor that receives from a debtor in full satisfaction of a receivable either (i) receivables from third parties, real estate, or other assets or (ii) shares of stock or other evidence of an equity interest in the debtor, or both, shall account for those assets (including an equity interest) at their fair value at the time of the restructuring ~~(see paragraph 13 for how to measure fair value).~~[16] A creditor that receives long-lived assets that will be sold from a debtor in full satisfaction of a receivable shall account for those assets at their fair value less cost to sell, as that term is used in paragraph 34 of FASB Statement No. 144, *Accounting for the Impairment or Disposal of Long-Lived Assets.* The excess of (i) the recorded investment in the receivable[17] satisfied over (ii) the fair value of assets received (less cost to sell, if required above) is a loss to be recognized. For purposes of this paragraph, losses, to the extent they are not offset against allowances for uncollectible amounts or other valuation accounts, shall be included in measuring net income for the period.

E6. FASB Statement No. 19, *Financial Accounting and Reporting by Oil and Gas Producing Companies,* is amended as follows:

a. Paragraph 47(l)(i), as effectively amended:

If satisfaction of the retained production payment is reasonably assured. The seller of the property, who retained the production payment, shall record the transaction as a sale, with recognition of any resulting gain or loss. The retained production payment shall be recorded as a receivable, with interest accounted for in accordance with the provisions of *APB Opinion No. 21,* "Interest on Receivables and Payables." The purchaser shall record as the cost of the assets acquired the cash consideration paid plus the present value ~~(determined in accordance with *APB Opinion No. 21)*~~ of the retained production payment, which shall be recorded as a payable. The oil and gas reserve estimates and production data, including those applicable to liquidation of the retained production payment, shall be reported by the purchaser of the property (paragraphs 59E–59L).

E7. FASB Statement No. 35, *Accounting and Reporting by Defined Benefit Pension Plans,* is amended as follows:

a. Paragraph 11, as amended, and its related footnotes 4a, as added previously, and 5:

Plan investments, whether equity or debt securities, real estate, or other (excluding insurance contracts) shall be presented at their fair value at the reporting date. ~~The fair value of an investment is the amount that the plan could reasonably expect to receive for it in a current sale between a willing buyer and a willing seller, that is, other than in a forced or liquidation sale. Fair value shall be measured by the market price if there is an active market for the investment. If there is not an active market for an investment but there is such a market for similar investments, selling prices in that market may be helpful in estimating fair value. If a market price is not available, a forecast of expected cash flows~~[4a] ~~may aid in estimating fair value, provided the expected cash flows are discounted at a rate commensurate with the risk involved.~~[5]

[4a]~~This pronouncement was issued prior to FASB Concepts Statement No. 7, *Using Cash Flow Information and Present Value in Accounting Measurements,* and therefore the term expected cash flows does not necessarily have the same meaning as that term in Concepts Statement 7.~~

[5]~~For an indication of factors to be considered in determining the discount rate, see paragraphs 13 and 14 of APB Opinion No. 21, *Interest on Receivables and Payables.* If significant,~~ †The fair value of an investment shall be reduced by ~~reflect the~~ brokerage commissions and other costs normally incurred in a sale if those costs are significant (similar to fair value less cost to sell).

E8. FASB Statement No. 60, *Accounting and Reporting by Insurance Enterprises,* is amended as follows:

a. Paragraph 19 and its related footnote 4a, as added previously:

Real estate acquired in settling mortgage guaranty and title insurance claims shall be reported at fair value. ~~; that is, the amount that reasonably could be expected to be received in a current sale between a willing buyer and a willing seller. If no market price is available, the expected cash flows~~[4a] ~~(anticipated sales price less maintenance and selling costs of the real estate) may aid in estimating fair value provided the cash flows are discounted at a rate commensurate with the risk involved.~~ Real estate acquired in settling claims shall be separately reported in the balance sheet and shall not be classified as an investment. Subsequent reductions in the reported amount and realized gains and losses on the sale of real estate acquired in settling claims shall be recognized as an adjustment to claim costs incurred.

[4a]~~This pronouncement was issued prior to FASB Concepts Statement No. 7, *Using Cash Flow Information and Present Value in Accounting Measurements,* and therefore the term expected cash flows does not necessarily have the same meaning as that term in Concepts Statement 7.~~

E9. FASB Statement No. 63, *Financial Reporting by Broadcasters,* is amended as follows:

a. Paragraph 4:

A licensee shall report the asset and liability for a broadcast license agreement either (a) at the ~~present value of the liability calculated in accordance with the provisions of APB Opinion No. 21, *Interest on Receivables and Payables,*~~ fair value of the liability or (b) at the gross amount of the liability. ~~If the present value approach is used~~ If a present value technique is used to measure fair value, the difference between the gross and net liability shall be accounted for as interest in accordance with ~~Opinion 21~~ APB Opinion No. 21, *Interest on Receivables and Payables.*

b. Paragraph 8:

Broadcasters may **barter** unsold advertising time for products or services. All barter transactions except those involving the exchange of advertising time for network programming[3] shall be reported at the estimated fair value of the product or service received~~, in accordance with the provisions of paragraph 25 of APB Opinion No. 29, *Accounting for Nonmonetary Transactions*~~. Barter revenue shall be reported when commercials are broadcast, and merchandise or services received shall be reported when received or used. If merchandise or services are received prior to the broadcast of the commercial, a liability shall be reported. Likewise, if the commercial is broadcast first, a receivable shall be reported.

c. Paragraph 38:

For purposes of imputing interest ~~in accordance with Opinion 21~~, it is assumed that the $1,000,000 payment on July 31, 19X1 and the $6,000,000 payments on January 1, 19X2 and 19X3 relate to films A and B and the $6,000,000 payment on January 1, 19X4 relates to films C and D. Other simplifying assumptions or methods of assigning the payments to the films could be made.

[For ease of use, the remainder of this paragraph, which is unaffected by this Statement, has been omitted.]

d. Paragraph 39:

Asset and Liability Recognition (~~Present Value Approach~~Fair Value Approach)

[For ease of use, the remainder of this paragraph, which is unaffected by this Statement, has been omitted.]

e. Paragraph 40:

Expense Recognition (~~Present Value Approach~~ Fair Value Approach)

[For ease of use, the remainder of this paragraph, which is unaffected by this Statement, has been omitted.]

E10. FASB Statement No. 65, *Accounting for Certain Mortgage Banking Activities,* is amended as follows:

a. Paragraph 4, as amended:

Mortgage loans held for sale shall be reported at the lower of cost or ~~market~~fair value, determined as of the balance sheet date. If a mortgage

loan has been the hedged item in a fair value hedge, the loan's "cost" basis used in lower-of-cost-or-~~market~~fair value accounting shall reflect the effect of the adjustments of its carrying amount made pursuant to paragraph 22(b) of Statement 133. The amount by which cost exceeds ~~market~~fair value shall be accounted for as a valuation allowance. Changes in the valuation allowances shall be included in the determination of net income of the period in which the change occurs. **Mortgage-backed securities** held by not-for-profit organizations shall be reported at fair value in accordance with the provisions of FASB Statement No. 124, *Accounting for Certain Investments Held by Not-for-Profit Organizations.*

b. Paragraph 6, as amended:

A mortgage loan transferred to a long-term-investment classification shall be transferred at the lower of cost or ~~market~~fair value on the transfer date. Any difference between the carrying amount of the loan and its outstanding principal balance shall be recognized as an adjustment to yield by the interest method.[2] A mortgage loan shall not be classified as a long-term investment unless the mortgage banking enterprise has both the ability and the intent to hold the loan for the foreseeable future or until maturity. After the securitization of a mortgage loan held for sale, any retained mortgage-backed securities shall be classified in accordance with the provisions of FASB Statement No. 115, *Accounting for Certain Investments in Debt and Equity Securities.* However, a mortgage banking enterprise must classify as trading any retained mortgage-backed securities that it commits to sell before or during the securitization process.

c. Paragraph 9, as amended:

The ~~market~~fair value of mortgage loans and mortgage-backed securities held for sale shall be determined by type of loan. At a minimum, separate determinations of ~~market~~fair value for residential (one- to four-family dwellings) and commercial mortgage loans shall be made. Either the aggregate or individual loan basis may be used in determining the lower of cost or ~~market~~fair value for each type of loan. ~~Market~~Fair value for loans subject to investor purchase commitments (committed loans) and loans held on a speculative basis (uncommitted loans)[3] shall be determined separately as follows:

a. *Committed Loans.* ~~Market value for m~~Mortgage loans covered by investor commitments shall be based on ~~fair values~~the fair values of the loans.

b. *Uncommitted Loans.* ~~Market~~Fair value for uncommitted loans shall be based on the market in which the mortgage banking enterprise normally operates. That determination would include consideration of the following:

   (1) [This subparagraph has been deleted. See Status page.]

   (2) Market prices and yields sought by the mortgage banking enterprise's normal market outlets

   (3) Quoted **Government National Mortgage Association (GNMA)** security prices or other public market quotations for long-term mortgage loan rates

   (4) **Federal Home Loan Mortgage Corporation (FHLMC)** and **Federal National Mortgage Association (FNMA)** current delivery prices

c. *Uncommitted Mortgage-Backed Securities.* Fair value for uncommitted mortgage-backed securities that are collateralized by a mortgage banking enterprise's own loans ordinarily shall be based on the ~~market~~fair value of the securities. If the trust holding the loans may be readily terminated and the loans sold directly, fair value for the securities shall be based on the ~~market~~fair value of the loans or the securities, depending on the mortgage banking enterprise's sales intent. Fair value for other uncommitted mortgage-backed securities shall be based on published mortgage-backed securities yields.

d. Paragraph 10, as amended:

Capitalized costs of acquiring rights to service mortgage loans, associated with the purchase or origination of mortgage loans (paragraph 13 of FASB Statement No. 140, *Accounting for Transfers and Servicing of Financial Assets and Extinguishments of Liabilities*), shall be excluded from the cost of mortgage loans for the purpose of determining the lower of cost or ~~market~~fair value.

e. Paragraph 12, as amended:

The carrying amount of mortgage loans to be sold to an **affiliated enterprise** shall be adjusted to the lower of cost or ~~market~~fair value of the loans as of the date management decides that a sale to an affiliated enterprise will occur. The date shall be determined based on, at a minimum, formal approval by an authorized representative of the purchaser, issuance of a commitment to purchase the loans, and acceptance of the commitment by the selling enterprise. The amount of any adjustment shall be charged to income.

f. Paragraph 29, as amended:

The method used in determining the lower of cost or ~~market~~fair value of mortgage loans (that is, aggregate or individual loan basis) shall be disclosed.

E11. FASB Statement No. 67, *Accounting for Costs and Initial Rental Operations of Real Estate Projects,* is amended as follows:

a. Paragraph 8 and its related footnote 6:

Accounting for costs of amenities shall be based on management's plans for the amenities in accordance with the following:

a. If an amenity is to be sold or transferred in connection with the sale of individual units, costs in excess of anticipated proceeds shall be allocated as **common costs** because the amenity is clearly associated with the development and sale of the project. The common costs include expected future operating costs to be borne by the developer until they are assumed by buyers of units in a project.

b. If an amenity is to be sold separately or retained by the developer, capitalizable costs of the amenity in excess of its estimated fair value as of the expected date of its substantial physical completion shall be allocated as common costs. For the purpose of determining the amount to be capitalized as common costs, the amount of cost previously allocated to the amenity shall not be revised after the amenity is substantially completed and available for use. A later sale of the amenity at more or less than its estimated fair value as of the date of substantial physical completion, less any accumulated depreciation, results in a gain or loss that shall be included in net income in the period in which the sale occurs.

Costs of amenities shall be allocated among land parcels[6] benefited and for which development is probable. A land parcel may be considered to be an individual lot or unit, an amenity, or a **phase.** The fair value of a parcel is affected by its physical characteristics, its highest and best use, and the time and cost required for the buyer to make such use of the property considering access, development plans, zoning restrictions, and market absorption factors.

---

[6]~~A land parcel may be considered to be an individual lot or unit, an amenity, or a phase.~~

b. Paragraph 28 (glossary):

~~**Fair Value**~~

~~The amount in cash or cash equivalent value of other consideration that a real estate parcel would yield in a current sale between a willing buyer and a willing seller (i.e., selling price), that is, other than in a forced or liquidation sale. The fair value of a parcel is affected by its physical characteristics, its probable ultimate use, and the time required for the buyer to make such use of the property considering access, development plans, zoning restrictions, and market absorption factors.~~

E12. FASB Statement No. 87, *Employers' Accounting for Pensions,* is amended as follows:

a. Paragraph 49, as amended, and its related footnotes 11a, as added previously, and 12:

For purposes of measuring the minimum liability required by the provisions of paragraph 36 and for purposes of the disclosures required by paragraphs 5 and 8 of FASB Statement No. 132 (revised 2003), *Employers' Disclosures about Pensions and Other Postretirement Benefits,* plan investments, whether equity or debt securities, real estate, or other, shall be measured at their fair value as of the **measurement date.** ~~The fair value of an investment is the amount that the plan could reasonably expect to receive for it in a current sale between a willing buyer and a willing seller, that is, other than in a forced~~

~~or liquidation sale. Fair value shall be measured by the market price if an active market exists for the investment. If no active market exists for an investment but such a market exists for similar investments, selling prices in that market may be helpful in estimating fair value. If a market price is not available, a forecast of expected cash flows[11a] may aid in estimating fair value, provided the expected cash flows are discounted at a current rate commensurate with the risk involved.[12]~~

[11a]~~This pronouncement was issued prior to FASB Concepts Statement No. 7, *Using Cash Flow Information and Present Value in Accounting Measurements,* and therefore the term expected cash flows does not necessarily have the same meaning as that term in Concepts Statement 7.~~

[12]~~For an indication of factors to be considered in determining the discount rate, refer to paragraphs 13 and 14 of APB Opinion No. 21, *Interest on Receivables and Payables.* If significant,~~ tThe fair value of an investment shall be reduced by ~~reflect the~~ brokerage commissions and other costs normally incurred in a sale if those costs are significant (similar to fair value less cost to sell).

b. Paragraph 264 (glossary):

~~**Fair value**~~

~~The amount that a pension plan could reasonably expect to receive for an investment in a current sale between a willing buyer and a willing seller, that is, other than in a forced or liquidation sale.~~

E13. FASB Statement No. 106, *Employers' Accounting for Postretirement Benefits Other Than Pensions,* is amended as follows:

a. Paragraph 65, as amended, and its related footnotes 20a, as added previously, and 21:

For purposes of the disclosures required by paragraphs 5 and 8 of FASB Statement No. 132 (revised 2003), *Employers' Disclosures about Pensions and Other Postretirement Benefits,* plan investments, whether equity or debt securities, real estate, or other, shall be measured at their fair value as of the measurement date. ~~The fair value of an investment is the amount that the plan could reasonably expect to receive for it in a current sale between a willing buyer and a willing seller, that is, other than in a forced or liquidation sale. Fair value shall be measured by the market price if an active market exists for the investment. If no active market exists for an investment but an active market exists for similar investments, selling prices in that market may be~~

~~helpful in estimating fair value. If a market price is not available, a forecast of expected cash flows~~[20a] ~~may aid in estimating fair value, provided the expected cash flows are discounted at a current rate commensurate with the risk involved.~~[21] (Refer to paragraph 71.)

[20a]~~This pronouncement was issued prior to FASB Concepts Statement No. 7, *Using Cash Flow Information and Present Value in Accounting Measurements,* and therefore the term expected cash flows does not necessarily have the same meaning as that term in Concepts Statement 7.~~

[21]~~For an indication of factors to be considered in determining the discount rate, refer to paragraphs 13 and 14 of APB Opinion No. 21, *Interest on Receivables and Payables.* If significant,~~ tThe fair value of an investment shall be reduced by ~~reflect the~~ brokerage commissions and other costs normally incurred in a sale if those costs are significant (similar to fair value less cost to sell).

b. Paragraph 518 (glossary):

Fair value

~~The amount that a plan could reasonably expect to receive for an investment in a current sale between a willing buyer and a willing seller, that is, other than a forced or liquidation sale.~~

E14. FASB Statement No. 107, *Disclosures about Fair Value of Financial Instruments,* is amended as follows:

a. Paragraph 5:

~~For purposes of this Statement, the fair value of a financial instrument is the amount at which the instrument could be exchanged in a current transaction between willing parties, other than in a forced or liquidation sale. If a quoted market price is available for an instrument, the fair value to be disclosed for that instrument is the product of the number of trading units of the instrument times that market price.~~

b. Paragraph 6:

~~Under the definition of fair value in paragraph 5, the quoted price for a single trading unit in the most active market is the basis for determining market price and reporting fair value. This is the case even if placing orders to sell all of an entity's holdings of an asset or to buy back all of a liability might affect the price, or if a market's normal volume for one day might not be sufficient to absorb the quantity held or owed by an entity.~~

c. Paragraph 9:

Generally accepted accounting principles already require disclosure of or subsequent measurement at fair value for many classes of financial instruments. ~~Although the definitions or the methods of estimation of fair value vary to some extent, and various terms such as market value, current value, or mark-to-market are used, the amounts computed under those requirements satisfy the requirements of this Statement and~~ tThose requirements are not superseded or modified by this Statement.

d. Paragraph 10, as amended:

An entity shall disclose, either in the body of the financial statements or in the accompanying notes,[3a] the fair value of financial instruments for which it is practicable to estimate that value. Fair value disclosed in the notes shall be presented together with the related carrying amount in a form that makes it clear whether the fair value and carrying amount represent assets or liabilities and how the carrying amounts relate to what is reported in the statement of financial position. An entity also shall disclose the method(s) and significant assumptions used to estimate the fair value of financial instruments.[3aa]

[3a]If disclosed in more than a single note, one of the notes shall include a summary table. The summary table shall contain the fair value and related carrying amounts and cross-references to the location(s) of the remaining disclosures required by this Statement, as amended.

[3aa]For financial instruments recognized at fair value in the statement of financial position, the disclosure requirements of FASB Statement No. 157, *Fair Value Measurements,* also apply.

e. Paragraph 11:

~~Quoted market prices, if available, are the best evidence of the fair value of financial instruments. If quoted market prices are not available, management's best estimate of fair value may be based on the quoted market price of a financial instrument with similar characteristics or on valuation techniques (for example, the present value of estimated future cash flows using a discount rate commensurate with the risks involved, option pricing models, or matrix pricing models). Appendix A of this Statement contains examples of procedures for estimating fair value.~~

f. Paragraphs 18–29 (Appendix A) are deleted. This appendix provided examples of procedures for estimating the fair value of financial instruments.

g. Paragraph 30:

The examples that follow are guides to implementation of the disclosure requirements of this Statement. Entities are not required to display the information contained herein in the specific manner illustrated. Alternative ways of disclosing the information are permissible as long as they satisfy the disclosure requirements of this Statement. ~~Paragraphs 12 and 21 of this Statement describe possible additional voluntary disclosures that may be appropriate in certain circumstances.~~In some cases, an entity's management may decide to provide further information about the fair value of a financial instrument. For example, an entity may want to explain that although the fair value of its long-term debt is less than the carrying amount, settlement at the reported fair value may not be possible or may not be a prudent management decision for other reasons, or the entity may want to state that potential taxes and other expenses that would be incurred in an actual sale or settlement are not taken into consideration.

h. Paragraph 31, section titled "Commitments to extend credit, standby letters of credit, and financial guarantees written" of Note V:

~~Commitments to extend credit, standby letters of credit, and financial guarantees written~~

~~The fair value of commitments is estimated using the fees currently charged to enter into similar agreements, taking into account the remaining terms of the agreements and the present creditworthiness of the counterparties. For fixed-rate loan commitments, fair value also considers the difference between current levels of interest rates and the committed rates. The fair value of guarantees and letters of credit is based on fees currently charged for similar agreements or on the estimated cost to terminate them or otherwise settle the obligations with the counterparties at the reporting date.~~

E15. FASB Statement No. 115, *Accounting for Certain Investments in Debt and Equity Securities,* is amended as follows:

a. Paragraph 3(a) and its related footnote 2:

The fair value of an equity security is readily determinable if sales prices or bid-and-asked quotations are currently available on a securities exchange registered with the Securities and Exchange Commission (SEC) or in the over-the-counter market, provided that those prices or quotations for the over-the-counter market are publicly reported by the National Association of Securities Dealers Automated Quotations systems or by ~~the National Quotation Bureau~~Pink Sheets LLC. Restricted stock[2] ~~does not meet that definition~~meets that definition if the restriction terminates within one year.

---

[2]The fair value of restricted stock shall be measured based on the quoted price of an otherwise identical unrestricted security of the same issuer, adjusted for the effect of the restriction, in accordance with the provisions of FASB Statement No. 157, *Fair Value Measurements.*~~Restricted stock, for the purpose of this Statement, means equity securities for which sale is restricted by governmental or contractual requirement (other than in connection with being pledged as collateral) except if that requirement terminates within one year or if the holder has the power by contract or otherwise to cause the requirement to be met within one year. Any portion of the security that can be reasonably expected to qualify for sale within one year, such as may be the case under Rule 144 or similar rules of the SEC, is not considered restricted.~~

b. Paragraph 137 (glossary), as amended:

~~Fair value~~

~~The amount at which an asset could be bought or sold in a current transaction between willing parties, that is, other than in a forced or liquidation sale. Quoted market prices in active markets are the best evidence of fair value and should be used as the basis for the measurement, if available. If a quoted market price is available, the fair value is the product of the number of trading units times that market price. If a quoted market price is not available, the estimate of fair value should be based on the best information available in the circumstances. The estimate of fair value should consider prices for similar assets and the results of valuation techniques to the extent available in the circumstances. Examples of valuation techniques include the present value of estimated expected future cash flows using a discount rate commensurate with the risks involved, option-pricing models, matrix pricing, option-adjusted spread models, and fundamental analysis. Valuation techniques for measuring assets should be consistent with the objective of measuring fair value. Those~~

~~techniques should incorporate assumptions that market participants would use in their estimates of values, including assumptions about interest rates, default, prepayment, and volatility.~~

E16. FASB Statement No. 116, *Accounting for Contributions Received and Contributions Made,* is amended as follows:

a. Paragraph 19:

~~Quoted market prices, if available, are the best evidence of the fair value of monetary and nonmonetary assets, including services. If quoted market prices are not available, fair value may be estimated based on quoted market prices for similar assets, independent appraisals, or valuation techniques, such as the present value of estimated future cash flows.~~ Contributions of services that create or enhance nonfinancial assets may be measured by referring to either the fair value of the services received or the fair value of the asset or of the asset enhancement resulting from the services. A major uncertainty about the existence of value may indicate that an item received or given should not be recognized.[7]

b. Paragraph 20:

~~The present value of estimated future cash flows using a discount rate commensurate with the risks involved is an appropriate measure of fair value of unconditional promises to give cash.~~[8] ~~S~~If a present value technique is used to measure the fair value of unconditional promises to give cash, subsequent accruals of the interest element shall be accounted for as contribution income by donees and contribution expense by donors. Not-for-profit organizations shall report the contribution income as an increase in either temporarily or permanently restricted net assets if the underlying promise to give is donor restricted.

---

[8]~~An entity may estimate the future cash flows of a portfolio of short-term promises resulting from a mass fund-raising appeal by using experience it gained from similar appeals.~~

c. Paragraph 184:

Mission G would recognize the contributed property as an asset and as support and measure that property at its fair value (paragraph 8). Information necessary to estimate the fair value of that property could be obtained from various sources, including ~~(a)~~ amounts recently paid for similar properties in the locality, ~~(b) estimates of the market value of the property by local appraisers or real estate brokers, (c) an estimate of the fair value of the property by the local tax assessor's office, or (d) estimates of its replacement cost~~ and estimates of its replacement cost adjusted to reflect the price that would be received for the contributed property ~~(paragraph 19)~~. This contribution is unrestricted support because the donated assets may be used for any purpose and Mission G does not have a policy of implying time restrictions on gifts of long-lived assets (paragraph 16). If Mission G's policy is to imply a time restriction, the contribution is temporarily restricted support and the restriction expires over the useful life of the building.

d. Paragraph 186:

If Museum H capitalizes its collections, Museum H would recognize the fair value of the contributed work of art received as revenue and capitalize it as an asset at its fair value (paragraph~~s~~ 13 ~~and 19~~). ~~The staff of Museum H is qualified to estimate the fair value of the contributed painting and evidence of its fair value exists.~~ If Museum H does not capitalize its collections, Museum H is precluded from recognizing the contribution (paragraph 13) and would provide the information required by paragraphs 26 and 27.

e. Paragraph 208:

The 19X0 communication between Individual R and Church S specified an intention to give. The ability to modify a will at any time prior to death is well established; thus in 19X0 Church S did not receive a promise to give and did not recognize a contribution received. When the probate court declares the will valid, Church S would recognize a receivable and revenue for an unconditional promise to give at the fair value of its interest in the estate (paragraphs 8, 20, and ~~19~~21). If the promise to give contained in the valid will was instead conditioned on a future and uncertain event, Church S would recognize the contribution when the condition was substantially met. A conditional promise in a valid will would be disclosed in notes to financial statements (paragraph 25).

E17. FASB Statement No. 124, *Accounting for Certain Investments Held by Not-for-Profit Organizations,* is amended as follows:

a. Paragraph 3(a) and its related footnote 3:

> Sales prices or bid-and-asked quotations for the security are currently available on a securities exchange registered with the Securities and Exchange Commission (SEC) or in the over-the-counter market, provided that those prices or quotations for the over-the-counter market are publicly reported by the National Association of Securities Dealers Automated Quotations systems or by Pink Sheets LLC~~the National Quotation Bureau~~. Restricted stock[3]~~does not meet that definition~~ meets that definition if the restriction terminates within one year.

> ---

> [3]The fair value of restricted stock shall be measured based on the quoted price of an otherwise identical unrestricted security of the same issuer, adjusted for the effect of the restriction, in accordance with the provisions of FASB Statement No. 157, *Fair Value Measurements.*~~For the purpose of this Statement, restricted stock means equity securities for which sale is restricted at acquisition by governmental or contractual requirement (other than in connection with being pledged as collateral) except if that requirement terminates within one year or if the holder has the power by contract or otherwise to cause the requirement to be met within one year. Any portion of the security that can be reasonably expected to qualify for sale within one year, such as may be the case under Rule 144 or similar rules of the SEC, is not considered restricted.~~

b. Paragraph 112 (glossary), as amended:

> ~~**Fair value**~~

> ~~The amount at which an asset could be bought or sold in a current transaction between willing parties, that is, other than in a forced or liquidation sale. Quoted market prices in active markets are the best evidence of fair value and should be used as the basis for the measurement, if available. If a quoted market price is available, the fair value is the product of the number of trading units times that market price. If a quoted market price is not available, the estimate of fair value should be based on the best information available in the circumstances. The estimate of fair value should consider prices for similar assets and the results of valuation techniques to the extent available in the circumstances. Examples of valuation techniques include the present value of estimated expected future cash flows using a discount rate commensurate with the risks involved,~~ ~~option-pricing models, matrix pricing, option-adjusted spread models, and fundamental analysis. Valuation techniques for measuring assets should be consistent with the objective of measuring fair value. Those techniques should incorporate assumptions that market participants would use in their estimates of values, including assumptions about interest rates, default, prepayment, and volatility.~~

E18. FASB Statement No. 133, *Accounting for Derivative Instruments and Hedging Activities,* is amended as follows:

a. Paragraph 16A, as added previously:

> ~~Any difference between a transaction price and the estimated fair value at the inception of a hybrid financial instrument for which the fair value election is applied shall not be recognized in earnings unless that estimated fair value is (a) obtained from a quoted market price in an active market, or (b) is evidenced by comparison to other observable current market transactions, or (c) is based on a valuation technique incorporating observable market data.~~

b. Paragraph 17, as amended, and its related footnote 6c, as added previously:

> An entity shall recognize all of its derivative instruments in its statement of financial position as either assets or liabilities depending on the rights or obligations under the contracts. All derivative instruments shall be measured at fair value. ~~The guidance in FASB Statement No. 107, *Disclosures about Fair Value of Financial Instruments,* as amended, shall apply in determining the fair value of a financial instrument (derivative or hedged item). If expected future cash flows are used to estimate fair value, those expected cash flows[6c] shall be the best estimate based on reasonable and supportable assumptions and projections. All available evidence shall be considered in developing estimates of expected future cash flows. The weight given to the evidence shall be commensurate with the extent to which the evidence can be verified objectively. If a range is estimated for either the amount or the timing of possible cash flows, the likelihood of possible outcomes shall be considered in determining the best estimate of future cash flows.~~

[6e]~~This Statement was issued prior to FASB Concepts State-~~
~~ment No. 7, *Using Cash Flow Information and Present Value in*~~
~~*Accounting Measurements,* and therefore the term *expected*~~
~~*cash flows* does not necessarily have the same meaning as that~~
~~term does in Concepts Statement 7.~~

c. Paragraph 540 (glossary):

~~**Fair value**~~

~~The amount at which an asset (liability)~~
~~could be bought (incurred) or sold (settled)~~
~~in a current transaction between willing par-~~
~~ties, that is, other than in a forced or liquida-~~
~~tion sale. Quoted market prices in active~~
~~markets are the best evidence of fair value~~
~~and should be used as the basis for the meas-~~
~~urement, if available. If a quoted market~~
~~price is available, the fair value is the prod-~~
~~uct of the number of trading units times that~~
~~market price. If a quoted market price is not~~
~~available, the estimate of fair value should~~
~~be based on the best information available in~~
~~the circumstances. The estimate of fair value~~
~~should consider prices for similar assets or~~
~~similar liabilities and the results of valuation~~
~~techniques to the extent available in the cir-~~
~~cumstances. Examples of valuation tech-~~
~~niques include the present value of estimated~~
~~expected future cash flows using discount~~
~~rates commensurate with the risks involved,~~
~~option-pricing models, matrix pricing,~~
~~option-adjusted spread models, and funda-~~
~~mental analysis. Valuation techniques for~~
~~measuring assets and liabilities should be~~
~~consistent with the objective of measuring~~
~~fair value. Those techniques should incorpo-~~
~~rate assumptions that market participants~~
~~would use in their estimates of values, future~~
~~revenues, and future expenses, including as-~~
~~sumptions about interest rates, default, pre-~~
~~payment, and volatility. In measuring for-~~
~~ward contracts, such as foreign currency~~
~~forward contracts, at fair value by discount-~~
~~ing estimated future cash flows, an entity~~
~~should base the estimate of future cash flows~~
~~on the changes in the forward rate (rather~~
~~than the spot rate). In measuring financial li-~~
~~abilities and nonfinancial derivatives that are~~
~~liabilities at fair value by discounting esti-~~
~~mated future cash flows (or equivalent out-~~
~~flows of other assets), an objective is to use~~
~~discount rates at which those liabilities could~~
~~be settled in an arm's-length transaction.~~

E19. FASB Statement No. 136, *Transfers of Assets
to a Not-for-Profit Organization or Charitable Trust
That Raises or Holds Contributions for Others,* is
amended as follows:

a. Summary:

This Statement requires that a specified beneficiary recognize its rights to the assets held by a
recipient organization as an asset unless the donor has explicitly granted the recipient organization variance power. Those rights are either an
interest in the net assets of the recipient organization, a beneficial interest, or a receivable. If
the beneficiary and the recipient organization are
financially interrelated organizations, the beneficiary is required to recognize its interest in the
net assets of the recipient organization and adjust that interest for its share of the change in net
assets of the recipient organization. If the beneficiary has an unconditional right to receive all or
a portion of the specified cash flows from a
charitable trust or other identifiable pool of assets, the beneficiary is required to recognize that
beneficial interest, measuring and subsequently
remeasuring it at fair value~~, using a valuation~~
~~technique such as the present value of the esti-~~
~~mated expected future cash flows~~. If the recipient organization is explicitly granted variance
power, the specified beneficiary does not recognize its potential for future distributions from the
assets held by the recipient organization. In all
other cases, a beneficiary recognizes its rights as
a receivable.

b. Paragraph 15:

A specified beneficiary shall recognize its rights
to the assets (financial or nonfinancial) held by a
recipient organization as an asset unless the recipient organization is explicitly granted variance power. Those rights are either an interest in
the net assets of the recipient organization, a
beneficial interest, or a receivable. If the beneficiary and the recipient organization are financially interrelated organizations, the beneficiary
shall recognize its interest in the net assets of the
recipient organization and adjust that interest for
its share of the change in net assets of the recipient organization.[6] If the beneficiary has an unconditional right to receive all or a portion of the
specified cash flows from a charitable trust or
other identifiable pool of assets, the beneficiary
shall recognize that beneficial interest, measuring and subsequently remeasuring it at fair

value, using a valuation technique such as the present value of the estimated expected future cash flows. In all other cases, a beneficiary shall recognize its rights to the assets held by a recipient organization as a receivable and contribution revenue in accordance with the provisions of Statement 116 for unconditional promises to give.[7]

c. Paragraph 36:

This Statement does not establish standards for the trustee, National Bank (paragraph 9). Because Museum is unable to influence the operating or financial decisions of the trustee, Museum and National Bank are not financially interrelated organizations (paragraph 13(a)). Therefore, Museum would recognize its asset (a beneficial interest in the trust) and contribution revenue that increases temporarily restricted net assets (paragraph 15). Museum would measure its beneficial interest at fair value, using a valuation technique such as the present value of the estimated expected future cash receipts from the trust's assets (paragraph 15). That value generally can be measured by the fair value of the assets contributed to the trust.

E20. FASB Statement No. 140, *Accounting for Transfers and Servicing of Financial Assets and Extinguishments of Liabilities,* is amended as follows:

a. Paragraph 11(c):

Initially measure at fair value assets obtained and liabilities incurred in a sale (paragraphs 68–70) or, if it is not practicable to estimate the fair value of an asset or a liability, apply alternative measures (paragraphs 71 and 72)

b. Paragraph 17(h), as amended:

If the entity has securitized financial assets during any period presented and accounts for that transfer as a sale, for each major asset type (for example, mortgage loans, credit card receivables, and automobile loans):

(1) Its accounting policies for initially measuring the interests that continue to be held by the transferor, if any, and servicing assets or servicing liabilities, if any, including the methodology (whether quoted market price, prices based on sales of similar assets

and liabilities, or prices based on valuation techniques) used in determining their fair value (paragraphs 68–70)

[For ease of use, the remainder of this subparagraph, which is unaffected by this Statement, has been omitted.]

c. Paragraph 17(i), as amended:

If the entity has interests that continue to be held by the transferor in financial assets that it has securitized or servicing assets or liabilities relating to assets that it has securitized, at the date of the latest statement of financial position presented, for each major asset type (for example, mortgage loans, credit card receivables, and automobile loans):

(1) Its accounting policies for subsequently measuring those retained interests, including the methodology (whether quoted market price, prices based on sales of similar assets and liabilities, or prices based on valuation techniques) used in determining their fair value (paragraphs 68–70)

(2) The key assumptions used in subsequently measuring the fair value of those interests (including, at a minimum, quantitative information about discount rates, expected prepayments including the expected weighted-average life of prepayable financial assets, and anticipated credit losses, including expected static pool losses,[9] if applicable)[9a]

---

[9]Expected static pool losses can be calculated by summing the actual and projected future credit losses and dividing the sum by the original balance of the pool of assets.

[9a]The timing and amount of future cash flows for retained interests in securitizations are commonly uncertain, especially if those interests are subordinate to more senior beneficial interests. Thus, estimates of future cash flows used for a fair value measurement depend heavily on assumptions about default and prepayment of all the assets securitized, because of the implicit credit or prepayment risk enhancement arising from the subordination.

[For ease of use, the remainder of this subparagraph, which is unaffected by this Statement, has been omitted.]

d. Paragraph 63(b):

Initially measure servicing assets and servicing liabilities at fair value, if practicable (paragraphs 10, 11(b), 11(c), 71, and 68–72).

e. Paragraphs 68–70 and the heading preceding paragraph 68 and footnotes 20 and 21 to paragraph 69, as amended:

~~Fair Value~~

~~68. The fair value of an asset (or liability) is the amount at which that asset (or liability) could be bought (or incurred) or sold (or settled) in a current transaction between willing parties, that is, other than in a forced or liquidation sale. Quoted market prices in active markets are the best evidence of fair value and shall be used as the basis for the measurement, if available. If a quoted market price is available, the fair value is the product of the number of trading units times that market price.~~

~~69. If quoted market prices are not available, the estimate of fair value shall be based on the best information available in the circumstances. The estimate of fair value shall consider prices for similar assets and liabilities and the results of valuation techniques to the extent available in the circumstances. Examples of valuation techniques include the present value of estimated future cash flows,~~[20] ~~option-pricing models, matrix pricing, option-adjusted spread models, and fundamental analysis. Valuation techniques for measuring financial assets and liabilities and servicing assets and liabilities shall be consistent with the objective of measuring fair value. Those techniques shall incorporate assumptions that market participants would use in their estimates of values, future revenues, and future expenses, including assumptions about interest rates, default, prepayment, and volatility.~~[21] ~~In measuring **financial liabilities** and servicing liabilities at fair value, the objective is to estimate the value of the assets required currently to (a) settle the liability with the holder or (b) transfer a liability to an entity of comparable credit standing.~~

~~70. Estimates of expected future cash flows, if used to estimate fair value, shall be based on reasonable and supportable assumptions and projections. All available evidence shall be considered in developing estimates of expected future cash flows. The weight given to the evidence shall be commensurate with the extent to which the evidence can be verified objectively. If a range is estimated for either the amount or timing of possible cash flows, the likelihood of pos-~~ ~~sible outcomes shall be considered either directly, if applying an expected cash flow approach, or indirectly through the risk-adjusted discount rate, if determining the best estimate of future cash flows.~~

~~[20]FASB Concepts Statement No. 7, *Using Cash Flow Information and Present Value in Accounting Measurements*, discusses the use of present value techniques in measuring the fair value of an asset (or liability) in paragraphs 42–54 and 75–88. The Board believes that an expected present value technique is superior to traditional "best-estimate" techniques, especially in situations in which the timing or amount of estimated cash flows is uncertain, as is often the case for interests that continue to be held by a transferor in transferred financial assets. Concepts Statement 7 also discusses in paragraph 44 the steps needed to complete a proper search for the "rate commensurate with the risk" in applying the traditional technique.~~

~~[21]The timing and amount of future cash flows for interests in securitizations that continue to be held by a transferor are commonly uncertain, especially if those interests are subordinate to more senior beneficial interests. Applying the present value approach depends heavily on assumptions about default and prepayment of all the assets securitized, because of the implicit credit or prepayment risk enhancement arising from the subordination.~~

f. Paragraph 364 (glossary):

~~**Fair value**~~

~~Refer to paragraphs 68–70.~~

E21. FASB Statement No. 141, *Business Combinations,* is amended as follows:

a. Paragraph F1 (glossary):

Fair value

~~The amount at which an asset (or liability) could be bought (or incurred) or sold (or settled) in a current transaction between willing parties, that is, other than in a forced or liquidation sale.~~

E22. FASB Statement No. 142, *Goodwill and Other Intangible Assets,* is amended as follows:

a. Paragraph 3:

Appendix A to this Statement provides implementation guidance on how intangible assets should be accounted for in accordance with this Statement. Appendix A is an integral part of the standards provided in this Statement. Appendix B provides background information and the basis for the Board's conclusions. Appendix C provides illustrations of some of the financial statement disclosures that this Statement requires. Appendix D lists other accounting pronouncements superseded or amended by this Statement. ~~Appendix E includes relevant excerpts from FASB Concepts Statement No. 7, *Using Cash Flow Information and Present Value in Accounting Measurements*.~~ Appendix F provides a glossary of terms used in this Statement.

b. Footnote 12 to paragraph 17:

~~The fair value of an intangible asset shall be estimated using the guidance in paragraphs 23–25 (except the guidance specific to estimating the fair value of a **reporting unit**).~~

c. Paragraph 19:

The first step of the goodwill impairment test, used to identify potential impairment, compares the fair value of a reporting unit with its carrying amount, including goodwill. ~~The guidance in paragraphs 23–25 shall be used to determine~~The guidance in paragraphs 23 and 25 shall be considered in determining the fair value of a reporting unit. If the fair value of a reporting unit exceeds its carrying amount, goodwill of the reporting unit is considered not impaired, thus the second step of the impairment test is unnecessary. If the carrying amount of a reporting unit exceeds its fair value, the second step of the goodwill impairment test shall be performed to measure the amount of impairment loss, if any.

d. Paragraph 23 and its related footnote 16:

~~The fair value of an asset (or liability) is the amount at which that asset (or liability) could be bought (or incurred) or sold (or settled) in a current transaction between willing parties, that is, other than in a forced or liquidation sale. Thus, the fair value of a reporting unit refers to the amount at which the unit as a whole could be bought or sold in a current transaction between willing parties.~~ The fair value of a reporting unit refers to the price that would be received to sell the unit as a whole in an orderly transaction between market participants at the measurement date. Quoted market prices in active markets are the best evidence of fair value and shall be used as the basis for the measurement, if available. However, the market price of an individual equity security (and thus the market capitalization

of a reporting unit with publicly traded equity securities) may not be representative of the fair value of the reporting unit as a whole.[16] Substantial value may arise from the ability to take advantage of synergies and other benefits that flow from control over another entity. Consequently, measuring the fair value of a collection of assets and liabilities that operate together in a controlled entity is different from measuring the fair value of that entity's individual equity securities. An acquiring entity often is willing to pay more for equity securities that give it a controlling interest than an investor would pay for a number of equity securities representing less than a controlling interest. That control premium may cause the fair value of a reporting unit to exceed its market capitalization. The quoted market price of an individual equity security, therefore, need not be the sole measurement basis of the fair value of a reporting unit.

---

[16]~~Substantial value may arise from the ability to take advantage of synergies and other benefits that flow from control over another entity. Consequently, measuring the fair value of a collection of assets and liabilities that operate together in a controlled entity is different from measuring the fair value of that entity's individual equity securities. An acquiring entity often is willing to pay more for equity securities that give it a controlling interest than an investor would pay for a number of equity securities representing less than a controlling interest. That control premium may cause the fair value of a reporting unit to exceed its market capitalization.~~

e. Paragraph 24:

~~If quoted market prices are not available, the estimate of fair value shall be based on the best information available, including prices for similar assets and liabilities and the results of using other valuation techniques. A present value technique is often the best available technique with which to estimate the fair value of a group of net assets (such as a reporting unit). If a present value technique is used to measure fair value, estimates of future cash flows used in that technique shall be consistent with the objective of measuring fair value. Those cash flow estimates shall incorporate assumptions that marketplace participants would use in their estimates of fair value. If that information is not available without undue cost and effort, an entity may use its own assumptions. Those cash flow estimates shall be based on reasonable and supportable assumptions and shall consider all available evidence. The weight given to the evidence shall be commensurate with the extent to which the evidence can be verified objectively. If a range is~~

~~estimated for the amounts or timing of possible cash flows, the likelihood of possible outcomes shall be considered. Concepts Statement 7 discusses the essential elements of a present value measurement (paragraph 23), provides examples of circumstances in which an entity's cash flows might differ from the market cash flows (paragraph 32), and discusses the use of present value techniques in measuring the fair value of an asset or a liability (paragraphs 39–54 and 75–88). Appendix E of this Statement incorporates those paragraphs of Concepts Statement 7.~~

f. Appendix E is deleted. This appendix provided excerpts from FASB Concepts Statement No. 7, *Using Cash Flow Information and Present Value in Accounting Measurements.*

g. Paragraph F1 (glossary):

    ~~**Fair value**~~

    ~~The amount at which an asset (or liability) could be bought (or incurred) or sold (or settled) in a current transaction between willing parties, that is, other than in a forced or liquidation sale.~~

E23. FASB Statement No. 143, *Accounting for Asset Retirement Obligations,* is amended as follows:

a. Paragraphs 6 and 7 and footnote 5 to paragraph 6:

    ~~6. Statement 5 and FASB Concepts Statement No. 7, *Using Cash Flow Information and Present Value in Accounting Measurements,* deal with uncertainty in different ways. Statement 5 deals with uncertainty about whether a loss has been incurred by setting forth criteria to determine when to *recognize* a loss contingency. Concepts Statement 7 addresses measurement of liabilities and provides a *measurement* technique to deal with uncertainties about the amount and timing of the future cash flows necessary to settle the liability. Paragraphs 55–61 of Concepts Statement 7[5] discuss, in detail, the relationship between the fair value measurement objective and expected cash flow approach that is articulated in Concepts Statement 7 and accounting for contingencies under Statement 5. The guidance in Statement 5 and FASB Interpretation No. 14, *Reasonable Estimation of the Amount of a Loss,* are not applicable to a liability for which the objective is to measure that liabil-~~ ~~ity at fair value. That is because in Statement 5 uncertainty is used to decide whether to recognize a liability, whereas in Concepts Statement 7 uncertainties in the amount and timing of settlement are incorporated into the fair value measurement of the recognized liability. This Statement requires that all asset retirement obligations within the scope of this Statement be recognized when a reasonable estimate of fair value can be made.~~

    ~~7. The fair value of a liability for an asset retirement obligation is the amount at which that liability could be settled in a current transaction between willing parties, that is, other than in a forced or liquidation transaction. Quoted market prices in active markets are the best evidence of fair value and shall be used as the basis for the measurement, if available. If quoted market prices are not available, the estimate of fair value shall be based on the best information available in the circumstances, including prices for similar liabilities and the results of present value (or other valuation) techniques.~~

~~[5]Appendix F incorporates those paragraphs.~~

b. Paragraph 8 and its related footnotes 6 and 7;

    An expected present value technique[6] will usually be the only appropriate ~~is often the best available~~ technique with which to estimate the fair value of a liability for an asset retirement obligation.[6a] An entity, when using that technique, shall discount the expected cash flows using a credit-adjusted risk-free rate. Thus, the effect of an entity's credit standing is reflected in the discount rate rather than in the expected cash flows. ~~If a present value technique is used to estimate fair value, estimates of future cash flows used in that technique shall be consistent with the objective of measuring fair value.[7] Concepts Statement 7 discusses two present value techniques: a traditional approach, in which a single set of estimated cash flows and a single interest rate (a rate commensurate with the risk) are used to estimate fair value, and an expected cash flow approach, in which multiple cash flow scenarios that reflect the range of possible outcomes and a credit-adjusted risk-free rate are used to estimate fair value. Although either present value technique could theoretically be used for a fair value measurement, the expected cash flow approach will usually be the only appropriate technique~~

~~for an asset retirement obligation. As discussed in paragraph 44 of Concepts Statement 7, proper application of a traditional approach entails analysis of at least two liabilities—one that exists in the marketplace and has an observable interest rate and the liability being measured. The appropriate rate of interest for the cash flows being measured must be inferred from the observable rate of interest of some other liability, and to draw that inference the characteristics of the cash flows must be similar to those of the liability being measured. It would be rare, if ever, that there would be an observable rate of interest for a liability that has cash flows similar to an asset retirement obligation being measured. In addition, an asset retirement obligation will usually have uncertainties in both timing and amount. In that circumstance, employing a traditional present value technique, where uncertainty is incorporated into the rate, will be difficult, if not impossible.~~

~~[6]Appendix F incorporates paragraphs 39–54 and 75–88 of Concepts Statement 7 that discuss present value techniques.~~

[6a]Proper application of a discount rate adjustment technique entails analysis of at least two liabilities—the liability that exists in the marketplace and has an observable interest rate and the liability being measured. The appropriate rate of interest for the cash flows being measured must be inferred from the observable rate of interest of some other liability, and to draw that inference the characteristics of the cash flows must be similar to those of the liability being measured. Rarely, if ever, would there be an observable rate of interest for a liability that has cash flows similar to an asset retirement obligation being measured. In addition, an asset retirement obligation usually will have uncertainties in both timing and amount. In that circumstance, employing a discount rate adjustment technique, where uncertainty is incorporated into the rate, will be difficult, if not impossible.

~~[7]Appendix F incorporates paragraph 23 of Concepts Statement 7 that discusses the essential elements of a fair value measurement.~~

c. Paragraph 9 and its related footnote 8:

~~The cash flows used in estimates of fair value shall incorporate assumptions that marketplace participants would use in their estimates of fair value whenever that information is available without undue cost and effort. Otherwise, an entity may use its own assumptions.[8] Those estimates shall be based on reasonable and supportable assumptions and shall consider all available evidence. The weight given to the evidence shall be commensurate with the extent to which the evidence can be verified objectively. If a range is estimated for the timing or the amount of possible cash flows, the likelihood of possible outcomes shall be considered. An entity, when using the expected cash flow technique, shall discount the estimated cash flows using a credit-adjusted risk-free rate. Thus, the effect of the entity's credit standing is reflected in the discount rate rather than in the estimated cash flows.~~

~~[8]Paragraph 32 of Concepts Statement 7 (included in Appendix F) provides reasons why an entity's assumptions may differ from those expected by others in the marketplace.~~

d. Footnote 12 to paragraph 14:

The subsequent measurement provisions require an entity to identify undiscounted estimated cash flows associated with the initial measurement of a liability. Therefore, an entity that obtains an initial measurement of fair value from a market price or from a technique other than ~~the expected cash flow approach described in Concepts Statement 7~~ an expected present value technique must determine the undiscounted cash flows and estimated timing of those cash flows that are embodied in that fair value amount for purposes of applying the subsequent measurement provisions. Appendix E includes an example of the subsequent measurement of a liability that is initially obtained from a market price.

e. Paragraph A19:

~~The objective of the initial measurement of a liability for an asset retirement obligation shall be fair value. Quoted market prices are the best representation of fair value. When market prices are not available, the amount of the liability must be estimated using some other measurement technique. The use of an expected present value technique in measuring the fair value of a liability is discussed in Concepts Statement 7.~~

f. Paragraph A20 and its related footnote 17:

In estimating the fair value of a liability for an asset retirement obligation using an expected present value technique, an entity shall begin by estimating the expected cash flows that reflect, to the extent possible, a marketplace assessment of the cost and timing of performing the required retirement activities. ~~The measurement objective is to determine the amount a third party[17] would demand to assume the obligation.~~ Considerations in estimating those expected cash flows include developing and incorporating explicit assumptions, to the extent possible, about all of the following:

a. The costs that a third party would incur in performing the tasks necessary to retire the asset

b. Other amounts that a third party would include in determining the price of ~~settlement~~ the transfer, including, for example, inflation, overhead, equipment charges, profit margin, and advances in technology

c. The extent to which the amount of a third party's costs or the timing of its costs would vary under different future scenarios and the relative probabilities of those scenarios

d. The price that a third party would demand and could expect to receive for bearing the uncertainties and unforeseeable circumstances inherent in the obligation, sometimes referred to as a market-risk premium.

It is expected that uncertainties about the amount and timing of future cash flows can be accommodated by using the expected ~~cash flow~~ present value technique and therefore will not prevent the determination of a reasonable estimate of fair value.

---

[17]~~In this context, a third party is meant to encompass participants (or hypothetical participants) that provide settlement of asset retirement obligations in a market.~~

g. Paragraph A21 and its related footnotes 18 and 19:

An entity shall discount ~~estimates of future~~ expected cash flows using an interest rate that equates to a risk-free interest rate adjusted for the effect of its credit standing (a credit-adjusted risk-free rate).[18] ~~The risk-free interest rate is the interest rate on monetary assets that are essentially risk free and that have maturity dates that coincide with the expected timing of the estimated cash flows required to satisfy the asset retirement obligation.[19] Concepts Statement 7 illustrates an adjustment to the risk-free interest rate to reflect the credit standing of the entity, but acknowledges that a~~ Adjustments for default risk can be reflected in either the discount rate or the ~~estimated~~ expected cash flows. The Board believes that in most situations, an entity will know the adjustment required to the risk-free interest rate to reflect its credit standing. Consequently, it would be easier and less complex to reflect that adjustment in the discount rate. In addition, be-

cause of the requirements in paragraph 15 relating to upward and downward adjustments in expected cash flows ~~cash flow estimates~~, it is essential to the operationality of this Statement that the credit standing of the entity be reflected in the ~~interest~~ discount rate. For those reasons, the Board chose to require that the risk-free rate be adjusted for the credit standing of the entity to determine the discount rate.

---

[18]In determining the adjustment for the effect of its credit standing, an entity should consider the effects of all terms, collateral, and existing guarantees ~~that would affect the amount required to settle~~ on the fair value of the liability.

[19]~~In the United States, the risk-free rate is the rate for zero-coupon U.S. Treasury instruments.~~

h. Paragraph A26:

Revisions to a previously recorded asset retirement obligation will result from changes in the assumptions used to estimate the expected cash flows required to settle the asset retirement obligation, including changes in estimated probabilities, amounts, and timing of the settlement of the asset retirement obligation, as well as changes in the legal requirements of an obligation. Any changes that result in upward revisions to the ~~undiscounted estimated~~ expected cash flows shall be treated as a new liability and discounted at the current rate. Any downward revisions to the ~~undiscounted estimated~~ expected cash flows will result in a reduction of the asset retirement obligation. For downward revisions, the amount of the liability to be removed from the existing accrual shall be discounted at the credit-adjusted risk-free rate that was used at the time the obligation to which the downward revision relates was originally recorded (or the historical weighted-average rate if the year(s) to which the downward revision applies cannot be determined).

i. Paragraph C1:

This appendix includes four examples that illustrate the recognition and measurement provisions of this Statement. Example 1 illustrates (a) initial measurement of a liability for an asset retirement obligation using an expected present value technique, (b) subsequent measurement assuming that there are no changes in ~~estimated~~ expected cash flows, and (c) settlement of the asset retirement obligation liability (ARO liability) at the end of its term. Example 2 is similar to

Example 1. However, Example 2 illustrates subsequent measurement of an ARO liability after a change in ~~estimated~~expected cash flows. Example 3 highlights the recognition and measurement provisions of this Statement for an ARO liability that is incurred over more than one reporting period. Example 4 illustrates accounting for asset retirement obligations that are conditional and that have a low likelihood of enforcement.

j. Paragraph C3(d):

A contractor would typically demand and receive a premium (market risk premium) for bearing the uncertainty and unforeseeable circumstances inherent in "locking in" today's price for a project that will not occur for 10 years. The entity estimates the amount of that premium to be 5 percent of the ~~estimated inflation-adjusted cash flows~~expected cash flows adjusted for inflation.

k. Paragraph C4:

On December 31, 2012, the entity settles its asset retirement obligation by using its internal workforce at a cost of $351,000. Assuming no changes during the 10-year period in the expected cash flows used to estimate the obligation, the entity would recognize a gain of $89,619 on settlement of the obligation:

Labor	$195,000
Allocated overhead and equipment charges (80 percent of labor)	156,000
Total costs incurred	351,000
ARO liability	440,619
Gain on settlement of obligation	$ 89,619

Initial Measurement of the ARO Liability at January 1, 2003

	Expected Cash Flows 1/1/03
Expected labor costs	$131,250
Allocated overhead and equipment charges (.80 × $131,250)	105,000
Contractor's markup [.20 × ($131,250 + $105,000)]	47,250
Expected cash flows before inflation adjustment	283,500
Inflation factor assuming 4 percent rate for 10 years	1.4802
Expected cash flows adjusted for inflation	419,637
Market-risk premium (.05 × $419,637)	20,982
Expected cash flows adjusted for market risk	$440,619
~~Expected P~~present value using credit-adjusted risk-free rate of 8.5 percent for 10 years	$194,879

[For ease of use, the rest of this example, which is unaffected by this Statement, has been omitted.]

l. Paragraph C6:

On December 31, 2004, the entity revises its estimate of labor costs to reflect an increase of 10 percent in the marketplace. In addition, it revises the probability assessments related to those labor costs. The change in labor costs results in an upward revision to the ~~undiscounted~~ expected cash flows; consequently, the incremental expected cash flows are discounted at the current credit-adjusted risk-free rate of 8 percent. All other assumptions remain unchanged. The revised estimate of expected cash flows for labor costs is as follows:

Cash Flow Estimate	Probability Assessment	Expected Cash Flows
$110,000	30%	$ 33,000
137,500	45	61,875
192,500	25	48,125
		$143,000

m. Paragraph C7:

[For ease of use, only the portion of this example affected by this Statement has been reproduced.]

Subsequent Measurement of the ARO Liability Reflecting a Change in Labor Cost Estimate as of December 31, 2004

	~~Revised~~ Incremental Expected Cash Flows 12/31/04
Incremental expected labor costs ($143,000 – $131,250)	$11,750
Allocated overhead and equipment charges (.80 × $11,750)	9,400
Contractor's markup [.20 × ($11,750 + $9,400)]	4,230
Expected cash flows before inflation adjustment	25,380
Inflation factor assuming 4 percent rate for 8 years	1.3686
Expected cash flows adjusted for inflation	34,735
Market-risk premium (.05 × $34,735)	1,737
Expected cash flows adjusted for market risk	$36,472
Expected Ppresent value of incremental liability using credit-adjusted risk-free rate of 8 percent for 8 years	$19,704

n. Paragraph C8:

Example 3 depicts an entity that places a nuclear utility plant into service on December 31, 2003. The entity is legally required to decommission the plant at the end of its useful life, which is estimated to be 20 years. Based on the requirements of this Statement, the entity recognizes a liability for an asset retirement obligation and capitalizes an amount for an asset retirement cost over the life of the plant as contamination occurs. The following schedule reflects the ~~un-discounted~~ expected cash flows and respective credit-adjusted risk-free rates used to measure each portion of the liability through December 31, 2005, at which time the plant is 90 percent contaminated.

Date	~~Undiscounted~~ Expected Cash Flows	Credit-Adjusted Risk-Free Rate
12/31/03	$23,000	9.0%
12/31/04	1,150	8.5
12/31/05	1,900	9.2

o. Paragraph C9:

On December 31, 2005, the entity increases by 10 percent its estimate of ~~undiscounted~~ expected cash flows that were used to measure those portions of the liability recognized on December 31, 2003, and December 31, 2004. ~~Because the change results in an upward revision to the undiscounted estimated cash flows, the incremental estimated cash flow is discounted at the current credit-adjusted risk-free rate of 9.2 percent. As a result, $2,300 (10 percent of $23,000) plus $115 (10 percent of $1,150) plus $1,900 (resulting from contamination in 2005), which totals $4,315 of incremental undiscounted cash flows are discounted at the then current credit-adjusted risk-free rate of 9.2 percent and recorded as a liability on December 31, 2005.,~~ which results in an upward revision to the expected cash flows. Accordingly, the incremental expected cash flows of $2,415 [$2,300 (10 percent of $23,000) plus $115 (10 percent of $1,150)] are discounted at the then-current credit-adjusted risk-free rate of 9.2 percent and recorded as a liability on December 31, 2005.

[For ease of use, only the portion of this example affected by this Statement has been reproduced.]

	Date Incurred		
	12/31/03	12/31/04	12/31/05
Initial measurement of the ARO liability:			
Expected cash flows adjusted for market risk	$23,000	$1,150	$1,900
Credit-adjusted risk-free rate	9.00%	8.50%	9.20%
Discount period in years	20	19	18
Expected present value	$4,104	$244	$390
Measurement of ~~incremental~~revision in expected cash flows occurring on December 31, 2005:			
~~Incremental~~Revision in expected cash flows (increase of 10 percent) ~~[($23,000 × 10%) + ($1,150 × 10%)]~~			$2,415
Credit-adjusted risk-free rate at December 31, 2005			9.20%
Discount period remaining in years			18
Expected present value			$495

Carrying Amount of Liability Incurred in 2005
Plus Effect of Change in ~~Estimated~~Expected Cash Flows

Year	Liability Balance 1/1	Accretion (9.2%)	Change in ~~Cash Flow~~ Estimate	New Liability	Liability Balance 12/31
2005			$495	$390	$885

Carrying Amount of Total Liability

Year	Liability Balance 1/1	Accretion	Change in ~~Cash Flow~~ Estimate	New Liability	Total Carrying Amount 12/31
2003				$4,104	$4,104
2004	$4,104	$369		244	4,717
2005	4,717	424	$495	390	6,026

p. Paragraph C11:

At the end of the first year, 20 percent of the timber has been harvested. The lessee estimates that the ~~fair value of~~possible cash flows associated with performing reforestation activities in 4 years for the portion of the land that has been harvested will be $300,000. When estimating the fair value of the ARO liability to be recorded (using an expected present value technique), the lessee incorporates the probability that the restoration provisions will not be enforced:

Possible Cash Flows ~~Estimate~~	Probability Assessment	Expected Cash Flows
$300,000	10%	$30,000
0	90	0
		$30,000

Expected ~~P~~present value using credit-adjusted risk-free rate of 8.5 percent for 4 years $21,647

q. Paragraph C12:

During the term of the lease, the lessee should reassess the likelihood that the lessor will require reforestation. For example, if the lessee subsequently determines that the likelihood of the lessor electing the reforestation option has increased, that change will result in a change in the ~~estimate of future~~ expected cash flows and be accounted for as illustrated in Example 2.

r. Appendix F is deleted. This appendix provided excerpts from Concepts Statement 7.

E24. FASB Statement No. 144, *Accounting for the Impairment or Disposal of LongLived Assets,* is amended as follows:

a. Paragraph 22 and its related footnote 12:

~~The fair value of an asset (liability) is the amount at which that asset (liability) could be bought (incurred) or sold (settled) in a current transaction between willing parties, that is, other than in a forced or liquidation sale.[12] Quoted market prices in active markets are the best evidence of fair value and shall be used as the basis for the measurement, if available. However, in many instances, quoted market prices in active markets will not be available for the long-lived assets (asset groups) covered by this Statement. In those instances, the estimate of fair value shall be based on the best information available, including prices for similar assets (groups) and the results of using other valuation techniques.~~

~~[12]The fair value of an asset or a disposal group refers to the amount at which the group as a whole could be bought or sold in a current single transaction. Therefore, the fair value of the group would not necessarily equate to the sum of the fair values of the individual assets and liabilities of the group.~~

b. Paragraph 23 and its related footnote 13:

~~A present value technique is often the best available valuation technique with which to estimate the fair value of a long-lived asset (asset group). Paragraphs 39–54 of FASB Concepts Statement No. 7, *Using Cash Flow Information and Present Value in Accounting Measurements*, discuss the use of two present value techniques to measure the fair value of an asset (liability).[13] The first is expected present value, in which multiple cash flow scenarios that reflect the range of possible outcomes and a risk-free rate are used to estimate fair value. The second is traditional present value, in which a single set of estimated cash flows and a single interest rate (a rate commensurate with the risk) are used to estimate fair value. Either present value technique can be used for a fair value measurement. However, f~~For long-lived assets (asset groups) that have uncertainties both in timing and amount, an expected present value technique will often be the appropriate technique with which to estimate fair value. (Example 4 of Appendix A illustrates the use of that technique.)

---

[13]~~Appendix E incorporates those paragraphs of Concepts Statement 7.~~

c. Paragraph 24 and its related footnote 14:

~~If a present value technique is used, estimates of future cash flows shall be consistent with the objective of measuring fair value. Assumptions that marketplace participants would use in their estimates of fair value shall be incorporated whenever that information is available without undue cost and effort.[14] Otherwise, the entity may use its own assumptions.~~

---

[14]~~Concepts Statement 7 discusses the essential elements of a present value measurement (paragraph 23) and provides reasons why an entity's estimates of cash flows might differ from~~ ~~those used by marketplace participants (paragraph 32). Appendix E incorporates those paragraphs.~~

d. Paragraph A6:

At December 31, 20X2, a manufacturing facility with a carrying amount of $48 million is tested for recoverability. At that date, 2 courses of action to recover the carrying amount of the facility are under consideration—sell in 2 years or sell in 10 years (at the end of its remaining useful life).~~of 10 years. The facility has identifiable cash flows that are largely independent of the cash flows of other assets.~~

e. Paragraph A7:

As indicated in the following table, the possible cash flows associated with each of those courses of action are $41 million and $48.7 million, respectively. They are developed based on entity-specific assumptions about future sales (volume and price) and costs in varying scenarios that consider the likelihood that existing customer relationships will continue, changes in economic (market) conditions, and other relevant factors.~~The following table shows the range and probability of possible estimated cash flows expected to result from the use and eventual disposition of the facility assuming that (a) it is sold at the end of 2 years or (b) it is sold at the end of 10 years. Among other things, the range of possible estimated cash flows considers future sales levels (volume and price) and associated manufacturing costs in varying scenarios that consider (a) the likelihood that existing customer relationships will continue and (b) future economic (market) conditions. The probability assessments consider all information available without undue cost and effort. Such assessments are by their nature subjective and, in many situations, may be limited to management's best judgment about the probabilities of the best, worst, and most-likely scenarios.~~

Course of Action	Cash Flows Estimate (Use)	Cash Flows Estimate (Disposition)	Cash Flows Estimate (Total)	Probability Assessment	Possible Cash Flows (Probability-Weighted) Cash Flows
			(in $ millions)		
Sell in 2 years	$ 8	$30	$38	20%	$ 7.6
	11	30	41	50	20.5
	13	30	43	30	12.9
					$41.0
Sell in 10 years	36	1	37	20	$ 7.4
	48	1	49	50	24.5
	55	1	56	30	16.8
					$48.7

f. Paragraph A8:

In computing the future cash flows used to test the facility for recoverability, the entity concludes that there is (a) a 60 percent probability that the facility will be sold at the end of 2 years and (b) a 40 percent probability that the facility will continue to be used for its remaining estimated useful life of 10 years.As further indicated in the following table, there is a 60 percent probability that the facility will be sold in 2 years and a 40 percent probability that the facility will be sold in 10 years. The following table shows the computation of future cash flows based on the probability of those alternative courses of action.[27] As shown, those futurethe expected cash flows are $44.1 million (undiscounted). Therefore, the carrying amount of the facility of $48 million would not be recoverable.

Course of Action	Possible Cash Flows (Probability-Weighted) Cash Flows	Probability Assessment (Course of Action)	Expected Cash Flows (Undiscounted)
		(in $ millions)	
Sell in 2 years	$41.0	60%	$24.6
Sell in 10 years	48.7	40	19.5
			$44.1

g. Paragraph A11 and its related footnote 28:

This example illustrates the application of an expected present value technique to estimate the fair value of a long-lived asset in an impairment situation.the absence of an observable market price (paragraph 23).[28] It is based on the facts provided for the manufacturing facility in Example 2.

[28]Present value is the current measure of an estimated future cash inflow, discounted at an interest rate for the number of periods between today and the date of the estimated cash flow. The present value of $X in n periods in the future and discounted at interest of i per period is computed using the formula $X / (1 + i)^n$. Because all of the risks are considered in the estimates of cash flows, the entity discounts the expected cash flows for each year using the risk-free rate of interest. The risk-free rate of interest is the interest rate on monetary assets that are essentially risk free and that have maturity dates that coincide with the expected timing of the cash flow. In the United

States, the risk-free rate is the rate for zero-coupon U.S. Treasury instruments. A yield curve for U.S. Treasury instruments may be used to determine the appropriate risk-free rates of interest.

h. Paragraph A12 and its related footnote 29:

Consistent with an objective of measuring fair value, the entity's estimates of future cash flows used to test the manufacturing facility for recoverability in Example 2 are adjusted to incorporate assumptions that, based on available information, marketplace participants would use in their estimates of the fair value of the asset. The net effect of those adjustments is to increase the entity's estimates of future cash flows (on an undiscounted basis) by approximately 15 percent.[29]

---

[29]In this example, a reliable estimate of the market risk premium is not available. Paragraph 62 of FASB Concepts Statement No. 7, *Using Cash Flow Information and Present Value in Accounting Measurements,* explains:

An estimate of fair value should include the price that marketplace participants are able to receive for bearing the uncertainties in cash flows—the adjustment for risk—if the amount is identifiable, measurable, and significant. An arbitrary adjustment for risk, or one that cannot be evaluated by comparison to marketplace information, introduces an unjustified bias into the measurement. On the other hand, excluding a risk adjustment (if it is apparent that mar-

ketplace participants include one) would not produce a measurement that faithfully represents fair value. There are many techniques for estimating a risk adjustment, including matrix pricing, option-adjusted spread models, and fundamental analysis. However, in many cases a reliable estimate of the market risk premium may not be obtainable or the amount may be small relative to potential measurement error in the estimated cash flows. In such situations, the present value of expected cash flows, discounted at a risk-free rate of interest, may be the best available estimate of fair value in the circumstances.

i. Paragraph A13:

The following table shows by year the computation of the expected cash flows used in the measurement. They reflect the possible cash flows (probability-weighted) used to test the manufacturing facility for recoverability in Example 2, adjusted for relevant marketplace assumptions, which increases the possible cash flows in total by approximately 15 percent.range and probability of possible cash flows expected to result from the use and eventual disposition of the facility over its remaining useful life of 10 years (Example 2), adjusted for market assumptions. It also shows by year the computation of expected cash flows.

Year	TotalPossible Cash Flows Estimate (Market)	Probability Assessment	Expected Cash Flows (Undiscounted)
	(in $ millions)		
1	$4.6	20%	$ .9
	6.3	50	3.2
	7.5	30	2.3
			$6.4
2	$4.6	20%	$ .9
	6.3	50	3.2
	7.5	30	2.3
			$6.4
3	$4.3	20%	$ .9
	5.8	50	2.9
	6.7	30	2.0
			$5.8
4	$4.3	20%	$ .9
	5.8	50	2.9
	6.7	30	2.0
			$5.8

Year	~~Total~~Possible Cash Flows ~~Estimate~~ (Market)	Probability Assessment	Expected Cash Flows (Undiscounted)
	(in $ millions)		
5	$4.0	20%	$ .8
	5.4	50	2.7
	6.4	30	1.9
			$5.4
6	$4.0	20%	$ .8
	5.4	50	2.7
	6.4	30	1.9
			$5.4
7	$3.9	20%	$ .8
	5.1	50	2.6
	5.6	30	1.7
			$5.1
8	$3.9	20%	$ .8
	5.1	50	2.6
	5.6	30	1.7
			$5.1
9	$3.9	20%	$ .8
	5.0	50	2.5
	5.5	30	1.7
			$5.0
10	$4.9	20%	$1.0
	6.0	50	3.0
	6.5	30	2.0
			$6.0

j. Paragraph A14:

The following table shows the computation of the expected present value; that is, the sum of the present values of the expected cash flows by year, each discounted at a risk-free interest rate determined from the yield curve for U.S. Treasury instruments.[29a] ~~The following table shows the computation of the present value of the expected cash flows; that is, the sum of the present values of the expected cash flows by year, which~~ ~~are calculated by discounting those cash flows at a risk-free rate.~~ As shown, the expected present value is $42.3 million, which is less than the carrying amount of $48 million. In accordance with paragraph 7, the entity would recognize an impairment loss of $5.7 million ~~($48 million less $42.3 million)~~.

[29a]In this example, a market risk premium is included in the expected cash flows; that is, the cash flows are certainty equivalent cash flows.

Year	Expected Cash Flows (Undiscounted)	Risk-Free Rate of Interest	Expected Present Value	~~Expected Present Value~~
		(in $ millions)		
1	$ 6.4	5.0%	$ 6.1	
2	6.4	5.1	5.8	
3	5.8	5.2	5.0	
4	5.8	5.4	4.7	
5	5.4	5.6	4.1	
6	5.4	5.8	3.9	
7	5.1	6.0	3.4	
8	5.1	6.2	3.2	
9	5.0	6.4	2.9	
10	6.0	6.6	3.2	
	$56.4		$42.3	~~$42.3~~

k. Appendix E is deleted. This appendix provided excerpts from Concepts Statement 7.

E25. FASB Statement No. 146, *Accounting for Costs Associated with Exit or Disposal Activities,* is amended as follows:

a. Paragraph 5:

~~The fair value of a liability is the amount at which that liability could be settled in a current transaction between willing parties, that is, other than in a forced or liquidation transaction. Quoted market prices in active markets are the best evidence of fair value and shall be used as the basis for the measurement, if available. If quoted market prices are not available, the estimate of fair value shall be based on the best information available in the circumstances, including prices for similar liabilities and the results of using other valuation techniques. (Certain valuation techniques are discussed in Appendix A.)~~

b. Paragraph A2 and its related footnote 13:

The objective of initial measurement of a liability for a cost associated with an exit or disposal activity is fair value (paragraph 3). A present value technique is often the best available valuation technique with which to estimate the fair value of a liability for a cost associated with an exit or disposal activity. For a liability that has uncertainties both in timing and amount, an expected present value technique generally will be the appropriate technique. ~~For a liability, fair value represents the amount that a willing third party of comparable credit standing would demand and could expect to receive to assume all of the duties, uncertainties, and risks inherent in the transferor's obligation, including a profit element or risk premium.~~[13]

~~[13]Paragraph 62 of FASB Concepts Statement No. 7, *Using Cash Flow Information and Present Value in Accounting Measurements,* explains:~~

~~An estimate of fair value should include the price that marketplace participants are able to receive for bearing the uncertainties in cash flows—the adjustment for risk—if the amount is identifiable, measurable, and significant. An arbitrary adjustment for risk, or one that cannot be evaluated by comparison to marketplace information, introduces an unjustified bias into the measurement. On the other hand, excluding a risk adjustment (if it is apparent that marketplace participants include one) would not produce a measurement that faithfully represents fair value. There are many techniques for estimating a risk adjustment, including matrix pricing, option-adjusted spread models, and fundamental analysis. However, in many cases a reliable estimate of the market risk premium may not be obtainable or the amount may be small relative to potential measurement error in the estimated cash flows. In such situations, the present value of expected cash flows, discounted at a risk-free rate of interest, may be the best available estimate of fair value in the circumstances.~~

c. Paragraph A4 and its related footnotes 14 and 15:

A present value technique often is the best available valuation technique with which to estimate the fair value of a liability. FASB Concepts Statement No. 7, *Using Cash Flow Information and Present Value in Accounting Measurements,* discusses two present value techniques.[14] The first technique is expected present value, in which multiple cash flow scenarios that reflect the range of possible outcomes and a risk-free rate adjusted for the entity's credit standing[15] are used to estimate fair value. The second technique is traditional present value, in which a single set of estimated cash flows and a single risk-adjusted interest rate are used to estimate fair value. In contrast to a traditional present value technique, which incorporates uncertainty in the amount and timing of cash flows in the interest rate, an expected present value technique incorporates that uncertainty in the estimated cash flows. Thus, an expected present value technique often will be the appropriate valuation technique if a liability for a cost associated with an exit or disposal activity has uncertainties in both the amount and timing of estimated cash flows.

[14]Paragraph 23 of Concepts Statement 7 discusses the essential elements of a present value measurement.

[15]When using an expected present value technique, the effect of an entity's credit standing can be reflected in either the discount rate or the estimated cash flows. However, it is usually easier and less complex to reflect that adjustment in the discount rate.

d. Paragraph A5 and its related footnote 16:

When using a present value technique, estimates of future cash flows should incorporate assumptions that marketplace participants would use in their estimates of fair value whenever that information is available without undue cost and effort. Otherwise, an entity may use its own estimates of future cash flows.[16]

[16]Paragraph 38 of Concepts Statement 7 explains:

As a practical matter, an entity that uses cash flows in accounting measurements often has little or no information about some or all of the assumptions that marketplace participants would use in assessing the fair value of an asset or a liability. In those situations, an entity must necessarily use the information that is available without undue cost and effort in developing cash flow estimates. The use of an entity's own assumptions about future cash flows is compatible with an estimate of fair value, as long as there are no contrary data indicating that marketplace participants

would use different assumptions. If such data exist, the entity must adjust its assumptions to incorporate that market information.

E26. FASB Statement No. 150, *Accounting for Certain Financial Instruments with Characteristics of both Liabilities and Equity,* is amended as follows:

a. Paragraph D1 (glossary):

Fair value

The amount at which an asset (liability) could be bought (incurred) or sold (settled) in a current transaction between willing parties, that is, other than in a forced or liquidation sale. Additional guidance on determining fair value is provided in other FASB Statements and FASB Concepts Statements.

E27. FASB Statement No. 156, *Accounting for Servicing of Financial Assets,* is amended as follows:

a. Paragraph 3(c):

Fair value

See paragraphs 68–70 of Statement 140.

E28. FASB Interpretation No. 45, *Guarantor's Accounting and Disclosure Requirements for Guarantees, Including Indirect Guarantees of Indebtedness of Others,* is amended as follows:

a. Paragraph 9(a):

When a guarantee is issued in a standalone arm's-length transaction with an unrelated party, the liability recognized at the inception of the guarantee should be the premium received or receivable by the guarantor as a practical expedient.

b. Paragraph 9(b):

When a guarantee is issued as part of a transaction with multiple elements with an unrelated party (such as in conjunction with selling an asset or entering into an operating lease), the liability recognized at the inception of the guarantee should be an estimate of the guarantee's fair value. In that circumstance, guarantors should consider what premium would be required by the guarantor to issue the same guarantee in a standalone arm's-length transaction with an unrelated party as a practical expedient. In the absence of observable transactions for identical or

~~similar guarantees, expected present value measurement techniques as set forth in FASB Concepts Statement No. 7,~~ *Using Cash Flow Information and Present Value in Accounting Measurements,* ~~will likely provide the best estimate of fair value. Concepts Statement 7 states in its glossary that "*expected present value* refers to the sum of the probability-weighted present values in a range of estimated cash flows, all discounted using the same interest rate convention." The general principles in paragraph 41 of Concepts Statement 7 are also relevant.~~

E29. Statement 133 Implementation Issue No. A23, "Definition of a Derivative: Prepaid Interest Rate Swaps," is amended as follows:

a. First paragraph of the Background section:

A *prepaid interest rate swap contract,* as that term is used in this Issue, obligates one party to make periodic payments to another party that are based on a variable interest rate applied to an effective notional amount. It is characterized as an at-the-money interest rate swap contract for which the fixed leg has been fully prepaid ~~(at its fair value—a discounted amount)~~, with the result that the party that receives the variable-leg-based payments has no obligation whatsoever to make any future payments under the contract. Under that characterization, the fair value of the fixed leg and the fair value of the variable leg are equal and offsetting because the at-the-money interest rate swap contract has an overall fair value of zero.

E30. Statement 133 Implementation Issue No. B13, "Embedded Derivatives: Accounting for Remarketable Put Bonds," is amended as follows:

a. Third paragraph of Structure 1 of the Response section:

Determination of the carrying value of the investor's freestanding call option: The carrying value of the investor's attached freestanding written call option to the investment bank should be its fair value in accordance with paragraph 17 of Statement 133. ~~The initial fair value allocated to the call option by the investor should be based on the initial proceeds paid by the investment bank for the purchase of that option.~~ The remaining proceeds would be allocated to the carrying amount of the puttable bond.

b. Third paragraph of Structure 2 of the Response section:

Determination of the carrying value of the investor's freestanding written call option: The carrying value of the investor's freestanding written call option to the investment bank should be its fair value in accordance with paragraph 17 of Statement 133. ~~The initial fair value allocated to the call option by the investor should be based on the initial proceeds paid by the investment bank for the purchase of that option.~~ The remaining proceeds would be allocated to the carrying amount of the puttable bond.

c. Third paragraph of Structure 5 of the Response section:

Determination of the carrying value of the investor's freestanding written call option: The carrying value of the investor's freestanding written call option to the investment bank should be its fair value in accordance with paragraph 17 of Statement 133. In the remarketing format, the transfer of the purchased call option is concurrent with the issuance of the bond. ~~Therefore, the initial fair value assigned to the call option should be based on the proceeds paid by the investment bank at the inception of the structure for the purchase of that option, and t~~The remaining proceeds would be allocated to the carrying amount of the puttable bond. The debtor recognizes no gain or loss upon the transfer of the option to the investment bank.

d. Third paragraph of Structure 6 of the Response section:

Determination of the carrying value of the investor's freestanding written call option: The carrying value of the investor's freestanding written call option to the investment bank should be its fair value in accordance with paragraph 17 of Statement 133 with the remaining proceeds allocated to the carrying amount of the puttable bond. In the assignment format, the transfer of the purchased call option by the debtor to the investment bank may not be concurrent with the issuance of the bond. ~~If the transfer of the purchased call option is concurrent with the issuance of the bond, consistent with the remarketing format, the initial fair value assigned to the call option should be based on the initial proceeds paid by the investment bank at the inception of the structure for the purchase of that option, with the remaining proceeds allocated to~~

the carrying amount of the puttable bond. The debtor recognizes no gain or loss upon the transfer of the call option. In transactions involving a delay between the issuance of the bond and the transfer of the assignable call option to the investment bank, the allocation of the initial proceeds to the carrying value of the option would be equal to the fair value of the option based on a market quote. Presumably, that market quote would be equal to the amount that would be paid by a third party (such as the investment bank) to purchase the call option under current market conditions. The remaining proceeds would be allocated to the carrying amount of the puttable bond. During any period of time between the initial issuance of the bond and the transfer of the call option to the investment bank, the call option must be measured at fair value with changes in value recognized in earnings as required by paragraph 18 of Statement 133. As a result of the requirement to measure the call option at fair value during the time period before it is assigned to the investment bank, the debtor would not recognize a gain or loss upon the assignment because the proceeds paid by the investment bank would be the option's current fair value on the date of the assignment, which would be the option's carrying amount at that point in time. Any change in the fair value of the option during the time period before it is assigned to the investment bank would be attributable to the passage of time and changes in market conditions.

E31. Statement 133 Implementation Issue No. B35, "Embedded Derivatives: Application of Statement 133 to a Not-for-Profit Organization's Obligation Arising from an Irrevocable Split-Interest Agreement," is amended as follows:

a. Second paragraph of the Response section:

The NFP organization's liability for its obligation under a split-interest agreement would typically not meet the definition of a derivative instrument in its entirety because it would not meet the criterion in paragraph 6(b). That criterion requires the contract to have no initial net investment or an initial net investment that is smaller than would be required for other types of contracts that would be expected to have a similar response to changes in market factors. In

contrast, the initial net investment for the liability recognized for typical split-interest agreements is its fair value (generally measured at the present value of the estimated future payments). If the NFP organization's liability for its obligation under the split-interest agreement does not in its entirety meet the definition of a derivative instrument in paragraph 6, that liability must be analyzed to determine whether it contains provisions that constitute an embedded derivative instrument that warrants separate accounting under paragraph 12. Generally, the liability representing an obligation under a split-interest agreement contains an embedded derivative that warrants separate accounting if the payments are variable and the agreement is period-certain (rather than life-contingent) unless a fair value election is made pursuant to Statement 155. The following examples, although not all-inclusive, provide an understanding of the applicability of paragraph 12 to various split-interest agreements.

E32. Statement 133 Implementation Issue No. I2, "Disclosures: Near-Term Reclassification of Gains and Losses That Are Reported in Accumulated Other Comprehensive Income," is amended as follows:

a. Second paragraph of the Background section:

When interest rate or commodity swaps are used for cash flow hedges, in effect a single derivative is being used to hedge multiple hedged forecasted transactions because a swap involves multiple cash flows (like a series of forward contracts). For instance, a five-year interest rate swap may be designated as the hedging instrument to hedge the variability in cash flows for each of the resets in a five-year variable-rate borrowing. The fair value of a swap may be the net of both positive discounted cash flows (that is, the right to receive future payments) and negative discounted cash flows (that is, the obligation to make future payments). This could happen, for example, if nearby forward rates were below the fixed rate on the swap and far-term forward rates were above the fixed rate on the swap, in which case an entity could have an expectation of having to make cash outflows on the swap for nearby exposures and to receive cash inflows on the swap for the far-term exposures.

Statement of Financial Accounting Standards No. 158 Employers' Accounting for Defined Benefit Pension and Other Postretirement Plans

an amendment of FASB Statements No. 87, 88,106, and 132(R)

STATUS

Issued: September 2006

Effective Date: An employer with publicly traded equity securities (as defined in paragraph 11) shall initially apply the requirement to recognize the funded status of a benefit plan (paragraph 4) and the disclosure requirements (paragraph 7) as of the end of the fiscal year ending after December 15, 2006; an employer without publicly traded equity securities shall initially apply the requirement to recognize the funded status of a benefit plan (paragraphs 4 and 8) and the disclosure requirements (paragraphs 7 and 10) as of the end of the fiscal year ending after June 15, 2007; an employer without publicly traded equity securities shall provide the disclosures in paragraph 14 in the notes to the financial statements for a fiscal year ending after December 15, 2006, but before June 16, 2007 unless it has applied the recognition provisions of this Statement in preparing those financial statements; the requirement to measure plan assets and benefit obligations as of the date of the employer's fiscal year-end statement of financial position (paragraphs 5, 6, and 9) shall be effective for fiscal years ending after December 15, 2008

Affects: Amends ARB 43, Chapter 3, paragraphs 4 and 7
Amends APB 28, paragraph 30(k)
Amends FAS 87, paragraphs 16, 20, 25, 26, 29, 32 through 34, 49, 52, 55, 74, and 264 and footnotes 5 and 6
Replaces FAS 87, paragraphs 28 and 35 through 38
Adds FAS 87, paragraphs 44A, 74A through 74D, and 261A
Deletes FAS 87, footnote 7
Amends FAS 88, paragraphs 9, 12, and 13 and footnote 2
Adds FAS 88, paragraphs 17A, 17B, and 57A
Effectively amends FAS 106, paragraphs 12 and 13
Amends FAS 106, paragraphs 22, 31, 46, 52, 53, 55, 56, 59, 60, 62, 72, 73, 88, 92, 93, 97, 98, and 518 and footnotes 18, 19, 25, 26, and 28
Adds FAS 106, paragraphs 31A, 44A, 44B, 103A through 103D, and 391A
Amends FAS 130, paragraphs 17, 19, 20, 130, and 131
Deletes FAS 130, paragraph 21
Effectively amends FAS 130, paragraph 39
Amends FAS 132(R), paragraphs 3, 5, 5(c), 5(h), 5(o), 6, 8, 8(g), 9, and C3
Replaces FAS 132(R), paragraphs 5(i) and 8(h)
Deletes FAS 132(R), paragraphs 5(k) and 8(j)
Adds FAS 132(R), paragraphs 10A through 10D
Amends FSP APB 18-1

Affected by: Paragraphs A15(a), A20(a), and A28(a) amended by FSP FAS 158-1, paragraph 14

Other Interpretive Release: FASB Staff Position FAS 146-1

Issues Discussed by FASB Emerging Issues Task Force (EITF)

Affects: Nullifies EITF Topic No. D-106
Modifies EITF Issue No. 03-2 and Topic No. D-36

Interpreted by: No EITF Issues

Related Issues: EITF Issues No. 84-35, 86-27, 88-1, 88-5, 88-23, 90-3, 91-7, 92-12, 92-13, 93-3, 93-4, 96-5, 97-14, 03-4, and 05-5 and Topic No. D-27

SUMMARY

This Statement improves financial reporting by requiring an employer to recognize the overfunded or underfunded status of a defined benefit postretirement plan (other than a multiemployer plan) as an asset or liability in its statement of financial position and to recognize changes in that funded status in the year in which the changes occur through comprehensive income of a business entity or changes in unrestricted net assets of a not-for-profit organization. This Statement also improves financial reporting by requiring an employer to measure the funded status of a plan as of the date of its year-end statement of financial position, with limited exceptions.

This Statement requires an employer that is a business entity and sponsors one or more single-employer defined benefit plans to:

a. Recognize the funded status of a benefit plan—measured as the difference between plan assets at fair value (with limited exceptions) and the benefit obligation—in its statement of financial position. For a pension plan, the benefit obligation is the projected benefit obligation; for any other postretirement benefit plan, such as a retiree health care plan, the benefit obligation is the accumulated postretirement benefit obligation.
b. Recognize as a component of other comprehensive income, net of tax, the gains or losses and prior service costs or credits that arise during the period but are not recognized as components of net periodic benefit cost pursuant to FASB Statement No. 87, *Employers' Accounting for Pensions,* or No. 106, *Employers' Accounting for Postretirement Benefits Other Than Pensions.* Amounts recognized in accumulated other comprehensive income, including the gains or losses, prior service costs or credits, and the transition asset or obligation remaining from the initial application of Statements 87 and 106, are adjusted as they are subsequently recognized as components of net periodic benefit cost pursuant to the recognition and amortization provisions of those Statements.
c. Measure defined benefit plan assets and obligations as of the date of the employer's fiscal year-end statement of financial position (with limited exceptions).
d. Disclose in the notes to financial statements additional information about certain effects on net periodic benefit cost for the next fiscal year that arise from delayed recognition of the gains or losses, prior service costs or credits, and transition asset or obligation.

This Statement also applies to a not-for-profit organization or other entity that does not report other comprehensive income. This Statement's reporting requirements are tailored for those entities.

This Statement amends Statement 87, FASB Statement No. 88, *Employers' Accounting for Settlements and Curtailments of Defined Benefit Pension Plans and for Termination Benefits,* Statement 106, and FASB Statement No. 132 (revised 2003), *Employers' Disclosures about Pensions and Other Postretirement Benefits,* and other related accounting literature. Upon initial application of this Statement and subsequently, an employer should continue to apply the provisions in Statements 87, 88, and 106 in measuring plan assets and benefit obligations as of the date of its statement of financial position and in determining the amount of net periodic benefit cost.

Reasons for Issuing This Statement

The Board issued this Statement to address concerns that prior standards on employers' accounting for defined benefit postretirement plans failed to communicate the funded status of those plans in a complete and understandable way. Prior standards did not require an employer to report in its statement of financial position the overfunded or underfunded status of a defined benefit postretirement plan. Those standards did not require an employer to recognize completely in earnings or other comprehensive income the financial effects of certain events affecting the plan's funded status when those events occurred.

Prior accounting standards allowed an employer to recognize in its statement of financial position an asset or liability arising from a defined benefit postretirement plan, which almost always differed from the plan's overfunded or underfunded status. Those standards allowed an employer to:

a. Delay recognition of economic events that affected the costs of providing postretirement benefits—changes in plan assets and benefit obligations—and recognize a liability that was sometimes significantly less than the underfunded status of the plan.
b. Recognize an asset in its statement of financial position, in some situations, for a plan that was underfunded.

Prior standards relegated information about the overfunded or underfunded status of a plan to the notes to financial statements. That information was in the form of a reconciliation of the overfunded or underfunded status to amounts recognized in an employer's statement of financial position. The Board was told that presenting such information only in the notes made it more difficult for users of financial statements to assess an employer's financial position and ability to satisfy postretirement benefit obligations.

The Board concluded that such reporting, together with other features of the existing standards, did not provide representationally faithful and understandable financial information and might lead to the inefficient allocation of resources in the capital markets. This Statement is the first step in a project to comprehensively reconsider Statements 87, 88, 106, 132(R), and related pronouncements.

How the Changes Improve Financial Reporting

This Statement improves financial reporting because the information reported by a sponsoring employer in its financial statements is more complete, timely, and, therefore, more representationally faithful. Thus, it will be easier for users of those financial statements to assess an employer's financial position and ability to satisfy postretirement benefit obligations.

This Statement results in financial statements that are more complete because it requires an employer that sponsors a single-employer defined benefit postretirement plan to report the overfunded or underfunded status of the plan in its statement of financial position rather than in the notes.

This Statement results in more timely financial information because it requires an employer to recognize all transactions and events affecting the overfunded or underfunded status of a defined benefit postretirement plan in comprehensive income (or changes in unrestricted net assets) in the year in which they occur. Moreover, this Statement requires that plan assets and benefit obligations be measured as of the date of an employer's fiscal year-end statement of financial position, thus eliminating the alternative of a measurement date that could be up to three months earlier.

This Statement results in financial reporting that is more understandable by eliminating the need for a reconciliation in the notes to financial statements.

How the Conclusions Underlying This Statement Relate to the FASB's Conceptual Framework

FASB Concepts Statements No. 1, *Objectives of Financial Reporting by Business Enterprises,* and No. 4, *Objectives of Financial Reporting by Nonbusiness Organizations,* explain that financial reporting should provide information that is useful in making business and resource allocation decisions. FASB Concepts Statement No. 2, *Qualitative Characteristics of Accounting Information,* explains that essential elements of decision usefulness are relevance and reliability. Information must be timely and complete for it to be relevant and reliable. This Statement results in financial information that is more complete, timely, and, therefore, more representationally faithful.

Benefits and Costs

The objective of financial reporting is to provide information that is useful to present and potential investors, creditors, and other capital market participants in making rational investment, credit, and similar resource allocation decisions. The Board recognizes that the benefits of providing information for that purpose should justify the related costs. After careful consideration, the Board concluded that the benefits of the improved financial reporting that result from this Statement outweigh the costs of its implementation.

The Board believes that this Statement provides financial statements that are more complete and easier to understand because information previously reported in the notes will be recognized in an employer's financial statements. Reporting the current funded status of a postretirement benefit plan as an asset or liability in an employer's statement of financial position allows users of those financial statements to assess an employer's financial position and its ability to satisfy the benefit obligations without referring to a reconciliation in the notes to financial statements. Likewise, recognizing transactions and events that affect the funded status in the financial statements in the year in which they occur enhances the timeliness and, therefore, the usefulness of the financial information.

The Board recognizes that employers will incur costs to implement this Statement. However, the Board believes that the expected benefits outweigh the costs. Several provisions of this Statement are intended to minimize the costs of implementation. For example, the Board decided not to require retrospective application of the changes after learning about the significant costs that some employers would incur in retrospectively revising financial statements of previous periods. Moreover, this Statement does not change the basic approach to measuring plan assets, benefit obligations, or annual net periodic benefit cost. Employers were previously required to disclose in the notes to financial statements amounts for a plan that, under the application of this Statement, are recognized in the statement of financial position. Therefore, no new information or new computations other than those related to income tax effects are required.

The Board acknowledges, however, that certain employers who previously did not use a fiscal year-end measurement date may incur incremental one-time costs when initially applying the requirement to measure plan assets and benefit obligations as of the date of the employer's year-end statement of financial position. Furthermore, some employers may have contractual arrangements that are affected because they reference financial statement metrics, such as book value. Those employers may incur costs associated with revising those contractual arrangements. To mitigate those costs, this Statement provides delayed effective dates for certain of its provisions and an alternative approach for initially applying the change in measurement date.

Effective Dates and Transition

The required date of adoption of the recognition and disclosure provisions of this Statement differs for an employer that is an issuer of publicly traded equity securities (as defined) and an employer that is not. For purposes of this Statement, an employer is deemed to have publicly traded equity securities if any of the following conditions is met:

a. The employer has issued equity securities that trade in a public market, which may be either a stock exchange (domestic or foreign) or an over-the-counter market, including securities quoted only locally or regionally.
b. The employer has made a filing with a regulatory agency in preparation for the sale of any class of equity securities in a public market.
c. The employer is controlled by an entity covered by (a) or (b).

An employer with publicly traded equity securities is required to initially recognize the funded status of a defined benefit postretirement plan and to provide the required disclosures as of the end of the fiscal year ending after December 15, 2006.

An employer without publicly traded equity securities is required to recognize the funded status of a defined benefit postretirement plan and to provide the required disclosures as of the end of the fiscal year ending after June 15, 2007.

However, an employer without publicly traded equity securities is required to disclose the following information in the notes to financial statements for a fiscal year ending after December 15, 2006, but before June 16, 2007, unless it has applied the recognition provisions of this Statement in preparing those financial statements:

a. A brief description of the provisions of this Statement
b. The date that adoption is required
c. The date the employer plans to adopt the recognition provisions of this Statement, if earlier.

The requirement to measure plan assets and benefit obligations as of the date of the employer's fiscal year-end statement of financial position is effective for fiscal years ending after December 15, 2008. If in the last quarter of the preceding fiscal year an employer enters into a transaction that results in a settlement or experiences an event that causes a curtailment of the plan, the related gain or loss pursuant to Statement 88 or 106 is required to be recognized in earnings or changes in unrestricted net assets of that quarter.

Earlier application of the recognition or measurement date provisions is encouraged; however, early application must be for all of an employer's benefit plans. Retrospective application of this Statement is not permitted.

Statement of Financial Accounting Standards No. 158

Employers' Accounting for Defined Benefit Pension and Other Postretirement Plans

an amendment of FASB Statements No. 87, 88, 106, and 132(R)

CONTENTS

OBJECTIVE

1. This Statement results from the initial phase of a comprehensive project to improve an employer's accounting for defined benefit pension and other postretirement plans. The objectives of this Statement are for an employer to:

a. Recognize the overfunded or underfunded status of a single-employer[1] defined benefit postretirement plan (benefit plan or plan) as an asset or liability in its statement of financial position and to recognize changes in that funded status in comprehensive income (for a business entity) or changes in unrestricted net assets (for a not-for-profit organization) in the year in which the changes occur.
b. Measure the funded status of a plan as of the date of its year-end statement of financial position, with limited exceptions.

This Statement does not change the accounting for a multiemployer plan.

2. The changes to an employer's accounting and reporting for benefit plans required by this Statement are described in paragraphs 4–22 below. The amendments to the recognition, measurement date, and disclosure requirements of FASB Statements No. 87, *Employers' Accounting for Pensions,* No. 88, *Employers' Accounting for Settlements and Curtailments of Defined Benefit Pension Plans and for Termination Benefits,* No. 106, *Employers' Accounting for Postretirement Benefits Other Than Pensions,* and No. 132 (revised 2003), *Employers' Disclosures about Pensions and Other Postretirement Benefits,* required to effect those changes are included in appendixes to this Statement. Those amendments are an integral part of this Statement. The definitions of terms used in this Statement are the same as those in Statements 87, 88, and 106 (as amended).

3. This Statement also amends Statements 87 and 106 to include guidance related to the selection of as-

sumed discount rates that was previously included in the basis for conclusions of Statement 106 (see Appendixes C and D).

STANDARDS OF FINANCIAL ACCOUNTING AND REPORTING

Reporting by a Business Entity

Recognition of the Funded Status of a Single-Employer Defined Benefit Postretirement Plan

4. A business entity that sponsors one or more single-employer defined benefit plans shall:

a. Recognize the funded status of a benefit plan—measured as the difference between the fair value of plan assets[2] and the benefit obligation—in its statement of financial position. For a pension plan, the benefit obligation shall be the projected benefit obligation; for any other postretirement benefit plan, such as a retiree health care plan, the benefit obligation shall be the accumulated postretirement benefit obligation.
b. Aggregate the statuses of all overfunded plans and recognize that amount as an asset in its statement of financial position. It also shall aggregate the statuses of all underfunded plans and recognize that amount as a liability in its statement of financial position. A business entity that presents a classified statement of financial position shall classify the liability for an underfunded plan as a current liability, a noncurrent liability, or a combination of both. The current portion (determined on a plan-by-plan basis) is the amount by which the actuarial present value of benefits included in the benefit obligation payable in the next 12 months, or operating cycle if longer, exceeds the fair value of plan assets. The asset for an overfunded plan shall be classified as a noncurrent asset in a classified statement of financial position.
c. Recognize as a component of other comprehensive income[3] the gains or losses and prior service

---

[1]Consistent with paragraph 71 of FASB Statement No. 87, *Employers' Accounting for Pensions,* and paragraph 84 of FASB Statement No. 106, *Employers' Accounting for Postretirement Benefits Other Than Pensions,* a multiple-employer plan shall be considered a single-employer plan rather than a multiemployer plan for purposes of this Statement.

[2]Paragraph 49 of Statement 87 and paragraph 65 of Statement 106 address measuring plan assets at fair value. Paragraph 51 of Statement 87 and paragraph 66 of Statement 106 provide an exception to measuring plan assets at fair value. Plan assets used in plan operations shall be measured at cost less accumulated depreciation or amortization. Paragraph 61 of Statement 87 and paragraph 69 of Statement 106 also provide for a non-fair-value measurement of participation rights in certain insurance contracts.

[3]A business entity that is not required to report other comprehensive income pursuant to FASB Statement No. 130, *Reporting Comprehensive Income,* shall apply the provisions of paragraphs 8–10 of this Statement in an analogous manner that is appropriate for its method of financial reporting.

costs or credits that arise during the period but are not recognized as components of net periodic benefit cost of the period pursuant to Statements 87 and 106.

d. Recognize corresponding adjustments in other comprehensive income when the gains or losses, prior service costs or credits, and transition assets or obligations remaining from the initial application of Statements 87 and 106 are subsequently recognized as components of net periodic benefit cost pursuant to the recognition and amortization provisions of Statements 87, 88, and 106.

e. Apply the provisions of FASB Statement No. 109, *Accounting for Income Taxes,* to determine the applicable income tax effects of items (a)–(d) above.

Measurement Date of Plan Assets and Benefit Obligations

5. A business entity shall measure plan assets and benefit obligations as of the date of its fiscal year-end statement of financial position unless:

a. The plan is sponsored by a subsidiary that is consolidated using a fiscal period that differs from its parent's, as permitted by ARB No. 51, *Consolidated Financial Statements.*

b. The plan is sponsored by an investee that is accounted for using the equity method of accounting under APB Opinion No. 18, *The Equity Method of Accounting for Investments in Common Stock,* using financial statements of the investee for a fiscal period that is different from the investor's, as permitted by Opinion 18.

In those cases, a business entity shall measure the subsidiary's plan assets and benefit obligations as of the date used to consolidate the subsidiary's statement of financial position and shall measure the investee's plan assets and benefit obligations as of the date of the investee's financial statements used to apply the equity method. For example, if a calendar year-end parent consolidates a subsidiary using the subsidiary's September 30 financial statements, the funded status of the subsidiary's benefit plan included in the consolidated financial statements shall be measured as of September 30.

6. Unless a business entity remeasures both its plan assets and benefit obligations during the fiscal year, the funded status it reports in its interim-period statement of financial position shall be the same asset or liability recognized in the previous year-end state-

ment of financial position adjusted for (a) subsequent accruals of net periodic benefit cost that exclude the amortization of amounts previously recognized in other comprehensive income (for example, subsequent accruals of service cost, interest cost, and return on plan assets) and (b) contributions to a funded plan, or benefit payments. Sometimes, a business entity remeasures both plan assets and benefit obligations during the fiscal year. That is the case, for example, when a significant event such as a plan amendment, settlement, or curtailment occurs that calls for a remeasurement. Upon remeasurement, a business entity shall adjust its statement of financial position in a subsequent interim period (on a delayed basis if the measurement date provisions of this Statement have not yet been implemented) to reflect the overfunded or underfunded status of the plan consistent with that measurement date.

Disclosure Requirements

7. A business entity that sponsors one or more benefit plans shall disclose the following information in the notes to its annual financial statements, separately for pension plans and other postretirement benefit plans:

a. For each annual statement of income presented, the amounts recognized in other comprehensive income, showing separately the net gain or loss and net prior service cost or credit. Those amounts shall be separated into amounts arising during the period and reclassification adjustments of other comprehensive income as a result of being recognized as components of net periodic benefit cost for the period.

b. For each annual statement of income presented, the net transition asset or obligation recognized as a reclassification adjustment of other comprehensive income as a result of being recognized as a component of net periodic benefit cost for the period.

c. For each annual statement of financial position presented, the amounts in accumulated other comprehensive income that have not yet been recognized as components of net periodic benefit cost, showing separately the net gain or loss, net prior service cost or credit, and net transition asset or obligation.

d. The amounts in accumulated other comprehensive income expected to be recognized as components of net periodic benefit cost over the fiscal year that follows the most recent annual statement of financial position presented, showing separately the net gain or loss, net prior service cost or credit, and net transition asset or obligation.

e. The amount and timing of any plan assets expected to be returned to the business entity during the 12-month period, or operating cycle if longer, that follows the most recent annual statement of financial position presented.

Reporting by a Not-for-Profit Organization

Recognition of the Funded Status of a Single-Employer Defined Benefit Postretirement Plan

8. A not-for-profit organization that sponsors one or more single-employer defined benefit plans (a not-for-profit employer) shall:

a. Recognize the funded status of a benefit plan—measured as the difference between the fair value of plan assets[4] and the benefit obligation—in its statement of financial position. For a pension plan, the benefit obligation shall be the projected benefit obligation; for any other postretirement benefit plan, such as a retiree health care plan, the benefit obligation shall be the accumulated postretirement benefit obligation.

b. Aggregate the statuses of all overfunded plans and recognize that amount as an asset in its statement of financial position. It also shall aggregate the statuses of all underfunded plans and recognize that amount as a liability in its statement of financial position. A not-for-profit employer that presents a classified statement of financial position shall report the liability for an underfunded plan as a current liability, a noncurrent liability, or a combination of both. The current portion (determined on a plan-by-plan basis) is the amount by which the actuarial present value of benefits included in the benefit obligation payable in the next 12 months, or operating cycle if longer, exceeds the fair value of plan assets. The asset recognized for an overfunded plan shall be presented as a noncurrent asset in a classified statement of financial position.

c. Recognize as a separate line item or items within changes in unrestricted net assets, apart from expenses, the gains or losses and the prior service costs or credits that arise during the period but are not recognized as components of net periodic benefit cost pursuant to Statements 87 and 106. Consistent with the provisions of FASB State-

ment No. 117, *Financial Statements of Not-for-Profit Organizations,* this Statement does not prescribe whether the separate line item or items shall be included within or outside an intermediate measure of operations or performance indicator, if one is presented. The AICPA Audit and Accounting Guide, *Health Care Organizations,* requires a not-for-profit organization within its scope to report items of other comprehensive income outside the performance indicator.

d. Reclassify to net periodic benefit cost a portion of the net gain or loss and prior service costs or credits previously recognized in a separate line item or items, pursuant to paragraph 8(c), and a portion of the transition asset or obligation remaining from the initial application of Statements 87 and 106, pursuant to the recognition and amortization provisions of Statements 87, 88, and 106. The contra adjustment or adjustments shall be reported in the same line item or items within changes in unrestricted net assets, apart from expenses, as the initially recognized amounts. Net periodic benefit cost shall be reported by functional classification pursuant to paragraph 26 of Statement 117.

e. Apply the provisions of Statement 109 to determine the applicable income tax effects, if any, of items (a)–(d) above.

Measurement Date of Plan Assets and Benefit Obligations

9. A not-for-profit employer shall measure plan assets and benefit obligations as of the date of its fiscal year-end statement of financial position, unless it meets one of the exceptions described in paragraph 5 for a business entity. Similarly, a not-for-profit employer shall report the funded status in interim-period financial statements (if presented) in an analogous manner to that described in paragraph 6 for a business entity.

Disclosure Requirements

10. A not-for-profit employer that sponsors one or more benefit plans shall disclose the following information in the notes to its annual financial statements, separately for pension plans and other postretirement benefit plans:

a. For each annual statement of activities presented, the net gain or loss and net prior service cost or

---

[4]See footnote 2.

credit recognized in the statement of activities apart from expenses. Those amounts shall be separated into amounts arising during the period and amounts reclassified as components of net periodic benefit cost of the period (unless they are separately reported pursuant to paragraphs 8(c) and 8(d)).

b. For each annual statement of activities presented, the net transition asset or obligation recognized as a component of net periodic benefit cost of the period (if not separately reported pursuant to paragraphs 8(c) and 8(d)).

c. For each annual statement of financial position presented, the amounts that have not yet been recognized as components of net periodic benefit cost, showing separately the net gain or loss, net prior service cost or credit, and net transition asset or obligation.

d. The amounts of net gain or loss, net prior service cost or credit, and net transition asset or obligation that arose previously and are expected to be recognized as components of net periodic benefit cost over the fiscal year that follows the most recent annual statement of financial position presented.

e. The amount and timing of any plan assets expected to be returned to the not-for-profit employer during the 12-month period, or operating cycle if longer, that follows the most recent annual statement of financial position presented.

Effective Dates

11. This Statement provides different effective dates for the recognition and related disclosure provisions and for the required change to a fiscal year-end measurement date. Also, the effective date of the recognition and disclosure provisions differs for an employer that is an issuer of publicly traded equity securities from one that is not. For purposes of this Statement, an employer is deemed to have publicly traded equity securities if any of the following conditions is met:

a. The employer has issued equity securities that trade in a public market, which may be either a stock exchange (domestic or foreign) or an over-the-counter market, including securities quoted only locally or regionally.

b. The employer has made a filing with a regulatory agency in preparation for the sale of any class of equity securities in a public market.

c. The employer is controlled by an entity covered by (a) or (b).

Effective Dates for Recognition and Related Disclosure Provisions

12. An employer with publicly traded equity securities shall initially apply the requirement to recognize the funded status of a benefit plan (paragraph 4) and the disclosure requirements (paragraph 7) as of the end of the fiscal year ending after December 15, 2006. Application as of the end of an earlier fiscal year is encouraged; however, early application shall be for all of an employer's benefit plans.

13. An employer without publicly traded equity securities shall initially apply the requirement to recognize the funded status of a benefit plan (paragraphs 4 and 8) and the disclosure requirements (paragraphs 7 and 10) as of the end of the fiscal year ending after June 15, 2007. Application as of the end of an earlier fiscal year is encouraged; however, early application shall be for all of an employer's benefit plans.

14. An employer without publicly traded equity securities shall disclose the following information in the notes to the financial statements for a fiscal year ending after December 15, 2006, but before June 16, 2007, unless it has applied the recognition provisions of this Statement in preparing those financial statements:

a. A brief description of the provisions of this Statement

b. The date that adoption is required

c. The date the employer plans to adopt the recognition provisions of this Statement, if earlier.

Effective Date for Measurement Date Provisions

15. The requirement to measure plan assets and benefit obligations as of the date of the employer's fiscal year-end statement of financial position (paragraphs 5, 6, and 9) shall be effective for fiscal years ending after December 15, 2008, and shall not be applied retrospectively. Earlier application is encouraged; however, early application shall be for all of an employer's benefit plans. The requirement in paragraphs 5(k) and 8(j) of Statement 132(R) to disclose the measurement date is eliminated, effective in the year the employer initially adopts the measurement date provisions of this Statement.

Transition

Recognition Provisions

16. An employer shall apply the recognition provisions of this Statement as of the end of the fiscal year

of initial application. Retrospective application is not permitted. The amounts recognized in an employer's statement of financial position as of the end of the fiscal year before applying this Statement, including amounts required to recognize any additional minimum pension liability, shall be adjusted so that:

a. For a business entity, gains or losses, prior service costs or credits, and transition assets or obligations that have not yet been included in net periodic benefit cost as of the end of the fiscal year in which the Statement is initially applied are recognized as components of the ending balance of accumulated other comprehensive income, net of tax. Any required adjustment shall be reported as an adjustment of the ending balance of accumulated other comprehensive income.

b. For a not-for-profit employer, gains or losses, prior service costs or credits, and transition assets or obligations that have not yet been included in net periodic benefit cost as of the end of the fiscal year in which this Statement is initially applied are included in the ending balance of unrestricted net assets, net of tax, if any. Any required adjustment shall be reported in the statement of activities, in a separate line item or items within changes in unrestricted net assets, apart from expenses and outside a performance indicator or other intermediate measure of operations, if one is presented.

Measurement Date Provisions

17. This Statement provides two approaches for an employer to transition to a fiscal year-end measurement date. In the first approach (paragraph 18), an employer remeasures plan assets and benefit obligations as of the beginning of the fiscal year that the measurement date provisions are applied. An employer uses those new measurements to determine the effects of the measurement date change as of the beginning of the fiscal year that the measurement date provisions are applied. In the second approach (paragraph 19), an employer continues to use the measurements determined for the prior fiscal year-end reporting to estimate the effects of the change.

18. Under the first approach, an employer shall measure plan assets and benefit obligations as of the beginning of the fiscal year that the measurement date provisions are applied. For an employer that is a business entity:

a. Net periodic benefit cost for the period between the measurement date that is used for the imme-

diately preceding fiscal year-end and the beginning of the fiscal year that the measurement date provisions are applied, exclusive of any curtailment or settlement gain or loss, shall be recognized, net of tax, as a separate adjustment of the opening balance of retained earnings. That is, the pretax amount recognized as an adjustment to retained earnings is the net periodic benefit cost that without a change in measurement date otherwise would have been recognized on a delayed basis during the first interim period for the fiscal year that the measurement date provisions are applied.

b. Any gain or loss arising from a curtailment or settlement between the measurement date that is used for the immediately preceding fiscal year-end and the beginning of the fiscal year that the measurement date provisions are applied shall be recognized in earnings in that period and not as an adjustment to retained earnings. This provision prohibits an employer from early application of the measurement date provisions when the employer has issued financial statements for the prior year without recognition of such a settlement or curtailment. For example, assume an employer with a June 30 year-end that used a March 31 measurement date curtailed its benefit plan on May 31, 2006, resulting in a curtailment loss. That employer would be able to apply early the measurement date provisions in fiscal year 2007 if it recognizes the May 31, 2006 curtailment loss in its financial statements for the year ending June 30, 2006. That would not be the case if its 2006 financial statements had been issued before it wished to early adopt for fiscal year 2007.

c. Other changes in the fair value of plan assets and the benefit obligations (for example, gains or losses) for the period between the measurement date that is used for the immediately preceding fiscal year-end and the beginning of the fiscal year that the measurement date provisions are applied shall be recognized, net of tax, as a separate adjustment of the opening balance of accumulated other comprehensive income for the fiscal year that the measurement date provisions are applied.

The guidance in this paragraph also shall apply to a not-for-profit employer, except that the adjustments that would be made to the opening balances of retained earnings and accumulated other comprehensive income shall instead be recognized as a change in unrestricted net assets in the statement of activities, net of tax, if any. Those amounts shall be reported in a separate line item or items apart from expenses and outside a performance indicator or other intermediate measure of operations, if one is presented.

19. In lieu of remeasuring plan assets and benefit obligations as of the beginning of the fiscal year that the measurement date provisions are applied, under the second approach, an employer shall use earlier measurements determined for the year-end reporting as of the fiscal year immediately preceding the year that the measurement date provisions are applied. For an employer that is a business entity:

a. Net periodic benefit cost for the period between the earlier measurement date and the end of the fiscal year that the measurement date provisions are applied, exclusive of any curtailment or settlement gain or loss, shall be allocated proportionately between amounts to be recognized as an adjustment of retained earnings and net periodic benefit cost for the fiscal year that the measurement date provisions are applied. For example, a calendar-year employer that uses a September 30 measurement date and has no settlement or curtailment during the period would allocate as an adjustment of retained earnings three-fifteenths of net periodic benefit cost determined for the period from September 30, 2007, to December 31, 2008. The remaining twelve-fifteenths would be recognized as net periodic benefit cost for the fiscal year that the measurement date provisions first are applied.

b. Any gain or loss arising from a curtailment or settlement between the measurement date that is used for the immediately preceding fiscal year-end and the beginning of the fiscal year that the measurement date provisions are applied shall be recognized in earnings in that period and not as an adjustment to retained earnings. This provision prohibits an employer from early application of the measurement date provisions when the employer has issued financial statements for the prior year without recognition of such a settlement or curtailment (see paragraph 18(b)).

c. Other changes in the fair value of plan assets and the benefit obligations (for example, gains or losses) for the period between the earlier measurement date and the end of the fiscal year that the measurement date provisions are applied

shall be recognized as other comprehensive income for the fiscal year that the measurement date provisions are applied.

That approach shall be adjusted if, during the period between the earlier measurement date and the beginning of the fiscal year that the change in measurement date occurs, an employer elects to remeasure plan assets and benefit obligations or there is an event, such as a settlement or curtailment, that requires an intervening measurement. In that case, a revised net periodic benefit cost for the remainder of that period is determined by prorating the revised net periodic benefit cost for the period from the date of the intervening remeasurement to the end of the fiscal year that the measurement date provisions are applied. The guidance in this paragraph also shall apply to a not-for-profit employer, except that the adjustment that would be made to retained earnings shall instead be recognized as a change in unrestricted net assets in the statement of activities, net of tax, if any. Those amounts shall be reported in a separate line item or items apart from expenses and outside a performance indicator or other intermediate measure of operations, if one is presented. The amounts that would be recognized in other comprehensive income shall be recognized pursuant to paragraph 8 of this Statement.

Disclosures Required in the Year of Application

20. In the year that the recognition provisions of this Statement are initially applied, an employer shall disclose, in the notes to the annual financial statements, the incremental effect of applying this Statement on individual line items in the year-end statement of financial position.

21. In the year that the measurement date provisions of this Statement are initially applied, a business entity shall disclose the separate adjustments of retained earnings and accumulated other comprehensive income from applying this Statement. A not-for-profit employer shall disclose the separate adjustment of unrestricted net assets from applying this Statement.

22. The disclosures specified by paragraphs 17 and 18 of FASB Statement No. 154, *Accounting Changes and Error Corrections,* are not required.

> **The provisions of this Statement need
> not be applied to immaterial items.**

*This Statement was adopted by the unanimous vote of the seven members of the Financial Accounting
Standards Board:*

Robert H. Herz,	G. Michael Crooch	Edward W. Trott
Chairman	Thomas J. Linsmeier	Donald M. Young
George J. Batavick	Leslie F. Seidman	

Appendix A

IMPLEMENTATION GUIDANCE

Introduction

A1. This appendix is an integral part of this Statement. It provides guidance illustrating the transition provisions of this Statement in simplified situations. Applying those provisions to actual situations will require judgment; this appendix is intended to aid in making those judgments. Certain assumptions, including benefit payments, employer contributions, and obligations settled, have not been included because those transactions are not affected by the provisions of this Statement. Therefore, the examples do not include all the assumptions necessary to reconcile between various stated assumptions or the beginning and ending balances of plan assets or benefit obligations. Examples 1 and 2 provide implementation guidance for a business entity that sponsors a defined benefit postretirement plan. Example 3 provides guidance for a not-for-profit organization that sponsors a defined benefit postretirement plan.

Example 1—Application of the Recognition Provisions of This Statement

A2. Company A adopts the recognition and disclosure requirements of this Statement as of the end of its fiscal year (December 31, 2006). For simplicity, this example assumes that Company A's annual report includes a statement of financial position and a statement of changes in stockholders' equity. An income statement is not presented in this example because it is not affected by the recognition provisions of this Statement. Additionally, this example does not consider the effects on financial reporting for interim

periods. In applying the recognition provisions of this Statement for transition, Company A adjusts the amounts recognized in the statement of financial position as of December 31, 2006, prior to application of this Statement, so that gains or losses, prior service costs or credits, and the transition asset or obligation that have not yet been included in net periodic benefit cost as of December 31, 2006, are recognized as a component of the ending balance of accumulated other comprehensive income, net of tax (illustrated in paragraph A4). The adjustment is reported as an adjustment of the ending balance of accumulated other comprehensive income (see paragraph A7).

A3. The funded status of Company A's defined benefit pension plan and the amounts not yet recognized as components of net periodic pension cost as of December 31, 2006, and December 31, 2007, are shown below. Company A measures plan assets and benefit obligations as of the date of its financial statements. Under the prior provisions of FASB Statement No. 87, *Employers' Accounting for Pensions,* Company A did not have an additional minimum pension liability at December 31, 2006. Company A is not required to amortize the cumulative net loss because it is less than 10 percent of the greater of the projected benefit obligation or the market-related value of plan assets for all years presented. No plan amendments affect the period from January 1, 2006, to December 31, 2007. Company A's applicable tax rate for 2006 and 2007 is 40 percent. All deferred tax assets recognized are evaluated by Company A, and no valuation allowance is considered necessary at any time. Under the prior provisions of Statement 87, Company A had a recognized liability of $45,000 at December 31, 2006, for the amount that past net periodic pension costs exceeded past contributions to the plan.

	12/31/06	12/31/07
	(in thousands)	
Projected benefit obligation	$(2,525)	$(2,700)
Plan assets at fair value	1,625	1,700
Funded status	$ (900)	$(1,000)

Items not yet recognized as a component of net periodic pension cost:

	12/31/06	12/31/07
Transition obligation	$ 240	$ 200
Prior service cost	375	350
Net loss	240	260
	$ 855	$ 810

A4. At December 31, 2006, Company A recognizes a liability for the underfunded status of its defined benefit pension plan and adjusts ending accumulated other comprehensive income, net of tax, for the transition obligation, prior service cost, and net loss that have not been recognized as a component of net periodic pension cost. The journal entry is shown below:

Accumulated other comprehensive income	855	
Deferred tax asset	342	
Deferred tax benefit—accumulated other comprehensive income		342
Liability for pension benefits		855

A5. The following table illustrates the adjustments made to Company A's statement of financial position for December 31, 2006. The table is not intended to illustrate the disclosure requirements of this Statement (see paragraph A6). This illustration assumes that plan assets exceed the actuarial present value of benefits to be paid over the next fiscal year. Therefore, the entire liability for pension benefits is classified as a long-term liability.

Company A
Statement of Financial Position
December 31, 2006
(in thousands)

	Before Application of Statement 158	Adjustments	After Application of Statement 158
Current assets:			
Cash	$ 40,000	$ 0	$ 40,000
Inventory	720,500	0	720,500
Total current assets	760,500	0	760,500
Intangible assets	100,000	0	100,000
Total assets	$860,500	$ 0	$860,500
Current liabilities	$ 60,000	$ 0	$ 60,000
Liability for pension benefits	45	855	900
Other long-term liabilities	99,955	0	99,955
Deferred income taxes	20,000	(342)	19,658
Total liabilities	180,000	513	180,513
Common stock	150,000	0	150,000
Paid-in capital	300,000	0	300,000
Retained earnings	205,500	0	205,500
Accumulated other comprehensive income	25,000	(513)	24,487
Total stockholders' equity	680,500	(513)	679,987
Total liabilities and stockholders' equity	$860,500	$ 0	$860,500

A6. The following table illustrates the disclosures required by paragraph 20 of this Statement in the year that the recognition provisions are initially adopted.

**Incremental Effect of Applying FASB Statement No. 158
on Individual Line Items in the Statement of Financial Position
December 31, 2006
(in thousands)**

	Before Application of Statement 158	Adjustments	After Application of Statement 158
Liability for pension benefits	$ 45	$ 855	$ 900
Deferred income taxes	20,000	(342)	19,658
Total liabilities	180,000	513	180,513
Accumulated other comprehensive income	25,000	(513)	24,487
Total stockholders' equity	680,500	(513)	679,987

A7. Company A's statement of changes in stockholders' equity for the year ended December 31, 2006, which includes the effects of applying the provisions of this Statement, follows. Brackets are used to highlight those effects. The table is not intended to illustrate the disclosure requirements of this Statement.

Company A
Statement of Changes in Stockholders' Equity
Year Ended December 31, 2006
(in thousands)

	Total	Comprehensive Income	Retained Earnings	Accumulated Other Comprehensive Income	Common Stock	Paid-in Capital
Balance at December 31, 2005	$612,979		$137,988	$24,991	$150,000	$300,000
Comprehensive income						
Net income for 2006	67,512	$67,512	67,512			
Other comprehensive income, net of tax						
Foreign currency translation gain	15	15				
Unrealized holding loss arising during period	(6)	(6)				
Other comprehensive income		9		9		
Comprehensive income		$67,521				
Adjustment to initially apply FASB Statement No. 158, net of tax	[(513)]			[(513)]		
Balance at December 31, 2006	$679,987		$205,500	$24,487	$150,000	$300,000

A8. In applying this Statement in 2007, Company A:

a. Adjusts other comprehensive income, net of tax, to recognize the amortization of the transition obligation in net periodic pension cost
b. Adjusts other comprehensive income, net of tax, to recognize the amortization of prior service cost in net periodic pension cost
c. Recognizes a pension liability for the additional net loss arising during the year, and a corresponding decrease in other comprehensive income, net of tax
d. Recognizes a pension liability and net periodic pension cost, net of tax, for the service cost, interest cost, and expected return on plan assets.

A9. The components of projected net periodic pension cost for the year ended December 31, 2007, are:

Service cost	$120
Interest cost	95
Expected return on plan assets	(80)
Amortization of prior service cost	25
Amortization of the transition obligation	40
Amortization of net (gain) loss	0
Net periodic benefit cost	$200

A10. For the year ending December 31, 2007, Company A makes the following journal entries in applying the recognition provisions of this Statement:

a. Recognize net periodic pension cost and a corresponding increase in other comprehensive income, net of tax, for amortization of the transition obligation (see paragraph A9):

Net periodic pension cost	40	
Deferred tax benefit—other comprehensive income	16	
Deferred tax benefit—net income		16
Other comprehensive income		40

b. Recognize net periodic pension cost and a corresponding increase in other comprehensive income, net of tax, for amortization of prior service cost (see paragraph A9):

Net periodic pension cost	25	
Deferred tax benefit—other comprehensive income	10	
Deferred tax benefit—net income		10
Other comprehensive income		25

c. Recognize a pension liability and net periodic pension cost, net of tax, for the service cost of $120, interest cost of $95, and the expected return on plan assets of $(80) (see paragraph A9):

Net periodic pension cost	135	
Deferred tax asset	54	
Deferred tax benefit—net income		54
Liability for pension benefits		135

d. Recognize a pension liability for the additional net loss arising during the year and a corresponding decrease in other comprehensive income, net of tax (this is the increase in net loss from $240 to $260 shown in paragraph A3):

Other comprehensive income	20	
Deferred tax asset	8	
Deferred tax benefit—other comprehensive income		8
Liability for pension benefits		20

Example 2(a)—Change in the Measurement Date and Plan Settlement

A11. Company B adopted the recognition provisions of this Statement in its December 31, 2006 financial statements. As required by this Statement, Company B changes the measurement date for its defined benefit pension plan from September 30 to

December 31 for its 2008 financial statements. Company B elects to implement that change by remeasuring plan assets and obligations as of December 31, 2007 (see paragraph 18). Company B has a plan settlement on November 30, 2007, and remeasures its plan assets and benefit obligations as of November 30, 2007, resulting in a settlement loss before taxes of $60,000, which is a portion of the net loss in accumulated other comprehensive income. However, the effects of remeasuring plan assets and obligations as of November 30, 2007, on the funded status reported in Company B's statement of financial position are not recognized until the following fiscal year because the change in measurement date has not been adopted at November 30, 2007. In recognizing the effects of the plan settlement and change in measurement date, Company B:

a. Recognizes the settlement loss in net income in the fourth quarter of 2007 and a corresponding decrease in the cumulative net loss in other comprehensive income (illustrated in paragraph A14)
b. Recognizes the net periodic pension cost incurred from October 1, 2007, to December 31, 2007, net of tax, as an adjustment to beginning retained earnings and beginning accumulated other comprehensive income for 2008 (illustrated in paragraph A15(a))
c. Recognizes any gains or losses arising during the period from October 1, 2007, to December 31, 2007, net of tax, as an adjustment to beginning accumulated other comprehensive income for 2008 (illustrated in paragraph A15(b))
d. Recognizes corresponding changes in its pension liability and deferred tax accounts for the above items.

A12. The funded statuses of Company B's plan as of September 30, 2007, November 30, 2007, December 31, 2007, and December 31, 2008, and amounts included in accumulated other comprehensive income to be recognized as a component of net periodic pension cost are shown below. Company B has no remaining transition asset or obligation. Company B is not required to amortize the cumulative net loss because it is less than 10 percent of the greater of the market-related value of plan assets or the projected benefit obligation for all years presented. Company B's applicable tax rate for 2007 and 2008 is 40 percent. All deferred tax assets recognized are evaluated by Company B, and no valuation allowance is considered necessary at any time.

	9/30/07	11/30/07	12/31/07	12/31/08
	(in thousands)			
Projected benefit obligation	$(3,660)	$(3,200)	$(3,210)	$(3,700)
Plan assets at fair value	2,600	2,200	2,225	2,200
Funded status	$(1,060)	$(1,000)	$ (985)	$(1,500)
Items not yet recognized as a component of net periodic pension cost:				
Prior service cost	$ 380	$ 360	$ 350	$ 230
Net loss	265	220	315	365
	$ 645	$ 580	$ 665	$ 595

A13. Based on actuarial valuations performed as of September 30, 2007, and November 30, 2007, Company B determines its net periodic pension cost for the two-month period from October 1, 2007, to November 30, 2007, and for the one-month period from December 1, 2007, to December 31, 2007, respectively, to be:

Net Periodic Pension Cost for:	2 Months	1 Month	Total
Service cost	$ 25	$ 15	$ 40
Interest cost	30	15	45
Expected return on plan assets	(30)	(15)	(45)
Total service cost, interest cost, and expected return on plan assets	25	15	40
Amortization of prior service cost	20	10	30
Amortization of net loss	0	0	0
Total amortization	20	10	30
Net periodic benefit cost	$ 45	$ 25	$ 70

A14. In the fourth quarter of 2007, Company B makes the following journal entry to recognize the settlement loss:

Net periodic pension cost (settlement loss)	60	
Deferred tax benefit—other comprehensive income	24	
Deferred tax benefit—net income		24
Other comprehensive income		60

A15. In 2008, Company B makes the following journal entries in applying the measurement date provisions of this Statement:

a. Adjust the beginning balances of retained earnings, accumulated other comprehensive income, pension liability, and deferred tax accounts for the amortization of prior service cost and the service cost, interest cost, and expected return on plan assets (see paragraph A13):

Retained earnings	70	
Deferred tax asset ($40 × 40%)	16	
Deferred tax benefit—accumulated other comprehensive income ($30 × 40%)	12	
Deferred tax benefit—retained earnings ($70 × 40%)		28
Accumulated other comprehensive income		30
Liability for pension benefits		40

b. Adjust the beginning balances of accumulated other comprehensive income, pension liability, and deferred tax accounts for the net loss arising during the period:

Accumulated other comprehensive income	110[a]	
Deferred tax asset	44	
Deferred tax benefit—accumulated other comprehensive income		44
Liability for pension benefits		110

---

[a]This is the net change in the cumulative net loss after recognition of the settlement loss, calculated as follows: Net loss at 12/31/07 of $315 – Net loss at 9/30/07 of $265 + Plan settlement loss of $60 = $110.

A16. Company B's statement of changes in stockholders' equity for 2007 and 2008, which shows the effects of the settlement loss and change in measurement date, follows. Brackets are used to highlight those effects. The table is not intended to illustrate the disclosure requirements of this Statement.

Company B
Statement of Changes in Stockholders' Equity
Years Ended December 31, 2007, and 2008
(in thousands)

	Total	Comprehensive Income	Retained Earnings	Accumulated Other Comprehensive Income	Common Stock	Paid-in Capital
Balance at December 31, 2006	$289,140		$55,000	$(360)	$195,000	$39,500
Comprehensive income						
Net income for 2007	5,464	[$5,464^b]	5,464			
Other comprehensive income, net of tax						
Settlement loss (see paragraph A14)	[36]	[36]				
Prior service cost	72	72				
Net loss	(99)	(99)				
Other comprehensive income		9		9		
Comprehensive income		$5,473				
Balance at December 31, 2007	294,613		60,464	(351)	195,000	39,500

Effects of changing pension plan measurement date pursuant to FASB Statement No. 158

Service cost, interest cost, and expected return on plan assets for October 1–December 31, net of tax (see paragraph A15(a))	[(24)]				
Amortization of prior service cost for October 1–December 31, net of tax (see paragraph A15(a))	0		[(18)]	[18]	
Additional loss for October 1–December 31, net of tax (see paragraph A15(b))	[(66)]		[(18)]	[(66)]	
Beginning balance, as adjusted	294,523		60,422	(399)	195,000
Comprehensive income					
Net income for 2008	12,000	$12,000	12,000		
Other comprehensive income, net of tax					
Prior service cost	72	72			
Net loss	(30)	(30)			
Other comprehensive income		42		42	42
Comprehensive income		$12,042			
Balance at December 31, 2008	$306,565		$72,422	$(357)	$195,000	39,500

---

bIncludes the settlement loss of $60 ($36, net of tax).

Example 2(b)—Change in the Measurement Date (Alternative Method)

A17. Company C adopted the recognition provisions of this Statement in its December 31, 2006 financial statements. As required by this Statement, Company C changes the measurement date for its defined benefit pension plan from September 30 to December 31 for its 2008 financial statements. Company C elects the alternative transition method (see paragraph 19). Based on the measurement of plan assets and benefit obligations as of September 30, 2007, Company C's actuary prepares a 15-month projection of net periodic pension cost to December 31, 2008. In recognizing the effects of the change in measurement date for its 2008 financial statements, Company C:

a. Allocates the net periodic pension cost for the 15-month period from October 1, 2007, to December 31, 2008, net of tax, proportionately between amounts to be recognized as an adjustment of retained earnings and net periodic pension cost for 2008 (illustrated in paragraphs A19, A20(a), and A20(b))

b. Recognizes any net gain or loss arising during the period from October 1, 2007, to December 31, 2008, net of tax, in other comprehensive income for 2008 (illustrated in paragraph A21)

c. Recognizes corresponding changes in its pension liability and deferred tax accounts for the above items.

A18. The funded statuses of Company C's plan as of September 30, 2007, and December 31, 2008, and amounts included in accumulated other comprehensive income to be recognized as components of net periodic pension cost are shown below. Company C has no remaining transition asset or obligation. Company C is not required to amortize the cumulative net loss because it is less than 10 percent of the greater of the market-related value of plan assets or the projected benefit obligation for all years presented. Company C's applicable tax rate for 2007 and 2008 is 40 percent. All deferred tax assets recognized are evaluated by Company C, and no valuation allowance is considered necessary at any time.

	9/30/07	12/31/08
	(in thousands)	
Projected benefit obligation	$(3,200)	$(3,500)
Plan assets at fair value	2,200	2,330
Funded status	$(1,000)	$(1,170)
Items not yet recognized as a component of net periodic pension cost:		
Prior service cost	$ 400	$ 275
Net loss	265	315
	$ 665	$ 590

A19. Based on an actuarial valuation performed as of September 30, 2007, Company C determines its net periodic pension cost for the 15-month period from October 1, 2007, to December 31, 2008, and allocates its net periodic pension cost proportionately between amounts to be recognized as an adjustment of retained earnings and net periodic pension cost for 2008 as follows:

Net Periodic Pension Cost for:	15 Months	3 Months	12 Months
Service cost	$ 130		
Interest cost	150		
Expected return on plan assets	(105)		
Total service cost, interest cost, and expected return on plan assets	175	$35	$140
Amortization of prior service cost	125		
Amortization of net loss	0		
Total amortization	125	25	100
Net periodic pension cost	$ 300	$60	$240

A20. In 2008, Company C makes the following journal entries in applying the measurement date provisions of this Statement:

a. Adjust retained earnings, accumulated other comprehensive income, pension liability, and deferred tax accounts for three-fifteenths of the net periodic pension cost projected for the 15-month period from October 1, 2007, to December 31, 2008 (see paragraph A19):

Retained earnings	60	
Deferred tax assets ($35 × 40%)	14	
Deferred tax benefit—accumulated other comprehensive income ($25 × 40%)	10	
Deferred tax benefit—retained earnings ($60 × 40%)		24
Accumulated other comprehensive income		25
Liability for pension benefits		35

b. Recognize net periodic pension cost for twelve-fifteenths of the net periodic pension cost projected for the 15-month period from October 1, 2007, to December 31, 2008, and make corresponding changes to the pension liability and deferred tax accounts (see paragraph A19):

Net periodic pension cost	240	
Deferred tax assets ($140 × 40%)	56	
Deferred tax benefit—other comprehensive income ($100 × 40%)	40	
Deferred tax benefit—net income ($240 × 40%)		96
Other comprehensive income		100
Liability for pension benefits		140

A21. In 2008, Company C adjusts other comprehensive income and pension liability for the entire net loss arising during the period from October 1, 2007, to December 31, 2008, because net gains or losses cannot be readily identifiable as arising in certain periods. The journal entry is as follows:

Other comprehensive income	50[a]	
Deferred tax asset	20	
Deferred tax benefit—other comprehensive income		20
Liability for pension benefits		50

---

[a]This is the net change in the cumulative net loss, calculated as follows: Net loss at 12/31/08 of $315 – Net loss at 9/30/07 of $265 = $50.

(This page intentionally left blank.)

A22. Company C's statement of changes in stockholders' equity for 2007 and 2008, which shows the effects of the change in measurement date, follows. Brackets are used to highlight those effects. The table is not intended to illustrate the disclosure requirements of this Statement.

Company C
Statement of Changes in Stockholders' Equity
Years Ended December 31, 2007, and 2008
(in thousands)

	Total	Comprehensive Income	Retained Earnings	Accumulated Other Comprehensive Income	Common Stock	Paid-in Capital
Balance at December 31, 2006	$559,800		$30,000	$(200)	$400,000	$130,000
Comprehensive income						
Net income for 2007	10,500	$10,500	10,500			
Other comprehensive income, net of tax						
Prior service cost	60	60				
Net loss	(39)	(39)				
Other comprehensive income		21		21		
Comprehensive income		$10,521				
Balance at December 31, 2007	570,321		40,500	(179)	400,000	130,000
Comprehensive income						
Net income for 2008 (see paragraph A20(b))	11,856	[11,856[b]]	11,856			
Other comprehensive income, net of tax						
Prior service cost (see paragraph A20(b))	[60]	[60]				
Net loss (see paragraph A21)	[(30)]	[(30)]				
Other comprehensive income	30	30		30		
Comprehensive income		$11,886				

Effects of changing the pension plan measurement date pursuant to FASB Statement No. 158

Service cost, interest cost, and expected return on plan assets for October 1–December 31, 2007, net of tax (see paragraph A20(a))	[21]	[21]		
Amortization of prior service cost for October 1–December 31, 2007, net of tax (see paragraph A20(a))	0	[(15)]	[15]	
	(21)	(36)	15	
Balance at December 31, 2008	$582,186	$52,320	$(134)	$400,000	$130,000

[b]Includes the net periodic pension cost of $240 ($144, net of tax).

Example 2(c)—Change in the Measurement Date (Alternative Method) and Plan Settlement

A23. Company D adopted the recognition provisions of this Statement in its December 31, 2006 financial statements. As required by this Statement, Company D changes the measurement date for its defined benefit pension plan from September 30 to December 31 for its 2008 financial statements. Company D elects the alternative transition method (see paragraph 19). As of September 30, 2007, Company D's actuary prepares a 15-month projection of net periodic pension cost to December 31, 2008. Company D has a plan settlement on November 30, 2007, resulting in new measurements of plan assets and obligations and recognition of a loss before taxes of $90,000, which is a portion of the net loss in accumulated other comprehensive income. As a result of the plan settlement, the actuary prepares a new projection of net periodic pension cost for the 13 months to December 31, 2008. Pursuant to paragraph 19, the loss from the plan settlement is recognized in the last quarter of 2007. However, the effects of remeasuring plan assets and obligations as of November 30, 2007, on the funded status reported in Company D's statement of financial position are not recognized until the following fiscal year because the change in measurement date has not been adopted at November 30, 2007. In recognizing the effects of the plan settlement and change in measurement date, Company D:

a. Recognizes the settlement loss in net income in the fourth quarter of 2007 and a corresponding decrease in the cumulative net loss in other comprehensive income (illustrated in paragraph A25)
b. Determines the net periodic pension cost for the period between September 30, 2007, and December 31, 2007, net of tax, to be recognized in 2008 as an adjustment of retained earnings by proportionately allocating projections of net periodic pension cost for 15 months and 13 months made as of September 30, 2007, and November 30, 2007, respectively (illustrated in paragraphs A27, A28(a), and A28(c))
c. Recognizes any net gain or loss arising during the period from October 1, 2007, to November 30, 2007, net of tax, as an adjustment of accumulated other comprehensive income and recognizes any net gain or loss arising during the period from December 1, 2007, to December 31, 2008, net of tax, as an adjustment of other comprehensive income for 2008 (illustrated in paragraphs A28(b) and A29)
d. Recognizes corresponding changes in its pension liability and deferred tax accounts for the above items.

A24. The funded statuses of Company D's plan as of September 30, 2007, November 30, 2007, and December 31, 2008, and amounts previously included in accumulated other comprehensive income that are to be recognized as a component of net periodic pension cost are shown below. Company D has no remaining transition asset or obligation. Company D is not required to amortize the cumulative net loss because it is less than 10 percent of the greater of the market-related value of plan assets or the projected benefit obligation for all years presented. Company D's applicable tax rate for 2007 and 2008 is 40 percent. All deferred tax assets recognized are evaluated by Company D, and no valuation allowance is considered necessary at any time.

	9/30/07	11/30/07	12/31/08
		(in thousands)	
Projected benefit obligation	$(3,550)	$(3,600)	$(3,610)
Plan assets at fair value	2,500	2,525	2,510
Funded status	$(1,050)	$(1,075)	$(1,100)
Items not yet recognized as a component of net periodic pension cost:			
Prior service cost	$ 400	$ 380	$ 250
Net loss	200	250	300
	$ 600	$ 630	$ 550

A25. In the fourth quarter of 2007, Company D makes the following journal entry to recognize the settlement loss:

Net periodic pension cost (settlement loss)	90	
Deferred tax benefit—other comprehensive income	36	
Deferred tax benefit—net income		36
Other comprehensive income		90

A26. Based on actuarial valuations performed as of September 30, 2007, and November 30, 2007, Company D determines its net periodic pension cost for the 2-month period from October 1, 2007, to November 30, 2007, and 13-month period from December 1, 2007, to December 31, 2008, respectively, to be:

Net Periodic Pension Cost for:	2 Months	13 Months
Service cost	$ 17	$ 110
Interest cost	20	140
Expected return on plan assets	(14)	(100)
Total service cost, interest cost, and expected return on plan assets	23	150
Amortization of prior service cost	20	130
Amortization of net (gain) loss	0	0
Total amortization	20	130
Net periodic pension cost	$ 43	$ 280

A27. Company D allocates its net periodic pension cost proportionately between the amounts to be recognized as an adjustment of retained earnings and net periodic pension cost for 2008 as follows:

Adjustment to Retained Earnings:	**2 Months**	**13 Months (above) × (1/13)**	**Total**
Service cost	$ 17	$ 8	$ 25
Interest cost	20	11	31
Expected return on plan assets	(14)	(7)	(21)
Total service cost, interest cost, and expected return on plan assets	23	12	35
Amortization of prior service cost	20	10	30
Amortization of net (gain) loss	0	0	0
Total amortization	20	10	30
Net periodic pension cost	$ 43	$22	$ 65

Adjustment to Net Periodic Pension Cost:	**13 Months (above) × (12/13)**
Service cost	$101
Interest cost	129
Expected return on plan assets	(92)
Total service cost, interest cost, and expected return on plan assets	138
Amortization of prior service cost	120
Amortization of net (gain) loss	0
Total amortization	120
Net periodic pension cost	$258

A28. In 2008, Company D makes the following journal entries in applying the measurement date provisions of this Statement:

a. Adjust retained earnings, accumulated other comprehensive income, pension liability, and deferred tax accounts for the net periodic pension cost for the 2-month period from October 1, 2007, to November 30, 2007, and one-thirteenth of the net periodic pension cost projected for the 13-month period from December 1, 2007, to December 31, 2008 (see paragraph A27):

Retained earnings	65	
Deferred tax assets ($35 × 40%)	14	
Deferred tax benefit—accumulated other comprehensive income ($30 × 40%)	12	
Deferred tax benefit—retained earnings ($65 × 40%)		26
Accumulated other comprehensive income		30
Liability for pension benefits		35

b. Adjust accumulated other comprehensive income, pension liability, and deferred tax accounts for the net loss arising during the two-month period from October 1, 2007, to November 30, 2007:

Accumulated other comprehensive income	140[a]	
Deferred tax assets	56	
Deferred tax benefit—accumulated other comprehensive income		56
Liability for pension benefits		140

c. Recognize net periodic pension cost, pension liability, and deferred tax assets for twelve-thirteenths of the net periodic pension cost projected for the 13-month period from December 1, 2007, to December 31, 2008 (see paragraph A27):

Net periodic pension cost	258	
Deferred tax assets ($138 × 40%)	55	
Deferred tax benefit—other comprehensive income ($120 × 40%)	48	
Deferred tax benefit—net income ($258 × 40%)		103
Other comprehensive income		120
Liability for pension benefits		138

A29. In 2008, Company D adjusts other comprehensive income and pension liability for the entire net loss arising during the period from December 1, 2007, to December 31, 2008, because net gains and losses cannot be readily identifiable as arising in certain periods. The journal entry is as follows:

Other comprehensive income	50[b]	
Deferred tax asset	20	
Deferred tax benefit—other comprehensive income		20
Liability for pension benefits		50

---

[a]This is the net change in the cumulative net loss after recognition of the settlement loss, calculated as follows: Net loss at 11/30/07 of $250 – Net loss at 9/30/07 of $200 + Plan settlement loss of $90 = $140.

[b]This is the net change in the cumulative net loss, calculated as follows: Net loss at 12/31/08 of $300 – Net loss at 11/30/07 of $250 = $50.

A30. The following is Company D's statement of changes in stockholders' equity for 2007 and 2008 that shows the effects of the change in measurement date. Brackets are used to highlight those effects. The table is not intended to illustrate the disclosure requirements of this Statement.

Company D
Statement of Changes in Stockholders' Equity
Years Ended December 31, 2006, 2007, and 2008
(in thousands)

	Total	Comprehensive Income	Retained Earnings	Accumulated Other Comprehensive Income	Common Stock	Paid-in Capital
Balance at December 31, 2006	$659,100		$100,000	$(900)	$500,000	$60,000
Comprehensive income						
Net income for 2007	20,446	[$20,446^c]	20,446			
Other comprehensive income, net of tax						
Settlement loss (see paragraph A25)		[54]				
Prior service cost		72				
Net loss		(60)				
Other comprehensive income	66	66		66		
Comprehensive income		$20,512				
Balance at December 31, 2007	679,612		120,446	(834)	500,000	60,000
Comprehensive income						
Net income for 2008 (see paragraph A28(c))	11,845	[$11,845^d]	11,845			
Other comprehensive income, net of tax						
Prior service cost	72	72				
Net loss (see paragraph A29)		[(30)]				
Other comprehensive income	42	42		42		
Comprehensive income		$11,887				

Effects of accounting change regarding pension plan measurement date pursuant to FASB Statement No. 158

Service cost, interest cost, and expected return on plan assets for October 1–December 31, 2007, net of tax (see paragraph A28(a))

Additional net loss for October 1–November 30, 2007 (see paragraph A28(b))

Amortization of prior service cost for October 1–December 31, 2007, net of tax (see paragraph A28(a))

Balance at December 31, 2008

			$60,000
			$500,000
	[21]	[84]	
		[18]	[18]
	(39)	(66)	
	$132,252	$(858)	
[21]			
[84]			
0			
(105)			
$691,394			

cIncludes the settlement loss of $90 ($54, net of tax).
dIncludes the net periodic pension cost of $258 ($155, net of tax).

A31. If Company D issues financial information about its financial position as of a date in 2008 but prior to December 31, 2008, the effects of remeasuring plan assets and obligations as of November 30, 2007, on the funded status reported in Company D's statement of financial position would be recognized prior to issuing that information as follows:

a. Adjust other comprehensive income for amortization of prior service cost:

Retained earnings	20	
Deferred tax benefit—other comprehensive income	8	
Deferred tax benefit—retained earnings		8
Other comprehensive income		20

b. Recognize the additional loss in other comprehensive income:

Other comprehensive income	140	
Deferred tax asset	56	
Deferred tax benefit—other comprehensive income		56
Liability for pension benefits		140

Example 3—Application of the Recognition Provisions and Early Adoption of the Measurement Date Provisions of This Statement by a Not-for-Profit Organization

Year of Initial Adoption

A32. Organization E, a not-for-profit, voluntary health and welfare organization, adopts the recognition provisions of this Statement at the end of its fiscal year (June 30, 2007). Organization E also elects to adopt early the measurement date provisions of this Statement and changes the measurement date for its defined benefit pension plan from March 31 to June 30 for its 2007 financial statements. Organization E is able to adopt early because it did not have any settlements or curtailments during the three-month period ended June 30, 2006, for which there would have been delayed recognition (see paragraphs 18(b) and 19(b)). Organization E elects the alternative transition method for the change in measurement date (see paragraph 19). Organization E's actuary prepares a 15-month projection of net periodic pension cost for April 1, 2006, to June 30, 2007 (based on the 12-month projection previously prepared for April 1, 2006, to March 31, 2007).

A33. In applying the recognition provisions of this Statement for transition, Organization E adjusts the amounts recognized in its statement of financial position as of June 30, 2007, prior to application of this Statement, so that gains or losses, prior service costs or credits, and the transition asset or obligation that have not yet been included in net periodic benefit cost as of June 30, 2007, are included in the ending balance of unrestricted net assets, net of tax, if any. Any required adjustment is reported in the statement of activities, in a separate line item or items within changes in unrestricted net assets, apart from expenses and outside a performance indicator or other intermediate measure of operations, if one is presented.

A34. The funded status of Organization E's defined benefit pension plan as of March 31, 2006, and June 30, 2007, and amounts to be recognized as components of net periodic pension cost are shown below. Under the prior provisions of Statement 87, Organization E would not have had an additional minimum pension liability at June 30, 2007. The cumulative net loss not yet recognized as a component of net periodic pension cost is less than 10 percent of the greater of the projected benefit obligation or the market-related value of plan assets for both years presented. No plan amendments affect the period from April 1, 2006, to June 30, 2007. Organization E is not subject to income taxes.

	3/31/06	6/30/07
	(in thousands)	
Projected benefit obligation	$(3,660)	$(3,670)
Plan assets at fair value	2,600	2,510
Funded status	$(1,060)	$(1,160)
Items not yet recognized as a component of net periodic pension cost:		
Transition obligation	$ 290	$ 240
Prior service cost	400	275
Net loss	265	315
	$ 955	$ 830
Components of projected 15 months' net periodic pension cost:		
Service cost	$ 130	
Interest cost	150	
Expected return on plan assets	(155)	
Amortization of prior service cost	125	
Amortization of net (gain) loss	0	
Amortization of transition obligation	50	
Net periodic pension cost	$ 300	

At June 30, 2007, Organization E recognizes a liability for the underfunded status of its defined benefit pension plan and adjusts the ending balance of unrestricted net assets for the transition obligation, prior service cost, and net loss that have not been recognized as components of net periodic pension cost. The journal entry is shown below:

Change in unrestricted net assets to initially apply the recognition provisions of FASB Statement No. 158	830	
Liability for pension benefits		830

A35. In recognizing the effects of the change in measurement date for its 2007 financial statements, Organization E allocates the net periodic pension cost for the 15-month period from April 1, 2006, to June 30, 2007, proportionately between amounts to be recognized as an adjustment of unrestricted net assets and net periodic pension cost for 2007 (illustrated in paragraph A36). The latter is reported within the appropriate functional expense categories.

A36. The 15-month projection of net periodic pension cost is allocated proportionately between amounts to be recognized as an adjustment of unrestricted net assets and net periodic pension cost for 2007:

	4/1/06–6/30/06	7/1/06–6/30/07
Net periodic pension cost	$300 × (3/15) = $60	$300 × (12/15) = $240

The journal entry to recognize the adjustment of unrestricted net assets is as follows:

Change in unrestricted net assets related to change in measurement date under FASB Statement No. 158	60	
Liability for pension benefits		60

A37. The following is Organization E's statement of activities, which includes an intermediate measure of operations. The estimated $240 of net periodic pension cost for 2007 is reported within the appropriate functional expense categories. The $890 decrease in unrestricted assets displayed as the effect of adoption of the recognition and measurement date provisions of this Statement comprises $830 of items not yet recognized in net periodic pension cost as of June 30, 2007 (transition obligation, prior service cost, and net loss), and $60 of net periodic pension cost allocated to the period from April 1, 2006, to June 30, 2006. Pursuant to paragraphs 16(b) and 19, Organization E recognizes the $890 accounting adjustment apart from expenses and outside its intermediate measure of operations. Because Organization E elects to present the accounting changes in a single line item, it discloses the individual components in the notes to financial statements (see paragraphs 10, 20, and 21).

Organization E
Statement of Activities
Year Ended June 30, 2007
(in thousands)

	Unrestricted	Temporarily Restricted	Permanently Restricted	Total
Operating:				
Revenues, gains, and other support:				
Private contributions, other than bequests	$ 65,000	$ 15,800		$ 80,800
Bequests	9,000			9,000
Government grants		7,000		7,000
Investment income used for operating activities	12,000	1,000		13,000
Sales of educational materials	1,000			1,000
Other	3,000			3,000
Net assets released from restrictions	15,000	(15,000)		0
Total revenues, gains, and other support	105,000	8,800		113,800
Expenses:				
Program services:				
Research and medical support	62,000			62,000
Public education	8,000			8,000
Community service	13,000			13,000
Total program services	83,000			83,000
Supporting services:				
Fund raising	9,000			9,000
Management and general	8,000			8,000
Total supporting services	17,000			17,000
Total expenses	100,000			100,000
Increase in net assets from operating activities	5,000	8,800		13,800
Nonoperating:				
Investment income in excess of amount used for operating activities	3,000			3,000
Contributions for endowment funds			$10,000	10,000
Increase in net assets before effect of adoption of FASB Statement No. 158	8,000	8,800	10,000	26,800
Effect of adoption of recognition and measurement date provisions of FASB Statement No. 158	(890)			(890)
Increase in net assets	7,110	8,800	10,000	25,910
Net assets, beginning of year	140,000	40,000	20,000	200,000
Net assets, end of year	$147,110	$ 48,800	$30,000	$225,910

Subsequent Year

A38. Organization E's actuary prepares a 12-month projection of net periodic pension cost for July 1, 2007, to June 30, 2008. The funded status of Organization E's defined benefit pension plan as of June 30, 2007 (repeated from above), and June 30, 2008, and amounts to be recognized as components of net periodic pension cost, are shown below. The cumulative net loss not yet recognized as a component of net periodic pension cost is less than 10 percent of the greater of the projected benefit obligation and the market-related value of plan assets. No plan amendments affect the period from July 1, 2007, to June 30, 2008. Assumptions about benefit payments and contributions made by Organization E have not been

included in this example because those transactions are not affected by the provisions of this Statement. During the fiscal year ending June 30, 2008, Organization E:

a. Recognizes the additional net loss as a change in unrestricted net assets and a change in the liability that reflects the underfunded status of the plan
b. Recognizes the amortization of the transition obligation as a component of net periodic pension cost
c. Recognizes the amortization of prior service cost as a component of net periodic pension cost
d. Recognizes net periodic pension cost for 2008, reported within the appropriate functional expense categories.

	6/30/07	6/30/08
	(in thousands)	
Projected benefit obligation	$(3,670)	$(3,600)
Plan assets at fair value	2,510	2,385
Funded status	$(1,160)	$(1,215)
Items not yet recognized as a component of net periodic pension cost:		
Transition obligation	$ 240	$ 200
Prior service cost	275	175
Net loss	315	365
	$ 830	$ 740
Components of projected 12 months' net periodic pension cost for fiscal year 2008:		
Service cost	$ 110	
Interest cost	120	
Expected return on plan assets	(125)	
Amortization of prior service cost	100	
Amortization of net (gain) loss	0	
Amortization of transition obligation	40	
Net periodic pension cost	$ 245	

A39. For the year ending June 30, 2008, Organization E recognizes the amortizations of the transition obligation and prior service cost as components of net periodic pension cost and recognizes the additional loss arising during the year. The journal entries are shown below:

a. Recognize the additional loss in unrestricted net assets:

Net loss not yet recognized in net periodic pension cost	50	
Liability for pension benefits		50

b. Recognize the amortization of the transition obligation in net periodic pension cost:

Net periodic pension cost (functionalized)	40	
Transition obligation not yet recognized in net periodic pension cost		40

c. Recognize the amortization of prior service cost in net periodic pension cost:

Net periodic pension cost (functionalized)	100	
Prior service cost not yet recognized in net periodic pension cost		100

d. Recognize service cost, interest cost, and the expected return on plan assets in net periodic pension cost:

Net periodic pension cost (functionalized)	105[a]	
Liability for pension benefits		105

In its statement of activities, Organization E chooses to present one combined separate line item (encompassing the net loss arising during the year and the amortizations of the transition obligation and prior service cost) apart from expenses. Organization E would disclose the components of that combined line item in the notes to financial statements, pursuant to paragraph 10 of this Statement.

---

[a]Equals $110 service cost + $120 interest cost – $125 expected return on plan assets.

A40. The following statement of activities reflects the presentation of the combined line item if Organization E chooses to present it outside its intermediate measure of operations:

Organization E
Statement of Activities
Year Ended June 30, 2008
(in thousands)

	Unrestricted	Temporarily Restricted	Permanently Restricted	Total
Operating:				
Revenues, gains, and other support:				
Private contributions, other than bequests	$ 60,000	$ 14,200		$ 74,200
Bequests	17,000			17,000
Government grants		9,000		9,000
Investment income used for operating activities	11,500	1,000		12,500
Sales of educational materials	2,000			2,000
Other	2,000			2,000
Net assets released from restrictions	17,000	(17,000)		0
Total revenues, gains, and other support	109,500	7,200		116,700
Expenses:				
Program services:				
Research and medical support	58,000			58,000
Public education	9,000			9,000
Community service	15,000			15,000
Total program services	82,000			82,000
Supporting services:				
Fund raising	15,000			15,000
Management and general	9,000			9,000
Total supporting services	24,000			24,000
Total expenses	106,000			106,000
Increase in net assets from operating activities	3,500	7,200		10,700
Nonoperating:				
Investment income in excess of amount used for operating activities	1,500			1,500
Contributions for endowment funds			$15,000	15,000
Pension-related changes other than net periodic pension cost	90[b]			90
Increase in net assets	5,090	7,200	15,000	27,290
Net assets, beginning of year	147,110	48,800	30,000	225,910
Net assets, end of year	$152,200	$ 56,000	$45,000	$253,200

---

[b]Equals $40 amortization of transition obligation + $100 amortization of prior service cost – $50 net loss.

A41. The following statement of activities reflects the presentation of the combined separate line item if, alternatively, Organization E chooses to present it within its intermediate measure of operations. This alternative would not be available to Organization E if it was within the scope of AICPA Audit and Accounting Guide, *Health Care Organizations,* and presented a performance indicator pursuant to the provisions of that Guide.

Organization E
Statement of Activities
Year Ended June 30, 2008
(in thousands)

	Unrestricted	Temporarily Restricted	Permanently Restricted	Total
Operating:				
Revenues, gains, and other support:				
Private contributions, other than bequests	$ 60,000	$ 14,200		$ 74,200
Bequests	17,000			17,000
Government grants		9,000		9,000
Investment income used for operating activities	11,500	1,000		12,500
Sales of educational materials	2,000			2,000
Other	2,000			2,000
Net assets released from restrictions	17,000	(17,000)		0
Total revenues, gains, and other support	109,500	7,200		116,700
Expenses:				
Program services:				
Research and medical support	58,000			58,000
Public education	9,000			9,000
Community service	15,000			15,000
Total program services	82,000			82,000
Supporting services:				
Fund raising	15,000			15,000
Management and general	9,000			9,000
Total supporting services	24,000			24,000
Total expenses	106,000			106,000
Pension-related changes other than net periodic pension cost	90[c]			90
Increase in net assets from operating activities	3,590	7,200		10,790
Nonoperating:				
Investment income in excess of amount used for operating activities	1,500			1,500
Contributions for endowment funds			$15,000	15,000
Increase in net assets	5,090	7,200	15,000	27,290
Net assets, beginning of year	147,110	48,800	30,000	225,910
Net assets, end of year	$152,200	$ 56,000	$45,000	$253,200

---

[c]Equals $40 amortization of transition obligation + $100 amortization of prior service cost – $50 net loss.

Appendix B

BACKGROUND INFORMATION AND BASIS FOR CONCLUSIONS

CONTENTS

Appendix B

BACKGROUND INFORMATION AND BASIS FOR CONCLUSIONS

Introduction

B1. This appendix summarizes considerations that Board members deemed significant in reaching the conclusions in this Statement. It includes reasons for accepting certain approaches and rejecting others. Individual Board members gave greater weight to some factors than to others.

Background Information

B2. In November 2005, the Board added a project to its agenda to comprehensively reconsider the guidance in FASB Statements No. 87, *Employers' Accounting for Pensions,* No. 88, *Employers' Accounting for Settlements and Curtailments of Defined Benefit Pension Plans and for Termination Benefits,* No. 106, *Employers' Accounting for Postretirement Benefits Other Than Pensions,* and No. 132 (revised 2003), *Employers' Disclosures about Pensions and Other Postretirement Benefits.* The project was undertaken because of concerns about the existing accounting requirements for defined benefit postretirement obligations, including pensions.

B3. Statement 87 was issued in 1985 and was effective for financial statements for fiscal years beginning after December 15, 1986. It establishes standards of financial reporting and accounting for an employer that offers pension benefits to its employees. Statement 87 prescribes the measurement of net periodic pension cost and required recognition of a liability that at least equaled the excess, if any, of the accumulated benefit obligation over the fair value of plan assets. Statement 87 also did not limit the amount that could be recognized as an employer's asset (for example, contributions to the plan in excess of net periodic pension cost recognized), even if the plan was significantly underfunded.

B4. Statement 106 was issued in 1990 and was effective for financial statements for fiscal years beginning after December 15, 1992. Before the issuance of that Statement, an employer generally recognized, on a cash basis, the costs arising from the exchange of employee service for postretirement benefits other than pensions (principally, retiree health care). That is, the costs were recognized when the obligation

was satisfied rather than when it was incurred. Statement 106 requires an employer to recognize the cost incurred over the periods in which employees render service in exchange for the promise to provide postretirement benefits. Statement 106 did not require that a minimum liability be recognized. Similar to Statement 87, it also did not limit the amount that could be recognized as an asset by an employer (for example, contributions to the plan in excess of net periodic postretirement benefit cost recognized).

B5. Statements 87 and 106 take similar approaches to the delayed recognition of certain economic events in measuring periodic benefit cost, to the net reporting of periodic benefit cost, and to the offsetting of assets and liabilities. Delayed recognition allows changes in the value of plan assets or in the benefit obligation (including changes resulting from plan amendments) that were not anticipated in measuring the net periodic benefit cost or benefit obligation to be recognized over subsequent periods instead of in the year they occur.

B6. The net reporting of periodic benefit cost means that the recognized consequences of different types of events and transactions affecting a postretirement benefit plan are aggregated into a single net amount (net periodic benefit cost) in an employer's financial statements. That reporting aggregates certain items that usually would be reported separately for any other part of an employer's operations, such as compensation cost of benefits promised, interest cost resulting from deferred payment of those benefits, and investment results from assets contributed to prefund the obligation.

B7. The offsetting of assets and liabilities refers to combining in an employer's statement of financial position the recognized effects of investing in plan assets and incurring liabilities for benefits. The assets and liabilities are offset, even though the liability has not been settled, the assets may still be largely controlled by the employer, and substantial risks and rewards associated with both of those amounts are borne by an employer.

B8. The primary criticisms of those and other features of the existing and past standards of accounting for postretirement benefit arrangements include the following:

a. An employer that sponsors a defined benefit plan is not required to recognize the economic events that affect the cost of providing postretirement benefits—the changes in plan assets and benefit obligations—as those changes take place.

b. Important information about postretirement plans is relegated to the notes to financial statements, in the form of a reconciliation of the overfunded or underfunded status to amounts recognized in the statement of financial position.

c. Net reporting of periodic benefit cost in an employer's reported results of operations obscures the individual effects of compensation, investing, and financing activities.

B9. The Board understood and acknowledged the first two of the above issues when it developed Statement 87. In Statement 87, the Board concluded that ". . . it would be conceptually appropriate and preferable to recognize a net pension liability or asset measured as the difference between the projected benefit obligation and plan assets, either with no delay in recognition of gains and losses, or perhaps with gains and losses reported currently in comprehensive income but not in earnings. However, it concluded that those approaches would be too great a change from past practice to be adopted at the present time" (paragraph 107). In Statement 87, the Board also noted that "because gains and losses may reflect refinements in estimates as well as real changes in economic values and because some gains in one period may be offset by losses in another or vice versa, this Statement does not require recognition of gains and losses as components of net pension cost of the period in which they arise" (paragraph 29; footnote reference omitted).

B10. The Board improved disclosures twice since Statements 87 and 106 were issued. FASB Statement No. 132, *Employers' Disclosures about Pensions and Other Postretirement Benefits,* issued in 1998, standardized the disclosure requirements for pensions and other postretirement benefits. Statement 132(R) added requirements for disclosures about the:

a. Types of plan assets held and the related investment strategy

b. Employer's annual measurement date(s) used in the accounting for the benefit arrangements

c. Plan obligations and expected near-term cash flows

d. Components of net periodic benefit cost recognized during interim periods.

B11. Some constituents believe the disclosures that are required by Statement 132(R) compensate for the lack of transparency that results from delayed recognition and net reporting. However, in Statement 87, the Board observed that:

Footnote disclosure is not an adequate substitute for recognition. The argument that the information is equally useful regardless of how it is presented could be applied to any financial statement element, but the usefulness and integrity of financial statements are impaired by each omission of an element that qualifies for recognition. . . . If the argument were valid, the consequences of recognition would not be different from those of not recognizing but disclosing the same information. . . . [paragraph 116]

B12. When issued, Statements 87 and 106 represented evolutionary improvements in accounting. However, many years have passed and requests for the Board to address issues related to employers' accounting for defined benefit postretirement plans have increased. Those requests were made by users of financial statements and others, including the SEC staff (in its June 2005 report to Congress on off-balance-sheet arrangements that was required by the Sarbanes-Oxley Act of 2002), members of the Board's Financial Accounting Standards Advisory Council and User Advisory Council, and representatives of the Pension Benefit Guaranty Corporation. Those constituents urged the Board to undertake a project that would improve the transparency and understandability of an employer's financial statements regarding the costs and obligations of providing postretirement benefits. Those improved financial statements would better serve the informational needs of equity owners, creditors, employees, retirees, donors, and other users.

B13. In light of the Board's discussions in the development of Statement 87, particularly the conclusions summarized in paragraph B9 of this Statement, as well as requests from certain constituents, the Board concluded that the accounting for defined benefit postretirement plans should be reconsidered. Although the trend of sponsoring defined benefit postretirement plans, particularly defined benefit pension plans, has declined in recent years, the Board decided to address the perceived deficiencies in the accounting because of the long-term nature and magnitude of existing arrangements.

B14. In March 2006, the Board issued an Exposure Draft, *Employers' Accounting for Defined Benefit Pension and Other Postretirement Plans,* and received comment letters from over 245 respondents. On June 27, 2006, the Board held 2 public roundtable meetings with a total of 33 constituents to discuss issues raised in the comment letters. At the roundtable meetings, constituents discussed several aspects of the Exposure Draft, including the scope and objective of the project; implementation of the proposed recognition provisions; measurement and effective date provisions; perceived economic consequences, including the effect of the proposed Statement on financial metrics referenced in contractual arrangements of nonpublic employers; and other matters.

B15. In July and August 2006, the Board redeliberated the issues raised by respondents to the Exposure Draft and by participants in the roundtable meetings. During redeliberations, the Board affirmed its conclusion that greater transparency and understandability of an employer's financial statements related to postretirement benefit obligations were necessary to better serve the needs of investors, creditors, donors, employees, retirees, and other capital market participants in making rational investment, credit, and similar resource allocation decisions.

Scope

B16. The Board intends to comprehensively reconsider the accounting for postretirement benefit plans. A project to improve and internationally converge the accounting will take years to complete. Thus, to provide timely and significant improvements in postretirement benefit accounting, the Board decided to conduct the project in phases. The first phase led to this Statement.

B17. The objective of this Statement is to improve the understandability and representational faithfulness of the amounts reported in an employer's statement of financial position by recognizing as an asset or a liability the overfunded or underfunded status of a single-employer defined benefit postretirement plan. This Statement does not change the accounting and reporting with respect to a multiemployer plan, and it does not change the amount of net periodic benefit cost recognized in earnings.

B18. This Statement does not change the basic approach to measuring plan assets, benefit obligations, or net periodic benefit cost. This Statement requires an employer to recognize the gains or losses and the prior service costs or credits that arise during the period but are not recognized as components of net periodic benefit cost of the period as a component of other comprehensive income, or other appropriate components of equity or net assets in the statement of financial position for an entity that does not report other comprehensive income. To more accurately reflect the funded statuses of defined benefit plans and to further improve the understandability of the financial statements, this Statement also requires that the measurement of plan assets and benefit obligations be as of the date of the employer's statement of financial position, not up to three months earlier as had been permitted by Statements 87 and 106.

B19. Some respondents suggested that the Board expand the scope of the first phase to include reconsideration of measurement of a benefit obligation before requiring recognition of the funded status of a defined benefit postretirement plan in an employer's statement of financial position. Others suggested that the Board address all proposed changes in a single comprehensive project to prevent multiple large adjustments to shareholders' equity should the Board later determine that recognition should be based on measures other than the projected benefit obligation (for pensions) and accumulated postretirement benefit obligation (for other postretirement benefits). They stated that a phased approach could result in confusing financial statements in the interim between the two phases.

B20. Many respondents, whether or not they supported a phased approach, considered the projected benefit obligation to be an inappropriate measure of the liability for pension benefit obligations because they believe it does not meet the definition of a liability under FASB Concepts Statement No. 6, *Elements of Financial Statements.* Specifically, they stated that because that measure reflects estimated future increases in compensation, it does not represent a present obligation. Of those respondents, most thought that the accumulated benefit obligation should be used to measure the liability for pension benefits because it does not reflect future increases in compensation and because it better reflects the amount the obligation could be settled for with a third party.

B21. Other respondents suggested that recognizing the funded status using the projected benefit obligation represented a change in measurement that was outside the scope of the first phase. They considered it to be a change in measurement because Statement 87 only required a minimum pension liability to be recognized when the accumulated benefit obligation was greater than the fair value of plan assets.

B22. During redeliberations, the Board affirmed its prior decision to conduct the project in phases. The objective of the first phase was to make meaningful, near-term improvements in an employer's financial reporting of pensions and other postretirement benefits by making the statement of financial position more complete, transparent, and understandable. In deciding to exclude measurement of the obligation from the scope of this Statement, the Board considered the following factors:

a. In Statement 87, the Board concluded after extensive debate that the pension obligation did meet Concepts Statement 6's definition of a liability and that the projected benefit obligation was the most relevant measure of the pension obligation. That conclusion was not one of the departures from the conceptually preferable alternatives acknowledged in Statement 87. The Board's current decision, therefore, is consistent with that conclusion. The Board decided to accept the Board's assessment in Statement 87 for purposes of the first phase of the project.

b. Most users of financial statements that commented on the Exposure Draft believe the projected benefit obligation reflects an employer's economic obligation and the terms of the substantive plan.

c. Using a measure of the obligation other than the projected benefit obligation might necessitate changing how other assumptions are determined, specifically the discount rate. Views on that issue are described in paragraphs 140–142 of Statement 87's basis for conclusions.

d. For most plans that provide postretirement benefits other than pensions, there is no measure of the obligation that is analogous to the accumulated benefit obligation in a pension plan. Therefore, if the Board was to require that the accumulated benefit obligation be used to measure the pension obligation, the Board also would have to determine the equivalent measure for other postretirement benefits. Thus, the issue is broader than pension plans alone.

e. There generally has been no criticism that the measure of net periodic pension cost should exclude the effects of future compensation increases. Paragraph 139 of Statement 87's basis for conclusions states:

> Among those respondents who argued that obligations dependent on future compensation increases are excluded by the definition of a liability, very few were prepared to accept a measure of net periodic pension cost that was based only on compensation to date. The Board notes

that under the double entry accounting system, recognition of an accrued cost as a charge against operations requires recognition of a liability for that accrued cost. Thus, excluding future compensation from the liability and including it in net periodic pension cost are conflicting positions.

B23. Furthermore, present measurements of the pension obligation, including the accumulated benefit obligation, reflect factors relating to expectations about the future, for example, future employee service and eligibility for actuarially unreduced early retirement benefits. The Board affirmed that the scope of the first phase of the project should exclude reconsidering which forward-looking information should be included in the measure of the obligation to be recognized. The Board noted that it would be inconsistent to reconsider some and not others.

B24. Some respondents did not support recognition of other postretirement benefits using the accumulated postretirement benefit obligation. Those respondents stated that retiree health care is a revocable commitment by an employer because an employer typically has the discretion to unilaterally freeze, reduce, or withdraw those benefits. Therefore, respondents suggested that obligations should only be recognized when participants become fully eligible for the benefits or when the obligation is legally enforceable.

B25. The Board acknowledges that the legal statuses of pension benefits and retiree health care benefits are generally different. However, that difference existed when Statement 106 was issued. Statement 106 focuses on substantive postretirement benefit plans. The issues raised by certain respondents to the Exposure Draft are fundamental to the accounting and are inconsistent with the assumption of an ongoing plan that underlies both Statements 87 and 106.

B26. For the reasons noted in paragraphs B22–B25, the Board affirmed its prior decision to require an employer to recognize the funded status—measured as the difference between the fair value of plan assets and the benefit obligation—in its statement of financial position. For a pension plan, the benefit obligation should be the projected benefit obligation; for any other postretirement benefit plan, such as a retiree health care plan, the benefit obligation should be the accumulated postretirement benefit obligation.

The Board's decision simply carries over the measurement principles from Statements 87 and 106 and the conclusion that the projected benefit obligation is the most relevant measure of a defined benefit pension obligation.

B27. The Board expects to readdress in the second phase of the project many issues that were initially addressed by Statements 87 and 106 as well as those that have been raised about the measurement of postretirement benefit obligations, such as the effects of evolving changes in benefit plan design (for example, cash balance pension plans and plans with lump-sum benefits payable upon an employee's termination). However, the Board's commitment to readdress those issues and the issues raised by respondents to the Exposure Draft should not be viewed as a conclusion that the present measurements of defined benefit postretirement obligations are inappropriate or will change. The issues about measurement of postretirement benefit obligations are complex, and considering them will require substantial time. Therefore, considering those issues as part of this Statement would have delayed other significant improvements the Board concluded should be made promptly. In the second multiyear phase of the project, the Board will comprehensively reconsider those and other accounting issues for postretirement benefit obligations, including:

a. How the items that affect the cost of providing postretirement benefits should be recognized and displayed in earnings or other comprehensive income
b. How to measure an employer's benefit obligations, including whether more or different guidance should be provided about measurement assumptions
c. Whether postretirement benefit trusts should be consolidated by the plan sponsor.

B28. The Board expects that the second phase of the project will benefit from:

a. Progress on the project to complete, improve, and converge the FASB's conceptual framework with the International Accounting Standards Board's (IASB) framework
b. Progress on the joint FASB-IASB project on financial statement presentation
c. Progress on researching and analyzing the accounting for cash balance pension plans and plans with lump-sum benefits payable upon an employee's termination.

However, the Board does not intend that progress on the second phase must await completion of any other project on its agenda.

Amendments Considered and Made

Recognition of the Funded Status

B29. The Board wished to implement significant improvements in financial reporting on a more timely basis than would be possible in the context of its comprehensive project described in paragraph B27. Therefore, the Board decided not to consider in this Statement changes in either the basic approach for measuring plan assets and benefit obligations or the basic approach for measuring and reporting the amount of net periodic benefit cost recognized in annual or interim financial statements. As described in paragraph B22, the Board concluded in Statement 87 that the projected benefit obligation is the conceptually appropriate and preferable measure of the benefit obligation. Statement 87's basis for conclusions explains the Board's reasons for that conclusion.

B30. The Board reasoned that financial reporting will be significantly improved by requiring recognition in an employer's statement of financial position of the funded statuses of its sponsored defined benefit postretirement plans other than multiemployer plans. The Board believes that recognition requirement will significantly improve the understandability of reported financial information, thereby facilitating analysis of an employer's financial reports.

B31. After determining that the funded statuses of all plans should be recognized, the Board considered how those recognized amounts should be displayed. The Board decided to require separate recognition of an asset for overfunded plans and separate recognition of a liability for underfunded plans. The Board rejected the alternative of aggregating all plans and reporting the net amount as a single net asset or net liability because an employer does not have the ability to offset excess assets of one plan against the underfunded obligations of another plan, other than through a legal merger that may or may not be possible. In reaching that conclusion, the Board affirmed paragraph 156 of Statement 87's basis for conclusions, which states:

> The Board believes that an employer with one well-funded plan and another less well funded or unfunded plan is in a different position than an employer with similar obligations and assets in a single plan. The Board

was not convinced that combining plans would be easy or even possible in many cases. For example, the Board believes it would be difficult to combine a qualified plan with an unqualified plan or a flat benefit plan with a final-pay plan. Further, netting all plans would be inconsistent with other standards that preclude offsetting assets and liabilities unless a right of offset exists.

Respondents generally agreed that the funded statuses of overfunded plans and underfunded plans should not be aggregated and recognized as a single net amount.

Gains and Losses

B32. Gains and losses are changes in measures of the benefit obligation or plan assets that occur during a period because of differences between experience and assumptions or that occur because of changes in one or more actuarial assumptions. For example, gains and losses can arise from differences between the expected return and actual return on plan assets, from changes in the benefit obligation due to changes in discount rates, or from changes in assumptions about future compensation, retirement dates, mortality rates, employee turnover, retiree participation rates, health care cost trend rates, or government subsidies.

B33. The Board acknowledges that before this Statement delayed recognition in net periodic benefit cost of gains and losses was often the principal reason why an employer had not recognized the overfunded or underfunded statuses of its postretirement benefit plans in its statement of financial position. In developing the provisions of this Statement, the Board considered how those previously unrecognized gains and losses should be recognized, specifically, whether they should be recognized by a business entity in other comprehensive income.

B34. The Board proposed that gains and losses arising during a period but not included as a component of net periodic benefit cost of that period be recognized as increases or decreases in other comprehensive income. Gains and losses initially recognized in other comprehensive income should be adjusted as they are subsequently recognized as a component of net periodic benefit cost based on the applicable recognition or amortization requirements of Statement 87, 88, or 106.

B35. Most respondents supported recognition through other comprehensive income. Respondents representing cooperative businesses stated that recognizing gains and losses in that manner would be a disadvantage to businesses with contractual arrangements that require an employer to buy or sell equity or membership interests at book value. They asked the Board to consider allowing recognition as an asset (a deferred charge) or as a liability (a deferred credit) amounts that would otherwise decrease or increase shareholders' equity. The Board considered that suggestion but concluded that it would not be representationally faithful to report losses and gains, such as those from the performance of plan assets, as deferred charges or credits because those items do not meet the definition of an asset or a liability in Concepts Statement 6.

B36. In affirming its conclusions about the recognition of previously unrecognized gains and losses, the Board noted that the recognition requirements of this Statement eliminate any need to recognize a minimum pension liability. In addition, recognition of previously unrecognized gains and losses through other comprehensive income is consistent with the prior required accounting for any net unrecognized gain or loss that was recognized when an additional minimum pension liability was recognized. Recognition of gains and losses in other comprehensive income is consistent with the objective of this Statement not to change how net periodic benefit cost is determined. This Statement does not change the past practice of delaying recognition of gains and losses as a component of net periodic benefit cost, reflecting the long-term nature of postretirement benefit arrangements. Furthermore, that treatment is consistent with the practice of including in other comprehensive income certain changes in value that have not been recognized in earnings (for example, unrealized gains or losses on available-for-sale equity securities). Decisions about such potential changes in the recognition of net periodic benefit cost will be considered in the second phase of the project.

Prior Service Costs and Credits

B37. Before this Statement, the effect of a plan amendment that retroactively changes benefits attributable to prior employee service was not fully recognized in net periodic benefit cost in the period the amendment was adopted. The Board considered the following two alternatives for a business entity for recognizing the remaining unamortized prior service costs or credits that result from previous plan amendments or initiations:

a. Recognition through other comprehensive income
b. Recognition as an intangible asset (or negative intangible asset that would be considered as a reduction of employee-related intangible assets, some of which are unrecognized).

B38. The Board members who supported the alternative to classify previously unrecognized prior service costs and credits in the statement of financial position on an aggregate basis for all plans as a net intangible asset (or net negative intangible asset) considered that approach to be consistent with the previous accounting required when an additional minimum pension liability was recognized and an intangible asset was recognized to the extent of any unrecognized prior service cost. Those Board members also noted that unrecognized prior service costs and credits are not characterized as losses or gains in Statements 87 and 106. Therefore, they are unlike other items presently recognized in other comprehensive income. Although those Board members questioned whether the effect of a plan amendment qualifies conceptually for recognition as an asset or negative asset, they concluded that the characterization of such an effect, as set forth in Statements 87 and 106, would best be reconsidered during the second phase of the project.

B39. The Board members who supported recognition through other comprehensive income noted the reasoning in paragraph 286 of Statement 106:

> Some Board members support immediate recognition of prior service cost as an expense, particularly the portion related to existing retirees. Although some intangible economic benefits of a plan initiation or amendment may be received in future periods from benefit improvements for active plan participants, they believe that those intangible benefits do not qualify for recognition as an asset. Therefore, they believe there is little basis for delaying recognition of the underlying prior service cost to future periods. Other Board members believe that a plan initiation or amendment is made with a view to benefiting the employer's future operations through reduced employee turnover, improved productivity, or reduced demands for increases in cash compensation.

B40. The Board decided to adopt the first alternative and require prior service costs and credits to be recognized initially through other comprehensive income and subsequently recognized as a component of net periodic benefit cost based on the existing recognition and amortization provisions of Statements 87, 88, and 106.

B41. That approach also is consistent with the treatment of previously unrecognized gains and losses. The Board reasoned that there is not a sufficient distinction between previously unrecognized gains and losses and prior service costs and credits to support different accounting treatment. In addition, the resulting accounting is simple, transparent, and symmetrical. The Board believes that an amendment that increases benefits attributable to service already rendered does not give rise to an asset and the reduction of benefits by a negative plan amendment does not give rise to a liability. The Board rejected the notion of a negative intangible asset on both conceptual and understandability grounds. The Board also concluded that recognition of prior service costs and credits related to both retired employees and active employees should be reconsidered in the second phase of the project. Doing so will take full advantage of the ongoing work in the conceptual framework project related to the definitions of an asset and a liability.

Transition Assets and Obligations

B42. Upon initial application of Statement 87 or 106, an employer typically had an unrecognized net asset or an unrecognized net obligation measured as the difference between the funded status of the plan and amounts recognized in the employer's statement of financial position. For postretirement benefits other than pensions, it often was a net obligation because those benefits are not typically funded by plan assets. Statement 87 required delayed recognition for the net transition asset or obligation by requiring prospective recognition (amortization) as part of net periodic benefit cost.

B43. The transition guidance in Statement 106 permitted, but did not require, an employer to delay recognition and amortize the transition asset or obligation on a basis similar to Statement 87's requirements. The Board observed that even though Statement 87 was issued in 1985, and Statement 106 was issued in 1990, certain employers have yet to completely amortize the transition asset or obligation.

B44. The Board considered various alternatives for a business entity to recognize any remaining transition asset or obligation upon initial application of this Statement, including:

a. Adjust retained earnings, similar to the accounting for changes in an accounting principle.
b. Recognize an intangible asset for a transition obligation or recognize a credit in accumulated other comprehensive income for a transition asset.
c. Recognize an increase or decrease in accumulated other comprehensive income, similar to the recognition treatment for unrecognized gains and losses.
d. Elect either alternative (a) or (b).

B45. The Board proposed the first alternative in the Exposure Draft, which would have required that any remaining transition amounts be recognized under the retrospective transition method proposed by the Exposure Draft as direct charges or credits to beginning retained earnings, net of applicable income taxes. Those amounts would not have been subsequently recognized as a component of net periodic benefit cost. The Board viewed any remaining transition asset or obligation as similar to the cumulative effect resulting from a change in accounting principle that should not affect current or future reported earnings. The Board believed that alternative would reduce recordkeeping costs and improve the comparability of ongoing net periodic benefit cost reported between an employer that elected immediate recognition of the transition amount for Statement 106 and one that did not.

B46. Some respondents stated that recognizing any remaining transition asset or obligation as an adjustment of retained earnings was inconsistent with the Board's stated objective of not changing net periodic benefit cost, since those amounts would no longer be amortized. Furthermore, some respondents indicated that the amount of the transition asset or obligation remaining after having been amortized for many years since initial adoption of Statements 87 and 106 generally was not significant and, therefore, the costs associated with changing accounting procedures should not be imposed by the Board. Other respondents were concerned with the proposed accounting's effects for rate regulated entities.

B47. As a result of respondents' feedback through comment letters and the roundtable meetings, the Board concluded that the benefits of recognizing any

remaining transition asset or obligation as an adjustment of retained earnings did not exceed the costs and was inconsistent with the Board's intent not to change amounts reported as net periodic benefit cost as part of the first phase of the project. Therefore, the Board decided that previously unrecognized transition assets or obligations resulting from the initial adoption of Statements 87 and 106 should be recognized in the same way as previously unrecognized net gains and losses and prior service costs and credits (the second alternative); that is, those previously unrecognized transition assets or obligations should be recognized as an adjustment to accumulated other comprehensive income with subsequent amortization as a component of net periodic benefit cost pursuant to the existing recognition and amortization provisions of Statements 87, 88, and 106.

Classification of Recognized Assets and Liabilities

B48. Respondents to the Exposure Draft asked the Board to clarify how net postretirement benefit liabilities would be reported in a classified statement of financial position. The Board decided to provide explicit guidance about the net postretirement assets and liabilities in a classified statement of financial position. The Board concluded that an employer that presents a classified statement of financial position should report the liability for an underfunded plan as a current liability, a noncurrent liability, or a combination of both. The current portion (determined on a plan-by-plan basis) is the amount by which the actuarial present value of benefits included in the benefit obligation payable in the next 12 months, or operating cycle if longer, exceeds the fair value of plan assets. If plan assets exceed the actuarial present value of those payments, the unfunded obligation should be classified as a noncurrent liability. The amount classified as a current liability is limited to the amount of the plan's unfunded status recognized in the employer's statement of financial position.

B49. The Board considered an alternative whereby a current liability would be based on the contributions required to prefund the plan over the next fiscal year or operating cycle if longer. Board members who supported that alternative reasoned that postretirement benefit plans are not consolidated and that the net liability recognized for an underfunded plan represents an employer's obligation to contribute assets to the plan.

B50. The Board rejected the alternative approach. The Board reasoned that the amount expected to be contributed to prefund the plan was substantively an intercompany transaction that should not affect the classification of the benefit payment liability. Because the net overfunded or underfunded status is based on the difference between the plan assets and benefit obligation, the plan assets and benefit obligation have been effectively consolidated and presented on a net basis for reporting purposes. The Board decided to place the emphasis on cash outflows from the employer to independent third parties. To the extent there are sufficient plan assets to cover benefit payments to plan participants and settlements of the obligation (for example, to a retiree or an insurance company), none of the net postretirement liability should be classified as current. To the extent there are insufficient plan assets, the employer would disburse cash to an independent third party (for example, a retiree). The amount of that expected disbursement should be classified as a current liability. The Board reasoned that net postretirement assets should be classified as noncurrent because their use is generally restricted to the payment of benefit obligations and because any refunds from the plan essentially represent a transfer of the employer's assets to itself. The Board decided to require disclosure of the amount and timing of any plan assets expected to be returned to the employer during the 12-month period, or operating cycle if longer, that follows the most recent statement of financial position presented in annual financial statements.

Measurement Date

B51. Statements 87 and 106 required that plan assets and benefit obligations be measured as of the date of an employer's fiscal year-end statement of financial position or, if used consistently from year to year, as of a date not more than three months before that date. The Exposure Draft proposed eliminating the choice of a measurement date other than the date of an employer's fiscal year-end statement of financial position. Measuring postretirement plans as of the date of an employer's fiscal year-end statement of financial position would improve the representational faithfulness of amounts recognized by eliminating delayed recognition of events and transactions arising between the measurement date and the fiscal year-end.

B52. Some respondents stated that any change in measurement date should be considered in the second phase of the project because it relates to measurement, which the Board stated was beyond the scope of the first phase. The Board noted that the notion of recognizing the overfunded or underfunded statuses of postretirement plans as of the fiscal year-

end is inseparable from measuring those statuses as of the same point in time. Therefore, aligning the measurement date with the date of an employer's statement of financial position is a prerequisite to recognizing the overfunded or underfunded status as of the reporting date. The Board acknowledges that a change in measurement date will affect net periodic benefit cost for some employers. However, those changes in amounts are not the result of a fundamental change in how the amounts are determined. Therefore, those changes are consistent with the objectives and scope of the first phase of the project.

B53. Many respondents to the Exposure Draft acknowledged the conceptual merit of measuring plan assets and benefit obligations as of the date of an employer's statement of financial position. However, a majority of respondents thought the costs would outweigh the benefits. Those respondents stated that collecting data related to certain plan assets and benefit obligations could be time-consuming. Determining the fair value of plan assets that do not have readily available market values (for example, private equity and real estate) and collecting data related to foreign plans can be particularly difficult. They also noted that the sequential nature of the flow of information from an investment manager to an actuary, and then to an employer and an auditor, adds a significant amount of time to the data collection and analysis process. Other respondents raised concerns that the proposed change would put additional stress on actuarial resources at the end of the calendar year and would likely increase the cost of services.

B54. Some respondents stated that aligning the measurement date and fiscal year-end would not result in more reliable measures of liabilities due to the long-term nature of postretirement benefit obligations. Respondents described the long-term nature of postretirement benefit obligations, the relative uncertainty associated with estimating future cash flows, and what they believed was an illusory improvement (false precision) associated with measuring benefit obligations as of the date of the statement of financial position.

B55. The Board reasoned that allowing alternative measurement dates added complexity and reduced understandability because potentially significant changes in plan assets and benefit obligations that arise after the measurement date but before the fiscal year-end are not recognized until the following period. The required note disclosures to reconcile plan assets and benefit obligations as of that earlier measurement date to amounts recognized in an employer's statement of financial position as of the reporting date also added complexity. Aligning the measurement date with the date of an employer's statement of financial position makes reported postretirement benefit information more representationally faithful and increases the comparability of financial statements of employers with similar fiscal years.

B56. During redeliberations, the Board considered an alternative to an explicit requirement that an employer measure plan assets and benefit obligations at the date of its statement of financial position. That alternative would have established an objective similar to IAS 19, *Employee Benefits,* which does not specify the date on which plan assets and benefit obligations are to be measured. Instead, IAS 19 requires that amounts recognized not be materially different from what they would be if they had been determined as of the date of an employer's statement of financial position. The Board noted that such a provision can raise issues about how to determine materiality and whether such a provision was intended to be different from, or in addition to, the materiality exemption set forth at the end of the standards section of this Statement. Further, that provision may often require an employer to measure plan assets and benefit obligations as of its fiscal year-end so it can assess the materiality of any differences between those amounts and amounts determined as of an earlier measurement date. The notion in IAS 19 could be applied to other amounts in an employer's statement of financial position; however, that notion is not present in other standards. Therefore, the Board decided against adopting that approach as an alternative to requiring that plan assets and benefit obligations be measured as of the employer's fiscal year-end.

B57. The Board noted that many employers already measure postretirement plan assets and obligations, at least for some of their plans, as of their fiscal year-ends, which suggests that it is often practicable to obtain the necessary data as of the reporting date. Furthermore, the Board noted that recognizing the funded statuses of postretirement plans in the statement of financial position increases the importance of measuring postretirement assets and obligations as of the same date as the employer's other reported assets and liabilities. Therefore, the Board affirmed its prior decision to require an employer to measure the funded status of a plan as of the date of its statement of financial position. However, the effective date for this change was delayed to fiscal years ending after

December 15, 2008, to provide more time for a preparer and its external resource providers to implement any necessary changes in systems and processes in an efficient manner.

Note Disclosures Required

Transitional Disclosures

B58. This Statement requires transitional disclosures for a fiscal year ending after December 15, 2006, and before June 16, 2007, if an employer has not implemented this Statement as a result of the delayed effective date allowed for an employer without publicly traded equity securities (paragraph 14). The Board decided that an employer should provide a brief description of the provisions of this Statement, the date that adoption is required, and the date that the employer plans to adopt the recognition provisions of this Statement, if earlier. That disclosure will provide users, particularly parties that have contractual or other relationships with an employer that might be affected by this Statement, with an early notice of any significant accounting changes resulting from this Statement. Such disclosure is similar to the disclosures required for SEC registrants pursuant to SEC Staff Accounting Bulletin No. 74, *Disclosure of the Impact That Recently Issued Accounting Standards Will Have on the Financial Statements of the Registrant When Adopted in a Future Period.*

B59. The Board agreed to explicitly require an employer to disclose in the notes to financial statements the incremental effect of applying this Statement on line items in the year-end statement of financial position for the year that the recognition provisions of this Statement are initially applied. The Board noted that this disclosure will give users a basis to isolate the effects of this Statement from other changes that occur during the year. The Board concluded that this Statement has the potential to affect several line items on an employer's statement of financial position and, therefore, it was important to provide users with clear information about this Statement's effects.

B60. The Board agreed that any other disclosures ordinarily required by FASB Statement No. 154, *Accounting Changes and Error Corrections,* would not apply to the recognition of the net overfunded or underfunded status or to changes in the measurement date required to measure plan assets and benefit obligations as of the date of an employer's statement of financial position. The Board concluded that the disclosures required by Statement 154 are not necessary for those changes. However, the Board decided that this Statement should require that the effects of the changes on retained earnings, accumulated other comprehensive income, and other comprehensive income not be obscured through aggregation of the effects with other unrelated items. Furthermore, the Board decided that a business entity should disclose, in the year the measurement date provisions of this Statement are initially adopted, the separate adjustments of retained earnings and accumulated other comprehensive income from applying this Statement. That disclosure may be made either by reporting the adjustments as separate line items within the statement of changes in shareholders' equity or by disclosing the adjustments in the notes to financial statements. A not-for-profit organization should disclose similarly the separate adjustments of unrestricted net assets either within the statement of activities or in the notes to financial statements.

Amendments to Existing Disclosure Requirements Made Necessary by Changes in Recognition

Reconciliation of the funded status to amounts recognized

B61. This Statement's recognition requirements for gains or losses, prior service costs or credits, and any remaining transition asset or obligation related to the initial application of Statement 87 or 106 eliminate all differences between a plan's funded status and amounts recognized in an employer's statement of financial position. Therefore, this Statement eliminates the previous requirement in paragraph 5(c) of Statement 132(R) to reconcile the funded status of the plan to amounts recognized in the employer's statement of financial position once the employer applies both the recognition provisions and measurement date provisions of this Statement. Likewise, this Statement eliminates the Statement 132(R) disclosures that reference the additional minimum pension liability (paragraphs 5(i), 8(g), and 8(h)) and measurement date (paragraphs 5(k) and 8(j)).

Disclosure by a business entity of amounts recognized in other comprehensive income and accumulated other comprehensive income

B62. The Board considered the items that are initially recognized in other comprehensive income pursuant to this Statement and subsequently recognized as components of net periodic benefit cost based on the recognition and amortization provisions of Statements 87, 88, and 106 and concluded that they

should be separately disclosed. That is, gains or losses and prior service costs or credits from plan amendments arising during the period and amortization of gains or losses, prior service costs or credits, and the transition asset or obligation for the period should be disclosed to provide information about the nature of the items affecting an employer's financial statements. The Board decided not to require separate disclosure of the amount recognized in other comprehensive income from application of the measurement date provisions of this Statement when the alternative transition approach (paragraph 19) is elected. Under the alternative approach for a change in measurement date, the net gain or loss associated with the change in measurement date cannot be separated from the net gain or loss recognized in other comprehensive income for the period. The Board concluded that requiring an employer that elects this method to allocate the net gain or loss recognized in other comprehensive income would result in disclosures that are based on arbitrary amounts that may not be representationally faithful.

B63. The Board recognizes that certain of those disclosures might be redundant with other standards, given paragraphs 17 and 24–26 of FASB Statement No. 130, *Reporting Comprehensive Income.* However, disclosure related to certain amounts reported in the statement of changes in shareholders' equity could be satisfied by cross-referencing to the postretirement benefits note, which would be more complete under the approach selected by the Board. Furthermore, Statement 130 allows alternative disclosure formats. Requiring certain disclosures in the notes describing postretirement benefits will result in more consistent disclosure of the information by all employers. It also will eliminate the need for a user to analyze multiple parts of the financial statements and notes to find all relevant information about the accounting for postretirement benefits.

Estimated amount of amortization for the next fiscal year

B64. Some respondents requested additional disclosures about the effect of the delayed recognition provisions of Statements 87 and 106 on net periodic benefit cost for future periods because they find it difficult to project the amortization of gains or losses and prior service costs or credits. Others asked the Board to consider requiring disclosure of all projected components, including service cost, interest cost, and investment returns. However, others noted that all elements of net periodic benefit cost already recognized are disclosed in interim-period financial reports. Therefore, projections for at least the remainder of the year should be enhanced.

The Board considered three alternatives:

a. Require separate disclosure of the amounts subject to amortization (that is, gains or losses beyond the corridor established by paragraphs 32 and 33 of Statement 87 and paragraphs 59 and 60 of Statement 106, respectively, and prior service costs or credits) and the average period over which each item is amortized
b. Require disclosure of the estimated portions of the net gain or loss and the prior service cost or credit in accumulated other comprehensive income that will be recognized as components of net periodic benefit cost over the fiscal year that follows the most recent annual statement of financial position presented
c. Permit an employer to choose either of the foregoing alternatives and require that disclosure only if the amount is expected to differ significantly from the current period.

B65. The Board evaluated those alternatives in light of its decision to make only those changes in disclosure requirements that are directly related to the changes to recognition made by this Statement. The Board noted that the first alternative might be of limited usefulness, and potentially misleading, if the reclassification pattern is other than straight line. Therefore, the Board affirmed the disclosure proposed in the Exposure Draft (the second alternative) because that alternative provides a straightforward and easily understood forecast (and not merely the information that could be used to form a forecast). Also, the data to prepare that forecast should be readily available to an employer. The Board decided that such disclosure should include all amounts subject to amortization and, therefore, also should include the estimated portion of any net transition asset or obligation that will be recognized as a component of net periodic benefit cost over the fiscal year that follows the most recent statement of financial position presented.

Excess or surplus plan assets

B66. Respondents asked the Board to provide additional guidance on the current-noncurrent classification of net postretirement benefit assets and liabilities recognized. The Board decided to provide additional guidance and to require disclosure of the amount and timing of any plan assets expected to be returned to the employer during the 12-month period, or operating cycle if longer, that follows the most recent statement of financial position presented (see paragraphs B48–B50).

Note Disclosures Considered but Not Required

B67. The Board considered, but decided not to require, the disclosures described in paragraphs B68–B74. Each proposed disclosure was rejected for reasons noted below as well as for one or more of the following reasons: the disclosed information would have limited usefulness, the disclosure was considered and rejected by the Board during previous projects, such as Statement 132(R), and the disclosure was outside the scope of the first phase of the project.

Disclosure of the Retroactive Effect of This Statement on the Prior Year's Statement of Financial Position

B68. To make year-to-year financial statements comparable, the Exposure Draft proposed requiring retrospective application of this Statement effective for fiscal years ending after December 15, 2006, for all changes except those that relate to the measurement date. Respondents argued that the costs associated with retrospective application would exceed the benefits that would be derived from year-to-year comparability. The Board determined in its redeliberations that retrospective application would not be required or permitted by this Statement.

B69. Some respondents suggested limited retrospective application, at least for the year immediately preceding the initial year the recognition provisions of this Statement are implemented. The Board considered whether to require disclosure of the effect that recognizing the funded statuses would have had on the individual line items in the statement of financial position for the end of the year immediately preceding the year of adoption. The Board considered the implementation issues associated with providing that disclosure, primarily those related to accounting for deferred income taxes. Preparers would still have to assess the realizability of any incremental deferred tax assets and possibly other issues as noted in paragraphs B89 and B90. Additionally, not all employers would be affected equally if the Board retained an impracticability exemption from the disclosure requirement because an employer was unable to assess the realizability of deferred tax assets for the prior year without considering information that subsequently became available.

B70. The Board considered allowing an employer to use information obtained after the end of the prior fiscal year in developing its forecast of the reversal of temporary differences and future taxable income. The Board decided, however, that determining the deferred tax accounting, including the realizability of deferred taxes on a retrospective basis, with or without the use of hindsight, was subject to sufficient implementation difficulties that made it not justifiable on a benefit-cost basis. The Board also concluded that there was extensive information already available in the notes to financial statements for that prior year.

Market-Related Value

B71. The market-related value of plan assets is used to determine the expected-return-on-plan-assets component of net periodic benefit cost. It also is used to establish the minimum annual amortization threshold (that is, 10 percent of the greater of the market-related value of plan assets or the benefit obligation) for gains or losses not yet recognized as a component of net periodic benefit cost. The Board considered, but decided not to require, disclosure of the market-related value of plan assets and the method used to determine it. Certain users of financial statements asked the Board to consider that disclosure because it would help them forecast the expected return on plan assets and future amortization of gains or losses. The Board observed that the new disclosures stated in paragraph 7 are responsive, in part, to that request. In addition, the Board observed that disclosure of the market-related value of plan assets would not add sufficient benefits to justify the additional costs of compliance. An aggregate market-related value would not necessarily be useful for an employer with multiple plans. To make the information more useful, an employer with several plans with different characteristics would need to provide disaggregated information about market-related values. The Board concluded that requiring that level of disclosure was beyond the limited scope of this Statement.

Sensitivity of the Postretirement Benefit Obligation to Changes in Interest Rates

B72. Certain respondents asked the Board to consider requiring disclosure of the sensitivity of the postretirement benefit obligation to changes in interest rates. Those respondents believe the potential volatility of amounts recognized from changes in interest rates should be quantified in the notes to financial statements. The Board acknowledges that the requirements of this Statement may increase both the amount and volatility of assets and liabilities recognized in an employer's statement of financial position. However, the Board reasoned that sensitivity analysis focusing only on a plan's postretirement benefit obligation could be misleading because some changes in plan obligations and assets have the same cause. For example, a change in interest rates would affect the amounts of both plan assets and benefit obligations, particularly if the plan has a dedicated bond portfolio. In addition, the Board observed that disclosure of sensitivity information was considered during the deliberations that led to the issuance of Statement 132(R). Therefore, that disclosure would be better addressed in the second phase of the project.

Alternative Amortization Method

B73. The Board was asked to require disclosure of the method used to amortize gains or losses if that method differs from the minimum amortization required by Statements 87 and 106. The Board observed that paragraph 5(o) of Statement 132(R) requires disclosure of any alternative methods used to amortize gains or losses or prior service costs or credits.

Contributions to the Plan

B74. The Board considered whether it should require disclosure of an employer's significant plan contributions that might be triggered under certain circumstances by the Employee Retirement Income Security Act or other funding requirements. The Board concluded that existing disclosures (that is, those required by FASB Statements and, for public companies, SEC regulations) should provide sufficient information about contributions to the plans over the fiscal year that follows the most recent statement of financial position presented. In developing disclosures that focus solely on certain U.S. regulatory or other requirements that apply only in limited circumstances, the Board would have had to consider whether there are similar requirements elsewhere in the world applicable to plans of multinational companies. That effort was beyond the scope of the project and was not considered necessary to meet the objectives of this Statement. After the Board completed its redeliberations, the Pension Protection Act of 2006 was enacted and will affect future funding by U.S. employers. The Board concluded that consideration of any additional disclosures associated with that legislation would have delayed issuance of this Statement. Therefore, the Board decided that disclosure of an employer's significant plan contributions should be considered in a separate project.

Reporting by a Not-for-Profit Organization or Other Entity That Does Not Report Other Comprehensive Income

B75. The Board employs a differences-based approach in setting accounting standards for not-for-profit organizations. Under that approach, the standards applicable to a business entity apply to a not-for-profit organization unless substantive transactional or reporting considerations justify different accounting or reporting. In the deliberations that led to Statements 87 and 106, the Board concluded that the guidance developed for a business entity also should apply to a not-for-profit organization. In the deliberations that led to the issuance of the Exposure Draft, the Board similarly concluded that the changes to Statements 87 and 106 made by this Statement for a business entity should apply equally to a not-for-profit organization. The Board concluded that reporting the funded statuses of postretirement benefit plans in the statement of financial position of a not-for-profit employer would make it easier for creditors, donors, and others to assess the not-for-profit organization's financial position and liquidity. Virtually no respondents suggested that not-for-profit organizations be excluded from the scope of this Statement. Thus, in its redeliberations, the Board affirmed the applicability of the basic recognition, measurement date, and disclosure provisions of this Statement to not-for-profit organizations.

B76. In its initial deliberations, the Board acknowledged that its decision to require recognition by a business entity of gains or losses and prior service costs or credits in other comprehensive income in the periods in which they arise could not be applied by a not-for-profit organization and other entities that are not required to report other comprehensive income. A not-for-profit organization that prepares financial statements under the provisions of FASB Statement No. 117, *Financial Statements of Not-for-Profit Organizations,* is explicitly excluded from the scope of Statement 130. Thus, this Statement contains additional application guidance that focuses on the reporting by a not-for-profit organization. Appendix A of this Statement includes an illustrative example to help constituents better understand the guidance for a not-for-profit organization.

B77. The key not-for-profit issue addressed in this Statement is where the gains or losses and prior service costs or credits recognized by a business entity in other comprehensive income should be reported within a not-for-profit organization's statement of activities, particularly in relation to any performance indicator or other intermediate measure of operations. In its initial deliberations, the Board noted that Statement 117 neither requires nor prohibits a not-for-profit organization from reporting an intermediate measure of operations (or performance indicator) within its statement of activities (statement of changes in net assets), nor does it prescribe the components of such a measure if it is presented. The Board also noted, however, that other authoritative accounting pronouncements (in particular, the AICPA's Statement of Position (SOP) 02-2, *Accounting for Derivative Instruments and Hedging Activities by Not-for-Profit Health Care Organizations, and Clarification of the Performance Indicator,* and its Audit and Accounting Guide, *Health Care Organizations*) require a not-for-profit health care provider to present a performance indicator that is the functional equivalent of income from continuing operations of a for-profit provider. Finally, the Board noted that other not-for-profit organizations may elect to present a performance indicator that is the functional equivalent of income from continuing operations. Although the Board was unaware of specific organizations outside the health care sector that were doing so, the Board decided that, for consistency, the Exposure Draft should provide similar guidance for both health care providers required to present a functionally equivalent performance indicator and other employers that voluntarily choose to present a similar operating measure. The Board decided that those employers should apply the provisions of the Exposure Draft in the same manner as a business entity, that is, by reporting gains or losses, prior service costs or credits, and the transition asset or obligation outside the performance indicator or other intermediate operating measure in the period in which they arise. Likewise, those employers should subsequently reclassify those amounts to net periodic benefit cost pursuant to the recognition and amortization provisions of Statements 87, 88, and 106.

B78. The Board also considered how this Statement would be applied by an organization that presents an intermediate measure of operations that is not the functional equivalent of income from continuing operations or by an organization that elects not to present an intermediate measure of operations. Consistent with the provisions of Statement 117, in the

Exposure Draft the Board decided not to prescribe how those organizations should report gains or losses and prior service costs or credits in the periods in which they arise. However, the Board decided to require that those amounts be reported in the statement of activities apart from functional expenses. The Board noted that the gains or losses and the prior service costs or credits could be significant and, thus, decided that separate reporting would make it easier for users to compare the financial statements of different organizations.

B79. Respondents generally agreed with the separate reporting proposed by the Exposure Draft. A couple of respondents, however, noted that some not-for-profit organizations present expenses by natural classification in their statements of activities and disclose expenses by functional classification in the notes to financial statements or in a separate statement of functional expenses. All of those alternatives are permitted by Statement 117. Those respondents suggested that the requirement for separate reporting be extended to apply to all presentations of expenses, whether by functional or natural category. The Board agreed. This Statement requires that the items be separately reported apart from all expenses. If the items are reported in the aggregate in the basic financial statements, the components should be disclosed in the notes.

B80. Some respondents disagreed with the approach described in paragraphs B77 and B78 and suggested that the Board require reported amounts to be presented outside any intermediate measure of operations or performance indicator. Other respondents agreed with the approach but asked for clarification of when an intermediate measure of operations is "functionally equivalent" to income from continuing operations of a business entity. Those respondents expressed their view that, absent clarification, the proposed requirement might not be adequately understood or consistently applied by other not-for-profit organizations.

B81. In its redeliberations, the Board rejected the suggested approach of always presenting the reported amounts outside an operating measure, noting that not-for-profit organizations are diverse, have diverse aims for an operating measure, and, therefore, may choose different components to include in an operating measure. The Board concluded that the requirement for separate reporting would help ensure

transparency whether presented within or outside such diverse operating measures. The Board concluded that there was no compelling reason to deviate from the spirit of Statement 117 by being more prescriptive on this matter. The Board also concluded that attempting to define a *functionally equivalent* operating measure was outside the scope of this Statement. The Board decided that this Statement should simply reference the existing guidance concerning operating measures and performance indicators and impose no new display requirements beyond presentation in a discrete line item or items apart from expenses.

B82. During its initial deliberations, the Board also addressed whether the amounts separately presented should be subsequently recognized as components of net periodic benefit cost. Because there are no equivalents to retained earnings or accumulated other comprehensive income in the financial statements of a not-for-profit organization, the Board considered amending Statements 87 and 106 to require that not-for-profit organizations report gains or losses and prior service costs or credits in net periodic benefit cost (and, therefore, expenses) in the period in which they arise. The Board decided that given the objective and scope of the project that led to this Statement (paragraphs B2–B28), it was preferable to include reconsideration of the measurement of net periodic benefit cost for this one sector in its broader reconsideration of the issue as part of the next phase of the project. Thus, the Exposure Draft changed neither the way in which a not-for-profit organization measures its net periodic benefit cost nor the way in which it reports that cost by expense category (functional or natural).

B83. Several respondents nevertheless asked the Board to reconsider its prior decision. In its redeliberations, the Board examined the possible consequences of amending Statements 87 and 106 either to allow immediate recognition in expenses (bypassing the separate line item recognition) or no recognition in expenses (retaining the separate line item recognition but eliminating the subsequent reclassification). In addition to not wanting to change the measure of net periodic benefit cost for not-for-profit organizations before a broad reconsideration, the Board also chose not to make those changes because of the possibility of unintended or undesirable consequences for not-for-profit organizations, including nontransparent volatility in expenses, circumvention of functional expense reporting for a portion of an organization's resources, and issues related to an organization's recoverability of such amounts under grants and contracts. Accordingly, the Board affirmed its prior decision on this matter.

B84. One respondent asked the Board to provide additional guidance concerning permissible display in the statement of financial position of the cumulative effect on unrestricted net assets of adopting the provisions of this Statement, in the absence of the separate component of equity (accumulated other comprehensive income) contained in a business entity's statement of financial position. The respondent was especially concerned about situations in which adoption of the Statement would largely or entirely eliminate a not-for-profit organization's reported unrestricted net assets. The Board, while understanding the concern, concluded that providing guidance beyond referring to Statement 117's flexibility of display within net asset classes was outside the scope of this Statement. The Board also noted that in such instances there also would generally be a certain degree of transparency from the presence in the statement of financial position of a large, noncurrent liability and other information provided by the notes to financial statements.

B85. The Board decided that for reasons similar to those described in paragraphs B75–B84, other entities that do not report other comprehensive income pursuant to Statement 130 should apply the guidance that is applicable to not-for-profit organizations in an analogous manner that is appropriate for how they report their results of operations and financial positions.

Guidance on Discount Rates

B86. The Board decided to amend Statements 87 and 106 to incorporate guidance on the selection of appropriate discount rates that previously resided in other literature (such as in paragraph 186 of Statement 106's basis for conclusions). The Board considered whether codifying only that guidance without considering completely other guidance on various aspects of Statements 87 and 106 was consistent with the Board's objectives for this Statement.

B87. The Board does not consider the codification to be a change to existing standards. Certain constituents advocated that the existing standards should provide all necessary guidance on the objective and method of selecting the discount rate assumptions and that codifying the guidance would improve consistency between Statements 87 and 106. They noted

that the wording in paragraph 186 was specifically cited in a September 22, 1993 letter from the SEC to the Chairman of the Emerging Issues Task Force (EITF). In that letter, the SEC staff stated its belief "that the guidance that is provided in paragraph 186 of Statement 106 for selecting discount rates to measure the postretirement benefit obligation also is appropriate guidance for measuring the pension benefit obligation." Paragraph 186 of Statement 106 was incorporated into the *Current Text* and EITF Topic No. D-36, "Selection of Discount Rates Used for Measuring Defined Benefit Pension Obligations and Obligations of Postretirement Benefit Plans Other Than Pensions." The Board believes its decision to incorporate the paragraph into Statements 87 and 106 is consistent with the objectives of both this project and its broader project on codification. The Board further decided to emphasize that the determination of the assumed discount rates is separate from the determination of the expected return on plan assets whenever the actual portfolio of plan assets differs from the hypothetical portfolio of high-quality fixed-income investments described in paragraph 44 of Statement 87, as amended, and paragraph 31 of Statement 106, as amended.

Effective Date and Transition

Recognition of the Funded Status

B88. The Exposure Draft proposed requiring retrospective application of this Statement effective for fiscal years ending after December 15, 2006, for all changes except those that relate to the measurement date (paragraphs B51–B57). The Board selected that effective date because most of the information needed to apply this Statement already is required for notes to financial statements and the Board wanted to implement improvements in financial reporting for postretirement benefits as soon as possible. Retrospective application was proposed because it is the transition method for a change in accounting principle generally required by Statement 154. That Statement generally requires that method because it improves interperiod comparability.

B89. Many respondents to the Exposure Draft stated that the costs of retrospectively applying this Statement would outweigh the benefits. Some noted that there would be significant complexities in assessing the realizability of any incremental deferred tax assets recognized in prior periods. Multiple years of financial statements and financial summaries would have to be restated, and the effects on financial metrics referenced in contractual arrangements would have to be assessed. Additional complications would arise if prior-period financial statements were audited by different auditors. Other respondents stated that retrospective application would not increase comparability because of the impracticability exemption related to deferred income taxes included in the Exposure Draft.

B90. The Board decided that retrospective application of this Statement would not ensure comparable financial statements from year to year for a single employer or between employers and would be costly to implement. Therefore, the Board decided that this Statement should be implemented on a prospective basis. The Board decided not to permit retrospective application so that all employers would apply the same method of transition, thereby enhancing comparability.

B91. Because of the implementation issues raised by respondents about retrospective application, the Board also concluded that the effect of initially applying the recognition provisions of this Statement should be recognized as an adjustment of accumulated other comprehensive income as of the end rather than as of the beginning of the year for an employer that is subject to Statement 130. A not-for-profit organization should report the effect as a change in unrestricted net assets in its statement of activities, in a separate line item or items apart from expenses and outside any performance indicator or other intermediate measure of operations.

B92. The Exposure Draft proposed no special provisions for a nonpublic employer regarding recognition provisions in this Statement. The Board did not consider the implementation issues for a nonpublic employer to be sufficiently different from those of a public employer to justify a delayed effective date. The Board concluded that because the information necessary to recognize the funded status of a defined benefit postretirement plan already is determined and generally included in note disclosures, a nonpublic employer would be able to apply the provisions of this Statement related to recognition for fiscal years ending after December 15, 2006. The Board decided to gather additional information through the notice for recipients of the Exposure Draft to determine whether nonpublic employers with contractual arrangements, other than debt covenants, that reference certain financial metrics, including book value, return on equity, or debt to equity, should be given a delayed effective date.

B93. Respondents to the Exposure Draft noted that reductions in equity that could result from recognizing the funded status of benefit plans pursuant to the provisions of this Statement would have significant effects on employers with contractual arrangements that reference book value. During redeliberations, the Board noted that the majority of employers with those arrangements included cooperative businesses that transact with member-owners on a book value basis, and other nonpublic employers that have compensation arrangements referencing book value. Therefore, the Board decided to delay the effective date to fiscal years ending after June 15, 2007, for those employers to provide them with additional time to address the effects of this Statement on the contractual arrangements noted above. Because a significant number of cooperatives issue publicly traded debt, which would result in their meeting the definition of the term *public* that is used in Statement 132(R), the Board decided to use an approach that focuses on issuance of equity securities and is similar to the definition of a nonpublic entity, defined in FASB Statement No. 123 (revised 2004), *Share-Based Payment,* as follows:

> Any entity other than one (a) whose equity securities trade in a public market either on a stock exchange (domestic or foreign) or in the over-the-counter market, including securities quoted only locally or regionally, (b) that makes a filing with a regulatory agency in preparation for the sale of any class of equity securities in a public market, or (c) that is controlled by an entity covered by (a) or (b). An entity that has only debt securities trading in a public market (or that has made a filing with a regulatory agency in preparation to trade only debt securities) is a nonpublic entity for purposes of this Statement.

B94. The Board concluded that the recognition provisions of this Statement should be implemented as soon as possible by employers that have issued publicly traded equity securities because of the use of their financial statements by participants in the public marketplace, the more limited arrangements that may be affected, and the greater resources they have to address issues with contractual arrangements. Therefore, the Board affirmed the effective date for fiscal years ending after December 15, 2006, for those employers with publicly traded equity securities. The Board decided to encourage early application of this Statement's recognition provisions; however, the

Board was concerned about the complexity and possible confusion for users if there were multiple accounting changes over different periods, which could result if it permitted early application on a plan-by-plan basis. Therefore, the Board decided that early application should be for all of an employer's benefit plans.

Measurement Date

B95. The Exposure Draft proposed that employers remeasure plan assets and benefit obligations as of the beginning of the fiscal year that the measurement date provisions are effective. In considering the implementation issues associated with performing a second measurement in the year the measurement date is changed, the Board noted that Statements 87 and 106 do not require that all measurement procedures related to postretirement obligations be performed as of the measurement date. In Statement 87, the Board stated that "as with other financial statement items requiring estimates, much of the information can be prepared as of an earlier date and projected forward to account for subsequent events . . ." (paragraph 52).

B96. Due to the costs noted in paragraph B53, the Board decided to allow an alternative approach for the transition to a fiscal year-end measurement date. In lieu of remeasuring plan assets and benefit obligations as of the beginning of the fiscal year that the measurement date provisions are effective, an employer may use earlier measurements determined for year-end reporting as of the fiscal year immediately preceding the year the measurement date provisions are initially applied. The adjustment to retained earnings is approximated by prorating a portion of net periodic benefit cost determined for the period beginning with the last measurement date used for the immediately preceding fiscal year and ending with the last day of the fiscal year that the measurement provisions are applied. For example, a calendar-year employer that uses a September 30 measurement date would allocate three-fifteenths of net period benefit cost determined for the period from September 30, 2007, to December 31, 2008. It is not possible to quantify adjustments to beginning accumulated other comprehensive income without a measurement as of the beginning of the fiscal year. Therefore, the effect of the change in measurement date on accumulated other comprehensive income is recognized during the fiscal year in other comprehensive income, not distinguishing the effects of changing the measurement date from other changes during the period.

Curtailment and settlement gains and losses are recognized in earnings as they arise. The Board concluded that alternative would simplify transition and reduce implementation costs because a second measurement of plan assets and benefit obligations would not be required during transition.

B97. The Board considered whether eliminating the earlier measurement date alternative should be applied retrospectively because that application necessitates conducting an additional measurement of plan assets and benefit obligations for each individual plan as of the financial reporting date for each prior year presented if an employer has been using an alternative measurement date. The Exposure Draft acknowledged that retrospective application could be impracticable because of the need to determine the fair value of certain plan assets. For that reason, and to reduce the costs of implementation, the Exposure Draft proposed not requiring or permitting retrospective application of the provision related to the change in measurement date. Respondents supported that approach and the Board affirmed that decision during its redeliberations.

B98. Before issuing the Exposure Draft, the Board considered two alternative effective dates for the change in measurement date for a public employer. Under the first alternative, the change would be effective for fiscal years beginning after December 15, 2006. Under the second alternative, the change would be effective for fiscal years ending after December 15, 2007. The Board preferred the first alternative because it required that net periodic benefit cost for that fiscal year be based on measurements as of the beginning of the year. Thus, results of operations for each interim period and the fiscal year would be more representationally faithful of the events occurring during those periods. The Board considered the costs that would be incurred to conduct the necessary measurements under both alternatives and concluded that the costs would likely be similar.

B99. Certain respondents expressed a concern about the short time frame expected between issuance of this Statement and the proposed effective date of fiscal years ending after December 15, 2006, for recognition of the funded status and the proposed effective date of years beginning after December 15, 2006, for the change in measurement date. Those respondents stated that it would be difficult and costly to implement both accounting changes simultaneously. The Board determined that recognition of the funded status is the most important provision in this Statement and decided to delay the effective date for the measurement date change to fiscal years ending after December 15, 2008, for all employers. That delay will provide sufficient time for preparers and resource providers to implement necessary system and process changes in an efficient manner. The Board decided to encourage early application of this Statement's measurement date provisions; however, the Board was concerned about the complexity and possible confusion for users if there were multiple accounting changes over different periods, which could result if it permitted early application on a plan-by-plan basis. Therefore, the Board decided that early application should be for all of an employer's benefit plans.

Amendments Considered but Not Made

Separate Line Item Presentation

B100. In developing the Exposure Draft, the Board considered whether to require that postretirement-benefit-related assets and liabilities be presented as separate line items in an employer's statement of financial position. That presentation would be consistent with this Statement's objective to increase the transparency of the funded statuses of the postretirement benefit plans in an employer's statement of financial position.

B101. The Board decided not to specify at this time the display of postretirement benefit assets or liabilities. The Board reasoned that required note disclosures provide adequate information about amounts recognized. In addition, SEC registrants already are subject to certain reporting requirements for significant assets and liabilities. Respondents did not comment on separate line-item presentation and the Board affirmed it prior decision.

Interim-Period Remeasurement

B102. Because the primary objective of the first phase of the project was recognition of the funded statuses of an employer's postretirement benefit plans, the Board considered whether the status of each plan should be measured each interim reporting period or whether interim-period recognition could be based on a limited remeasurement approach. Limited remeasurement might involve updating certain, but not all, assumptions and other valuation short-

cuts. The Board decided not to require that plan assets and benefit obligations be remeasured for interim-period reporting because:

a. There would be additional costs to implement that change.
b. It would raise additional issues not addressed by Statement 87 or 106.
c. It would represent a fundamental change in the measurement of net periodic benefit cost, and measurement issues were beyond the scope and objectives of this Statement.

The Board observed that employers can establish a consistent policy for periodic measurements of plan assets and benefit obligation pursuant to Statements 87 and 106. The Board also decided not to allow a limited remeasurement approach because doing so would inevitably necessitate the need for the Board to address issues about measurement that were beyond the scope of this Statement. The Board noted that unless an employer remeasures both its plan assets and benefit obligations during the fiscal year, the amount it reports in interim-period financial statements should be the same asset or liability recognized in the previous year-end statement of financial position adjusted for (a) subsequent accruals of net periodic benefit cost, other than the amortization of amounts previously recognized in accumulated other comprehensive income (that is, those amounts are reclassified from accumulated other comprehensive income as components of net periodic benefit cost and do not affect the asset or liability recognized in the statement of financial position) and (b) contributions to a funded plan, or benefit payments. However, sometimes an employer remeasures both the benefit obligation and plan assets during the fiscal year. That is the case, for example, when a significant event, such as a plan amendment, settlement, or curtailment occurs that calls for a remeasurement. Upon remeasurement, the employer should adjust its statement of financial position (on a delayed basis until the measurement date provisions of this Statement have been implemented) to reflect the overfunded or underfunded status of the defined benefit plan as of that remeasurement date. Until the measurement date provisions of this Statement have been adopted, the employer should continue to recognize the overfunded or underfunded status of its plans on a delayed basis (for example, on a three-month lag for a calendar-year employer that measures plan assets and benefit obligations as of September 30). The Board will deliberate the accounting issues related to interim periods during the second phase of the project.

Implementation Guidance

B103. When they were issued, Statements 87, 88, and 106 represented fundamental changes in the accounting for defined benefit postretirement plans, changes in the depiction of those plans, and changes in their effects on an employer's financial statements. Those Statements include examples to illustrate the application of certain accounting and disclosure requirements.

B104. Many of the illustrations would have required extensive changes to implement the provisions of this Statement. The Board concluded that the changes that would be necessary included eliminating reconciliations of the funded status to amounts recognized in an employer's statement of financial position, eliminating references to the additional minimum pension liability, and eliminating references to unrecognized gains or losses, unrecognized prior service costs or credits, and the unrecognized transition asset or obligation to reflect that those items now would be recognized in accumulated other comprehensive income.

B105. The Board believes the original need for those illustrations, particularly those relating to the transition provisions of Statements 87 and 106, are not essential to understanding or applying the provisions of this Statement. The Board decided to consider further those illustrations included in Statements 87, 88, and 106 and to update those that have continuing relevance following the issuance of this Statement.

B106. The Board believes many of the staff Q&As contained in FASB Special Reports, *A Guide to Implementation of Statement 87 on Employers' Accounting for Pensions; A Guide to Implementation of Statement 88 on Employers' Accounting for Settlements and Curtailments of Defined Benefit Pension Plans and for Termination Benefits;* and *A Guide to Implementation of Statement 106 on Employers' Accounting for Postretirement Benefits Other Than Pensions,* are not essential to understanding or applying the provisions of this Statement. Additionally, the Board believes the need for those Q&As has diminished over the many years since Statements 87, 88, and 106 were first issued. The Board decided to consider further those Q&As and to update those that have continuing relevance following the issuance of this Statement.

Benefit-Cost Considerations

B107. The objective of financial reporting is to provide information that is useful to present and potential investors, creditors, donors, and other capital market participants in making rational investment, credit, and similar resource allocation decisions. However, the benefits of providing information for that purpose should justify the related costs. Investors, creditors, donors, and other users of financial information benefit from improvements in financial reporting, while the costs to implement a new standard are borne primarily by the preparer. The Board's assessment of the costs and benefits of issuing an accounting standard is unavoidably more qualitative than quantitative because there is no method to objectively measure the costs to implement an accounting standard or to quantify the value of improved information in financial statements.

Benefits

B108. The benefits of this Statement are as follows:

a. Reporting of postretirement benefit obligations in statements of financial position will be more complete. Under the prior accounting standards, significant obligations were not recognized in the statement of financial position. Important information about the nature and amount of an employer's obligations for postretirement benefits, including those for retiree health care plans (which are not usually funded), was relegated to the notes to financial statements.

b. The understandability of financial statements will be improved. Users of financial statements will be better able to assess an employer's financial position and its ability to carry out the obligations of its pension and other postretirement benefit plans.

c. The timeliness of recognition in the financial statements will be improved, either as net periodic benefit cost or other comprehensive income. Also improved will be the timeliness of recognizing the effects of the events that affect the costs of providing postretirement benefits, including changes in plan assets and benefit obligations that occur during a period because of differences between experience and assumptions, or that occur as a result of changes in one or more actuarial assumptions.

d. The comparability of financial statements between employers will be improved, and the representational faithfulness of statements of financial position enhanced, by requiring that plan assets and benefit obligations be measured as of the date of an employer's year-end statement of financial position, not up to three months earlier as was previously permitted.

B109. This Statement requires the recognition of information about events that affect postretirement benefit obligations and plan assets that previously was included only in note disclosures. The Board believes that disclosure is not a substitute for recognition in financial reporting. The changes in accounting for postretirement benefits that are required by this Statement provide a benefit because of the increased credibility and representational faithfulness of financial reporting that results from requiring the recognition (and not merely the disclosure) of the funded statuses of an employer's postretirement benefit obligations. Furthermore, this Statement should reduce or eliminate the effort required by users that adjust financial statements to include unrecognized benefit obligations or plan assets on a pro forma basis in an employer's statement of financial position.

Costs

B110. Based on input from constituents, the Board believes that the incremental costs of implementing the principal provisions of this Statement will not be significant because the information needed to recognize a plan's funded status (that is, gains or losses, prior service costs or credits, and the transition asset or obligation) is already needed to determine net periodic benefit cost and is included in annual note disclosures.

B111. In addition, the Board took certain steps to reduce the costs of implementation. For example, this Statement requires prospective application rather than retrospective application. This Statement also provides an alternative transition for the requirement to measure plan assets and benefit obligations as of the date of an employer's year-end statement of financial position. An employer that previously used an earlier measurement date (that is, up to three months earlier pursuant to the prior provisions of Statements 87 and 106) would ordinarily need to perform an additional measurement in the year the new requirement is implemented to align the measurement date with the date of an employer's year-end statement of financial position. For example, to have beginning balances for the year that the change in

measurement date provision is effective, an employer with a calendar year-end that used September 30 as its measurement date would need to perform an additional measurement at December 31. Time and other resources would be needed to collect, process, and validate information used in that measurement.

B112. Incremental one-time costs associated with measuring plan assets as of the financial reporting date (that is, if plan assets and benefit obligations are not already being measured as of that date) may include the following:

a. Costs to implement changes in systems and processes used to gather and roll forward demographic information and other data related to measurement assumptions
b. Fees paid to external consultants involved in the measurement of benefit obligations or the valuation of plan assets
c. Fees paid to external auditors to audit the results of a second measurement of plan assets, benefit obligations, and related effects on net periodic benefit cost.

In addition to the alternative approach (see paragraph B96), the Board delayed the effective date for the change in measurement date to alleviate those costs.

B113. The Board acknowledges there still will be incremental one-time costs. However, the Board believes the ongoing financial reporting benefits derived from measuring postretirement benefit assets and obligations included in an employer's year-end statement of financial position as of the same date as all other assets and liabilities included in that statement will exceed those one-time costs.

Potential Economic Consequences of Recognition of the Funded Status

B114. Some respondents to the Exposure Draft said that required recognition of the funded statuses of an employer's plans may have undesirable economic consequences. They suggested that such recognition is likely to cause some employers to reduce, eliminate, or otherwise revise their postretirement benefit plans. Some also contended that recognition will raise the cost of capital for employers whose plans are significantly underfunded.

B115. The Board is aware that changes in the behavior of lenders, employers, and others may occur as a result of this Statement. However, it is not the Board's intention to affect the likelihood of any changes in those behaviors. FASB Concepts Statement No. 2, *Qualitative Characteristics of Accounting Information*, explains neutrality. It states:

> Neutrality means that either in formulating or implementing standards, the primary concern should be the relevance and reliability of the information that results, not the effect that the new rule may have on a particular interest.

> To be neutral, accounting information must report economic activity as faithfully as possible, without coloring the image it communicates for the purpose of influencing behavior in *some particular direction*. [paragraphs 98 and 100]

B116. Neutrality does not imply that improved financial reporting should have no economic consequences. To the contrary, a change in accounting standards that results in financial statements that are more relevant and representationally faithful, and thus more useful for decision making, presumably will have economic consequences. For example, required recognition of a plan's funded status and the events that affect that plan's status based on the provisions of this Statement results in recognizing to a greater degree the difference between a defined benefit plan and a defined contribution plan.

B117. The Board believes it is the economic nature of postretirement benefit arrangements that determines decisions made by employers, lenders, investors, donors, and others. That economic nature is not affected by the financial accounting treatment of those arrangements. However, the decision usefulness of information about those arrangements is affected by the reporting standards that govern how those arrangements are depicted in the financial statements. This Statement results in a more relevant, complete, representationally faithful, and comparable depiction of postretirement benefit plans in an employer's financial statements.

International Accounting Comparison

B118. The U.S. and international accounting standards for employers' accounting for defined benefit postretirement plans are similar regarding delayed recognition of certain events in measuring net periodic benefit cost, net periodic benefit cost reporting, and offsetting of liabilities and assets. Under those standards, returns on invested assets are recognized based on an expected long-term rate of return, the individual elements of net periodic benefit cost are combined and reported as a single amount in an employer's financial statements, and the values of assets contributed and liabilities recognized are shown net in an employer's statement of financial position. The U.S. and international accounting standards differ in some areas, including the following:

a. Statements 87 and 106 require, at a minimum, that gains and losses be amortized as a component of net periodic benefit cost if the accumulated amount exceeds 10 percent of the greater of the market-related value of plan assets or the benefit obligation. Under IAS 19 amortization requires using a similar formula except that in applying the threshold plan assets are measured at fair value, not at market-related value.

b. IAS 19 requires that prior service costs be recognized as a component of net periodic benefit cost over the vesting period. If the benefits vest immediately, the cost is recognized immediately. Statements 87 and 106 require that the cost (for vested and nonvested benefits) generally be recognized as a component of net periodic benefit cost over the active plan participants' future service periods.

c. IAS 19 requires that plan assets be measured at fair value for purposes of determining the expected return on plan assets; Statements 87 and 106 allow the use of fair values that are averaged over a period of up to five years (that is, market-related values).

B119. This Statement was issued as a result of a limited-scope phase of a comprehensive project conducted by the FASB. The IASB recently added to its agenda a project to review pension accounting standards. The IASB's project will be conducted in two phases. The first phase is aimed at making targeted improvements to pension accounting. The second phase is a fundamental review of accounting for postretirement benefits. The goal of the second phase is to converge with the FASB. The objective of phase two for both Boards is to develop a single, converged, and high-quality accounting standard that will cover all aspects of employers' accounting for defined benefit postretirement plans.

B120. The limited amendments adopted by this Statement that relate to recognition of the funded statuses of postretirement benefit plans differ from the provisions of IAS 19. This Statement requires that gains or losses and prior service costs or credits not recognized by a business entity as part of net periodic benefit cost be recognized as increases or decreases in an employer's assets or liabilities and as corresponding adjustments to other comprehensive income. IAS 19 does not require recognition of all gains or losses. However, it permits an employer to adopt a policy of recognizing all gains or losses, subject to certain limitations on the recognition of assets, in the period in which they occur—but outside profit or loss—"in a statement of changes in equity titled statement of recognized income and expense" (IAS 19, paragraphs 58, 93B, and 93C).

B121. This Statement's requirement to measure plan assets and benefit obligations as of the date of an employer's year-end statement of financial position is similar to IAS 19, which requires that measurements of plan assets and benefit obligations be determined with sufficient regularity to ensure that the amounts recognized in the financial statements do not differ materially from those that would be determined at the date of the year-end statement of financial position.

Appendix C

AMENDMENTS TO STATEMENTS 87 AND 88

C1. This appendix contains the amendments to FASB Statements No. 87, *Employers' Accounting for Pensions,* and No. 88, *Employers' Accounting for Settlements and Curtailments of Defined Benefit Pension Plans and for Termination Benefits,* as a result of this Statement. The following principal topics are addressed:

a. Amendments related to the recognition of the funded status of a defined benefit plan in an employer's statement of financial position, that is, recognition of gains or losses, prior service costs or credits, and the transition asset or obligation remaining from the initial adoption of Statement 87 that were previously unrecognized as of the date this Statement is initially applied.
b. Amendments to codify into Statement 87 the guidance from the basis for conclusions of FASB Statement No. 106, *Employers' Accounting for Postretirement Benefits Other Than Pensions,*

that describes the objective of selecting assumed discount rates from a portfolio of high-quality debt instruments.
c. Amendments related to measuring plan assets and benefit obligations as of the date of an employer's year-end statement of financial position, eliminating the alternative of selecting a measurement date not more than three months prior to the date of an employer's year-end statement of financial position.
d. Amendments to conform the terms in the glossary of Statement 87 to this Statement.
e. Amendments needed to provide additional guidance for applying the amendments noted in (a) above to a not-for-profit organization or other entity that does not report other comprehensive income pursuant to FASB Statement No. 130, *Reporting Comprehensive Income.*

C2. Statement 87 is amended as follows: [Added text is underlined and deleted text is ~~struck out~~.]

a. Paragraph 16:

Net periodic pension cost has often been viewed as a single homogeneous amount, but in fact it is made up of several *components* that reflect different aspects of the employer's financial arrangements as well as the cost of benefits earned by employees. The cost of a benefit can be determined without regard to how the employer decides to finance the plan. The **service cost component** of net periodic pension cost is the **actuarial present value** of benefits attributed by the plan's benefit formula to services rendered by employees during the period. The service cost component is conceptually the same for an unfunded plan, a plan with minimal funding, and a well-funded plan. The other components of net periodic pension cost are **interest cost**[4] (interest on the **projected benefit obligation,** which is a discounted amount), **actual return on plan assets, amortization** of any ~~unrecognized~~ **prior service cost** or credit included in accumulated other comprehensive income, and **gain or loss,** which includes, to the extent recognized, amortization of the net gain or loss included in accumulated other comprehensive income. Both the return on plan assets and interest cost components are in substance financial items rather than employee compensation costs.

b. Paragraph 20:

The following components shall be included in the net pension cost recognized for a period by an employer **sponsoring** a defined benefit pension plan:

a. Service cost

b. Interest cost

c. Actual return on plan assets, if any

d. Amortization of any prior service cost or credit included in accumulated other comprehensive income~~Amortization of unrecognized prior service cost, if any~~

e. Gain or loss (including the effects of changes in assumptions) to the extent recognized (paragraph 34)

f. Amortization of any net transition asset or obligation existing at the date of initial application of this Statement and remaining in accumulated other comprehensive income (paragraph 77).~~Amortization of the unrecognized net obligation (and loss or cost) or unrecognized net asset (and gain) existing at the date of initial application of this Statement (paragraph 77).~~

c. Paragraph 25:

~~The cost of retroactive benefits (including benefits that are granted to retirees) is the increase in the projected benefit obligation at the date of the amendment.~~A plan amendment that retroactively increases benefits (including benefits that are granted to retirees) increases the projected benefit obligation. The cost of the benefit improvement shall be recognized as a charge to other comprehensive income at the date of the amendment. Except as specified in paragraphs 26 and 27, that prior service cost shall be amortized as a component of net periodic pension cost by assigning an equal amount to each future period of service of each employee active at the date of the amendment who is expected to receive benefits under the plan. If all or almost all of a plan's **participants** are inactive, the cost of retroactive plan amendments affecting benefits of inactive participants shall be amortized based on the remaining life expectancy of those participants instead of based on the remaining service period. Other comprehensive income is adjusted each period as prior service cost is amortized.

d. Paragraph 26:

To reduce the complexity and detail of the computations required, consistent use of an alternative ~~amortization~~ approach that more rapidly ~~reduces~~amortizes the ~~unrecognized~~ cost of retroactive amendments is acceptable. For example, a straight-line amortization of the cost over the average remaining service period of employees expected to receive benefits under the plan is acceptable. The alternative method used shall be disclosed.

e. Paragraph 28:

A plan amendment that retroactively reduces, rather than increases, benefits decreases the projected benefit obligation. The reduction in benefits shall be recognized as a credit (prior service credit) to other comprehensive income that shall be used first to reduce any remaining prior service cost included in accumulated other comprehensive income. Any remaining prior service credit shall be amortized as a component of net periodic pension cost on the same basis as the cost of a benefit increase.~~A plan amendment can reduce, rather than increase, the projected benefit obligation. Such a reduction shall be used to reduce any existing unrecognized prior service cost, and the excess, if any, shall be amortized on the same basis as the cost of benefit increases.~~

f. Paragraph 29 and its related footnote 5:

Gains and losses are changes in the amount of either the projected benefit obligation or plan assets resulting from experience different from that assumed and from changes in assumptions. This Statement does not distinguish between those sources of gains and losses. Gains and losses include amounts that have been realized, for example by sale of a security, as well as amounts that are unrealized. Because gains and losses may reflect refinements in estimates as well as real changes in economic values and because some gains in one period may be offset by losses in another or vice versa, this Statement does not require recognition of gains and losses as components of net pension cost of the period in which they arise.[5] Gains and losses that are not recognized immediately as a component of net periodic pension cost shall be recognized as increases or decreases in other comprehensive income as they arise.

[5]Accounting for **plan terminations** and **curtailments** and other circumstances in which recognition of gains and losses as a component of net periodic pension cost might not be delayed is addressed in FASB Statement No. 88, *Employers' Accounting for Settlements and Curtailments of Defined Benefit Pension Plans and for Termination Benefits.*

g. Paragraph 32 and its related footnote 6:

As a minimum, amortization of ~~an unrecognized net gain or loss~~ a net gain or loss included in accumulated other comprehensive income (excluding asset gains and losses not yet reflected in market-related value) shall be included as a component of net pension cost for a year if, as of the beginning of the year, that ~~unrecognized~~ net gain or loss exceeds 10 percent of the greater of the projected benefit obligation or the market-related value of plan assets. If amortization is required, the minimum amortization[6] shall be that excess divided by the average remaining service period of active employees expected to receive benefits under the plan. If all or almost all of a plan's participants are inactive, the average remaining life expectancy of the inactive participants shall be used instead of average remaining service.

[6]The amortization must always reduce the beginning-of-the-year balance. Amortization of a net ~~unrecognized~~ gain results in a decrease in net periodic pension cost; amortization of a net ~~unrecognized~~ loss results in an increase in net periodic pension cost.

h. Paragraph 33:

Any systematic method of ~~amortizing~~amortization of unrecognized gains or losses may be used in lieu of the minimum specified in the previous paragraph provided that (a) the minimum is used in any period in which the minimum amortization is greater (reduces the net balance included in accumulated other comprehensive income by more), (b) the method is applied consistently, (c) the method is applied similarly to both gains and losses, and (d) the method used is disclosed.

i. Paragraph 34:

The gain or loss component of net periodic pension cost shall consist of (a) the difference between the actual return on plan assets and the expected return on plan assets and (b) amortization of the ~~unrecognized~~ net gain or loss included in accumulated other comprehensive income~~from previous periods~~.

j. Paragraph 35:

If the projected benefit obligation exceeds the fair value of plan assets, the employer shall recognize in its statement of financial position a liability that equals the **unfunded projected benefit obligation.** If the fair value of plan assets exceeds the projected benefit obligation, the employer shall recognize in its statement of financial position an asset that equals the overfunded projected benefit obligation.~~A liability (unfunded accrued pension cost) is recognized if net periodic pension cost recognized pursuant to this Statement exceeds amounts the employer has contributed to the plan. An asset (**prepaid pension cost**) is recognized if net periodic pension cost is less than amounts the employer has contributed to the plan.~~

k. Paragraph 36:

The employer shall aggregate the statuses of all overfunded plans and recognize that amount as an asset in its statement of financial position. It also shall aggregate the statuses of all underfunded plans and recognize that amount as a liability in its statement of financial position. An employer that presents a classified statement of financial position shall classify the liability for an underfunded plan as a current liability, a noncurrent liability, or a combination of both. The current portion (determined on a plan-by-plan basis) is the amount by which the actuarial present value of benefits included in the benefit obligation payable in the next 12 months, or operating cycle if longer, exceeds the fair value of plan assets. The asset for an overfunded plan shall be classified as a noncurrent asset in a classified statement of financial position.~~If the accumulated benefit obligation exceeds the fair value of plan assets, the employer shall recognize in the statement of financial position a liability (including unfunded accrued pension cost) that is at least equal to the **unfunded accumulated benefit obligation.** Recognition of an additional minimum liability is required if an unfunded accumulated benefit obligation exists and (a) an asset has been recognized as prepaid pension cost, (b) the liability already recognized as unfunded accrued pension cost is less than the unfunded accumulated benefit obligation, or (c) no accrued or prepaid pension cost has been recognized.~~

l. Paragraph 37, as amended, and its related footnote 7:

> The asset or liability that is recognized pursuant to paragraph 35 may result in a temporary difference, as defined in FASB Statement No. 109, *Accounting for Income Taxes.* The deferred tax effects of any temporary differences shall be recognized in income tax expense or benefit for the year and shall be allocated to various financial statement components, including other comprehensive income, pursuant to paragraphs 35–39 of Statement 109.~~If an additional minimum liability is recognized pursuant to paragraph 36, an equal amount shall be recognized as an intangible asset, provided that the asset recognized shall not exceed the amount of unrecognized prior service cost.~~[7] ~~If an additional liability required to be recognized exceeds unrecognized prior service cost, the excess (which would represent a net loss not yet recognized as net periodic pension cost) shall be reported in other comprehensive income, net of any tax benefits that result from considering such losses as temporary differences for purposes of applying the provisions of FASB Statement No. 109, Accounting for Income Taxes.~~

> ~~[7]For purposes of this paragraph, an unrecognized net obligation existing at the date of initial application of this Statement (paragraph 77) shall be treated as unrecognized prior service cost.~~

m. Paragraph 38, as amended:

> If a new determination of the funded status of a plan to be recognized as an asset or a liability in the employer's statement of financial position is made (paragraph 52), or when net gains or losses, prior service costs or credits, or the net transition asset or obligation existing at the date of initial application of this Statement are amortized as components of net periodic pension cost, the related balances for those net gains or losses, prior service costs or credits, and transition asset or obligation in accumulated other comprehensive income shall be adjusted as necessary and reported in other comprehensive income.~~When a new determination of the amount of additional liability is made to prepare a statement of financial position, the related intangible asset and the balance accumulated in a separate component of equity shall be eliminated or adjusted as necessary. Eliminations of or adjustments to that balance shall be reported in other comprehensive income.~~

n. Paragraph 44A is added as follows:

> Pursuant to paragraph 44, an employer may look to rates of return on high-quality fixed-income investments in determining assumed discount rates. The objective of selecting assumed discount rates using that method is to measure the single amount that, if invested at the measurement date in a portfolio of high-quality debt instruments, would provide the necessary future cash flows to pay the pension benefits when due. Notionally, that single amount, the projected benefit obligation, would equal the current market value of a portfolio of high-quality zero coupon bonds whose maturity dates and amounts would be the same as the timing and amount of the expected future benefit payments. Because cash inflows would equal cash outflows in timing and amount, there would be no reinvestment risk in the yields to maturity of the portfolio. However, in other than a zero coupon portfolio, such as a portfolio of long-term debt instruments that pay semiannual interest payments or whose maturities do not extend far enough into the future to meet expected benefit payments, the assumed discount rates (the yield to maturity) need to incorporate expected reinvestment rates available in the future. Those rates shall be extrapolated from the existing yield curve at the measurement date. The determination of the assumed discount rate is separate from the determination of the expected rate of return on plan assets whenever the actual portfolio differs from the hypothetical portfolio above. Assumed discount rates shall be reevaluated at each measurement date. If the general level of interest rates rises or declines, the assumed discount rates shall change in a similar manner.

o. Paragraph 49, as amended:

> For purposes of ~~measuring the minimum liability required by~~applying the provisions of paragraph ~~35~~36 and for purposes of the disclosures required by paragraphs 5 and 8 of FASB Statement No. 132 (revised 2003), *Employers' Disclosures about Pensions and Other Postretirement Benefits,* plan investments, whether equity or debt securities, real estate, or other, shall be measured at their fair value as of the measurement date.[12]

Note: FASB Statement No. 157, *Fair Value Measurements,* amended paragraph 49 prior to the issuance of this Statement, eliminating additional guidance about the measurement of plan assets at fair value. The preexisting guidance is effective for an employer until it adopts Statement 157. The changes to paragraph 49, as previously amended, and its related footnotes 11a, as previously added, and 12 made by Statement 157 and this Statement are shown below:

For purposes of ~~measuring the minimum liability required by~~applying the provisions of paragraph 35~~36~~ and for purposes of the disclosures required by paragraphs 5 and 8 of FASB Statement No. 132 (revised 2003), *Employers' Disclosures about Pensions and Other Postretirement Benefits,* plan investments, whether equity or debt securities, real estate, or other, shall be measured at their fair value as of the measurement date. ~~The fair value of an investment is the amount that the plan could reasonably expect to receive for it in a current sale between a willing buyer and a willing seller, that is, other than in a forced or liquidation sale. Fair value shall be measured by the market price if an active market exists for the investment. If no active market exists for an investment but such a market exists for similar investments, selling prices in that market may be helpful in estimating fair value. If a market price is not available, a forecast of expected cash flows~~[11a] ~~may aid in estimating fair value, provided the expected cash flows are discounted at a current rate commensurate with the risk involved.~~[12]

[11a]~~This pronouncement was issued prior to FASB Concepts Statement No. 7, *Using Cash Flow Information and Present Value in Accounting Measurements,* and therefore the term expected cash flows does not necessarily have the same meaning as that term in Concepts Statement 7.~~

[12]~~For an indication of factors to be considered in determining the discount rate, refer to paragraphs 13 and 14 of APB Opinion No. 21, *Interest on Receivables and Payables.* If significant,~~ fThe fair value of an investment shall be reduced by ~~reflect the~~ brokerage commissions and other costs normally incurred in a sale if those costs are significant (similar to fair value less cost to sell).

p. Paragraph 52:

The measurements of plan assets and benefit obligations required by this Statement shall be as of the date of the employer's fiscal year-end statement of financial position unless (a) the plan is sponsored by a subsidiary that is consolidated using a fiscal period that differs from its parent's, as permitted by ARB No. 51, *Consolidated Financial Statements,* or (b) the plan is sponsored by an investee that is accounted for using the equity method of accounting under APB Opinion No. 18, *The Equity Method of Accounting for Investments in Common Stock,* using financial statements of the investee for a fiscal period that is different from the investor's, as permitted by Opinion 18. In those cases, the employer shall measure the subsidiary's plan assets and benefit obligations as of the date used to consolidate the subsidiary's statement of financial position and shall measure the investee's plan assets and benefit obligations as of the date of the investee's financial statements used to apply the equity method.~~financial statements or, if used consistently from year to year, as of a date not more than three months prior to that date.~~ Requiring that the pension measurements be as of a particular date is not intended to require that all procedures be performed after that date. As with other financial statement items requiring estimates, much of the information can be prepared as of an earlier date and projected forward to account for subsequent events (for example, employee service). Unless a business entity remeasures both its plan assets and benefit obligations during the fiscal year, the funded status it reports in its interim-period statement of financial position shall be the same asset or liability recognized in the previous year-end statement of financial position adjusted for (1) subsequent accruals of net periodic pension cost that exclude the amortization of amounts previously recognized in other comprehensive income (for example, subsequent accruals of service cost, interest cost, and return on plan assets) and (2) contributions to a funded plan, or benefit payments. Sometimes, a business entity remeasures both plan assets and benefit obligations during the fiscal year. That is the case, for example, when a significant event such as a plan amendment, settlement, or curtailment occurs that calls for a remeasurement. Upon remeasurement, a business entity shall adjust its statement of financial position in a subsequent interim period (on a delayed basis if the measurement date provisions of FASB Statement No. 158, *Employers' Accounting for Defined Benefit Pension and Other Postretirement Plans,* have not yet been implemented) to reflect the overfunded or underfunded status of the plan consistent with that measurement date. ~~The additional minimum~~

~~liability reported in interim financial statements shall be the same additional minimum liability (paragraph 36) recognized in the previous year-end statement of financial position, adjusted for subsequent accruals and contributions, unless measures of both the obligation and plan assets are available as of a more current date or a significant event occurs, such as a plan amendment, that would ordinarily call for such measurements.~~

q. Paragraph 55:

An employer that sponsors two or more separate defined benefit pension plans shall determine net periodic pension cost, liabilities, and assets by separately applying the provisions of this Statement to each plan. In particular, unless an employer clearly has a right to use the assets of one plan to pay benefits of another, a liability required to be recognized pursuant to paragraph 35 ~~or 36~~ for one plan shall not be reduced or eliminated because ~~another plan has~~the employer has recognized an asset for another plan that has assets in excess of its ~~accumulated~~ projected benefit obligation ~~or because the employer has prepaid pension cost related to another plan~~.

r. Paragraph 74, as amended:

When an employer is acquired in a business combination and that employer sponsors a single-employer defined benefit pension plan, the assignment of the purchase price to individual assets acquired and liabilities assumed shall include a liability for the projected benefit obligation in excess of plan assets or an asset for plan assets in excess of the projected benefit obligation, thereby eliminating any previously existing ~~unrecognized~~ net gain or loss, ~~unrecognized~~ prior service cost or credit, or transition asset or obligation recognized in accumulated other comprehensive income. ~~or unrecognized net obligation or net asset existing at the date of initial application of this Statement. Subsequently, to the extent that those amounts are considered in determining the amounts of contributions, differences between the purchaser's net pension cost and amounts contributed will reduce the liability or asset recognized at the date of the combination.~~If it is expected that the plan will be terminated or curtailed, the effects of those actions shall be considered in measuring the projected benefit obligation.

s. Paragraphs 74A–74D and the related heading are added as follows:

Not-for-Profit Organizations and Other Entities That Do Not Report Other Comprehensive Income

74A. A not-for-profit employer shall recognize as a separate line item or items within changes in unrestricted net assets, apart from expenses, the gains or losses and the prior service costs or credits that would be recognized in other comprehensive income pursuant to paragraphs 25, 28, and 29 of this Statement. Consistent with the provisions of FASB Statement No. 117, *Financial Statements of Not-for-Profit Organizations,* this Statement does not prescribe whether the separate line item or items shall be included within or outside an intermediate measure of operations or performance indicator, if one is presented. The AICPA Audit and Accounting Guide, *Health Care Organizations,* requires a not-for-profit organization within its scope to report items of other comprehensive income outside the performance indicator.

74B. A not-for-profit employer shall reclassify to net periodic pension cost a portion of the net gain or loss and prior service costs or credits previously recognized in a separate line item or items and a portion of the transition asset or obligation remaining from the initial application of this Statement, pursuant to the recognition and amortization provisions of paragraphs 24–34 and 77. The contra adjustment or adjustments shall be reported in the same line item or items within changes in unrestricted net assets, apart from expenses, as the initially recognized amounts. Net periodic pension cost shall be reported by functional classification pursuant to paragraph 26 of Statement 117.

74C. In applying the provisions of this Statement to a not-for-profit employer, the references to accumulated other comprehensive income or a separate component of equity in paragraphs 20(d), 20(f), 28, 32–34, 38, 74, and 264, and the references to amounts previously recognized in other comprehensive income in paragraphs 52 and 264, shall instead be to the gains or losses, the prior service costs or credits, and the transition asset or obligation that have been recognized as changes in unrestricted net assets arising from a defined benefit plan but not yet reclassified as components of net periodic pension cost.

74D. An employer other than a not-for-profit employer that does not report other comprehensive income pursuant to FASB Statement No. 130, *Reporting Comprehensive Income,* shall apply the provisions of paragraphs 74A–74C in an analogous manner that is appropriate for its method of reporting financial performance and financial position.

t. Paragraph 261A and its related footnote 17 are added as follows:

The illustrations included in this appendix demonstrate the application of the requirements of this Statement prior to the amendments required by FASB Statement No. 158, *Employers' Accounting for Defined Benefit Pension and Other Postretirement Plans.* Many of those illustrations would require changes to implement the provisions of Statement 158. Those changes include eliminating reconciliations of the funded status to amounts recognized in an employer's statement of financial position, eliminating references to the additional minimum pension liability, and eliminating references to unrecognized gains and losses, unrecognized prior service costs and credits, and unrecognized transition assets and obligations to reflect that those items would be recognized in accumulated other comprehensive income pursuant to Statement 158.[17] Those illustrations remain applicable until the provisions of Statement 158 are applied. The provisions of Statement 158 are illustrated in Appendix A of that Statement.

[17]The Board has a project on its technical agenda to consider further the illustrations included in this appendix and to supersede those that become irrelevant after the provisions of Statement 158 are applied and to amend those that have continuing relevance.

u. Paragraph 264 (glossary):

Amortization
Usually refers to the process of reducing a recognized liability systematically by recognizing revenues or reducing a recognized asset systematically by recognizing expenses or costs. In pension accounting, amortization is also used to refer to the systematic recognition in net pension cost over several periods of amounts previously recognized in other comprehensive income, that is, prior service costs or credits, gains or losses, ~~previously *unrecognized* amounts, including un-~~

~~recognized prior service cost and unrecognized net gain or loss~~ and the transition asset or obligation existing at the date of initial application of this Statement.

Gain or loss
A change in the value of either the projected benefit obligation or the plan assets resulting from experience different from that assumed or from a change in an actuarial assumption. Gains and losses that are not recognized in net periodic pension cost when they arise are recognized in other comprehensive income. Those gains or losses are subsequently recognized as a component of net periodic pension cost based on the amortization provisions of this Statement.~~See also **Unrecognized net gain or loss.**~~

Gain or loss component (of net periodic pension cost)
The sum of (a) the difference between the actual return on plan assets and the expected return on plan assets and (b) the amortization of the ~~unrecognized~~ net gain or loss recognized in accumulated other comprehensive income~~from previous periods~~. The gain or loss component is the net effect of delayed recognition of gains and losses in determining net periodic pension cost (the net change in the gain or loss) in accumulated other comprehensive income~~(the net change in the unrecognized net gain or loss)~~ except that it does not include changes in the projected benefit obligation occurring during the period and deferred for later recognition in net periodic pension cost.

~~**Measurement date**~~
~~The date as of which plan assets and obligations are measured.~~

Net periodic pension cost
The amount recognized in an employer's financial statements as the cost of a pension plan for a period. Components of net periodic pension cost are service cost, interest cost, actual return on plan assets, gain or loss, amortization of ~~unrecognized~~ prior service cost or credit, and amortization of the ~~unrecognized net~~ transition asset or obligation ~~or asset~~ existing at the date of initial application of this Statement. This Statement uses the term *net periodic pension cost* instead of *net pension expense* because part of

the cost recognized in a period may be capitalized along with other costs as part of an asset such as inventory.

Prior service cost
The cost of retroactive benefits granted in a plan amendment. ~~See also~~ ~~Unrecognized prior service cost.~~

~~Unfunded accumulated benefit obligation~~
~~The excess of the accumulated benefit obligation over plan assets.~~

~~Unrecognized net gain or loss~~
~~The cumulative net gain or loss that has not been recognized as a part of net periodic pension cost. See~~ ~~Gain or loss.~~

~~Unrecognized prior service cost~~
~~That portion of prior service cost that has not been recognized as a part of net periodic pension cost.~~

C3. Statement 87 represented fundamental changes in how defined benefit postretirement pension plans were measured and recognized in an employer's financial statements. Appendix B of Statement 87 includes various illustrations that described how certain aspects of the accounting requirements were to be applied.

C4. Many of the illustrations would have required extensive changes to implement the provisions of this Statement. The Board concluded that necessary changes included eliminating the following:

a. Reconciliations of the funded status to amounts recognized in the employer's statement of financial position
b. References to the additional minimum pension liability
c. References to unrecognized gains and losses and unrecognized prior service costs and credits to reflect that those items should be recognized in accumulated other comprehensive income.

C5. The Board believes that many of those illustrations are not essential to understanding or applying the provisions of this Statement. Additionally, the Board believes the need for examples of how to apply Statement 87 has diminished over the many years since Statement 87 was first issued. The Board decided to consider further those illustrations in Statement 87 and in related guidance and to update those that have continuing relevance following the issuance of this Statement.

C6. Statement 88 is amended as follows:

a. Paragraph 9 and its related footnote 2:

For purposes of this Statement, the maximum gain or loss subject to recognition in earnings when a pension obligation is settled is the ~~unrecognized~~ net gain or loss <u>remaining in accumulated other comprehensive income</u> defined in paragraph 29 of Statement 87[2] plus any ~~remaining unrecognized net asset existing at the date of~~<u>transition asset remaining in accumulated other comprehensive income from</u> initial application of Statement 87 ~~(as discussed in paragraph 21 of this Statement)~~. That maximum amount includes any gain or loss first measured at the time of settlement. The maximum amount shall be recognized in earnings if the entire projected benefit obligation is settled. If only part of the projected benefit obligation is settled, the employer shall recognize in earnings a pro rata portion of the maximum amount equal to the percentage reduction in the projected benefit obligation.

---

[2]Paragraph 29 of Statement 87 states:

Gains and losses are changes in the amount of either the projected benefit obligation or plan assets resulting from experience different from that assumed and from changes in assumptions. This Statement does not distinguish between those sources of gains and losses. Gains and losses include amounts that have been realized, for example by sale of a security, as well as amounts that are unrealized. Because gains and losses may reflect refinements in estimates as well as real changes in economic values and because some gains in one period may be offset by losses in another or vice versa, this Statement does not require recognition of gains and losses as components of net pension cost of the period in which they arise. <u>Gains and losses that are not recognized immediately as a component of net periodic pension cost shall be recognized as increases or decreases in other comprehensive income as they arise.</u> [Footnote reference omitted.]

b. Paragraph 12:

The ~~unrecognized~~ prior service cost <u>included in accumulated other comprehensive income</u> associated with years of service no longer expected to be rendered as the result of a curtailment is a loss. For example, if a curtailment eliminates half of the estimated remaining future years of service of those who were employed at the date of a prior plan amendment and were expected to receive benefits under the plan, then the loss associated with the curtailment is half of the ~~remaining unrecognized~~ prior service cost <u>included in accumulated other comprehensive</u>

income related to that amendment that has not been amortized as a component of net periodic pension cost~~related to that plan amendment~~. For purposes of applying the provisions of this paragraph, ~~unrecognized~~ prior service cost includes the cost of retroactive plan amendments (refer to paragraphs 24–25 of Statement 87) and any ~~remaining unrecognized net obligation existing at the date of~~ transition obligation remaining in accumulated other comprehensive income from initial application of Statement 87.~~initial application of Statement 87 (as discussed in paragraph 21 of this Statement).~~

c. Paragraph 13:

The projected benefit obligation may be decreased (a gain) or increased (a loss) by a curtailment.[4]

a. To the extent that such a gain exceeds any ~~unrecognized~~ net loss included in accumulated other comprehensive income (or the entire gain, if ~~an unrecognized net gain~~ a net gain exists), it is a *curtailment gain*

b. To the extent that such a loss exceeds any ~~unrecognized~~ net gain included in accumulated other comprehensive income (or the entire loss, if ~~an unrecognized net loss~~ a net loss exists), it is a *curtailment loss.*

For purposes of applying the provisions of this paragraph, any transition asset remaining in accumulated other comprehensive income from initial application of Statement 87 ~~remaining unrecognized net asset existing at the date of initial application of Statement 87 (as discussed in paragraph 21 of this Statement)~~ shall be treated as ~~an unrecognized net gain~~ a net gain and shall be combined with the ~~unrecognized~~ net gain or loss arising subsequent to transition to Statement 87.

d. Paragraphs 17A and 17B and the related heading are added as follows:

Not-for-Profit Organizations and Other Entities That Do Not Report Other Comprehensive Income

17A. Not-for-profit employers and other employers that do not report other comprehensive income in accordance with the provisions of FASB Statement No. 130, *Reporting Comprehensive Income,* shall apply the provisions of paragraphs 9, 10, and 14 of this Statement in an analogous manner that is appropriate for their method of reporting financial performance and financial position.

17B. For such employers, the references to accumulated other comprehensive income in paragraphs 9, 12, and 13 of this Statement shall instead be to the gains or losses, the prior service costs or credits, and the transition asset or obligation that have been recognized as changes in unrestricted net assets arising from a defined benefit plan but not yet reclassified as components of net periodic pension cost. In footnote 2 to paragraph 9, the reference to paragraph 29 of Statement 87 shall also be to paragraph 74A of that Statement.

e. Paragraph 57A and its related footnote 6a are added as follows:

The illustrations included in this appendix demonstrate the application of the requirements of this Statement prior to the amendments required by FASB Statement No. 158, *Employers' Accounting for Defined Benefit Pension and Other Postretirement Plans.* Many of those illustrations would require changes to implement the provisions of Statement 158. Those changes include eliminating reconciliations of the funded status to amounts recognized in an employer's statement of financial position, eliminating references to the additional minimum pension liability, and eliminating references to unrecognized gains and losses, unrecognized prior service costs and credits, and unrecognized transition assets and obligations to reflect that those items would be recognized in accumulated other comprehensive income pursuant to Statement 158.[6a] Those illustrations remain applicable until the provisions of Statement 158 are applied. The provisions of Statement 158 are illustrated in Appendix A of that Statement.

[6a]The Board has a project on its technical agenda to consider further the illustrations included in this appendix and to supersede those that become irrelevant after the provisions of Statement 158 are applied and to amend those that have continuing relevance.

C7. Statement 88 represented fundamental changes in how defined benefit postretirement plans were measured and recognized in an employer's financial statements when settled or curtailed or when employers offered benefits to employees in connection with their termination of employment. Appendix B of Statement 88 includes various illustrations that described how certain aspects of the accounting requirements were to be applied.

C8. Many of the illustrations would have required extensive changes to implement the provisions of this Statement. The Board concluded that necessary changes included eliminating the following:

a. Reconciliations of the funded status to amounts recognized in the employer's statement of financial position
b. References to additional minimum pension liability
c. References to unrecognized gains and losses and unrecognized prior service costs and credits to reflect that those items should be recognized in accumulated other comprehensive income.

C9. The Board believes that many of those illustrations are not essential to understanding or applying the provisions of this Statement. Additionally, the Board believes the need for examples of how to apply Statement 88 has diminished over the many years since Statement 88 was first issued. The Board decided to consider further those illustrations included in Statement 88 and in related guidance and to update those that have continuing relevance following the issuance of this Statement.

Appendix D

AMENDMENTS TO STATEMENT 106

D1. This appendix contains the amendments to FASB Statement No. 106, *Employers' Accounting for Postretirement Benefits Other Than Pensions,* as a result of this Statement. The following principal topics are addressed:

a. Amendments related to the recognition of the funded status of a defined benefit plan in an employer's statement of financial position, that is, recognition of gains or losses, prior service costs or credits, and the transition asset or obligation remaining from the initial adoption of Statement 106 that were previously unrecognized as of the date this Statement is initially applied.

b. Amendments to codify into the standards section the guidance from the basis for conclusions of Statement 106 that describes the objective of selecting the assumed discount rates from a portfolio of high-quality debt instruments.
c. Amendments related to measuring plan assets and benefit obligations as of the date of an employer's year-end statement of financial position, eliminating the alternative of selecting a measurement date not more than three months prior to the date of an employer's year-end statement of financial position.
d. Amendments to conform the terms in the glossary of Statement 106 to this Statement.
e. Amendments needed to provide additional guidance for applying the amendments noted in (a) above to a not-for-profit organization or other entity that does not report other comprehensive income pursuant to FASB Statement No. 130, *Reporting Comprehensive Income.*

D2. Statement 106 is amended as follows: [Added text is underlined and deleted text is struck out.]

a. Paragraph 22:

Net periodic postretirement benefit cost comprises several components that reflect different aspects of the employer's financial arrangements. The **service cost** component of net periodic postretirement benefit cost is the actuarial present value of benefits attributed to services rendered by employees during the period (the portion of the expected postretirement benefit obligation attributed to service in the period). The service cost component is the same for an unfunded plan, a plan with minimal funding, and a well-funded plan. The other components of net periodic postretirement benefit cost are **interest cost**[8] (interest on the accumulated postretirement benefit obligation, which is a discounted amount), **actual return on plan assets, amortization** of ~~unrecognized~~any **prior service cost** or credit included in accumulated other comprehensive income, amortization of the **transition obligation** or **transition asset,** and the **gain or loss component,** which includes, to the extent recognized, amortization of the net gain or loss included in accumulated other comprehensive income.

b. Paragraph 31:

Assumed discount rates shall reflect the time value of money as of the ~~measurement date~~ measurement date in determining the present value of future cash outflows currently expected to be required to satisfy the postretirement benefit obligation. In making that assumption, employers shall look to rates of return on high-quality fixed-income investments currently available whose cash flows match the timing and amount of expected benefit payments. If settlement of the obligation with third-party insurers is possible (for example, the purchase of nonparticipating life insurance contracts to provide death benefits), the interest rates inherent in the amount at which the postretirement benefit obligation could be settled are relevant in determining the assumed discount rates. Assumed discount rates are used in measurements of the expected and accumulated postretirement benefit obligations and the service cost and interest cost components of net periodic postretirement benefit cost.

c. Paragraph 31A is added as follows:

Pursuant to paragraph 31, an employer shall look to rates of return on high-quality fixed-income investments in determining assumed discount rates. The objective of selecting assumed discount rates using that method is to measure the single amount that, if invested at the measurement date in a portfolio of high-quality debt instruments, would provide the necessary future cash flows to pay the postretirement benefits when due. Notionally, that single amount, the accumulated postretirement benefit obligation, would equal the current market value of a portfolio of high-quality zero coupon bonds whose maturity dates and amounts would be the same as the timing and amount of the expected future benefit payments. Because cash inflows would equal cash outflows in timing and amount, there would be no reinvestment risk in the yields to maturity of the portfolio. However, in other than a zero coupon portfolio, such as a portfolio of long-term debt instruments that pay semiannual interest payments or whose maturities do not extend far enough into the future to meet expected benefit payments, the assumed discount rates (the yield to maturity) need to incorporate expected reinvestment rates available in the future. Those rates shall be extrapolated from the existing yield curve at the measurement date. The determination of the assumed discount rate is separate from the determination of the expected rate of return on plan assets whenever the actual portfolio differs from the hypothetical portfolio described above. Assumed discount rates shall be reevaluated at each measurement date. If the general level of interest rates rises or declines, the assumed discount rates shall change in a similar manner.

d. Paragraphs 44A and 44B and the related heading are added as follows:

Recognition of liabilities and assets

44A. An employer that sponsors one or more single-employer defined benefit postretirement plans other than pensions shall recognize in its statement of financial position the funded statuses of those plans. The status for each plan shall be measured as the difference between the fair value of plan assets and the accumulated postretirement benefit obligation as it is defined in this Statement.

44B. The employer shall aggregate the statuses of all overfunded plans and recognize that amount as an asset in its statement of financial position. It also shall aggregate the statuses of all underfunded plans and recognize that amount as a liability in its statement of financial position. An employer that presents a classified statement of financial position shall classify the liability for an underfunded plan as a current liability, a noncurrent liability, or a combination of both. The current portion (determined on a plan-by-plan basis) is the amount by which the actuarial present value of benefits included in the benefit obligation payable in the next 12 months, or operating cycle if longer, exceeds the fair value of plan assets. The asset for an overfunded plan shall be classified as a noncurrent asset in a classified statement of financial position.

e. Paragraph 46 and its related footnote 18:

The following components shall be included in the net postretirement benefit cost recognized for a period by an employer sponsoring a defined benefit postretirement plan:

a. Service cost (paragraph 47)
b. Interest cost (paragraph 48)

c. Actual return on plan assets, if any (paragraph 49)

d. Amortization of any prior service cost or credit included in accumulated other comprehensive income to the extent required by paragraphs 50–55~~Amortization of unrecognized prior service cost, if any (paragraphs 50–55)~~

e. **Gain or loss** (including the effects of changes in assumptions) to the extent recognized (paragraphs 56–62)

f. Amortization of any obligation or asset existing at the date of initial application of this Statement, hereinafter referred to as the transition obligation[18] or transition asset remaining in accumulated other comprehensive income (paragraphs 110 and 112). ~~Amortization of the unrecognized obligation or asset existing at the date of initial application of this Statement, hereinafter referred to as the **unrecognized transition obligation**[18] or **unrecognized transition asset** (paragraphs 110 and 112).~~

---

[18]Amortization of the ~~unrecognized~~ transition obligation or asset will be adjusted prospectively to recognize the effects of (a) a negative plan amendment pursuant to paragraph 55, (b) a constraint on immediate recognition of a net gain or loss pursuant to paragraph 60, (c) settlement accounting pursuant to paragraphs 92 and 93, (d) plan curtailment accounting pursuant to paragraphs 97–99, and (e) a constraint on delayed ~~recognition~~ amortization of the ~~unrecognized~~ transition obligation pursuant to paragraph 112.

f. Paragraph 52:

~~The cost of benefit improvements (including improved benefits that are granted to **fully eligible plan participants**) is the increase in the accumulated postretirement benefit obligation as a result of the plan amendment, measured at the date of the amendment.~~ A plan amendment that retroactively increases benefits (including benefits that are granted to **fully eligible plan participants**) increases the accumulated postretirement benefit obligation. The cost of the benefit improvement shall be recognized as a charge to other comprehensive income at the date of the amendment. Except as specified in the next sentence and in paragraphs 53 and 54, that prior service cost shall be amortized as a component of net periodic postretirement benefit cost by assigning an equal amount to each remaining year of service to the full eligibility date of each plan participant active at the date of the amendment who was not yet fully eligible for benefits at that

date. If all or almost all of a plan's participants are fully eligible for benefits, the prior service cost shall be amortized based on the remaining life expectancy of those plan participants rather than on the remaining years of service to the full eligibility dates of the active plan participants. Other comprehensive income is adjusted as a result of amortizing prior service cost.

g. Paragraph 53:

To reduce the complexity and detail of the computations required, consistent use of an alternative ~~amortization~~ approach that more rapidly ~~reduces~~ amortizes the~~unrecognized~~ prior service cost recognized in accumulated other comprehensive income is permitted. For example, a straight-line amortization of the cost over the average remaining years of service to full eligibility for benefits of the active plan participants is acceptable.

h. Paragraph 55:

A plan amendment ~~can reduce, rather than increase,~~that retroactively reduces, rather than increases, benefits decreases the accumulated postretirement benefit obligation. The reduction in benefits shall be recognized as a corresponding credit (prior service credit) to other comprehensive income that ~~A reduction in that obligation~~ shall be used first to reduce any remaining ~~existing unrecognized~~ prior service cost included in accumulated other comprehensive income, then to reduce any ~~remaining unrecognized~~ transition obligation remaining in accumulated other comprehensive income. The excess, if any, shall be amortized as a component of net periodic postretirement benefit cost on the same basis as specified in paragraph 52 for prior service cost. Immediate recognition of the excess is not permitted.

i. Paragraph 56:

Gains and losses are changes in the amount of either the accumulated postretirement benefit obligation or plan assets resulting from experience different from that assumed or from changes in assumptions. This Statement generally does not distinguish between those sources of gains and losses. Gains and losses include amounts that have been realized, for example, by the sale of a security, as well as amounts that are unrealized. Because gains and losses may reflect refinements in estimates as well as real changes in economic values and because some gains in one period may be offset by losses in another or vice versa, this Statement does not require recognition of gains and losses as components of net postretirement benefit cost in the period in which they arise, except as described in paragraph 61. Gains and losses that are not recognized immediately as a component of net periodic postretirement benefit cost shall be recognized as increases or decreases in other comprehensive income as they arise. (Gain and loss recognition in accounting for settlements and curtailments is addressed in paragraphs 90–99.)

j. Paragraph 59 and its related footnote 19:

As a minimum, amortization of ~~an unrecognized net gain or loss~~ a net gain or loss included in accumulated other comprehensive income (excluding plan asset gains and losses not yet reflected in market-related value) shall be included as a component of net periodic postretirement benefit cost for a year if, as of the beginning of the year, that ~~unrecognized~~ net gain or loss exceeds 10 percent of the greater of the accumulated postretirement benefit obligation or the market-related value of plan assets. If amortization is required, the minimum amortization[19] shall be that excess divided by the average remaining service period of active plan participants. If all or almost all of a plan's participants are inactive, the average remaining life expectancy of the inactive participants shall be used instead of the average remaining service period.

---

[19]The amortization must always reduce the beginning-of-the-year balance included in accumulated other comprehensive income. Amortization of ~~an unrecognized net gain~~ a net gain included in accumulated other comprehensive income results in a decrease in net periodic postretirement benefit cost; amortization of ~~an unrecognized net loss~~ a net loss included in accumulated other comprehensive income results in an increase in net periodic postretirement benefit cost.

k. Paragraph 60:

Any systematic method of ~~amortization of unrecognized~~ amortizing gains and losses included in accumulated other comprehensive income may be used in place of the minimum amortization specified in paragraph 59 provided that (a) the minimum amortization is recognized in any period in which it is greater (reduces the ~~unrecognized amount~~ net gain or loss balance by

more) than the amount that would be recognized under the method used, (b) the method is applied consistently, (c) the method is applied similarly to both gains and losses, and (d) the method used is disclosed. If an enterprise uses a method of consistently recognizing gains and losses immediately, any gain that does not offset a loss previously recognized in income pursuant to this paragraph shall first offset any ~~unrecognized~~ transition obligation remaining in accumulated other comprehensive income; any loss that does not offset a gain previously recognized in income pursuant to this paragraph shall first offset any ~~unrecognized~~ transition asset remaining in accumulated other comprehensive income.

l. Paragraph 62:

The gain or loss component of net periodic postretirement benefit cost shall consist of (a) the difference between the actual return on plan assets and the expected return on plan assets, (b) any gain or loss immediately recognized or the amortization of the ~~unrecognized~~ net gain or loss ~~from previous periods~~ included in accumulated other comprehensive income, and (c) any amount immediately recognized as a gain or loss pursuant to paragraph 61.

m. Paragraph 65:

Note: FASB Statement No. 157, *Fair Value Measurements,* amended paragraph 65 prior to the issuance of this Statement, eliminating additional guidance about the measurement of plan assets at fair value. The preexisting guidance is effective for an employer until it adopts Statement 157. The changes to paragraph 65, as previously amended, and its related footnotes 20a, as previously added, and 21 made by Statement 157 are shown below:

For purposes of the disclosures required by paragraphs 5 and 8 of FASB Statement No. 132 (revised 2003), *Employers' Disclosures about Pensions and Other Postretirement Benefits,* plan investments, whether equity or debt securities, real estate, or other, shall be measured at their fair value as of the measurement date. ~~The fair value of an investment is the amount that the plan could reasonably expect to receive for it in a current sale between a willing buyer and a willing seller, that is, other than in a forced or liquidation sale.~~ Fair value shall be measured by the market price if an active market exists for the investment. If no active market exists for an investment but an active market exists for similar investments, selling prices in that market may be helpful in estimating fair value. If a market price is not available, a forecast of expected cash flows[20a] may aid in estimating fair value, provided the expected cash flows are discounted at a current rate commensurate with the risk involved.[21] (Refer to paragraph 71.)

[20a]This pronouncement was issued prior to FASB Concepts Statement No. 7, *Using Cash Flow Information and Present Value in Accounting Measurements,* and therefore the term expected cash flows does not necessarily have the same meaning as that term in Concepts Statement 7.

[21]For an indication of factors to be considered in determining the discount rate, refer to paragraphs 13 and 14 of APB Opinion No. 21, *Interest on Receivables and Payables.* If significant, tThe fair value of an investment shall be reduced by reflect the brokerage commissions and other costs normally incurred in a sale if those costs are significant (similar to fair value less cost to sell).

n. Paragraph 72:

The measurements of *plan assets and benefit obligations* required by this Statement shall be as of the date of the employer's fiscal year-end statement of financial position, unless (a) the plan is sponsored by a subsidiary that is consolidated using a fiscal period that differs from its parent's, as permitted by ARB No. 51, *Consolidated Financial Statements,* or (b) the plan is sponsored by an investee that is accounted for using the equity method of accounting under APB Opinion No. 18, *The Equity Method of Accounting for Investments in Common Stock,* using financial statements of the investee for a fiscal period that is different from the investor's, as permitted by Opinion 18. In those cases, the employer shall measure the subsidiary's plan assets and benefit obligations as of the date used to consolidate the subsidiary's statement of financial position and shall measure the investee's plan assets and benefit obligations as of the date of the investee's financial statements used to apply the equity method.financial statements or, if used consistently from year to year, as of a date not more than three months prior to that date. Even though the postretirement benefit measurements are required as of a particular date, all procedures are not required to be performed after that date. As with other financial statement items requiring estimates, much of the informa-

tion can be prepared as of an earlier date and projected forward to account for subsequent events (for example, employee service).

o. Paragraph 73:

Measurements of *net periodic postretirement benefit cost* for both interim and annual financial statements generally shall be based on the assumptions at the beginning of the year (assumptions used for the previous year-end measurements of plan assets and obligations) unless more recent measurements of both plan assets and the accumulated postretirement benefit obligation are available. For example, if a significant event occurs, such as a plan amendment, settlement, or curtailment, that ordinarily would call for remeasurement, the assumptions used for those later measurements shall be used to remeasure net periodic postretirement benefit cost from the date of the event to the year-end measurement date. Unless an employer remeasures both its plan assets and benefit obligations during the fiscal year, the funded status it reports in its interim-period statement of financial position shall be the same asset or liability recognized in the previous year-end statement of financial position adjusted for (a) subsequent accruals of net periodic postretirement benefit cost that exclude the amortization of amounts previously recognized in other comprehensive income (for example, subsequent accruals of service cost, interest cost, and return on plan assets) and (b) contributions to a funded plan, or benefit payments. Upon remeasurement, a business entity shall adjust its statement of financial position in a subsequent interim period (on a delayed basis if the measurement date provisions of FASB Statement No. 158, *Employers' Accounting for Defined Benefit Pension and Other Postretirement Plans,* have not yet been implemented) to reflect the overfunded or underfunded status of the plan consistent with that measurement date.

p. Paragraph 88:

As a result of applying the provisions of paragraphs 86 and 87, any previously existing unrecognized net gain or loss, unrecognized prior service cost or credit, orunrecognized transition obligation or transition asset remaining in accumulated other comprehensive income is eliminated for the acquired employer's plan. Subsequently, to the extent that the net obligation assumed or net assets acquired are considered in determining the amounts of contributions to the plan, differences between the purchaser's net periodic postretirement benefit cost and amounts it contributes will reduce the liability or asset recognized at the date of the combination.

q. Paragraph 92:

For purposes of this Statement, the maximum gain or loss subject to recognition in income when a postretirement benefit obligation is settled is the unrecognized net gain or loss included in accumulated other comprehensive income defined in paragraphs 56–60 plus any remaining unrecognized transition asset remaining in accumulated other comprehensive income. That maximum gain or loss includes any gain or loss resulting from remeasurements of plan assets and the accumulated postretirement benefit obligation at the time of settlement.

r. Paragraph 93 and its related footnotes 25 and 26:

If the entire accumulated postretirement benefit obligation is settled and the maximum amount subject to recognition is a gain, the settlement gain shall first reduce any remaining unrecognized transition obligation remaining in accumulated other comprehensive income;[25] any excess gain shall be recognized in income.[26] If the entire accumulated postretirement benefit obligation is settled and the maximum amount subject to recognition is a loss, the maximum settlement loss shall be recognized in income. If only part of the accumulated postretirement benefit obligation is settled, the employer shall recognize in income the excess of the pro rata portion (equal to the percentage reduction in the accumulated postretirement benefit obligation) of the maximum settlement gain over any remaining unrecognized transition obligation or a pro rata portion of the maximum settlement loss.

---

[25]As discussed in paragraph 112, in measuring the gain or loss subject to recognition in income when a postretirement benefit obligation is settled, it shall first be determined whether amortization recognition of an additional amount of any unrecognized transition obligation is required.

[26]Because the plan is the unit of accounting, the determination of the effects of a settlement considers only the unrecognized net gain or loss and transition obligation or asset included in accumulated other comprehensive income and unrecognized transition obligation or asset related to the plan for which all or a portion of the accumulated postretirement benefit obligation is being settled.

s. Paragraph 97 and its related footnote 28:

The unrecognized prior service cost included in accumulated other comprehensive income associated with the portion of the future years of service that had been expected to be rendered, but as a result of a curtailment are no longer expected to be rendered, is a loss. For purposes of measuring the effect of a curtailment, unrecognized prior service cost includes the cost of plan amendments and any remaining unrecognized transition obligation. For example, a curtailment may result from the termination of a significant number of employees who were plan participants at the date of a prior plan amendment.[28] The loss associated with that curtailment is measured as (a) the portion of the remaining unrecognized prior service cost included in accumulated other comprehensive income related to that (and any prior) plan amendment attributable to the previously expected remaining future years of service of the employees who were terminated and (b) the portion of the remaining unrecognized transition obligation attributable to the previously expected remaining future years of service of the terminated employees who were plan participants at the date of transition.

---

[28]A curtailment also may result from terminating the accrual of additional benefits for the future services of a significant number of employees. The loss in that situation is (a) a proportionate amount of the remaining unrecognized prior service cost included in accumulated other comprehensive income based on the portion of the remaining expected years of service in the amortization period that originally was attributable to those employees who were plan participants at the date of the plan amendment and whose future accrual of benefits has been terminated and (b) a proportionate amount of the remaining unrecognized transition obligation remaining in accumulated other comprehensive income based on the portion of the remaining years of service of all participants active at the date of transition that originally was attributable to the remaining expected future years of service of the employees whose future accrual of benefits has been terminated.

t. Paragraph 98:

The accumulated postretirement benefit obligation may be decreased (a gain) or increased (a loss) by a curtailment.[29] That (gain) loss shall reduce any unrecognized net loss (gain) included in accumulated other comprehensive income.

a. To the extent that such a gain exceeds any unrecognized net loss included in accumulated other comprehensive income (or the entire gain, if an unrecognized net gain a net gain exists), it is a curtailment gain.

b. To the extent that such a loss exceeds any ~~unrecognized~~ net gain included in accumulated other comprehensive income (or the entire loss, if ~~an unrecognized net loss~~a net loss exists), it is a curtailment loss.

For purposes of applying the provisions of this paragraph, any ~~remaining unrecognized~~ transition asset remaining in accumulated other comprehensive income shall be treated as ~~an unrecognized net gain~~a net gain and shall be combined with the ~~unrecognized~~ net gain or loss arising subsequent to transition to this Statement.

u. Paragraphs 103A–103D and the related heading are added as follows:

Not-for-Profit Organizations and Other Entities That Do Not Report Other Comprehensive Income

103A. A not-for-profit employer shall recognize as a separate line item or items within changes in unrestricted net assets, apart from expenses, the gains or losses and the prior service costs or credits that would be recognized in other comprehensive income pursuant to paragraphs 52, 55, and 56 of this Statement. Consistent with the provisions of FASB Statement No. 117, *Financial Statements of Not-for-Profit Organizations,* this Statement does not prescribe whether the separate line item or items shall be included within or outside an intermediate measure of operations or performance indicator, if one is presented. The AICPA Audit and Accounting Guide, *Health Care Organizations,* requires a not-for-profit organization within its scope to report items of other comprehensive income outside the performance indicator.

103B. A not-for-profit employer shall reclassify to net periodic postretirement benefit cost a portion of the net gain or loss and prior service costs or credits previously recognized in a separate line item or items and a portion of the transition asset or obligation remaining from the initial application of this Statement, pursuant to the recognition and amortization provisions of paragraphs 50–62, 112, and 113. The contra adjustment or adjustments shall be reported in the same line item or items within changes in unrestricted net assets, apart from expenses, as the initially recognized amounts. Net periodic postretirement benefit cost shall be reported by functional classification pursuant to paragraph 26 of Statement 117.

103C. In applying the provisions of this Statement to not-for-profit employers, the references to accumulated other comprehensive income in paragraphs 22, 46(d), 46(f), 53, 55, 59 (and its related footnote 19), 60, 62, 88, 92, 93 (and its related footnote 26), 97 (and its related footnote 28), 98, and 518, and the references to amounts previously recognized in other comprehensive income in paragraphs 73 and 518, shall instead be to the gains or losses, prior service costs or credits, and transition obligation or asset that have been recognized as changes in unrestricted net assets arising from a postretirement benefit plan but not yet reclassified as components of net periodic postretirement benefit cost.

103D. An employer other than a not-for-profit employer that does not report other comprehensive income pursuant to FASB Statement No. 130, *Reporting Comprehensive Income,* shall apply the provisions of paragraphs 103A–103C in an analogous manner that is appropriate for its method of reporting financial performance and financial position.

v. Paragraph 391A and its related footnote 38 are added as follows:

The illustrations included in this appendix demonstrate the application of the requirements of this Statement prior to the amendments required by FASB Statement No. 158, *Employers' Accounting for Defined Benefit Pension and Other Postretirement Plans.* Many of those illustrations would require changes to implement the provisions of Statement 158. Those changes include eliminating reconciliations of the funded status to amounts recognized in an employer's statement of financial position, eliminating references to the additional minimum pension liability, and eliminating references to unrecognized gains and losses, unrecognized prior service costs and credits, and unrecognized transition assets and obligations to reflect that those items would be recognized in accumulated other comprehensive income pursuant to Statement 158.[38] Those illustrations remain applicable until the provisions of Statement 158 are applied. The provisions of Statement 158 are illustrated in Appendix A of that Statement.

---

[38]The Board has a project on its technical agenda to consider further the illustrations included in this appendix and to supersede those that become irrelevant after the provisions of Statement 158 are applied and to amend those that have continuing relevance.

w. Paragraph 518 (glossary):

Amortization

Usually refers to the process of reducing a recognized liability systematically by recognizing revenues or of reducing a recognized asset systematically by recognizing expenses or costs. In accounting for postretirement benefits, amortization is also used to refer to the systematic recognition in net periodic postretirement benefit cost over several periods of amounts previously recognized in other comprehensive income previously *unrecognized* amounts, including unrecognized prior service cost, unrecognized net gain or loss, that is, gains or losses, prior service cost or credits, and any unrecognized transition obligation or asset.

Gain or loss

A change in the value of either the accumulated postretirement benefit obligation or the plan assets resulting from experience different from that assumed or from a change in an actuarial assumption, or the consequence of a decision to temporarily deviate from the substantive plan. Gains or losses that are not recognized in net periodic postretirement benefit cost when they arise are recognized in other comprehensive income. Those gains or losses are subsequently recognized as a component of net periodic postretirement benefit cost based on the recognition and amortization provisions of this Statement. Also refer to **Unrecognized net gain or loss.**

Gain or loss component (of net periodic postretirement benefit cost)

The sum of (a) the difference between the actual return on plan assets and the expected return on plan assets, (b) any gain or loss immediately recognized or the amortization of the unrecognized net gain or loss recognized in accumulated other comprehensive income from previous periods, and (c) any

amount immediately recognized as a gain or loss pursuant to a decision to temporarily deviate from the substantive plan. The gain or loss component is generally the net effect of delayed recognition in determining net periodic postretirement benefit cost of gains and losses (the net change in the unrecognized net gain or loss recognized in accumulated other comprehensive income) except that it does not include changes in the accumulated postretirement benefit obligation occurring during the period and deferred for later recognition in net periodic postretirement benefit cost.

Measurement date

The date of the financial statements or, if used consistently from year to year, a date not more than three months prior to that date, as of which plan assets and obligations are measured.

Net periodic postretirement benefit cost

The amount recognized in an employer's financial statements as the cost of a postretirement benefit plan for a period. Components of net periodic postretirement benefit cost include service cost, interest cost, actual return on plan assets, gain or loss, amortization of unrecognized prior service cost or credit, and amortization of the unrecognized transition obligation or asset.

Prior service cost

The cost of benefit improvements attributable to plan participants' prior service pursuant to a plan amendment or a plan initiation that provides benefits in exchange for plan participants' prior service. Also refer to **Unrecognized prior service cost.**

Transition asset

The unrecognized amount, as of the date this Statement is initially applied, of (a) the fair value of plan assets plus any recognized accrued postretirement benefit cost or less any recognized prepaid postretirement benefit cost in excess of (b) the accumulated postretirement benefit obligation.

Transition obligation

The unrecognized amount, as of the date this Statement is initially applied, of (a) the accumulated postretirement benefit obligation in excess of (b) the fair value of plan assets plus any recognized accrued postretirement benefit cost or less any recognized prepaid postretirement benefit cost.

Unrecognized net gain or loss

~~The cumulative net gain or loss that has not been recognized as a part of net periodic postretirement benefit cost or as a part of the accounting for the effects of a settlement or a curtailment. Also refer to **Gain or loss.**~~

Unrecognized prior service cost

~~The portion of prior service cost that has not been recognized as a part of net periodic postretirement benefit cost, as a reduction of the effects of a negative plan amendment, or as a part of the accounting for the effects of a curtailment.~~

Unrecognized transition asset

~~The portion of the transition asset that has not been recognized either immediately as the effect of a change in accounting or on a delayed basis as a part of net periodic postretirement benefit cost, as an offset to certain losses, or as a part of accounting for the effects of a settlement or a curtailment.~~

Unrecognized transition obligation

~~The portion of the transition obligation that has not been recognized either immediately as the effect of a change in accounting or on a delayed basis as a part of net periodic postretirement benefit cost, as an offset to certain gains, or as a part of accounting for the effects of a settlement or a curtailment.~~

D3. Statement 106 represented fundamental changes in how defined benefit postretirement plans other than pensions were measured and recognized in an employer's financial statements. Appendix C of Statement 106 includes various illustrations that described how certain aspects of the accounting requirements were to be applied.

D4. Many of the illustrations would have required extensive changes to implement the provisions of this Statement. The Board concluded that necessary changes included eliminating the following:

a. Reconciliations of the funded status to amounts recognized in the employer's statement of financial position

b. References to unrecognized gains and losses and unrecognized prior service costs and credits to reflect that those items should be recognized in accumulated other comprehensive income.

D5. The Board believes that many of those illustrations are not essential to understanding or applying the provisions of this Statement. Additionally, the Board believes the need for examples of how to apply Statement 106 has diminished over the many years since Statement 106 was first issued. The Board decided to consider further those illustrations included in Statement 106 and in related guidance and to update those that have continuing relevance following the issuance of this Statement.

Appendix E

AMENDMENTS TO STATEMENT 132(R)

E1. FASB Statement No. 132 (revised 2003), *Employers' Disclosures about Pensions and Other Postretirement Benefits,* is amended as follows: [Added text is underlined and deleted text is ~~struck out~~.]

a. Paragraph 3:

This Statement incorporates all of the disclosure requirements of FASB Statement No. 132, *Employers' Disclosures about Pensions and Other Postretirement Benefits.* This Statement amends APB Opinion No. 28, *Interim Financial Reporting,* to require interim-period disclosure of the components of net periodic benefit cost and, if significantly different from previously disclosed amounts, the amounts of contributions and projected contributions to fund pension plans and other postretirement benefit plans. Information required to be disclosed about pension plans should not be combined with information required to be disclosed about other postretirement benefit plans except as permitted by paragraph 12 of this Statement. Public and nonpublic entities shall provide the disclosures required in paragraphs 5–9, as applicable. Paragraphs 10A–10D describe how those requirements shall be applied to not-for-profit organizations and other entities that do not report other comprehensive income.~~The disclosures that are new or have been changed are identified with an asterisk (*).~~ Appendix A provides background information and the basis for the Board's conclusions in this Statement. Appendix B provides background information and the basis for the Board's conclusions as originally contained in Statement 132. Appendix C provides illustrations of the required disclosures. Appendix D provides information about the impact of this Statement on the consensuses reached on EITF Issues relating to disclosures about pension plans and other postretirement benefit plans. Appendix E provides a glossary of terms that are used in this Statement.

b. Paragraph 5:

Certain terms used in this Statement, such as **projected benefit obligation,**[3] **accumulated benefit obligation, accumulated postretirement benefit obligation,** and *net pension cost,* are defined in Statements 87 and 106. An employer that sponsors one or more defined benefit pension plans or one or more other defined benefit postretirement plans shall provide the following information, separately for pension plans and other postretirement benefit plans. Amounts related to the employer's results of operations (including items of other comprehensive income) shall be disclosed for each period for which a statement of income is presented. Amounts related to the employer's statement of financial position, ~~unless otherwise stated,~~ shall be disclosed as of the ~~measurement~~ date of ~~used for~~ each statement of financial position presented.

---

[3]Terms defined in Appendix E are set in **boldface type** the first time they appear.

c. Paragraph 5(c):

The funded status of the plans, ~~the amounts not recognized in the statement of financial position,~~ and the amounts recognized in the statement of financial position, ~~including:~~showing separately the assets and current and noncurrent liabilities recognized.

(1) ~~The amount of any unamortized prior service cost.~~

(2) ~~The amount of any unrecognized net gain or loss (including asset gains and losses not yet reflected in market-related value).~~

(3) ~~The amount of any remaining unamortized, unrecognized net obligation or net asset existing at the initial date of application of Statement 87 or Statement 106.~~

(4) ~~The net pension or other postretirement benefit prepaid assets or accrued liabilities.~~

(5) ~~Any intangible asset and the amount of accumulated other comprehensive income recognized pursuant to paragraph 37 of Statement 87, as amended.~~

d. Paragraph 5(h):

The amount of net periodic benefit cost recognized, showing separately the service cost component, the interest cost component, the expected return on plan assets for the period, the gain or loss component, the prior service cost or credit component, the transition asset or obligation component, and the gain or loss recognized due to settlements or curtailments.~~the amortization of the unrecognized transition obligation or transition asset, the amount of recognized gains or losses, the amount of prior service cost recognized, and the amount of gains or losses recognized due to a settlement or curtailment.~~

e. Paragraph 5(i):

~~The amount included within other comprehensive income for the period arising from a change in the additional minimum pension liability recognized pursuant to paragraph 37 of Statement 87, as amended.~~Separately the net gain or loss and net prior service cost or credit recognized in other comprehensive income for the period pursuant to paragraphs 25 and 29 of Statement 87 and paragraphs 52 and 56 of Statement 106, as amended, and reclassification adjustments of other comprehensive income for the period, as those amounts, including amortization of the net transition asset or obligation, are recognized as components of net periodic benefit cost.

f. Paragraph 5(ii) is added as follows:

The amounts in accumulated other comprehensive income that have not yet been recognized as components of net periodic benefit cost, showing separately the net gain or loss, net prior service cost or credit, and net transition asset or obligation.

g. Paragraph 5(k):

~~The measurement date(s) used to determine pension and other postretirement benefit measurements for the pension plans and other postretirement benefit plans that make up at least the majority of plan assets and benefit obligations.~~*

h. Paragraph 5(o):

If applicable, any alternative method used to amortize prior service amounts or ~~unrecognized~~ net gains and losses pursuant to paragraphs 26 and 33 of Statement 87 or paragraphs 53 and 60 of Statement 106.

i. Paragraph 5(s) is added as follows:

The amounts in accumulated other comprehensive income expected to be recognized as components of net periodic benefit cost over the fiscal year that follows the most recent annual statement of financial position presented, showing separately the net gain or loss, net prior service cost or credit, and net transition asset or obligation.

j. Paragraph 5(t) is added as follows:

The amount and timing of any plan assets expected to be returned to the employer during the 12-month period, or operating cycle if longer, that follows the most recent annual statement of financial position presented.

k. Paragraph 6:

The disclosures required by this Statement shall be aggregated for all of an employer's defined benefit pension plans and for all of an employer's other defined benefit postretirement plans unless disaggregating in groups is considered to provide useful information or is otherwise required by this paragraph and paragraph 7 of this Statement. ~~Unless otherwise stated, d~~Disclosures shall be as of the ~~measurement~~ date ~~for~~of each statement of financial position presented. ~~Disclosure of amounts recognized in the statement of financial position shall present prepaid benefit costs and accrued benefit liabilities separately.~~ Disclosures about pension plans with assets in excess of the accumulated benefit obligation generally may be aggregated with disclosures about pension plans with accumulated benefit obligations in excess of assets. The same aggregation is permitted for other postretirement benefit plans. If aggregate disclosures are presented, an employer shall disclose:

a. The aggregate benefit obligation and aggregate fair value of plan assets for plans with benefit obligations in excess of plan assets as of the measurement date of each statement of financial position presented

b. The aggregate pension accumulated benefit obligation and aggregate fair value of plan assets for pension plans with accumulated benefit obligations in excess of plan assets.

l. Paragraph 8:

A **nonpublic entity** is not required to disclose the information required by paragraphs 5(a)–(c), 5(h), 5(m), and 5(o)–(r) of this Statement. A nonpublic entity that sponsors one or more defined benefit pension plans or one or more other defined benefit postretirement plans shall provide the following information, separately for pension plans and other postretirement benefit plans. Amounts related to the employer's results of operations (including items of other comprehensive income) shall be disclosed for each period for which a statement of income is presented. Amounts related to the employer's statement of financial position shall be disclosed as of the ~~measurement date used for~~date of each statement of financial position presented.

m. Paragraph 8(g):

The amounts recognized in the statements of financial position, showing separately the postretirement benefit assets and current and noncurrent postretirement benefit liabilities.~~including net pension and other postretirement benefit prepaid assets or accrued liabilities and any intangible asset and the amount of accumulated other comprehensive income recognized pursuant to paragraph 37 of Statement 87, as amended.~~

n. Paragraph 8(h):

~~The amount of net periodic benefit cost recognized and the amount included within other comprehensive income arising from a change in the minimum pension liability recognized pursuant to paragraph 37 of Statement 87, as amended.~~Separately, the net gain or loss and net prior service cost or credit recognized in other comprehensive income for the period pursuant to paragraphs 25 and 29 of Statement 87 and paragraphs 52 and 56 of Statement 106, as amended, and reclassification adjustments of other comprehensive income for the period, as those amounts, including amortization of the net transition asset or obligation, are recognized as components of net periodic benefit cost.

o. Paragraph 8(hh) is added as follows:

The amounts in accumulated other comprehensive income that have not yet been recognized as components of net periodic benefit cost, showing separately the net gain or loss, net prior service cost or credit, and net transition asset or obligation.

p. Paragraph 8(j):

~~The measurement date(s) used to determine pension and other postretirement benefit measurements for the pension plans and other postretirement benefit plans that make up at least the majority of plan assets and benefit obligations.~~*

q. Paragraph 8(n) is added as follows:

The amounts in accumulated other comprehensive income expected to be recognized as components of net periodic benefit cost over the fiscal year that follows the most recent annual statement of financial position presented, showing separately the net gain or loss, net prior service cost or credit, and net transition asset or obligation.

r. Paragraph 8(o) is added as follows:

The amount and timing of any plan assets expected to be returned to the employer during the 12-month period, or operating cycle if longer, that follows the most recent annual statement of financial position presented.

s. Paragraph 9:

A **publicly traded entity** shall disclose the following information in its interim financial statements that include a statement of income:

a. The amount of net periodic benefit cost recognized, for each period for which a statement of income is presented, showing separately the service cost component, the interest cost component, the expected return on plan assets for the period, ~~the amortization of the unrecognized transition obligation or transition asset, the amount of recognized gains or losses~~ the gain or loss component, the ~~amount of~~ prior service cost or credit component ~~recognized~~, the transition asset or obligation component, and the

~~amount of~~ gain or loss recognized due to a settlement or curtailment*

b. The total amount of the employer's contributions paid, and expected to be paid, during the current fiscal year, if significantly different from amounts previously disclosed pursuant to paragraph 5(g) of this Statement. Estimated contributions may be presented in the aggregate combining (1) contributions required by funding regulations or laws, (2) discretionary contributions, and (3) non-cash contributions.*

t. Paragraphs 10A–10D and the related heading are added as follows:

Not-for-Profit Organizations and Other Entities That Do Not Report Other Comprehensive Income

10A. For not-for-profit employers and other employers that do not report other comprehensive income in accordance with FASB Statement No. 130, *Reporting Comprehensive Income,* the references to the net gain or loss, net prior service cost or credit, and net transition asset or obligation recognized in other comprehensive income in paragraphs 5(i) and 8(h) of this Statement shall instead be to such amounts recognized as changes in unrestricted net assets arising from a defined benefit plan but not yet included in net periodic benefit cost.

10B. For those employers, the references to reclassification adjustments of other comprehensive income in paragraphs 5(i) and 8(h) of this Statement shall instead be to reclassifications to net periodic benefit cost of amounts previously recognized as changes in unrestricted net assets arising from a defined benefit plan but not included in net periodic benefit cost when they arose.

10C. For those employers, the references to the net gain or loss, net prior service cost or credit, and net transition asset or obligation recognized in accumulated other comprehensive income in paragraphs 5(ii), 5(s), 8(hh), and 8(n) of this Statement shall instead be to such amounts that have been recognized as changes in unrestricted net assets arising from a defined benefit plan but not yet reclassified as components of net periodic benefit cost.

10D. For those employers, the references to results of operations (including items of other comprehensive income) in paragraphs 5 and 8 shall instead be to changes in unrestricted net assets and the references to a statement of income in those paragraphs shall instead be to a statement of activities.

u. Paragraph C3:

During 20X3, Company A acquired FV Industries and amended its plans. ~~For one of the defined benefit pension plans, the accumulated benefit obligation exceeds the fair value of plan assets, and Company A recognized an additional minimum liability in accordance with the provisions of paragraphs 36 and 37 of Statement 87.~~

Notes to Financial Statements

Pension and Other Postretirement Benefit Plans

Company A has both funded and unfunded noncontributory defined benefit pension plans that together cover substantially all of its employees. The plans provide defined benefits based on years of service and final average salary.

Company A also has other postretirement benefit plans covering substantially all of its employees. The health care plans are contributory with participants' contributions adjusted annually; the life insurance plans are noncontributory. The accounting for the health care plans anticipates future cost-sharing changes to the written plans that are consistent with the company's expressed intent to increase retiree contributions each year by 50 percent of health care cost increases in excess of 6 percent. The postretirement health care plans include a limit on the company's share of costs for recent and future retirees.

Company A acquired FV Industries on December 27, 20X3, including its pension plans and other postretirement benefit plans. Amendments made at the end of 20X3 to Company A's plans increased the pension benefit obligations by $70 and reduced the other postretirement benefit obligations by $75.

~~Company A uses a December 31 measurement date for the majority of its plans.~~

Obligations and Funded Status

At December 31	Pension Benefits		Other Benefits	
	20X3	20X2	20X3	20X2
Change in benefit obligation				
Benefit obligation at beginning of year	$1,246	$1,200	$ 742	$ 712
Service cost	76	72	36	32
Interest cost	90	88	55	55
Plan participants' contributions			20	13
Amendments	70		(75)	
Actuarial loss	20		25	
Acquisition	900		600	
Benefits paid	(125)	(114)	(90)	(70)
Benefit obligation at end of year	2,277	1,246	1,313	742
Change in plan assets				
Fair value of plan assets at beginning of year	1,068	894	206	87
Actual return on plan assets	29	188	5	24
Acquisition	1,000		25	
Employer contributions	75	100	137	152
Plan participants' contributions			20	13
Benefits paid	(125)	(114)	(90)	(70)
Fair value of plan assets at end of year	2,047	1,068	303	206
Funded status at end of year	$ (230)	$ (178)	$(1,010)	$(536)
~~Unrecognized net actuarial loss (gain)~~	~~94~~	~~18~~	~~(11)~~	~~(48)~~
~~Unrecognized prior service cost (benefit)~~	~~210~~	~~160~~	~~(92)~~	~~(22)~~
~~Net amount recognized~~	~~$ 74~~	~~$ 0~~	~~$(1,113)~~	~~$(606)~~

Note: Nonpublic entities are not required to provide information in the above tables; they are required to disclose the employer's contributions, participants' contributions, benefit payments, and the funded status, ~~and the net amount recognized~~.

Amounts recognized in the statement of financial position consist of:

	Pension Benefits		Other Benefits	
	20X3	20X2	20X3	20X2
~~Prepaid benefit cost~~Noncurrent assets	$ 227	$ 127	$ 0	$ 0
~~Accrued benefit cost~~	~~(236)~~	~~(180)~~	~~(1,113)~~	~~(606)~~
Current liabilities	(125)	(125)	(150)	(150)
Noncurrent liabilities	(332)	(180)	(860)	(386)
~~Intangible assets~~	~~50~~	~~53~~	~~0~~	~~0~~
~~Accumulated other comprehensive income~~	~~33~~	~~0~~	~~0~~	~~0~~
~~Net amounts recognized~~	~~$ 74~~	~~$ 0~~	~~$(1,113)~~	~~$(606)~~
	$(230)	$(178)	$(1,010)	$(536)

Amounts recognized in accumulated other comprehensive income consist of:

	Pension Benefits		Other Benefits	
	20X3	20X2	20X3	20X2
Net loss (gain)	$ 94	$ 18	$ (11)	$(48)
Prior service cost (credit)	210	160	(92)	(22)
	$304	$178	$(103)	$(70)

The accumulated benefit obligation for all defined benefit pension plans was $1,300 and $850 at December 31, 20X3, and 20X2, respectively.

Information for pension plans with an
accumulated benefit obligation in excess
of plan assets

	December 31	
	20X3	20X2
Projected benefit obligation	$263	$247
Accumulated benefit obligation	237	222
Fair value of plan assets	84	95

Components of Net Periodic Benefit Cost and Other Amounts Recognized in Other Comprehensive Income

Net Periodic Benefit Cost	Pension Benefits		Other Benefits	
	20X3	20X2	20X3	20X2
Service cost	$ 76	$ 72	$ 36	$ 32
Interest cost	90	88	55	55
Expected return on plan assets	(85)	(76)	(17)	(8)
Amortization of prior service cost	20	16	(5)	(5)
Amortization of net (gain) loss	0	0	0	0
Net periodic benefit cost	$101	$100	$ 69	$ 74

Other Changes in Plan Assets and Benefit Obligations Recognized in Other Comprehensive Income

	Pension Benefits		Other Benefits	
Net loss (gain)	$ 76	$112	$ 37	$(48)
Prior service cost (credit)	70	0	(75)	(27)
Amortization of prior service cost	(20)	(16)	5	5
Total recognized in other comprehensive income	126	96	(33)	(70)
Total recognized in net periodic benefit cost and other comprehensive income	$227	$196	$ 36	$ 4

The estimated net loss and prior service cost for the defined benefit pension plans that will be amortized from accumulated other comprehensive income into net periodic benefit cost over the next fiscal year are $4 and $27, respectively. The estimated prior service credit for the other defined benefit postretirement plans that will be amortized from accumulated other comprehensive income into net periodic benefit cost over the next fiscal year is $10.

Note: Nonpublic entities are not required to separately disclose components of net periodic benefit cost.

Additional Information

	Pension Benefits		Other Benefits	
	20X3	20X2	20X3	20X2
Increase in minimum liability included in other comprehensive income	$33	$0	N/A	N/A

[Note: The remaining sections of Illustration 1 are omitted because they are unaffected by this Statement.]

Appendix F

AMENDMENTS TO OTHER EXISTING PRONOUNCEMENTS

F1. This appendix includes substantive amendments to existing pronouncements other than those contained in Appendixes C–E of this Statement that have been altered as a direct result of the guidance contained in this Statement. [Added text is underlined and deleted text is struck out.]

F2. ARB No. 43, Chapter 3, "Working Capital," is amended, as follows:

a. Paragraph 4, as amended:

For accounting purposes, the term *current assets* is used to designate cash and other assets or resources commonly identified as those which are reasonably expected to be realized in cash or sold or consumed during the normal operating cycle of the business. Thus the term comprehends in general such resources as (a) cash available for current operations and items which are the equivalent of cash; (b) inventories of merchandise, raw materials, goods in process, finished goods, operating supplies, and ordinary maintenance material and parts; (c) trade accounts, notes, and acceptances receivable; (d) receivables from officers, employees, affiliates, and others, if collectible in the ordinary course of business within a year; (e) instalment or deferred accounts and notes receivable if they conform generally to normal trade practices and terms within the business; (f) marketable securities representing the investment of cash available for current operations, including investments in debt and equity securities classified as trading securities under FASB Statement No. 115, *Accounting for Certain Investments in Debt and Equity Securities;* and (g) prepaid expenses such as insurance, interest, rents, taxes, unused royalties, current paid advertising service not yet received, and operating supplies. Prepaid expenses are not current assets in the sense that they will be converted into cash but in the sense that, if not paid in advance, they would require the use of current assets during the operating cycle. An asset representing the overfunded status of a single-employer defined benefit postretirement plan shall be classified pursuant to

FASB Statement No. 158, *Employers' Accounting for Defined Benefit Pension and Other Postretirement Plans.*

b. Paragraph 7, as amended:

The term *current liabilities* is used principally to designate obligations whose liquidation is reasonably expected to require the use of existing resources properly classifiable as current assets, or the creation of other current liabilities. As a balance-sheet category, the classification is intended to include obligations for items which have entered into the operating cycle, such as payables incurred in the acquisition of materials and supplies to be used in the production of goods or in providing services to be offered for sale; collections received in advance of the delivery of goods or performance of services[2]; and debts which arise from operations directly related to the operating cycle, such as accruals for wages, salaries, commissions, rentals, royalties, and income and other taxes. Other liabilities whose regular and ordinary liquidation is expected to occur within a relatively short period of time, usually twelve months, are also intended for inclusion, such as short-term debts arising from the acquisition of capital assets, serial maturities of long-term obligations, amounts required to be expended within one year under sinking fund provisions, and agency obligations arising from the collection or acceptance of cash or other assets for the account of third persons.[3] The current liability classification is also intended to include obligations that, by their terms, are due on demand or will be due on demand within one year (or operating cycle, if longer) from the balance sheet date, even though liquidation may not be expected within that period. It is also intended to include long-term obligations that are or will be callable by the creditor either because the debtor's violation of a provision of the debt agreement at the balance sheet date makes the obligation callable or because the violation, if not cured within a specified grace period, will make the obligation callable. Accordingly, such callable obligations shall be classified as current liabilities unless one of the following conditions is met:

a. The creditor has waived[3a] or subsequently lost[3b] the right to demand repayment for more than one year (or operating cycle, if longer) from the balance sheet date.

b. For long-term obligations containing a grace period within which the debtor may cure the violation, it is probable[3c] that the violation will be cured within that period, thus preventing the obligation from becoming callable.

If an obligation under (b) above is classified as a long-term liability (or, in the case of an unclassified balance sheet, is included as a long-term liability in the disclosure of debt maturities), the circumstances shall be disclosed. Short-term obligations that are expected to be refinanced on a long-term basis, including those callable obligations discussed herein, shall be classified in accordance with FASB Statement No. 6, *Classification of Short-Term Obligations Expected to Be Refinanced.* A liability representing the underfunded status of a single-employer defined benefit postretirement plan shall be classified pursuant to Statement 158.

F3. APB Opinion No. 28, *Interim Financial Reporting,* is amended as follows:

a. Paragraph 30(k), as amended:

The following information about defined benefit pension plans and other defined benefit postretirement benefit plans, disclosed for all periods presented pursuant to the provisions of FASB Statement No. 132 (revised 2003), *Employers' Disclosures about Pensions and Other Postretirement Benefits:*

(1) The amount of net periodic benefit cost recognized, for each period for which a statement of income is presented, showing separately the service cost component, the interest cost component, the expected return on plan assets for the period, the gain or loss component, the prior service cost or credit component, the transition asset or obligation component, and the gain or loss recognized due to a settlement or curtailment.the amortization of the unrecognized transition obligation or transition asset, the amount of recognized gains or losses, the amount of prior service cost recognized, and the amount of gain or loss recognized due to a settlement or curtailment.*

(2) The total amount of the employer's contributions paid, and expected to be paid, during the current fiscal year, if significantly

different from amounts previously disclosed pursuant to paragraph 5(g) of Statement 132(R). Estimated contributions may be presented in the aggregate combining (a) contributions required by funding regulations or laws, (b) discretionary contributions, and (c) noncash contributions.*

F4. FASB Statement No. 130, *Reporting Comprehensive Income,* is amended as follows:

a. Paragraph 17:

Items included in other comprehensive income shall be classified based on their nature. For example, under existing accounting standards, other comprehensive income shall be classified separately into foreign currency items, gains or losses associated with pension or other postretirement benefits, prior service costs or credits associated with pension or other postretirement benefits, transition assets or obligations associated with pension or other postretirement benefits,minimum pension liability adjustments, and unrealized gains and losses on certain investments in debt and equity securities. Additional classifications or additional items within current classifications may result from future accounting standards.

b. Paragraph 19:

An enterprise shall determine reclassification adjustments for each classification of other comprehensive income, except minimum pension liability adjustments. The requirement for a reclassification adjustment for Statement 52 foreign currency translation adjustments is limited to translation gains and losses realized upon sale or upon complete or substantially complete liquidation of an investment in a foreign entity.

c. Paragraph 20:

An enterprise may display reclassification adjustments on the face of the financial statement in which comprehensive income is reported, or it may disclose reclassification adjustments in the notes to the financial statements. Therefore, for all classifications of other comprehensive income other than minimum pension liability adjustments, an enterprise may use either (a) a gross display on the face of the financial statement or (b) a net display on the face of the financial statement and disclose the gross change in the notes to the financial statements.[6] Gross and net displays are illustrated in Appendix B. An example of the calculation of reclassification adjustments for Statement 115 available-for-sale securities is included in Appendix C.

d. Paragraph 21:

~~An enterprise shall not determine a reclassification adjustment for minimum pension liability adjustments. Therefore, an enterprise shall use a net display for that classification.~~

e. Paragraph 130:

Brackets are used to highlight certain basic totals that must be displayed in financial statements to comply with the provisions of this Statement. This Statement requires not only displaying

those certain basic totals but also reporting components of those aggregates. For example, it requires reporting information about unrealized gains and losses on available-for-sale securities, foreign currency items, <u>gains or losses associated with pension or other postretirement benefits, prior service costs or credits associated with pension or other postretirement benefits, and transition assets or obligations associated with pension or other postretirement benefits</u>~~and minimum pension liability adjustments~~.

f. Paragraph 131, as amended:

Note: Only the illustrations in paragraph 131 have been affected by this Statement. Therefore, they are the only part of paragraph 131 that has been reproduced here.

Format A: One-Statement Approach

Enterprise
Statement of Income and Comprehensive Income
Year Ended December 31, ~~19X9~~20X9

Revenues		$140,000
Expenses		(25,000)
Other gains and losses		8,000
Gain on sale of securities		2,000
Income from operations before tax		125,000
Income tax expense		(31,250)
Income before extraordinary item ~~and cumulative effect of accounting change~~*		93,750
Extraordinary item, net of tax		~~(28,000)~~
		(30,500)
~~Income before cumulative effect of accounting change*~~		~~65,750~~
~~Cumulative effect of accounting change,*net of tax~~		~~(2,500)~~
[Net income		63,250]
Other comprehensive income, net of tax:		
Foreign currency translation adjustments[a]		8,000
Unrealized gains on securities:[b]		
Unrealized holding gains arising during period	$13,000	
Less: reclassification adjustment for gains included in net income	(1,500)	11,500
Defined benefit pension plans:[c]		
~~Minimum pension liability adjustment[e]~~		~~(2,500)~~
Prior service cost arising during period	(1,600)	
Net loss arising during period	(1,000)	
Less: amortization of prior service cost included in net periodic pension cost	100	(2,500)
Other comprehensive income		17,000
[Comprehensive income		$ 80,250]

Alternatively, components of other comprehensive income could be displayed before tax with one amount shown for the aggregate income tax expense or benefit:

Other comprehensive income, before tax:		
Foreign currency translation adjustments[a]		$10,666
Unrealized gains on securities:[b]		
Unrealized holding gains arising during period	$17,333	
Less: reclassification adjustment for gains included in		
net income	(2,000)	15,333
Defined benefit pension plans:[c]		
~~Minimum pension liability adjustment~~[e]		~~(3,333)~~
Prior service cost arising during period	(2,133)	
Net loss arising during period	(1,333)	
Less: amortization of prior service cost included in		
net periodic pension cost	133	(3,333)
Other comprehensive income, before tax		22,666
[Income tax expense related to items of other comprehensive income		(5,666)]
Other comprehensive income, net of tax		$17,000

~~[e]After the effective date of FASB Statement No. 154, *Accounting Changes and Error Corrections*, voluntary changes in accounting principle will no longer be reported via a cumulative-effect adjustment through the income statement of the period of change.~~

[a]It is assumed that there was no sale or liquidation of an investment in a foreign entity. Therefore, there is no reclassification adjustment for this period.

[b]This illustrates the gross display. Alternatively, a net display can be used, with disclosure of the gross amounts (current-period gain and reclassification adjustment) in the notes to the financial statements.

[c]This illustrates the gross display~~required net display for this classification~~. Alternatively, a net display can be used, with disclosure of the gross amounts (prior service cost and net loss for the defined benefit pension plans less amortization of prior service cost) in the notes to financial statements.

Format B: Two-Statement Approach

Enterprise
Statement of Income
Year Ended December 31, ~~19X9~~20X9

Revenues	$140,000
Expenses	(25,000)
Other gains and losses	8,000
Gain on sale of securities	2,000
Income from operations before tax	125,000
Income tax expense	(31,250)
Income before extraordinary item ~~and cumulative effect of accounting change~~*	93,750
Extraordinary item, net of tax	~~(28,000)~~
	(30,500)
~~Income before cumulative effect of accounting change*~~	~~65,750~~
~~Cumulative effect of accounting change,*net of tax~~	~~(2,500)~~
[Net income	$ 63,250]

Enterprise
Statement of Comprehensive Income
Year Ended December 31, ~~19X9~~20X9

[Net income		$63,250]
Other comprehensive income, net of tax:		
Foreign currency translation adjustments[a]		8,000
Unrealized gains on securities:[b]		
Unrealized holding gains arising during period	$13,000	
Less: reclassification adjustment for gains included in net income	(1,500)	11,500
Defined benefit pension plans:[c]		
~~Minimum pension liability adjustment[e]~~		~~(2,500)~~
Prior service cost arising during period	(1,600)	
Net loss arising during period	(1,000)	
Less: amortization of prior service cost included in net periodic pension cost	100	(2,500)
Other comprehensive income		17,000
[Comprehensive income		$80,250]

Alternatively, components of other comprehensive income could be displayed before tax with one amount shown for the aggregate income tax expense or benefit as illustrated in Format A.

---

*After the effective date of Statement 154, voluntary changes in accounting principle will no longer be reported via a cumulative-effect adjustment through the income statement of the period of change.

[a]It is assumed that there was no sale or liquidation of an investment in a foreign entity. Therefore, there is no reclassification adjustment for this period.

[b]This illustrates the gross display. Alternatively, a net display can be used, with disclosure of the gross amounts (current-period gain and reclassification adjustment) in the notes to the financial statements.

[c]This illustrates the gross display. required net display for this classification. Alternatively, a net display can be used, with disclosure of the gross amounts (prior service cost and net loss for defined benefit pension plans less amortization of prior service cost) in the notes to financial statements.

(This page intentionally left blank.)

Format C: Statement-of-Changes-in-Equity Approach (Alternative 1)

Enterprise
Statement of Changes in Equity
Year Ended December 31, ~~19X9~~20X9

	Total	Comprehensive Income[a]	Retained Earnings	Accumulated Other Comprehensive Income	Common Stock	Paid-in Capital
Beginning balance	~~$563,500~~ 561,500		$ 88,500	~~$25,000~~ 23,000	$150,000	$300,000
Comprehensive income						
Net income	63,250	$63,250	63,250			
Other comprehensive income, net of tax						
Unrealized gains on securities, net of reclassification adjustment (see disclosure)	11,500	11,500				
Foreign currency translation adjustments	8,000	8,000				
Defined benefit pension plans:						
Net prior service cost (see disclosure)	(1,500)	(1,500)				
Net loss	(1,000)	(1,000)				
~~Minimum pension liability adjustment~~	~~(2,500)~~	~~(2,500)~~				
Other comprehensive income		17,000		17,000		
Comprehensive income		$80,250				
Common stock issued	150,000				50,000	100,000
Dividends declared on common stock	(10,000)		(10,000)			
Ending balance	~~$783,750~~ 781,750		$141,750	~~$42,000~~ 40,000	$200,000	$400,000

Disclosure of reclassification amount:[b]

Unrealized holding gains arising during period	$13,000
Less: reclassification adjustment for gains included in net income	(1,500)
Net unrealized gains on securities	$11,500
Prior service cost from plan amendment during period	$ (1,600)
Less: amortization of prior service cost included in net periodic pension cost	100
Net prior service cost arising during period	(1,500)
Net loss arising during period	(1,000)
Defined benefit pension plans, net	$ (2,500)

[a] Alternatively, an enterprise can omit the separate column labeled "Comprehensive Income" by displaying an aggregate amount for comprehensive income ($80,250) in the "Total" column.

[b] It is assumed that there was no sale or liquidation of an investment in a foreign entity. Therefore, there is no reclassification adjustment for this period.

Format D: Statement-of-Changes-in-Equity Approach (Alternative 2)

Enterprise
Statement of Changes in Equity
Year Ended December 31, ~~19X9~~20X9

Retained earnings				
Balance at January 1	$ 88,500			
Net income	63,250	[	$63,250	]
Dividends declared on common stock	(10,000)			
Balance at December 31	141,750			
Accumulated other comprehensive income[a]				
Balance at January 1	~~25,000~~			
	23,000			
Unrealized gains on securities, net of reclassification adjustment (see disclosure)			11,500	
Foreign currency translation adjustments			8,000	
Defined benefit pension plans:				
Net prior service cost (see disclosure)			(1,500)	
Net loss			(1,000)	
~~Minimum pension liability adjustment~~			~~(2,500)~~	
Other comprehensive income	17,000		17,000	
Comprehensive income		[	$80,250	]
Balance at December 31	~~42,000~~			
	40,000			
Common stock				
Balance at January 1	150,000			
Shares issued	50,000			
Balance at December 31	200,000			
Paid-in capital				
Balance at January 1	300,000			
Common stock issued	100,000			
Balance at December 31	400,000			
Total equity	$~~783,750~~			
	781,750			

Disclosure of reclassification amount:[b]

Unrealized holding gains arising during period	$ 13,000
Less: reclassification adjustment for gains included in net income	(1,500)
Net unrealized gains on securities	$ 11,500
Prior service cost from plan amendment during period	$ (1,600)
Less: amortization of prior service cost included in net periodic pension cost	100
Net prior service cost arising during period	(1,500)
Net loss arising during period	(1,000)
Defined benefit pension plans, net	$ (2,500)

---

[a]All items of other comprehensive income are displayed net of tax.

[b]It is assumed that there was no sale or liquidation of an investment in a foreign entity. Therefore, there is no reclassification adjustment for this period.

All Formats: Required Disclosure of Related Tax Effects Allocated to Each Component of Other Comprehensive Income

Enterprise
Notes to Financial Statements
Year Ended December 31, ~~19X9~~20X9

	Before-Tax Amount	Tax (Expense) or Benefit	Net-of-Tax Amount
Foreign currency translation adjustments	$10,666	$(2,666)	$ 8,000
Unrealized gains on securities:			
Unrealized holding gains arising during period	17,333	(4,333)	13,000
Less: reclassification adjustment for gains realized in net income	(2,000)	500	(1,500)
Net unrealized gains	15,333	(3,833)	11,500
Defined benefit pension plans:			
~~Minimum pension liability adjustment~~	~~(3,333)~~	~~833~~	~~(2,500)~~
Prior service cost from plan amendment during period	(2,133)	533	(1,600)
Less: amortization of prior service cost included in net periodic pension cost	133	(33)	100
Net prior service cost arising during period	(2,000)	500	(1,500)
Net loss arising during period	(1,333)	333	(1,000)
Defined benefit pension plans, net	(3,333)	833	(2,500)
Other comprehensive income	$22,666	$(5,666)	$17,000

Alternatively, the tax amounts for each component can be displayed parenthetically on the face of the financial statement in which comprehensive income is reported.

All Formats: Disclosure of Accumulated Other Comprehensive Income Balances

Enterprise
Notes to Financial Statements
Year Ended December 31, ~~19X9~~ 20X9

	Foreign Currency Items	Unrealized Gains on Securities	Defined Benefit Pension Plans	Minimum Pension Liability Adjustment	Accumulated Other Comprehensive Income
Beginning balance	$ (500)	$25,500	$(2,000)	$ ~~—0~~	~~$25,000~~ 23,000
Current-period change	8,000	11,500	(2,500)	~~(2,500)~~	17,000
Ending balance	$7,500	$37,000	$(4,500)	~~$(2,500)~~	~~$42,000~~ 40,000

Alternatively, the balances of each classification within accumulated other comprehensive income can be displayed in a statement of changes in equity or in a statement of financial position.

All Formats: Accompanying Statement of Financial Position

Enterprise
Statement of Financial Position
December 31, ~~19X9~~20X9

Assets:

Cash	$ 150,000
Accounts receivable	175,000
Available-for-sale securities	112,000
Plant and equipment	985,000
Total assets	$1,422,000

Liabilities:

Accounts payable	$ 112,500
Accrued liabilities	~~79,250~~
	78,583
~~Pension l~~Liability for pension benefits	~~128,000~~
	130,667
Notes payable	318,500
Total liabilities	$ ~~638,250~~
	640,250

Equity:

Common stock	$ 200,000
Paid-in capital	400,000
Retained earnings	141,750
[Accumulated other comprehensive income	~~42,000~~]
	40,000
Total equity	~~783,750~~
	781,750
Total liabilities and equity	$1,422,000

Appendix G

IMPACT ON RELATED LITERATURE

G1. This appendix addresses the impact of this Statement on authoritative accounting literature included in categories *(b), (c),* and *(d)* in the GAAP hierarchy discussed in AICPA Statement on Auditing Standards No. 69, *The Meaning of* Present Fairly in Conformity With Generally Accepted Accounting Principles.

G2. The Board believes many of the staff Q&As contained in FASB Special Reports, *A Guide to Implementation of Statement 87 on Employers' Accounting for Pensions; A Guide to Implementation of Statement 88 on Employers' Accounting for Settlements and Curtailments of Defined Benefit Pension Plans and for Termination Benefits;* and *A Guide to Implementation of Statement 106 on Employers' Accounting for Postretirement Benefits Other Than Pensions,* are not essential to understanding or applying the provisions of this Statement. Additionally, the Board believes the need for those Q&As has diminished over the many years since Statements 87, 88, and 106 were first issued. The Board decided to consider further those Q&As and to update those that have continuing relevance following the issuance of this Statement.

G3. The following tables list Emerging Issues Task Force (EITF) Issues and Topics, FASB Staff Positions (FSPs), guidance issued by the American Institute of Certified Public Accountants (AICPA) or its staff, and guidance issued by the SEC or its staff relating to postretirement benefit obligations, including pensions, and indicate (a) the status of that literature after issuance of this Statement and (b) the impact of this Statement on that literature (if any). (**Note:** The *EITF Abstracts* will be updated accordingly following issuance of this Statement.)

G4. Decisions about whether to amend AICPA guidance are made by the FASB in conjunction with the AICPA. (**Note:** The AICPA will make the changes until there is an FASB codification.)

G5. Decisions about whether to amend SEC or SEC staff guidance are made by the SEC and its staff.

G6. The following guidance is related to the accounting for pensions or other postretirement benefits but is either outside the scope of this Statement or unaffected by this Statement:

Literature	Title
Issue 84-35	Business Combinations: Sale of Duplicate Facilities and Accrual of Liabilities
Issue 86-27	Measurement of Excess Contributions to a Defined Contribution Plan or Employee Stock Ownership Plan
Issue 88-1	Determination of Vested Benefit Obligation for a Defined Benefit Pension Plan
Issue 88-5	Recognition of Insurance Death Benefits
Issue 88-23	Lump-Sum Payments under Union Contracts
Issue 90-3	Accounting for Employers' Obligations for Future Contributions to a Multiemployer Pension Plan
Issue 91-7	Accounting for Pension Benefits Paid by Employers after Insurance Companies Fail to Provide Annuity Benefits
Issue 92-12	Accounting for OPEB Costs by Rate-Regulated Enterprises
Issue 92-13	Accounting for Estimated Payments in Connection with the Coal Industry Retiree Health Benefit Act of 1992
Issue 93-3	Plan Assets under FASB Statement No. 106
Issue 93-4	Accounting for Regulatory Assets
Issue 96-5	Recognition of Liabilities for Contractual Termination Benefits or Changing Benefit Plan Assumptions in Anticipation of a Business Combination
Issue 97-14	Accounting for Deferred Compensation Arrangements Where Amounts Earned Are Held in a Rabbi Trust and Invested

Literature	Title
Issue 03-4	Determining the Classification and Benefit Attribution Method for a "Cash Balance" Pension Plan
Issue 05-5	Accounting for Early Retirement or Postemployment Programs with Specific Features (Such As Terms Specified in Altersteilzeit Early Retirement Arrangements)
Topic D-27	Accounting for the Transfer of Excess Pension Assets to a Retiree Health Care Benefits Account
FSP FAS 146-1	Determining Whether a One-Time Termination Benefit Offered in Connection with an Exit or Disposal Activity Is, in Substance, an Enhancement to an Ongoing Benefit Arrangement

G7. The following guidance is affected by the issuance of this Statement:

Status Legend

Nullified	Guidance is deemed unnecessary upon adoption of this Statement.
Modified	Guidance is partially nullified and replaced upon adoption of this Statement.

Literature	Title	Status	Description
EITF Issues and Topics			
Issue 03-2	Accounting for the Transfer to the Japanese Government of the Substitutional Portion of Employee Pension Fund Liabilities	Modified	Issue 03-2 clarifies how an employer should account for the separation of the government-required portion (similar to social security) of the benefit obligation of a Japanese Employee Pension Fund from the employer's discretionary portion. It also clarifies how to account for the transfer of the government-required portion and related assets to the Japanese government as authorized under the June 2001 amendment to the Japanese Welfare Pension Insurance Law. It states that subsequent to this separation, accounting should continue to be in accordance with Statements 87 and 88.

This Statement eliminates minimum pension liability adjustments and requires the recognition of gains or losses, prior service costs or credits, and transition assets and obligations in other comprehensive income to the extent not yet recognized as components of net periodic benefit cost. |

Literature	Title	Status	Description
Topic D-36	Selection of Discount Rates Used for Measuring Defined Benefit Pension Obligations and Obligations of Postretirement Benefit Plans Other Than Pensions	Modified	Topic D-36 presents the SEC staff position on the selection of discount rates for Statements 87 and 106, including the guidance in paragraph 186 of Statement 106. This Statement incorporates paragraph 186 of Statement 106 into the standards section of both Statements 87 and 106. Therefore, the duplicate guidance is eliminated.
Topic D-106	Clarification of Q&A No. 37 of FASB Special Report, *A Guide to Implementation of Statement 87 on Employers' Accounting for Pensions*	Nullified	Topic D-106 clarifies the guidance in Q&A No. 37 on how to determine an additional minimum liability when the report date is December 31 and the measurement date is September 30. This Statement eliminates the provisions related to an additional minimum liability. Therefore, Topic D-106 is nullified.

FASB FSPs and Statement 133 Implementation Issues

| FSP APB 18-1 | Accounting by an Investor for Its Proportionate Share of Accumulated Other Comprehensive Income of an Investee Accounted for under the Equity Method in Accordance with APB Opinion No. 18 upon a Loss of Significant Influence | Modified | FSP APB 18-1 provides guidance on how an investor should account for its proportionate share of an investee's equity adjustments for other comprehensive income upon a loss of significant influence. FSP APB 18-1 includes minimum pension liability adjustments as an example of one of the investee's equity adjustments related to other comprehensive income.

This Statement eliminates minimum pension liability adjustments and requires the recognition of gains or losses, prior service costs or credits, and transition assets or obligations in other comprehensive income to the extent not yet recognized as components of net periodic benefit cost. The background and issue section in FSP APB 18-1 is amended by eliminating the reference to minimum pension liability adjustments and adding the recognition of gains or losses, prior service costs or credits, and transition assets or obligations as some of the investee's equity adjustments related to other comprehensive income. |

Literature	Title	Status	Description
AICPA Literature			
AICPA Audit and Accounting Guide	*Health Care Organizations*, 2005	Modified	The Guide on health care organizations assists preparers of financial statements in preparing financial statements in conformity with GAAP and assists auditors in auditing and reporting on such financial statements in accordance with generally accepted auditing standards. The Guide requires health care organizations to report an earnings measure (performance indicator) that is the functional equivalent of income from continuing operations of a for-profit enterprise. Paragraph 10.21(e) requires health care organizations to report separately from the performance indicator "items that are required to be reported in or reclassified from other comprehensive income. …." Minimum pension liabilities are included as an example of those items. This Statement eliminates minimum pension liability adjustments and requires the recognition of gains or losses, prior service costs or credits, and transition assets or obligations in other comprehensive income to the extent not yet recognized as components of net periodic benefit cost. Paragraph 10.21(e) of the Guide is amended to eliminate the references to minimum pension liabilities and to add references to gains or losses, prior service costs or credits, and transition assets or obligations recognized in accordance with Statements 87, as amended, and 106, as amended.

AICPA Audit and Accounting Guide	Life and Health Insurance Entities, 2005	Modified	The Guide on life and health insurance entities assists preparers of financial statements in preparing financial statements in conformity with GAAP and assists auditors in auditing and reporting on such financial statements in accordance with generally accepted auditing standards. The Guide is directed primarily to the aspects of the preparation and audit of life and health insurance entities' financial statements that are unique to those organizations and are considered significant to them. Paragraph 14.70(f) states that a reporting entity that uses an actuarial valuation as of a date prior to the financial statement date to measure plan assets and obligations, and determines that an additional minimum liability is required to be established in accordance with paragraph 37 of Statement 87, and if the reporting entity contributes amounts to the plan to fund that additional minimum liability prior to the financial statement date, such amount funded may be used to reduce the additional minimum liability recognized in the reporting entity's financial statements. This Statement eliminates the provisions in Statements 87 and 106 that permit plan assets and benefit obligations to be measured as of a date that is not more than three months prior to the date of the employer's statement of financial position. Therefore, paragraph 14.70(f) is eliminated.

Literature	Title	Status	Description
SOP 02-2	*Accounting for Derivative Instruments and Hedging Activities by Not-for-Profit Health Care Organizations, and Clarification of the Performance Indicator*	Modified	Among other matters, SOP 02-2 amended the Guide on health care organizations to clarify that the performance indicator reported by not-for-profit health care organizations excludes items required by Statement 130 to be reported as items of other comprehensive income, and to clarify that any changes to guidance on other comprehensive income would trigger conforming changes to the definition of *performance indicator* in the Guide. This Statement eliminates minimum pension liability adjustments and requires the recognition of gains or losses, prior service costs or credits, and transition assets or obligations in other comprehensive income to the extent not yet recognized as components of net periodic benefit cost. Paragraphs 9 and 19 of SOP 02-2 are amended to eliminate the references to minimum pension liability adjustments and to add references to gains or losses, prior service costs or credits, and transition assets or obligations recognized in other comprehensive income. Additionally, footnote 5 is amended to state that the Statement 87 guidance referred to in that note has been amended by this Statement.

Statement of Financial Accounting Standards No. 159
The Fair Value Option for Financial Assets and Financial Liabilities

Including an amendment of FASB Statement No. 115

STATUS

Issued: February 2007

Effective Date: As of the beginning of each reporting entity's first fiscal year that begins after November 15, 2007; this Statement should not be applied retrospectively to fiscal years beginning prior to the effective date, except as permitted in paragraph 30 for early adoption.

Affects: Amends APB 21, paragraph 16
Amends FAS 57, paragraph 24(f)
Amends FAS 95, paragraphs 15 through 17 and footnote 8c
Effectively amends FAS 95, footnote 5
Amends FAS 102, paragraph 8
Amends FAS 115, paragraphs 4, 17, and 18
Effectively amends FAS 123(R), paragraph E1
Amends FAS 124, paragraph 6
Amends FAS 133, paragraphs 42 and 44A
Effectively amends FAS 140, paragraph 364
Effectively amends FAS 141, paragraph F1

Affected by: No other pronouncements

SUMMARY

Why Is the FASB Issuing This Statement?

This Statement permits entities to choose to measure many financial instruments and certain other items at fair value. The objective is to improve financial reporting by providing entities with the opportunity to mitigate volatility in reported earnings caused by measuring related assets and liabilities differently without having to apply complex hedge accounting provisions. This Statement is expected to expand the use of fair value measurement, which is consistent with the Board's long-term measurement objectives for accounting for financial instruments.

What Is the Scope of This Statement—Which Entities Does It Apply to and What Does It Affect?

This Statement applies to all entities, including not-for-profit organizations. Most of the provisions of this Statement apply only to entities that elect the fair value option. However, the amendment to FASB Statement No. 115, *Accounting for Certain Investments in Debt and Equity Securities,* applies to all entities with available-for-sale and trading securities. Some requirements apply differently to entities that do not report net income.

The following are eligible items for the measurement option established by this Statement:

1. Recognized financial assets and financial liabilities except:

    a. An investment in a subsidiary that the entity is required to consolidate
    b. An interest in a variable interest entity that the entity is required to consolidate

   c. Employers' and plans' obligations (or assets representing net overfunded positions) for pension benefits, other postretirement benefits (including health care and life insurance benefits), postemployment benefits, employee stock option and stock purchase plans, and other forms of deferred compensation arrangements, as defined in FASB Statements No. 35, *Accounting and Reporting by Defined Benefit Pension Plans,* No. 87, *Employers' Accounting for Pensions,* No. 106, *Employers' Accounting for Postretirement Benefits Other Than Pensions,* No. 112, *Employers' Accounting for Postemployment Benefits,* No. 123 (revised December 2004), *Share-Based Payment,* No. 43, *Accounting for Compensated Absences,* No. 146, *Accounting for Costs Associated with Exit or Disposal Activities,* and No. 158, *Employers' Accounting for Defined Benefit Pension and Other Postretirement Plans,* and APB Opinion No. 12, *Omnibus Opinion—1967*

   d. Financial assets and financial liabilities recognized under leases as defined in FASB Statement No. 13, *Accounting for Leases* (This exception does not apply to a guarantee of a third-party lease obligation or a contingent obligation arising from a cancelled lease.)

   e. Deposit liabilities, withdrawable on demand, of banks, savings and loan associations, credit unions, and other similar depository institutions

   f. Financial instruments that are, in whole or in part, classified by the issuer as a component of shareholder's equity (including "temporary equity"). An example is a convertible debt security with a noncontingent beneficial conversion feature.

2. Firm commitments that would otherwise not be recognized at inception and that involve only financial instruments

3. Nonfinancial insurance contracts and warranties that the insurer can settle by paying a third party to provide those goods or services

4. Host financial instruments resulting from separation of an embedded nonfinancial derivative instrument from a nonfinancial hybrid instrument.

How Will This Statement Change Current Accounting Practices?

The fair value option established by this Statement permits all entities to choose to measure eligible items at fair value at specified election dates. A business entity shall report unrealized gains and losses on items for which the fair value option has been elected in earnings (or another performance indicator if the business entity does not report earnings) at each subsequent reporting date. A not-for-profit organization shall report unrealized gains and losses in its statement of activities or similar statement.

The fair value option:

1. May be applied instrument by instrument, with a few exceptions, such as investments otherwise accounted for by the equity method

2. Is irrevocable (unless a new election date occurs)

3. Is applied only to entire instruments and not to portions of instruments.

How Does This Statement Contribute to International Convergence?

The fair value option in this Statement is similar, but not identical, to the fair value option in IAS 39, *Financial Instruments: Recognition and Measurement.* The international fair value option is subject to certain qualifying criteria not included in this standard, and it applies to a slightly different set of instruments.

What Is the Effective Date of This Statement?

This Statement is effective as of the beginning of an entity's first fiscal year that begins after November 15, 2007. Early adoption is permitted as of the beginning of a fiscal year that begins on or before November 15, 2007, provided the entity also elects to apply the provisions of FASB Statement No. 157, *Fair Value Measurements.*

No entity is permitted to apply this Statement retrospectively to fiscal years preceding the effective date unless the entity chooses early adoption. The choice to adopt early should be made after issuance of this Statement but within 120 days of the beginning of the fiscal year of adoption, provided the entity has not yet issued financial statements, including required notes to those financial statements, for any interim period of the fiscal year of adoption.

This Statement permits application to eligible items existing at the effective date (or early adoption date).

Statement of Financial Accounting Standards No. 159

The Fair Value Option for Financial Assets and Financial Liabilities

Including an amendment of FASB Statement No. 115

CONTENTS

OBJECTIVE

1. This Statement permits entities to choose to measure many financial instruments and certain other items at fair value that are not currently required to be measured at fair value. The objective is to improve financial reporting by providing entities with the opportunity to mitigate volatility in reported earnings caused by measuring related assets and liabilities differently without having to apply complex hedge accounting provisions. This Statement is expected to expand the use of fair value measurement, which is consistent with the Board's long-term measurement objectives for accounting for financial instruments. In addition, it is similar to a measurement choice permitted in International Financial Reporting Standards.

2. This Statement also establishes presentation and disclosure requirements designed to facilitate comparisons between entities that choose different measurement attributes for similar types of assets and liabilities. This Statement does not affect any existing accounting literature that requires certain assets and liabilities to be carried at fair value. This Statement does not establish requirements for recognizing and measuring dividend income, interest income, or interest expense. This Statement does not eliminate disclosure requirements included in other accounting standards, including requirements for disclosures about fair value measurements included in FASB Statements No. 157, *Fair Value Measurements,* and No. 107, *Disclosures about Fair Value of Financial Instruments.*

STANDARDS OF FINANCIAL ACCOUNTING AND REPORTING

The Fair Value Option

3. This Statement permits all entities to choose, at specified election dates, to measure eligible items at fair value (the "fair value option"). A business entity shall report unrealized gains and losses on items for which the fair value option has been elected in earnings (or another performance indicator if the business entity does not report earnings) at each subsequent reporting date. Upfront costs and fees related to items for which the fair value option is elected shall be recognized in earnings as incurred and not deferred.

4. The requirements related to earnings and some of the other requirements of this Statement apply differently to not-for-profit organizations. Paragraph 23 explains the differences.

5. The decision about whether to elect the fair value option:

a. Is applied instrument by instrument, except as discussed in paragraph 12
b. Is irrevocable (unless a new election date occurs, as discussed in paragraph 9)
c. Is applied only to an entire instrument and not to only specified risks, specific cash flows, or portions of that instrument.

Key Terms

6. The following terms are used in this Statement with the following definitions:

a. **Fair value**—The price that would be received to sell an asset or paid to transfer a liability in an orderly transaction between market participants at the measurement date.
b. **Financial asset**—Cash, evidence of an ownership interest in an entity, or a contract that conveys to one entity a right (1) to receive cash or another financial instrument from a second entity or (2) to exchange other financial instruments on potentially favorable terms with the second entity.
c. **Financial liability**—A contract that imposes on one entity an obligation (1) to deliver cash or another financial instrument to a second entity or (2) to exchange other financial instruments on potentially unfavorable terms with the second entity.
d. **Firm commitment**—An agreement with an unrelated party, binding on both parties and usually legally enforceable, with the following characteristics:
   (1) The agreement specifies all significant terms, including the quantity to be exchanged, a fixed price, and the timing of the transaction. The fixed price may be expressed as a specified amount of an entity's functional currency or of a foreign currency. It may also be expressed as a specified interest rate or specified effective yield.

(2) The agreement includes a disincentive for nonperformance that is sufficiently large to make performance probable.

Applying the Fair Value Option

Scope of Eligible Items

7. All entities may elect the fair value option for the following items (eligible items):

a. A recognized financial asset and financial liability, except any listed in paragraph 8

b. A firm commitment that would otherwise not be recognized at inception and that involves only financial instruments (An example is a forward purchase contract for a loan that is not readily convertible to cash. That commitment involves only financial instruments—a loan and cash—and would not otherwise be recognized because it is not a derivative instrument.)

c. A written loan commitment

d. The rights and obligations under an insurance contract that is not a financial instrument (because it requires or permits the insurer to provide goods or services rather than a cash settlement) but whose terms permit the insurer to settle by paying a third party to provide those goods or services

e. The rights and obligations under a warranty that is not a financial instrument (because it requires or permits the warrantor to provide goods or services rather than a cash settlement) but whose terms permit the warrantor to settle by paying a third party to provide those goods or services

f. A host financial instrument resulting from the separation of an embedded nonfinancial derivative instrument from a nonfinancial hybrid instrument under paragraph 12 of FASB Statement No. 133, *Accounting for Derivative Instruments and Hedging Activities,* subject to the scope exceptions in paragraph 8. (An example of such a nonfinancial hybrid instrument is an instrument in which the value of the bifurcated embedded derivative is payable in cash, services, or merchandise but the debt host is payable only in cash.)

Recognized Financial Assets and Financial Liabilities That Are Not Eligible Items

8. No entity may elect the fair value option for the following financial assets and financial liabilities:

a. An investment in a subsidiary that the entity is required to consolidate

b. An interest in a variable interest entity that the entity is required to consolidate

c. Employers' and plans' obligations (or assets representing net overfunded positions) for pension benefits, other postretirement benefits (including health care and life insurance benefits), postemployment benefits, employee stock option and stock purchase plans, and other forms of deferred compensation arrangements, as defined in FASB Statements No. 35, *Accounting and Reporting by Defined Benefit Pension Plans,* No. 87, *Employers' Accounting for Pensions,* No. 106, *Employers' Accounting for Postretirement Benefits Other Than Pensions,* No. 112, *Employers' Accounting for Postemployment Benefits,* No. 123 (revised December 2004), *Share-Based Payment,* No. 43, *Accounting for Compensated Absences,* No. 146, *Accounting for Costs Associated with Exit or Disposal Activities,* and No. 158, *Employers' Accounting for Defined Benefit Pension and Other Postretirement Plans,* and APB Opinion No. 12, *Omnibus Opinion—1967*

d. Financial assets and financial liabilities recognized under leases as defined in FASB Statement No. 13, *Accounting for Leases* (This exception does not apply to a guarantee of a third-party lease obligation or a contingent obligation arising from a cancelled lease.)

e. Deposit liabilities, withdrawable on demand, of banks, savings and loan associations, credit unions, and other similar depository institutions

f. Financial instruments that are, in whole or in part, classified by the issuer as a component of shareholder's equity (including "temporary equity"). An example is a convertible debt security with a noncontingent beneficial conversion feature.

Election Dates

9. An entity may decide whether to elect the fair value option for each eligible item on its election date. Alternatively, an entity may elect the fair value option according to a preexisting policy for specified types of eligible items. An entity may choose to elect the fair value option for an eligible item only on the date that one of the following occurs:

a. The entity first recognizes the eligible item.

b. The entity enters into an eligible firm commitment.

c. Financial assets that have been reported at fair value with unrealized gains and losses included in earnings because of specialized accounting principles cease to qualify for that specialized accounting. (An example is a transfer of assets from a subsidiary subject to the AICPA Audit and Accounting Guide, *Investment Companies,* to another entity within the consolidated reporting entity not subject to that Guide.)

d. The accounting treatment for an investment in another entity changes because:

(1) The investment becomes subject to the equity method of accounting. (For example, the investment may previously have been reported as a security accounted for under either FASB Statement No. 115, *Accounting for Certain Investments in Debt and Equity Securities,* or the fair value option in this Statement.)

(2) The investor ceases to consolidate a subsidiary or variable interest entity but retains an interest (for example, because the investor no longer holds a majority voting interest but continues to hold some common stock).

e. An event that requires an eligible item to be measured at fair value at the time of the event but does not require fair value measurement at each reporting date after that, excluding the recognition of impairment under lower-of-cost-or-market accounting or other-than-temporary impairment. (See paragraph 10.)

10. Some of the events that require remeasurement of eligible items at fair value, initial recognition of eligible items, or both, and thereby create an election date for the fair value option as discussed in paragraph 9(e) are:

a. Business combinations, as defined in FASB Statement No. 141, *Business Combinations*

b. Consolidation or deconsolidation of a subsidiary or variable interest entity

c. Significant modifications of debt, as defined in EITF Issue No. 96-19, "Debtor's Accounting for a Modification or Exchange of Debt Instruments."

11. An acquirer, parent, or primary beneficiary decides whether to apply the fair value option to eligible items of an acquiree, subsidiary, or consolidated variable interest entity, but that decision applies only in the consolidated financial statements. Fair value option choices made by an acquired entity, subsidiary, or variable interest entity continue to apply in separate financial statements of those entities if they issue separate financial statements.

Instrument-by-Instrument Application

12. The fair value option may be elected for a single eligible item without electing it for other identical items with the following four exceptions:

a. If multiple advances are made to one borrower pursuant to a single contract (such as a line of credit or a construction loan) and the individual advances lose their identity and become part of a larger loan balance, the fair value option shall be applied only to the larger balance and not to each advance individually.

b. If the fair value option is applied to an investment that would otherwise be accounted for under the equity method of accounting, it shall be applied to all of the investor's financial interests in the same entity (equity and debt, including guarantees) that are eligible items.

c. If the fair value option is applied to an eligible insurance or reinsurance contract, it shall be applied to all claims and obligations under the contract.

d. If the fair value option is elected for an insurance contract (base contract) for which integrated or nonintegrated contract features or coverages[1] (some of which are called riders) are issued either concurrently or subsequently, the fair value option also must be applied to those features or coverages. The fair value option cannot be elected for only the nonintegrated contract features or coverages, even though those features or coverages are accounted for separately under AICPA Statement of Position 05-1, *Accounting by Insurance Enterprises for Deferred Acquisition Costs in Connection With Modifications or Exchanges of Insurance Contracts.*

13. The fair value option need not be applied to all instruments issued or acquired in a single transaction (except as required by paragraph 12(a) or 12(b)). For example, investors in shares of stock and registered bonds might apply the fair value option to only some

---

[1]AICPA Statement of Position 05-1, *Accounting by Insurance Enterprises for Deferred Acquisition Costs in Connection With Modifications or Exchanges of Insurance Contracts,* defines a *nonintegrated contract feature* in an insurance contract. For purposes of applying this Statement, neither an integrated contract feature or coverage nor a nonintegrated contract feature or coverage qualifies as a separate instrument.

of the shares or bonds issued or acquired in a single transaction. For this purpose, an individual bond is considered to be the minimum denomination of that debt security. A financial instrument that is legally a single contract may not be separated into parts for purposes of applying the fair value option. In contrast, a loan syndication arrangement may result in multiple loans to the same borrower by different lenders. Each of those loans is a separate instrument, and the fair value option may be elected for some of those loans but not others.

14. An investor in an equity security may elect the fair value option for its entire investment in that equity security, including any fractional shares issued by the investee (for example, fractional shares that are acquired in a dividend reinvestment program).

Presentation of Items Measured at Fair Value under This Statement

Statement of Financial Position

15. Entities shall report assets and liabilities that are measured at fair value pursuant to the fair value option in this Statement in a manner that separates those reported fair values from the carrying amounts of similar assets and liabilities measured using another measurement attribute. To accomplish that, an entity shall either:

a. Present the aggregate of fair value and non-fair-value amounts in the same line item in the statement of financial position and parenthetically disclose the amount measured at fair value included in the aggregate amount
b. Present two separate line items to display the fair value and non-fair-value carrying amounts.

Cash Flow Statement

16. Entities shall classify cash receipts and cash payments related to items measured at fair value according to their nature and purpose as required by FASB Statement No. 95, *Statement of Cash Flows* (as amended).

Disclosures Applicable to This Statement and Statement 155

17. The principal objectives of the disclosures required by paragraphs 18–22 are to facilitate comparisons (a) between entities that choose different measurement attributes for similar assets and liabilities and (b) between assets and liabilities in the financial statements of an entity that selects different measurement attributes for similar assets and liabilities. Those disclosure requirements are expected to result in the following:

a. Information to enable users of its financial statements to understand management's reasons for electing or partially electing the fair value option
b. Information to enable users to understand how changes in fair values affect earnings for the period
c. The same information about certain items (such as equity investments and nonperforming loans) that would have been disclosed if the fair value option had not been elected
d. Information to enable users to understand the differences between fair values and contractual cash flows for certain items.

To meet those objectives, the disclosures described in paragraphs 18–22 are required for items measured at fair value under the option in this Statement and the option in paragraph 16 of Statement 133 (as amended by FASB Statement No. 155, *Accounting for Certain Hybrid Financial Instruments*). Those disclosures are not required for securities classified as trading securities under Statement 115, life settlement contracts measured at fair value pursuant to FASB Staff Position FTB 85-4-1, "Accounting for Life Settlement Contracts by Third-Party Investors," or servicing rights measured at fair value pursuant to FASB Statement No. 156, *Accounting for Servicing of Financial Assets*.[2] Entities shall provide the disclosures required by paragraphs 18–22 in both interim and annual financial statements. Entities are encouraged but are not required to present the disclosures required by this Statement in combination with related fair value information required to be disclosed by other Statements (for example, Statement 107 and Statement 157).

---

[2]Those standards include some disclosure requirements that are not affected by this Statement.

Required Disclosures as of Each Date for Which an Interim or Annual Statement of Financial Position Is Presented

18. As of each date for which a statement of financial position is presented, entities shall disclose the following:

a. Management's reasons for electing a fair value option for each eligible item or group of similar eligible items

b. If the fair value option is elected for some but not all eligible items within a group of similar eligible items:
   (1) A description of those similar items and the reasons for partial election
   (2) Information to enable users to understand how the group of similar items relates to individual line items on the statement of financial position

c. For each line item in the statement of financial position that includes an item or items for which the fair value option has been elected:
   (1) Information to enable users to understand how each line item in the statement of financial position relates to major categories of assets and liabilities presented in accordance with Statement 157's fair value disclosure requirements[3]
   (2) The aggregate carrying amount of items included in each line item in the statement of financial position that are not eligible for the fair value option, if any

d. The difference between the aggregate fair value and the aggregate unpaid principal balance of:
   (1) Loans and long-term receivables (other than securities subject to Statement 115) that

have contractual principal amounts and for which the fair value option has been elected
   (2) Long-term debt instruments that have contractual principal amounts and for which the fair value option has been elected

e. For loans held as assets for which the fair value option has been elected:
   (1) The aggregate fair value of loans that are 90 days or more past due
   (2) If the entity's policy is to recognize interest income separately from other changes in fair value, the aggregate fair value of loans in nonaccrual status
   (3) The difference between the aggregate fair value and the aggregate unpaid principal balance for loans that are 90 days or more past due, in nonaccrual status, or both

f. For investments that would have been accounted for under the equity method if the entity had not chosen to apply the fair value option,[4] the information required by paragraph 20 of APB Opinion No. 18, *The Equity Method of Accounting for Investments in Common Stock* (excluding the disclosures in paragraphs 20(a)(3), 20(b), and 20(e) of that Opinion).[5]

Required Disclosures for Each Period for Which an Interim or Annual Income Statement Is Presented

19. For each period for which an income statement is presented, entities shall disclose the following about items for which the fair value option has been elected:

a. For each line item in the statement of financial position, the amounts of gains and losses from fair value changes included in earnings during the

---

[3]Paragraph 10 of Statement 107 also requires an entity to relate carrying amounts that are disclosed in accordance with that Statement to what is reported in the statement of financial position.

[4]This disclosure applies to investments in common stock, investments in in-substance common stock, and other investments (for example, partnerships and certain limited liability corporations) that (a) would otherwise be required to be accounted for under the equity method under other generally accepted accounting principles (GAAP) and (b) would be required to satisfy the disclosure requirements of paragraph 20 of Opinion 18.

[5]The following guidance from paragraph 20 and subparagraphs (a) and (d) of Opinion 18 is applicable:

   The significance of an investment to the investor's financial position and results of operations should be considered in evaluating the extent of disclosures of the financial position and results of operations of an investee. If the investor has more than one investment in common stock, disclosures wholly or partly on a combined basis may be appropriate. The following disclosures are generally applicable to the equity method of accounting for investments in common stock:

   a. Financial statements of an investor should disclose parenthetically, in notes to financial statements, or in separate statements or schedules (1) the name of each investee and percentage of ownership of common stock, [and] (2) the accounting policies of the investor with respect to investments in common stock. . . .
   d. When investments in common stock of corporate joint ventures or other investments accounted for under the equity method are, in the aggregate, material in relation to the financial position or results of operations of an investor, it may be necessary for summarized information as to assets, liabilities, and results of operations of the investees to be presented in the notes or in separate statements, either individually or in groups, as appropriate. [Footnote reference omitted.]

period and in which line in the income statement those gains and losses are reported (This Statement does not preclude an entity from meeting this requirement by disclosing amounts of gains and losses that include amounts of gains and losses for other items measured at fair value, such as items required to be measured at fair value.)

b. A description of how interest and dividends are measured and where they are reported in the income statement (This Statement does not address the methods used for recognizing and measuring the amount of dividend income, interest income, and interest expense for items for which the fair value option has been elected.)

c. For loans and other receivables held as assets:

    (1) The estimated amount of gains or losses included in earnings during the period attributable to changes in instrument-specific credit risk

    (2) How the gains or losses attributable to changes in instrument-specific credit risk were determined

d. For liabilities with fair values that have been significantly affected during the reporting period by changes in the instrument-specific credit risk:

    (1) The estimated amount of gains and losses from fair value changes included in earnings that are attributable to changes in the instrument-specific credit risk

    (2) Qualitative information about the reasons for those changes

    (3) How the gains and losses attributable to changes in instrument-specific credit risk were determined.

20. The disclosure requirements in paragraphs 18 and 19 do not eliminate disclosure requirements included in other GAAP pronouncements, including other disclosure requirements relating to fair value measurement.

Other Required Disclosures

21. In annual periods only, an entity shall disclose the methods and significant assumptions used to estimate the fair value of items for which the fair value option has been elected.[6]

22. If an entity elects the fair value option at the time one of the events in paragraphs 9(d) and 9(e) occurs, the entity shall disclose the following in financial statements for the period of the election:

a. Qualitative information about the nature of the event

b. Quantitative information by line item in the statement of financial position indicating which line items in the income statement include the effect on earnings of initially electing the fair value option for an item.

Application by Not-for-Profit Organizations

23. Not-for-profit organizations shall apply the provisions of this Statement with the following modifications:

a. References to an income statement should be replaced with references to a statement of activities, statement of changes in net assets, or statement of operations. References to earnings should be replaced with references to changes in net assets, except as indicated in paragraph 23(b).

b. Health care organizations subject to the AICPA Audit and Accounting Guide, *Health Care Organizations,* shall report unrealized gains and losses on items for which the fair value option has been elected within the performance indicator or as a part of discontinued operations, as appropriate.[7] Consistent with the provisions of FASB Statement No. 117, *Financial Statements*

---

[6]Paragraph 10 of Statement 107 already requires an entity to disclose annually the methods and significant assumptions used to estimate the fair value of financial instruments. Thus, the effect of this disclosure requirement is essentially limited to instruments outside the scope of Statement 107 (for example, certain insurance contracts) for which the fair value option has been elected.

[7]Unlike other not-for-profit organizations, organizations subject to the health care Guide present performance indicators analogous to income from continuing operations.

of Not-for-Profit Organizations, not-for-profit organizations may present such gains and losses either within or outside other intermediate measures of operations unless such gains or losses are part of discontinued operations.[8]

c. The disclosure requirements in paragraph 19 shall apply not only with respect to the effect on performance indicators or other intermediate measures of operations, if presented, but also with respect to the effect on the change in each of the net asset classes (unrestricted, temporarily restricted, and permanently restricted), as applicable.

Effective Date

24. This Statement shall be effective as of the beginning of each reporting entity's first fiscal year that begins after November 15, 2007. This Statement should not be applied retrospectively to fiscal years beginning prior to the effective date, except as permitted in paragraph 30 for early adoption.

Application to Eligible Items Existing at the Effective Date

25. At the effective date, an entity may elect the fair value option for eligible items that exist at that date. The entity shall report the effect of the first remeasurement to fair value as a cumulative-effect adjustment to the opening balance of retained earnings. A not-for-profit organization shall report such cumulative-effect adjustment as a separate line item within the changes in the appropriate net asset class or classes in its statement of activities, outside of any performance indicator or other intermediate measure of operations.

26. The difference between the carrying amount and the fair value of eligible items for which the fair value option is elected at the effective date shall be removed from the statement of financial position and included in the cumulative-effect adjustment. Those differences may include, but are not limited to:

a. Unamortized deferred costs, fees, premiums, and discounts
b. Valuation allowances (for example, allowances for loan losses)
c. Accrued interest, which would be reported as part of the fair value of the eligible item.

27. An entity that elects the fair value option for items existing at the effective date shall provide the following in its annual and first-interim-period financial statements for the fiscal year that includes the effective date:

a. A schedule that presents the following by line item in the statement of financial position:
  (1) The pretax portion of the cumulative-effect adjustment to retained earnings (or appropriate class or classes of net assets) for items on that line
  (2) The fair value at the effective date of eligible items for which the fair value option is elected and the carrying amount of those same items immediately before electing the fair value option
b. The net effect on the entity's deferred tax assets and liabilities of electing the fair value option
c. Management's reasons for electing the fair value option for each existing eligible item or group of similar eligible items
d. If the fair value option is elected for some but not all eligible items within a group of similar eligible items:
  (1) A description of those similar items and the reasons for partial election
  (2) Information to enable users to understand how the group of similar items relates to individual line items on the statement of financial position
e. The amount of valuation allowances that were removed from the statement of financial position because they related to items for which the fair value option was elected.

Available-for-Sale and Held-to-Maturity Securities

28. Available-for-sale and held-to-maturity securities held at the effective date are eligible for the fair value option at that date. If the fair value option is elected for any of those securities at the effective date, cumulative unrealized gains and losses at that date shall be included in the cumulative-effect adjustment. The amount of unrealized gains and losses reclassified from accumulated other comprehensive income (for available-for-sale securities) and the amount of unrealized gains and losses that was previously unrecognized (for held-to-maturity securities) shall be separately disclosed. If Statement 157 is adopted at the same time that this Statement is

---

[8]This includes intermediate measures of operations presented by not-for-profit organizations other than health care organizations and any additional intermediate measures of operations presented within the performance indicator by not-for-profit health care organizations.

adopted, any change in an existing eligible item's recorded fair value at the effective date due to application of the guidance in Statement 157 (such as for an available-for-sale security) shall be included in the cumulative-effect adjustment if the fair value option was elected for that eligible item.

29. If an entity elects the fair value option for a held-to-maturity or available-for-sale security in conjunction with the adoption of this Statement, that security shall be reported as a trading security under Statement 115, but the accounting for a transfer to the trading category under paragraph 15(b) of Statement 115 does not apply. Electing the fair value option for an existing held-to-maturity security will not call into question the intent of an entity to hold other debt securities to maturity in the future.

Early Adoption

30. An entity may adopt this Statement and elect the fair value option for existing eligible items as of the beginning of a fiscal year that begins on or before November 15, 2007, subject to the following conditions:

a. The choice to adopt early shall be made after issuance of this Statement but within 120 days of the beginning of the fiscal year of adoption.
b. The entity also adopts all of the requirements of Statement 157 at this Statement's early adoption date (the first day of the fiscal year of adoption) or earlier.
c. At the time the entity chooses to adopt this Statement early, the entity has not yet issued financial statements, including required notes to those financial statements, for any interim period of the fiscal year that includes the early adoption date.
d. The choices to apply or not apply the fair value option to eligible items existing at the early adoption date are retroactive to the early adoption date.
e. For eligible items with an election date (as specified in paragraph 9) occurring after the early adoption date but before the date of the entity's choice to apply early, the election for those items is retroactive to their election date.
f. All other requirements that would normally apply as of the required effective date also apply as of the early adoption date.

The provisions of this Statement need not be applied to immaterial items.

This Statement was adopted by the affirmative votes of five members of the Financial Accounting Standards Board. Messrs. Linsmeier and Young dissented.

Mr. Linsmeier dissents from issuance of this Statement because he believes a fair value option generally will not result in financial reporting that achieves many of the objectives for issuing this Statement given in paragraph A3. Mr. Linsmeier agrees with paragraph A3(a)—that the effect on earnings from using mixed measurement attributes under GAAP in the United States may not be representative of the economics of the reporting entity's activities. In addition, he agrees with paragraph A3(b)—that a fair value option will enable entities to mitigate reporting volatility in earnings that results from using different measurement attributes in reporting related financial assets and financial liabilities. However, providing entities with an instrument-by-instrument option that often will result in the reporting at fair value of only some instruments within the scope of this Statement will not result in reporting that is more

representative of entities' economic exposures and will provide an opportunity for entities to report significantly less earnings volatility than they are exposed to.

Mr. Linsmeier also agrees with paragraph A3(d)—that fair values for financial assets and financial liabilities provide more relevant and understandable information than cost or cost-based measures. However, an instrument-by-instrument option that results in partial adoption of fair values for only some financial (and other) instruments significantly reduces the relevance of the resulting reporting by failing to portray the earnings effects of financial (and other) instruments' exposures in the same reporting period and increases users' costs in processing the information by introducing treatment alternatives that reduce the comparability of reported results within and across reporting entities and line items. For these reasons, Mr. Linsmeier does not agree that this Statement represents a cost-beneficial interim step toward measuring all financial instruments at fair value—a long-term goal stated by the Board in Statement 133. Rather, he believes users of financial statements would be better served by accelerating efforts to issue a Statement requiring all financial instruments to be measured at fair value each reporting period with changes in those fair values reported in earnings.

Mr. Young dissents from the issuance of this Statement because it will not improve financial reporting for the following reasons:

1. The provision of an option for fair value is likely to delay the adoption of consistent use of fair value measurement for financial instruments.
2. This Statement introduces a fragmented approach to reporting financial instruments at fair value instead of a conceptually coherent framework. It permits the continued use of non-fair-value measurement of financial instruments that will result in financial statements that are not representationally faithful. It also impairs consistency and comparability, which will reduce understandability of financial statements and increase complexity for users.
3. The application of the fair value option to financial liabilities that are part of an entity's capital structure, without any qualifying criteria (such as correcting an existing measurement mismatch), can result in misleading financial reporting.
4. While the preparers of financial statements will realize benefits in reduced volatility of reported earnings or reduction in the cost to achieve reduced volatility, those benefits are not justified by the cost that users will incur from increases in complexity and reduction in understandability.

This Statement does not meet the objective of financial reporting; it reduces understandability and increases costs for users. It provides benefits to preparers in managing volatility in earnings, which is not an objective of financial reporting.

Mr. Young believes the fair value option will further delay a comprehensive fair value measurement requirement for financial instruments. He believes the assumption in paragraph A3(d) cannot be supported by past experience or empirical evidence. He believes the more likely outcome of this Statement is a very limited expansion in the use of fair value for financial instruments and a delay in the broader requirement for fair value for financial instruments.

With more than a decade of preparers' meeting the requirement for disclosure of fair values for financial instruments (Statement 107) and electing the option of trading classification for marketable securities (Statement 115), it is unlikely that any significant incremental preparer experience using fair value will

be gained from this Statement that will facilitate adoption of a fair value requirement for financial instruments.

With the fair value option, a preparer can manage volatility that would otherwise exist from the mixed-attribute accounting model. With this benefit secured, there will only be greater resistance from the preparer community to wider adoption of a fair value measurement for financial instruments. Without a fair value option, the preparer community would be more supportive of a fair value measurement requirement for financial instruments. Therefore, the introduction of elective fair value can only result in further delay and resistance to the requirement for fair value measurement of financial instruments.

Mr. Young disagrees with the Board's decision to permit free choice between different initial and subsequent measurement attributes for financial instruments. Mr. Young agrees with the Board's acknowledgment, in the discussion relating the conclusions in this Statement to the conceptual framework, that the Board's decision impairs comparability and consistency, two desirable qualitative characteristics of financial information in its conceptual framework. Mr. Young believes that the disclosures required by this Statement, taken together with disclosure requirements in other GAAP, are not a substitute for consistent and comparable measurement of similar items.

Reporting financial instruments at fair value and including unrealized changes in fair value in earnings would reflect the economic events in the periods in which they occur and faithfully represent the underlying economics—a key objective of the conceptual framework. Providing an "option" to continue the use of historical-cost-based measurement will lead to accounting that potentially misrepresents the underlying economics.

Mr. Young believes that most users do not expect revaluation of the entity's securities (which are part of an entity's overall capital structure) to be a component of operating performance. In his view, the changes in the entity's overall capital structure (both debt capital and equity capital), particularly from the effect of changes in the entity's own creditworthiness, should not be reflected in business performance. Recognizing changes in an entity's own creditworthiness in earnings could mislead users and potentially misrepresent or conceal operating performance issues. At a minimum, eligibility criteria should be required when the fair value option is elected for the debt portion of an entity's capital structure.

Mr. Young disagrees that the fair value option reduces complexity and costs as discussed in paragraph A3(b). Instead, he believes complexity and cost are shifted from the preparer to the user. He believes the user will be required to expend more cost and effort to compare financial statements prepared using the fair value option with financial statements prepared using a different measurement basis. It is not clear that the same level of user understanding can be achieved at any cost.

With regard to the cost-benefit criterion of the Board's conceptual framework, Mr. Young notes that the incremental burden that would be imposed on preparers by a requirement to measure all financial instruments that are within the scope of this Statement at fair value would not be large, given the requirements of existing accounting guidance. Statement 107 already requires certain fair value measurements of financial instruments for disclosure purposes. Therefore, the ability to measure many financial instruments at fair value should already be in place. Mr. Young believes a far greater benefit to financial reporting at a much lower cost to users and preparers would result from a requirement to measure financial instruments, as defined in the scope of this Statement or the scope of Statement 107 or Statement 115, at fair value.

Members of the Financial Accounting Standards Board:

Robert H. Herz,
Chairman
George J. Batavick

G. Michael Crooch
Thomas J. Linsmeier
Leslie F. Seidman

Edward W. Trott
Donald M. Young

Appendix A

BACKGROUND INFORMATION AND BASIS FOR CONCLUSIONS

CONTENTS

Appendix A

BACKGROUND INFORMATION AND BASIS FOR CONCLUSIONS

Introduction

A1. This appendix summarizes considerations that Board members deemed significant in reaching the conclusions in this Statement. It includes reasons for accepting certain views and rejecting others. Individual Board members gave greater weight to some factors than to others.

Background Information

A2. In Statements 155 and 156 and FSP FTB 85-4-1, the Board decided to permit entities to elect fair value as the subsequent measurement attribute with changes in fair value included in earnings for certain hybrid instruments, servicing rights, and life settlement contracts, respectively. The Board received requests from constituents to explore creating a more broadly applicable fair value option. In May 2004, knowing that the IASB had incorporated a fair value option in IAS 39, *Financial Instruments: Recognition and Measurement,* the Board added a project to its agenda to consider whether entities should be permitted a one-time election, at the initial recognition of an item, to report financial instruments, and perhaps certain nonfinancial instruments that are similar to financial instruments, at fair value with the changes in fair value included in earnings. Work on this project was initially deferred until the IASB concluded its reconsideration of possible modifications to the fair value option in IAS 39. In June 2005, the IASB issued *The Fair Value Option,* an amendment to IAS 39. In January 2006, the Board issued an Exposure Draft, *The Fair Value Option for Financial Assets and Financial Liabilities,* for a 75-day comment period. Approximately 80 organizations and individuals responded to the Exposure Draft.

Basis for Conclusions

Reasons for Permitting a Fair Value Option

A3. The Board decided to permit entities to elect a fair value option for financial assets and financial liabilities for the following reasons:

a. A fair value option would enable entities to mitigate the volatility in earnings that results from using different measurement attributes in reporting related financial assets and financial liabilities. The effect on earnings from using mixed measurement attributes under GAAP in the United States may not be representative of the economics of the reporting entity's activities. Although special hedge accounting under Statement 133 compensates in part for the mismatch of measurement attributes, only certain hedging relationships can qualify for hedge accounting and only derivatives can be used as the hedging instrument under Statement 133.

b. A fair value option would enable entities to achieve consistent accounting and, potentially, an offsetting effect for the changes in the fair values of related assets and liabilities without having to apply complex hedge accounting provisions, thereby providing greater simplicity in the application of accounting guidance. A fair value option would enable entities to avoid the time, effort, and systems needed to document fair value hedging relationships and demonstrate their effectiveness to qualify for continued hedge accounting. That is, rather than designating a fair value hedging relationship under Statement 133, entities could elect to apply the fair value option to the hedged item at its inception. However, the offset resulting from the application of the fair value option is based on the fair value of the entire financial asset or liability and not selected risks inherent in those financial assets or financial liabilities.

c. A fair value option would achieve further convergence with the IASB, which has incorporated a fair value option for financial instruments in IAS 39.

d. A fair value option would expand the use of the fair value measurement attribute for financial instruments. The Board believes fair values for financial assets and financial liabilities provide more relevant and understandable information than cost or cost-based measures. The Board considers fair value measurements of financial instruments to be more relevant to financial statement users than cost-based measurements because fair value reflects the current cash equivalent of the entity's financial instruments rather than the price of a past transaction. The Board also believes that, with the passage of time, historical prices become irrelevant in assessing an entity's current financial position.

Some respondents to the Exposure Draft, primarily users of financial statements, objected to the elective nature of this Statement and urged the Board to require, rather than permit, fair value accounting for all financial instruments. The Board continues to believe that fair value is the most relevant measurement attribute for financial instruments. However, the Board concluded that it has more work to do before fair value measurement can be required for all financial instruments. There are several unresolved issues, including how to measure fair value (which has been addressed through the issuance of Statement 157), what is included in the scope, how to present changes in fair value, whether to continue to permit hedge accounting for forecasted transactions, whether additional disclosures should be required, and the relationship with the existing Statement on transfers and extinguishments of financial instruments. Those issues are being addressed as part of the Board's research project on financial instruments, which is being conducted jointly with the IASB. The Board views the fair value option as an interim step that can mitigate existing reporting issues and expand the use of fair value measurements for financial instruments.

Scope

A4. In undertaking the fair value option project, the Board initially planned to address not only financial assets and financial liabilities but also certain nonfinancial assets and nonfinancial liabilities that are similar to financial items. However, the Board decided that additional input was needed from constituents about the use of fair value in accounting for nonfinancial assets and nonfinancial liabilities. The Board decided to split the project into two phases and use the notice for recipients in the Exposure Draft for Phase 1 to solicit information about the potential application of the fair value option to nonfinancial assets and nonfinancial liabilities. Consequently, Phase 1 addresses the fair value option for certain financial assets and financial liabilities, and Phase 2 will consider permitting the fair value option to be elected for certain nonfinancial assets, nonfinancial liabilities, and some of the financial assets and financial liabilities excluded from the scope of Phase 1.

A5. Some respondents questioned whether insurance contracts are financial instruments. Some insurance contracts require the payment of cash to settle a claim (and thus are financial instruments in the scope of this Statement), whereas others may permit settlement of a claim by either a cash payment or the provision of goods or services (by the insurance company or by a third party that is compensated by the insurance company), in which case the insurance

contract would not meet the definition of a financial instrument. Some respondents noted that scrutinizing individual contracts to determine whether they are financial instruments would be quite burdensome, as would be the case in determining whether warranty rights and obligations meet the definition of a financial instrument. The Board decided to expand the scope of this Statement slightly by including insurance and reinsurance contracts as well as warranty rights and obligations that permit or require settlement of a claim by providing goods or services if settlement of the related obligation is permitted by payment to a third-party provider of goods or services rather than only by the insurer's or warrantor's providing goods or services directly to the insured or other claimant.

A6. The Board also considered the case of a hybrid nonfinancial instrument for which bifurcation of an embedded derivative would be required by paragraph 12 of Statement 133. If that bifurcation results in the nonfinancial features of the hybrid instrument being included entirely in the embedded derivative, the resulting host contract would be a financial instrument that would be accounted for separately. The Board decided that in that case, the host financial instrument would be eligible for election of the fair value option subject to the scope exceptions in paragraph 8 of this Statement.

A7. The Board discussed whether the fair value option should be permitted for financial assets and financial liabilities that would otherwise not be recognized at inception under existing GAAP. The Board determined that under Phase 1 of the project, the fair value option should be permitted at inception for unrecognized firm commitments that involve only financial instruments. This Statement uses the definition of *firm commitment* as set forth in Statement 133, which requires that the terms of the agreement include a disincentive for nonperformance that is sufficiently large to make performance probable. The Board notes that Statement 133 Implementation Issue No. F3, "Firm Commitments—Statutory Remedies for Default Constituting a Disincentive for Nonperformance," clarifies that the binding provisions of a firm commitment are regarded to include those legal rights and obligations codified in the laws to which such an agreement is subject.

A8. The Board considered whether the fair value option should not be permitted for certain financial assets and financial liabilities. The Board's discussions focused on items that have historically been excluded from pronouncements that address financial instruments broadly, particularly the scope exceptions in Statement 107. The Board supported a broad application of the fair value option and decided to keep scope exceptions to a minimum. The Board decided to exclude from the scope of this Statement the following financial assets and financial liabilities for the reasons indicated:

a. An interest in an entity (principally an investment in a subsidiary or a primary beneficiary's variable interest in a variable interest entity) that would otherwise be consolidated. The Board believes the fair value option project should not be used to make significant changes to consolidation practices.
b. Employers' and plans' financial obligations (or assets representing net overfunded positions) for pension benefits, other postretirement benefits (including health care and life insurance benefits), postemployment benefits, employee stock option and stock purchase plans, and other forms of deferred compensation arrangements as defined in Statements 35, 87, 106, 112, 123(R), 43, 146, and 158 and Opinion 12. The Board believes that any modifications should be part of a reconsideration of those individual areas. (The Board revised this scope exception to clarify that the fair value option is not available for the asset or liability that represents the net overfunded or underfunded status of a benefit plan.)
c. Financial assets and financial liabilities recognized under lease contracts as defined in Statement 13. (This exclusion does not include a contingent obligation arising out of a cancelled lease and a guarantee of a third-party lease obligation.) The Board believes that lease accounting provisions should not be changed by the fair value option project without a comprehensive reconsideration of the accounting for lease contracts.
d. Deposit liabilities, withdrawable on demand, of banks, savings and loan associations, credit unions, and other similar depository institutions. The Board will include those liabilities in the deliberations of Phase 2 because the fair value of those liabilities are often significantly affected by nonfinancial components.
e. Financial instruments that are, in whole or in part, classified by the issuer as components of shareholder's equity (including "temporary equity"). The changes in the fair value of any contract that, for whatever reason, is reported in shareholders' equity, in whole or in part, should not affect earnings. The current standard for convertible debt

with noncontingent beneficial conversion features requires separate recognition as part of additional paid-in capital (in the shareholders' equity section of the statement of financial position) of the intrinsic value of the embedded beneficial conversion features.

A9. The scope of the Exposure Draft excluded written loan commitments that are not accounted for as derivatives under Statement 133. Consideration of those loan commitments had been deferred to Phase 2 of the fair value option project. Many respondents disagreed with that scope exception, noting that there is no substantive difference between those loan commitments currently in the scope of Statement 133 and those excluded from Statement 133's fair value accounting requirement. The Board agreed with those observations and decided that written loan commitments that are not accounted for as derivatives under Statement 133 should be included within the scope of Phase 1 and removed the scope exception.

A10. The Board also affirmed that the election of the fair value option is not permitted for current or deferred income tax assets or liabilities because those assets and liabilities are not contractual. Thus, they are not financial assets or financial liabilities.

A11. The Board discussed whether the fair value option election should be prohibited for nonpublic entities that have elected the exception under FASB Statement No. 126, *Exemption from Certain Required Disclosures about Financial Instruments for Certain Nonpublic Entities*, from having to disclose fair values under Statement 107. The Board noted a significant difference between a nonpublic company's election not to be subject to Statement 107, which requires fair value disclosures of **all** of an entity's financial assets and liabilities (if practicable), and a nonpublic company's desire to elect the fair value option for selected financial assets and financial liabilities. Because the fair value option may be applied on an instrument-by-instrument basis, the Board believes that the fair value option should be available to nonpublic entities that have elected the Statement 126 exception.

Election of the Fair Value Option

A12. The Exposure Draft indicated that the election of the fair value option should be made at initial recognition of the financial asset or financial liability or upon a remeasurement event that gives rise to new-basis accounting at fair value for that item. The

Board noted that an election after initial recognition would permit entities to recognize gains or losses in earnings after those gains and losses had occurred and, consequently, is not permitted.

A13. A few respondents to the Exposure Draft requested that the Board modify that provision to permit the fair value option election when (a) the legal form and substance of the item changes or (b) a change in risk management strategy occurs. However, those respondents did not provide the Board with any information that had not been considered in the Board's deliberations prior to the Exposure Draft; therefore, the Board did not add those two suggested events as circumstances that would permit a new choice about whether to elect the fair value option.

A14. The Board also discussed whether an entity may elect the fair value option for financial assets that have been reported at fair value (with changes included in earnings) under specialized accounting principles but, at a point in time, become no longer subject to that required reporting because they no longer qualify for those specialized accounting principles. The Board decided that, consistent with the reasons in paragraph A3, the consolidated reporting entity should be able to continue its reporting at fair value (with changes included in earnings). Consequently, the Board decided that an entity may elect the fair value option in that circumstance even though the election would not be made at the date of initial recognition.

A15. When a contract is modified (or a rider added to it) after it has been initially recognized, the question arises as to whether that modification would permit election of the fair value option for the related asset or liability. The Board decided that the availability of the fair value option should be based on whether, under GAAP, the modification is accounted for as the continuation of the original contract or as the termination of the original contract and the origination of a new contract. If the modification is considered the origination of a new contract, the fair value option could be elected on the date of its initial recognition. Otherwise, the entity's previous decision about electing the fair value option for the original contract would govern the accounting for the continuation of that original contract.

A16. The Board also decided that an entity may elect the fair value option at the time that an entity becomes subject to the equity method of accounting, even though that point in time is not necessarily the date of initial recognition of the investment in the investee.

A17. A respondent requested that the Board clarify whether the fair value option should be elected at the trade date or the settlement date of an asset or liability. The Board considered that request and noted that an entity would elect the fair value option at the time of initial recognition, which could occur at the trade date or the settlement date depending on relevant GAAP. For example, if an entity was required to initially recognize a contract on the trade date, the fair value option would also need to be elected on the trade date and not the settlement date.

A18. The Exposure Draft permitted the election of the fair value option on a contract-by-contract (that is, instrument-by-instrument) basis. Some respondents supported a contract-by-contract election, noting that entities could better align their accounting practices with their risk management activities. They noted that this accounting symmetry would allow preparers to mitigate some of the earnings volatility associated with a mixed-attribute model. Many respondents expressed concerns about permitting a contract-by-contract election. One concern was that having the contract as the unit of account would unduly constrain the determination of fair value. (Statement 157, which was issued after the Exposure Draft, provides guidance on determining fair value; under that Statement, the unit of valuation need not be the unit of account.) Another concern was that such an election approach would allow for abuse in applying the rules in order to obtain a desired outcome. Moreover, that technique could exacerbate noncomparability in reporting between similar entities. Some respondents suggested either an entity-wide election for all financial assets and financial liabilities or an option to measure all or none of a category or type of asset or liability at fair value (an election by type).

A19. The Board believes that the election of the fair value option on an instrument-by-instrument basis is more consistent with the reasons in paragraph A3 for permitting a fair value option than either an entity-wide election or an election by type. Because entities typically use their hedging activities to mitigate a portion of their risks rather than eliminate all their risks, an instrument-by-instrument election is consistent with this Statement's objective to achieve an offsetting accounting effect for the changes in the fair values of related financial assets and financial liabilities without having to apply complex hedge accounting provisions of Statement 133. An instrument-by-instrument election also accomplishes further convergence with the IASB's fair value option for financial instruments in IAS 39. To provide entities with greater flexibility in obtaining benefits from the fair value option, the Board decided to permit election on an instrument-by-instrument basis. To minimize the potential for abuse, the Board decided that once an entity elects the fair value option for an asset or liability, it could not subsequently discontinue the use of the fair value measurement treatment for reporting that asset or liability.

Qualifying criteria

A20. To provide entities with greater flexibility in obtaining the benefits of the fair value option, the Board decided not to impose any eligibility requirements in the Exposure Draft. Respondents generally agreed with that decision. However, several respondents recommended that the Board incorporate eligibility requirements that are the same or similar to the eligibility requirements in IAS 39. They asserted that the suggested modification would provide further convergence with international standards and result in more relevant information.

A21. The Board concluded that the absence of those eligibility requirements would not lead to substantive divergence with international standards. Furthermore, the Board concluded that including eligibility requirements for the fair value option would conflict with the objectives of this Statement. That is, it would reduce the use of the fair value measurement attribute for financial instruments, increase complexity, and hinder entities' ability to mitigate accounting mismatches through the use of a flexible and easy-to-implement fair value option. However, the Board was mindful of those respondents' concerns as it reconsidered the disclosure requirements.

Documentation requirements

A22. Respondents to the Exposure Draft stated that documentation of the fair value option was an internal control matter and did not require accounting guidance from the Board. Those respondents also stated that the Board's documentation requirements set forth in the Exposure Draft were overly burdensome and detracted from the benefits of the fair value option election, mainly, its simplicity. In its redeliberations, the Board decided that it is sufficient for this Statement to indicate the timing of requirements for making the election and provide an acknowledgment that an entity could establish a policy to elect the fair value option for specified classes of assets or liabilities. The Board agreed that maintaining evidence of

compliance with the requirements of this Statement is a matter of internal control and decided not to prescribe how that evidence should be created and maintained.

Use of Non-Fair-Value Measures

A23. In its initial deliberations, the Board discussed whether entities should be permitted to elect (outside of the hedge accounting provided in Statement 133) to recognize in earnings the change in an asset's or liability's fair value attributable to only certain selected risks (rather than the total change in fair value). The Board rejected recognizing the fair value changes that are attributable to only selected risks because that would be inconsistent with expanding the use of the fair value measurement attribute and international convergence. Moreover, the resulting measurement would not represent the fair value of the asset or liability as a whole.

A24. The Board also considered whether to curtail the debtor's recognizing in earnings the effect of changes in its creditworthiness in reporting liabilities at fair value when the fair value option has been elected. For example, the debtor might exclude the effects of the change in its creditworthiness from the liability's carrying amount, resulting in a non-fair-value measure. The Board agreed that liability remeasurements at fair value should include the effect of changes in creditworthiness so that the estimate reflects the amount that would be observed in an exchange between willing parties of the same credit quality. The Exposure Draft provided no special treatment for the effect of changes in the debtor's creditworthiness in reporting the debtor's liabilities when the fair value option is elected.

A25. Some respondents disagreed with reporting the effect of changes in the issuer's own creditworthiness as gains and losses in the issuer's financial statements. Some respondents suggested the change in fair value should be split: the change in fair value attributable to changes in the debtor's creditworthiness should be reported in other comprehensive income (until realized) and the remaining change in fair value should be reported in earnings. Under that suggestion, the assets or liabilities would still be reported at fair value. Other respondents objected to including the change in fair value attributable to changes in the debtor's creditworthiness in other comprehensive income, which they stated would misstate shareholders' equity. Under that suggestion, liabilities would be reported at a non-fair-value measure. The Board concluded that there is no justification, conceptual or otherwise, for curtailing the debtor's recognizing in earnings the effect of changes in its creditworthiness in reporting liabilities at fair value. However, the Board decided to require additional disclosures that would help users of financial statements understand the related reporting. The Board decided to focus on the effect of changes in instrument-specific credit risk on fair value, rather than on the effect of changes in the debtor's creditworthiness. If, in any period presented, changes in instrument-specific credit risk cause significant changes in the fair values of financial liabilities for which the fair value option has been elected, the entity must disclose its estimate of the portion of the change in fair value of those liabilities that is due to changes in instrument-specific credit risk. The entity also must disclose qualitative information about the reasons for those changes (which are included in current-period earnings), as discussed in paragraph A36.

A26. Some respondents to the Exposure Draft suggested that to meet some of the Board's stated objectives for this Statement, the fair value option should be permitted for a portion of an asset or liability. Those respondents stated that electing the fair value option for a portion of an asset or liability would enable them to (a) mitigate volatility in reported earnings that is caused by an accounting model that uses multiple measurement attributes and (b) achieve an offset accounting effect for the changes in the fair values of related financial assets and financial liabilities without having to apply complex hedge accounting provisions.

A27. As discussed above, the Board rejected recognizing fair value changes that are attributable to only selected risks and fair value changes that exclude the effects of an entity's own creditworthiness. The Board views permitting a fair value option election for only a portion of an asset or a liability as similar to those other issues. The Board believes that a fair value election for only a portion of an asset or a liability would not meet its objectives of expanding the use of fair value measurement for financial instruments and international convergence. Therefore, the Board rejected respondents' requests to permit election of the fair value option for only a portion of an asset or a liability.

Financial Statement Presentation and Disclosures

A28. The Board observed that several accounting pronouncements permit an entity to elect to measure certain items at fair value. The Board determined that an entity that elects the fair value option under Statement 155's amendment of paragraph 16 of Statement 133 should provide the disclosures required by this Statement for those elections. The Board determined that the disclosures required by this Statement are not required to be applied to securities classified as trading securities under Statement 115, life settlement contracts that are accounted for under the fair value method under FSP FTB 85-4-1, or servicing assets or liabilities measured at fair value under Statement 156.

A29. The Board considered whether any special display guidance for the statement of financial position or income statement or additional disclosures were needed to compensate for the lack of comparability that will arise from the use of the fair value option. The Board decided that special display guidance is needed on the statement of financial position with respect to the elective use of fair values. Assets and liabilities that are subsequently measured at fair value pursuant to the election of the fair value option under this Statement should be reported separately from the carrying amounts of assets and liabilities subsequently measured using another measurement attribute on the face of the statement of financial position. To accomplish that separate reporting, an entity may either (a) display separate line items for the fair value and non-fair-value carrying amounts or (b) present amounts that aggregate those fair value and non-fair-value amounts and disclose parenthetically the amount of fair value included in the aggregate amount for that line item.

A30. The Board considered the interaction between the fair value option project and its project on financial statement presentation and decided not to specify how an entity should report in its income statement the changes in the fair values of assets and liabilities subsequently measured at fair value as a result of electing the fair value option. The Board determined that an entity should disclose, by line item in the statement of financial position, the amounts of gains and losses included in earnings during each period and in which line item in the income statement those gains and losses are reported. The Board determined that the above disclosure is required for items for which the fair value option has been elected but emphasized that this Statement does not preclude an entity from satisfying that requirement by disclosing amounts of gains and losses that include gains and losses for other items measured at fair value, such as items that are required to be measured at fair value under GAAP. The Board believes that presenting such disclosures using a tabular format will be more easily understood. The Board, however, did not require tabular presentation.

A31. The Board observed that several accounting pronouncements require disclosures about fair value measurements for financial instruments. The Board encourages entities to combine the fair value information disclosed under this Statement with the fair value information disclosed under other pronouncements, where meaningful. The Board concluded that having those disclosures in one place would enhance users' understanding about fair value and the use of fair value in financial reporting, although the Board did not mandate that presentation.

A32. The Board deliberated whether a reporting entity should disclose quantitative information about the extent to which (a) fair value is used to subsequently measure assets and liabilities, (b) the fair value option has or has not been elected, and (c) items were or were not eligible for the fair value option. The Board determined that this Statement's requirement to separately display elective fair value amounts in the statement of financial position and Statement 157's requirement to disclose fair value measurements by level within the fair value hierarchy would provide meaningful information to users. The Board also determined that if a line item in the statement of financial position includes an item or items for which the fair value option has been elected and includes an item or items that were not eligible for the fair value option at initial recognition or upon the occurrence of an election event specified in paragraphs 9(d) and 9(e), an entity must disclose the carrying amount of those ineligible items as of the reporting date. The Board noted that Statement 157's fair value hierarchy disclosures must be presented by major category of assets and liabilities. The Board determined that for each line item in the statement of financial position that includes an item or items for which the fair value option has been elected, an entity must disclose information to enable users to relate the line item in the statement of financial position to the major categories of assets and liabilities presented in accordance with Statement 157's fair value disclosure requirements. The Board considered fair value disclosures required by Statement 107 and noted that Statement 107 already requires an entity to relate amounts disclosed pursuant to that Statement's disclosure requirements to what is reported in the statement of financial position.

A33. Users of financial statements requested additional information about management's reasons for electing the fair value option and, for instances in which an entity elects the fair value option for only certain instruments within a group of similar instruments, disclosure of management's reasons for only partial election. The Board agreed but decided not to provide guidance on how to define groups of similar instruments. Rather, the Board decided that an entity should provide information to enable users to relate groups of similar items to specific line items in the statement of financial position.

A34. The Exposure Draft required disclosure of (a) information sufficient to allow users of financial statements to understand the effect on earnings of changes in the fair values of assets and liabilities subsequently measured at fair value as a result of a fair value election and (b) quantitative information by line item indicating where in the income statement gains and losses are reported that arise from changes in the fair value of financial assets and financial liabilities for which the fair value option has been elected. Some respondents urged the Board to require entities to disclose the cumulative effect on assets and liabilities of electing the fair value option. Users requested additional information about changes in fair values during the period to enhance their ability to assess the quality of an entity's earnings. Users also requested additional information about an entity's methods and significant assumptions used to estimate fair value. Some respondents questioned whether separate disclosure of unrealized gains or losses was required.

A35. The Board determined that preparers should not be required to maintain two sets of accounting records, one reflecting fair value measurements and one without the effects of the fair value election. The Board considered the disclosure requirements of Statement 157, noting that for assets and liabilities that are measured at fair value on a recurring basis using significant unobservable inputs (Level 3 measurements), an entity is required by Statement 157 to (a) separately present changes during the period attributable to total gains or losses included in earnings and describe where those gains and losses are reported in the income statement, (b) disclose the valuation techniques used to measure fair value, and (c) disclose information about unrealized gains and losses relating to the assets and liabilities that are still held at the end of a reporting period. The Board believes that those disclosures will provide meaningful information to users. As stated in paragraph A30, the

Board determined during its redeliberations that an entity should disclose, by line item in the statement of financial position, the amounts of gains and losses from fair value changes included in earnings during each period and in which line item in the income statement those gains and losses are reported. The Board specified that that requirement applies to fair value changes for all items for which the fair value option has been elected, regardless of the level within the fair value hierarchy. The Board believes that the additional disaggregation of information about changes in fair value during the period will enhance a user's ability to assess the quality of an entity's earnings. The Board determined that the general requirement in the Exposure Draft to provide sufficient information to allow users to understand how changes in fair values of assets and liabilities affect earnings for the period was unnecessary because the disclosure requirements in Statement 157 and this Statement produce that information.

A36. Respondents noted that an entity's deteriorating creditworthiness may reduce the fair value of the entity's debt and increase its earnings, and they questioned the relevance of the reduced value of the debt if it is not realizable due to the entity's liquidity constraints. For long-term debt instruments that have contractual principal amounts and for which the fair value option has been elected, the Board decided to require disclosure of the difference between the aggregate fair value carrying amount and the aggregate unpaid principal amount the entity would be contractually required to pay to the holders of those obligations. This disclosure is similar to one required by the IASB and will give users of financial statements relevant information about the relationship between current value and the related required cash payments. In addition, for liabilities for which the fair value option has been elected and whose fair values have been significantly affected during the reporting period by changes in instrument-specific credit risk, the Board determined that an entity should disclose, by line item in the statement of financial position, the estimated amount of gains and losses included in earnings that are attributable to changes in the instrument-specific credit risk. The Board also decided that qualitative information about the reasons for those changes must be disclosed. The Board decided not to provide (a) guidance about when a change in instrument-specific credit risk is considered significant or (b) detailed computational guidance about how to determine the approximation of the amount of the liabilities' fair value change attributable to the change in instrument-specific credit risk. Rather, the

Board decided to require that an entity disclose how it determines gains and losses attributable to instrument-specific credit risk.

A37. Respondents suggested that disclosure requirements about assets for which the fair value option has been elected should be similar to the disclosure requirements for liabilities for which the fair value option has been elected. The Board determined that for any loans and long-term receivables (other than securities subject to Statement 115) that have contractual principal amounts and for which the fair value option has been elected, an entity must disclose the difference between the aggregate fair value carrying amount and the aggregate unpaid principal amount the entity would be contractually entitled to receive from the issuers of the obligations.

A38. Some respondents to the Exposure Draft requested that disclosures about loans measured at fair value due to election of the fair value option provide the same information as if those loans were measured using an amortized cost method with a corresponding allowance for loan losses. The Board noted that existing accounting guidance about loan charge-offs and the allowance for loan losses is not applicable to loans measured at fair value. The Board reviewed those existing disclosure requirements and determined that the following disclosures about loans measured at fair value due to election of the fair value option would provide useful information to financial statement users: (a) the aggregate fair value of loans that are 90 days or more past due, (b) the aggregate fair value of loans that are in nonaccrual status when the entity's policy is to recognize interest income separately from other changes in fair value, and (c) for loans that are 90 days or more past due, in nonaccrual status, or both, the difference between the aggregate fair value and the aggregate unpaid principal amount the entity would be contractually entitled to receive from the issuers of those obligations through maturity. In addition, for loans and other receivables measured at fair value due to the election of the fair value option, the Board determined that an entity should disclose separately the estimated amount of change in fair value of those assets attributable to changes in instrument-specific credit risk from all other changes in fair value for those assets. The Board decided not to provide guidance on how to determine the approximation of the amount of fair value change attributable to the change in instrument-specific credit risk. Rather, the Board decided to require that an entity disclose how it determines gains and losses attributable to instrument-specific credit risk. The Board considered whether disclosures about loans for which the fair value option has been elected should be provided in a disaggregated manner, such as by major loan type or geographical characteristics. The Board noted that the issue of disaggregating loan disclosure information is not new and should not be addressed in this project.

A39. The Board reviewed the existing disclosure requirements in paragraph 20 of Opinion 18 that apply to equity method investments and decided to continue to require most of those disclosures for investments that would have been accounted for under the equity method if the entity had chosen not to elect the fair value option. The Board decided that the disclosure requirements in paragraphs 20(a)(3), 20(b), and 20(e) of that Opinion should not be required for investments measured at fair value that would otherwise be accounted for under the equity method. The information required by those paragraphs was not necessary for investments reported at fair value.

A40. The Board decided that if an entity elects the fair value option when one of the events described in paragraphs 9(d) and 9(e) occurs, the entity should provide (a) qualitative information about the nature of the event and (b) quantitative information by line item in the statement of financial position about which line items in the income statement include the effect on earnings of initially electing the fair value option for an item.

A41. The Board considered whether to provide guidance on how reported interest should be determined for receivables and payables reported at fair value pursuant to the fair value option. The Board noted that the issue of determining interest when financial assets and financial liabilities are measured at fair value is not new and would best be resolved in a different project. During its redeliberations, the Board affirmed that the fair value option project does not address methods for recognizing and measuring the amount of interest and dividend income and that an entity should provide a description indicating how interest and dividends are measured and reported in the income statement. However, the Board clarified that origination fees and costs related to items for which the fair value option is elected should be expensed as incurred. No amendment to FASB Statement No. 91, *Accounting for Nonrefundable Fees and Costs Associated with Originating or Acquiring Loans and Initial Direct Costs of Leases,* is required because that Statement does not apply to loans measured at fair value with changes reported in earnings.

Cash Flow Reporting

A42. The Board considered whether the cash receipts and cash payments related to financial assets and financial liabilities for which the fair value option has been elected should be classified as operating activities in the statement of cash flows, since that classification is required for trading securities under Statement 115. The Board decided that the required classification as operating activities for trading securities is inappropriate because Statement 115 permits securities to be classified as trading even though they are not being held for sale in the near term. The Board concluded that the cash receipts and cash payments related to trading securities as well as to financial assets and financial liabilities for which the fair value option has been elected should be classified pursuant to Statement 95 (as amended) based on the nature and purpose for which the related financial assets and financial liabilities were acquired or incurred. The Board decided that Statements 95 and 115 as well as FASB Statement No. 102, *Statement of Cash Flows—Exemption of Certain Enterprises and Classification of Cash Flows from Certain Securities Acquired for Resale,* should be amended to reflect those conclusions.

A43. The Board considered amending Statement 95 to require a reconciling line item for changes in fair value when the indirect method is followed in presenting the statement of cash flows, but it decided that amendment would not be necessary because paragraph 29 of Statement 95 requires separate line items for major reconciling items.

Amendments Related to the Fair Value Election

A44. In addition to the amendments to Statements 95, 102, and 115 about the classification of the cash receipts and cash payments related to trading securities discussed in paragraph A42, the Board considered whether other amendments were warranted. The Board decided that the special display requirements for the statement of financial position with respect to the elective use of fair values should apply to the use of the trading category under Statement 115. As a result, two further amendments to Statement 115 are warranted:

a. To require entities to either display separate line items in an entity's statement of financial position for the fair value and non-fair-value carrying amounts for investments in debt and equity securities or present amounts that aggregate those fair value and non-fair-value amounts provided that the amount of fair value for available-for-sale and trading securities included in the aggregate amount for that line item is separately disclosed parenthetically on the face of the entity's statement of financial position

b. To revise the phrasing of paragraph 4 about scope to reflect the availability of the fair value option for investments in equity securities that would otherwise be accounted for under the equity method.

A similar amendment of the definition of *related parties* in FASB Statement No. 57, *Related Party Disclosures,* is also warranted. Those modifications of Statement 57 and paragraph 4 of Statement 115 do not change the original definition of *related parties* or the original scope of Statement 115. The Board also decided that a further amendment of Statement 133 is warranted to clarify that a nonderivative financial instrument (such as a foreign-currency-denominated liability) that is reported at fair value cannot be designated as hedging the foreign currency exposure of a net investment in a foreign operation. A foreign-currency-denominated financial asset or liability that is reported at fair value does not give rise to any foreign currency transaction gain or loss, as that term is used in FASB Statement No. 52, *Foreign Currency Translation.* That clarification of Statement 133 is warranted because the measurement of liabilities at fair value is newly available on a broad basis under this Statement. The definitions of *financial asset* and *financial liability* in this Statement reflect minor clarifying changes to the definitions of those terms in FASB Statement No. 140, *Accounting for Transfers and Servicing of Financial Assets and Extinguishments of Liabilities,* and Statement 141. The Board decided that a formal amendment of Statements 140 and 141 is not necessary because the changes are only editorial.

Effective Date and Transition

A45. The Board initially decided that this Statement should be effective as of the beginning of each reporting entity's first fiscal year that begins after December 15, 2006, with earlier adoption permitted as of the beginning of an entity's earlier fiscal year that begins after issuance of this Statement (thereby resulting in an earlier effective date). Many respondents asked for a delay in the effective date to allow more time to review existing positions and risk management strategies. Some respondents recommended that the Board delay the effective date to be either concurrent with or later than the effective date for Statement 157. The Board decided that this Statement should be effective as of the beginning of each reporting entity's first fiscal year that begins after November 15, 2007, the same effective date as Statement 157.

A46. The Exposure Draft permitted an entity to elect the fair value option for existing financial assets and financial liabilities that are within the scope of this Statement, rather than limit its application to only newly recognized financial assets and financial liabilities. The Board had decided that retrospective application of this Statement to fiscal years preceding the effective date, which would involve restatement of previously issued financial statements, should not be permitted because of the elective nature of this Statement and the benefit of hindsight. Therefore, the effect of the initial adoption of this Statement attributable to the election of the fair value option for selected financial assets and financial liabilities existing at the effective date should be accounted for as a cumulative-effect adjustment of retained earnings as of the effective date, not the beginning of the earliest year presented. Respondents were supportive of those provisions and no changes have been made for that reporting.

A47. Respondents that requested a delay in the effective date also generally favored permitting early adoption of this Statement. Some entities particularly wanted to be able to adopt it at the beginning of fiscal year 2007. To facilitate early adoption as of the beginning of fiscal years beginning after November 15, 2006, the Board decided to change the provision in the Exposure Draft that limited early adoption to the beginning of an entity's earlier fiscal year that begins after issuance of this Statement. The Board decided that an entity may make the decision to adopt this Statement early (which would necessarily include the decision whether to elect the fair value option for each of its existing eligible assets and liabilities) within 120 days of the beginning of the reporting entity's fiscal year, thereby making that election retroactive to the beginning of the fiscal year (or to the date of initial recognition, if later for certain assets and liabilities). Although the Board prefers not to permit entities to make retroactive elections that can have a significant retroactive effect on earnings of the current year in which the election is made, the Board believes that the early adoption of the fair value option warrants permitting retroactive elections within the first 120 days of the fiscal year. The 120-day retroactive election provision does not apply to entities that do not choose early adoption of this Statement.

A48. Though supportive of permitting such retroactive early adoption, the Board decided that two conditions were important in establishing the 120-day retroactive election provision:

a. The entity also must adopt all of the requirements of Statement 157 concurrent with or prior to the early adoption of this Statement. The Board's willingness to permit a fair value option under this Statement was implicitly premised on the improved guidance being developed for determining fair value measurements. Now that the guidance in Statement 157 has been finalized, it must be used in applying the fair value option.

b. At the time it decides to adopt this Statement early, the entity has not yet issued financial statements, including required notes to those financial statements, for any interim period of the fiscal year that includes the early adoption date. The Board had decided that the initial application of this Statement should not involve restatement of previously issued financial statements.

A49. To facilitate users' understanding of how the fair value option was elected at initial adoption with respect to existing assets and liabilities, the Board decided to require a detailed analysis of the cumulative-effect adjustment to the opening balance of retained earnings (or appropriate class or classes of net assets) as of the date of initial adoption, including a comparison of the previous carrying amount and the new fair value carrying amount for the affected assets and liabilities. That cumulative-effect adjustment would include removing from the statement of financial position the difference between the carrying amount and fair value of eligible items for which the fair value option is elected at the effective date. Those differences may include, but are not limited to, any unamortized deferred costs (including deferred acquisition costs for insurance contracts), fees, premiums, discounts, valuation allowances (such as an allowance for loan losses), and accrued interest related to existing assets and liabilities for which the fair value option has been elected at the initial application of this Statement. To further facilitate users' understanding, the Board also decided to require disclosure of additional information about management's reasons for electing the fair value option, and, for instances in which an entity elects the fair value option

for only certain instruments within a group of similar instruments, disclosure of management's reasons for only partial election.

A50. The Board considered whether to permit election of the fair value option for available-for-sale and held-to-maturity securities previously accounted for under Statement 115. The Board decided to permit an entity to elect the fair value option for those securities upon the initial adoption of this Statement, which has the effect of reclassifying those securities into the trading category. However, the Board decided that the amount of the effect of that reclassification into the trading category should be included in the cumulative-effect adjustment of retained earnings and that the amount of the effect of that reclassification should be separately disclosed. The effect of that reclassification into the trading category arising from the initial adoption of this Statement should not be included in current-period earnings as a transfer between categories under Statement 115.

Similarities and Differences with International Accounting Standards

A51. The IASB has included a fair value option for financial instruments in IAS 39. The provisions in IAS 39 are similar to those in this Statement insofar as the fair value options in both pronouncements require that the election:

a. Be made at the initial recognition of the financial asset or financial liability

b. Is irrevocable

c. Results in the changes in fair value being recognized in earnings (referred to as "profit or loss" in IAS 39) as those changes occur.

A52. The differences between the provisions in this Statement and international standards pertain principally to disclosures, scope exceptions, and whether certain eligibility criteria must be met to elect the fair value option.

Benefits and Costs

A53. The mission of the FASB is to establish and improve standards of financial accounting and reporting to provide information that is useful to users of financial statements (present and potential investors, creditors, donors, and other capital market participants) in making rational investment, credit, and similar resource allocation decisions. In fulfilling that mission, the Board endeavors to determine that a proposed standard will fill a significant need and that the costs imposed to meet that standard, as compared with other alternatives, are justified in relation to the overall benefits of the resulting information. Although the costs to implement a new standard may not be borne evenly, users of financial statements benefit from improvements in financial reporting, thereby facilitating the functioning of markets for capital and credit and the efficient allocation of resources in the economy.

A54. The Board's assessment of the benefits and costs of establishing a fair value option was based on discussions with preparers, auditors, regulators, and users of financial statements. The Board considered the costs associated with decreased comparability as a result of allowing a choice between fair value and the non-fair-value measurement attribute otherwise required by GAAP. The Board also considered the benefits arising from mitigating problems of volatility in reported earnings caused by an accounting model that uses multiple measurement attributes; achieving an offsetting accounting effect for the changes in the fair values of related assets and liabilities without having to apply complex hedge accounting provisions, thereby simplifying the application of

accounting guidance; and expanding the use of the fair value measurement attribute for financial instruments. The Board concluded that the financial reporting benefits would outweigh the costs of noncomparability, particularly since the improved disclosures required by this Statement would enable users to compare entities that make different decisions about use of the fair value option.

Appendix B

ILLUSTRATIVE FAIR VALUE DISCLOSURES

B1. The examples below illustrate selected disclosure requirements for items reported at fair value under this Statement and include selected disclosures required by Statements 157 and 107. The examples represent suggested forms for presenting disclosure information. While the suggested forms of presentation illustrate selected required disclosures, the suggested forms of presentation are not mandated by this Statement. Aggregation of related fair value disclosures is encouraged but not required.

B2. The statement of financial position for Company XYZ as of December 31, 2008, after the adoption of this Statement, is provided to assist in understanding the illustrative fair value disclosure examples set forth below:

Company XYZ
Statement of Financial Position
($ in 000s)

Description		At December 31, 2008
Assets		
Cash and due from banks		$ 38
Deposits with banks		22
Fed funds sold and securities purchased under resale agreements		134
Securities borrowed		75
Trading securities		115
Securities available-for-sale		75
Securities held-to-maturity		32
Loans and lease receivables ($150 at fair value)	$560	
Allowance for loan and lease losses	(10)	
Loans, net of allowance for loan and lease losses		550
Derivatives		60
Private equity investments ($75 at fair value)		125
Premises and equipment		10
Other assets		20
Total assets		$1,256
Liabilities		
Non-interest-bearing deposits		$ 143
Interest-bearing deposits		412
Fed funds purchased and securities sold under repurchase agreements		130
Accounts payable		110
Short-term borrowings		128
Long-term debt ($60 at fair value)		200
Total liabilities		1,123
Shareholders' equity		
Common stock (authorized 5,000,000 shares; issued 3,550,000 shares)		4
Capital surplus		88
Retained earnings		42
Accumulated other comprehensive income (loss)		(1)
Total shareholders' equity		133
Total liabilities and shareholders' equity		$1,256

Example 1—Initial Adoption of Fair Value Option (FVO)

B3. This Statement requires that an entity provide information about the extent to which the fair value option is elected for existing eligible items at the time of initial adoption in a manner that reconciles to the cumulative-effect adjustment to retained earnings. That information might be presented as follows: [Disclosures required by paragraphs 27(a), 27(b), and 27(e) of this Statement are illustrated below.]

($ in 000s) Description	Balance Sheet 1/1/08 prior to Adoption	Net Gain/(Loss) upon Adoption	Balance Sheet 1/1/08 after Adoption of FVO
Loans net	$120	$(20)	$100
Private equity investments	50	(10)	40
Long-term debt	(70)	4	(66)
Pretax cumulative effect of adoption of the fair value option		(26)	
Increase in deferred tax asset		8	
Cumulative effect of adoption of the fair value option (charge to retained earnings)		$(18)	

The $20,000 net loss for loans that was recorded as part of the cumulative-effect adjustment to retained earnings upon initial adoption of this Statement includes $3,000, which was removed from the allowance for loan and lease losses.

B4. An entity might provide the following additional disclosures required by paragraphs 27(c) and 27(d) of this Statement in this same note: (a) management's reasons for electing the fair value option for each existing eligible item or group of similar eligible items and (b) if the fair value option is elected for some but not all eligible items within a group of similar eligible items, (1) a description of those similar items and the reasons for partial election and (2) information to enable users to understand how the group of similar items relates to individual line items on the statement of financial position.

Example 2—Fair Value Measurements and Changes in Fair Values Included in Current-Period Earnings

B5. The objective is to provide information about (a) assets and liabilities measured at fair value on a recurring basis (as required by Statement 157), (b) changes in fair values of assets and liabilities for which the fair value option has been elected in a manner that relates to the statement of financial position (as required by this Statement), and (c) fair value estimates and corresponding carrying amounts for major categories of assets and liabilities that include items measured at fair value on a recurring basis (in accordance with Statement 107).

B6. Table 1 represents the fair value hierarchy table set forth in Statement 157, supplemented to (a) provide information about where in the income statement changes in fair values of assets and liabilities reported at fair value are included in earnings[9] and (b) voluntarily integrate selected disclosures required annually by Statement 107. [Disclosures required by paragraphs 19(a) and 18(c) of this Statement are illustrated below.]

---

[9]Paragraph 19(a) of this Statement requires an entity to disclose the amounts of gains and losses included in earnings from fair value changes for assets and liabilities for which the fair value option has been elected but does not preclude an entity from meeting that disclosure requirement by disclosing amounts of gains and losses that include amounts of gains and losses for other items measured at fair value through earnings, such as items required to be measured at fair value.

Table 1
($ in 000s)

Description	Total Carrying Amount in Statement of Financial Position 12/31/08[10]	Statement 107 Fair Value Estimate 12/31/08[11]	Assets/ Liabilities Measured at Fair Value 12/31/08	Fair Value Measurements at December 31, 2008, Using			Changes in Fair Values for the 12-Month Period Ended December 31, 2008, for Items Measured at Fair Value Pursuant to Election of the Fair Value Option				
				Quoted Prices in Active Markets for Identical Assets (Level 1)	Significant Other Observable Inputs (Level 2)	Significant Unobservable Inputs (Level 3)	Trading Gains and Losses	Other Gains and Losses	Interest Income on Loans	Interest Expense on Long-Term Debt	Total Changes in Fair Values Included in Current-Period Earnings
Trading securities	$ 115	$ 115	$115	$105	$ 10		$10[12]				$10
Available-for-sale securities	75	75	75	75							
Loans, net	400	412	150	0	100	$ 50		$ (3)	$10		7
Derivatives	60	60	60	25	15	20	5[13]				5
Private equity investments	125	138	75*	0	25	50		(18)			(18)
Long-term debt	(200)	(206)	(60)	(30)	(10)	(20)		13		$(4)	9

*Represents investments that would otherwise be accounted for under the equity method of accounting.

Loans are included in loans and lease receivables in the statement of financial position. As of December 31, 2008, approximately $160,000 of lease receivables are included in loans and lease receivables in the statement of financial position and are not eligible for the fair value option.

[10] This column discloses carrying amount information required annually by Statement 107 only for major categories of assets and liabilities that include items measured at fair value.

[11] This column discloses fair value estimates required annually by Statement 107 only for major categories of assets and liabilities that include items measured at fair value. Statement 107 requires an entity to disclose fair value estimates and related carrying amounts for all financial instruments within the scope of that Statement, if practicable. Footnote 3a of Statement 107 requires that if an entity discloses the fair value of financial instruments in more than a single note, one of the notes shall include a summary table (not presented in this appendix).

[12] This Statement does not require disclosure of this amount, nor does it preclude disclosure of this amount. This amount is shown here for completeness.

[13] Refer to note 12.

B7. An entity might provide the following additional disclosures required by paragraphs 18(a) and 18(b) of this Statement here: (a) management's reasons for electing a fair value option for each eligible item or group of similar eligible items and (b) if the fair value option is elected for some but not all eligible items within a group of similar eligible items, (1) a description of those similar items and the reasons for partial election and (2) information to enable users to understand how the group of similar items relates to individual line items on the statement of financial position.

B8. Table 2 is an alternative illustrative example that does not integrate disclosures required annually by Statement 107 or the additional gain and loss amounts voluntarily displayed in Table 1. Table 2 represents the fair value hierarchy table set forth in Statement 157, supplemented to provide information about where in the income statement changes in fair values of assets and liabilities for which the fair value option has been elected are included in earnings. [Disclosures required by paragraphs 19(a) and 18(c) of this Statement are illustrated below.]

Table 2
($ in 000s)

Description	Fair Value Measurements 12/31/08	Fair Value Measurements at December 31, 2008, Using			Changes in Fair Values for the 12-Month Period Ended December 31, 2008, for Items Measured at Fair Value Pursuant to Election of the Fair Value Option			
		Quoted Prices in Active Markets for Identical Assets (Level 1)	Significant Other Observable Inputs (Level 2)	Significant Unobservable Inputs (Level 3)	Other Gains and Losses	Interest Income on Loans	Interest Expense on Long-Term Debt	Total Changes in Fair Values Included in Current-Period Earnings
Trading securities	$115	$105	$ 10					
Available-for-sale securities	75	75						
Loans	150	0	100	$ 50	$ (3)	$10		$ 7
Derivatives	60	25	15	20				
Private equity investments*	75	0	25	50	(18)			(18)
Long-term debt	(60)	(30)	(10)	(20)	13		$(4)	9

*Represents investments that would otherwise be accounted for under the equity method of accounting.

Loans are included in loans and lease receivables in the statement of financial position. As of December 31, 2008, approximately $160,000 of lease receivables are included in loans and lease receivables in the statement of financial position and are not eligible for the fair value option.

B9. An entity might provide the following additional disclosures required by paragraphs 18(a) and 18(b) of this Statement here: (a) management's reasons for electing a fair value option for each eligible item or group of similar eligible items and (b) if the fair value option is elected for some but not all eligible items within a group of similar eligible items, (1) a description of those similar items and the reasons for partial election and (2) information to enable users to understand how the group of similar items relates to individual line items on the statement of financial position.

Appendix C

AMENDMENTS TO EXISTING PRONOUNCEMENTS

C1. APB Opinion 21, *Interest on Receivables and Payables,* is amended as follows: [Added text is underlined and deleted text is struck out.]

a. Paragraph 16, as amended:

Statement presentation of discount and premium. The discount or premium resulting from the determination of present value in cash or non-cash transactions is not an asset or liability separable from the note which gives rise to it. Therefore, the discount or premium should be reported in the balance sheet as a direct deduction from or addition to the face amount of the note. It should not be classified as a deferred charge or deferred credit. The description of the note should include the effective interest rate; the face amount should also be disclosed in the financial statements or in the notes to the statements.[9] Amortization of discount or premium should be reported as interest expense. Issue costs should be reported in the balance sheet as deferred charges. This paragraph does not apply to the amortization of premium and discount and the debt issuance costs of liabilities that are reported at fair value.

C2. FASB Statement No. 57, *Related Party Disclosures,* is amended as follows:

a. Paragraph 24(f):

Related parties. Affiliates of the enterprise; entities for which investments in their equity securities would, absent the election of the fair value

option under FASB Statement No. 159, *The Fair Value Option for Financial Assets and Financial Liabilities,* be required to be are accounted for by the equity method by the enterprise; trusts for the benefit of employees, such as pension and profit-sharing trusts that are managed by or under the trusteeship of management; principal owners of the enterprise; its management; members of the immediate families of principal owners of the enterprise and its management; and other parties with which the enterprise may deal if one party controls or can significantly influence the management or operating policies of the other to an extent that one of the transacting parties might be prevented from fully pursuing its own separate interests. Another party also is a related party if it can significantly influence the management or operating policies of the transacting parties or if it has an ownership interest in one of the transacting parties and can significantly influence the other to an extent that one or more of the transacting parties might be prevented from fully pursuing its own separate interests.

C3. FASB Statement No. 95, *Statement of Cash Flows,* is amended as follows:

a. Paragraph 15, as amended:

Investing activities include making and collecting loans and acquiring and disposing of debt or equity instruments and property, plant, and equipment and other productive assets, that is, assets held for or used in the production of goods or services by the enterprise (other than materials that are part of the enterprise's inventory). Investing activities exclude acquiring and disposing of certain loans or other debt or equity instruments that are acquired specifically for resale, as discussed in Statement 102, and securities that are classified as trading securities as discussed in FASB Statement No. 115, *Accounting for Certain Investments in Debt and Equity Securities*.

b. Paragraph 16, as amended:

Cash inflows from investing activities are:[5]

a. Receipts from collections or sales of loans made by the enterprise and of other entities' debt instruments (other than cash equivalents, and certain debt instruments that are acquired specifically for resale as discussed in Statement 102, ~~and securities classified as trading securities as discussed in Statement 115~~) that were purchased by the enterprise

b. Receipts from sales of equity instruments of other enterprises (other than certain equity instruments carried in a trading account as described in Statement 102, ~~and certain securities classified as trading securities as discussed in Statement 115~~) and from returns *of investment* in those instruments

c. Receipts from sales of property, plant, and equipment and other productive assets.

c. Paragraph 17, as amended:

Cash outflows for investing activities are:

a. Disbursements for loans made by the enterprise and payments to acquire debt instruments of other entities (other than cash equivalents, and certain debt instruments that are acquired specifically for resale as discussed in Statement 102, ~~and securities classified as trading securities as discussed in Statement 115~~)

b. Payments to acquire equity instruments of other enterprises (other than certain equity instruments carried in a trading account as described in Statement 102 ~~and certain securities classified as trading securities as discussed in Statement 115~~)

c. Payments at the time of purchase or soon before or after purchase[6] to acquire property, plant, and equipment and other productive assets.[7]

d. Footnote 8c, as added, to paragraph 22:

The term *goods* includes certain loans and other debt and equity instruments of other enterprises that are acquired specifically for resale, as discussed in Statement 102, ~~and securities that are classified as trading securities as discussed in Statement 115~~.

C4. FASB Statement No. 102, *Statement of Cash Flows—Exemption of Certain Enterprises and Classification of Cash Flows from Certain Securities Acquired for Resale,* is amended as follows:

a. Paragraph 8, as amended:

Banks, brokers and dealers in securities, and other enterprises may carry securities and other

assets in a trading account.[3] Cash receipts and cash payments resulting from purchases and sales of securities classified as trading securities as discussed in FASB Statement No. 115, *Accounting for Certain Investments in Debt and Equity Securities,* shall be classified pursuant to Statement 95 (as amended) based on the nature and purpose for which the securities were ac~~quired as operating cash flows~~. Cash receipts and cash payments resulting from purchases and sales of other securities and other assets shall be classified as operating cash flows if those assets are acquired specifically for resale and are carried at market value in a trading account. Cash flows from purchases, sales, and maturities of available-for-sale securities shall be classified as cash flows from investing activities and reported gross in the statement of cash flows.

C5. FASB Statement No. 115, *Accounting for Certain Investments in Debt and Equity Securities,* is amended as follows:

a. Paragraph 4, as amended:

This Statement does not apply to investments in equity securities that, absent the election of the fair value option under FASB Statement No. 159, *The Fair Value Option for Financial Assets and Financial Liabilities,* would be required to be accounted for under the equity method nor to investments in consolidated subsidiaries. This Statement does not apply to enterprises whose specialized accounting practices include accounting for substantially all investments in debt and equity securities at market value or fair value, with changes in value recognized in earnings (income) or in the change in net assets. Examples of those enterprises are brokers and dealers in securities, defined benefit pension plans, and investment companies. This Statement applies to cooperatives and mutual enterprises, including credit unions and mutual insurance companies, but does not apply to not-for-profit organizations. FASB Statement No. 124, *Accounting for Certain Investments Held by Not-for-Profit Organizations,* establishes standards for not-for-profit organizations. This Statement does not apply to investments in derivative instruments that are subject to the requirements of FASB Statement No. 133, *Accounting for Derivative Instruments and Hedging Activities.* If an investment would otherwise be in the scope of this Statement and it has within it an embedded derivative that is subject to Statement 133, the host instrument (as described in Statement 133) remains within the scope of this Statement. A transaction gain or loss on a held-to-maturity foreign-currency-denominated debt security shall be accounted for pursuant to FASB Statement No. 52, *Foreign Currency Translation.*

b. Paragraph 17, as amended:

An enterprise shall report its investments in available-for-sale securities and trading securities separately from similar assets that are subsequently measured using another measurement attribute on the face of the statement of financial position. To accomplish that, an entity shall either (a) present the aggregate of those fair value and non-fair-value amounts in the same line item and parenthetically disclose the amount of fair value included in the aggregate amount or (b) present two separate line items to display the fair value and non-fair-value carrying amounts. An enterprise that presents a classified statement of financial position shall report individual held-to-maturity securities, individual available-for-sale securities, and individual trading securities as either current or noncurrent, as appropriate, under the provisions of ARB No. 43, Chapter 3A, "Working Capital—Current Assets and Current Liabilities."[5]

c. Paragraph 18:

Cash flows from purchases, sales, and maturities of available-for-sale securities and held-to-maturity securities shall be classified as cash flows from investing activities and reported gross for each security classification in the statement of cash flows. Cash flows from purchases, sales, and maturities of trading securities shall be classified based on the nature and purpose for which the securities were acquired as cash flows from operating activities.

C6. FASB Statement No. 124, *Accounting for Certain Investments Held by Not-for-Profit Organizations,* is amended as follows:

a. Paragraph 6, as amended:

Generally accepted accounting principles other than those discussed in this Statement also apply to investments held by not-for-profit organizations. For example, not-for-profit organizations must disclose information required by FASB Statements No. 107, *Disclosures about Fair Value of Financial Instruments,* and No. Statement 133, and FASB Statement No. 159, *The Fair Value Option for Financial Assets and Financial Liabilities.*

C7. FASB Statement No. 133, *Accounting for Derivative Instruments and Hedging Activities,* is amended as follows:

a. Paragraph 42, as amended:

A derivative instrument or a nonderivative financial instrument that may give rise to a foreign currency transaction gain or loss under Statement 52 can be designated as hedging the foreign currency exposure of a net investment in a foreign operation provided the conditions in paragraphs 40(a) and 40(b) are met. (A nonderivative financial instrument that is reported at fair value does not give rise to a foreign currency transaction gain or loss under Statement 52 and, thus, cannot be designated as hedging the foreign currency exposure of a net investment in a foreign operation.) The gain or loss on a hedging derivative instrument (or the foreign currency transaction gain or loss on the nonderivative hedging instrument) that is designated as, and is effective as, an economic hedge of the net investment in a foreign operation shall be reported in the same manner as a translation adjustment to the extent it is effective as a hedge. The hedged net investment shall be accounted for consistent with Statement 52; the provisions of this Statement for recognizing the gain or loss on assets designated as being hedged in a fair value hedge do not apply to the hedge of a net investment in a foreign operation.

b. Paragraph 44A, as added:

In each statement of financial position presented, an entity shall report hybrid financial instruments measured at fair value under the election and under the practicability exception in paragraph 16 of this Statement in a manner that separates those reported fair values from the carrying amounts of assets and liabilities subsequently measured using another measurement attribute on the face of the statement of financial position. To accomplish that separate reporting, an entity may either (a) display separate line items for the fair value and non-fair-value carrying amounts or (b) present the aggregate of those fair value and non-fair-value amounts and parenthetically disclose the amount of fair value included in the aggregate amount. For those hybrid financial instruments measured at fair value under the election and under the practicability exception in paragraph 16, an entity shall also disclose the information specified in paragraphs 18–22 of FASB Statement No. 159, *The Fair Value Option for Financial Assets and Financial Liabilities.*